STEIFF

S O R T I M E N T

1947-1999

STEIFF

A S S O R T M E N T

1947-1999

Günther Pfeiffer

Vom geliebten Spielzeug

From dearly loved toys

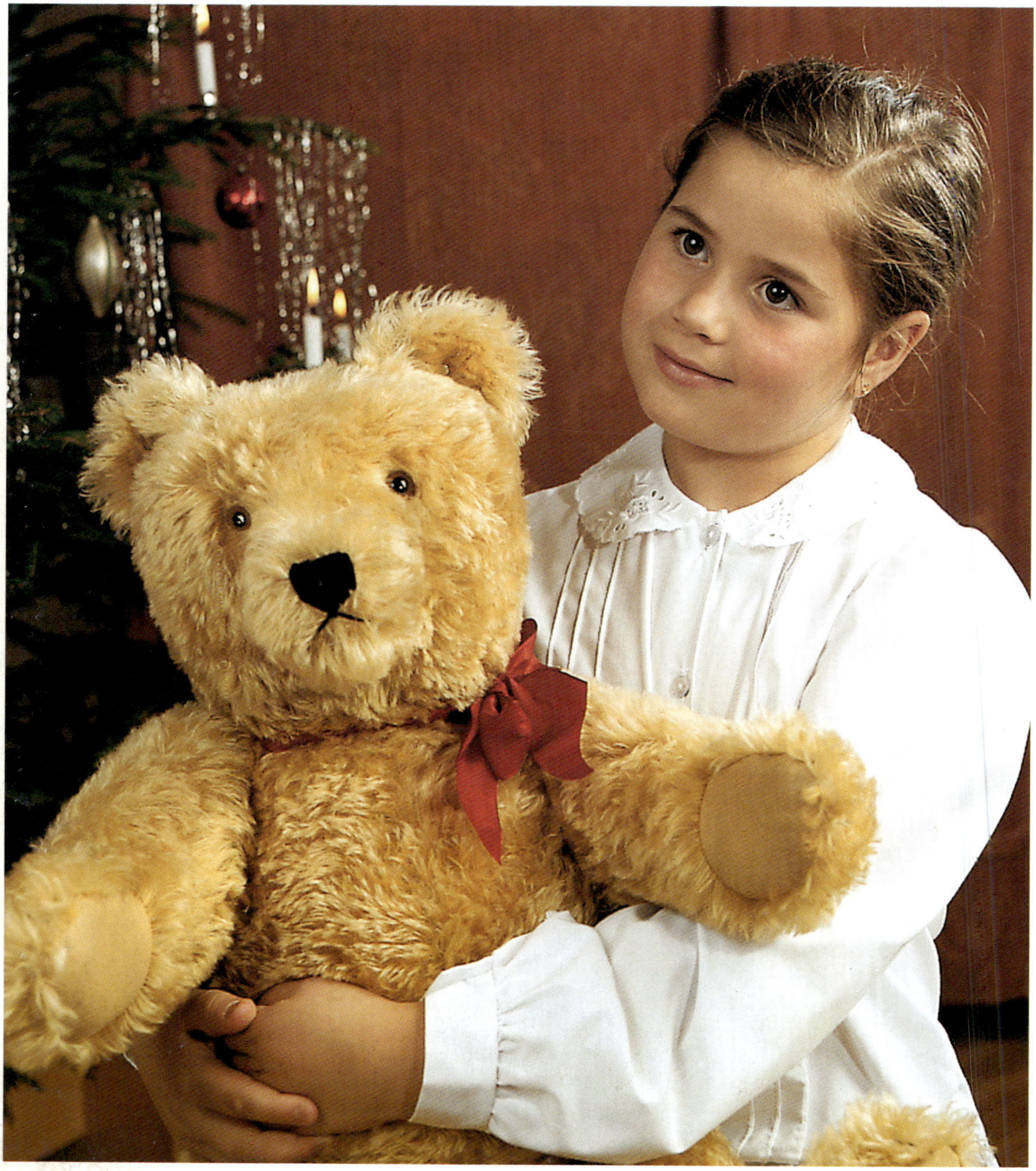

ZUM BEGEHRTEN SAMMLEROBJEKT

TO DESIRABLE COLLECTIBLES

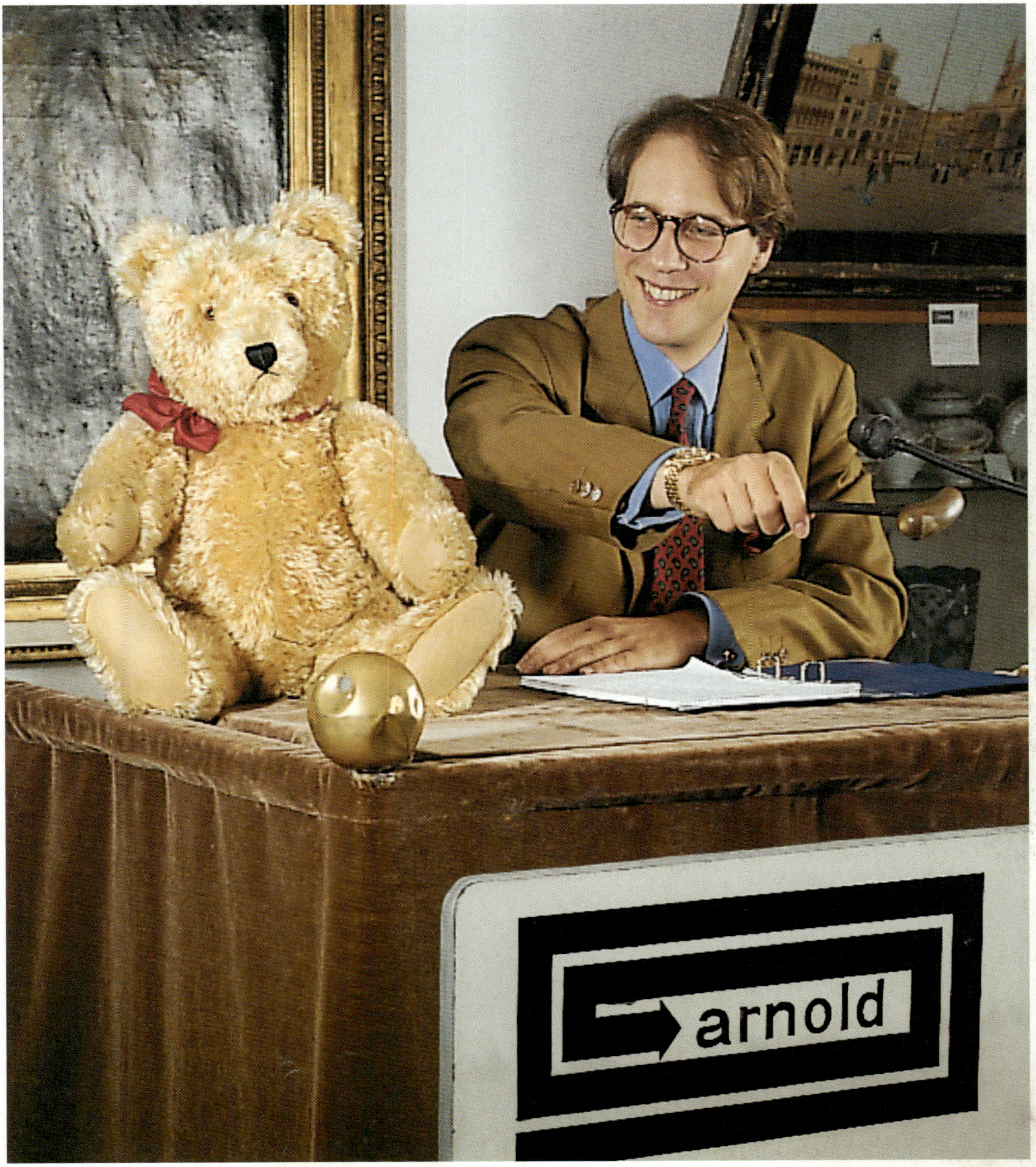

Verlag/publishing house GAF Günther Pfeiffer GmbH, Taunusstein 1999

Hergestellt in Deutschland/Produced and Printed in Germany

Fotografien/photographers
Manuela Heymann-Baxendale, GAF Günther Pfeiffer GmbH

Satz und Layout/Typesetting and Layout
Monika Hochmuth, Dresden

Englische Übersetzung/English translation
PS Translation, Germersheim

Druck/Print
Media-Print GmbH, Paderborn

Kunstdruck (80er Raster)/Fine art printing (80 screen type)

ISBN 3-9804712-2-5

INHALT
TABLE OF CONTENTS

Über dieses Buch

Es hat sich viel bewegt.

Vor Ihnen liegt der komplett überarbeitete und ergänzte Nachfolger des 1995 erstmals herausgegebenen Buches über das Steiff Sortiment seit 1947.

In den letzten vier Jahren ist dieses wunderschöne Sammelgebiet endgültig seinen Kinderschuhen entwachsen und hat seine Stellung auf dem Sammlermarkt weiter ausbauen und etablieren können.

Verschiedene Faktoren haben zu dieser Entwicklung beigetragen. Weltweite Kontakte, die z.B. durch das Internet vereinfacht wurden, wunderschöne Präsentationen in Museen und natürlich auch herausragende Ergebnisse, die Steiff Tiere auf internationalen Auktionen erzielten, haben für Aufsehen gesorgt.

Nicht zuletzt hat auch die Margarete Steiff GmbH, durch völlig neue Kreationen und innovative Produkte - auch und gerade in den letzten Jahren - dazu beigetragen, dass der Sammler heute aus einer Vielzahl von Produkten seine Favoriten auswählen und seiner Sammlung hinzufügen kann. Es ist geradezu phänomenal, wie es dieser Marke gelungen ist, sich innerhalb von nur wenigen Jahren auf einem völlig neuen Markt zu orientieren ohne ihre Wurzeln zu vernachlässigen oder gar zu vergessen. Bis zum heutigen Tag wurde in vorbildlicher Weise die Balance zwischen alt und neu sowie zwischen Sammlerartikeln und Kinderspielzeug gefunden. Die so häufig zitierte Devise der Margarete Steiff „für Kinder ist nur das Beste gut genug" hat heute, wie schon vor mehr als 100 Jahren, uneingeschränkte Gültigkeit.

Auch wir haben uns bemüht, unseren Anteil dazu beizutragen und die für Sammler und Liebhaber von Steiff Produkten unverzichtbare Fachliteratur auf den aktuellen Stand zu bringen.

Die Textpassagen erscheinen erstmals sowohl in deutscher als auch in englischer Sprache.

Freuen Sie sich auf ca. 8.600 Produkte, die mit mehr als 3.800 Farbfotografien auf den folgenden 600 Seiten gezeigt werden.

Es erwarten Sie viele neue Artikel, sowohl aktuelle Neuheiten als auch ältere Stücke, die aufgrund von Recherchen erst jetzt wieder entdeckt wurden.

Die detaillierte Beschreibung zur Anwendung dieses Buches soll Ihnen dabei helfen, dieses Nachschlagewerk zu einem stetigen und zuverlässigen Begleiter werden zu lassen.

About this Book

Much has changed.

In your hands you hold the completely revised and expanded edition of the book that was originally published in 1995 on the Steiff product range dating back as far as 1947.

This fabulous collectors' field has finally left its infancy and, during the last four years, has been able to further expand and consolidate its position in the collectors' market.

Various factors have contributed to this development. The simplification of global contacts by, for example, the Internet; beautiful displays in museums; and, of course, the excellent prices that Steiff animals have been able to achieve at international auctions have all caused a stir.

With completely new creations and innovative products, Margarete Steiff GmbH has – particularly in the last few years – greatly contributed to the fact that a collector can today choose his favorites from a variety of products, in order to add to his/her collection. It is absolutely phenomenal how this brand has managed, within the space of just a few years, to gain a foothold in a completely new market, without neglecting or even completely losing sight of its roots. Right up until the present day, in an exemplary fashion, a balance has been achieved between old and new, as well as between collectors' items and children's toys. Margarete Steiff's often-cited phrase, "Only the best is good enough for children" is as valid today as it was 100 years ago.

We too have made our contribution by updating the indispensable literature on which collectors' and enthusiasts of Steiff products rely.

For the first time, text passages appear in both English and German.

Enjoy the approximately 8,600 products that are depicted in more than 3,800 color photographs on the following 600 pages.

Many new products await you, including current novelties, as well as older items that have only just been rediscovered as the result of research.

The detailed description of how to use this book is intended to help make it an indispensable work of reference, as well as a reliable, constant companion.

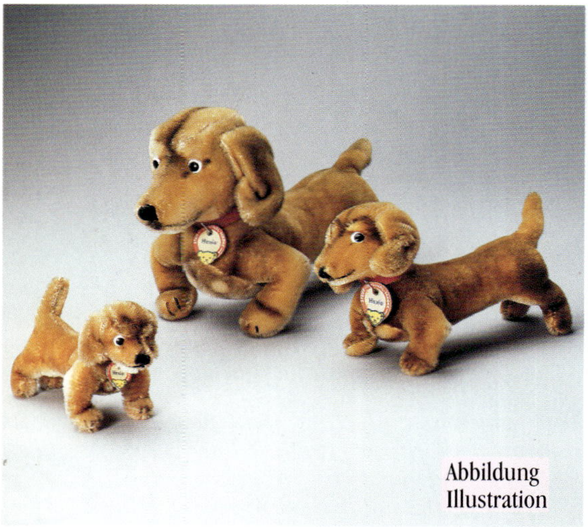

Abbildung
Illustration

Dackel **Hexie** - ***Hexie*** *Dachshund*

Kurzhaar-Mohair, braun/gelb, stehend, Kopf drehbar, Stimme - *short-hair mohair, brown/yellow, standing, head swivels, press voice*

SERIE	ART.-NO	PERIOD	PR.	INFO
18	**1309,0**	1954-1958	3	9 cm
180	**1309,00**	1959-1964	3	
418	**1309,00**	1965-1967	3	
	4180/09	1968-1972	2-3	
18	**1313,0**	1954-1958	3	13 cm
180	**1313,00**	1959-1963	3	
418	**1313,00**	1965-1967	3	
	4180/13	1968-1974	2-3	
18	**1320,0**	1956-1958	3	20 cm
180	**1320,00**	1959-1963	3	
418	**1320,00**	1965-1967	3	
	4180/20	1968-1974	3	
18	**1325,0**	1958-1958	3	25 cm
180	**1325,00**	1959-1963	3	
418	**1325,00**	1965-1967	3	
	4180/25	1968-1973	3	

Anwendung

Im folgenden Beispiel wird der Aufbau der einzelnen Artikeldarstellungen und -beschreibungen erläutert.

Abbildung: Aus Gründen der Übersicht bzw. Verfügbarkeit können nicht immer alle Größen oder Farben des jeweiligen Artikels abgebildet werden. Sollten Abweichungen nicht im Foto dargestellt sein, erfolgt ein Hinweis im Text.

Hier wird der **Steiff-Artikelname** angegeben. Ist dieser **fett** gedruckt, bedeutet dies, dass er auch auf dem Brustschild so wiedergegeben wird. Aber auch bei Tieren mit eigenem Namen wird der sonst übliche Brustschildtext „Original Steiff" nicht selten werkseitig verwendet.

Artikelbeschreibung: Hier werden die aus den Katalogen entnommenen Angaben über Material, Farbe, Ausstattung usw. wiedergegeben.

In der Spalte **„SERIE"** wird die Steiff-Seriennummer und 1986 bis 1990 die EAN-Nummer genannt.

Die Spalte **„ART.-NO"** zeigt die Steiff-Artikelnummer (ab 1991 EAN-Nummer) **fett** gedruckt, wenn diese auf der Fahne verwendet wird.

Der Zeitraum **„PERIOD"** entspricht den Angaben in den Katalogen. Sind hier Lücken, wurde der Artikel in den entsprechenden Katalogen nicht angeboten.

Unter **„PR."** stehen die Preisgruppen, wie im folgenden näher beschrieben.

Die Kategorie **„INFO"** gibt hauptsächlich Größen bzw. Farben an, darüber hinaus Abweichungen zu der Artikelbeschreibung.

Usage

*Writing in **italic print** indicates the English language.*

The following example explains how each article is presented and described.

***Illustration**: Due to clearness and availability not all existing sizes or colors can always be shown on the photographs. If any variations are not shown they are referred to in the text caption.*

*This is the **Steiff article name** in German and English. If it is in **bold** print, then it also appears on the Steiff name tag. But even if the animals have their own names, the factory has sometimes used the name tag "Original Steiff".*

***Description**: This reflects the information taken from the various Steiff catalogs about the material used, the color, accessories, etc.*

*The column entitled **"SERIE"** indicates the Steiff serial number. From 1986 to 1990, the EAN number is printed.*

*The column entitled **"ART.-NO"** indicates the Steiff article number (from 1991, the EAN number) in **bold** print if used on the label.*

*The column entitled **"PERIOD"** indicates the time-period the article was listed in the Steiff catalogs. If there are any gaps within the years, then the article was not offered in the catalogs of these years.*

*The column entitled **"PR."** indicates the price groups, which are more fully explained below.*

*The column entitled **"INFO"** mainly indicates sizes, colors, and any variations.*

Preisgruppen

Die Einteilung in Preisgruppen lautet:

1		bis	25,00 €
1-2	12,50 €	bis	37,50 €
2	25,00 €	bis	50,00 €
2-3	37,50 €	bis	75,00 €
3	50,00 €	bis	125,00 €
3-4	75,00 €	bis	187,50 €
4	125,00 €	bis	250,00 €
4-5	187,50 €	bis	375,00 €
5	250,00 €	bis	500,00 €
5-6	375,00 €	bis	875,00 €
6	500,00 €	bis	1.250,00 €
6-7	875,00 €	bis	1.875,00 €
7	1.250,00 €	bis	2.500,00 €
7-8	1.875,00 €	bis	3.750,00 €
8	2.500,00 €	bis	5.000,00 €
8-9	3.750,00 €	bis	6.250,00 €
9		über	6.250,00 €

Die Preisgruppen wurden gegenüber der Ausgabe 1995 angepasst. Alle Preise werden jetzt in € (Euro) angegeben.

Artikel aus dem laufenden Steiff Programm werden erstmals bewertet. Die Einordnung erfolgt in der Preisgruppe, die den Händlerverkaufspreis beinhaltet.

Durch die Einführung von Zwischengruppen wurde ein größerer Spielraum, der noch konkretere Einordnungen zulässt, geschaffen.

Ab Preisgruppe 6 wurden die Preisangaben allgemein erhöht. So wurde die nach oben offene Preisgruppe 9 auf „mehr als € 6.250,00", dies entspricht DM 12.223,94, angehoben. Artikel können damit bis zu diesem Betrag in die Gruppen eingeordnet werden. Dies ist aufgrund der aktuellen Preisentwicklung notwendig geworden.

Selbstverständlich ändert dies nichts daran, dass Angebot und Nachfrage, Qualität und persönliche Prioritäten entscheidenden Einfluss auf die Preise haben.

Ein perfekt erhaltenes Steiff Tier, das zudem noch Knopf, Fahne und Brustschild vorweist, wird mit Sicherheit einen wesentlich höheren Preis erzielen, als ein bespieltes Exemplar der gleichen Art.

Das heißt jedoch nicht, dass nur perfekte Stücke sammelwürdig sind. Ein gut erhaltenes Steiff Tier, bleibt auch ohne diese Zeichen zweifelsfrei erkennbar und besitzt ebenso seinen Charme, seinen Charakter und seinen Wert.

Jeder muss für sich, seinen Geschmack und seinen Geldbeutel eine eigene Entscheidung treffen. Ein

Price Categories

The price categories are divided as follows:

1		*up to*	*25.00 €*
1-2	*12.50 €*	*up to*	*37.50 €*
2	*25.00 €*	*up to*	*50.00 €*
2-3	*37.50 €*	*up to*	*75.00 €*
3	*50.00 €*	*up to*	*125.00 €*
3-4	*75.00 €*	*up to*	*187.50 €*
4	*125.00 €*	*up to*	*250.00 €*
4-5	*187.50 €*	*up to*	*375.00 €*
5	*250.00 €*	*up to*	*500.00 €*
5-6	*375.00 €*	*up to*	*875.00 €*
6	*500.00 €*	*up to*	*1,250.00 €*
6-7	*875.00 €*	*up to*	*1,875.00 €*
7	*1,250.00 €*	*up to*	*2,500.00 €*
7-8	*1,875.00 €*	*up to*	*3,750.00 €*
8	*2,500.00 €*	*up to*	*5,000.00 €*
8-9	*3,750.00 €*	*up to*	*6,250.00 €*
9		*over*	*6,250.00 €*

Price categories have been subjected to changes from those cited in the 1995 edition. All prices are now quoted in € (Euro).

For the first time, items from the current Steiff range have also been categorized. Products are assigned to a particular category on the basis of their retail sales price.

The introduction of subcategories has provided more flexibility, and thus more accurate grouping.

From price category 6 upwards, prices have been subject to a general increase. For example, the open-ended price category 9 was increased to "more than € 6,250.00", corresponding to DM 12,223.94. It is therefore possible to categorize items up to this limit. This step was necessary due to the general inflation in prices.

Of course, this does not change the fact that supply and demand, quality and personal priorities have a considerable impact on prices.

A perfectly preserved animal by Steiff that also still has its button, tag and chest tag will certainly obtain a much higher price than one of the same model in used condition.

Of course, this does not mean that only perfect examples are collectors' items. Even without the above markings, a well-preserved animal from Steiff remains undeniably recognizable and also possesses its charm, character and value.

Individual decisions must be taken based on personal taste and financial situation. A price in

Katalogpreis kann immer nur eine Orientierung sein.

Bitte beachten Sie, dass beim grenzüberschreitenden Handel evtl. Frachtkosten, Zölle und Einfuhrsteuern entstehen. Diese Kosten haben wir nicht berücksichtigt.

Die Wechselkurse von Euro zu den jeweiligen Landeswährungen können Sie z.B. dem Wirtschaftsteil Ihrer Zeitung entnehmen. Der Wechselkurs € zu DM lautet: 1 € = 1,95583 DM.

a catalogue can only serve as a guide.

Please note that foreign trade may incur freight costs, customs charges and import duties, which are not included in the above prices.

The exchange rate of the Euro (€) to currencies in other countries can, for example, be taken from the business pages in local newspapers. The Deutschmark exchange rate to the Euro € is: 1 € = 1.95583 DM.

Zeitliche Einordnung von Steiff-Erzeugnissen aufgrund der Markenzeichen: Knopf, Fähnchen und Brustschild

Classification of Steiff products according to year of production based on trademarks: button, label, and chest tag

Ab 1947

Die **US-Zonen-Fahne** wurde am Körper angebracht, eingenäht in eine Naht, meist am rechten Arm oder Bein. Verwendung von 1947-1953.

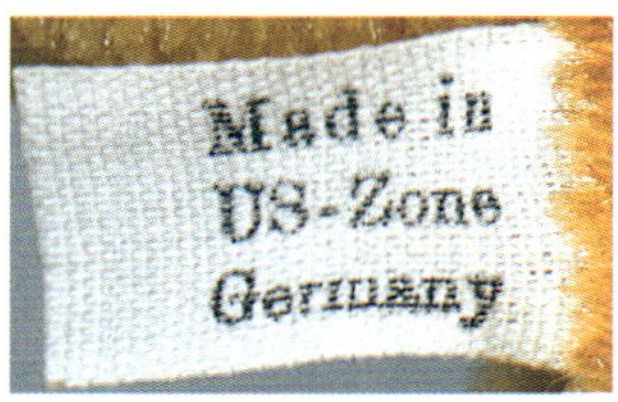

From 1947

*The **US Zone label** was sewn into one of the body seams, usually on the right arm or leg. It was used from 1947 -1953.*

Zu dieser Zeit wurde eine Vielzahl von **Knöpfen** verwendet. Zum einen die Restbestände aus der Zeit vor 1942 (heruntergezogenes „f“),

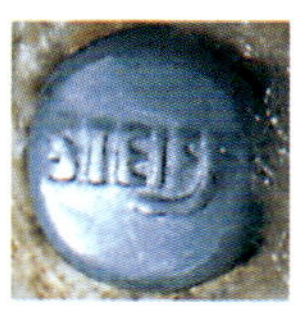
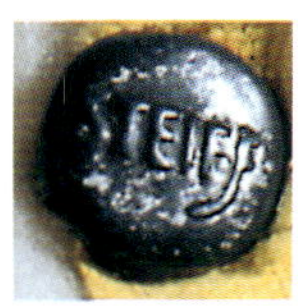

*During this time, a number of different **buttons** were used. One of these was the button left over from the production period prior to 1942 (note that the "f" is underscored),*

weiterhin ein blanker **Knopf** - diesen auch in blau bemalter Version,

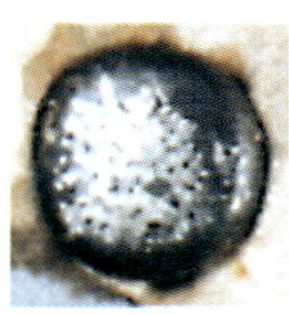

*a blank **button** was also used, somtimes painted blue.*

sowie einen **Knopf** mit „STEIFF“ in Groß-Druckbuchstaben, ohne heruntergezogenes „f“.

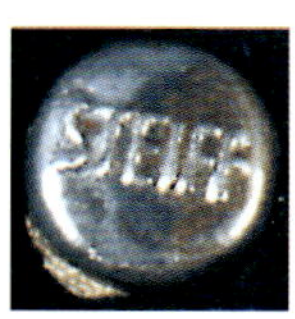
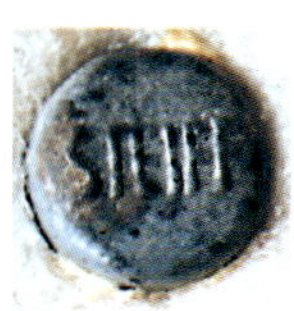

*and a **button** with the word "STEIFF" printed in block capitals, without descending "f"s.*

Die durch den Knopf befestigte Fahne war zwischen 1947 und 1952 gelb, in wenigen Fällen auch weiß (1948 - 1950), anfangs aus Papier, später aus Leinengewebe und zeigt den Namen STEIFF sowie den weiteren Text in Druckschrift. Ab ca. 1950 wurden auf der Rückseite der Fahne Informationen über das verwendete Material gedruckt.

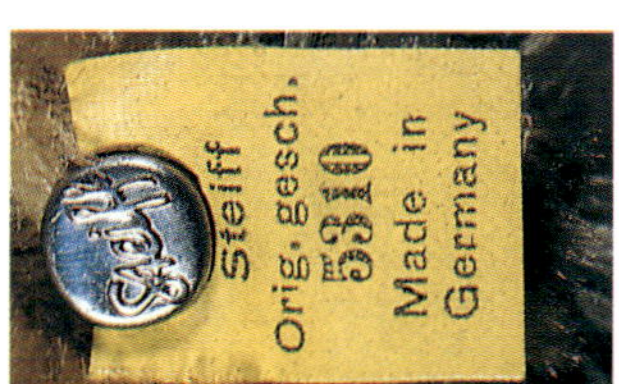

Between 1947 and 1952, a yellow label fastened with the button was used. Occasionally it was white (from 1948 - 1950). At first it was made of paper, then later of linen fabric. It shows the name STEIFF, along with the additional text in block letters. From about 1950, information about the material used was printed on the reverse side.

Von ca. 1952 ist die nebenstehende **Fahne** mit der etwas veränderten Druckschrift. Sie zeigt, dass zu dieser Zeit auch Buchstabenzusätze (hier „M" für Mecki „Maid") hinter der Artikel-Nummer angegeben wurden.

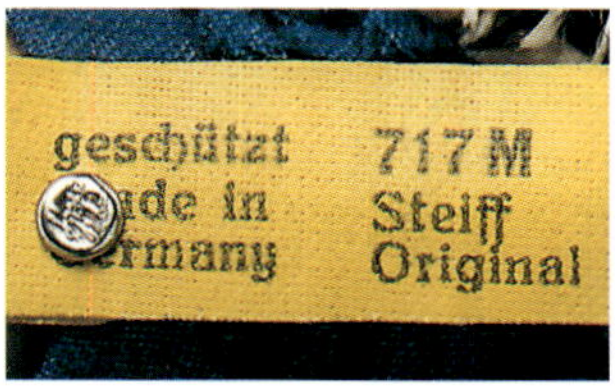

*The **label** shown at the left is from approximately 1952. The printing is somewhat different, and clearly shows that in this phase, also letters were added to the tag after the article number (See: "M" for Mecki "Maid").*

Auch bei den **Brustschildern** wurde auf die bis ca. 1941 verwendeten Exemplare zurückgegriffen, d.h. es wurde der eckige Bärenkopf mit der angedeuteten Schnauze, sowie Nase und Mund, verwendet. Die Schrift für Tiername bzw. „Original Steiff" ist rotbraun.

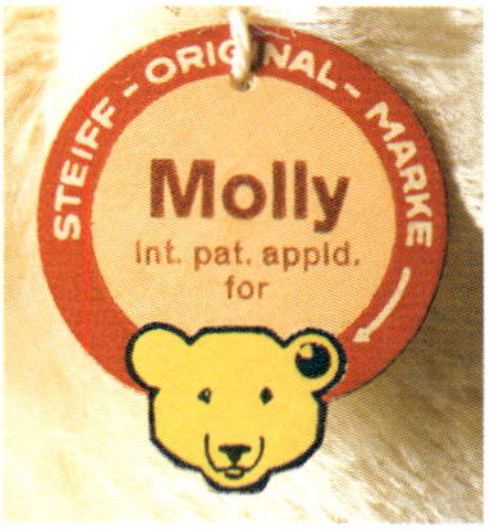

*The **chest tags** which were used up to about 1941 were also used during this period. Note the angular bear´s head with the muzzle, nose, and mouth drawn in. The name of the animal or "Steiff Original" is printed in reddish-brown.*

Ab 1952/53

Neben diesem alten Bärenkopf-**Brustschild** gibt es noch eine neuere Version. Diese zeigt einen oben abgerundeten Kopf, nur noch mit Nase und Mund. Auch bei diesem Zeichen ist die Schrift rotbraun.

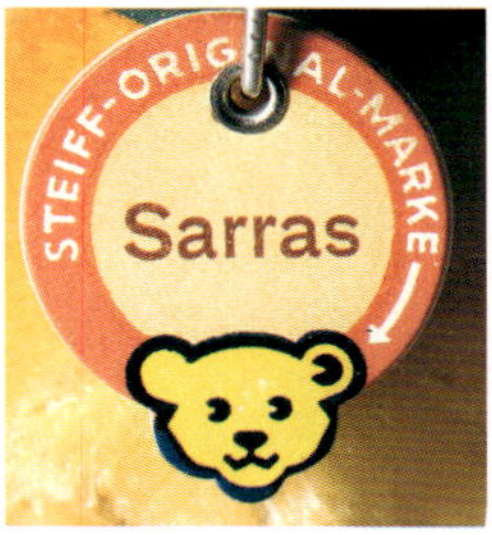

From 1952/53

*A newer version of this old bear´s head **chest tag** also exists. On this one, the bear´s head is rounded at the top, and it only has a nose and mouth. The letters are also in reddish-brown.*

Der Nickel-**Knopf** mit dem „Steiff"-Schriftzug in Schreibschrift wird eingeführt. Dieser bleibt bis zum Ende der 60er-Jahre in Verwendung, d.h. auch nach Einführung der neuen Artikel-Nummer mit Schrägstrich wird dieser Knopf noch benutzt.

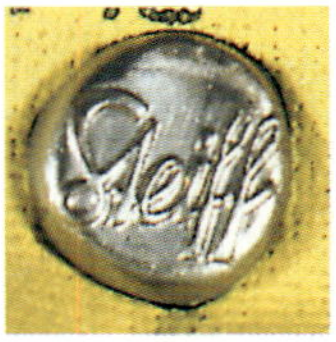

*The nickel **button** with the word "Steiff" written in script is now introduced. This button was used up to the end of the 1960s. Its use was continued even after introduction of the new article numbers separated by a slash.*

Ab Mitte der 60er-Jahre wird der Schreibschrift-**Knopf** leicht verändert. Der Schriftzug ist insgesamt etwas fetter und die Bögen der beiden „f" sind kürzer.

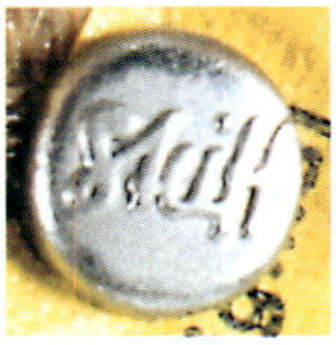

*In the mid 1960s, the script style used for the word STEIFF on the **button** was changed somewhat. The script became a little thicker and the loops of both of the Steiff "fs" are shorter.*

Auch die **Fahne** verändert sich zu diesem Zeitpunkt. Das Material ist jetzt ausschließlich Leinengewebe. Der Namenszug „Steiff" wird jetzt in Schreibschrift gedruckt. Der Zusatz „geschützt" entfällt.

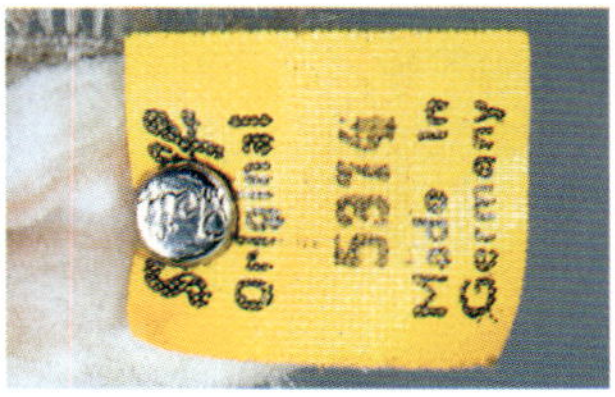

*The **label** was also changed at the same time and was henceforth made exclusively from linen. The STEIFF name is now in script and the word "registered" has been deleted.*

Ab Mitte der 50er-Jahre wird diese **Fahne** um das Feld „Preis" verlängert. Sie wird bis ca. 1970 verwendet. Oftmals fehlt dieser Teil, da er beim Kauf oder später abgetrennt wurde. Anhand der unterschiedlichen Schrift bei der Artikelnummer läßt sich dies jedoch leicht feststellen.

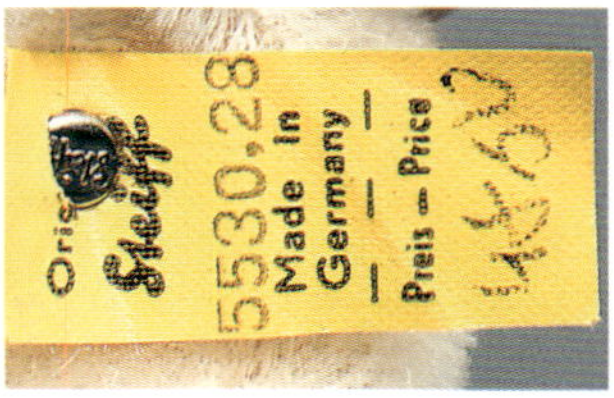

*From the mid 1950s onward, the **label** was lengthened to have more room for a price section. This label remained in use until approx. 1970. Often, the price portion of the label was removed by the buyer after purchase. The different typeset used for the article number is still an easy means of identifying the production date.*

1953 wird erstmals ein verändertes **Brustschild** verwendet. Der Bärenkopf ist jetzt gänzlich in runden Formen gehalten. Das Schild trägt eine blaue Aufschrift (die rotbraune Schrift kommt nur noch 1953 in einigen Fällen vor). Dieser Typ Brustschild bleibt bis 1971 unverändert.

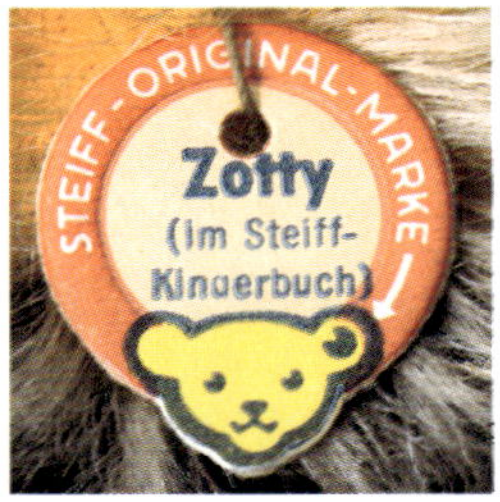

*In 1953, a new **chest tag** was introduced for the first time. The shape of the bear´s head is totally round. The writing on the tag is blue (the red-brown letters were only used very seldom in 1953). This chest tag remained unchanged until 1971.*

Ab 1969

Wieder ein neuer **Knopf**, der sogenannte Linsenknopf, eine Hohlniete aus Nickel, wird eingeführt. Die Verwendung dauert bis ca. 1977.

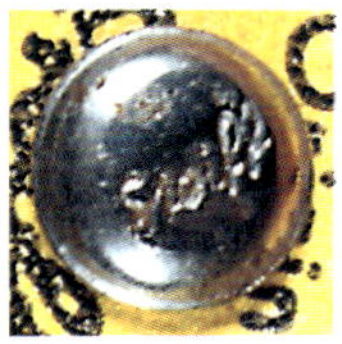

From 1969

*Another new **button** was introduced - the so-called "lentil" button - which was a hollow nickel rivet. This button was used until approx. 1977.*

1969/70 gibt es auch eine Veränderung der **Fahne**. Das Zusatzfeld „Preis" entfällt wieder. Dafür wird die Fläche, auf der die Artikel-Nummer gedruckt ist entsprechend länger. Dieses letzte Leinenfähnchen wird bis 1980 verwendet.

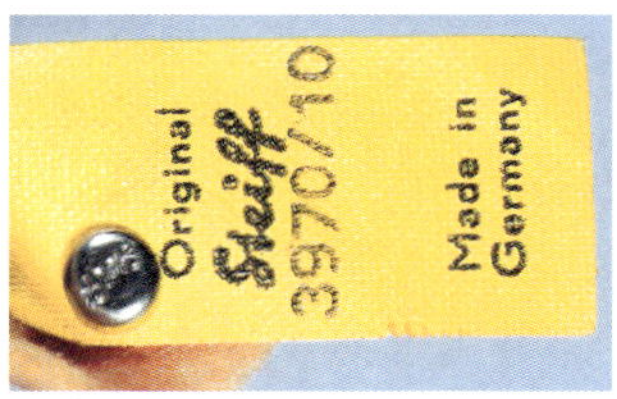

*In 1969/70 the **label** was also changed. The "price" field was deleted again and the space where the article number was printed was lengthened instead. This last linen label was used until 1980.*

Ab 1972 gibt es das neue, bis heute noch in Verwendung befindliche, **Brustschild**. Die Marke ist jetzt rund und in eine gelbe und eine rote Hälfte geteilt.

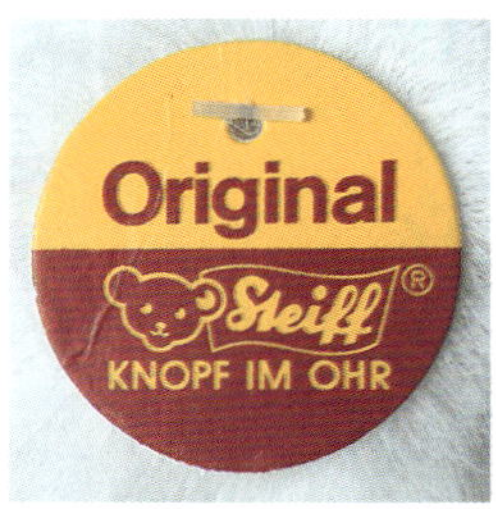

*In 1972 a new **chest tag** was introduced, which is still in use today. The trademark is now round, with one half yellow and one half red.*

Ab 1978

Ein zweiteiliger Messingknopf, wieder mit eingeprägtem „Steiff" Schriftzug, wird eingeführt. Bis 1982 hat dieser **Knopf** einen Durchmesser von 8, ab 1983 9mm. Es handelt sich dabei um den heute noch aktuellen Knopf.

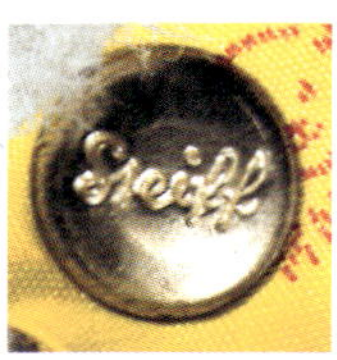

From 1978

*A riveted brass button was introduced again, with the name "Steiff" stamped in script letters. Up to 1982, the **button** diameter was 8mm. From 1983, the button diameter was 9mm. This button is still used today.*

Gleichzeitig wird für nur kurze Zeit zwischen 1978 und 1980 ein goldfarbener **Knopf**, der dem Schreibschriftknopf aus den 50er und 60er-Jahren gleicht, verwendet.

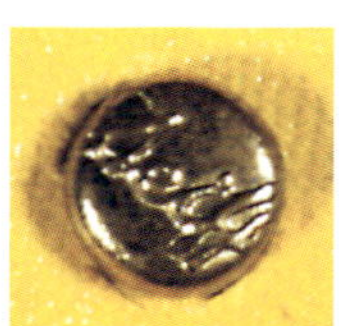

*A gold-colored **button** was used simultaneously for a short time, between 1978 and 1980. It resembled the script button used in the 50s and 60s.*

Ab 1981 wird eine doppelt gelegte Stoff-**Fahne** in gelb mit roter Aufschrift verwendet. 1981 ist die Artikel-Nummer in sehr kleiner Form eingewebt.

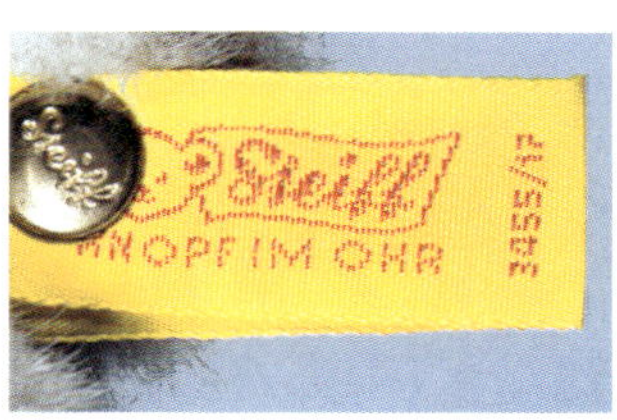

*From 1981 onwards, a double cloth **label** in yellow with red lettering was used. And also in 1981, the article number is woven into the cloth in very small figures.*

1982 bis zum Ende der Verwendung in 1987 wird auf der Stoff-**Fahne** die Artikel-Nummer wesentlich größer dargestellt.

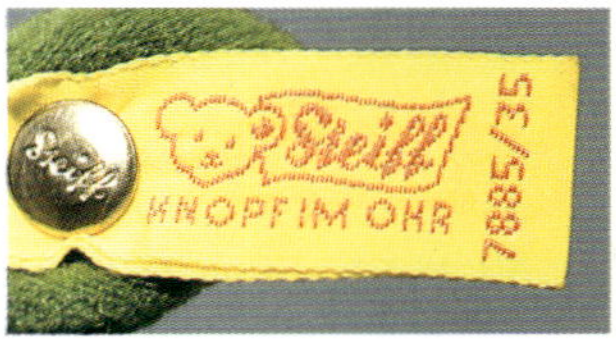

*In 1982 until the end of its use in 1987, the article number appears a lot larger on the cloth **label**.*

1986/87 wird ein neues Material für die **Fahne** verwendet, ein sogenanntes Printband. Bis 1989 wird die Artikel-Nummer, ab 1990 die neu eingeführte EAN-Nummer aufgedruckt. Diese Fahne wird noch heute verwendet.

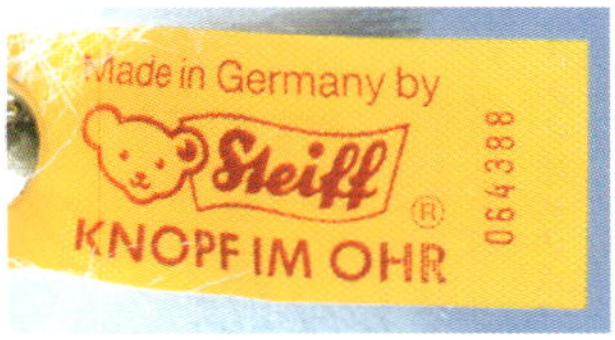

*In 1986/87 a different material was introduced for the **label** - so-called printed tape. Up to 1989 the article number was printed on it. In 1990, the new EAN number was introduced and printed on the tag. This tag is still in use today.*

Weiterhin gibt bzw. gab es folgende Knöpfe, Fahnen bzw. Brustschilder

The following buttons, labels, and chest tags were/are also used.

Der zweiteilige Messing**knopf**, jedoch ohne eingeprägten „Steiff" Schriftzug, wird ab 1984 zur Kennzeichnung der 2. Wahl verwendet.

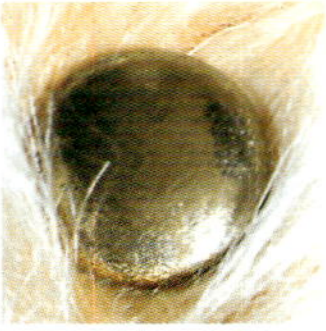

*The riveted brass **button**, without the stamped "Steiff" legend was used to identify "second class" articles from 1984 onwards.*

Für Repliken wird ab 1980 eine doppelt gelegte Stoff-Fahne in weiß mit schwarzer Aufschrift verwendet. Bis 1981 ist die Artikel-Nummer in sehr kleiner Form eingewebt.

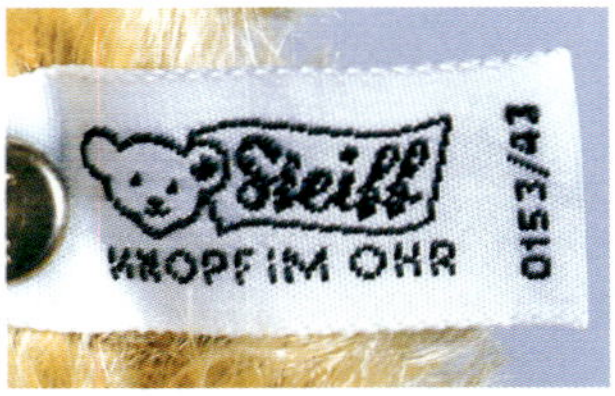

From 1980 onwards, a white double cloth label with black lettering was used for replicas. Until 1981, the article number was woven into it using very small figures.

1982 bis zum Ende der Verwendung in 1986 wird auf der Stoff-**Fahne** die Artikel-Nummer wesentlich größer dargestellt.

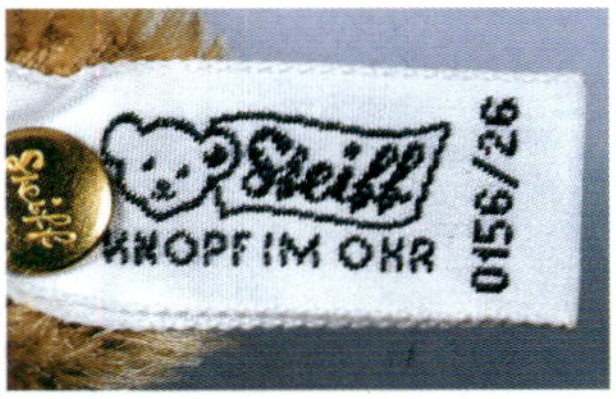

*From 1982 until the end of its use in 1986, the article number was shown a lot larger on the cloth **label**.*

1987 wird ein neues Material für die **Fahne** verwendet, ein sogenanntes Printband. Bis 1989 wird die Artikel-Nummer, ab 1990 die neu eingeführte EAN-Nummer aufgedruckt. Diese Fahne wird noch heute für Repliken verwendet.

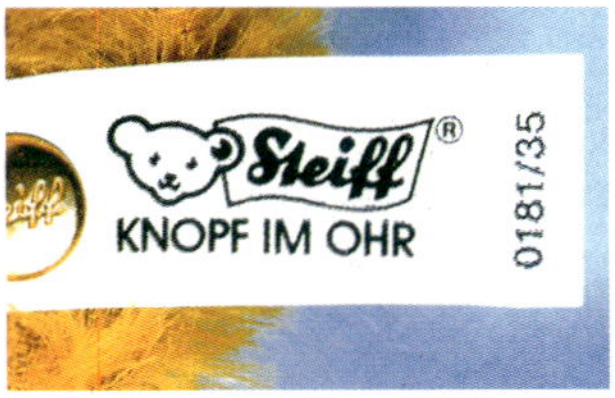

*In 1987 a new material was used for the **label** - so-called print tape. Up to 1989, the article number was printed on it. In 1990, the new EAN number was introduced. This tag is still used for replicas today.*

Ab 1994 wird die Printband-**Fahne** auch zur Kennzeichnung von Sonderserien verwendet. Im Gegensatz zu den offiziellen Steiff-Repliken ist die Druckfarbe rot.

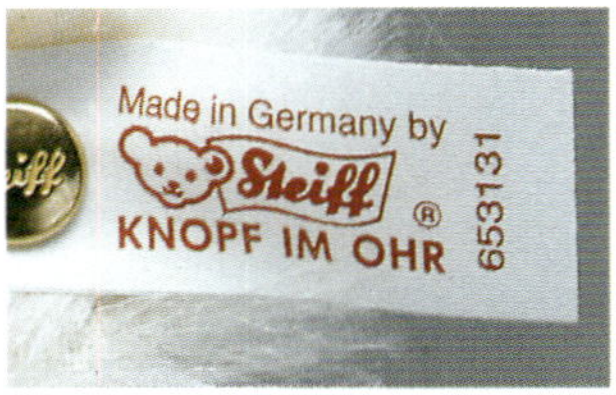

*The print tape **label** has been in use since 1994, also to identify special series production. Contrary to the label for official Steiff replicas, the print is in red.*

Für Repliken und Sonderausgaben werden sehr häufig Nachbildungen der Original-Brustschilder aus der jeweiligen Zeit verwendet. Es gibt jedoch auch die unterschiedlichsten Anhänger, wie z.B. Plaketten, kleine Heftchen mit Beschreibungen und anderes. Ein detailliertes Aufführen würde an dieser Stelle zu weit führen. In den meisten Fällen können sie jedoch bei den Abbildungen im entsprechenden Kapitel deutlich erkannt werden.

Die Rückseiten von Fahnen und Brustschildern enthalten ebenfalls Angaben, z.B. über verwendete Materialien, Stückzahlen von Limitierungen, Kundenname oder enthaltenen Mottenschutz. Die bisherigen Erkenntnisse reichen jedoch nicht aus, um eine lückenlose zeitliche Erfassung vornehmen zu können.

Alle gezeigten und genannten Informationen können Ihnen - zusammen mit den exakten Angaben bei den jeweiligen Artikeln betr. die Sortimentszugehörigkeit - dabei helfen, eine relativ genaue zeitliche Zuordnung zu treffen.

Bitte beachten Sie jedoch, dass die Termine, zu denen neue Knöpfe, Fahnen oder Brustschilder eingeführt wurden, nie exakt an einem Stichtag begonnen haben oder endeten.

Very often, reproductions of the original chest tags of a particular time period are used for replicas and special editions. There are, however, a number of different things attached such as little plaques, information booklets, etc. It's not possible to go into great detail here, but you will find that, in most cases, they are easily recognizable in the photographs shown.

The reverse sides of labels and chest tags also include information about what material was used, limited edition quantities, customer names or even moth protection. Current knowledge on this subject is not sufficient to provide a perfect chronological assessment.

All of the information given - along with the exact details shown next to each article about its respective assortment properties – can, however, provide you with enough information to be able to judge relatively precisely to which time period an article belongs.

Please note, however, that the dates listed for the introduction of new buttons, labels, or chest tags are not precise, as they were never officially introduced or discontinued on specifically determined dates.

Erläuterungen zu den verwendeten Serien-/Artikelnummern bis zur aktuellen Europäischen Artikel-Nummer (EAN)

Das von **1947 bis 1958** verwendete Nummernsystem entspricht dem aus der Zeit bis 1941.

Die ersten beiden Ziffern stehen für die Serie (Tiergattung), so z. B. 18 für Dackel, 44 für Katzen, 64 für Schweine, 71 für Wollminiaturen, 79 für Handspieltiere usw.

Teilweise wird ein Buchstabe als 3. Stelle hinzugefügt um eine weitere Unterteilung zu ermöglichen, so z. B. 44 G für Katze Susy oder 44 K für Katze Kitty. Sie wird auf 2 x 2 Ziffern erweitert, wenn zwei Serien betroffen sind, z. B. 71 64 für ein Woll-Schwein oder 79 44 für eine Handspiel-Katze. Auf der Fahne wird die Seriennummer nur in einem bestimmten Zeitraum vor 1941 angegeben.

Die vierstellige Artikel-Nummer hat folgende Bedeutung:

1. Stelle (Tausender) gibt die Stellung an:
   - 1 = stehend
   - 2 = liegend
   - 3 = sitzend
   - 4 = aufwartend
   - 5 = gegliedert

Information about the use of the serial and article numbers, up to introduction of the current European Article Number (EAN)

*The numbering system used from **1947 to 1958** is identical to that used up to 1941.*

The first two numbers represent the series (type of species). For example: 18 for dachshund, 44 for cats, 64 for pigs, 71 for wool miniatures, 79 for glove puppets, etc.

Sometimes, a letter was introduced as the third digit, in order to create a further classification. For example: 44 G for Susy Cat or 44 K for Kitty Cat. The numbers were expanded to two double digits to represent two different series. For example: 71 64 for a wool pig or 79 44 for a hand-cat. The serial number only appears on the label for a certain period prior to 1941.

The four-digit article number is explained as follows:

1st digit (thousands) indicates the animal's position:
- *1 = standing*
- *2 = lying*
- *3 = sitting*
- *4 = sitting up (begging)*
- *5 = jointed*

6 = jung
7 = karikiert

2. Stelle (Hunderter) gibt die Stoffart an:
1 = Filz
3 = Mohair
4 = Samt
5 = Wollplüsch
6 = Kunstseidenplüsch (bis 1950) bzw. Dralonplüsch (ab 1955)
8 = Holz
9 = Stahl

3. & 4. Stelle (Zehner & Einer) geben die Höhe in cm an: z. B.
10 = 10 cm Kopfhöhe oder
35 = 35 cm Kopfhöhe.

Hinter dem Komma stehenden Zahlen oder Buchstaben bedeuten:
0 = ohne Räder
1 = Druckstimme
2 = Doppeldruck-, Brumm- oder Ziehstimme
3 = mit Musikwerk
ST = mit Steuerung
ex = Exzenterräder

Die Buchstaben br, c, g oder w stehen für die Farben braun, caramel, gold oder weiß, die Buchstaben M und B für Maid und Bub.

Diese Einteilung bedeutet, dass eine Unterscheidung bei gleichgroßen und gleich ausgestatteten Artikeln nur über die Serie möglich ist, denn der gegliederte, aus Mohair hergestellte Bär mit 43 cm Größe und einer Brummstimme trägt die Artikelnummer 5343,2 ebenso wie der entsprechende Schimpanse. Mit Seriennummer wird es aber eindeutig, denn der Bär hat die Nummer 12 5343,2, der Affe 9 5343,2.

Ab **1959** gibt es ein geändertes Nummernsystem. Die Serie (Tiergattung) wird auf drei Ziffern erweitert. Dies ist notwendig geworden, um für neu ins Sortiment aufgenommene Tierarten freie Nummern zu haben. Weiterhin wurden die Buchstabenergänzungen sowie zwei gleichzeitig verwendete Seriennummern (s.o.) in die neuen Seriennummern eingearbeitet. Bestehende Nummern wurden meist durch das Anhängen einer „0“ erweitert. So steht jetzt 180 für Dackel, 440 für Katzen usw.

Die Artikel-Nummer ist weiterhin vierstellig und behält weitgehend ihre bisherige Bedeutung:

1. Stelle (Tausender) = Stellung, bei Wagen und Fahrzeugen Zahl der Räder:

0 = Handspieltiere 8 = Puppen & Figuren
1 bis 7 wie bis 1958 9 = Mechanik

2. Stelle (Hunderter) = Stoffart:
0 = Filz
1 & 2 reserviert für Größenangaben bis 299 cm

6 = young
7 = in caricature

2nd Digit (hundreds) indicates the type of fabric:
1 = felt
3 = mohair
4 = velvet
5 = wool plush
6 = artificial silk plush (up to 1950) resp. Dralon plush from 1955
8 = wood
9 = steel

3rd and 4th Digits (tens and ones) indicate the size in cm. For example:
10 = 10 cm tall, or
35 = 35 cm tall.

Numbers or letters after the decimal indicate:
0 = without wheels
1 = squeaker (press voice)
2 = double press voice, growler, or pull cord voice
3 = with musical box
ST = steering
ex = on eccentric wheels

The letters br, c, g or w stand for the colors brown, caramel, gold, or white. The letters M and B stand for girl (Maid) and Boy (Bub).

With this method of classification, the only means of differentiating between articles of the same size and equipment/accessories is by the serial number. A jointed mohair bear, 43 cm tall, which growls has the article number 5343.2, just like the chimpanzee. But the serial number differentiates between the two, because the bear has number 12 5343.2 and the ape number 9 5343.2.

The numbering system was changed in ***1959****. The series (species) was expanded to include three digits. This was necessary in order to have numbers available for newly introduced animals. Supplementary letters as well as two simultaneously used serial numbers (see above) have also been covered with the new system. Existing numbers were usually supplemented by attaching an “0” to them. That's why we now have the number 180 for dachshund, and 440 for cats, etc.*

The article number still has four digits and, generally speaking, represents the same information as previously:

1st Digit (thousands) = position, number of wheels for wagons and vehicles:

0 = glove puppet 8 = dolls and figures
1 to 7 same as before 1958 9 = mechanical

2nd Digit (hundreds) = type of fabric:
0 = felt

3 = Mohair
4 = Samt
5 = Wollplüsch
6 = Dralonplüsch
7 = Kunststoff, Gummi
8 = Holz
9 = Eisen

3. & 4. Stelle (Zehner & Einer) = Kopfhöhe in cm

1. Stelle nach dem Komma:
0 = ohne Räder
1 = Fahrtiere, Nachziehtiere
2 = Reittiere mit starren Rädern
3 = Reittiere mit Lenkung
4 = Wolltiere
5 = Ersatzteile
6 = Musiktiere
7 = Bub
8 = Mädel
9 = Schautiere, Sonderausführungen

2. Stelle nach dem Komma = Farbe:
0 = Normal
1 = Gold
2 = Caramel
3 = Braun
4 = Weiß
5 = Grau
6 = Schwarz
7 = Bunt
8 = Rot
9 = Gefleckt

Auch bei diesem System wird die Seriennummer benötigt, um eindeutig ein Tier zu bezeichnen.

Bereits **1965** findet eine erneute Änderung des Nummernsystems statt. Allerdings wird nur die dreistellige Seriennummer komplett neu vergeben.

Bisher wurden z. B. alle Dackel unter der Seriennummer 180 geführt. Jetzt wird folgende Aufteilung vorgenommen: 414 = Waldi, 415 = Zieh-Waldi, 416 = Bazi, 418 = Hexie, 419 = Raudi und 420 = Lumpi.

Alle anderen Teile des Nummernsystems bleiben unverändert. Für die auf der Fahne gedruckte Artikelnummer ändert sich folglich auch nichts.

Nur drei Jahre später, nämlich **1968**, wird das Nummernsystem komplett neu organisiert. Die Seriennummer entfällt völlig. Es gibt nur noch eine vierstellige Artikelnummer über die jeder Artikel eindeutig zu identifizieren ist. Es folgt, getrennt durch einen Schrägstrich, die zweistellige Größenangabe in cm.

Während der Umstellungsphase in den Jahren 1968/69 wurde jedoch relativ häufig die neue Artikelnummer statt mit Schrägstrich weiterhin mit einem Komma als Trennzeichen zur Größenangabe gedruckt.

1 & 2 reserved for size indications up to 299 cm
3 = mohair
4 = velvet
5 = wool plush
6 = Dralon plush
7 = synthetic, rubber
8 = wood
9 = iron

3rd & 4th Digits (tens and ones) = height in cm

1st Digit after Decimal:
0 = without wheels
1 = moving animals, pull-type animals
2 = riding animals with rigid wheels
3 = riding animals with steering
4 = wool animals
5 = spare parts
6 = musical animals
7 = boy
8 = girl
9 = Display animals, special editions

2nd Digit after Decimal = color:
0 = normal
1 = gold
2 = caramel
3 = brown
4 = white
5 = grey
6 = black
7 = bright and colorful
8 = red
9 = spotted

With this system, the serial number was essential to clearly identify an animal.

*The numbering system was changed again in **1965** already, but only the three-digit serial number was newly allocated.*

Up to then, for example, all dachshunds were given the serial number 180. The new system set up the following classification: 414 = Waldi, 415 = Pull-type Waldi, 416 = Bazi, 418 = Hexie, 419 = Raudi and 420 = Lumpi.

All other parts of the numbering system remained unchanged, as did the article number printed on the label.

*But only three years later, in **1968**, the numbering system was completely re-organized, and the serial number completely deleted. Now there is only a 4-digit article number which allows the unambiguous identification of each article. Only the 2-digit size designation in cm, which is separated by a slash, follows this number.*

During the transition phase in 1968/69, the new article number was, however, often printed with a comma separating the size information from

1986 wird erstmals die EAN (Europäische Artikel Nummer) im Katalog angegeben. Bis 1990 wird jedoch parallel dazu weiterhin die seit 1968 verwendete Artikelnummer gedruckt. Erst ab **1991** wird ausschließlich die EAN-Nummer verwendet. Es handelt sich dabei um eine sechsstellige Zahl, die für jeden Artikel getrennt vergeben wird. Aus der Zahl allein sind für den Sammler keine detaillierten Daten über den Artikel abzulesen.

the number, instead of using a slash.

*In 1986 the EAN (European Article Number) was used in the catalog for the first time. However, up to 1990, the article numbers in use since 1968, are also printed in parallel. Exclusive use of the EAN numbers began in **1991**. This is a six-digit number which is individually allocated to each article. The number alone does not give the collector any information about the article.*

Erläuterungen zu den verwendeten Materialien innerhalb der Produktionszeit 1947-1999

Welche Materialien im Einzelnen verwendet wurden, lässt sich bei den Beschreibungen zu den jeweiligen Artikeln nachlesen.

An dieser Stelle möchte ich noch einige Hinweise geben, die es ermöglichen, eine zeitliche Einordnung mit Hilfe der Materialien zu präzisieren.

Kunstseidenplüsch wurde nur noch kurze Zeit nach der Wiederaufnahme der Spielzeugproduktion verwendet. Nach 1950 werden keine Tiere aus diesem Material mehr hergestellt.

Ab 1955 werden erstmals Tiere aus Dralon (später auch Orlon, Dolan etc.) angeboten. Dieses Material spielt bis zum Ende der 70er-Jahre eine Rolle.

Ebenfalls ab 1955 gibt es die ersten Schaumgummi-Füllungen. Bis zu diesem Zeitpunkt wird Holzwolle, bei weichen Tieren Holzwolle gemischt mit Watte, verwendet.

Diese ersten Schaumgummi-Füllungen haben mit den Schaumstoff-Flocken-Füllungen vom Anfang der 60er-Jahre gemeinsam, dass sie sich nach einiger Zeit zersetzen.

Formgeschäumte Artikel, d. h. die Füllung besteht aus einem speziell gefertigten Schäumling, gibt es erst ab Ende der 60er-Jahre.

Die Umstellung von Glas- auf Kunststoffaugen erfolgt nach und nach in den 60er-Jahren.

Im gleichen Zeitraum werden die bisher verwendeten Stimmen aus Pappe und Leinen von Kunststoffstimmen abgelöst. Die Farbe des Leinens bei den von der Fa. Steiff verwendeten Stimmen ist immer rot.

The materials used in production from 1947-1999

The exact materials used for each animal are indicated next to the description of each article.

In this section, I would like to provide you with some additional information to help you identify specific time periods based on the materials used.

Synthetic plush (artificial silk or rayon) was only used for a short time when production was resumed after the war. After 1950, this material was no longer used.

In 1955, Dralon was used for the first time. (later also called Orlon, Dolan etc.) This material was used until the end of the 70s.

In 1955, the first foam rubber stuffings were used. Up to that time, excelsior (wood wool) was used, and soft animals were filled with a mixture of excelsior (wood shavings) and cotton.

The foam rubber stuffing and the foam flakes used in the early 60s both disintegrated after a while.

Pre-formed foam articles, where the stuffing consisted of special foam, were only introduced at the end of the 60s.

The transition from glass eyes to plastic eyes, was made slowly and successively in the 60s.

At the same time, the voice boxes which were made of cardboard and linen, were replaced by synthetic ones. The color of the linen STEIFF uses for the voice boxes is always red.

Baeren & Teddybaeren

Bears & Teddy bears

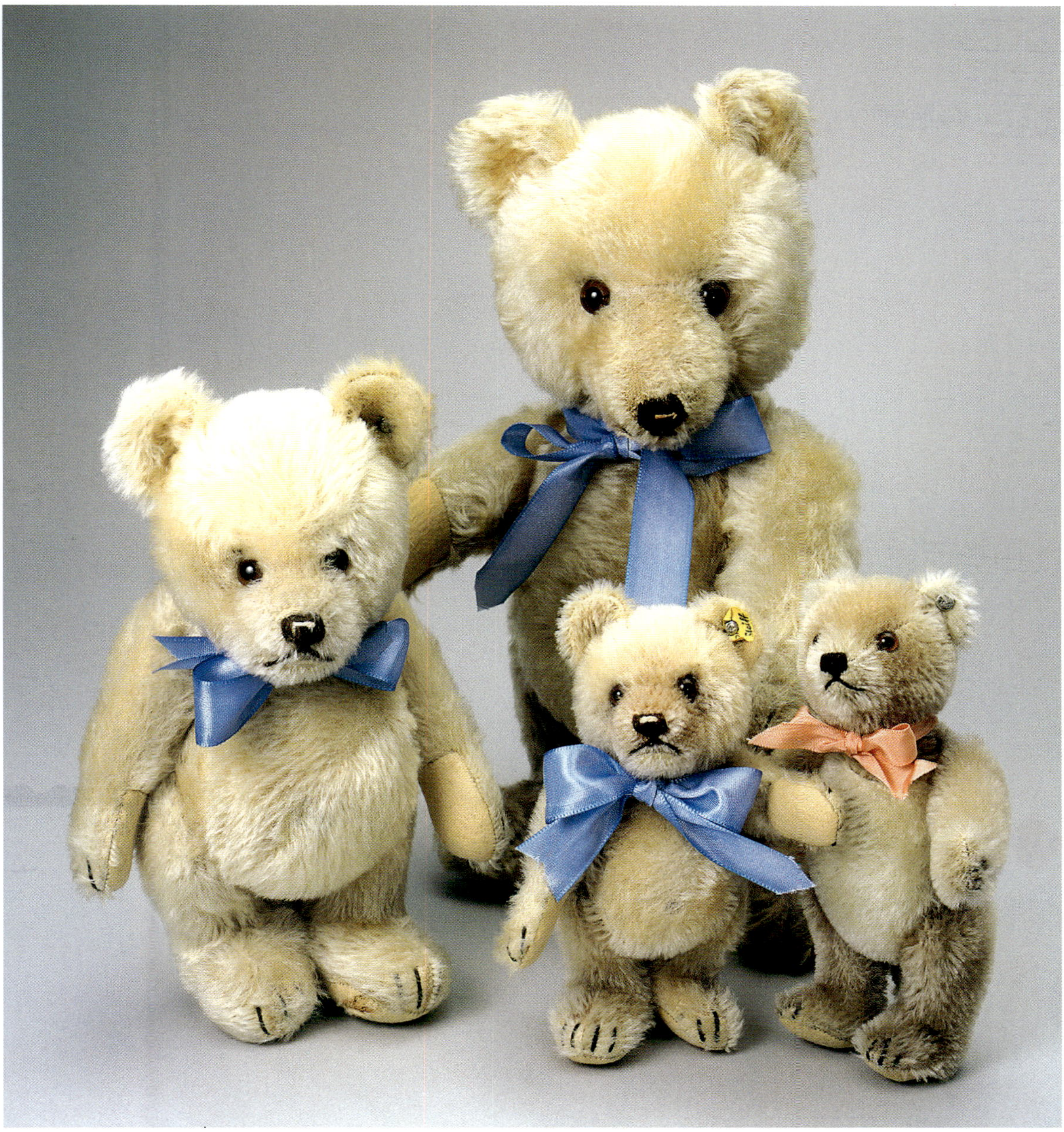

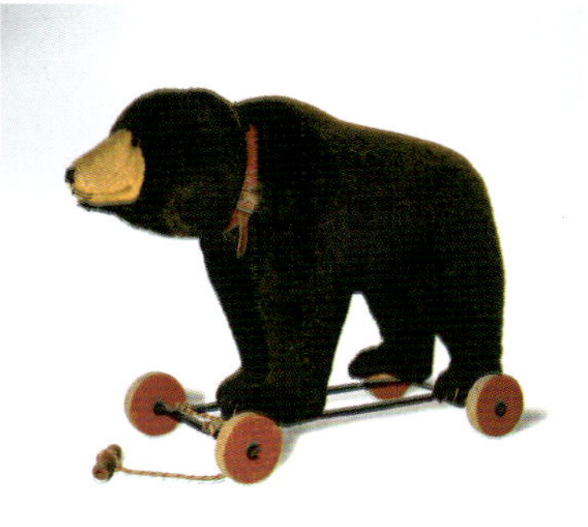

Baer auf Raedern, Reitbaer - *Bear on Wheels, Riding Bear*

Mohair, Eisengerippe, rotes Lederhalsband, dunkelbraun, hellbraune Schnauze, stehend auf Holzrollen, ab Groesse 35 cm mit Verbindungsschienen, ab Groesse 43 cm auf Metallscheibenraedern mit Gummireifen, Groessen 28 und 35 cm Druckstimme, ab Groesse 43 cm Zugstimme, Groessen 28 bis 80 cm bereits vor 1940 im Programm - *mohair, iron frame, red leather collar, dark brown, light brown muzzle, on wooden wheels, connecting frame from 35 cm size, metal disc wheels & rubber tires from 43 cm, 28 & 35 cm with press voice, pull cord voice from 43 cm, 28 - 80 cm already in production prior to 1940*

SERIE	ART.-NO	PERIOD	PR.	INFO
12	**1328,2**	1950-1950	5-6	28 cm
12	**1335,2**	1950-1950	5-6	35 cm
12	**1343,2**	1950-1957	6	43 cm, auch als 1343,2 ST (ab 1956) mit Steuerung - *also as 1343,2 ST (from 1956) with steering*
12	**1344,2**	1949-1949	6	44 cm, lackierte Holzraeder - *painted wooden wheels*
12	**1350,2**	1949-1957	6	50 cm, auch als 1350,2 ST (ab 1953) mit Steuerung - *also as 1350,2 ST (from 1953) with steering*
12	**1360,2**	1949-1957	6	60 cm, auch als 1360,2 ST (ab 1956) mit Steuerung - *also as 1360,2 ST (from 1956) with steering*
12	**1380,2**	1950-1957	6	80 cm, auch als 1380,2 ST (ab 1956) mit Steuerung - *also as 1380,2 ST (from 1956) with steering*
12	**13100,2**	1951-1957	6	100 cm

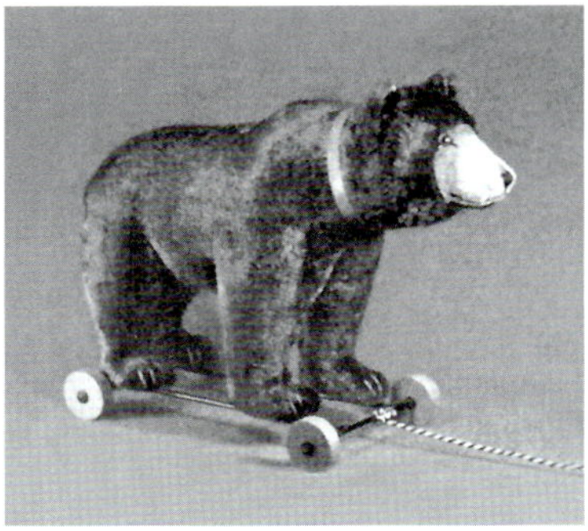

Reitbaer - *Riding Bear*

Seidenpluesch, Eisengerippe, braun, hellbraune Schnauze, Lederhalsband, Zugstimme, stehend auf Holzraedern, mit Verbindungsschienen - *silk plush, iron frame, brown, light brown muzzle, leather collar, pull cord voice, on wooden wheels, with connecting frame*

SERIE	ART.-NO	PERIOD	PR.	INFO
12	**1644,2**	1949-1949	6	44 cm
12	**1650,2**	1949-1949	6	50 cm

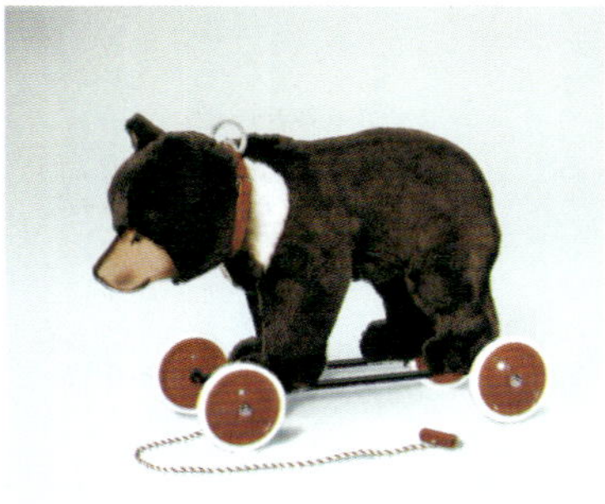

Reitbaer - *Riding Bear*

Dralon, dunkelbraun, weisser Kragen, Stahlgerippe, starre Scheibenraeder/Gummireifen, ab 1967 Plastikreifen, ab 1968 Schlepplenkung, (auch genannt: schwenkbare Vorderraeder), Kunststofflager, Haltegriff, Zugstimme, abwaschbar - *dralon, dark brown, white collar, steel frame, rigid disc wheels/rubber, from 1967 plastic tires, from 1968 pull-type steering (also called swivelling front wheels), plastic bearings, grip handle, pull cord voice, surface washable*

SERIE	ART.-NO	PERIOD	PR.	INFO
040	**1643,33**	1967-1967	4-5	43 cm
	0410/43	1968-1976	4	
040	**1650,23**	1966-1967	4-5	50 cm
	0410/50	1968-1980	4	
	8155/50	1981-1983	4	
	0410/60	1969-1977	4-5	60 cm

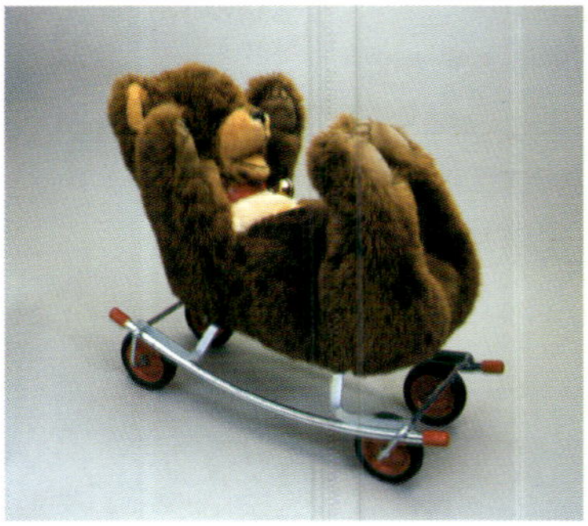

Reitbaer - *Riding Bear*

Webpelz, Metallwiege mit Raedern, zum Fahren und Schaukeln, Sitzflaeche = Bauch - *woven fur, on metal cradle with wheels, for riding & rocking, stomach is used to sit on*

SERIE	ART.-NO	PERIOD	PR.	INFO
	8010/40	1980-1980	4	40 cm
481307	**8150/40**	1981-1986	4	

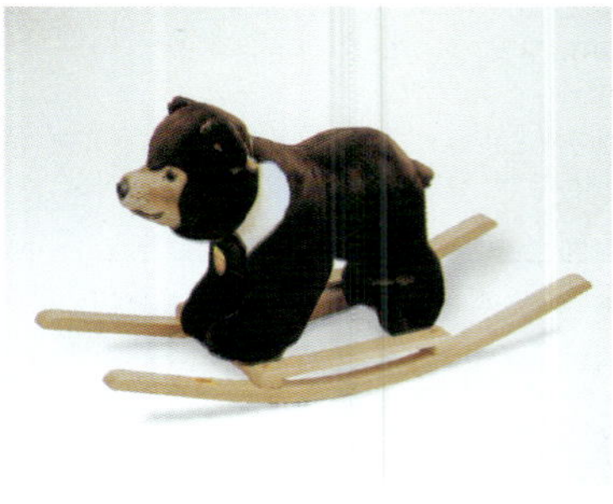

Schaukel Baer - *Rocking Bear*

Webpelz, Holzwiege, stehend, abwaschbar - *woven fur, on wooden cradle, standing, surface washable*

SERIE	ART.-NO	PERIOD	PR.	INFO
480300	**8130/50**	1982-1990	4	50 cm

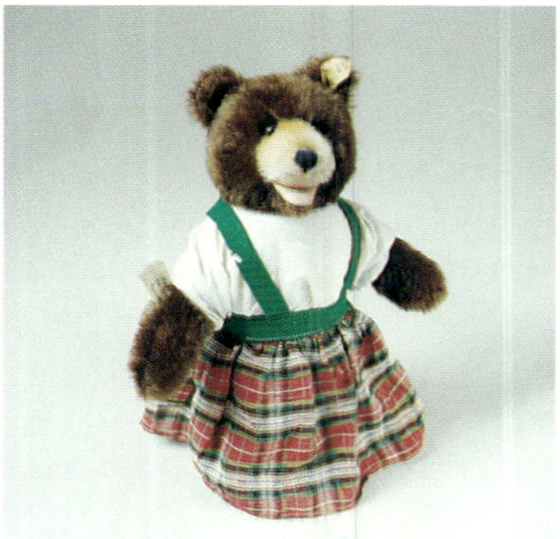

Musik-Baer - *Music Bear*

Kopf Mohairpluesch, offener Mund, dunkelbraun, rotkarierter Rock mit gruenen Traegern, weisse Bluse, Schweizer Musikwerk zum Druecken - *mohair head, open mouth, dark brown, red plaid skirt &*

green suspenders, white blouse, Swiss music box

SERIE	ART.-NO	PERIOD	PR.	INFO
97 12	**9325**	1950-1951	8	25 cm

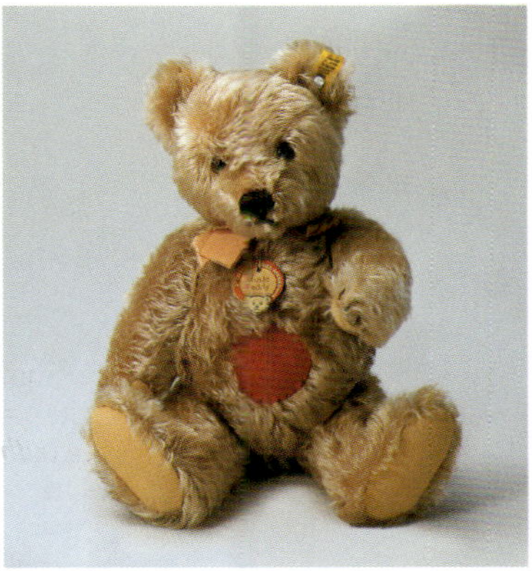

Music Teddy

Mohair, caramel, gegliedert, Schweizer-Drueckerwerk, aufgenaehte rote Filzflaeche am Bauch traegt die Aufschrift "Music" in weiss - *mohair, caramel, jointed, Swiss music box, red felt patch stitched to stomach with word "Music" in white*

SERIE	ART.-NO	PERIOD	PR.	INFO
97 12	**9335,3**	1951-1957	8	35 cm

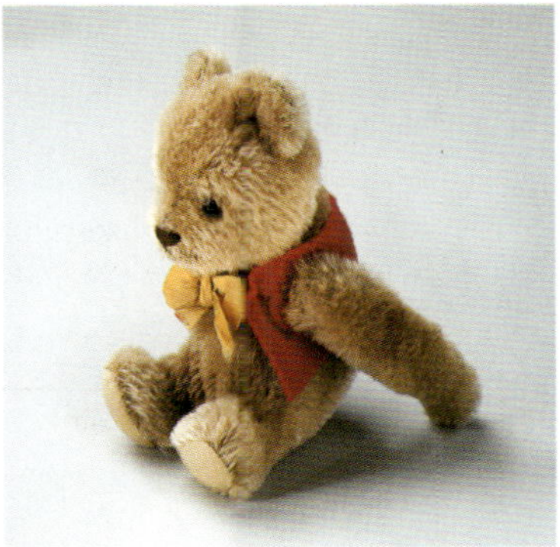

Turbo Teddy Purzelbaer - *Turbo Teddy Somersault Bear*

Mohair, caramel, Uhrwerk mit Armaufzug - *mohair, caramel, winding mechanism operated by winding arm*

SERIE	ART.-NO	PERIOD	PR.	INFO
96 12	**9315,4**	1951-1951	8	15 cm

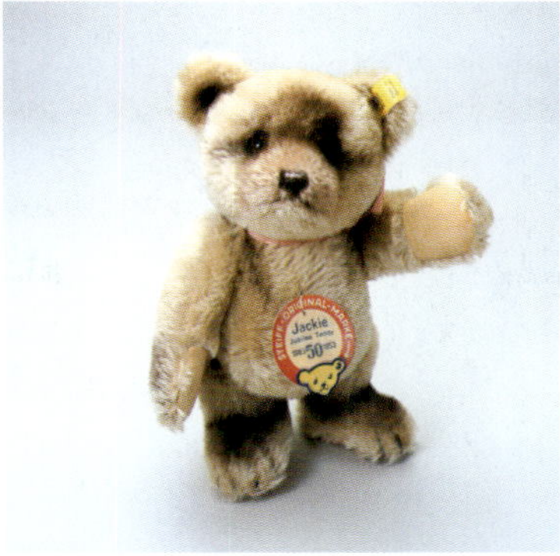

Jackie

Jubilaeums Teddy "50 Jahre Teddy", Mohair, hellblond, gegliedert, weich, ab Groesse 25 cm mit Druckstimme, Groesse 75 cm wurde nur als Schaustueck produziert - *anniversary Teddy "50 Years of Teddy", mohair, light blond, jointed, soft, from 25 cm size with press voice, 75 cm only produced as display item*

SERIE	ART.-NO	PERIOD	PR.	INFO
12B	**5317**	1953-1955	7-8	17 cm
12B	**5325**	1953-1955	7-8	25 cm, ab 1954 auch 5325,2 - *from 1954 also 5325,2*
12B	**5335**	1953-1955	8	35 cm, ab 1954 auch 5335,2 - *from 1954 also 5335,2*
12B	**5375**	1953-1953	9	75 cm

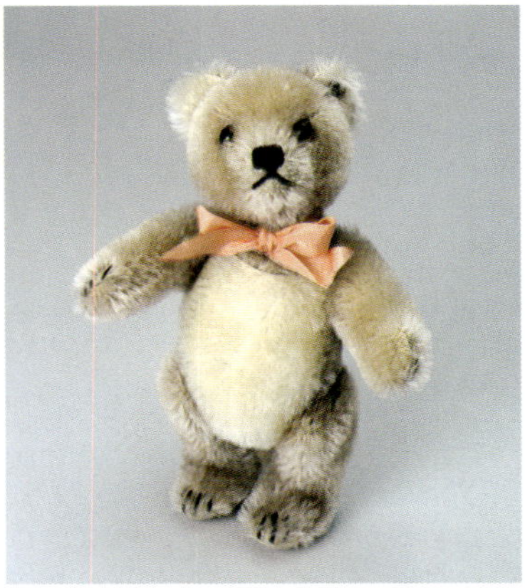

Original Teddybaer mit Halsmechanik - *Original Teddybear with neck mechanism*

Mohairpluesch, caramel, gegliedert, Halsmechanik vom Schwanz aus zu betaetigen - *mohair, caramel, jointed, mechanical neck operated by tail*

SERIE	ART.-NO	PERIOD	PR.	INFO
12	**5318** H	1955-1955	7	18 cm
12	**5325** H	1955-1955	7	25 cm

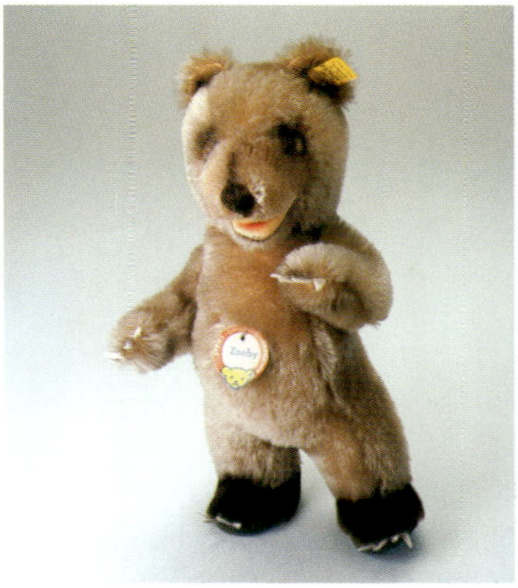

Zoo-Baer **Zooby** - ***Zooby*** *Zoo Bear*

Mohair, braun, aufwartend, Kopf & Arme gegliedert Krallen aus Filz an Fuessen und Pfoten - *mohair, brown, sitting up, head & arms jointed, felt claws on paws & feet*

SERIE	ART.-NO	PERIOD	PR.	INFO
120	**4328,02**	1964-1964	6	28 cm
033	**4328,02**	1966-1966	6	

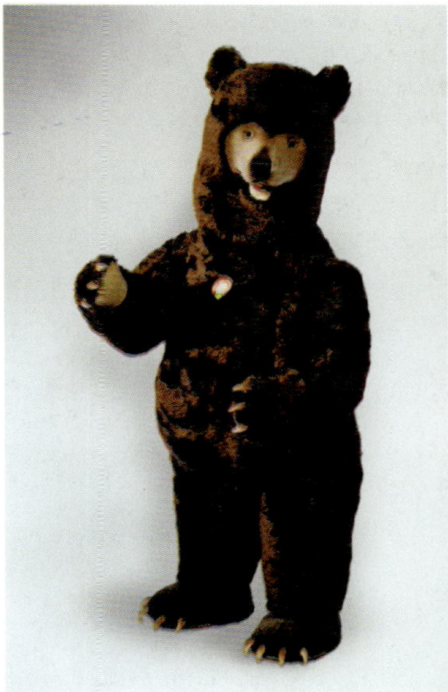

Zoo-Baer - *Zoo Bear*

Mohair, Schautier, braun, aufwartend, Kopf & Arme gegliedert, Krallen an Fuessen und Pfoten - *mohair, display animal, brown, sitting up, head & arms jointed, claws on paws and feet*

SERIE	ART.-NO	PERIOD	PR.	INFO
	0339/12	1967-1967	6	120 cm

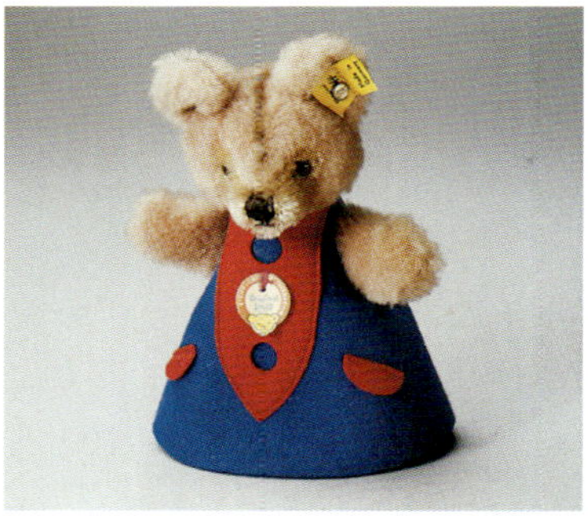

Betthupferlteddy - *Nightcap Teddy*

Kopf & Arme Mohair, dunkelblaue/rote Filzkleidung, Drehkopf, innen hohl zur Abdeckung kleiner Praesente - *head & arms mohair, dark blue/red felt clothing, swivel head, hollow interior to cover small gifts*

SERIE	ART.-NO	PERIOD	PR.	INFO
	3170/15	1969-1974	4	15 cm

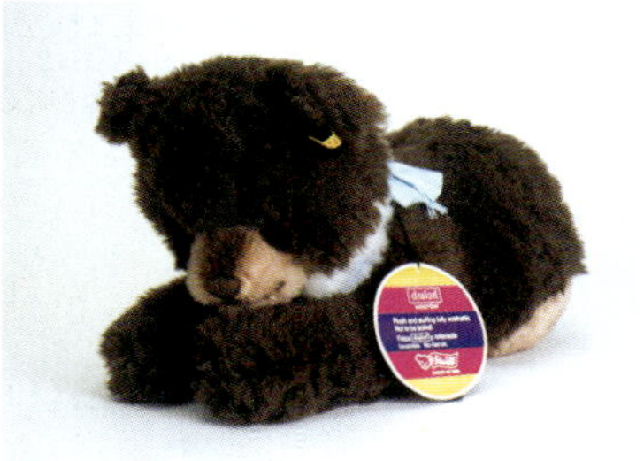

Wiggi

Dralon, liegend, sehr weich - *dralon, lying, very soft*

SERIE	ART.-NO	PERIOD	PR.	INFO
	5200/23	1970-1974	3	23 cm

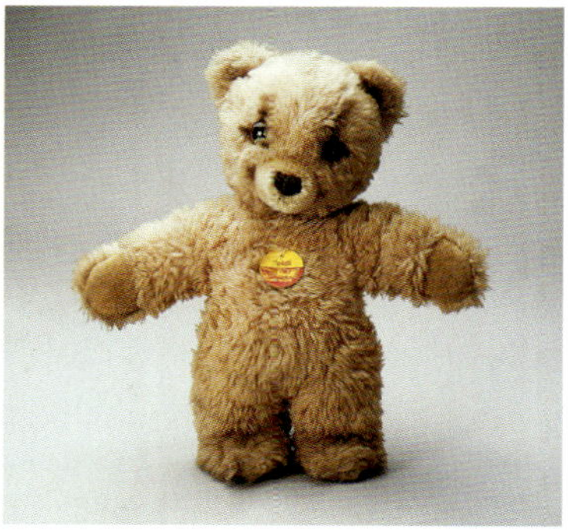

Weich-Baer **Toldy** - ***Toldy*** *Soft Bear*

Dralon, formgeschaeumt, blaue Weste (fehlt auf Foto), Schlenkerkopf, sehr weich, vollwaschbar - *dralon, foam stuffing, blue vest (not shown in photo), floppy head, very soft, fully washable*

SERIE	ART.-NO	PERIOD	PR.	INFO
	6200/30	1970-1979	3	30 cm
	6200/40	1970-1979	3	40 cm

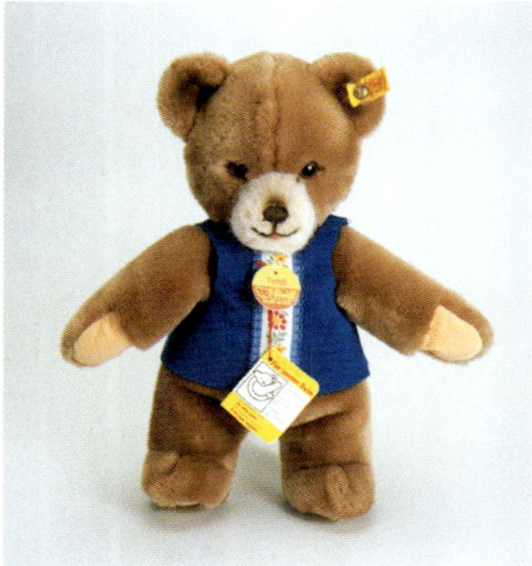

Toldi

Webpelz, sehr weich, 20 cm Koerper blau gefaerbt, 30 cm mit blauer Weste, waschmaschinenfest - *woven fur, very soft, 20 cm body dyed blue, 30 cm wearing blue vest, machine washable*

SERIE	ART.-NO	PERIOD	PR.	INFO
	6242/20	1982-1983	2	20 cm
	6242/30	1982-1984	2-3	30 cm

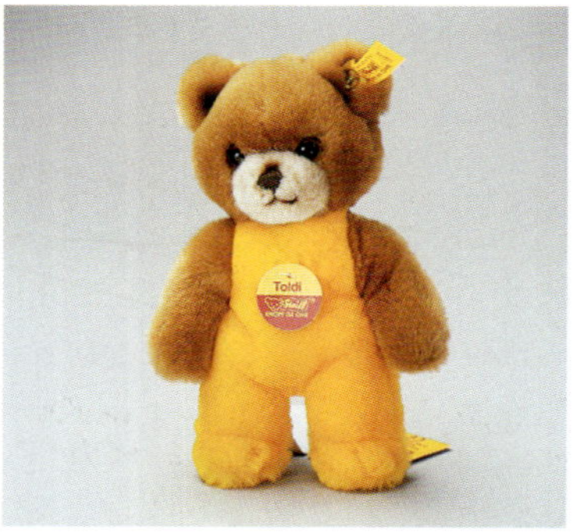

Toldi

Webpelz, Pieps-Stimme, waschmaschinenfest - *woven fur, squeaker, machine washable*

SERIE	ART.-NO	PERIOD	PR.	INFO
080104	**6250/22**	1984-1990	2	22 cm

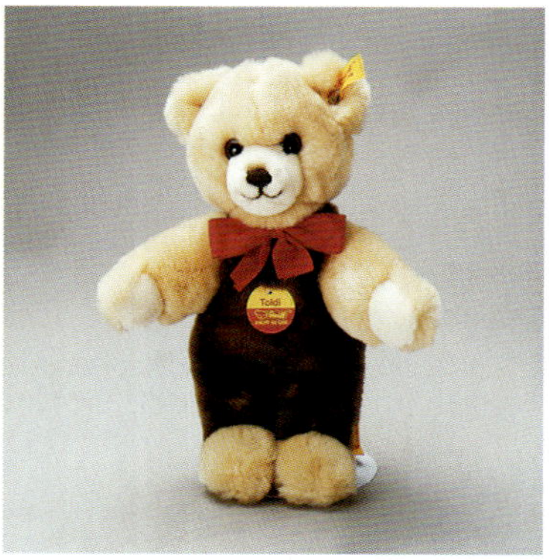

Toldi

Webpelz, Pieps-Stimme, waschmaschinenfest - *woven fur, squeaker, machine washable*

SERIE	ART.-NO	PERIOD	PR.	INFO
080739	**6270/27**	1988-1988	2-3	27 cm

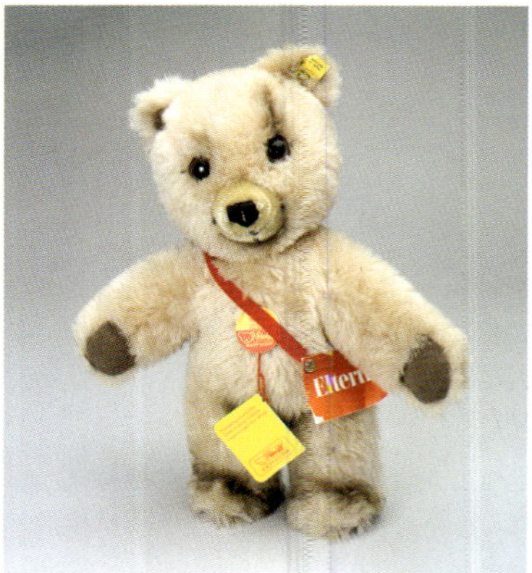

Toddel

Dralon, beige, roter Umhaenger mit Aufschrift "Toddel"oder "Eltern", aus der Zeitschrift "ELTERN", Cop. Sintenis, ab 1976 formgeschaeumt, superweich, abwaschbar - *dralon, beige, red shoulder strap & label with name "Toddel" or 'Eltern" of magazine "ELTERN", copyr. Sintenis, from 1976 foam stuffing, super soft, surface washable*

SERIE	ART.-NO	PERIOD	PR.	INFO
	0290/32	1971-1982	3-4	32 cm

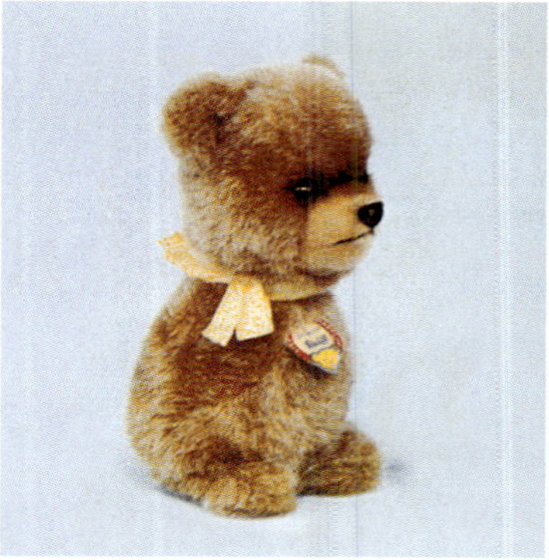

Buzzel

Dralon, formgeschaeumt, superweich, vollwaschbar - *dralon, foam stuffing, super soft, fully washable*

SERIE	ART.-NO	PERIOD	PR.	INFO
	6150/20	1971-1975	3	20 cm

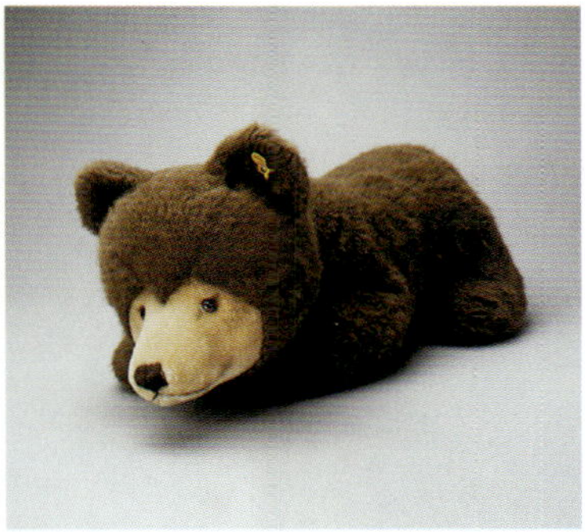

Schlummi

Pelzimitation, nougat, liegend, superweich, abwaschbar - *imitation fur, nougat, lying, super soft, surface washable*

SERIE	ART.-NO	PERIOD	PR.	INFO
	5300/50	1972-1977	3	50 cm

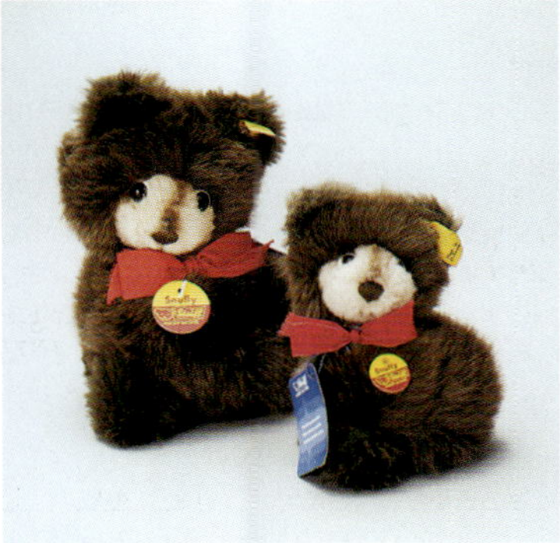

Snuffy

Pelz-Imitation (ab 1978 Synthetik-Webpelz), braun, geringe Farbunterschiede zwischen den Artikel-Nr. 3510 & 3511, abwaschbar - *imitation fur (from 1978 synthetic woven fur), brown, small color variations between article no. 3510 & 3511, surface washable*

SERIE	ART.-NO	PERIOD	PR.	INFO
	3510/14	1974-1977	2	14 cm
	3511/14	1978-1980	2	
	3510/18	1974-1977	2	18 cm
	3511/18	1978-1980	2	

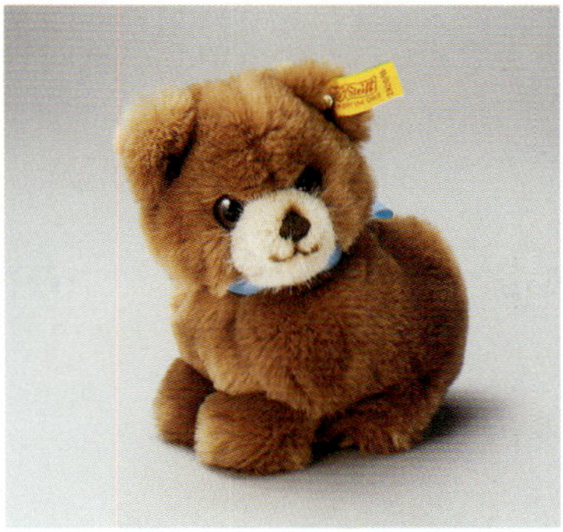

Snuffy

Webpelz, braun, waschmaschinenfest - *woven fur, brown, machine washable*

SERIE	ART.-NO	PERIOD	PR.	INFO
077326	**2920/16**	1983-1987	2	16 cm

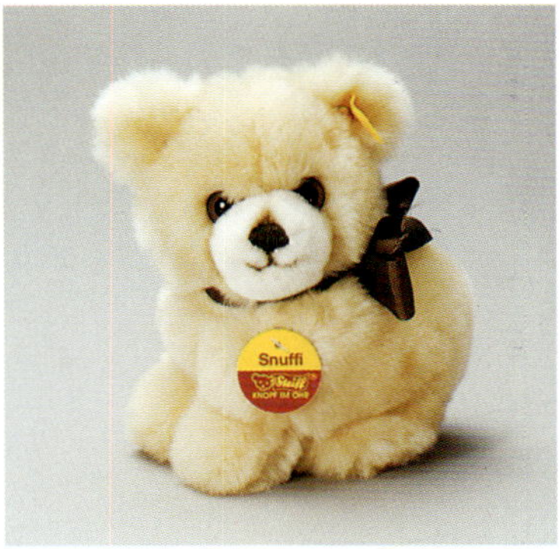

Snuffi

Webpelz, blond, waschmaschinenfest - *woven fur, blond, machine washable*

SERIE	ART.-NO	PERIOD	PR.	INFO
077302	**2921/16**	1987-1990	2	16 cm
	077302	1991-1999	2	

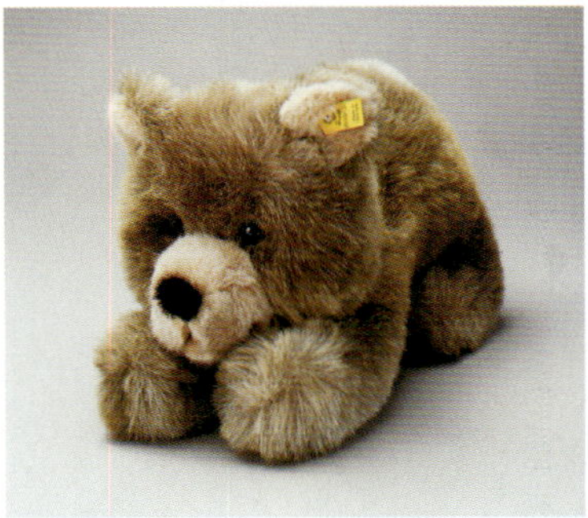

Junior

Pelzimitation, ab 1978 Synthetik-Webpelz, liegend, abwaschbar - *imitation fur, from 1978 synthetic woven fur, lying, surface washable*

SERIE	ART.-NO	PERIOD	PR.	INFO
	2880/35	1975-1979	2-3	35 cm

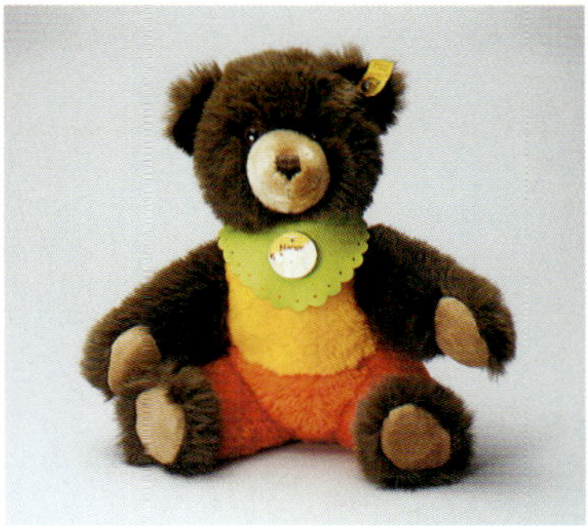

Happy

Pelzimitation, ab 1978 Webpelz, sitzend, gruenes Laetzchen, formgeschaeumt, vollwaschbar - *imitation fur, from 1978 woven fur, sitting, green bib, foam stuffing, fully washable*

SERIE	ART.-NO	PERIOD	PR.	INFO
	6110/35	1975-1979	3	35 cm

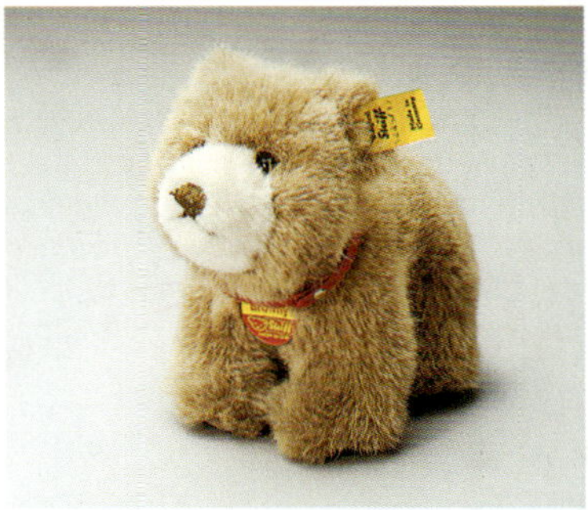

Browny

Nerzimitation, ab 1978 Synthetik-Webpelz, stehend, abwaschbar - *imitation mink, from 1978 synthetic woven fur, standing, surface washable*

SERIE	ART.-NO	PERIOD	PR.	INFO
	1445/12	1977-1984	2	12 cm

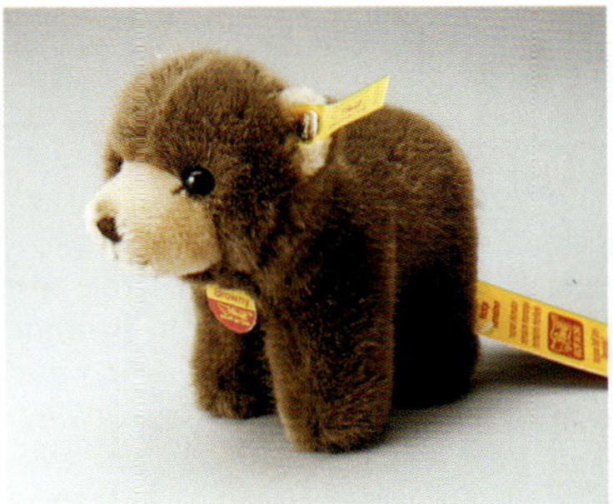

Browny

Webpelz, abwaschbar - *woven fur, surface washable*

SERIE	ART.-NO	PERIOD	PR.	INFO
040207	**1444/12**	1985-1990	2	14 cm
	040207	1991-1999	2	

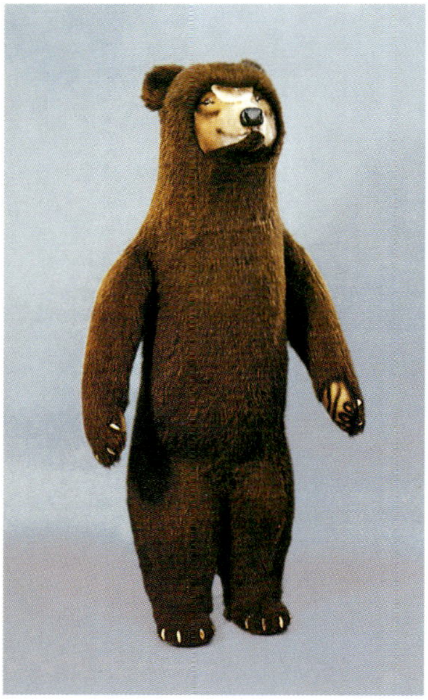

Braunbaer - *Brown Bear*

Synthetik-Wirkpluesch, ab 1979 Wirkpelz, aufwartend, abwaschbar, dieser Baer wurde bereits 1972 in USA angeboten - *synthetic knitted plush, from 1979 knitted fur, sitting up, surface washable, in 1972 this bear was sold in the USA only*

SERIE	ART.-NO	PERIOD	PR.	INFO
	0409/19	1972-1980	5-6	190 cm

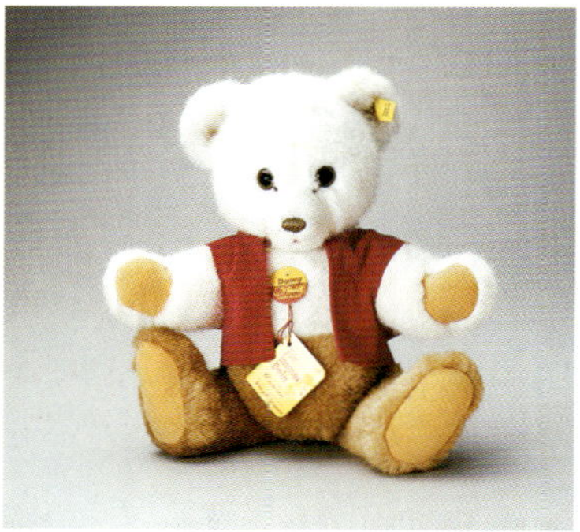

Dormy

Webpelz, Kopf, Arme & Oberkoerper weiss, Beine & Unterkoerper hellbraun, rote oder blaue Weste, Beine beweglich, Brummstimme, abwaschbar - *woven fur, head, arms & upper body white, legs & lower body light brown, red or blue vest, legs movable, growler, surface washable*

SERIE	ART.-NO	PERIOD	PR.	INFO
	0215/35	1979-1983	3-4	35 cm

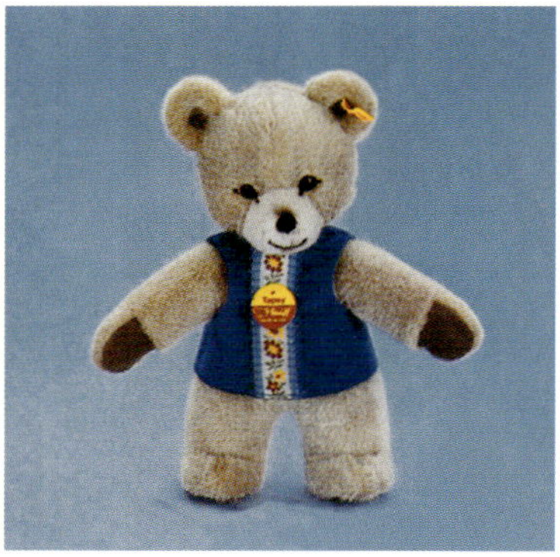

Weichbaer-**Tapsy** - ***Tapsy*** *Soft Bear*

Webpelz, blaue Weste, abwaschbar - *woven fur, blue vest, surface washable*

SERIE	ART.-NO	PERIOD	PR.	INFO
	6210/30	1980-1982	3	30 cm

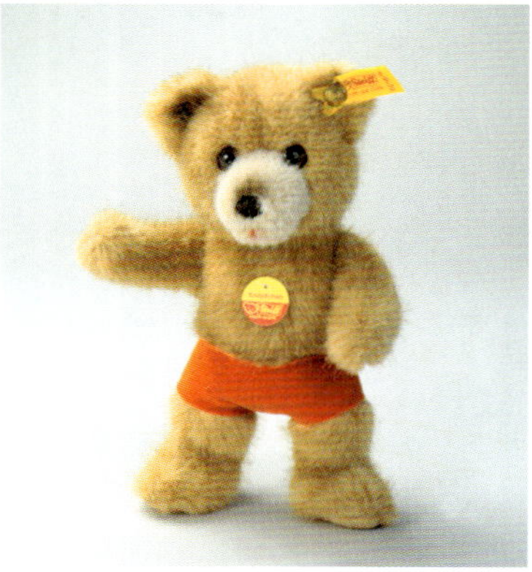

Knoepfchen

Webpelz, rote Hose, abwaschbar - *woven fur, red shorts, surface washable*

SERIE	ART.-NO	PERIOD	PR.	INFO
	0218/16	1981-1984	3-4	16 cm

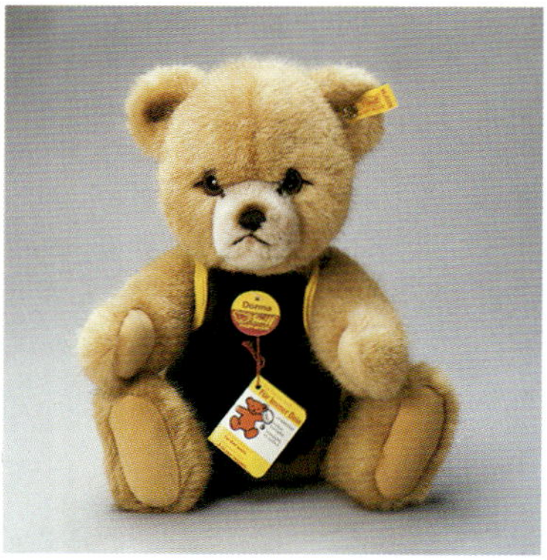

Dorma

Webpelz, gegliedert, Brummstimme, mit Schuerze, abwaschbar - *woven fur, jointed, growler, apron, surface washable*

SERIE	ART.-NO	PERIOD	PR.	INFO
017902	**0217/34**	1981-1986	3-4	34 cm

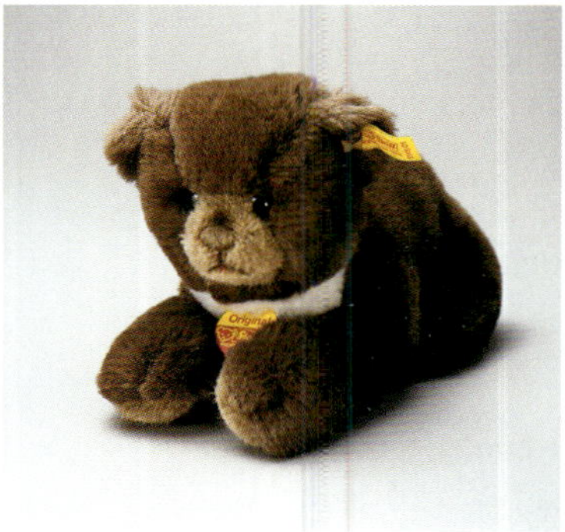

Kuschel

Webpelz, Schaumstoff-Fuellung, superweich, waschmaschinenfest - *woven fur, foam stuffing, super soft, machine washable*

SERIE	ART.-NO	PERIOD	PR.	INFO
	5505/25	1981-1983	2-3	25 cm

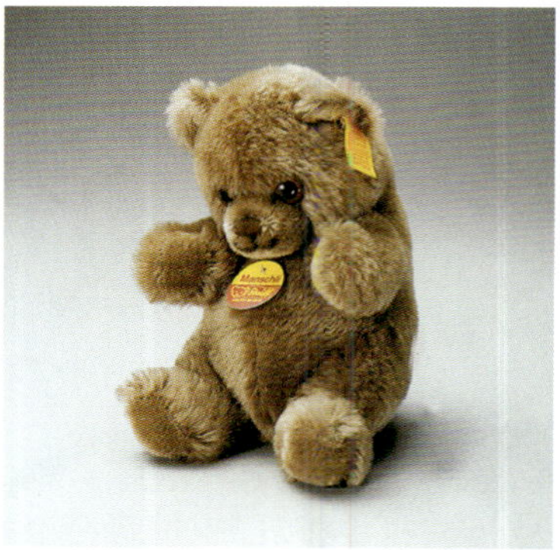

Manschli

Mohair Webpelz, abwaschbar - *mohair woven fur, surface washable*

SERIE	ART.-NO	PERIOD	PR.	INFO
	0310/19	1983-1985	4-5	19 cm

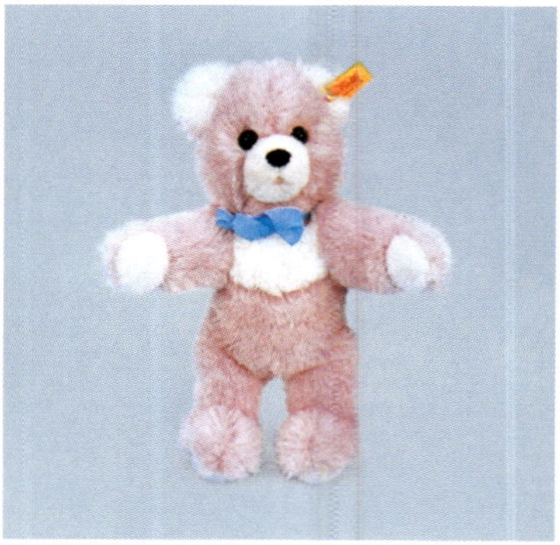

Baby Teddy

Webpelz, Druckstimme, waschmaschinenfest, 26 cm - *woven fur, press voice, machine washable, 26 cm*

SERIE	ART.-NO	PERIOD	PR.	INFO
201059	**5683/26**	1983-1986	1-2	rosa - *pink*
201080	**5684/26**	1983-1986	1-2	blau - *blue*

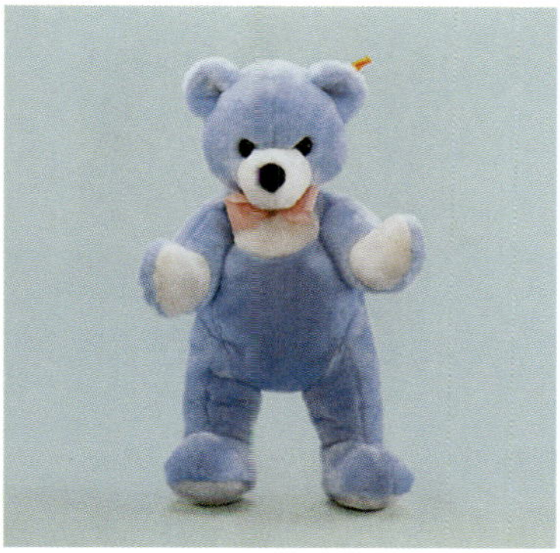

Baby Teddy

Webpelz, Druckstimme, waschmaschinenfest, 60 cm - *woven fur, press voice, machine washable, 60 cm*

SERIE	ART.-NO	PERIOD	PR.	INFO
	5675/60	1984-1985	2	blau - *blue*
	5676/60	1984-1985	2	rosa - *pink*

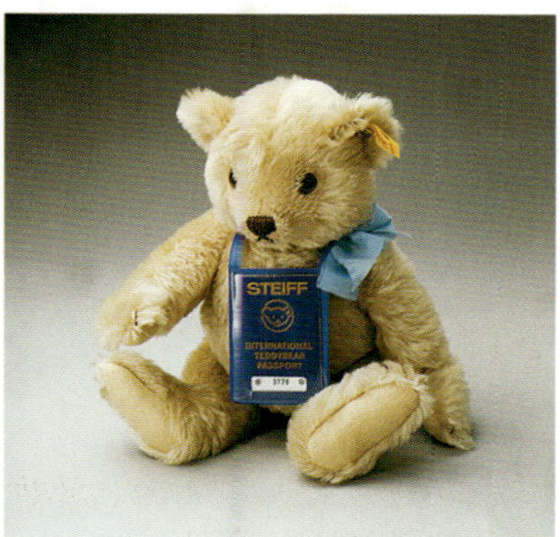

Passport-Baer - *Passport-Bear*

Mohair Webpelz, gegliedert, Druckstimme, abwaschbar - *mohair woven fur, jointed, press voice, surface washable*

SERIE	ART.-NO	PERIOD	PR.	INFO
011504	**0245/40**	1985-1988	4	40 cm

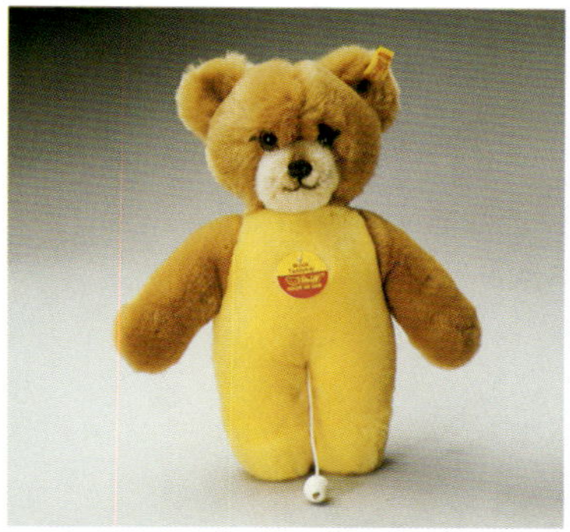

Musik Teddybaer - *Musical Teddybear*

Spieluhr, Webpelz, formgeschaeumt, Musikwerk austauschbar, ohne Musikwerk waschbar - *musical clock, woven fur, preformed foam stuffing, music box can be exchanged, washable without music box*

SERIE	ART.-NO	PERIOD	PR.	INFO
231100	**6350/26**	1986-1990	2	26 cm
	231100	1991-1993	2	

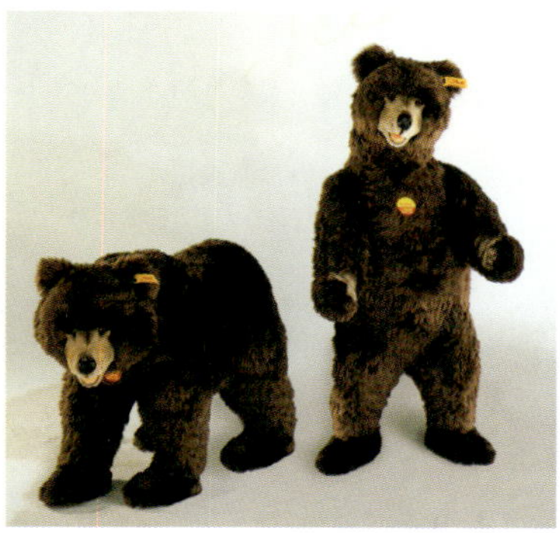

Studio Baer - *Studio Bear*

Webpelz, abwaschbar - *woven fur, surface washable*

SERIE	ART.-NO	PERIOD	PR.	INFO
500503	**0327/85**	1987-1990	7	160 cm, stehend - *standing*
	500503	1991-1999	7	
500558	**0328/99**	1987-1990	7	160 cm, aufwartend - *sitting up*
	500558	1991-1999	7	

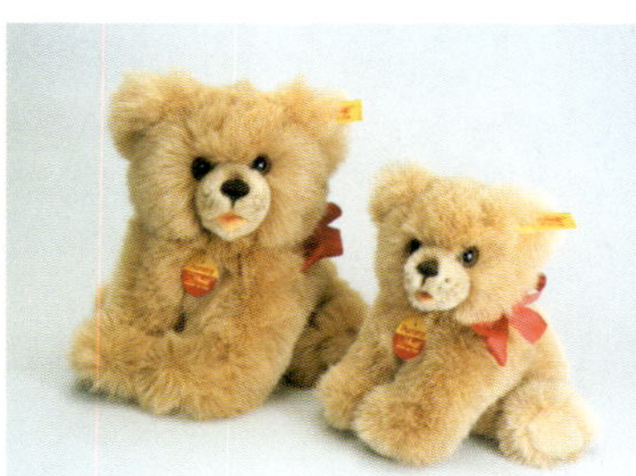

Pummy Baer - ***Pummy*** *Bear*

Webpelz, waschmaschinenfest - *woven fur, machine washable*

SERIE	ART.-NO	PERIOD	PR.	INFO
083006	**5050/17**	1989-1990	2	17 cm
	083006	1991-1991	2	
083020	**5050/21**	1989-1990	2	21 cm
	083020	1991-1992	2	

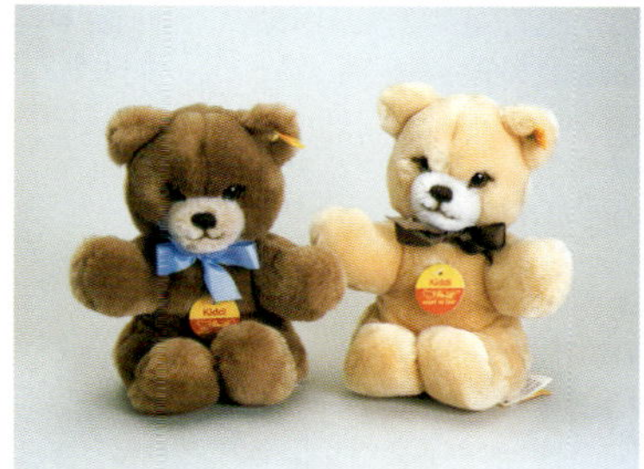

Kiddi Baer - ***Kiddi*** *Bear*

Webpelz, blond oder beige, Pieps-Stimme, waschmaschinenfest - *woven fur, blond or beige, press voice, machine washable*

SERIE	ART.-NO	PERIOD	PR.	INFO
082627	**5701/20**	1989-1990	2	20 cm, blond
	082627	1991-1999	2	
082658	**5702/20**	1989-1990	2	20 cm, beige
	082658	1991-1991	2	

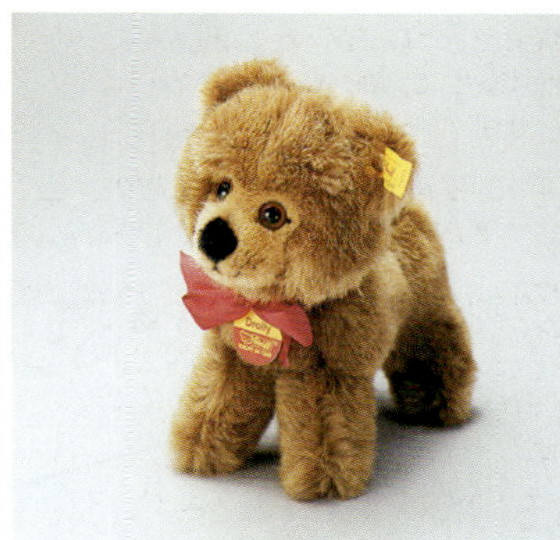

Drolly Baer - ***Drolly*** *Bear*

Webpelz, braun, stehend, waschmaschinenfest - *woven fur, brown, standing, machine washable*

SERIE	ART.-NO	PERIOD	PR.	INFO
081255	**5750/22**	1990-1990	2	22 cm
	081255	1991-1991	2	

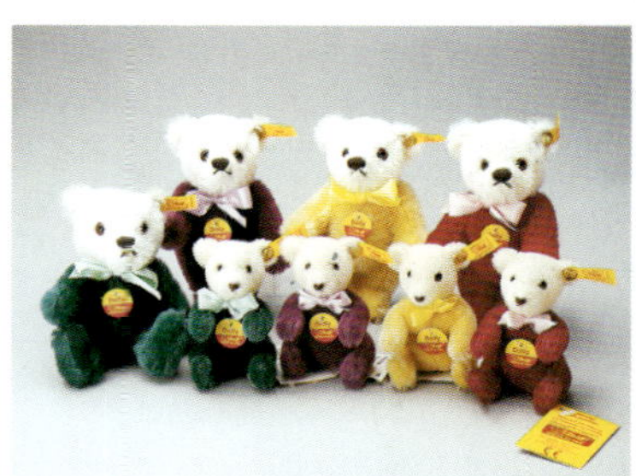

Dolly Teddy

Mohair Webpelz, 12 cm mit drehbarem

Kopf, 15 cm gegliedert, abwaschbar - *mohair woven fur, 12 cm with swivel head, 15 cm jointed, surface washable*

EAN-No.	Period	Pr.	Info
030604	1991-1992	3	12 cm, rot/weiss - *red/white*
030628	1991-1992	3	15 cm
030659	1991-1992	3	12 cm, gelb/weiss - *yellow/white*
030673	1991-1992	3	15 cm
030703	1991-1992	3	12 cm, gruen/weiss - *green/white*
030727	1991-1992	3	15 cm
030758	1991-1992	3	12 cm, violett/weiss - *violet/white*
030772	1991-1992	3	15 cm

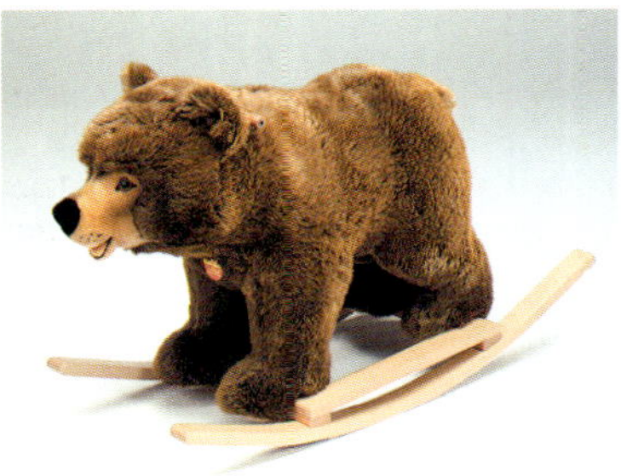

Reit-Baer - *Riding Bear*

Webpelz, Metall-Innengestell, Holzschaukel, abwaschbar - *woven fur, iron frame, wooden rocker, surface washable*

EAN-No.	Period	Pr.	Info
480355	1991-1997	5	70 cm

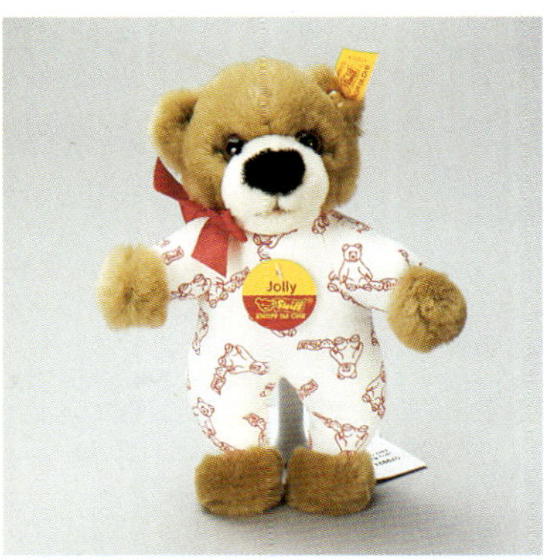

Jolly Baer - ***Jolly*** *Bear*

Webpelz/Baumwollstoff, waschmaschinenfest - *woven fur & cotton, machine washable*

EAN-No.	Period	Pr	Info
079900	1991-1991	2	18 cm, rot/braun - *red/brown*
079917	1991-1991	2	26 cm
079924	1991-1991	2	18 cm, weiss/braun - *white/brown*
079931	1991-1991	2	26 cm

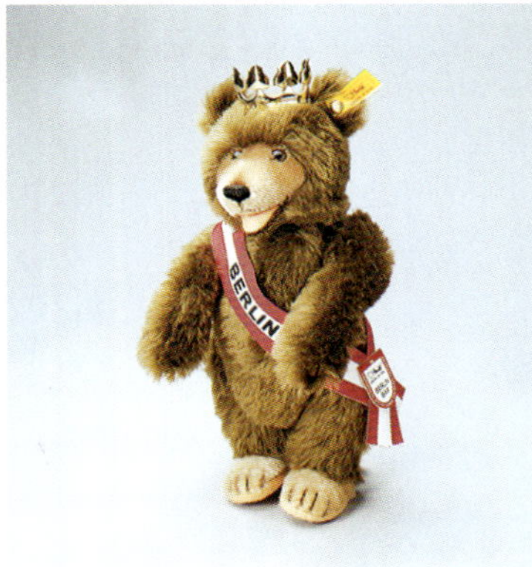

Berlin-Baer - *Berlin Bear*

Mohair Webpelz, braun, mit Krone, abwaschbar - *mohair woven fur, brown, crown, surface washable*

EAN-No.	Period	Pr.	Info
010057	1993-1994	3	29 cm

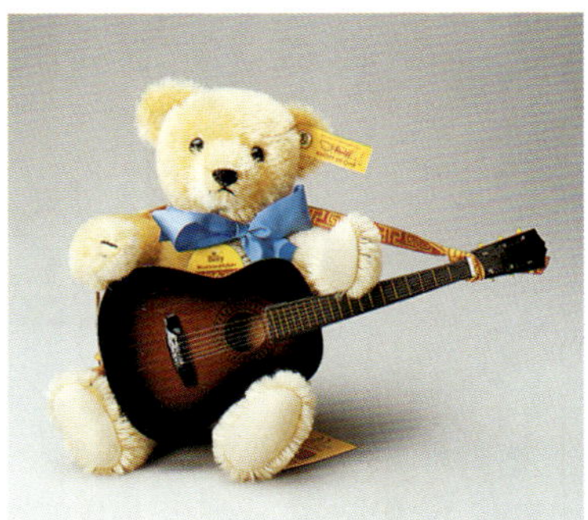

Billy Musikteddybaer - *Billy the Musical Teddybear*

Mohair Webpelz, blond, mit Gitarre und Musikwerk, abwaschbar - *mohair woven fur, blond, with guitar & music box, surface washable*

EAN-No.	Period	Pr.	Info
027505	1993-1994	3-4	25 cm

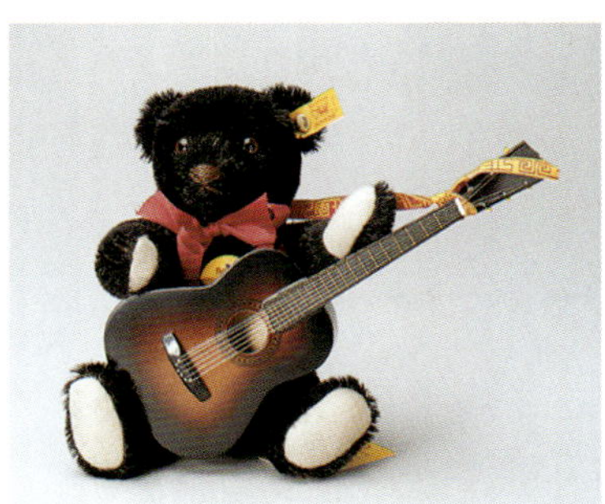

Bobby Musikteddybaer - *Bobby the Musical Teddybear*

Mohair Webpelz, schwarz, mit Gitarre und Musikwerk, abwaschbar - *mohair woven fur, black, with guitar & music Box, surface washable*

EAN-No.	Period	Pr.	Info
027529	1993-1997	3-4	25 cm

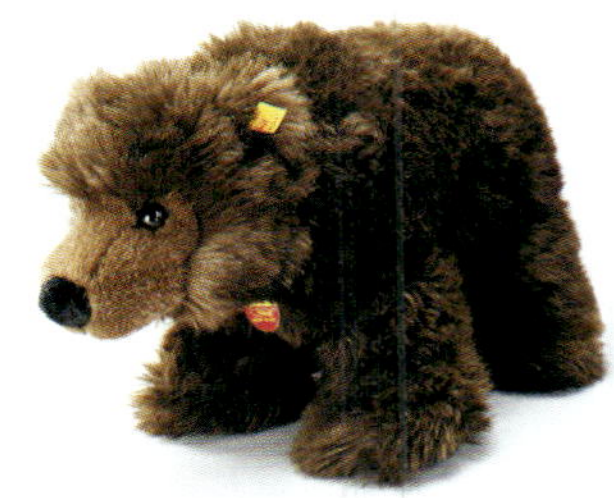

Petz Braunbaer - *Brown Bear* ***Petz***

Webpelz, dunkelbraun, stehend, abwaschbar - *woven fur, dark brown, standing, surface washable*

EAN-No.	Period	Pr.	Info
069710	1993-1994	3	43 cm
069734	1993-1994	3	55 cm
069758	1993-1994	3	70 cm

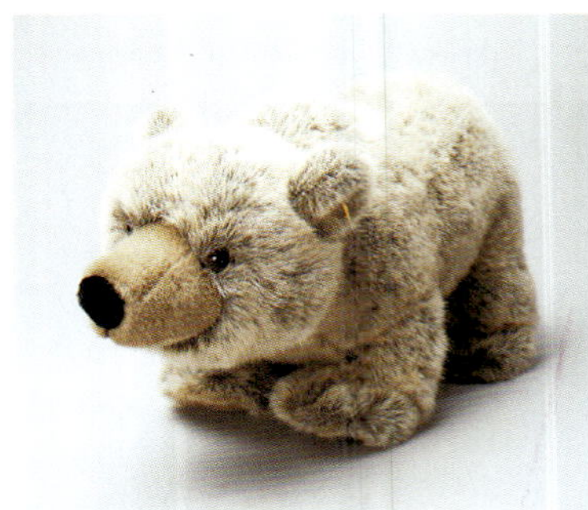

Urs Braunbaer - *Brown Bear* ***Urs***

Webpelz, grau/beige, stehend, abwaschbar - *woven fur, grey/beige, standing, surface washable*

EAN-No.	Period	Pr.	Info
069772	1993-1997	2-3	43 cm
069796	1993-1995	3	55 cm

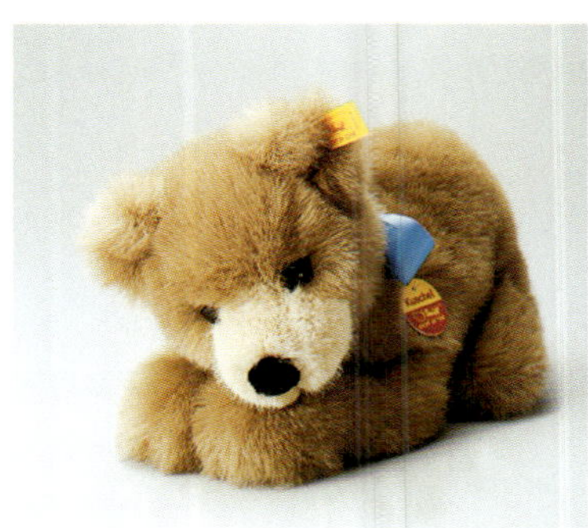

Kuschel Baer - ***Kuschel*** *Bear*

Webpelz, hellbraun, waschmaschinenfest - *woven fur, light brown, machine washable*

EAN-No.	Period	Pr.	Info
099854	1993-1996	2	30 cm

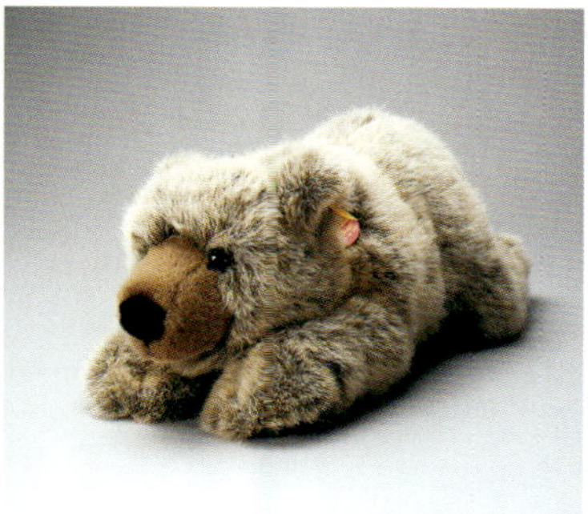

Urs Braunbaer - *Brown Bear* ***Urs***

Webpelz, grau/beige, liegend, abwaschbar - *woven fur, grey/beige, lying, surface washable*

EAN-No.	Period	Pr.	Info
069826	1994-1998	2-3	50 cm
069840	1994-1994	3	75 cm
069864	1994-1996	3-4	110 cm

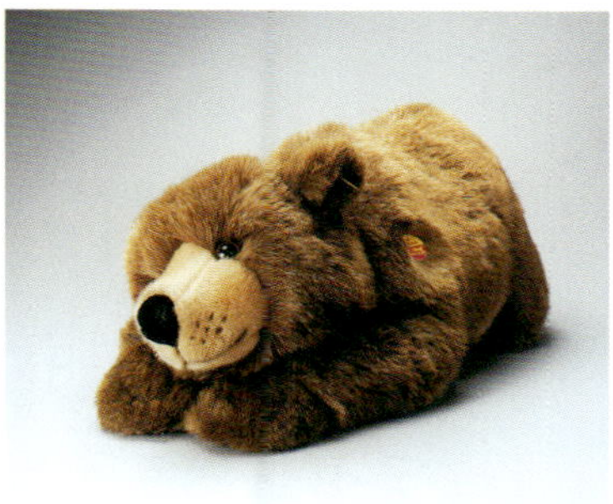

Bruno Braunbaer - *Brown Bear* ***Bruno***

Webpelz, braun, liegend, abwaschbar - *woven fur, brown lying, surface washable*

EAN-No.	Period	Pr.	Info
069949	1994-1997	2-3	50 cm
069963	1994-1996	3	75 cm
069987	1994-1996	3-4	110 cm

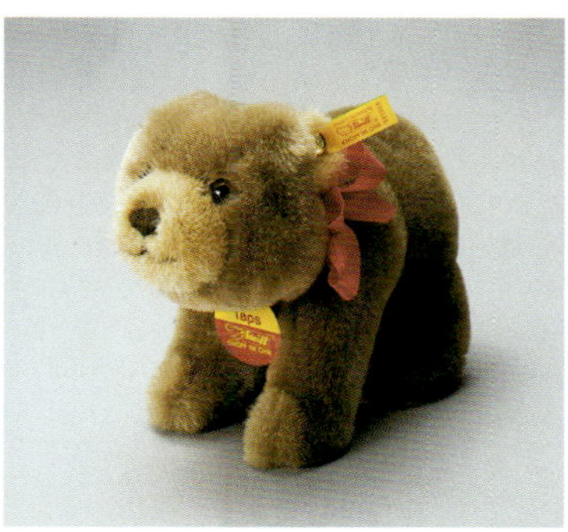

Taps

Webpelz, braun, stehend, waschmaschinenfest - *woven fur, brown, standing, machine washable*

EAN-No.	Period	Pr.	Info
081668	1994-1995	2	16 cm

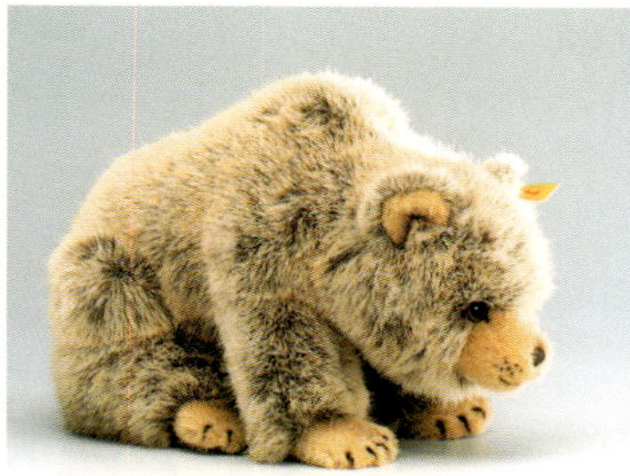

Siro Braunbaer - *Brown Bear* ***Siro***

Webpelz, grau/beige, sitzend, handwaschbar - *woven fur, grey/beige, sitting, hand washable*

EAN-No.	Period	Pr.	Info
069413	1995-1998	3	28 cm

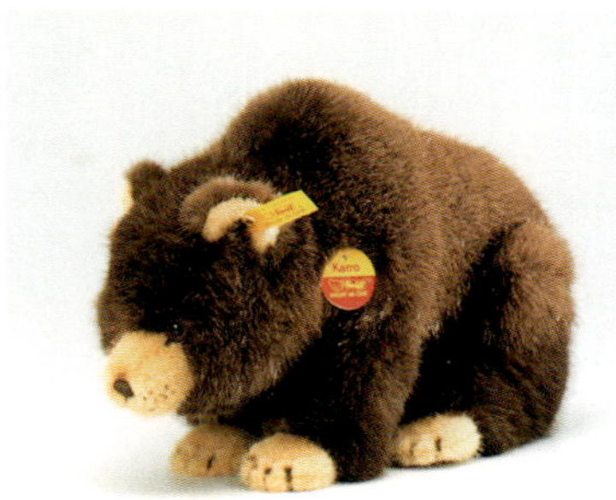

Karro Braunbaer - *Brown Bear* ***Karro***

Webpelz, dunkelbraun, sitzend, handwaschbar - *woven fur, dark brown, sitting, hand washable*

EAN-No.	Period	Pr.	Info
069451	1995-1998	3	28 cm

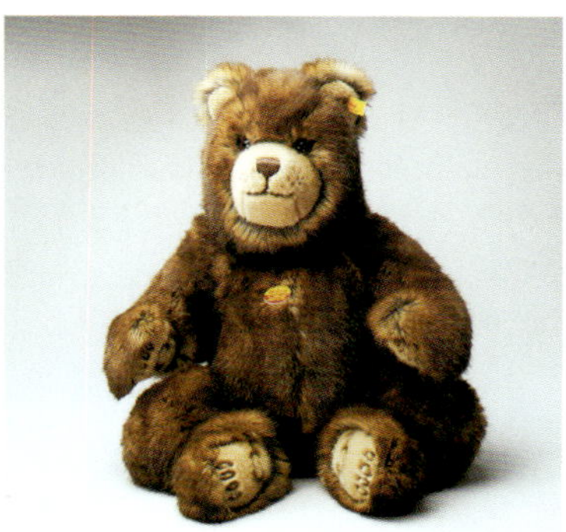

Baer - *Bear*

Webpelz, braun gespitzt, sitzend, handwaschbar - *woven fur, brown tipped, sitting down, hand washable*

EAN-No.	Period	Pr.	Info
069529	1995-1997	3-4	43 cm
069567	1995-1998	4	60 cm

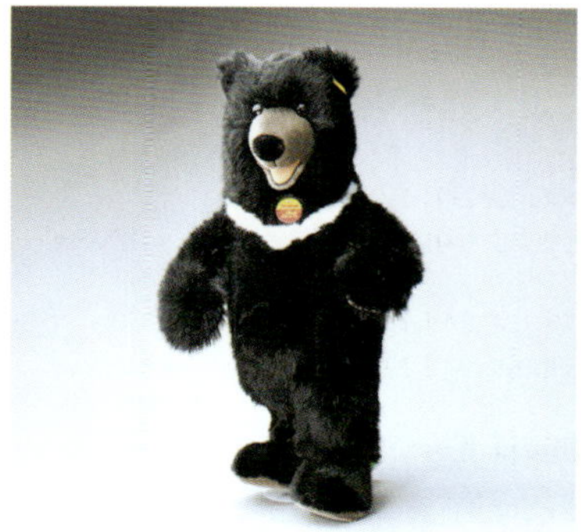

Kragenbaer - *Collar Bear*

Webpelz, schwarz, aufwartend, abwaschbar - *woven fur, black, begging, surface washable*

EAN-No.	Period	Pr.	Info
069604	1995-1996	3-4	53 cm

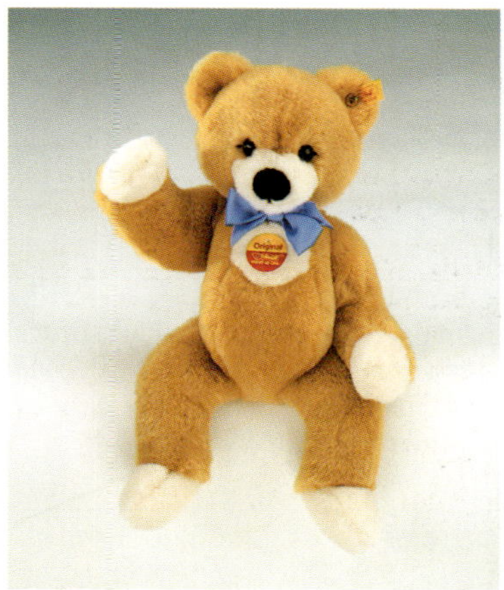

Schlenker Teddy - *Dangling Teddy*

Webpelz waschmaschinenfest - *woven fur, machine washable*

EAN-No.	Period	Pr.	Info
123757	1996-1998	3	30 cm

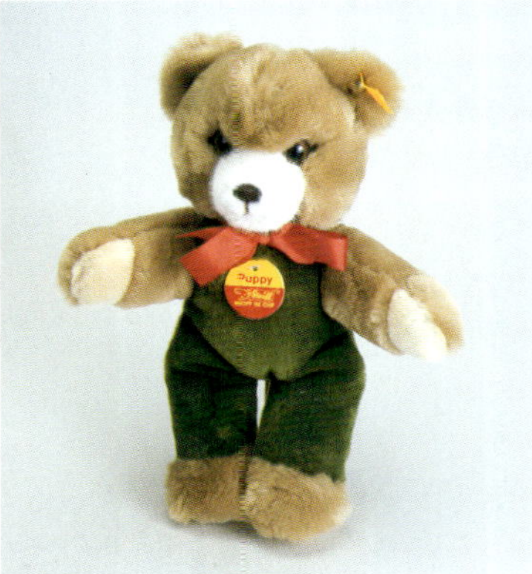

Puppy Baer - ***Puppy** Bear*

Webpelz, gruen/braun, Pieps-Stimme, waschmaschinenfest - *woven fur, green/brown, squeaker, machine washable*

EAN-No.	Period	Pr.	Info
124600	1996-1997	2	28 cm

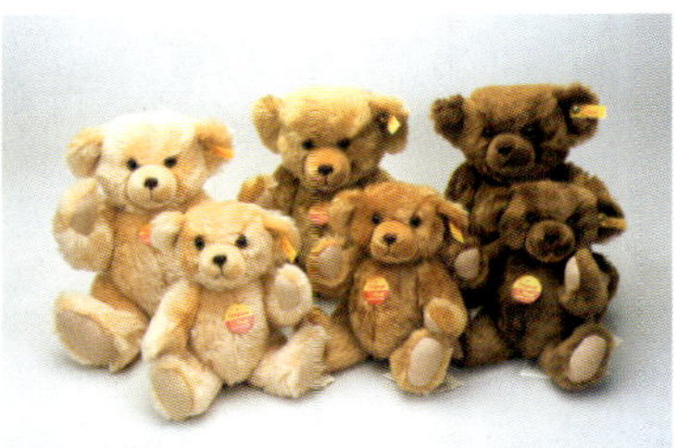

Teddybaer - *Teddybear*

Mohair Webpelz, hellblond, goldblond oder rotbraun, gegliedert, abwaschbar, Druckstimme - *mohair woven fur, light blond, gold blond or reddish brown, jointed, surface washable, press voice*

EAN-No.	Period	Pr.	Info
004018	1997-1998	2-3	26 cm, hellblond - *light blond*
004025	1997-1998	3	33 cm
004117	1997-1998	2-3	26 cm, goldblond - *gold blond*
004124	1997-1998	3	33 cm
004216	1997-1998	2-3	26 cm, rotbraun - *reddish brown*
004223	1997-1998	3	33 cm

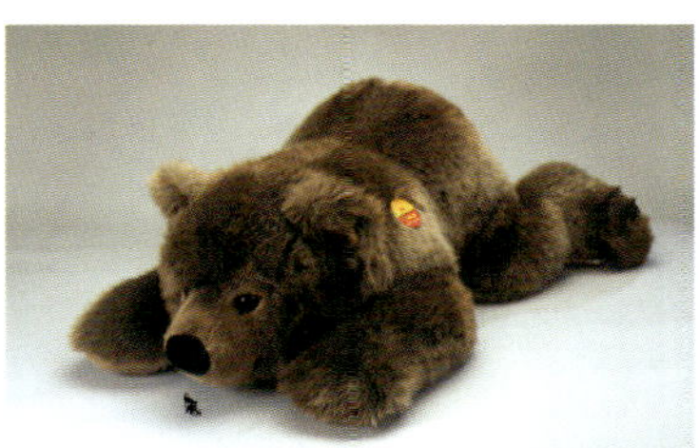

Urs Braunbaer - ***Urs** Brown Bear*

Webpelz, liegend - *woven fur, lying*

EAN-No.	Period	Pr.	Info
069666	1998-1999	3	45 cm
069673	1997-1999	3-4	55 cm
069680	1997-1999	4	90 cm
069697	1998-1999	5	120 cm

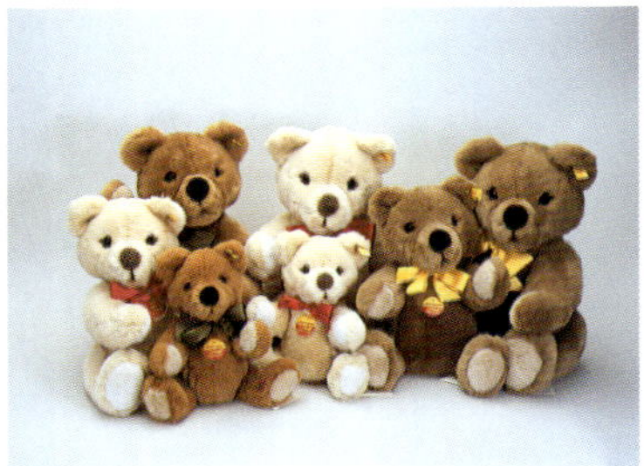

Bobby Teddybaer - ***Bobby** Teddybear*

Webpelz, gegliedert, Druck-Stimme, waschmaschinenfest - *woven fur, jointed, press voice, machine washable*

EAN-No.	Period	Pr.	Info
023200	1998-1999	2-3	28 cm, blond
023224	1998-1999	3	35 cm
023248	1998-1998	3	45 cm
023309	1998-1999	2-3	28 cm, whisky
023323	1998-1999	3	35 cm
023347	1998-1998	3	45 cm
023408	1998-1999	2-3	28 cm, braun - *brown*
023422	1998-1999	3	35 cm
023446	1998-1998	3	45 cm

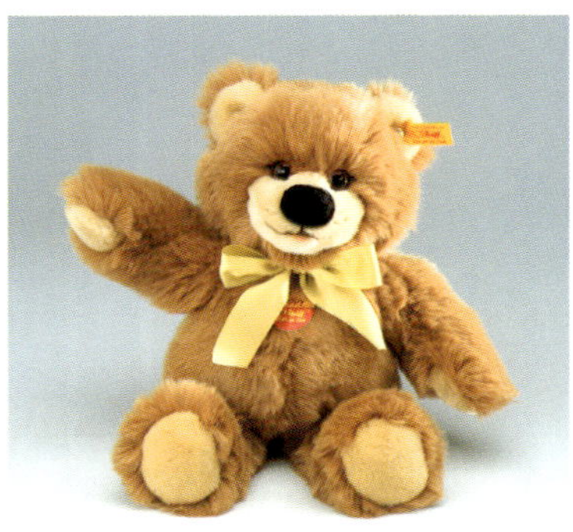

Poppy Baer - ***Poppy** Bear*

Webpelz, hellbraun, waschmaschinenfest - *woven fur, light brown, machine washable*

EAN-No.	Period	Pr.	Info
123740	1998-1999	2-3	30 cm

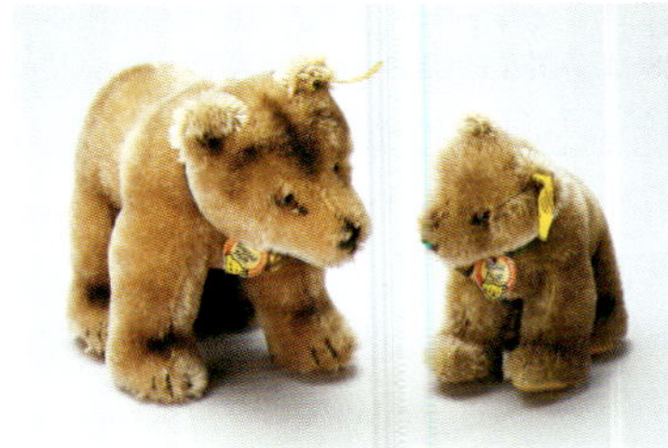

Jungbaer - *Bear Cub*

Mohair, caramel, stehend, Kopf drehbar, Lederhalsband mit Glocke - *mohair, caramel, standing, head swivels, leather collar with bell*

Serie	Art.-No	Period	Pr.	Info
12a	**1312,0**	1950-1958	4	12 cm
128	**1312,02**	1959-1964	4	
040	**1312,02**	1965-1967	4	
	0400/12	1968-1972	3-4	
12a	**1317,0**	1952-1953	4	17 cm
12a	**1317,02**	1954-1958	4	
128	**1317,02**	1961-1961	4	
040	**1317,02**	1965-1967	4	
	0400/17	1968-1972	3-4	
12a	**1325,01**	1952-1953	4	25 cm
12a	**1325,02**	1954-1958	4	
128	**1325,02**	1961-1961	4	
040	**1325,02**	1965-1966	4	

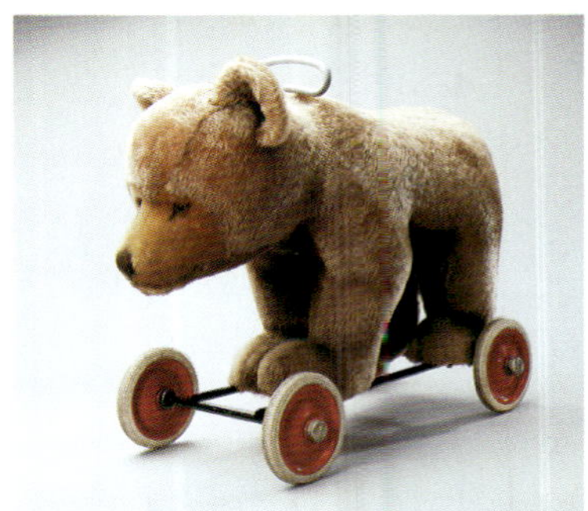

Jungbaer auf Raedern, ab 35 cm Reit-Jungbaer - *Bear Cub on wheels, from 35 cm Young Riding Bear*

Mohair, Eisengerippe, caramel, gruenes Lederhalsband, stehend auf Raedern, ab 35 cm gummibereifte Scheibenraeder mit Verbindungsschienen, ab 1967 Plastikreifen & Kunststofflager, ab 1968 Schlepplenkung, ab 43 cm Zugstimme & Haltegriff, abwaschbar - *mohair, metal frame, caramel, green leather collar, standing on wheels, from 35 cm rubber tires, disc wheels and connecting rods, from 1967 plastic tires & plastic bearings, from 1968 steered by a pull cord, from 43 cm pull voice & grip handle, surface washable*

Serie	Art.-No	Period	Pr.	Info
12a	**1328,1**	1950-1957	4	28 cm, Druckstimme, Holzraeder - *press voice, wooden wheels*
128	**1328,12**	1961-1961	4	

12a	**1335,1**	1950-1957	4	35 cm
128	**1335,12**	1961-1961	4	
128	**1343,22**	1960-1964	4-5	43 cm
040	**1343,22**	1965-1967	4-5	
	0400/43	1968-1976	4	
12a	**1350,2 J**	1951-1958	4-5	50 cm, ab 1953 auch mit Zusatz "ST" Steuerung - *from 1953 also available with steering "ST"*
128	**1350,22**	1959-1963	4-5	auch als 1350,32 mit Steuerung - *also 1350,32 with steering*
040	**1350,22**	1965-1967	4-5	
	0400/50	1968-1977	4-5	
12a	**1360,2 J**	1952-1958	5	60 cm, ab 1953 auch mit Zusatz "ST" Steuerung - *from 1953 also available with steering "ST"*
128	**1360,22**	1959-1963	5	auch als 1360,32 mit Steuerung - *also 1360,32 with steering*
040	**1360,22**	1965-1967	5	
	0400/60	1968-1976	5	
128	**1380,22**	1960-1963	5-6	80 cm
040	**1380,22**	1965-1967	5-6	
	0400/80	1968-1975	5-6	
128	**1399,22**	1962-1962	6	100 cm
040	**1399,22**	1966-1966	6	

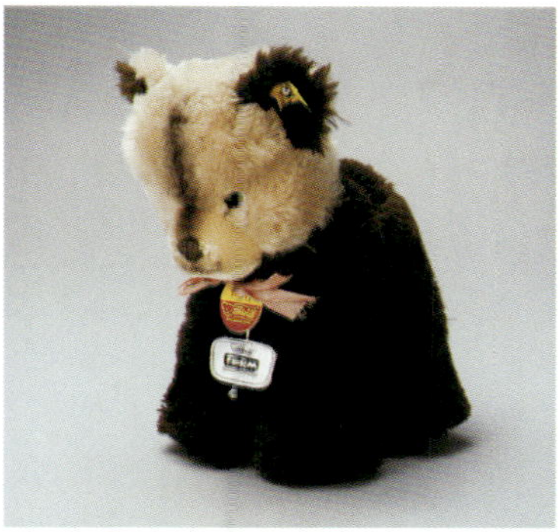

Jungbaer **Tapsy** - ***Tapsy** Bear Cub*

Dralon, formgeschaeumt, superweich, braun, stehend, abwaschbar - *dralon, stuffed with pre-formed foam, super soft, brown, standing, surface washable*

SERIE	ART.-NO	PERIOD	PR.	INFO
	6425/18	1973-1976	3	18 cm
	6425/25	1972-1978	3	25 cm

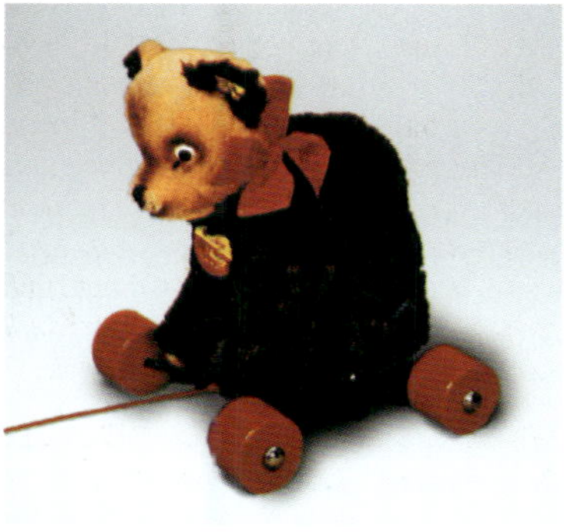

Rattler Jungbaer - ***Rattler** Bear Cub*

Dralon, auf Holz-Raeder, abwaschbar - *dralon, on wooden wheels, surface washable*

SERIE	ART.-NO	PERIOD	PR.	INFO
	0410/20	1973-1976	3-4	20 cm

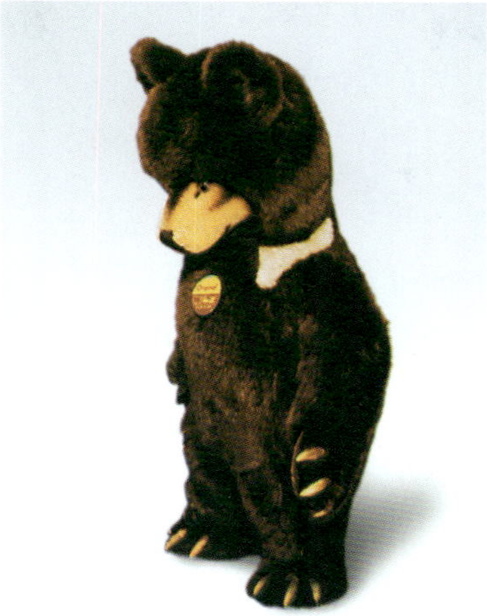

Jungbaer - *Bear Cub*

Pelzimitation, aufwartend, abwaschbar, dieser Baer wurde 1972 nur in USA angeboten - *imitation fur, sitting up, surface washable, in 1972 this bear was sold in the USA only*

SERIE	ART.-NO	PERIOD	PR.	INFO
	0418/80	1972-1975	5	80 cm

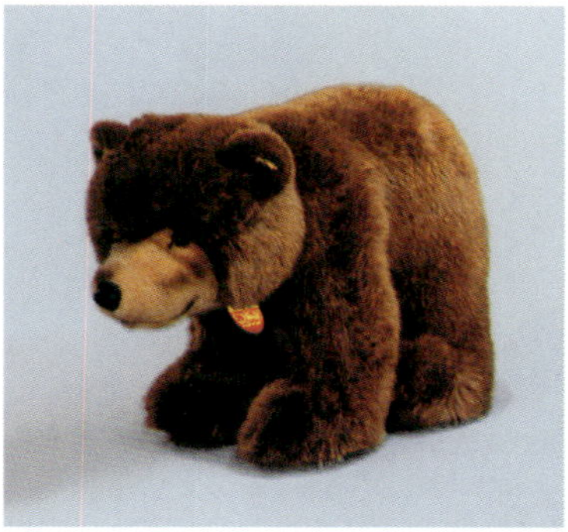

Jung Braunbaer - *Young Brown Bear*

Webpelz, stehend, abwaschbar - *woven fur, standing, surface washable*

SERIE	ART.-NO	PERIOD	PR.	INFO
	0417/60	1981-1983	3-4	60 cm

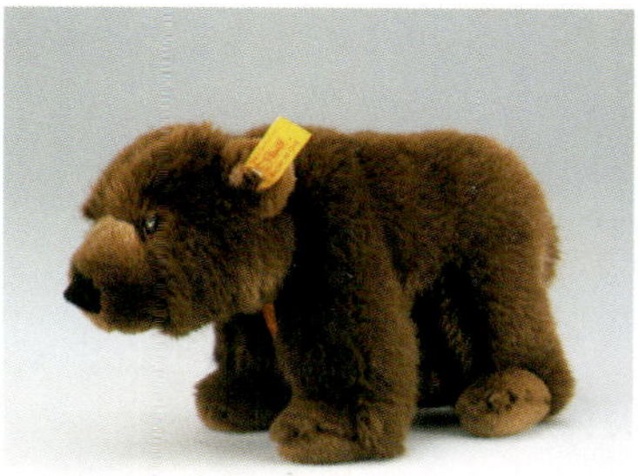

Baby Braunbaer - *Baby Brown Bear*

Webpelz, stehend, waschmaschinenfest - *woven fur, standing, machine washable*

EAN-NO.	PERIOD	PR.	INFO
069307	1997-1998	2	20 cm

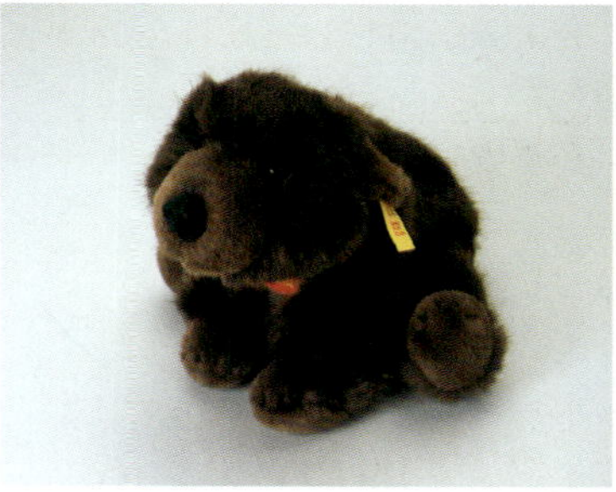

Baby Braunbaer - *Baby Brown Bear*

Webpelz, sitzend, waschmaschinenfest - *woven fur, sitting, machine washable*

EAN-NO.	PERIOD	PR.	INFO
069314	1997-1999	2-3	20 cm

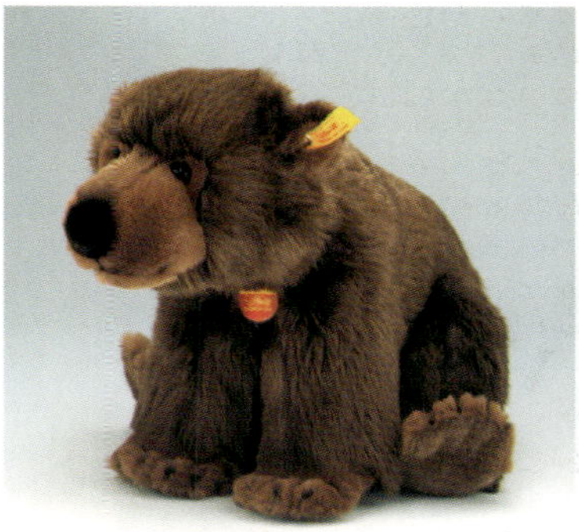

Braunbaer - *Brown Bear*

Webpelz, sitzend, waschmaschinenfest - *woven fur, sitting, machine washable*

EAN-NO.	PERIOD	PR.	INFO
069321	1997-1997	3	30 cm

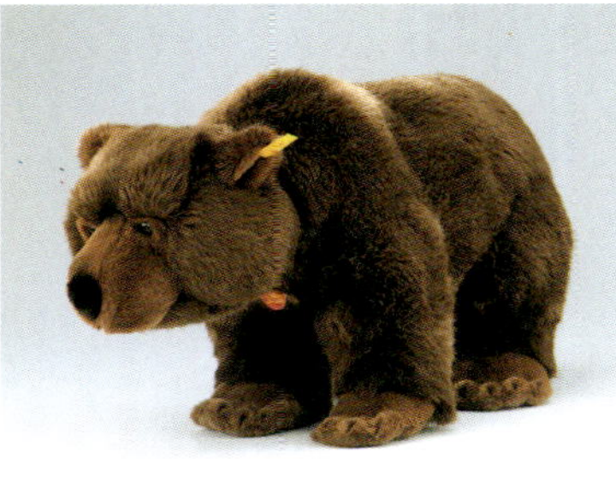

Braunbaer - *Brown Bear*

Webpelz, stehend, handwaschbar - *woven fur, standing, hand washable*

EAN-No.	Period	Pr.	Info
069338	1997-1997	3	45 cm

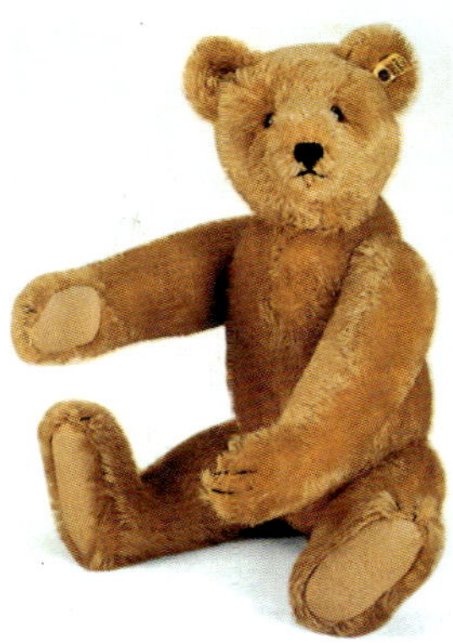

Original Teddy

blond, wie bereits bis 1940 im Programm, Mohair, gegliedert, ab Groesse 25 cm Doppeldruckstimme, ab Groesse 43 cm automatische Brummstimme - *blond, identical to the one produced prior to 1940, mohair, jointed, from 25 cm double press voice, from 43 cm automatic growler*

Serie	Art.-No	Period	Pr.	Info
12	**5310** bl	1949-1949	5-6	10 cm
12	**5315** bl	1949-1949	5-6	15 cm
12	**5323** bl	1949-1949	6	23 cm
12	**5325,2** bl	1949-1949	6	25 cm
12	**5330,2** bl	1949-1949	6-7	30 cm
12	**5335,2** bl	1949-1949	7	35 cm
12	**5343,2** bl	1949-1949	7	43 cm
12	**5350,2** bl	1949-1949	7-8	50 cm

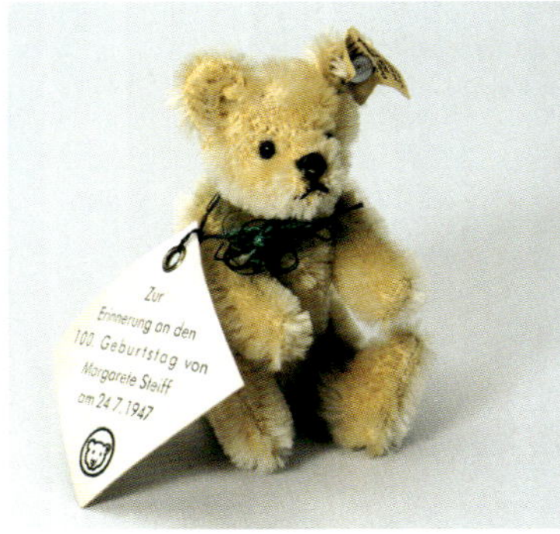

Original Teddy

Mohair, hellblond, gegliedert, Sonderausgabe zum 100. Geburtstag der Margarete Steiff, mit Anhaenger "Zur Erinnerung an den 100. Geburtstag von Margarete Steiff am 24.7.1947" - *mohair, light blond, jointed, special edition on the occasion of the 100. birthday of Margarete Steiff, with label "Zur Erinnerung an den 100. Geburtstag von Margarete Steiff am 24.7.1947"*

Serie	Art.-No	Period	Pr.	Info
12	**5310**	1947-1947	7	10 cm

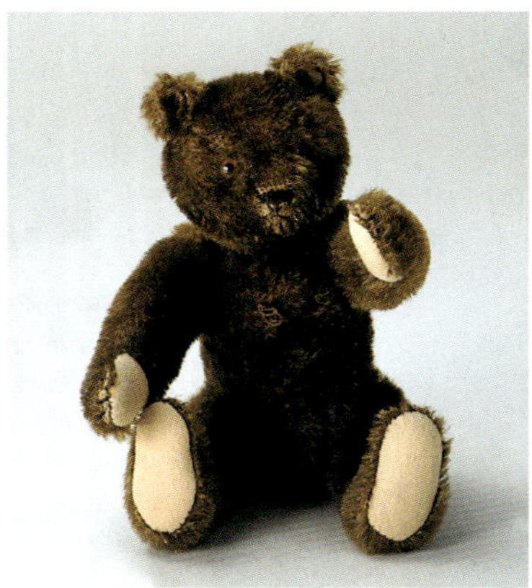

Original Teddy

dunkelbraun, wie bereits bis 1940 im Programm, Mohair, gegliedert, ab Groesse 25 cm Doppeldruckstimme, ab Groesse 43 cm automatische Brummstimme - *dark brown, identical to the one produced prior to 1940, mohair, jointed, from 25 cm double press voice, from 43 cm automatic growler*

Serie	Art.-No	Period	Pr.	Info
12	**5310** br	1949-1949	6	10 cm
12	**5315** br	1949-1949	6	15 cm
12	**5323** br	1949-1949	6	23 cm
12	**5325,2** br	1949-1949	6	25 cm
12	**5330,2** br	1949-1949	6-7	30 cm
12	**5335,2** br	1949-1949	7	35 cm
12	**5343,2** br	1949-1949	7-8	43 cm
12	**5350,2** br	1949-1949	8	50 cm

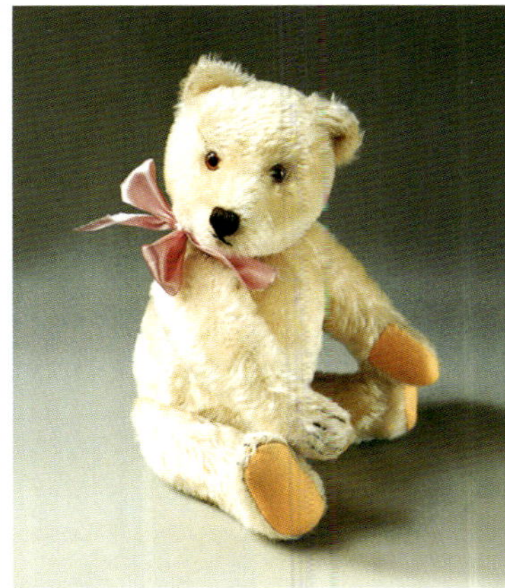

Original Teddy

weiss, wie bereits bis 1940 im Programm, Mohair, gegliedert, ab Groesse 25 cm Doppeldruckstimme, ab Groesse 43 cm automatische Brummstimme - *white, identical to the one produced prior to 1940, mohair, jointed, from 25 cm double press voice, from 43 cm automatic growler*

Serie	Art.-No	Period	Pr.	Info
12	**5310** w	1949-1949	6	10 cm
12	**5315** w	1949-1949	6	15 cm
12	**5323** w	1949-1949	6-7	23 cm
12	**5325,2** w	1949-1949	6-7	25 cm
12	**5330,2** w	1949-1949	7	30 cm
12	**5335,2** w	1949-1949	7-8	35 cm
12	**5343,2** w	1949-1949	8	43 cm
12	**5350,2** w	1949-1949	8	50 cm

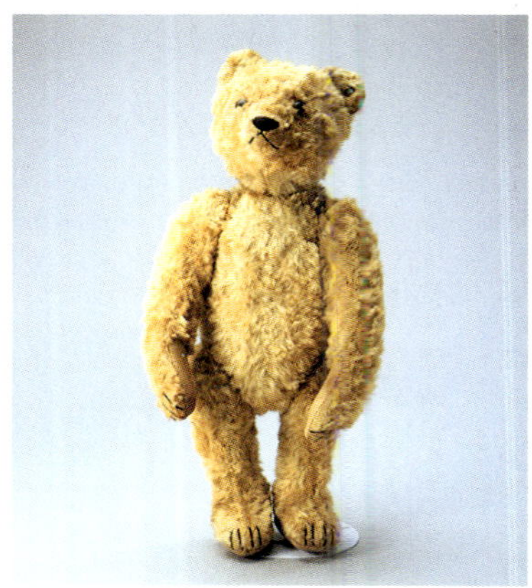

Original Teddy

Kunstseidenpluesch, blond, gegliedert, Druckstimme, ab Groesse 43 cm automatische Brummstimme - *artificial silk plush, blond, jointed, press voice, from 43 cm automatic growler*

Serie	Art.-No	Period	Pr.	Info
12	**5625,2**	1949-1949	6	25 cm
12	**5630,2**	1948-1949	6	30 cm
12	**5635,2**	1948-1949	6-7	35 cm

12	**5643,2**	1949-1949	7	43 cm
12	**5650,2**	1949-1949	7-8	50 cm

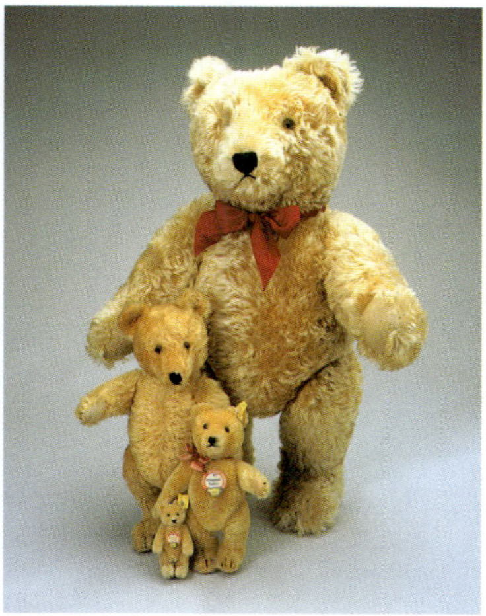

Original Teddy

Mohair, gold oder blond, gegliedert, ab 22 cm Druckstimme, ab 43 cm Automatik-Stimme (Ausnahmen siehe Tabelle), ab 18 cm mit Filzfuessen, ab 22 cm Filzpfoten & -fuesse, bis 15 cm Nase quer - ab 18 cm laengs gestickt - *mohair, gold or blond, jointed, from 22 cm press voice, from 43 cm automatic voice (see chart for exceptions), from 18 cm felt covered sole, from 22 cm felt covered paws & sole, nose is stitched horizontally up to 15 cm, from 18 cm stitched vertically*

SERIE	ART.-NO	PERIOD	PR.	INFO
12	**5310** g	1950-1958	5-6	10 cm
120	**5310,01**	1959-1964	5	
020	**5311,01**	1965-1966	3	11 cm, Biegeglieder - *flexible limbs*
12	**5315** g	1950-1958	5-6	15 cm
120	**5315,01**	1959-1964	5	
020	**5315,01**	1965-1966	5	
12	**5318** g	1954-1958	6	18 cm
120	**5318,01**	1959-1964	5-6	Druckstimme - *press voice*
020	**5318,01**	1965-1965	5-6	
12	**5322** g	1950-1953	6	22 cm
12	**5322,2** g	1954-1958	6	
120	**5322,01**	1959-1964	6	
020	**5322,01**	1965-1965	6	
12	**5325,2** g	1951-1958	6	25 cm
120	**5325,01**	1959-1964	6	
020	**5325,01**	1965-1966	6	
12	**5328,2** g	1950-1958	6	28 cm
120	**5328,01**	1959-1964	6	
020	**5328,01**	1965-1965	6	
12	**5335,2** g	1950-1958	6-7	35 cm
120	**5335,01**	1959-1964	6	
020	**5335,01**	1965-1966	6	autom. Kippstimme - *growler*
12	**5340,2** g	1956-1958	6-7	40 cm
120	**5340,01**	1959-1964	6-7	
020	**5340,01**	1965-1966	6-7	autom. Kippstimme - *growler*
12	**5343,2** g	1950-1958	7	43 cm
120	**5343,01**	1959-1964	7	
020	**5343,01**	1965-1966	7	
12	**5350,2** g	1950-1958	7	50 cm
120	**5350,01**	1959-1964	7	
020	**5350,01**	1965-1966	7	
12	**5365,2** g	1950-1958	7-8	65 cm
120	**5365,01**	1959-1964	7-8	
020	**5365,01**	1965-1965	7-8	
12	**5375,2** g	1950-1958	8	75 cm
120	**5375,01**	1959-1964	8	
020	**5375,01**	1965-1965	8	

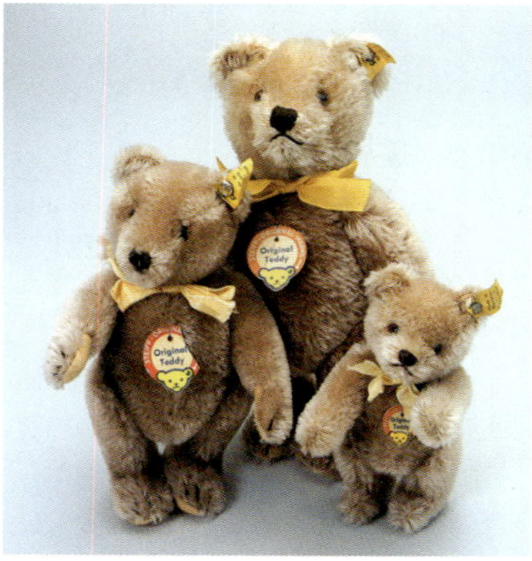

Original Teddy

Mohair, caramel, gegliedert, ab 22 cm Druckstimme, ab 43 cm Automatik-Stimme (Ausnahmen siehe Tabelle), ab 18 cm mit Filzfuessen, ab 22 cm Filzpfoten & -fuesse, bis 15 cm Nase quer - ab 18 cm laengs gestickt - *mohair, caramel, jointed, from 22 cm press voice, from 43 cm automatic voice (see chart for exceptions), from 18 cm felt covered sole, from 22 cm felt covered paws & sole, nose is stitched horizontally up to 15 cm, from 18 cm stitched vertically*

SERIE	ART.-NO	PERIOD	PR.	INFO
12	**5310** c	1951-1958	4-5	10 cm
120	**5310,02**	1959-1964	4-5	
021	**5311,02**	1965-1966	3	11 cm, Biegeglieder - *flexible limbs*
12	**5315** c	1951-1958	5	15 cm
120	**5315,02**	1959-1964	5	
021	**5315,02**	1965-1966	5	
12	**5318** c	1954-1958	5	18 cm
120	**5318,02**	1959-1964	5	Druckstimme - *press voice*
021	**5318,02**	1965-1966	5	
12	**5322** c	1951-1953	5-6	22 cm
12	**5322,2** c	1954-1958	5-6	
120	**5322,02**	1959-1964	5-6	
021	**5322,02**	1965-1966	5-6	
12	**5325,2** c	1951-1958	5-6	25 cm
120	**5325,02**	1959-1964	5-6	
021	**5325,02**	1965-1966	5-6	
12	**5328,2** c	1951-1958	5-6	28 cm
120	**5328,02**	1959-1964	5-6	
021	**5328,02**	1965-1966	5-6	
12	**5335,2** c	1951-1958	6	35 cm
120	**5335,02**	1959-1964	6	
021	**5335,02**	1965-1966	6	autom. Kippstimme - *growler*
12	**5340,2** c	1956-1958	6-7	40 cm
120	**5340,02**	1959-1964	6	
021	**5340,02**	1965-1966	6	autom. Kippstimme - *growler*
12	**5343,2** c	1951-1958	6-7	43 cm
120	**5343,02**	1959-1964	6-7	
021	**5343,02**	1965-1966	6-7	
12	**5350,2** c	1951-1958	7	50 cm
120	**5350,02**	1959-1964	7	
021	**5350,02**	1965-1966	7	
12	**5365,2** c	1951-1958	7-8	65 cm
120	**5365,02**	1959-1964	7	
021	**5365,02**	1965-1966	7	
12	**5375,2** c	1951-1958	7-8	75 cm
120	**5375,02**	1959-1964	7-8	
021	**5375,02**	1965-1966	7-8	
	0209/10	1967-1967	8	100 cm, Schautier - *display animal*

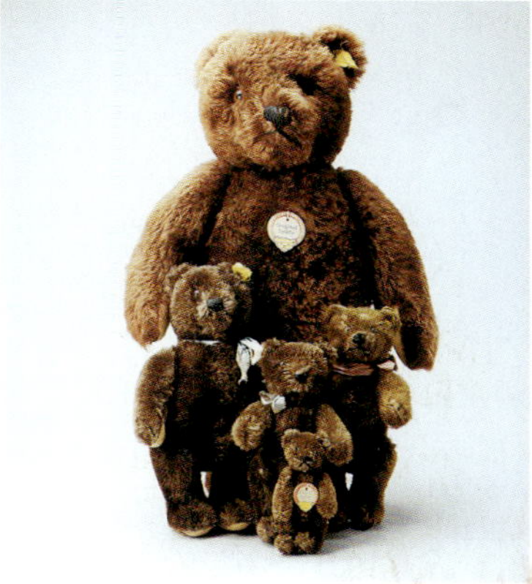

Original Teddy

Mohair, dunkelbraun, gegliedert, ab 22 cm Druckstimme, ab 43 cm Automatik-Stimme (Ausnahmen siehe Tabelle), ab 18 cm mit Filzfuessen, ab 22 cm Filzpfoten & -fuesse, bis 15 cm Nase quer - ab 18 cm laengs gestickt - *mohair, dark brown, jointed, from 22 cm press voice, from 43 cm automatic voice (see chart for exceptions), from 18 cm felt covered sole, from 22 cm felt covered paws & sole, nose is stitched horizontally up to 15 cm, from 18 cm stitched vertically*

SERIE	ART.-NO	PERIOD	PR.	INFO
12	**5310** br	1950-1958	5-6	10 cm
120	**5310,03**	1959-1964	5	
12	**5315** br	1950-1958	5-6	15 cm
120	**5315,03**	1959-1964	5	
12	**5318** br	1954-1958	6	18 cm
120	**5318,03**	1959-1964	6	Druckstimme - *press voice*
12	**5322** br	1950-1953	6	22 cm
12	**5322,2** br	1954-1958	6	
120	**5322,03**	1959-1964	6	
12	**5325,2** br	1951-1958	6-7	25 cm
120	**5325,03**	1959-1964	6-7	
12	**5328,2** br	1950-1958	6-7	28 cm
120	**5328,03**	1959-1964	6-7	
12	**5335,2** br	1950-1958	6-7	35 cm
120	**5335,03**	1959-1964	6-7	

12	**5340,2** br	1956-1958	7	40 cm
120	**5340,03**	1959-1964	7	
12	**5343,2** br	1950-1958	7	43 cm
120	**5343,03**	1959-1964	7	
12	**5350,2** br	1950-1958	7-8	50 cm
120	**5350,03**	1959-1964	7-8	
12	**5365,2** br	1950-1958	8	65 cm
120	**5365,03**	1959-1964	8	
12	**5375,2** br	1950-1958	8	75 cm
120	**5375,03**	1959-1964	8	

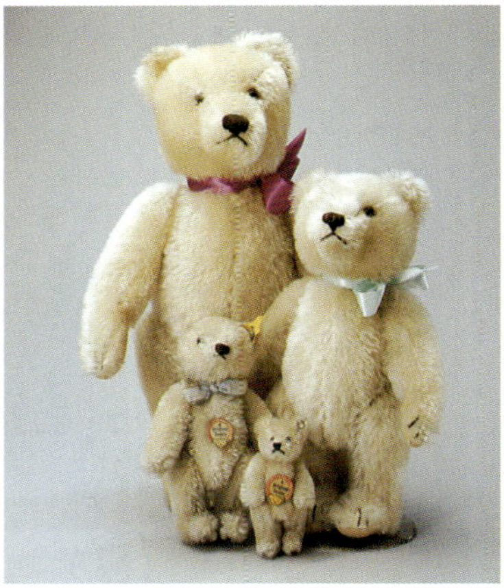

Original Teddy

Mohair, weiss, gegliedert, ab 22 cm Druckstimme, ab 43 cm Automatik-Stimme (Ausnahmen siehe Tabelle), ab 18 cm mit Filzfuessen, ab 22 cm Filzpfoten & -fuesse, bis 15 cm Nase quer - ab 18 cm laengs gestickt - *mohair, white, jointed, from 22 cm press voice, from 43 cm automatic voice (see chart for exceptions), from 18 cm felt covered sole, from 22 cm felt covered paws & sole, nose is stitched horizontally up to 15 cm, from 18 cm stitched vertically*

SERIE	ART.-NO	PERIOD	PR.	INFO
12	**5310** w	1950-1958	5-6	10 cm
120	**5310,04**	1959-1964	5-6	
12	**5315** w	1950-1958	5-6	15 cm
120	**5315,04**	1959-1964	5-6	
12	**5318** w	1954-1958	6	18 cm
120	**5318,04**	1959-1964	6	Druckstimme - *press voice*
12	**5322** w	1950-1953	6	22 cm
12	**5322,2** w	1954-1958	6	
120	**5322,04**	1959-1964	6	
12	**5325,2** w	1951-1958	6	25 cm
120	**5325,04**	1959-1964	6	
12	**5328,2** w	1950-1958	6-7	28 cm
120	**5328,04**	1959-1964	6-7	
12	**5335,2** w	1950-1958	7	35 cm
120	**5335,04**	1959-1964	7	
12	**5340,2** w	1956-1958	7	40 cm
120	**5340,04**	1959-1964	7	
12	**5343,2** w	1950-1958	7	43 cm
120	**5343,04**	1959-1964	7	
12	**5350,2** w	1950-1958	7-8	50 cm
120	**5350,04**	1959-1964	7-8	
12	**5365,2** w	1950-1958	8	65 cm

120	**5365,04**	1959-1964	8	
12	**5375,2** w	1950-1958	8-9	75 cm
120	**5375,04**	1959-1964	8-9	

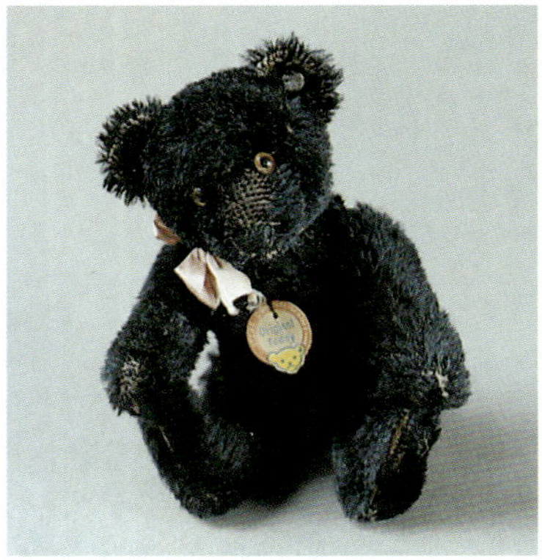

Original Teddy

Mohair, schwarz, gegliedert, Prototyp, kein Katalognachweis - *mohair, black, jointed, development piece, no reference in catalogs*

SERIE	ART.-NO	PERIOD	PR.	INFO
12	**5310** s	1950-1950	8	10 cm
12	**5315** s	1950-1950	8	15 cm

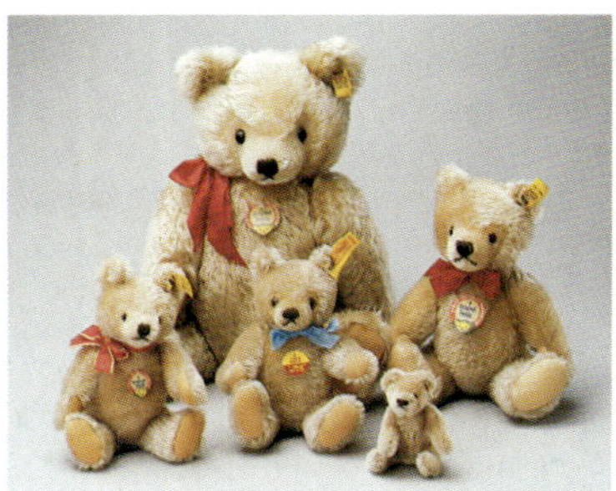

Original Teddybaer - *Original Teddybear*

Mohair, ab 1983 Mohair-Webpelz, honig (1993 blond), gegliedert, Maskengesicht, ab 18 cm Druckstimme, ab 36 cm Automatic-Stimme, ab 18 cm mit Filzpfoten & -fuessen, ab 1970 Pfoten & Fuesse mit Synthetik-Velours, bis 1970 Holzwolle-Stopfung (es gibt mit Holzwolle gestopfte Baeren, die Synthetik-Velours Pfoten & Fuesse haben), 11 cm Nase quer - alle anderen Groessen laengs gestickt, abwaschbar - *mohair, from 1983 mohair woven fur, honey (1993 blond), jointed, masked face, from 18 cm press voice, from 36 cm automatic voice, from 18 cm felt paws & feet, from 1970 paws & feet are covered with synthetic velvet, up to 1970 stuffed with excelsior (there are bears stuffed with excelsior which have synthetic velvet paws & feet), 11 cm nose stitched horizontally, all other sizes nose stitched vertically, surface washable*

SERIE	ART.-NO	PERIOD	PR.	INFO
020	**5311,01**	1966-1967	3	11 cm, Biegeglieder - *flexible limbs*
001086	**0201/11**	1968-1990	2-3	
001154	**0201/18**	1983-1990	2-3	18 cm
	001154	1991-1993	2-3	
020	**5319,01**	1966-1967	4	19 cm
	0201/19	1968-1975	3-4	
020	**5326,01**	1966-1967	4	26 cm
001208	**0201/26**	1968-1990	3	
	001208	1991-1993	3	
020	**5336,01**	1966-1967	4	36 cm
001253	**0201/36**	1968-1990	3-4	
	001253	1991-1993	3	
020	**5341,01**	1966-1967	4-5	41 cm
	0201/41	1968-1977	3-4	
001307	**0201/41**	1982-1990	3-4	
	001307	1991-1993	3	
020	**5351,01**	1966-1967	4-5	51 cm
	0201/51	1968-1976	4	
001352	**0201/51**	1982-1990	4	
	001352	1991-1992	3-4	
020	**5366,01**	1966-1967	5	66 cm
	0201/66	1968-1975	4-5	
001406	**0201/75**	1983-1989	5	75 cm
001451	**0201/99**	1982-1988	6	100 cm

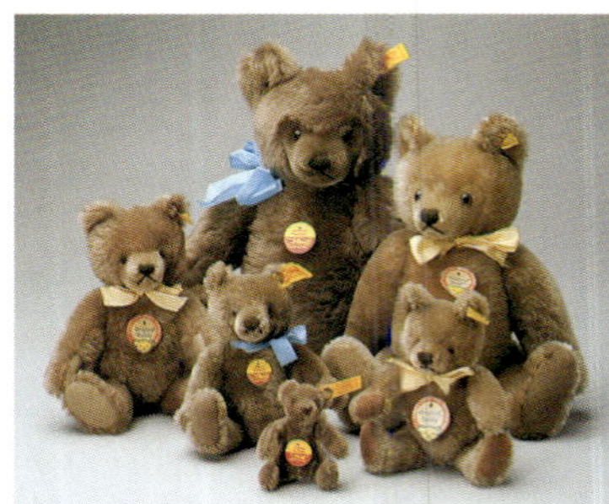

Original Teddybaer - *Original Teddybear*

Mohair, ab 1984 Mohair-Webpelz, caramel, gegliedert, Maskengesicht, ab 18 cm Druckstimme, ab 36 cm Automatic-Stimme, ab 18 cm mit Filzpfoten & -fuessen, ab 1970 Pfoten & Fuesse mit Synthetik-Velours, bis 1970 Holzwolle-Stopfung (es gibt mit Holzwolle gestopfte Baeren, die Synthetik-Velours Pfoten & Fuesse haben), 11 cm Nase quer - alle anderen Groessen laengs gestickt, abwaschbar - *mohair, from 1984 mohair woven fur, caramel, jointed, masked face, from 18 cm press voice, from 36 cm automatic voice, from 18 cm felt paws & feet, from 1970, paws & feet synthetic velvet, up to 1970 stuffed with excelsior (there are bears stuffed with excelsior which have synthetic velvet paws & feet), 11 cm nose stitched horizontally, all other sizes nose stitched vertically, surface washable*

SERIE	ART.-NO	PERIOD	PR.	INFO
021	**5311,02**	1966-1967	3	11 cm, Biegeglieder - *flexible limbs*
002083	**0202/11**	1968-1990	2-3	

002151	**0202/18**	1983-1990	2-3	18 cm
	002151	1991-1993	2-3	
021	**5319,02**	1966-1967	4	19 cm
	0202/19	1968-1975	3	
021	**5326,02**	1966-1967	4	26 cm
002205	**0202/26**	1968-1990	3	
	002205	1991-1993	3	
021	**5336,02**	1966-1967	4	36 cm
002250	**0202/36**	1968-1990	3-4	
	002250	1991-1993	3	
021	**5341,02**	1966-1967	4-5	41 cm
002304	**0202/41**	1968-1990	3-4	
	002304	1991-1992	3	
021	**5351,02**	1966-1967	5	51 cm
002359	**0202/51**	1968-1990	4	
	002359	1991-1992	3-4	
021	**5366,02**	1966-1967	5	66 cm
	0202/66	1968-1975	4-5	
002403	**0202/75**	1983-1989	5	75 cm
002458	**0202/99**	1983-1988	6	100 cm

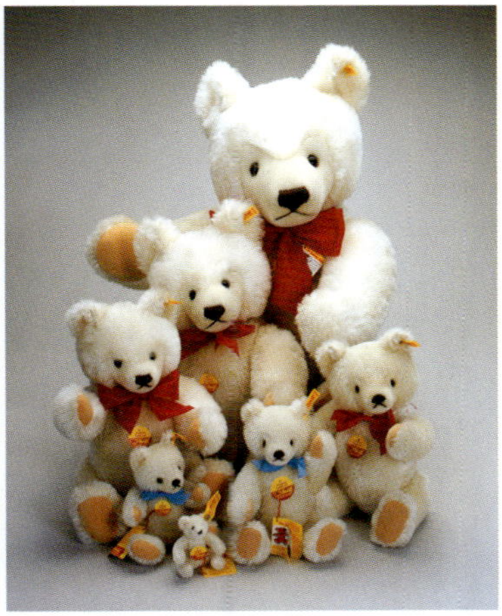

Original Teddybaer - *Original Teddybear*

Mohair-Webpelz, weiss, gegliedert, Maskengesicht, ab 18 cm Druckstimme, ab 36 cm Brummstimme, ab 18 cm mit Synthetik-Velours Pfoten & Fuessen, 11 cm Nase quer - alle anderen Groessen laengs gestickt, abwaschbar - *mohair woven fur, white, jointed, masked face, from 18 cm press voice, from 36 cm growler, from 18 cm synthetic velvet paws & feet, 11cm nose stitched horizontally, all other sizes nose stitched vertically, surface washable*

SERIE	ART.-NO	PERIOD	PR.	INFO
003080	**0203/11**	1983-1987	3	11 cm, Biegeglieder - *flexible limbs*
003158	**0203/18**	1983-1987	3	18 cm
003202	**0203/26**	1983-1987	3	26 cm
003257	**0203/36**	1983-1987	4	36 cm
003301	**0203/41**	1983-1987	4	41 cm
003356	**0203/51**	1983-1987	4-5	51 cm
	0203/75	1983-1984	5	75 cm
	0203/99	1983-1984	6	100 cm

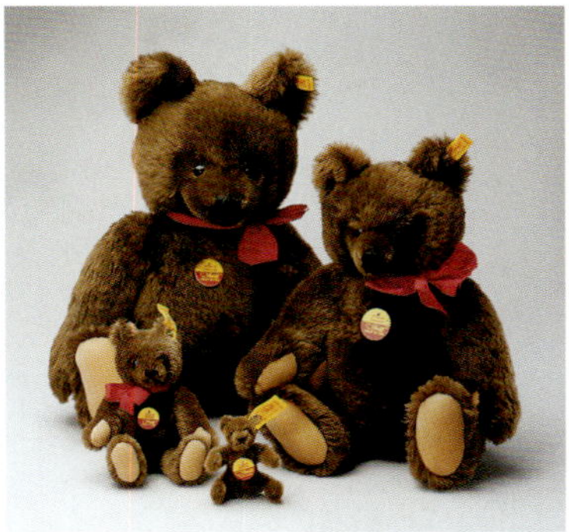

Original Teddybaer - *Original Teddybear*

Mohair-Webpelz, braun, gegliedert, Maskengesicht, ab 18 cm Druckstimme, ab 36 cm Brummstimme, ab 18 cm mit Synthetik-Velours Pfoten & Fuessen, 11 cm Nase quer - alle anderen Groessen laengs gestickt, abwaschbar - *mohair woven fur, brown, jointed, masked face, from 18 cm press voice, from 36 cm growler, from 18 cm synthetic velvet paws & feet, 11 cm nose stitched horizontally, all other sizes nose stitched vertically, surface washable*

SERIE	ART.-NO	PERIOD	PR.	INFO
006081	**0206/11**	1984-1990	2-3	11 cm, Biegeglieder - *flexible limbs*
006159	**0206/18**	1984-1990	2-3	18 cm
006203	**0206/26**	1984-1990	3	26 cm
006258	**0206/36**	1984-1990	3-4	36 cm
006302	**0206/41**	1984-1990	4	41 cm
006357	**0206/51**	1984-1990	4	51 cm

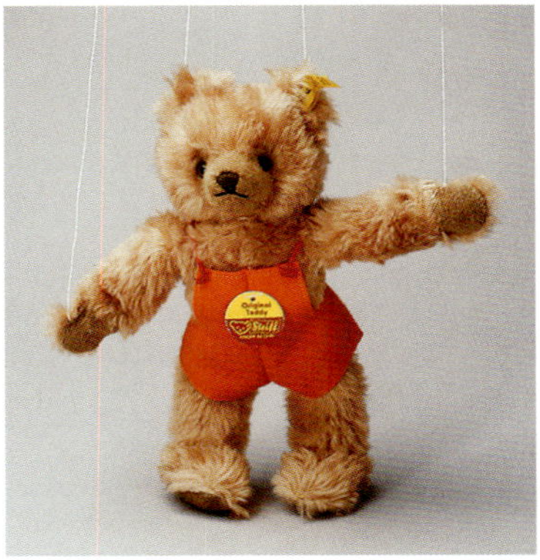

Original Teddybaer Marionette - *Original Teddybear puppet*

Dralon, hellbraun, Filzbekleidung, abwaschbar - *dralon, light brown, felt fabric clothes, surface washable*

SERIE	ART.-NO	PERIOD	PR.	INFO
	7726/25	1974-1975	4	25 cm

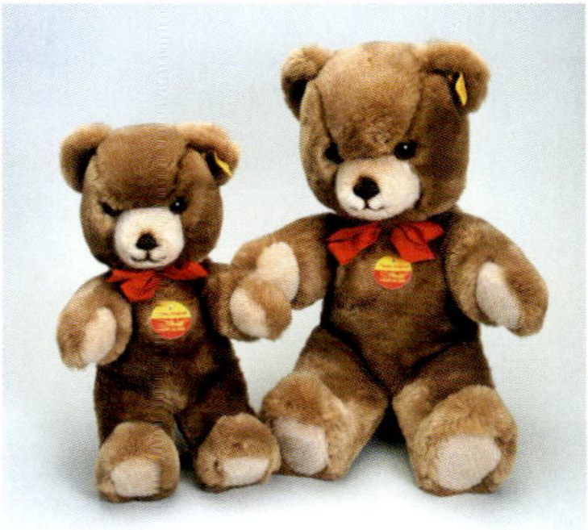

Teddy Original

Nerzimitation, ab 1978 Synthetik-Webpelz, Koerper formgeschaeumt, Arme & Beine biegsam, abwaschbar - *imitation mink fur, synthetic woven fur from 1978, body stuffed with pre-formed foam, arms & legs are flexible, surface washable*

SERIE	ART.-NO	PERIOD	PR.	INFO
018503	**0205/26**	1976-1988	2-3	26 cm
018558	**0205/35**	1976-1988	2-3	35 cm
	0205/50	1976-1984	2-3	50 cm

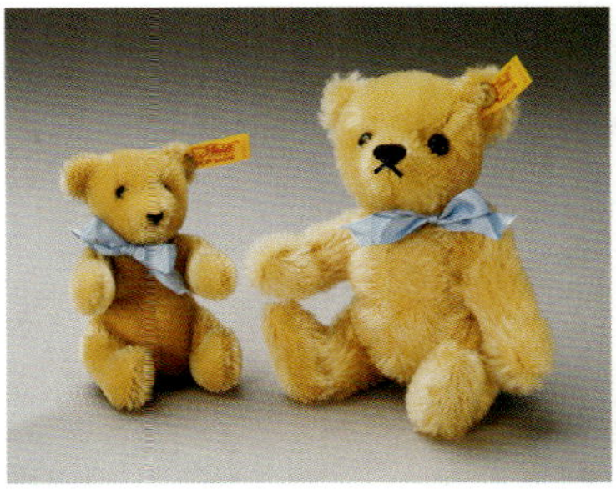

Original Teddybaer - *Original Teddybear*

Mohair Webpelz, blond, 12 cm Kopf drehbar, 15 cm gegliedert, abwaschbar - *mohair woven fur, blond, 12 cm swivel head, 15 cm jointed, surface washable*

SERIE	ART.-NO	PERIOD	PR.	INFO
030222	**0210/12**	1989-1990	2	12 cm
	030222	1991-1999	2	
030246	**0210/15**	1989-1990	2-3	15 cm
	030246	1991-1999	2-3	

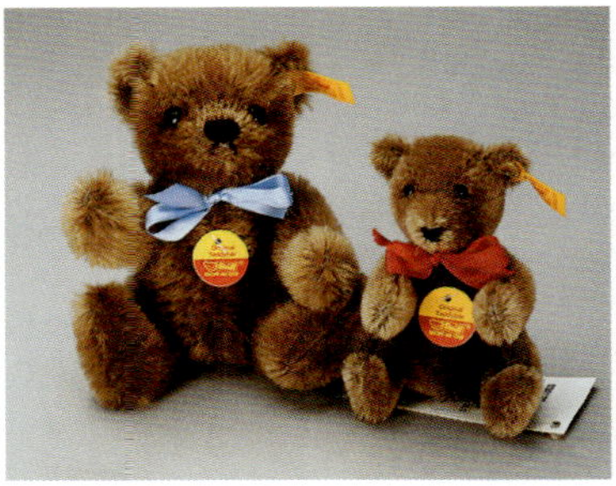

Original Teddybaer - *Original Teddybear*

Mohair Webpelz, caramel, 12 cm Kopf drehbar, 15 cm gegliedert, abwaschbar - *mohair woven fur, caramel, 12 cm swivel head, 15 cm jointed, surface washable*

SERIE	ART.-NO	PERIOD	PR.	INFO
030123	**0202/12**	1989-1990	2	12 cm
	030123	1991-1999	2	
030147	**0202/15**	1989-1990	2-3	15 cm
	030147	1991-1999	2-3	

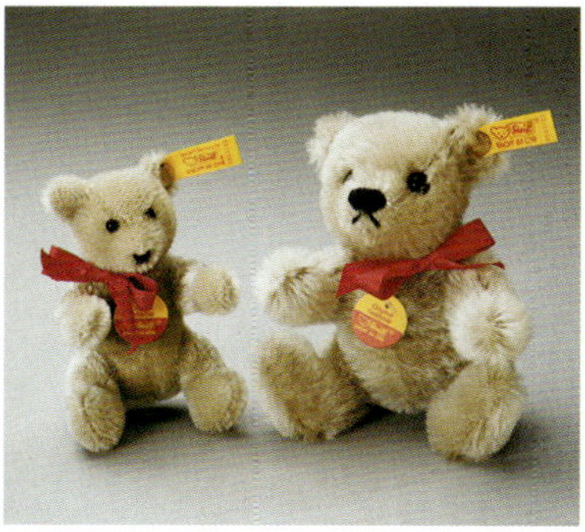

Original Teddybaer - *Original Teddybear*

Mohair Webpelz, grau, 12 cm Kopf drehbar, 15 cm gegliedert, abwaschbar - *mohair woven fur, grey, 12 cm swivel head, 15 cm jointed, surface washable*

SERIE	ART.-NO	PERIOD	PR.	INFO
030321	**0207/12**	1990-1990	2	12 cm
	030321	1991-1993	2	
030345	**0207/15**	1990-1990	2-3	15 cm
	030345	1991-1993	2-3	

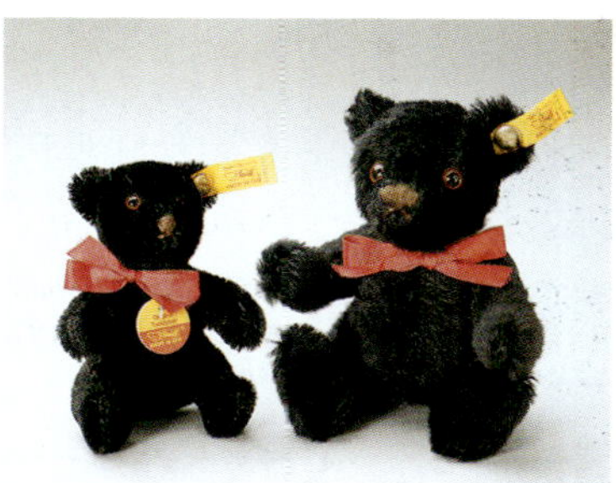

Original Teddybaer - *Original Teddybear*

Mohair Webpelz, schwarz, 12 cm Kopf drehbar, 15 cm gegliedert, abwaschbar - *mohair woven fur, black, 12 cm swivel head, 15 cm jointed, surface washable*

SERIE	ART.-NO	PERIOD	PR.	INFO
030529	**0209/12**	1990-1990	2	12 cm
	030529	1991-1993	2	
030543	**0209/15**	1990-1990	2-3	15 cm
	030543	1991-1993	2-3	

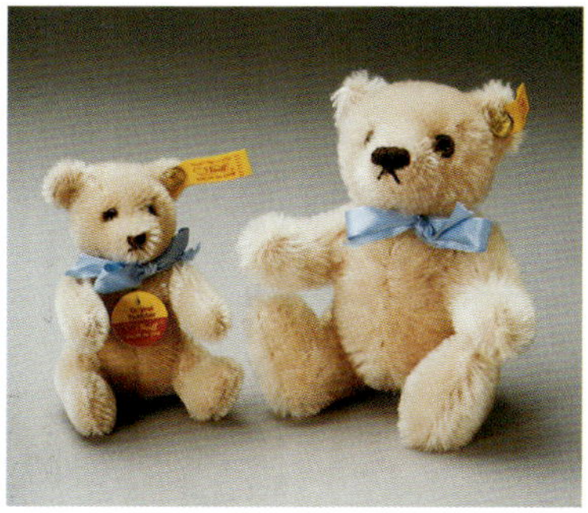

Original Teddybaer - *Original Teddybear*

Mohair Webpelz, rosé, 12 cm Kopf drehbar, 15 cm gegliedert, abwaschbar - *mohair woven fur, rose, 12 cm swivel head, 15 cm jointed, surface washable*

SERIE	ART.-NO	PERIOD	PR.	INFO
030420	**0211/12**	1990-1990	2	12 cm
	030420	1991-1993	2	
030444	**0211/15**	1990-1990	2-3	15 cm
	030444	1991-1993	2-3	

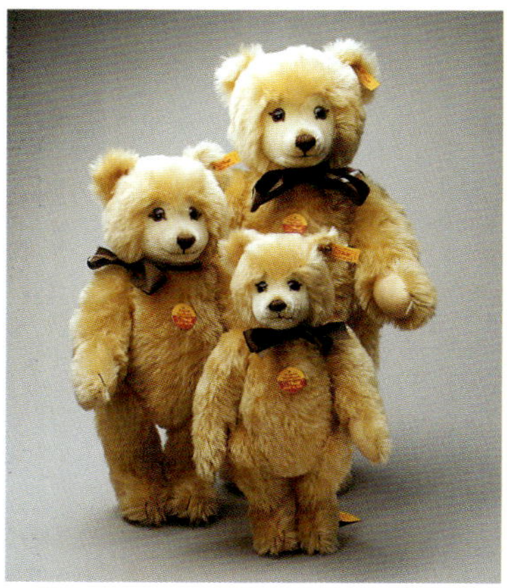

Original Steiffteddy

Mohair Webpelz, blond, gegliedert, Brumm-Stimme, abwaschbar - *mohair woven fur, blond, jointed, growler, surface washable*

EAN-NO.	PERIOD	PR.	INFO
010354	1991-1994	3	36 cm
010408	1991-1995	3-4	43 cm
010453	1991-1996	4	55 cm

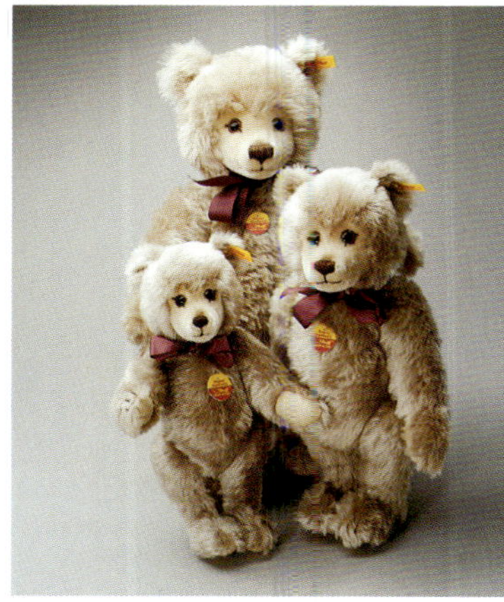

Original Steiffteddy

Mohair Webpelz, dunkelblond, gegliedert, Brumm-Stimme, abwaschbar - *mohair woven fur, dark blond, jointed, growler, surface washable*

EAN-NO.	PERIOD	PR.	INFO
010859	1991-1993	3	36 cm
010903	1991-1993	3-4	43 cm
010958	1991-1993	4	55 cm

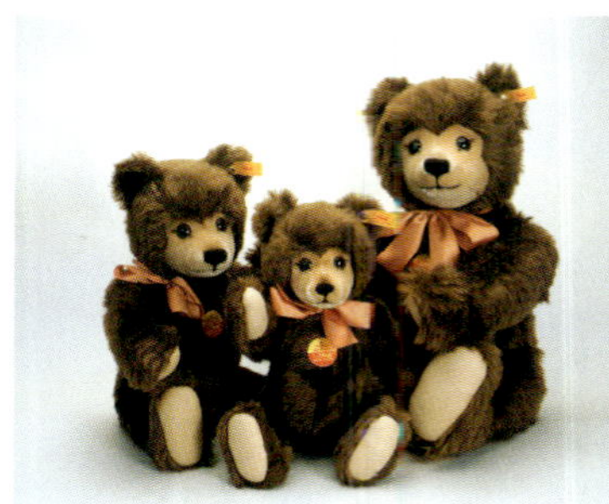

Original Steiffteddy

Mohair Webpelz, braun, gegliedert, Brumm-Stimme, abwaschbar - *mohair woven fur, brown, jointed, growler, surface washable*

EAN-NO.	PERIOD	PR.	INFO
011054	1992-1993	3	36 cm
011108	1992-1993	3-4	43 cm
011153	1992-1993	4	55 cm

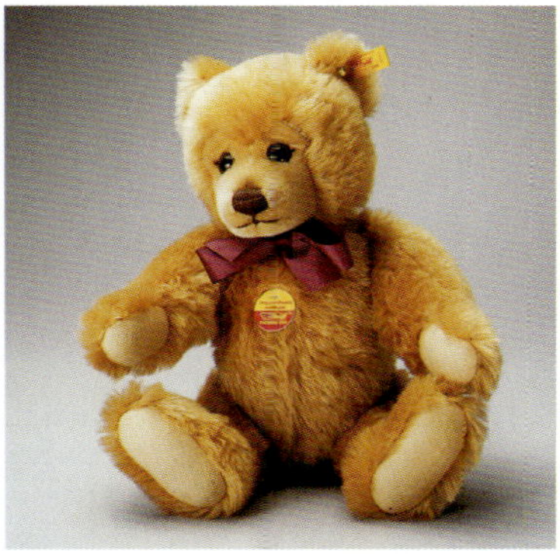

Original Steiffteddy mit Musik - *Original Musical Steiff Teddy*

Mohair Webpelz, mit Musikwerk, 39 cm, gegliedert, abwaschbar - *mohair woven fur, with music box, 39 cm, jointed, surface washable*

EAN-No.	Period	Pr.	Info
011184	1992-1993	3-4	altrosa - *old rose*
011214	1992-1993	3-4	rotblond - *sandy*

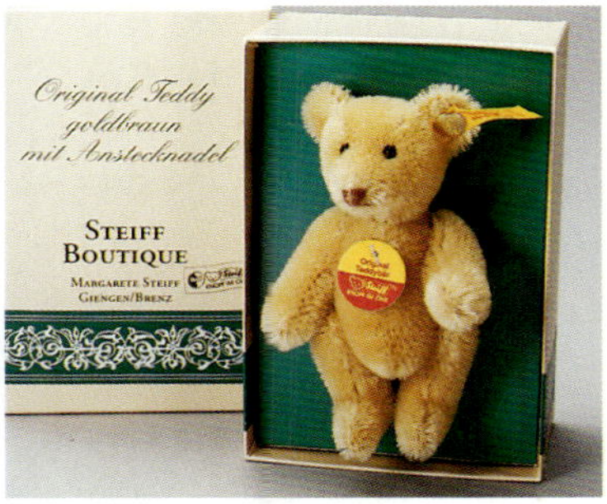

Original Teddybaer - *Original Teddy Bear*

Mohair Webpelz, 10 cm, gegliedert, mit Ansteckadel, abwaschbar - *mohair woven fur, with pin fastening, 10 cm, jointed, surface washable*

EAN-No.	Period	Pr.	Info
604683	1994-1995	3	silbergrau - *silver grey*
604713	1994-1995	3	goldbraun - *gold brown*
604744	1994-1995	3	gelb - *yellow*

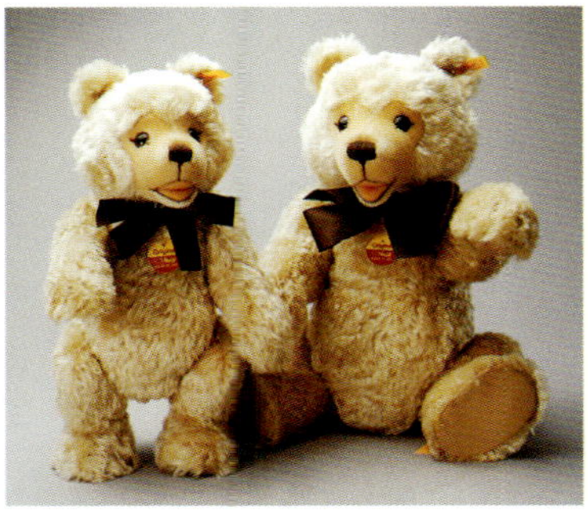

Teddybaer - *Teddy Bear*

Mohair Webpelz, hellblond, gegliedert, Brumm-Stimme, abwaschbar - *mohair woven fur, light blond, jointed, growler, surface washable*

EAN-No.	Period	Pr.	Info
008016	1995-1998	3-4	38 cm
008078	1995-1998	4	46 cm

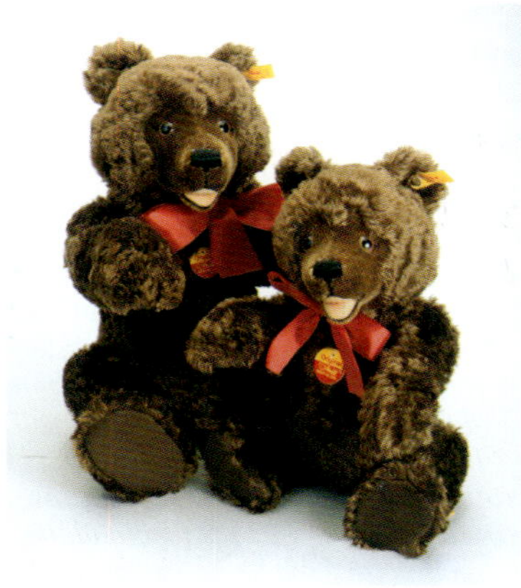

Teddybaer - *Teddy Bear*

Mohair Webpelz, rotbraun, gegliedert, Brumm-Stimme, abwaschbar - *mohair woven fur, red brown, jointed, growler, surface washable*

EAN-No.	Period	Pr.	Info
008504	1995-1998	3-4	38 cm
008542	1995-1996	4	46 cm

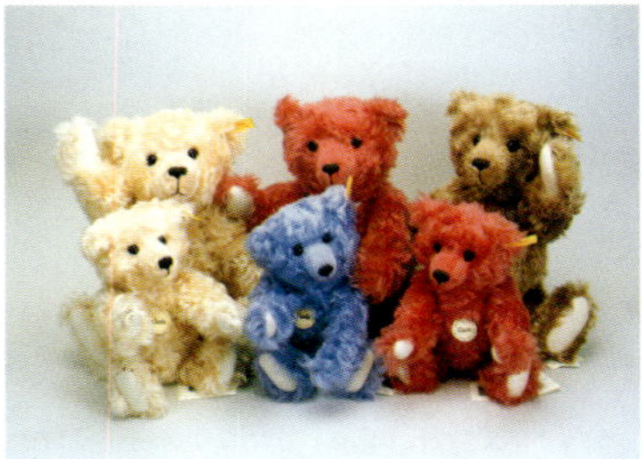

Classic Teddybaer - ***Classic*** *Teddybear*

Mohair Webpelz, gegliedert, abwaschbar, 28 cm Druck-, 40 cm Brumm-Stimme - *mohair woven fur, jointed, surface washable, 28 cm press voice, 40 cm tilt-me voice*

EAN-No.	Period	Pr.	Info
005015	1998-1999	3	28 cm, apricot
005022	1998-1999	3-4	40 cm
005060	1998-1999	3	28 cm, hellblau - *light blue*
005077	1998-1999	3-4	40 cm
005114	1998-1999	3	28 cm, zimt - *cinnamon*
005121	1998-1999	3-4	40 cm
005152	1998-1999	3	28 cm, rot - *red*
005169	1998-1999	3-4	40 cm

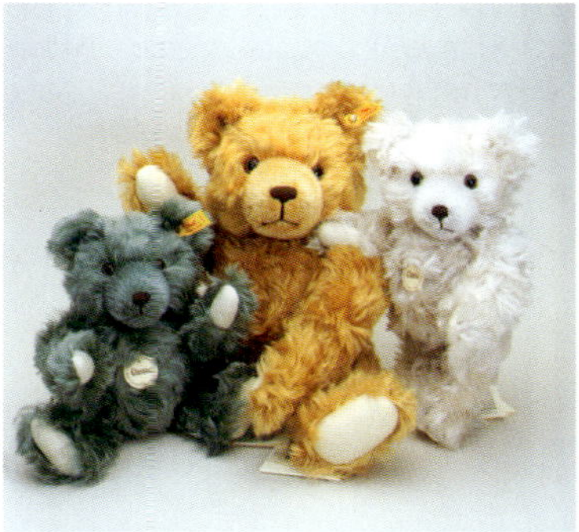

Classic Teddybaer - ***Classic*** *Teddybear*

Mohair Webpelz, gegliedert, abwaschbar, Brumm-Stimme - *mohair woven fur, jointed, surface washable, tilt-me voice*

EAN-No.	Period	Pr.	Info
005206	1998-1999	3	28 cm, goldblond - *gold blond*
005213	1998-1999	3-4	40 cm
005251	1998-1999	3	28 cm, silbergrau - *silver-grey*
005268	1998-1999	3-4	40 cm
005305	1998-1999	3	28 cm, gruen - *green*
005312	1998-1999	3-4	40 cm

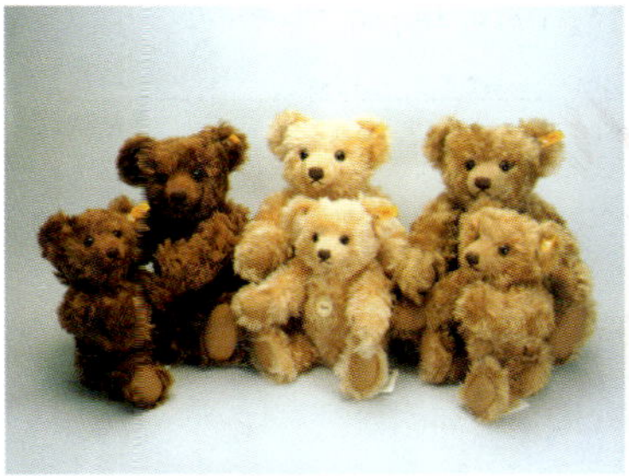

Classic Teddybaer - *Classic Teddybear*

Mohair Webpelz, gegliedert, abwaschbar, Kippstimme - *mohair woven fur, jointed, surface washable, tilt-me voice*

EAN-No.	Period	Pr.	Info
004421	1999-1999	3	35 cm, rotblond - *reddish blond*
004445	1999-1999	4	45 cm
004490	1999-1999	3	35 cm, rotbraun - *reddish brown*
004513	1999-1999	4	45 cm
004353	1999-1999	3	35 cm, hellblond - *light blond*
004377	1999-1999	4	45 cm

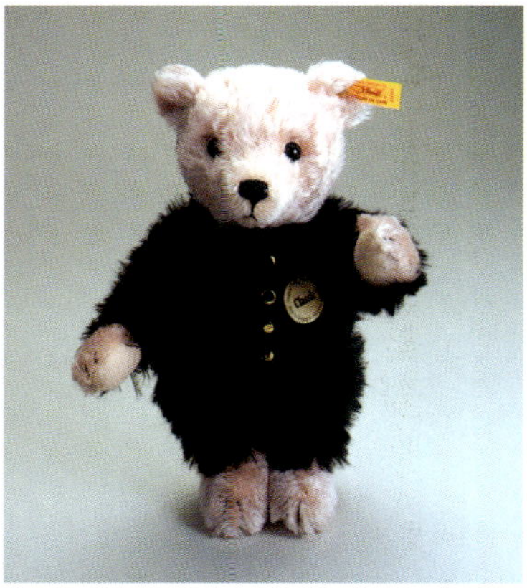

Classic Teddybaer - ***Classic*** *Teddybear*

Mohair Webpelz, rosé/schwarz, gegliedert, abwaschbar, Kippstimme - *mohair woven fur, rose/black, jointed, surface washable, tilt-me voice*

EAN-No.	Period	Pr.	Info
028304	1999-1999	3-4	32 cm

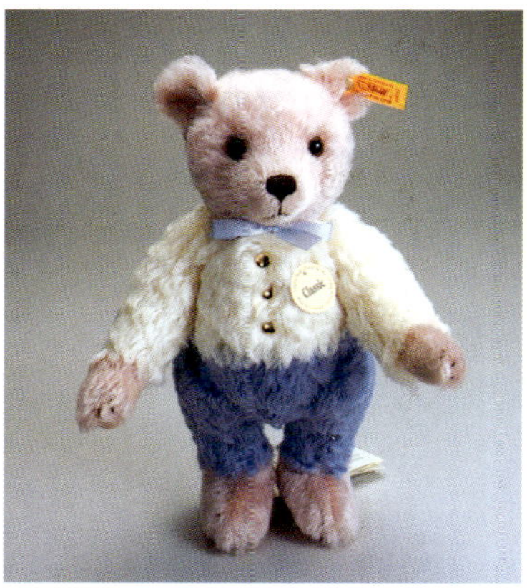

Classic Teddybaer - ***Classic*** *Teddybear*

Mohair Webpelz, rosé/bleu/weiss, gegliedert, abwaschbar, Kippstimme - *mohair woven fur, rose/baby blue/white, jointed, surface washable, tilt-me voice*

EAN-No.	Period	Pr.	Info
028311	1999-1999	3-4	32 cm

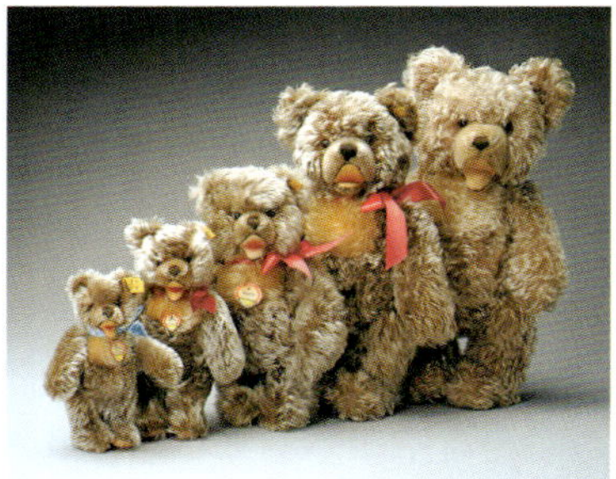

Zottelbaer **Zotty** - *Zottelbear* ***Zotty***

Mohair, langhaarig, caramel gespitzt, gegliedert, sehr weich, bis Groesse 35 cm Druckstimme, ab Groesse 43 cm Brummstimme (Ausnahmen siehe Tabelle), zwischen 1965 und 1967 auch mit Zusatz "im Steiff-Kinderbuch", abwaschbar - *long hair mohair, caramel, light tipped, jointed, very soft, up to 35 cm press voice, from 43 cm growler (see chart for exceptions), between 1965 & 1967 also with additional comment "im Steiff-Kinderbuch", surface washable*

Serie	Art.-No	Period	Pr.	Info
12Z	**6317,1**	1952-1958	4	17 cm
121	**6317,00**	1959-1959	4	
121	**6317,02**	1960-1961	4	
121	**6318,02**	1963-1964	4	18 cm
030	**6318,02**	1965-1967	4	
	0300/18	1968-1975	3-4	
12Z	**6322,1**	1952-1958	4-5	22 cm
121	**6322,00**	1959-1959	4-5	
121	**6322,02**	1960-1964	4-5	
030	**6322,02**	1965-1967	4-5	
	0300/22	1968-1978	4	
12Z	**6328,1**	1951-1958	5	28 cm
121	**6328,00**	1959-1959	4-5	
121	**6328,02**	1960-1964	4-5	
030	**6328,02**	1965-1967	4-5	
	0300/28	1968-1978	4	
12Z	**6335,1**	1951-1958	5	35 cm
121	**6335,00**	1959-1959	4-5	
121	**6335,02**	1960-1964	4-5	
030	**6335,02**	1965-1967	4-5	Brummstimme - *growler*
	0300/35	1968-1978	4	
12Z	**6343,2**	1951-1958	5	43 cm
121	**6343,00**	1959-1959	4-5	
121	**6343,02**	1960-1964	4-5	
030	**6343,02**	1965-1967	4-5	
	0300/43	1968-1978	4	
12Z	**6350,2**	1951-1958	6	50 cm
121	**6350,00**	1959-1959	5-6	
121	**6350,02**	1960-1964	5-6	
030	**6350,02**	1965-1967	5-6	
	0300/50	1968-1977	5	
	0309/08	1967-1967	6	80 cm, Schautier - *display animal*
	0309/10	1967-1967	6	100 cm, Schautier - *display animal*

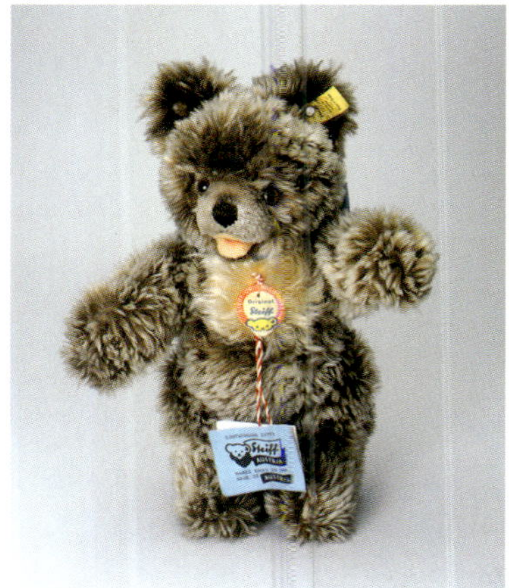

Dolan-Zotty

Dolan, caramel gespitzt, gegliedert, abwaschbar, nur in Oesterreich-Katalogen - *dolan, caramel, light tipped, jointed, surface washable, exclusively in Austrian catalogs*

Serie	Art.-No	Period	Pr.	Info
	0312/28	1970-1976	4-5	28 cm
	0312/35	1970-1976	4-5	35 cm
	0312/43	1970-1972	5	43 cm

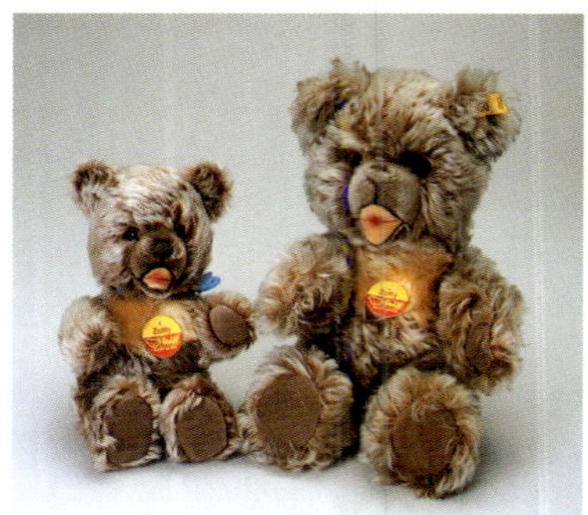

Zotty Baer - ***Zotty*** *Bear*

Mohair, Koerper formgeschaeumt, Arme & Beine biegsam, abwaschbar - *mohair, body stuffed with pre-formed foam, flexible arms & legs, surface washable*

Serie	Art.-No	Period	Pr.	Info
	0305/22	1976-1982	3	22 cm
	0305/32	1976-1982	3	32 cm
	0305/45	1976-1982	3-4	45 cm

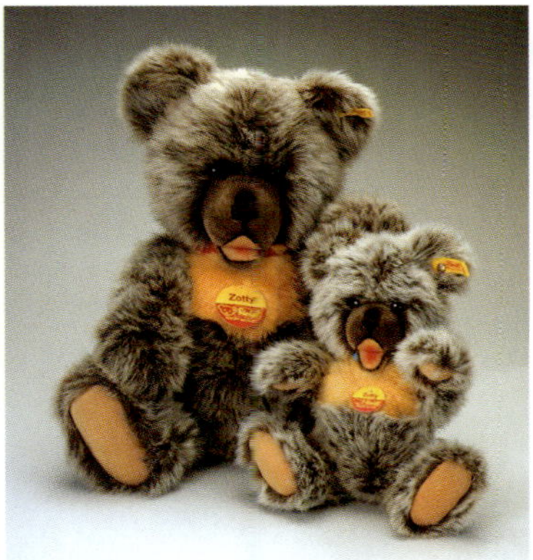

Zotty Baer - ***Zotty** Bear*

Webpelz, gegliedert, Brummstimme, abwaschbar - *woven fur, jointed, growler, surface washable*

SERIE	ART.-NO	PERIOD	PR.	INFO
	0302/30	1979-1985	3	30 cm
	0302/40	1979-1985	3	40 cm
	0302/50	1979-1985	3-4	50 cm

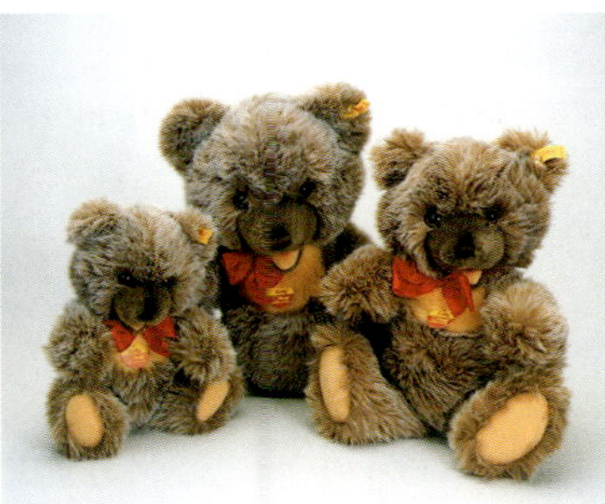

Zotty Baer - ***Zotty** Bear*

Webpelz, caramel gespitzt, gegliedert, Druckstimme, abwaschbar - *woven fur, caramel tipped, jointed, press voice, surface washable*

SERIE	ART.-NO	PERIOD	PR.	INFO
018107	**0305/30**	1985-1990	3	30 cm
	018107	1991-1999	3	
018206	**0305/40**	1985-1990	3-4	40 cm
	018206	1991-1997	3-4	
018305	**0305/50**	1985-1990	4	50 cm
	018305	1991-1995	4	

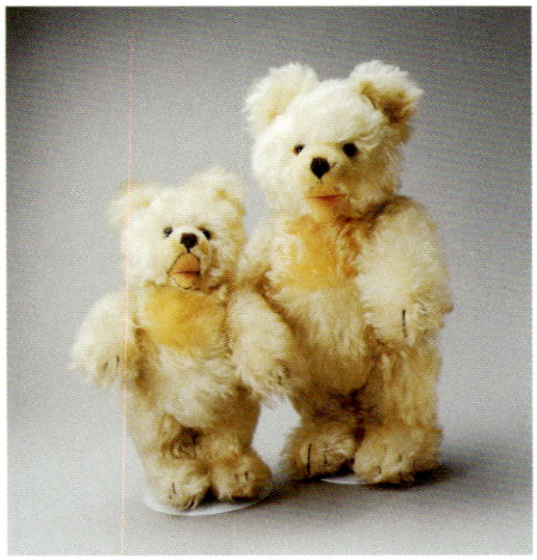

Zotty Baer - ***Zotty** Bear*

Langhaar-Mohair, weiss, gegliedert, weich, Doppeldruckstimme, abwaschbar - *long hair mohair, white, jointed, soft, double press voice, surface washable*

SERIE	ART.-NO	PERIOD	PR.	INFO
121	**6328,04**	1960-1961	6-7	28 cm
121	**6335,04**	1960-1961	7	35 cm

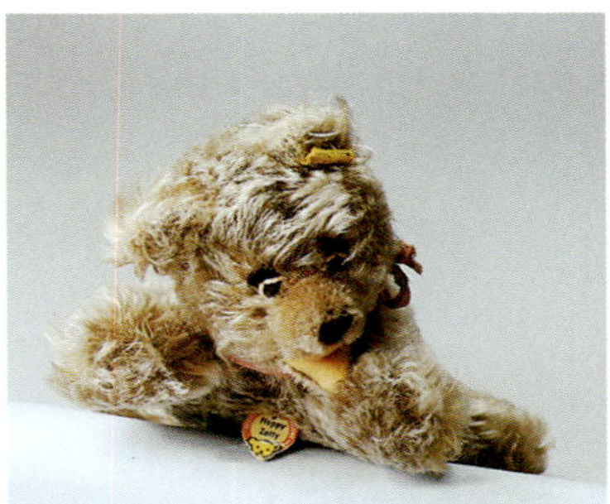

Floppy Zotty

Mohair, Augen gestickt, caramel gespitzt, flach liegend, sehr weich, Schlaftier, abwaschbar - *mohair, eyes embroidered, caramel with light tips, lying flat, very soft, sleeping animal, surface washable*

SERIE	ART.-NO	PERIOD	PR.	INFO
85 12	**7317**	1954-1958	3	17 cm
850 121	**7317,00**	1959-1964	3	
550	**7317,00**	1965-1967	3	
	5500/17	1968-1969	2	
85 12	**7328**	1953-1958	3	28 cm
850 121	**7328,00**	1959-1964	3	
550	**7328,00**	1965-1967	3	
	5500/28	1968-1969	2	

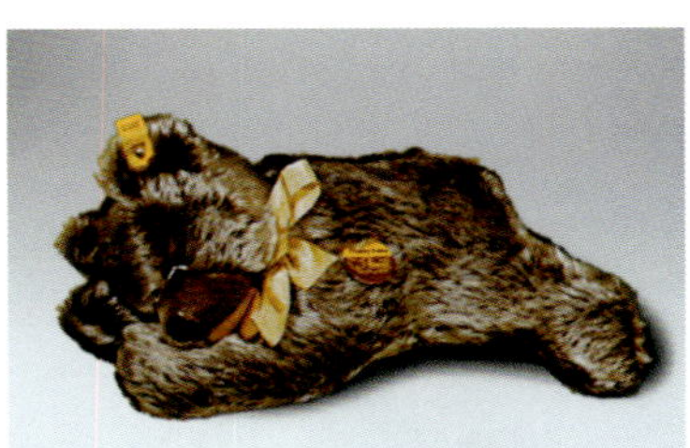

Floppy Zotty

Mohair, formgeschaeumt, Augen gestickt, liegend, Schlaftier, sehr weich, vollwaschbar - *mohair, stuffed with pre-formed foam, eyes are embroidered, lying, sleeping animal, very soft, fully washable*

SERIE	ART.-NO	PERIOD	PR.	INFO
	5507/17	1970-1977	2	17 cm
	5507/28	1970-1977	2	28 cm

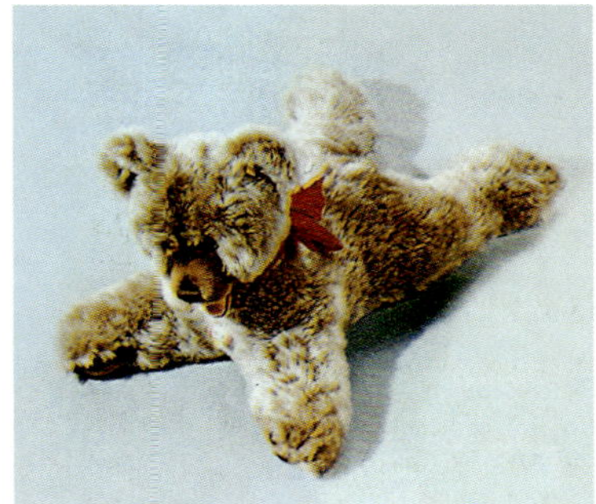

Racker Zotty-Baer - *Racker Zotty Bear*

Mohair, liegend, zum Spielen & Sitzen - *mohair, lying, to sit on or play animal*

SERIE	ART.-NO	PERIOD	PR.	INFO
822 121	**2345,00**	1960-1961	5	45 cm

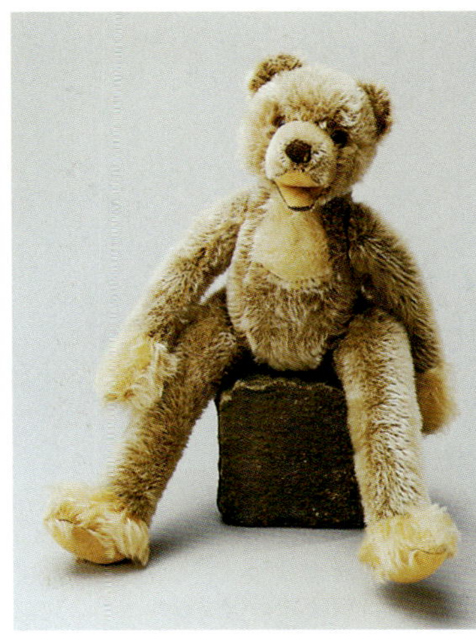

Zotty **Zolac**

Mohair, caramel, Haende, Fuesse & Brust blond, Schlenkertier, gegliedert - *mohair, caramel, hands, feet & chest are blond, floppy animal, jointed*

SERIE	ART.-NO	PERIOD	PR.	INFO
121	**7340,00**	1964-1964	6	40 cm
580	**7340,00**	1966-1966	6	

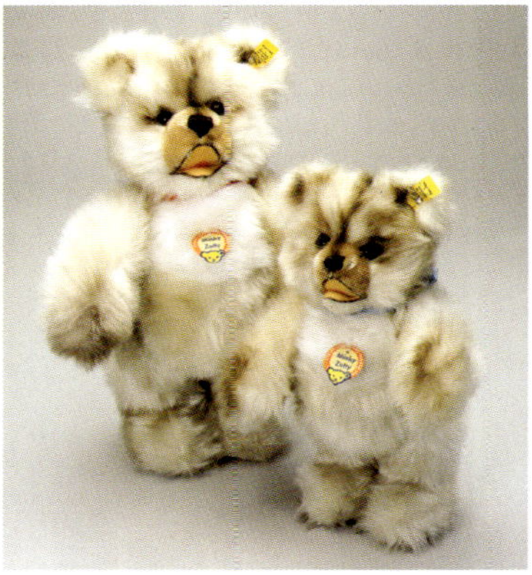

Minky Zotty

pelzartiges Material, ab 1974 Pelzimitation, formgeschaeumt, hellbeige, gegliedert, Stimme, sehr weich & leicht, abwaschbar - *fur-like material, from 1974 called imitation fur, stuffed with pre-formed foam, light beige, jointed, voice, very soft & light, surface washable*

SERIE	ART.-NO	PERIOD	PR.	INFO
	0301/28	1969-1976	4-5	28 cm
	0301/35	1969-1977	4-5	35 cm

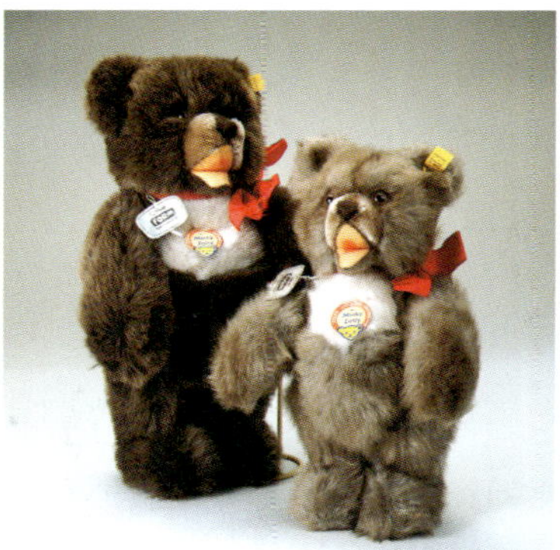

Minky Zotty

pelzartiges Material, ab 1974 Pelzimitation, formgeschaeumt, caramel, gegliedert, Stimme, sehr weich & leicht, abwaschbar - *fur-like material, from 1974 called imitation fur, stuffed with pre-formed foam, caramel, jointed, voice, very soft & light, surface washable*

SERIE	ART.-NO	PERIOD	PR.	INFO
	0302/28	1969-1976	4-5	28 cm
	0302/35	1969-1977	4-5	35 cm

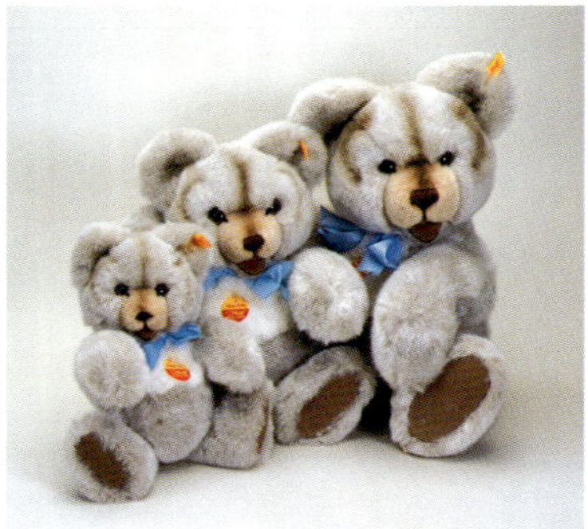

Minky Zotty

Webpelz, gegliedert, Druck-Stimme, waschmaschinenfest - *woven fur, jointed, press voice, machine washable*

SERIE	ART.-NO	PERIOD	PR.	INFO
018350	**0312/30**	1988-1990	2-3	30 cm
	018350	1991-1992	2-3	
018404	**0312/40**	1988-1990	3	40 cm
	018404	1991-1992	3	
018459	**0312/50**	1988-1990	3-4	50 cm
	018459	1991-1992	3-4	

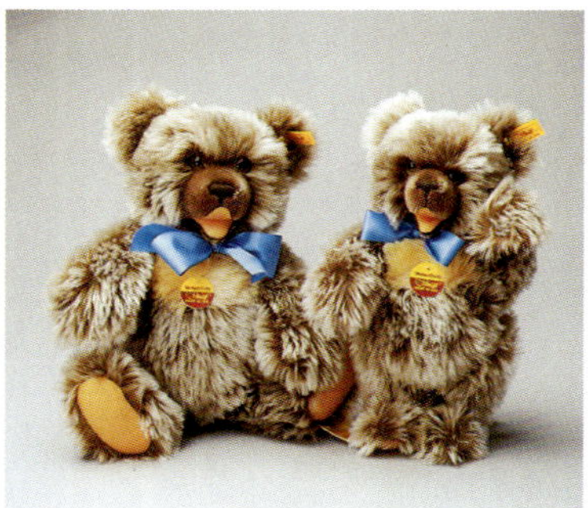

Mohair Zotty

Mohair Webpelz, gegliedert, 30 cm mit Druckstimme, ab 40 cm Brummstimme, abwaschbar - *mohair woven fur, jointed, 30 cm press voice, from 40 cm growler, surface washable*

EAN-NO.	PERIOD	PR.	INFO
009204	1993-1996	3	30 cm
009259	1993-1996	3-4	40 cm
009303	1993-1996	4	50 cm

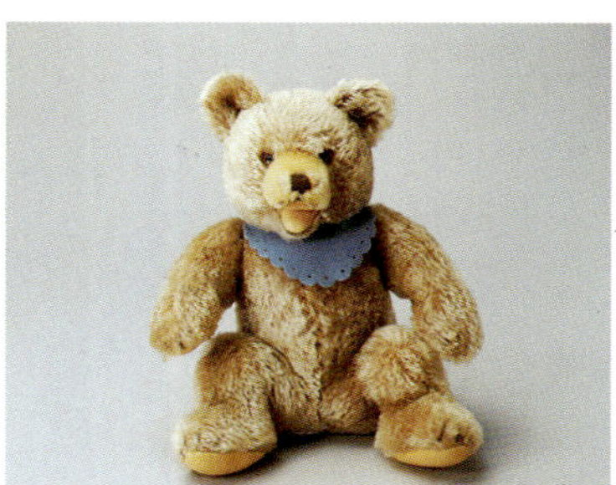

Weichbaer **Orsi** - *Soft Bear* ***Orsi***

Mohair, caramel, aufwartend, blaues Laetzchen, Kopf & Arme gegliedert, superweich - *mohair, caramel, sitting up, blue bib, head & arms jointed, super soft*

SERIE	ART.-NO	PERIOD	PR.	INFO
12	**4322,1**	1952-1958	4-5	22 cm
122	**4322,00**	1959-1962	4-5	
12	**4335,1**	1958-1958	5	35 cm
122	**4335,00**	1959-1962	5	

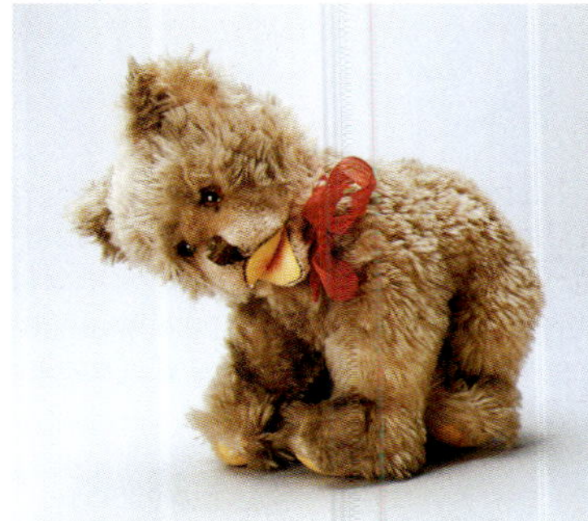

Cosy Orsi

Dralon Pluesch, Schaumgummi-Fuellung, caramel, stehend, offener Mund, sehr weich, waschbar - *dralon plush, stuffed with foam rubber, caramel, standing, open mouth, very soft, washable*

SERIE	ART.-NO	PERIOD	PR.	INFO
83 12	**6620**	1955-1958	3	20 cm
830 128	**6620,00**	1959-1964	3	
484	**6620,00**	1965-1967	3	
	4840/20	1968-1978	2-3	

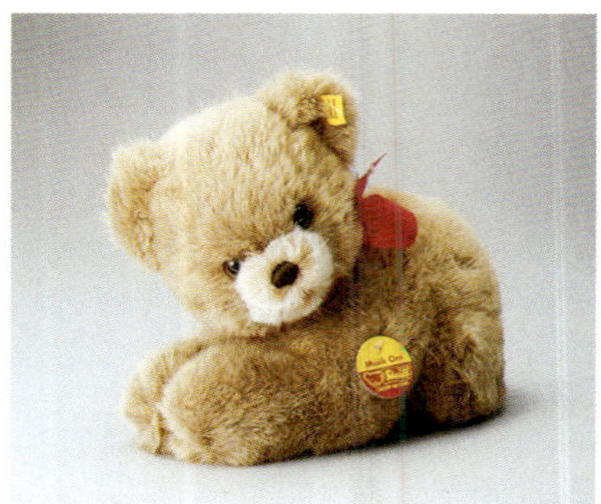

Musik Orsi - *Music Orsi*

Webpelz, Koerper formgeschaeumt, austauschbares Musikwerk, vollwaschbar - *woven fur, body stuffed with pre-formed foam, music box can be exchanged, fully washable*

SERIE	ART.-NO	PERIOD	PR.	INFO
	6370/22	1978-1985	2-3	22 cm

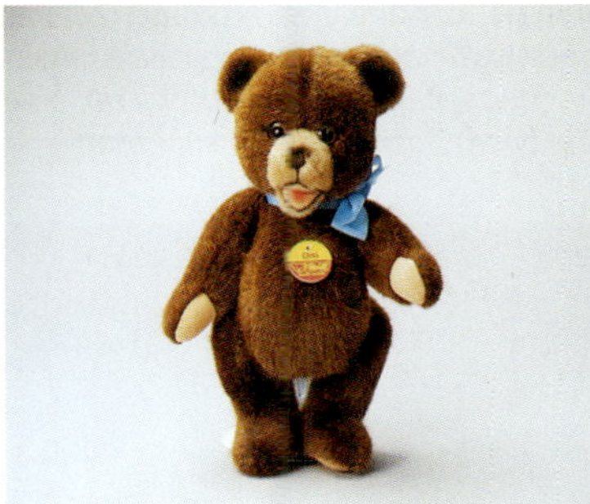

Orsi

Webpelz, caramel, aufwartend, Kopf & Arme gegliedert, superweich, abwaschbar - *woven fur, caramel, sitting up, head & arms jointed, super soft, surface washable*

SERIE	ART.-NO	PERIOD	PR.	INFO
	0220/30	1980-1983	3-4	30 cm

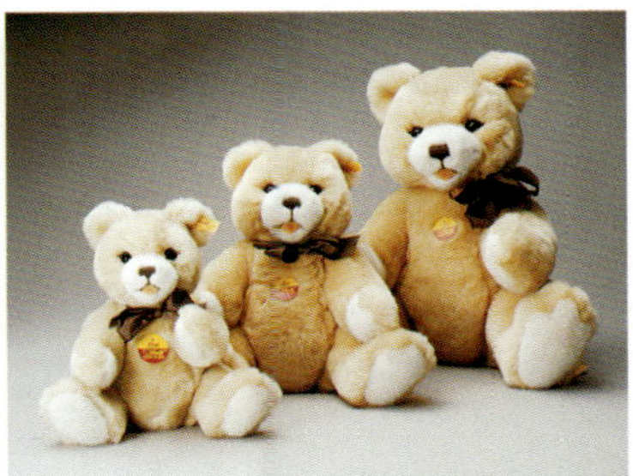

Orsi

Webpelz, blond, gegliedert, 30 cm mit Pieps-Stimme, ab 40 cm Druckstimme, waschmaschinenfest - *woven fur, blond, jointed, 30 cm squeaker, from 40 cm press voice, machine washable*

EAN-NO.	PERIOD	PR.	INFO
013058	1993-1995	2-3	30 cm
013089	1993-1995	3	40 cm
013119	1993-1996	3	50 cm

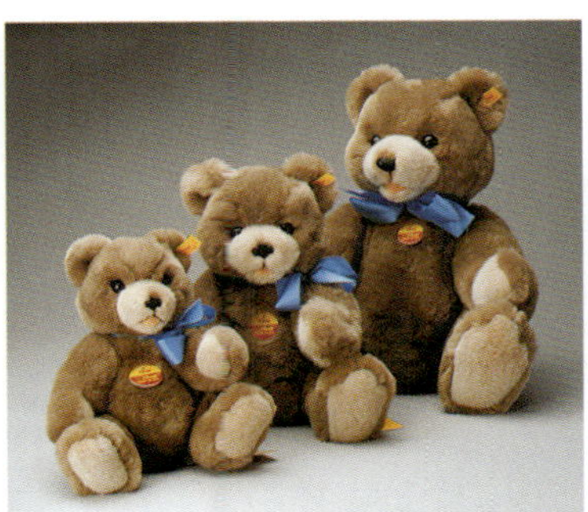

Orsi

Webpelz, braun, gegliedert, 30 cm mit Pieps-Stimme, ab 40 cm Druckstimme, waschmaschinenfest - *woven fur, brown, jointed, 30 cm squeaker, from 40 cm press voice, machine washable*

EAN-NO.	PERIOD	PR.	INFO
013256	1993-1999	3	30 cm
013287	1993-1997	3	40 cm
013317	1993-1996	3	50 cm

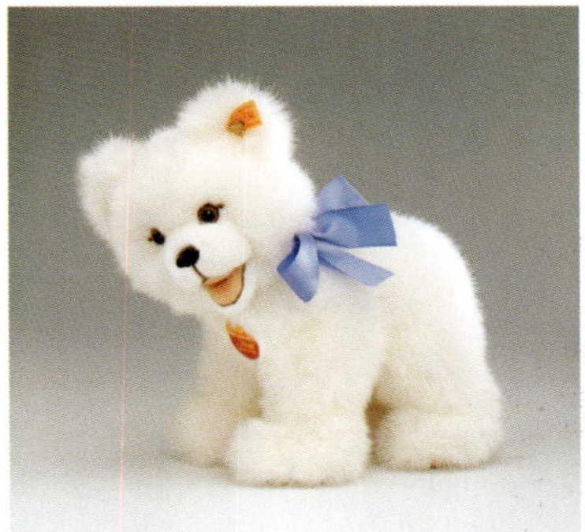

Cosy Orsy Jungbaer - ***Cosy Orsy** Cub*

Webpelz, weiss, stehend, handwaschbar - *woven fur, white, standing, hand washable*

EAN-NO.	PERIOD	PR.	INFO
085918	1999-1999	2-3	25 cm

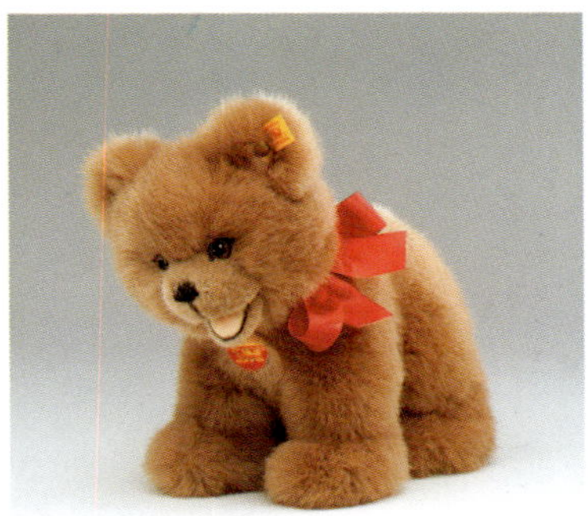

Cosy Orsy Jungbaer - ***Cosy Orsy** Cub*

Webpelz, hellbraun, stehend, handwaschbar - *woven fur, light brown, standing, hand washable*

EAN-NO.	PERIOD	PR.	INFO
085925	1999-1999	2-3	25 cm

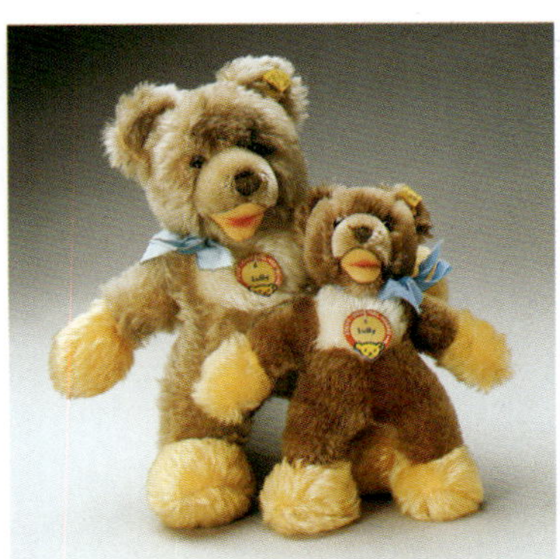

Lully Baby Baer - ***Lully** Baby Bear*

Mohairpluesch, caramel, stehend, Kopf drehbar, Druckstimme, weich, abwaschbar - *mohair, caramel, standing, head swivels, press voice, soft, surface washable*

SERIE	ART.-NO	PERIOD	PR.	INFO
12	**7322**	1955-1958	4	22 cm
123	**7322,00**	1961-1961	4	
035	**7322,00**	1966-1967	4	
	0350/22	1968-1977	3-4	
12	**7330**	1955-1958	4	30 cm
123	**7330,00**	1961-1961	4	
035	**7330,00**	1966-1967	4	
	0350/30	1968-1977	3-4	

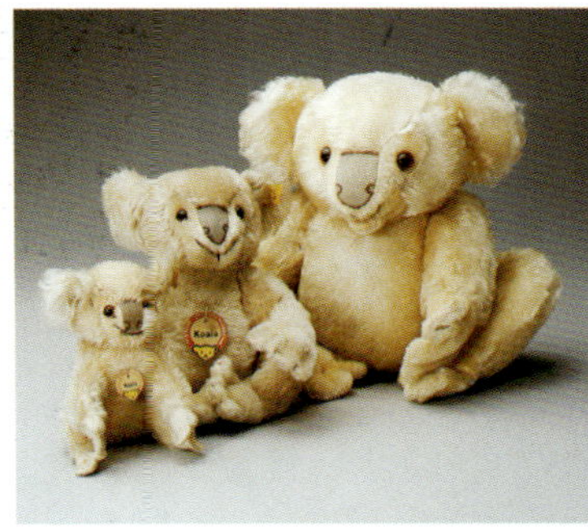

Koala

Mohair, braun/weiss, ab 22 cm gegliedert, weich - *mohair, brown/white, jointed from 22 cm, soft*

SERIE	ART.-NO	PERIOD	PR.	INFO
12K	**4312**	1955-1958	4-5	12 cm
124	**4312,00**	1959-1961	4-5	
12K	**5322**	1955-1958	5	22 cm
124	**5322,00**	1959-1961	5	
12K	**5335,2**	1955-1958	5-6	35 cm
124	**5335,00**	1959-1961	5-6	

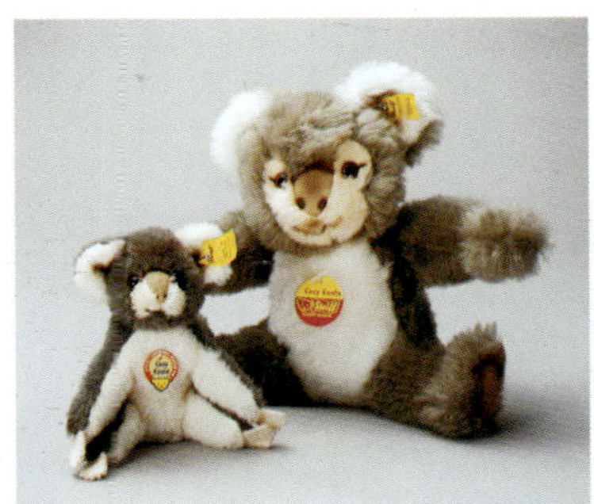

Cosy Koala

Dralon, gefuellt mit synthet. Fasern & Schaumstoff, sitzend, sehr weich, vollwaschbar - *dralon, stuffed with synthetic fibers & foam, sitting, very soft, fully washable*

SERIE	ART.-NO	PERIOD	PR.	INFO
	4770/12	1970-1975	3	12 cm
	4770/22	1970-1975	3	22 cm

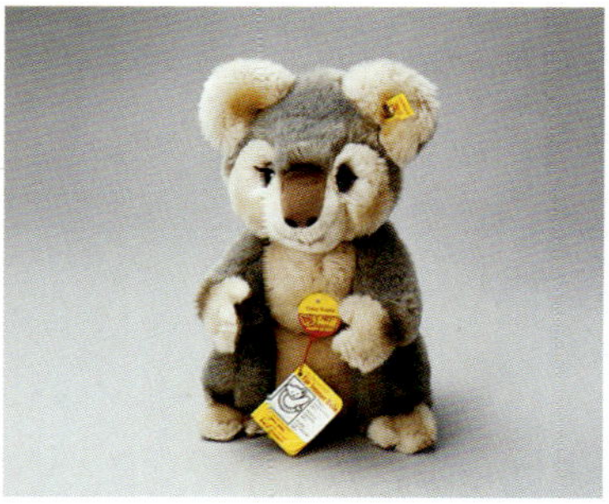

Cosy Koala

Webpelz, aufwartend, kuschelweich, waschmaschinenfest - *woven fur, begging, soft & cuddly, machine washable*

SERIE	ART.-NO	PERIOD	PR.	INFO
	5358/27	1982-1985	2-3	27 cm

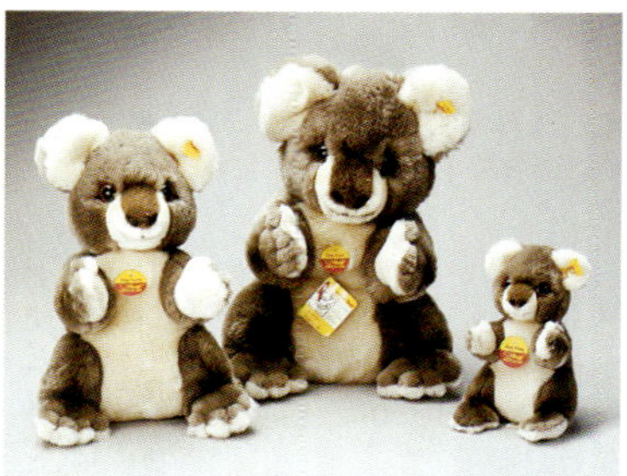

Cosy Koala

Webpelz, aufwartend, superweich, waschmaschinenfest - *woven fur, begging, super soft, machine washable*

SERIE	ART.-NO	PERIOD	PR.	INFO
085611	**5358/18**	1986-1989	2	18 cm
085635	**5358/28**	1986-1989	2-3	28 cm
085659	**5358/38**	1986-1987	3	38 cm
085673	**5358/50**	1986-1986	3-4	50 cm

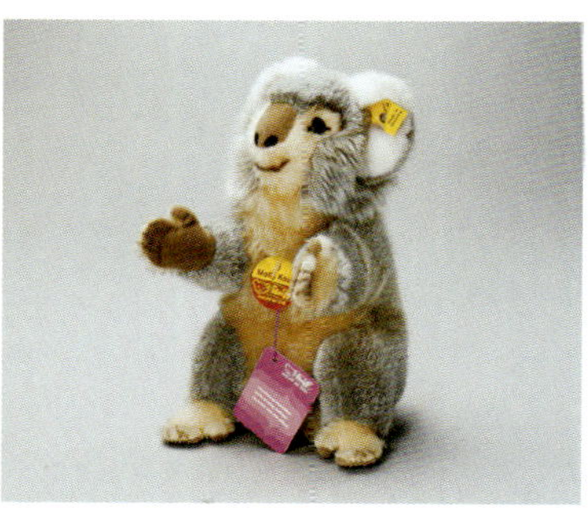

Molly Koala

Nerzimitation, ab 1978 Webpelz, mollig weich, abwaschbar - *imitation mink fur, from 1978 woven fur, soft & cuddly, surface washable*

SERIE	ART.-NO	PERIOD	PR.	INFO
	0331/22	1976-1982	2-3	22 cm
	0331/40	1973-1980	3	40 cm

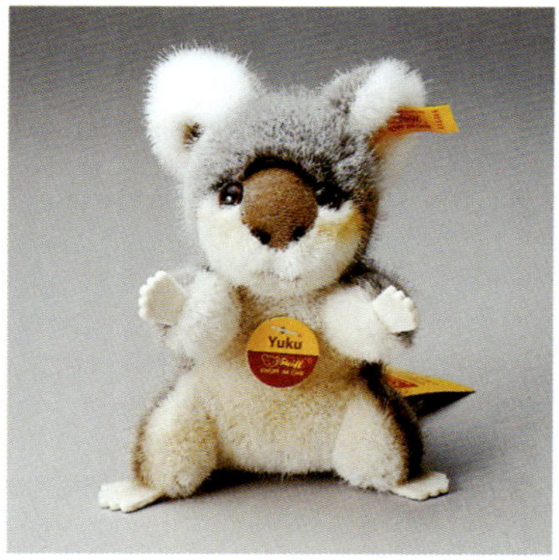

Yuku Koalabaer - ***Yuku*** *Koala Bear*

Webpelz, aufwartend, abwaschbar - *woven fur, sitting up, surface washable*

SERIE	ART.-NO	PERIOD	PR.	INFO
040306	**1446/11**	1981-1990	2	11 cm
	040306	1991-1999	2	

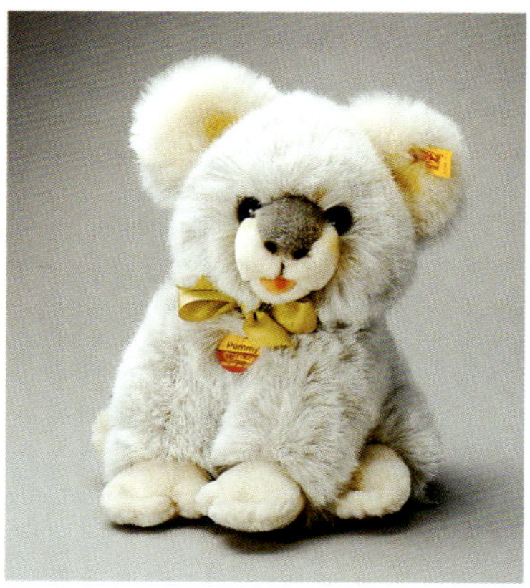

Pummy Koala

Webpelz, sitzend, waschmaschinenfest - *woven fur, sitting, machine washable*

SERIE	ART.-NO	PERIOD	PR.	INFO
083105	**5035/17**	1989-1990	2-3	17 cm
	083105	1991-1991	2-3	
083129	**5035/21**	1989-1990	2-3	21 cm

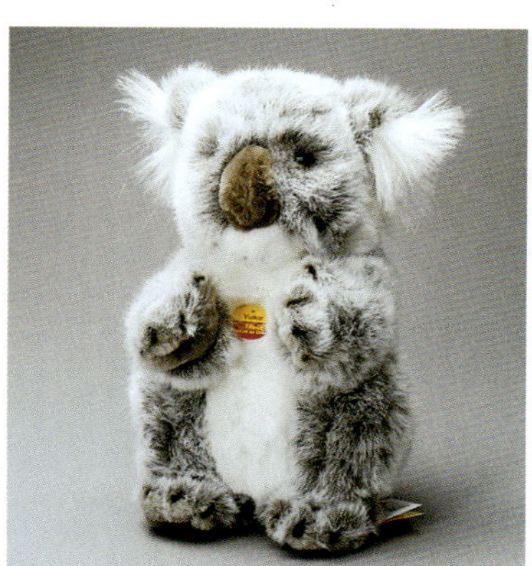

Yuku Koala

Webpelz, aufwartend, waschmaschinenfest - *woven fur, begging, machine washable*

EAN-NO.	PERIOD	PR.	INFO
060052	1992-1996	3	30 cm

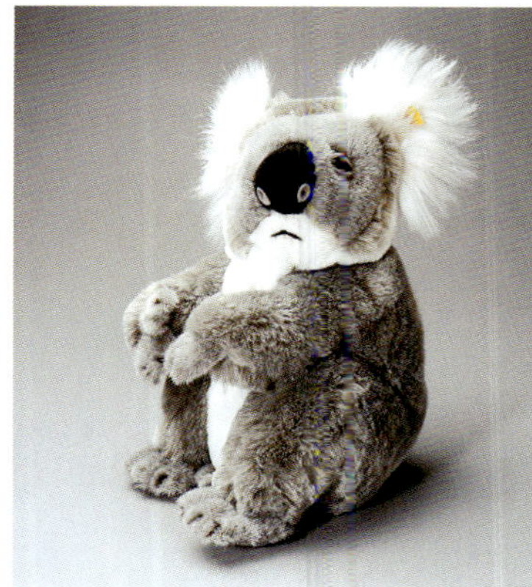

Colo Koala

Webpelz, handwaschbar - *woven fur, hand washable*

EAN-NO.	PERIOD	PR.	INFO
060106	1995-1999	3-4	32 cm

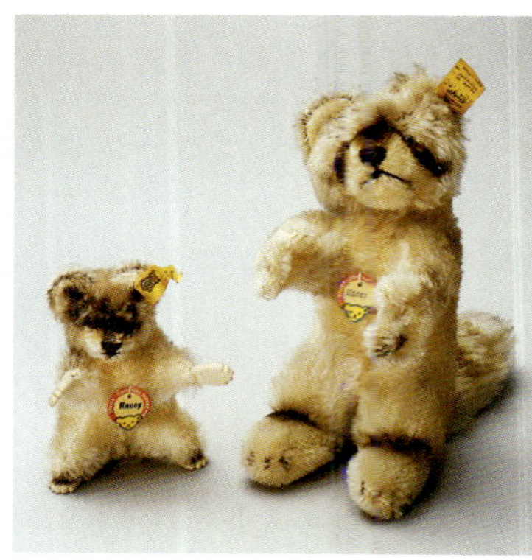

Raccy Waschbaer - ***Raccy*** *Racoon*

Mohairpluesch, grau/weiss/braun, aufwartend, Kopf drehbar - *mohair, grey/white/brown, sitting up, head swivels*

SERIE	ART.-NO	PERIOD	PR.	INFO
12W	**4310**	1957-1958	3-4	10 cm
126	**4310,00**	1959-1964	3	
12W	**4317**	1957-1958	4	17 cm
126	**4317,00**	1960-1962	3-4	

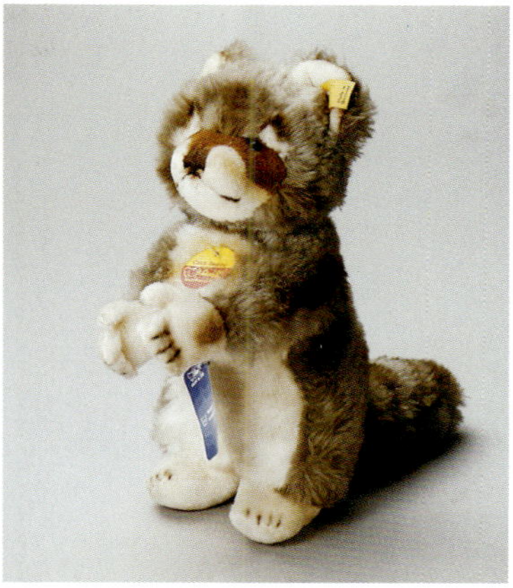

Cosy Raccy, ab 1974 **Cosy Raggy** - ***Cosy Raccy**, from 1974 **Cosy Raggy***

Dralon-Pluesch, Schaumstoff-Flocken-Fuellung, aufwartend, grau/weiss/braun, sehr weich, waschbar - *dralon plush, stuffed with foam, sitting up, grey/white/brown, very soft, washable*

SERIE	ART.-NO	PERIOD	PR.	INFO
83 12W	**6620**	1957-1958	3	20 cm
830 126	**6620,00**	1959-1963	3	
482	**6620,00**	1965-1967	3	
	4820/20	1968-1978	2-3	

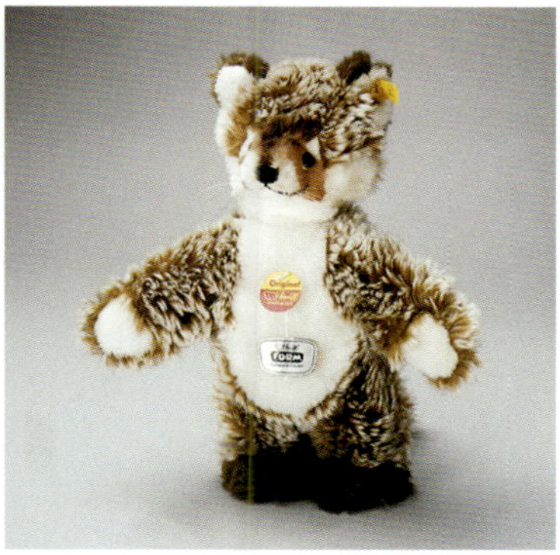

Weich-Waschbaer - *Soft Racoon*

Dolan & Dralon, formgeschaeumt, Schlenkerkopf, vollwaschbar - *dolan & dralon, stuffed with pre-formed foam, floppy head, fully washable*

SERIE	ART.-NO	PERIOD	PR.	INFO
	6205/30	1972-1979	2-3	30 cm
	6205/40	1972-1979	3	40 cm

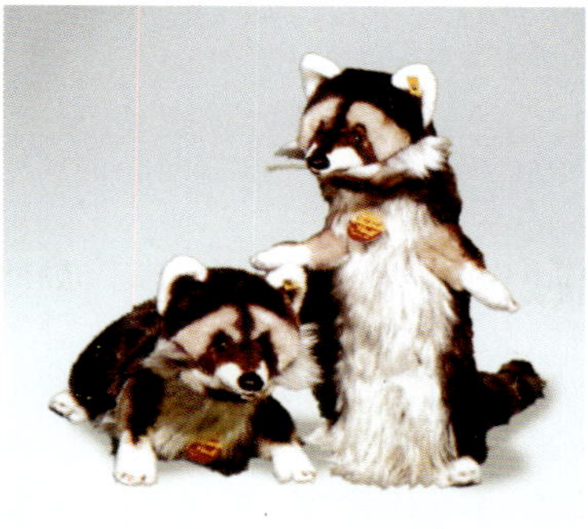

Waschbaer - *Racoon*

Pelzimitation, abwaschbar - *imitation fur, surface washable*

SERIE	ART.-NO	PERIOD	PR.	INFO
	0478/50	1973-1977	3-4	50 cm

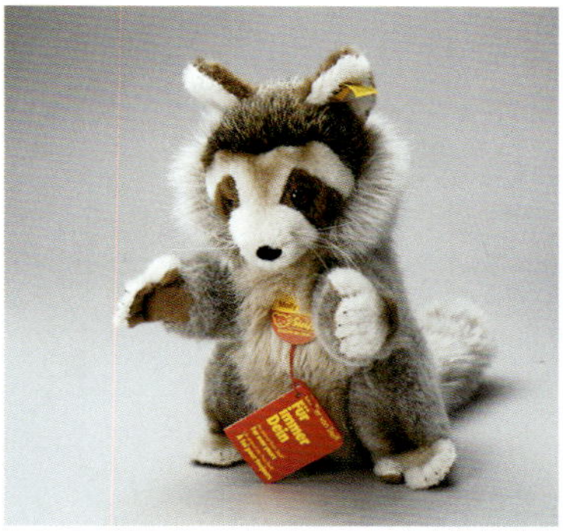

Molly Raggy

Pelzimitation, ab 1978 Synthetik-Webware, aufwartend, mollig weich, abwaschbar - *imitation fur, from 1978 synthetic woven fur, sitting up, soft & cuddly, surface washable*

SERIE	ART.-NO	PERIOD	PR.	INFO
	0348/22	1977-1982	2-3	22 cm
	0348/40	1977-1979	3	40 cm

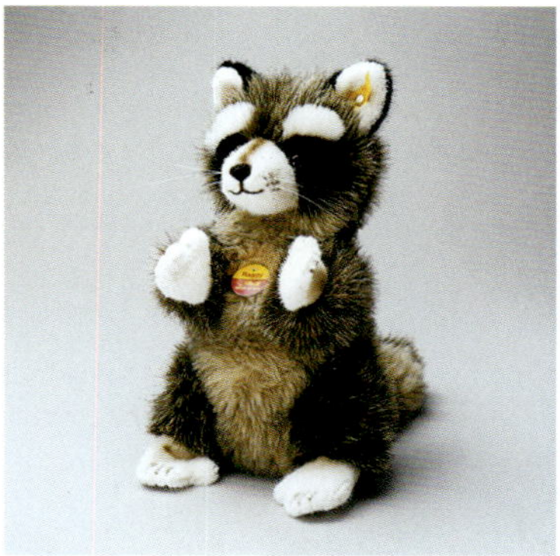

Raggy Waschbaer - ***Raggy** Raccoon*

Webpelz, 25 cm stehend, 35 cm aufwartend, abwaschbar - *woven fur, standing 25 cm, sitting up 35 cm, surface washable*

SERIE	ART.-NO	PERIOD	PR.	INFO
071454	**2050/25**	1987-1990	2-3	25 cm
	071454	1991-1993	2-3	
071485	**2055/35**	1987-1990	3	35 cm
	071485	1991-1997	3	

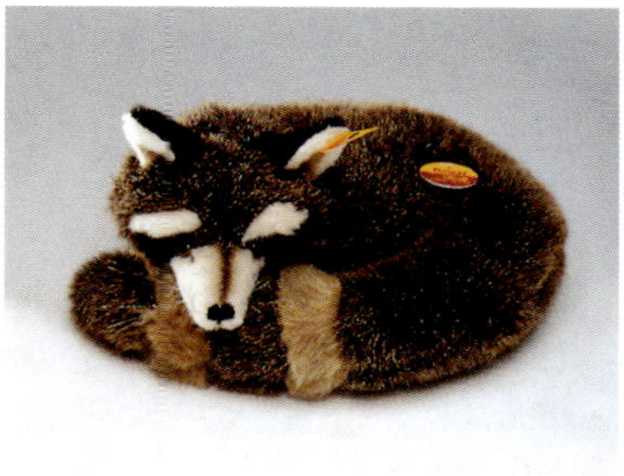

Raggy Ringelwaschbaer - ***Raggy** Ringed Raccoon*

Webpelz, abwaschbar - *woven fur, surface washable*

SERIE	ART.-NO	PERIOD	PR.	INFO
071508	**2060/20**	1987-1990	2	20 cm
	071508	1991-1993	2	

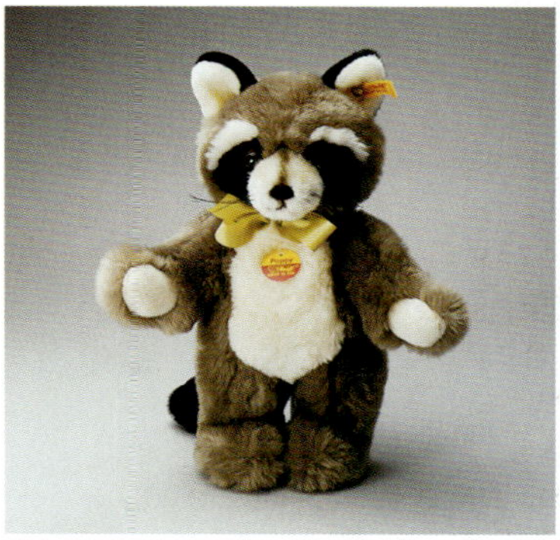

Poppy Waschbaer - ***Poppy** Raccoon*

Webpelz, Pieps-Stimme, waschmaschinenfest - *woven fur, squeaker, machine washable*

SERIE	ART.-NO	PERIOD	PR.	INFO
125157	**6020/32**	1989-1990	2	32 cm
	125157	1991-1991	2	
	083990	1992-1993	2	

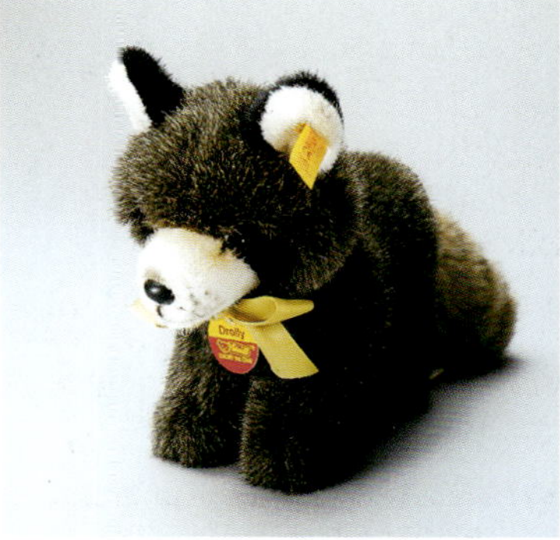

Drolly Waschbaer - ***Drolly** Raccoon*

Webpelz, stehend, waschmaschinenfest - *woven fur, standing, machine washable*

EAN-No.	Period	Pr.	Info
081354	1992-1995	2	22 cm

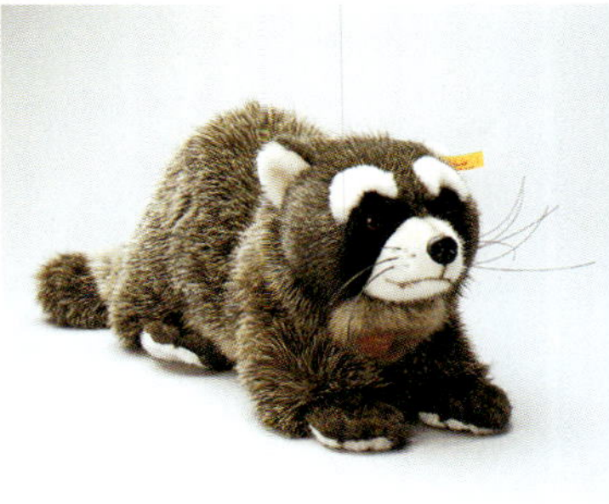

Pummy Waschbaer - ***Pummy** Raccoon*

Webpelz, stehend, waschmaschinenfest - *woven fur, standing, machine washable*

EAN-No.	Period	Pr.	Info
071515	1993-1995	2-3	35 cm

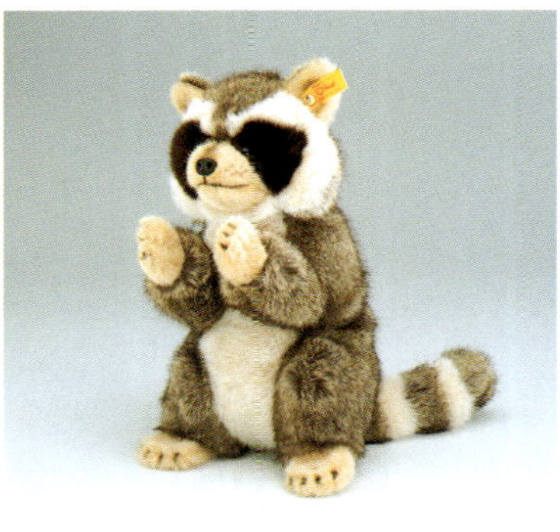

Raggy Waschbaer - ***Raggy** Raccoon*

Webpelz, beige gespitzt, aufwartend, waschmaschinenfest - *woven fur, beige tipped, begging, machine washable*

EAN-No.	Period	Pr.	Info
071522	1997-1997	3	26 cm

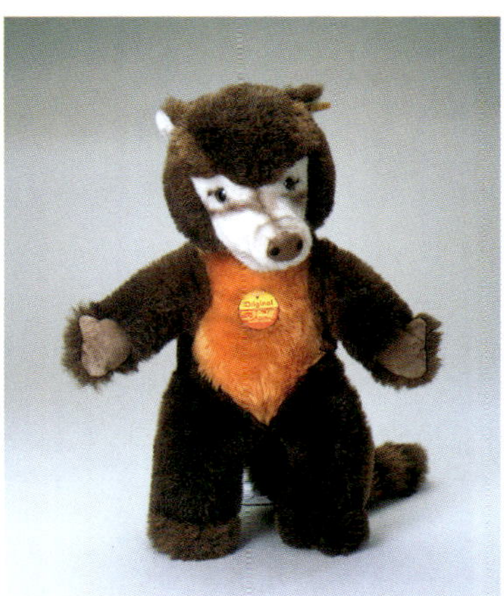

Nasenbaer - *Honey Bear*

Wirkpluesch, abwaschbar - *knitted plush, surface washable*

Serie	Art.-No	Period	Pr.	Info
	0475/40	1976-1977	4	40 cm

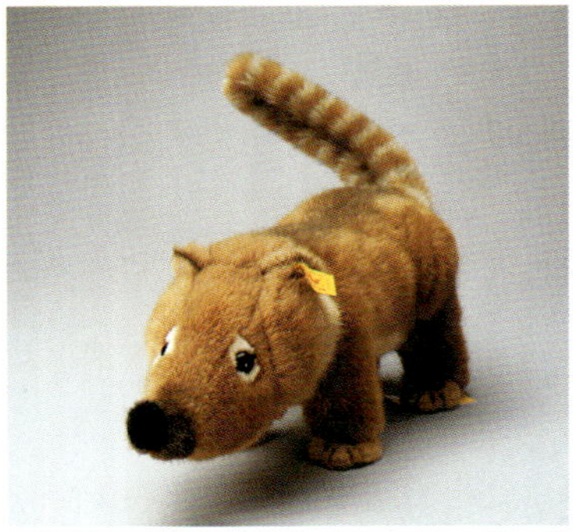

Nasenbaer - *Honey Bear*

Webpelz, braun, stehend, handwaschbar - *woven fur, brown, standing, hand washable*

EAN-No.	Period	Pr.	Info
120008	1995-1995	3	45 cm

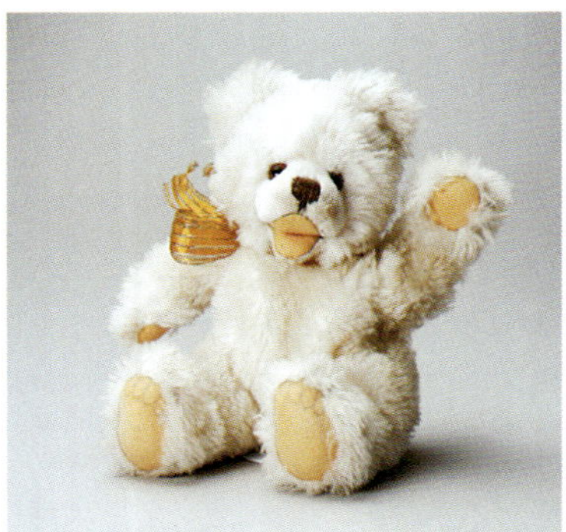

Cosy Teddy

Dralon-Pluesch, Schaumstoff-Fuellung, weiss, sitzend, Arme & Kopf gegliedert, Filz an Fuessen & Haenden bemalt, offener Mund, sehr weich, waschbar - *dralon plush, stuffed with foam, white, sitting, head & arms jointed, felt on feet & paws painted, open mouth, very soft, washable*

Serie	Art.-No	Period	Pr.	Info
83 12	**5622**	1955-1958	4	22 cm
830 120	**5622,00**	1959-1963	3-4	
476	**5622,00**	1965-1966	3-4	

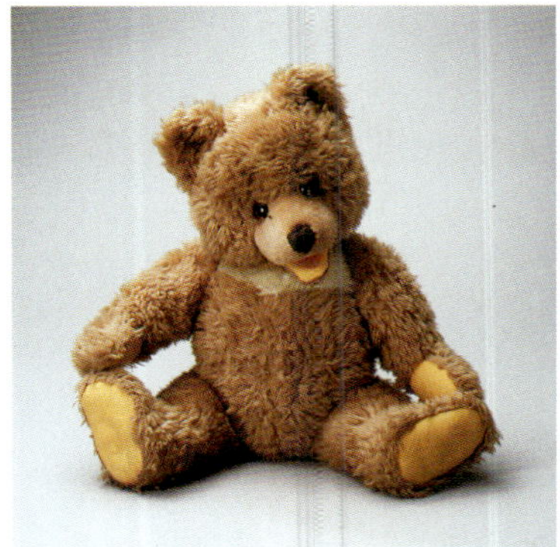

Cosy Teddy

Dralon-Pluesch, Schaumgummi-Fuellung, caramel, weisse Brust, gegliedert, offener Mund, sehr weich, vollwaschbar - *dralon plush, stuffed with foam rubber, caramel, upper chest white, jointed, open mouth, very soft, washable*

Serie	Art.-No	Period	Pr.	Info
476	**5620,00**	1965-1967	3-4	20 cm
	4762/20	1968-1976	3	
83 12	**5630**	1956-1958	4	30 cm
830 120	**5630,00**	1959-1963	3-4	
476	**5630,00**	1965-1967	3-4	
	4762/30	1968-1976	3	
830 120	**5640,00**	1963-1964	4	40 cm
476	**5640,00**	1965-1967	4	
	4762/40	1968-1975	3-4	

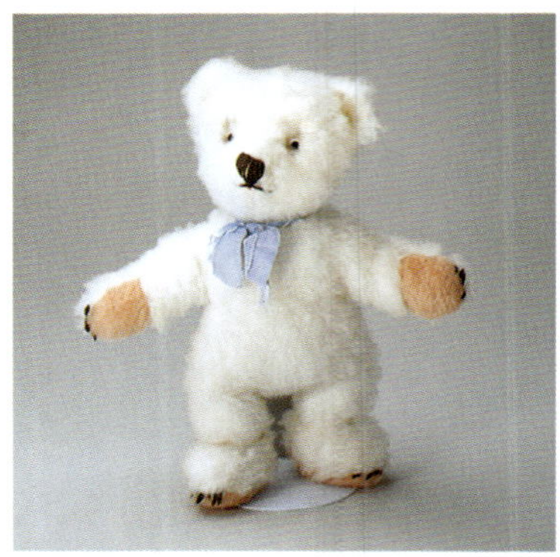

Cosy Teddy

Dralon, weiss, Filz-Krallen an Haenden & Fuessen, geschlossener Mund, waschbar - *dralon, white, felt claws on paws & feet, mouth closed, washable*

Serie	Art.-No	Period	Pr.	Info
830 120	**6628,04**	1964-1964	4-5	28 cm

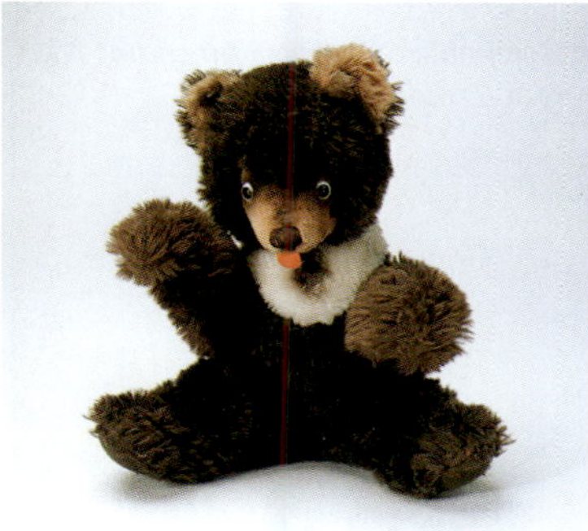

Cosy Bruni Kragenbaer - ***Cosy Bruni*** *Collar Bear*

Dralon-Pluesch, Schaumstoff-Flocken-Fuellung, braun, weisser Kragen, sitzend, Kopf & Arme gegliedert, waschbar - *dralon plush, stuffed with foam flakes, brown, white collar, sitting, head & arms jointed, washable*

SERIE	ART.-NO	PERIOD	PR.	INFO
477	**5625,03**	1965-1966	4	25 cm

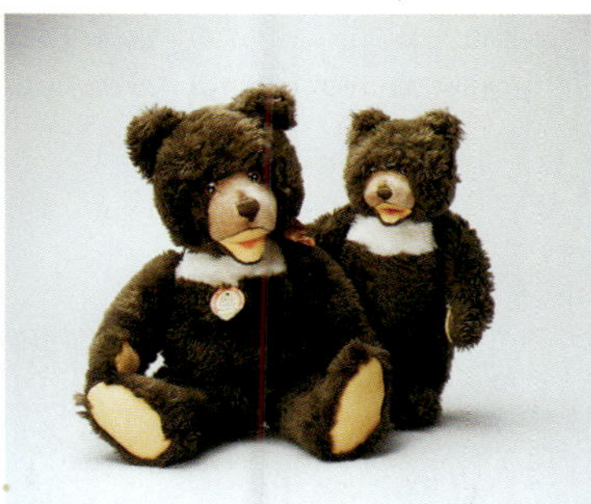

Cosy Teddy

Dralon-Pluesch, Schaumgummi-Fuellung, dunkelbraun, weisse Brust, gegliedert, offener Mund, sehr weich, vollwaschbar, - *dralon plush, stuffed with foam rubber, dark brown, upper chest white, jointed, open mouth, very soft, washable*

SERIE	ART.-NO	PERIOD	PR.	INFO
	4763/20	1968-1973	4	20 cm
476	**5630,03**	1966-1967	4	30 cm
	4763/30	1968-1973	3-4	
476	**5640,03**	1967-1967	4	40 cm
	4763/40	1968-1973	3-4	

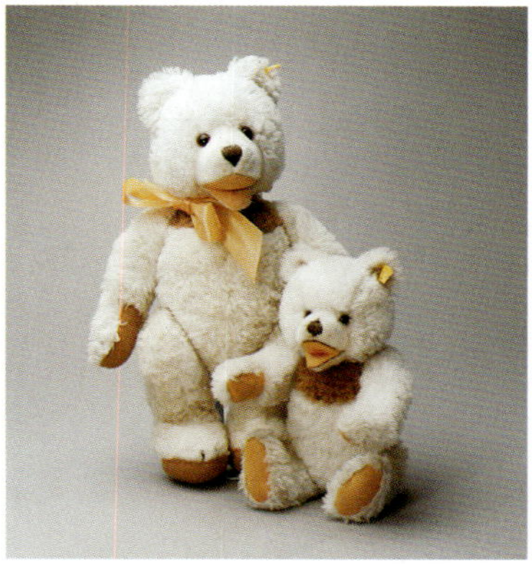

Cosy Teddy

Dralon-Pluesch, Schaumgummi-Fuellung, weiss, Brust caramel, gegliedert, offener Mund, sehr weich, vollwaschbar, - *dralon plush, stuffed with foam rubber, white, upper chest caramel, jointed, open mouth, very soft, washable*

SERIE	ART.-NO	PERIOD	PR.	INFO
	4764/20	1968-1975	4	20 cm
476	**5630,04**	1966-1967	4-5	30 cm
	4764/30	1968-1975	4	
476	**5640,04**	1967-1967	4-5	40 cm
	4764/40	1968-1975	4	

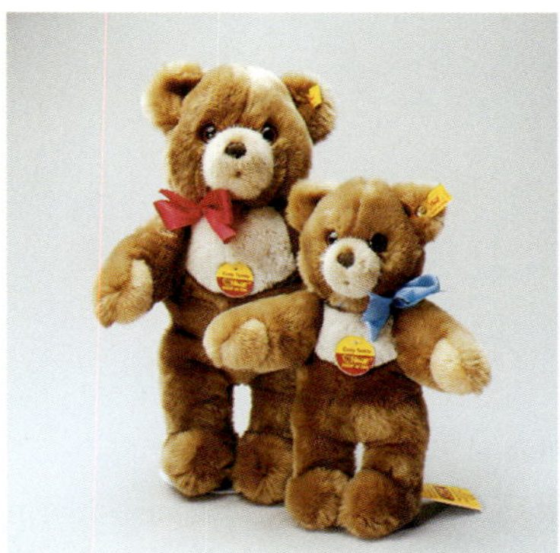

Cosy Teddy

Webpelz, braun/beige oder rotbraun, superweich, waschmaschinenfest - *woven fur, brown/beige or red-brown, super soft, machine washable*

SERIE	ART.-NO	PERIOD	PR.	INFO
018657	**5355/26**	1981-1990	2	26 cm, braun/beige - *brown/beige*
	018657	1991-1999	2	
018701	**5355/36**	1981-1990	2-3	36 cm
	018701	1991-1999	2-3	
	018718	1997-1999	2	26 cm, rotbraun - *red-brown*
	018725	1997-1999	2-3	36 cm

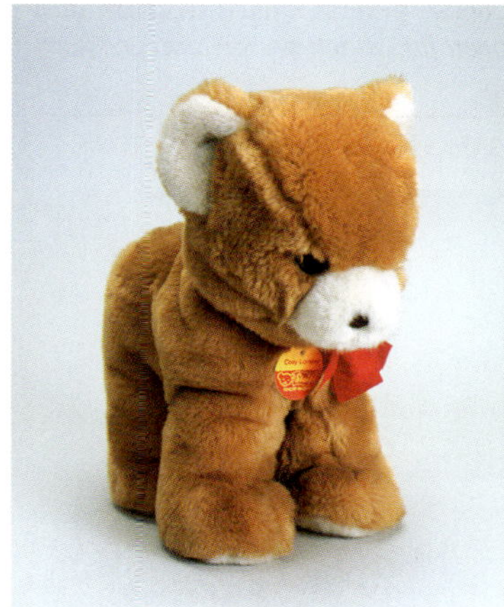

Cosy Lommy

Webpelz, blond, stehend, kuschelweich, waschmaschinenfest - *woven fur, blond, standing, soft & cuddly, machine washable*

SERIE	ART.-NO	PERIOD	PR.	INFO
	5353/25	1982-1984	2-3	25 cm

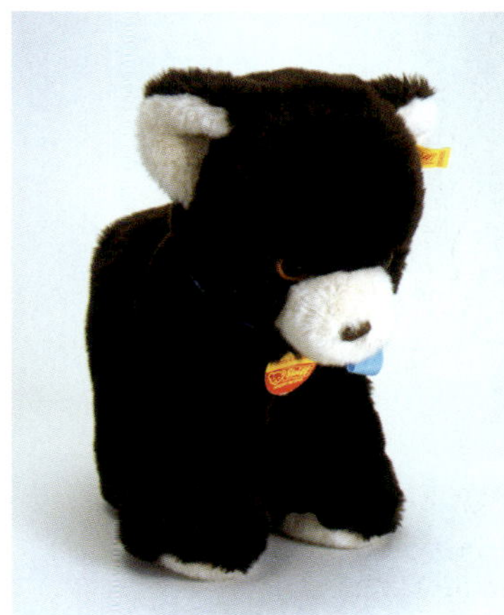

Cosy Lommy

Webpelz, braun, stehend, kuschelweich, waschmaschinenfest - *woven fur, brown, standing, soft & cuddly, machine washable*

SERIE	ART.-NO	PERIOD	PR.	INFO
	5354/25	1982-1984	2-3	25 cm

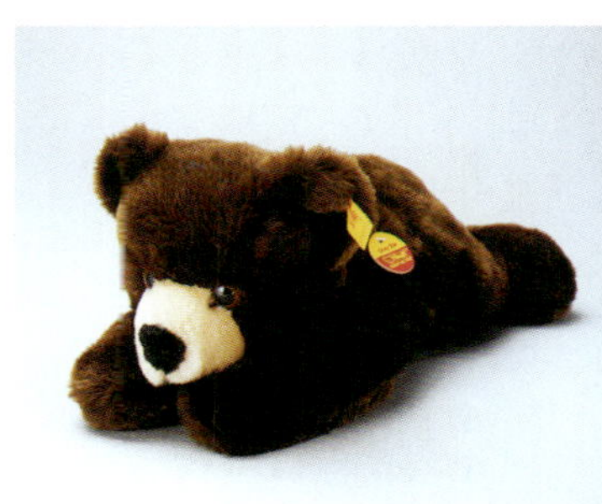

Cosy Baer - *Cosy Bear*

Webpelz, liegend, waschmaschinenfest - *woven fur, lying, machine washable*

SERIE	ART.-NO	PERIOD	PR.	INFO
085406	**5352/33**	1988-1989	2-3	33 cm

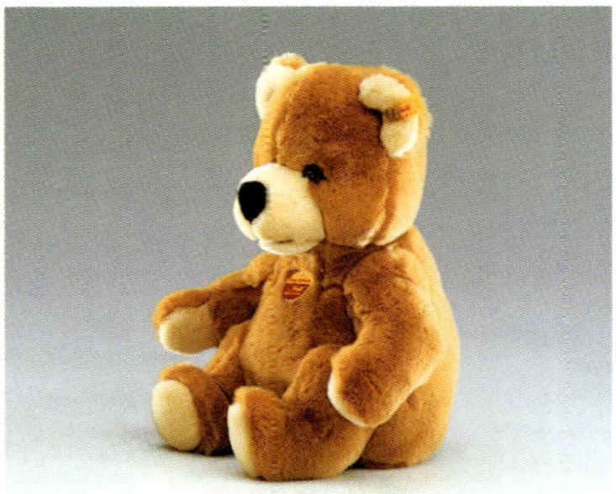

Cosy Browny Baer - *Cosy Browny Bear*

Webpelz, hellbraun, sitzend, waschmaschinenfest - *woven fur, light brown, sitting, machine washable*

EAN-NO.	PERIOD	PR.	INFO
085284	1996-1997	2-3	28 cm

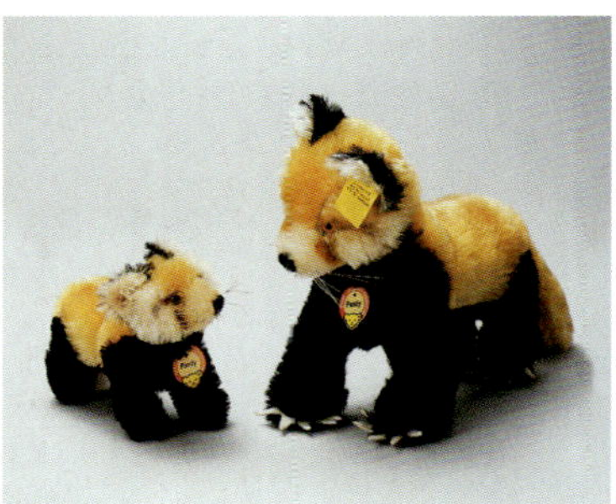

Pandy Indischer Panda - ***Pandy** Indian Panda*

Mohairpluesch, rot/schwarz, stehend, Kopf drehbar, ab 17 cm je fuenf Filzkrallen an den Fuessen - *mohair, red/black, standing, head swivels, from 17 cm five felt claws attached to feet*

SERIE	ART.-NO	PERIOD	PR.	INFO
132	**1310,00**	1963-1964	4-5	10 cm
132	**1317,00**	1963-1963	5	17 cm
132	**1325,00**	1963-1963	5-6	25 cm

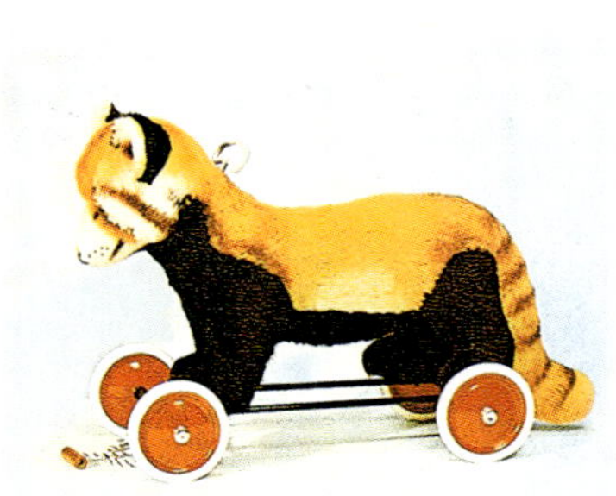

Reit-**Pandy** - *Riding **Pandy***

Mohairpluesch, rot/schwarz, stehend auf Metallscheibenraedern mit Gummireifen, Haltegriff, Zugstimme - *mohair, red/black, standing on metal disc wheels with rubber tires, grip handle, pull cord voice*

SERIE	ART.-NO	PERIOD	PR.	INFO
132	**1350,20**	1963-1963	6-7	50 cm

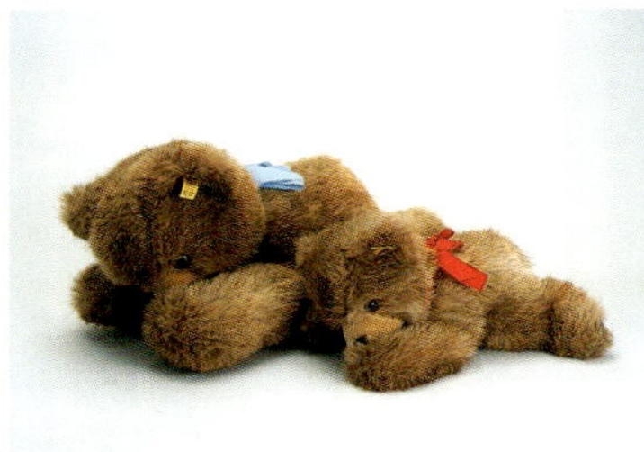

Floppy Teddy

Synthetik-Webpelz, formgeschaeumt, liegend, vollwaschbar - *synthetic woven fur, stuffed with pre-formed foam, lying, fully washable*

SERIE	ART.-NO	PERIOD	PR.	INFO
	5700/20	1978-1982	1-2	20 cm
	5700/30	1978-1982	2	30 cm

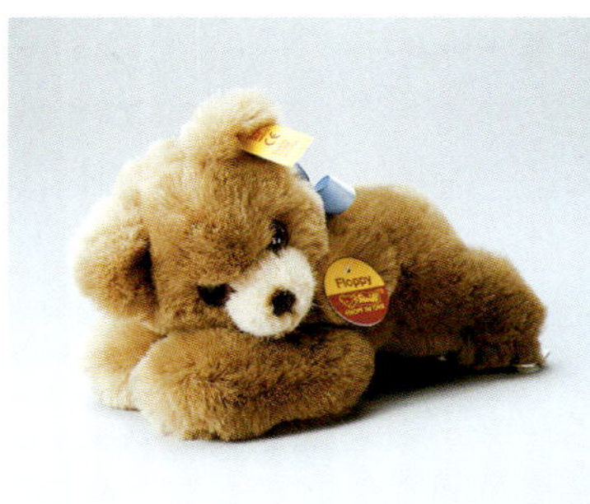

Floppy Baer - ***Floppy** Bear*

Webpelz, mollig weich, waschmaschinenfest - *woven fur, soft & cozy, machine washable*

SERIE	ART.-NO	PERIOD	PR.	INFO
082108	**5600/18**	1983-1990	2	20 cm
	082108	1991-1999	2	
082122	**5600/25**	1983-1988	2	25 cm

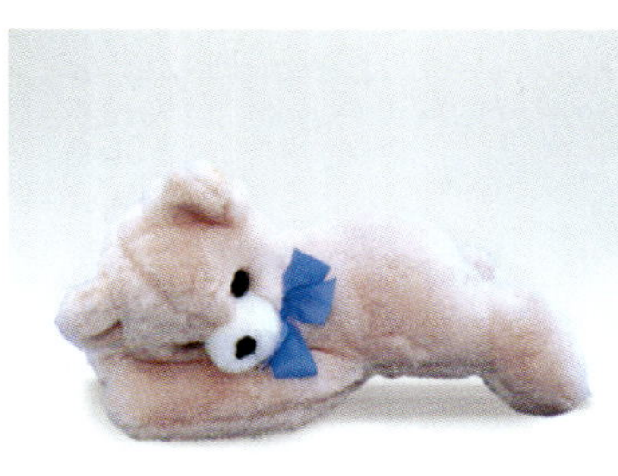

Baby Floppy Baer - *Baby Floppy Bear*

Webpelz, rosa, liegend, sehr weich, waschmaschinenfest - *woven fur, pink, lying, very soft, machine washable*

SERIE	ART.-NO	PERIOD	PR.	INFO
	5650/18	1983-1985	2	18 cm
	5650/25	1983-1985	2	25 cm

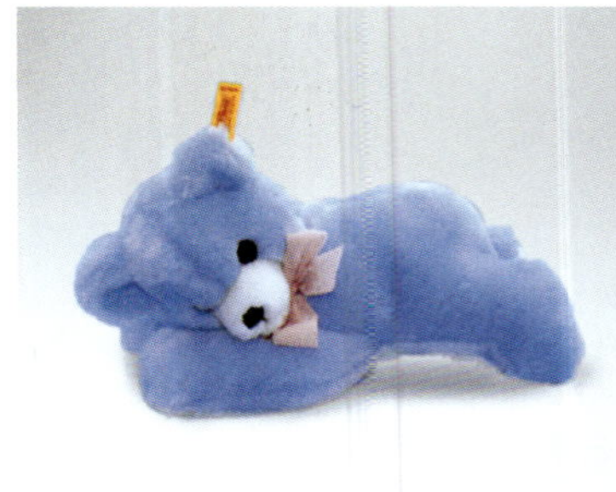

Baby Floppy Baer - *Baby Floppy Bear*

Webpelz, blau, liegend, sehr weich, waschmaschinenfest - *woven fur, blue, lying, very soft, machine washable*

SERIE	ART.-NO	PERIOD	PR.	INFO
	5651/18	1983-1985	2	18 cm
	5651/25	1983-1985	2	25 cm

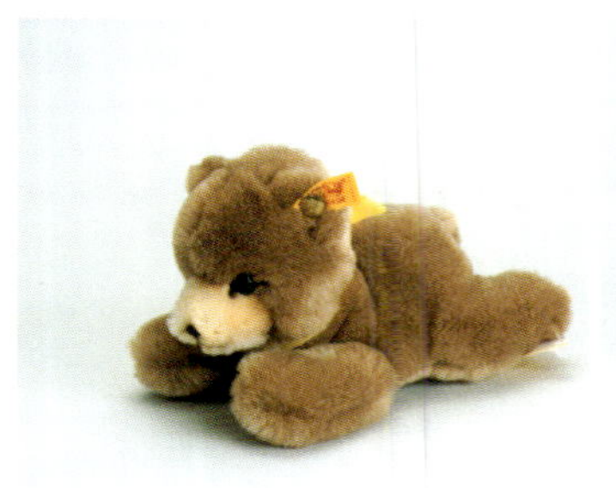

Mini Floppy Baer - ***Mini Floppy** Bear*

Webpelz, zimt, liegend, waschmaschinenfest - *woven fur, cinnamon, lying, machine washable*

SERIE	ART.-NO	PERIOD	PR.	INFO
081811	**5651/16**	1989-1990	2	16 cm
	081811	1991-1991	2	

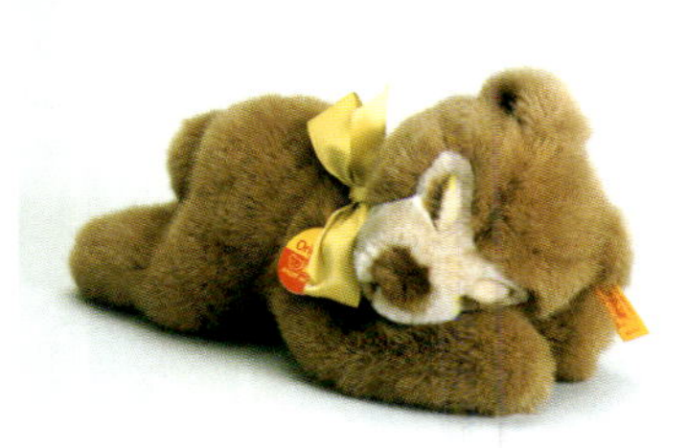

Schlafbaer - *Bedtime Bear*

Webpelz, zimt, liegend, waschmaschinenfest - *woven fur, cinnamon, lying, machine washable*

EAN-No.	Period	Pr.	Info
082511	1991-1997	2	22 cm

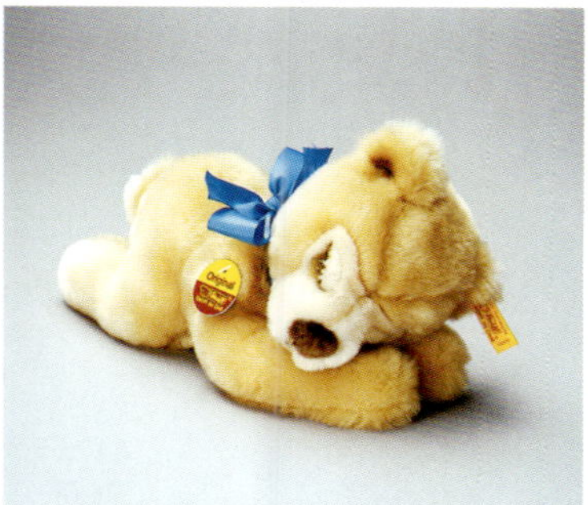

Schlafbaer - *Bedtime Bear*

Webpelz, blond, liegend, waschmaschinenfest - *woven fur, blond, lying, machine washable*

EAN-No.	Period	Pr.	Info
082535	1991-1999	2	28 cm

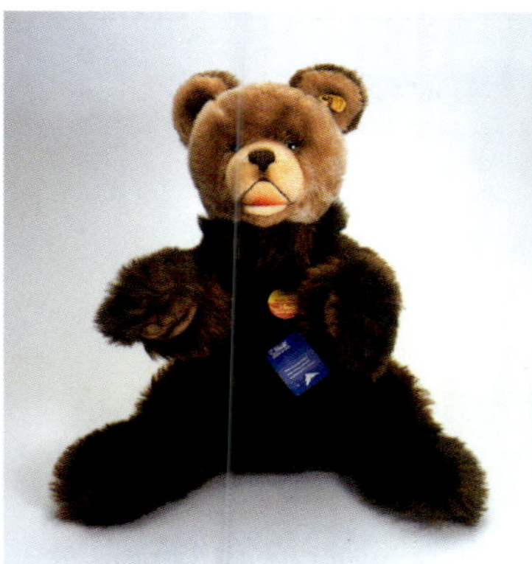

Molly Baer - *Molly Bear*

Dralon-Wirkpluesch, ab 1978 Webpelz, braun, offener Mund, bemalte Pfoten, abwaschbar - *dralon knitted plush, from 1978 woven fur, brown, open mouth, paws painted, surface washable*

Serie	Art.-No	Period	Pr.	Info
	0330/40	1973-1977	3	40 cm
	0330/70	1974-1984	4	70 cm

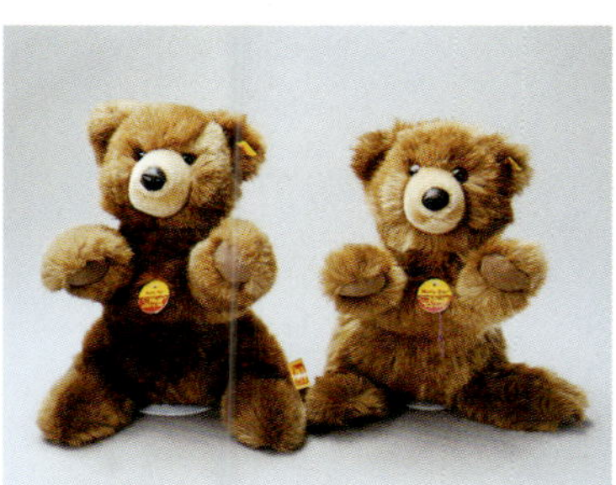

Molly Baer - *Molly Bear*

Pelzimitation, ab 1978 Webpelz, geschlossener Mund, mollig weich, abwaschbar - *imitation fur, from 1978 woven fur, mouth closed, very soft, surface washable*

Serie	Art.-No	Period	Pr.	Info
101250	**0330/32**	1977-1989	2-3	32 cm
101304	**0330/45**	1977-1988	3	45 cm

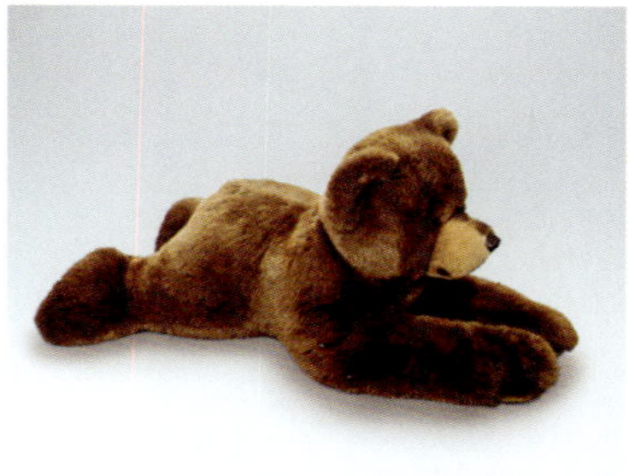

Super Molly Baer - ***Super Molly*** *Bear*

Webpelz, liegend, mollig weich, abwaschbar - *woven fur, lying, soft & cozy, surface washable*

Serie	Art.-No	Period	Pr.	Info
	0341/99	1980-1982	4	130 cm

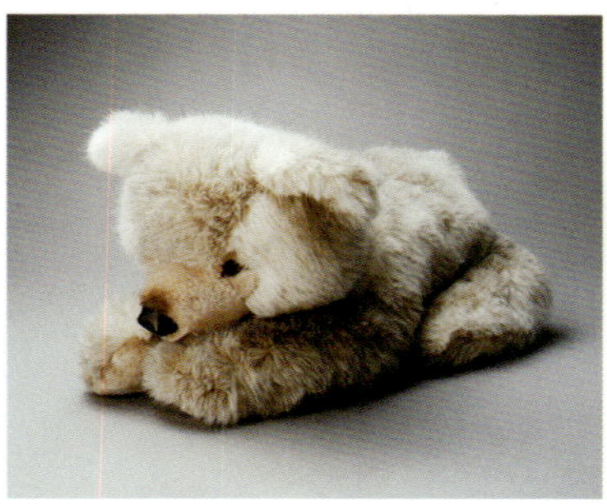

Molly Grisly Baer - *Molly Grizzly Bear*

Webpelz, liegend, mollig weich, abwaschbar - *woven fur, lying, soft & cozy, surface washable*

Serie	Art.-No	Period	Pr.	Info
	0333/35	1981-1983	2-3	35 cm
	0333/55	1981-1982	3	55 cm

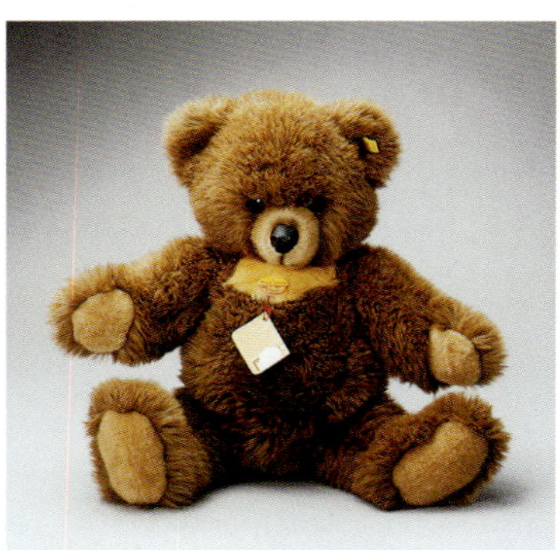

Molly Teddy

Webpelz, braun, mollig weich, abwaschbar - *woven fur, brown, soft & cozy, surface washable*

Serie	Art.-No	Period	Pr.	Info
	0320/55	1981-1982	4	55 cm

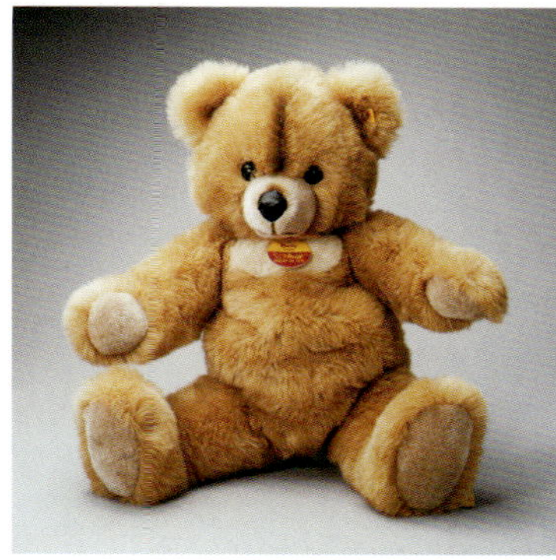

Molly Teddy

Webpelz, beigebraun, mollig weich, abwaschbar - *woven fur, beige/brown, soft & cozy, surface washable*

Serie	Art.-No	Period	Pr.	Info
019203	**0320/65**	1981-1990	3	65 cm
	019203	1991-1991	3	

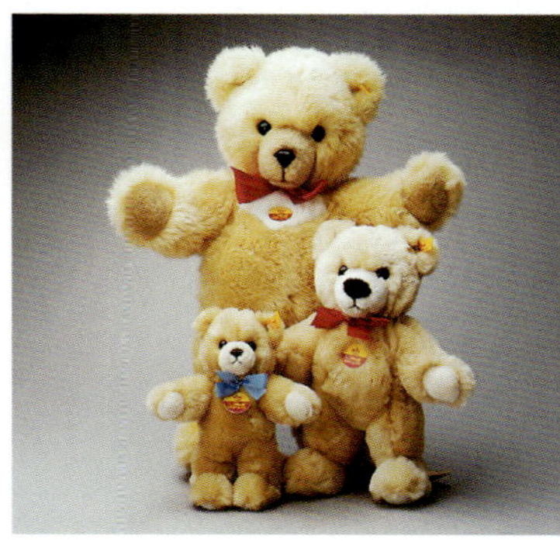

Molly Teddy

Webpelz, sekt, sehr weich - *woven fur, champagne, very soft*

Serie	Art.-No	Period	Pr.	Info
019333	**0321/22**	1988-1990	2	22 cm
	019333	1991-1999	2	
019357	**0321/32**	1988-1990	2-3	32 cm
	019357	1991-1999	2-3	
019401	**0321/55**	1983-1990	3	55 cm
	019401	1991-1999	3	

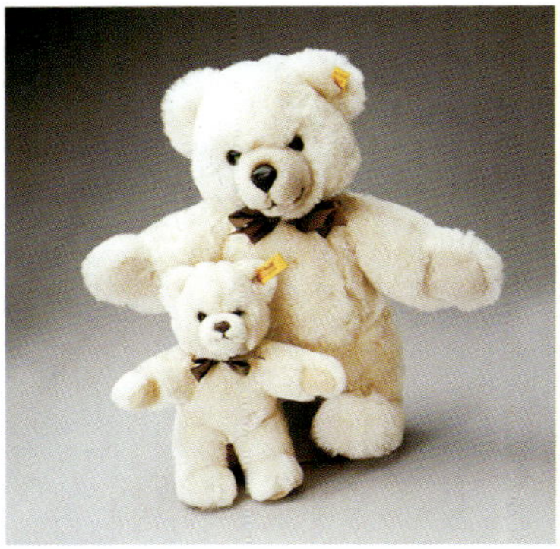

Molly Teddy

Webpelz, creme, waschmaschinenfest - *woven fur, cream, machine washable*

SERIE	ART.-NO	PERIOD	PR.	INFO
019555	**0322/22**	1988-1990	2	22 cm
	019555	1991-1999	2	
019579	**0322/32**	1988-1990	2-3	32 cm
	019579	1991-1999	2-3	
019609	**0322/40**	1984-1990	3	40 cm
	019609	1991-1999	3	

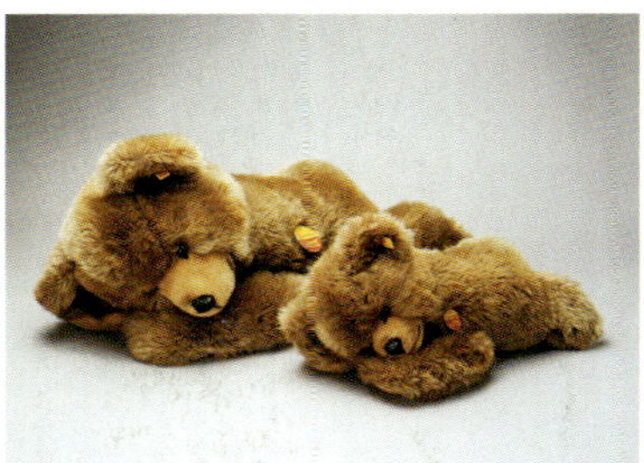

Super Molly Baer - ***Super Molly** Bear*

Webpelz, liegend, mollig weich, abwaschbar - *woven fur, lying, soft, surface washable*

SERIE	ART.-NO	PERIOD	PR.	INFO
102042	**0341/40**	1983-1990	3	40 cm
102073	**0341/65**	1983-1990	3-4	65 cm
102110	**0341/90**	1983-1989	4	90 cm
102134	**0341/98**	1983-1987	4	115 cm

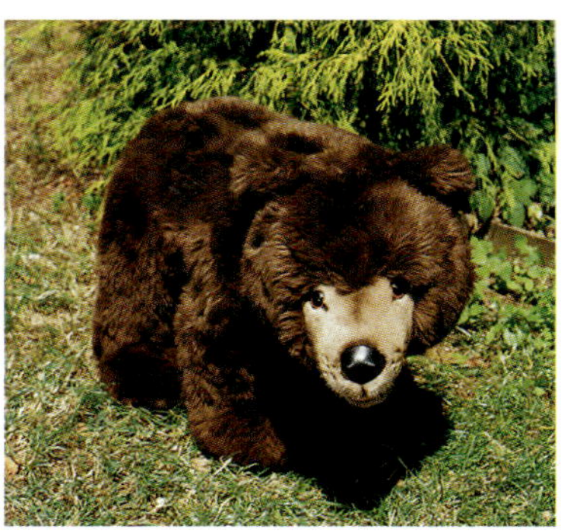

Super Molly Jungbaer - ***Super Molly** Cub*

Webpelz, stehend, abwaschbar - *woven fur, standing, surface washable*

SERIE	ART.-NO	PERIOD	PR.	INFO
100802	**0323/50**	1987-1988	4	50 cm

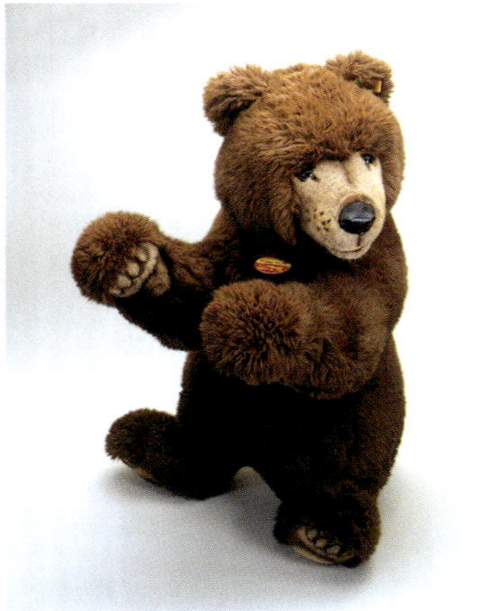

Super Molly Jungbaer - ***Super Molly** Cub*

Webpelz, aufwartend, abwaschbar - *woven fur, sitting up, surface washable*

SERIE	ART.-NO	PERIOD	PR.	INFO
100901	**0324/60**	1987-1988	4	60 cm

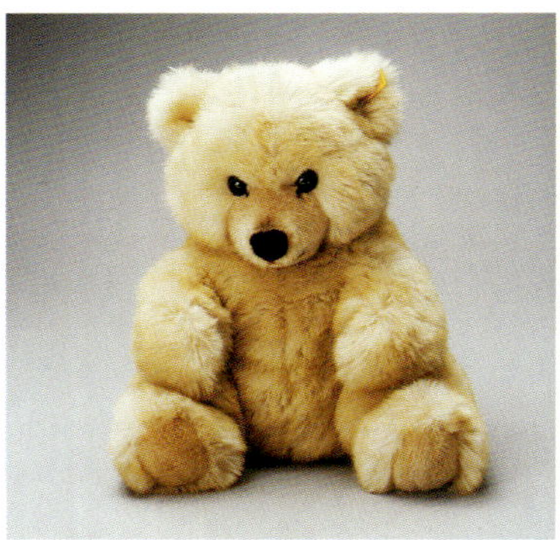

Molly Baer - *Molly Bear*

Webpelz, sitzend, abwaschbar - *woven fur, sitting, surface washable*

SERIE	ART.-NO	PERIOD	PR.	INFO
101359	**0331/33**	1988-1989	3	33 cm

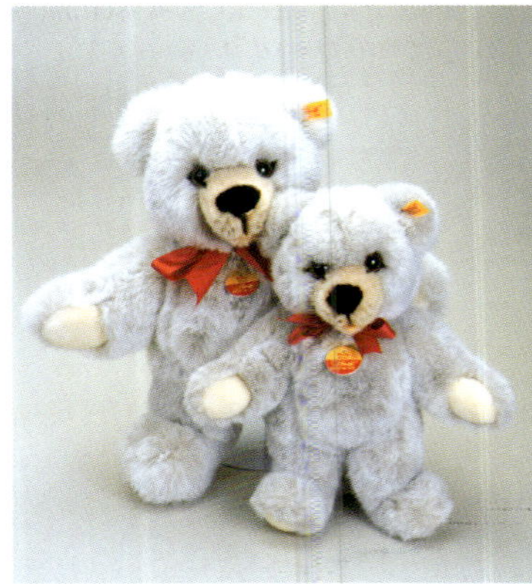

Molly Minky

Webpelz, grau, Pieps-Stimme, waschmaschinenfest - *woven fur, grey, squeaker, machine washable*

SERIE	ART.-NO	PERIOD	PR.	INFO
020049	**0318/32**	1989-1990	2-3	32 cm
	020049	1991-1996	2-3	
020087	**0318/42**	1989-1990	3	42 cm
	020087	1991-1995	3	

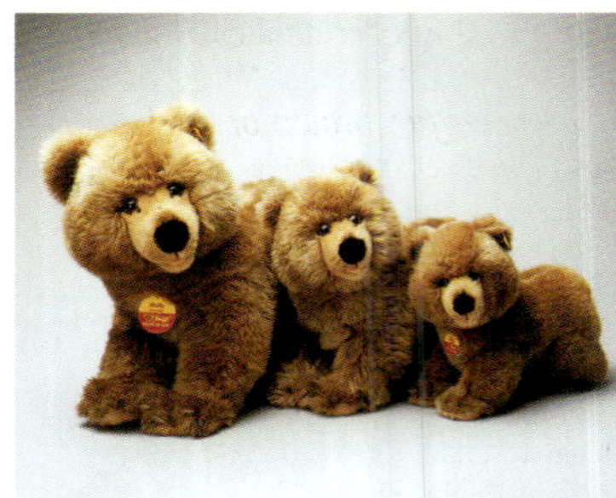

Molly Braunbaer - *Molly Brown Bear*

Webpelz, braun, stehend, abwaschbar - *woven fur, brown, standing, surface washable*

SERIE	ART.-NO	PERIOD	PR.	INFO
100048	**0343/25**	1989-1990	2-3	25 cm
	100048	1991-1993	2-3	
100079	**0343/32**	1989-1990	3	32 cm
	100079	1991-1993	3	
100116	**0343/40**	1989-1990	3	40 cm
	100116	1991-1991	3	

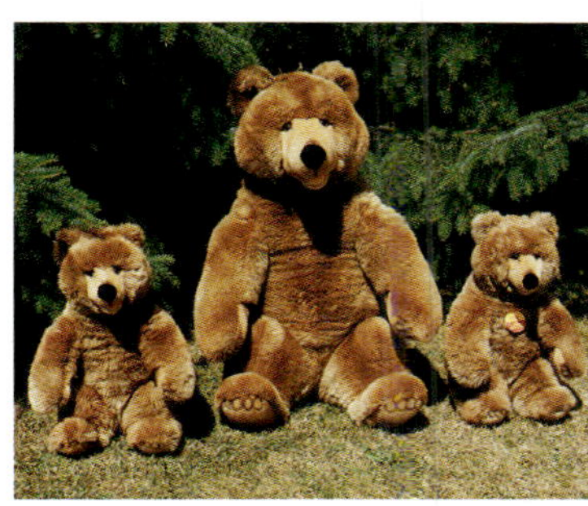

Molly Braunbaer - *Molly Brown Bear*

Webpelz, braun, sitzend, abwaschbar - *woven fur, brown, sitting, surface washable*

SERIE	ART.-NO	PERIOD	PR.	INFO
100376	**0345/35**	1989-1990	3	35 cm
	100376	1991-1993	3	
100413	**0345/45**	1989-1990	3	45 cm
	100413	1991-1992	3	
100451	**0345/60**	1989-1990	3-4	60 cm
	100451	1991-1991	3-4	
100482	**0345/80**	1989-1990	4	80 cm
	100482	1991-1991	4	

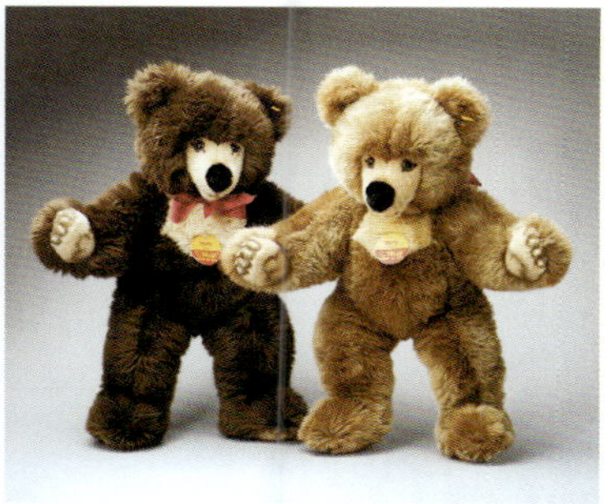

Molly Teddy

Webpelz, braun oder dunkelbraun, Pfoten & Fuesse bemalt, offener Mund, abwaschbar - *woven fur, brown or dark brown, paws & feet are painted, open mouth, surface washable*

SERIE	ART.-NO	PERIOD	PR.	INFO
019722	**0323/60**	1990-1990	3	60 cm, braun - *brown*
	019722	1991-1992	3	
019746	**0323/75**	1990-1990	3-4	75 cm
	019746	1991-1992	3-4	
019784	**0323/99**	1990-1990	4	110 cm
	019784	1991-1991	4	
019920	**0324/60**	1990-1990	3	60 cm, dunkelbraun - *dark brown*
	019920	1991-1992	3	
019944	**0324/75**	1990-1990	3-4	75 cm
	019944	1991-1992	3-4	

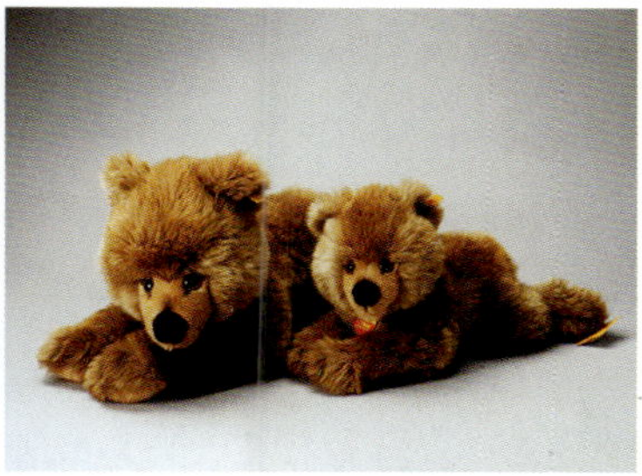

Molly Braunbaer - *Molly Brown Bear*

Webpelz, liegend, abwaschbar - *woven fur, lying, surface washable*

SERIE	ART.-NO	PERIOD	PR.	INFO
100574	**0347/40**	1990-1990	3	40 cm
	100574	1991-1991	3	
100611	**0347/55**	1990-1990	3	55 cm
	100611	1991-1991	3	
100659	**0347/75**	1990-1990	3-4	75 cm
	100659	1991-1991	3-4	
100697	**0347/96**	1990-1990	4	100 cm
	100697	1991-1991	4	
100734	**0347/98**	1990-1990	4	125 cm
	100734	1991-1991	4	

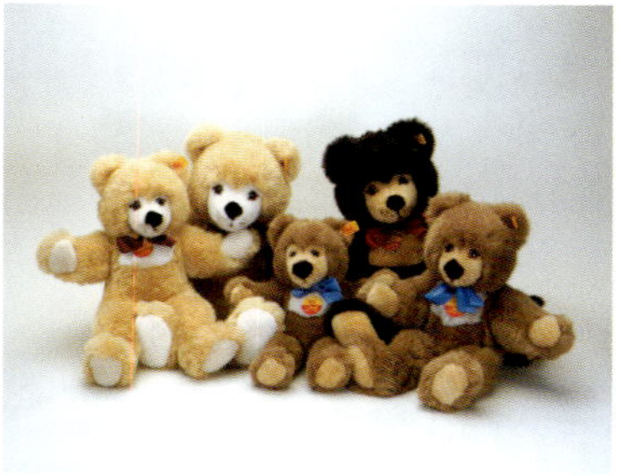

Molly Teddy

Webpelz, blond, zimt oder braun, geschlossener Mund, Pieps-Stimme, waschmaschinenfest - *woven fur, blond, cinnamon or brown, mouth closed, squeaker, machine washable*

EAN-NO.	PERIOD	PR.	INFO
021039	1992-1994	2-3	28 cm, blond
021053	1991-1992	2-3	36 cm
021107	1991-1992	3	48 cm
021237	1992-1994	2-3	28 cm, zimt - *cinnamon*
021251	1991-1993	2-3	36 cm
021305	1991-1992	3	48 cm
021435	1992-1993	2-3	28 cm, braun - *brown*
021459	1991-1992	2-3	36 cm
021503	1991-1992	3	48 cm

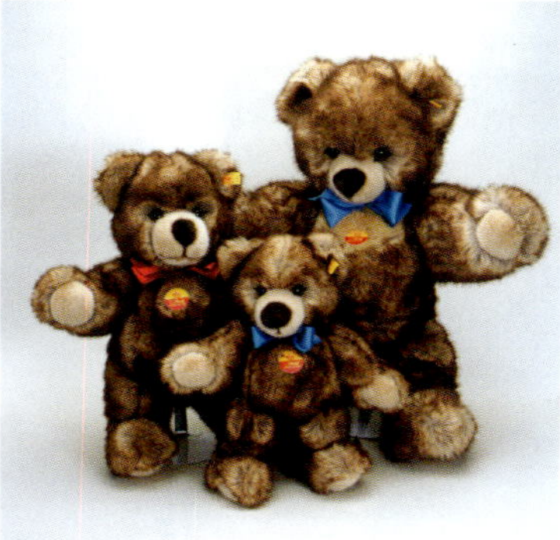

Molly Teddy

Webpelz, braun, gespitzt, geschlossener Mund, waschmaschinenfest - *woven fur, brown, light tipped, mouth closed, machine washable*

EAN-NO.	PERIOD	PR.	INFO
021558	1994-1997	2-3	32 cm
021565	1994-1996	2-3	40 cm
021572	1994-1996	3	55 cm

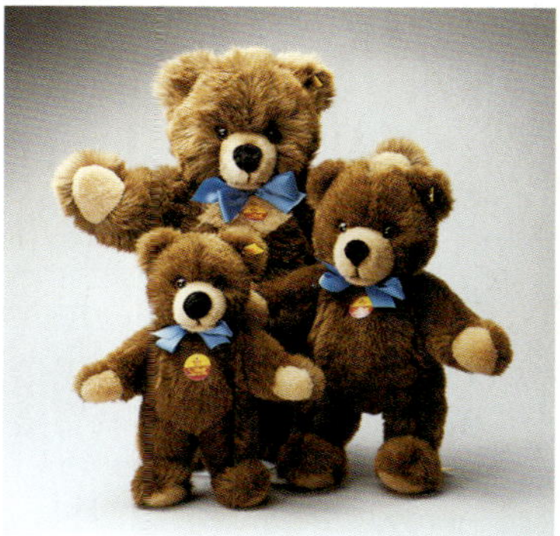

Molly Teddy

Webpelz, dunkelbraun, geschlossener Mund, waschmaschinenfest - *woven fur, dark brown, mouth closed, machine washable*

EAN-NO.	PERIOD	PR.	INFO
021701	1994-1999	2-3	32 cm
021725	1994-1996	2-3	40 cm
021749	1994-1996	3	55 cm
021763	1994-1999	4	70 cm

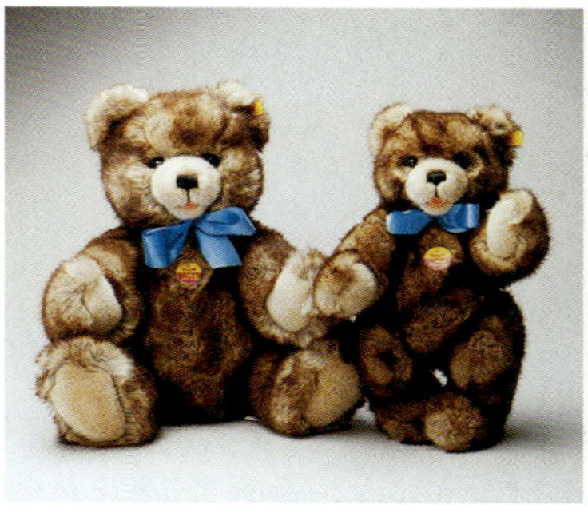

Knuffi Teddybaer - ***Knuffi** Teddy Bear*

Webpelz, braun, gespitzt, gegliedert, Druckstimme, waschmaschinenfest - *woven fur, brown, light tipped, jointed, press voice, machine washable*

EAN-NO.	PERIOD	PR.	INFO
017803	1994-1997	3-4	40 cm
017827	1994-1995	3-4	50 cm

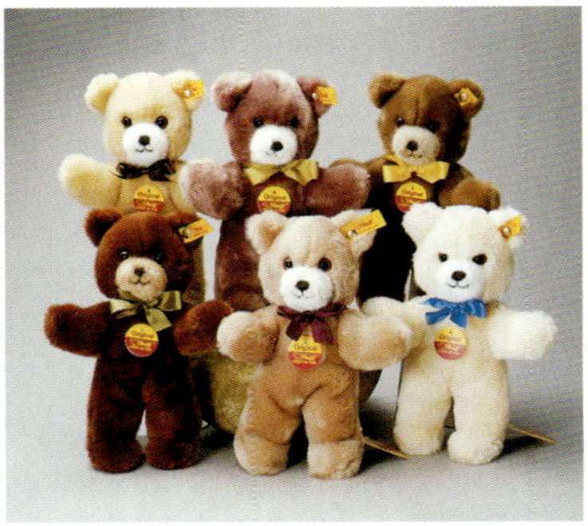

Teddybaer - *Teddybear*

Webpelz, 22 cm, waschmaschinenfest - *woven fur, 22cm, machine washable*

EAN-No.	Period	Pr.	Info
023057	1995-1999	2	elfenbein - *ivory*
023071	1995-1999	2	beige
023095	1995-1999	2	hellrosa - *light pink*
023118	1995-1996	2	altrosa - *rose*
023132	1995-1999	2	hellbraun - *light brown*
023156	1995-1999	2	cognac - *brandy*

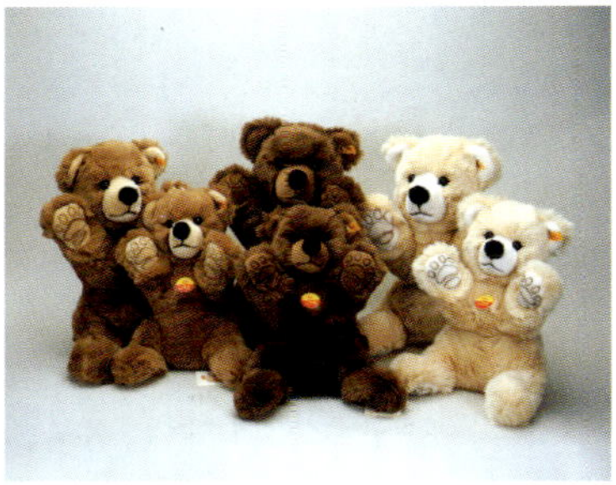

Molly Teddybaer - ***Molly Teddy**bear*

Webpelz, abwaschbar, geschlossener Mund - *woven fur, surface washable, mouth closed*

EAN-No.	Period	Pr.	Info
022012	1996-1997	2-3	38 cm, blond
022029	1996-1997	3	48 cm
022067	1996-1997	2-3	38 cm, hellbraun - *light brown*
022074	1996-1997	3	48 cm
022111	1996-1997	2-3	38 cm, dunkelbraun - *dark brown*
022128	1996-1997	3	48 cm

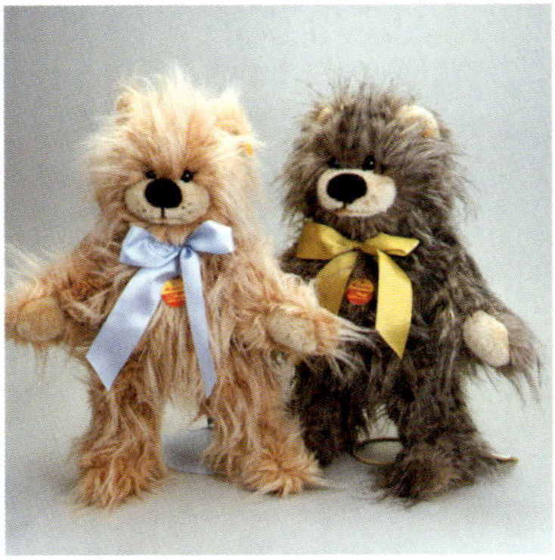

Wuschel Teddy

Webpelz, rotblond, caramel oder grau gespitzt, 40 cm, handwaschbar - *woven fur, sandy, caramel or grey tipped, 40 cm, hand washable*

EAN-No.	Period	Pr.	Info
022500	1997-1997	3	rotblond - *sandy*
022555	1997-1997	3	caramel
022609	1997-1997	3	grau gespitzt - *grey tipped*

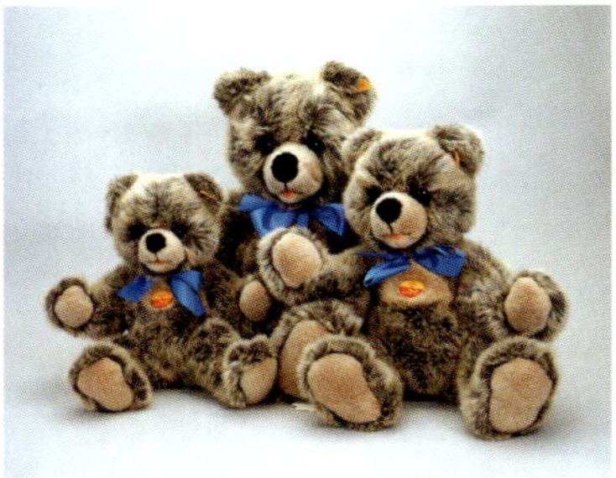

Molly Baer - *Molly Bear*

Webpelz, dunkelbraun/beige gespitzt, waschmaschinenfest - *woven fur, dark brown/beige tipped, machine washable*

EAN-No.	Period	Pr.	Info
123764	1997-1999	3	40 cm
123771	1997-1998	3	50 cm
123788	1997-1997	3-4	60 cm

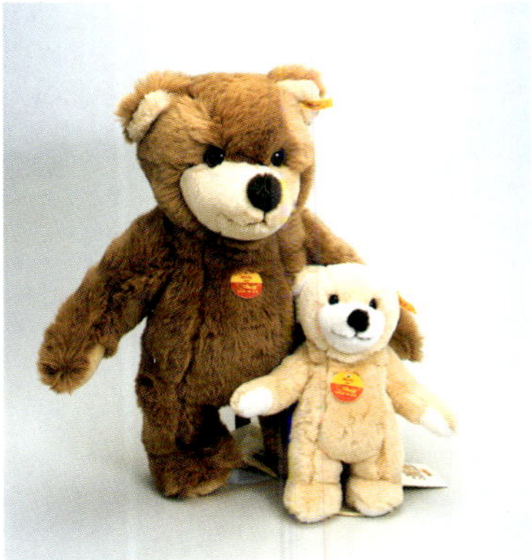

Molly Baer - *Molly Bear*

Webpelz, blond oder braun, waschmaschinenfest - *woven fur, blond or brown, machine washable*

EAN-No.	Period	Pr.	Info
100123	1998-1999	2	24 cm, blond
100130	1998-1998	2-3	34 cm
100147	1998-1998	3	44 cm
100185	1998-1999	2	24 cm, braun - *brown*
100192	1998-1998	2-3	34 cm
100208	1998-1998	3	44 cm

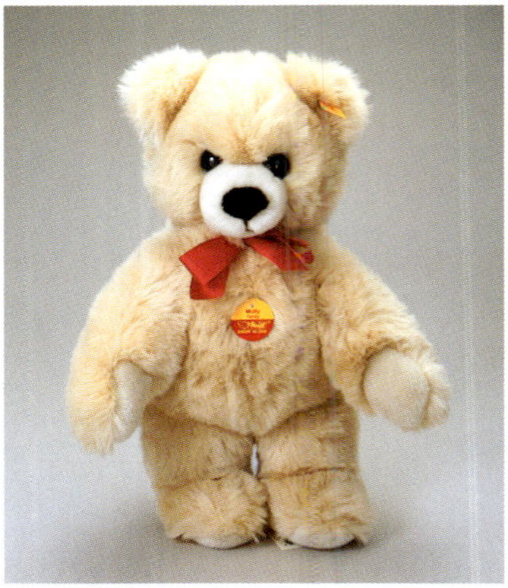

Molly Schlenker-Teddybaer - ***Molly** Dangling Teddybear*

Webpelz, waschmaschinenfest - *woven fur, machine washable*

EAN-No.	Period	Pr.	Info
019425	1999-1999	2-3	35 cm, blond
019432	1999-1999	3	45 cm
019623	1999-1999	2-3	35 cm, whisky
019630	1999-1999	3	45 cm
019975	1999-1999	2-3	35 cm, braun - *brown*
019982	1999-1999	3	45 cm

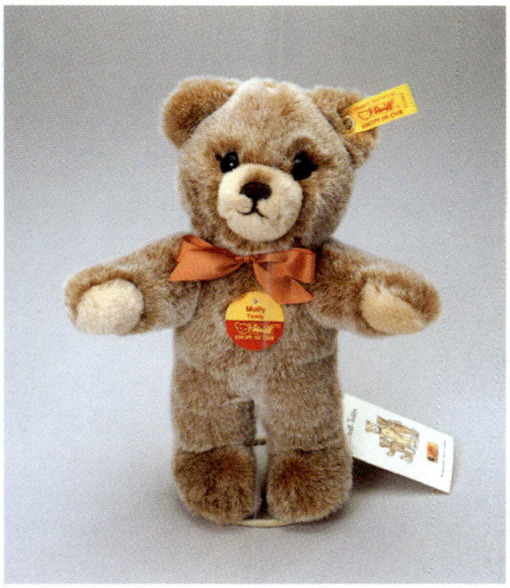

Molly Teddybaer - *Molly Teddybear*

Webpelz, hellbraun/beige gespitzt, waschmaschinenfest - *woven fur, light brown/ beige tipped, machine washable*

EAN-No.	Period	Pr.	Info
019500	1999-1999	2	22 cm

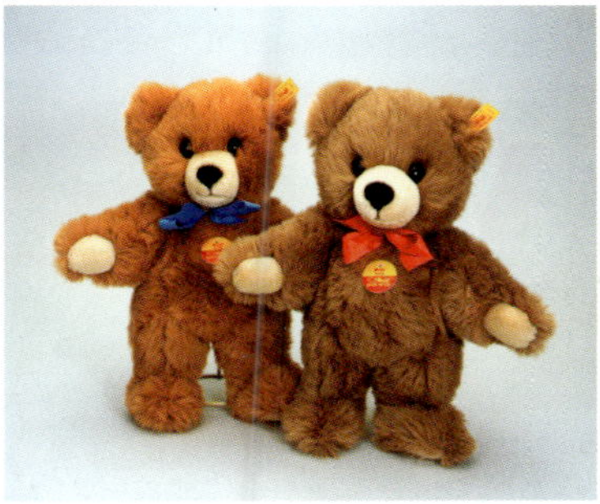

Molly Teddybaer - *Molly Teddybear*

Webpelz, waschmaschinenfest - *woven fur, machine washable*

EAN-No.	Period	Pr.	Info
019647	1999-1999	2	22 cm, braun - *brown*
019661	1999-1999	2-3	32 cm
019807	1999-1999	2	22 cm, whisky
019821	1999-1999	2-3	32 cm

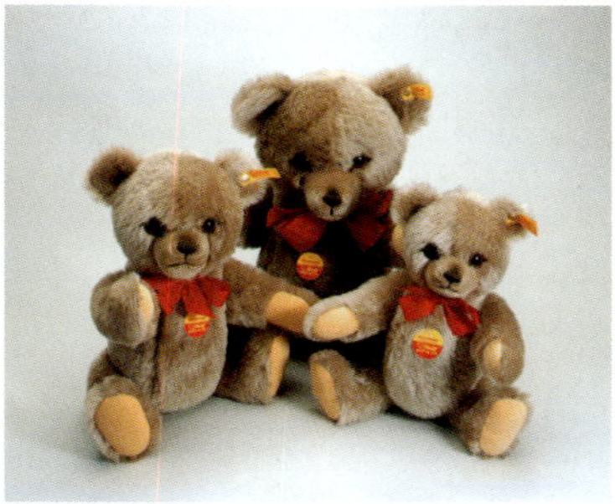

Steiff **Brummbaer** - *Steiff Growler Bear*

Mohair Webpelz, dunkelblond, gegliedert, 28 cm mit Druck-Stimme - sonst Brummstimme, abwaschbar - *mohair woven fur, dark blond, jointed, 28 cm press voice, from 33 cm growler, surface washable*

Serie	Art.-No	Period	Pr.	Info
011535	**0228/28**	1990-1990	2-3	28 cm
	011535	1991-1993	2-3	
011559	**0228/33**	1987-1990	2-3	33 cm
	011559	1991-1999	2-3	
011580	**0228/38**	1987-1990	3	38 cm
	011580	1991-1999	3	
011627	**0228/48**	1987-1990	3	48 cm
	011627	1991-1994	3	

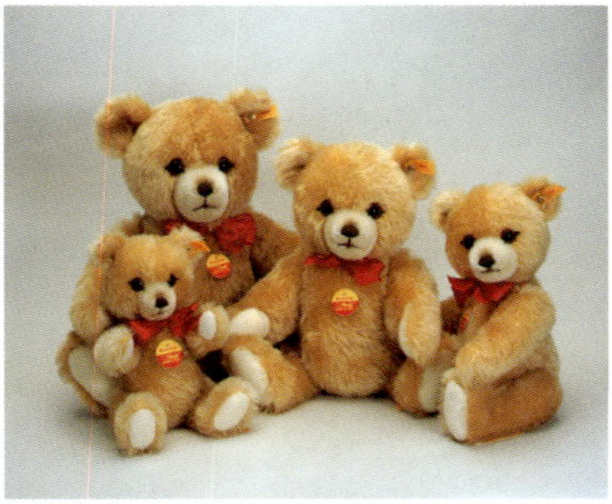

Steiff **Brummbaer** - *Steiff Growler Bear*

Mohair Webpelz, blond, gegliedert, 28 cm mit Druck-Stimme - sonst Brummstimme, abwaschbar - *mohair woven fur, blond, jointed, 28 cm press voice, from 33 cm growler, surface washable*

Serie	Art.-No	Period	Pr.	Info
011733	**0226/28**	1990-1990	2-3	28 cm
	011733	1991-1993	2-3	
011757	**0226/33**	1990-1990	2-3	33 cm
	011757	1991-1999	2-3	
011788	**0226/38**	1990-1990	3	38 cm
	011788	1991-1999	3	
011825	**0226/48**	1990-1990	3	48 cm
	011825	1991-1994	3	

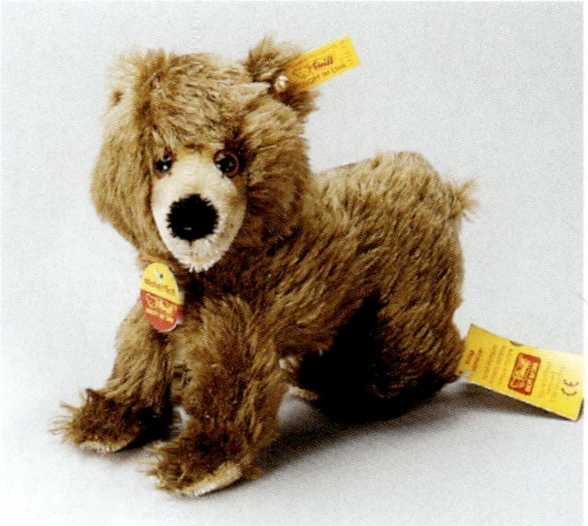

Mohair Soft Baer - ***Mohair Soft** Bear*

Mohair Webpelz, dunkelbraun, stehend, handwaschbar - *mohair woven fur, dark brown, standing, hand washable*

Serie	Art.-No	Period	Pr.	Info
034251	**1210/25**	1990-1990	2-3	25 cm
	034251	1991-1992	2-3	

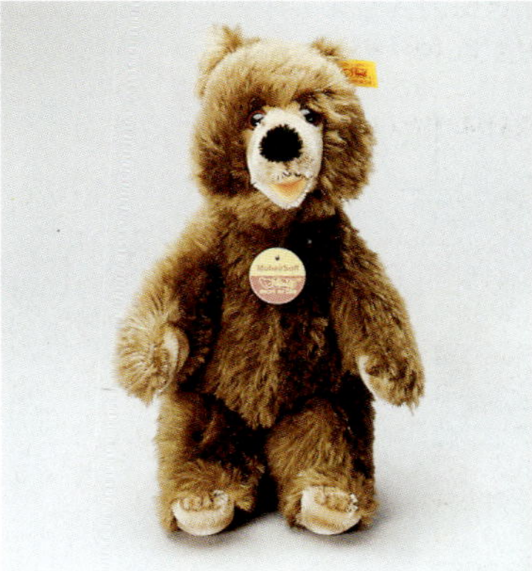

Mohair Soft Baer - ***Mohair Soft** Bear*

Mohair Webpelz, dunkelbraun, sitzend, handwaschbar - *mohair woven fur, dark brown, sitting, hand washable*

Serie	Art.-No	Period	Pr.	Info
034350	**1212/25**	1990-1990	3	25 cm
	034350	1991-1991	3	

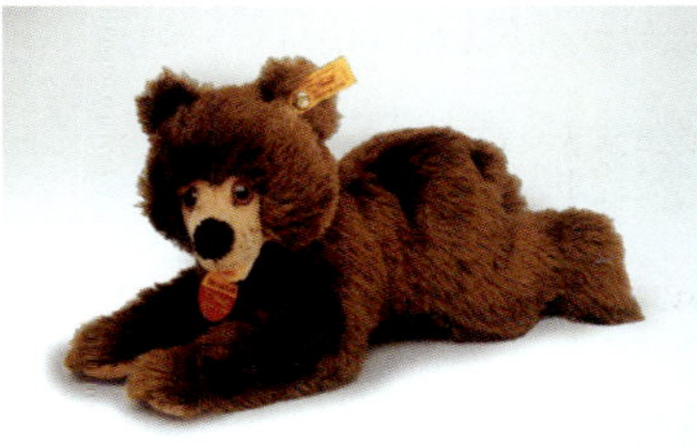

Mohair Soft Baer - ***Mohair Soft** Bear*

Mohair Webpelz, dunkelbraun, liegend, handwaschbar - *mohair woven fur, dark brown, lying, hand washable*

Serie	Art.-No	Period	Pr.	Info
034459	**1215/25**	1990-1990	2-3	25 cm
	034459	1991-1992	2-3	

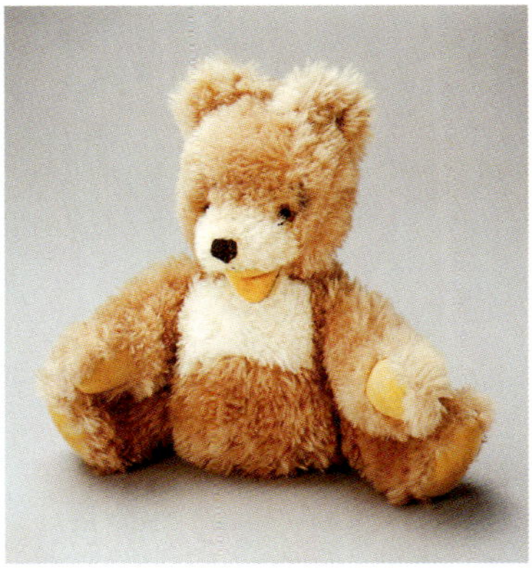

Petsy Baer - ***Petsy** Bear*

Dralon, braun, Brustansatz weiss, bemalte Pfoten, offener Mund, sehr weich - *dralon, brown, white chest, painted paws, open mouth, very soft*

SERIE	ART.-NO	PERIOD	PR.	INFO
119	**6625,03**	1951-1963	4	25 cm
119	**6635,03**	1961-1963	4	35 cm
119	**6645,03**	1961-1963	4-5	45 cm

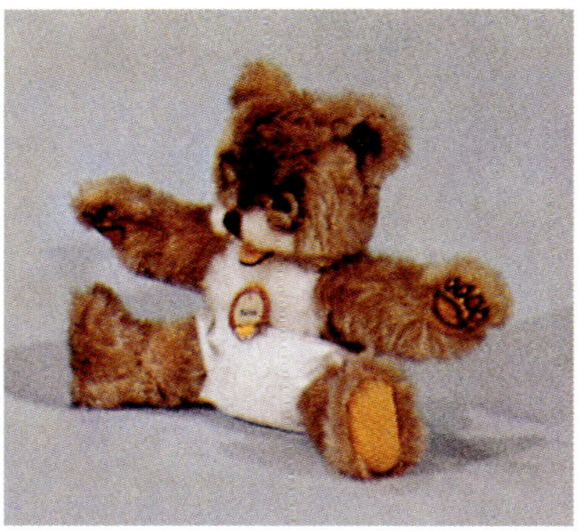

Cosy **Petsy** mit Hoeschen - *Cozy **Petsy** with Shorts*

Dralon, hellbraun, Brustansatz weiss, bemalte Pfoten, weisses Hoeschen, offener Mund, sehr weich - *dralon, light brown, white chest, paws painted, white shorts, open mouth, very soft*

SERIE	ART.-NO	PERIOD	PR.	INFO
830 119	**6625,03**	1964-1964	5	25 cm

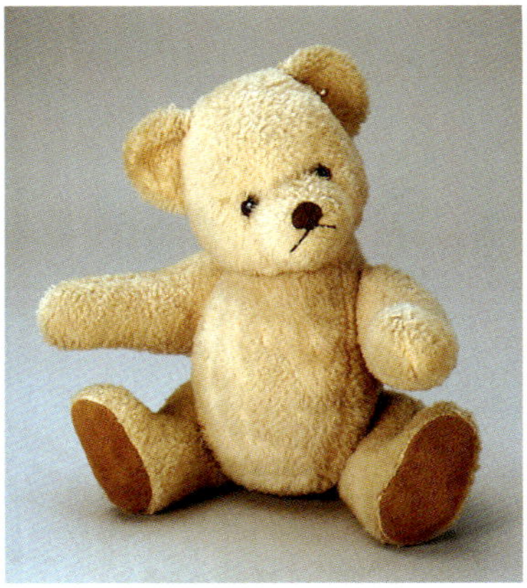

Dralon Teddy **Petsy**

Dralon, hellbeige, gegliedert, 38 cm mit Brummstimme, abwaschbar - *dralon, light beige, jointed, 38 cm with growler, surface washable*

SERIE	ART.-NO	PERIOD	PR.	INFO
	0240/24	1970-1974	4-5	24 cm
	0240/30	1970-1974	4-5	30 cm
	0240/38	1970-1974	4-5	38 cm

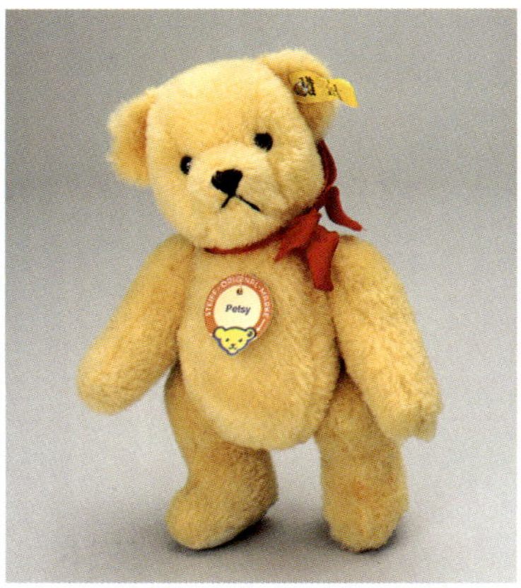

Dralon Teddy **Petsy**

Dralon, gold, gegliedert, 38 cm mit Brummstimme, abwaschbar - *dralon, gold, jointed, 38 cm with growler, surface washable*

SERIE	ART.-NO	PERIOD	PR.	INFO
	0241/24	1970-1973	4-5	24 cm
	0241/30	1970-1973	4-5	30 cm
	0241/38	1970-1974	4-5	38 cm

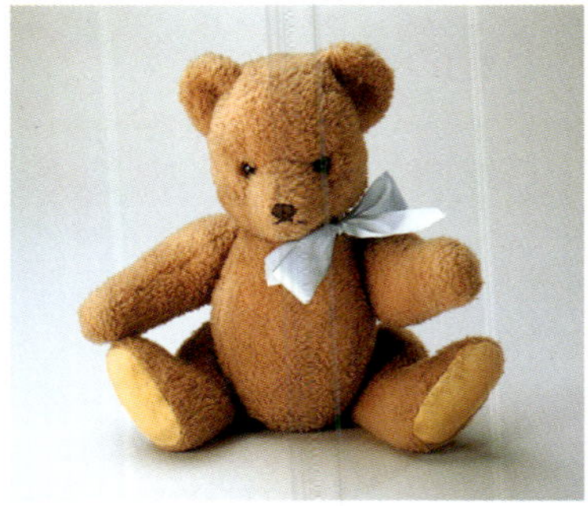

Dralon Teddy **Petsy**

Dralon, caramel, gegliedert, 38 cm mit Brummstimme, abwaschbar - *dralon, caramel, jointed, 38 cm with growler, surface washable*

SERIE	ART.-NO	PERIOD	PR.	INFO
	0242/24	1970-1976	4-5	24 cm
	0242/30	1970-1976	4-5	30 cm
	0242/38	1970-1976	4-5	38 cm

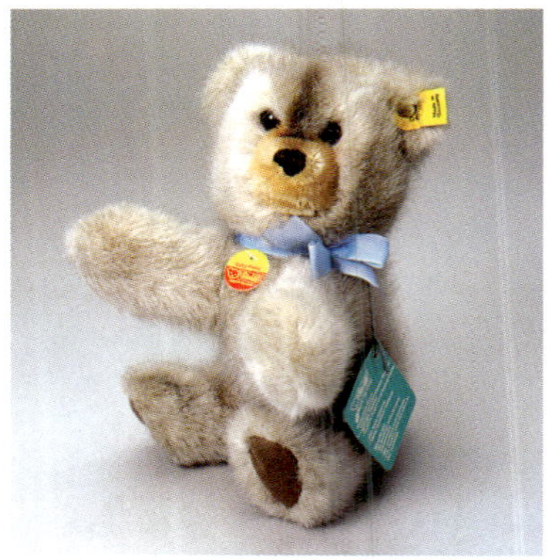

Baby-Petsy

Pelzimitation, ab 1978 Synthetik-Wirkpelz, formgeschaeumt, aufwartend, vollwaschbar - *imitation fur, from 1978 synthetic knitted fur, stuffed with pre-formed foam, sitting up, fully washable*

SERIE	ART.-NO	PERIOD	PR.	INFO
	5740/16	1977-1979	2-3	16 cm

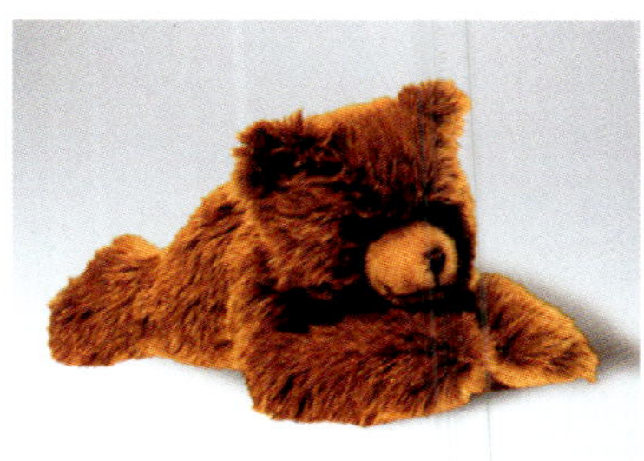

Molly Petsy

Webpelz, liegend, mollig weich, abwaschbar - *woven fur, lying, soft & cozy, surface washable*

SERIE	ART.-NO	PERIOD	PR.	INFO
	0332/45	1981-1984	2-3	45 cm

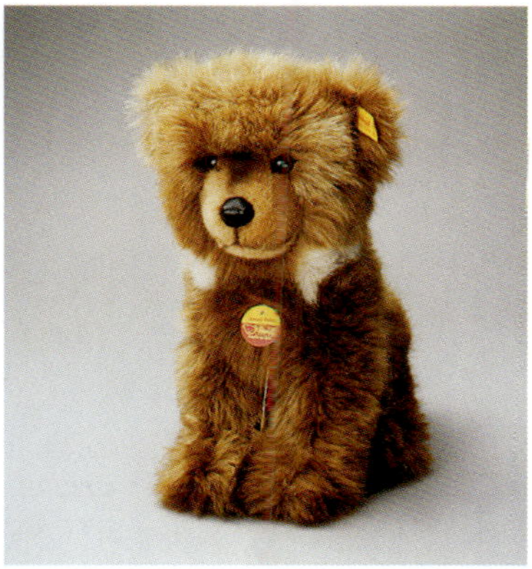

Junior Petsy

Webpelz, sitzend, abwaschbar - *woven fur, sitting, surface washable*

SERIE	ART.-NO	PERIOD	PR.	INFO
	2877/30	1982-1983	2-3	30 cm

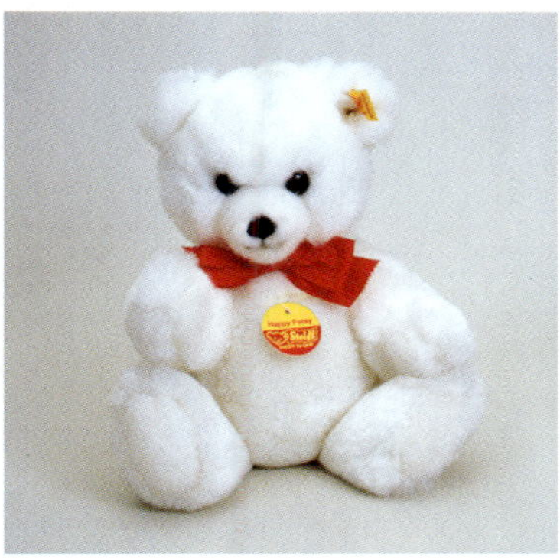

Happy Petsy

Webpelz, weiss, gegliedert, Druckstimme, waschmaschinenfest - *woven fur, white, jointed, press voice, machine washable*

SERIE	ART.-NO	PERIOD	PR.	INFO
	5740/20	1984-1984	4	20 cm
	5740/28	1984-1984	4	28 cm

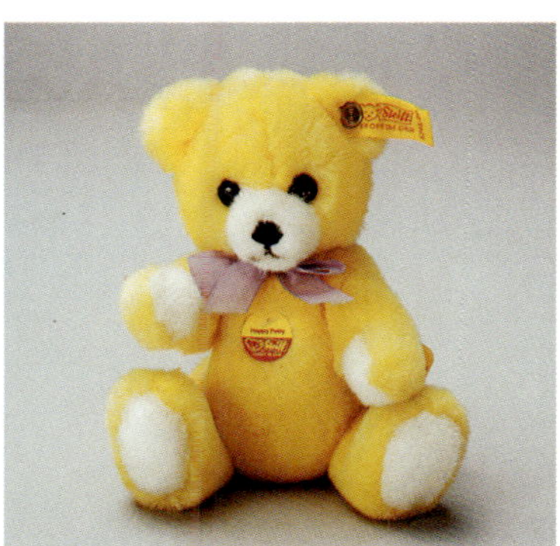

Happy Petsy

Webpelz, dottergelb, gegliedert, Druckstimme, waschmaschinenfest - *woven fur, egg yellow, jointed, press voice, machine washable*

SERIE	ART.-NO	PERIOD	PR.	INFO
	5745/20	1984-1984	4	20 cm
	5745/28	1984-1984	4	28 cm

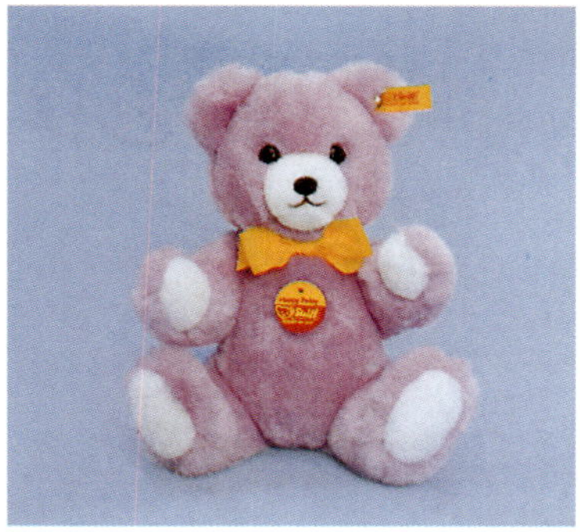

Happy Petsy

Webpelz, lila, gegliedert, Druckstimme, waschmaschinenfest - *woven fur, lavender, jointed, press voice, machine washable*

SERIE	ART.-NO	PERIOD	PR.	INFO
	5748/20	1984-1984	4	20 cm
	5748/28	1984-1984	4	28 cm

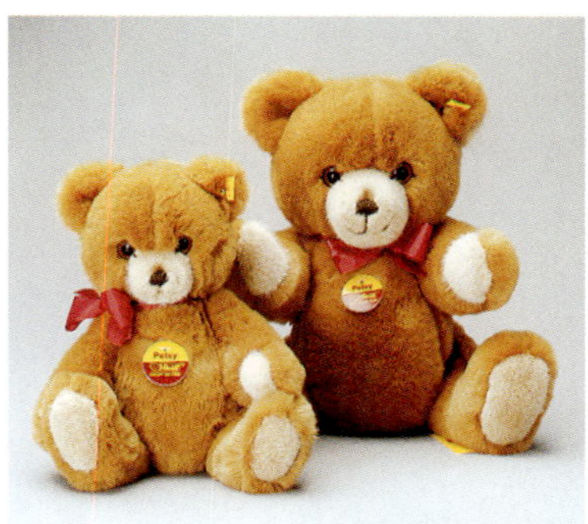

Teddy **Petsy**

Webpelz, hellbraun, mit Stimme, gegliedert, waschmaschinenfest - *woven fur, light brown, voice, jointed, machine washable*

SERIE	ART.-NO	PERIOD	PR.	INFO
	0230/20	1984-1984	3	20 cm
012051	**0230/28**	1984-1990	2-3	28 cm
	012051	1991-1999	2-3	
012082	**0230/35**	1984-1990	3	35 cm
	012082	1991-1999	3	
012129	**0230/45**	1984-1990	3	45 cm
	012129	1991-1999	3	

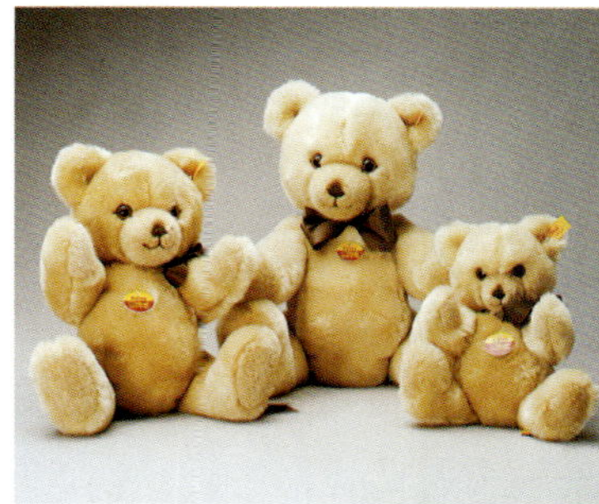

Teddy **Petsy**

Webpelz, blond, mit Stimme, gegliedert, waschmaschinenfest - *woven fur, blond, voice, jointed, machine washable*

SERIE	ART.-NO	PERIOD	PR.	INFO
	0233/20	1984-1984	3	20 cm
012259	**0233/28**	1984-1990	2-3	28 cm
	012259	1991-1999	2-3	
012280	**0233/35**	1984-1990	3	35 cm
	012280	1991-1999	3	
012327	**0233/45**	1984-1990	3	45 cm
	012327	1991-1999	3	
012365	**0233/80**	1985-1987	4	80 cm

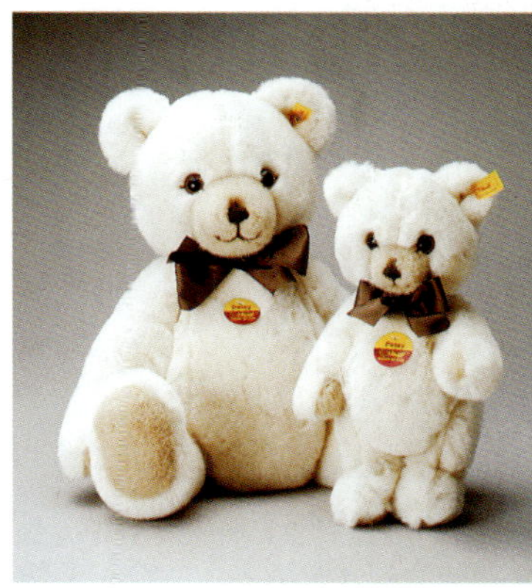

Teddy **Petsy**

Webpelz, creme, mit Stimme, gegliedert, waschmaschinenfest - *woven fur, cream, voice, jointed, machine washable*

SERIE	ART.-NO	PERIOD	PR.	INFO
	0235/20	1984-1984	3	20 cm
012457	**0235/28**	1984-1990	2-3	28 cm
	012457	1991-1999	2-3	
012488	**0235/35**	1984-1990	3	35 cm
	012488	1991-1999	3	
012525	**0235/45**	1984-1990	3	45 cm
	012525	1991-1999	3	

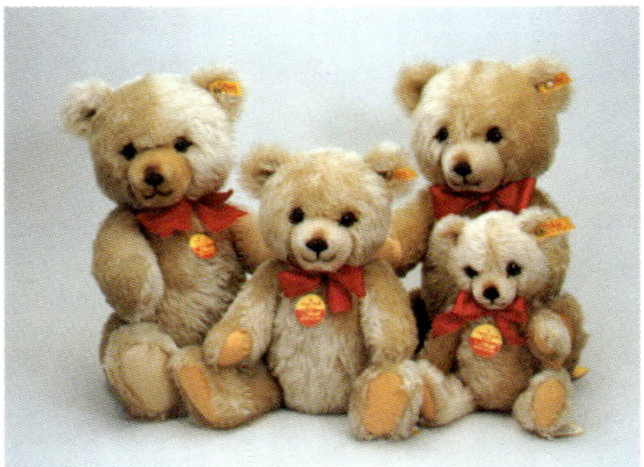

Petsy Soft Mohair

Mohair Webpelz, blond, gegliedert, 28 cm Pieps-Stimme, ab 35 cm Druckstimme, handwaschbar - *mohair woven fur, blond, jointed, 28 cm squeaker, from 35 cm press voice, hand washable*

SERIE	ART.-NO	PERIOD	PR.	INFO
011856	**0224/28**	1990-1990	3	28 cm
	011856	1991-1993	3	
011887	**0224/35**	1990-1990	3	35 cm
	011887	1991-1993	3	
011900	**0224/45**	1990-1990	3	45 cm
	011900	1991-1992	3	

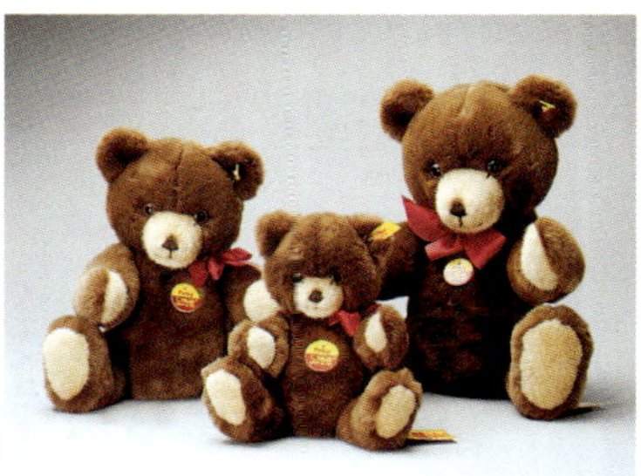

Teddy **Petsy**

Webpelz, braun, gegliedert, 28 cm Druckstimme, waschmaschinenfest - *woven fur, brown, jointed, 28 cm press voice, machine washable*

SERIE	ART.-NO	PERIOD	PR.	INFO
012556	**0238/28**	1990-1990	2-3	28 cm
	012556	1991-1999	2-3	
012587	**0238/35**	1990-1990	3	35 cm
	012587	1991-1999	3	
012624	**0238/45**	1990-1990	3	45 cm
	012624	1991-1999	3	

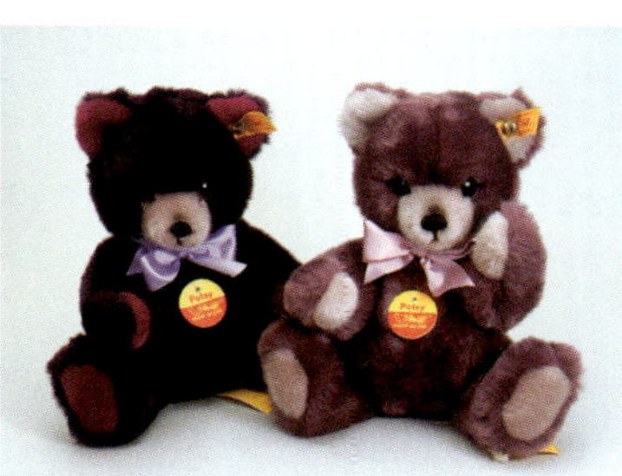

Teddy **Petsy**

Webpelz, gegliedert, Pieps-Stimme, waschmaschinenfest - *woven fur, jointed, squeaker, machine washable*

SERIE	ART.-NO	PERIOD	PR.	INFO
012754	**0236/28**	1990-1990	3	28 cm, aubergine - *purple*
012853	**0237/28**	1990-1990	3	28 cm, brombeer - *blackberry*

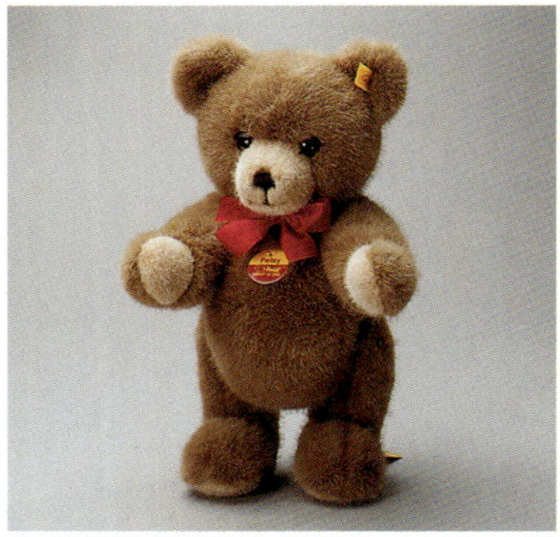

Teddy **Petsy**

Webpelz, zimt, gegliedert, waschmaschinenfest - *woven fur, cinnamon, jointed, machine washable*

EAN-NO.	PERIOD	PR.	INFO
012174	1995-1999	3	35 cm

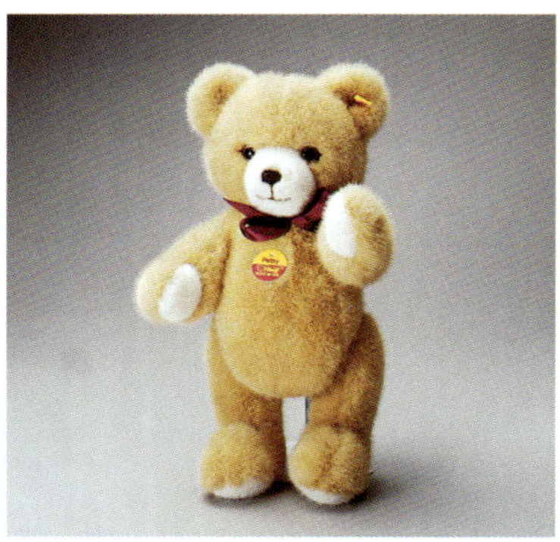

Teddy **Petsy**

Webpelz, dunkelblond, gegliedert, waschmaschinenfest - *woven fur, dark blond, jointed, machine washable*

EAN-NO.	PERIOD	PR.	INFO
012396	1995-1997	3	35 cm

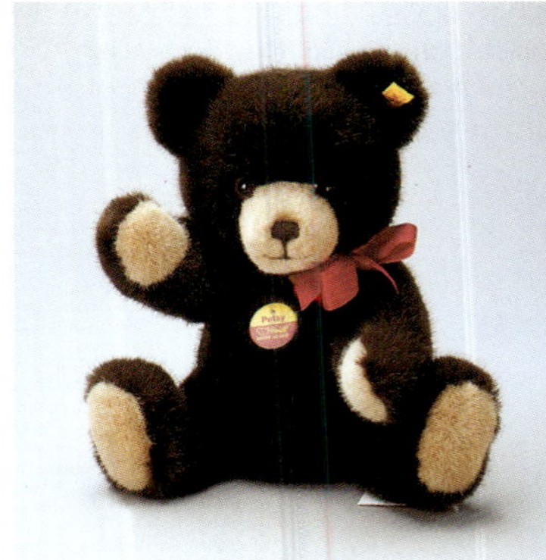

Teddy **Petsy**

Webpelz, dunkelbraun, gegliedert, waschmaschinenfest - *woven fur, dark brown, jointed, machine washable*

EAN-NO.	PERIOD	PR.	INFO
012679	1995-1997	3	35 cm

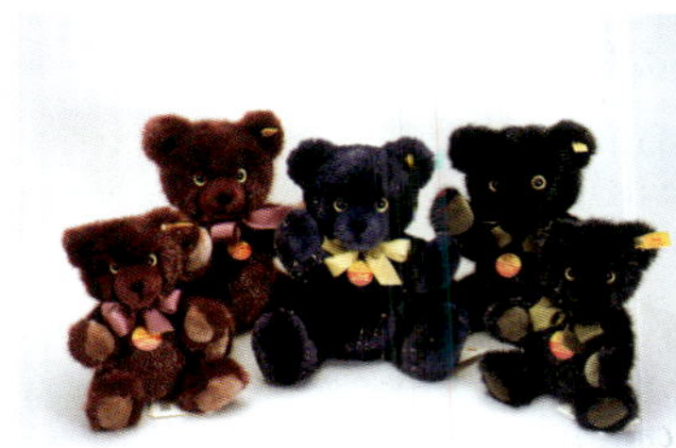

Teddy **Petsy**

Webpelz, gegliedert, waschmaschinenfest - *woven fur, jointed, machine washable*

EAN-NO.	PERIOD	PR.	INFO
012907	1996-1998	2-3	28 cm, dunkelblau - *dark blue*
012921	1996-1998	3	35 cm
012945	1998-1998	2-3	28 cm, dunkelgruen - *dark green*
012952	1998-1998	3	35 cm
012976	1998-1998	2-3	28 cm, dunkelrot - *dark red*
012983	1998-1998	3	35 cm

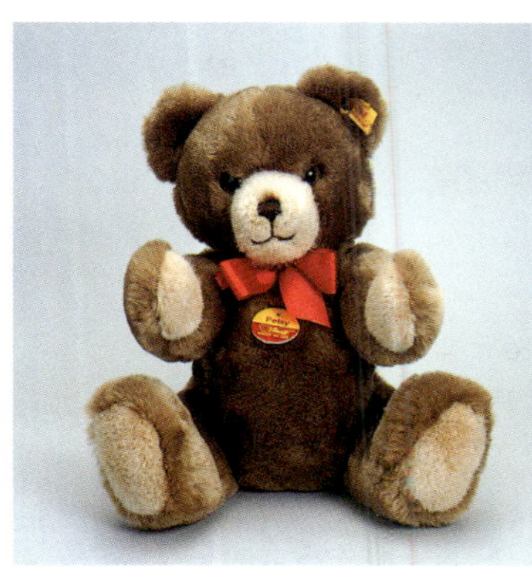

Teddy **Petsy**

Webpelz, caramel, gegliedert, waschmaschinenfest, 28 cm Pieps-Stimme - *woven fur, caramel, jointed, 28 cm press voice, machine washable*

EAN-No.	Period	Pr.	Info
012419	1997-1999	2-3	28 cm
012426	1997-1999	3	35 cm
012433	1997-1999	3	45 cm

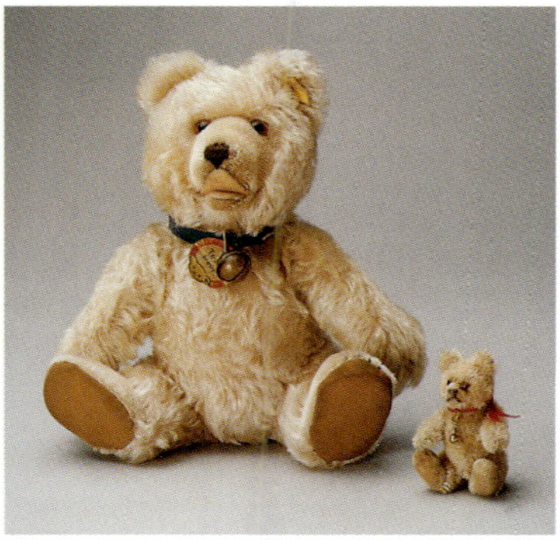

Teddy Baby

Mohairpluesch, mais oder honig, gegliedert, freistehend, Lederhalsband mit Glocke (ausser 9 cm), ausser 28 cm alle Groessen bereits bis 1940 im Programm - *mohair, corn yellow or honey, jointed, free-standing, leather collar with bell (except 9 cm), all sizes were already in production prior to 1940 except the 28cm size*

Serie	Art.-No	Period	Pr.	Info
12G	**7309** m	1949-1957	6	9 cm
12G	**7322** m	1949-1953	6-7	22 cm
12G	**7322,2** m	1954-1957	6-7	
12G	**7328,2** m	1951-1957	7	28 cm
12G	**7330,2** m	1949-1950	7	30 cm
12G	**7340,2** m	1949-1957	7-8	40 cm

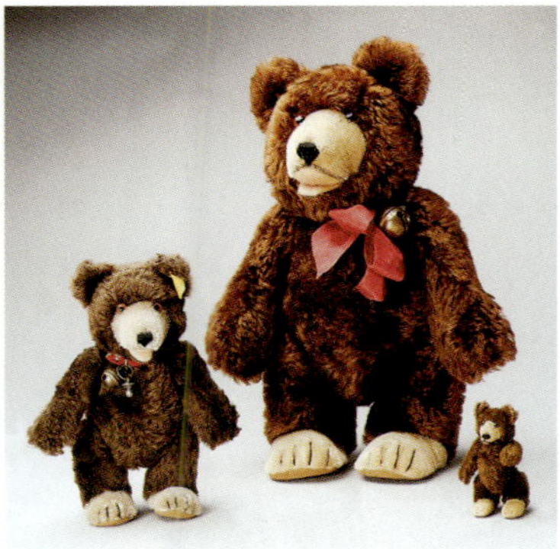

Teddy Baby

Mohairpluesch, dunkelbraun, gegliedert, freistehend, Lederhalsband mit Glocke (ausser 9 cm), ausser 28 cm alle Groessen bereits bis 1940 im Programm - *mohair, dark brown, jointed, free-standing, leather collar with bell (except 9 cm), all sizes were already in production prior to 1940 except the 28 cm size*

Serie	Art.-No	Period	Pr.	Info
12G	**7309 br**	1949-1957	6	9 cm
12G	**7322** br	1949-1953	6-7	22 cm
12G	**7322,2** br	1954-1957	6-7	
12G	**7328,2** br	1951-1957	7	28 cm
12G	**7330,2** br	1949-1950	7	30 cm
12G	**7340,2** br	1949-1957	7-8	40 cm

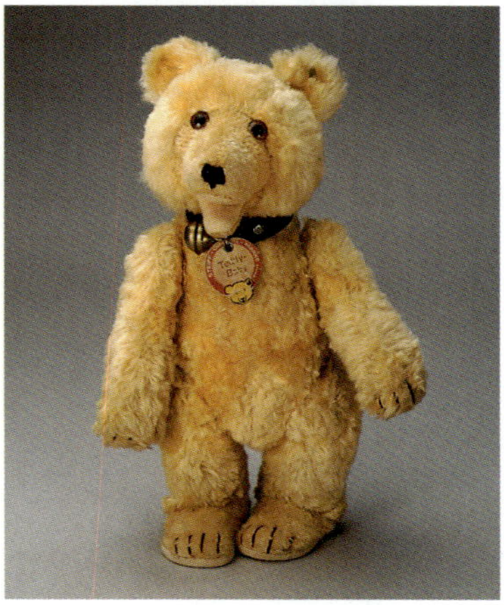

Teddy Baby

Kunstseidenpluesch, 30 cm, gegliedert, freistehend, Lederhalsband mit Glocke - *artificial silk plush, 30 cm, jointed, free-standing, leather collar with bell*

Serie	Art.-No	Period	Pr.	Info
12G	**7630,2** bl	1948-1949	7	
	salmblond - *salmon gold*			
12G	**7630,2** br	1949-1949	7	
	dunkelbraun - *dark brown*			

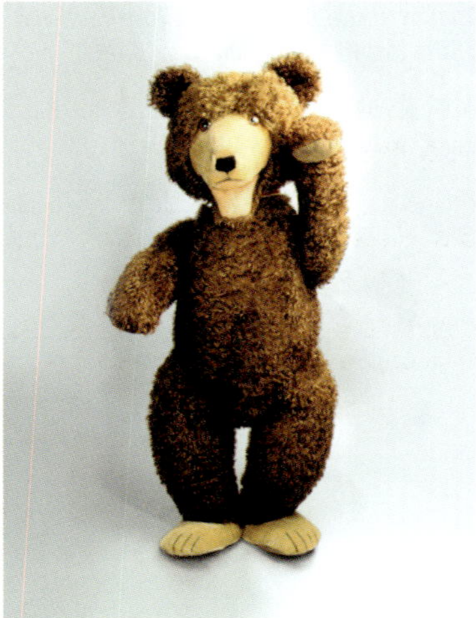

Teddy Baby

Schautier, Mohair, gegliedert, dunkelbraun - *display animal, mohair, jointed, dark brown*

Serie	Art.-No	Period	Pr.	Info
129	**4150,93**	1960-1960	8	150 cm
	0339/15	1967-1967	8	

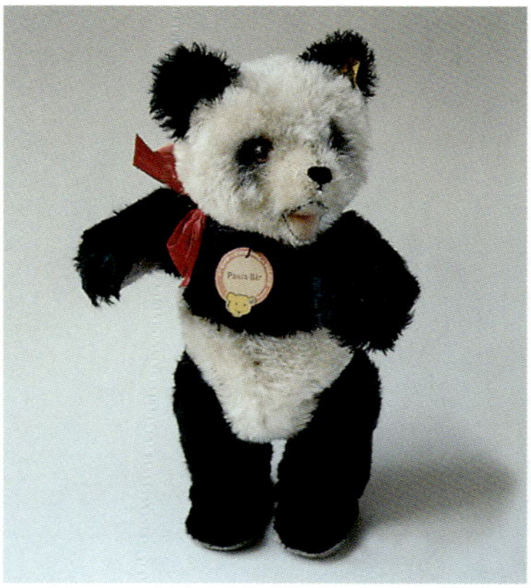

Panda

Mohairpluesch, schwarz/weiss, gegliedert, der drollige indische Bambusbaer, Fortsetzung des bis 1940 angebotenen Modelles - *mohair, black/white, jointed, cute little Indian bamboo bear, continuation of model offered up to 1940*

Serie	Art.-No	Period	Pr.	Info
12P	**5330,2**	1949-1950	7-8	30 cm

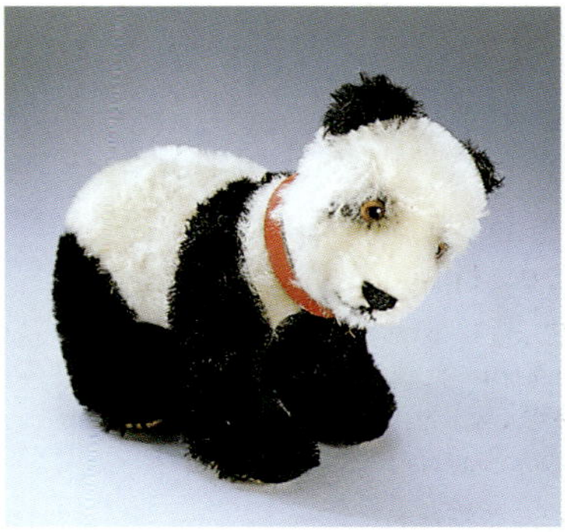

Panda

Mohair, schwarz/weiss, stehend, Drehkopf - *mohair, black/white, standing, head swivels*

Serie	Art.-No	Period	Pr.	Info
12P	**1312,0**	1955-1958	4	12 cm

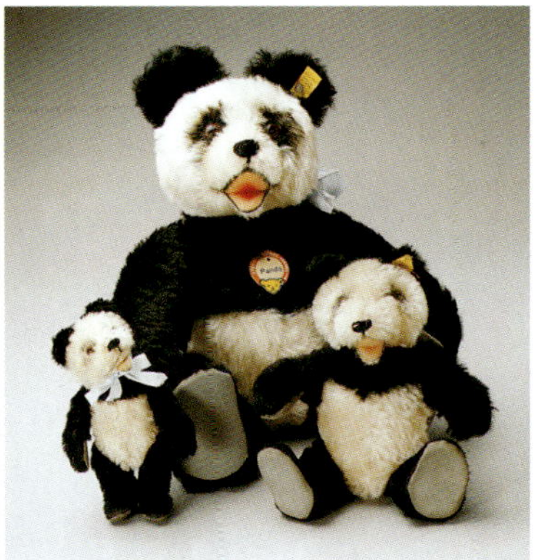

Panda

Mohairpluesch, schwarz/weiss, gegliedert, ab 22 cm mit Stimme - *mohair, black/white, jointed, from 22 cm with voice*

SERIE	ART.-NO	PERIOD	PR.	INFO
12P	**5315**	1951-1958	7	15 cm
125	**5315,00**	1959-1961	6-7	
12P	**5322**	1951-1953	6-7	22 cm
12P	**5322,2**	1954-1958	6-7	
125	**5322,00**	1959-1961	6-7	
12P	**5328,2**	1951-1956	7	28 cm
12P	**5335,2**	1951-1958	7	35 cm
125	**5335,00**	1959-1961	7	
12P	**5343,2**	1951-1956	7-8	43 cm
12P	**5350,2**	1951-1958	8	50 cm
125	**5350,00**	1959-1961	8	

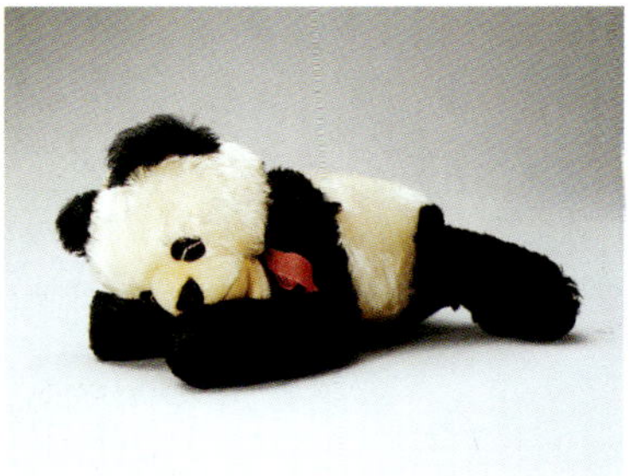

Floppy Panda

Mohairpluesch, Augen gestickt, schwarz/weiss, liegend, sehr weich und schmiegsam - *mohair, eyes embroidered, black/white, lying, very soft & cuddly*

SERIE	ART.-NO	PERIOD	PR.	INFO
85 12P	**7317**	1954-1958	4	17 cm
850 125	**7317,00**	1959-1961	4	
85 12P	**7328**	1953-1958	4	28 cm
850 125	**7328,00**	1959-1961	4	

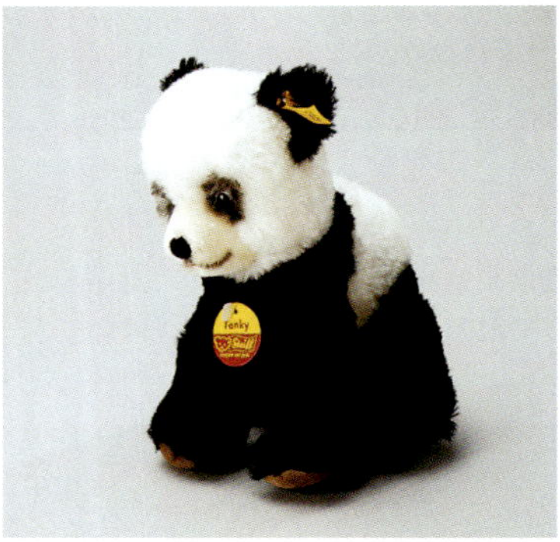

Jungpanda **Tanky** - *Young Panda* ***Tanky***

Dralon, stehend, abwaschbar - *dralon, standing, surface washable*

SERIE	ART.-NO	PERIOD	PR.	INFO
	6426/18	1973-1976	3	18 cm

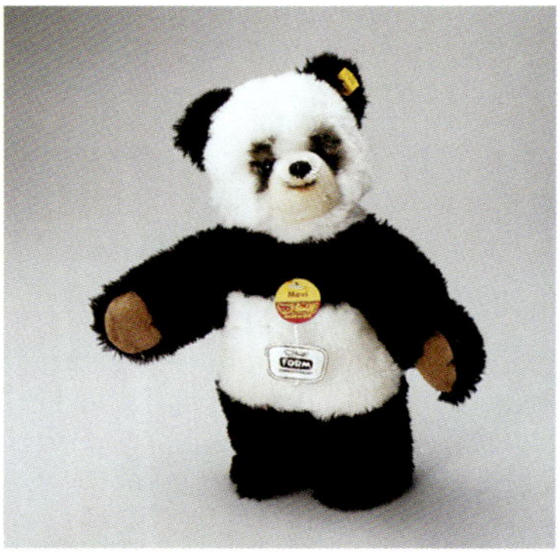

Weich-Panda, ab 1975 **Movi** - *Soft Panda, from 1975* ***Movi***

Dralon, formgeschaeumt, schwarz/weiss, Schlenkerkopf, vollwaschbar - *dralon, stuffed with pre-formed foam, black/white, floppy head, fully washable*

SERIE	ART.-NO	PERIOD	PR.	INFO
	6202/30	1973-1976	3	30 cm
	6202/40	1973-1976	3	40 cm

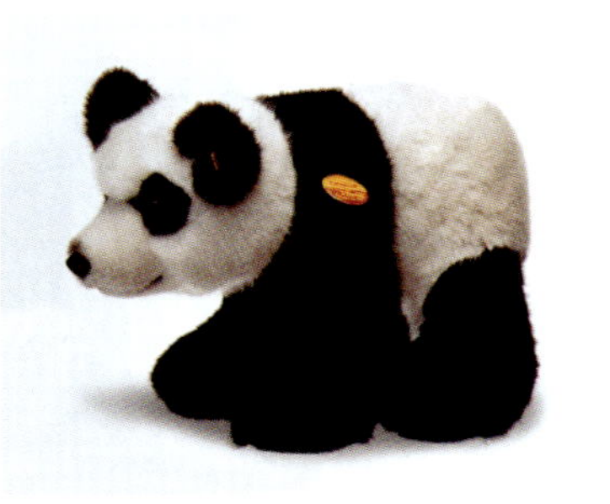

Jung Panda - *Young Panda*

Webpelz, stehend, abwaschbar - *woven fur, standing, surface washable*

SERIE	ART.-NO	PERIOD	PR.	INFO
	0477/60	1981-1983	4	60 cm

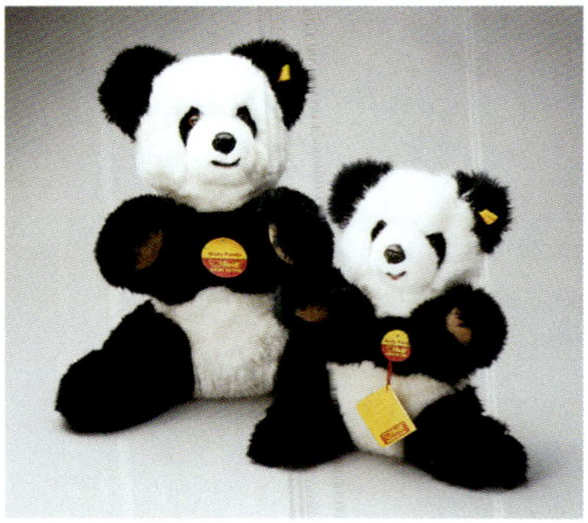

Molly Panda

Webpelz, schwarz/weiss, aufwartend, abwaschbar - *woven fur, black/white, sitting up, surface washable*

SERIE	ART.-NO	PERIOD	PR.	INFO
101052	**0326/32**	1978-1989	3	32 cm
101106	**0326/45**	1978-1989	3	45 cm

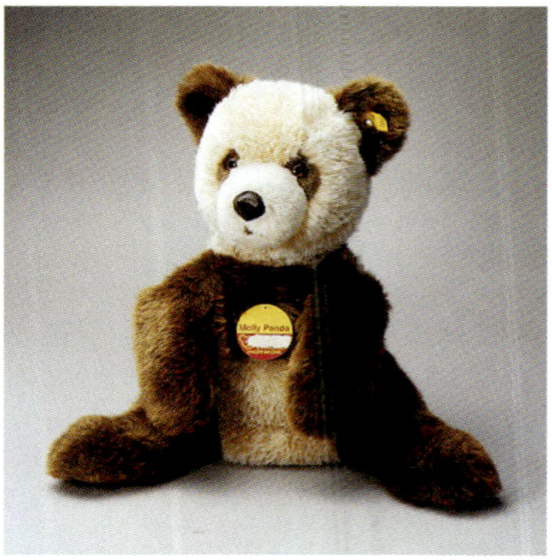

Molly Panda

Wirkpelz, braun/beige, aufwartend, abwaschbar - *knitted fur, brown/beige, sitting up, surface washable*

SERIE	ART.-NO	PERIOD	PR.	INFO
	0327/32	1978-1981	3	32 cm
	0327/45	1978-1981	3	45 cm

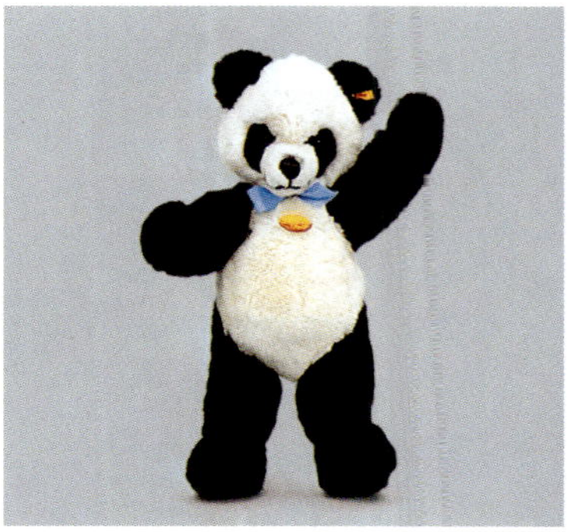

Molly Panda

Webpelz, mollig weich, abwaschbar - *woven fur, soft & cuddly, surface washable*

SERIE	ART.-NO	PERIOD	PR.	INFO
	0323/65	1981-1983	4	65 cm

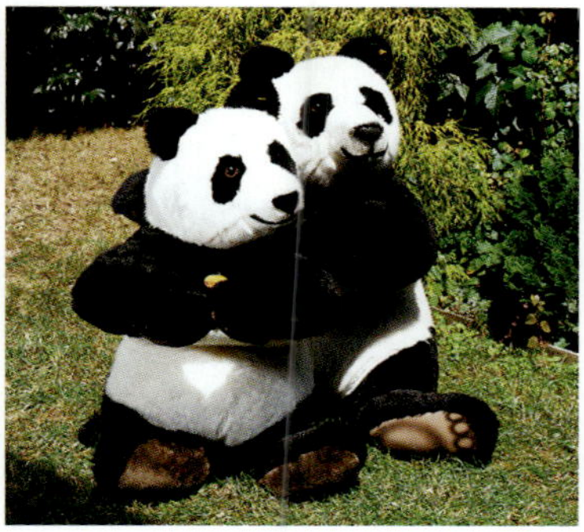

Super Molly Panda

Webpelz, abwaschbar - *woven fur, surface washable*

SERIE	ART.-NO	PERIOD	PR.	INFO
104053	**0438/70**	1985-1987	4	70 cm
104084	**0438/98**	1985-1986	5	112 cm

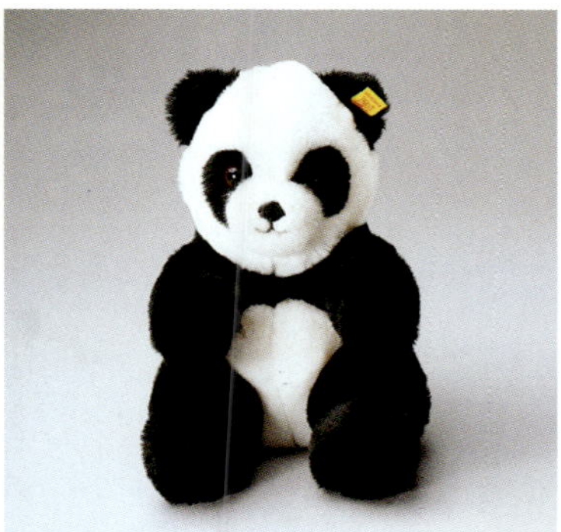

Cosy Panda

Webpelz, superweich, waschmaschinenfest - *woven fur, super soft, machine washable*

SERIE	ART.-NO	PERIOD	PR.	INFO
085505	**5357/25**	1984-1988	3	25 cm

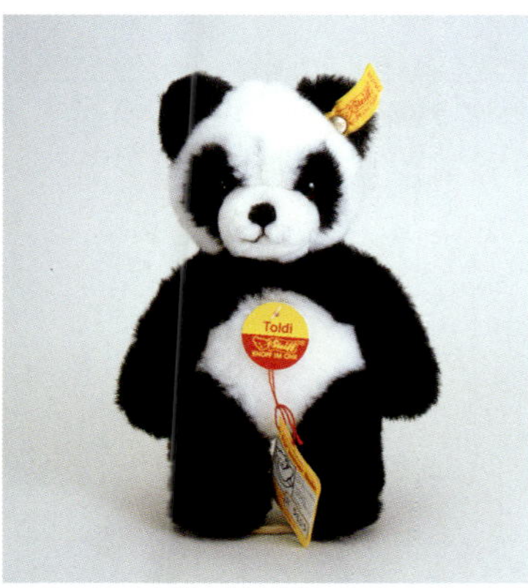

Toldi Panda

Wirkpelz, Pieps-Stimme, waschmaschinenfest - *knitted fur, squeaker, machine washable*

SERIE	ART.-NO	PERIOD	PR.	INFO
080159	**6251/22**	1986-1986	2-3	22 cm

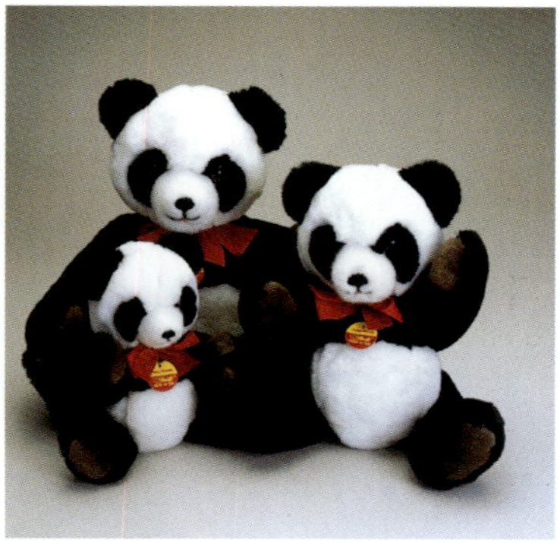

Petsy Panda

Webpelz, schwarz/weiss, gegliedert, Pieps-Stimme, waschmaschinenfest - *woven fur, black/white, jointed, squeaker, machine washable*

SERIE	ART.-NO	PERIOD	PR.	INFO
013454	**0240/28**	1986-1990	2-3	28 cm
	013454	1991-1999	2-3	
013485	**0240/35**	1986-1989	3	35 cm
013522	**0240/45**	1986-1988	3	45 cm

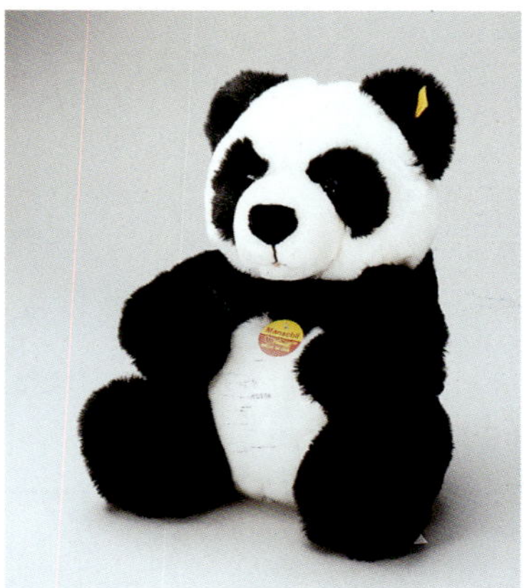

Manschli Panda

Webpelz, sitzend, waschmaschinenfest - *woven fur, sitting, machine washable*

EAN-NO.	PERIOD	PR.	INFO
060151	1992-1994	3	30 cm

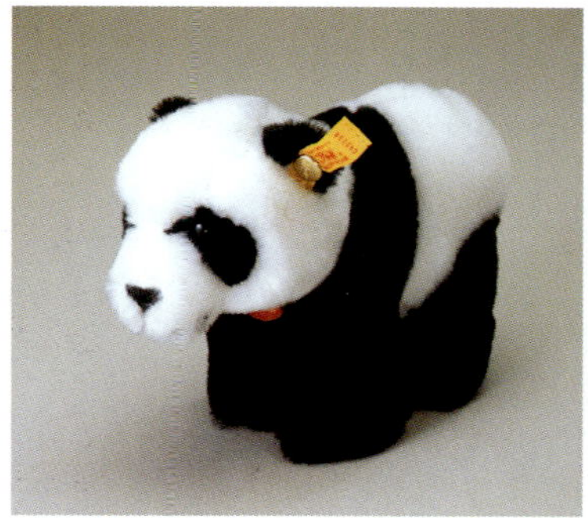

Panda

Webpelz, stehend, waschmaschinenfest - *woven fur, standing, machine washable*

EAN-NO.	PERIOD	PR.	INFO
040238	1997-1999	2	16 cm

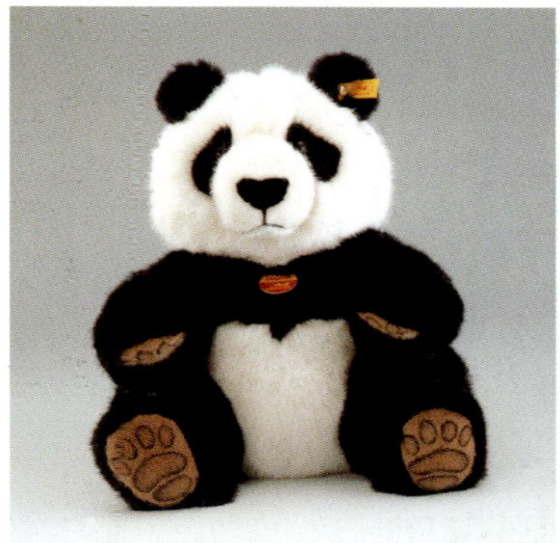

Panda

Webpelz, sitzend, waschmaschinenfest - *woven fur, sitting, machine washable*

EAN-NO.	PERIOD	PR.	INFO
060168	1997-1999	3-4	35 cm

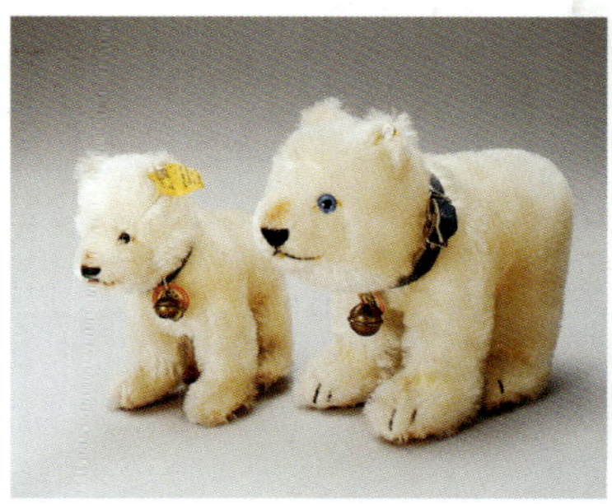

Eisbaer - *Polar Bear*

Mohair, weiss, stehend, Kopf drehbar, Lederhalsband mit Glocke - *mohair, white, standing, head swivels, leather collar with bell*

SERIE	ART.-NO	PERIOD	PR.	INFO
13	**1312,0**	1950-1958	4	12 cm
130	**1312,04**	1959-1961	4	
046	**1312,04**	1965-1967	4	
	0460/12	1968-1972	3-4	

13	**1317,0**	1952-1953	4	17 cm
13	**1317,02**	1954-1958	4	
130	**1317,04**	1959-1961	4	
046	**1317,04**	1966-1967	4	
	0460/17	1968-1972	4	
13	**1325,01**	1952-1953	4-5	25 cm
13	**1325,02**	1954-1958	4-5	
130	**1325,04**	1959-1961	4-5	

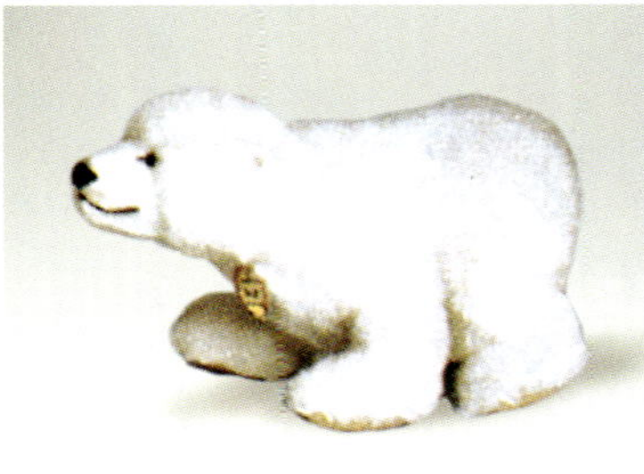

Cosy Nauty

Dralon, Schaumgummi-Fuellung, stehend, waschbar - *dralon, stuffed with foam rubber, standing, washable*

SERIE	ART.-NO	PERIOD	PR.	INFO
830 130	**6622,00**	1963-1964	3	22 cm
486	**6622,00**	1965-1966	3	

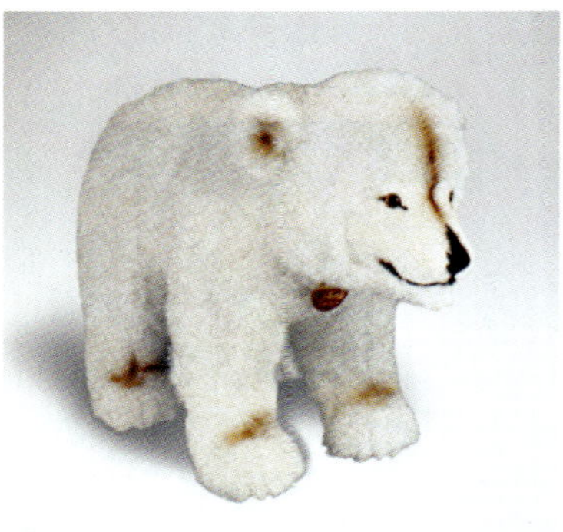

Eisbaer - *Polar Bear*

Pelzimitation, stehend, abwaschbar - *imitation fur, standing, surface washable*

SERIE	ART.-NO	PERIOD	PR.	INFO
	0468/40	1973-1976	3	40 cm

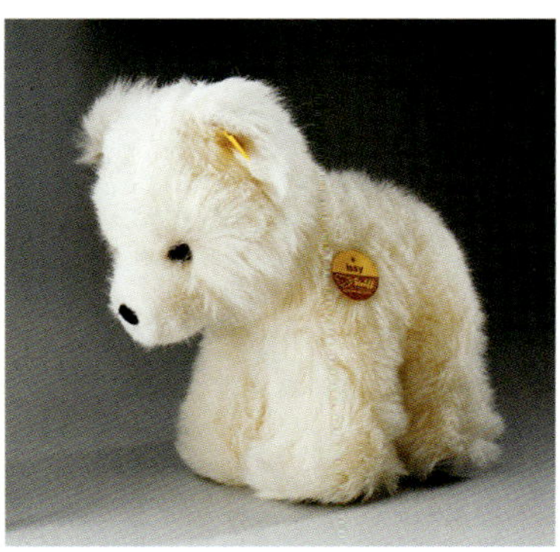

Issy Eisbaer - ***Issy** Polar Bear*

Webpelz, ab 1981 Wirkpelz, formgeschaeumt, weiss, stehend, vollwaschbar - *woven fur, from 1981 knitted fur, stuffed with pre-formed foam, white, standing, fully washable*

SERIE	ART.-NO	PERIOD	PR.	INFO
	0467/23	1978-1982	2-3	23 cm

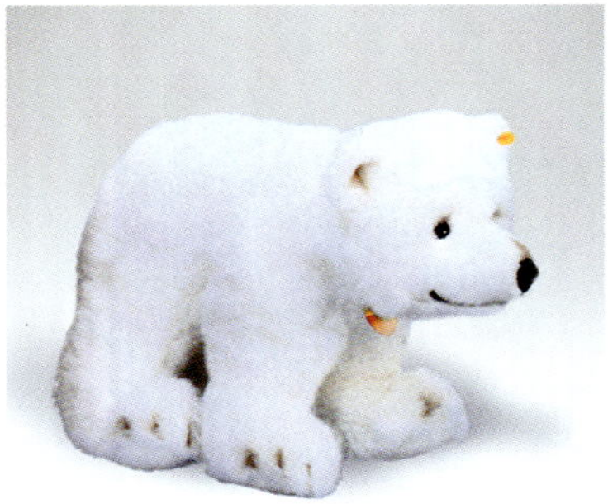

Jung Eisbaer - *Polar Bear Cub*

Webpelz, stehend - *woven fur, standing*

SERIE	ART.-NO	PERIOD	PR.	INFO
	0468/60	1981-1983	4	60 cm

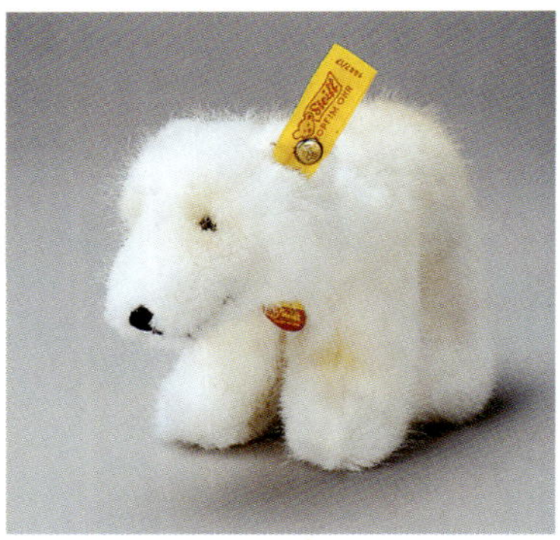

Starly Eisbaer - ***Starly** Polar Bear*

Webpelz, stehend, abwaschbar - *woven fur, standing, surface washable*

SERIE	ART.-NO	PERIOD	PR.	INFO
	1447/17	1981-1983	2-3	17 cm

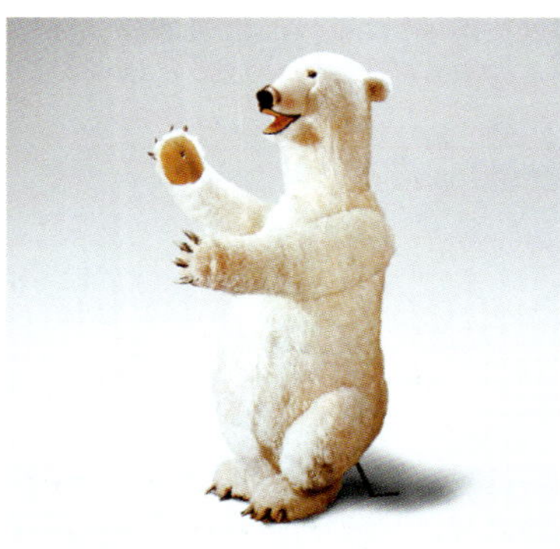

Eisbaer - *Polar Bear*

Schautier, Mohair, weiss, gegliedert - *display animal, mohair, white, jointed*

SERIE	ART.-NO	PERIOD	PR.	INFO
130	**4180,94**	1960-1960	8	180 cm
	0469/18	1967-1967	8	

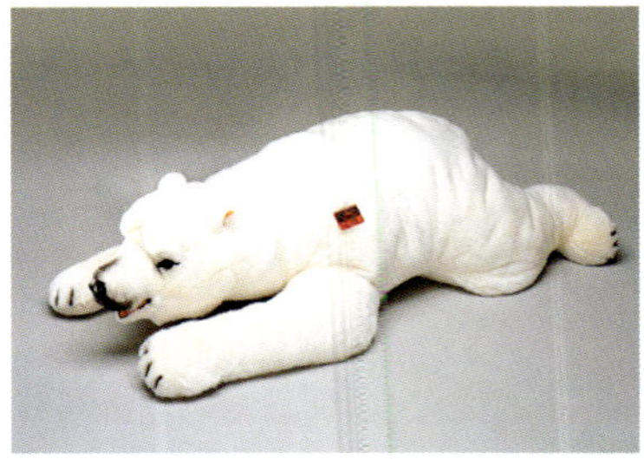

Eisbaer - *Polar Bear*

Studiotier, 160 cm liegend, Webpelz, 200 cm stehend, Mohair, abwaschbar - *studio animal, lying 160 cm, woven fur, standing 200 cm, mohair, surface washable*

SERIE	ART.-NO	PERIOD	PR.	INFO
501500	**0472/99**	1982-1990	6	160 cm
	501500	1991-1999	6	
	0470/99	1982-1983	6	200 cm

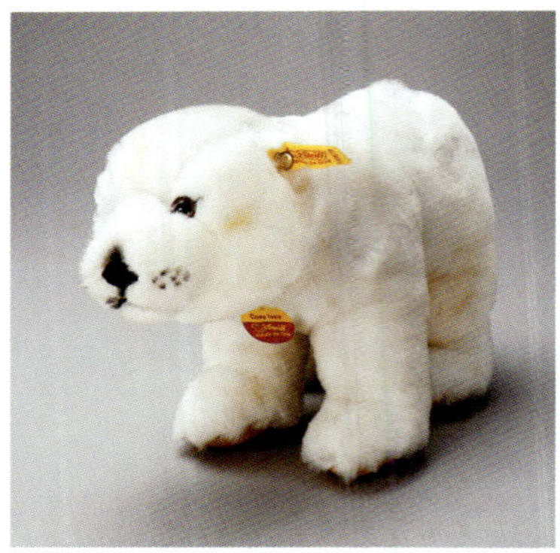

Cosy Issy Eisbaer - ***Cosy Issy** Polar Bear*

Webpelz, superweich, waschmaschinenfest - *woven fur, very soft, machine washable*

SERIE	ART.-NO	PERIOD	PR.	INFO
094309	**5405/17**	1984-1986	2-3	17 cm
094330	**5405/30**	1983-1990	2-3	30 cm
	094330	1991-1991	2-3	

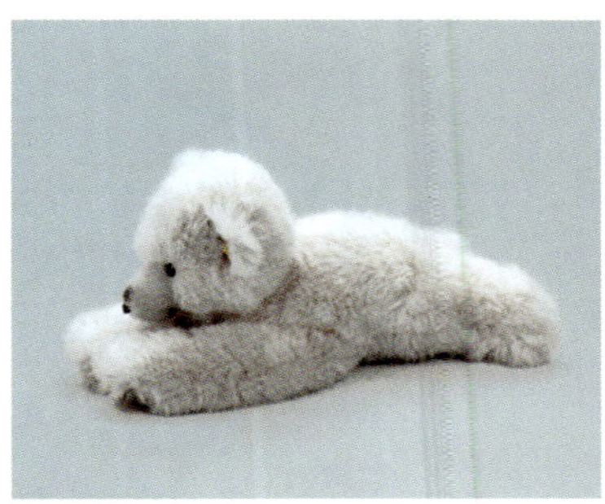

Molly Eisbaer - *Molly Polar Bear*

Webpelz, liegend, mollig weich, abwaschbar - *woven fur, lying, soft & cuddly, surface washable*

SERIE	ART.-NO	PERIOD	PR.	INFO
	0334/45	1981-1983	3	45 cm
	0334/55	1981-1982	3	55 cm

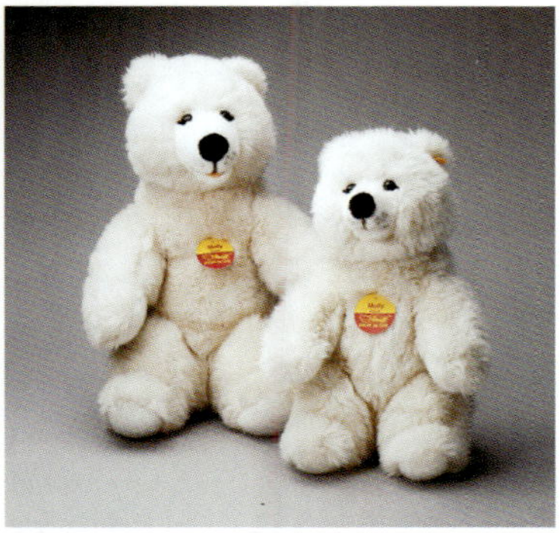

Molly Eisbaer - *Molly Polar Bear*

Webpelz, sitzend, abwaschbar - *woven fur, sitting, surface washable*

SERIE	ART.-NO	PERIOD	PR.	INFO
101007	**0355/35**	1990-1990	3	35 cm
	101007	1991-1992	3	
101021	**0355/45**	1990-1990	3-4	45 cm
	101021	1991-1992	3-4	
101069	**0355/60**	1990-1990	4	60 cm
	101069	1991-1991	4	

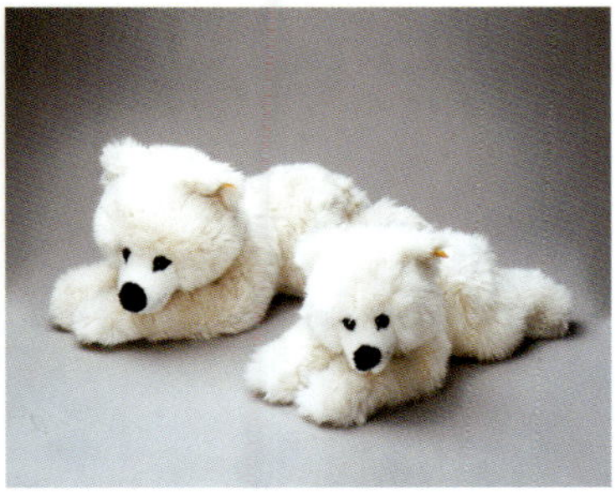

Molly Eisbaer - *Molly Polar Bear*

Webpelz, liegend, abwaschbar - *woven fur, lying, surface washable*

SERIE	ART.-NO	PERIOD	PR.	INFO
101151	**0357/40**	1990-1990	3	40 cm
	101151	1991-1991	3	
101182	**0357/55**	1990-1990	3	55 cm
	101182	1991-1991	3	
101212	**0357/75**	1990-1990	4	75 cm
	101212	1991-1991	4	

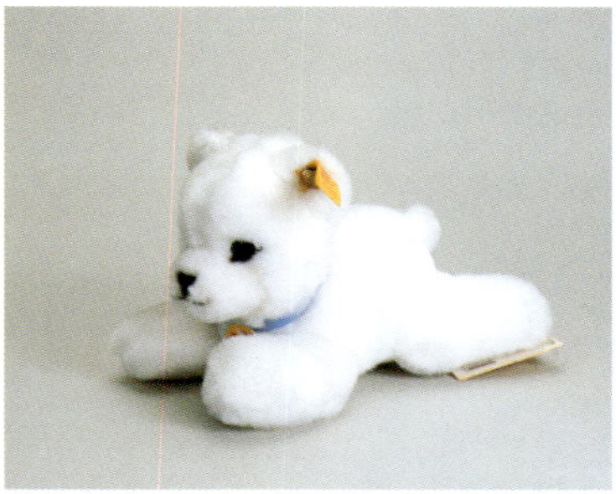

Mini Floppy Eisbaer - ***Mini Floppy*** *Polar Bear*

Webpelz, liegend, waschmaschinenfest - *woven fur, lying, machine washable*

SERIE	ART.-NO	PERIOD	PR.	INFO
081835	**5652/16**	1989-1990	2	16 cm

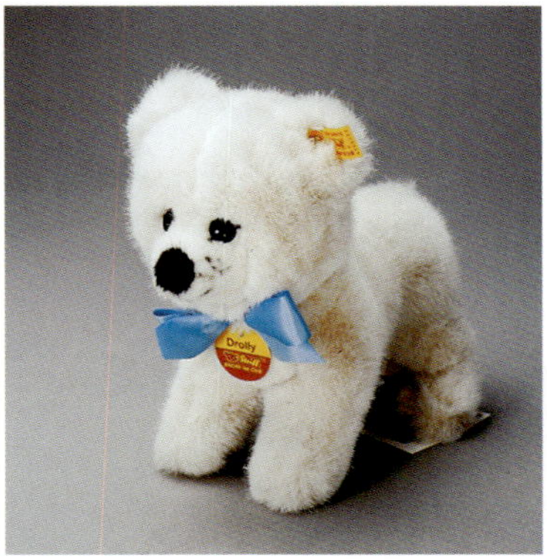

Drolly Eisbaer - ***Drolly*** *Polar Bear*

Webpelz, weiss, stehend, waschmaschinenfest - *woven fur, white, standing, machine washable*

SERIE	ART.-NO	PERIOD	PR.	INFO
081286	**5755/22**	1990-1990	2	22 cm
	081286	1991-1993	2	

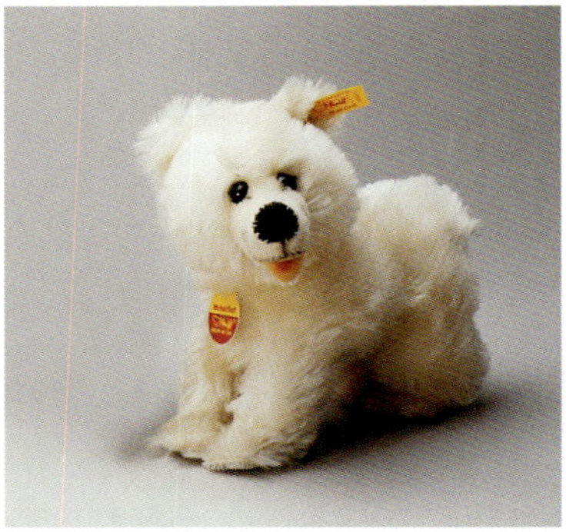

Mohair Soft Eisbaer - ***Mohair Soft*** *Polar Bear*

Mohair Webpelz, weiss, stehend, handwaschbar - *mohair woven fur, white, standing, hand washable*

SERIE	ART.-NO	PERIOD	PR.	INFO
034657	**1220/25**	1990-1990	3	25 cm
	034657	1991-1992	3	

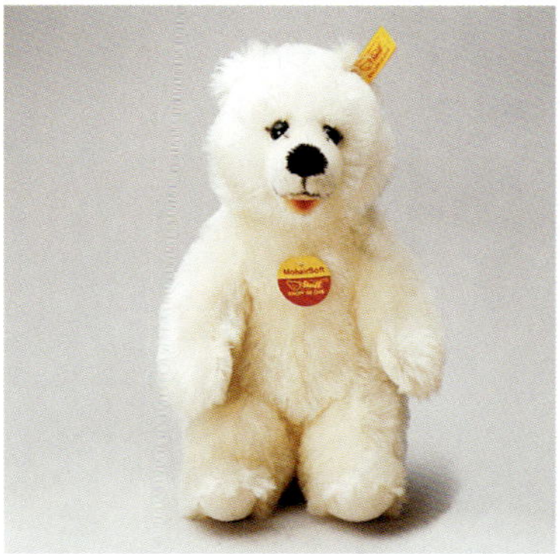

Mohair Soft Eisbaer - ***Mohair Soft*** *Polar Bear*

Mohair Webpelz, weiss, sitzend, handwaschbar - *mohair woven fur, white, sitting, hand washable*

SERIE	ART.-NO	PERIOD	PR.	INFO
034756	**1222/25**	1990-1990	3	25 cm
	034756	1991-1991	3	

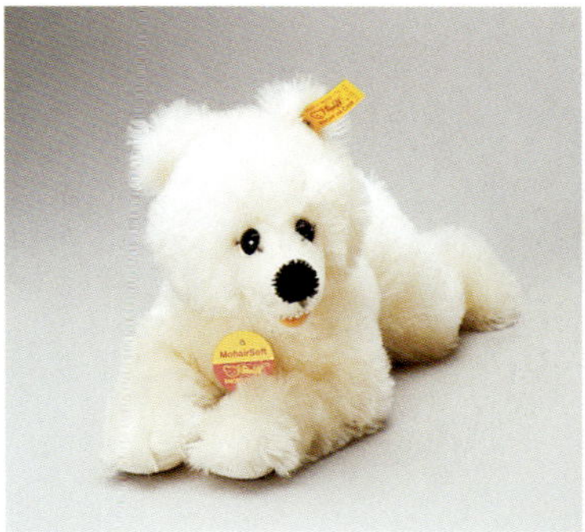

Mohair Soft Eisbaer - ***Mohair Soft*** *Polar Bear*

Mohair Webpelz, weiss, liegend, handwaschbar - *mohair woven fur, white, lying, hand washable*

SERIE	ART.-NO	PERIOD	PR.	INFO
034855	**1225/25**	1990-1990	3	25 cm
	034855	1991-1992	3	

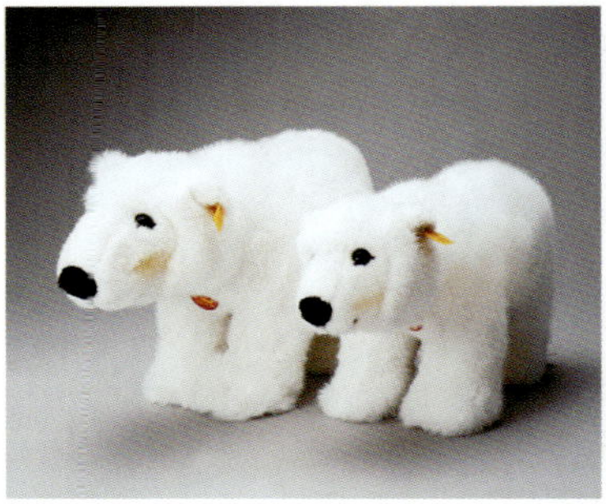

Issy Eisbaer - ***Issy*** *Polar Bear*

Webpelz, weiss, stehend, waschmaschinenfest - *woven fur. white, standing, machine washable*

EAN-No.	Period	Pr.	Info
062803	1993-1996	2-3	35 cm
062827	1993-1996	3	45 cm

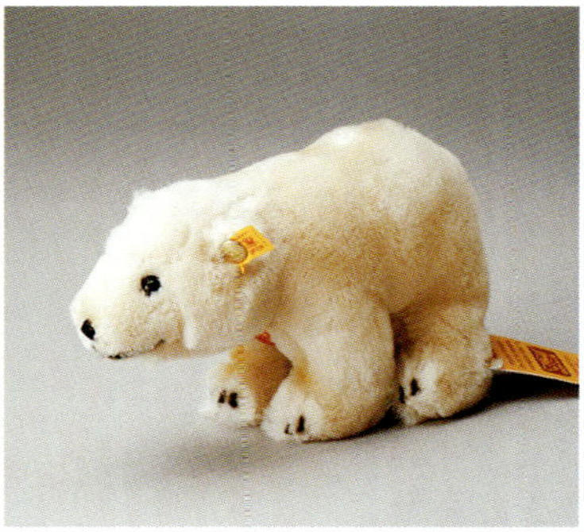

Lommy Eisbaer - ***Lommy*** *Polar Bear*

Webpelz, stehend, waschmaschinenfest - *woven fur, standing, machine washable*

EAN-No.	Period	Pr.	Info
047152	1994-1999	2	18 cm

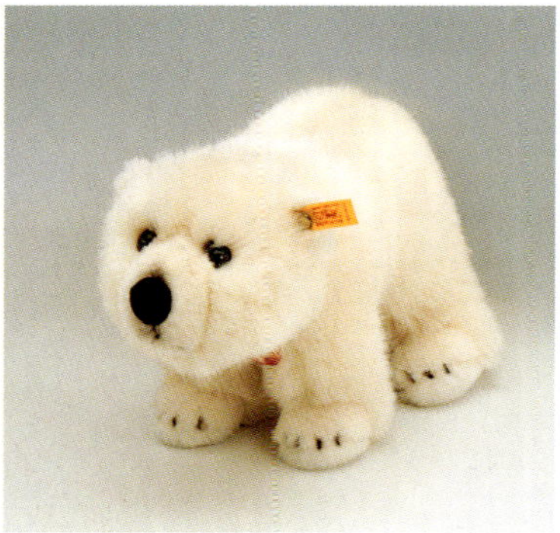

Baby Eisbaer - *Baby Polar Bear*

Webpelz, stehend, waschmaschinenfest - *woven fur, standing, machine washable*

EAN-No.	Period	Pr.	Info
062841	1996-1999	2-3	22 cm

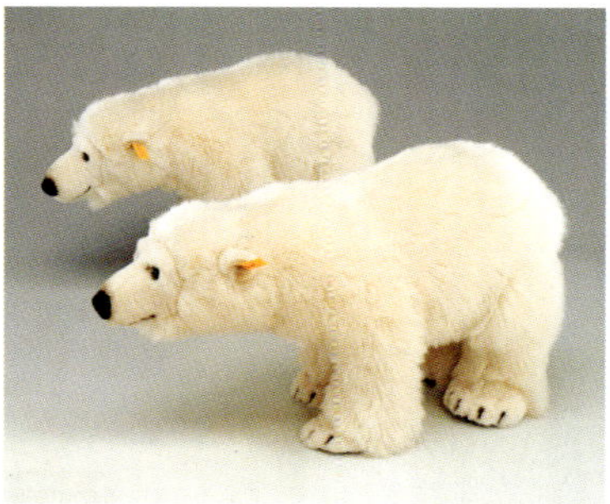

Eisbaer - *Polar Bear*

Webpelz, stehend, abwaschbar - *woven fur, standing, surface washable*

EAN-No.	Period	Pr.	Info
062858	1996-1997	3	40 cm
062865	1996-1998	3	47 cm

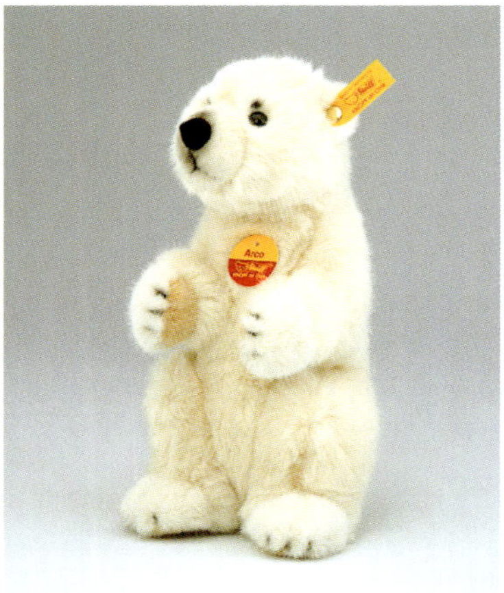

Arco Baby Eisbaer - ***Arco*** *Baby Polar Bear*

Webpelz, aufwartend, waschmaschinenfest - *woven fur, begging, machine washable*

EAN-No.	Period	Pr.	Info
062872	1997-1999	2-3	25 cm

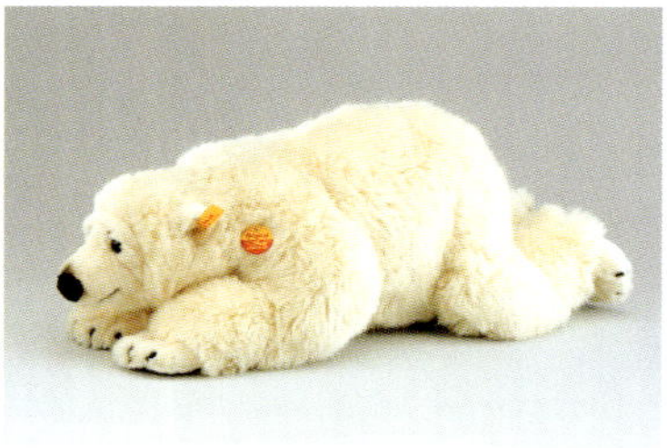

Eisbaer - *Polar Bear*

Webpelz, liegend, abwaschbar - *woven fur, lying, surface washable*

EAN-No.	Period	Pr.	Info
062896	1997-1998	3-4	60 cm

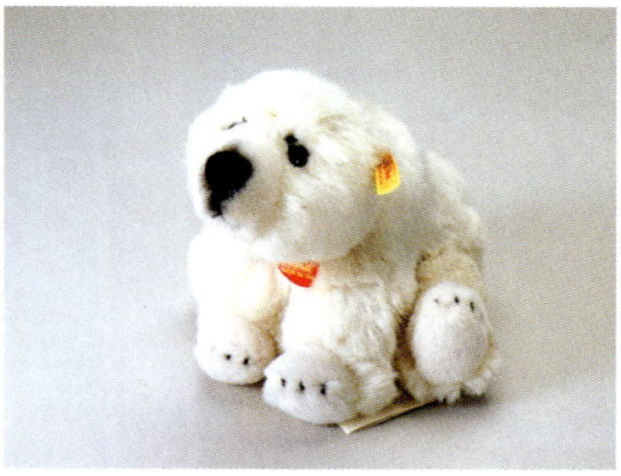

Arco Baby Eisbaer - ***Arco*** *Baby Polar Bear*

Webpelz, sitzend, waschmaschinenfest - *woven fur, sitting, machine washable*

EAN-No.	Period	Pr.	Info
062797	1998-1999	2-3	20 cm

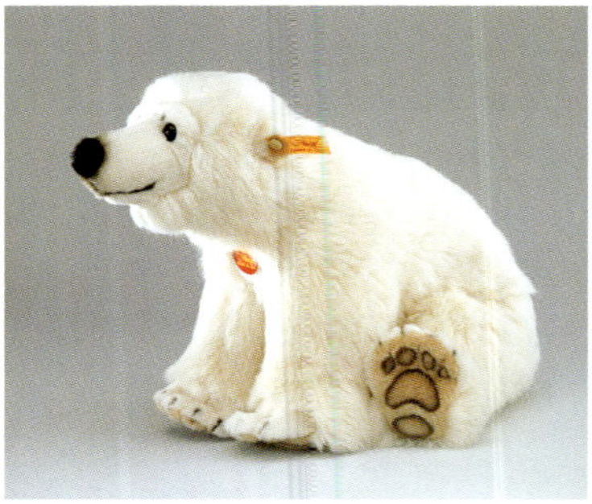

Arco Eisbaer - ***Arco*** *Polar Bear*

Webpelz, sitzend, abwaschbar - *woven fur, sitting, surface washable*

EAN-No.	Period	Pr.	Info
062810	1998-1999	3	32 cm

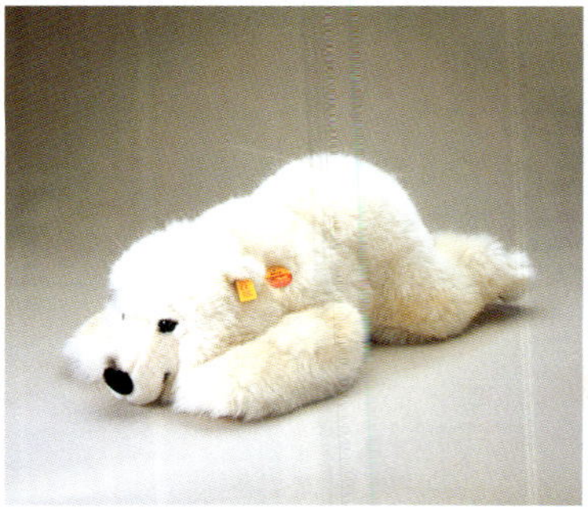

Arco Eisbaer - ***Arco*** *Polar Bear*

Webpelz, liegend - *woven fur, lying*

EAN-No.	Period	Pr.	Info
062919	1999-1999	3-4	60 cm
062926	1999-1999	3-4	70 cm
062933	1999-1999	4	90 cm
062940	1999-1999	5	120 cm

HUNDE

DOGS

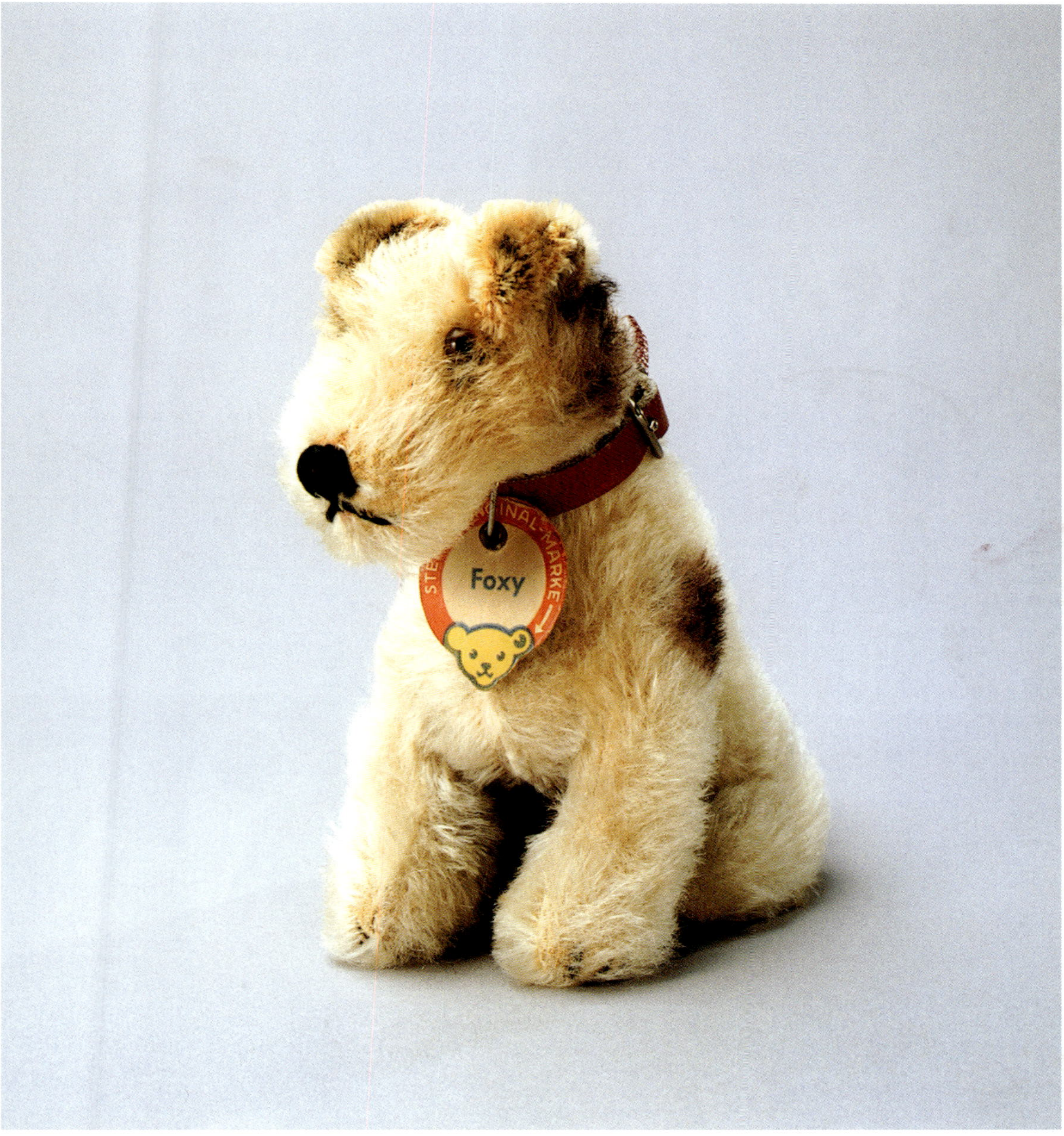

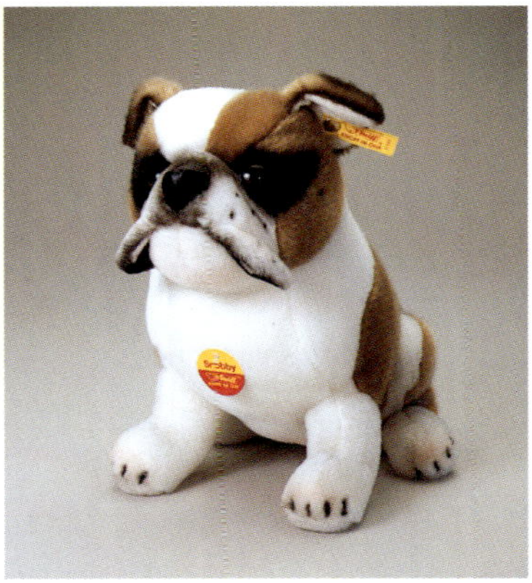

Snobby Bulldogge - ***Snobby** Bulldog*

Webpelz, weiss/braun, sitzend, waschmaschinenfest - *woven fur, white/brown, sitting, machine washable*

EAN-No.	Period	Pr.	Info
079450	1998-1999	3	25 cm

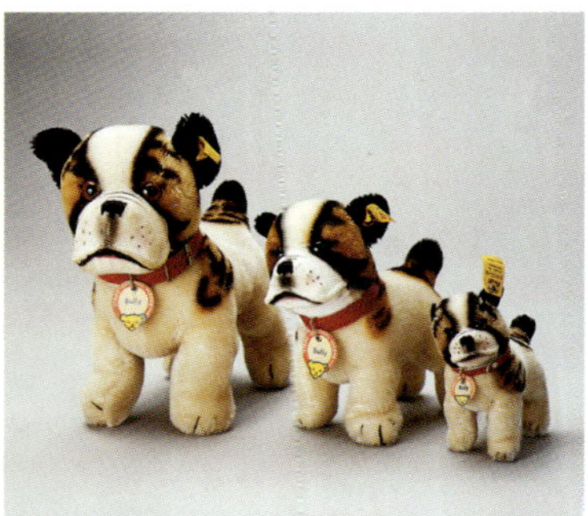

Bully

Mohairpluesch, weiss gefleckt, stehend, abwaschbar - *mohair, white, spotted, standing, surface washable*

Serie	Art.-No	Period	Pr.	Info
11	**1310,0**	1951-1958	4	10 cm
110	**1310,00**	1959-1962	3-4	
400	**1310,00**	1966-1967	3-4	
	4000/10	1968-1974	3	
11	**1317,0**	1952-1958	4-5	17 cm
110	**1317,00**	1959-1962	4	
400	**1317,00**	1966-1967	4	
	4000/17	1968-1974	3-4	
11	**1322,0**	1952-1953	4-5	22 cm
11	**1322,02**	1954-1958	4	
110	**1322,00**	1959-1962	4	

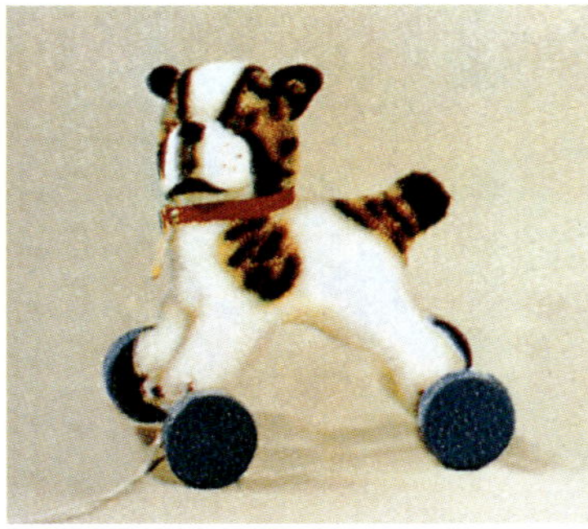

Bully Nachziehtier - ***Bully** Pull type toy*

Mohairpluesch, weiss gefleckt, stehend auf Exzenter-Raedern - *mohair, white, spotted, standing on eccentric wheels*

Serie	Art.-No	Period	Pr.	Info
81 11	**1310** ex	1954-1957	4-5	10 cm
810 110	**1310,10**	1960-1960	4-5	

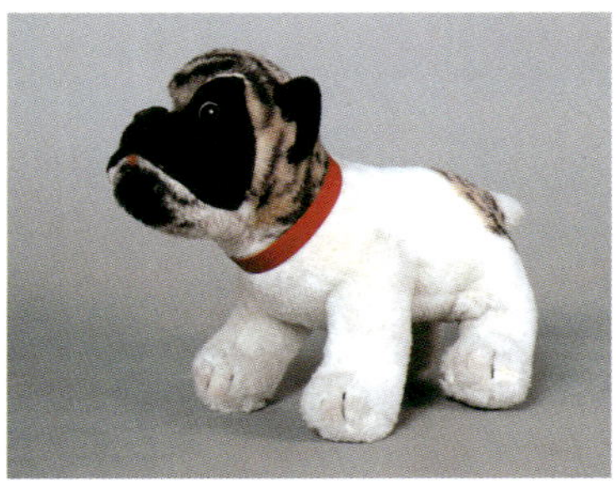

Cosy Bully

Dralon, stehend - *dralon, standing*

Serie	Art.-No	Period	Pr.	Info
110	**1622,00**	1962-1962	3-4	22 cm

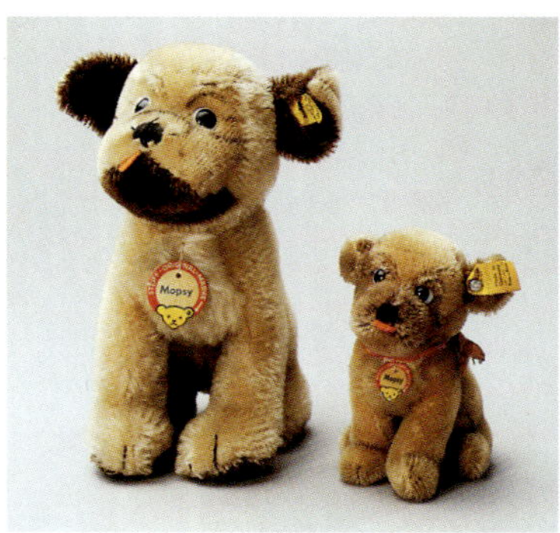

Mopsy

Mohairpluesch, hellbraun, sitzend, abwaschbar - *mohair, light brown, sitting, surface washable*

Serie	Art.-No	Period	Pr.	Info
113	**3312,00**	1960-1964	3	12 cm
401	**3312,00**	1965-1967	3	
	4010/12	1968-1981	3	
113	**3322,00**	1960-1964	3-4	22 cm
401	**3322,00**	1965-1967	3	
	4010/22	1968-1977	3	

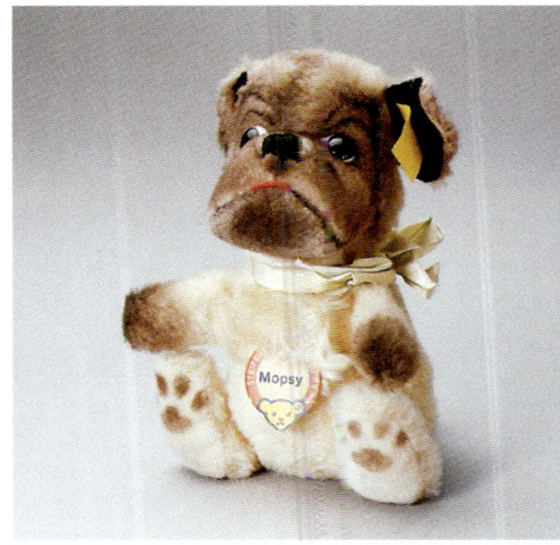

Mopsy Ball Hund - ***Mopsy** Ball Dog*

Dralonpluesch, weich, mit Stimme - *dralon, soft, press voice*

Serie	Art.-No	Period	Pr.	Info
815 113	**4616,00**	1960-1961	5	16 cm

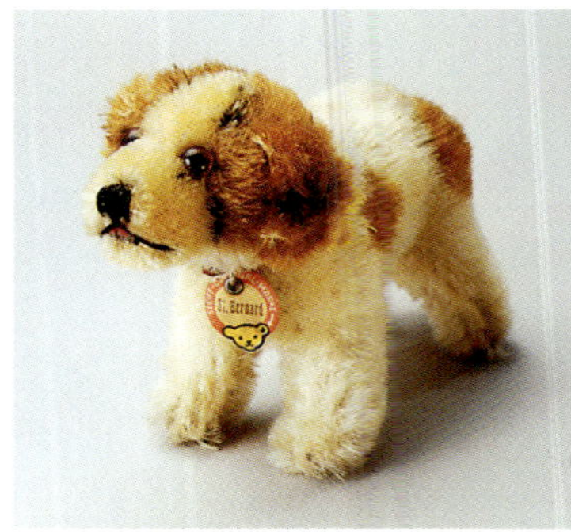

St. Bernhard

Mohair, weiss/braun, stehend, Groesse 22 cm ab 1954 mit Druckstimme - *mohair, white/brown, standing, 22 cm from 1954 press voice*

Serie	Art.-No	Period	Pr.	Info
14	**1310,0**	1953-1957	5	10 cm
14	**1314,0**	1953-1957	5	14 cm
14	**1322,0**	1953-1953	5	22 cm
14	**1322,02**	1954-1957	5	

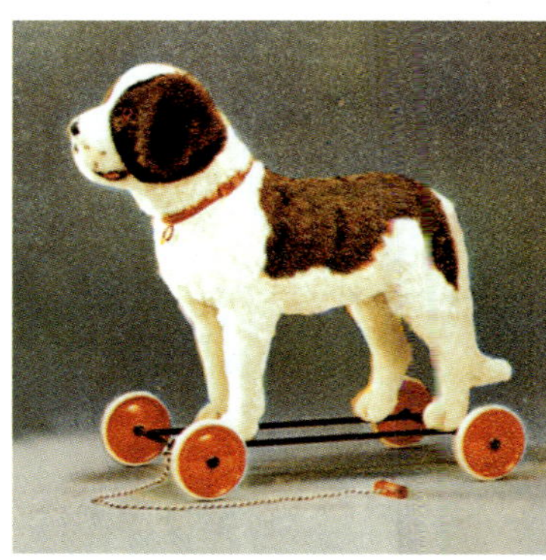

Reit-St. Bernhard, ab 1951 Reit-Bernhardiner - *Riding St. Bernard, from 1951: Riding Bernhardiner*

Mohairpluesch, Eisengerippe, Zugstimme, braun/weiss, stehend auf Scheibenraedern mit Gummireifen, VK-Modell mit Holzraedern, mit Verbindungsschienen - *mohair, iron frame, pull cord voice, brown/ white, standing on disc wheels with rubber tires, prewar model has wooden wheels, with connecting bars*

SERIE	ART.-NO	PERIOD	PR.	INFO
14	**1343,2**	1949-1957	5-6	43 cm
14	**1350,2**	1949-1957	5-6	50 cm
14	**1360,2**	1950-1957	5-6	60 cm
14	**1362,2**	1949-1949	5-6	62 cm

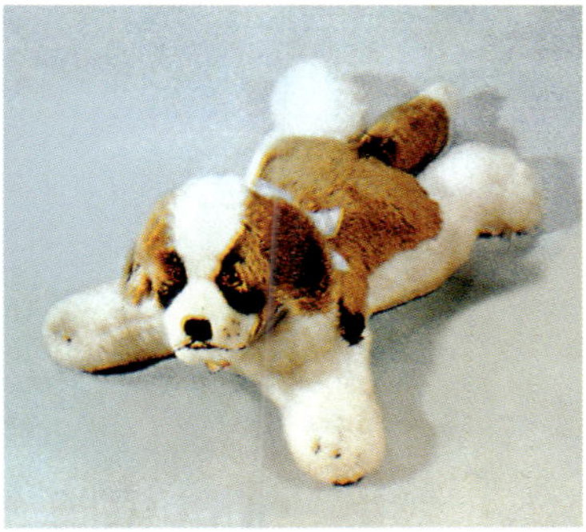

Racker St. Bernhard Berni

Mohair, liegend, Sitz- und Spieltier - *mohair, lying, either a sitting or playing animal*

SERIE	ART.-NO	PERIOD	PR.	INFO
822 140	**2345,00**	1960-1961	5	45 cm

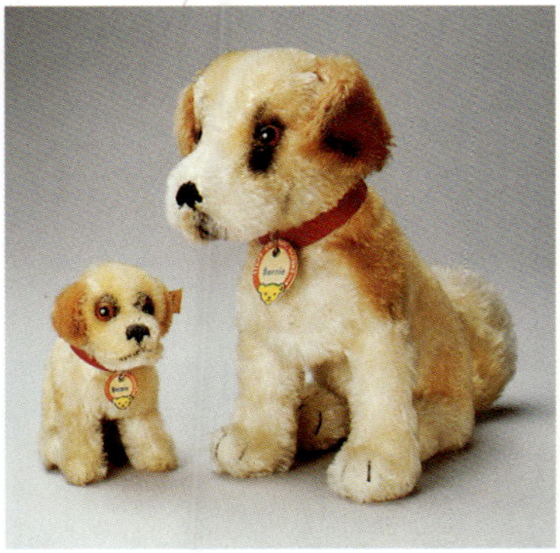

Bernie Bernhardiner

Mohairpluesch, weiss/braun, sitzend - *mohair, white/brown, sitting*

SERIE	ART.-NO	PERIOD	PR.	INFO
140	**3312,00**	1963-1963	3	12 cm
404	**3312,00**	1966-1967	3	
	4040/12	1968-1970	3	
140	**3322,00**	1963-1963	3-4	22 cm
404	**3322,00**	1966-1967	3-4	
	4040/22	1968-1970	3-4	

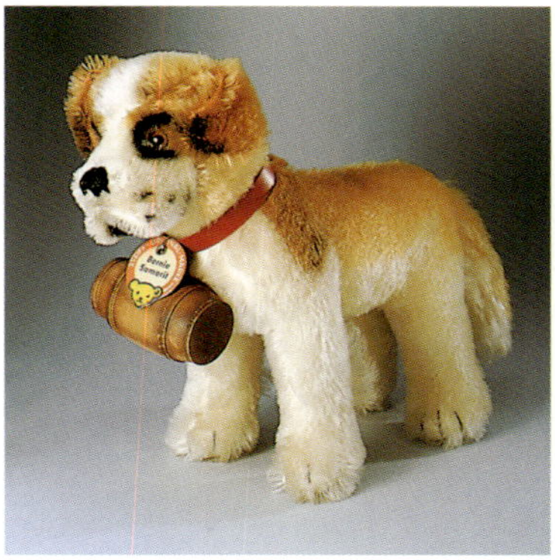

Bernie Samarit

Mohair, hellbraun/weiss gefleckt, stehend, mit Fass am Halsband - *mohair, light brown/white spotted, standing, with cask fastened to its collar*

SERIE	ART.-NO	PERIOD	PR.	INFO
140	**1322,09**	1964-1964	5	22 cm
404	**1322,09**	1965-1966	5	

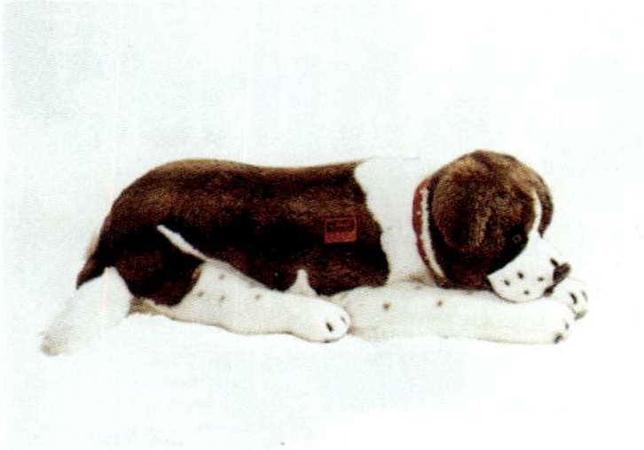

Bernhardiner

Studio-Tier, Pelz-Imitation, ab 1978 Synthetik-Webpelz, liegend, abwaschbar - *studio animal, imitation fur, from 1978 synthetic woven fur, lying, surface washable*

SERIE	ART.-NO	PERIOD	PR.	INFO
	4040/99	1973-1983	4-5	125 cm

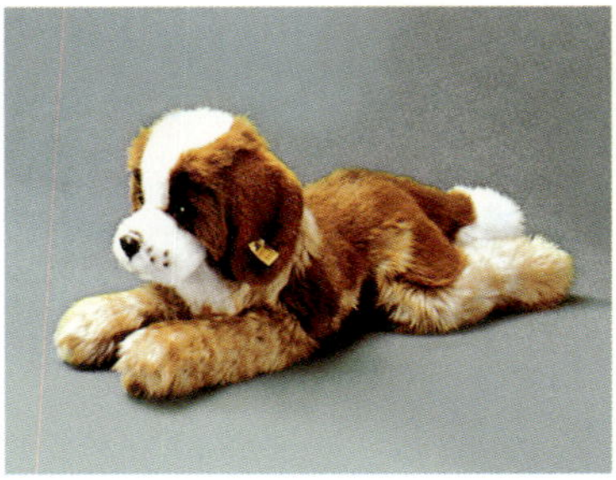

Junior Bernie

Wirkflor, ab 1978 Synthetik-Webpelz, liegend, abwaschbar - *knitted pile, from 1978 synthetic woven fur, lying, surface washable*

SERIE	ART.-NO	PERIOD	PR.	INFO
	2888/35	1976-1983	2-3	35 cm

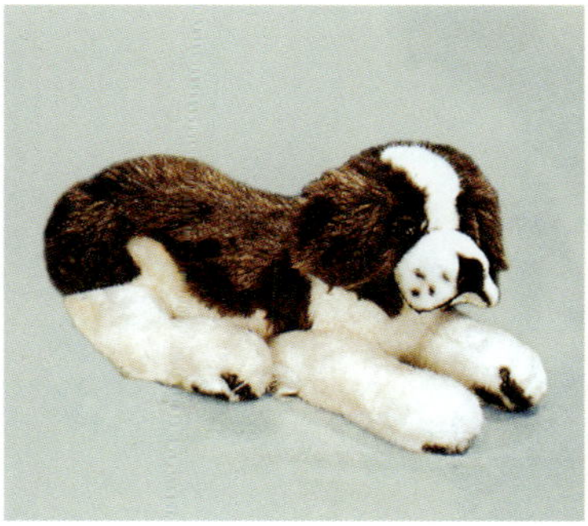

Molly Bernie

Pelz-Imitation, 1978 Synthetik-Webpelz, abwaschbar - *imitation fur, 1978 synthetic woven fur, surface washable*

SERIE	ART.-NO	PERIOD	PR.	INFO
	0333/40	1973-1978	2-3	40 cm

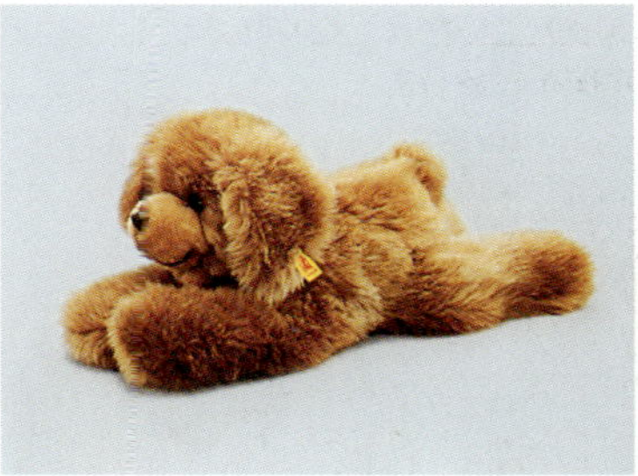

Molly Barry

Webpelz, mollig-weich, abwaschbar - *woven fur, soft & cuddly, surface washable*

SERIE	ART.-NO	PERIOD	PR.	INFO
	0350/45	1981-1984	3	46 cm
	0350/65	1981-1983	3	66 cm

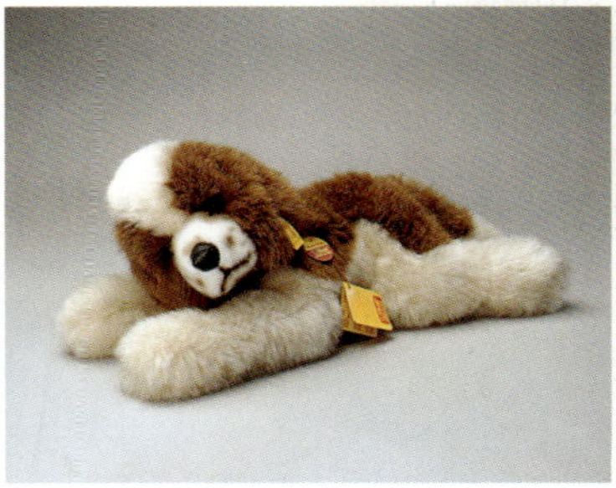

Super Molly Bernie

Webpelz, abwaschbar - *woven fur, surface washable*

SERIE	ART.-NO	PERIOD	PR.	INFO
102547	**0342/40**	1984-1986	3	40 cm
102578	**0342/60**	1984-1986	3	60 cm
	0342/80	1984-1985	3-4	80 cm
	0342/98	1984-1985	4	105 cm

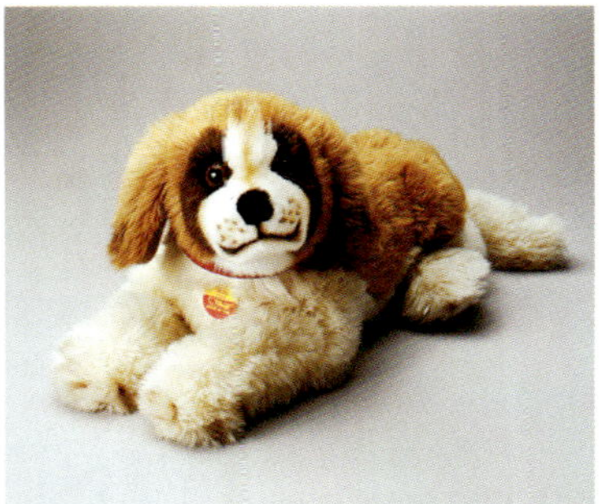

Molly Barry Bernhardiner - ***Molly Barry*** *St. Bernhard*

Webpelz, Lederhalsband, mittelbraun, liegend, abwaschbar - *woven fur, leather collar, medium brown, lying, surface washable*

Serie	Art.-No	Period	Pr.	Info
104756	**0455/45**	1990-1990	3	45 cm
	104756	1991-1991	3	
104787	**0455/55**	1990-1990	3	55 cm
	104787	1991-1991	3	
104817	**0455/65**	1990-1990	3	65 cm
	104817	1991-1991	3	
104848	**0455/98**	1990-1990	3-4	125 cm
	104848	1991-1991	3-4	

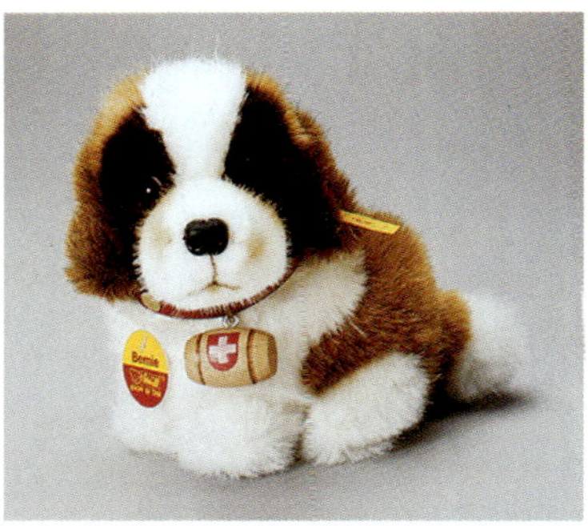

Bernie Bernhardiner - ***Bernie*** *St. Bernhard*

Webpelz, Lederhalsband mit Faesschen, ohne Halsband waschmaschinenfest - *woven fur, leather collar with cask attached, machine washable if collar & cask are removed*

EAN-No.	Period	Pr.	Info
078217	1992-1999	2	16 cm

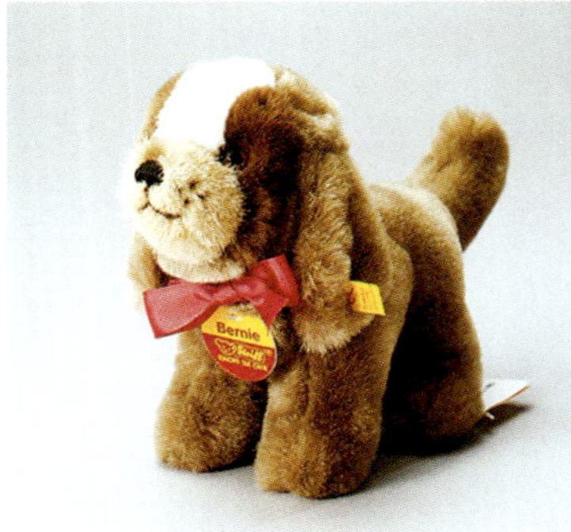

Bernie

Webpelz, braun, stehend, waschmaschinenfest - *woven fur, brown, standing, machine washable*

EAN-No.	Period	Pr.	Info
081767	1994-1996	2	16 cm

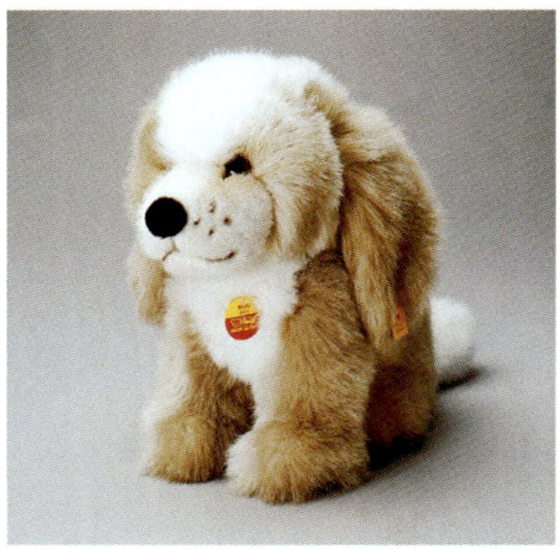

Molly Barry Junghund - ***Molly Barry*** *Puppy*

Webpelz, sitzend, handwaschbar - *woven fur, sitting, hand washable*

EAN-No.	Period	Pr.	Info
104862	1994-1996	2-3	25 cm

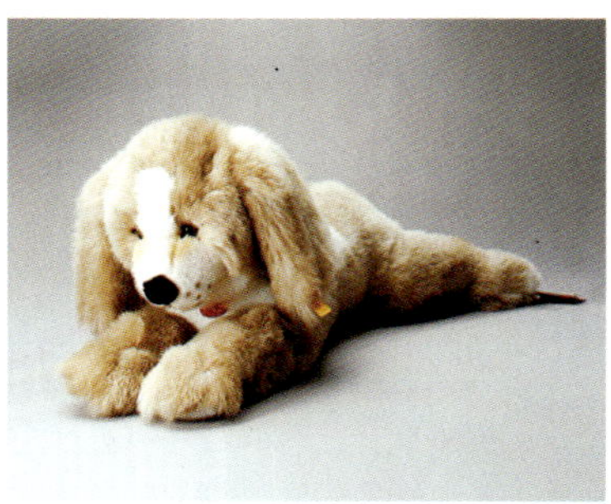

Molly Barry

Webpelz, liegend, handwaschbar - *woven fur, lying, hand washable*

EAN-No.	Period	Pr.	Info
104893	1994-1997	3	70 cm

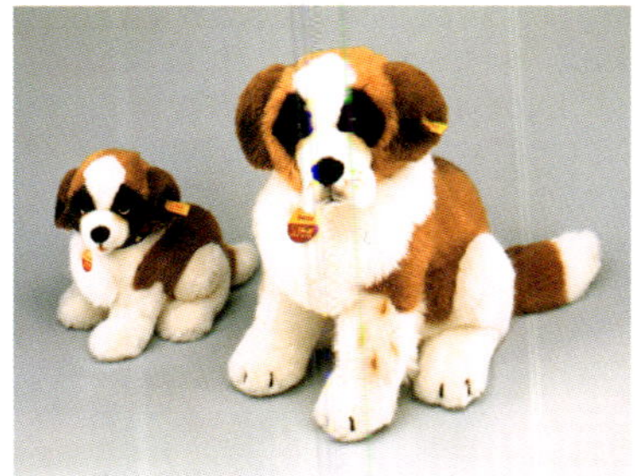

Bernie

Webpelz, sitzend, mit Lederhalsband, weiss/braun - *woven fur, sitting, leather collar, white/brown*

EAN-No.	Period	Pr.	Info
078224	1995-1996	3	27 cm
078255	1995-1996	4	48 cm

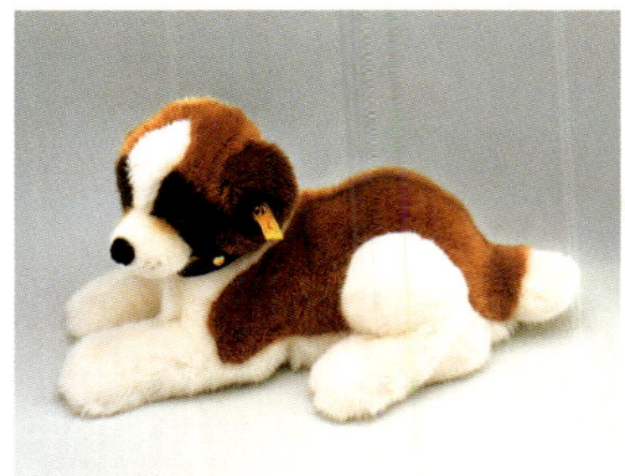

Bernie

Webpelz, weiss/braun, liegend, Lederhalsband, ohne Halsband waschmaschinenfest - *woven fur, white/brown, lying, leather collar, without leather collar hand washable*

EAN-No.	Period	Pr.	Info
078231	1995-1997	3	40 cm

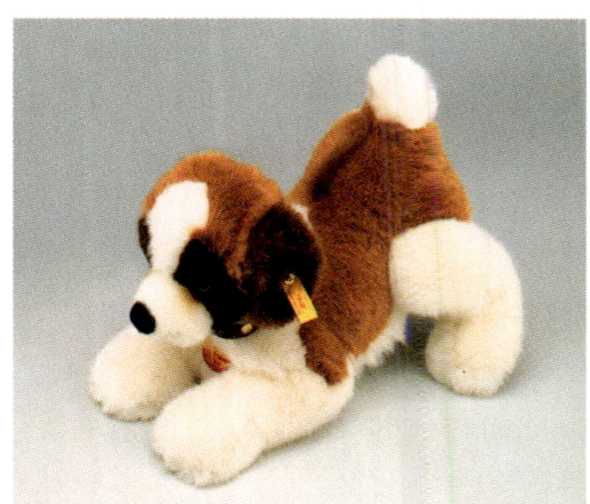

Bernie

Webpelz, weiss/braun, spielend, Lederhalsband, ohne Halsband handwaschbar - *woven fur, white/brown, playing, leather collar, without leather collar hand washable*

EAN-No.	Period	Pr.	Info
078248	1995-1999	3	32 cm

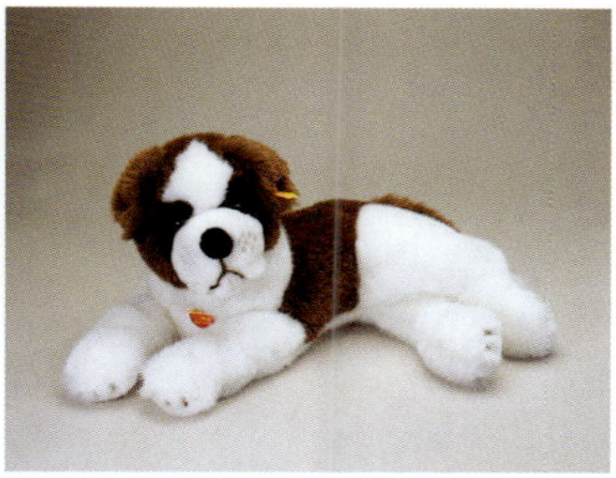

Bernhardiner - *St. Bernhard*

Webpelz, seitlich liegend, waschmaschinenfest - *woven fur, lying aside, machine washable*

EAN-No.	Period	Pr.	Info
105050	1998-1999	3-4	50 cm

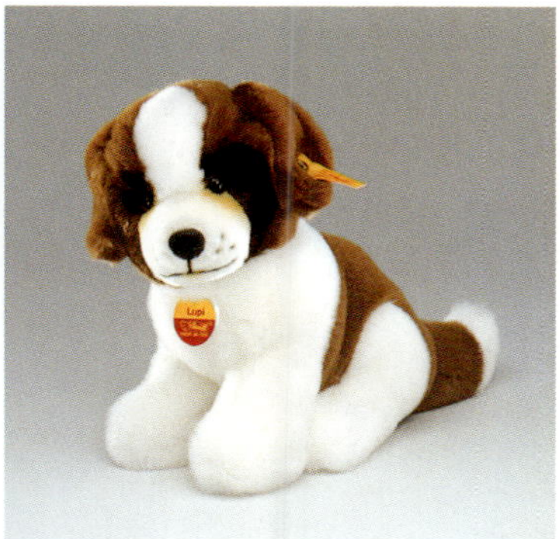

Lupi Bernhardiner - ***Lupi*** *St. Bernhard*

Webpelz, sitzend, waschmaschinenfest - *woven fur, sitting, machine washable*

EAN-No.	Period	Pr.	Info
078279	1999-1999	2-3	22 cm

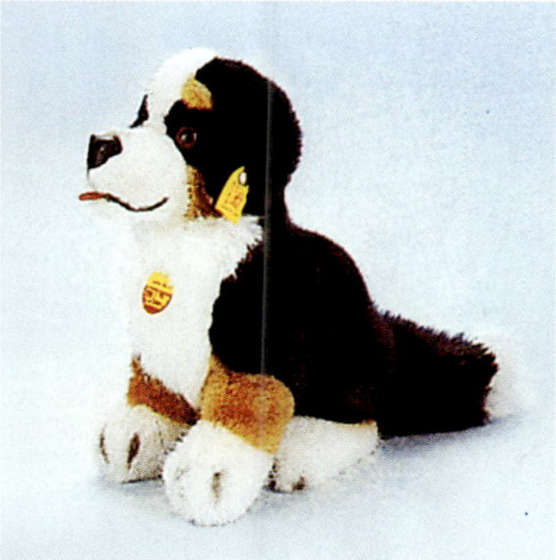

Junior Senni

Webpelz, sitzend, abwaschbar - *woven fur, sitting, surface washable*

Serie	Art.-No	Period	Pr.	Info
	2887/26	1981-1983	3	26 cm

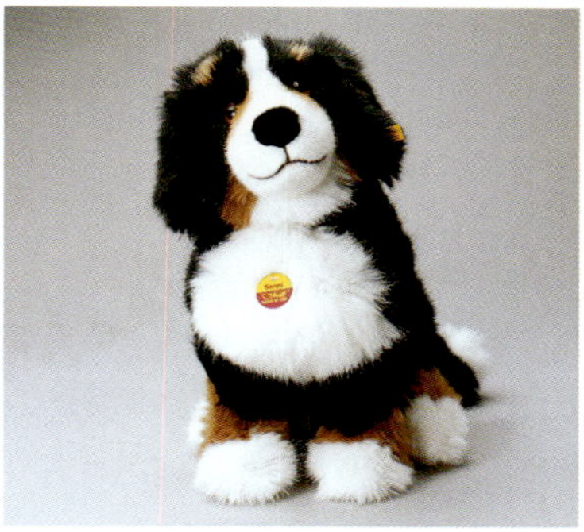

Senni Berner Sennenhund - ***Senni***
Bernese Mountain Dog

Webpelz, sitzend, abwaschbar - *woven fur, sitting, surface washable*

EAN-No.	Period	Pr.	Info
078453	1992-1995	3	45 cm

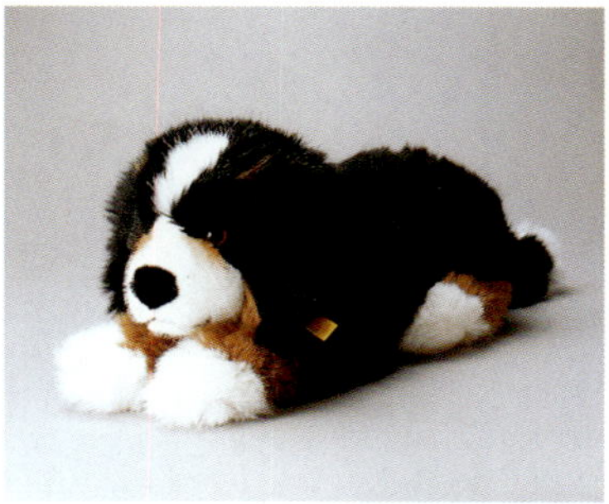

Senni Berner Sennenhund - ***Senni***
Bernese Mountain Dog

Webpelz, liegend, abwaschbar - *woven fur, lying, surface washable*

EAN-No.	Period	Pr.	Info
078477	1992-1995	3	45 cm

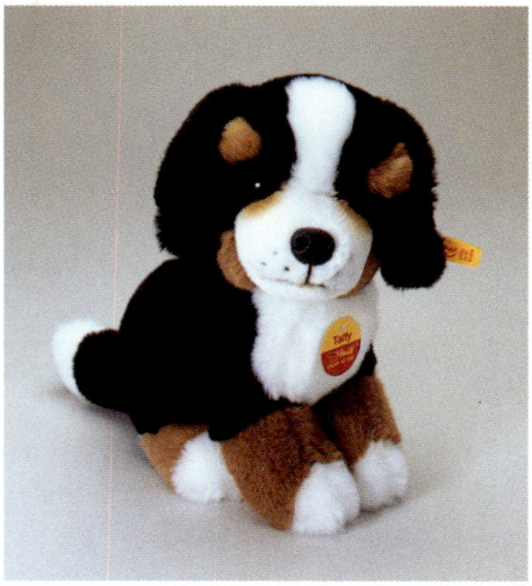

Taffy Berner Sennenhund - ***Taffy***
Bernese Mountain Dog

Webpelz, sitzend, waschmaschinenfest - *woven fur, sitting, machine washable*

EAN-No.	Period	Pr.	Info
078446	1999-1999	3	22 cm

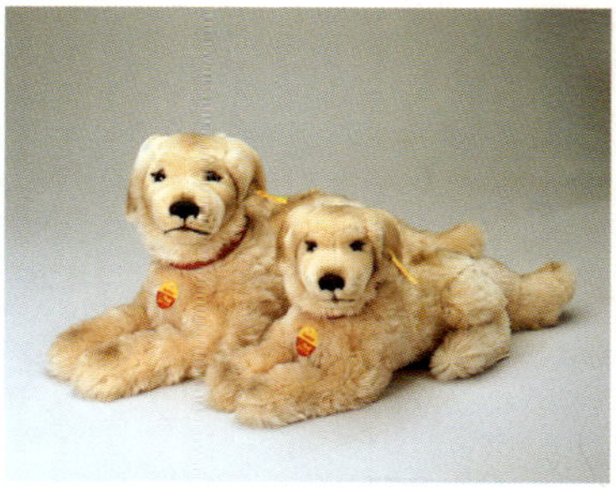

Hektor Golden Retriever

Webpelz, blond, liegend, Lederhalsband, ohne Halsband waschmaschinenfest - *woven fur, blond, lying, leather collar, machine washable without collar*

EAN-No.	Period	Pr.	Info
078484	1997-1999	3	33 cm
078491	1997-1999	3	42 cm

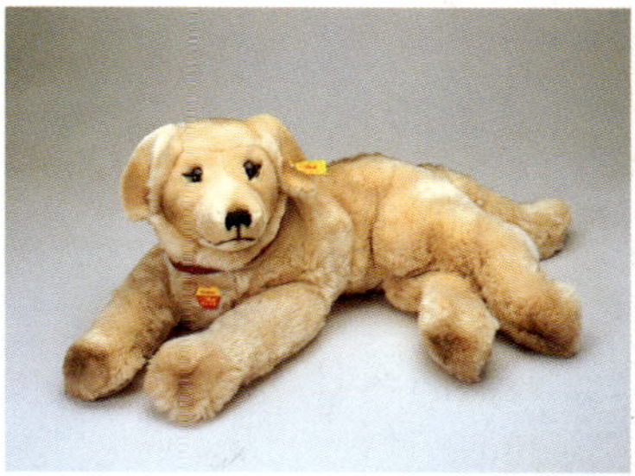

Hektor Golden Retriever

Webpelz, blond, seitlich liegend, Lederhalsband, ohne Halsband waschmaschinenfest - *woven fur, blond, lying aside, leather collar, machine washable without collar*

EAN-No.	Period	Pr.	Info
078514	1999-1999	2-3	60 cm

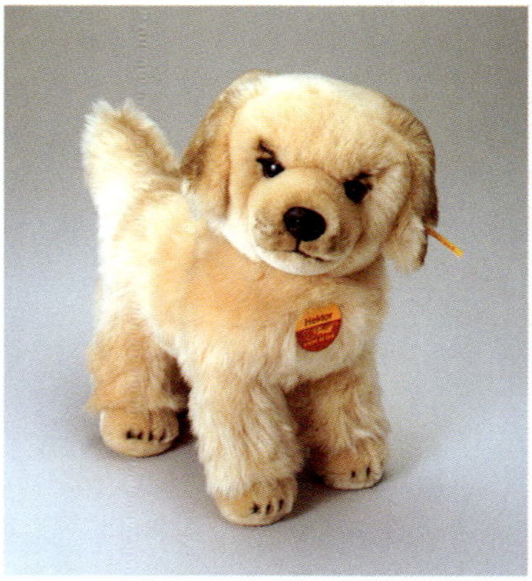

Hektor Golden Retriever

Webpelz, blond, stehend, waschmaschinenfest - *woven fur, blond, standing, machine washable*

EAN-No.	Period	Pr.	Info
080647	1999-1999	3	25 cm

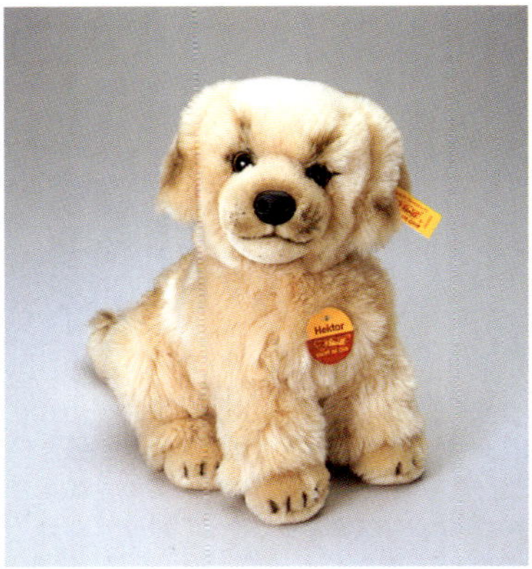

Hektor Golden Retriever

Webpelz, blond, sitzend, waschmaschinenfest - *woven fur, blond, sitting, machine washable*

EAN-No.	Period	Pr.	Info
080654	1999-1999	3	22 cm

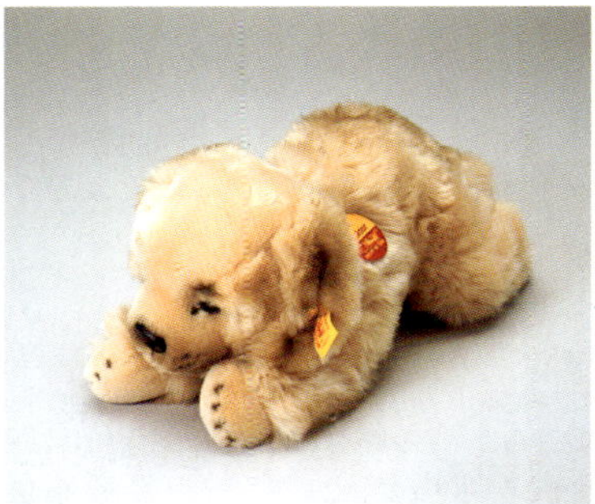

Hektor Golden Retriever

Webpelz, blond, liegend, waschmaschinenfest - *woven fur, blond, lying, machine washable*

EAN-No.	Period	Pr.	Info
080661	1999-1999	3	28 cm

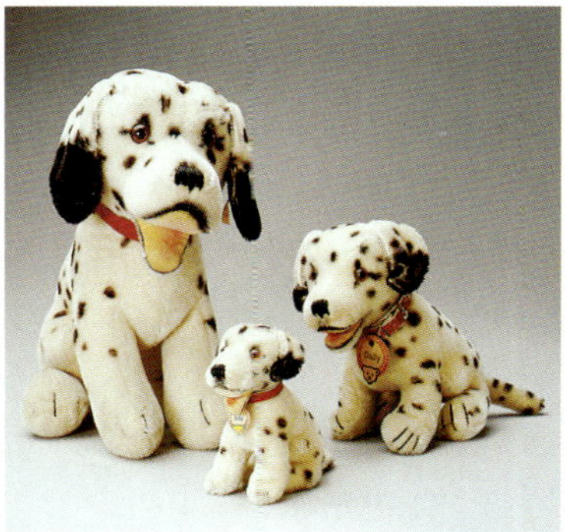

Dally Dalmatiner - ***Dally** Dalmatian*

Mohair, weiss/schwarz, rotes Lederhalsband, sitzend, beweglicher Kopf - *mohair, white/black, red leather collar, sitting, movable head*

Serie	Art.-No	Period	Pr.	Info
15	**3310**	1953-1958	4	10 cm
150	**3310,00**	1959-1964	4	
406	**3310,00**	1965-1967	4	
	4060/10	1968-1969	3-4	
15	**3317**	1953-1958	4	17 cm
150	**3317,00**	1959-1963	4	
406	**3317,00**	1966-1967	4	
	4060/17	1968-1969	4	
15	**3328**	1953-1953	4-5	28 cm
15	**3328,2**	1954-1958	4-5	
150	**3328,00**	1959-1963	4-5	

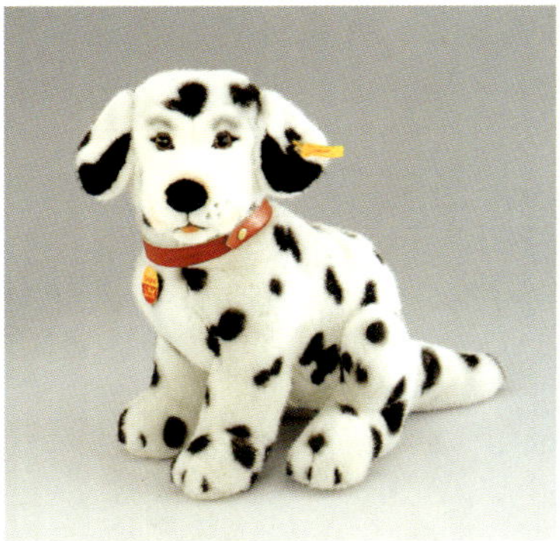

Dalmatiner - *Dalmatian*

Webpelz, sitzend, Lederhalsband, ohne Halsband handwaschbar - *woven fur, sitting, leather collar, hand washable without collar*

EAN-No.	Period	Pr.	Info
078361	1997-1999	3	32 cm

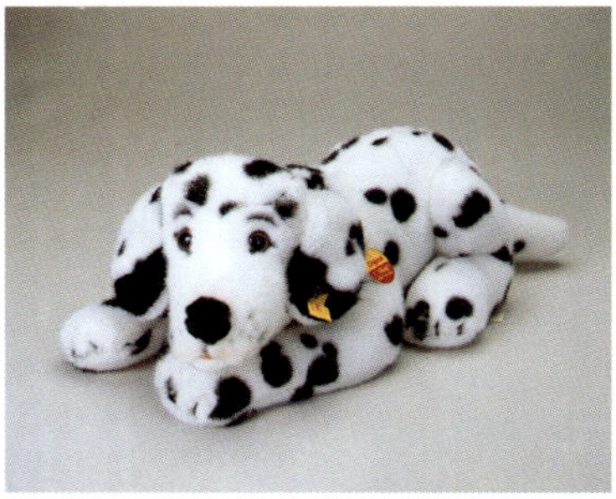

Dalmatiner - *Dalmatian*

Webpelz, liegend, Lederhalsband, ohne Halsband waschmaschinenfest - *woven fur, lying, leather collar, hand washable without collar*

EAN-No.	Period	Pr.	Info
078385	1997-1999	3	35 cm

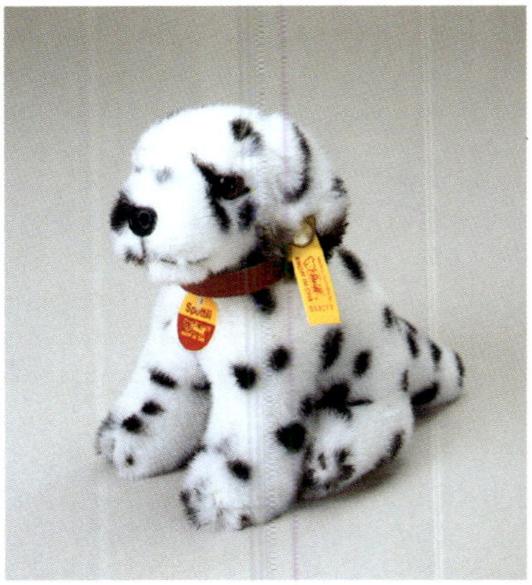

Spottili Dalmatiner - ***Spottili** Dalmatian*

Webpelz, sitzend, Halsband, ohne Halsband waschmaschinenfest - *woven fur, sitting, collar, machine washable without collar*

EAN-No.	Period	Pr.	Info
053177	1998-1999	2	12 cm

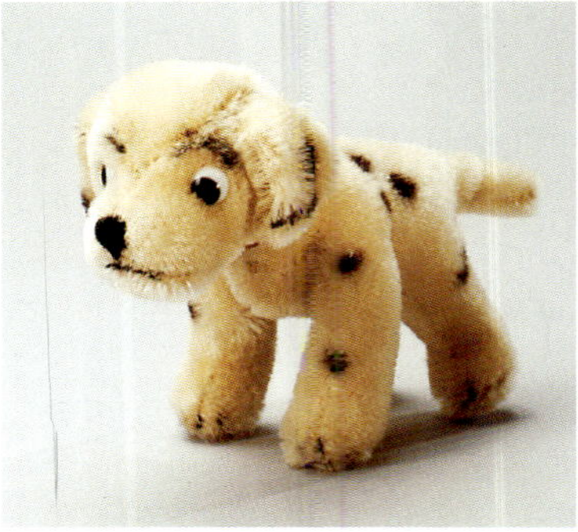

Rolly Dalmatiner - ***Rolly** Dalmation*

Mohair, weiss, schwarz gepunktet, stehend, Copyr. 1961 W. Disney Prod. - *mohair, white with black spots, standing, Copyr. 1961 W. Disney Prod.*

Serie	Art.-No	Period	Pr.	Info
152	**1312,00**	1962-1962	5	12 cm
152	**1322,00**	1962-1962	5-6	22 cm

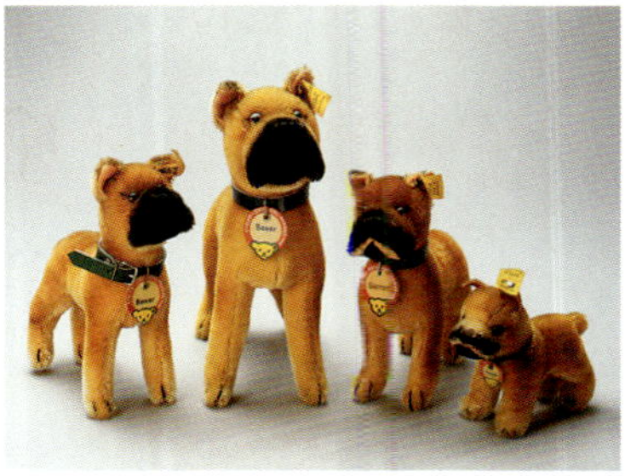

Sarras ab 1958 **Boxer** - ***Sarras** from 1958 **Boxer***

Mohairpluesch, braun, schwarz schattiert, stehend - *mohair, brown with black shading, standing*

SERIE	ART.-NO	PERIOD	PR.	INFO
16	**1310,0**	1954-1958	5	10 cm
160	**1310,00**	1959-1963	3	
410	**1310,00**	1966-1967	3	
	4100/10	1968-1970	3	
16	**1317,0**	1950-1957	5	17 cm
160	**1317,00**	1959-1963	3-4	
410	**1317,00**	1966-1967	3-4	
	4100/17	1968-1970	3	
16	**1322,0**	1950-1957	5-6	22 cm
160	**1322,00**	1959-1963	4	

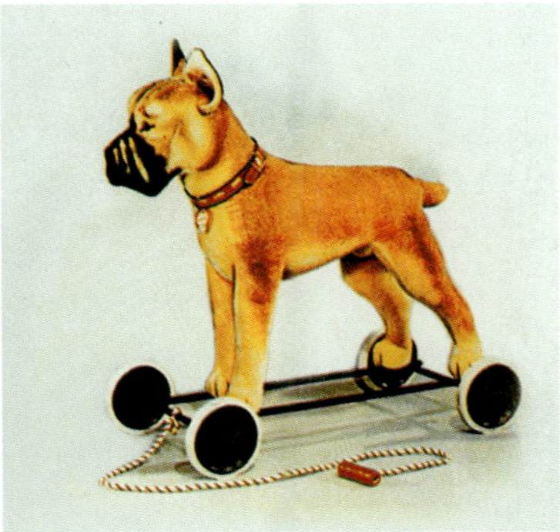

Reit **Sarras** ab 1958 **Boxer** - *Riding* ***Sarras*** *from1958* ***Boxer***

Mohairpluesch, Eisengerippe, Zugstimme, braun/schwarz, stehend auf Scheibenraedern mit Gummi - *mohair, iron frame, pull cord voice, brown/black, standing on disc wheels with rubber tires*

SERIE	ART.-NO	PERIOD	PR.	INFO
16	**1350,2**	1950-1957	5-6	50 cm
160	**1350,20**	1961-1961	5	

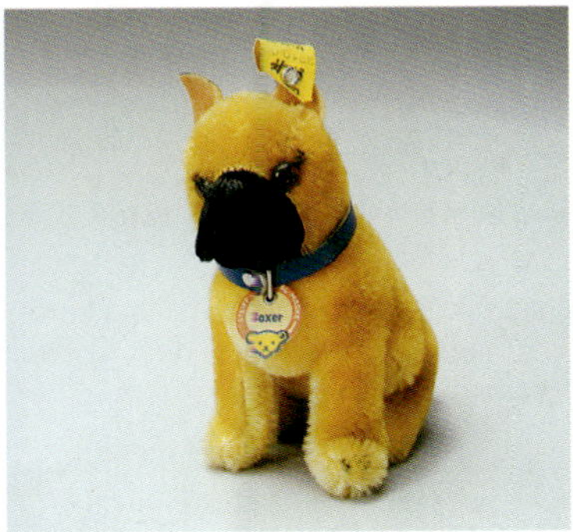

Sarras ab 1958 **Boxer** - ***Sarras*** *from 1958* ***Boxer***

Mohair, braun/schwarz, sitzend, drehbarer Kopf - *mohair, brown/black, sitting, head swivels*

SERIE	ART.-NO	PERIOD	PR.	INFO
16	**3310**	1951-1958	5	10 cm
160	**3310,00**	1959-1961	3-4	
16	**3314**	1951-1958	5	14 cm
160	**3314,00**	1959-1961	4	

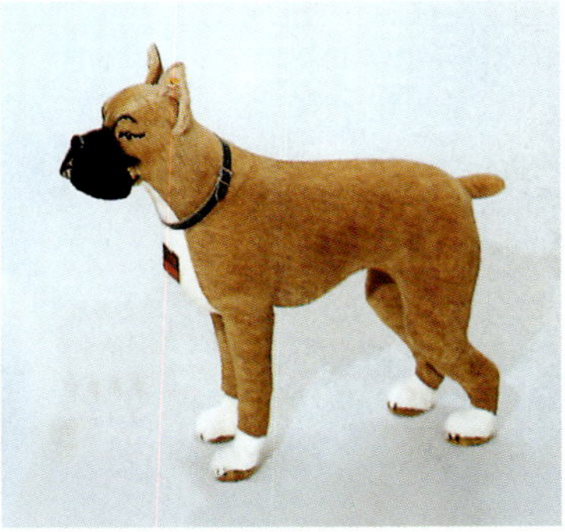

Hector Boxer

Studio-Tier, Webpelz, stehend, abwaschbar - *studio animal, woven fur, standing, surface washable*

SERIE	ART.-NO	PERIOD	PR.	INFO
	4075/60	1978-1984	4-5	60 cm

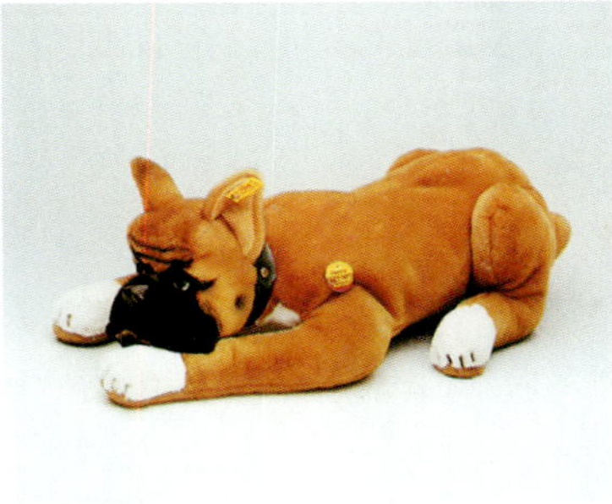

Hector Boxer

Webpelz, liegend, waschbar - *woven fur, lying, washable*

SERIE	ART.-NO	PERIOD	PR.	INFO
078156	**4045/50**	1982-1989	3	50 cm

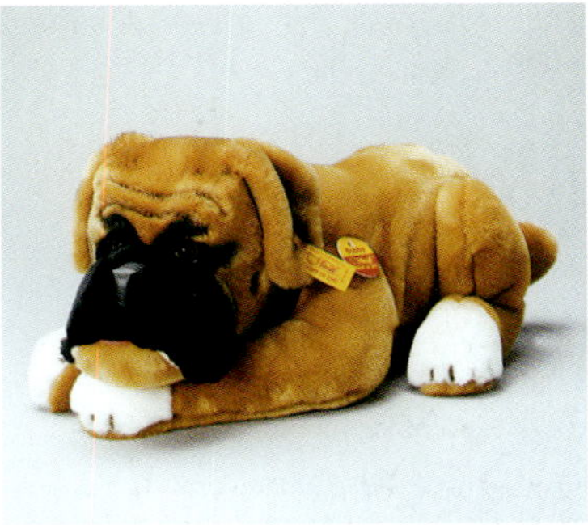

Bobby Jungboxer - ***Bobby*** *Young Boxer*

Webpelz, liegend, abwaschbar - *woven fur, lying, surface washable*

SERIE	ART.-NO	PERIOD	PR.	INFO
078101	**4045/35**	1983-1990	3	35 cm
	078101	1991-1996	3	

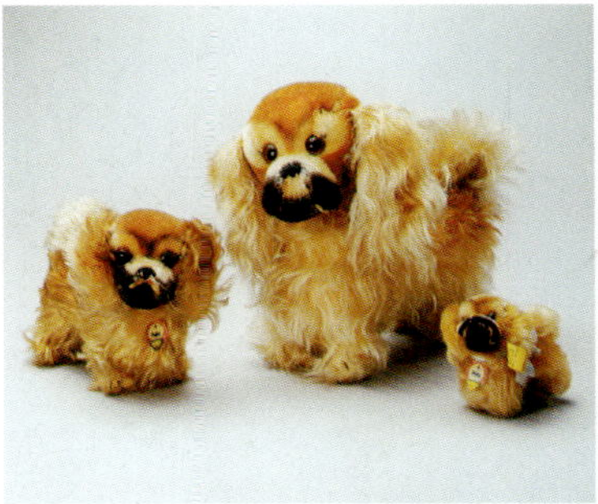

Pekinese **Peky**

Mohair, langhaarig, hellbraun, schwarze Schnauze, stehend, beweglicher Kopf, abwaschbar - *long-hair mohair, light brown, black muzzle, standing, head swivels, surface washable*

SERIE	ART.-NO	PERIOD	PR.	INFO
17a	**1308,0**	1953-1958	3-4	8 cm
172	**1308,00**	1959-1964	3	
412	**1308,00**	1965-1967	3	
	4120/08	1968-1972	2-3	
17a	**1310,0**	1953-1958	3-4	10 cm
172	**1310,00**	1959-1964	3	
412	**1310,00**	1965-1967	3	
	4120/10	1968-1976	2-3	
17a	**1314,0**	1953-1958	4	14 cm
172	**1314,00**	1959-1964	3	
412	**1314,00**	1965-1967	3	
	4120/14	1968-1977	3	
17a	**1322,0**	1953-1953	4	22 cm
17a	**1322,02**	1954-1958	3-4	
172	**1322,00**	1959-1964	3-4	
412	**1322,00**	1965-1967	3-4	
	4120/22	1968-1976	3	

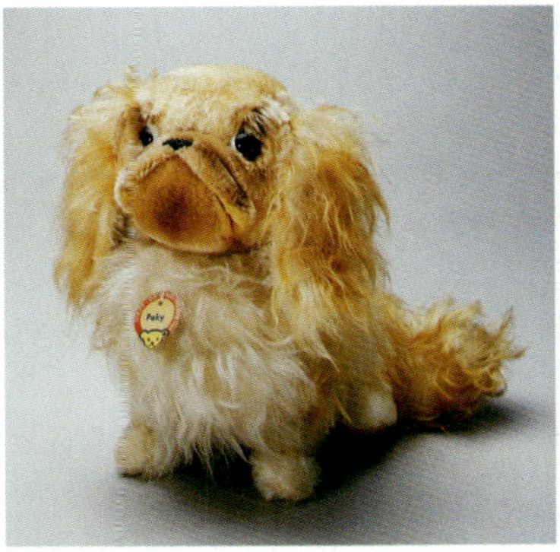

Pekinese **Peky**

Mohair, langhaarig, hellbraun, sitzend, Drehkopf, abwaschbar - *long-hair mohair, light brown, sitting, head swivels, surface washable*

SERIE	ART.-NO	PERIOD	PR.	INFO
412	**3330,00**	1965-1967	3	30 cm
	4120/30	1968-1976	3	

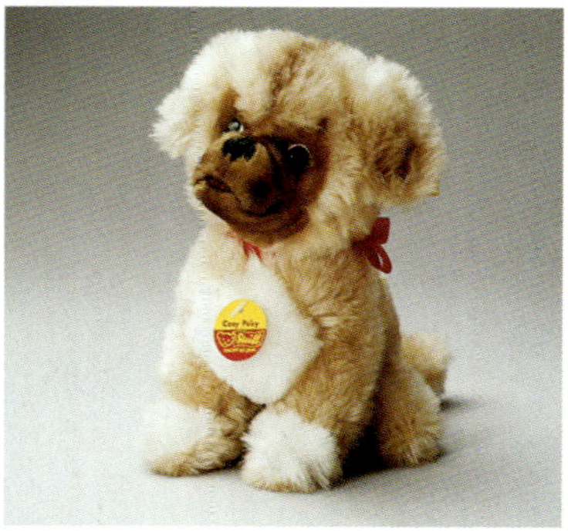

Cosy Peky Pekinese

Dralon, gefuellt mit synthetischen Fasern & Schaumstoff, beige, sitzend, sehr weich, vollwaschbar - *dralon, stuffed with synthetic fiber & foam, beige, sitting, very soft, fully washable*

SERIE	ART.-NO	PERIOD	PR.	INFO
	5070/20	1968-1978	2-3	20 cm

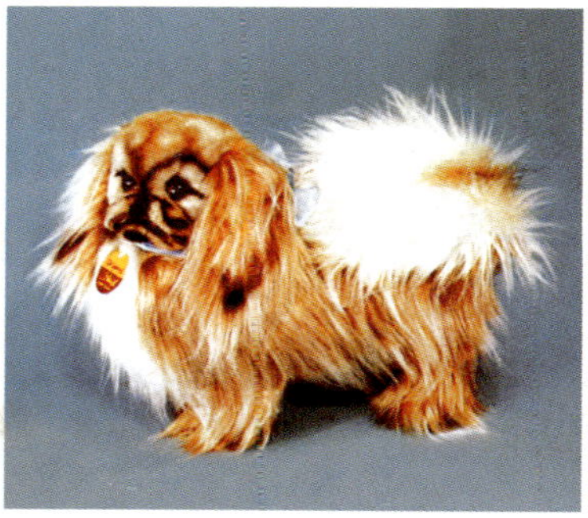

Peky Pekinese

Crylor, stehend, abwaschbar - *crylor, standing, surface washable*

SERIE	ART.-NO	PERIOD	PR.	INFO
	4128/40	1973-1975	2-3	40 cm

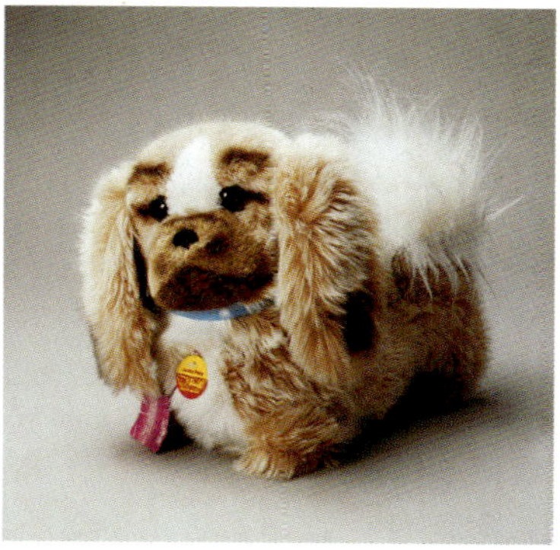

Junior Peky Pekinese

Pelzimitation, ab 1978 Synthetik-Webpelz, stehend, abwaschbar - *imitation fur, from 1978 synthetic woven fur, standing, surface washable*

SERIE	ART.-NO	PERIOD	PR.	INFO
076152	**2890/22**	1977-1987	2-3	22 cm
	2890/30	1977-1981	2-3	30 cm

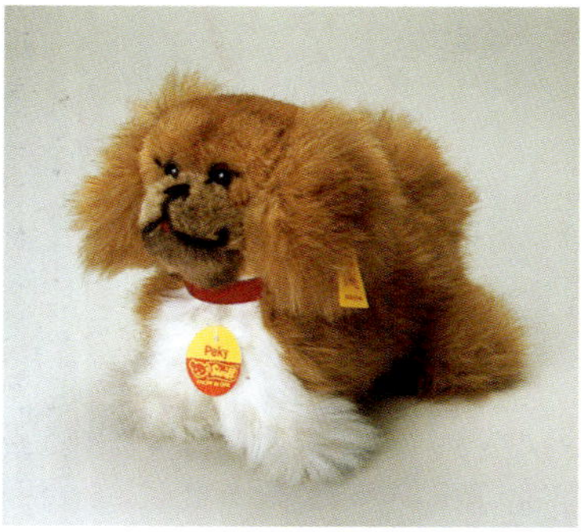

Peky Pekinese

Webpelz, stehend, abwaschbar - *woven fur, standing, surface washable*

SERIE	ART.-NO	PERIOD	PR.	INFO
	4030/14	1980-1985	2	14 cm

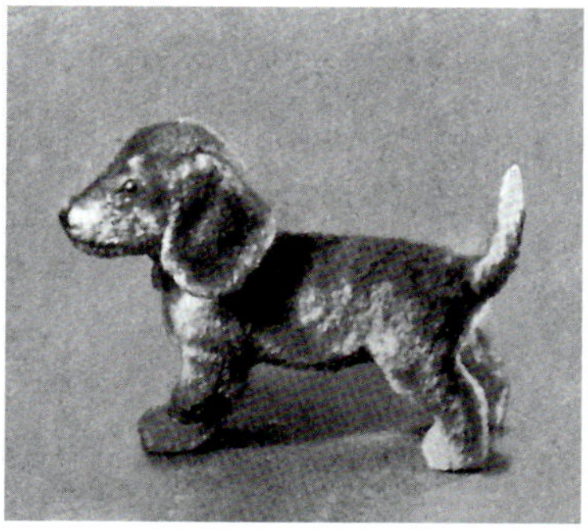

Bazi Jungdackel - ***Bazi** Dachshund Puppy*

Seidenpluesch, hellbraun, stehend, Halsband - *silk plush, light brown, standing, collar*

SERIE	ART.-NO	PERIOD	PR.	INFO
18	**1614,0**	1949-1949	4	14 cm

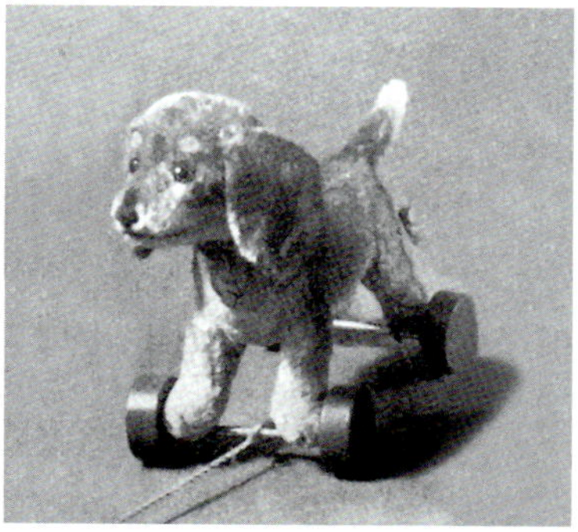

Bazi Jungdackel - ***Bazi** Dachshund Puppy*

Seidenpluesch, hellbraun, stehend auf Exzenterraedern, Halsband - *silk plush, light brown, standing on eccentric wheels, collar*

SERIE	ART.-NO	PERIOD	PR.	INFO
18	**1614** ex	1949-1949	4-5	14 cm

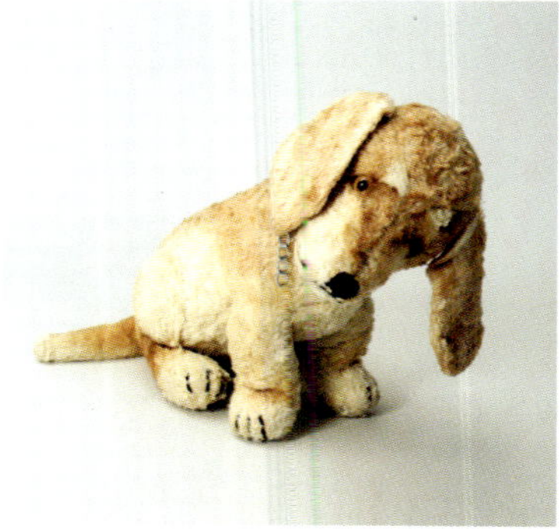

Bazi Jungdackel - ***Bazi** Dachshund Puppy*

Seidenpluesch, hellbraun, sitzend, Drehkopf, Halsband - *silk plush, light brown, sitting, head swivels, collar*

SERIE	ART.-NO	PERIOD	PR.	INFO
18	**3614**	1949-1949	4	14 cm
18	**3617**	1948-1949	4	17 cm

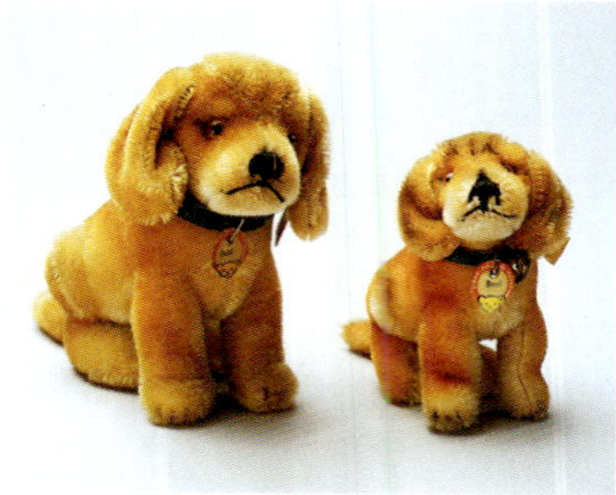

Bazi Jungdackel - ***Bazi** Dachshund Puppy*

Mohairpluesch, kurzhaarig, hellbraun, sitzend, Kopf drehbar - *short-hair mohair, light brown, sitting, head swivels*

SERIE	ART.-NO	PERIOD	PR.	INFO
18	**3310**	1950-1958	3-4	10 cm
180	**3310,00**	1959-1961	3	
416	**3310,00**	1966-1967	3	
	4165/10	1968-1969	3	
18	**3314**	1949-1957	4	14 cm
180	**3314,00**	1960-1961	4	
18	**3317**	1950-1957	4	17 cm
180	**3317,00**	1960-1961	3-4	
416	**3317,00**	1966-1967	3-4	
	4165/17	1968-1969	3	

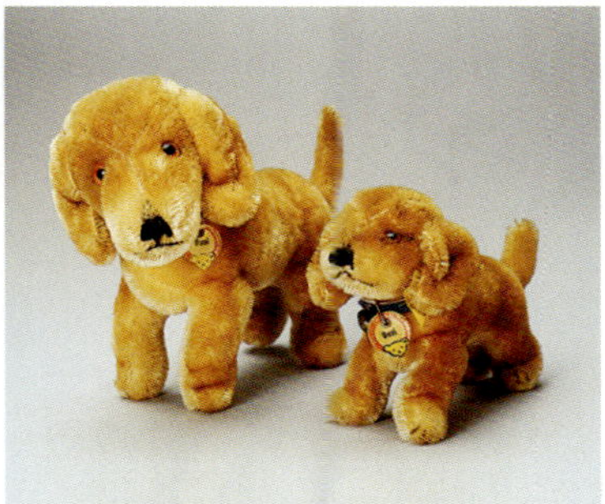

Bazi Jungdackel - ***Bazi** Dachshund Puppy*

Mohairpluesch, kurzhaarig, hellbraun, stehend, abwaschbar - *short-hair mohair, light brown, standing, surface washable*

SERIE	ART.-NO	PERIOD	PR.	INFO
18	**1310,0**	1950-1958	3-4	10 cm
180	**1310,00**	1961-1961	3	
416	**1310,00**	1966-1967	3	
	4160/10	1968-1975	2-3	
18	**1314,0**	1950-1957	3-4	14 cm
180	**1314,00**	1961-1961	3	
416	**1314,00**	1966-1967	3	
	4160/14	1968-1975	2-3	

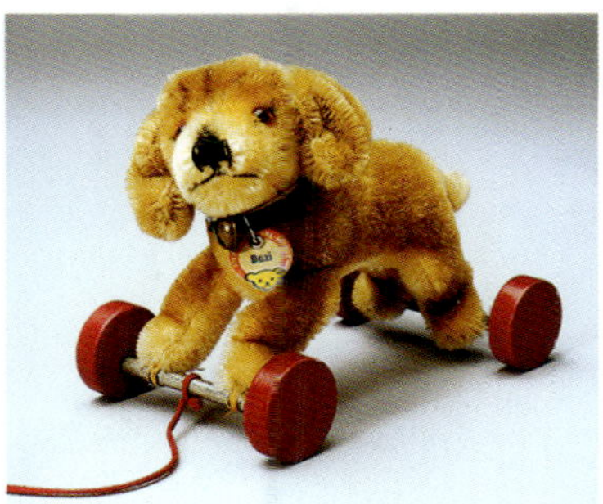

Nachzieh-**Bazi** - *Pull toy **Bazi***

Mohair, kurzhaarig, hellbraun, stehend, auf Exzenterraedern - *short-hair mohair, light brown, standing on eccentric wheels*

SERIE	ART.-NO	PERIOD	PR.	INFO
81 18	**1310** ex	1954-1957	4-5	10 cm
810 180	**1310,10**	1960-1960	4-5	
18	**1314** ex	1950-1957	4-5	14 cm
180	**1314,10**	1961-1961	4-5	

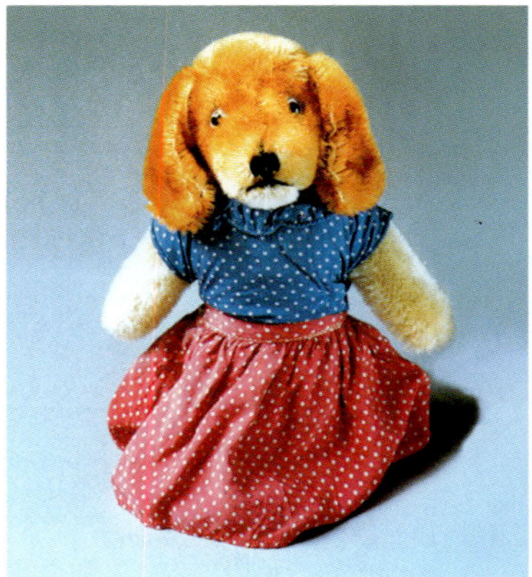

Musik-Bazi - *Music Bazi*

Kopf Mohairpluesch, braun, roter Rock, blaue Bluse, Schweizer Musikwerk zum Druecken - *head is mohair, brown, red skirt & blue blouse, with Swiss music box (press voice)*

SERIE	ART.-NO	PERIOD	PR.	INFO
97 18	**9325**	1950-1951	6-7	25 cm

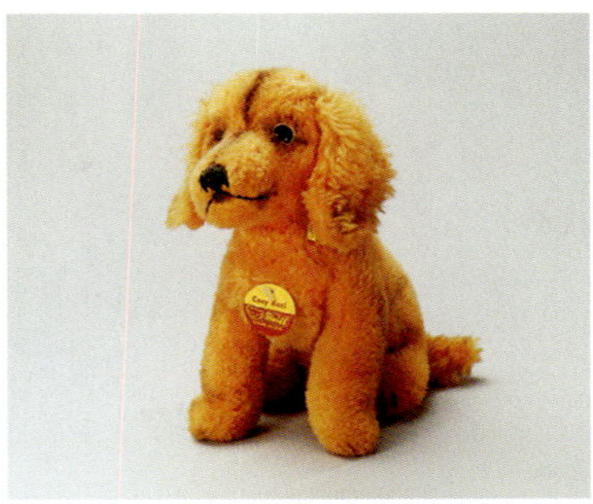

Cosy Bazi Dackel - *Cozy Bazi Dachshund*

Dralon, gefuellt mit synthetischen Fasern & Schaumstoff, sitzend, sehr weich, vollwaschbar - *dralon, stuffed with synthetic fiber & foam, sitting, very soft, fully washable*

SERIE	ART.-NO	PERIOD	PR.	INFO
503	**3620,00**	1966-1967	2-3	20 cm
	5030/20	1968-1977	2-3	

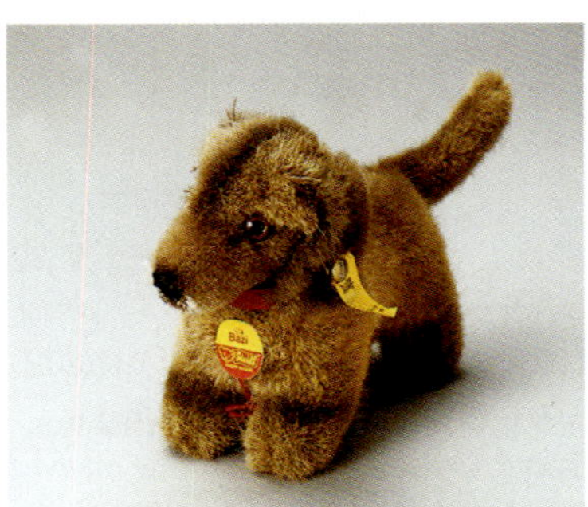

Bazi Dackel - ***Bazi** Dachshund*

Webpelz, Halsband, stehend, abwaschbar - *woven fur, collar, standing, surface washable*

SERIE	ART.-NO	PERIOD	PR.	INFO
078521	**4144/12**	1979-1986	2	12 cm

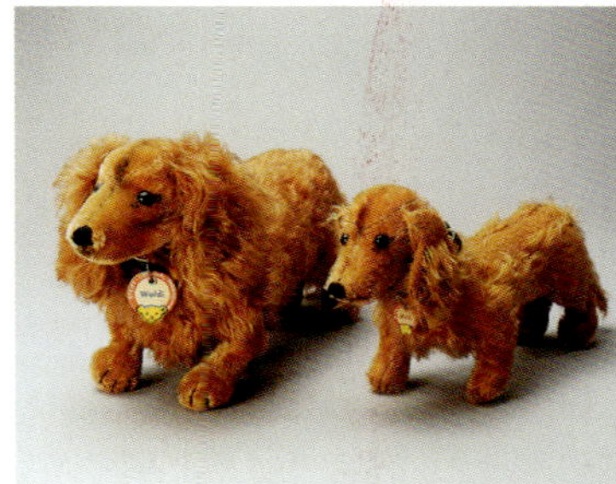

Dachshund **Waldi**

Langhaar-Mohair, kupferbraun, Lederhalsband, stehend, abwaschbar - *longhair mohair, copper brown, leather collar, standing, surface washable*

SERIE	ART.-NO	PERIOD	PR.	INFO
18	**1317,02**	1949-1958	3-4	17 cm
180	**1317,00**	1960-1964	3	
414	**1317,00**	1965-1967	3	
	4140/17	1968-1980	2-3	
18	**1322,02**	1951-1958	3-4	22 cm
180	**1322,00**	1960-1964	3	
414	**1322,00**	1965-1967	3	
	4140/22	1968-1980	3	
18	**1328,02**	1951-1958	3-4	28 cm
180	**1328,00**	1960-1964	3	
414	**1328,00**	1965-1967	3	
	4140/28	1968-1977	3	

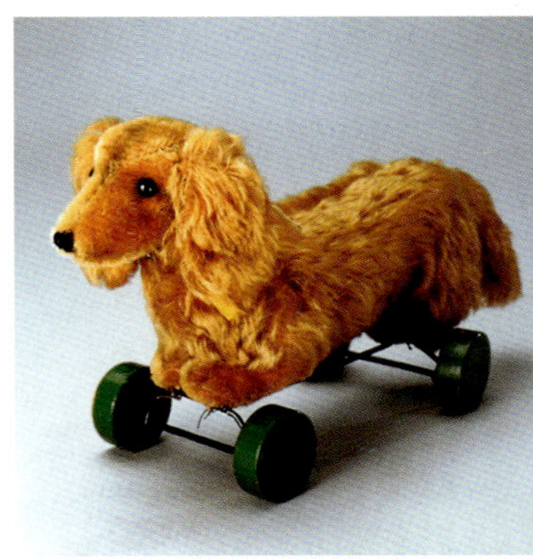

Dachshund **Waldi**

Langhaar-Mohair, kupferbraun, stehend, auf Exzenterraedern - *longhair mohair, copper brown, standing, on eccentric wheels*

SERIE	ART.-NO	PERIOD	PR.	INFO
18	**1317** ex	1949-1957	4-5	17 cm
180	**1317,10**	1959-1961	4	
415	**1317,10**	1966-1967	4	
	4150/17	1968-1970	4	
18	**1322** ex	1951-1957	4-5	22 cm
180	**1322,10**	1959-1959	4-5	

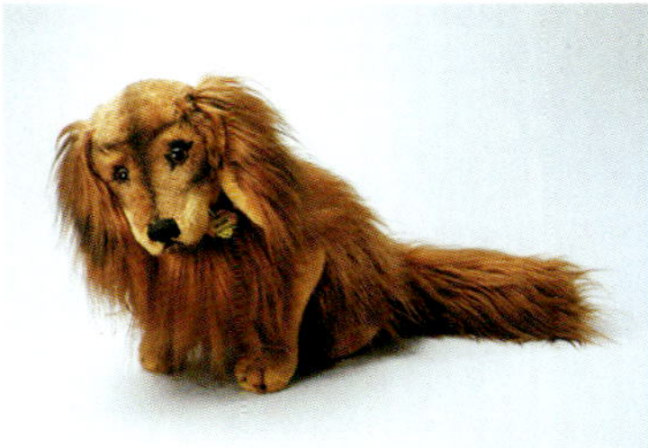

Waldi Langhaardackel - ***Waldi** Long-Hair Dachshund*

Crylor, langhaarig, ab 1978 Dralonpluesch, rotbraun, sitzend, Drehkopf, abwaschbar - *crylor, longhair, from 1978 dralon plush, red-brown, sitting, head swivels, surface washable*

SERIE	ART.-NO	PERIOD	PR.	INFO
414	**3635,03**	1967-1967	3	35 cm
	4140/35	1968-1978	3	

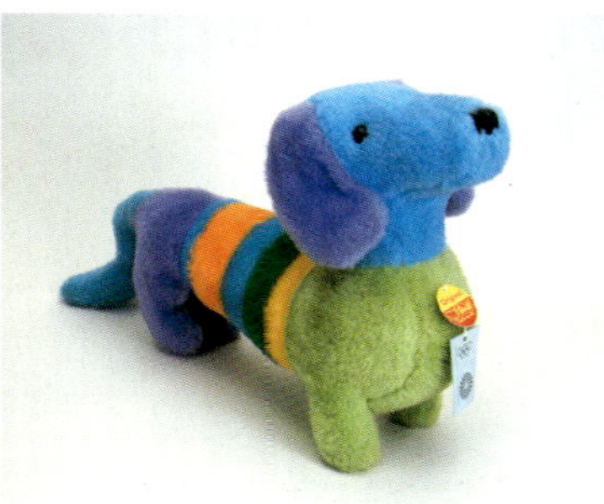

Olympia Waldi - *Olympic Waldi*

Dralon, stehend, offizielles Maskottchen der Olympischen Spiele 1972 in Muenchen - *dralon, standing, official mascot of the 1972 Olympic Games in Munich*

SERIE	ART.-NO	PERIOD	PR.	INFO
	4150/25	1971-1971	3-4	25 cm

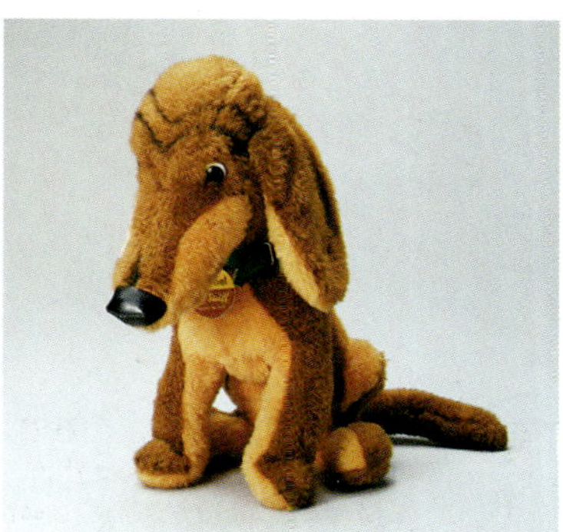

Waldi Dackel - ***Waldi** Dachshund*

Dralon, Lederhalsband, Plastiknase, sitzend, abwaschbar - *dralon, leather collar, plastic nose, sitting, surface washable*

SERIE	ART.-NO	PERIOD	PR.	INFO
	4145/25	1971-1974	3	25 cm

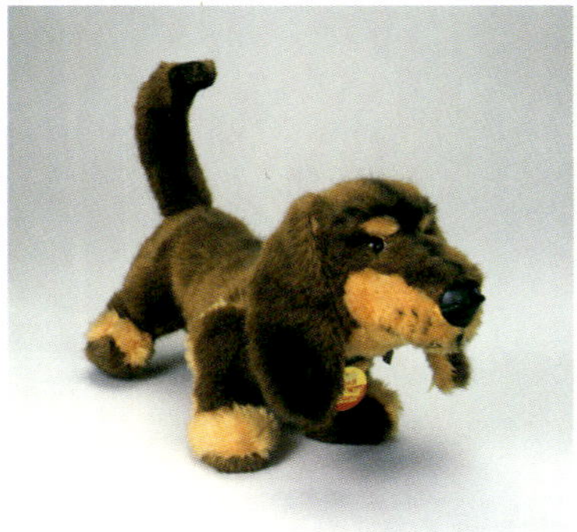

Waldi Dackel - ***Waldi** Dachshund*

Nerzimitation, ab 1978 Synthetik-Webpelz, abwaschbar - *imitation mink, from1978 synthetic woven fur, surface washable*

SERIE	ART.-NO	PERIOD	PR.	INFO
	4142/20	1976-1978	3	20 cm
	4142/28	1976-1978	3	28 cm

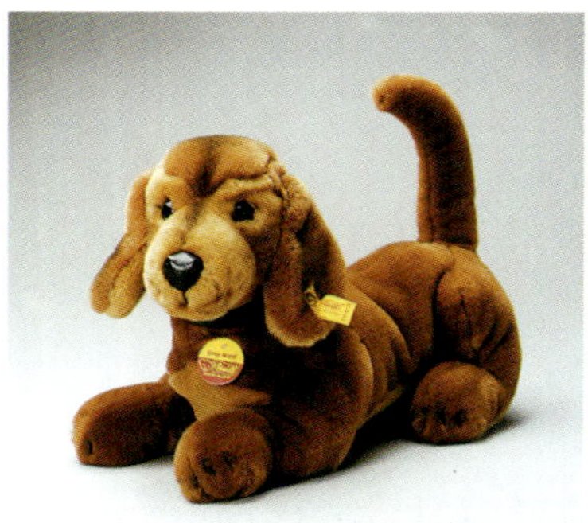

Cosy Waldi

Webpelz, weich, waschmaschinenfest - *woven fur, soft, machine washable*

SERIE	ART.-NO	PERIOD	PR.	INFO
096631	**5460/35**	1982-1988	3	35 cm

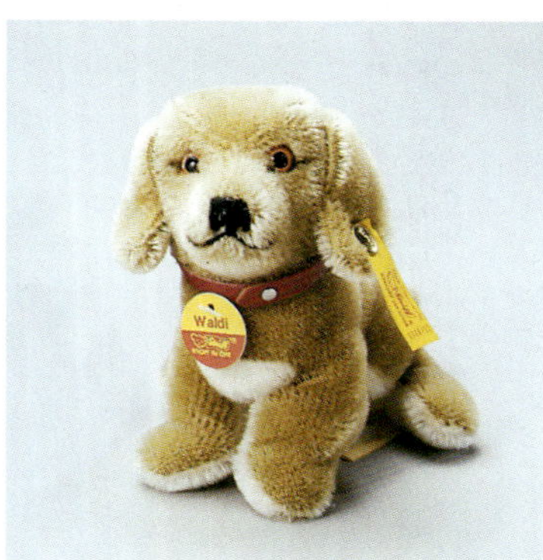

Waldi Hund - ***Waldi** Dog*

Mohair Webpelz, hellbraun, Lederhalsband, sitzend, Kopf drehbar, abwaschbar - *mohair woven fur, light brown, leather collar, sitting, head swivels, surface washable*

SERIE	ART.-NO	PERIOD	PR.	INFO
031427	**1306/12**	1990-1990	2	12 cm
	031427	1991-1992	2	

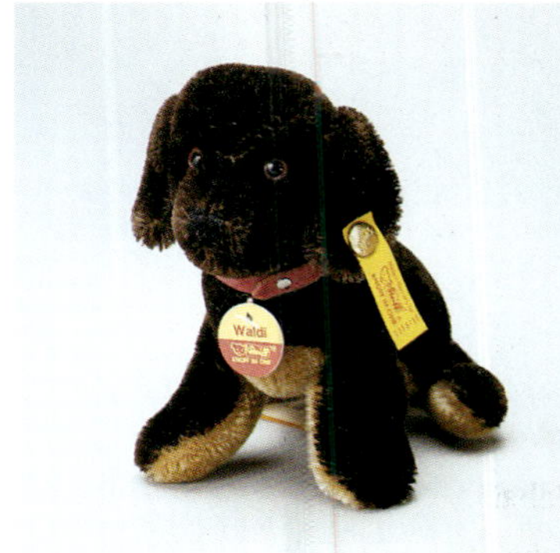

Waldi Hund - ***Waldi** Dog*

Mohair Webpelz, dunkelbraun, Lederhalsband, sitzend, Kopf drehbar, abwaschbar - *mohair woven fur, dark brown, leather collar, sitting, head swivels, surface washable*

SERIE	ART.-NO	PERIOD	PR.	INFO
031526	**1313/12**	1990-1990	2	12 cm
	031526	1991-1992	2	

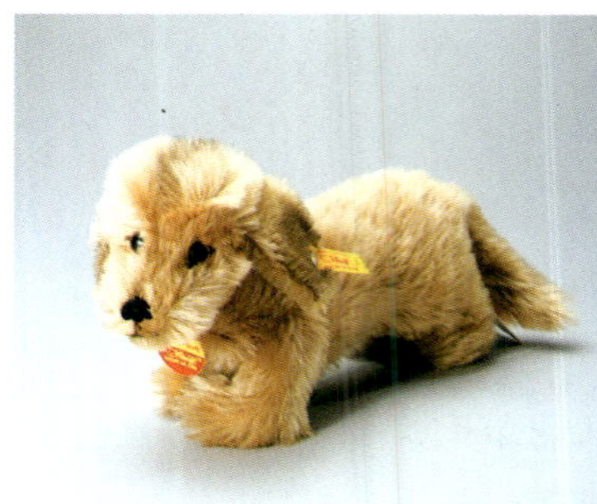

Mohair Soft Waldi

Mohair Webpelz, Lederhalsband, stehend, handwaschbar - *mohair woven fur, leather collar, standing, hand washable*

EAN-NO.	PERIOD	PR.	INFO
036057	1991-1992	2	25 cm

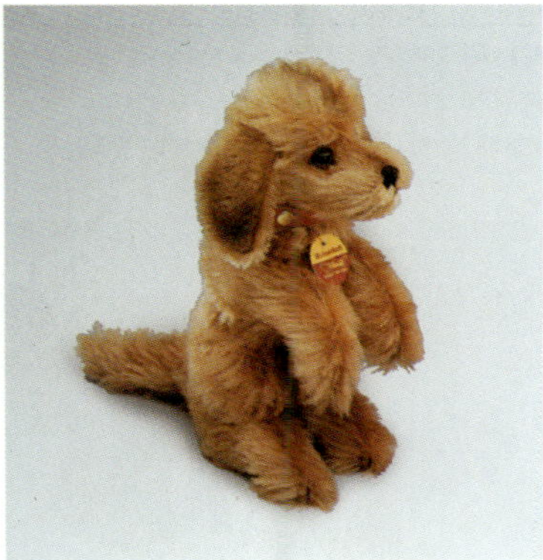

Mohair Soft Waldi

Mohair Webpelz, Lederhalsband, aufwartend, handwaschbar - *mohair woven fur, leather collar, sitting up, hand washable*

EAN-No.	Period	Pr.	Info
036156	1991-1992	2	25 cm

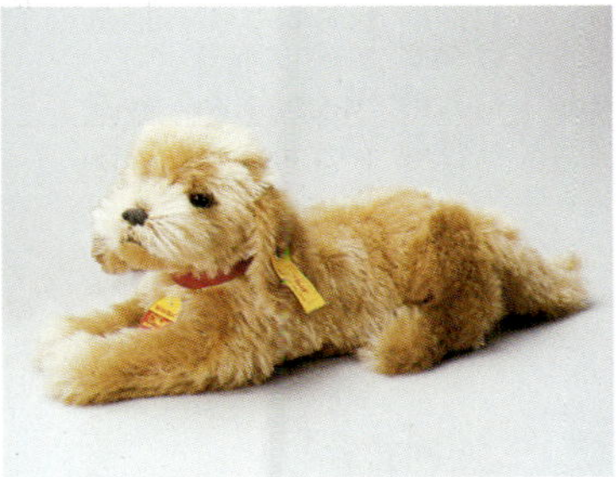

Mohair Soft Waldi

Mohair Webpelz, Lederhalsband, liegend, handwaschbar - *mohair woven fur, leather collar, lying, hand washable*

EAN-No.	Period	Pr.	Info
036255	1991-1992	2	25 cm

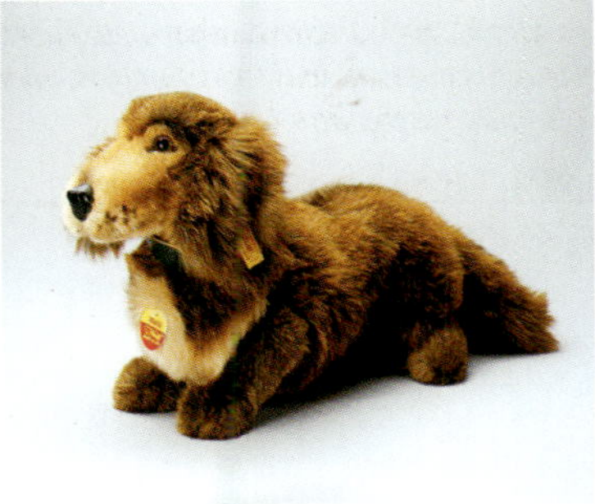

Waldi Langhaardackel - ***Waldi** Long Hair Dachshund*

Webpelz, Lederhalsband, stehend, abwaschbar - *woven fur, leather collar, standing, surface washable*

EAN-No.	Period	Pr.	Info
078569	1991-1995	2-3	35 cm
078583	1991-1993	3	45 cm

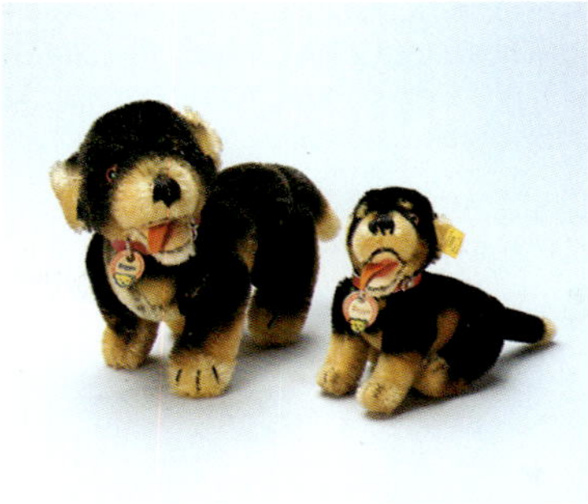

Dackel **Beppo** - *Dachshund **Beppo***

Mohair, schwarz/braun, gegliedert, 17 cm mit Druckstimme - *mohair, black/brown, jointed, 17 cm with press voice*

Serie	Art.-No	Period	Pr.	Info
18	**5310**	1952-1957	4	10 cm
180	**5310,00**	1961-1961	4	
18	**5317**	1952-1957	4	17 cm
180	**5317,00**	1961-1961	4	

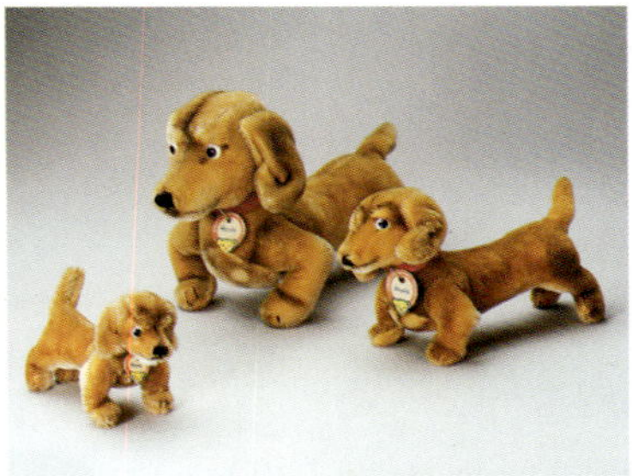

Dackel **Hexie** - ***Hexie** Dachshund*

Kurzhaar-Mohair, braun/gelb, stehend, Kopf drehbar, Stimme - *short-hair mohair, brown/yellow, standing, head swivels, press voice*

Serie	Art.-No	Period	Pr.	Info
18	**1309,0**	1954-1958	3	9 cm
180	**1309,00**	1959-1964	3	
418	**1309,00**	1965-1967	3	
	4180/09	1968-1972	2-3	
18	**1313,0**	1954-1958	3	13 cm
180	**1313,00**	1959-1963	3	
418	**1313,00**	1965-1967	3	
	4180/13	1968-1974	2-3	
18	**1320,0**	1956-1958	3	20 cm
180	**1320,00**	1959-1963	3	
418	**1320,00**	1965-1967	3	
	4180/20	1968-1974	3	
18	**1325,0**	1958-1958	3	25 cm
180	**1325,00**	1959-1963	3	
418	**1325,00**	1965-1967	3	
	4180/25	1968-1973	3	

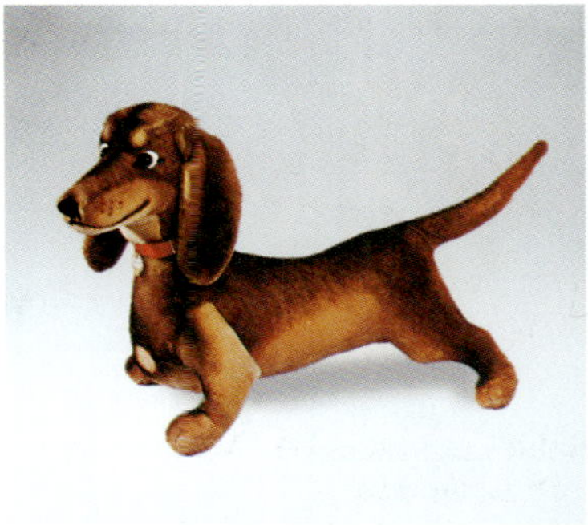

Hexie Dackel - ***Hexie** Dachshund*

Schautier, Mohair, stehend - *display animal, mohair, standing*

Serie	Art.-No	Period	Pr.	Info
180	**1350,90**	1960-1960	5	50 cm

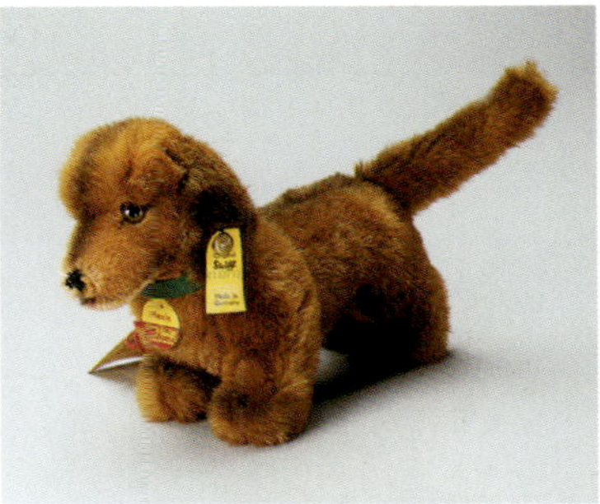

Hexie Dackel - ***Hexie** Dachshund*

Webpelz, stehend, abwaschbar - *woven fur, standing, surface washable*

Serie	Art.-No	Period	Pr.	Info
078507	**4142/12**	1979-1986	2	12 cm

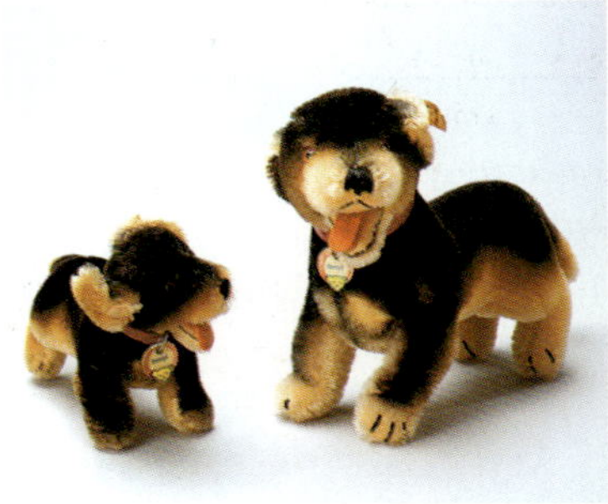

Dackel **Lumpi** - ***Lumpi** Dachshund*

Mohair, schwarz/braun, springend, Drehkopf, offene Schnauze, abwaschbar - *mohair, black/brown, jumping, head swivels, open mouth, surface washable*

Serie	Art.-No	Period	Pr.	Info
180	**1311,06**	1963-1964	3-4	11 cm
420	**1311,06**	1965-1967	3-4	
	4200/11	1968-1974	3	
180	**1318,06**	1963-1964	3-4	18 cm
420	**1318,06**	1965-1967	3-4	
	4200/18	1968-1974	3	

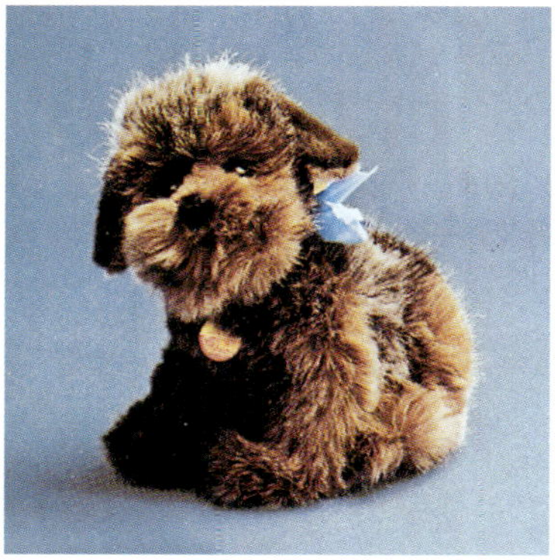

Junior Lumpi

Pelzimitation, ab 1978 Synthetik-Webpelz, sitzend, abwaschbar - *imitation fur, from 1978 synthetic woven fur, sitting, surface washable*

SERIE	ART.-NO	PERIOD	PR.	INFO
	2885/28	1976-1981	2	28 cm

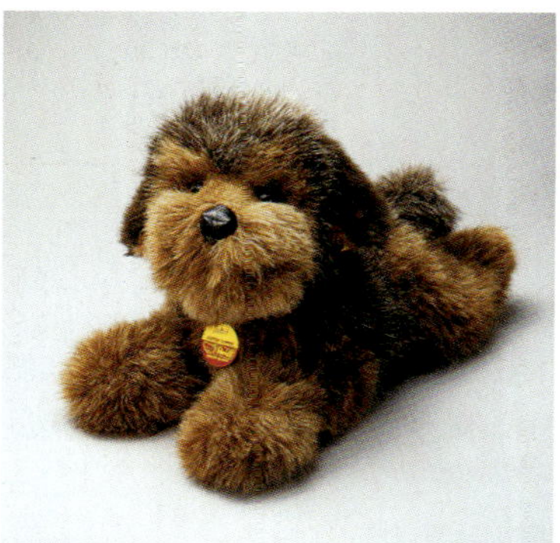

Junior Lumpi

Pelzimitation, ab 1978 Synthetik-Webpelz, liegend, abwaschbar - *imitation fur, from 1978 synthetic woven fur, lying, surface washable*

SERIE	ART.-NO	PERIOD	PR.	INFO
	2886/28	1976-1981	2	28 cm

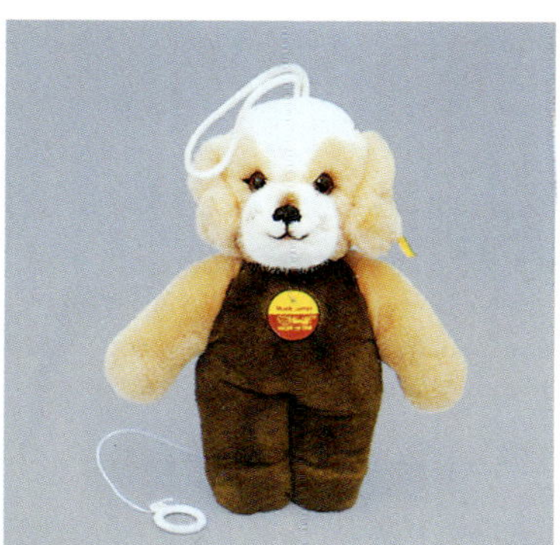

Musik Lumpi Hund - *Musical Lumpi Dog*

Webpelz, formgeschaeumt, Musikwerk austauschbar, waschbar - *woven fur, stuffed with pre-formed foam, music box may be exchanged, washable*

SERIE	ART.-NO	PERIOD	PR.	INFO
231209	**6352/26**	1986-1987	2	26 cm

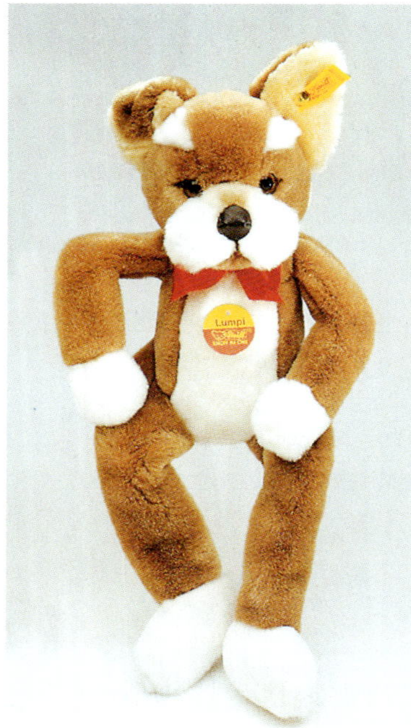

Lumpi Schlenker-Hund - ***Lumpi*** *Dangling Dog*

Webpelz, Pieps-Stimme, waschmaschinenfest - *woven fur, squeaker, machine washable*

SERIE	ART.-NO	PERIOD	PR.	INFO
123252	**6291/32**	1986-1988	2-3	32 cm

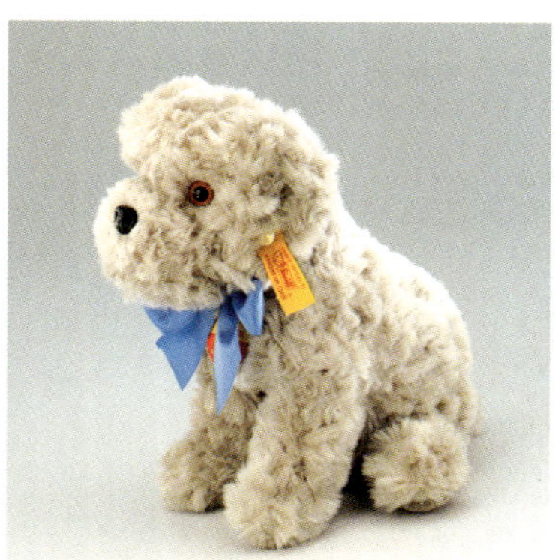

Lumpi Junghund - ***Lumpi*** *Puppy*

Webpelz, 20 cm, sitzend, waschmaschinenfest - *woven fur, 20 cm, sitting, machine washable*

EAN-NO.	PERIOD	PR.	INFO
078163	1997-1998	2	creme - *cream*
078170	1997-1998	2	grau - *grey*
078187	1997-1998	2	hellbraun - *light brown*

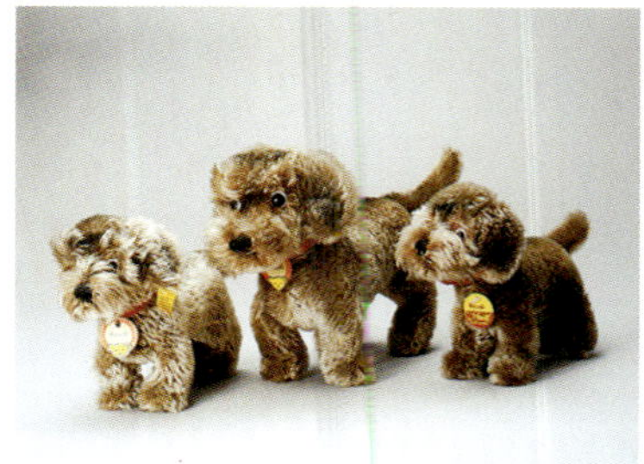

Rauhhaardackel **Raudi** - ***Raudi*** *Dachshund*

Mohair, grau/braun gespitzt, Halsband - *mohair, grey/brown light tipped, collar*

SERIE	ART.-NO	PERIOD	PR.	INFO
419	**1317,07** **4190/17**	1965-1967 1968-1978	3-4 3	17 cm
419	**1323,07** **4190/23**	1965-1967 1968-1978	3-4 3	23 cm

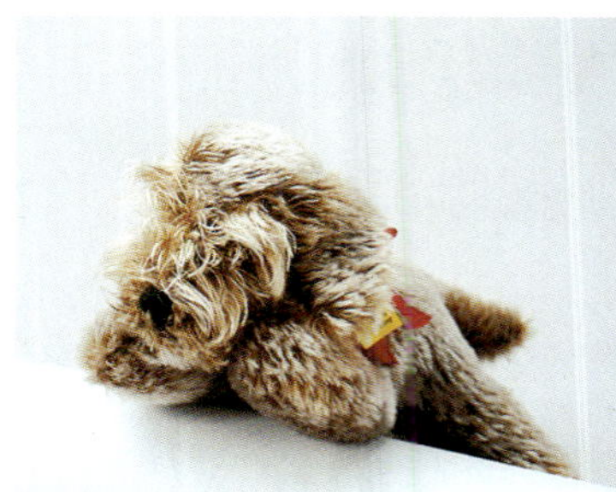

Floppy Raudi

Mohair, formgeschaeumt, Augen gestickt, liegend, Schlaftier, sehr weich, vollwaschbar - *mohair, stuffed with pre-formed foam, eyes embroidered, lying, sleeping toy, very soft, fully washable*

SERIE	ART.-NO	PERIOD	PR.	INFO
	5637/17	1970-1977	2	17 cm
	5637/28	1970-1977	2	28 cm

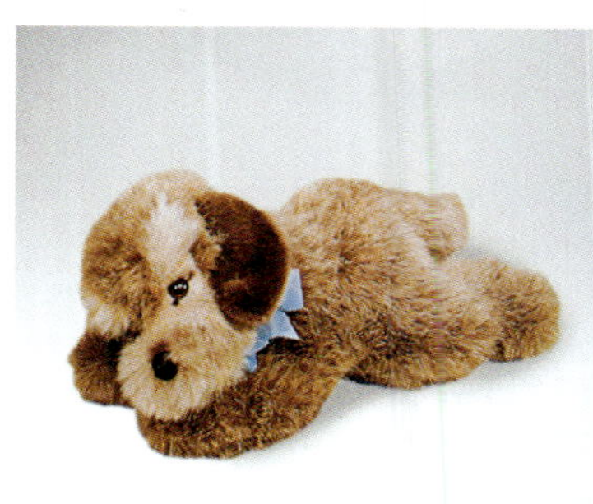

Floppy Raudi

Synthetik-Webpelz, formgeschaeumt, liegend, vollwaschbar - *synthetic woven fur, stuffed with pre-formed foam, lying, fully washable*

SERIE	ART.-NO	PERIOD	PR.	INFO
	5717/20	1978-1981	1-2	20 cm
	5717/30	1978-1981	2	30 cm

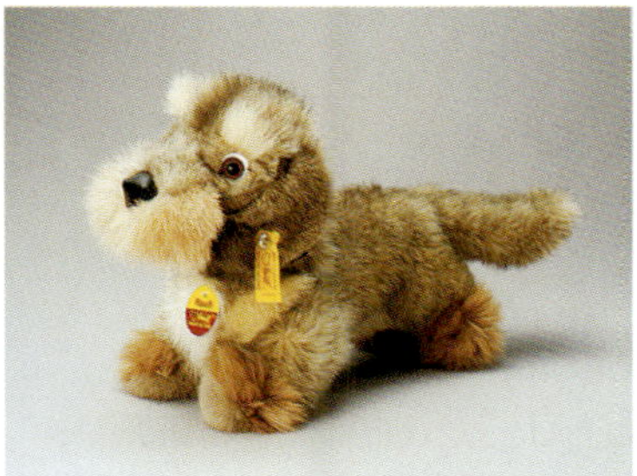

Raudi Dachshund

Webpelz, sandgrau, stehend, abwaschbar - *woven fur, sandy grey, standing, surface washable*

SERIE	ART.-NO	PERIOD	PR.	INFO
078606	**4150/25**	1986-1990	2-3	25 cm
	078606	1991-1996	2-3	
078620	**4150/40**	1986-1990	3	40 cm
	078620	1991-1991	3	

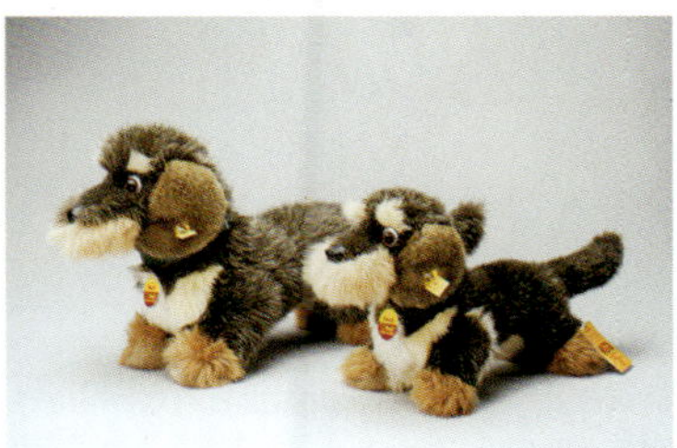

Raudi Dachshund

Webpelz, graubraun, stehend, abwaschbar - *woven fur, grey-brown, standing, surface washable*

SERIE	ART.-NO	PERIOD	PR.	INFO
078651	**4151/25**	1986-1990	3	25 cm
	078651	1991-1999	3	
078675	**4151/40**	1986-1990	3	40 cm
	078675	1991-1996	3	

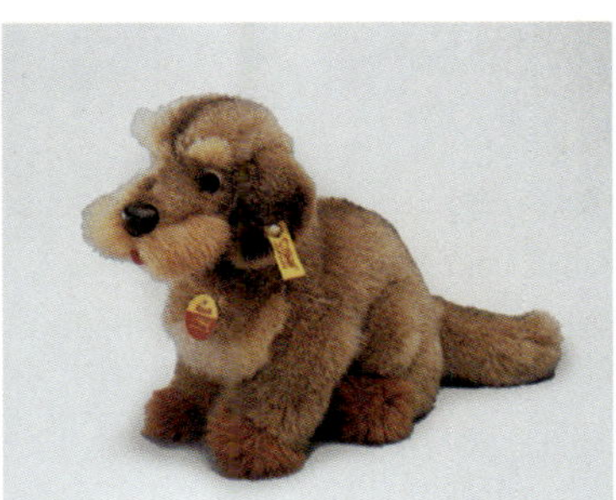

Raudi Dachshund

Webpelz, sandgrau, Halsband, sitzend - *woven fur, sandy grey, collar, sitting*

SERIE	ART.-NO	PERIOD	PR.	INFO
078705	**4152/25**	1990-1990	2-3	25 cm
	078705	1991-1993	2-3	

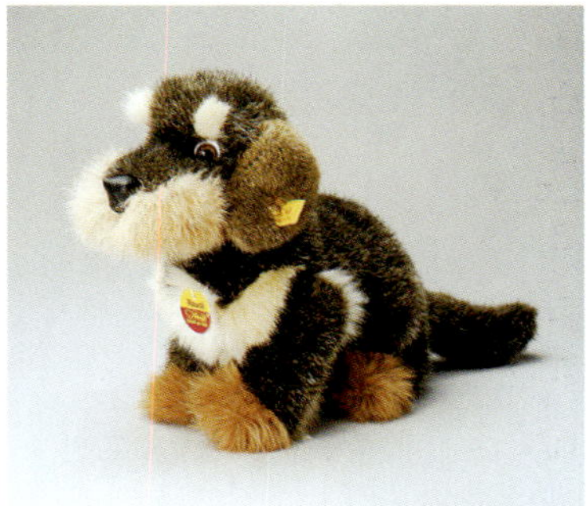

Raudi Dachshund

Webpelz, graubraun, Halsband, sitzend - *woven fur, grey/brown, collar, sitting*

SERIE	ART.-NO	PERIOD	PR.	INFO
078750	**4153/25**	1990-1990	2-3	25 cm
	078750	1991-1995	2-3	

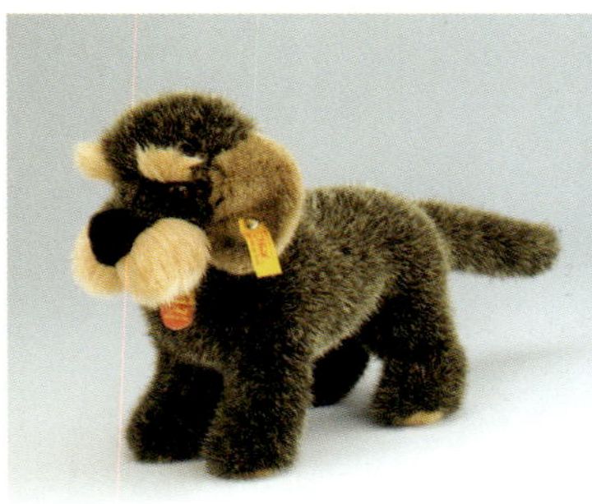

Bobby Hund - *Bobby Dog*

Webpelz, grau/braun, stehend, Lederhalsband, ohne Halsband waschmaschinenfest - *woven fur, grey/brown, standing, leather collar, machine washable without collar*

EAN-NO.	PERIOD	PR.	INFO
078682	1997-1997	2-3	28 cm

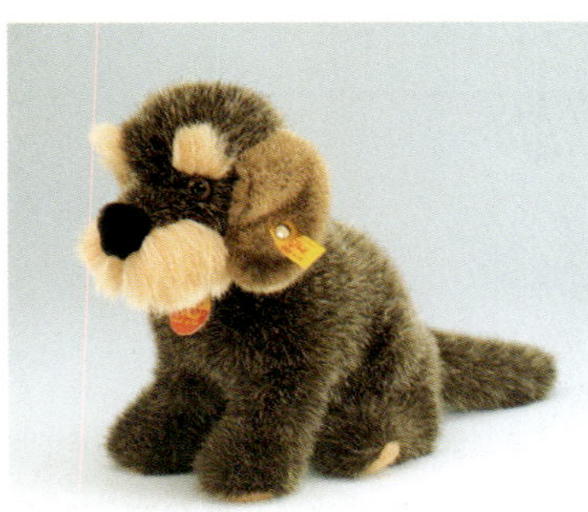

Bobby Hund - *Bobby Dog*

Webpelz, grau/braun, sitzend, Lederhalsband, ohne Halsband waschmaschinenfest - *woven fur, grey/brown, sitting, leather collar, machine washable without collar*

EAN-NO.	PERIOD	PR.	INFO
078699	1997-1997	2-3	25 cm

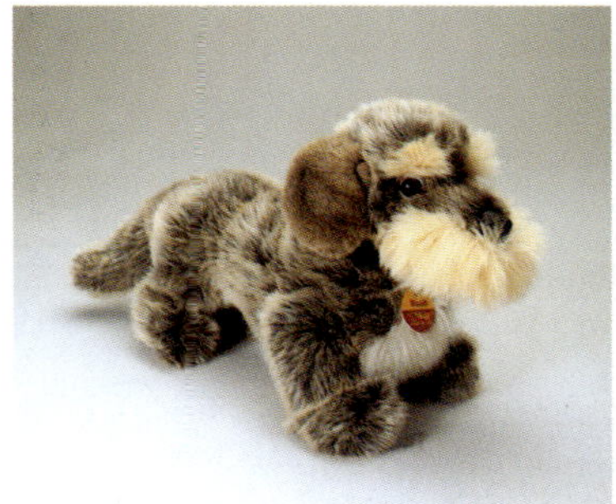

Raudi Rauhhaardackel - ***Raudi** Dachshund*

Webpelz, grau/braun, stehend, Lederhalsband, ohne Halsband handwaschbar - *woven fur, grey/brown, standing, leather collar, hand washable without collar*

EAN-NO.	PERIOD	PR.	INFO
078590	1998-1999	3	28 cm

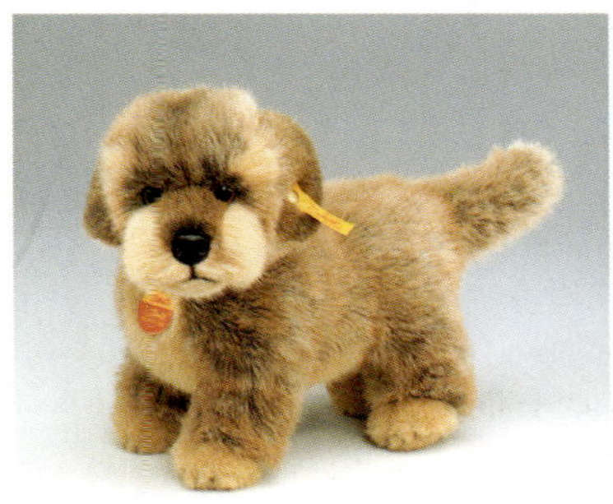

Raudi Rauhhaardackel - ***Raudi** Dachshund*

Webpelz beige/braun, stehend, waschmaschinenfest - *woven fur, beige/brown, standing, machine washable*

EAN-NO.	PERIOD	PR.	INFO
080791	1999-1999	2-3	25 cm

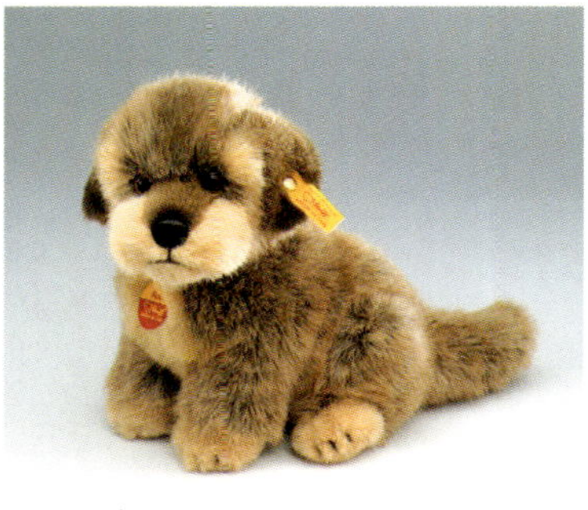

Raudi Rauhhaardackel - ***Raudi*** *Dachshund*

Webpelz, beige/braun, sitzend, waschmaschinenfest - *woven fur, beige/brown, sitting, machine washable*

EAN-No.	Period	Pr.	Info
080807	1999-1999	2-3	22 cm

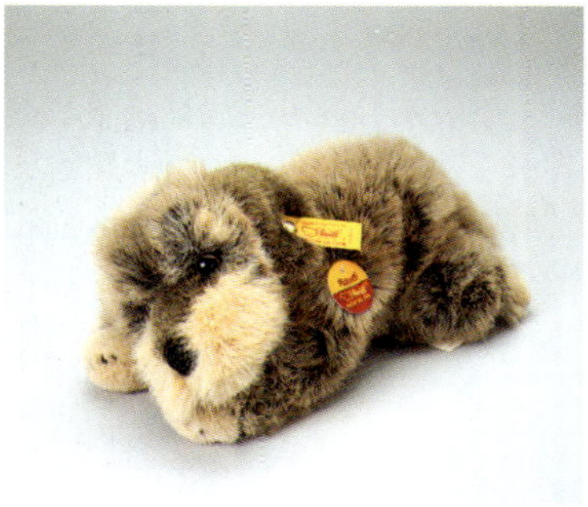

Raudi Rauhhaardackel - ***Raudi*** *Dachshund*

Webpelz, beige/braun, liegend, waschmaschinenfest - *woven fur, beige/brown, lying, machine washable*

EAN-No.	Period	Pr.	Info
080814	1999-1999	2-3	28 cm

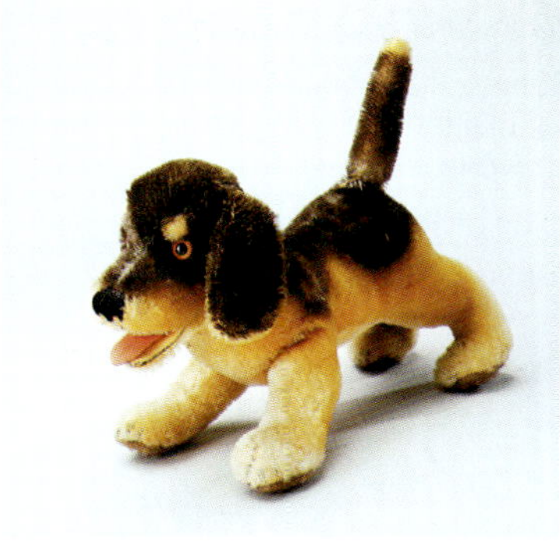

Hoppeldackel ohne Wagen - *Jumping Dog without Wagon*

Mohair, braun/schwarz, Pfoten mit Klettenplatten, stehend, Cosy Tier - *mohair, brown/black, paws have velcro surface, standing, cozy animal*

Serie	Art.-No	Period	Pr.	Info
575	**1328,00**	1967-1967	3-4	28 cm
	5750/28	1968-1970	3-4	

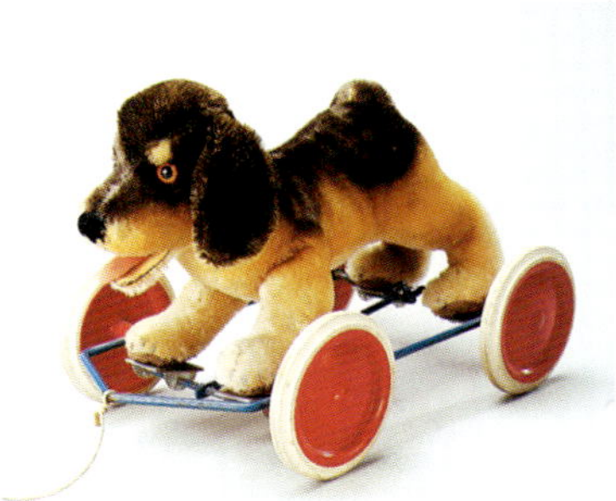

Hoppeldackel mit Wagen - *Jumping Dog with Wagon*

Mohair, braun/schwarz, Pfoten mit Klettenplatten, vom Fahrgestell abnehmbar - *mohair, brown/black, paws have velcro surface, can be removed from its frame*

Serie	Art.-No	Period	Pr.	Info
575	**1328,10**	1967-1967	4	33 cm
	5750/33	1968-1970	4	

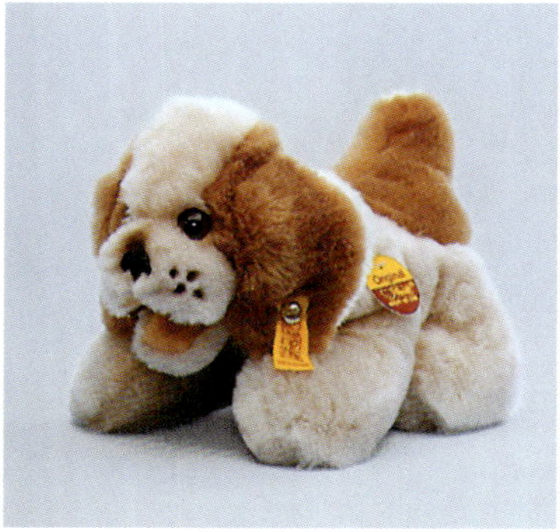

Kuschel Hund - ***Kuschel*** *Dog*

Webpelz, Schaumstoff-Fuellung, superweich, waschmaschinenfest - *woven fur, stuffed with foam, super soft, machine washable*

Serie	Art.-No	Period	Pr.	Info
099984	**5530/25**	1981-1987	2	25 cm

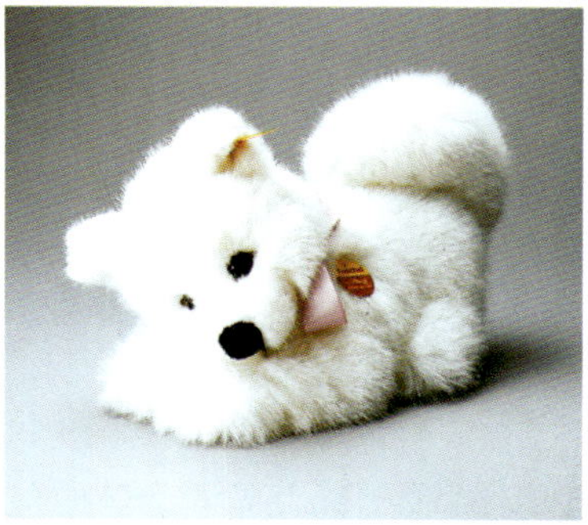

Kuschel Hund - ***Kuschel*** *Dog*

Webpelz, weiss, waschmaschinenfest - *woven fur, white, machine washable*

EAN-No.	Period	Pr.	Info
099878	1993-1994	2	30 cm

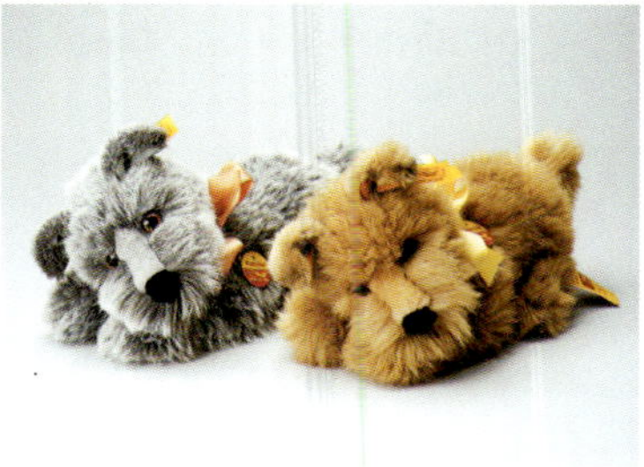

Kuschel Hund - ***Kuschel*** *Dog*

Webpelz, 30 cm, waschmaschinenfest - *woven fur, 30 cm, machine washable*

EAN-No.	Period	Pr.	Info
099885	1993-1995	2	braun - *brown*
099892	1993-1995	2	grau - *grey*

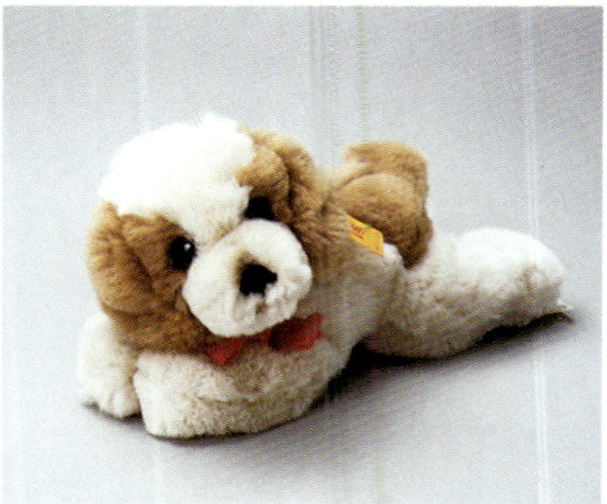

Floppy Hund - ***Floppy*** *Dog*

Webpelz, mollig weich, waschmaschinenfest - *woven fur, soft & cozy, machine washable*

Serie	Art.-No	Period	Pr.	Info
082306	**5610/18**	1983-1988	1-2	18 cm
082320	**5610/25**	1983-1988	1-2	25 cm

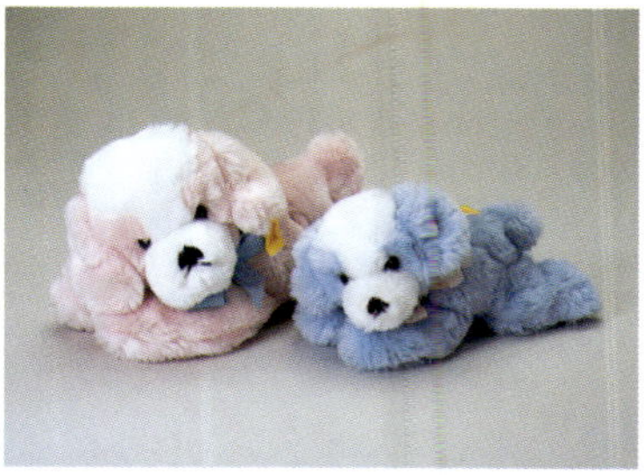

Baby Floppy Hund - *Baby Floppy Dog*

Webpelz, weich, waschmaschinenfest - *woven fur, soft, machine washable*

Serie	Art.-No	Period	Pr.	Info
	5660/18	1983-1985	1-2	18 cm, rosa - *pink*
	5660/25	1983-1985	1-2	25 cm

	5661/18	1983-1985	1-2	18 cm, blau - *blue*
	5661/25	1983-1985	1-2	25 cm

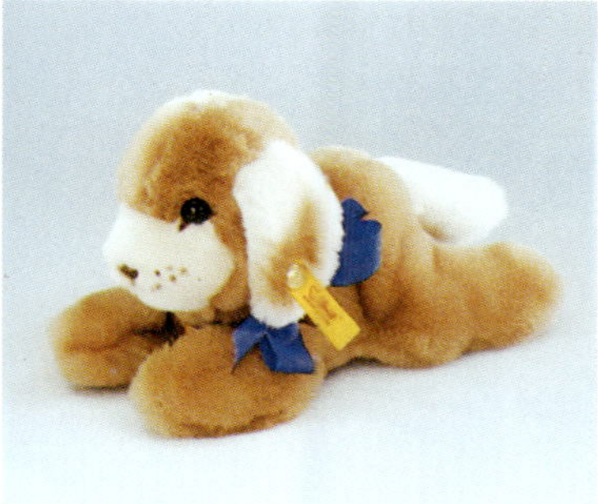

Mini Floppy Hund - ***Mini Floppy** Dog*

Webpelz, waschmaschinenfest - *woven fur, machine washable*

SERIE	ART.-NO	PERIOD	PR.	INFO
081941	**5662/16**	1989-1990	1-2	16 cm
	081941	1991-1991	1-2	

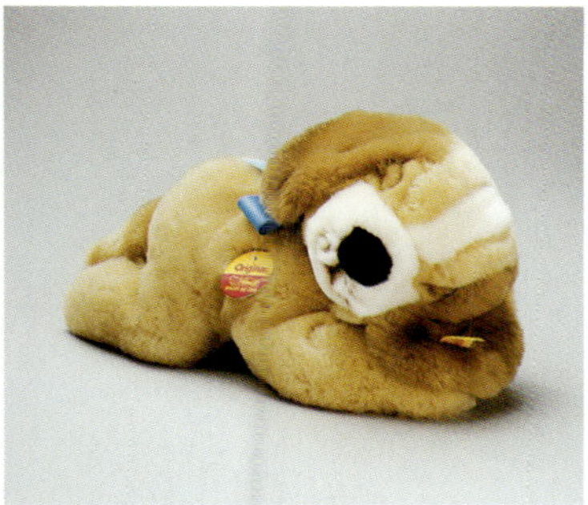

Schlafhund - *Bedtime Dog*

Webpelz, liegend, waschmaschinenfest - *woven fur, lying, machine washable*

EAN-NO.	PERIOD	PR.	INFO
082580	1991-1999	2	28 cm

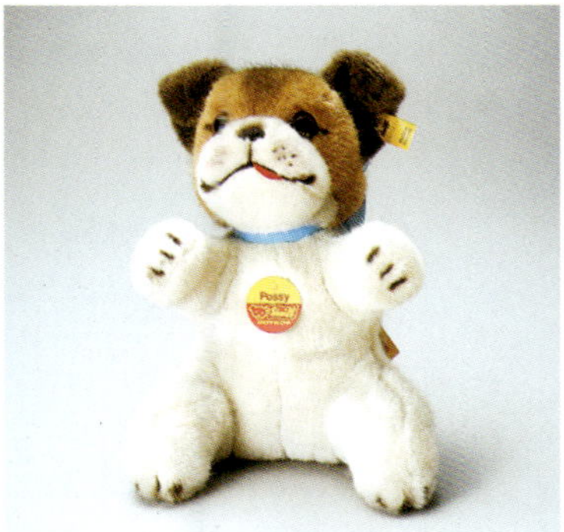

Possy Hund - ***Possy** Dog*

Webpelz, aufwartend, abwaschbar - *woven fur, sitting up, surface washable*

SERIE	ART.-NO	PERIOD	PR.	INFO
	5820/22	1980-1981	3	22 cm

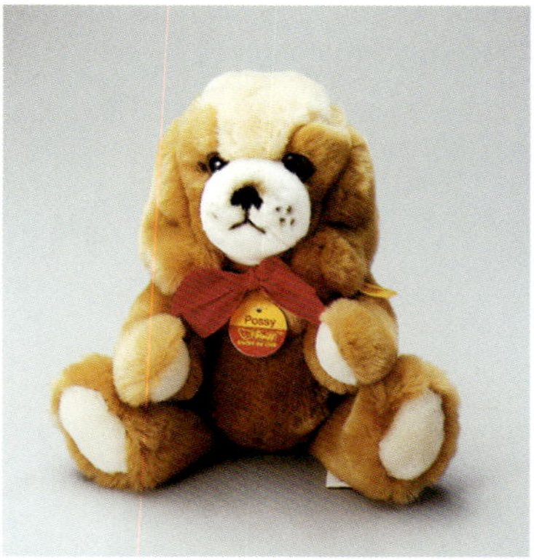

Possy Hund - ***Possy** Dog*

Webpelz, gegliedert, Pieps-Stimme, waschmaschinenfest - *woven fur, jointed, squeaker, machine washable*

SERIE	ART.-NO	PERIOD	PR.	INFO
081705	**6230/28**	1988-1989	2-3	28 cm

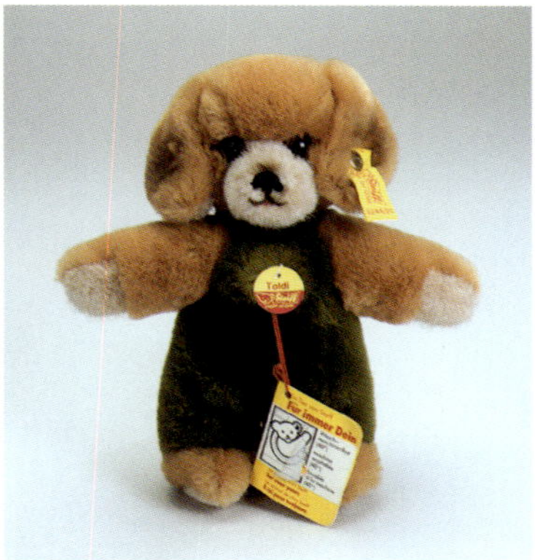

Toldi Hund - ***Toldi** Dog*

Webpelz, weich, waschmaschinenfest - *woven fur, soft, machine washable*

SERIE	ART.-NO	PERIOD	PR.	INFO
	6244/20	1982-1983	2	20 cm

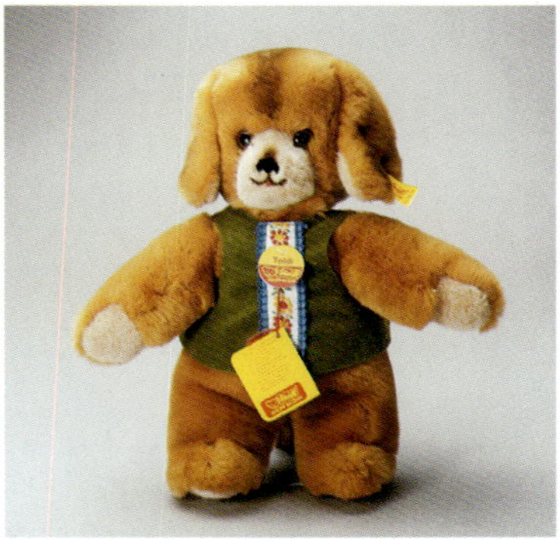

Toldi Hund - ***Toldi** Dog*

Webpelz, weich, mit Blouson, waschmaschinenfest - *woven fur, soft, vest, machine washable*

SERIE	ART.-NO	PERIOD	PR.	INFO
	6244/30	1982-1984	2	30 cm

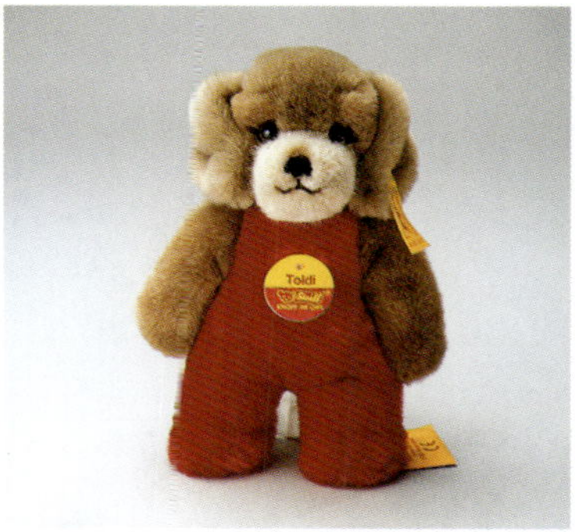

Toldi Hund - ***Toldi** Dog*

Webpelz, Pieps-Stimme, waschmaschinenfest - *woven fur, press voice, machine washable*

SERIE	ART.-NO	PERIOD	PR.	INFO
080401	**6253/22**	1984-1990	2	22 cm

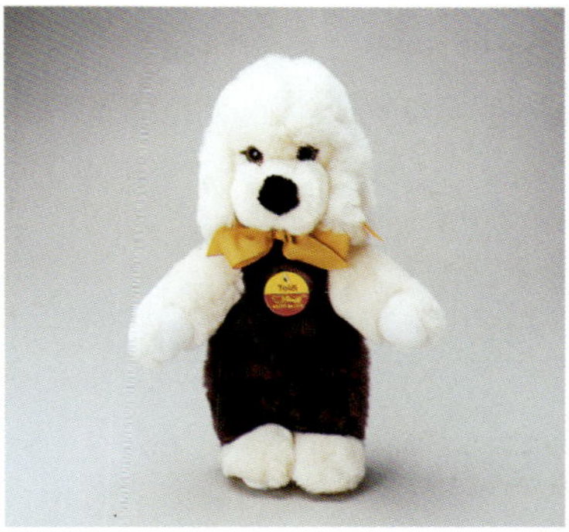

Toldi Hund - ***Toldi** Dog*

Webpelz Pieps-Stimme, waschmaschinenfest - *woven fur, press voice, machine washable*

SERIE	ART.-NO	PERIOD	PR.	INFO
081033	**6276/27**	1988-1989	2	27 cm

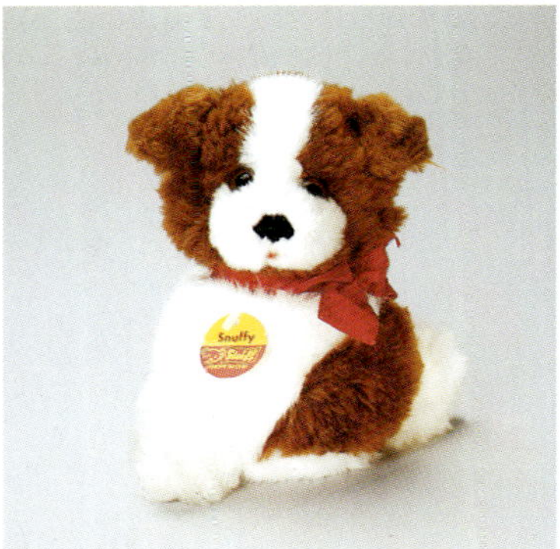

Snuffy Hund - ***Snuffy*** *Dog*

Pelz-Imitation, ab 1978 Synthetik-Webpelz, weiss/braun, sitzend, abwaschbar - *imitation fur, from 1978 synthetic woven fur, white/brown, sitting, surface washable*

SERIE	ART.-NO	PERIOD	PR.	INFO
	3525/14	1974-1977	1-2	14 cm
	3526/14	1978-1980	1-2	
	3525/18	1974-1977	2	18 cm
	3526/18	1978-1981	2	

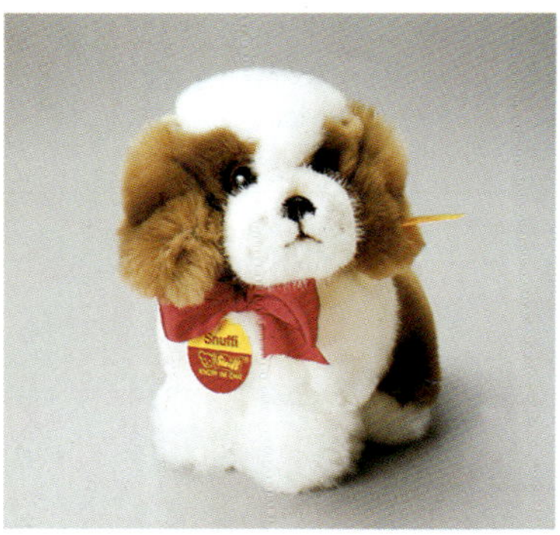

Snuffi Hund - ***Snuffi*** *Dog*

Webpelz, sitzend, waschmaschinenfest - *woven fur, sitting, machine washable*

SERIE	ART.-NO	PERIOD	PR.	INFO
077340	**2923/16**	1983-1990	2	16 cm
	077340	1991-1999	2	

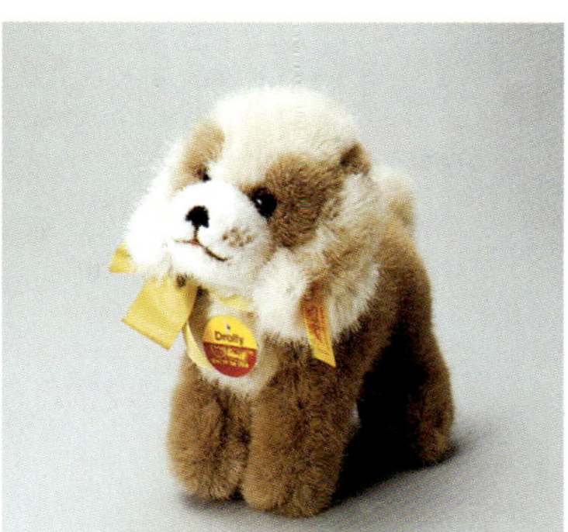

Drolly Hund - ***Drolly*** *Dog*

Webpelz, beige, stehend, waschmaschinenfest - *woven fur, beige, standing, machine washable*

SERIE	ART.-NO	PERIOD	PR.	INFO
081316	**5770/22**	1990-1990	2	22 cm
	081316	1991-1995	2	

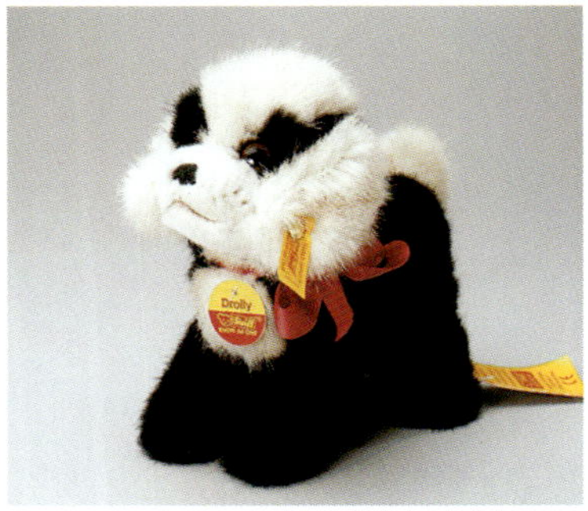

Drolly Hund - ***Drolly*** *Dog*

Webpelz, schwarz/beige, stehend, waschmaschinenfest - *woven fur, black/beige, standing, machine washable*

EAN-NO.	PERIOD	PR.	INFO
081323	1991-1993	2	22 cm

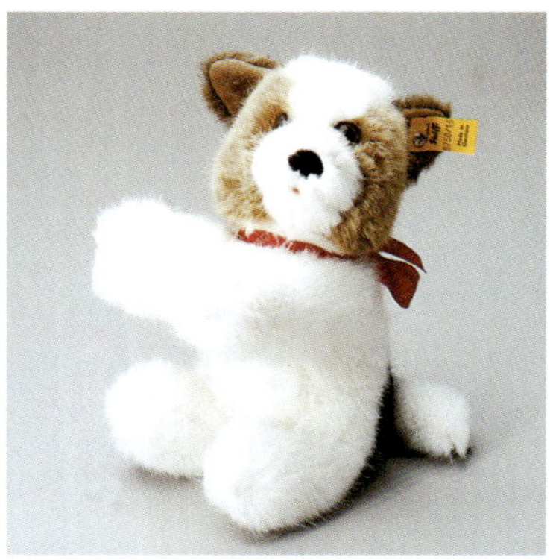

Baby Bello Hund - ***Baby Bello*** *Dog*

Pelzimitation, ab 1978 Synthetik-Webpelz, formgeschaeumt, vollwaschbar - *imitation fur, from1978 synthetic woven fur, stuffed with pre-formed foam, fully washable*

SERIE	ART.-NO	PERIOD	PR.	INFO
	5750/16	1977-1979	2-3	16 cm

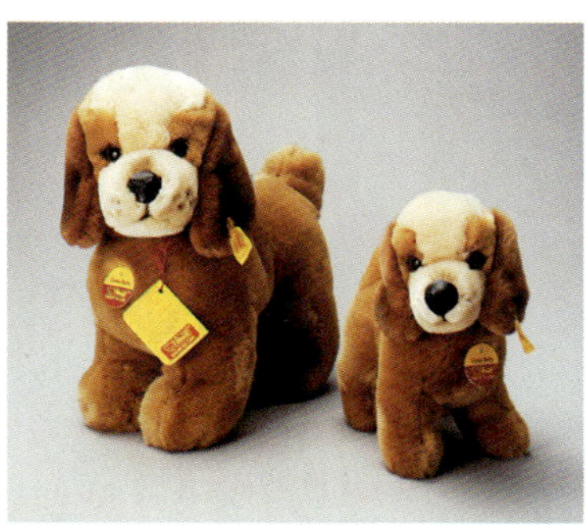

Cosy Bello Hund - ***Cosy Bello*** *Dog*

Webpelz, weich, waschmaschinenfest - *woven fur, soft, machine washable*

SERIE	ART.-NO	PERIOD	PR.	INFO
096549	**5457/27**	1984-1986	2	27 cm
096525	**5457/20**	1986-1988	2	20 cm

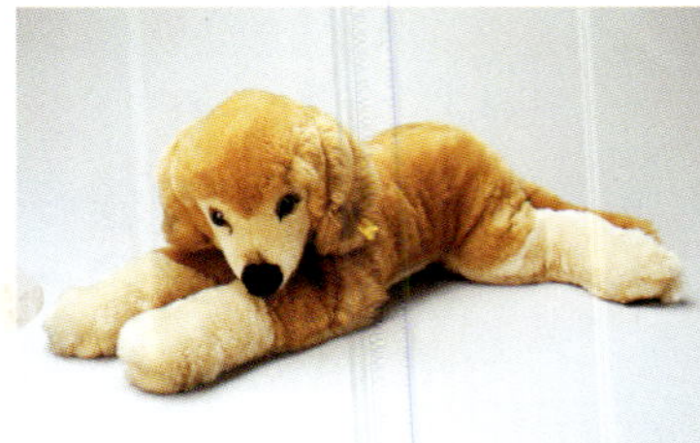

Molly Bello

Webpelz, abwaschbar - *woven fur, surface washable*

SERIE	ART.-NO	PERIOD	PR.	INFO
102653	**0343/50**	1987-1987	3	50 cm

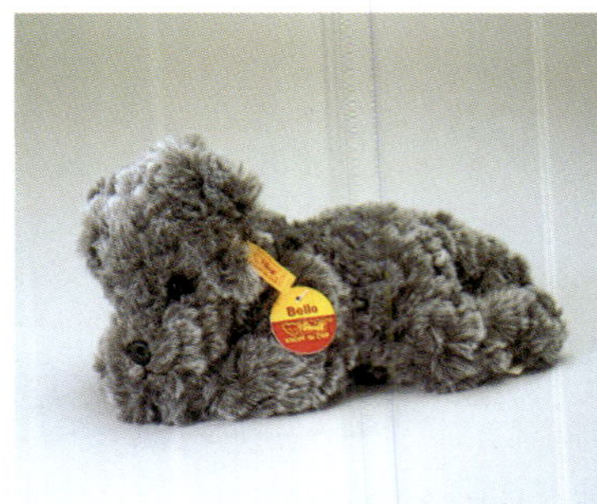

Bello Hund - ***Bello*** *Dog*

Webpelz, grau, waschmaschinenfest - *woven fur, grey, machine washable*

EAN-NO.	PERIOD	PR.	INFO
082313	1997-1998	2	22 cm

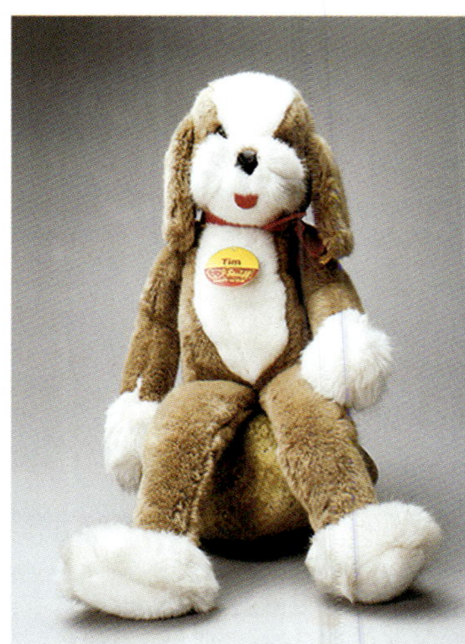

Tim Schlenkerhund - ***Tim*** *Dangling Dog*

Webpelz, Schlenkerglieder, abwaschbar - *woven fur, floppy joints, surface washable*

SERIE	ART.-NO	PERIOD	PR.	INFO
	6284/60	1978-1981	3	60 cm

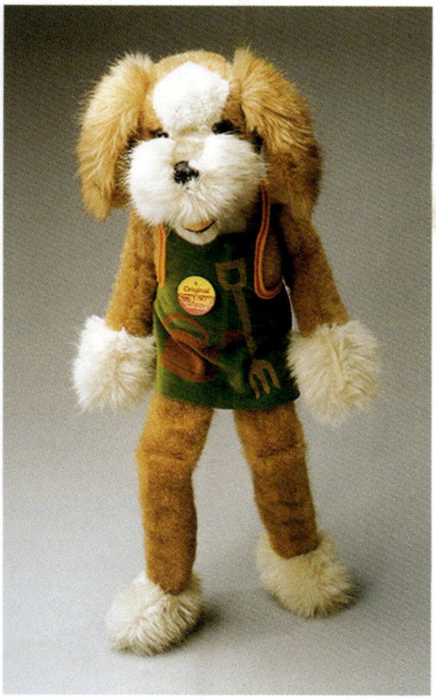

Schlenkerhund - *Dangling Dog*

Webpelz, gruene Schuerze, Schlenkerglieder, abwaschbar - *woven fur, green apron, floppy joints, surface washable*

SERIE	ART.-NO	PERIOD	PR.	INFO
	6287/50	1981-1985	3	50 cm

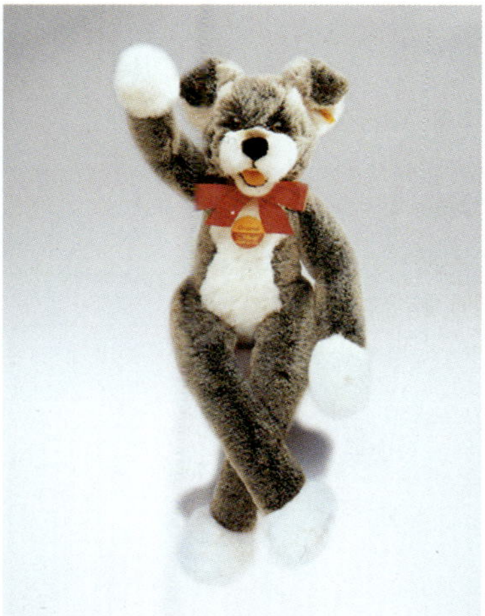

Schlenkerhund - *Dangling Dog*

Webpelz, grau, abwaschbar - *woven fur, grey, surface washable*

SERIE	ART.-NO	PERIOD	PR.	INFO
122224	**6287/70**	1990-1990	3	70 cm
	122224	1991-1992	3	
122262	**6287/99**	1990-1990	3	100 cm
	122262	1991-1992	3	

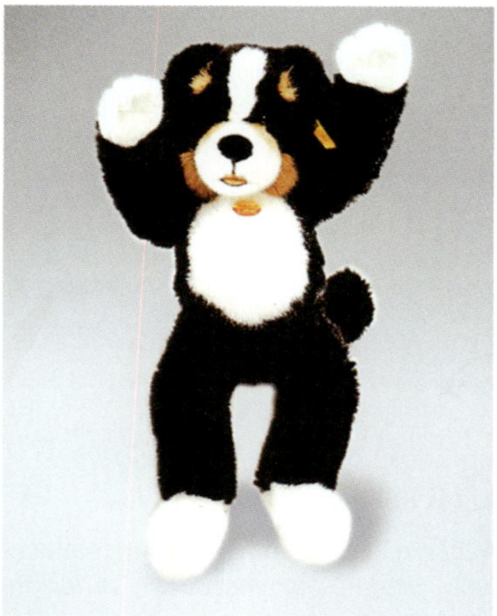

Schlenkerhund - *Dangling Dog*

Webpelz, waschmaschinenfest - *woven fur, machine washable*

EAN-NO.	PERIOD	PR.	INFO
123535	1993-1994	3	50 cm

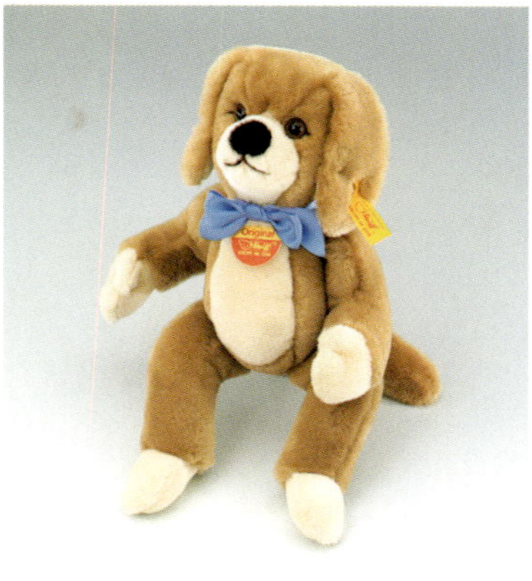

Schlenker Hund - *Dangling Dog*

Webpelz, waschmaschinenfest - *woven fur, machine washable*

EAN-NO.	PERIOD	PR.	INFO
122217	1997-1998	2-3	22 cm

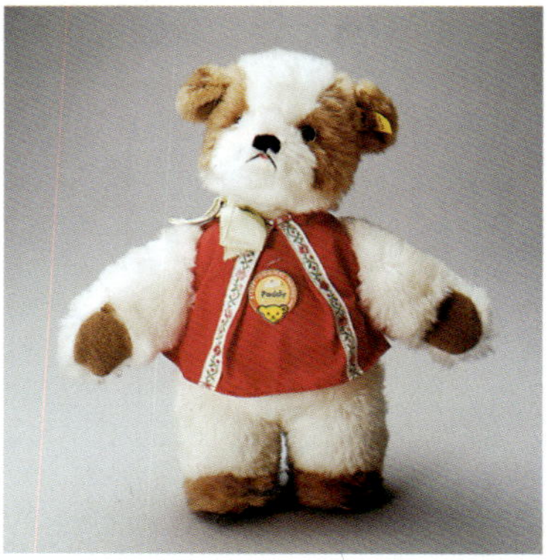

Weich-Hund **Paddy** - *Soft Dog* ***Paddy***

Dralon, formgeschaeumt, rote Weste, sehr weich, vollwaschbar - *dralon, stuffed with pre-formed foam, red vest, very soft, fully washable*

SERIE	ART.-NO	PERIOD	PR.	INFO
	6250/30	1970-1977	2-3	30 cm
	6250/40	1970-1975	2-3	40 cm

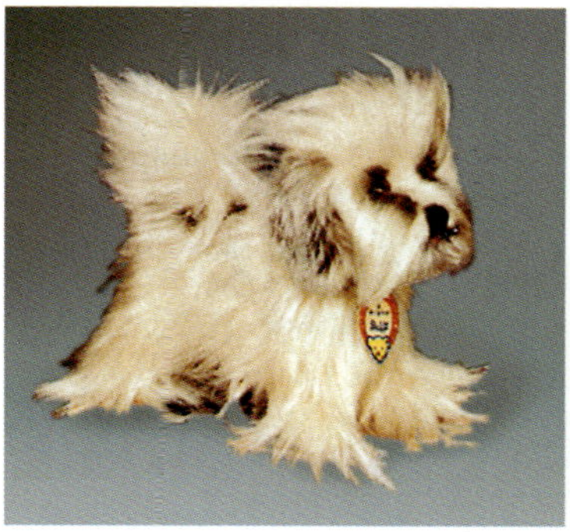

Hund Theophil - *Dog Theophil*

"Der kleine Tierversand", im Kaefigkarton, mit Tiersteckbrief, Dralon, stehend, abwaschbar - *"Der kleine Tierversand", packed in small cardboard dog crate, with animal information label, dralon, standing, surface washable*

SERIE	ART.-NO	PERIOD	PR.	INFO
	5840/15	1971-1974	3	15 cm

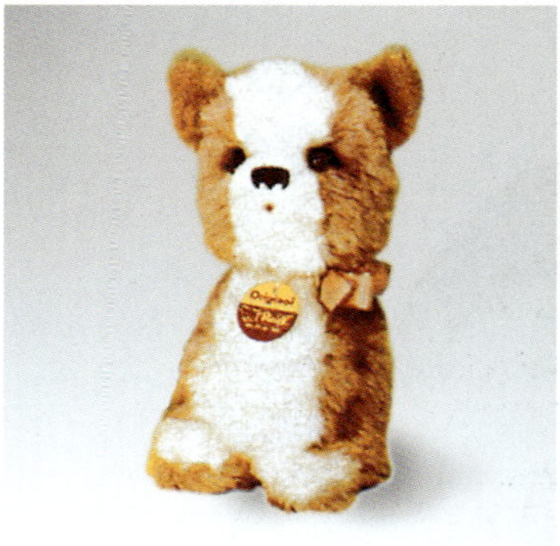

Buzzel Hund - *Buzzel Dog*

Dralon, formgeschaeumt, superweich, vollwaschbar - *dralon, stuffed with pre-formed foam, super soft, fully washable*

SERIE	ART.-NO	PERIOD	PR.	INFO
	6170/20	1971-1975	2	28 cm

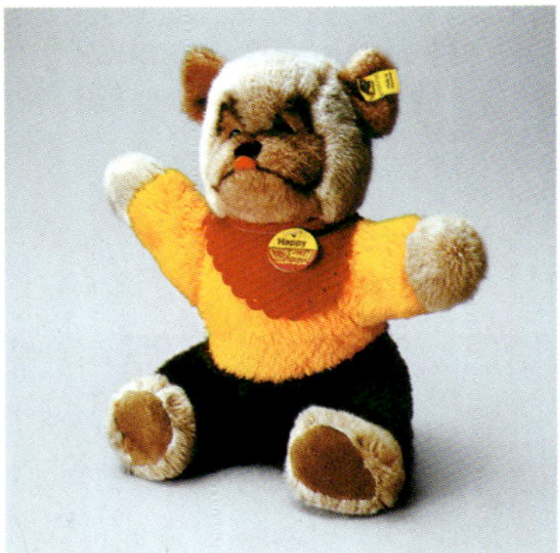

Happy Hund - ***Happy*** *Dog*

Pelzimitation, ab 1978 Dralon, formgeschaeumt, rotes Laetzchen, sitzend, vollwaschbar - *imitation fur, from 1978 dralon, stuffed with pre-formed foam, red bib, sitting, fully washable*

SERIE	ART.-NO	PERIOD	PR.	INFO
	6127/35	1975-1979	2-3	35 cm

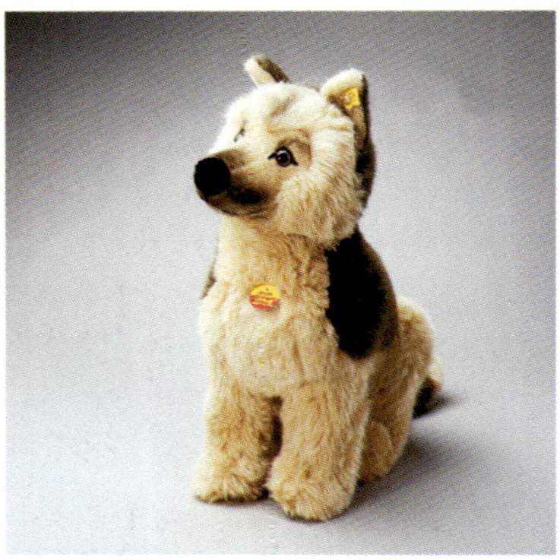

Wolfi Hund - ***Wolfi*** *Dog*

Webpelz, sitzend, abwaschbar - *woven fur, sitting, surface washable*

SERIE	ART.-NO	PERIOD	PR.	INFO
078934	**4165/45**	1987-1988	2-3	45 cm

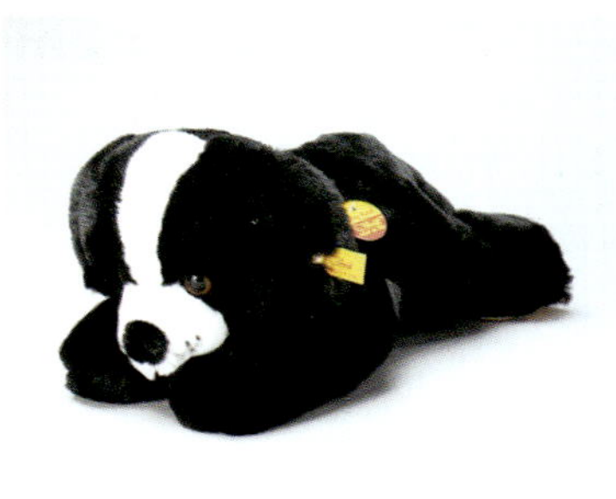

Cosy Hund - *Cosy Dog*

Webpelz, liegend, waschmaschinenfest - *woven fur, lying, machine washable*

SERIE	ART.-NO	PERIOD	PR.	INFO
088209	**5368/33**	1988-1990	2	33 cm

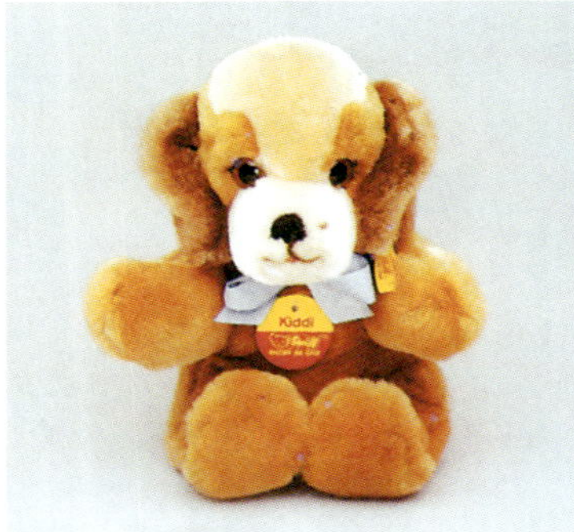

Kiddi Hund - ***Kiddi*** *Dog*

Webpelz, Pieps-Stimme, waschmaschinenfest - *woven fur, squeaker, machine washable*

SERIE	ART.-NO	PERIOD	PR.	INFO
082740	**5712/20**	1989-1990	2	20 cm
	082740	1991-1991	2	

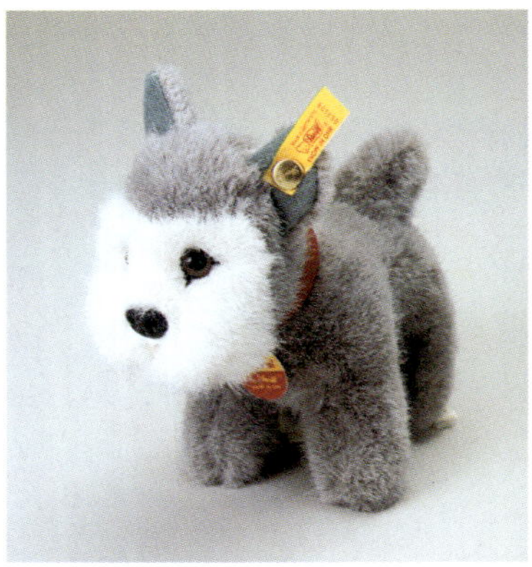

Hund - *Dog*

Webpelz, grau, stehend, Halsband, ohne Halsband waschmaschinenfest - *woven fur, grey, standing, collar, machine washable without collar*

EAN-NO.	PERIOD	PR.	INFO
053108	1996-1998	1-2	14 cm

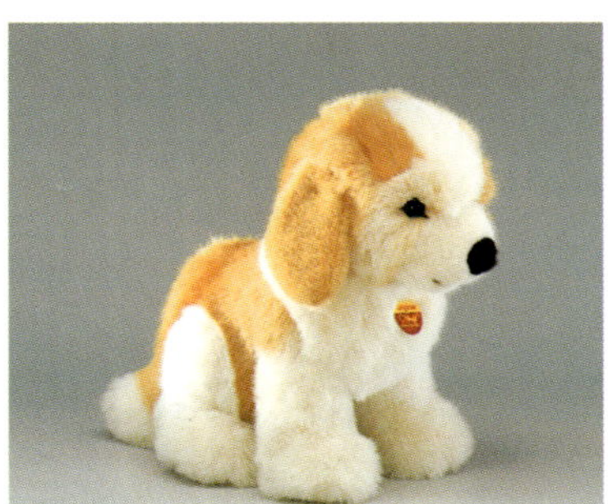

Junghund - *Puppy Dog*

Webpelz, hellbraun/weiss, sitzend, waschmaschinenfest - *woven fur, light brown/white, sitting, machine washable*

EAN-NO.	PERIOD	PR.	INFO
078132	1996-1996	2-3	25 cm

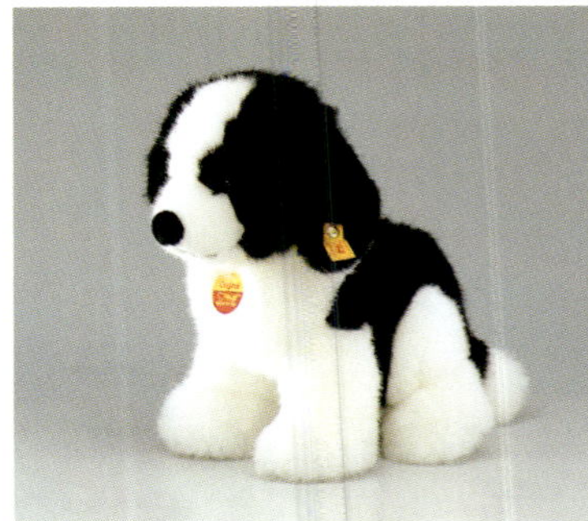

Junghund - *Puppy Dog*

Webpelz, schwarz/weiss, sitzend, waschmaschinenfest - *woven fur, black/white, sitting, machine washable*

EAN-NO.	PERIOD	PR.	INFO
078149	1996-1997	2-3	25 cm

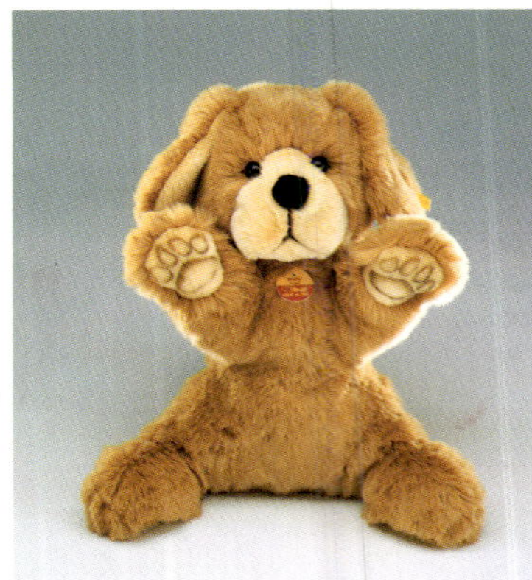

Molly Hund - *Molly Dog*

Webpelz, braun, abwaschbar - *woven fur, brown, surface washable*

EAN-NO.	PERIOD	PR.	INFO
106101	1996-1997	2-3	38 cm

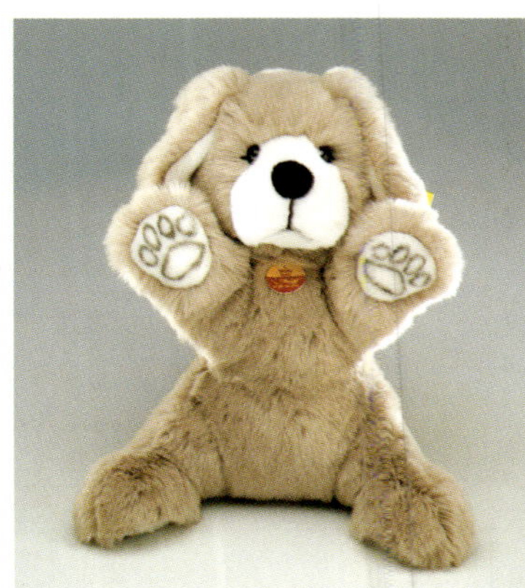

Molly Hund - *Molly Dog*

Webpelz, grau, abwaschbar - *woven fur, grey, surface washable*

EAN-No.	Period	Pr.	Info
106156	1996-1996	2-3	38 cm

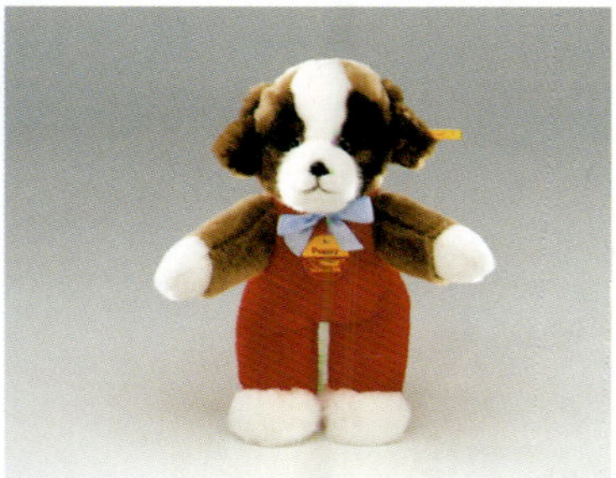

Puppy Hund - ***Puppy*** *Dog*

Webpelz, rot/braun, Pieps-Stimme, waschmaschinenfest - *woven fur, red/brown, squeaker, machine washable*

EAN-No.	Period	Pr.	Info
124808	1996-1997	2	28 cm

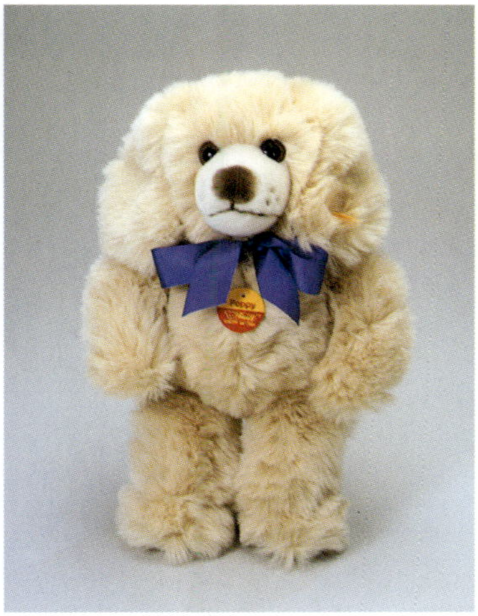

Poppy Hund - ***Poppy*** *Dog*

Webpelz, blond, waschmaschinenfest - *woven fur, blond, machine washable*

EAN-No.	Period	Pr.	Info
123269	1999-1999	2-3	30 cm

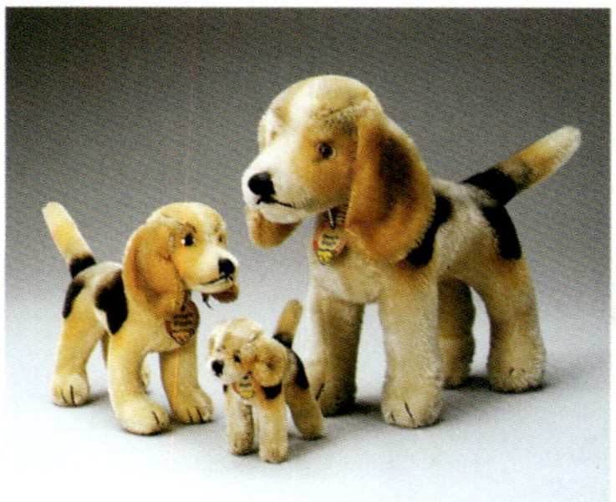

Biggie Beagle

Mohairpluesch, weiss/gold/grau, stehend, ab 17 cm mit Stimme - *mohair, white/gold/grey, standing, from 17 cm size press voice*

Serie	Art.-No	Period	Pr.	Info
23	**1310,0**	1958-1958	4	10 cm
230	**1310,00**	1959-1961	4	
23	**1317,0**	1958-1958	4	17 cm
230	**1317,00**	1959-1961	4	
23	**1325,0**	1958-1958	4-5	25 cm
230	**1325,00**	1959-1961	4-5	

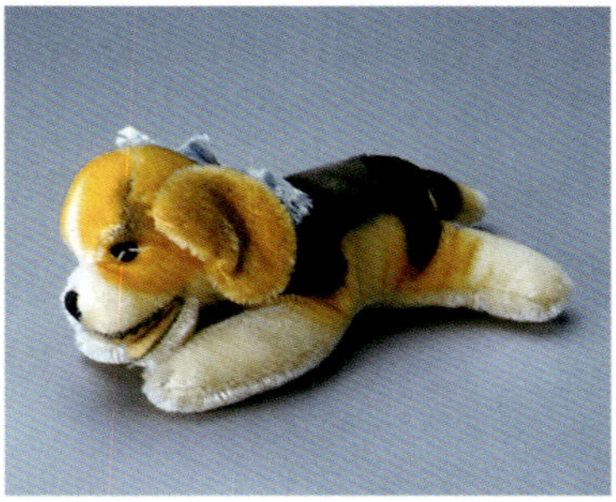

Floppy Biggie Beagle

Schlaftier, Mohair, Augen gestickt, weiss/schwarz/gold, liegend, sehr weich - *sleeping toy, mohair, eyes embroidered, white/black/gold, lying, very soft*

Serie	Art.-No	Period	Pr.	Info
850 230	**7317,00**	1959-1961	3-4	17 cm

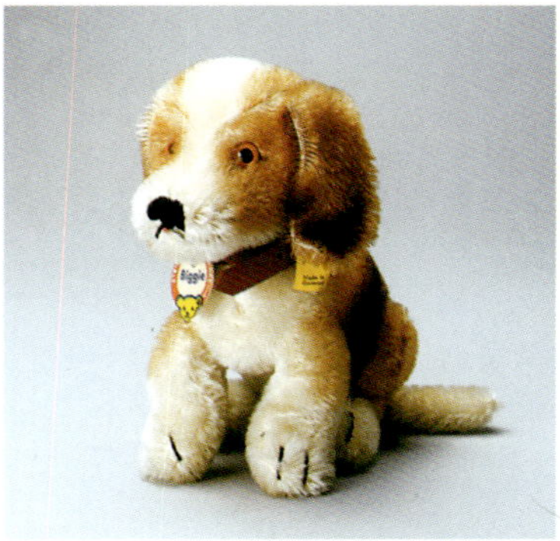

Biggie Beagle

Mohair, weiss, braun, sitzend, Drehkopf - *mohair, white, brown, sitting, head swivels*

Serie	Art.-No	Period	Pr.	Info
409	**3310,00**	1965-1967	3-4	10 cm
	4090/10	1968-1975	3	
409	**3318,00**	1965-1967	4	18 cm
	4090/18	1968-1975	3-4	

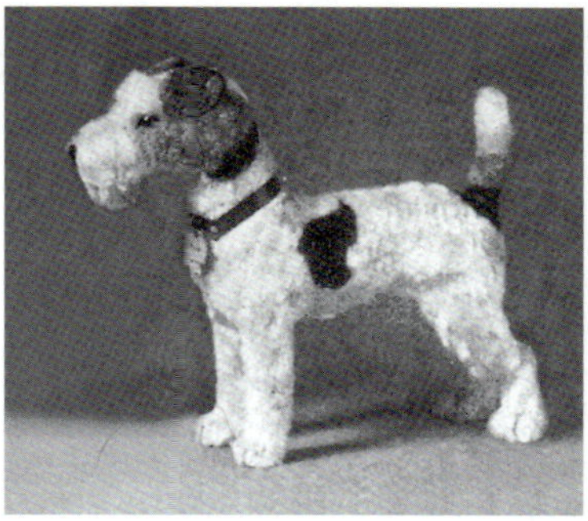

Foxterrier

Seidenpluesch, Halsband, weiss, schwarz/braun gefleckt, stehend ohne Raeder, Groesse 29 cm mit Stimme - *silk plush, collar, white, black/brown spotted, standing without wheels, size 29 cm voice*

Serie	Art.-No	Period	Pr.	Info
26	**1610,0**	1949-1949	4	10 cm
26	**1618,0**	1949-1949	4	18 cm
26	**1623,0**	1948-1949	4	23 cm
26	**1629,02**	1948-1949	4	29 cm

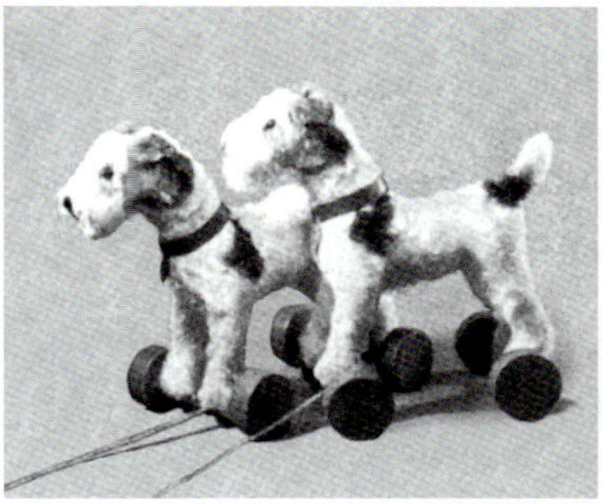

Foxterrier

Seidenpluesch, stehend auf Exzenterraedern - *silk plush, standing on eccentric wheels*

Serie	Art.-No	Period	Pr.	Info
26	**1618** ex	1949-1949	4-5	18 cm

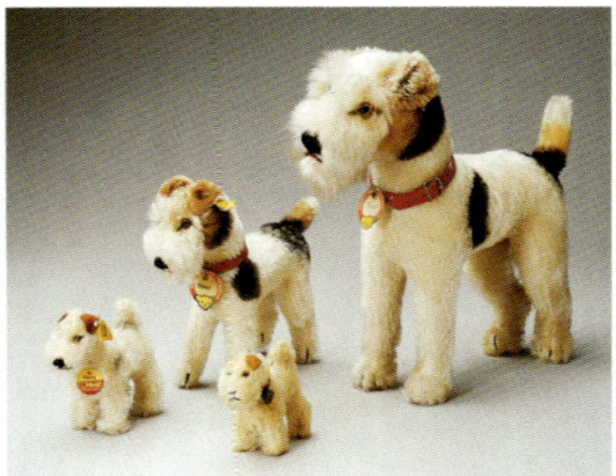

Fox ab 1954 **Foxy** Foxterrier - ***Fox*** *from 1954* ***Foxy*** *Foxterrier*

Mohairpluesch, weiss, schwarz/gelb gefleckt, stehend ohne Raeder, ab 22 cm mit Stimme - *mohair, white, black/yellow spotted, standing without wheels, voice from 22 cm*

SERIE	ART.-NO	PERIOD	PR.	INFO
26	**1307,0**	1949-1949	4	7 cm
26	**1308,0**	1950-1957	3-4	8 cm
260	**1308,04**	1959-1959	3-4	
26	**1310,0**	1949-1958	3-4	10 cm
260	**1310,00**	1959-1964	3	
422	**1310,00**	1965-1967	3	
	4220/10	1958-1975	2-3	
26	**1317,0**	1950-1957	4	17 cm
260	**1317,00**	1959-1962	3-4	
422	**1317,00**	1966-1967	3-4	
	4220/17	1968-1975	3	
26	**1318,0**	1949-1949	4-5	18 cm
26	**1322,0**	1950-1958	4	22 cm
260	**1322,00**	1959-1959	4	
26	**1323,02**	1949-1949	4-5	23 cm
26	**1328,02**	1950-1957	4	28 cm
260	**1328,00**	1959-1962	3-4	
422	**1328,00**	1966-1967	3-4	
	4220/28	1968-1974	3	
26	**1329,02**	1949-1949	4-5	29 cm
26	**1335,02**	1950-1958	4	35 cm
260	**1335,00**	1959-1962	3-4	
422	**1335,00**	1966-1966	3-4	
26	**1336,02**	1949-1949	4-5	36 cm

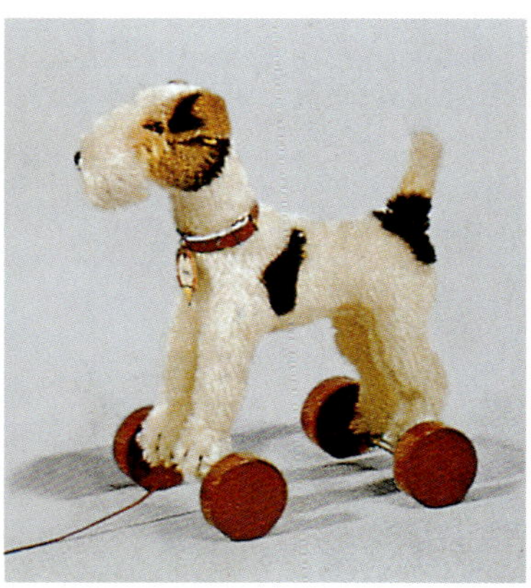

Foxy Foxterrier

Mohairpluesch, weiss, schwarz/gelb gefleckt, stehend auf Exzenterraedern - *mohair, white, black/yellow spotted, standing on eccentric wheels*

SERIE	ART.-NO	PERIOD	PR.	INFO
26	**1317** ex	1949-1957	4-5	17 cm
260	**1317,10**	1959-1961	4-5	
26	**1322** ex	1949-1957	4-5	22 cm
260	**1322,10**	1959-1959	4-5	

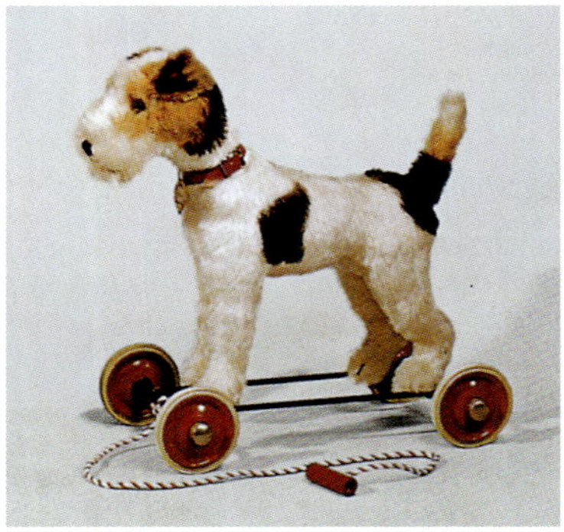

Foxy Foxterrier / Reit-**Foxy** - ***Foxy*** *Foxterrier / Riding* ***Foxy***

Mohair, Eisengerippe, weiss, schwarz/gelb gefleckt, stehend, auf Metallscheibenraedern mit Gummireifen, 28 & 35 cm Druckstimme, ab 43 cm Zugstimme - *mohair, iron frame, white, black/yellow spotted, standing on metal disc wheels with rubber tires, 28 & 35 cm press voice, from 43 cm pull cord voice*

SERIE	ART.-NO	PERIOD	PR.	INFO
26	**1328,2**	1950-1950	4-5	28 cm
26	**1328,1**	1951-1957	4-5	
260	**1328,10**	1961-1961	4-5	
26	**1335,2**	1950-1950	4-5	35 cm
26	**1335,1**	1951-1957	4-5	
260	**1335,10**	1961-1961	4-5	
26	**1343,2**	1949-1958	4-5	43 cm
260	**1343,20**	1961-1961	4-5	
423	**1343,20**	1966-1966	4-5	
26	**1350,2**	1949-1958	5	50 cm
260	**1350,20**	1961-1961	5	

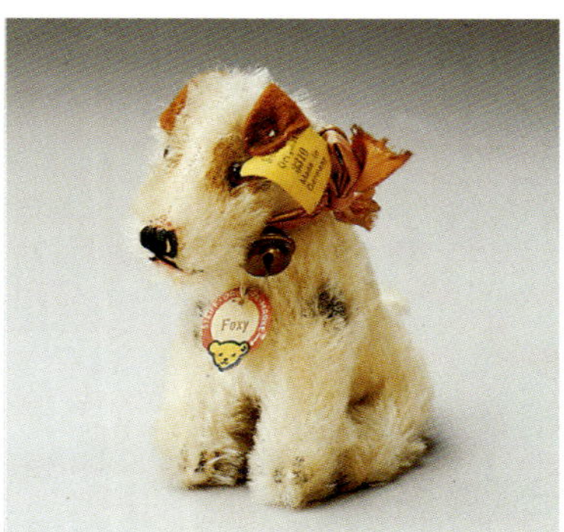

Foxy Foxterrier

Mohairpluesch, weiss, schwarz/gelb gefleckt, sitzend - *mohair, white, black/yellow spotted, sitting*

SERIE	ART.-NO	PERIOD	PR.	INFO
26	**3310**	1953-1954	5	10 cm
26	**3314**	1953-1955	5	14 cm
26	**3317**	1953-1955	5	17 cm

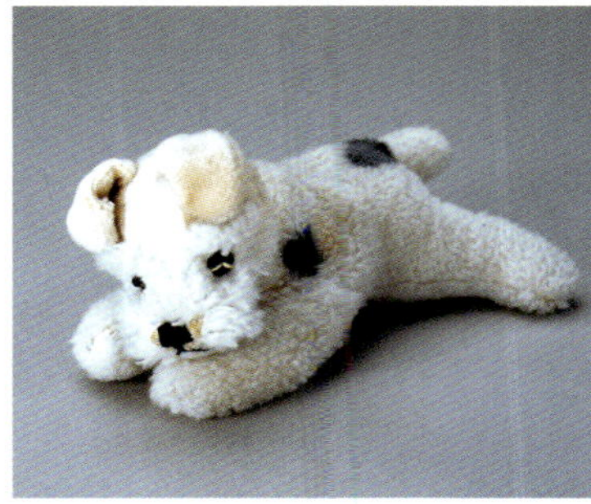

Cosy Foxy Foxterrier

Cosy Waschtier, Dralon-Pluesch, Schaumgummi Fuellung, weiss, braun/schwarz gefleckt, liegend, sehr weich, vollwaschbar - *cozy washable animal, dralon, stuffed with foam rubber, white, black/yellow spotted, lying, very soft, fully washable*

SERIE	ART.-NO	PERIOD	PR.	INFO
83 26	**7617**	1958-1958	3	17 cm
830 260	**7617,00**	1959-1963	3	

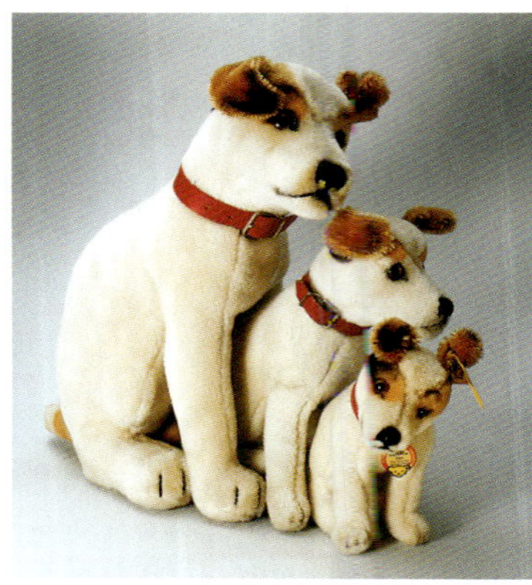

Elektrola Fox

Dralon, Ohren Mohair, rotes Halsband, sitzend, "die Stimme seines Herrn" - *dralon, mohair ears, sitting, red collar, "His master´s voice"*

SERIE	ART.-NO	PERIOD	PR.	INFO
	4420/12	1968-1974	6	12 cm
	4420/17	1968-1969	6	17 cm
	4420/25	1968-1970	6	25 cm
	4420/45	1968-1968	6-7	45 cm, Schautier - *display animal*

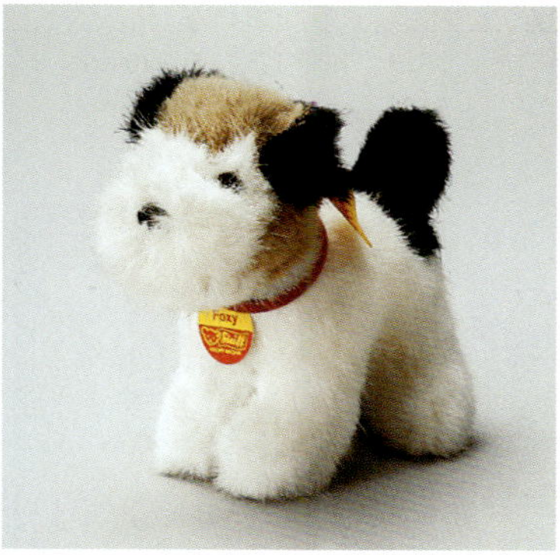

Foxy Terrier

Nerzimitation, ab 1978 Synthetik-Webpelz, weiss, schwarz/braun, stehend, abwaschbar - *imitation mink, from 1978 synthetic woven fur, white, black/brown, standing, surface washable*

SERIE	ART.-NO	PERIOD	PR.	INFO
	1528/11	1977-1985	2	11 cm

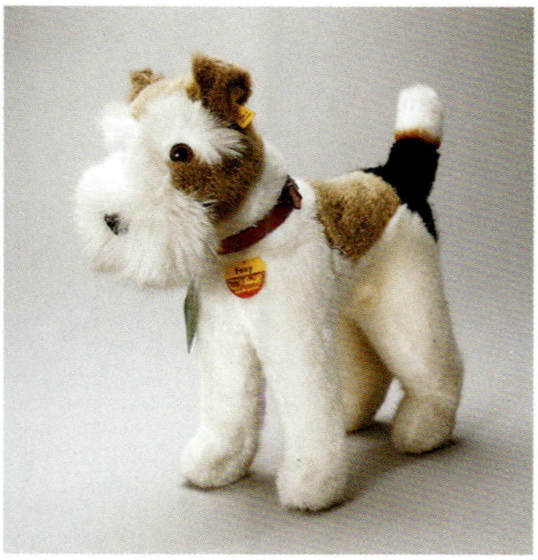

Foxy Terrier

Nerzimitation, ab 1978 Synthetik-Webpelz, weiss, schwarz/braun, stehend, abwaschbar - *imitation mink, from 1978 synthetic woven fur, white, black/brown, standing, surface washable*

SERIE	ART.-NO	PERIOD	PR.	INFO
	4215/21	1977-1981	2-3	21 cm
	4215/30	1977-1980	2-3	30 cm

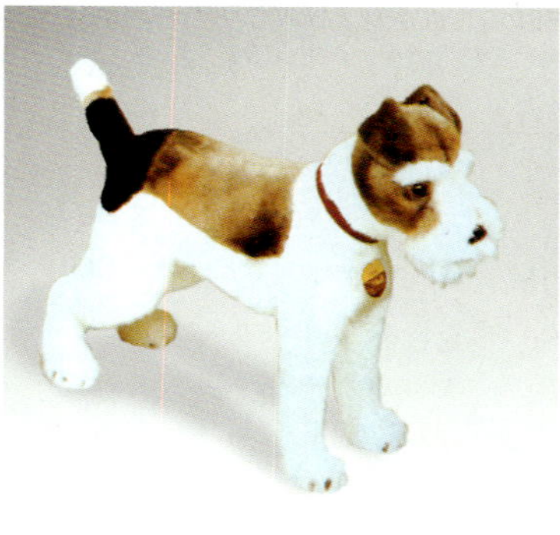

Foxy Terrier

Studio-Tier, Webpelz, stehend, abwaschbar - *studio animal, woven fur, standing, surface washable*

SERIE	ART.-NO	PERIOD	PR.	INFO
	4080/50	1978-1984	3	50 cm

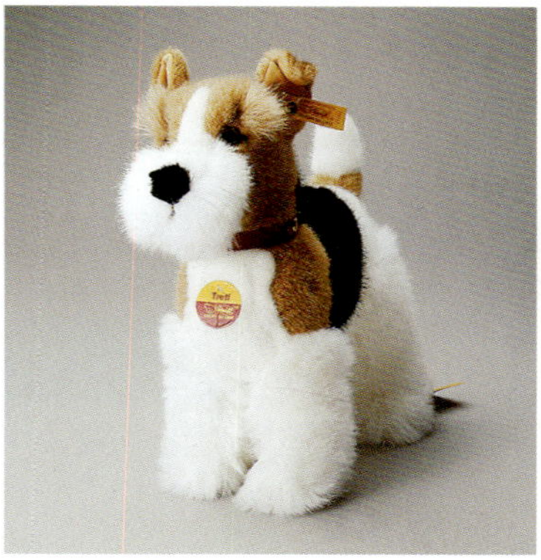

Treff Foxterrier

Webpelz, stehend, abwaschbar - *woven fur, standing, surface washable*

SERIE	ART.-NO	PERIOD	PR.	INFO
078552	**4140/30**	1988-1990	2-3	30 cm
	078552	1991-1996	2-3	

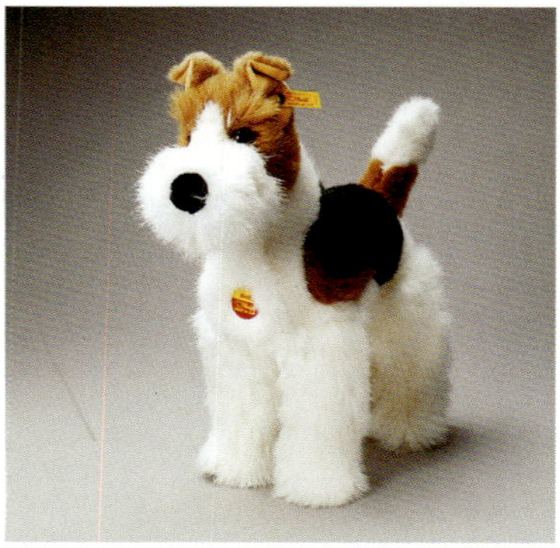

Bello Foxterrier ab 1996 **Yello** - ***Bello*** *Foxterrier from 1996* ***Yello***

Webpelz, stehend, abwaschbar - *woven fur, standing, surface washable*

EAN-NO.	PERIOD	PR.	INFO
078545	1995-1998	3	45 cm

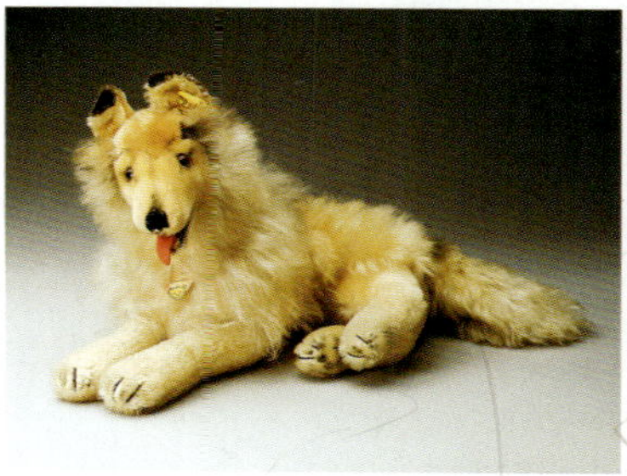

Collie

Mohair, Langhaar-Mohair-Maehne, braun/schwarz/weiss, rote Filzzunge, liegend - *mohair, with long mohair mane, brown/black/white, red felt tongue, lying*

SERIE	ART.-NO	PERIOD	PR.	INFO
270	**2325,00**	1960-1964	4	25 cm
425	**2325,00**	1965-1967	4	
	4250,25	1968-1975	3-4	
270	**2343,00**	1960-1964	4	43 cm
425	**2343,00**	1965-1967	4	
	4250/43	1968-1975	3-4	

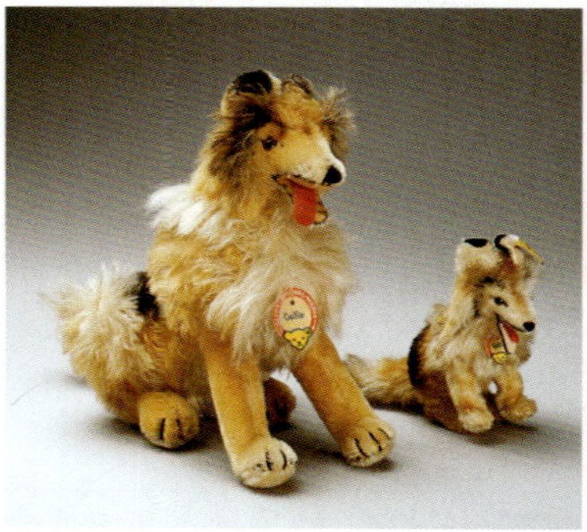

Collie

Mohair, Langhaar-Mohair-Maehne, braun/schwarz/weiss, rote Filzzunge, sitzend, 1960 nur in USA, ab 1962 mit veraenderter Artikel-Nummer weltweit - *mohair, with long mohair mane, brown/black/white, red felt tongue, sitting, 1960 only in USA, from 1962 with different art.no worldwide*

SERIE	ART.-NO	PERIOD	PR.	INFO
270	**3312,90**	1960-1960	4	12 cm
270	**3312,00**	1962-1963	4	
425	**3312,00**	1966-1967	4	
	4255/12	1968-1969	4	
270	**3322,90**	1960-1960	4	22 cm
270	**3322,00**	1962-1963	4	
425	**3322,00**	1966-1967	4	
	4255/22	1968-1969	4	

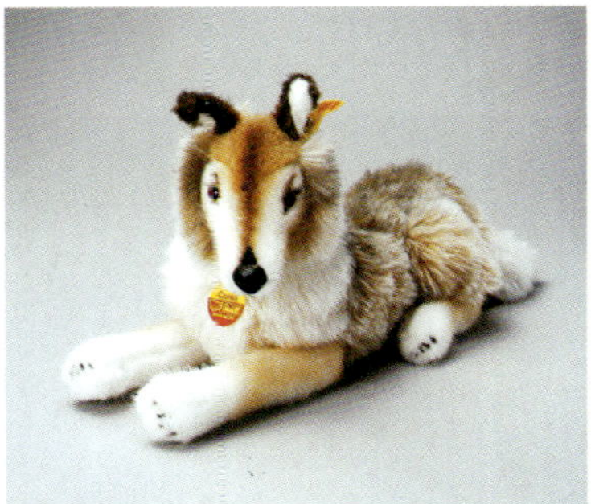

Corso Collie

Webpelz, abwaschbar - *woven fur, surface washable*

SERIE	ART.-NO	PERIOD	PR.	INFO
078309	**4090/40**	1983-1988	3	40 cm

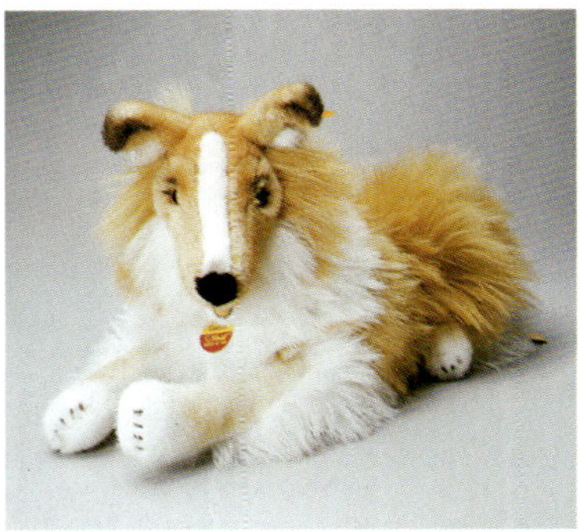

Corso Collie

Webpelz, blond/weiss, liegend, abwaschbar - *woven fur, blond/white, lying, surface washable*

EAN-NO.	PERIOD	PR.	INFO
079757	1992-1996	3-4	40 cm
079771	1992-1993	3-4	50 cm

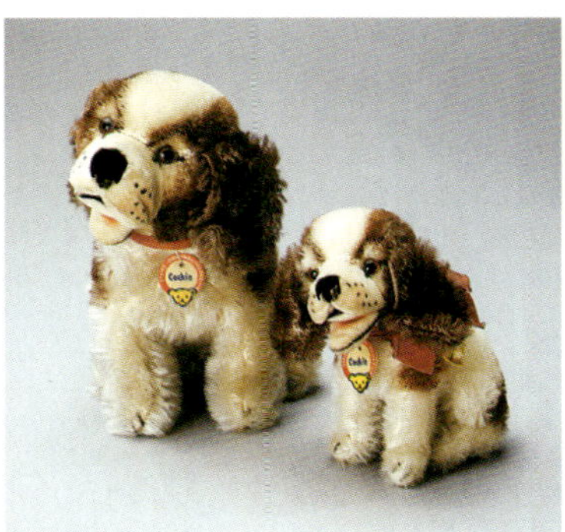

Cockie Cocker Spaniel

Mohair, weiss/braun, sitzend, Kopf drehbar, Samtschnauze, 1957er Modell (25 & 30 cm) Mohairschnauze - *mohair, white/brown, sitting, head swivels, velvet muzzle, 1957 model (25 & 30cm) have mohair muzzle*

SERIE	ART.-NO	PERIOD	PR.	INFO
29	**3310**	1951-1958	4	10 cm
290	**3310,00**	1959-1959	4	
29	**3314**	1951-1958	4	14 cm
290	**3314,00**	1959-1959	4	
29	**3317**	1951-1955	4	17 cm
29	**3322,2**	1951-1956	4-5	22 cm
29	**3325**	1957-1958	4-5	25 cm
290	**3325,00**	1959-1959	4-5	
29	**3328,2**	1951-1956	4-5	28 cm
29	**3330**	1957-1958	4-5	30 cm
290	**3330,00**	1959-1959	4-5	

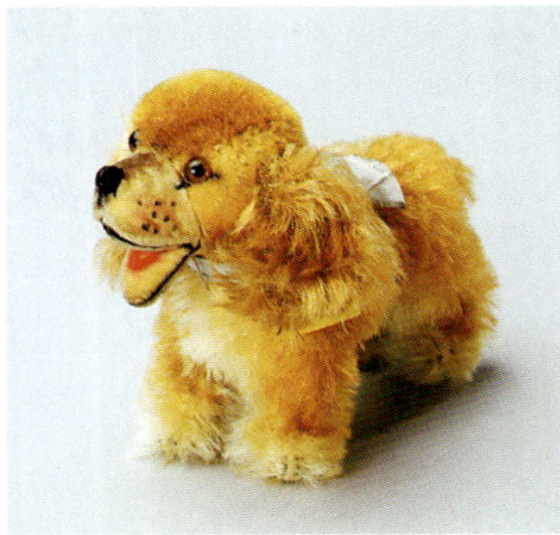

Cocker Spaniel **Cockie**

Mohair, mittelbraun, stehend, Drehkopf, offene Schnauze - *mohair, medium brown, standing, head swivels, open mouth*

SERIE	ART.-NO	PERIOD	PR.	INFO
29	**1310,0**	1952-1957	4	10 cm
29	**1317,0**	1952-1957	4	17 cm
29	**1325,02**	1952-1957	4	25 cm

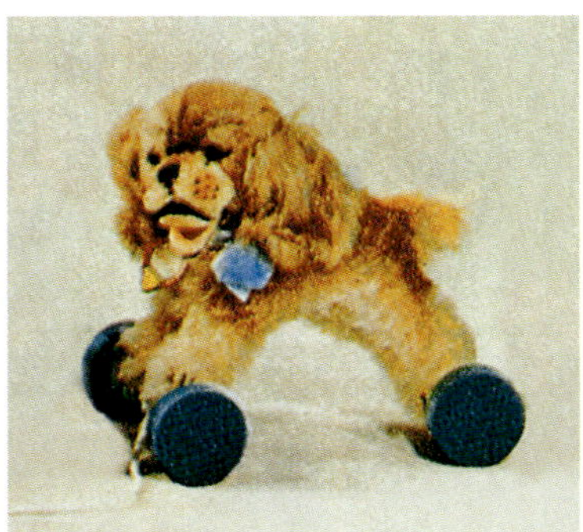

Nachzieh-**Cockie** - *Pull Toy **Cockie***

Mohair, mittelbraun, stehend auf Exzenterraedern - *mohair, medium brown, standing on eccentric wheels*

SERIE	ART.-NO	PERIOD	PR.	INFO
81 29	**1310** ex	1954-1957	4-5	10 cm
810 290	**1310,10**	1960-1960	4-5	

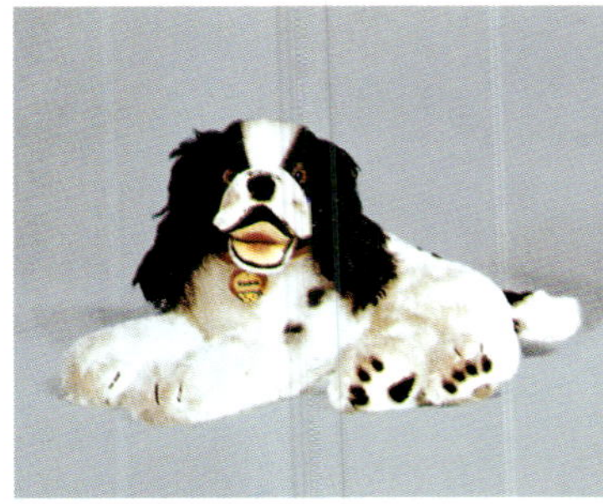

Cockie Cocker Spaniel

Mohairpluesch, weiss/schwarz, liegend, offener Mund, Doppelstimme, sehr weich - *mohair, white/black, lying, open mouth, double press voice, very soft*

SERIE	ART.-NO	PERIOD	PR.	INFO
29	**2335,1**	1955-1958	4	35 cm
290	**2335,06**	1959-1964	4	
428	**2335,06**	1965-1966	4	

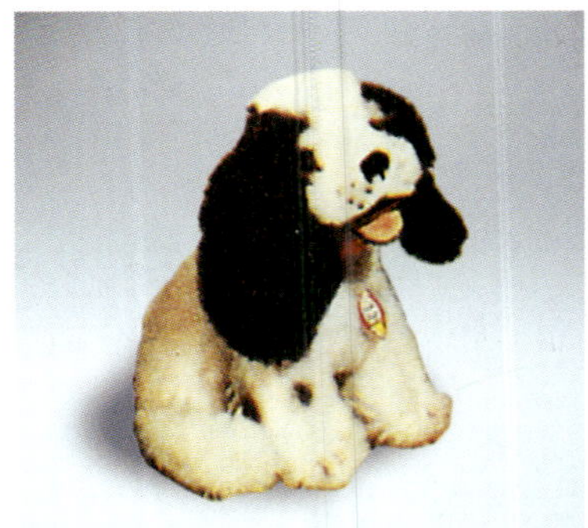

Cockie Cocker Spaniel

Halsmechanik, Mohair, schwarz/weiss, sitzend, offener Mund - *neck mechanism, mohair, black/white, sitting, open mouth*

SERIE	ART.-NO	PERIOD	PR.	INFO
29	**3310** H	1955-1955	5-6	10 cm
29	**3314** H	1955-1955	5-6	14 cm

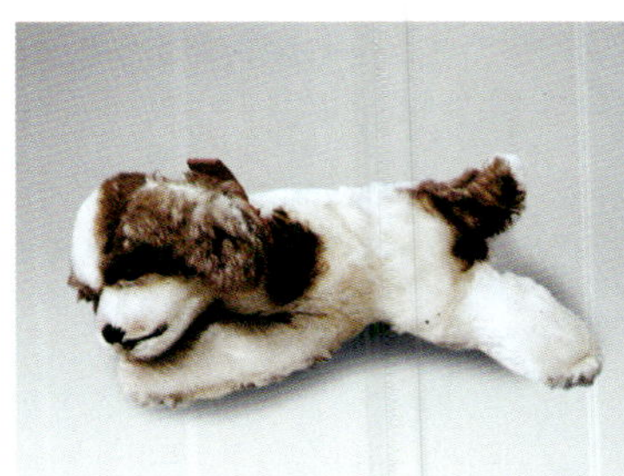

Floppy Cockie

Schlaftier, Mohair, Augen gestickt, weiss/braun, flach liegend, sehr weich, ab 1970 formgeschaeumt - *sleeping toy, mohair, eyes embroidered, white/brown, lying flat, very soft, from 1970 filled with pre-formed foam*

SERIE	ART.-NO	PERIOD	PR.	INFO
85 29	**7317**	1954-1958	2-3	17 cm
850 290	**7317,00**	1959-1964	2-3	
556	**7317,00**	1965-1967	2-3	
	5560/17	1968-1969	2	
	5567/17	1970-1977	1-2	
85 29	**7328**	1953-1958	2-3	28 cm
850 290	**7328,00**	1959-1964	2-3	
556	**7328,00**	1965-1967	2-3	
	5560/28	1968-1969	2	
	5567/28	1970-1977	1-2	

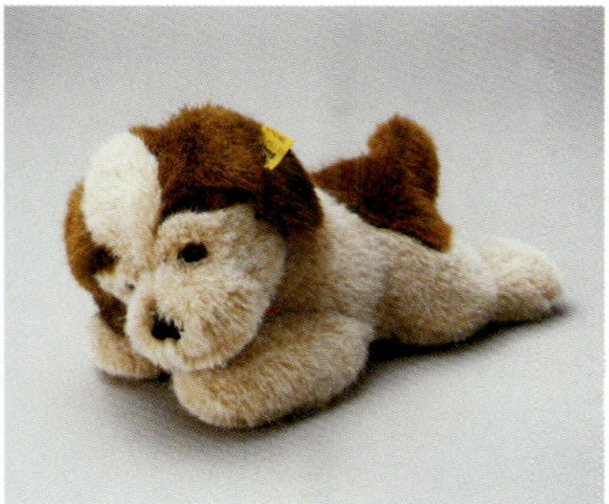

Floppy Cockie

Synthetik-Webpelz, formgeschaeumt, liegend, vollwaschbar - *synthetic woven fur, stuffed with pre-formed foam, lying, fully washable*

SERIE	ART.-NO	PERIOD	PR.	INFO
	5715/20	1978-1982	2	20 cm
	5715/30	1978-1982	2	30 cm

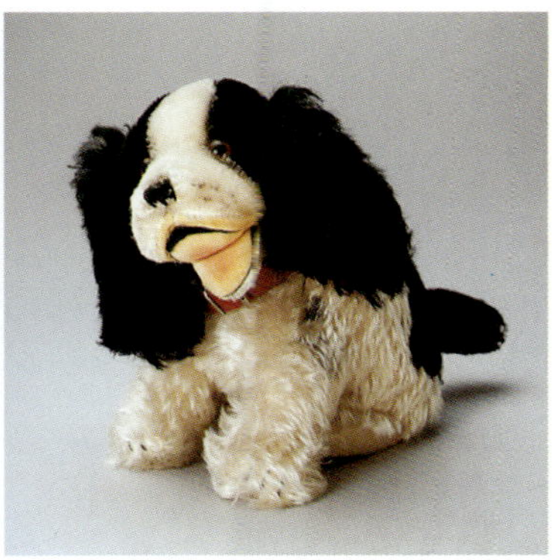

Musik Cockie - *Music Cockie*

Mohair, Schweizer Musikwerk mit Schwanz gekoppelt, schwarz/weiss, sitzend, offener Mund, Kopf drehbar - *mohair, Swiss music box which is connected to the tail, black/white, sitting, open mouth, head swivels*

SERIE	ART.-NO	PERIOD	PR.	INFO
97 29	**3317,3**	1955-1957	5	17 cm
860 290	**3317,60**	1961-1961	5	

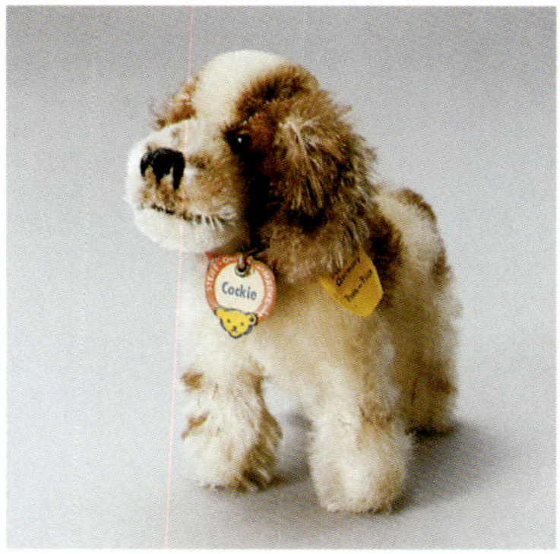

Cockie Cocker Spaniel

Mohairpluesch, weiss/braun, stehend, Kopf drehbar - *mohair, white/brown, standing, head swivels*

SERIE	ART.-NO	PERIOD	PR.	INFO
29	**1311,0**	1957-1958	4	11 cm
290	**1311,00**	1959-1959	4	
29	**1318,0**	1957-1958	4-5	18 cm
290	**1318,00**	1959-1959	4-5	
29	**1328,0**	1957-1958	4-5	28 cm
290	**1328,00**	1959-1959	4-5	

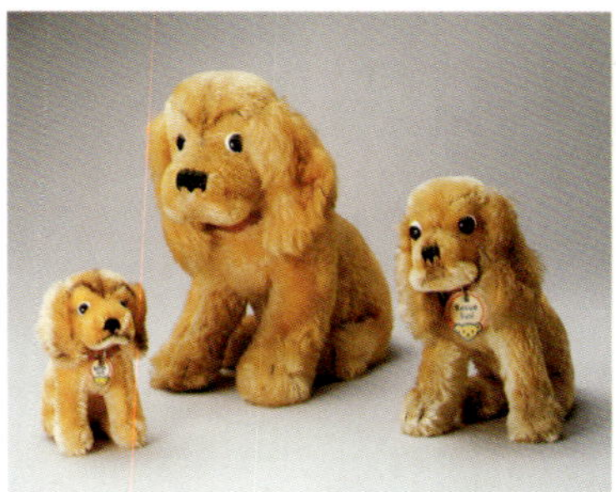

Revue Susi

Mohair, braun, sitzend, Drehkopf - *mohair, brown, sitting, head swivels*

SERIE	ART.-NO	PERIOD	PR.	INFO
290	**3312,03**	1959-1964	3	12 cm
430	**3312,03**	1965-1967	3	
	4300/12	1968-1976	2-3	
290	**3317,03**	1959-1964	3	17 cm
430	**3317,03**	1965-1967	3	
	4300/17	1968-1977	2-3	
290	**3328,03**	1959-1964	3-4	28 cm
430	**3328,03**	1965-1967	3-4	
	4300/28	1968-1976	3	
290	**3335,03**	1964-1964	3-4	35 cm
430	**3335,03**	1965-1967	3-4	
	4300/35	1968-1975	3	

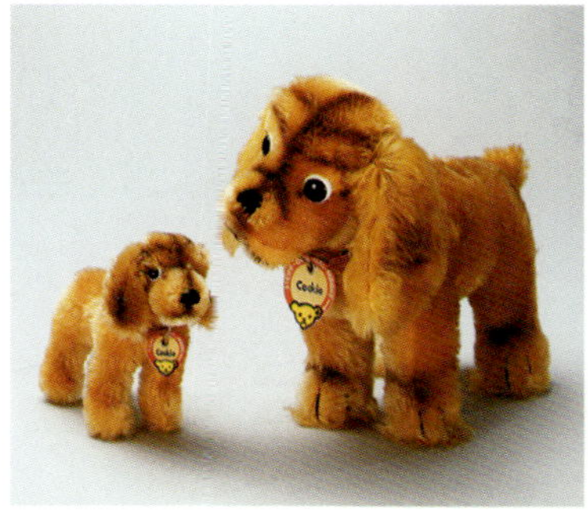

Cockie Cocker Spaniel

Mohair, braun, stehend, abwaschbar, geschlossene Schnauze - *mohair, brown, standing, surface washable, mouth closed*

SERIE	ART.-NO	PERIOD	PR.	INFO
290	**1312,03**	1960-1964	3	12 cm
427	**1312,03**	1965-1967	3	
	4273/12	1968-1975	2-3	
290	**1319,03**	1960-1964	3	19 cm
427	**1319,03**	1966-1967	3	
	4273/19	1968-1976	3	
290	**1329,03**	1960-1964	3-4	29 cm
427	**1329,03**	1966-1967	3-4	
	4273/29	1968-1976	3	

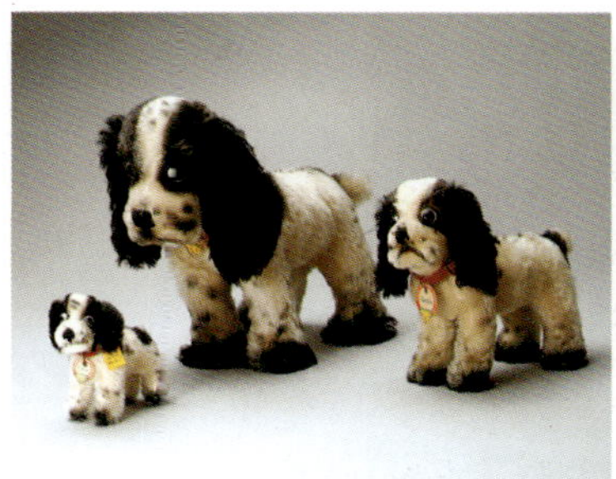

Cockie Cocker Spaniel

Mohair, schwarz/weiss, stehend, abwaschbar - *mohair, black/white, standing, surface washable*

SERIE	ART.-NO	PERIOD	PR.	INFO
290	**1312,06**	1960-1964	3-4	12 cm
428	**1312,06**	1965-1967	3-4	
	4276/12	1968-1976	3	
290	**1319,06**	1960-1964	4	19 cm
428	**1319,06**	1965-1967	4	
	4276/19	1968-1976	3-4	
290	**1329,06**	1960-1964	4	29 cm
428	**1329,06**	1965-1967	4	
	4276/29	1968-1976	4	

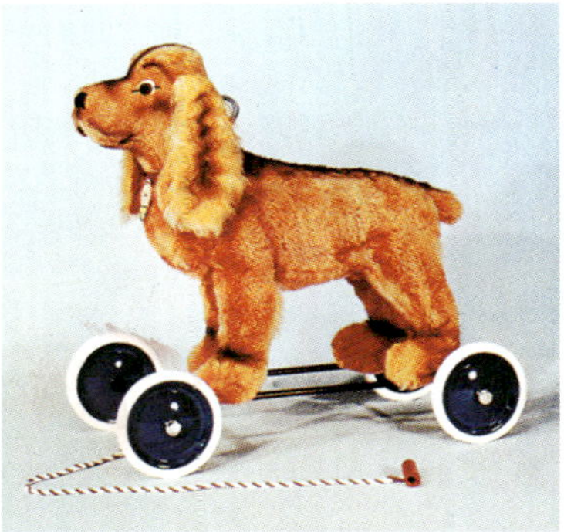

Reit-**Cockie** - *Riding **Cockie***

Dralon, rotbraun, Stahlgerippe, Haltegriff, stehend, gummibereifte Metallscheibenraeder, ab 1967 Plastikreifen und Kunststofflager, Zugstimme - *dralon, red-brown, steel frame, grip handle, standing, metal disc wheels & rubber tires, from 1967 plastic tires & plastic bearings, pull cord voice*

SERIE	ART.-NO	PERIOD	PR.	INFO
290	**1650,23**	1962-1964	5	50 cm
428	**1650,23**	1965-1967	5	
	4273/50	1968-1975	4-5	

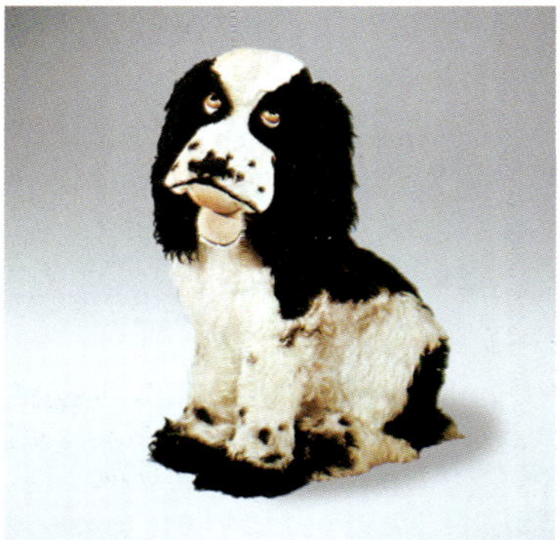

Cockie

Schautier, Mohair, schwarz/weiss, sitzend - *display animal, mohair, black/white, sitting*

SERIE	ART.-NO	PERIOD	PR.	INFO
290	**3375,90**	1960-1960	5-6	75 cm
	4279/08	1967-1967	5-6	

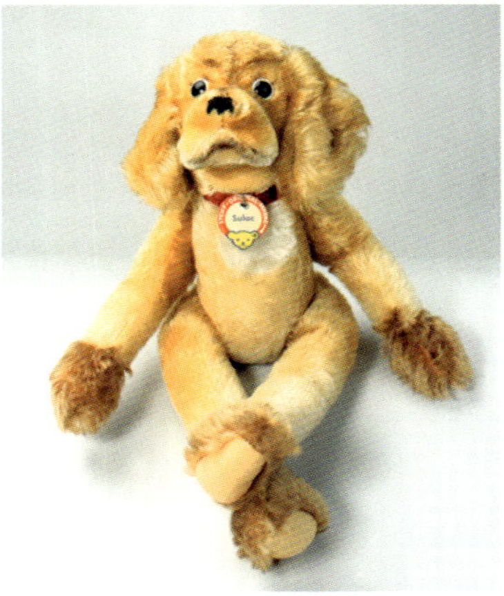

Susi Hund Sulac - ***Susi** Dog Sulac*

Mohair, Schlenkertier, gegliedert - *mohair, dangling animal, jointed*

SERIE	ART.-NO	PERIOD	PR.	INFO
290	**7340,00**	1964-1964	5	40 cm

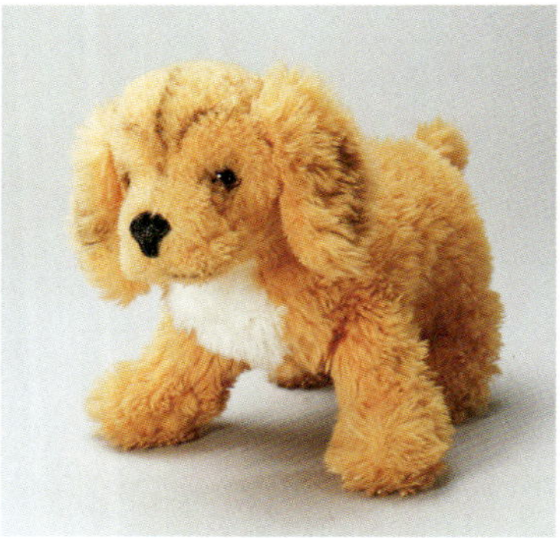

Cosy Cockie

Dralon-Pluesch, Schaumgummi-Fuellung, rotbraun/weiss, stehend, sehr weich - *dralon, stuffed with foam rubber, red-brown/white, standing, very soft*

SERIE	ART.-NO	PERIOD	PR.	INFO
830 290	**1622,00**	1962-1963	2-3	22 cm
500	**1622,00**	1965-1967	2-3	
	5000/22	1968-1977	2	

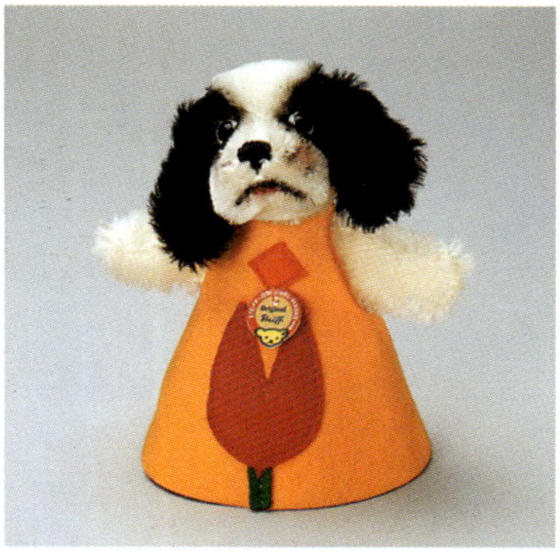

Betthupferl-Cockie - *Nightcap Cockie*

Kopf & Arme Mohair, orange Filzkleidung, Drehkopf, innen hohl zur Abdeckung kleiner Praesente - *head & arms mohair, orange felt clothes, head swivels, hollow interior to cover small gifts*

SERIE	ART.-NO	PERIOD	PR.	INFO
	3178/15	1969-1974	4	15 cm

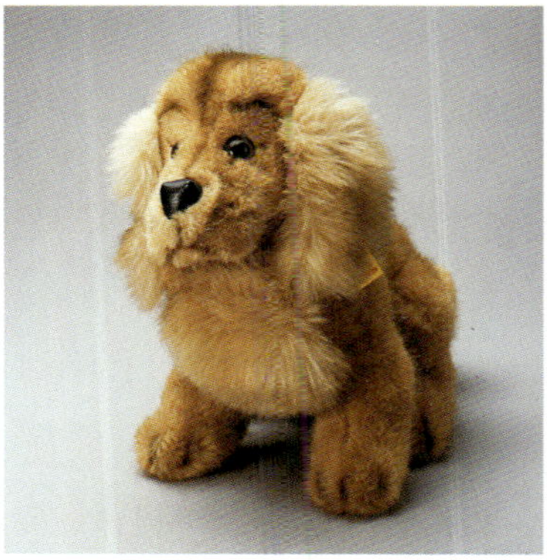

Junior Cockie

Webpelz, sitzend, abwaschbar - *woven fur, sitting, surface washable*

SERIE	ART.-NO	PERIOD	PR.	INFO
	2884/26	1981-1983	2-3	26 cm

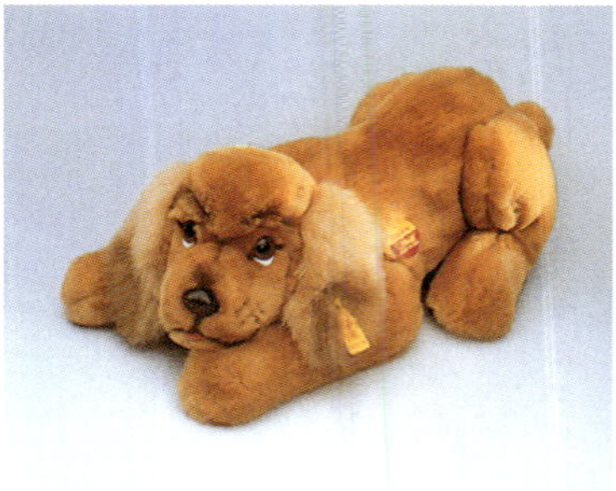

Cockie Spaniel

Webpelz, abwaschbar - *woven fur, surface washable*

SERIE	ART.-NO	PERIOD	PR.	INFO
078057	**4035/38**	1984-1989	2-3	38 cm

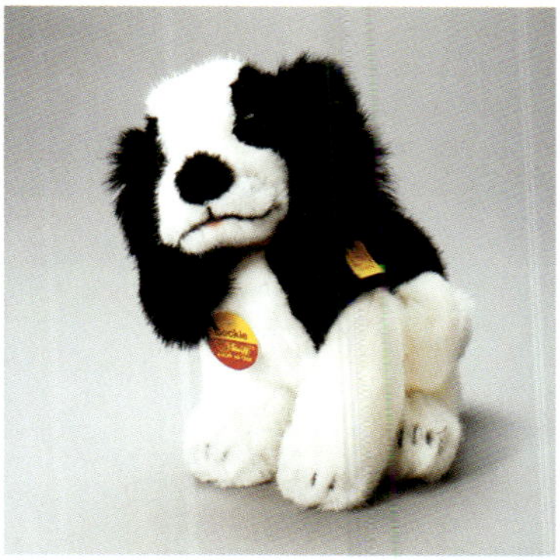

Cockie Spaniel

Webpelz, Lederhalsband, schwarz/weiss, sitzend, abwaschbar - *woven fur, leather collar, black & white, sitting, surface washable*

SERIE	ART.-NO	PERIOD	PR.	INFO
079214	**4026/21**	1990-1990	2	21 cm
	079214	1991-1991	2	

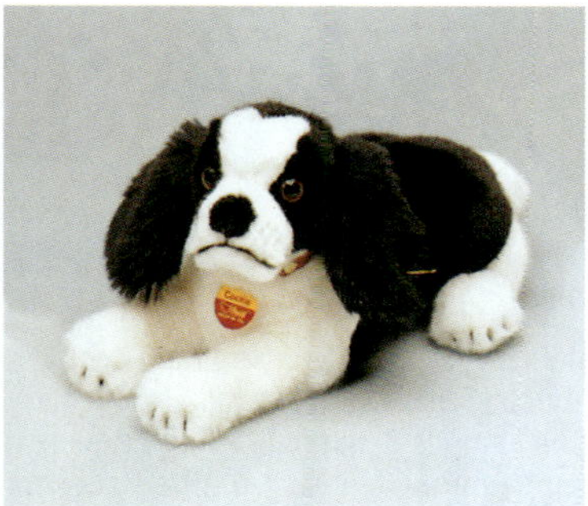

Cockie Spaniel

Webpelz, Lederhalsband, schwarz/weiss, liegend, abwaschbar - *woven fur, leather collar, black & white, lying, surface washable*

SERIE	ART.-NO	PERIOD	PR.	INFO
079252	**4028/32**	1990-1990	2-3	32 cm
	079252	1991-1991	2-3	

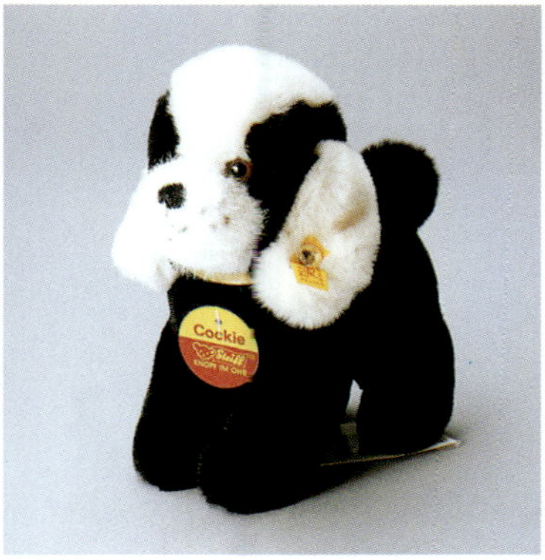

Cockie Hund - ***Cockie** Dog*

Webpelz, schwarz/creme, stehend, waschmaschinenfest - *woven fur, black/cream, standing, machine washable*

EAN-NO.	PERIOD	PR.	INFO
081750	1994-1996	2	16 cm

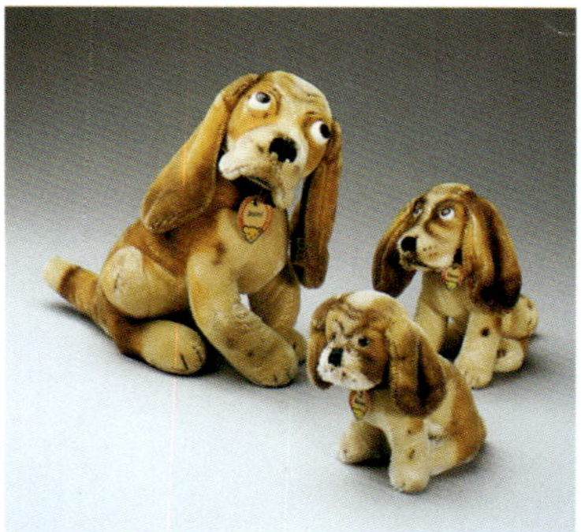

Basset

Mohair, braun/weiss, sitzend, Drehkopf - *mohair, brown/white, sitting, head swivels*

SERIE	ART.-NO	PERIOD	PR.	INFO
380	**3312,00**	1961-1963	4-5	12 cm
380	**3314,00**	1961-1962	5	14 cm
380	**3322,00**	1961-1962	5	22 cm

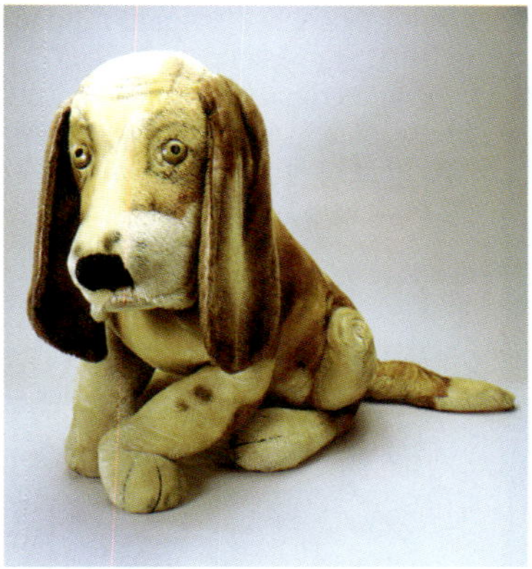

Basset

Schautier, Mohairpluesch, braun/weiss, sitzend - *display animal, mohair, brown/white, sitting*

SERIE	ART.-NO	PERIOD	PR.	INFO
380	**3375,90**	1960-1960	5-6	75 cm
	4089/08	1967-1967	5-6	

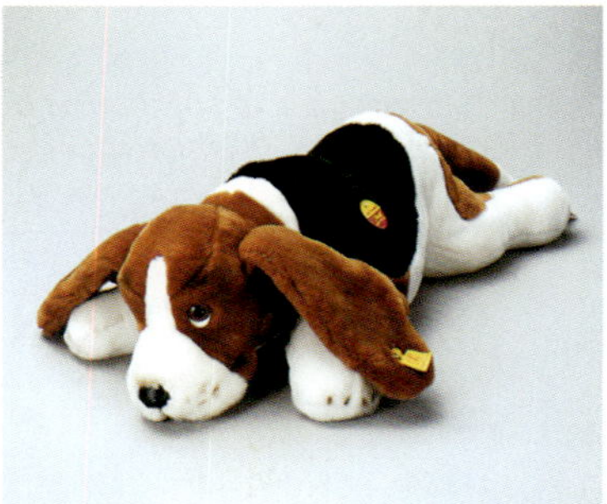

Cosy Basset

Webpelz, superweich, waschmaschinenfest - *woven fur, super soft, machine washable*

SERIE	ART.-NO	PERIOD	PR.	INFO
096686	**5463/50**	1984-1988	3	50 cm

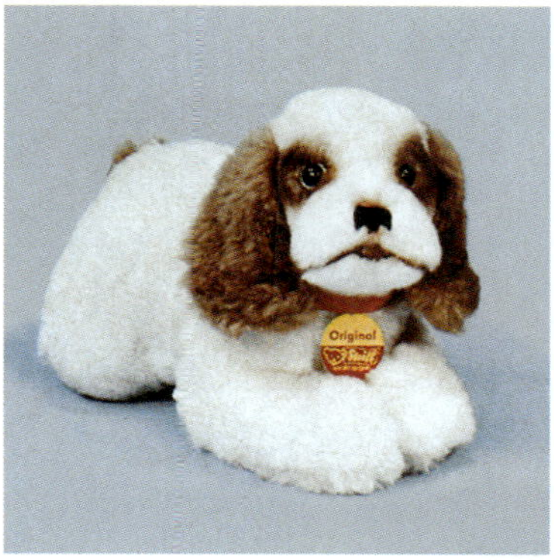

Treff

Dralon, liegend, vollwaschbar - *dralon, lying, fully washable*

SERIE	ART.-NO	PERIOD	PR.	INFO
	5220,23	1970-1973	2	23 cm

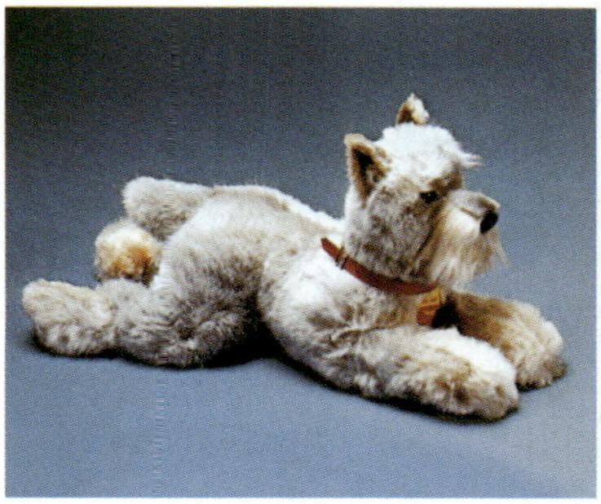

Molly Treff

Pelzimitation, ab 1978 Webpelz, liegend, abwaschbar - *imitation fur, from 1978 woven fur, lying, surface washable*

SERIE	ART.-NO	PERIOD	PR.	INFO
	0337/50	1976-1981	3	50 cm

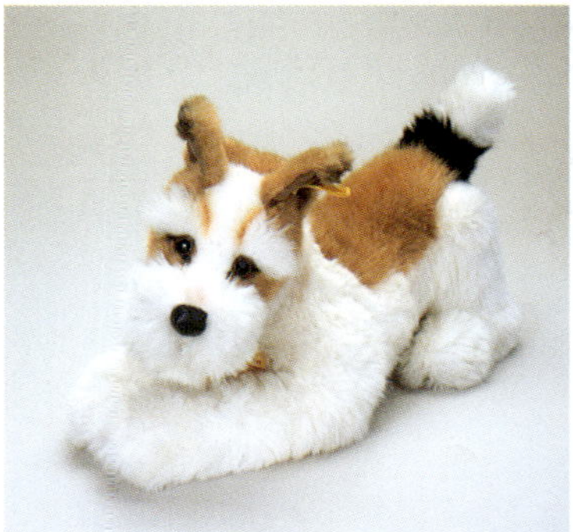

Junior Treff Terrier

Webpelz, abwaschbar - *woven fur, surface washable*

SERIE	ART.-NO	PERIOD	PR.	INFO
076053	**2882/35**	1982-1986	2-3	35 cm

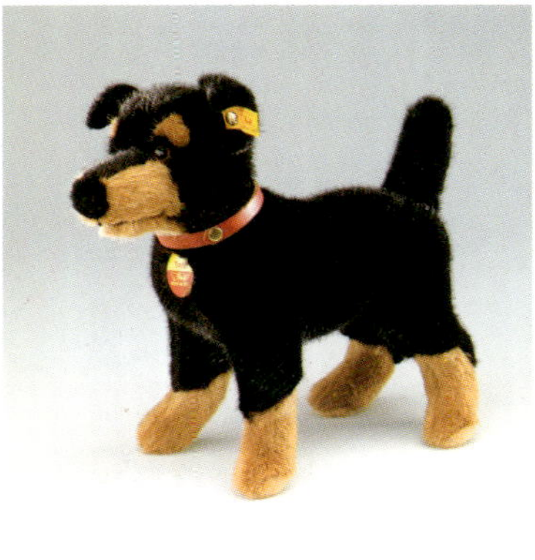

Treff Jagdterrier - ***Treff*** *Hunting Terrier*

Webpelz, schwarz/braun, stehend, Lederhalsband, ohne Halsband waschmaschinenfest - *woven fur, black/brown, standing, leather collar, machine washable without collar*

EAN-No.	Period	Pr.	Info
079597	1998-1998	3	28 cm

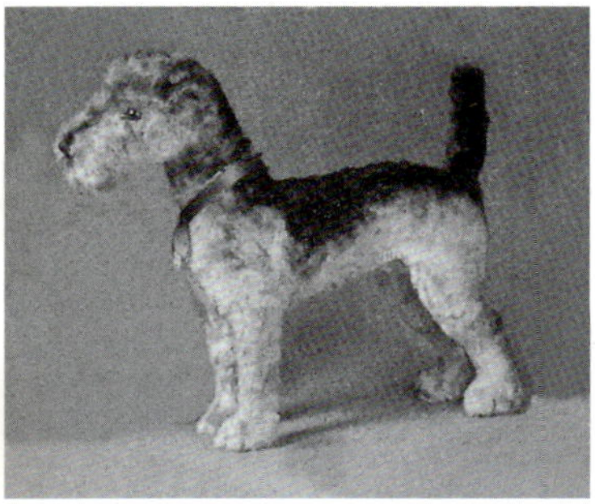

Fellow Airedale Terrier

Kunstseidenpluesch, Halsband, hellbraun/schwarz, stehend ohne Raeder - *artificial silk plush, collar, light brown & black, standing without wheels*

Serie	Art.-No	Period	Pr.	Info
40	**1622,0**	1948-1949	4	22 cm
40	**1628,02**	1948-1949	4	28 cm

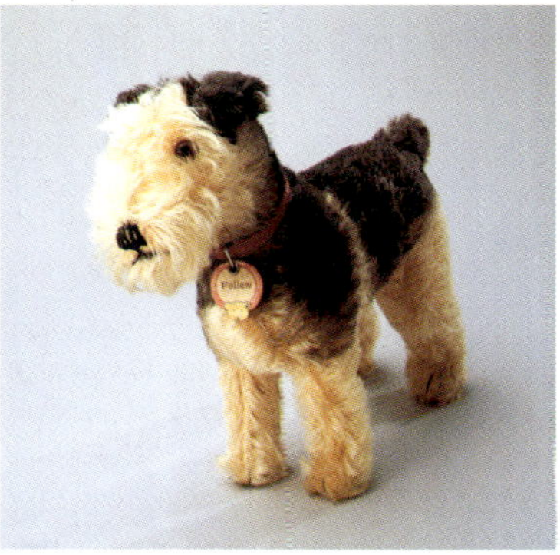

Fellow Airedale Terrier

Mohairpluesch, dunkelbraun, hellbraun verlaufend, stehend ohne Raeder - *mohair, dark brown, blending into light brown, standing without wheels*

Serie	Art.-No	Period	Pr.	Info
40	**1322,0**	1949-1949	4-5	22 cm
40	**1328,02**	1949-1949	4-5	28 cm

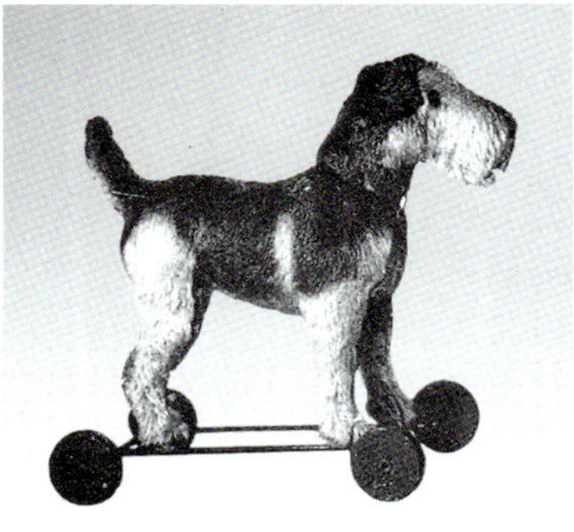

Reit-**Fellow** - *Riding* ***Fellow***

Mohairpluesch, Eisengerippe, dunkelbraun, hellbraun verlaufend, stehend auf Raedern mit Verbindungsschienen, Zugstimme - *mohair, iron frame, dark brown, blending into light brown, standing on wheels, connecting bars, pull cord voice*

Serie	Art.-No	Period	Pr.	Info
40	**1343,2**	1949-1950	5	43 cm
40	**1350,2**	1949-1950	5	50 cm

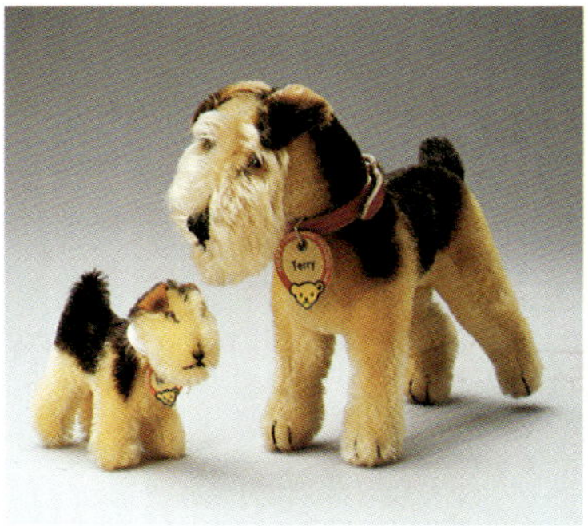

Terry Airedale Terrier

Mohair, hellbraun/schwarz, stehend, ab 28 cm Druckstimme - *mohair, light brown & black, standing, from 28 cm press voice*

Serie	Art.-No	Period	Pr.	Info
40	**1308,0**	1951-1957	4	8 cm
40	**1310,0**	1951-1957	3-4	10 cm
400	**1310,00**	1961-1961	3-4	
40	**1317,0**	1951-1957	4	17 cm
400	**1317,00**	1960-1961	4	
40	**1322,0**	1950-1957	4	22 cm
40	**1328,02**	1950-1957	4	28 cm
400	**1328,00**	1960-1961	4	
40	**1335,02**	1951-1957	4	35 cm
400	**1335,00**	1960-1961	4	

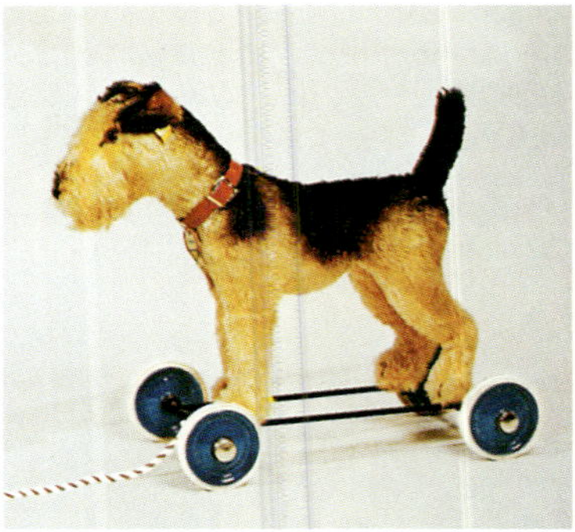

(Reit-)**Terry** Airedale Terrier - *(Riding-)* ***Terry*** *Airdale Terrier*

Mohair, Eisengerippe, hellbraun/schwarz, stehend, Druckstimme, auf Holzraedern, ab 43 cm als Reittier auf Scheibenraedern mit Gummireifen, Zugstimme - *mohair, iron frame, light brown & black, press voice, standing on wooden wheels, from 43cm riding toy with disc wheels & rubber tires, pull cord voice*

Serie	Art.-No	Period	Pr.	Info
40	**1328,2**	1950-1950	4-5	28 cm
40	**1328,1**	1951-1957	4-5	
400	**1328,10**	1961-1961	4-5	
40	**1335,2**	1950-1950	4-5	35 cm
40	**1335,1**	1951-1957	4-5	
400	**1335,10**	1961-1961	4-5	
40	**1343,2**	1951-1957	4-5	43 cm
400	**1343,20**	1961-1961	4-5	
40	**1350,2**	1951-1957	5	50 cm
400	**1350,20**	1961-1961	5	

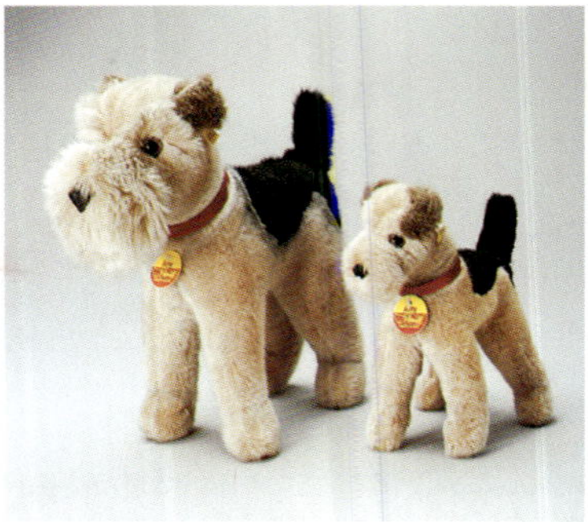

Arry Airedale Terrier

Nerzimitation, ab 1978 Synthetik-Webpelz, stehend, abwaschbar - *imitation fur, from 1978 synthetic woven fur, standing, surface washable*

Serie	Art.-No	Period	Pr.	Info
	4216/21	1977-1981	2-3	21 cm
	4216/30	1977-1981	2-3	30 cm

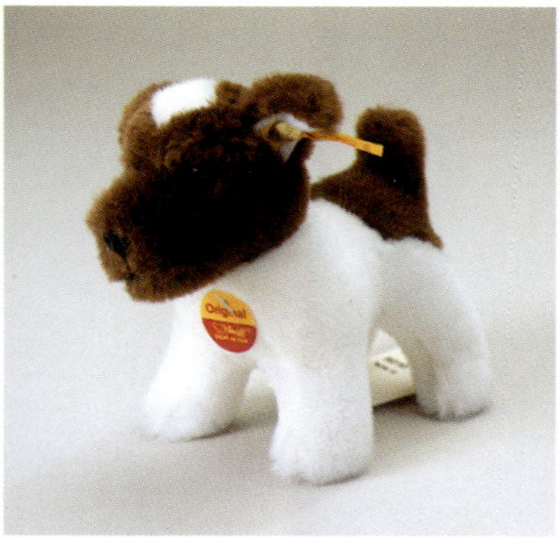

Terrier

Webpelz, weiss/braun, stehend, waschmaschinenfest - *woven fur, white/brown, standing, machine washable*

EAN-No.	Period	Pr.	Info
053153	1997-1999	2	14 cm

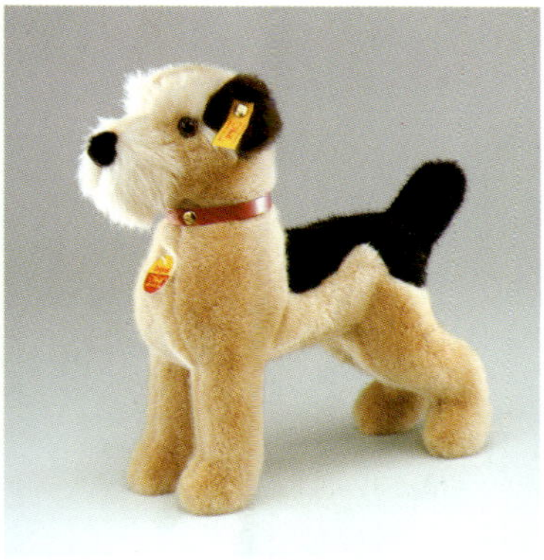

Terrier

Webpelz, beige, stehend, Lederhalsband, ohne Halsband waschmaschinenfest - *woven fur, beige, standing, leather collar, machine washable without collar*

EAN-No.	Period	Pr.	Info
079603	1998-1998	2-3	28 cm

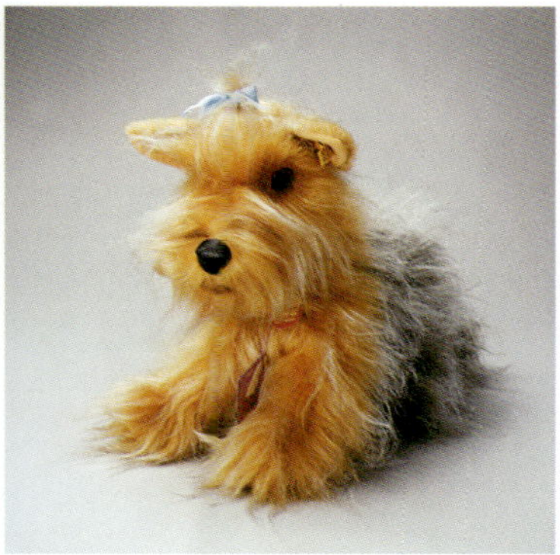

Terry Terrier

Wirkpelz, sitzend, abwaschbar - *knitted fur, sitting, surface washable*

Serie	Art.-No	Period	Pr.	Info
	4085/28	1978-1982	2-3	28 cm

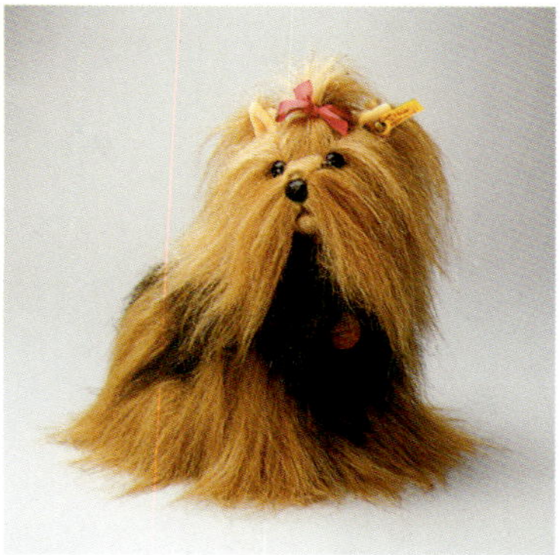

Taffy Yorkshire Terrier

Wirkpelz, sitzend, abwaschbar - *knitted fur, sitting, surface washable*

Serie	Art.-No	Period	Pr.	Info
079306	**4192/25**	1987-1990	2-3	25 cm
	079306	1991-1995	2-3	

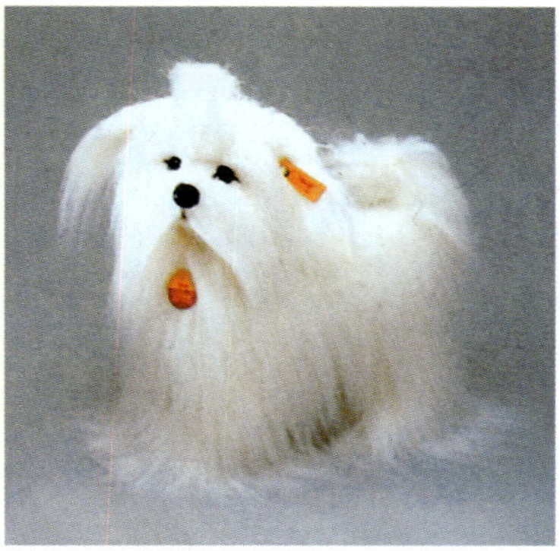

Issy Malteserhund - ***Issy** Maltese Dog*

Wirkpelz, stehend, abwaschbar - *knitted fur, standing, surface washable*

Serie	Art.-No	Period	Pr.	Info
079405	**4195/32**	1988-1989	2-3	32 cm

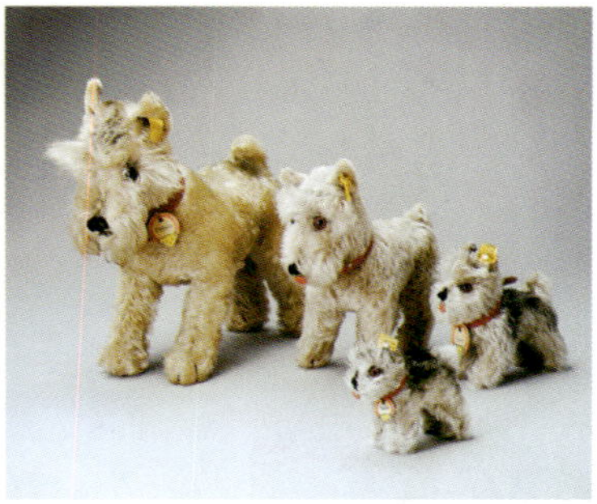

Schnauzer **Tessie**

Mohair, hellgrau, stehend, Kopf drehbar, abwaschbar - *mohair, light grey, standing, head swivels, surface washable*

Serie	Art.-No	Period	Pr.	Info
47	**1310,0**	1954-1958	3-4	10 cm
470	**1310,00**	1959-1964	3	
432	**1310,00**	1965-1967	3	
	4320/10	1968-1970	2-3	
47	**1314,0**	1954-1958	3-4	14 cm
470	**1314,00**	1959-1964	3	
432	**1314,00**	1965-1967	3	
	4320/14	1968-1976	3	
47	**1322,0**	1954-1958	4	22 cm
470	**1322,00**	1959-1964	3-4	
432	**1322,05**	1965-1967	3-4	
	4320/22	1968-1976	3	
470	**1328,00**	1959-1964	4	28 cm
432	**1328,05**	1965-1967	4	
	4320/28	1968-1976	3-4	

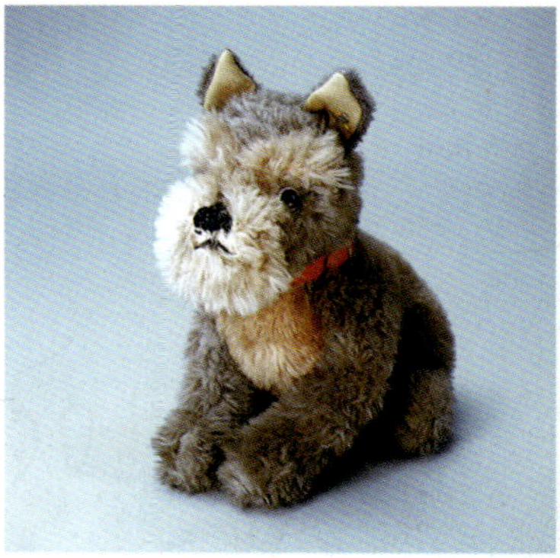

Cosy Schnauz

Dralon-Pluesch, Schaumstoff-Flocken-Fuellung, grau, sitzend, waschbar - *dralon, stuffed with foam flakes, grey, sitting, washable*

Serie	Art.-No	Period	Pr.	Info
505	**3625,05**	1965-1967	2-3	25 cm
	5050/25	1968-1976	2	

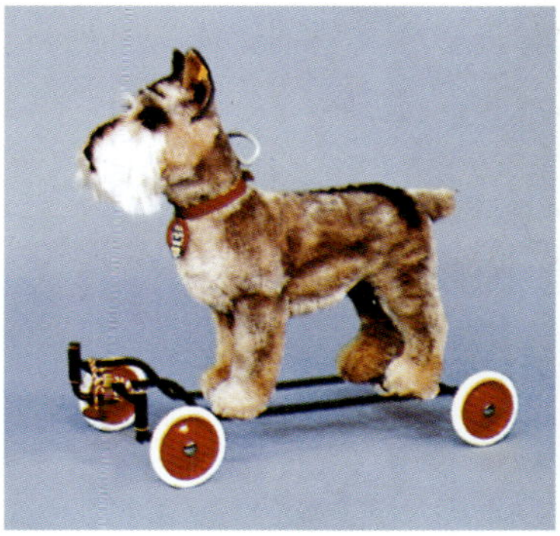

Reit-Schnauzer - *Riding Schnauzer*

Dralon, Stahlrohrgestell, Kunststofflager, Plastikreifen, Schlepplenkung, abwaschbar - *dralon, steel frame, plastic bearings, plastic tires, pull-type steering, surface washable*

Serie	Art.-No	Period	Pr.	Info
	4320/50	1970-1975	4	50 cm

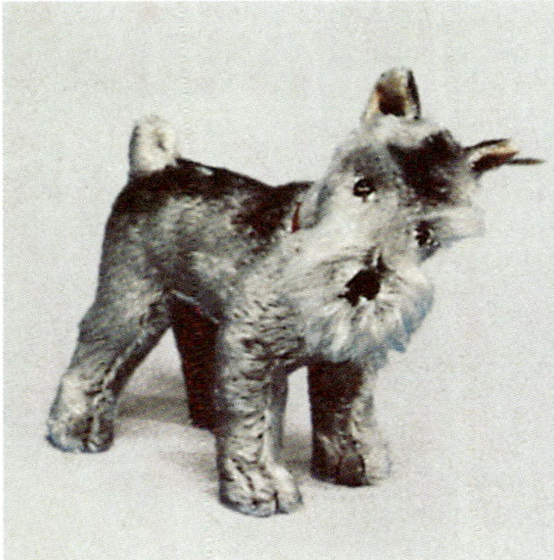

Schnauzer Tessie

Dralon, stehend, abwaschbar - *dralon, standing, surface washable*

SERIE	ART.-NO	PERIOD	PR.	INFO
	4328/50	1973-1975	4	50 cm

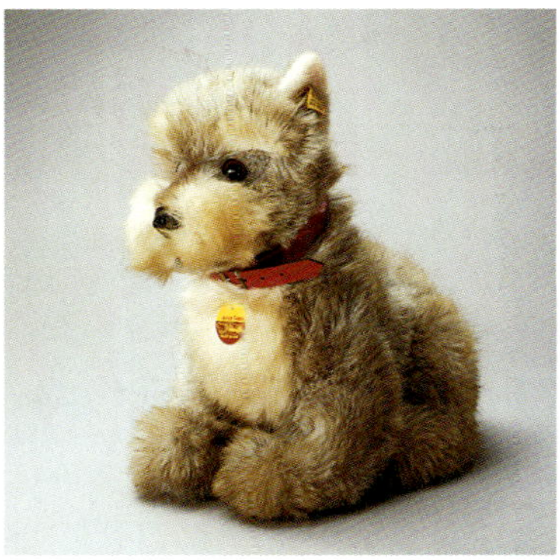

Junior-Tessie

Pelzimitation, ab 1978 Synthetik-Webpelz, grau/weiss, sitzend, abwaschbar - *imitation fur, from 1978 synthetic woven fur, grey/white, sitting, surface washable*

SERIE	ART.-NO	PERIOD	PR.	INFO
	2883/30	1977-1980	3	30 cm

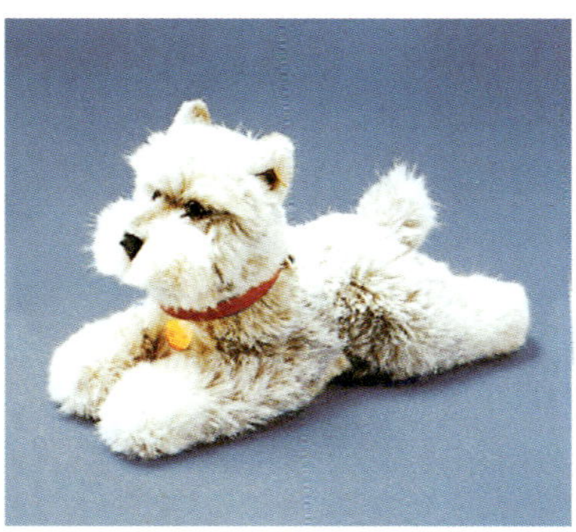

Junior-Tessie

Pelzimitation, ab 1978 Synthetik-Webpelz, grau/weiss, liegend, abwaschbar - *imitation fur, from 1978 synthetic woven fur, grey/white, lying, surface washable*

SERIE	ART.-NO	PERIOD	PR.	INFO
	2884/30	1977-1980	2-3	30 cm

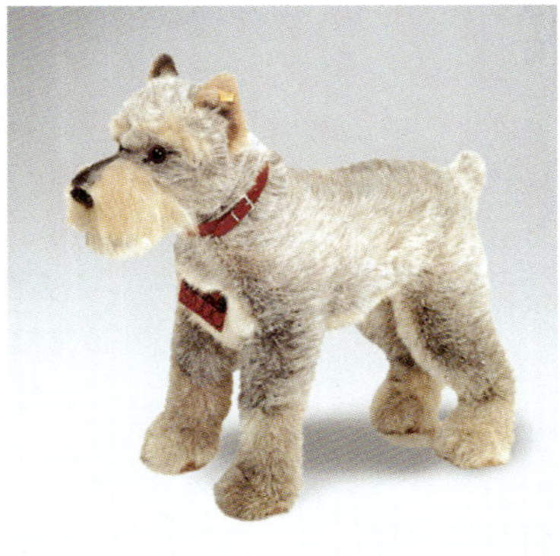

Schnauzer Tessie

Studio-Tier, Webpelz, stehend, abwaschbar - *studio animal, woven fur, standing, surface washable*

SERIE	ART.-NO	PERIOD	PR.	INFO
	4070/55	1978-1984	4	55 cm

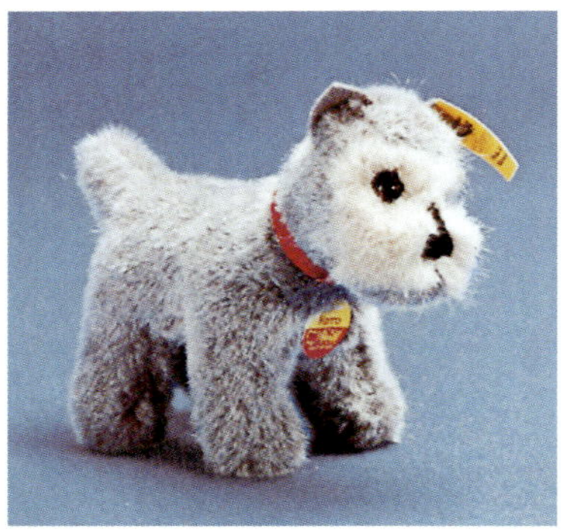

Harro Schnauzer

Webpelz, stehend, abwaschbar - *woven fur, standing, surface washable*

SERIE	ART.-NO	PERIOD	PR.	INFO
	1530/12	1978-1981	2	12 cm

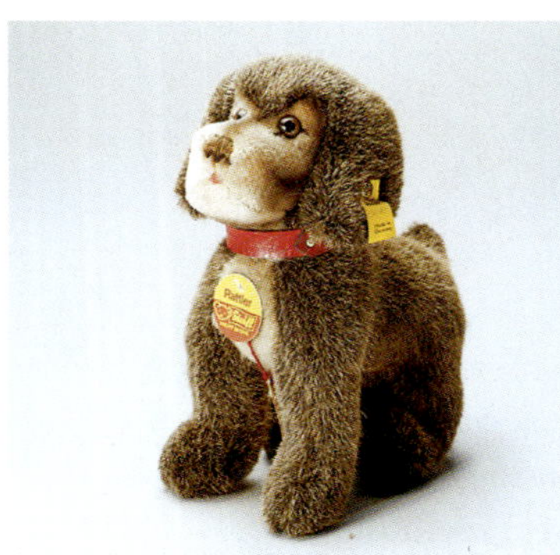

Rattler

Webpelz, stehend, abwaschbar - *woven fur, standing, surface washable*

SERIE	ART.-NO	PERIOD	PR.	INFO
	4020/20	1979-1981	2-3	20 cm

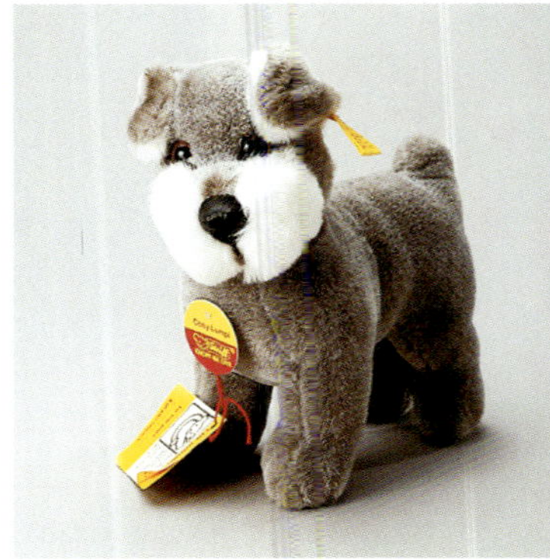

Cosy Lumpi Schnauzer

Webpelz, stehend, waschmaschinenfest - *woven fur, standing, machine washable*

SERIE	ART.-NO	PERIOD	PR.	INFO
096716	**5465/16**	1985-1988	2	18 cm
096730	**5465/27**	1985-1988	2	27 cm

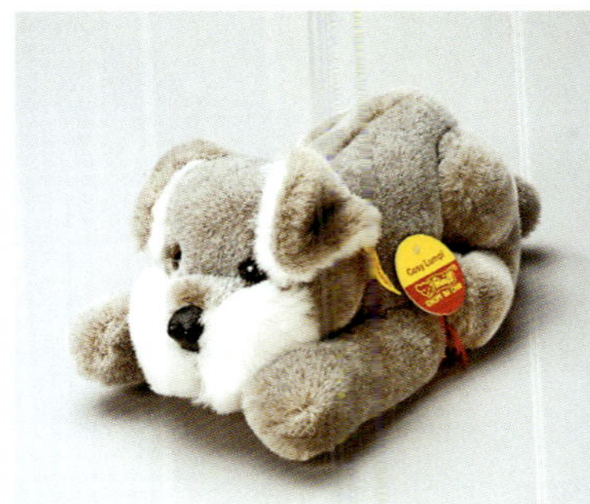

Cosy Lumpi Schnauzer

Webpelz, liegend, waschmaschinenfest - *woven fur, lying, machine washable*

SERIE	ART.-NO	PERIOD	PR.	INFO
096815	**5466/16**	1985-1988	2	22 cm

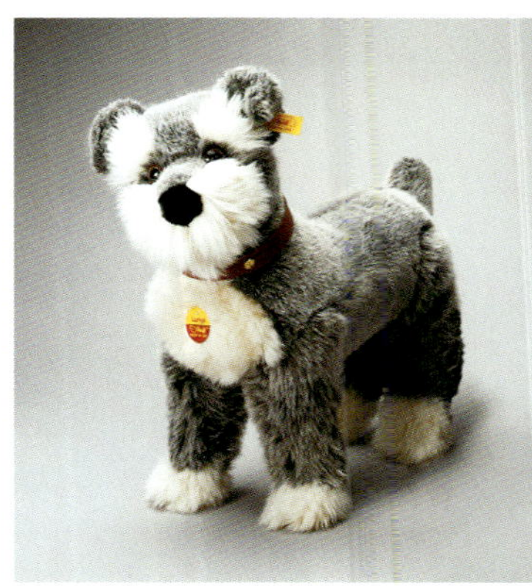

Lumpi Schnauzer

Webpelz, Lederhalsband, grau, stehend - *woven fur, leather collar, grey, standing*

EAN-No.	Period	Pr.	Info
078811	1993-1994	2-3	40 cm

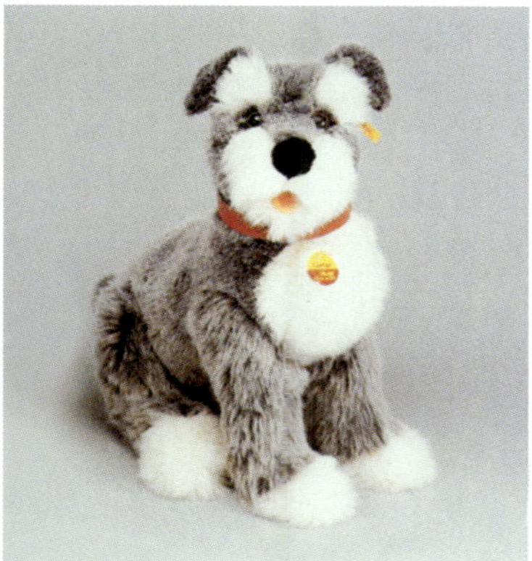

Lumpi Schnauzer

Webpelz, Lederhalsband, grau, sitzend - *woven fur, leather collar, grey, sitting*

EAN-No.	Period	Pr.	Info
078828	1993-1994	2-3	40 cm

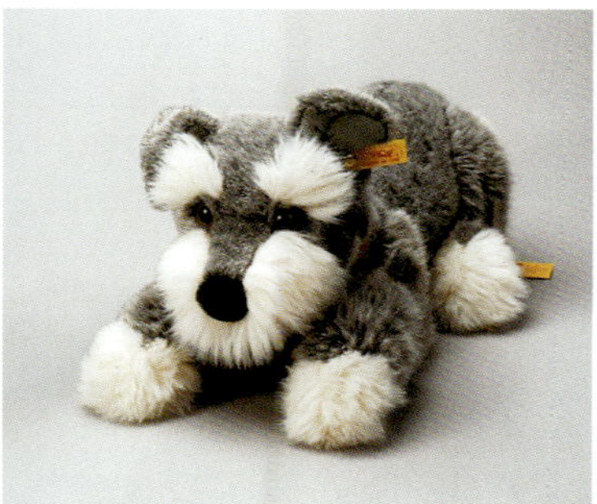

Lumpi Schnauzer

Webpelz, Lederhalsband, grau, liegend - *woven fur, leather collar, grey, lying*

EAN-No.	Period	Pr.	Info
078835	1993-1994	2-3	40 cm

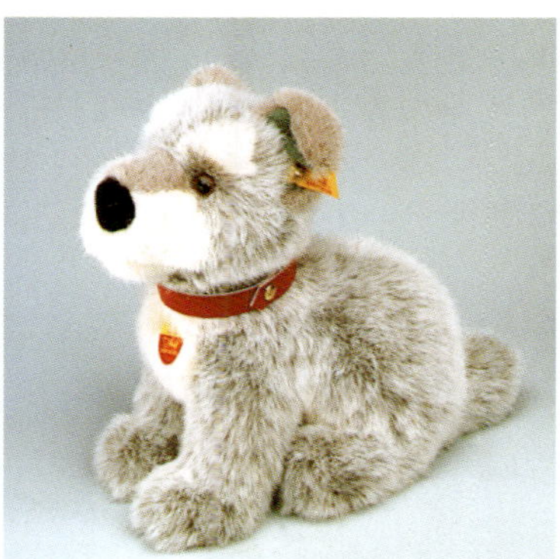

Molly Schnauzer

Webpelz, Lederhalsband, grau, sitzend - *woven fur, leather collar, grey, sitting*

EAN-No.	Period	Pr.	Info
104640	1995-1998	2-3	22 cm

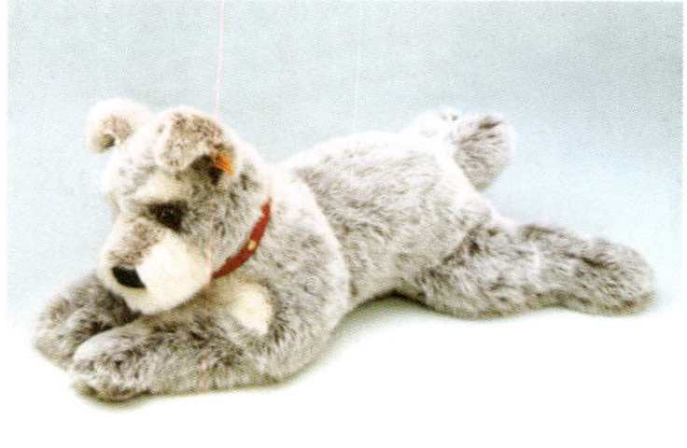

Molly Schnauzer

Webpelz, Lederhalsband, grau, liegend - *woven fur, leather collar, grey, lying*

EAN-No.	Period	Pr.	Info
104657	1995-1998	2-3	35 cm
104701	1995-1998	3	60 cm

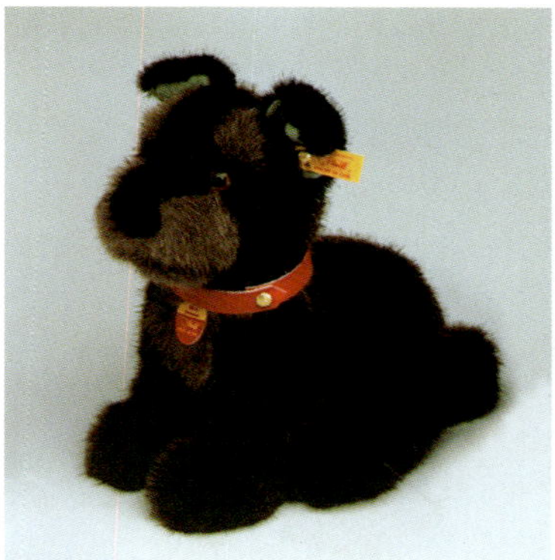

Molly Schnauzer

Webpelz, Lederhalsband, braun, sitzend - *woven fur, leather collar, brown, sitting*

EAN-No.	Period	Pr.	Info
104664	1995-1997	2-3	22 cm

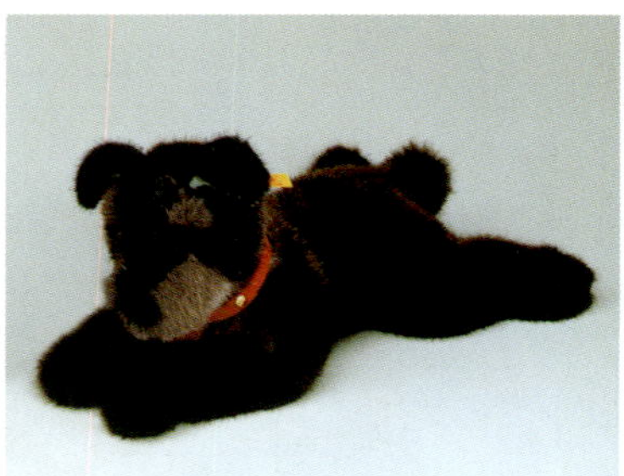

Molly Schnauzer

Webpelz, Lederhalsband, braun, liegend - *woven fur, leather collar, brown, lying*

EAN-No.	Period	Pr.	Info
104671	1995-1996	2-3	35 cm

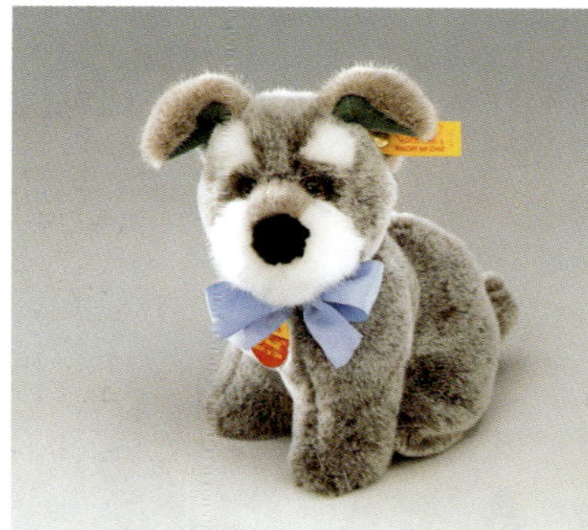

Snuffi Schnauzer

Webpelz, sitzend, waschmaschinenfest - *woven fur, sitting, machine washable*

EAN-No.	Period	Pr.	Info
077357	1996-1997	2	16 cm

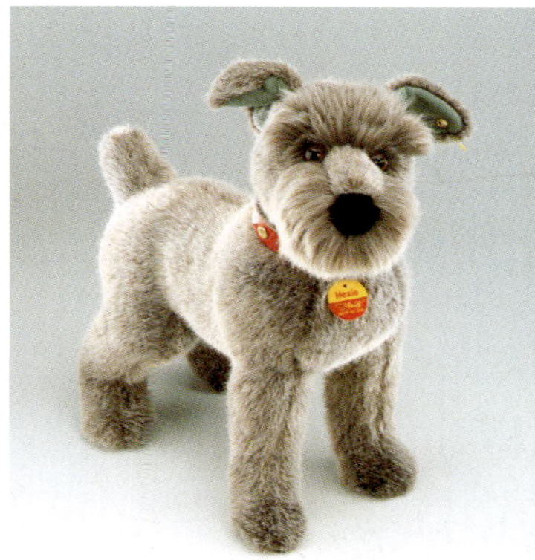

Hexie Mittelschnauzer - ***Hexie*** *Schnauzer*

Webpelz, grau, stehend, Lederhalsband, ohne Halsband waschmaschinenfest - *woven fur, grey, standing, leather collar, machine washable without collar*

EAN-No.	Period	Pr.	Info
078842	1998-1998	3	35 cm

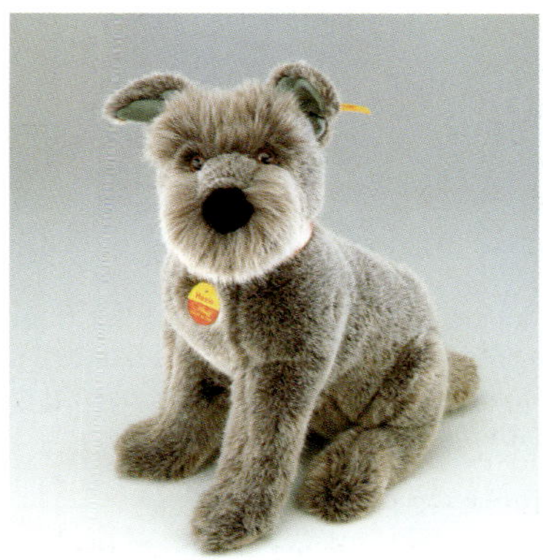

Hexie Mittelschnauzer - ***Hexie*** *Schnauzer*

Webpelz, grau, sitzend, Lederhalsband, ohne Halsband waschmaschinenfest - *woven fur, grey, sitting, leather collar, machine washable without collar*

EAN-No.	Period	Pr.	Info
078866	1998-1998	3	30 cm

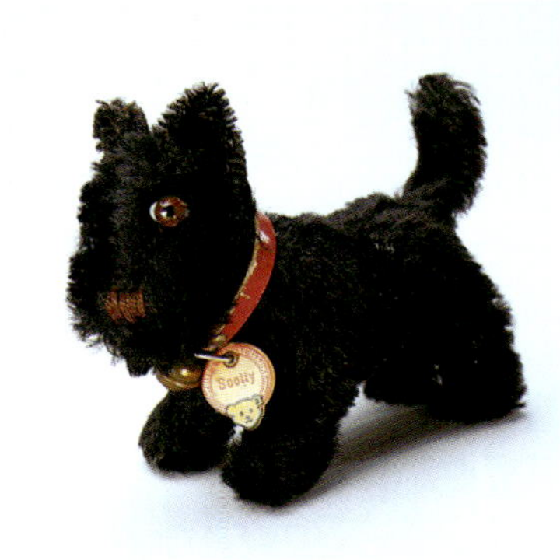

Scotty

Mohairpluesch, tiefschwarz, rotes Halsband, stehend ohne Raeder, Kopf drehbar, ab 17 cm mit Druckstimme - *mohair, deep black, red collar, standing without wheels, head swivels, press voice from 17 cm*

Serie	Art.-No	Period	Pr.	Info
51	**1310,0**	1950-1957	4	10 cm
51	**1314,0**	1949-1957	4	14 cm
51	**1317,02**	1949-1955	4-5	17 cm
51	**1322,02**	1949-1957	4-5	22 cm
51	**1325,02**	1951-1954	5	25 cm
51	**1328,02**	1951-1954	5	28 cm
51	**1335,02**	1951-1957	5	35 cm

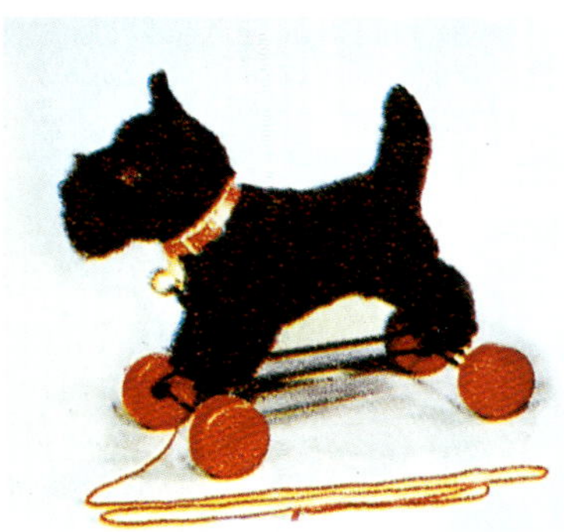

Scotty

Mohair, Holzrollen, schwarz, rotes Halsband, stehend, auf Exzenter-Raedern - *mohair, wooden wheels, black, red collar, standing on eccentric wheels*

Serie	Art.-No	Period	Pr.	Info
51	**1314** ex	1950-1957	5	14 cm
51	**1317** ex	1949-1954	5	17 cm

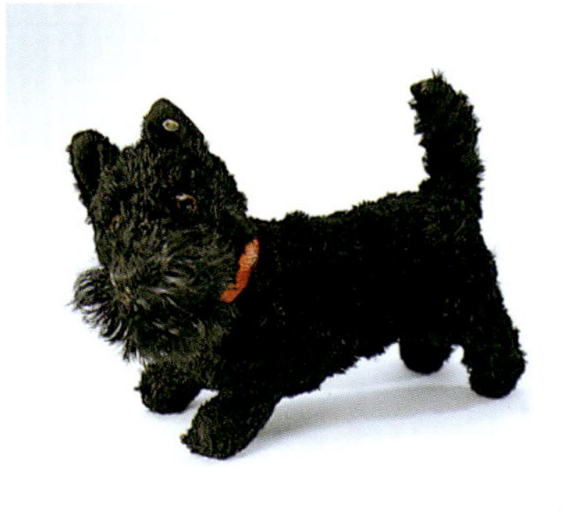

Scotty

Seidenpluesch, Halsband, schwarz, stehend ohne Raeder, Drehkopf - *silk plush, collar, black, standing without wheels, head swivels*

Serie	Art.-No	Period	Pr.	Info
51	**1614,0**	1949-1949	4-5	14 cm
51	**1617,0**	1949-1949	4-5	17 cm

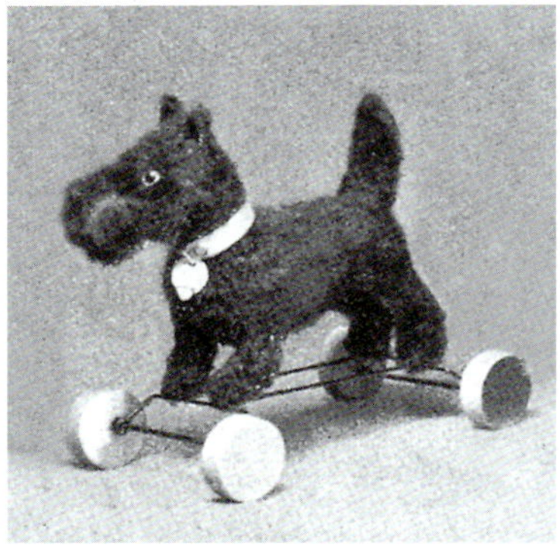

Scotty

Seidenpluesch, Halsband, schwarz, stehend auf Exzenterraedern, Drehkopf - *silk plush, collar, black, standing on eccentric wheels, head swivels*

Serie	Art.-No	Period	Pr.	Info
51	**1614** ex	1949-1949	4-5	14 cm

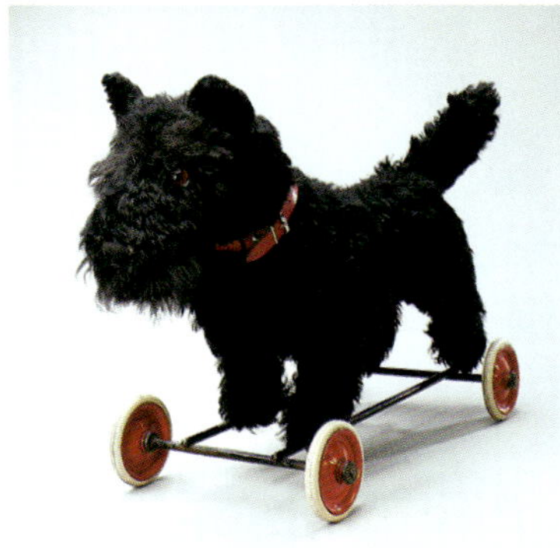

Reit-**Scotty** - *Riding **Scotty***

Mohair, Eisengerippe, schwarz, Metallscheibenraeder/Gummireifen, Zugstimme (bis 1951) - *mohair, iron frame, black, metal disc wheels & rubber tires, pull cord voice (up to 1951)*

Serie	Art.-No	Period	Pr.	Info
51	**1343,2**	1950-1951	5	43 cm
51	**1343**	1953-1957	5	
510	**1343,20**	1961-1961	5	

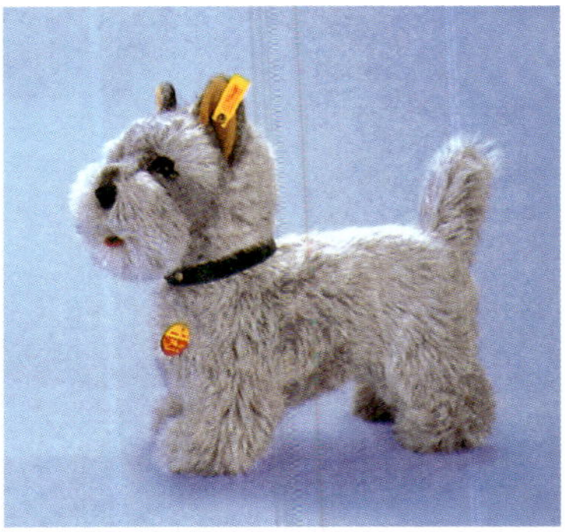

Junior Raudi Scotchterrier

Webpelz, abwaschbar - *woven fur, surface washable*

Serie	Art.-No	Period	Pr.	Info
	2893/30	1982-1984	2-3	30 cm

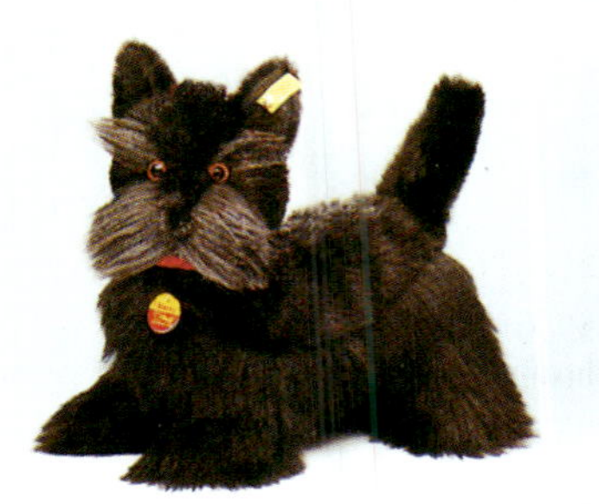

Blacky Scotch Terrier

Webpelz, Lederhalsband, schwarz, stehend, abwaschbar - *woven fur, leather collar, black, standing, surface washable*

Serie	Art.-No	Period	Pr.	Info
079504	**4184/35**	1989-1990	3	35 cm

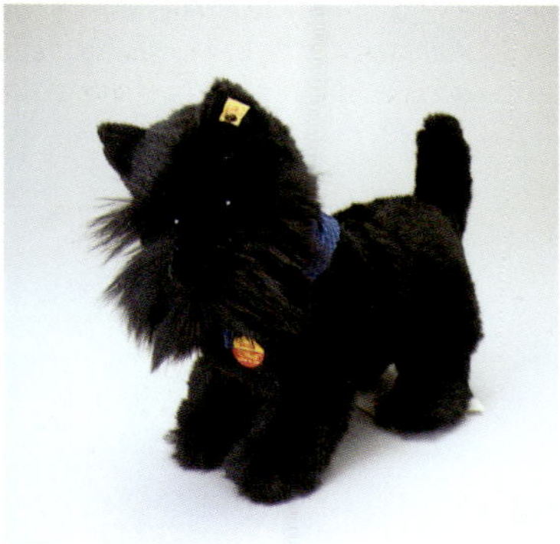

Scoty Scotch Terrier

Webpelz, schwarz, waschmaschinenfest, blau-schwarz kariertes Halstuch - *woven fur, black, machine washable, blue-black chequered scarf*

EAN-No.	Period	Pr.	Info
079580	1997-1999	3	35 cm

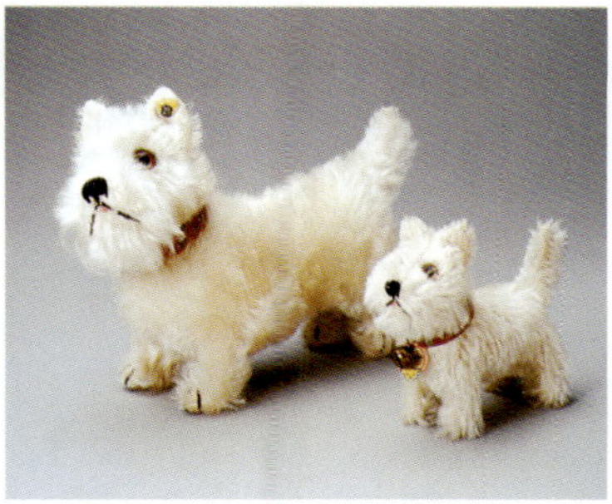

Sealyham

Mohairpluesch, weiss, rotes Halsband, stehend ohne Raeder, Kopf drehbar, ab 17 cm mit Druckstimme - *mohair, white, red collar, standing without wheels, head swivels, press voice from 17 cm size*

Serie	Art.-No	Period	Pr.	Info
51a	**1310,0**	1950-1957	4	10 cm
51a	**1314,0**	1949-1957	4	14 cm
51a	**1317,02**	1949-1954	4-5	17 cm
51a	**1322,02**	1949-1957	4-5	22 cm
51a	**1325,02**	1951-1954	5	25 cm
51a	**1328,02**	1951-1954	5	28 cm
51a	**1335,02**	1951-1957	5	35 cm

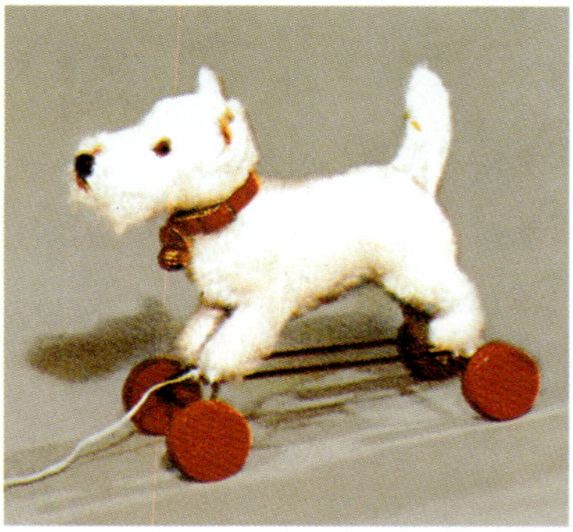

Sealyham

Mohair, Holzrollen, weiss, rotes Halsband, stehend auf Exzenterraedern - *mohair, wooden wheels, white, red collar, standing on eccentric wheels*

Serie	Art.-No	Period	Pr.	Info
51a	**1314** ex	1950-1954	5	14 cm
51a	**1317** ex	1949-1954	5	17 cm

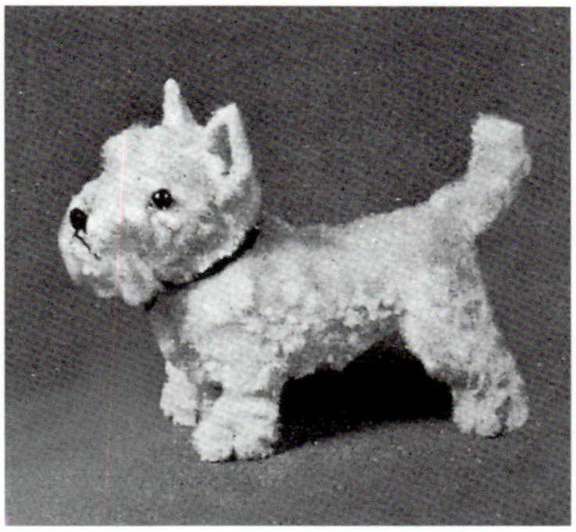

Sealyham

Seidenpluesch, Halsband, weiss, stehend ohne Raeder, Drehkopf, 17 cm mit Stimme - *silk plush, collar, white, standing without wheels, head swivels, 17 cm with voice*

Serie	Art.-No	Period	Pr.	Info
51a	**1614,0**	1948-1949	4-5	14 cm
51a	**1617,02**	1948-1949	4-5	17 cm

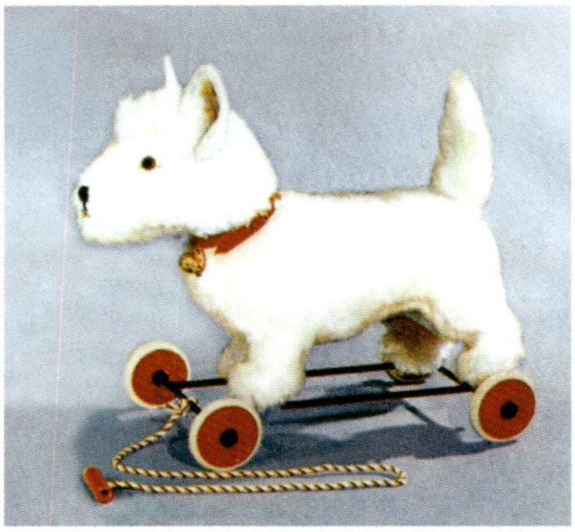

Reit-**Sealyham** - *Riding **Sealyham***

Mohair, Eisengerippe, weiss, rotes Halsband, stehend, Metallscheibenraeder mit Gummireifen, bis 1951 Zugstimme - *mohair, iron frame, white, red collar, standing, metal disc wheels with rubber tires, pull cord voice up to 1951*

Serie	Art.-No	Period	Pr.	Info
51a	**1343,2**	1950-1951	5	43 cm
51a	**1343**	1953-1957	5	

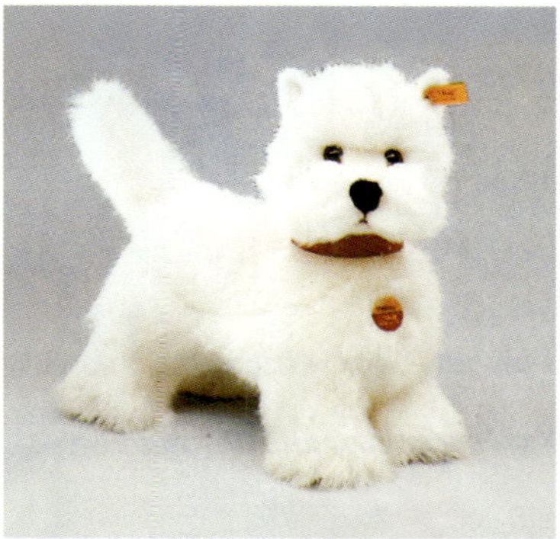

Whitey West Highland White Terrier

Webpelz, Lederhalsband, weiss, stehend, abwaschbar - *woven fur, leather collar, white, standing, surface washable*

Serie	Art.-No	Period	Pr.	Info
079535	**4135/35**	1989-1990	3	35 cm
	079535	1991-1991	3	

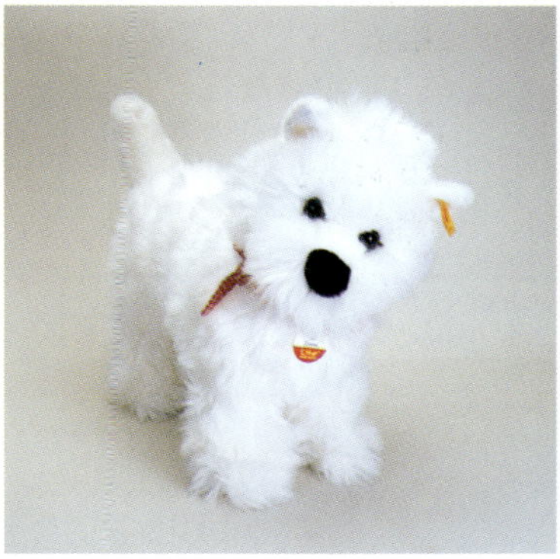

Tommi West Highland White Terrier

Webpelz, rot-weiss kariertes Halstuch, waschmaschinenfest - *woven fur, red-white chequered scarf, machine washable*

EAN-No	Period	Pr.	Info
079542	1997-1999	3	35 cm

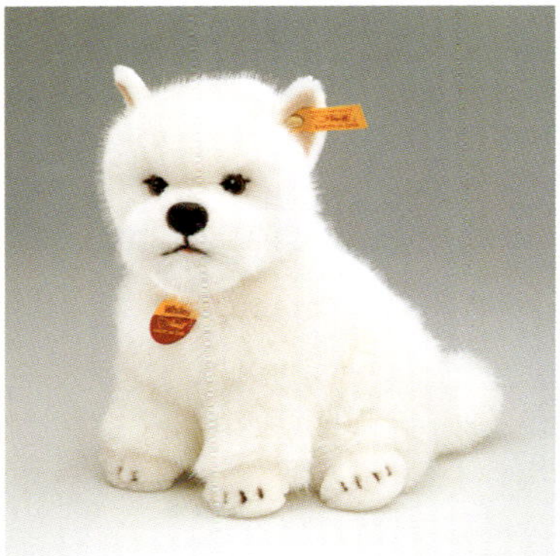

Whitey West Highland White Terrier

Webpelz, sitzend, waschmaschinenfest - *woven fur, sitting, machine washable*

EAN-No.	Period	Pr.	Info
080722	1999-1999	2-3	22 cm

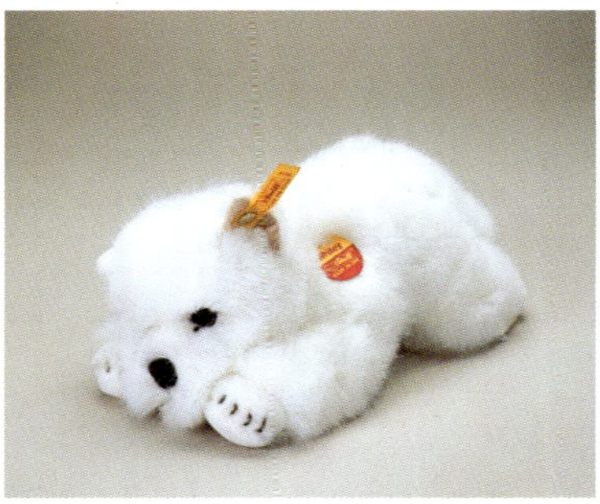

Whitey West Highland White Terrier

Webpelz, liegend, waschmaschinenfest - *woven fur, lying, machine washable*

EAN-No.	Period	Pr.	Info
080746	1999-1999	2-3	28 cm

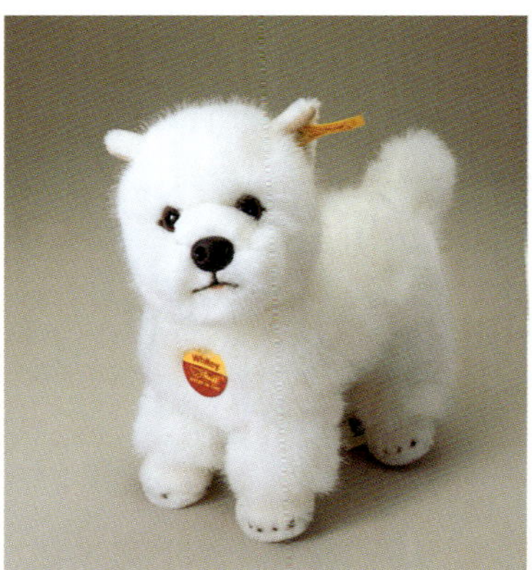

Whitey West Highland White Terrier

Webpelz, stehend, waschmaschinenfest - *woven fur, standing, machine washable*

EAN-No.	Period	Pr.	Info
080715	1999-1999	2-3	25 cm

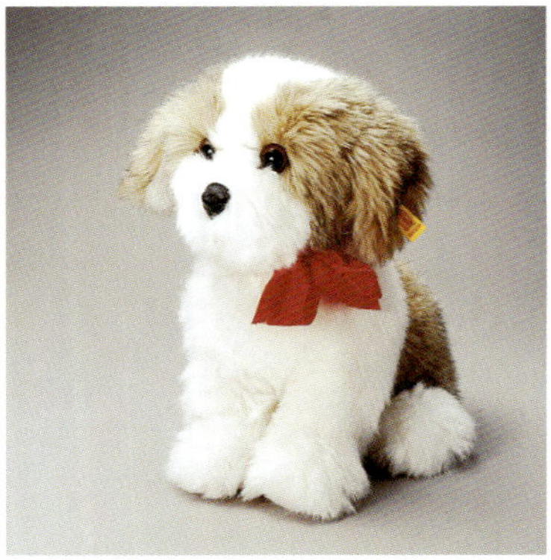

Junior Charly Bobtail

Webpelz, abwaschbar - *woven fur, surface washable*

Serie	Art.-No	Period	Pr.	Info
076107	**2883/35**	1982-1986	3	35 cm

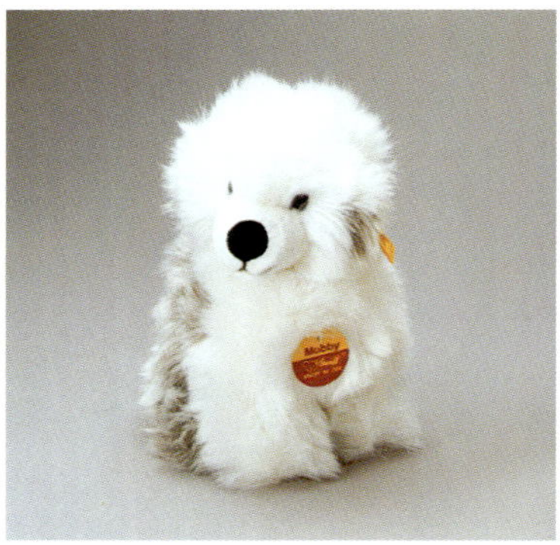

Mobby Bobtail

Webpelz, sitzend, abwaschbar - *woven fur, sitting, surface washable*

Serie	Art.-No	Period	Pr.	Info
078354	**4130/20**	1988-1989	2-3	20 cm

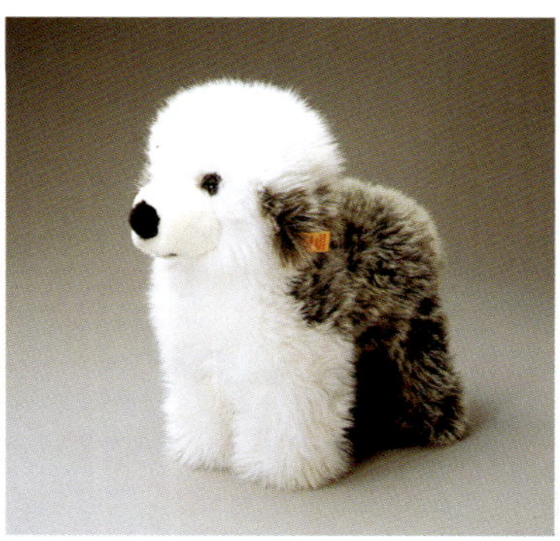

Mobby Bobtail

Webpelz, stehend, abwaschbar - *woven fur, standing, surface washable*

Serie	Art.-No	Period	Pr.	Info
078408	**4132/20**	1988-1989	2-3	20 cm
078422	**4132/24**	1988-1989	3	30 cm

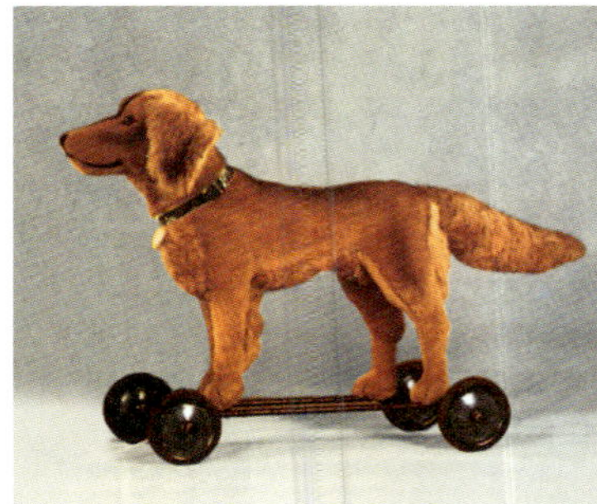

Reit-Setter - *Riding Setter*

Mohair, Eisengerippe, Zugstimme, rot- oder kupferbraun, Metallscheibenraeder mit Gummireifen, Verbindungsschienen - *mohair, iron frame, pull cord voice, red- or copper-brown, metal disc wheels with rubber tires, connecting bar frame*

Serie	Art.-No	Period	Pr.	Info
66	**1343,2**	1950-1954	5	43 cm
66	**1350,2**	1950-1954	5	50 cm

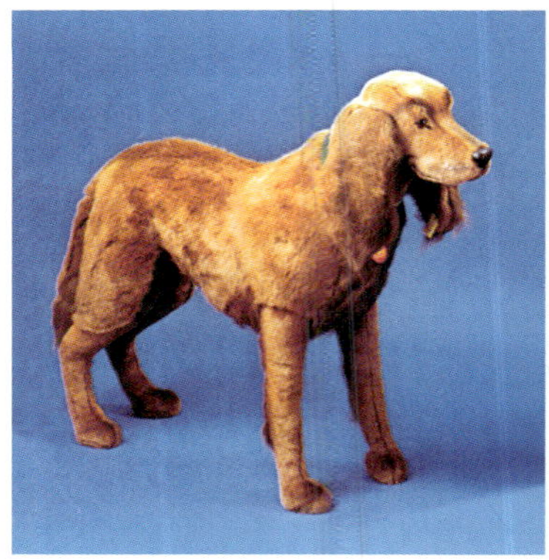

Pranko Setter

Studio-Tier, Webpelz, stehend, abwaschbar - *studio animal, woven fur, standing, surface washable*

Serie	Art.-No	Period	Pr.	Info
	4060/80	1978-1981	4-5	80 cm

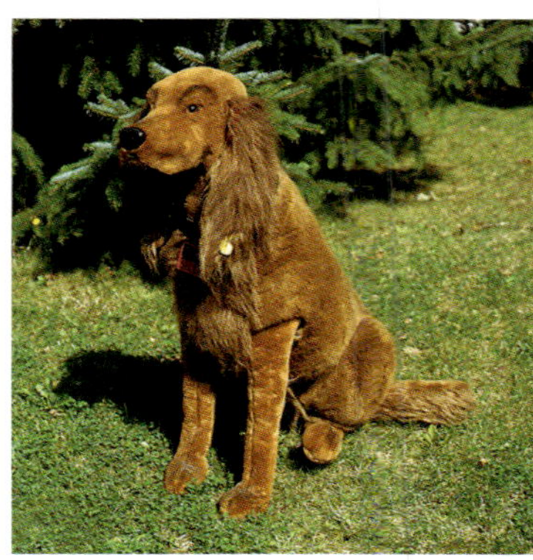

Bosco Setter

Studio-Tier, Webpelz, sitzend, abwaschbar - *studio animal, woven fur, sitting, surface washable*

SERIE	ART.-NO	PERIOD	PR.	INFO
	4061/80	1979-1983	5	80 cm

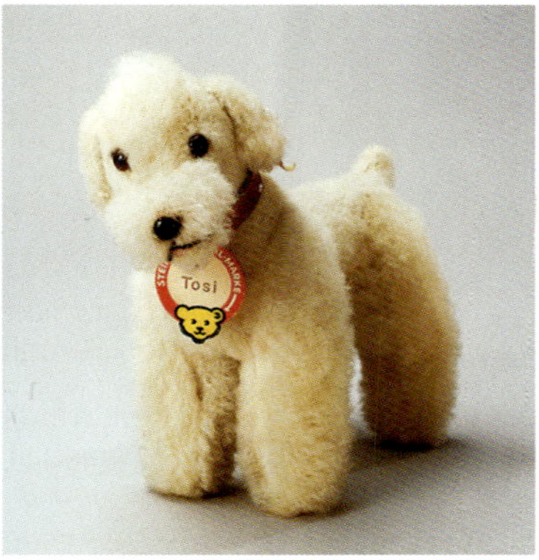

Tosi Pudel - ***Tosi*** *Poodle*

Wollpluesch, schwarz oder weiss, stehend ohne Raeder, Karakulschur - *wool plush, black or white, standing without wheels, Karakul trim*

SERIE	ART.-NO	PERIOD	PR.	INFO
58	**1514,0** s	1950-1953	4	14 cm, schwarz - *black*
58	**1517,0** s	1950-1953	4-5	17 cm
58	**1522,0** s	1950-1953	4-5	22 cm
58	**1528,01** s	1950-1950	5	28 cm
58	**1528,02** s	1951-1953	5	
58	**1514,0** w	1950-1953	4	14 cm, weiss - *white*
58	**1517,0** w	1950-1953	4-5	17 cm
58	**1522,0** w	1950-1953	4-5	22 cm
58	**1528,01** w	1950-1950	5	28 cm
58	**1528,02** w	1951-1953	5	

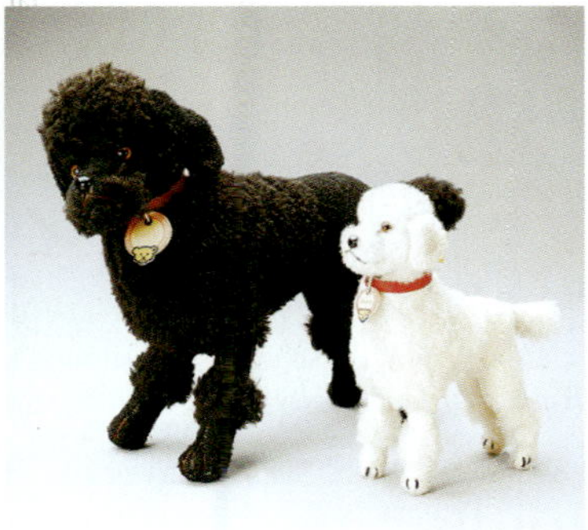

Pudel **Snobby** - *Poodle* ***Snobby***

Wollpluesch, schwarz oder weiss, stehend, franzoesische Schur, 28 cm Kopf drehbar - *wool plush, black or white, standing, French trim, 28 cm head swivels*

SERIE	ART.-NO	PERIOD	PR.	INFO
58	**6517,0** s	1952-1952	5	17 cm, schwarz - *black*
58	**6528,0** s	1952-1952	5	28 cm
58	**6517,0** w	1952-1952	5	17 cm, weiss - *white*
58	**6528,0** w	1952-1952	5	28 cm

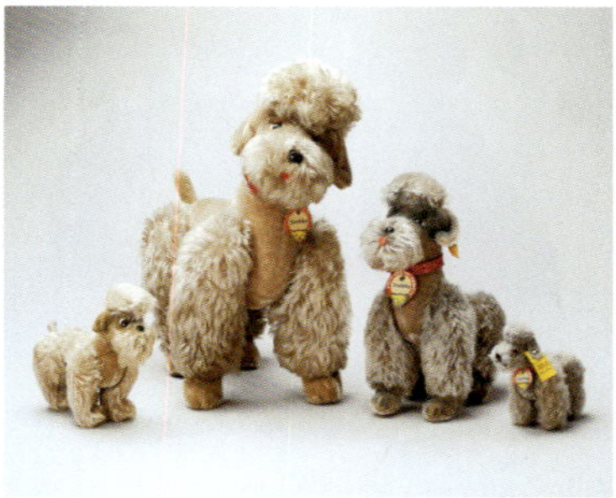

Pudel **Snobby** - *Poodle* ***Snobby***

Mohair, grau, gegliedert, moderne Schur, ab 22 cm Kopf drehbar - *mohair, grey, jointed, modern trim, head swivels from 22cm size*

SERIE	ART.-NO	PERIOD	PR.	INFO
58	**5310** gr	1956-1958	3	10 cm
580	**5310,05**	1959-1964	2-3	
443	**5310,05**	1965-1967	2-3	
	4435/10	1968-1972	2-3	
58	**5314** gr	1954-1958	3	14 cm
580	**5314,05**	1959-1963	2-3	
443	**5314,05**	1965-1967	2-3	
	4435/14	1968-1974	2-3	
58	**5322** gr	1954-1958	3-4	22 cm
580	**5322,05**	1959-1963	3	
443	**5322,05**	1965-1967	3	
	4435/22	1968-1974	2-3	
58	**5335** gr	1954-1954	3-4	35 cm
58	**5335,2**	1955-1958	3	
580	**5335,05**	1959-1963	3	
443	**5335,05**	1965-1967	3	
	4435/35	1968-1974	3	
58	**5343,2** gr	1955-1958	4	43 cm
580	**5343,05**	1959-1963	3-4	
443	**5343,05**	1965-1967	3-4	
	4435/43	1968-1968	3	

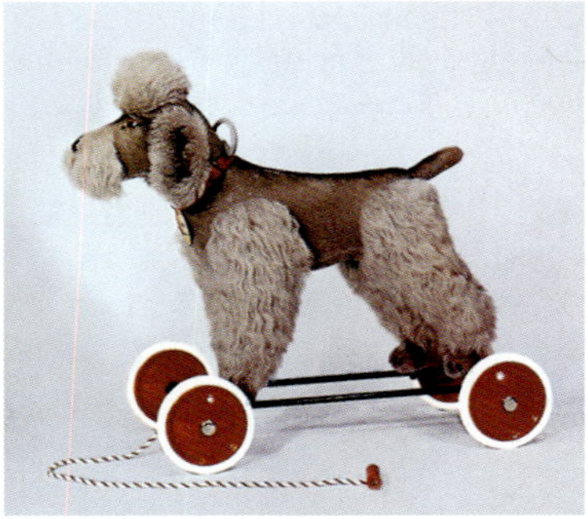

Reit-Pudel **Snobby** - *Riding Poodle* ***Snobby***

Mohair, Stahlskelett, Zugstimme, grau, stehend auf gummibereiften Metallscheibenraedern, ab 1967 Plastikreifen, Verbindungsschienen, Haltegriff, Schlepplenkung - *mohair, steel frame, pull cord voice, grey, standing on metal disc wheels with rubber tires, from 1967 plastic tires, connecting bars frame, grip handle & pull type steering*

SERIE	ART.-NO	PERIOD	PR.	INFO
58	**1350,2** gr	1956-1958	4-5	50 cm
580	**1350,25**	1959-1964	4-5	
446	**1350,25**	1965-1967	4-5	
	4435/50	1968-1969	4-5	

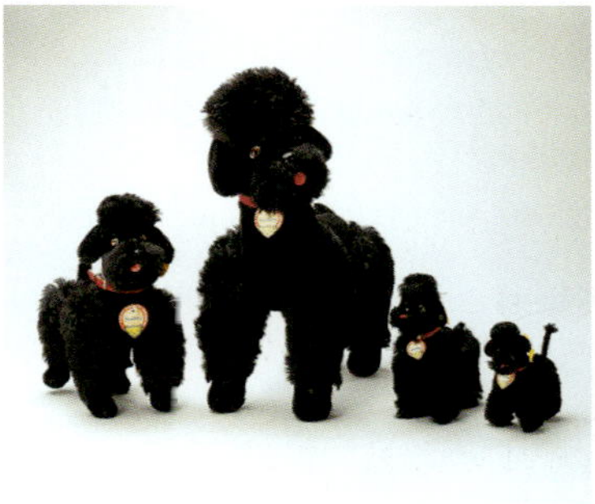

Pudel **Snobby** - *Poodle* ***Snobby***

Mohair, schwarz, gegliedert, moderne Schur, ab 22 cm Kopf drehbar - *mohair, black, jointed, modern trim, head swivels from 22 cm size*

SERIE	ART.-NO	PERIOD	PR.	INFO
58	**5310** s	1956-1958	3	10 cm
580	**5310,06**	1959-1964	2-3	
444	**5310,06**	1965-1967	2-3	
	4436/10	1968-1972	2-3	
58	**5314** s	1953-1958	3	14 cm
580	**5314,06**	1959-1963	2-3	
444	**5314,06**	1965-1967	2-3	
	4436/14	1968-1974	2-3	
58	**5322** s	1953-1958	3-4	22 cm
580	**5322,06**	1959-1963	3	
444	**5322,06**	1965-1967	3	
	4436/22	1968-1974	2-3	
58	**5335** s	1953-1953	3-4	35 cm
58	**5335,2** s	1954-1958	3	
580	**5335,06**	1959-1963	3	
444	**5335,06**	1965-1967	3	
	4436/35	1968-1973	3	
58	**5343,2** s	1955-1958	4	43 cm
580	**5343,06**	1959-1963	3-4	
444	**5343,06**	1965-1967	3-4	
	4436/43	1968-1968	3	

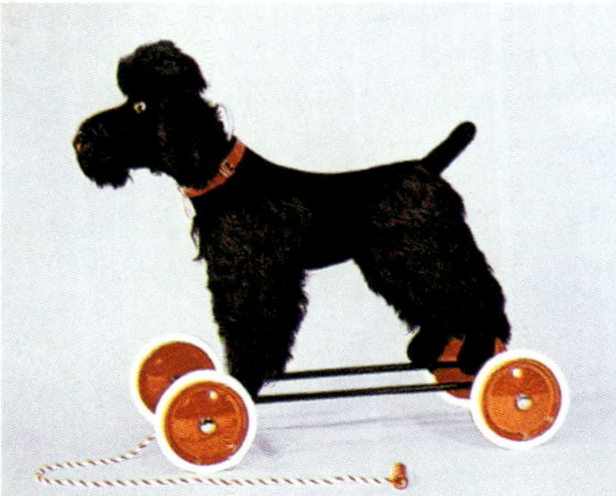

Reit-Pudel **Snobby** - *Riding Poodle* ***Snobby***

Mohair, Stahlskelett, Zugstimme, schwarz, stehend auf gummibereiften Metallscheibenraedern, ab 1967 Plastikreifen, Verbindungsschienen, Haltegriff, Schlepplenkung - *mohair, steel frame, pull cord voice, black, standing on metal disc wheels with rubber tires, from 1967 plastic tires, connecting bars frame, grip handle & pull type steering*

Serie	Art.-No	Period	Pr.	Info
58	**1350,2** s	1956-1958	4-5	50 cm
580	**1350,26**	1959-1964	4-5	
446	**1350,26**	1965-1967	4-5	
	4436/50	1968-1969	4-5	

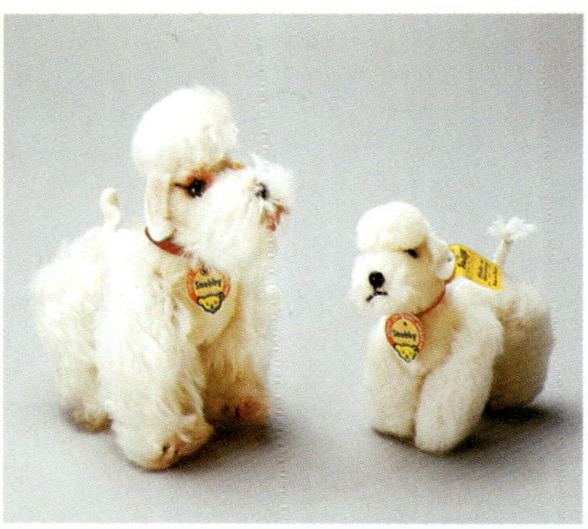

Pudel **Snobby** - *Poodle* ***Snobby***

Mohair, weiss, gegliedert, moderne Schur, ab 22 cm Kopf drehbar - *mohair, white, jointed, modern trim, head swivels from 22 cm size*

Serie	Art.-No	Period	Pr.	Info
58	**5310** w	1956-1958	4	10 cm
580	**5310,04**	1959-1964	3-4	
58	**5314** w	1953-1958	4	14 cm
580	**5314,04**	1959-1963	3-4	
58	**5322** w	1953-1958	4	22 cm
580	**5322,04**	1959-1963	3-4	
58	**5335** w	1953-1953	4	35 cm
58	**5335,2**	1954-1958	4	
580	**5335,04**	1959-1963	4	
58	**5343,2** w	1955-1958	4	43 cm
580	**5343,04**	1959-1963	4	

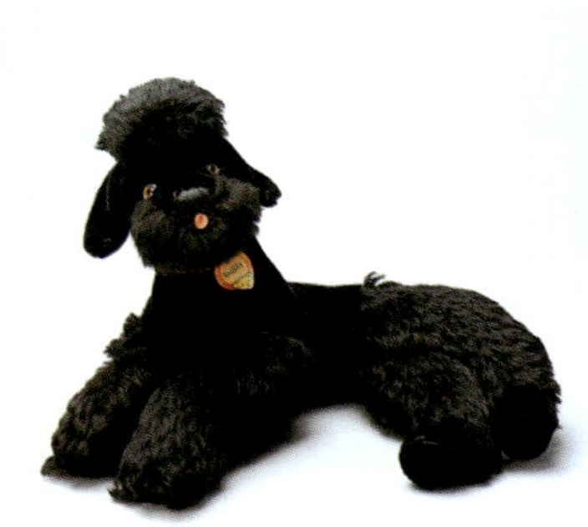

Snobby Pudel - ***Snobby*** *Poodle*

Mohairpluesch, grau oder schwarz, 35 cm, liegend, Stimme, weich - *mohair, grey or black, 35 cm, lying, voice, soft*

Serie	Art.-No	Period	Pr.	Info
58	**2335,1** gr	1955-1958	3	grau - *grey*
580	**2335,05**	1959-1964	3	
440	**2335,05**	1965-1967	3	
58	**2335,1** s	1955-1958	3	schwarz - *black*
580	**2335,06**	1959-1964	3	
440	**2335,06**	1966-1967	3	

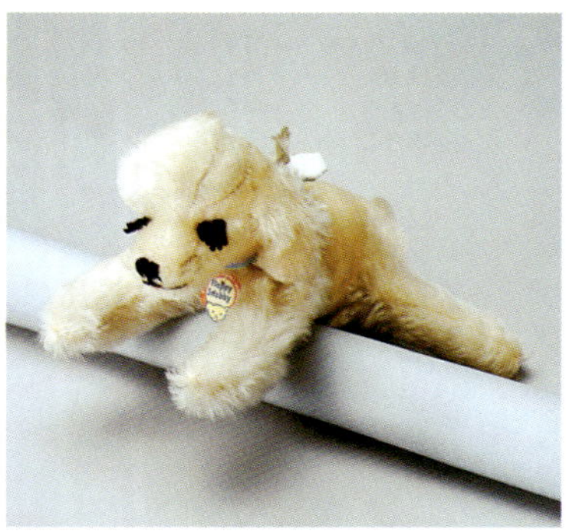

Floppy Snobby Pudel - ***Floppy Snobby*** *Poodle*

Schlaftier, Mohair, Augenwimpern aus Filz, weiss, liegend, sehr weich - *sleeping toy, mohair, felt eyelashes, white, lying, very soft*

Serie	Art.-No	Period	Pr.	Info
850 580	**7317,04**	1959-1963	3-4	17 cm
850 580	**7328,04**	1959-1963	3-4	28 cm

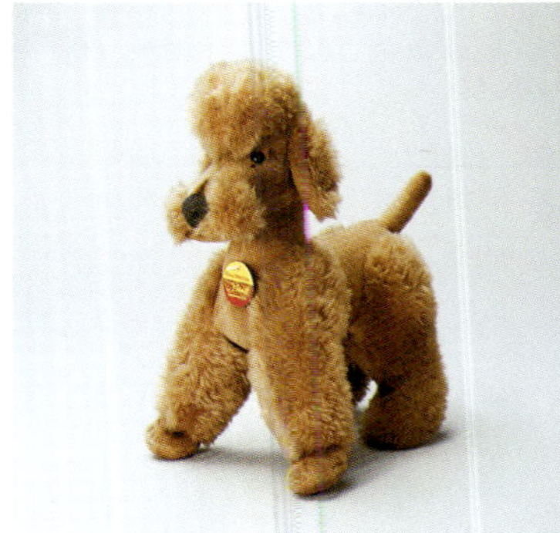

Cosy Snobby Pudel - ***Cosy Snobby*** *Poodle*

Dralon, braun oder weiss, 28 cm, gefuellt mit synthetischen Fasern & Schaumstoff, stehend, sehr weich, vollwaschbar - *dralon, brown or white, 28 cm, stuffed with synthetic fibers & foam, standing, very soft, fully washable*

Serie	Art.-No	Period	Pr.	Info
830 580	**6628,03**	1961-1963	2	braun - *brown*
502	**6628,03**	1965-1967	2	
	5020/28	1968-1977	2	
830 580	**6628,04**	1961-1963	2-3	weiss - *white*

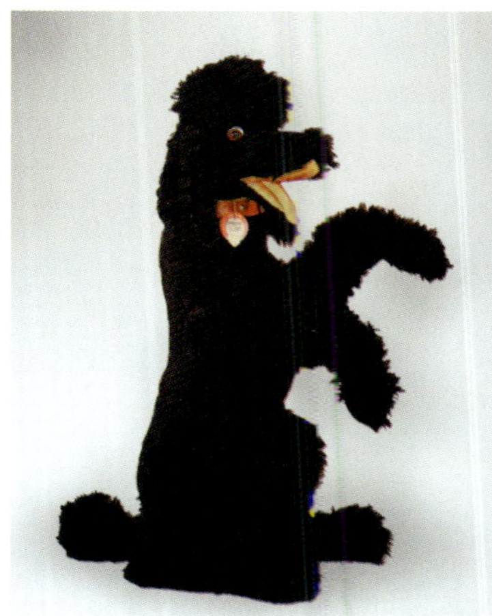

Snobby Pudel - *Snobby Poodle*

Schautier, Mohair, schwarz, aufwartend - *display animal, mohair, black, sitting up*

Serie	Art.-No	Period	Pr.	Info
	4439/08	1967-1967	5-6	80 cm

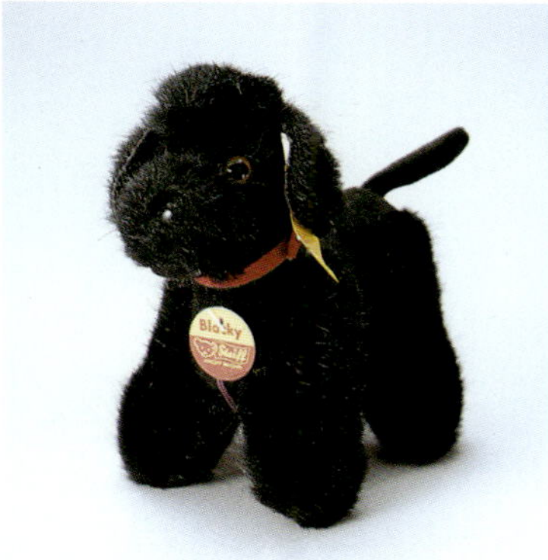

Blacky Pudel - ***Blacky** Poodle*

Webpelz, schwarz, stehend, abwaschbar - *woven fur, black, standing, surface washable*

SERIE	ART.-NO	PERIOD	PR.	INFO
	1532/12	1978-1984	1-2	12 cm

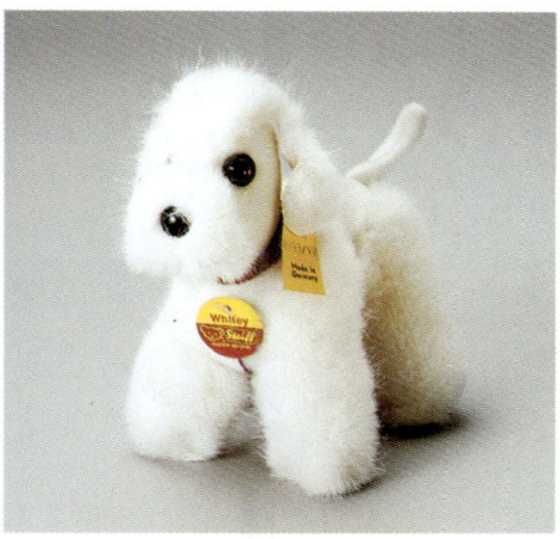

Whitey Pudel - ***Whitey** Poodle*

Webpelz, weiss, stehend, abwaschbar - *woven fur, white, standing, surface washable*

SERIE	ART.-NO	PERIOD	PR.	INFO
	1533/12	1978-1984	1-2	12 cm

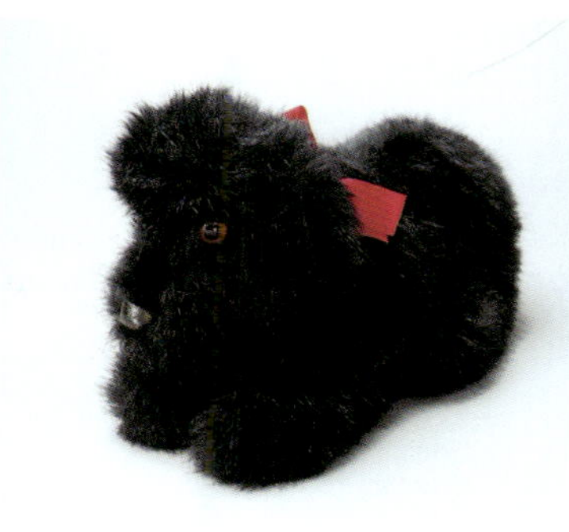

Bobby Pudel - ***Bobby** Poodle*

Webpelz, schwarz, liegend, abwaschbar - *woven fur, black, lying, surface washable*

SERIE	ART.-NO	PERIOD	PR.	INFO
	4160/35	1978-1981	2-3	35 cm

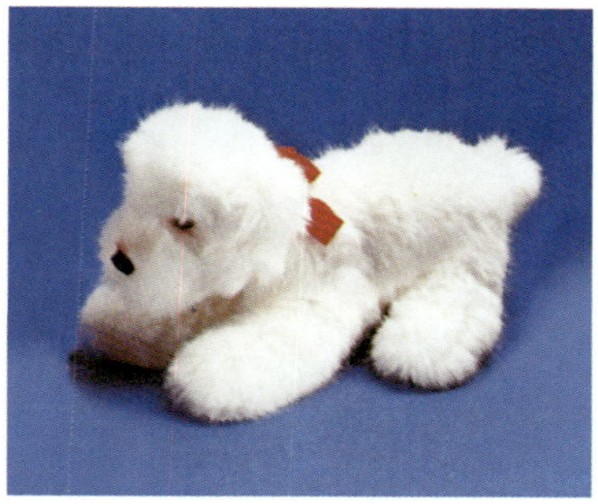

Tobby Pudel - ***Tobby** Poodle*

Webpelz, weiss, liegend, abwaschbar - *woven fur, white, lying, surface washable*

SERIE	ART.-NO	PERIOD	PR.	INFO
	4161/35	1978-1981	2-3	35 cm

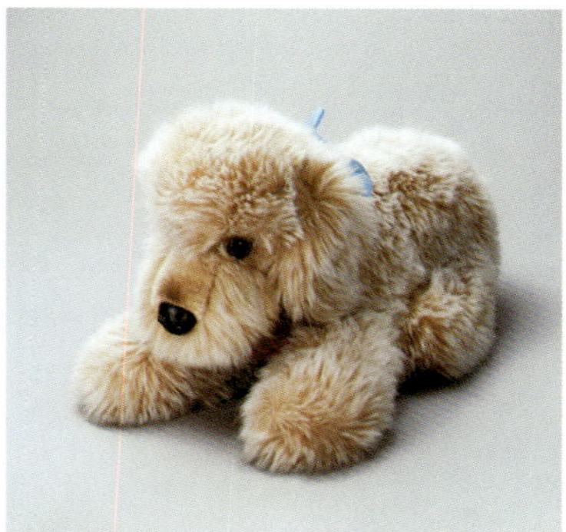

Nobby Pudel - ***Nobby** Poodle*

Webpelz, apricot, liegend, abwaschbar - *woven fur, apricot, lying, surface washable*

SERIE	ART.-NO	PERIOD	PR.	INFO
	4162/35	1978-1981	2-3	35 cm

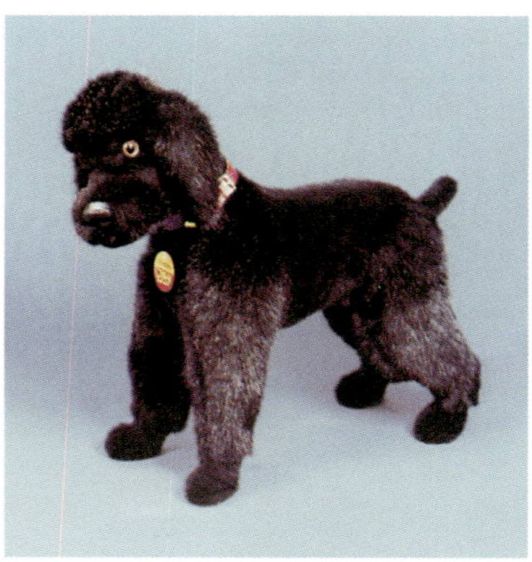

Snobby Pudel - ***Snobby** Poodle*

Studio-Tier, Webpelz, schwarz, stehend, abwaschbar - *studio animal, woven fur, black, standing, surface washable*

SERIE	ART.-NO	PERIOD	PR.	INFO
	4157/50	1978-1984	4-5	50 cm

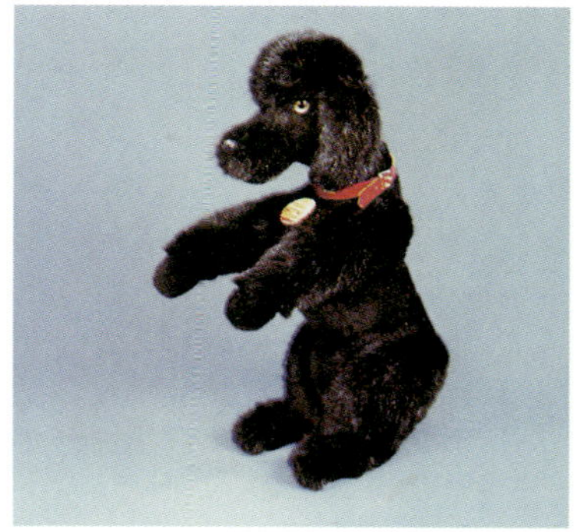

Mobby Pudel - ***Mobby** Poodle*

Studio-Tier, Webpelz, schwarz, aufwartend, abwaschbar - *studio animal, woven fur, black, sitting up, surface washable*

SERIE	ART.-NO	PERIOD	PR.	INFO
	4158/50	1978-1981	4	50 cm

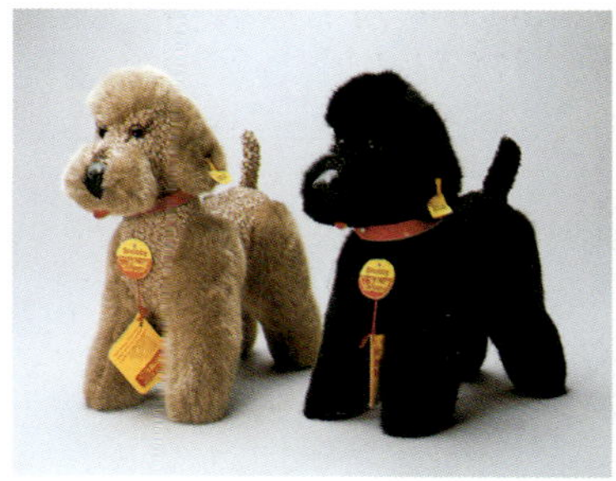

Snobby Pudel - ***Snobby** Poodle*

Webpelz, stehend, 26 cm, abwaschbar - *woven fur, standing, 26 cm, surface washable*

SERIE	ART.-NO	PERIOD	PR.	INFO
	4156/26	1980-1984	2-3	braun - *brown*
	4157/26	1980-1984	2-3	schwarz - *black*

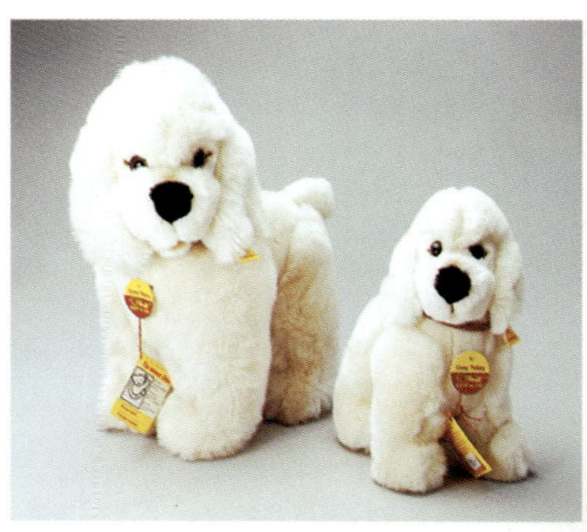

Cosy Tobby Pudel - ***Cosy Tobby** Poodle*

Webpelz, apricot, stehend, superweich - *woven fur, apricot, standing, super soft*

SERIE	ART.-NO	PERIOD	PR.	INFO
096020	**5445/20**	1986-1988	2	20 cm
096044	**5445/28**	1986-1988	2-3	28 cm

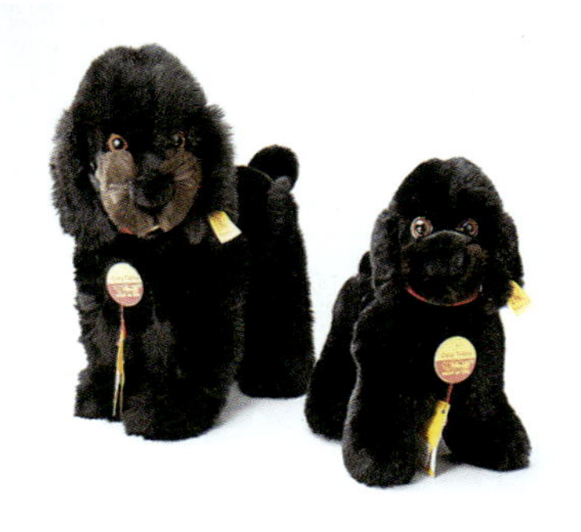

Cosy Tobby Pudel - ***Cosy Tobby** Poodle*

Webpelz, schwarz, stehend, superweich - *woven fur, black, standing, super soft*

SERIE	ART.-NO	PERIOD	PR.	INFO
096068	**5447/20**	1986-1988	2	20 cm
096082	**5447/28**	1986-1988	2-3	28 cm

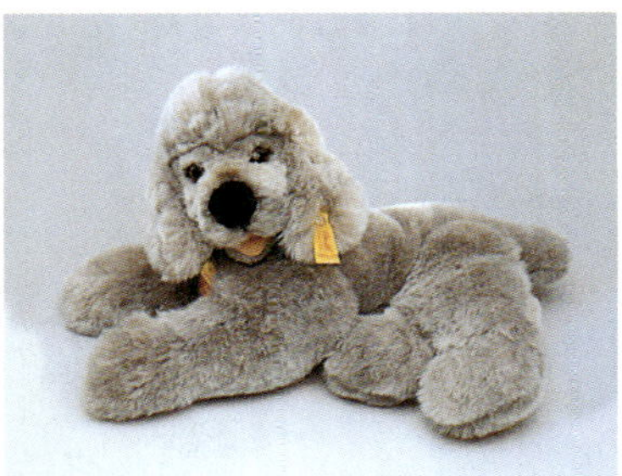

Cosy Nobby Pudel - ***Cosy Nobby** Poodle*

Webpelz, grau, liegend, superweich, waschmaschinenfest - *woven fur, grey, lying, super soft, machine washable*

SERIE	ART.-NO	PERIOD	PR.	INFO
096143	**5452/28**	1986-1989	2-3	28 cm

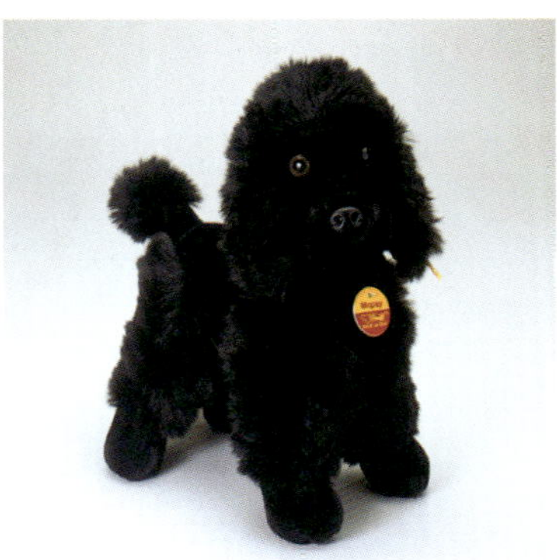

Mopsy Pudel - ***Mopsy** Poodle*

Webpelz, 28 cm, stehend, waschmaschinenfest - *woven fur, 28 cm, standing, machine washable*

EAN-NO.	PERIOD	PR.	INFO
079382	1998-1999	3	weiss - *white*
079399	1998-1999	3	schwarz - *black*

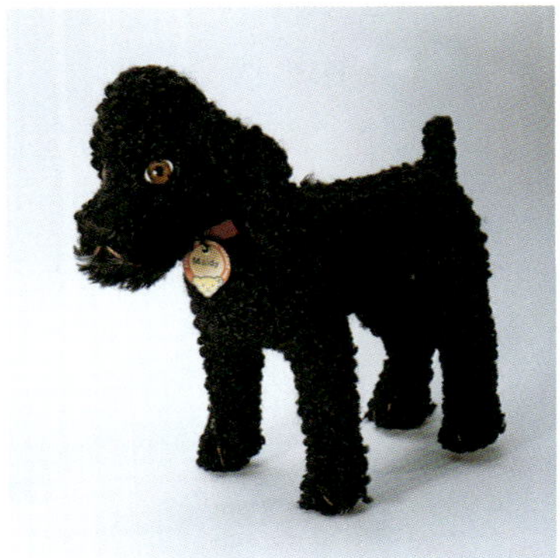

Maidy Zwergpudel - ***Maidy** Miniature Poodle*

Mohairpluesch, schwarz, stehend, Kopf drehbar - *mohair, black, standing, head swivels*

SERIE	ART.-NO	PERIOD	PR.	INFO
581	**1325,06**	1959-1959	5-6	25 cm
581	**1330,06**	1959-1959	5-6	30 cm

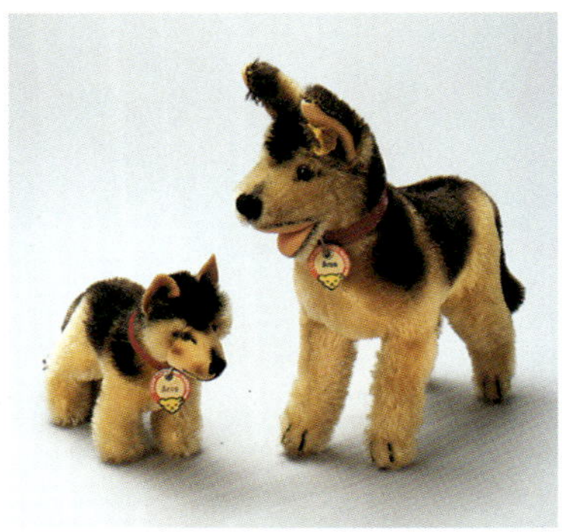

Schaeferhund **Arco** - *German Shepherd **Arco***

Mohair, braun/schwarz, stehend, 10 cm geschlossener Mund, ab 17 cm offener Mund ohne Zunge - *mohair, brown/black, standing, 10 cm mouth closed, from 17 cm mouth open, no tongue*

SERIE	ART.-NO	PERIOD	PR.	INFO
61	**1310,0**	1951-1956	4-5	10 cm
61	**1317,0**	1951-1956	5	17 cm
61	**1322,02**	1951-1956	5	22 cm

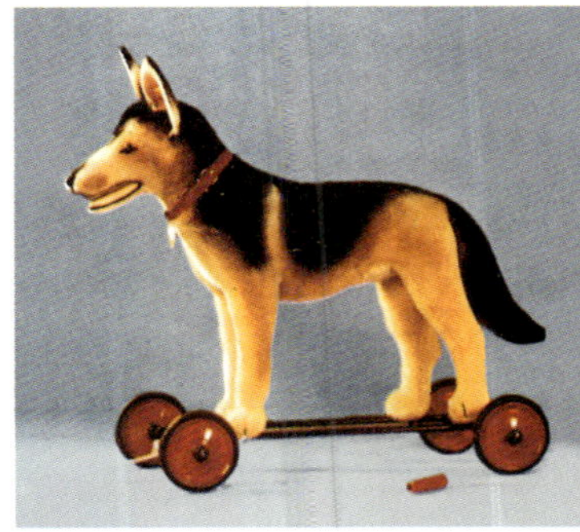

Reit-**Arco** - *Riding **Arco***

Mohairpluesch, Eisengerippe, Zugstimme, hellbraun/schwarz, stehend auf Holzraedern, ab 1950 Metallscheibenraeder mit Gummi, mit Verbindungsschienen, offener Mund ohne Zunge - *mohair, iron frame, pull cord voice, light brown & black, standing on wooden wheels, from 1950 metal disc wheels with rubber tires, with connecting bar frame, open mouth, no tongue*

SERIE	ART.-NO	PERIOD	PR.	INFO
61	**1343,2**	1949-1956	5-6	43 cm
61	**1350,2**	1950-1956	5-6	50 cm

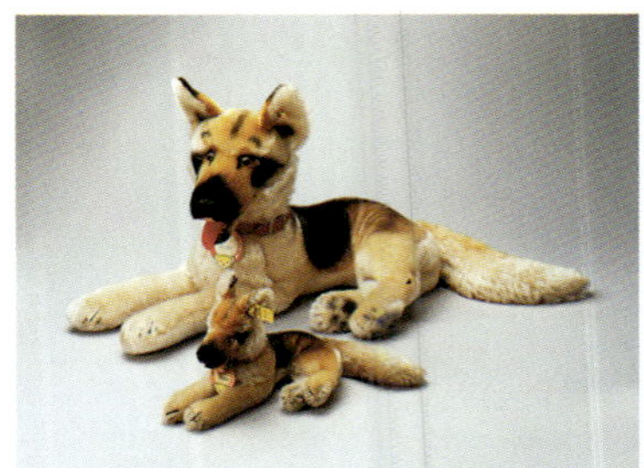

Schaeferhund **Arco** - *German Shepherd **Arco***

Mohairpluesch, braun/schwarz/weiss, liegend - *mohair, brown/black/white, lying*

SERIE	ART.-NO	PERIOD	PR.	INFO
61	**2322,1**	1957-1958	4	22 cm
610	**2322,00**	1959-1964	4	
434	**2322,00**	1965-1967	4	
	4340/22	1968-1976	3-4	
61	**2335,1**	1957-1958	4	35 cm
610	**2335,00**	1959-1964	4	
434	**2335,00**	1965-1967	4	
	4340/35	1968-1976	3-4	
61	**2350,1**	1957-1958	4	50 cm
610	**2350,00**	1959-1964	4	
434	**2350,00**	1965-1967	4	
	4340/50	1968-1974	3-4	

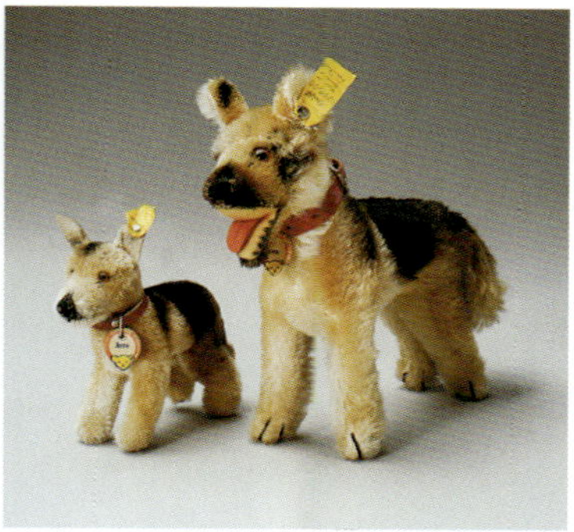

Schaeferhund **Arco** - *German Shepherd* ***Arco***

Mohair, braun/schwarz, stehend, 10 cm geschlossener Mund, ab 17 cm offener Mund mit roter Filz-Zunge - *mohair, brown/black, standing, 10 cm mouth closed, from 17 cm open mouth with red felt tongue*

SERIE	ART.-NO	PERIOD	PR.	INFO
61	**6310,0**	1957-1958	4	10 cm
610	**6310,00**	1959-1961	4	
61	**6317,0**	1957-1958	4	17 cm
610	**6317,00**	1959-1961	4	
61	**6322,0**	1957-1958	4-5	22 cm
610	**6322,00**	1959-1961	4-5	
61	**6335,0**	1957-1958	5	35 cm
610	**6335,00**	1959-1961	5	

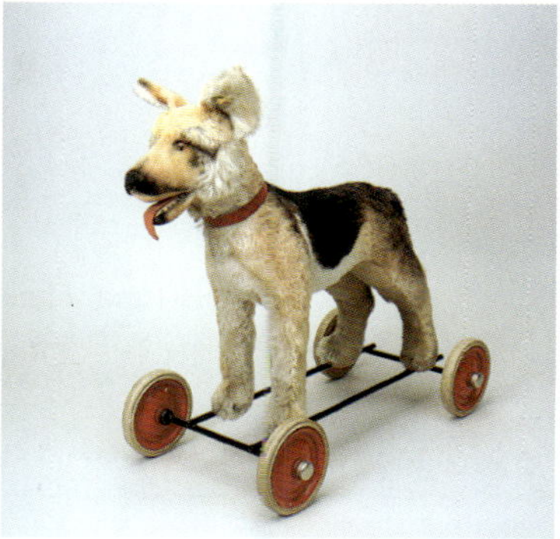

Reit-**Arco** - *Riding* ***Arco***

Mohair, Eisengerippe, Zugstimme, hellbraun/schwarz, stehend auf Metallscheibenraedern mit Gummireifen, ab 1967 Plastikreifen & Schlepplenkung, mit Verbindungsschienen, offener Mund mit roter Filz-Zunge - *mohair, iron frame, pull cord voice, light brown/black, standing on metal disc wheels with rubber tires, from 1967 plastic tires & pull type steering, with connecting bar frame, open mouth with red felt tongue*

SERIE	ART.-NO	PERIOD	PR.	INFO
61	**6343,2**	1957-1958	5	43 cm
610	**6343,20**	1959-1961	5	
61	**6350,2**	1957-1958	5	50 cm
610	**6350,20**	1959-1961	5	
434	**6350,20**	1966-1967	5	
	4340/55	1968-1970	5	

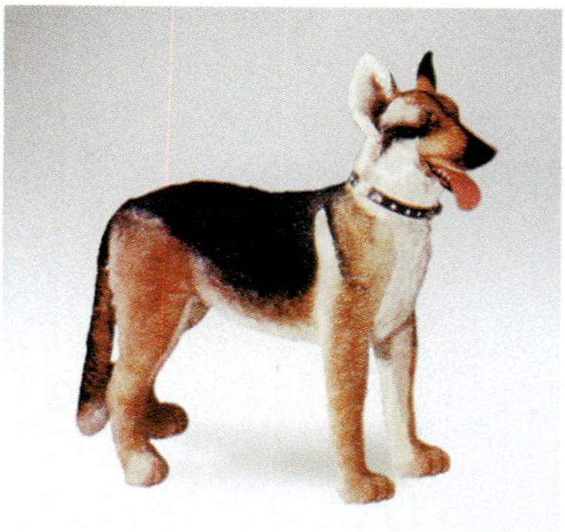

Schaeferhund - *German Shepherd*

Schautier, Mohair, stehend - *display animal, mohair, standing*

SERIE	ART.-NO	PERIOD	PR.	INFO
434	**1385,90**	1966-1966	5-6	85 cm
	4349/09	1967-1967	5-6	

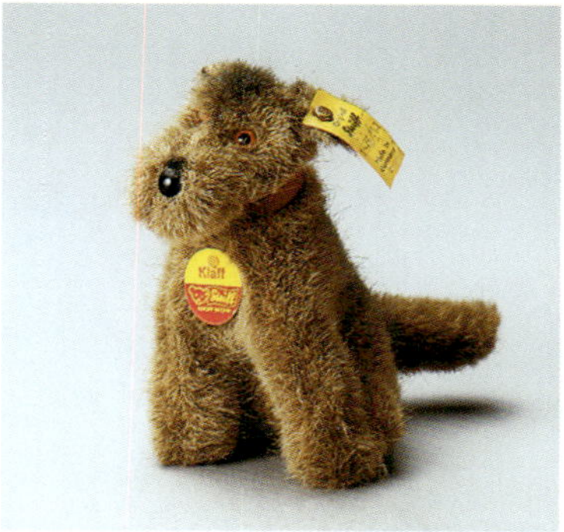

Klaeff Schaeferhund - ***Klaeff*** *German Shepherd*

Synthetik-Webpelz, sitzend, abwaschbar - *synthetic woven fur, sitting, surface washable*

SERIE	ART.-NO	PERIOD	PR.	INFO
	1526/11	1978-1981	2	11 cm

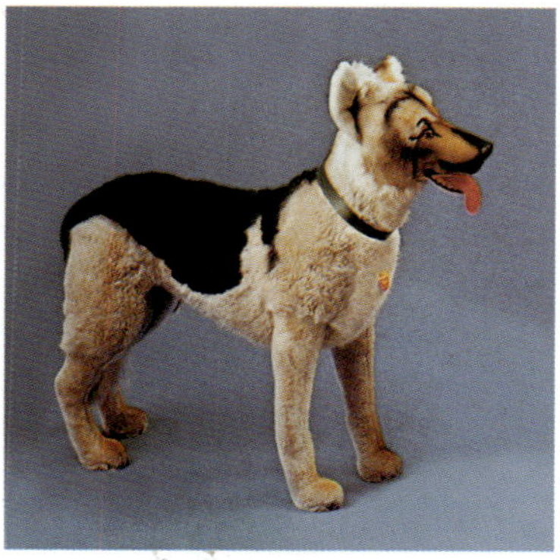

Arco Schaeferhund - ***Arco*** *German Shepherd*

Studio-Tier, Webpelz, stehend, abwaschbar - *studio animal, woven fur, standing, surface washable*

SERIE	ART.-NO	PERIOD	PR.	INFO
	4050/80	1978-1984	5	80 cm

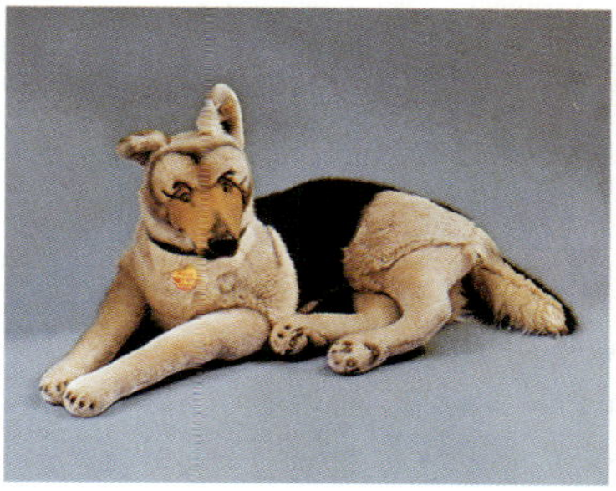

Hasso Schaeferhund - ***Hasso*** *German Shepherd*

Studio-Tier, Webpelz, liegend, abwaschbar - *studio animal, woven fur, lying, surface washable*

SERIE	ART.-NO	PERIOD	PR.	INFO
	4052/80	1978-1984	4-5	80 cm

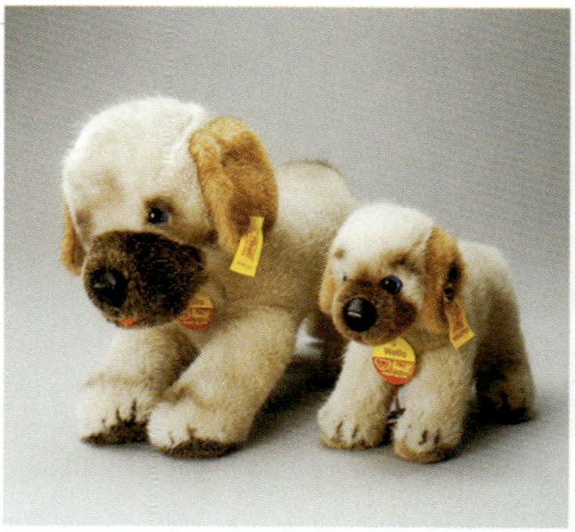

Welfo Schaeferhundwelpe - ***Welfo*** *German Shepherd Puppy*

Webpelz, stehend, abwaschbar - *woven fur, standing, surface washable*

SERIE	ART.-NO	PERIOD	PR.	INFO
	4053/23	1978-1985	2	23 cm
	4053/20	1983-1985	2-3	20 cm

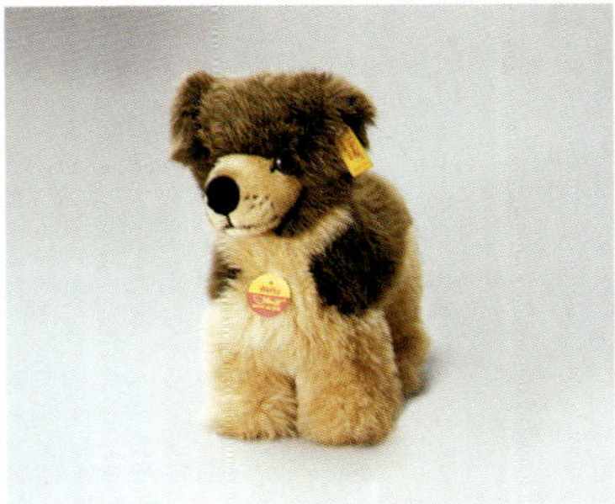

Welfo Welpe - ***Welfo*** *Puppy*

Webpelz, stehend, abwaschbar - *woven fur, standing, surface washable*

SERIE	ART.-NO	PERIOD	PR.	INFO
078804	**4160/24**	1987-1989	2	24 cm

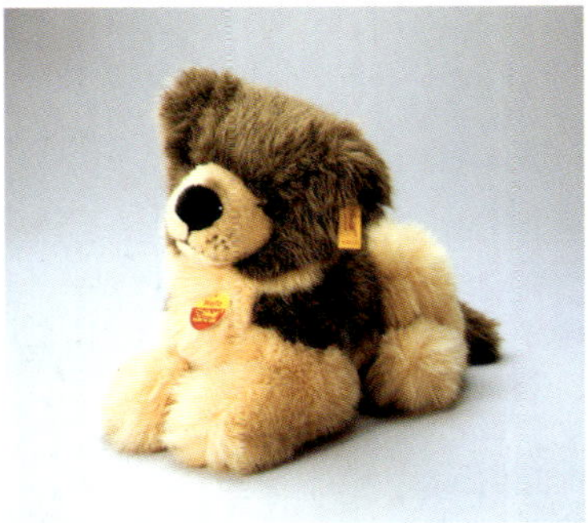

Welfo Welpe - ***Welfo*** *Puppy*

Webpelz, liegend, abwaschbar - *woven fur, lying, surface washable*

SERIE	ART.-NO	PERIOD	PR.	INFO
078859	**4162/22**	1987-1989	2	22 cm

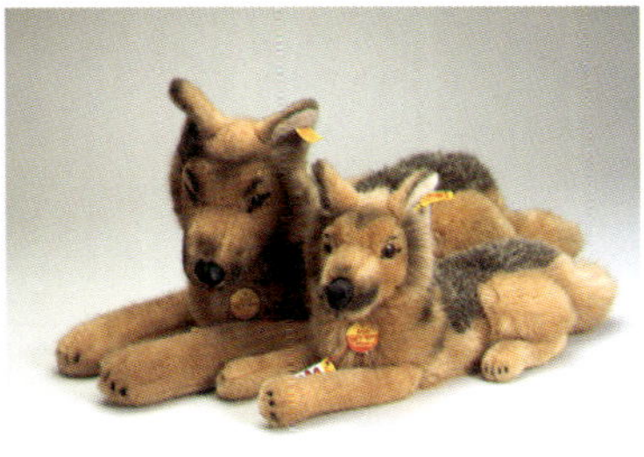

Arco Schaeferhund - ***Arco*** *German Shepherd*

Webpelz, abwaschbar - *woven fur, surface washable*

SERIE	ART.-NO	PERIOD	PR.	INFO
	4048/40	1983-1985	3	40 cm
078200	**4048/50**	1982-1988	3	50 cm

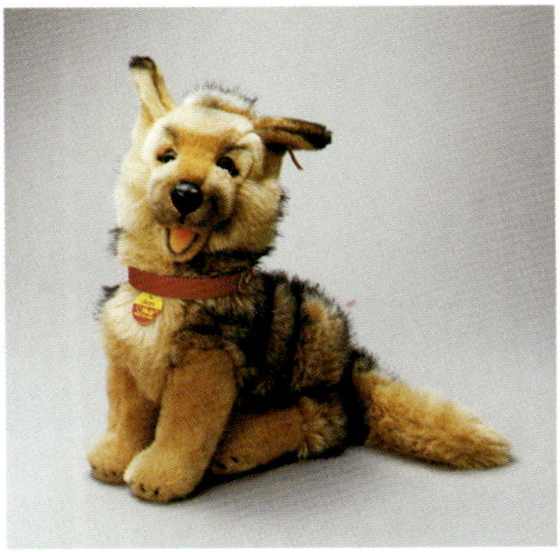

Arco Schaeferhund - ***Arco*** *German Shepherd*

Webpelz, Lederhalsband, blond, sitzend, abwaschbar - *woven fur, leather collar, blond, sitting, surface washable*

SERIE	ART.-NO	PERIOD	PR.	INFO
078880	**4167/40**	1990-1990	3	40 cm
	078880	1991-1995	3	

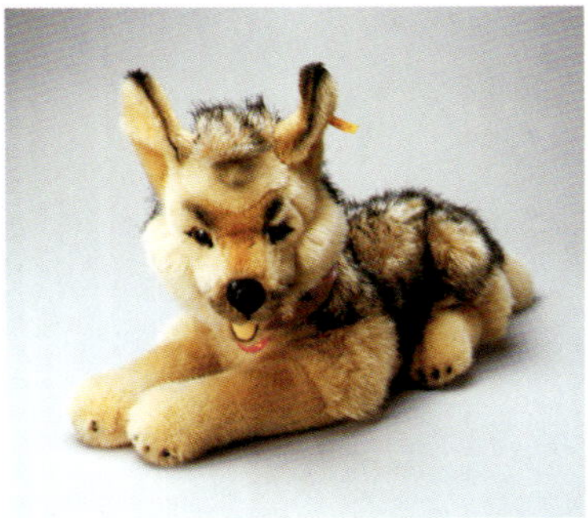

Arco Schaeferhund - ***Arco*** *German Shepherd*

Webpelz, Lederhalsband, blond, liegend, abwaschbar - *woven fur, leather collar, blond, lying, surface washable*

SERIE	ART.-NO	PERIOD	PR.	INFO
078903	**4168/45**	1990-1990	3	45 cm
	078903	1991-1995	3	

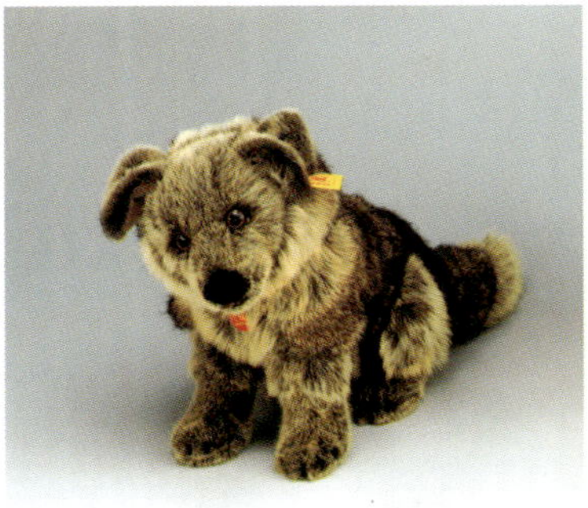

Hassan Schaeferhund Welpe - *Hassan German Shepherd Puppy*

Webpelz, sitzend, handwaschbar - *woven fur, sitting, hand washable*

EAN-NO.	PERIOD	PR.	INFO
078927	1996-1997	3	28 cm

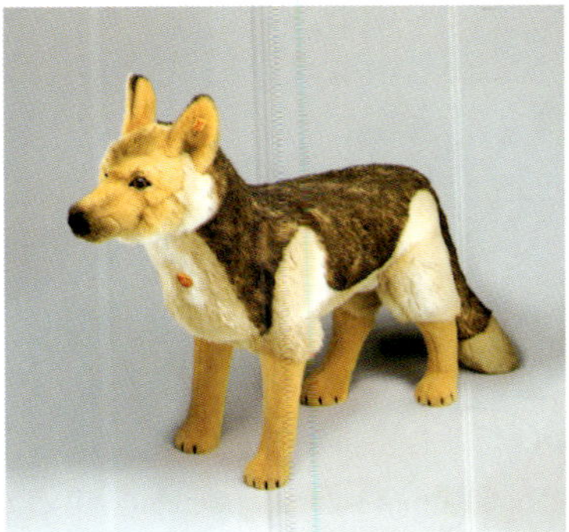

Hasso Schaeferhund - ***Hasso*** *German Shepherd*

Webpelz, stehend, abwaschbar - *woven fur, standing, surface washable*

EAN-NO.	PERIOD	PR.	INFO
078910	1996-1996	5	70 cm

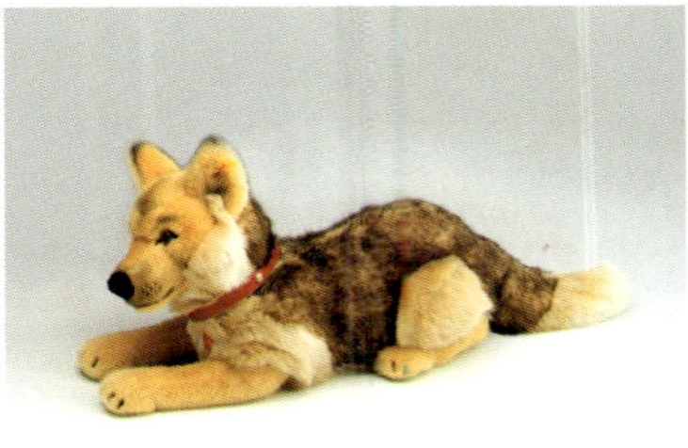

Hasso Schaeferhund - ***Hasso*** *German Shepherd*

Webpelz, liegend, Lederhalsband, ohne Halsband handwaschbar - *woven fur, lying, leather collar, hand washable without collar*

EAN-NO.	PERIOD	PR.	INFO
078965	1996-1999	3-4	55 cm

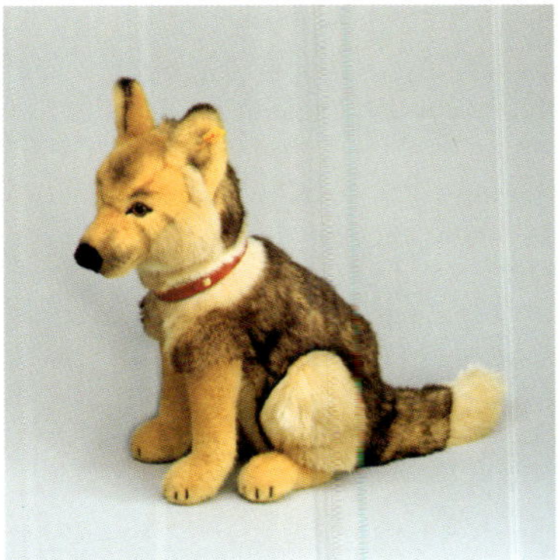

Hasso Schaeferhund - ***Hasso*** *German Shepherd*

Webpelz, sitzend, Lederhalsband, abwaschbar - *woven fur, sitting, leather collar, surface washable*

EAN-No.	Period	Pr.	Info
078941	1996-1997	3-4	40 cm

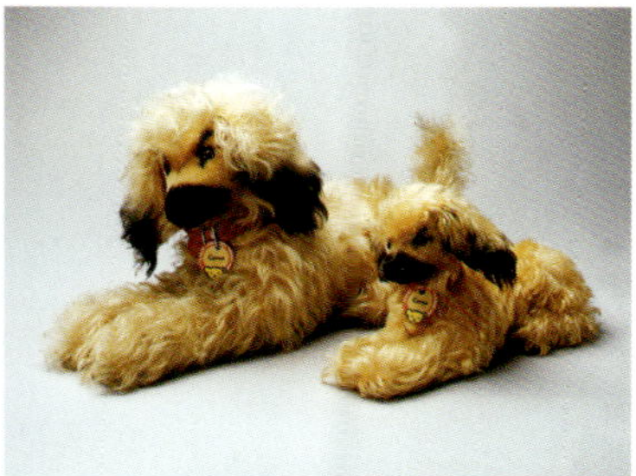

Afghane **Corso** - *Afghan Hound* ***Corso***

Mohair, langhaarig, rotbraun/schwarz, liegend - *long-hair mohair, red-brown/black, lying*

Serie	Art.-No	Period	Pr.	Info
438	**2322,00**	1966-1967	4-5	22 cm
	4380/22	1968-1968	4-5	
438	**2335,00**	1966-1967	5	35 cm
	4380/35	1968-1968	5	

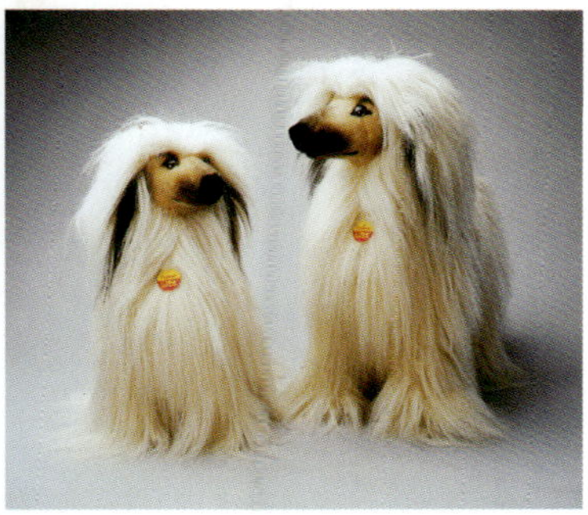

Hassan Afghane - ***Hassan*** *Afghan Hound*

Wirkpelz, abwaschbar - *knitted fur, surface washable*

Serie	Art.-No	Period	Pr.	Info
079108	**4180/45**	1987-1988	3	45 cm, stehend - *standing*
079160	**4182/40**	1987-1988	3	40 cm, sitzend - *sitting*

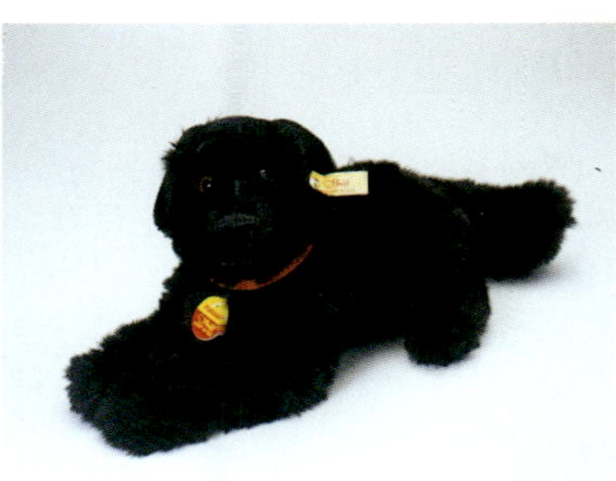

Hassan Labrador

Webpelz, schwarz, liegend, Lederhalsband, ohne Halsband waschmaschinenfest - *woven fur, black, lying, leather collar, machine washable without collar*

EAN-No.	Period	Pr.	Info
079184	1998-1999	3	33 cm
079191	1998-1999	3	42 cm

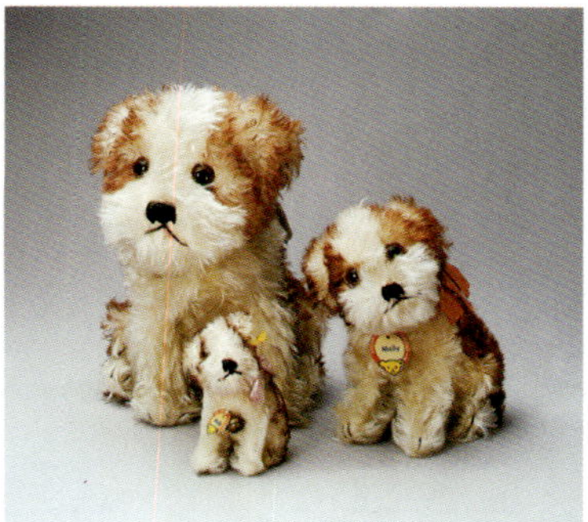

Molly Junghund - ***Molly*** *Puppy*

Mohairpluesch, Groesse 10 cm 1949 auch Seidenpluesch, braun, weiss gespitzt, sitzend, Drehkopf - *mohair, 10 cm 1949 also in artificial silk plush, brown, white tipped, sitting, head swivels*

Serie	Art.-No	Period	Pr.	Info
68	**3610**	1949-1949	4	10 cm, Seidenpluesch - *silk plush*
68	**3310**	1949-1958	4	Mohair
680	**3310,00**	1959-1961	4	
436	**3310,00**	1966-1967	4	
	4360/10	1968-1969	3-4	
68	**3314**	1949-1955	4-5	14 cm
68	**3317**	1949-1958	4-5	17 cm
680	**3317,00**	1959-1961	4	
436	**3317,00**	1966-1967	4	
	4360/17	1968-1969	4	
68	**3322,2**	1949-1954	5	22 cm
68	**3325,2**	1949-1958	5	25 cm
680	**3325,00**	1959-1961	4-5	
436	**3325,00**	1966-1967	4-5	
	4360/25	1968-1969	4	

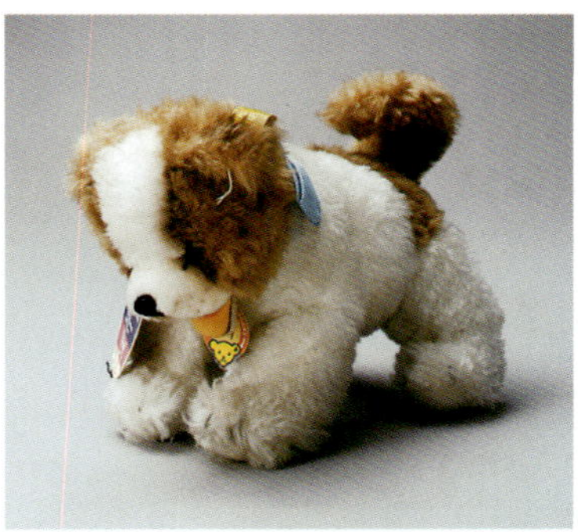

Cosy Molly Hund - ***Cosy Molly*** *Dog*

Dralon Pluesch (Bayer), Schaumgummi-Fuellung, weiss/braun, stehend, offener Mund, sehr weich, vollwaschbar - *dralon (Bayer), stuffed with foam rubber, white/brown, standing, open mouth, very soft, fully washable*

Serie	Art.-No	Period	Pr.	Info
83 68	**6620**	1955-1958	3	20 cm
830 680	**6620,00**	1959-1964	3	
504	**6620,00**	1965-1967	3	
	5040/20	1968-1977	2-3	

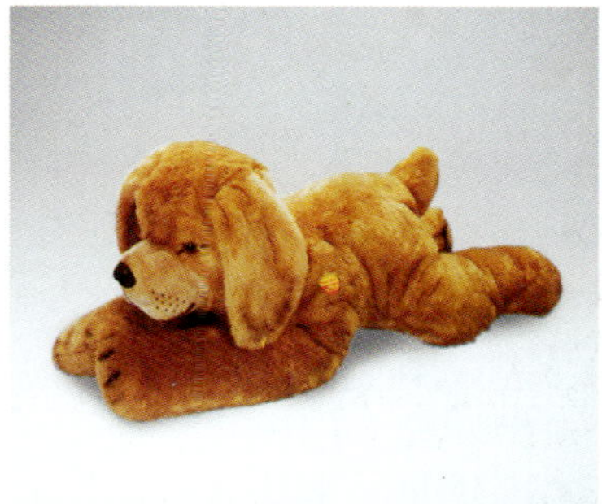

Super Molly Hund - ***Super Molly*** *Dog*

Webpelz, mollig weich, abwaschbar - *woven fur, soft & cuddly, surface washable*

Serie	Art.-No	Period	Pr.	Info
	0342/99	1980-1983	3	125 cm

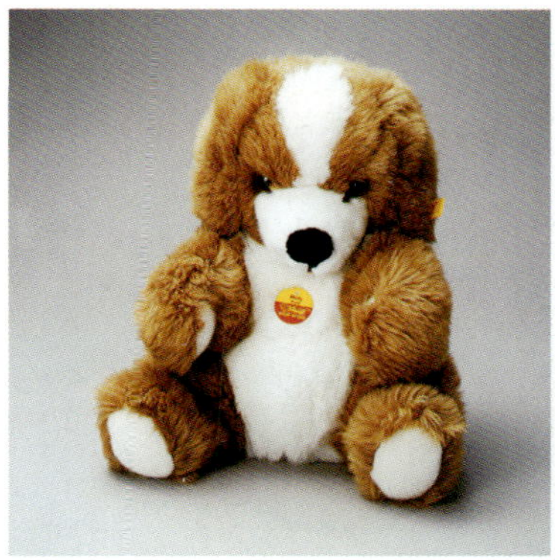

Molly Hund - *Molly Dog*

Webpelz, sitzend, handwaschbar - *woven fur, sitting, hand washable*

Serie	Art.-No	Period	Pr.	Info
101441	**0332/33**	1989-1989	2-3	33 cm

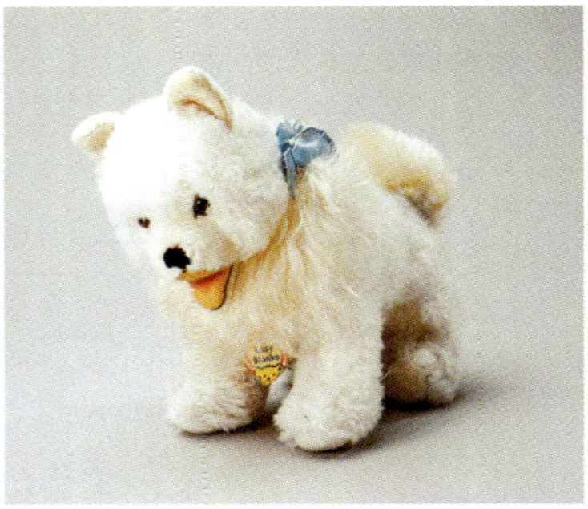

Cosy Spitz **Blanko** - ***Cosy** Spitz **Blanko***

Dralon-Pluesch, Schaumgummi-Fuellung, weiss, stehend, sehr weich, waschbar - *dralon, stuffed with foam rubber, white, standing, very soft, washable*

SERIE	ART.-NO	PERIOD	PR.	INFO
830 690	**1622,00**	1960-1963	3	22 cm
506	**1622,00**	1965-1967	3	
	5060/22	1968-1973	3	

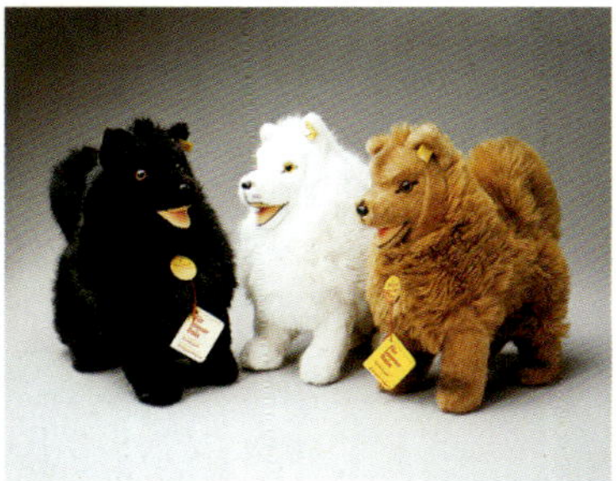

Spitz - *Pomeranian*

Webpelz, 30 cm, stehend, abwaschbar - *woven fur, 30cm, standing, surface washable*

SERIE	ART.-NO	PERIOD	PR.	INFO
	4120/30	1980-1983	3	schwarz - *black*
	4121/30	1980-1983	3	weiss - *white*
	4122/30	1980-1983	3	rotbraun - *red-brown*

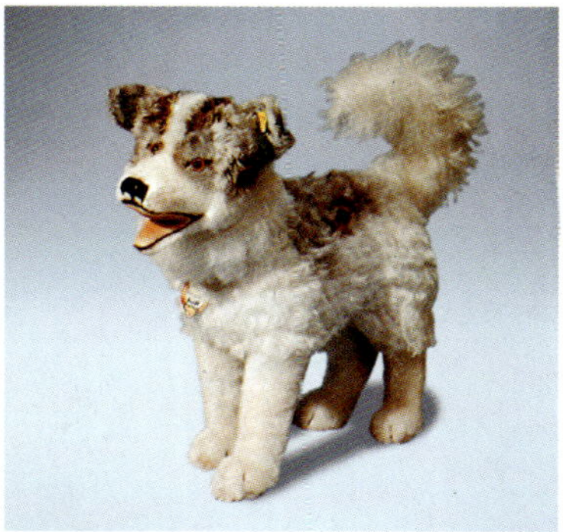

Polarspitz

Schautier, Mohair, stehend - *display animal, mohair, standing*

SERIE	ART.-NO	PERIOD	PR.	INFO
693	**1360,90**	1960-1960	6	60 cm
	4519/06	1967-1967	6	

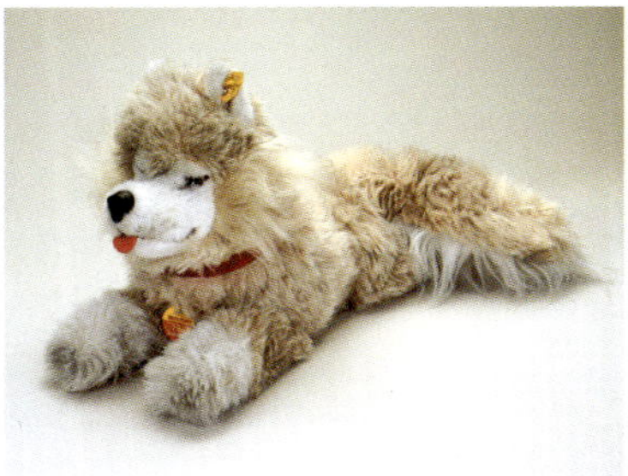

Molly Husky

Pelzimitation, ab 1978 Webpelz, abwaschbar - *imitation fur, from1978 woven fur, surface washable*

SERIE	ART.-NO	PERIOD	PR.	INFO
	0340/35	1976-1981	2-3	35 cm
	0340/60	1975-1981	2-3	60 cm

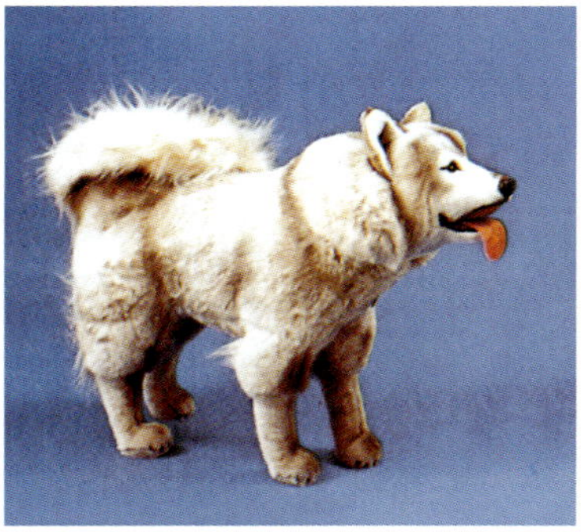

Husky Polarhund - *Husky Polar Dog*

Studio-Tier, Webpelz, stehend, abwaschbar - *display animal, woven fur, standing, surface washable*

SERIE	ART.-NO	PERIOD	PR.	INFO
	4055/65	1978-1981	5	65 cm

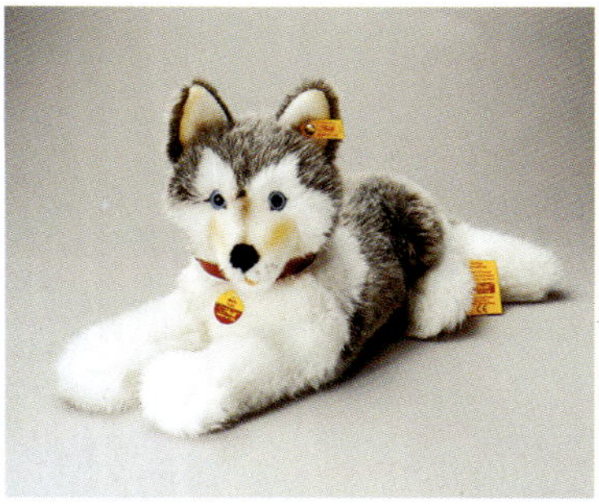

Molly Husky

Webpelz, Lederhalsband, liegend - *woven fur, leather collar, lying*

SERIE	ART.-NO	PERIOD	PR.	INFO
104916	**0460/45**	1989-1990	3	45 cm
	104916	1991-1999	3	
104947	**0460/60**	1989-1990	3-4	60 cm
	104947	1991-1999	3-4	

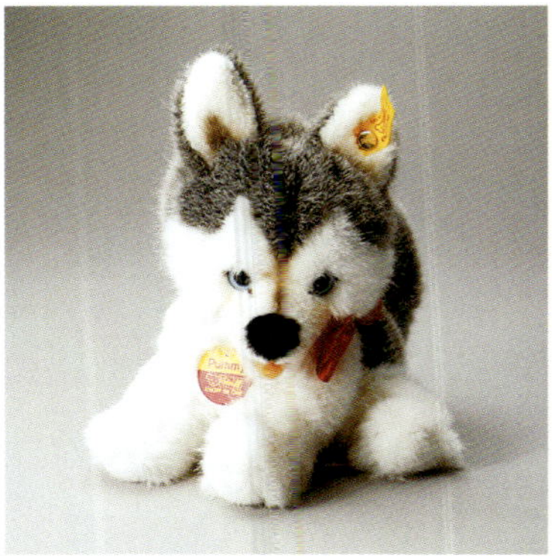

Pummy Husky

Webpelz, waschmaschinenfest - *woven fur, machine washable*

SERIE	ART.-NO	PERIOD	PR.	INFO
083600	**5070/17**	1989-1990	2-3	17 cm
	083600	1991-1996	2-3	
083624	**5070/21**	1989-1990	2-3	21 cm
	083624	1991-1991	2-3	

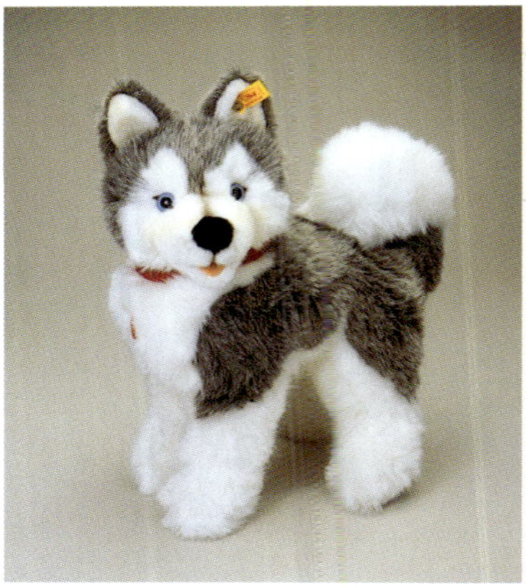

Husky

Webpelz, grau/weiss, stehend, Lederhalsband, ohne Halsband handwaschbar - *woven fur, grey/white, standing, leather collar, hand washable without collar*

EAN-NO.	PERIOD	PR.	INFO
079634	1997-1999	3-4	35 cm

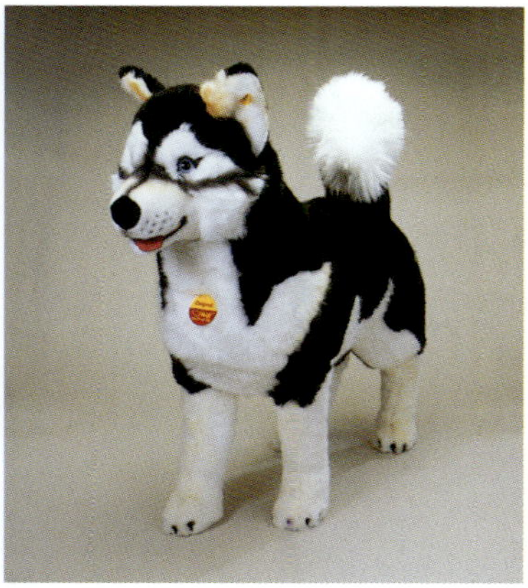

Husky

Studio-Tier, Webpelz, 80 cm, stehend, abwaschbar - *studio animal, woven fur, 80 cm, standing, surface washable*

EAN-NO.	PERIOD	PR.	INFO
524417	1998-1999	6	schwarz - *black*
524394	1998-1999	6	grau - *grey*
524363	1998-1999	6	dunkelbraun - *dark brown*

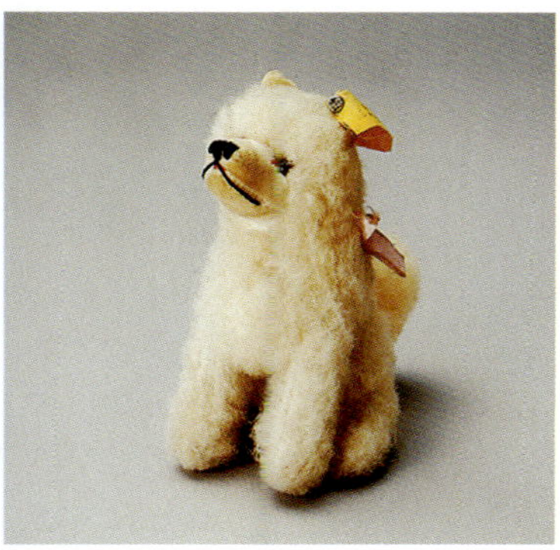

Chow Chow

Wollpluesch, weiss, sitzend - *wool plush, white, sitting*

SERIE	ART.-NO	PERIOD	PR.	INFO
69	**3510**	1951-1957	4	10 cm

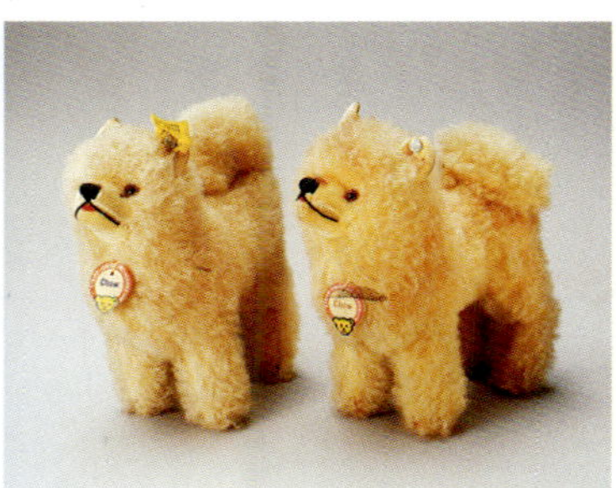

Chow Chow

Wollpluesch, mais, stehend - *wool plush, corn yellow, standing*

SERIE	ART.-NO	PERIOD	PR.	INFO
69	**1512,0**	1951-1957	3	12 cm
691	**1512,00**	1959-1959	3	
69	**1517,0**	1952-1954	4	17 cm
69	**1525,02**	1952-1954	4	25 cm

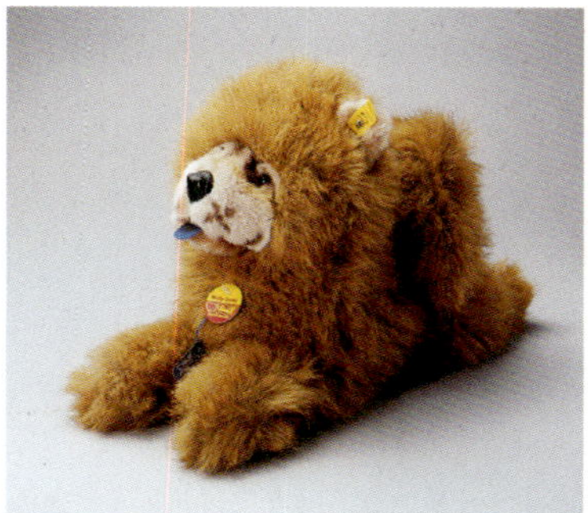

Molly Corso

Pelzimitation, ab 1978 Webpelz, abwaschbar - *imitation fur, from 1978 woven fur, surface washable*

SERIE	ART.-NO	PERIOD	PR.	INFO
	0338/35	1976-1981	2-3	35 cm
	0338/60	1975-1981	2-3	60 cm

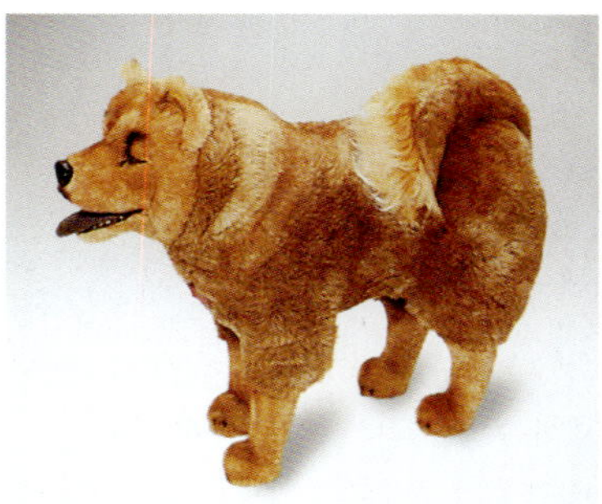

Corso Chow Chow

Studio-Tier, Webpelz, stehend, abwaschbar - *studio animal, woven fur, standing, surface washable*

SERIE	ART.-NO	PERIOD	PR.	INFO
	4065/65	1978-1984	5	65 cm

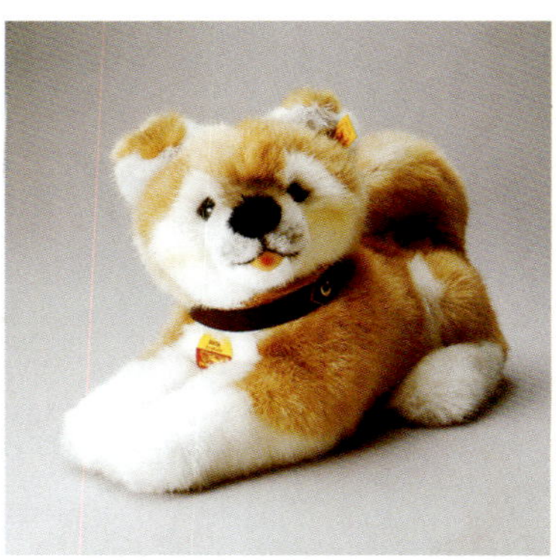

Akita Junghund - ***Akita** Puppy*

Webpelz, liegend, Lederhalsband, ohne Halsband waschmaschinenfest - *woven fur, lying, leather collar, machine washable without collar*

EAN-NO.	PERIOD	PR.	INFO
079726	1992-1995	2-3	30 cm
079740	1991-1994	3	40 cm
079764	1991-1993	3	50 cm

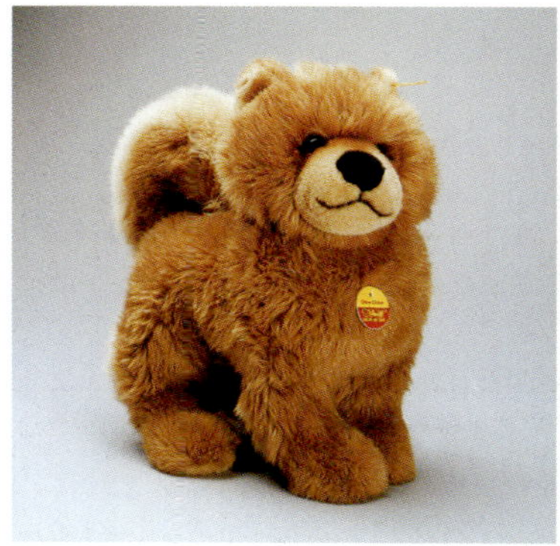

Chow Chow

Webpelz, stehend, abwaschbar - *woven fur, standing, surface washable*

EAN-NO.	PERIOD	PR.	INFO
079375	1992-1993	2-3	35 cm

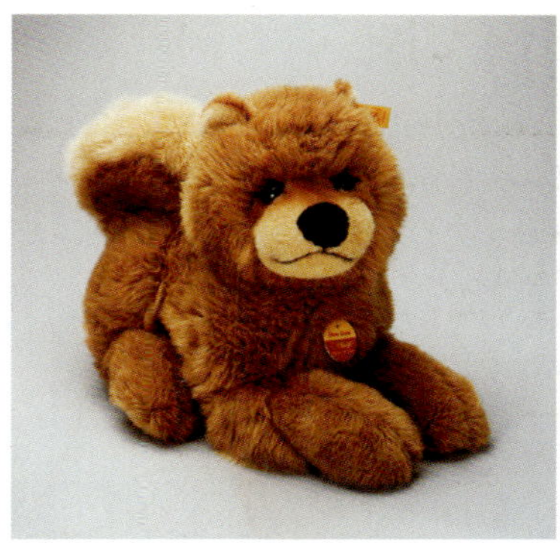

Chow Chow

Webpelz, liegend, abwaschbar - *woven fur, lying, surface washable*

EAN-NO.	PERIOD	PR.	INFO
079474	1992-1993	2-3	35 cm

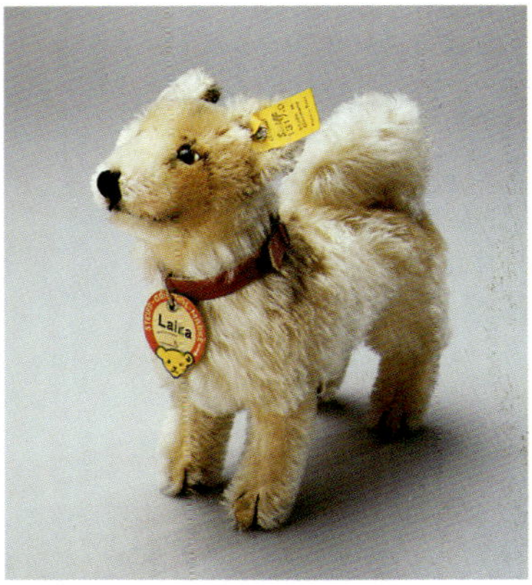

Laika Weltraumhund - ***Laika*** *the Space Dog*

Mohair, langhaarig, stehend, Druckstimme - *long-hair mohair, standing, press voice*

Serie	Art.-No	Period	Pr.	Info
69a	**1317,0**	1958-1958	6	17 cm
695	**1317,00**	1959-1959	6	
69a	**1325,0**	1958-1958	6	25 cm
695	**1325,00**	1959-1959	6	

Katzen

Cats

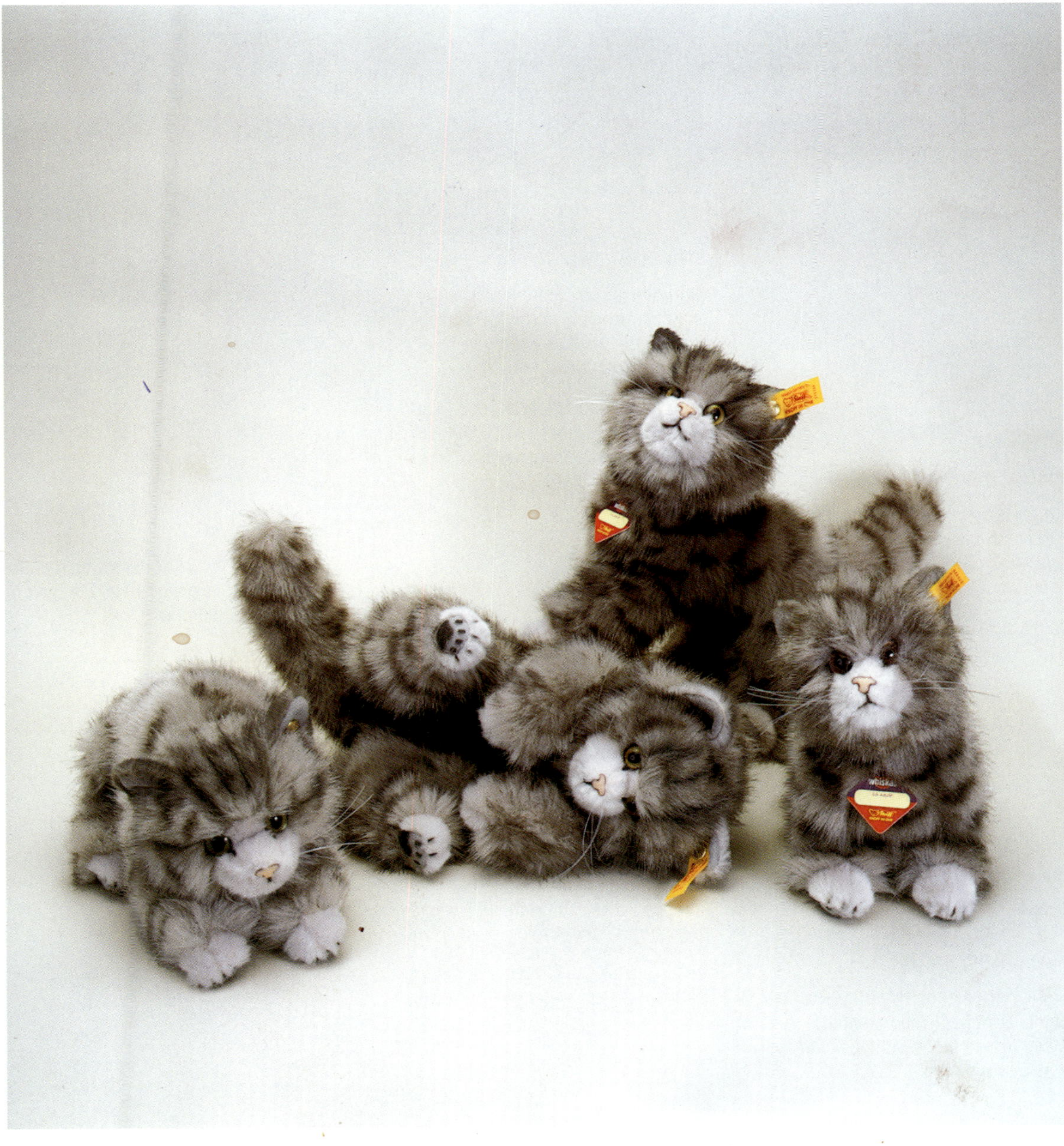

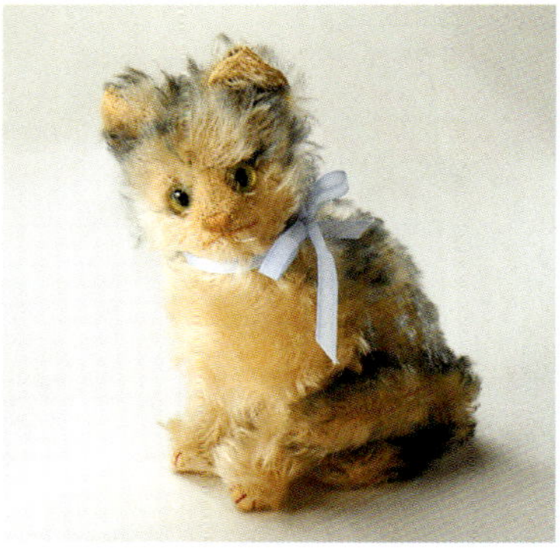

Fluffy Katze - ***Fluffy** Cat*

Mohairpluesch, grau/weiss, sitzend - *mohair, grey/white, sitting*

SERIE	ART.-NO	PERIOD	PR.	INFO
44F	**3314**	1949-1950	5	14 cm
44F	**3317**	1949-1950	5	17 cm
44F	**3322,2**	1949-1950	5	22 cm

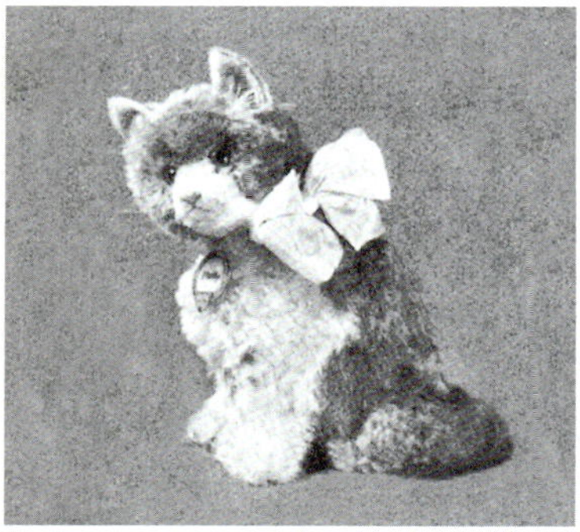

Fluffy Katze - ***Fluffy** Cat*

langhaariger Seidenpluesch, Seidenhalsband, grau/weiss, sitzend, Drehkopf - *long-hair silk plush, silk ribbon collar, grey & white, sitting, head swivels*

SERIE	ART.-NO	PERIOD	PR.	INFO
44F	**3622,2**	1949-1949	5	22 cm

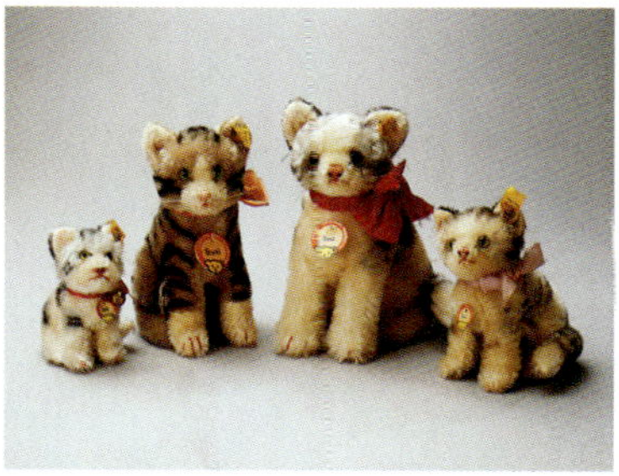

Susi Katze - ***Susi** Cat*

Mohairpluesch, weiss/grau gestromelt, sitzend, Drehkopf, abwaschbar - *mohair, white & grey tabby, sitting, head swivels, surface washable*

SERIE	ART.-NO	PERIOD	PR.	INFO
44G	**3310**	1950-1958	4	10 cm
440	**3310,00**	1959-1964	3-4	
278	**3310,00**	1965-1967	3-4	
	2780/10	1968-1975	3	
44G	**3312**	1950-1954	5	12 cm
44G	**3314**	1949-1957	4	14 cm
44G	**3314,2**	1958-1958	4	
440	**3314,00**	1959-1963	3-4	
278	**3314,00**	1965-1967	3-4	
	2780/14	1968-1978	3	
44G	**3317,2**	1949-1955	5	17 cm
44G	**3322,2**	1949-1958	4	22 cm
440	**3322,00**	1959-1963	3-4	
278	**3322,00**	1965-1967	3-4	
	2780/22	1968-1978	3	

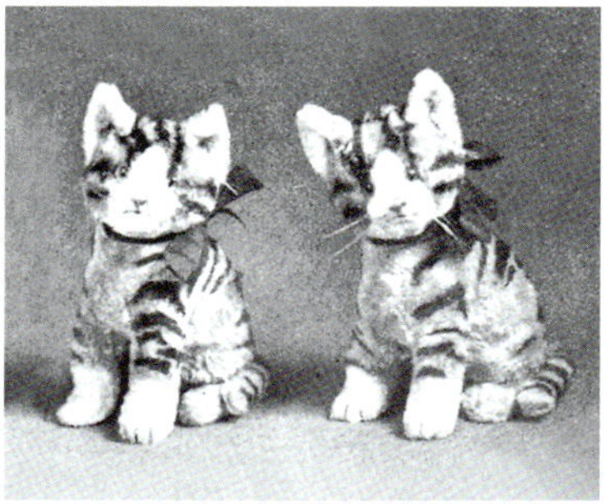

Susi Katze - ***Susi** Cat*

Seidenpluesch, Seidenhalsband, grau/weiss, gestromelt, sitzend, Drehkopf - *silk plush, silk ribbon collar, grey & white tabby, sitting, head swivels*

SERIE	ART.-NO	PERIOD	PR.	INFO
44G	**3614**	1949-1949	4-5	14 cm
44G	**3617**	1948-1949	4-5	17 cm
44G	**3622,2**	1949-1949	4-5	22 cm

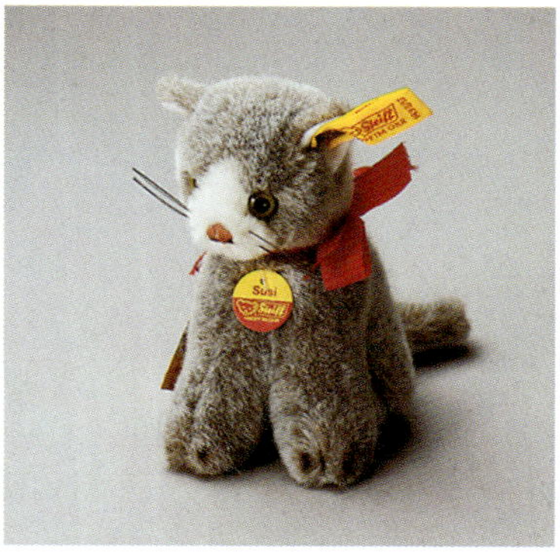

Susi Katze - ***Susi** Cat*

Webpelz, grau, abwaschbar - *woven fur, grey, surface washable*

SERIE	ART.-NO	PERIOD	PR.	INFO
049101	**1493/13**	1982-1988	2	14 cm

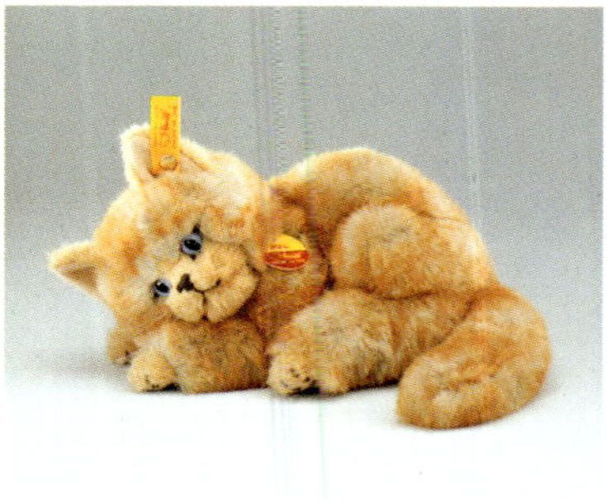

Susi Katze - ***Susi** Cat*

Webpelz, 22 cm, seitlich liegend, waschmaschinenfest - *woven fur, 22 cm, lying aside, machine washable*

EAN-NO.	PERIOD	PR.	INFO
074998	1998-1999	3	rot gestromelt - *red striped*
075025	1998-1999	3	braun gefleckt - *brown spotted*
075056	1998-1999	3	weiss - *white*

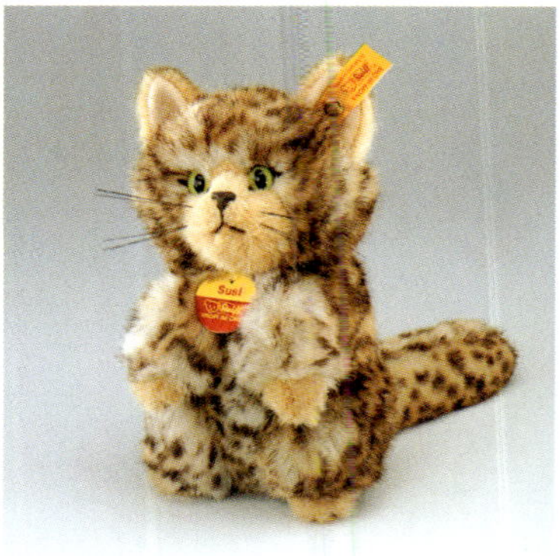

Susi Katze - ***Susi** Cat*

Webpelz, 20 cm, aufwartend, waschmaschinenfest - *woven fur, 20 cm, sitting up, machine washable*

EAN-NO.	PERIOD	PR.	INFO
075018	1998-1998	2-3	rot gestromelt - *red striped*
075049	1998-1998	2-3	braun gefleckt - *brown spotted*
075070	1998-1998	2-3	weiss - *white*

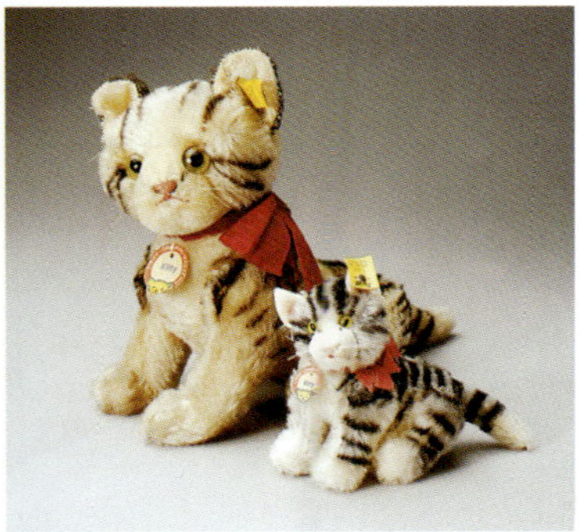

Kitty Katze, 1965-1967 auch mit Zusatz **im Steiff-Kinderbuch** - ***Kitty** Cat, 1965-1967 also with supplement **im Steiff-Kinderbuch***

Mohairpluesch, weiss/grau gestromelt, gegliedert - *mohair, white & grey tabby, jointed*

SERIE	ART.-NO	PERIOD	PR.	INFO
44K	**5310**	1951-1958	4	10 cm
440	**5310,00**	1959-1964	3-4	
280	**5310,00**	1965-1967	3-4	
	2800/10	1968-1969	3-4	
44K	**5317**	1949-1958	4	17 cm
440	**5317,00**	1959-1964	3-4	
280	**5317,00**	1965-1967	3-4	
	2800/17	1968-1970	3-4	
44K	**5322**	1949-1953	4	22 cm
44K	**5322,2**	1954-1958	4	
440	**5322,00**	1959-1964	3-4	
280	**5322,00**	1965-1967	3-4	
	2800/22	1968-1970	3-4	

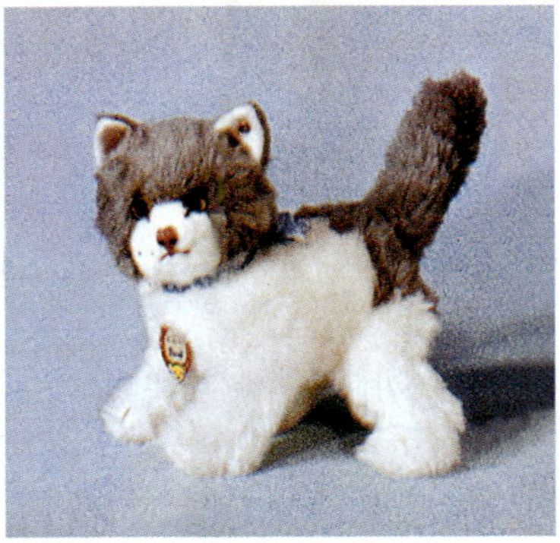

Cosy Kitty Katze - ***Cosy Kitty** Cat*

Dralon-Pluesch, Schaumgummi-Fuellung, ab 1968 gefuellt mit synthetischen Fasern & Schaumstoff, weiss/grau, sehr weich - *dralon, stuffed with foam rubber, from 1968 stuffed with synthetic fibers & foam, white & grey, very soft*

SERIE	ART.-NO	PERIOD	PR.	INFO
83 44	**6620**	1955-1958	2-3	20 cm
830 440	**6620,00**	1959-1964	2-3	
510	**6620,00**	1965-1967	2-3	
	5100/20	1968-1978	2	

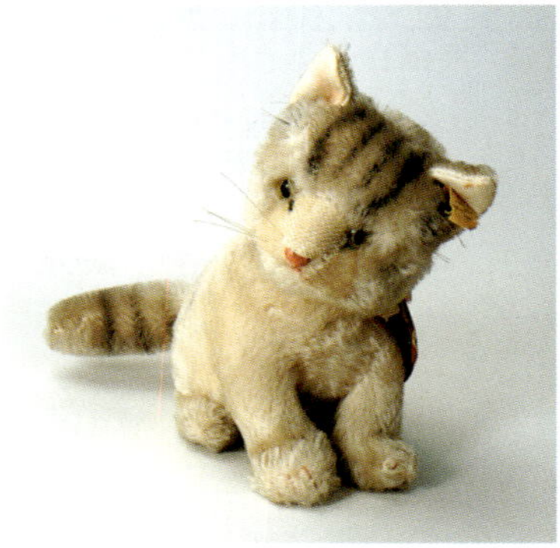

Musik Kitty Katze - ***Musik Kitty** Cat*

Mohair, weiss/grau gestreift, sitzend, Schweizer Aufziehwerk mit Schwanz gekoppelt - *mohair, white/grey striped, sitting, Swiss music box which is connected to the tail*

SERIE	ART.-NO	PERIOD	PR.	INFO
97 44	**3317,3**	1955-1957	5	17 cm
860 440	**3317,60**	1961-1961	5	

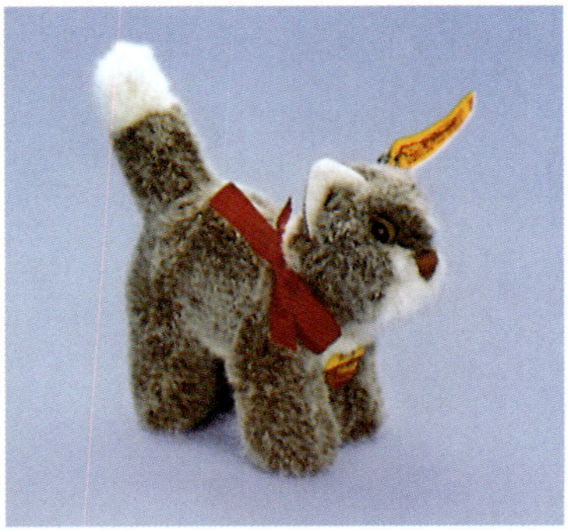

Kitty Katze - ***Kitty** Cat*

Nerzimitation, ab 1978 Synthetik-Webpelz, grau/weiss - *imitation mink, from 1978 synthetic woven fur, grey & white*

SERIE	ART.-NO	PERIOD	PR.	INFO
	1495/10	1977-1982	2	10 cm

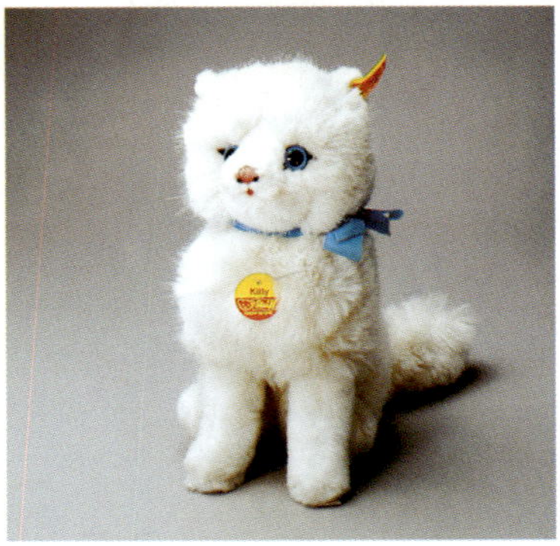

Kitty Angorakatze - ***Kitty** Angora Cat*

Webpelz, weiss, abwaschbar - *woven fur, white, surface washable*

SERIE	ART.-NO	PERIOD	PR.	INFO
	2753/26	1982-1985	2-3	26 cm

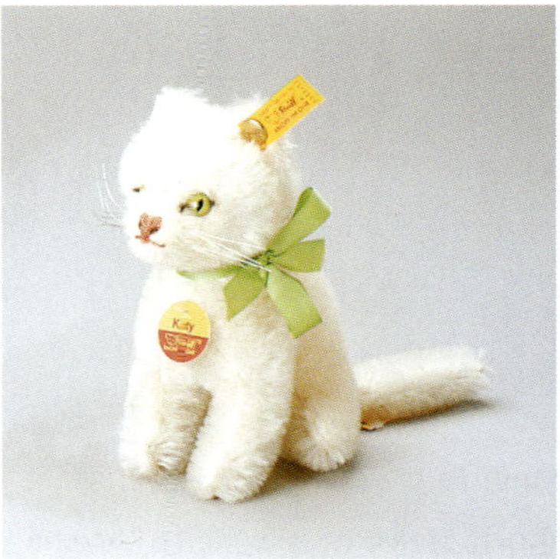

Kitty Katze - ***Kitty** Cat*

Mohair Webpelz, weiss, sitzend, Kopf drehbar, abwaschbar - *mohair woven fur, white, sitting, head swivels, surface washable*

SERIE	ART.-NO	PERIOD	PR.	INFO
031724	**1307/12**	1990-1990	2	12 cm
	031724	1991-1993	2	

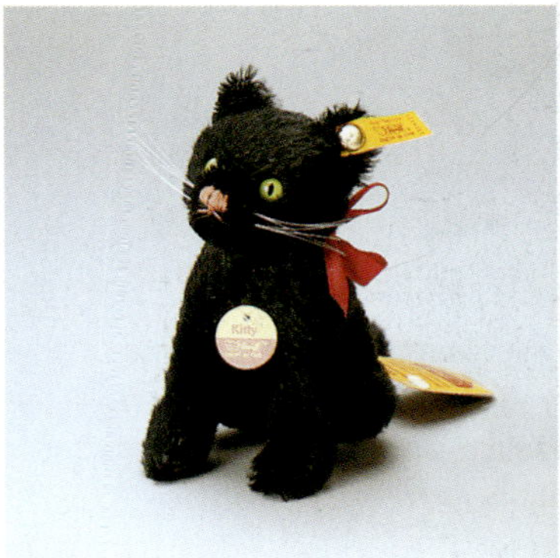

Kitty Katze - ***Kitty** Cat*

Mohair Webpelz, schwarz, sitzend, Kopf drehbar, abwaschbar - *mohair woven fur, black sitting, head swivels, surface washable*

SERIE	ART.-NO	PERIOD	PR.	INFO
031922	**1314/12**	1990-1990	2	12 cm
	031922	1991-1993	2	

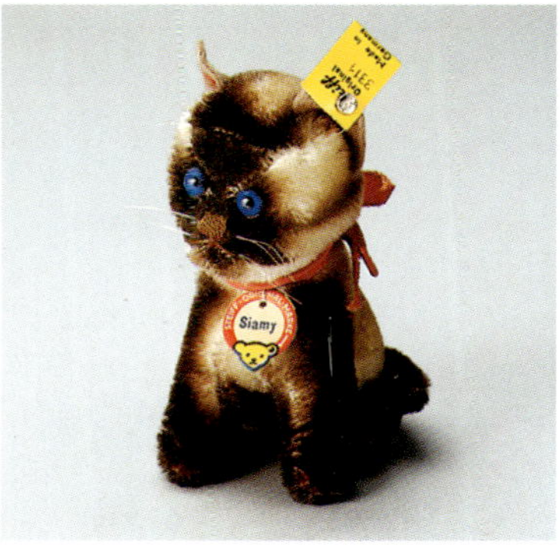

Siamy Katze - ***Siamy** Cat*

Mohair, hellbraun, schokolade, sitzend - *mohair, light brown, chocolate, sitting*

SERIE	ART.-NO	PERIOD	PR.	INFO
44S	**3311**	1953-1954	5	11 cm
44S	**3315**	1953-1954	5	15 cm
44S	**3323,2**	1953-1954	5-6	23 cm

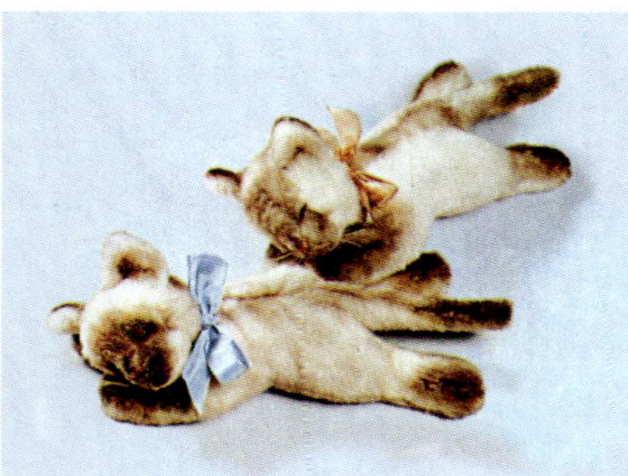

Cosy Siamy Katze - ***Cosy Siamy** Cat*

Dralon-Pluesch (Bayer), Schaumgummi-Fuellung, braun (Toene), liegend, sehr weich, waschbar - *dralon (Bayer), stuffed with foam rubber, brown (tones), lying very soft, washable*

SERIE	ART.-NO	PERIOD	PR.	INFO
830 440	**7617,00**	1959-1961	3	17 cm

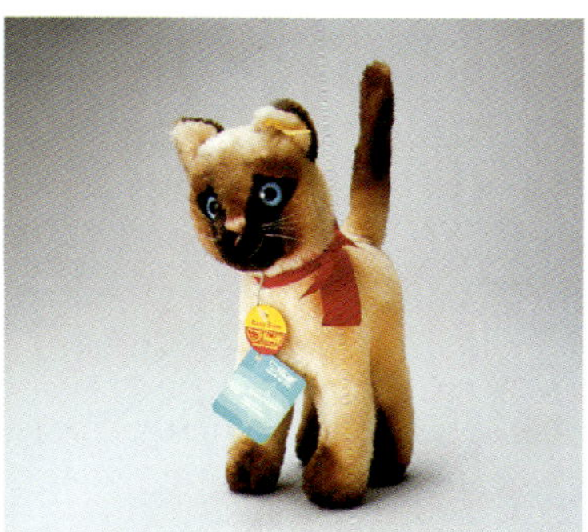

Cosy Siam Katze - ***Cosy Siamy** Cat*

Dralon, gefuellt mit synthetischen Fasern & Schaumstoff, stehend, sehr weich, vollwaschbar - *dralon, stuffed with synthetic fibers & foam, standing, very soft, fully washable*

SERIE	ART.-NO	PERIOD	PR.	INFO
	5110/22	1970-1979	3	22 cm

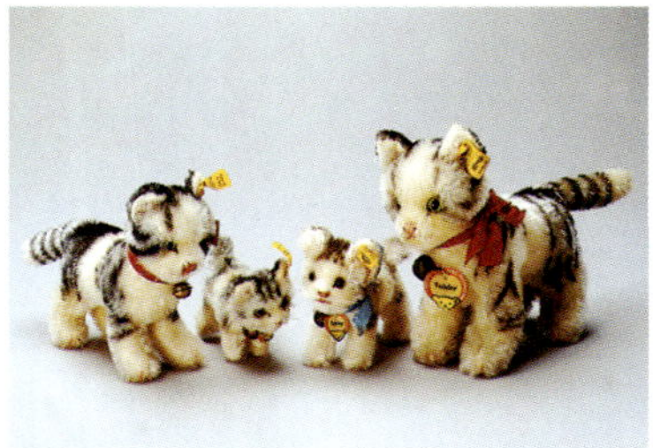

Katze **Tabby** - *Cat **Tabby***

Mohairpluesch, grau, gestromelt, ab 1951 weiss/grau gestromelt, stehend ohne Raeder, abwaschbar - *mohair, grey tabby, from 1951 white/grey tabby, standing without wheels, surface washable*

SERIE	ART.-NO	PERIOD	PR.	INFO
44	**1307,0**	1949-1958	4	7 cm
440	**1307,00**	1959-1964	3	
270	**1307,00**	1965-1967	3	
	2700/07	1968-1973	2-3	
44	**1310,0**	1949-1958	4	10 cm
440	**1310,00**	1959-1964	3	
270	**1310,00**	1965-1967	3	
	2700/10	1968-1976	2-3	
44	**1314,0**	1949-1958	4	14 cm
440	**1314,00**	1959-1964	3	
270	**1314,00**	1965-1967	3	
	2700/14	1968-1977	2-3	
44	**1317,0**	1949-1958	4	17 cm
440	**1317,00**	1959-1964	3	
270	**1317,00**	1965-1967	3	
	2700/17	1968-1977	3	

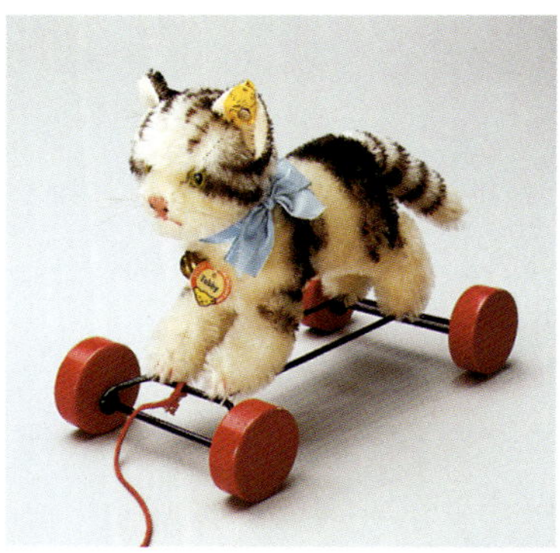

Nachzieh-**Tabby** - *Pull Toy **Tabby***

Mohairpluesch, weiss/grau gestromelt, stehend auf Exzenter-Raedern - *mohair, white/grey tabby, standing on eccentric wheels*

SERIE	ART.-NO	PERIOD	PR.	INFO
81 44	**1310** ex	1955-1957	4-5	10 cm
810 440	**1310,10**	1960-1960	4-5	
44	**1314** ex	1950-1957	4-5	14 cm
440	**1314,10**	1961-1961	4-5	
272	**1314,10**	1966-1967	4-5	
	2720/14	1968-1969	4-5	
44	**1317** ex	1949-1957	5	17 cm

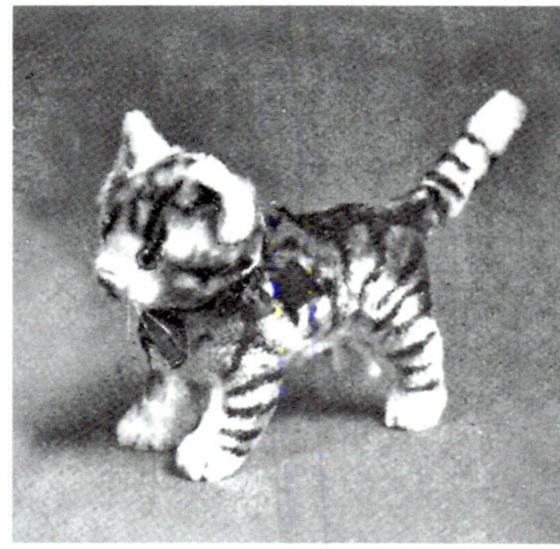

Katze **Tabby** - *Cat **Tabby***

Kunstseidenpluesch, Seidenhalsband, grau/weiss, gestromelt, stehend ohne Raeder - *artificial silk plush, silk ribbon collar, grey/white, tabby, standing without wheels*

SERIE	ART.-NO	PERIOD	PR.	INFO
44	**1610,0**	1949-1949	4	10 cm
44	**1614,0**	1948-1949	4	14 cm
44	**1617,0**	1948-1949	4	17 cm

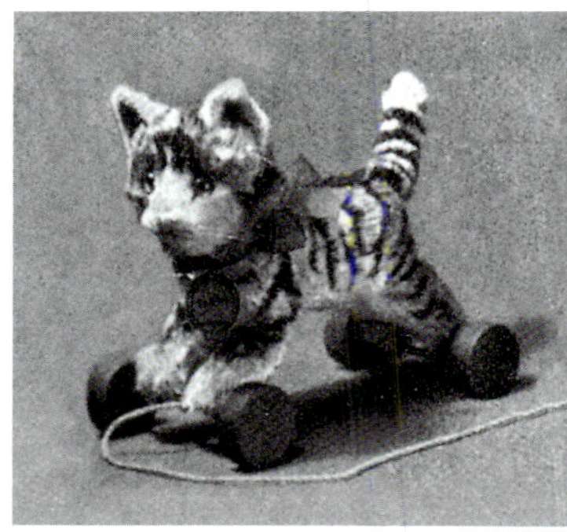

Katze **Tabby** - *Cat **Tabby***

Seidenpluesch, Seidenhalsband, grau/weiss, gestromelt, stehend auf Exzenterraedern - *silk plush, silk ribbon collar, grey/white, tabby, standing on eccentric wheels*

SERIE	ART.-NO	PERIOD	PR.	INFO
44	**1617** ex	1949-1949	4-5	17 cm

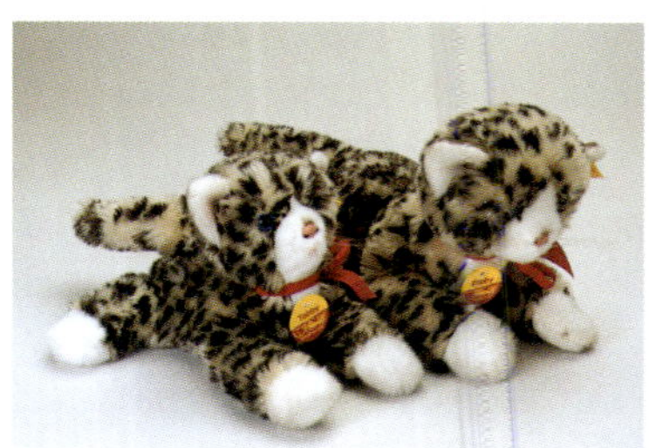

Katze **Tabby** - *Cat **Tabby***

Wirkpelz, liegend, abwaschbar - *knitted fur, lying, surface washable*

SERIE	ART.-NO	PERIOD	PR.	INFO
	2732/17	1979-1983	1-2	17 cm
	2732/22	1979-1983	1-2	22 cm

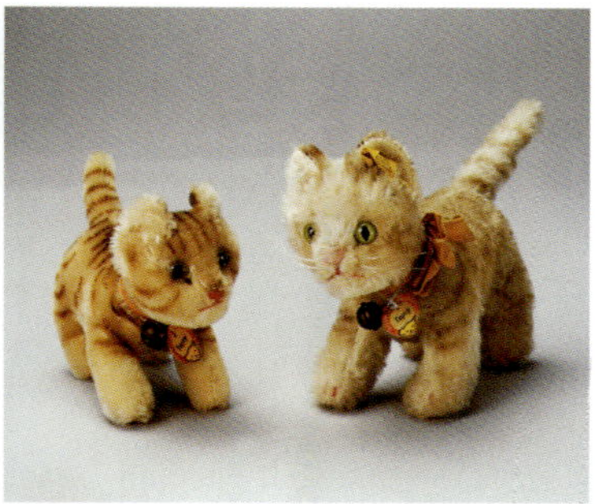

Katze **Tapsy** - *Cat* ***Tapsy***

Mohairpluesch, weiss/grau in grau gestreift, stehend - *mohair, white & grey, with grey stripes, standing*

SERIE	ART.-NO	PERIOD	PR.	INFO
440	**1308,00**	1959-1964	3-4	8 cm
274	**1308,00**	1965-1966	3-4	
440	**1311,00**	1959-1962	3-4	11 cm
274	**1311,00**	1966-1966	3-4	
440	**1315,00**	1959-1963	4	15 cm
274	**1315,00**	1966-1966	4	
440	**1318,00**	1959-1963	4	18 cm
274	**1318,00**	1966-1966	4	

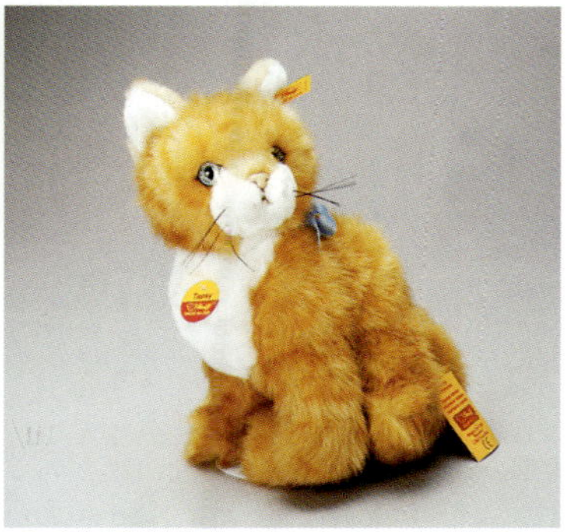

Katze **Tapsy** - *Cat* ***Tapsy***

Webpelz, roetlich gestromelt, sitzend, waschmaschinenfest - *woven fur, reddish tabby, sitting, machine washable*

SERIE	ART.-NO	PERIOD	PR.	INFO
074486	**2742/23**	1988-1990	2	23 cm
	074486	1991-1994	2	

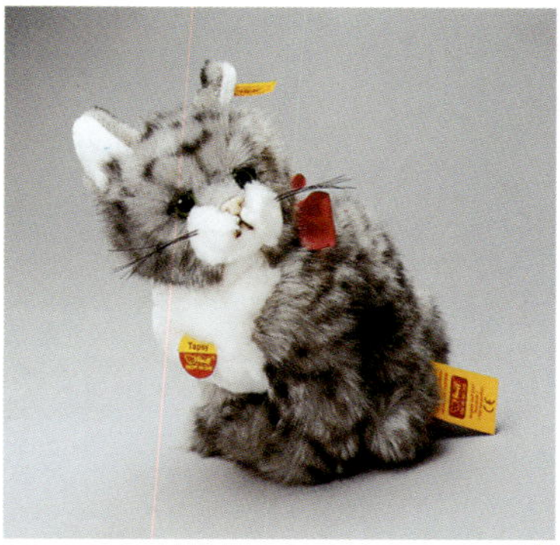

Katze **Tapsy** - *Cat* ***Tapsy***

Webpelz, grau gestromelt, sitzend, waschmaschinenfest - *woven fur, grey tabby, sitting, machine washable*

SERIE	ART.-NO	PERIOD	PR.	INFO
074455	**2740/23**	1989-1990	2-3	23 cm
	074455	1991-1996	2-3	

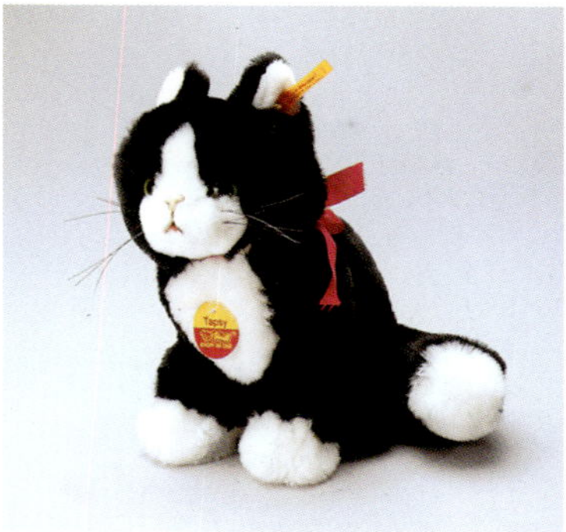

Katze **Tapsy** - *Cat* ***Tapsy***

Webpelz, schwarz/weiss, sitzend, waschmaschinenfest - *woven fur, black & white, sitting, machine washable*

EAN-NO.	PERIOD	PR.	INFO
074400	1991-1995	2-3	20 cm
074424	1991-1992	2-3	25 cm

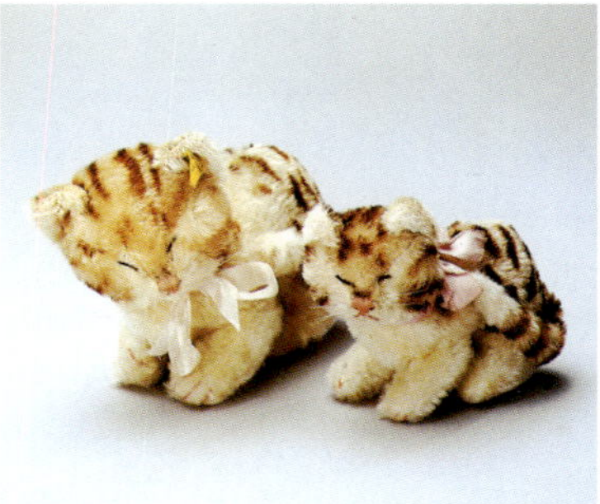

Katze **Snurry** - *Cat* ***Snurry***

Mohair, Augen gestickt, braun gestromelt, liegend, Drehkopf - *mohair, eyes embroidered, brown tabby, lying, head swivels*

SERIE	ART.-NO	PERIOD	PR.	INFO
440	**2315,03**	1964-1964	3-4	15 cm
276	**2315,03**	1965-1966	3-4	
440	**2320,03**	1964-1964	3-4	20 cm
276	**2320,03**	1965-1966	3-4	
440	**2325,03**	1964-1964	4	25 cm
276	**2325,03**	1965-1966	4	

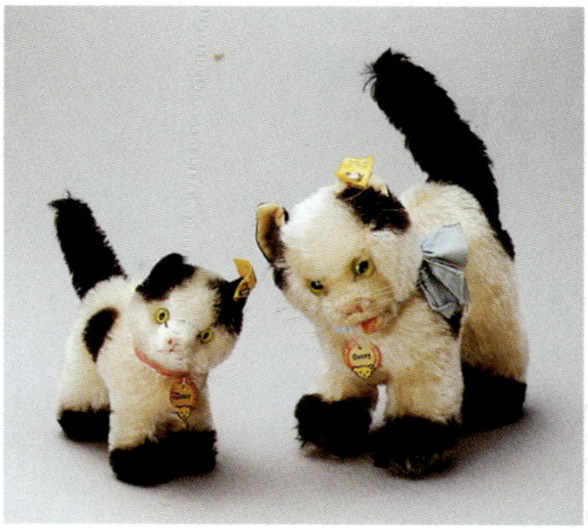

Junges Kaetzchen **Gussy** - *Young Kitty* ***Gussy***

Mohair, weiss/schwarz gefleckt, Kopf drehbar, stehend, weich - *mohair, white / black spotted, head swivels, standing, soft*

SERIE	ART.-NO	PERIOD	PR.	INFO
44	**6312,0**	1952-1958	4	12 cm
440	**6312,00**	1959-1964	3-4	
282	**6312,00**	1965-1967	3-4	
	2820/12	1968-1969	3-4	
44	**6317,0**	1952-1958	4	17 cm
440	**6317,00**	1960-1962	3-4	
282	**6317,00**	1966-1967	3-4	
	2820/17	1968-1969	3-4	

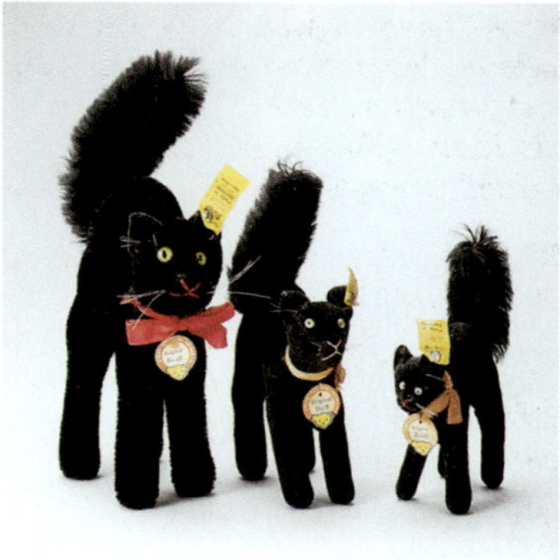

Schwarzer Kater - *Black Tom Cat*

8 & 10 cm Samt, ab 14 cm Mohairpluesch, schwarz, stehend, karikiert - *8 & 10 cm velvet, from 14 cm mohair, black, standing, in caricature form*

SERIE	ART.-NO	PERIOD	PR.	INFO
44	**7408**	1950-1958	3-4	8 cm
440	**7408,00**	1959-1964	3	
285	**7408,00**	1965-1966	3	
44	**7410**	1950-1958	3-4	10 cm
440	**7410,00**	1959-1961	3	
285	**7410,00**	1966-1967	3	
	2860/10	1968-1973	3	

44	**7314**	1950-1958	4	14 cm
440	**7314,00**	1959-1962	3-4	
286	**7314,00**	1965-1967	3-4	
	2860/14	1968-1976	3	
44	**7317**	1950-1955	4-5	17 cm
44	**7322**	1950-1958	4-5	22 cm
440	**7322,00**	1959-1962	4	
286	**7322,00**	1965-1967	4	
	2860/22	1968-1974	3-4	

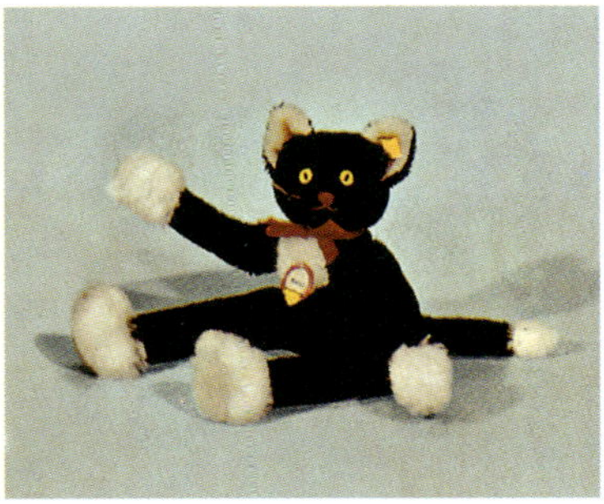

Kater **Kalac** - *Tom Cat **Kalac***

Mohair, Schlenkertier, gegliedert, schwarz/weiss - *mohair, dangling animal, jointed, black & white*

SERIE	ART.-NO	PERIOD	PR.	INFO
440	**7340,00**	1964-1964	5	40 cm
582	**7340,00**	1966-1966	5	

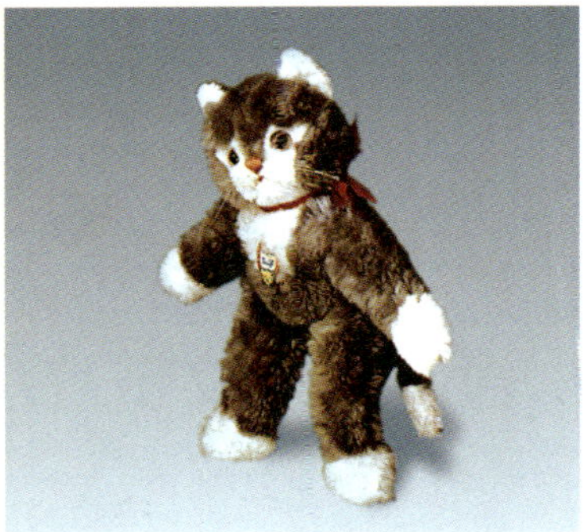

Schlenker-Kater - *Dangling Tom Cat*

Dralon, grau, Schlenkerglieder, Kopf drehbar, abwaschbar - *dralon, grey, floppy joints, head swivels, surface washable*

SERIE	ART.-NO	PERIOD	PR.	INFO
	2870/32	1969-1976	2-3	32 cm

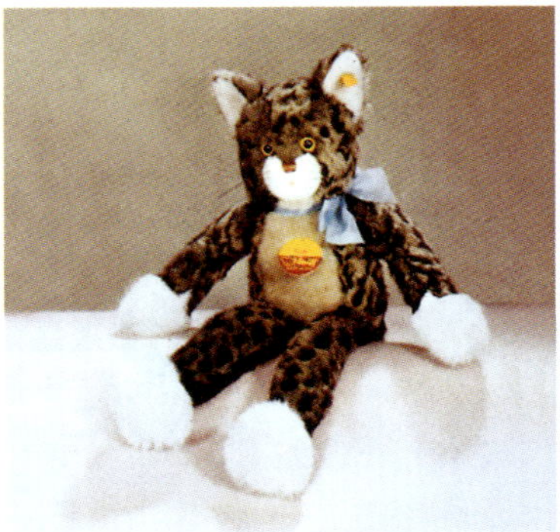

Tom Schlenkerkater - *Dangling **Tom** Cat*

Webpelz, Schlenkerglieder, abwaschbar - *woven fur, floppy joints, surface washable*

SERIE	ART.-NO	PERIOD	PR.	INFO
	6285/60	1978-1980	3	60 cm

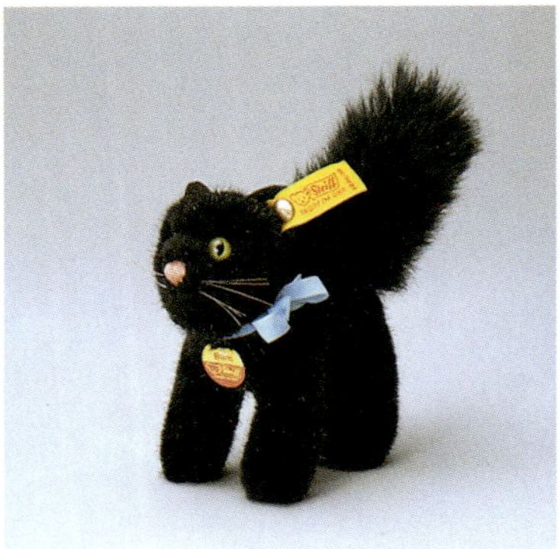

Burri Kater - ***Burri** Tom Cat*

Webpelz, schwarz, stehend, abwaschbar - *woven fur, black, standing, surface washable*

SERIE	ART.-NO	PERIOD	PR.	INFO
	1496/10	1979-1984	1-2	10 cm

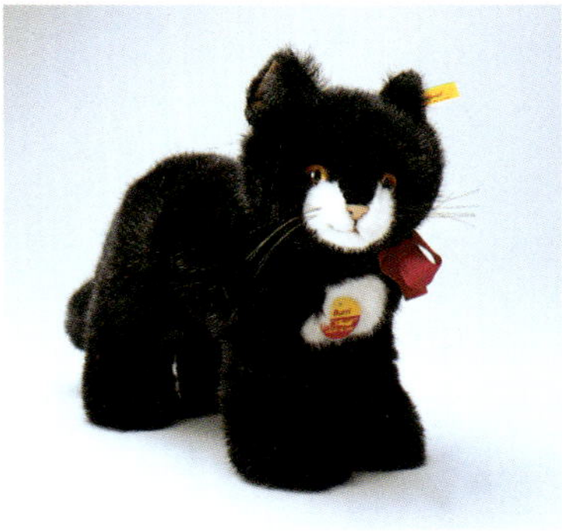

Burri Kater - ***Burri** Tom Cat*

Webpelz, schwarz, stehend, handwaschbar - *woven fur, black, standing, hand washable*

EAN-NO.	PERIOD	PR.	INFO
074394	1994-1996	2-3	25 cm

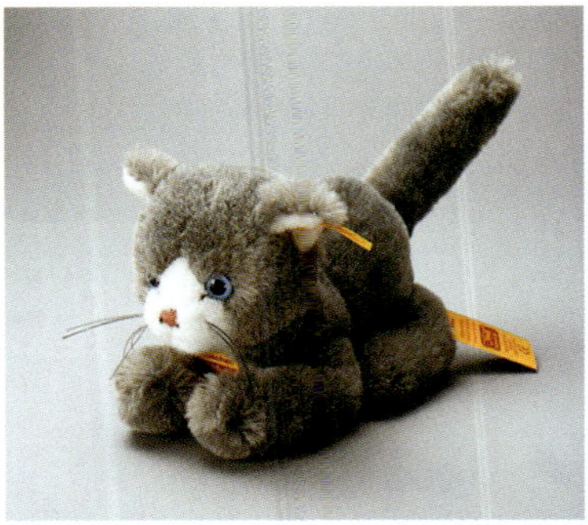

Kuschel Katze - ***Kuschel** Cat*

Webpelz, Schaumstoff-Fuellung, grau, superweich, waschmaschinenfest - *woven fur, stuffed with foam, grey, super soft, machine washable*

SERIE	ART.-NO	PERIOD	PR.	INFO
099960	**5520/25**	1981-1990	2	25 cm
	099960	1991-1996	2	

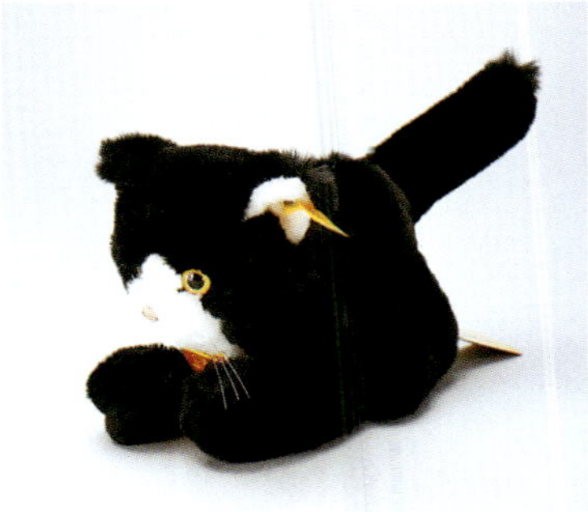

Kuschel Katze - ***Kuschel** Cat*

Webpelz, Schaumstoff-Fuellung, schwarz, superweich, waschmaschinenfest - *woven fur, stuffed with foam, black, super soft, machine washable*

SERIE	ART.-NO	PERIOD	PR.	INFO
099977	**5522/25**	1981-1990	2	23 cm
	099977	1991-1999	2	

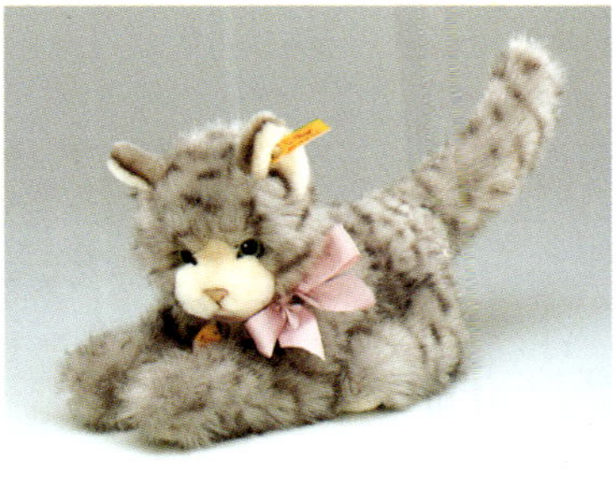

Kuschel Katze - ***Kuschel** Cat*

Webpelz, grau gestromelt, waschmaschinenfest - *woven fur, grey tabby, machine washable*

EAN-NO.	PERIOD	PR.	INFO
099939	1992-1995	2	25 cm

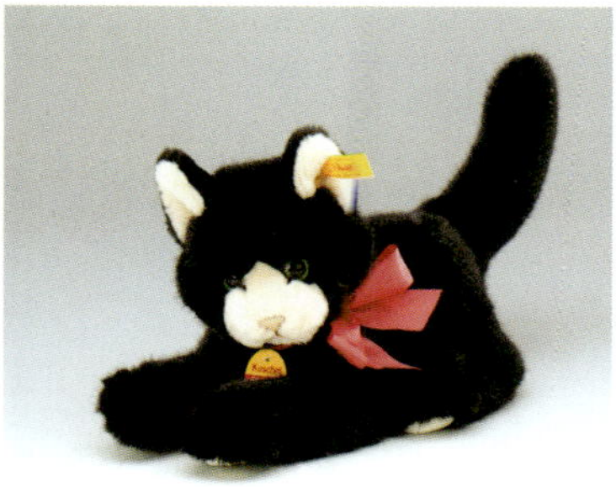

Kuschel Katze - ***Kuschel*** *Cat*

Webpelz, schwarz, waschmaschinenfest - *woven fur, black, machine washable*

EAN-No.	Period	Pr.	Info
099946	1992-1997	2	25 cm

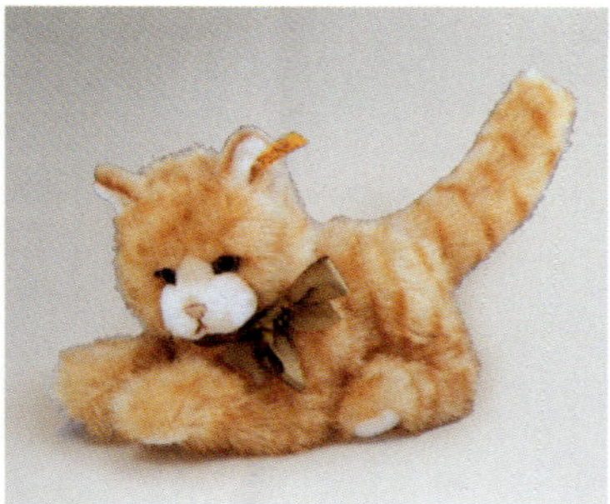

Kuschel Katze - ***Kuschel*** *Cat*

Webpelz, rot gestromelt, waschmaschinenfest - *woven fur, red tabby, machine washable*

EAN-No.	Period	Pr.	Info
099953	1992-1993	2	25 cm

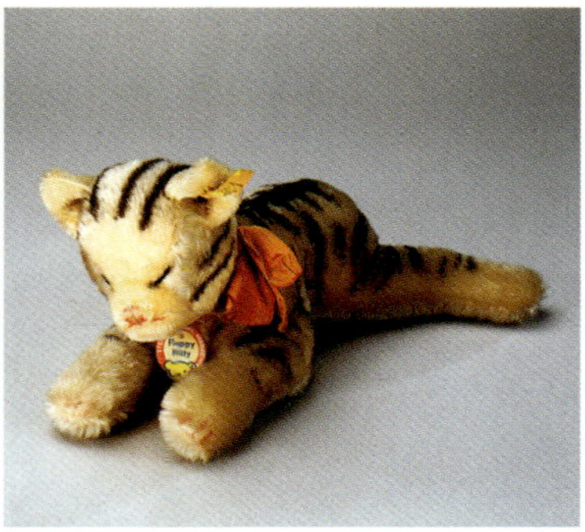

Floppy Kitty Katze (ab 1956 Floppy Katze) - ***Floppy Kitty*** *Cat (from 1956 Floppy Cat)*

Mohair, Augen gestickt, schwarz/weiss gestromt, liegend, Schlaftier, sehr weich, flach - *mohair, eyes are embroidered, black / white tabby, lying, sleeping toy, very soft & flat*

Serie	Art.-No	Period	Pr.	Info
85 44	**7317**	1954-1958	3-4	17 cm
850 440	**7317,00**	1959-1964	3	
560	**7317,00**	1965-1967	3	
	5600/17	1968-1969	3	
85 44	**7328**	1953-1958	3-4	28 cm
850 440	**7328,00**	1959-1964	3	
560	**7328,00**	1965-1967	3	
	5600/28	1968-1969	3	

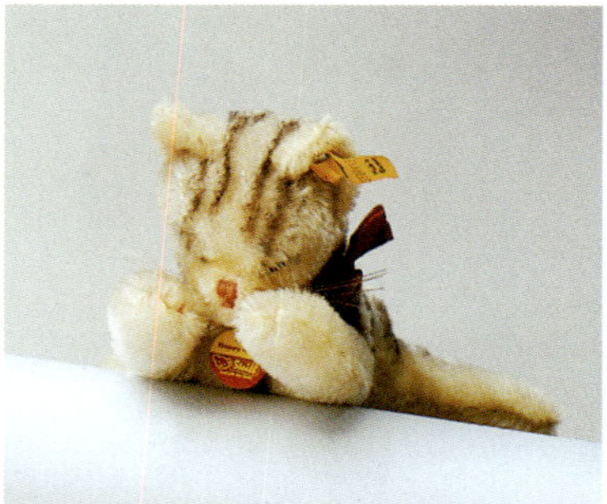

Floppy Katze - *Floppy Cat*

Mohair, formgeschaeumt, Augen gestickt, liegend, Schlaftier, sehr weich, vollwaschbar - *mohair, stuffed with pre-formed foam, eyes embroidered, lying, sleeping toy, very soft, fully washable*

Serie	Art.-No	Period	Pr.	Info
	5607/17	1970-1977	2	17 cm
	5607/28	1970-1977	2	28 cm

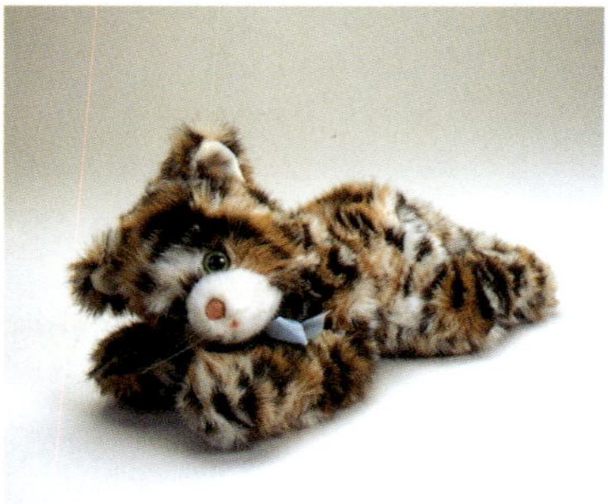

Floppy Mizzi

Synthetik-Webpelz, formgeschaeumt, liegend, vollwaschbar - *synthetic woven fur, stuffed with pre-formed foam, lying, fully washable*

Serie	Art.-No	Period	Pr.	Info
	5720/20	1978-1982	2	20 cm
	5720/30	1978-1981	2	30 cm

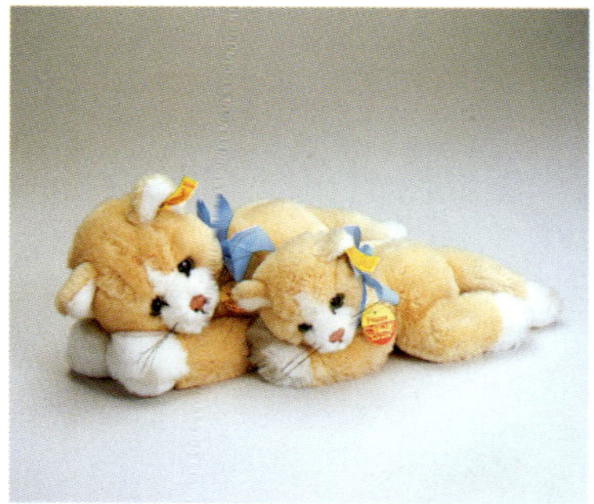

Floppy Katze - ***Floppy*** *Cat*

Webpelz, mollig weich, waschmaschinenfest - *woven fur, soft & cuddly, machine washable*

Serie	Art.-No	Period	Pr.	Info
082405	**5620/18**	1983-1990	2	22 cm
	082405	1991-1999	2	
082429	**5620/25**	1983-1989	2	25 cm

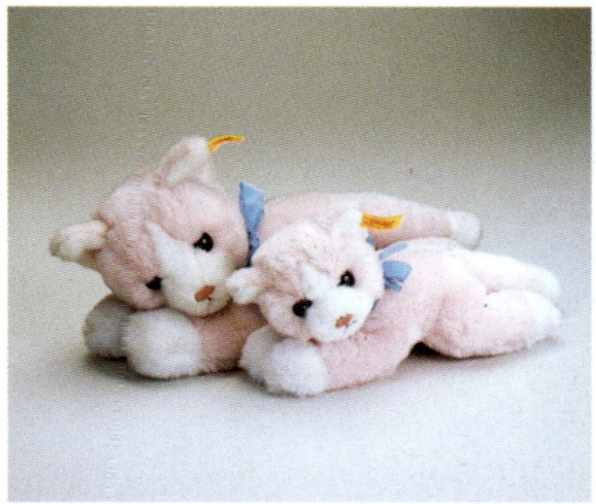

Baby Floppy Katze - *Baby Floppy Cat*

Webpelz, rosa, mollig weich, waschmaschinenfest - *woven fur, pink, soft & cuddly, machine washable*

Serie	Art.-No	Period	Pr.	Info
	5665/18	1983-1985	1-2	18 cm
	5665/25	1983-1985	1-2	25 cm

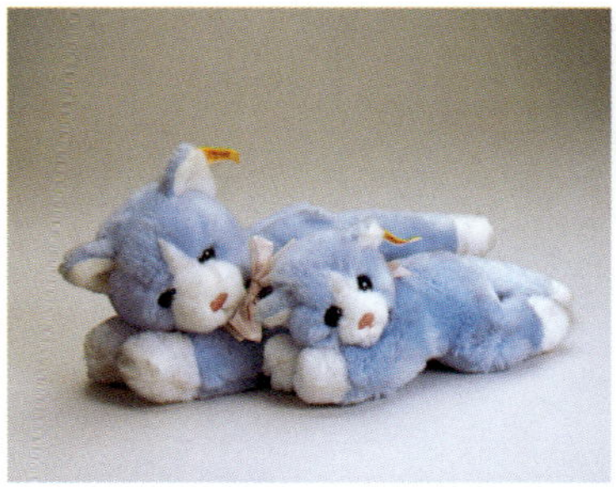

Baby Floppy Katze - *Baby Floppy Cat*

Webpelz, blau, mollig weich, waschmaschinenfest - *woven fur, blue, soft & cuddly, machine washable*

Serie	Art.-No	Period	Pr.	Info
	5666/18	1983-1985	1-2	18 cm
	5666/25	1983-1985	1-2	25 cm

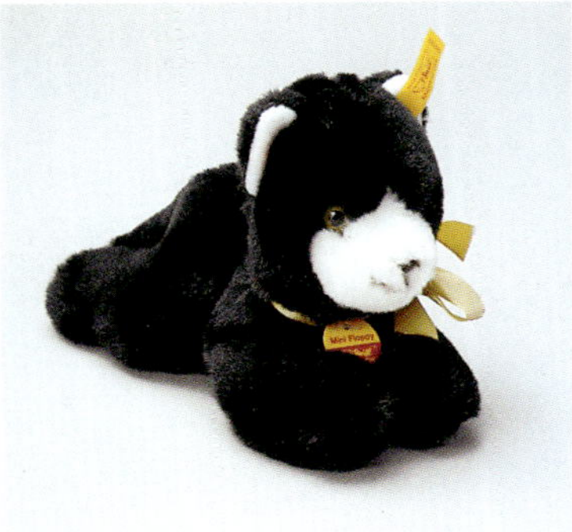

Mini Floppy Katze - ***Mini Floppy** Cat*

Webpelz, waschmaschinenfest - *woven fur, machine washable*

SERIE	ART.-NO	PERIOD	PR.	INFO
081989	**5665/16**	1989-1990	1-2	16 cm

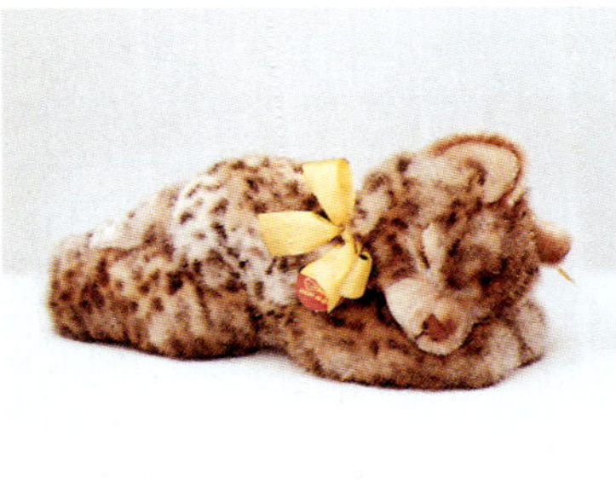

Schlafkatze - *Sleeping Cat*

Webpelz, liegend, waschmaschinenfest - *woven fur, lying, machine washable*

EAN-NO.	PERIOD	PR.	INFO
082597	1991-1993	2	22 cm

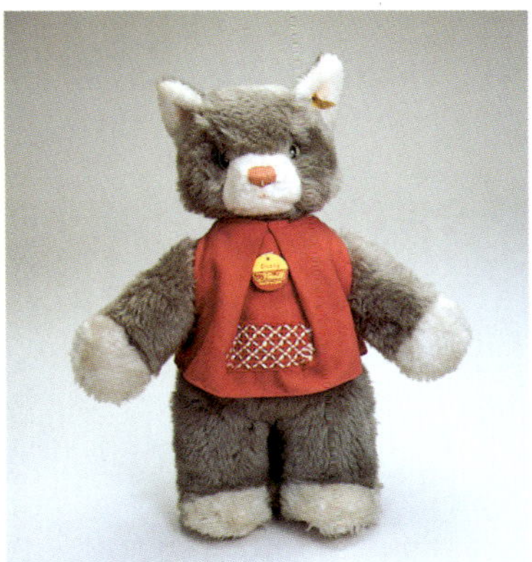

Weich-Katze **Dossy** - *Soft Cat **Dossy***

Dralon, formgeschaeumt, rote Weste, Schlenkerkopf, vollwaschbar - *dralon, stuffed with pre-formed foam, red vest, floppy head, fully washable*

SERIE	ART.-NO	PERIOD	PR.	INFO
	6230/30	1970-1978	2-3	30 cm
	6230/40	1970-1976	2-3	40 cm

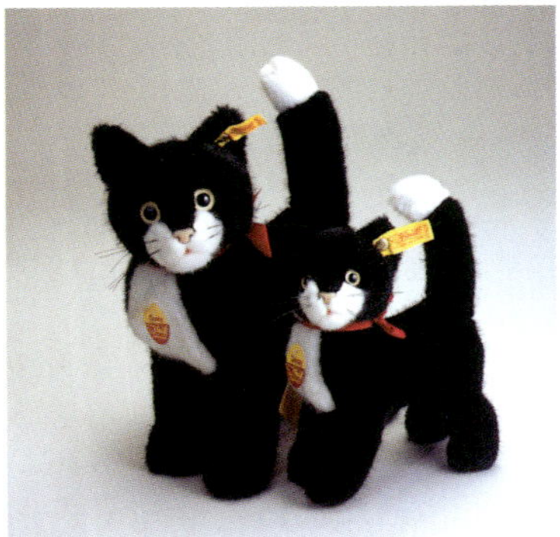

Dossy Katze - ***Dossy** Cat*

Webpelz, schwarz, abwaschbar - *woven fur, black, surface washable*

SERIE	ART.-NO	PERIOD	PR.	INFO
074301	**2738/16**	1984-1989	2	16 cm
074325	**2738/26**	1984-1990	2-3	26 cm

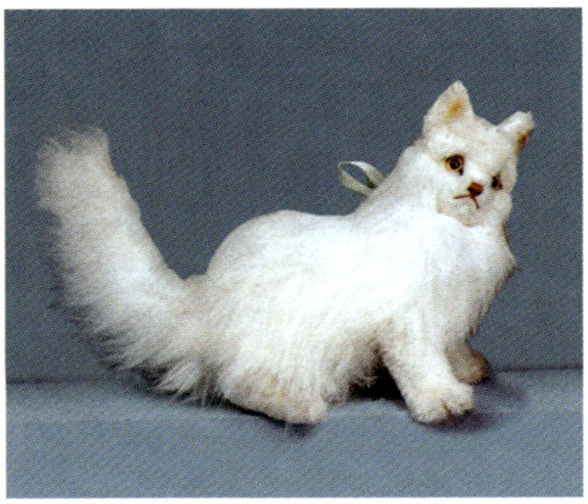

Perserkatze Diva - *Persian Cat Diva*

Drehkopf, Crylor, 1978 Dralonpluesch, langhaarig, weiss, sitzend, abwaschbar - *head swivels, crylor, in 1978 dralon, long-hair, white, sitting, surface washable*

SERIE	ART.-NO	PERIOD	PR.	INFO
283	**3635,04**	1967-1967	3	35 cm
	2834/35	1968-1978	3	

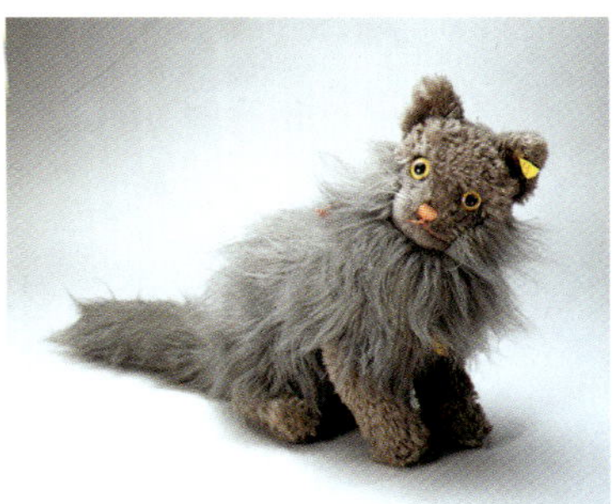

Perserkatze Diva - *Persian Cat Diva*

Drehkopf, Crylor, 1978 Dralonpluesch, langhaarig, grau, sitzend, abwaschbar - *head swivels, crylor, in 1978 dralon, long-hair, grey, sitting, surface washable*

SERIE	ART.-NO	PERIOD	PR.	INFO
283	**3635,05**	1967-1967	3	35 cm
	2835/35	1968-1978	3	

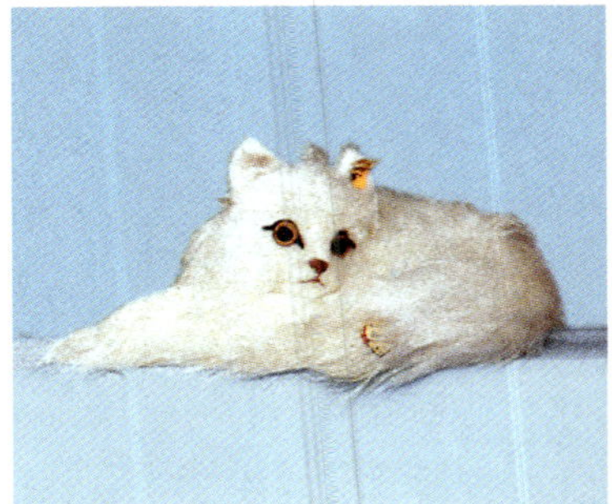

Angorakatze Diva - *Angora Cat Diva*

Crylor, langhaarig, 30 cm, weiss oder grau, liegend, abwaschbar - *crylor, long-hair, 30 cm, white or grey, lying, surface washable*

SERIE	ART.-NO	PERIOD	PR.	INFO
	2844/30	1968-1974	3	weiss - *white*
	2845/30	1968-1974	3	grau - *grey*

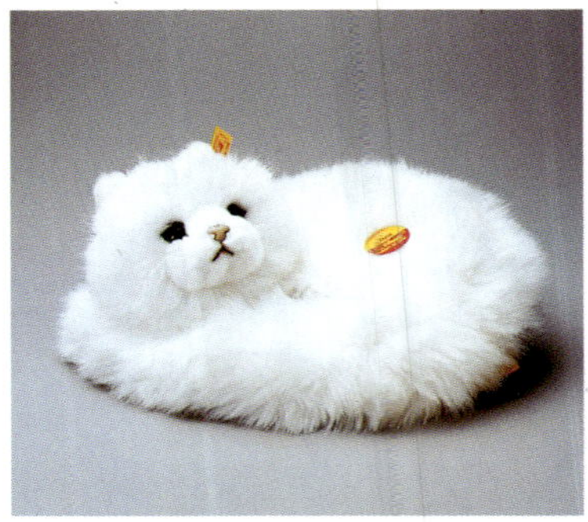

Diva Perserkatze - ***Diva** Persian Cat*

Webpelz, weiss, geringelt, waschmaschinenfest - *woven fur, white, curled up, machine washable*

EAN-NO.	PERIOD	PR.	INFO
074981	1991-1996	2-3	30 cm

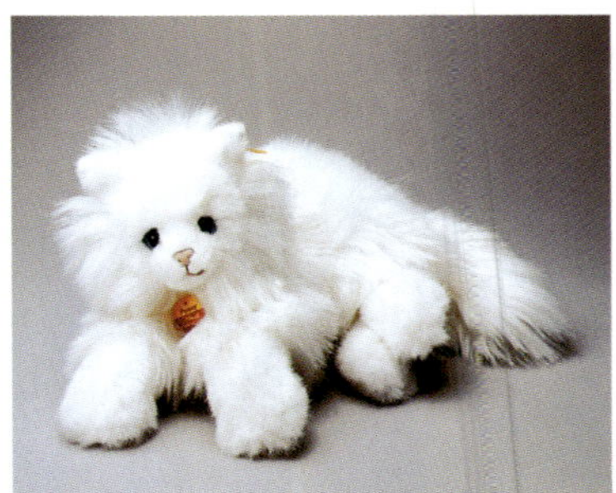

Pussy Perserkatze - ***Pussy** Persian Cat*

Webpelz, weiss, liegend, abwaschbar - *woven fur, white, lying, surface washable*

EAN-NO.	PERIOD	PR.	INFO
074974	1994-1998	3-4	45 cm

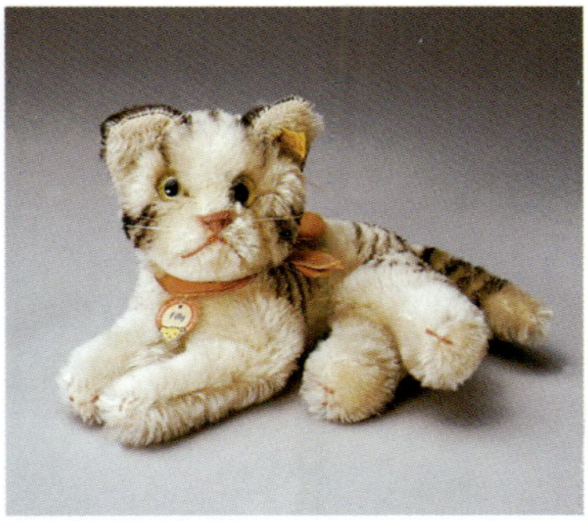

Fiffy Katze - ***Fiffy** Cat*

Mohairpluesch, weiss/grau gestromelt, liegend, Kopf drehbar - *mohair, white/grey tabby, lying, head swivels*

SERIE	ART.-NO	PERIOD	PR.	INFO
44	**2312**	1955-1956	4	12 cm
44	**2317**	1955-1958	4	17 cm
440	**2317,00**	1959-1962	4	
44	**2325,1**	1955-1958	4	25 cm
440	**2325,00**	1959-1962	4	

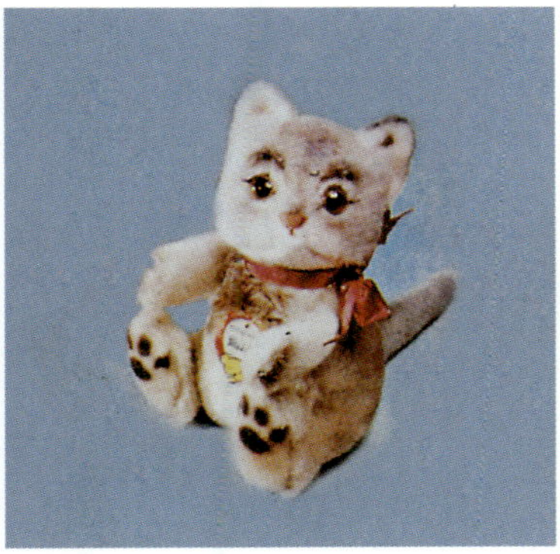

Ball Katze Sulla - *Ball Cat Sulla*

Dralon-Pluesch, Schaumstoff-Flocken-Fuellung, weich, Druckstimme - *dralon, stuffed with foam flakes, soft, press voice*

SERIE	ART.-NO	PERIOD	PR.	INFO
815 440	**4616,00**	1960-1961	4-5	16 cm

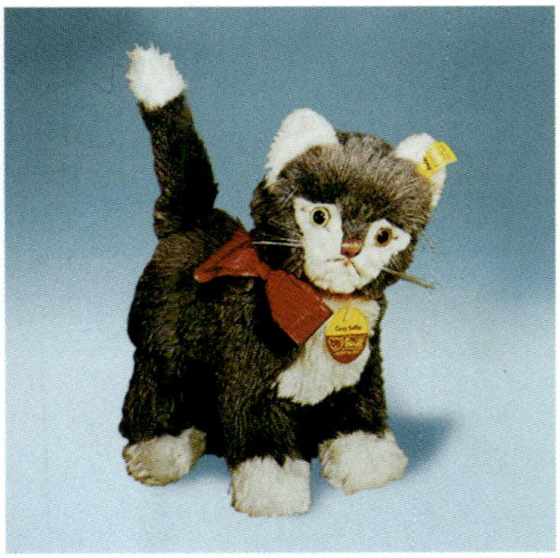

Cosy Sulla Katze - ***Cosy Sulla** Cat*

Dralon-Pluesch, Schaumstoff-Flocken-Fuellung, grau/weiss, stehend, Drehkopf, waschbar - *dralon, stuffed with foam flakes, grey & white, standing, head swivels, washable*

SERIE	ART.-NO	PERIOD	PR.	INFO
510	**1625,05**	1965-1967	2-3	25 cm
	5100/25	1968-1978	2	

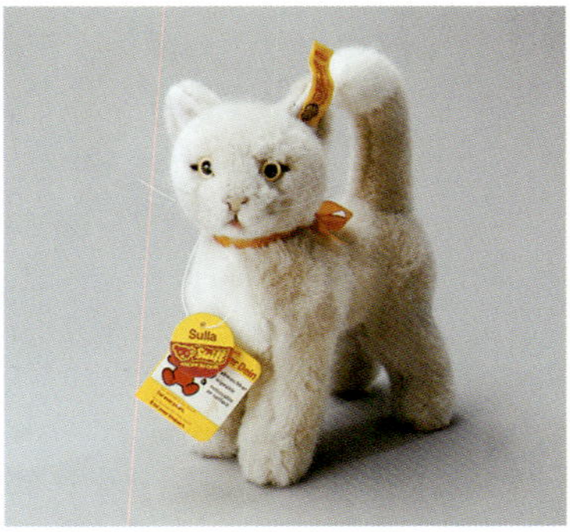

Sulla Katze - ***Sulla** Cat*

Webpelz, creme, abwaschbar - *woven fur, cream, surface washable*

SERIE	ART.-NO	PERIOD	PR.	INFO
074202	**2735/16**	1984-1986	2	16 cm
074226	**2735/26**	1984-1986	2	26 cm

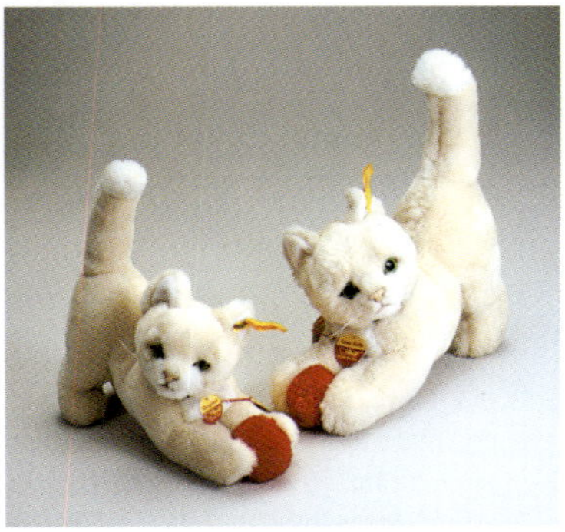

Cosy Sulla Katze - ***Cosy Sulla** Cat*

Webpelz, creme, mit Ball, waschmaschinenfest - *woven fur, cream, playing with ball, machine washable*

SERIE	ART.-NO	PERIOD	PR.	INFO
095054	**5440/16**	1985-1987	2	16 cm
095085	**5440/22**	1985-1987	2	22 cm

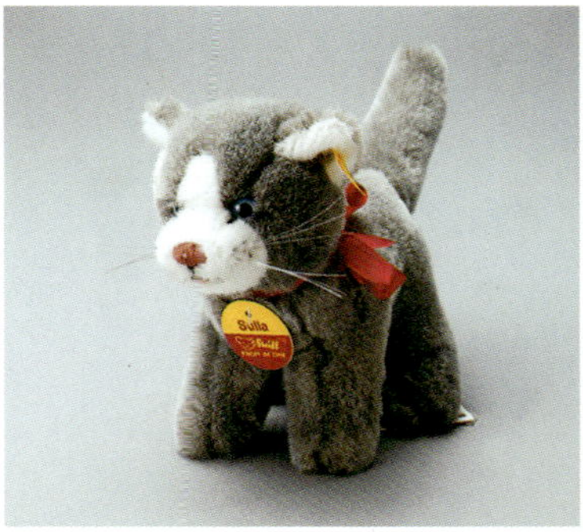

Sulla Katze - ***Sulla** Cat*

Webpelz, grau, stehend, waschmaschinenfest - *woven fur, grey, standing, machine washable*

EAN-NO.	PERIOD	PR.	INFO
081798	1994-1995	1-2	16 cm

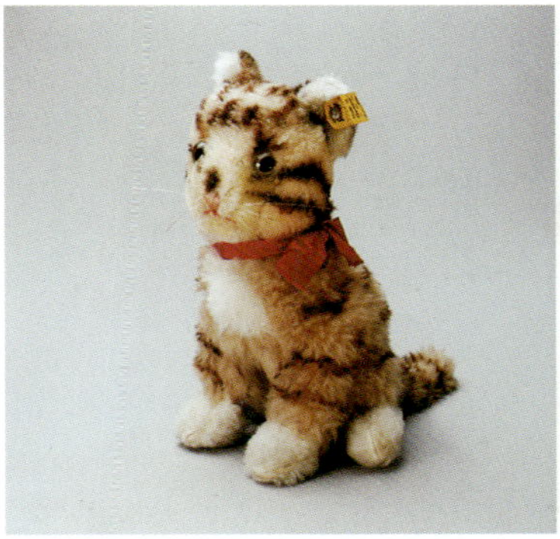

Katze **Cattie** - *Cat **Cattie***

Dralon, braun, sitzend, abwaschbar - *dralon, brown, sitting, surface washable*

SERIE	ART.-NO	PERIOD	PR.	INFO
	2770/18	1969-1976	2	18 cm
	2770/23	1969-1976	2	23 cm

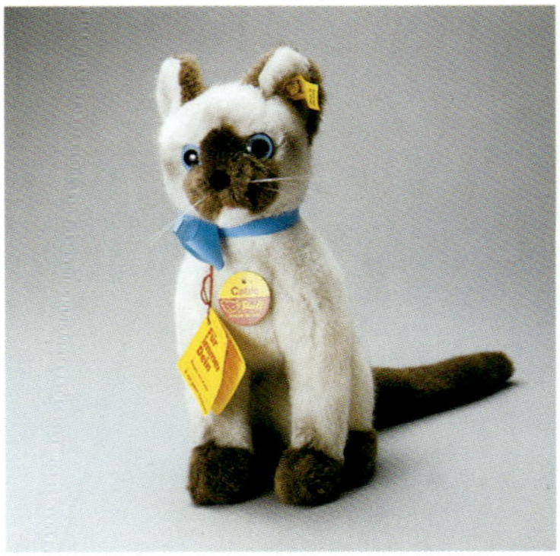

Cattie Siamkatze - ***Cattie** Siamese Cat*

Webpelz, sitzend, abwaschbar - *woven fur, sitting, surface washable*

SERIE	ART.-NO	PERIOD	PR.	INFO
	2740/25	1980-1983	2-3	25 cm

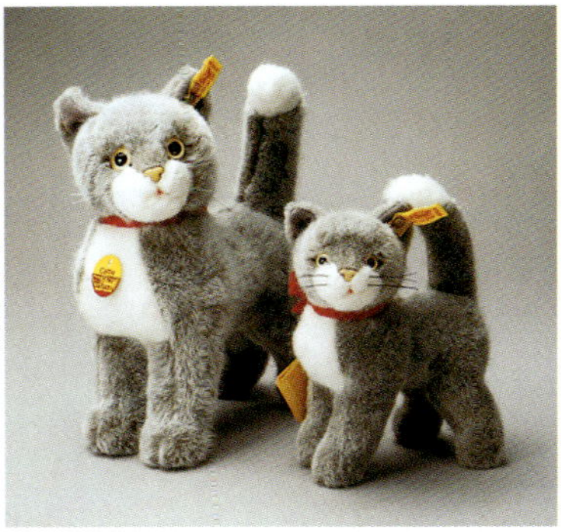

Cattie Katze - ***Cattie*** *Cat*

Webpelz, grau, abwaschbar - *woven fur, grey, surface washable*

SERIE	ART.-NO	PERIOD	PR.	INFO
074257	**2736/16**	1984-1988	2	16 cm
074271	**2736/26**	1984-1988	2-3	26 cm

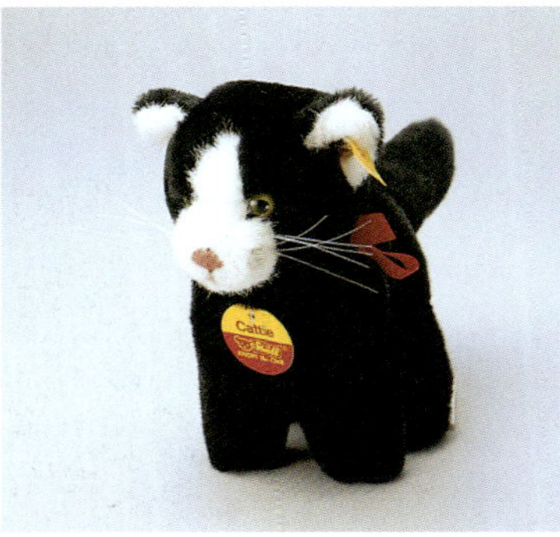

Cattie Katze - ***Cattie*** *Cat*

Webpelz, schwarz, stehend, waschmaschinenfest - *woven fur, black, standing machine washable*

EAN-NO.	PERIOD	PR.	INFO
081781	1994-1995	1-2	16 cm

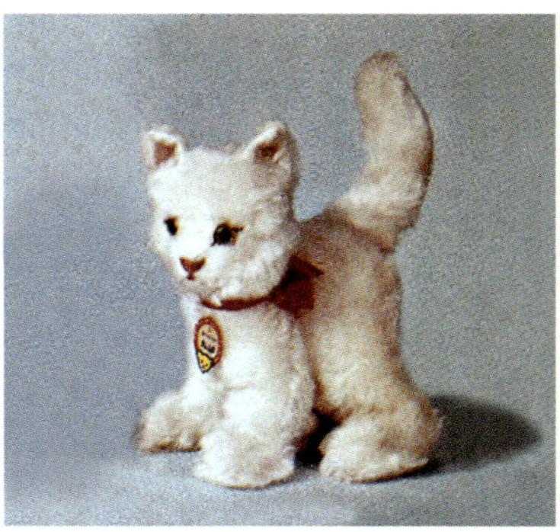

Cosy Minka Katze - ***Cosy Minka*** *Cat*

Dralon, Kunstfaser-Fuellung, weiss, stehend, sehr weich, waschbar - *dralon, stuffed with synthetic fibers, white, standing, very soft, washable*

SERIE	ART.-NO	PERIOD	PR.	INFO
830 440	**6622,04**	1961-1964	2-3	22 cm
510	**6622,04**	1966-1966	2-3	

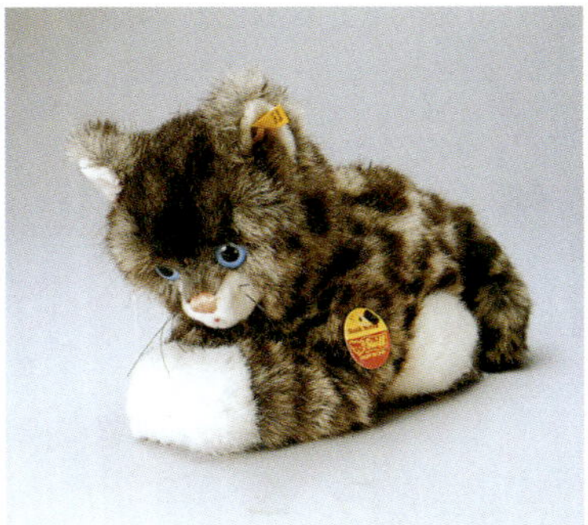

Musik Minka Katze - *Musical Minka Cat*

Webpelz, austauschbares Musikwerk, waschbar - *woven fur, exchangeable music box, washable*

SERIE	ART.-NO	PERIOD	PR.	INFO
	6371/22	1978-1980	3	22 cm

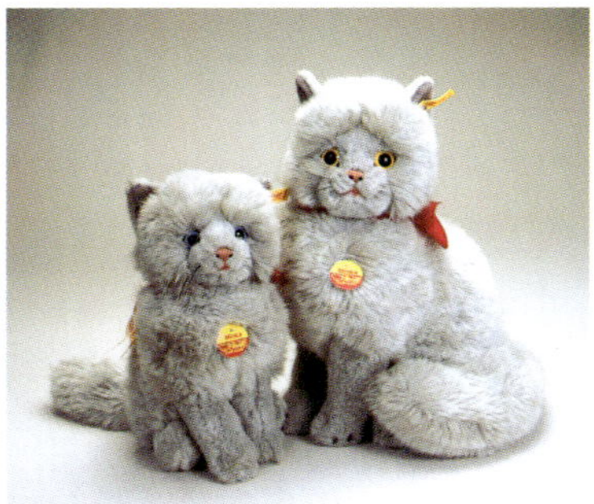

Minka Perserkatze - ***Minka*** *Persian Cat*

Webpelz, grau, 26 cm Augen blau, 35 cm gelb, geringe Modellunterschiede - *woven fur, grey, 26 cm blue eyes, 35 cm yellow eyes, small discrepancies between the two sizes*

SERIE	ART.-NO	PERIOD	PR.	INFO
	2752/26	1982-1985	2-3	26 cm
	2752/35	1982-1984	2-3	35 cm

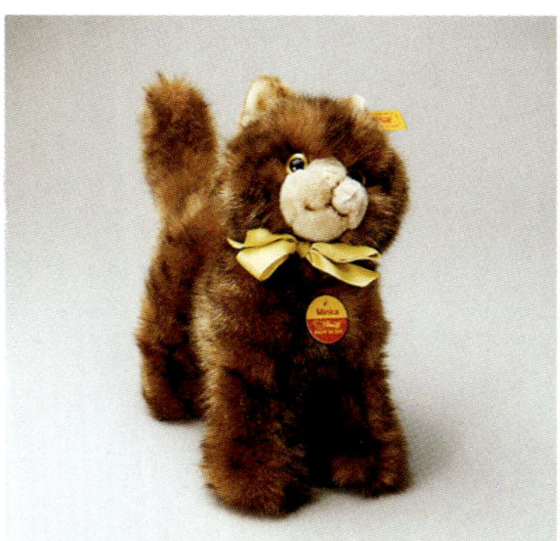

Minka Katze - ***Minka*** *Cat*

Webpelz, braun gestromelt, stehend, waschmaschinenfest - *woven fur, brown tabby, standing, machine washable*

SERIE	ART.-NO	PERIOD	PR.	INFO
074196	**2710/28**	1990-1990	2	28 cm
	074196	1991-1991	2	

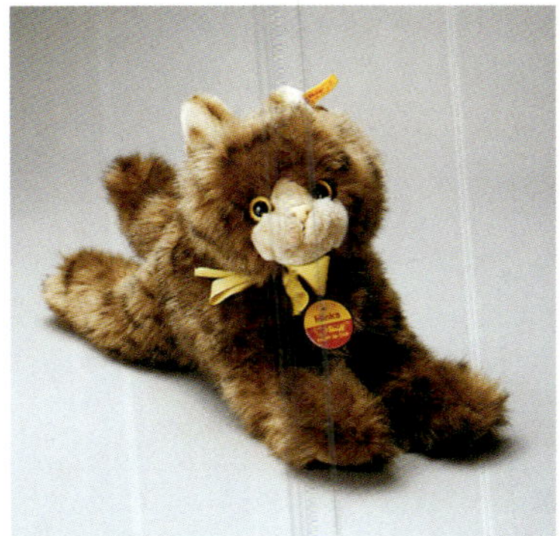

Minka Katze - ***Minka*** *Cat*

Webpelz, braun gestromelt, liegend, waschmaschinenfest - *woven fur, brown tabby, lying, machine washable*

SERIE	ART.-NO	PERIOD	PR.	INFO
074240	**2715/35**	1990-1990	2	35 cm
	074240	1991-1991	2	

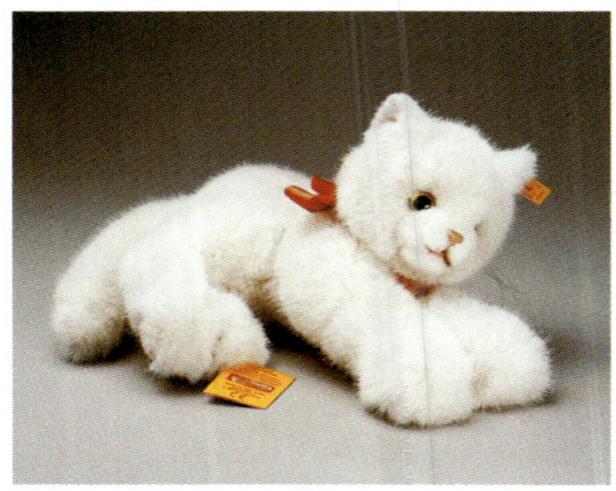

Minka Katze - ***Minka*** *Cat*

Webpelz, creme, liegend, waschmaschinenfest - *woven fur, cream, lying, machine washable*

EAN-NO.	PERIOD	PR.	INFO
075063	1993-1995	2	30 cm

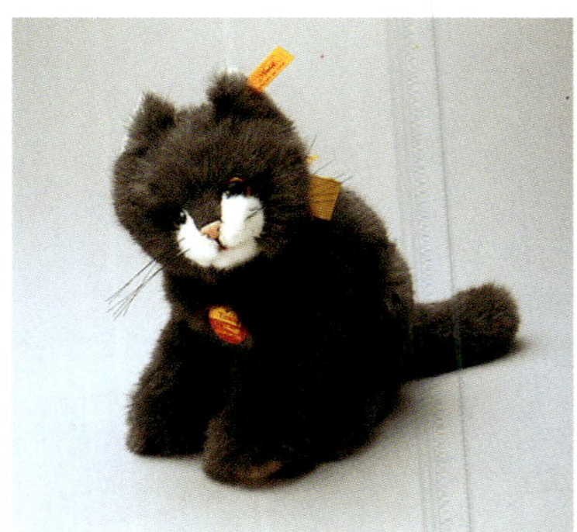

Tinka Katze - ***Tinka*** *Cat*

Webpelz, grau, sitzend, waschmaschinenfest - *woven fur, grey, sitting, machine washable*

EAN-No.	Period	Pr.	Info
075032	1993-1994	2	25 cm

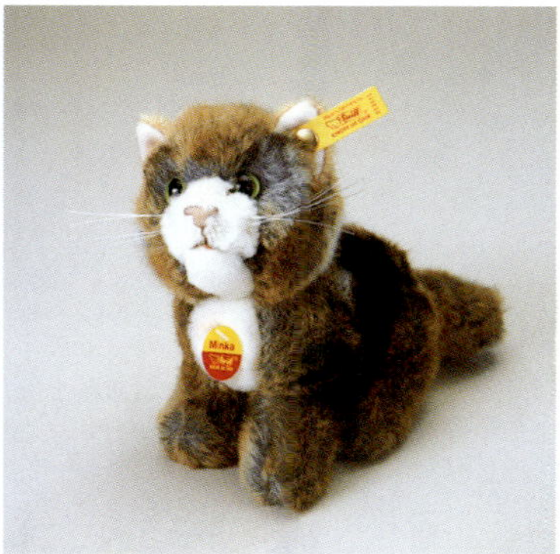

Minka Kaetzchen - ***Minka** Kitten*

Webpelz, braun gefleckt, sitzend, waschmaschinenfest - *woven fur, brown spotted, sitting, machine washable*

EAN-No.	Period	Pr.	Info
053511	1998-1999	2	14 cm

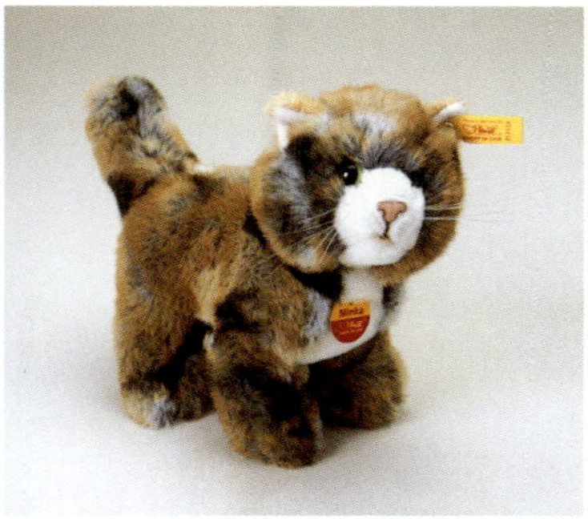

Minka Kaetzchen - ***Minka** Kitten*

Webpelz, braun gefleckt, stehend, waschmaschinenfest - *woven fur, brown spotted, standing, machine washable*

EAN-No.	Period	Pr.	Info
053528	1998-1999	2	16 cm

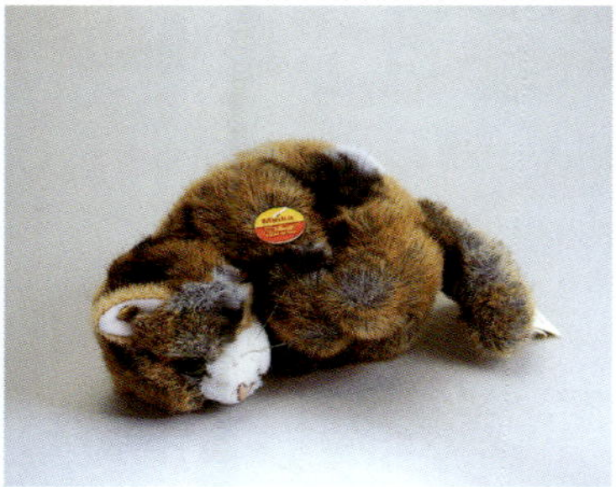

Minka Kaetzchen - ***Minka** Kitten*

Webpelz, braun gefleckt, liegend, waschmaschinenfest - *woven fur, brown spotted, lying, machine washable*

EAN-No.	Period	Pr.	Info
053535	1998-1999	2	16 cm

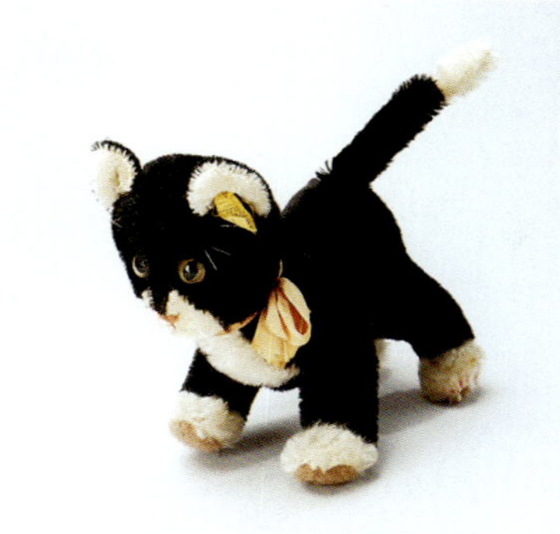

Hoppelkatze ohne Wagen - *Hopping Cat without Wagon*

Mohair, Pfoten mit Klettenplatten, schwarz/weiss, stehend, Cosy Tier - *mohair, paws have Velcro pads, black & white, standing, cozy animal*

Serie	Art.-No	Period	Pr.	Info
571	**1330,00**	1967-1967	3-4	30 cm
	5710/30	1968-1970	3-4	

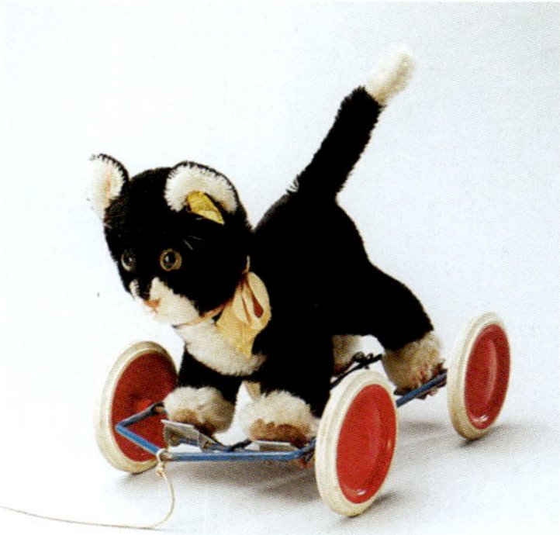

Hoppelkatze mit Wagen - *Hopping Cat with Wagon*

Mohair, Pfoten mit Klettenplatten, vom Fahrgestell abnehmbar als Cosy Tier - *mohair, paws have Velcro pads, can be removed from the wheel frame & used as a cozy animal*

Serie	Art.-No	Period	Pr.	Info
571	**1330,10**	1967-1967	4	35 cm
	5710/35	1968-1970	4	

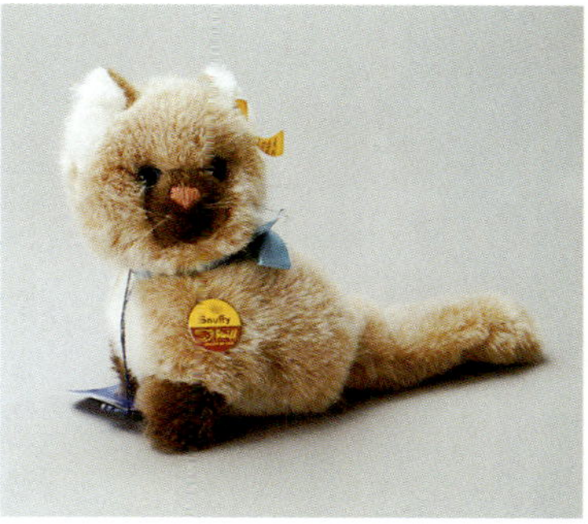

Snuffy Katze - ***Snuffy** Cat*

Pelz-Imitation, ab 1978 Synthetik-Webpelz, sitzend, abwaschbar - *imitation fur, from 1978 synthetic woven fur, sitting, surface washable*

Serie	Art.-No	Period	Pr.	Info
	3520/12	1974-1982	1-2	12 cm, beige
	3520/17	1974-1982	2	17 cm
	3521/12	1974-1982	1-2	12 cm, grau - *grey*
	3521/17	1974-1982	2	17 cm

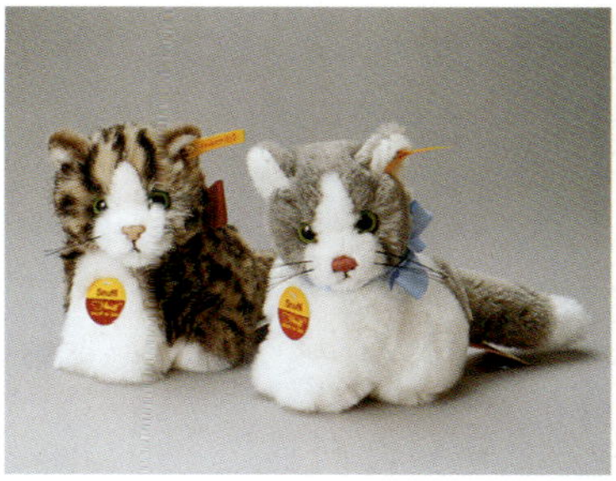

Snuffi Katze - ***Snuffi** Cat*

Webpelz, waschmaschinenfest, 16 cm - *woven fur, machine washable, 16cm*

Serie	Art.-No	Period	Pr.	Info
077364	**2926/16**	1983-1990	2	grau - *grey*
	077364	1991-1999	2	
077388	**2927/16**	1983-1987	2	rot - *red*
077395	**2928/16**	1987-1990	2	gestromelt - *tabby*
	077395	1991-1999	2	

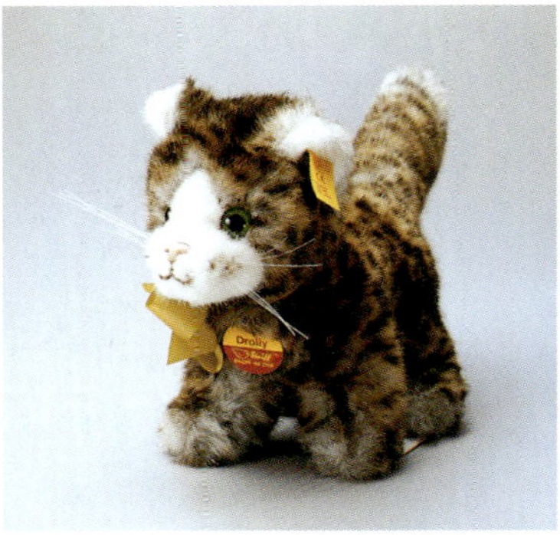

Drolly Katze - ***Drolly** Cat*

Webpelz, gefleckt, stehend, waschmaschinenfest - *woven fur, spotted, standing, machine washable*

SERIE	ART.-NO	PERIOD	PR.	INFO
081347	**5780/22**	1990-1990	2-3	22 cm
	081347	1991-1999	2-3	

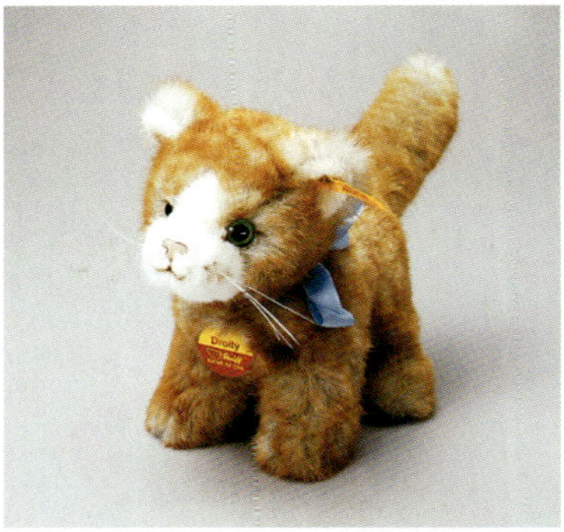

Drolly Katze - ***Drolly** Cat*

Webpelz, stehend, waschmaschinenfest, 22 cm - *woven fur, standing, machine washable, 22cm*

EAN-NO.	PERIOD	PR.	INFO
081613	1993-1997	2	rot geflammt - *flame red*
081620	1993-1995	2	grau - *grey*
081637	1993-1995	2	schwarz - *black*

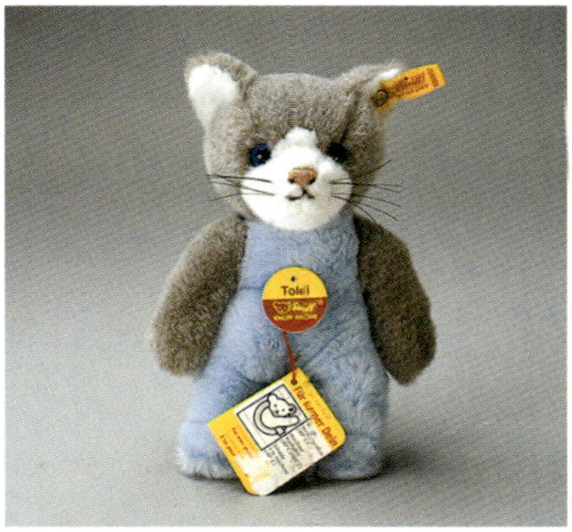

Toldi Katze - ***Toldi** Cat*

Webpelz, Pieps-Stimme, waschmaschinenfest - *woven fur, squeaker, machine washable*

SERIE	ART.-NO	PERIOD	PR.	INFO
080456	**6260/22**	1984-1989	2	22 cm

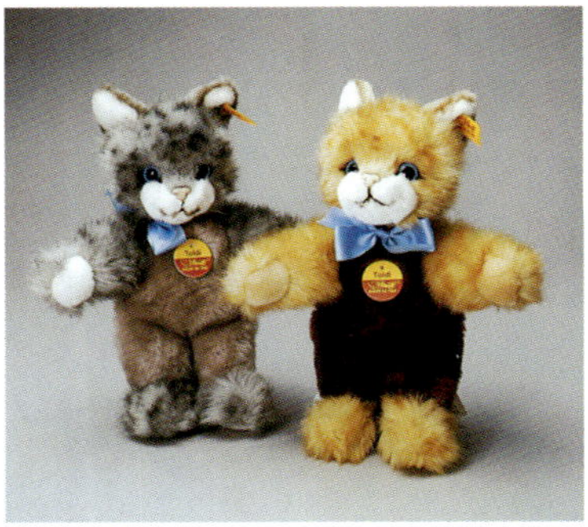

Toldi Katze - ***Toldi** Cat*

Webpelz, gestromelt, Pieps-Stimme, waschmaschinenfest, 27 cm - *woven fur, tabby, squeaker, machine washable, 27cm*

SERIE	ART.-NO	PERIOD	PR.	INFO
081002	**6265/27**	1989-1990	2-3	grau - *grey*
080982	**6275/27**	1988-1990	2-3	roetlich - *reddish*

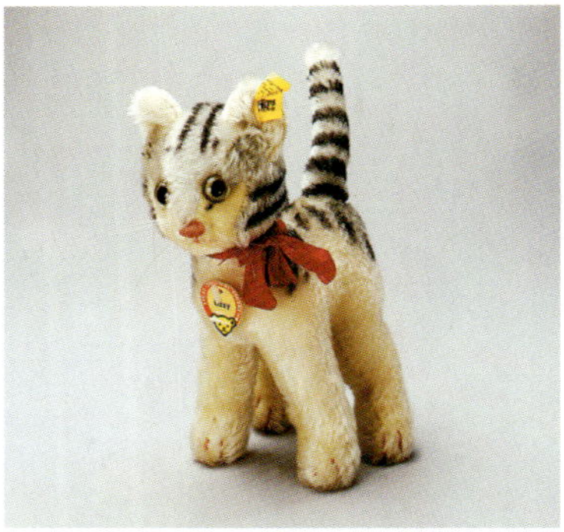

Katze **Lizzy** - *Cat **Lizzy***

Mohair, weiss/grau, stehend, abwaschbar - *mohair, white & grey, standing, surface washable*

SERIE	ART.-NO	PERIOD	PR.	INFO
	2713/15	1968-1976	2-3	15 cm
	2713/22	1968-1976	3	22 cm

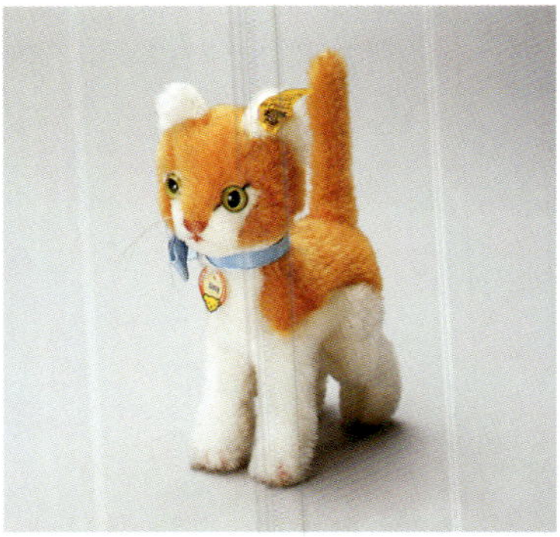

Katze **Lizzy** - *Cat **Lizzy***

Dralon, weiss/braun, stehend, abwaschbar - *dralon, white & brown, standing, surface washable*

SERIE	ART.-NO	PERIOD	PR.	INFO
	2716/15	1968-1972	2-3	15 cm
	2716/22	1968-1972	2-3	22 cm

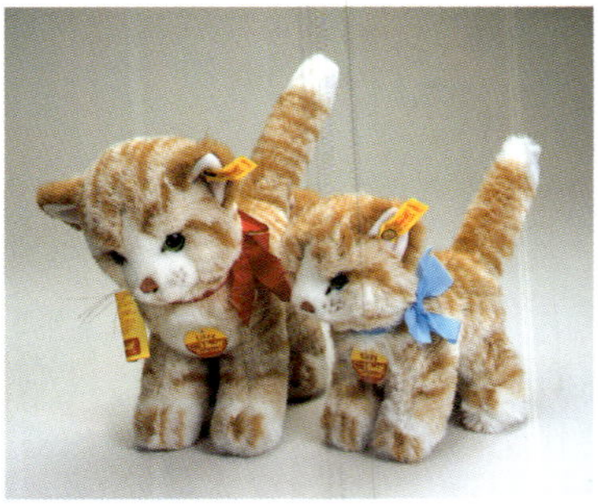

Lizzy Katze - ***Lizzy** Cat*

Wirkpelz, stehend, abwaschbar - *knitted fur, standing, surface washable*

SERIE	ART.-NO	PERIOD	PR.	INFO
074158	**2728/17**	1979-1990	2	17 cm
074172	**2728/22**	1979-1989	2	22 cm

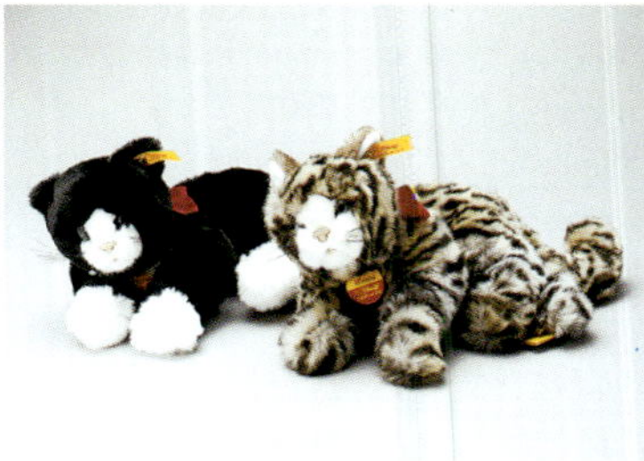

Minou Katze - ***Minou** Cat*

Webpelz, liegend, waschmaschinenfest - *woven fur, lying, machine washable*

SERIE	ART.-NO	PERIOD	PR.	INFO
074509	**2754/25**	1986-1990 creme - *cream*	3	25 cm,
074554	**2754/40**	1986-1989	3	40 cm
074608	**2755/25**	1986-1988 grau - *grey*	3	25 cm,

074653	**2755/40**	1986-1988	3	40 cm
074707	**2756/25**	1986-1990	3	25 cm, schwarz - *black*
	074707	1991-1999	3	
074752	**2756/40**	1986-1989	3	40 cm
074806	**2757/25**	1987-1990	3	25 cm, gestromelt - *tabby*
	074806	1991-1999	3	
074851	**2757/40**	1987-1990	3	40 cm
	074851	1991-1995	3	

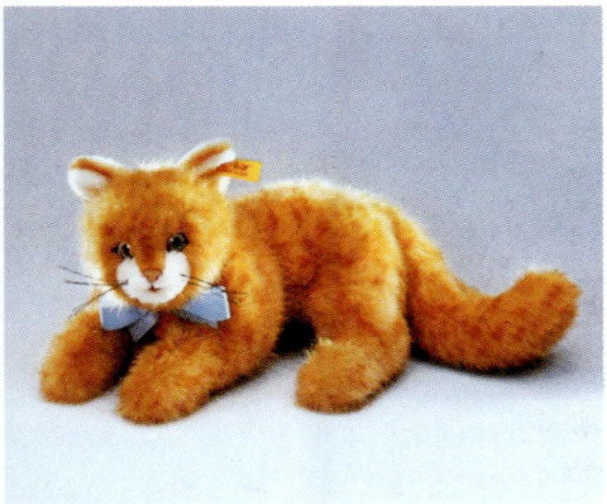

Minou Katze - ***Minou** Cat*

Webpelz, roetlich gestromelt, liegend, waschmaschinenfest - *woven fur, reddish tabby, lying, machine washable*

SERIE	ART.-NO	PERIOD	PR.	INFO
074950	**2758/40**	1988-1990	2-3	40 cm
	074950	1991-1993	2-3	

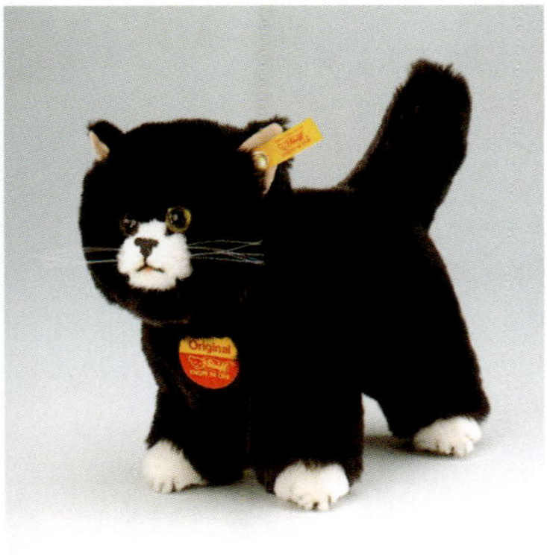

Jungkatze - *Kitten*

Webpelz, 16 cm, stehend, waschmaschinenfest - *woven fur, 16 cm, standing, machine washable*

EAN-NO.	PERIOD	PR.	INFO
074875	1996-1998	2-3	grau gestromelt - *grey striped*
074912	1996-1999	2-3	rot gestromelt - *red striped*
074790	1997-1999	2-3	braun gestromelt - *brown striped*
074837	1997-1998	2-3	schwarz - *black*

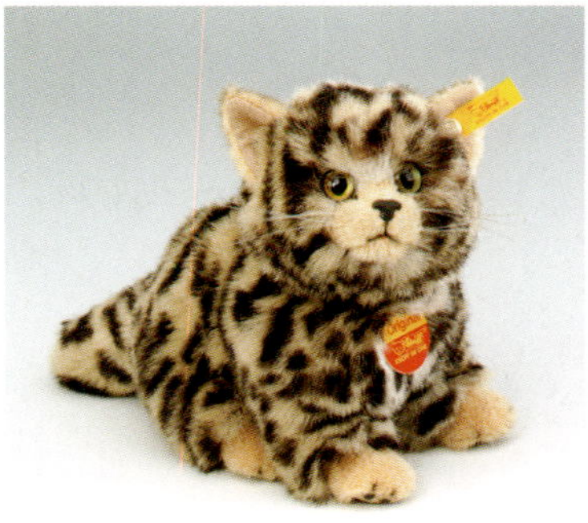

Jungkatze - *Kitten*

Webpelz, 16 cm, sitzend, waschmaschinenfest - *woven fur, 16 cm, sitting, machine washable*

EAN-NO.	PERIOD	PR.	INFO
074882	1996-1998	2-3	grau gestromelt - *grey striped*
074813	1997-1999	2-3	braun gestromelt - *brown striped*
074844	1997-1999	2-3	schwarz - *black*

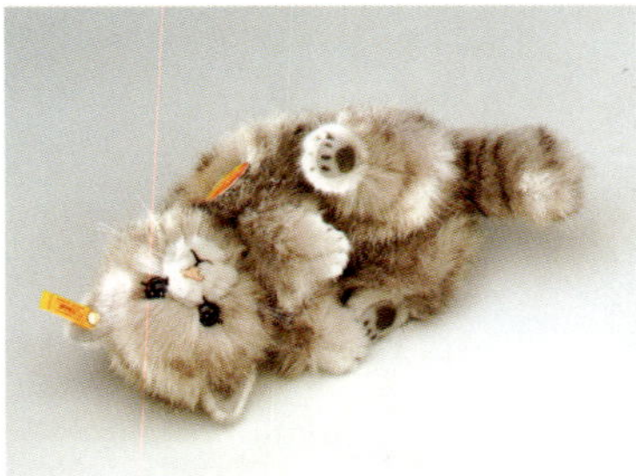

Jungkatze - *Kitten*

Webpelz, 20 cm, seitlich liegend, waschmaschinenfest - *woven fur, 20 cm, lying aside, machine washable*

EAN-NO.	PERIOD	PR.	INFO
074899	1996-1998	2-3	grau gestromelt - *grey striped*
074936	1996-1999	2-3	rot gestromelt - *red striped*
074820	1997-1999	2-3	braun gestromelt - *brown striped*
074868	1997-1999	2-3	schwarz - *black*

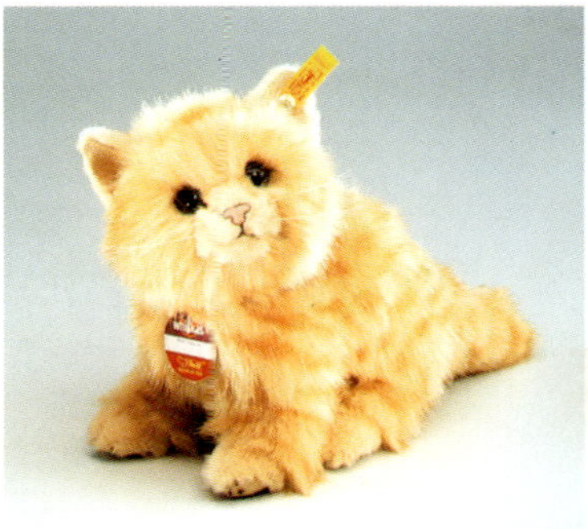

Whiskas-Katze - *Whiskas-Cat*

Webpelz, 16 cm, sitzend, waschmaschinenfest - *woven fur, 16 cm, sitting, machine washable*

EAN-NO.	PERIOD	PR.	INFO
074929	1996-1999	2-3	rot gestromelt - *red striped*
075322	1999-1999	2-3	grau - *grey*

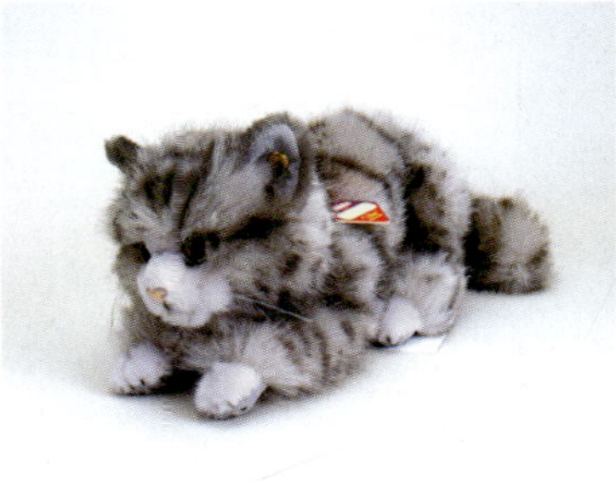

Whiskas-Katze - *Whiskas-Cat*

Webpelz, grau gestromelt, kauernd, waschmaschinenfest - *woven fur, grey striped, crouching, machine washable*

EAN-NO.	PERIOD	PR.	INFO
075094	1998-1999	3	22 cm

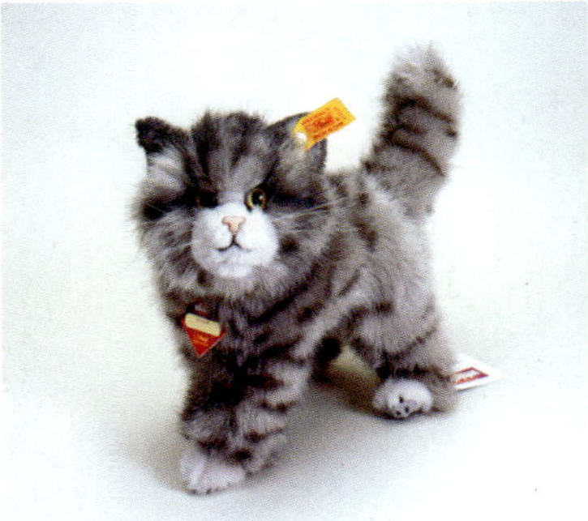

Whiskas-Katze - *Whiskas-Cat*

Webpelz, grau, stehend, waschmaschinenfest - *woven fur, grey, standing, machine washable*

EAN-NO.	PERIOD	PR.	INFO
075339	1999-1999	3	22 cm

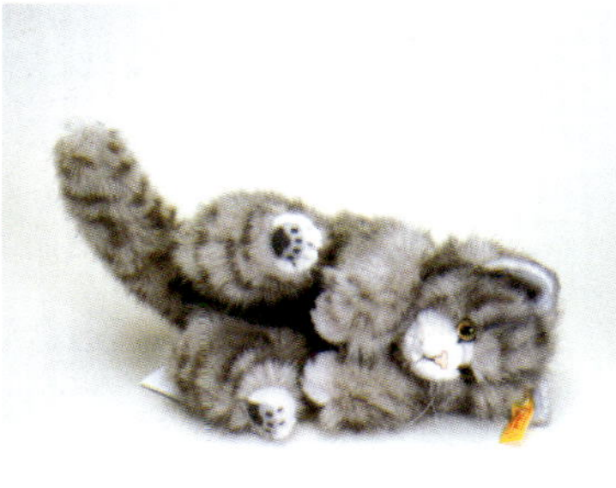

Whiskas-Katze - *Whiskas-Cat*

Webpelz, grau, liegend, waschmaschinenfest - *woven fur, grey, lying aside, machine washable*

EAN-No.	Period	Pr.	Info
075346	1999-1999	3	22 cm

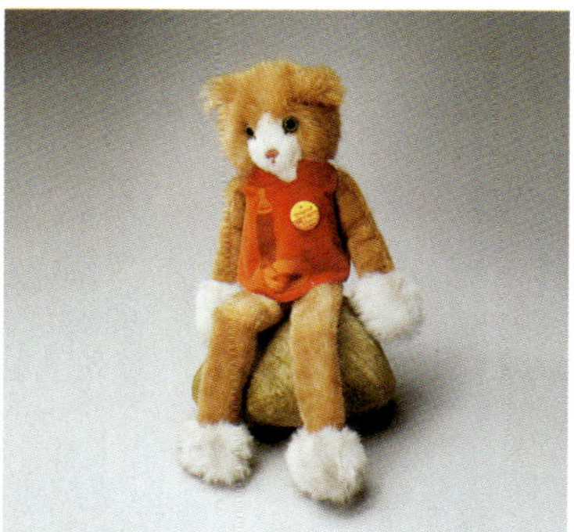

Schlenkerkatze - *Dangling Cat*

Webpelz, oranges Blouson, Schlenkerglieder, abwaschbar - *woven fur, orange top, floppy joints, surface washable*

Serie	Art.-No	Period	Pr.	Info
	6286/50	1981-1985	2-3	50 cm

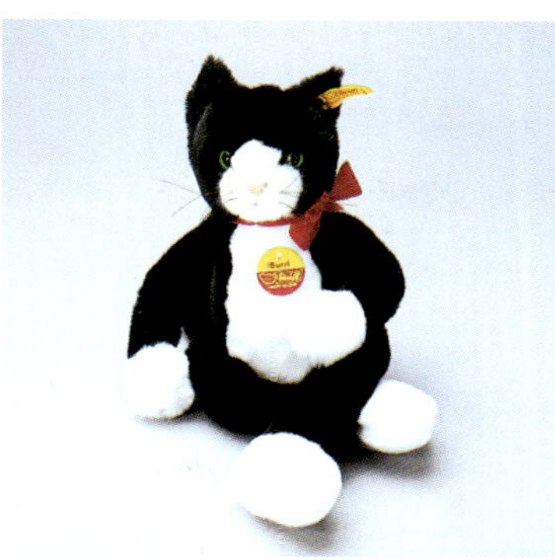

Burri Schlenker-Katze - ***Burri** Dangling Cat*

Webpelz, Pieps-Stimme, waschmaschinenfest - *woven fur, squeaker, machine washable*

Serie	Art.-No	Period	Pr.	Info
123153	**6290/32**	1986-1988	2-3	32 cm

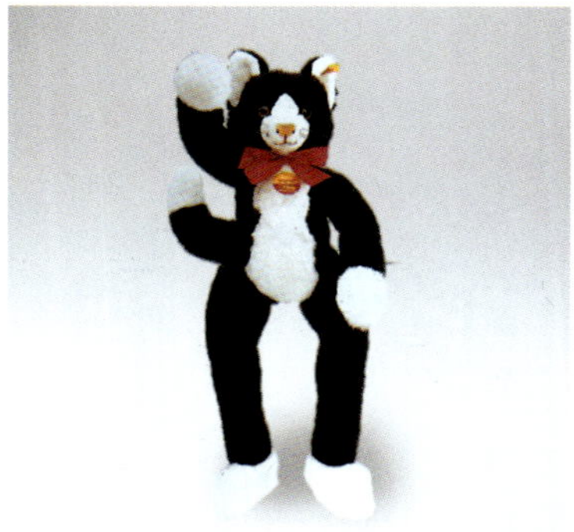

Schlenkerkatze - *Dangling Cat*

Webpelz, schwarz, abwaschbar - *woven fur, black, surface washable*

Serie	Art.-No	Period	Pr.	Info
122323	**6285/70**	1990-1990	3	70 cm
	122323	1991-1993	3	
122361	**6285/99**	1990-1990	3-4	100 cm
	122361	1991-1992	3-4	

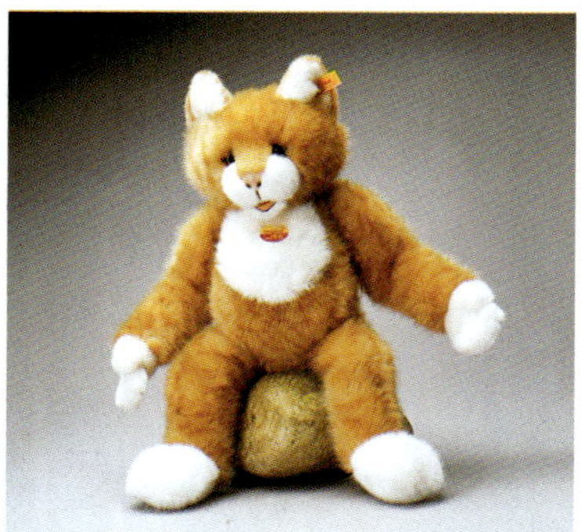

Schlenker Katze - *Dangling Cat*

Webpelz, waschmaschinenfest - *woven fur, machine washable*

EAN-No.	Period	Pr.	Info
123580	1993-1995	3	50 cm

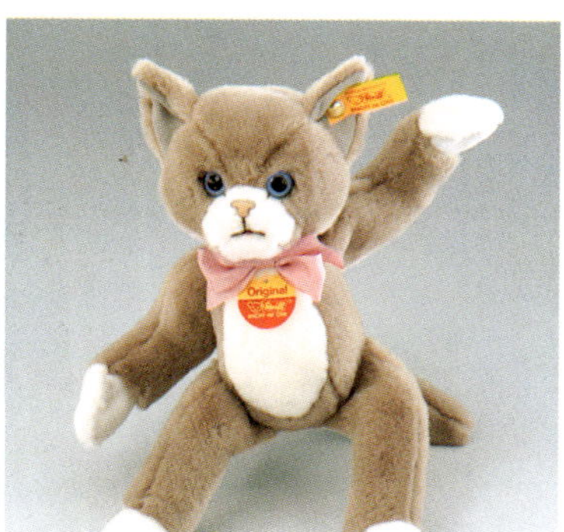

Schlenker Katze - *Dangling Cat*

Webpelz, waschmaschinenfest - *woven fur, machine washable*

EAN-No.	Period	Pr.	Info
122330	1997-1998	2-3	22 cm

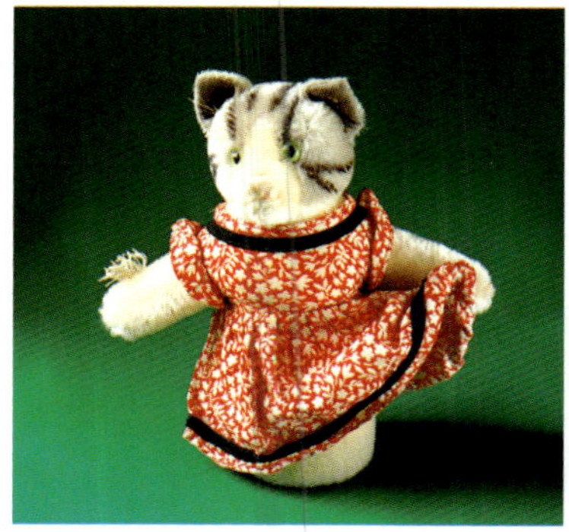

Musik Katze - *Musical Cat*

Kopf Mohairpluesch, Schweizer Musikwerk, zum Druecken, grau/weiss, rotes Kleid - *head is mohair, Swiss music box (squeeze type), grey & white, red dress*

Serie	Art.-No	Period	Pr.	Info
97 44	**9325**	1950-1951	6-7	25 cm

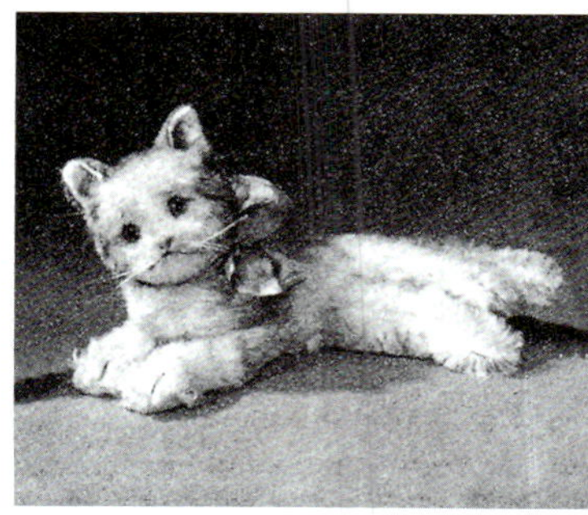

Katze - *Cat*

Mohair, grau/weiss, liegend, weich, Miau-Stimme - *mohair, grey & white, lying, soft, meow voice*

Serie	Art.-No	Period	Pr.	Info
44	**2322,1**	1952-1953	4-5	22 cm

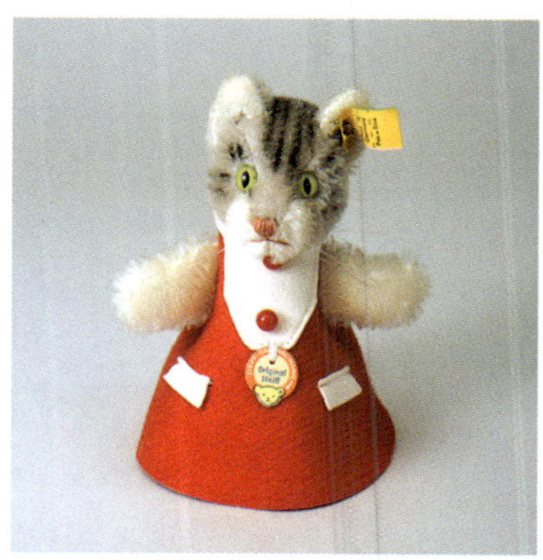

Betthupferlkatze - *Pillow Cat*

Kopf & Arme Mohair, Filzkleidung, rot, Drehkopf, innen hohl zur Abdeckung kleiner Praesente - *head & arms mohair, red felt clothing, head swivels, hollow interior to cover small gifts*

Serie	Art.-No	Period	Pr.	Info
	3177/15	1969-1974	4	15 cm

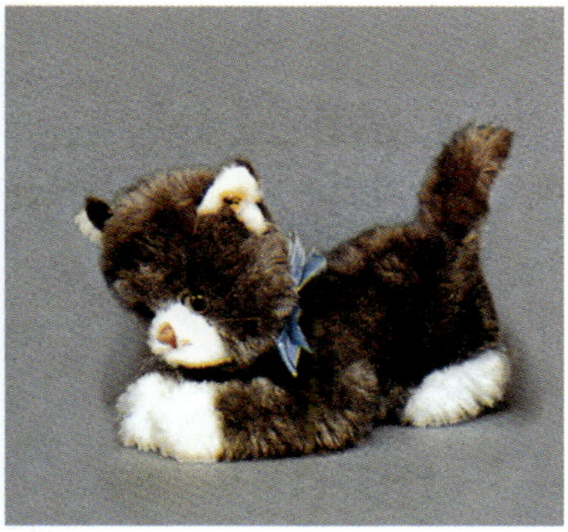

Dralon-Katze **Sigi** - *Dralon Cat **Sigi***

Dralon, liegend, vollwaschbar - *dralon, lying, fully washable*

Serie	Art.-No	Period	Pr.	Info
	5210/23	1970-1973	2	23 cm

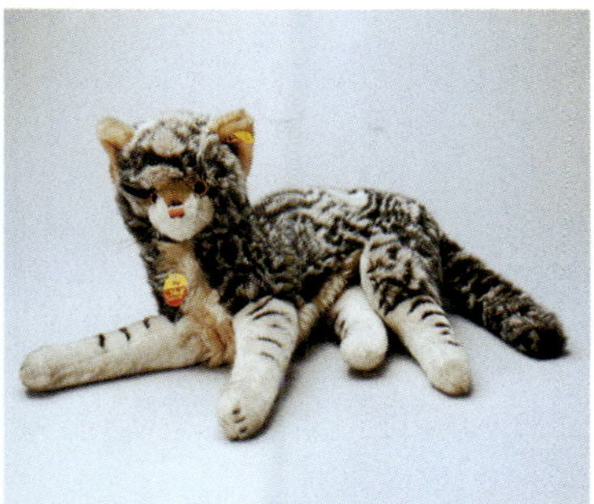

Sigi Katze - ***Sigi** Cat*

Wirkflor, ab 1978 Synthetik-Webpelz, abwaschbar - *knitted fur, 1978 synthetic woven fur, surface washable*

Serie	Art.-No	Period	Pr.	Info
	2820/35	1976-1979	2-3	35 cm

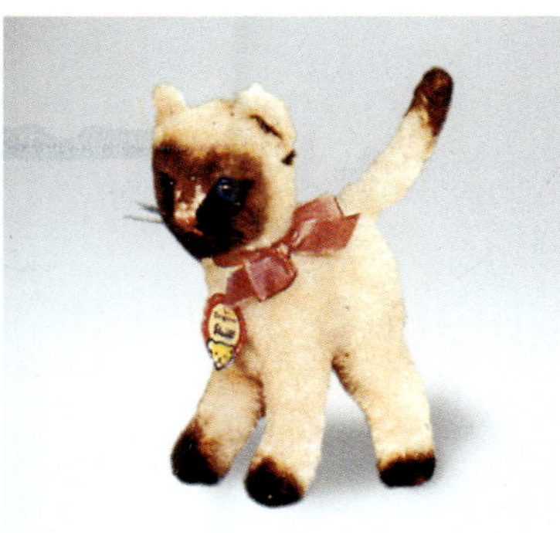

Katze Aram - *Cat Aram*

"Der kleine Tierversand", Dralon, im Kaefigkarton, stehend, mit Tiersteckbrief, abwaschbar - *"Der kleine Tierversand", dralon, packed in small animal box, standing, with information label, surface washable*

Serie	Art.-No	Period	Pr.	Info
	5830/16	1971-1974	4	16 cm

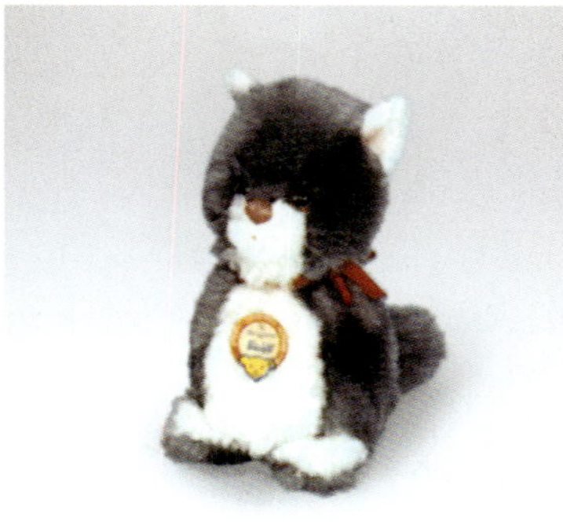

Buzzel Katze - *Buzzel Cat*

Dralon, formgeschaeumt, superweich, vollwaschbar - *dralon, stuffed with pre-formed foam, super soft, fully washable*

Serie	Art.-No	Period	Pr.	Info
	6155/20	1971-1975	1-2	20 cm

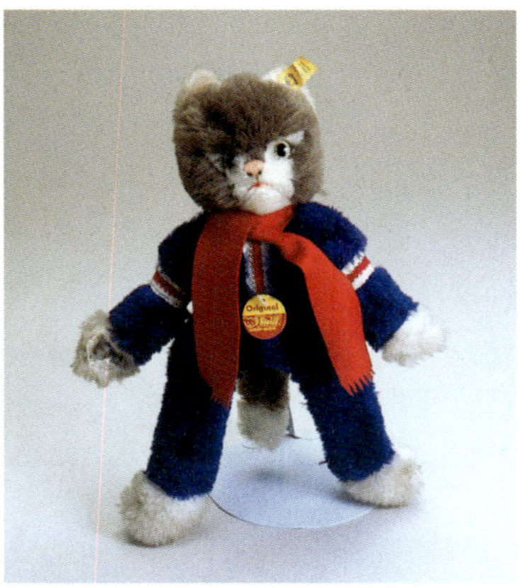

Schlenker-Kater - *Dangling Tom Cat*

Orlon/Dralon, grau/weiss, Koerper, Arme & Beine blau, sehr weich, abwaschbar - *orlon/dralon, grey & white / body, arms & legs blue, very soft, surface washable*

Serie	Art.-No	Period	Pr.	Info
	7827/32	1972-1977	3	32 cm

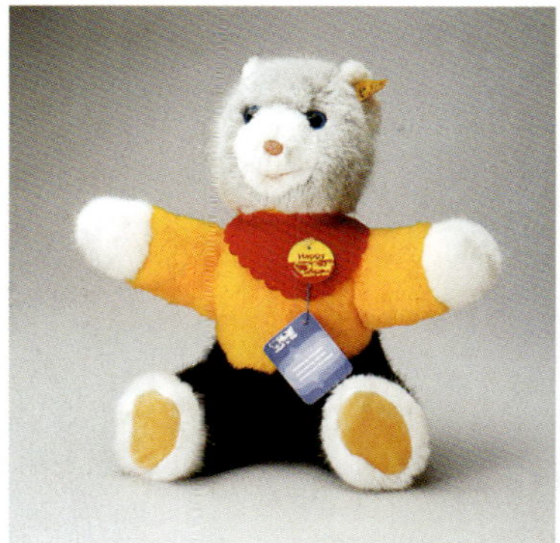

Happy Katze - ***Happy** Cat*

Pelzimitation, ab 1978 Dralon, formgeschaeumt, rotes Laetzchen, sitzend, vollwaschbar - *imitation fur, from 1978 dralon, stuffed with pre-formed foam, red bib, sitting, fully washable*

Serie	Art.-No	Period	Pr.	Info
	6118/35	1975-1979	2-3	35 cm

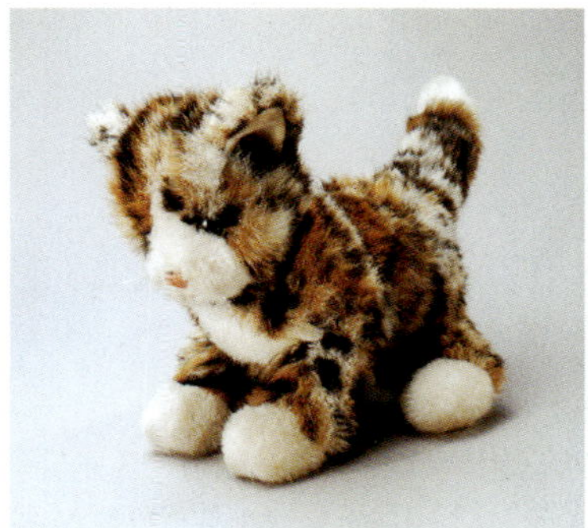

Mizzi Katze - ***Mizzi** Cat*

Pelzimitation, ab 1978 Synthetik-Webpelz, formgeschaeumt, 22 cm, abwaschbar - *imitation fur, from 1978 synthetic woven fur, stuffed with pre-formed foam, 22 cm, surface washable*

Serie	Art.-No	Period	Pr.	Info
	2720/22	1976-1980	2	grau - *grey*
	2723/22	1976-1980	2	rot - *red*
	2725/22	1976-1981	2	bunt - *multi-colored*

SERIE	ART.-NO	PERIOD	PR.	INFO
	2750/22	1981-1983	2	22 cm

SERIE	ART.-NO	PERIOD	PR.	INFO
095153	**5442/16**	1985-1987	2	16 cm
095184	**5442/22**	1985-1987	2	22 cm

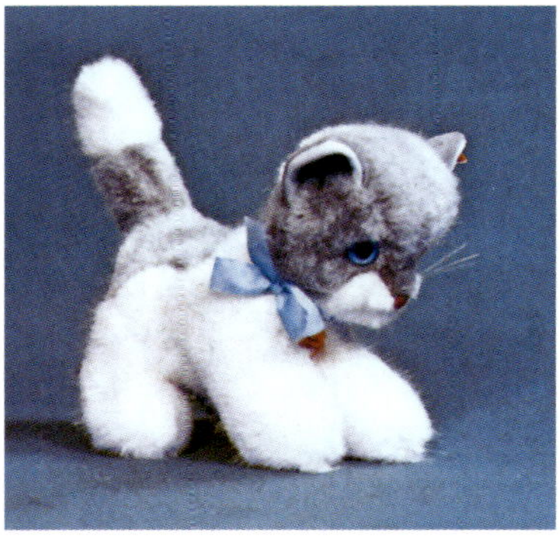

Baby-Muschi Katze - *Baby Muschi Cat*

Pelzimitation, ab 1978 Synthetik-Webpelz, formgeschaeumt, stehend, vollwaschbar - *imitation fur, from 1978 synthetic woven fur, stuffed with pre-formed foam, standing, fully washable*

SERIE	ART.-NO	PERIOD	PR.	INFO
	5755/16	1977-1979	2	16 cm

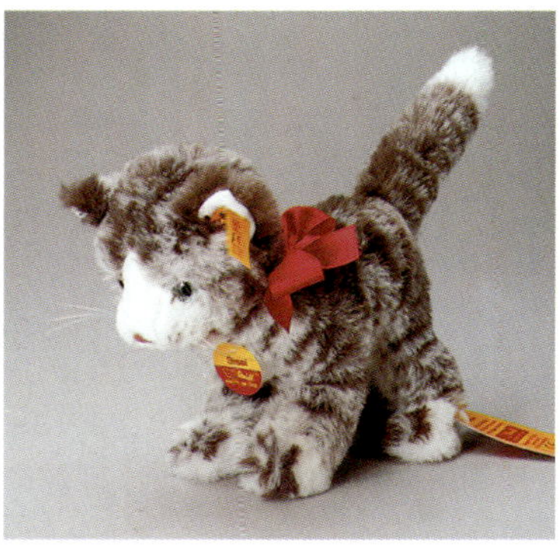

Sissi Katze - ***Sissi** Cat*

Wirkpelz, stehend, abwaschbar - *knitted fur, standing, surface washable*

SERIE	ART.-NO	PERIOD	PR.	INFO
074103	**2726/17**	1979-1990	2	17 cm
	074103	1991-1998	2	
074127	**2726/22**	1979-1990	2	22 cm
	074127	1991-1992	2	

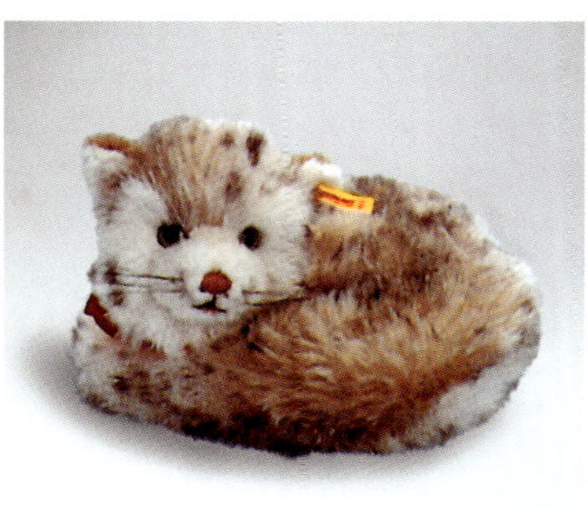

Ringelkatze - *Curled Cat*

Webpelz, liegend, abwaschbar - *woven fur, lying, surface washable*

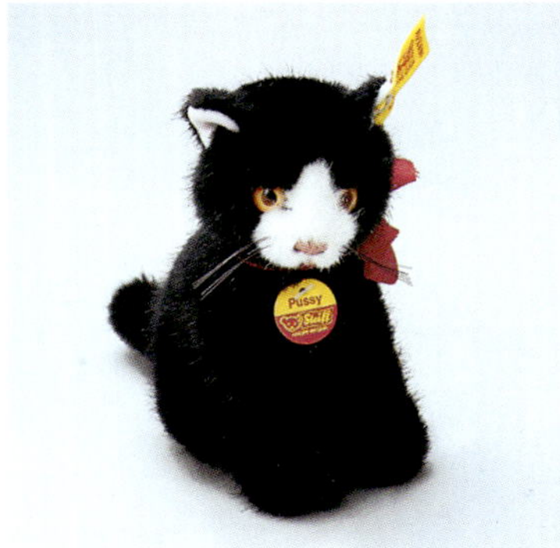

Pussy Katze - ***Pussy** Cat*

Webpelz, schwarz, abwaschbar - *woven fur, black, surface washable*

SERIE	ART.-NO	PERIOD	PR.	INFO
	1493/14	1982-1984	2	14 cm

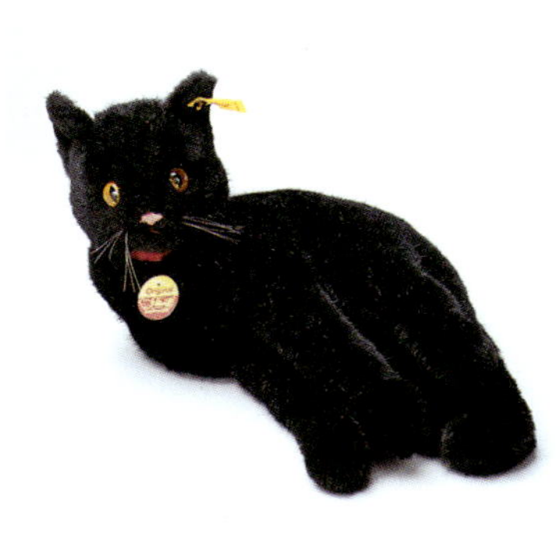

Katze - *Cat*

Wirkpelz, liegend, abwaschbar - *knitted fur, lying, surface washable*

SERIE	ART.-NO	PERIOD	PR.	INFO
	2745/30	1983-1984	3	30 cm

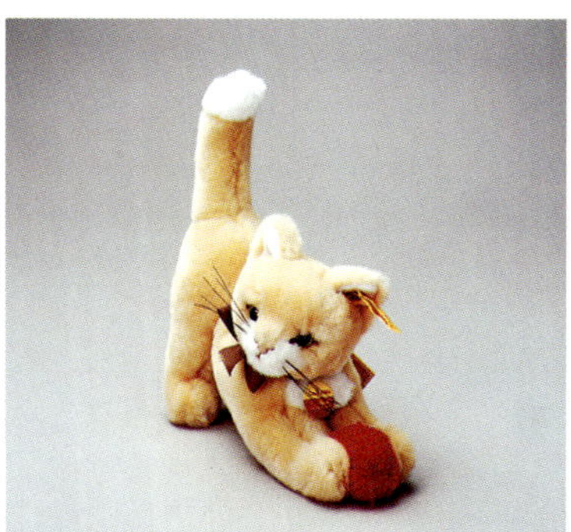

Cosy Milla Katze - ***Cosy Milla** Cat*

Webpelz, blond, mit Ball, waschmaschinenfest - *woven fur, blond, playing with ball, machine washable*

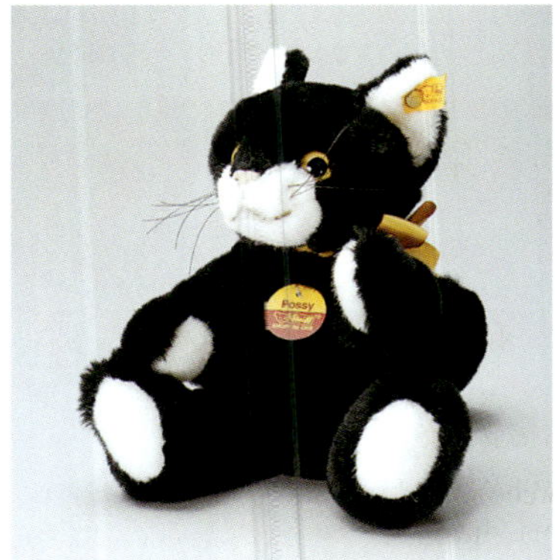

Possy Katze - ***Possy** Cat*

Webpelz, gegliedert, Pieps-Stimme, waschmaschinenfest - *woven fur, jointed, squeaker, machine washable*

SERIE	ART.-NO	PERIOD	PR.	INFO
081606	**6225/28**	1988-1990	2-3	28 cm

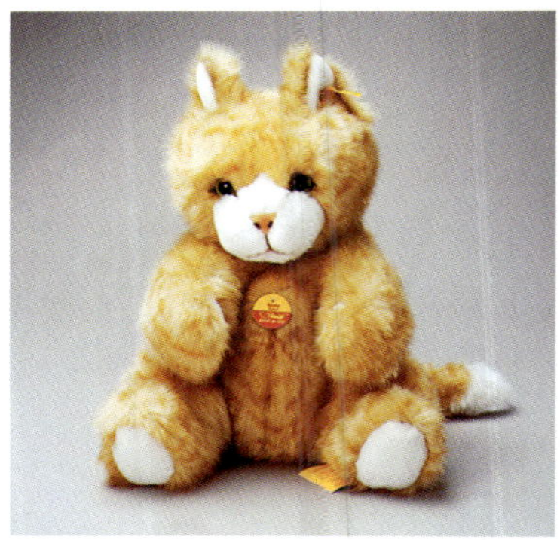

Molly Katze - ***Molly** Cat*

Webpelz, sitzend, handwaschbar - *woven fur, sitting, hand washable*

SERIE	ART.-NO	PERIOD	PR.	INFO
101472	**0334/33**	1989-1989	2-3	33 cm

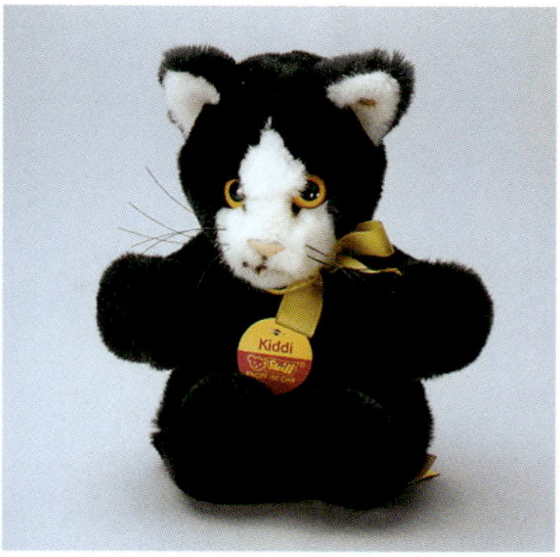

Kiddi Katze - ***Kiddi** Cat*

Webpelz, schwarz, Pieps-Stimme, waschmaschinenfest - *woven fur, black, squeaker, machine washable*

SERIE	ART.-NO	PERIOD	PR.	INFO
082801	**5717/20**	1989-1990	1-2	20 cm

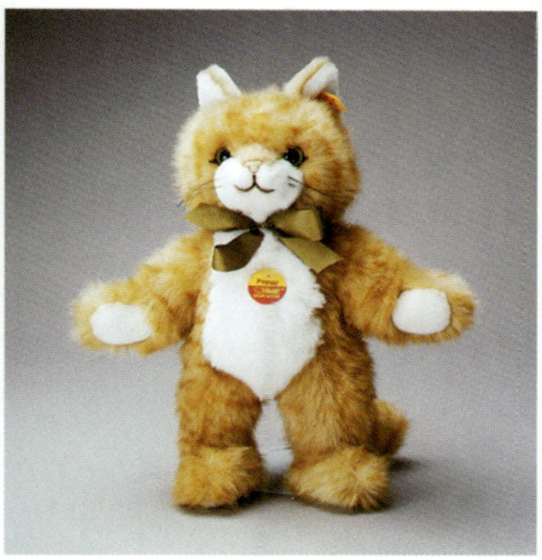

Poppy Katze - ***Poppy** Cat*

Webpelz, rot gestromelt, Pieps-Stimme, waschmaschinenfest - *woven fur, red tabby, squeaker, machine washable*

SERIE	ART.-NO	PERIOD	PR.	INFO
125959	**6080/32**	1989-1990	2-3	32 cm

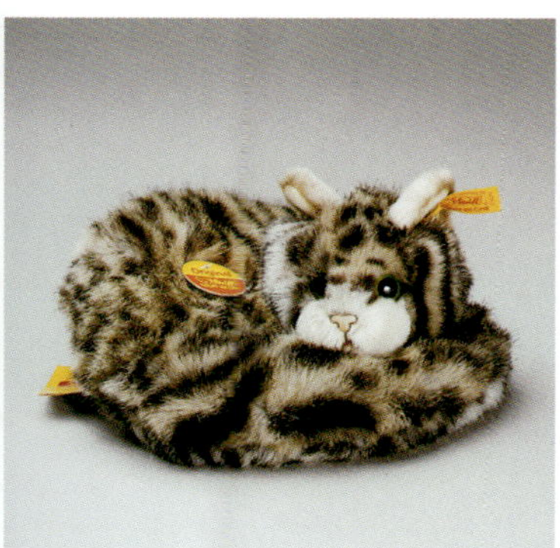

Ringelkatze - *Curled Cat*

Webpelz, getigert, waschmaschinenfest - *woven fur, imitation tiger, machine washable*

EAN-NO.	PERIOD	PR.	INFO
074189	1992-1999	2	18 cm

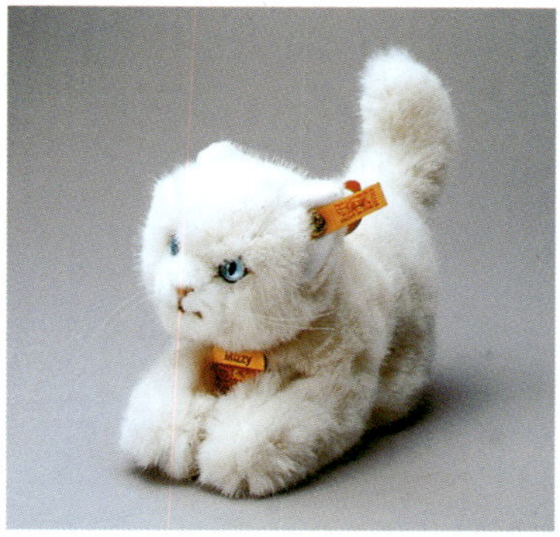

Mizzy Jungkatze - ***Mizzy** Kitten*

Webpelz, creme, liegend, waschmaschinenfest - *woven fur, cream, lying, machine washable*

EAN-NO.	PERIOD	PR.	INFO
074363	1994-1996	2	20 cm

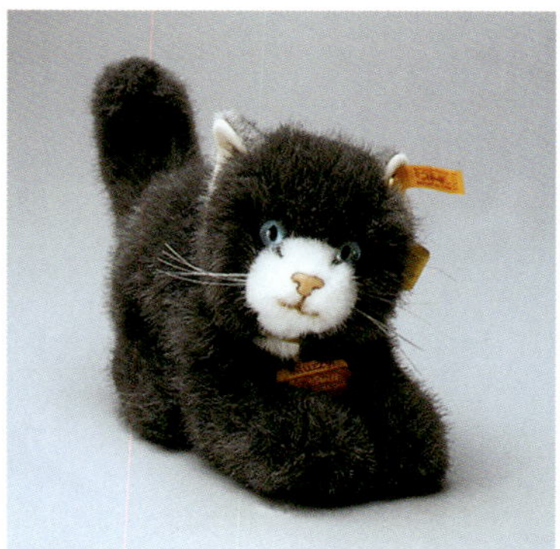

Muzzy Jungkatze - ***Muzzy** Kitten*

Webpelz, dunkelgrau, liegend, waschmaschinenfest - *woven fur, dark grey, lying, machine washable*

EAN-NO.	PERIOD	PR.	INFO
074370	1994-1997	2	20 cm

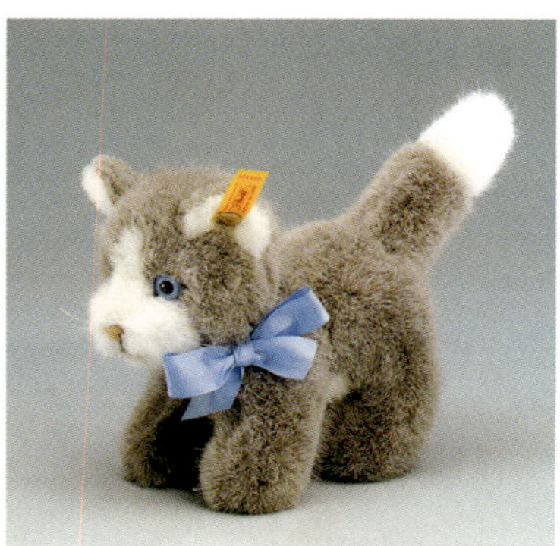

Katze - *Cat*

Webpelz, grau, stehend, waschmaschinenfest - *woven fur, grey, standing, machine washable*

EAN-NO.	PERIOD	PR.	INFO
053504	1996-1998	2	14 cm

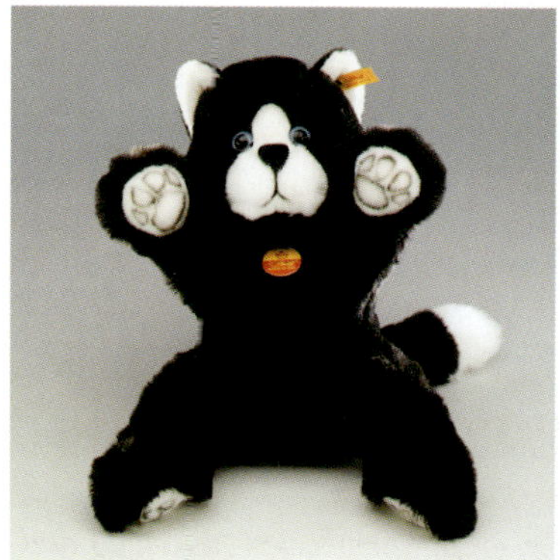

Molly Katze - ***Molly** Cat*

Webpelz, schwarz, abwaschbar - *woven fur, black, surface washable*

EAN-NO.	PERIOD	PR.	INFO
106200	1996-1998	2-3	38 cm

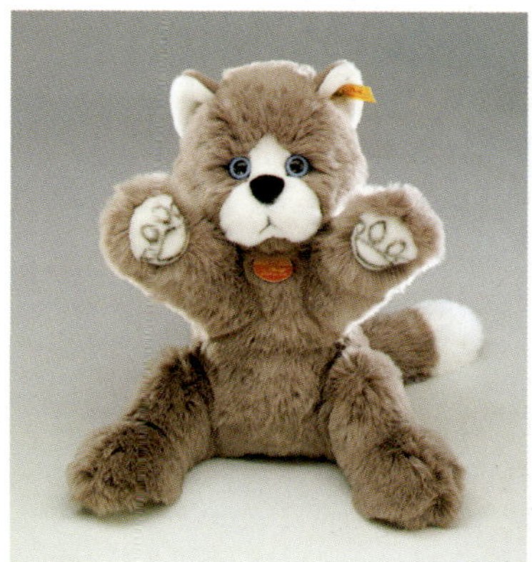

Molly Katze - ***Molly** Cat*

Webpelz, grau, abwaschbar - *woven fur, grey, surface washable*

EAN-NO.	PERIOD	PR.	INFO
106255	1996-1996	2-3	38 cm

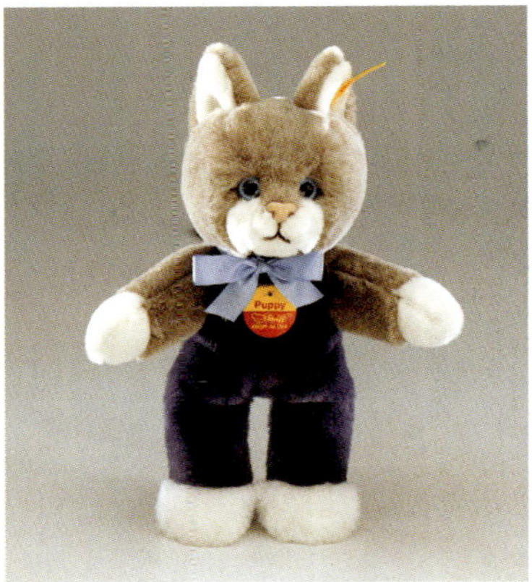

Puppy Katze - ***Puppy*** *Cat*

Webpelz, dunkelblau/grau, mit Pieps-Stimme, waschmaschinenfest - *woven fur, dark blue/grey, squeaker, machine washable*

EAN-No.	Period	Pr.	Info
124907	1996-1998	2	28 cm

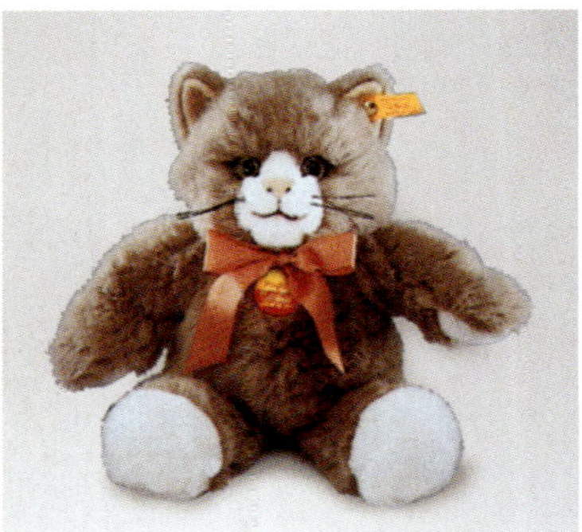

Poppy Katze - ***Poppy*** *Cat*

Webpelz, hellgrau, waschmaschinenfest - *woven fur, light grey, machine washable*

EAN-No.	Period	Pr.	Info
123160	1998-1999	2-3	30 cm

Haus- & Hoftiere

House & Farm animals

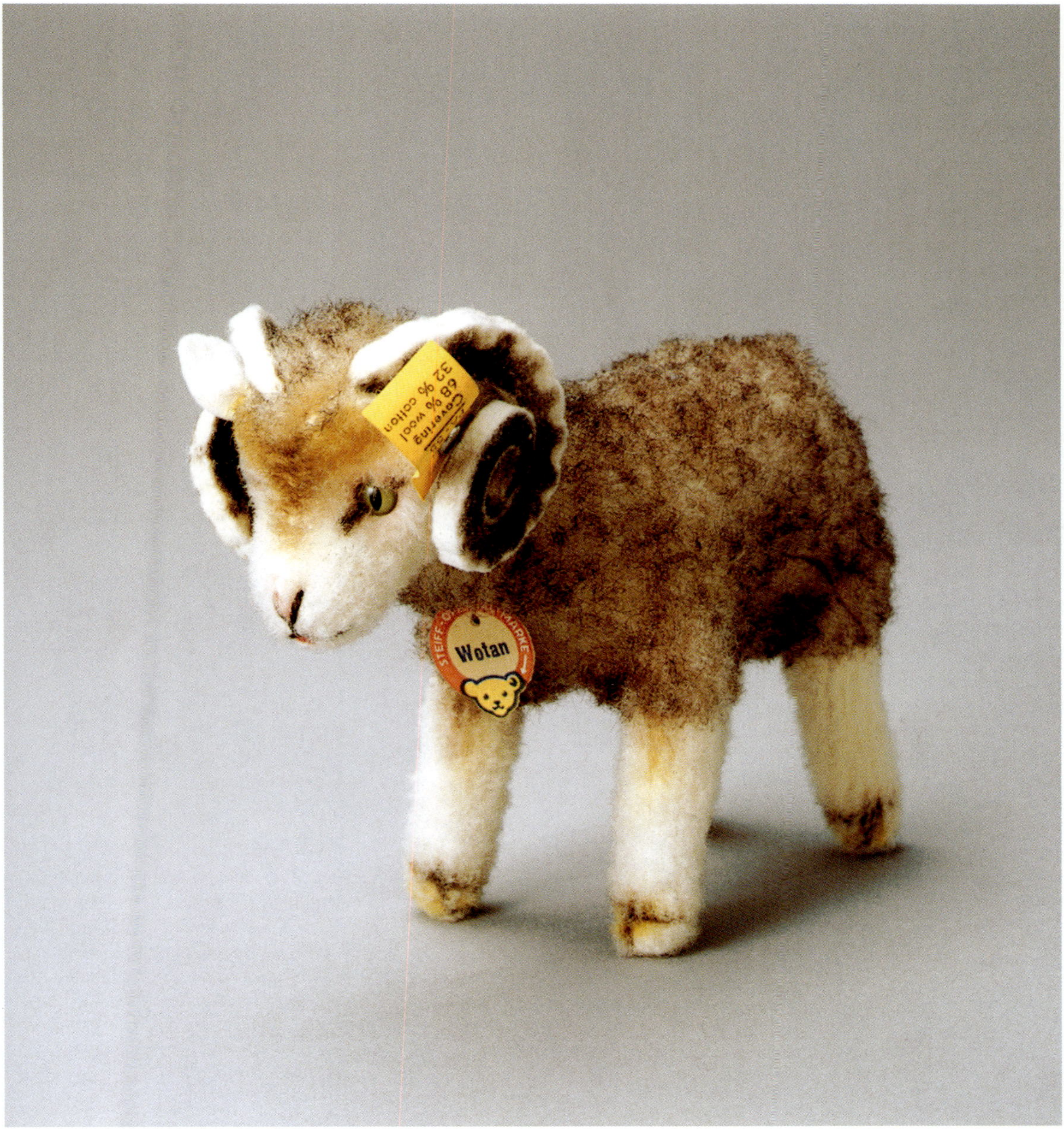

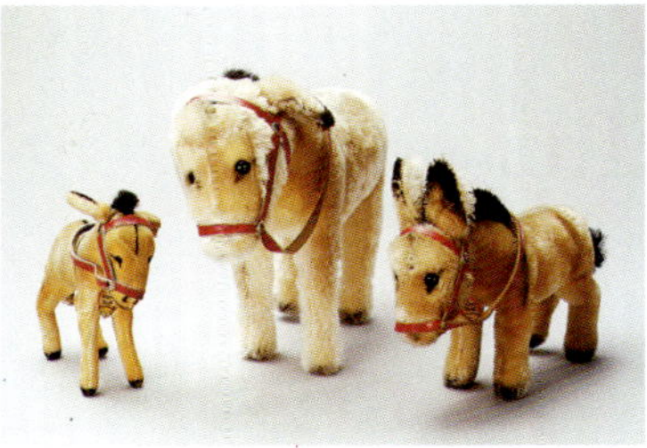

Esel - *Donkey*

12 cm Samt (1950/51 mit Decke), ab 14 cm Mohair, Lederzuegel - *12 cm velvet (1950/51 with blanket), from 14 cm mohair, leather bridle & reins*

SERIE	ART.-NO	PERIOD	PR.	INFO
24	**1412,0**	1950-1958	4-5	12 cm
240	**1412,00**	1959-1964	4	
361	**1412,00**	1965-1967	4	
	3610/12	1968-1969	3-4	
24	**1314,0**	1954-1958	4-5	14 cm
240	**1314,00**	1959-1961	4-5	
24	**1322,0**	1950-1958	4-5	22 cm
240	**1322,00**	1959-1961	4-5	
24	**1328,0**	1950-1958	5	28 cm
240	**1328,00**	1959-1961	5	

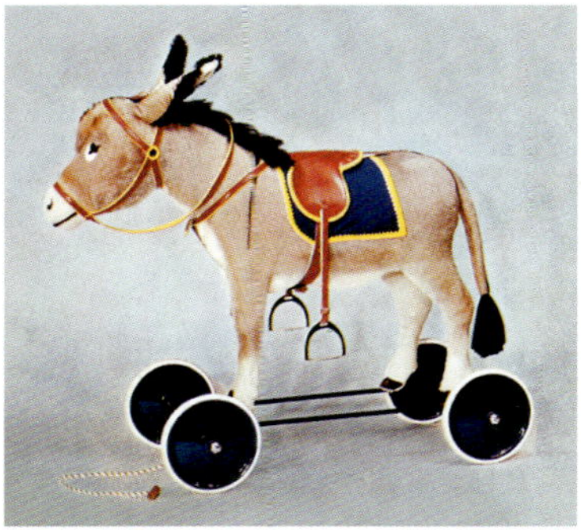

Reit-Esel - *Riding Donkey*

Mohair, Eisengerippe, grau/weiss, stehend auf Metallscheibenraedern mit Gummireifen, ab 1967 Plastikreifen & Kunststofflager, rotes Ledergeschirr und Sattel, 44 cm Holzräder, 35 cm Druckstimme, ab 43 cm Zugstimme, ab 50 cm Steigbuegel & Haltegriff - *mohair, iron frame, grey & white, standing on metal disc wheels with rubber tires, from 1967 plastic tires & plastic bearings, red leather harness & saddle, 44 cm with wooden wheels, 35 cm press voice, from 43 cm pull cord voice, from 50 cm stirrups & grip handles*

SERIE	ART.-NO	PERIOD	PR.	INFO
24	**1335,2**	1950-1950	5	35 cm
24	**1335,1**	1951-1957	5	
240	**1335,10**	1961-1961	5	
24	**1343,2**	1950-1958	5	43 cm, ab 1953 auch 1343,2 ST mit Lenkung - *from 1953 also 1343,2 ST with steering*
240	**1343,20**	1959-1964	5	
24	**1344,2**	1949-1949	5-6	44 cm
24	**1350,2**	1950-1958	5	50 cm, ab 1953 auch 1350,2 ST mit Lenkung - *from 1953 also 1350,2 ST with steering*
240	**1350,20**	1959-1964	5	ab 1961 auch 1350,30 mit Lenkung - *from 1961 also 1350,30 with steering*
360	**1350,20**	1966-1966	5	
24	**1380,2**	1951-1958	5-6	80 cm, ab 1956 auch 1380,2 ST mit Lenkung - *from 1956 also 1380,2 ST with steering*
240	**1380,20**	1959-1961	5-6	
360	**1380,20**	1966-1967	5-6	
	3600/80	1968-1975	5	
24	**13100,2**	1951-1957	5-6	100 cm
240	**1399,20**	1961-1961	5-6	
360	**1399,20**	1966-1966	5-6	

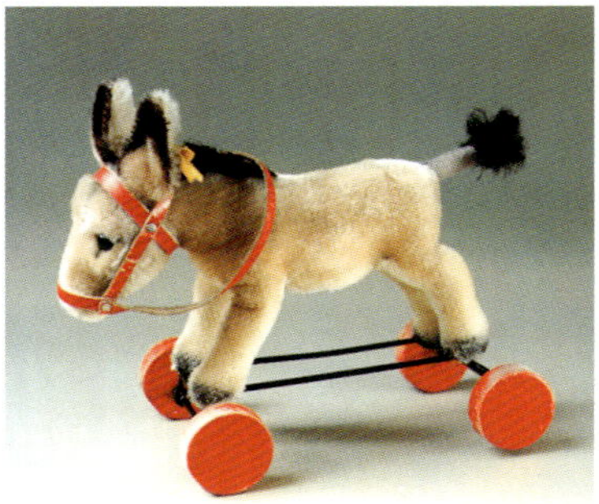

Esel - *Donkey*

Mohairpluesch, grau schattiert, stehend auf Exzenter-Raedern - *mohair, shaded in grey, standing on eccentric wheels*

SERIE	ART.-NO	PERIOD	PR.	INFO
24	**1314** ex	1954-1957	5	14 cm
240	**1314,10**	1961-1961	5	

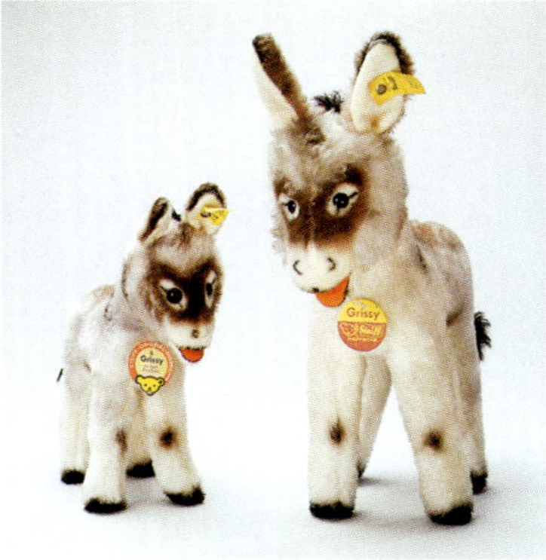

Grissy Esel - ***Grissy*** *Donkey*

Dralonpluesch, grau/weiss, stehend, 1965 bis 1967 auch mit Zusatz "im Steiff Kinderbuch", weich, abwaschbar - *dralon, grey & white, standing, 1965 till 1967 also with supplement "im Steiff-Kinderbuch", soft, surface washable*

SERIE	ART.-NO	PERIOD	PR.	INFO
240	**1617,00**	1963-1964	3	17 cm
361	**1617,00**	1965-1967	3	
	3610/17	1968-1975	2-3	
240	**1622,00**	1960-1964	3	22 cm
361	**1622,00**	1965-1967	3	
	3610/22	1968-1976	2-3	
240	**1635,00**	1960-1964	3	35 cm
361	**1635,00**	1965-1967	3	
	3610/35	1968-1975	3	
240	**1650,00**	1960-1964	3	50 cm
361	**1650,00**	1965-1967	3	
	3610/50	1968-1974	3	

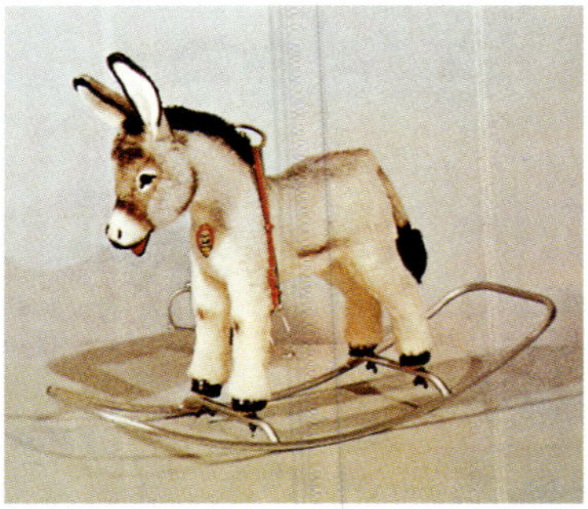

Wiegen **Grissy** - *Rocking* ***Grissy***

Dralon, grau/weiss, Stahlgerippe, abnehmbare Stahlwiege - tauschbar gegen Wechselrahmen 8220/55, Haltegriff, Steigbuegel - *dralon, grey & white, steel frame, removable steel rocker, can be exchanged for alternating frame 8220/55, grip handle, stirrups*

SERIE	ART.-NO	PERIOD	PR.	INFO
240	**1655,95**	1960-1964	4	55 cm
362	**1655,05**	1965-1967	4	
	3620/55	1968-1969	4	

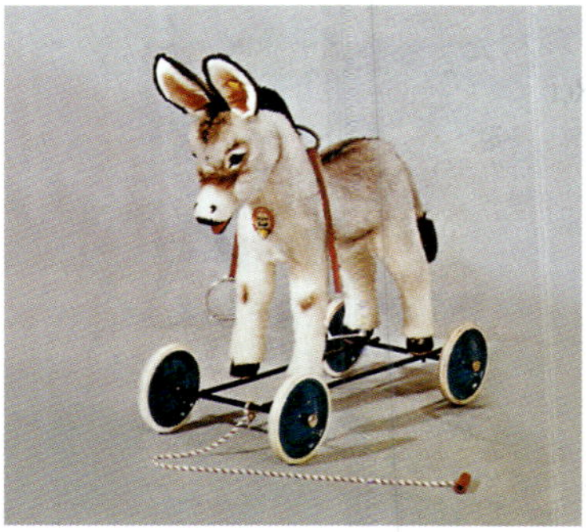

Reit-Esel **Grissy** - *Riding Donkey* ***Grissy***

Dralon, grau/weiss, Stahlgerippe, gummibereifte Scheibenraeder, ab 1967 Plastikreifen & Kunststofflager, Haltegriff, Steigbuegel, Schlepplenkung, abwaschbar - *dralon, grey & white, steel frame, disc wheels with rubber tires, from 1967 plastic tires & plastic bearings, grip handle, stirrups, pull type steering, surface washable*

SERIE	ART.-NO	PERIOD	PR.	INFO
240	**1660,25**	1960-1964	4	60 cm
362	**1660,25**	1965-1967	4	
	3620/60	1968-1980	4	

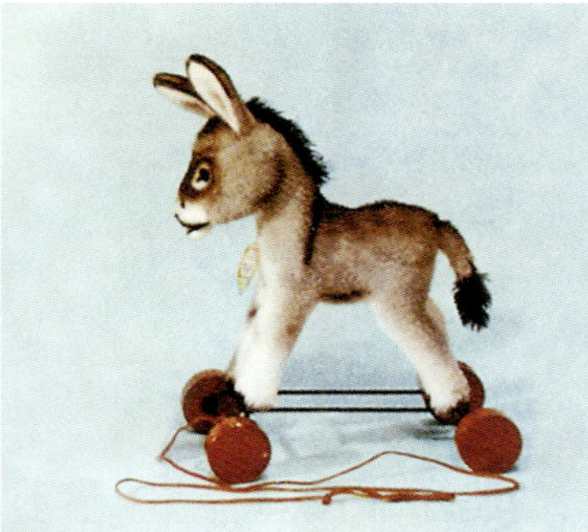

Grissy

Dralon, grau/weiss, stehend auf Exzenterraedern, weich, abwaschbar - *dralon, grey & white, standing on eccentric wheels, soft. surface washable*

SERIE	ART.-NO	PERIOD	PR.	INFO
240	**1620,10**	1963-1963	4	20 cm

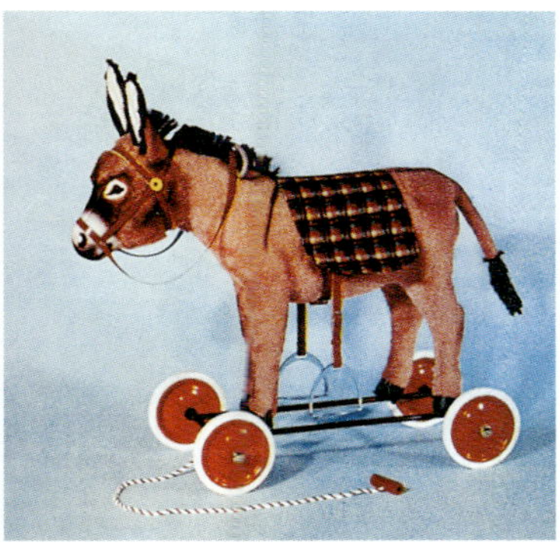

Reit-Esel - *Riding Donkey*

Dralon, hellbraun, Stahlgerippe, gummibereifte Scheibenraeder, ab 1967 Plastikreifen & Kunststofflager, Haltegriff, Satteldecke, Zugstimme, Steigbuegel, Schlepplenkung, abwaschbar - *dralon, light brown, steel frame, disc wheels with rubber tires, from 1967 plastic tires & plastic bearings, grip handle, saddle blanket, stirrups, pull type steering, pull cord voice, surface washable*

SERIE	ART.-NO	PERIOD	PR.	INFO
360	**1650,22**	1966-1967	4	50 cm
	3600/50	1968-1970	4	

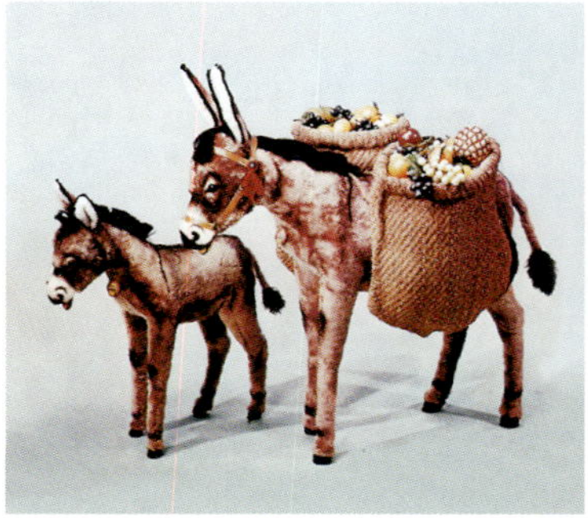

Bergesel - *Mountain Donkey*

Schautier, Dralon, grau, stehend - Bastsaecke (ohne Fruechte), hellbraun, als Zubehoer - *display animal, dralon, grey, standing - bast sacks (without fruit), light brown, accessories for mountain donkey*

SERIE	ART.-NO	PERIOD	PR.	INFO
363	**6685,90**	1966-1966	5-6	85 cm
	3639/09	1967-1967	5-6	
363	**6115,90**	1966-1966	6	115 cm
	3639/12	1967-1967	6	
363	**0624,90**	1966-1966	3	Bastsaecke - *bast sacks*
	3639/07	1967-1967	3	

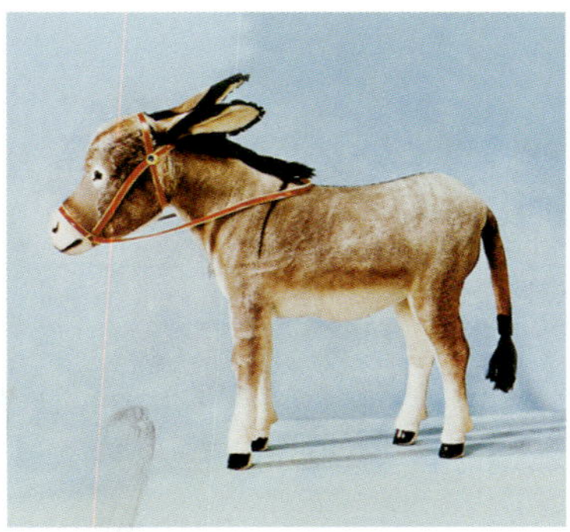

Esel - *Donkey*

Schautier, Mohair, Lederzuegel, 100 cm zusaetzlich mit Sattel, grau, stehend - *display animal, mohair, leather bridle and reins, 100 cm also with saddle, grey, standing*

SERIE	ART.-NO	PERIOD	PR.	INFO
	3609/10	1967-1967	6	100 cm
240	**1120,90**	1960-1960	6	120 cm
	3609/12	1967-1967	6	

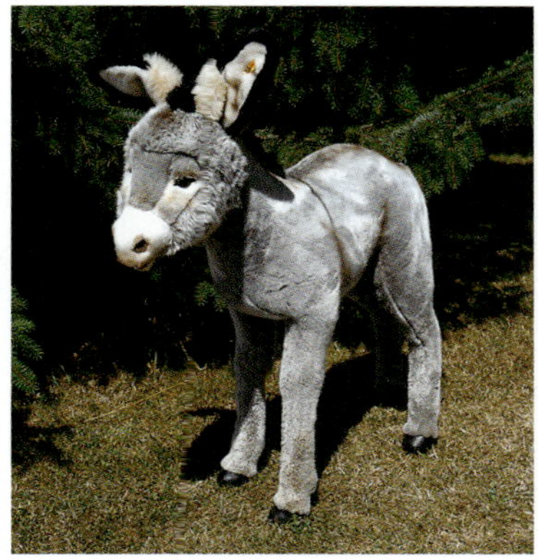

Eselchen - *Little Donkey*

Studio-Tier, Webpelz, abwaschbar - *studio animal, woven fur, surface washable*

SERIE	ART.-NO	PERIOD	PR.	INFO
502538	**0453/75**	1989-1990	6-7	80 cm
	502538	1991-1999	6-7	

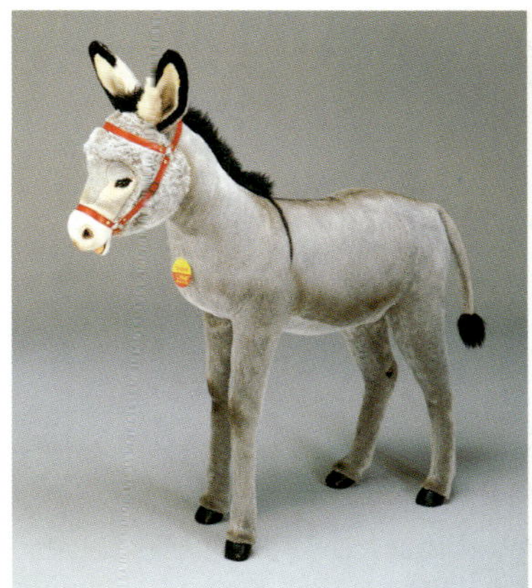

Esel - *Donkey*

Studio-Tier, Webpelz, abwaschbar - *studio animal, woven fur, surface washable*

SERIE	ART.-NO	PERIOD	PR.	INFO
502507	**0450/99**	1989-1990	6	110 cm
	502507	1991-1994	6	

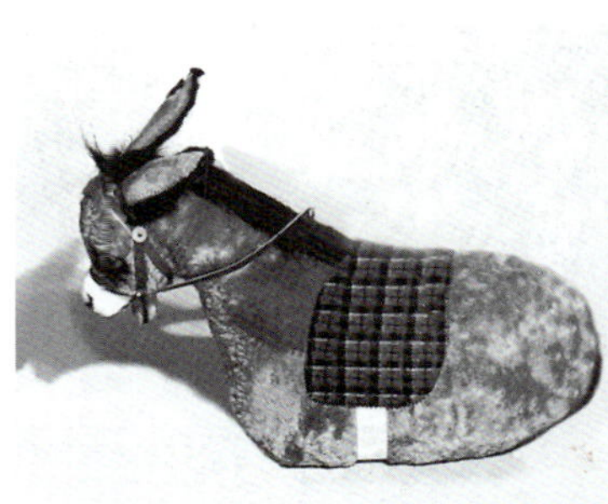

Racker-Esel - *Racker Donkey*

Racker Tier, liegend, zum Spielen und Sitzen - *racker animal, in lying position, for playing & sitting on*

SERIE	ART.-NO	PERIOD	PR.	INFO
	6100/50	1969-1969	5	50 cm

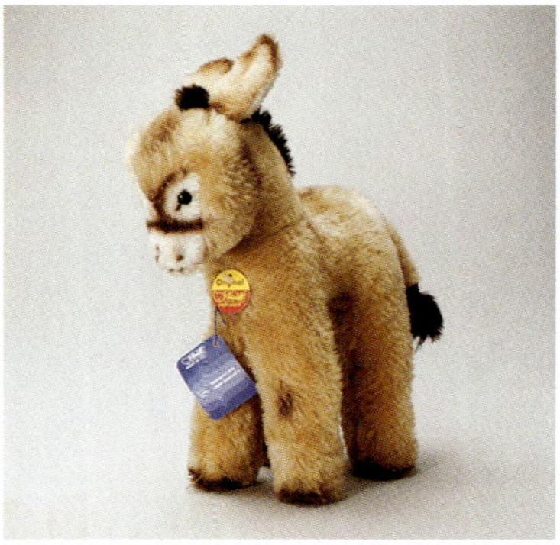

Esel **Grissy** - *Donkey **Grissy***

Dralon, formgeschaeumt, stehend, vollwaschbar - *dralon, stuffed with pre-formed foam, standing, fully washable*

SERIE	ART.-NO	PERIOD	PR.	INFO
	3615/30	1971-1978	2-3	30 cm

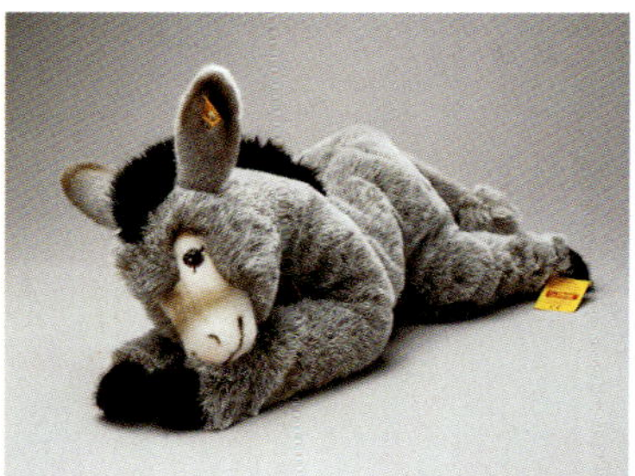

Molly Esel - *Molly Donkey*

Pelz-Imitation, ab 1978 Synthetik-Webpelz, grau, liegend, weich abwaschbar - *imitation fur, from 1978 synthetic woven fur, grey, lying, soft, surface washable*

SERIE	ART.-NO	PERIOD	PR.	INFO
101458	**0335/55**	1981-1990	3	58 cm
	101458	1991-1999	3	
	0335/80	1974-1981	3	80 cm

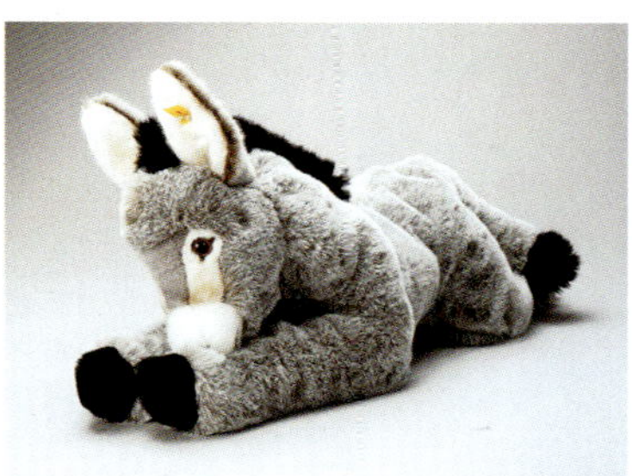

Molly Esel - *Molly Donkey*

Webpelz, waschmaschinenfest - *woven fur, machine washable*

EAN-NO.	PERIOD	PR.	INFO
101526	1992-1999	3	70 cm

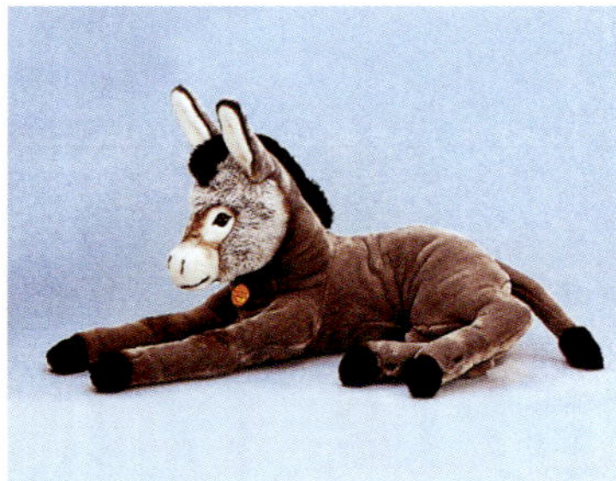

Super Molly Esel - ***Super Molly** Donkey*

Webpelz, mollig weich, abwaschbar - *woven fur, soft & cuddly, surface washable*

SERIE	ART.-NO	PERIOD	PR.	INFO
	0367/99	1983-1985	3-4	110 cm

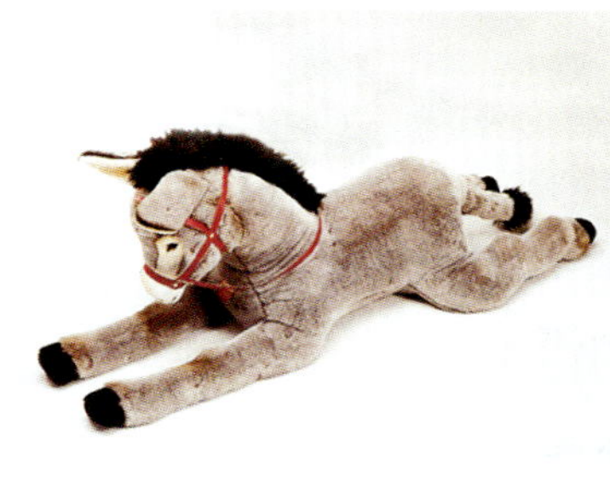

Super Molly Esel - ***Super Molly** Donkey*

Webpelz, Leder-Kopfgeschirr, liegend, abwaschbar - *woven fur, leather bridle & reins, lying, surface washable*

EAN-NO.	PERIOD	PR.	INFO
103360	1991-1992	4	125 cm

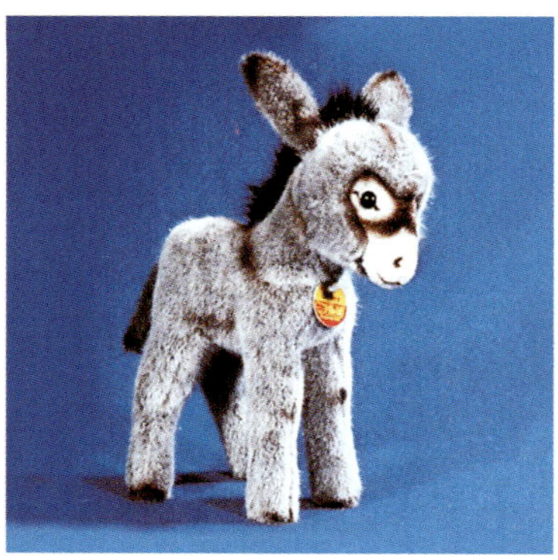

Esel **Grissy** - *Donkey **Grissy***

Nerzimitation, ab 1978 Synthetik-Webpelz, stehend, abwaschbar - *imitation mink, from 1978 synthetic woven fur, standing, surface washable*

SERIE	ART.-NO	PERIOD	PR.	INFO
	3605/20	1976-1982	2-3	20 cm
	3605/27	1976-1981	2-3	27 cm

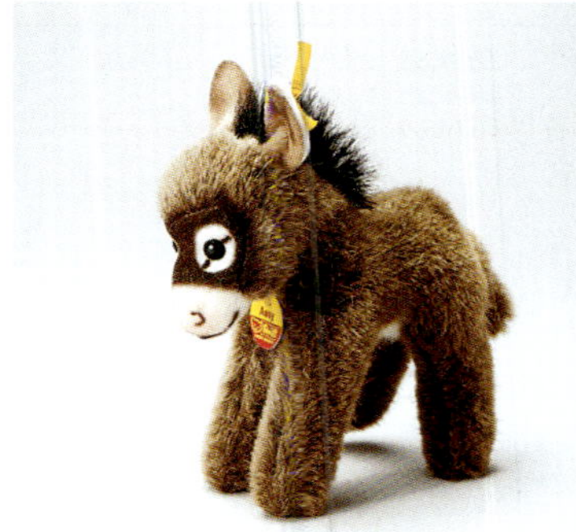

Assy Esel - ***Assy** Donkey*

Nerzimitation, ab 1978 Synthetik-Webpelz, stehend, abwaschbar - *imitation mink, from 1978 synthetic woven fur, standing, surface washable*

SERIE	ART.-NO	PERIOD	PR.	INFO
	1510/14	1977-1985	2	14 cm

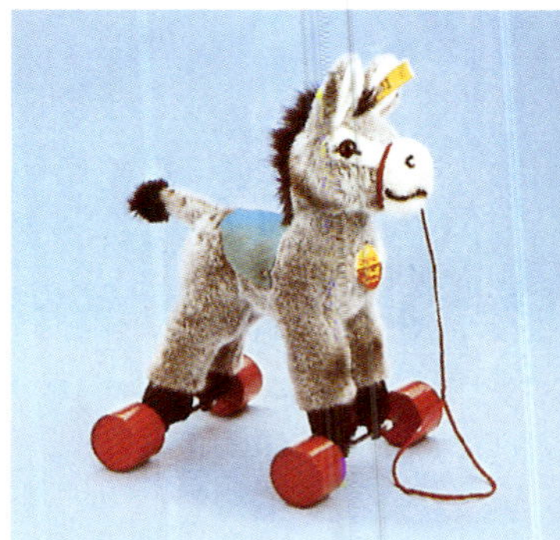

Nachziehesel - *Pull Toy Donkey*

Webpelz, auf Holz-Raedern, abwaschbar - *woven fur, on wooden wheels, surface washable*

SERIE	ART.-NO	PERIOD	PR.	INFO
	6422/24	1980-1982	3	24 cm

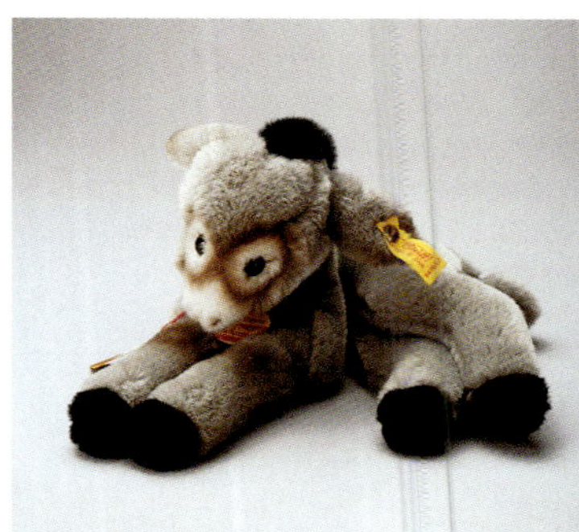

Cosy Grissy Esel - ***Cosy Grissy** Donkey*

Webpelz, kuschelweich, waschmaschinenfest - *woven fur, soft & cuddly, machine washable*

SERIE	ART.-NO	PERIOD	PR.	INFO
	5470/27	1983-1985	2	27 cm

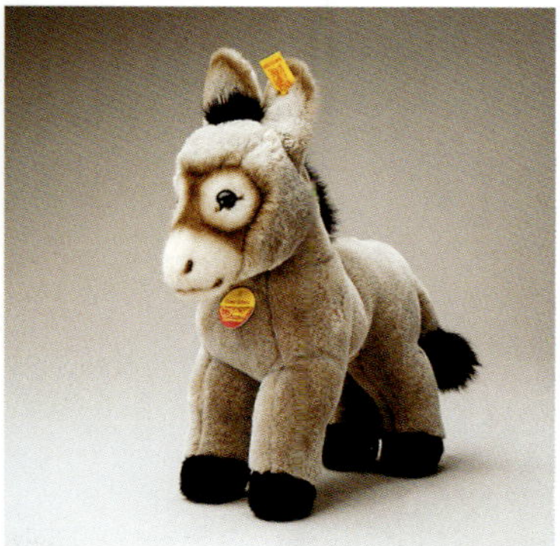

Cosy Grissy Esel - ***Cosy Grissy*** *Donkey*

Webpelz, stehend, superweich, waschmaschinenfest - *woven fur, standing, super soft, machine washable*

SERIE	ART.-NO	PERIOD	PR.	INFO
097140	**5472/28**	1984-1987	2	28 cm

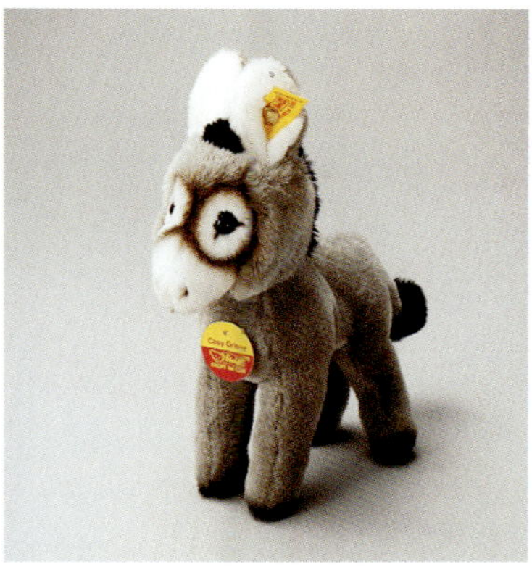

Cosy Grissy Esel - ***Cosy Grissy*** *Donkey*

Webpelz, stehend, superweich, waschmaschinenfest - *woven fur, standing, super soft, machine washable*

SERIE	ART.-NO	PERIOD	PR.	INFO
097126	**5472/20**	1986-1989	2	20 cm

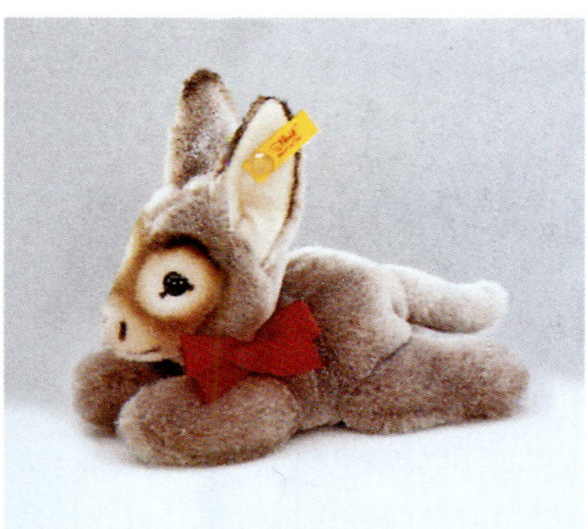

Mini Floppy Esel - ***Mini Floppy*** *Donkey*

Webpelz, waschmaschinenfest - *woven fur, machine washable*

SERIE	ART.-NO	PERIOD	PR.	INFO
082047	**5672/16**	1989-1990	1-2	16 cm
	082047	1991-1991	1-2	

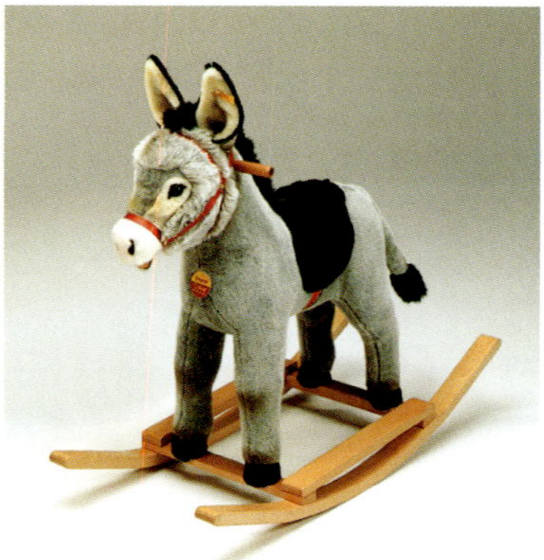

Reit-Esel - *Riding Donkey*

Webpelz, Metall-Innengestell, Holzschaukel, Kopfgeschirr, abwaschbar - *woven fur, metal frame, wooden rocker, bridle, surface washable*

EAN-NO.	PERIOD	PR.	INFO
480805	1991-1994	4	80 cm

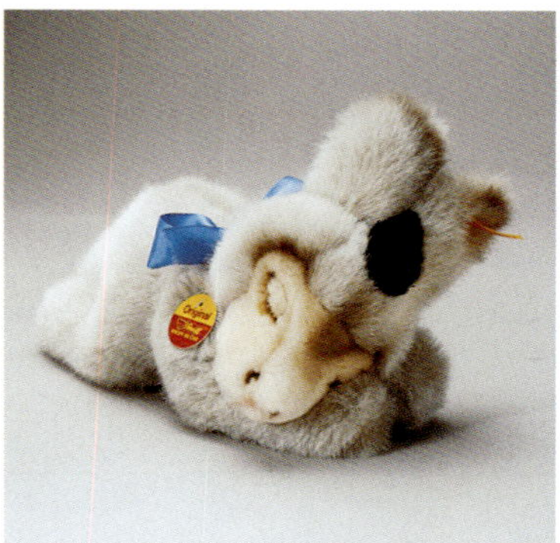

Schlafesel - *Sleeping Donkey*

Webpelz, waschmaschinenfest - *woven fur, machine washable*

EAN-NO.	PERIOD	PR.	INFO
082573	1991-1995	2	22 cm

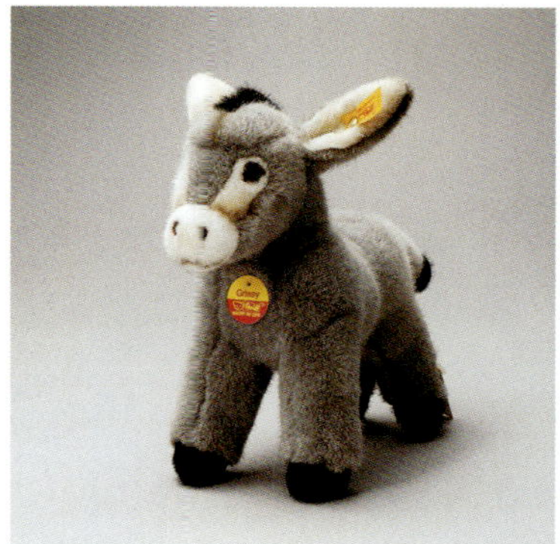

Esel **Grissy** - *Donkey* ***Grissy***

Webpelz, stehend, waschmaschinenfest - *woven fur, standing, machine washable*

EAN-NO.	PERIOD	PR.	INFO
072802	1992-1996	2	30 cm
072826	1992-1994	2-3	40 cm

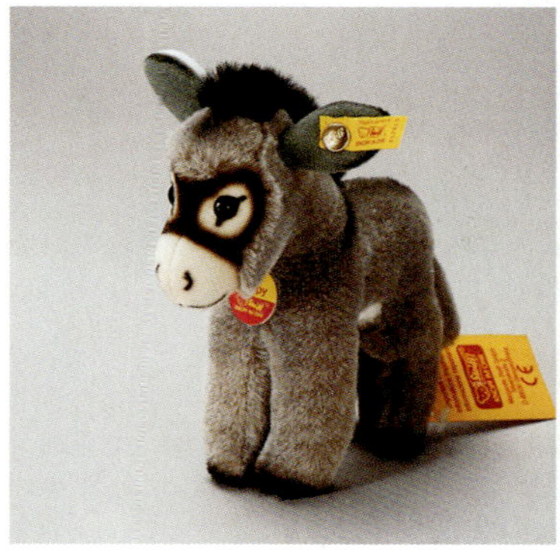

Stupy Esel, ab 1996 **Strupy** - ***Stupy*** *Donkey from 1996* ***Strupy***

Webpelz, stehend, waschmaschinenfest - *woven fur, standing, machine washable*

EAN-NO.	PERIOD	PR.	INFO
052859	1994-1999	2	15 cm

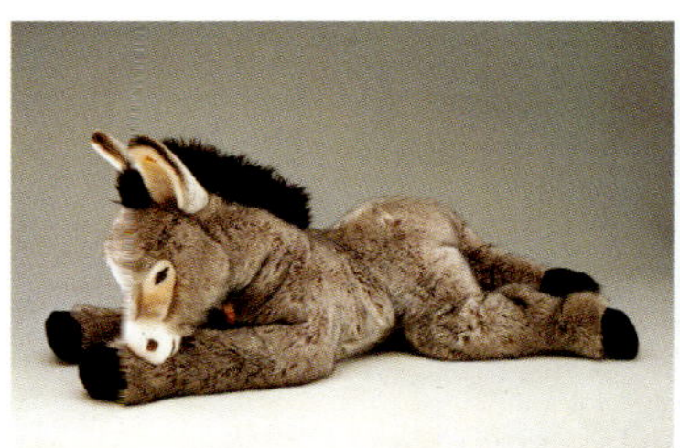

Molly Esel - ***Molly*** *Donkey*

Webpelz, grau, liegend, abwaschbar - *woven fur, grey, lying, surface washable*

EAN-NO.	PERIOD	PR.	INFO
103391	1996-1999	4	100 cm

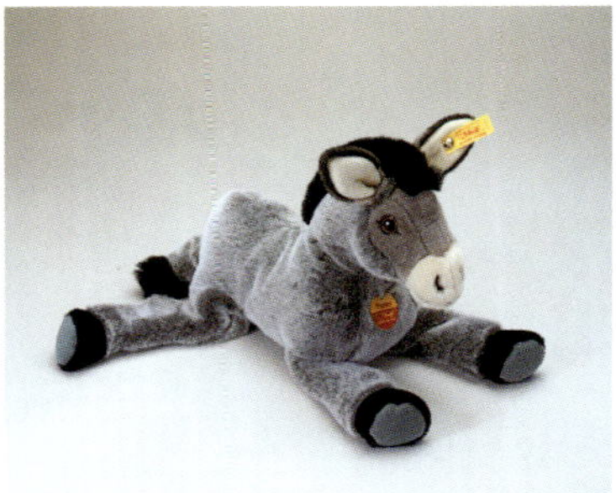

Poppy Esel - ***Poppy*** *Donkey*

Webpelz, grau, waschmaschinenfest - *woven fur, grey, machine washable*

EAN-No.	Period	Pr.	Info
124129	1998-1999	2-3	35 cm

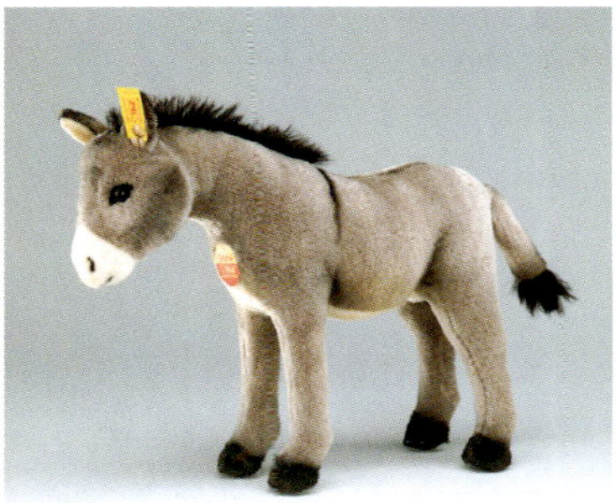

Esel - *Donkey*

Webpelz, grau, stehend, abwaschbar - *woven fur, grey, standing, surface washable*

EAN-No.	Period	Pr.	Info
072796	1998-1999	3	30 cm

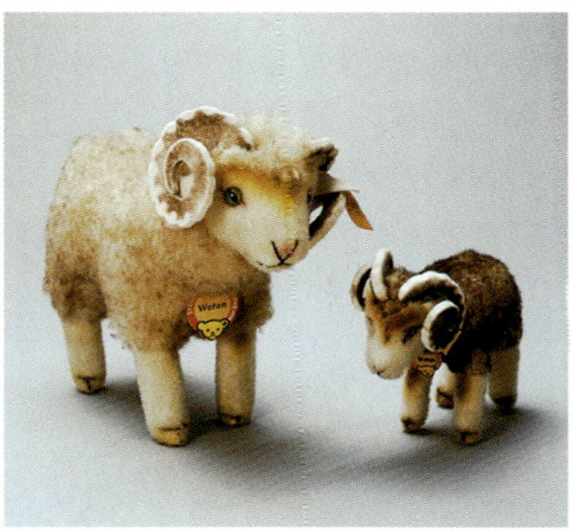

Widder **Wotan** - *Ram* ***Wotan***

Wollpluesch, weiss/braun gespitzt, stehend - *plush wool, white/brown tipped, standing*

Serie	Art.-No	Period	Pr.	Info
347	**1512,00**	1966-1967	4	12 cm
	3470/12	1968-1973	3-4	
347	**1522,00**	1966-1967	4-5	22 cm
	3470/22	1968-1972	4	

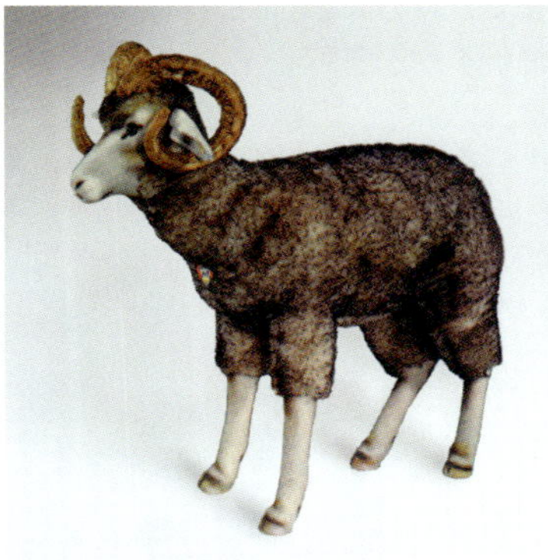

Widder - *Ram*

Schautier, Wollpluesch, stehend - *display animal, plush wool, standing*

Serie	Art.-No	Period	Pr.	Info
347	**1590,90**	1966-1966	5-6	95 cm
	3459/10	1967-1967	5-6	

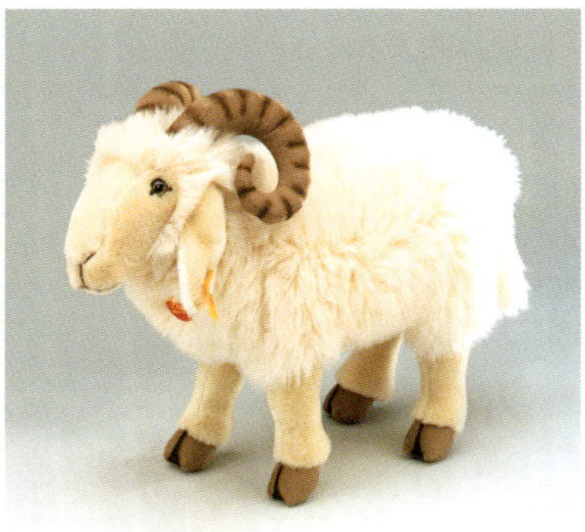

Widder - *Ram*

Webpelz, wollweiss, stehend, abwaschbar - *woven fur, wool-white, standing, surface washable*

EAN-No.	Period	Pr.	Info
073236	1996-1998	3	45 cm

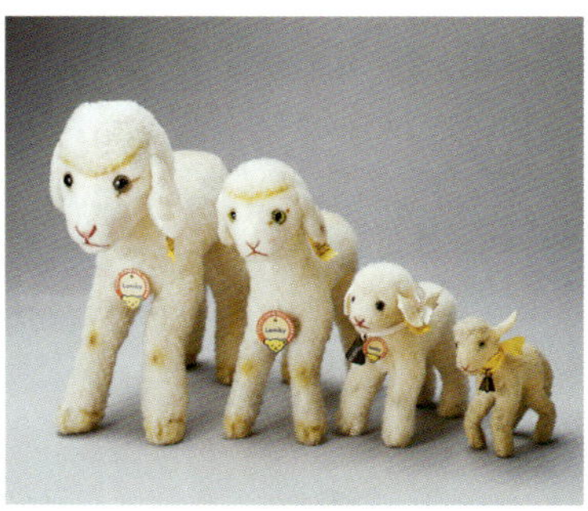

Lamm ab 1954 **Lamby** - *Lamb from 1954* ***Lamby***

Wollpluesch - auch Lammpluesch genannt, Seidenhalsband & Glocke, weiss, stehend ohne Raeder, jung - *plush (lambs) wool, silk ribbon with bell, white, standing without wheels, young*

Serie	Art.-No	Period	Pr.	Info
46	**6510,0**	1953-1958	3	10 cm
460	**6510,04**	1959-1964	2-3	
345	**6510,04**	1965-1967	2-3	
	3450/10	1968-1974	2	
46	**6514,0**	1949-1958	3	14 cm
460	**6514,04**	1959-1964	3	
345	**6514,04**	1965-1967	3	
	3450/14	1968-1976	2-3	
46	**6517,0**	1949-1951	4	17 cm
46	**6522,0**	1948-1958	3-4	22 cm
460	**6522,04**	1959-1964	3-4	
345	**6522,04**	1965-1967	3-4	
	3450/22	1968-1976	3	
46	**6528,0**	1949-1958	4	28 cm
460	**6528,04**	1959-1964	3-4	
345	**6528,04**	1965-1967	3-4	
	3450/28	1968-1973	3	
46	**6535,02**	1953-1958	4	35 cm
460	**6535,04**	1959-1964	3-4	
345	**6535,04**	1965-1967	3-4	
	3450/35	1968-1973	3	

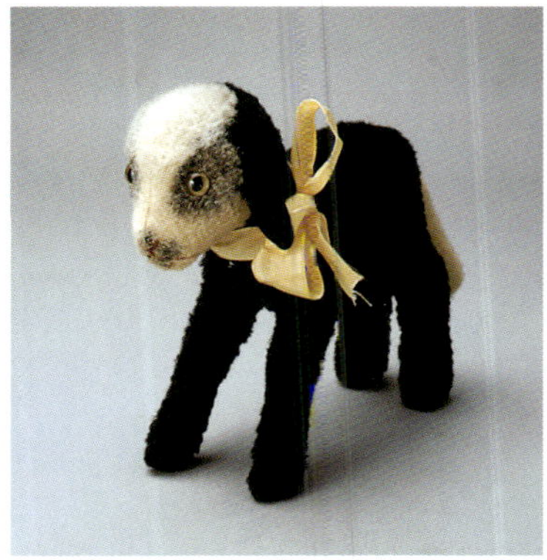

Lamby

Wollpluesch, schwarz, stehend - *plush wool, black, standing*

Serie	Art.-No	Period	Pr.	Info
46	**6510,0** s	1954-1956	4-5	10 cm
46	**6514,0** s	1954-1956	4-5	14 cm
46	**6522,0** s	1954-1956	4-5	22 cm

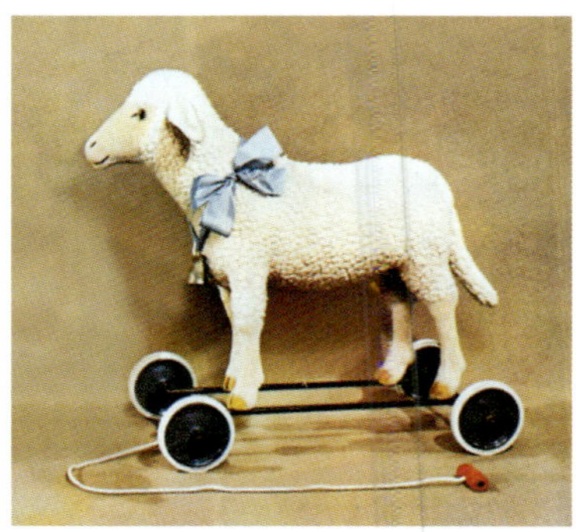

Reit-Lamm - *Riding Lamb*

Noppen-Wollpluesch, Eisengerippe, Seidenhalsband, Glocke, Zugstimme, weiss, stehend, Metallscheibenraeder mit Gummi, 1967 Plastikreifen und Haltegriff - *curled plush wool, iron frame, silk ribbon with bell, pull cord voice, white, standing, metal disc wheels with rubber tires, in 1967 plastic tires & grip handle*

SERIE	ART.-NO	PERIOD	PR.	INFO
46	**1543,2**	1950-1957	5	43 cm
460	**1543,24**	1961-1961	5	
46	**1550,2**	1950-1957	5	50 cm
460	**1550,24**	1961-1961	5	
345	**1550,24**	1966-1967	5	

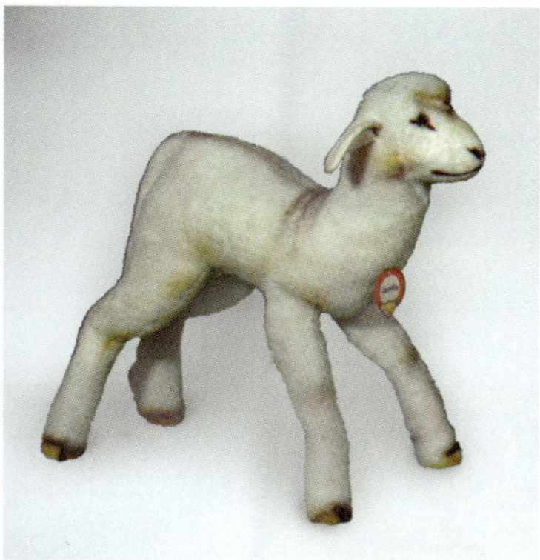

Lamm - *Lamb*

Schautier, Wollpluesch, stehend - *display animal, plush wool, standing*

SERIE	ART.-NO	PERIOD	PR.	INFO
345	**1555,90**	1966-1966	5	55 cm
	3459/06	1957-1967	5	

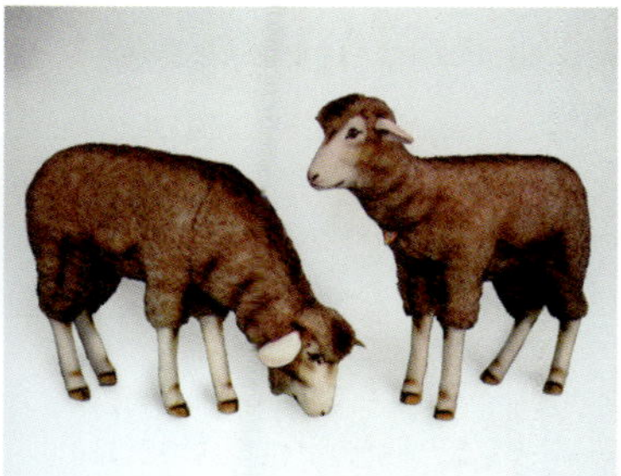

Schaf - *Sheep*

Schautiere, Wollpluesch, grasend (80 cm) bzw. stehend (90 cm) - *display animals, plush wool, grazing (80 cm) or standing (90 cm)*

SERIE	ART.-NO	PERIOD	PR.	INFO
345	**1589,90**	1966-1966	5-6	80 cm
	3459/08	1967-1967	5-6	
345	**1590,90**	1966-1966	5-6	90 cm
	3459/09	1967-1967	5-6	

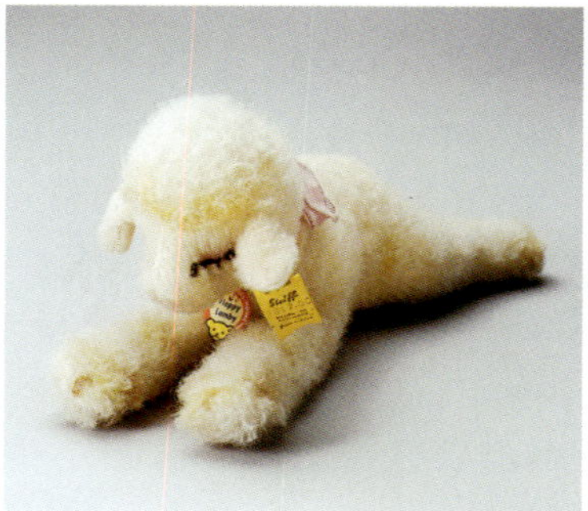

Floppy Lamby

Schlaftier, Wollpluesch, Augen gestickt, weiss, liegend, sehr weich und schmiegsam - *sleeping animal, plush wool, eyes embroidered, white, lying, very soft & snuggly*

SERIE	ART.-NO	PERIOD	PR.	INFO
85 46	**7517**	1954-1958	3	17 cm
850 460	**7517,00**	1959-1964	2-3	
562	**7517,00**	1965-1967	2-3	
	5620/17	1968-1971	2	
85 46	**7528**	1953-1958	3	28 cm
850 460	**7528,00**	1959-1964	2-3	
562	**7528,00**	1965-1967	2-3	
	5620/28	1968-1971	2	

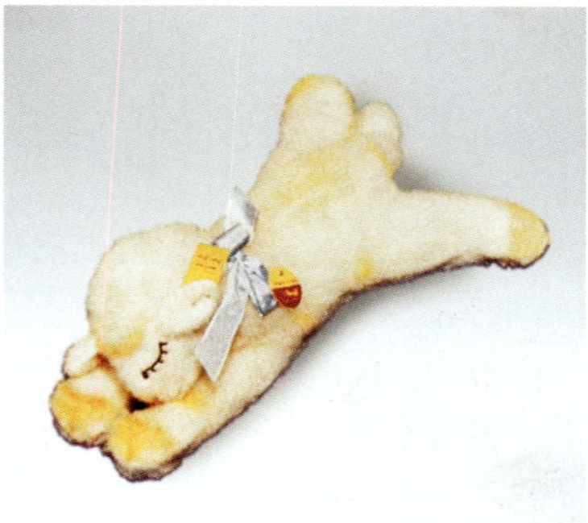

Floppy Lamm ab 1972 **Floppy Lamby** - *Floppy Lamb from 1972* ***Floppy Lamby***

Schlaftier, Wollpluesch, formgeschaeumt, Augen gestickt, liegend, sehr weich, vollwaschbar - *sleeping animal, plush wool, stuffed with pre-formed foam, eyes embroidered, lying, very soft, fully washable*

SERIE	ART.-NO	PERIOD	PR.	INFO
	5627/17	1970-1977	2	17 cm
	5627/28	1970-1977	2	28 cm

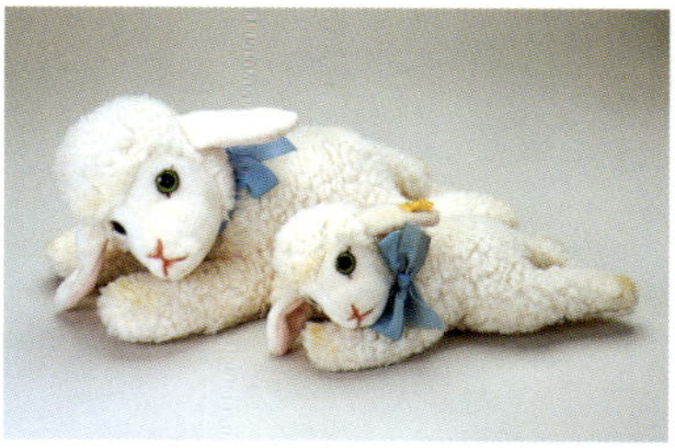

Floppy Lamby

Synthetik-Wirkpelz, formgeschaeumt, liegend, vollwaschbar - *synthetic knitted fur, stuffed with pre-formed foam, lying, fully washable*

SERIE	ART.-NO	PERIOD	PR.	INFO
	5725/20	1978-1982	1-2	20 cm
	5725/30	1978-1982	1-2	30 cm

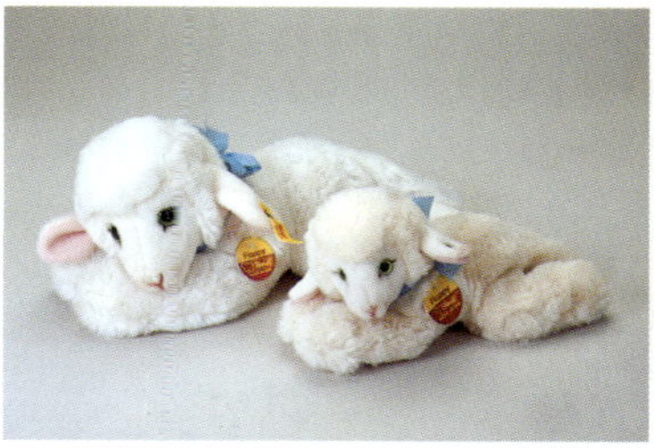

Floppy Lamm - ***Floppy*** *Lamb*

Webpelz, mollig weich, waschmaschinenfest - *woven fur, soft & cuddly, machine washable*

SERIE	ART.-NO	PERIOD	PR.	INFO
082504	**5625/18**	1983-1990	1-2	22 cm
	082504	1991-1999	1-2	
082528	**5625/25**	1983-1989	1-2	25 cm

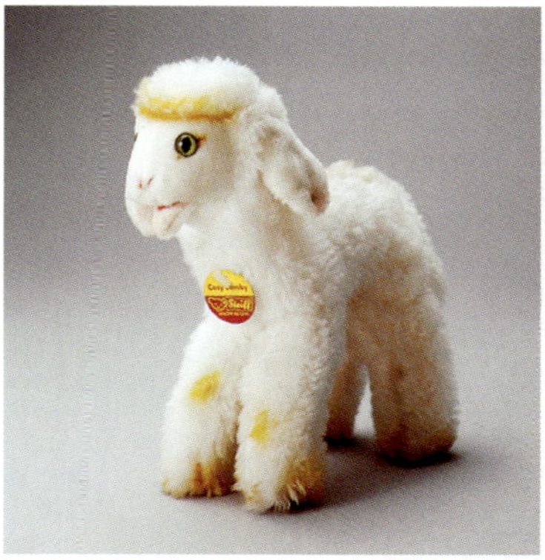

Cosy Lamby

Dralon-Pluesch, Schaumgummi-Fuellung, weiss, stehend, sehr weich, waschbar - *dralon, stuffed with foam rubber, white, standing, very soft, washable*

SERIE	ART.-NO	PERIOD	PR.	INFO
830 460	**1622,04**	1963-1964	2-3	22 cm
514	**1622,04**	1965-1967	2-3	
	5140/22	1968-1978	2	

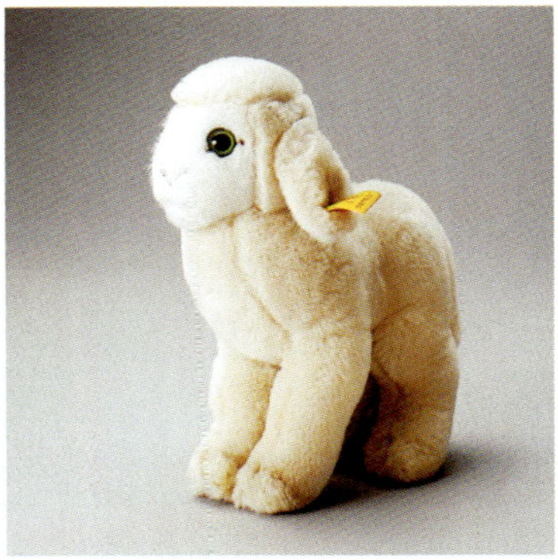

Cosy Lamby

Webpelz, weiss, stehend, abwaschbar - *woven fur, white, standing, surface washable*

SERIE	ART.-NO	PERIOD	PR.	INFO
097324	**5474/21**	1985-1988	2	21 cm
097348	**5474/27**	1985-1988	2	27 cm

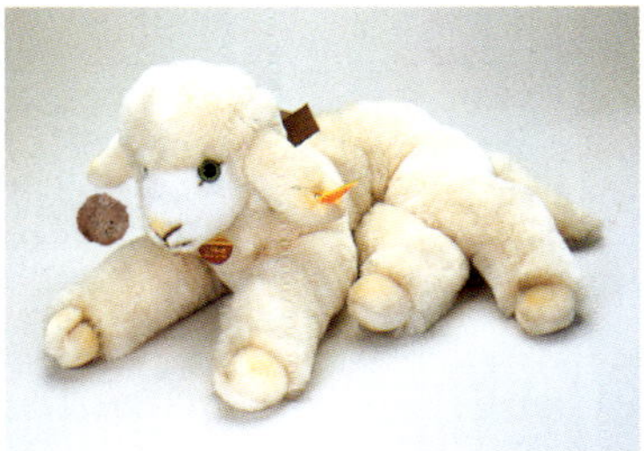

Cosy Lamby

Webpelz, liegend, waschmaschinenfest - *woven fur, lying, machine washable*

SERIE	ART.-NO	PERIOD	PR.	INFO
097232	**5473/25**	1986-1989	2-3	25 cm
097256	**5473/40**	1986-1989	3	40 cm

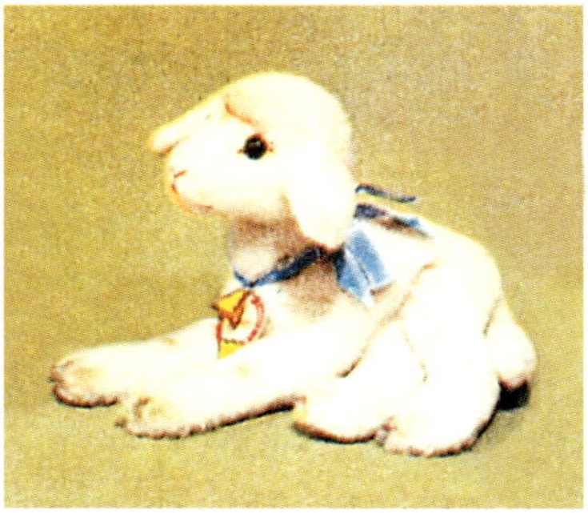

Lamm - *Lamb*

Wollpluesch, weiss, liegend - *plush wool, white, lying*

SERIE	ART.-NO	PERIOD	PR.	INFO
46	**2510**	1954-1955	4	10 cm
46	**2514**	1954-1955	4	14 cm

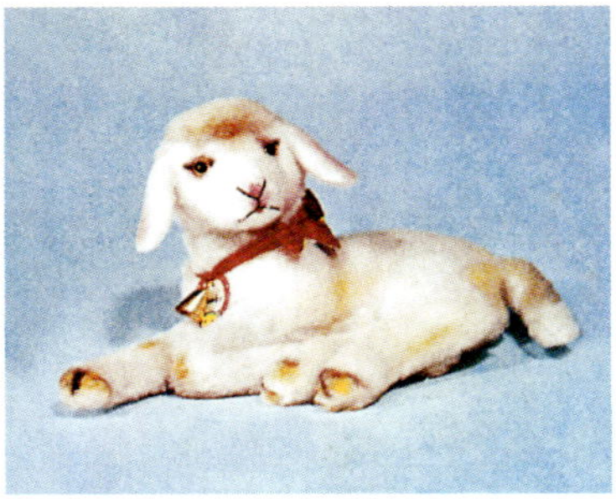

Lamby

Wollpluesch, weiss, liegend - *plush wool, white, lying*

SERIE	ART.-NO	PERIOD	PR.	INFO
345	**2525,04**	1966-1967	3	25 cm
	3455/25	1968-1972	3	

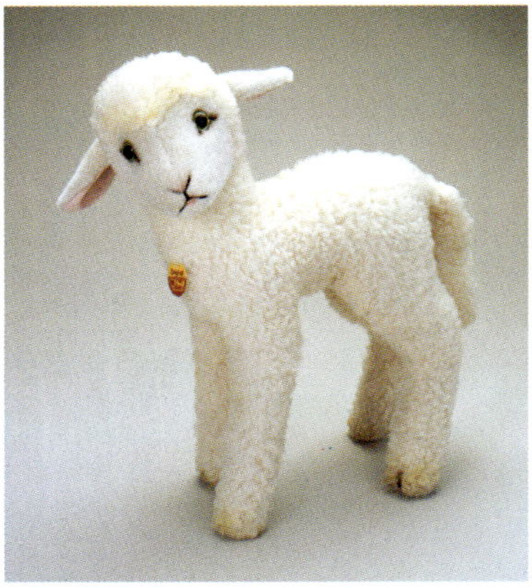

Lamby

Wirkpelz, stehend, abwaschbar - *knitted fur, standing, surface washable*

SERIE	ART.-NO	PERIOD	PR.	INFO
	1834/40	1978-1980	2-3	40 cm

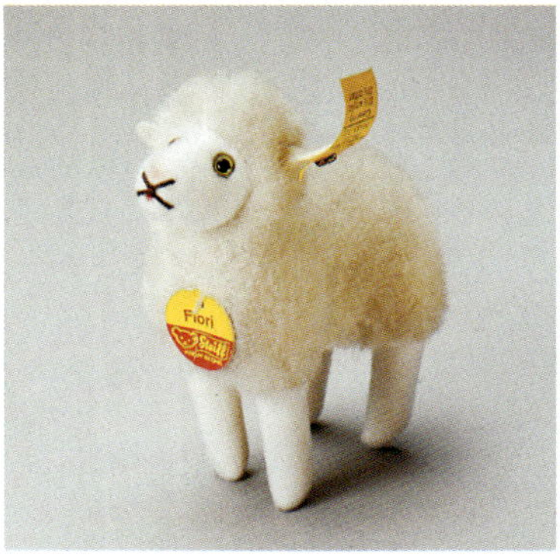

Flori Schaf - ***Flori** Sheep*

Synthetik-Webpelz, stehend, abwaschbar - *synthetic woven fur, standing, surface washable*

SERIE	ART.-NO	PERIOD	PR.	INFO
052286	**1518/11**	1978-1987	2	11 cm

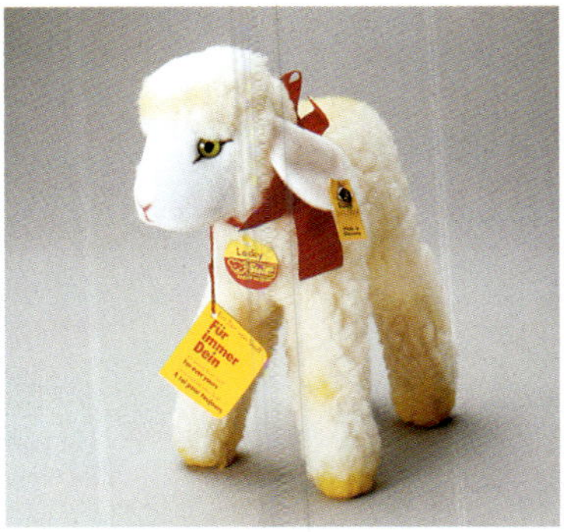

Locky Lamm - ***Locky** Lamb*

Wirkpelz, stehend, abwaschbar - *knitted fur, standing, surface washable*

SERIE	ART.-NO	PERIOD	PR.	INFO
	3450/22	1979-1981	2	22 cm

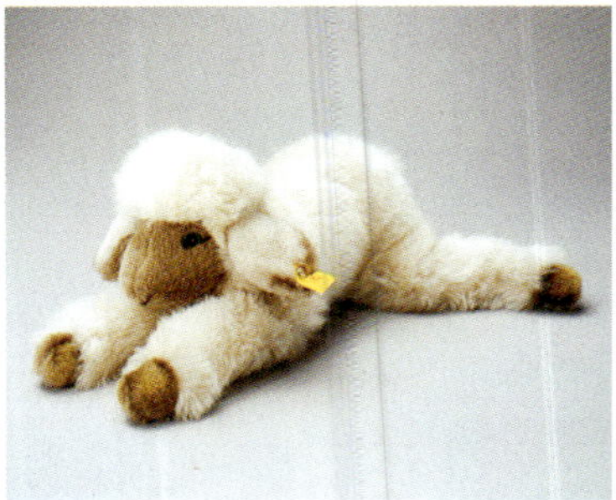

Molly Lamby

Webpelz, liegend - *woven fur, lying*

SERIE	ART.-NO	PERIOD	PR.	INFO
	0370/40	1981-1984	2	40 cm

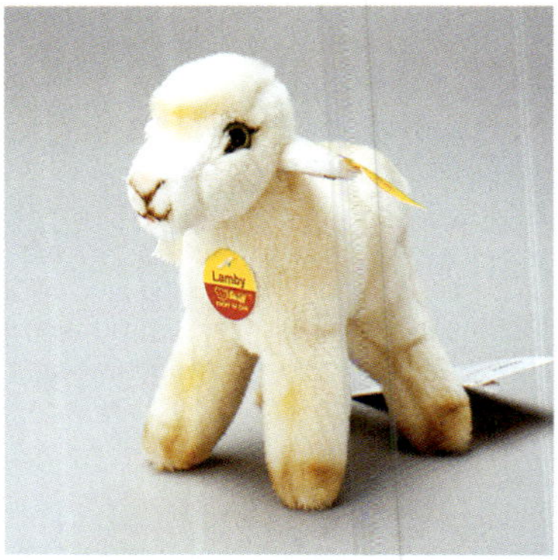

Lamby Lamm - ***Lamby** Lamb*

Webpelz, waschmaschinenfest - *woven fur, machine washable*

SERIE	ART.-NO	PERIOD	PR.	INFO
052804	**1527/12**	1987-1990	2	12 cm

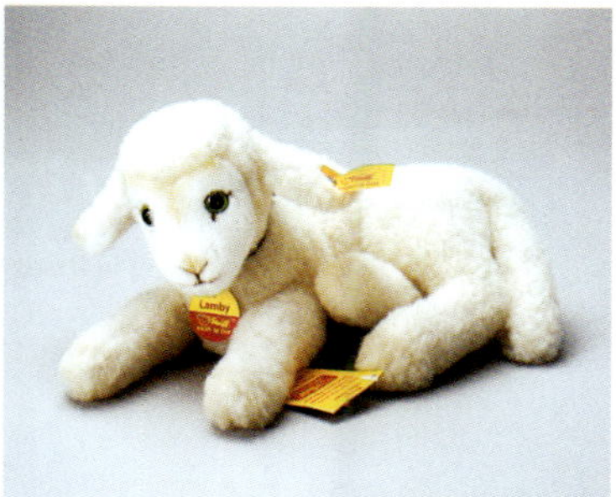

Lamby Lamm - ***Lamby** Lamb*

Woll-Wirkpelz, weiss, liegend, handwaschbar - *knitted wool fur, white, lying, hand washable*

Serie	Art.-No	Period	Pr.	Info
073151	**3460/25**	1989-1990	2	25 cm
	073151	1991-1997	2	
073182	**3460/30**	1989-1990	2	30 cm
	073182	1991-1991	2	

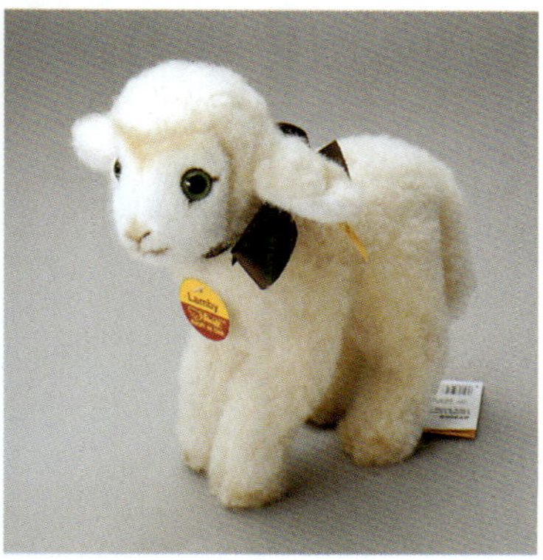

Lamby Lamm - ***Lamby** Lamb*

Woll-Wirkpelz, weiss, stehend, handwaschbar - *knitted wool fur, white, standing, hand washable*

Serie	Art.-No	Period	Pr.	Info
073069	**3462/22**	1989-1990	2	22 cm
	073069	1991-1997	2	

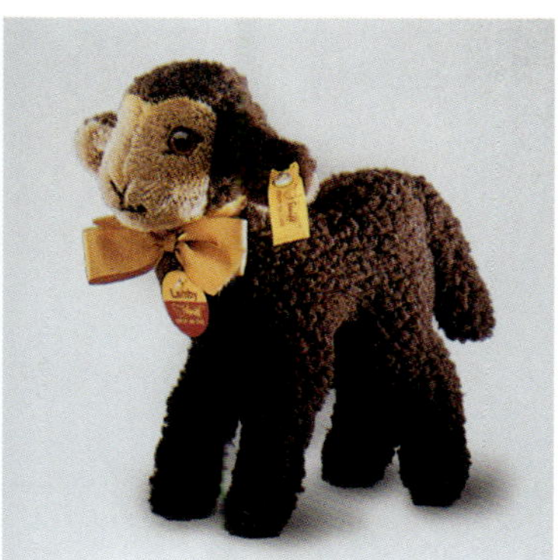

Lamby Lamm - ***Lamby** Lamb*

Woll-Wirkpelz, braun, stehend, handwaschbar - *knitted wool fur, brown, standing, hand washable*

Serie	Art.-No	Period	Pr.	Info
073366	**3464/22**	1989-1990	2	22 cm
	073366	1991-1991	2	

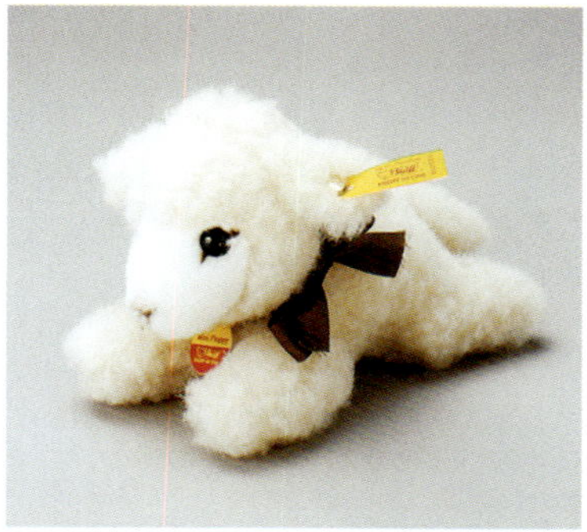

Mini Floppy Lamm - ***Mini Floppy** Lamb*

Woll-Wirkpelz, handwaschbar - *knitted wool fur, hand washable*

Serie	Art.-No	Period	Pr.	Info
082023	**5668/16**	1989-1990	1-2	16 cm
	082023	1991-1991	1-2	

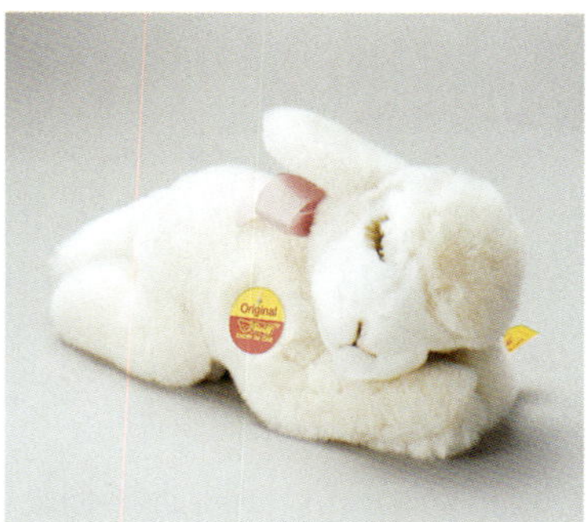

Schlaflamm - *Bedtime Lamb*

Webpelz, waschmaschinenfest - *woven fur, machine washable*

Serie	Art.-No	Period	Pr.	Info
082566	**5646/22**	1990-1990	2	28 cm
	082566	1991-1999	2	

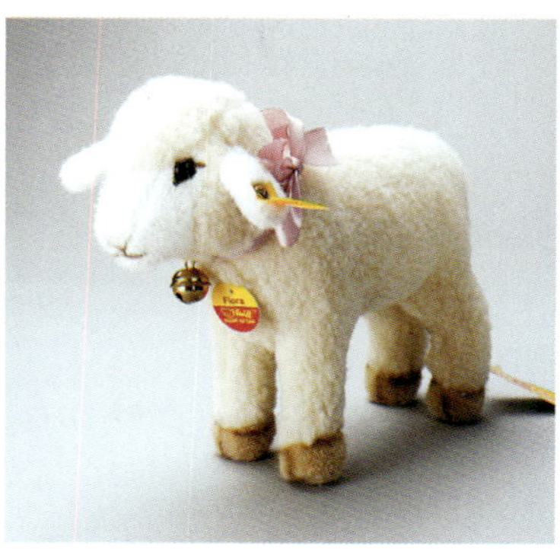

Flora Schaf - ***Flora** Sheep*

Woll-Webpelz, stehend, handwaschbar - *wool woven fur, standing, hand washable*

EAN-No.	Period	Pr.	Info
073427	1991-1993	2-3	25 cm

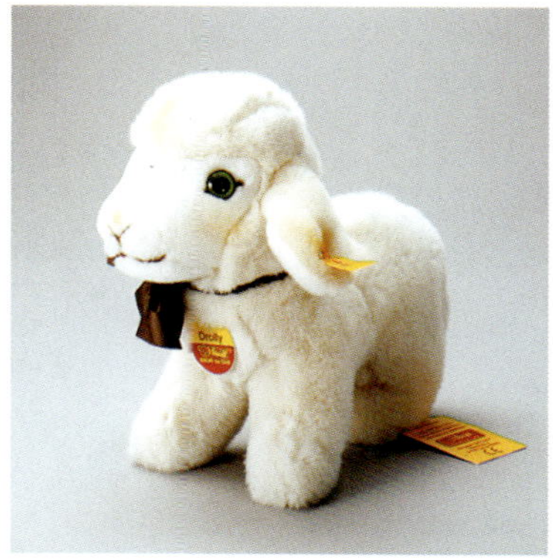

Drolly Lamm - ***Drolly** Lamb*

Webpelz, waschmaschinenfest - *woven fur, machine washable*

EAN-No.	Period	Pr.	Info
081576	1992-1997	2	22 cm

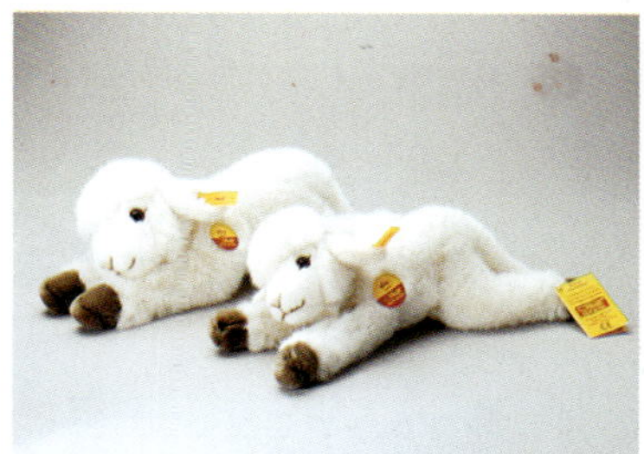

Molly Lamm - *Molly Lamb*

Webpelz, liegend, waschmaschinenfest - *woven fur, lying, machine washable*

EAN-No.	Period	Pr.	Info
103063	1994-1999	2-3	30 cm
103087	1994-1997	2-3	40 cm
103100	1993-1996	2-3	50 cm
103124	1993-1998	3	60 cm

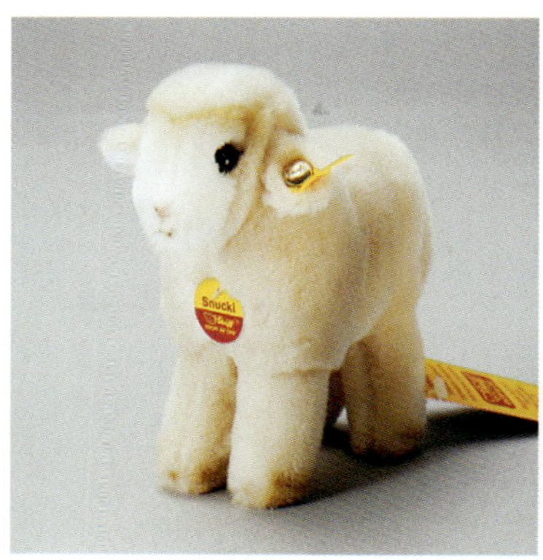

Snucki Schaf - ***Snucki** Sheep*

Webpelz, stehend, waschmaschinenfest - *woven fur, standing, machine washable*

EAN-No.	Period	Pr.	Info
052811	1994-1997	1-2	16 cm

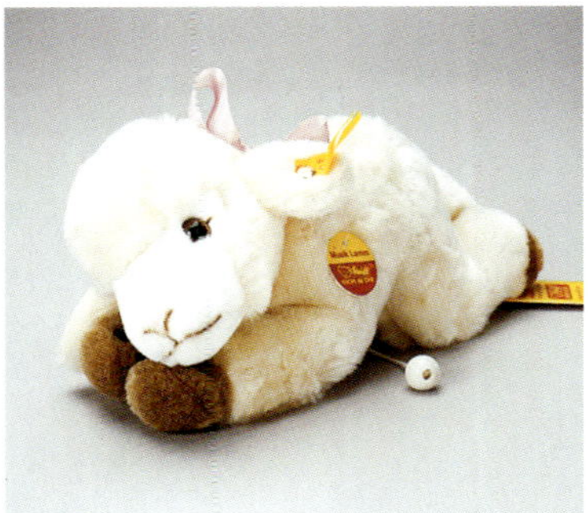

Musik Schlaf**lamm** - *Music Sleeping Lamb*

Webpelz, mit Musikwerk SKS (Schlaf, Kindlein, schlaf), abwaschbar - *woven fur, with music box "sleep little child, sleep", surface washable*

EAN-No.	Period	Pr.	Info
231544	1995-1999	2-3	28 cm

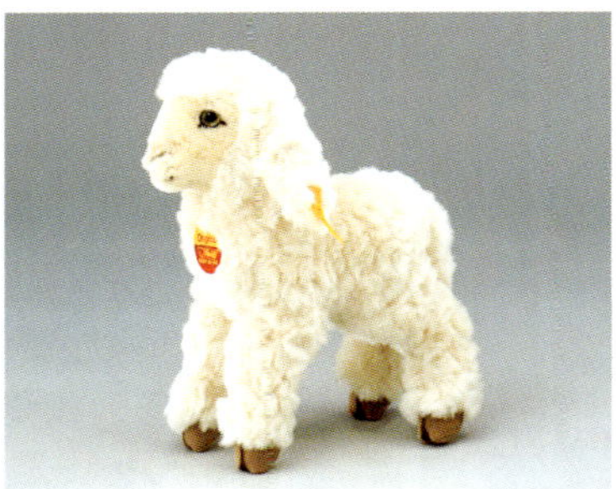

Lamm - *Lamb*

Webpelz, wollweiss, stehend, waschmaschinenfest - *woven fur, wool-white, standing, machine washable*

EAN-No.	Period	Pr.	Info
073168	1996-1998	2-3	22 cm

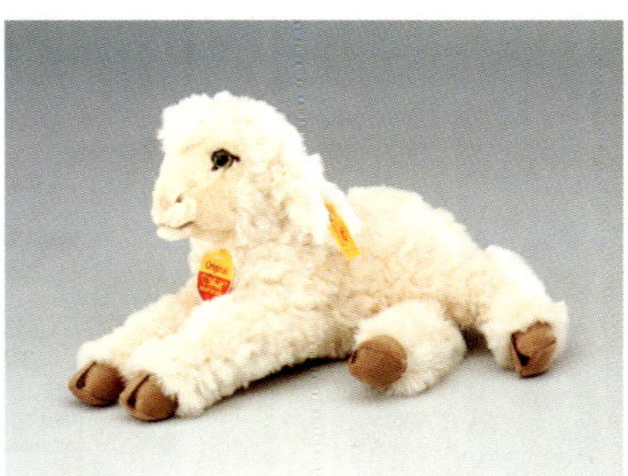

Lamm - *Lamb*

Webpelz, wollweiss, seitlich liegend, waschmaschinenfest - *woven fur, wool-white, lying aside, machine washable*

EAN-No.	Period	Pr.	Info
073175	1996-1998	2-3	24 cm

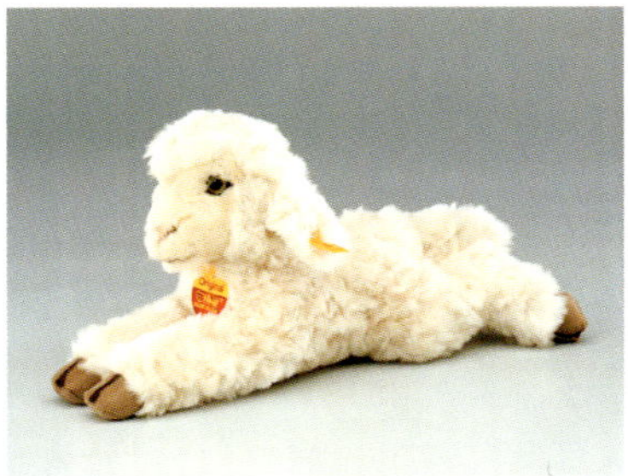

Lamm - *Lamb*

Webpelz, wollweiss, liegend, waschmaschinenfest - *woven fur, wool-white, lying, machine washable*

EAN-No.	Period	Pr.	Info
073199	1996-1998	2-3	28 cm

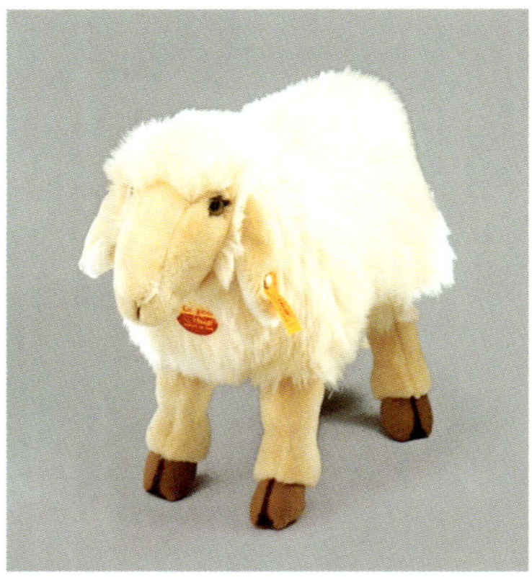

Bea Schaf - ***Bea** Sheep*

Webpelz, wollweiss, stehend, abwaschbar - *woven fur, wool-white, standing, surface washable*

EAN-No.	Period	Pr.	Info
073212	1996-1998	3	40 cm

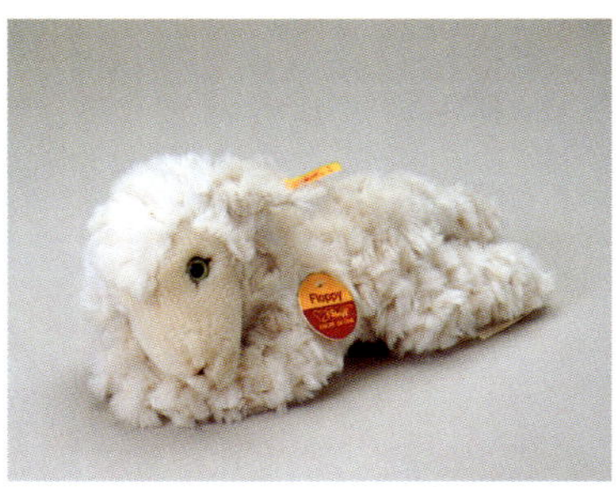

Lamm - *Lamb*

Webpelz, waschmaschinenfest - *woven fur, machine washable*

EAN-No.	Period	Pr.	Info
082498	1997-1999	2	22 cm

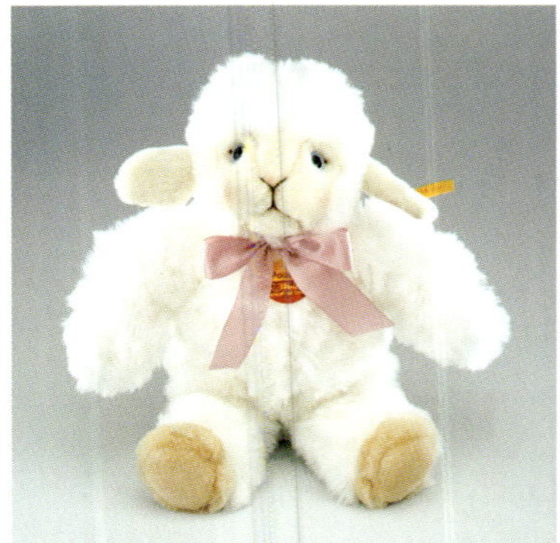

Poppy Lamm - ***Poppy** Lamb*

Webpelz, weiss, waschmaschinenfest - *woven fur, white, machine washable*

EAN-No.	Period	Pr.	Info
123061	1998-1999	2-3	30 cm

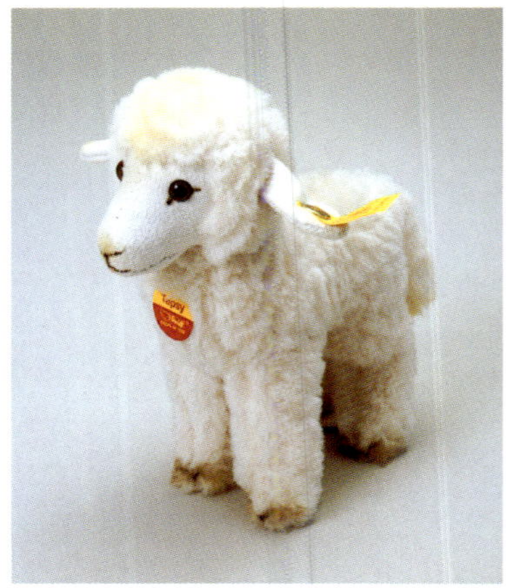

Tapsy Laemmchen - ***Tapsy** Baby-lamb*

Webpelz, wollweiss, stehend, waschmaschinenfest - *woven fur, wool-white, standing, machine washable*

EAN-No.	Period	Pr.	Info
052828	1998-1999	2	14 cm

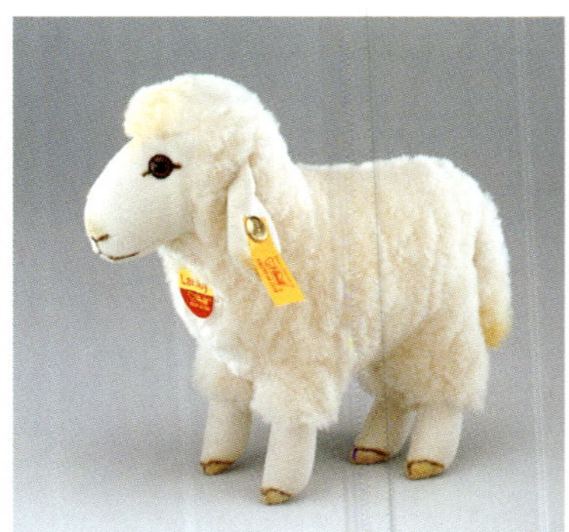

Lamby Schaf - ***Lamby** Sheep*

Webpelz, wollweiss, stehend, waschmaschinenfest - *woven fur, wool-white, standing, machine washable*

EAN-No.	Period	Pr.	Info
052835	1998-1999	2	16 cm

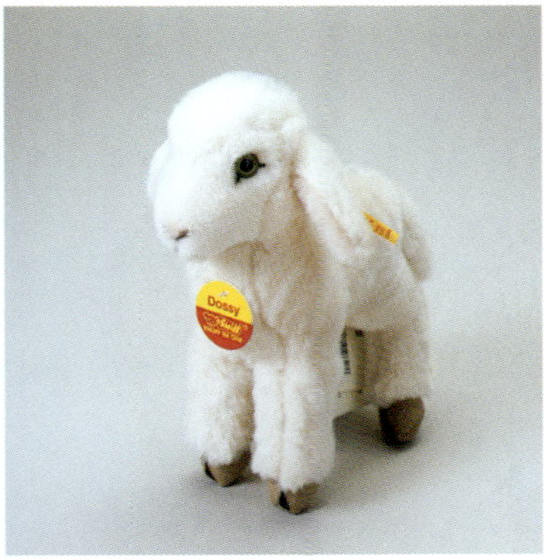

Dossy Lamm - ***Dossy** Lamb*

Webpelz, wollweiss oder dunkelbraun, 18 cm, stehend, waschmaschinenfest - *woven fur, wool-white or dark brown, 18 cm, standing, machine washable*

EAN-No.	Period	Pr.	Info
073076	1998-1999	2-3	wollweiss - *wool-white*
073083	1998-1998	2-3	dunkelbraun - *dark brown*

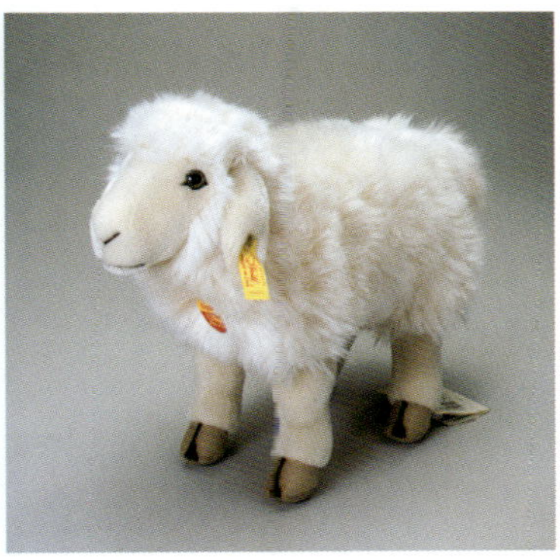

Siglinde Schaf - ***Siglinde** Sheep*

Webpelz, wollweiss, stehend, handwaschbar - *woven fur, wool-white, standing, machine washable*

EAN-No.	Period	Pr.	Info
073229	1998-1999	3	35 cm

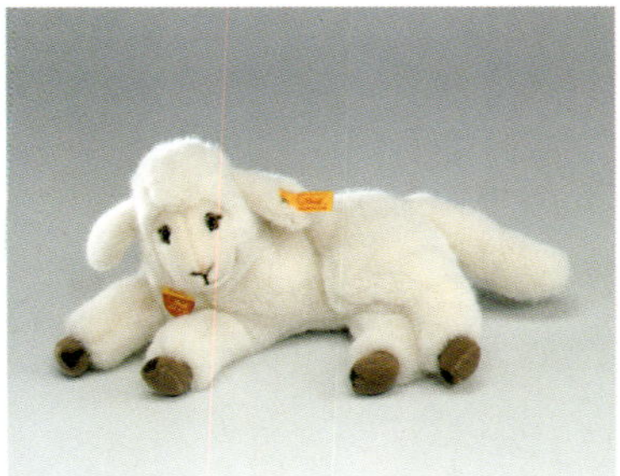

Flocky Lamm - ***Flocky** Lamb*

Webpelz, seitlich liegend, waschmaschinenfest - *woven fur, lying aside, machine washable*

EAN-No.	Period	Pr.	Info
103131	1999-1999	2-3	25 cm

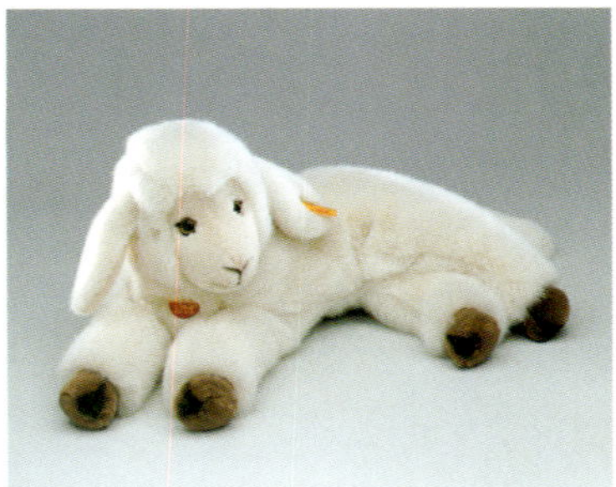

Flora Lamm - ***Flora** Lamb*

Webpelz, seitlich liegend, waschmaschinenfest - *woven fur, lying aside, machine washable*

EAN-No.	Period	Pr.	Info
103148	1999-1999	3	45 cm

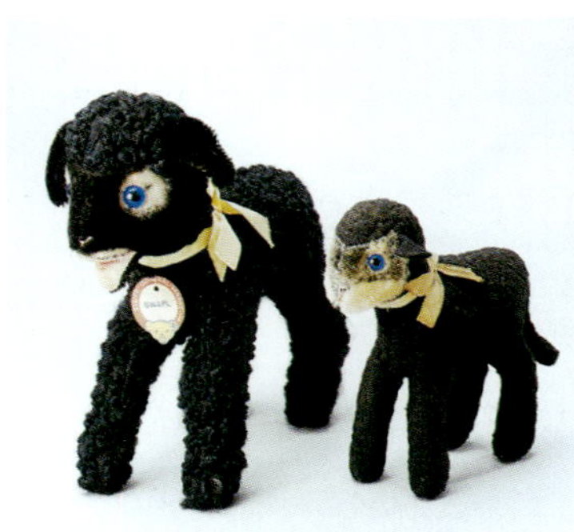

Swapl Persianer Lamm - ***Swapl** Persian Lamb*

Wollpluesch, ab 22 cm Mohair-Kraeuselpluesch, schwarz, stehend - *plush wool, from 22 cm mohair curly plush, black, standing*

Serie	Art.-No	Period	Pr.	Info
46a	**6510,0**	1957-1958	3-4	10 cm
461	**6510,06**	1959-1964	3-4	
46a	**6514,0**	1957-1958	3-4	14 cm
461	**6514,06**	1959-1964	3-4	
46a	**6322,0**	1957-1958	4-5	22 cm
461	**6322,06**	1959-1962	4-5	
46a	**6328,0**	1957-1958	4-5	28 cm
461	**6328,06**	1959-1960	4-5	
46a	**6335,0**	1957-1958	5	35 cm
461	**6335,06**	1959-1960	5	

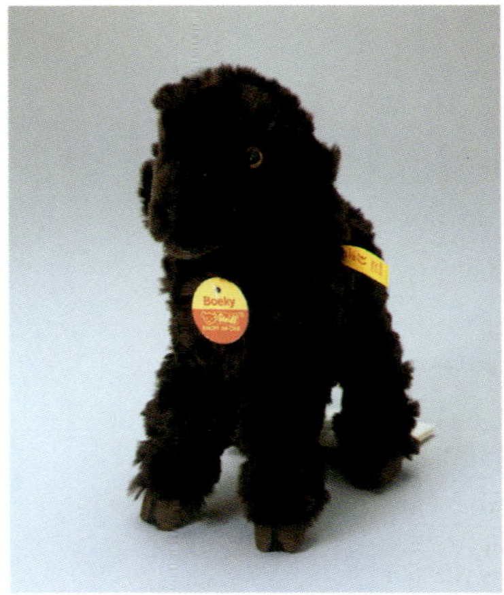

Boeky Lamm - ***Boeky** Lamb*

Webpelz, dunkelbraun, stehend, waschmaschinenfest - *woven fur, dark brown, standing, machine washable*

EAN-No.	Period	Pr.	Info
073267	1997-1999	2-3	22 cm

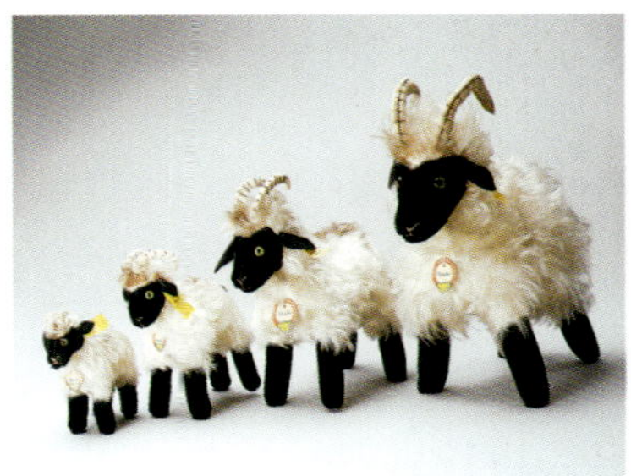

Heideschaf **Snucki** - *Mountain Sheep **Snucki***

Mohair, weiss, Beine & Kopf schwarz, stehend - *mohair, white, legs & head black, standing*

Serie	Art.-No	Period	Pr.	Info
462	**1312,00**	1959-1964	3	12 cm
350	**1312,00**	1965-1967	3	
	3500/12	1968-1969	2-3	
462	**1317,00**	1959-1964	3	17 cm
350	**1317,00**	1965-1967	3	
	3500/17	1968-1974	3	
462	**1322,00**	1959-1964	3-4	22 cm
350	**1322,00**	1965-1967	3-4	
	3500/22	1968-1974	3-4	
462	**1328,00**	1964-1964	4	28 cm
350	**1328,00**	1965-1966	4	

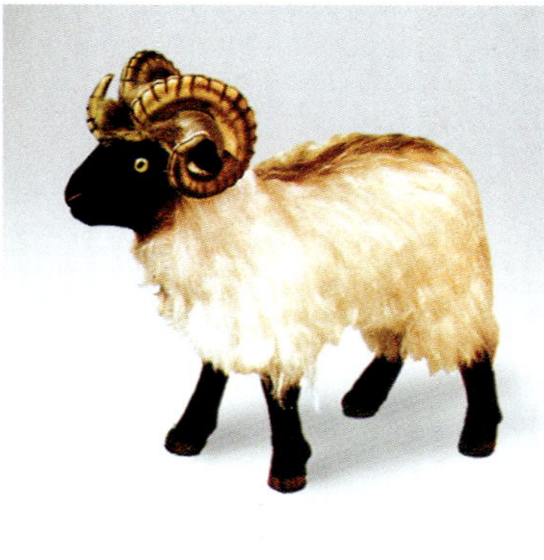

Heideschaf - *Moorland Sheep*

Schautier, Mohair - *display animal, mohair*

SERIE	ART.-NO	PERIOD	PR.	INFO
462	**1350,90**	1960-1960	5-6	50 cm

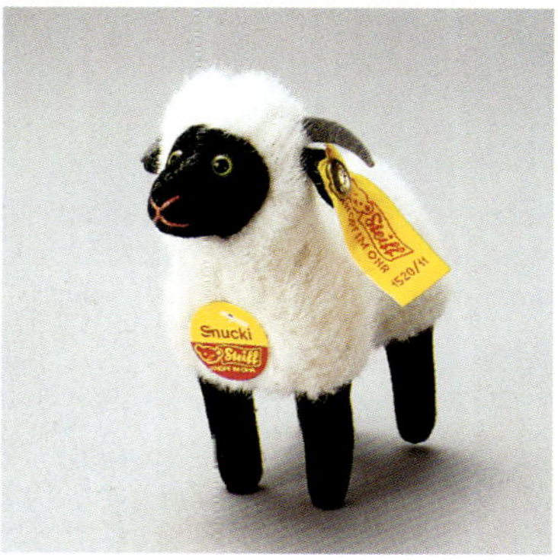

Snucki Heideschaf - ***Snucki*** *Moorland Sheep*

Synthetik-Webpelz, stehend, abwaschbar - *synthetic woven fur, standing, surface washable*

SERIE	ART.-NO	PERIOD	PR.	INFO
052293	**1520/11**	1978-1987	3	11 cm

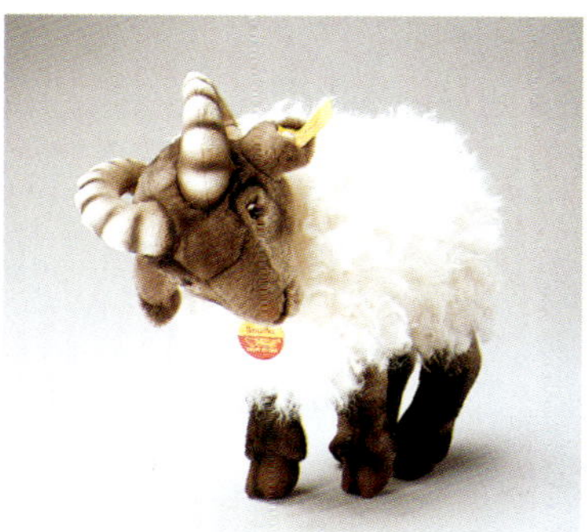

Snucki Heidschnucke - ***Snucki*** *Moorland Sheep*

Webpelz, stehend, Brumm-Stimme, abwaschbar - *woven fur, standing, growler, surface washable*

EAN-NO.	PERIOD	PR.	INFO
073465	1991-1992	3	28 cm

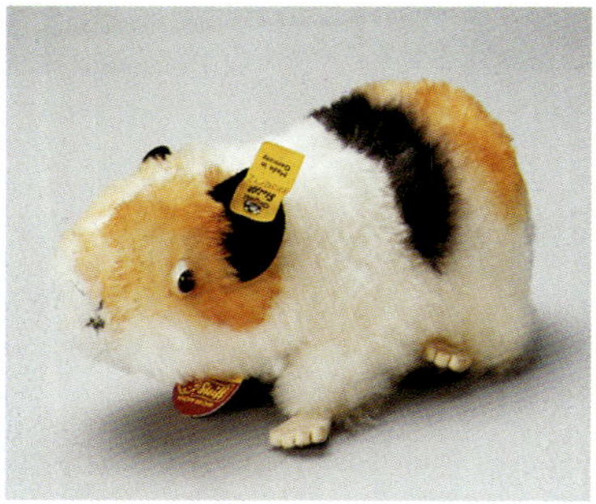

Meerschwein **Swinny** - *Guinea Pig* ***Swinny***

Dralon-Pluesch, weiss/gelb/schwarz, abwaschbar - *dralon, white/yellow/black, surface washable*

SERIE	ART.-NO	PERIOD	PR.	INFO
507	**2609,00**	1962-1963	3	9 cm
225	**2609,00**	1965-1967	3	
	2250/09	1968-1979	2-3	
507	**2612,00**	1962-1963	3	12 cm
225	**2612,00**	1966-1967	3	
	2250/12	1968-1979	2-3	

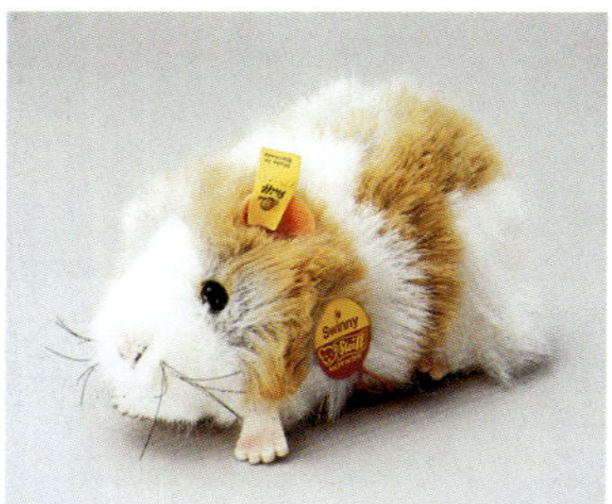

Swinny Meerschweinchen - ***Swinny*** *Guinea Pig*

Pelzimitation, ab 1978 Synthetik-Webpelz, stehend, abwaschbar - *imitation fur, from 1978 synthetic woven fur, standing, surface washable*

SERIE	ART.-NO	PERIOD	PR.	INFO
	2255/15	1976-1981	2-3	15 cm

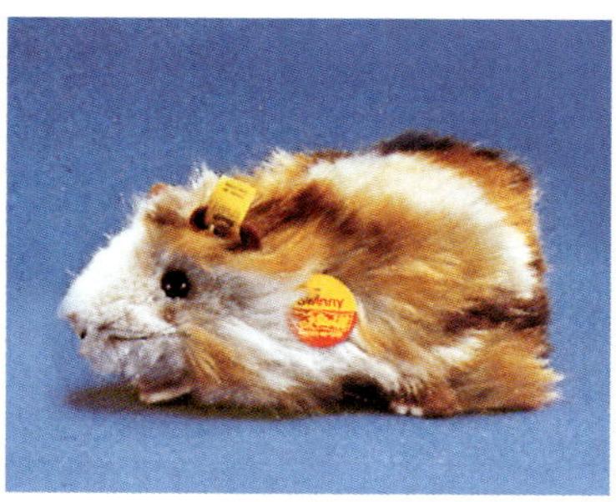

Swinny Meerschweinchen - ***Swinny*** *Guinea Pig*

Pelzimitation, ab 1978 Synthetik-Webpelz, stehend, abwaschbar - *imitation fur, from 1978 synthetic woven fur, standing, surface washable*

SERIE	ART.-NO	PERIOD	PR.	INFO
	2256/15	1976-1983	2-3	15 cm

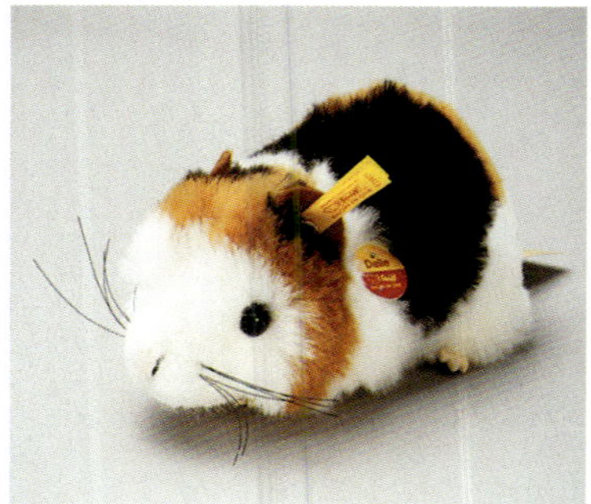

Dalle Meerschweinchen - ***Dalle*** *Guinea Pig*

Wirkpelz, stehend, abwaschbar - *knitted fur, standing, surface washable*

SERIE	ART.-NO	PERIOD	PR.	INFO
071805	**2252/10**	1980-1990	1-2	15 cm
	071805	1991-1999	1-2	

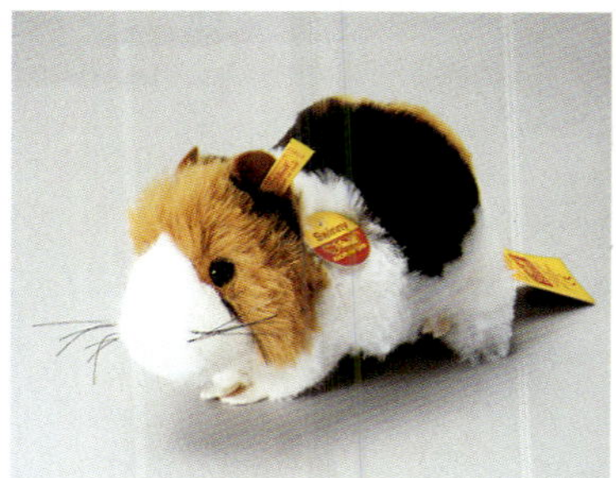

Swinny Meerschweinchen - ***Swinny*** *Guinea Pig*

Webpelz, Druckstimme, abwaschbar - *woven fur, press voice, washable*

SERIE	ART.-NO	PERIOD	PR.	INFO
071850	**2254/15**	1984-1990	1-2	20 cm
	071850	1991-1999	1-2	

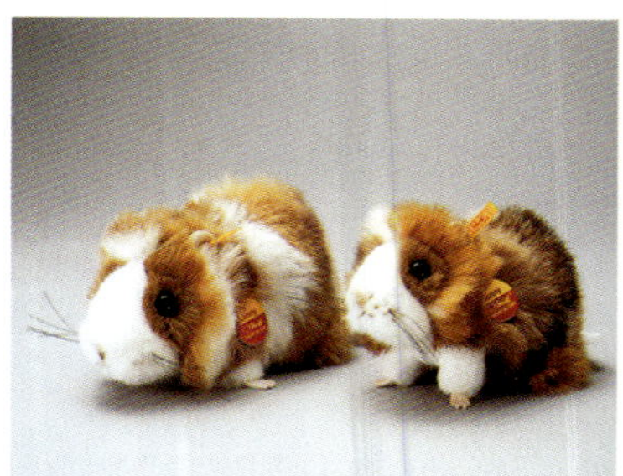

Ginny Meerschweinchen - ***Ginny*** *Guinea Pig*

Webpelz, gefleckt, stehend, Pieps-Stimme, waschmaschinenfest - *woven fur, spotted, standing, press voice, machine washable*

SERIE	ART.-NO	PERIOD	PR.	INFO
071911	**2251/18**	1990-1990	2	18 cm
	071911	1991-1999	2	
071935	**2251/22**	1990-1990	2	22 cm
	071935	1991-1999	2	

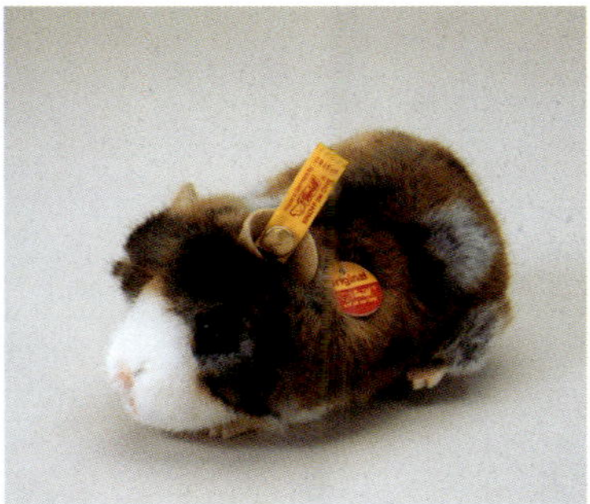

Meerschweinchen - *Guinea Pig*

Webpelz, braun gefleckt, waschmaschinenfest - *woven fur, brown spotted, machine washable*

EAN-NO.	PERIOD	PR	INFO
053702	1996-1999	1-2	14 cm

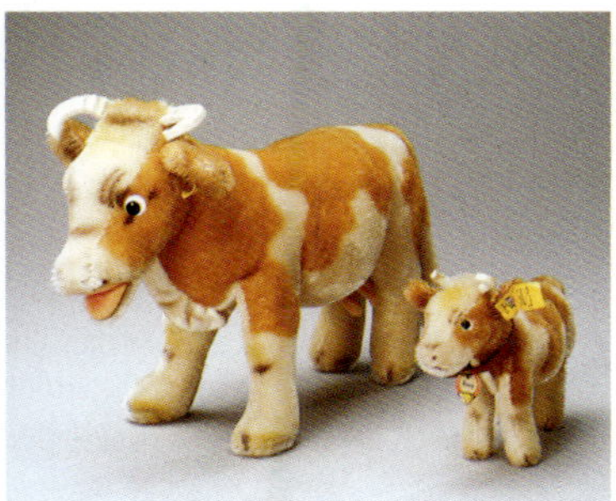

Kuh **Bessy** - *Cow **Bessy***

Mohairpluesch, Halsband mit Glocke, weiss/braun, stehend, 12 cm geschlossenes Maul, ab 17 cm offenes Maul, abwaschbar - *mohair, collar with bell, white & brown, standing, 12 cm mouth closed, from 17 cm open mouth, surface washable*

SERIE	ART.-NO	PERIOD	PR.	INFO
52	**1312,0**	1958-1958	3-4	12 cm
520	**1312,03**	1959-1961	3-4	
391	**1312,03**	1966-1967	3-4	
	3910/12	1968-1973	3	
52	**1317,0**	1958-1958	4	17 cm
520	**1317,03**	1959-1961	4	
391	**1317,03**	1966-1967	4	
	3910/17	1968-1973	3-4	
52	**1325,0**	1958-1958	4-5	25 cm
520	**1325,03**	1959-1963	4-5	

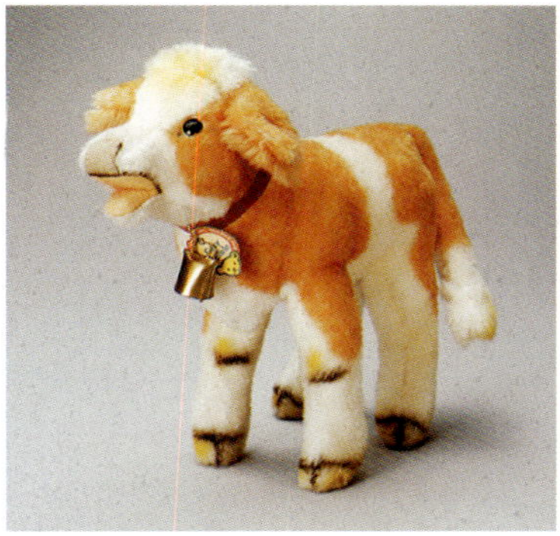

Cosy Kaelble - *Cosy Little Calf*

Dralon, gefuellt mit synthetischen Fasern & Schaumstoff, rostbraun/weiss, stehend, sehr weich, vollwaschbar - *dralon, stuffed with synthetic fibers & foam, rust brown & white, standing, very soft, fully washable*

SERIE	ART.-NO	PERIOD	PR.	INFO
518	**6628,00**	1967-1967	3	28 cm
	5180/28	1968-1975	3	

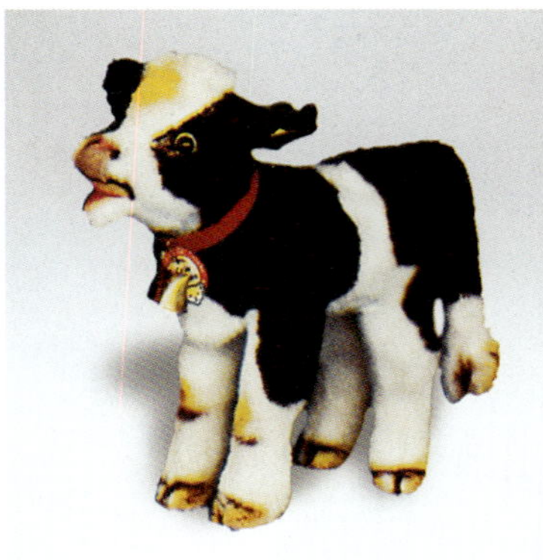

Cosy Kaelble - *Cosy Little Calf*

Dralon, schwarz/weiss, stehend, waschbar, sehr weich - *dralon, black & white, standing, washable, very soft*

SERIE	ART.-NO	PERIOD	PR.	INFO
	5186/28	1970-1971	3	28 cm

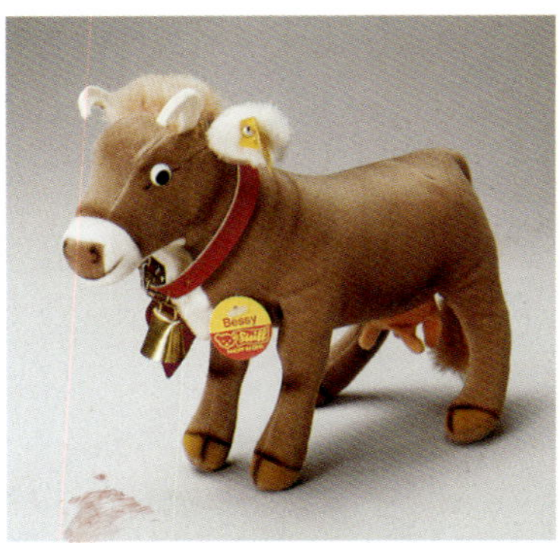

Bessy Kuh - ***Bessy** Cow*

Trevirasamt, abwaschbar - *trevira velvet, surface washable*

SERIE	ART.-NO	PERIOD	PR.	INFO
	3915/20	1976-1979	3	20 cm

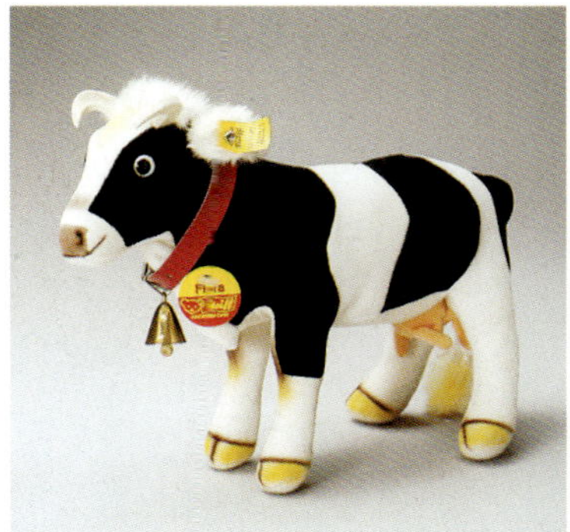

Flora Kuh - ***Flora** Cow*

Trevirasamt, schwarz/weiss, stehend, abwaschbar - *trevira velvet, black & white, standing, surface washable*

SERIE	ART.-NO	PERIOD	PR.	INFO
	3916/20	1976-1978	3	20 cm

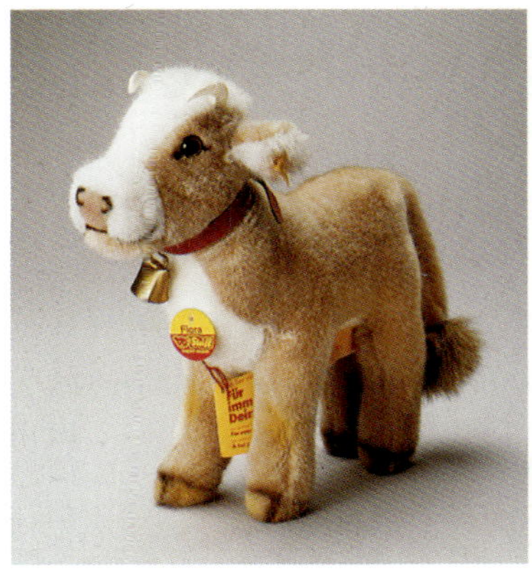

Flora Kuh - ***Flora** Cow*

Wirkpelz, stehend, abwaschbar - *knitted fur, standing, surface washable*

SERIE	ART.-NO	PERIOD	PR.	INFO
	3792/25	1980-1983	3	25 cm

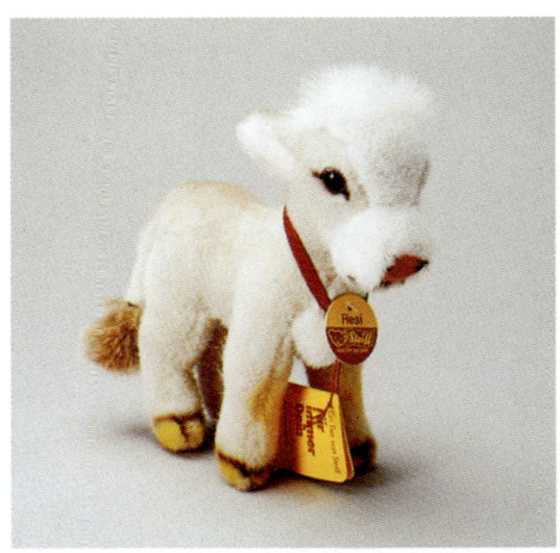

Resi Kalb - ***Resi** Calf*

Webpelz, stehend, abwaschbar - *woven fur, standing, surface washable*

SERIE	ART.-NO	PERIOD	PR.	INFO
	3790/18	1980-1982	3	18 cm

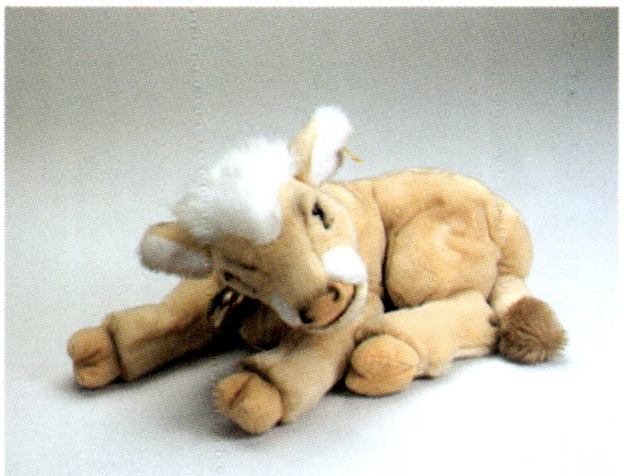

Kalb - *Calf*

Webpelz, liegend, waschbar - *woven fur, lying, washable*

SERIE	ART.-NO	PERIOD	PR.	INFO
077968	**3795/27**	1982-1987	2-3	27 cm

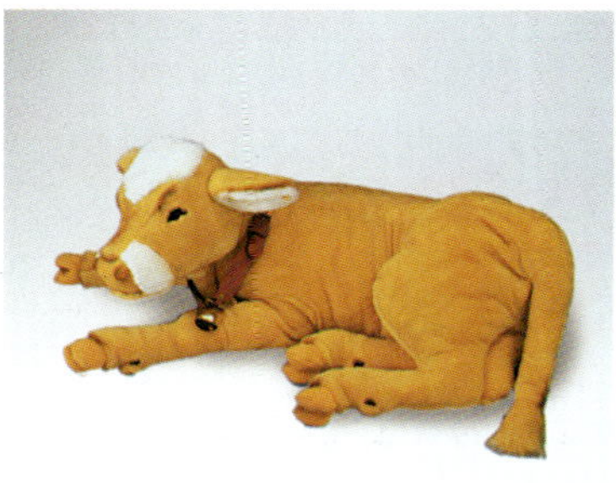

Super Molly Kalb - ***Super Molly*** *Calf*

Webpelz, mollig weich, abwaschbar - *woven fur, soft & cuddly, surface washable*

SERIE	ART.-NO	PERIOD	PR.	INFO
	0365/99	1983-1985	4	100 cm

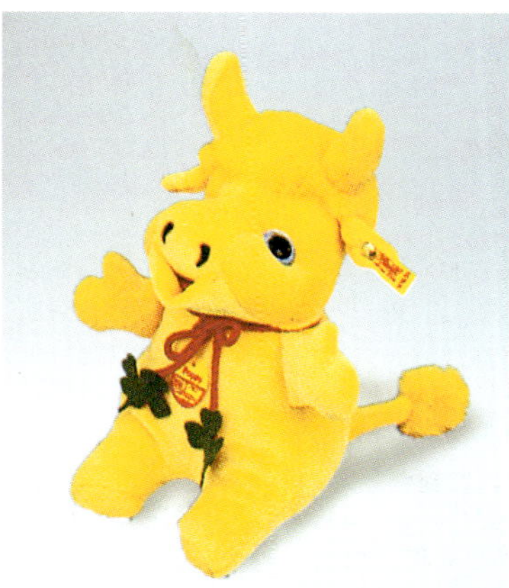

Poppy Kuh - ***Poppy*** *Cow*

Nicki-Stoff, abwaschbar - *nicki velvet, surface washable*

SERIE	ART.-NO	PERIOD	PR.	INFO
	7878/26	1984-1984	3-4	26 cm

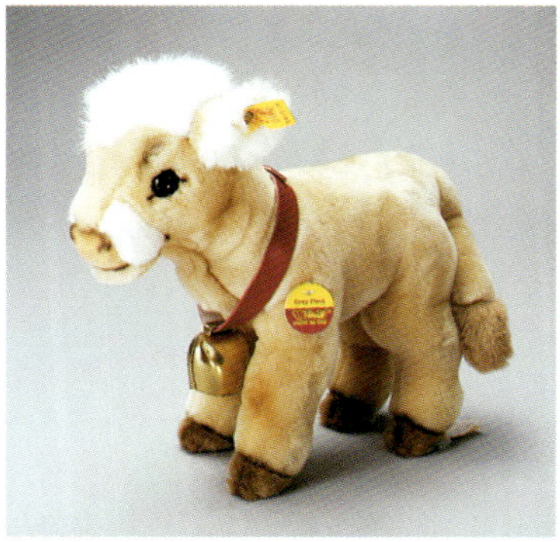

Cosy Flora Kalb - ***Cosy Flora*** *Calf*

Webpelz, stehend, waschmaschinenfest - *woven fur, standing, machine washable*

SERIE	ART.-NO	PERIOD	PR.	INFO
097744	**5477/25**	1985-1988	3	28 cm

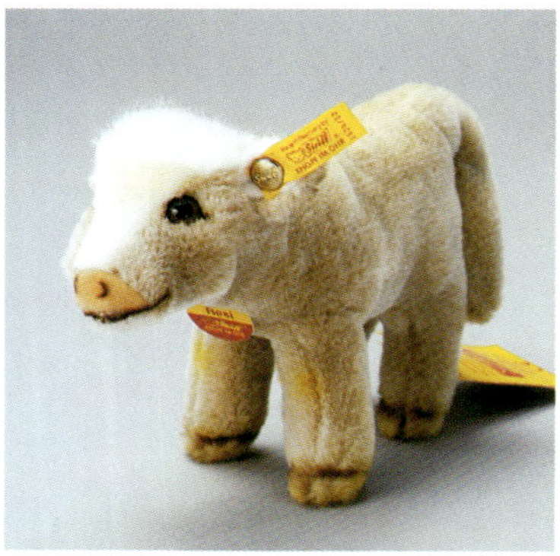

Resi Kalb - ***Resi*** *Calf*

Webpelz, waschmaschinenfest - *woven fur, machine washable*

SERIE	ART.-NO	PERIOD	PR.	INFO
052651	**1524/12**	1987-1990	2-3	12 cm

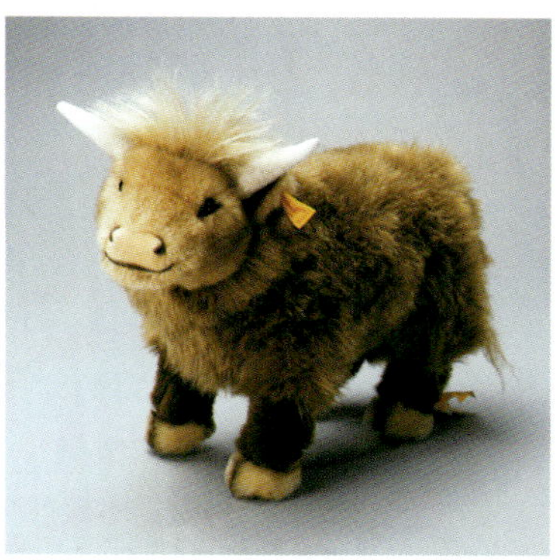

Schottisches Hochlandrind - *Scottish Highland Ox*

Webpelz, abwaschbar - *woven fur, surface washable*

SERIE	ART.-NO	PERIOD	PR.	INFO
072505	**2690/32**	1988-1989	3	32 cm

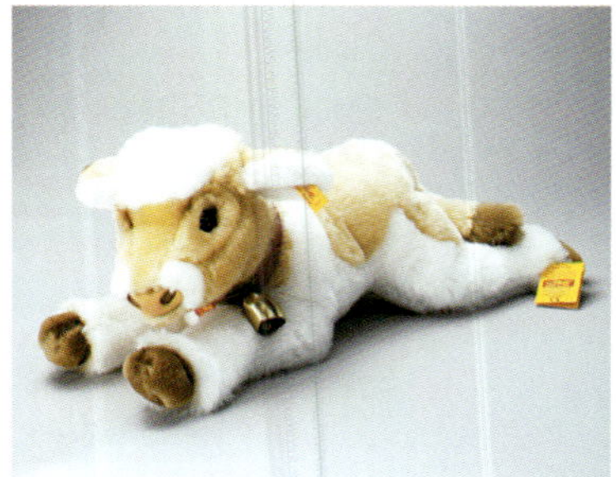

Molly Kalb - *Molly Calf*

Webpelz, Lederhalsband, ohne Halsband waschmaschinenfest - *woven fur, leather collar, machine washable without collar*

EAN-NO.	PERIOD	PR.	INFO
103407	1991-1995	3	45 cm
103414	1991-1993	3	60 cm

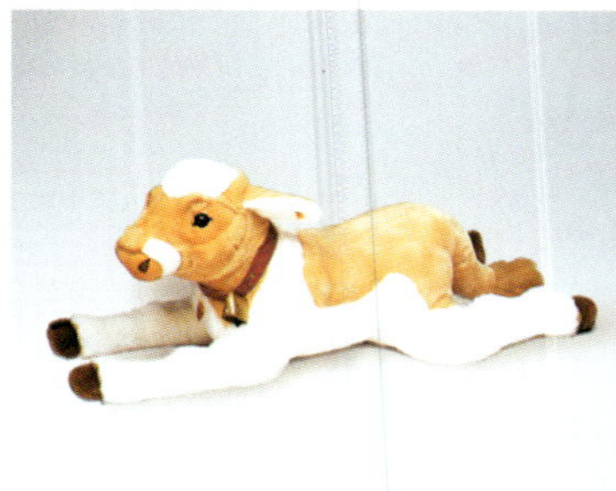

Super Molly Kalb - ***Super Molly*** *Calf*

Webpelz, Leder-Halsband mit Glocke, liegend, abwaschbar - *woven fur, leather collar with bell, lying, surface washable*

EAN-NO.	PERIOD	PR.	INFO
103445	1991-1993	4	125 cm

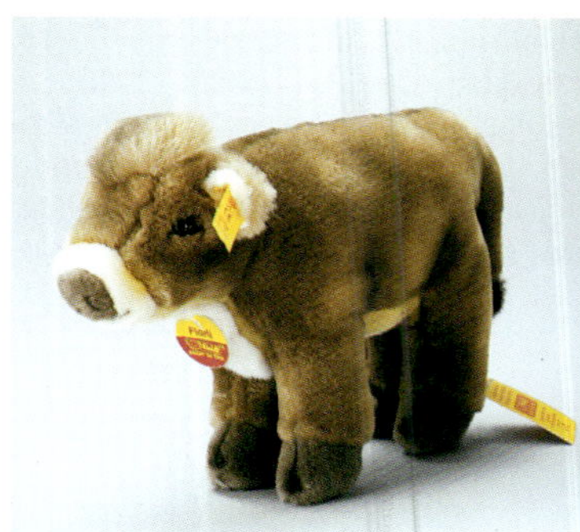

Florli Kalb - ***Florli*** *Calf*

Webpelz, stehend, waschmaschinenfest - *woven fur, standing, machine washable*

EAN-NO.	PERIOD	PR.	INFO
072956	1993-1996	2	25 cm

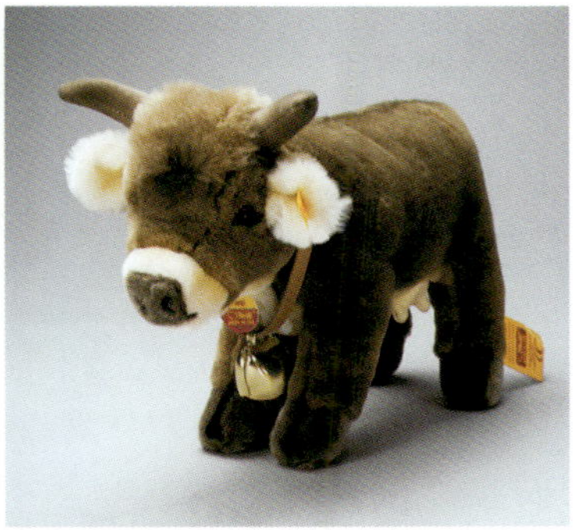

Resi Kuh - ***Resi** Cow*

Webpelz, Lederhalsband und Glocke, stehend, ohne Halsband waschmaschinenfest - *woven fur, leather collar with bell, standing, machine washable without collar*

EAN-No.	Period	Pr.	Info
072901	1993-1999	3	40 cm

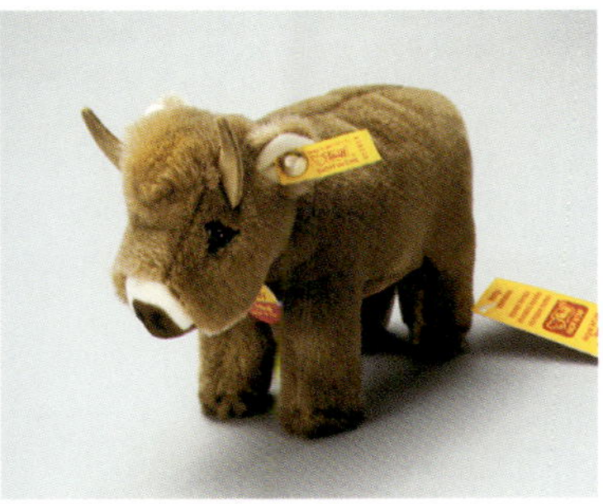

Bessy Kuh - ***Bessy** Cow*

Webpelz, stehend, waschmaschinenfest - *woven fur, standing, machine washable*

EAN-No.	Period	Pr.	Info
052668	1994-1998	2	18 cm

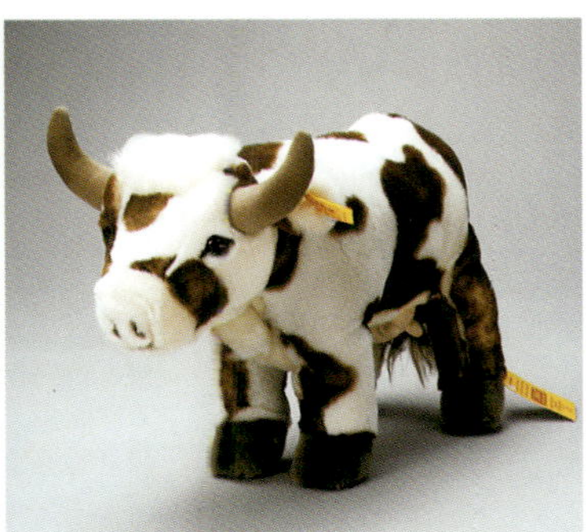

Lena Kuh ab 1996 **Bertha** - ***Lena** Cow from 1996 **Bertha***

Webpelz, weiss/braun gefleckt, stehend, handwaschbar - *woven fur, spotted brown & white, standing, hand washable*

EAN-No.	Period	Pr.	Info
072970	1995-1997	3	45 cm

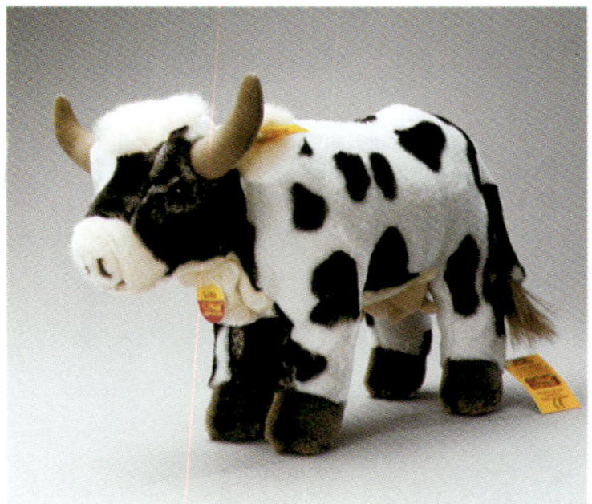

Lotte Kuh 1996 **Ulla** - ***Lotte** Cow in 1996 **Ulla***

Webpelz, weiss/schwarz gefleckt, stehend, handwaschbar - *woven fur, spotted black & white, standing, hand washable*

EAN-No.	Period	Pr.	Info
072994	1995-1996	3	45 cm

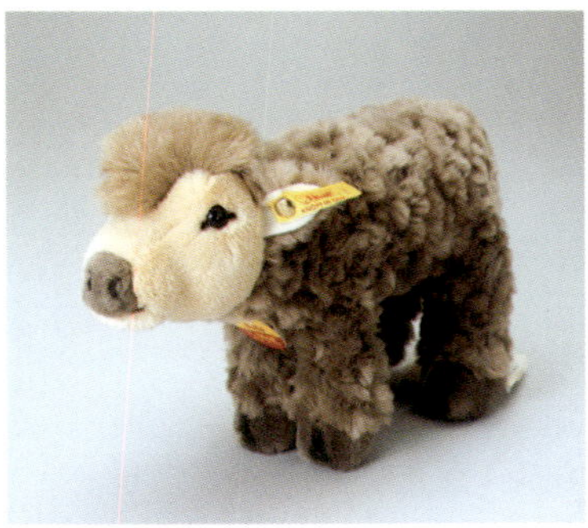

Sulla Kalb - ***Sulla** Calf*

Webpelz, stehend, waschmaschinenfest - *woven fur, standing, machine washable*

EAN-No.	Period	Pr.	Info
072857	1997-1999	2-3	27 cm

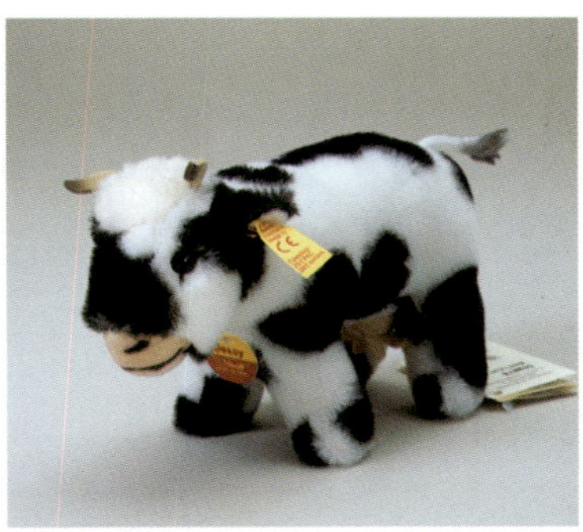

Bessy Kuh - ***Bessy** Cow*

Webpelz, schwarz/weiss gefleckt, stehend, waschmaschinenfest - *woven fur, black/white spotted, standing, machine washable*

EAN-No.	Period	Pr.	Info
052675	1998-1999	2	18 cm

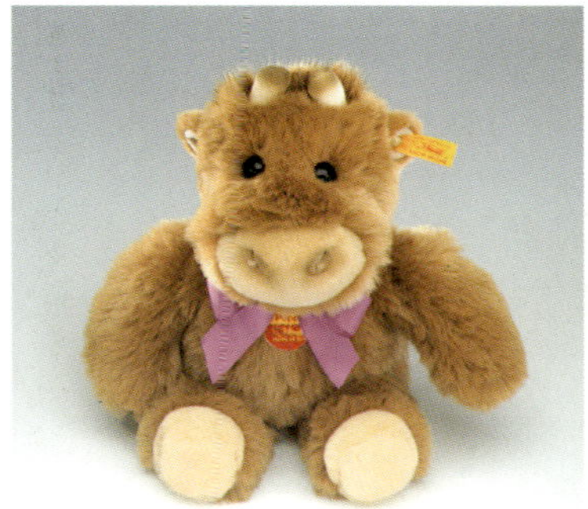

Poppy Kuh - ***Poppy** Cow*

Webpelz, hellbraun, waschmaschinenfest - *woven fur, light brown, machine washable*

EAN-No.	Period	Pr.	Info
123399	1999-1999	2-3	30 cm

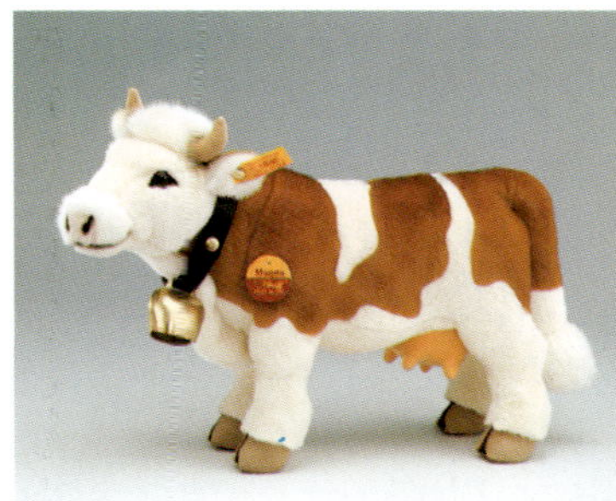

Magda Kuh - ***Magda** Cow*

Webpelz, weiss/braun gefleckt, stehend, Lederhalsband & Glocke, abwaschbar - *woven fur, white/brown spotted, standing, leather collar & bell, surface washable*

EAN-No.	Period	Pr.	Info
072918	1999-1999	3	32 cm

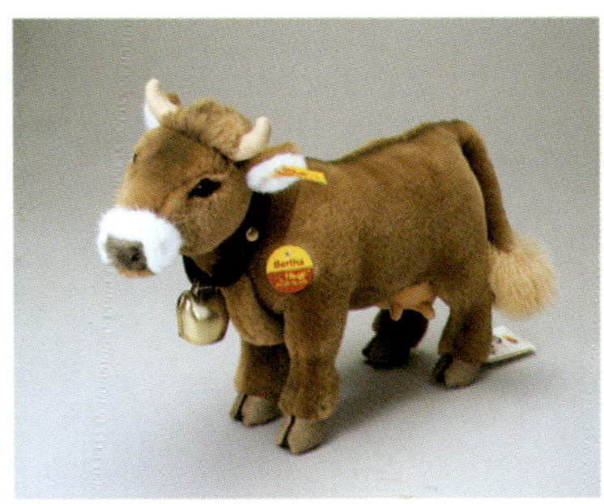

Bertha Kuh - ***Bertha** Cow*

Webpelz, hellbraun, stehend, Lederhalsband & Glocke, abwaschbar - *woven fur, light brown, standing, leather collar & bell, surface washable*

EAN-No.	Period	Pr.	Info
072925	1999-1999	3	32 cm

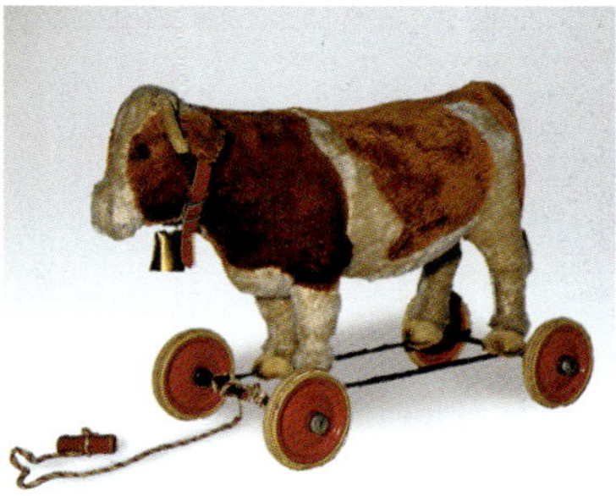

Reit-Ochse - *Riding Ox*

Mohair, Eisengerippe, Zugstimme, Lederhalfter & Glocke, braun/weiss, stehend, auf Holzraedern, ab 1950 Metallscheibenraeder mit Gummireifen, Verbindungsschienen - *mohair, iron frame, pull cord voice, leather collar & bell, brown & white, standing, wooden wheels (from 1950 metal disc wheels with rubber tires), connecting frame*

SERIE	ART.-NO	PERIOD	PR.	INFO
52	**1343,2**	1949-1957	5-6	43 cm
521	**1343,20**	1961-1961	5-6	
52	**1350,2**	1950-1957	5-6	50 cm
521	**1350,20**	1961-1961	5-6	

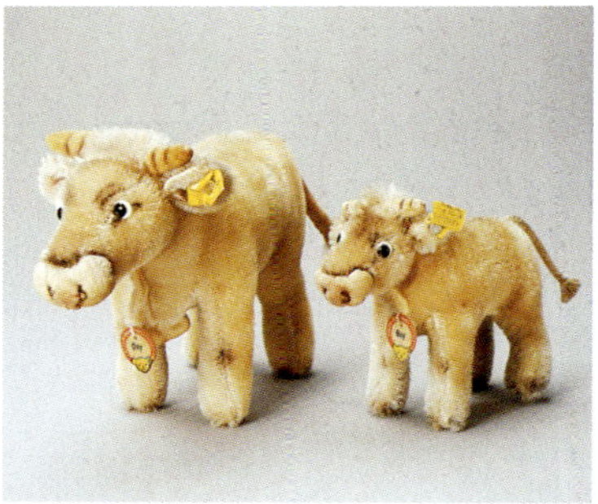

Ochse **Oxy** - *Ox* ***Oxy***

Mohair, weiss/grau/braun, stehend, ab 14 cm Druckstimme - *mohair, white/grey/ brown, standing, from 14 cm press voice*

SERIE	ART.-NO	PERIOD	PR.	INFO
52	**1310,0**	1953-1957	4-5	10 cm
52	**1314,0**	1953-1957	4-5	14 cm
52	**1322,0**	1953-1953	5	22 cm
52	**1322,02**	1954-1957	5	

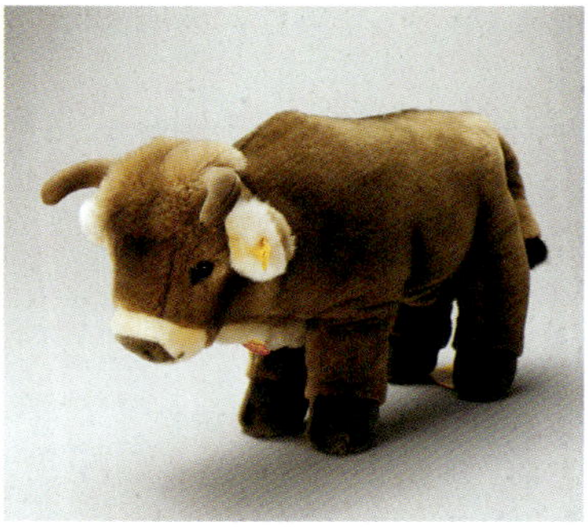

Bully Stier - ***Bully*** *Steer*

Webpelz, stehend, waschmaschinenfest - *woven fur, standing, machine washable*

EAN-NO.	PERIOD	PR.	INFO
072888	1993-1995	3	48 cm

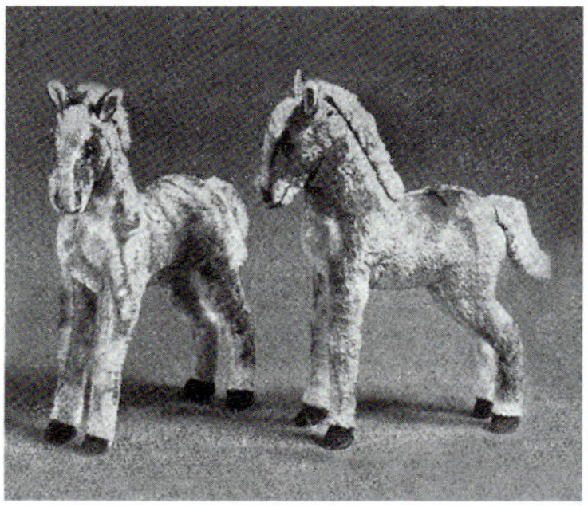

Fohlen - *Foal*

Kunstseidenpluesch, hellbraun schattiert, stehend, ohne Raeder - *artificial silk plush, shaded light brown, standing, without wheels*

SERIE	ART.-NO	PERIOD	PR.	INFO
56	**6628,0**	1948-1948	4	28 cm

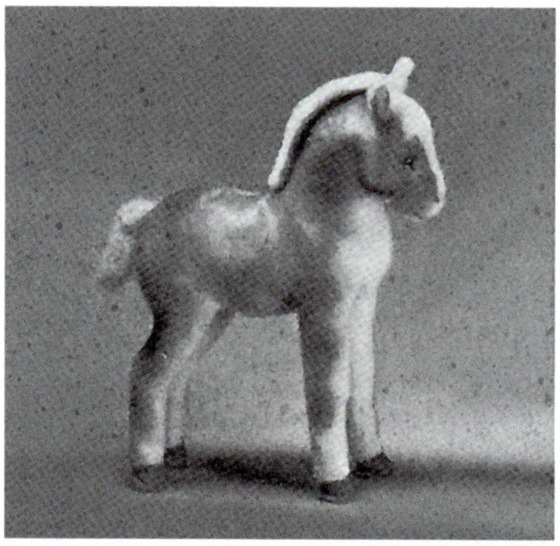

Fohlen - *Foal*

Wollpluesch, braun/weiss, hellbraun schattiert, stehend, ohne Raeder - *plush wool, brown & white, light brown shading, standing, without wheels*

SERIE	ART.-NO	PERIOD	PR.	INFO
56	**6528,0**	1949-1951	4	28 cm

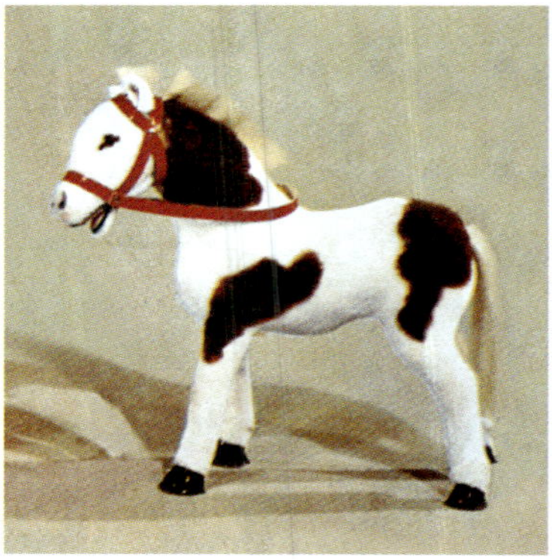

Pferd - *Horse*

Mohair, weiss/braun gefleckt, stehend, Lederzuegel - *mohair, white/brown spotted, standing, bridle & reins*

SERIE	ART.-NO	PERIOD	PR.	INFO
56	**1322,0**	1952-1958	4	22 cm
560	**1322,04**	1959-1959	4	
56	**1328,0**	1952-1957	4-5	28 cm
56	**1328,02**	1958-1958	4-5	
560	**1328,04**	1959-1959	4-5	
56	**1335,0**	1953-1953	5	35 cm
56	**1335,02**	1954-1958	5	
560	**1335,04**	1959-1959	5	

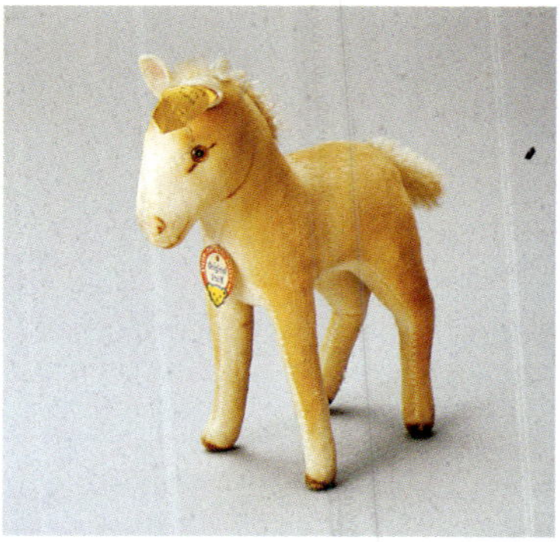

Fohlen - *Foal*

14 cm Samtpluesch, 28 cm Mohair, hellbraun/weiss, stehend - *14 cm plush velvet, 28 cm mohair, light brown & white, standing*

SERIE	ART.-NO	PERIOD	PR.	INFO
56	**6414,0**	1952-1958	4	14 cm
560	**6414,03**	1959-1961	4	
56	**6328,0**	1953-1957	4-5	28 cm

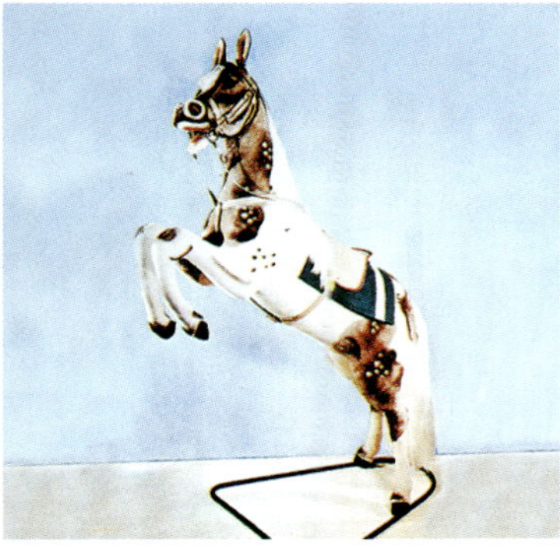

Pferd - *Horse*

Schautier - *display animal*

SERIE	ART.-NO	PERIOD	PR.	INFO
560	**4250,90**	1960-1960	7	250 cm

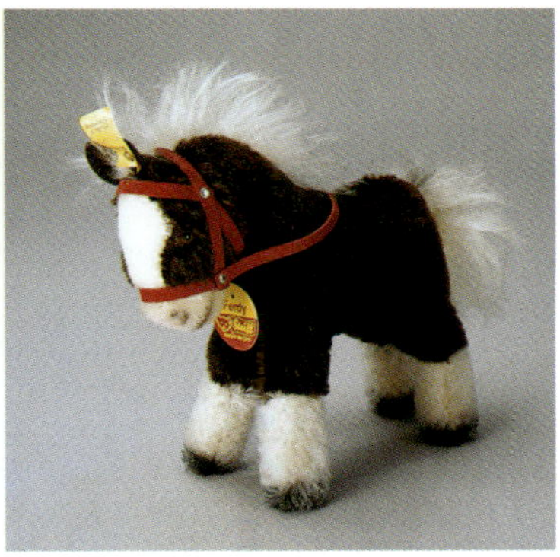

Spielpferd **Ferdy** - *Play Horse* ***Ferdy***

Mohair, braun/weiss, stehend, Lederzuegel, abwaschbar - *mohair, brown & white, standing, leather bridle & reins, surface washable*

SERIE	ART.-NO	PERIOD	PR.	INFO
375	**1318,03**	1965-1967	3	18 cm
	3750/18	1968-1981	3	
375	**1325,03**	1965-1967	3	25 cm
	3750/25	1968-1978	3	

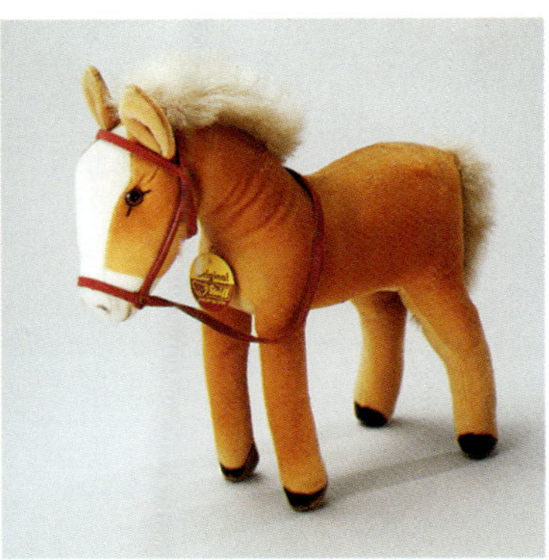

Pferd - *Horse*

Trevirasamt, abwaschbar - *trevira velvet, surface washable*

SERIE	ART.-NO	PERIOD	PR.	INFO
	3770/22	1976-1978	3	22 cm

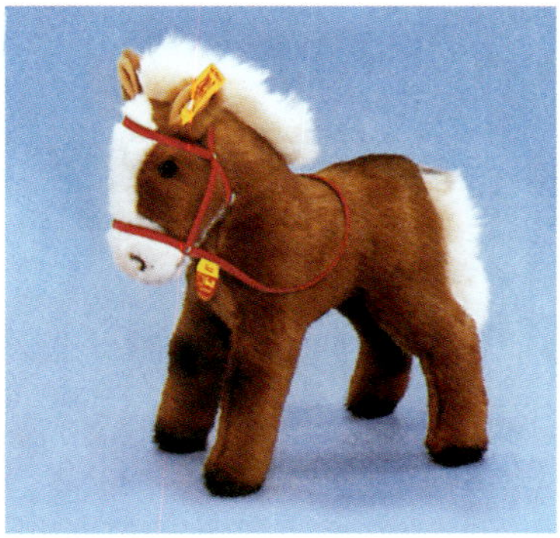

Rico Pferd - ***Rico*** *Horse*

Webpelz, stehend, abwaschbar - *woven fur, standing, surface washable*

SERIE	ART.-NO	PERIOD	PR.	INFO
	3760/25	1979-1985	2-3	25 cm

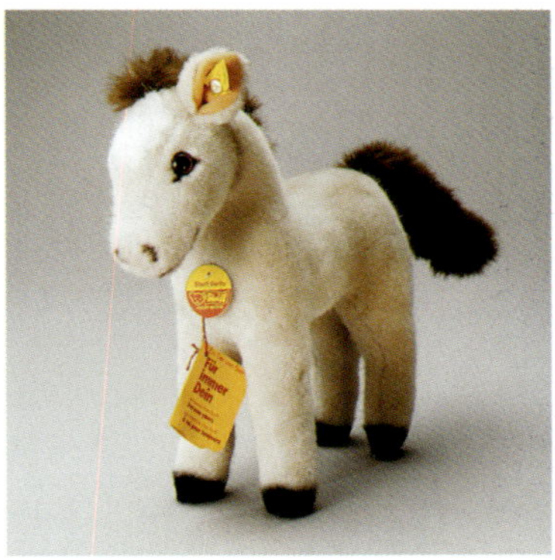

Steiff Derby Pferd - ***Steiff Derby*** *Horse*

Webpelz, falb, stehend, abwaschbar - *woven fur, dun colored, standing, surface washable*

SERIE	ART.-NO	PERIOD	PR.	INFO
	3785/25	1980-1983	3	25 cm

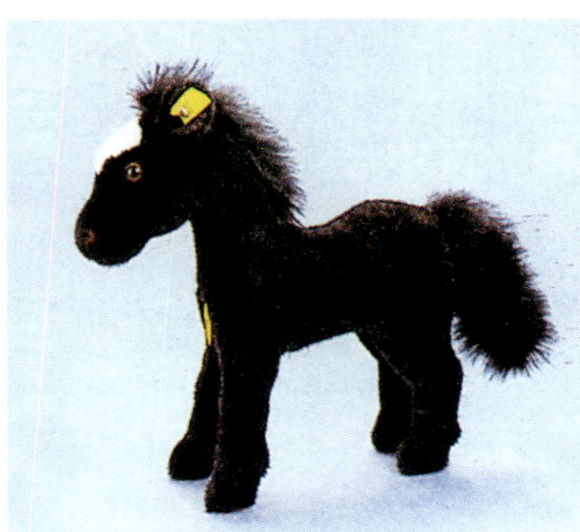

Racy Pferd - ***Racy*** *Horse*

Webpelz, schwarz, stehend, abwaschbar - *woven fur, black, standing, surface washable*

SERIE	ART.-NO	PERIOD	PR.	INFO
	3780/25	1980-1984	2-3	25 cm

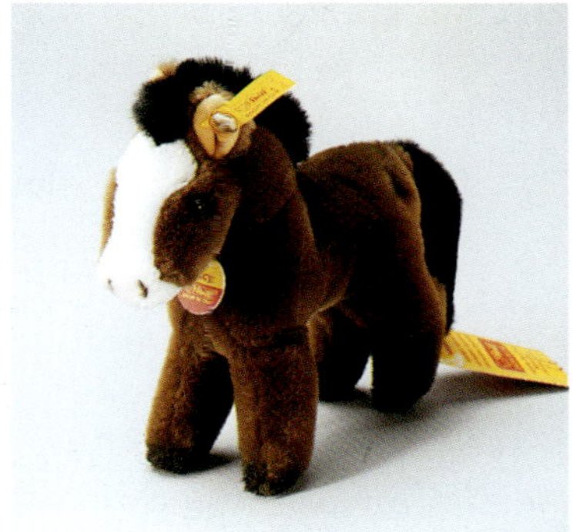

Racy Pferd - ***Racy*** *Horse*

Webpelz, stehend, waschmaschinenfest - *woven fur, standing, machine washable*

SERIE	ART.-NO	PERIOD	PR.	INFO
052552	**1522/14**	1987-1990	2	14 cm
	052552	1991-1999	2	

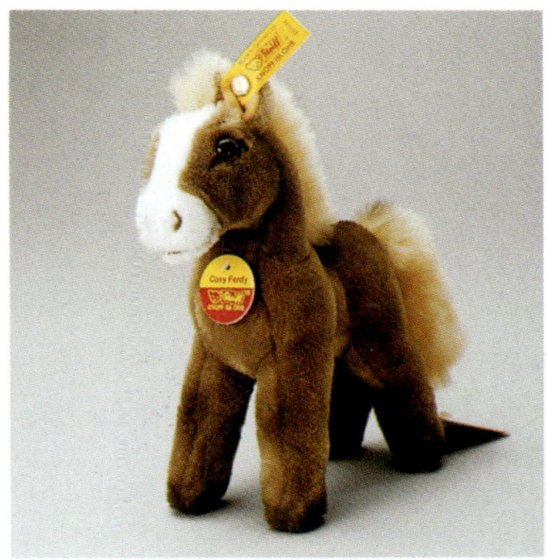

Cosy Ferdy Pferd - ***Cosy Ferdy*** *Horse*

Webpelz, braun, stehend, superweich, waschmaschinenfest - *woven fur, brown, standing, super soft, machine washable*

SERIE	ART.-NO	PERIOD	PR.	INFO
097522	**5475/20**	1986-1990	2	20 cm
	097522	1991-1999	2	
097546	**5475/28**	1985-1990	2-3	28 cm
	097546	1991-1999	2-3	

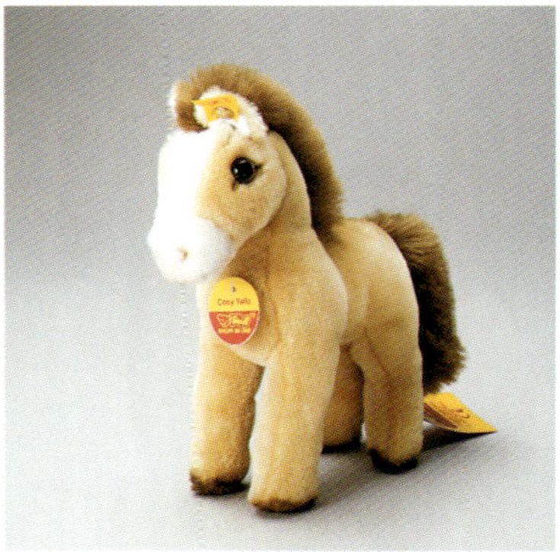

Cosy Yello Pferd - ***Cosy Yello*** *Horse*

Webpelz, beige, stehend, superweich, waschmaschinenfest - *woven fur, beige, standing, super soft, machine washable*

SERIE	ART.-NO	PERIOD	PR.	INFO
097621	**5476/20**	1986-1990	2	20 cm
	097621	1991-1996	2	

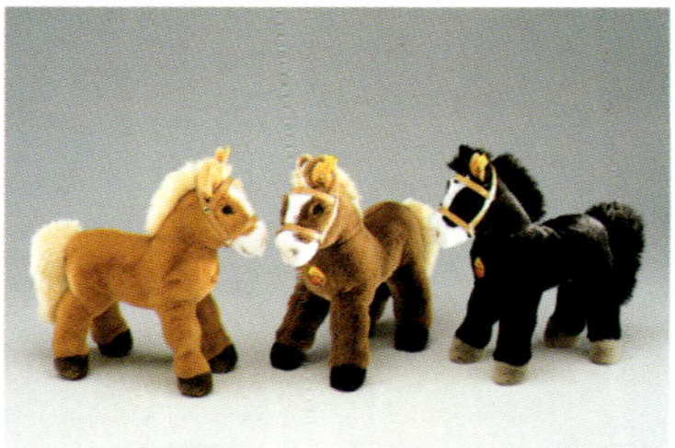

Ferdy Pferd - ***Ferdy*** *Horse*

Webpelz, blond, braun oder schwarz, Leder-Kopfgeschirr, stehend, ohne Kopfgeschirr waschmaschinenfest - *woven fur, blond, brown or black, leather harness, standing, machine washable without harness*

EAN-NO.	PERIOD	PR.	INFO
072642	1992-1999	3	34 cm, blond
072666	1992-1995	3	44 cm
072703	1992-1999	3	34 cm, braun - *brown*
072727	1992-1995	3	44 cm
072765	1993-1999	3	34 cm, schwarz - *black*
072789	1993-1995	3	44 cm

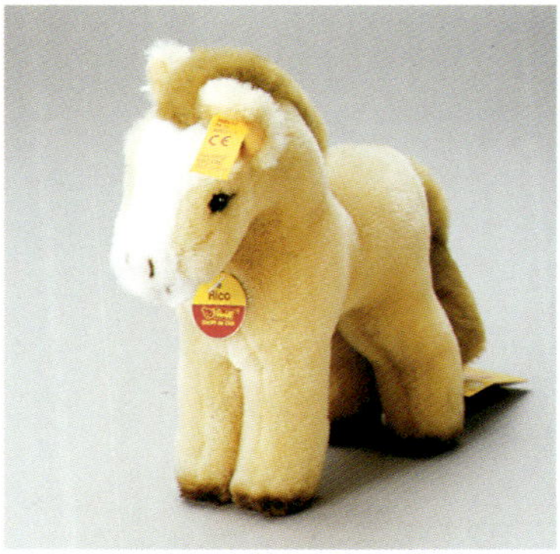

Rico Pferd - ***Rico*** *Horse*

Webpelz, blond, waschmaschinenfest - *woven fur, blond, machine washable*

EAN-NO.	PERIOD	PR.	INFO
052576	1994-1996	1-2	16 cm

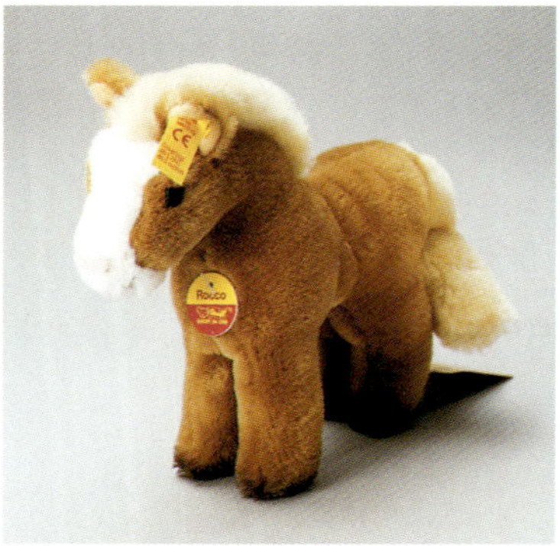

Rocco Pferd - ***Rocco*** *Horse*

Webpelz, hellbraun, waschmaschinenfest - *woven fur, light brown, machine washable*

EAN-NO.	PERIOD	PR.	INFO
052590	1994-1999	2	15 cm

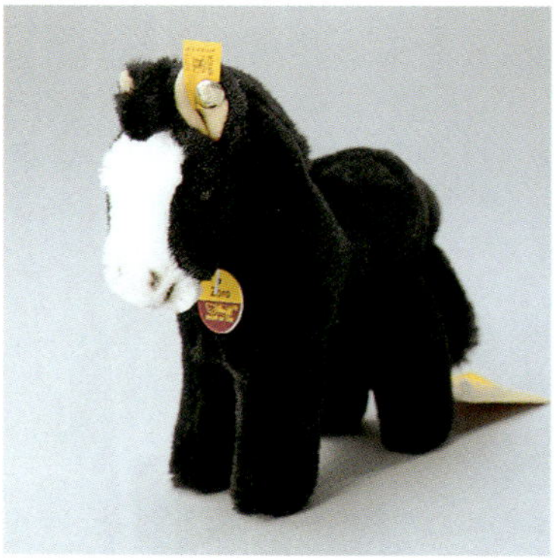

Zoro Pferd - ***Zoro*** *Horse*

Webpelz, schwarz, waschmaschinenfest - *woven fur, black, machine washable*

EAN-NO.	PERIOD	PR.	INFO
052613	1994-1996	1-2	16 cm

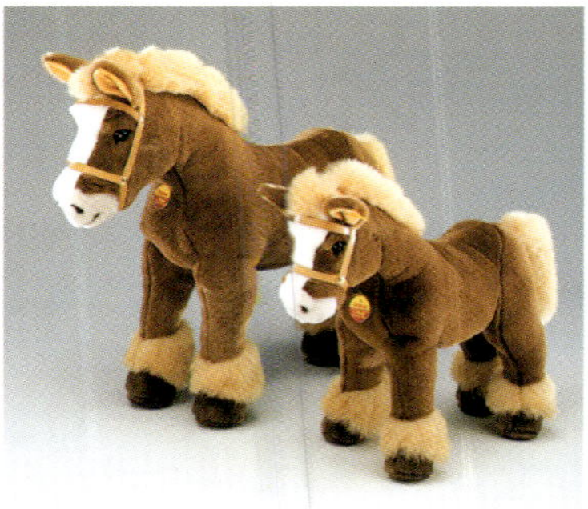

Pferd - *Horse*

Webpelz, braun, stehend, 37 cm hand-, 47 cm abwaschbar, mit Zaumzeug aus Leder - *woven fur, brown, standing, leather harness, 37 cm hand-, 47 cm surface washable without harness*

EAN-NO.	PERIOD	PR.	INFO
072611	1996-1997	3	37 cm
072628	1996-1997	3-4	47 cm

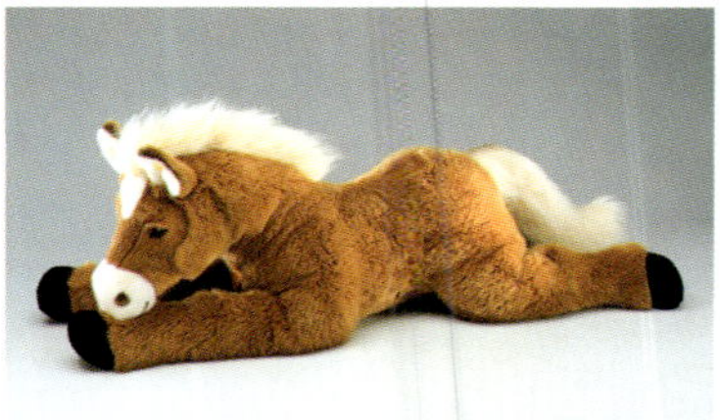

Molly Pferd - ***Molly*** *Horse*

Webpelz, braun, liegend, abwaschbar - *woven fur, brown, lying, surface washable*

EAN-NO.	PERIOD	PR.	INFO
103278	1996-1997	4	100 cm

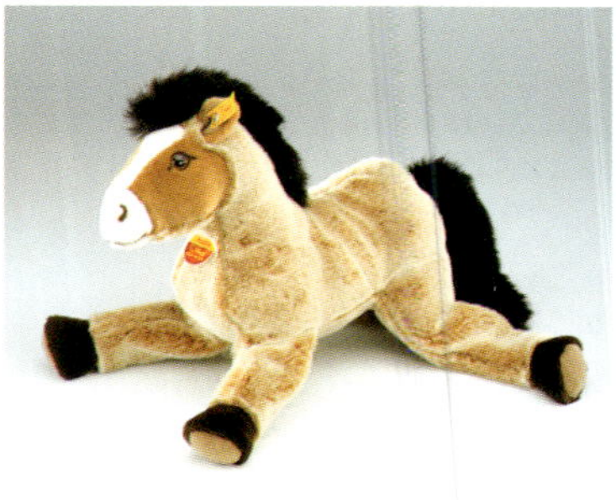

Poppy Pferd - ***Poppy*** *Horse*

Webpelz, hellbraun, waschmaschinenfest - *woven fur, light brown, machine washable*

EAN-NO.	PERIOD	PR.	INFO
124112	1998-1999	2-3	35 cm

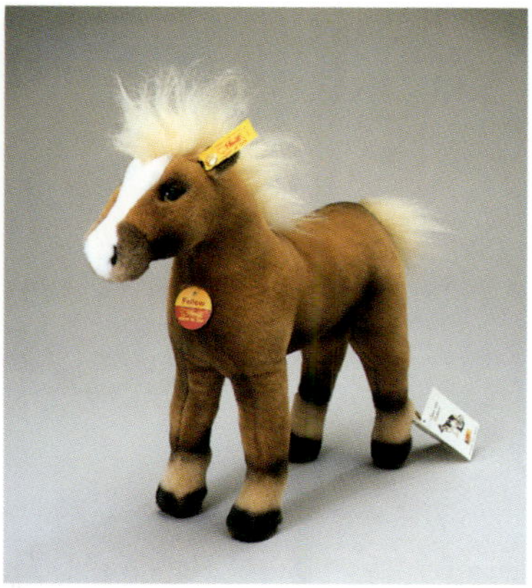

Fellow Pferd - ***Fellow** Horse*

Webpelz, hellbraun, stehend, abwaschbar - *woven fur, light brown, standing, surface washable*

EAN-No.	Period	Pr.	Info
072772	1999-1999	3	35 cm

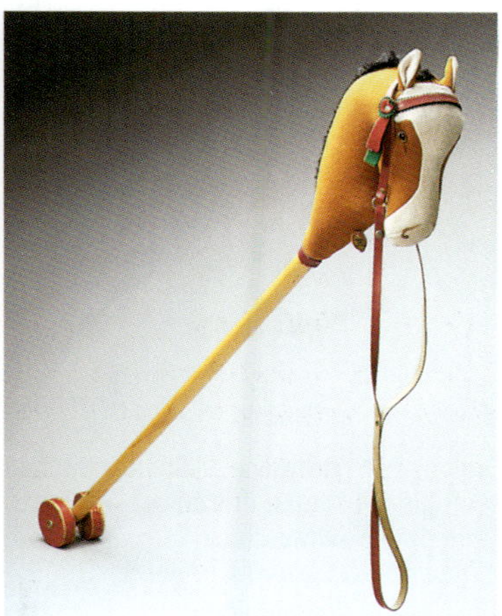

Steckenpferd - *Hobby-Horse*

Filz, Lederzuegel, braun/weiss, 2 Laufrollen am Stockende - *felt, leather reins, brown & white, two wheels at the end of the stick*

Serie	Art.-No	Period	Pr.	Info
56	**150**	1949-1957	4	100 cm
561	**7050,00**	1961-1961	4	
378	**7050,00**	1966-1967	4	
	3780/50	1968-1970	4	

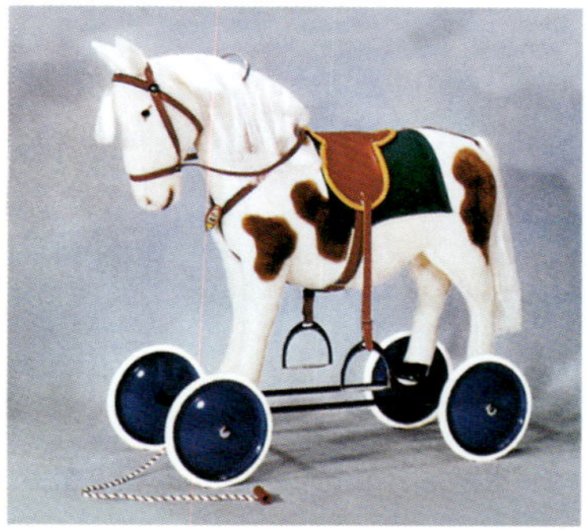

Reit-Pony - *Riding Pony*

Mohairpluesch, Eisengerippe, weiss, braun gefleckt, 1949 mit Holzrollen, ab 1950 Metallscheibenraeder mit Gummi-, ab 1967 Plastikreifen & Kunststofflager, Ledersattel & -zuegel, Zugstimme, Haltegriff, ab 50 cm Steigbuegel, ab 1953 auch mit Lenkung erhaeltlich (,34 statt ,24), ab 1968 Schlepplenkung - *mohair, metal frame, white/brown spotted, 1949 wooden wheels, from 1950 metal disc wheels with rubber tires, from 1967 plastic tires & bearings, leather saddle & reins, pull cord voice, grip handle, from 50 cm with stirrups, from 1953 also available with steering (,34 instead ,24), from 1968 pull type steering*

Serie	Art.-No	Period	Pr.	Info
56	**1342** bw	1949-1949	6	42 cm
56	**1343,2** w	1950-1958	5-6	43 cm
560	**1343,24**	1959-1962	5-6	
372	**1343,24**	1966-1967	5-6	
	3704/43	1968-1969	5	
56	**1349** bw	1949-1949	6	49 cm
56	**1350,2** w	1950-1958	5-6	50 cm
560	**1350,24**	1959-1962	5-6	
372	**1350,24**	1966-1967	5-6	
	3704/50	1968-1970	5	
56	**1360,2** w	1950-1958	6	60 cm
560	**1360,24**	1959-1962	5-6	
372	**1360,24**	1966-1967	5-6	
	3704/60	1968-1970	5	
56	**1380,2** w	1951-1957	6	80 cm
560	**1380,24**	1961-1961	5-6	
372	**1380,24**	1966-1967	5-6	
	3704/80	1968-1970	5-6	
56	**13100,2** w	1951-1957	6	100 cm
560	**1399,24**	1961-1961	5-6	
372	**1399,24**	1966-1966	5-6	

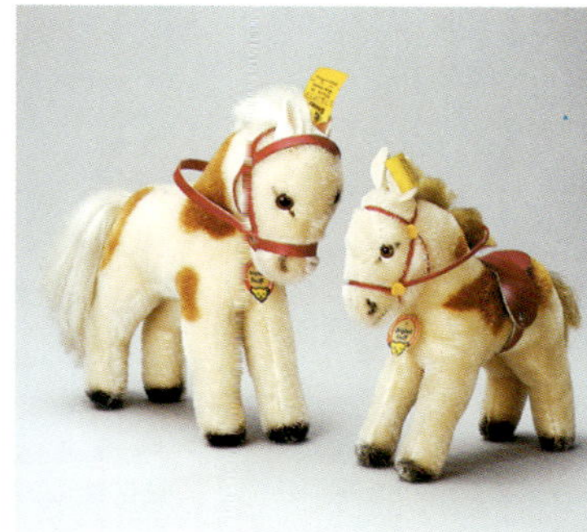

Pony

Mohair, weiss, braun gefleckt, stehend, 12 cm mit Ledersattel, Garnhalfter & Kunststoffzuegel, 17 cm Lederhalfter & -zuegel, abwaschbar - *mohair, white/brown spotted, standing, 12 cm leather saddle, knitted halter & plastic reins, 17 cm leather halter & reins, surface washable*

Serie	Art.-No	Period	Pr.	Info
56	**1312,0**	1951-1958	4	12 cm
560	**1312,00**	1959-1964	3-4	
375	**1312,00**	1965-1967	3-4	
	3750/12	1968-1976	3	
56	**1317,0**	1952-1957	4	17 cm
560	**1317,00**	1960-1961	4	
375	**1317,00**	1966-1967	4	
	3750/17	1968-1976	3-4	

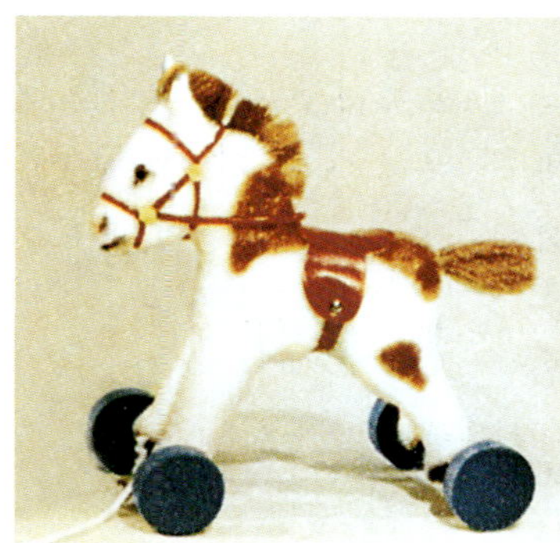

Nachzieh-Pony - *Pull Toy Pony*

Mohair, weiss, braun gefleckt, stehend auf Exzenterraedern - *mohair, white/brown spotted, standing, on eccentric wheels*

Serie	Art.-No	Period	Pr.	Info
81 56	**1312** ex	1954-1957	4-5	12 cm
810 560	**1312,10**	1960-1960	4-5	

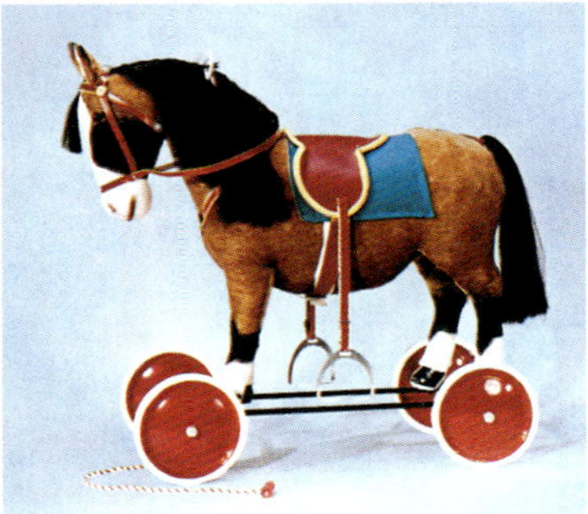

Reit-Pony - *Riding Pony*

bis 1954 auch als "Luxusausfuehrung" bezeichnet, Mohairpluesch, Eisengerippe, braun/schwarz/weiss, Metallscheibenraeder mit Gummireifen, Ledersattel & -zuegel, Zugstimme, Haltegriff, ab 50 cm Steigbuegel, ab 1953 auch mit Lenkung erhaeltlich (,33 statt ,23) - *up to 1954, also called the "luxury model", mohair, metal frame, brown/black/white, metal disc wheels & rubber tires, leather saddle & reins, pull cord voice, grip handle, from 50 cm with stirrups, from 1953 also available with steering (,33 instead of ,23)*

SERIE	ART.-NO	PERIOD	PR.	INFO
56	**1343,2** br	1951-1958	5-6	43 cm
560	**1343,23**	1959-1964	5-6	
370	**1343,23**	1966-1966	5-6	
56	**1350,2** br	1951-1958	5-6	50 cm
560	**1350,23**	1959-1964	5-6	
370	**1350,23**	1966-1966	5-6	
56	**1360,2** br	1951-1958	5-6	60 cm
560	**1360,23**	1959-1964	5-6	
370	**1360,23**	1966-1966	5-6	
56	**1380,2** br	1951-1957	6	80 cm
560	**1380,23**	1961-1961	5-6	
370	**1380,23**	1966-1966	5-6	
56	**13100,2** br	1951-1957	6	100 cm
560	**1399,23**	1961-1961	5-6	
370	**1399,23**	1966-1966	5-6	

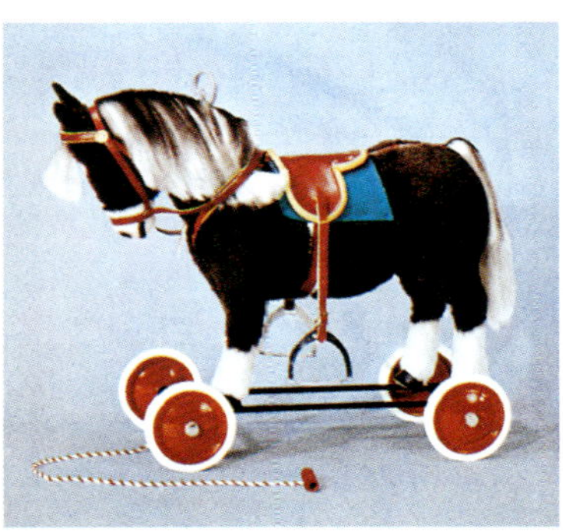

Reit-Pony - *Riding Pony*

Dralon, Stahlgerippe, braun, roter Ledersattel, Steigbuegel, Haltegriff, gummibereifte Scheibenraeder, ab 1967 Plastikreifen & Kunststofflager, Zugstimme, Schlepplenkung, abwaschbar - *dralon, metal frame, brown, red leather saddle, stirrups, grip handle, disc wheels with rubber tires, from 1967 plastic tires & bearings, pull cord voice, pull type steering, surface washable*

SERIE	ART.-NO	PERIOD	PR.	INFO
370	**1643,23**	1965-1967	4	43 cm
	3703/43	1968-1975	4	
370	**1650,23**	1965-1967	4	50 cm
	3703/50	1968-1975	4	
370	**1660,23**	1965-1967	4	60 cm
	3703/60	1968-1975	4	
370	**1680,23**	1965-1967	4-5	80 cm
	3703/80	1968-1975	4-5	

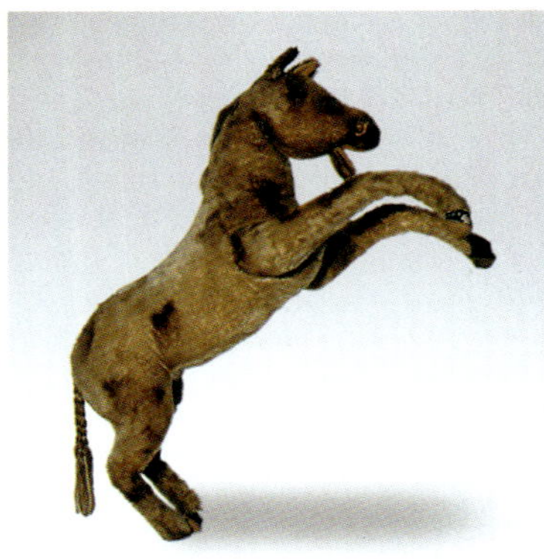

Studio Pony

Mohair, weiss/hellbraun, offener Mund, kein Katalognachweis bekannt - *mohair, white/ light brown, open mouth, no catalog information available*

EAN-NO.	PERIOD	PR.	INFO
	1960-1960	5	85 cm

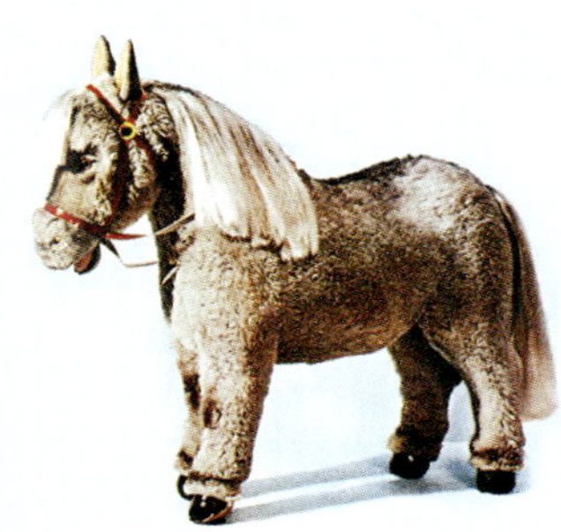

Shetland Pony

Schautier, Alpaka, grau/schwarz, stehend - *display animal, Alpaca, grey/black, standing*

SERIE	ART.-NO	PERIOD	PR.	INFO
562	**1599,96**	1960-1960	6	100 cm
	3769/10	1967-1967	6	

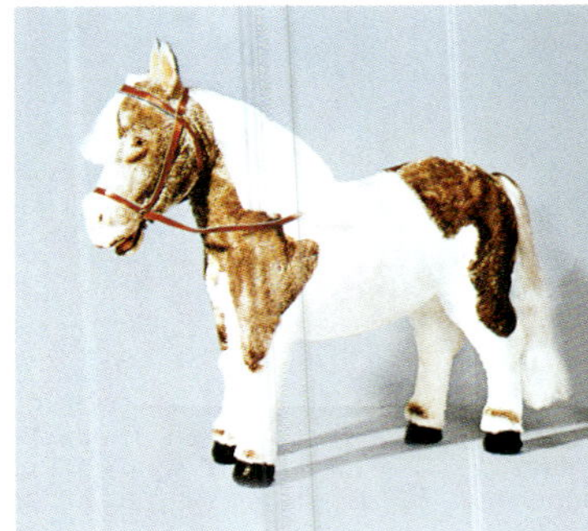

Shetland Pony

Schautier, Dralon, weiss, braun gefleckt, stehend - *display animal, dralon, white/ brown spotted, standing*

SERIE	ART.-NO	PERIOD	PR.	INFO
562	**1699,94**	1960-1960	6	100 cm
	3779/10	1967-1967	6	

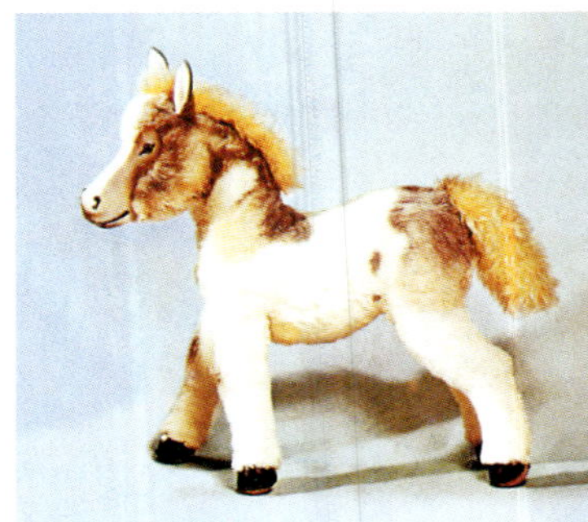

Shetland Pony **Sheddy**

Dralon, weiss/hellbraun, stehend, zwischen 1965 bis 1967 auch mit Zusatz "im Steiff-Kinderbuch", abwaschbar - *dralon, white & light brown, standing, between 1965 & 1967 also with supplement "im Steiff-Kinderbuch", surface washable*

SERIE	ART.-NO	PERIOD	PR.	INFO
562	**1622,00**	1960-1964	3	22 cm
376	**1622,00**	1965-1967	3	
	3760/22	1968-1974	2-3	
562	**1635,00**	1960-1964	3-4	35 cm
376	**1635,00**	1965-1967	3-4	
	3760/35	1968-1973	3	
562	**1650,00**	1960-1964	4	50 cm
376	**1650,00**	1965-1967	4	
	3760/50	1968-1968	4	

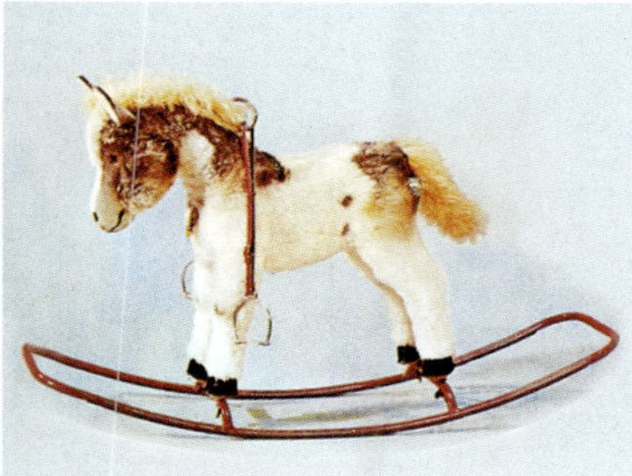

Wiegen-Pony **Sheddy** - *Rocking Pony* ***Sheddy***

Dralon, Stahlgerippe, weiss/hellbraun, abnehmbare Stahlrohr-Wiege, Haltegriff & Steigbuegel - *dralon, metal frame, white & light brown, removable steel tube rocker, grip handle & stirrups*

SERIE	ART.-NO	PERIOD	PR.	INFO
562	**1655,99**	1960-1964	4	55 cm
376	**1655,09**	1965-1967	4	
	3760/55	1968-1969	3-4	

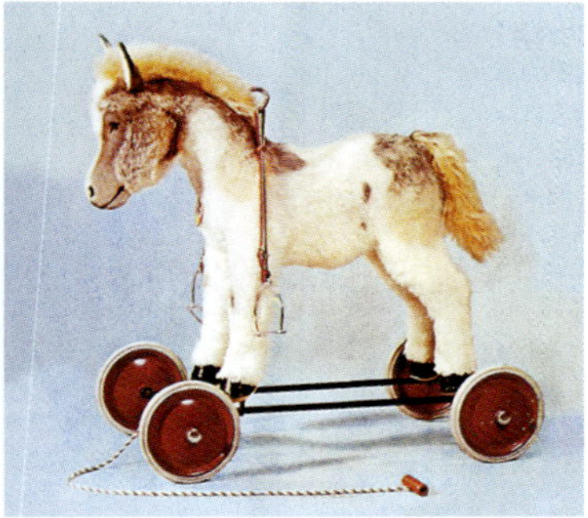

Reit-Pony **Sheddy** - *Riding Pony* ***Sheddy***

Dralon, Stahlgerippe, weiss/hellbraun, Steigbuegel, Haltegriff, gummibereifte Metallscheibenraeder, ab 1967 Plastikreifen & Kunststofflager, abwaschbar - *dralon, metal frame, white & light brown, stirrups, grip handle, metal disc wheels with rubber, from 1967 plastic tires & bearings, surface washable*

SERIE	ART.-NO	PERIOD	PR.	INFO
562	**1660,29**	1960-1964	4	60 cm
376	**1660,29**	1965-1967	4	
	3760/60	1968-1976	4	

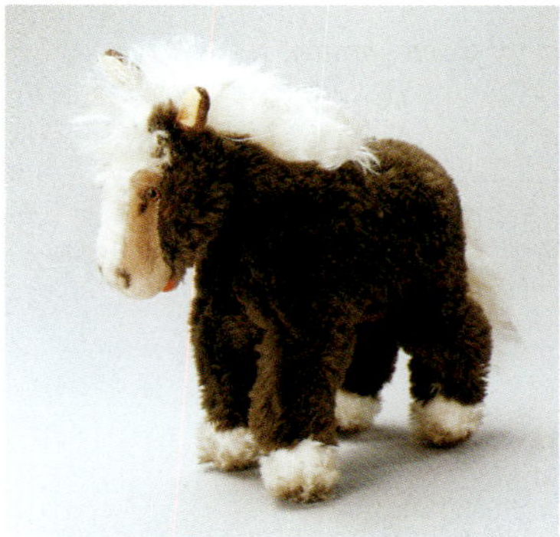

Cosy Pony

Dralon-Pluesch, Schaumgummi-Fuellung, dunkelbraun/weiss, stehend, offener Mund, sehr weich, waschbar - *dralon, stuffed with foam rubber, dark brown & white, standing, open mouth, very soft, washable*

SERIE	ART.-NO	PERIOD	PR.	INFO
830 562	**1628,03**	1964-1964	2-3	28 cm
516	**1628,03**	1965-1967	2-3	
	5160/28	1968-1978	2	

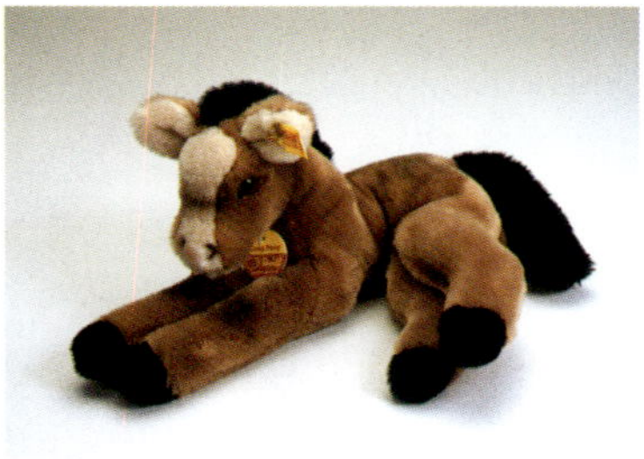

Cosy Pony

Webpelz, liegend, kuschelweich, waschmaschinenfest - *woven fur, lying, soft & cuddly, machine washable*

SERIE	ART.-NO	PERIOD	PR.	INFO
	5360/25	1982-1985	2	25 cm
	5360/40	1980-1984	2-3	40 cm

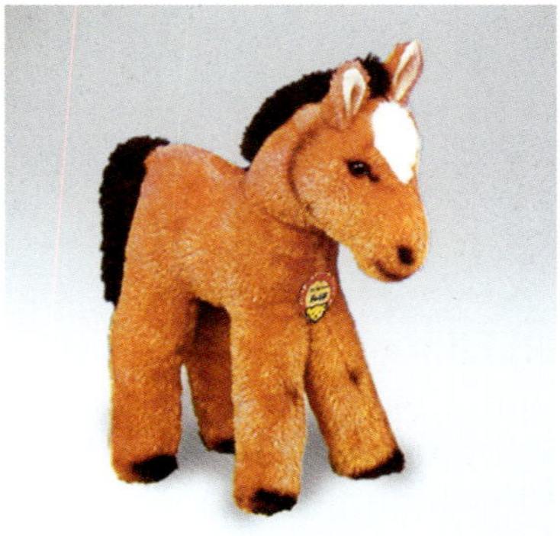

Pony

Dralon, geschaeumt, hellbraun, stehend, vollwaschbar - *dralon, stuffed with foam, light brown, standing, fully washable*

SERIE	ART.-NO	PERIOD	PR.	INFO
	3745/30	1971-1976	2-3	30 cm

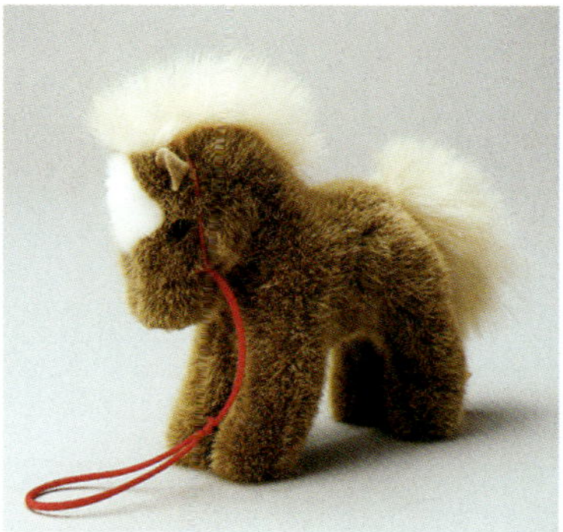

Stompy Pony

Nerzimitation, ab 1978 Synthetik-Webpelz, stehend, abwaschbar - *imitation mink, from 1978 synthetic woven fur, standing, surface washable*

SERIE	ART.-NO	PERIOD	PR.	INFO
052200	**1516/14**	1977-1986	2	14 cm

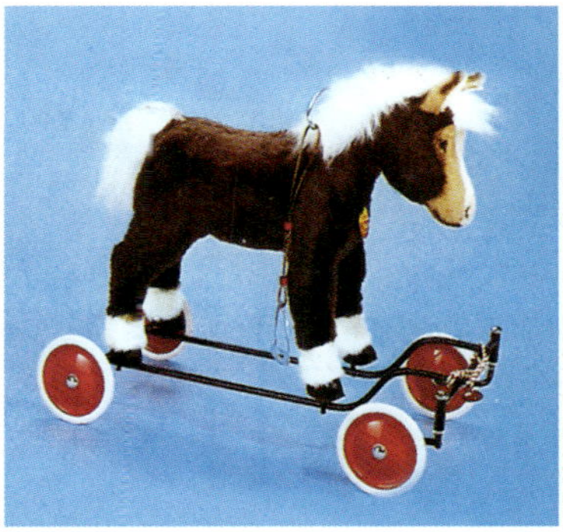

Reit-Pony - *Riding Pony*

Dralon, Stahlrohrgestell, dunkelbraun, Schlepplenkung, Scheibenraeder mit Plastikreifen, abwaschbar - *dralon, steel tubular frame, dark brown, pull type steering, disc wheels with plastic tires, surface washable*

SERIE	ART.-NO	PERIOD	PR.	INFO
	3710/60	1971-1980	4	60 cm
	8175/60	1981-1983	4	

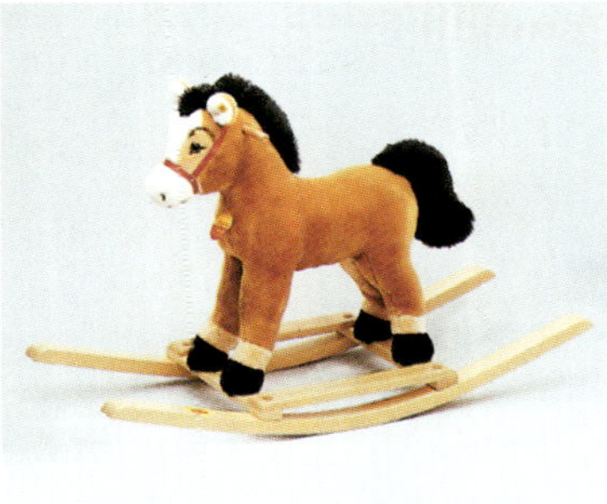

Schaukel Pony - *Rocking Pony*

Webpelz, Holzwiege, abwaschbar - *woven fur, wooden rocker, surface washable*

SERIE	ART.-NO	PERIOD	PR.	INFO
480508	**8135/50**	1982-1990	4-5	50 cm

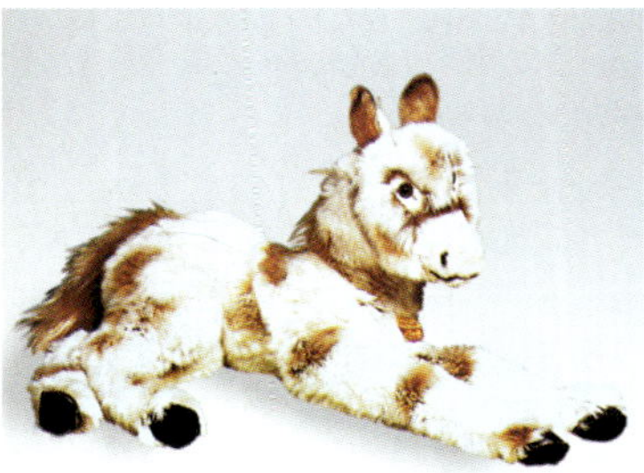

Molly Pony

Pelz-Imitation, abwaschbar - *imitation fur, surface washable*

SERIE	ART.-NO	PERIOD	PR.	INFO
	0336/80	1974-1977	3	80 cm

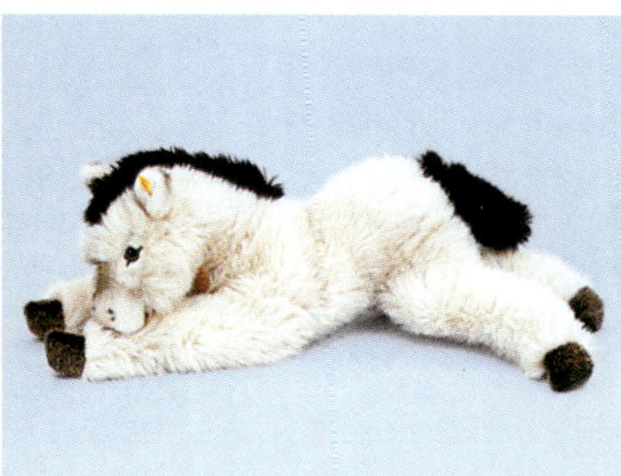

Molly Pony

Webpelz, mollig weich, abwaschbar - *woven fur, soft & cozy, surface washable*

SERIE	ART.-NO	PERIOD	PR.	INFO
	0336/55	1981-1984	2-3	55 cm

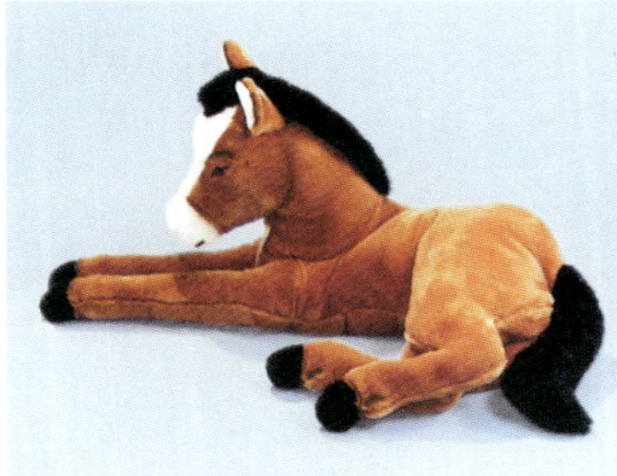

Super Molly Pony

Webpelz, mollig weich, abwaschbar - *woven fur, soft & cozy, surface washable*

SERIE	ART.-NO	PERIOD	PR.	INFO
103353	**0366/99**	1983-1986	3-4	110 cm

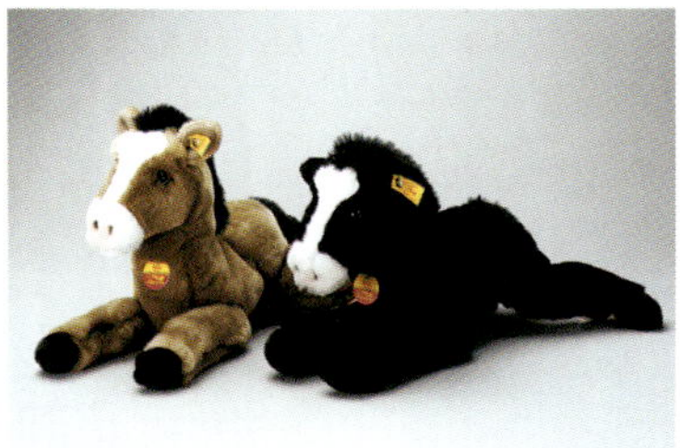

Molly Pony

Webpelz, braun oder schwarz, waschmaschinenfest - *woven fur, brown or black, machine washable*

SERIE	ART.-NO	PERIOD	PR.	INFO
103308	**0365/40**	1988-1990	2-3	40 cm, braun - *brown*
	103308	1991-1999	2-3	
103322	**0365/50**	1987-1990	2-3	50 cm
103384	**0367/40**	1988-1990	2-3	40 cm, schwarz - *black*
	103384	1991-1999	2-3	

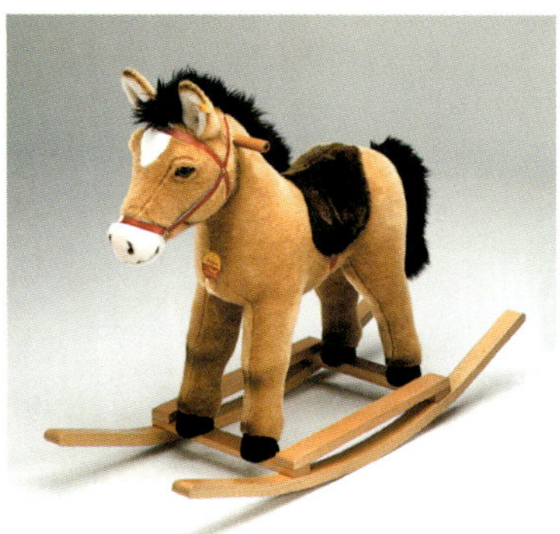

Reit-Pony - *Riding Pony*

Webpelz, Metall-Innengestell, Holzschaukel, Kopfgeschirr, abwaschbar - *woven fur, metal frame, wooden rocker, harness, surface washable*

EAN-NO.	PERIOD	PR.	INFO
480607	1991-1999	5-6	80 cm

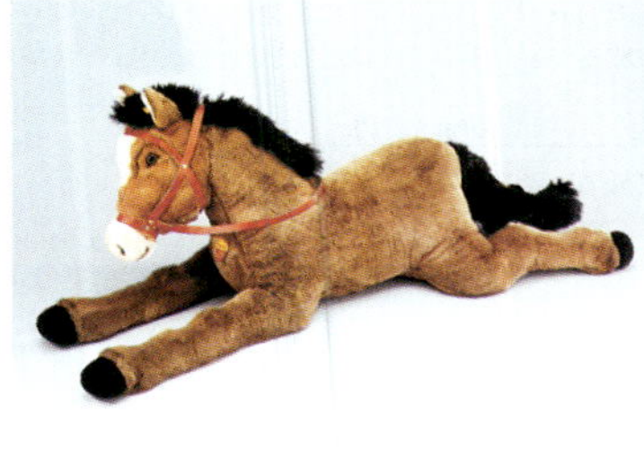

Super Molly Pony

Webpelz, Leder-Kopfgeschirr, liegend, abwaschbar - *woven fur, leather bridle & reins, lying, surface washable*

EAN-NO.	PERIOD	PR.	INFO
103346	1991-1993	4	125 cm

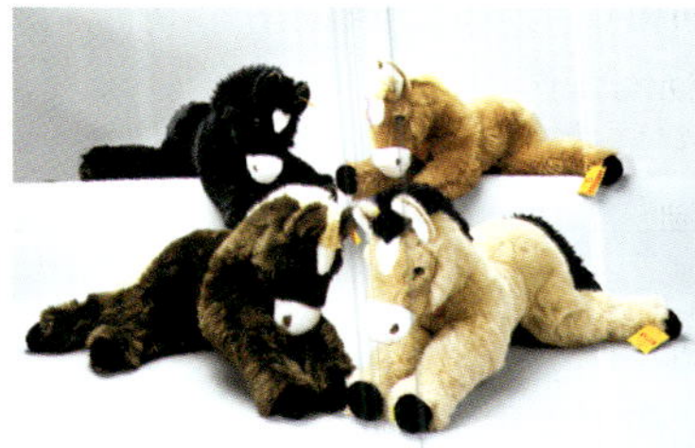

Molly Pony

Webpelz, blond, braun, dunkelbraun oder schwarz, liegend, waschmaschinenfest - *woven fur, blond, brown, dark brown or black, lying, machine washable*

EAN-NO.	PERIOD	PR.	INFO
101601	1992-1996	3	50 cm, blond
101625	1992-1997	3	60 cm
101656	1992-1999	3	50 cm, braun - *brown*
101670	1992-1996	3	60 cm
101700	1993-1995	3	50 cm, dunkelbraun - *dark brown*
101724	1993-1996	3	60 cm
101779	1995-1999	3	50 cm, schwarz - *black*

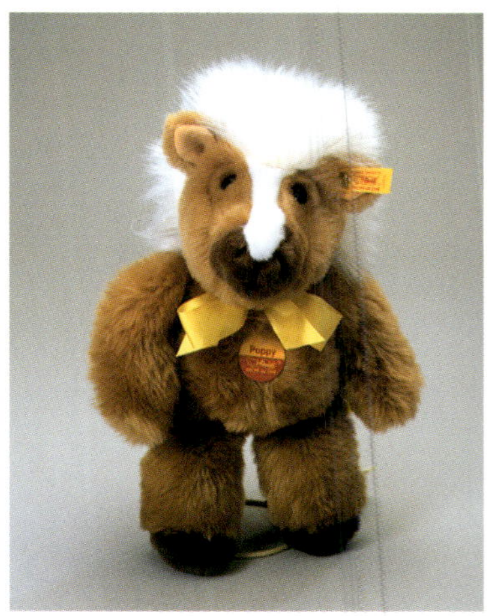

Poppy Pony

Webpelz, hellbraun, waschmaschinenfest - *woven fur, light brown, machine washable*

EAN-No.	Period	Pr.	Info
123214	1999-1999	2-3	30 cm

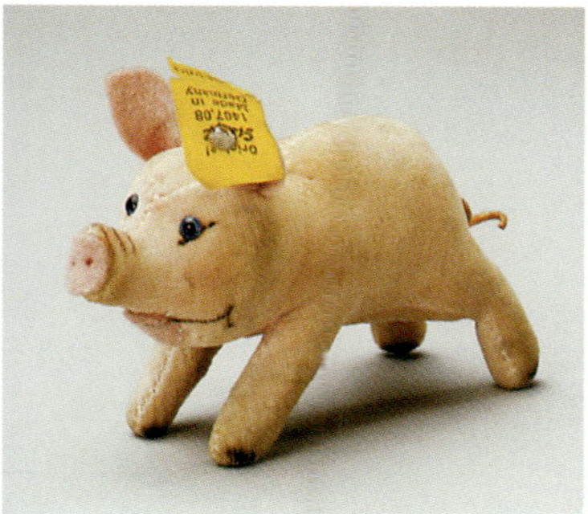

Jolanthe Schwein - ***Jolanthe** Pig*

Samt, rosa, stehend, keine Halsmarke - *velvet, pink, standing, no chest label*

Serie	Art.-No	Period	Pr.	Info
64	**1407,01**	1952-1958	3-4	7 cm
640	**1407,08**	1959-1964	3-4	
396	**1407,08**	1965-1967	3-4	
	3970/07	1963-1975	3	

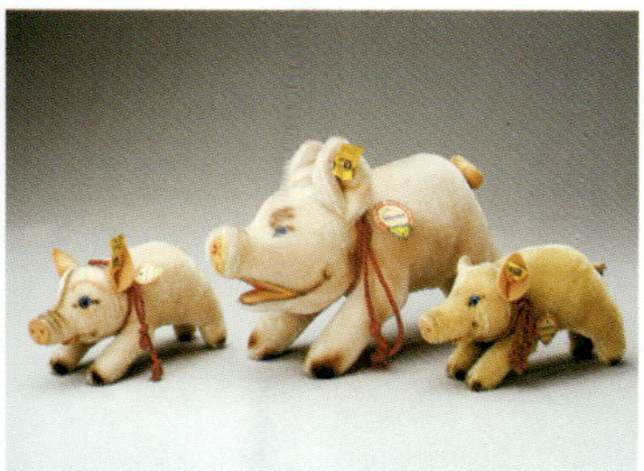

Jolanthe Schwein - ***Jolanthe** Pig*

Mohair, rosa, stehend, gruene oder rote Kordel, abwaschbar - *mohair, pink, standing, green or red neck cord, surface washable*

Serie	Art.-No	Period	Pr.	Info
64	**1310,0**	1951-1957	3-4	10 cm
640	**1310,03**	1960-1963	3	
397	**1310,08**	1966-1967	3	
	3970/10	1968-1977	3	
64	**1317,01**	1952-1957	4-5	17 cm
640	**1317,08**	1960-1961	4-5	
397	**1317,08**	1966-1967	4-5	
	3970/17	1968-1972	4	
64	**1322,01**	1952-1957	5	22 cm
640	**1322,08**	1960-1961	4-5	

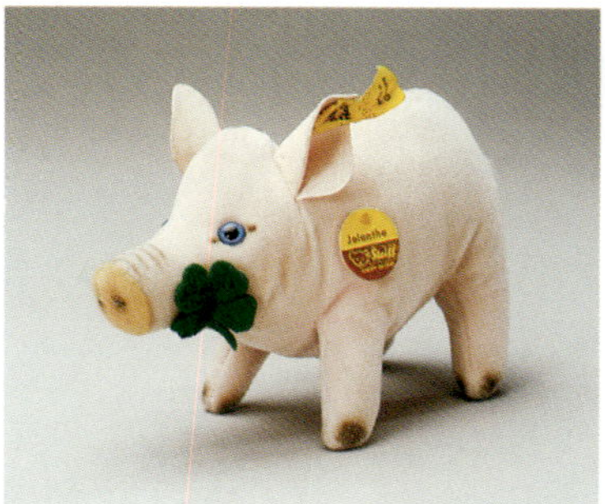

Jolanthe Schwein - ***Jolanthe** Pig*

Trevirasamt, rosa, stehend, abwaschbar - *trevira velvet, pink, standing, surface washable*

Serie	Art.-No	Period	Pr.	Info
	3970/10	1978-1978	3	10 cm

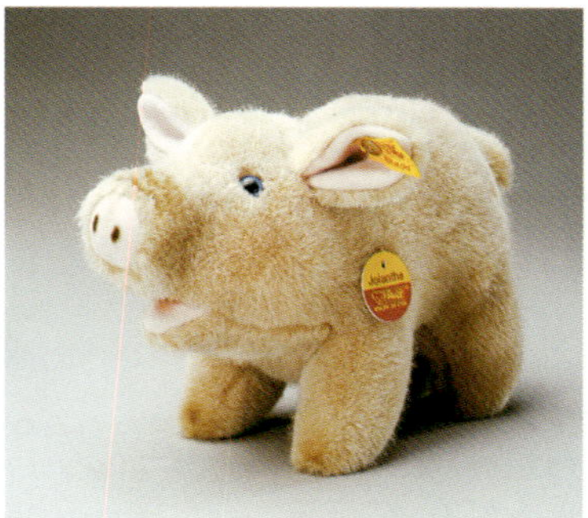

Jolanthe Schwein - ***Jolanthe** Pig*

Webpelz, stehend, abwaschbar - *woven fur, standing, surface washable*

Serie	Art.-No	Period	Pr.	Info
077982	**3810/17**	1979-1990	2	17 cm
	077982	1991-1992	2	
	072406	1993-1993	2	

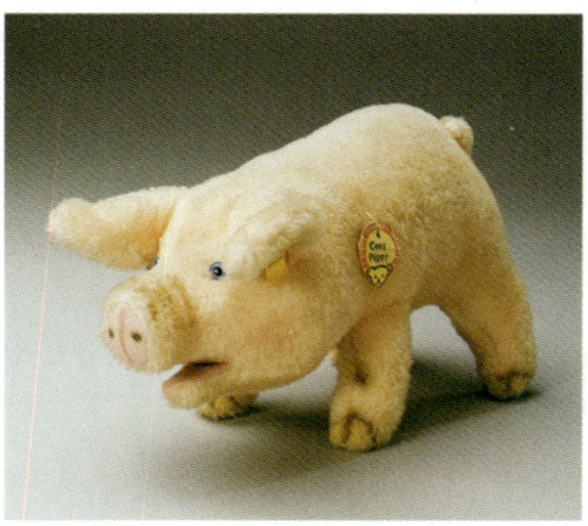

Cosy Piggy Schwein - ***Cosy Piggy** Pig*

Dralon, gefuellt mit synthetischen Fasern, rosa, stehend, waschbar - *dralon, stuffed with synthetic fibers, pink, standing, washable*

Serie	Art.-No	Period	Pr.	Info
497	**1620,00**	1966-1967	3-4	20 cm
	4970/20	1968-1968	3-4	

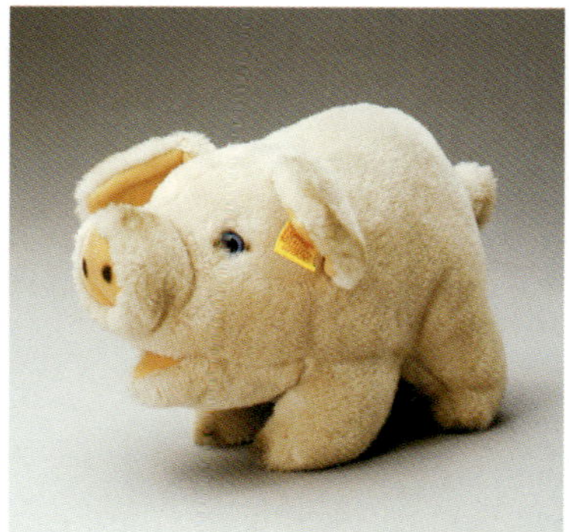

Cosy Piggy Schwein - ***Cosy Piggy** Pig*

Webpelz, stehend, waschmaschinenfest - *woven fur, standing, machine washable*

Serie	Art.-No	Period	Pr.	Info
094507	**5414/18**	1985-1990	2	18 cm
	094507	1991-1999	2	

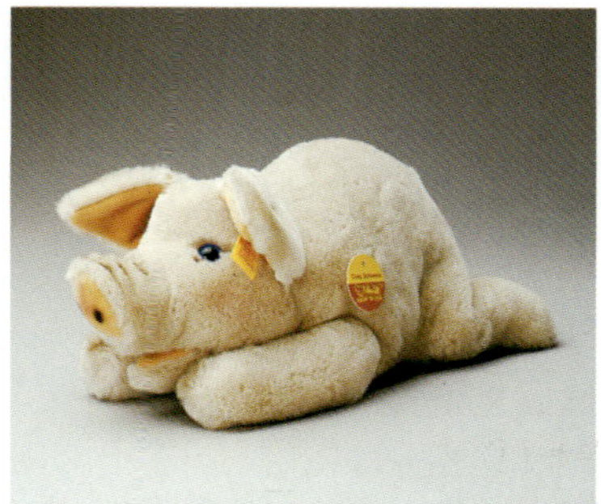

Cosy Schwein - *Cosy Pig*

Webpelz, kuschelweich, waschmaschinenfest - *woven fur, soft & cuddly, machine washable*

Serie	Art.-No	Period	Pr.	Info
094606	**5415/28**	1982-1990	2-3	28 cm
	094606	1991-1996	2-3	

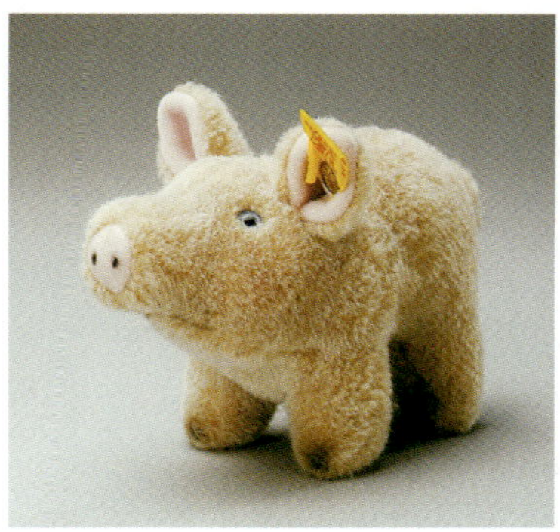

Piggy Schwein - ***Piggy** Pig*

Webpelz, stehend, abwaschbar - *woven fur, standing, surface washable*

Serie	Art.-No	Period	Pr.	Info
052101	**1505/10**	1981-1990	1-2	13 cm
	052101	1991-1999	1-2	

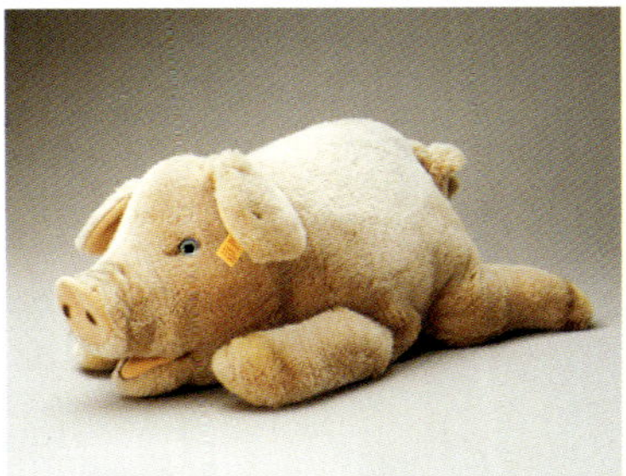

Molly Schwein - *Molly Pig*

Webpelz, mollig weich, abwaschbar - *woven fur, soft & cozy, surface washable*

SERIE	ART.-NO	PERIOD	PR.	INFO
103254	**0360/45**	1981-1990	3	50 cm
	103254	1991-1996	3	

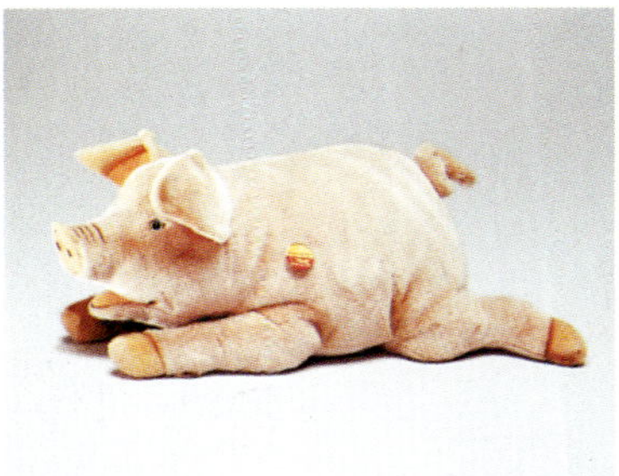

Super Molly Schwein - ***Super Molly*** *Pig*

Webpelz, mollig weich, abwaschbar - *woven fur, soft & cozy, surface washable*

SERIE	ART.-NO	PERIOD	PR.	INFO
103285	**0361/90**	1983-1990	3-4	90 cm
	103285	1991-1991	3-4	

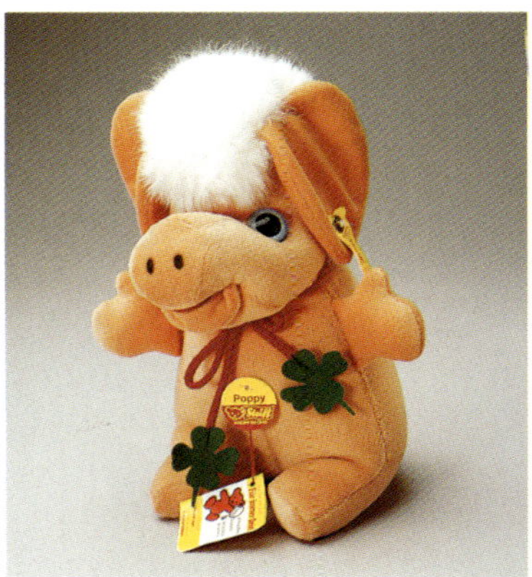

Poppy Schwein - ***Poppy*** *Pig*

Nicki-Stoff, abwaschbar - *nicki velvet, surface washable*

SERIE	ART.-NO	PERIOD	PR.	INFO
	7877/26	1984-1984	3-4	26 cm

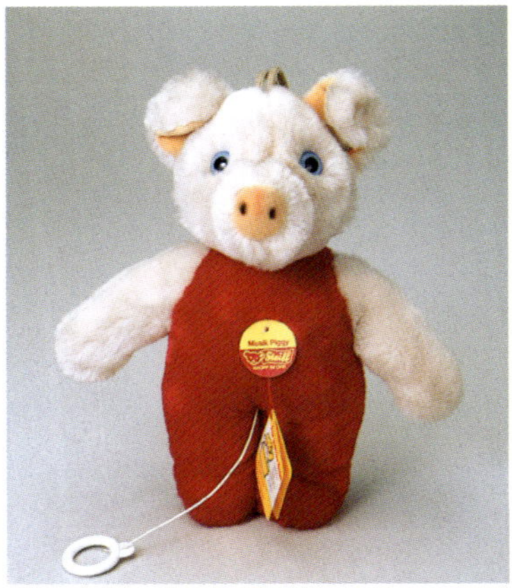

Musik Piggy Schwein - *Music Piggy Pig*

Webpelz, Musikwerk austauschbar, waschbar - *woven fur, music box can be exchanged, washable*

SERIE	ART.-NO	PERIOD	PR.	INFO
231254	**6353/26**	1984-1986	3	26 cm

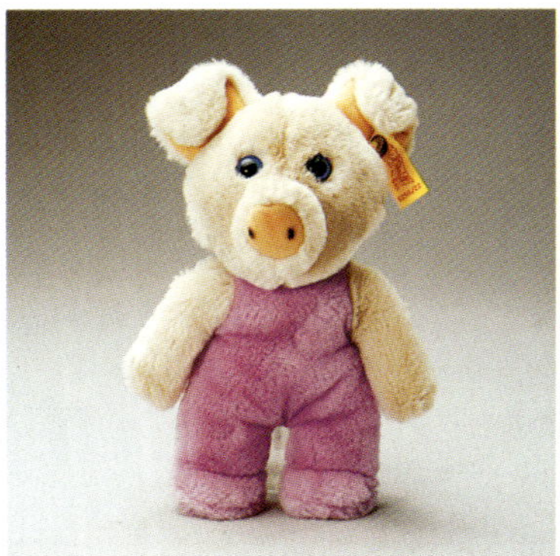

Toldi Schwein - ***Toldi*** *Pig*

Webpelz, Pieps-Stimme, waschmaschinenfest - *woven fur, squeaker, machine washable*

SERIE	ART.-NO	PERIOD	PR.	INFO
080357	**6256/22**	1984-1988	2	22 cm

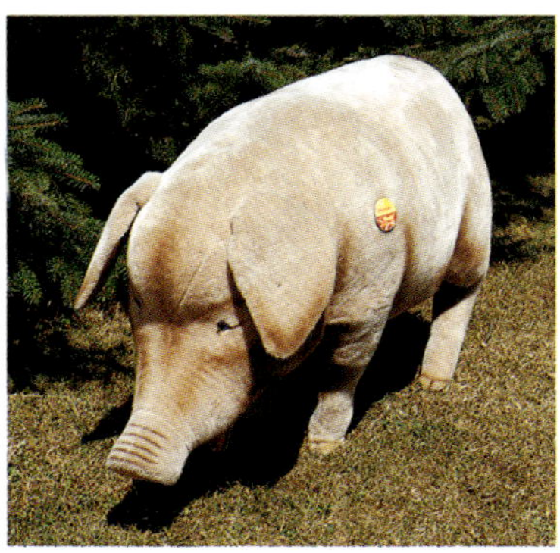

Schwein - *Pig*

Studiotier, Webpelz, ohne Katalognachweis - *studio animal, woven fur, no catalog information available*

SERIE	ART.-NO	PERIOD	PR.	INFO
	7943/70	1980-1980	6	70 cm

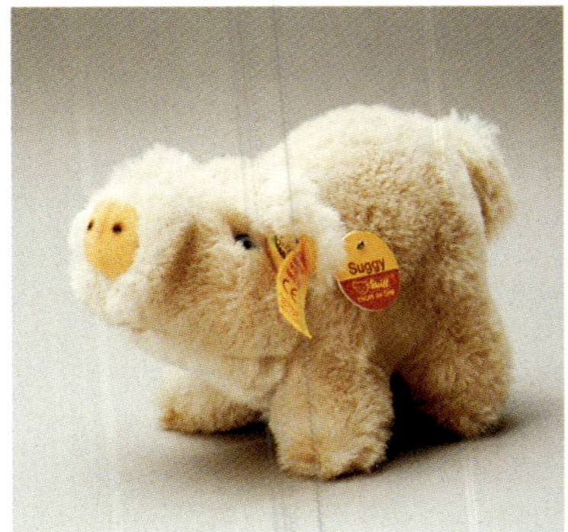

Suggy Schwein - ***Suggy*** *Pig*

Webpelz, waschmaschinenfest - *woven fur, machine washable*

SERIE	ART.-NO	PERIOD	PR.	INFO
052705	**1525/08**	1987-1990	1-2	10 cm
	052705	1991-1999	1-2	

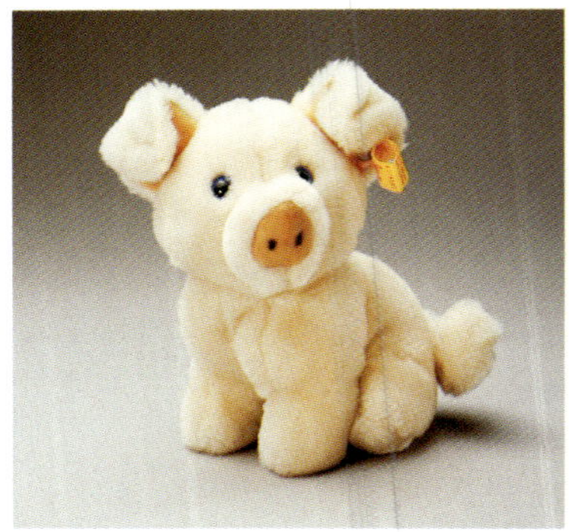

Snuffy Schwein - ***Snuffy*** *Pig*

Webpelz, waschmaschinenfest - *woven fur, machine washable*

SERIE	ART.-NO	PERIOD	PR.	INFO
077265	**2918/18**	1987-1989	2	18 cm

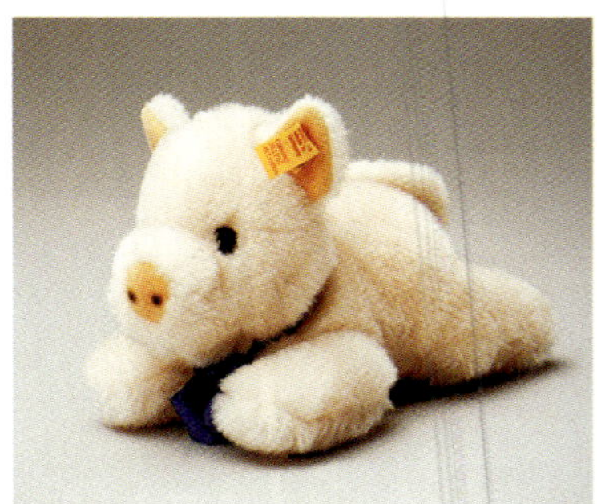

Mini Floppy Schwein - ***Mini Floppy*** *Pig*

Webpelz, waschmaschinenfest - *woven fur, machine washable*

Serie	Art.-No	Period	Pr.	Info
082061	**5675/16**	1989-1990	2	16 cm
	082061	1991-1991	2	

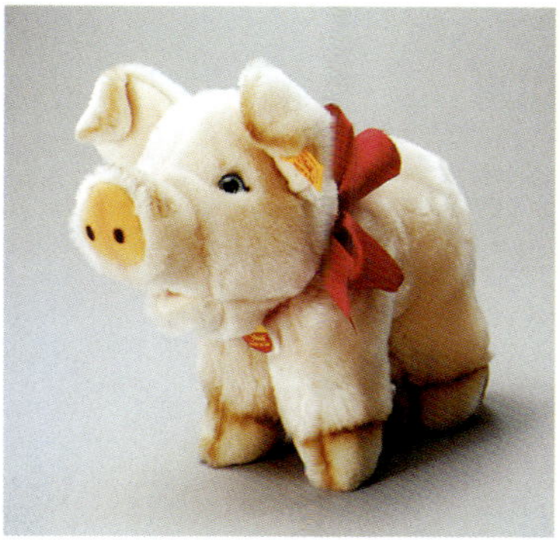

Piggy Schwein - ***Piggy*** *Pig*

Webpelz, stehend, waschmaschinenfest - *woven fur, standing, machine washable*

EAN-No.	Period	Pr.	Info
072413	1992-1999	2	18 cm
072444	1992-1997	2-3	30 cm

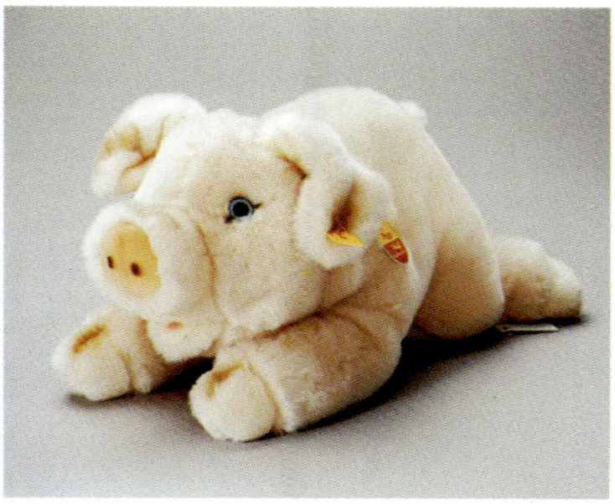

Piggy Schwein - ***Piggy*** *Pig*

Webpelz, liegend, waschmaschinenfest, 90 cm abwaschbar - *woven fur, lying, machine washable, 90 cm surface washable*

EAN-No.	Period	Pr.	Info
072543	1992-1999	2-3	35 cm
072581	1992-1999	3-4	65 cm
072598	1992-1996	4	90 cm

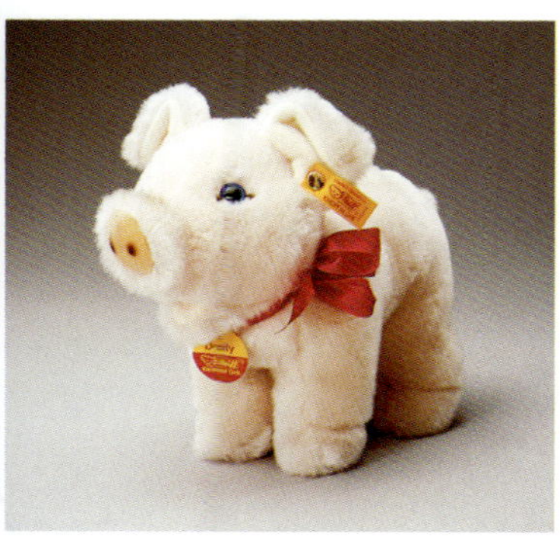

Drolly Schwein - ***Drolly*** *Pig*

Webpelz, waschmaschinenfest - *woven fur, machine washable*

EAN-No.	Period	Pr.	Info
081590	1992-1999	2-3	22 cm

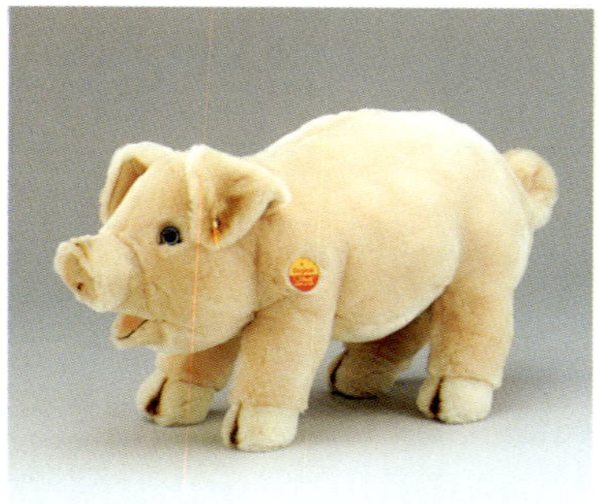

Hausschwein - *Pig*

Webpelz, stehend, handwaschbar - *woven fur, standing, hand washable*

EAN-No.	Period	Pr.	Info
072482	1996-1999	3	50 cm

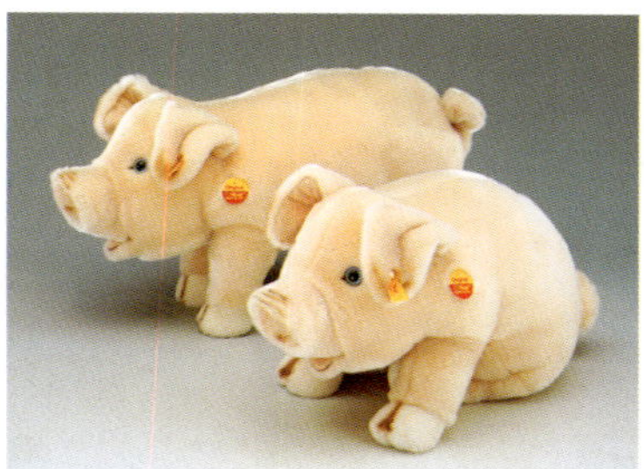

Hausschwein - *Pig*

Webpelz, sitzend, handwaschbar - *woven fur, sitting, hand washable*

EAN-No.	Period	Pr.	Info
072390	1996-1998	3	30 cm

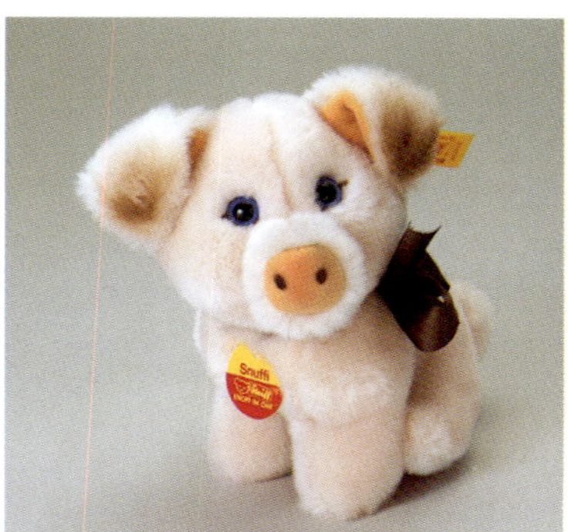

Snuffi Schwein - ***Snuffi*** *Pig*

Webpelz, sitzend, waschmaschinenfest - *woven fur, sitting, machine washable*

EAN-No.	Period	Pr.	Info
077289	1996-1999	2	16 cm

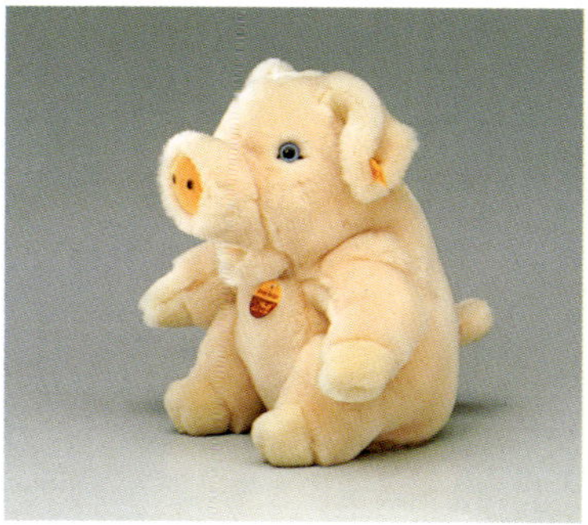

Cosy Suggy Sau - ***Cosy Suggy*** *Pig*

Webpelz, sitzend, waschmaschinenfest - *woven fur, sitting, machine washable*

EAN-No.	Period	Pr.	Info
085512	1996-1997	2-3	28 cm

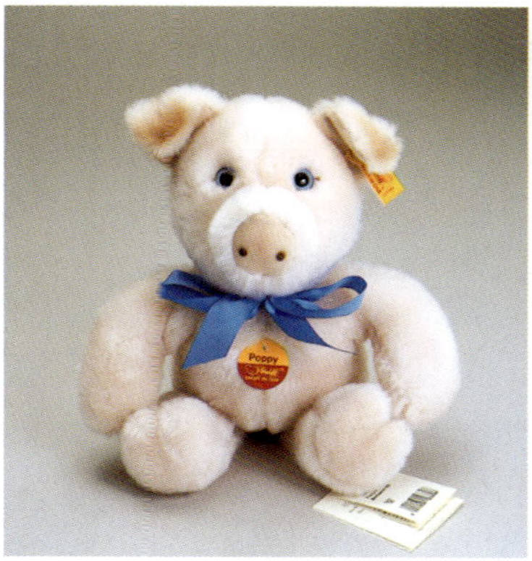

Poppy Schwein - ***Poppy*** *Pig*

Webpelz, waschmaschinenfest - *woven fur, machine washable*

EAN-No.	Period	Pr.	Info
123306	1999-1999	2-3	30 cm

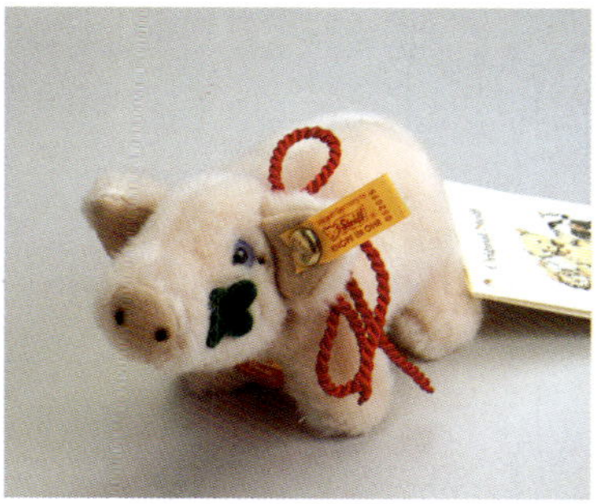

Gluecksschwein - *Lucky Pig*

Webpelz, rosa, stehend, Kleeblatt aus gruenem Filz in der Schnauze, waschmaschinenfest - *woven fur, pink, standing, with green felt cloverleaf in its mouth, machine washable*

EAN-No.	Period	Pr.	Info
052095	1999-1999	1-2	10 cm

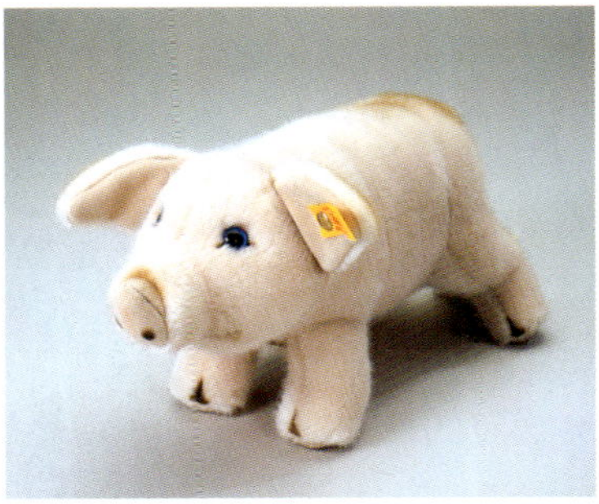

Jolanthe Schwein - ***Jolanthe*** *Pig*

Webpelz, stehend, waschmaschinenfest - *woven fur, standing, machine washable*

EAN-No.	Period	Pr.	Info
072499	1999-1999	2-3	27 cm

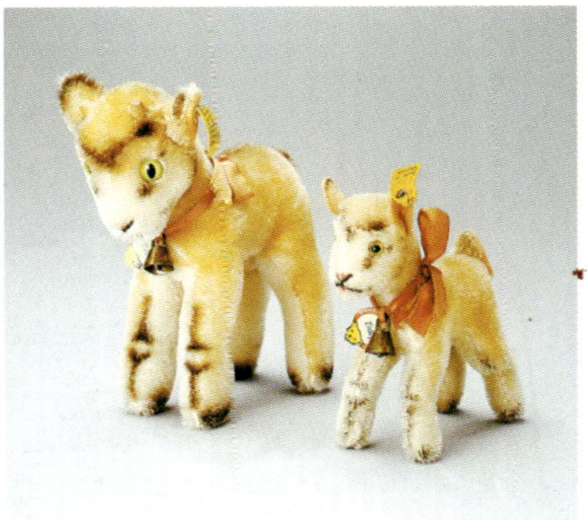

Zicky Ziege - ***Zicky*** *Goat*

Mohair, braun/weiss, stehend - *mohair, brown & white, standing*

Serie	Art.-No	Period	Pr.	Info
74	**6310,0**	1952-1958	3-4	10 cm
740	**6310,00**	1959-1964	3	
355	**6310,00**	1965-1967	3	
	3550/10	1968-1970	3	
74	**6314,0**	1953-1958	3-4	14 cm
740	**6314,00**	1959-1964	3	
355	**6314,00**	1965-1967	3	
	3550/14	1968-1972	3	
74	**6322,0**	1953-1958	4	22 cm
740	**6322,00**	1959-1964	3-4	
355	**6322,00**	1965-1967	3-4	
	3550/22	1968-1971	3-4	
74	**6328,02**	1953-1955	5	28 cm
74	**6335,02**	1953-1958	4-5	35 cm
740	**6335,00**	1959-1964	4-5	

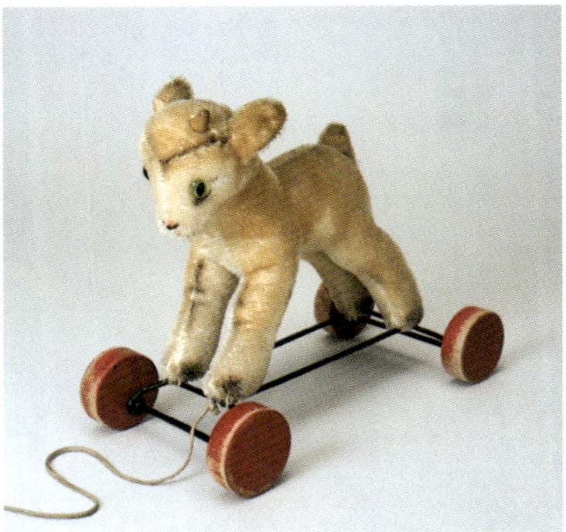

Nachzieh-Ziege - *Pull Toy Goat*

Mohair, braun/weiss, stehend auf Exzenter-Raedern - *mohair, brown & white, standing on eccentric wheels*

Serie	Art.-No	Period	Pr.	Info
74	**6314** ex	1953-1957	4-5	14 cm

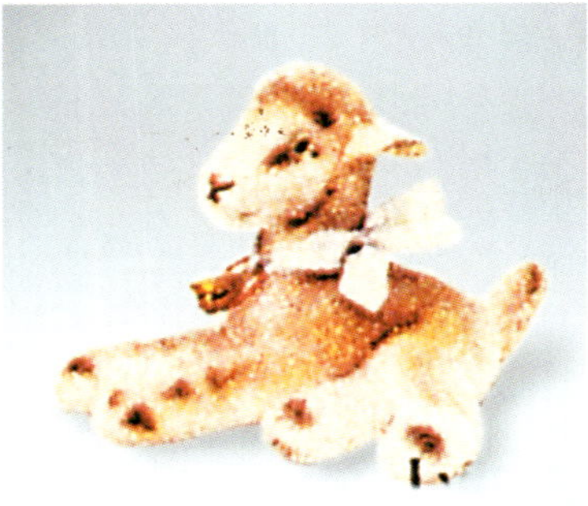

Ziege - *Goat*

Mohair, braun/weiss, liegend - *mohair, brown & white, lying*

Serie	Art.-No	Period	Pr.	Info
74	**2310**	1954-1956	4	10 cm
74	**2314**	1954-1956	4	14 cm

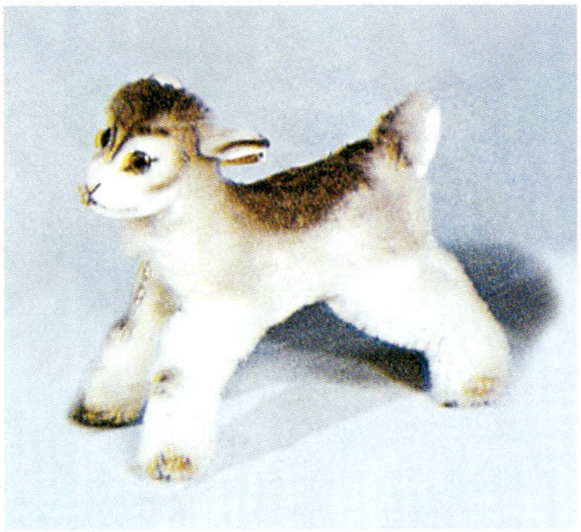

Cosy Boeky

Dralon-Pluesch, Schaumstoff-Fuellung, stehend, sehr weich, waschbar - *dralon, stuffed with foam, standing, very soft, washable*

Serie	Art.-No	Period	Pr.	Info
830 740	**1622,00**	1960-1962	2-3	22 cm

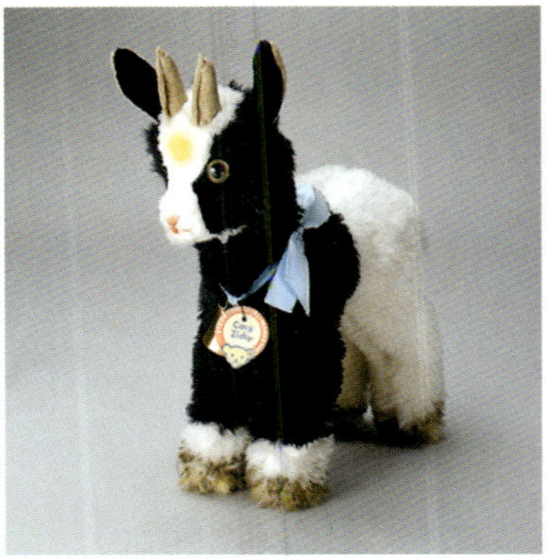

Cosy Zicky Ziege - ***Cosy Zicky*** *Goat*

Dralon, gefuellt mit synthet. Material, schwarz/weiss, stehend, sehr weich, vollwaschbar - *dralon, stuffed with synthetic material, black & white, standing, very soft, fully washable*

Serie	Art.-No	Period	Pr.	Info
496	**6625,00**	1967-1967	3	25 cm
	4960/25	1968-1975	2-3	

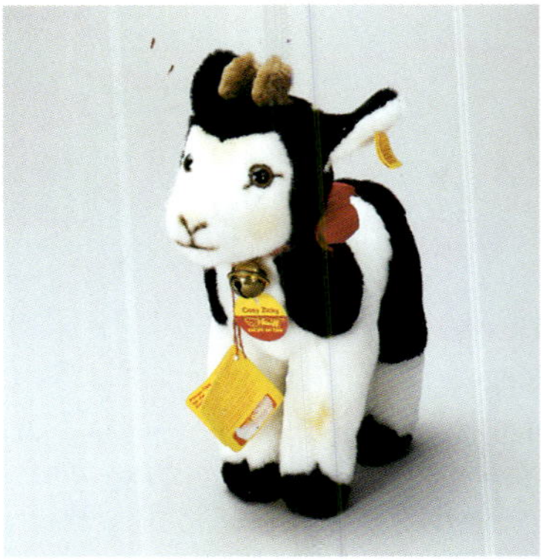

Cosy Zicky Ziege - ***Cosy Zicky*** *Goat*

Webpelz, schwarz/weiss, waschmaschinenfest - *woven fur, black & white, machine washable*

Serie	Art.-No	Period	Pr.	Info
097805	**5480/22**	1987-1988	2	22 cm

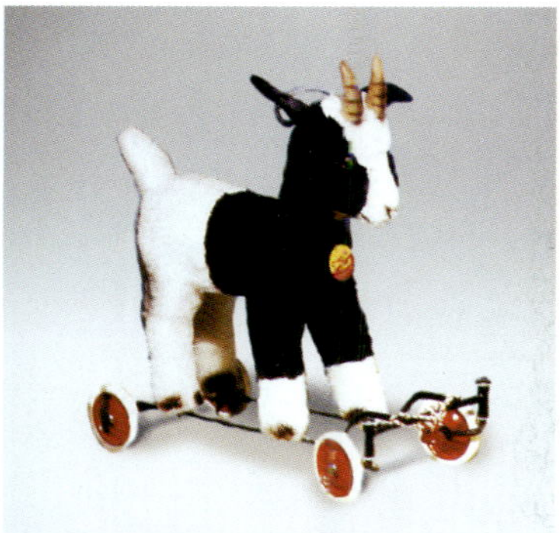

Reit-Ziege **Zicky** - *Riding Goat* ***Zicky***

Dralon, Stahlrohrgestell, Scheibenraeder mit Plastikreifen, abwaschbar - *dralon, steel tubular frame, disc wheels with plastic tires, surface washable*

SERIE	ART.-NO	PERIOD	PR.	INFO
	3560/50	1971-1974	4-5	50 cm

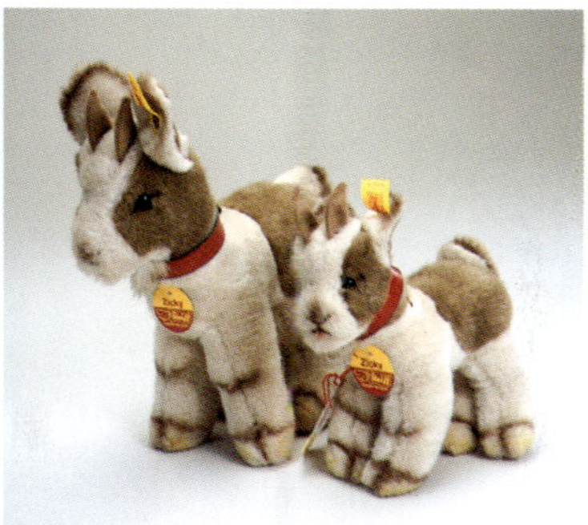

Zicky Ziege - ***Zicky*** *Goat*

Webpelz, stehend, abwaschbar - *woven fur, standing, surface washable*

SERIE	ART.-NO	PERIOD	PR.	INFO
	3455/17	1981-1984	2	17 cm
	3455/23	1981-1984	2	23 cm

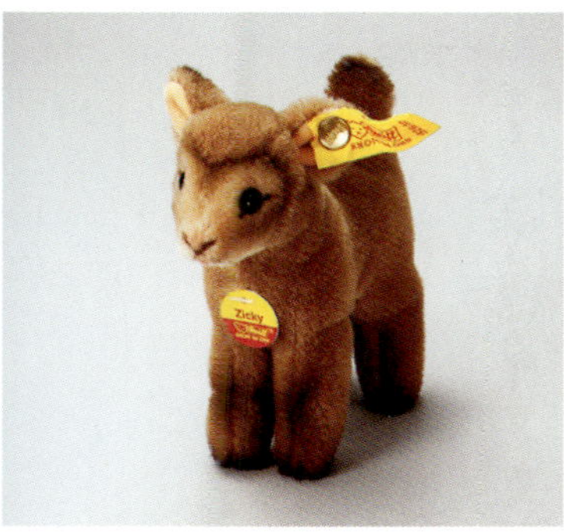

Zicky Ziege - ***Zicky*** *Goat*

Webpelz, waschmaschinenfest - *woven fur, machine washable*

SERIE	ART.-NO	PERIOD	PR.	INFO
052750	**1526/12**	1987-1990	2	12 cm

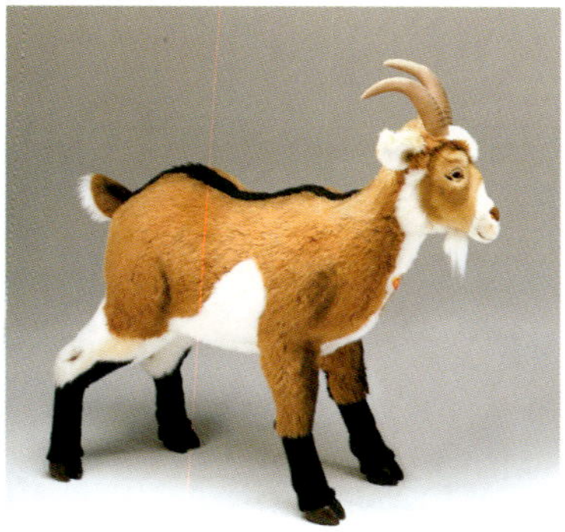

Ziege - *Goat*

Studio-Tier, Webpelz, braun/weiss, abwaschbar - *studio animal, woven fur, brown & white, surface washable*

SERIE	ART.-NO	PERIOD	PR.	INFO
502408	**0440/99**	1989-1990	7	100 cm
	502408	1991-1999	7	

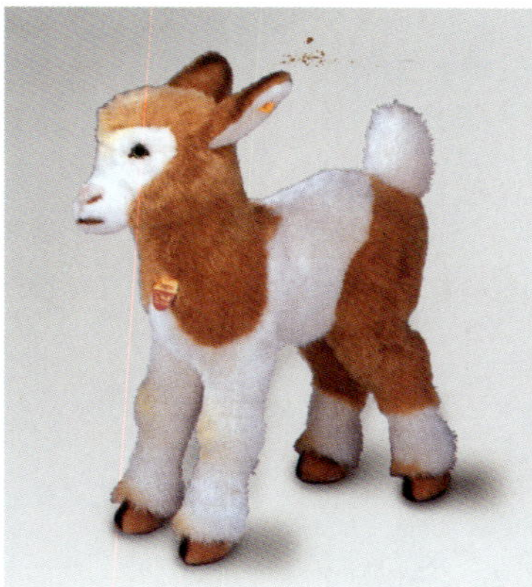

Zicklein - *Goat Kid*

Studio-Tier, Webpelz, braun/weiss, abwaschbar - *studio animal, woven fur, brown & white, surface washable*

SERIE	ART.-NO	PERIOD	PR.	INFO
502453	**0445/60**	1989-1990	5	60 cm
	502453	1991-1993	5	

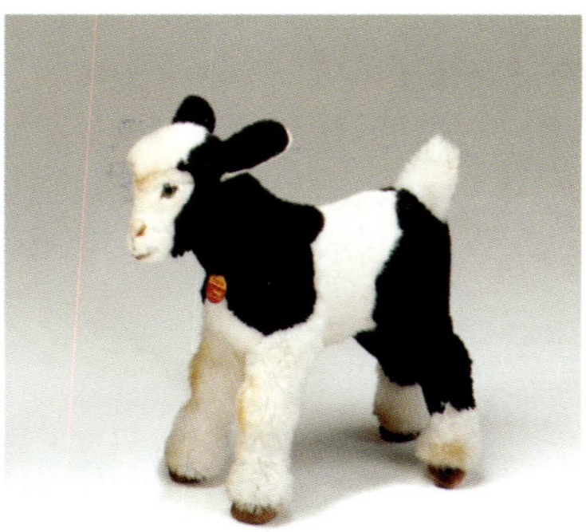

Zicklein - *Goat Kid*

Studio-Tier, Webpelz, schwarz/weiss, abwaschbar - *studio animal, woven fur, black & white, surface washable*

SERIE	ART.-NO	PERIOD	PR.	INFO
502460	**0446/60**	1989-1990	5	60 cm
	502460	1991-1999	5	

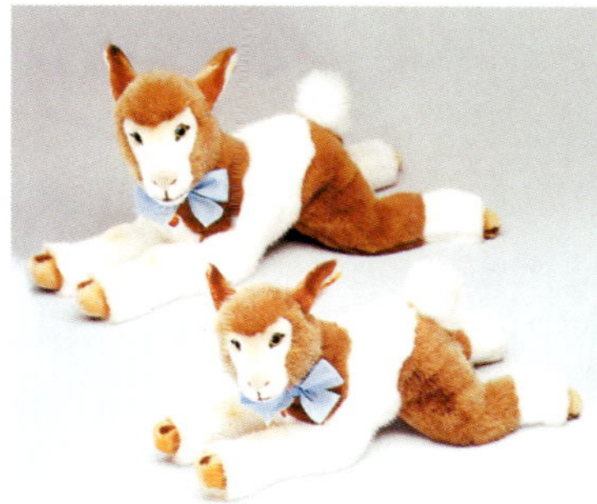

Molly Zicky Ziege - ***Molly Zicky*** *Goat*

Webpelz, braun/weiss, waschmaschinenfest - *woven fur, brown & white, machine washable*

SERIE	ART.-NO	PERIOD	PR.	INFO
103209	**0363/40**	1990-1990	2-3	40 cm
	103209	1991-1991	2-3	
103223	**0363/50**	1990-1990	2-3	50 cm
	103223	1991-1992	2-3	

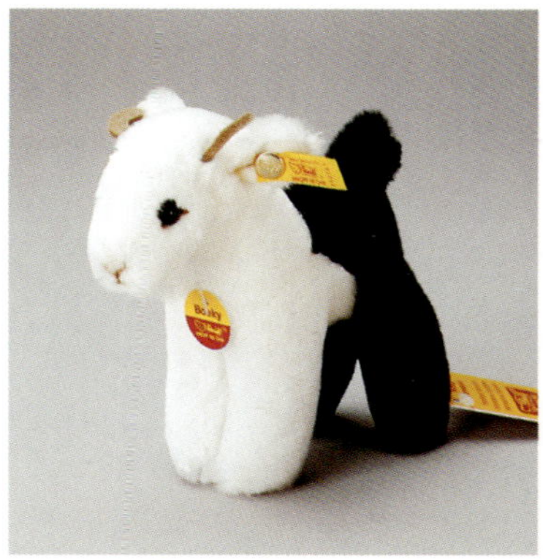

Boecky Ziege - ***Boecky*** *Goat*

Webpelz, stehend, handwaschbar - *woven fur, standing, hand washable*

EAN-NO.	PERIOD	PR.	INFO
052767	1994-1995	1-2	16 cm

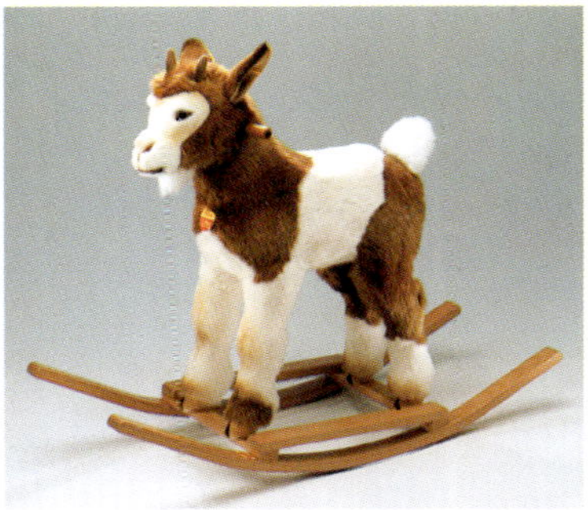

Reit-Ziege - *Riding Goat*

Webpelz, Holzwippe, abwaschbar - *woven fur, wooden rocker, surface washable*

EAN-No.	Period	Pr.	Info
480706	1994-1995	5	80 cm

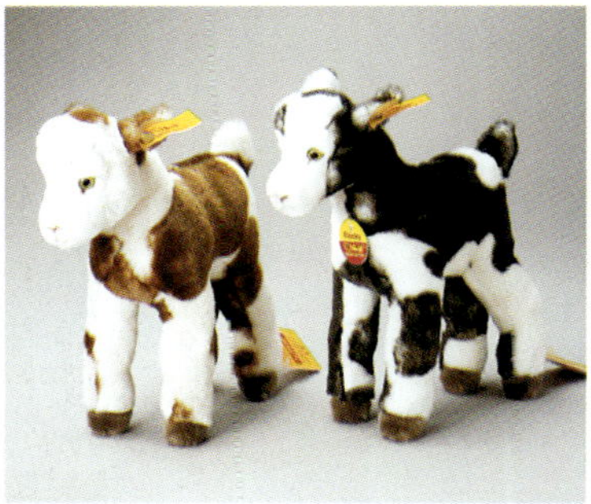

Flocky Ziege - ***Flocky*** *Goat*

Webpelz, 22 cm, weiss/braun oder weiss/schwarz, stehend, waschmaschinenfest - *woven fur, 22 cm, brown & white or black & white, standing, machine washable*

EAN-No.	Period	Pr.	Info
073014	1995-1997	2-3	weiss/braun - *white/brown*
073021	1995-1997	2-3	weiss/schwarz - *white/black*

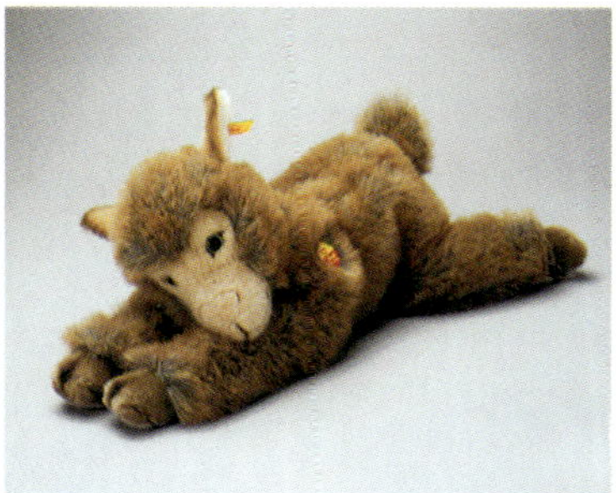

Molly Ziege - *Molly Goat*

Webpelz, 60 cm, weiss oder braun, liegend, waschmaschinenfest - *woven fur, 60 cm, white or brown, lying, machine washable*

EAN-No.	Period	Pr.	Info
103162	1995-1997	3	weiss - *white*
103186	1995-1997	3	braun - *brown*

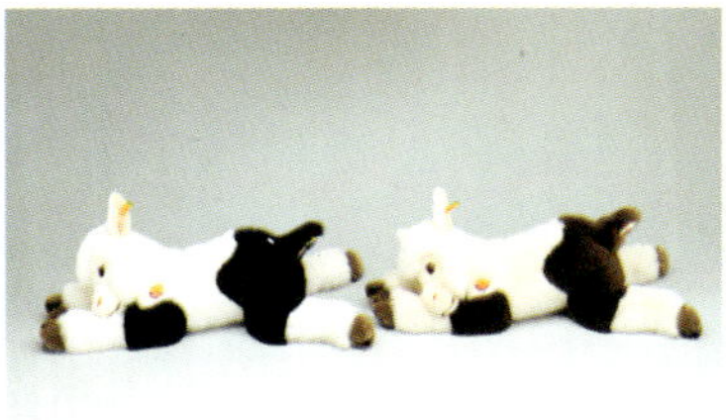

Molly Ziege - *Molly Goat*

Webpelz, 75 cm, schwarz/weiss oder braun/weiss, liegend, waschmaschinenfest - *woven fur, 75 cm, brown & white or black & white, lying, machine washable*

EAN-No.	Period	Pr.	Info
103230	1995-1997	3-4	schwarz/weiss - *black/white*
103247	1995-1997	3-4	braun/weiss - *brown/white*

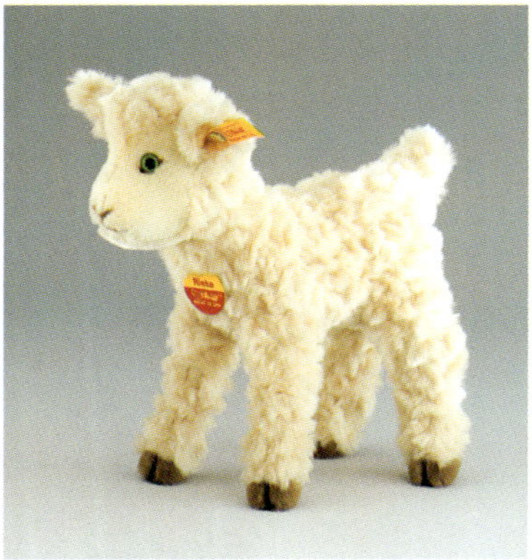

Rieke Ziege - ***Rieke*** *Goat*

Webpelz, stehend, waschmaschinenfest - *woven fur, standing, machine washable*

EAN-No.	Period	Pr.	Info
073038	1997-1998	2-3	22 cm

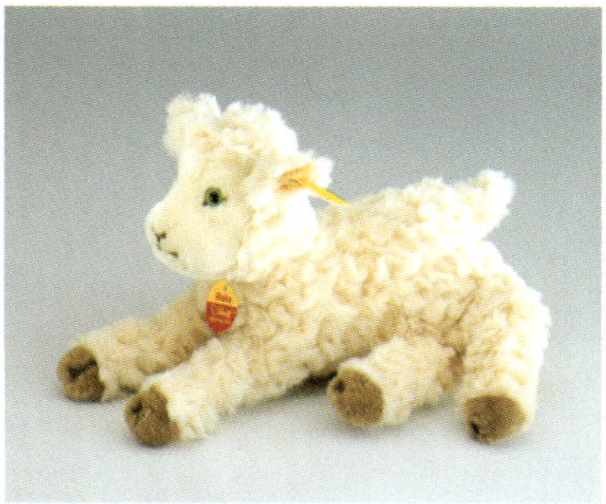

Rieke Ziege - ***Rieke*** *Goat*

Webpelz, liegend, waschmaschinenfest - *woven fur, lying, machine washable*

EAN-No.	Period	Pr.	Info
073045	1997-1998	2-3	25 cm

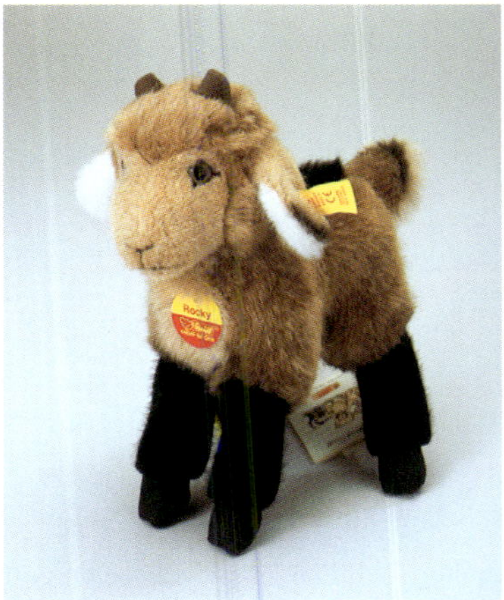

Rocky Zwergzicklein - ***Rocky*** *Goat Kid*

Webpelz, braun, stehend, waschmaschinenfest - *woven fur, brown, standing, machine washable*

EAN-No.	Period	Pr.	Info
073052	1998-1999	2-3	22 cm

Hasen

Rabbits

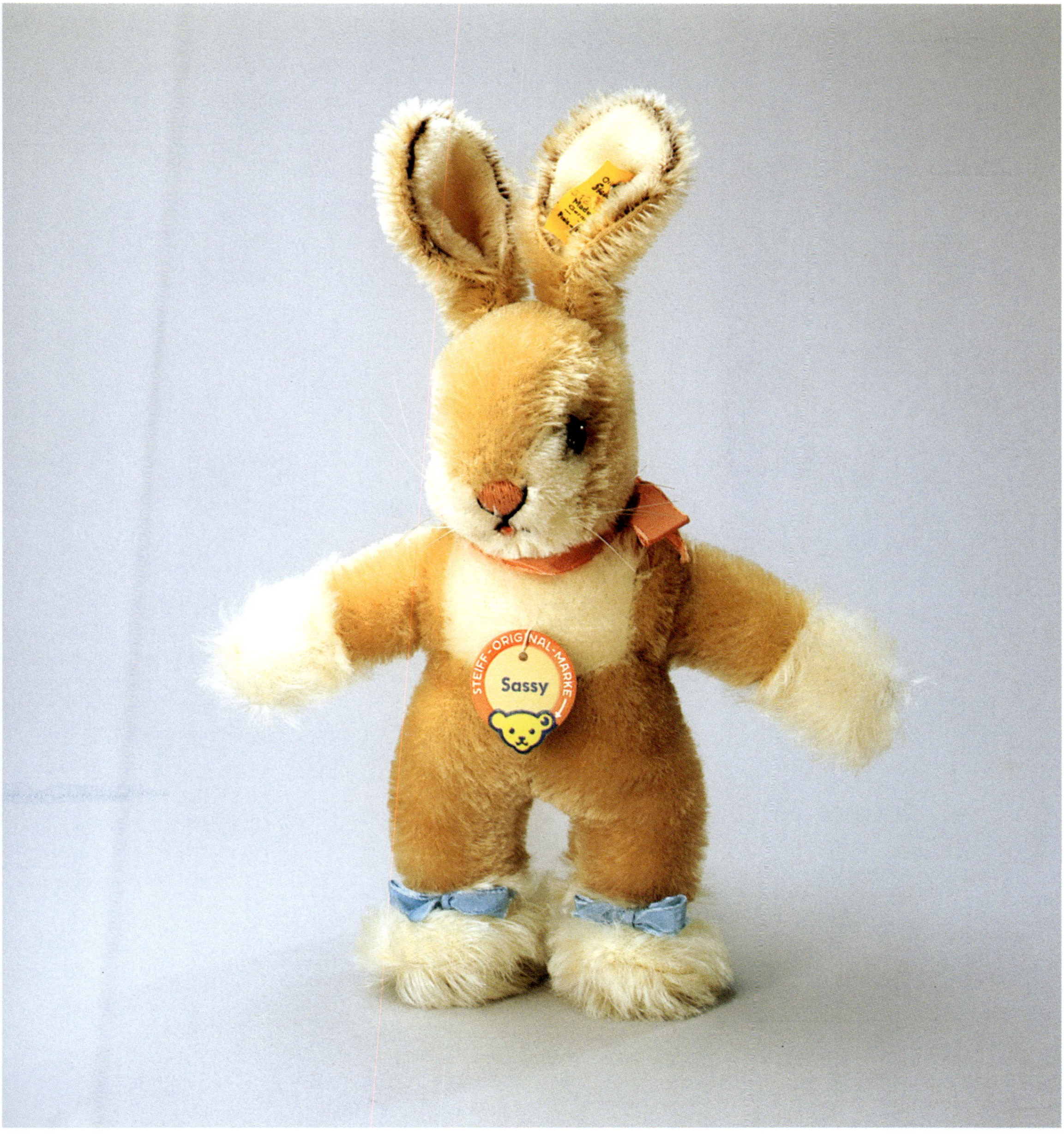

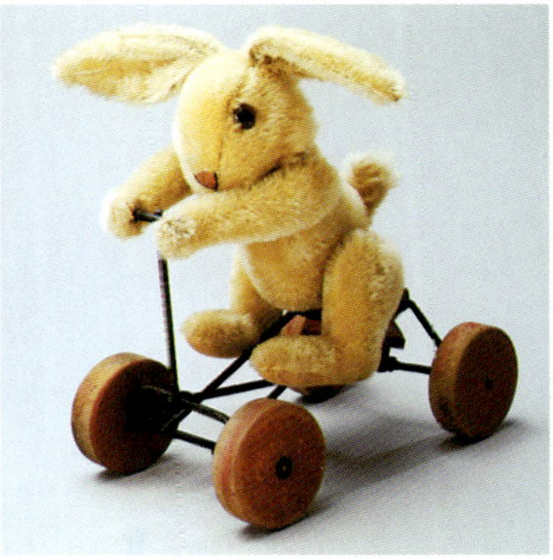

Record-Hase ab 1951 Record Hansi - *Record Rabbit from 1951 Record Hansi*

Mohairpluesch, offener Mund, hellbraun, ab 1951 braun/weiss, auf Selbstfahrer mit automat. Bewegung und Stimme - *mohair, open mouth, light brown, from 1951 brown/white, in riding position, with automatic movements & voice*

SERIE	ART.-NO	PERIOD	PR.	INFO
36	**325**	1949-1958	5-6	25 cm
360	**9325,10**	1959-1964	5	

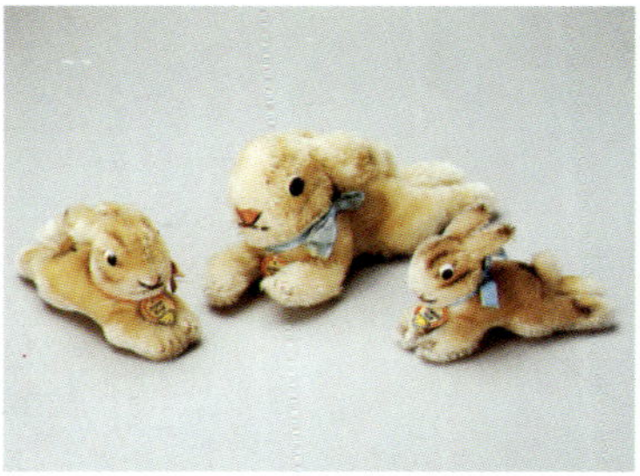

Lieg Hase - *Lying Rabbit*

Mohair, braun/weiss, liegend - *mohair, brown & white, lying*

SERIE	ART.-NO	PERIOD	PR.	INFO
36	**2306**	1953-1958	3-4	6 cm
360	**2306,00**	1959-1964	3	
296	**2306,00**	1965-1967	3	
	2960/06	1968-1970	3	
36	**2309**	1953-1958	3-4	9 cm
360	**2309,00**	1959-1964	3	
296	**2309,00**	1965-1967	3	
	2960/09	1968-1970	3	
36	**2312**	1953-1958	3-4	12 cm
360	**2312,00**	1959-1964	3	
296	**2312,00**	1965-1967	3	
	2960/12	1968-1970	3	

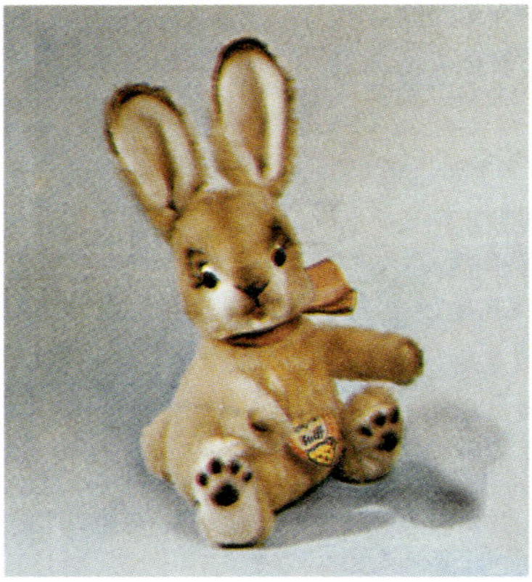

Ball Hase - *Ball Rabbit*

Dralonpluesch, weich, Druckstimme - *dralon, soft, press voice*

SERIE	ART.-NO	PERIOD	PR.	INFO
815 360	**4616,00**	1960-1961	4-5	16 cm

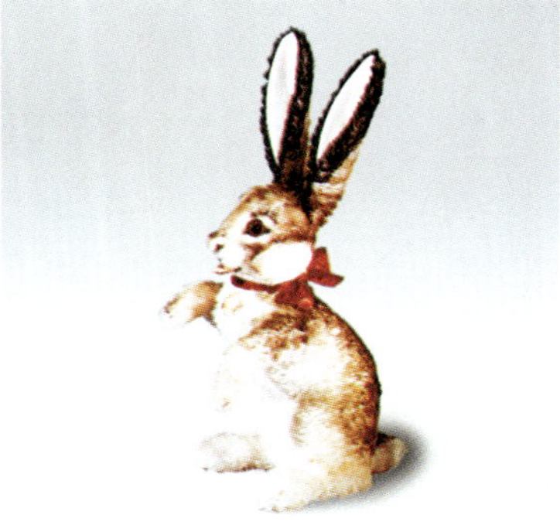

Hase - *Rabbit*

Schautier, Mohair, aufwartend - *displyay animal, mohair, sitting up*

SERIE	ART.-NO	PERIOD	PR.	INFO
360	**4375,90**	1960-1960	5	75 cm
	3029/08	1967-1967	5	

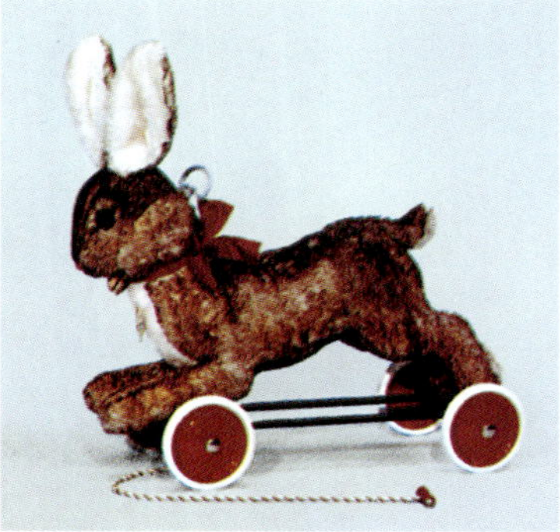

Reit-Hase - *Riding Rabbit*

Mohair, braun gespitzt, stehend auf Scheibenraedern mit Gummi- ab 1967 Plastikreifen, Eisengerippe, Haltegriff - *mohair, brown tipped, standing on disc wheels with rubber tires, in 1967 plastic tires, iron frame, grip handle*

SERIE	ART.-NO	PERIOD	PR.	INFO
360	**1350,20**	1964-1964	4	50 cm
294	**1350,20**	1965-1967	4	

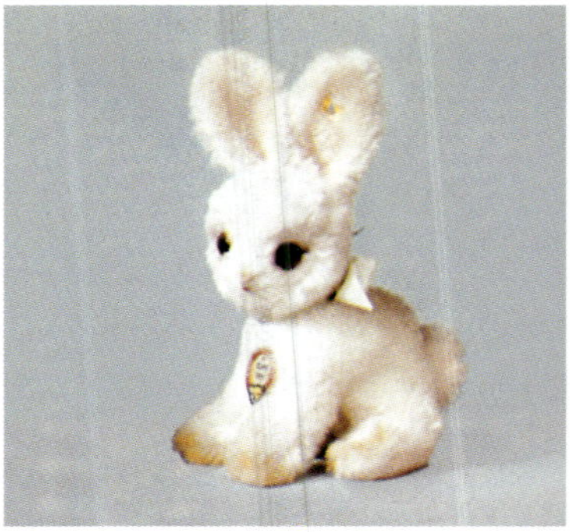

Cosy Issy Hase - ***Cosy Issy*** *Rabbit*

Dralon-Pluesch, Schaumstoff-Flocken-Fuellung, weiss, waschbar, sitzend - *dralon, stuffed with foam flakes, white, washable, sitting*

SERIE	ART.-NO	PERIOD	PR.	INFO
830 360	**6622,04**	1961-1964	2	22 cm
494	**6622,04**	1965-1967	2	
	4940/22	1968-1976	2	

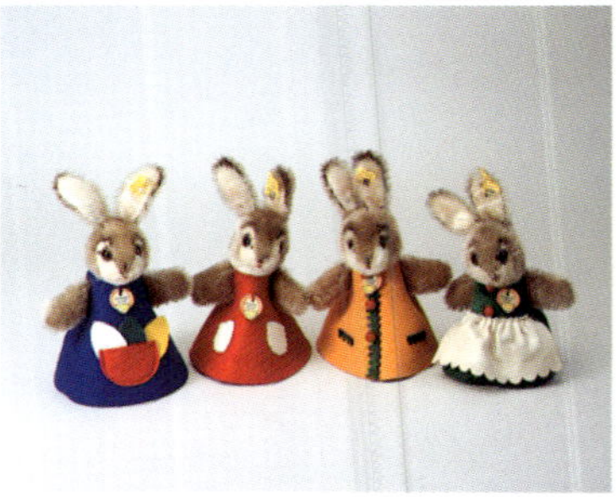

Betthupferlhase - *Nightcap Rabbit*

Kopf & Arme Mohair, Filzkleidung, Kopf drehbar, innen hohl zur Abdeckung kleiner Praesente, 15 cm - *head & arms mohair, felt clothing, swivel head, hollow interior to cover small gifts, 15 cm*

SERIE	ART.-NO	PERIOD	PR.	INFO
	3171/15	1968-1973	4	orange
	3172/15	1968-1972	4	rot - *red*
	3173/15	1968-1973	4	gruen - *green*
	3174/15	1968-1973	4	blau - *blue*

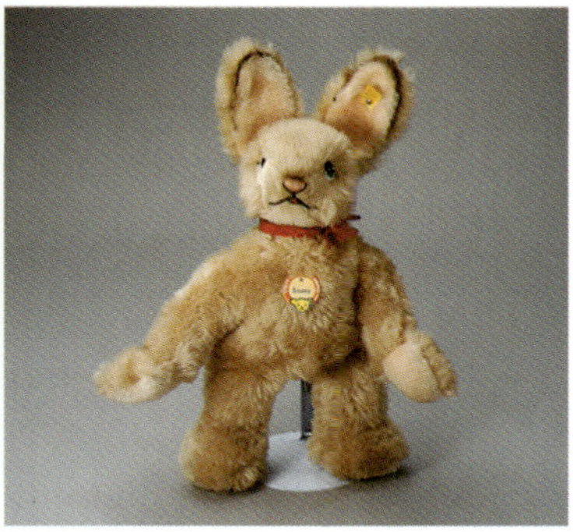

Sitzhase **Lausy** - *Sitting Rabbit **Lausy***

Dralon, Schlenkerbeine, beige, Drehkopf, sehr weich, abwaschbar - *dralon, floppy legs, beige, head swivels, very soft, surface washable*

SERIE	ART.-NO	PERIOD	PR.	INFO
	3150/35	1968-1978	2-3	35 cm

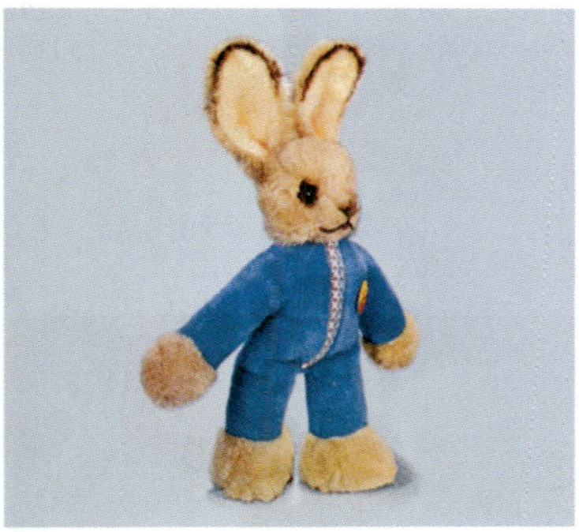

Schlenkerhase - *Dangling Rabbit*

Dralon, Koerper, Arme & Beine tuerkis, abwaschbar - *dralon, body, arms & legs turquoise, surface washable*

SERIE	ART.-NO	PERIOD	PR.	INFO
	7830/35	1973-1978	3	35 cm

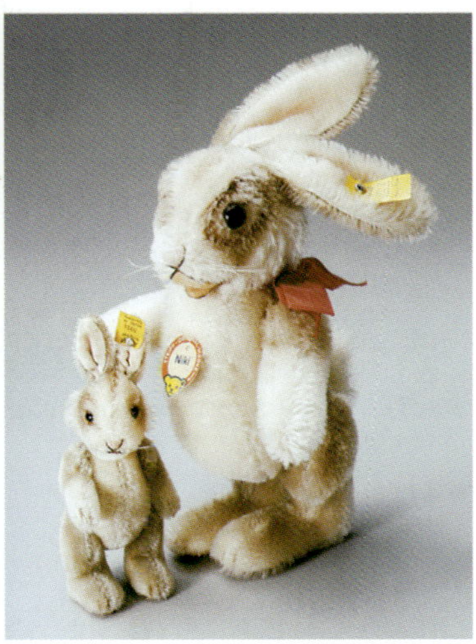

Niki-Hase - ***Niki** Rabbit*

Mohair, grau/weiss, gegliedert, 14 & 17 cm geschlossener Mund, ab 22 cm offener Mund - *mohair, grey & white, jointed, 14 & 17 cm mouth closed, from 22 cm open mouth*

SERIE	ART.-NO	PERIOD	PR.	INFO
36	**5314**	1952-1958	4-5	14 cm
360	**5314,00**	1959-1964	4	
36	**5317**	1951-1958	4-5	17 cm
360	**5317,00**	1959-1960	4	
36	**5322**	1951-1958	4-5	22 cm
360	**5322,00**	1959-1964	4	
36	**5328,2**	1951-1958	4-5	28 cm
360	**5328,00**	1959-1964	4	
36	**5335,2**	1953-1957	5	35 cm
360	**5335,00**	1960-1964	4-5	

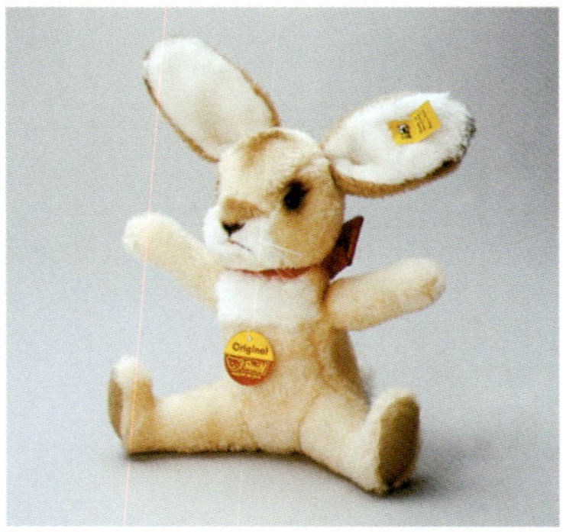

Sitz-Hase Niki - *Sitting Rabbit Niki*

Dralon, beige, Drehkopf, sehr weich, abwaschbar - *dralon, beige, head swivels, very soft, surface washable*

SERIE	ART.-NO	PERIOD	PR.	INFO
	3160/25	1969-1974	2-3	25 cm

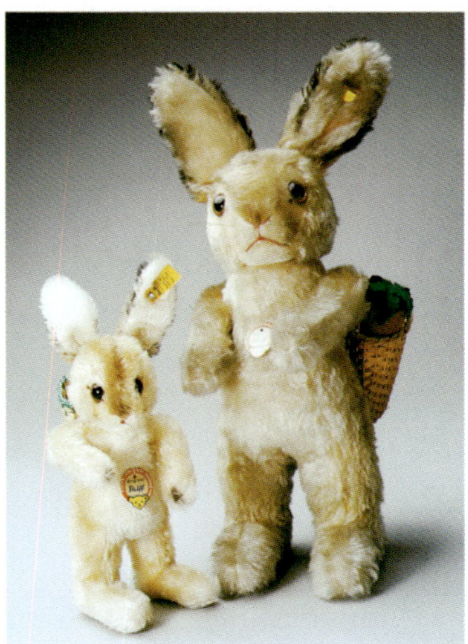

Osterhase - *Easter Rabbit*

Mohair, braun/weiss, aufwartend, Drehkopf, mit Korb - *mohair, brown & white, sitting up, head swivels, basket*

SERIE	ART.-NO	PERIOD	PR.	INFO
293	**4325,00**	1967-1967	4	25 cm
	2930/25	1968-1969	4	
293	**4340,00**	1967-1967	4	40 cm
	2930/40	1968-1969	4	

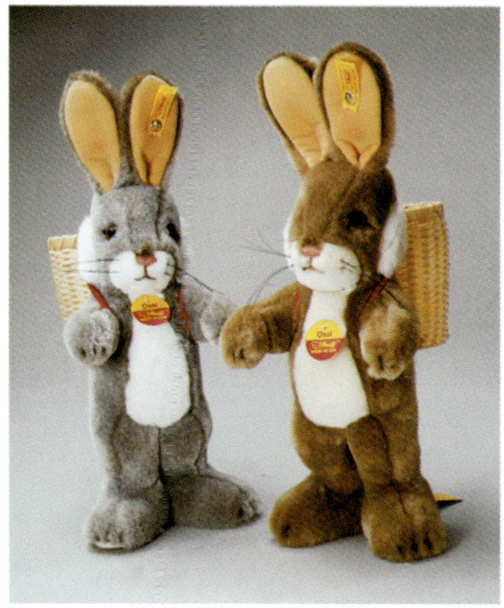

Ossi Osterhase - ***Ossi** Easter Rabbit*

Webpelz, braun oder grau, 30 cm, mit Weidenkiepe, handwaschbar - *woven fur, brown or grey, 30 cm, wicker basket, hand washable*

EAN-NO.	PERIOD	PR.	INFO
349300	1994-1995	2-3	braun - *brown*
349324	1994-1995	2-3	grau - *grey*

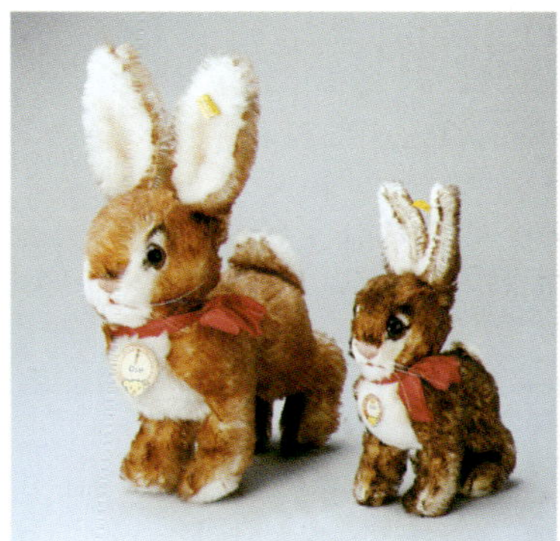

Ossi Hase - ***Ossi** Rabbit*

Langhaar-Mohair, braun gespitzt, huepfend, abwaschbar - *long-hair mohair, brown tipped, hopping, surface washable*

SERIE	ART.-NO	PERIOD	PR.	INFO
360	**1318,00**	1962-1964	3	18 cm
294	**1318,00**	1965-1967	3	
	2940/18	1968-1976	2-3	
360	**1323,00**	1962-1964	3	23 cm
294	**1323,00**	1965-1967	3	
	2940/23	1968-1976	2-3	

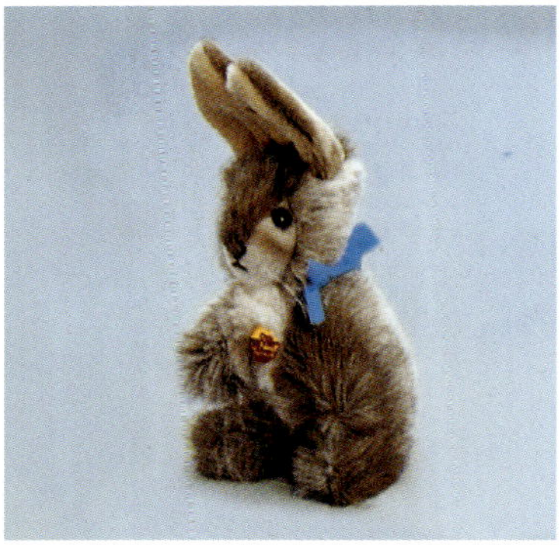

Ossi Hase - ***Ossi*** *Rabbit*

Synthetik-Webpelz, aufwartend - *synthetic woven fur, sitting up*

SERIE	ART.-NO	PERIOD	PR.	INFO
	2947/35	1978-1982	2-3	35 cm

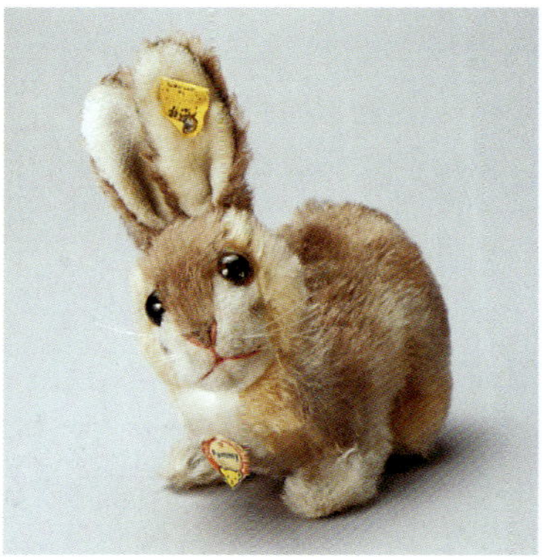

Pummy Hase - ***Pummy*** *Rabbit*

Mohair, weiss/grau/braun, hockend, Drehkopf, abwaschbar - *mohair, white/grey/ brown, crouching, head swivels, surface washable*

SERIE	ART.-NO	PERIOD	PR.	INFO
360	**2315,05**	1963-1964	3	15 cm
296	**2315,05**	1965-1967	3	
	2960/15	1968-1976	2-3	
360	**2325,05**	1963-1964	3	25 cm
296	**2325,05**	1965-1967	3	
	2960/25	1968-1976	2-3	

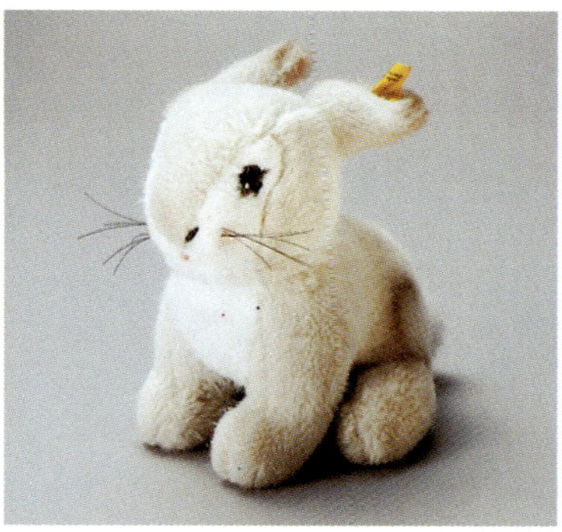

Pummy Hase - ***Pummy*** *Rabbit*

Webpelz, beige, sitzend, abwaschbar - *woven fur, beige, sitting, surface washable*

SERIE	ART.-NO	PERIOD	PR.	INFO
	2963/16	1980-1983	2	16 cm

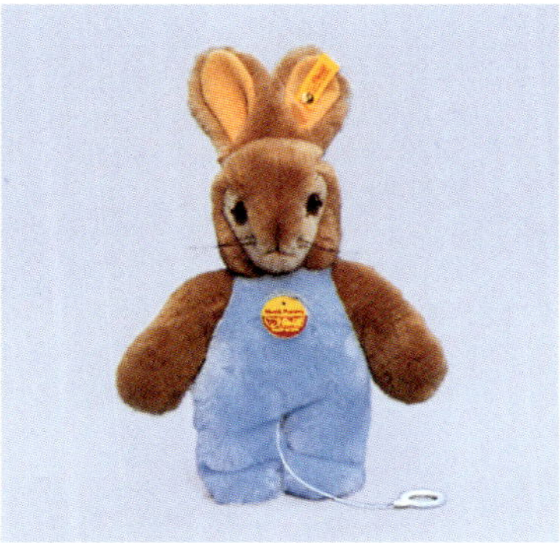

Musik Pummy Hase - *Pummy Music Rabbit*

Webpelz, formgeschaeumt, Musikwerk austauschbar, ohne Musikwerk waschbar - *woven fur, stuffed with pre-formed foam, music box can be exchanged, washable if music box removed*

SERIE	ART.-NO	PERIOD	PR.	INFO
231155	**6351/26**	1984-1987	2	26 cm

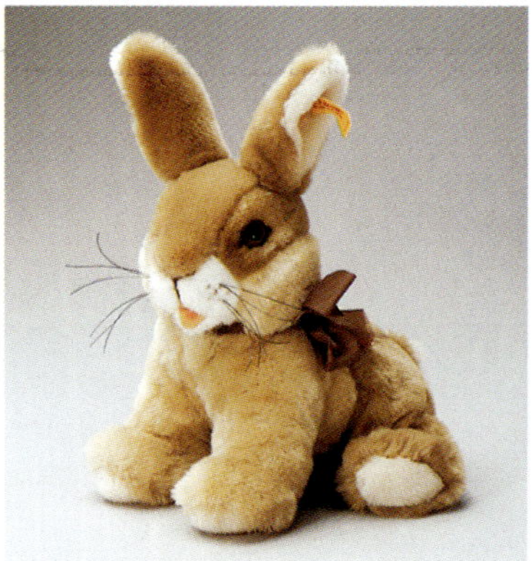

Pummy Hase - ***Pummy*** *Rabbit*

Webpelz, waschmaschinenfest - *woven fur, machine washable*

SERIE	ART.-NO	PERIOD	PR.	INFO
083303	**5060/17**	1989-1990	2	17 cm, beige/creme - *beige/cream*
	083303	1991-1991	2	
083327	**5060/21**	1989-1990	2	21 cm
083358	**5063/17**	1989-1990	2	17 cm, braun/creme - *brown/cream*
	083358	1991-1991	2	
083372	**5063/21**	1989-1990	2	21 cm
083402	**5067/17**	1989-1990	2	17 cm, grau/ weiss - *grey/white*
	083402	1991-1991	2	
083426	**5067/21**	1989-1990	2	21 cm

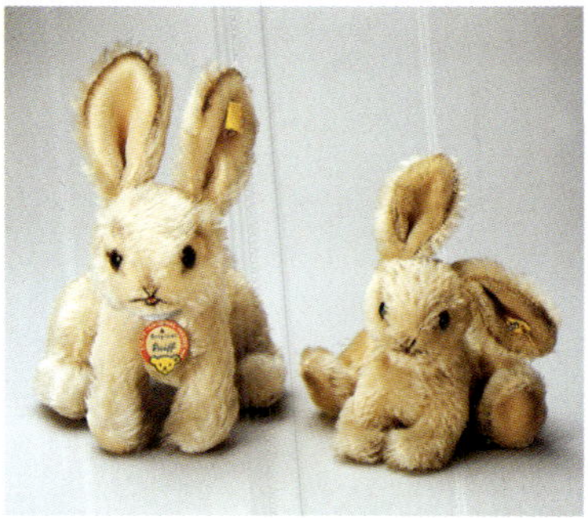

Verwandlungshase - *Changeable Rabbit*

Mohair, weiss/gelb/braun, laeuft, sitzt, steht aufrecht, Hinterbeine & Kopf gegliedert, rund & weich - *mohair, white/yellow/ brown, may be put into running, sitting or upright positions, hind legs & head are jointed, round & soft*

SERIE	ART.-NO	PERIOD	PR.	INFO
36	**6317**	1957-1958	4	17 cm
360	**6317,00**	1959-1964	3-4	
307	**6317,00**	1965-1967	3-4	
	3070/17	1968-1970	3	
36	**6325**	1957-1958	4	25 cm
360	**6325,00**	1959-1964	3-4	
307	**6325,00**	1965-1967	3-4	
	3070/25	1968-1970	3-4	

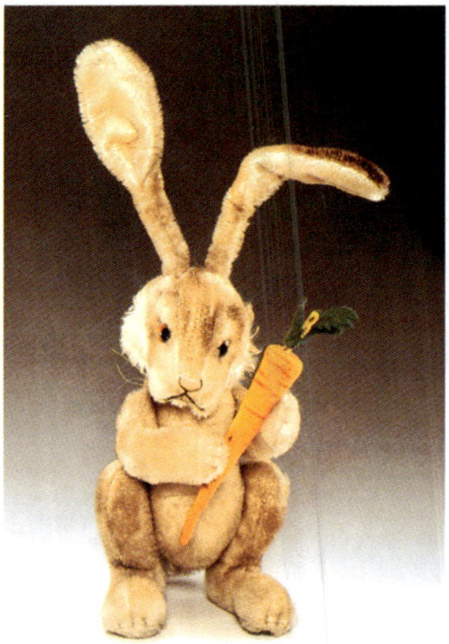

Ruebenhase - *Carrot Rabbit*

Mohair, gegliedert, verschiedene Groessen bekannt, kein Katalognachweis - *mohair, jointed, varying sizes known, no catalog information available*

EAN-NO.	PERIOD	PR.	INFO
	1954-1954	7-8	

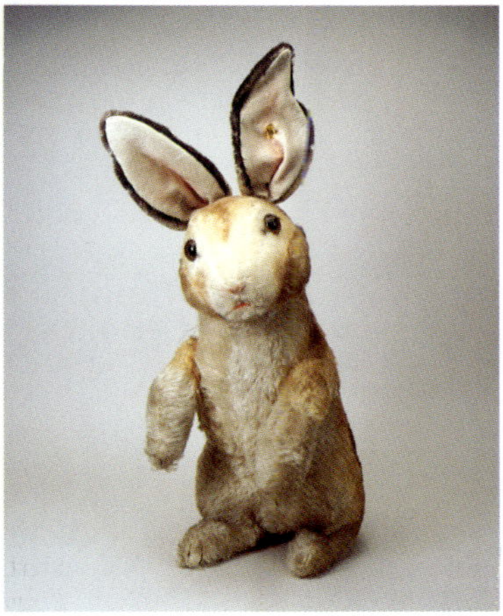

Hase - *Rabbit*

Mohair, hellbraun/weiss, aufwartend, geschlossener Mund, Drehkopf, ab 22 cm Druckstimme - *mohair, light brown & white, sitting up, mouth closed, head swivels, from 22 cm press voice*

SERIE	ART.-NO	PERIOD	PR.	INFO
36	**4310**	1950-1958	4	10 cm
360	**4310,00**	1959-1960	4	
36	**4317**	1949-1958	4	17 cm
360	**4317,00**	1959-1960	4	
36	**4322,2**	1949-1953	4-5	22 cm
36	**4328,2**	1949-1958	4-5	28 cm
360	**4328,00**	1959-1960	4-5	
36	**4335,2**	1951-1953	5	35 cm
36	**4350,2**	1951-1958	5	50 cm
360	**4350,00**	1959-1960	5	
36	**4365,2**	1951-1957	5-6	65 cm

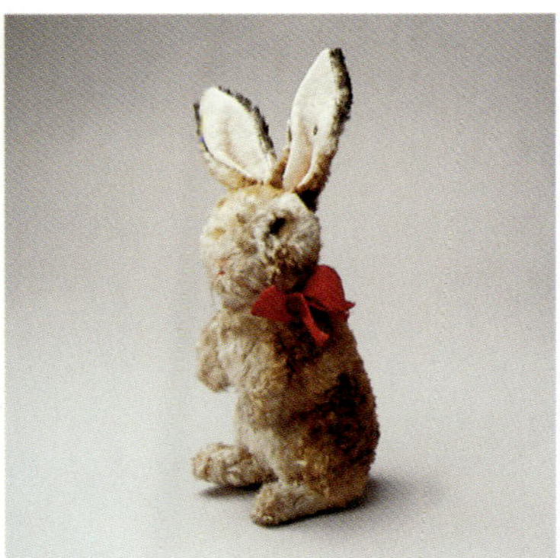

Hase - *Rabbit*

Kunstseidenpluesch, hellbraun/weiss, bemalt, aufwartend, Drehkopf, Druckstimme - *artificial silk plush, light brown & white, painted, sitting up, head swivels, press voice*

SERIE	ART.-NO	PERIOD	PR.	INFO
36	**4623,2**	1949-1949	4	23 cm
36	**4629,2**	1948-1949	4	29 cm

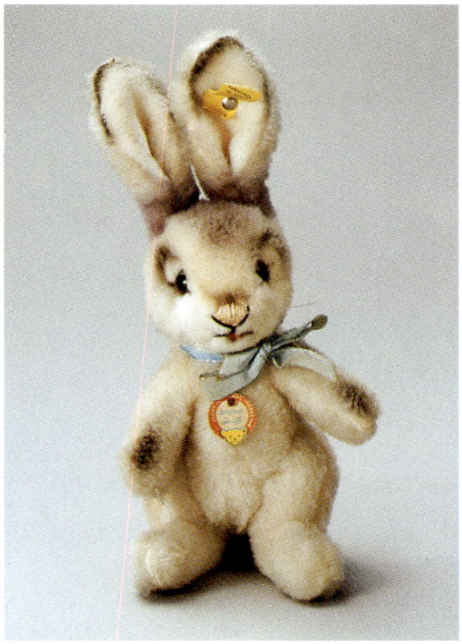

Dralon-Hase - *Dralon Rabbit*

waschbarer Dralon-Pluesch (Bayer), weiss/gelb/graubraun, aufwartend, Drehkopf, sehr weich - *dralon (Bayer), white/yellow/grey-brown, sitting up, head swivels, very soft, washable*

SERIE	ART.-NO	PERIOD	PR.	INFO
36	**4617**	1956-1958	3	17 cm
360	**4617,00**	1959-1964	3	
304	**4617,00**	1965-1967	3	
	3040/17	1968-1974	2-3	
36	**4625**	1956-1958	3	25 cm
360	**4625,00**	1959-1964	3	
304	**4625,00**	1965-1967	3	
	3040/25	1968-1974	2-3	

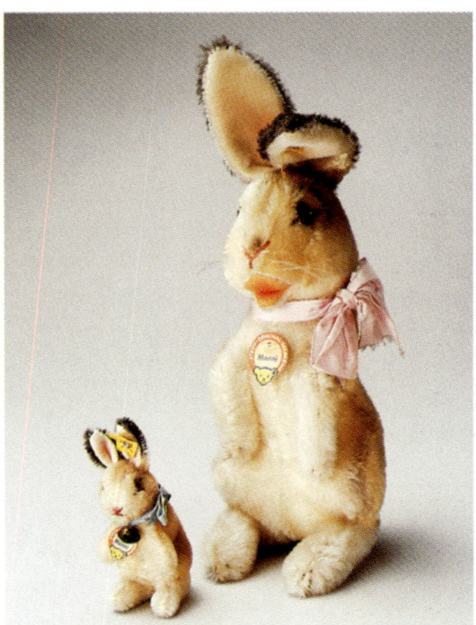

Manni Hase - ***Manni** Rabbit*

Mohair, braun/weiss, aufwartend, Drehkopf, 10 cm geschlossener Mund, ab 20 cm offener Mund, abwaschbar - *mohair, brown & white, sitting up, head swivels, 10 cm mouth closed, from 20 cm open mouth, surface washable*

SERIE	ART.-NO	PERIOD	PR.	INFO
360	**4310,03**	1961-1964	3-4	10 cm
302	**4310,03**	1965-1967	3-4	
	3020/10	1968-1974	3	
360	**4320,03**	1961-1964	4	20 cm
302	**4320,03**	1965-1967	4	
	3020/20	1968-1976	3-4	
360	**4330,03**	1961-1964	4	30 cm
302	**4330,03**	1965-1967	4	
	3020/30	1968-1976	4	
360	**4340,03**	1961-1964	4-5	40 cm
302	**4340,03**	1965-1967	4-5	
	3020/40	1968-1973	4	
360	**4355,03**	1961-1964	5	55 cm
302	**4355,03**	1965-1967	5	
	3020/55	1968-1973	4-5	

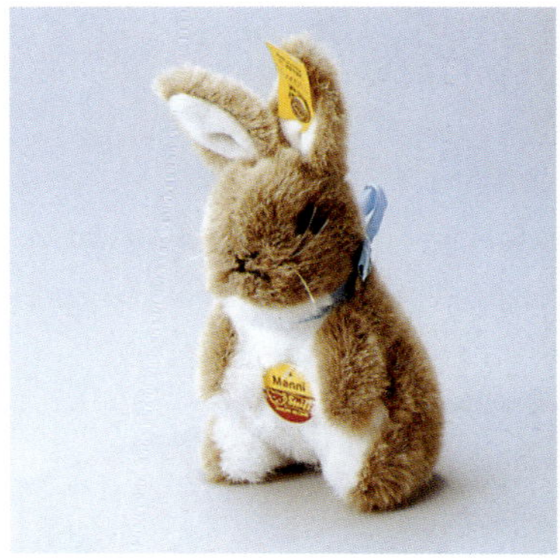

Manni Hase - ***Manni** Rabbit*

Nerzimitation, ab 1978 Synthetik-Webpelz, 10 cm, aufwartend, abwaschbar - *imitation mink, from 1978 synthetic woven fur, 10 cm, sitting up, surface washable*

SERIE	ART.-NO	PERIOD	PR.	INFO
	1502/10	1977-1981 - *brown/white*	2	braun/weiss
	1503/10	1977-1981	2	grau/weiss - *grey/white*

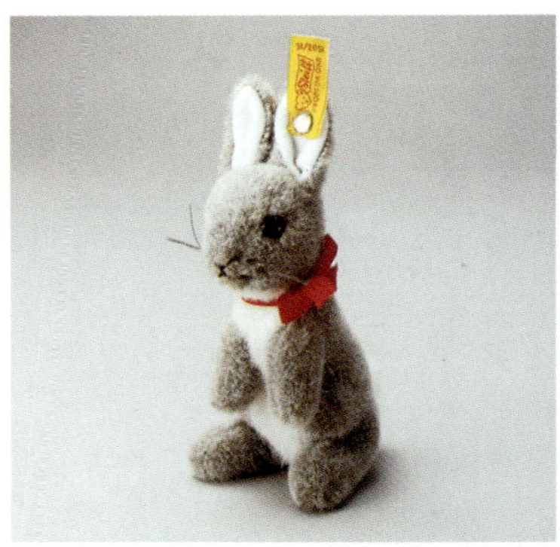

Manni Hase - ***Manni** Rabbit*

Webpelz, 15 cm, abwaschbar - *woven fur, 15 cm, surface washable*

SERIE	ART.-NO	PERIOD	PR.	INFO
050305	**1502/15**	1984-1987	2	beige
050404	**1503/15**	1984-1987	2	grau - *grey*

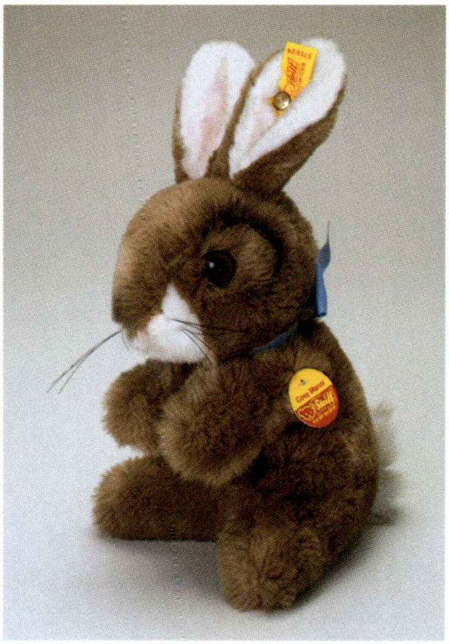

Cosy Manni Hase - ***Cosy Manni*** *Rabbit*

Webpelz, superweich, waschmaschinenfest - *woven fur, super soft, machine washable*

SERIE	ART.-NO	PERIOD	PR.	INFO
	5361/24	1982-1984	2	24 cm

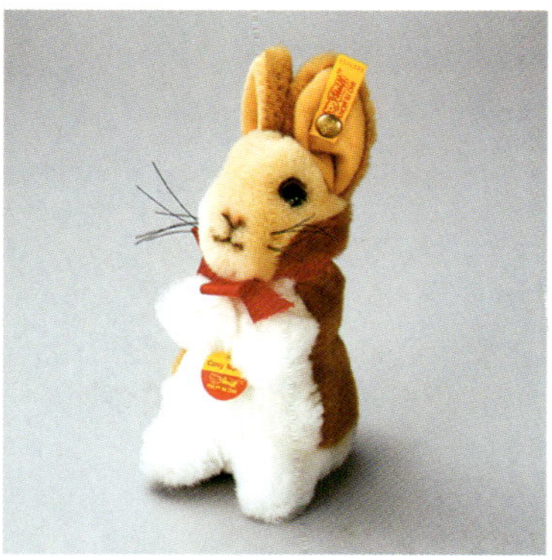

Cosy Manni Hase - ***Cosy Manni*** *Rabbit*

Webpelz, hellbraun/weiss oder braun/creme, 15 cm, waschmaschinenfest - *woven fur, light brown/white or brown/cream, 15 cm, machine washable*

SERIE	ART.-NO	PERIOD	PR.	INFO
098413	**5507/15**	1988-1990	2	hellbraun/weiss - *light brown/white*
	098413	1991-1991	2	
098468	**5508/15**	1988-1990	2	braun/creme - *brown/cream*
	098468	1991-1991	2	

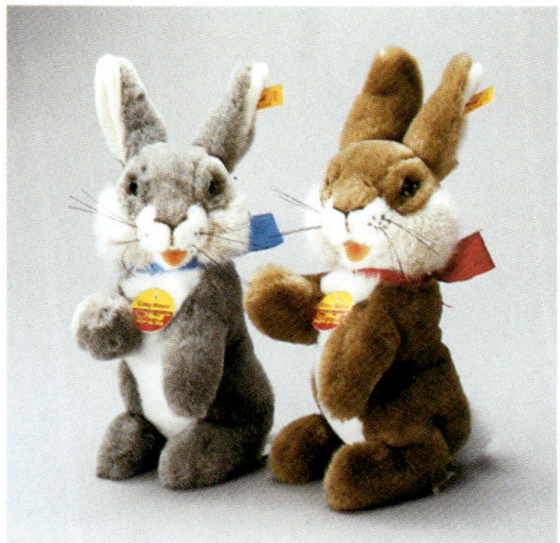

Cosy Manni Hase - ***Cosy Manni*** *Rabbit*

Webpelz, creme, grau oder hellbraun, 27 cm, aufwartend, waschmaschinenfest - *woven fur, cream, grey or light brown, 27 cm, sitting up, machine washable*

EAN-NO.	PERIOD	PR.	INFO
087004	1995-1997	2-3	creme - *cream*
087028	1995-1999	2-3	grau - *grey*
087042	1995-1998	2-3	hellbraun - *light brown*

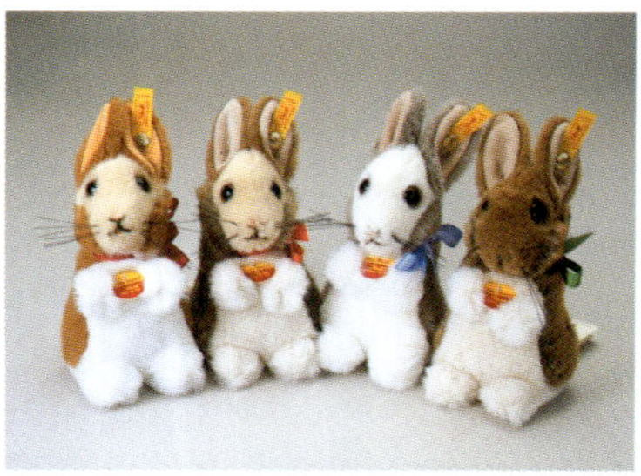

Cosy Manni Hase - ***Cosy Manni*** *Rabbit*

Webpelz, 16 cm, waschmaschinenfest - *woven fur, 16 cm, machine washable*

EAN-NO.	PERIOD	PR.	INFO
086953	1999-1999	1-2	weiss/braun gefleckt - *white/brown spotted*
086960	1999-1999	1-2	weiss/braun gespitzt - *white/brown tipped*
086977	1999-1999	1-2	weiss/braun - *white/brown*
086984	1999-1999	1-2	weiss/grau - *white/grey*

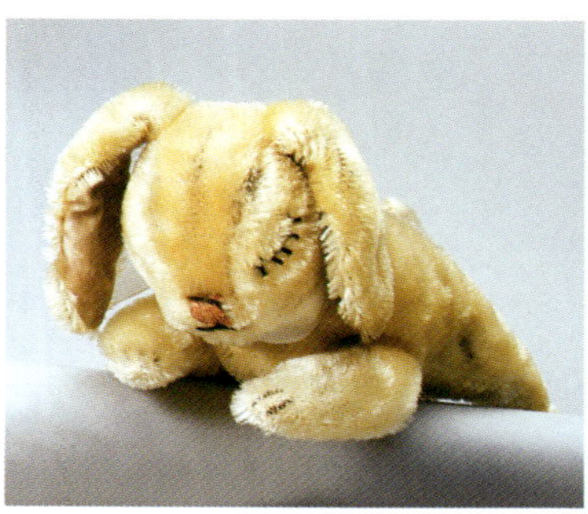

Floppy Hase ab 1965 **Floppy Hansi** - *Floppy Rabbit from 1965* ***Floppy Hansi***

Schlaftier, Mohair, Augen gestickt, weiss/hellbraun, flach liegend, sehr weich und schmiegsam - *sleeping toy, mohair, eyes embroidered, white/light brown, lying flat, very soft & cozy*

SERIE	ART.-NO	PERIOD	PR.	INFO
85 36	**7317**	1954-1958	3	17 cm
850 360	**7317,00**	1959-1964	2-3	
552	**7317,00**	1965-1967	2-3	
	5520/17	1968-1971	2	
85 36	**7328**	1953-1958	3	28 cm
850 360	**7328,00**	1959-1964	2-3	
552	**7328,00**	1965-1967	2-3	
	5520/28	1968-1971	2	

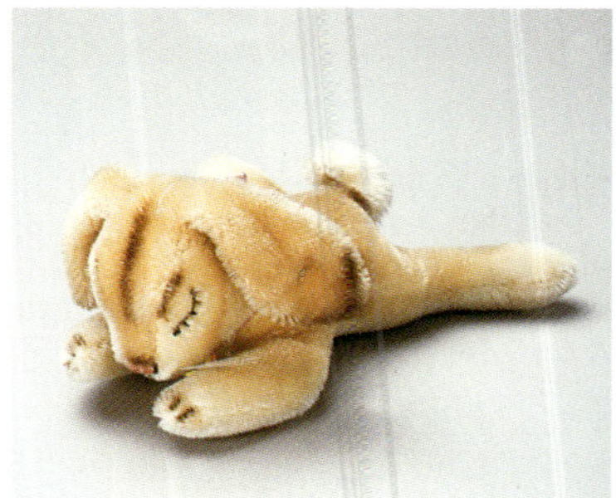

Floppy Hansi

Mohair (1978 Synthetik-Webpelz, formgeschaeumt), Augen gestickt, liegend, Schlaftier, sehr weich, vollwaschbar - *mohair (1978 synthetic woven fur, stuffed with pre-formed foam), eyes embroidered, lying, sleeping toy, very soft, fully washable*

SERIE	ART.-NO	PERIOD	PR.	INFO
	5527/17	1970-1977	2	17 cm
	5727/17	1978-1978	2	
	5527/28	1970-1977	2	28 cm
	5727/28	1978-1978	2	

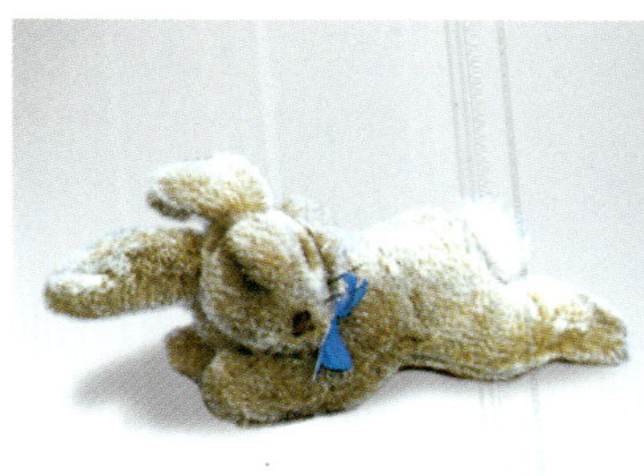

Floppy Hase - ***Floppy*** *Rabbit*

Webpelz, formgeschaeumt, liegend, vollwaschbar - *woven fur, stuffed with pre-formed foam, lying, fully washable*

SERIE	ART.-NO	PERIOD	PR.	INFO
	5705/20	1979-1982	2	20 cm
	5705/30	1979-1982	2	30 cm

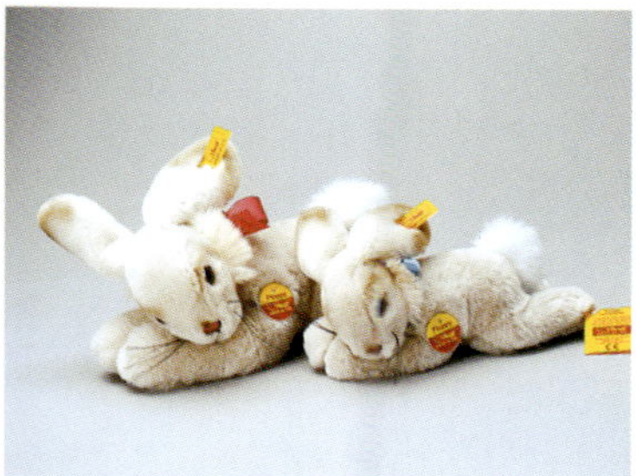

Floppy Hase - ***Floppy*** *Rabbit*

Webpelz, mollig weich, waschmaschinenfest - *woven fur, soft & cuddly, machine washable*

SERIE	ART.-NO	PERIOD	PR.	INFO
082207	**5605/18**	1983-1990	2	22 cm
	082207	1991-1999	2	
082221	**5605/25**	1983-1990	2-3	30 cm
	082221	1991-1999	2-3	

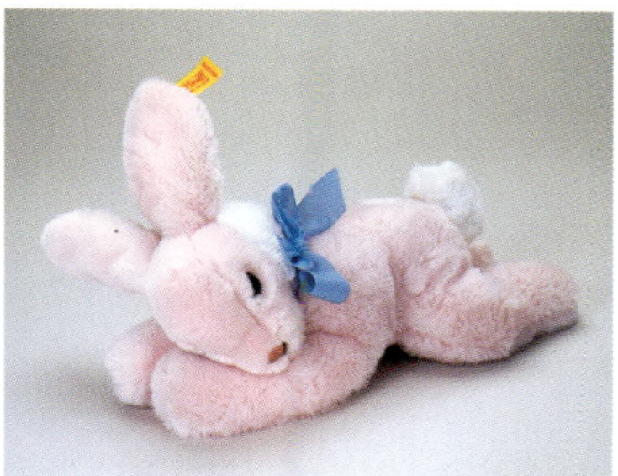

Baby Floppy Hase - *Baby Floppy Rabbit*

Webpelz, rosa oder blau, mollig weich, waschmaschinenfest - *woven fur, pink or blue, soft & cuddly, machine washable*

SERIE	ART.-NO	PERIOD	PR.	INFO
	5655/18	1983-1985	1-2	18 cm, rosa - *pink*
	5655/25	1983-1985	1-2	25 cm
	5656/18	1983-1985	1-2	18 cm, blau - *blue*
	5656/25	1983-1985	1-2	25 cm

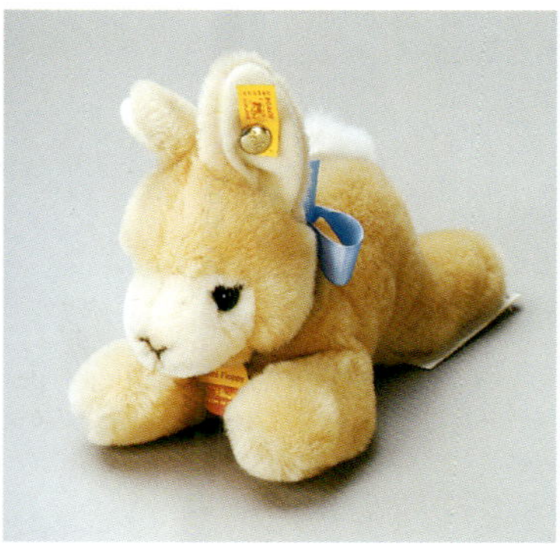

Mini Floppy Hase - ***Mini Floppy*** *Rabbit*

Webpelz, waschmaschinenfest - *woven fur, machine washable*

SERIE	ART.-NO	PERIOD	PR.	INFO
081903	**5658/16**	1989-1990	1-2	16 cm
	081903	1991-1991	1-2	

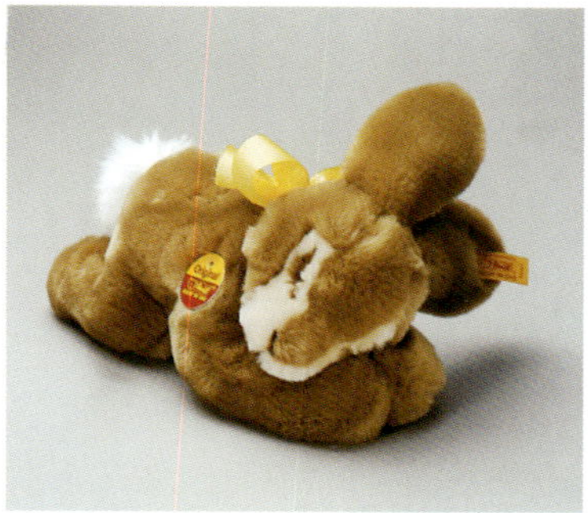

Schlafhase - *Bedtime Rabbit*

Webpelz, waschmaschinenfest - *woven fur, machine washable*

SERIE	ART.-NO	PERIOD	PR.	INFO
082542	**5644/22**	1990-1990	2	28 cm
	082542	1991-1999	2	

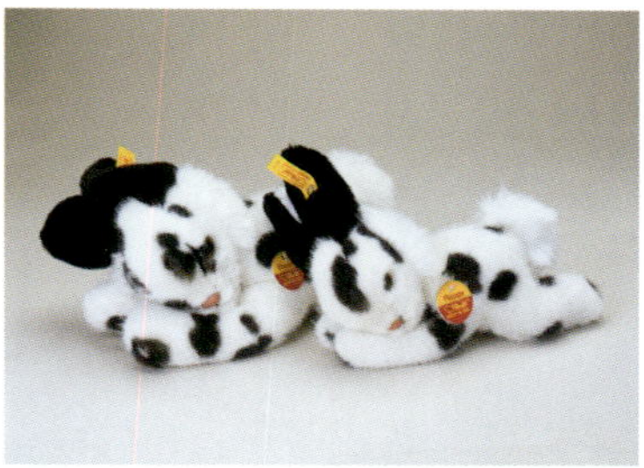

Floppy Hase - ***Floppy*** *Rabbit*

Webpelz, weiss/schwarz gefleckt, waschmaschinenfest - *woven fur, white/black spotted, machine washable*

EAN-NO.	PERIOD	PR.	INFO
082238	1999-1999	2	22 cm
082245	1999-1999	2-3	30 cm

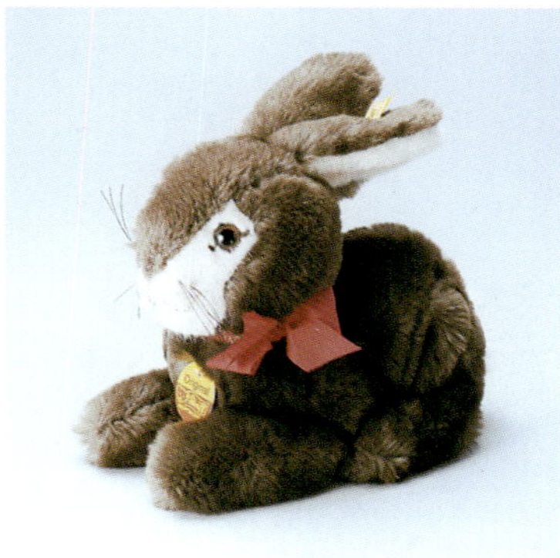

Kuschel Hase - *Cuddly Rabbit*

Webpelz, Schaumstoff-Fuellung, sitzend, superweich, waschmaschinenfest - *woven fur, stuffed with foam, sitting, super soft, machine washable*

SERIE	ART.-NO	PERIOD	PR.	INFO
	5525/25	1981-1984	2	25 cm

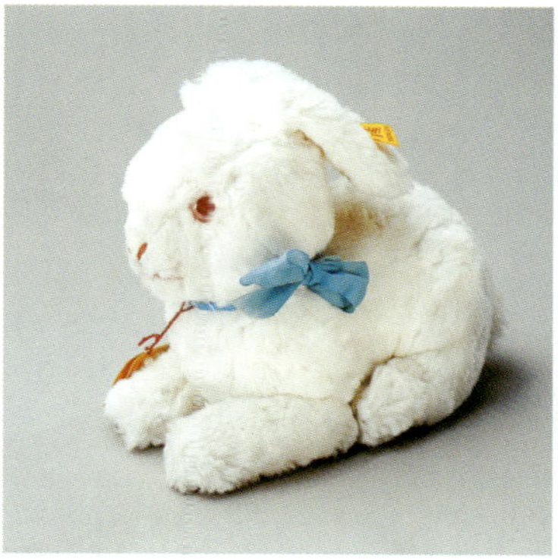

Kuschel Ango - *Cuddly Ango*

Webpelz, Schaumstoff-Fuellung, sitzend, superweich, waschmaschinenfest - *woven fur, stuffed with foam, sitting, super soft, machine washable*

SERIE	ART.-NO	PERIOD	PR.	INFO
	5526/25	1981-1984	2	25 cm

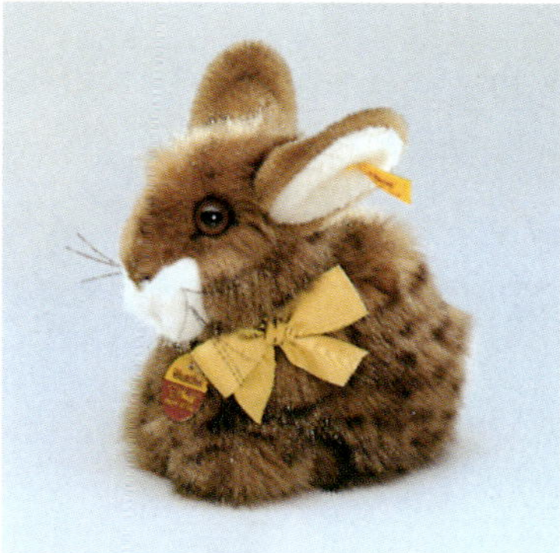

Wuschel Hase - ***Wuschel*** *Rabbit*

Webpelz, 15 cm, waschmaschinenfest - *woven fur, 15 cm, machine washable*

EAN-NO.	PERIOD	PR.	INFO
077418	1991-1993	2	braun - *brown*
077425	1991-1993	2	grau - *grey*
077449	1991-1993	2	graubraun - *grey-brown*
077456	1991-1993	2	blond

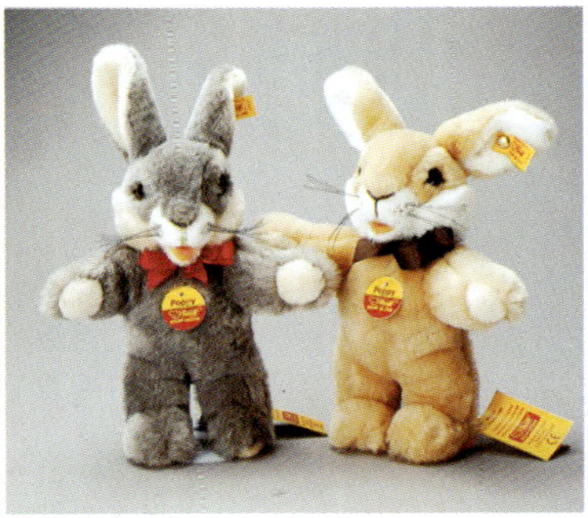

Poppy Hase - ***Poppy*** *Rabbit*

Webpelz, Pieps-Stimme, blond, zimt oder grau, waschmaschinenfest - *woven fur, squeaker, blond, cinnamon or grey, machine washable*

SERIE	ART.-NO	PERIOD	PR.	INFO
125539	**6060/24**	1989-1990	2-3	24 cm, blond
	125539	1991-1991	2-3	
125553	**6060/32**	1989-1990	2-3	32 cm
	125553	1991-1991	2-3	
125638	**6062/24**	1989-1990	2-3	24 cm, zimt - *cinnamon*
	125638	1991-1991	2-3	
125652	**6062/32**	1989-1990	2-3	32 cm
125737	**6067/24**	1989-1990	2-3	24 cm, grau - *grey*
	125737	1991-1991	2-3	
125751	**6067/32**	1989-1990	2-3	32 cm
	125751	1991-1991	2-3	

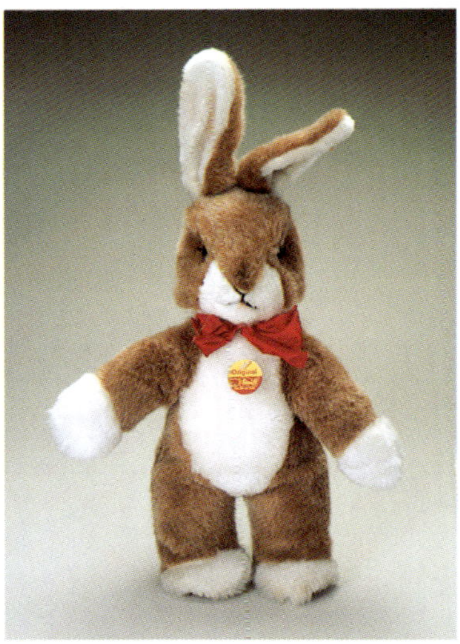

Weich-Hase - *Soft Rabbit*

Dralon, formgeschaeumt, sehr weich, Schlenkerkopf, vollwaschbar - *dralon, stuffed with pre-formed foam, very soft, floppy head, fully washable*

SERIE	ART.-NO	PERIOD	PR.	INFO
	6235/30	1971-1979	2-3	30 cm
	6235/40	1971-1979	2-3	40 cm

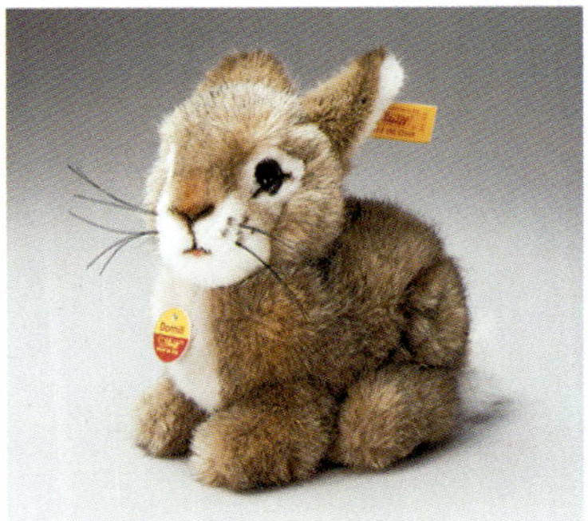

Dormili Hase - ***Dormili*** *Rabbit*

Webpelz, sitzend, abwaschbar - *woven fur, sitting, surface washable*

SERIE	ART.-NO	PERIOD	PR.	INFO
077708	**2974/16**	1986-1990	2	16 cm
	077708	1991-1999	2	

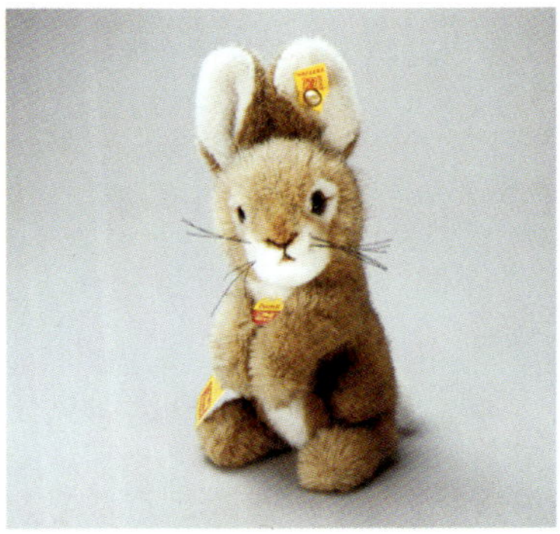

Dormili Hase - ***Dormili*** *Rabbit*

Webpelz, aufwartend, abwaschbar - *woven fur, sitting up, surface washable*

SERIE	ART.-NO	PERIOD	PR.	INFO
077807	**2977/20**	1986-1988	2	20 cm

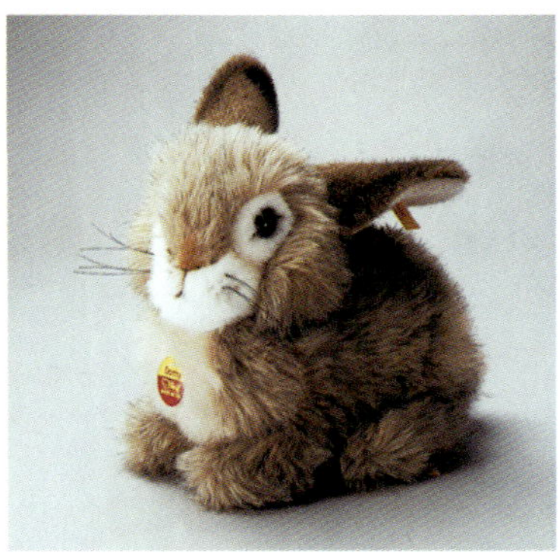

Dormy Hase - ***Dormy*** *Rabbit*

Webpelz, sitzend, sehr weich, abwaschbar - *woven fur, sitting, very soft, surface washable*

SERIE	ART.-NO	PERIOD	PR.	INFO
077753	**2975/25**	1985-1990	2-3	25 cm
	077753	1991-1997	2-3	

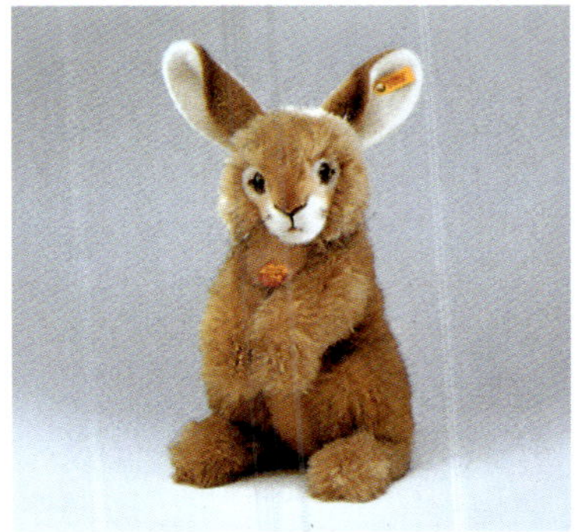

Dormy Hase - ***Dormy*** *Rabbit*

Webpelz, aufwartend, abwaschbar - *woven fur, sitting up, surface washable*

SERIE	ART.-NO	PERIOD	PR.	INFO
077821	**2978/35**	1987-1990	2-3	35 cm

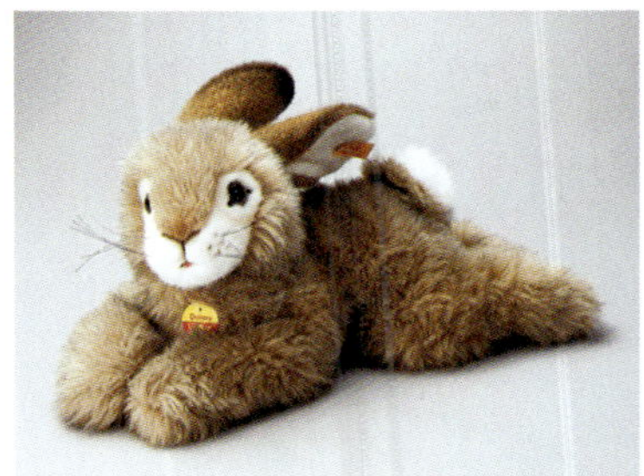

Dormy Hase - ***Dormy*** *Rabbit*

Webpelz, liegend, abwaschbar - *woven fur, lying, surface washable*

SERIE	ART.-NO	PERIOD	PR.	INFO
077678	**2972/40**	1988-1990	2-3	40 cm
	077678	1991-1995	2-3	

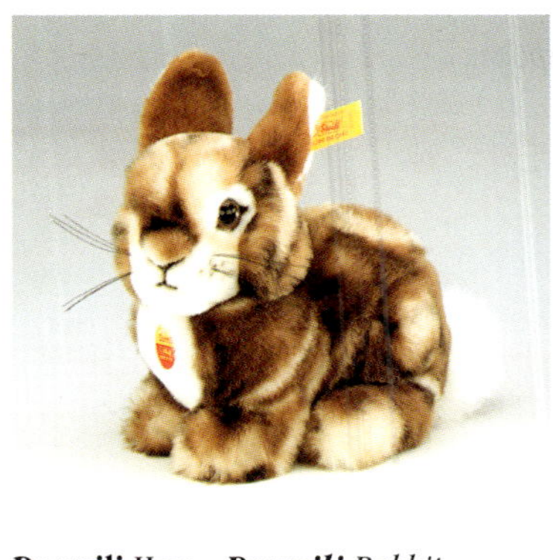

Dormili Hase - ***Dormili*** *Rabbit*

Webpelz, 16 cm, senf, grau oder braun gefleckt, sitzend, waschmaschinenfest - *woven fur, 16 cm, mustard, grey or brown spotted, sitting, machine washable*

EAN-NO.	PERIOD	PR.	INFO
077593	1996-1999	2	senf - *mustard*
077616	1996-1999	2	grau - *grey*
077630	1996-1999	2	braun - *brown*

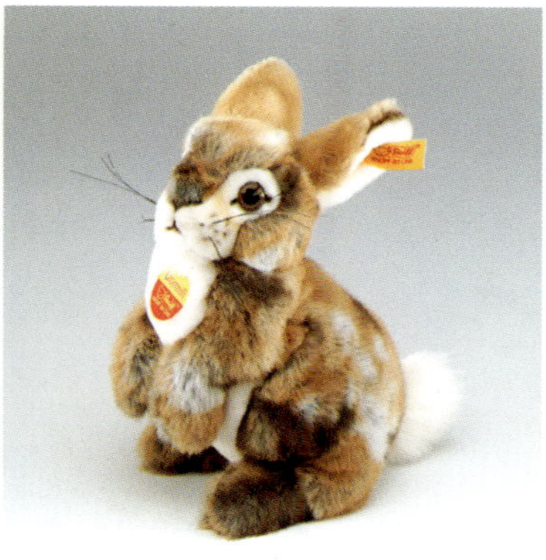

Dormili Hase - ***Dormili*** *Rabbit*

Webpelz, braun gefleckt, aufwartend, waschmaschinenfest - *woven fur, brown spotted, sitting up, machine washable*

EAN-No.	Period	Pr.	Info
077715	1998-1999	2-3	20 cm

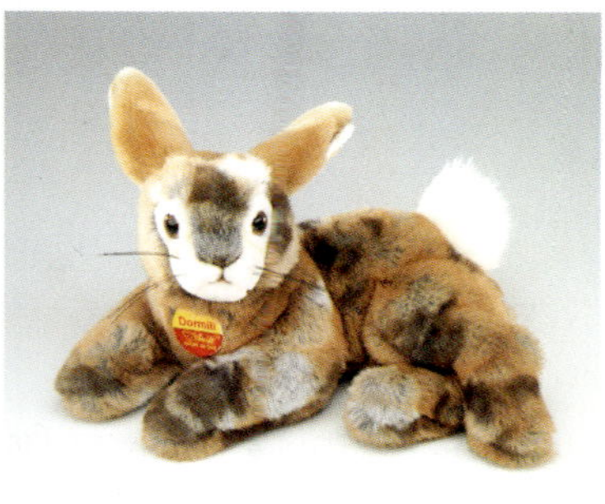

Dormili Hase - ***Dormili*** *Rabbit*

Webpelz, braun gefeckt, seitlich liegend, waschmaschinenfest - *woven fur, brown spotted, lying aside, machine washable*

EAN-No.	Period	Pr.	Info
077739	1998-1999	2-3	20 cm

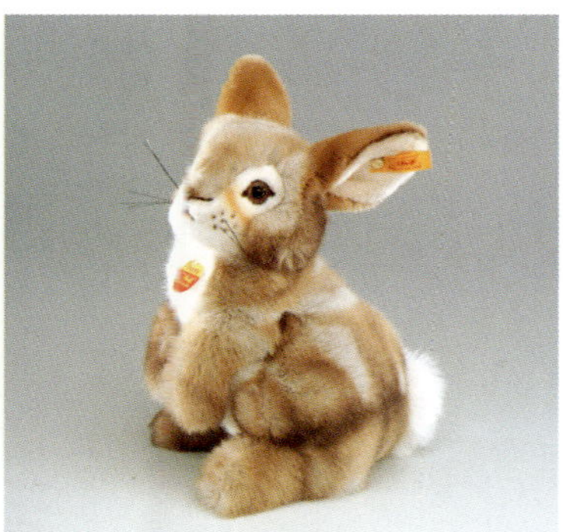

Dormy Hase - ***Dormy*** *Rabbit*

Webpelz, braun gefleckt, aufwartend, waschmaschinenfest - *woven fur, brown spotted, sitting up, machine washable*

EAN-No.	Period	Pr.	Info
078040	1998-1999	2-3	25 cm

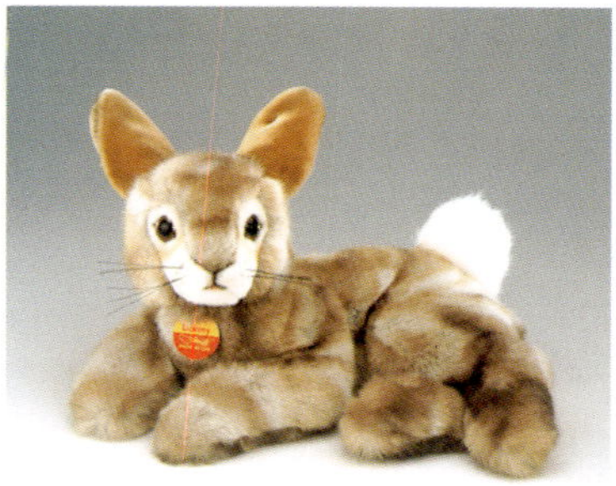

Dormy Hase - ***Dormy*** *Rabbit*

Webpelz, braun gefleckt, seitlich liegend, waschmaschinenfest - *woven fur, brown spotted, lying aside, machine washable*

EAN-No.	Period	Pr.	Info
078064	1998-1999	2-3	28 cm

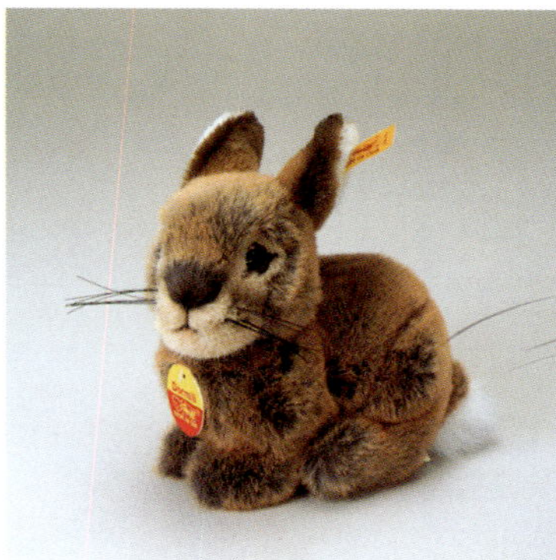

Dormili Hase - ***Dormili*** *Rabbit*

Webpelz, braun gespitzt, sitzend, waschmaschinenfest - *woven fur, brown tipped, sitting, machine washable*

EAN-No.	Period	Pr.	Info
080111	1999-1999	2	16 cm

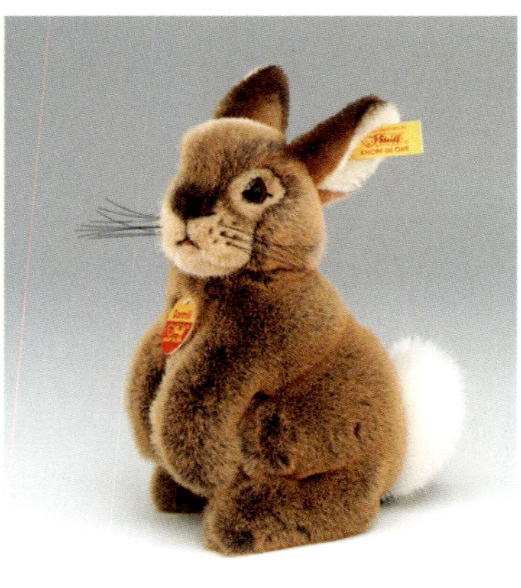

Dormili Hase - ***Dormili*** *Rabbit*

Webpelz, braun gespitzt, aufwartend, waschmaschinenfest - *woven fur, brown tipped, sitting up, machine washable*

EAN-No.	Period	Pr.	Info
080128	1999-1999	2	18 cm

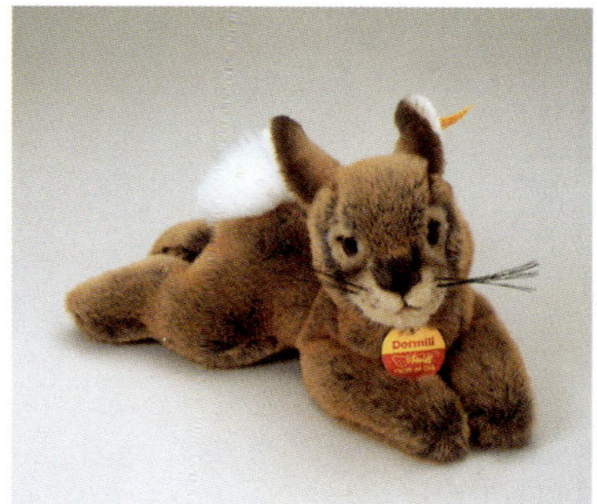

Dormili Hase - ***Dormili*** *Rabbit*

Webpelz, braun gespitzt, liegend, waschmaschinenfest - *woven fur, brown tipped, lying, machine washable*

EAN-No.	Period	Pr.	Info
080135	1999-1999	2	22 cm

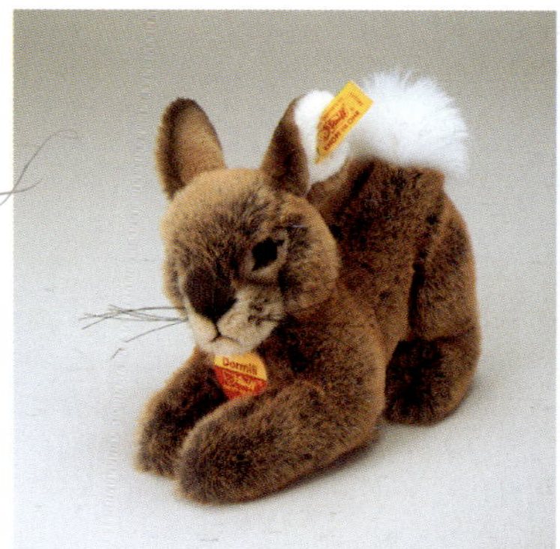

Dormili Hase - ***Dormili*** *Rabbit*

Webpelz, braun gespitzt, spielend, waschmaschinenfest - *woven fur, brown tipped, playing, machine washable*

EAN-No.	Period	Pr.	Info
080142	1999-1999	2	18 cm

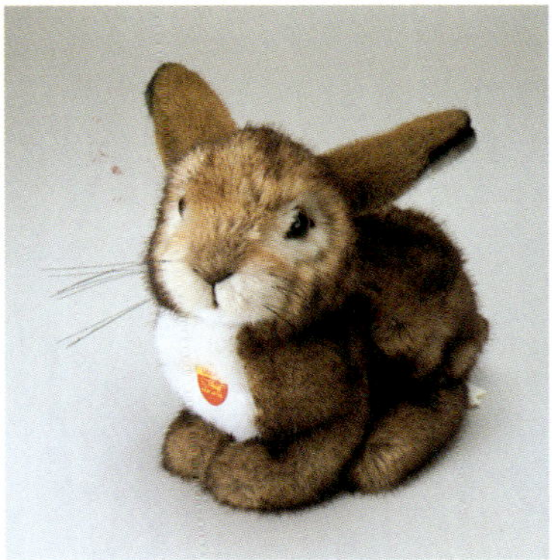

Dormy Hase - ***Dormy** Rabbit*

Webpelz, braun gefleckt, sitzend, waschmaschinenfest - *woven fur, brown spotted, sitting, machine washable*

EAN-No.	Period	Pr.	Info
080326	1999-1999	2-3	25 cm

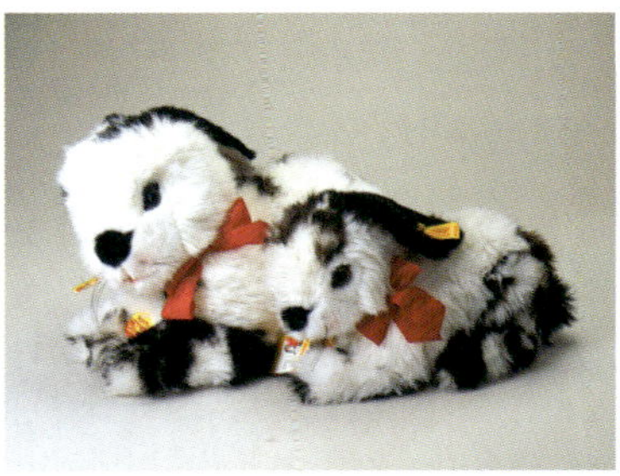

Spotty Hase - ***Spotty** Rabbit*

Pelzimitation, ab 1978 Synthetik-Webpelz, liegend, abwaschbar - *imitation fur, from 1978 synthetic woven fur, lying, surface washable*

Serie	Art.-No	Period	Pr.	Info
	2970/23	1977-1984	2-3	23 cm
	2970/30	1977-1984	2-3	30 cm

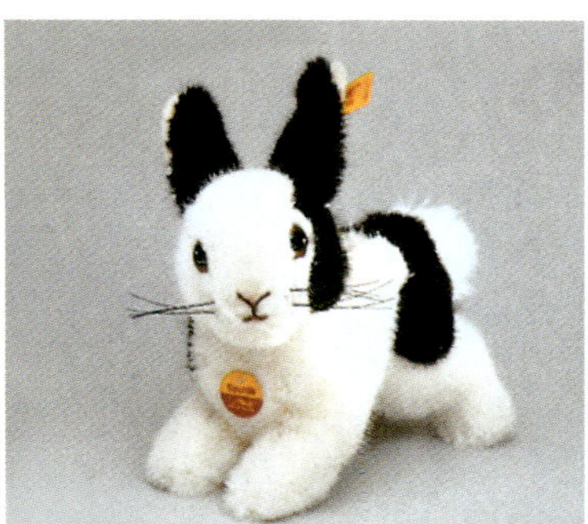

Spottili Hase - ***Spottili** Rabbit*

Webpelz, schwarz/weiss oder grau/weiss, 17 cm, springend, abwaschbar - *woven fur, black/white or grey/white 17 cm, jumping, surface washable*

Serie	Art.-No	Period	Pr.	Info
077845	**2982/17**	1987-1990	2	schwarz/weiss - *black/white*
077906	**2992/17**	1987-1989	2	grau/weiss - *grey/white*

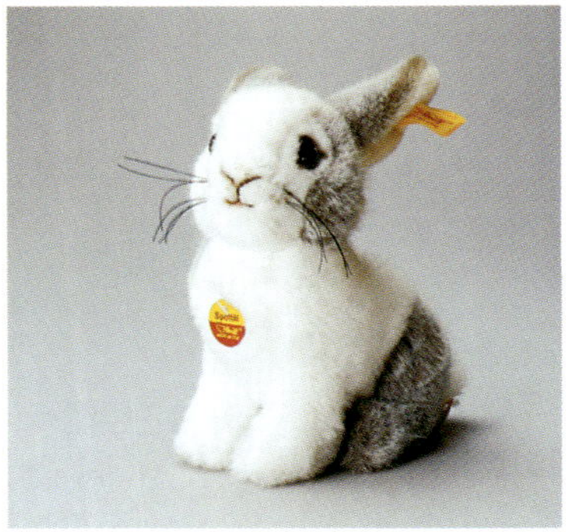

Spottili Hase - ***Spottili** Rabbit*

Webpelz, schwarz/weiss oder grau/weiss, 17 cm, sitzend, abwaschbar - *woven fur, black/white or grey/white, 17 cm, sitting, surface washable*

Serie	Art.-No	Period	Pr.	Info
077869	**2984/17**	1987-1990	2	schwarz/weiss - *black/white*
077937	**2994/17**	1987-1989	2	grau/weiss - *grey/white*

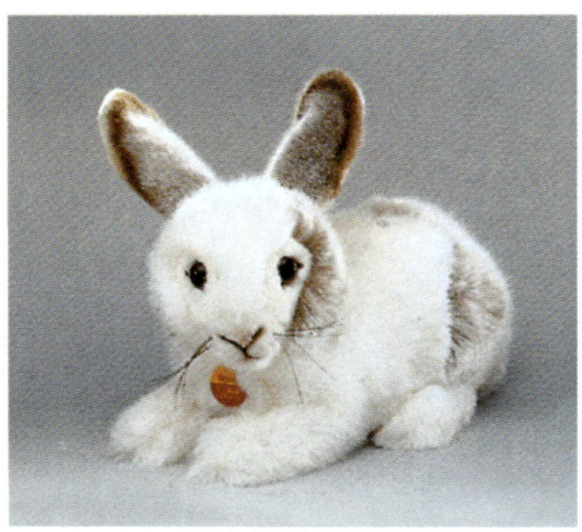

Spotty Hase - ***Spotty** Rabbit*

Webpelz, schwarz/weiss oder grau/weiss, 30 cm, liegend, abwaschbar - *woven fur, black/white or grey/white, 30 cm, lying, surface washable*

Serie	Art.-No	Period	Pr.	Info
077883	**2985/30**	1987-1988	2-3	schwarz/weiss - *black/white*
077951	**2995/30**	1987-1989	2-3	grau/weiss - *grey/white*

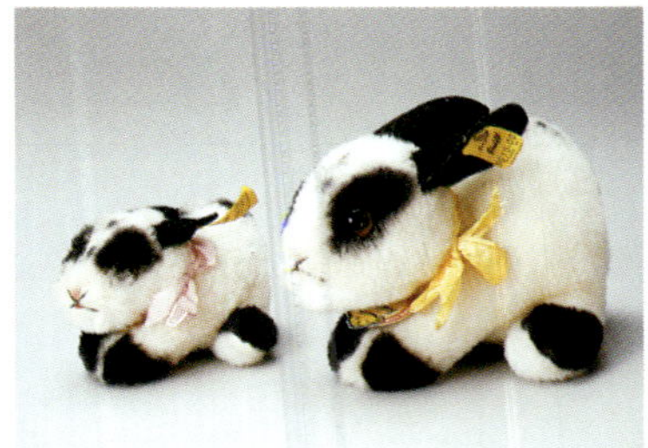

Timmy Hase - ***Timmy** Rabbit*

Dralon, weiss/schwarz gefleckt, liegend - *dralon, white/black spotted, lying*

Serie	Art.-No	Period	Pr.	Info
305	**6610,00**	1965-1967	3	10 cm
	3050/10	1968-1974	2-3	
305	**6615,00**	1965-1967	3	15 cm
	3050/15	1968-1974	2-3	

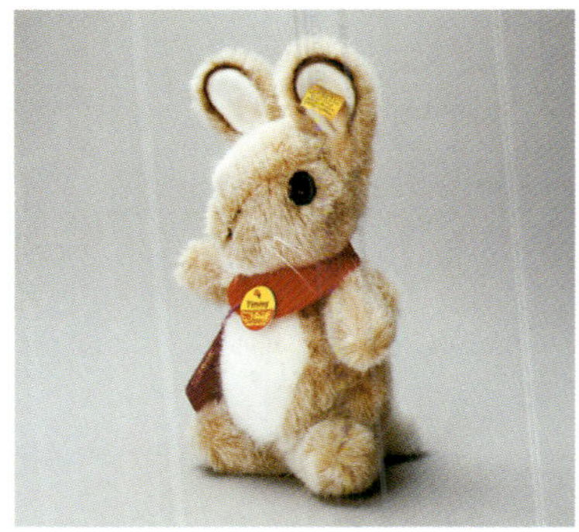

Timmy Hase - ***Timmy** Rabbit*

Nerzimitation, ab 1978 Synthetik-Webpelz, beige/weiss oder grau/weiss, 16 cm, aufwartend, abwaschbar - *imitation mink, from 1978 synthetic woven fur, beige/white or grey/white, 16 cm, sitting up, surface washable*

Serie	Art.-No	Period	Pr.	Info
	3155/16	1977-1983	2	beige/weiss - *beige/white*
	3156/16	1977-1983	2	grau/weiss - *grey/white*

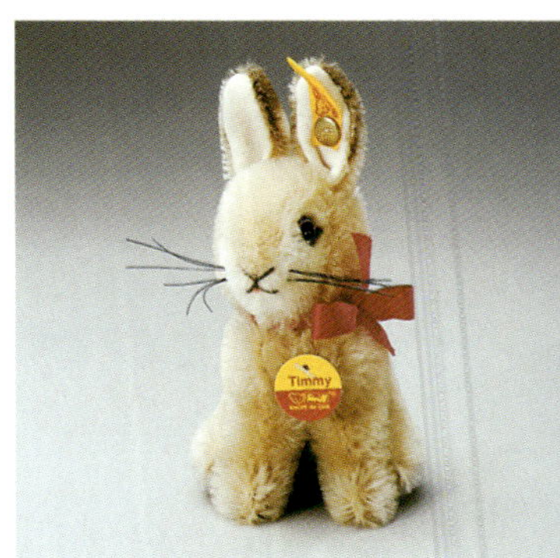

Timmy Hase - ***Timmy** Rabbit*

Mohair-Webpelz, braun, sitzend, Kopf drehbar - *mohair woven fur, brown, sitting, head swivels*

SERIE	ART.-NO	PERIOD	PR.	INFO
032707	**1350/10**	1989-1990	2	10 cm
	032707	1991-1992	2	
032721	**1350/12**	1989-1990	2	12 cm
	032721	1991-1992	2	

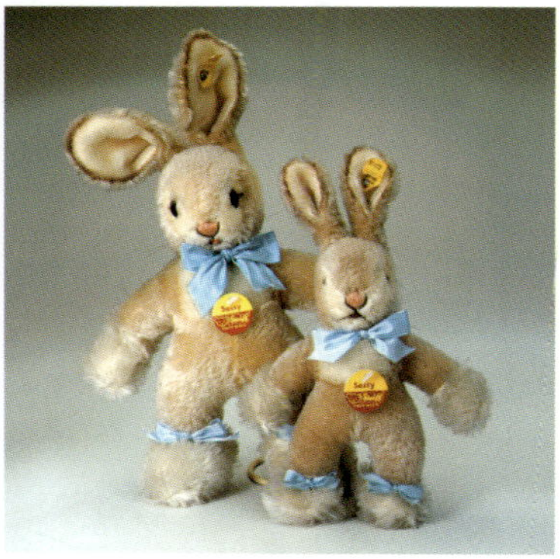

Baby Hase **Sassy** - *Baby Rabbit **Sassy***

Mohairpluesch, caramel, Pfoten weiss (nur 1959-60 rosa), Kopf drehbar, sehr weich, Druckstimme, abwaschbar - *mohair, caramel with white paws (only 1959-60 pink paws), head swivels, very soft, press voice, surface washable*

SERIE	ART.-NO	PERIOD	PR.	INFO
36	**7322**	1955-1958	4	22 cm. Pfoten weiss - *white paws*
360	**7322,04**	1959-1964	3-4	
312	**7322,04**	1965-1967	3-4	
	3120/22	1968-1977	3	
36	**7330**	1955-1958	4	30 cm
360	**7330,04**	1959-1964	3-4	
312	**7330,04**	1965-1967	3-4	
	3120/30	1968-1978	3	
360	**7322,08**	1959-1960	4	22 cm, Pfoten rosa - *pink paws*
360	**7330,08**	1959-1960	4	30 cm

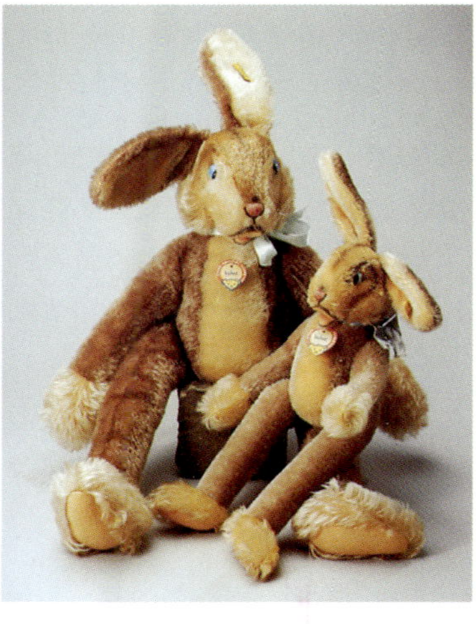

Lulac Schlenkerhase - ***Lulac** Floppy Rabbit*

Mohair, caramel, gegliedert, lange Glieder, superweich, Druckstimme, abwaschbar - *mohair, caramel, jointed, very long limbs, super soft, press voice, surface washable*

SERIE	ART.-NO	PERIOD	PR.	INFO
36	**7343,1**	1952-1958	5	43 cm
360	**7343,00**	1959-1964	5	
314	**7343,00**	1965-1967	5	
	3140/43	1968-1974	4-5	
360	**7360,00**	1964-1964	5	60 cm
314	**7360,00**	1965-1966	5	

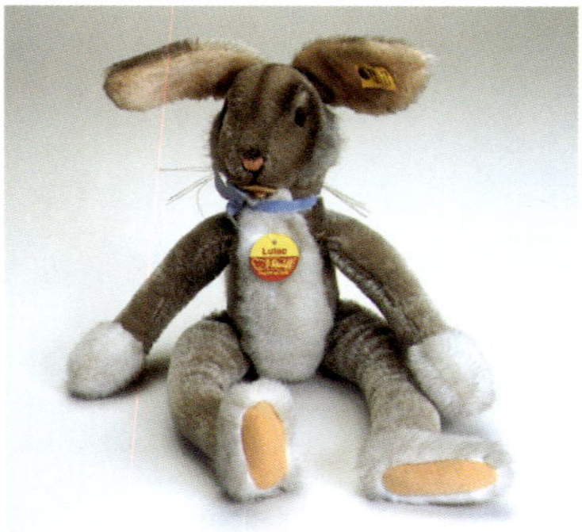

Lulac Hase - ***Lulac** Rabbit*

Mohair, hellbraun (ab 1976 genannt honig) oder grau, 43 cm, Schlenkerglieder, abwaschbar - *mohair, light brown (from 1976 called honey) or grey, 43 cm, floppy joints, surface washable*

SERIE	ART.-NO	PERIOD	PR.	INFO
	3141/43	1974-1981	3	hellbraun - *light brown*
	3142/43	1974-1980	3	grau - *grey*

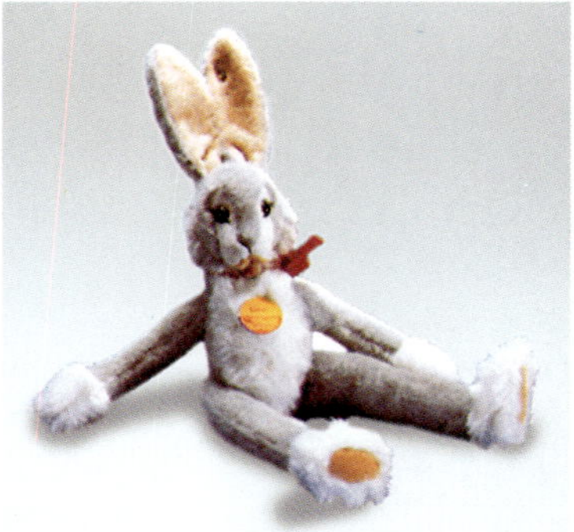

Lulac Hase - ***Lulac** Rabbit*

Pelz-Imitation, ab 1978 Synthetik-Webpelz, beige oder grau, Schlenkerglieder, abwaschbar - *imitation fur, from 1978 synthetic woven fur, beige or grey, floppy joints, surface washable*

SERIE	ART.-NO	PERIOD	PR.	INFO
	3143/60	1974-1978	3	60 cm, beige
	3143/80	1974-1978	3	80 cm
	3144/60	1974-1979	3	60 cm, grau - *grey*
	3144/80	1974-1977	3	80 cm

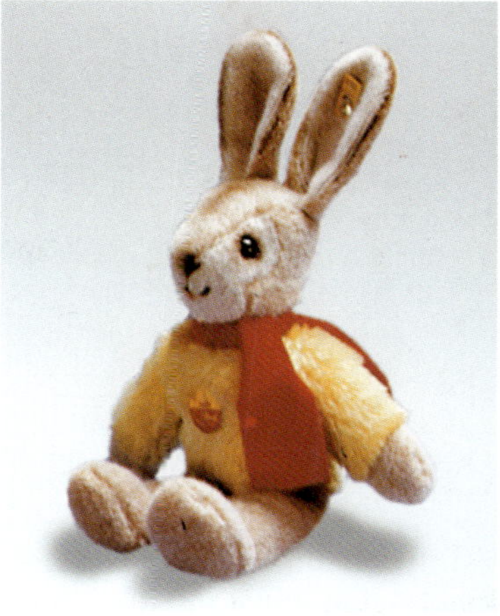

Lully Schlenkerhase - ***Lully** Floppy Rabbit*

Webpelz, roter Schal, Schlenkerglieder, abwaschbar - *woven fur, red scarf, floppy joints, surface washable*

SERIE	ART.-NO	PERIOD	PR.	INFO
	6280/40	1979-1981	3	40 cm

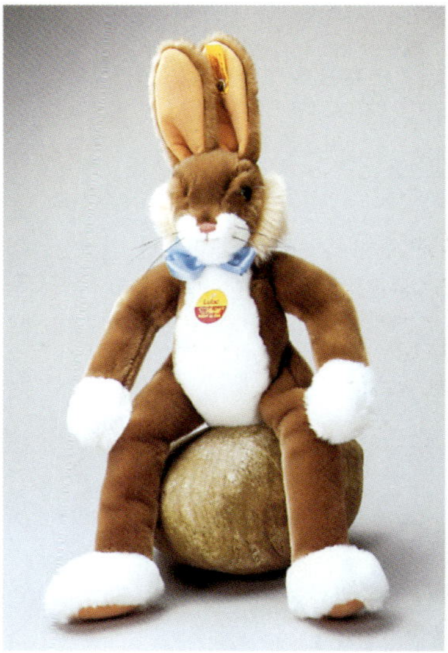

Lulac Schlenkerhase - ***Lulac** Dangling Rabbit*

Webpelz, zimt, abwaschbar - *woven fur, cinnamon, surface washable*

SERIE	ART.-NO	PERIOD	PR.	INFO
122804	**6283/50**	1983-1990	2-3	45 cm
	122804	1991-1999	2-3	

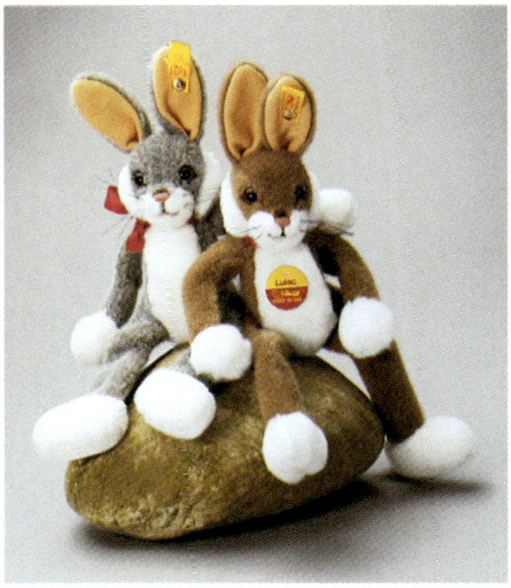

Lulac Schlenkerhase - ***Lulac*** *Dangling Rabbit*

Webpelz, grau oder beige, abwaschbar - *woven fur, grey or beige, surface washable*

SERIE	ART.-NO	PERIOD	PR.	INFO
122552	**6281/25**	1984-1990	2-3	30 cm, grau - *grey*
	122552	1991-1999	2-3	
122606	**6281/75**	1987-1990	4	75 cm
	122606	1991-1999	4	
122651	**6282/25**	1984-1990	2-3	30 cm, beige
	122651	1991-1999	2-3	
122705	**6282/75**	1987-1989	3	75 cm

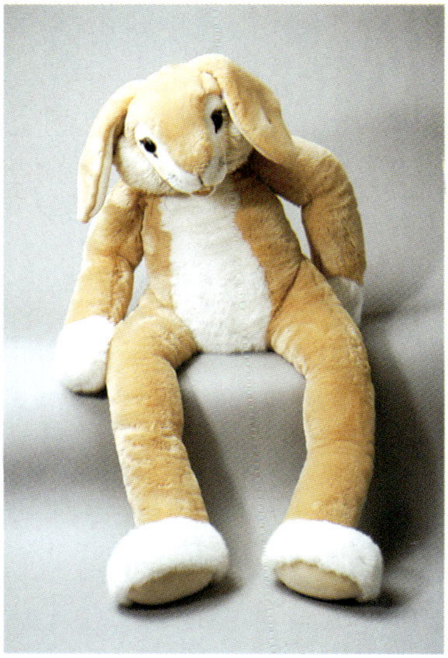

Lulac Hase - ***Lulac*** *Rabbit*

Webpelz, creme, abwaschbar - *woven fur, cream, surface washable*

SERIE	ART.-NO	PERIOD	PR.	INFO
122507	**6284/99**	1989-1990	4-5	120 cm
	122507	1991-1999	4-5	

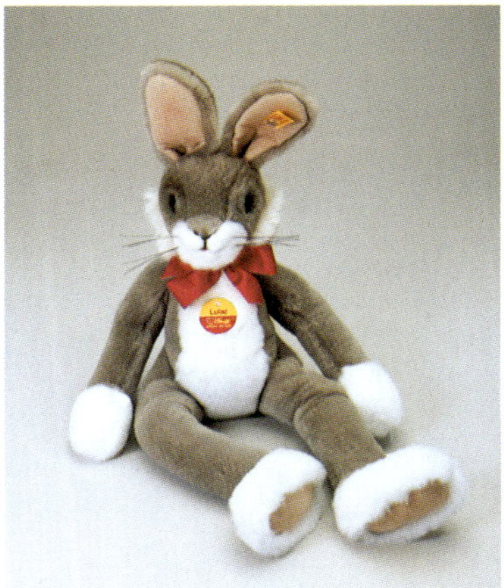

Lulac Schlenkerhase - ***Lulac*** *Dangling Rabbit*

Webpelz, grau, waschmaschinenfest - *woven fur, grey, machine washable*

EAN-NO.	PERIOD	PR.	INFO
122798	1999-1999	2-3	45 cm

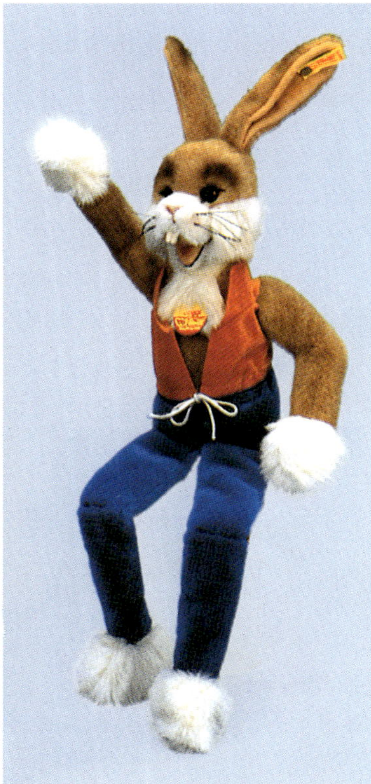

Joggi Hase - ***Joggi*** *Rabbit*

Webpelz, orange Weste, blaue Beine, Schlenkerglieder, abwaschbar - *woven fur, orange vest, blue legs, floppy joints, surface washable*

SERIE	ART.-NO	PERIOD	PR.	INFO
	3145/55	1981-1985	3-4	55 cm

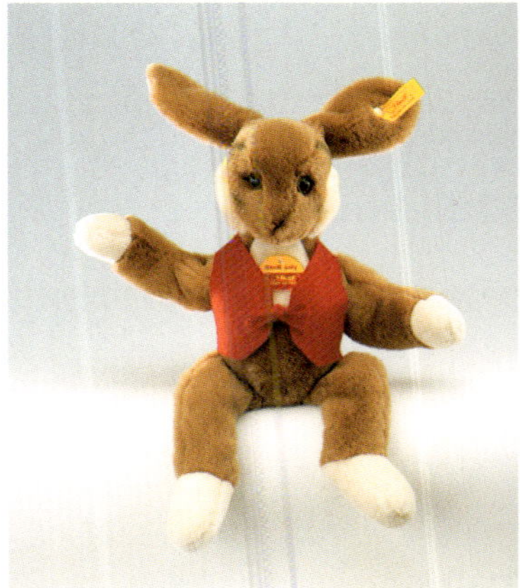

Steiff Jolly Hase - ***Steiff Jolly*** *Rabbit*

Webpelz, braun oder grau, rote Filzweste, ohne Weste waschmaschinenfest - *woven fur, brown or grey, red felt-waistcoat, machine washable without waistcoat*

EAN-NO.	PERIOD	PR.	INFO
122903	1998-1999	2-3	32 cm, braun - *brown*
122828	1997-1998	3	45 cm
122910	1998-1998	2-3	32 cm, grau - *grey*
122842	1997-1998	3	45 cm

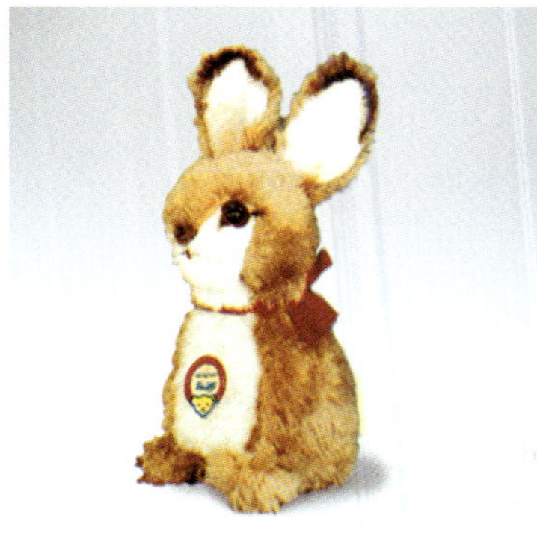

Buzzel Hase - *Buzzel Rabbit*

Dralon, formgeschaeumt, superweich - *dralon, stuffed with pre-formed foam, super soft*

SERIE	ART.-NO	PERIOD	PR.	INFO
	6156/20	1971-1978	1-2	20 cm

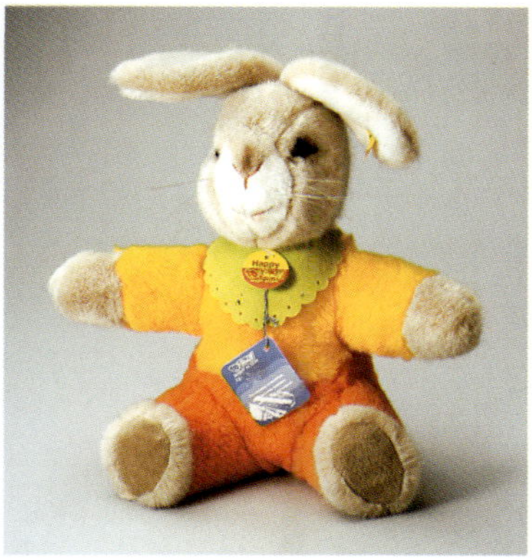

Happy Hase - ***Happy** Rabbit*

Pelzimitation, formgeschaeumt, ab 1978 Wirkpluesch, orange & gelb, gruenes Laetzchen, sitzend - *imitation fur, stuffed with pre-formed foam, from 1978 knitted plush, orange & yellow, green bib, sitting*

SERIE	ART.-NO	PERIOD	PR.	INFO
	6120/35	1975-1979	2-3	35 cm

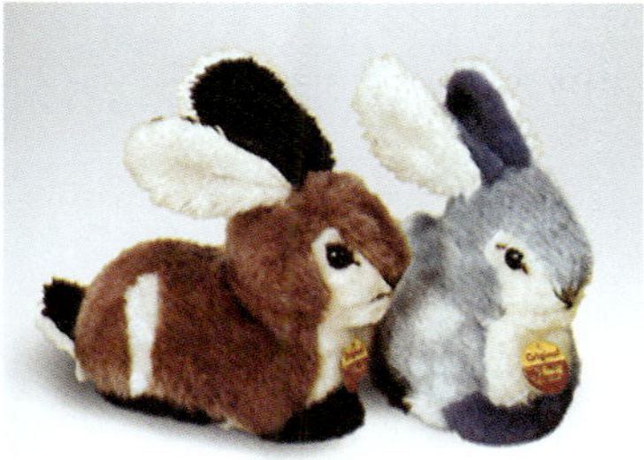

Hase - *Rabbit*

Dralon, formgeschaeumt, beige/weiss oder hellblau/weiss, 22 cm, sitzend, abwaschbar - *dralon, stuffed with pre-formed foam, beige/white or light blue/white, 22 cm, sitting, surface washable*

SERIE	ART.-NO	PERIOD	PR.	INFO
	3165/22	1972-1978	2	beige/weiss - *beige/white*
	3166/22	1972-1975	2	hellblau/ weiss - *light blue/white*

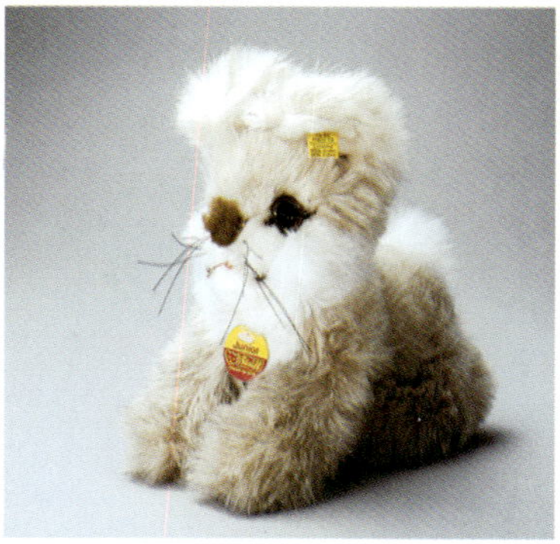

Junior Hase - ***Junior** Rabbit*

Pelzimitation, ab 1978 Synthetik-Webpelz, liegend, abwaschbar - *imitation fur, from 1978 synthetic woven fur, lying, surface washable*

SERIE	ART.-NO	PERIOD	PR.	INFO
	2882/25	1975-1980	2	25 cm
	2882/35	1975-1980	2	35 cm

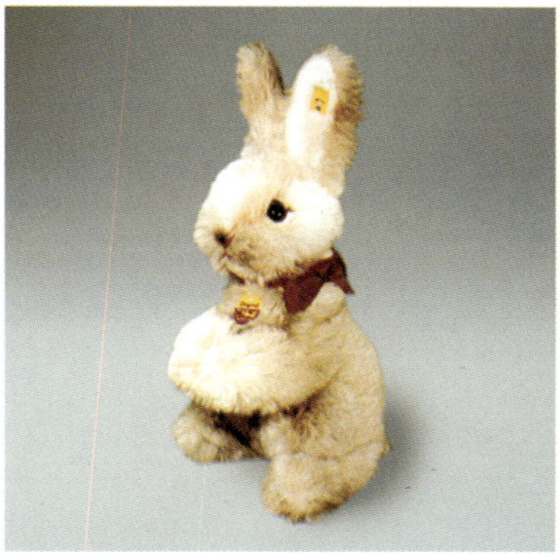

Hase - *Rabbit*

Pelzimitation, superweich, aufwartend, abwaschbar - *imitation fur, super soft, sitting up, surface washable*

SERIE	ART.-NO	PERIOD	PR.	INFO
	2950/30	1975-1978	2	30 cm

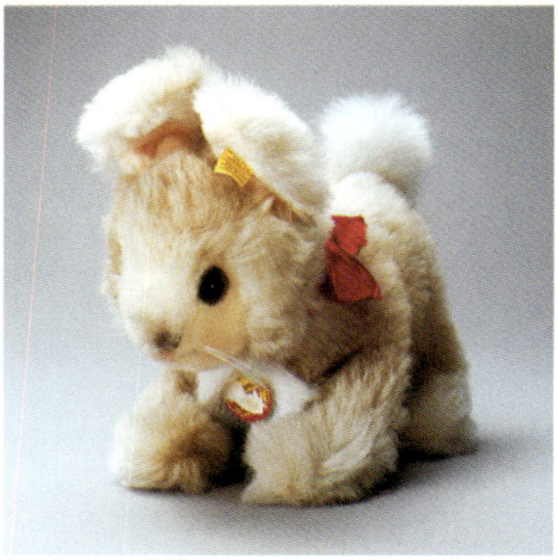

Muemmel Hase - ***Muemmel** Rabbit*

Pelzimitation, ab 1978 Wirkflor, formgeschaeumt, stehend, abwaschbar - *imitation fur, from 1978 knitted pile, stuffed with pre-formed foam, standing, surface washable*

SERIE	ART.-NO	PERIOD	PR.	INFO
	2945/25	1976-1982	2	25 cm

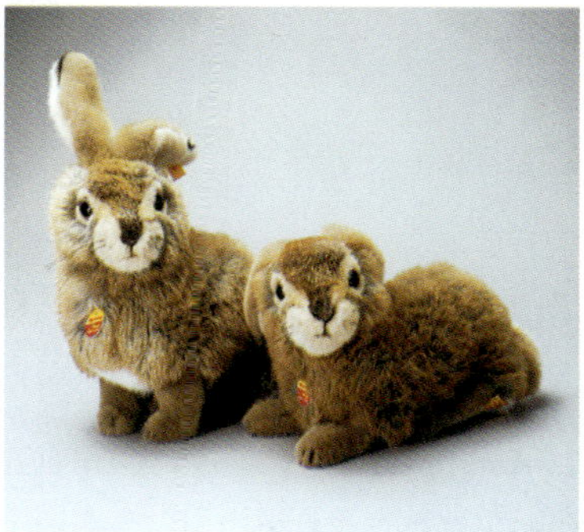

Muemmel Feldhase - ***Muemmel** Wild Rabbit*

Webpelz, goldbraun, 40 cm, abwaschbar - *woven fur, golden brown, 40 cm, surface washable*

EAN-NO.	PERIOD	PR.	INFO
077654	1994-1999	3	sitzend - *sitting*
077661	1994-1997	3	liegend - *lying*

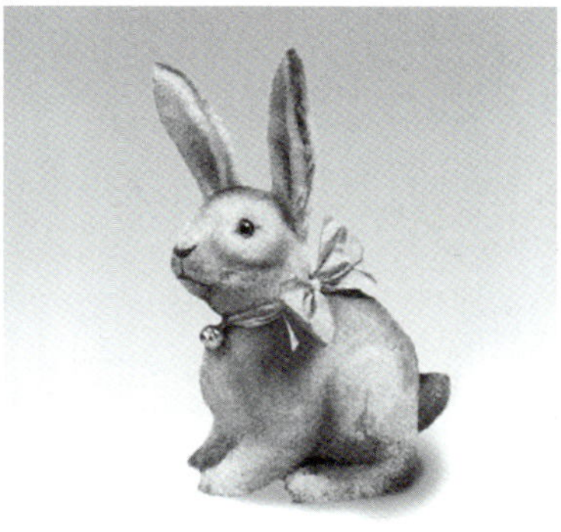

Hase - *Rabbit*

Mohairpluesch, mais oder weiss, sitzend, Drehkopf - *mohair, corn yellow or white, sitting, head swivels*

SERIE	ART.-NO	PERIOD	PR.	INFO
36	**3315** m	1949-1949	4-5	15 cm, mais - *corn yellow*
36	**3318** m	1949-1949	4-5	18 cm
36	**3315** w	1949-1949	4-5	15 cm, weiss - *white*
36	**3318** w	1949-1949	4-5	18 cm

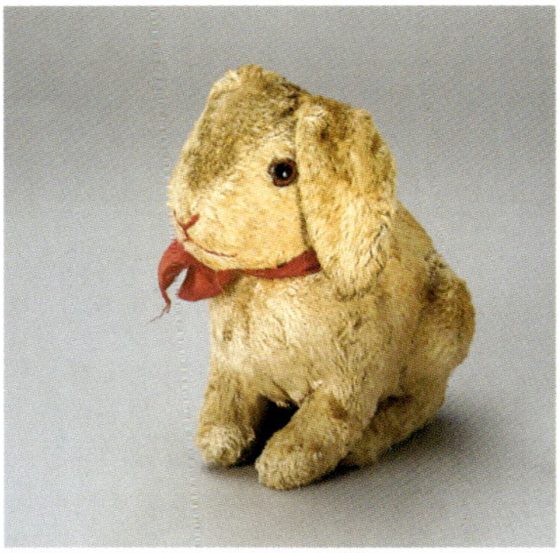

Hase - *Rabbit*

Kunstseidenpluesch, hellbraun, bemalt, sitzend, Drehkopf - *artificial silk plush, light brown, painted, sitting, head swivels*

SERIE	ART.-NO	PERIOD	PR.	INFO
36	**3616**	1949-1949	4	16 cm
36	**3619**	1948-1949	4	19 cm

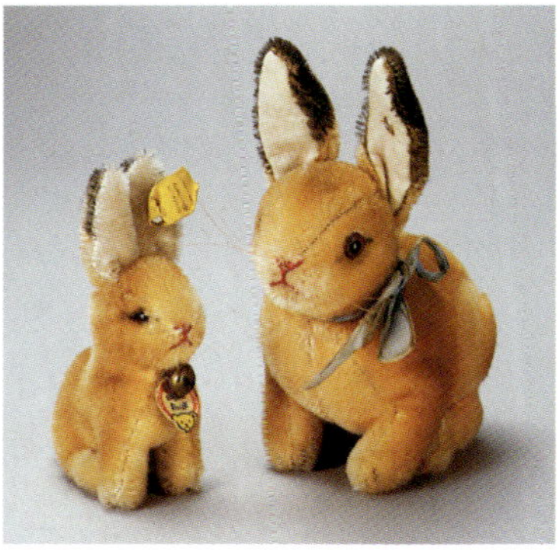

Hase ab 1967 **Sonny** Hase - *Rabbit from 1967* ***Sonny*** *Rabbit*

Mohairpluesch, hellbraun/weiss, schattiert, sitzend, Drehkopf - *mohair, light brown/ white, shaded, sitting, head swivels*

SERIE	ART.-NO	PERIOD	PR.	INFO
36	**3308**	1950-1958	3-4	8 cm
360	**3308,00**	1959-1964	3	
299	**3308,03**	1965-1967	3	
	2990/08	1968-1974	3	
36	**3309**	1951-1958	3-4	9 cm
360	**3309,00**	1959-1964	3	
299	**3309,03**	1965-1967	3	
	2990/09	1968-1968	3	
36	**3315**	1950-1958	4	15 cm
360	**3315,00**	1959-1964	3-4	
36	**3318**	1950-1958	4	18 cm
360	**3318,00**	1959-1964	3-4	

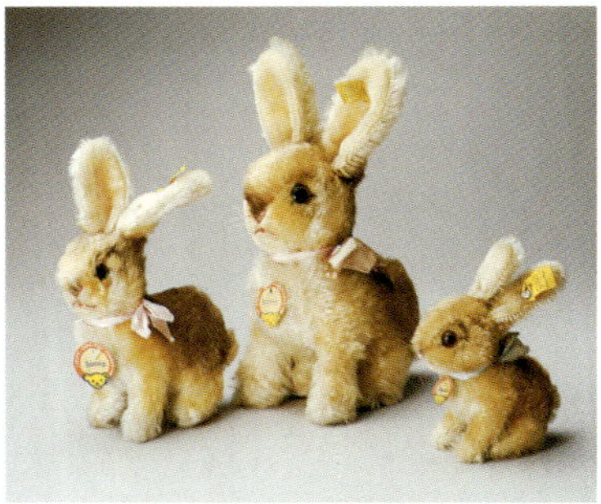

Sonny Hase - ***Sonny*** *Rabbit*

Mohair, weiss/braun, sitzend, Drehkopf, abwaschbar - *mohair, white/brown, sitting, head swivels, surface washable*

SERIE	ART.-NO	PERIOD	PR.	INFO
360	**3310,03**	1964-1964	3	10 cm
299	**3310,03**	1965-1967	3	
	2990/10	1968-1976	2	
360	**3317,03**	1964-1964	3	17 cm
299	**3317,03**	1965-1967	3	
	2990/17	1968-1976	2-3	
360	**3322,03**	1964-1964	3	22 cm
299	**3322,03**	1965-1967	3	
	2990/22	1968-1974	2-3	

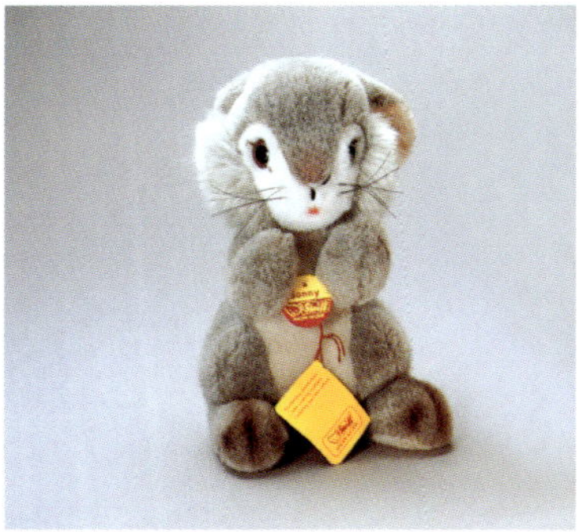

Sonny Hase - ***Sonny*** *Rabbit*

Webpelz, grau, aufwartend, abwaschbar - *woven fur, grey, sitting up, surface washable*

SERIE	ART.-NO	PERIOD	PR.	INFO
077500	**2960/22**	1979-1987	2	22 cm

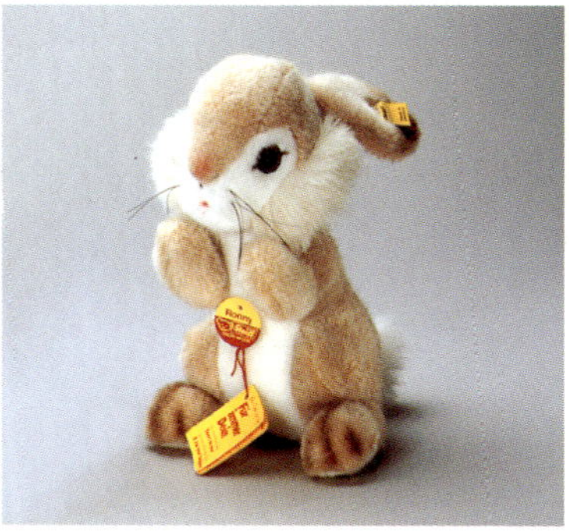

Ronny Hase - ***Ronny*** *Rabbit*

Webpelz, beige, aufwartend, abwaschbar - *woven fur, beige, sitting up, surface washable*

SERIE	ART.-NO	PERIOD	PR.	INFO
077555	**2961/22**	1979-1987	2	22 cm

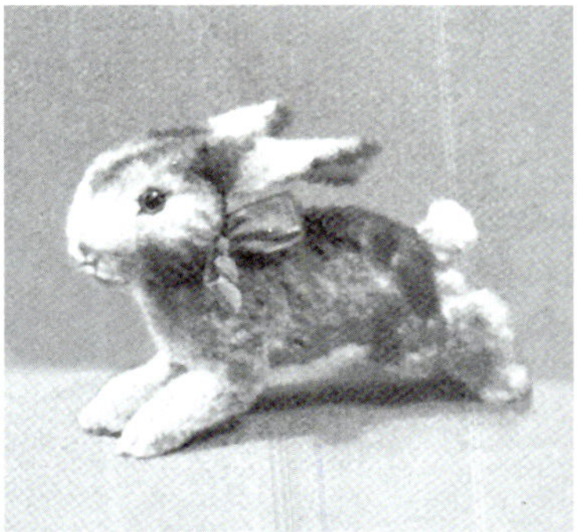

Hase - *Rabbit*

Seidenpluesch, hellbraun, bemalt, springend, ohne Raeder - *artificial silk plush, light brown, painted, hopping, without wheels*

SERIE	ART.-NO	PERIOD	PR.	INFO
36	**1614,0**	1949-1949	4	14 cm

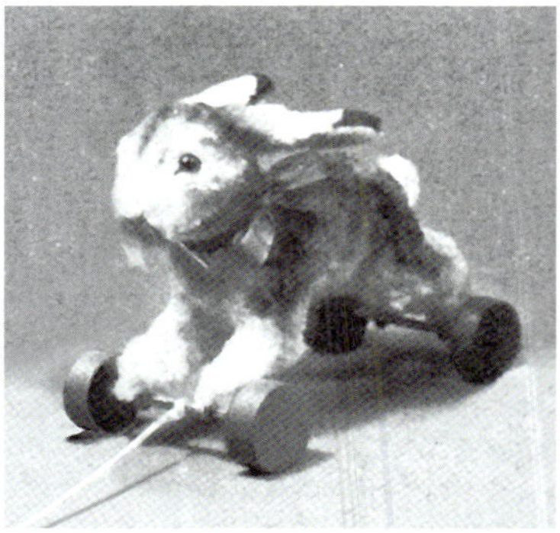

Hase - *Rabbit*

Seidenpluesch, hellbraun, bemalt, springend auf Exzenterraedern - *artificial silk plush, light brown, painted, hopping, on eccentric wheels*

SERIE	ART.-NO	PERIOD	PR.	INFO
36	**1614** ex	1949-1949	4-5	14 cm

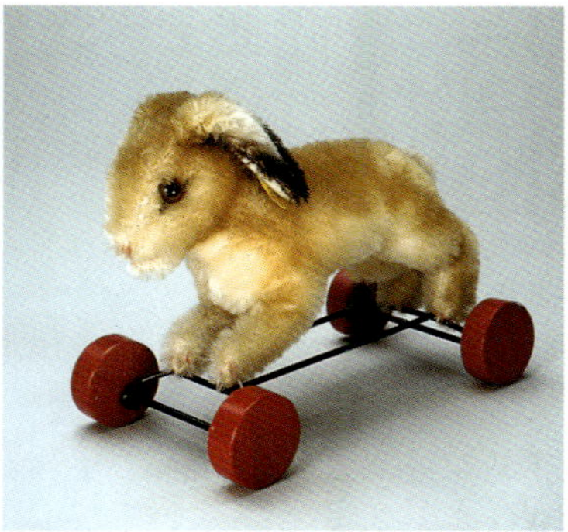

Nachzieh-Hase / Hoppel-Hase - *Pull toy Rabbit / Hopping Rabbit*

Mohair, braun/weiss, springend, auf Exzenterraedern - *mohair, brown/white, hopping, on eccentric wheels*

SERIE	ART.-NO	PERIOD	PR.	INFO
81 36	**1308** ex	1955-1957	4-5	8 cm
810 360	**1308,10**	1959-1960	4-5	
36	**1314** ex	1950-1958	4-5	14 cm
360	**1314,10**	1960-1964	4	
292	**1314,10**	1965-1967	4	
	2920/14	1968-1969	4	
36	**1317** ex	1949-1957	4-5	17 cm
360	**1317,10**	1959-1961	4-5	

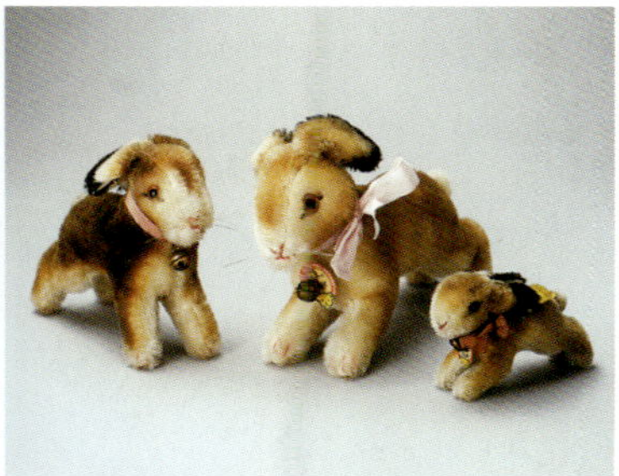

Hase ab 1974 **Hoppy** Hase - *Rabbit from 1974* ***Hoppy*** *Rabbit*

Mohair, braun/weiss, springend, abwaschbar - *mohair, brown/white, hopping, surface washable*

SERIE	ART.-NO	PERIOD	PR.	INFO
36	**1308,0**	1950-1958	4	8 cm
360	**1308,00**	1959-1964	3-4	
290	**1308,00**	1965-1967	3-4	
	2900/08	1968-1974	3	
36	**1314,0**	1949-1958	4	14 cm
360	**1314,00**	1959-1964	3-4	
290	**1314,00**	1965-1967	3-4	
	2900/14	1968-1976	3	
36	**1317,0**	1949-1958	4-5	17 cm
360	**1317,00**	1959-1964	4	
290	**1317,00**	1965-1967	4	
	2900/17	1968-1976	3-4	

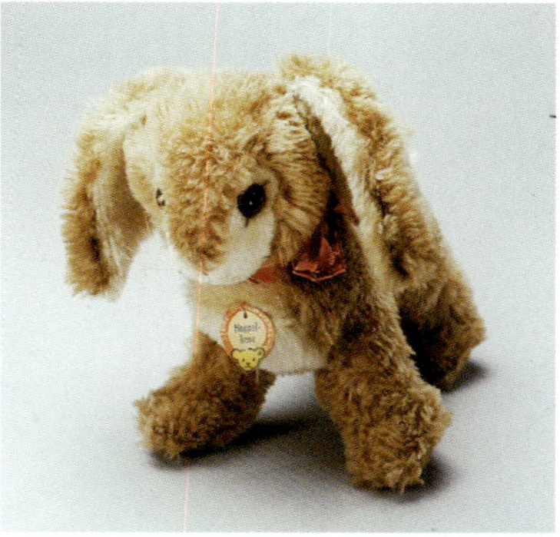

Hoppelhase - *Hopping Rabbit*

Cosy-Tier, Dralon, Pfoten mit Klettenplatten, braun, ohne Wagen, stehend - *Cozy animal, dralon, Velcro strips on paws, brown, without wagon, standing*

SERIE	ART.-NO	PERIOD	PR.	INFO
573	**1630,00**	1967-1967	3	30 cm
	5730/30	1968-1970	3	

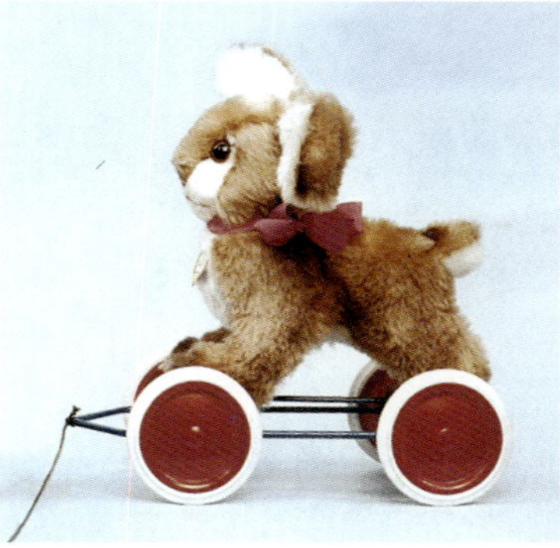

Hoppelhase mit Wagen - *Hopping Rabbit with Wagon*

Dralon, Pfoten mit Klettenplatten, braun, vom Fahrgestell abnehmbar als Cosy-Tier - *dralon, Velcro strips on paws, brown, can be removed from the wagon & used as a cozy toy*

SERIE	ART.-NO	PERIOD	PR.	INFO
573	**1630,10**	1967-1967	3-4	35 cm
	5730/35	1968-1971	3-4	

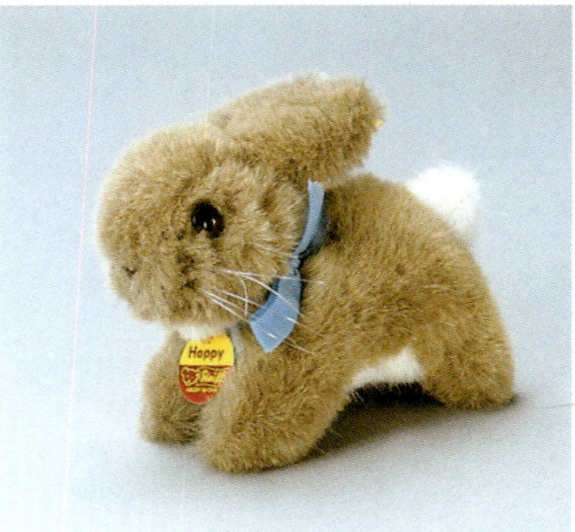

Hoppy Hase - ***Hoppy*** *Rabbit*

Nerzimitation, ab 1978 Synthetik-Webpelz, braun oder grau, 9 cm, springend - *imitation mink from 1978 synthetic woven fur, brown or grey, 9 cm, hopping*

SERIE	ART.-NO	PERIOD	PR.	INFO
	1500/09	1977-1983	1-2	braun - *brown*
	1501/09	1977-1983	1-2	grau - *grey*

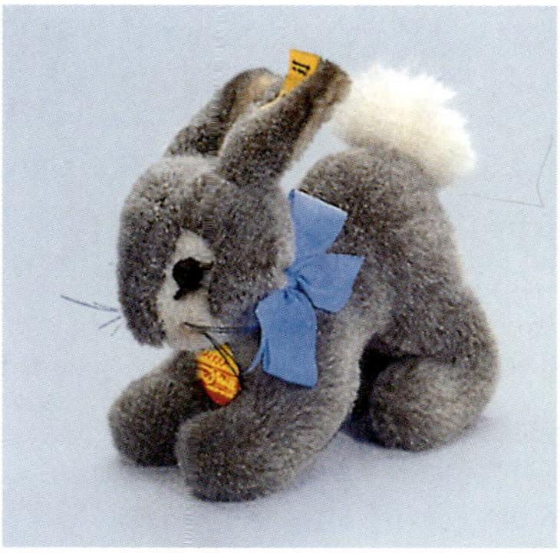

Hoppel Hase - ***Hoppel*** *Rabbit*

Webpelz, grau, springend, abwaschbar - *woven fur, grey, hopping, surface washable*

SERIE	ART.-NO	PERIOD	PR.	INFO
	2957/13	1980-1983	2	13 cm

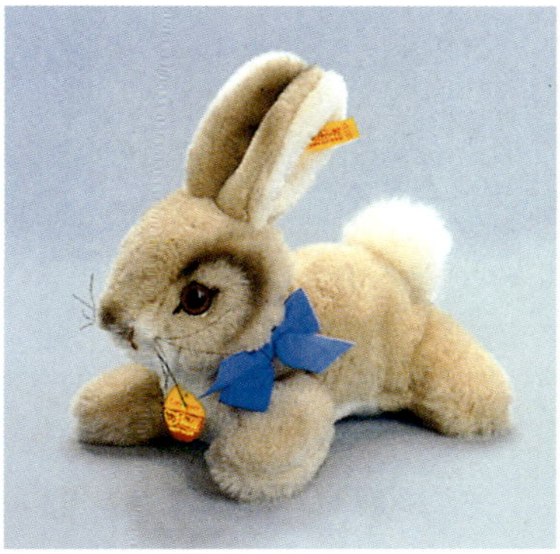

Cosy Hoppy Hase - ***Cosy Hoppy*** *Rabbit*

Webpelz, superweich, waschmaschinenfest - *woven fur, super soft, machine washable*

SERIE	ART.-NO	PERIOD	PR.	INFO
	5362/24	1982-1985	2	24 cm

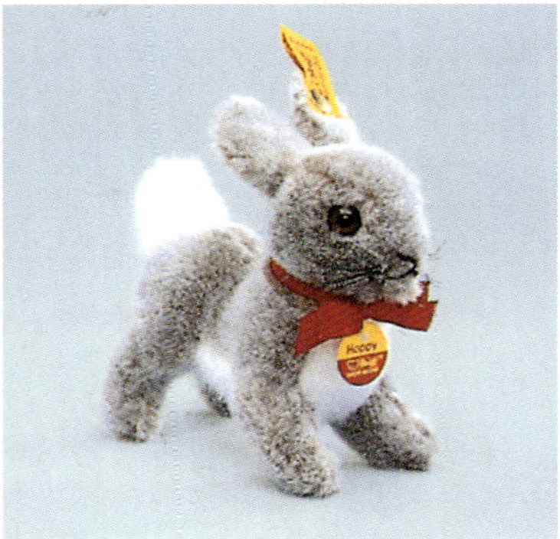

Hoppy Hase - ***Hoppy*** *Rabbit*

Webpelz, beige oder grau, 13 cm, abwaschbar - *woven fur, beige or grey, 13 cm, surface washable*

SERIE	ART.-NO	PERIOD	PR.	INFO
050107	**1500/13**	1984-1987	2	beige
050206	**1501/13**	1984-1987	2	grau - *grey*

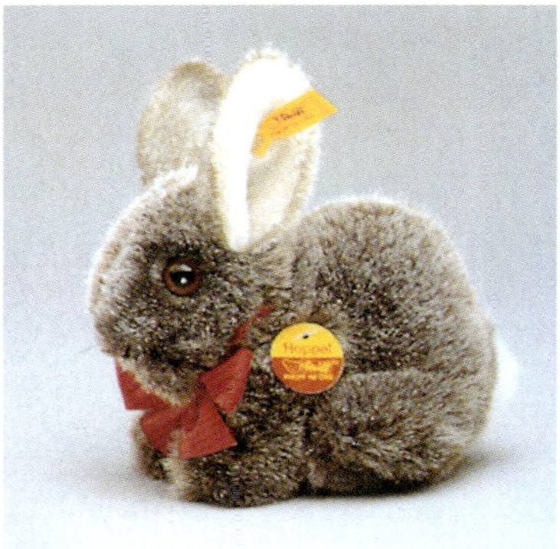

Hoppel Hase - ***Hoppel*** *Rabbit*

Webpelz, grau, kauernd, abwaschbar - *woven fur, grey, crouching, surface washable*

SERIE	ART.-NO	PERIOD	PR.	INFO
077586	**2956/16**	1990-1990	2	16 cm
	077586	1991-1993	2	

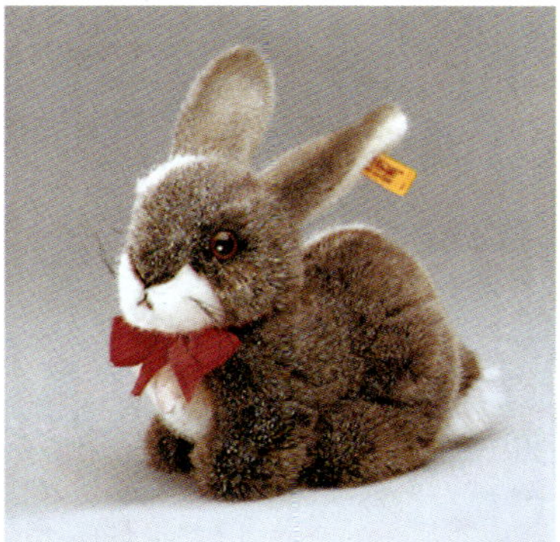

Hoppel Hase - ***Hoppel*** *Rabbit*

Webpelz, grau, sitzend, abwaschbar - *woven fur, grey, sitting, surface washable*

SERIE	ART.-NO	PERIOD	PR.	INFO
077623	**2957/22**	1990-1990	2	22 cm
	077623	1991-1991	2	

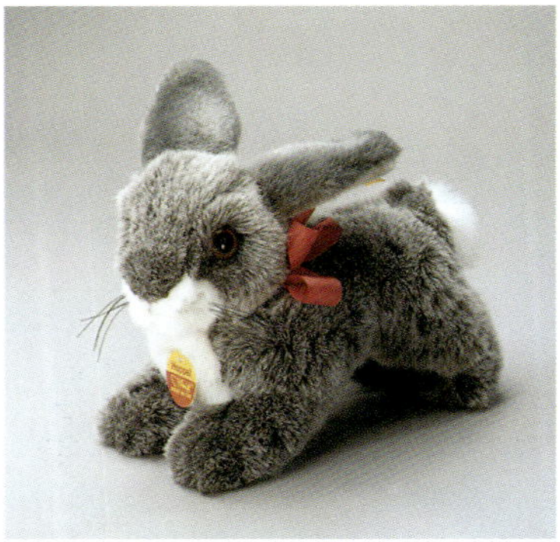

Hoppel Hase - ***Hoppel*** *Rabbit*

Webpelz, grau, springend, abwaschbar - *woven fur, grey, hopping, surface washable*

SERIE	ART.-NO	PERIOD	PR.	INFO
077647	**2958/25**	1990-1990	2	25 cm
	077647	1991-1991	2	

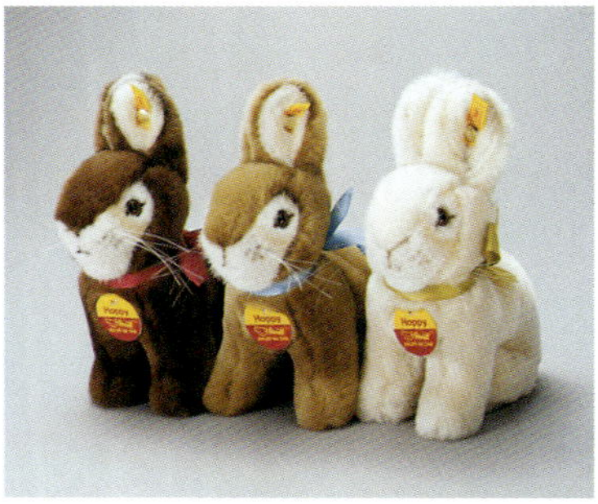

Hoppy Hase - ***Hoppy*** *Rabbit*

Webpelz, 16 cm, sitzend, waschmaschinenfest - *woven fur, 16 cm, sitting, machine washable*

EAN-NO.	PERIOD	PR.	INFO
081699	1994-1995	1-2	grau - *grey*
081712	1994-1995	1-2	braun - *brown*
081729	1994-1995	1-2	beige
081736	1994-1995	1-2	creme - *cream*

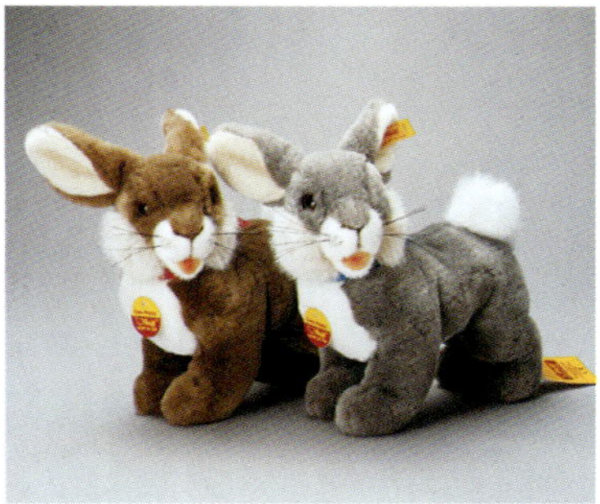

Cosy Hoppy Hase - ***Cosy Hoppy*** *Rabbit*

Webpelz, 24 cm, springend, waschmaschinenfest - *woven fur, 24 cm, hopping, machine washable*

EAN-NO.	PERIOD	PR.	INFO
086809	1995-1996	2-3	creme - *cream*
086823	1995-1997	2-3	grau - *grey*
086847	1995-1997	2-3	hellbraun - *light brown*

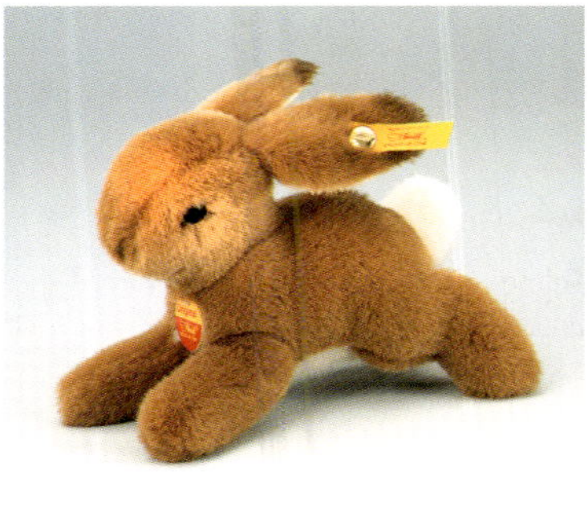

Hase - *Rabbit*

Webpelz, 14 cm, waschmaschinenfest - *woven fur, 14 cm, machine washable*

EAN-NO.	PERIOD	PR.	INFO
050114	1997-1997	1-2	weiss - *white*
050121	1997-1997	1-2	grau - *grey*
050138	1997-1997	1-2	hellbraun - *light brown*
050145	1997-1997	1-2	dunkelbraun - *dark brown*

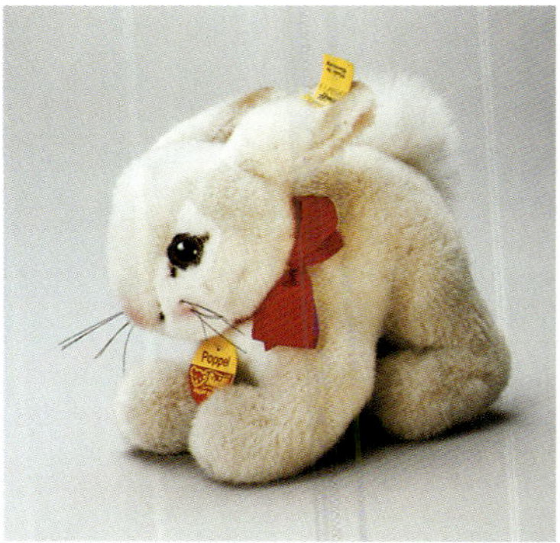

Poppel Hase - ***Poppel*** *Rabbit*

Webpelz, beige, springend, abwaschbar - *woven fur, beige, hopping, surface washable*

SERIE	ART.-NO	PERIOD	PR.	INFO
	2958/13	1980-1983	2	13 cm

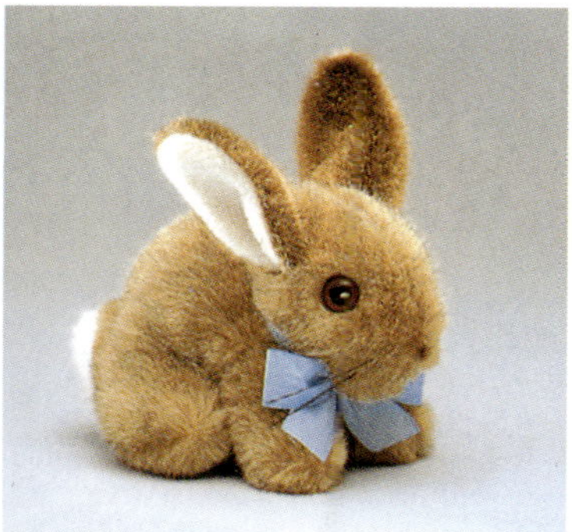

Poppel Hase - ***Poppel** Rabbit*

Webpelz, braun, kauernd, abwaschbar - *woven fur, brown, crouching, surface washable*

SERIE	ART.-NO	PERIOD	PR.	INFO
077685	**2960/16**	1990-1990	2	16 cm
	077685	1991-1992	2	

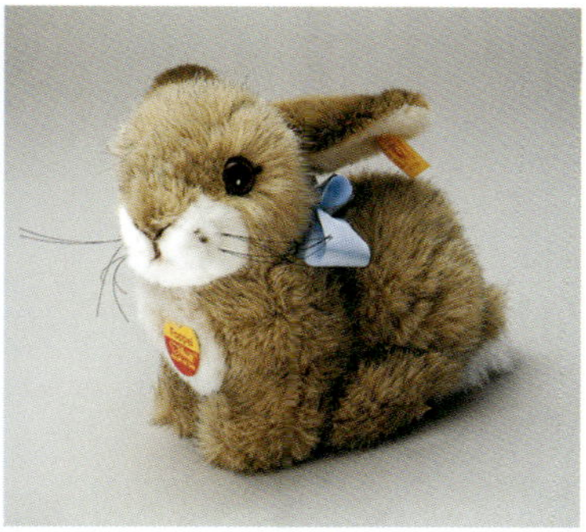

Poppel Hase - ***Poppel** Rabbit*

Webpelz, braun, sitzend, abwaschbar - *woven fur, brown sitting, surface washable*

SERIE	ART.-NO	PERIOD	PR.	INFO
077722	**2961/22**	1990-1990	2	22 cm
	077722	1991-1993	2	

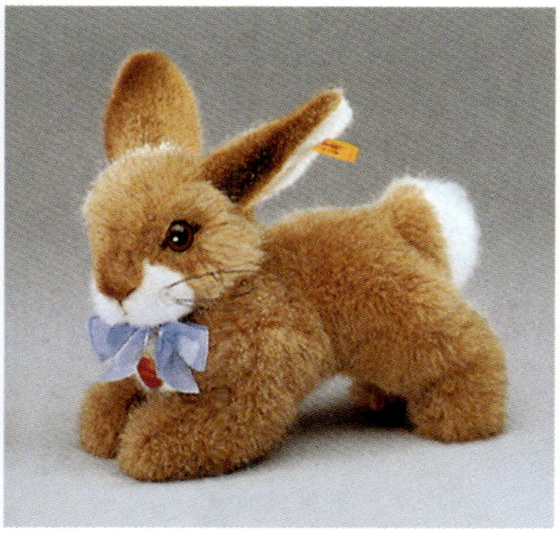

Poppel Hase - ***Poppel** Rabbit*

Webpelz, braun, springend, abwaschbar - *woven fur, brown, hopping, surface washable*

SERIE	ART.-NO	PERIOD	PR.	INFO
077746	**2962/25**	1990-1990	2	25 cm
	077746	1991-1991	2	

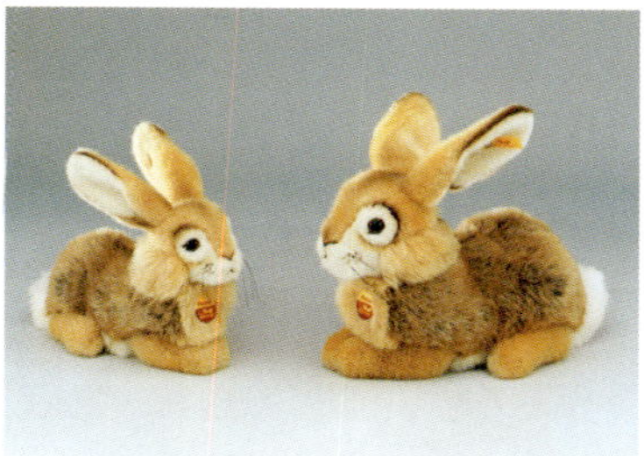

Poppel Hase - ***Poppel** Rabbit*

Webpelz, braun, kauernd, waschmaschinenfest - *woven fur, brown, crouching, machine washable*

EAN-NO.	PERIOD	PR.	INFO
077760	1996-1998	2-3	20 cm
077777	1996-1997	3	28 cm

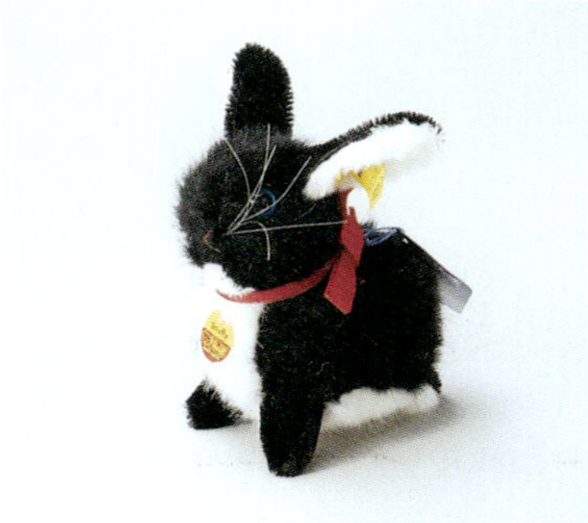

Snuffy Hase - ***Snuffy** Rabbit*

Pelz-Imitation, ab 1978 Synthetik-Webpelz, beige, grau oder schwarz, sitzend - *imitation fur, from 1978 synthetic woven fur, beige, grey or black, sitting*

SERIE	ART.-NO	PERIOD	PR.	INFO
	2910/12	1974-1982	1-2	12 cm, beige
	2910/18	1974-1982	1-2	18 cm
	2911/12	1974-1982	1-2	12 cm, grau - *grey*
	2911/18	1974-1982	1-2	18 cm
	2912/12	1974-1982	1-2	12 cm, schwarz - *black*
	2912/18	1974-1982	1-2	18 cm

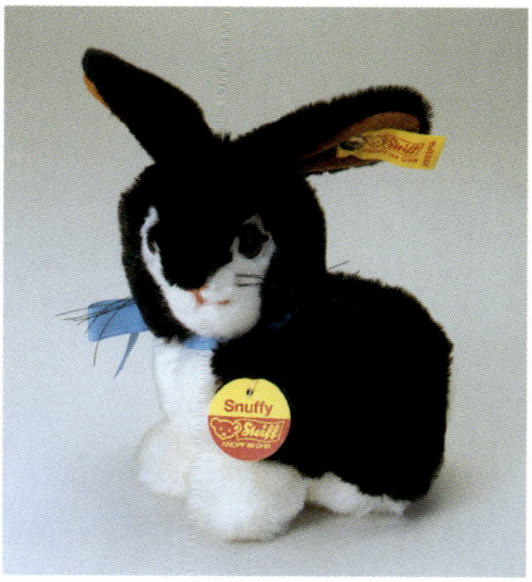

Snuffy Hase - ***Snuffy** Rabbit*

Webpelz, 16 cm, waschmaschinenfest - *woven fur, 16 cm, machine washable*

SERIE	ART.-NO	PERIOD	PR.	INFO
077401	**2931/16**	1983-1988	2	beige
077432	**2932/16**	1983-1988	2	caramel
077470	**2933/16**	1983-1988	2	braun - *brown*

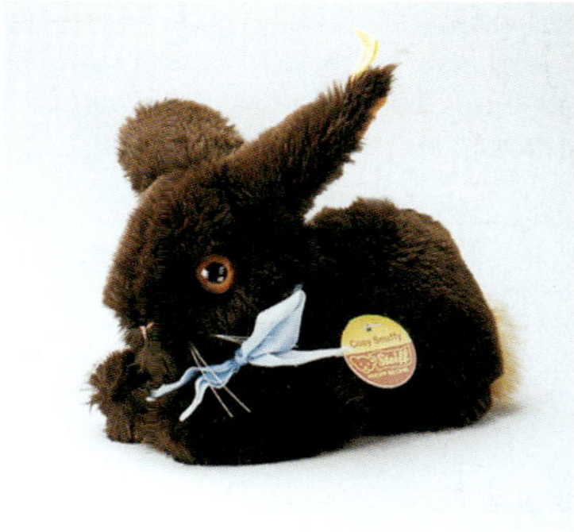

Cosy Snuffy Hase - ***Cosy Snuffy** Rabbit*

Webpelz, 16 cm, superweich - *woven fur, 16 cm, super soft*

SERIE	ART.-NO	PERIOD	PR.	INFO
088452	**5363/16**	1982-1987	1-2	beige
088469	**5364/16**	1982-1987	1-2	caramel
088476	**5365/16**	1982-1987	1-2	braun - *brown*

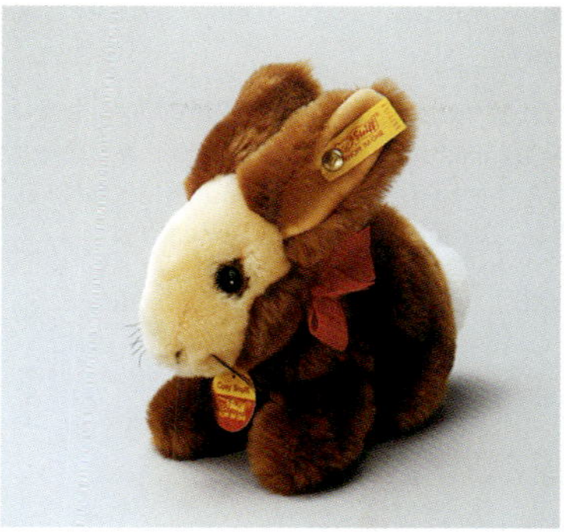

Cosy Snuffi Hase - ***Cosy Snuffi** Rabbit*

Webpelz, hellbeige/weiss oder rost/beige, 18 cm, waschmaschinenfest - *woven fur, light beige/white or rust brown/beige, 18 cm, machine washable*

SERIE	ART.-NO	PERIOD	PR.	INFO
098505	**5511/18**	1988-1989	2	hellbeige/ weiss - *light beige/white*
098550	**5512/18**	1988-1989	2	rost/beige - *rust brown/beige*

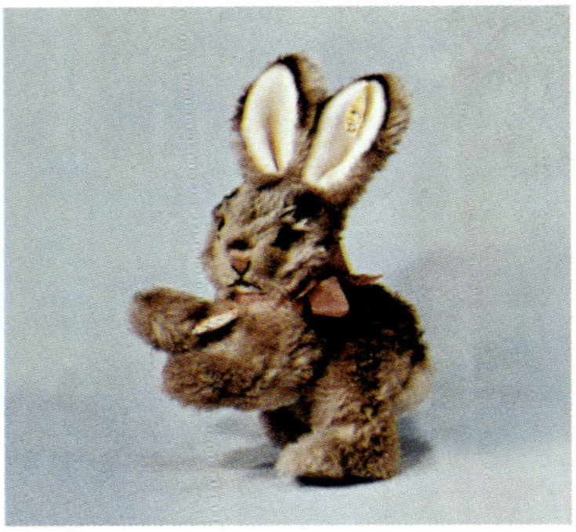

Cosy Mummy Hase - ***Cosy Mummy** Rabbit*

Dralon, caramel, Schaumgummi-Fuellung, stehend, sehr weich, voll waschbar - *dralon, caramel, stuffed with foam rubber, standing, very soft, fully washable*

SERIE	ART.-NO	PERIOD	PR.	INFO
83 36	**6620**	1955-1958	3	20 cm
830 360	**6620,00**	1959-1964	2-3	
494	**6620,00**	1965-1967	2-3	
	4940/20	1968-1978	2	

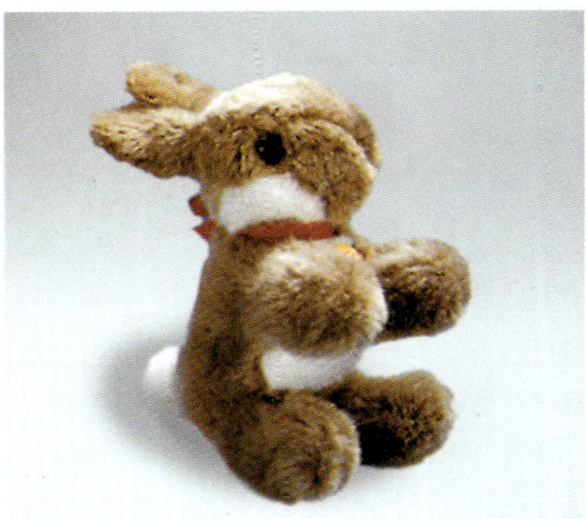

Baby Mummy Hase - ***Baby Mummy** Rabbit*

Pelzimitation, ab 1978 Synthetik-Webpelz, formgeschaeumt, aufwartend - *imitation fur, from 1978 synthetic woven fur, stuffed with pre-formed foam, sitting up*

SERIE	ART.-NO	PERIOD	PR.	INFO
	5745/16	1977-1979	2	16 cm

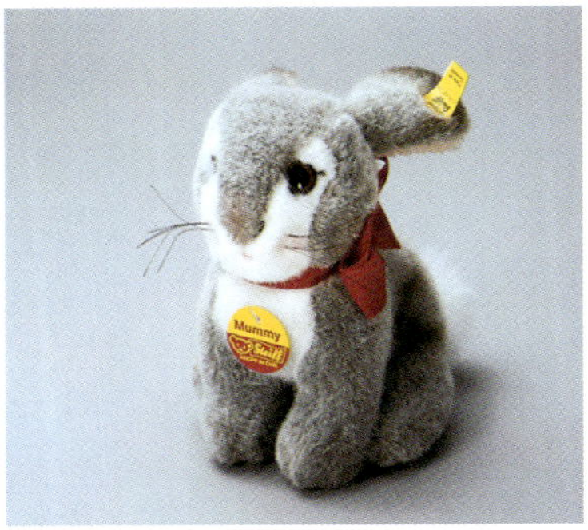

Mummy Hase - ***Mummy** Rabbit*

Webpelz, grau, sitzend, abwaschbar - *woven fur, grey, sitting, surface washable*

SERIE	ART.-NO	PERIOD	PR.	INFO
	2962/16	1980-1983	2	16 cm

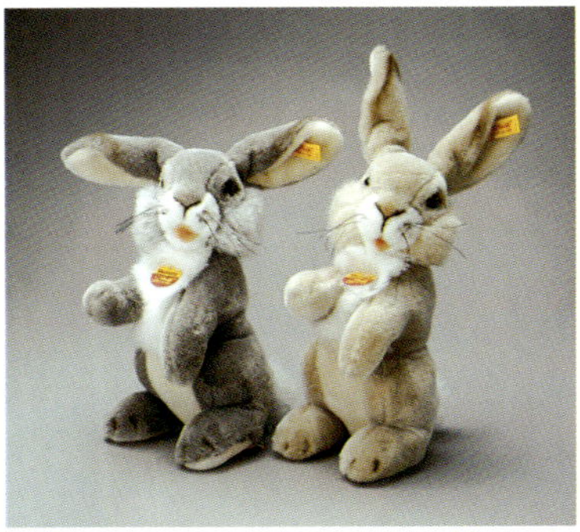

Mummy Hase - ***Mummy** Rabbit*

Webpelz, beige oder grau, 32 cm, aufwartend - *woven fur, beige or grey, 32 cm, sitting up*

SERIE	ART.-NO	PERIOD	PR.	INFO
077517	**2950/32**	1988-1990	2-3	beige
077562	**2955/32**	1988-1989	2-3	grau - *grey*

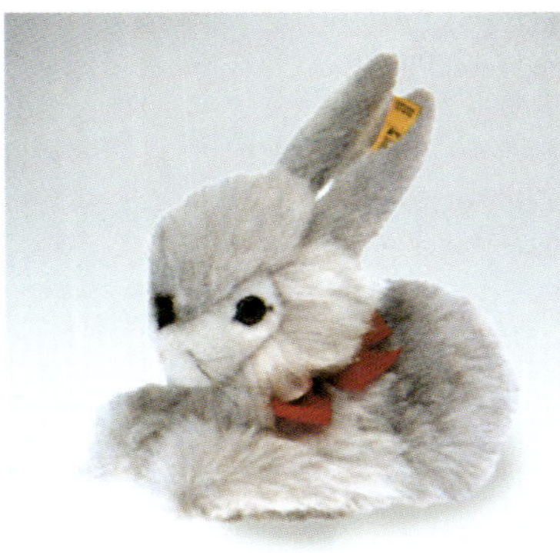

Winni Hase - ***Winni** Rabbit*

Synthetik-Webpelz, grau, liegend, abwaschbar - *synthetic woven fur, grey, lying, surface washable*

SERIE	ART.-NO	PERIOD	PR.	INFO
	2955/18	1978-1981	2	18 cm

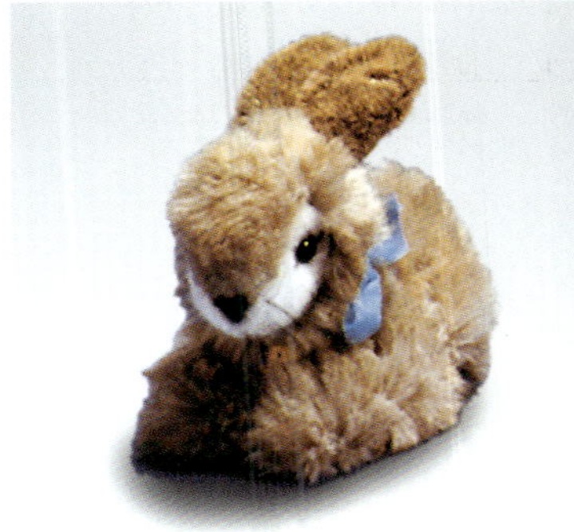

Wunni Hase - ***Wunni** Rabbit*

Synthetik-Webpelz, hellbeige, liegend, abwaschbar - *synthetic woven fur, light beige, lying, surface washable*

SERIE	ART.-NO	PERIOD	PR.	INFO
	2956/18	1978-1981	2	18 cm

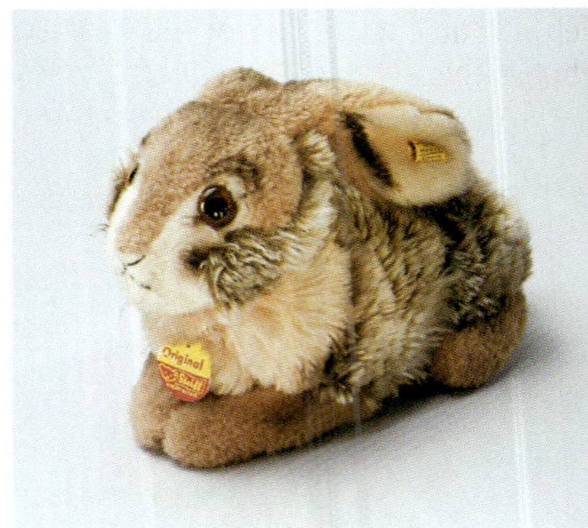

Duerer-Hase - *Duerer Rabbit*

Dralon, liegend, abwaschbar - *dralon, lying, surface washable*

SERIE	ART.-NO	PERIOD	PR.	INFO
	2965/20	1973-1982	2-3	20 cm
	2965/25	1972-1981	2-3	25 cm

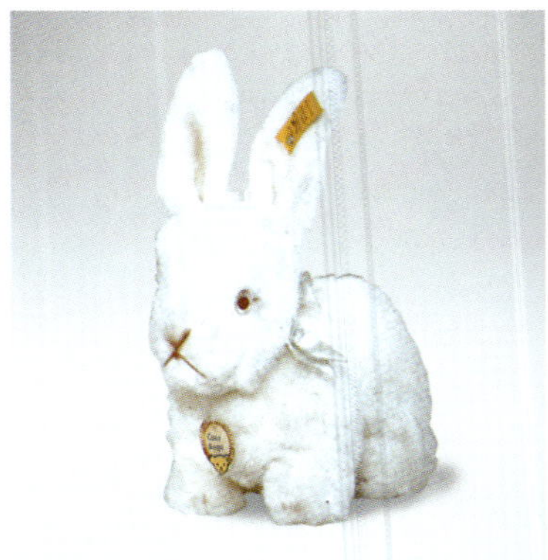

Cosy Ango Angorahase - ***Cosy Ango** Angora Rabbit*

Dralon, gefuellt mit synthetischen Fasern, vollwaschbar, weiss, rote Augen, sitzend - *dralon, stuffed with synthetic fibers, fully washable, white, red eyes, sitting*

SERIE	ART.-NO	PERIOD	PR.	INFO
495	**6620,04**	1966-1967	2	20 cm
	4950/20	1968-1974	2	

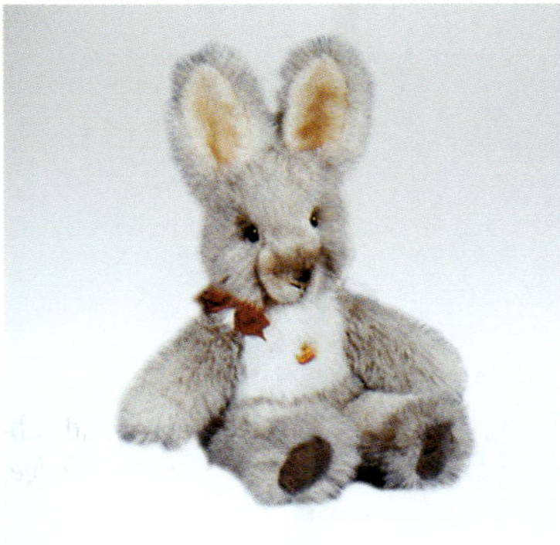

Ango Hase ab 1981 Cosy Ango - *Ango Rabbit from 1981 Cosy Ango*

Pelzimitation, ab 1978 Synthetik-Webpelz, abwaschbar - *imitation fur, from1978 synthetic woven fur, surface washable*

SERIE	ART.-NO	PERIOD	PR.	INFO
	3135/45	1976-1982	2-3	45 cm

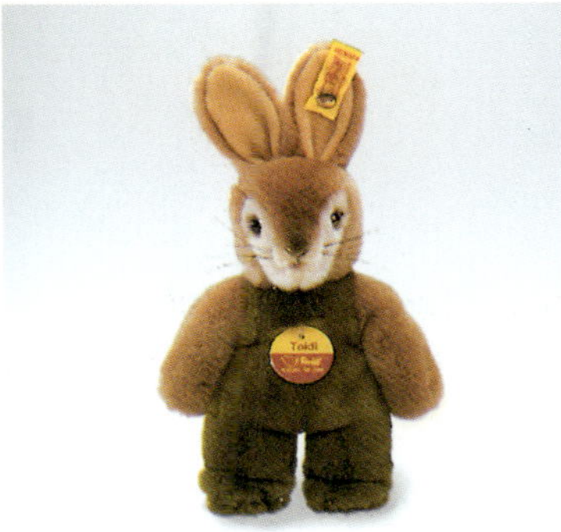

Toldi Hase - ***Toldi** Rabbit*

Webpelz, Pieps-Stimme, waschmaschinenfest - *woven fur, squeaker, machine washable*

SERIE	ART.-NO	PERIOD	PR.	INFO
080302	**6254/22**	1984-1990	2	22 cm

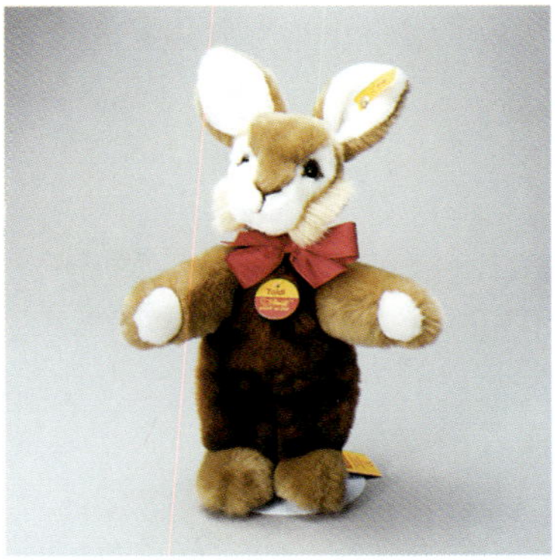

Toldi Hase - ***Toldi** Rabbit*

Webpelz, Pieps-Stimme, waschmaschinenfest - *woven fur, squeaker, machine washable*

SERIE	ART.-NO	PERIOD	PR.	INFO
081095	**6266/27**	1989-1990	2	27 cm

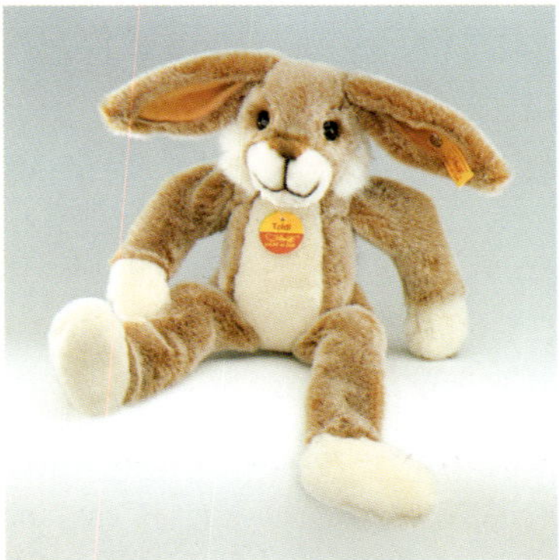

Toldi Kuschelhase - ***Toldi** Cuddly Rabbit*

Webpelz, braun oder grau gespitzt, 30 oder 35 cm, waschmaschinenfest - *woven fur, brown or grey tipped, 30 or 35 cm, machine washable*

EAN-NO.	PERIOD	PR.	INFO
122378	1998-1999	2-3	30 cm, braun - *brown*
122408	1998-1998	2-3	35 cm
122385	1998-1998	2-3	30 cm, grau - *grey*
122415	1998-1998	2-3	35 cm

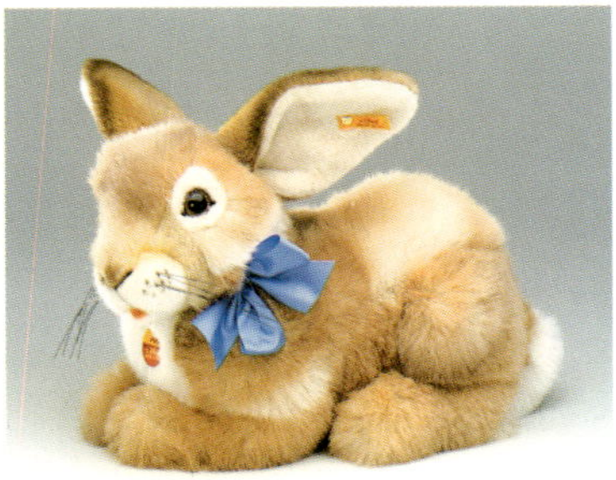

Putsi Hase - ***Putsi** Rabbit*

Webpelz, kauernd, waschmaschinenfest - *woven fur, crouching, machine washable*

EAN-NO.	PERIOD	PR.	INFO
077784	1992-1995	2-3	40 cm

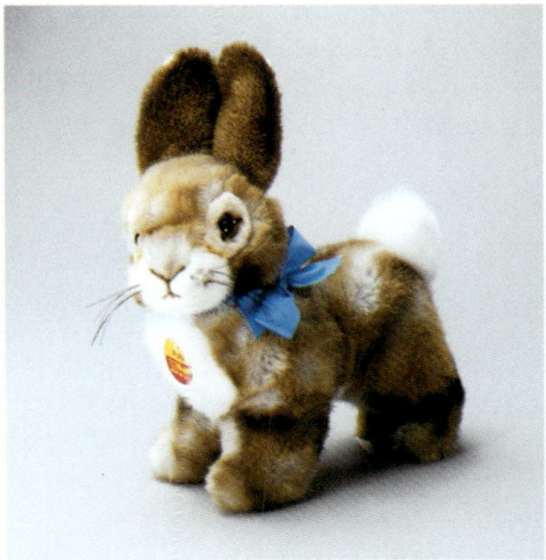

Putsi Hase - ***Putsi** Rabbit*

Webpelz, springend, waschmaschinenfest - *woven fur, hopping, machine washable*

EAN-NO.	PERIOD	PR.	INFO
077838	1992-1995	2-3	27 cm

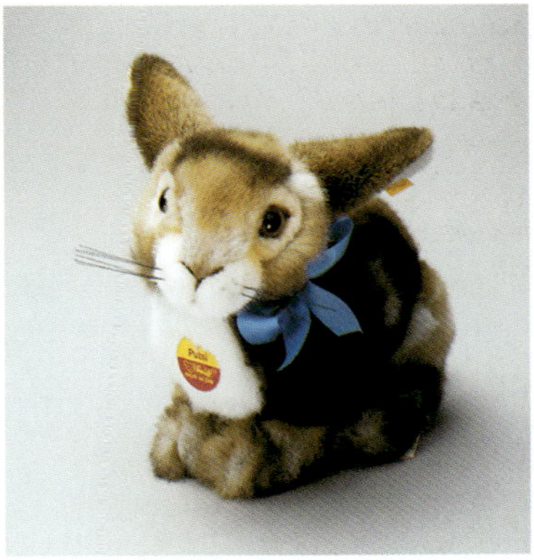

Putsi Hase - ***Putsi** Rabbit*

Webpelz, sitzend, waschmaschinenfest - *woven fur, sitting, machine washable*

EAN-NO.	PERIOD	PR.	INFO
077890	1992-1997	2-3	27 cm

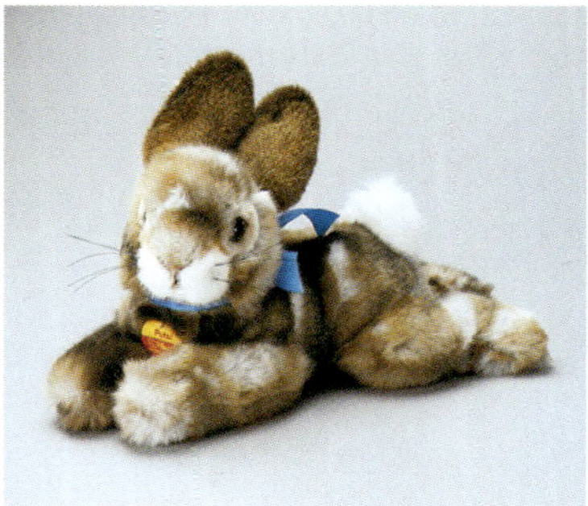

Putsi Hase - ***Putsi** Rabbit*

Webpelz, liegend, waschmaschinenfest - *woven fur, lying, machine washable*

EAN-No.	Period	Pr.	Info
077913	1992-1999	2-3	33 cm

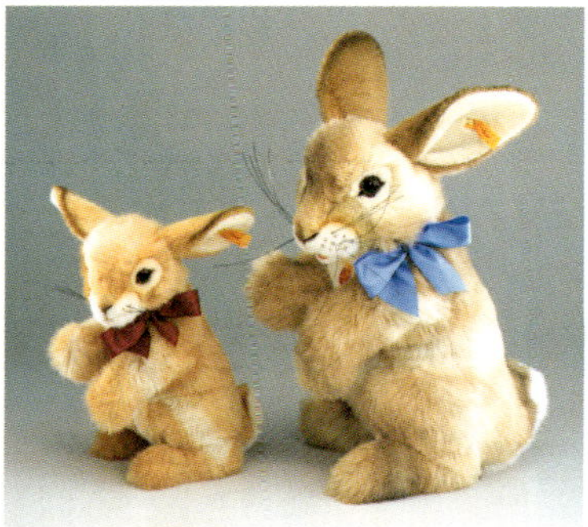

Putsi Hase - ***Putsi** Rabbit*

Webpelz, aufwartend, waschmaschinenfest - *woven fur, sitting up, machine washable*

EAN-No.	Period	Pr.	Info
077852	1993-1996	2-3	28 cm, rotblond - *red blond*
077876	1993-1997	3	40 cm, graubeige - *grey-beige*

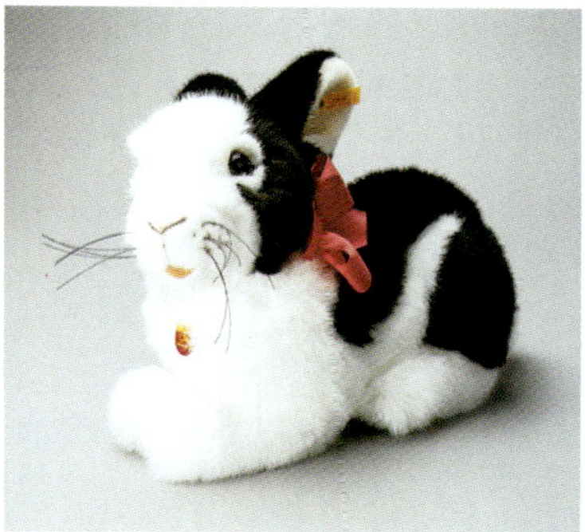

Putsi Hase - ***Putsi** Rabbit*

Webpelz, dunkelbraun/weiss, kauernd, waschmaschinenfest - *woven fur, dark brown/white, crouching, machine washable*

EAN-No.	Period	Pr.	Info
077791	1995-1997	3	40 cm

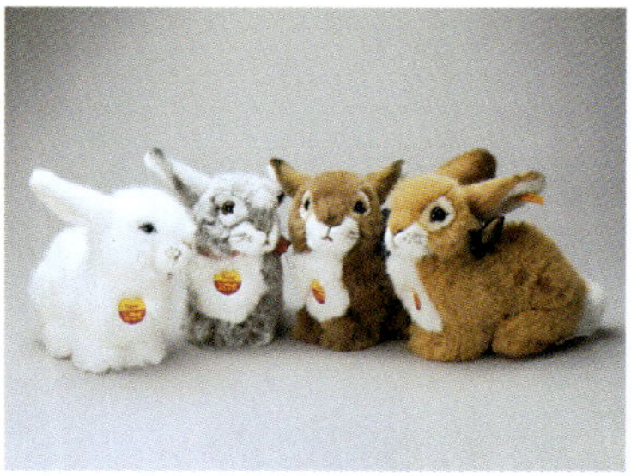

Topsi Hase - ***Topsi** Rabbit*

Webpelz, 27 cm, sitzend, waschmaschinenfest - *woven fur, 27 cm, sitting, machine washable*

EAN-No.	Period	Pr.	Info
078002	1993-1995	2-3	weiss - *white*
078019	1993-1997	2-3	grau - *grey*
078026	1993-1996	2-3	hellbraun - *light brown*
078033	1993-1997	2-3	beige

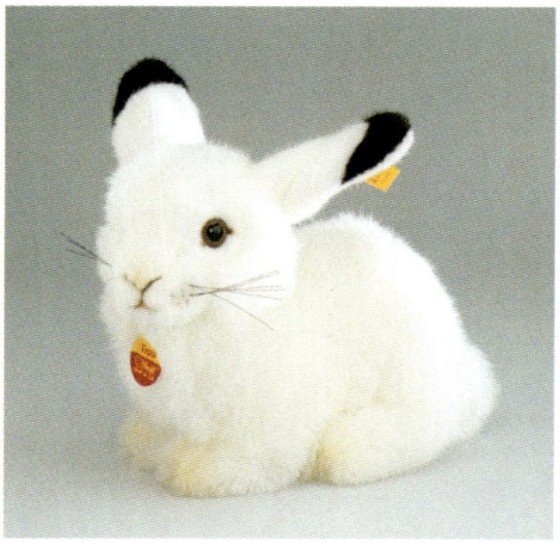

Topsi Schneehase ab 1998 **Hoppel** - ***Topsi** Blue Hare from 1998* ***Hoppel***

Webpelz, weiss, sitzend, waschmaschinenfest - *woven fur, white, sitting, machine washable*

EAN-No.	Period	Pr.	Info
077944	1997-1999	2-3	23 cm

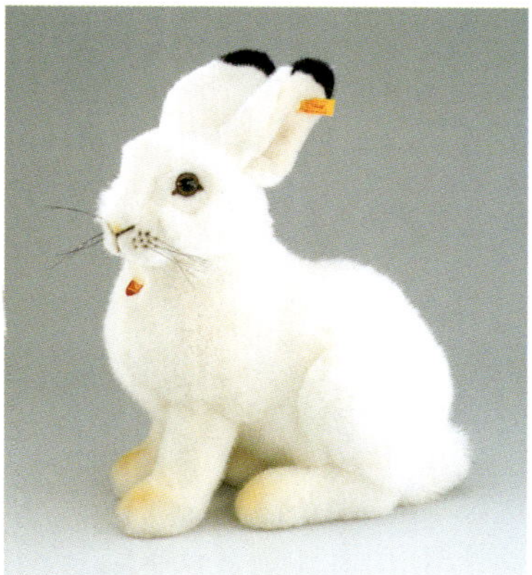

Topsi Schneehase ab 1998 **Hoppel** - ***Topsi** Blue Hare from 1998* ***Hoppel***

Webpelz, weiss, sitzend, waschmaschinenfest - *woven fur, white, sitting, machine washable*

EAN-No.	Period	Pr.	Info
077975	1997-1999	3-4	40 cm

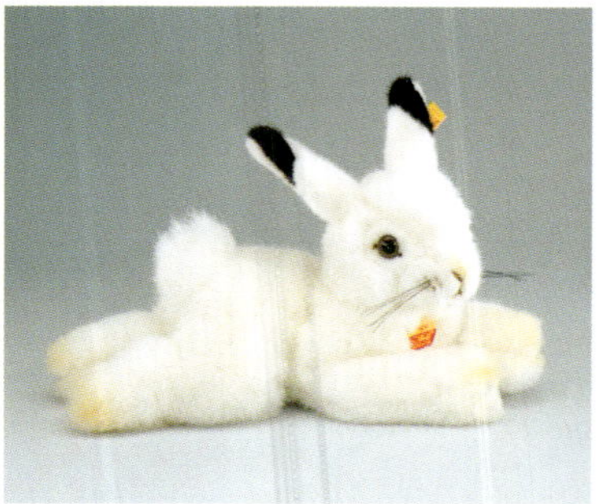

Topsi Schneehase ab 1998 **Hoppel** - ***Topsi** Blue Hare from 1998* ***Hoppel***

Webpelz, weiss, liegend, waschmaschinenfest - *woven fur, white, lying, machine washable*

EAN-No.	Period	Pr.	Info
077999	1997-1999	2-3	35 cm

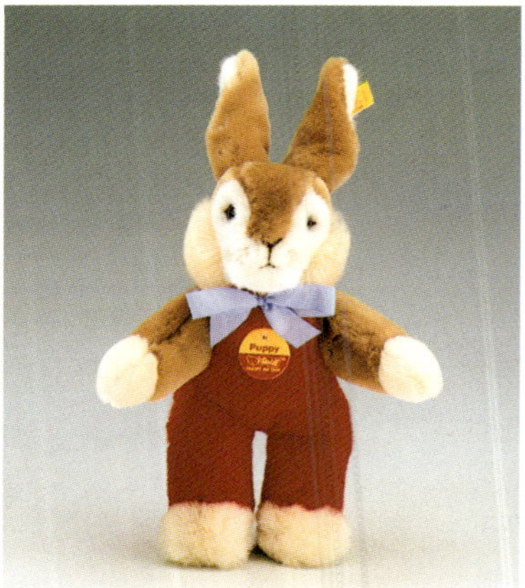

Puppy Hase - ***Puppy** Rabbit*

Webpelz, 28 cm, Pieps-Stimme, waschmaschinenfest - *woven fur, 28 cm, squeaker, machine washable*

EAN-No.	Period	Pr.	Info
124709	1996-1998	2	gruen/braun - *green/brown*
124716	1996-1998	2	rot/braun - *red/brown*
124723	1996-1997	2	braun/beige - *brown/beige*
124730	1996-1997	2	dunkelblau/grau - *darkblue/grey*
124747	1996-1997	2	gelb/braun - *yellow/brown*

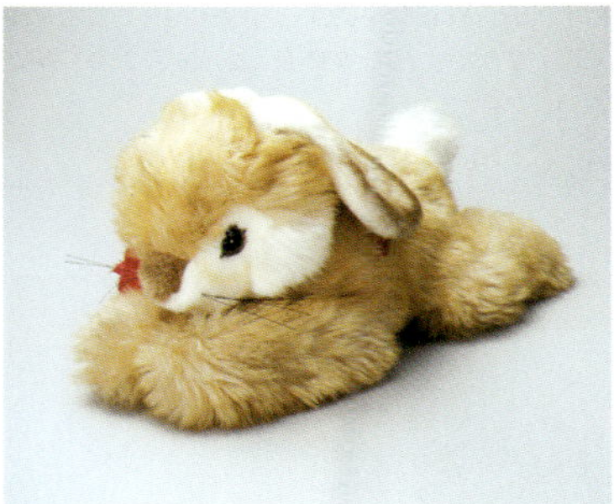

Molly Hase - ***Molly** Rabbit*

Webpelz, liegend, mollig weich, abwaschbar - *woven fur, lying, soft & cuddly, surface washable*

SERIE	ART.-NO	PERIOD	PR.	INFO
101489	**0338/34**	1981-1987	2	34 cm

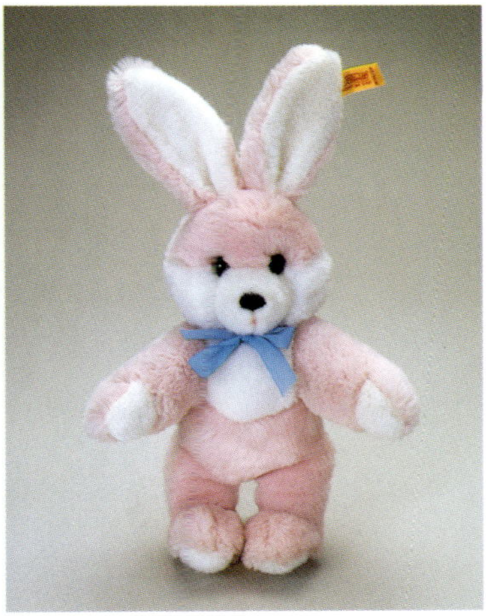

Baby Hase - *Baby Rabbit*

Webpelz, rosa, Druckstimme - *woven fur, pink, press voice*

SERIE	ART.-NO	PERIOD	PR.	INFO
201158	**5686/28**	1983-1986	2	28 cm

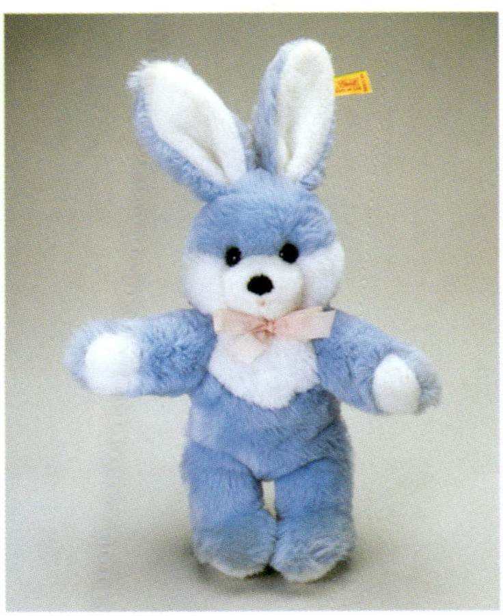

Baby Hase - *Baby Rabbit*

Webpelz, blau, Druckstimme - *woven fur, blue, press voice*

SERIE	ART.-NO	PERIOD	PR.	INFO
201189	**5687/28**	1983-1986	2	28 cm

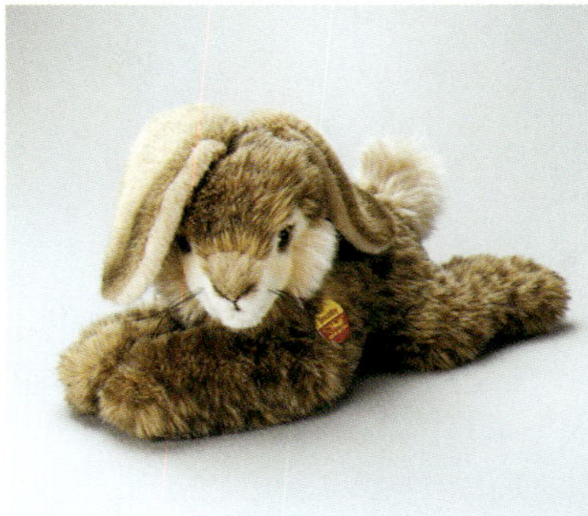

Snobby Hase - ***Snobby** Rabbit*

Webpelz, abwaschbar - *woven fur, surface washable*

SERIE	ART.-NO	PERIOD	PR.	INFO
077609	**2968/35**	1983-1988	2-3	35 cm

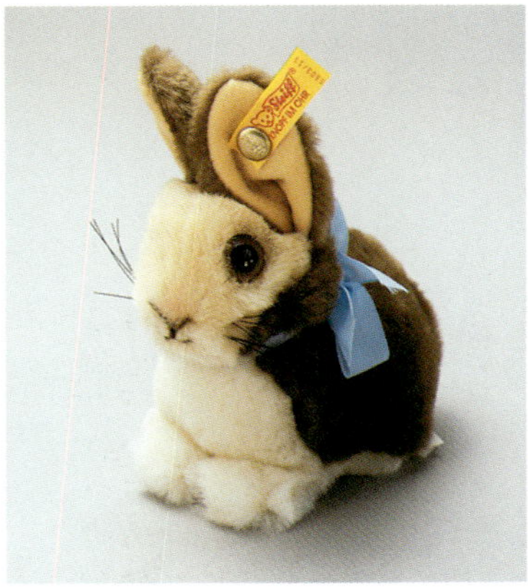

Cosy Minni Hase - ***Cosy Minni** Rabbit*

Webpelz, 13 cm, waschmaschinenfest - *woven fur, 13cm, machine washable*

SERIE	ART.-NO	PERIOD	PR.	INFO
098239	**5502/13**	1988-1990	1-2	beige/weiss - *beige/white*
	098239	1991-1991	1-2	
098260	**5503/13**	1988-1990	1-2	braun/creme - *brown/cream*
098307	**5504/13**	1988-1990	1-2	grau/weiss - *grey/white*
098338	**5505/13**	1988-1990	1-2	schwarz/weiss - *black/white*
	098338	1991-1991	1-2	

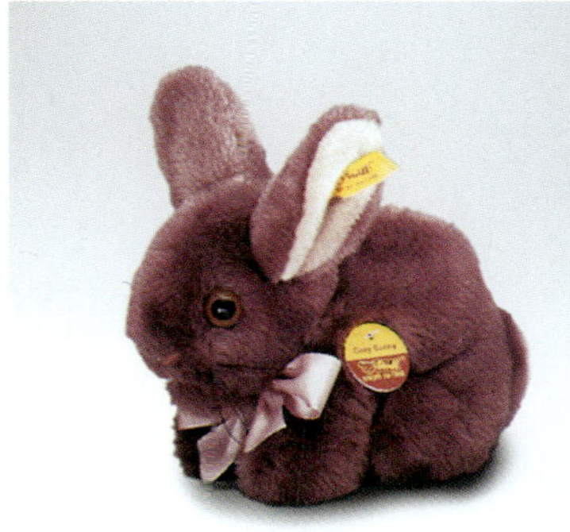

Cosy Bunny Hase - ***Cosy Bunny** Rabbit*

Webpelz, aubergine oder brombeer, 16 cm - *woven fur, purple or blackberry, 16 cm*

SERIE	ART.-NO	PERIOD	PR.	INFO
098703	**5513/16**	1990-1990	2	aubergine - *purple*
098758	**5514/16**	1990-1990	2	brombeer - *blackberry*

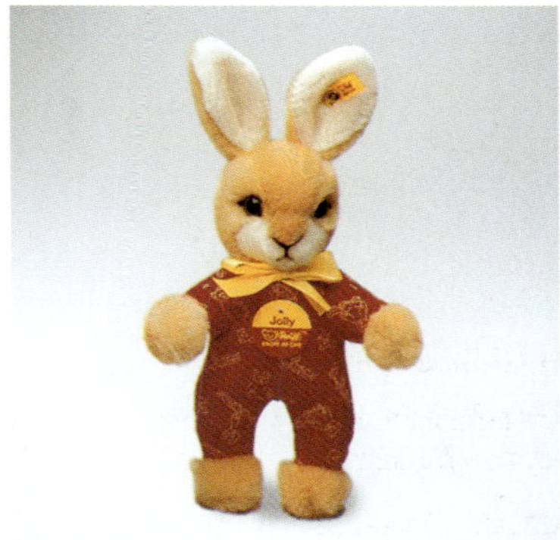

Jolly Hase - ***Jolly** Rabbit*

Webpelz/Baumwollstoff, waschmaschinenfest - *woven fur & cotton, machine washable*

EAN-NO.	PERIOD	PR.	INFO
079948	1991-1991	2	18 cm, rot/blond - *red/blond*
079955	1991-1991	2	26 cm
079962	1991-1991	2	18 cm, weiss/blond - *white/blond*
079979	1991-1991	2	26 cm

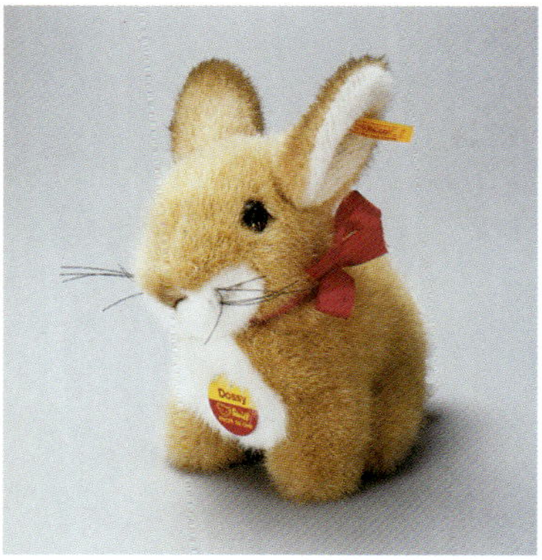

Dossy Hase - ***Dossy** Rabbit*

Webpelz, 18 cm, sitzend, waschmaschinenfest - *woven fur, 18 cm, sitting, machine washable*

EAN-No.	Period	Pr.	Info
077487	1993-1995	2	hellgrau - *light grey*
077494	1993-1995	2	hellbraun - *light brown*
077524	1993-1994	2	hellbeige - *light beige*

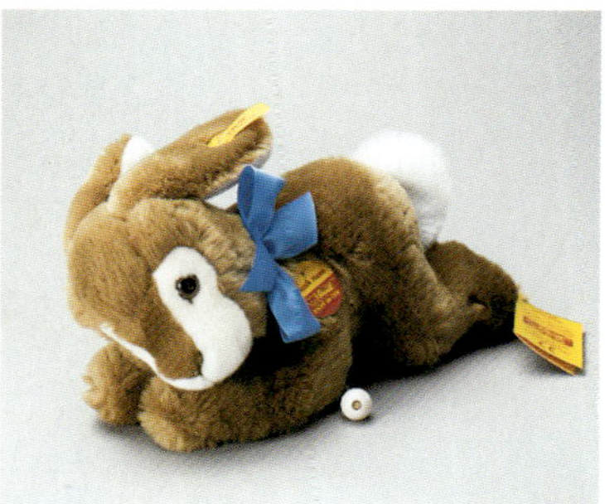

Musik Schlaf Hase - *Music Sleeping Rabbit*

Webpelz, mit Musikwerk SMP (Schlafe mein Prinzchen), abwaschbar - *woven fur, music box playing "sleep my Prince", surface washable*

EAN-No.	Period	Pr.	Info
231407	1995-1997	2-3	26 cm

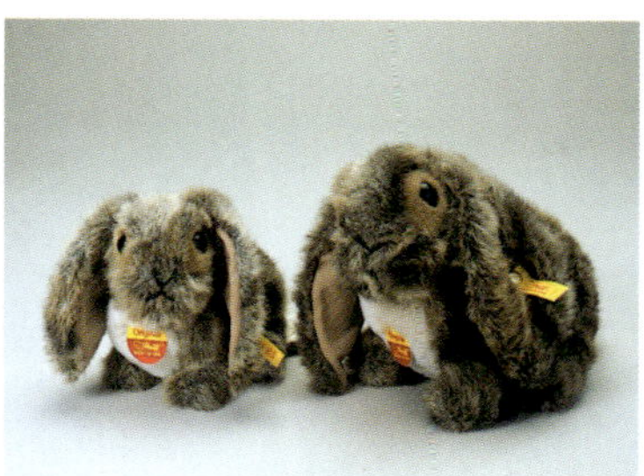

Widderkaninchen - *Ram Rabbit*

Webpelz, braun gefleckt, sitzend, waschmaschinenfest - *woven fur, brown spotted, sitting, machine washable*

EAN-No.	Period	Pr.	Info
078071	1999-1999	2-3	18 cm
078088	1999-1999	2-3	22 cm

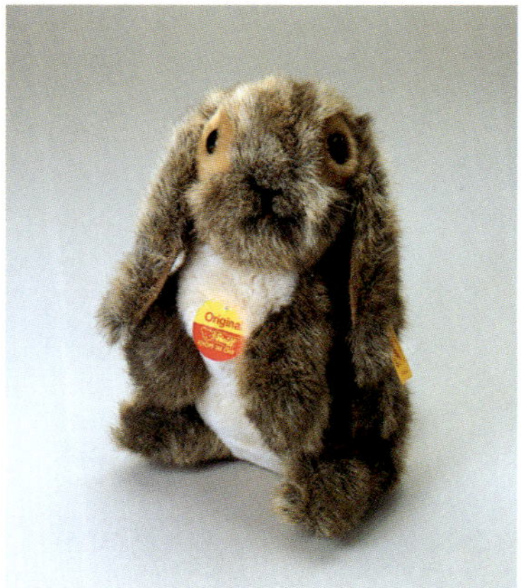

Widderkaninchen - *Ram Rabbit*

Webpelz, braun gefleckt, aufwartend, waschmaschinenfest - *woven fur, brown spotted, sitting up, machine washable*

EAN-No.	Period	Pr.	Info
078095	1999-1999	2-3	20 cm

Wald- & Feldtiere

Field & Forest animals

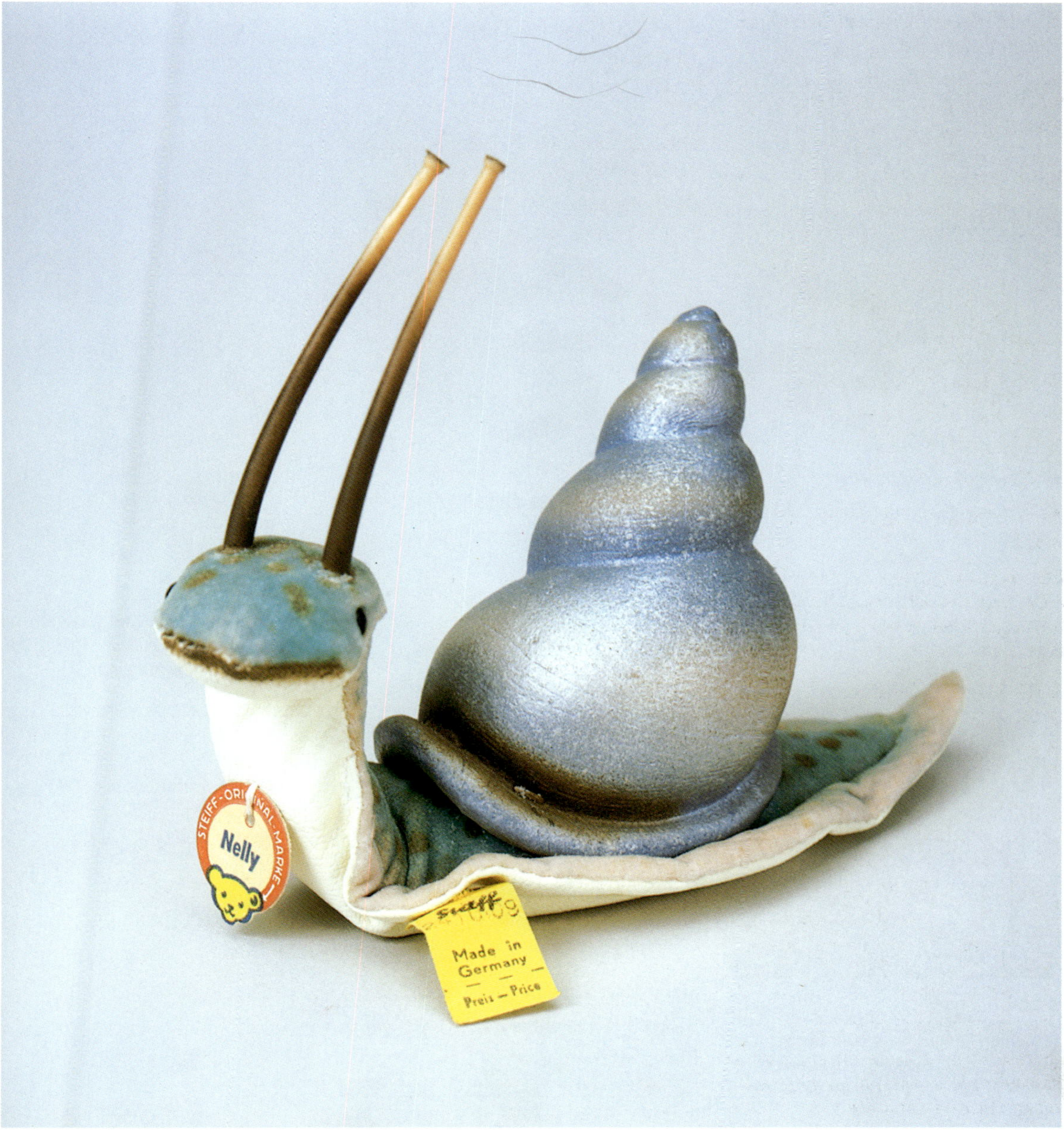

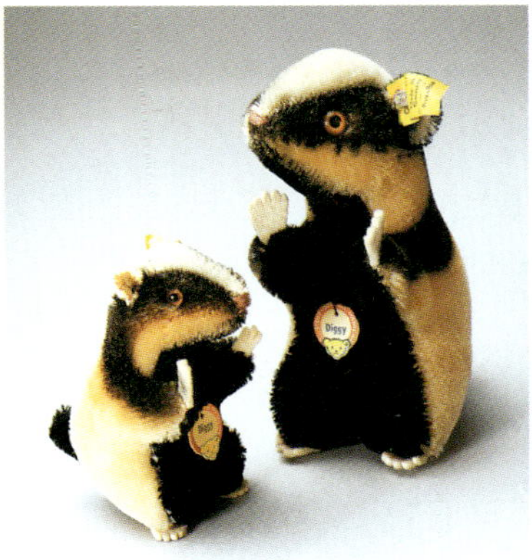

Diggy Dachs - ***Diggy** Badger*

Mohair, schwarz/weiss/gelb, aufwartend - *mohair, black/white/yellow, sitting up*

SERIE	ART.-NO	PERIOD	PR.	INFO
185	**4310,00**	1959-1964	3	10 cm
210	**4310,00**	1965-1966	3	
185	**4315,00**	1959-1962	3-4	15 cm
210	**4315,00**	1966-1966	3-4	

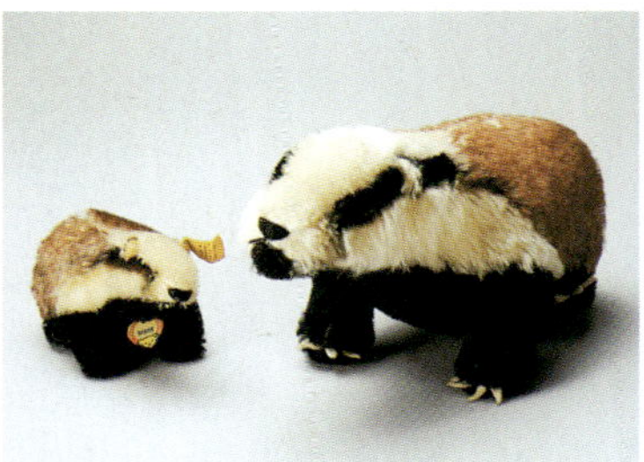

Diggy Dachs - ***Diggy** Badger*

Mohairpluesch, braun/schwarz/weiss, gespitzt, stehend - *mohair, brown/black/white, tipped fur, standing*

SERIE	ART.-NO	PERIOD	PR.	INFO
185	**1310,00**	1963-1964	4	10 cm
185	**1317,00**	1963-1963	4-5	17 cm

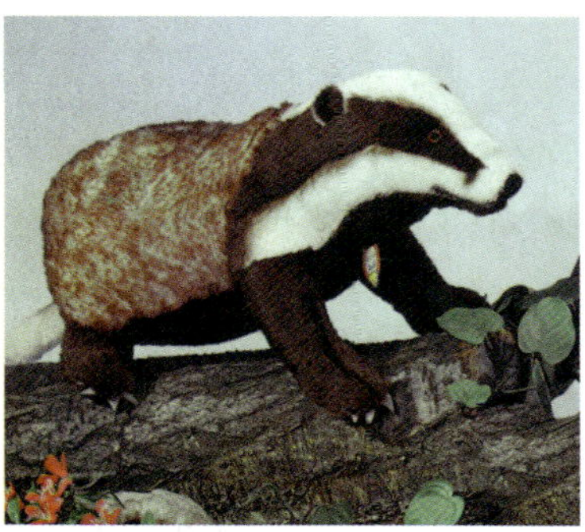

Dachs - *Badger*

Schautier, Mohairpluesch, braun/schwarz/weiss, gespitzt, stehend - *display animal, mohair, brown/black/white, tipped, standing*

SERIE	ART.-NO	PERIOD	PR.	INFO
	2109/04	1967-1967	5-6	40 cm

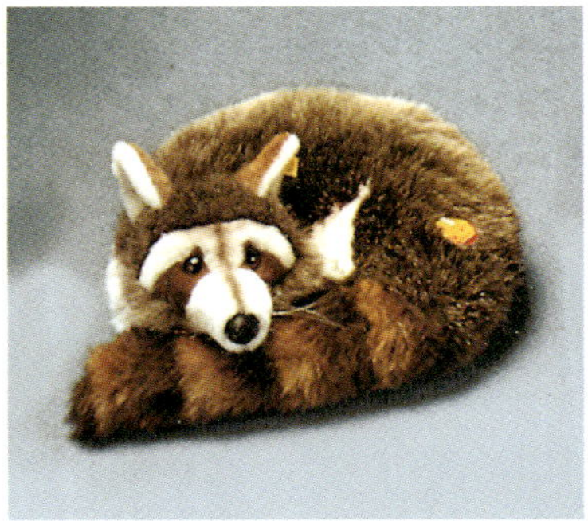

Ringel **Raggy** Dachs - *Curled up **Raggy** Badger*

Pelzimitation, ab 1978 Synthetik-Webpelz, geringelt liegend, abwaschbar - *imitation fur, from 1978 synthetic woven fur, lying curled up, surface washable*

SERIE	ART.-NO	PERIOD	PR.	INFO
	1543/35	1977-1980	2-3	35 cm

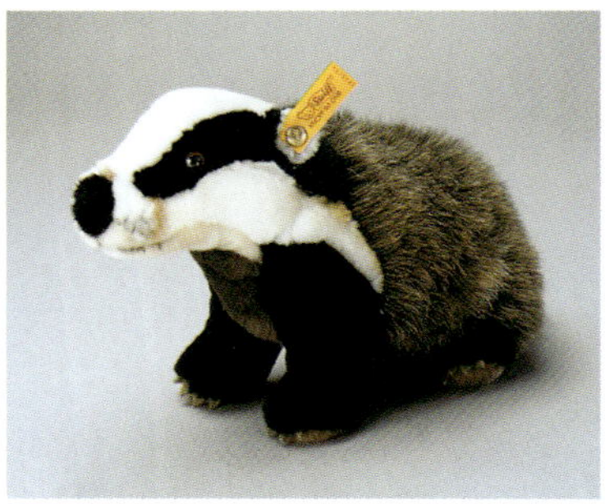

Diggy Dachs - ***Diggy** Badger*

Webpelz, stehend, abwaschbar - *woven fur, standing, surface washable*

SERIE	ART.-NO	PERIOD	PR.	INFO
071256	**1840/26**	1986-1988	2-3	26 cm
071287	**1840/36**	1986-1988	3	36 cm

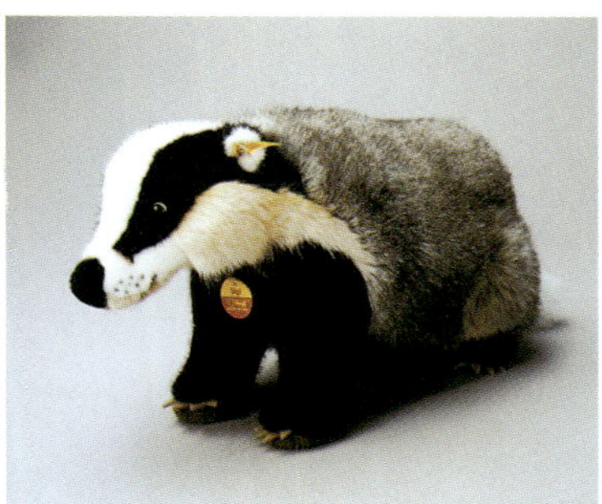

Sigi Dachs - ***Sigi** Badger*

Webpelz, stehend, abwaschbar - *woven fur, standing, surface washable*

EAN-NO.	PERIOD	PR.	INFO
071294	1994-1997	3	45 cm

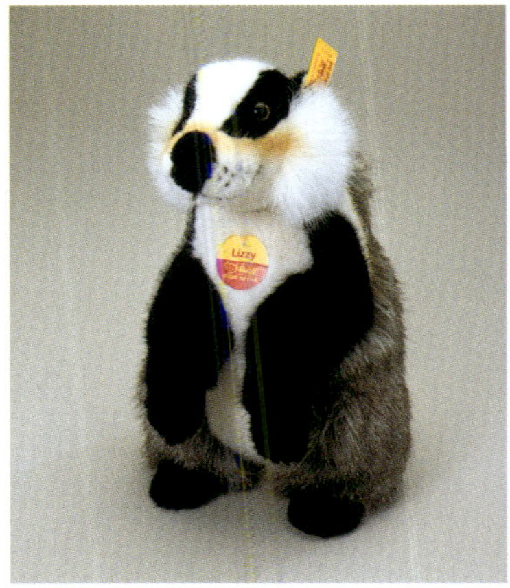

Lizzy Dachs - ***Lizzy** Badger*

Webpelz, aufwartend, waschmaschinenfest - *woven fur, sitting up, machine washable*

EAN-NO.	PERIOD	PR.	INFO
071270	1999-1999	2-3	25 cm

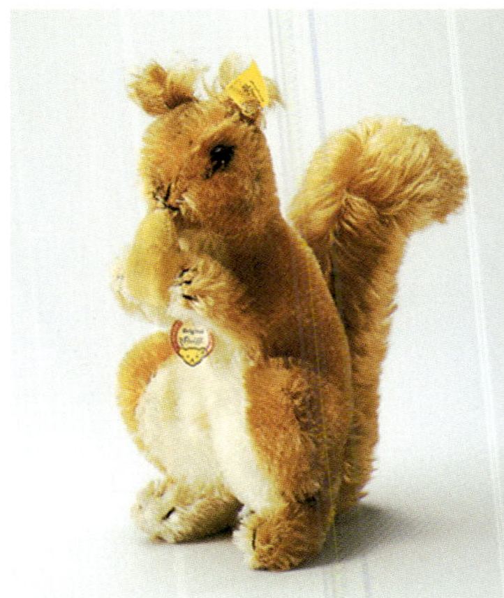

Eichhorn - *Squirrel*

Mohairpluesch, 20 cm, aufwartend, mit Samtnuss - *mohair, 20 cm, sitting up, holding a velvet nut in its paws*

SERIE	ART.-NO	PERIOD	PR.	INFO
19	**4320** br	1949-1956	4-5	rotbraun/weiss - *red-brown/white*
19	**4320** gr	1949-1956	4-5	grau/weiss - *grey/white*

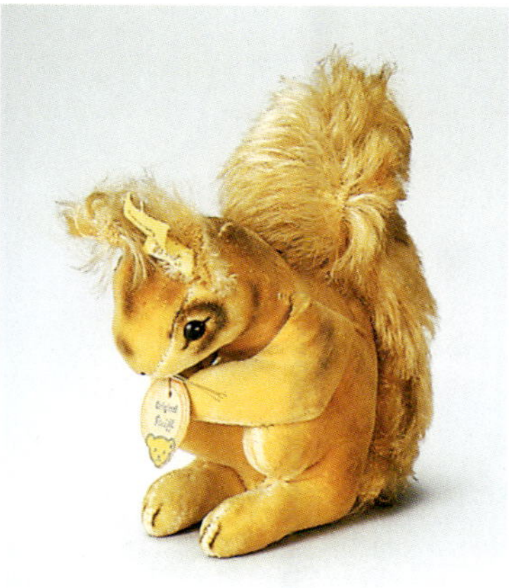

Eichhorn - *Squirrel*

Samt, 10 cm, aufwartend - *velvet, 10 cm, sitting up*

SERIE	ART.-NO	PERIOD	PR.	INFO
19	**4410** br	1950-1956	4	braun - *brown*
19	**4410** gr	1951-1956	4	grau - *grey*

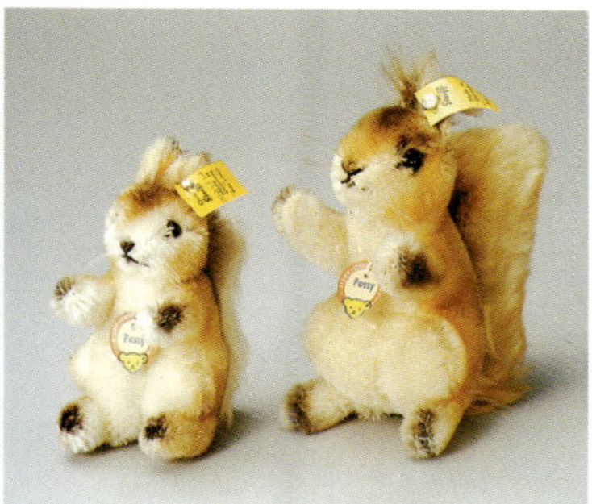

Possy Eichhoernchen - ***Possy*** *Squirrel*

Mohairpluesch, braun/weiss, aufwartend, buschiger Schwanz, abwaschbar - *mohair, brown/white, sitting up, bushy tail, surface washable*

SERIE	ART.-NO	PERIOD	PR.	INFO
19	**4310** br	1957-1958	3-4	10 cm
190	**4310,01**	1959-1964	3	
200	**4310,01**	1965-1967	3	
	2001/10	1968-1976	2-3	
19	**4314** br	1957-1958	3-4	14 cm
190	**4314,01**	1959-1964	3	
200	**4314,01**	1965-1967	3	
	2001/14	1968-1976	2-3	
19	**4322** br	1957-1958	4	22 cm
190	**4322,01**	1959-1964	3-4	
200	**4322,01**	1965-1967	3-4	
	2001/22	1968-1976	3	

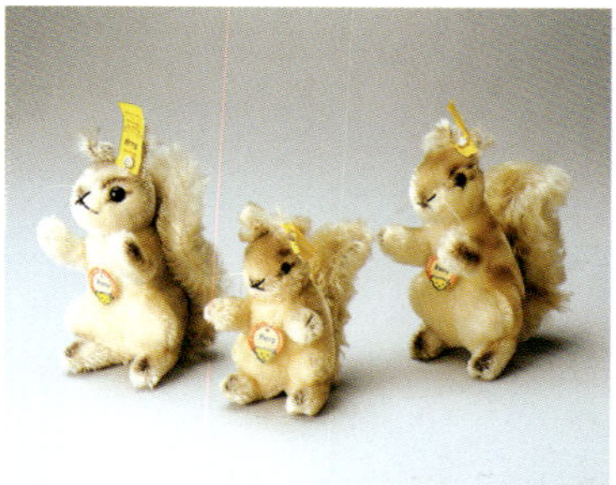

Possy Eichhoernchen - ***Possy*** *Squirrel*

Mohairpluesch, grau/weiss, auch mit Streifen, aufwartend, buschiger Schwanz - *mohair, grey & white, also with stripes, sitting up, bushy tail*

SERIE	ART.-NO	PERIOD	PR.	INFO
19	**4310** gr	1957-1958	3-4	10 cm
190	**4310,05**	1959-1964	3	
202	**4310,05**	1965-1967	3	
	2005/10	1968-1970	2-3	
19	**4314** gr	1957-1958	3-4	14 cm
190	**4314,05**	1959-1964	3	
202	**4314,05**	1965-1967	3	
	2005/14	1968-1969	2-3	
19	**4322** gr	1957-1958	4	22 cm
190	**4322,05**	1959-1964	3-4	
202	**4322,05**	1965-1967	3-4	
	2005/22	1968-1970	3	

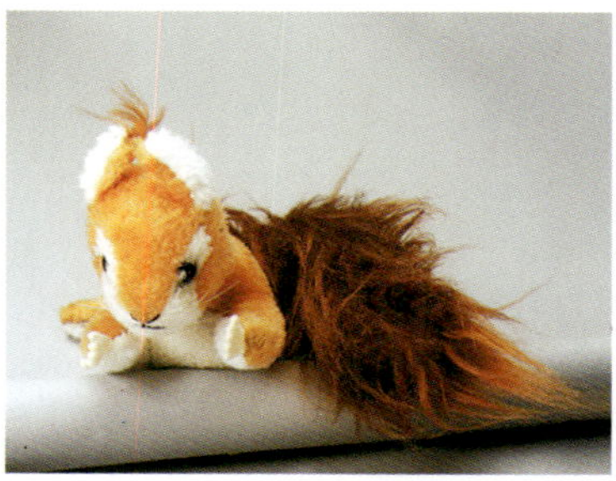

Cosy Eich

Dralon, gefuellt mit synthetischen Fasern & Schaumstoff, aufwartend, sehr weich, waschbar - *dralon, stuffed with synthetic fibers & foam, sitting up, very soft, washable*

SERIE	ART.-NO	PERIOD	PR.	INFO
	4910/22	1968-1974	2	22 cm

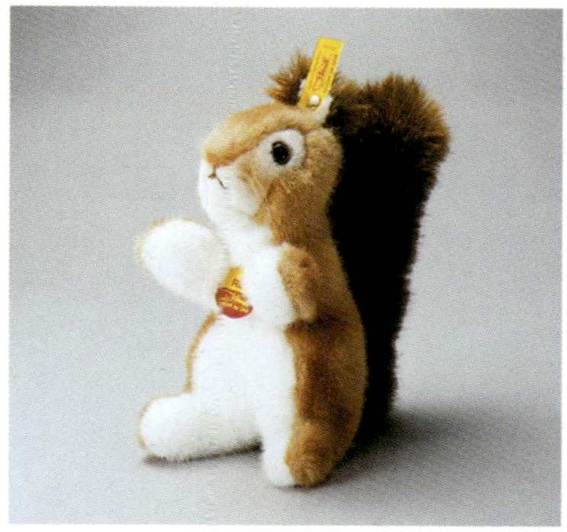

Ricky Eichhoernchen - ***Ricky*** *Squirrel*

Nerzimitation, ab 1978 Synthetik-Webpelz, aufwartend, abwaschbar - *imitation fur, from 1978 synthetic woven fur, sitting up, surface washable*

SERIE	ART.-NO	PERIOD	PR.	INFO
071324	**2030/20**	1977-1990	2	20 cm
	071324	1991-1999	2	

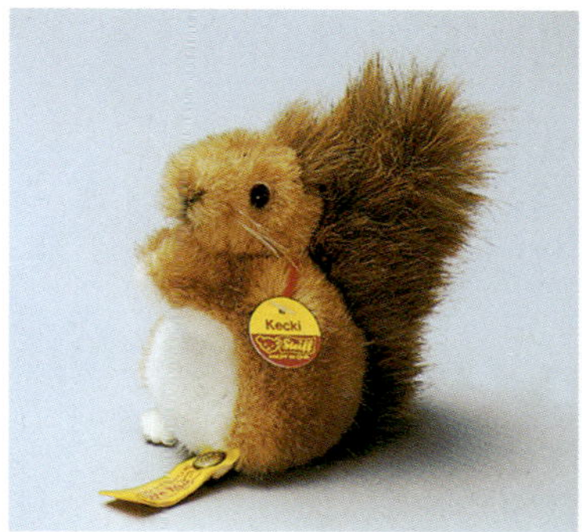

Kecki Eichhoernchen - ***Kecki*** *Squirrel*

Webpelz, aufwartend, abwaschbar - *woven fur, sitting up, surface washable*

SERIE	ART.-NO	PERIOD	PR.	INFO
	1467/10	1978-1985	1-2	10 cm

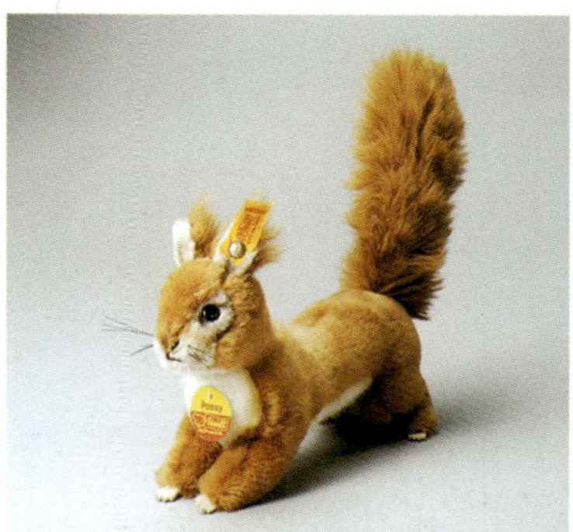

Possy Eichhoernchen - ***Possy*** *Squirrel*

Webpelz, stehend, abwaschbar - *woven fur, standing, surface washable*

SERIE	ART.-NO	PERIOD	PR.	INFO
	2032/25	1982-1985	2-3	25 cm

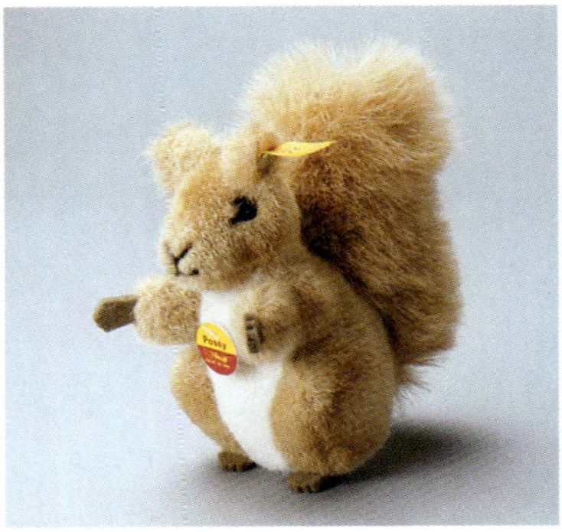

Possy Eichhoernchen - ***Possy*** *Squirrel*

Webpelz, aufwartend, abwaschbar - *woven fur, siting up, surface washable*

Serie	Art.-No	Period	Pr.	Info
045103	**1466/12**	1986-1990	1-2	12 cm
	045103	1991-1999	1-2	

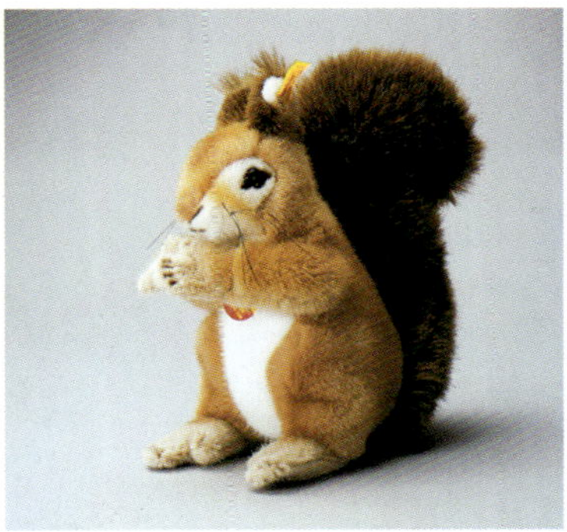

Kecki Eichhoernchen - ***Kecki*** *Squirrel*

Webpelz, aufwartend, abwaschbar - *woven fur, siting up, surface washable*

Serie	Art.-No	Period	Pr.	Info
071317	**2015/24**	1988-1990	3	24 cm
	071317	1991-1999	3	

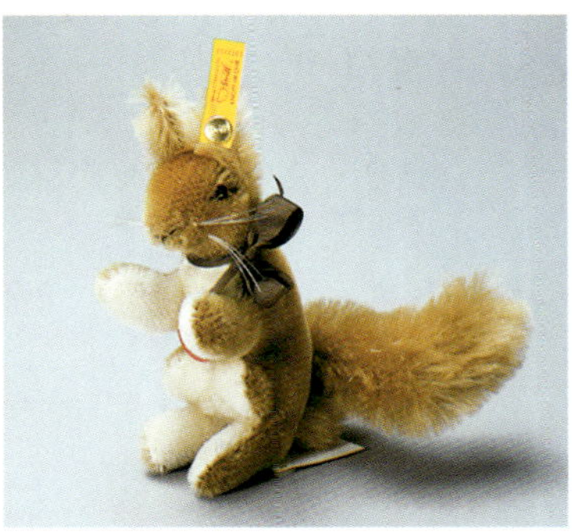

Possy Eichhoernchen - ***Possy*** *Squirrel*

Mohair-Webpelz, braun, aufwartend, abwaschbar - *mohair woven fur, brown, sitting up, surface washable*

Serie	Art.-No	Period	Pr.	Info
032325	**1312/12**	1990-1990	2	12 cm
	032325	1991-1993	2	

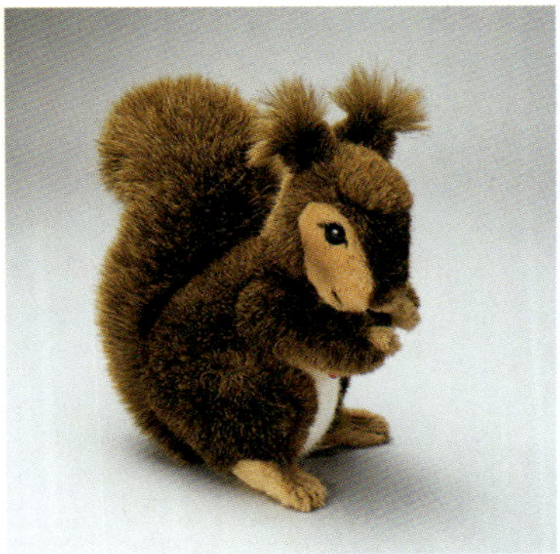

Toffy Eichhoernchen - ***Toffy*** *Squirrel*

Webpelz, dunkelbraun, aufwartend, abwaschbar - *woven fur, dark brown, sitting up, surface washable*

EAN-No.	Period	Pr.	Info
071331	1993-1997	2-3	25 cm

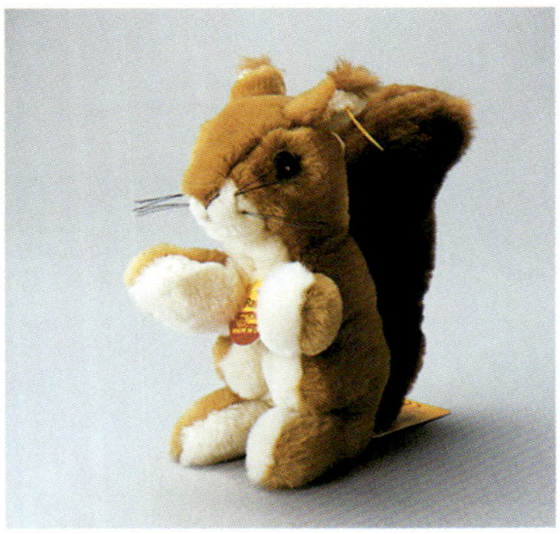

Raggi Eichhoernchen - ***Raggi*** *Squirrel*

Webpelz, aufwartend, waschmaschinenfest - *woven fur, sitting up, machine washable*

EAN-No.	Period	Pr.	Info
081828	1994-1996	2	16 cm

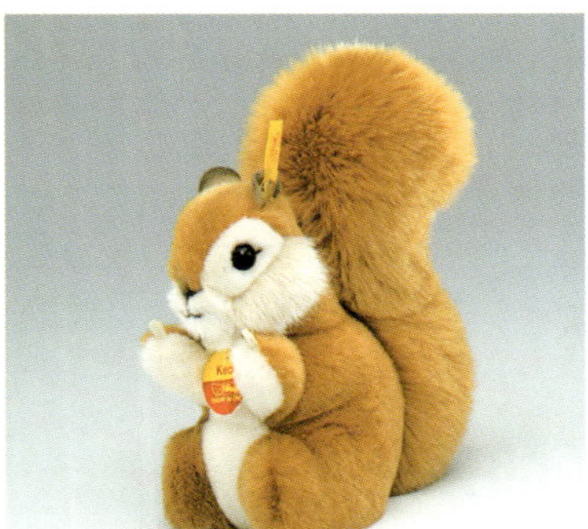

Kecki Eichhoernchen - ***Kecki*** *Squirrel*

Webpelz, aufwartend, waschmaschinenfest - *woven fur, sitting up, machine washable*

EAN-No.	Period	Pr.	Info
045110	1999-1999	2	18 cm

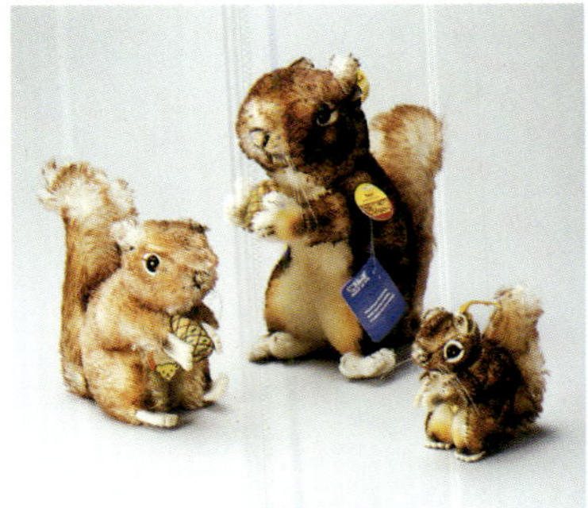

Perri Eichhoernchen - ***Perri*** *Squirrel*

Mohairpluesch, braun/weiss gespitzt, aufwartend, Copyr. Walt Disney Productions, abwaschbar - *mohair, brown/white tipped, sitting up, Copyr. Walt Disney Productions, surface washable*

Serie	Art.-No	Period	Pr.	Info
191	**4312,03**	1959-1964	3	12 cm
204	**4312,03**	1965-1967	3	
	2040/12	1968-1983	2-3	
191	**4317,03**	1959-1964	3	17 cm
204	**4317,03**	1965-1967	3	
	2040/17	1968-1980	2-3	
191	**4322,03**	1960-1964	3-4	22 cm
204	**4322,03**	1965-1967	3-4	
	2040/22	1968-1978	3	

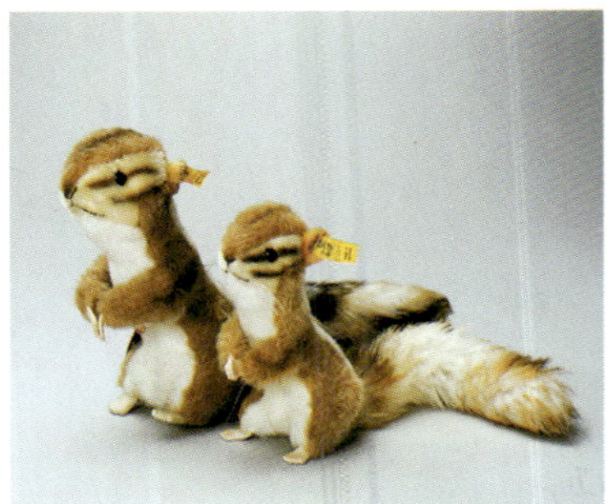

Chippy Streifenhoernchen - ***Chippy*** *Chipmunk*

Dralon, aufwartend, abwaschbar - *dralon, sitting up, surface washable*

Serie	Art.-No	Period	Pr.	Info
	2050/15	1975-1981	2-3	15 cm
	2050/20	1975-1981	2-3	20 cm

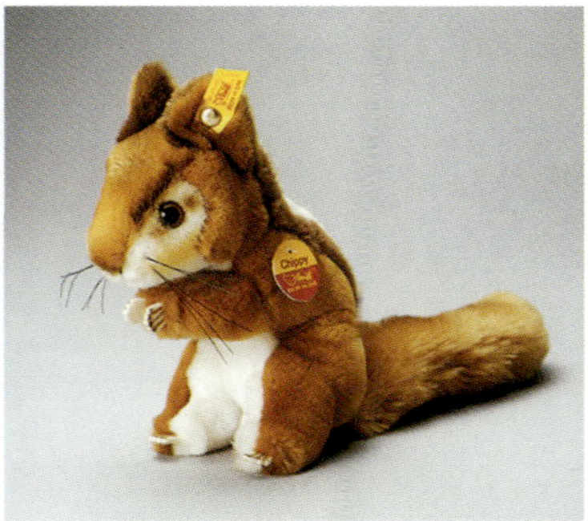

Chippy Streifenhoernchen - ***Chippy*** *Chipmunk*

Webpelz/Wirkpelz, aufwartend, waschmaschinenfest - *woven fur/knitted fur, sitting up, machine washable*

SERIE	ART.-NO	PERIOD	PR.	INFO
071355	**2025/18**	1989-1990	2-3	18 cm
	071355	1991-1997	2-3	

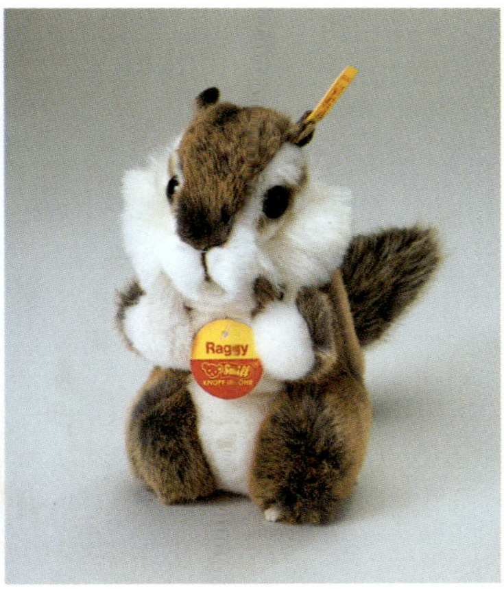

Raggi Streifenhoernchen - ***Raggi*** *Chipmunk*

Webpelz, aufwartend, waschmaschinenfest - *woven fur, sitting up, surface washable*

EAN-NO.	PERIOD	PR.	INFO
045158	1999-1999	2	15 cm

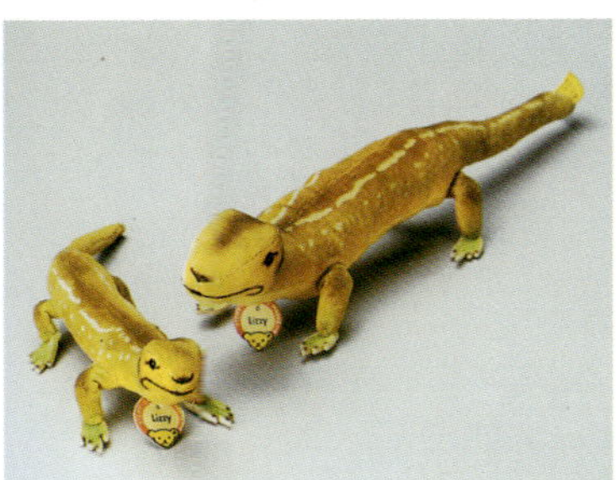

Lizzy Eidechse - ***Lizzy*** *Lizard*

Samtpluesch, gruen/braun, stehend - *plush velvet, green/brown, standing*

SERIE	ART.-NO	PERIOD	PR.	INFO
195	**1404,00**	1959-1961	4-5	4 cm
195	**1406,00**	1959-1961	5	6 cm

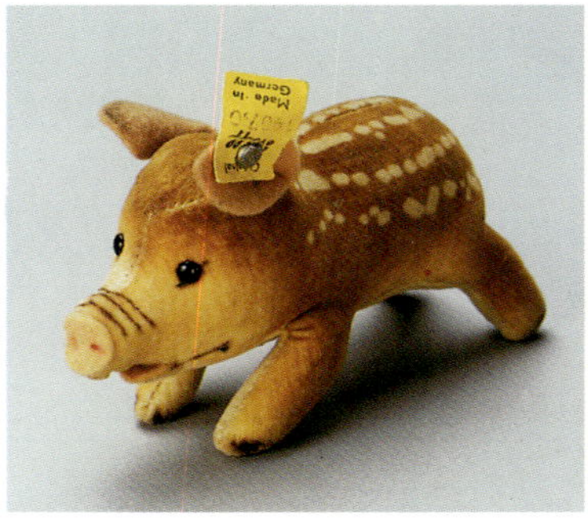

Wildschwein-Frischling - *Young Wild Boar*

Samt, braun, hell getupft, stehend, kein Brustschild - *velvet, brown with light speckles, standing, no chest tag*

SERIE	ART.-NO	PERIOD	PR.	INFO
64	**1407,0** br	1952-1958	3-4	7 cm
640	**1407,03**	1959-1964	3	
266	**1407,03**	1965-1967	3	
	2670/07	1968-1973	3	

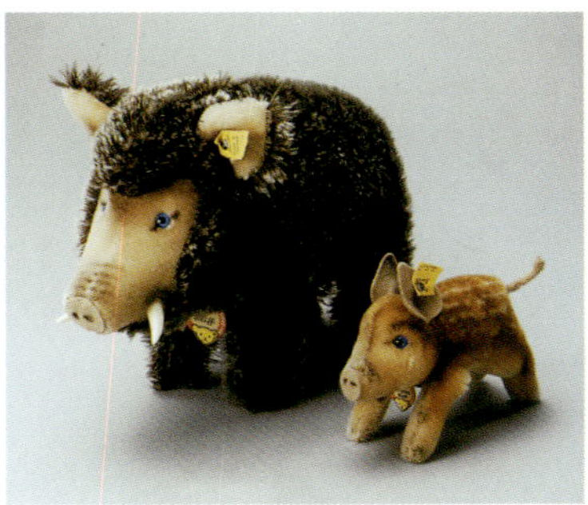

Wildschwein ab 1974 **Dalle** - *Wild Boar from 1974* ***Dalle***

Mohair, braun, ab 15 cm Igel-Mohair, gespitzt, stehend, Stosszaehne, abwaschbar - *mohair, brown, from 15 cm spiky mohair, tipped, standing, with tusks, surface washable*

SERIE	ART.-NO	PERIOD	PR.	INFO
640	**1310,03**	1961-1964	3	10 cm
267	**1310,03**	1965-1967	3	
	2670/10	1968-1975	3	
	2670/15	1969-1976	3	15 cm
640	**1320,03**	1961-1964	3-4	20 cm
267	**1320,03**	1965-1967	3-4	
	2670/20	1968-1976	3	

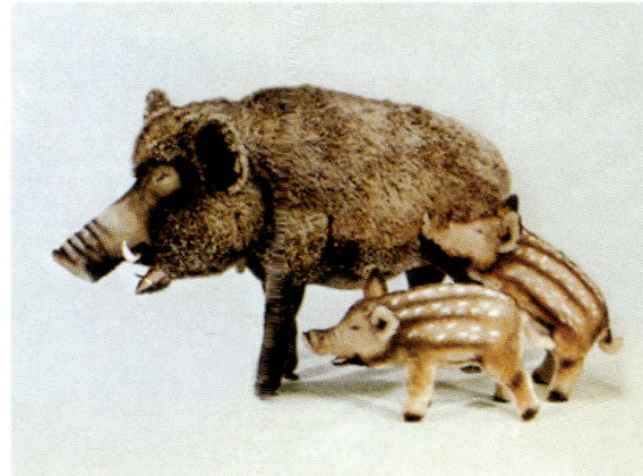

Frischling / Wildschwein - *Young Boar / Wild Boar*

Schautiere, Mohair, natur, stehend, offenes Maul, Frischling, 35 cm, mit Streifen & Punkten, Wildschwein, 80 cm, mit 2 Hauern - *display animals, mohair, natural color, standing, open mouth, young boar, 35 cm, with stripes & speckles, wild boar, 80 cm, with two tusks*

SERIE	ART.-NO	PERIOD	PR.	INFO
640	**1335,90**	1963-1963	4-5	35 cm
267	**1335,90**	1966-1966	4-5	
	2679/04	1967-1967	4-5	
640	**1380,90**	1963-1963	6	80 cm
267	**1380,90**	1966-1966	6	
	2679/08	1967-1967	6	

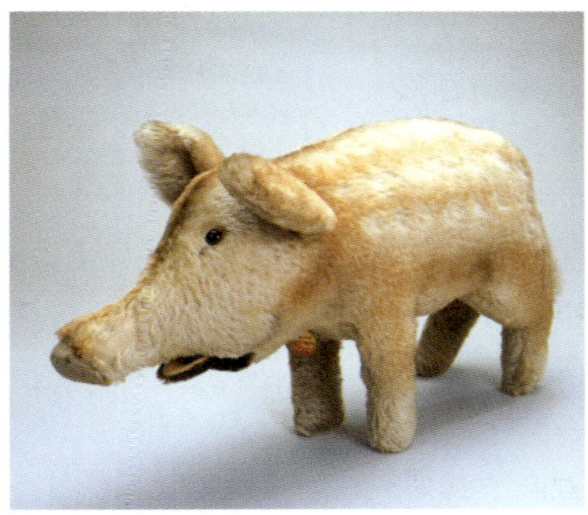

Frischling - *Young Boar*

Mohair, stehend, abwaschbar - *mohair, standing, surface washable*

SERIE	ART.-NO	PERIOD	PR.	INFO
	2678/40	1973-1973	4-5	40 cm

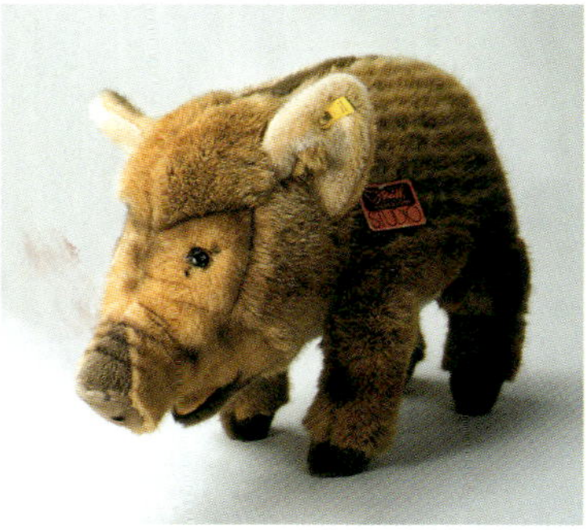

Frischling - *Young Boar*

Studio-Tier, Webpelz, stehend, abwaschbar - *studio-animal, woven fur, standing, surface washable*

SERIE	ART.-NO	PERIOD	PR.	INFO
	2678/50	1981-1984	4	50 cm

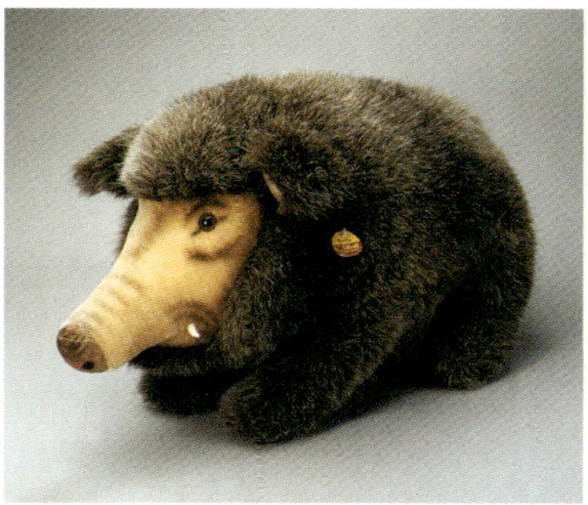

Dalle Wildschwein - ***Dalle*** *Wild Boar*

Pelz-Imitation, ab 1978 Synthetik-Webpelz, stehend, abwaschbar - *imitation fur, from 1978 synthetic woven fur, standing, surface washable*

SERIE	ART.-NO	PERIOD	PR.	INFO
	2677/40	1974-1978	4	40 cm

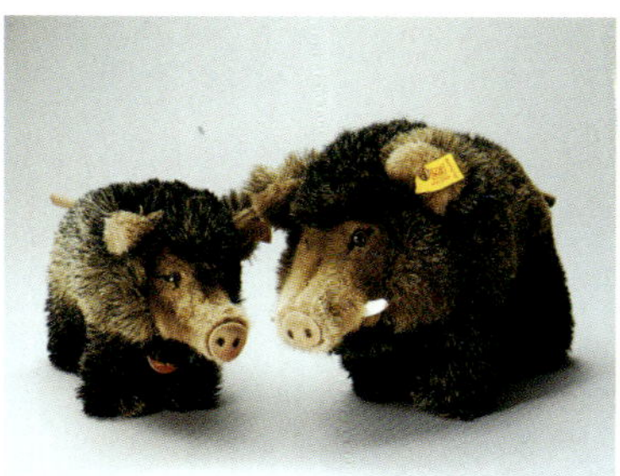

Wutzi Wildschwein - ***Wutzi*** *Wild Boar*

Wirkpluesch, ab 1978 Synthetik-Webpelz, stehend, abwaschbar - *Knitted plush, from 1978 synthetic woven fur, standing, surface washable*

SERIE	ART.-NO	PERIOD	PR.	INFO
072208	**2675/15**	1977-1987	2	15 cm
072222	**2675/20**	1977-1987	2	20 cm

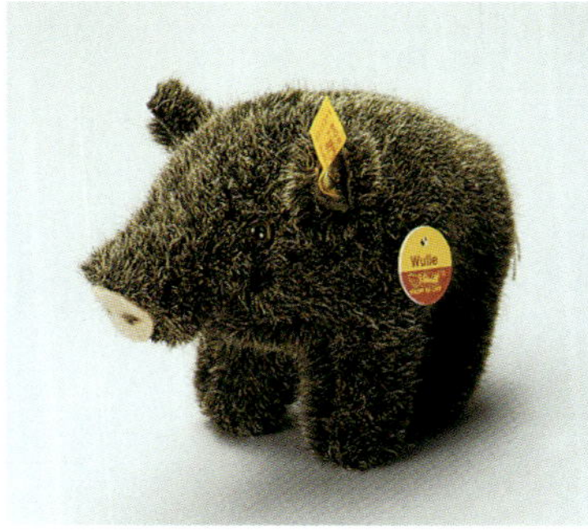

Wulle Wildschwein ab 1996 **Wutzi** - ***Wulle*** *Wild Boar from 1996* ***Wutzi***

Webpelz, stehend, abwaschbar - *woven fur, standing, surface washable*

SERIE	ART.-NO	PERIOD	PR.	INFO
045400	**1468/10**	1978-1990	1-2	14 cm
	045400	1991-1999	1-2	

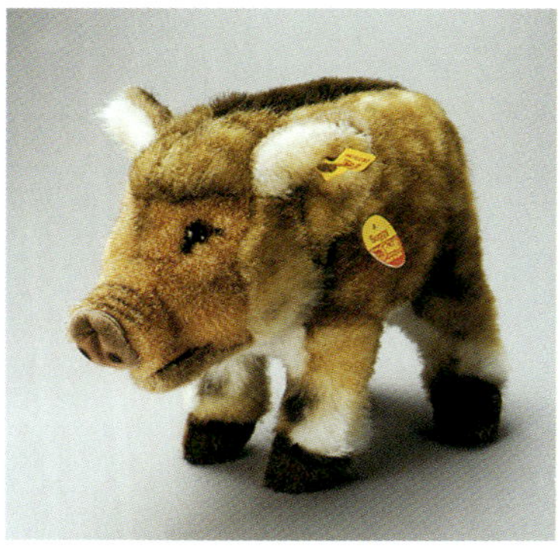

Suggy Frischling - ***Suggy*** *Young Boar*

Webpelz, stehend, abwaschbar - *woven fur, standing, surface washable*

SERIE	ART.-NO	PERIOD	PR.	INFO
072352	**2677/30**	1982-1986	3	30 cm

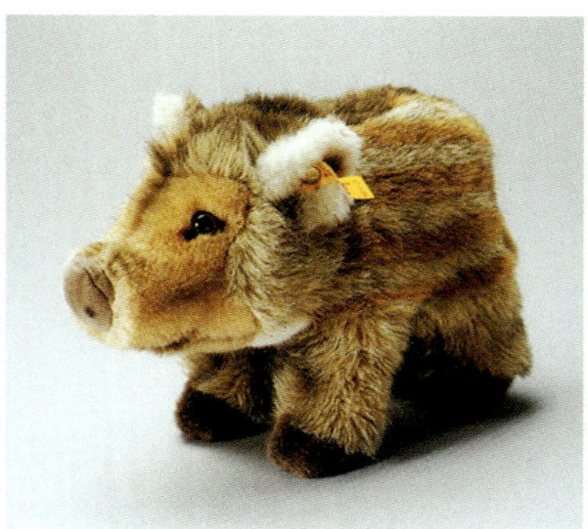

Suggy Frischling - ***Suggy*** *Young Boar*

Webpelz, stehend, abwaschbar - *woven fur, standing, surface washable*

SERIE	ART.-NO	PERIOD	PR.	INFO
072192	**2650/23**	1988-1990	2-3	23 cm
	072192	1991-1995	2-3	

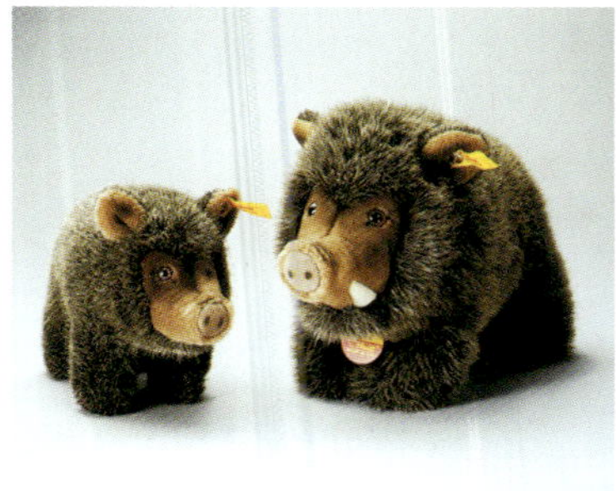

Bora Wildschwein - ***Bora*** *Wild Boar*

Webpelz, stehend, abwaschbar - *woven fur, standing, surface washable*

SERIE	ART.-NO	PERIOD	PR.	INFO
072253	**2660/20**	1987-1990	2	22 cm
	072253	1991-1999	2	
072284	**2660/30**	1987-1990	2-3	30 cm
	072284	1991-1996	2-3	

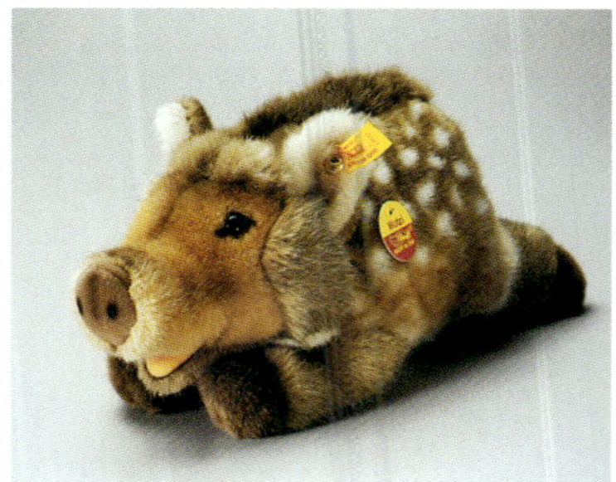

Wutzi Frischling - ***Wutzi*** *Young Boar*

Webpelz, hellbraun, liegend, Pieps-Stimme, abwaschbar - *woven fur, light brown, lying, squeaker, surface washable*

SERIE	ART.-NO	PERIOD	PR.	INFO
072215	**2655/28**	1990-1990	2	28 cm
	072215	1991-1993	2	
072239	**2655/40**	1990-1990	2-3	40 cm
	072239	1991-1994	2-3	

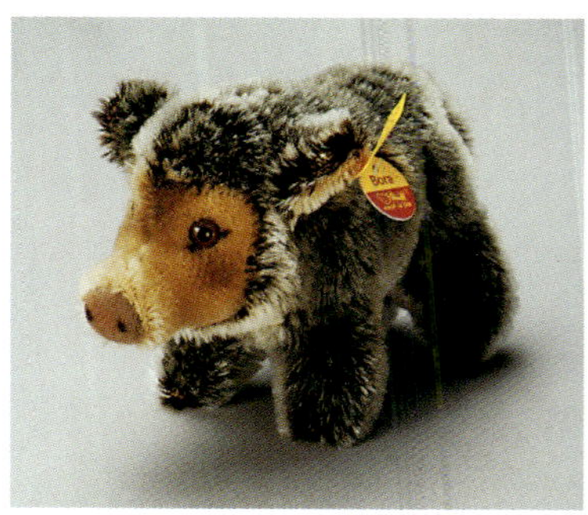

Bora Wildschwein - ***Bora*** *Wild Boar*

Mohair Webpelz, stehend, abwaschbar - *mohair woven fur,standing, surface washable*

EAN-NO.	PERIOD	PR.	INFO
032356	1991-1993	1-2	10 cm

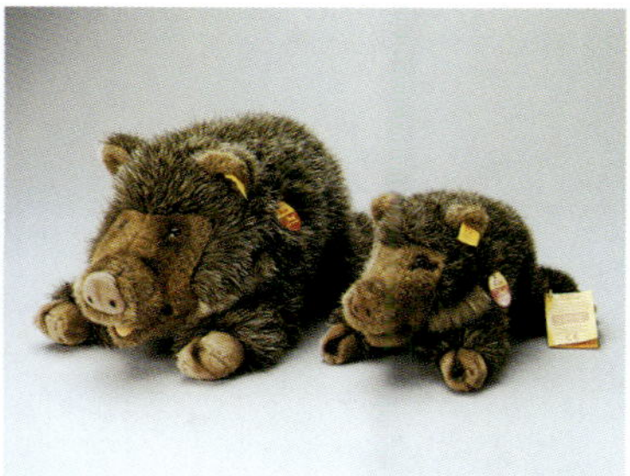

Wulle Wildschwein ab 1996 **Wutzi** - ***Wulle*** *Wild Boar from 1966* ***Wutzi***

Webpelz, liegend, hand-/ abwaschbar - *woven fur, lying, hand-/ surface washable*

EAN-No.	Period	Pr.	Info
072307	1994-1999	2-3	22 cm
072321	1994-1995	2-3	30 cm
072345	1993-1996	3	45 cm
072369	1993-1997	3-4	60 cm
072383	1993-1995	4	90 cm

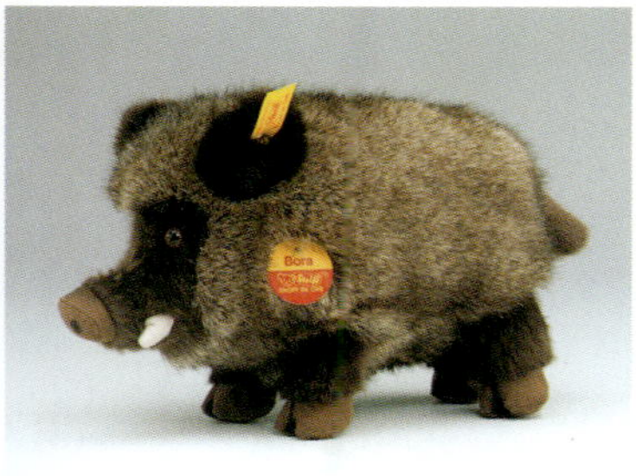

Bora Wildschwein - ***Bora*** *Wild Boar*

Webpelz, stehend, abwaschbar - *woven fur, standing, surface washable*

EAN-No.	Period	Pr.	Info
072260	1999-1999	2-3	22 cm

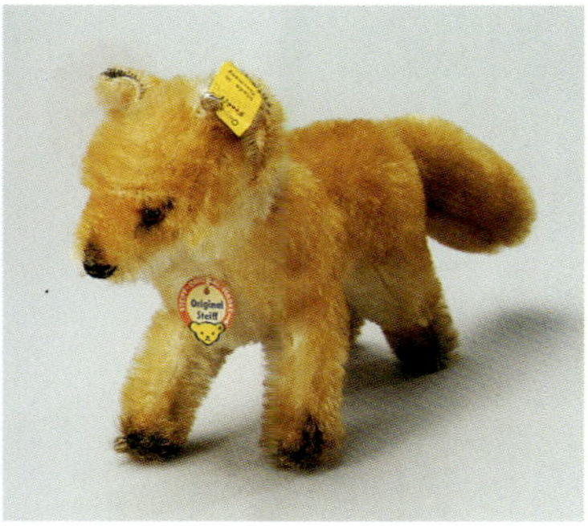

Fuchs - *Fox*

Mohairpluesch, rotbraun/weiss, stehend - *mohair, reddish-brown/white, standing*

Serie	Art.-No	Period	Pr.	Info
28	**1310,0**	1950-1957	4	10 cm
28	**1314,0**	1949-1957	4	14 cm
28	**1317,0**	1949-1957	4	17 cm

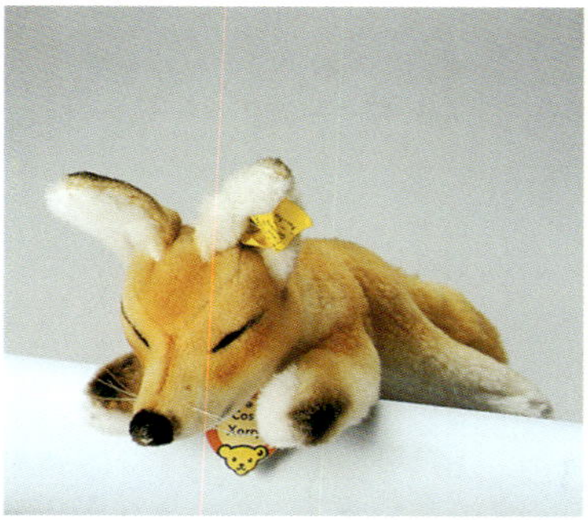

Cosy Xorry Fuchs - ***Cosy Xorry*** *Fox*

Dralon-Pluesch, Schaumgummi-Fuellung, braun, liegend, sehr weich, waschbar - *dralon, stuffed with foam rubber, brown, lying, very soft, washable*

Serie	Art.-No	Period	Pr.	Info
83 28	**7617**	1958-1958	3	17 cm
830 280	**7617,00**	1959-1963	3	

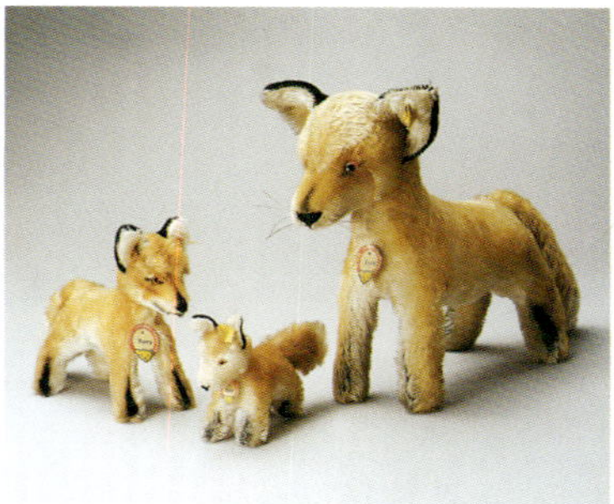

Xorry Fuchs - ***Xorry*** *Fox*

Mohair, rotbraun/weiss, stehend - *mohair, reddish-brown/white, standing*

Serie	Art.-No	Period	Pr.	Info
280	**1311,00**	1960-1964	3	11 cm
150	**1311,00**	1965-1967	3	
	1500/11	1968-1969	3	
280	**1318,00**	1960-1964	3-4	18 cm
150	**1318,00**	1965-1967	3-4	
	1500/18	1968-1969	3	
280	**1328,00**	1960-1964	3-4	28 cm
150	**1328,00**	1965-1967	3-4	
	1500/28	1968-1968	3	

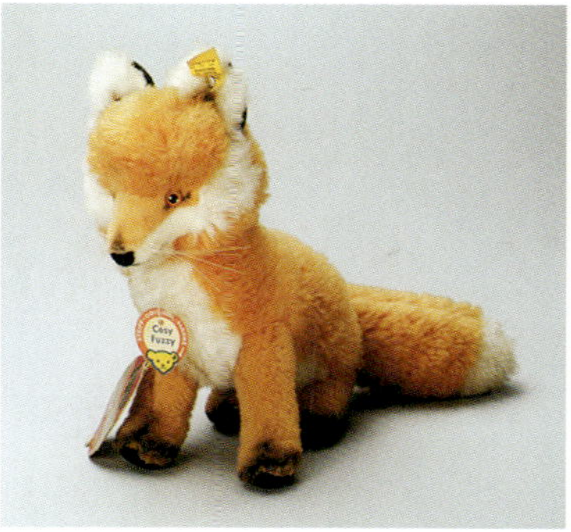

Cosy Fuzzy Fuchs - ***Cosy Fuzzy*** *Fox*

Dralon, Schaumgummi-Fuellung, rotbraun/weiss, sitzend, sehr weich, waschbar - *dralon, stuffed with foam, red-brown/ white, sitting, very soft, washable*

Serie	Art.-No	Period	Pr.	Info
830 280	**3622,00**	1963-1964	2-3	22 cm
490	**3622,00**	1965-1967	2-3	
	4900/22	1968-1980	2	

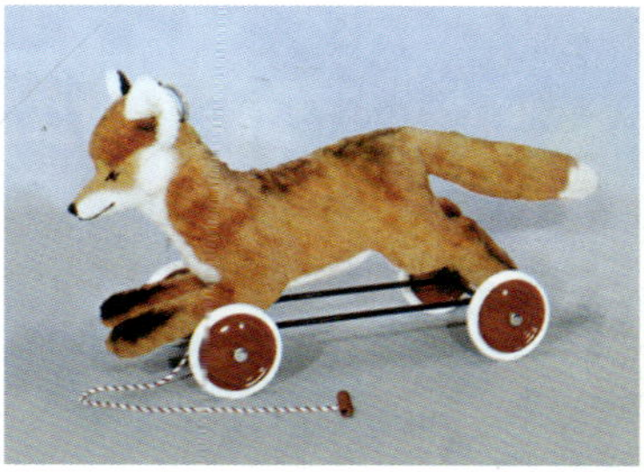

Reit-Fuchs - *Riding Fox*

Dralon, rotbraun/weiss, stehend, Metallscheibenraeder mit Gummireifen, Eisengriff - *dralon, reddish-brown/white, standing, disc wheels with rubber tires, metal grip handle*

Serie	Art.-No	Period	Pr.	Info
150	**1650,20**	1965-1966	4	50 cm

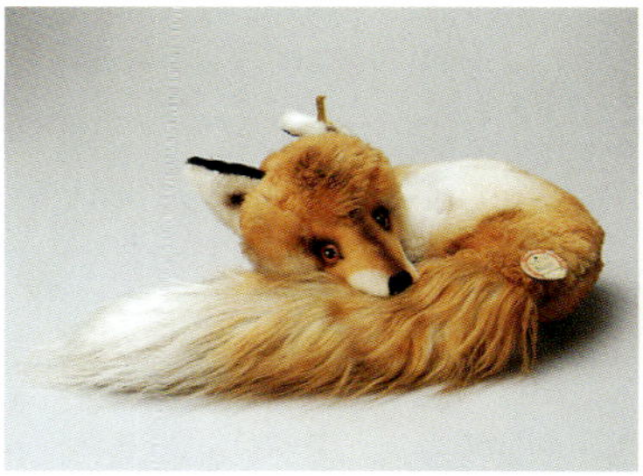

Ringel-Fuchs - *Curled Up Fox*

Dralon, rotbraun, liegend, abwaschbar - *dralon, reddish-brown, lying, surface washable*

Serie	Art.-No	Period	Pr.	Info
	1540/30	1968-1976	2-3	30 cm

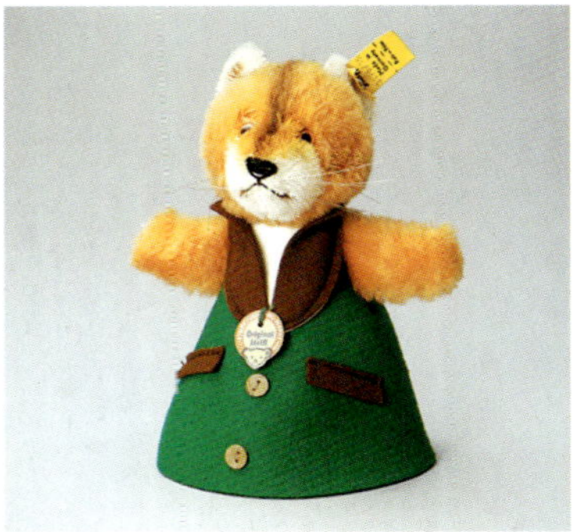

Betthupferlfuchs - *Nightcap Fox*

Kopf & Arme Mohair, Filzkleidung, gruen, Drehkopf, innen hohl zur Abdeckung kleiner Praesente - *head & arms mohair, felt clothing, green, head swivels, hollow interior to cover small gifts*

Serie	Art.-No	Period	Pr.	Info
	3176/15	1969-1974	4	15 cm

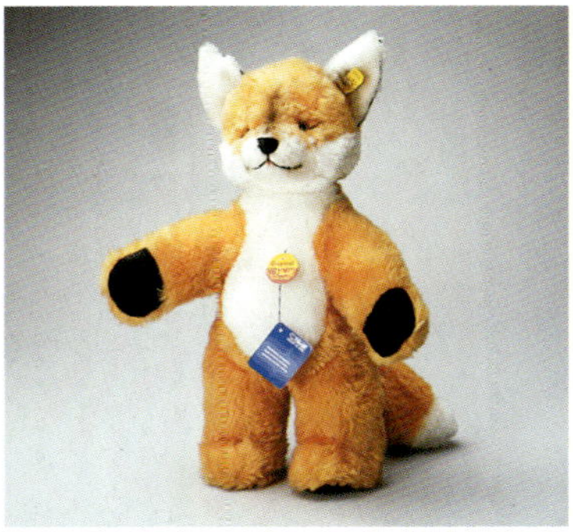

Weich-Fuchs - *Soft Fox*

Dralon, formgeschaeumt, sehr weich, Schlenkerkopf, vollwaschbar - *dralon, stuffed with pre-formed foam, very soft, floppy head, fully washable*

Serie	Art.-No	Period	Pr.	Info
	6215/30	1971-1978	2-3	30 cm
	6215/40	1971-1977	2-3	40 cm

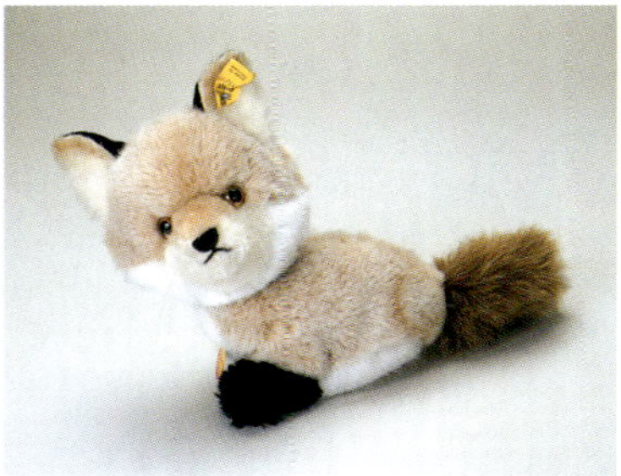

Snuffy Fuchs - ***Snuffy*** *Fox*

Pelz-Imitation, ab 1978 Synthetik-Webpelz, sitzend, abwaschbar - *imitation fur, from 1978 synthetic woven fur, sitting, surface washable*

Serie	Art.-No	Period	Pr.	Info
	3515/14	1974-1981	1-2	14 cm
	3515/18	1974-1981	1-2	18 cm

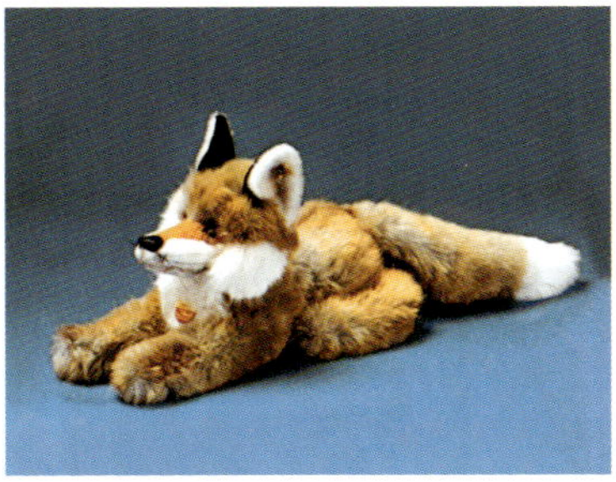

Junior Fuchs - *Junior Fox*

Pelzimitation, ab 1978 Synthetik-Webpelz, liegend, abwaschbar - *imitation fur, from 1978 synthetic woven fur, lying, surface washable*

Serie	Art.-No	Period	Pr.	Info
	2881/35	1975-1981	3	35 cm

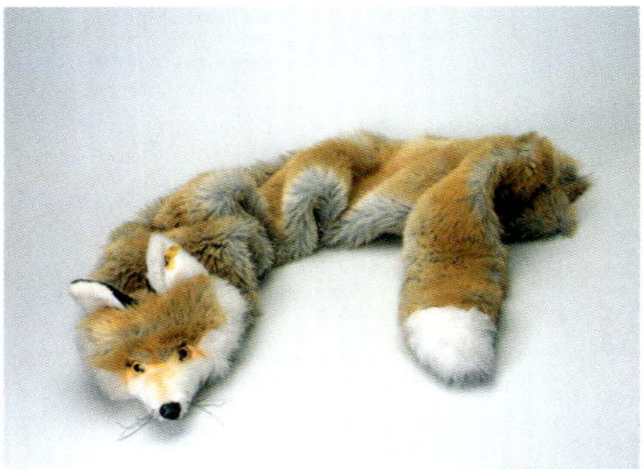

Rotfuchs - *Red Fox*

Pelzimitation, abwaschbar - *imitation fur, surface washable*

Serie	Art.-No	Period	Pr.	Info
	1545/99	1976-1977	3-4	99 cm

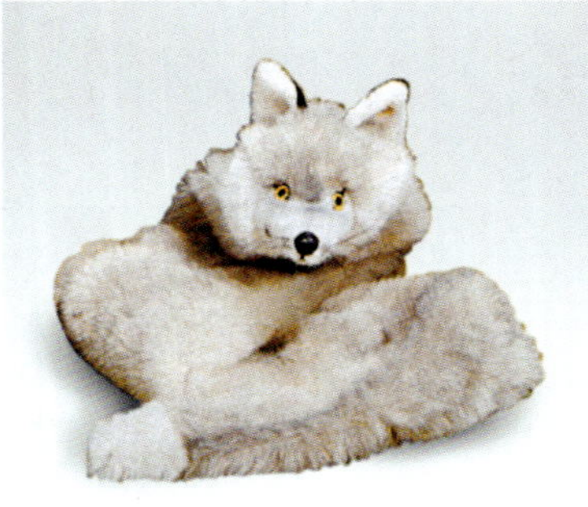

Silberfuchs - *Silver Fox*

Pelzimitation, abwaschbar - *imitation fur, surface washable*

Serie	Art.-No	Period	Pr.	Info
	1546/99	1976-1977	3-4	99 cm

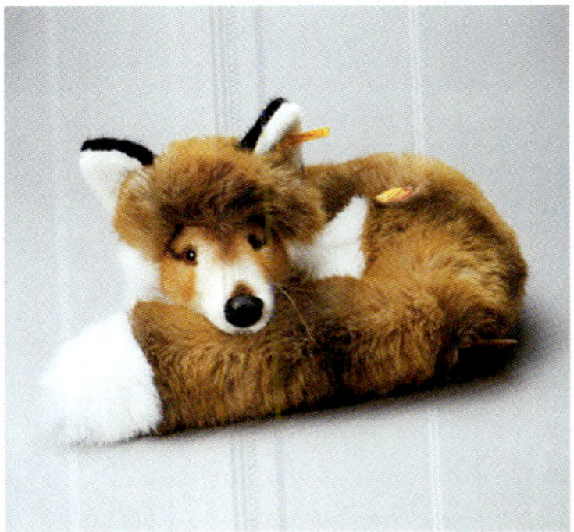

Ringel-**Fuzzy** - *Curled Up* ***Fuzzy***

Pelzimitation, ab 1978 Synthetik-Webpelz, geringelt liegend, abwaschbar - *imitation fur, from 1978 synthetic woven fur, lying curled up, surface washable*

Serie	Art.-No	Period	Pr.	Info
070105	**1542/35**	1977-1990	2-3	35 cm
	070105	1991-1996	2-3	

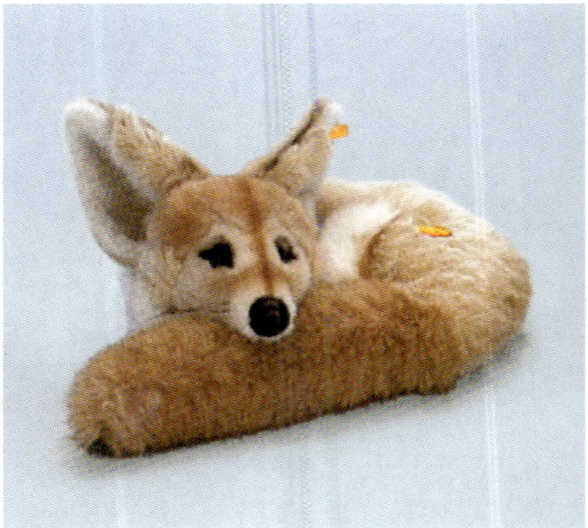

Ringel-**Xorry** - *Curled Up* ***Xorry***

Wirkpluesch, ab 1978 Synthetik-Webpelz, geringelt liegend, abwaschbar - *knitted plush, from 1978 synthetic woven fur, lying curled up, surface washable*

Serie	Art.-No	Period	Pr.	Info
	1544/35	1977-1983	2-3	35 cm

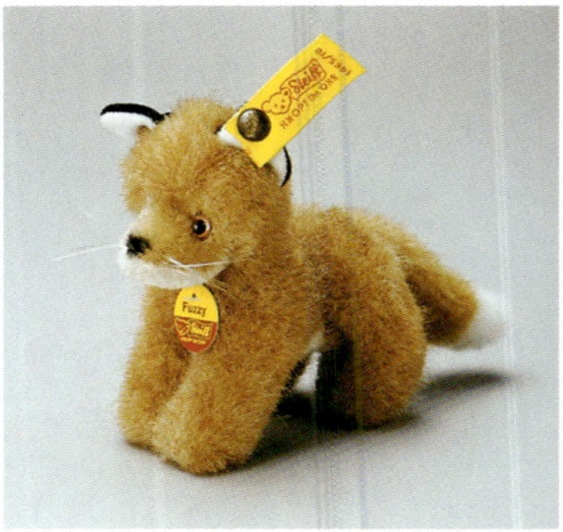

Fuzzy Fuchs - ***Fuzzy*** *Fox*

Webpelz, stehend, abwaschbar - *woven fur, standing, surface washable*

SERIE	ART.-NO	PERIOD	PR.	INFO
	1465/10	1978-1985	1-2	10 cm

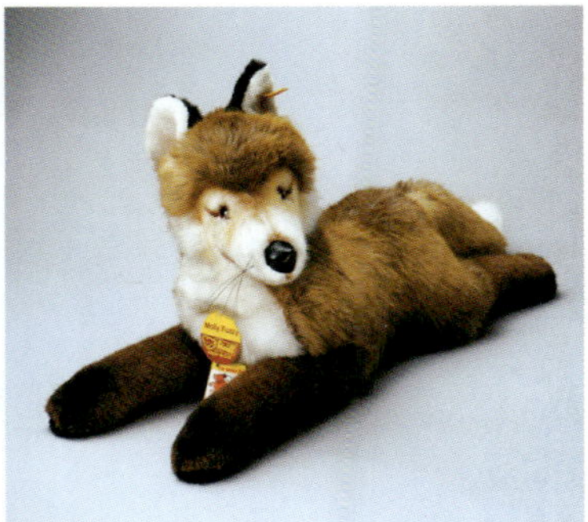

Molly Fuzzy Fuchs - ***Molly Fuzzy** Fox*

Webpelz, liegend, mollig weich, abwaschbar - *woven fur, lying, soft & cuddly, surface washable*

SERIE	ART.-NO	PERIOD	PR.	INFO
103155	**0347/55**	1981-1987	3	55 cm

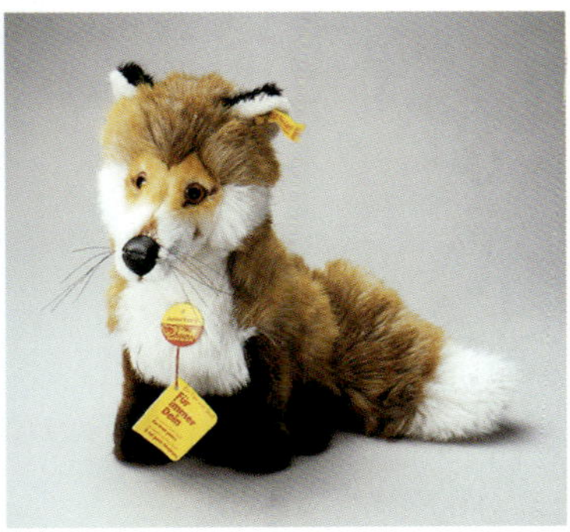

Junior Fuzzy

Webpelz, sitzend, abwaschbar - *woven fur, sitting, surface washable*

SERIE	ART.-NO	PERIOD	PR.	INFO
	2892/28	1981-1983	2-3	28 cm

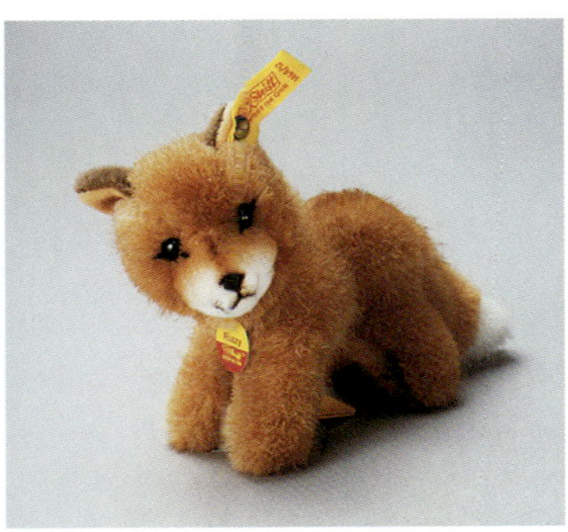

Fuzzy Fuchs - ***Fuzzy** Fox*

Webpelz, stehend, abwaschbar - *woven fur, standing, surface washable*

SERIE	ART.-NO	PERIOD	PR.	INFO
045059	**1464/12**	1986-1988	1-2	12 cm

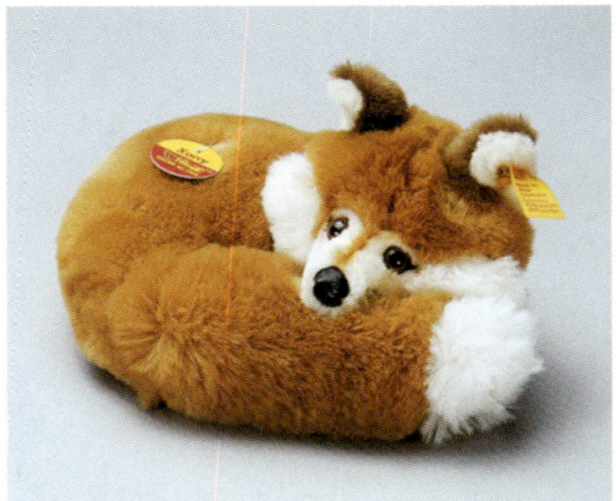

Xorry Ringelfuchs - ***Xorry** Curled Up Fox*

Wirkpelz, geringelt liegend, waschmaschinenfest - *knitted fur, lying curled up, machine washable*

SERIE	ART.-NO	PERIOD	PR.	INFO
070051	**1540/20**	1986-1990	2	20 cm
	070051	1991-1999	2	

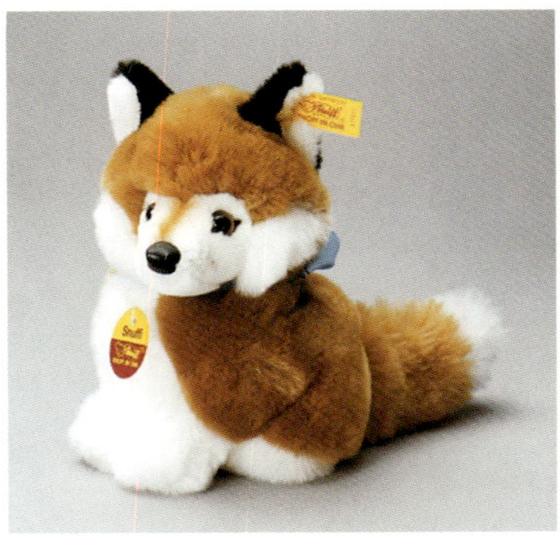

Snuffi Fuchs - ***Snuffi** Fox*

Webpelz, sitzend, waschmaschinenfest - *woven fur, sitting, machine washable*

SERIE	ART.-NO	PERIOD	PR.	INFO
077227	**2916/16**	1987-1990	2	16 cm
	077227	1991-1999	2	

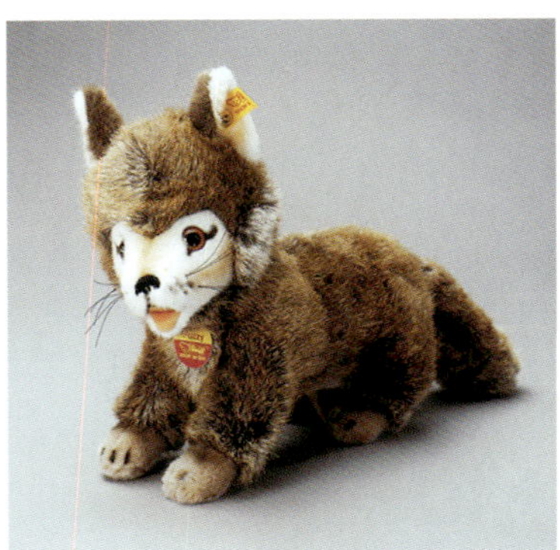

Fuzzy Fuchs - ***Fuzzy** Fox*

Webpelz, stehend, handwaschbar - *woven fur, standing, hand washable*

SERIE	ART.-NO	PERIOD	PR.	INFO
070150	**1548/25**	1989-1990	2	25 cm
	070150	1991-1991	2	

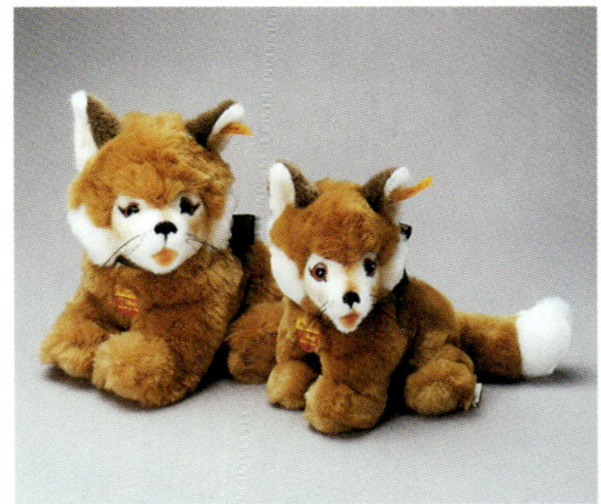

Pummy Fuchs - ***Pummy** Fox*

Webpelz, waschmaschinenfest - *woven fur, machine washable*

SERIE	ART.-NO	PERIOD	PR.	INFO
083952	**5250/17**	1989-1990	2	17 cm
	083952	1991-1991	2	
083976	**5250/21**	1989-1990	2	21 cm

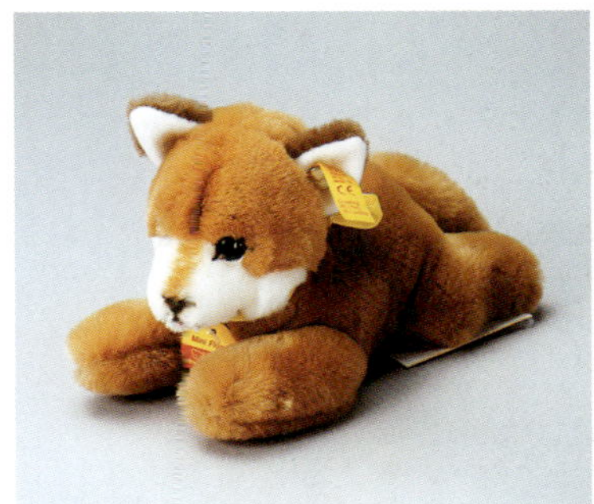

Mini Floppy Fuchs - ***Mini Floppy** Fox*

Webpelz, liegend, waschmaschinenfest - *woven fur, lying, machine washable*

SERIE	ART.-NO	PERIOD	PR.	INFO
082085	**5678/16**	1989-1990	1-2	16 cm
	082085	1991-1991	1-2	

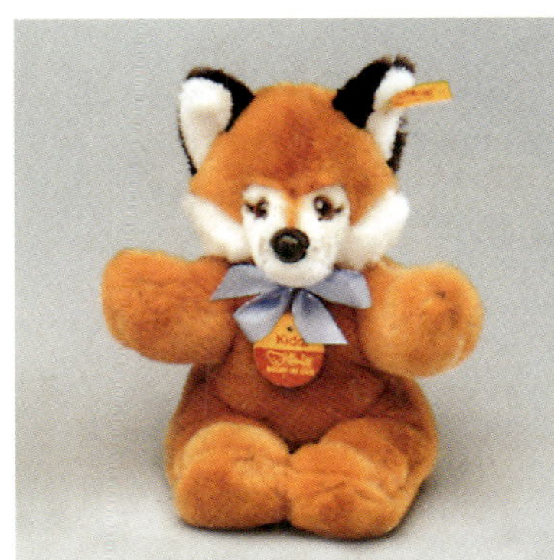

Kiddi Fuchs - ***Kiddi** Fox*

Webpelz, Pieps-Stimme, waschmaschinenfest - *woven fur, squeaker, machine washable*

SERIE	ART.-NO	PERIOD	PR.	INFO
082924	**5728/20**	1989-1990	2	20 cm

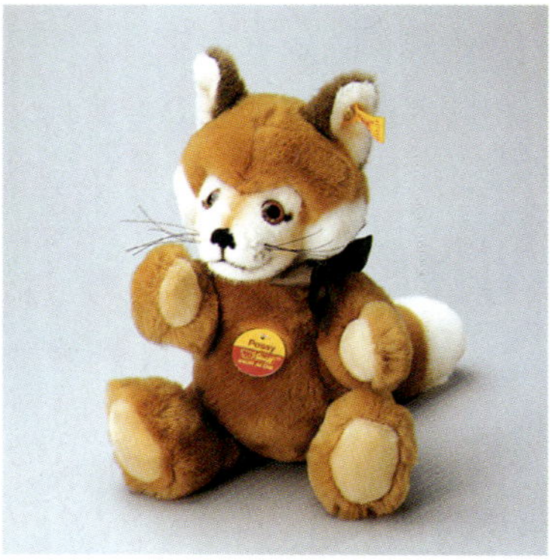

Possy Fuchs - ***Possy*** *Fox*

Webpelz, gegliedert, Pieps-Stimme, waschmaschinenfest - *woven fur, jointed, squeaker, machine washable*

SERIE	ART.-NO	PERIOD	PR.	INFO
081743	**6240/28**	1989-1990	2-3	28 cm

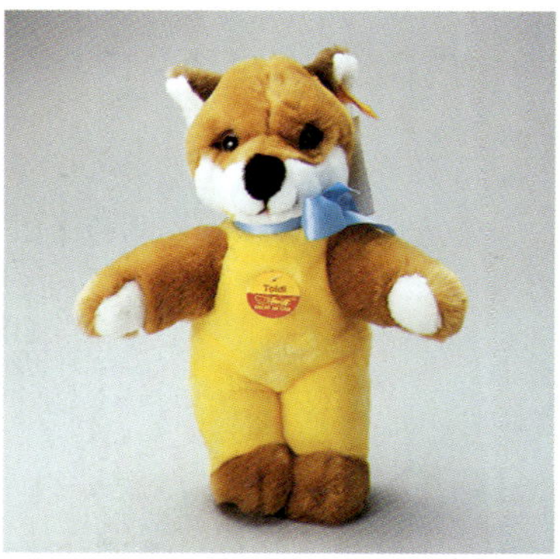

Toldi Fuchs - ***Toldi*** *Fox*

Webpelz, Pieps-Stimme, waschmaschinenfest - *woven fur, squeaker, machine washable*

SERIE	ART.-NO	PERIOD	PR.	INFO
081156	**6267/27**	1989-1990	2	27 cm

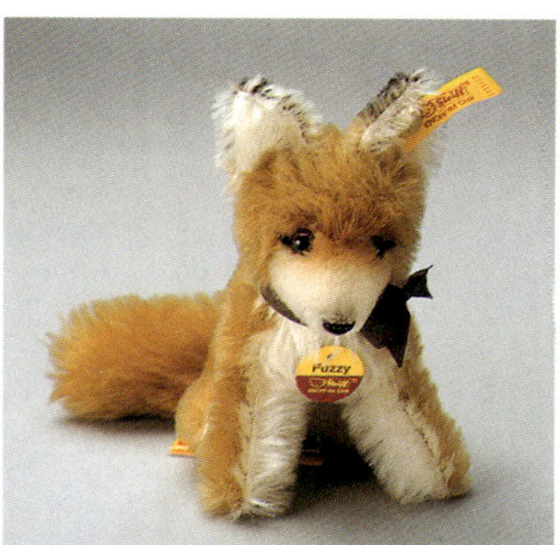

Fuzzy Fuchs - ***Fuzzy*** *Fox*

Mohair Webpelz, rotbraun, sitzend, abwaschbar - *mohair woven fur, reddish-brown, sitting, surface washable*

SERIE	ART.-NO	PERIOD	PR.	INFO
032424	**1311/12**	1990-1990	2-3	12 cm
	032424	1991-1993	2-3	

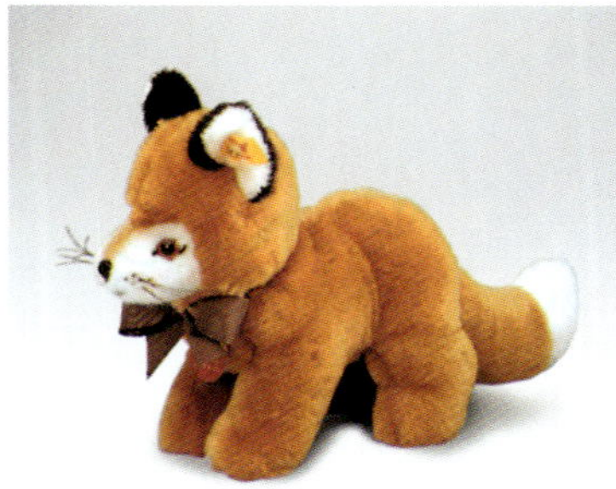

Drolly Fuchs - ***Drolly*** *Fox*

Webpelz, rotbraun, stehend, waschmaschinenfest - *woven fur, reddish-brown, standing, machine washable*

SERIE	ART.-NO	PERIOD	PR.	INFO
081378	**5790/22**	1990-1990	2	22 cm
	081378	1991-1993	2	

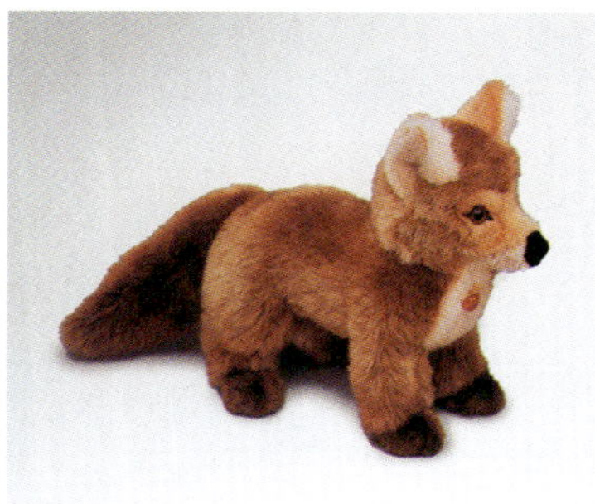

Fuzzy Fuchs - ***Fuzzy*** *Fox*

Webpelz, stehend, abwaschbar - *woven fur, standing, surface washable*

EAN-NO.	PERIOD	PR.	INFO
070204	1992-1993	2-3	40 cm

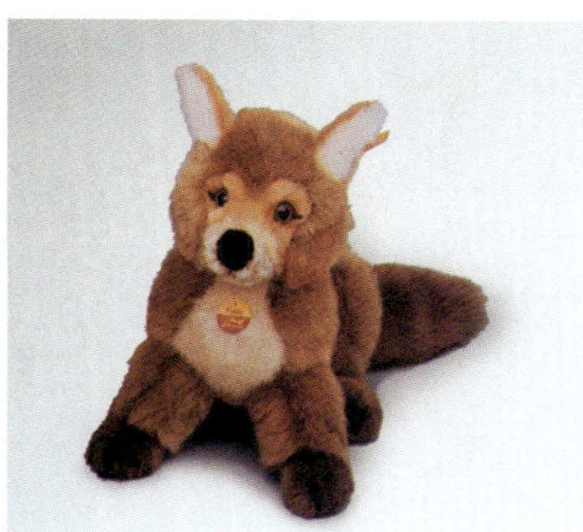

Fuzzy Fuchs - ***Fuzzy*** *Fox*

Webpelz, sitzend, abwaschbar - *woven fur, sitting, surface washable*

EAN-NO.	PERIOD	PR.	INFO
070259	1992-1993	2-3	40 cm

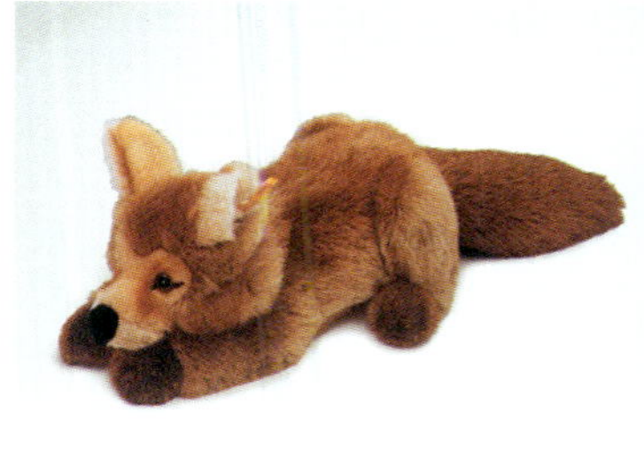

Fuzzy Fuchs - ***Fuzzy*** *Fox*

Webpelz, liegend, abwaschbar - *woven fur, lying, surface washable*

EAN-NO.	PERIOD	PR.	INFO
070303	1992-1993	2-3	40 cm

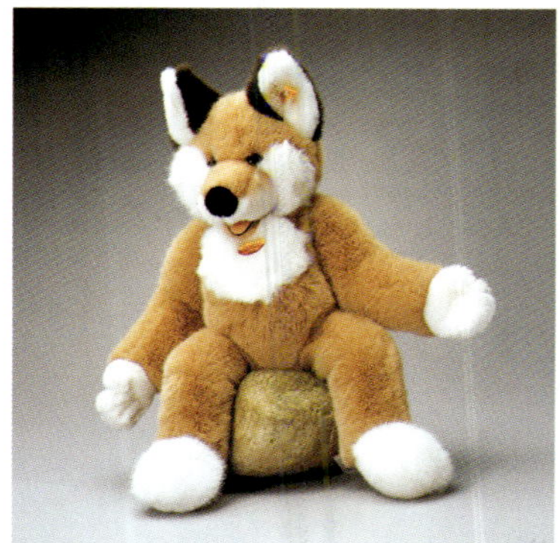

Schlenker Fuchs - *Dangling Fox*

Webpelz, waschmaschinenfest - *woven fur, machine washable*

EAN-NO.	PERIOD	PR.	INFO
123634	1993-1996	3	50 cm

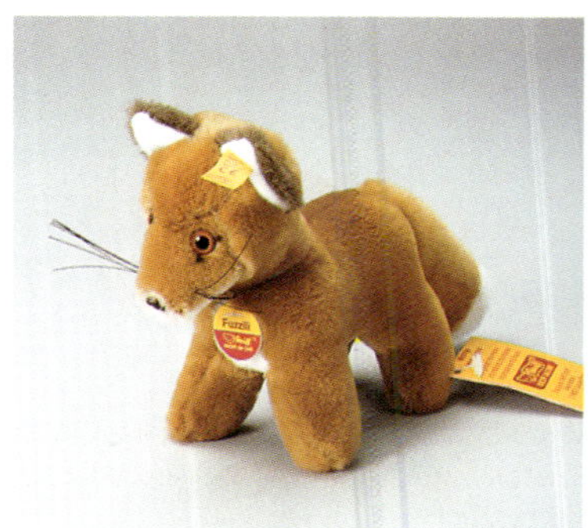

Fuzzili Fuchs - ***Fuzzili*** *Fox*

Webpelz, stehend, handwaschbar - *woven fur, standing, hand washable*

EAN-NO.	PERIOD	PR.	INFO
045066	1994-1996	2	18 cm

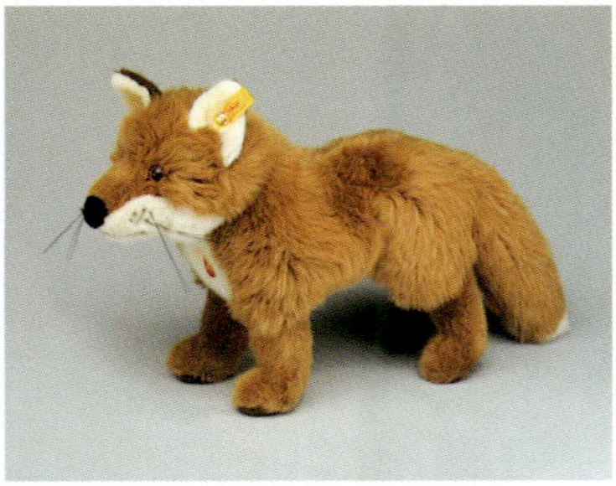

Snorry Jungfuchs - ***Snorry** Fox Cub*

Webpelz, stehend, abwaschbar - *woven fur, standing, surface washable*

EAN-No.	Period	Pr.	Info
070327	1994-1997	3	45 cm

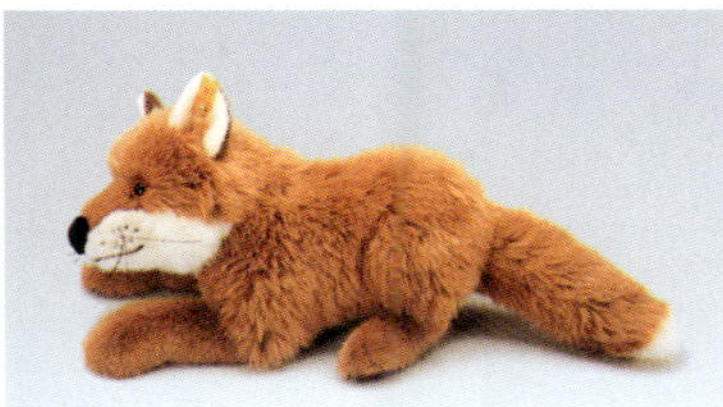

Snorry Jungfuchs - ***Snorry** Fox Cub*

Webpelz, liegend, abwaschbar - *woven fur, lying, surface washable*

EAN-No.	Period	Pr.	Info
070365	1994-1995	2-3	45 cm

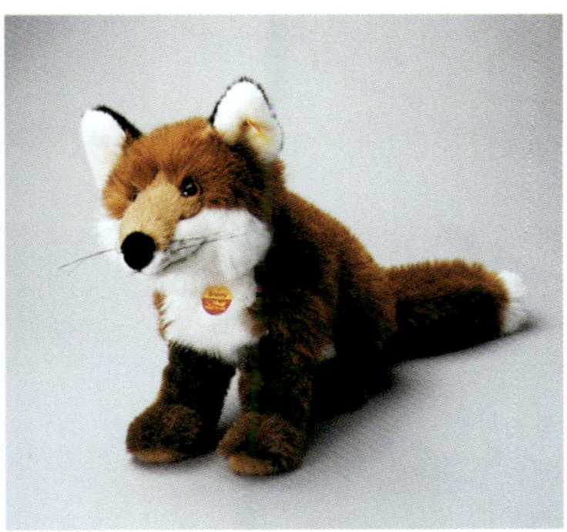

Snorry Fuchs - ***Snorry** Fox*

Webpelz, braun/weiss, sitzend, abwaschbar - *woven fur, brown/white, sitting, surface washable*

EAN-No.	Period	Pr.	Info
070426	1994-1996	3	60 cm

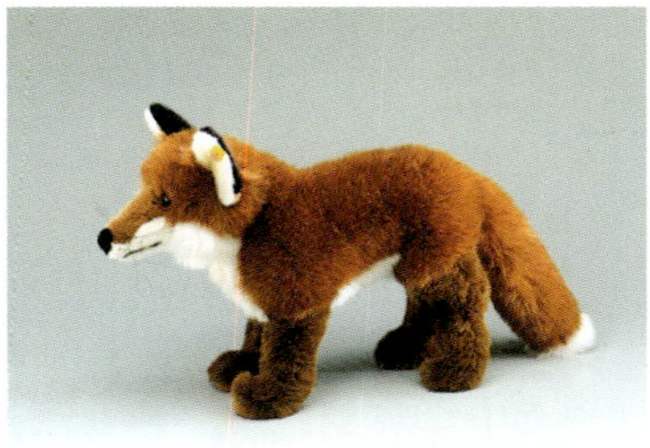

Snorry Fuchs - ***Snorry** Fox*

Webpelz, braun/weiss, stehend, abwaschbar - *woven fur, brown/white, standing, surface washable*

EAN-No.	Period	Pr.	Info
070402	1995-1995	3	60 cm

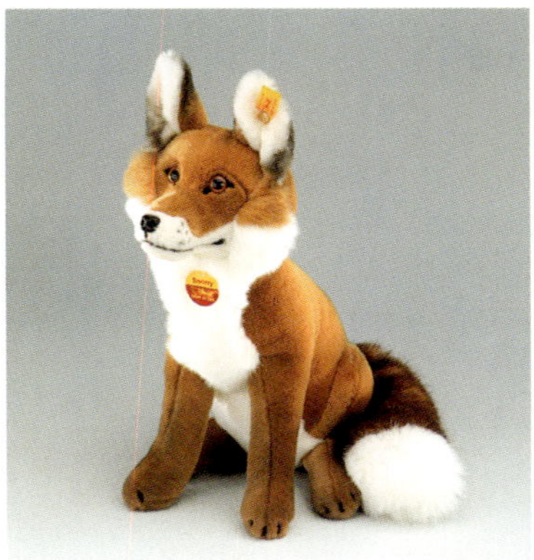

Snorry Fuchs - ***Snorry** Fox*

Webpelz, sitzend, waschmaschinenfest - *woven fur, sitting, machine washable*

EAN-No.	Period	Pr.	Info
070266	1998-1999	3	32 cm

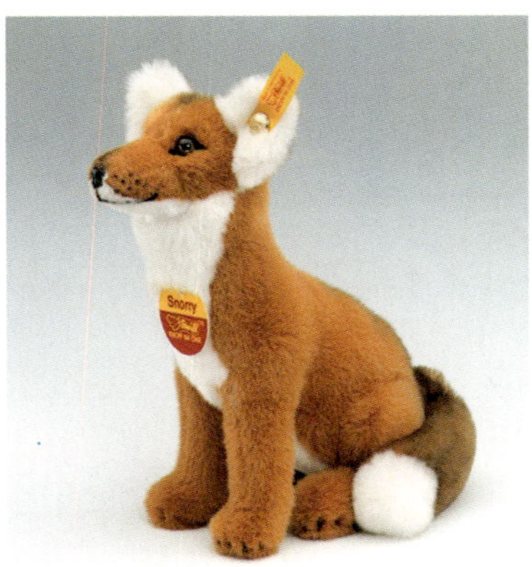

Snorry Fuchs - ***Snorry** Fox*

Webpelz, sitzend, abwaschbar - *woven fur, sitting, surface washable*

EAN-No.	Period	Pr.	Info
070242	1999-1999	2-3	17 cm

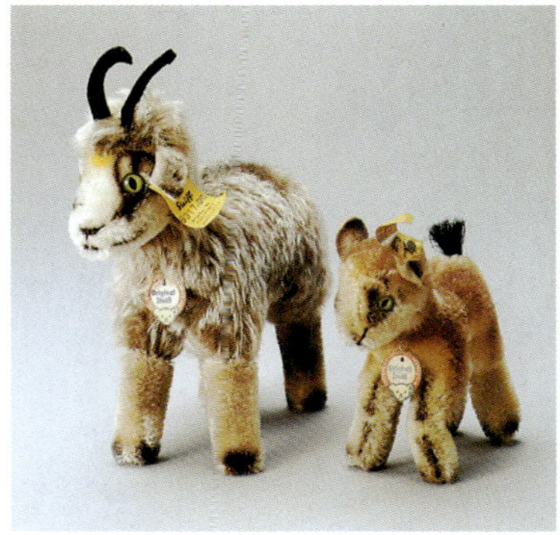

Gemse - *Chamois Buck*

Mohair, braun/schwarz, 17 cm Langhaar-Mohair, mit typischer Zeichnung, stehend - *mohair, brown/black, 17 cm, long-hair mohair, with typical markings, standing*

Serie	Art.-No	Period	Pr.	Info
305	**6312,00**	1961-1963	3-4	12 cm
160	**6312,00**	1966-1967	3-4	
	1600/12	1968-1970	3	
305	**6317,00**	1961-1963	4	17 cm
160	**6317,00**	1966-1967	4	
	1600/17	1968-1973	3	

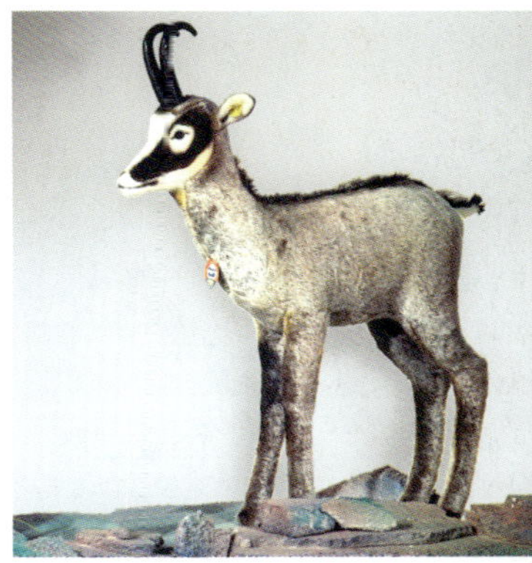

Gemse / Gamskitz - *Chamois Buck / Chamois Kid*

Schautiere, Mohair, braun/beige, stehend - *display animals, mohair, brown/beige, standing*

Serie	Art.-No	Period	Pr.	Info
	1609/06	1967-1967	5-6	60 cm
	1609/09	1967-1967	6-7	90 cm

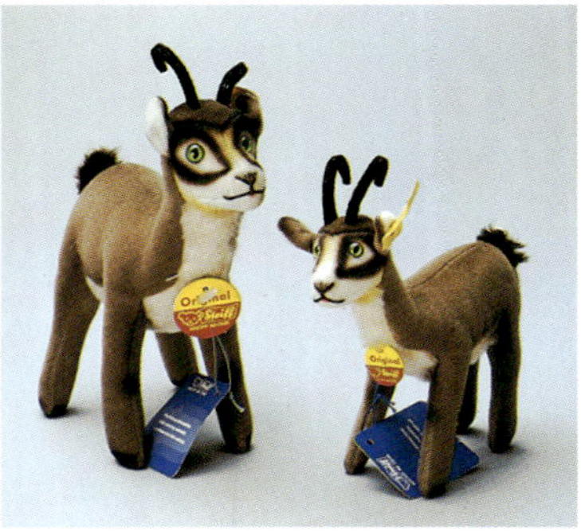

Gemse - *Chamois Buck*

Trevirasamt, stehend, abwaschbar - *trevira velvet, standing, surface washable*

Serie	Art.-No	Period	Pr.	Info
	1610/14	1976-1981	3	14 cm
	1610/22	1976-1982	3	22 cm

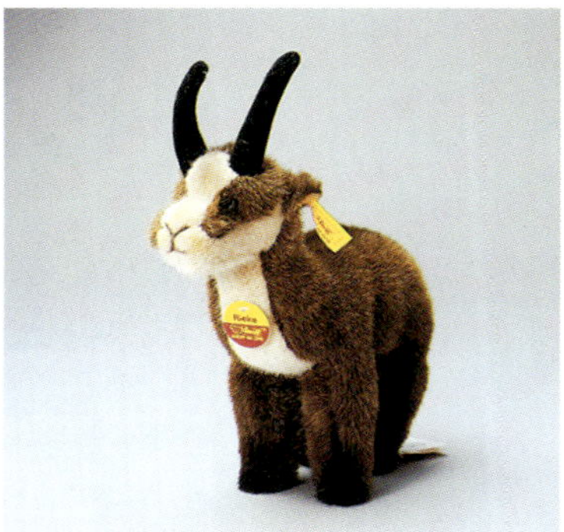

Rieke Gemse - ***Rieke*** *Chamois Buck*

Webpelz, stehend, abwaschbar - *woven fur, standing, surface washable*

EAN-No.	Period	Pr.	Info
070983	1994-1995	2-3	30 cm

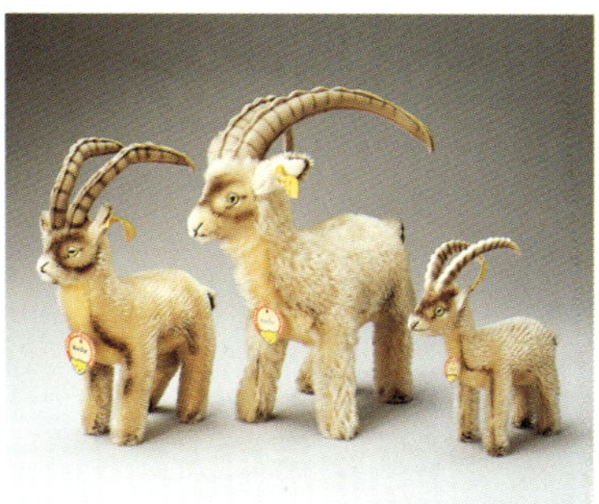

Rocky Steinbock - ***Rocky*** *Capricorn Goat*

Mohairpluesch, hellbraun, stehend, Figur a. d. Tierkreiszeichen - *mohair, light brown, standing, figure from the signs of the Zodiac*

Serie	Art.-No	Period	Pr.	Info
307	**1314,00**	1963-1964	3-4	14 cm
162	**1314,00**	1965-1967	3-4	
	1620/14	1968-1974	3	
307	**1322,00**	1963-1963	3-4	22 cm
162	**1322,00**	1965-1967	3-4	
	1620/22	1968-1976	3	
307	**1328,00**	1963-1963	4	28 cm
162	**1328,00**	1965-1967	4	
	1620/28	1968-1976	3	

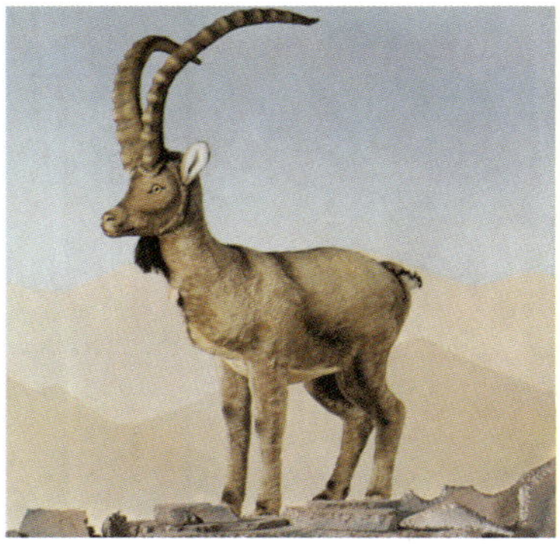

Steinbock - *Capricorn Goat*

Schautier, Mohairpluesch, hellbraun, stehend - *display animal, mohair, light brown, standing*

Serie	Art.-No	Period	Pr.	Info
	1629/15	1967-1967	6-7	150 cm

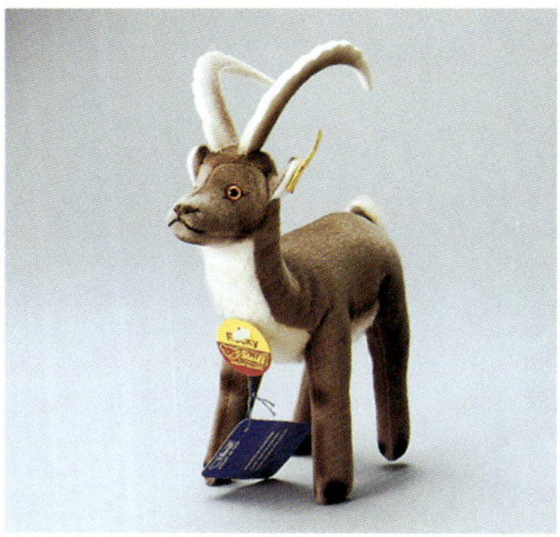

Rocky Steinbock - ***Rocky*** *Capricorn Goat*

Trevirasamt, stehend, abwaschbar - *trevira velvet, standing, surface washable*

Serie	Art.-No	Period	Pr.	Info
	1630/14	1976-1979	3	14 cm
	1630/22	1976-1981	3	22 cm

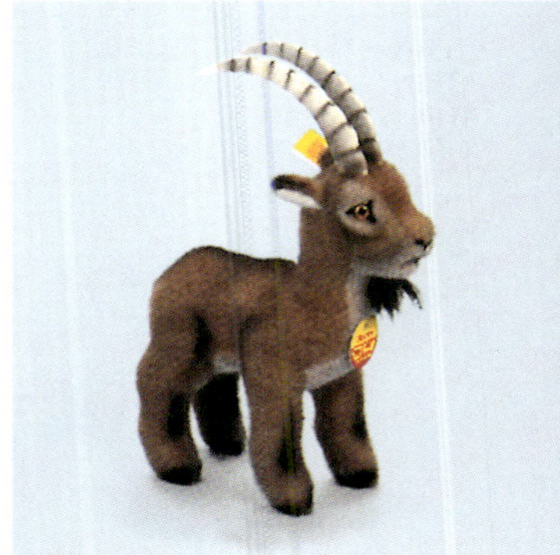

Rocky Steinbock - ***Rocky*** *Capricorn Goat*

Webpelz, stehend, abwaschbar - *woven fur, standing, surface washable*

Serie	Art.-No	Period	Pr.	Info
	3460/20	1982-1984	2-3	20 cm

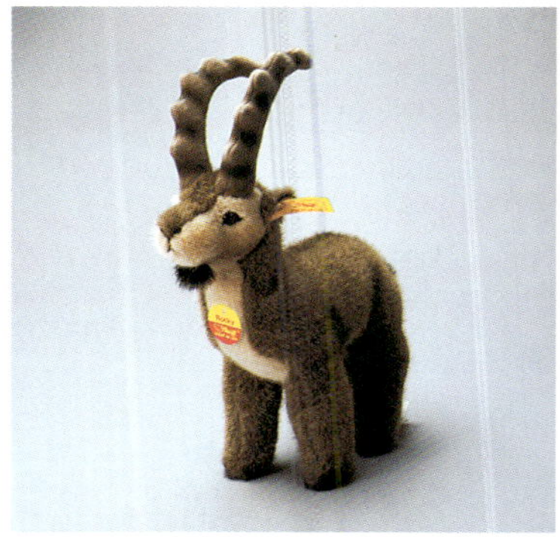

Rocky Steinbock - ***Rocky*** *Capricorn Goat*

Webpelz, stehend, abwaschbar - *woven fur, standing, surface washable*

EAN-No.	Period	Pr.	Info
070990	1993-1995	2-3	30 cm

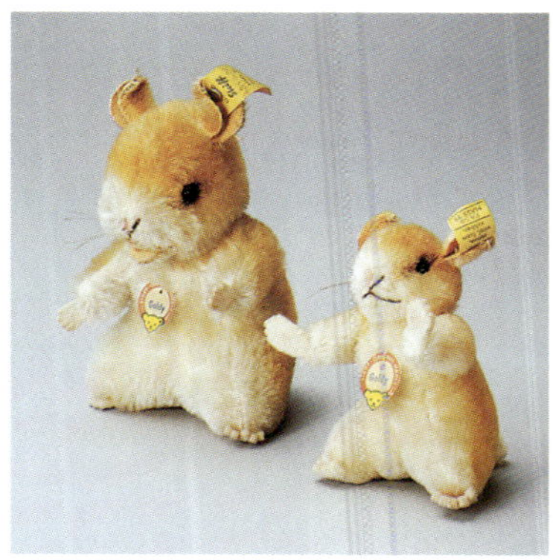

Goldy Hamster

Mohairpluesch, gold/weiss, aufwartend, Kopf drehbar - *mohair, gold/white, sitting up, head swivels*

SERIE	ART.-NO	PERIOD	PR.	INFO
33	**4310**	1955-1958	3	10 cm
330	**4310,00**	1959-1964	3	
215	**4310,00**	1965-1967	3	
	2150/10	1968-1974	2-3	
33	**4314**	1955-1958	3-4	14 cm
330	**4314,00**	1961-1964	3	
215	**4314,00**	1966-1967	3	
	2150/14	1968-1974	3	

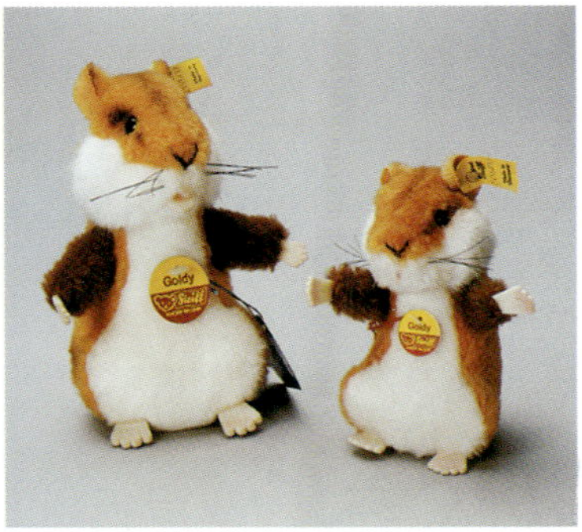

Goldy Hamster

Dralon, aufwartend, abwaschbar - *dralon, sitting up, surface washable*

SERIE	ART.-NO	PERIOD	PR.	INFO
	2155/12	1975-1984	2	12 cm
	2155/17	1975-1984	2	17 cm

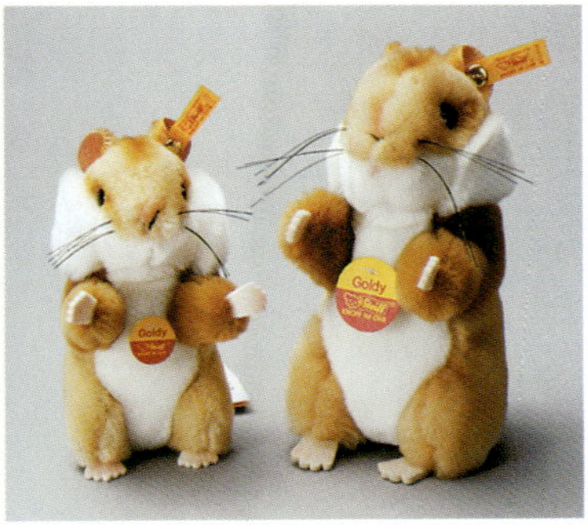

Goldy Hamster

Webpelz, aufwartend, abwaschbar - *woven fur, sitting up, surface washable*

SERIE	ART.-NO	PERIOD	PR.	INFO
071607	**2150/12**	1985-1990	1-2	13 cm
	071607	1991-1999	1-2	
071638	**2150/16**	1985-1990	2	16 cm
	071638	1991-1996	2	

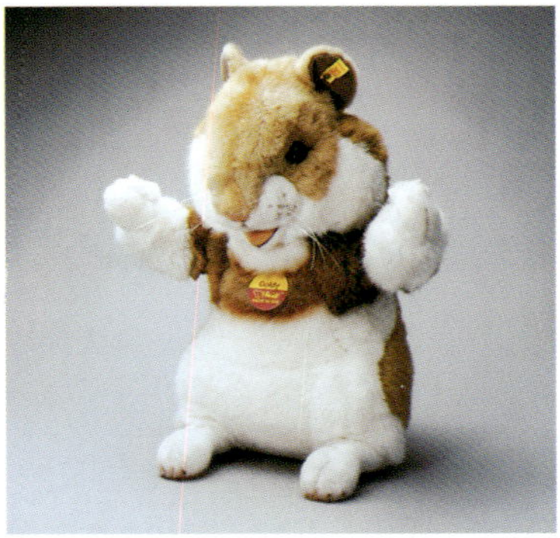

Super **Goldy** Hamster

Webpelz, aufwartend, abwaschbar - *woven fur, sitting up, surface washable*

SERIE	ART.-NO	PERIOD	PR.	INFO
071683	**2150/50**	1985-1986	4	50 cm

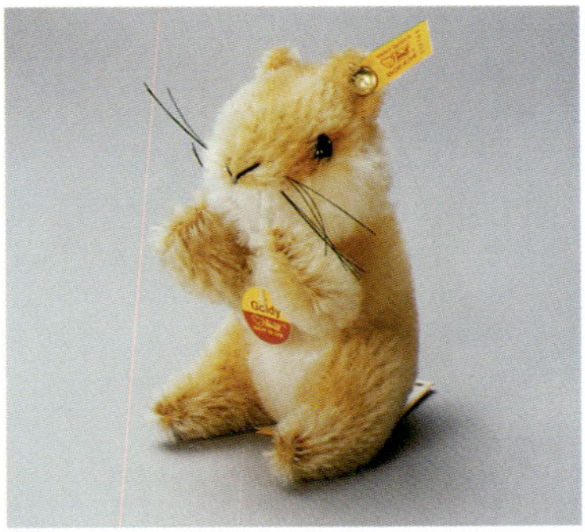

Goldy Hamster

Mohair Webpelz, aufwartend, abwaschbar - *mohair woven fur, sitting up, surface washable*

EAN-NO.	PERIOD	PR.	INFO
032769	1991-1993	2	12 cm

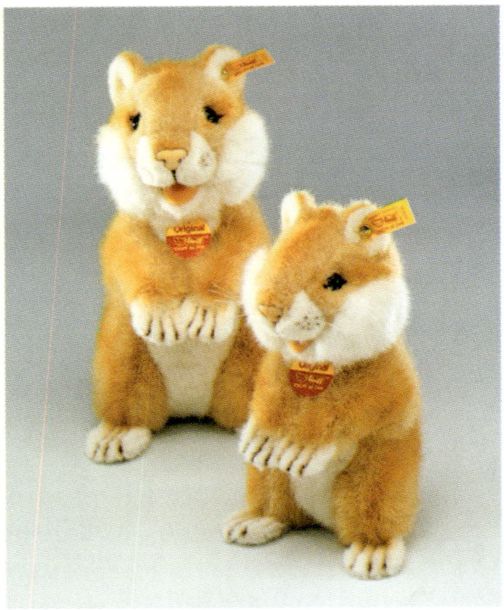

Goldhamster - *Gold Hamster*

Webpelz, aufwartend, waschmaschinenfest - *woven fur, sitting up, machine washable*

EAN-NO.	PERIOD	PR.	INFO
071690	1996-1998	2-3	20 cm
071706	1996-1998	3	25 cm

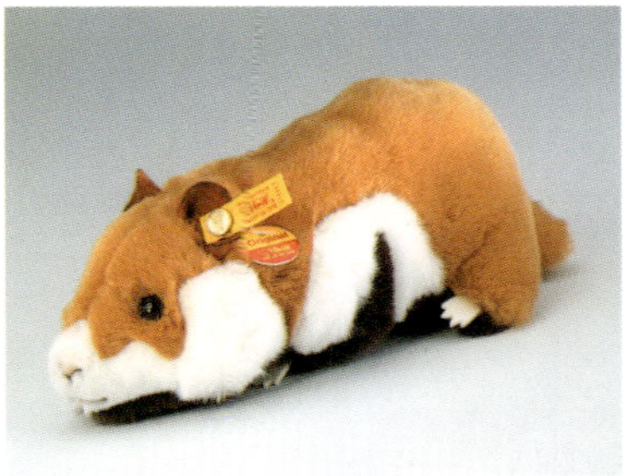

Feldhamster - *Field Hamster*

Webpelz, waschmaschinenfest - *woven fur, machine washable*

EAN-NO.	PERIOD	PR.	INFO
070907	1997-1999	2	20 cm

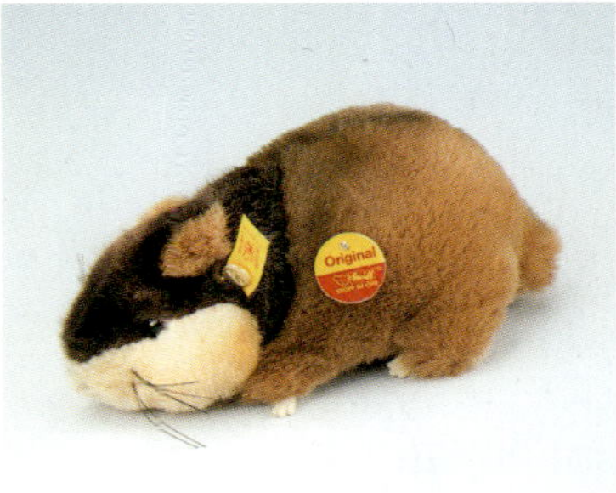

Lemming

Webpelz, braun, waschmaschinenfest - *woven fur, brown, machine washable*

EAN-NO.	PERIOD	PR.	INFO
070846	1997-1999	1-2	15 cm

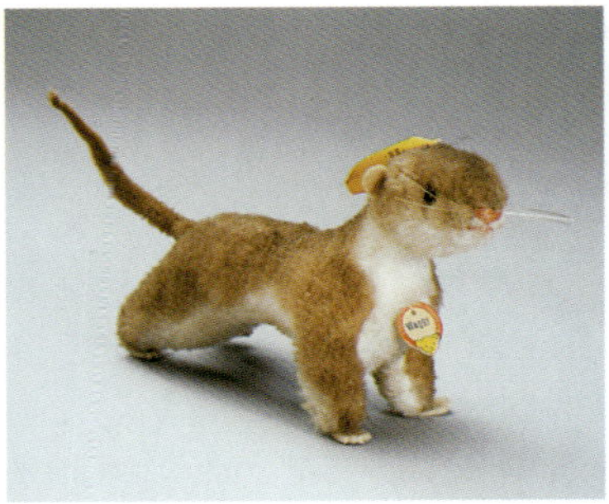

Waggy Wiesel - ***Waggy*** *Weasel*

Dralon, braun/weiss, stehend - *dralon, brown/white, standing*

SERIE	ART.-NO	PERIOD	PR.	INFO
335	**1612,03**	1962-1962	4	12 cm

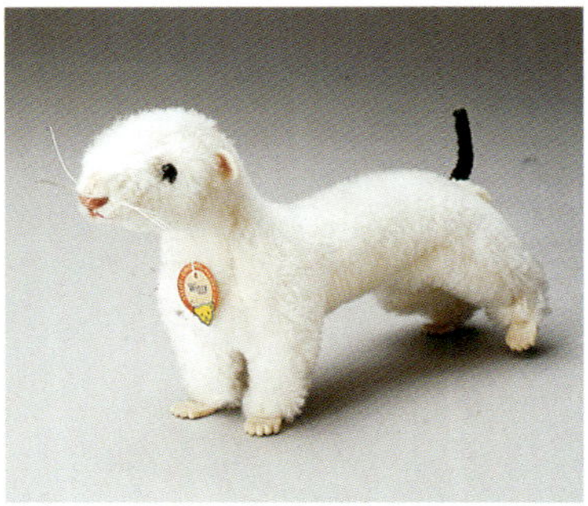

Hermelin **Wiggy** - *Ermine* ***Wiggy***

Dralon, weiss, stehend - *dralon, white, standing*

SERIE	ART.-NO	PERIOD	PR.	INFO
335	**1612,04**	1962-1962	4	12 cm

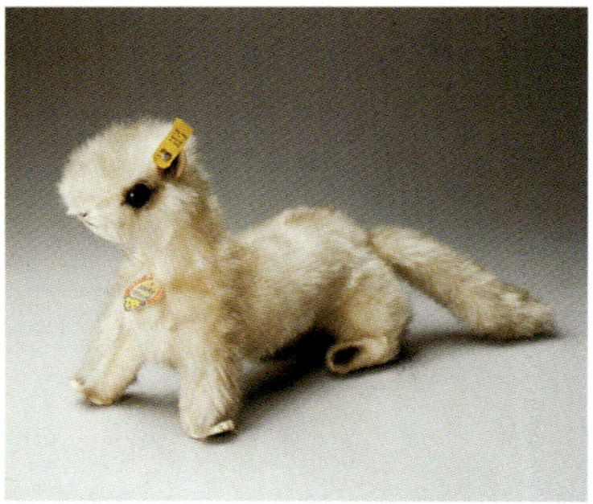

Minky Wiesel - *Minky Weasel*

pelzartiges Material, hellbeige, stehend - *fur-like material, light beige, standing*

SERIE	ART.-NO	PERIOD	PR.	INFO
	2230/22	1969-1972	3-4	50 cm

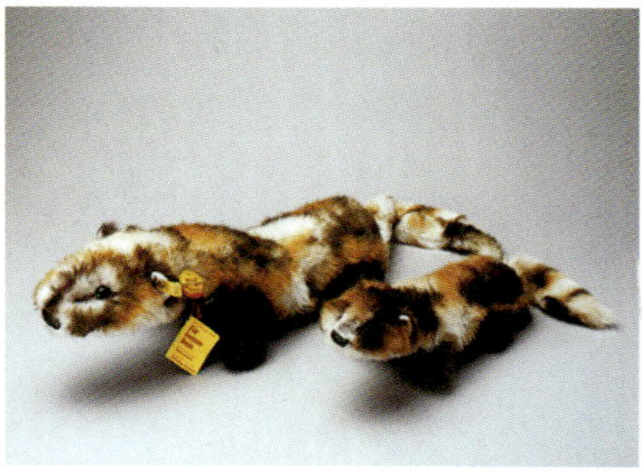

Wizzi Iltis - ***Wizzi*** *Ferret*

Pelzimitation, ab 1978 Synthetik-Webpelz, abwaschbar - *imitation fur, from 1978 synthetic woven fur, surface washable*

SERIE	ART.-NO	PERIOD	PR.	INFO
	2270/25	1976-1980	3	25 cm
	2270/35	1976-1980	3	35 cm

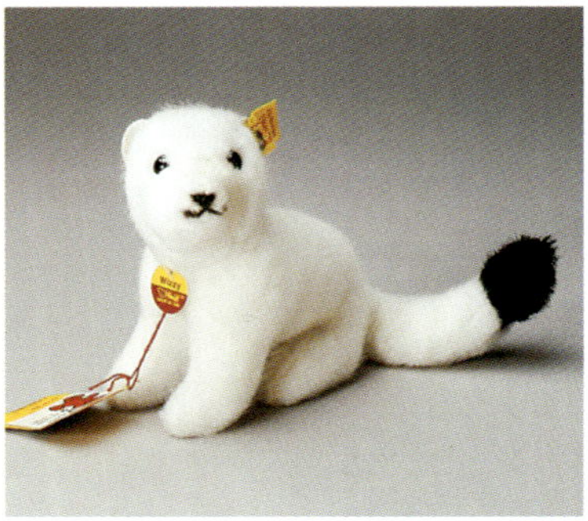

Wizzy Hermelin - ***Wizzy*** *Ermine*

Webpelz, abwaschbar - *woven fur, surface washable*

SERIE	ART.-NO	PERIOD	PR.	INFO
045301	**1480/12**	1986-1987	2-3	12 cm

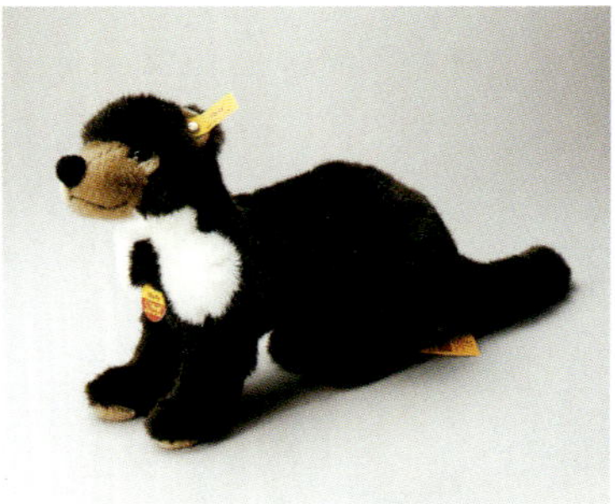

Marty Steinmarder - ***Marty*** *Marten*

Webpelz, dunkelbraun, waschmaschinenfest - *woven fur, dark brown, machine washable*

EAN-NO.	PERIOD	PR.	INFO
071218	1993-1998	3	40 cm

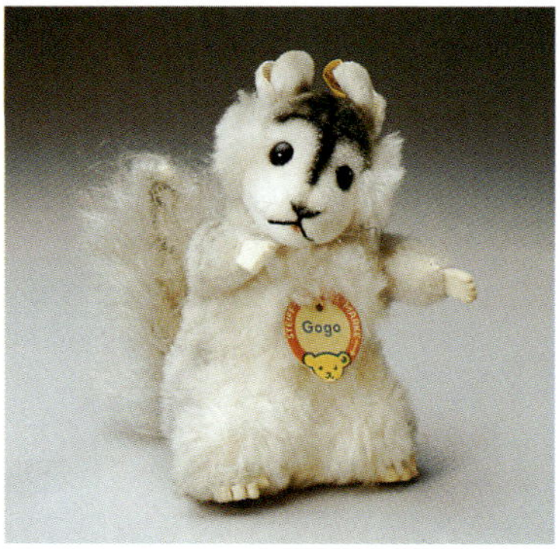

Gogo Chinchilla

Dralon, grau/weiss, aufwartend, aus "Around the world with Gogo", Kopf drehbar - *dralon, grey/white, sitting up, taken from "Around the World with Gogo", head swivels*

SERIE	ART.-NO	PERIOD	PR.	INFO
227	**4615,00**	1965-1967	4	15 cm

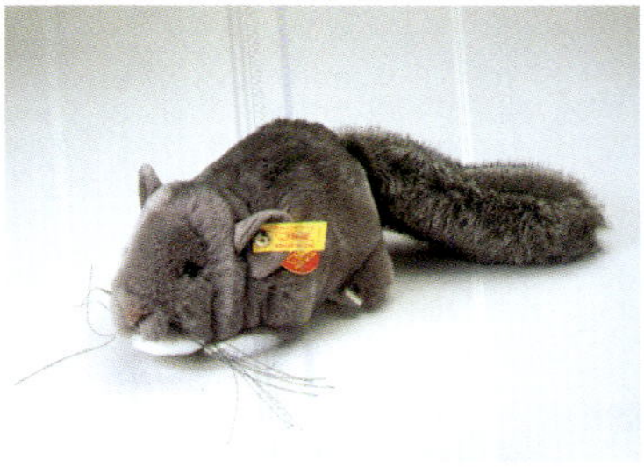

Chinchilla

Webpelz, grau, waschmaschinenfest - *woven fur, grey, machine washable*

EAN-NO.	PERIOD	PR.	INFO
070860	1997-1999	2	20 cm

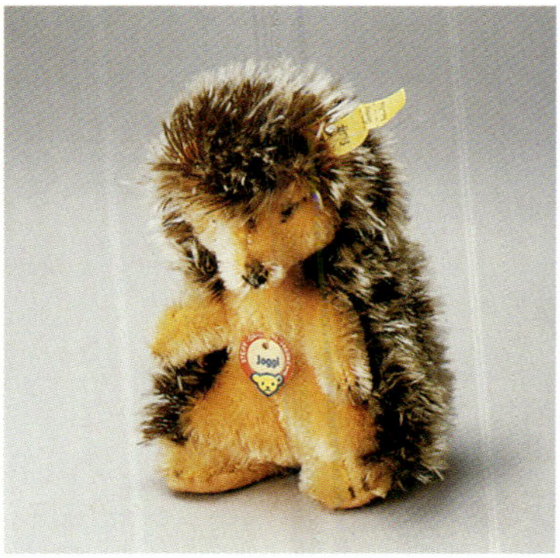

Joggi Igel - ***Joggi*** *Hedgehog*

Mohair, ab 1978 Dralon/Mohair, braun gespitzt, aufwartend - *mohair, from 1978 dralon/mohair, brown tipped, sitting up*

SERIE	ART.-NO	PERIOD	PR.	INFO
37	**4312**	1951-1958	3-4	12 cm
370	**4312,00**	1959-1964	3	
167	**4312,00**	1965-1967	3	
	1680/12	1968-1985	2	

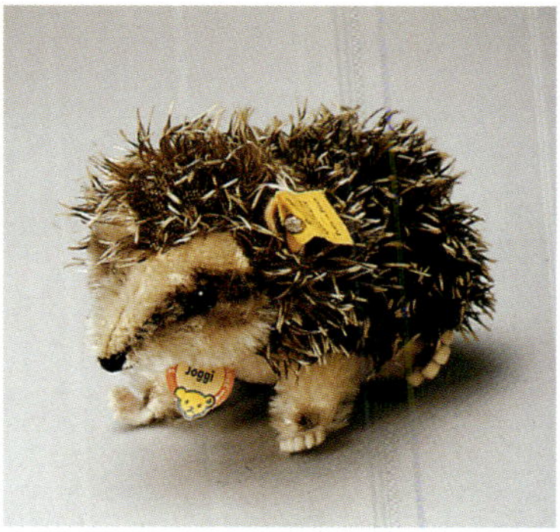

Igel **Joggi** - *Hedgehog* ***Joggi***

Mohair, braun gespitzt, liegend - *mohair, brown tipped, lying*

SERIE	ART.-NO	PERIOD	PR.	INFO
370	**2312,00**	1961-1964	3	12 cm
167	**2312,00**	1965-1966	3	

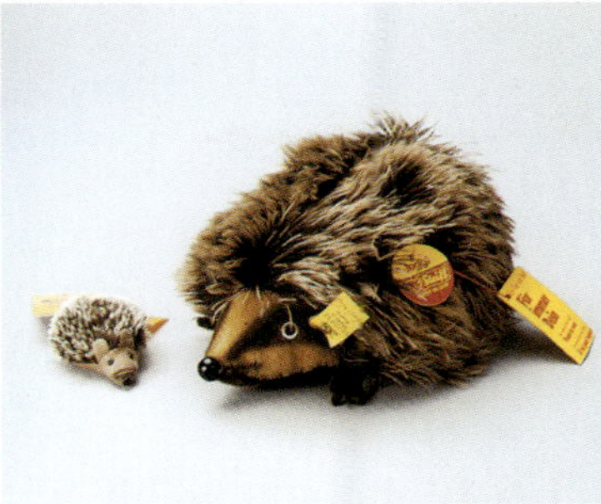

Joggi Igel - ***Joggi** Hedgehog*

Igel-Mohair, liegend, abwaschbar - *spiky mohair, lying, surface washable*

SERIE	ART.-NO	PERIOD	PR.	INFO
167	**2306,00**	1966-1967	1	6 cm
056109	**1670/06**	1968-1990	1	
	056109	1991-1999	1	
167	**2310,00**	1966-1967	2	10 cm
	1670/10	1968-1985	1	
167	**2317,00**	1966-1967	2	17 cm
	1670/17	1968-1985	1-2	

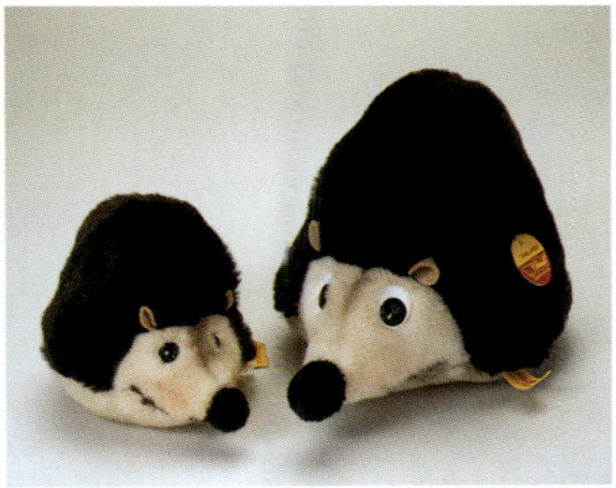

Cosy Joggi Igel - ***Cosy Joggi** Hedgehog*

Webpelz, superweich, waschmaschinenfest - *woven fur, super soft, machine washable*

SERIE	ART.-NO	PERIOD	PR.	INFO
	5397/15	1981-1985	1-2	15 cm
	5397/25	1981-1984	2	25 cm

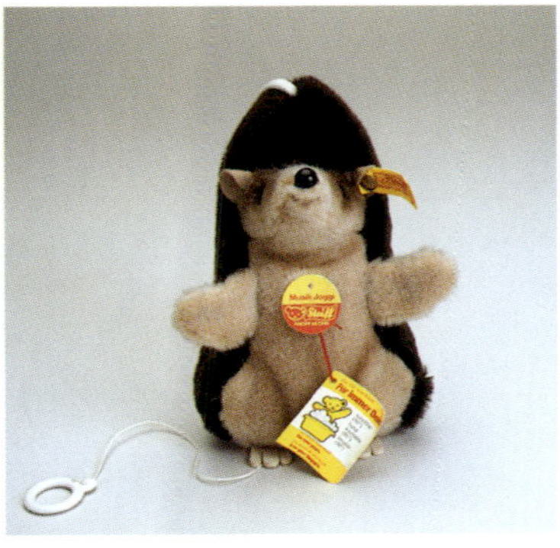

Musik Joggi Igel - *Musical Joggi Hedgehog*

Webpelz, Musikwerk austauschbar, waschbar - *woven fur, music box can be exchanged, washable*

SERIE	ART.-NO	PERIOD	PR.	INFO
	6373/18	1983-1985	2-3	18 cm

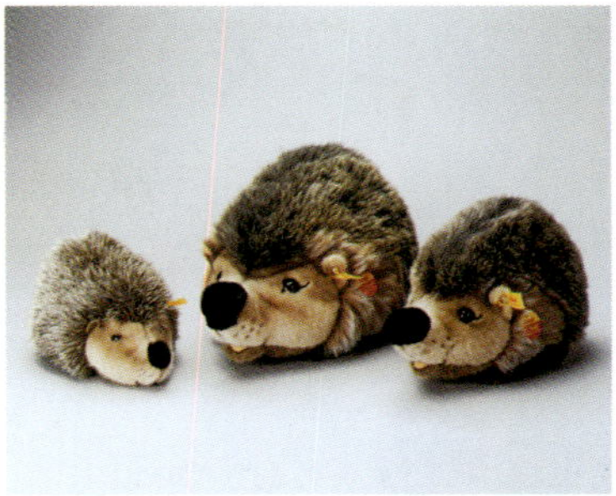

Joggi Igel - ***Joggi** Hedgehog*

Webpelz, graubraun, stehend, ab 25 cm offener Mund, abwaschbar - *woven fur, greyish-brown, from 25 cm mouth open, surface washable, standing*

SERIE	ART.-NO	PERIOD	PR.	INFO
070501	**1675/12**	1985-1990	1	16 cm
	070501	1991-1999	1	
070556	**1675/18**	1985-1990	1-2	22 cm
	070556	1991-1999	1-2	
070570	**1675/25**	1990-1990	2-3	25 cm
	070570	1991-1999	2-3	
070594	**1675/35**	1990-1990	2-3	35 cm
	070594	1991-1995	2-3	
070600	**1675/45**	1986-1990	3	45 cm
	070600	1991-1992	3	
070655	**1675/70**	1986-1988	3-4	70 cm

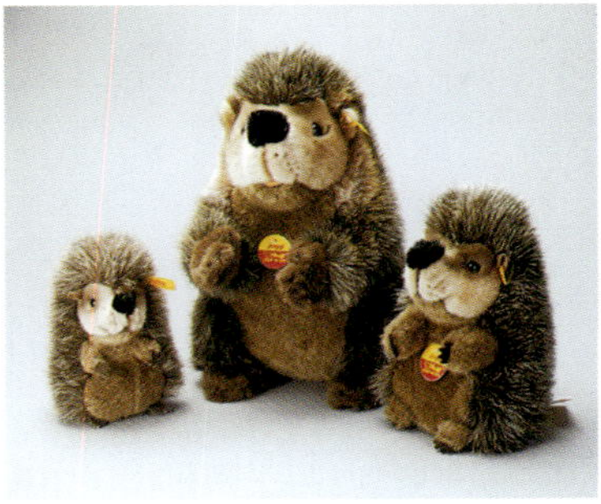

Joggi Igel - ***Joggi** Hedgehog*

Webpelz, graubraun, aufwartend, ab 32 cm offener Mund, abwaschbar - *woven fur, greyish-brown, sitting up, from 32 cm open mouth, surface washable*

SERIE	ART.-NO	PERIOD	PR.	INFO
070709	**1677/14**	1985-1990	1-2	15 cm
	070709	1991-1999	1-2	
070730	**1677/20**	1990-1990	2	20 cm
	070730	1991-1999	2	
	070754	1994-1999	3	32 cm
	070785	1994-1995	3	40 cm
070778	**1677/50**	1988-1990	3-4	50 cm
	070778	1991-1996	3-4	

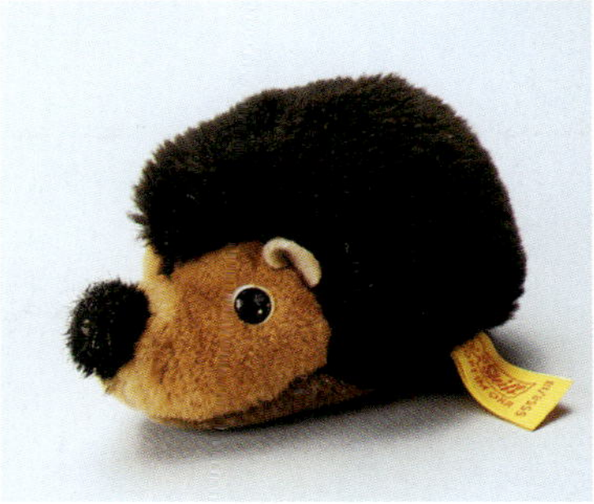

Mini Cosy Igel - *Mini Cozy Hedgehog*

Webpelz, superweich, waschmaschinenfest - *woven fur, super soft, machine washable*

SERIE	ART.-NO	PERIOD	PR.	INFO
084300	**5558/10**	1986-1990	1	10 cm
	084300	1991-1999	1	

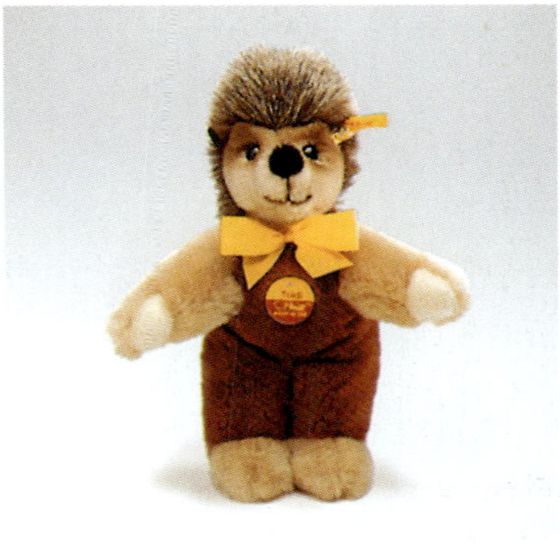

Toldi Igel - ***Toldi** Hedgehog*

Webpelz, Pieps-Stimme, waschmaschinenfest - *woven fur, squeaker, machine washable*

SERIE	ART.-NO	PERIOD	PR.	INFO
080883	**5273/27**	1988-1990	2	27 cm

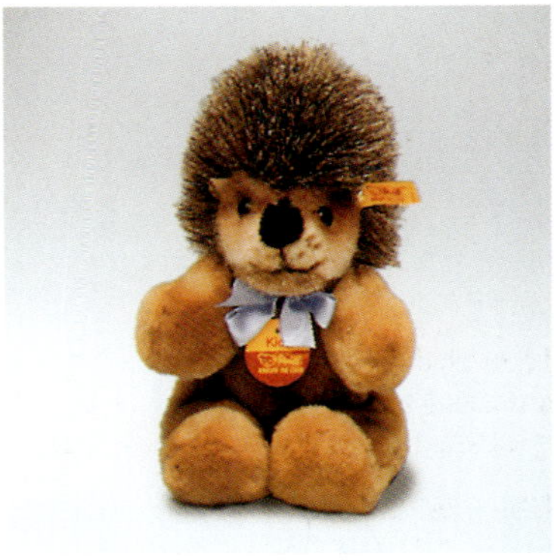

Kiddi Igel - ***Kiddi** Hedgehog*

Webpelz, Pieps-Stimme, waschmaschinenfest - *woven fur, squeaker, machine washable*

SERIE	ART.-NO	PERIOD	PR.	INFO
082894	**5725/20**	1989-1990	2	20 cm

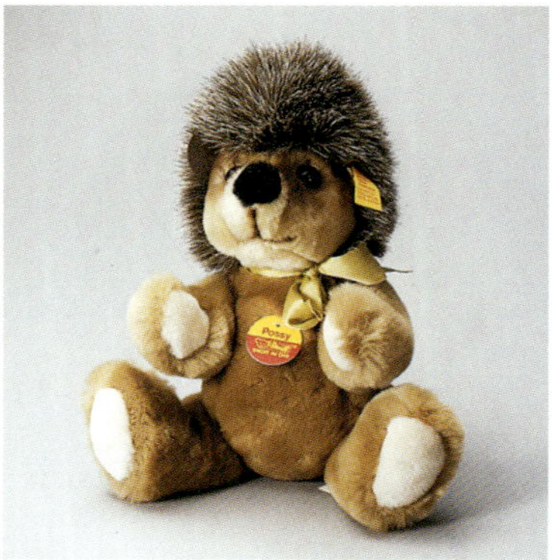

Possy Igel - ***Possy*** *Hedgehog*

Webpelz, gegliedert, Pieps-Stimme, waschmaschinenfest - *woven fur, jointed, squeaker, machine washable*

Serie	Art.-No	Period	Pr.	Info
081774	**6245/28**	1989-1990	2-3	28 cm

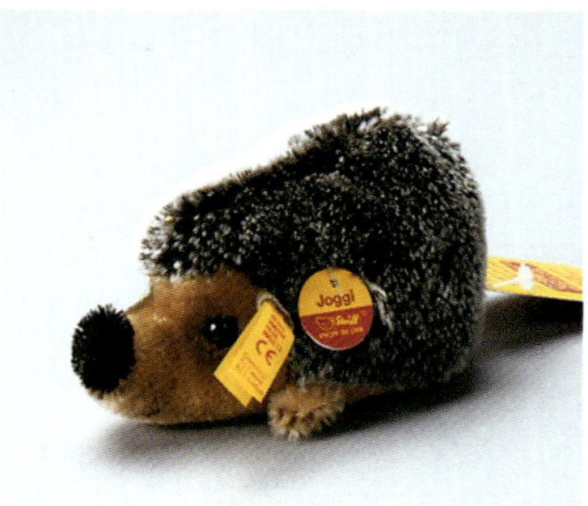

Joggi Igel - ***Joggi*** *Hedgehog*

Mohair Webpelz, sitzend, abwaschbar - *mohair woven fur, sitting, surface washable*

EAN-No.	Period	Pr.	Info
032257	1991-1995	1-2	7 cm

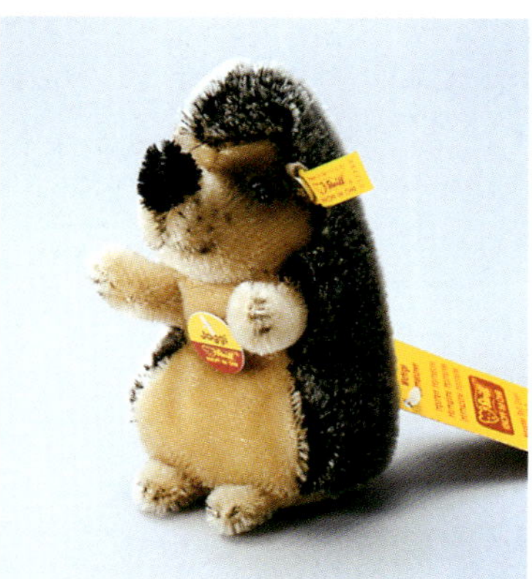

Joggi Igel - ***Joggi*** *Hedgehog*

Mohair Webpelz, aufwartend, abwaschbar - *mohair woven fur, sitting up, surface washable*

EAN-No.	Period	Pr.	Info
032288	1991-1995	1-2	12 cm

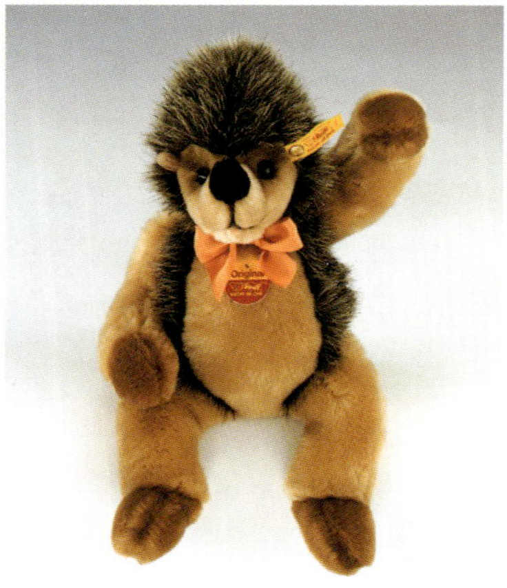

Schlenker Igel - *Dangling Hedgehog*

Webpelz, waschmaschinenfest - *woven fur, machine washable*

EAN-No.	Period	Pr.	Info
123856	1996-1998	2-3	30 cm

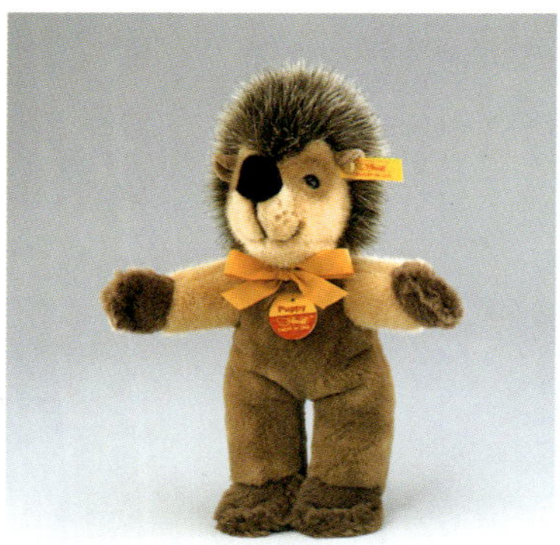

Puppy Igel - ***Puppy*** *Hedgehog*

Webpelz, beige/braun, waschmaschinenfest, Pieps-Stimme - *woven fur, beige/brown, machine washable, squeaker*

EAN-No.	Period	Pr.	Info
124952	1997-1998	2	28 cm

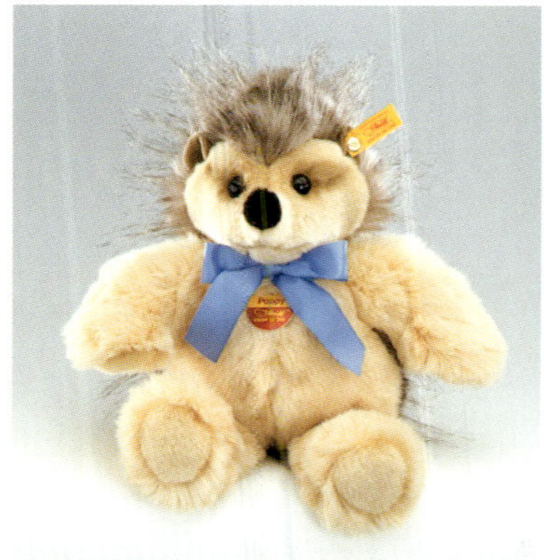

Poppy Igel - ***Poppy*** *Hedgehog*

Webpelz, grau/beige, waschmaschinenfest - *woven fur, grey/beige, machine washable*

EAN-No.	Period	Pr.	Info
123863	1998-1999	2-3	30 cm

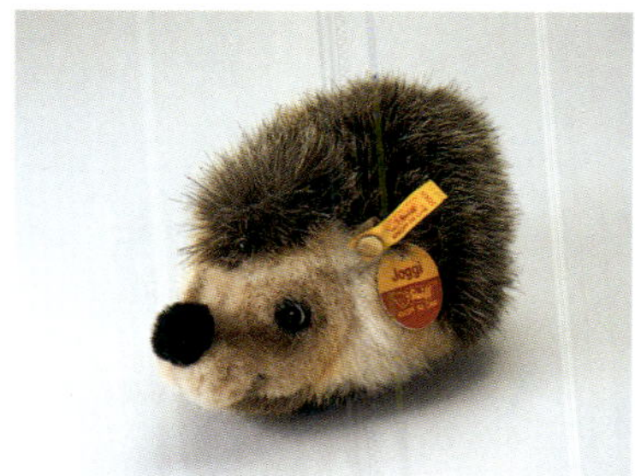

Joggi Igel - ***Joggi*** *Hedgehog*

Webpelz, stehend, waschmaschinenfest - *woven fur, standing, machine washable*

EAN-No.	Period	Pr.	Info
070624	1999-1999	1-2	17 cm

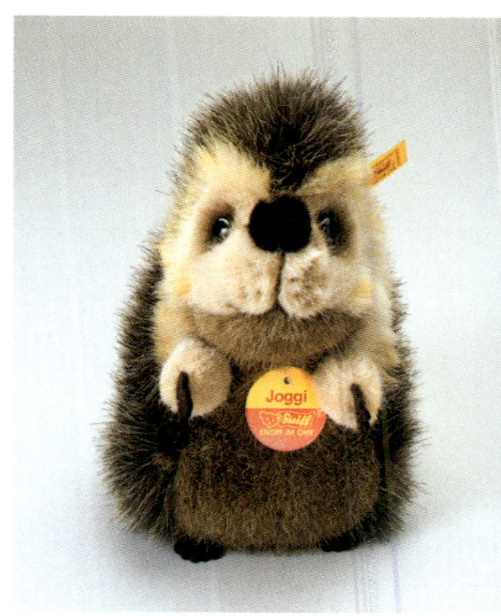

Joggi Igel - ***Joggi*** *Hedgehog*

Webpelz, aufwartend, waschmaschinenfest - *woven fur, sitting up, machine washable*

EAN-No.	Period	Pr.	Info
070662	1999-1999	1-2	16 cm

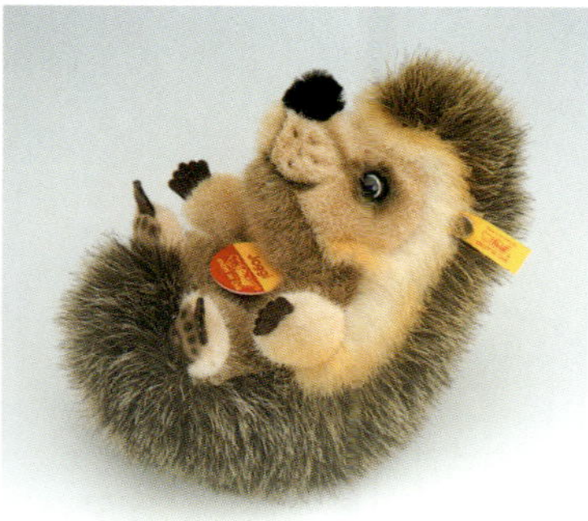

Joggi Igel - ***Joggi** Hedgehog*

Webpelz, rueckenliegend, waschmaschinenfest - *woven fur, lying on his back, machine washable*

EAN-No.	Period	Pr.	Info
070761	1999-1999	2	18 cm

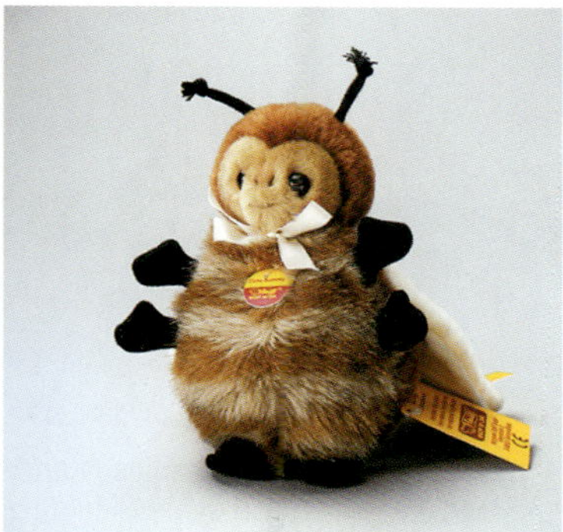

Cosy Summy Biene - ***Cosy Summy** Bee*

Webpelz, waschmaschinenfest - *woven fur, machine washable*

EAN-No.	Period	Pr.	Info
093913	1995-1997	2	20 cm

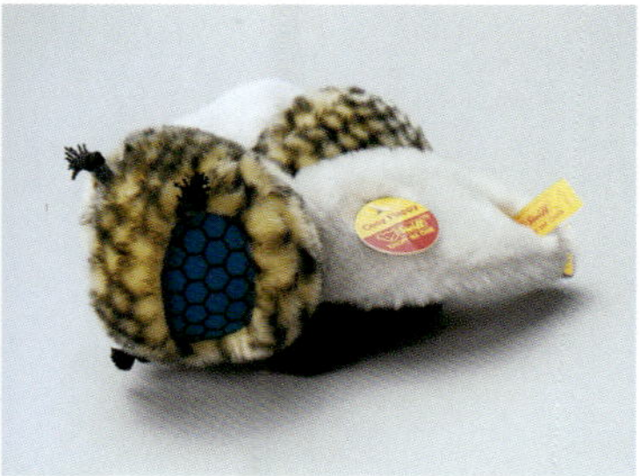

Cosy Flappy Fliege - ***Cosy Flappy** Fly*

Webpelz, 20 cm, waschmaschinenfest - *woven fur, 20 cm, machine washable*

EAN-No.	Period	Pr.	Info
099519	1994-1994	2-3	rot - *red*
099533	1994-1994	2-3	gelb - *yellow*
099540	1994-1994	2-3	gruen - *green*
099557	1994-1994	2-3	blau - *blue*
099588	1994-1994	2-3	braun - *brown*

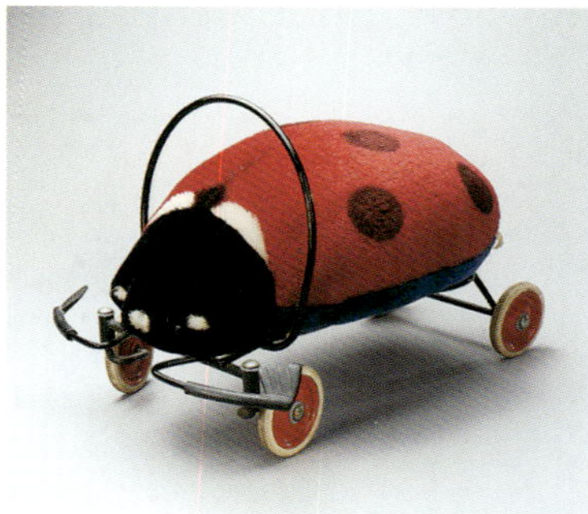

Reit-Marienkaefer - *Riding Ladybird*

Mohairpluesch, rot/blau/schwarz, Stahlgestell, Fussrasten, Haltegriff, abwaschbar, Scheibenraeder mit Gummi, ab 1967 Plastikreifen & Kunststofflager, Schlepplenkung (=schwenkbare Vorderraeder) - *mohair, red/blue/black, steel frame, footrests, grip handle, surface washable, disc wheels with rubber tires, from 1967 plastic tires & bearings, pull-type steering (=front wheels swivel)*

Serie	Art.-No	Period	Pr.	Info
39	**1330**	1950-1958	4-5	30 cm
390	**1330,20**	1959-1964	4	
246	**1330,20**	1965-1967	4	
	2460/30	1968-1980	3-4	
481703	**8190/30**	1981-1990	3-4	

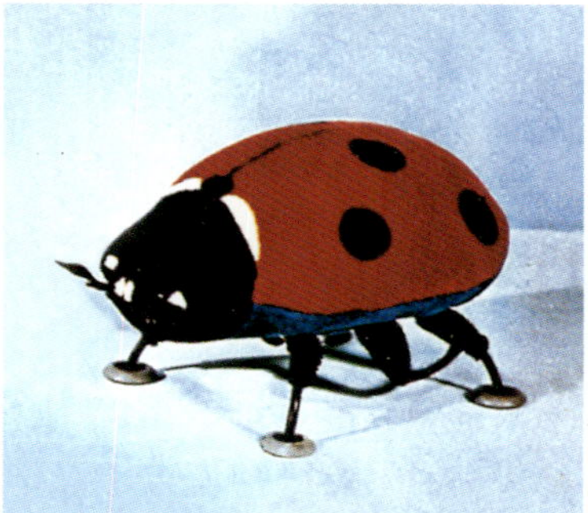

Sitz-Marienkaefer - *Sitting Ladybird*

Mohair, schwarz/rot, Stahlgestell mit Gummifuessen, abwaschbar - *mohair, black/red, steel frame with rubber feet. surface washable*

Serie	Art.-No	Period	Pr.	Info
820 390	**2330,00**	1961-1964	4	30 cm
602	**2330,00**	1965-1967	4	
	6020/30	1968-1974	4	

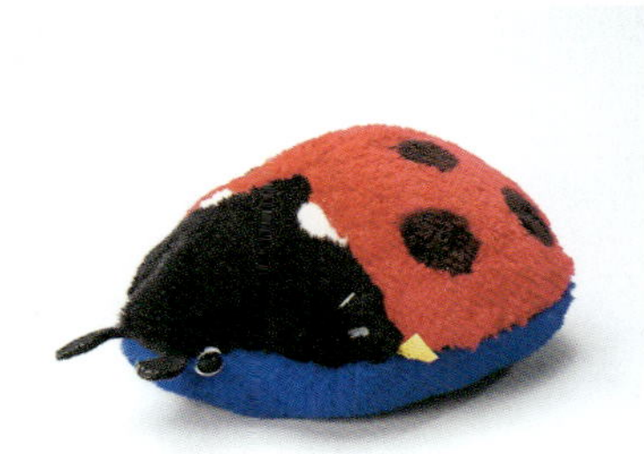

Cosy Marienkaefer ab 1974 **Cosy Crabby** - *Cozy Ladybird from 1974 **Cosy Crabby***

Dralon, rot/schwarz/blau, formgeschaeumt, vollwaschbar - *dralon, red/black/blue, stuffed with pre-formed foam, fully washable*

Serie	Art.-No	Period	Pr.	Info
	4935/24	1972-1981	1	24 cm

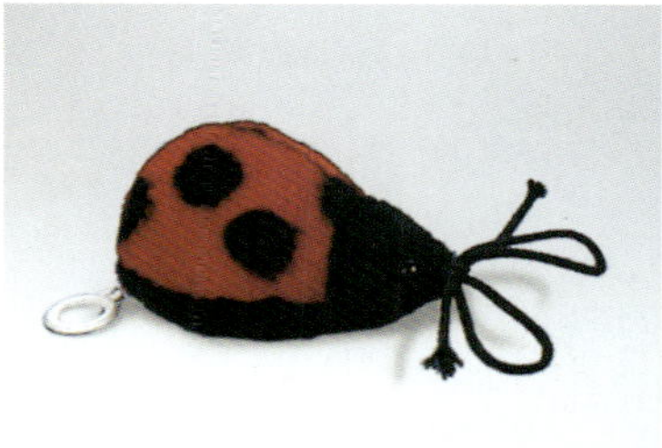

Musik-Marienkaefer - *Musical Ladybird*

Webpelz, Koerper formgeschaeumt, Musikwerk austauschbar (SKS, WWS, GAN), waschbar, 18 cm - *woven fur, body stuffed with pre-formed foam, music box can be changed (SKS, WWS, GAN), washable, 18 cm*

Serie	Art.-No	Period	Pr.	Info
233708	**6381/18**	1977-1986	1-2	SKS (Schlaf Kindlein schlaf) - *SKS (Sleep Little Child Sleep)*
233746	**6382/18**	1977-1986	1-2	WWS (Weisst Du wieviel Sternlein) - *WWS (Twinkle, Twinkle Little Star)*
233784	**6383/18**	1977-1986	1-2	GAN (Guten Abend, gute Nacht) - *GAN (Good Evening, Goodnight)*

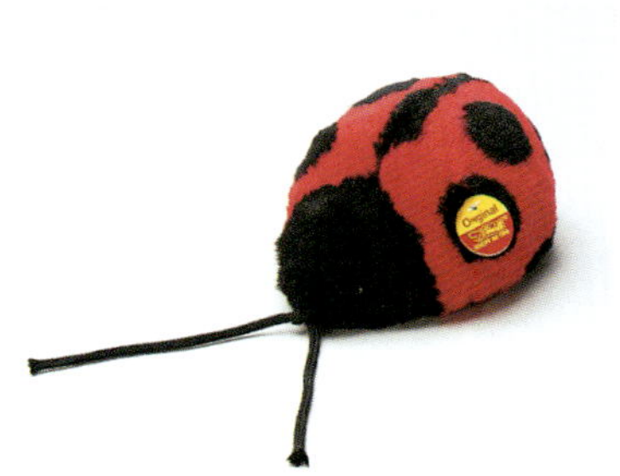

Musik-Marienkaefer - *Musical Ladybird*

Wirkpelz, Koerper formgeschaeumt, Musikwerk austauschbar (SKS, WWS, GAN), ohne Musikwerk waschbar, 20 cm - *knitted fur, body stuffed with pre-formed foam, music box can be changed (SKS, WWS, GAN), washable without music box, 20 cm*

SERIE	ART.-NO	PERIOD	PR.	INFO
233715	**6381/20**	1986-1990	1-2	SKS (Schlaf Kindlein schlaf) - *SKS (Sleep Little Child Sleep)*
	233715	1991-1997	1-2	
233753	**6382/20**	1986-1990	1-2	WWS (Weisst Du wieviel Sternlein) - *WWS (Twinkle, Twinkle Little Star)*
	233753	1991-1997	1-2	
233791	**6383/20**	1986-1990	1-2	GAN (Guten Abend, gute Nacht) - *GAN (Good Evening, Goodnight)*
	233791	1991-1997	1-2	

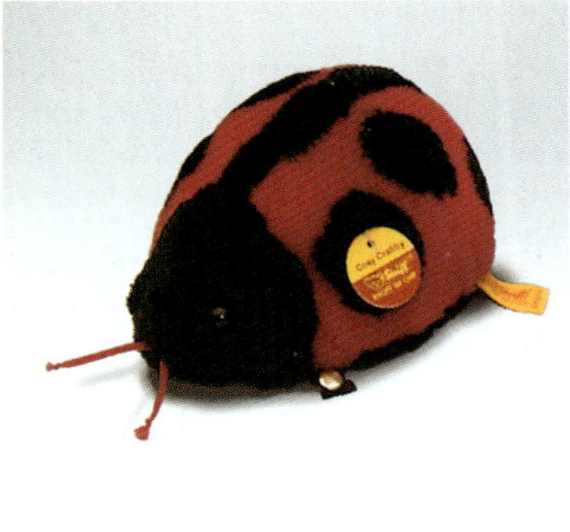

Cosy Crabby Marienkaefer - ***Cosy Crabby*** *Ladybird*

Wirkpelz, superweich, waschmaschinenfest - *knitted fur, super soft, machine washable*

SERIE	ART.-NO	PERIOD	PR.	INFO
093944	**5400/16**	1986-1988	1	16 cm

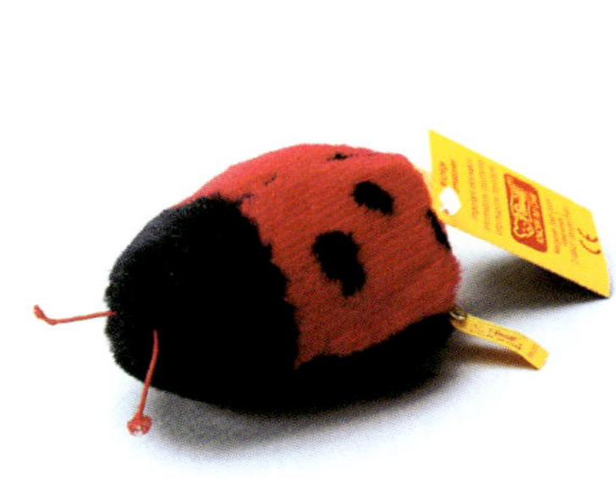

Mini Cosy Marienkaefer - *Mini Cosy Ladybird*

Webpelz, superweich, waschmaschinenfest - *woven fur, super soft, machine washable*

SERIE	ART.-NO	PERIOD	PR.	INFO
084201	**5557/10**	1986-1990	1	10 cm
	084201	1991-1998	1	

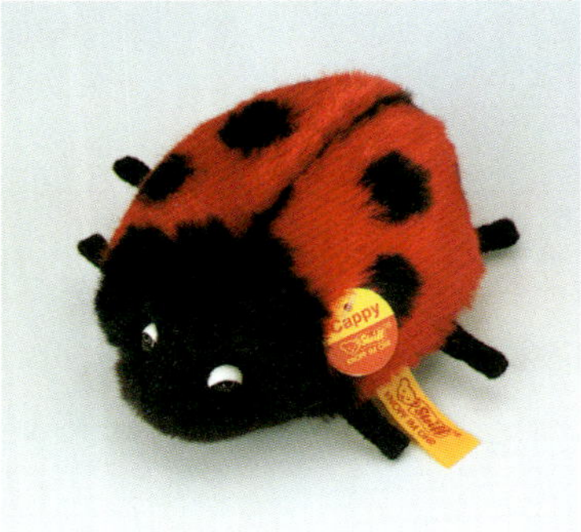

Cappy Marienkaefer - ***Cappy*** *Ladybird*

Webpelz, waschmaschinenfest - *woven fur, machine washable*

EAN-NO.	PERIOD	PR.	INFO
084218	1997-1999	1	10 cm

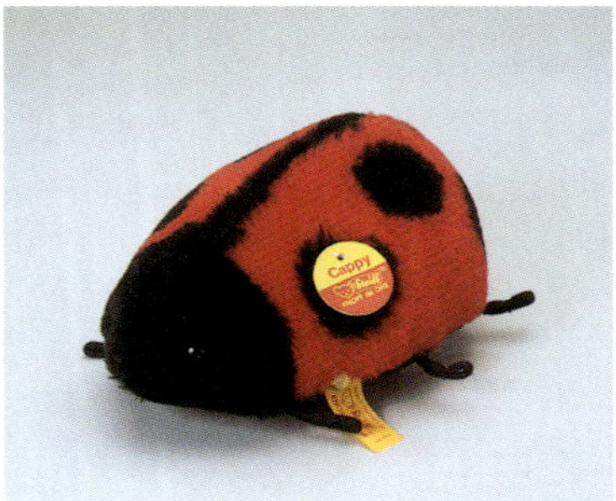

Cappy Marienkaefer - ***Cappy*** *Ladybird*

Webpelz, waschmaschinenfest - *woven fur, machine washable*

EAN-NO.	PERIOD	PR.	INFO
091704	1997-1999	1-2	18 cm

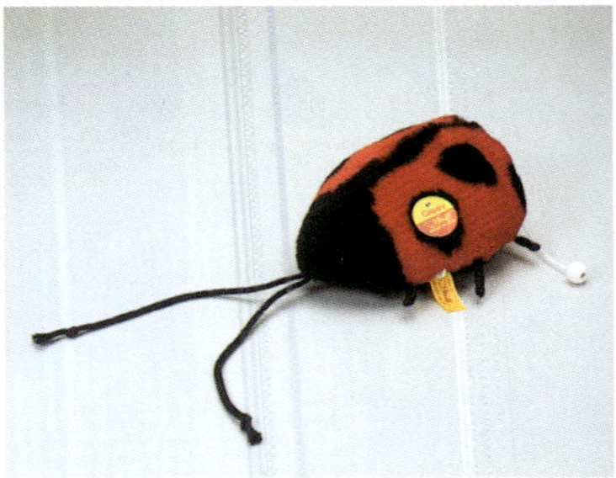

Cappy Musik-Marienkaefer - ***Cappy*** *Musical-Ladybird*

Webpelz, abwaschbar, Musikwerk SMP (Schlafe mein Prinzchen) - *woven fur, surface washable, music-box SMP (sleep my little prince)*

EAN-NO.	PERIOD	PR.	INFO
233807	1997-1999	1-2	18 cm

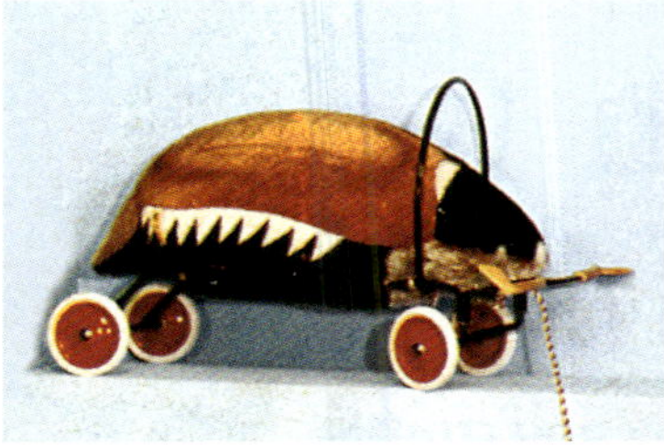

Reit-Maikaefer - *Riding May-Beetle*

Mohair, Stahlgestell, Plastikreifen, Kunststofflager, braun/schwarz, Schlepplenkung, Haltegriff - *mohair, steel frame, plastic tires & bearings, brown/black, pull-type steering, grip handle*

SERIE	ART.-NO	PERIOD	PR.	INFO
	2470/30	1968-1970	5	30 cm

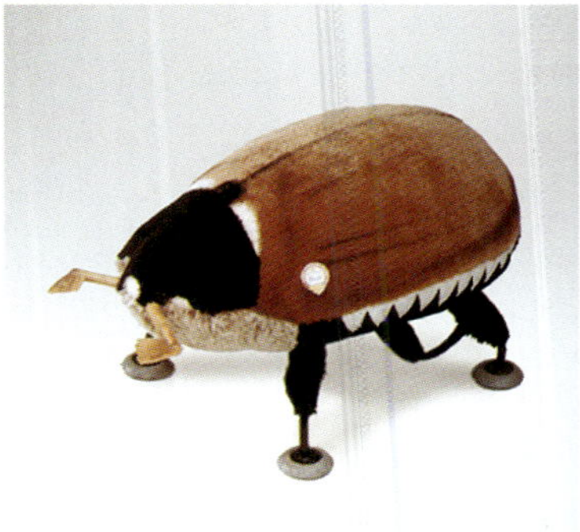

Snuggy-Maikaefer - *Snuggy May-Beetle*

Mohair, Eisengestell mit Gummifuessen, braun/schwarz, Sitztier - *mohair, iron frame with rubber feet, brown/black, sitting animal*

SERIE	ART.-NO	PERIOD	PR.	INFO
	6050/30	1968-1969	5	30 cm

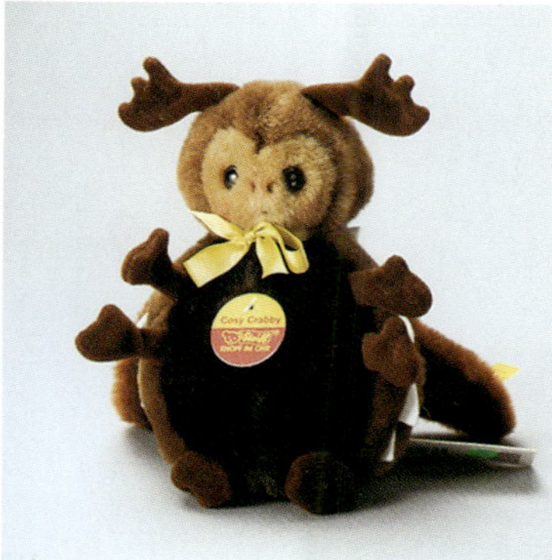

Cosy Crabby Maikaefer - ***Cosy Crabby*** *May-Beetle*

Webpelz, waschmaschinenfest - *woven fur, machine washable*

EAN-No.	Period	Pr.	Info
094002	1995-1996	2	20 cm

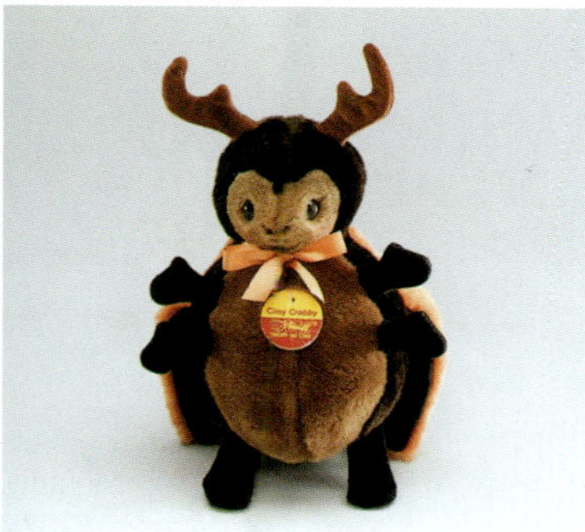

Cosy Crabby Hirschkaefer - ***Cosy Crabby*** *Stag Beetle*

Webpelz, waschmaschinenfest - *woven fur, machine washable*

EAN-No.	Period	Pr.	Info
093975	1995-1997	2	20 cm

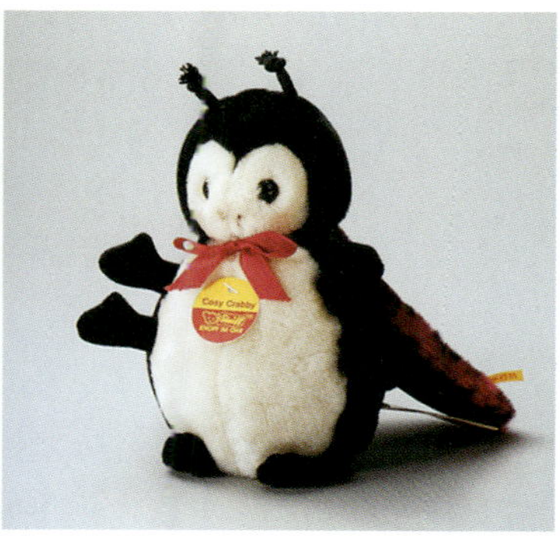

Cosy Crabby Kaefer - ***Cosy Crabby*** *Beetle*

Webpelz, 20 cm, waschmaschinenfest - *woven fur, 20 cm, machine washable*

EAN-No.	Period	Pr.	Info
099625	1992-1996	2	rot - *red*
099656	1992-1994	2	gruen - *green*
099687	1992-1994	2	aubergine - *purple*
099724	1992-1993	2	braun - *brown*
099755	1992-1993	2	blau - *blue*
099786	1992-1994	2	rosé - *rose*

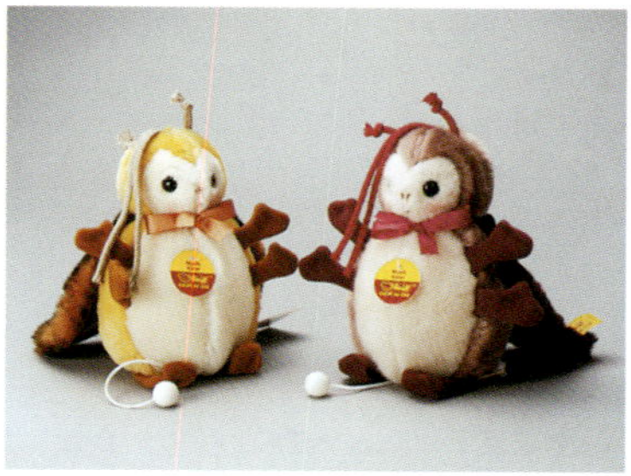

Musik Kaefer - *Musical Beetle*

Webpelz, 20 cm, Musikwerk, abwaschbar - *woven fur, 20 cm, music box, surface washable*

EAN-No.	Period	Pr.	Info
231452	1994-1995	2	honig, "Guter Mond" - *honey, "Good Moon"*
231469	1994-1995	2	hellblau, "Weisst Du wieviel Sternlein" - *light blue, "Twinkle, Twinkle Little Star"*
231476	1994-1995	2	altrosa, "Guten Abend, gute Nacht" - *rose, "Good Evening, Goodnight"*

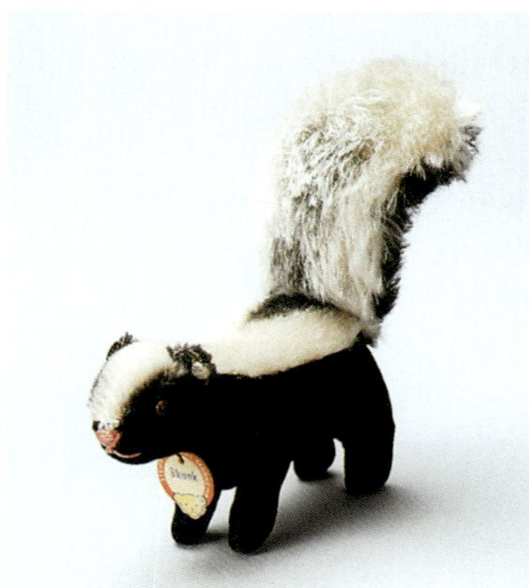

Skunk

Samt, Mohairschwanz, schwarz/weiss, stehend - *velvet, mohair tail, black/white, standing*

Serie	Art.-No	Period	Pr.	Info
450	**1410,00**	1962-1963	4	10 cm

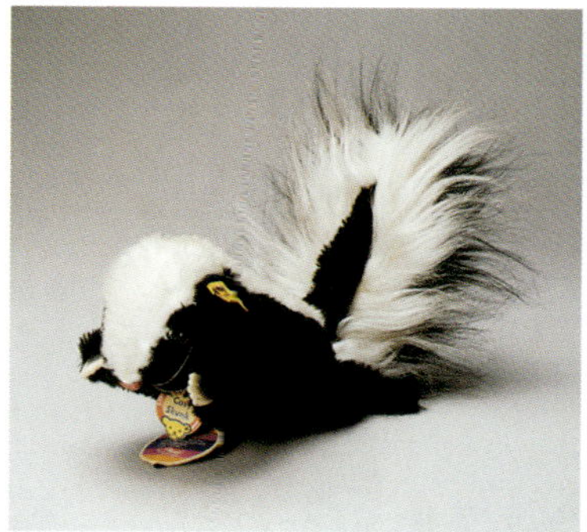

Cosy Skunk

Dralon, gefuellt mit synthetischen Fasern und Schaumstoff, schwarz/weiss, aufwartend, sehr weich, vollwaschbar - *dralon, stuffed with synthetic fibers & foam, black/white, sitting up, very soft, fully washable*

Serie	Art.-No	Period	Pr.	Info
	4920,22	1969-1974	2-3	22 cm

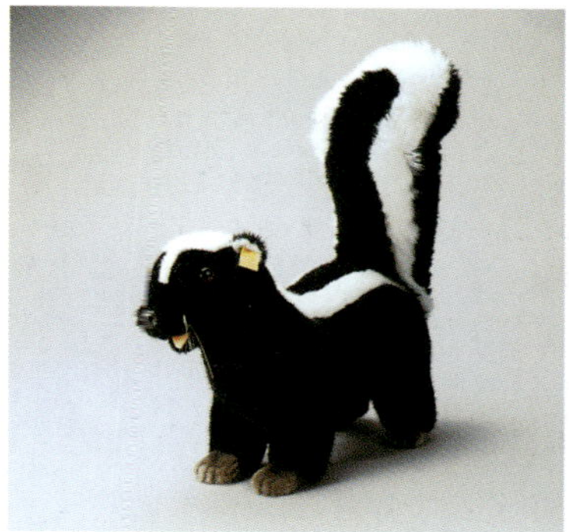

Skunk

Webpelz, stehend, schwarz/weiss, handwaschbar - *woven fur, standing, black/white, hand washable*

Serie	Art.-No	Period	Pr.	Info
071744	**2080/35**	1989-1990	2-3	35 cm
	071744	1991-1994	2-3	

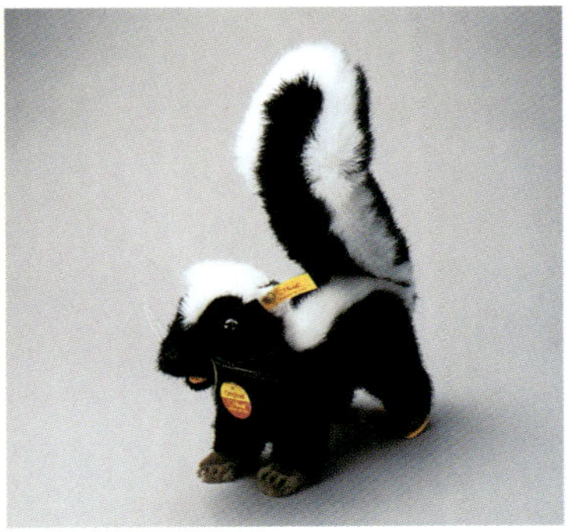

Skunk

Webpelz, stehend, schwarz/weiss, waschmaschinenfest - *woven fur, standing, black/white, machine washable*

EAN-No.	Period	Pr.	Info
071713	1995-1999	3	28 cm

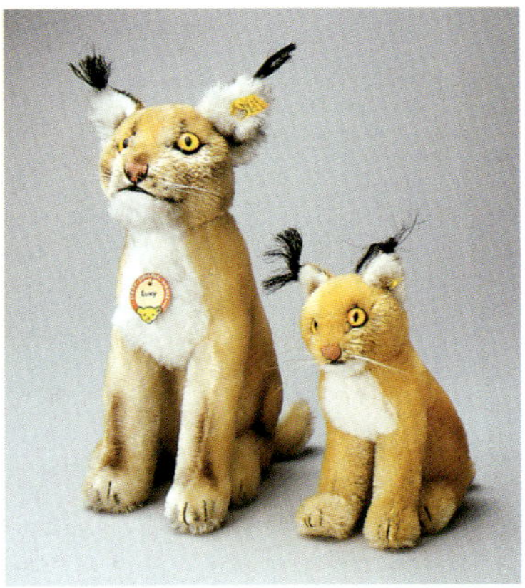

Luxy Luchs - ***Luxy*** *Lynx*

Mohairpluesch, braun/weiss, sitzend - *mohair, brown/white, sitting*

Serie	Art.-No	Period	Pr.	Info
490	**3317,00**	1963-1963	5	17 cm
490	**3325,00**	1963-1963	5-6	25 cm

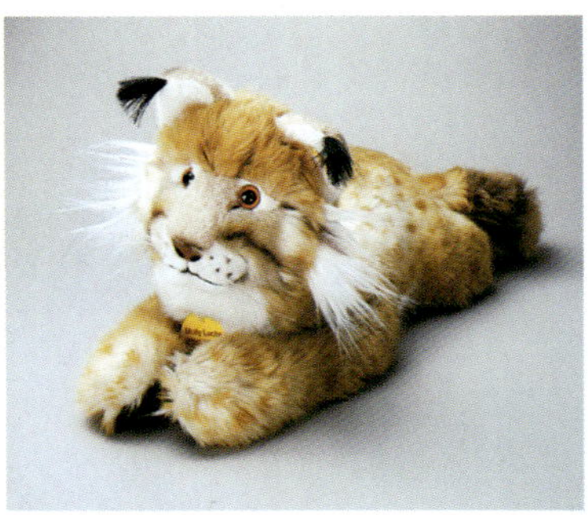

Molly Luchs - *Molly Lynx*

Pelzimitation, liegend, ab 1978 Synthetik-Webpelz, abwaschbar - *imitation fur, from 1978 synthetic woven fur, surface washable*

Serie	Art.-No	Period	Pr.	Info
	0345/50	1976-1981	3	50 cm

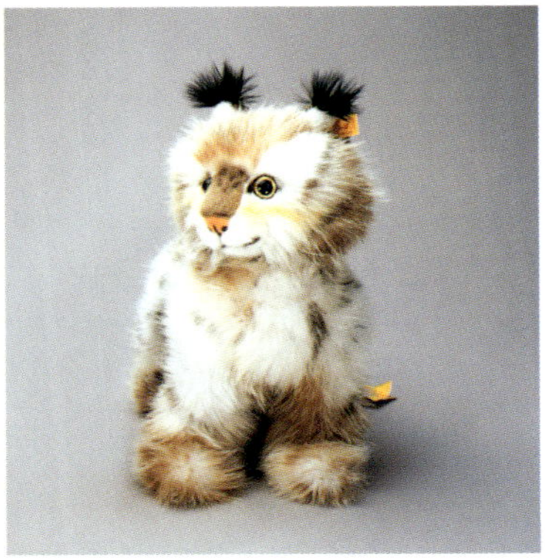

Molly Baby Luchs - *Molly Baby Lynx*

Webpelz, stehend, abwaschbar - *woven fur, standing, surface washable*

EAN-No.	Period	Pr.	Info
102561	1991-1993	3	30 cm

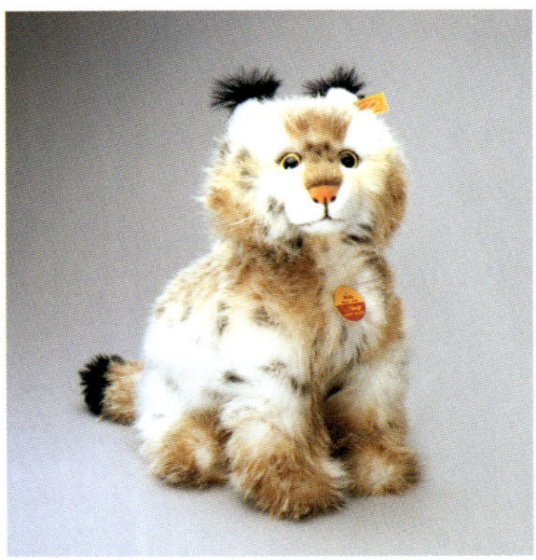

Molly Baby Luchs - *Molly Baby Lynx*

Webpelz, sitzend, abwaschbar - *woven fur, sitting, surface washable*

EAN-No.	Period	Pr.	Info
102615	1991-1994	3	30 cm

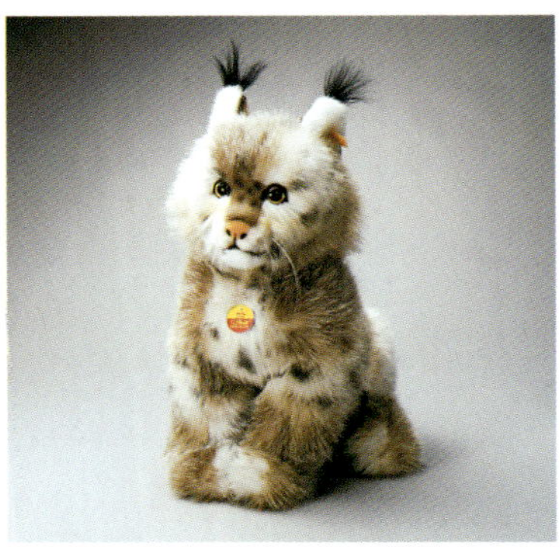

Molly Luchs - *Molly Lynx*

Webpelz, sitzend, abwaschbar - *woven fur, sitting, surface washable*

EAN-No.	Period	Pr.	Info
102707	1991-1993	3	40 cm

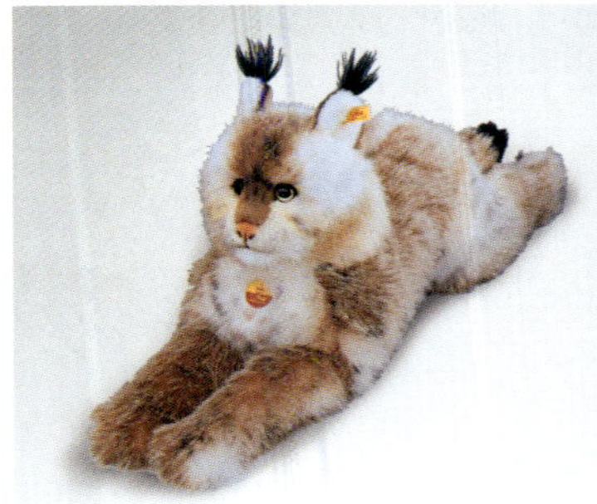

Molly Luchs - *Molly Lynx*

Webpelz, liegend, abwaschbar - *woven fur, lying, surface washable*

EAN-No.	Period	Pr.	Info
102752	1991-1993	3	50 cm

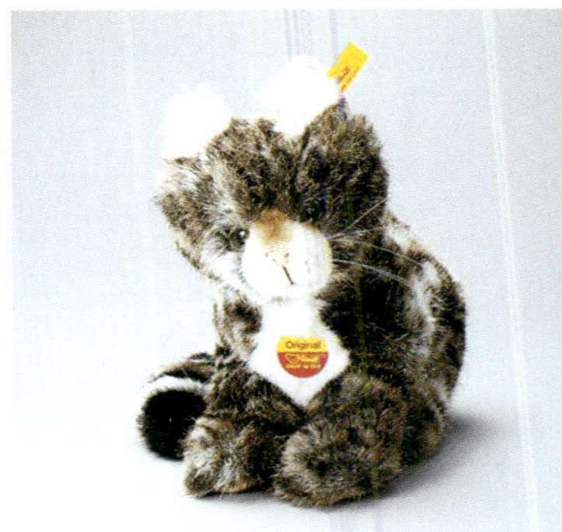

Wildkatze - *Wildcat*

Webpelz, 25 cm, gefleckt, sitzend, abwaschbar - *woven fur, 25 cm, spotted, sitting, surface washable*

EAN-No.	Period	Pr.	Info
075155	1995-1999	3	grau - *grey*
075193	1995-1998	3	braun - *brown*

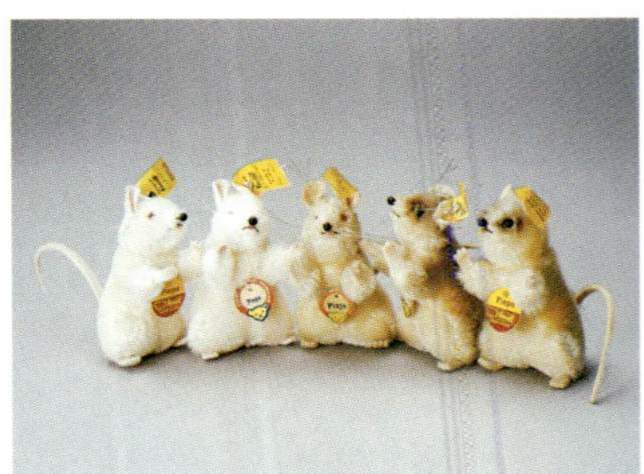

Pieps Maus - ***Pieps*** *Mouse*

Mohairpluesch, 8 cm, aufwartend, abwaschbar - *mohair, 8 cm, sitting up, surface washable*

Serie	Art.-No	Period	Pr.	Info
50	**4308** w	1958-1958	3	weiss - *white*
500	**4308,04**	1959-1964	2-3	

217	**4308,04**	1965-1967	2-3	
	2174/08	1968-1978	2	
50	**4308** gr	1958-1958	3	grau - *grey*
500	**4308,05**	1959-1964	2-3	
217	**4308,05**	1965-1967	2-3	
	2175/08	1968-1978	2	

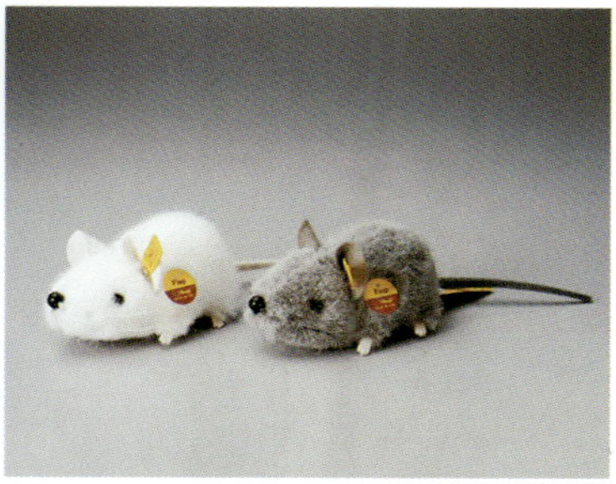

Fiep Maus - ***Fiep** Mouse*

Nerzimitation, 1978/79 Dralon, ab 1980 Webpelz, 12 cm, Filzohren & -schwanz, Filzpfoten, stehend, abwaschbar - *imitation mink, 1978/79 dralon, from 1980 woven fur, 12 cm, felt ears & tail, felt paws, standing, surface washable*

SERIE	ART.-NO	PERIOD	PR.	INFO
056208	**2170/10**	1976-1990	1	weiss - *white*
	056208	1991-1999	1	
056253	**2171/10**	1976-1990	1	grau - *grey*
	056253	1991-1999	1	

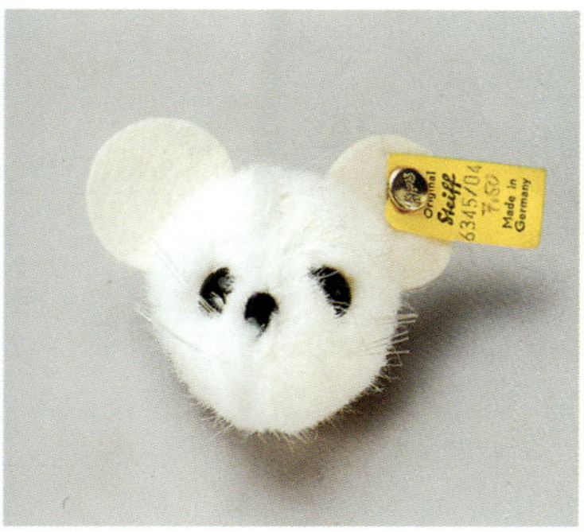

Ansteckmaeuschen - *Mouse Pin*

Webpelz, weiss, abwaschbar - *woven fur, white, surface washable*

SERIE	ART.-NO	PERIOD	PR.	INFO
	6345/04	1979-1983	2-3	4 cm

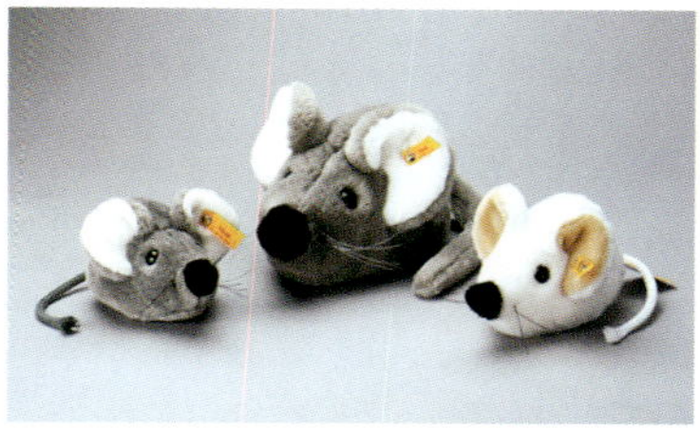

Cosy Fiep Maus - ***Cosy Fiep** Mouse*

Webpelz, weiss oder grau, superweich, waschmaschinenfest - *woven fur, white or grey, super soft, machine washable*

SERIE	ART.-NO	PERIOD	PR.	INFO
093234	**5393/15**	1981-1990	1	16 cm, weiss - *white*
	093234	1991-1999	1	
093258	**5393/30**	1985-1990	1-2	30 cm
093265	**5393/45**	1987-1987	2	45 cm
093289	**5393/80**	1985-1986	2-3	80 cm
093333	**5394/15**	1981-1990	1	16 cm, grau - *grey*
	093333	1991-1999	1	
093357	**5394/30**	1985-1990	1-2	30 cm
	093357	1991-1999	1-2	
093364	**5394/45**	1987-1988	2	45 cm
093388	**5394/80**	1985-1986	2-3	80 cm

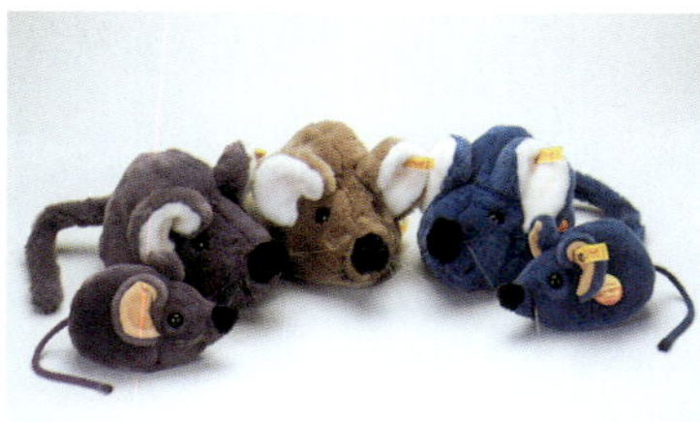

Cosy Fiep Maus - ***Cosy Fiep** Mouse*

Webpelz, blau, violett, oliv, gelb, aubergine oder gelboliv, superweich, waschmaschinenfest - *woven fur, blue, violet, olive green, yellow, aubergine or yellowish olive green, super soft, machine washable*

SERIE	ART.-NO	PERIOD	PR.	INFO
	5390/15	1981-1985	1	15 cm, blau - *blue*
	5390/30	1981-1984	1-2	30 cm
	5391/15	1981-1985	1	15 cm, violett - *violet*
	5391/30	1981-1984	1-2	30 cm
093135	**5392/15**	1981-1988	1	15 cm, oliv - *olive green*
093159	**5392/30**	1981-1988	1-2	30 cm
093166	**5392/45**	1987-1987	2	45 cm
093036	**5388/15**	1986-1988	1	15 cm, gelb - *yellow*
093050	**5388/30**	1986-1988	1-2	30 cm
093074	**5390/15**	1988-1990	1	15 cm, aubergine
093104	**5391/15**	1988-1990	1	15 cm, gelboliv - *yellowish olive green*

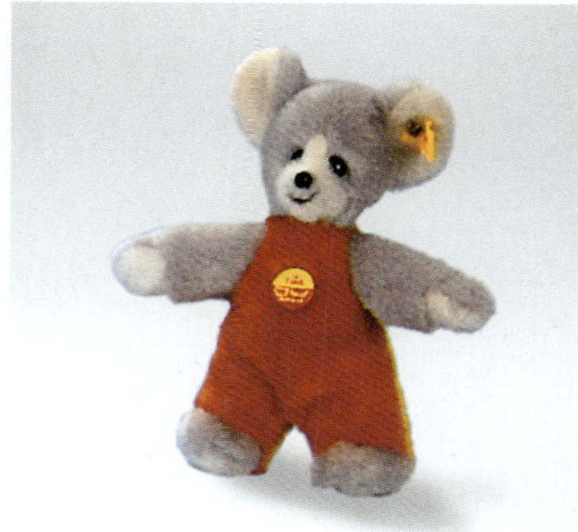

Toldi Maus - ***Toldi** Mouse*

Webpelz, sehr weich, waschmaschinenfest - *woven fur, very soft, machine washable*

SERIE	ART.-NO	PERIOD	PR.	INFO
	6248/20	1982-1983	2	20 cm

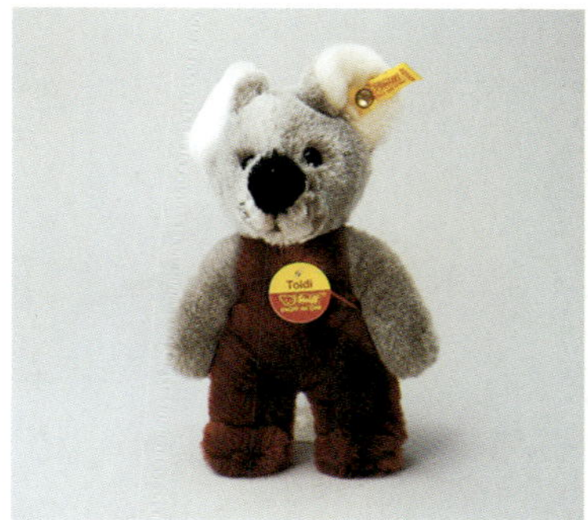

Toldi Maus - ***Toldi** Mouse*

Webpelz, Pieps-Stimme, waschmaschinenfest - *woven fur, squeaker, machine washable*

SERIE	ART.-NO	PERIOD	PR.	INFO
080500	**6261/22**	1986-1987	2	22 cm

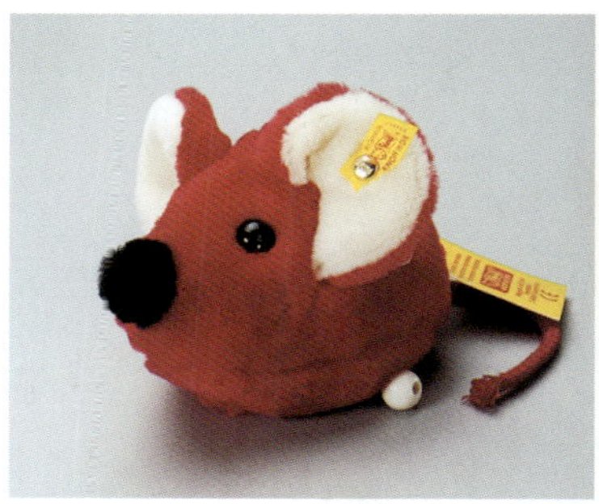

Musik Fiep Maus - *Musical Fiep Mouse*

Webpelz, formgeschaeumt, 17 cm, Musikwerk austauschbar, waschbar - *woven fur, stuffed with pre-formed foam, 17 cm, music box exchangeable, washable*

SERIE	ART.-NO	PERIOD	PR.	INFO
233609	**6378/15**	1985-1986	1-2	weiss - *white*
233647	**6380/15**	1985-1990	1-2	rot - *red*
	233647	1991-1996	1-2	

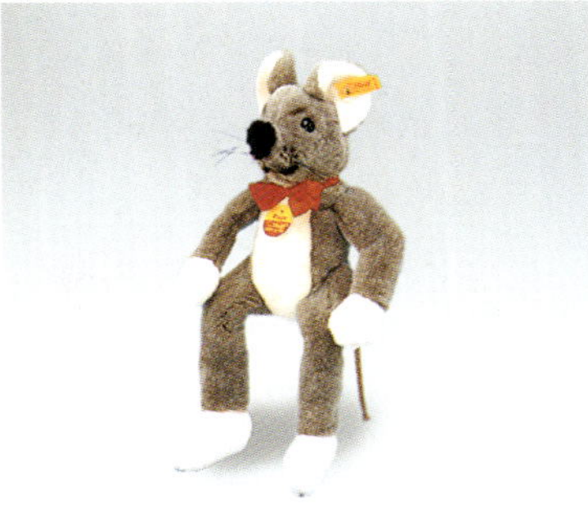

Pieps Schlenker-Maus - ***Pieps*** *Dangling Mouse*

Webpelz, Pieps-Stimme, waschmaschinenfest - *woven fur, squeaker, machine washable*

SERIE	ART.-NO	PERIOD	PR.	INFO
123450	**6294/32**	1986-1987	2-3	32 cm

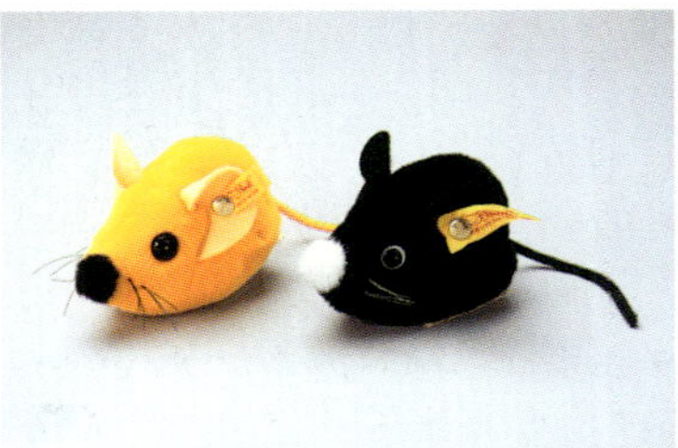

Mini Cosy Maus - *Mini Cozy Mouse*

Webpelz, 10 cm, superweich, waschmaschinenfest - *woven fur, 10 cm, super soft, machine washable*

SERIE	ART.-NO	PERIOD	PR.	INFO
084102	**5550/10**	1986-1989	1	gelb - *yellow*
084157	**5552/10**	1986-1989	1	schwarz - *black*

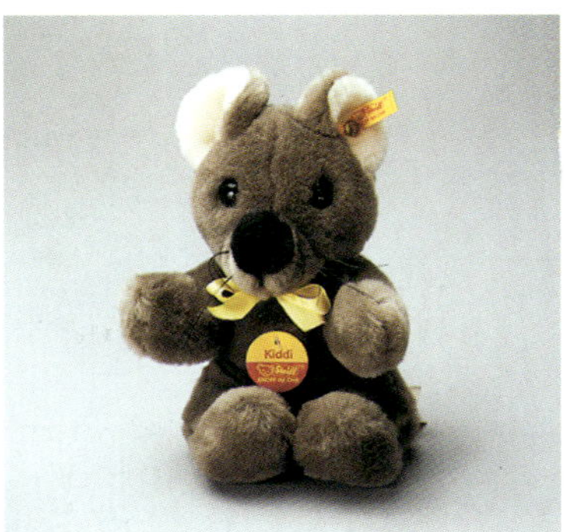

Kiddi Maus - ***Kiddi*** *Mouse*

Webpelz, Pieps-Stimme, waschmaschinenfest - *woven fur, squeaker, machine washable*

SERIE	ART.-NO	PERIOD	PR.	INFO
082863	**5722/20**	1989-1990	2	20 cm

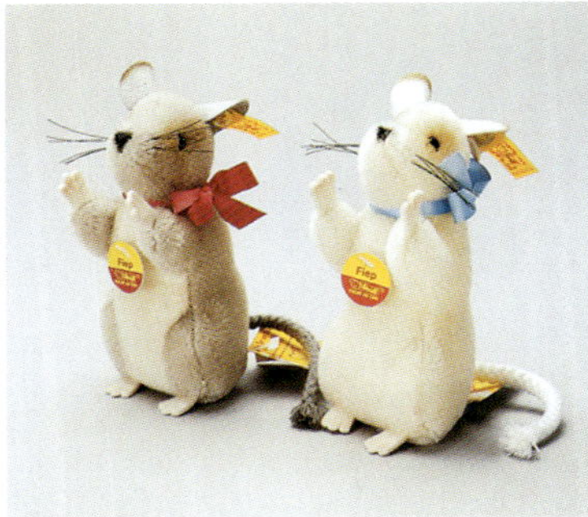

Fiep Maus - ***Fiep*** *Mouse*

Mohair Webpelz, 12 cm, aufwartend, abwaschbar - *mohair woven fur, 12 cm, sitting up, surface washable*

SERIE	ART.-NO	PERIOD	PR.	INFO
032226	**1308/12**	1990-1990	1-2	grau - *grey*
	032226	1991-1993	1-2	
032127	**1310/12**	1990-1990	1-2	weiss - *white*
	032127	1991-1992	1-2	

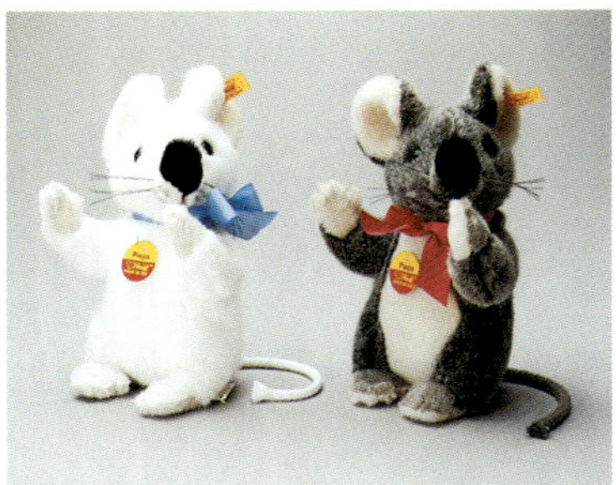

Pieps Maus - ***Pieps*** *Mouse*

Webpelz, 22 cm, aufwartend, Pieps-Stimme, waschmaschinenfest - *woven fur, 22 cm, sitting up, squeaker, machine washable*

SERIE	ART.-NO	PERIOD	PR.	INFO
070877	**2270/22**	1990-1990	1-2	grau - *grey*
	070877	1991-1992	1-2	
070976	**2275/22**	1990-1990	1-2	weiss - *white*
	070976	1991-1992	1-2	

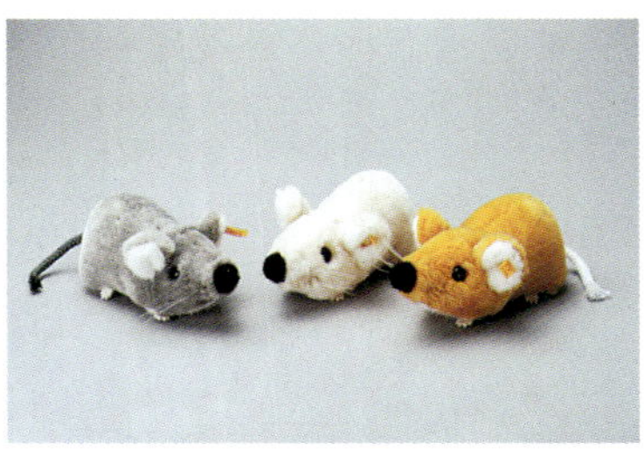

Cosy Sniffy Maus - ***Cosy Sniffy*** *Mouse*

Webpelz, 18 cm, Pieps-Stimme, waschmaschinenfest - *woven fur, 18 cm, squeaker, machine washable*

EAN-NO.	PERIOD	PR.	INFO
093067	1995-1997	1-2	weiss - *white*
093081	1995-1995	1-2	gelb - *yellow*
093098	1995-1995	1-2	himbeer - *raspberry*
093128	1995-1995	1-2	violett - *violet*
093142	1995-1995	1-2	blau - *blue*
093173	1995-1997	1-2	grau - *grey*

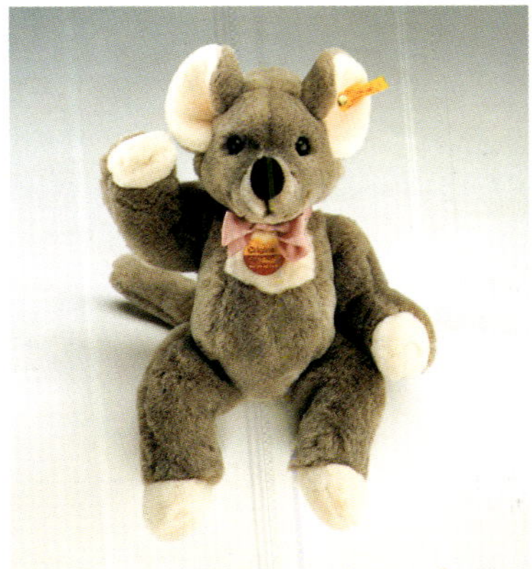

Schlenker Maus - *Dangling Mouse*

Webpelz, waschmaschinenfest - *woven fur, machine washable*

EAN-NO.	PERIOD	PR.	INFO
123443	1996-1998	2-3	30 cm

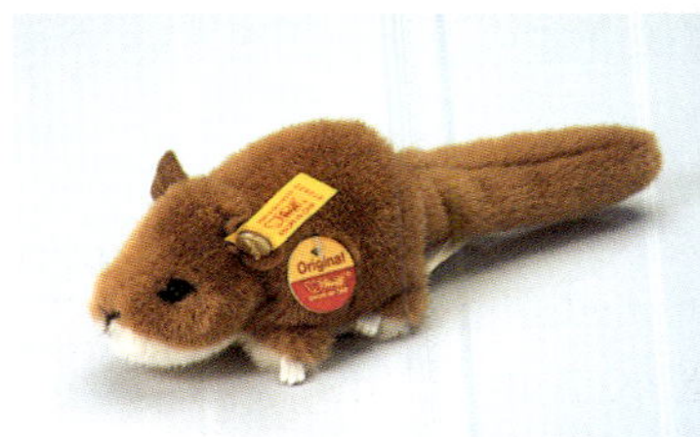

Haselmaus - *Dormouse*

Webpelz, braun, waschmaschinenfest - *woven fur, brown, machine washable*

EAN-NO.	PERIOD	PR.	INFO
070822	1997-1999	1	10 cm

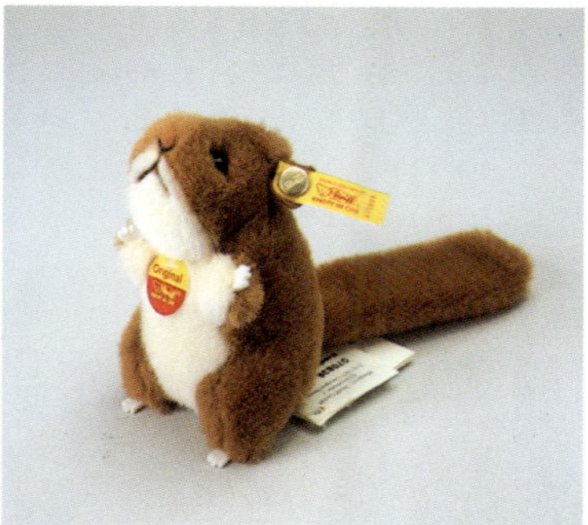

Haselmaus - *Dormouse*

Webpelz, braun, aufwartend, waschmaschinenfest - *woven fur, brown, sitting up, machine washable*

EAN-No.	Period	Pr.	Info
070839	1999-1999	1	10 cm

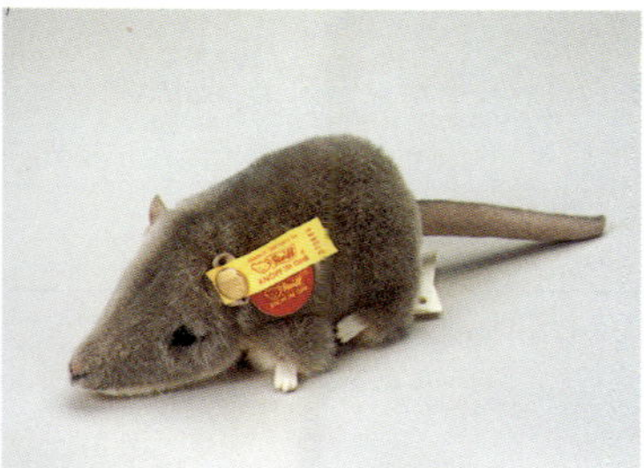

Spitzmaus - *Shrew*

Webpelz, grau, waschmaschinenfest - *woven fur, grey, machine washable*

EAN-No.	Period	Pr.	Info
070884	1997-1999	1	12 cm

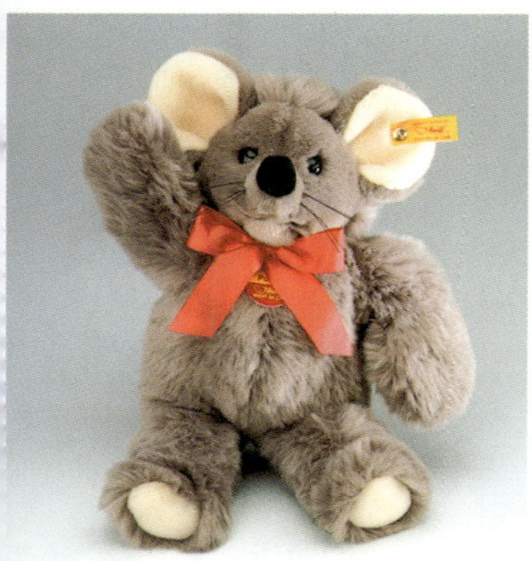

Poppy Maus - ***Poppy** Mouse*

Webpelz, grau, waschmaschinenfest - *woven fur, grey, machine washable*

EAN-No.	Period	Pr.	Info
123467	1998-1999	2-3	30 cm

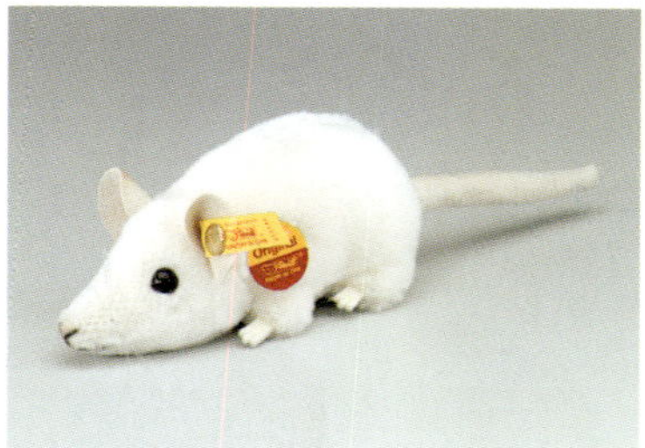

Hausmaus - *Farm Mouse*

Webpelz, 12 cm, weiss oder grau, waschmaschinenfest - *woven fur, 12 cm, white or grey, machine washable*

EAN-No.	Period	Pr.	Info
056185	1998-1999	1-2	weiss - *white*
056192	1998-1999	1-2	grau - *grey*

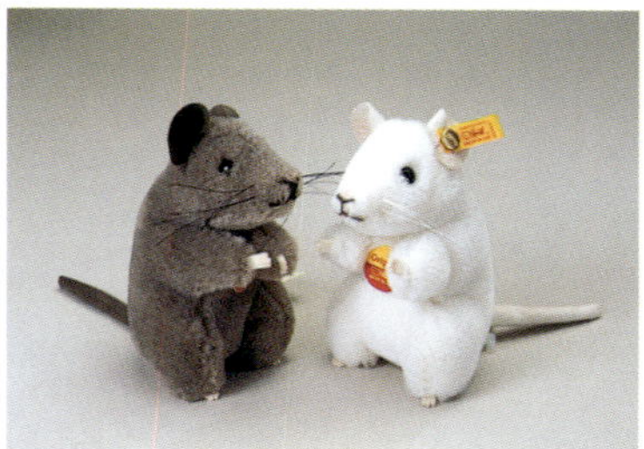

Hausmaus - *Farm Mouse*

Webpelz, 12 cm, aufwartend, waschmaschinenfest - *woven fur, 12 cm, sitting up, machine washable*

EAN-No.	Period	Pr.	Info
056147	1999-1999	1-2	weiss - *white*
056154	1999-1999	1-2	grau - *grey*

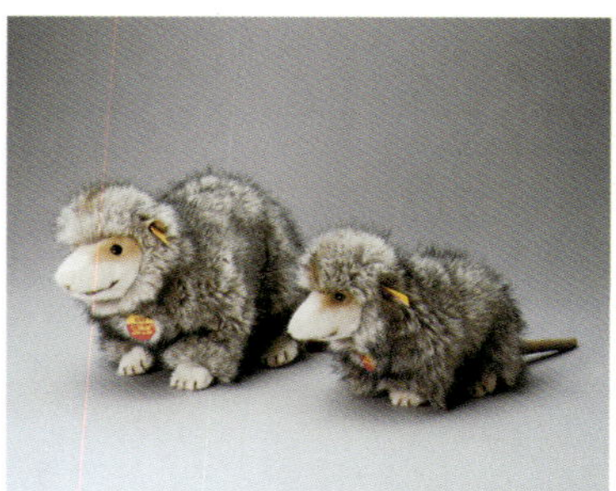

Billy Opossum

Webpelz, waschmaschinenfest - *woven fur, machine washable*

EAN-No.	Period	Pr.	Info
072000	1991-1993	3	25 cm
072024	1991-1992	3	35 cm

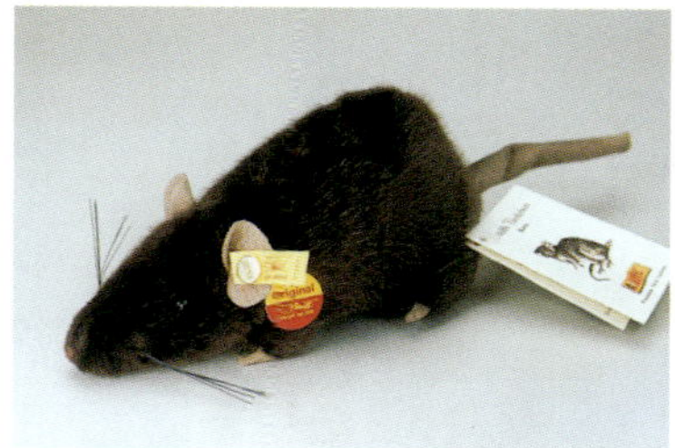

Ratte - *Rat*

Webpelz, graubraun, waschmaschinenfest - *woven fur, grey-brown, machine washable*

EAN-No.	Period	Pr.	Info
070891	1998-1999	1-2	16 cm

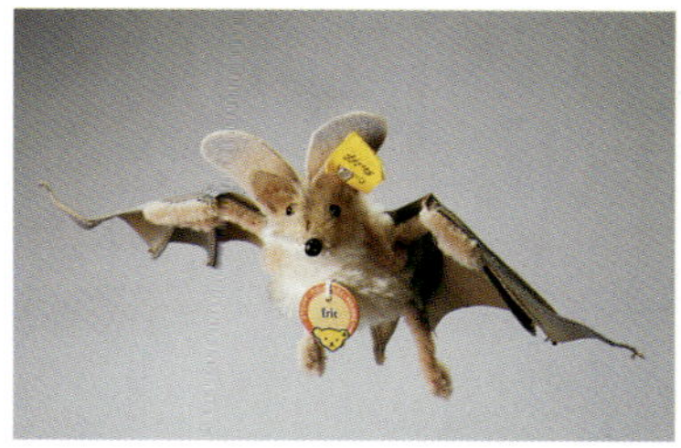

Eric Fledermaus - ***Eric** Bat*

Mohair, Kunststoff-Fluegel, graubraun, stehend - *mohair, synthetic wings, grey-brown, standing*

Serie	Art.-No	Period	Pr.	Info
502	**1310,00**	1960-1962	5	10 cm
502	**1317,00**	1960-1961	5-6	17 cm

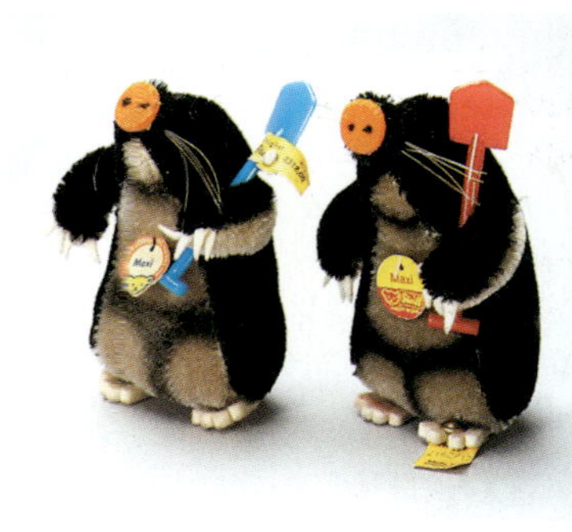

Maxi Maulwurf ab 1996 **Bazi** - ***Maxi** Mole from 1996 **Bazi***

Mohair, ab 1978 Synthetik-Webpelz, schwarz/grau, aufwartend, mit rotem oder blauem Spaten, abwaschbar - *mohair, from 1978 synthetic woven fur, black/grey, sitting up, holding a red or blue spade, surface washable*

Serie	Art.-No	Period	Pr.	Info
504	**4312,00**	1964-1964	3	12 cm
218	**4312,00**	1965-1967	3	
056307	**2180/12**	1968-1990	2	
	056307	1991-1999	1	
056352	**2180/15**	1976-1989	2	15 cm

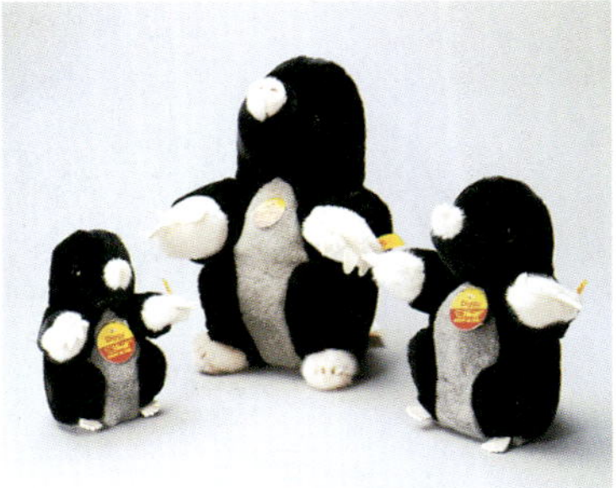

Diggy Maulwurf - ***Diggy*** *Mole*

Webpelz, aufwartend, waschmaschinenfest - *woven fur, sitting up, machine washable*

SERIE	ART.-NO	PERIOD	PR.	INFO
071768	**2185/13**	1990-1990	1-2	14 cm
	071768	1991-1999	1-2	
071782	**2185/16**	1990-1990	1-2	18 cm
	071782	1991-1999	1-2	
	071799	1995-1999	2-3	25 cm

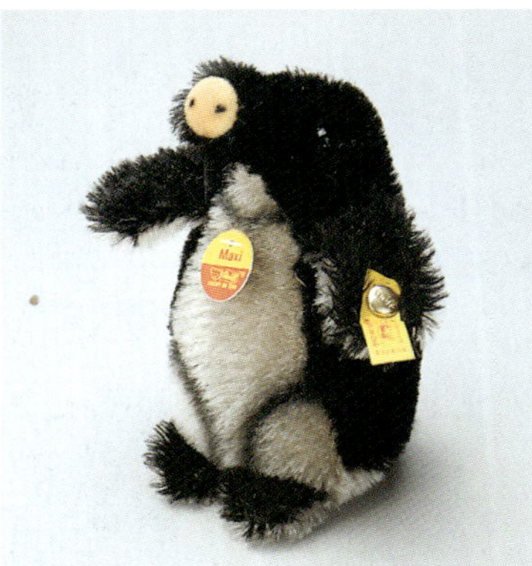

Maxi Maulwurf - ***Maxi*** *Mole*

Mohair Webpelz, aufwartend, abwaschbar - *mohair woven fur, sitting up, surface washable*

EAN-NO.	PERIOD	PR.	INFO
032806	1991-1995	2	12 cm

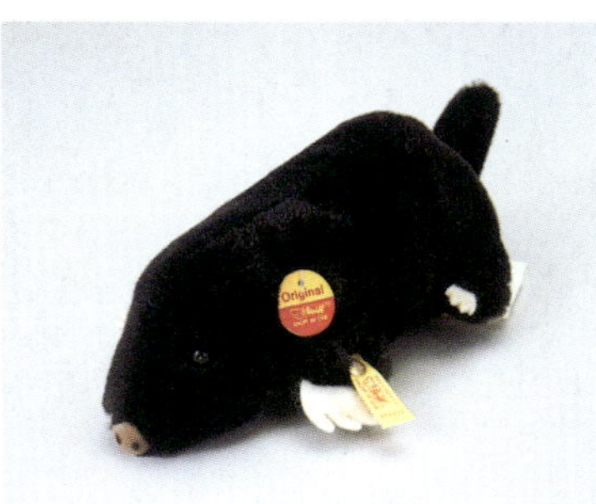

Maulwurf - *Mole*

Webpelz, waschmaschinenfest - *woven fur, machine washable*

EAN-NO.	PERIOD	PR.	INFO
070921	1997-1999	1	18 cm

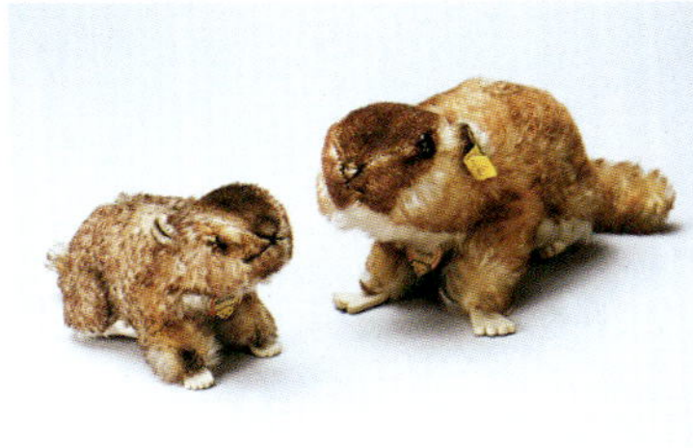

Murmy Murmeltier - ***Murmy*** *Marmot*

Mohair, braun, liegend - *mohair, brown, lying*

SERIE	ART.-NO	PERIOD	PR.	INFO
505	**2310,00**	1960-1964	3-4	10 cm
505	**2314,00**	1960-1962	3-4	14 cm

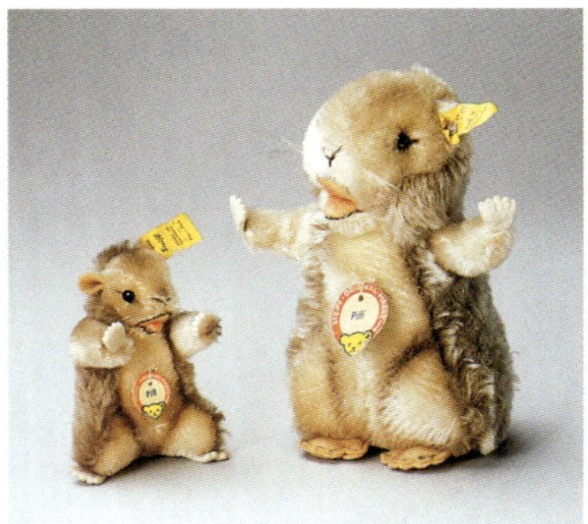

Piff Murmeltier - ***Piff*** *Marmot*

Mohair, grau/weiss/gelb, aufwartend, Drehkopf, zwischen 1965 & 1967 auch mit Zusatz "im Steiff-Kinderbuch", abwaschbar - *mohair, grey/white/yellow, sitting up, head swivels, between 1965 & 1967 also with additional comment "im Steiff Kinderbuch", surface washable*

SERIE	ART.-NO	PERIOD	PR.	INFO
505	**4310,00**	1961-1964	3	10 cm
220	**4310,00**	1965-1967	3	
	2200/10	1968-1969	3	
505	**4317,00**	1961-1962	3	17 cm
220	**4317,00**	1966-1967	3	
	2200/17	1968-1969	3	

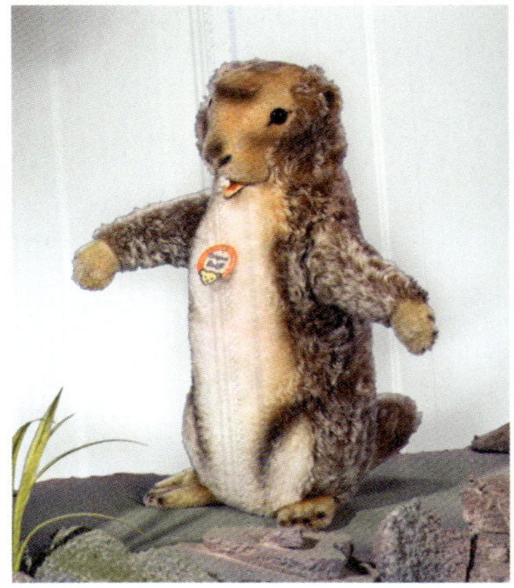

Murmeltier - *Marmot*

Schautier, Mohair, grau/weiss/gelb, aufwartend - *display animal, mohair, grey/white/yellow, sitting up*

SERIE	ART.-NO	PERIOD	PR.	INFO
	2209/06	1967-1967	5-6	60 cm

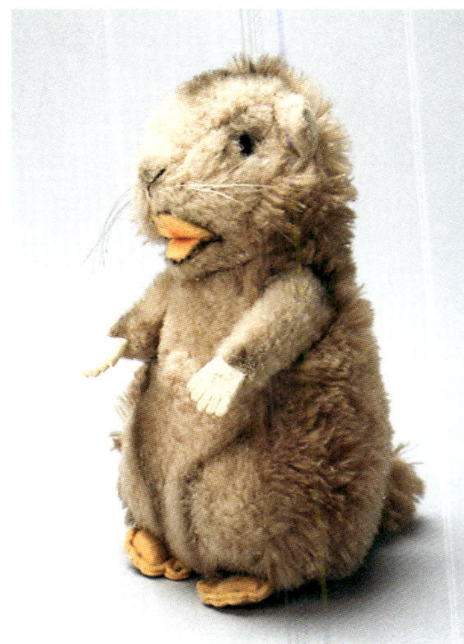

Piff Murmeltier - ***Piff*** *Marmot*

Dralon, grau/weiss/gelb, aufwartend, Drehkopf, abwaschbar, 17 cm ab 1972 Filzhaende und Fuesse - *dralon, grey/white/yellow, sitting up, head swivels, surface washable, 17 cm from 1972 felt hands & feet*

SERIE	ART.-NO	PERIOD	PR.	INFO
	2200/10	1970-1977	2	10 cm
	2200/17	1970-1977	2	17 cm

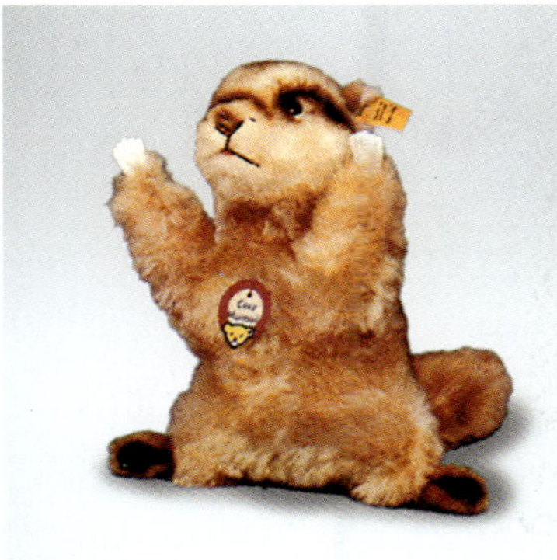

Cosy Murmel

Dralon, gefuellt mit synthetischen Fasern und Schaumstoff, aufwartend, sehr weich, vollwaschbar - *dralon, stuffed with synthetic fibers & foam, sitting up, very soft, fully washable*

SERIE	ART.-NO	PERIOD	PR.	INFO
	4850/22	1969-1977	2	22 cm

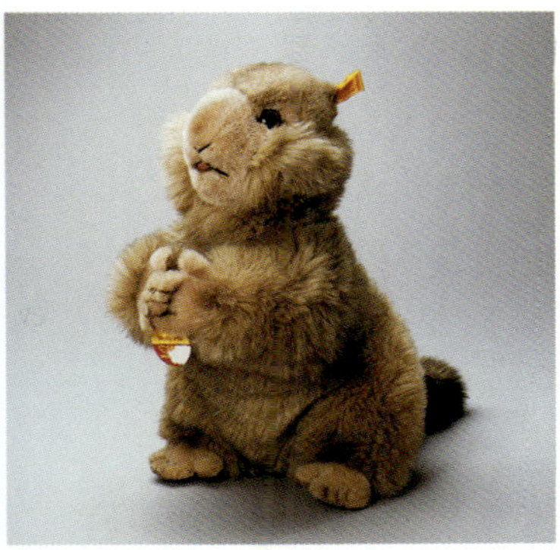

Molly Piff Murmeltier - ***Molly Piff*** *Marmot*

Pelzimitation, ab 1978 Synthetik-Webpelz, mollig weich, abwaschbar - *imitation fur, from 1978 synthetic woven fur, soft & cuddly, surface washable*

SERIE	ART.-NO	PERIOD	PR.	INFO
103056	**0346/30**	1976-1990	2	30 cm
	103056	1991-1993	2	

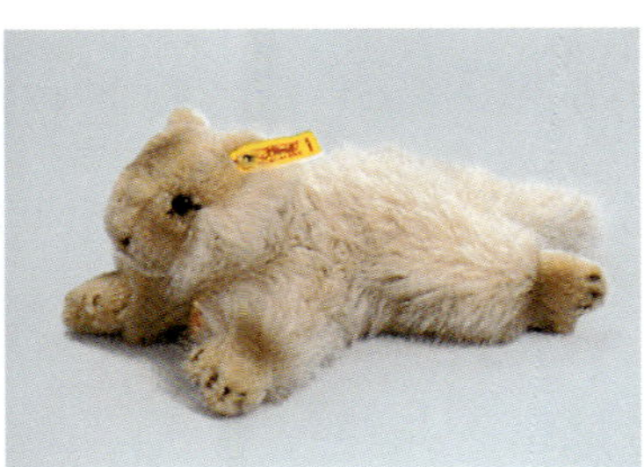

Molly Murmel

Webpelz, liegend, mollig weich, abwaschbar - *woven fur, lying, soft & cuddly, surface washable*

SERIE	ART.-NO	PERIOD	PR.	INFO
	0345/25	1981-1984	2	29 cm

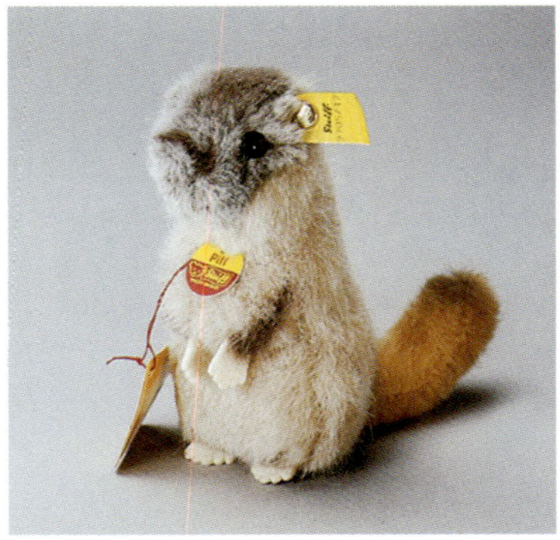

Piff Murmeltier - ***Piff*** *Marmot*

Webpelz, aufwartend, abwaschbar - *woven fur, sitting up, surface washable*

SERIE	ART.-NO	PERIOD	PR.	INFO
	2205/12	1978-1985	2	12 cm

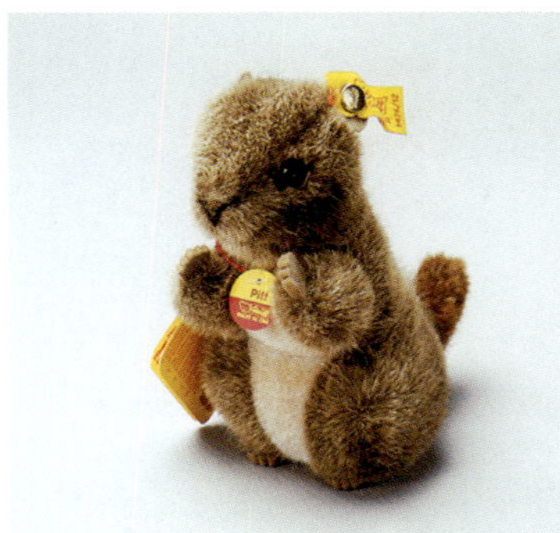

Piff Murmeltier - ***Piff*** *Marmot*

Webpelz, aufwartend, abwaschbar - *woven fur, sitting up, surface washable*

SERIE	ART.-NO	PERIOD	PR.	INFO
045202	**1476/12**	1986-1989	2	12 cm

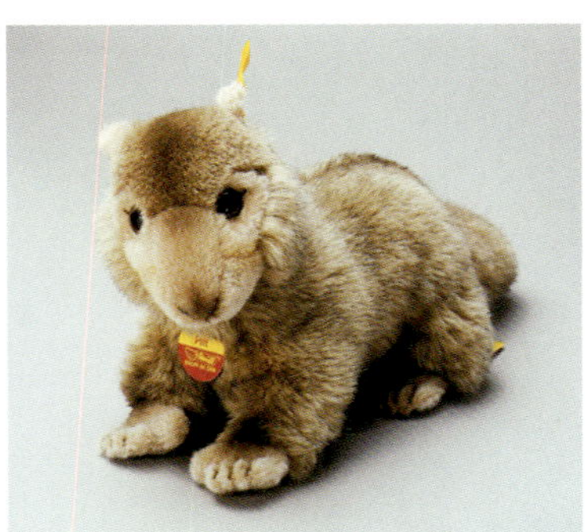

Piff Murmeltier - ***Piff*** *Marmot*

Webpelz, stehend, abwaschbar - *woven fur, standing, surface washable*

SERIE	ART.-NO	PERIOD	PR.	INFO
071546	**2070/25**	1987-1989	2	25 cm

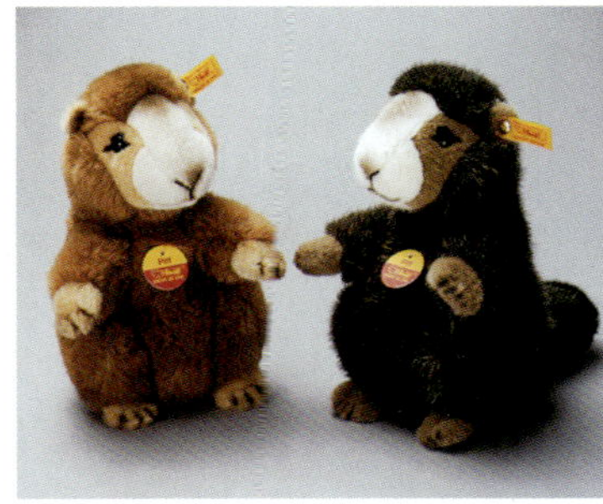

Piff Murmeltier - ***Piff*** *Marmot*

Webpelz, 24 cm, aufwartend, Pieps-Stimme, waschmaschinenfest - *woven fur, 24 cm, sitting up, squeaker, machine washable*

SERIE	ART.-NO	PERIOD	PR.	INFO
071362	**2041/24**	1990-1990	2	rotbraun - *reddish-brown*
	071362	1991-1991	2	
071416	**2042/24**	1990-1990	2	graubraun - *grey-brown*
	071415	1991-1993	2	

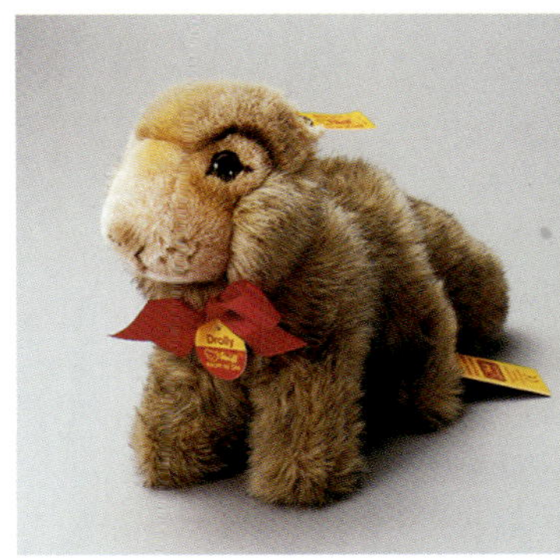

Drolly Murmeltier - ***Drolly*** *Marmot*

Webpelz, stehend, waschmaschinenfest - *woven fur, standing, machine washable*

EAN-NO.	PERIOD	PR.	INFO
081392	1992-1993	2	22 cm

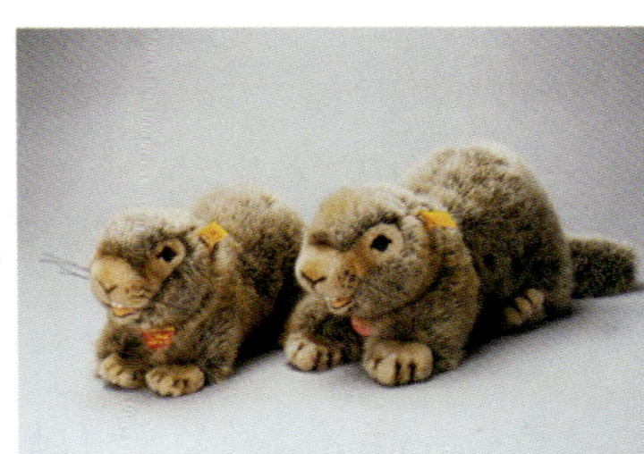

Piff Murmel - ***Piff*** *Marmot*

Webpelz, stehend, waschmaschinenfest - *woven fur, standing, machine washable*

EAN-NO.	PERIOD	PR.	INFO
071379	1993-1995	2-3	25 cm
071393	1993-1998	3	30 cm

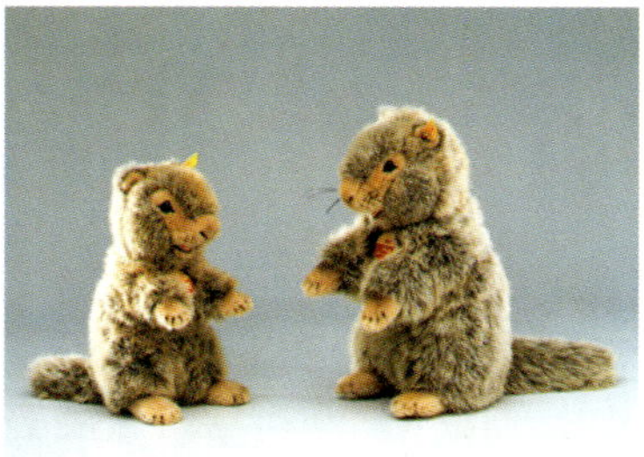

Piff Murmel - ***Piff*** *Marmot*

Webpelz, aufwartend, handwaschbar - *woven fur, sitting up, hand washable*

EAN-No.	Period	Pr.	Info
071423	1995-1997	2-3	23 cm
071447	1995-1998	3	27 cm

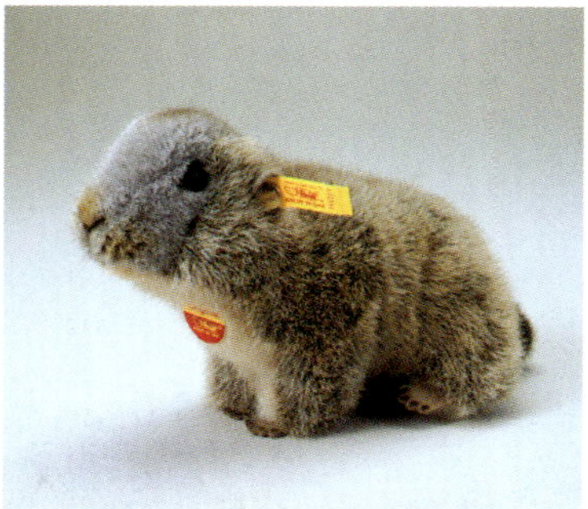

Murmeltier - *Marmot*

Webpelz, stehend, waschmaschinenfest - *woven fur, standing, machine washable*

EAN-No.	Period	Pr.	Info
045219	1996-1999	2	18 cm

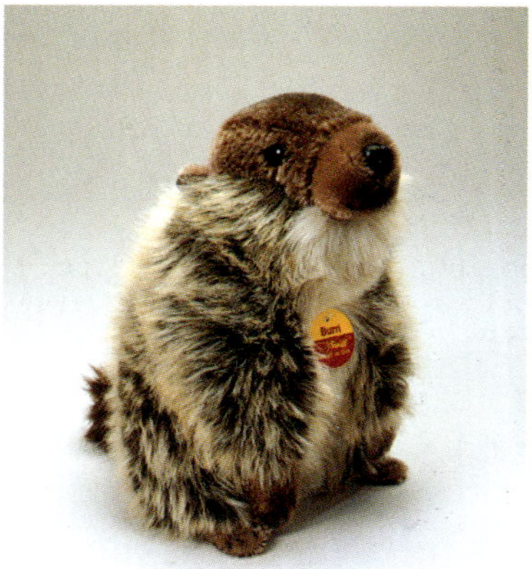

Burri Murmeltier - ***Burri*** *Marmot*

Webpelz, aufwartend, handwaschbar - *woven fur, sitting up, hand washable*

EAN-No.	Period	Pr.	Info
071461	1998-1999	2-3	23 cm

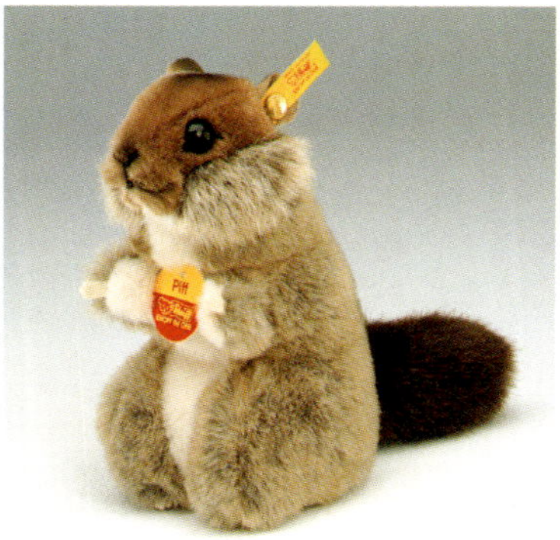

Piff Murmeltier - ***Piff*** *Marmot*

Webpelz, aufwartend, waschmaschinenfest - *woven fur, sitting up, machine washable*

EAN-No.	Period	Pr.	Info
045226	1999-1999	2	15 cm

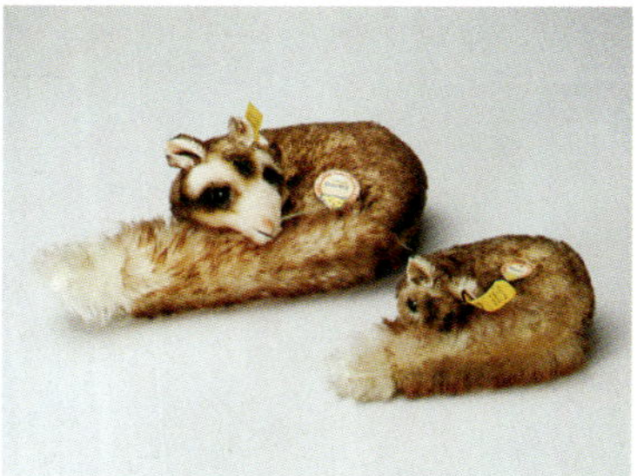

Dormy Siebenschlaefer - ***Dormy*** *Dormouse*

Mohair, braun gespitzt, liegend, weich gestopft, abwaschbar - *mohair, brown tipped, lying, very soft, surface washable*

Serie	Art.-No	Period	Pr.	Info
222	**2312,00**	1966-1967	3-4	12 cm
	2220/12	1968-1974	3	
222	**2320,00**	1966-1967	3-4	20 cm
	2220/20	1968-1974	3	

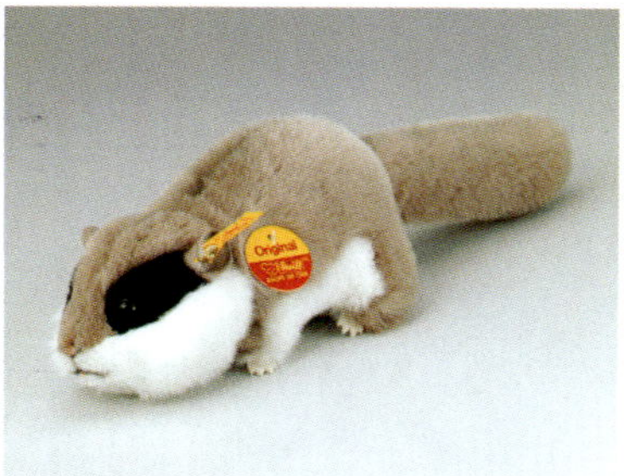

Siebenschlaefer - *Edible Dormouse*

Webpelz, grau, waschmaschinenfest - *woven fur, grey, machine washable*

EAN-No.	Period	Pr.	Info
070808	1997-1998	1-2	20 cm

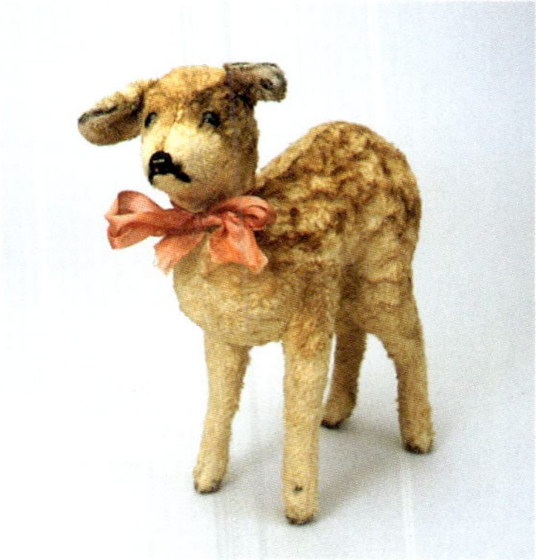

Jungreh - *Fawn*

Seidenpluesch, hellbraun getupft, stehend ohne Raeder - *artificial silk plush, light brown with speckles, standing, without wheels*

Serie	Art.-No	Period	Pr.	Info
60	**6617,0**	1949-1949	4-5	17 cm
60	**6622,0**	1948-1949	4-5	22 cm

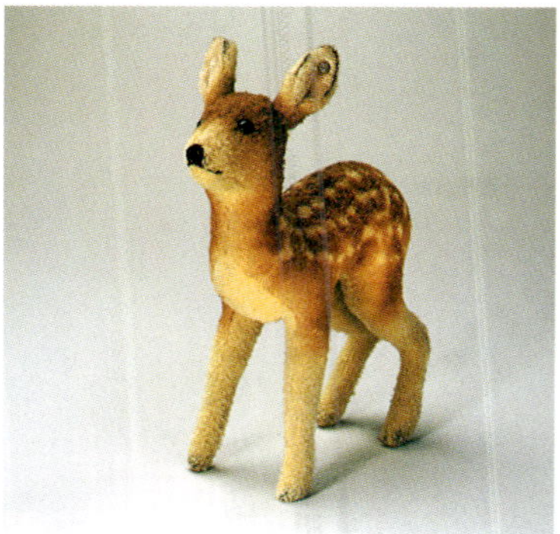

Jungreh - *Fawn*

Wollpluesch (bis 1939 & ab 1954 Mohairpluesch), hellbraun, hell getupft, stehend, ohne Raeder - *plush wool (up to 1939 & from 1954 mohair), light brown with light speckles, standing, without wheels*

Serie	Art.-No	Period	Pr.	Info
60	**6517,0**	1949-1953	4-5	17 cm
60	**6522,0**	1949-1953	4-5	22 cm

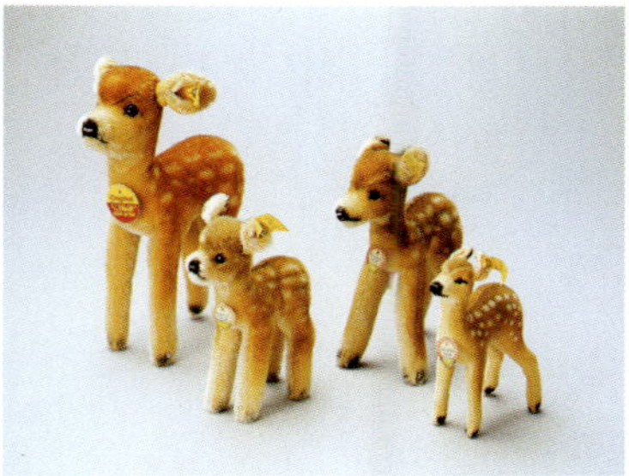

Jungreh - *Fawn*

12 cm Samt, ab 14 cm Mohair (bis 1953 Wollpluesch), hellbraun, gefleckt, stehend ohne Raeder - *12 cm velvet, from 14 cm mohair (up to 1953 plush wool), light brown with light speckles, standing, without wheels*

SERIE	ART.-NO	PERIOD	PR.	INFO
60	**6412,0**	1949-1958	3-4	12 cm
600	**6412,00**	1959-1964	3	
180	**6412,00**	1965-1967	3	
	1810/12	1968-1972	3	
60	**6314,0**	1954-1958	3-4	14 cm
600	**6314,00**	1959-1964	3	
181	**6314,00**	1965-1967	3	
	1810/14	1968-1969	3	
60	**6317,0**	1954-1958	3-4	17 cm
600	**6317,00**	1959-1964	3	
181	**6317,00**	1965-1967	3	
	1810/17	1968-1978	3	
60	**6322,0**	1954-1958	3-4	22 cm
600	**6322,00**	1960-1964	3	
181	**6322,00**	1965-1967	3	
	1810/22	1968-1973	3	

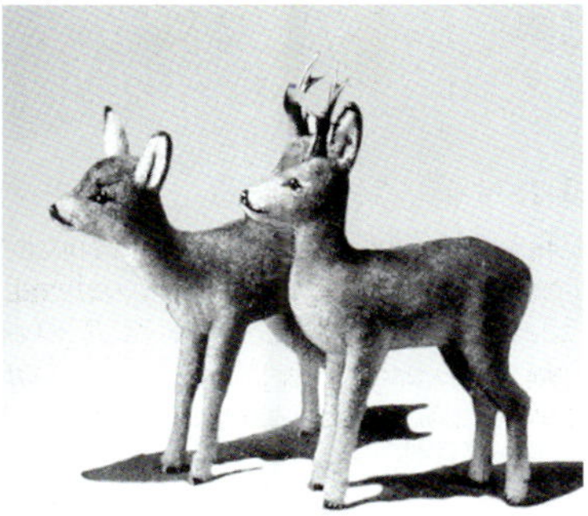

Rehbock / Rehgeiss - *Roebuck / Doe*

Wollpluesch (bis 1939 Wollmohair), braun verlaufend, stehend, ohne Raeder, Bock, 35 cm, mit Gehoern - *plush wool (up to 1939 wool mohair), brown, blended, standing, without wheels, buck, 35 cm, with antlers*

SERIE	ART.-NO	PERIOD	PR.	INFO
60	**1528,0**	1949-1953	4-5	28 cm
60	**1535,0**	1949-1953	4-5	35 cm

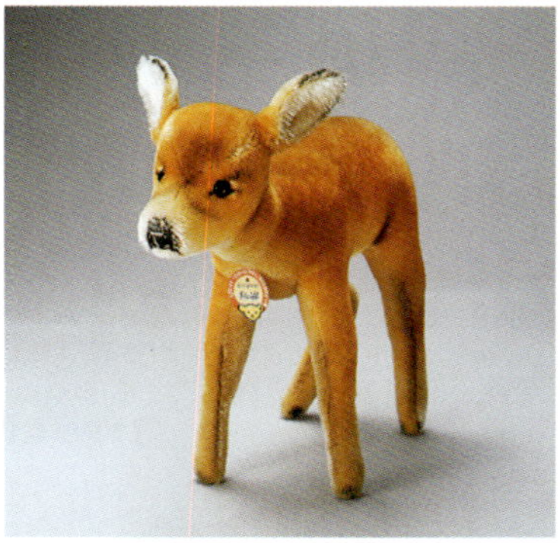

Rehgeiss - *Doe*

Mohair (bis 1953 Wollpluesch), hellbraun, stehend - *mohair (up to 1953 plush wool), light brown, standing*

SERIE	ART.-NO	PERIOD	PR.	INFO
60	**1328,0**	1954-1958	4	28 cm
600	**1328,00**	1959-1964	3-4	
182	**1328,00**	1965-1967	3-4	
	1820/28	1968-1970	3-4	

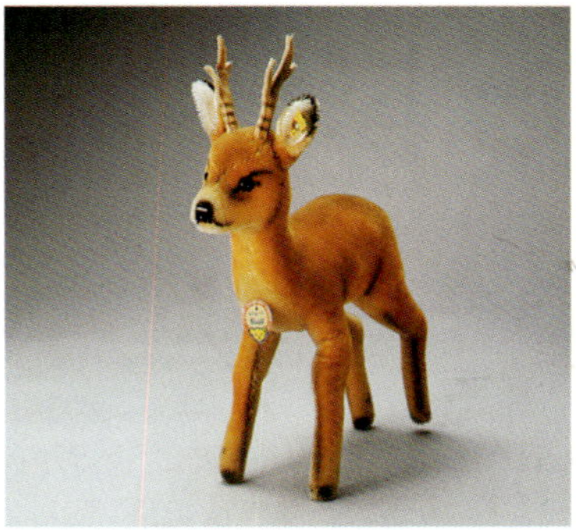

Rehbock - *Roebuck*

Mohair (bis 1953 Wollpluesch), hellbraun, stehend, abwaschbar - *mohair (up to 1953 plush wool), light brown, standing, surface washable*

SERIE	ART.-NO	PERIOD	PR.	INFO
60	**1335,0**	1954-1958	4	35 cm
600	**1335,00**	1959-1964	3-4	
182	**1335,00**	1965-1967	3-4	
	1820/35	1968-1974	3-4	

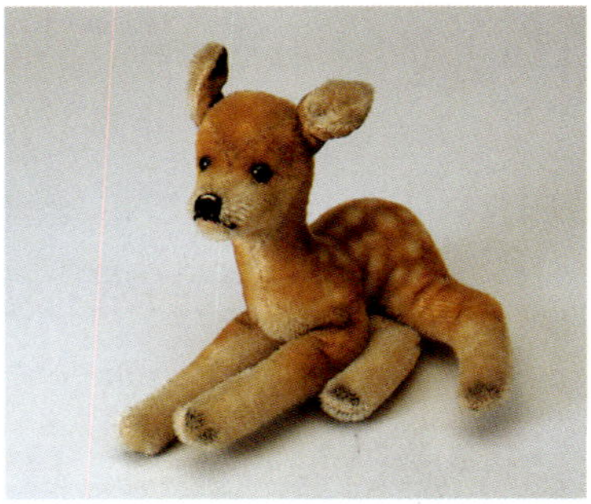

Reh - *Fawn*

Mohair, liegend - *mohair, lying*

SERIE	ART.-NO	PERIOD	PR.	INFO
60	**2314**	1954-1955	4-5	14 cm
60	**2317**	1954-1955	4-5	17 cm

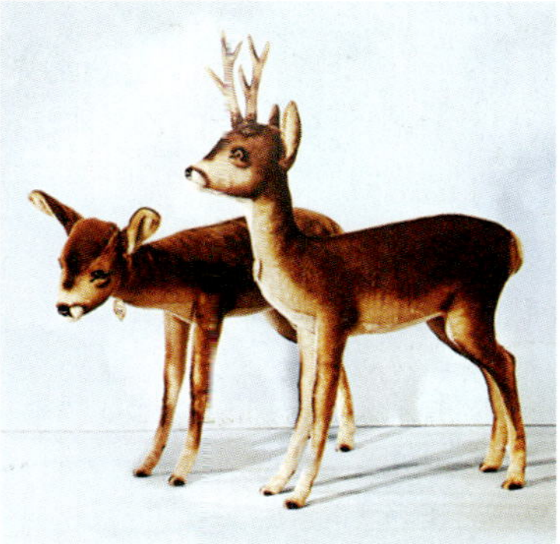

Rehgeiss / Rehbock - *Doe / Roebuck*

Schautiere, Wollpluesch, braun, stehend - *display animals, plush wool, brown, standing*

SERIE	ART.-NO	PERIOD	PR.	INFO
600	**1395,90**	1960-1960	6	95 cm
	1829/09	1967-1967	6	
600	**1399,90**	1960-1960	6	100 cm
	1829/10	1967-1967	6	

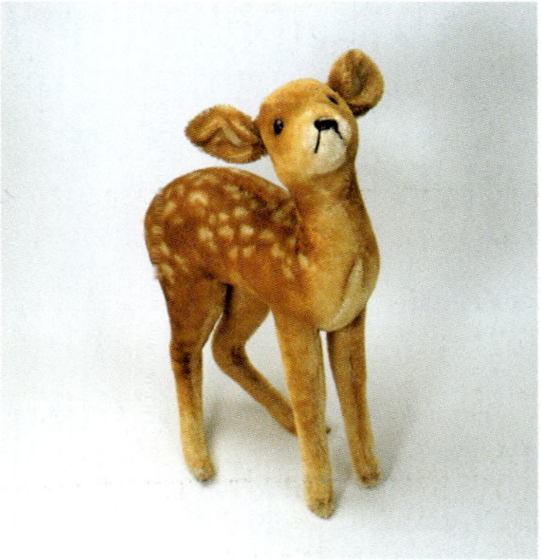

Rehkitz - *Fawn*

Schautier, Mohair, braun, weiss gepunktet, stehend - *display animal, mohair, brown, white dots, standing*

SERIE	ART.-NO	PERIOD	PR.	INFO
600	**6355,90**	1960-1960	5	55 cm
	1829/06	1967-1967	5	

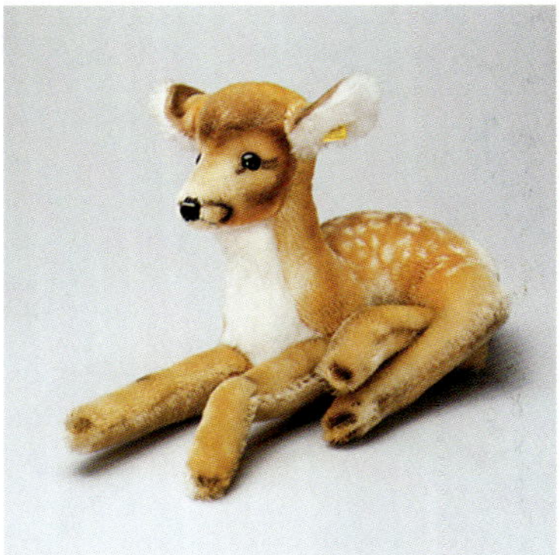

Rehkitz - *Fawn*

Mohair, braun, hell getupft, liegend, abwaschbar - *mohair, brown, light speckles, lying, surface washable*

SERIE	ART.-NO	PERIOD	PR.	INFO
182	**2335,00**	1965-1967	3	35 cm
	1823/35	1968-1975	3	

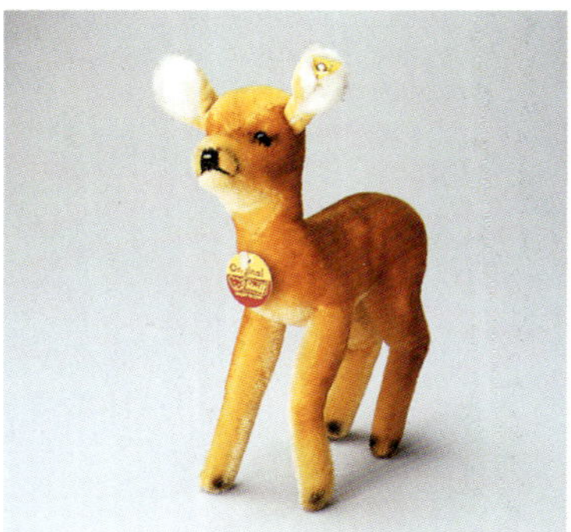

Rehgeiss - *Doe*

Mohair, stehend, abwaschbar - *mohair, standing, surface washable*

SERIE	ART.-NO	PERIOD	PR.	INFO
	1811/21	1971-1978	2-3	21 cm

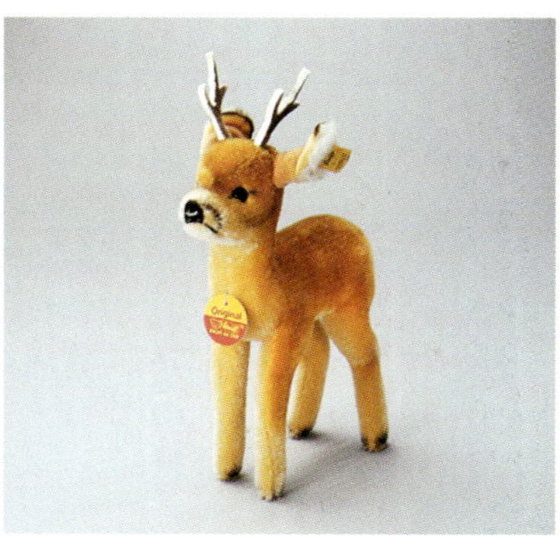

Rehbock ab 1975 **Boecky** - *Roebuck from 1975* ***Boecky***

Mohair, stehend, mit Gehoern, abwaschbar - *mohair, standing, with antlers, surface washable*

SERIE	ART.-NO	PERIOD	PR.	INFO
	1811/22	1971-1977	2-3	22 cm

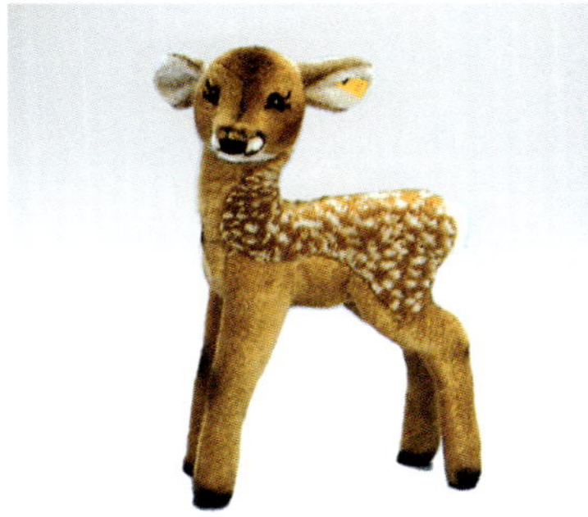

Elfi Reh - ***Elfi*** *Deer*

Webpelz, stehend, abwaschbar - *woven fur, standing, surface washable*

SERIE	ART.-NO	PERIOD	PR.	INFO
	1830/40	1978-1982	3	40 cm

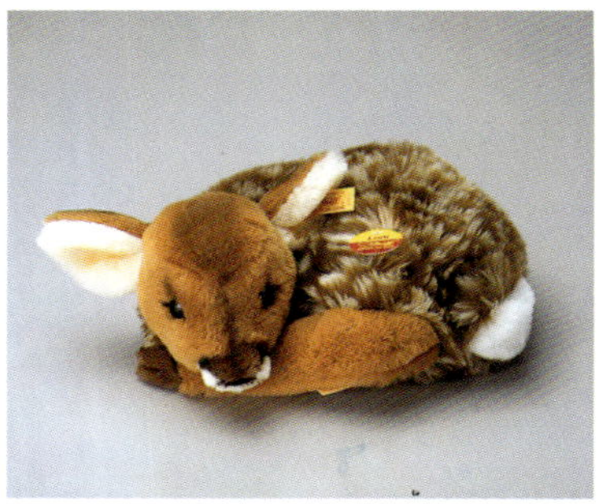

Lorli Rehkitz - ***Lorli*** *Fawn*

Wirkpelz, liegend, waschmaschinenfest - *knitted fur, lying, machine washable*

SERIE	ART.-NO	PERIOD	PR.	INFO
071171	**1831/20**	1988-1990	2	22 cm
	071171	1991-1999	2	

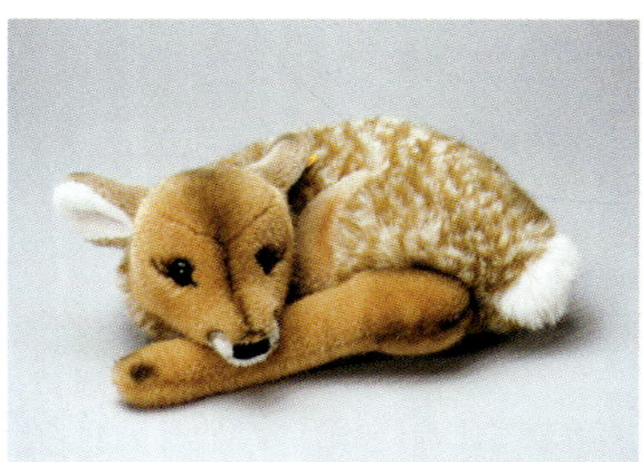

Lorli Reh - ***Lorli*** *Deer*

Webpelz, liegend, abwaschbar - *woven fur, lying, surface washable*

SERIE	ART.-NO	PERIOD	PR.	INFO
071188	**1831/38**	1978-1989	2	38 cm

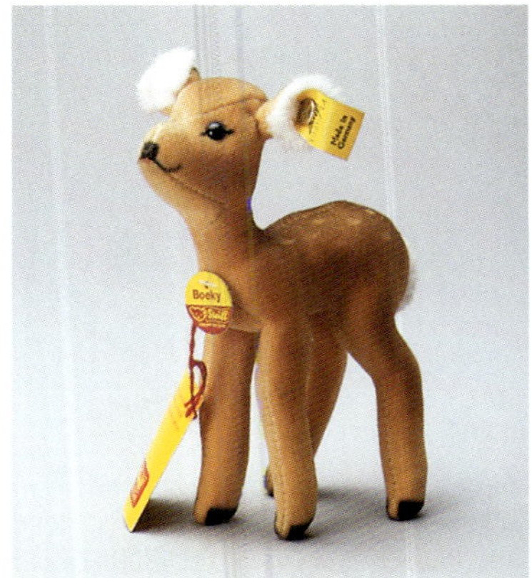

Boeky Rehkitz - ***Boeky*** *Fawn*

Trevira, stehend, abwaschbar - *trevira, standing, surface washable*

SERIE	ART.-NO	PERIOD	PR.	INFO
	1820/14	1980-1983	2	14 cm

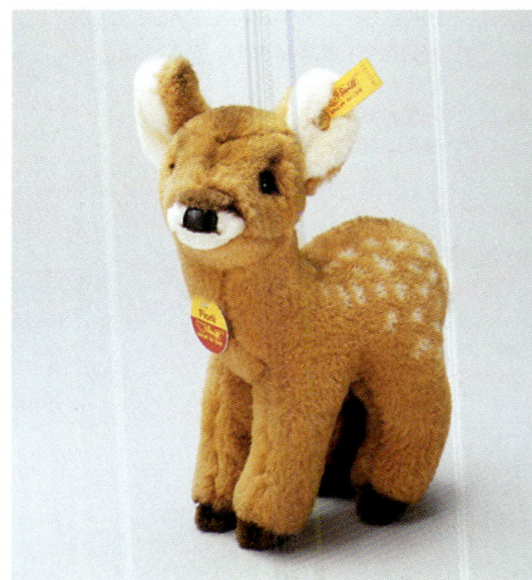

Florli Rehkitz - ***Florli*** *Fawn*

Wirkpelz, stehend, waschmaschinenfest - *knitted fur, standing, machine washable*

SERIE	ART.-NO	PERIOD	PR.	INFO
071003	**1835/22**	1988-1990	2	22 cm
	071003	1991-1993	2	

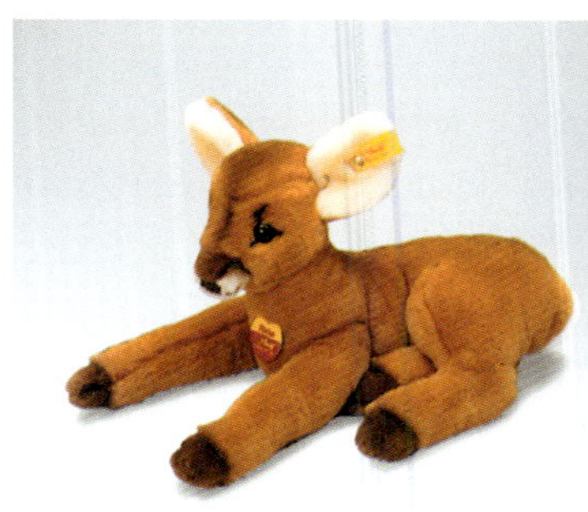

Rieke Reh - ***Rieke*** *Deer*

Webpelz, liegend, waschmaschinenfest - *woven fur, lying, machine washable*

SERIE	ART.-NO	PERIOD	PR.	INFO
071140	**1837/30**	1988-1990	2-3	30 cm

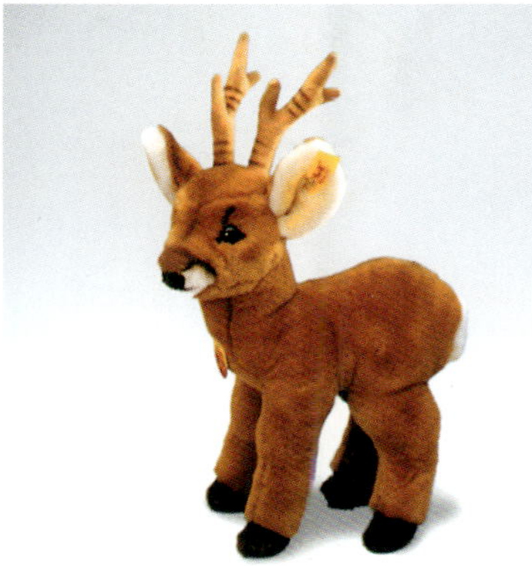

Boeky Rehbock - ***Boeky*** *Roebuck*

Webpelz, stehend, waschmaschinenfest - *woven fur, standing, machine washable*

SERIE	ART.-NO	PERIOD	PR.	INFO
071102	**1838/30**	1988-1990	2-3	30 cm

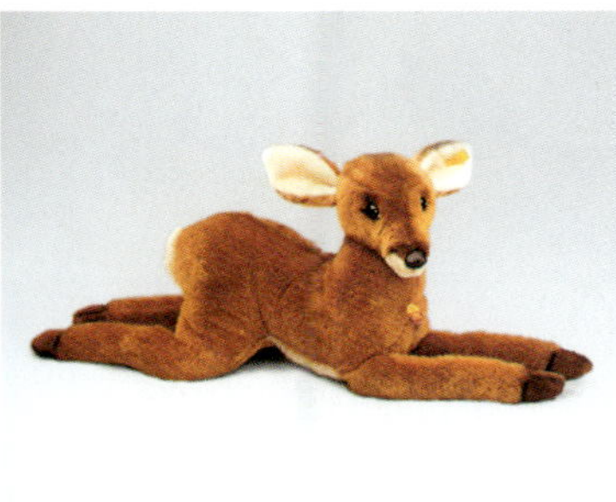

Molly Reh - *Molly Deer*

Webpelz, liegend, abwaschbar - *woven fur, lying, surface washable*

EAN-NO.	PERIOD	PR.	INFO
104602	1991-1992	3	60 cm

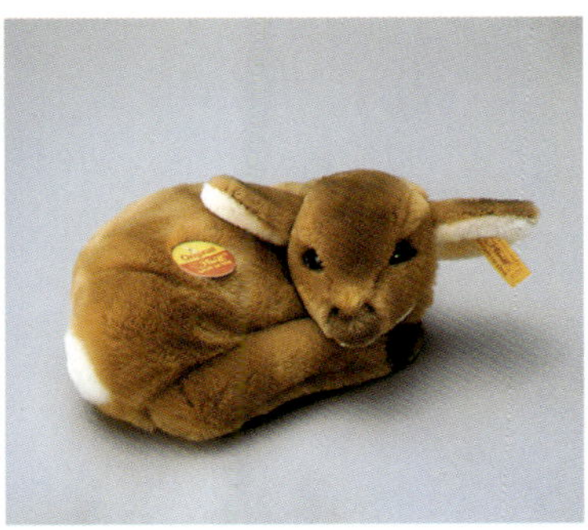

Ringelreh - *Curled Up Fawn*

Webpelz, liegend, waschmaschinenfest - *woven fur, lying, machine washable*

EAN-NO.	PERIOD	PR.	INFO
071157	1992-1997	2	18 cm

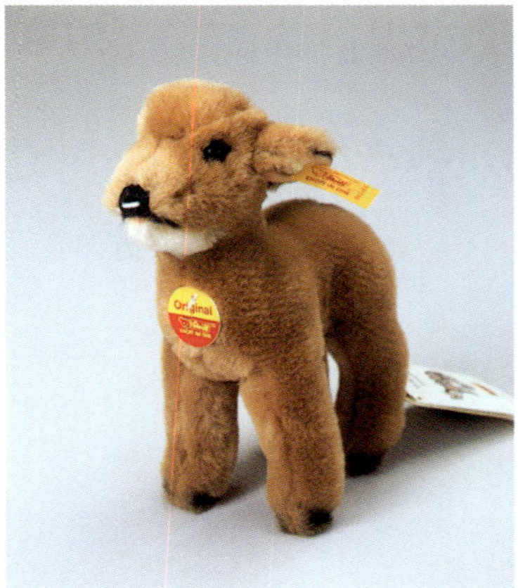

Reh - *Deer*

Webpelz, stehend, waschmaschinenfest - *woven fur, standing, machine washable*

EAN-NO.	PERIOD	PR.	INFO
045455	1996-1999	2	15 cm

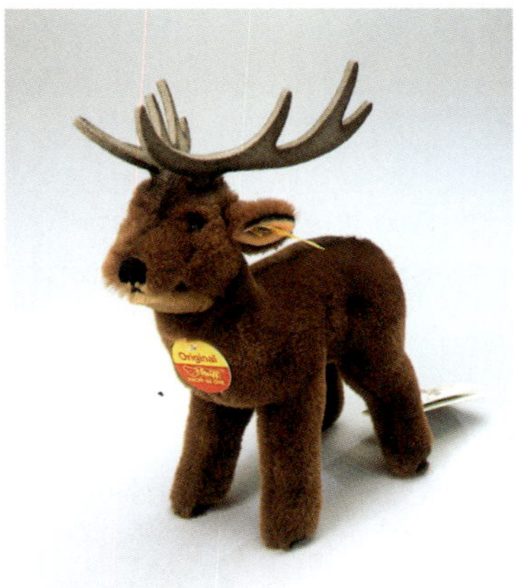

Hirsch - *Stag*

Webpelz, stehend, abwaschbar - *woven fur, standing, surface washable*

EAN-NO.	PERIOD	PR.	INFO
045479	1996-1998	2-3	18 cm

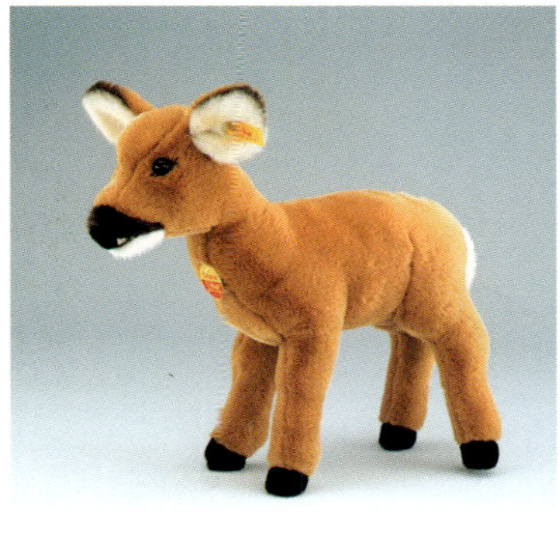

Reh - *Deer*

Webpelz, stehend, abwaschbar - *woven fur, standing, surface washable*

EAN-NO.	PERIOD	PR.	INFO
071010	1997-1998	2-3	35 cm

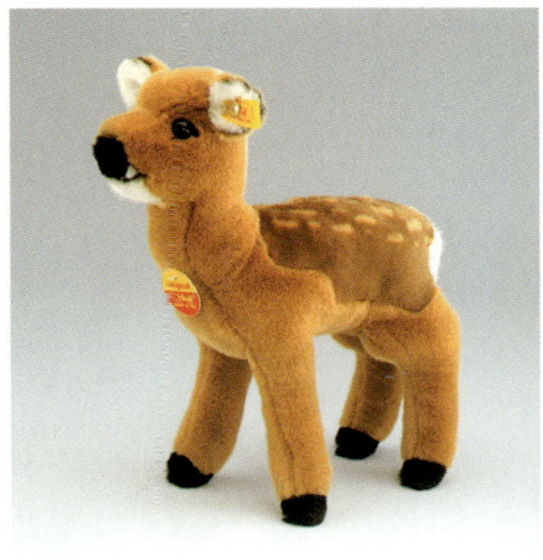

Rehkitz - *Fawn*

Webpelz, stehend, waschmaschinenfest - *woven fur, standing, machine washable*

EAN-NO.	PERIOD	PR.	INFO
071034	1997-1998	2-3	25 cm

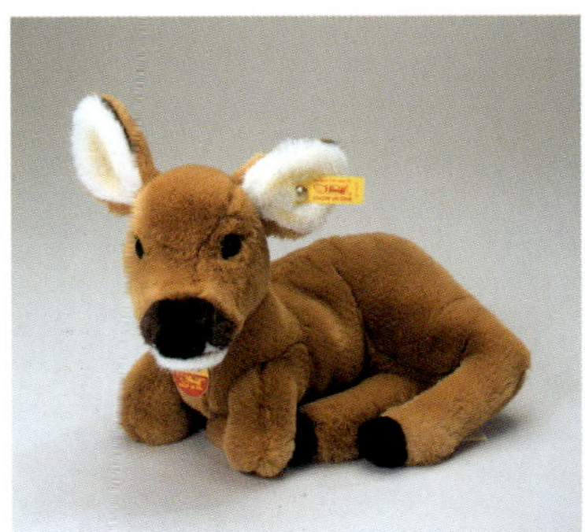

Reh - *Deer*

Webpelz, liegend, waschmaschinenfest - *woven fur, lying, machine washable*

EAN-NO.	PERIOD	PR.	INFO
071027	1997-1998	2-3	30 cm

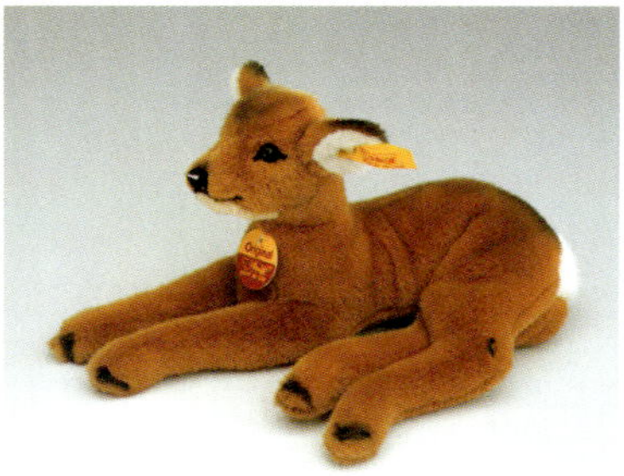

Reh - *Deer*

Webpelz, liegend, waschmaschinenfest - *woven fur, lying, machine washable*

EAN-No.	Period	Pr.	Info
071041	1999-1999	2-3	25 cm

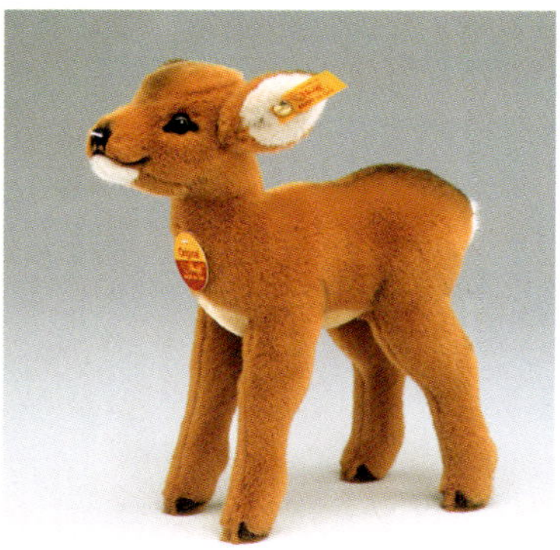

Reh - *Deer*

Webpelz, stehend, abwaschbar - *woven fur, standing, surface washable*

EAN-No.	Period	Pr.	Info
071058	1999-1999	2-3	25 cm

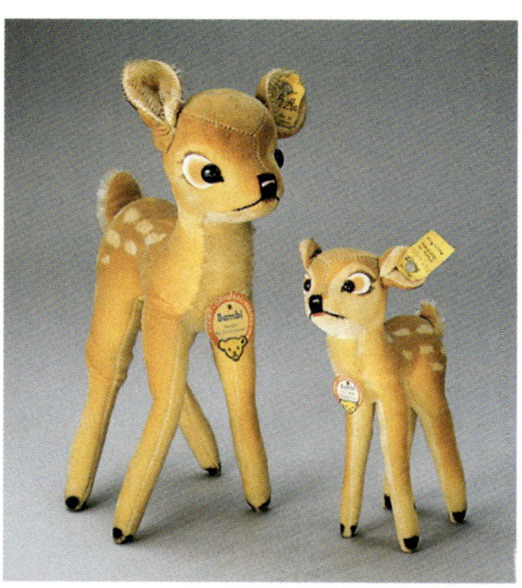

Bambi Reh - ***Bambi*** *Deer*

Samt, hellbraun getupft, stehend, Copyr. Walt Disney, dieser Artikel wurde nicht weltweit angeboten - *velvet, light brown with speckles, standing, Copyr. Walt Disney, this article was not sold worldwide*

Serie	Art.-No	Period	Pr.	Info
60	**7414,0**	1952-1958	3-4	14 cm
602	**7414,00**	1959-1964	3	
184	**7414,00**	1965-1967	3	
	1840/14	1968-1972	3	
60	**7422,0**	1951-1958	3-4	22 cm
602	**7422,00**	1959-1964	3	
184	**7422,00**	1966-1967	3	
	1840/22	1968-1972	3	

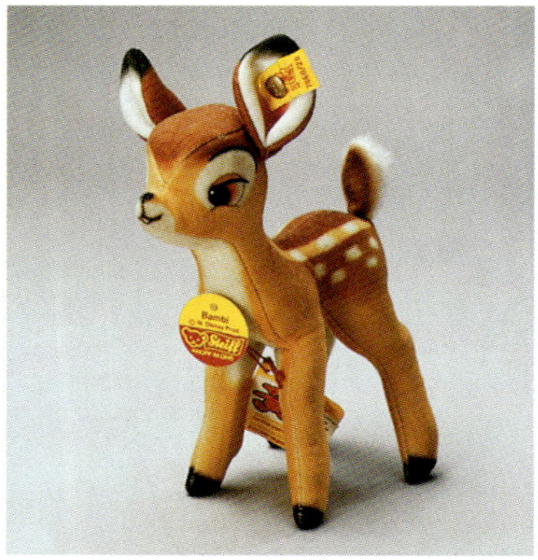

Bambi

Trevirasamt, stehend, abwaschbar - *trevira velvet, standing, surface washable*

Serie	Art.-No	Period	Pr.	Info
059506	**7860/20**	1984-1986	3	20 cm

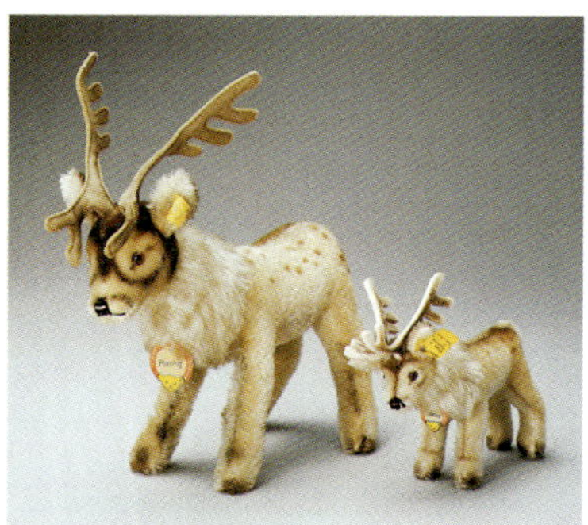

Renny Rentier - ***Renny*** *Reindeer*

Mohairpluesch, braun/weiss, stehend - *mohair, brown/white, standing*

Serie	Art.-No	Period	Pr.	Info
60a	**1314,0**	1956-1958	3-4	14 cm
603	**1314,00**	1959-1963	3-4	
185	**1314,00**	1965-1967	3-4	
	1850/14	1968-1970	3	
60a	**1322,0**	1956-1958	4	22 cm
603	**1322,00**	1959-1963	3-4	
185	**1322,00**	1965-1967	3-4	
	1850/22	1968-1970	3	

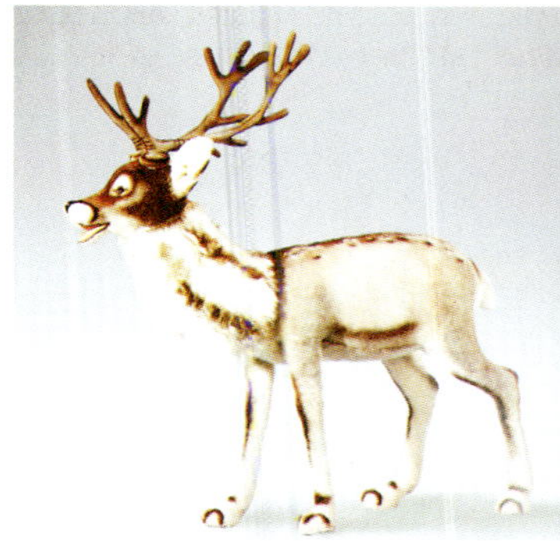

Rentier - *Reindeer*

Schautier, stehend - *display animal, standing*

Serie	Art.-No	Period	Pr.	Info
603	**1150,90**	1960-1960	6-7	150 cm
	1859/15	1967-1967	6-7	

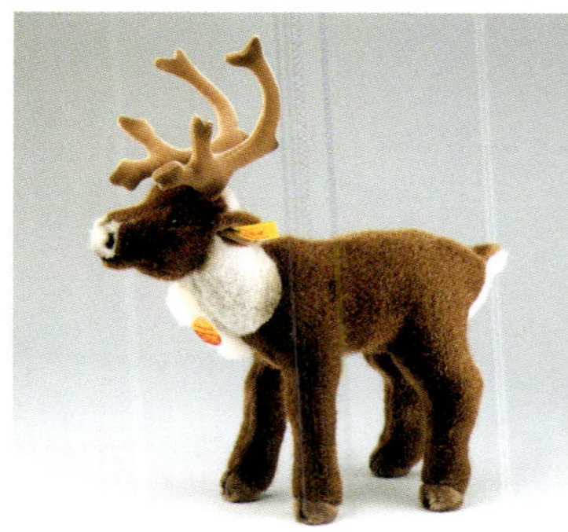

Karibu - *Caribou*

Webpelz, grau/braun, stehend, abwaschbar - *woven fur, grey/brown, standing, surface washable*

EAN-No.	Period	Pr.	Info
069208	1997-1998	3	32 cm

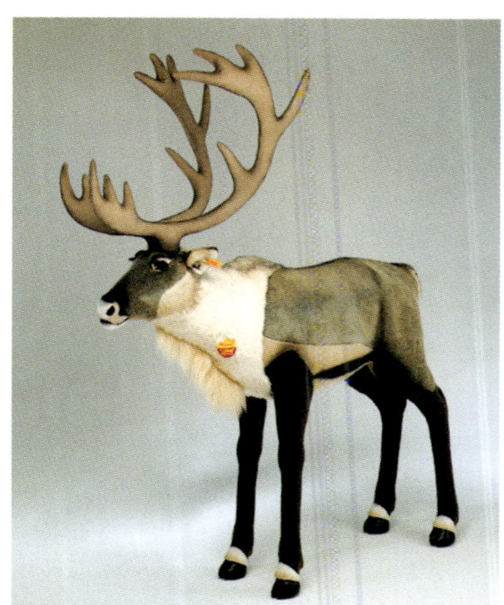

Rentier - *Reindeer*

Studio-Tier, Webpelz, stehend, abwaschbar - *studio-animal, woven fur, standing, washable*

EAN-No.	Period	Pr.	Info
524165	1999-1999	8	175 cm

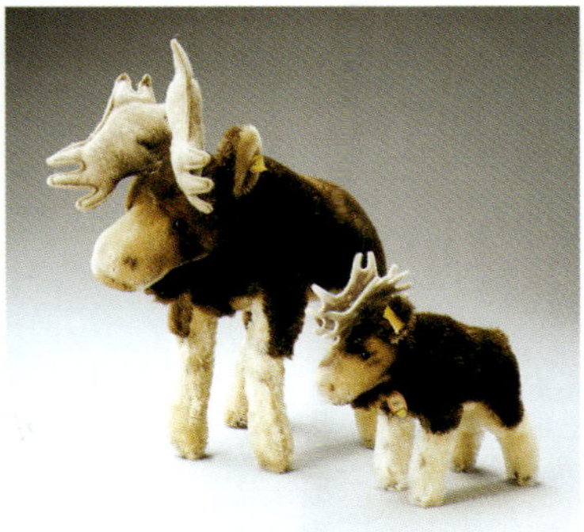

Moosy Elch - ***Moosy*** *Moose*

Mohairpluesch, braun/weiss, stehend, nur fuer USA - *mohair, brown/white, standing, only for USA*

Serie	Art.-No	Period	Pr.	Info
604	**1314,90**	1960-1960	4-5	14 cm
604	**1325,90**	1960-1960	5	25 cm

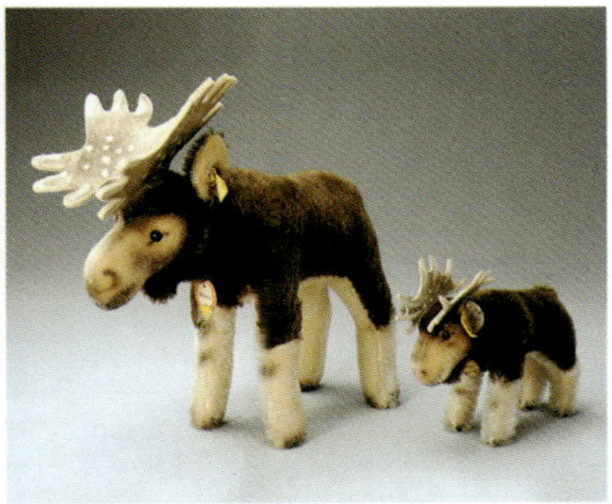

Moosy Elch - ***Moosy*** *Moose*

Mohairpluesch, braun/weiss, stehend - *mohair, brown/white, standing*

Serie	Art.-No	Period	Pr.	Info
604	**1314,00**	1963-1964	4-5	14 cm
604	**1325,00**	1963-1964	5	25 cm

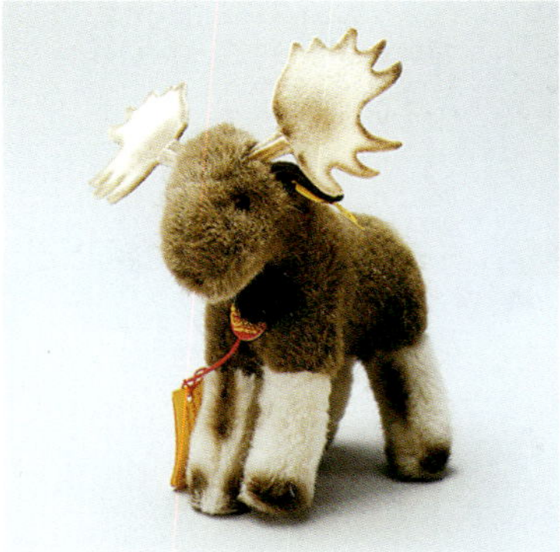

Mosy Elch - ***Mosy*** *Elk*

Webpelz, stehend, abwaschbar - *woven fur, standing, surface washable*

Serie	Art.-No	Period	Pr.	Info
	1457/14	1979-1982	2	14 cm

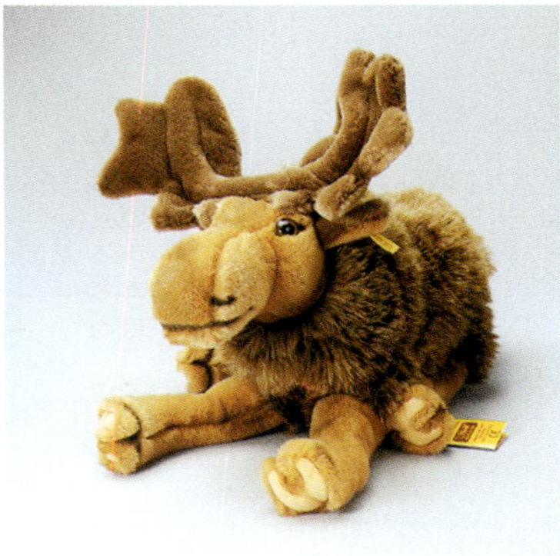

Molly Elch - ***Molly*** *Elk*

Webpelz, liegend, waschmaschinenfest - *woven fur, lying, machine washable*

Serie	Art.-No	Period	Pr.	Info
104558	**0420/40**	1989-1990	3	40 cm
	104558	1991-1996	3	

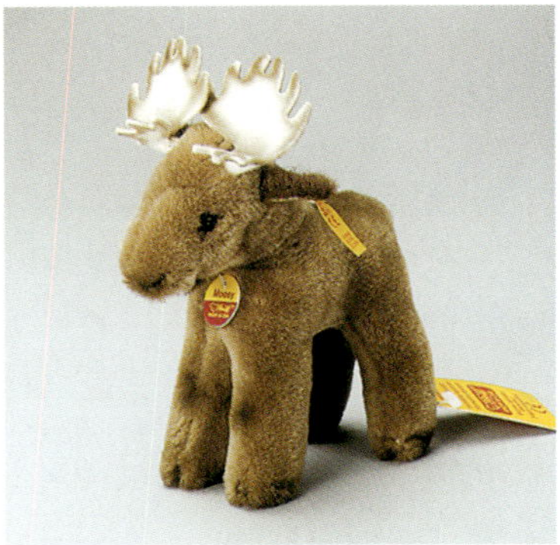

Moosy Elch - ***Moosy*** *Elk*

Webpelz, stehend, handwaschbar - *woven fur, standing, hand washable*

EAN-No.	Period	Pr.	Info
045004	1994-1997	2	16 cm

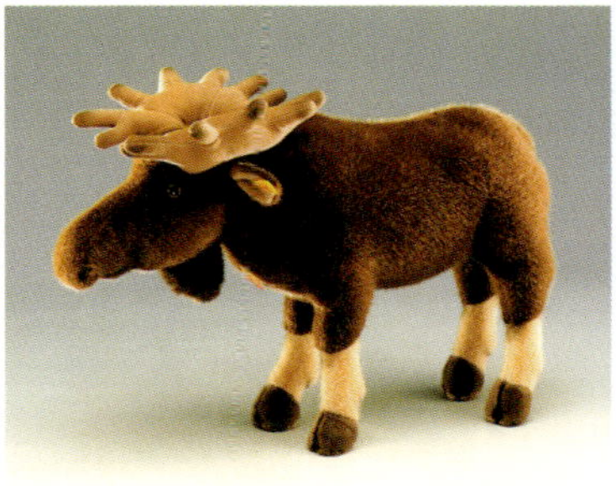

Elch - *Elk*

Webpelz, stehend, abwaschbar - *woven fur, standing, surface washable*

EAN-No.	Period	Pr.	Info
069185	1996-1996	3	42 cm

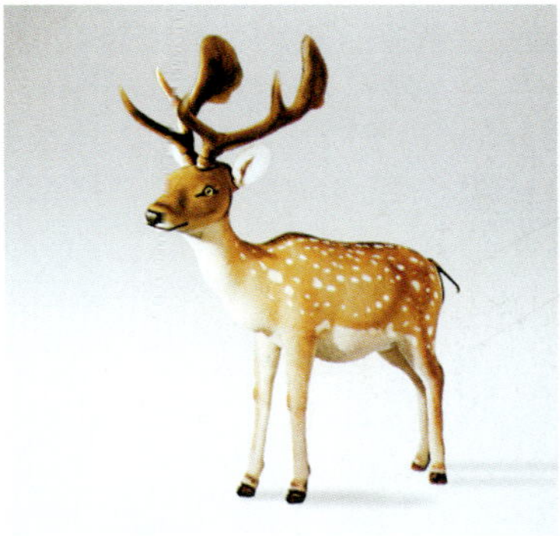

Damhirsch - *Fallow Deer*

Schautier, stehend - *display animal, standing*

Serie	Art.-No	Period	Pr.	Info
605	**1150,90**	1963-1963	6-7	150 cm
	1909/15	1967-1967	6-7	

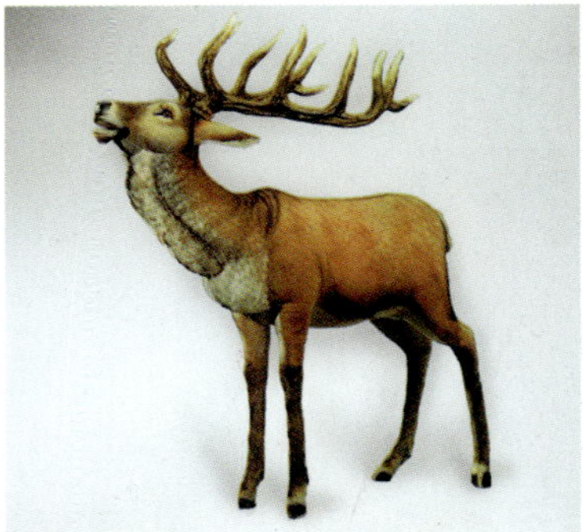

Rothirsch - *Red Stag*

Schautier, Mohair, rotbraun, stehend - *display animal, mohair, red-brown, standing*

Serie	Art.-No	Period	Pr.	Info
	1909/19	1967-1967	7	190 cm

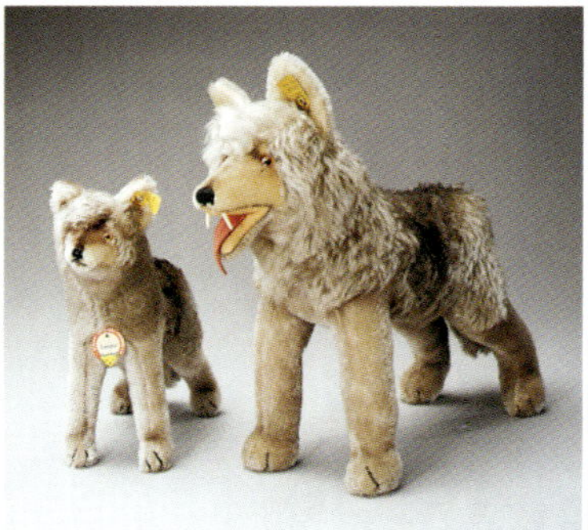

Loopy Wolf

Mohair, grau, stehend, 25 cm geschlossene, 35 cm offene Schnauze - *mohair, grey, standing, 25 cm muzzle closed, 35 cm muzzle open*

SERIE	ART.-NO	PERIOD	PR.	INFO
612	**1325,00**	1964-1964	6-7	25 cm
612	**1335,00**	1964-1964	7	35 cm

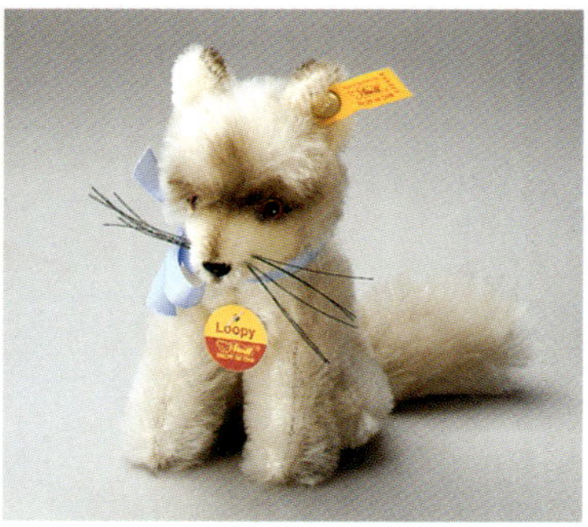

Loopy Wolf

Mohair Webpelz, sitzend, Kopf drehbar, abwaschbar - *mohair woven fur, sitting, head swivels, surface washable*

EAN-NO.	PERIOD	PR.	INFO
032455	1991-1993	2	12 cm

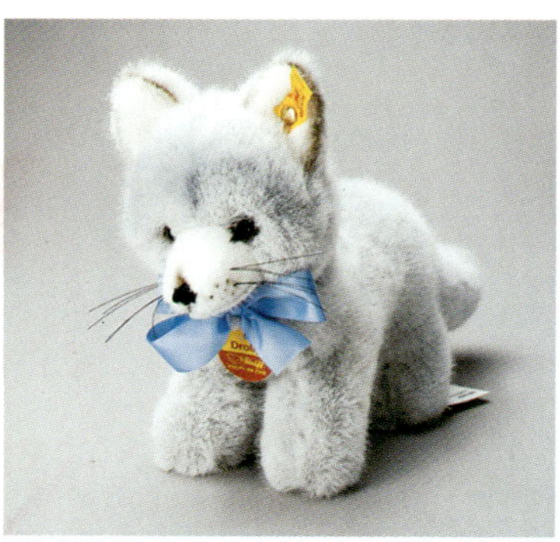

Drolly Wolf

Webpelz, stehend, waschmaschinenfest - *woven fur, standing, machine washable*

EAN-NO.	PERIOD	PR.	INFO
081552	1991-1993	1-2	22 cm

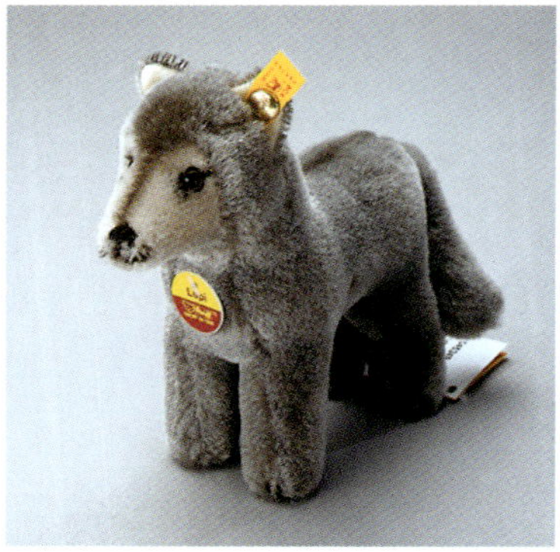

Lupi Wolf

Webpelz, stehend, handwaschbar - *woven fur, standing, hand washable*

EAN-NO.	PERIOD	PR.	INFO
045349	1994-1995	1-2	18 cm

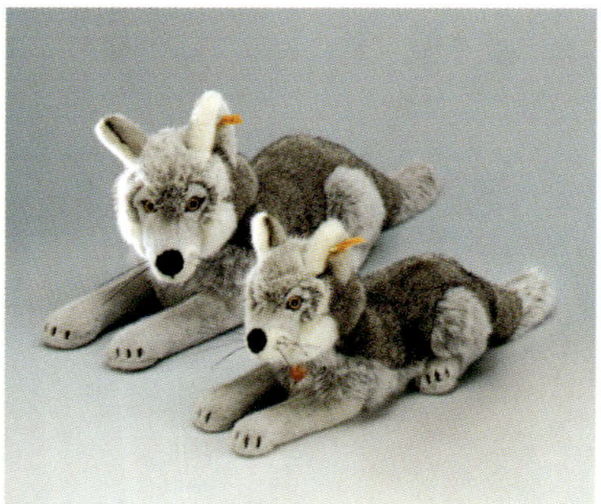

Jungwolf - *Young Wolf*

Webpelz, grau, liegend, waschmaschinenfest - *woven fur, grey, lying, machine washable*

EAN-NO.	PERIOD	PR.	INFO
069253	1996-1997	3	45 cm

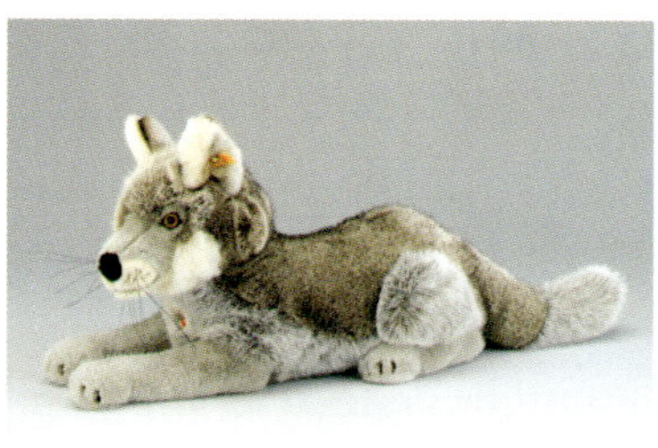

Wolf

Webpelz, grau, liegend, handwaschbar - *woven fur, grey, lying, hand washable*

EAN-NO.	PERIOD	PR.	INFO
069260	1996-1998	3-4	60 cm

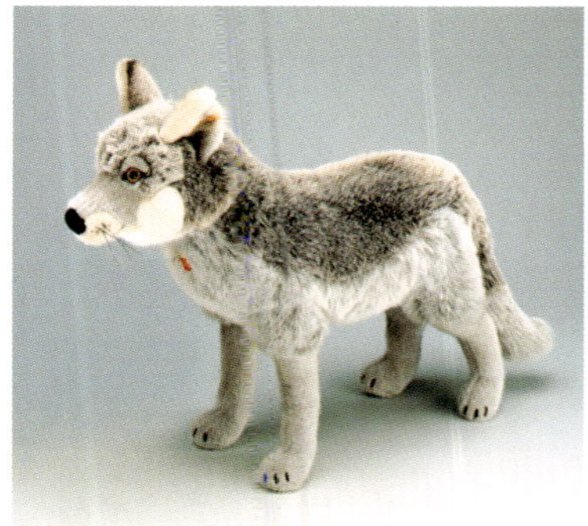

Wolf

Webpelz, grau, stehend, abwaschbar - *woven fur, grey, standing, surface washable*

EAN-NO.	PERIOD	PR.	INFO
069222	1996-1998	4	60 cm

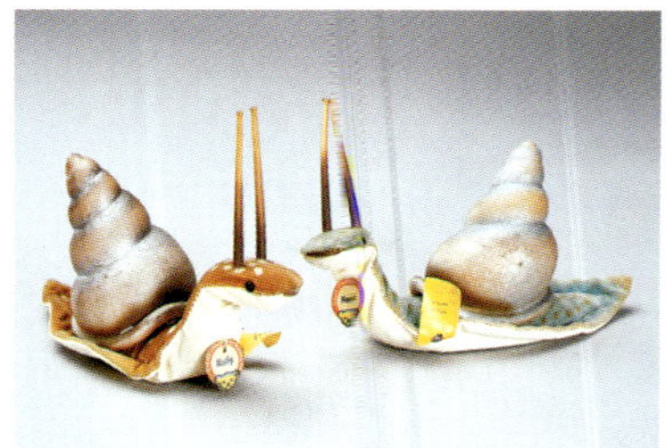

Nelly Schnecke - *Nelly Snail*

Samt, Haus aus Plastik, gefleckt, 10 cm, liegend - *velvet body, plastic shell, speckled, 10 cm, lying*

SERIE	ART.-NO	PERIOD	PR.	INFO
653	**2410,03**	1961-1963	5	braun - *brown*
653	**2410,09**	1961-1963	5	gruen - *green*

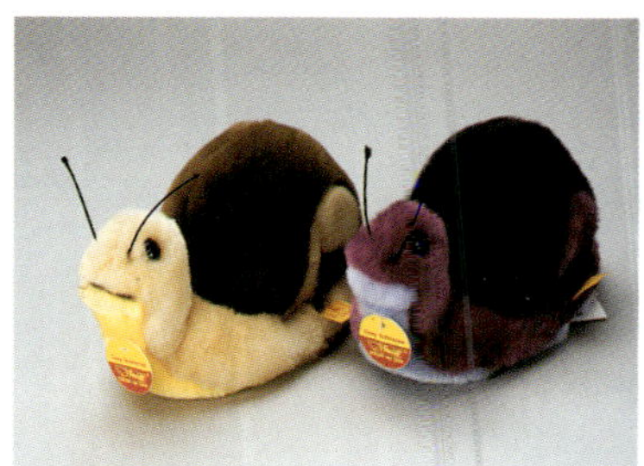

Cosy Schnecke - *Cosy Snail*

Webpelz, 20 cm, waschmaschinenfest - *woven fur, 20 cm, machine washable*

SERIE	ART.-NO	PERIOD	PR.	INFO
094866	**5432/20**	1988-1990	1-2	aubergine
	094866	1991-1995	1-2	
094880	**5434/20**	1988-1990	1-2	braun - *brown*
	094880	1991-1996	1-2	

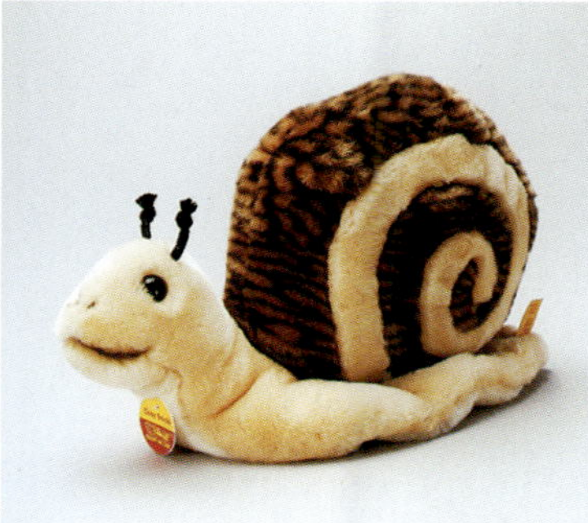

Cosy Snicki Schnecke - ***Cosy Snicki*** *Snail*

Webpelz, 28 cm, waschmaschinenfest - *woven fur, 28 cm, machine washable*

EAN-No.	Period	Pr.	Info
094910	1993-1994	2	lila - *lavender*
094927	1993-1995	2	braun - *brown*

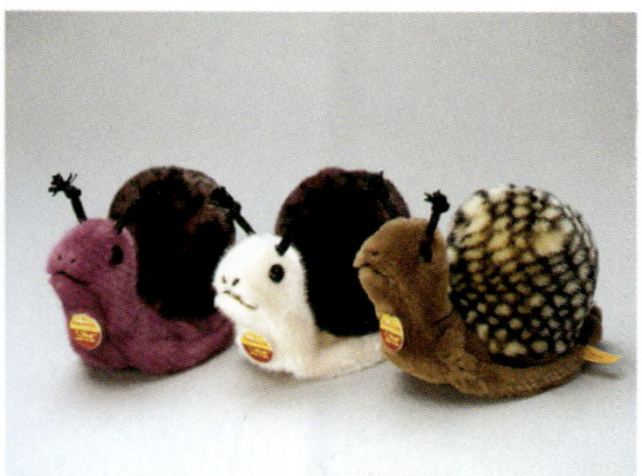

Cosy Snickili Schnecke - ***Cosy Snickili*** *Snail*

Webpelz, 16 cm, waschmaschinenfest - *woven fur, 16 cm, machine washable*

EAN-No.	Period	Pr.	Info
094934	1994-1995	1	gelb-braun - *yellow-brown*
094941	1994-1996	1	rosè-violett - *rose-violet*
094958	1994-1996	1	aubergine-pflaume - *purple-plum*
094972	1994-1995	1	braun-gelb - *brown-yellow*
094996	1994-1995	1	beige-gruen - *beige-green*
095016	1994-1995	1	dunkelblau-hellblau - *dark blue-light blue*

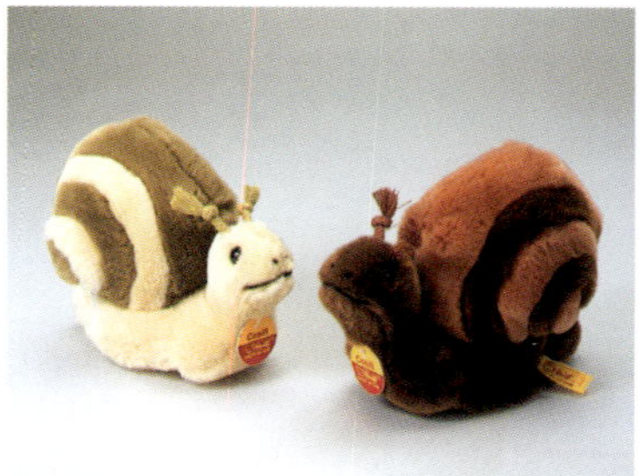

Cosili Schnecke - ***Cosili*** *Snail*

Webpelz, 16 cm, waschmaschinenfest - *woven fur, 16 cm, machine washable*

EAN-No.	Period	Pr.	Info
094811	1999-1999	1-2	braun - *brown*
094835	1999-1999	1-2	beige

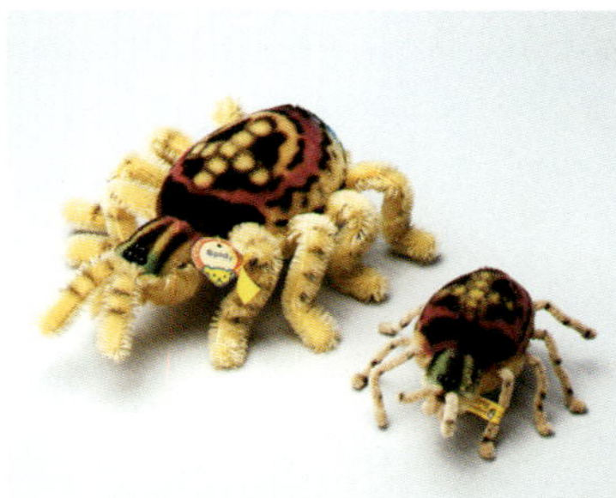

Spidy Spinne - ***Spidy*** *Spider*

Mohair, stehend - *mohair, standing*

Serie	Art.-No	Period	Pr.	Info
655	**2312,00**	1960-1961	5	12 cm
655	**2322,00**	1960-1961	5-6	22 cm

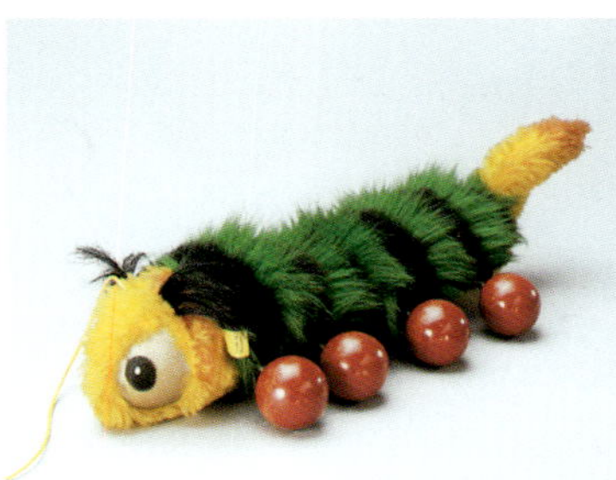

Nachziehraupe - *Pull Toy Caterpillar*

Wirkpelz, gruen/schwarz, Kopf & Schwanz gelb, auf 4 Raederpaaren, abwaschbar - *knitted fur, green/black, head & tail yellow, on four pairs of wheels, surface washable*

Serie	Art.-No	Period	Pr.	Info
	6424/43	1980-1983	3	43 cm

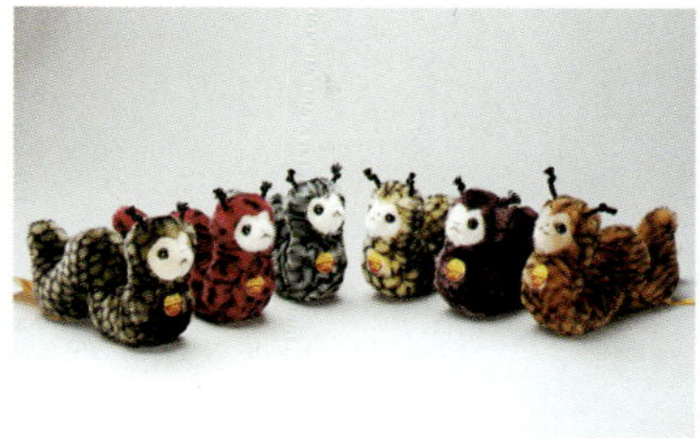

Cosy Fluppy Raupe - ***Cosy Fluppy*** *Caterpillar*

Webpelz, 20 cm, waschmaschinenfest - *woven fur, 20 cm, machine washable*

EAN-No.	Period	Pr.	Info
091407	1995-1997	1	rot - *red*
091414	1995-1997	1	gelb - *yellow*
091421	1995-1996	1	gruen - *green*
091438	1995-1996	1	blau - *blue*
091445	1995-1996	1	aubergine
091452	1995-1997	1	braun - *brown*

Wassertiere & Vögel

Aquatic animals & Birds

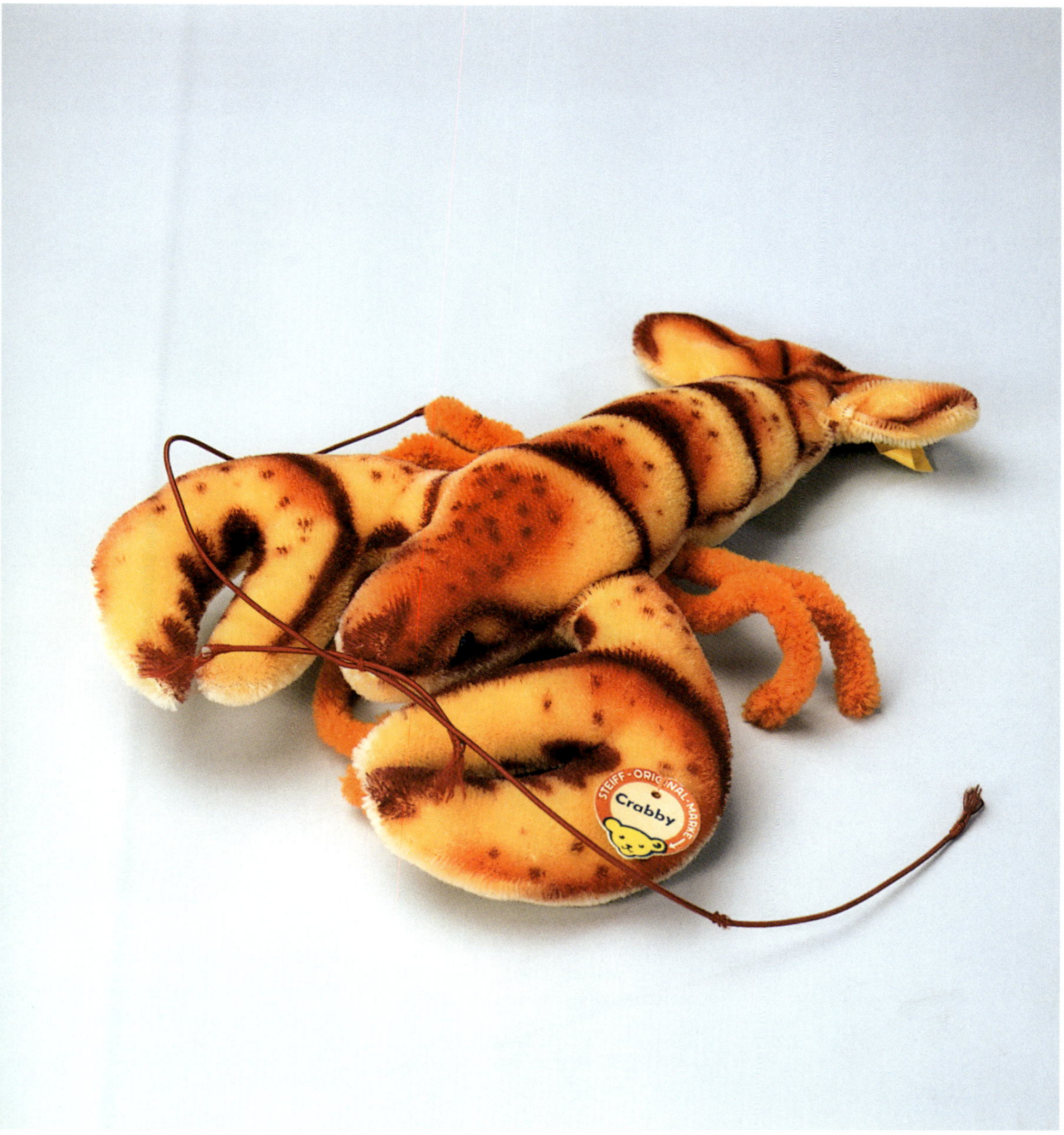

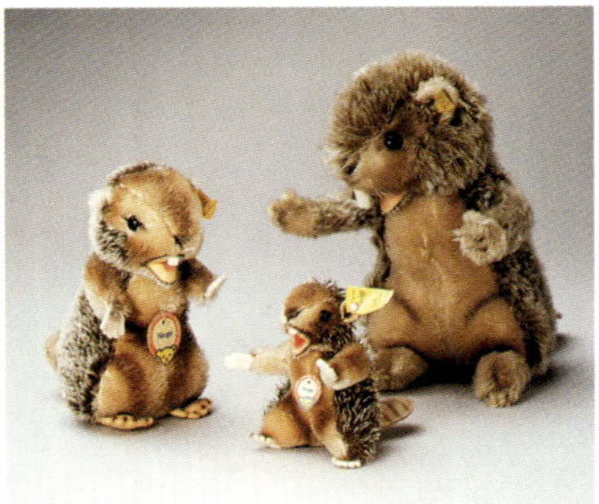

Nagy Biber - ***Nagy*** *Beaver*

Mohairpluesch/Igel-Mohair, naturfarben, aufwartend, Kopf drehbar, abwaschbar - *mohair/spiky mohair, natural color, sitting up, head swivels, surface washable*

SERIE	ART.-NO	PERIOD	PR.	INFO
19a	**4310**	1958-1958	3-4	10 cm
194	**4310,00**	1959-1964	3	
212	**4310,00**	1965-1967	3	
	2120/10	1968-1978	2-3	
19a	**4317**	1958-1958	3-4	17 cm
194	**4317,00**	1959-1964	3	
212	**4317,00**	1965-1967	3	
	2120/17	1968-1978	3	
194	**4325,00**	1960-1964	3-4	25 cm
212	**4325,00**	1965-1966	3-4	

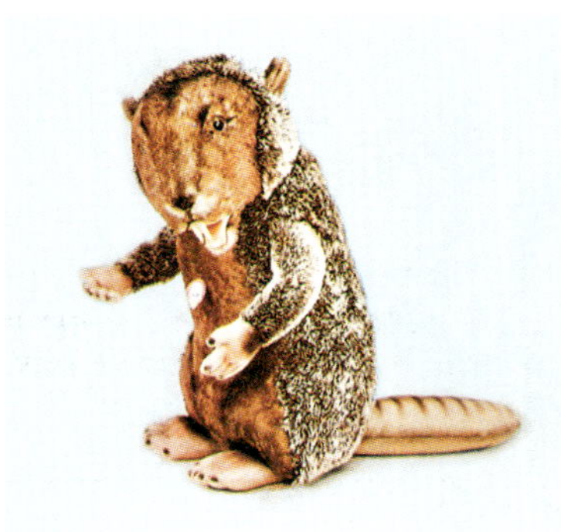

Biber - *Beaver*

Schautier, Mohair, aufwartend - *display animal, mohair, sitting up*

SERIE	ART.-NO	PERIOD	PR.	INFO
194	**4385,90**	1960-1960	5-6	90 cm
	2129/09	1967-1967	5-6	

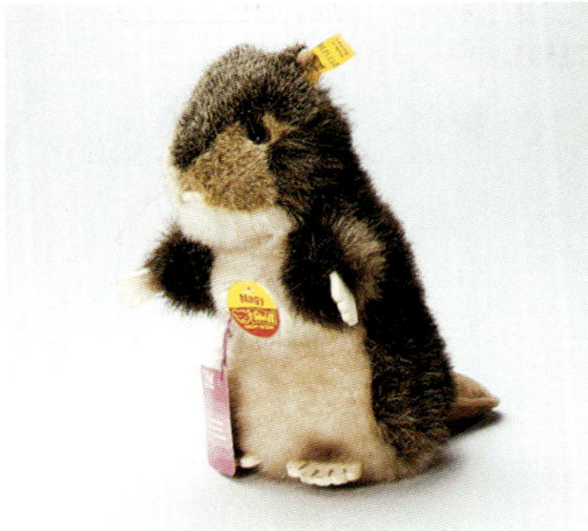

Nagy Biber - ***Nagy*** *Beaver*

Nerzimitation, ab 1978 Synthetik-Wirkpelz, aufwartend, abwaschbar - *imitation mink, from 1978 synthetic knitted fur, sitting up, surface washable*

SERIE	ART.-NO	PERIOD	PR.	INFO
	2121/18	1977-1980	2	18 cm

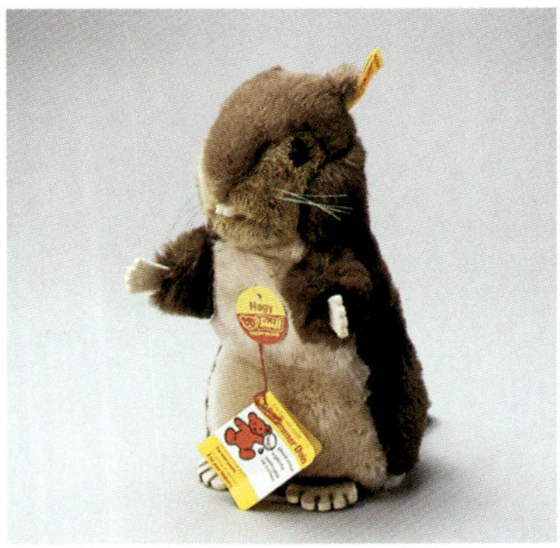

Nagy Biber - ***Nagy*** *Beaver*

Webpelz, aufwartend, abwaschbar - *woven fur, sitting up, surface washable*

SERIE	ART.-NO	PERIOD	PR.	INFO
	2125/20	1981-1985	2	20 cm

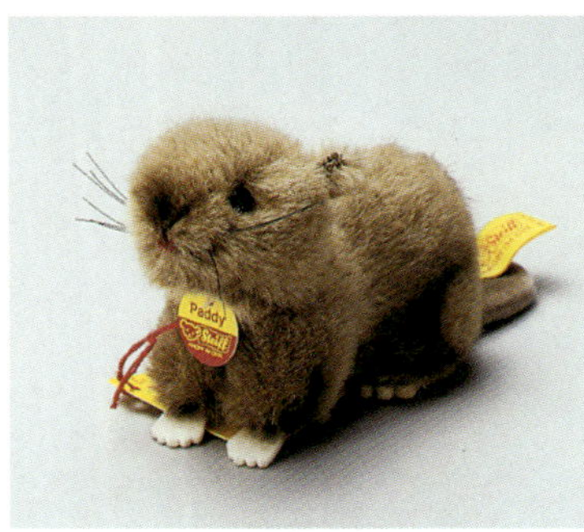

Paddy Biber - ***Paddy*** *Beaver*

Webpelz, stehend, abwaschbar - *woven fur, standing, surface washable*

SERIE	ART.-NO	PERIOD	PR.	INFO
045509	**1470/12**	1981-1989	2	12 cm

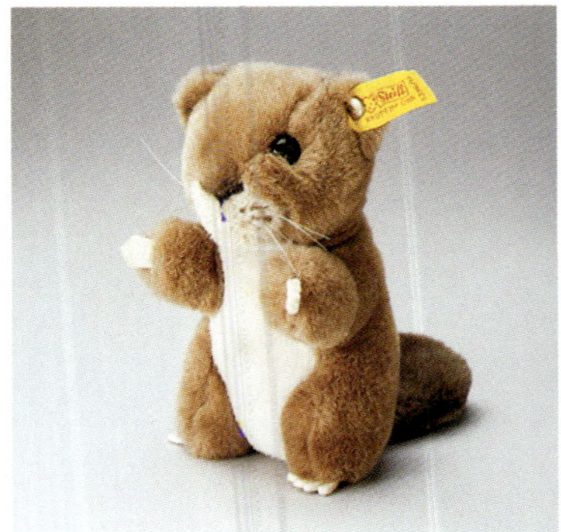

Cosy Nagy Biber - ***Cosy Nagy*** *Beaver*

Webpelz, waschmaschinenfest - *woven fur, machine washable*

SERIE	ART.-NO	PERIOD	PR.	INFO
093524	**5396/17**	1986-1990	2	17 cm
	093524	1991-1996	2	
093548	**5396/22**	1986-1988	2	22 cm

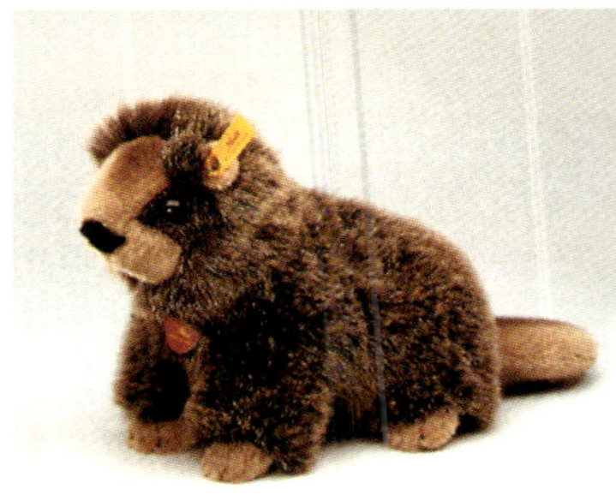

Paddy Biber - ***Paddy*** *Beaver*

Webpelz, stehend, abwaschbar - *woven fur, standing, surface washable*

EAN-NO.	PERIOD	PR.	INFO
071560	1991-1992	2	25 cm

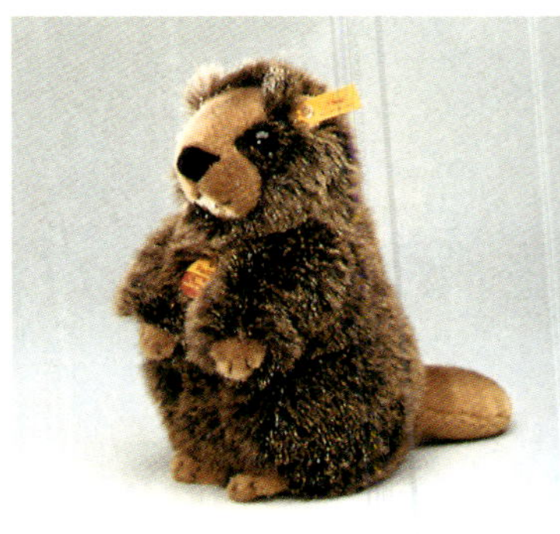

Paddy Biber - ***Paddy*** *Beaver*

Webpelz, aufwartend, abwaschbar - *woven fur, sitting up, surface washable*

EAN-NO.	PERIOD	PR.	INFO
071584	1991-1993	2-3	27 cm

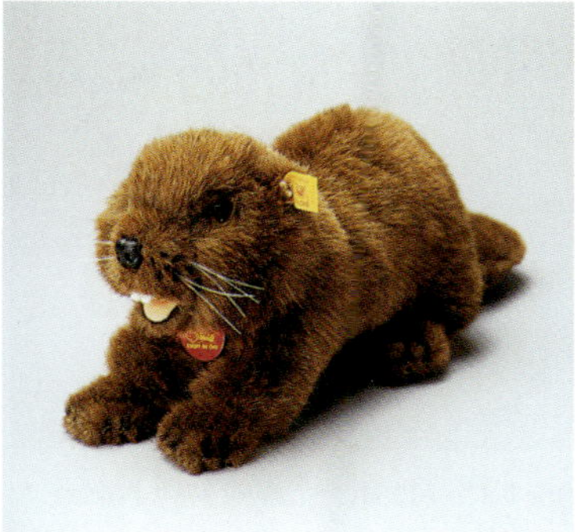

Nagy Biber - ***Nagy*** *Beaver*

Webpelz, stehend, waschmaschinenfest - *woven fur, standing, machine washable*

EAN-No.	Period	Pr.	Info
071539	1993-1998	2-3	25 cm
071553	1993-1998	3	30 cm

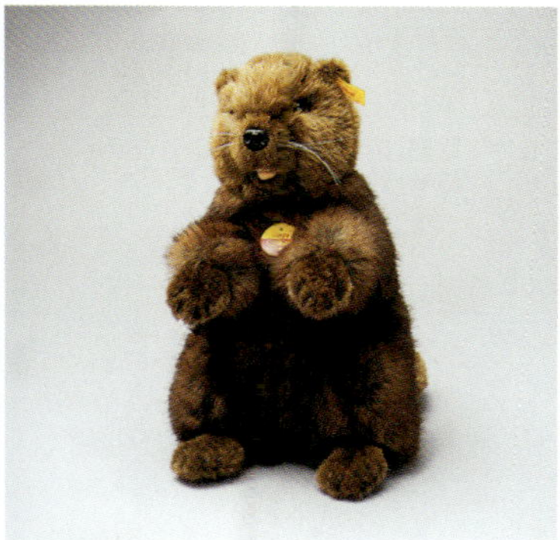

Nagy Biber - ***Nagy*** *Beaver*

Webpelz, aufwartend, waschmaschinenfest - *woven fur, sitting up, machine washable*

EAN-No.	Period	Pr.	Info
071577	1993-1996	3	30 cm

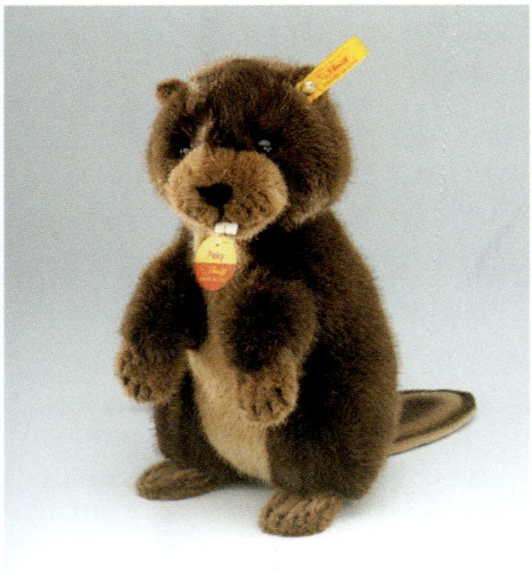

Peky Biber - ***Peky*** *Beaver*

Webpelz, braun, aufwartend, Kopf drehbar, waschmaschinenfest - *woven fur, brown, sitting up, head turnable, machine washable*

EAN-No.	Period	Pr.	Info
071591	1998-1998	2-3	25 cm

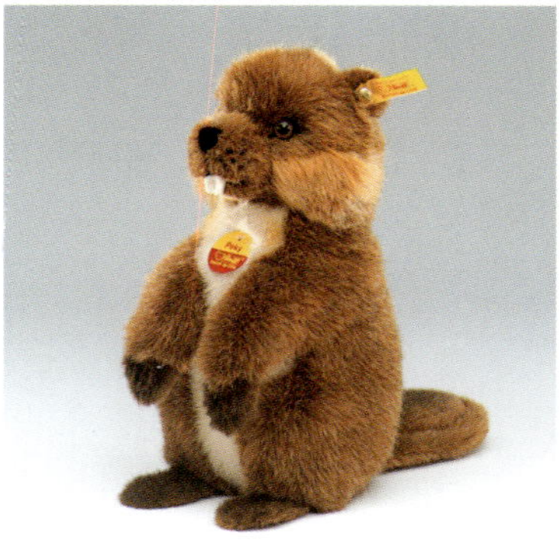

Peky Biber - ***Peky*** *Beaver*

Webpelz, aufwartend, waschmaschinenfest - *woven fur, sitting up, machine washable*

EAN-No.	Period	Pr.	Info
076251	1999-1999	2-3	25 cm

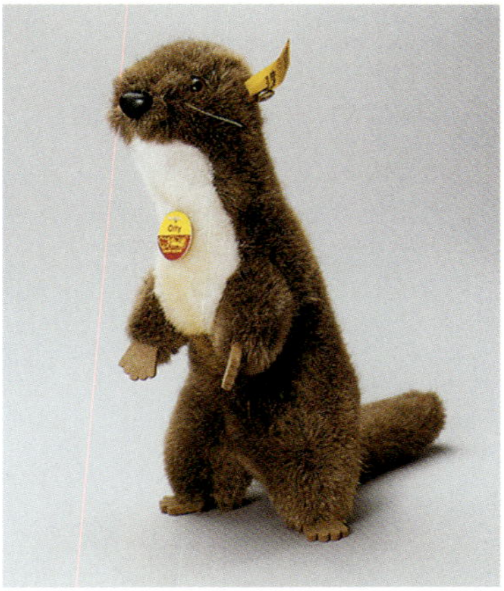

Otty Fischotter - ***Otty*** *Otter*

Webpelz, aufwartend, abwaschbar - *woven fur, sitting up, surface washable*

Serie	Art.-No	Period	Pr.	Info
	2160/20	1979-1982	3-4	20 cm

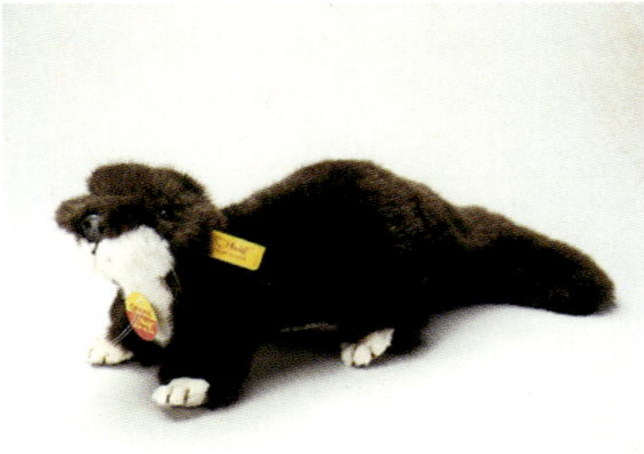

Putsi Fischotter - ***Putsi*** *Otter*

Webpelz, stehend, abwaschbar - *woven fur, standing, surface washable*

Serie	Art.-No	Period	Pr.	Info
071409	**2040/25**	1987-1988	3-4	25 cm

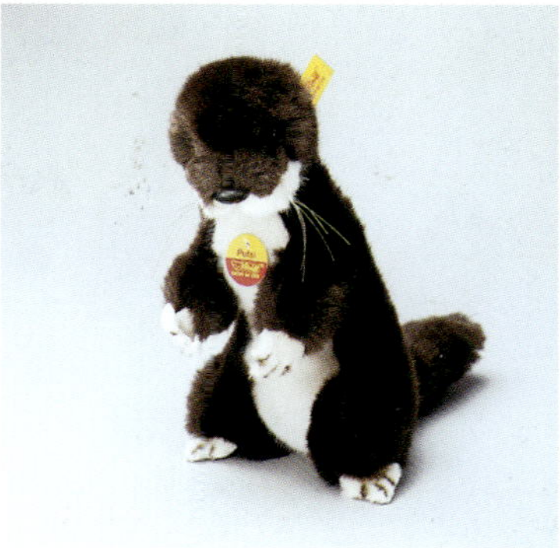

Putsi Fischotter - ***Putsi*** *Otter*

Webpelz, aufwartend, abwaschbar - *woven fur, sitting up, surface washable*

Serie	Art.-No	Period	Pr.	Info
071430	**2045/25**	1987-1988	3-4	25 cm

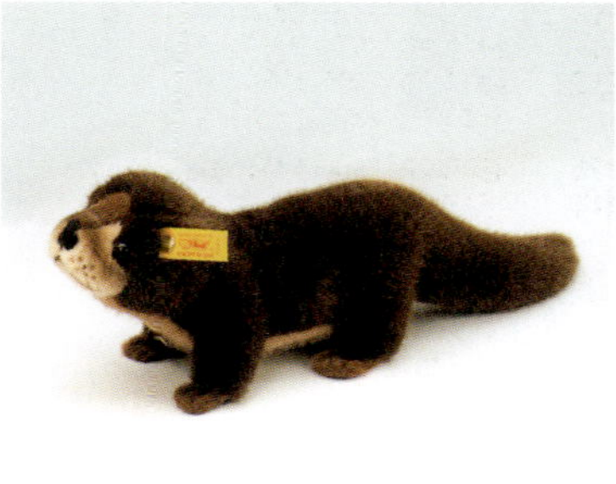

Baby Fischotter - *Baby Otter*

Webpelz, dunkelbraun, stehend, waschmaschinenfest - *woven fur, dark brown, standing, machine washable*

EAN-No.	Period	Pr.	Info
071942	1996-1997	2	22 cm

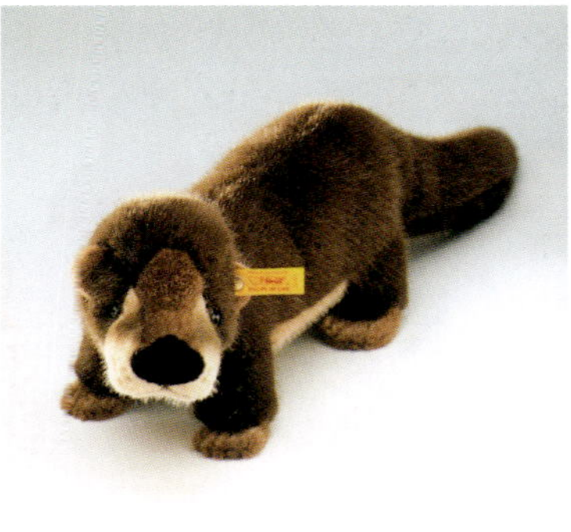

Fischotter - *Otter*

Webpelz, dunkelbraun, stehend, waschmaschinenfest - *woven fur, dark brown, standing, machine washable*

EAN-No.	Period	Pr.	Info
071959	1996-1997	2-3	32 cm

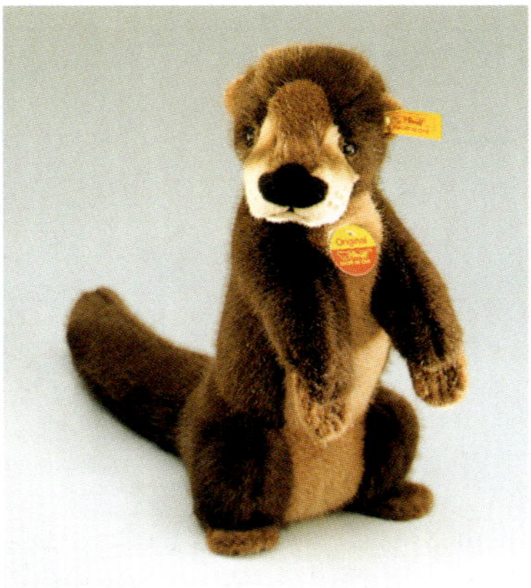

Fischotter - *Otter*

Webpelz, dunkelbraun, aufwartend, waschmaschinenfest - *woven fur, dark brown, sitting up, machine washable*

EAN-No.	Period	Pr.	Info
071966	1996-1998	2-3	32 cm

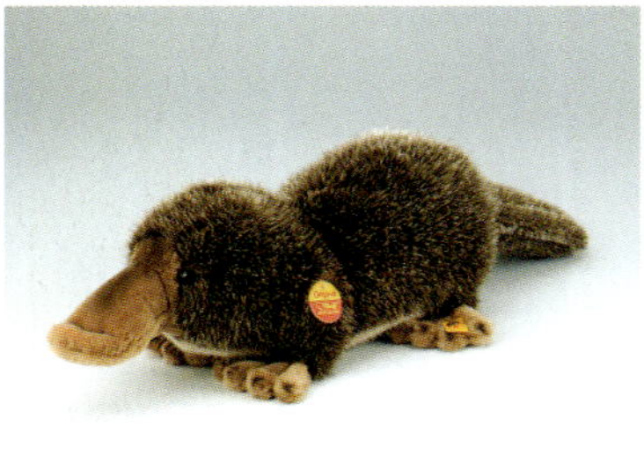

Schnabeltier - *Duckbill*

Webpelz, braun, stehend, waschmaschinenfest - *woven fur, brown, standing, machine washable*

EAN-No.	Period	Pr.	Info
064913	1996-1997	3	35 cm

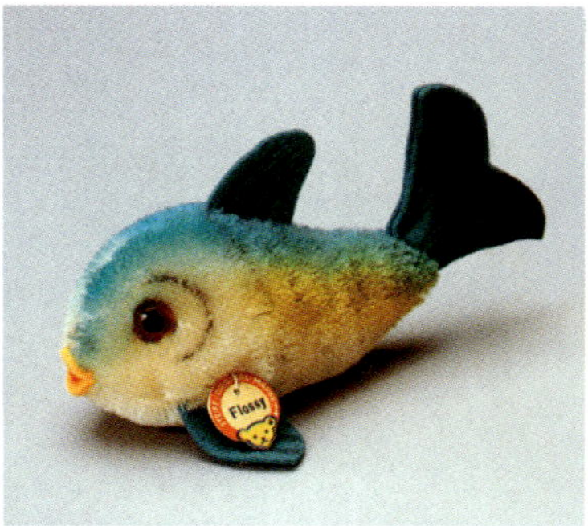

Flossy Fisch - ***Flossy** Fish*

Mohair, blau, liegend, abwaschbar - *mohair, blue, lying, surface washable*

Serie	Art.-No	Period	Pr.	Info
250	**2310,00**	1960-1964	3	13 cm
230	**2310,00**	1965-1967	3	
	2300/10	1968-1981	2	
250	**2322,00**	1960-1964	3	28 cm
230	**2322,00**	1965-1967	3	
	2300/22	1968-1978	2-3	
250	**2350,00**	1960-1964	3-4	66 cm
230	**2350,00**	1965-1967	3-4	
	2300/50	1968-1975	3	

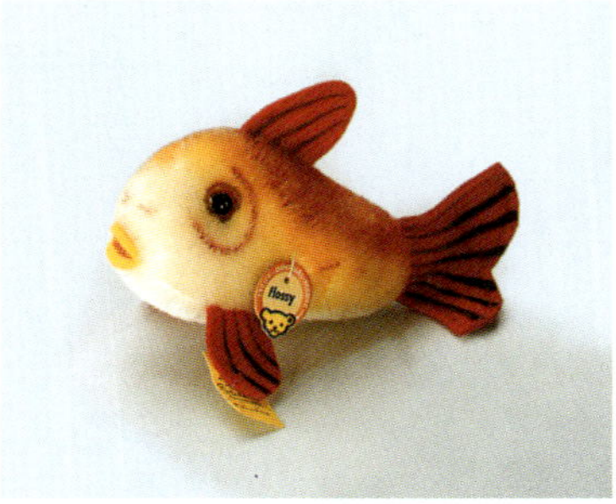

Flossy Fisch - ***Flossy** Fish*

Mohair, gold (rot), liegend, abwaschbar - *mohair, gold (red), lying, surface washable*

Serie	Art.-No	Period	Pr.	Info
250	**2310,01**	1960-1964	3	13 cm
231	**2310,01**	1965-1967	3	
	2301/10	1968-1981	2	
250	**2322,01**	1960-1964	3	28 cm
231	**2322,01**	1965-1967	3	
	2301/22	1968-1978	2	
250	**2350,01**	1960-1964	3-4	66 cm
231	**2350,01**	1965-1967	3-4	
	2301/50	1968-1975	3	

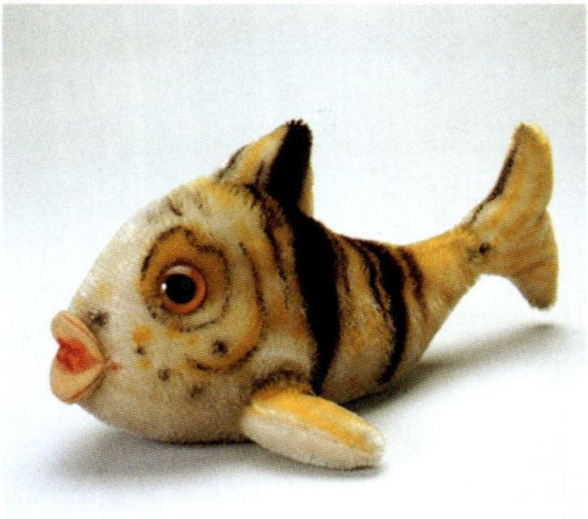

Flossy Fisch - ***Flossy** Fish*

Mohair, bunt (gelb), liegend, abwaschbar - *mohair, multi-colored (yellow), lying, surface washable*

Serie	Art.-No	Period	Pr.	Info
250	**2310,07**	1960-1964	4	13 cm
250	**2322,07**	1960-1964	4	28 cm
250	**2350,07**	1960-1964	4	66 cm

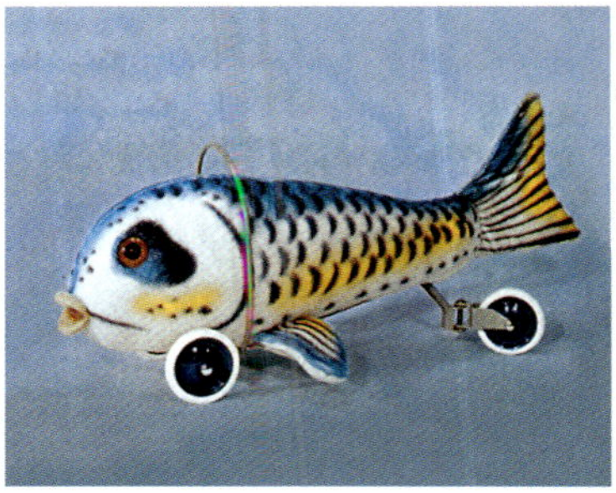

Reit-Fisch **Flossy** - *Riding Fish **Flossy***

Mohair, blau, Stahlgerippe, lenkbar durch Spornrad, auf Scheibenraedern mit Gummi, ab 1967 Plastikreifen & Kunststofflager, Haltegriff, Fussrasten, ab 1969 neues Modell mit Schlepplenkung, abwaschbar - *mohair, blue, iron frame, steered by tail wheel, disc wheels with rubber tires (from 1967 plastic tires & bearings), grip handle, foot rests, from 1969 new model with pull-type steering, surface washable*

Serie	Art.-No	Period	Pr.	Info
230	**2355,20**	1965-1967	4-5	55 cm
	2300/55	1968-1974	4	

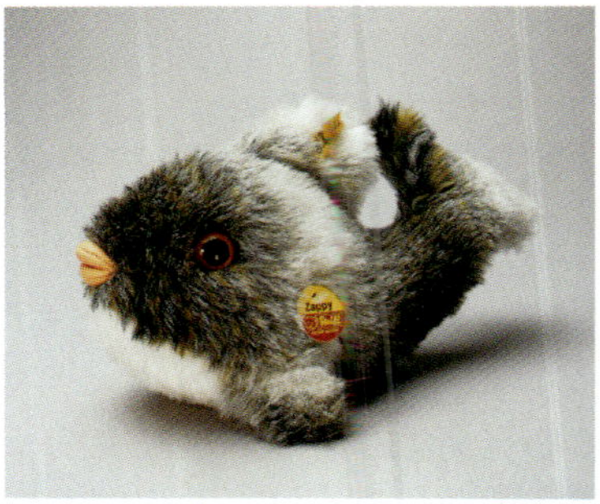

Zappy Fisch - ***Zappy** Fish*

Dralon-Wirkpluesch, ab 1978 Wirkflor, 25 cm, abwaschbar - *dralon knitted plush, from 1978 knitted pile, 25 cm, surface washable*

Serie	Art.-No	Period	Pr.	Info
	2310/25	1976-1979	2	rot - *red*
	2311/25	1976-1979	2	gruen - *green*

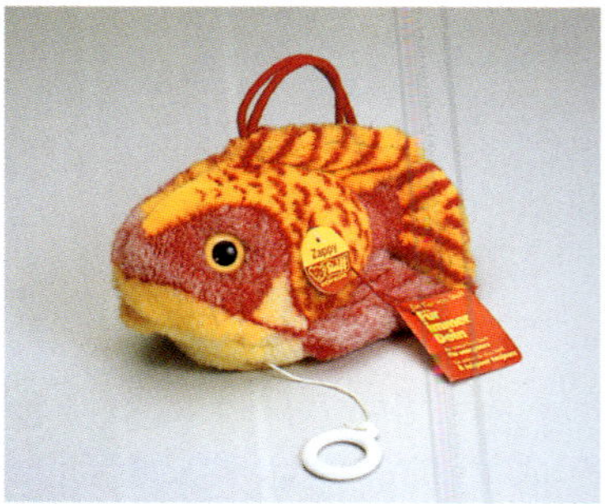

Zappy Musik-Fisch - ***Zappy** Musical Fish*

Wirkpelz, Koerper formgeschaeumt, 20 cm, Musikwerk (Weisst Du wieviel Sternlein stehen) austauschbar, abwaschbar - *knitted fur, stuffed with pre-formed foam, 20 cm, music box (Twinkle, Twinkle Little Star) is exchangeable, surface washable*

SERIE	ART.-NO	PERIOD	PR.	INFO
	6377/20	1980-1983	2-3	rot - *red*
	6378/20	1980-1983	2-3	gruen - *green*

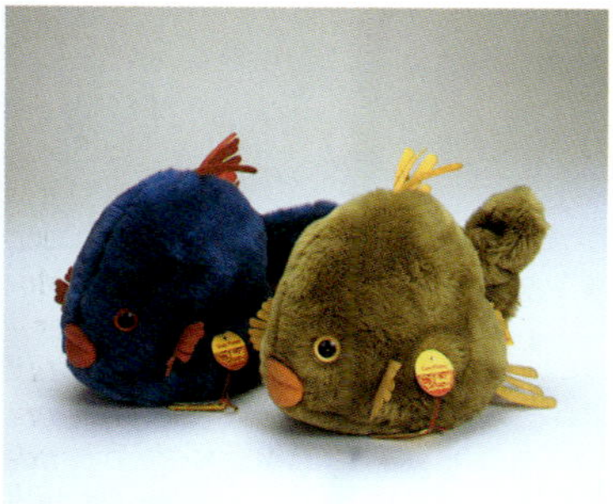

Cosy Flossy

Webpelz, superweich, waschmaschinenfest - *woven fur, super soft, machine washable*

SERIE	ART.-NO	PERIOD	PR.	INFO
	5384/16	1981-1984	2	16 cm, blau - *blue*
	5384/25	1981-1984	2	25 cm
	5385/16	1981-1984	2	16 cm, gruen - *green*
	5385/25	1981-1985	2	25 cm

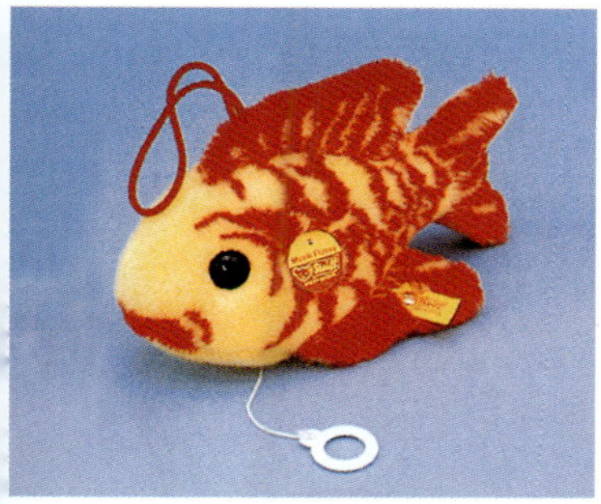

Musik Flossy Fisch - *Musical Flossy Fish*

Wirkpelz, formgeschaeumt, 20 cm, Musikwerk austauschbar, waschbar - *knitted fur, stuffed with pre-formed foam, 20 cm, music box exchangeable, washable*

SERIE	ART.-NO	PERIOD	PR.	INFO
233104	**6367/20**	1986-1987	2	rot - *red*
233159	**6368/20**	1986-1987	2	gruen - *green*

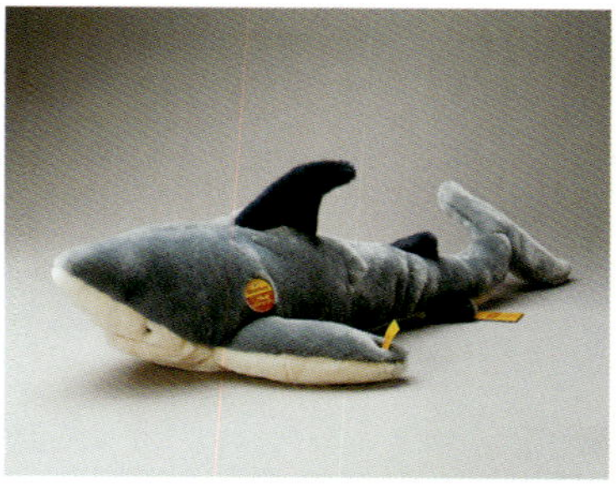

Sharkey Hai - ***Sharkey*** *Shark*

Webpelz, waschmaschinenfest - *woven fur, machine washable*

EAN-NO.	PERIOD	PR.	INFO
063305	1995-1999	3	70 cm

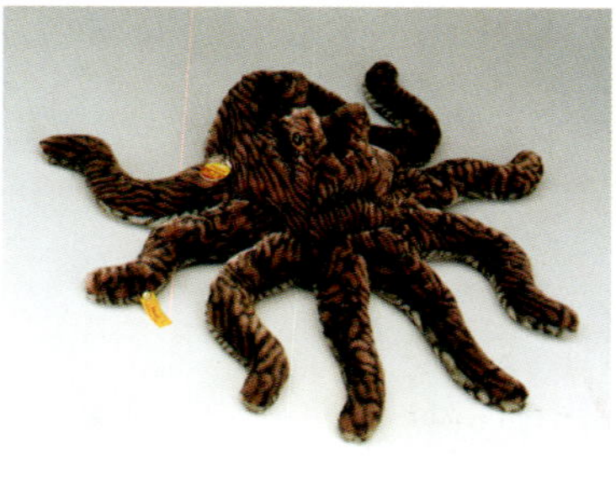

Tintenfisch - *Octopus*

Webpelz, 50 cm, eingearbeitete Tasche im Koerper, waschmaschinenfest - *woven fur, 50 cm, a pocket is sewn into the body, machine washable*

EAN-NO.	PERIOD	PR.	INFO
068614	1995-1995	3	rot/beige - *red/beige*
068638	1995-1996	3	blau/pflaume - *blue/plum*

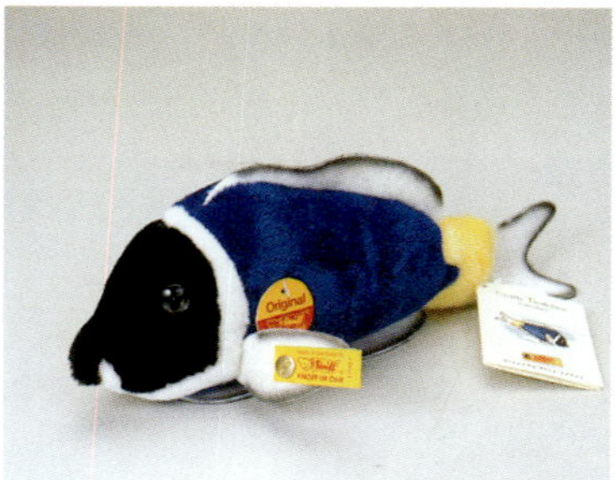

Kaiserfisch ab 1998 Weisskehldoktorfisch - *Imperial Fish from 1998 Butterfly-Fish*

Webpelz, blau, handwaschbar - *woven fur, blue, hand washable*

EAN-NO.	PERIOD	PR.	INFO
121807	1996-1999	1-2	27 cm

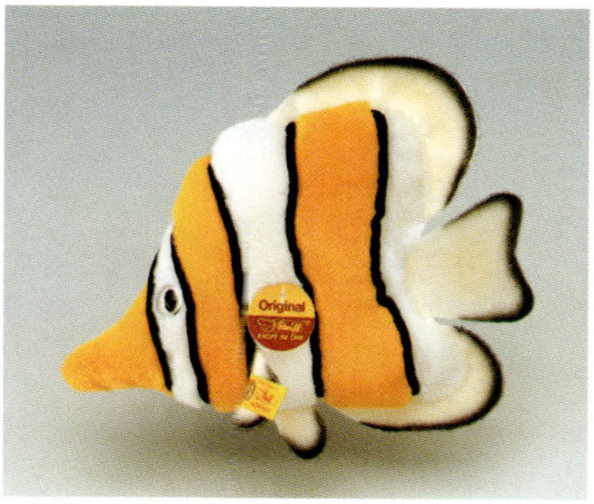

Pinzett-Fisch - *Pincette Fish*

Webpelz, gelb/weiss, handwaschbar - *woven fur, yellow/white, hand washable*

EAN-NO.	PERIOD	PR.	INFO
121821	1996-1997	2	22 cm

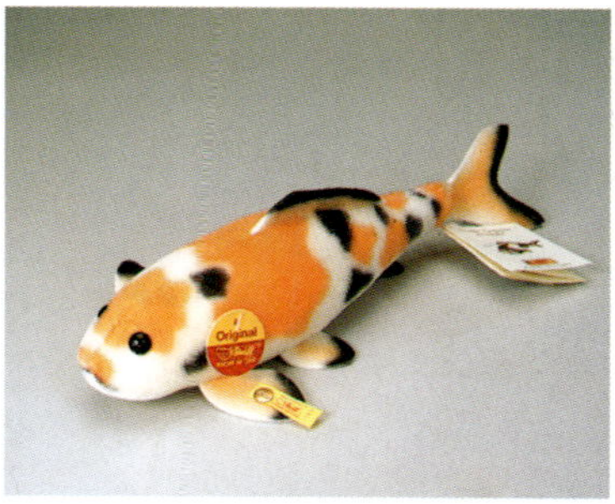

Koi Karpfen - *Koi Carp*

Mohair Webpelz, orange gefleckt, abwaschbar - *mohair woven fur, orange spotted, surface washable*

EAN-NO.	PERIOD	PR.	INFO
121838	1998-1999	1-2	28 cm

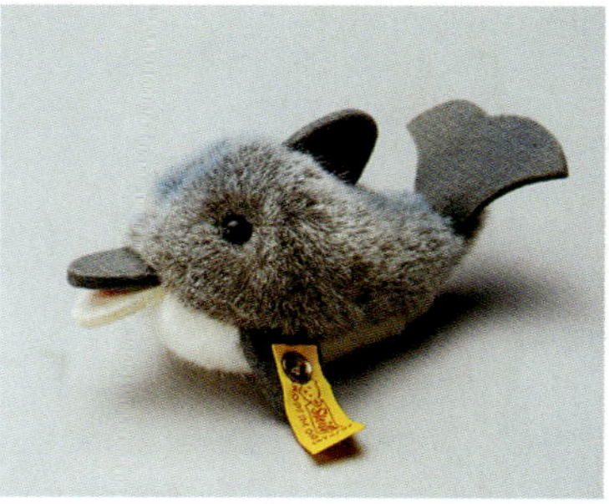

Clippy Delphin - ***Clippy*** *Dolphin*

Nerzimitation, ab 1978 Synthetik-Webpelz, abwaschbar - *imitation mink, from 1978 synthetic woven fur, surface washable*

SERIE	ART.-NO	PERIOD	PR.	INFO
047107	**1472/07**	1977-1989	1-2	7 cm

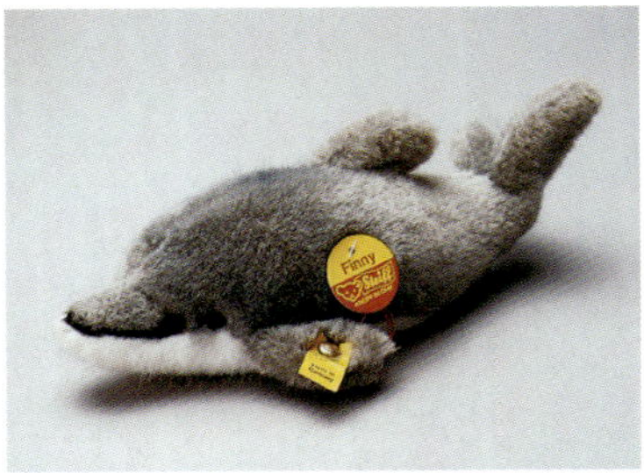

Finny Delphin - ***Finny** Dolphin*

Webpelz, liegend, abwaschbar - *woven fur, lying, surface washable*

SERIE	ART.-NO	PERIOD	PR.	INFO
063305	**2320/25**	1980-1986	2	25 cm
	2320/35	1980-1983	2-3	35 cm

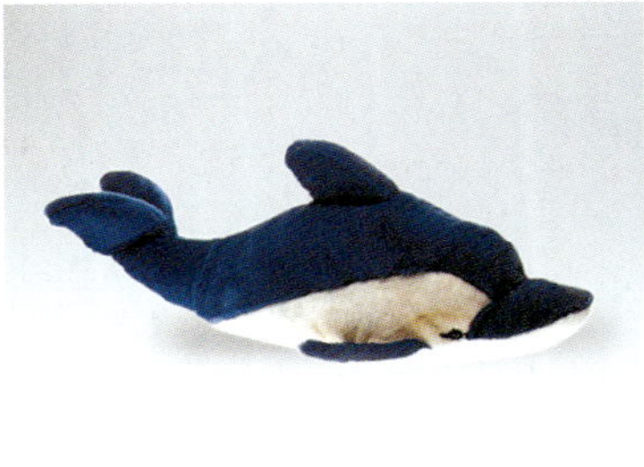

Cosy Delphin - *Cosy Dolphin*

Webpelz, abwaschbar - *woven fur, surface washable*

SERIE	ART.-NO	PERIOD	PR.	INFO
	5410/80	1981-1981	3	80 cm

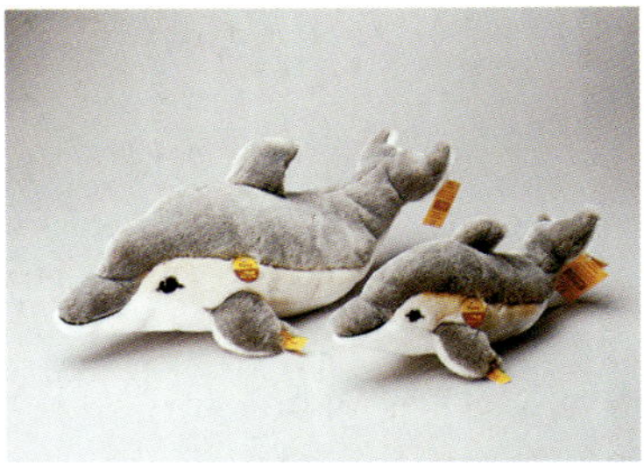

Finny Delphin - ***Finny** Dolphin*

Webpelz, Piepsstimme, waschmaschinenfest, 135 cm abwaschbar - *woven fur, squeaker, machine washable, 135 cm surface washable*

SERIE	ART.-NO	PERIOD	PR.	INFO
063329	**2322/35**	1987-1990	2	35 cm
	063329	1991-1999	2	
063350	**2322/50**	1987-1990	2-3	50 cm
	063350	1991-1999	2-3	
063381	**2322/99**	1987-1989	3	135 cm

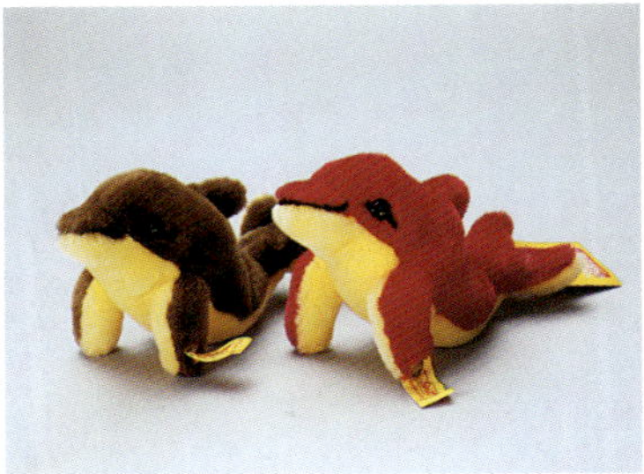

Mini Cosy Delphin - *Mini Cosy Dolphin*

Webpelz, 15 cm, waschmaschinenfest - *woven fur, 15 cm, machine washable*

SERIE	ART.-NO	PERIOD	PR.	INFO
084836	**5583/15**	1987-1988	1-2	rot - *red*
084850	**5585/15**	1987-1988	1-2	blau - *blue*
084874	**5587/15**	1987-1988	1-2	braun - *brown*
084881	**5588/15**	1987-1988	1-2	grau - *grey*

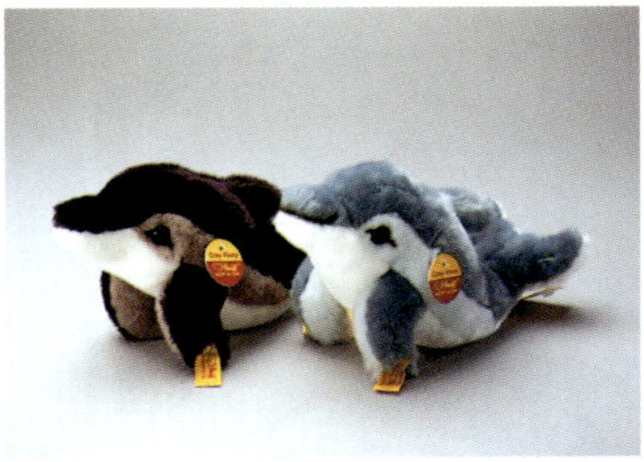

Cosy Finny Delphin - ***Cosy Finny** Dolphin*

Webpelz, 25 cm, Pieps-Stimme, waschmaschinenfest - *woven fur, 25 cm, squeaker, machine washable*

SERIE	ART.-NO	PERIOD	PR.	INFO
095009	**5436/25**	1988-1990	1-2	aubergine
095023	**5438/25**	1988-1990	1-2	eisblau - *ice blue*
	095023	1991-1999	1-2	

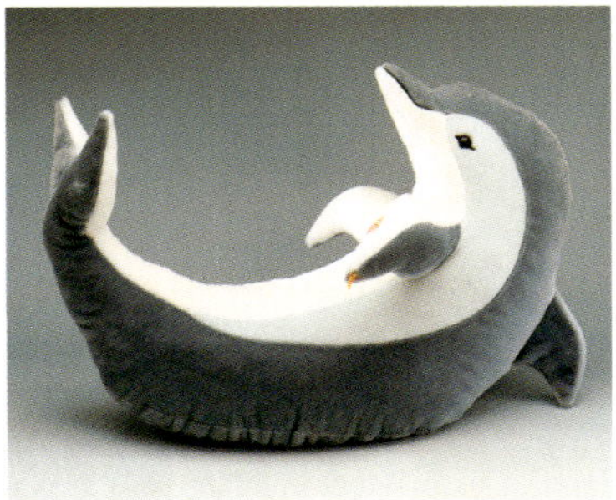

Sitz-Delphin - *Sitting Dolphin*

Webpelz, mit Stimme im Maul, abwaschbar - *woven fur, voice in its mouth, surface washable*

EAN-NO.	PERIOD	PR.	INFO
482359	1995-1996	4-5	100 cm

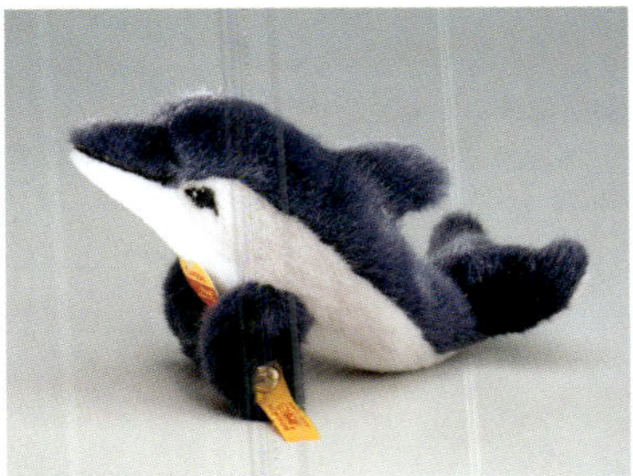

Clippy Delphin - ***Clippy** Dolphin*

Webpelz, waschmaschinenfest - *woven fur, machine washable*

EAN-NO.	PERIOD	PR	INFO
047404	1996-1999	1	15 cm

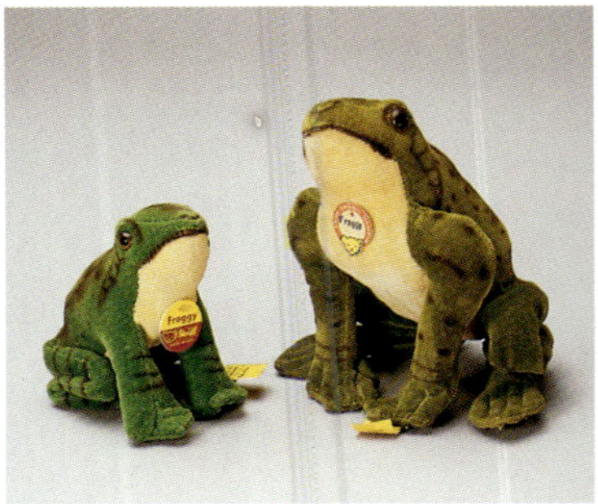

Frosch **Froggy** - *Frog **Froggy***

Samt, gruen/gelb, sitzend, ab 1978 Trevira-Samt (geaendertes Modell), abwaschbar - *velvet, green/yellow, sitting, from 1978 trevira velvet (altered model), surface washable*

SERIE	ART.-NO	PERIOD	PR.	INFO
31	**3408**	1953-1958	3-4	8 cm
310	**3408,00**	1959-1964	3	
237	**3408,00**	1965-1967	3	
056505	**2370/08**	1968-1986	2	
31	**3410**	1953-1958	4	10 cm
310	**3410,00**	1959-1964	3-4	
237	**3410,00**	1965-1967	3-4	
	2370/10	1968-1975	2-3	

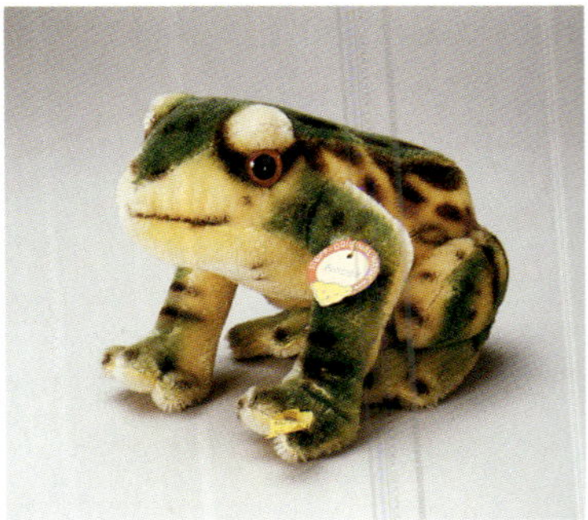

Froggy Frosch - ***Froggy** Frog*

Mohair, bunt, sitzend, 28 cm mit Stimme - *mohair, multi-colored, sitting, 28 cm with voice*

SERIE	ART.-NO	PERIOD	PR.	INFO
310	**3320,00**	1960-1964	4	20 cm
238	**3320,00**	1965-1967	4	
	2380/20	1968-1973	3-4	
310	**3328,00**	1959-1964	4	28 cm

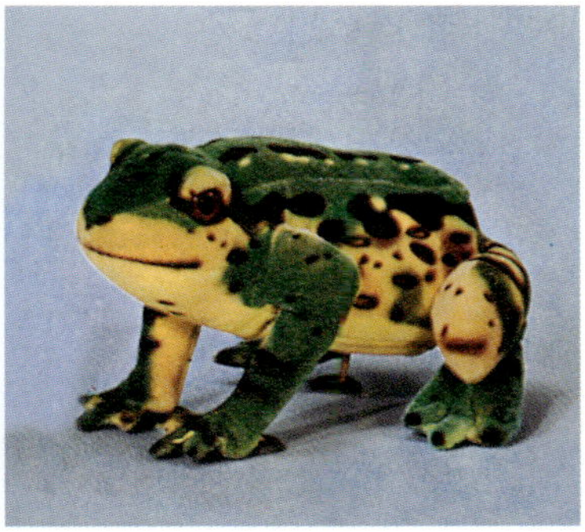

Snuggy Froggy

Sitztier, Mohairpluesch, Stahlgestell mit Gummifuessen - *sitting animal, mohair, steel frame with rubber feet*

SERIE	ART.-NO	PERIOD	PR.	INFO
820 310	**3340,00**	1959-1963	5	40 cm
601	**3340,00**	1966-1966	5	

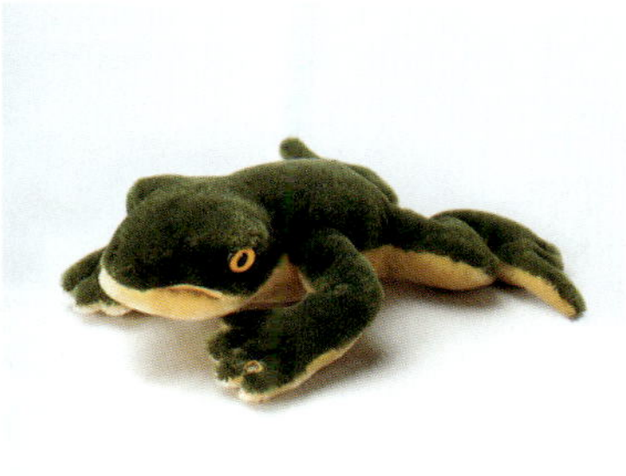

Frosch **Froggy** - *Frog* ***Froggy***

ab 1968 "Krabbelfrosch", Mohair, liegend, gruen/gelb, sehr weich, abwaschbar - *from 1968 "crawling frog", mohair, lying flat, green/yellow, very soft, surface washable*

SERIE	ART.-NO	PERIOD	PR.	INFO
310	**2322,00**	1962-1964	3	22 cm
236	**2322,00**	1965-1967	3	
	2360/22	1968-1978	2-3	

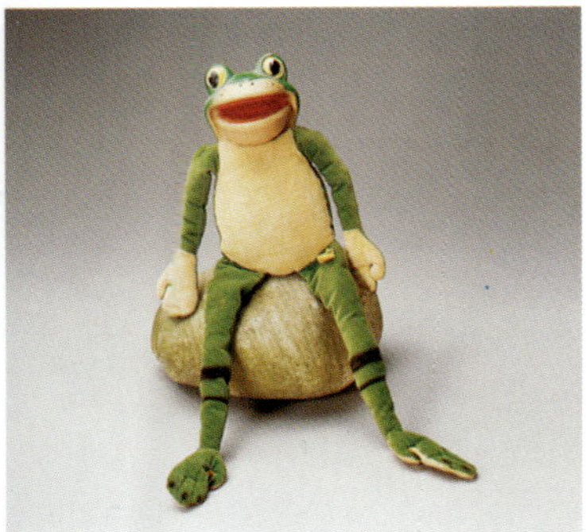

Schlenkerfrosch - *Dangling Frog*

PVC-Kopf, Samt, gruen/mais, Schlenkerglieder, abwaschbar - *PVC head, velvet, green/corn yellow, floppy joints, surface washable*

SERIE	ART.-NO	PERIOD	PR.	INFO
	2390/35	1970-1974	4	35 cm

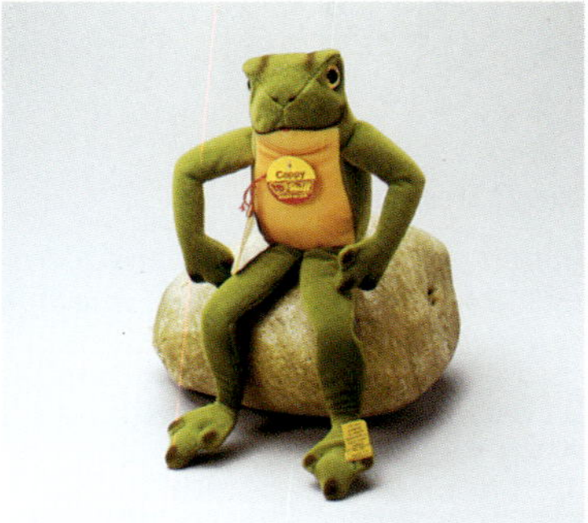

Cappy Schlenkerfrosch - ***Cappy*** *Dangling Frog*

Trevirasamt, Schlenkerglieder, abwaschbar - *trevira velvet, floppy joints, surface washable*

SERIE	ART.-NO	PERIOD	PR.	INFO
	2380/32	1979-1984	3	32 cm

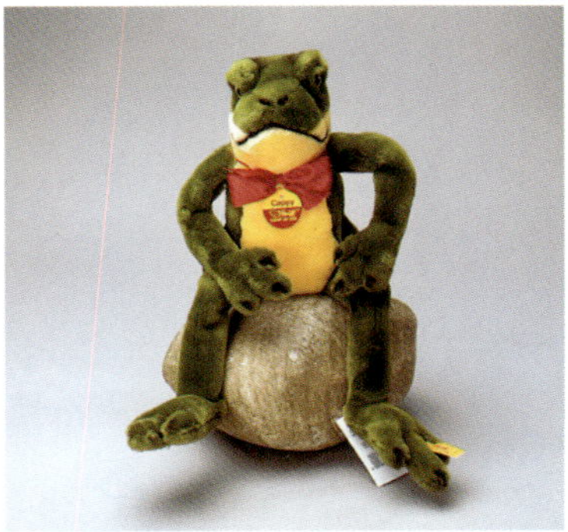

Cappy Schlenkerfrosch - ***Cappy*** *Dangling Frog*

Webpelz, Pieps-Stimme, waschmaschinenfest - *woven fur, squeaker, machine washable*

SERIE	ART.-NO	PERIOD	PR.	INFO
123351	**6292/32**	1986-1990	3	32 cm
	123351	1991-1995	3	

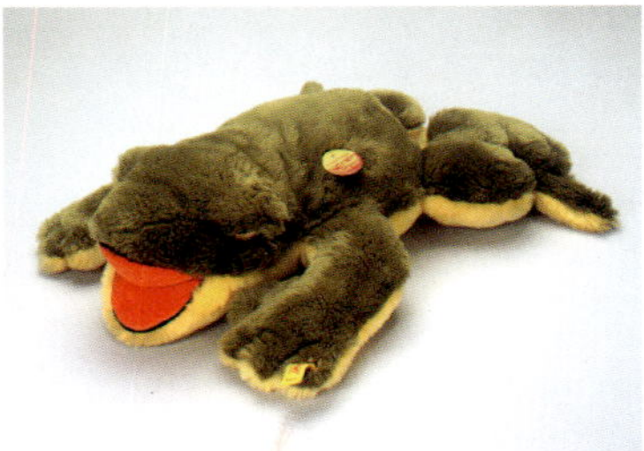

Cosy Froggy

Webpelz, liegend, superweich, waschmaschinenfest - *woven fur, lying flat, super soft, machine washable*

SERIE	ART.-NO	PERIOD	PR.	INFO
	5382/43	1981-1983	2-3	43 cm

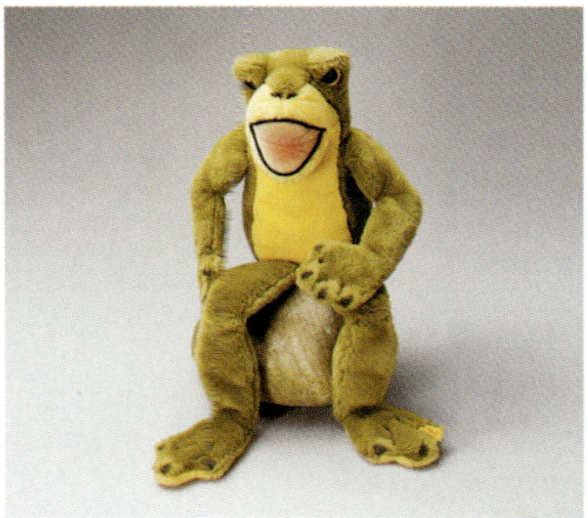

Cosy Cappy

Webpelz, Schlenkerglieder, superweich, waschmaschinenfest - *woven fur, floppy joints, super soft, machine washable*

SERIE	ART.-NO	PERIOD	PR.	INFO
	5383/60	1981-1984	3	60 cm

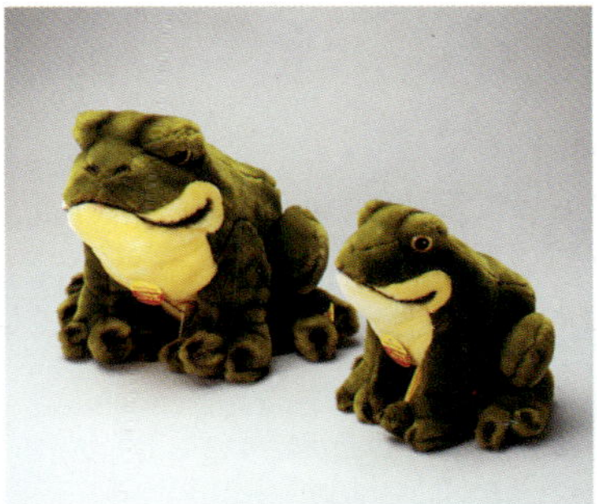

Cosy Froggy Frosch - ***Cosy Froggy*** *Frog*

Webpelz, superweich, waschmaschinenfest - *woven fur, super soft, machine washable*

SERIE	ART.-NO	PERIOD	PR.	INFO
092053	**5384/16**	1986-1990	2	15 cm
	092053	1991-1999	2	
092107	**5384/20**	1985-1987	2	18 cm
092138	**5384/28**	1985-1987	2-3	25 cm
092183	**5384/50**	1986-1987	3	50 cm

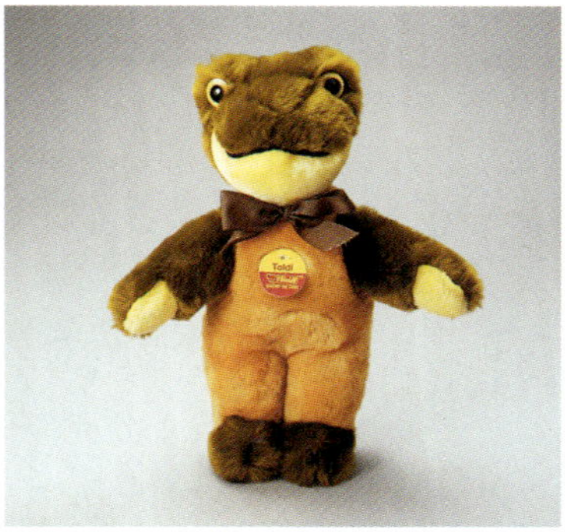

Toldi Frosch - ***Toldi** Frog*

Webpelz, Pieps-Stimme, waschmaschinenfest - *woven fur, squeaker, machine washable*

SERIE	ART.-NO	PERIOD	PR.	INFO
080937	**6274/27**	1988-1989	2	27 cm

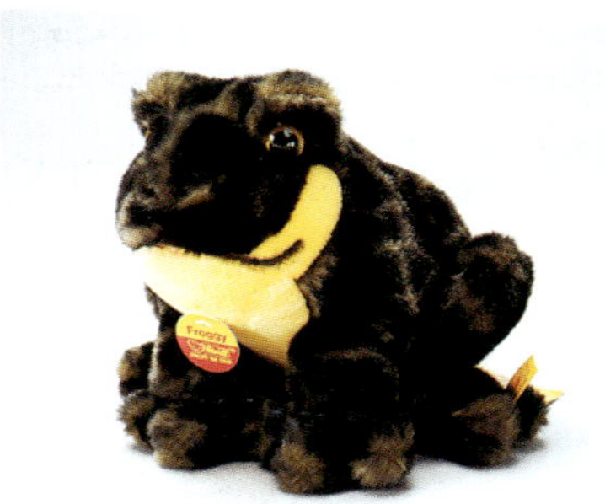

Froggy Frosch - ***Froggy** Frog*

Webpelz, 20 cm, waschmaschinenfest - *woven fur, 20 cm, machine washable*

EAN-NO.	PERIOD	PR.	INFO
073472	1992-1993	2	braun - *brown*
073489	1992-1995	2	gruen - *green*
073496	1992-1993	2	rot - *red*

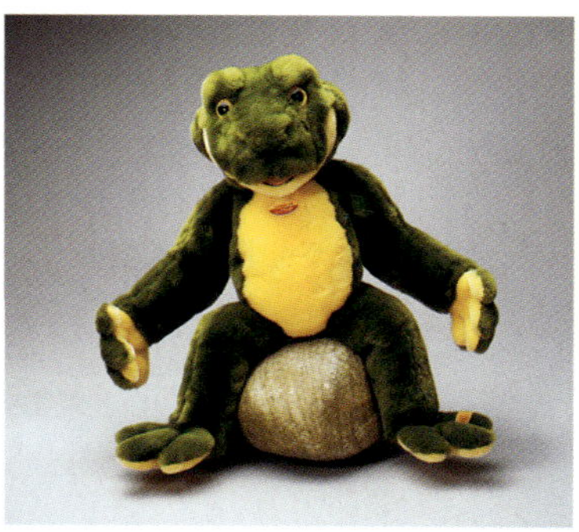

Schlenkerfrosch - *Dangling Frog*

Schlenkerglieder, Webpelz, waschmaschinenfest - *floppy joints, woven fur, machine washable*

EAN-NO.	PERIOD	PR.	INFO
123689	1993-1996	3	50 cm

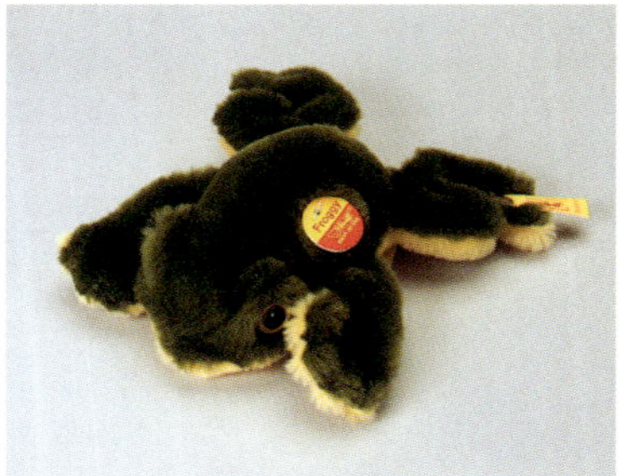

Froggy Frosch - ***Froggy** Frog*

Webpelz, gruen, liegend, waschmaschinenfest - *woven fur, green, lying, machine washable*

EAN-NO.	PERIOD	PR.	INFO
056529	1996-1999	1	14 cm

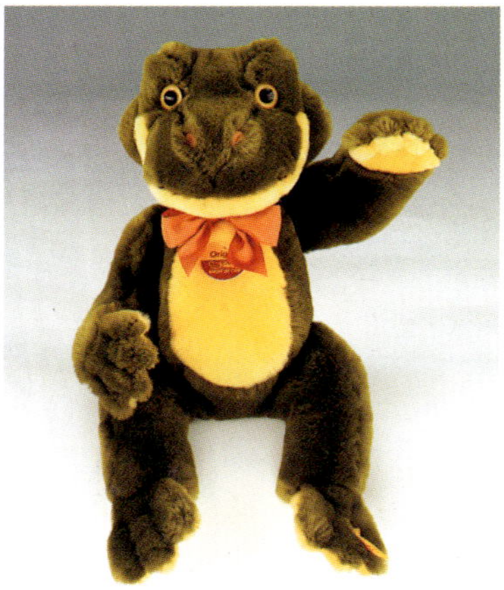

Schlenker Frosch - *Dangling Frog*

Webpelz, waschmaschinenfest - *woven fur, machine washable*

EAN-NO.	PERIOD	PR.	INFO
123672	1996-1997	2-3	30 cm

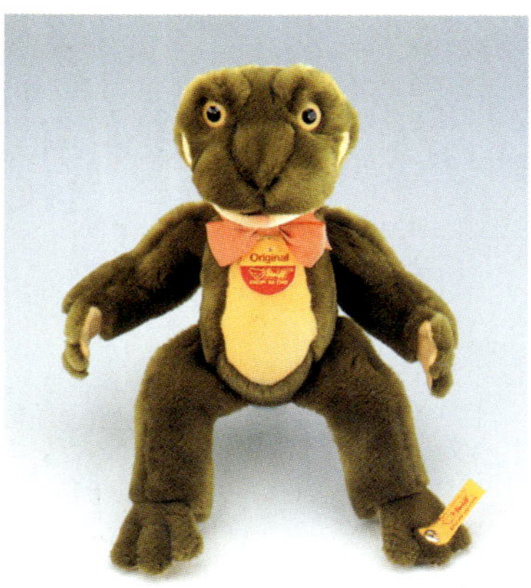

Schlenker Frosch - *Dangling Frog*

Webpelz, waschmaschinenfest - *woven fur, machine washable*

EAN-NO.	PERIOD	PR.	INFO
123665	1997-1998	2-3	22 cm

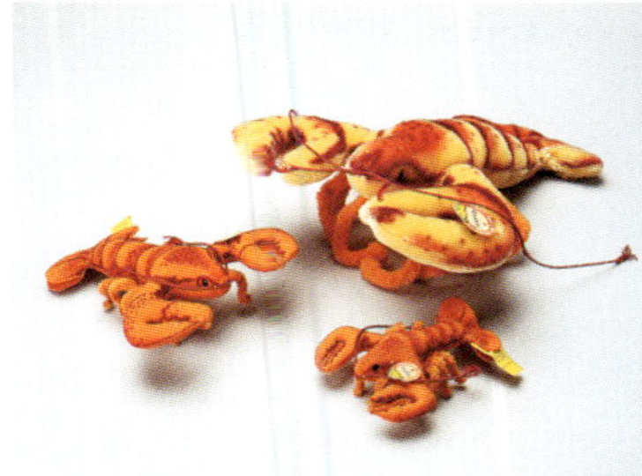

Crabby Hummer - ***Crabby** Lobster*

"Figur aus den Tierkreiszeichen", Filz, Groesse 28 cm Mohair, rot/schwarz, stehend - *figure from the "signs of the Zodiac", felt, size 28 cm mohair, red/black, standing*

SERIE	ART.-NO	PERIOD	PR.	INFO
338	**2010,00**	1963-1964	4	10 cm
240	**2010,00**	1965-1966	4	
338	**2017,00**	1963-1964	4	17 cm
240	**2017,00**	1965-1966	4	
338	**2328,00**	1963-1964	6	28 cm
240	**2328,00**	1965-1965	6	

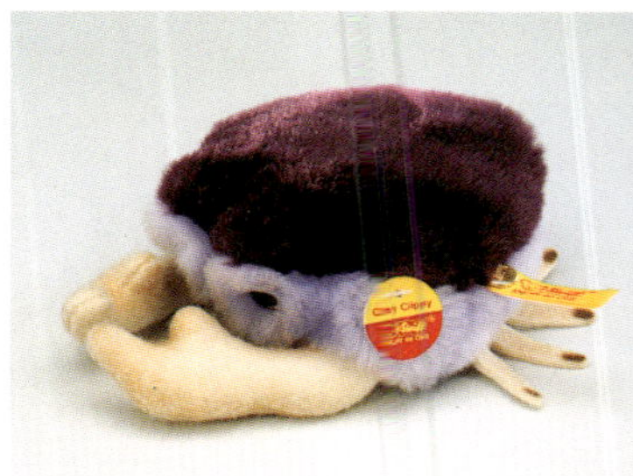

Cosy Clippy Krabbe - ***Cosy Clippy** Crab*

Webpelz, 10 cm, waschmaschinenfest - *woven fur, 10 cm, machine washable*

EAN-NO.	PERIOD	PR.	INFO
095856	1995-1996	1	violett - *violet*
095863	1995-1996	1	gelb - *yellow*
095870	1995-1996	1	rot - *red*
095887	1995-1996	1	oliv - *olive green*
095894	1995-1996	1	aubergine
095900	1995-1996	1	himbeer - *raspberry*

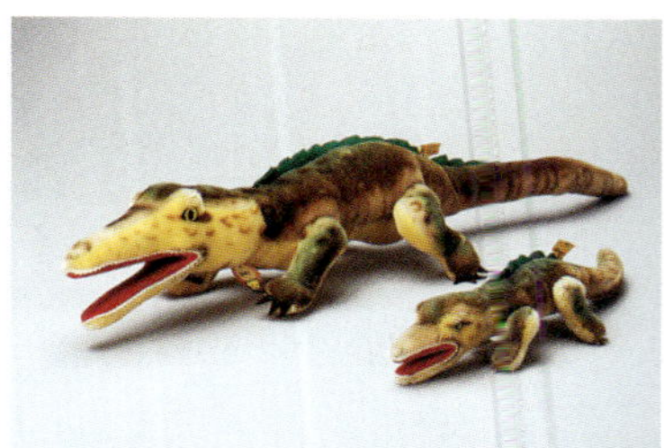

Gaty Krokodil - ***Gaty** Crocodile*

Mohairpluesch, gelb/gruen/braun, bis 1958 mit Stimme, stehend, abwaschbar - *mohair, yellow/green/brown, up to 1958 press voice, standing, surface washable*

Serie	Art.-No	Period	Pr.	Info
41	**2315**	1957-1958	3-4	15 cm
410	**2315,00**	1959-1964	3	
097	**2315,00**	1965-1967	3	
	0970/15	1968-1974	2-3	
41	**2330**	1957-1958	4	30 cm
410	**2330,00**	1959-1964	3-4	
097	**2330,00**	1965-1967	3-4	
	0970/30	1968-1974	3	

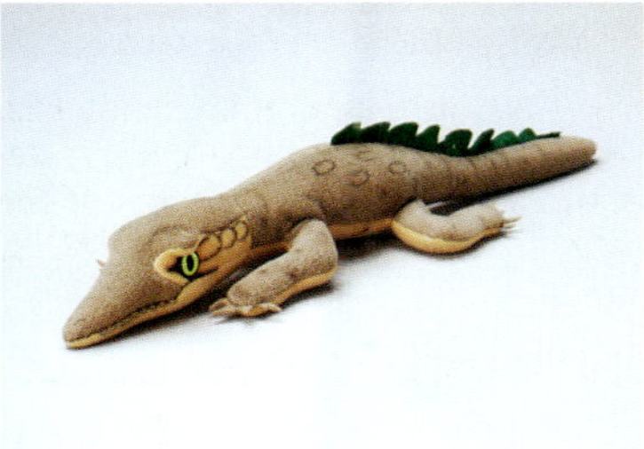

Gaty Krokodil - ***Gaty*** *Crocodile*

Trevirasamt, liegend, vollwaschbar - *trevira velvet, lying flat, fully washable*

Serie	Art.-No	Period	Pr.	Info
	0980/15	1975-1978	2-3	15 cm
	0980/30	1975-1978	3	30 cm

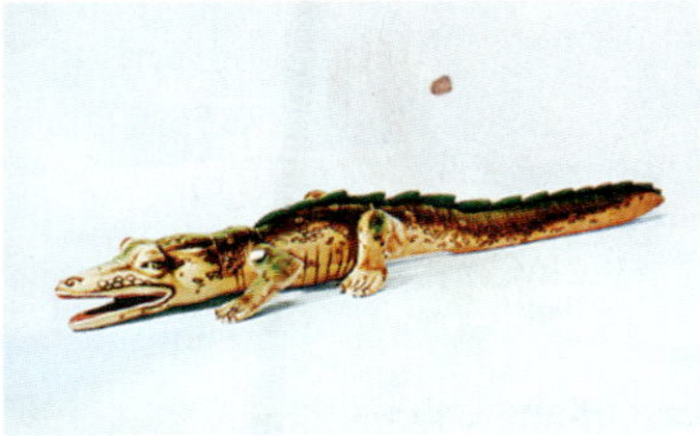

Krokodil - *Crocodile*

Schautier, Mohair, stehend - *display animal, mohair, standing*

Serie	Art.-No	Period	Pr.	Info
410	**2380,90**	1960-1960	6	250 cm
	0979/25	1967-1967	6	

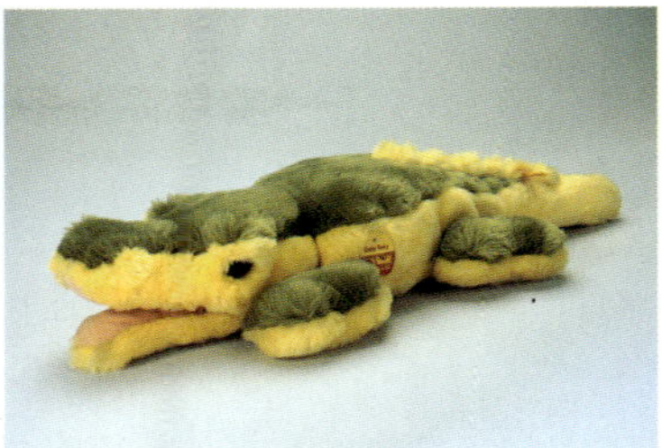

Cosy Gaty Krokodil - ***Cosy Gaty*** *Crocodile*

Webpelz, kuschelweich, waschmaschinenfest - *woven fur, soft & cuddly, machine washable*

Serie	Art.-No	Period	Pr.	Info
094903	**5425/50**	1983-1990	2-3	50 cm

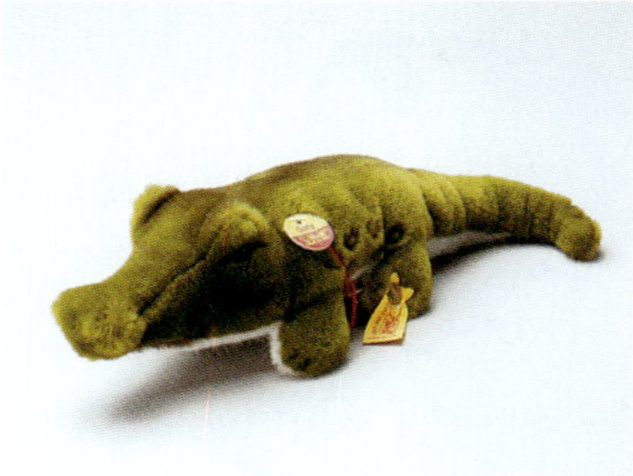

Gaty Krokodil - ***Gaty*** *Crocodile*

Webpelz, stehend, abwaschbar - *woven fur, standing, surface washable*

Serie	Art.-No	Period	Pr.	Info
040900	**1463/18**	1985-1990	1-2	28 cm
	040900	1991-1995	1-2	

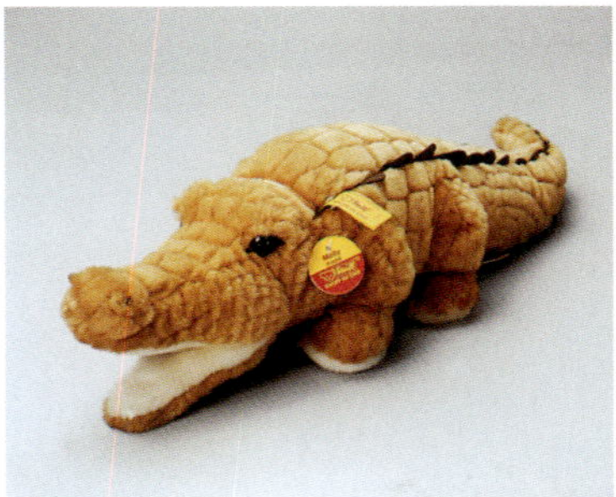

Molly Kroko

Webpelz, braun oder schwarz, liegend, waschmaschinenfest - *woven fur, brown or black, lying, machine washable*

Serie	Art.-No	Period	Pr.	Info
104442	**0430/50**	1990-1990	2-3	50 cm, braun - *brown*
	104442	1991-1992	2-3	
104466	**0430/90**	1990-1990	3	90 cm
	104466	1991-1992	3	
104480	**0430/99**	1990-1990	3-4	120 cm
	104480	1991-1991	3-4	
104503	**0432/50**	1990-1990	2-3	50 cm, schwarz - *black*
	104503	1991-1991	2-3	
104527	**0432/90**	1990-1990	3	90 cm
	104527	1991-1991	3	

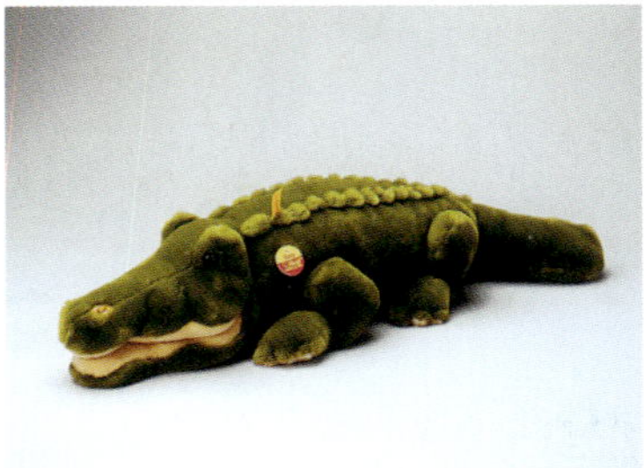

Gaty Krokodil - ***Gaty*** *Crocodile*

Webpelz, gruen, 100 cm dunkelgruen gemustert, handwaschbar - *woven fur, green, 100 cm patterned in dark green, hand washable*

EAN-No.	Period	Pr.	Info
068225	1992-1995	3	75 cm
068256	1992-1994	3-4	100 cm

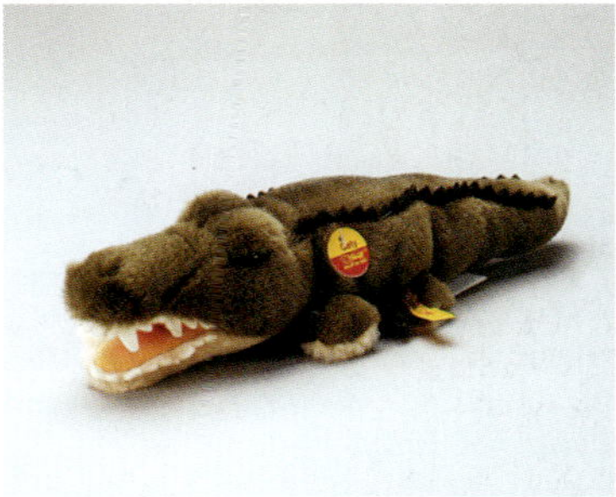

Gaty Krokodil - ***Gaty*** *Crocodile*

Webpelz, mit Zaehnen, handwaschbar - *woven fur, with teeth, hand washable*

EAN-No.	Period	Pr.	Info
040894	1995-1996	1-2	20 cm

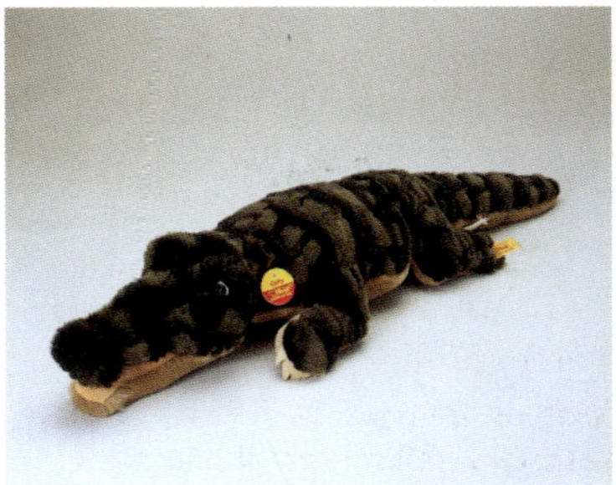

Gaty Krokodil - ***Gaty*** *Crocodile*

Webpelz, gruen, waschmaschinenfest - *woven fur, green, machine washable*

EAN-No.	Period	Pr.	Info
095450	1997-1999	2-3	65 cm

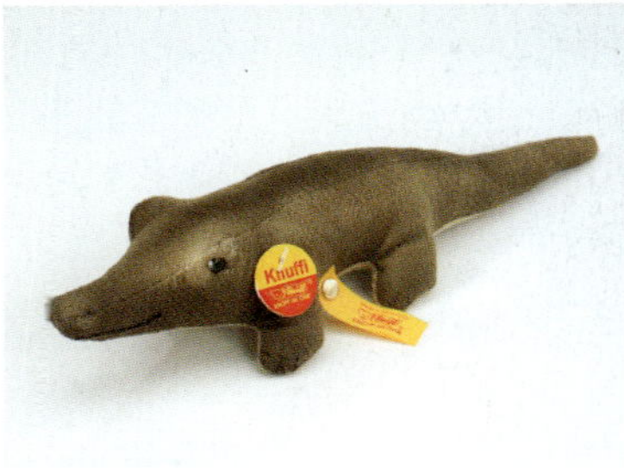

Knuffi Krokodil - ***Knuffi*** *Crocodile*

Microfaser-Vlies, gruen, handwaschbar - *micro fibre fleece, green, hand washable*

EAN-No.	Period	Pr.	Info
067778	1997-1997	1-2	15 cm

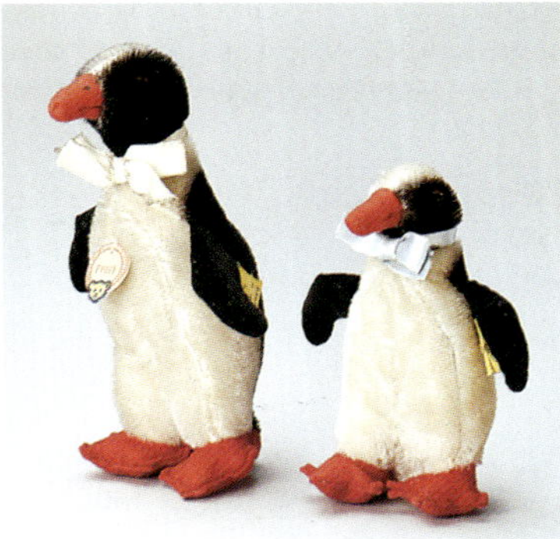

Peggy Pinguin - ***Peggy*** *Penguin*

Mohair, weiss/schwarz, Fuesse & Schnabel rot, aufwartend - *mohair, white/black, feet & beak red, sitting up*

SERIE	ART.-NO	PERIOD	PR.	INFO
54	**4310**	1952-1956	4-5	10 cm
54	**4314**	1952-1956	4-5	14 cm
54	**4322**	1952-1956	5	22 cm

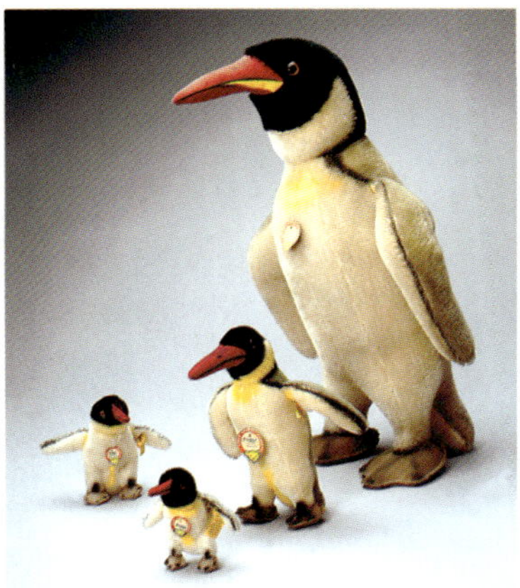

Peggy Pinguin - ***Peggy*** *Penguin*

Mohair, weiss/grau/gelb, roter Schnabel, aufwartend, Kopf drehbar, abwaschbar - *mohair, white/grey/yellow, red beak, sitting up, head swivels, surface washable*

SERIE	ART.-NO	PERIOD	PR.	INFO
54	**4310**	1956-1958	3-4	10 cm
540	**4310,07**	1959-1964	3	
250	**4310,07**	1965-1967	3	
	2500/10	1968-1972	2-3	
54	**4314**	1956-1958	3-4	14 cm
540	**4314,07**	1959-1964	3	
250	**4314,07**	1965-1967	3	
	2500/14	1968-1975	2-3	
54	**4322**	1956-1958	3-4	22 cm
540	**4322,07**	1959-1964	3	
250	**4322,07**	1965-1967	3	
	2500/22	1968-1975	3	
54	**4335**	1956-1958	4	35 cm
540	**4335,07**	1959-1964	3-4	
250	**4335,07**	1965-1967	3-4	
	2500/35	1968-1975	3	
540	**4350,07**	1959-1964	4-5	50 cm
250	**4350,07**	1965-1967	4-5	
	2500/50	1968-1974	4	

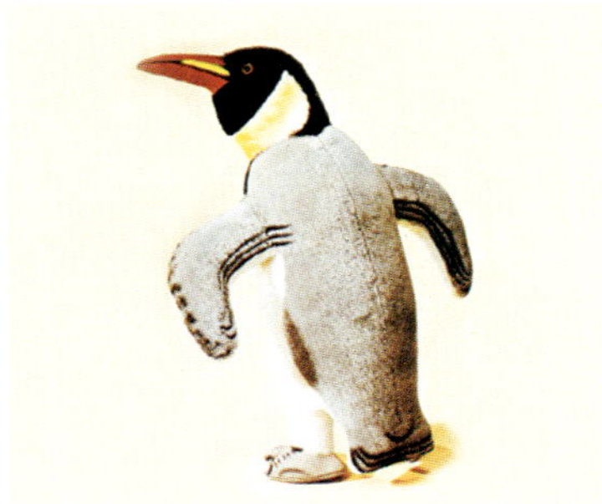

Pinguin - *Penguin*

Schautier, Mohair, aufwartend - *display animal, mohair, sitting up*

SERIE	ART.-NO	PERIOD	PR.	INFO
540	**4380,90**	1960-1960	5	80 cm
	2509/08	1967-1967	5	

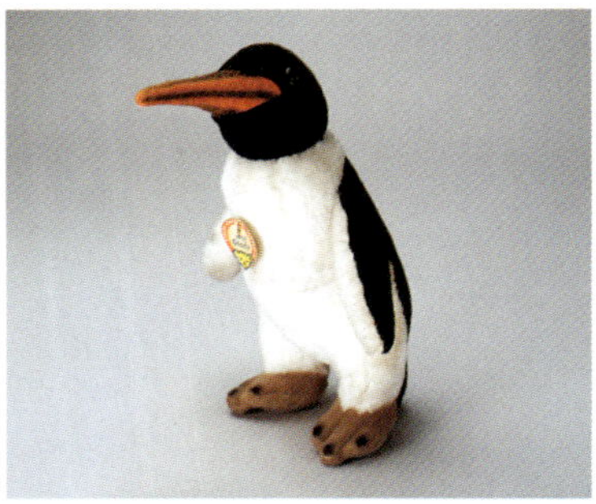

Cosy Charly

Dralon-Pluesch, schwarz/weiss, Drehkopf, aufwartend, Schaumstoff-Flocken-Fuellung, ab 1968 gefuellt mit synthetischen Fasern und Schaumstoff, sehr weich, waschbar - *dralon, black/white, head swivels, sitting up, stuffed with foam flakes, from 1968 stuffed with synthetic fibers & foam, very soft, washable*

SERIE	ART.-NO	PERIOD	PR.	INFO
515	**4625,06**	1965-1967	3	25 cm
	5150/25	1968-1975	2-3	

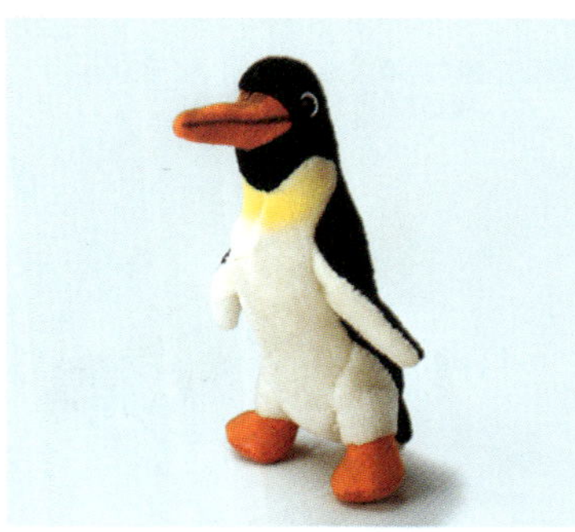

Pinni Pinguin - *Pinni Penguin*

"Der kleine Tierversand", Dralon, im Kaefigkarton, mit Tiersteckbrief, aufwartend, abwaschbar - *"Der kleine Tierversand", dralon, packed in a card-board animal crate, complete with animal shipping label, sitting up, surface washable*

SERIE	ART.-NO	PERIOD	PR.	INFO
	5825/17	1971-1974	3-4	17 cm

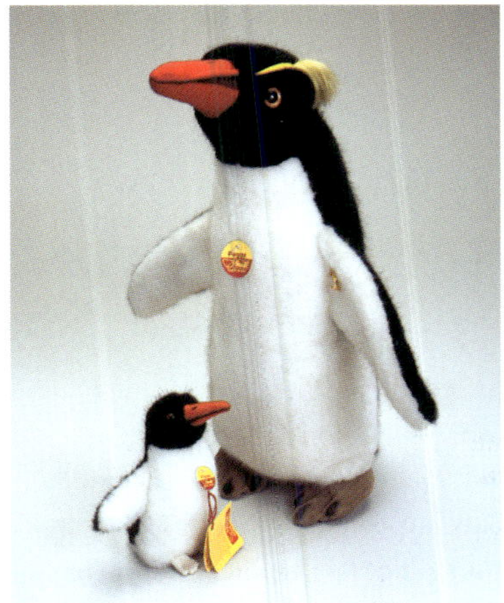

Peggy Pinguin - ***Peggy*** *Penguin*

Nerzimitation, ab 1978 Synthetik-Webpelz, aufwartend, abwaschbar - *imitation mink, from 1978 synthetic woven fur, sitting up, surface washable*

SERIE	ART.-NO	PERIOD	PR.	INFO
057502	**2505/12**	1976-1990	1	12 cm
	057502	1991-1999	1	
	2505/27	1976-1982	2-3	27 cm
	2505/40	1976-1981	3	40 cm

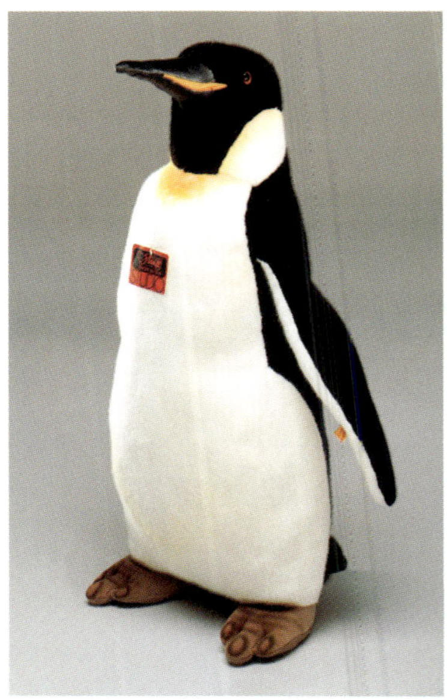

Koenigspinguin - *King Penguin*

Studio-Tier, Synthetik-Webpelz, aufwartend, abwaschbar - *studio animal, synthetic woven fur, sitting up, surface washable*

SERIE	ART.-NO	PERIOD	PR.	INFO
505034	**2509/09**	1978-1990	5	90 cm
	505034	1991-1999	5	

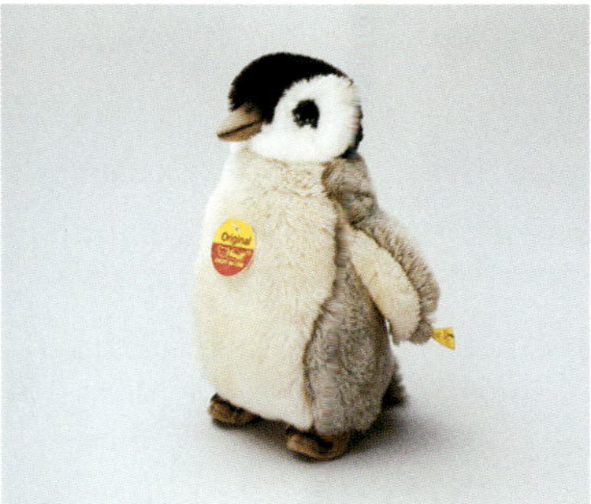

Jung Pinguin - *Young Penguin*

Webpelz, waschmaschinenfest - *woven fur, machine washable*

SERIE	ART.-NO	PERIOD	PR.	INFO
063404	**2507/20**	1983-1989	2	20 cm
063459	**2507/38**	1982-1988	2-3	38 cm

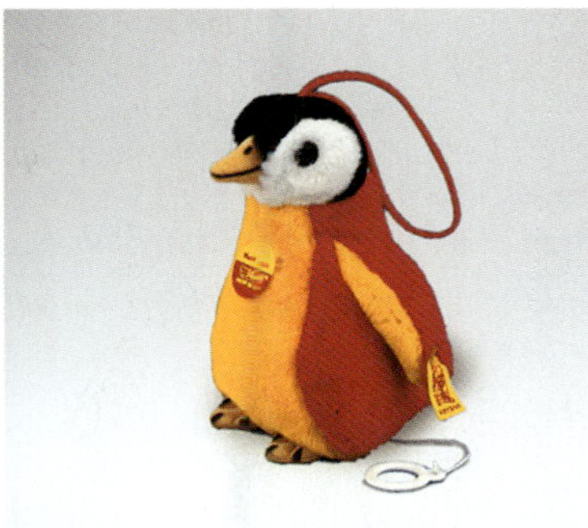

Musik Peggy Pinguin - *Musical Peggy Penguin*

Webpelz, formgeschaeumt, Musikwerk austauschbar, waschbar - *woven fur, stuffed with pre-formed foam, music box exchangeable, washable*

SERIE	ART.-NO	PERIOD	PR.	INFO
233456	**6377/17**	1985-1986	2-3	17 cm

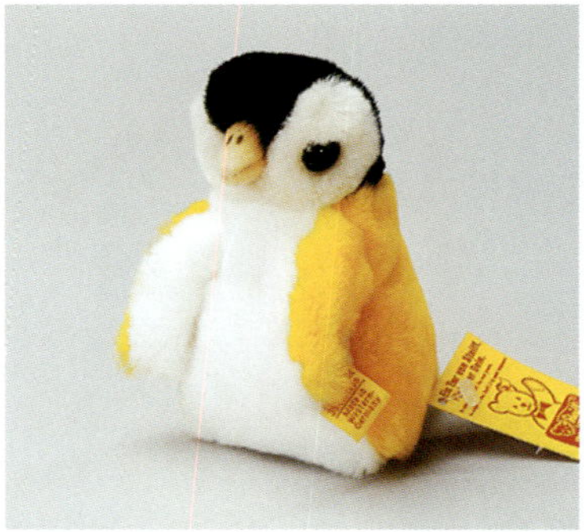

Mini Cosy Pinguin - *Mini Cosy Penguin*

Webpelz, 11 cm, waschmaschinenfest - *woven fur, 11 cm, machine washable*

SERIE	ART.-NO	PERIOD	PR.	INFO
084737	**5573/11**	1987-1988	1-2	rot - *red*
084744	**5574/11**	1987-1988	1-2	gelb - *yellow*
084751	**5575/11**	1987-1988	1-2	blau - *blue*
084782	**5578/11**	1987-1989	1-2	grau - *grey*

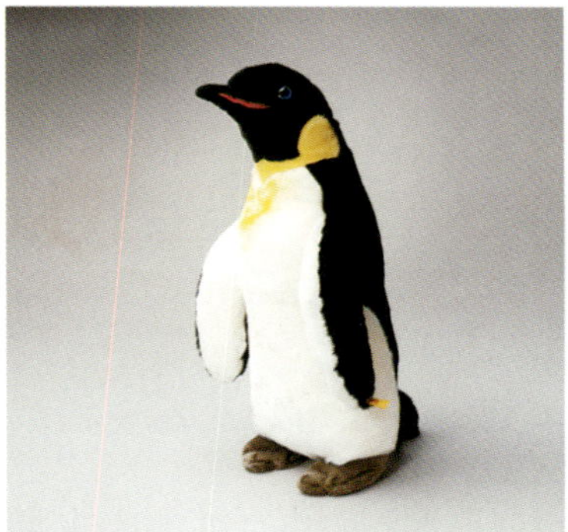

Charly Pinguin - ***Charly** Penguin*

Webpelz, waschmaschinenfest - *woven fur, machine washable*

SERIE	ART.-NO	PERIOD	PR.	INFO
063541	**2510/40**	1987-1990	3	40 cm
	063541	1991-1999	3	

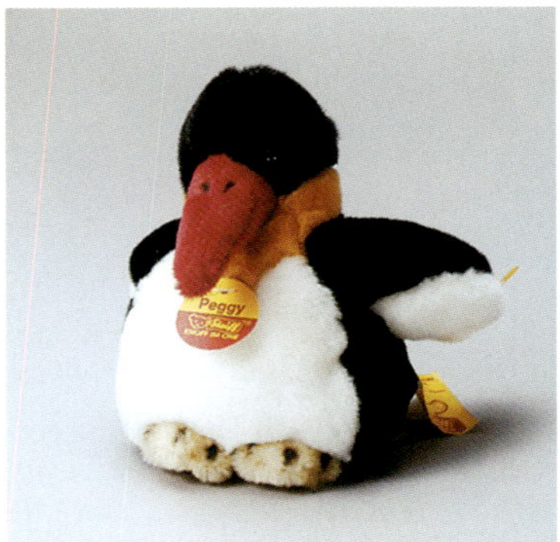

Peggy Pinguin - ***Peggy** Penguin*

Webpelz, waschmaschinenfest - *woven fur, machine washable*

SERIE	ART.-NO	PERIOD	PR.	INFO
064517	**2570/14**	1990-1990	1-2	14 cm
	064517	1991-1991	1-2	

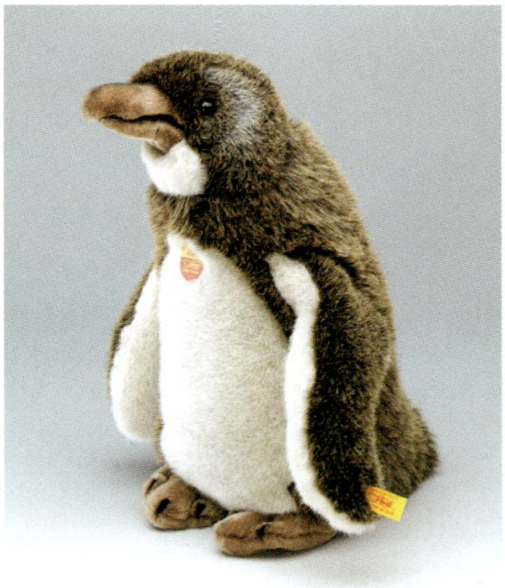

Maggy Jungpinguin - ***Maggy** Young Penguin*

Webpelz, waschmaschinenfest - *woven fur, machine washable*

EAN-NO.	PERIOD	PR.	INFO
063602	1992-1995	2-3	34 cm

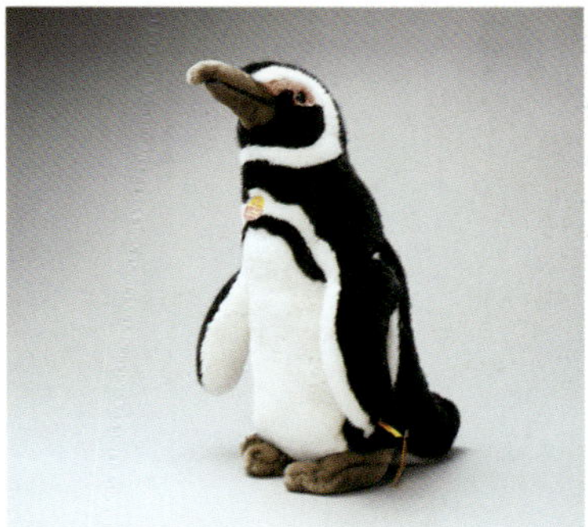

Maggy Pinguin - ***Maggy** Penguin*

Webpelz, waschmaschinenfest - *woven fur, machine washable*

EAN-NO.	PERIOD	PR.	INFO
063657	1992-1996	3	44 cm

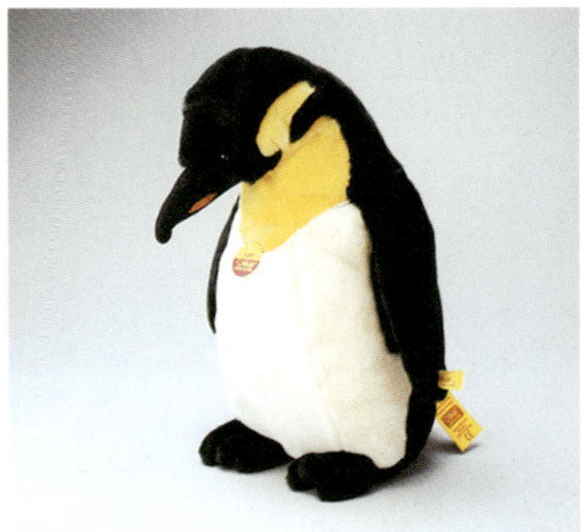

Lari Pinguin - ***Lari** Penguin*

Webpelz, waschmaschinenfest - *woven fur, machine washable*

EAN-No.	Period	Pr.	Info
063558	1994-1996	2-3	35 cm

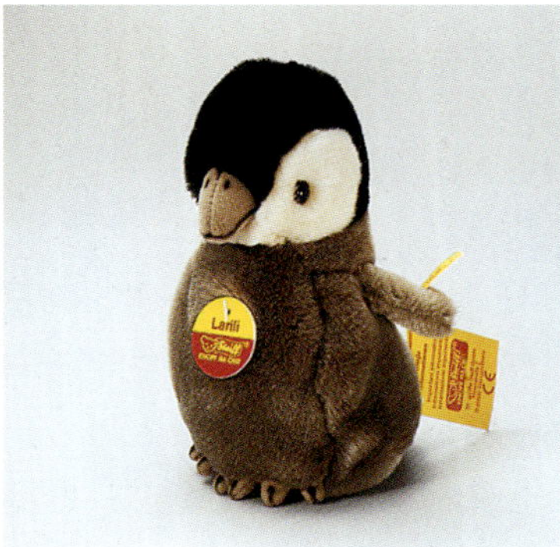

Larili Pinguin Baby - ***Larili** Penguin Baby*

Webpelz, waschmaschinenfest - *woven fur, machine washable*

EAN-No.	Period	Pr.	Info
063572	1994-1999	1-2	18 cm

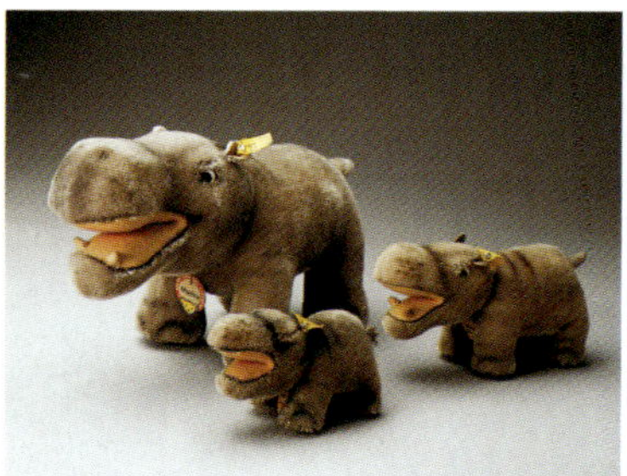

Mockie Nilpferd - ***Mockie** Hippopotamus*

Mohairpluesch, grau, stehend, ab 14 cm Holzzaehne - *mohair, grey, standing, from 14 cm wooden teeth*

Serie	Art.-No	Period	Pr.	Info
55a	**1310,0**	1954-1958	3-4	10 cm
552	**1310,00**	1959-1964	3	
55a	**1314,0**	1954-1958	4	14 cm
552	**1314,00**	1959-1963	3-4	
55a	**1322,0**	1956-1958	4-5	22 cm
552	**1322,00**	1959-1963	4	

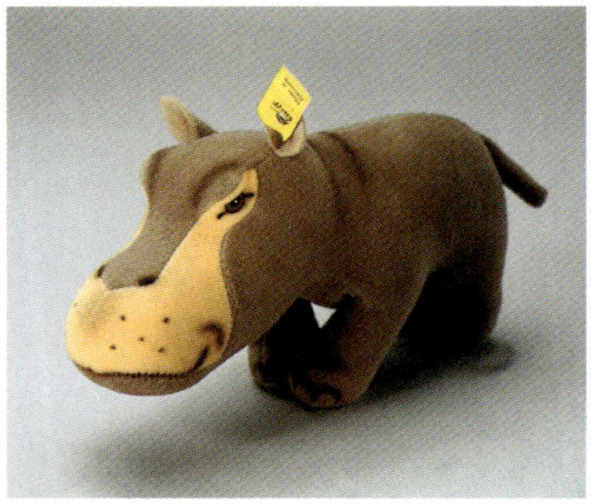

Mockie Nilpferd - ***Mockie** Hippopotamus*

Trevirasamt, stehend, vollwaschbar - *trevira velvet, standing, fully washable*

Serie	Art.-No	Period	Pr.	Info
	1120/14	1975-1978	3	14 cm
	1120/20	1975-1978	3	20 cm

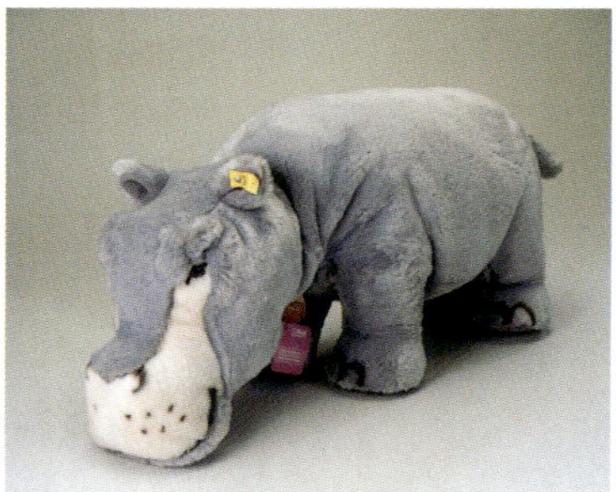

Mockie Nilpferd - ***Mockie** Hippopotamus*

Synthetik-Webpluesch, grau, stehend, abwaschbar - *synthetic woven fur, grey, standing, surface washable*

Serie	Art.-No	Period	Pr.	Info
	6304/50	1977-1979	3	50 cm

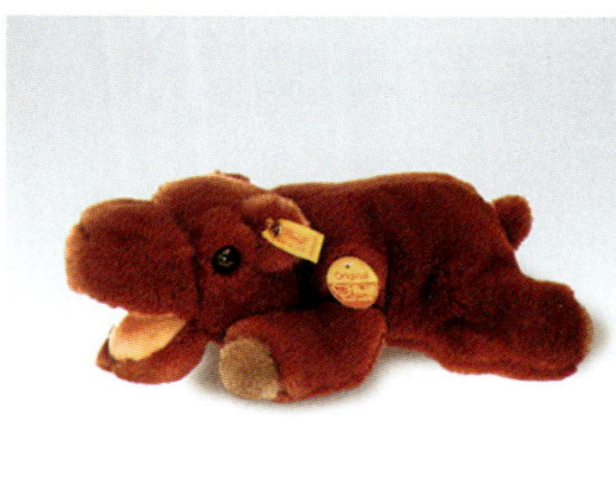

Kuschel Nilpferd - *Cuddly Hippopotamus*

Webpelz, Schaumstoff-Fuellung, superweich, waschmaschinenfest - *woven fur, stuffed with foam, super soft, machine washable*

Serie	Art.-No	Period	Pr.	Info
	5515/25	1981-1982	2	25 cm

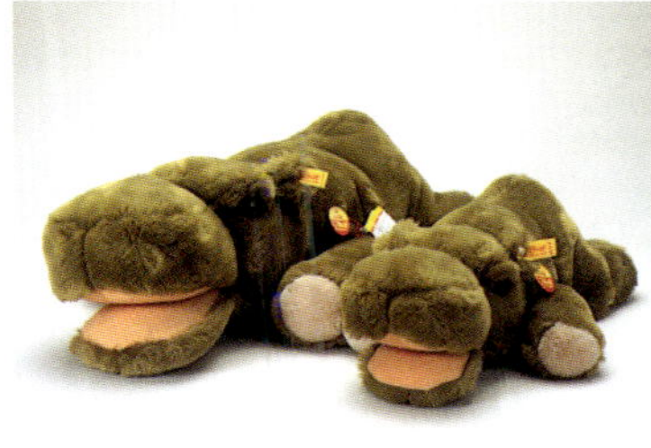

Linda Nilpferd - ***Linda** Hippopotamus*

Webpelz, gruen, waschmaschinenfest - *woven fur, green, machine washable*

Serie	Art.-No	Period	Pr.	Info
	5517/25	1983-1985	2	25 cm
	5517/35	1983-1985	2-3	35 cm
	5517/55	1983-1985	3	55 cm

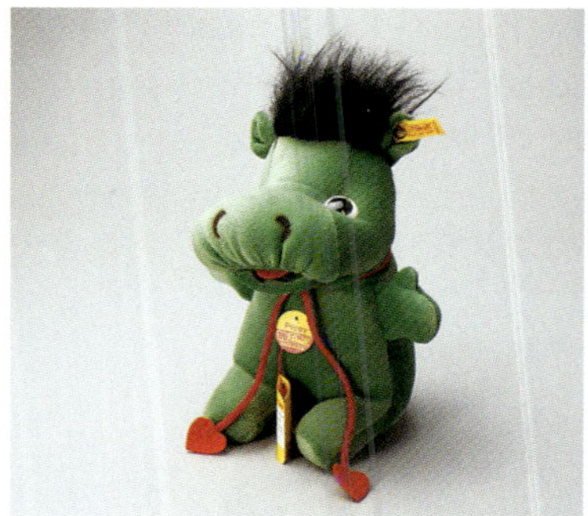

Poppy Nilpferd - ***Poppy** Hippopotamus*

Nicki-Stoff, abwaschbar - *nicki velvet, surface washable*

Serie	Art.-No	Period	Pr.	Info
	7882/26	1984-1984	3-4	26 cm

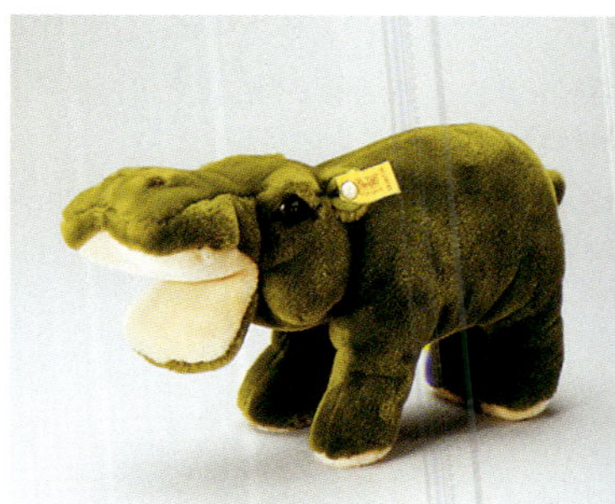

Cosy Hippo Nilpferd - ***Cosy Hippo** Hippopotamus*

Webpelz, superweich, waschmaschinenfest - *woven fur, super soft, machine washable*

Serie	Art.-No	Period	Pr.	Info
098543	**5510/30**	1986-1987	2-3	30 cm
098567	**5510/40**	1986-1987	3	40 cm
098581	**5510/50**	1986-1987	3	50 cm

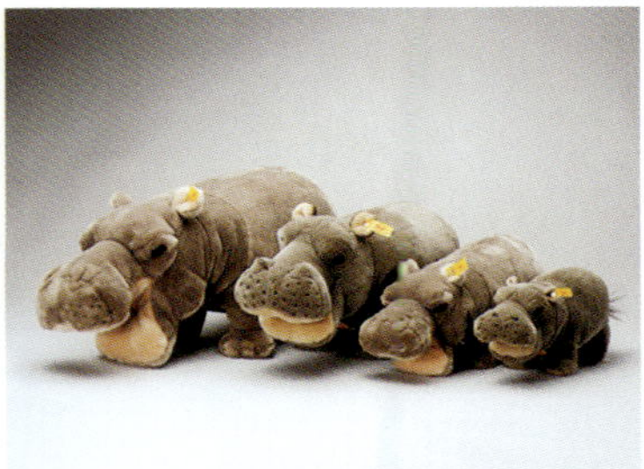

Mocky Nilpferd - ***Mocky*** *Hippopotamus*

Webpelz, stehend, waschmaschinenfest, geringe Unterschiede zwischen 92er- und 94er-Modell - *woven fur, standing, machine washable, small differences between the 92/94 models*

EAN-No.	Period	Pr.	Info
063428	1992-1992	2-3	25 cm
063466	1994-1996	3	35 cm
063442	1992-1992	3	45 cm
063480	1994-1999	3-4	60 cm

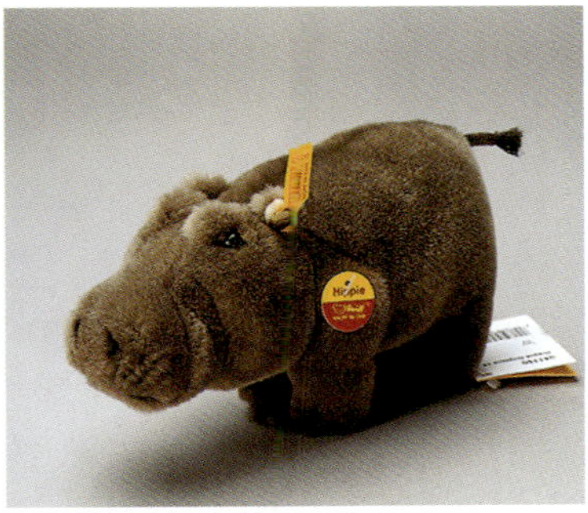

Hippie Nilpferd - ***Hippie*** *Hippopotamus*

Webpelz, stehend, waschmaschinenfest - *woven fur, standing, machine washable*

EAN-No.	Period	Pr.	Info
041150	1995-1999	1-2	18 cm

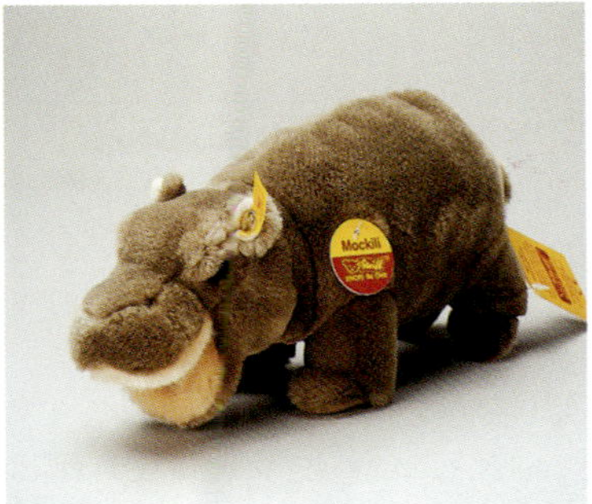

Mockili Baby Nilpferd - ***Mockili*** *Baby Hippopotamus*

Webpelz, stehend, waschmaschinenfest - *woven fur, standing, machine washable*

EAN-No.	Period	Pr.	Info
063497	1995-1997	2	22 cm

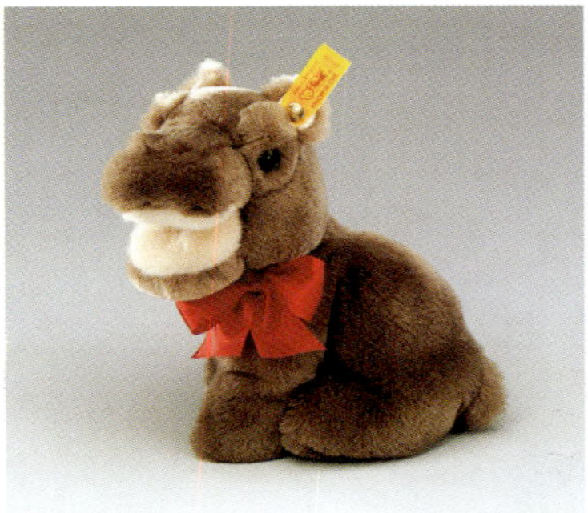

Snuffi Nilpferd - ***Snuffi*** *Hippopotamus*

Webpelz, sitzend, waschmaschinenfest - *woven fur, sitting, machine washable*

EAN-No.	Period	Pr.	Info
077166	1996-1997	2	16 cm

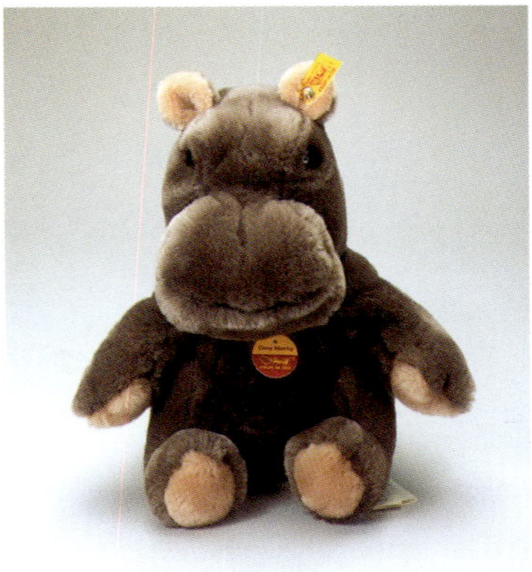

Cosy Mocky Nilpferd - ***Cosy Mocky*** *Hippopotamus*

Webpelz, sitzend, waschmaschinenfest - *woven fur, sitting, machine washable*

EAN-No.	Period	Pr.	Info
085413	1996-1999	2-3	28 cm

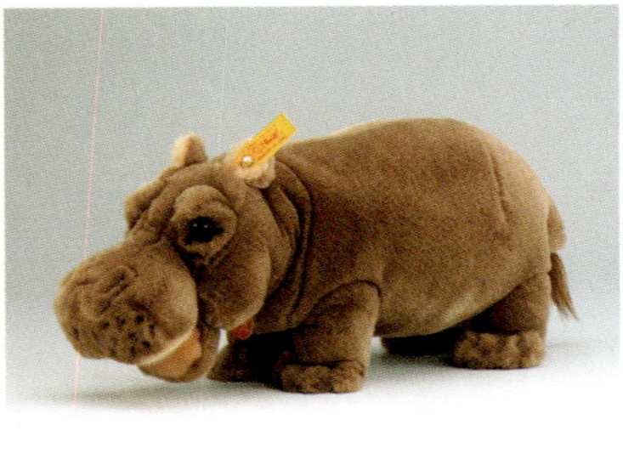

Mocky Nilpferd - ***Mocky*** *Hippopotamus*

Webpelz, stehend, waschmaschinenfest - *woven fur, standing, machine washable*

EAN-No.	Period	Pr.	Info
085420	1997-1998	3	32 cm

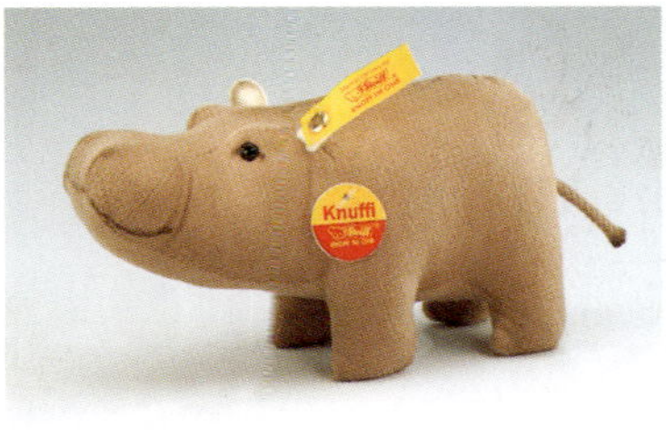

Knuffi Nilpferd - *Knuffi Hippopotamus*

Microfaser-Vlies, hellbraun, handwaschbar - *micro fibre fleece, light brown, hand washable*

EAN-No.	Period	Pr.	Info
067747	1997-1997	1-2	14 cm

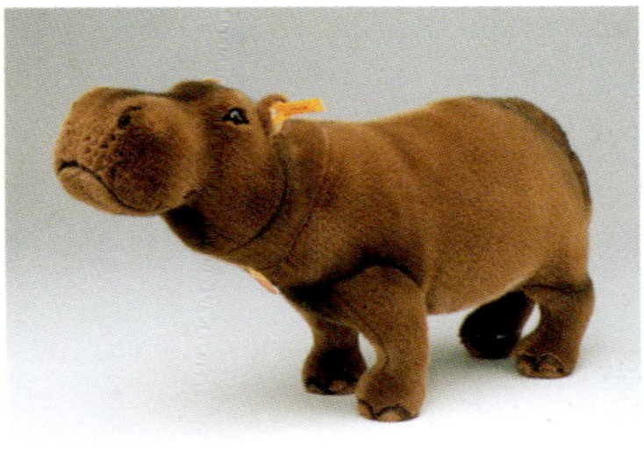

Nilpferd - *Hippopotamus*

Webpelz, stehend, abwaschbar - *woven fur, standing, surface washable*

EAN-No.	Period	Pr.	Info
063435	1999-1999	3	40 cm

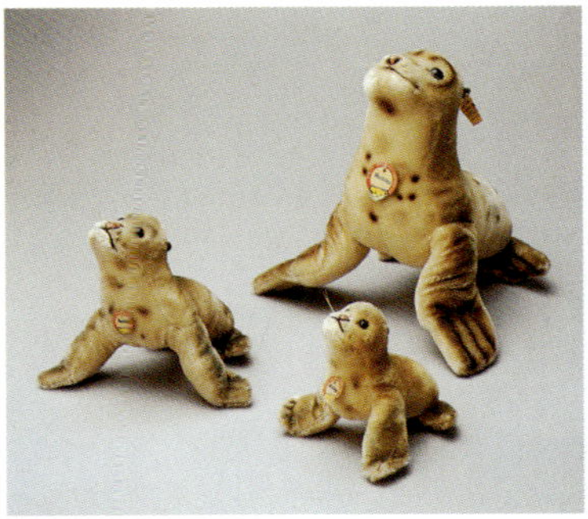

Robby Seehund - ***Robby*** *Seal*

Mohair, weiss, grau/gruen bemalt, aufwartend, abwaschbar - *mohair, white, painted with grey/green markings, sitting up, surface washable*

Serie	Art.-No	Period	Pr.	Info
63	**4310**	1954-1958	3-4	10 cm
630	**4310,00**	1959-1964	3	
117	**4310,00**	1965-1967	3	
	1170/10	1968-1974	2-3	
63	**4314**	1954-1958	3-4	14 cm
630	**4314,00**	1959-1963	3	
117	**4314,00**	1966-1967	3	
	1170/14	1968-1974	3	
63	**4322**	1958-1958	4	22 cm
630	**4322,00**	1959-1963	4	

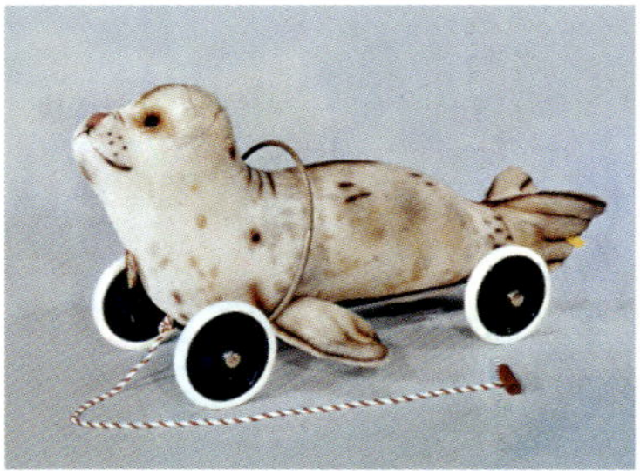

Reit-**Robby** - *Riding **Robby***

Mohair, Haltegriff & Fussrasten, grau, bemalt, gummibereifte Scheibenraeder, Zugstimme, ab 1967 Plastikreifen, Schlepplenkung - *mohair, grip handle & foot-rests, grey, painted markings, disc wheels with rubber tires, pull cord voice, from 1967 plastic tires & pull type steering*

SERIE	ART.-NO	PERIOD	PR.	INFO
630	**2350,20**	1962-1964	5	50 cm
117	**2350,20**	1965-1967	5	
	1170/50	1968-1970	5	

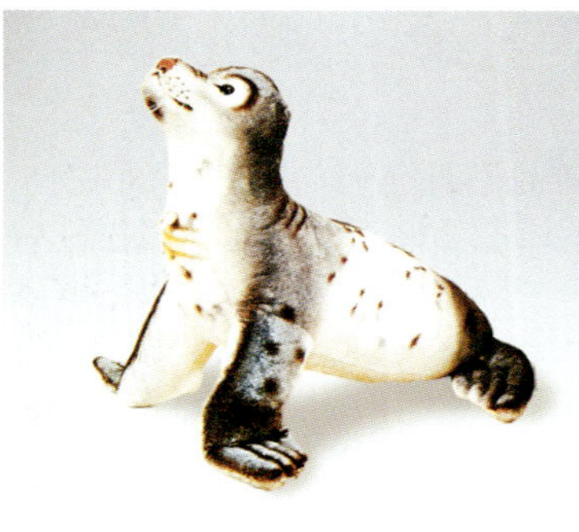

Seehund - *Seal*

Schautier, Mohair, aufwartend - *display animal, mohair, sitting up*

SERIE	ART.-NO	PERIOD	PR.	INFO
630	**4380,90**	1960-1960	5-6	80 cm
	1179/08	1967-1967	5-6	

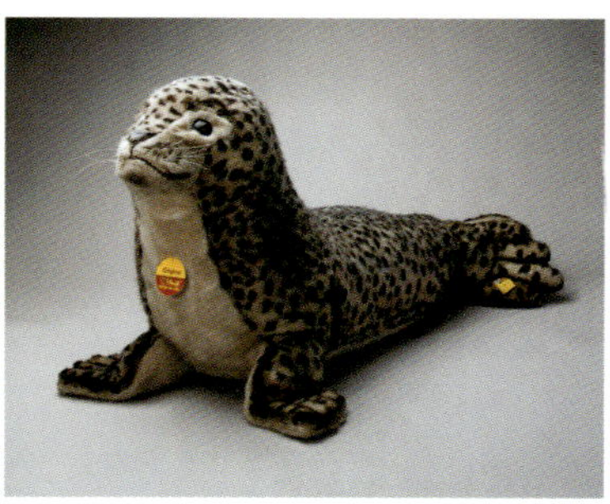

Robbe - *Seal*

Schautier, Webpelz, gefleckt, ohne Katalognachweis - *display animal, woven fur, speckled, no catalog information available*

EAN-NO.	PERIOD	PR.	INFO
	1960-1960	5	80 cm

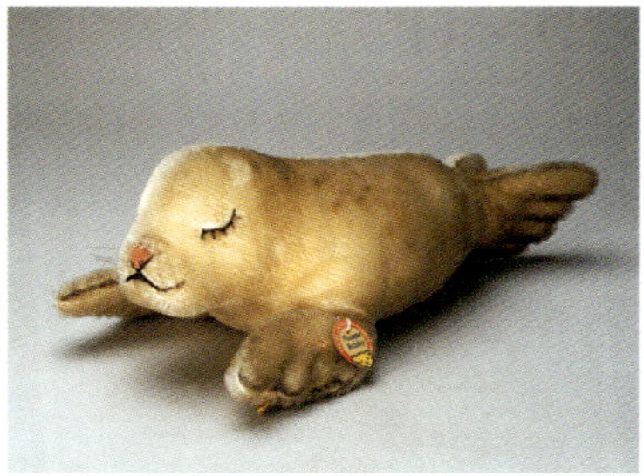

Floppy Robby

Mohair, grau/weiss, Augen gestickt, liegend, sehr weich - *mohair, grey/white, eyes embroidered, lying flat, very soft*

SERIE	ART.-NO	PERIOD	PR.	INFO
850 630	**7328,00**	1964-1964	3	28 cm
564	**7328,00**	1965-1967	3	
	5640/28	1968-1969	3	

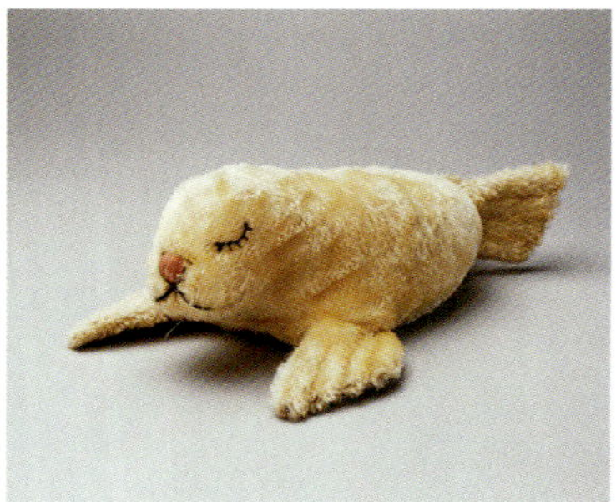

Floppy Robby

Mohair, formgeschaeumt, Augen gestickt, liegend, sehr weich, vollwaschbar - *mohair, stuffed with pre-formed foam, eyes embroidered, lying flat, very soft, fully washable*

SERIE	ART.-NO	PERIOD	PR.	INFO
	5647/28	1970-1976	2-3	28 cm

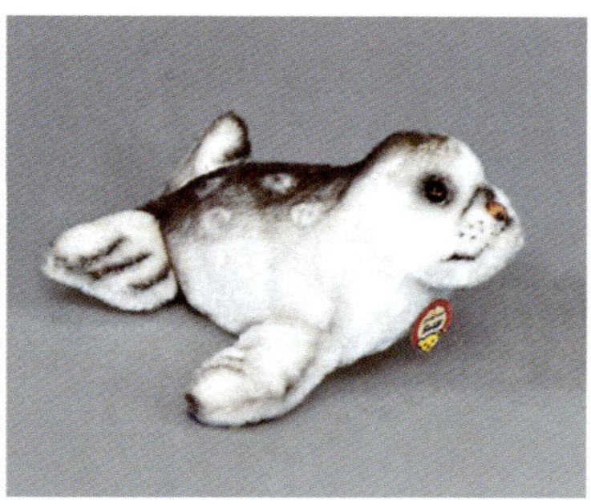

Cosy Robby Seehund - *Cosy Robby Seal*

Dralon, gefuellt mit synthetischen Fasern & Schaumstoff, aufwartend, sehr weich, vollwaschbar - *dralon, stuffed with synthetic fibers & foam, sitting up, very soft, fully washable*

SERIE	ART.-NO	PERIOD	PR.	INFO
	4897/20	1971-1975	1-2	20 cm

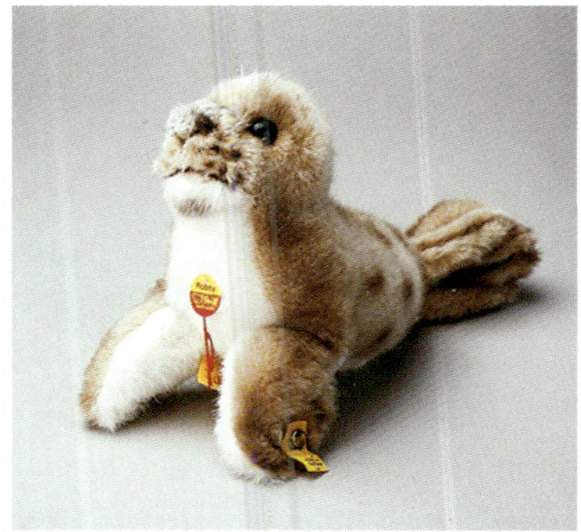

Robby Seehund - ***Robby** Seal*

Nerzimitation, formgeschaeumt, ab 1978 Synthetik-Webpelz, aufwartend, abwaschbar - *imitation mink, stuffed with pre-formed foam, from 1978 synthetic woven fur, sitting up, surface washable*

SERIE	ART.-NO	PERIOD	PR.	INFO
	1175/14	1975-1985	2	14 cm
	1175/20	1975-1982	2	20 cm

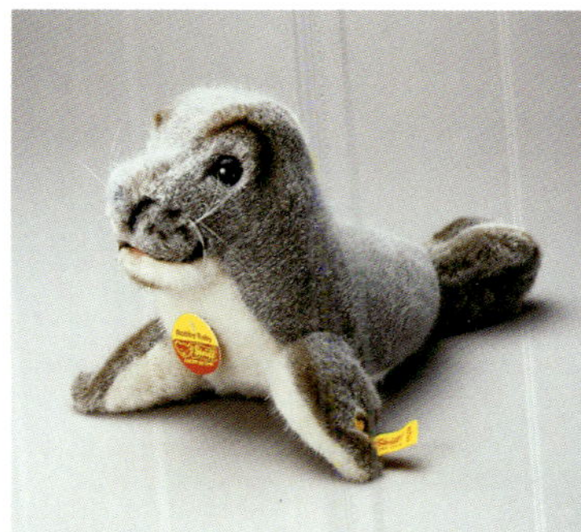

Robby Baby

Nerzimitation, ab 1978 Synthetik-Webpelz, aufwartend, Druckstimme, abwaschbar - *imitation mink, from 1978 synthetic woven fur, sitting up, press voice, surface washable*

SERIE	ART.-NO	PERIOD	PR.	INFO
063008	**1178/14**	1976-1987	1-2	14 cm

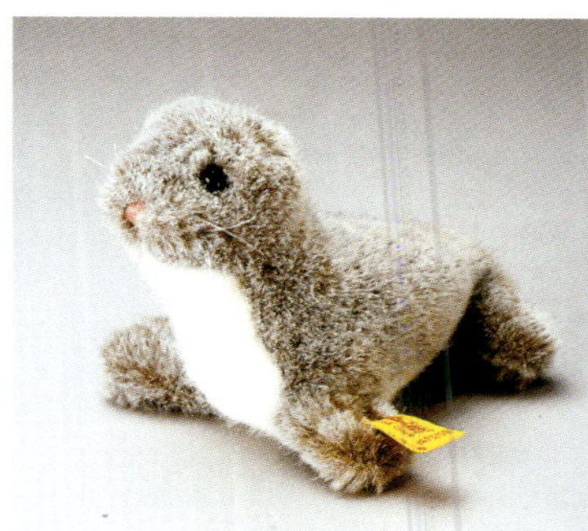

Olly Seehund - ***Olly** Seal*

Nerzimitation, ab 1978 Synthetik-Webpelz,

aufwartend, abwaschbar - *imitation mink, from 1978 synthetic woven fur, sitting up, surface washable*

SERIE	ART.-NO	PERIOD	PR.	INFO
047206	**1473/09**	1977-1990	1	15 cm
	047206	1991-1999	1	

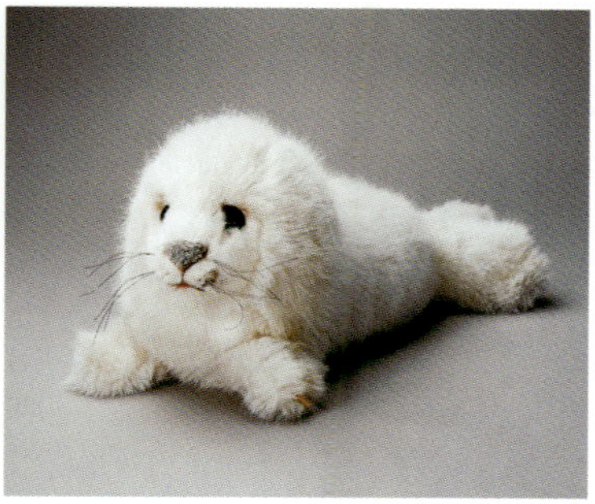

Heuler - *Seal Pup*

Synthetik-Webpelz, aufwartend, 70 cm Schautier, abwaschbar - *synthetic woven fur, sitting up, 70 cm display animal, surface washable*

SERIE	ART.-NO	PERIOD	PR.	INFO
	1179/04	1978-1982	2-3	40 cm
	1179/07	1980-1980	3-4	70 cm

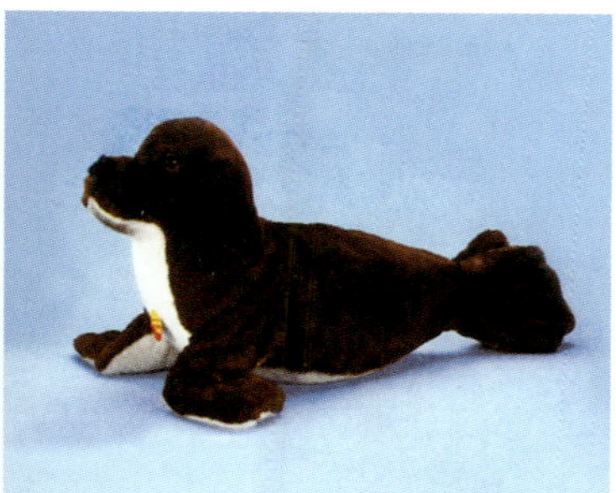

Super Molly Robbe - ***Super Molly** Seal*

Webpelz, mollig weich, abwaschbar - *woven fur, soft & cuddly, surface washable*

SERIE	ART.-NO	PERIOD	PR.	INFO
	0343/80	1980-1983	3	80 cm

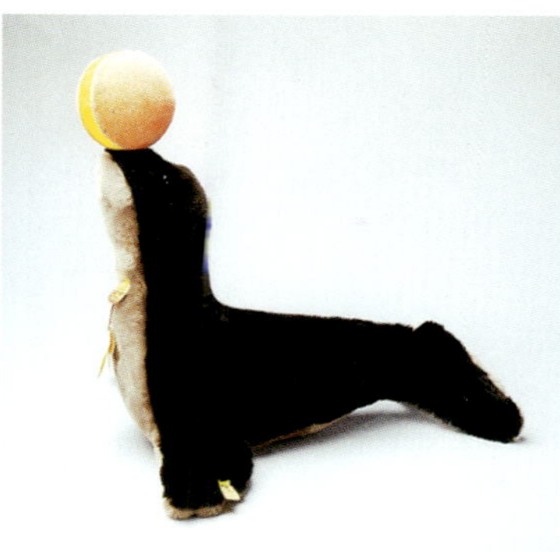

Cosy Movi Seehund - ***Cosy Movi** Seal*

Webpelz, mit Ball, aufwartend, superweich, waschmaschinenfest - *woven fur, with ball, sitting up, super soft, machine washable*

SERIE	ART.-NO	PERIOD	PR.	INFO
	5376/50	1981-1982	3-4	50 cm

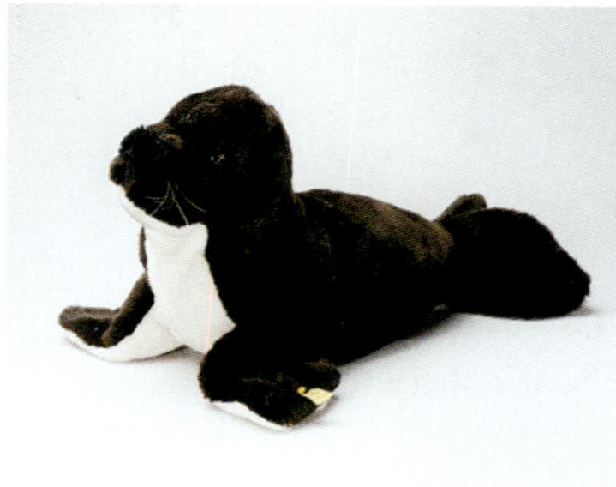

Cosy Robby

Webpelz, kuschelweich, waschmaschinenfest - *woven fur, soft & cuddly, machine washable*

SERIE	ART.-NO	PERIOD	PR.	INFO
090301	**5375/57**	1982-1990	3	57 cm

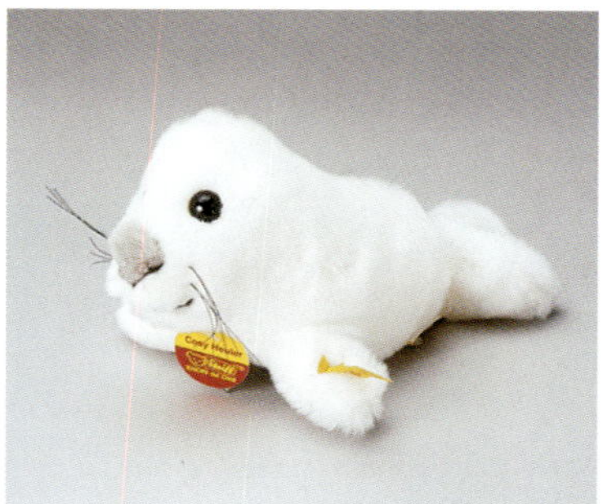

Cosy Heuler - ***Cosy** Seal Pup*

Webpelz, superweich, waschmaschinenfest - *woven fur, super soft, machine washable*

SERIE	ART.-NO	PERIOD	PR.	INFO
090103	**5374/17**	1984-1990	1-2	18 cm
	090103	1991-1999	1-2	
090158	**5374/35**	1982-1990	2	35 cm
	090158	1991-1995	2	

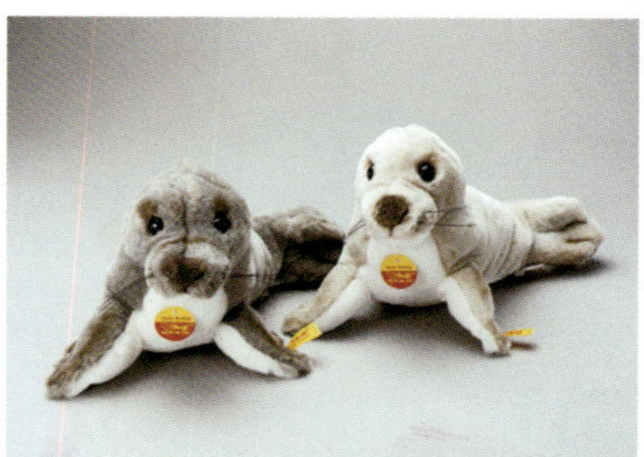

Cosy Robby Seehund - ***Cosy Robby** Seal*

Webpelz, 30 cm, Pieps-Stimme, superweich, waschmaschinenfest - *woven fur, 30 cm, squeaker, super soft, machine washable*

SERIE	ART.-NO	PERIOD	PR.	INFO
090202	**5375/30**	1986-1990	2	grau - *grey*
	090202	1991-1999	2	
090257	**5375/31**	1986-1990	2	beige
	090257	1991-1992	2	

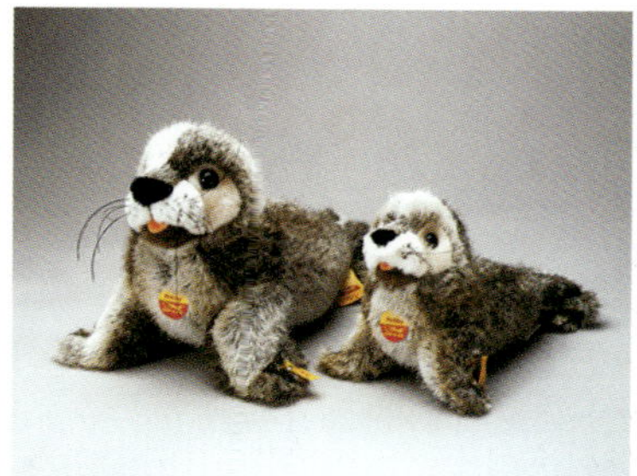

Robby Seehund - ***Robby** Seal*

Webpelz, gefleckt, liegend, Pieps-Stimme, waschmaschinenfest - *woven fur, spotted, lying, squeaker, machine washable*

SERIE	ART.-NO	PERIOD	PR.	INFO
	063077	1991-1999	2-3	32 cm
063107	**1150/45**	1990-1990	3	45 cm
	063107	1991-1997	3	
	063121	1991-1995	3	60 cm

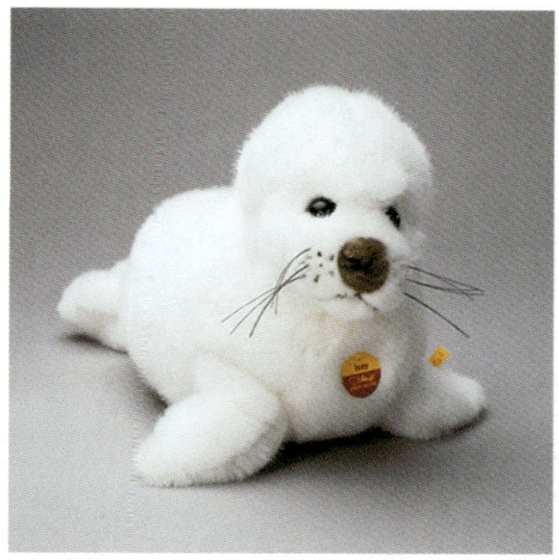

Issy Heuler - ***Issy** Seal Pup*

Webpelz, weiss, waschmaschinenfest - *woven fur, white, machine washable*

EAN-NO.	PERIOD	PR.	INFO
063152	1992-1999	2-3	34 cm
063176	1992-1995	3	40 cm
063190	1992-1993	3	50 cm

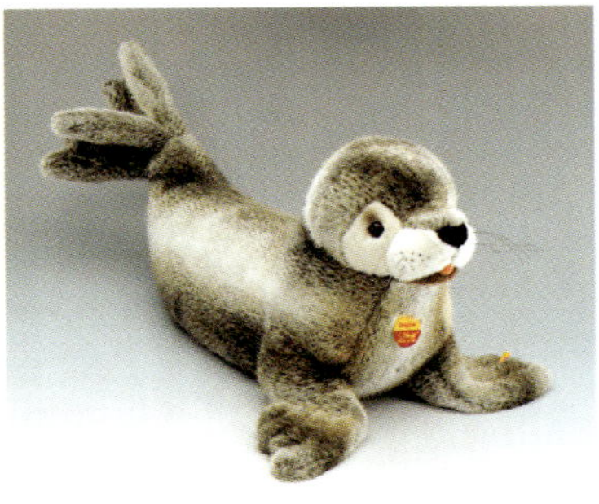

Sitz-Seehund - *Sitting Seal*

Webpelz, abwaschbar - *woven fur, surface washable*

EAN-No.	Period	Pr.	Info
482304	1995-1996	4	100 cm

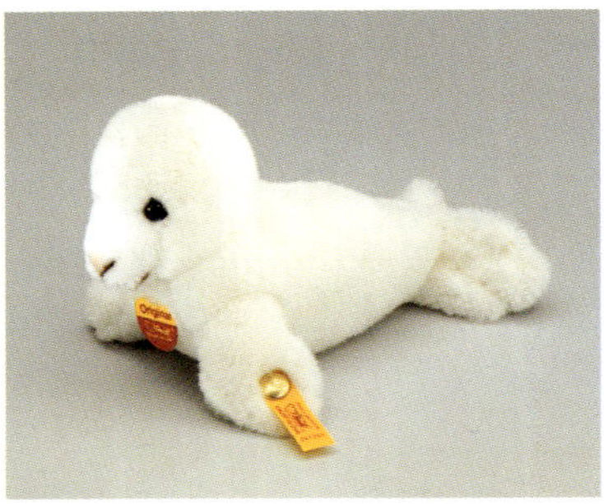

Heuler - *Newborn Seal*

Webpelz, weiss, waschmaschinenfest - *woven fur, white, machine washable*

EAN-No.	Period	Pr.	Info
047305	1996-1999	1-2	15 cm

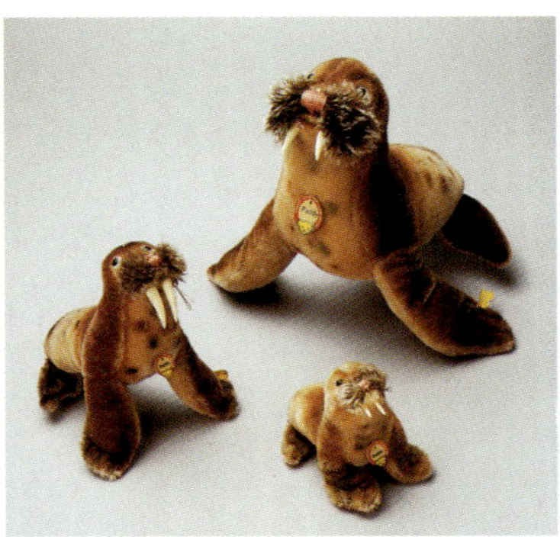

Paddy Walross - ***Paddy*** *Walrus*

Mohairpluesch, grau/braun schattiert, aufwartend, mit Zaehnen - *mohair, shaded brown & grey, sitting up, with tusks*

Serie	Art.-No	Period	Pr.	Info
631	**4310,00**	1959-1964	4	10 cm
115	**4310,00**	1965-1965	4	
631	**4314,00**	1959-1964	4	14 cm
115	**4314,00**	1965-1965	4	
631	**4322,00**	1959-1964	4-5	22 cm

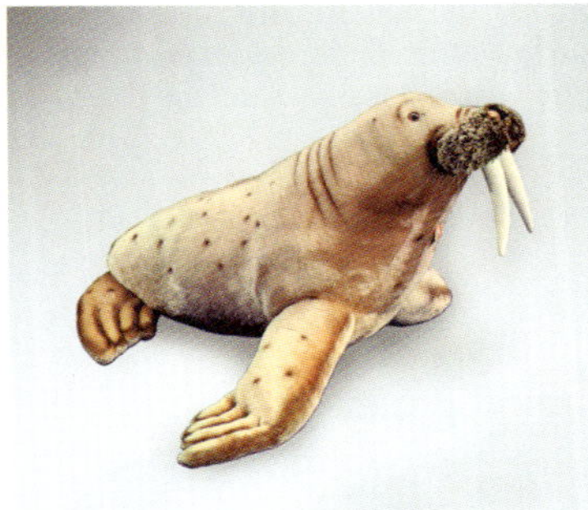

Walross - *Walrus*

Schautier, Mohairpluesch, beige/braun gefleckt, aufwartend, mit Zaehnen - *display animal, mohair, beige/brown spotted, begging, with tusks*

Serie	Art.-No	Period	Pr.	Info
	1159/10	1967-1967	6	100 cm

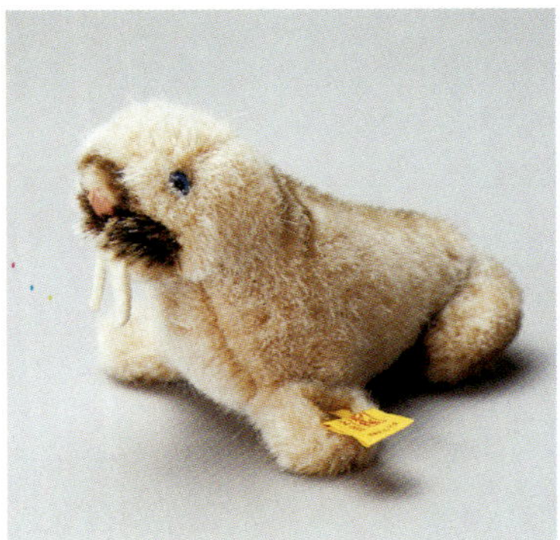

Wally Walross - ***Wally*** *Walrus*

Webpelz, aufwartend, abwaschbar - *woven fur, sitting up, surface washable*

Serie	Art.-No	Period	Pr.	Info
	1474/10	1979-1984	2	10 cm

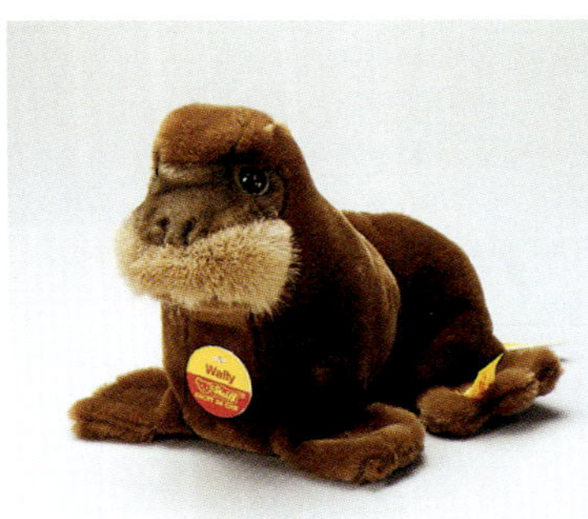

Wally Walross - ***Wally*** *Walrus*

Webpelz, waschmaschinenfest - *woven fur, machine washable*

Serie	Art.-No	Period	Pr.	Info
062902	**1170/16**	1988-1990	2	16 cm
	062902	1991-1997	2	

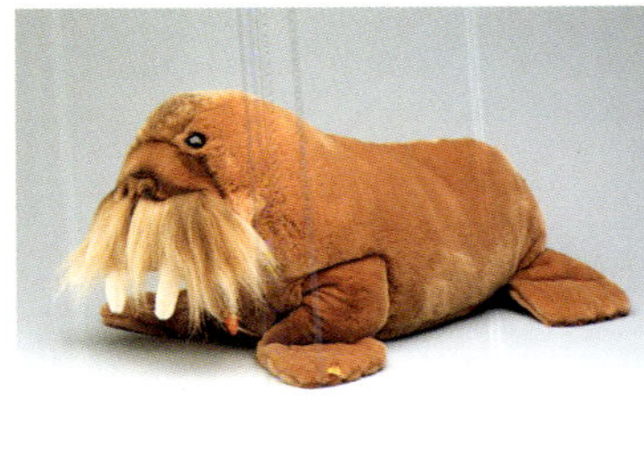

Wally Walross - ***Wally*** *Walrus*

Webpelz, abwaschbar - *woven fur, surface washable*

Serie	Art.-No	Period	Pr.	Info
062957	**1172/80**	1988-1990	3-4	80 cm
	062957	1991-1995	3-4	
062964	**1172/99**	1988-1989	4	140 cm

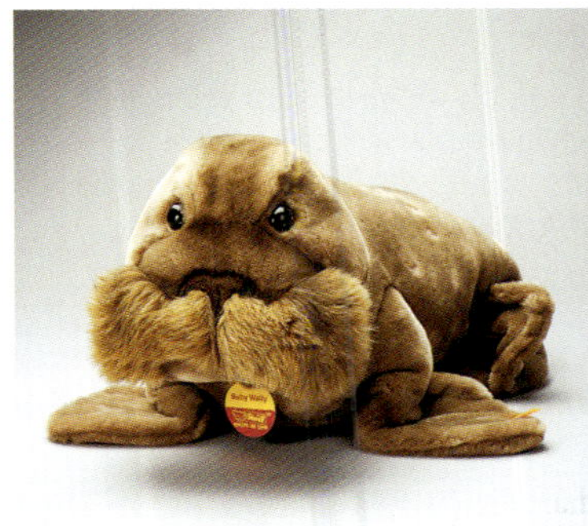

Baby Wally Walross - ***Baby Wally*** *Walrus*

Webpelz, waschmaschinenfest - *woven fur, machine washable*

Serie	Art.-No	Period	Pr.	Info
062988	**1174/55**	1988-1990	3-4	55 cm
	062988	1991-1995	3-4	

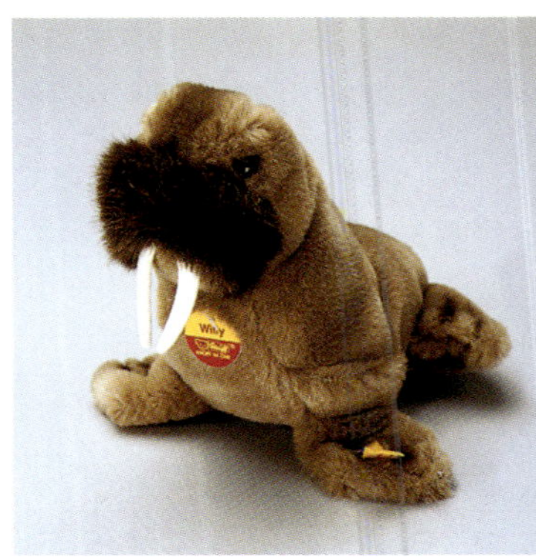

Willy Walross ab 1997 **Wally** - ***Willy*** *Walrus in 1997* ***Wally***

Webpelz, stehend, waschmaschinenfest - *woven fur, standing, machine washable*

EAN-No.	Period	Pr.	Info
047251	1994-1997	1-2	16 cm

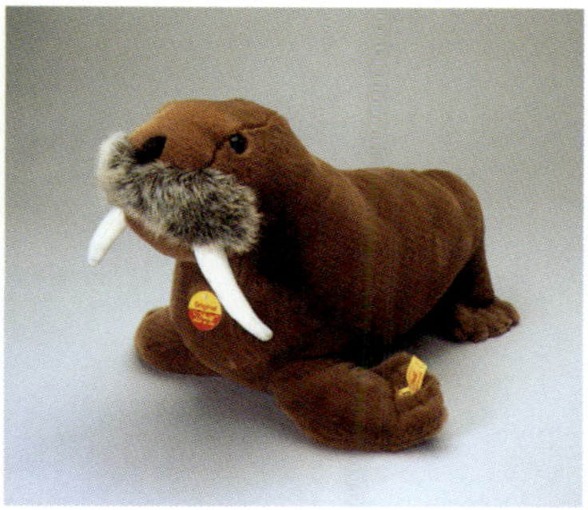

Walross - *Walrus*

Webpelz, braun, waschmaschinenfest - *woven fur, brown, machine washable*

EAN-No.	Period	Pr.	Info
047268	1998-1999	3	40 cm

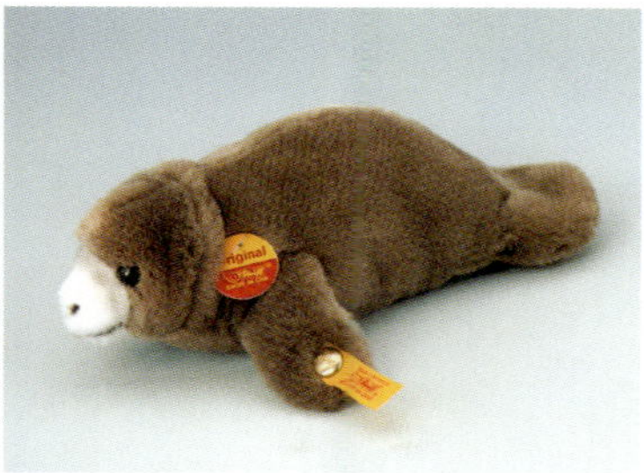

Manati - *Manatee*

Webpelz, waschmaschinenfest - *woven fur, machine washable*

EAN-No.	Period	Pr.	Info
047602	1997-1999	1	15 cm

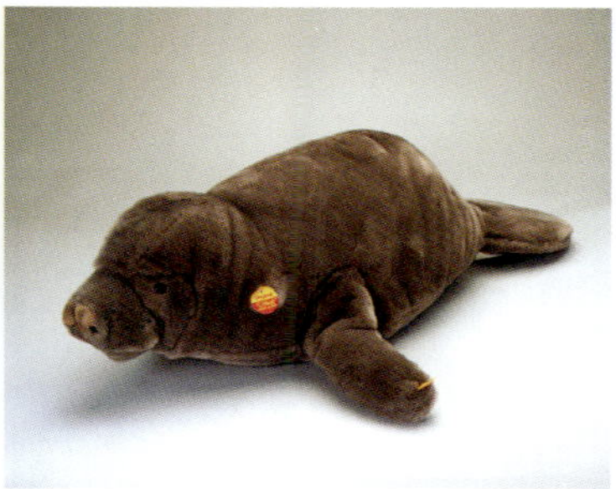

Manati - *Manatee*

Webpelz, liegend, handwaschbar - *woven fur, lying, hand washable*

EAN-No.	Period	Pr.	Info
062773	1997-1999	3	85 cm

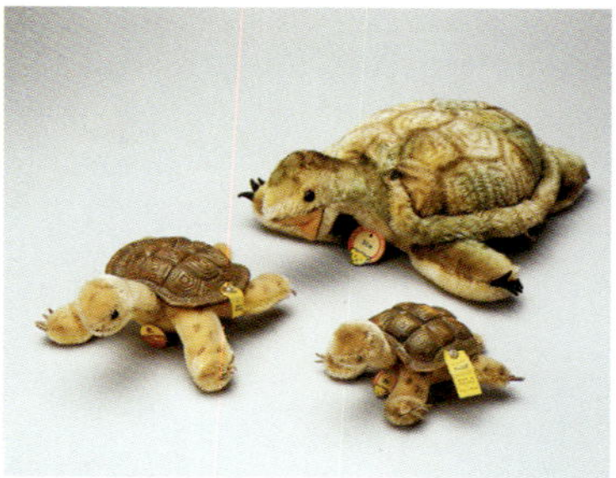

Slo Schildkroete - ***Slo** Turtle*

Mohairpluesch, gelb/braun, Gummi-/Plastikpanzer, 22 cm kpl. Mohair, abwaschbar - *mohair, yellow/brown, with rubber/plastic shell, 22 cm mohair, surface washable*

Serie	Art.-No	Period	Pr.	Info
65	**2310**	1955-1958	3	10 cm
650	**2310,00**	1959-1964	2-3	
245	**2310,00**	1965-1967	2-3	
	2450/10	1968-1975	2	
65	**2314**	1955-1958	3	14 cm
650	**2314,00**	1961-1964	3	
245	**2314,00**	1965-1967	3	
	2450/14	1968-1975	2-3	
65	**2322**	1958-1958	4	22 cm
650	**2322,00**	1959-1964	3-4	
245	**2322,00**	1965-1967	3-4	
	2450/22	1968-1975	3	

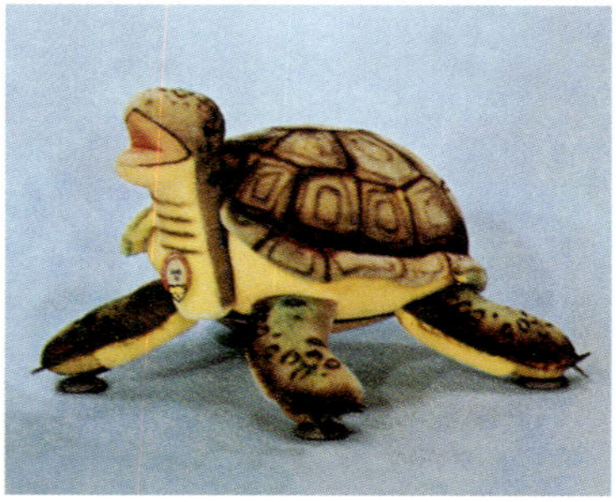

Snuggy Slo

Mohairpluesch, gruen/gelb/schwarz, Sitztier auf Stahlgestell mit Gummifuessen - *mohair, green/yellow/black, sitting animal with steel frame & rubber feet*

Serie	Art.-No	Period	Pr.	Info
82 65	**2343**	1957-1958	5	43 cm
820 650	**2343,00**	1959-1964	4-5	
603	**2343,00**	1965-1967	4-5	
	6030/43	1968-1974	4	

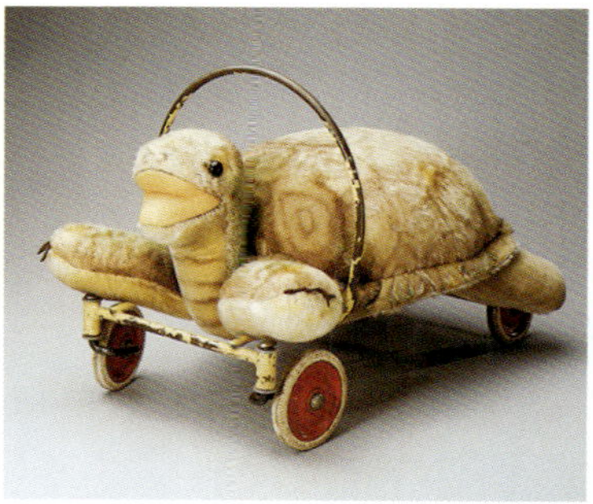

Reit-Schildkroete **Slo** - *Riding Turtle **Slo***

Mohairpluesch, gelb/braun, bemalt, Druckstimme, Stahlrohrgestell, Haltegriff, Fussrasten, auf Scheibenraedern mit Gummi-, ab 1967 Plastikreifen, ab 1968 Kunststofflager, Schleppienkung, abwaschbar - *mohair, yellow/brown, painted, press voice, iron frame, grip handle, foot-rests, disc wheels with rubber tires, from 1967 plastic tires, from 1968 plastic bearings, pull-type steering, surface washable*

Serie	Art.-No	Period	Pr.	Info
650	**2335,20**	1959-1964	4	35 cm
245	**2335,20**	1965-1967	4	
	2450/35	1968-1975	4	

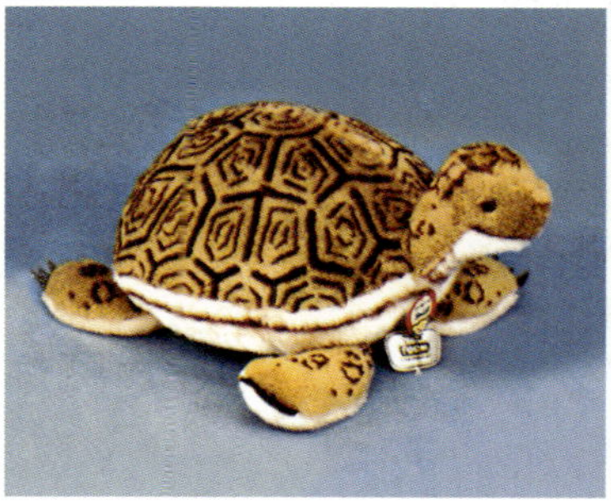

Cosy Slo Schildkroete - ***Cosy Slo** Turtle*

Dralon, gefuellt mit synthetischen Fasern und Schaumstoff, stehend, sehr weich, vollwaschbar - *dralon, stuffed with synthetic fibers & foam, standing, very soft, fully washable*

Serie	Art.-No	Period	Pr.	Info
	4930/24	1971-1976	2	24 cm

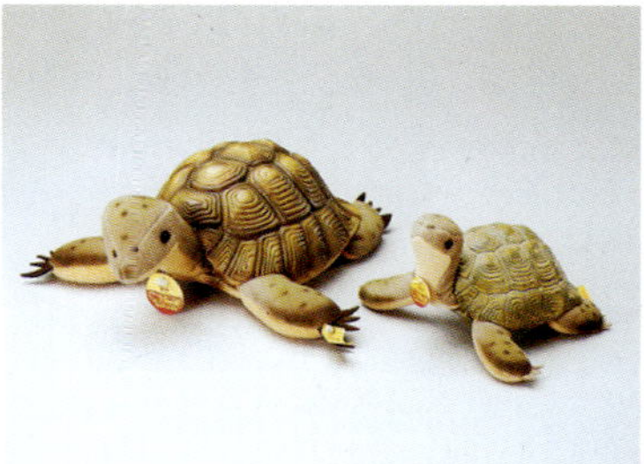

Slo Schildkroete - ***Slo** Turtle*

Trevirasamt, PVC-Panzer, stehend, abwaschbar - *trevira velvet, shell made of PVC, standing, surface washable*

Serie	Art.-No	Period	Pr.	Info
	2455/14	1976-1984	2-3	14 cm
	2455/22	1976-1980	3	22 cm

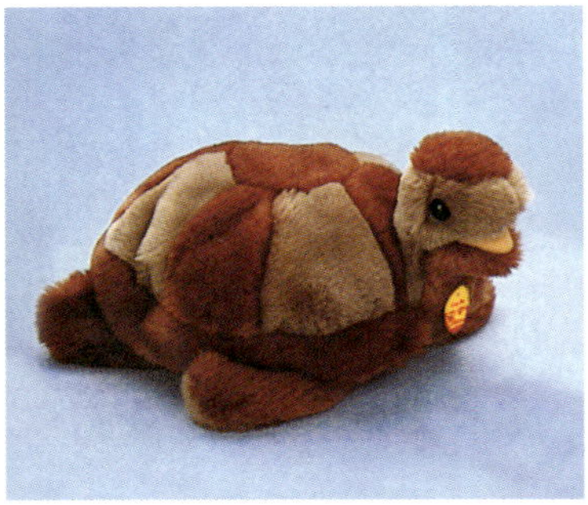

Cosy Slo Schildkroete - ***Cosy Slo** Turtle*

Webpelz, superweich, waschmaschinenfest - *woven fur, super soft, machine washable*

Serie	Art.-No	Period	Pr.	Info
	5420/32	1981-1983	2	32 cm

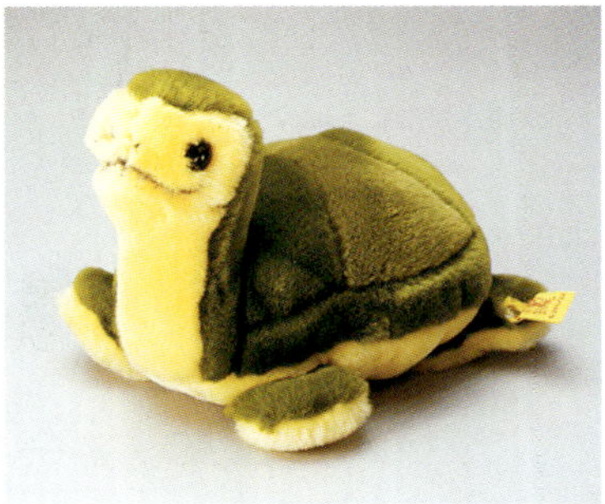

Cosy Slo Schildkroete - ***Cosy Slo** Turtle*

Webpelz, waschmaschinenfest - *woven fur, machine washable*

Serie	Art.-No	Period	Pr.	Info
092305	**5386/22**	1985-1990	2	20 cm
	092305	1991-1997	2	

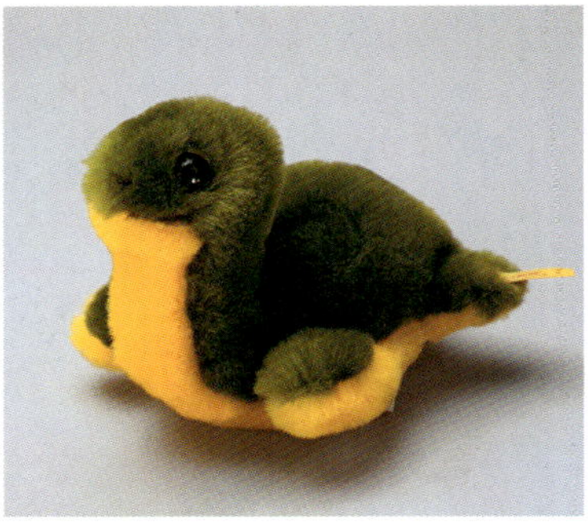

Mini Cosy Schildkroete - *Mini Cosy Turtle*

Webpelz, 14 cm, waschmaschinenfest - *woven fur, 14 cm, machine washable*

Serie	Art.-No	Period	Pr.	Info
084935	**5593/14**	1987-1988	1	rot - *red*
084942	**5594/14**	1987-1989	1	gelb - *yellow*
084966	**5596/14**	1987-1990	1	gruen - *green*
	084966	1991-1999	1	
084973	**5597/14**	1987-1988	1	braun - *brown*

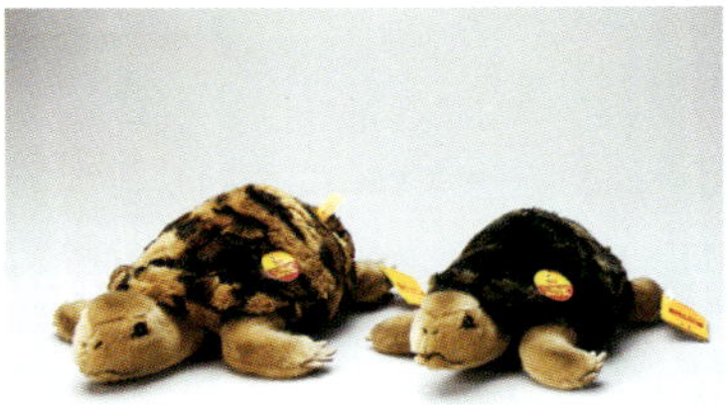

Slo Schildkroete - ***Slo** Turtle*

Webpelz, waschmaschinenfest - *woven fur, machine washable*

EAN-No.	Period	Pr.	Info
068300	1993-1995	2-3	27 cm, gruen - *green*
068324	1993-1996	2-3	35 cm
068348	1993-1996	2-3	27 cm, braun - *brown*
068362	1993-1994	2-3	35 cm

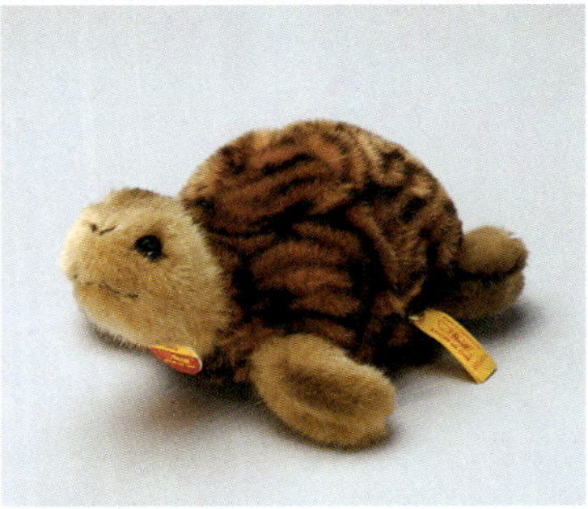

Slo Schildkroete - ***Slo** Turtle*

Webpelz, 16 cm, gefleckt, waschmaschinenfest - *woven fur, 16 cm, spotted, machine washable*

EAN-No.	Period	Pr.	Info
068393	1995-1999	1-2	gruen - *green*
068416	1995-1999	1-2	braun - *brown*
068430	1995-1999	1-2	gelb - *yellow*
068454	1995-1996	1-2	rost - *rust*

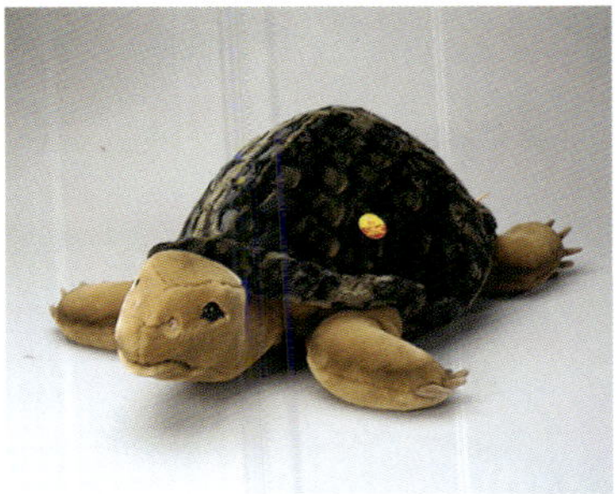

Slo Schildkroete - ***Slo** Turtle*

Webpelz, gruen gefleckt, abwaschbar - *woven fur, green with speckles, surface washable*

EAN-No.	Period	Pr.	Info
068478	1995-1999	4	70 cm

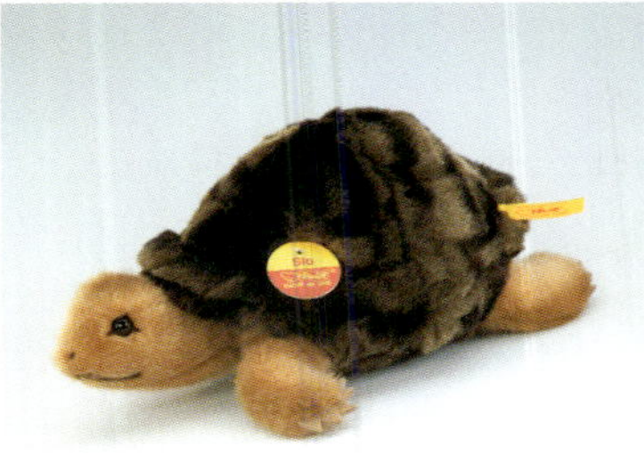

Slo Schildkroete - ***Slo** Turtle*

Webpelz, 22 cm, waschmaschinenfest - *woven fur, 22 cm, machine washable*

EAN-No.	Period	Pr.	Info
068409	1997-1999	2-3	gruen - *green*
068423	1997-1997	2-3	braun - *brown*

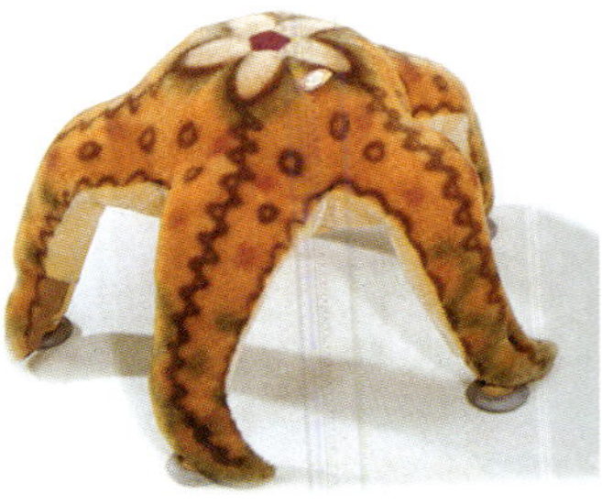

Seestern **Snuggy Starly** - *Starfish **Snuggy Starly***

Sitztier, Mohairpluesch, auf Stahlgestell mit Gummifuessen - *sitting animal, mohair, on steel frame with rubber feet*

Serie	Art.-No	Period	Pr.	Info
820 660	**2335,00**	1959-1964	5	35 cm
604	**2335,00**	1965-1967	5	
	6040/35	1968-1969	5	

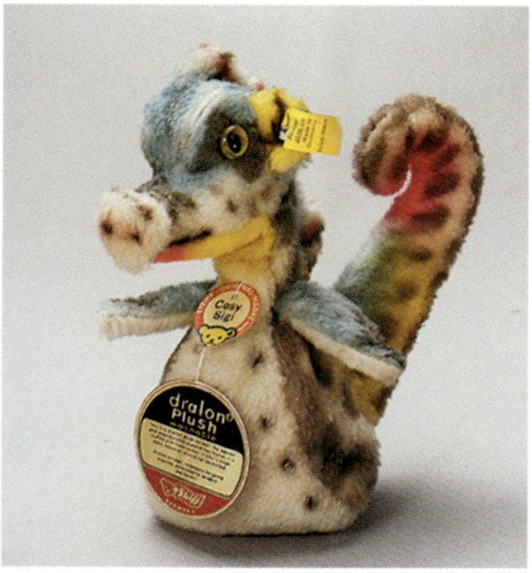

Seepferd **Cosy Sigi** - *Seahorse **Cosy Sigi***

Dralon, Schaumstoff-Fuellung, blau/gruen/gelb/schwarz, aufwartend, sehr weich, waschbar - *dralon, stuffed with foam, blue/green/yellow/black, sitting up, very soft, washable*

SERIE	ART.-NO	PERIOD	PR.	INFO
830 665	**4620,00**	1959-1959	6	20 cm
830 665	**4628,00**	1959-1959	6	28 cm

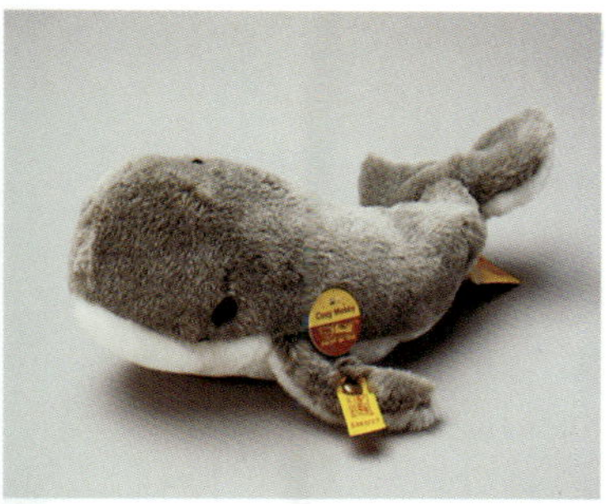

Cosy Mobby Wal - ***Cosy Mobby** Whale*

Webpelz, kuschelweich, waschmaschinenfest - *woven fur, soft & cuddly, machine washable*

SERIE	ART.-NO	PERIOD	PR.	INFO
092909	**5387/27**	1983-1989	2	27 cm

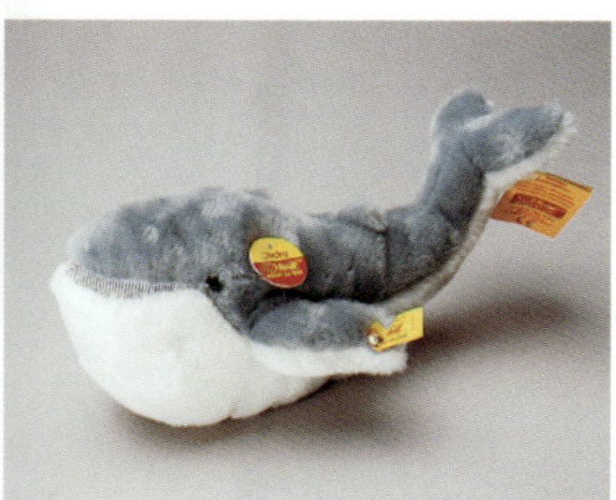

Dicky Blauwal - ***Dicky** Blue Whale*

Webpelz, eisblau, waschmaschinenfest - *woven fur, ice blue, machine washable*

SERIE	ART.-NO	PERIOD	PR.	INFO
063220	**1180/30**	1990-1990	1-2	30 cm
	063220	1991-1996	1-2	
063251	**1180/60**	1990-1990	2-3	60 cm
	063251	1991-1991	2-3	

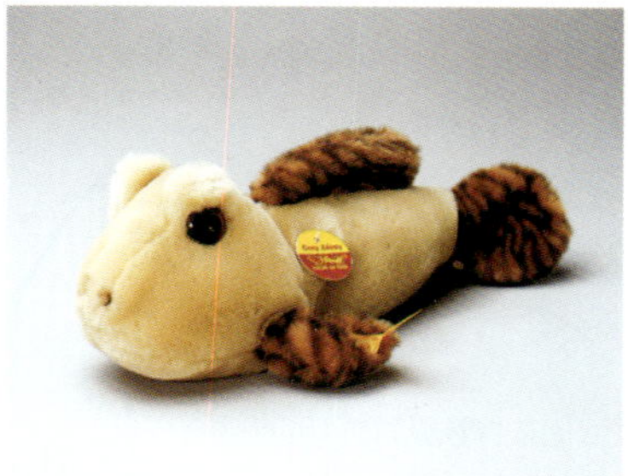

Cosy Zappy Schlammspringer - ***Cosy Zappy** Mud Puppy*

Webpelz, 30 cm, waschmaschinenfest - *woven fur, 30 cm, machine washable*

EAN-NO.	PERIOD	PR.	INFO
095214	1993-1993	3	rosé - *rose*
095221	1993-1993	3	gelb - *yellow*
095238	1993-1993	3	beige
095245	1993-1993	3	gruen - *green*

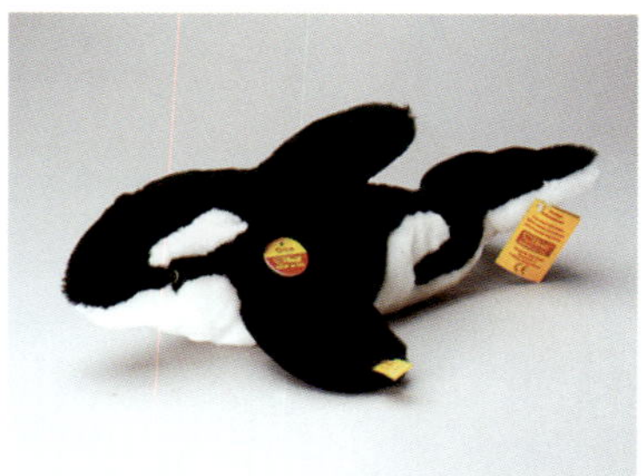

Orca Schwertwal - ***Orca** Sword Whale*

Webpelz, waschmaschinenfest, 75 cm handwaschbar - *woven fur, machine washable, 75 cm hand washable*

EAN-NO.	PERIOD	PR.	INFO
063275	1993-1999	2-3	40 cm
063299	1993-1999	3	55 cm
063268	1996-1999	3	75 cm

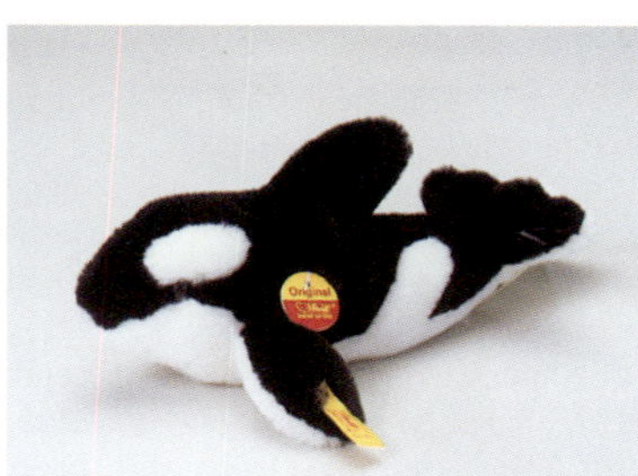

Schwertwal - *Sword Whale*

Webpelz, waschmaschinenfest - *woven fur, machine washable*

EAN-NO.	PERIOD	PR.	INFO
047367	1997-1999	1-2	15 cm

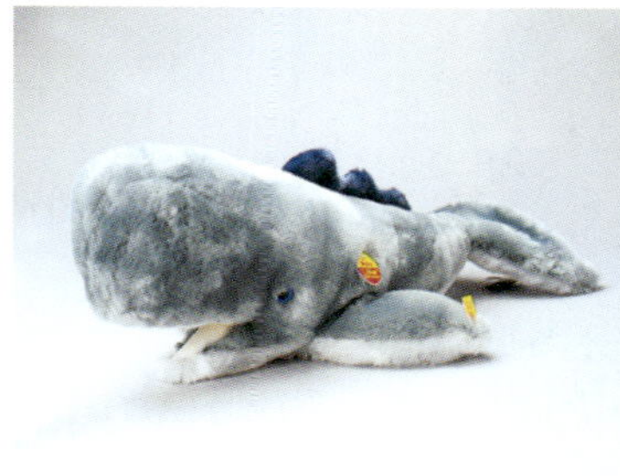

Moby Pottwal ab 1996 **Mobby** - ***Moby** Whale from 1996 **Mobby***

Webpelz, waschmaschinenfest - *woven fur, machine washable*

EAN-NO.	PERIOD	PR.	INFO
063206	1994-1997	2-3	55 cm

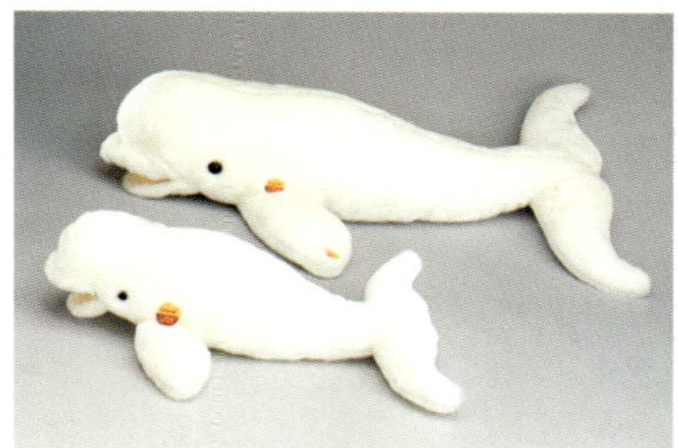

Belugawal - *Belugawhale*

Webpelz, weiss, Druck-Stimme, handwaschbar - *woven fur, white, press voice, hand washable*

EAN-NO.	PERIOD	PR.	INFO
063237	1996-1997	2-3	55 cm
063244	1995-1997	3	80 cm

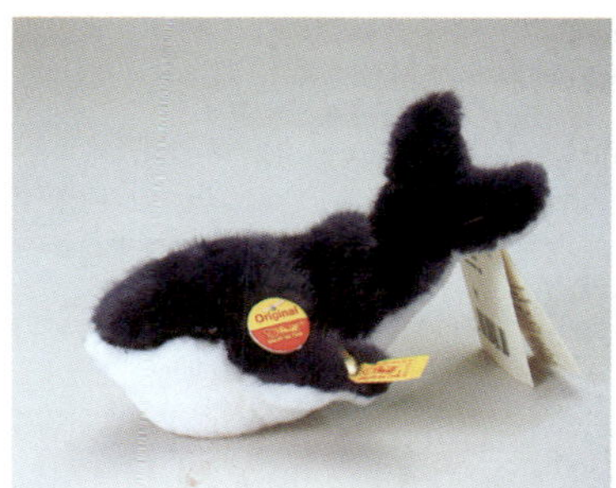

Blauwal - *Blue Whale*

Webpelz waschmaschinenfest - *woven fur, machine washable*

EAN-NO.	PERIOD	PR.	INFO
047350	1997-1999	1	15 cm

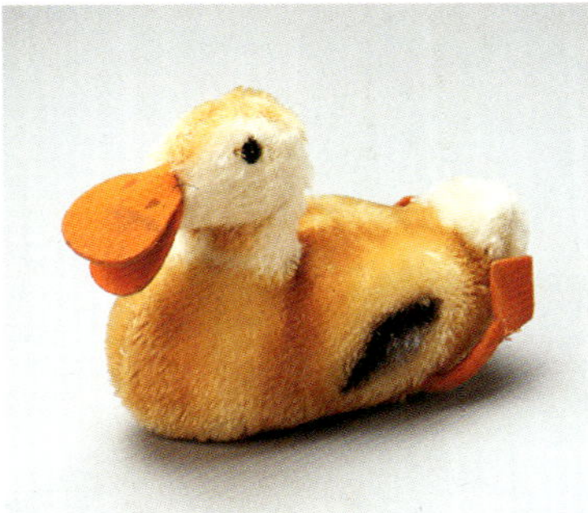

Spiel-Ente - *Play Duck*

Mohairpluesch, hellbraun, bunt bemalt, liegend, weich, Druckstimme, abwaschbar - *mohair, light brown, painted in bright colors, lying, soft, press voice, surface washable*

SERIE	ART.-NO	PERIOD	PR.	INFO
22	**2312**	1949-1958	3-4	12 cm
220	**2312,03**	1959-1964	3	
320	**2312,03**	1965-1967	3	
	3200/12	1968-1975	3	

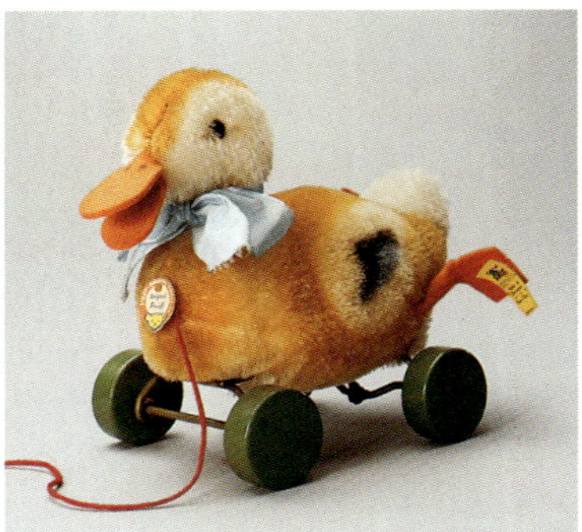

Piep-Ente - *Quacking Duck*

Mohairpluesch, hellbraun, bunt bemalt, liegend, Nachzieh-Tier auf Exzenterraedern, automat. Piepstimme, abwaschbar - *mohair, light brown, painted in bright colors, lying, pull type animal on eccentric wheels, automatic voice, surface washable*

SERIE	ART.-NO	PERIOD	PR.	INFO
22	**2314,2** ex	1949-1958	4-5	14 cm
220	**2314,13**	1959-1964	4	
320	**2314,13**	1965-1967	4	
	3200/14	1968-1974	3-4	

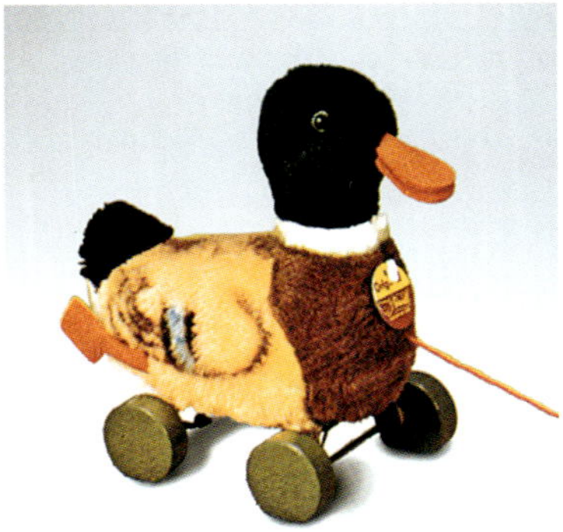

Ziehente - *Pull Type Duck*

Dralon, Holzraeder, abwaschbar - *dralon, wooden wheels, surface washable*

SERIE	ART.-NO	PERIOD	PR.	INFO
	3201/14	1974-1976	3	14 cm

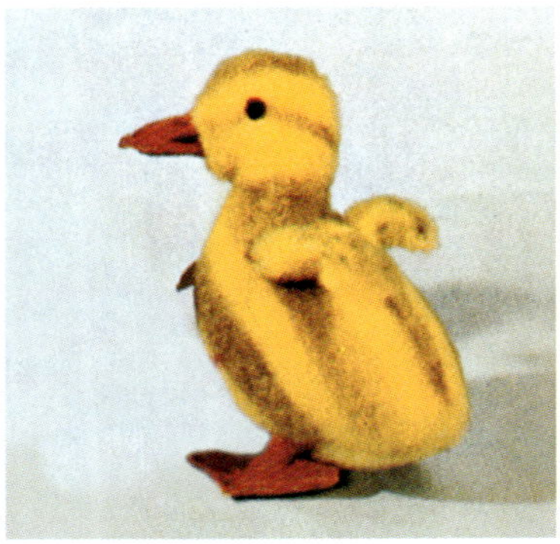

Jung-Ente - *Young Duckling*

Wollpluesch, gelb schattiert, aufrecht stehend, weich - *plush wool, yellow with shading, standing upright, soft*

SERIE	ART.-NO	PERIOD	PR.	INFO
22	**6514**	1949-1958	4	14 cm
220	**6514,01**	1959-1961	3-4	

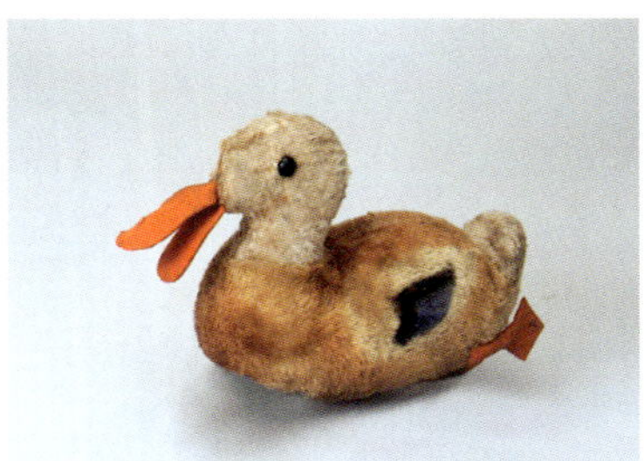

Spielente - *Play Duck*

Seidenpluesch, hellbraun, bemalt, liegend, weich, Druckstimme - *artificial silk plush, light brown, painted, lying, soft, press voice*

SERIE	ART.-NO	PERIOD	PR.	INFO
22	**2612**	1949-1949	4	12 cm

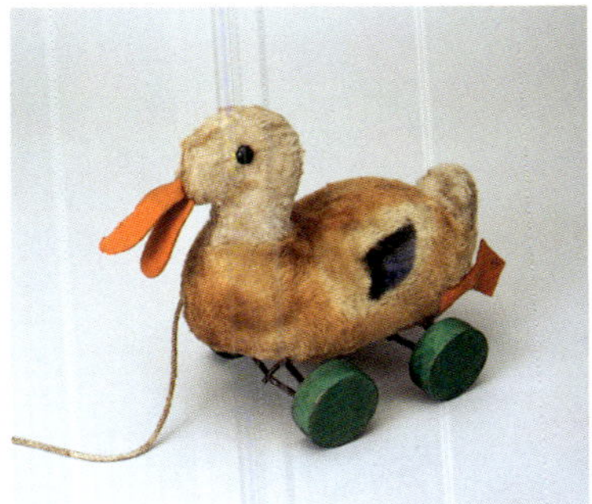

Piep-Ente - *Quacking Duck*

Seidenpluesch, hellbraun, bemalt, auf Exzenterraedern, mit automatischer Piepstimme - *artificial silk plush, light brown, painted, on eccentric wheels, with automatic voice*

SERIE	ART.-NO	PERIOD	PR.	INFO
22	**2614,2** ex	1949-1949	4-5	14 cm

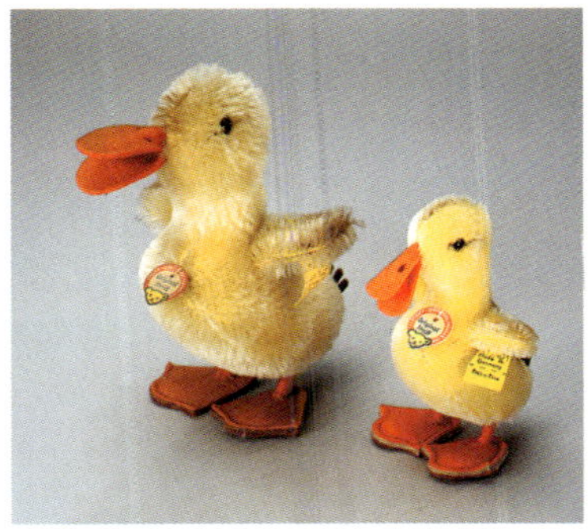

Ente - *Duck*

Mohair, gelb, stehend, offene Fluegel, abwaschbar - *mohair, yellow, standing, wings open, surface washable*

SERIE	ART.-NO	PERIOD	PR.	INFO
22	**6310**	1952-1958	3-4	10 cm
220	**6310,01**	1959-1964	3	
325	**6310,01**	1965-1967	3	
	3250/10	1968-1975	2-3	
22	**6317**	1952-1958	4	17 cm
220	**6317,01**	1959-1964	3-4	
325	**6317,01**	1965-1967	3-4	
	3250/17	1968-1976	3	

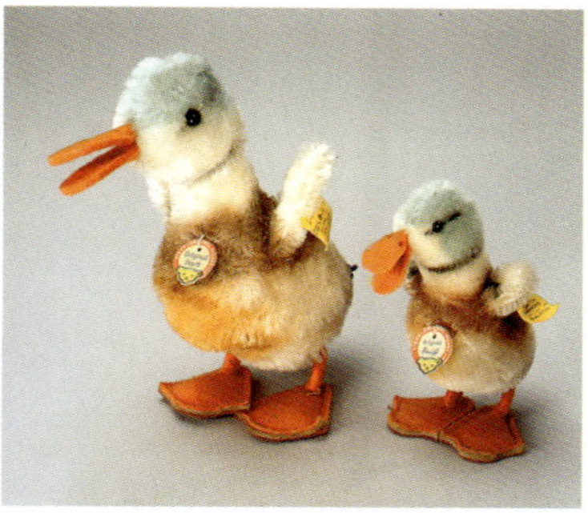

Ente - *Duck*

Mohair, bunt, stehend, offene Fluegel, abwaschbar - *mohair, multi-colored, standing, wings open, surface washable*

SERIE	ART.-NO	PERIOD	PR.	INFO
22	**6311**	1952-1958	3-4	11 cm
220	**6311,07**	1959-1964	3	
327	**6311,07**	1965-1967	3	
	3270/11	1968-1975	2-3	
22	**6318**	1952-1958	4	18 cm
220	**6318,07**	1959-1964	3-4	
327	**6318,07**	1965-1967	3-4	
	3270/18	1968-1976	3	

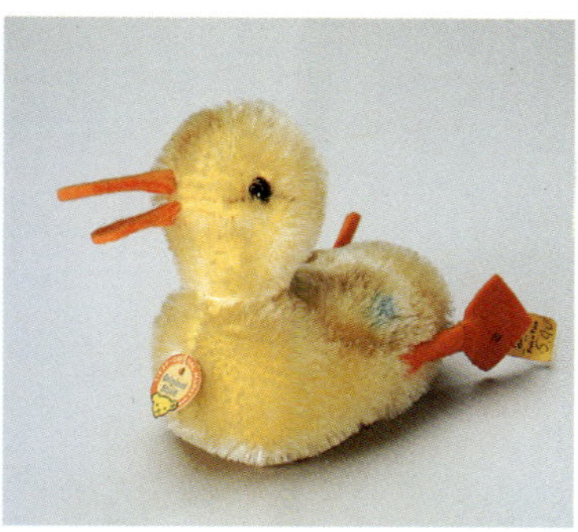

Spiel-Ente - *Play Duck*

Mohair, gelb, liegend, weich, abwaschbar - *mohair, yellow, lying, soft, surface washable*

SERIE	ART.-NO	PERIOD	PR.	INFO
22	**2310**	1953-1958	3-4	10 cm
220	**2310,01**	1959-1964	3	
321	**2310,01**	1965-1967	3	
	3210/10	1968-1978	2-3	
22	**2313**	1953-1958	4	13 cm
220	**2313,01**	1959-1964	3-4	
321	**2313,01**	1965-1967	3-4	
	3210/13	1968-1978	3	

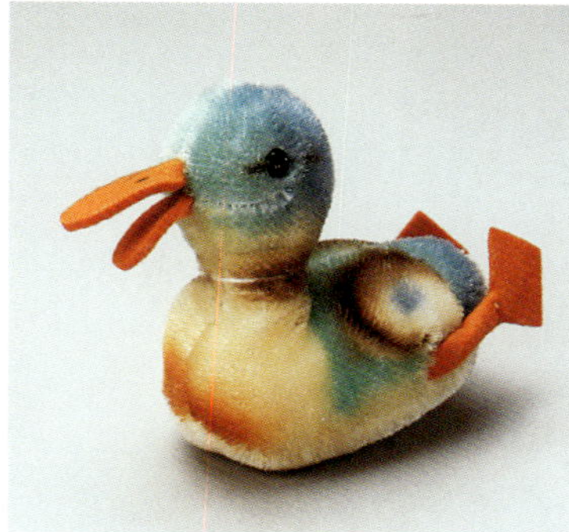

Spiel-Ente - *Play Duck*

Mohair, bunt, liegend, weich, abwaschbar - *mohair, multi-colored, lying, soft, surface washable*

SERIE	ART.-NO	PERIOD	PR.	INFO
22	**2311**	1953-1958	3-4	11 cm
220	**2311,07**	1959-1964	3	
323	**2311,07**	1965-1967	3	
	3230/11	1968-1977	2-3	
22	**2314**	1953-1958	4	14 cm
220	**2314,07**	1959-1964	3-4	
323	**2314,07**	1965-1967	3-4	
	3230/14	1968-1978	3	

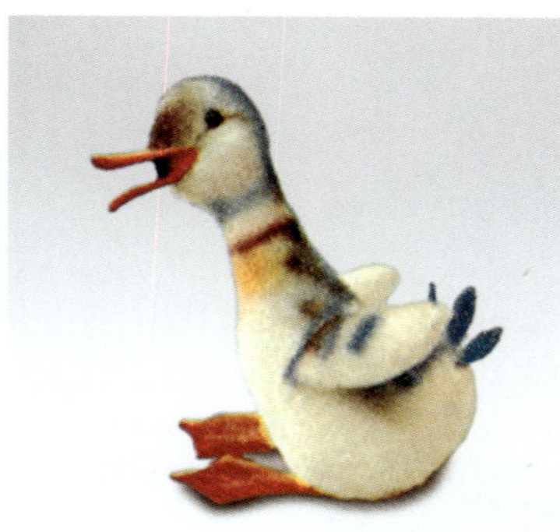

Ente - *Duck*

Mohair, bunt, liegend, weich, Druckstimme - *mohair, multi-colored, lying, soft, press voice*

SERIE	ART.-NO	PERIOD	PR.	INFO
22	**7322,1**	1953-1957	4	22 cm

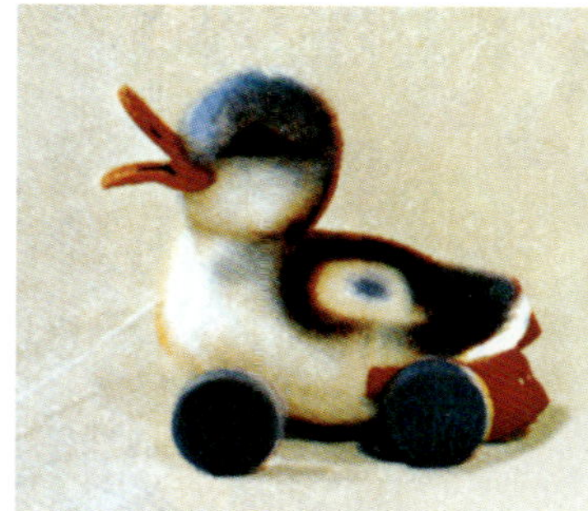

Nachzieh-Ente - *Pull Type Duck*

Mohair, liegend, auf Exzenterraedern - *mohair, lying, on eccentric wheels*

SERIE	ART.-NO	PERIOD	PR.	INFO
81 22	**2311** ex	1954-1957	4-5	11 cm
810 220	**2311,10**	1960-1960	4-5	

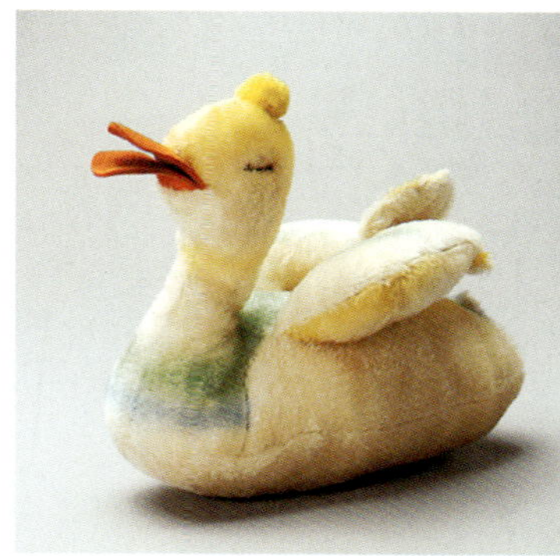

Floppy Ente - *Floppy Duck*

Mohair, liegend, sehr weich - *mohair, lying, very soft*

SERIE	ART.-NO	PERIOD	PR.	INFO
85 22	**7317**	1958-1958	4	17 cm
850 220	**7317,00**	1959-1959	4	
85 22	**7328**	1958-1958	4	28 cm
850 220	**7328,00**	1959-1959	4	

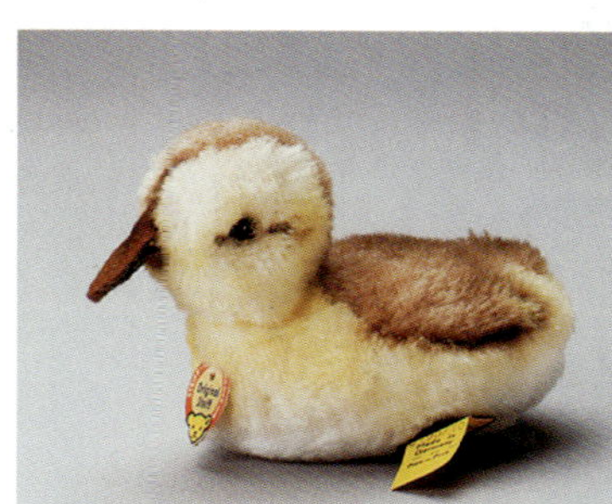

Entenkueken - *Duckling*

Dralon, liegend, sehr weich, abwaschbar - *dralon, lying, very soft, surface washable*

SERIE	ART.-NO	PERIOD	PR.	INFO
	3190/06	1968-1974	1-2	6 cm
	3190/10	1968-1976	1-2	10 cm

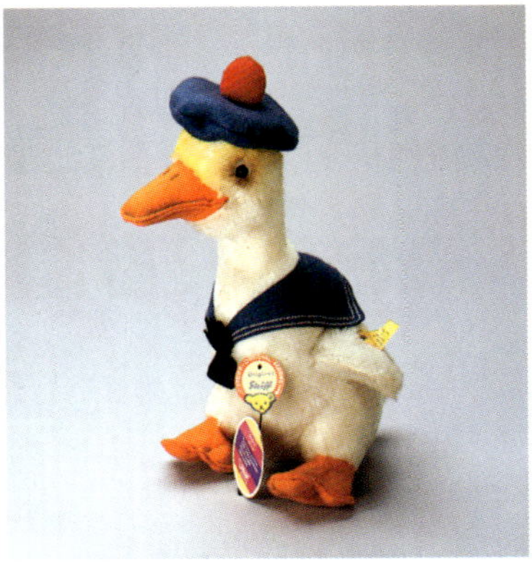

Cosy Ente Bub - *Cozy Duck Boy*

Dralon, gefuellt mit synthetischen Fasern & Schaumstoff, stehend, sehr weich, vollwaschbar - *dralon, stuffed with synthetic fibers & foam, standing, very soft, fully washable*

SERIE	ART.-NO	PERIOD	PR.	INFO
	4907/25	1970-1973	3-4	25 cm

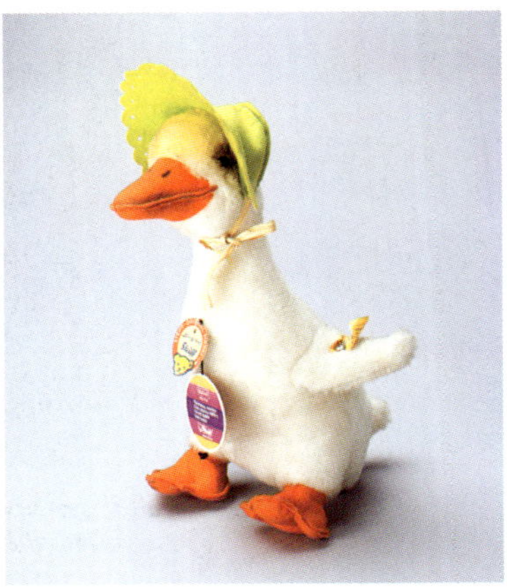

Cosy Ente Maid - *Cozy Duck Maid*

Dralon, gefuellt mit synthetischen Fasern & Schaumstoff, stehend, sehr weich, vollwaschbar - *dralon, stuffed with synthetic fibers & foam, standing, very soft, fully washable*

SERIE	ART.-NO	PERIOD	PR.	INFO
	4908/25	1970-1973	3-4	25 cm

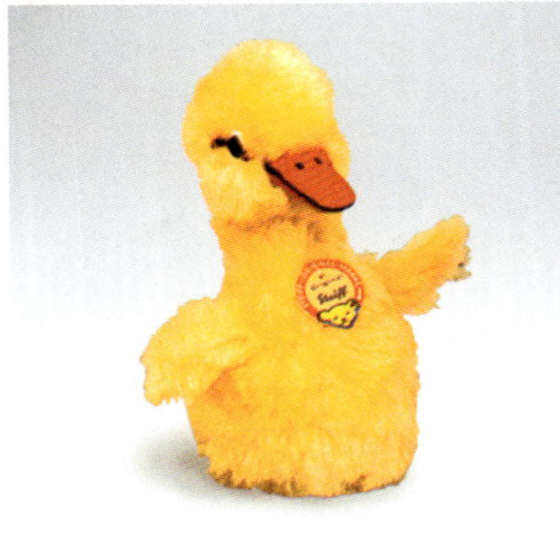

Buzzel Ente - *Buzzel Duck*

Dralon, formgeschaeumt, superweich, vollwaschbar - *dralon, stuffed with pre-formed foam, super soft, fully washable*

SERIE	ART.-NO	PERIOD	PR.	INFO
	6157/20	1971-1977	2	20 cm

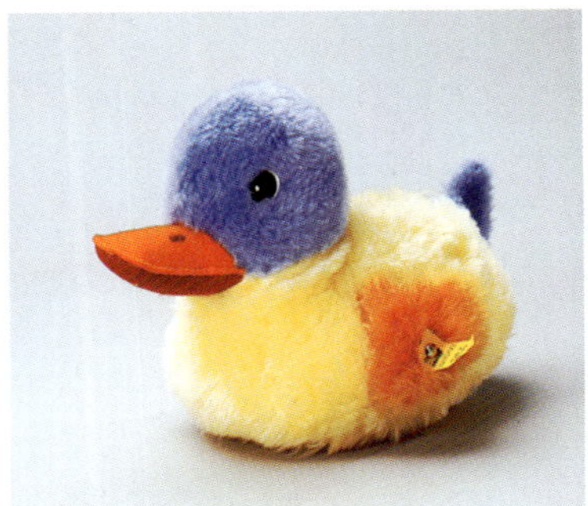

Ente **Waggi** - *Duck* ***Waggi***

Dralon, formgeschaeumt, 22 cm, liegend, abwaschbar - *dralon, stuffed with pre-formed foam, 22 cm, lying, surface washable*

SERIE	ART.-NO	PERIOD	PR.	INFO
	3280/22	1972-1980	1-2	hellblau - *light blue*
	3281/22	1972-1981	1-2	rostbraun - *rust brown*

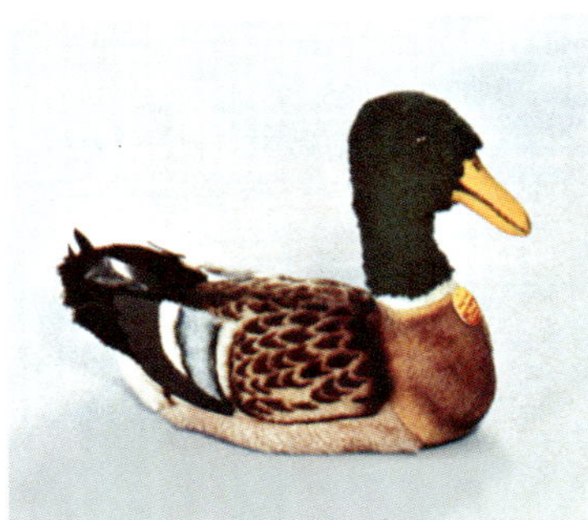

Erpel ab 1974 **Starli** - *Drake from 1974* ***Starli***

Dralon, liegend, abwaschbar - *dralon, lying, surface washable*

SERIE	ART.-NO	PERIOD	PR.	INFO
	3288/30	1973-1976	3	30 cm

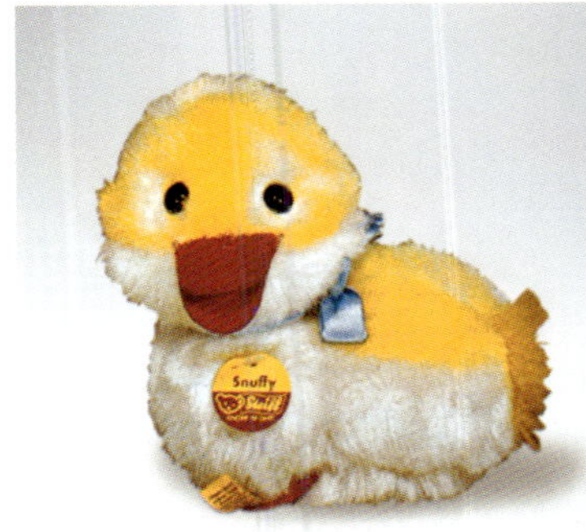

Snuffy Ente - ***Snuffy*** *Duck*

Pelzimitation, ab 1978 Synthetik-Webpelz, formgeschaeumt, liegend, abwaschbar - *imitation fur, from 1978 synthetic woven fur, stuffed with pre-formed foam, lying, surface washable*

SERIE	ART.-NO	PERIOD	PR.	INFO
	3524/12	1975-1978	2	12 cm
	3524/17	1975-1978	2	17 cm

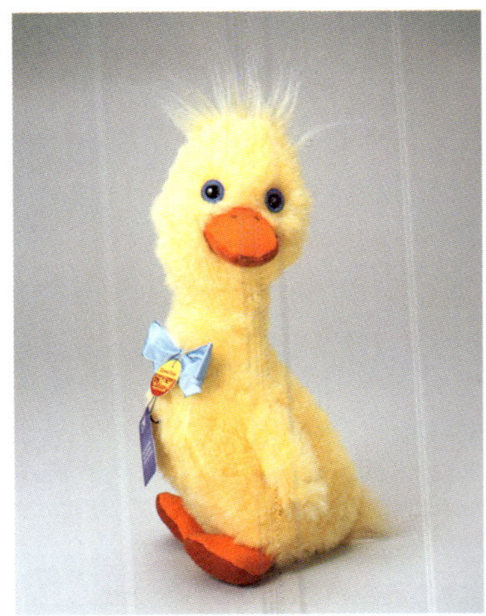

Comic Ente - *Comic Duck*

Dralonpluesch, 1978 Wirkflor, formgeschaeumt, gelb, Fuesse & Schnabel orange, blaue Schleife, stehend, vollwaschbar - *dralon plush, 1978 knitted pile, stuffed with pre-formed foam, yellow, feet & bill orange, blue ribbon, standing, fully washable*

SERIE	ART.-NO	PERIOD	PR.	INFO
	3275/35	1976-1978	3-4	35 cm

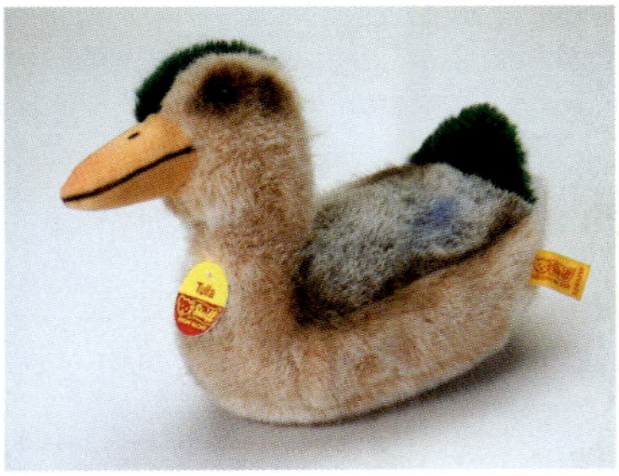

Tulla Ente - ***Tulla** Duck*

Nerzimitation, ab 1978 Synthetik-Webpelz, formgeschaeumt, liegend, Druckstimme, abwaschbar - *imitation mink, from 1978 synthetic woven fur, stuffed with preformed foam, lying, press voice, surface washable*

Serie	Art.-No	Period	Pr.	Info
077920	**3205/15**	1976-1987	2	15 cm

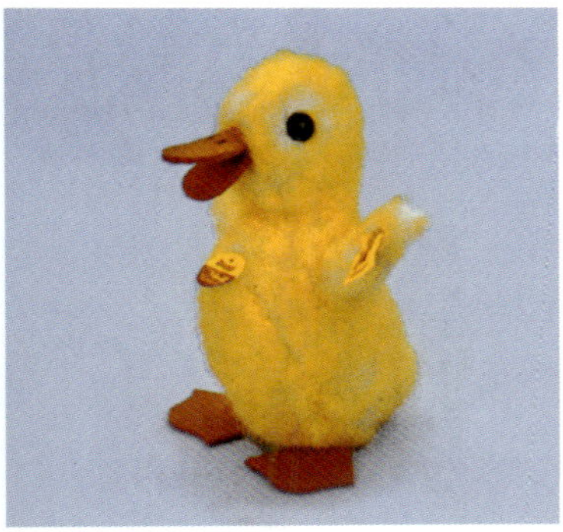

Daggi Ente - ***Daggi** Duck*

Pelzimitation, ab 1978 Synthetik-Webpelz, formgeschaeumt, gelb, stehend, vollwaschbar - *imitation fur, from 1978 synthetic woven fur, stuffed with preformed foam, yellow, standing, fully washable*

Serie	Art.-No	Period	Pr.	Info
	3240/17	1977-1982	2	17 cm

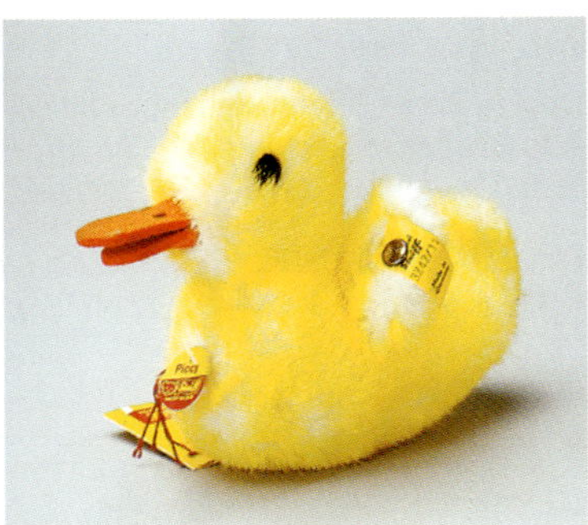

Piccy Ente - ***Piccy** Duck*

Synthetik-Webpelz, gelb, liegend, abwaschbar - *synthetic woven fur, yellow, lying, surface washable*

Serie	Art.-No	Period	Pr.	Info
	3242/08	1978-1982	1	8 cm
	3242/11	1978-1983	1-2	11 cm

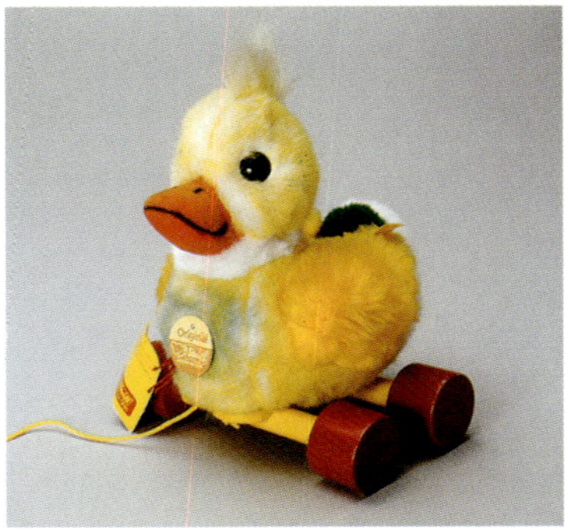

Nachziehente - *Pull Type Duck*

Webpelz/Dralon, Fahrgestell abnehmbar, abwaschbar - *woven fur/dralon, removable wheels & framework, surface washable*

Serie	Art.-No	Period	Pr.	Info
	6420/18	1980-1985	3	18 cm

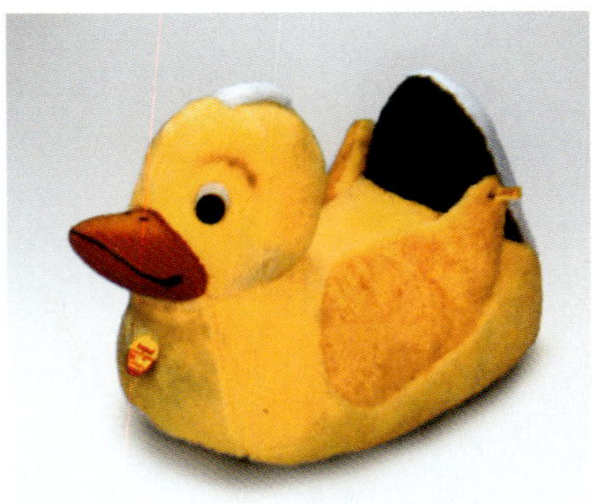

Schaukelente - *Rocking Duck*

Webpelz, gelb, abwaschbar - *woven fur, yellow, surface washable*

Serie	Art.-No	Period	Pr.	Info
	8020/45	1980-1980	3	45 cm
481857	**8195/45**	1981-1987	3	

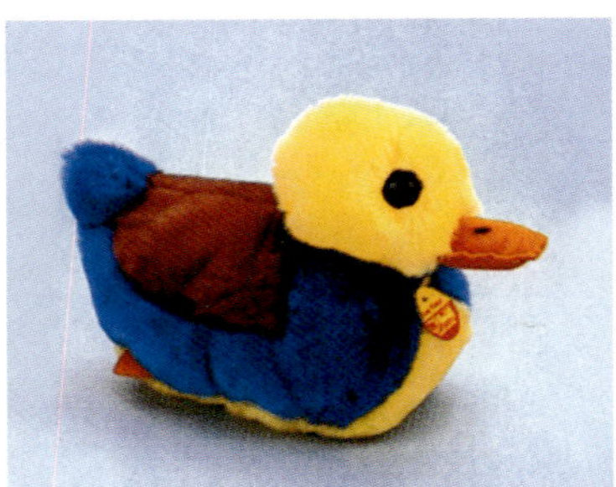

Cosy Waggi

Webpelz, Druckstimme, liegend, superweich, waschmaschinenfest - *woven fur, press voice, lying, super soft, machine washable*

Serie	Art.-No	Period	Pr.	Info
091254	**5380/26**	1981-1987	2	26 cm

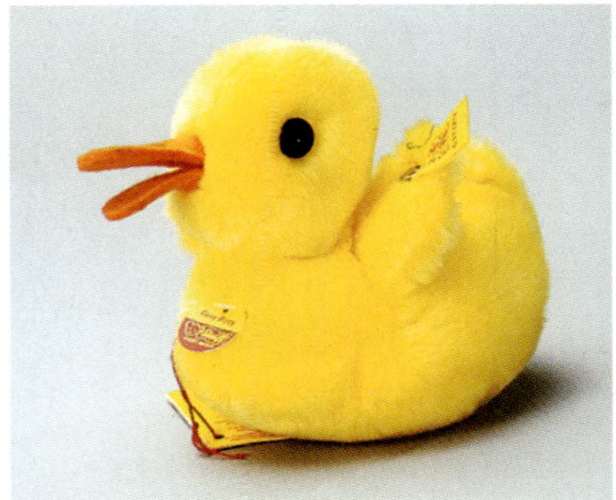

Cosy Piccy Ente - ***Cosy Piccy** Duck*

Webpelz, gelb, superweich, waschmaschinenfest - *woven fur, yellow, super soft, machine washable*

Serie	Art.-No	Period	Pr.	Info
091155	**5377/12**	1982-1990	1	12 cm
	091155	1991-1998	1	
	091261	1996-1999	1-2	18 cm

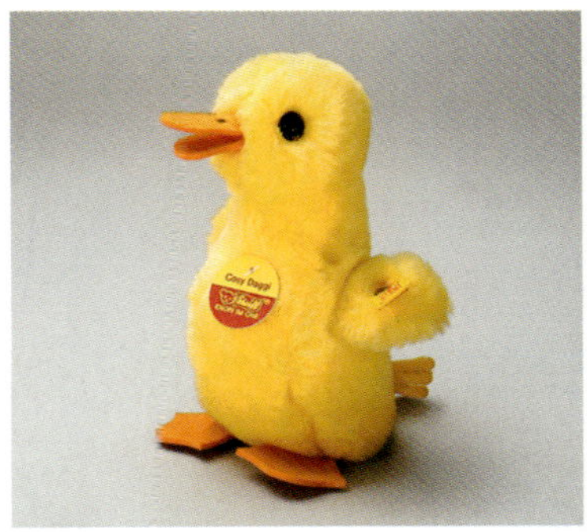

Cosy Daggi Ente - ***Cosy Daggi** Duck*

Webpelz, superweich, waschmaschinenfest - *woven fur, super soft, machine washable*

Serie	Art.-No	Period	Pr.	Info
091209	**5378/17**	1982-1986	2	17 cm

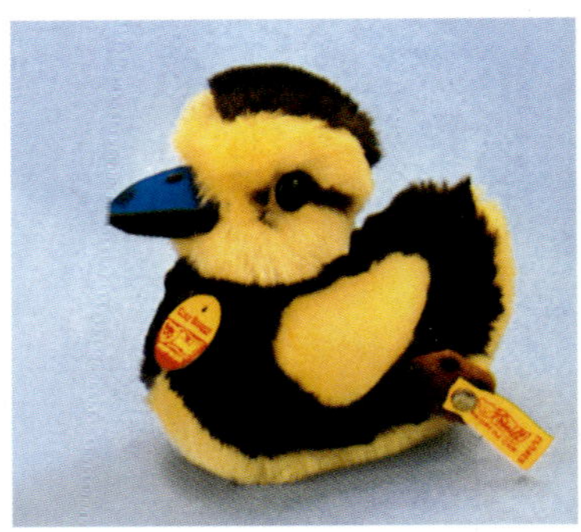

Cosy Snuggy Ente - ***Cosy Snuggy** Duck*

Webpelz, superweich, waschmaschinenfest - *woven fur, super soft, machine washable*

Serie	Art.-No	Period	Pr.	Info
	5381/13	1982-1985	1-2	13 cm

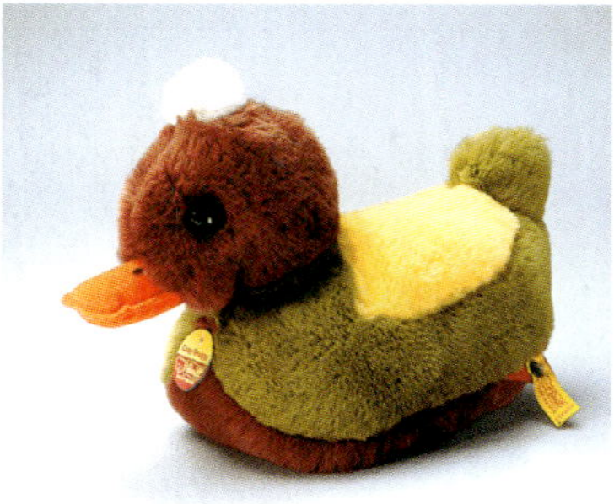

Cosy Snuggy Erpel - ***Cosy Snuggy*** *Drake*

Webpelz, Druckstimme, superweich, waschmaschinenfest - *woven fur, press voice, super soft, machine washable*

SERIE	ART.-NO	PERIOD	PR.	INFO
	5381/27	1982-1985	2	27 cm

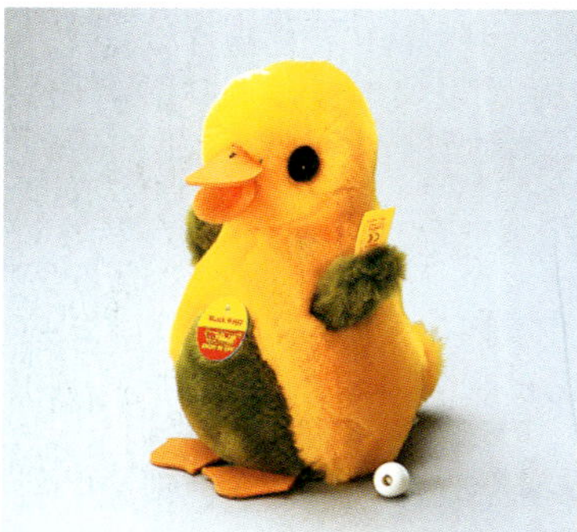

Musik Waggi Ente - *Musical Waggi Duck*

Webpelz, Koerper formgeschaeumt, Musikwerk austauschbar, ohne Musikwerk waschbar - *woven fur, body stuffed with pre-formed foam, music box exchangeable, washable if music box removed*

SERIE	ART.-NO	PERIOD	PR.	INFO
233302	**6372/18**	1983-1990	2	18 cm
	233302	1991-1997	2	

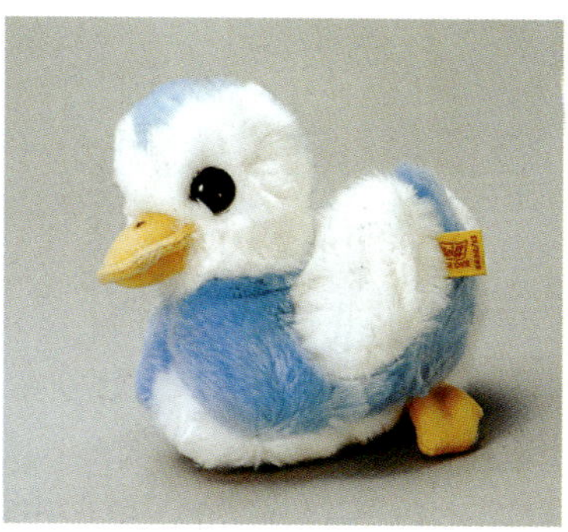

Baby Snuggy Ente - *Baby Snuggy Duck*

Webpelz, 13 cm, Druckstimme, waschmaschinenfest - *woven fur, 13 cm, press voice, machine washable*

SERIE	ART.-NO	PERIOD	PR.	INFO
201530	**5691/13**	1983-1986	1-2	rosa - *pink*
201585	**5692/13**	1983-1986	1-2	blau - *blue*

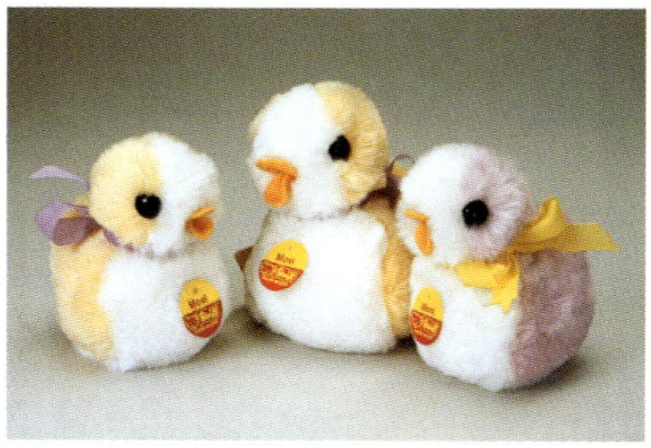

Movi Ente - ***Movi*** *Duck*

Webpelz, im Koerbchen, waschmaschinenfest - *woven fur, sitting in a basket, machine washable*

SERIE	ART.-NO	PERIOD	PR.	INFO
201837	**5705/12**	1984-1987 - *corn yellow*	2	12 cm, mais
201875	**5705/15**	1984-1987	2	15 cm
201936	**5708/12**	1984-1986 flieder - *lavender*	2	12 cm,
201974	**5708/15**	1984-1987	2	15 cm

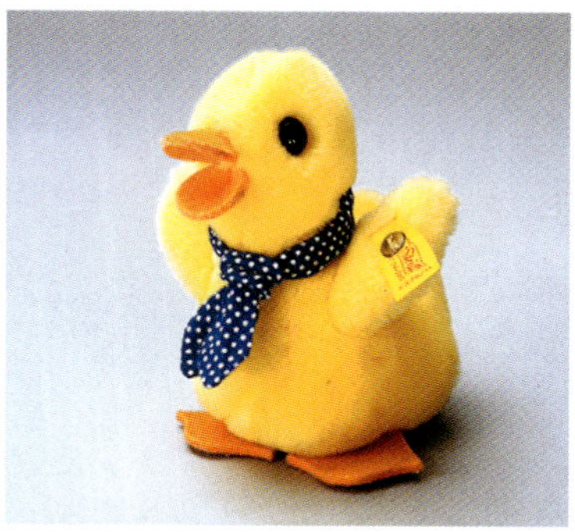

Cosy Movi Ente - ***Cosy Movi*** *Duck*

Webpelz, 12 cm, mit Krawatte oder Tuch, Pieps-Stimme, waschmaschinenfest - *woven fur, 12 cm, tie or scarf, squeaker, machine washable*

SERIE	ART.-NO	PERIOD	PR.	INFO
091100	**5376/11**	1985-1988	2	Krawatte - *tie*
091124	**5376/12**	1985-1988	2	Tuch - *scarf*

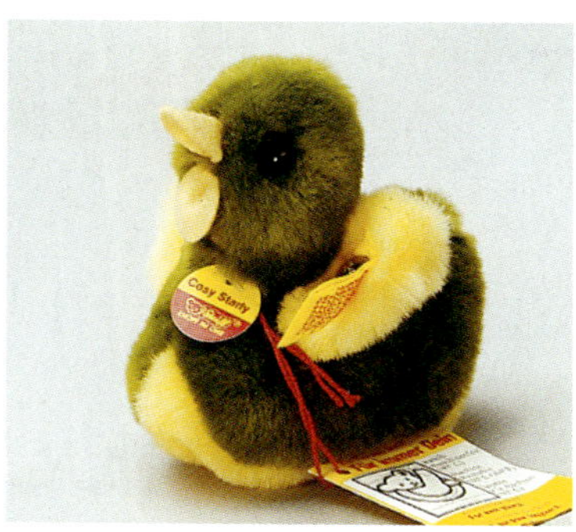

Cosy Starly Ente - ***Cosy Starly*** *Duck*

Webpelz, ab 12 cm Pieps-Stimme, waschmaschinenfest - *woven fur, from 12 cm squeaker, machine washable*

SERIE	ART.-NO	PERIOD	PR.	INFO
091322	**5382/09**	1986-1990	1	10 cm
	091322	1991-1999	1	
091346	**5382/12**	1986-1989	1-2	12 cm
091360	**5382/18**	1985-1987	2	18 cm

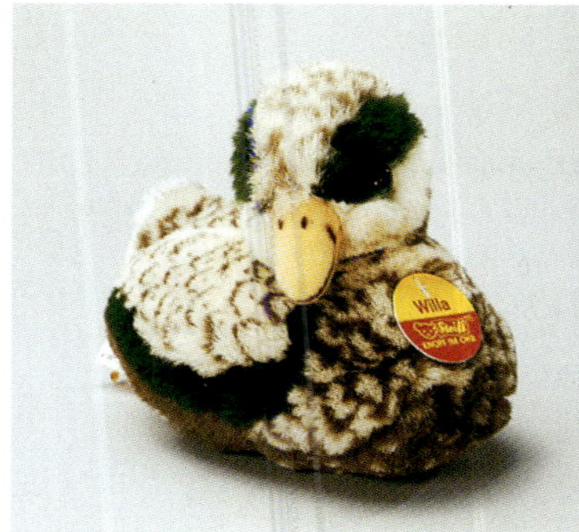

Willa Ente - ***Willa*** *Duck*

Wirkpelz, gruen, Pieps-Stimme, waschmaschinenfest - *knitted fur, green, squeaker, machine washable*

SERIE	ART.-NO	PERIOD	PR.	INFO
073502	**3210/16**	1988-1990	2	16 cm
	073502	1991-1994	2	
073526	**3210/22**	1988-1990	2	22 cm
	073526	1991-1993	2	

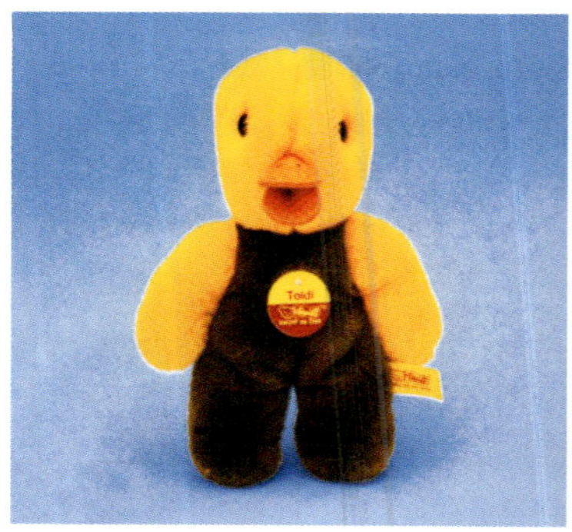

Toldi Ente - ***Toldi*** *Duck*

Webpelz, Pieps-Stimme, waschmaschinenfest - *woven fur, squeaker, machine washable*

SERIE	ART.-NO	PERIOD	PR.	INFO
080555	**6264/22**	1986-1987	2	22 cm

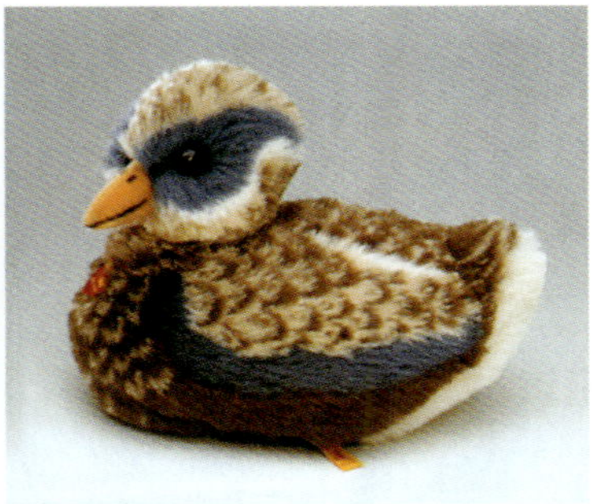

Pilla Ente - ***Pilla*** *Duck*

Wirkpelz, blau, Pieps-Stimme, waschmaschinenfest - *knitted fur, blue, squeaker, machine washable*

SERIE	ART.-NO	PERIOD	PR.	INFO
073557	**3211/16**	1988-1990	2	16 cm
073571	**3211/22**	1988-1990	2	22 cm

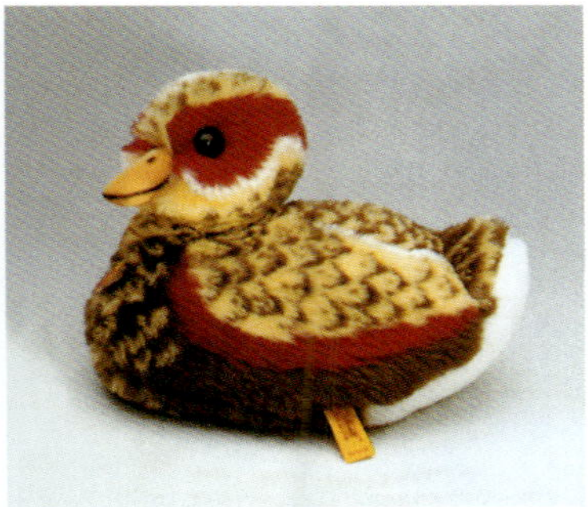

Trulla Ente - ***Trulla*** *Duck*

Wirkpelz, rot, Pieps-Stimme, waschmaschinenfest - *knitted fur, red, squeaker, machine washable*

SERIE	ART.-NO	PERIOD	PR.	INFO
073700	**3215/16**	1988-1989	2	16 cm
073724	**3215/22**	1988-1989	2	22 cm

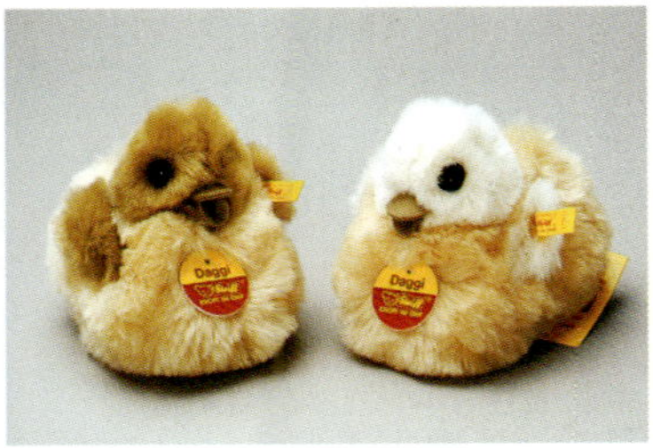

Daggi Entenkueken - ***Daggi*** *Duckling*

Webpelz, 11 cm, Pieps-Stimme, waschmaschinenfest - *woven fur, 11 cm, squeaker, machine washable*

SERIE	ART.-NO	PERIOD	PR.	INFO
073809	**3230/11**	1989-1990	1	creme - *cream*
	073809	1991-1997	1	
073854	**3232/11**	1989-1990	1	beige
	073854	1991-1997	1	

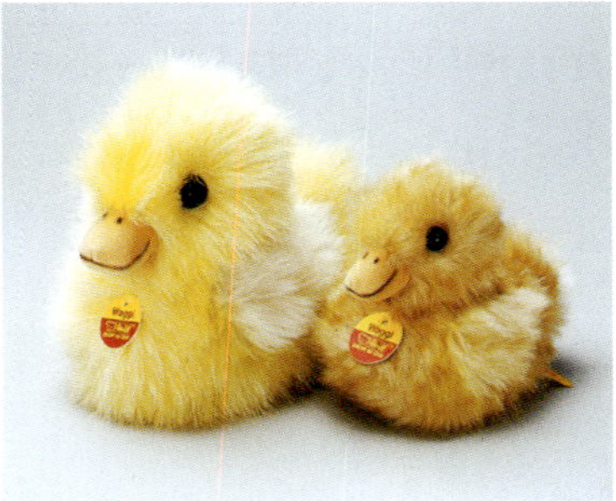

Waggi Ente - ***Waggi*** *Duck*

Webpelz, Pieps-Stimme, waschmaschinenfest - *woven fur, squeaker, machine washable*

SERIE	ART.-NO	PERIOD	PR.	INFO
073908	**3240/16**	1990-1990	1-2	16 cm, gelb - *yellow*
	073908	1991-1995	1-2	
073915	**3240/20**	1990-1990	2	20 cm
	073915	1991-1994	2	
073939	**3241/16**	1990-1990	1-2	16 cm, rost - *rust*
	073939	1991-1994	1-2	
073953	**3242/16**	1990-1990	1-2	grau - *grey*
	073953	1991-1993	1-2	
073977	**3243/16**	1990-1990	1-2	braun - *brown*
	073977	1991-1993	1-2	
073984	**3243/20**	1990-1990	2	20 cm
	073984	1991-1991	2	

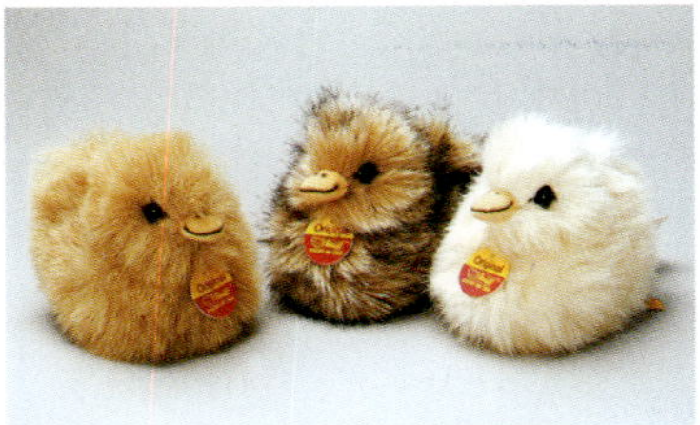

Entenkueken - *Duckling*

Webpelz, 15 cm, Pieps-Stimme, waschmaschinenfest - *woven fur, 15 cm, squeaker, machine washable*

EAN-NO.	PERIOD	PR.	INFO
073694	1992-1995	1	creme - *cream*
073717	1992-1995	1	beige
073731	1992-1997	1	beige gespitzt - *beige tipped*
073786	1992-1994	1	lila - *lavender*
073793	1992-1994	1	violett - *violet*

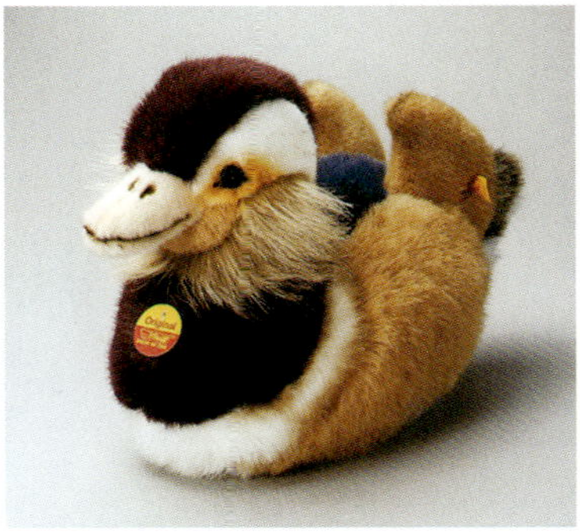

Mandarin Ente - *Mandarin Duck*

Webpelz, Pieps-Stimme, waschmaschinenfest - *woven fur, squeaker, machine washable*

EAN-NO.	PERIOD	PR.	INFO
073618	1992-1995	2-3	35 cm

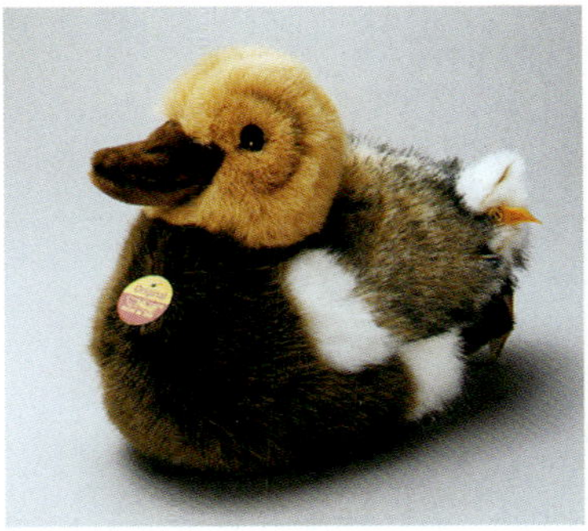

Ente - *Duck*

Webpelz, braun, Pieps-Stimme, waschmaschinenfest - *woven fur, brown, squeaker, machine washable*

EAN-NO.	PERIOD	PR.	INFO
073656	1992-1995	2-3	30 cm

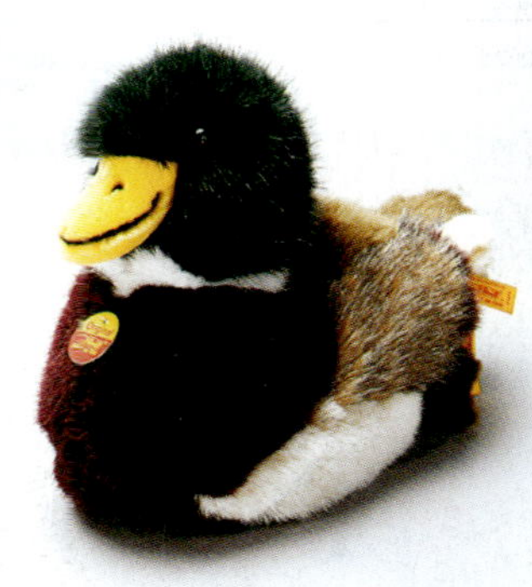

Erpel - *Drake*

Webpelz, Pieps-Stimme, waschmaschinenfest - *woven fur, squeaker, machine washable*

EAN-NO.	PERIOD	PR.	INFO
073670	1992-1994	2-3	30 cm

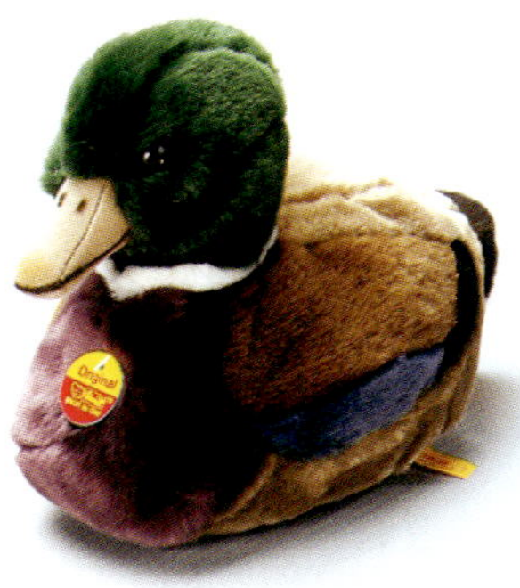

Erpel - *Drake*

Webpelz, braun/gruen, Pieps-Stimme, abwaschbar - *woven fur, brown/green, squeaker, surface washable*

EAN-No.	Period	Pr.	Info
073519	1995-1997	2-3	25 cm
073533	1995-1998	3	50 cm

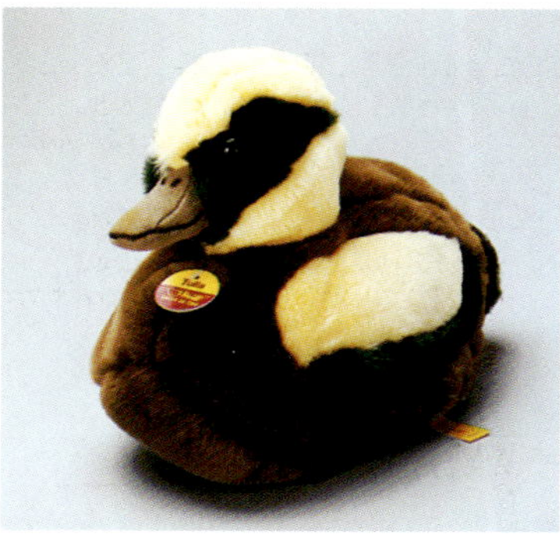

Tulla Ente - ***Tulla** Duck*

Webpelz, 25 cm, Pieps-Stimme, waschmaschinenfest - *woven fur, 25 cm, squeaker, machine washable*

EAN-No.	Period	Pr.	Info
073540	1995-1997	2-3	lila/rosé - *lavender/ rose*
073564	1995-1997	2-3	braun/gruen - *brown/ green*
073588	1995-1997	2-3	braun/gelb - *brown/ yellow*

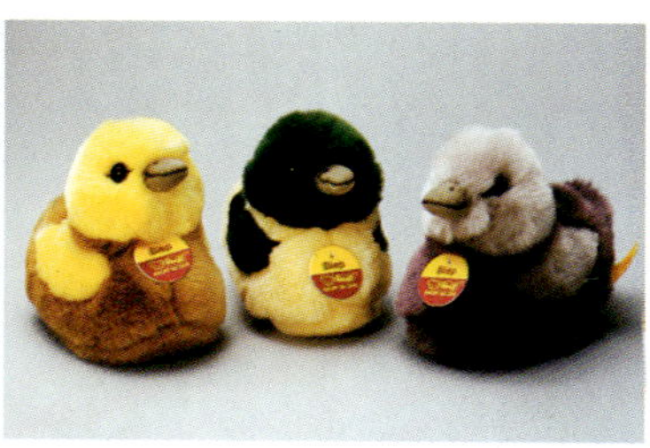

Biep Kueken - ***Biep** Duckling*

Webpelz, 16 cm, Pieps-Stimme, waschmaschinenfest - *woven fur, 16 cm, squeaker, machine washable*

EAN-No.	Period	Pr.	Info
073755	1995-1997	2	lila/rosé - *lavender/ rose*
073762	1995-1997	2	gelb/gruen - *yellow/ green*
073779	1995-1997	2	braun/gelb - *brown/ yellow*

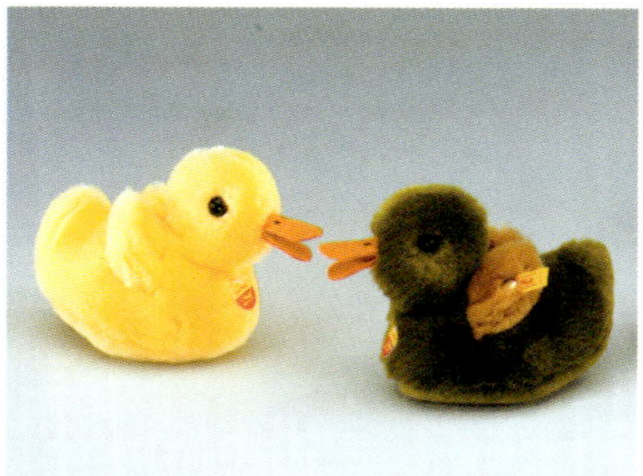

Cosy Piccy Ente - ***Cosy Piccy** Duck*

Webpelz, dottergelb, gruen, blau oder hellbraun, 13 / 18 cm, Pieps-Stimme, waschmaschinenfest - *woven fur, yolk yellow, green, blue or light brown, 13 cm / 18 cm, squeaker, machine washable*

EAN-No.	Period	Pr.	Info
091162	1996-1999	1	13 cm, dottergelb - *yolk yellow*
091179	1996-1997	1	13 cm, gruen - *green*
091285	1996-1997	1-2	18 cm
091186	1996-1997	1	13 cm, blau - *blue*
091278	1996-1997	1-2	18 cm
091193	1996-1998	1	13 cm, hellbraun - *light brown*

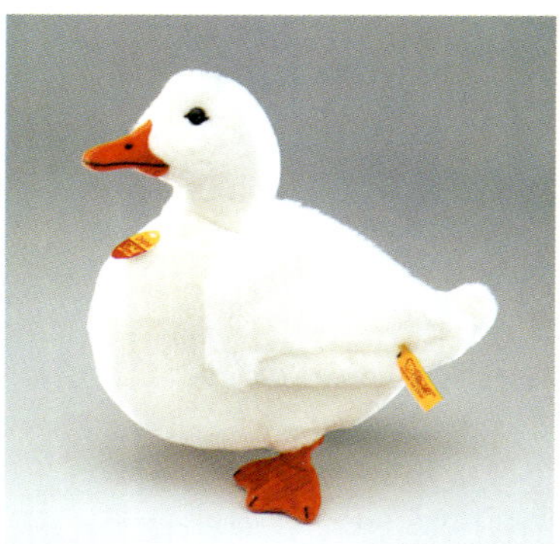

Hausente - *House Duck*

Webpelz, 25 cm, stehend, handwaschbar - *woven fur, 25 cm standing, hand washable*

EAN-No.	Period	Pr.	Info
076015	1998-1998	2-3	weiss - *white*
076022	1998-1999	2-3	grau - *grey*

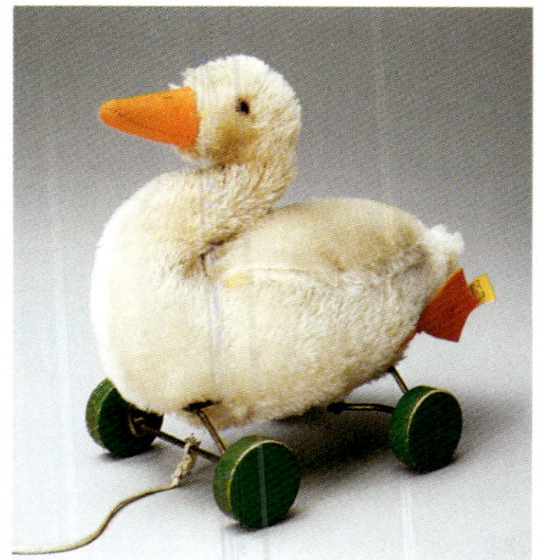

Gans - *Goose*

Mohairpluesch, grau/weiss, auf Exzenterraedern, automatische Pfeifstimme - *mohair, grey/white, on eccentric weels, automatic voice*

Serie	Art.-No	Period	Pr.	Info
30	**6317,2** ex	1949-1958	4-5	17 cm
300	**6317,10**	1959-1964	4-5	

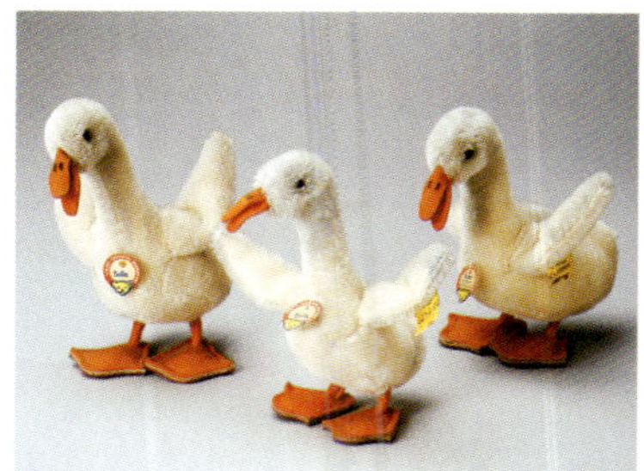

Gans ab 1967 **Tulla** - *Goose from 1967* ***Tulla***

Mohair, weiss, stehend, offene Fluegel, 1965 bis 1967 auch mit Zusatz "im Steiff Kinderbuch", abwaschbar - *mohair, white, standing, wings open, between 1965 & 1967 also with additional comment "im Steiff Kinderbuch", surface washable*

Serie	Art.-No	Period	Pr.	Info
30	**6312**	1952-1958	4	12 cm
300	**6312,00**	1959-1964	3	
330	**6312,00**	1965-1967	3	
	3300/12	1968-1973	3	
30	**6317**	1952-1958	4	17 cm
300	**6317,00**	1959-1964	3-4	
330	**6317,00**	1965-1967	3-4	
	3300/17	1968-1974	3-4	
30	**6328,0**	1958-1958	5	28 cm
300	**6328,00**	1959-1964	5	

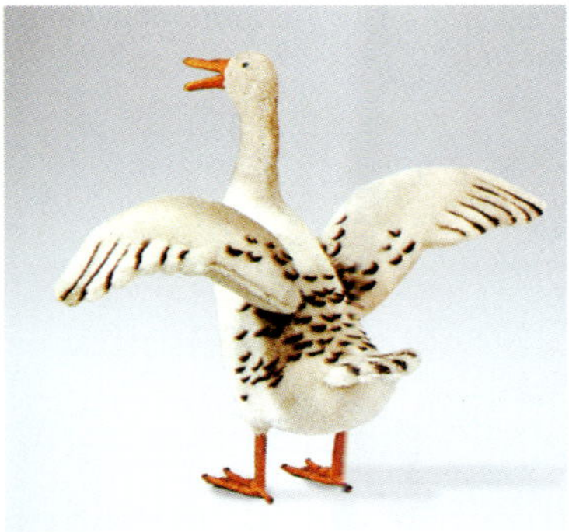

Gans - *Goose*

Schautier, Mohair, stehend, offene Fluegel, abwaschbar - *display animal, mohair, standing, wings open, surface washable*

SERIE	ART.-NO	PERIOD	PR.	INFO
300	**1360,90**	1960-1960	6	60 cm
	3309/06	1967-1967	6	

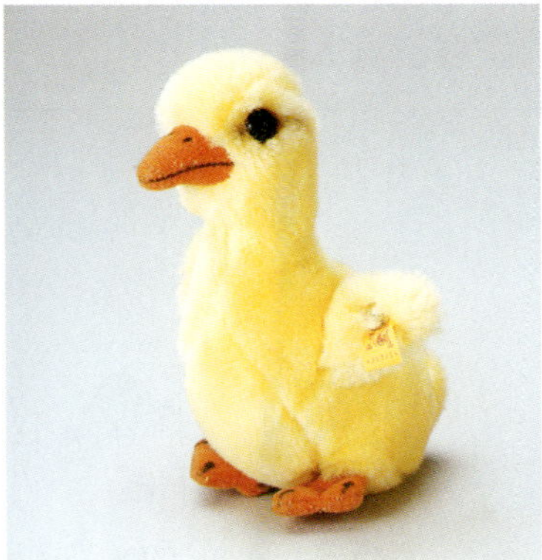

Friedericke Gans - ***Friedericke*** *Goose*

Webpelz, gelb, waschmaschinenfest - *woven fur, yellow, machine washable*

SERIE	ART.-NO	PERIOD	PR.	INFO
079801	**6202/14**	1988-1990	1-2	14 cm
	079801	1991-1999	1-2	

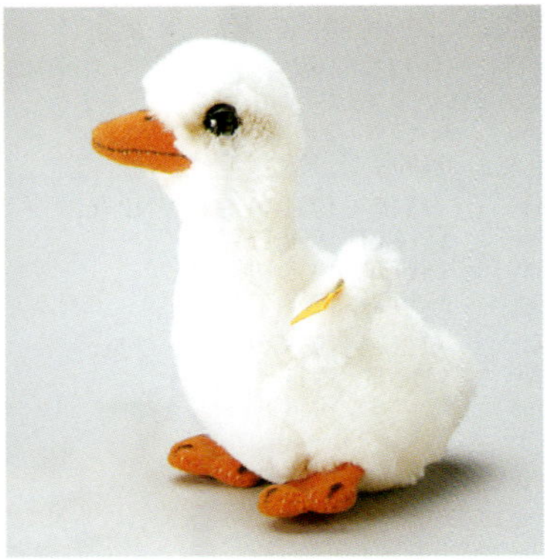

Frederic Gaenserich - ***Frederic*** *Gander*

Webpelz, weiss, waschmaschinenfest - *woven fur, white, machine washable*

SERIE	ART.-NO	PERIOD	PR.	INFO
079856	**6205/14**	1988-1990	1-2	14 cm
	079856	1991-1992	1-2	

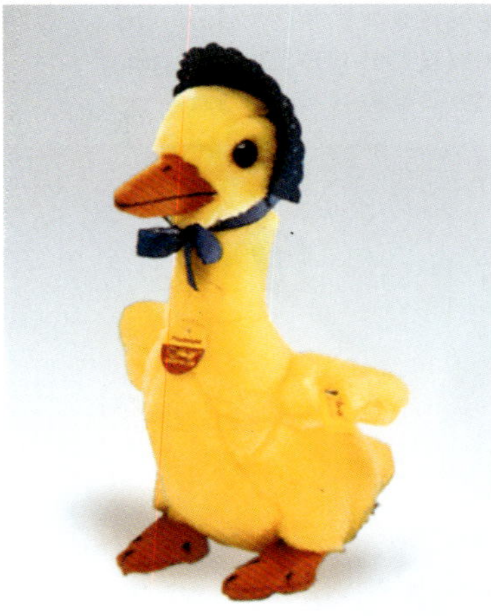

Friedericke Gans - ***Friedericke*** *Goose*

Webpelz, gelb, Pieps-Stimme, Kopftuch, waschmaschinenfest - *woven fur, yellow, squeaker, head scarf, machine washable*

SERIE	ART.-NO	PERIOD	PR.	INFO
079825	**6203/26**	1988-1990	3	26 cm

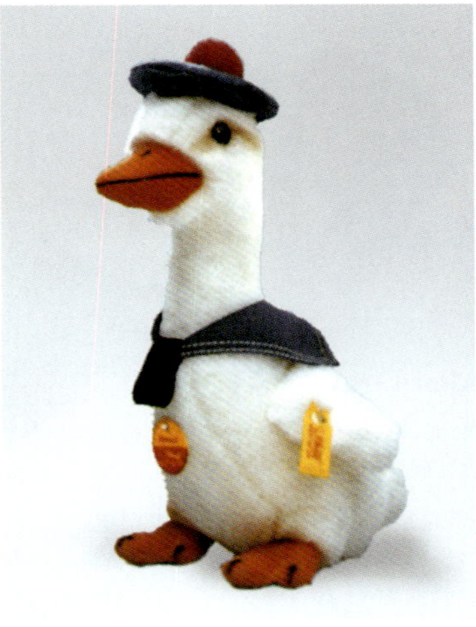

Frederic Gaenserich - ***Frederic*** *Gander*

Webpelz, weiss, Pieps-Stimme, Hut & Kragen, waschmaschinenfest - *woven fur, white, squeaker, hat & collar, machine washable*

SERIE	ART.-NO	PERIOD	PR.	INFO
079870	**6206/26**	1988-1990	3	26 cm

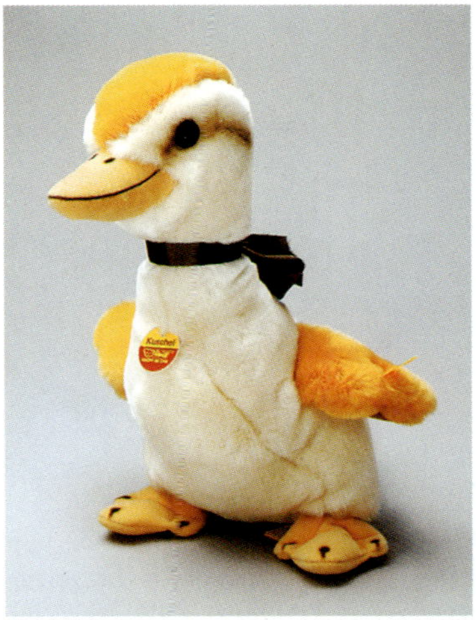

Kuschel Gans - ***Kuschel*** *Goose*

Webpelz, Pieps-Stimme, waschmaschinenfest - *woven fur, squeaker, machine washable*

SERIE	ART.-NO	PERIOD	PR.	INFO
098055	**6210/20**	1989-1990	2	20 cm, gelb - *yellow*
	098055	1991-1994	2	
098086	**6210/32**	1989-1990	2-3	32 cm
098154	**6212/20**	1989-1990	2	20 cm, braun - *brown*
	098154	1991-1994	2	
098185	**6212/32**	1989-1990	2-3	32 cm
	098185	1991-1991	2-3	
098208	**6212/50**	1989-1990	3	50 cm
	098208	1991-1992	3	

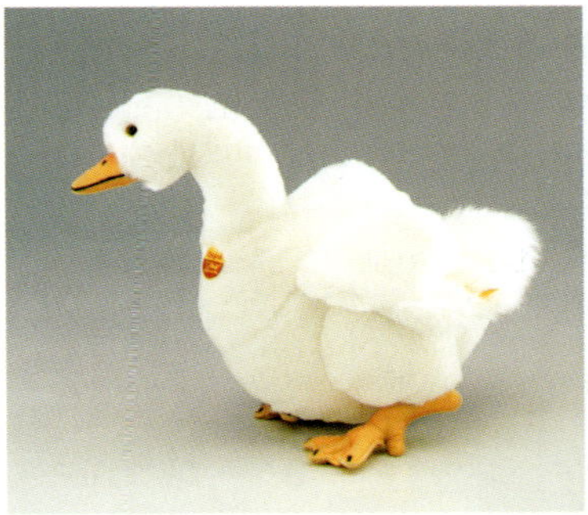

Hausgans - *House Goose*

Webpelz, weiss, stehend, abwaschbar - *woven fur, white, standing, surface washable*

EAN-NO.	PERIOD	PR.	INFO
074066	1996-1998	3	32 cm

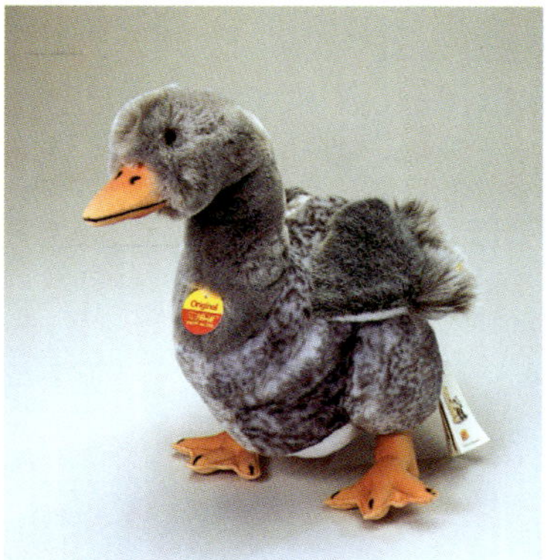

Graugans - *Grey Goose*

Webpelz, stehend, abwaschbar - *woven fur, standing, surface washable*

EAN-No.	Period	Pr.	Info
074080	1996-1999	3	32 cm

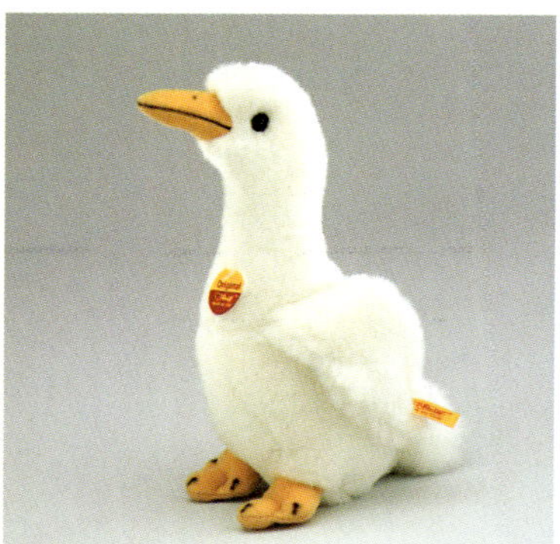

Gans - *Goose*

Webpelz, weiss, waschmaschinenfest - *woven fur, white, machine washable*

EAN-No.	Period	Pr.	Info
057557	1997-1998	2	16 cm

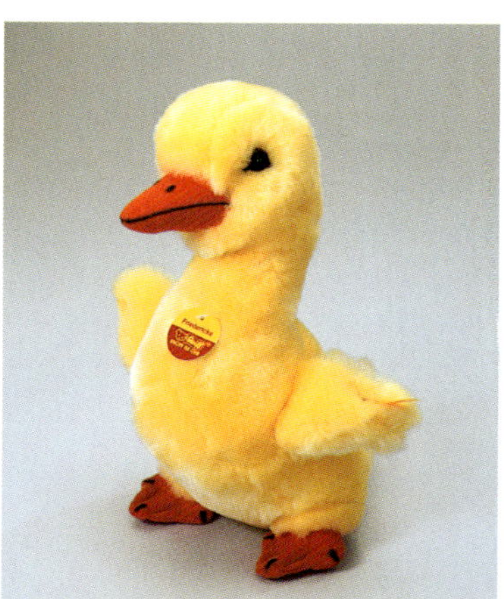

Friedericke Gans - ***Friedericke*** *Goose*

Webpelz, 25 cm, Pieps-Stimme, waschmaschinenfest - *woven fur, 25 cm, squeaker, machine washable*

EAN-No.	Period	Pr.	Info
079818	1997-1998	2	weiss - *white*
079832	1997-1999	2	gelb - *yellow*
079849	1997-1998	2	grau - *grey*

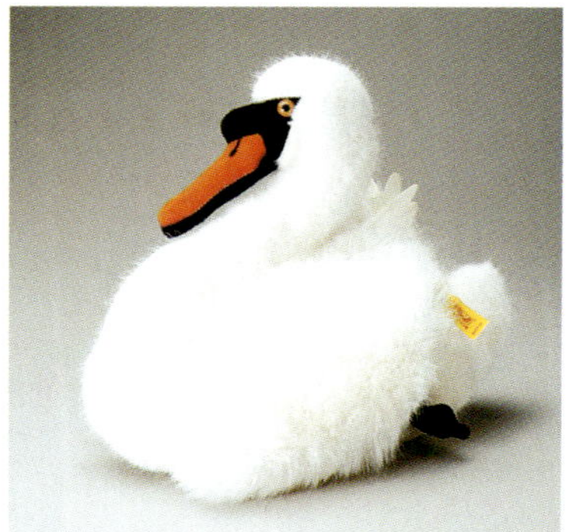

Schwan - *Swan*

Webpelz, weiss, Hals biegsam, abwaschbar - *woven fur, white, flexible neck, surface washable*

Serie	Art.-No	Period	Pr.	Info
	3247/26	1980-1983	3	26 cm

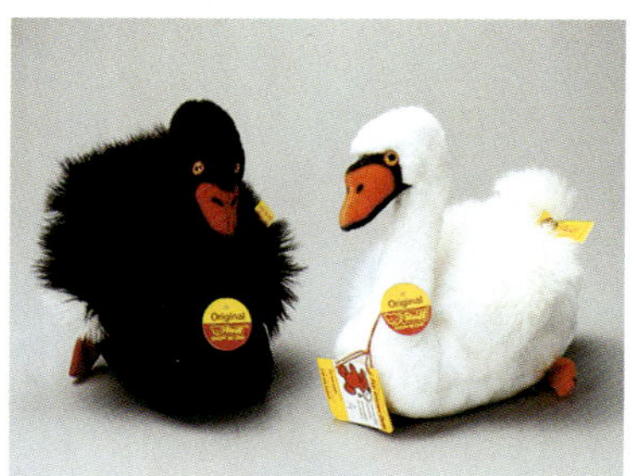

Schwan - *Swan*

Webpelz, 20 cm, abwaschbar - *woven fur, 20 cm, surface washable*

Serie	Art.-No	Period	Pr.	Info
	2612/20	1983-1985	2-3	weiss - *white*
	2613/20	1983-1985	2-3	schwarz - *black*

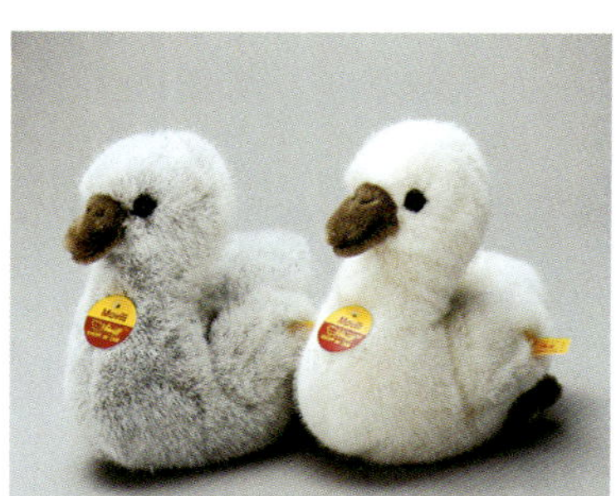

Movili Jungschwan - ***Movili*** *Young Swan*

Webpelz, 25 cm, waschmaschinenfest - *woven fur, 25 cm, machine washable*

EAN-No.	Period	Pr.	Info
074004	1994-1995	2	grau - *grey*
074011	1994-1995	2	beige

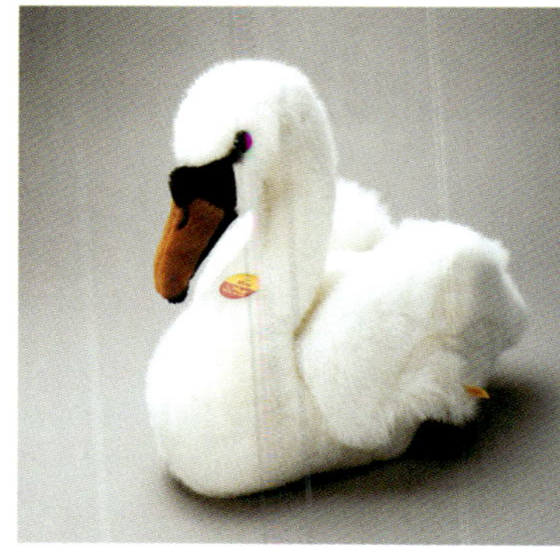

Movi Schwan - ***Movi*** *Swan*

Webpelz, handwaschbar - *woven fur, hand washable*

EAN-No.	Period	Pr.	Info
074042	1994-1997	3	50 cm

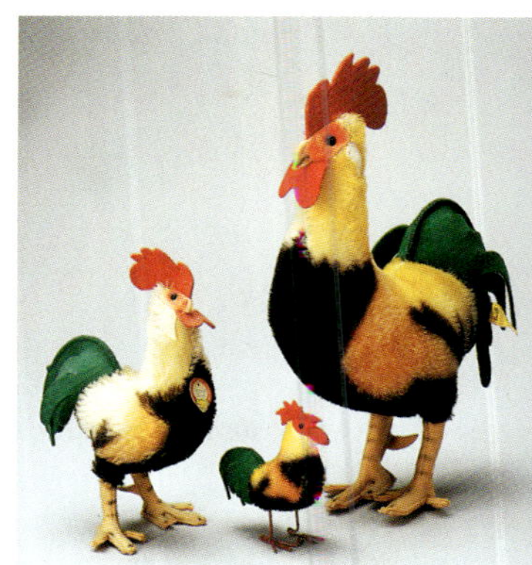

Hahn - *Rooster*

Mohair/Filz, 10 cm mit Metallbeinen, bunt, stehend, abwaschbar - *mohair/felt, 10 cm with metal legs, multi-colored, standing, surface washable*

Serie	Art.-No	Period	Pr.	Info
34	**1310**	1953-1958	3-4	10 cm
340	**1310,07**	1959-1964	3	
335	**1310,07**	1965-1967	3	
	3350/10	1968-1974	3	
34	**1317**	1953-1958	4	17 cm
340	**1317,07**	1959-1964	3-4	
335	**1317,07**	1965-1967	3-4	
	3350/17	1968-1978	3	
34	**1328**	1953-1958	4-5	28 cm
340	**1328,07**	1959-1964	4	
335	**1328,07**	1965-1967	4	
	3350/28	1968-1978	4	

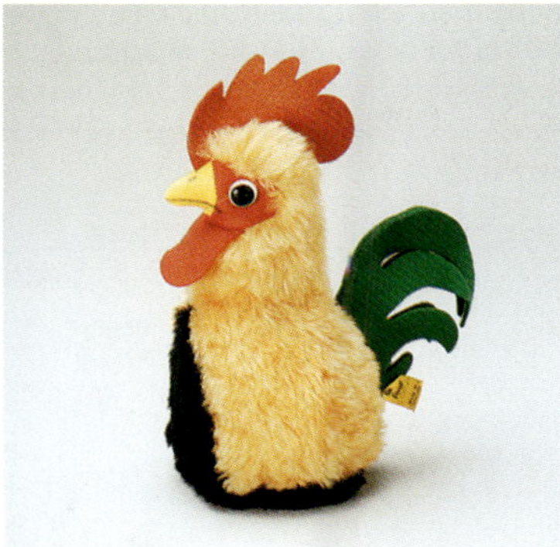

Buzzel Hahn - *Buzzel Rooster*

Dralon, formgeschaeumt, superweich, vollwaschbar - *dralon, stuffed with pre-formed foam, super soft, fully washable*

SERIE	ART.-NO	PERIOD	PR.	INFO
	6158/20	1971-1976	2	20 cm

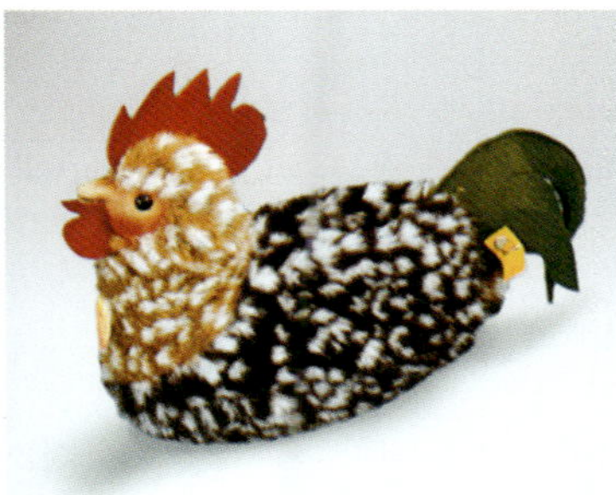

Kiki Hahn - *Kiki Rooster*

Wirkpelz, mit Rueckentasche, z.B. als Eierwaermer, vollwaschbar - *knitted fur, with pocket sewn into the back to be used as an egg warmer, fully washable*

SERIE	ART.-NO	PERIOD	PR.	INFO
	3355/20	1978-1981	3	20 cm

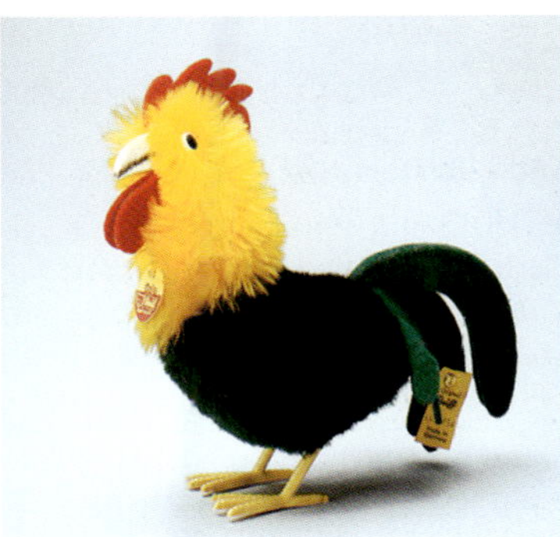

Gallo Hahn - ***Gallo** Rooster*

Dralon, stehend, abwaschbar - *dralon, standing, surface washable*

SERIE	ART.-NO	PERIOD	PR.	INFO
	3362/14	1979-1981	2	14 cm

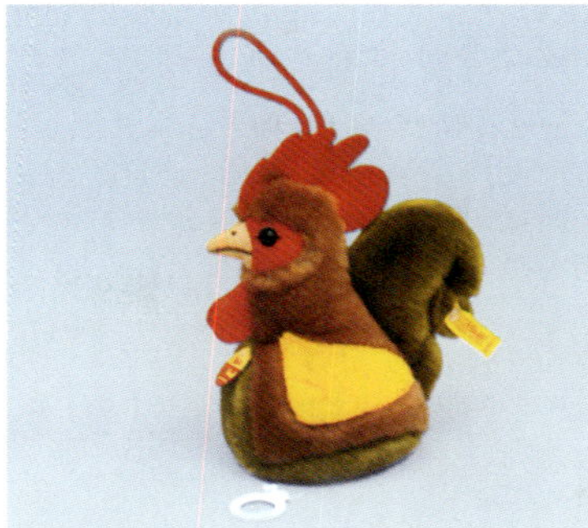

Gallo Musik-Hahn - ***Gallo** Musical Rooster*

Webpelz, formgeschaeumt, Musikwerk austauschbar, waschbar - *woven fur, stuffed with pre-formed foam, music box is exchangeable, washable*

SERIE	ART.-NO	PERIOD	PR.	INFO
233401	**6376/18**	1985-1987	2-3	18 cm

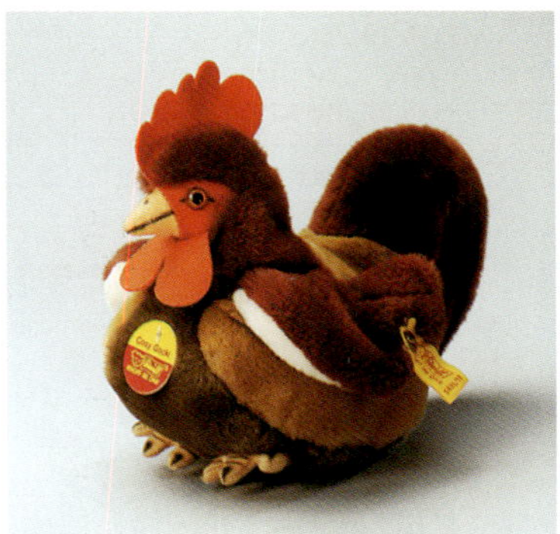

Cosy Gocki Hahn - ***Cosy Gocki** Rooster*

Webpelz, 18 cm, waschmaschinenfest - *woven fur, 18 cm, machine washable*

SERIE	ART.-NO	PERIOD	PR.	INFO
097850	**5490/18**	1987-1989	2	rot/schwarz - *red/black*
097881	**5491/18**	1987-1989	2	rot/braun - *red/brown*

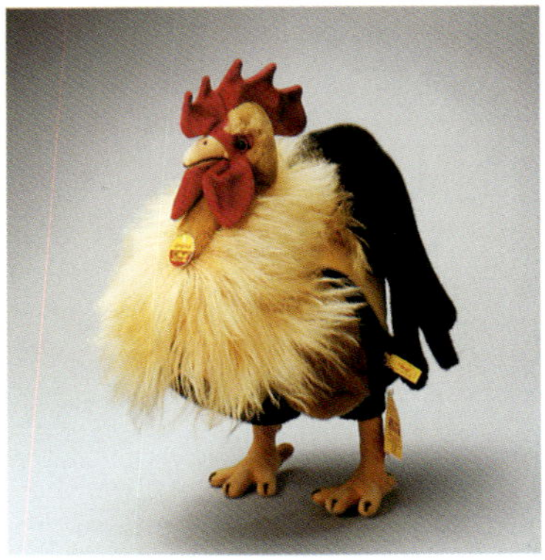

Hahn - *Rooster*

Webpelz/Mohair, gruen, stehend, abwaschbar - *woven fur/mohair, green, standing, surface washable*

EAN-NO.	PERIOD	PR.	INFO
502347	1994-1999	4	40 cm

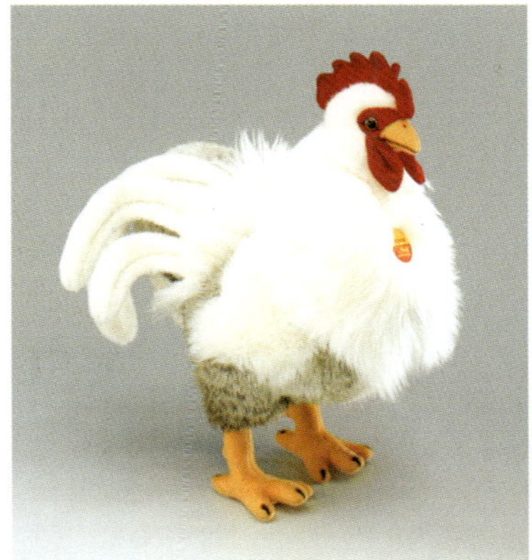

Hahn - *Rooster*

Webpelz, grau/weiss, stehend, abwaschbar - *woven fur, grey/white, standing, surface washable*

EAN-NO.	PERIOD	PR.	INFO
075605	1996-1996	3-4	36 cm

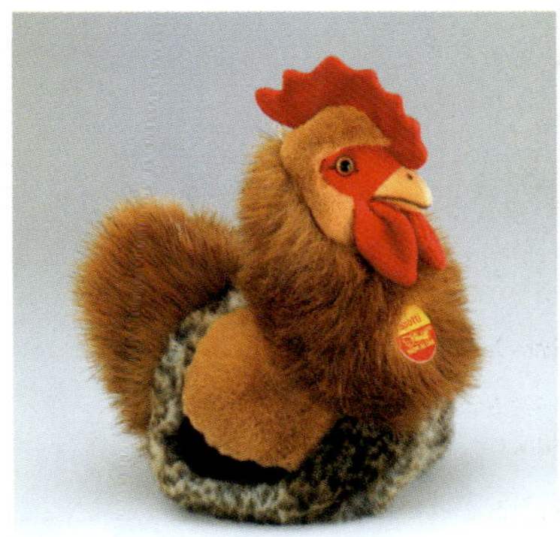

Spotti Hahn - ***Spotti** Rooster*

Webpelz, braun, waschmaschinenfest - *woven fur, brown, surface washable*

EAN-NO.	PERIOD	PR.	INFO
075582	1997-1999	2-3	20 cm

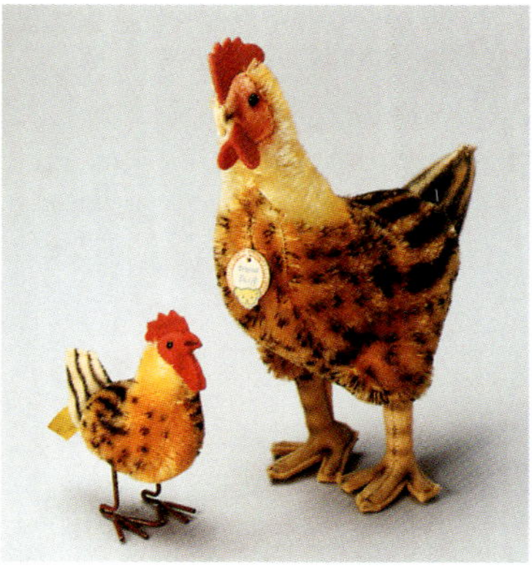

Huhn - *Hen*

Mohair/Filz, 10 cm mit Metallbeinen, gelb/braun/schwarz, stehend, abwaschbar - *mohair/felt, 10 cm with metal legs, yellow/brown/black, standing, surface washable*

SERIE	ART.-NO	PERIOD	PR.	INFO
35	**1310**	1953-1958	3-4	10 cm
350	**1310,04**	1959-1964	3	
337	**1310,04**	1965-1967	3	
	3370/10	1968-1974	3	
35	**1317**	1953-1958	4-5	17 cm
350	**1317,04**	1959-1964	4	

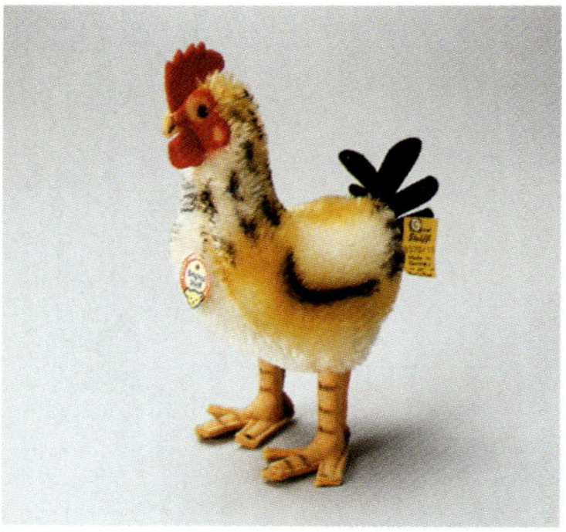

Huhn - *Hen*

Mohair, weiss, gelb/schwarz, stehend, abwaschbar - *mohair, white, yellow/black, standing, surface washable*

SERIE	ART.-NO	PERIOD	PR.	INFO
337	**1316,04**	1965-1967	3	16 cm
	3370/16	1968-1976	3	
337	**1325,04**	1965-1967	4	25 cm
	3370/25	1968-1976	3-4	

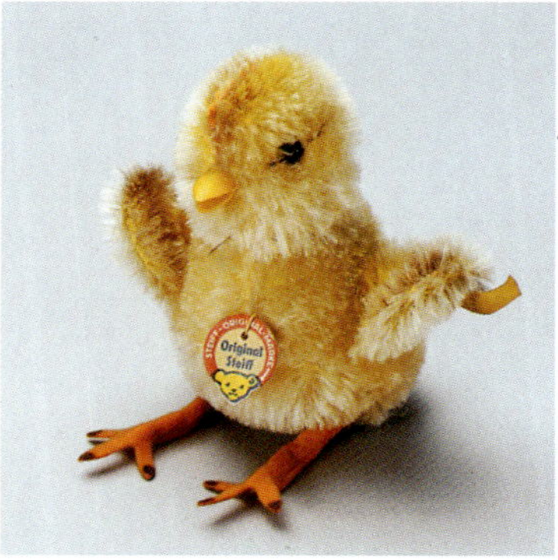

Kuecken - *Chick*

Mohair, gelb, ballartig, superweich, Stimme - *mohair, yellow, very round, super soft, press voice*

SERIE	ART.-NO	PERIOD	PR.	INFO
35	**3310**	1955-1958	3-4	10 cm
350	**3310,01**	1959-1964	3	
339	**3310,01**	1965-1967	3	
	3390/10	1968-1968	3	
35	**3314**	1955-1958	4	14 cm
350	**3314,01**	1959-1964	3-4	
339	**3314,01**	1965-1967	3-4	
	3390/14	1968-1968	3	

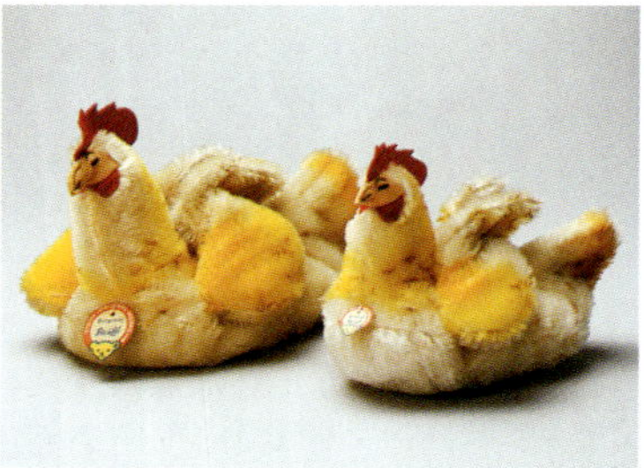

Floppy-Huhn - *Floppy Hen*

Mohair, Schlaftier, sehr weich - *mohair, sleeping animal, very soft*

SERIE	ART.-NO	PERIOD	PR.	INFO
85 35	**7317**	1958-1958	4	17 cm
850 350	**7317,00**	1959-1959	4	
85 35	**7328**	1958-1958	4	28 cm
850 350	**7328,00**	1959-1962	4	

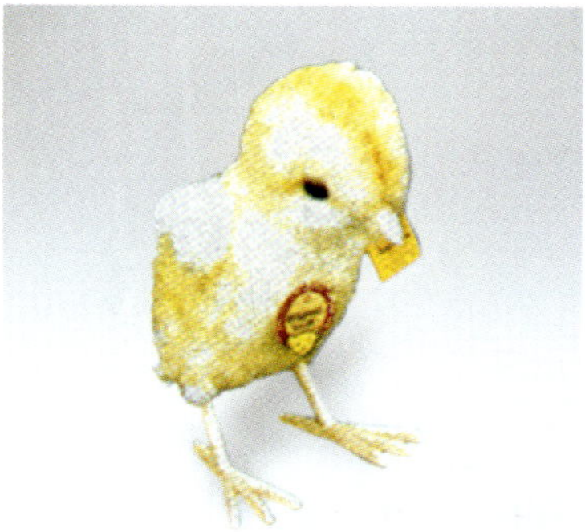

Kueken - *Chick*

Mohair, ab 1971 Dralon, 12 cm, Plastikfuesse, stehend, Stimme, abwaschbar - *mohair, from 1971 dralon, 12 cm, plastic feet, standing, press voice, surface washable*

SERIE	ART.-NO	PERIOD	PR.	INFO
	3380/12	1969-1974	2	gelb - *yellow*
	3385/12	1969-1974	2	braun - *brown*

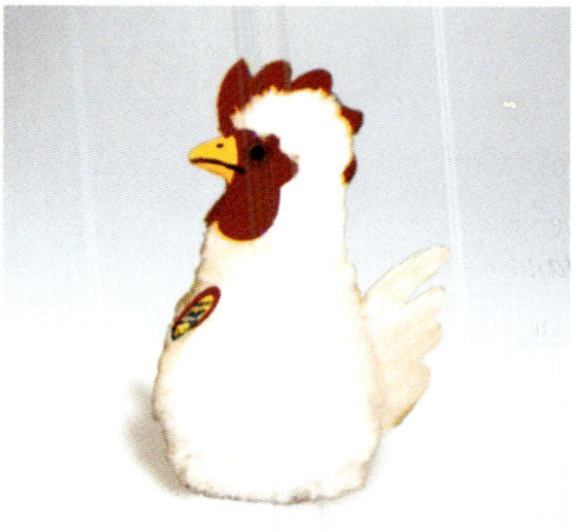

Buzzel Huhn - *Buzzel Hen*

Dralon, formgeschaeumt, superweich, vollwaschbar - *dralon, stuffed with pre-formed foam, super soft, fully washable*

SERIE	ART.-NO	PERIOD	PR.	INFO
	6158/19	1971-1974	2	19 cm

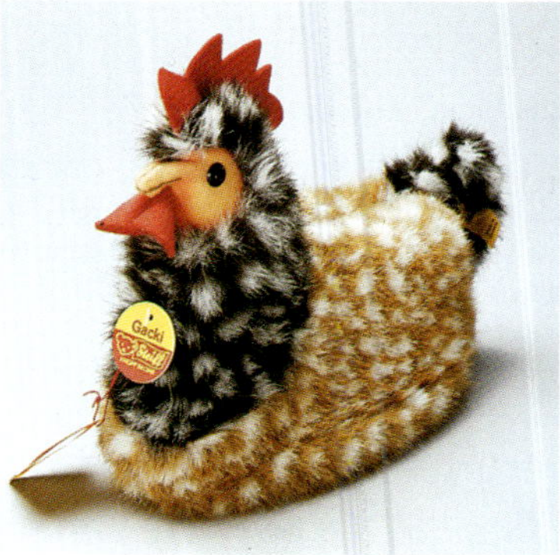

Gacki Huhn - ***Gacki*** *Hen*

Wirkpelz, mit Rueckentasche, z.B. als Eierwaermer, vollwaschbar - *knitted fur, with pocket sewn into the back to be used as an egg warmer, fully washable*

SERIE	ART.-NO	PERIOD	PR.	INFO
	3360/20	1978-1981	3	20 cm

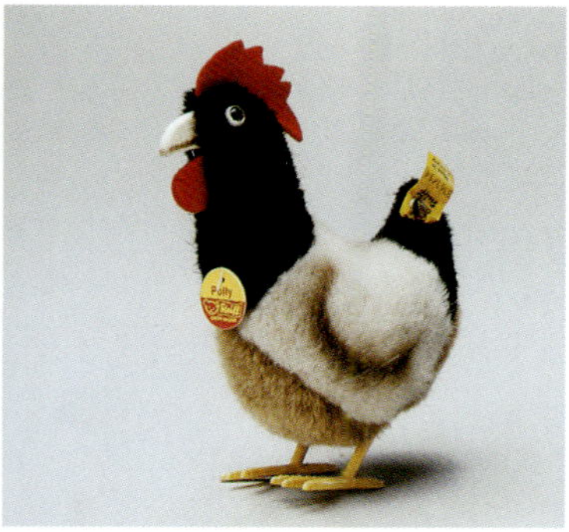

Polly Huhn - ***Polly** Hen*

Webpelz, stehend, abwaschbar - *woven fur, standing, surface washable*

SERIE	ART.-NO	PERIOD	PR.	INFO
	3363/14	1979-1981	2	14 cm

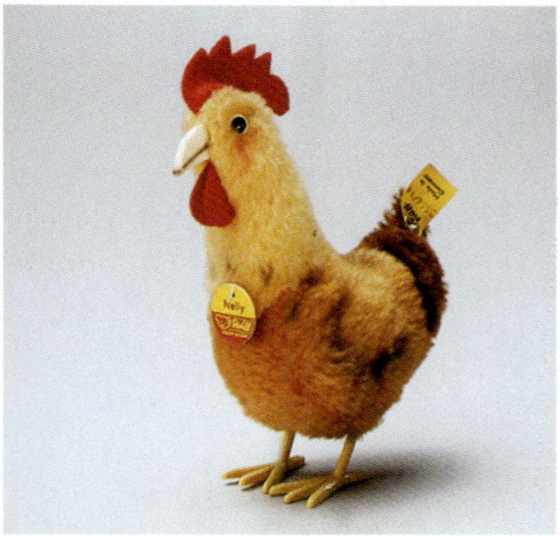

Nelly Huhn - ***Nelly** Hen*

Dralon, stehend, abwaschbar - *dralon, standing, surface washable*

SERIE	ART.-NO	PERIOD	PR.	INFO
	3364/14	1979-1981	2	14 cm

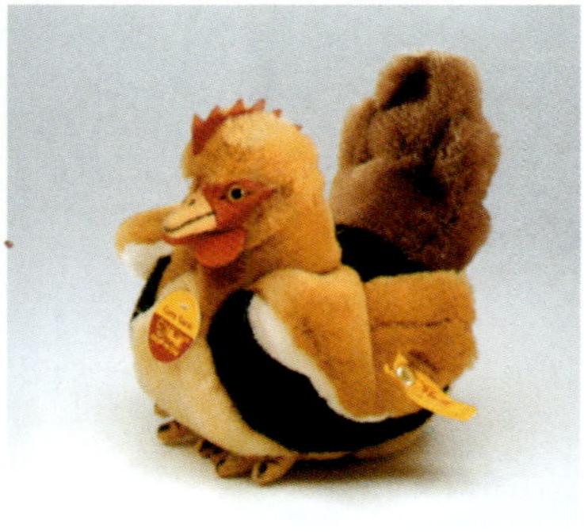

Cosy Gacki Huhn - ***Cosy Gacki** Hen*

Webpelz, 18 cm, waschmaschinenfest - *woven fur, 18 cm, machine washable*

SERIE	ART.-NO	PERIOD	PR.	INFO
097904	**5494/18**	1987-1989	2	braun/schwarz - *brown/black*
097928	**5495/18**	1987-1989	2	rost/braun - *rust/brown*

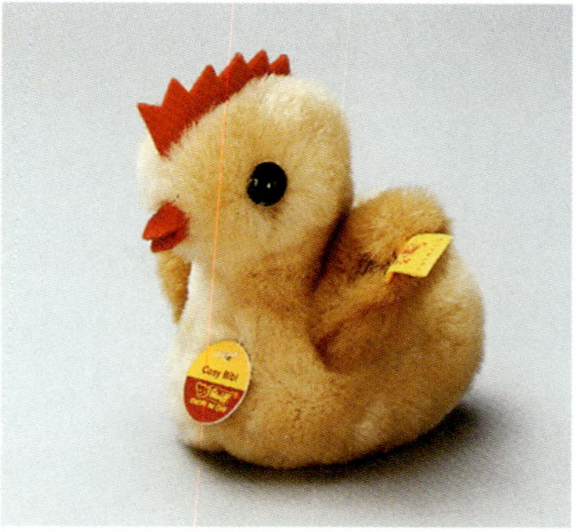

Cosy Bibi Kueken - ***Cosy Bibi** Chick*

Webpelz, 10 cm, waschmaschinenfest - *woven fur, 10 cm, machine washable*

SERIE	ART.-NO	PERIOD	PR.	INFO
097959	**5497/10**	1987-1990	1-2	rot - *red*
097973	**5498/10**	1987-1989	1-2	blond

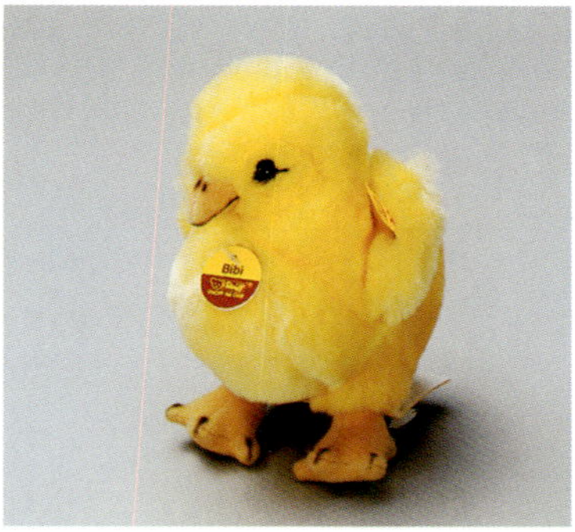

Bibi Kueken - ***Bibi** Chick*

Webpelz, 14 cm, Druck-Stimme, waschmaschinenfest - *woven fur, 14 cm, press voice, machine washable*

EAN-NO.	PERIOD	PR.	INFO
075551	1994-1995	1-2	hellbraun - *light brown*
075568	1994-1994	1-2	beige
075575	1994-1995	1-2	gelb - *yellow*

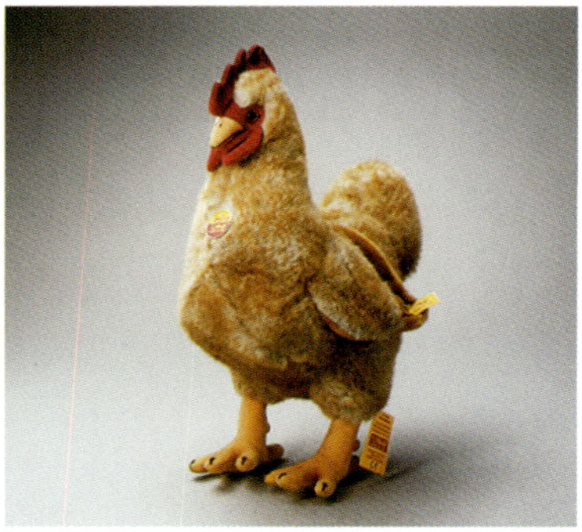

Henne - *Hen*

Webpelz, 40 cm, stehend, abwaschbar - *woven fur, 40 cm, standing, surface washable*

EAN-NO.	PERIOD	PR.	INFO
502378	1994-1999	3-4	braun - *brown*
502392	1994-1999	3-4	grau - *grey*

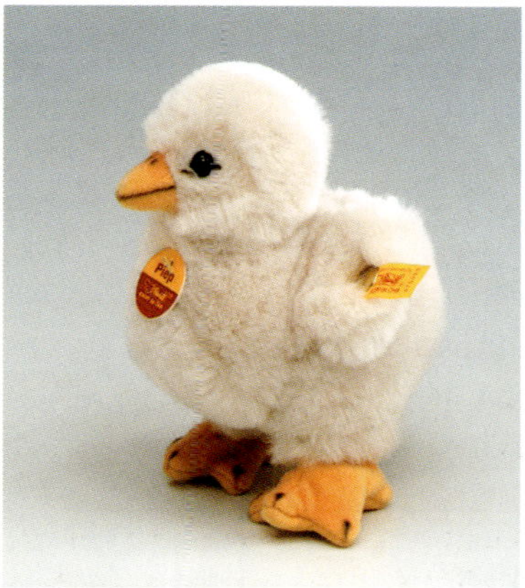

Piep Kueken - ***Piep** Chick*

Webpelz, 12 cm, waschmaschinenfest - *woven fur, 12 cm, machine washable*

EAN-NO.	PERIOD	PR.	INFO
075469	1996-1999	1-2	hellgrau - *light grey*
075476	1996-1998	1-2	wollweiss - *wool white*

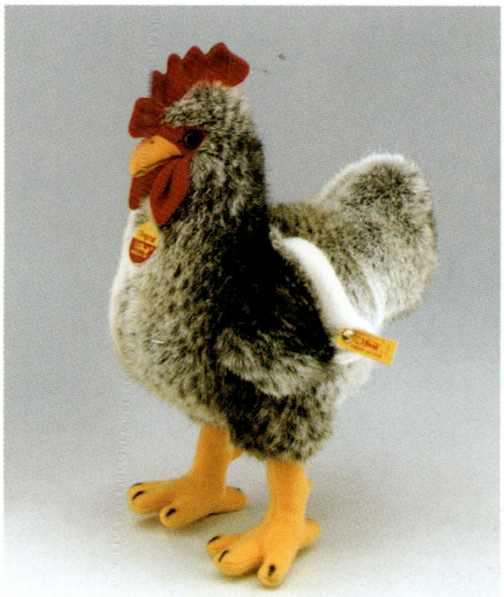

Huhn - *Hen*

Webpelz, grau, stehend, abwaschbar - *woven fur, grey, standing, surface washable*

EAN-NO.	PERIOD	PR.	INFO
075612	1996-1996	3	32 cm

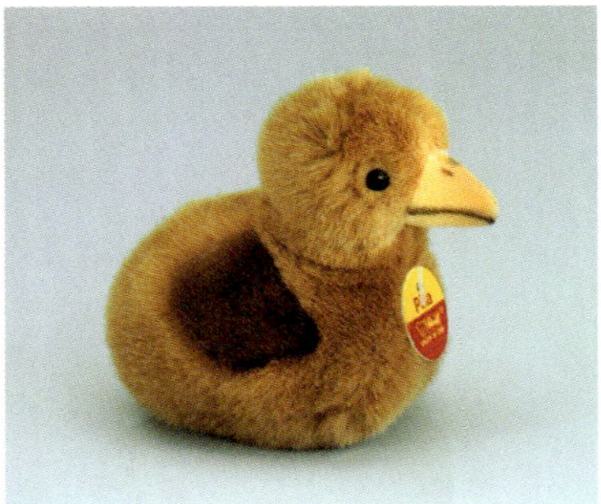

Pilla Kueken - ***Pilla*** *Chick*

Webpelz, 7 cm, waschmaschinenfest - *woven fur, 7 cm, machine washable*

EAN-No.	Period	Pr.	Info
075421	1997-1999	1	hellbeige - *light beige*
075445	1997-1998	1	hellbraun - *light brown*
075438	1997-1999	1	gelb - *yellow*

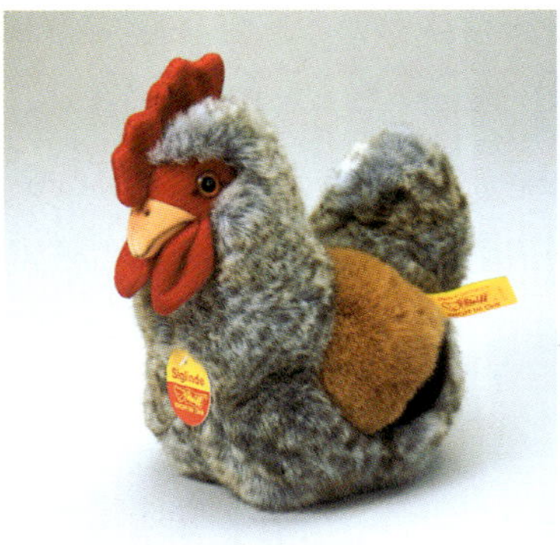

Siglinde Huhn - ***Siglinde*** *Hen*

Webpelz, braun, waschmaschinenfest - *woven fur, brown, machine washable*

EAN-No.	Period	Pr.	Info
075599	1997-1999	2-3	16 cm

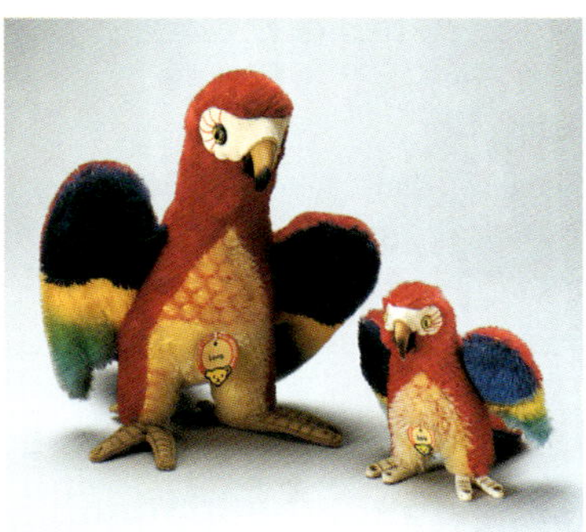

Papagei **Lora** - *Parrot* ***Lora***

Mohair, rot/blau/gelb, stehend, ausgebreitete Fluegel, abwaschbar - *mohair, red/blue/yellow, standing, wings open, surface washable*

Serie	Art.-No	Period	Pr.	Info
530	**1312,08**	1962-1964	3	12 cm
252	**1312,08**	1965-1967	3	
	2520/12	1968-1976	3	
530	**1322,08**	1962-1964	3-4	22 cm
252	**1322,08**	1965-1967	3-4	
	2520/22	1968-1974	3-4	

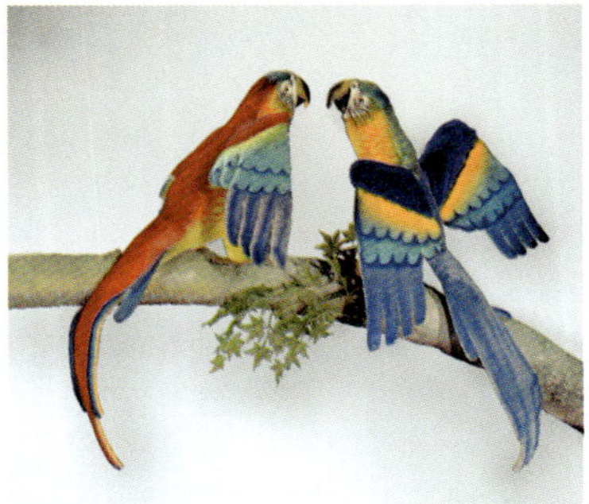

Papagei Ara - *Parrot Ara*

Schautiere, 50 cm, Mohair/Filz, Grundfarben blau bzw. rot, stehend - *display animals, 50 cm, mohair/felt, main color blue or red, standing*

Serie	Art.-No	Period	Pr.	Info
	2579/05	1967-1967	5-6	blau - *blue*
	2589/05	1967-1967	5-6	rot - *red*

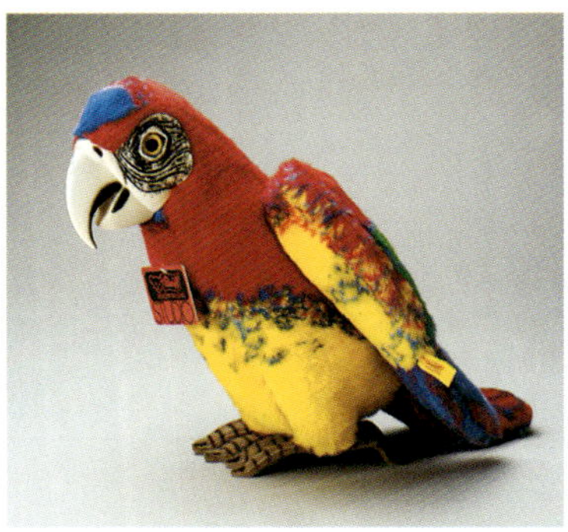

Lora Papagei - *Lora Parrot*

Studio-Tier, Wirkpelz, rot, stehend, abwaschbar - *studio animal, knitted fur, red, standing, surface washable*

Serie	Art.-No	Period	Pr.	Info
505058	**2540/30**	1979-1986	3	30 cm

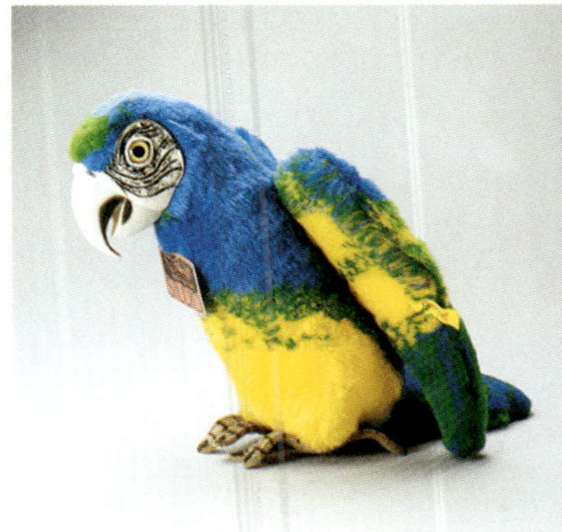

Yuku Papagei - *Yuku Parrot*

Studio-Tier, Wirkpelz, blau, stehend, abwaschbar - *studio animal, knitted fur, blue, standing, surface washable*

Serie	Art.-No	Period	Pr.	Info
505072	**2541/30**	1979-1986	3	30 cm

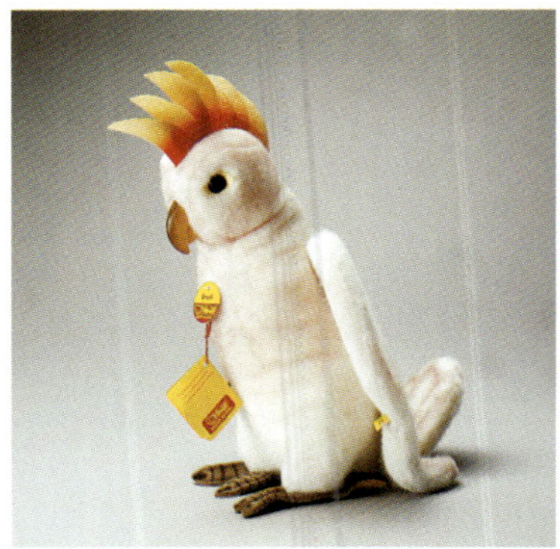

Starli Kakadu - ***Starli*** *Cockatoo*

Studio-Tier, Webpelz, abwaschbar - *studio animal, woven fur, surface washable*

Serie	Art.-No	Period	Pr.	Info
	2545/30	1979-1984	3	30 cm

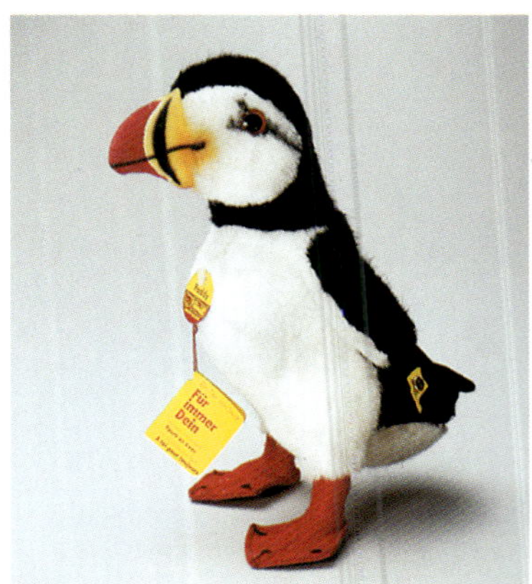

Paddy Papageientaucher - ***Paddy*** *Puffin*

Studio-Tier, Webpelz, stehend, abwaschbar - *studio animal, woven fur, standing, surface washable*

SERIE	ART.-NO	PERIOD	PR.	INFO
	2511/26	1979-1981	3	26 cm

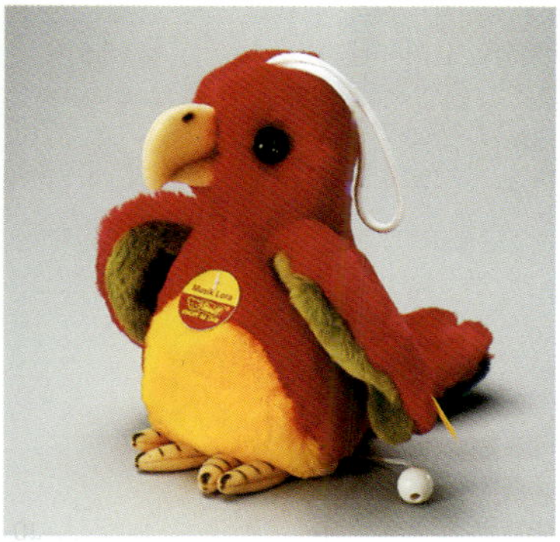

Musik Lora Papagei - *Musical Lora Parrot*

Webpelz, Musikwerk austauschbar, ohne Musikwerk waschbar - *woven fur, music box exchangeable, washable without music box*

SERIE	ART.-NO	PERIOD	PR.	INFO
233203	**6371/18**	1983-1990	2-3	18 cm
	233203	1991-1999	2-3	

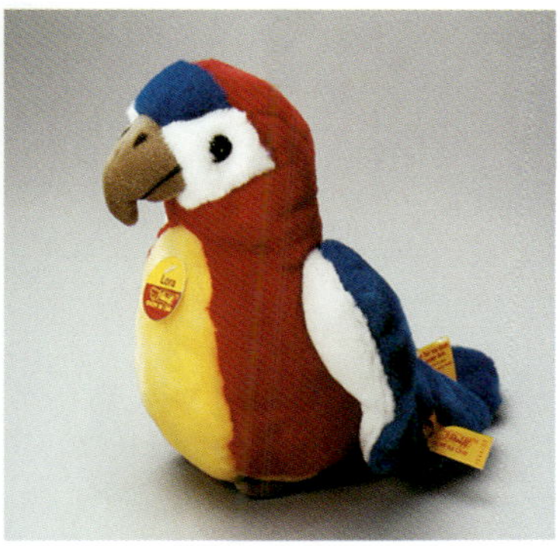

Lora Papagei - ***Lora** Parrot*

Webpelz, rot, waschmaschinenfest - *woven fur, red, machine washable*

SERIE	ART.-NO	PERIOD	PR.	INFO
064005	**2544/30**	1987-1988	2-3	30 cm

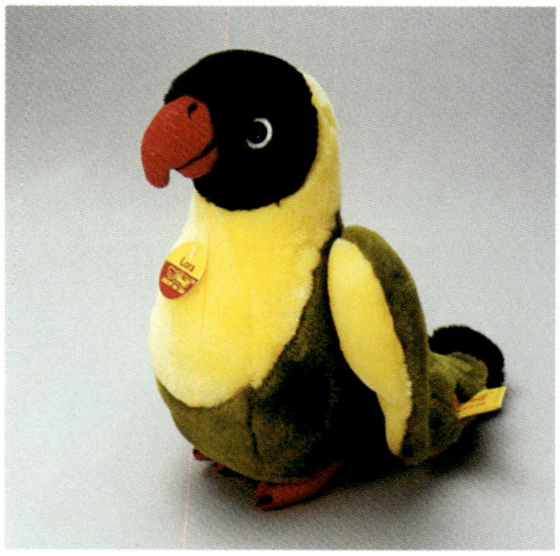

Lora Papagei - ***Lora** Parrot*

Webpelz, gruen, waschmaschinenfest - *woven fur, green, machine washable*

SERIE	ART.-NO	PERIOD	PR.	INFO
064159	**2550/30**	1987-1988	2-3	30 cm

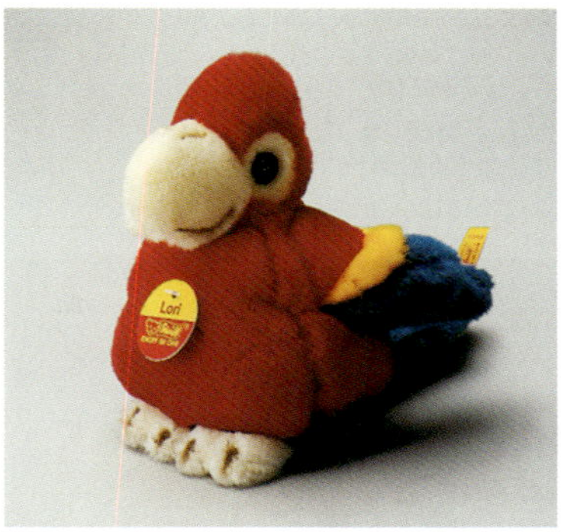

Lori Papagei - ***Lori** Parrot*

Webpelz, waschmaschinenfest - *woven fur, machine washable*

SERIE	ART.-NO	PERIOD	PR.	INFO
064616	**2555/14**	1990-1990	1-2	14 cm
	064616	1991-1995	1-2	

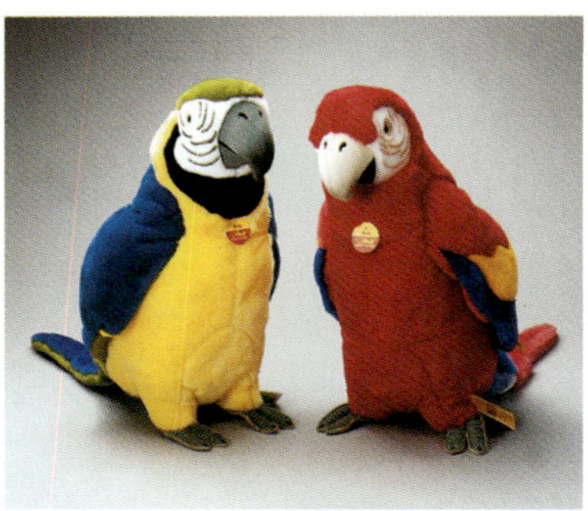

Ara Papagei - ***Ara** Parrot*

Webpelz, 50 cm, abwaschbar - *woven fur, 50 cm, surface washable*

EAN-NO.	PERIOD	PR.	INFO
063909	1992-1995	4	rot - *red*
063947	1992-1995	4	blau - *blue*

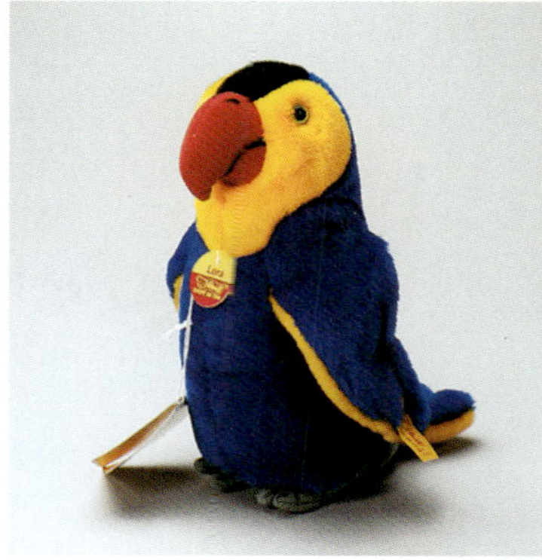

Lora Lori

Webpelz, 22 cm, waschmaschinenfest - *woven fur, 22 cm, machine washable*

EAN-NO.	PERIOD	PR.	INFO
064029	1993-1994	2-3	rot - *red*
064043	1993-1995	2-3	gruen - *green*
064067	1993-1994	2-3	blau - *blue*
064081	1993-1993	2-3	grau - *grey*

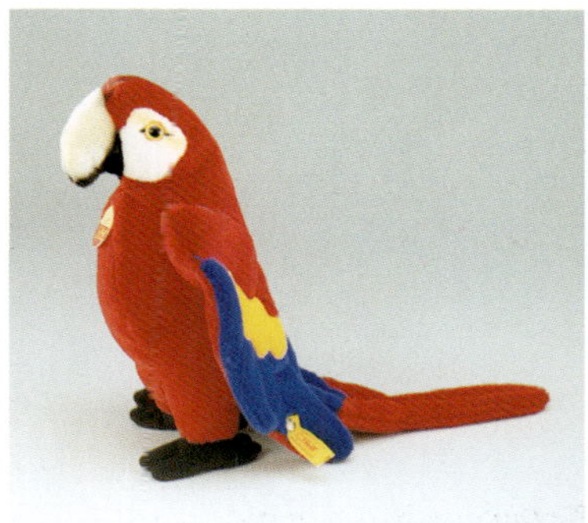

Lore Papagei - ***Lore** Parrot*

Webpelz, rot, stehend, waschmaschinenfest - *woven fur, red, standing, machine washable*

EAN-NO.	PERIOD	PR.	INFO
063817	1998-1999	2-3	25 cm

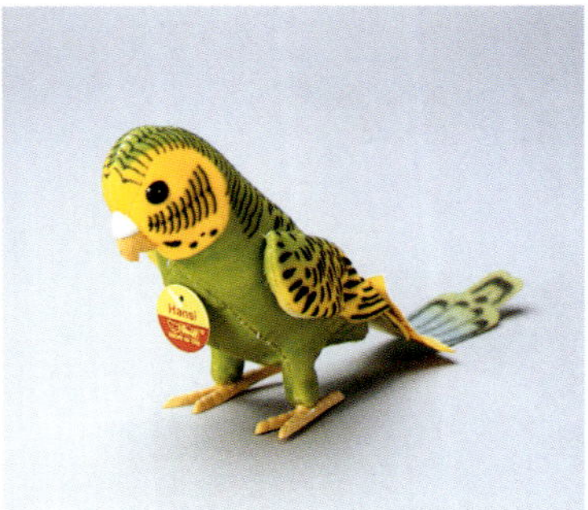

Hansi Wellensittich - ***Hansi** Parakeet*

Samt, ab 1979 Trevirasamt, gruen/gelb, Fuesse & Schnabel Plastik, stehend, abwaschbar - *velvet, from 1979 trevira velvet, green/yellow, feet & beak plastic, standing, surface washable*

SERIE	ART.-NO	PERIOD	PR.	INFO
253	**1413,01**	1967-1967	2-3	13 cm
057601	**2531/13**	1968-1990	1-2	
	057601	1991-1999	1-2	

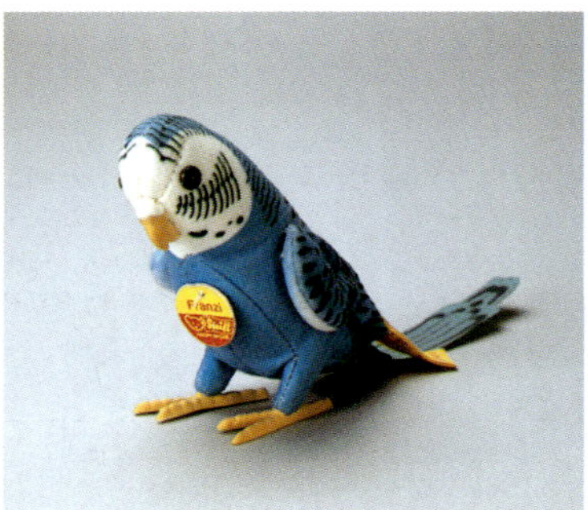

Franzi Wellensittich - ***Franzi** Parakeet*

Samt, ab 1979 Trevirasamt, blau/weiss, Fuesse & Schnabel Plastik, stehend, abwaschbar - *velvet, from 1979 trevira velvet, blue/white, feet & beak plastic, standing, surface washable*

SERIE	ART.-NO	PERIOD	PR.	INFO
253	**1413,04**	1967-1967	2-3	13 cm
057656	**2534/13**	1968-1990	1-2	
	057656	1991-1999	1-2	

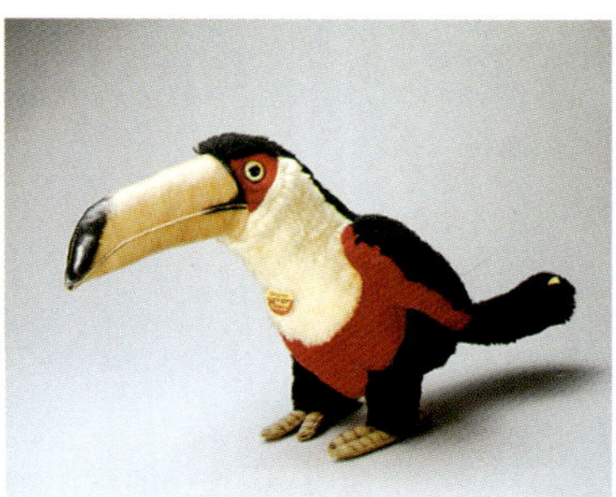

Studio Tukan - *Studio Tucan*

Webpelz, Schnabel aus Kunstleder, stehend, kein Katalognachweis - *woven fur, beak made of synthetic leather, standing, no catalog information available*

SERIE	ART.-NO	PERIOD	PR.	INFO
	2569/04	1970-1970	3-4	30 cm

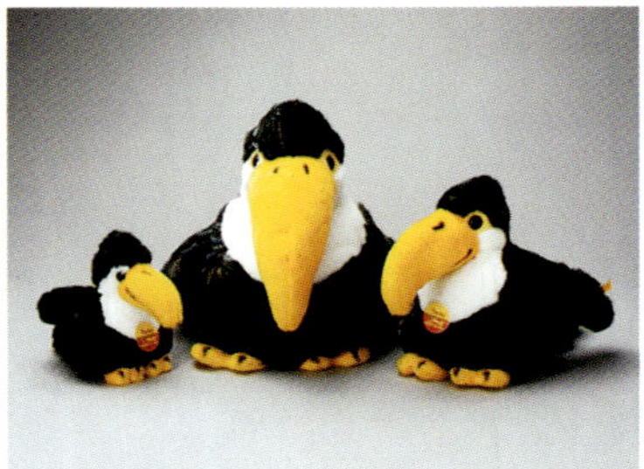

Tucky Tukan - ***Tucky** Tucan*

Webpelz, waschmaschinenfest - *woven fur, machine washable*

SERIE	ART.-NO	PERIOD	PR.	INFO
064210	**2560/14**	1990-1990	2	14 cm
	064210	1991-1993	2	
064234	**2560/20**	1989-1990	2	20 cm
	064234	1991-1993	2	
064272	**2560/30**	1989-1990	2-3	30 cm

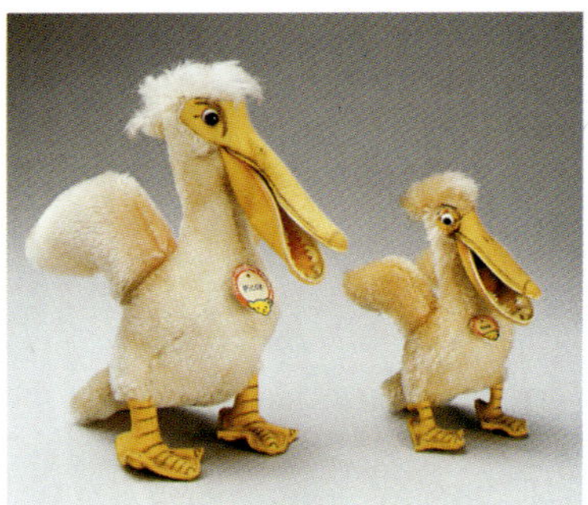

Piccy Pelikan - ***Piccy** Pelican*

Mohair, weiss/rosa, stehend - *mohair, white/pink, standing*

SERIE	ART.-NO	PERIOD	PR.	INFO
545	**1317,00**	1959-1961	4-5	17 cm
545	**1325,00**	1959-1961	5-6	25 cm

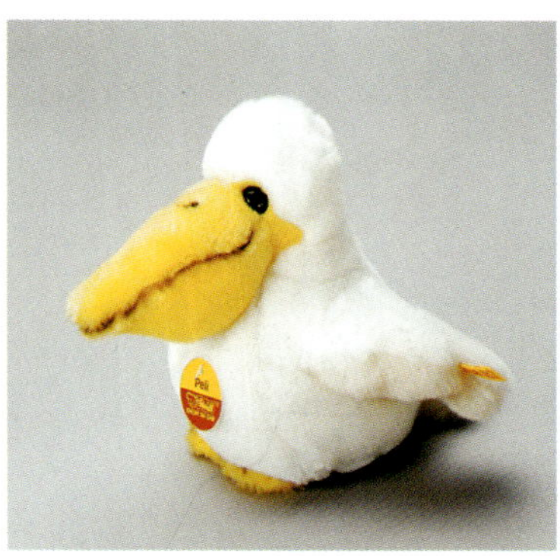

Peli Pelikan - ***Peli** Pelican*

Webpelz, waschmaschinenfest - *woven fur, machine washable*

SERIE	ART.-NO	PERIOD	PR.	INFO
064319	**2565/14**	1990-1990	2	14 cm
	064319	1991-1992	2	
064333	**2565/20**	1989-1990	2	20 cm
064371	**2565/30**	1989-1990	2-3	30 cm

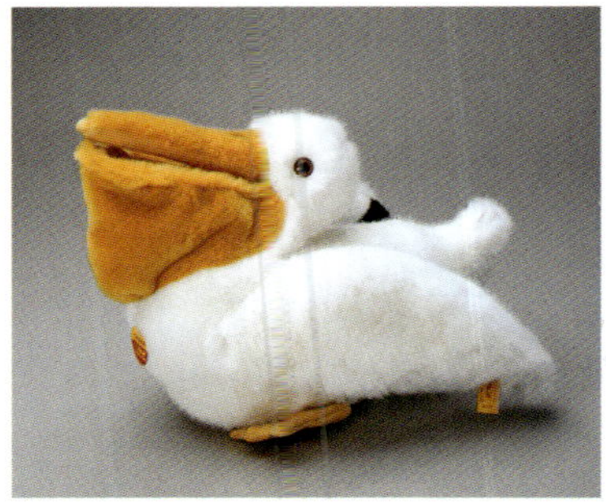

Pelikan - *Pelican*

Webpelz, weiss, eingearbeitete Tasche im Schnabel, waschmaschinenfest - *woven fur, white, pocket sewn into the beak, machine washable*

EAN-NO.	PERIOD	PR.	INFO
064388	1995-1998	3	35 cm

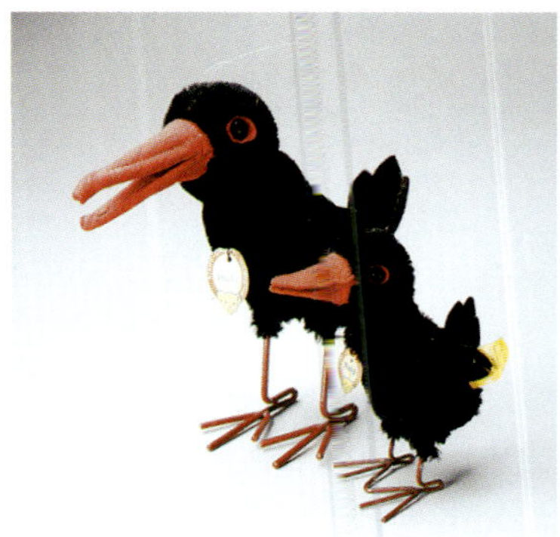

Hucky Rabe - ***Hucky** Raven*

Mohair, Metallbeine, ab 1973 Plastik, schwarz, roter Schnabel, stehend, lustiger Ausdruck, abwaschbar - *mohair, metal legs, from 1973 plastic, black, red beak, standing, funny facial expression, surface washable*

SERIE	ART.-NO	PERIOD	PR.	INFO
62	**7312**	1952-1958	3-4	12 cm
620	**7312,00**	1960-1964	3	
255	**7312,00**	1965-1967	3	
	2550/12	1968-1976	3	
62	**7317**	1952-1958	4	17 cm
620	**7317,00**	1960-1963	3-4	
255	**7317,00**	1966-1967	3-4	
	2550/17	1968-1974	3-4	

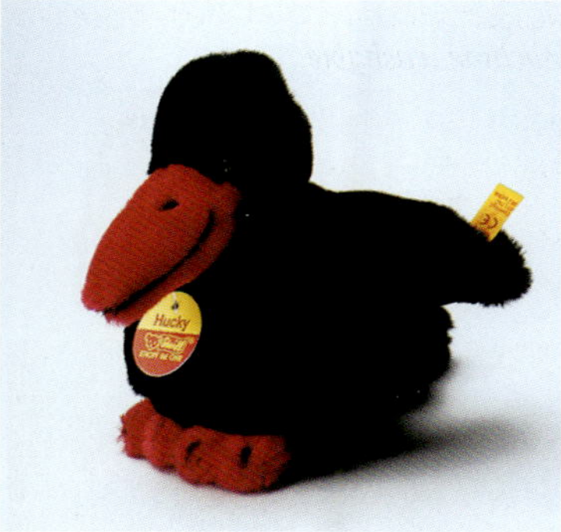

Hucky Rabe - ***Hucky** Raven*

Webpelz, waschmaschinenfest - *woven fur, machine washable*

Serie	Art.-No	Period	Pr.	Info
064418	**2580/14**	1990-1990	1-2	14 cm
	064418	1991-1996	1-2	
064432	**2580/20**	1989-1990	2	20 cm
	064432	1991-1994	2	

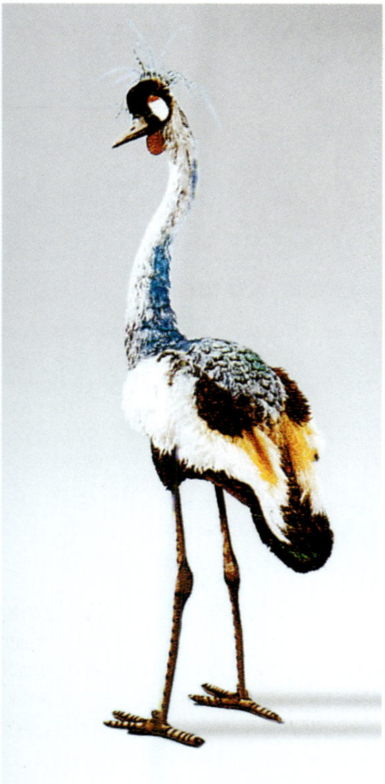

Kronen-Kranich - *Crowned Crane*

Schautier, Mohair, Beine mit Filzueberzug, Hals abnehmbar - *display animal, mohair, legs are covered with felt, neck is detachable*

Serie	Art.-No	Period	Pr.	Info
624	**1140,90**	1961-1961	6	140 cm
	1219/14	1967-1967	6	

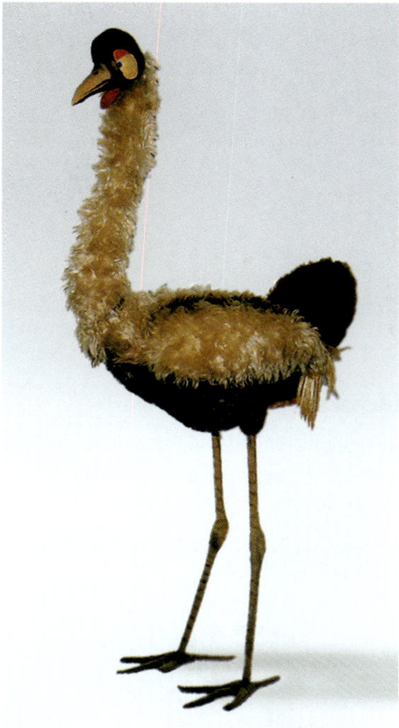

Emu

Mohair, kein Katalognachweis bekannt - *mohair, no catalog information available*

EAN-No.	Period	Pr.	Info
	1961-1961	6	140 cm

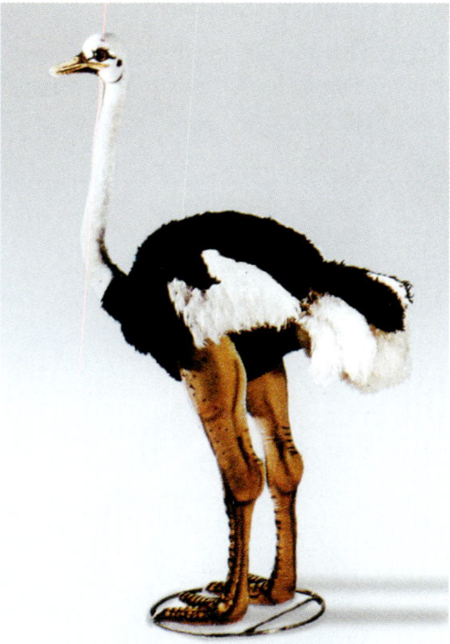

Strauss - *Ostrich*

Schautier, Mohair, Hals abnehmbar, stehend auf Standring - *display animal, mohair, neck is detachable, with stand ring*

Serie	Art.-No	Period	Pr.	Info
624	**1220,90**	1961-1961	6-7	220 cm
	1239/22	1967-1967	6-7	

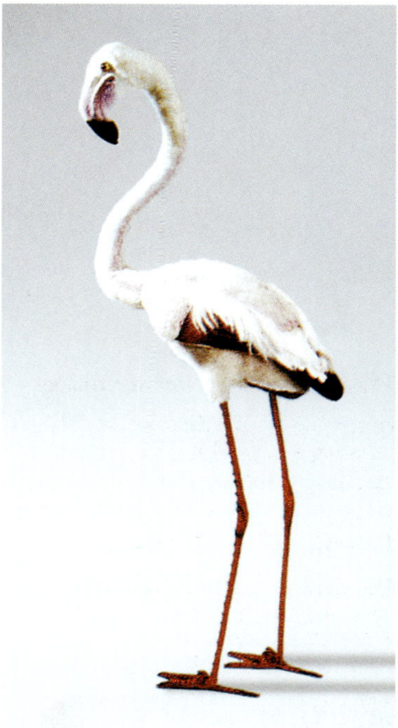

Flamingo

Schautier, Dralon, Mohair, Filz, Beine mit Kunststoffueberzug, Hals abnehmbar - *display animal, dralon, mohair, felt, legs are covered with synthetic material, neck is detachable*

Serie	Art.-No	Period	Pr.	Info
625	**1160,90**	1961-1961	6	160 cm
	1229/16	1967-1967	6	

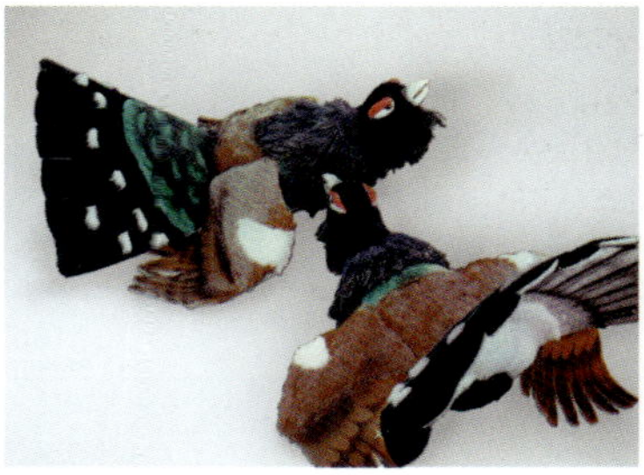

Auerhahn - *Grouse*

Schautier, Mohair, stehend, ausgebreitete Fluegel - *display animal, mohair, standing, wings open*

Serie	Art.-No	Period	Pr.	Info
	2639/05	1968-1968	5-6	50 cm

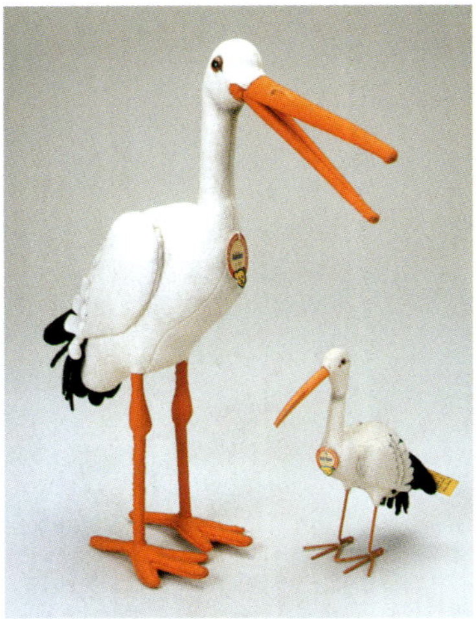

Storch **Adebar** - *Stork* ***Adebar***

Filz, schwarz/weiss/rot, stehend - *Felt, black/white/red, standing*

SERIE	ART.-NO	PERIOD	PR.	INFO
67	**1117**	1953-1958	4	17 cm
670	**1017,00**	1961-1961	3-4	
256	**1017,00**	1966-1967	3-4	
	2560/17	1968-1969	3	
67	**1135**	1953-1957	4-5	35 cm
670	**1035,00**	1961-1961	4	
256	**1035,00**	1966-1966	4	
67	**1160**	1953-1957	5-6	60 cm
670	**1060,00**	1961-1961	5	
256	**1060,00**	1966-1966	5	

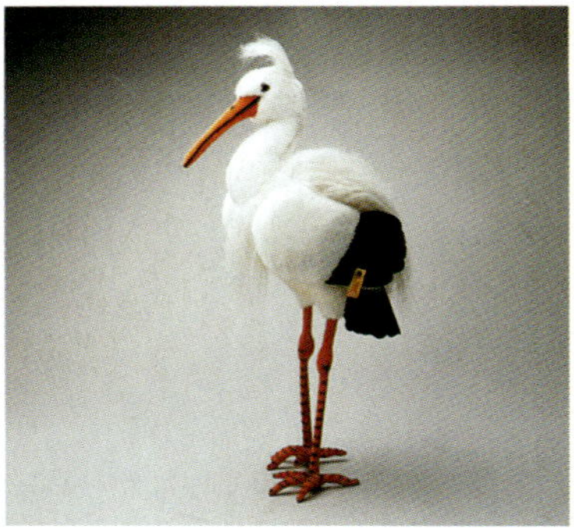

Storch - *Stork*

Studio-Tier, stehend, abwaschbar - *studio animal, standing, surface washable*

SERIE	ART.-NO	PERIOD	PR.	INFO
	2608/50	1980-1984	3	50 cm

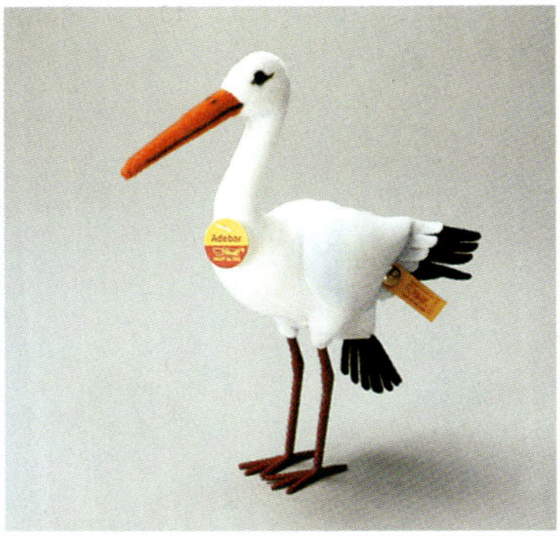

Adebar Storch - ***Adebar*** *Stork*

Trevirasamt/Wollfilz, abwaschbar - *trevira velvet/wool felt, surface washable*

EAN-NO.	PERIOD	PR.	INFO
057700	1991-1993	2	18 cm

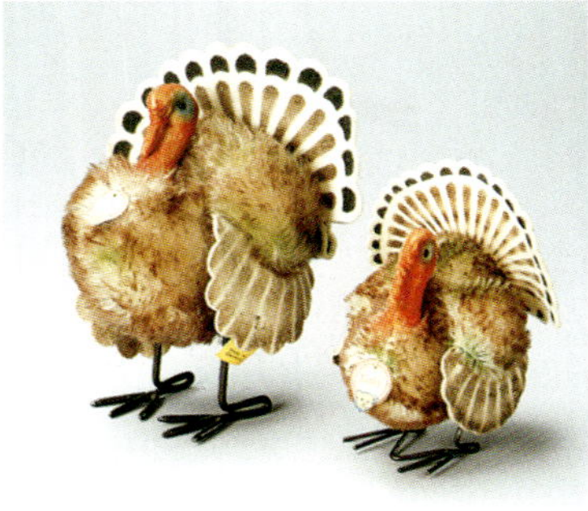

Tucky Truthahn - ***Tucky*** *Turkey*

Mohair, Filz, Metallbeine, braun/gruen/rot, stehend - *mohair, felt, metal legs, brown/green/red, standing*

SERIE	ART.-NO	PERIOD	PR.	INFO
67a	**1310,0**	1952-1958	4	10 cm
672	**1310,00**	1961-1961	4	
67a	**1314,0**	1952-1957	4	14 cm
672	**1314,00**	1961-1961	4	

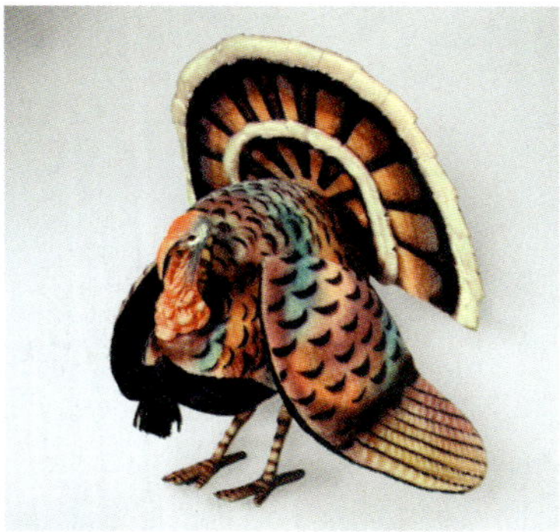

Truthahn - *Turkey*

Schautier, stehend - *display animal, standing*

SERIE	ART.-NO	PERIOD	PR.	INFO
	3339/08	1967-1967	6	80 cm

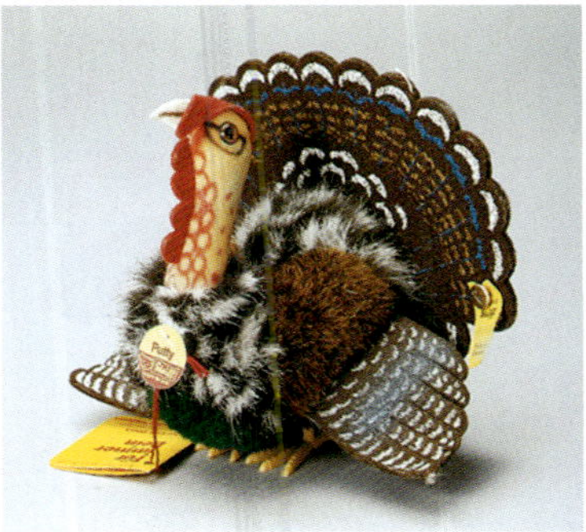

Putty Truthahn - ***Putty*** *Turkey*

Wirkpelz, Filz, Plastikbeine, abwaschbar - *knitted fur, felt, plastic legs, surface washable*

SERIE	ART.-NO	PERIOD	PR.	INFO
	3367/14	1979-1983	2-3	14 cm

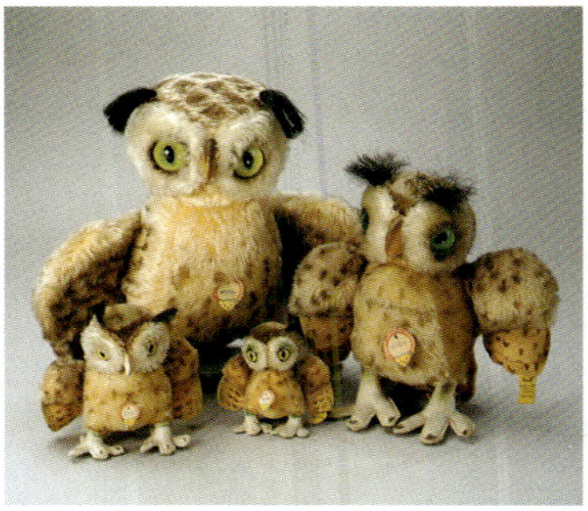

Uhu **Wittie** - *Owl* ***Wittie***

Mohair, Filzfuesse, stehend, ausgebreitete Fluegel, abwaschbar - *mohair, felt feet, standing, wings open, surface washable*

SERIE	ART.-NO	PERIOD	PR.	INFO
67b	**4310**	1954-1958	3-4	10 cm
674	**4310,00**	1959-1964	3	
262	**4310,00**	1965-1967	3	
	2620/10	1968-1976	3	
67b	**4314**	1954-1958	3-4	14 cm
674	**4314,00**	1959-1964	3	
262	**4314,00**	1965-1967	3	
	2620/14	1968-1978	3	
67b	**4322**	1955-1958	4	22 cm
674	**4322,00**	1959-1964	3-4	
262	**4322,00**	1965-1967	3-4	
	2620/22	1968-1977	3-4	
674	**4335,00**	1964-1964	4	35 cm
262	**4335,00**	1965-1967	4	
	2620/35	1968-1977	4	

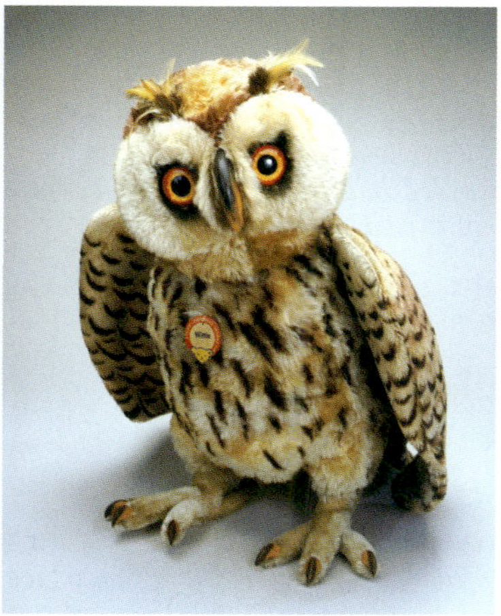

Uhu **Wittie** - *Owl* ***Wittie***

Schautier, Mohair, ausgebreitete Fluegel - *display animal, mohair, wings open*

SERIE	ART.-NO	PERIOD	PR.	INFO
674	**4380,90**	1963-1963	6	80 cm
	2629/08	1967-1967	6	

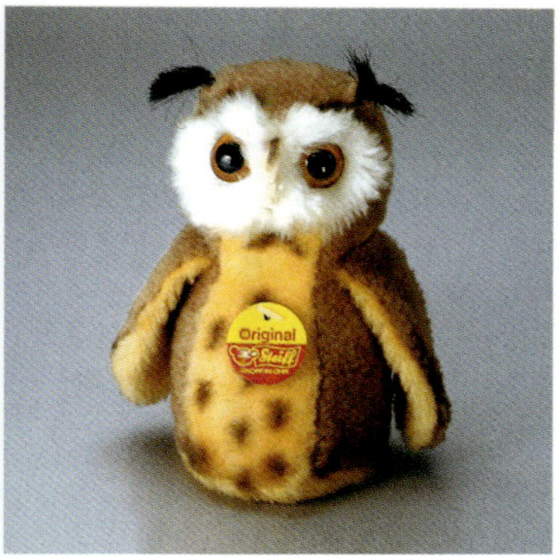

Buzzel Uhu - *Buzzel Owl*

Dralon, formgeschaeumt, superweich, vollwaschbar - *dralon, stuffed with pre-formed foam, super soft, fully washable*

SERIE	ART.-NO	PERIOD	PR.	INFO
	6154/20	1971-1978	2	20 cm

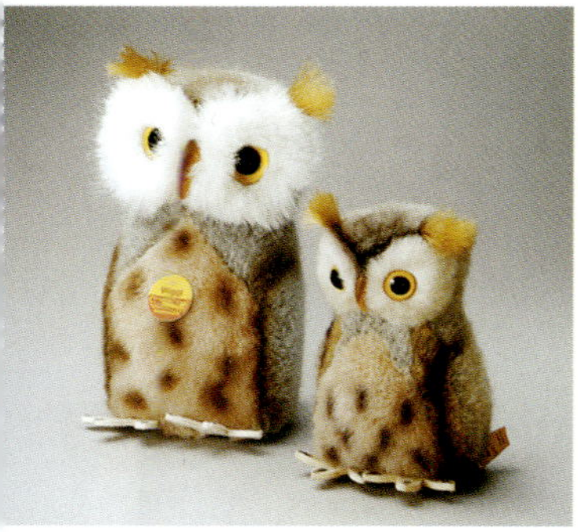

Wiggi Uhu - ***Wiggi*** *Owl*

Nerzimitation, ab 1978 Synthetik-Webpelz, formgeschaeumt, stehend, abwaschbar - *imitation mink, from 1978 synthetic woven fur, stuffed with pre-formed foam, standing, surface washable*

SERIE	ART.-NO	PERIOD	PR.	INFO
072154	**2625/15**	1976-1987	2	15 cm
	2625/25	1976-1983	2	25 cm

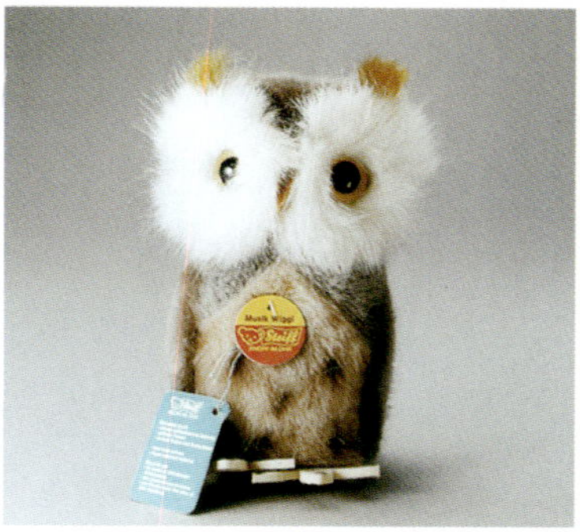

Musik Wiggi - *Musical Wiggi*

Webpelz, Koerper formgeschaeumt, Musikwerk austauschbar, waschbar - *woven fur, body stuffed with pre-formed foam, music box exchangeable, washable*

SERIE	ART.-NO	PERIOD	PR.	INFO
	6376/18	1978-1983	2-3	22 cm

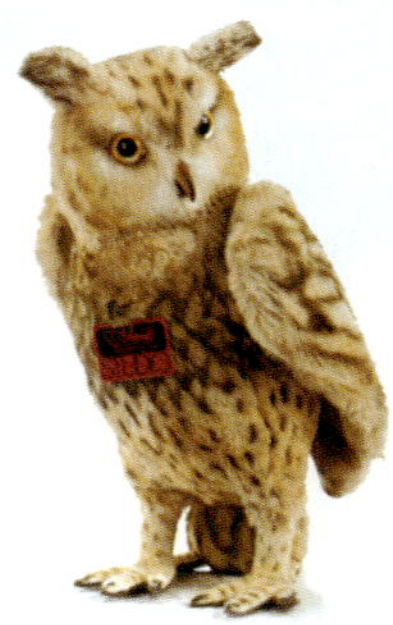

Studio Uhu - *Studio Owl*

Wirkpelz - *knitted fur*

SERIE	ART.-NO	PERIOD	PR.	INFO
	2590/50	1981-1981	4	50 cm

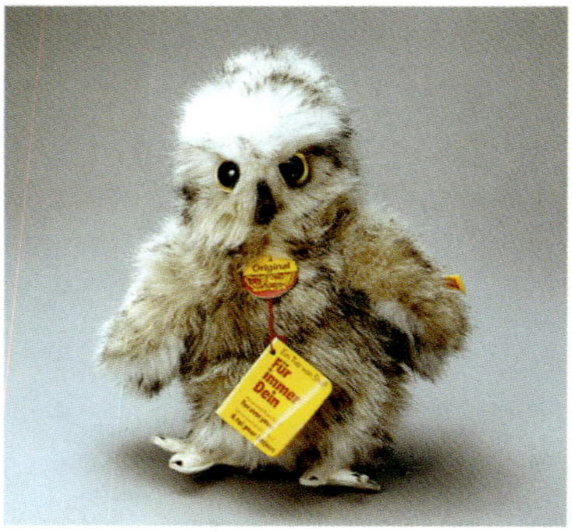

Jung Uhu - *Young Owl*

Webpelz, stehend, abwaschbar - *woven fur, standing, surface washable*

SERIE	ART.-NO	PERIOD	PR.	INFO
072055	**2591/22**	1981-1989	2	22 cm

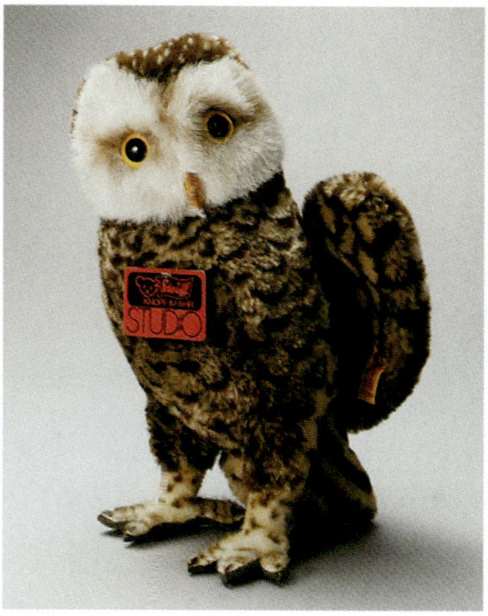

Studio Kauz - *Studio Screech Owl*

Wirkpelz - *knitted fur*

SERIE	ART.-NO	PERIOD	PR.	INFO
505201	**2593/28**	1981-1988	3	28 cm

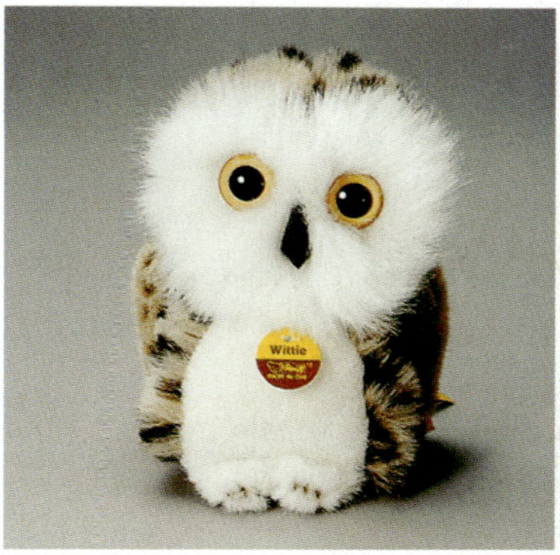

Wittie Eule - ***Wittie*** *Owl*

Wirkpelz, stehend, abwaschbar - *knitted fur, standing, surface washable*

SERIE	ART.-NO	PERIOD	PR.	INFO
045608	**1550/12**	1986-1990	1-2	12 cm
	045608	1991-1999	1-2	

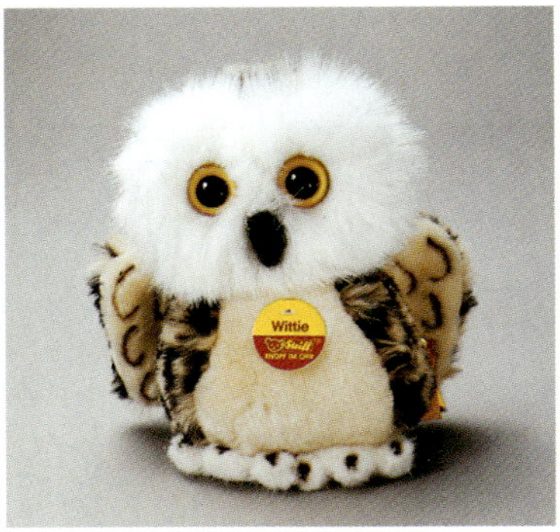

Wittie Junguhu - ***Wittie** Owlet*

Wirkpelz, abwaschbar - *knitted fur, surface washable*

SERIE	ART.-NO	PERIOD	PR.	INFO
072109	**2622/18**	1987-1990	2	18 cm
	072109	1991-1999	2	
072123	**2622/24**	1987-1988	2	24 cm

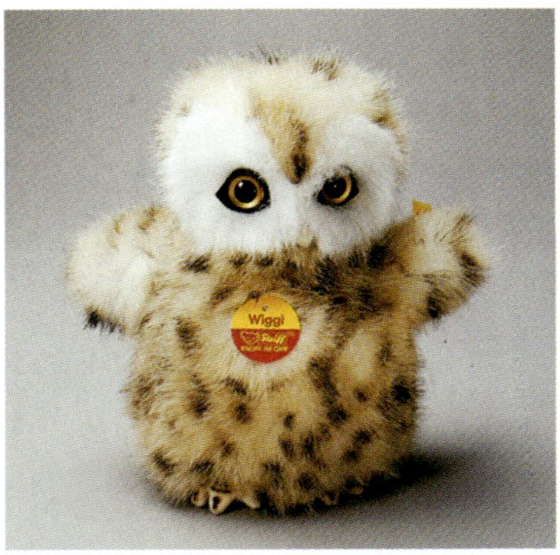

Wiggi Baby Eule - ***Wiggi** Baby Owlet*

Webpelz, creme gefleckt, handwaschbar - *woven fur, cream with speckles, hand washable*

SERIE	ART.-NO	PERIOD	PR.	INFO
072079	**2592/20**	1990-1990	2	20 cm
	072079	1991-1996	2	
072086	**2592/25**	1990-1990	2-3	25 cm
	072086	1991-1992	2-3	

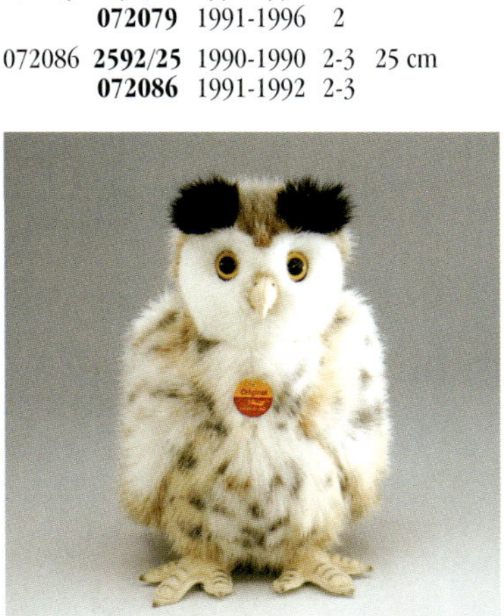

Junguhu - *Young Owlet*

Webpelz, sitzend, abwaschbar - *woven fur, sitting, surface washable*

EAN-NO.	PERIOD	PR.	INFO
072130	1997-1997	3-4	30 cm

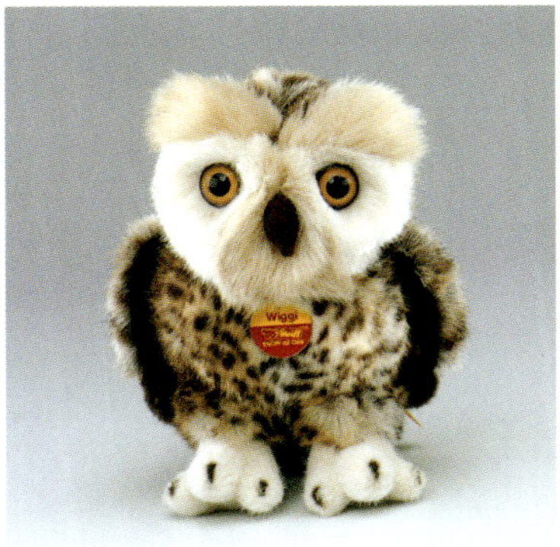

Wiggi Eule - ***Wiggi** Owlet*

Webpelz, waschmaschinenfest - *woven fur, machine washable*

EAN-NO.	PERIOD	PR.	INFO
072093	1998-1999	3	20 cm

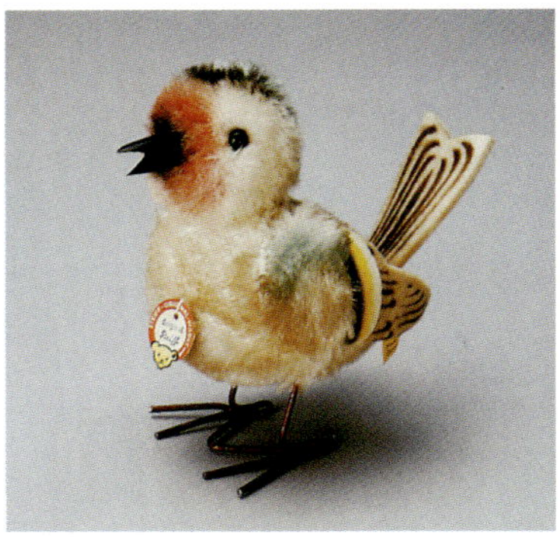

Fink - *Finch*

Mohair, Metallbeine, farbig, stehend - *mohair, metal legs, multi-colored, standing*

SERIE	ART.-NO	PERIOD	PR.	INFO
62a	**1312,3**	1955-1957	4	12 cm
62a	**1317,3**	1955-1957	4-5	17 cm

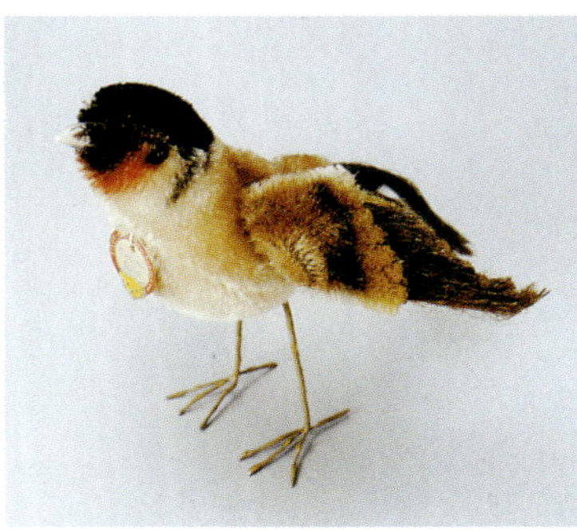

Fink - *Finch*

Singvogel, Mohair, braun/schwarz/rot, Fluegel & Schwanz aus versteiften Haartressen, biegbar, Metallbeine mit Plastikueberzug - *songbird, mohair, brown/black/red, wings & tail made of stiffened braided hair, flexible, metal legs are plastic coated*

SERIE	ART.-NO	PERIOD	PR.	INFO
622	**6310,03**	1959-1961	4-5	10 cm

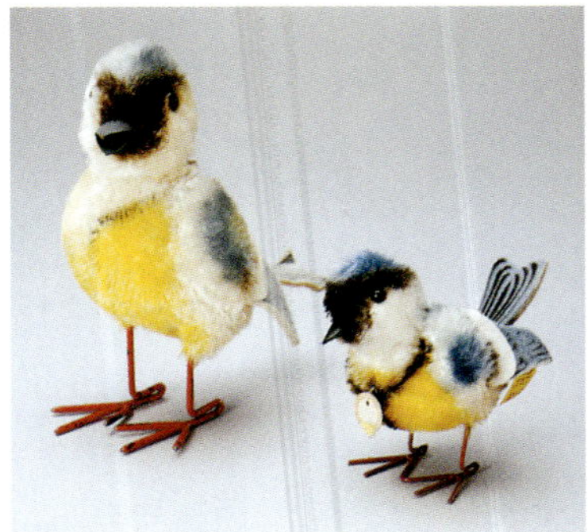

Meise - *Tit*

Mohairpluesch, weiss, schwarz/gelb gefleckt, Metallbeine - *mohair, white with black & yellow markings, metal legs*

SERIE	ART.-NO	PERIOD	PR.	INFO
62a	**1312,4**	1955-1957	4	12 cm
62a	**1317,4**	1955-1957	4-5	17 cm

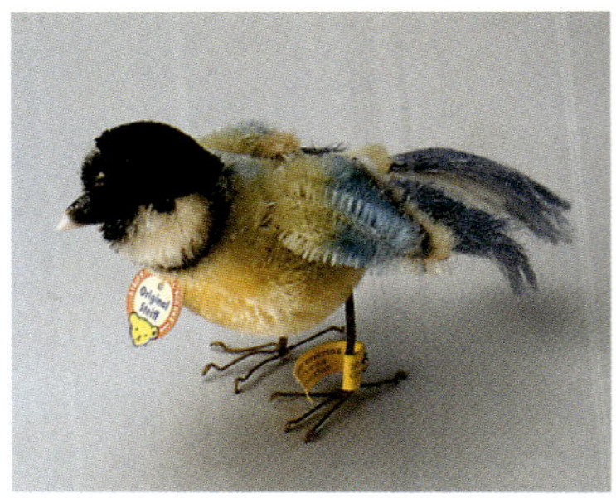

Blaumeise - *Blue Tit*

Mohair, blau/gelb, flexibel, auf Drahtbeinen mit Plastikummantelung - *mohair, blue/yellow, flexible, wire legs with plastic jacketing*

SERIE	ART.-NO	PERIOD	PR.	INFO
622	**6310,04**	1959-1961	4-5	10 cm

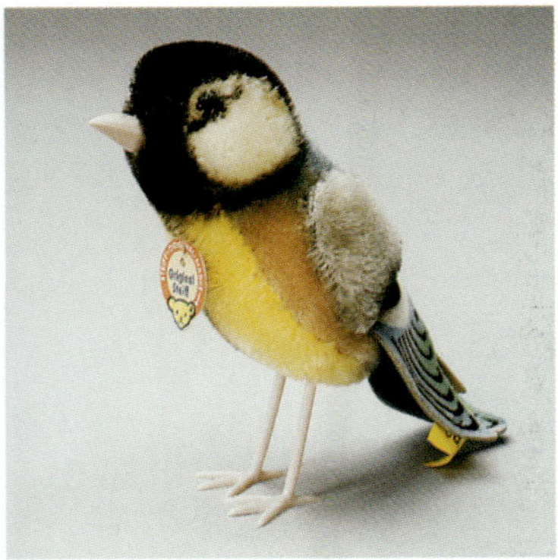

Meise - *Tit*

Mohair & Samt, Plastikfuesse, gelb/blau, stehend - *mohair & velvet, plastic feet, yellow/blue, standing*

Serie	Art.-No	Period	Pr.	Info
	2542/10	1969-1972	3	10 cm

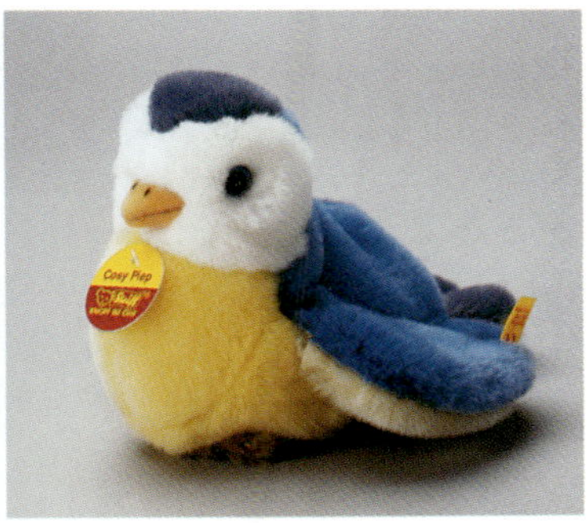

Cosy Piep Blaumeise - ***Cosy Piep*** *Blue Tit*

Webpelz, waschmaschinenfest - *woven fur, machine washable*

EAN-No.	Period	Pr.	Info
092565	1993-1996	1-2	15 cm

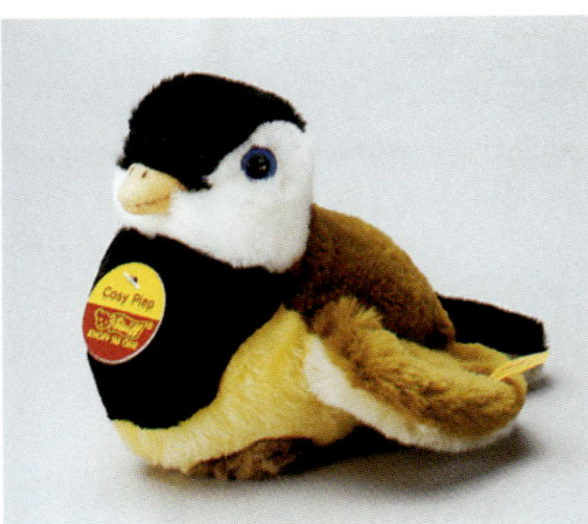

Cosy Piep Kohlmeise - ***Cosy Piep*** *Cabbage Tit*

Webpelz, waschmaschinenfest - *woven fur, machine washable*

EAN-No.	Period	Pr.	Info
092626	1993-1997	1-2	15 cm

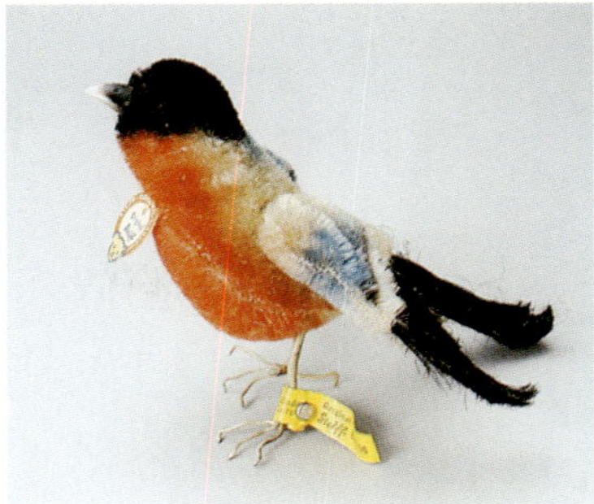

Gimpel - *Bullfinch*

Mohair, grau/schwarz/rot, flexibel, auf Drahtbeinen mit Plastikummantelung - *mohair, grey/black/red, flexible, wire legs with plastic jacketing*

Serie	Art.-No	Period	Pr.	Info
622	**6310,06**	1959-1961	4-5	10 cm

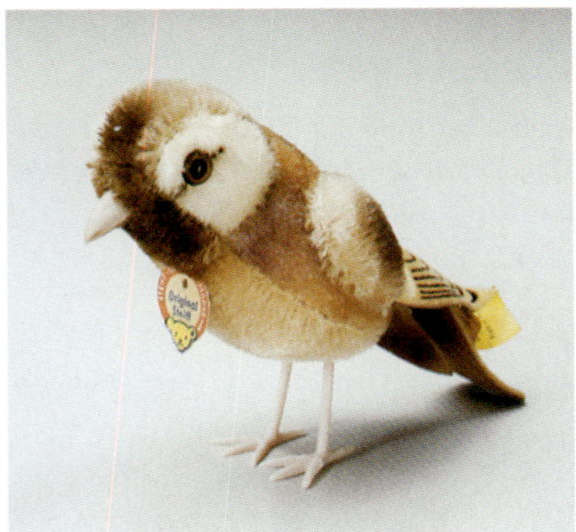

Spatz - *Sparrow*

Mohair & Samt, Plastikfuesse, braun, stehend - *mohair & velvet, plastic feet, brown, standing*

Serie	Art.-No	Period	Pr.	Info
	2540/10	1969-1972	3	10 cm

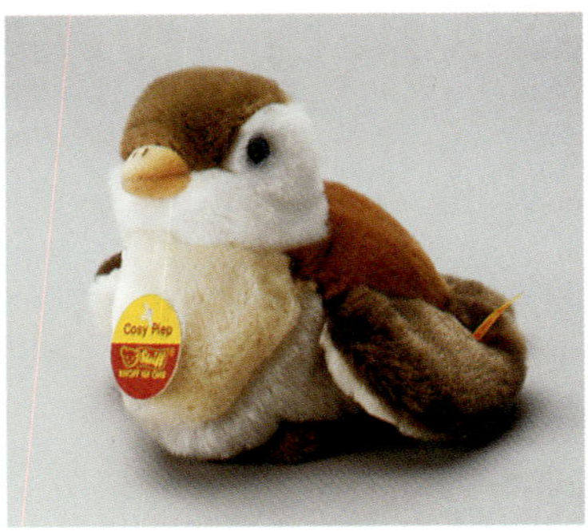

Cosy Piep Spatz - ***Cosy Piep*** *Sparrow*

Webpelz, waschmaschinenfest - *woven fur, machine washable*

EAN-No.	Period	Pr.	Info
092527	1993-1997	1-2	15 cm

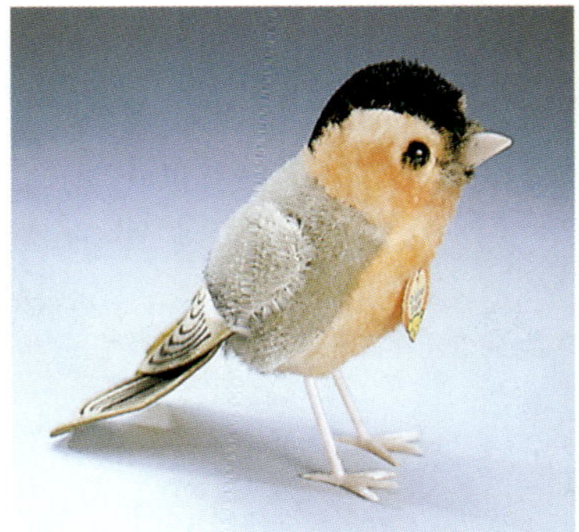

Dompfaff - *Bullfinch*

Mohair & Samt, Plastikfuesse, rot/grau, stehend - *mohair & velvet, plastic feet, red/grey, standing*

Serie	Art.-No	Period	Pr.	Info
	2544/10	1969-1972	3	10 cm

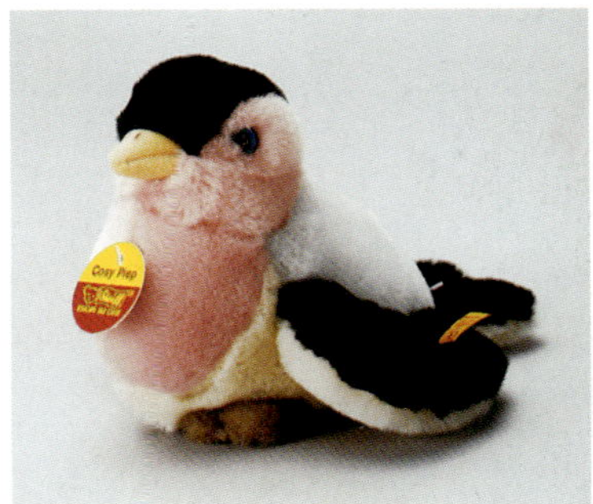

Cosy Piep Dompfaff - ***Cosy Piep*** *Bullfinch*

Webpelz waschmaschinenfest - *woven fur, machine washable*

EAN-No.	Period	Pr.	Info
092602	1993-1994	1-2	15 cm

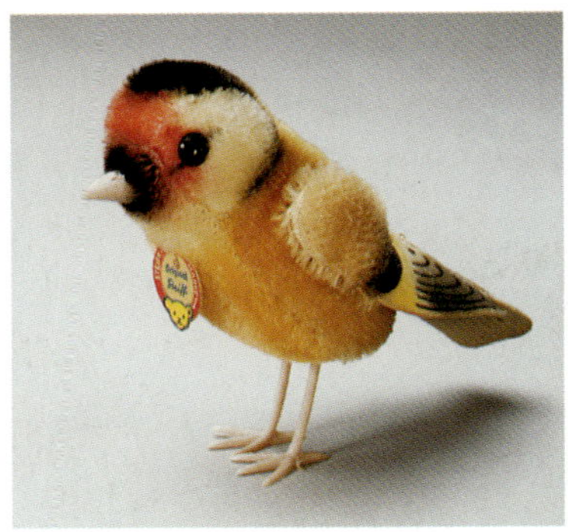

Distelfink - *Goldfinch*

Mohair/Samt, Plastikbeine, beige/grau, stehend - *mohair & velvet, plastic legs, beige/grey, standing*

Serie	Art.-No	Period	Pr.	Info
	2546/10	1969-1973	3	10 cm

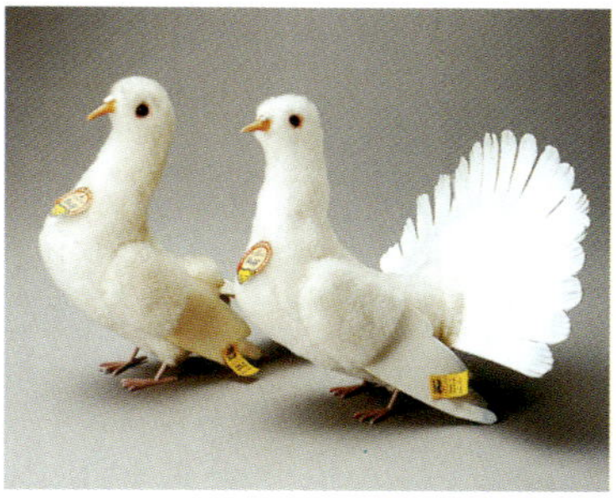

Taube - *Dove*

Dralon & Samt, Plastikfuesse, weiss, stehend - *dralon & velvet, plastic feet, white, standing*

SERIE	ART.-NO	PERIOD	PR.	INFO
	2564/25	1969-1972	3-4	25 cm

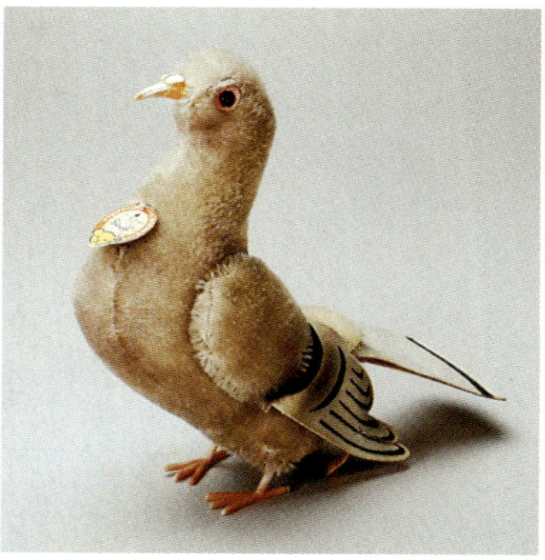

Taube - *Dove*

Dralon & Samt, Plastikfuesse, grau, stehend - *dralon & velvet, plastic feet, grey, standing*

SERIE	ART.-NO	PERIOD	PR.	INFO
	2565/25	1969-1973	3-4	25 cm

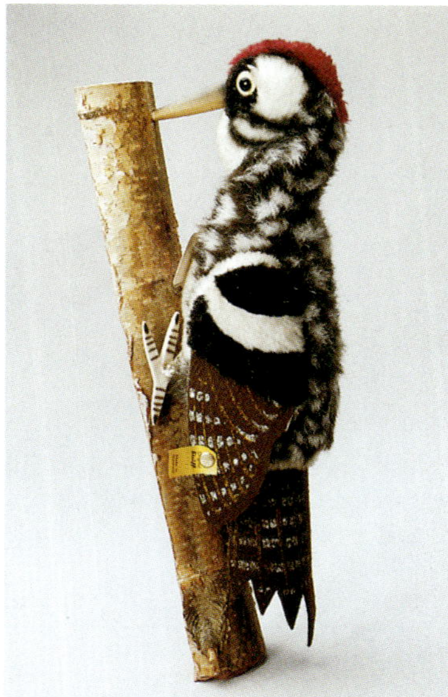

Buntspecht - *Spotted Woodpecker*

Studio-Tier, mit Wandhalterung, abwaschbar - *studio animal, complete with wall fastenings, surface washable*

SERIE	ART.-NO	PERIOD	PR.	INFO
	2603/28	1980-1981	3-4	28 cm

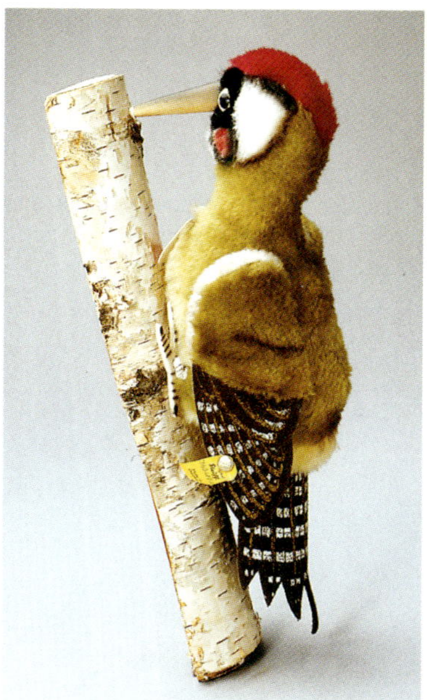

Gruenspecht - *Green Woodpecker*

Studio-Tier, mit Wandhalterung, abwaschbar - *studio animal, complete with wall fastenings, surface washable*

SERIE	ART.-NO	PERIOD	PR.	INFO
	2604/28	1980-1981	3-4	28 cm

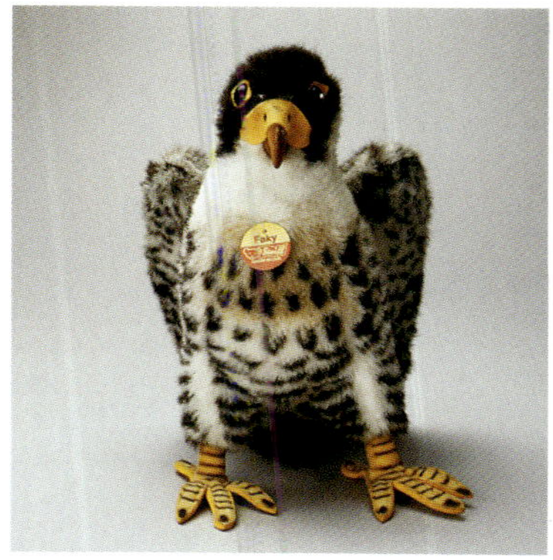

Faky Falke - ***Faky** Falcon*

Studio-Tier, Wirkpelz, stehend, ausgebreitete Fluegel, abwaschbar - *studio animal, knitted fur, standing, wings open, surface washable*

SERIE	ART.-NO	PERIOD	PR.	INFO
505256	**2615/28**	1979-1988	3-4	28 cm

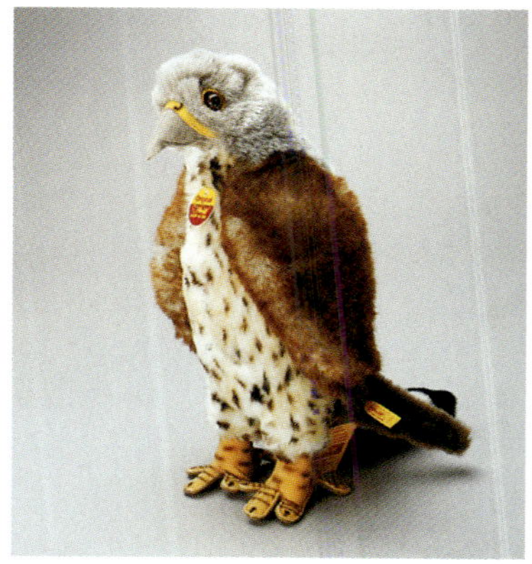

Turmfalke - *Kestrel*

Studio-Tier, Webpelz, abwaschbar - *studio animal, woven fur, surface washable*

EAN-NO.	PERIOD	PR.	INFO
505287	1994-1996	3	35 cm

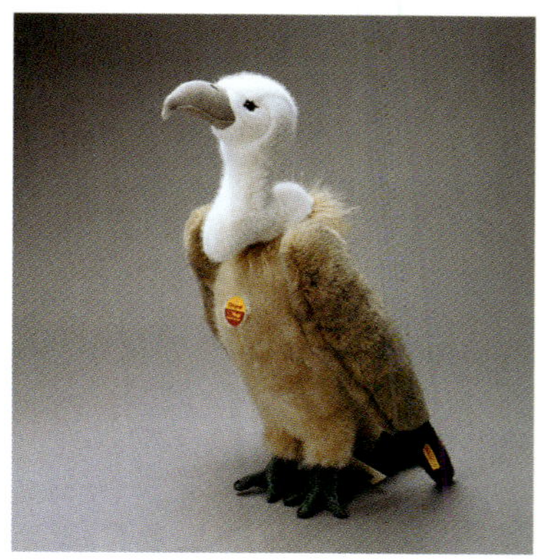

Studio Geier - *Studio Vulture*

Studio-Tier, Webpelz, abwaschbar - *studio*

animal, woven fur, surface washable

EAN-No.	Period	Pr.	Info
505096	1995-1999	3	45 cm

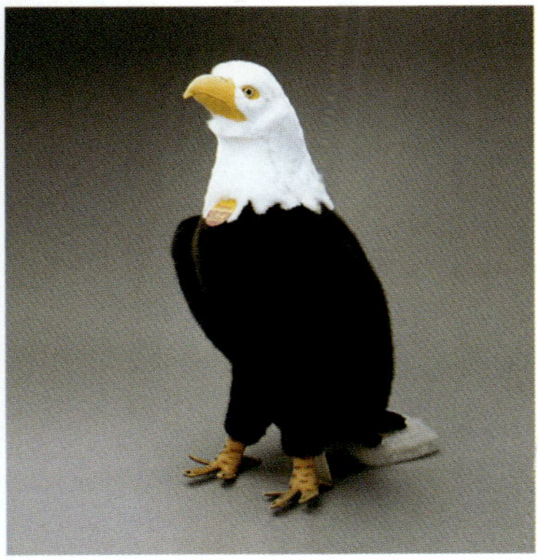

Weisskopfadler - *Bald Eagle*

Studio-Tier, Webpelz, abwaschbar - *studio animal, woven fur, surface washable*

EAN-No.	Period	Pr.	Info
505232	1994-1999	4	50 cm

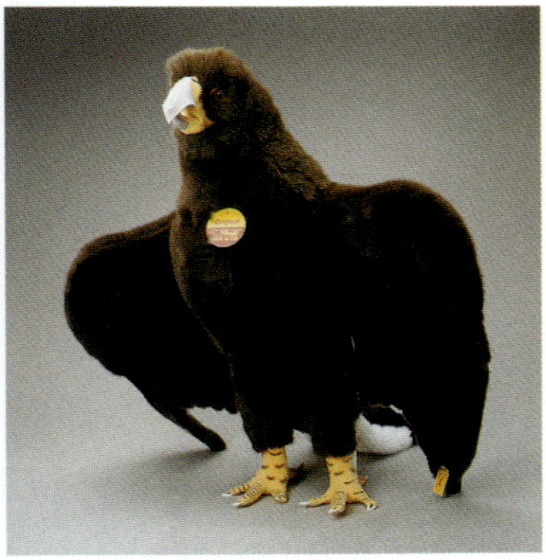

Studio Steinadler - *Studio Golden Eagle*

Studio-Tier, Webpelz, dunkelbraun, stehend, ausgebreitete Fluegel, abwaschbar - *studio animal, woven fur, dark brown, standing, wings open, surface washable*

EAN-No.	Period	Pr.	Info
505218	1995-1999	4	60 cm

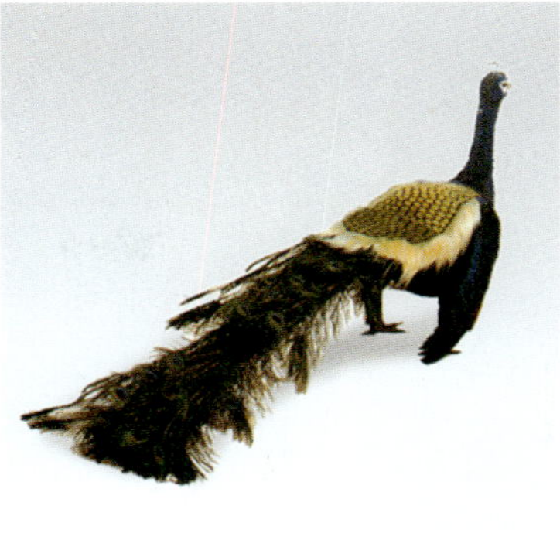

Pfau ohne Rad - *Peacock without Fantail*

Studio-Tier, Webpelz/Dralon - *studio animal, woven fur & dralon*

Serie	Art.-No	Period	Pr.	Info
	2621/80	1979-1984	4	80 cm

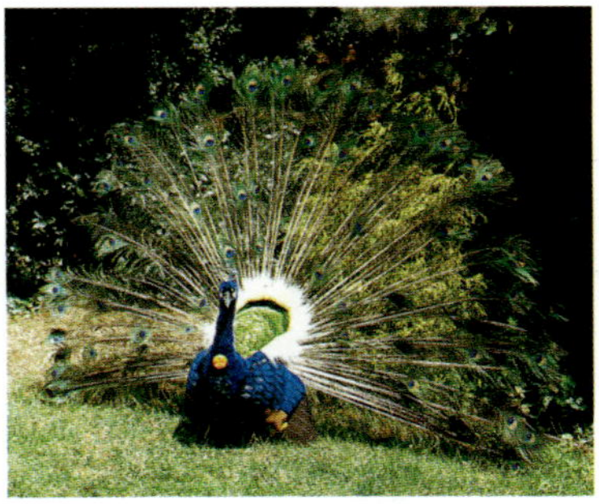

Pfau mit Rad - *Peacock with Fantail*

Studio-Tier, Webpelz/Dralon - *studio animal, woven fur & dralon*

Serie	Art.-No	Period	Pr.	Info
505300	**2620/99**	1979-1990	4-5	130 cm
	505300	1991-1993	4-5	

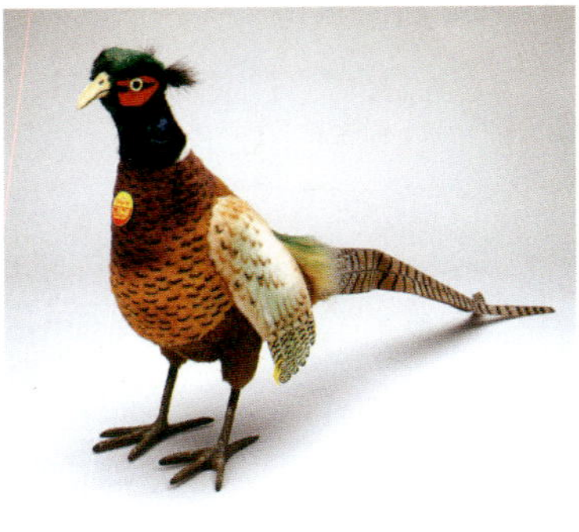

Fasan - *Pheasant*

Studio-Tier, Webpelz/Dralon, stehend - *studio animal, woven fur & dralon, standing*

Serie	Art.-No	Period	Pr.	Info
	2622/40	1979-1984	4-5	40 cm

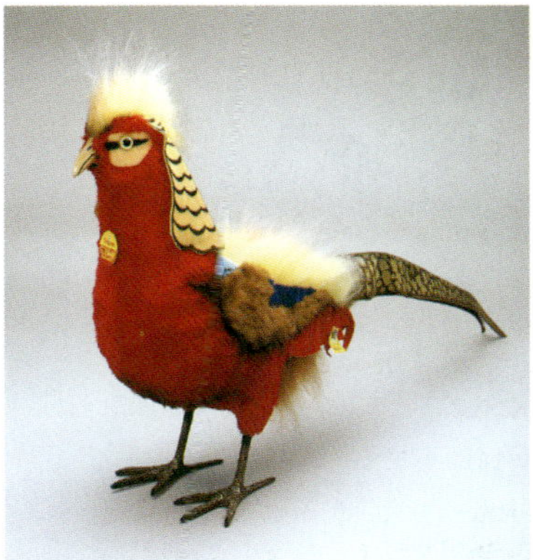

Goldfasan - *Golden Pheasant*

Studio-Tier, Webpelz/Dralon, stehend - *studio animal, woven fur & dralon, standing*

Serie	Art.-No	Period	Pr.	Info
	2623/40	1979-1984	4-5	40 cm

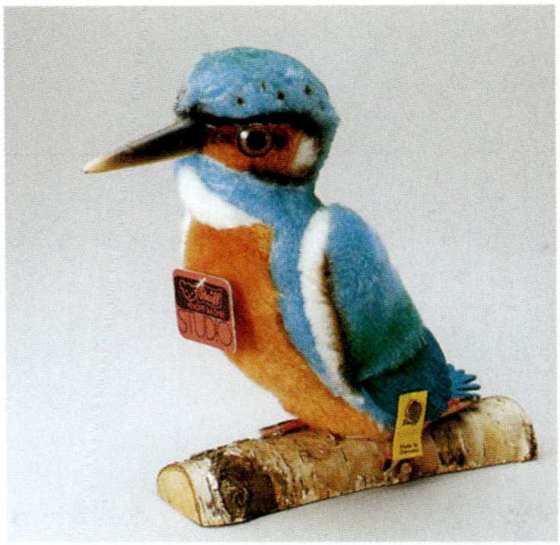

Eisvogel - *Kingfisher*

Studio-Tier, mit Holzsockel, abwaschbar - *studio animal, with wooden base, surface washable*

Serie	Art.-No	Period	Pr.	Info
	2605/20	1980-1981	3	20 cm

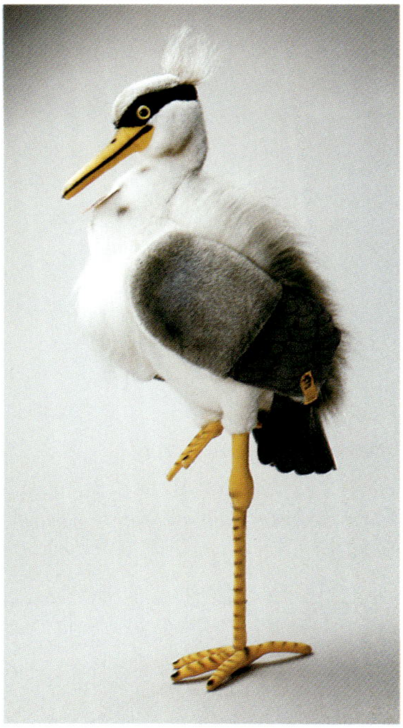

Fischreiher - *Grey Heron*

Studio-Tier, auf einem Bein stehend, abwaschbar - *studio animal, standing on one leg, surface washable*

SERIE	ART.-NO	PERIOD	PR.	INFO
	2606/50	1980-1984	4	50 cm

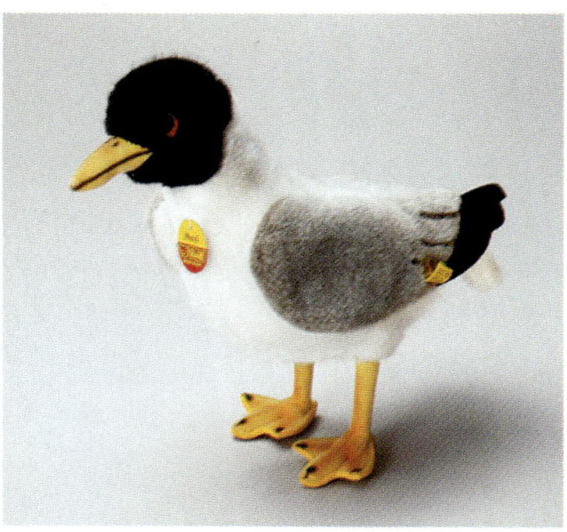

Movi Moewe - ***Movi** Seagull*

Studio-Tier, Webpelz, stehend, abwaschbar - *studio animal, woven fur, standing, surface washable*

SERIE	ART.-NO	PERIOD	PR.	INFO
	2525/28	1979-1981	3	28 cm

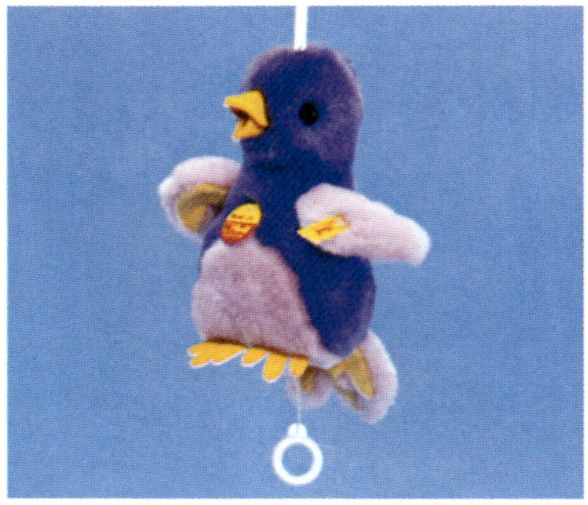

Musik Lari Vogel - *Musical Lari Bird*

Webpelz, lila, Musikwerk austauschbar, waschbar - *woven fur, lavender, music box exchangeable, washable*

SERIE	ART.-NO	PERIOD	PR.	INFO
231308	**6355/18**	1984-1986	2	18 cm

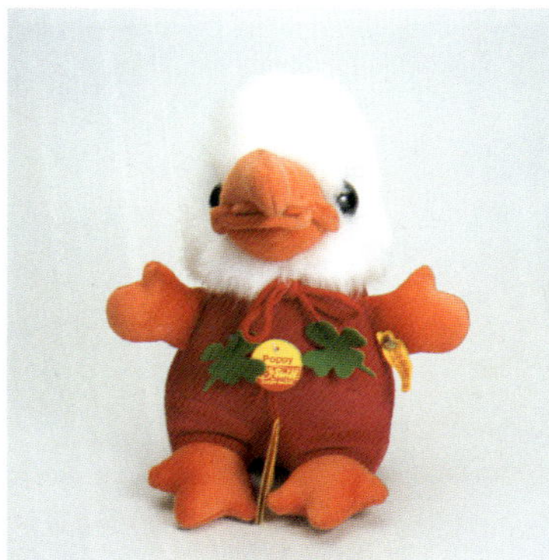

Poppy Vogel - ***Poppy** Bird*

Nicki-Stoff, abwaschbar - *nicki velvet, surface washable*

SERIE	ART.-NO	PERIOD	PR.	INFO
	7881/26	1984-1984	3-4	26 cm

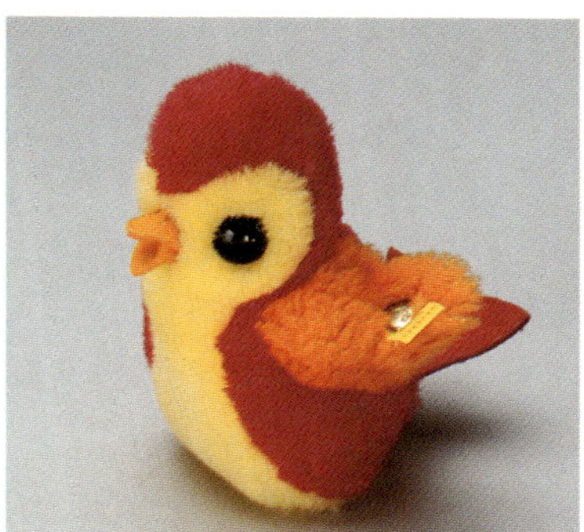

Mini Cosy Vogel - *Mini Cozy Bird*

Webpelz, 10 cm, waschmaschinenfest - *woven fur, 10 cm, machine washable*

SERIE	ART.-NO	PERIOD	PR.	INFO
084638	**5563/10**	1987-1989	1	rot - *red*
084645	**5564/10**	1987-1989	1	gelb - *yellow*
084652	**5565/10**	1987-1989	1	blau - *blue*
084676	**5567/10**	1987-1989	1	braun - *brown*

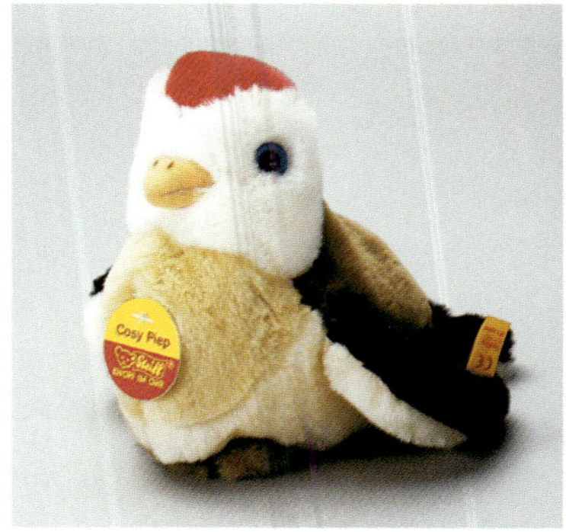

Cosy Piep Stieglitz - ***Cosy Piep** Goldfinch*

Webpelz, waschmaschinenfest - *woven fur, machine washable*

EAN-NO.	PERIOD	PR.	INFO
092541	1993-1995	1-2	15 cm

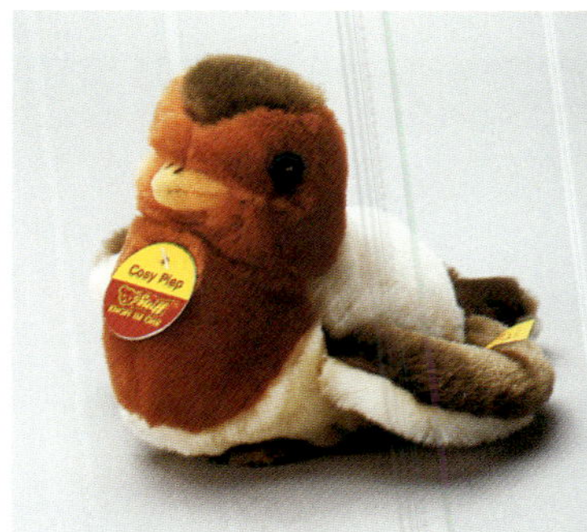

Cosy Piep Rotkehlchen - ***Cosy Piep** Red Breasted Robin*

Webpelz, waschmaschinenfest - *woven fur, machine washable*

EAN-NO.	PERIOD	PR.	INFO
092589	1993-1996	1-2	15 cm

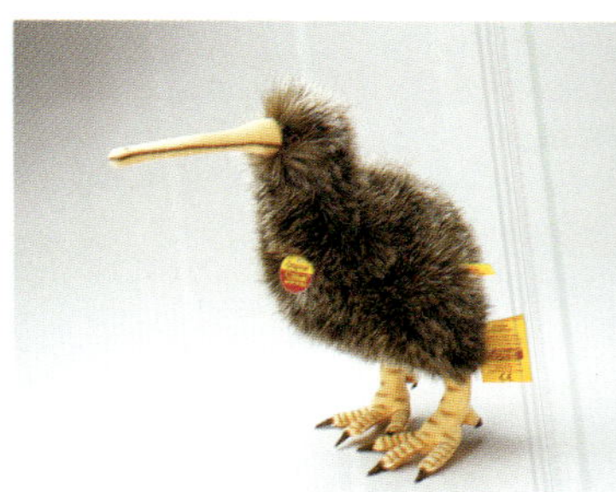

Kiwi

Webpelz, stehend, handwaschbar - *woven fur, standing, hand washable*

EAN-NO.	PERIOD	PR.	INFO
120015	1995-1999	3	25 cm

WILDNISTIERE

WILD ANIMALS

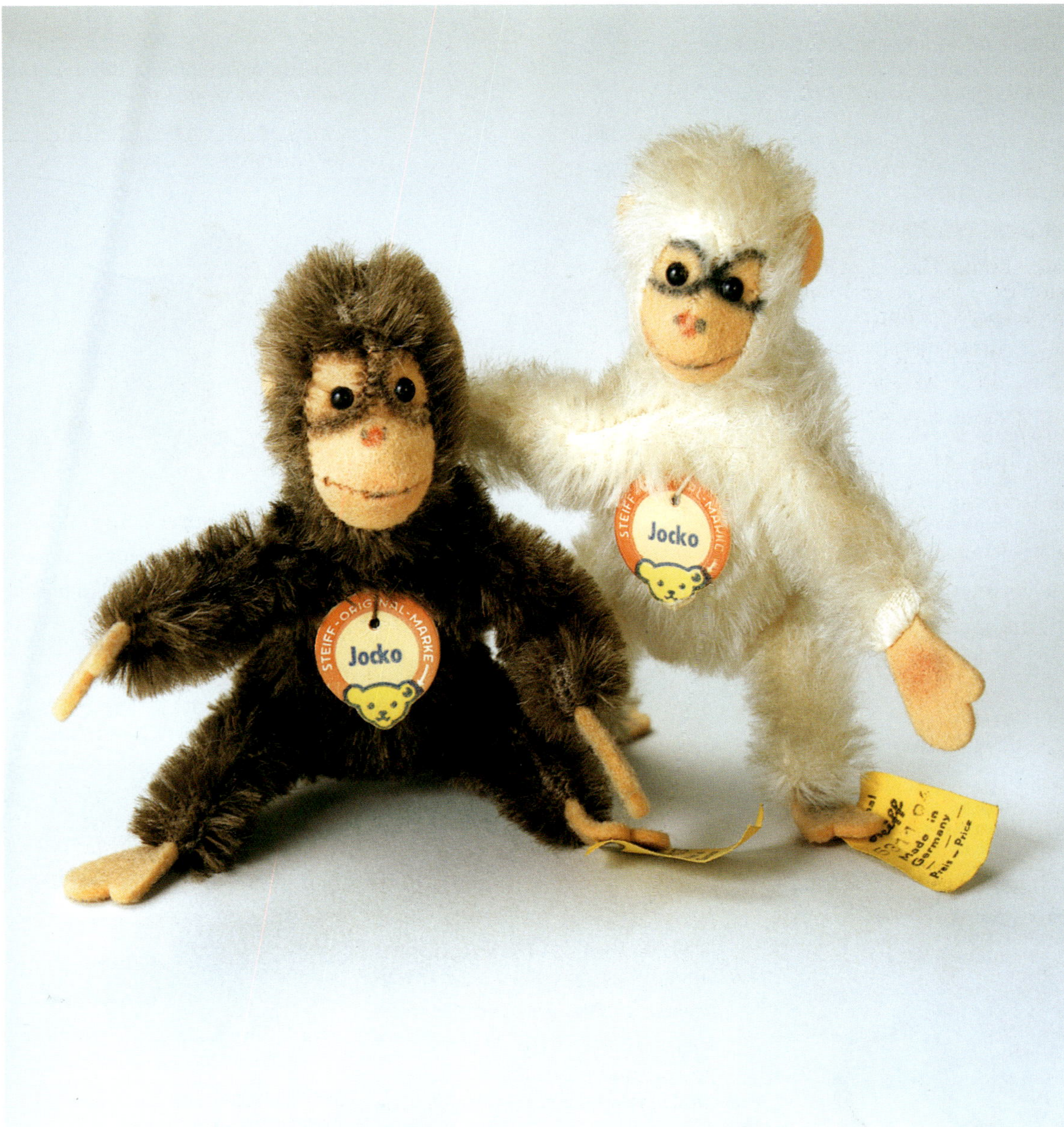

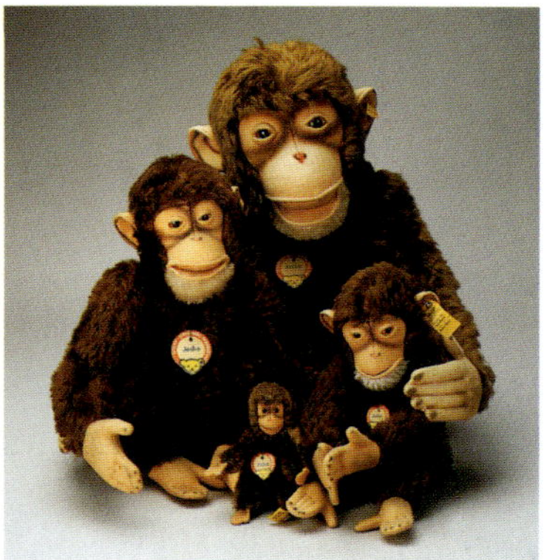

Jocko Schimpanse - ***Jocko*** *Chimpanzee*

Mohairpluesch, braun, gegliedert, 11 & 16 cm Biegeglieder, ab 1974 Groessen ab 25 cm Material Pelzimitation/Webpelz sowie Schlenkerglieder, mit Stimme, abwaschbar - *mohair, brown, jointed, 11 & 16 cm sizes have flexible joints, from 1974 imitation fur/woven fur & floppy joints introduced for 25 cm size & above, press voice, surface washable*

SERIE	ART.-NO	PERIOD	PR.	INFO
9	**5310** br	1949-1958	3-4	10 cm
090	**5310,03**	1959-1964	3-4	
002	**5311,03**	1965-1967	2-3	11 cm
060205	**0020/11**	1968-1990	1-2	
9	**5315** br	1949-1958	4	15 cm
090	**5315,03**	1959-1964	3-4	
002	**5315,03**	1965-1966	3-4	
002	**5316,03**	1967-1967	2-3	16 cm
	0020/16	1968-1981	2	
9	**5325** br	1949-1958	4	25 cm
090	**5325,03**	1959-1964	3-4	
002	**5325,03**	1965-1967	3-4	
	0020/25	1968-1981	2-3	
9	**5335** br	1949-1957	4	35 cm
9	**5335,2**	1958-1958	4	
090	**5335,03**	1959-1964	3-4	
002	**5335,03**	1965-1967	3-4	
	0020/35	1968-1981	3	
9	**5350** br	1949-1953	4-5	50 cm
9	**5350,2**	1954-1958	4-5	
090	**5350,03**	1959-1964	4	
002	**5350,03**	1965-1967	4	
	0020/50	1968-1981	3-4	
9	**5360** br	1950-1953	4-5	60 cm
9	**5360,2**	1954-1958	4-5	
090	**5360,03**	1959-1961	4-5	
002	**5360,03**	1965-1967	4-5	
	0020/60	1968-1981	3-4	
9	**5380** br	1950-1953	5	80 cm
9	**5380,2**	1954-1958	5	
090	**5380,03**	1959-1961	5	
002	**5380,03**	1966-1967	5	
	0020/80	1968-1973	4	

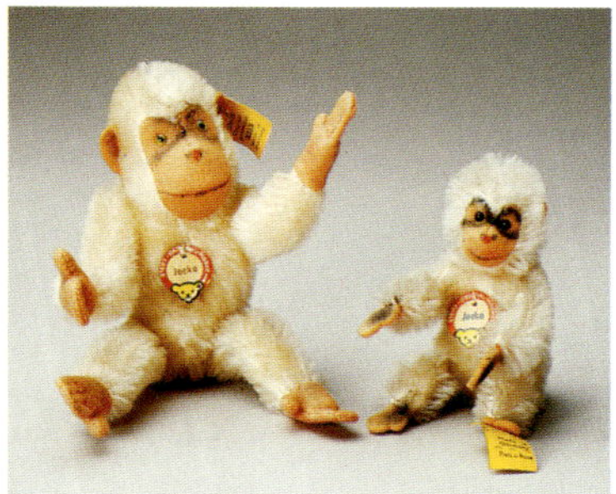

Jocko Schimpanse - ***Jocko*** *Chimpanzee*

Mohairpluesch, weiss, gegliedert, 11 cm Biegeglieder - *mohair, white, jointed, 11 cm flexible joints*

SERIE	ART.-NO	PERIOD	PR.	INFO
9	**5310** w	1949-1958	4-5	10 cm
090	**5310,04**	1959-1961	4	
001	**5311,04**	1966-1966	3-4	11 cm
9	**5315** w	1949-1958	4-5	15 cm
090	**5315,04**	1959-1961	4	

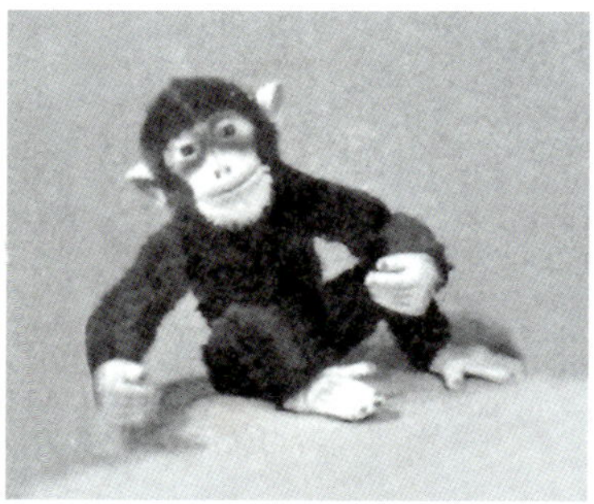

Schimpanse - *Chimpanzee*

Seidenpluesch, braun, gegliedert - *artificial silk plush, brown, jointed*

SERIE	ART.-NO	PERIOD	PR.	INFO
9	**5625**	1949-1949	5	25 cm

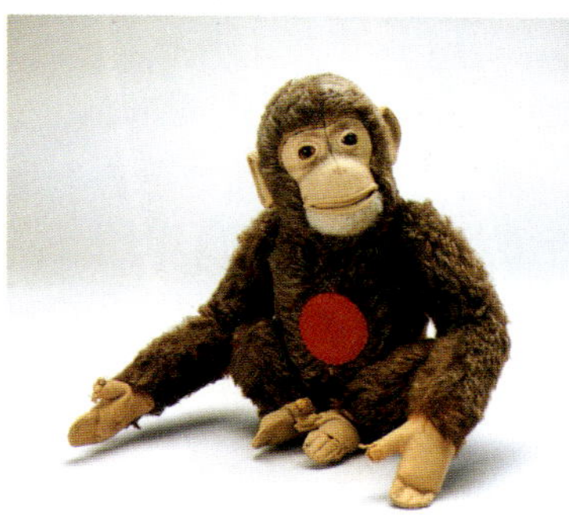

Music-Schimpanse - *Musical Chimpanzee*

Mohair, braun, gegliedert, Schweizer Drueckerwerk - *mohair, brown, jointed, Swiss squeeze music box*

SERIE	ART.-NO	PERIOD	PR.	INFO
97 9	**9335,3**	1951-1957	6-7	35 cm

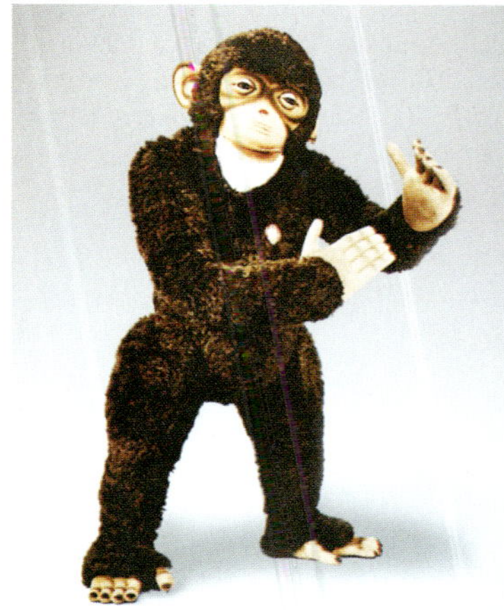

Studio-Schimpanse - *Studio Chimpanzee*

Schautier, Mohair, braun, stehend - *display animal, mohair, brown standing*

SERIE	ART.-NO	PERIOD	PR.	INFO
090	**4150,93**	1960-1960	7	150 cm
	0029/15	1967-1967	7	

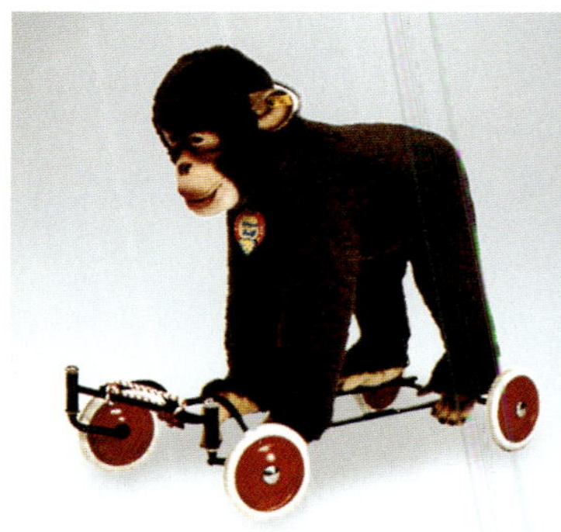

Reit-Schimpanse - *Riding Chimpanzee*

Dralon, Stahlrohrgestell, Plastikreifen, braun, Schlepplenkung, Haltegriff - *dralon, steel tubular frame, plastic tires, brown, pull type steering, grip handle*

SERIE	ART.-NO	PERIOD	PR.	INFO
	0022/50	1969-1972	4-5	50 cm

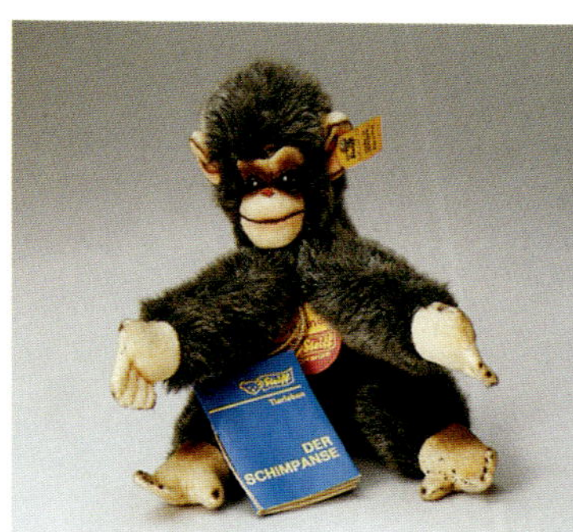

Toccolino Schimpanse - *Toccolino Chimpanzee*

"Der kleine Tierversand", Dralon, im Kaefigkarton, mit Tiersteckbrief, abwaschbar - *"Der kleine Tierversand", dralon, inside its own cardboard crate, with animal information label, surface washable*

SERIE	ART.-NO	PERIOD	PR.	INFO
	5805/15	1971-1974	4	15 cm

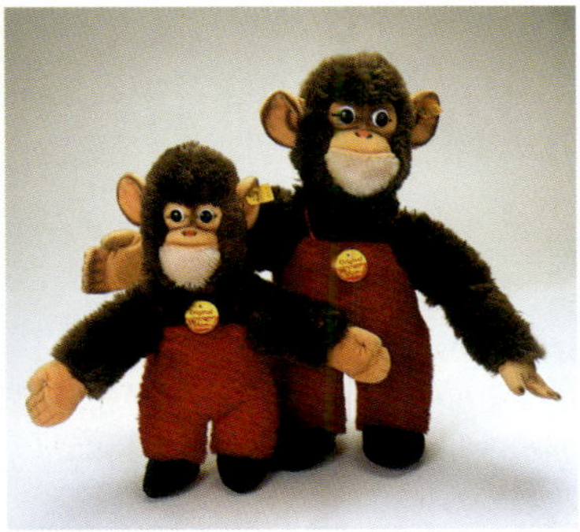

Weich-Schimpanse - *Soft Chimpanzee*

Dralon, formgeschaeumt, braun/rot, sehr weich, Schlenkerkopf, vollwaschbar - *dralon, stuffed with pre-formed foam, brown/red, very soft, floppy head, fully washable*

SERIE	ART.-NO	PERIOD	PR.	INFO
	6190/30	1971-1981	2	30 cm
	6190/40	1971-1982	2	40 cm

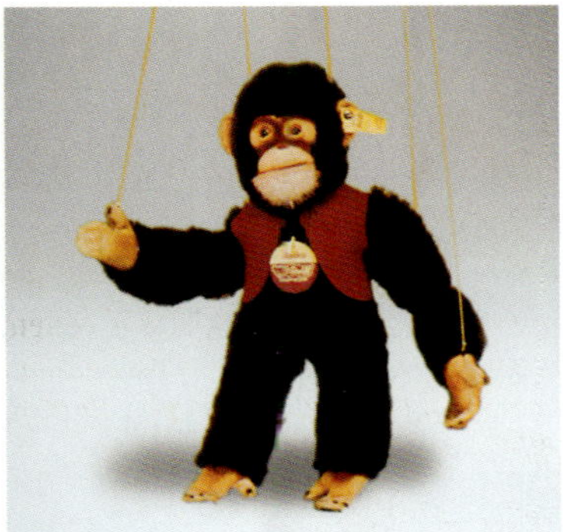

Jocko Schimpanse - ***Jocko** Chimpanzee*

Marionette, Dralon, braun, rote Weste, abwaschbar - *puppet, dralon, brown, red vest, surface washable*

SERIE	ART.-NO	PERIOD	PR.	INFO
	7725/25	1974-1975	4	25 cm

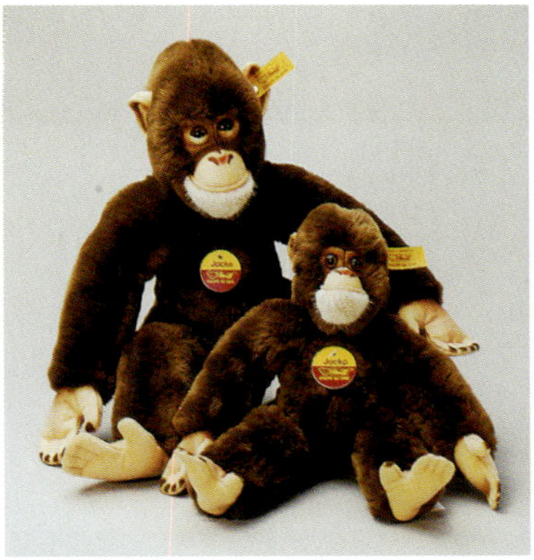

Jocko Schimpanse - ***Jocko** Chimpanzee*

Webpelz, waschmaschinenfest - *woven fur, machine washable*

SERIE	ART.-NO	PERIOD	PR.	INFO
060250	**0022/26**	1982-1990	2	26 cm
	060250	1991-1999	2	
060281	**0022/36**	1982-1990	2-3	36 cm
	060281	1991-1999	2-3	
060359	**0022/52**	1982-1990	3	52 cm
	060359	1991-1991	3	

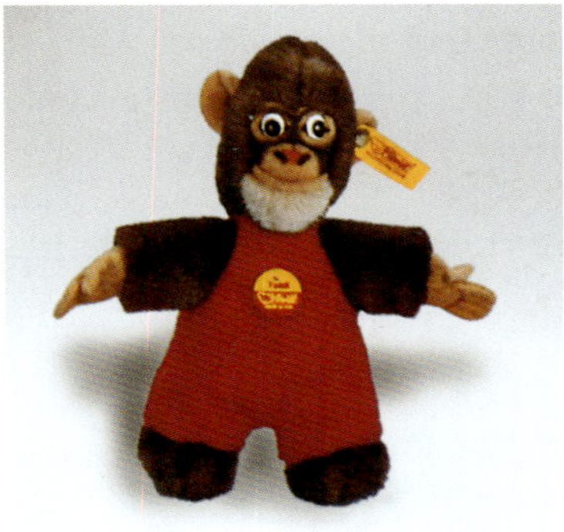

Toldi Schimpanse - ***Toldi** Chimpanzee*

Webpelz, sehr weich, waschmaschinenfest - *woven fur, very soft, machine washable*

SERIE	ART.-NO	PERIOD	PR.	INFO
	6240/20	1982-1983	2	20 cm

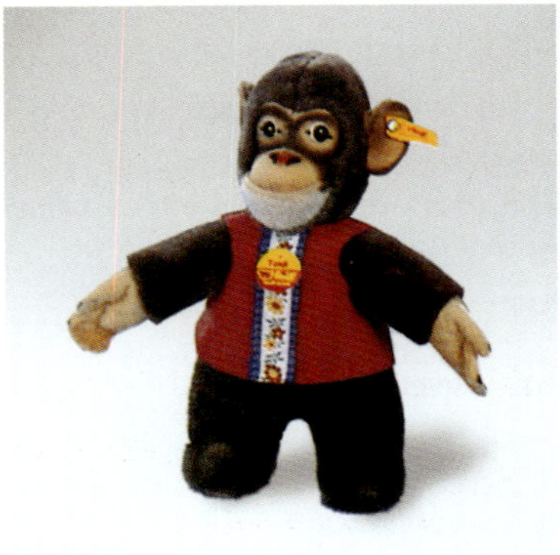

Toldi Schimpanse - ***Toldi** Chimpanzee*

Webpelz, sehr weich, waschmaschinenfest - *woven fur, very soft, machine washable*

SERIE	ART.-NO	PERIOD	PR.	INFO
	6240/30	1982-1983	2-3	30 cm

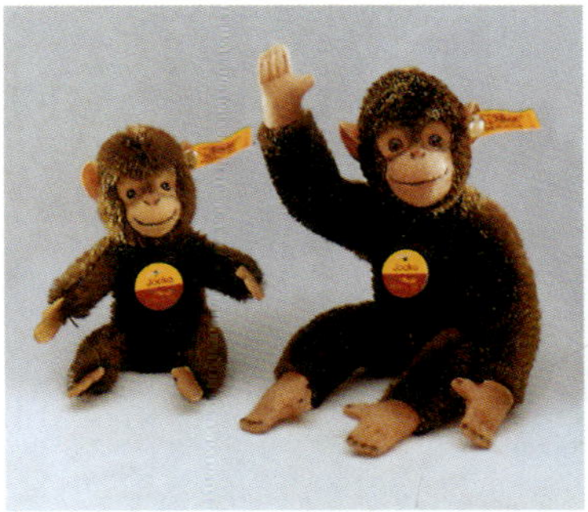

Jocko Schimpanse - ***Jocko** Chimpanzee*

Mohair Webpelz, braun, Kopf drehbar, abwaschbar - *mohair woven fur, brown, head swivels, surface washable*

SERIE	ART.-NO	PERIOD	PR.	INFO
030833	**0020/13**	1989-1990	2	13 cm
	030833	1991-1991	2	
030857	**0021/17**	1989-1990	2	17 cm
	030857	1991-1992	2	

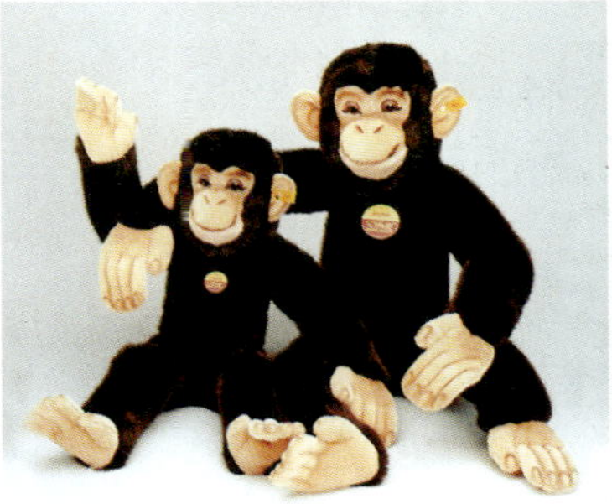

Jocko Schimpanse - ***Jocko** Chimpanzee*

Webpelz, abwaschbar, Finger- & Fussnaegel nur angedeutet - *woven fur, surface washable, fingernails & toenails are only outlined*

EAN-NO.	PERIOD	PR.	INFO
060656	1991-1993	3	55 cm
060700	1991-1992	3	70 cm

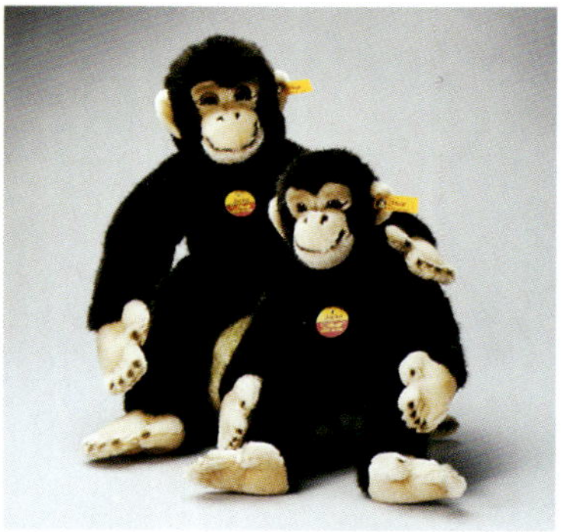

Jocko Schimpanse - ***Jocko*** *Chimpanzee*

Webpelz, dunkelbraun, Pieps-Stimme, waschmaschinenfest, Finger- & Fussnaegel als dunkle Flaeche - *woven fur, dark brown, squeaker, machine washable, fingernails & toenails are shown as darkened areas*

EAN-No.	Period	Pr.	Info
060731	1992-1999	3	35 cm
060755	1992-1996	3	44 cm

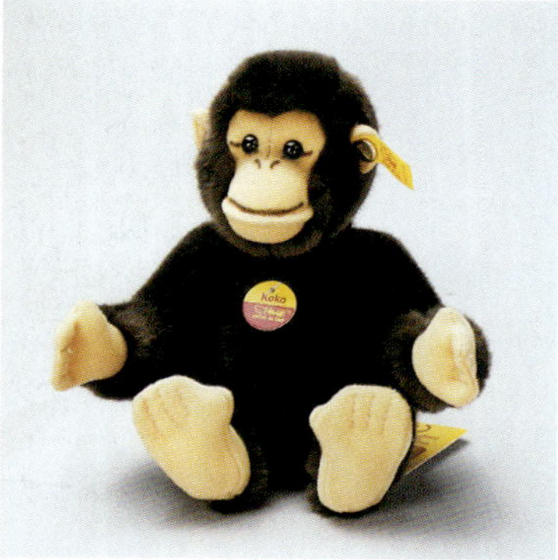

Koko Schimpanse ab 1996 **Coco** - ***Koko*** *Chimpanzee from 1996* ***Coco***

Webpelz, dunkelbraun, sitzend, waschmaschinenfest - *woven fur, dark brown, sitting, machine washable*

EAN-No.	Period	Pr.	Info
043178	1995-1999	2-3	15 cm

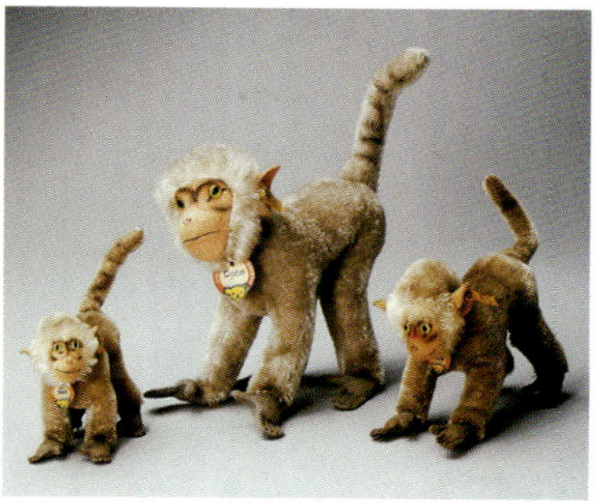

Pavian **Coco** - *Baboon* ***Coco***

Mohair, grau/weiss, stehend - *mohair, grey/white, standing*

Serie	Art.-No	Period	Pr.	Info
9a	**1310,0**	1952-1958	4	10 cm
091	**1310,00**	1959-1964	3-4	
003	**1310,00**	1965-1967	3-4	
	0030/10	1968-1970	3	
9a	**1314,0**	1952-1958	4	14 cm
091	**1314,00**	1959-1964	3-4	
003	**1314,00**	1965-1967	3-4	
	0030/14	1968-1970	3	
9a	**1322,0**	1952-1958	4-5	22 cm
091	**1322,00**	1959-1964	4	
003	**1322,00**	1965-1965	4	

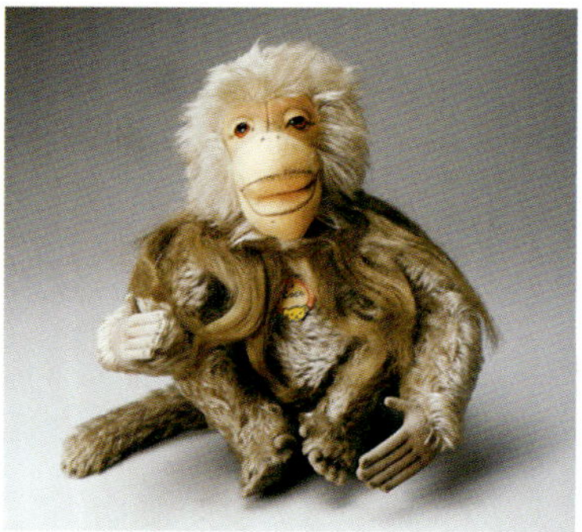

Pavian **Coco** - *Baboon* ***Coco***

Mohair, silbergrau, gegliedert, mit Haarmantel - *mohair, silver grey, jointed, with long-hair collar*

Serie	Art.-No	Period	Pr.	Info
9a	**5335**	1951-1958	5-6	35 cm
091	**5335,00**	1961-1961	5-6	

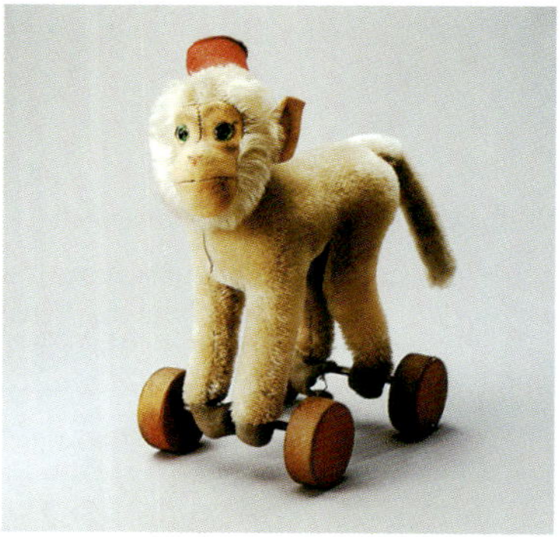

Pavian **Coco** - *Baboon* ***Coco***

Mohair, grau/weiss, stehend, auf Exzenterraedern - *mohair, grey/white, standing, on eccentric wheels*

Serie	Art.-No	Period	Pr.	Info
9a	**1325** ex	1951-1957	5	25 cm
091	**1325,10**	1959-1961	5	

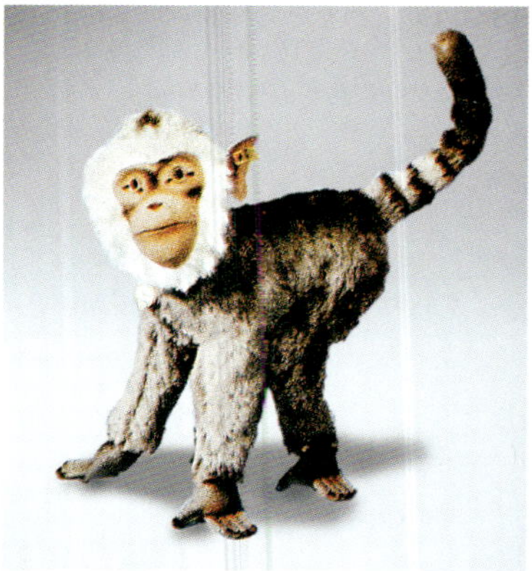

Coco Pavian - *Coco Baboon*

Schautier, Mohairpluesch, stehend - *display animal, mohair, standing*

Serie	Art.-No	Period	Pr.	Info
9a	**1350,0**	1953-1953	6	50 cm
091	**1350,90**	1960-1960	6	
	0039/05	1967-1967	6	

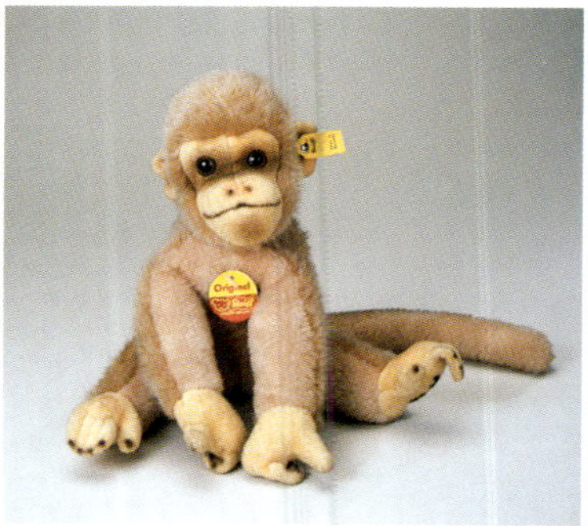

Pavian Baby - *Baboon Baby*

Dralonpelz, 1981 Webpelz, abwaschbar - *dralon fur, in 1981 woven fur, surface washable*

Serie	Art.-No	Period	Pr.	Info
	0079/03	1978-1981	2	30 cm

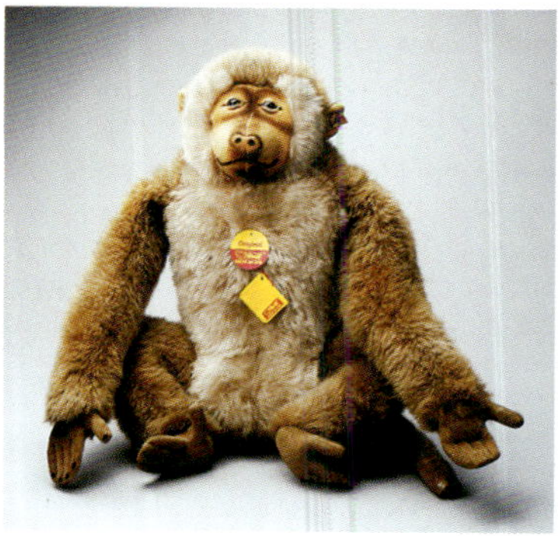

Pavian - *Baboon*

Studiotiere, Synthetik-Webpelz, 50 cm, abwaschbar, (0079/07: Kopf drehbar - kein Katalognachweis) - *studio animals, synthetic woven fur, 50 cm, surface washable, (0079/07: head swivels - no catalog information available)*

SERIE	ART.-NO	PERIOD	PR.	INFO
	0079/05	1978-1983	4	stehend - *standing*
	0079/07	1980-1980	4	sitzend - *sitting*

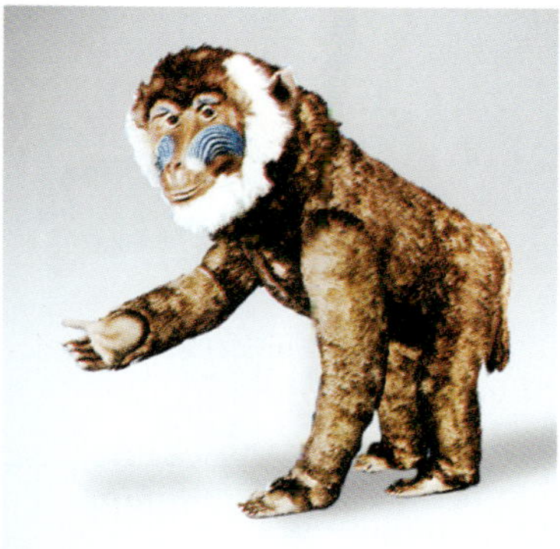

Mandrill

Schautier, Mohair - *display animal, mohair*

SERIE	ART.-NO	PERIOD	PR.	INFO
092	**1399,90**	1960-1960	6-7	100 cm

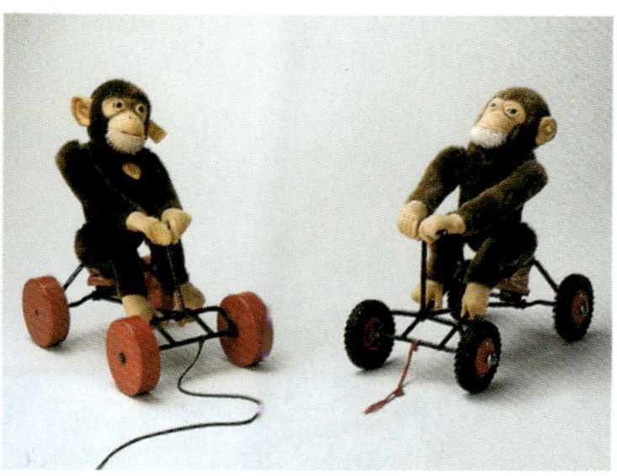

Record Peter - *Record-Peter*

bereits bis 1940 im Sortiment, Seidenpluesch mit Holzraedern, Mohairpluesch, Holzraeder, ab 1966 Gummiraeder, 25 cm, braun, Selbstfahrer mit Stimme (bewegt sich und pfeift automatisch beim Ziehen) - *already prior to 1940 in the assortment, silk plush with wooden wheels, mohair, wooden wheels, from 1966 rubber, 25 cm, brown, driving their carts themselves (they move automatically when pulled)*

SERIE	ART.-NO	PERIOD	PR.	INFO
10	**625**	1949-1949	5	Seidenpluesch - *silk plush*
10	**325**	1949-1957	5-6	Mohair
100	**9325,10**	1959-1961	5	
010	**9325,10**	1966-1967	4-5	
	0100/25	1968-1970	4-5	

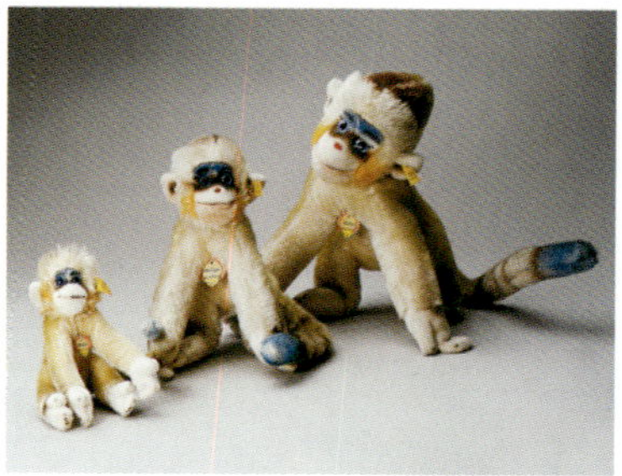

Buntaffe **Mungo** - *Multi-Colored Monkey* ***Mungo***

Mohairpluesch, stehend, Kopf drehbar, langer Schwanz - *mohair, standing, head swivels, long tail*

SERIE	ART.-NO	PERIOD	PR.	INFO
9b	**1317,0**	1957-1958	3-4	17 cm
102	**1317,07**	1959-1964	3-4	
004	**1317,07**	1966-1967	3-4	
	0040/17	1968-1970	3	
9b	**1325,0**	1957-1958	3-4	25 cm
102	**1325,07**	1959-1964	3-4	
004	**1325,07**	1965-1967	3-4	
	0040/25	1968-1971	3	
9b	**1335,0**	1958-1958	4	35 cm
102	**1335,07**	1959-1964	4	
004	**1335,07**	1966-1967	4	
	0040/35	1968-1971	3-4	

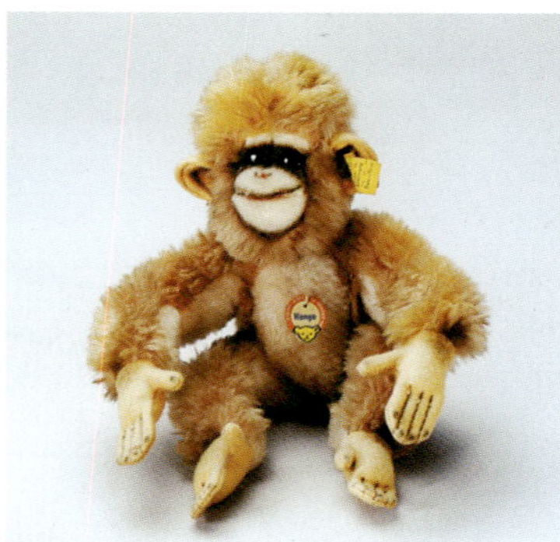

Buntaffe **Hango** - *Multi-Colored Monkey* ***Hango***

Dralonpluesch, hellbraun/gelb, Drehkopf, Schwanz & Glieder biegbar - *dralon, light brown/yellow, head swivels, tail & joints are flexible*

SERIE	ART.-NO	PERIOD	PR.	INFO
102	**5622,01**	1963-1964	2-3	22 cm
005	**5622,01**	1965-1966	2-3	

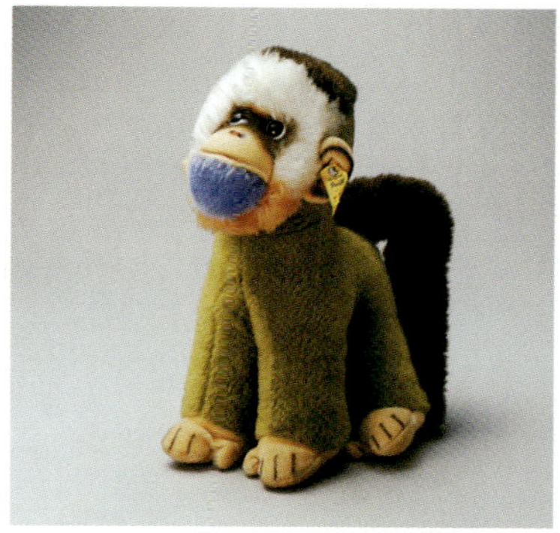

Buntaffe **Mungo** Jungtier - ***Mungo*** *Multi-Colored Young Monkey*

Dralon, formgeschaeumt, 25 cm, stehend, superweich, vollwaschbar - *dralon, stuffed with pre-formed foam, 25 cm, standing, super soft, fully washable*

SERIE	ART.-NO	PERIOD	PR.	INFO
	6420/25	1972-1977	2	gruen - *green*
	6421/25	1972-1977	2	blau - *blue*

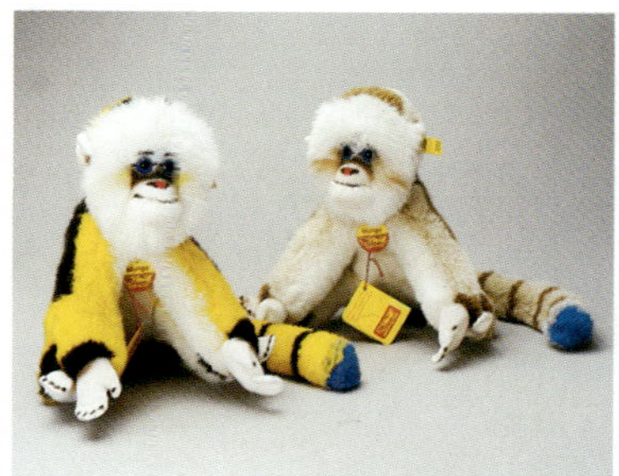

Mungo Buntaffe - ***Mungo*** *Multi-Colored Monkey*

Wirkpelz, 23 cm, abwaschbar - *knitted fur, 23 cm, surface washable*

SERIE	ART.-NO	PERIOD	PR.	INFO
	0025/23	1980-1982	2-3	braun - *brown*
	0026/23	1980-1983	2-3	gelb - *yellow*

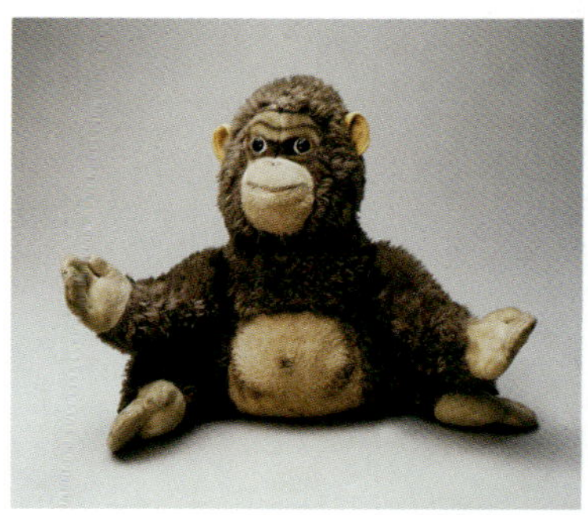

Gorilla **Gora**

Dralon, dunkelgrau, sitzend, Schlenkerarme, sehr weich - *dralon, dark grey, sitting, floppy arms, very soft*

SERIE	ART.-NO	PERIOD	PR.	INFO
103	**6625,05**	1961-1963	2-3	25 cm
103	**6635,05**	1961-1963	2-3	35 cm
103	**6645,05**	1961-1963	2-3	45 cm

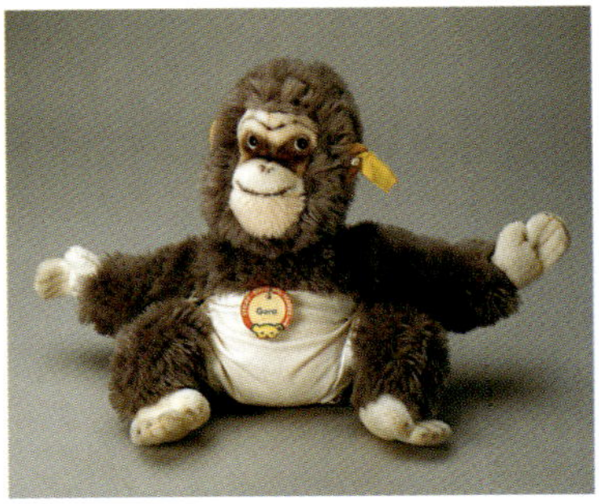

Cosy **Gora** mit Hoeschen - *Cozy **Gora** with Shorts*

Dralon-Pluesch, Schaumstoff-Flocken-Fuellung, dunkelgrau, weisses Hoeschen, waschbar - *dralon, stuffed with foam flakes, dark grey, white shorts, washable*

SERIE	ART.-NO	PERIOD	PR.	INFO
830 103	**6625,05**	1964-1964	3-4	25 cm
470	**6625,05**	1965-1966	3-4	

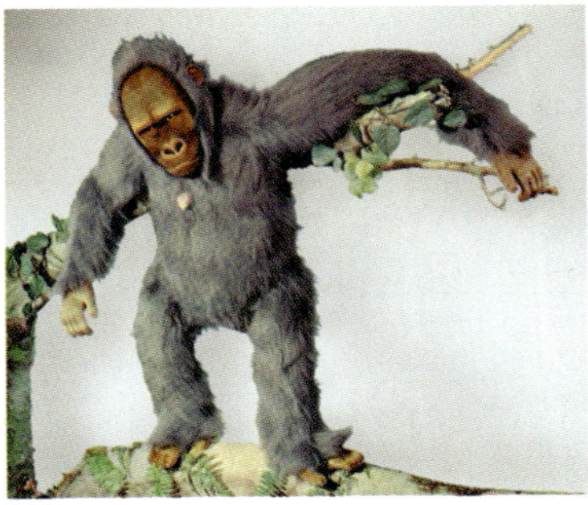

Gorilla

Schautier, grau - *display animal, grey*

SERIE	ART.-NO	PERIOD	PR.	INFO
	0029/13	1967-1967	6-7	130 cm

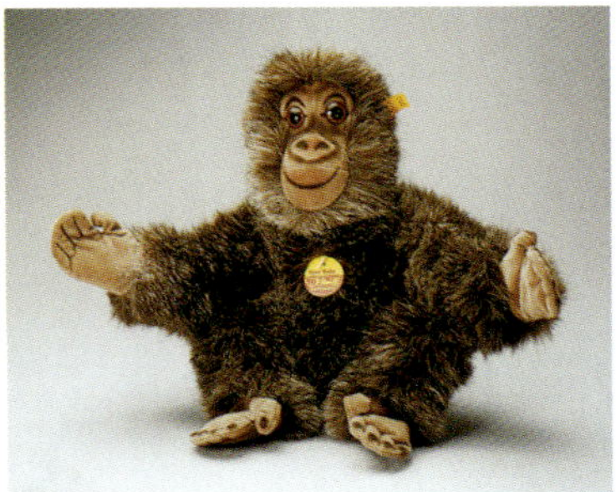

Gora Baby

Pelzimitation, ab 1978 Webpelz, abwaschbar - *imitation fur, from 1978 woven fur, surface washable*

SERIE	ART.-NO	PERIOD	PR.	INFO
	0035/35	1977-1981	2-3	35 cm

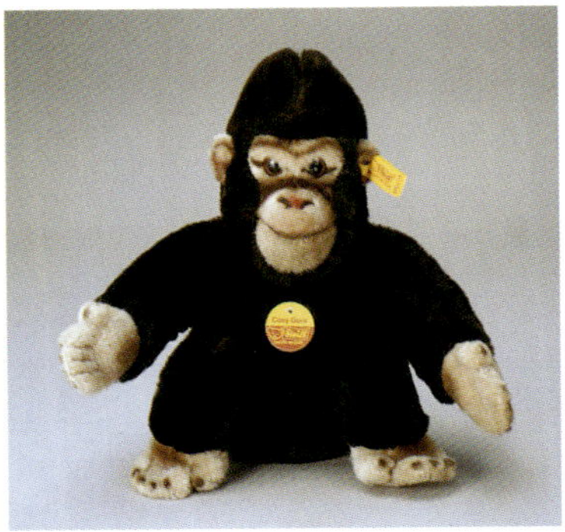

Cosy Gora Gorilla - *Cozy Gora Gorilla*

Webpelz, superweich, waschmaschinenfest - *woven fur, super soft, machine washable*

SERIE	ART.-NO	PERIOD	PR.	INFO
	5450/27	1981-1983	2	27 cm

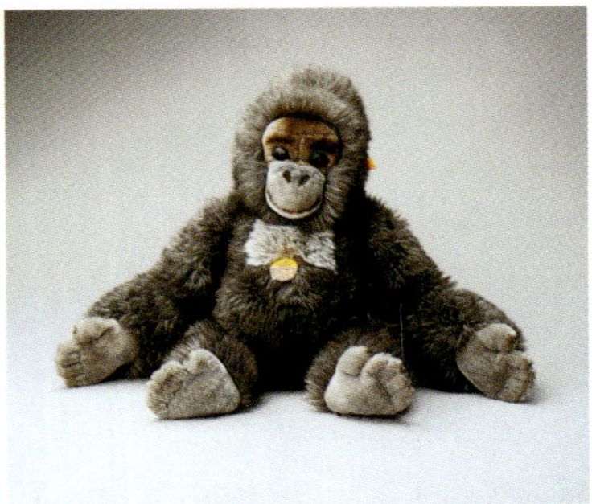

Gora Gorilla

Webpelz, abwaschbar - *woven fur, surface washable*

SERIE	ART.-NO	PERIOD	PR.	INFO
062407	**0540/45**	1987-1990	3	45 cm
	062407	1991-1993	3	
062445	**0540/60**	1987-1990	3	60 cm

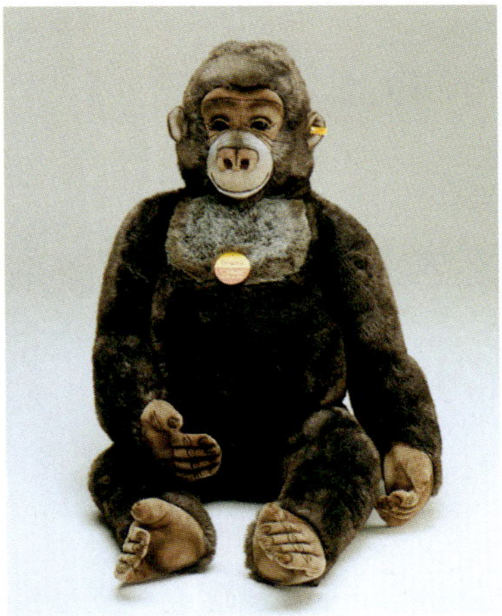

Gora Gorilla

Studio-Tier, Webpelz, abwaschbar - *studio animal, woven fur, surface washable*

SERIE	ART.-NO	PERIOD	PR.	INFO
501906	**0544/99**	1989-1990	6	160 cm
	501906	1991-1999	6	

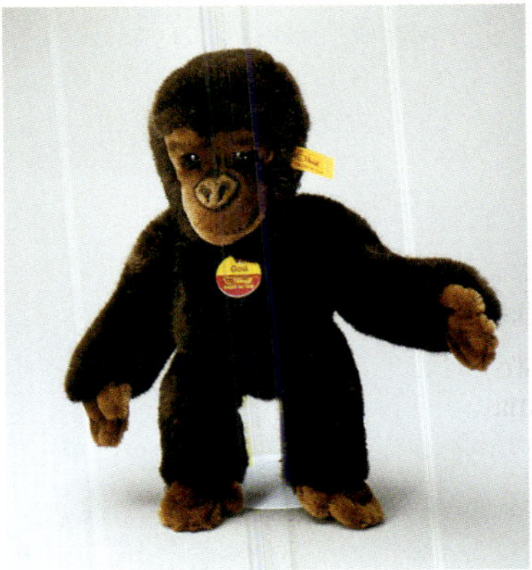

Gori Baby Gorilla

Webpelz, dunkelbraun, waschmaschinenfest - *woven fur, dark brown, machine washable*

SERIE	ART.-NO	PERIOD	PR.	INFO
062308	**0535/32**	1990-1990	2-3	35 cm
	062308	1991-1999	2-3	
062315	**0535/40**	1990-1990	3	40 cm
	062315	1991-1993	3	

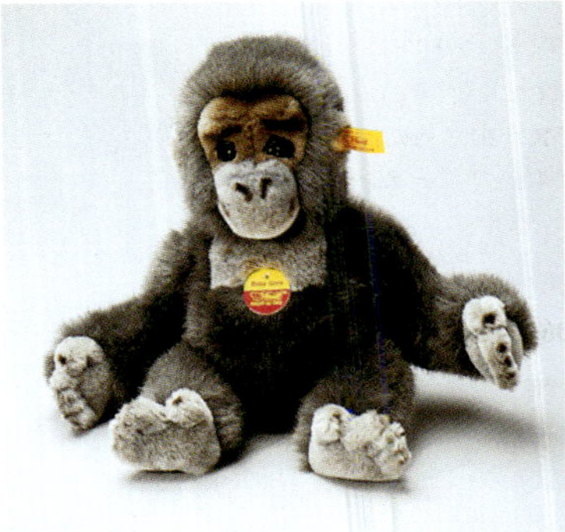

Baby Gora Gorilla

Webpelz, 32 cm, Pieps-Stimme, waschmaschinenfest - *woven fur, 32 cm, squeaker, machine washable*

EAN-NO.	PERIOD	PR.	INFO
062353	1991-1996	3	weiss - *white*
062452	1991-1999	3	grau - *grey*

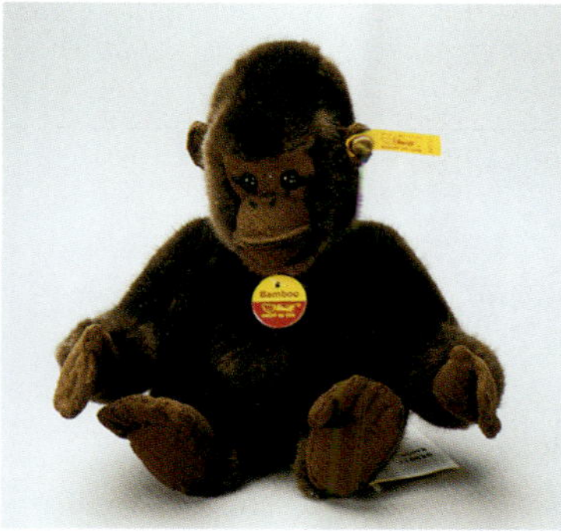

Bamboo Gorilla

Webpelz, dunkelbraun, sitzend, waschmaschinenfest - *woven fur, dark brown, sitting, machine washable*

EAN-No.	Period	Pr.	Info
043017	1995-1999	2-3	15 cm

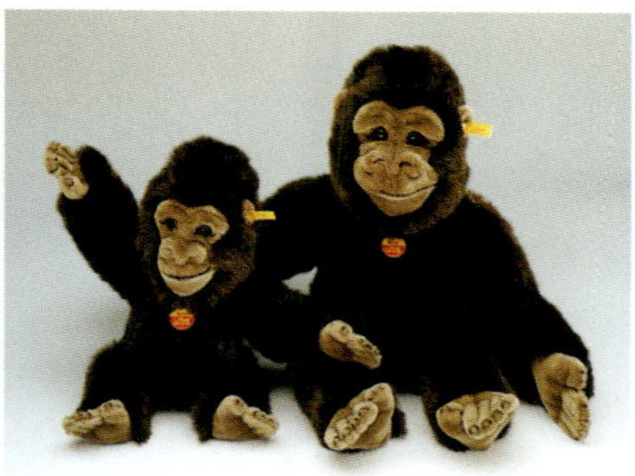

Gora Gorilla

Webpelz, dunkelbraun, sitzend, handwaschbar - *woven fur, dark brown, sitting, hand washable*

EAN-No.	Period	Pr.	Info
062209	1995-1997	3	40 cm
062230	1995-1996	3-4	60 cm

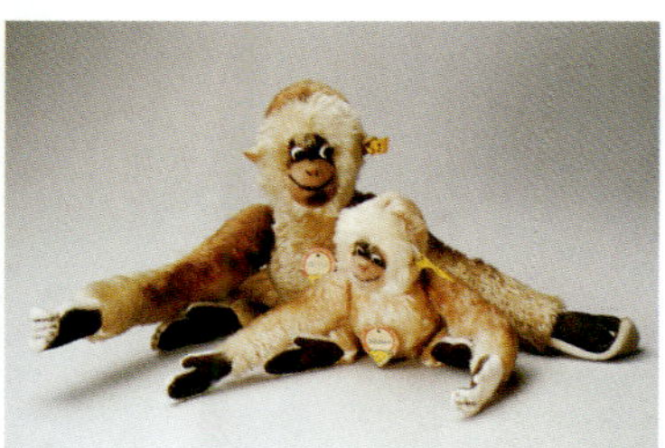

Gibbon

Mohairpluesch, hellbraun, Schlenkerglieder - *mohair, light brown, floppy joints*

Serie	Art.-No	Period	Pr.	Info
104	**7320,00**	1962-1964	4	20 cm
006	**7320,00**	1965-1966	4	
104	**7340,00**	1962-1964	4-5	40 cm
006	**7340,00**	1965-1966	4-5	

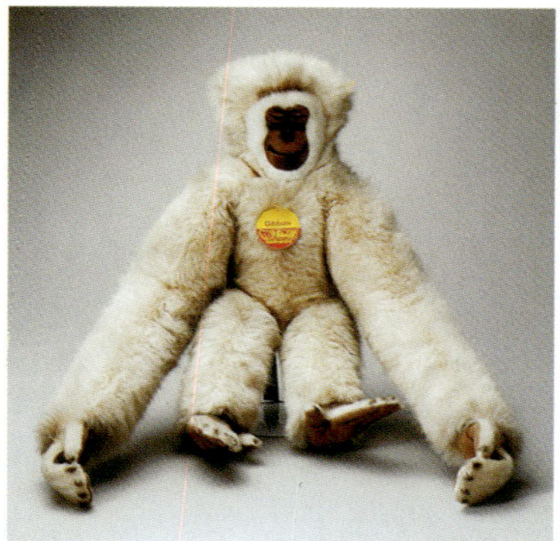

Gibbon Affe - ***Gibbon** Monkey*

Pelzimitation, ab 1978 Webpelz, beige, Schlenkertier, abwaschbar - *imitation fur, from 1978 woven fur, beige, dangling animal, surface washable*

Serie	Art.-No	Period	Pr.	Info
060502	**0040/60**	1974-1987	3	60 cm

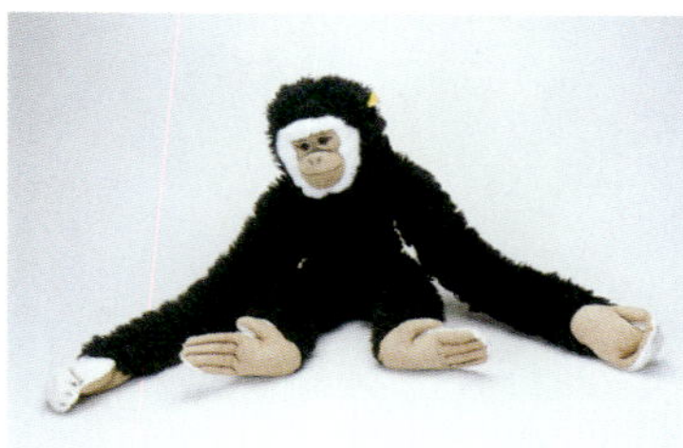

Gibbon Affe - ***Gibbon** Monkey*

Pelzimitation, ab 1978 Webpelz, schwarz, abwaschbar, Schlenkertier - *imitation fur, from 1978 woven fur, black, dangling animal, surface washable*

Serie	Art.-No	Period	Pr.	Info
	0041/60	1974-1978	3	60 cm

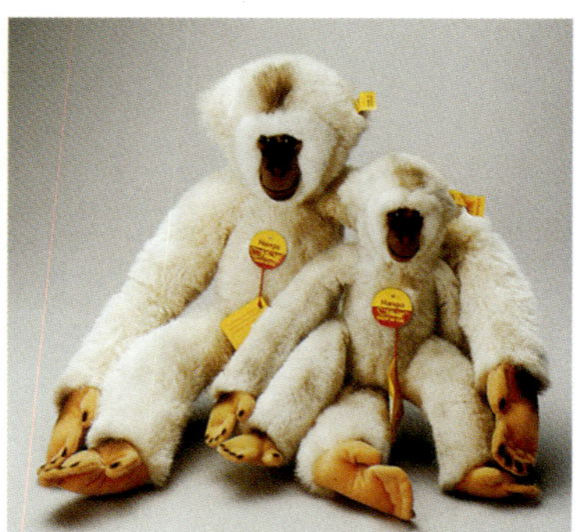

Hango Gibbon Baby

Web-/Wirkpelz, Schlenkertier, abwaschbar - *woven/knitted fur, dangling animal, surface washable*

Serie	Art.-No	Period	Pr.	Info
060403	**0040/28**	1980-1989	2-3	28 cm
060458	**0040/45**	1979-1989	3	45 cm

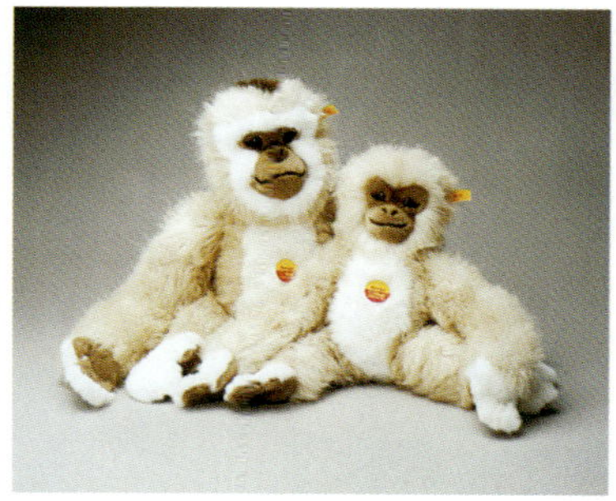

Bongo Gibbon

Webpelz, hell, handwaschbar - *woven fur, pale color, hand washable*

EAN-No.	Period	Pr.	Info
060489	1991-1995	3	40 cm
060526	1991-1994	3	55 cm

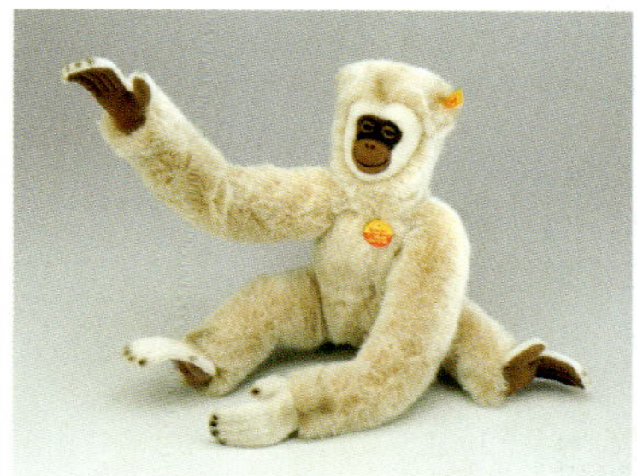

Bongo Gibbon

Webpelz, beige, handwaschbar - *Webpelz, beige, handwaschbar*

EAN-No.	Period	Pr.	Info
061509	1997-1998	3	45 cm

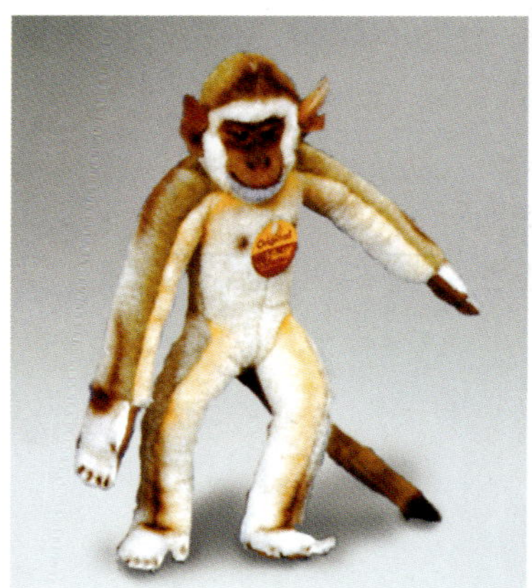

Meerkatze - *Long-Tailed Monkey*

Synthetik-Webpelz, stehend - *synthetic woven fur, standing*

Serie	Art.-No	Period	Pr.	Info
	0049/05	1978-1979	3	50 cm

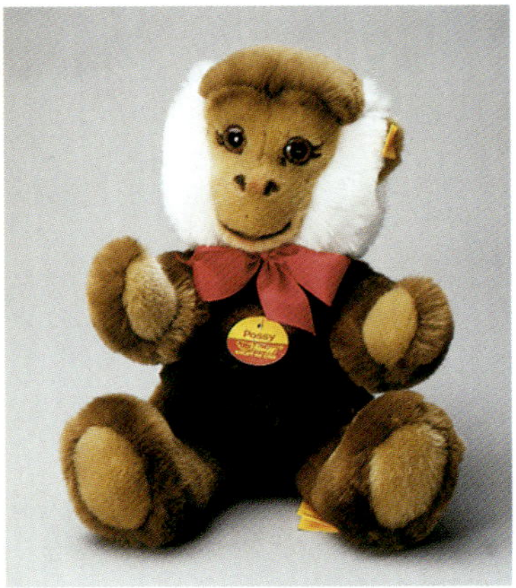

Possy Meerkatze - ***Possy*** *Long-Tailed Monkey*

Webpelz, gegliedert, Pieps-Stimme, waschmaschinenfest - *woven fur, jointed, squeaker, machine washable*

SERIE	ART.-NO	PERIOD	PR.	INFO
081477	**6215/28**	1989-1990	3	28 cm

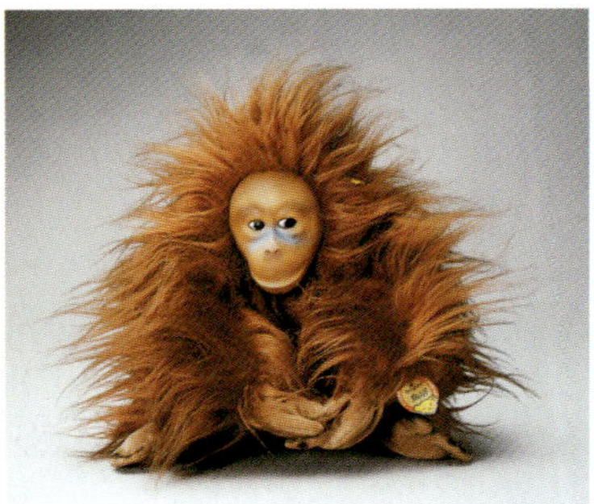

Schlenker-Orang - *Cosy Orang*

Plastikgesicht, Crylor, langhaarig, rotbraun, Schlenkerglieder, abwaschbar - *plastic face, crylor, long-hair, reddish-brown, dangling animal, surface washable*

SERIE	ART.-NO	PERIOD	PR.	INFO
	0060/30	1970-1974	4	30 cm

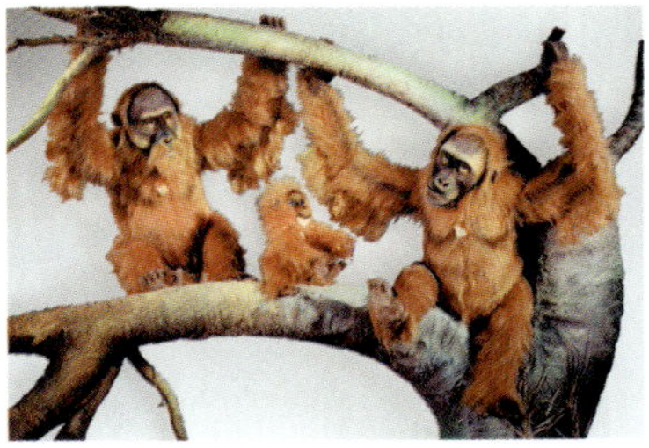

Orang Familie - *Orang Family*

Schautiere, Crylor, rotbraun - *display animals, crylor, red-brown*

SERIE	ART.-NO	PERIOD	PR.	INFO
	0089/04	1967-1967	4	40 cm
	0089/12	1967-1967	6	120 cm
	0089/13	1967-1967	6	130 cm

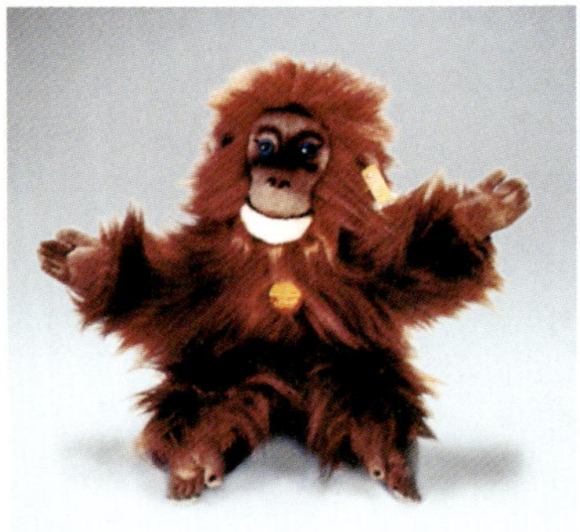

Orang Baby

Crylor, rotbraun, abwaschbar - *crylor, red-brown, surface washable*

SERIE	ART.-NO	PERIOD	PR.	INFO
	0088/40	1973-1975	3-4	40 cm

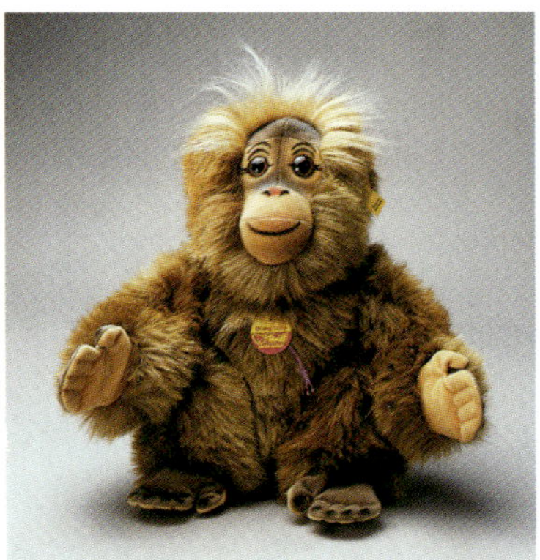

Orang Baby

Pelzimitation, ab 1978 Webpelz, braun, abwaschbar - *imitation fur, from 1978 woven fur, brown, surface washable*

SERIE	ART.-NO	PERIOD	PR.	INFO
	0030/35	1977-1980	2-3	35 cm

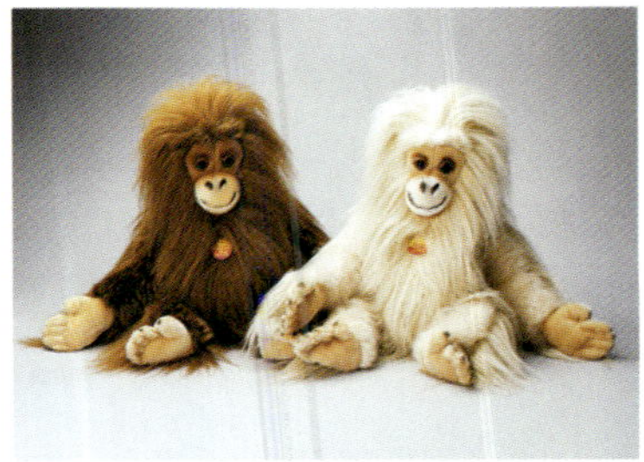

Bongo Orang

Wirk-/Webpelz, 50 cm, abwaschbar - *knitted/woven fur, 50 cm, surface washable*

SERIE	ART.-NO	PERIOD	PR.	INFO
062056	**0520/50**	1987-1989	3	rot - red
062254	**0525/50**	1987-1989	3	creme - *cream*

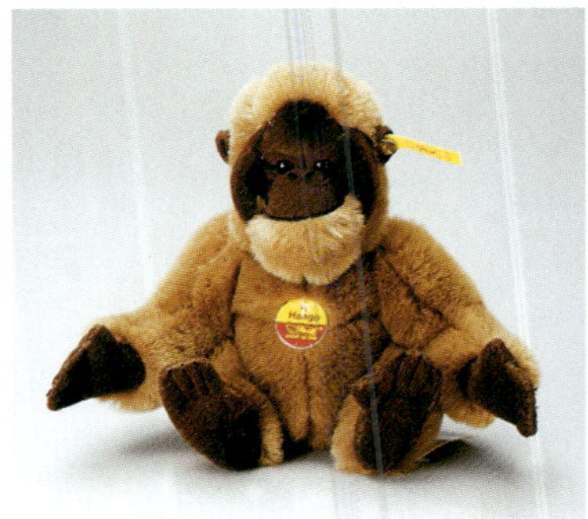

Hango Orang-Utan

Webpelz, braun, sitzend, waschmaschinenfest - *woven fur, brown, sitting, machine washable*

EAN-NO.	PERIOD	PR.	INFO
043338	1995-1999	2-3	15 cm

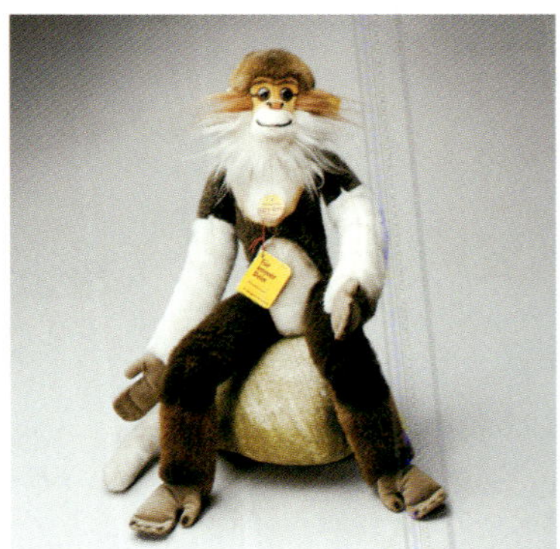

Kleideraffe - *Clothed Ape*

Webpelz, Schlenkertier, abwaschbar - *woven fur, dangling animal, surface washable*

SERIE	ART.-NO	PERIOD	PR.	INFO
	0045/50	1980-1983	3-4	50 cm

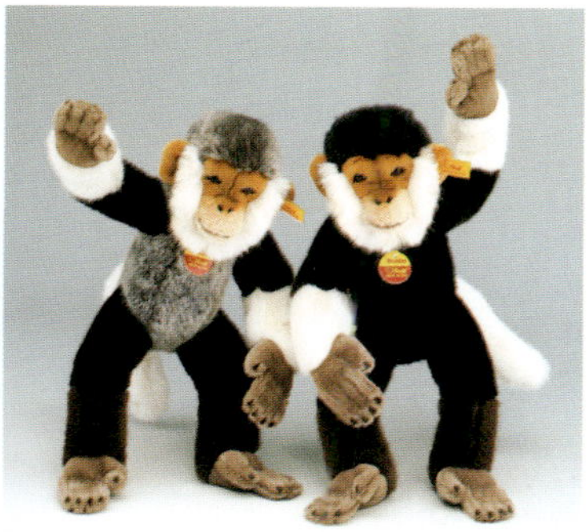

Bonbo Kleideraffe - ***Bonbo*** *Clothed Ape*

Webpelz, 38 cm, waschmaschinenfest - *woven fur, 38 cm, machine washable*

EAN-No.	Period	Pr.	Info
061202	1993-1996	3	grau - *grey*
061257	1993-1997	3	schwarz - *black*

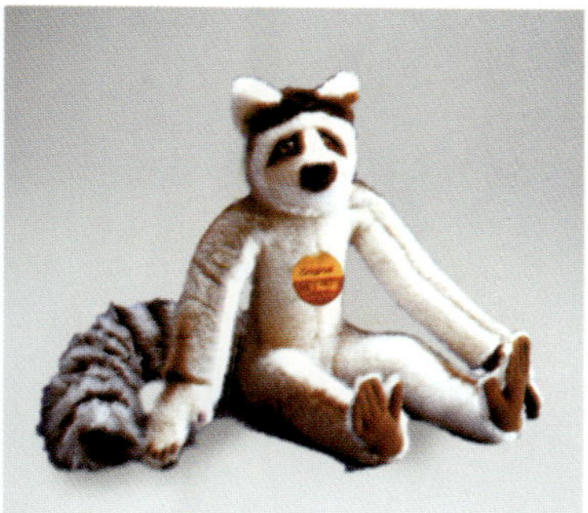

Lemur Katta

Synthetik-Webpelz, sitzend, abwaschbar - *synthetic woven fur, sitting, surface washable*

Serie	Art.-No	Period	Pr.	Info
	0059/05	1978-1979	3-4	50 cm

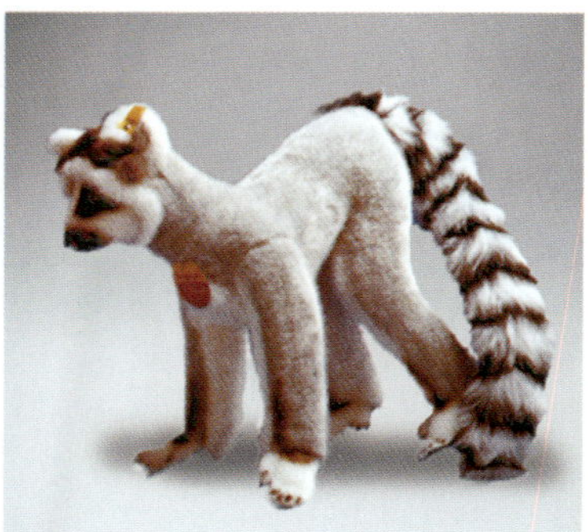

Lemur Katta

Synthetik-Webpelz, stehend, abwaschbar - *synthetic woven fur, standing, surface washable*

Serie	Art.-No	Period	Pr.	Info
	0059/06	1978-1979	3-4	60 cm

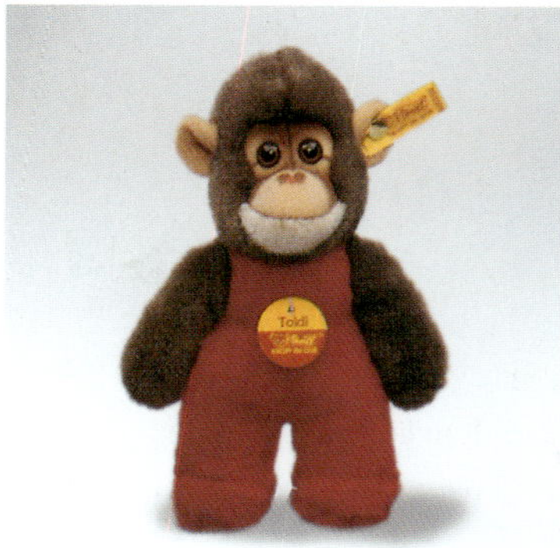

Toldi Affe - ***Toldi*** *Monkey*

Webpelz, Pieps-Stimme, waschmaschinenfest - *woven fur, squeaker, machine washable*

Serie	Art.-No	Period	Pr.	Info
080258	**6253/22**	1986-1990	2	22 cm

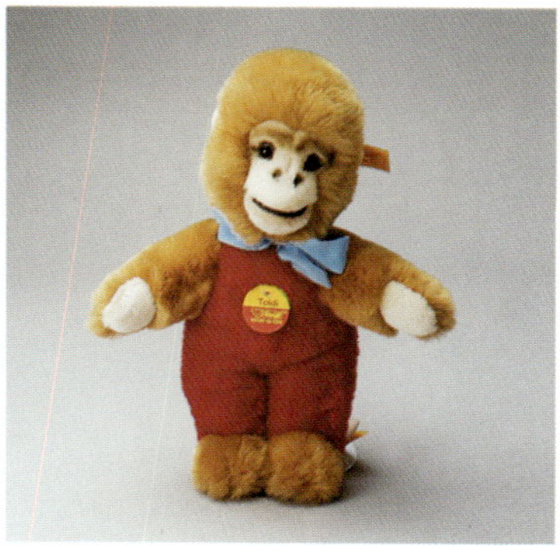

Toldi Affe - ***Toldi*** *Monkey*

Webpelz, Pieps-Stimme, waschmaschinenfest - *woven fur, squeaker, machine washable*

Serie	Art.-No	Period	Pr.	Info
080838	**6272/27**	1988-1989	2	27 cm

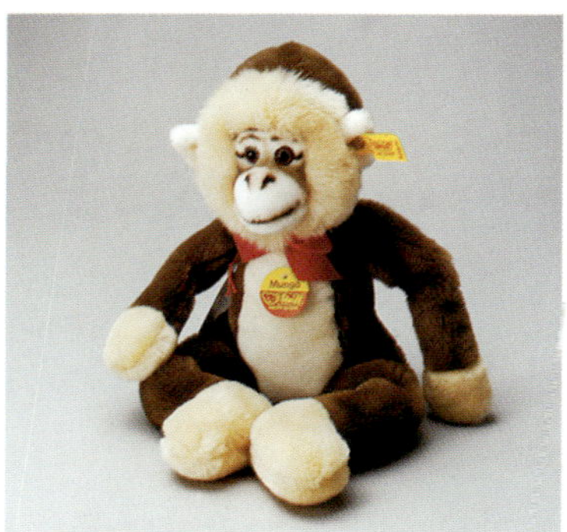

Mungo Schlenker-Affe - ***Mungo*** *Dangling Monkey*

Webpelz, Pieps-Stimme, waschmaschinenfest - *woven fur, squeaker, machine washable*

Serie	Art.-No	Period	Pr.	Info
123054	**6288/32**	1985-1987	2-3	32 cm

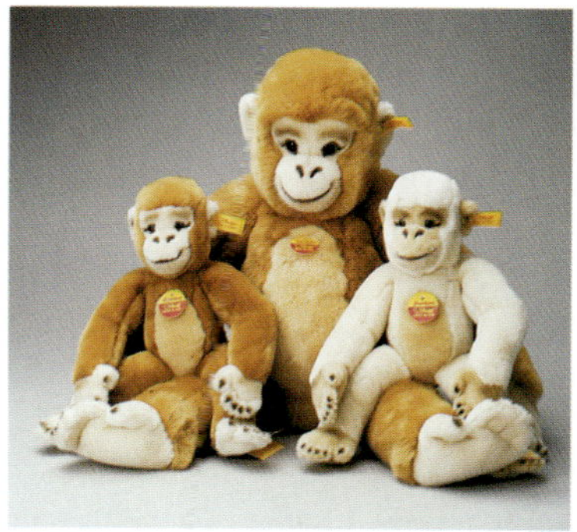

Bamboo Affe - ***Bamboo*** *Ape*

Webpelz, Pieps-Stimme, hellbraun oder braun, waschmaschinenfest - *woven fur, light brown or brown, squeaker, machine washable*

Serie	Art.-No	Period	Pr.	Info
061059	**0500/30**	1987-1988	2-3	30 cm, hellbraun - *light brown*
061080	**0500/45**	1987-1988	3	45 cm
061127	**0500/55**	1987-1988	3	55 cm
061356	**0505/30**	1987-1988	2-3	30 cm, creme - *cream*
061387	**0505/45**	1987-1988	3	45 cm
061424	**0505/55**	1987-1988	3	55 cm

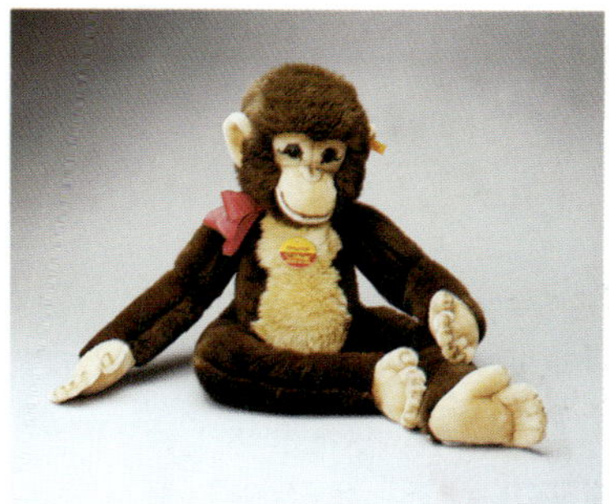

Schlenkeraffe - *Dangling Monkey*

Webpelz, dunkelbraun, abwaschbar - *woven fur, dark brown, surface washable*

Serie	Art.-No	Period	Pr.	Info
122026	**6280/70**	1990-1990	3	70 cm
	122026	1991-1993	3	
122064	**6280/99**	1990-1990	3-4	100 cm
	122064	1991-1992	3-4	

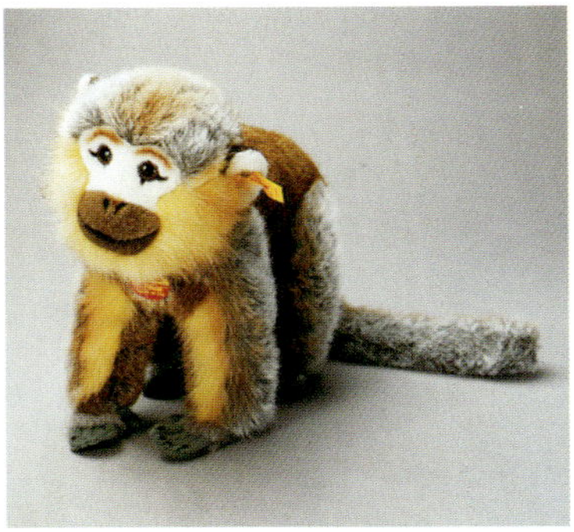

Springaffe - *Jumping Monkey*

Webpelz, grau/braun, stehend, handwaschbar - *woven fur, grey/brown, standing, hand washable*

EAN-No.	Period	Pr.	Info
120053	1995-1999	3-4	35 cm
120060	1995-1995	4	50 cm

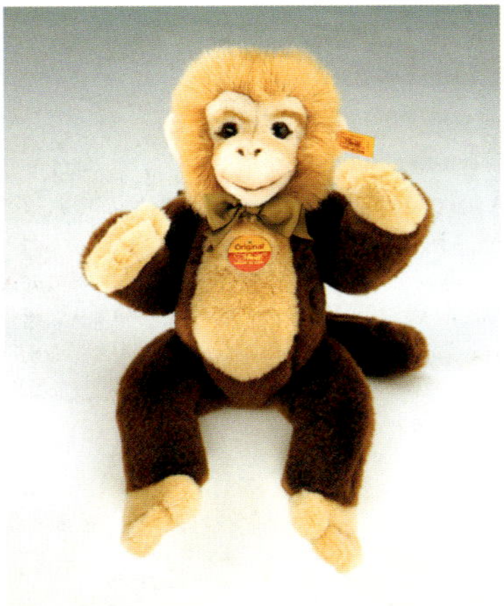

Schlenker Affe - *Dangling Monkey*

Webpelz, waschmaschinenfest - *woven fur, machine washable*

EAN-No.	Period	Pr.	Info
122040	1996-1997	2-3	30 cm

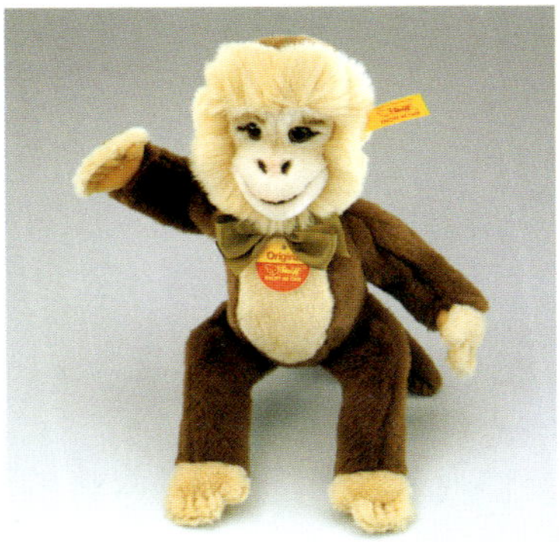

Schlenker Affe - *Dangling Monkey*

Webpelz, waschmaschinenfest - *woven fur, machine washable*

EAN-No.	Period	Pr.	Info
122019	1997-1998	2-3	22 cm

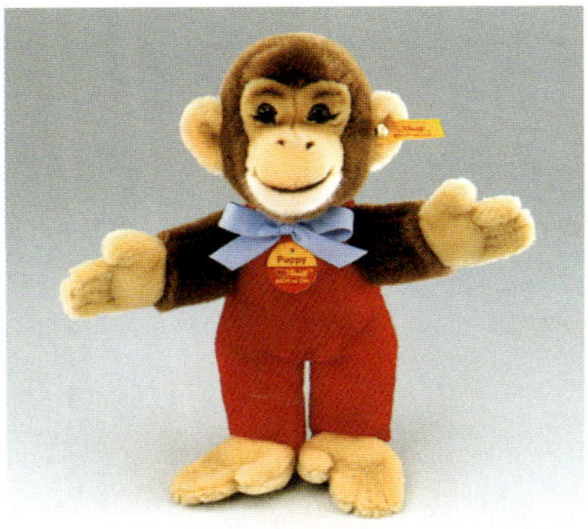

Puppy Affe - ***Puppy** monkey*

Webpelz, rot/braun, Pieps-Stimme, waschmaschinenfest - *woven fur, red/brown, squeaker, machine washable*

EAN-No.	Period	Pr.	Info
124662	1997-1998	2	28 cm

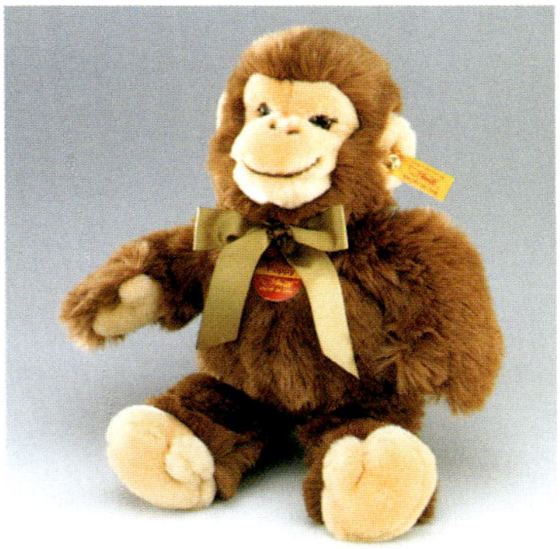

Poppy Affe - ***Poppy** Monkey*

Webpelz, braun, waschmaschinenfest - *woven fur, brown, machine washable*

EAN-No.	Period	Pr.	Info
123047	1998-1999	2-3	30 cm

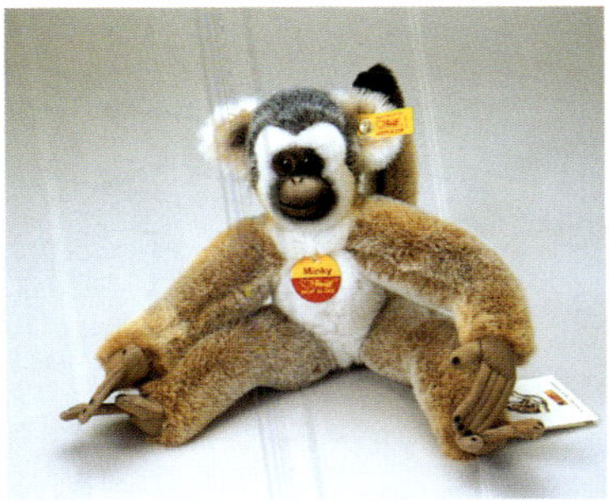

Minky Rotrueckentotenkopfaeffchen - ***Minky** Red-backed Squirrel Monkey*

Webpelz, abwaschbar - *woven fur, surface washable*

EAN-No.	Period	Pr.	Info
061554	1999-1999	3	28 cm

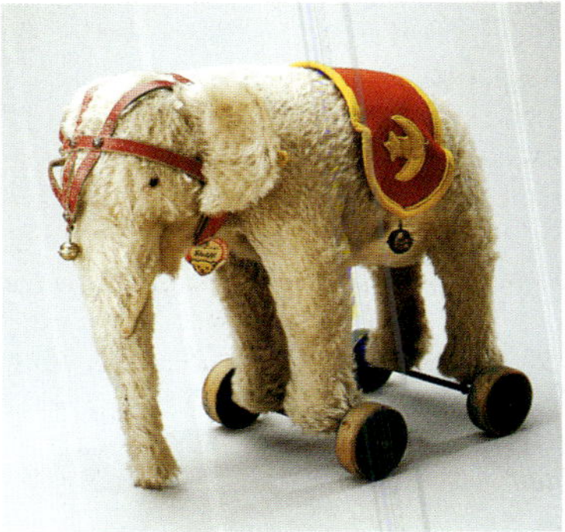

Zieh-Elefant - *Pull Toy Elephant*

Mohairpluesch, hellgrau, Lederkopfschmuck, rote Schabracke, stehend, Eisengerippe, 1949 lackierte Hartholz-Raeder, ab 1950 Scheibenraeder mit Gummi, ab 1967 Plastikreifen & Kunststofflager, 35 cm mit Verbindungsschienen, abwaschbar - *mohair, light grey, leather halter, red saddle cloth, standing, iron frame, 1949 on wooden wheels, from 1950 metal disc wheels with rubber tires, from 1967 plastic tires & bearings, 35 cm with connecting frame, voice, surface washable*

Serie	Art.-No	Period	Pr.	Info
20	**1328,2**	1950-1950	5-6	28 cm
20	**1328,1**	1951-1957	5-6	
200	**1328,10**	1961-1961	5	
20	**1335**	1949-1949	5-6	35 cm
20	**1335,2**	1950-1950	5-6	
20	**1335,1**	1951-1957	5-6	
200	**1335,10**	1961-1961	5	

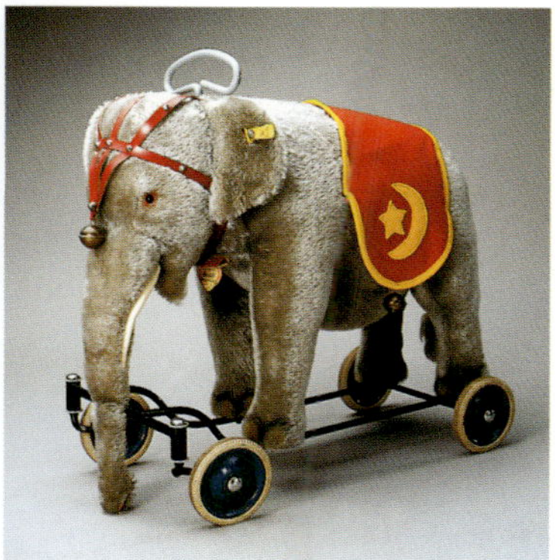

Reit-Elefant - *Riding Elephant*

Mohairpluesch, hellgrau, Lederkopfschmuck, rote Schabracke, Zugstimme & Haltegriff, Eisengerippe, stehend, abwaschbar, 1949 Holzraeder, ab 1950 Metallscheibenraeder mit Gummireifen, ab 1967 Plastikreifen & Kunststofflager, ab 1954 auch mit Lenkung erhaeltlich (Zusatz ST bzw. ,30 statt ,20), ab 1968 mit Schlepplenkung - *mohair, light grey, leather halter, red saddle cloth, pull cord voice & grip handle, iron frame, standing, surface washable, 1949 wooden wheels, from 1950 metal disc wheels with rubber tires, from 1967 plastic tires and bearings, from 1954 also available with steering (supplement ST or ,30 instead of ,20), from 1968 pull type steering*

Serie	Art.-No	Period	Pr.	Info
20	**1343,2**	1950-1958	5-6	43 cm
200	**1343,20**	1959-1964	5	
054	**1343,20**	1965-1967	5	
	0540/43	1968-1974	4-5	
20	**1344,2**	1949-1949	5-6	44 cm
20	**1350,2**	1950-1958	5-6	50 cm
200	**1350,20**	1959-1964	5	
054	**1350,20**	1965-1967	5	
	0540/50	1968-1974	5	
20	**1352,2**	1949-1949	5-6	52 cm
20	**1360,2**	1949-1958	5-6	60 cm
200	**1360,20**	1959-1964	5-6	
054	**1360,20**	1965-1967	5-6	
	0540/60	1968-1972	5	
20	**1380,2**	1950-1957	6	80 cm
200	**1380,20**	1961-1961	5-6	
054	**1380,20**	1966-1967	5-6	
	0540/80	1968-1972	5	
20	**13100,2**	1951-1957	6	100 cm
200	**1399,20**	1961-1961	6	
054	**1399,20**	1966-1966	6	

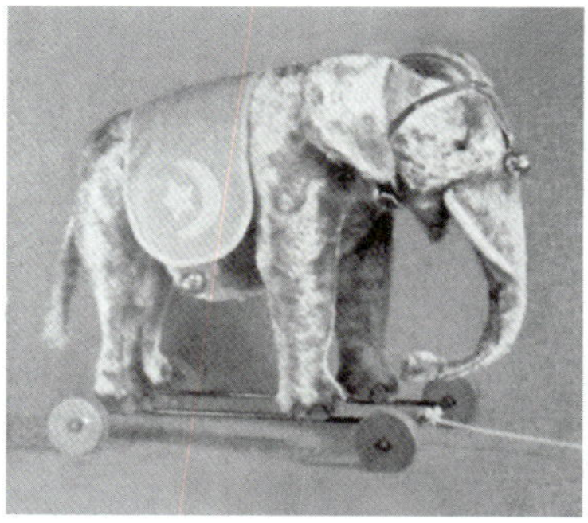

Reit-Elefant - *Riding Elephant*

Seidenpluesch, hellgrau, rote Filzschabracke, Lederkopfschmuck, stehend, auf Raedern, Eisengerippe mit Verbindungsschienen, Zugstimme - *silk plush, light grey, red felt saddle cloth, leather harness, standing, on wheels, iron frame & connecting rods, pull cord voice*

Serie	Art.-No	Period	Pr.	Info
20	**1644,2**	1949-1949	5-6	44 cm
20	**1652,2**	1949-1949	5-6	52 cm

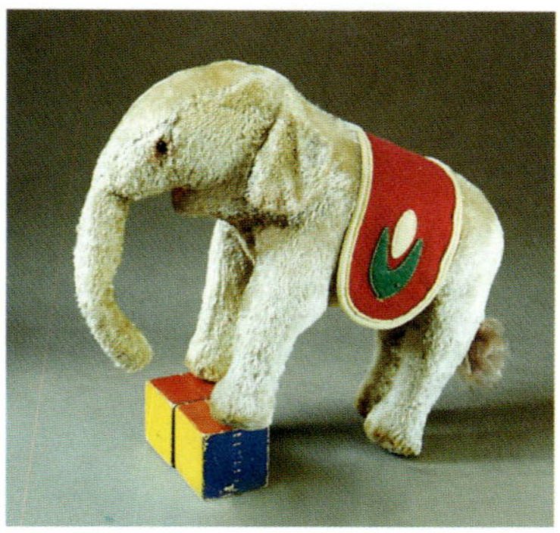

Spiel-Elefant - *Play Elephant*

weicher Kunstseidenpluesch, hellgrau, rote Schabracke (Filzdecke), stehend - *soft artificial silk plush, light grey, red saddle cloth (felt blanket), standing*

Serie	Art.-No	Period	Pr.	Info
20	**6622,0**	1948-1949	5	22 cm

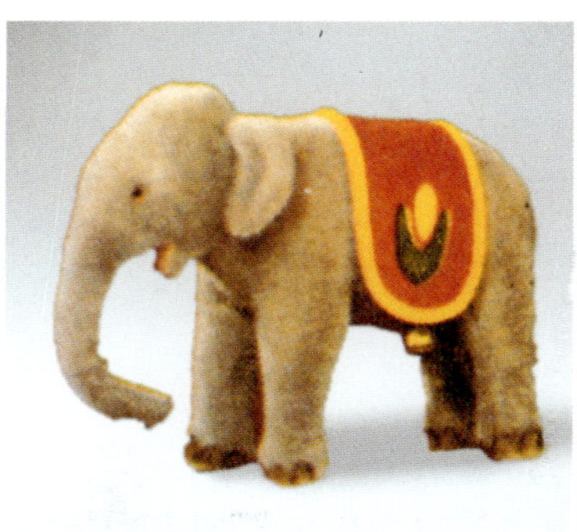

Jung-Elefant - *Young Elephant*

Mohair, grau, rote Decke mit gruenem liegendem Halbmond und gelbem Oval sowie Saeumung, stehend - *mohair, grey, red blanket with a green half moon & yellow oval & yellow edging, standing*

Serie	Art.-No	Period	Pr.	Info
20	**6322,0**	1950-1951	5	22 cm

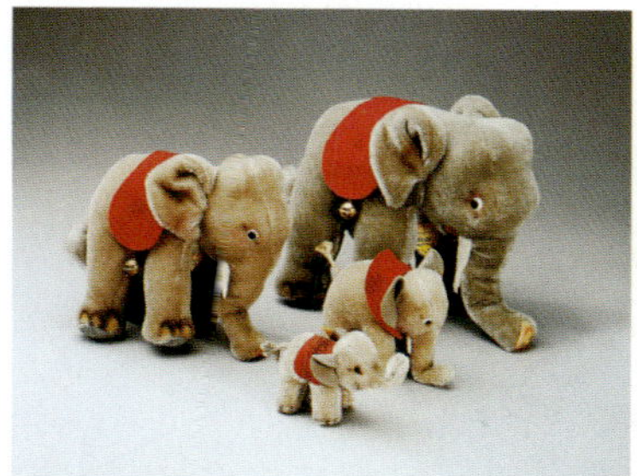

Elefant - *Elephant*

Mohairpluesch, grau, rote Satteldecke aus Filz, stehend, weich, abwaschbar, ab 17 cm 2 Kunststoff-Stosszaehne & Satteldecke mit 2 Gloeckchen, 7 & 10 cm mit Filzohren & Kordelschwanz, 7 cm Satteldecke mit Aufdruck "Steiff" - 1955 als Jubilaeumsausgabe mit Aufdruck "75 Jahre 1880-1955" - *mohair, grey, red felt saddle cloth, standing, soft, surface washable, from 17 cm two plastic tusks & saddle cloth with two bells, 7 & 10 cm felt ears & cord type tail, 7 cm has saddle cloth with "Steiff" imprinted, 1955 anniversary edition with "75 Jahre 1880-1955" imprinted*

Serie	Art.-No	Period	Pr.	Info
20	**6307,0**	1955-1955	3-4	7 cm, mit Jubilaeumsaufdruck - *anniversary imprint*
20	**6307,0**	1956-1958	3	7 cm, mit Aufdruck "Steiff" - *with "Steiff" imprint*
200	**6307,00**	1959-1964	2-3	
050	**6307,00**	1965-1967	2-3	
	0500/07	1968-1976	2	
	0500/07	1977-1977	2	leicht geaendertes Modell - *slightly altered model*
20	**6310,0**	1950-1958	3-4	10 cm
200	**6310,00**	1959-1964	3	
050	**6310,00**	1965-1967	3	
	0500/10	1968-1978	2-3	
20	**6317,0**	1952-1957	4	17 cm
20	**6317,01**	1958-1958	4	
200	**6317,00**	1959-1964	3-4	
050	**6317,00**	1965-1967	3-4	
	0500/17	1968-1976	3	
20	**6322,01**	1952-1958	4	22 cm
200	**6322,00**	1959-1964	3-4	
050	**6322,00**	1965-1967	3-4	
	0500/22	1968-1975	3	
20	**6335,0**	1956-1956	4	35 cm
20	**6335,01**	1957-1958	4	
200	**6335,00**	1959-1964	4	
050	**6335,00**	1965-1967	4	
	0500/35	1968-1968	4	

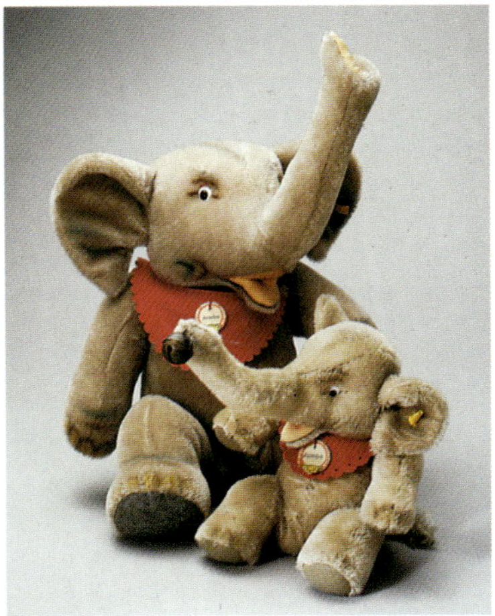

Weich-Elefant **Jumbo** - *Soft Elephant* ***Jumbo***

Mohair, grau, rotes Laetzchen, aufwartend, Kopf & Arme drehbar, superweich, abwaschbar - *mohair, grey, red bib, sitting up position, head & arms swivel, super soft, surface washable*

SERIE	ART.-NO	PERIOD	PR.	INFO
20	**4322,1**	1952-1958	4-5	22 cm
200	**4322,00**	1959-1962	4	
052	**4322,00**	1966-1967	4	
	0520/22	1968-1975	3-4	
20	**4335,1**	1958-1958	5	35 cm
200	**4335,00**	1959-1961	4-5	
052	**4335,00**	1966-1967	4-5	
	0520/35	1968-1974	4	

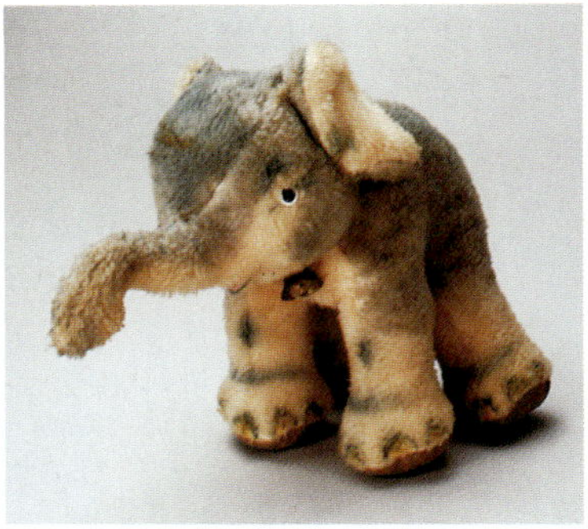

Cosy Trampy - *Cosy-Trampy*

Dralon, gefuellt mit synthetischen Fasern & Schaumstoff, sehr weich, grau, stehend, offener Mund, Halsband mit Gloeckchen, waschbar - *dralon, stuffed with synthetic fibers and foam, very soft, grey, standing, open mouth, collar with bell, washable*

SERIE	ART.-NO	PERIOD	PR.	INFO
83 20	**6620**	1956-1958	3	20 cm
830 200	**6620,00**	1959-1964	2-3	
488	**6620,00**	1965-1967	2-3	
	4880/20	1968-1978	2	

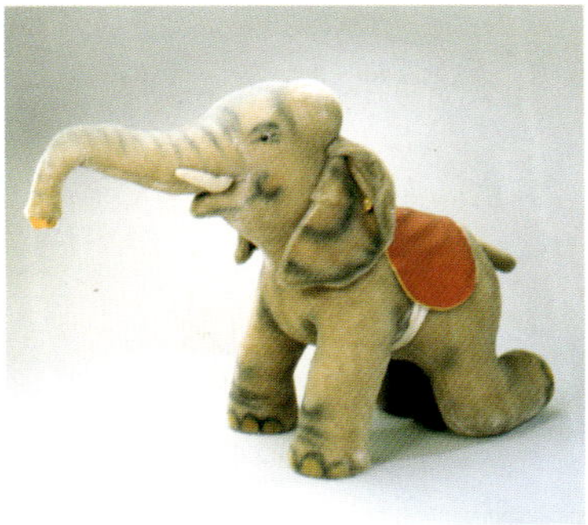

Snuggy Jumbo

Mohair, grau, Sitztier, Eisengestell mit Gummifuessen, roter Sattel - *mohair, grey, sitting animal, iron frame with rubber feet, red saddle*

SERIE	ART.-NO	PERIOD	PR.	INFO
82 20	**7355,0**	1957-1957	6	55 cm
820 200	**1355,00**	1961-1963	6	
600	**1355,00**	1966-1966	6	

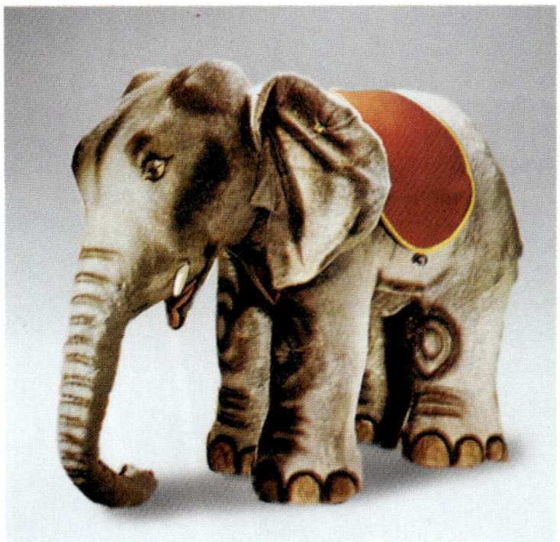

Elefant - *Elephant*

Schautier, Mohair, grau, stehend - *display animal, mohair, grey, standing*

SERIE	ART.-NO	PERIOD	PR.	INFO
200	**1155,90**	1960-1960	7	150 cm
	0539/15	1967-1967	7	

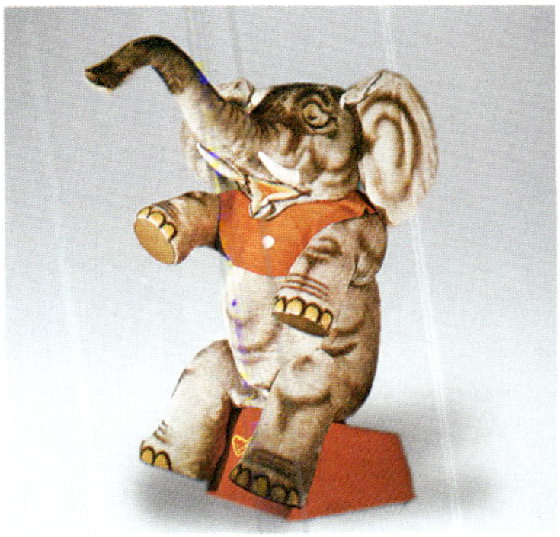

Elefant - *Elephant*

Schautier, Mohair, grau, aufwartend - *display animal, mohair, grey, sitting up*

SERIE	ART.-NO	PERIOD	PR.	INFO
200	**4150,90**	1960-1960	7	150 cm
	0529/15	1967-1967	7	

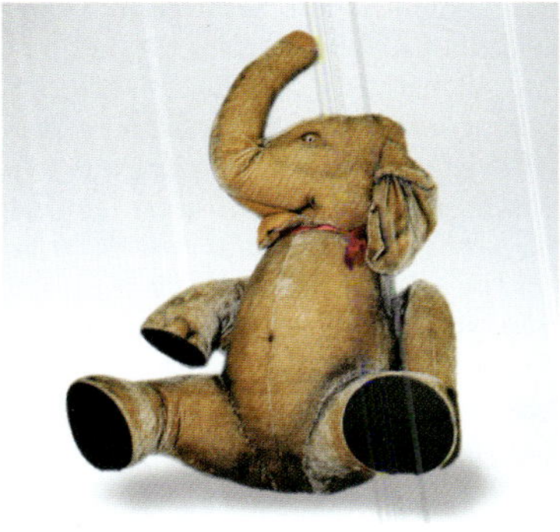

Elefant - *Elephant*

Schautier, Mohair, grau, aufwartend - *display animal, mohair, grey, sitting up*

SERIE	ART.-NO	PERIOD	PR.	INFO
200	**4399,90**	1960-1960	6	100 cm
	0529/10	1967-1967	6	

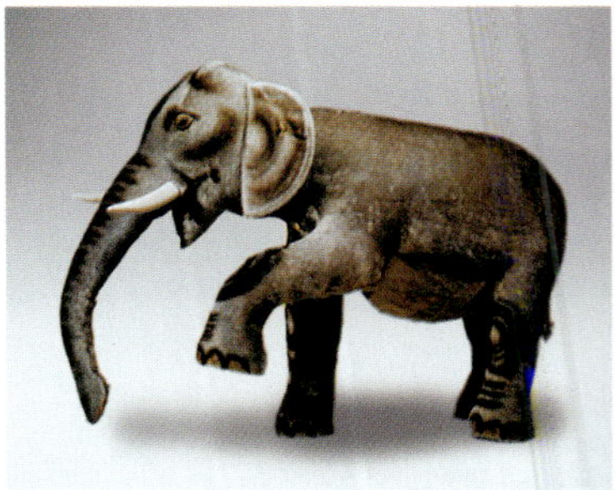

Elefant - *Elephant*

Schautier, Mohair, grau, stehend - *display animal, mohair, grey, standing*

SERIE	ART.-NO	PERIOD	PR.	INFO
200	**6150,90**	1960-1960	7	150 cm
	0549/15	1967-1967	7	

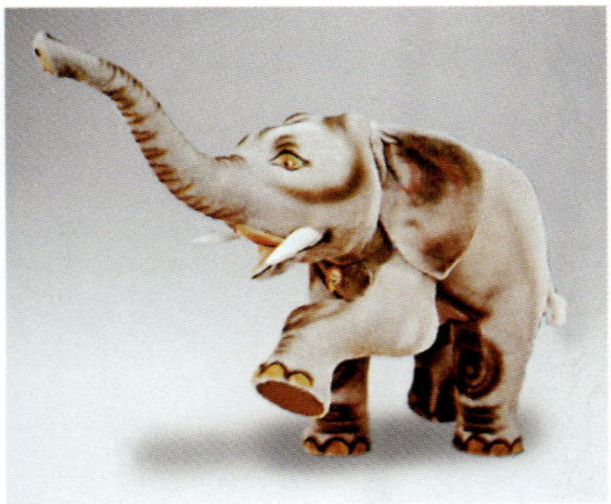

Elefant - *Elephant*

Schautier, Mohair, grau, stehend - *display animal, mohair, grey, standing*

SERIE	ART.-NO	PERIOD	PR.	INFO
200	**6375,90**	1960-1960	6	75 cm
	0509/08	1967-1967	6	

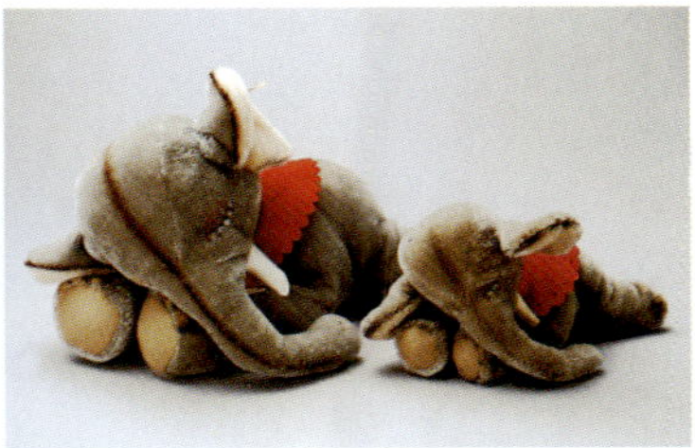

Floppy Ele

Mohair, Augen gestickt, grau, liegend, ab 1970 formgeschaeumt, sehr weich & schmiegsam, vollwaschbar - *mohair, eyes embroidered, grey, lying, from 1970 stuffed with pre-formed foam, very soft & cuddly, fully washable*

SERIE	ART.-NO	PERIOD	PR.	INFO
553	**7317,00**	1967-1967	2	17 cm
	5530/17	1968-1969	2	
	5537/17	1970-1977	2	
553	**7328,00**	1967-1967	2	28 cm
	5530/28	1968-1969	2	
	5537/28	1970-1977	2	

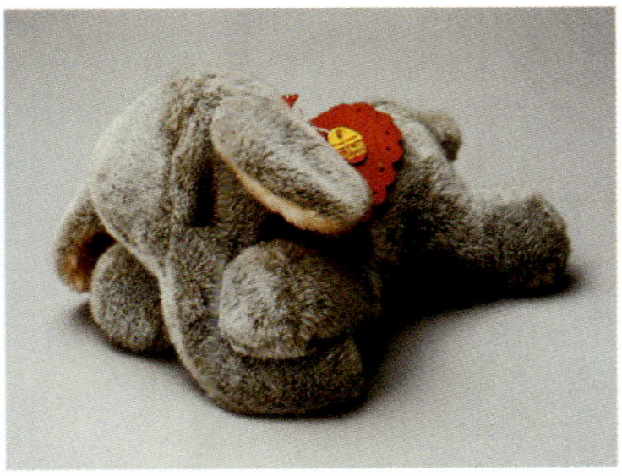

Floppy Jumbo

Synthetik-Webpelz, formgeschaeumt, vollwaschbar - *synthetic woven fur, stuffed with pre-formed foam, fully washable*

SERIE	ART.-NO	PERIOD	PR.	INFO
	5710/20	1978-1980	1-2	20 cm
	5710/30	1977-1981	2	30 cm

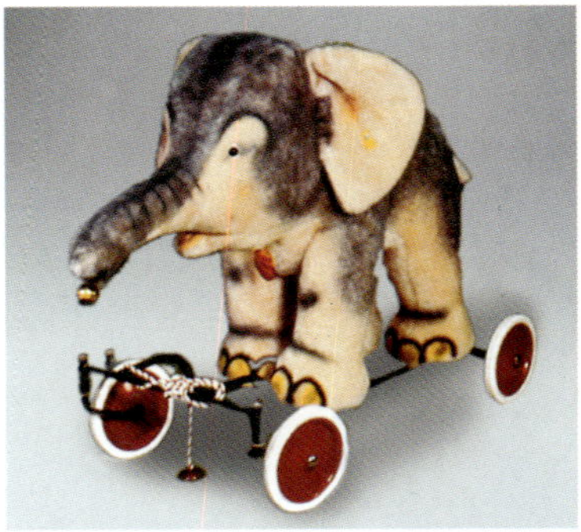

Reit-Trampy - *Riding Trampy*

Dralon, Stahlrohrgestell, Plastikreifen, Kunststofflager, Schlepplenkung, abwaschbar - *dralon, steel frame, plastic tires & bearings, pull type steering, surface washable*

SERIE	ART.-NO	PERIOD	PR.	INFO
	0550/60	1970-1975	4-5	60 cm

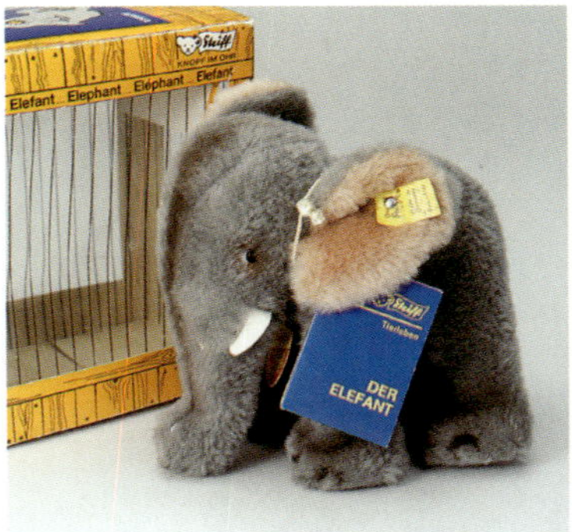

Elefant Jacobombo - *Elephant Jacobombo*

"Der kleine Tierversand", Dralon, stehend, im Kaefigkarton, mit Tiersteckbrief, abwaschbar - *"Der kleine Tierversand", dralon, standing, in its own cardboard crate, with information label, surface washable*

SERIE	ART.-NO	PERIOD	PR.	INFO
	5810/15	1971-1974	4	15 cm

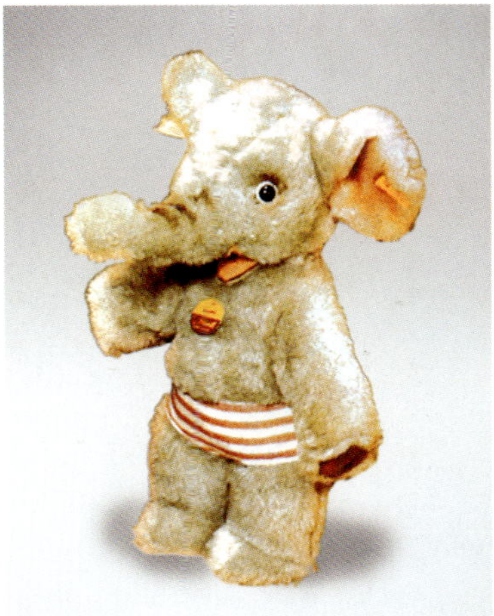

Weich-Ele Elefant ab 1974 Weich-Elefant **Burry** - *Soft Ele Elephant from 1974 Soft Elephant **Burry***

Dralon, formgeschaeumt, grau, rot/weisse Badehose, sehr weich, Schlenkerkopf, vollwaschbar - *dralon, stuffed with pre-formed foam, grey, red & white swimming trunks, very soft, floppy head, fully washable*

SERIE	ART.-NO	PERIOD	PR.	INFO
	6210/30	1971-1978	2	30 cm
	6210/40	1971-1975	2	40 cm

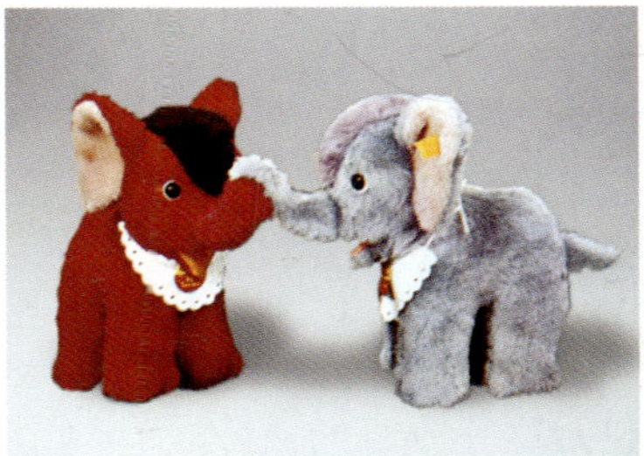

Jungelefant **Diggi** - *Baby Elephant **Diggi***

Dralon, formgeschaeumt, weisses Laetzchen, stehend, superweich, abwaschbar - *dralon, stuffed with pre-formed foam, white bib, standing, super soft, surface washable*

SERIE	ART.-NO	PERIOD	PR.	INFO
	6431/18	1973-1977	2	18 cm, rot - *red*
	6430/25	1972-1978	2	25 cm
	6431/25	1972-1975	2	25 cm, blau - *blue*

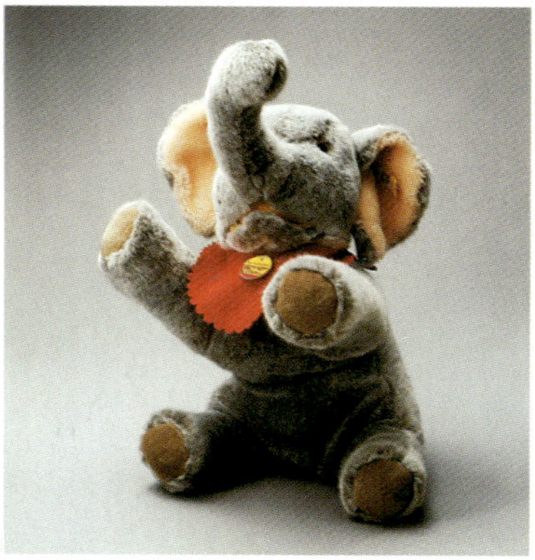

Molly Elefant - *Molly Elephant*

Pelz-Imitation, grau, abwaschbar - *imitation fur, grey, surface washable*

SERIE	ART.-NO	PERIOD	PR.	INFO
	0334/40	1974-1977	2-3	40 cm
	0334/70	1974-1977	3	70 cm

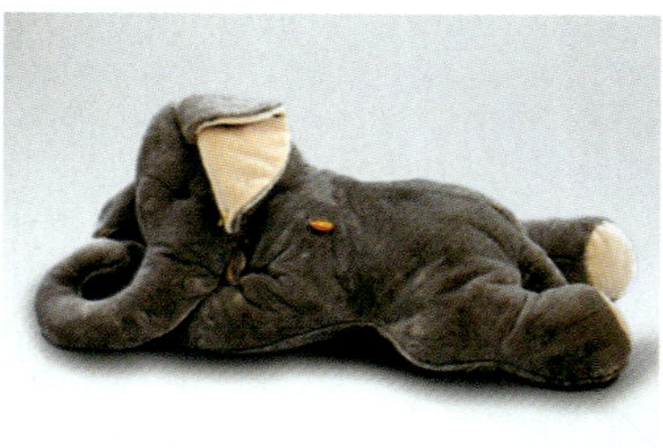

Super Molly Elefant - ***Super Molly** Elephant*

Webpelz, abwaschbar - *woven fur, surface washable*

SERIE	ART.-NO	PERIOD	PR.	INFO
102936	**0344/99**	1984-1986	4	115 cm

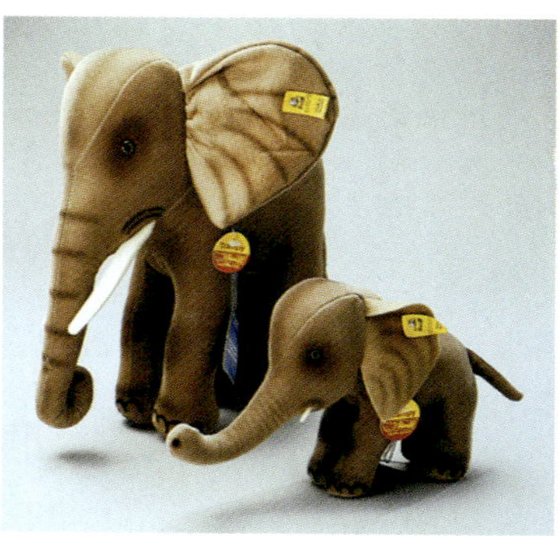

Trampy Elefant - ***Trampy** Elephant*

Trevirasamt, stehend, vollwaschbar - *trevira velvet, standing, fully washable*

SERIE	ART.-NO	PERIOD	PR.	INFO
	0510/17	1975-1978	3	17 cm
	0510/28	1975-1978	3-4	28 cm

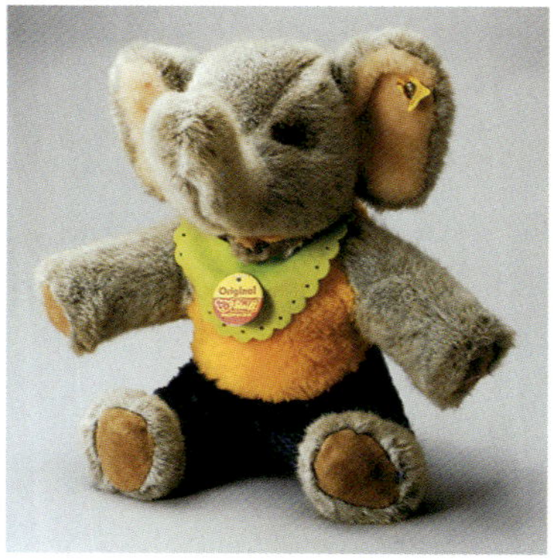

Happy Elefant - ***Happy** Elephant*

Pelzimitation, ab 1978 Webpelz, formgeschaeumt, gruenes Laetzchen, sitzend, vollwaschbar - *imitation fur, from 1978 woven fur, stuffed with pre-formed foam, green bib, sitting, fully washable*

SERIE	ART.-NO	PERIOD	PR.	INFO
	6112/35	1975-1979	3	35 cm

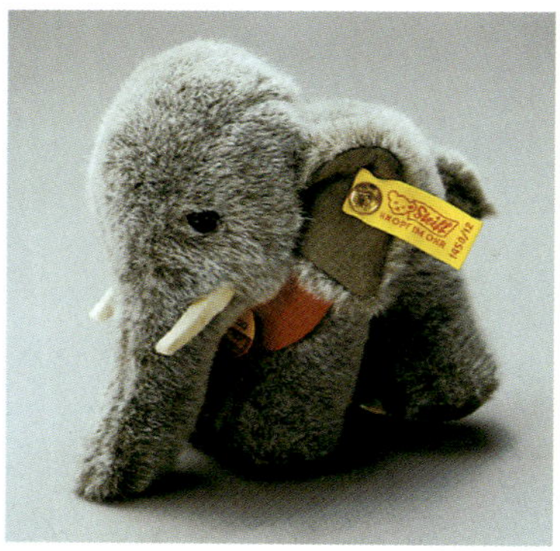

Jumbo Elefant - ***Jumbo** Elephant*

Nerzimitation, ab 1978 Synthetik-Webpelz, grau, stehend, Stosszaehne, abwaschbar - *imitation mink, from 1978 synthetic woven fur, grey, standing, tusks, surface washable*

SERIE	ART.-NO	PERIOD	PR.	INFO
	1450/12	1977-1984	1-2	12 cm

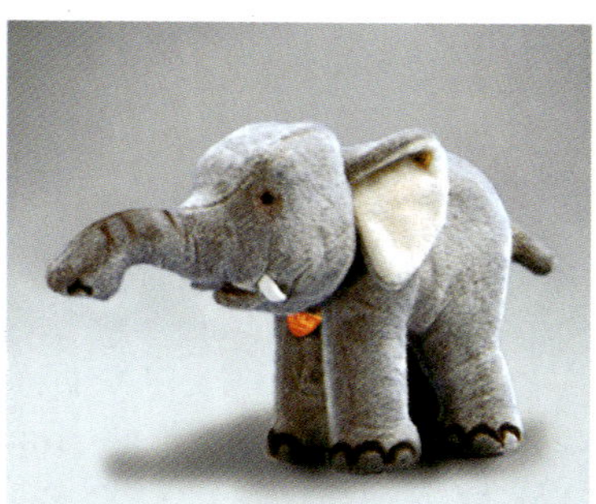

Trampy Elefant - ***Trampy** Elephant*

Synthetik-Webpluesch, grau, stehend, abwaschbar - *synthetic woven plush, grey, standing, surface washable*

SERIE	ART.-NO	PERIOD	PR.	INFO
	6300/60	1977-1979	3	60 cm

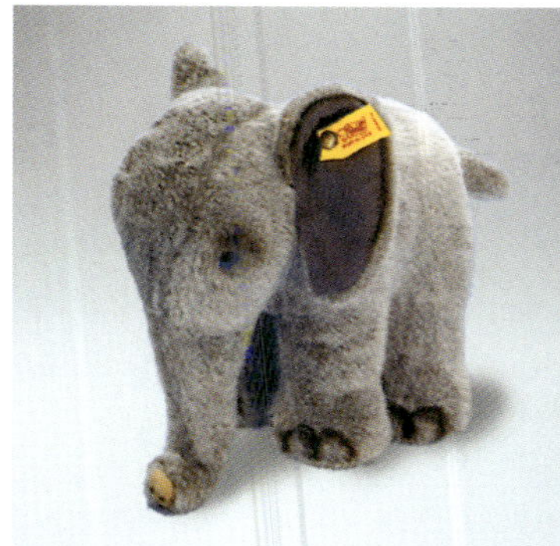

Diggy Elefant - ***Diggy** Elephant*

Webpelz, stehend, abwaschbar - *woven fur, standing, surface washable*

SERIE	ART.-NO	PERIOD	PR.	INFO
	0505/18	1979-1983	2	18 cm

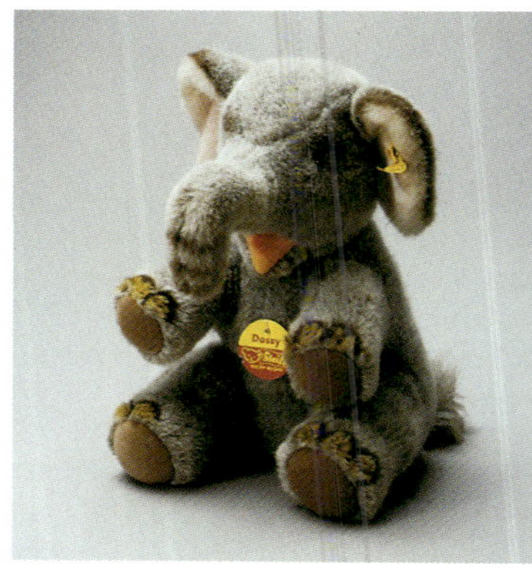

Dossy Elefant - ***Dossy** Elephant*

Webpelz, aufwartend, abwaschbar - *woven fur, sitting up, surface washable*

SERIE	ART.-NO	PERIOD	PR.	INFO
	5810/22	1980-1984	2-3	22 cm

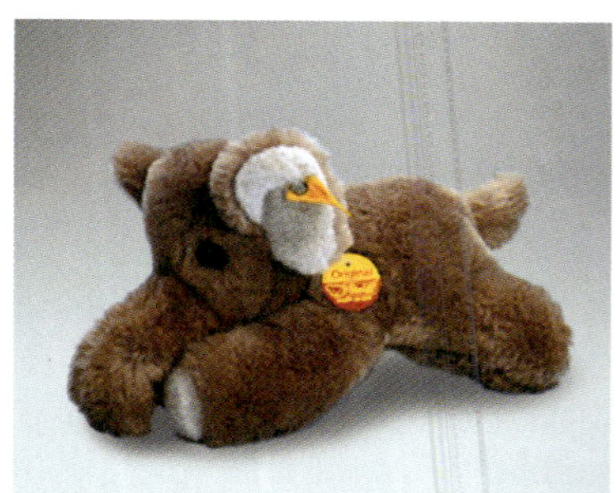

Kuschel Elefant - ***Kuschel** Elephant*

Webpelz, Schaumstoff-Fuellung, superweich, waschmaschinenfest - *woven fur, stuffed with foam, super soft, machine washable*

SERIE	ART.-NO	PERIOD	PR.	INFO
	5510/25	1981-1984	2	25 cm

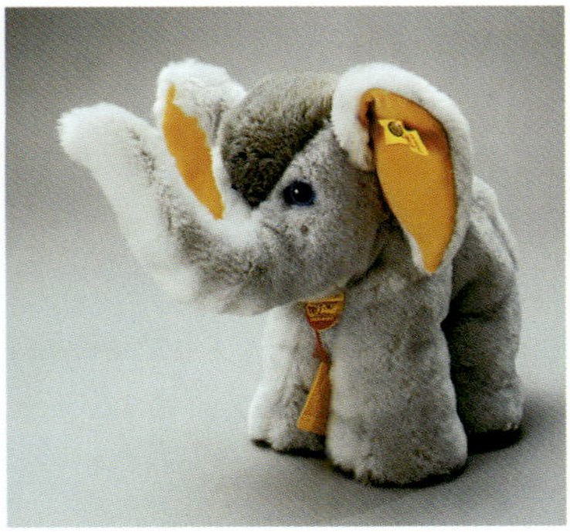

Cosy Trampy

Webpelz, kuschelweich, waschmaschinenfest - *woven fur, soft & cuddly, machine washable*

SERIE	ART.-NO	PERIOD	PR.	INFO
	5352/25	1982-1983	2-3	25 cm

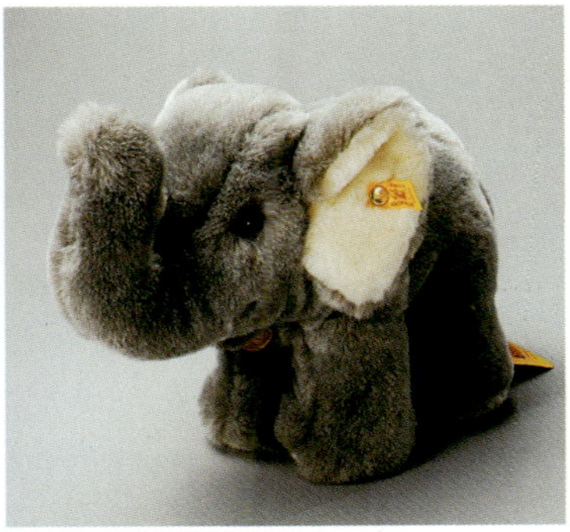

Cosy Jumbo ab 1998 Cosy Elefant - ***Cosy Jumbo*** *from 1998 Cosy Elephant*

Webpelz, Druckstimme, superweich, waschmaschinenfest - *woven fur, press voice, super soft, machine washable*

SERIE	ART.-NO	PERIOD	PR.	INFO
085109	**5350/15**	1984-1990	1-2	18 cm
	085109	1991-1999	1-2	
085123	**5350/22**	1984-1990	2-3	22 cm
	085123	1991-1996	2-3	
085154	**5350/30**	1984-1988	2-3	30 cm

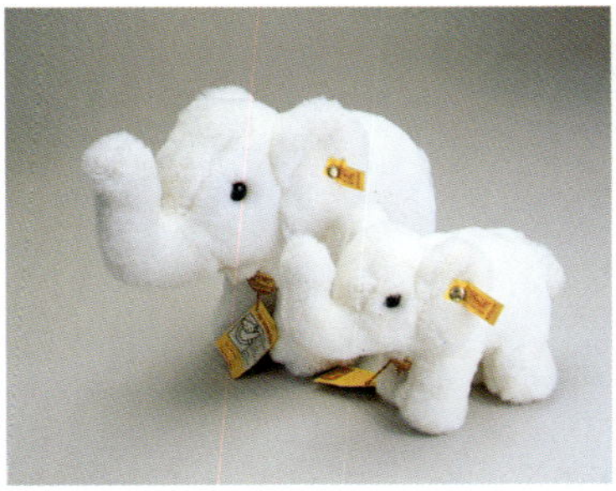

Happy 1986 **Cosy Jumbo**

Webpelz, weiss, Druckstimme, waschmaschinenfest - *woven fur, white, press voice, machine washable*

SERIE	ART.-NO	PERIOD	PR.	INFO
085208	**5750/15**	1984-1986	2-3	15 cm
085222	**5750/22**	1984-1986	2-3	22 cm

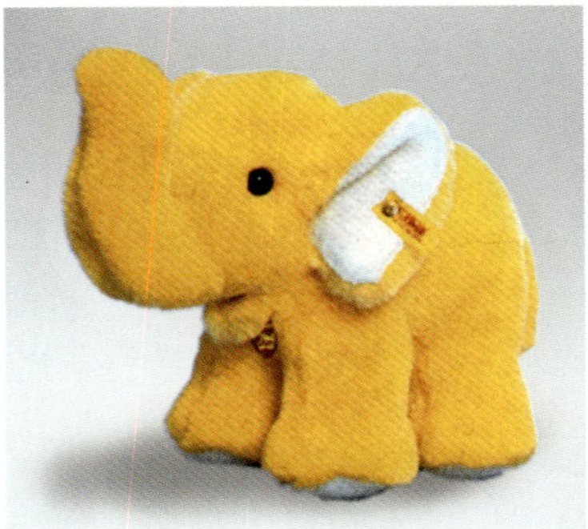

Happy Jumbo

Webpelz, dottergelb, Druckstimme, waschmaschinenfest - *woven fur, egg yellow, press voice, machine washable*

SERIE	ART.-NO	PERIOD	PR.	INFO
	5755/15	1984-1984	2-3	15 cm
	5755/22	1984-1984	2-3	22 cm

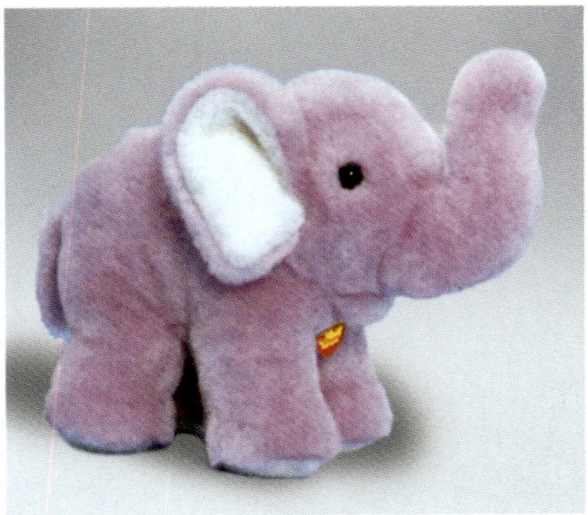

Happy Jumbo

Webpelz, lila, Druckstimme, waschmaschinenfest - *woven fur, lavender, press voice, machine washable*

SERIE	ART.-NO	PERIOD	PR.	INFO
	5758/15	1984-1984	2-3	15 cm
	5758/22	1984-1984	2-3	22 cm

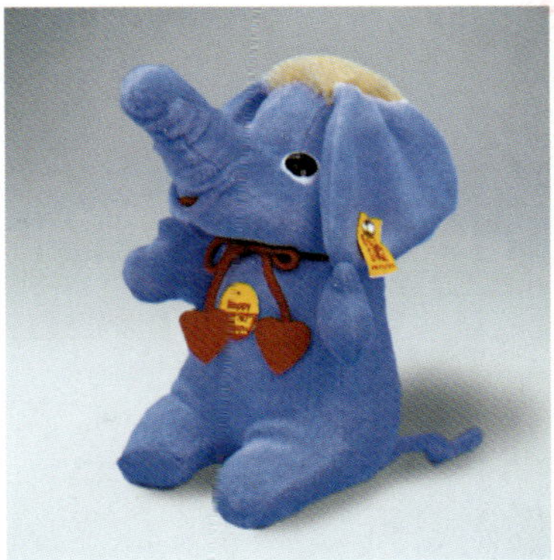

Poppy Elefant - ***Poppy*** *Elephant*

Poppy-Figur, Nicki-Stoff, abwaschbar - *Poppy figure, nicky velvet, surface washable*

SERIE	ART.-NO	PERIOD	PR.	INFO
	7875/26	1984-1984	3-4	26 cm

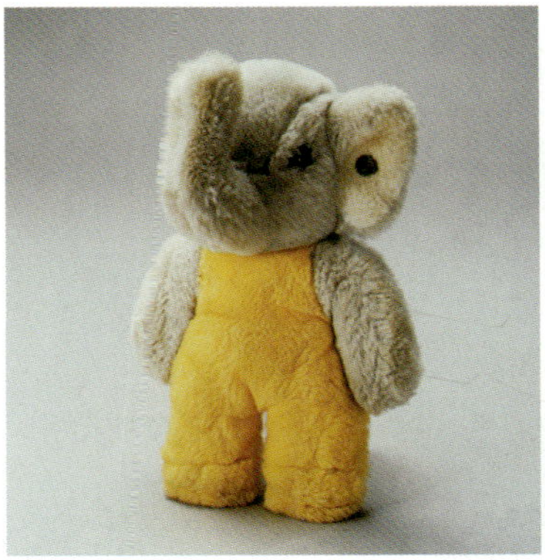

Toldi Elefant - ***Toldi*** *Elephant*

Webpelz, Pieps-Stimme, waschmaschinenfest - *woven fur, squeaker, machine washable*

SERIE	ART.-NO	PERIOD	PR.	INFO
080203	**6252/22**	1984-1988	2	22 cm

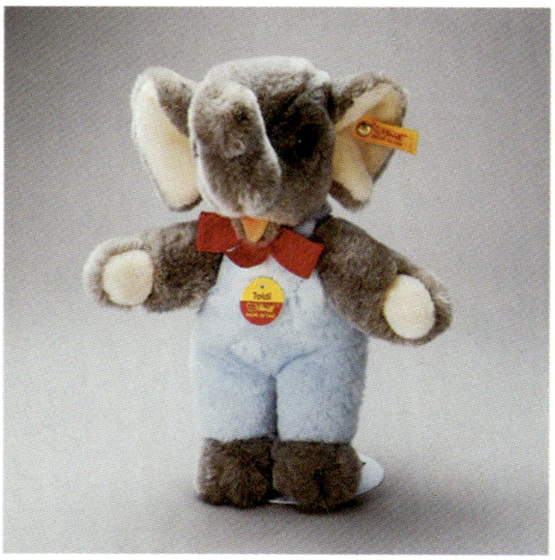

Toldi Elefant - ***Toldi*** *Elephant*

Webpelz, Pieps-Stimme, waschmaschinenfest - *woven fur, squeaker, machine washable*

SERIE	ART.-NO	PERIOD	PR.	INFO
080784	**6271/27**	1988-1989	2-3	27 cm

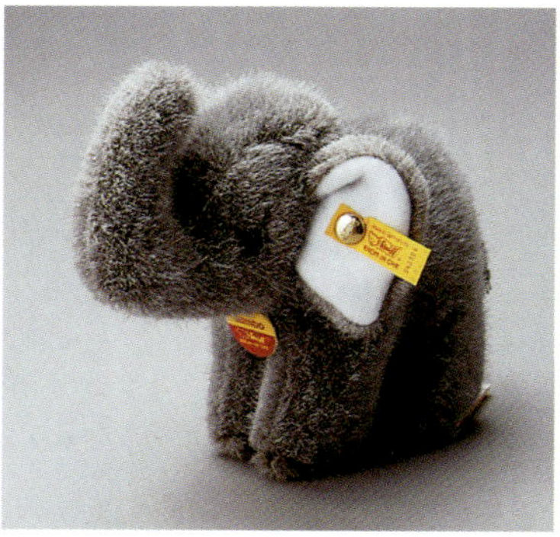

Jumbo Elefant - ***Jumbo*** *Elephant*

Webpelz, stehend, abwaschbar - *woven fur, standing, surface washable*

SERIE	ART.-NO	PERIOD	PR.	INFO
040504	**1451/12**	1985-1990	1-2	14 cm
	040504	1991-1999	1-2	

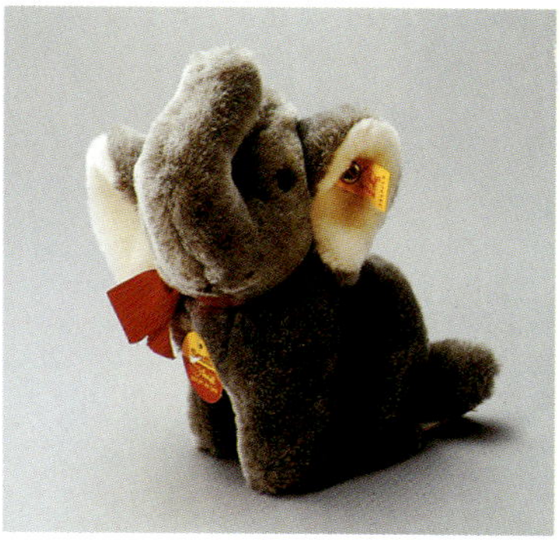

Snuffy Elefant - ***Snuffy*** *Elephant*

Webpelz, waschmaschinenfest - *woven fur, machine washable*

SERIE	ART.-NO	PERIOD	PR.	INFO
077142	**2912/18**	1987-1989	2	18 cm

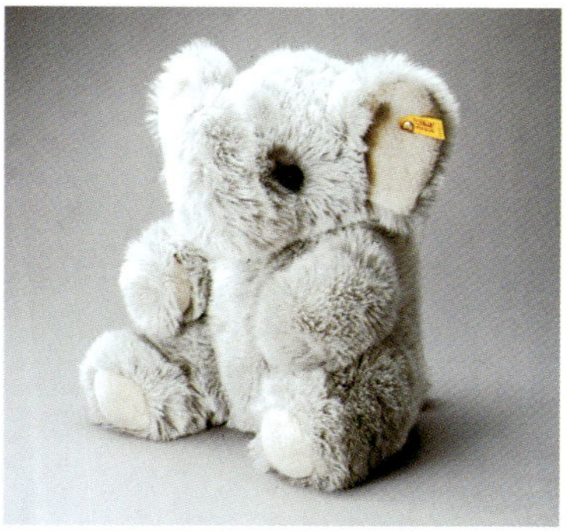

Molly Elefant - *Molly Elephant*

Webpelz, sitzend, abwaschbar - *woven fur, sitting, surface washable*

SERIE	ART.-NO	PERIOD	PR.	INFO
101403	**0333/33**	1988-1990	2	33 cm

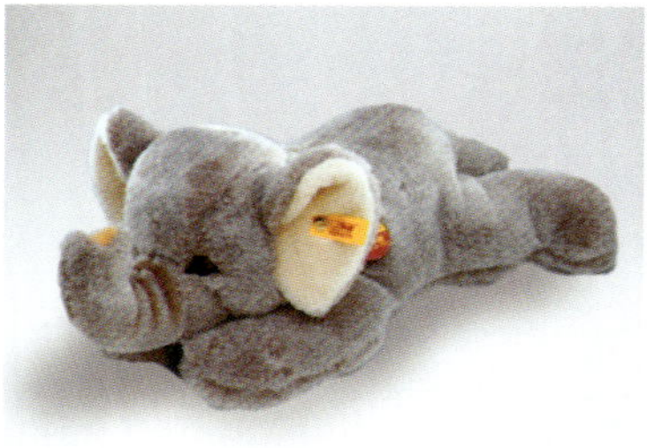

Cosy Elefant - *Cosy Elephant*

Webpelz, liegend, waschmaschinenfest - *woven fur, lying, machine washable*

SERIE	ART.-NO	PERIOD	PR.	INFO
085307	**5340/33**	1988-1990	2	33 cm

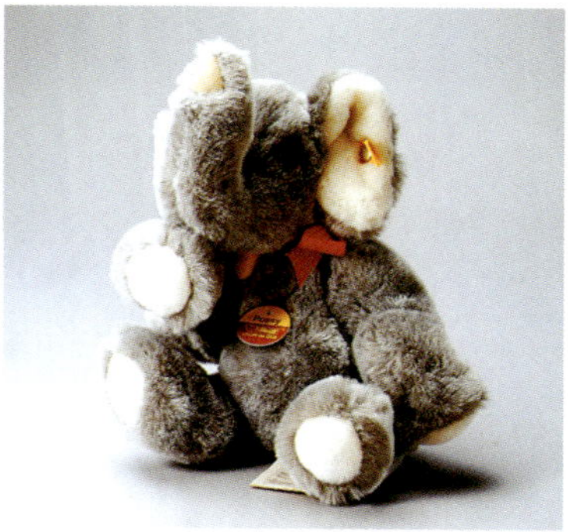

Possy Elefant - ***Possy*** *Elephant*

Webpelz, gegliedert, Pieps-Stimme, waschmaschinenfest - *woven fur, jointed, squeaker, machine washable*

SERIE	ART.-NO	PERIOD	PR.	INFO
081507	**6220/28**	1988-1989	2-3	28 cm

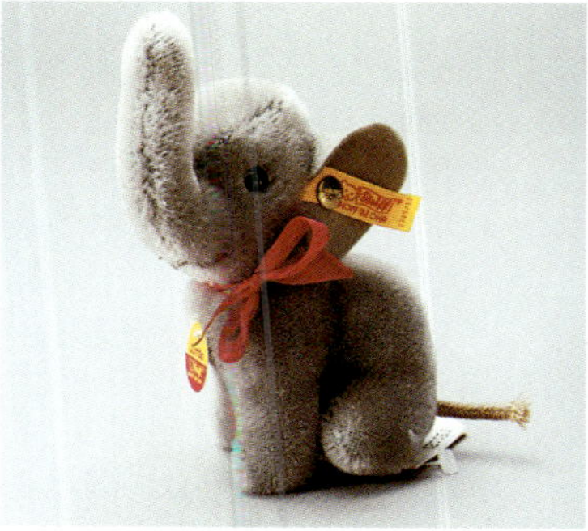

Jumbo Elefant - ***Jumbo*** *Elephant*

Webpelz, grau, sitzend, Kopf drehbar, abwaschbar - *woven fur, grey, sitting, head swivels, surface washable*

SERIE	ART.-NO	PERIOD	PR.	INFO
031106	**1305/09**	1989-1990	1-2	9 cm
	031106	1991-1991	1-2	
031120	**1305/12**	1989-1990	1-2	12 cm
	031120	1991-1992	1-2	

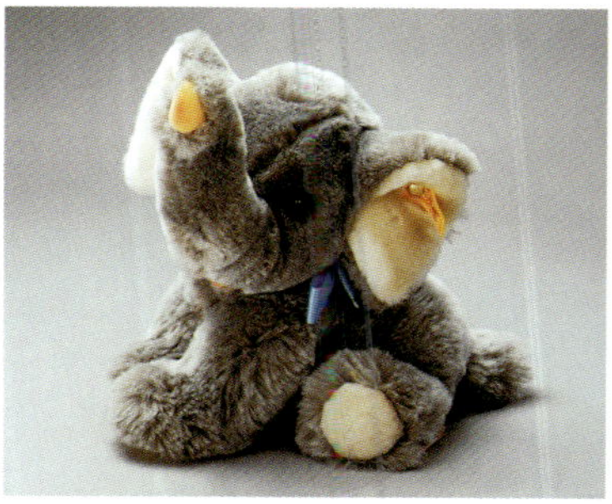

Pummy Elefant - ***Pummy*** *Elephant*

Webpelz, waschmaschinenfest - *woven fur, machine washable*

SERIE	ART.-NO	PERIOD	PR.	INFO
083204	**5040/17**	1989-1990	2-3	18 cm
	083204	1991-1999	2-3	
083228	**5040/21**	1989-1990	2-3	21 cm
	083228	1991-1992	2-3	

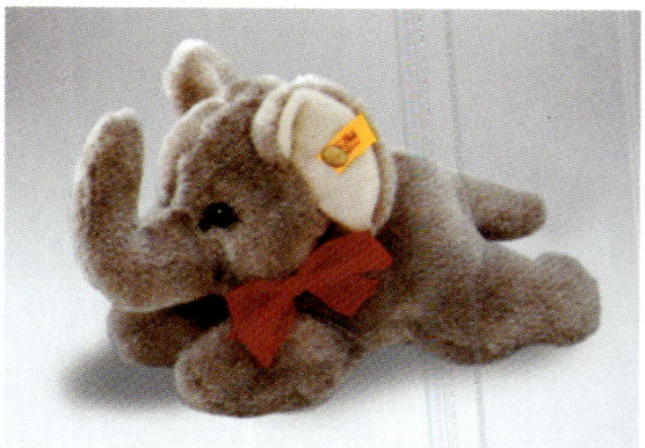

Mini Floppy Elefant - ***Mini Floppy*** *Elephant*

Webpelz, waschmaschinenfest - *woven fur, machine washable*

SERIE	ART.-NO	PERIOD	PR.	INFO
081866	**5655/16**	1989-1990	1	16 cm
	081866	1991-1991	1	

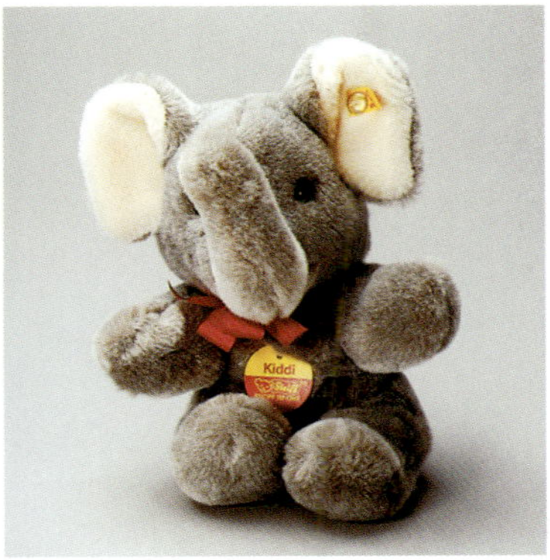

Kiddi Elefant - ***Kiddi** Elephant*

Webpelz, Pieps-Stimme, waschmaschinenfest - *woven fur, squeaker, machine washable*

SERIE	ART.-NO	PERIOD	PR.	INFO
082689	**5706/20**	1989-1990	2	20 cm

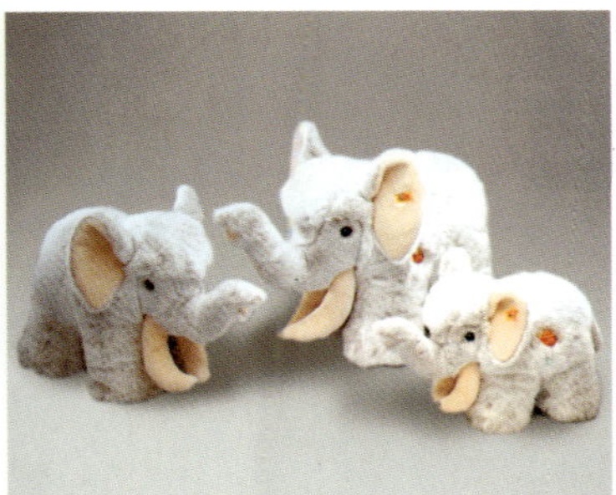

Jumbo Elefant - ***Jumbo** Elephant*

Webpelz, hellgrau, stehend, waschmaschinenfest - *woven fur, light grey, standing, machine washable*

SERIE	ART.-NO	PERIOD	PR.	INFO
062551	**0600/35**	1990-1990	2-3	35 cm
	062551	1991-1992	2-3	
062582	**0600/45**	1990-1990	3	45 cm
	062582	1991-1992	3	
062612	**0600/60**	1990-1990	3	60 cm
	062612	1991-1991	3	

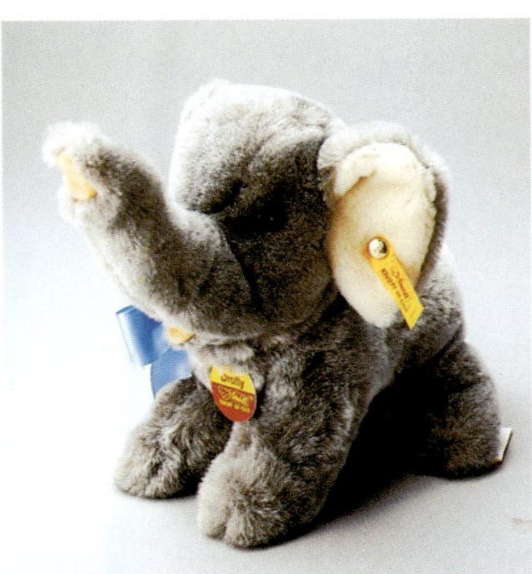

Drolly Elefant - ***Drolly** Elephant*

Webpelz, stehend, waschmaschinenfest - *woven fur, standing, machine washable*

EAN-NO.	PERIOD	PR.	INFO
081408	1991-1998	2	22 cm

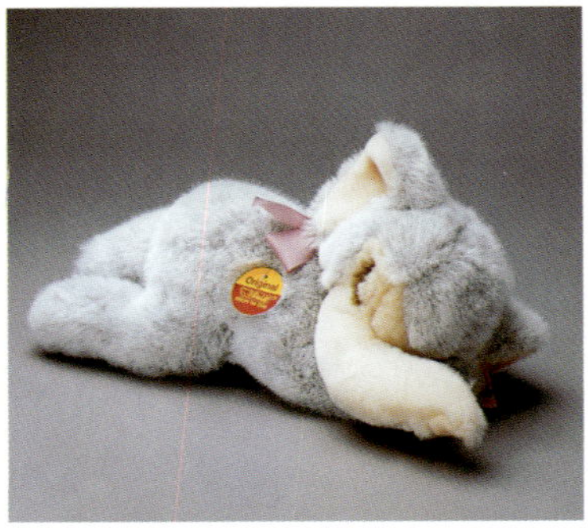

Schlafelefant - *Bedtime Elephant*

Webpelz, waschmaschinenfest - *woven fur, machine washable*

EAN-NO.	PERIOD	PR.	INFO
082559	1991-1993	1	22 cm

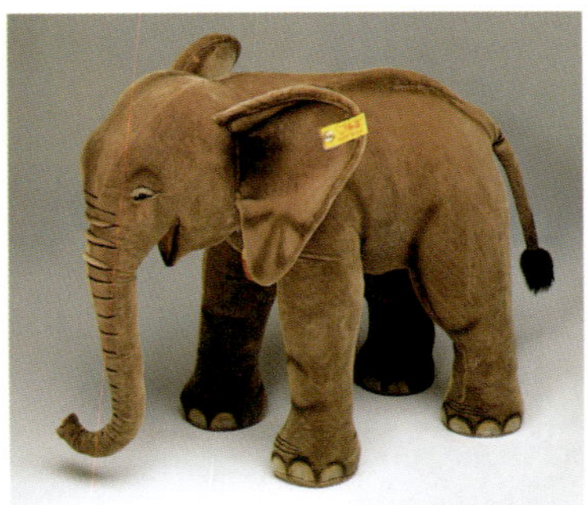

Studio Baby Elefant - *Studio Baby Elephant*

Webpelz, stehend, abwaschbar - *woven fur, standing, surface washable*

EAN-NO.	PERIOD	PR.	INFO
500701	1992-1999	7-8	120 cm

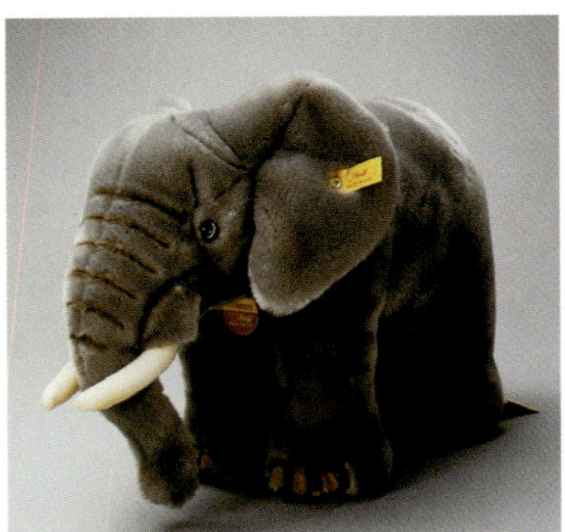

Trampy Elefant - ***Trampy** Elephant*

Webpelz, stehend, waschmaschinenfest - *woven fur, standing, machine washable*

EAN-NO.	PERIOD	PR.	INFO
063367	1993-1996	3	45 cm
063398	1993-1996	3-4	55 cm

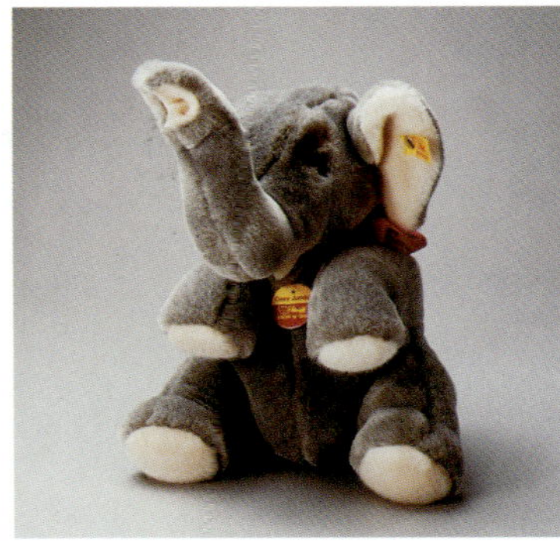

Cosy Jumbo ab 1998 **Cosy** Elefant - ***Cosy Jumbo** from 1998 **Cosy** Elephant*

Webpelz, sitzend, waschmaschinenfest - *woven fur, sitting, machine washable*

EAN-NO.	PERIOD	PR.	INFO
085215	1995-1998	3	25 cm
085239	1994-1998	3	32 cm

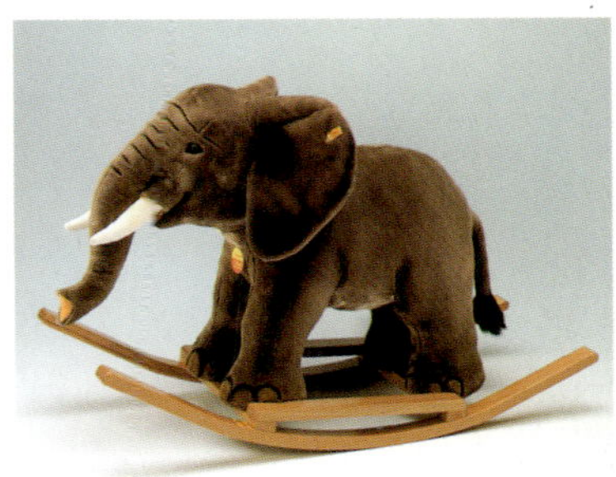

Reit-Elefant - *Riding Elephant*

Webpelz, Holzwippe, abwaschbar - *woven fur, wooden rocker, surface washable*

EAN-NO.	PERIOD	PR.	INFO
480102	1994-1999	5-6	70 cm

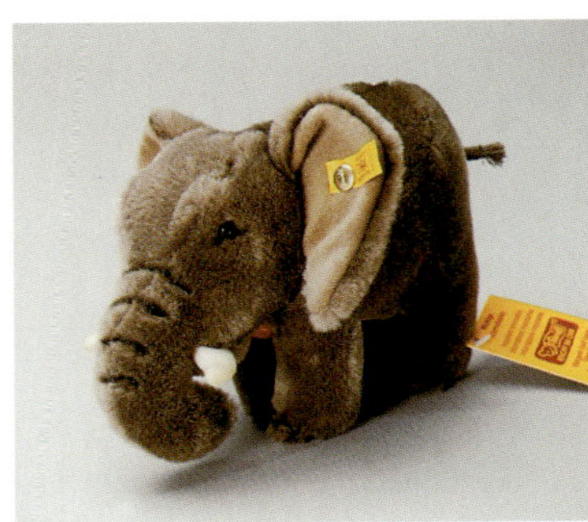

Eli Elefant - ***Eli** Elephant*

Webpelz, stehend, waschmaschinenfest - *woven fur, standing, machine washable*

EAN-NO.	PERIOD	PR.	INFO
040511	1995-1997	2	16 cm

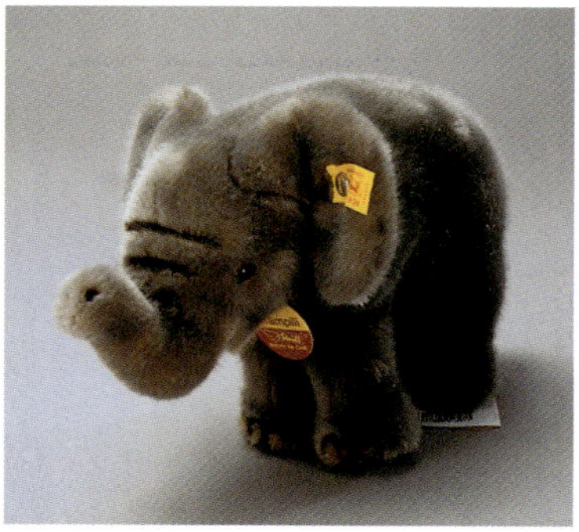

Trampili Baby Elefant - ***Trampili*** *Baby Elephant*

Webpelz, stehend, waschmaschinenfest - *woven fur, standing, machine washable*

EAN-No.	Period	Pr.	Info
063411	1995-1998	2-3	25 cm

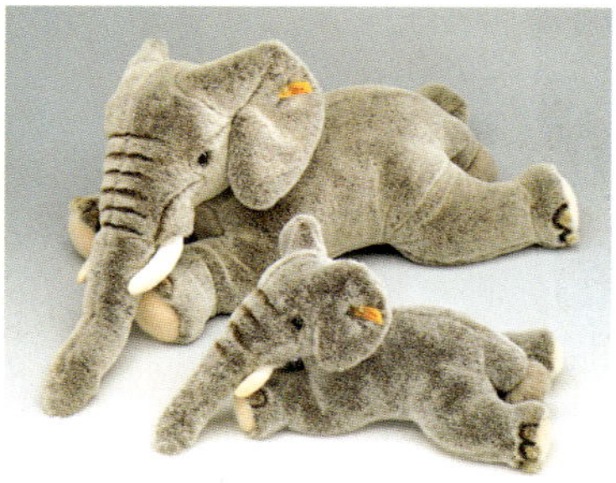

Molly Elefant - *Molly Elephant*

Webpelz, grau, liegend, waschmaschinenfest - *woven fur, grey, lying, machine washable*

EAN-No.	Period	Pr.	Info
101380	1995-1997	3	32 cm
101397	1995-1996	3-4	70 cm

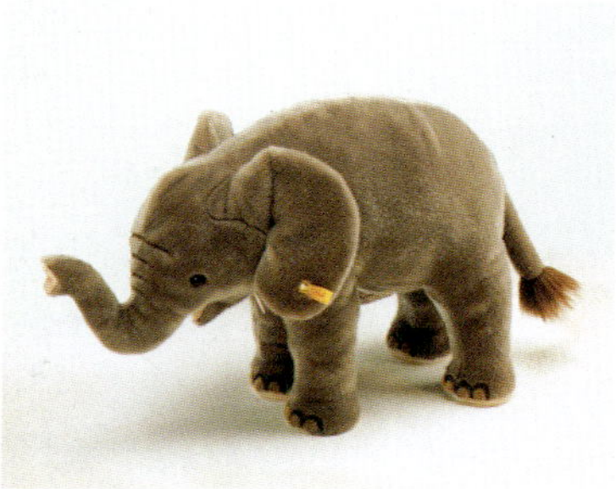

Baby Elefant - *Baby Elephant*

Studiotier, Webpelz, stehend, abwaschbar - *studio animal, woven fur, standing, surface washable*

EAN-No.	Period	Pr.	Info
500732	1995-1998	4	50 cm

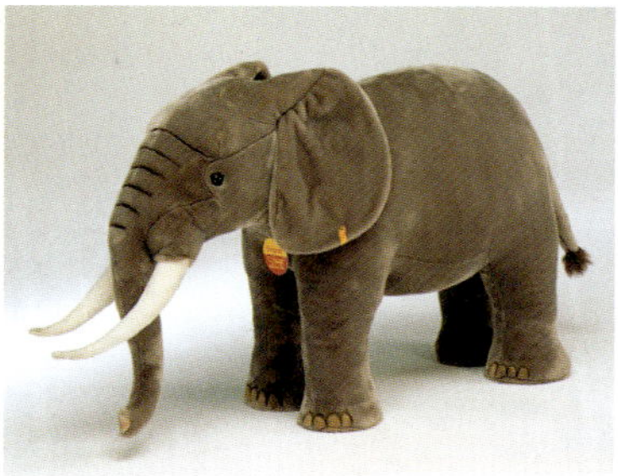

Elefant - *Elephant*

Studiotier, Webpelz, stehend, abwaschbar - *studio animal, woven fur, standing, surface washable*

EAN-No.	Period	Pr.	Info
500756	1995-1999	6-7	100 cm

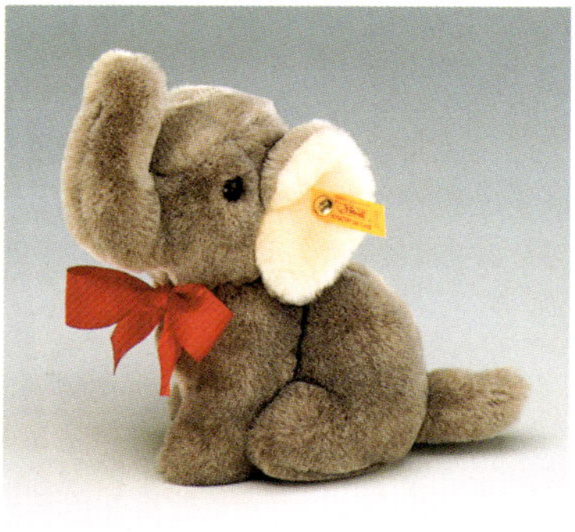

Snuffi Elefant - ***Snuffi*** *Elephant*

Webpelz, sitzend, waschmaschinenfest - *woven fur, sitting, machine washable*

EAN-No.	Period	Pr.	Info
077159	1996-1999	2	16 cm

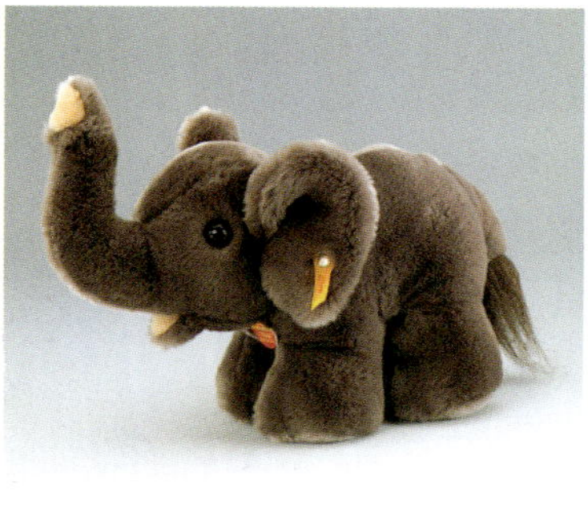

Elefant - *Elephant*

Webpelz, stehend, waschmaschinenfest - *woven fur, standing, machine washable*

EAN-No.	Period	Pr.	Info
085086	1997-1999	2-3	30 cm
085093	1997-1998	3	40 cm

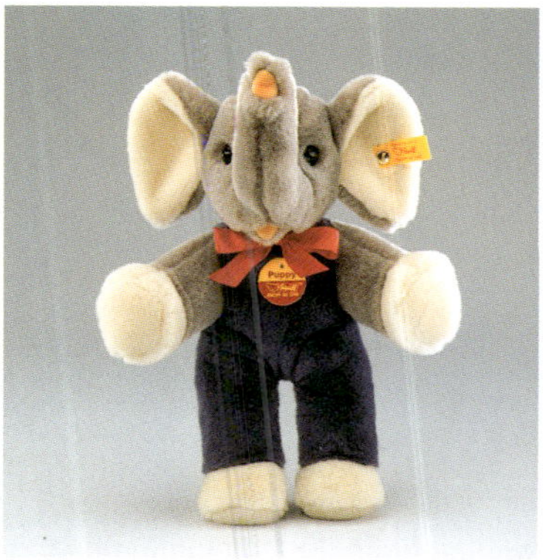

Puppy Elefant - ***Puppy*** *Elephant*

Webpelz, dunkelblau/grau, Pieps-Stimme, waschmaschinenfest - *woven fur, dark blue / grey, squeaker, machine washable*

EAN-No.	Period	Pr.	Info
124631	1997-1998	2	28 cm

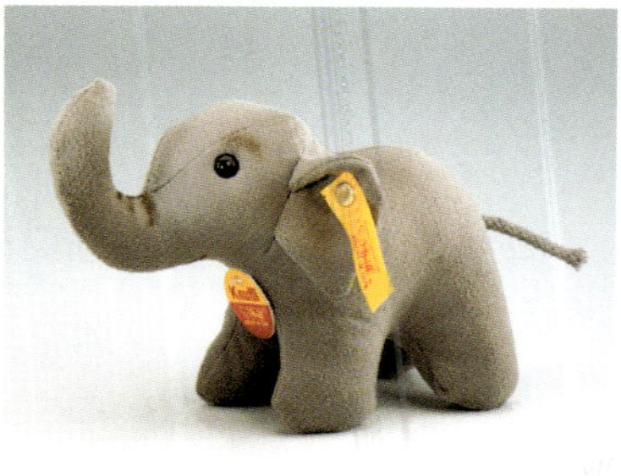

Knuffi Elefant - ***Knuffi*** *Elephant*

Microfaser-Vlies, grau, handwaschbar - *micro fibre fleece, grey, surface washable*

EAN-No.	Period	Pr.	Info
067716	1997-1997	1-2	10 cm

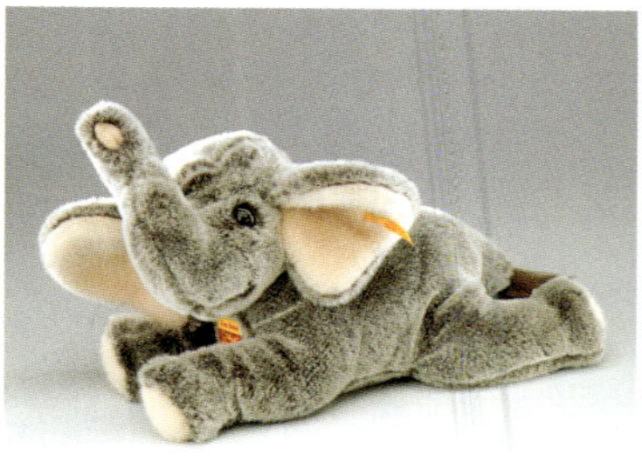

Cosy Elefant - ***Cosy*** *Elephant*

Webpelz, liegend, waschmaschinenfest - *woven fur, lying, machine washable*

EAN-No.	Period	Pr.	Info
085253	1998-1999	2-3	35 cm

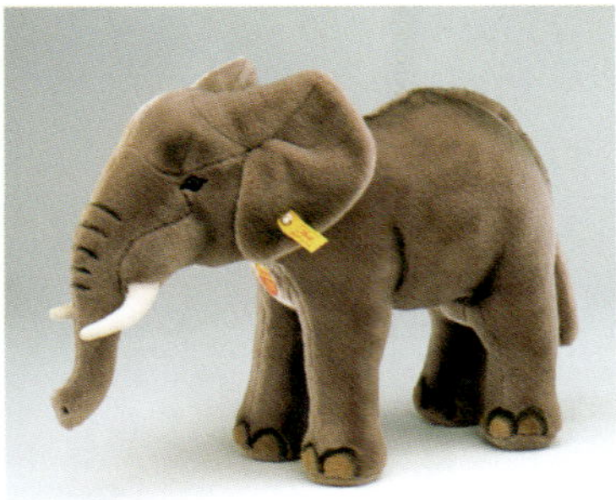

Elefant - *Elephant*

Webpelz, grau, stehend, abwaschbar - *woven fur, grey, standing, surface washable*

EAN-No.	Period	Pr.	Info
062513	1999-1999	3	40 cm

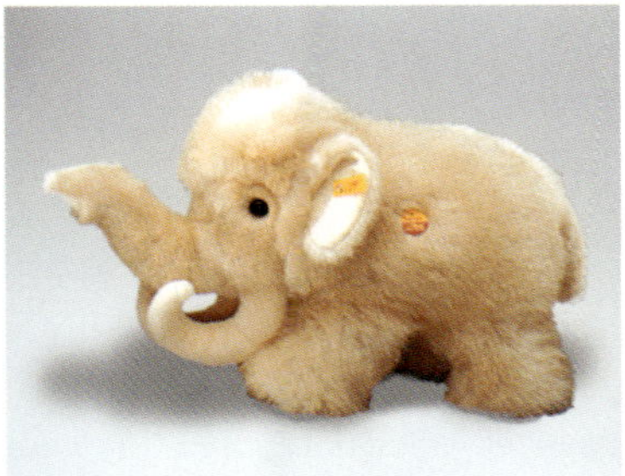

Trampy Mammut - ***Trampy*** *Mammoth*

Webpelz, creme, stehend, waschmaschinenfest - *woven fur, cream, standing, machine washable*

Serie	Art.-No	Period	Pr.	Info
062476	**0595/35**	1990-1990	2-3	35 cm
	062476	1991-1991	2-3	
062483	**0595/50**	1990-1990	3	50 cm
	062483	1991-1991	3	

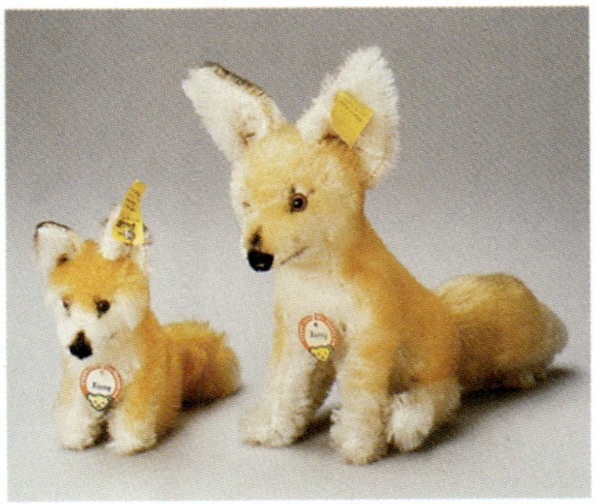

Wuestenfuchs **Xorry** - *Desert Fox* ***Xorry***

Mohairpluesch, sitzend, lange Ohren, naturfarben - *mohair, sitting, long ears, natural color*

Serie	Art.-No	Period	Pr.	Info
28	**3312**	1957-1958	3-4	12 cm
281	**3312,00**	1959-1962	3	
152	**3312,00**	1965-1967	3	
	1520/12	1968-1970	3	

28	**3317**	1957-1958	4	17 cm
281	**3317,00**	1959-1962	3-4	
152	**3317,00**	1966-1967	3-4	
	1520/17	1968-1970	3-4	

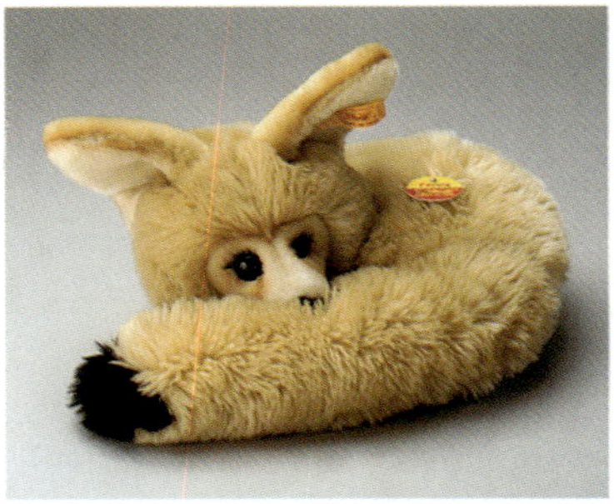

Fenny Wuestenfuchs - ***Fenny*** *Desert Fox*

Webpelz, creme, liegend, waschmaschinenfest - *woven fur, cream, lying, machine washable*

Serie	Art.-No	Period	Pr.	Info
070013	**1543/25**	1990-1990	2	25 cm
	070013	1991-1993	2	

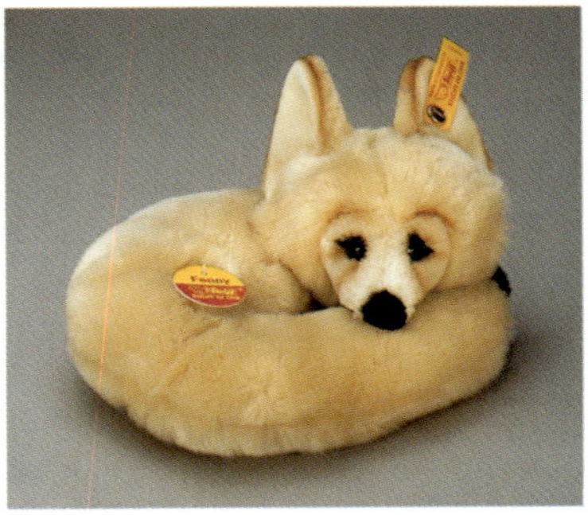

Fenny Wuestenfuchs - ***Fenny*** *Desert Fox*

Webpelz, creme, liegend, waschmaschinenfest - *woven fur, cream, lying, machine washable*

EAN-No.	Period	Pr.	Info
070006	1992-1996	2	20 cm

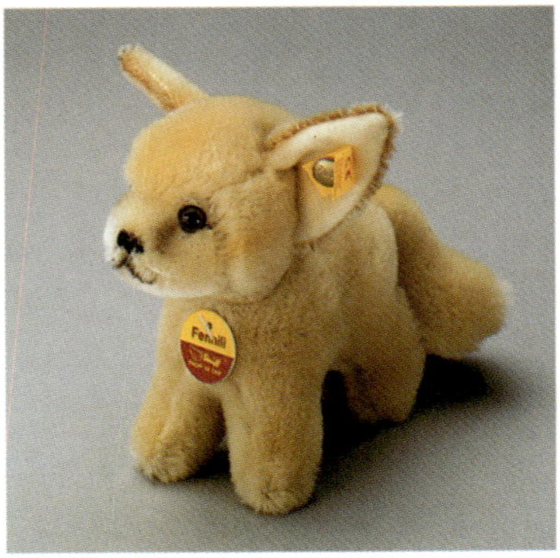

Fennili Wuestenfuchs - ***Fennili*** *Desert Fox*

Webpelz, hellbeige, stehend, handwaschbar - *woven fur, light beige, standing, hand washable*

EAN-No.	Period	Pr.	Info
045073	1995-1996	1-2	12 cm

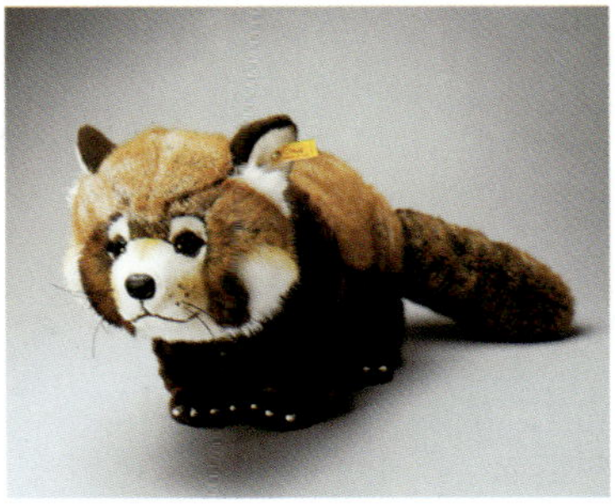

Katzenbaer - *Red Panda Bear*

Webpelz, roetlich gespitzt, stehend, abwaschbar - *woven fur, reddish tipped, standing, surface washable*

EAN-No.	Period	Pr.	Info
120039	1995-1996	4	60 cm

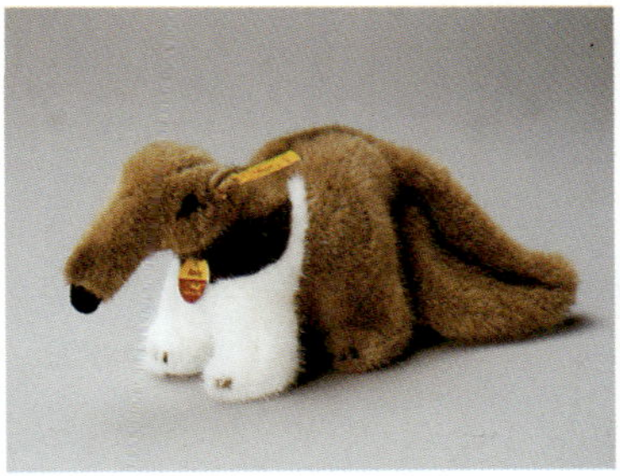

Andy Ameisenbaer - ***Andy*** *Ant Eater*

Webpelz, stehend, waschmaschinenfest - *woven fur, standing, machine washable*

EAN-No.	Period	Pr.	Info
040955	1994-1996	2	16 cm

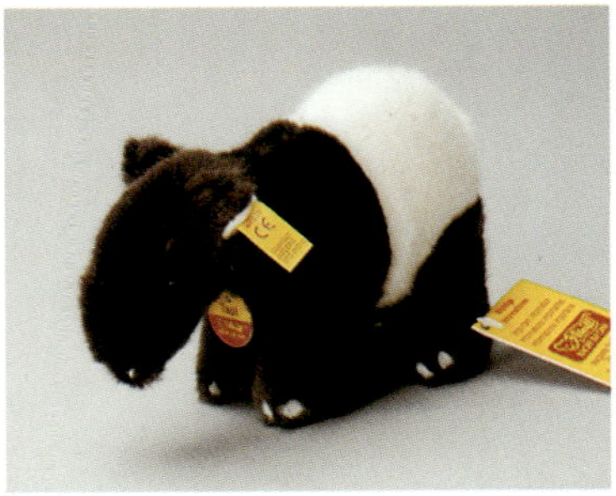

Tapi Tapir

Webpelz, stehend, waschmaschinenfest - *woven fur, standing, hand washable*

EAN-No.	Period	Pr.	Info
040986	1994-1995	2	16 cm

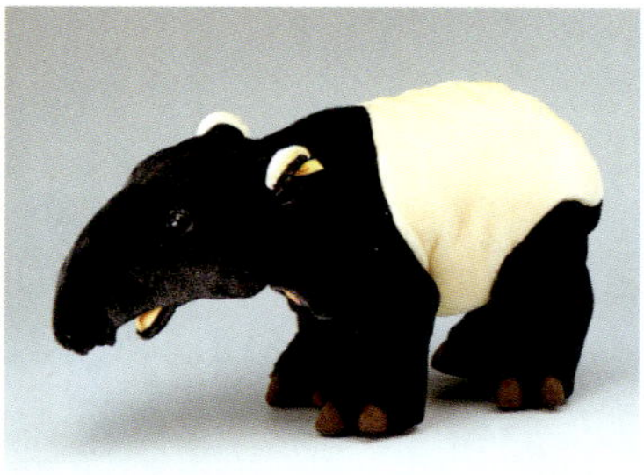

Tapi Tapir

Webpelz, stehend, handwaschbar - *woven fur, standing, machine washable*

EAN-No.	Period	Pr.	Info
068904	1995-1995	3	50 cm

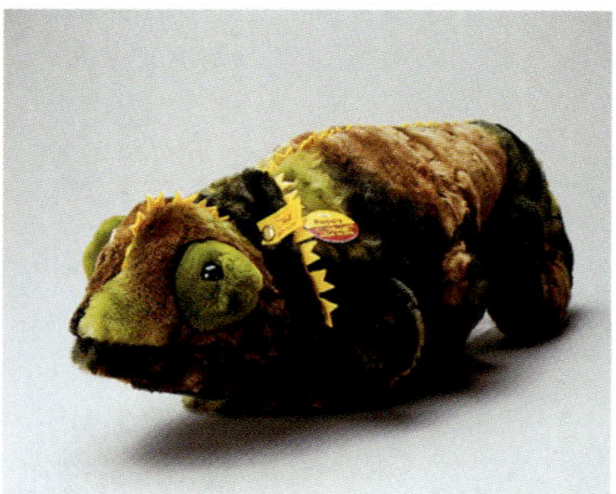

Poppy Chamaeleon - ***Poppy** Chameleon*

Webpelz, 45 cm, handwaschbar - *woven fur 45 cm, hand washable*

EAN-No.	Period	Pr.	Info
067259	1995-1996	3	rot - *red*
067273	1995-1995	3	gruen - *green*
067297	1995-1995	3	blau - *blue*

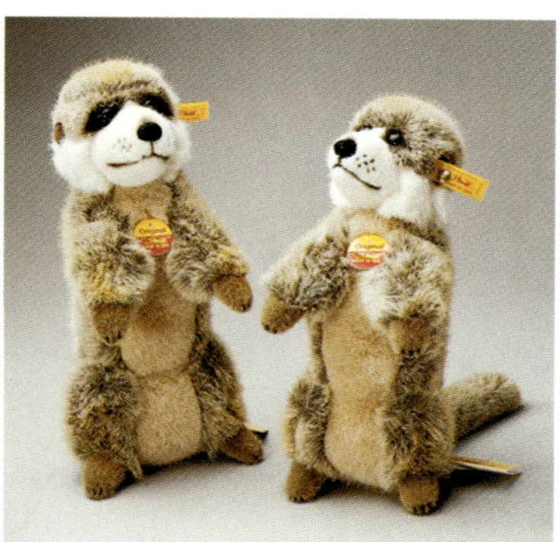

Erdmaennchen - *Siender-Tailed-Mierkat*

Webpelz, grau/beige gespitzt, aufwartend, waschmaschinenfest - *woven fur, grey/beige tipped, sitting up, machine washable*

EAN-No.	Period	Pr.	Info
070464	1995-1999	2-3	28 cm
070457	1995-1996	2-3	32 cm

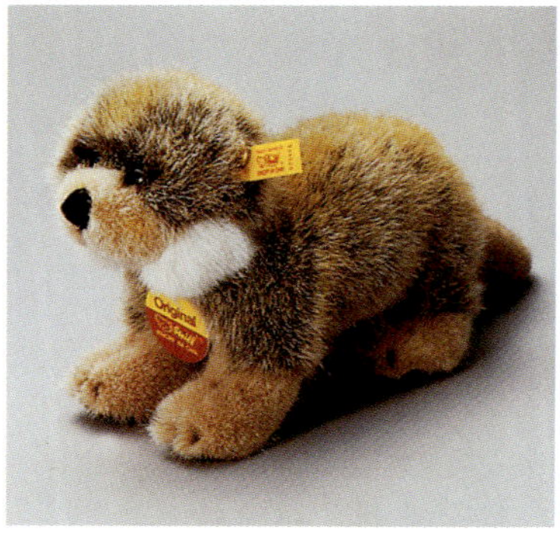

Erdmaennchen Baby - *Siender-Tailed-Mierkat Baby*

Webpelz, grau/beige gespitzt, stehend, waschmaschinenfest - *woven fur, grey/beige tipped, standing, machine washable*

EAN-No.	Period	Pr.	Info
070471	1995-1997	2	18 cm

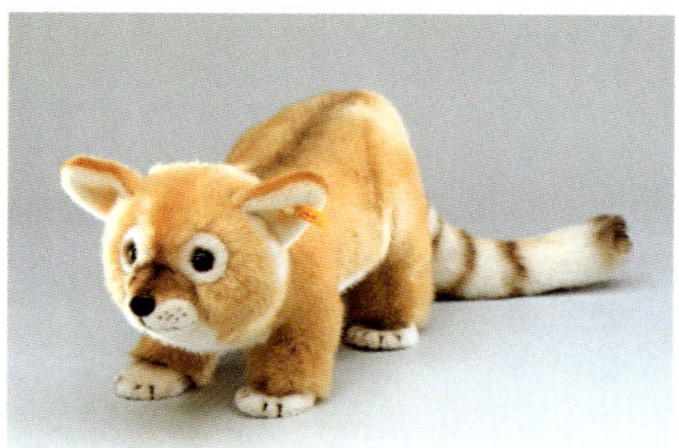

Katzenfrett - *Ringtail*

Webpelz, hellbeige, stehend, handwaschbar - *woven fur, light beige, standing, hand washable*

EAN-No.	Period	Pr.	Info
120046	1995-1996	3	40 cm

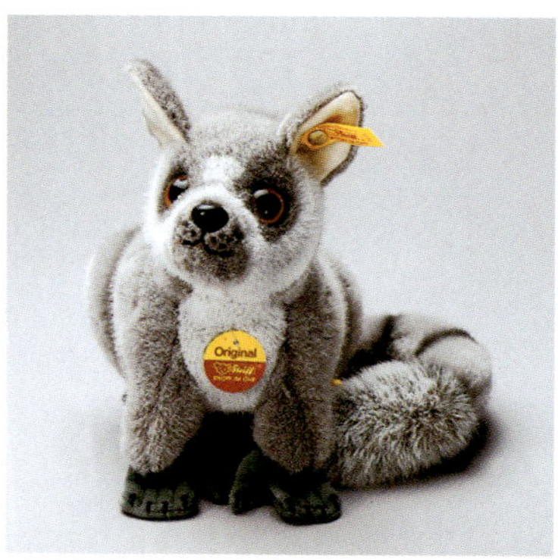

Busch-Baby - *Bush Baby*

Webpelz, sitzend, waschmaschinenfest - *woven fur, sitting, machine washable*

EAN-No.	Period	Pr.	Info
120022	1995-1996	3	20 cm

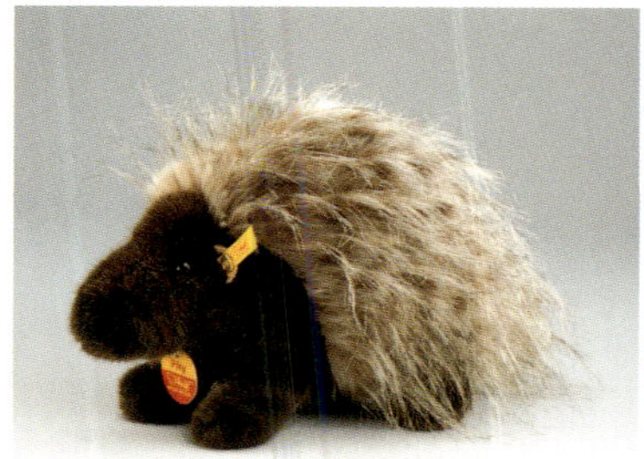

Piky Stachelschwein - ***Piky** Porcupine*

Webpelz, handwaschbar - *woven fur, surface washable*

EAN-No.	Period	Pr.	Info
064968	1997-1998	2-3	28 cm

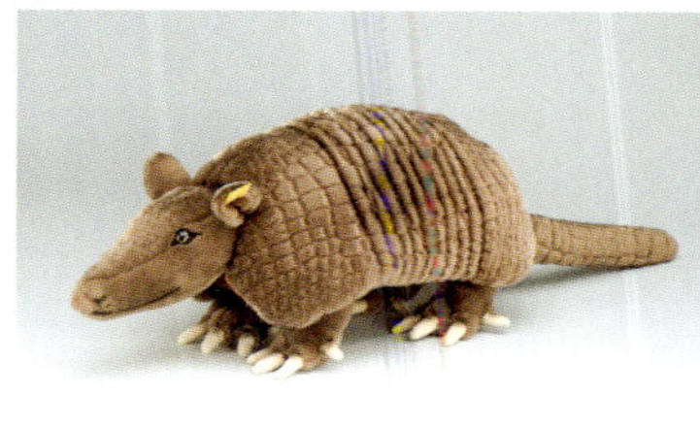

Guerteltier - *Armadillo*

Webpelz, grau, stehend, handwaschbar - *woven fur, grey, standing, hand washable*

EAN-No.	Period	Pr.	Info
120077	1998-1998	3-4	40 cm

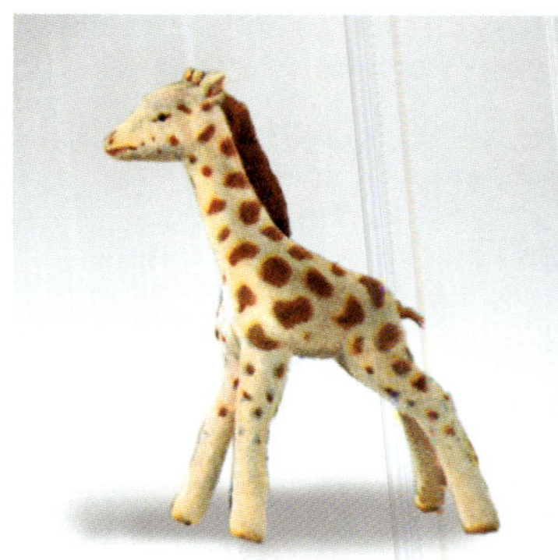

Giraffe

Samt, hellbraun, stehend - *velvet, light brown, standing*

Serie	Art.-No	Period	Pr.	Info
32	**6417,0**	1951-1952	4	17 cm

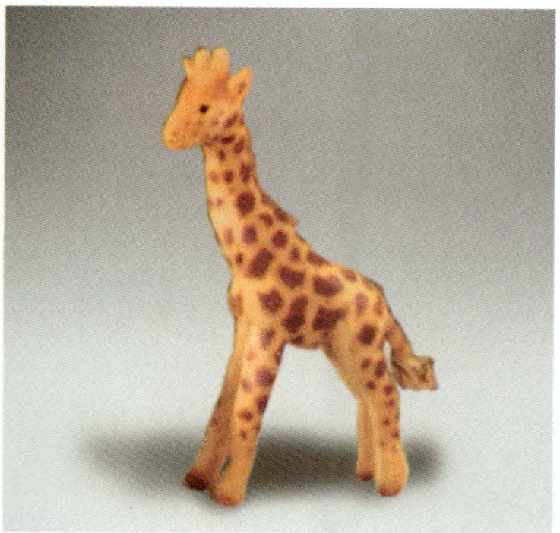

Giraffe

Wollpluesch, sandgelb bemalt, stehend, ohne Raeder - *plush wool, sandy gold with painted markings, standing, without wheels*

SERIE	ART.-NO	PERIOD	PR.	INFO
32	**6528,0**	1949-1953	4-5	28 cm
32	**6535,0**	1951-1953	4-5	35 cm
32	**6550,0**	1952-1953	4-5	50 cm

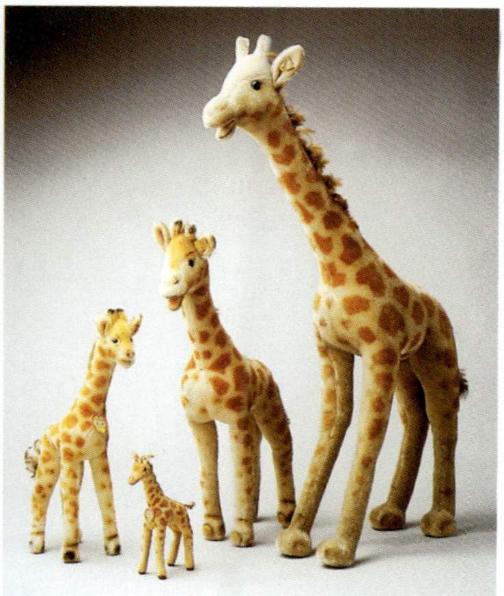

Giraffe

Samt-, ab 28 cm Mohairpluesch, natur bemalt, stehend, ab 35 cm offener Mund, abwaschbar - *velvet, from 28 cm mohair, natural coloring, standing, from 35 cm open mouth, surface washable*

SERIE	ART.-NO	PERIOD	PR.	INFO
32	**6414,0**	1953-1958	3-4	14 cm
320	**6414,00**	1959-1964	3-4	
074	**6414,00**	1965-1967	3-4	
	0750/14	1968-1972	3	
32	**6328,0**	1954-1958	4	28 cm
320	**6328,00**	1959-1964	3-4	
075	**6328,00**	1965-1967	3-4	
	0750/28	1968-1974	3	
32	**6335,0**	1954-1958	4	35 cm
320	**6335,00**	1959-1964	3-4	
075	**6335,00**	1965-1967	3-4	
	0750/35	1968-1974	3-4	
32	**6350,0**	1954-1958	4-5	50 cm
320	**6350,00**	1959-1964	4	
075	**6350,00**	1965-1967	4	
	0750/50	1968-1974	4	

320	**6375,00**	1959-1964	4	75 cm
075	**6375,00**	1965-1967	4	
	0750/75	1968-1974	4	

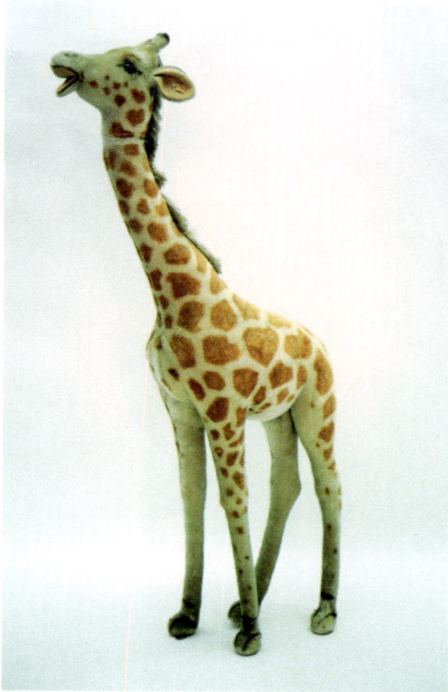

Giraffe

Schautier, Mohair, natur, stehend, abwaschbar, 240 cm bis 1984 & 150 cm bis Anfang 90er-Jahre mit offenem Mund - *display animal, mohair, natural coloring, standing, surface washable, 240 cm until 1984 & 150 cm up to the early 90´s with open mouth*

SERIE	ART.-NO	PERIOD	PR.	INFO
320	**6150,90**	1960-1960	6-7	150 cm
074	**6150,90**	1966-1966	6-7	
502200	**0759/15**	1968-1990	6-7	
	502200	1991-1999	6-7	
320	**6240,90**	1960-1960	7	240 cm
074	**6240,90**	1966-1966	7	
502309	**0759/24**	1968-1990	7	
	502309	1991-1999	7	

ab 1994 255 cm - *from 1994 255 cm*

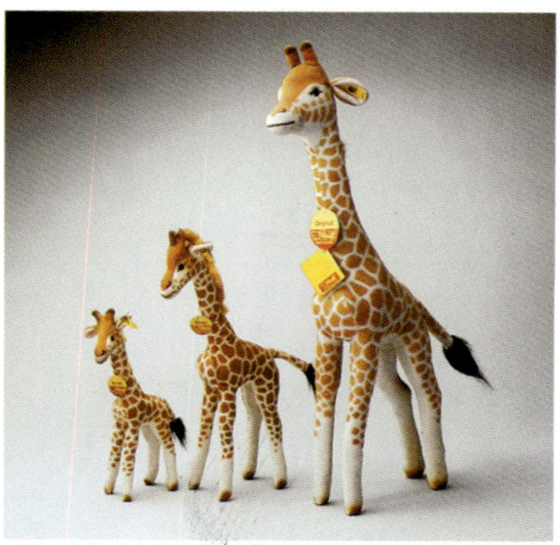

Bendy Giraffe

Trevirasamt, stehend, vollwaschbar - *trevira velvet, standing, fully washable*

SERIE	ART.-NO	PERIOD	PR.	INFO
	0755/28	1975-1985	2-3	28 cm
	0755/40	1975-1985	3	40 cm
	0755/60	1975-1985	3-4	60 cm

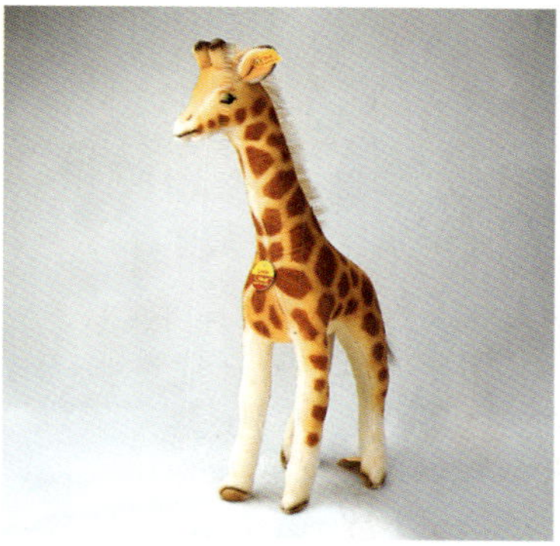

Linda Giraffe

Mohair Webpelz, stehend, abwaschbar - *mohair woven fur, standing, surface washable*

EAN-NO.	PERIOD	PR.	INFO
068072	1994-1999	3	50 cm

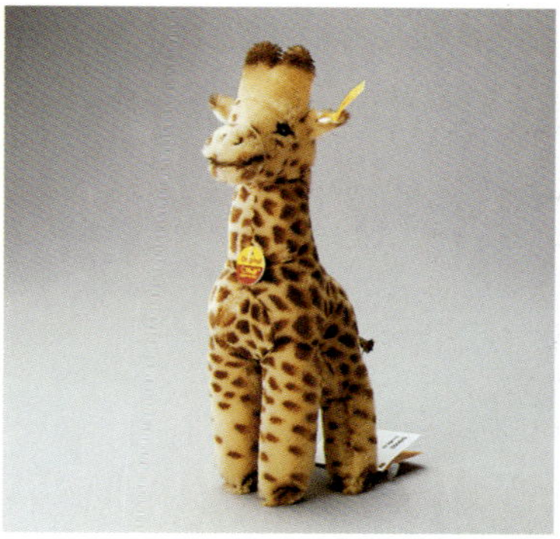

Giraffe

Webpelz, stehend, waschmaschinenfest - *woven fur, standing, machine washable*

EAN-NO.	PERIOD	PR.	INFO
042003	1995-1998	2	23 cm

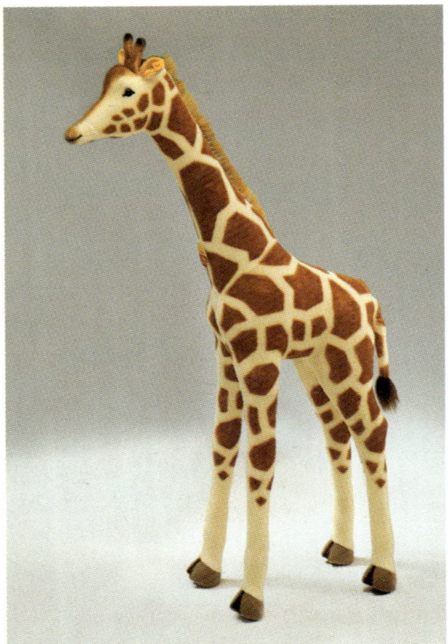

Studio Giraffe

Mohair Webpelz, stehend, abwaschbar - *mohair woven fur, standing, surface washable*

EAN-No.	Period	Pr.	Info
502187	1995-1999	6	110 cm

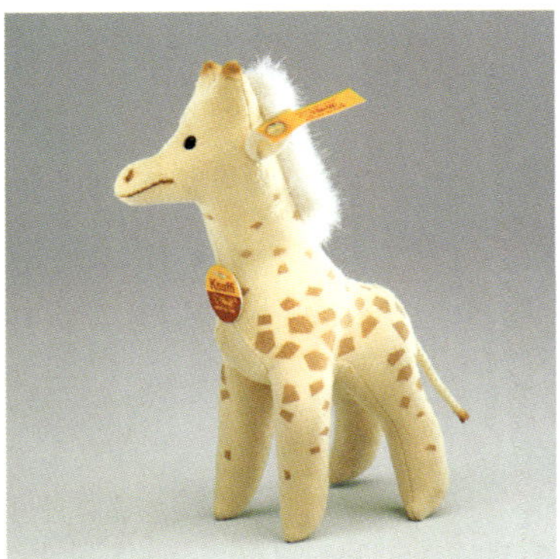

Knuffi Giraffe

Microfaser-Vlies, beige/braun gefleckt, handwaschbar - *micro fibre fleece, beige/ brown spotted, hand washable*

EAN-No.	Period	Pr.	Info
067723	1997-1997	1-2	15 cm

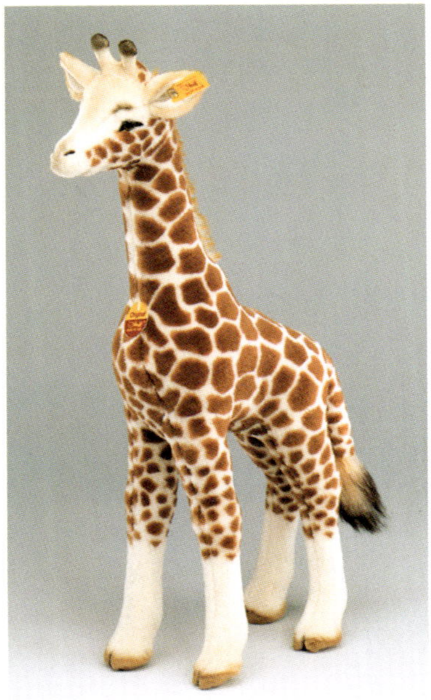

Giraffe

Webpelz, stehend, abwaschbar - *woven fur, standing, surface washable*

EAN-No.	Period	Pr.	Info
068089	1999-1999	3	50 cm

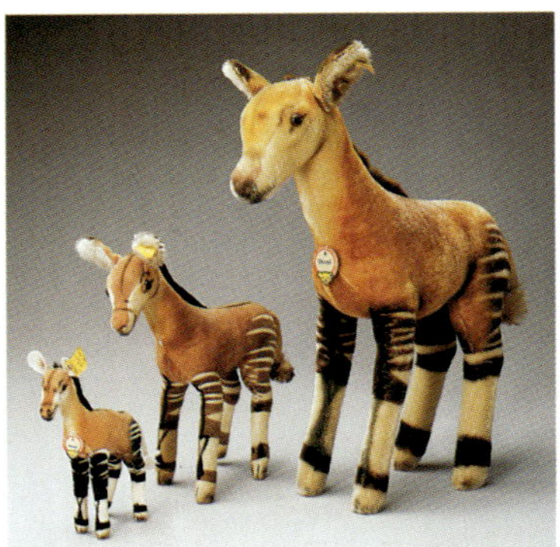

Okapi

Samt, 43 cm Mohair, braun, Beine schwarz/ weiss, stehend - *velvet, 43 cm mohair, brown, legs are black & white, standing*

Serie	Art.-No	Period	Pr.	Info
32a	**6414,0**	1958-1958	3-4	14 cm
324	**6414,00**	1959-1964	3-4	
077	**6414,00**	1965-1967	3-4	
	0770/14	1968-1970	3	
32a	**6428,0**	1958-1958	4	28 cm
324	**6428,00**	1959-1964	4	
077	**6428,00**	1965-1967	4	
	0770/28	1968-1970	3-4	
32a	**6343,0**	1958-1958	5	43 cm
324	**6343,00**	1959-1964	4-5	
077	**6343,00**	1965-1965	4-5	

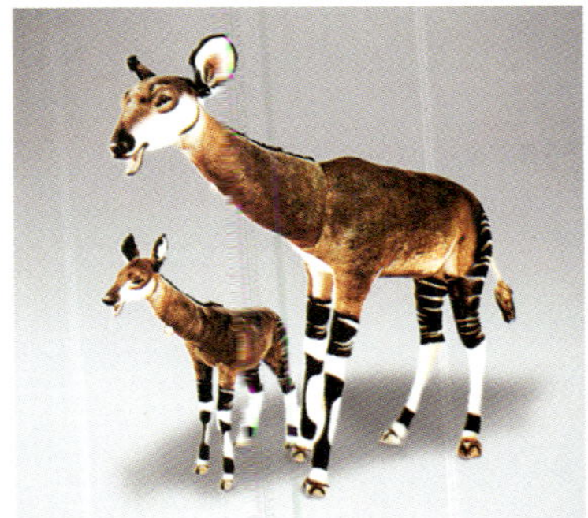

Okapi

Schautiere, Mohair, stehend - *display animals, mohair, standing*

Serie	Art.-No	Period	Pr.	Info
324	**1120,90**	1960-1960	6	120 cm
	0779/12	1967-1967	6	
324	**1200,90**	1960-1960	7	200 cm
	0779/20	1967-1967	7	

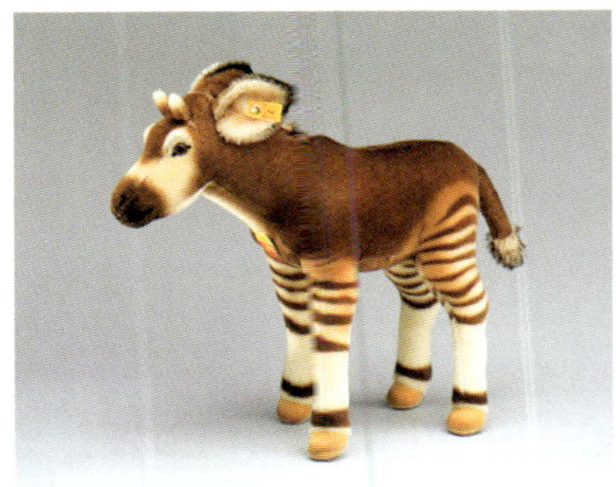

Kiwu Okapi

Mohair Webpelz, stehend, abwaschbar - *mohair woven fur, standing, surface washable*

EAN-No.	Period	Pr.	Info
067709	1995-1995	3	35 cm

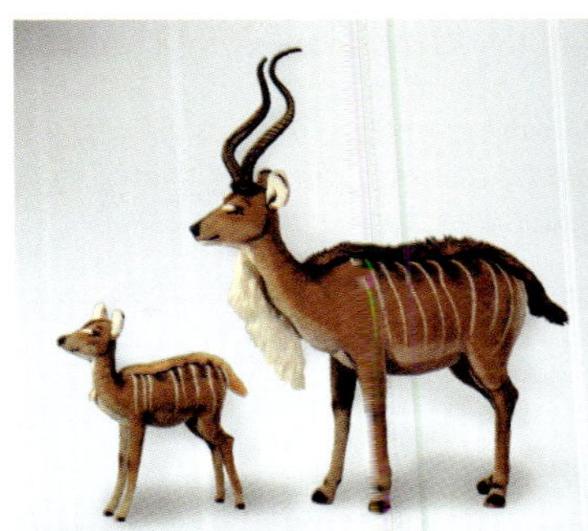

Kudu

Schautiere, braun, weisse Streifen, stehend - *display animals, brown, white striped, standing*

Serie	Art.-No	Period	Pr.	Info
	1279/10	1967-1967	6	100 cm
	1279/16	1967-1967	5-7	160 cm

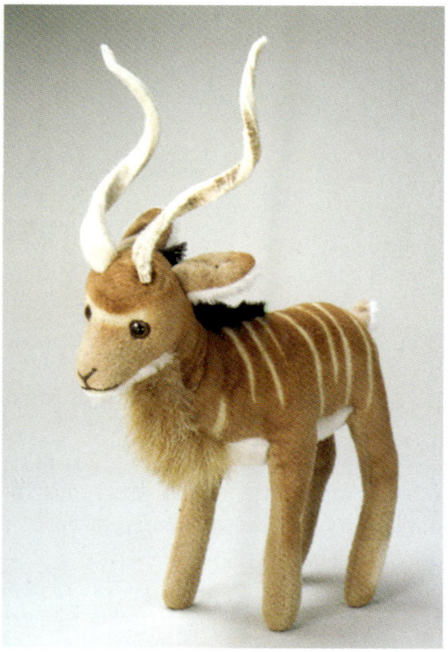

Kudu

Trevirasamt, braun, weisse Streifen, stehend, Filzhoerner, aus Sonderserie fuer Schaustuecke - *trevira velvet, brown, white striped, standing, felt horns, from special series for display animals*

EAN-No.	Period	Pr.	Info
	1969-1969	4-5	28 cm

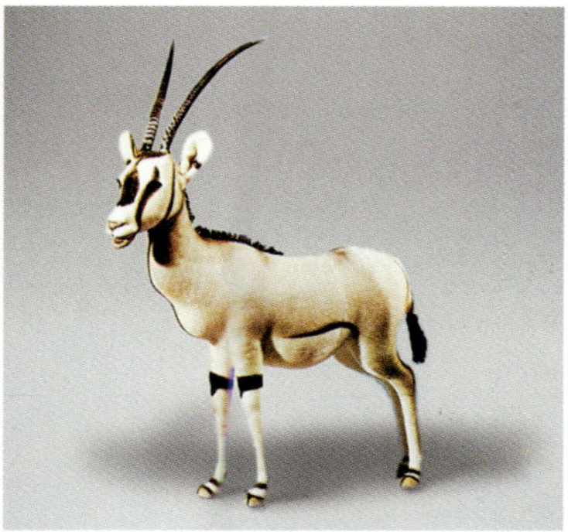

Antilope - *Antelope*

Schautier, stehend - *display animal, standing*

Serie	Art.-No	Period	Pr.	Info
326	**1150,90**	1960-1960	6-7	150 cm
	1259/15	1967-1967	6-7	

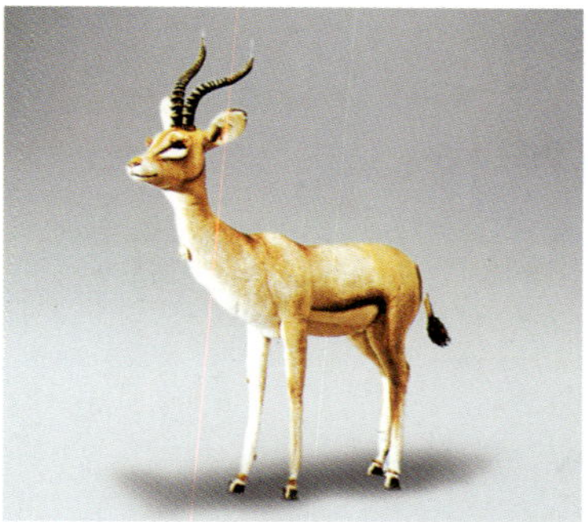

Gazelle

Schautier, stehend - *display animal, standing*

Serie	Art.-No	Period	Pr.	Info
327	**1120,90**	1960-1960	6	120 cm
	1269/12	1967-1967	6	

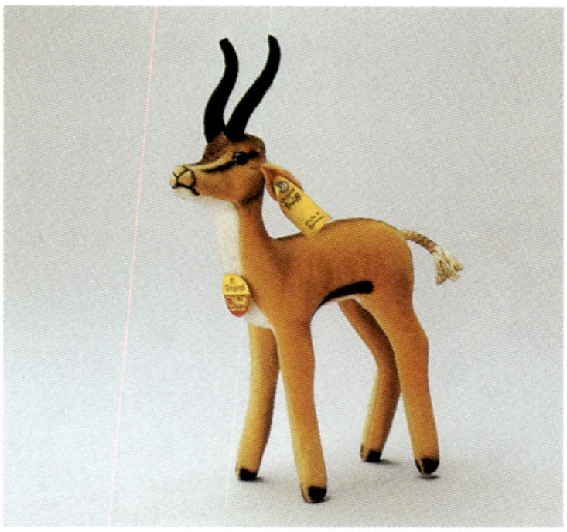

Gazelle

Trevira-Samt, Kordelschwanz, stehend, ohne Katalognachweis - *trevira velvet, tail made of braided cord, standing, no catalog information available*

Serie	Art.-No	Period	Pr.	Info
	1269/02	1970-1970	3-4	20 cm

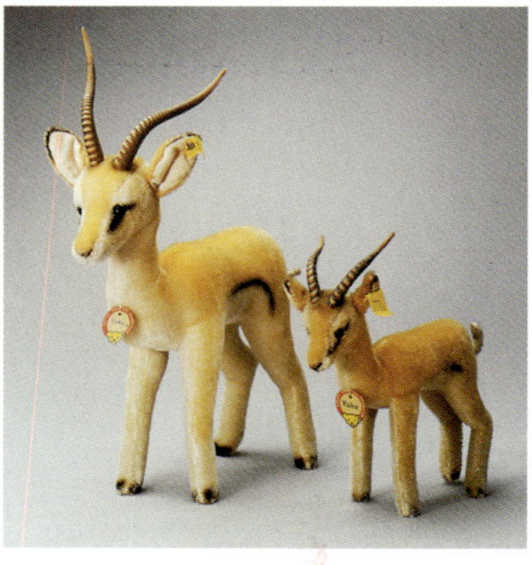

Springbock **Yuku** - *Pronghorn Antelope* ***Yuku***

Mohair, sandfarben mit schwarz, stehend - *mohair, tawny colored with black markings, standing*

Serie	Art.-No	Period	Pr.	Info
606	**1322,00**	1962-1963	4-5	22 cm
606	**1335,00**	1962-1963	5	35 cm

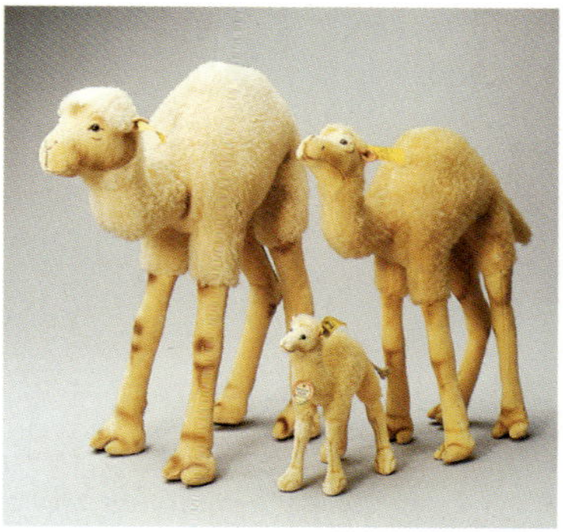

Dromedar - *Dromedary*

Wollpluesch 14 & 17 cm mit Kordelschwanz, hellbraun, stehend - *plush wool, 14 & 17 cm with braided cord tail, light brown, standing*

Serie	Art.-No	Period	Pr.	Info
42	**1514,0**	1953-1958	3-4	14 cm
420	**1514,00**	1959-1964	3	
060	**1514,00**	1965-1967	3	
	0600/14	1968-1969	3	
42	**1517,0**	1952-1952	5	17 cm
42	**1528,0**	1950-1958	4-5	28 cm
420	**1528,00**	1959-1962	4	
060	**1528,00**	1966-1967	4	
	0600/28	1968-1969	4	
42	**1535,0**	1950-1958	4-5	35 cm
420	**1535,00**	1959-1962	4-5	

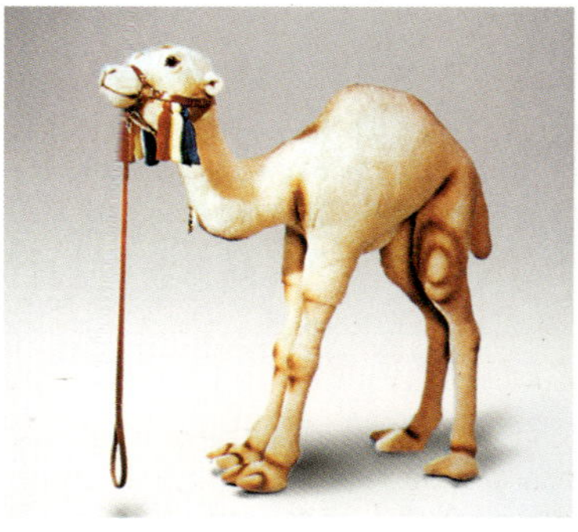

Dromedar - *Dromedary*

Schautier, Wollpluesch, stehend - *display animal, plush wool, standing*

Serie	Art.-No	Period	Pr.	Info
420	**1580,90**	1960-1960	5-6	80 cm
	0609/08	1967-1967	5-6	
	0609/10	1967-1967	6	100 cm

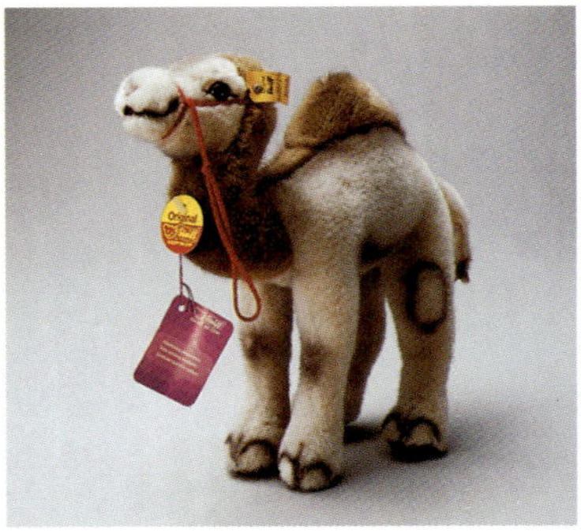

Dromedar - *Dromedary*

Nerzimitation, ab 1978 Synthetik-Webpelz, stehend, abwaschbar - *imitation mink, from 1978 synthetic woven fur, standing, surface washable*

SERIE	ART.-NO	PERIOD	PR.	INFO
	0600/24	1977-1979	2-3	24 cm
	0600/32	1977-1980	2-3	32 cm

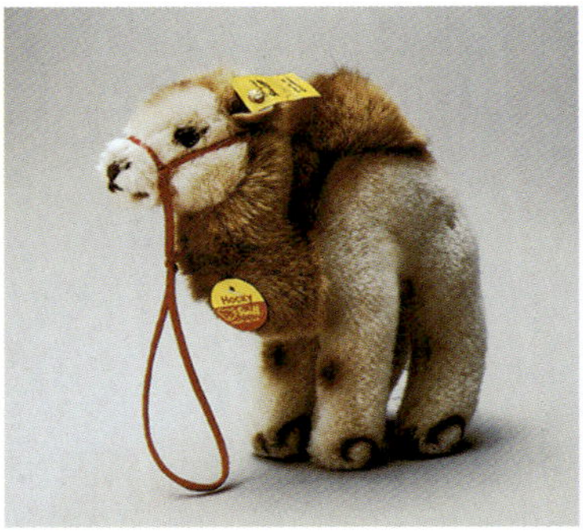

Hocky Dromedar - ***Hocky*** *Dromedary*

Nerzimitation, ab 1978 Synthetik-Webpelz, stehend, abwaschbar - *imitation mink, from 1978 synthetic woven fur, standing, surface washable*

SERIE	ART.-NO	PERIOD	PR.	INFO
	1453/14	1977-1983	1-2	14 cm

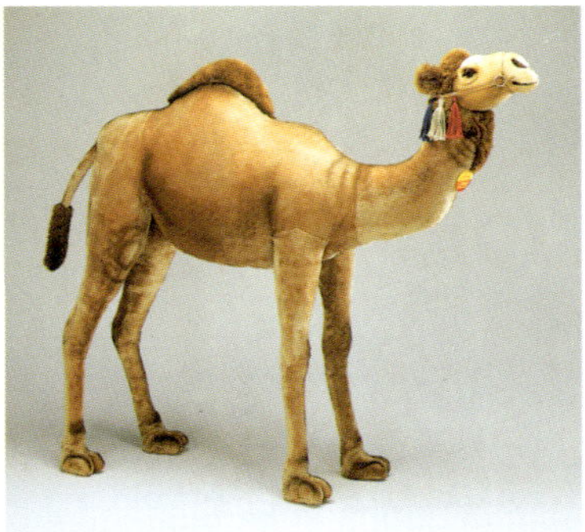

Dromedar - *Dromedary*

Studio-Tier, Dralonpluesch, stehend, abwaschbar - *studio animal, dralon, standing, surface washable*

SERIE	ART.-NO	PERIOD	PR.	INFO
502101	**0609/16**	1978-1990	7-8	160 cm
	502101	1991-1999	7-8	

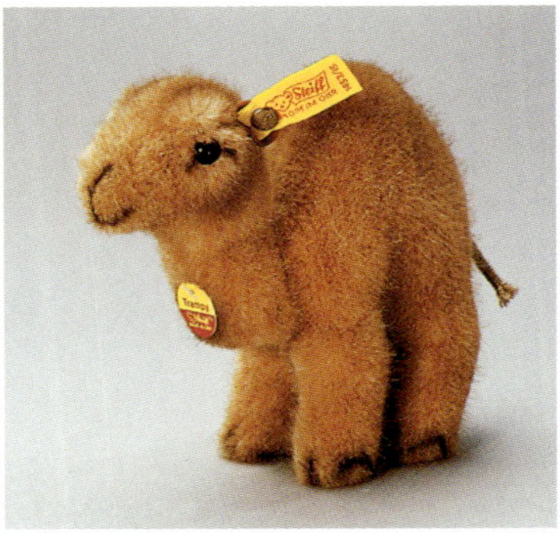

Trampy Dromedar - ***Trampy*** *Dromedary*

Webpelz, abwaschbar - *woven fur, surface washable*

SERIE	ART.-NO	PERIOD	PR.	INFO
040603	**1453/15**	1985-1988	1-2	15 cm

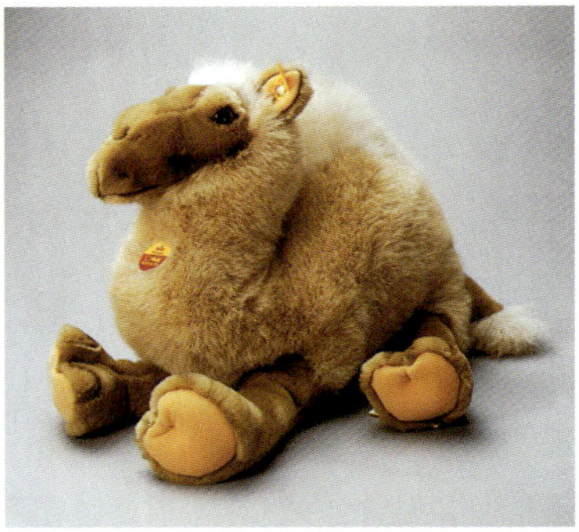

Molly Dromedar - ***Molly Dromedary***

Webpelz, liegend, waschmaschinenfest - *woven fur, lying, machine washable*

EAN-NO.	PERIOD	PR.	INFO
104091	1991-1996	3	40 cm

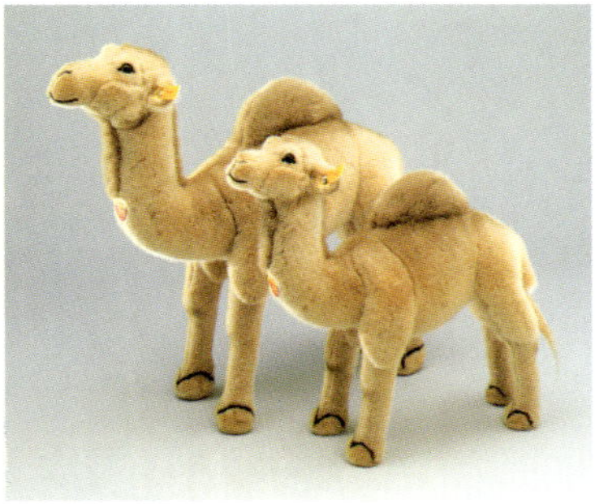

Hocky Dromedar - ***Hocky*** *Dromedary*

Webpelz, stehend, handwaschbar - *woven fur, standing, hand washable*

EAN-NO.	PERIOD	PR.	INFO
066900	1994-1999	3	35 cm
066924	1994-1999	3-4	50 cm

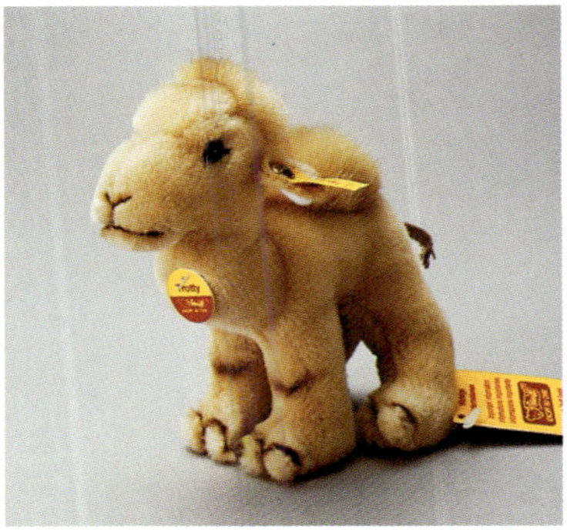

Trotty Dromedar - ***Trotty*** *Dromedary*

Webpelz, hellbeige, stehend, waschmaschinenfest - *woven fur, light beige, standing, machine washable*

EAN-NO.	PERIOD	PR.	INFO
040610	1995-1999	2	14 cm

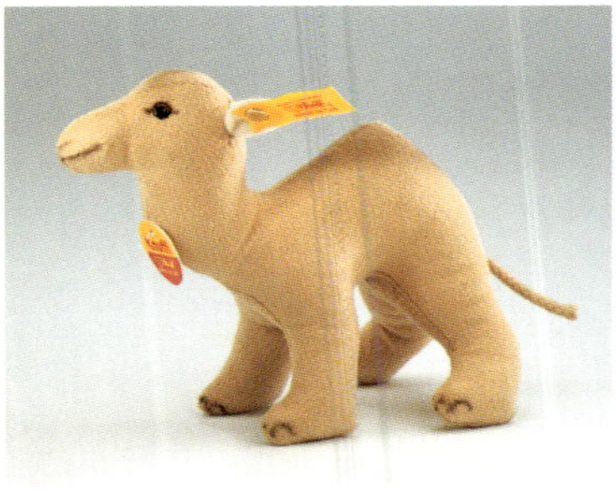

Knuffi Dromedar - ***Knuffi*** *Dromedary*

Microfaser-Vlies, beige, handwaschbar - *micro fibre fleece, beige, hand washable*

EAN-NO.	PERIOD	PR.	INFO
067761	1997-1997	1-2	12 cm

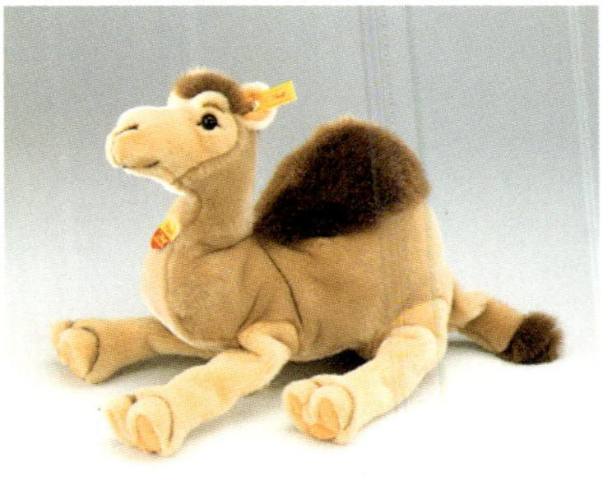

Poppy Dromedar - ***Poppy*** *Dromedary*

Webpelz, beige, waschmaschinenfest - *woven fur, beige, machine washable*

EAN-NO.	PERIOD	PR.	INFO
124136	1998-1998	3	35 cm

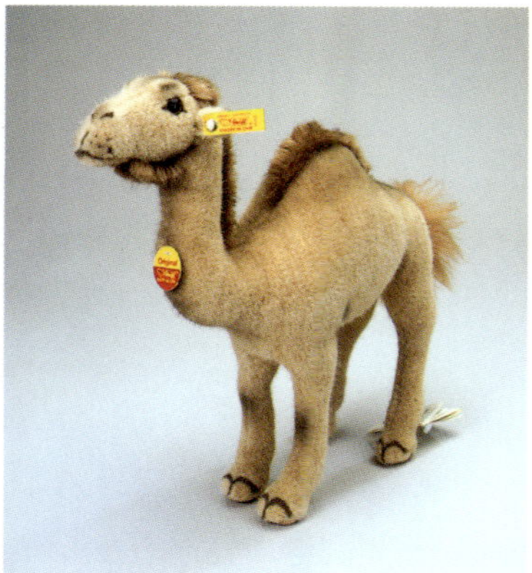

Dromedar - *Dromedary*

Webpelz, stehend, abwaschbar - *woven fur, standing, surface washable*

EAN-No.	Period	Pr.	Info
066948	1999-1999	3	35 cm

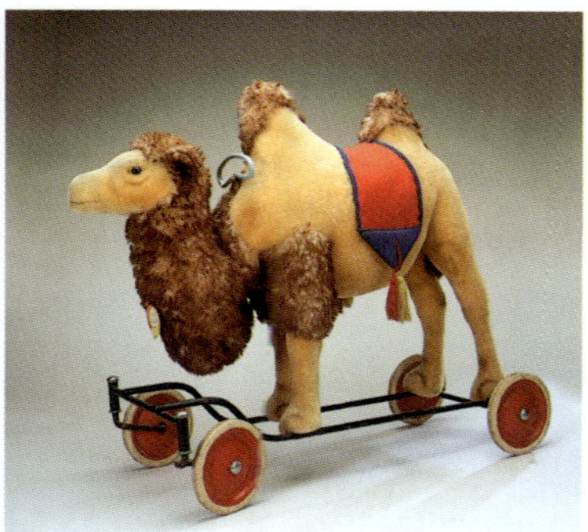

Reit-Kamel - *Riding Camel*

Mohairpluesch, Eisengerippe, Lederhalfter, hellbraun & braun gespitzt, stehend, 1949/50 Holzraeder, ab 1951 Metallscheibenraeder mit Gummireifen, ab 1967 Plastikreifen, Verbindungsschienen, Kopfschmuck & Schabracke, Zugstimme, Haltegriff, ab 1968 Schlepplenkung, abwaschbar - *mohair, iron frame, leather halter, light brown & brown tipped, standing, 1949/50 wooden wheels, from 1951 metal disc wheels with rubber tires, from 1967 plastic tires, connecting frame, head dress & saddle cloth, pull cord voice, grip handle, from 1968 pull type steering, surface washable*

Serie	Art.-No	Period	Pr.	Info
42	**1343**	1949-1950	5-6	43 cm
42	**1343**	1951-1957	5	
421	**1343,20**	1961-1961	5	
42	**1360,2**	1951-1951	5	60 cm
42	**1360**	1952-1957	5	
421	**1360,20**	1961-1961	5	
062	**1360,20**	1966-1967	5	
	0620/60	1968-1972	5	

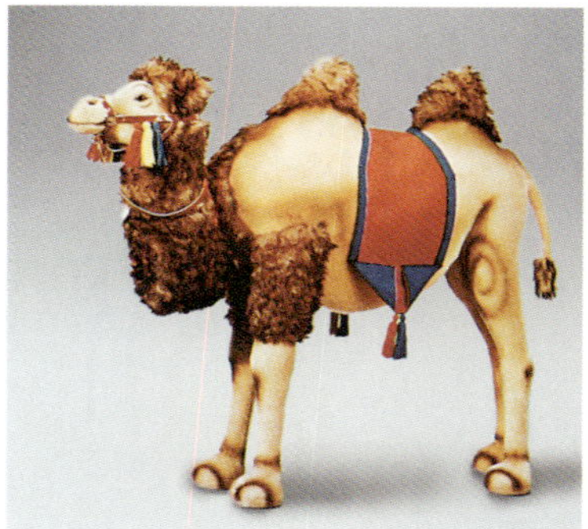

Kamel - *Camel*

Schautier, Mohair, hellbeige, stehend - *display animal, mohair, light beige, standing*

Serie	Art.-No	Period	Pr.	Info
421	**1399,90**	1960-1960	6	100 cm
	0629/10	1967-1967	6	

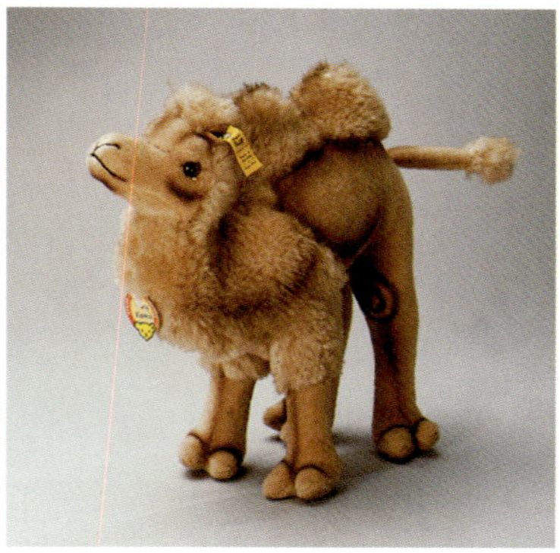

Cosy Kamel - *Cosy Camel*

Dralon, gefuellt mit synthetischen Fasern & Schaumstoff, stehend, sehr weich, vollwaschbar - *dralon, stuffed with synthetic fibers & foam, standing, very soft, fully washable*

Serie	Art.-No	Period	Pr.	Info
	4890/28	1968-1976	3	28 cm

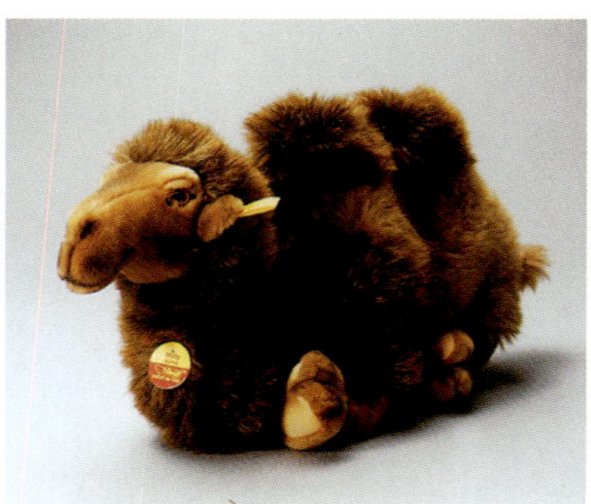

Molly Kamel - *Molly Camel*

Webpelz, abwaschbar - *woven fur, surface washable*

Serie	Art.-No	Period	Pr.	Info
104107	**0405/40**	1988-1990	2-3	40 cm
104138	**0405/60**	1988-1989	3	60 cm

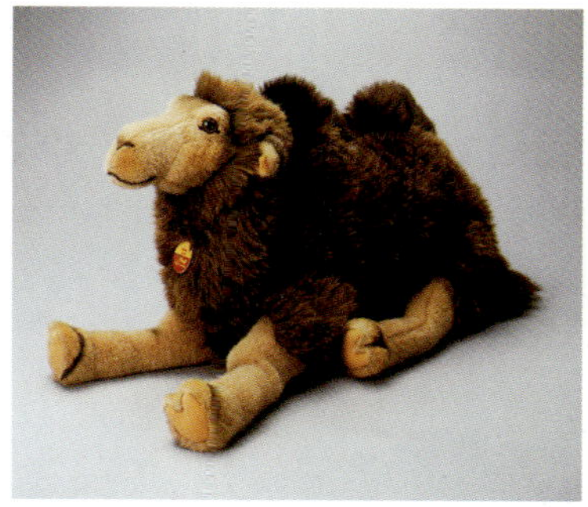

Molly Kamel - *Molly Camel*

Webpelz, liegend, waschmaschinenfest - *woven fur, lying, machine washable*

EAN-No.	Period	Pr.	Info
104114	1995-1997	3-4	50 cm
104121	1994-1999	4	70 cm

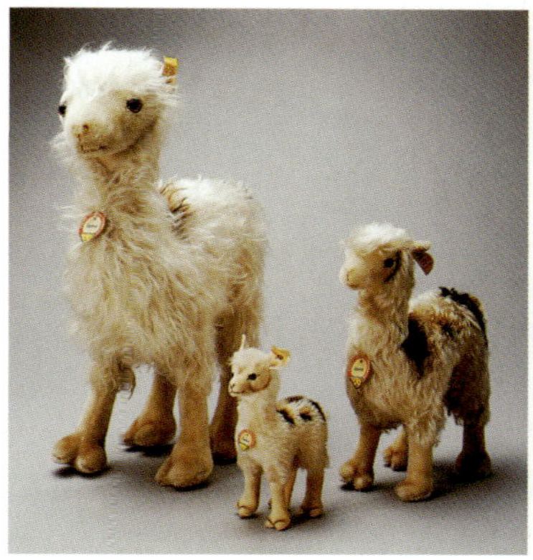

Lama - ***Llama***

Langhaar-Mohair, stehend, weiss, grau/braun gefleckt - *long-hair mohair, standing, white, grey/brown spotted*

Serie	Art.-No	Period	Pr.	Info
42a	**1317,0**	1957-1958	4	17 cm
425	**1317,00**	1959-1964	3-4	
065	**1317,00**	1965-1967	3-4	
	0650/17	1968-1969	3	
42a	**1328,0**	1957-1958	4	28 cm
425	**1328,00**	1959-1964	3-4	
065	**1328,00**	1965-1967	3-4	
	0650/28	1968-1969	3	
42a	**1343,0**	1957-1958	4-5	43 cm
425	**1343,00**	1959-1964	4	
065	**1343,00**	1965-1966	4	

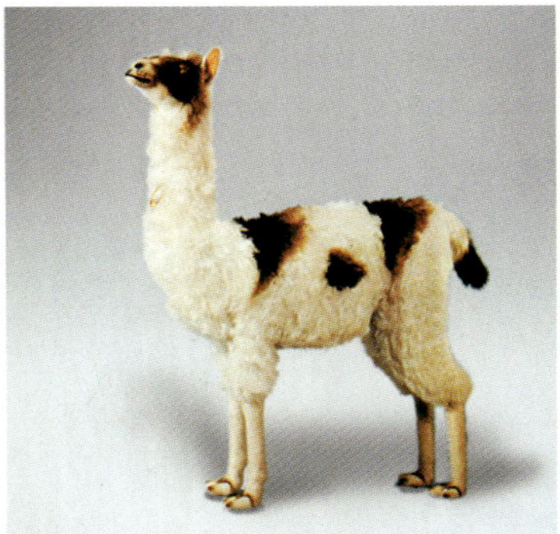

Lama - *Llama*

Schautier, Mohair, stehend - *display animal, mohair, standing*

SERIE	ART.-NO	PERIOD	PR.	INFO
425	**1399,90**	1960-1960	6	100 cm
	0659/10	1967-1967	6	
	0659/15	1967-1967	6	150 cm

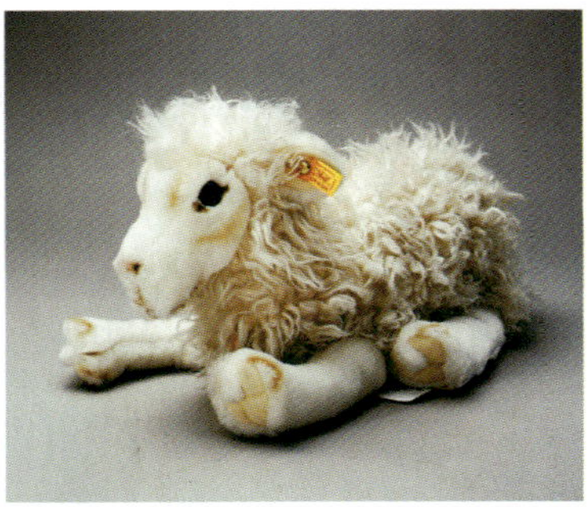

Molly Lama - *Molly Llama*

Webpelz, liegend, waschmaschinenfest - *woven fur, lying, machine washable*

EAN-NO.	PERIOD	PR.	INFO
104152	1991-1993	2-3	40 cm

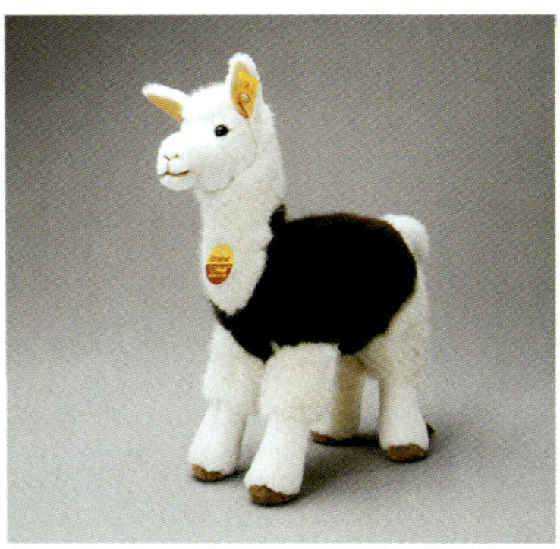

Lama - *Llama*

Webpelz, weiss/braun, stehend, handwaschbar - *woven fur, white/brown, standing, hand washable*

EAN-NO.	PERIOD	PR.	INFO
069161	1995-1998	2-3	32 cm

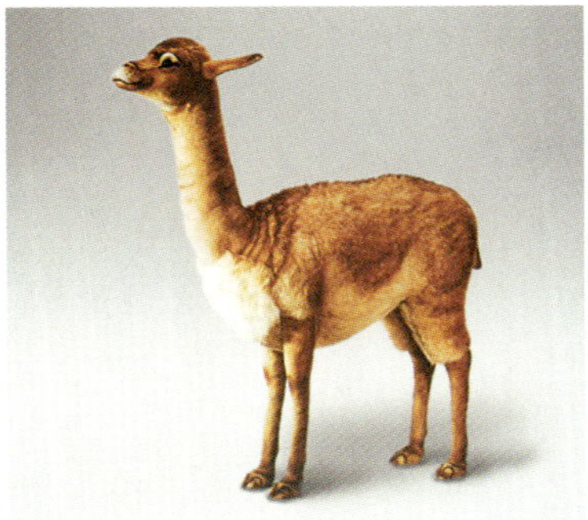

Vicuna

Schautier - *display animal*

SERIE	ART.-NO	PERIOD	PR.	INFO
427	**1150,90**	1960-1960	6	150 cm

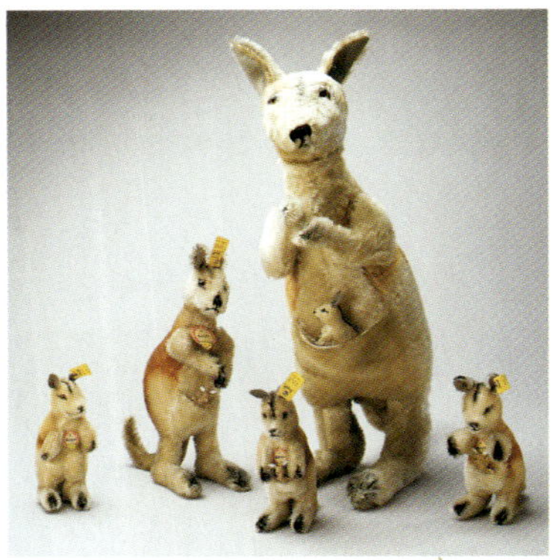

Kaenguruh **Kangoo** - *Kangaroo* ***Kangoo***

Mohair, weiss/grau/braun, aufwartend, Drehkopf, 14 & 28 cm Kunststoff-Baby, 50 cm Samt-Baby, 65 cm Mohair-Baby, ab 1965 auch mit Zusatz "im Steiff-Kinderbuch", auch ohne Bauchtasche hergestellt - *mohair, white/grey/brown, sitting up, head swivels, 14 & 28 cm plastic baby, 50 cm velvet baby, 65 cm mohair baby, from 1965 also with supplement "im Steiff-Kinderbuch", also manufactured without its pouch*

SERIE	ART.-NO	PERIOD	PR.	INFO
43	**4314**	1953-1958	3-4	14 cm
430	**4314,00**	1959-1964	3	
070	**4314,00**	1965-1966	3	
43	**4328**	1953-1958	4	28 cm
430	**4328,00**	1959-1964	3-4	
070	**4328,00**	1965-1966	3-4	
43	**4350**	1953-1958	4-5	50 cm
430	**4350,00**	1959-1964	4-5	
070	**4350,00**	1965-1966	4-5	
43	**4365**	1958-1958	5	65 cm
430	**4365,00**	1959-1964	5	
070	**4365,00**	1965-1966	5	

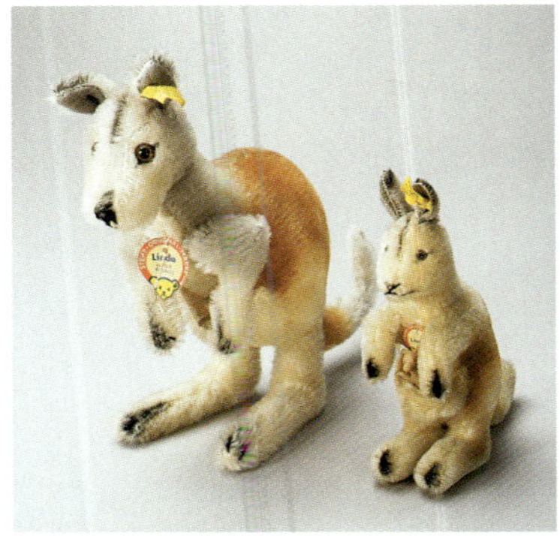

Kaenguruh **Linda** - *Kangaroo* ***Linda***

Mohair, weiss/grau/braun, aufwartend, Drehkopf, 14 & 28 cm Kunststoff-Baby, 50 cm Samt-Baby, abwaschbar - *mohair, white/grey/brown, sitting up, head swivels, 14 & 28 cm plastic baby, 50 cm velvet baby, surface washable*

SERIE	ART.-NO	PERIOD	PR.	INFO
070	**4314,00**	1967-1967	3	14 cm
	0700/14	1968-1974	3	
070	**4328,00**	1967-1967	3-4	28 cm
	0700/28	1968-1974	3	
070	**4350,00**	1967-1967	4-5	50 cm
	0700/50	1968-1974	4	

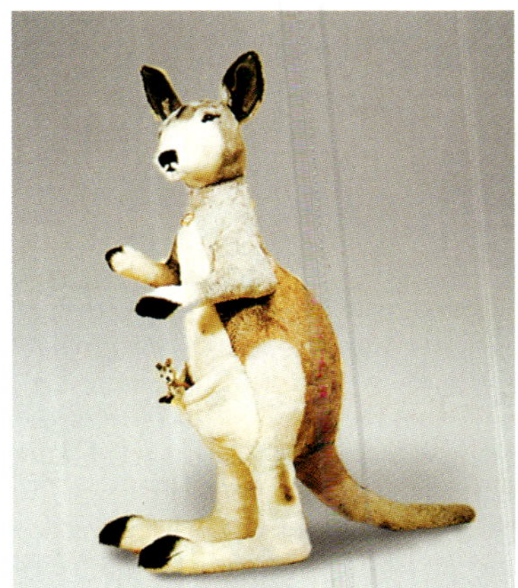

Kaenguruh - *Kangaroo*

Schautier, Mohair, weiss/grau/braun, aufwartend, Kopf & Arme gegliedert - *display animal, mohair, white/grey/brown, sitting up, head & arms jointed*

SERIE	ART.-NO	PERIOD	PR.	INFO
	0709/12	1967-1967	6	120 cm
430	**4150,90**	1960-1960	6	150 cm
	0709/15	1967-1967	6	

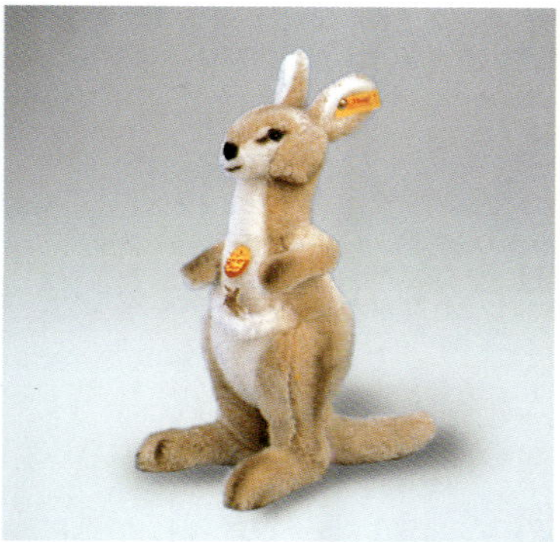

Linda Kaenguruh - ***Linda** Kangaroo*

Pelzimitation, ab 1978 Webpelz, aufwartend, mit Jungem (35 cm Plastik, 45 cm Samt) im Beutel, abwaschbar - *imitation fur, from 1978 woven fur, sitting up, with Baby (35 cm plastic, 45 cm velvet) in its pouch, surface washable*

SERIE	ART.-NO	PERIOD	PR.	INFO
	0710/35	1975-1985	2-3	35 cm
	0710/45	1975-1979	2-3	45 cm

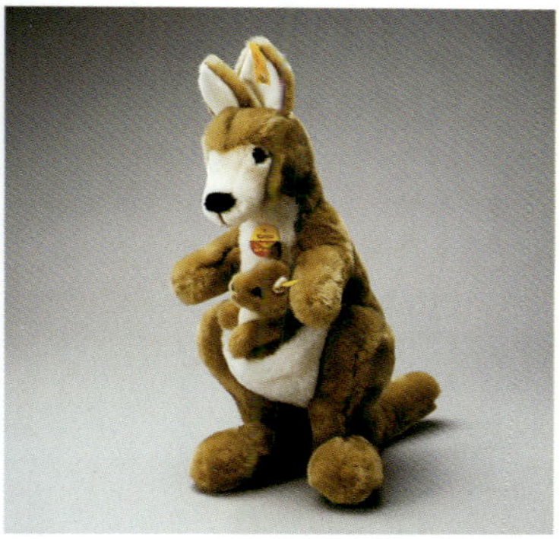

Kango Kaenguruh - ***Kango** Kangaroo*

mit Baby, Webpelz, waschmaschinenfest - *with Baby, woven fur, machine washable*

SERIE	ART.-NO	PERIOD	PR.	INFO
062711	**0892/40**	1989-1990	3	40 cm
	062711	1991-1999	3	

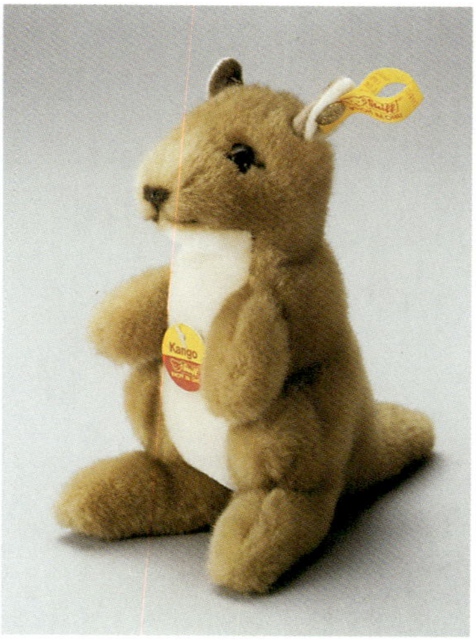

Kango Kaenguruh - ***Kango** Kangaroo*

Webpelz, aufwartend, waschmaschinenfest - *woven fur, sitting up, machine washable*

SERIE	ART.-NO	PERIOD	PR.	INFO
040351	**1448/13**	1989-1990	1-2	13 cm
	040351	1991-1999	1-2	

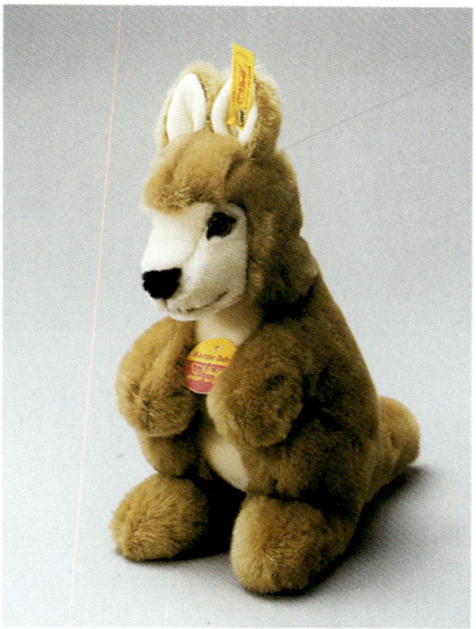

Kango Baby Kaenguruh - ***Kango Baby** Kangaroo*

Webpelz, waschmaschinenfest - *woven fur, machine washable*

EAN-NO.	PERIOD	PR.	INFO
062728	1991-1999	2	22 cm

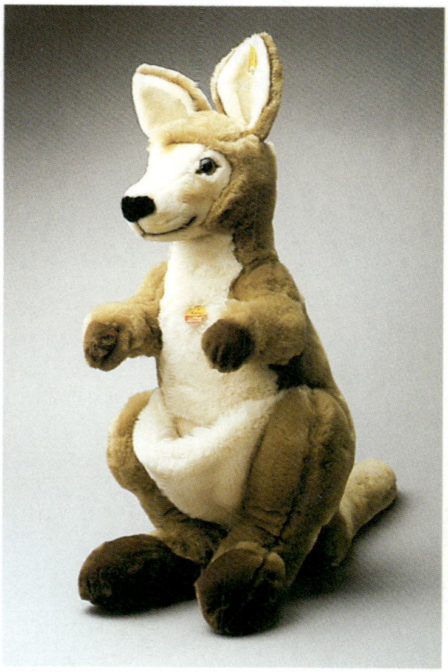

Kango Kaenguruh - ***Kango** Kangaroo*

Webpelz, abwaschbar - *woven fur, surface washable*

EAN-NO.	PERIOD	PR.	INFO
062759	1991-1995	3-4	60 cm

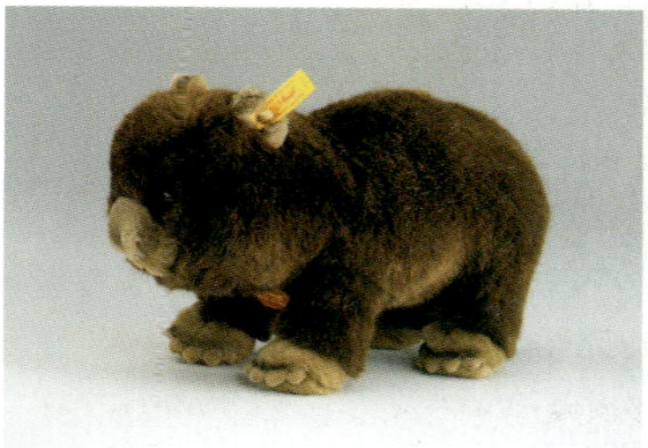

Womby Wombat

Webpelz, braun, stehend, waschmaschinenfest - *woven fur, brown, standing, machine washable*

EAN-NO.	PERIOD	PR.	INFO
064937	1997-1998	3	30 cm

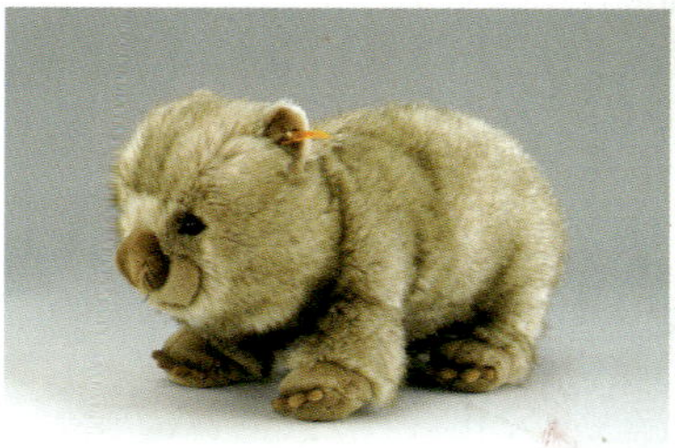

Womby Wombat

Webpelz, braun gespitzt, stehend, handwaschbar - *woven fur, brown tipped, standing, hand washable*

EAN-NO.	PERIOD	PR.	INFO
064944	1997-1997	3	42 cm

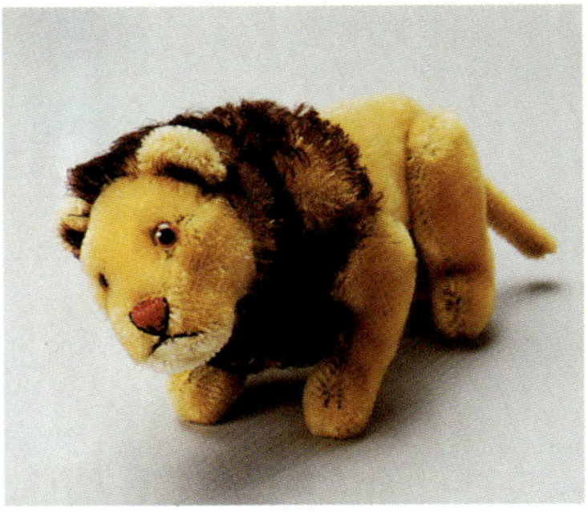

Loewen-Papa - *Papa Lion*

Mohair, mit Maehne, gelbbraun, gegliedert - *mohair, with mane, tawny colored, jointed*

SERIE	ART.-NO	PERIOD	PR.	INFO
48	**5314**	1951-1958	5	14 cm
480	**5314,00**	1959-1959	5	
48	**5322**	1949-1954	5	22 cm
48	**5322,2**	1955-1958	5	
480	**5322,00**	1959-1961	5	

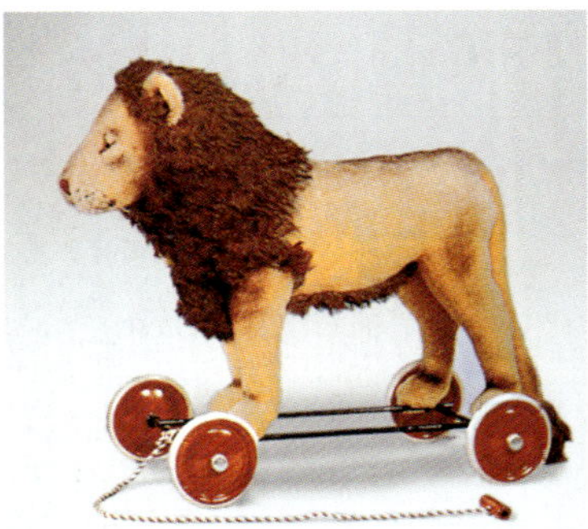

Reit-Loewe - *Riding Lion*

Mohairpluesch, mit Maehne, Eisengerippe, stehend auf Holzrollen, ab 1950 Metallscheibenraeder mit Gummireifen, Verbindungsschienen, hellbraun, Zugstimme, Haltegriff - *mohair, with mane, iron frame, wooden wheels, from 1950 metal disc wheels with rubber tires, connecting frame, light brown, pull cord voice, grip handle*

SERIE	ART.-NO	PERIOD	PR.	INFO
48	**1343,2**	1949-1949	5-6	43 cm
48	**1343,2**	1950-1957	5-6	
480	**1343,20**	1961-1961	5-6	
48	**1350,2**	1950-1957	5-6	50 cm
480	**1350,20**	1961-1964	5-6	
080	**1350,20**	1965-1966	5-6	

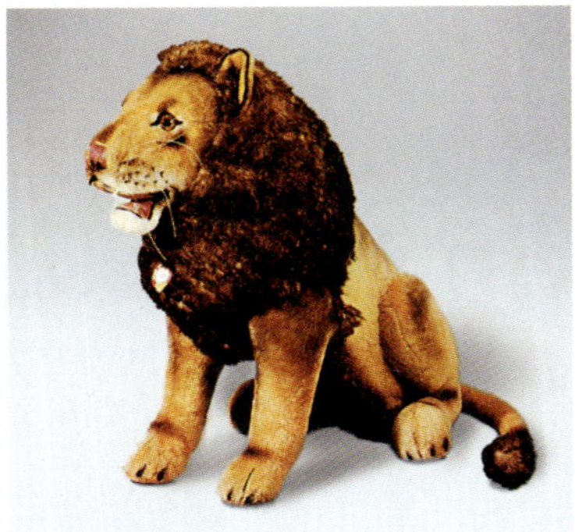

Loewe - *Lion*

Schautier, Mohair-Pluesch, sitzend - *display animal, mohair, sitting*

SERIE	ART.-NO	PERIOD	PR.	INFO
	0829/06	1967-1967	6	60 cm
48	**3390**	1953-1953	7	90 cm
480	**3390,90**	1960-1960	6-7	
	0829/09	1967-1967	6	
480	**3120,90**	1960-1960	6-7	120 cm
	0829/12	1967-1967	6	

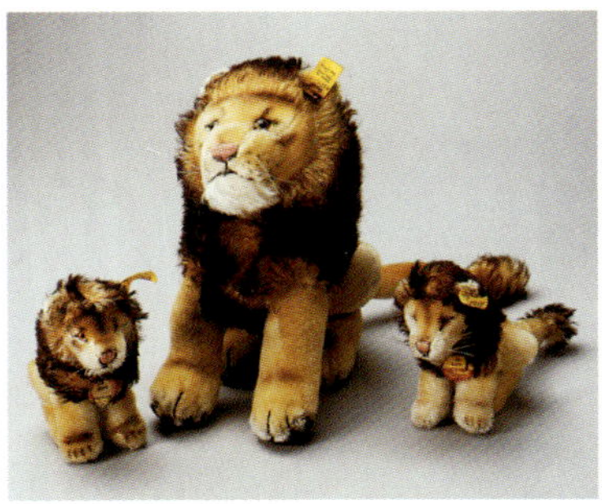

Loewe **Leo** - ***Leo** Lion*

Mohairpluesch, gelb/weiss, sitzend, mit Maehne, abwaschbar - *mohair, yellow/white, sitting, with mane, surface washable*

SERIE	ART.-NO	PERIOD	PR.	INFO
48	**3312**	1956-1958	3-4	12 cm
480	**3312,00**	1959-1964	3	
080	**3312,00**	1965-1967	3	
	0820/12	1968-1976	2-3	
48	**3322**	1958-1958	4	22 cm
480	**3322,00**	1959-1963	3-4	
080	**3322,00**	1966-1967	3-4	
	0820/22	1968-1974	3	

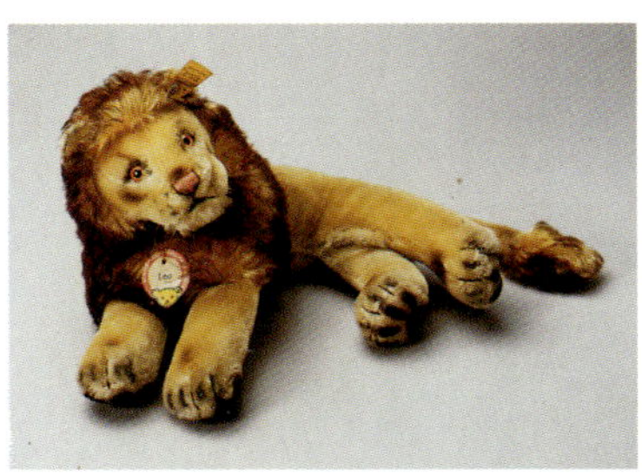

Loewe **Leo** - ***Leo** Lion*

Mohair, mit Maehne, gelb/weiss, liegend, Stimme, weich, abwaschbar - *mohair, with mane, yellow/white, lying, voice, soft, surface washable*

SERIE	ART.-NO	PERIOD	PR.	INFO
48	**2322,1**	1956-1958	3-4	22 cm
480	**2322,00**	1959-1964	3	
080	**2322,00**	1965-1967	3	
	0810/22	1968-1977	3	
48	**2335,1**	1955-1958	3-4	35 cm
480	**2335,00**	1959-1964	3-4	
080	**2335,00**	1965-1967	3-4	
	0810/35	1968-1977	3	
48	**2350,1**	1956-1958	4	50 cm
480	**2350,00**	1959-1964	3-4	
080	**2350,00**	1965-1967	3-4	
	0810/50	1968-1975	3-4	

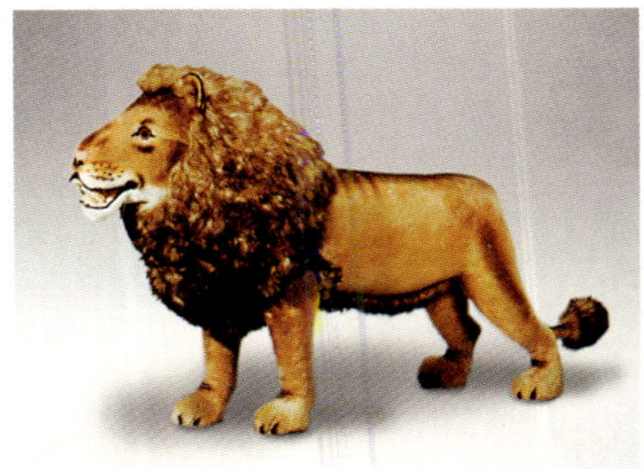

Loewe - *Lion*

Schautier, Mohair, naturfarben, stehend - *display animal, mohair, natural colors, standing*

SERIE	ART.-NO	PERIOD	PR.	INFO
480	**1399,90**	1960-1960	6-7	100 cm
080	**1399,90**	1966-1966	6-7	
	0809/10	1967-1967	6	

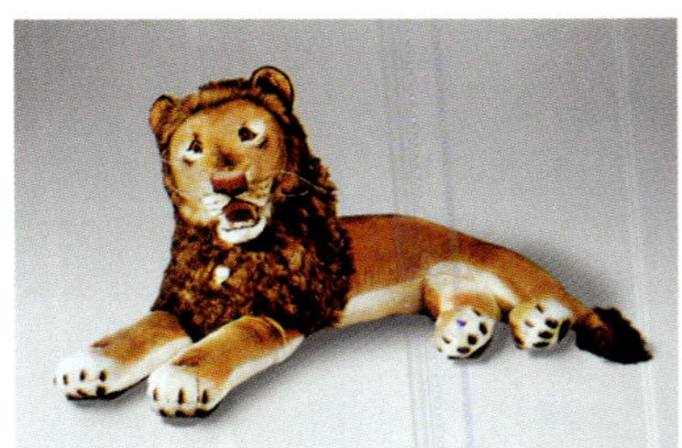

Loewe - *Lion*

Schautiere, Mohair, liegend - *display animal, mohair, lying*

SERIE	ART.-NO	PERIOD	PR.	INFO
	0819/09	1967-1967	6	90 cm
480	**2110,90**	1960-1960	6	110 cm
	0819/11	1967-1967	6	

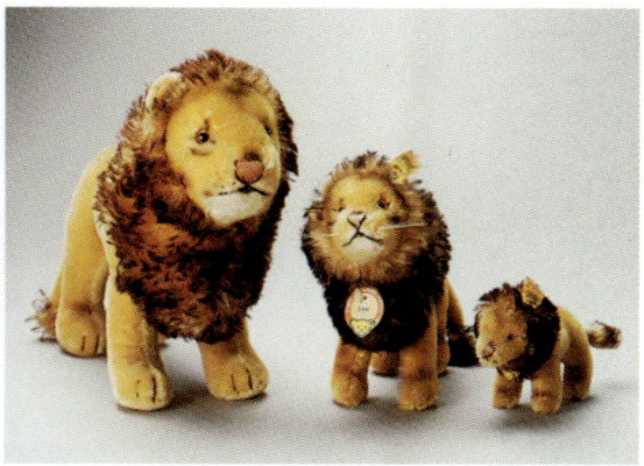

Loewe **Leo** - *Lion **Leo***

Mohair, gelbbraun, stehend, mit Maehne, abwaschbar - *mohair, tawny colored, standing, with mane, surface washable*

SERIE	ART.-NO	PERIOD	PR.	INFO
480	**1310,00**	1964-1964	3	10 cm
080	**1310,00**	1965-1967	3	
	0800/10	1968-1975	2-3	
480	**1317,00**	1964-1964	3	17 cm
080	**1317,00**	1965-1967	3	
	0800/17	1968-1975	2-3	
480	**1328,00**	1964-1964	3-4	28 cm
080	**1328,00**	1965-1967	3-4	
	0800/28	1968-1973	3	

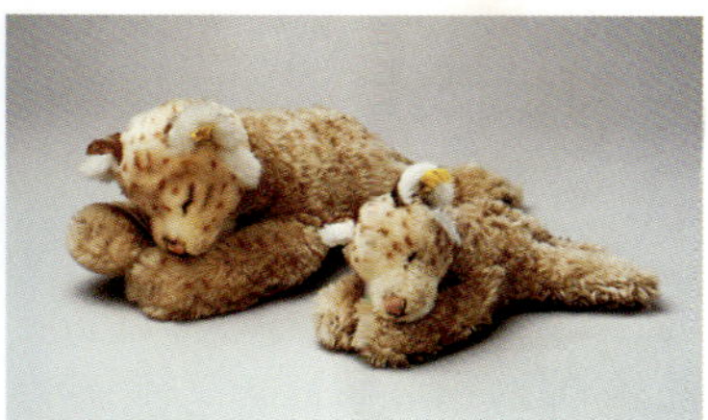

Floppy Leo Loewe - ***Floppy Leo** Lion*

Dralon, Schlaftier, liegend, sehr weich, ab 1970 formgeschaeumt, Augen gestickt, vollwaschbar - *dralon, sleeping animal, lying, very soft, from 1970 stuffed with pre-formed foam, eyes are embroidered, fully washable*

SERIE	ART.-NO	PERIOD	PR.	INFO
	5610/17	1969-1969	2	17 cm
	5617/17	1970-1977	2	
	5610/28	1969-1969	2	28 cm
	5617/28	1970-1977	2	

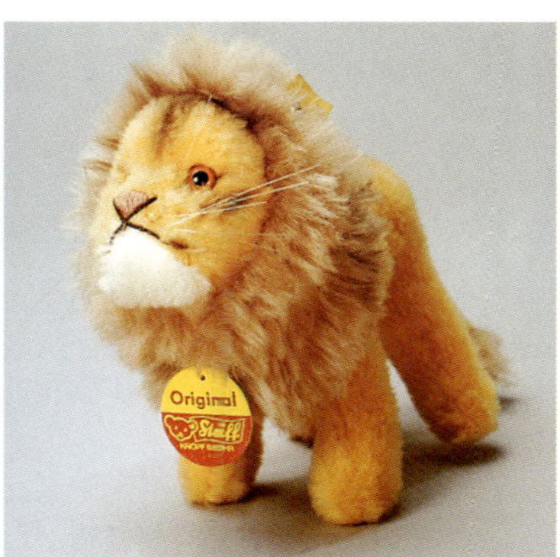

Simba

"Der kleine Tierversand", im Kaefigkarton, stehend, mit Tiersteckbrief, Dralon, abwaschbar - *"Der kleine Tierversand", in its own animal crate, standing, with information label, dralon, surface washable*

SERIE	ART.-NO	PERIOD	PR.	INFO
	5815/15	1971-1974	2	15 cm

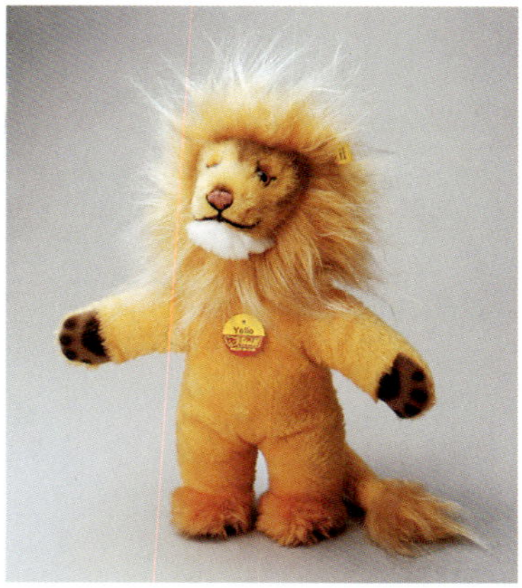

Weich-Loewe ab 1975 **Yello** - *Soft Lion from 1975 **Yello***

Dralon, formgeschaeumt, sehr weich, Schlenkerkopf, vollwaschbar - *dralon, stuffed with pre-formed foam, very soft, floppy head, fully washable*

SERIE	ART.-NO	PERIOD	PR.	INFO
	6212/30	1971-1978	2-3	30 cm
	6212/40	1971-1976	2-3	40 cm

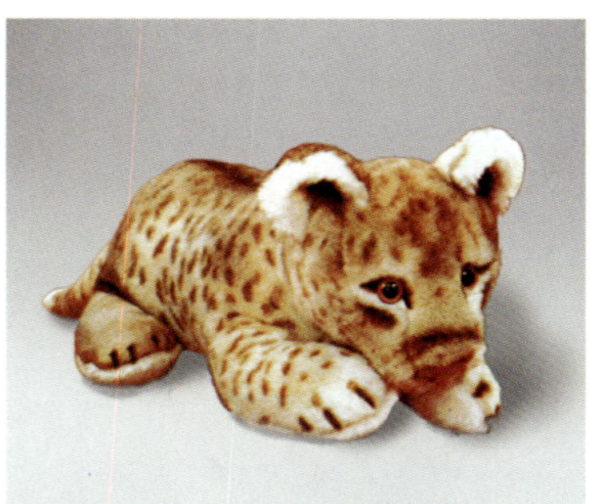

Lommy Loewe - ***Lommy** Lion*

Pelzimitation, beige, liegend, superweich, abwaschbar - *imitation fur, beige, lying, super soft, surface washable*

SERIE	ART.-NO	PERIOD	PR.	INFO
	5305/50	1972-1976	3	50 cm

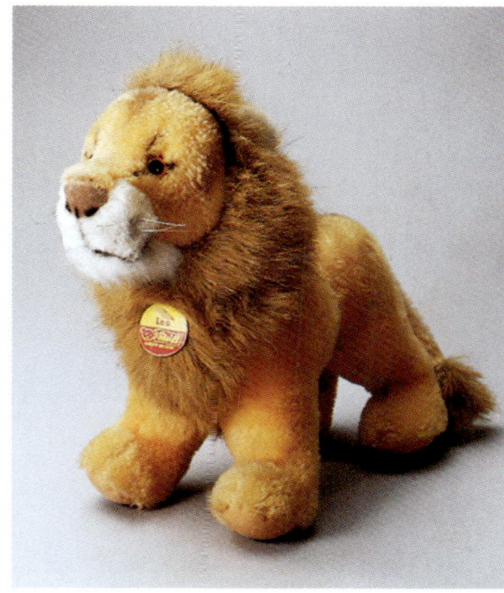

Leo Loewe - ***Leo** Lion*

Dralon, stehend, abwaschbar - *dralon, standing, surface washable*

SERIE	ART.-NO	PERIOD	PR.	INFO
	0805/18	1975-1980	2-3	18 cm
	0805/25	1975-1981	2-3	26 cm

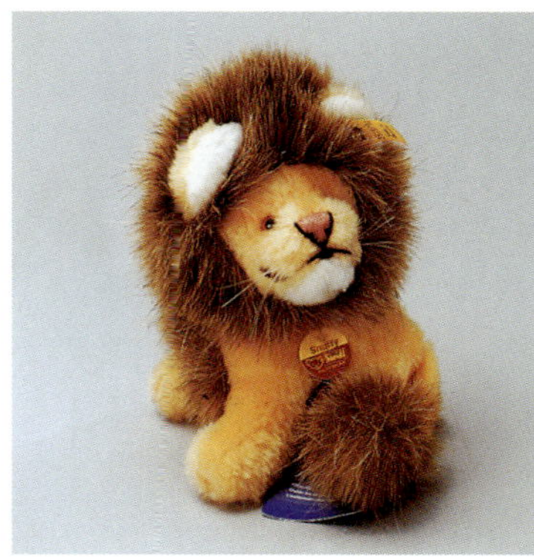

Snuffy Loewe - ***Snuffy** Lion*

Dralon, sitzend, abwaschbar - *dralon, sitting, surface washable*

SERIE	ART.-NO	PERIOD	PR.	INFO
	3518/14	1975-1982	2	14 cm
	3518/18	1975-1982	2	18 cm

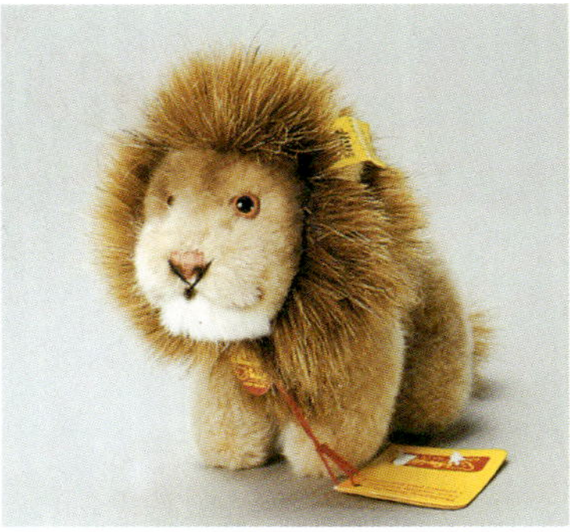

Leo Loewe - ***Leo** Lion*

Nerzimitation, ab 1978 Synthetik-Webpelz, stehend, abwaschbar - *imitation mink, from 1978 synthetic woven fur, standing, surface washable*

SERIE	ART.-NO	PERIOD	PR.	INFO
	1460/13	1977-1984	1-2	13 cm

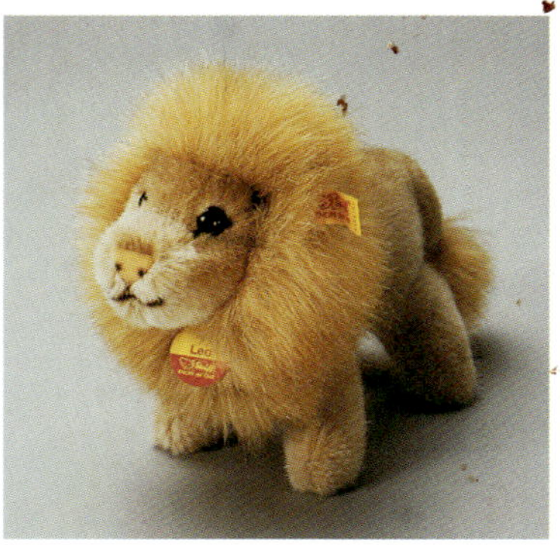

Leo Loewe - ***Leo** Lion*

Webpelz, stehend, abwaschbar - *woven fur, standing, surface washable*

SERIE	ART.-NO	PERIOD	PR.	INFO
040801	**1461/12**	1985-1990	1-2	14 cm
	040801	1991-1999	1-2	

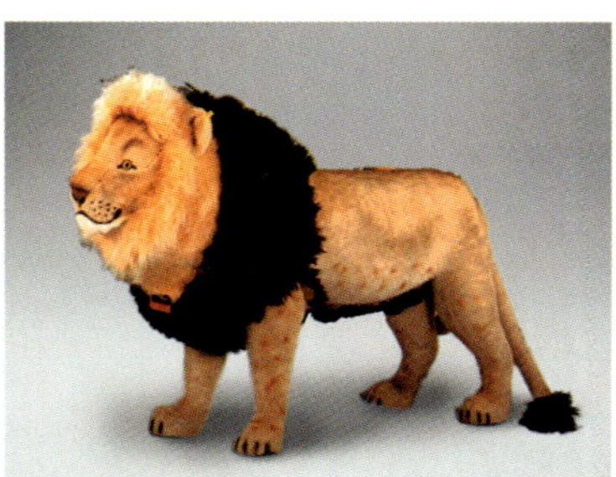

Studio Loewe - *Studio Lion*

Synthetik-Webpelz, stehend, abwaschbar - *synthetic woven fur, standing, surface washable*

SERIE	ART.-NO	PERIOD	PR.	INFO
502606	**0809/11**	1978-1986	6	110 cm

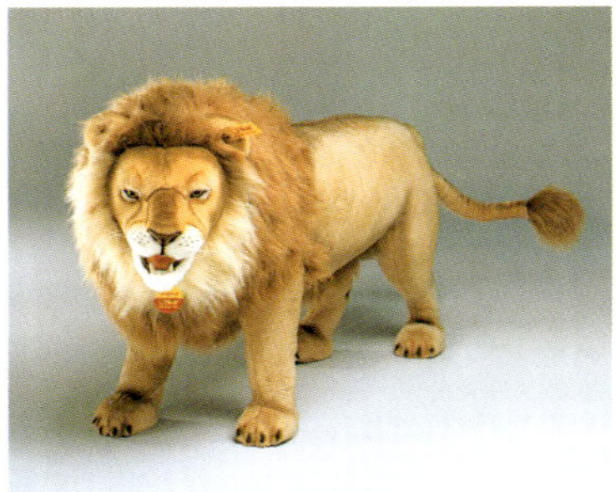

Studio Loewe - *Studio Lion*

Webpelz, stehend, abwaschbar - *woven fur, standing, surface washable*

SERIE	ART.-NO	PERIOD	PR.	INFO
502651	**0805/99**	1987-1990	7-8	110 cm
	502651	1991-1999	7-8	

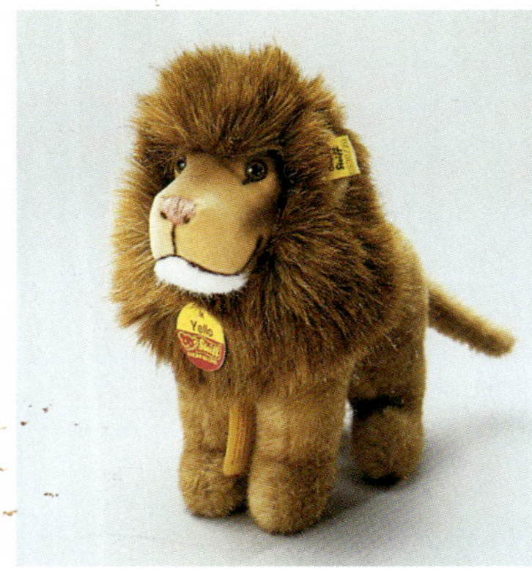

Yello Loewe - ***Yello** Lion*

Webpelz, stehend, abwaschbar - *woven fur, standing, surface washable*

SERIE	ART.-NO	PERIOD	PR.	INFO
	0800/20	1979-1981	2-3	20 cm

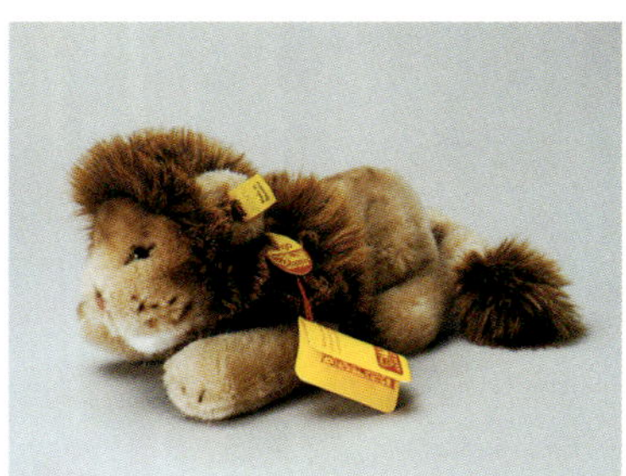

Rango Loewe - ***Rango** Lion*

Webpelz, liegend, abwaschbar - *woven fur, lying, surface washable*

SERIE	ART.-NO	PERIOD	PR.	INFO
	0812/16	1980-1983	2	16 cm

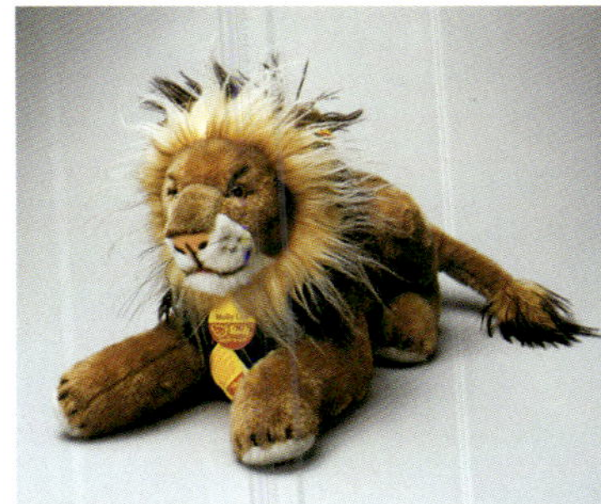

Molly Leo - *Molly Lion*

Webpelz, mollig weich, abwaschbar - *woven fur, soft & cuddly, surface washable*

SERIE	ART.-NO	PERIOD	PR.	INFO
103469	**0375/45**	1981-1986	3	45 cm

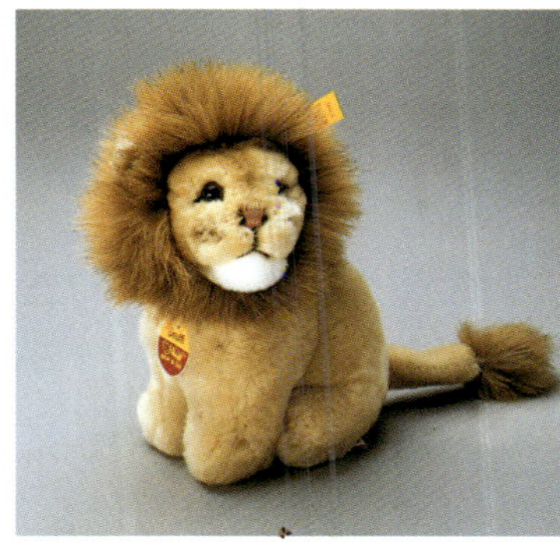

Snuffi Loewe - ***Snuffi** Lion*

Webpelz, sitzend, waschmaschinenfest - *woven fur, sitting, machine washable*

SERIE	ART.-NO	PERIOD	PR.	INFO
077180	**2914/18**	1987-1990	2	16 cm
	077180	1991-1999	2	

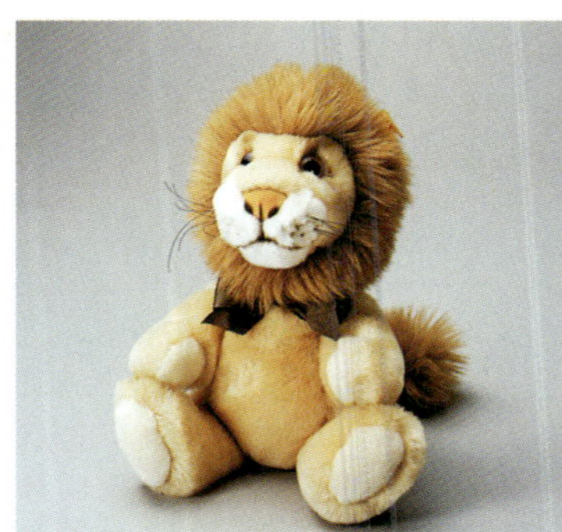

Possy Loewe - ***Possy** Lion*

Webpelz, gegliedert, Pieps-Stimme, waschmaschinenfest - *woven fur, jointed, squeaker, machine washable*

SERIE	ART.-NO	PERIOD	PR.	INFO
081675	**6228/28**	1989-1990	2-3	28 cm

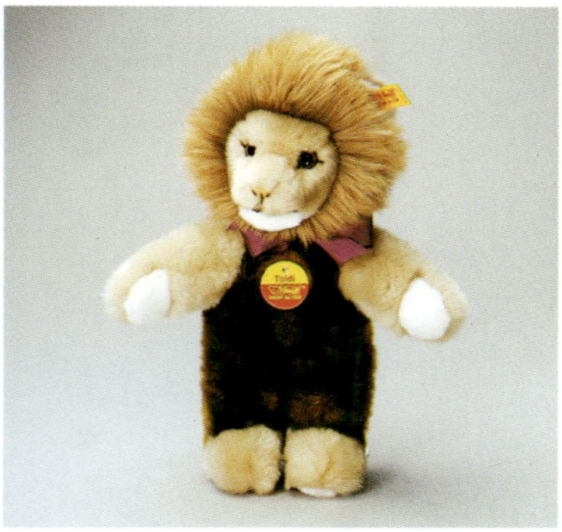

Toldi Loewe - ***Toldi*** *Lion*

Webpelz, Pieps-Stimme, waschmaschinenfest - *woven fur, squeaker, machine washable*

SERIE	ART.-NO	PERIOD	PR.	INFO
081217	**6264/27**	1989-1990	2	27 cm

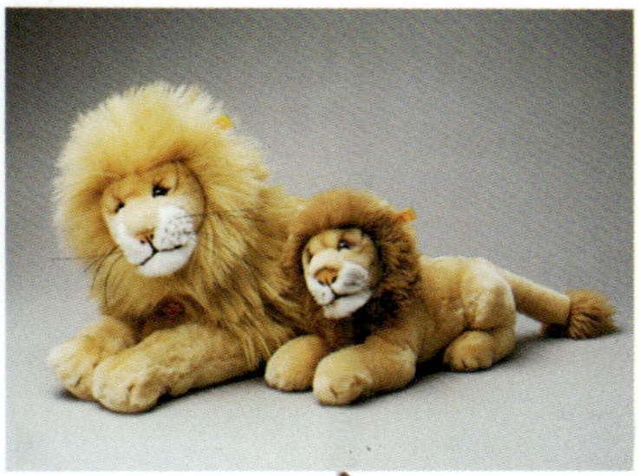

Molly Leo Loewe - *Molly Leo Lion*

Webpelz, liegend, abwaschbar - *woven fur, lying, surface washable*

SERIE	ART.-NO	PERIOD	PR.	INFO
103438	**0370/30**	1986-1990	3	30 cm
	103438	1991-1999	3	
	103452	1992-1999	3-4	50 cm
103483	**0370/70**	1987-1990	3-4	70 cm
	103483	1991-1993	3-4	

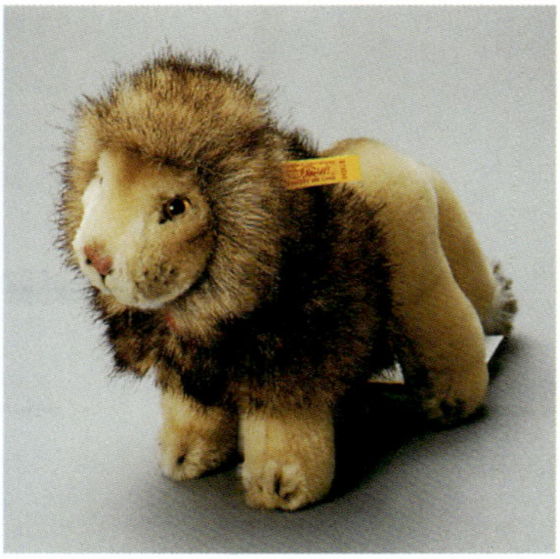

Leo Loewe - ***Leo*** *Lion*

Webpelz, stehend, waschmaschinenfest - *woven fur, standing, machine washable*

EAN-NO.	PERIOD	PR.	INFO
040818	1995-1996	2	20 cm

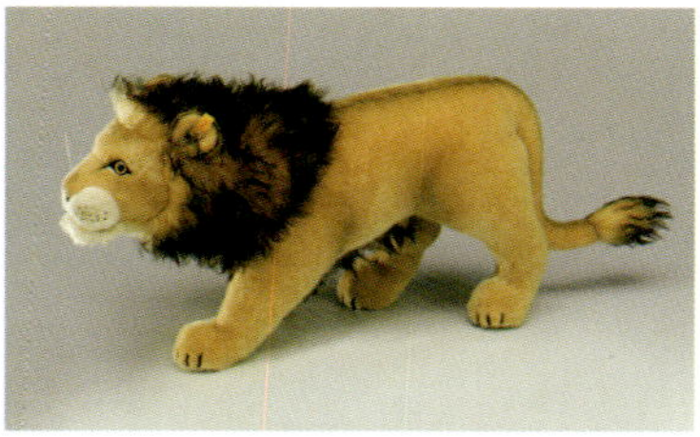

Studio Loewe - *Studio Lion*

Webpelz, stehend, abwaschbar - *woven fur, standing, surface washable*

EAN-NO.	PERIOD	PR.	INFO
502637	1995-1998	4-5	80 cm

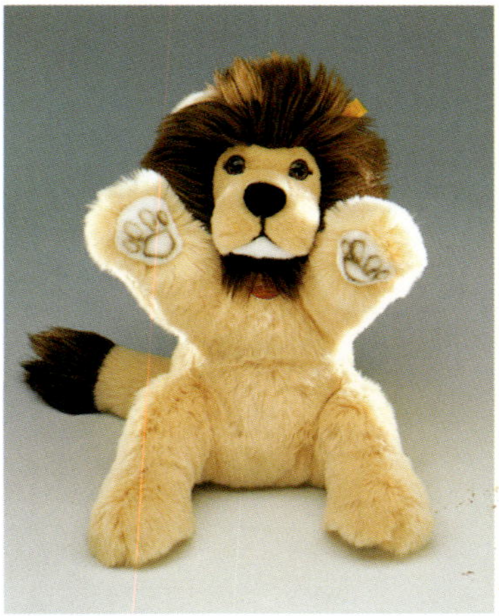

Molly Loewe - *Molly Lion*

Webpelz, abwaschbar - *woven fur, surface washable*

EAN-NO.	PERIOD	PR.	INFO
106552	1996-1997	3	38 cm

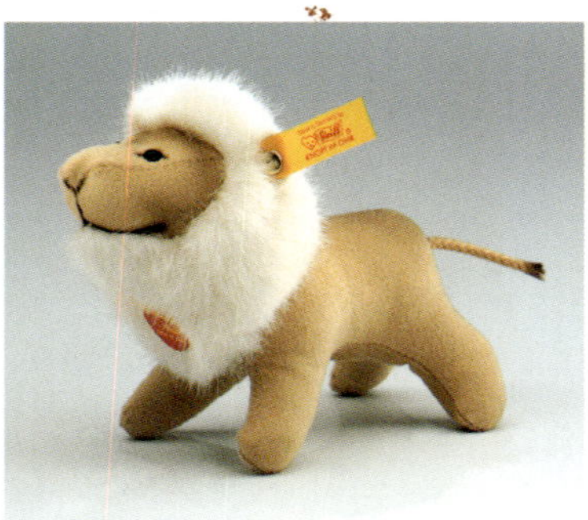

Knuffi Loewe - ***Knuffi*** *Lion*

Microfaser-Vlies, beige, handwaschbar - *micro fibre fleece, beige, hand washable*

EAN-NO.	PERIOD	PR.	INFO
067754	1997-1997	1-2	10 cm

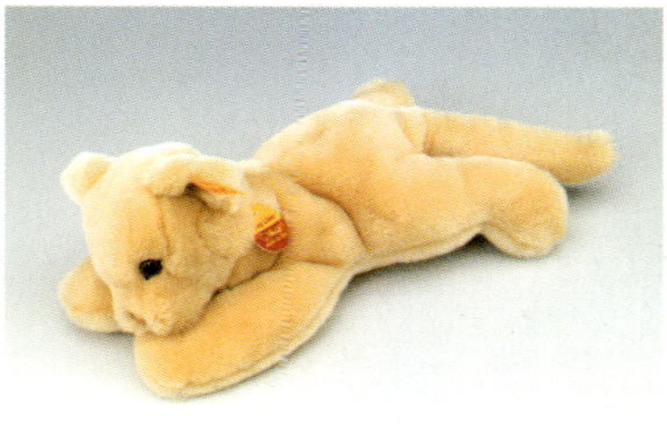

Cosy Loewe - ***Cosy*** *Lion*

Webpelz, liegend, waschmaschinenfest - *woven fur, lying, machine washable*

EAN-NO.	PERIOD	PR.	INFO
088810	1998-1999	2-3	28 cm

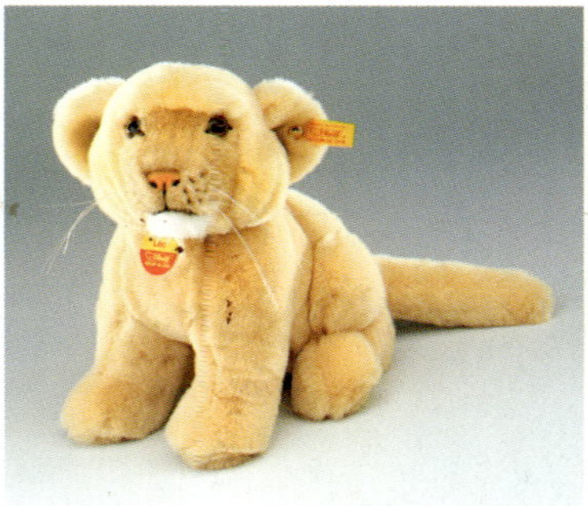

Leo Loewe - ***Leo*** *Lion*

Webpelz, sitzend, waschmaschinenfest - *woven fur, sitting, machine washable*

EAN-NO.	PERIOD	PR.	INFO
066740	1998-1999	3	25 cm

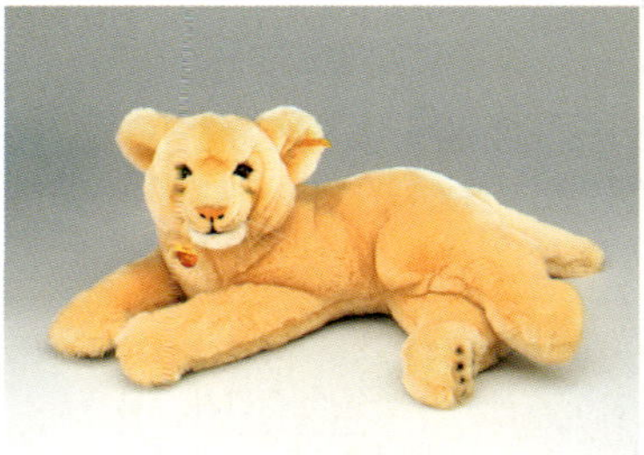

Barry Loewe - ***Barry*** *Lion*

Webpelz, seitlich liegend, waschmaschinenfest - *woven fur, lying aside, machine washable*

EAN-NO.	PERIOD	PR.	INFO
103469	1998-1999	3	45 cm

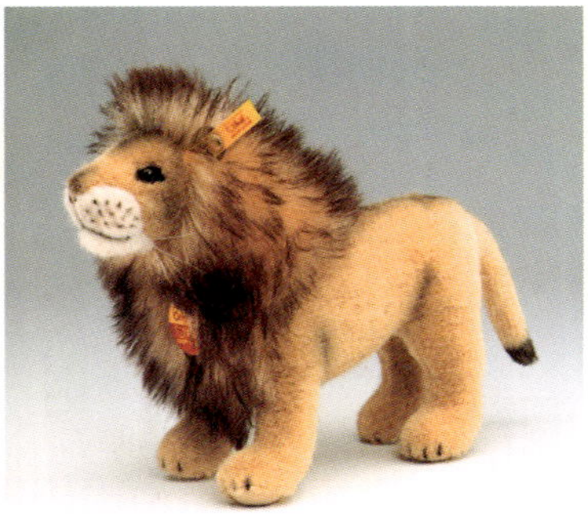

Loewe - *Lion*

Webpelz, stehend, abwaschbar - *woven fur, standing, surface washable*

EAN-No.	Period	Pr.	Info
066757	1999-1999	2-3	25 cm

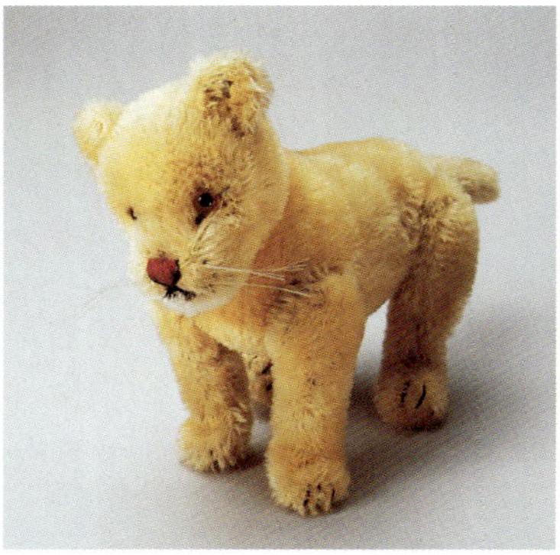

Loewen-Mama - *Mama Lioness*

Mohair, gelbbraun, gegliedert - *mohair, tawny colored, jointed*

Serie	Art.-No	Period	Pr.	Info
48	**5312**	1951-1957	4-5	12 cm
48	**5321**	1949-1954	4-5	21 cm
48	**5321,2**	1955-1957	4-5	

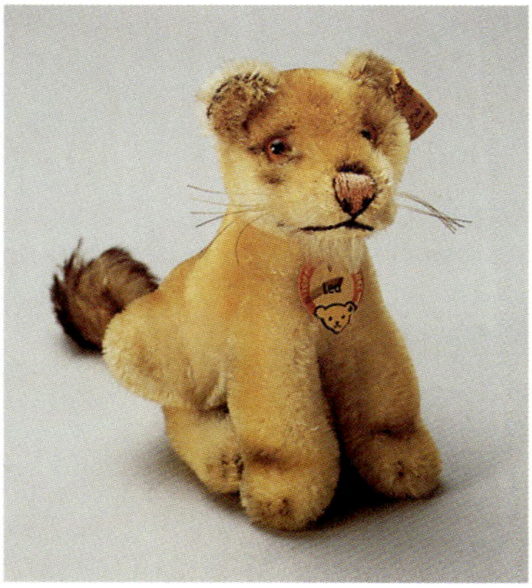

Loewin **Lea** - *Lioness **Lea***

Mohairpluesch, gelb/weiss, sitzend - *mohair, yellow/white, sitting*

Serie	Art.-No	Period	Pr.	Info
48	**3311**	1956-1958	4	11 cm
481	**3311,00**	1959-1964	3-4	
082	**3311,00**	1965-1967	3-4	
	0840/11	1968-1969	3	

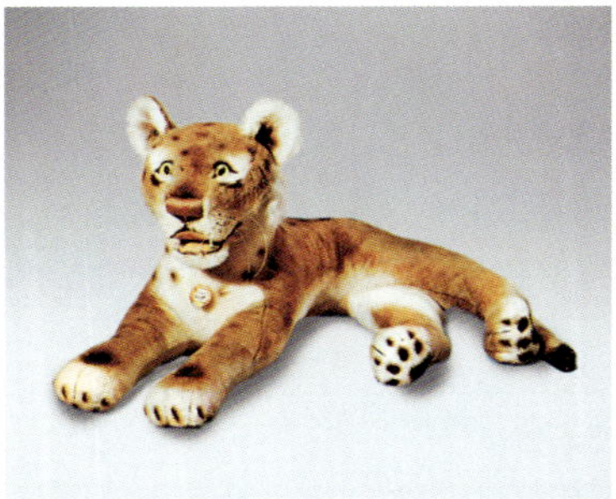

Loewin - *Lioness*

Schautier, Mohair, liegend - *display animal, mohair, lying*

Serie	Art.-No	Period	Pr.	Info
481	**2380,90**	1960-1960	6	80 cm
	0839/08	1967-1967	6	

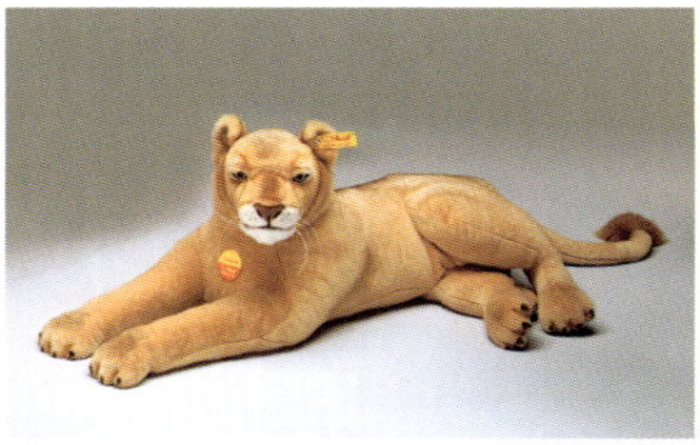

Studio Loewin - *Studio Lioness*

Webpelz, liegend, abwaschbar - *woven fur, lying, surface washable*

Serie	Art.-No	Period	Pr.	Info
502750	**0807/99**	1987-1990	6-7	140 cm
	502750	1991-1999	6-7	

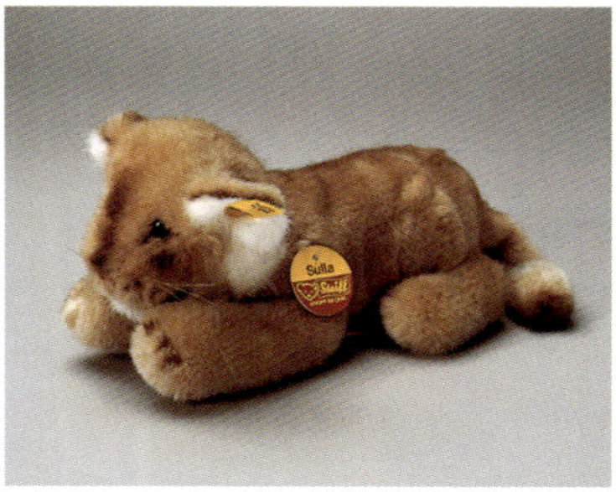

Sulla Loewin - ***Sulla** Lioness*

Webpelz, liegend, abwaschbar - *woven fur, lying, surface washable*

Serie	Art.-No	Period	Pr.	Info
	0815/15	1980-1982	2	15 cm

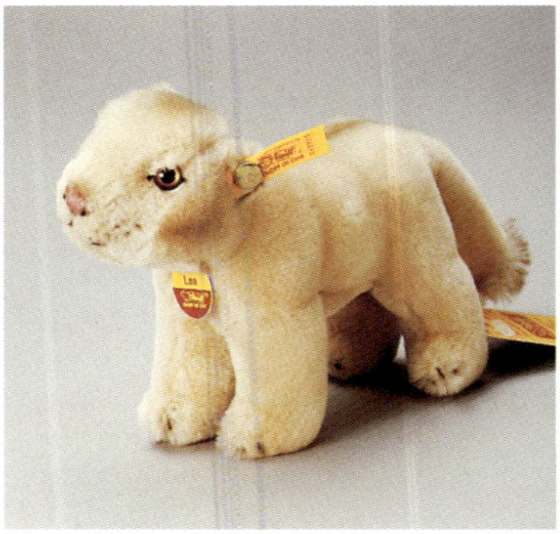

Lea Loewin - ***Lea** Lioness*

Webpelz, stehend, waschmaschinenfest - *woven fur, standing, machine washable*

EAN-No.	Period	Pr.	Info
040825	1995-1996	2	18 cm

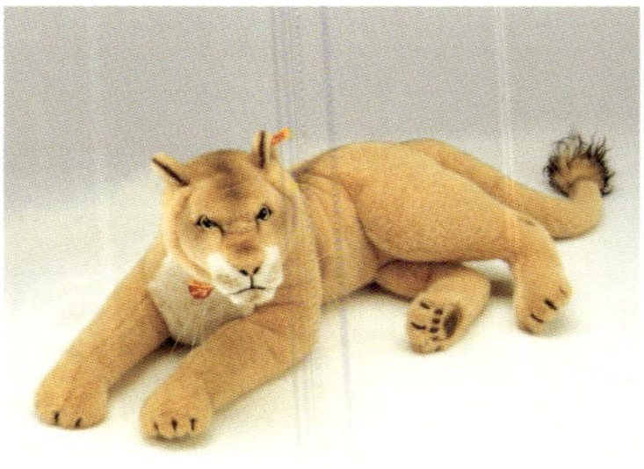

Studio Loewin - *Studio Lioness*

Webpelz, liegend, abwaschbar - *woven fur, lying, surface washable*

EAN-No.	Period	Pr.	Info
502729	1995-1998	4	70 cm

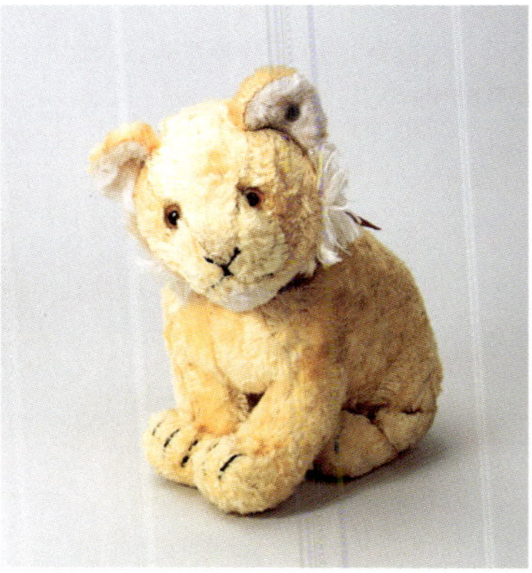

Jungloewe - *Young Lion*

Kunstseidenpluesch, gelbbraun, getupft, sitzend, Drehkopf - *artificial silk plush, tawny color with speckles, sitting, head swivels*

Serie	Art.-No	Period	Pr.	Info
48	**3617**	1948-1949	4-5	17 cm

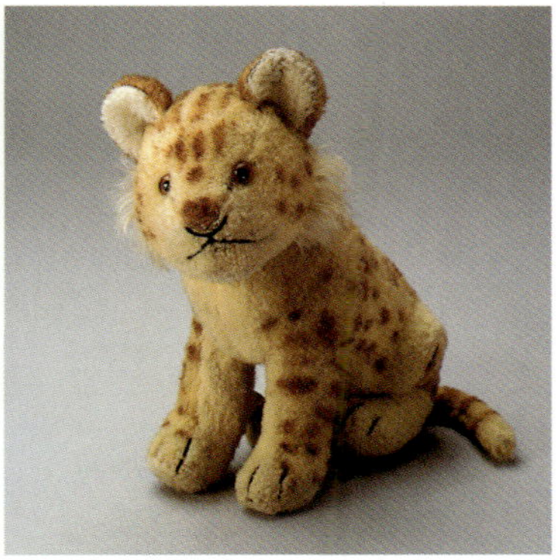

Jungloewe - *Young Lion*

Wollpluesch, gelb/braun gefleckt, sitzend, Drehkopf, sehr weich - *Plush wool, tawny colored with speckles, sitting, head swivels, very soft*

SERIE	ART.-NO	PERIOD	PR.	INFO
48	**3510**	1950-1954	4-5	10 cm
48	**3517**	1949-1954	4-5	17 cm

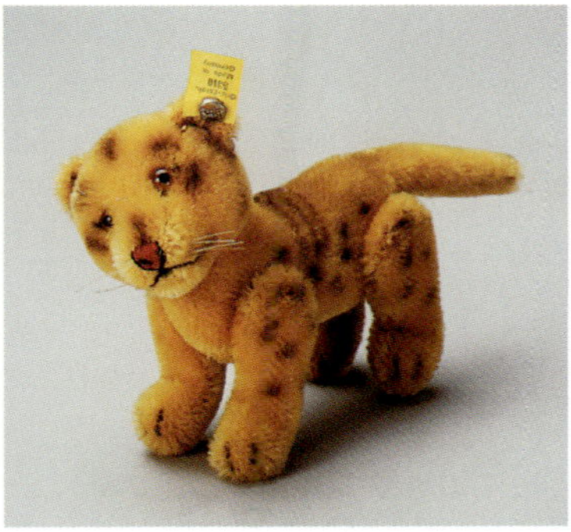

Loewen-Junges - *Young Lion*

Mohair, gelbbraun, gegliedert - *mohair, tawny colored, jointed*

SERIE	ART.-NO	PERIOD	PR.	INFO
48	**5310**	1951-1957	4-5	10 cm
48	**5316**	1949-1957	4-5	16 cm

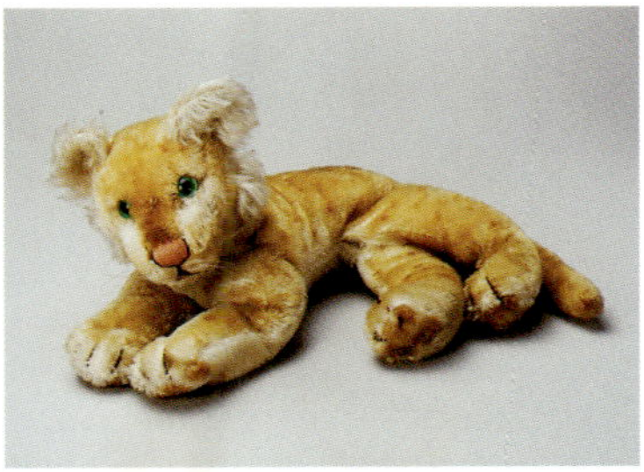

Jungloewe - *Young Lion*

Mohair, hellbraun, getupft, liegend, weich - *mohair, light brown, speckles, lying, soft*

SERIE	ART.-NO	PERIOD	PR.	INFO
48	**2317,1**	1954-1958	3-4	17 cm
482	**2317,00**	1959-1959	3-4	
48	**2328**	1953-1953	3-4	28 cm
48	**2328,1**	1954-1958	3-4	
482	**2328,00**	1959-1959	3-4	
48	**2343,1**	1954-1958	4	43 cm
482	**2343,00**	1959-1959	4	
48	**2360**	1953-1953	4	60 cm
48	**2360,1**	1954-1958	4	
482	**2360,00**	1959-1959	4	

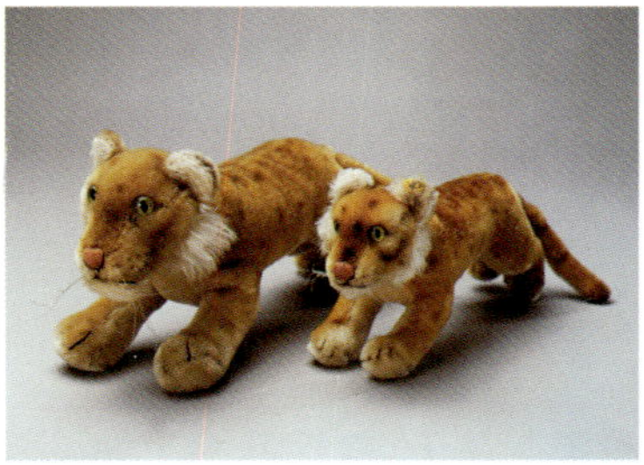

Jungloewe - *Young Lion*

Mohair, gelbbraun, stehend - *mohair, tawny colored, standing*

SERIE	ART.-NO	PERIOD	PR.	INFO
48	**1310,0**	1954-1957	4-5	10 cm
48	**1314,0**	1954-1957	4-5	14 cm
48	**1317,0**	1954-1957	4-5	17 cm

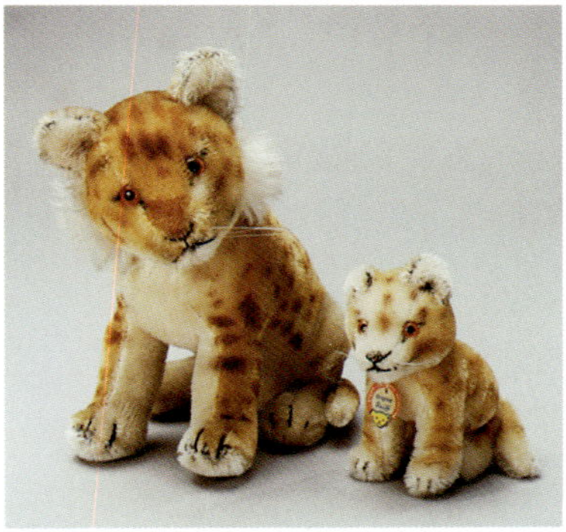

Jungloewe - *Young Lion*

Mohairpluesch, naturfarben, sitzend, drehbarer Kopf - *mohair, natural coloring, sitting, head swivels*

SERIE	ART.-NO	PERIOD	PR.	INFO
48	**3310**	1956-1958	4-5	10 cm
482	**3310,00**	1959-1961	4-5	
48	**3317**	1955-1958	4-5	17 cm

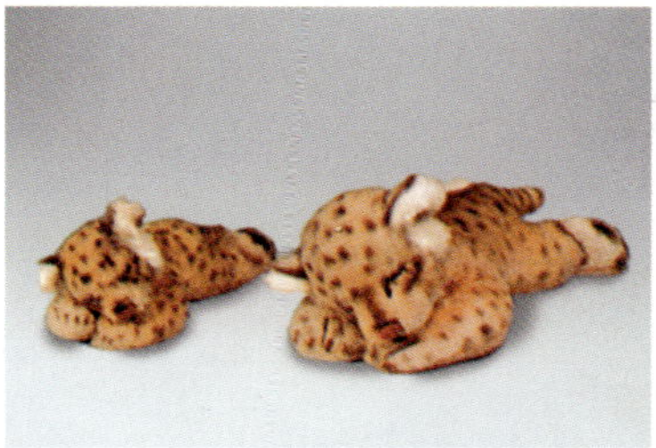

Floppy Loewenbaby - ***Floppy** Lion Baby*

Dralon-Pluesch, Augen gestickt, liegend, sehr weich - *dralon, eyes are embroidered, lying, very soft*

SERIE	ART.-NO	PERIOD	PR.	INFO
850 482	**7617,00**	1963-1963	2-3	17 cm
850 482	**7628,00**	1963-1963	2-3	28 cm

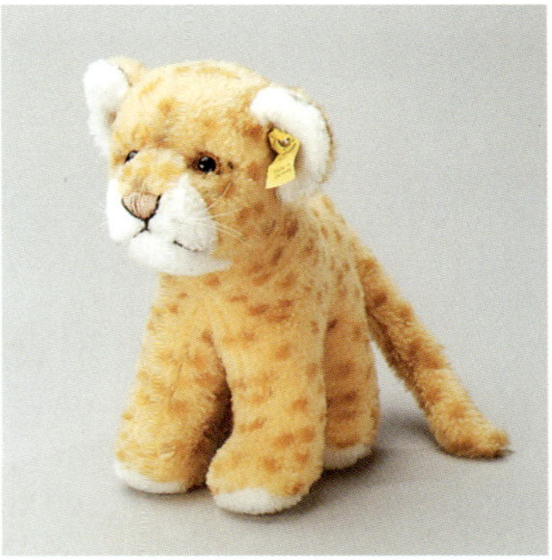

Jungloewe **Rango** - *Lion Cub **Rango***

Dralon, formgeschaeumt, stehend, abwaschbar - *dralon, stuffed with pre-formed foam, standing, surface washable*

SERIE	ART.-NO	PERIOD	PR.	INFO
	6435/18	1973-1977	2	18 cm
	6435/25	1972-1977	2	25 cm

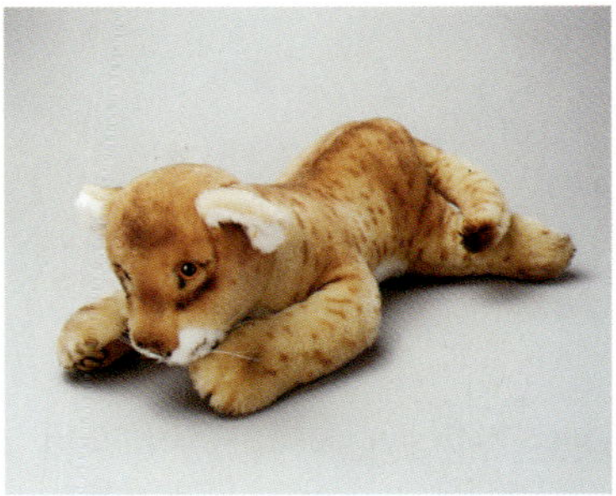

Molly Loewe - *Molly Lion*

Dralon-Wirkpluesch, 1978 Dralonpluesch, abwaschbar - *dralon knitted plush, in 1978 dralon plush, surface washable*

SERIE	ART.-NO	PERIOD	PR.	INFO
	0332/40	1973-1978	2	40 cm

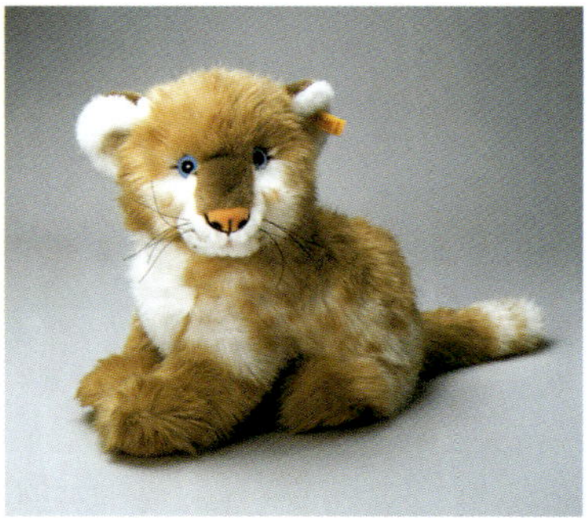

Junior Leo Loewe - ***Junior Leo** Lion*

Webpelz, abwaschbar - *woven fur, surface washable*

SERIE	ART.-NO	PERIOD	PR.	INFO
076206	**2897/30**	1982-1989	2-3	30 cm

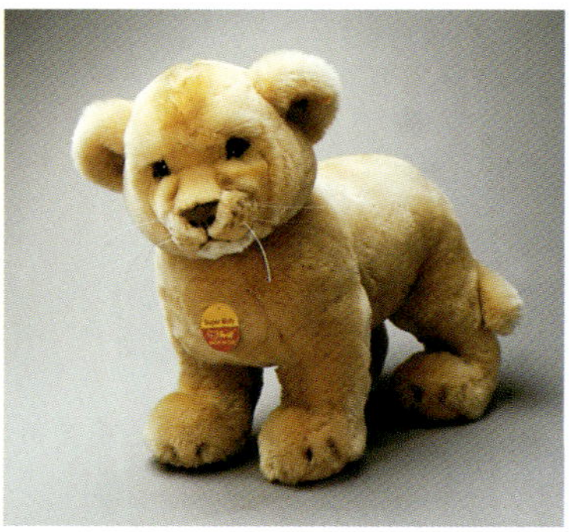

Super Molly Jungloewe - ***Super Molly** Lion Cub*

Webpelz, stehend, abwaschbar - *woven fur, standing, surface washable*

SERIE	ART.-NO	PERIOD	PR.	INFO
102974	**0381/50**	1987-1989	3	50 cm

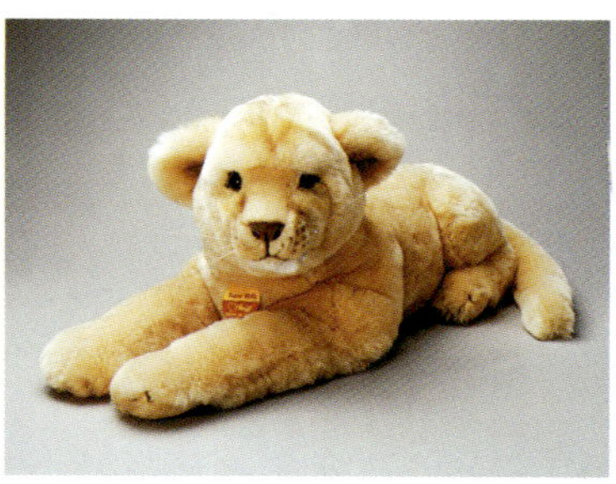

Super Molly Jungloewe - ***Super Molly** Lion Cub*

Webpelz, liegend, abwaschbar - *woven fur, lying, surface washable*

SERIE	ART.-NO	PERIOD	PR.	INFO
103025	**0382/60**	1987-1989	3	60 cm

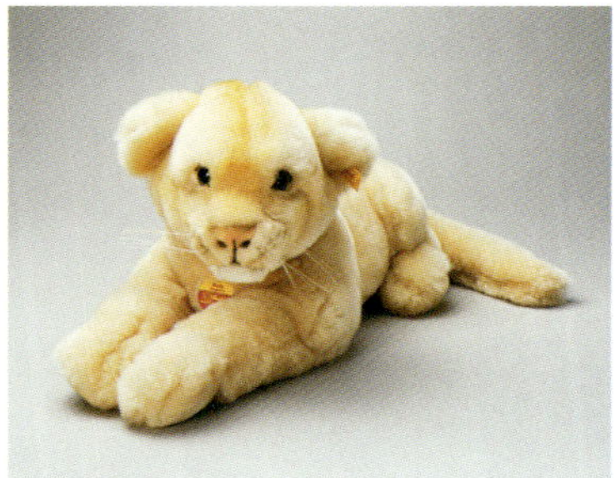

Molly Jungloewe - *Molly Lion Cub*

Webpelz, waschmaschinenfest - *woven fur, machine washable*

SERIE	ART.-NO	PERIOD	PR.	INFO
103001	**0372/45**	1989-1990	3	45 cm
	103001	1991-1999	3	

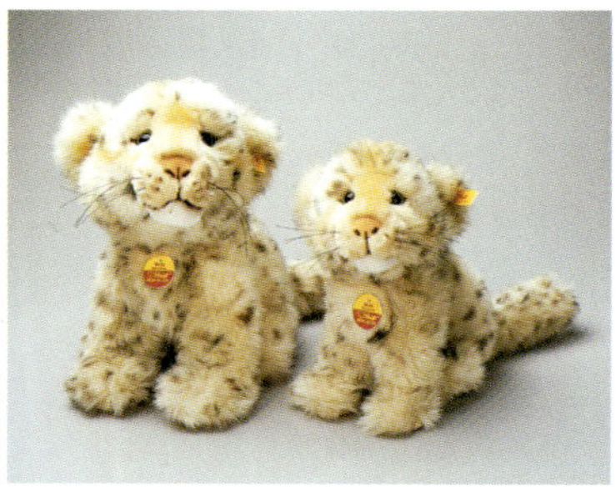

Molly Baby Loewe - *Molly Baby Lion*

Webpelz, gefleckt, sitzend, handwaschbar - *woven fur, speckled, sitting, hand washable*

SERIE	ART.-NO	PERIOD	PR.	INFO
102806	**0371/22**	1990-1990	2-3	22 cm
	102806	1991-1995	2-3	
102813	**0371/30**	1990-1990	2-3	30 cm
	102813	1991-1991	2-3	

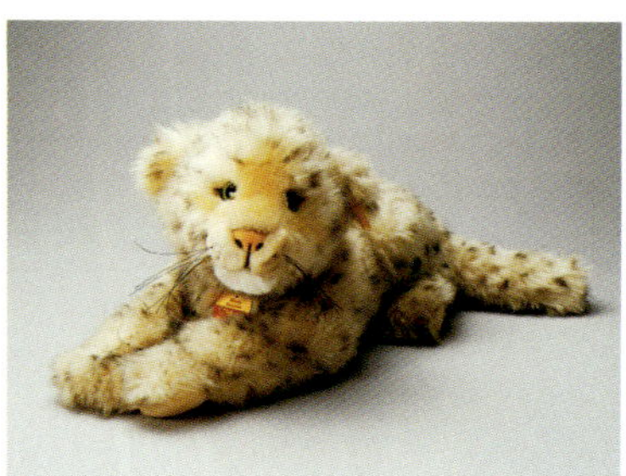

Molly Baby Loewe - *Molly Baby Lion*

Webpelz, gefleckt, liegend, handwaschbar - *woven fur, speckled, lying, hand washable*

SERIE	ART.-NO	PERIOD	PR.	INFO
102844	**0373/35**	1990-1990	3	35 cm
	102844	1991-1996	3	
102851	**0368/45**	1989-1990	3	45 cm
	102851	1991-1992	3	

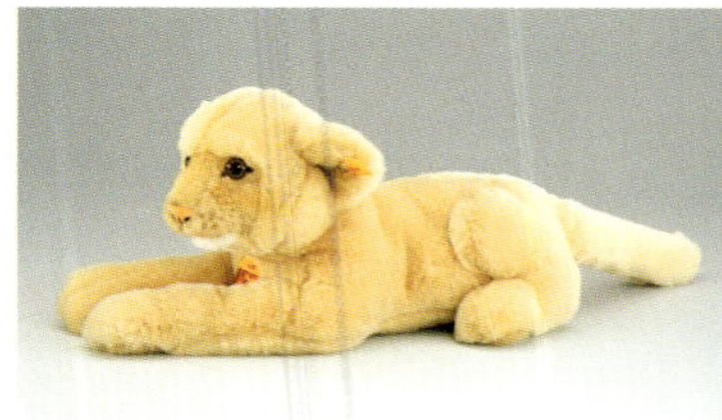

Leo Loewe - ***Leo** Lion*

Webpelz, liegend, waschmaschinenfest - *woven fur, lying, machine washable*

EAN-NO.	PERIOD	PR.	INFO
066702	1997-1999	3	35 cm

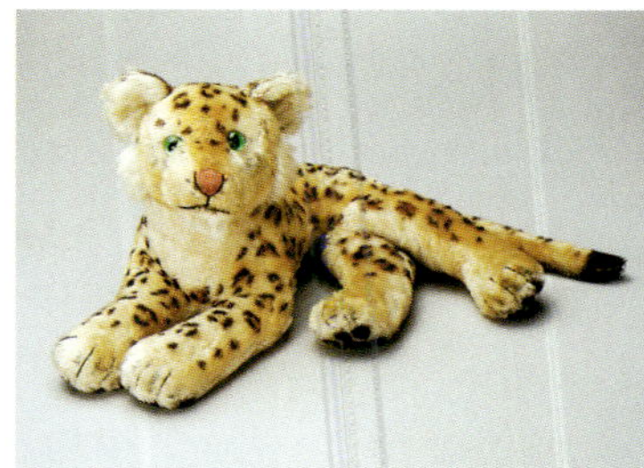

Leopard

Mohair, natuerliche Zeichnung, liegend, weich - *mohair, natural colored, lying, soft*

SERIE	ART.-NO	PERIOD	PR.	INFO
48a	**2317,1**	1954-1958	4	17 cm
483	**2317,00**	1959-1961	3-4	
48a	**2328**	1953-1953	4-5	28 cm
48a	**2328,1**	1954-1958	4	
483	**2328,00**	1959-1961	4	
48a	**2343,1**	1954-1958	4-5	43 cm
483	**2343,00**	1959-1959	4-5	
48a	**2360**	1953-1953	5	60 cm
48a	**2360,1**	1954-1958	4-5	
483	**2360,00**	1959-1959	4-5	

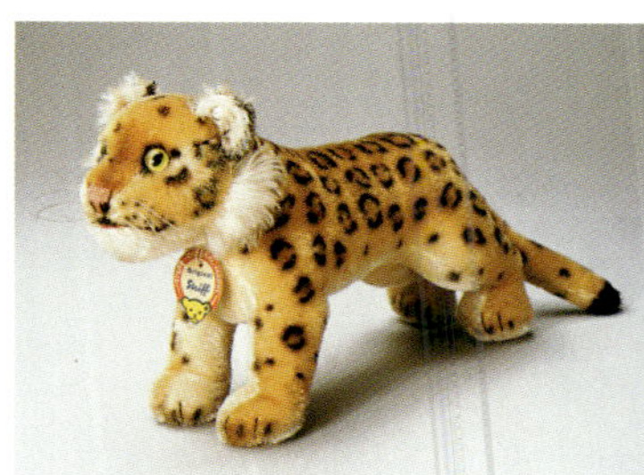

Leopard

Mohairpluesch, weiss, schwarz/gelb gefleckt, stehend - *mohair, white, black/ yellow spotted, standing*

SERIE	ART.-NO	PERIOD	PR.	INFO
48a	**1310,0**	1955-1958	4	10 cm
483	**1310,00**	1959-1961	3-4	
48a	**1314,0**	1956-1958	4	14 cm
48a	**1317,0**	1955-1958	4	17 cm
483	**1317,00**	1961-1961	4	

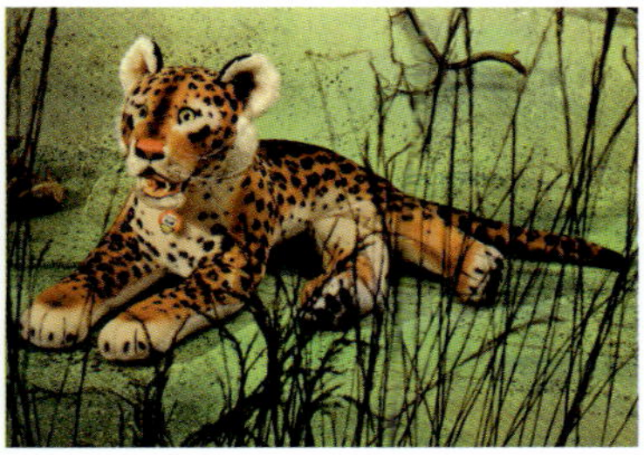

Leopard

Schautier, Mohair, naturfarben, liegend - *display animal, mohair natural-colored, lying*

Serie	Art.-No	Period	Pr.	Info
	0889/08	1967-1967	5-6	80 cm

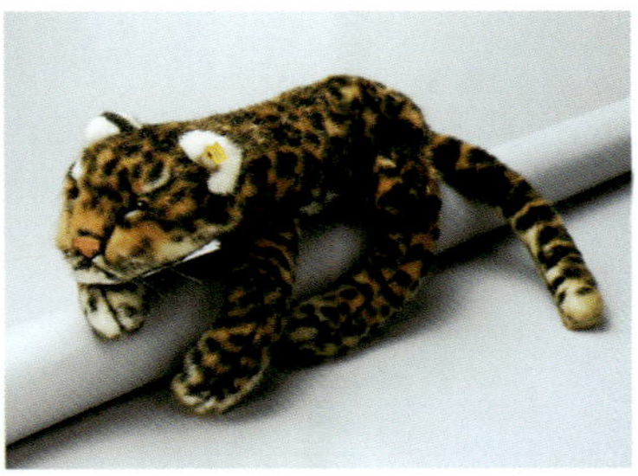

Lieg-Leopard - *Lying Leopard*

Dralon-Pelz, naturfarben, liegend, superweich, abwaschbar - *dralon fur, natural colored, lying, super soft, surface washable*

Serie	Art.-No	Period	Pr.	Info
	5320/35	1972-1977	2-3	35 cm
	5320/50	1972-1977	3	50 cm

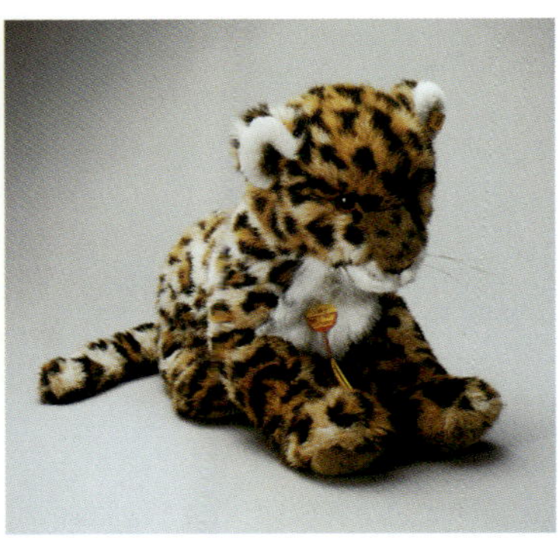

Taky Leopard

Pelzimitation, ab 1978 Wirkpluesch, sitzend, abwaschbar - *imitation fur, from 1978 knitted plush, sitting, surface washable*

Serie	Art.-No	Period	Pr.	Info
	0890/40	1976-1983	3	40 cm

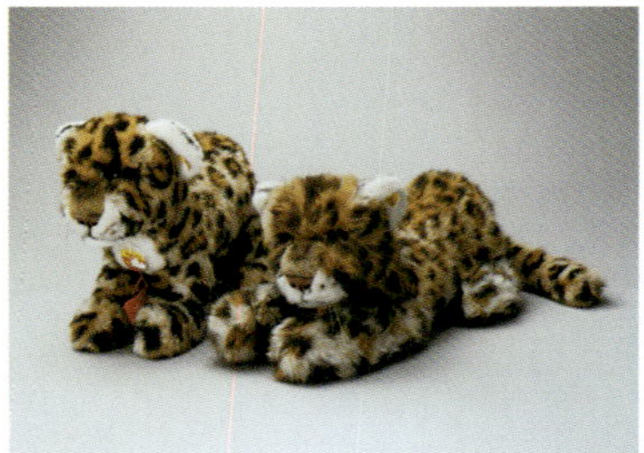

Patchy Jungleopard - ***Patchy*** *Young Leopard*

Wirkpluesch, ab 1978 Synthetik-Wirkpelz, abwaschbar, 30 cm liegend, 40 cm stehend - *knitted plush, from 1978 synthetic knitted fur, surface washable, 30 cm lying, 40 cm standing*

Serie	Art.-No	Period	Pr.	Info
	6320/30	1977-1981	2-3	30 cm
	6320/40	1977-1980	2-3	40 cm

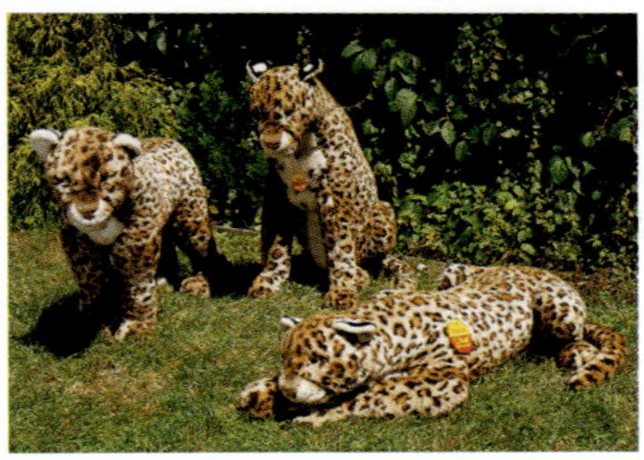

Leopard

Studiotiere, Wirkpluesch, ab 1978 Synthetik-Wirkpelz, abwaschbar - *studio animals, knitted plush, from 1978 synthetic knitted fur, surface washable*

Serie	Art.-No	Period	Pr.	Info
	6320/99	1977-1985	5	99 cm, liegend - *lying*
505379	**6321/99**	1977-1986	5-6	99 cm, stehend - *standing*
505386	**6322/99**	1980-1986	6	73 cm, sitzend - *sitting*

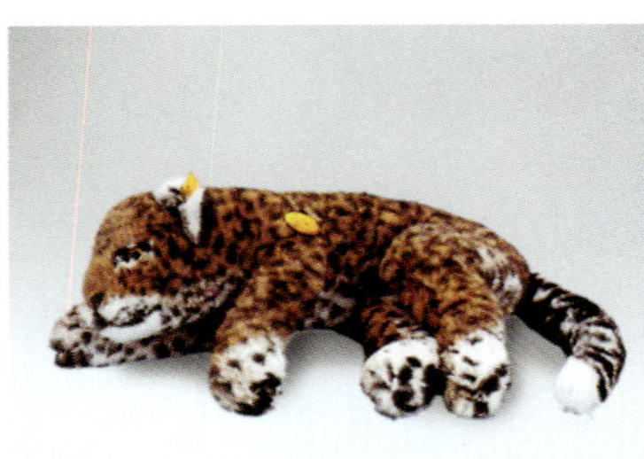

Pardy Leopard

Wirkpelz, liegend, abwaschbar - *knitted fur, lying, surface washable*

Serie	Art.-No	Period	Pr.	Info
	5351/40	1979-1982	3	40 cm

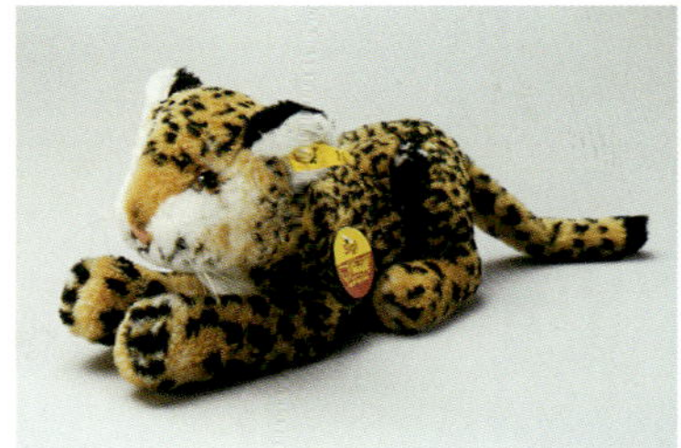

Sigi Leopard

Wirkpelz, liegend, abwaschbar - *knitted fur, lying, surface washable*

Serie	Art.-No	Period	Pr.	Info
	0825/16	1980-1983	2-3	16 cm

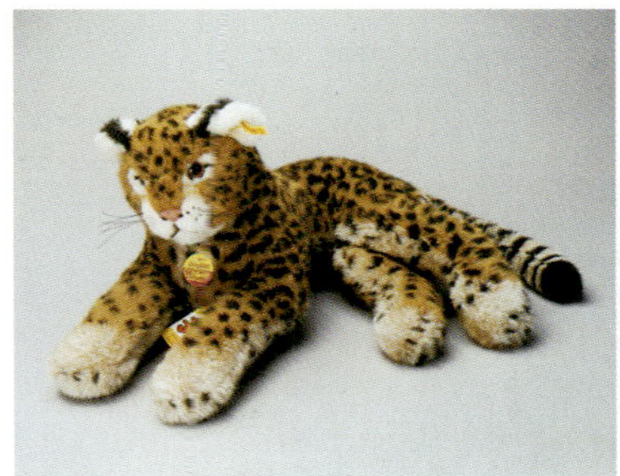

Leopard

Wirkpelz, liegend, abwaschbar - *knitted fur, lying, surface washable*

Serie	Art.-No	Period	Pr.	Info
	0885/50	1982-1985	3	50 cm

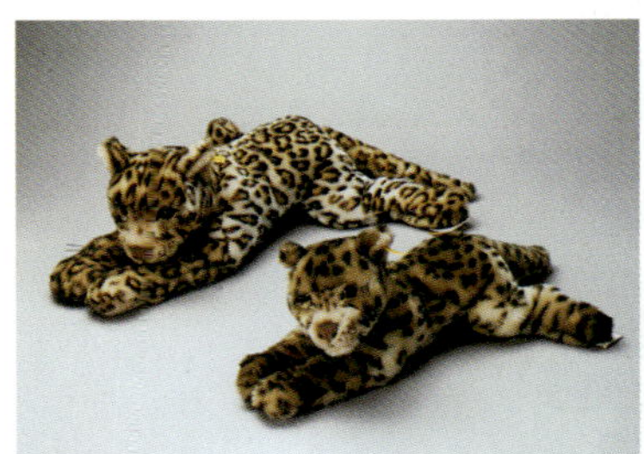

Molly Leopard

Webpelz, liegend, waschmaschinenfest - *woven fur, lying, machine washable*

Serie	Art.-No	Period	Pr.	Info
103926	**0390/40**	1988-1990	3	40 cm
	103926	1991-1999	3	
103957	**0390/50**	1987-1990	3-4	50 cm
	103957	1991-1997	3-4	

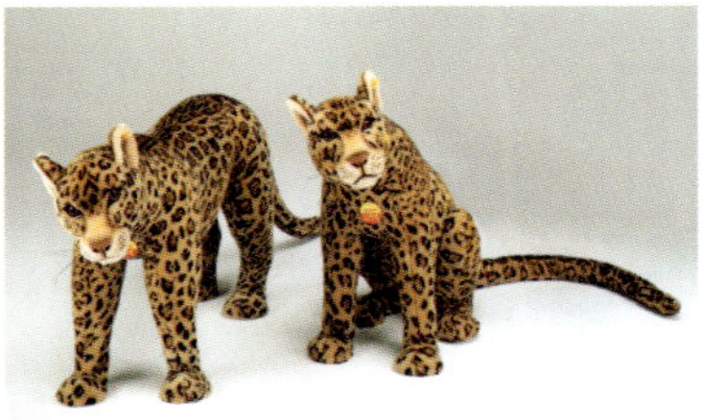

Studio Leopard

Webpelz, abwaschbar - *woven fur, surface washable*

Serie	Art.-No	Period	Pr.	Info
502903	**0850/99**	1990-1990	5-6	100 cm stehend - *standing*
	502903	1991-1996	5-6	
502934	**0854/99**	1990-1990	5-6	70 cm sitzend - *sitting*
	502934	1991-1996	5-6	

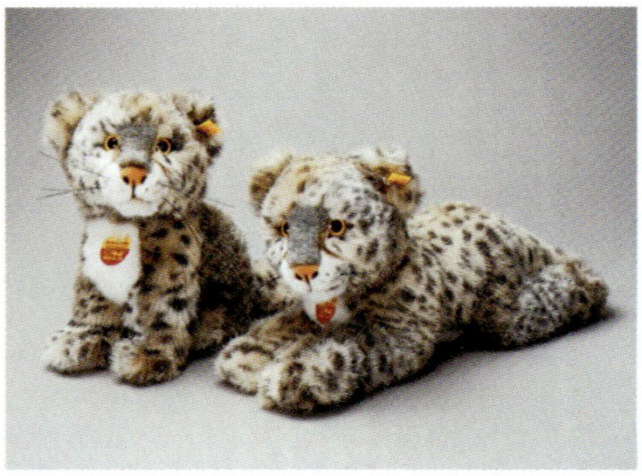

Snobby Baby Schneeleopard - *Snobby Baby Snow Leopard*

Webpelz, handwaschbar - *woven fur, hand washable*

EAN-No.	Period	Pr.	Info
065750	1991-1995	2-3	25 cm, sitzend - *sitting*
065804	1991-1996	3	30 cm, liegend - *lying*

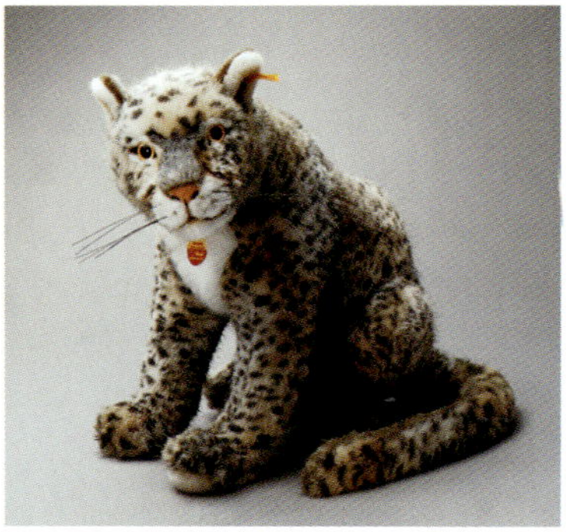

Snobby Schneeleopard - *Snobby Snow Leopard*

Webpelz, sitzend, abwaschbar - *woven fur, sitting, surface washable*

EAN-No.	Period	Pr.	Info
065552	1991-1994	3-4	45 cm

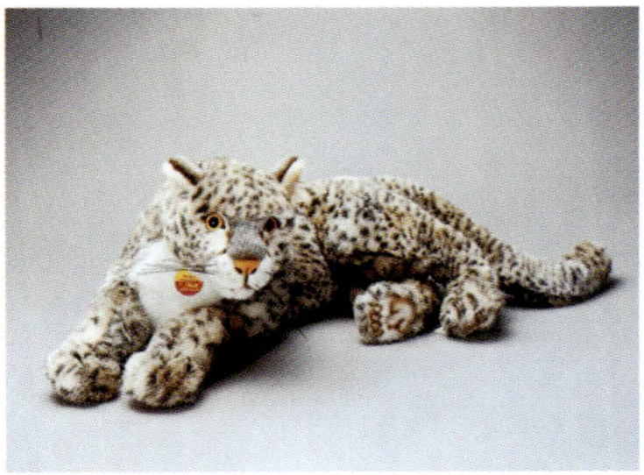

Snobby Schneeleopard - *Snobby Snow Leopard*

Webpelz, liegend, abwaschbar - *woven fur, lying, surface washable*

EAN-No.	Period	Pr.	Info
065606	1991-1993	3	45 cm

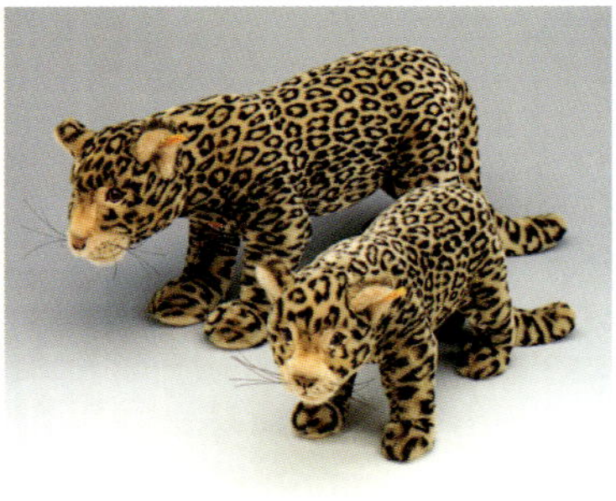

Pardy Leopard ab 1996 **Paddy** - ***Pardy*** *Leopard from 1996* ***Paddy***

Webpelz, stehend, abwaschbar - *woven fur, standing, surface washable*

EAN-No.	Period	Pr.	Info
065507	1995-1999	3	50 cm
065514	1995-1999	4	60 cm

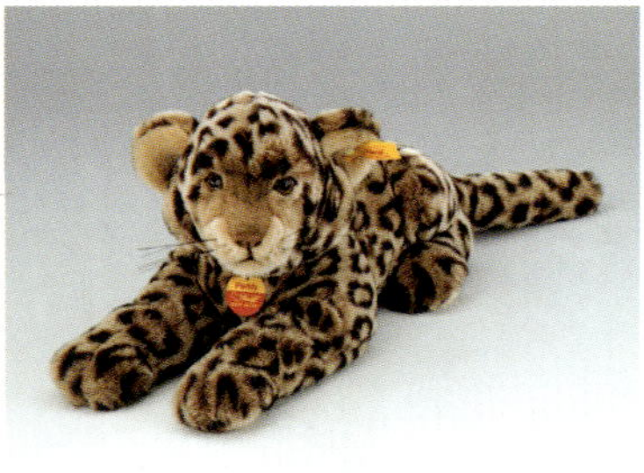

Paddy Leopard

Webpelz, liegend, waschmaschinenfest - *woven fur, lying, machine washable*

EAN-No.	Period	Pr.	Info
065477	1997-1999	3	35 cm

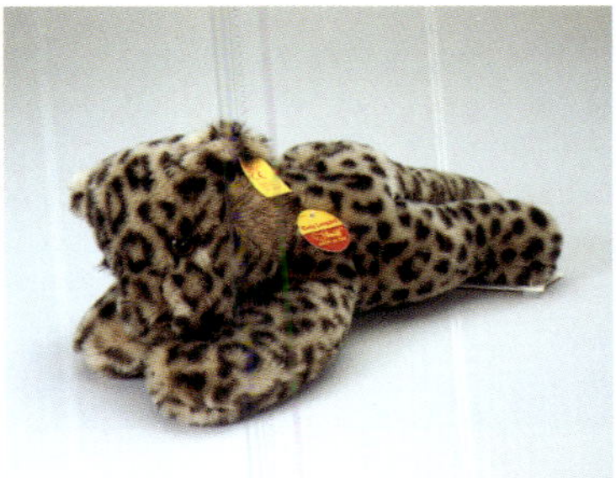

Cosy Leopard

Webpelz, liegend, waschmaschinenfest - *woven fur, lying, machine washable*

EAN-No.	Period	Pr.	Info
089039	1998-1999	2-3	28 cm

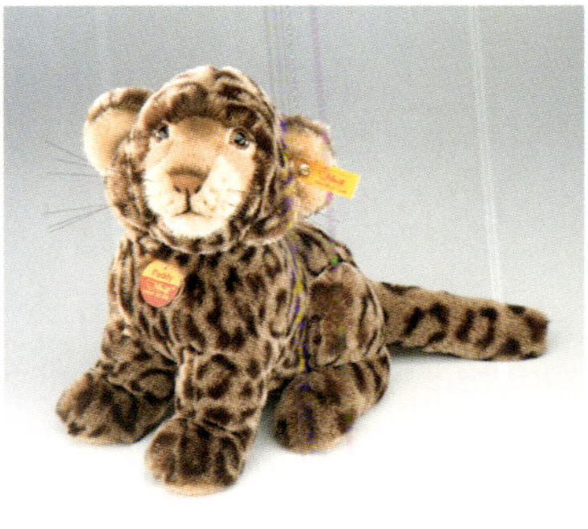

Paddy Leopard

Webpelz, sitzend, waschmaschinenfest - *woven fur, sitting, machine washable*

EAN-No.	Period	Pr.	Info
065521	1998-1999	3	25 cm

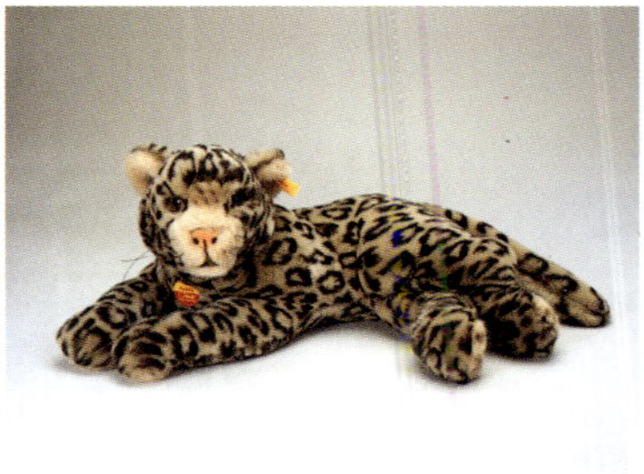

Paddy Leopard

Webpelz, seitlich liegend, waschmaschinenfest - *woven fur, lying aside, machine washable*

EAN-No.	Period	Pr.	Info
103933	1999-1999	3	45 cm

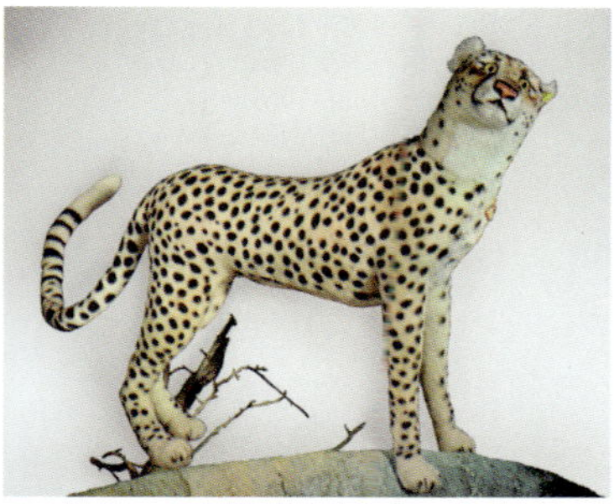

Gepard - *Cheetah*

Schautier, Mohair, stehend, Kopf drehbar - *display animal, mohair, standing, head swivels*

Serie	Art.-No	Period	Pr.	Info
	0899/10	1967-1967	6	100 cm

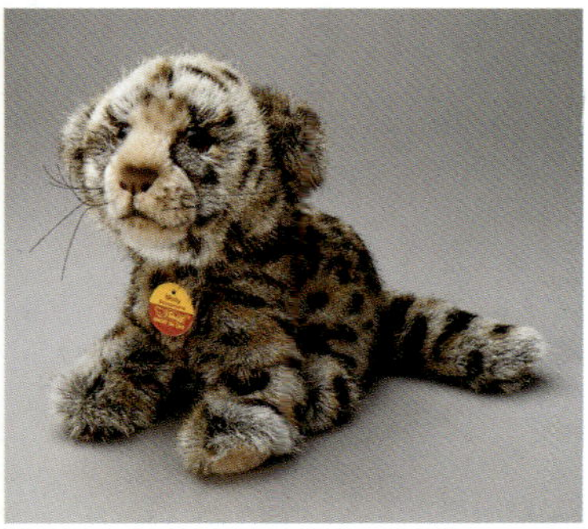

Molly Baby Gepard - ***Molly Baby*** *Cheetah*

Webpelz, sitzend, handwaschbar - *woven fur, sitting, hand washable*

Serie	Art.-No	Period	Pr.	Info
102905	**0392/22**	1990-1990	2	22 cm
	102905	1991-1994	2	
102929	**0392/30**	1990-1990	2	30 cm
	102929	1991-1993	2	

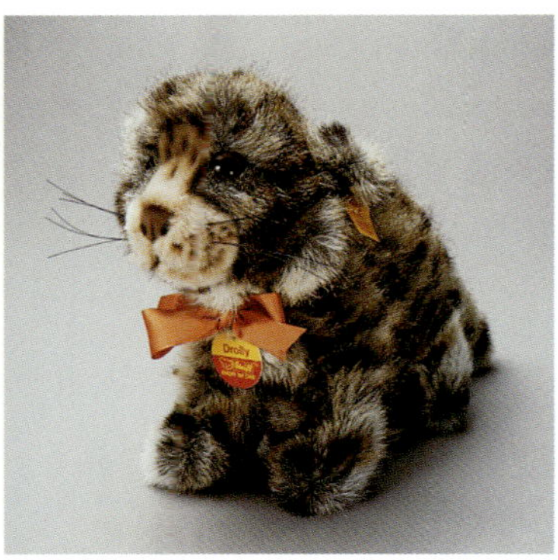

Drolly Gepard - ***Drolly*** *Cheetah*

Webpelz, stehend, waschmaschinenfest - *woven fur, standing, machine washable*

EAN-No.	Period	Pr.	Info
081439	1991-1994	2	22 cm

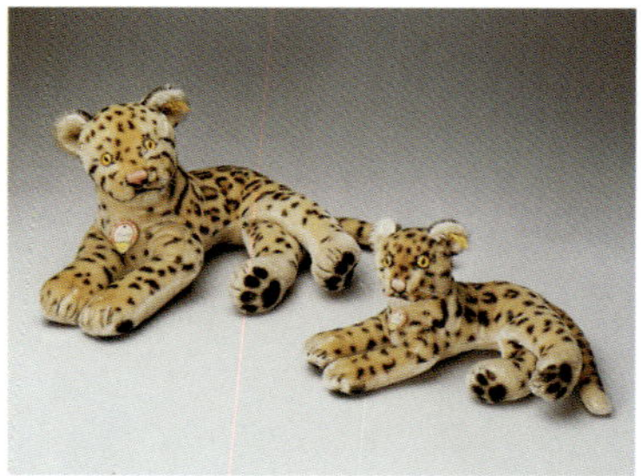

Ozelot - *Ocelot*

Mohair, natuerliche Zeichnung, liegend - *mohair, natural markings, lying*

Serie	Art.-No	Period	Pr.	Info
486	**2317,00**	1964-1964	4-5	17 cm
087	**2317,00**	1965-1967	4-5	
486	**2328,00**	1964-1964	4-5	28 cm
087	**2328,00**	1965-1967	4-5	

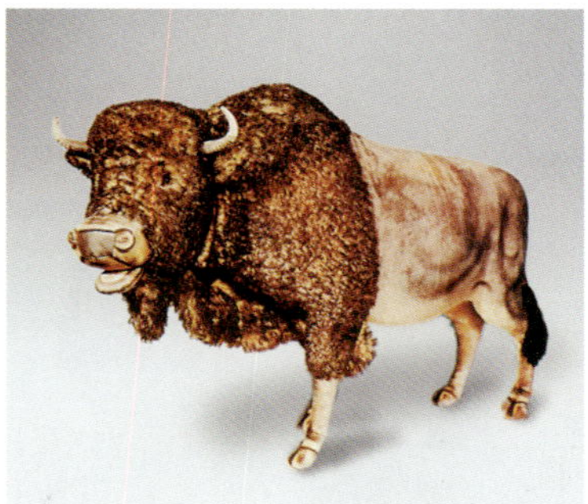

Bison

Schautier, Mohair - *display animal, mohair*

Serie	Art.-No	Period	Pr.	Info
523	**1200,90**	1960-1960	7	200 cm

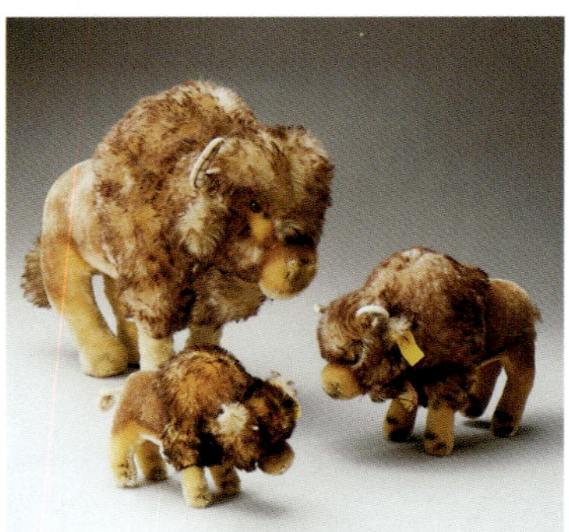

Bison

Mohairpluesch, braun, stehend - *mohair, brown, standing*

Serie	Art.-No	Period	Pr.	Info
523	**1312,90**	1960-1960	4	12 cm, nur USA - *USA only*
523	**1312,00**	1962-1963	4	12 cm
523	**1317,90**	1960-1960	4-5	17 cm, nur USA - *USA only*
523	**1317,00**	1962-1963	4-5	17 cm
523	**1330,90**	1960-1960	5	30 cm, nur USA - *USA only*
523	**1330,00**	1962-1963	5	30 cm

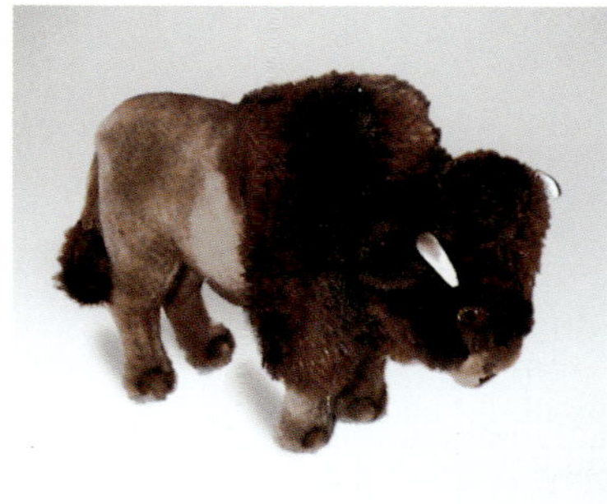

Bully Bison

Studio-Tier, Nerzimitation, ab 1978 Synthetik-Webpelz, braun, stehend, abwaschbar - *studio animal, imitation mink, from 1978 synthetic woven fur, brown, standing, surface washable*

Serie	Art.-No	Period	Pr.	Info
	6310,60	1977-1984	3-4	60 cm

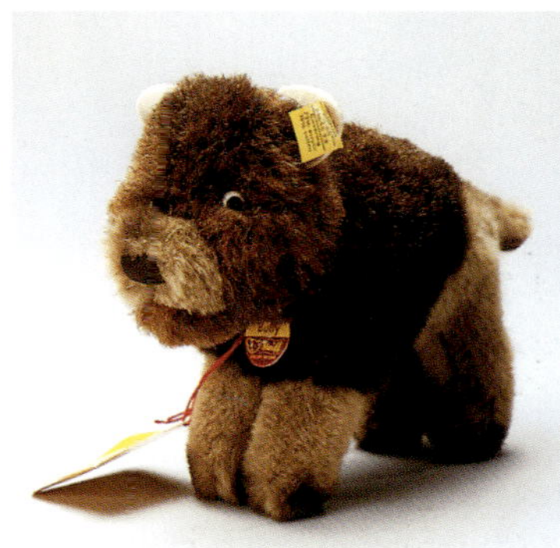

Bully Bison

Web-/Wirkpelz, stehend, abwaschbar - *woven/knitted fur, standing, surface washable*

Serie	Art.-No	Period	Pr.	Info
	1458/12	1979-1982	2	12 cm

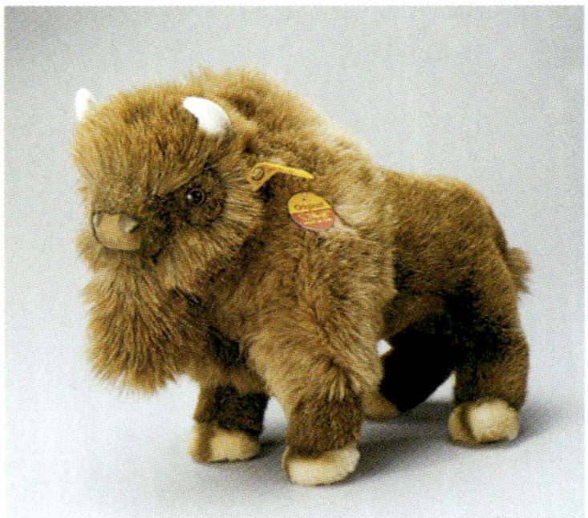

Bison

Webpelz, abwaschbar - *woven fur, surface washable*

SERIE	ART.-NO	PERIOD	PR.	INFO
072550	**2695/35**	1988-1989	3	35 cm

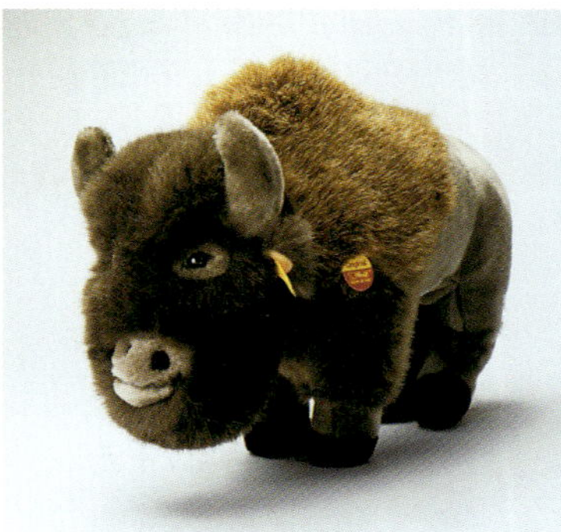

Bison

Webpelz, abwaschbar - *woven fur, surface washable*

EAN-NO.	PERIOD	PR.	INFO
068928	1993-1999	3-4	50 cm

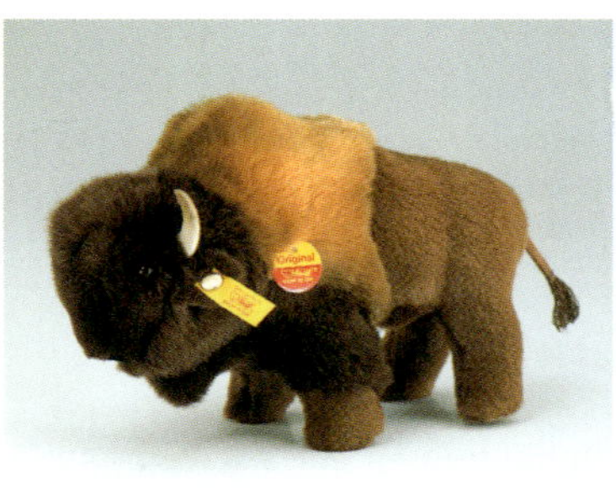

Bison

Webpelz, stehend, waschmaschinenfest - *woven fur, standing, machine washable*

EAN-NO.	PERIOD	PR.	INFO
044908	1997-1999	2	20 cm

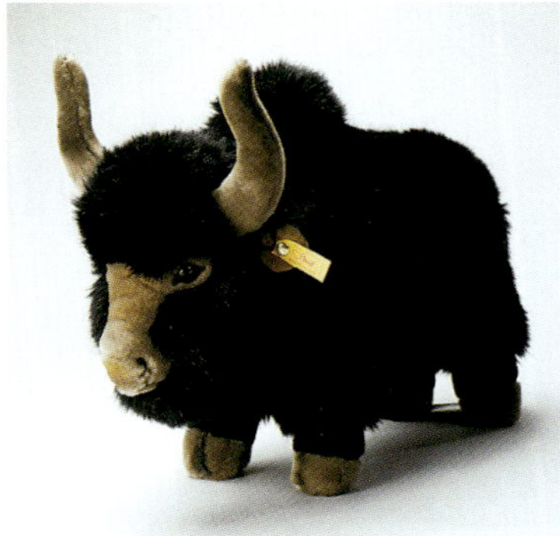

Yak

tibetanisches Hochlandrind, Webpelz, abwaschbar - *Highland Ox from Tibet, woven fur, surface washable*

EAN-NO.	PERIOD	PR.	INFO
068959	1993-1998	3-4	50 cm

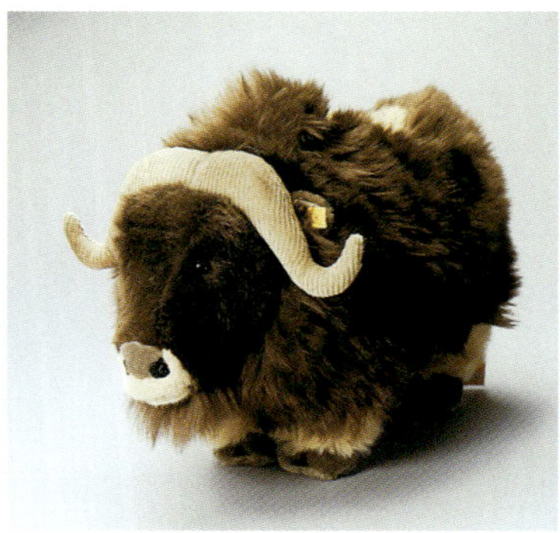

Moschusochse - *Musk Ox*

Webpelz, stehend, abwaschbar - *woven fur, standing, surface washable*

EAN-NO.	PERIOD	PR.	INFO
069055	1995-1998	4	50 cm

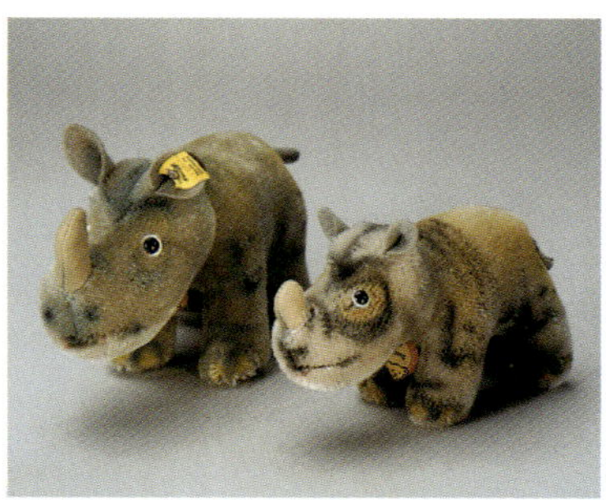

Nashorn **Nosy** - *Rhinoceros **Nosy***

Mohair, grau, stehend, abwaschbar - *mohair, grey, standing, surface washable*

SERIE	ART.-NO	PERIOD	PR.	INFO
55	**1310,0**	1954-1958	3-4	10 cm
550	**1310,00**	1959-1964	3	
110	**1310,00**	1966-1967	3	
	1100/10	1968-1974	2-3	

55	**1314,0**	1954-1958	3-4	14 cm
550	**1314,00**	1959-1964	3	
110	**1314,00**	1965-1967	3	
	1100/14	1968-1974	3	
55	**1322,0**	1956-1958	4	22 cm
550	**1322,00**	1959-1964	4	
110	**1322,00**	1965-1965	4	

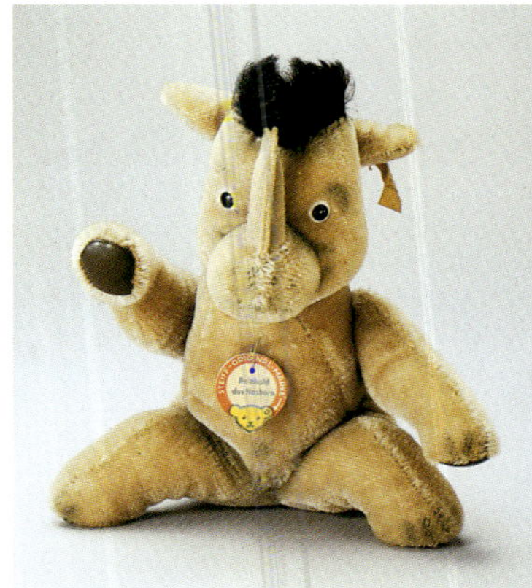

Reinhold das Nashorn - *Reinhold the Rhinoceros*

Mohair, grau, aufwartend, Drehkopf, aus Zeitschrift "Stern" - *mohair, grey, sitting up, head swivels, taken from "Stern" magazine*

SERIE	ART.-NO	PERIOD	PR.	INFO
550	**4322,05**	1964-1964	5-6	22 cm

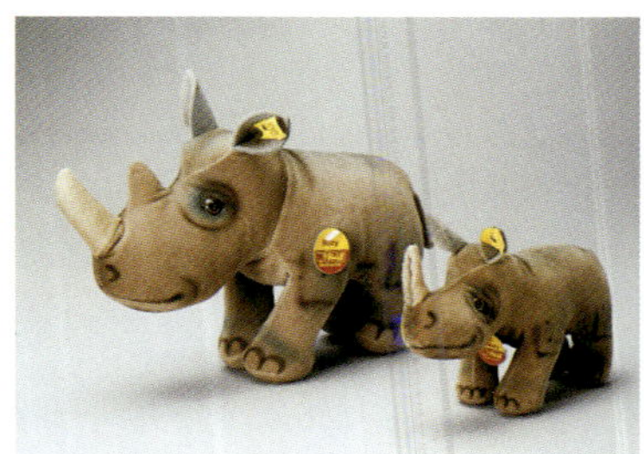

Nosy Nashorn - ***Nosy** Rhinoceros*

Trevirasamt, stehend, vollwaschbar - *trevira velvet, standing, fully washable*

SERIE	ART.-NO	PERIOD	PR.	INFO
	1110/12	1975-1978	2-3	12 cm
	1110/18	1975-1978	2-3	18 cm

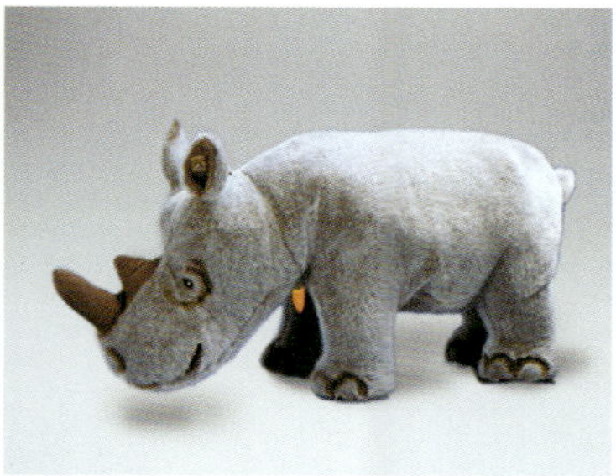

Nosy Nashorn - ***Nosy** Rhinoceros*

Synthetik-Webpluesch, grau, stehend, abwaschbar - *synthetic woven plush, grey, standing, surface washable*

SERIE	ART.-NO	PERIOD	PR.	INFO
	6305/50	1977-1979	3	50 cm

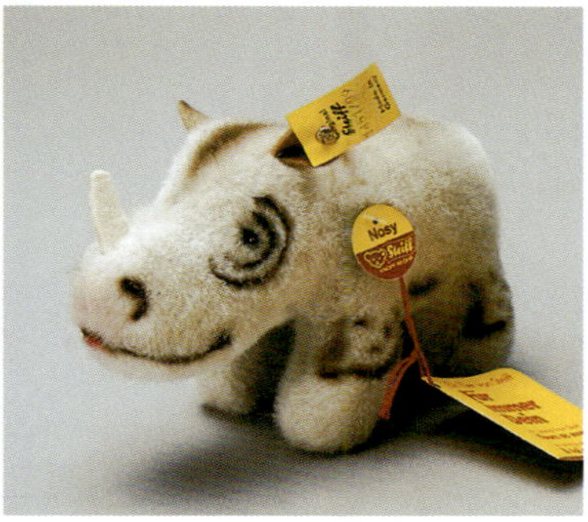

Nosy Nashorn - ***Nosy** Rhinoceros*

Webpelz, stehend, abwaschbar - *woven fur, standing, surface washable*

SERIE	ART.-NO	PERIOD	PR.	INFO
	1451/09	1979-1983	2	9 cm

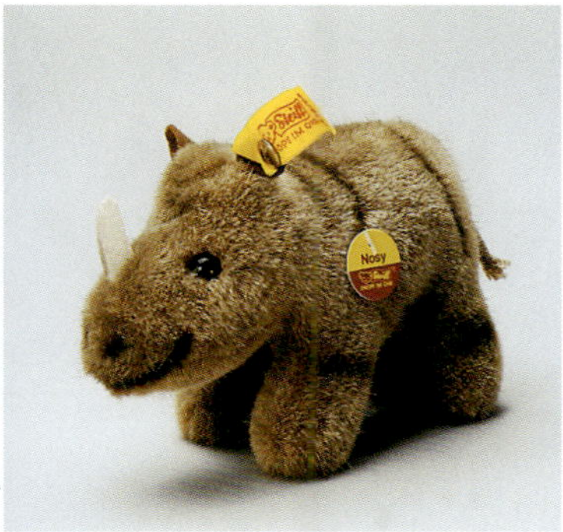

Nosy Nashorn - ***Nosy** Rhinoceros*

Webpelz, abwaschbar - *woven fur, surface washable*

SERIE	ART.-NO	PERIOD	PR.	INFO
040702	**1456/09**	1985-1988	1-2	9 cm

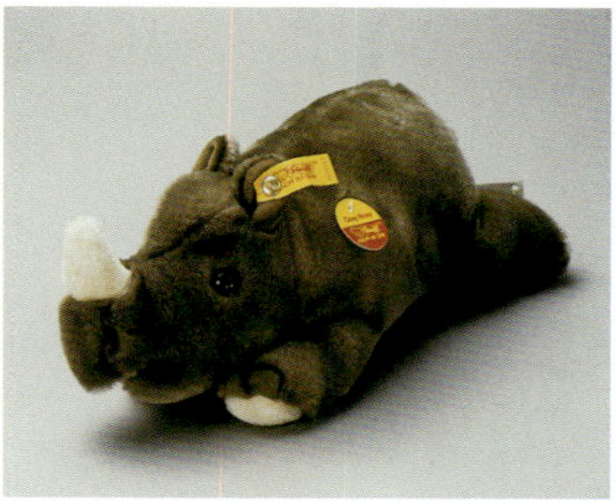

Cosy Nosy Nashorn - ***Cosy Nosy** Rhinoceros*

Webpelz, liegend, abwaschbar - *woven fur, lying, surface washable*

SERIE	ART.-NO	PERIOD	PR.	INFO
094712	**5420/19**	1988-1990	2	25 cm
094750	**5420/75**	1988-1988	3	75 cm
094767	**5420/99**	1988-1988	3-4	140 cm

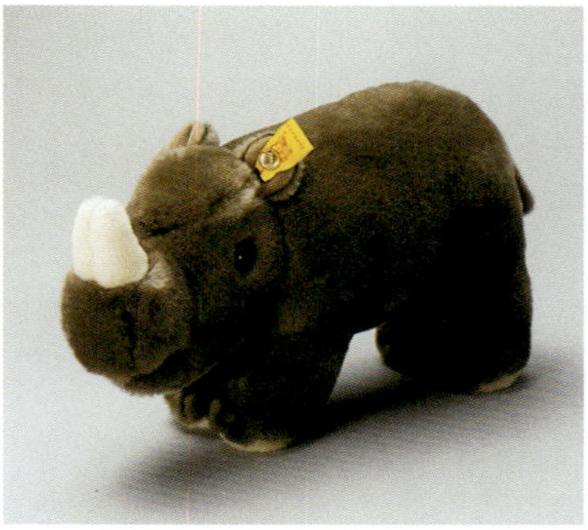

Cosy Nosy Nashorn - ***Cosy Nosy** Rhinoceros*

Webpelz, stehend, waschmaschinenfest - *woven fur, standing, machine washable*

SERIE	ART.-NO	PERIOD	PR.	INFO
094774	**5422/20**	1988-1989	2	25 cm
094798	**5422/40**	1988-1989	2-3	40 cm

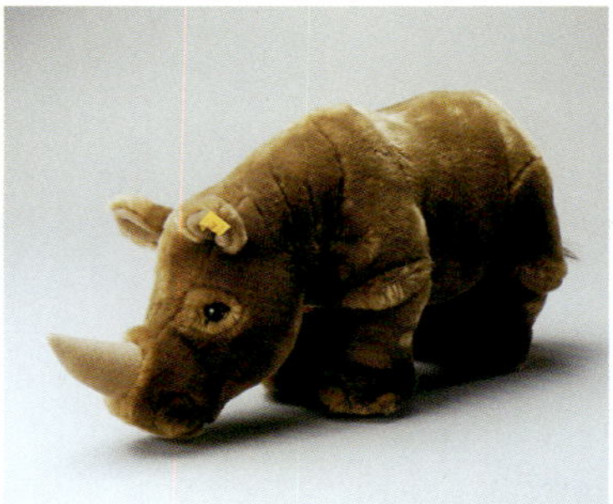

Nosy Nashorn - ***Nosy** Rhinoceros*

Webpelz, stehend, waschmaschinenfest - *woven fur, standing, machine washable*

EAN-NO.	PERIOD	PR.	INFO
063503	1993-1997	3	40 cm
063527	1993-1999	3-4	50 cm

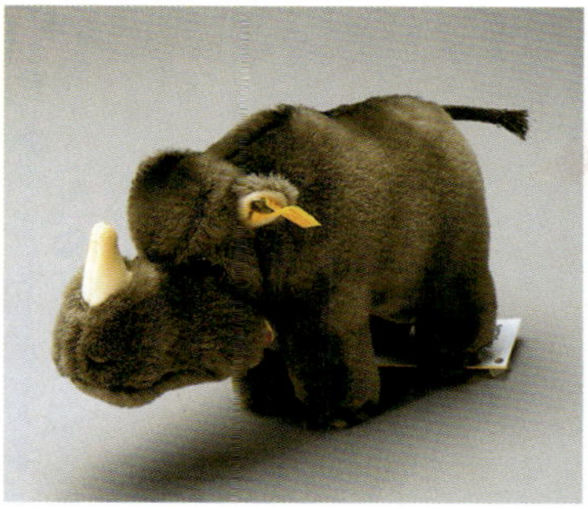

Rino Nashorn - ***Rino** Rhinoceros*

Webpelz, stehend, waschmaschinenfest - *woven fur, standing, machine washable*

EAN-NO.	PERIOD	PR.	INFO
040719	1995-1997	1-2	16 cm

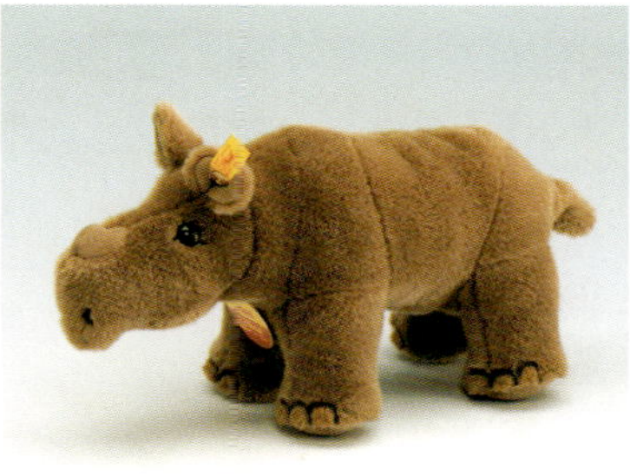

Nosili Baby Nashorn - ***Nosili** Baby Rhinoceros*

Webpelz, stehend, waschmaschinenfest - *woven fur, standing, machine washable*

EAN-NO.	PERIOD	PR.	INFO
063534	1995-1996	2	22 cm

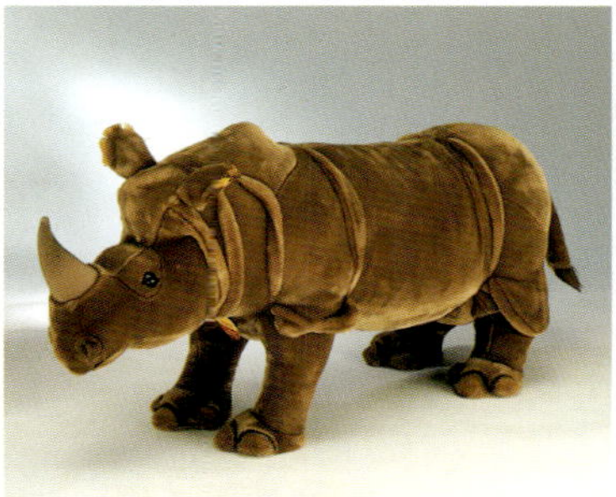

Studio Nashorn - *Studio Rhinoceros*

Webpelz, stehend, abwaschbar - *woven fur, standing, surface washable*

EAN-NO.	PERIOD	PR.	INFO
500855	1995-1999	6-7	100 cm

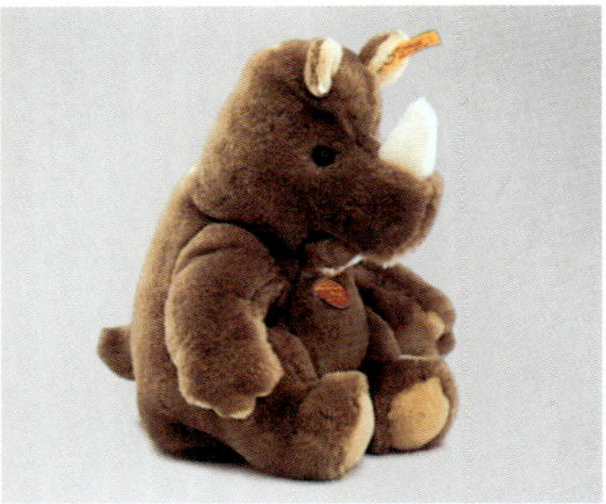

Cosy Nosy Nashorn - ***Cosy Nosy*** *Rhinoceros*

Webpelz, sitzend, waschmaschinenfest - *woven fur, sitting, machine washable*

EAN-No.	Period	Pr.	Info
085468	1996-1997	2-3	28 cm

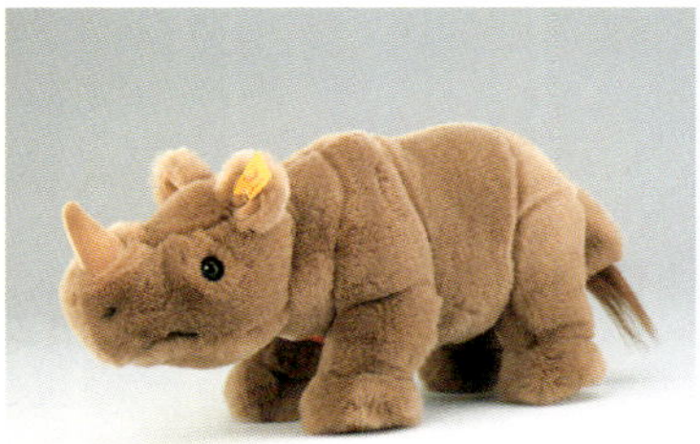

Nosy Nashorn - *Nosy Rhinoceros*

Webpelz, stehend, waschmaschinenfest - *woven fur, standing, machine washable*

EAN-No.	Period	Pr.	Info
085475	1997-1997	3	30 cm

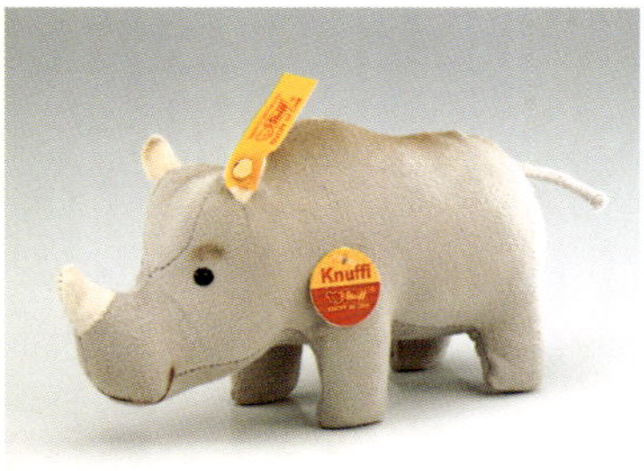

Knuffi Nashorn - ***Knuffi*** *Rhinoceros*

Microfaser-Vlies, grau, handwaschbar - *micro fibre fleece, grey, hand washable*

EAN-No.	Period	Pr.	Info
067730	1997-1997	1-2	14 cm

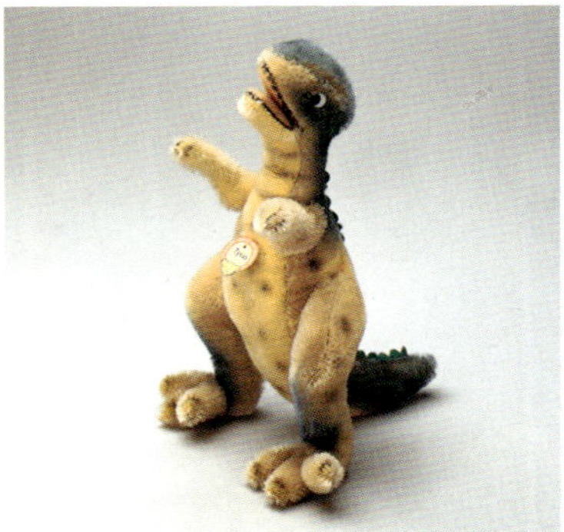

Tysus Tyrannosaurus Rex

Mohair, Arme gegliedert, aufwartend, kein Katalognachweis, weitere Groessen bekannt - *mohair, arms jointed, sitting up, no catalog information available, varying sizes known*

Serie	Art.-No	Period	Pr.	Info
635	**4317,90**	1959-1959	6	17 cm

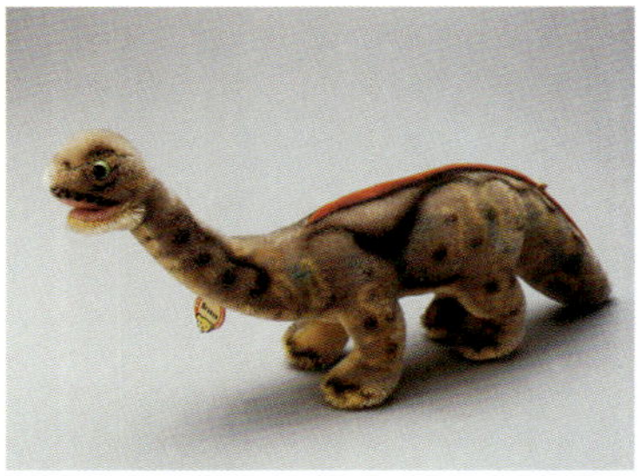

Brosus Brontosaurus

Mohair, stehend, kein Katalognachweis - *mohair, standing, no catalog information available*

Serie	Art.-No	Period	Pr.	Info
635	**1315,90**	1959-1959	6	15 cm
635	**1360,90**	1959-1959	6	60 cm

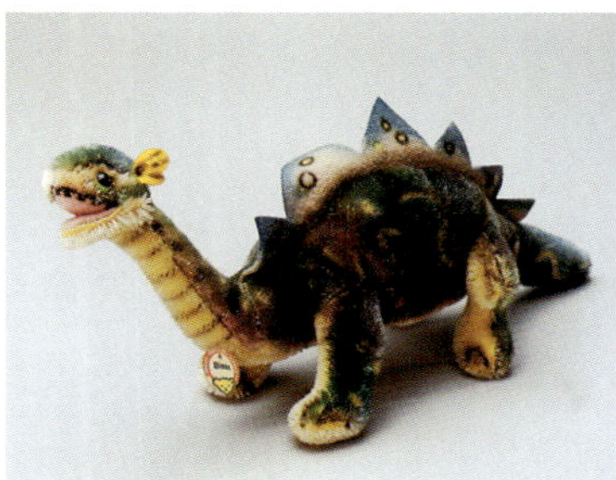

Dinos Stegosaurus

Mohair, stehend, kein Katalognachweis, weitere Groessen bekannt - *mohair, standing, no catalog information available, varying sizes known*

Serie	Art.-No	Period	Pr.	Info
635	**1312,90**	1959-1959	6	12 cm

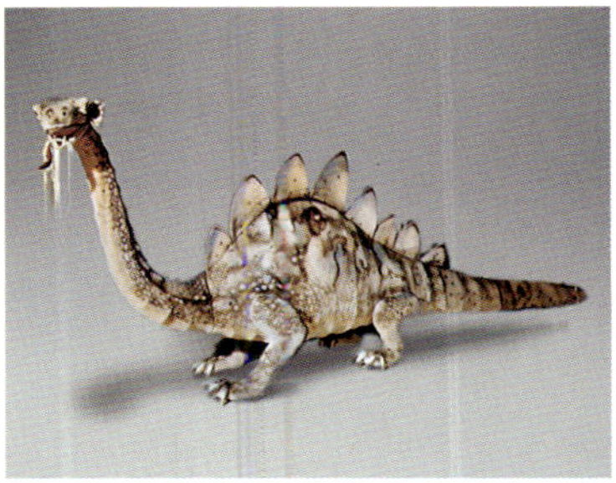

Dinosaurier - *Dinosaur*

Schautier - *display animal*

Serie	Art.-No	Period	Pr.	Info
635	**1299,90**	1960-1960	8	4 m lang - *4 m long*

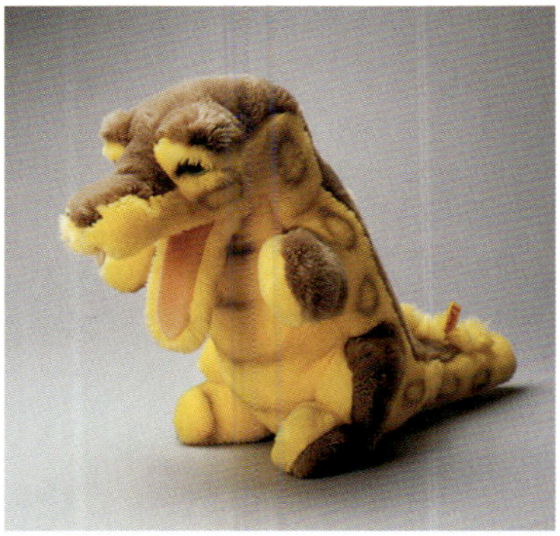

Cosy Nessy Drache - ***Cosy Nessy*** *Dragon*

Webpelz, superweich, waschmaschinenfest - *woven fur, super soft, machine washable*

Serie	Art.-No	Period	Pr.	Info
094989	**5430/50**	1981-1988	2-3	50 cm

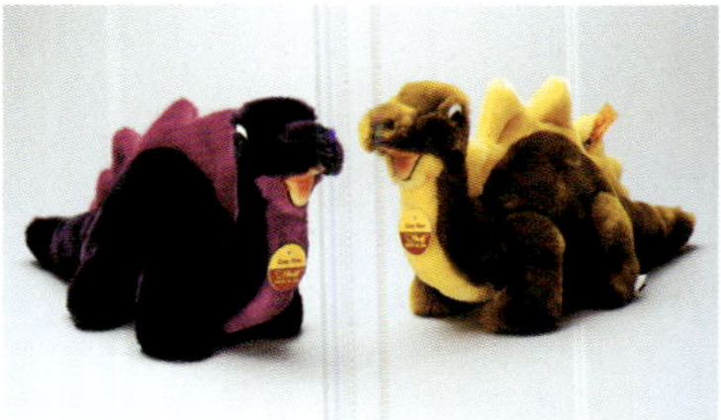

Cosy Dino Dinosaurier - ***Cosy Dino*** *Dinosaur*

Webpelz, 33 cm, waschmaschinenfest - *woven fur, 33 cm, machine washable*

Serie	Art.-No	Period	Pr.	Info
094804	**5426/33**	1988-1990	2	aubergine
	094804	1991-1995	2	
094842	**5428/33**	1988-1990	2	gelboliv - *yellowish-olive green*
	094842	1991-1995	2	

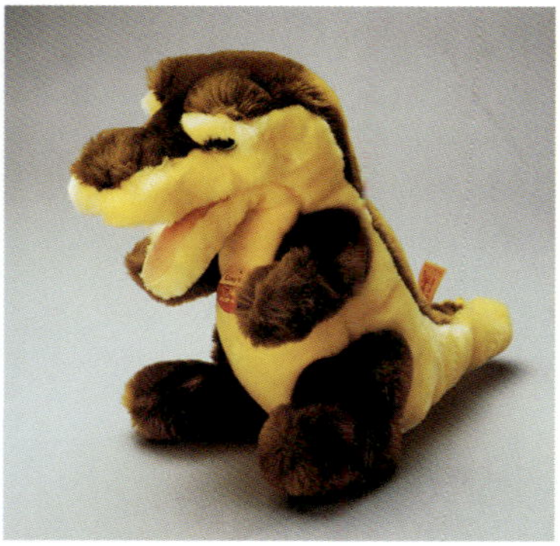

Cosy Nessy

Webpelz, gelboliv, waschmaschinenfest - *woven fur, yellowish-olive green, machine washable*

SERIE	ART.-NO	PERIOD	PR.	INFO
094965	**5431/33**	1988-1990	2	33 cm

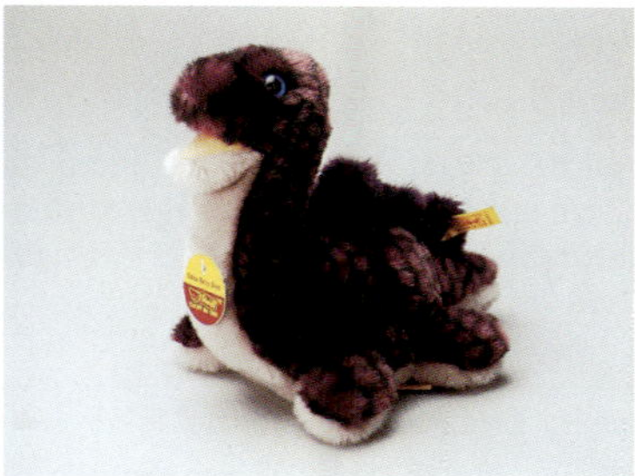

Cosy Baby Dino

Webpelz, 15 cm, Pieps-Stimme, waschmaschinenfest - *woven fur, 15 cm, squeaker, machine washable*

EAN-No.	PERIOD	PR.	INFO
094644	1993-1994	1-2	rot - *red*
094651	1993-1995	1-2	gelb - *yellow*
094668	1993-1995	1-2	gruen - *green*
094675	1993-1995	1-2	blau - *blue*
094682	1993-1995	1-2	violett - *violet*
094699	1993-1994	1-2	braun - *brown*

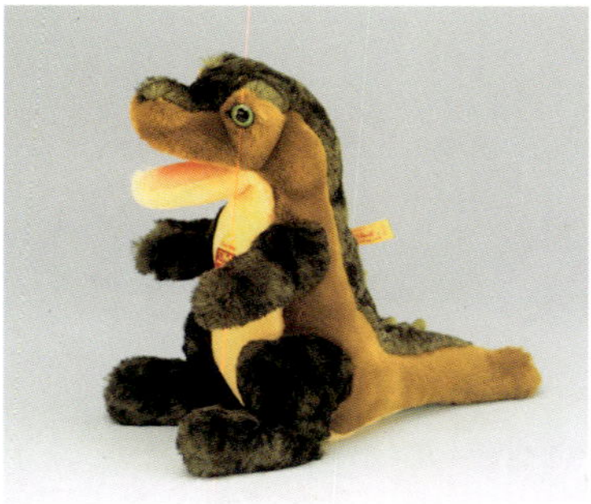

Cosy Nessy

Webpelz, aufwartend, waschmaschinenfest - *woven fur, sitting up, machine washable*

EAN-No.	PERIOD	PR.	INFO
095467	1994-1995	2	25 cm, gruen - *green*
095597	1994-1994	2-3	35 cm, rostbraun - *rusty brown*

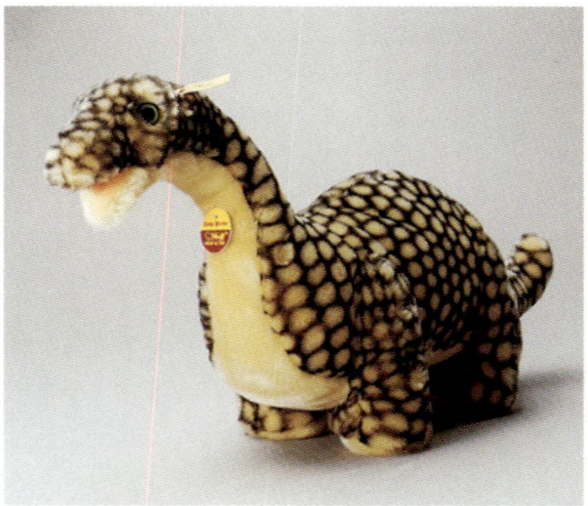

Cosy Bronto Brontosaurus

Webpelz, gelb, stehend, waschmaschinenfest - *woven fur, yellow, standing, machine washable*

EAN-No.	PERIOD	PR.	INFO
095733	1994-1995	3	50 cm

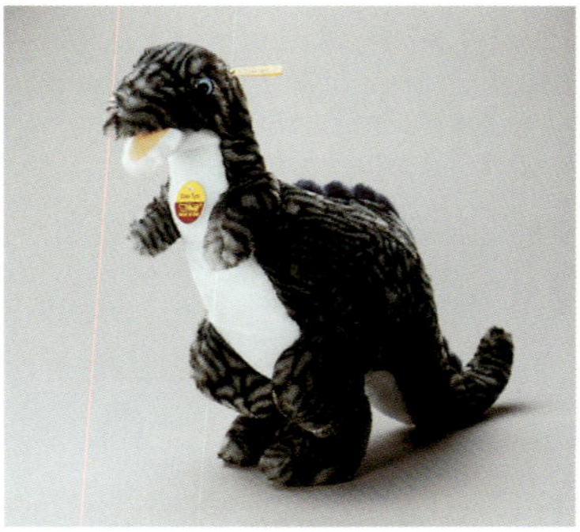

Cosy Tyro Tyrannosaurus Rex

Webpelz, blau, aufwartend, waschmaschinenfest - *woven fur, blue, sitting up, machine washable*

EAN-No.	PERIOD	PR.	INFO
095757	1994-1995	3	50 cm

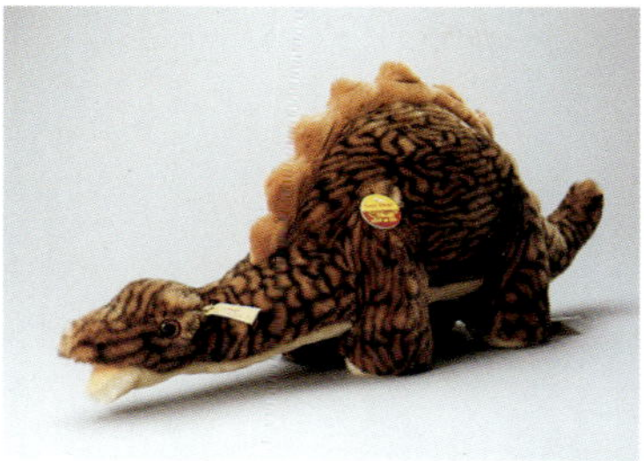

Cosy Stego Stegosaurus

Webpelz, braun, stehend, waschmaschinenfest - *woven fur, brown, standing, machine washable*

EAN-No.	PERIOD	PR.	INFO
095771	1994-1995	3	50 cm

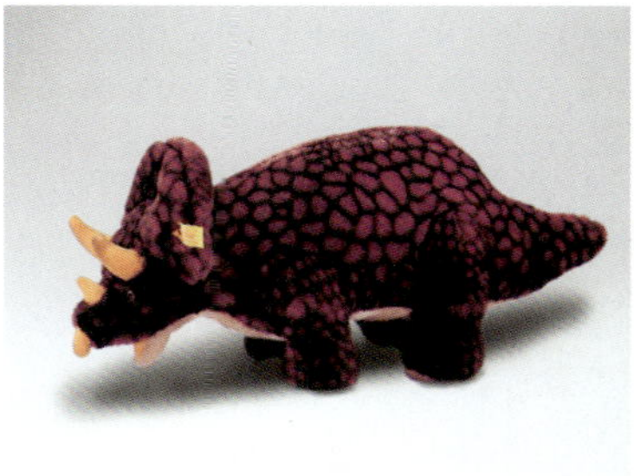

Cosy Rato Triceratops

Webpelz, violett, stehend, waschmaschinenfest - *woven fur, violet, standing, machine washable*

EAN-No.	PERIOD	PR.	INFO
095795	1994-1994	3	45 cm

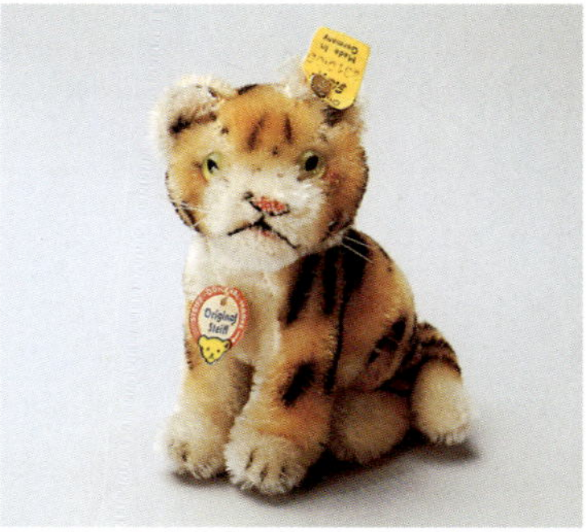

Tiger

Mohair, natuerlich gestreift, sitzend, Kopf drehbar - *mohair, naturally striped, sitting, head swivels*

SERIE	ART.-NO	PERIOD	PR.	INFO
70	**3310**	1951-1958	4-5	10 cm
700	**3310,00**	1959-1961	4-5	

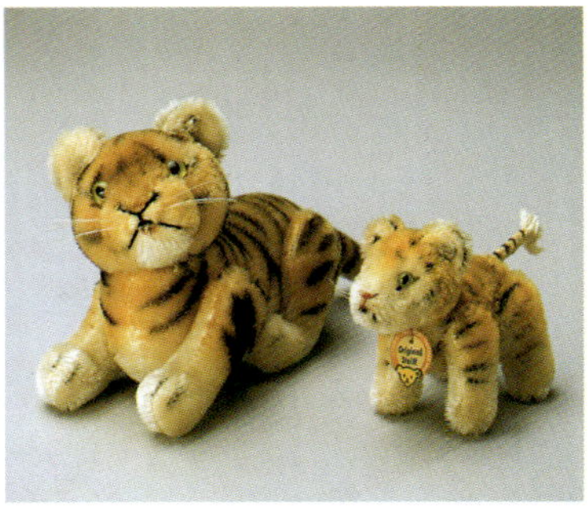

Tiger

Mohair, gelb/schwarz/weiss, getigert, gegliedert, 10 cm mit Kordelschwanz - *mohair, yellow/black/white with tiger stripes, jointed, 10 cm size has a cord tail*

SERIE	ART.-NO	PERIOD	PR.	INFO
70	**5310**	1952-1958	4-5	10 cm
700	**5310,00**	1959-1959	4-5	
70	**5314**	1952-1957	4-5	14 cm

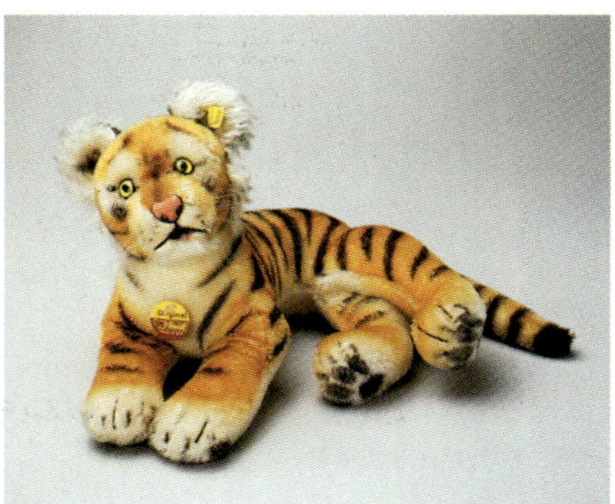

Jungtiger - *Tiger Cub*

Mohair, naturfarben, liegend, weich, abwaschbar - *mohair, natural color & markings, lying, soft, surface washable*

SERIE	ART.-NO	PERIOD	PR.	INFO
70	**2317,1**	1954-1958	3-4	17 cm
700	**2317,00**	1959-1964	3	
090	**2317,00**	1965-1967	3	
	0910/17	1968-1978	2-3	
70	**2328**	1953-1953	4	28 cm
70	**2328,1**	1954-1958	3-4	
700	**2328,00**	1959-1964	3	
090	**2328,00**	1965-1967	3	
	0910/28	1968-1977	2-3	
70	**2343,1**	1954-1958	4	43 cm
700	**2343,00**	1959-1964	3-4	
090	**2343,00**	1965-1967	3-4	
	0910/43	1968-1976	3	
70	**2360**	1953-1953	4	60 cm
70	**2360,1**	1954-1958	4	
700	**2360,00**	1959-1964	4	
090	**2360,00**	1965-1967	4	
	0910/60	1968-1977	3-4	

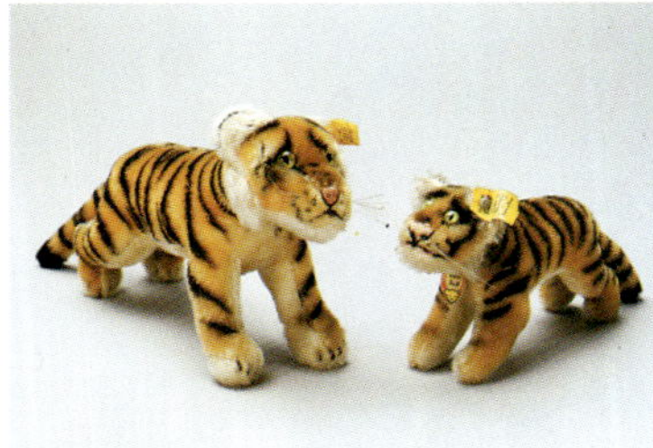

Jungtiger - *Tiger Cub*

Mohair, gelb/weiss, schwarz getigert, stehend - *mohair, tawny yellow/white, black tiger stripes, standing*

SERIE	ART.-NO	PERIOD	PR.	INFO
70	**1310,0**	1954-1958	3-4	10 cm
700	**1310,00**	1959-1964	3	
090	**1310,00**	1965-1967	3	
	0900/10	1968-1975	2-3	
70	**1314,0**	1954-1958	4	14 cm
700	**1314,00**	1959-1964	3-4	
090	**1314,00**	1965-1967	3-4	
	0900/14	1968-1975	3	
70	**1317,0**	1954-1958	4	17 cm
700	**1317,00**	1959-1964	4	
090	**1317,00**	1965-1965	4	

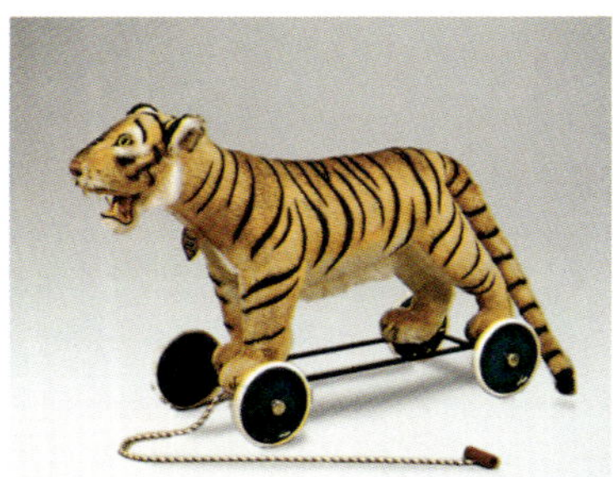

Reit Tiger - *Riding Tiger*

Mohair, gelb/braun, getigert, Eisengestell, Scheibenraeder mit Gummi, Druckstimme, offener Mund mit Zaehnen - *mohair, tawny with tiger stripes, iron frame, disc wheels with rubber tires, press voice, open mouth with teeth*

SERIE	ART.-NO	PERIOD	PR.	INFO
70	**1350,2**	1956-1958	5-6	50 cm
700	**1350,20**	1959-1964	5-6	

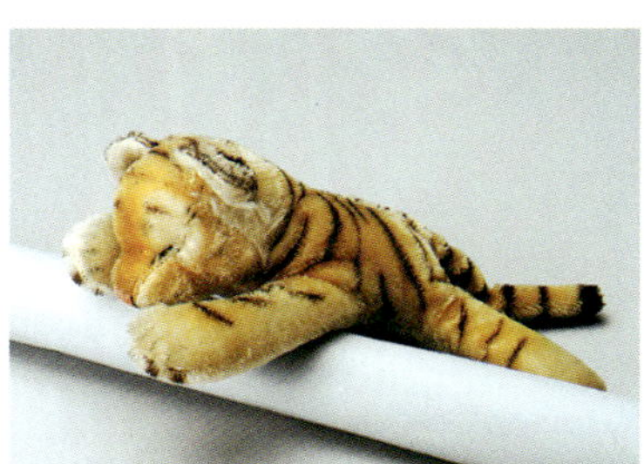

Floppy Tiger

Mohair, Augen gestickt, gelb/braun, getigert, flach liegend, sehr weich und schmiegsam - *mohair, eyes are embroidered, tawny colored with tiger stripes, lying flat, very soft & cuddly*

SERIE	ART.-NO	PERIOD	PR.	INFO
85 70	**7317**	1956-1958	3	17 cm
850 700	**7317,00**	1959-1961	3	
85 70	**7328**	1956-1958	3	28 cm
850 700	**7328,00**	1959-1961	3	

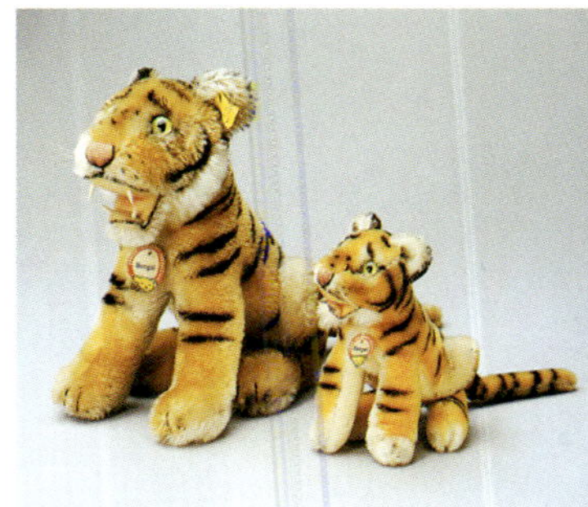

Bengal

Mohair, getigert, sitzend, offener Mund, ab 22 cm mit Zaehnen - *mohair, tiger stripes, sitting, open mouth, from 22 cm with teeth*

SERIE	ART.-NO	PERIOD	PR.	INFO
700	**3314,00**	1959-1961	5	14 cm
700	**3322,00**	1959-1961	5-6	22 cm
700	**3343,00**	1959-1961	6	43 cm

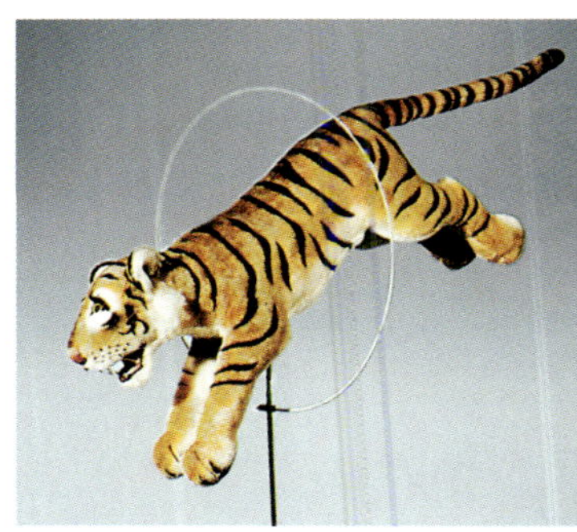

Tiger

Schautier, Mohair-Pluesch, springend - *display animal, mohair, jumping*

SERIE	ART.-NO	PERIOD	PR.	INFO
70	**1380,0**	1953-1953	6-7	80 cm
700	**1380,90**	1960-1960	6	
	0909/08	1967-1967	6	

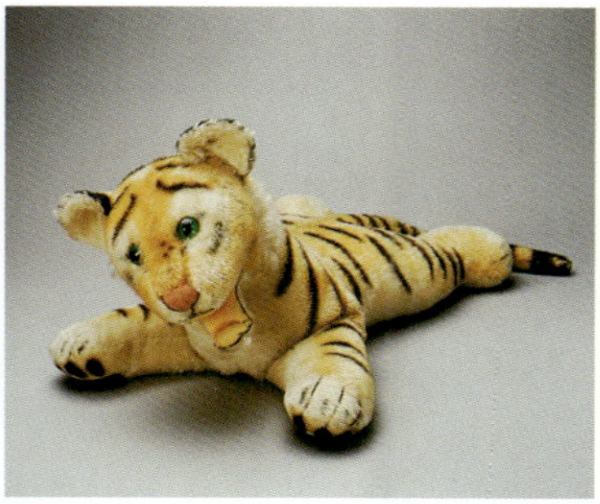

Racker Tiger

Mohair, liegend, zum Spielen & Sitzen - *mohair, lying, for playing & sitting*

SERIE	ART.-NO	PERIOD	PR.	INFO
822 700	**2345,00**	1960-1961	4-5	45 cm

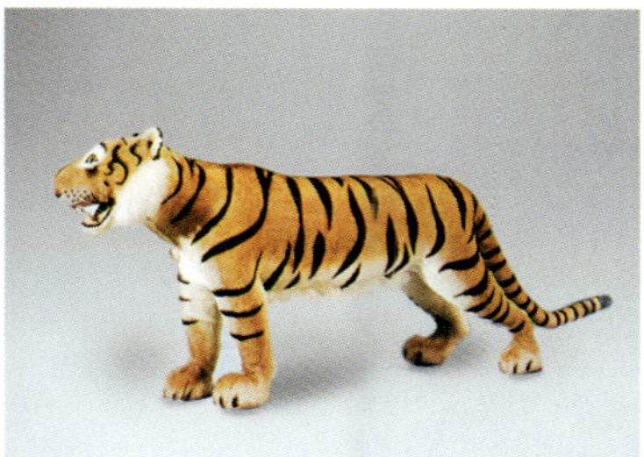

Tiger

Schautier, Mohair, naturfarben, stehend - *display animal, mohair, natural coloring & markings, standing*

SERIE	ART.-NO	PERIOD	PR.	INFO
700	**1399,90**	1960-1960	6	100 cm
090	**1399,90**	1966-1966	6	
	0909/10	1967-1967	6	

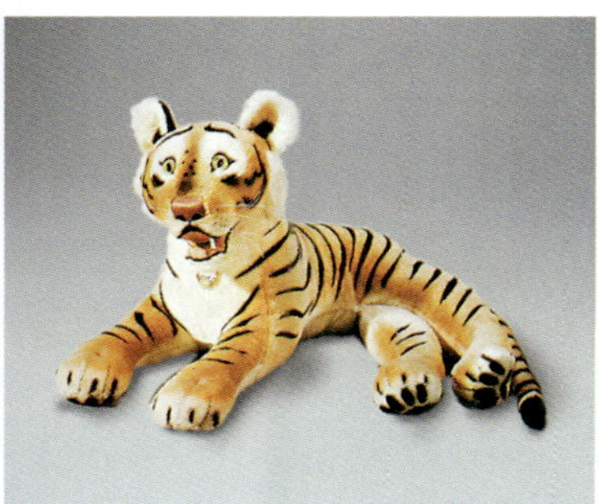

Tiger

Schautier, Mohair, naturfarben, liegend - *display animal, mohair, natural coloring & markings, lying*

SERIE	ART.-NO	PERIOD	PR.	INFO
700	**2380,90**	1960-1960	5-6	80 cm
	0919/08	1967-1967	5-6	

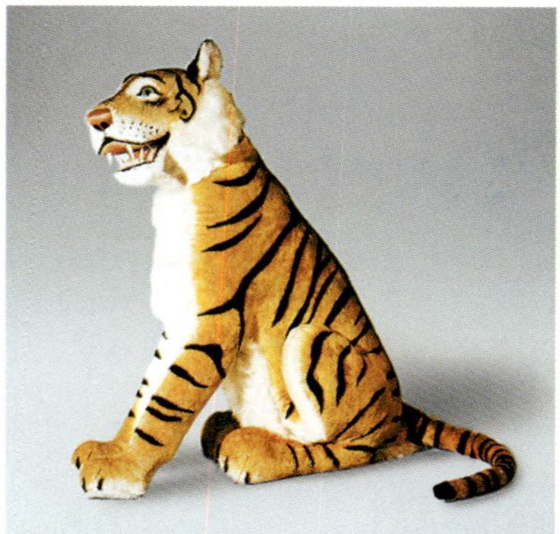

Tiger

Schautier, Mohair, naturfarben, sitzend - *display animal, mohair, natural coloring & markings, sitting*

SERIE	ART.-NO	PERIOD	PR.	INFO
700	**3360,90**	1960-1960	6	60 cm
	0929/06	1967-1967	5-6	
	0929/09	1967-1967	6	90 cm
700	**3120,90**	1960-1960	6-7	120 cm
	0929/12	1967-1967	6	

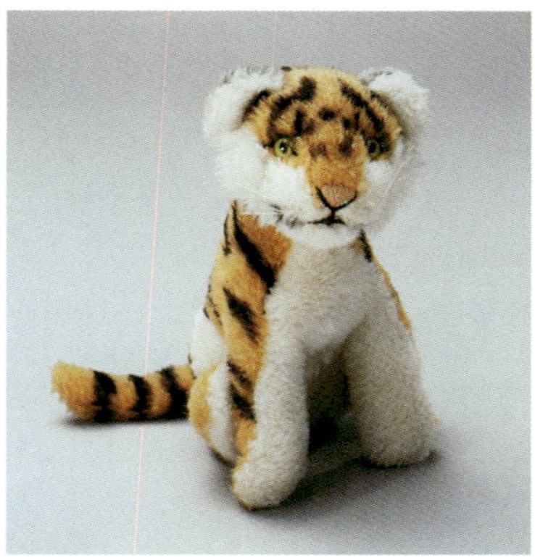

Tiger Ponx

"Der kleine Tierversand", im Kaefigkarton, mit Tiersteckbrief, Dralon, abwaschbar - *"Der kleine Tierversand", in its own animal crate, with information label, dralon, surface washable*

SERIE	ART.-NO	PERIOD	PR.	INFO
	5818/17	1971-1974	3	17 cm

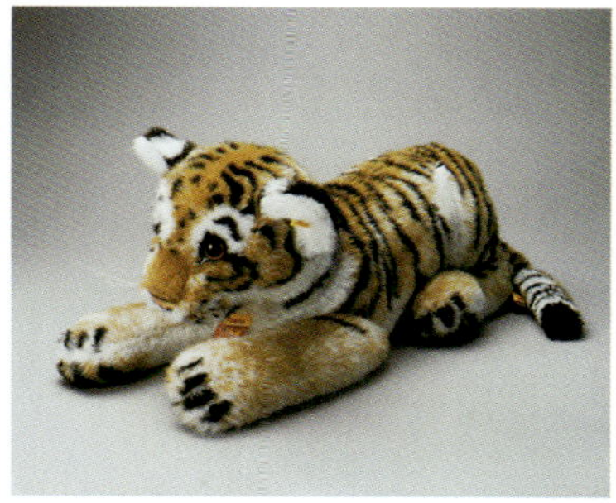

Pascha Jungtiger - ***Pascha*** *Tiger Cub*

Wirkpelz, liegend abwaschbar - *knitted fur, lying, surface washable*

SERIE	ART.-NO	PERIOD	PR.	INFO
	6314/60	1978-1983	2-3	60 cm
062506	**0870/60**	1984-1989	2-3	

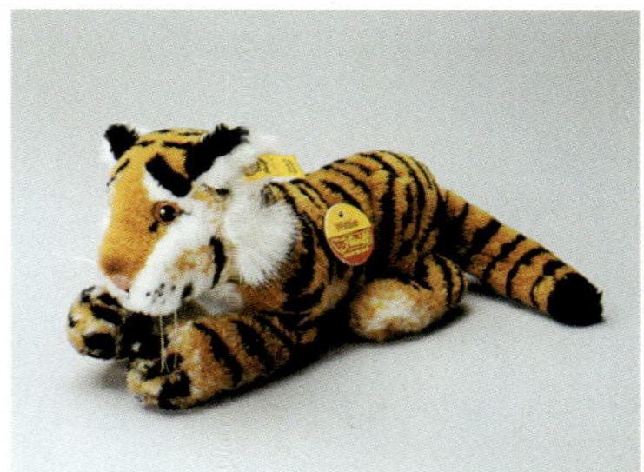

Wittie Tiger

Wirkpelz, liegend, abwaschbar - *knitted fur, lying, surface washable*

SERIE	ART.-NO	PERIOD	PR.	INFO
	0820/16	1980-1983	2	16 cm

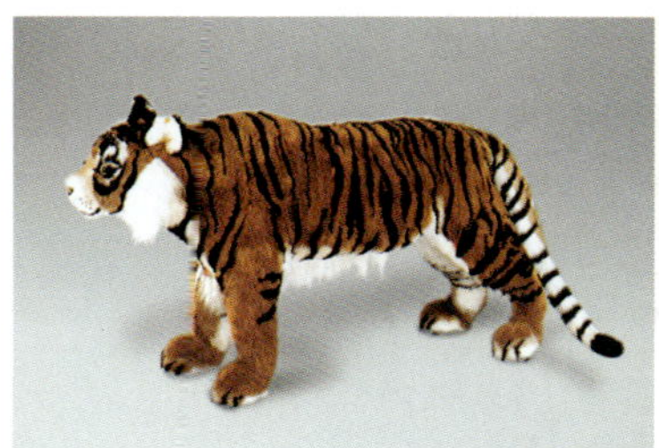

Tiger

Studio-Tier, stehend, abwaschbar - *studio animal, standing, surface washable*

SERIE	ART.-NO	PERIOD	PR.	INFO
502880	**0822/99**	1980-1986	6	150 cm

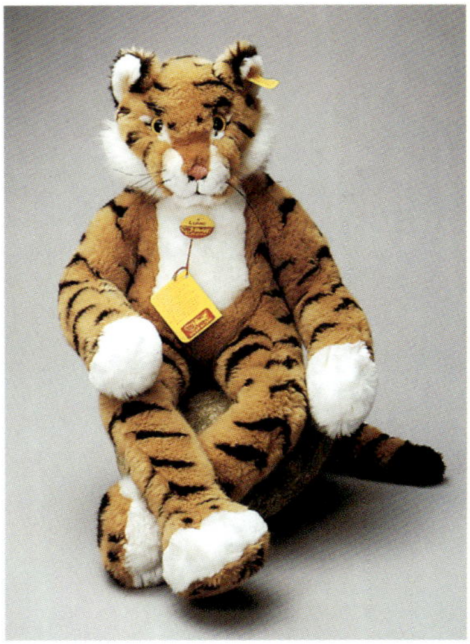

Lulac Schlenkertiger - ***Lulac** Dangling Tiger*

Wirkpelz, abwaschbar - *knitted fur, surface washable*

SERIE	ART.-NO	PERIOD	PR.	INFO
	6285/55	1982-1985	3-4	55 cm

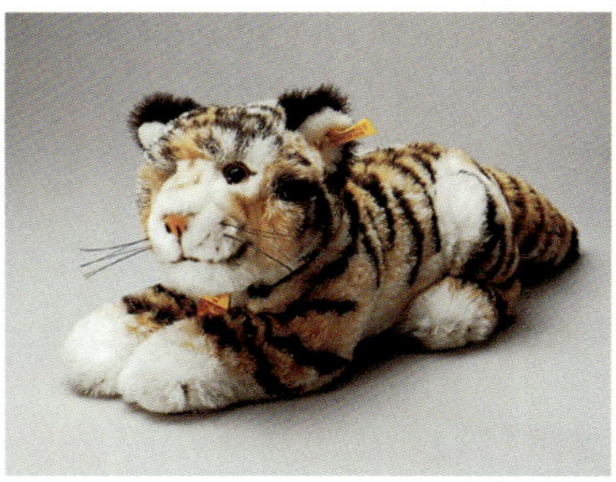

Molly Taky Tiger

Wirkpelz, waschmaschinenfest - *knitted fur, machine washable*

SERIE	ART.-NO	PERIOD	PR.	INFO
103537	**0380/30**	1986-1990	2	30 cm
	103537	1991-1995	2	

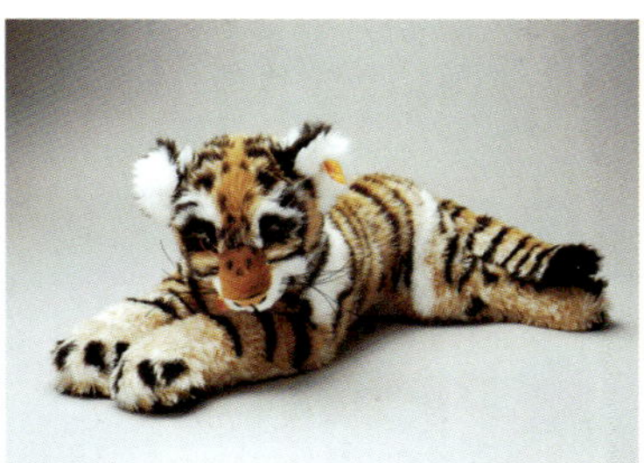

Molly Tiger

Wirkpelz, waschmaschinenfest - *knitted fur, machine washable*

SERIE	ART.-NO	PERIOD	PR.	INFO
103506	**0378/60**	1988-1990	2-3	60 cm

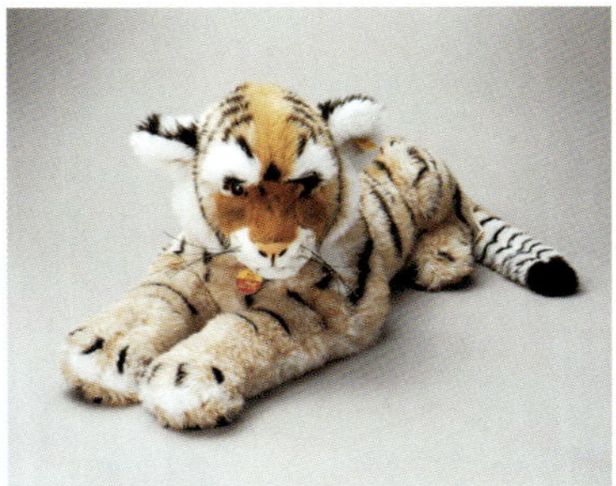

Molly Jungtiger - *Molly Tiger Cub*

Wirkpelz, abwaschbar - *knitted fur, surface washable*

SERIE	ART.-NO	PERIOD	PR.	INFO
103636	**0376/45**	1989-1990	2-3	45 cm
	103636	1991-1995	2-3	
103674	**0376/60**	1989-1990	2-3	60 cm

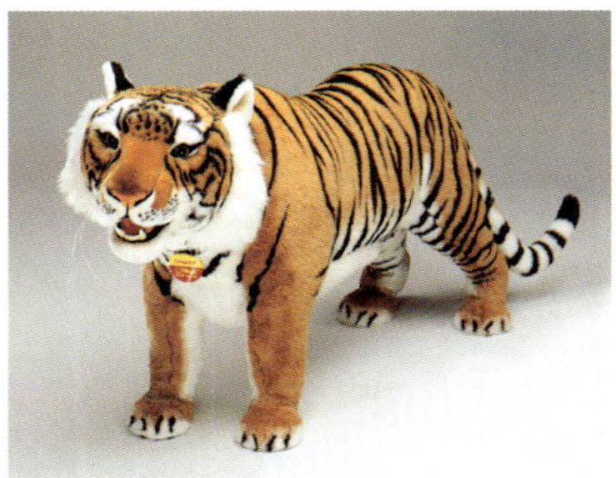

Studio Tiger

Wirkpluesch, 160 cm stehend, 150 cm liegend - *knitted plush, 160 cm standing, 150 cm lying*

SERIE	ART.-NO	PERIOD	PR.	INFO
502804	**0830/99**	1990-1990	7	160 cm
	502804	1991-1999	7	
502859	**0837/99**	1990-1990	6	150 cm

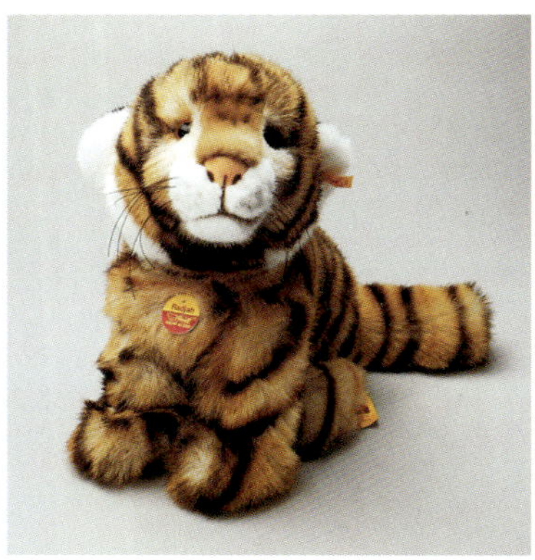

Radjah Jungtiger - ***Radjah** Tiger Cub*

Webpelz, sitzend, handwaschbar - *woven fur, sitting, hand washable*

EAN-NO.	PERIOD	PR.	INFO
066207	1992-1996	3	30 cm

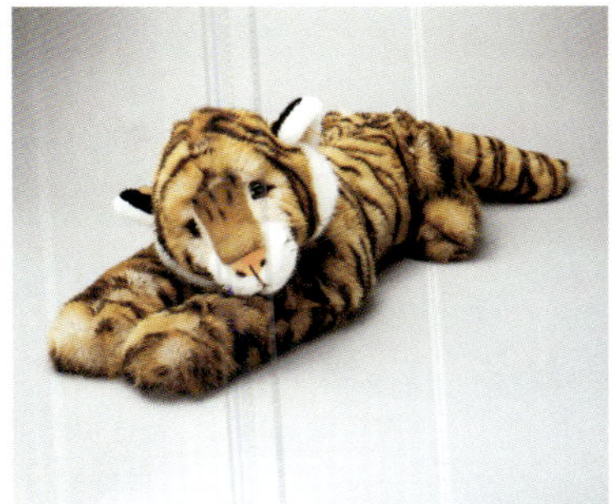

Radjah Jungtiger - ***Radjah** Tiger Cub*

Webpelz, liegend, handwaschbar - *woven fur, lying, hand washable*

EAN-NO.	PERIOD	PR.	INFO
066252	1992-1996	3	45 cm
066283	1992-1994	3	60 cm

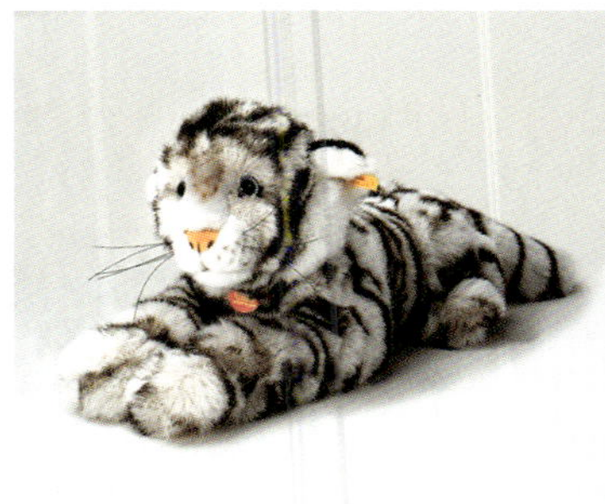

Schadah Jungtiger - ***Schadah** Tiger Cub*

Webpelz, weiss, schwarz gestreift, liegend, handwaschbar - *woven fur, white, black striped, lying, hand washable*

EAN-NO.	PERIOD	PR.	INFO
066504	1993-1996	3	45 cm
066528	1993-1995	3	60 cm

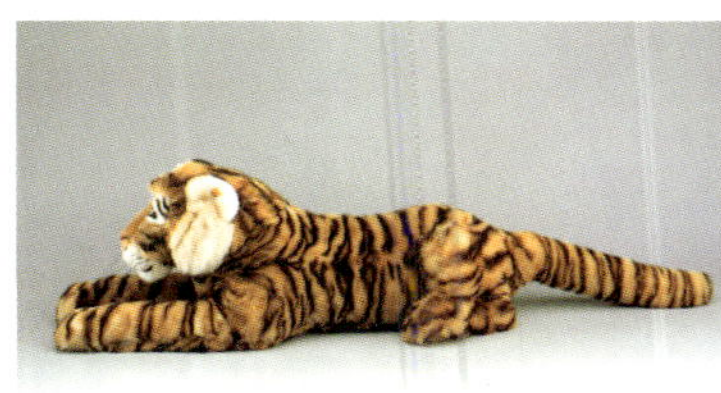

Radjah Tiger

Webpelz, braun, liegend, handwaschbar - *woven fur, brown, lying, hand washable*

EAN-NO.	PERIOD	PR.	INFO
066375	1993-1996	4	80 cm

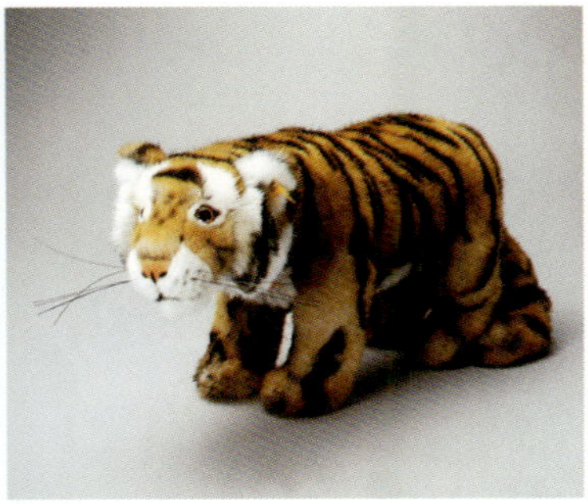

Radjah Tiger

Webpelz, braun, stehend, abwaschbar - *woven fur, brown, standing, surface washable*

EAN-No.	Period	Pr.	Info
066399	1995-1999	3-4	50 cm
066412	1995-1995	4	60 cm

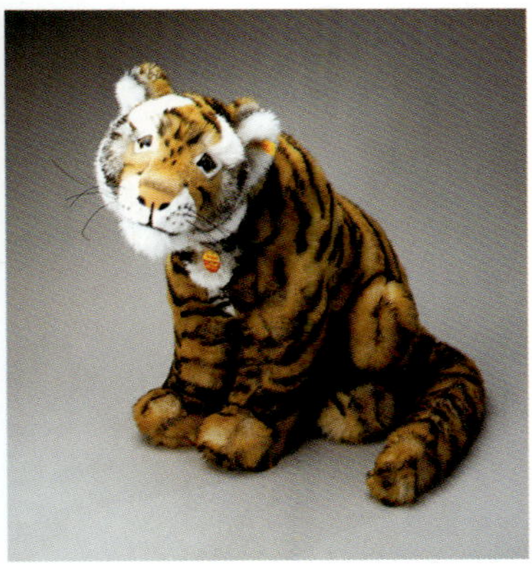

Radjah Tiger

Webpelz, braun, sitzend, abwaschbar - *woven fur, brown, sitting, surface washable*

EAN-No.	Period	Pr.	Info
066436	1995-1997	5	70 cm

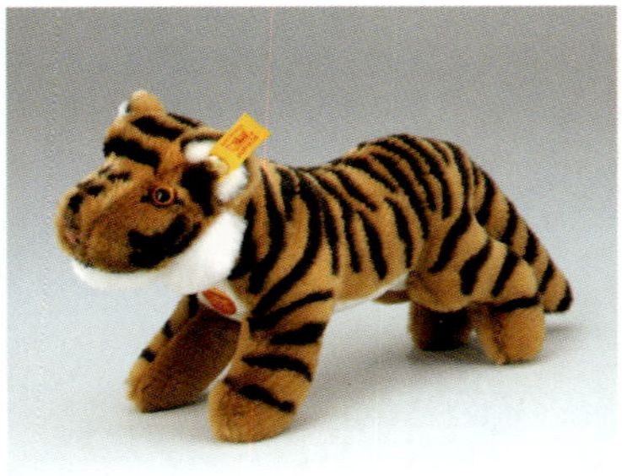

Tiger

Webpelz, stehend, waschmaschinenfest - *woven fur, standing, machine washable*

EAN-No.	Period	Pr.	Info
041457	1997-1998	2	20 cm

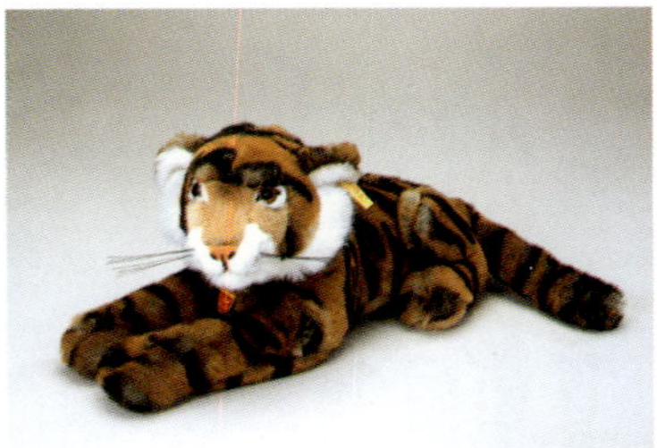

Radjah Tiger

Webpelz, liegend, waschmaschinenfest - *woven fur, lying, machine washable*

EAN-No.	Period	Pr.	Info
066184	1997-1999	3	35 cm

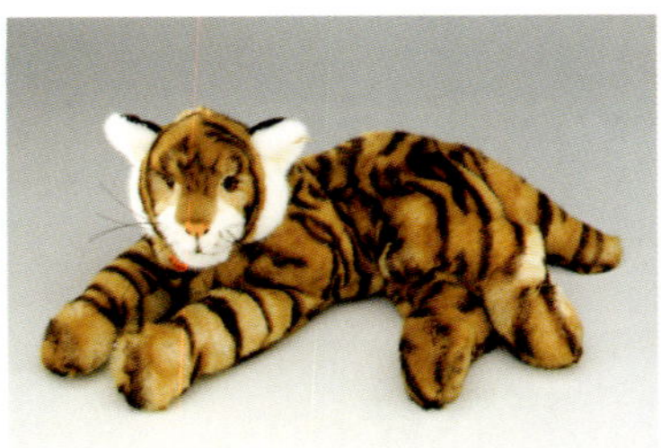

Schadah Tiger

Webpelz, seitlich liegend, waschmaschinenfest - *woven fur, lying aside, machine washable*

EAN-No.	Period	Pr.	Info
103513	1998-1999	3	45 cm

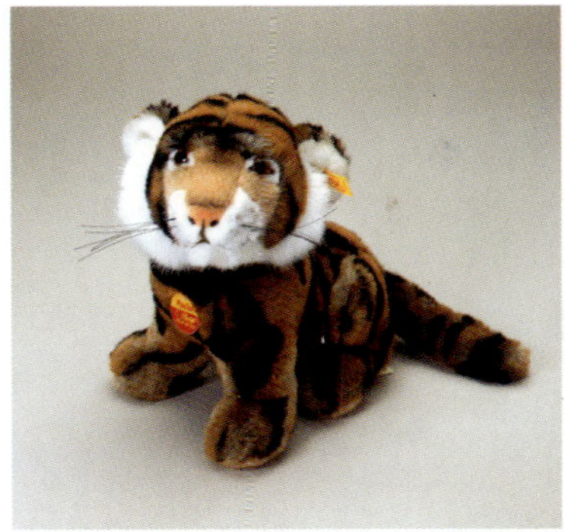

Radjah Tiger

Webpelz, sitzend, waschmaschinenfest - *woven fur, sitting, machine washable*

EAN-No.	Period	Pr.	Info
066238	1998-1999	3	25 cm

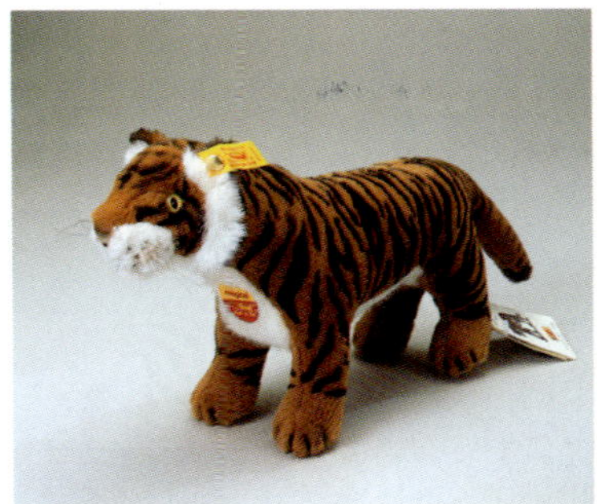

Tiger

Webpelz, stehend, abwaschbar - *woven fur, standing, surface washable*

EAN-No.	Period	Pr.	Info
066160	1999-1999	2-3	27 cm

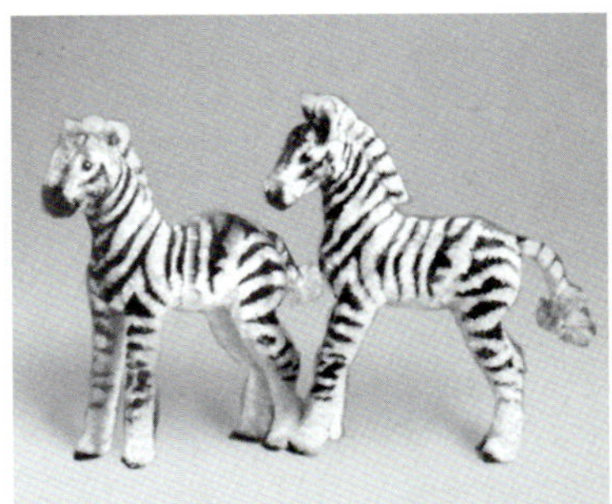

Zebra

Kunstseidenpluesch, weiss/schwarz gestreift, bemalt, stehend, ohne Raeder - *artificial silk plush, black/white striped, painted, standing, without wheels*

Serie	Art.-No	Period	Pr.	Info
72	**6022,0**	1948-1948	4	22 cm

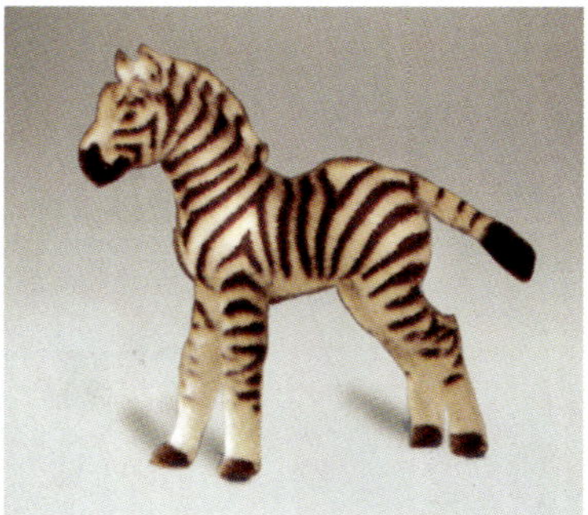

Zebra

Wollpluesch, weiss/schwarz gestreift, bemalt, stehend, ohne Raeder, jung & weich - *plush wool, black/white striped, painted, standing, without wheels, young foal & soft*

SERIE	ART.-NO	PERIOD	PR.	INFO
72	**6522,0**	1949-1951	4	22 cm
72	**6528,0**	1951-1951	4	28 cm

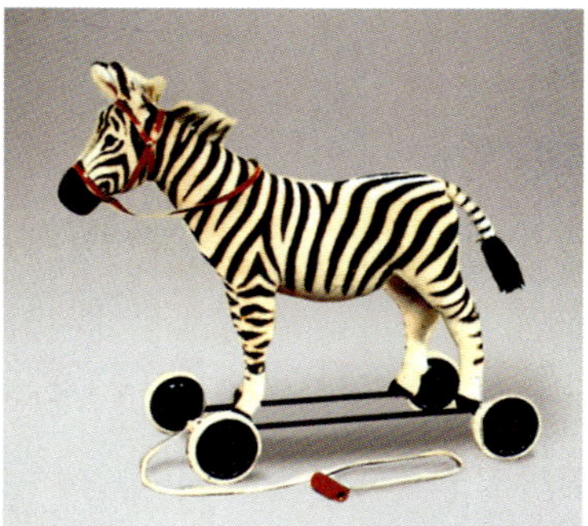

Reit-Zebra - *Riding Zebra*

Mohairpluesch, Eisengerippe, Zugstimme, weiss/schwarz gestreift, stehend auf Metallscheibenraedern mit Gummi - *mohair, iron frame, pull cord voice, black/white striped, standing on metal disc wheels with rubber tyres*

SERIE	ART.-NO	PERIOD	PR.	INFO
72	**1343,2**	1950-1957	5-6	43 cm
720	**1343,20**	1961-1961	5-6	
72	**1350,2**	1950-1957	5-6	50 cm
720	**1350,20**	1961-1961	5-6	

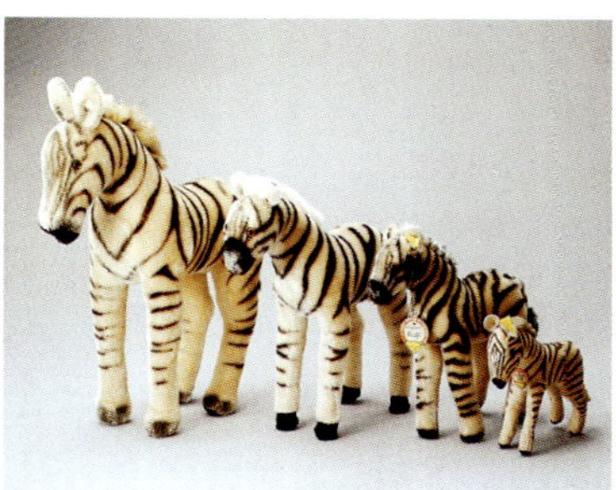

Zebra

Samt, ab 22 cm Mohair, schwarz/weiss gestreift, stehend - *velvet, from 22 cm mohair, black/white striped, standing*

SERIE	ART.-NO	PERIOD	PR.	INFO
72	**6412,0**	1951-1958	3-4	12 cm
720	**6412,00**	1959-1964	3	
141	**6412,00**	1965-1967	3	
	1420/12	1968-1973	2-3	
72	**6322,0**	1953-1958	4	22 cm
720	**6322,00**	1959-1962	3-4	
142	**6322,00**	1966-1967	3-4	
	1420/22	1968-1977	3	
72	**6328,0**	1953-1958	4	28 cm
720	**6328,00**	1959-1962	4	
72	**6335,0**	1956-1958	4	35 cm
720	**6335,00**	1959-1962	4	

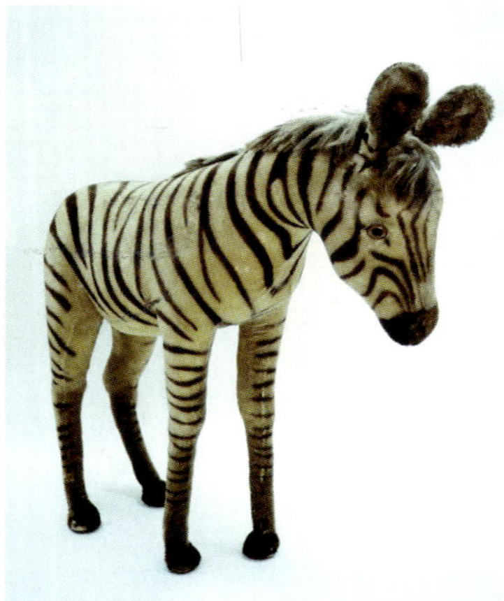

Zebra

Schautier, schwarz/weiss, stehend - *display animal, black/white, standing*

SERIE	ART.-NO	PERIOD	PR.	INFO
	1429/10	1967-1967	6	100 cm
720	**1150,90**	1960-1960	6	150 cm
	1429/15	1967-1967	6	

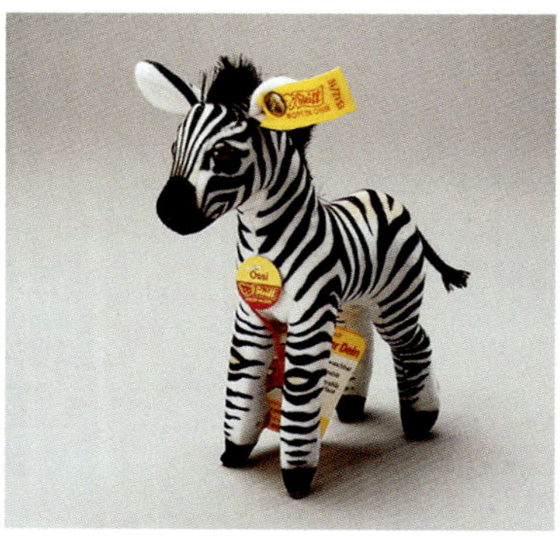

Ossi Zebra

Trevirasamt, abwaschbar - *trevira velvet, surface washable*

SERIE	ART.-NO	PERIOD	PR.	INFO
052132	**1512/16**	1982-1987	2	16 cm

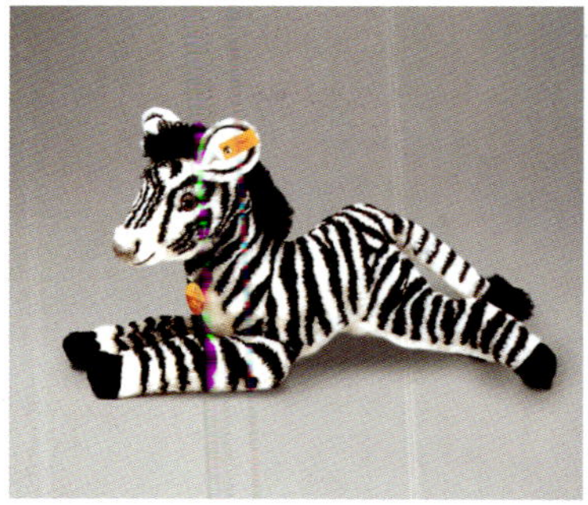

Molly Zebra

Wirkpelz, waschmaschinenfest - *knitted fur, machine washable*

SERIE	ART.-NO	PERIOD	PR.	INFO
104329	**0411/40**	1988-1990	2-3	40 cm
	104329	1991-1994	2-3	

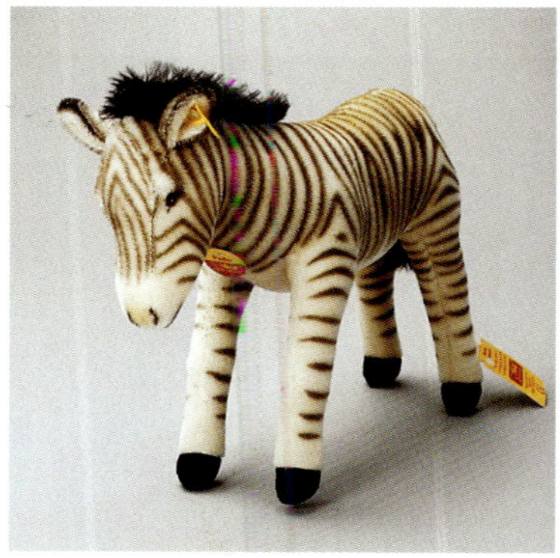

Fello Zebra

Mohair Webpelz, stehend, abwaschbar - *mohair woven fur, standing, surface washable*

EAN-NO.	PERIOD	PR.	INFO
067549	1995-1998	3	30 cm

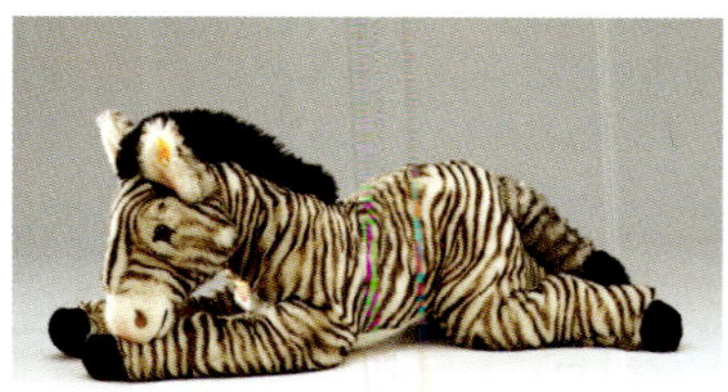

Molly Zebra

Webpelz, liegend, waschmaschinenfest - *woven fur, lying, machine washable*

EAN-NO.	PERIOD	PR.	INFO
104343	1995-1997	3-4	55 cm

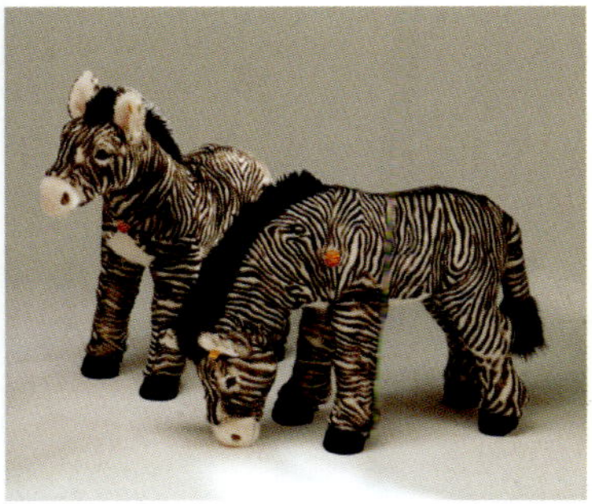

Studio Zebra

Webpelz, 60 cm, abwaschbar - *woven fur, 60 cm, surface washable*

EAN-No.	Period	Pr.	Info
502323	1995-1998	5	stehend - *standing*
502330	1995-1998	5	grasend - *grazing*

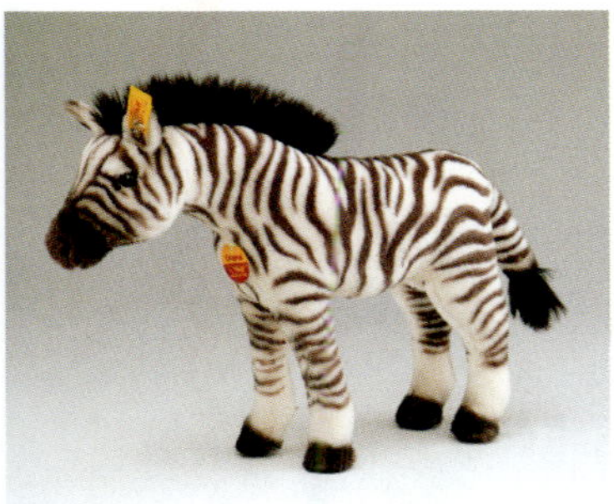

Zebra

Webpelz, stehend, abwaschbar - *woven fur, standing, surface washable*

EAN-No.	Period	Pr.	Info
067556	1999-1999	3	35 cm

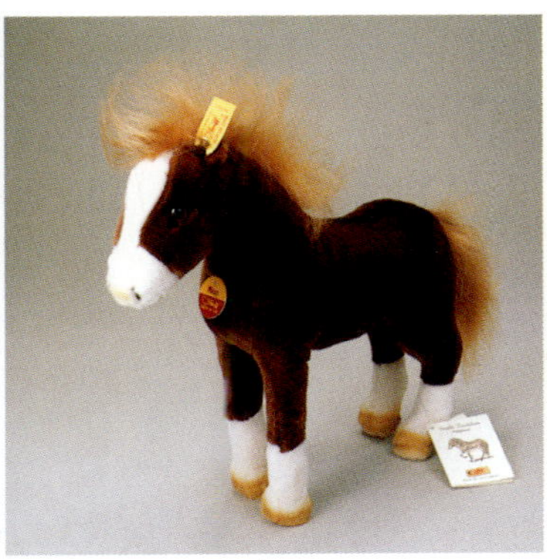

Rico Wildpferd - ***Rico*** *Wild Horse*

Webpelz, rotbraun, stehend, abwaschbar - *woven fur, reddish brown, standing, surface washable*

EAN-No.	Period	Pr.	Info
067617	1998-1999	3	32 cm

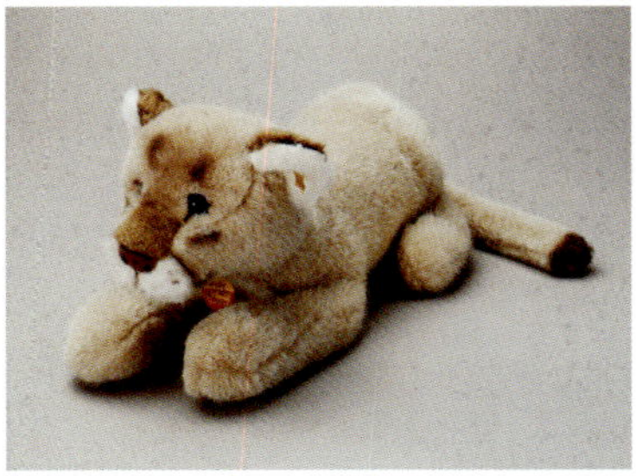

Drolly Jungpuma - ***Drolly*** *Puma Cub*

Pelzimitation, ab 1978 Synthetik-Webpelz, liegend, abwaschbar - *imitation fur, from 1978 synthetic woven fur, lying, surface washable*

Serie	Art.-No	Period	Pr.	Info
	6315/30	1977-1980	2-3	30 cm

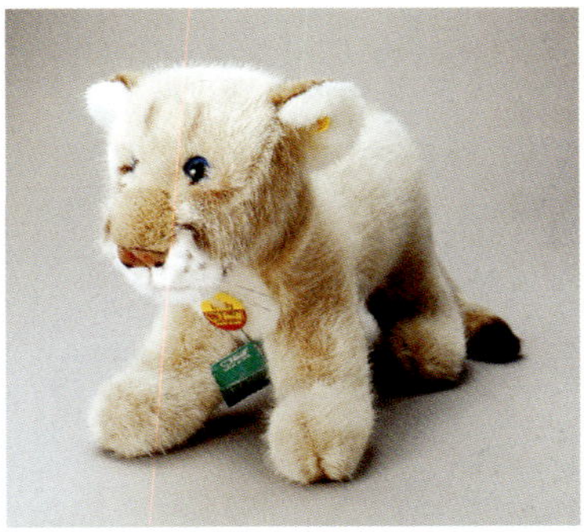

Drolly Jungpuma - ***Drolly*** *Puma Cub*

Pelzimitation, ab 1978 Synthetik-Webpelz, stehend, abwaschbar - *imitation fur, from 1978 synthetic woven fur, standing, surface washable*

Serie	Art.-No	Period	Pr.	Info
	6315/40	1977-1981	2-3	40 cm

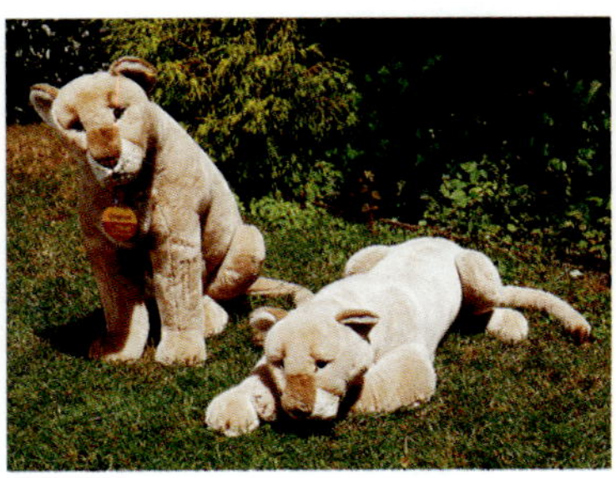

Puma

Studio-Tier, Pelzimitation, ab 1978 Synthetik-Webpelz, abwaschbar - *studio animal, imitation fur, from 1978 synthetic woven fur, surface washable*

Serie	Art.-No	Period	Pr.	Info
	6315/99	1977-1984	5	99 cm, liegend - *lying*
	6316/99	1977-1984	5-6	73 cm, sitzend - *sitting*

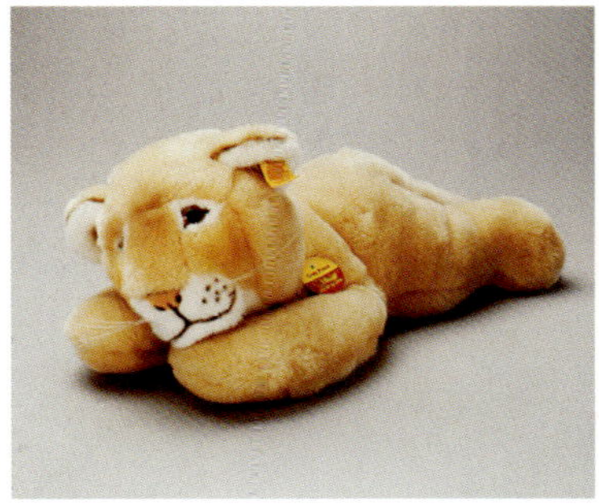

Cosy Puma

Webpelz, liegend, superweich, waschmaschinenfest - *woven fur, lying, super soft, machine washable*

Serie	Art.-No	Period	Pr.	Info
088575	**5372/33**	1981-1988	2	33 cm

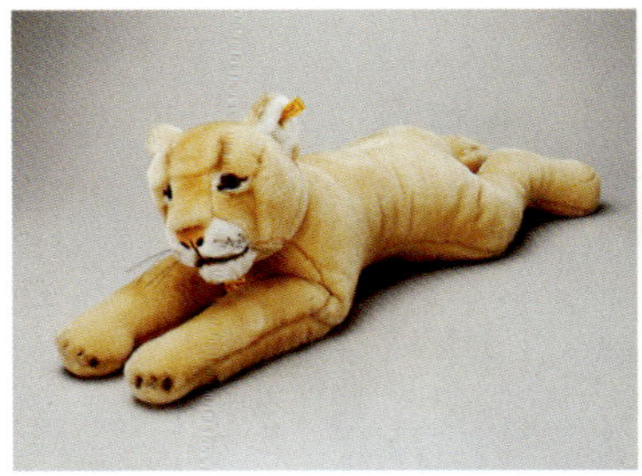

Molly Puma

Webpelz, abwaschbar - *woven fur, surface washable*

Serie	Art.-No	Period	Pr.	Info
103773	**0385/75**	1984-1988	3-4	75 cm
103797	**0385/98**	1985-1986	4	112 cm

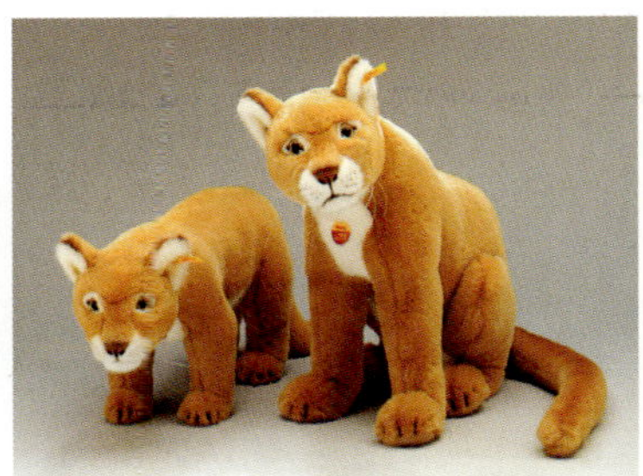

Monty Puma ab 1996 **Ango** - ***Monty*** *Puma from 1996* ***Ango***

Webpelz, 50 cm, abwaschbar - *woven fur, 50 cm, surface washable*

EAN-No	Period	Pr.	Info
066016	1995-1999	3-4	stehend - *standing*
066023	1995-1999	4	sitzend - *sitting*

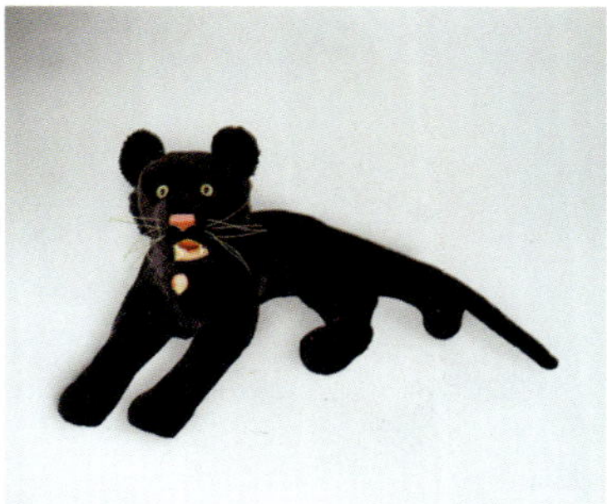

Panther

Schautier, Pelzimitation, schwarz, liegend - *display animal, imitation fur, black, lying*

SERIE	ART.-NO	PERIOD	PR.	INFO
	0949/08	1967-1967	5-6	80 cm

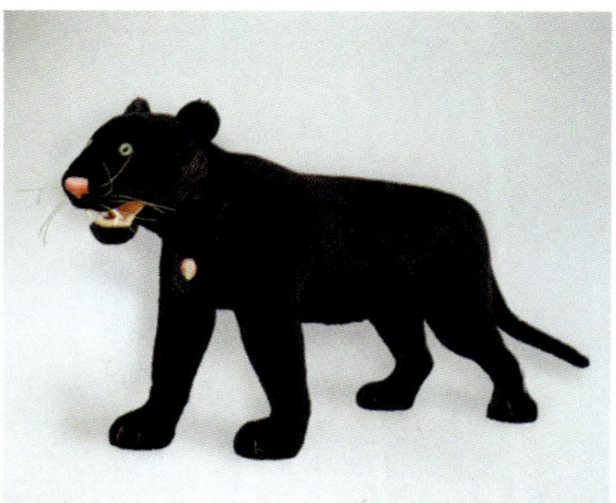

Panther

Schautier, Pelzimitation, schwarz, stehend - *display animal, imitation fur, black, standing*

SERIE	ART.-NO	PERIOD	PR.	INFO
	0949/10	1967-1967	6	100 cm

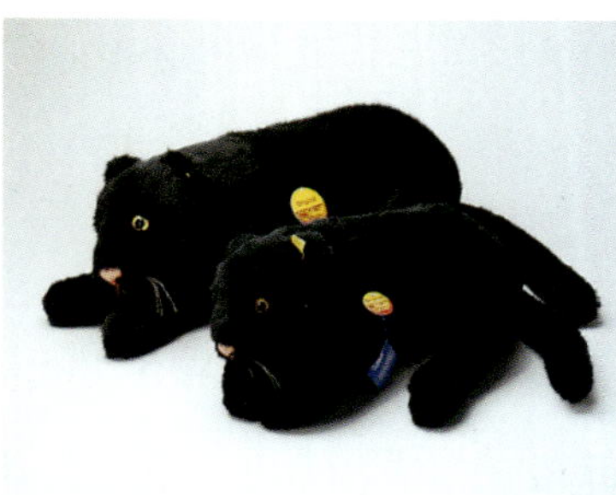

Lieg-Panther - *Lying Panther*

Dralon-Pelz, schwarz, superweich, abwaschbar - *dralon fur, black, super soft, surface washable*

SERIE	ART.-NO	PERIOD	PR.	INFO
	5322/35	1972-1981	2-3	35 cm
	5322/50	1972-1980	3	50 cm

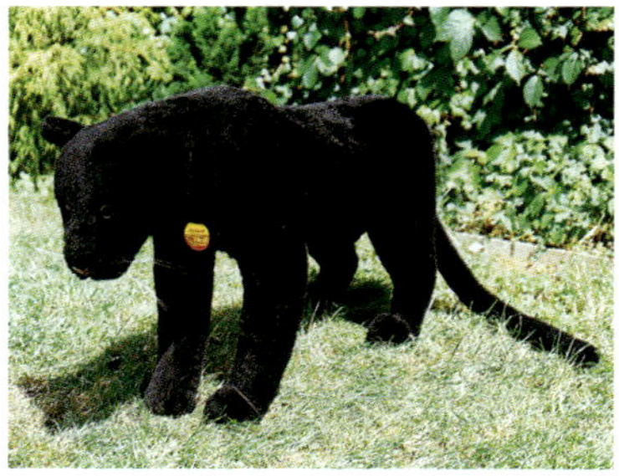

Panther

Studio-Tiere, Pelzimitation, ab 1978 Dralon, schwarz, 99 cm, abwaschbar - *studio animals, imitation fur, from 1978 dralon, black, 99 cm, surface washable*

SERIE	ART.-NO	PERIOD	PR.	INFO
	6323/99	1977-1984	5	liegend - *lying*
	6325/99	1977-1984	5-6	stehend - *standing*

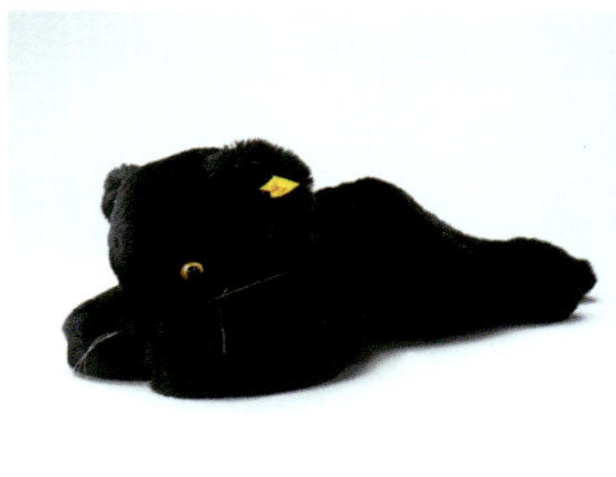

Cosy Panther

Webpelz, liegend, superweich, waschmaschinenfest - *woven fur, lying, super soft, machine washable*

SERIE	ART.-NO	PERIOD	PR.	INFO
088520	**5370/28**	1980-1990	2-3	35 cm
	088520	1991-1999	2-3	

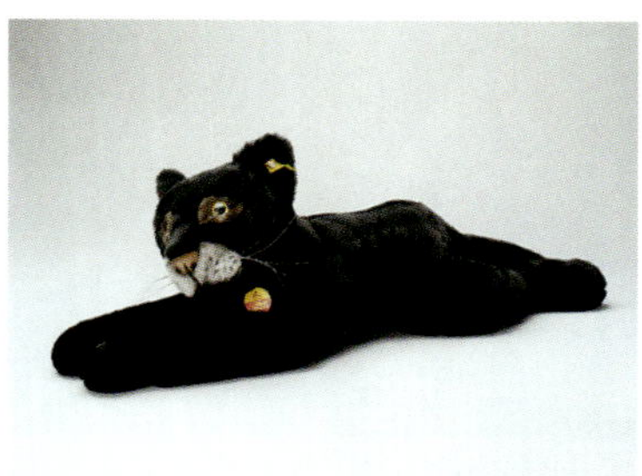

Molly Panther

Webpelz, abwaschbar - *woven fur, surface washable*

SERIE	ART.-NO	PERIOD	PR.	INFO
103872	**0387/75**	1984-1990	3-4	75 cm
	103872	1991-1994	3-4	
103896	**0387/98**	1985-1986	4	112 cm

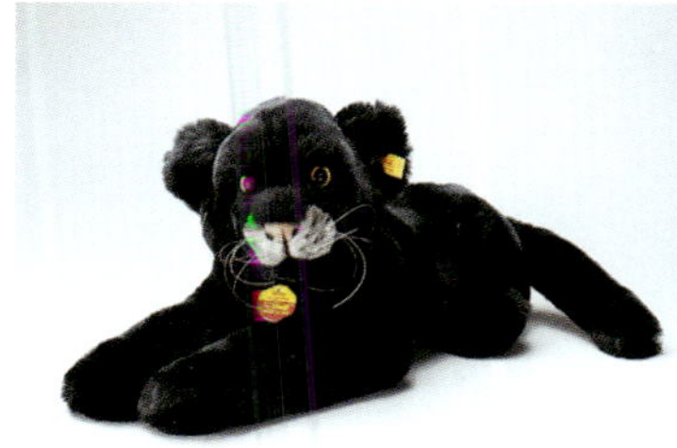

Molly Jungpanther - *Molly Panther Cub*

Webpelz, liegend, waschmaschinenfest - *woven fur, lying, machine washable*

SERIE	ART.-NO	PERIOD	PR.	INFO
103834	**0388/45**	1989-1990	3	45 cm
	103834	1991-1999	3	
103858	**0388/60**	1989-1990	3-4	60 cm
	103858	1991-1996	3-4	

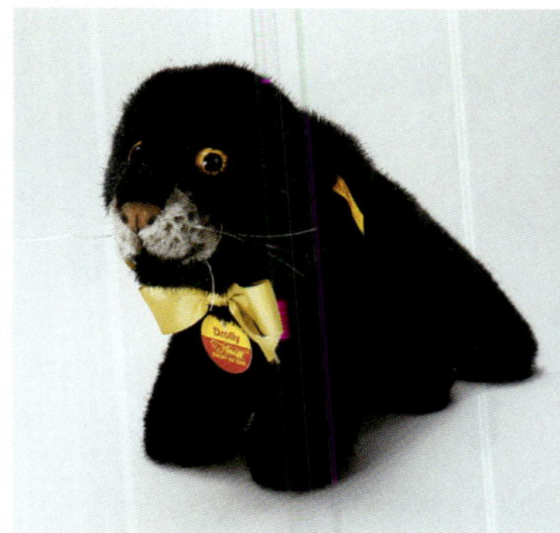

Drolly Panther

Webpelz, stehend, waschmaschinenfest - *woven fur, standing, machine washable*

EAN-NO.	PERIOD	PR.	INFO
081453	1991-1995	2	22 cm

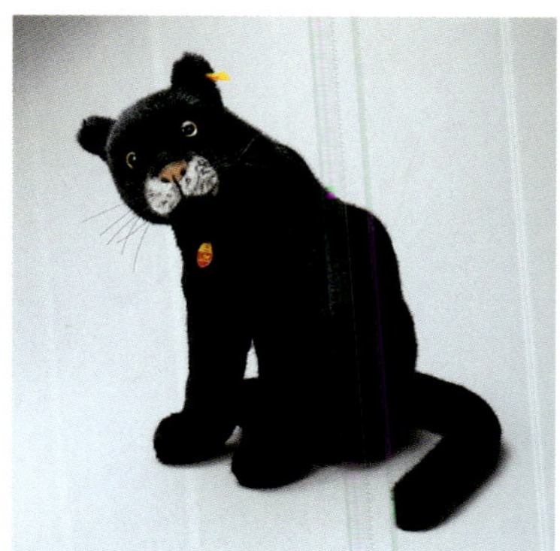

Taky Panther

Webpelz, schwarz, sitzend, abwaschbar - *woven fur, black, sitting, surface washable*

EAN-NO.	PERIOD	PR.	INFO
065156	1992-1994	3	45 cm

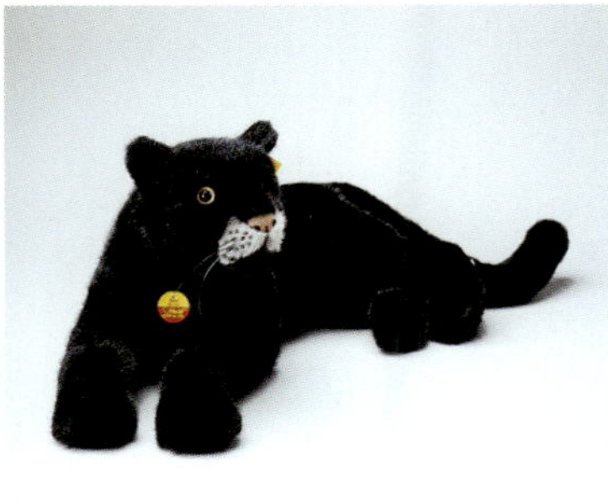

Taky Panther

Webpelz, schwarz, liegend, abwaschbar - *woven fur, black, lying, surface washable*

EAN-No.	Period	Pr.	Info
065200	1992-1999	3-4	45 cm

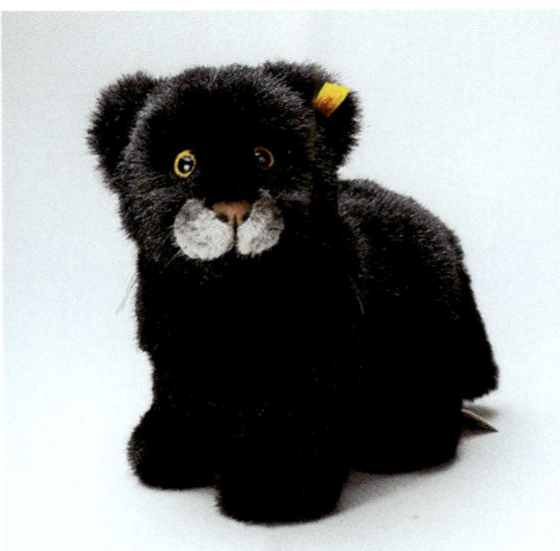

Taky Baby Panther

Webpelz, schwarz, stehend, waschmaschinenfest - *woven fur, black, standing, machine washable*

EAN-No.	Period	Pr.	Info
065309	1992-1995	2-3	30 cm

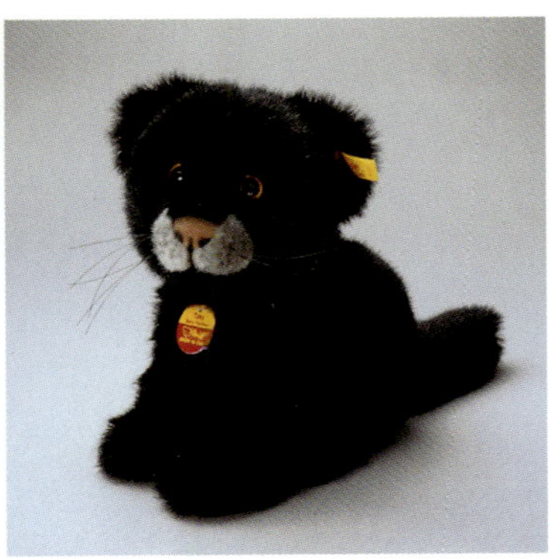

Taky Baby Panther

Webpelz, schwarz, sitzend, waschmaschinenfest - *woven fur, black, sitting, machine washable*

EAN-No.	Period	Pr.	Info
065408	1992-1995	2-3	25 cm

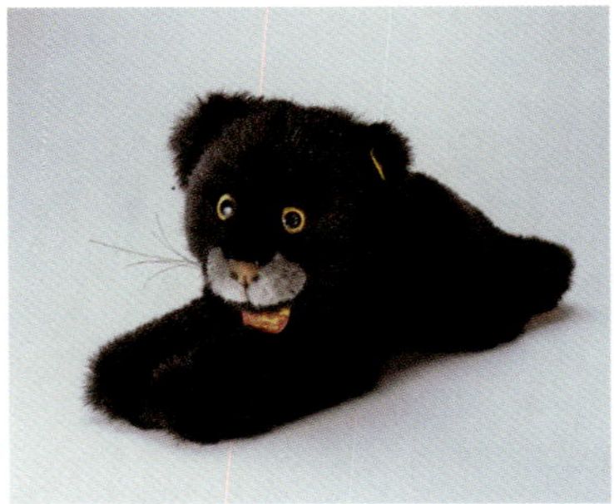

Taky Baby Panther

Webpelz, schwarz, liegend, waschmaschinenfest - *woven fur, black, lying, machine washable*

EAN-No.	Period	Pr.	Info
065453	1992-1997	3	30 cm

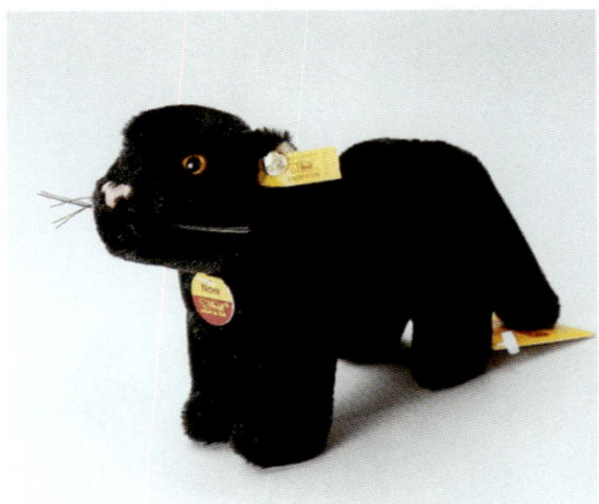

Nora Panther

Webpelz, schwarz, stehend, waschmaschinenfest - *woven fur, black, standing, machine washable*

EAN-No.	Period	Pr.	Info
041426	1995-1998	1-2	18 cm

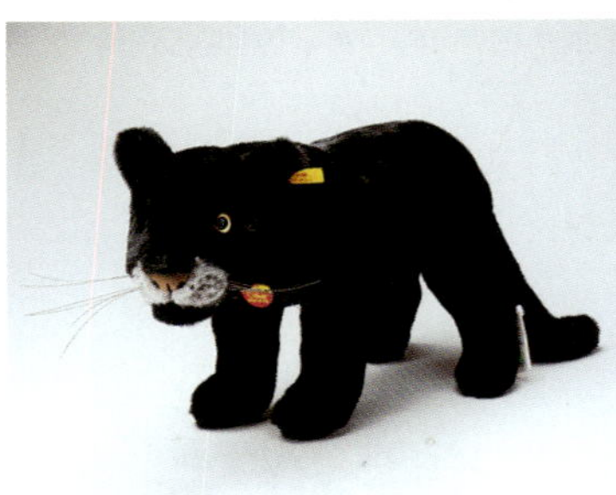

Taky Panther

Webpelz, schwarz, stehend, abwaschbar - *woven fur, black, standing, surface washable*

EAN-No.	Period	Pr.	Info
065057	1995-1999	3	50 cm
065064	1995-1999	4	60 cm

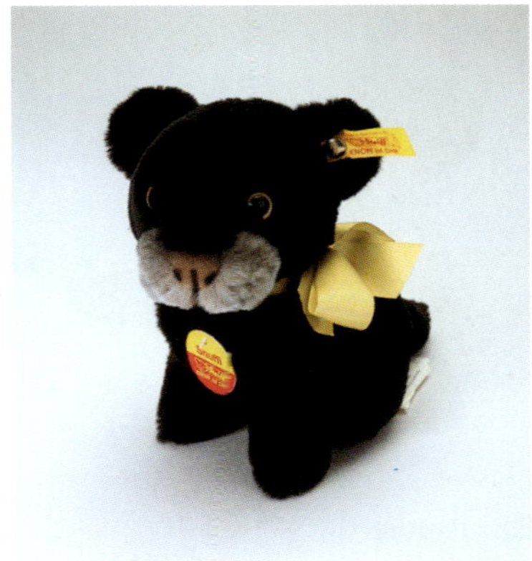

Snuffi Panther

Webpelz, sitzend, waschmaschinenfest - *woven fur, sitting, machine washable*

EAN-No.	Period	Pr.	Info
077203	1996-1999	2	16 cm

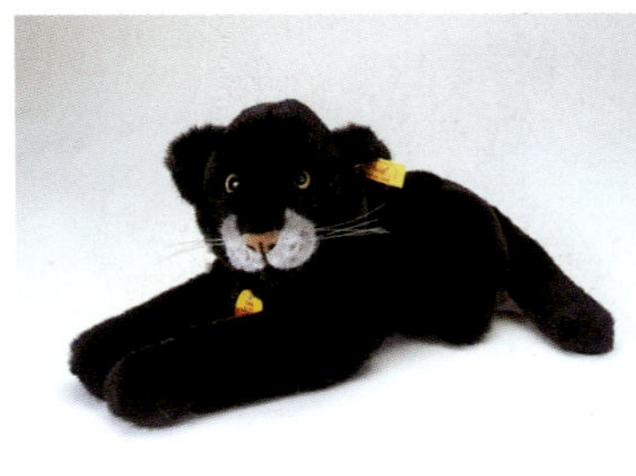

Taky Panther

Webpelz, liegend, waschmaschinenfest - *woven fur, lying, machine washable*

EAN-No.	Period	Pr.	Info
065026	1997-1999	3	35 cm

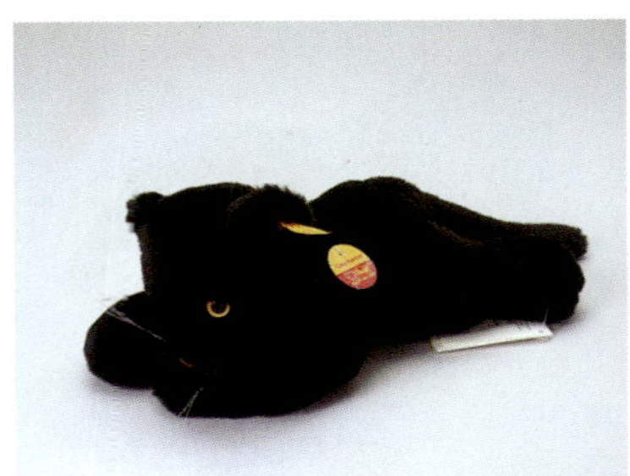

Cosy Panther

Webpelz, schwarz, liegend, waschmaschinenfest - *woven fur, black, lying, machine washable*

EAN-No.	Period	Pr.	Info
088513	1998-1999	2-3	28 cm

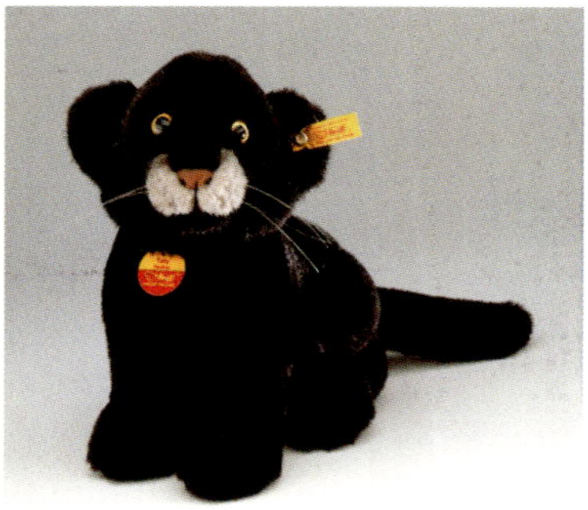

Taky Panther

Webpelz, sitzend, waschmaschinenfest - *woven fur, sitting, machine washable*

EAN-No.	Period	Pr.	Info
065071	1998-1999	3	25 cm

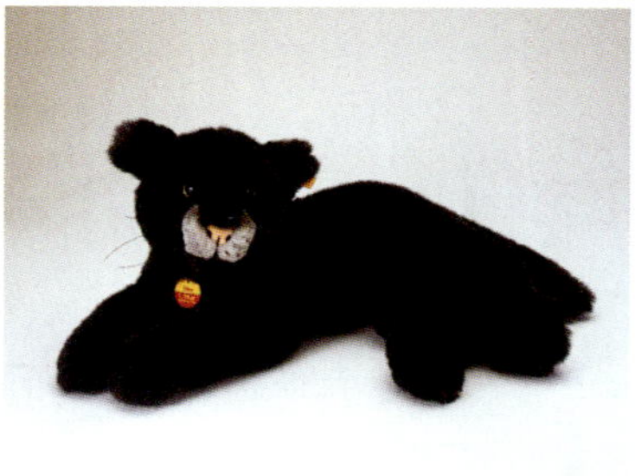

Oko Panther

Webpelz, seitlich liegend, waschmaschinenfest - *woven fur, lying aside, machine washable*

EAN-No.	Period	Pr.	Info
103889	1998-1999	3	45 cm

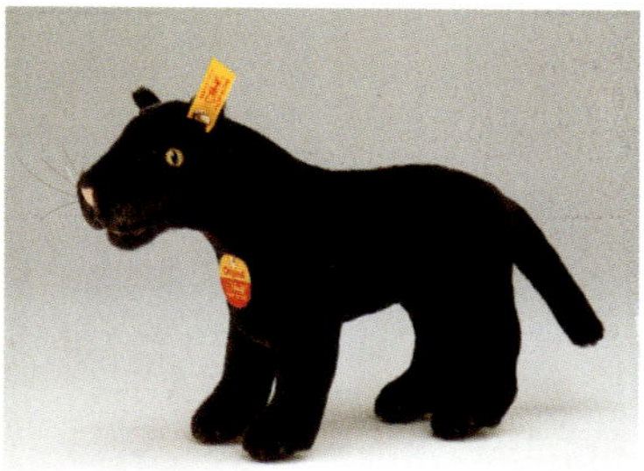

Panther

Webpelz, stehend, abwaschbar - *woven fur, standing, surface washable*

EAN-No.	Period	Pr.	Info
065019	1999-1999	2-3	25 cm

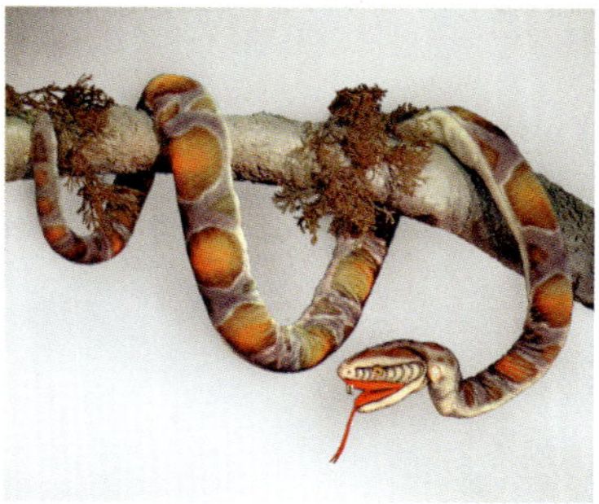

Schlange - *Snake*

Schautier - *display animal*

Serie	Art.-No	Period	Pr.	Info
	2439/29	1967-1967	6-7	290 cm

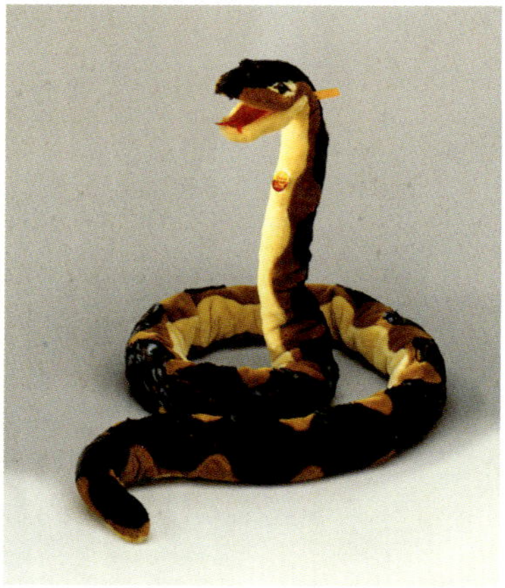

Studio Schlange - *Studio Snake*

Webpelz, abwaschbar - *woven fur, surface washable*

EAN-No.	Period	Pr.	Info
505966	1995-1995	4	250 cm

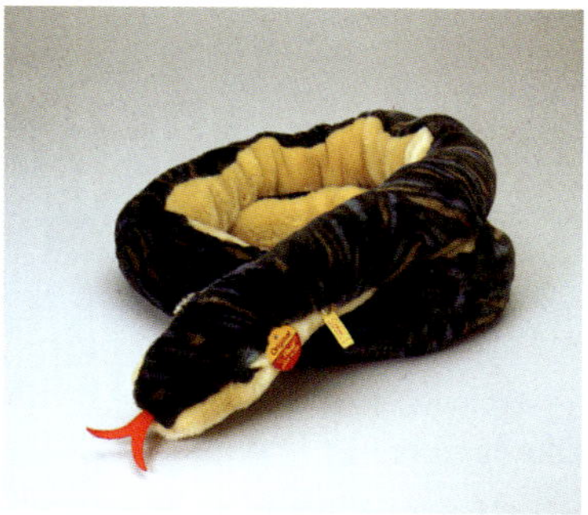

Schlange - *Snake*

Webpelz, waschmaschinenfest - *woven fur, machine washable*

EAN-No.	Period	Pr.	Info
067389	1997-1999	2-3	150 cm

Wollminiaturen

Woolen miniatures

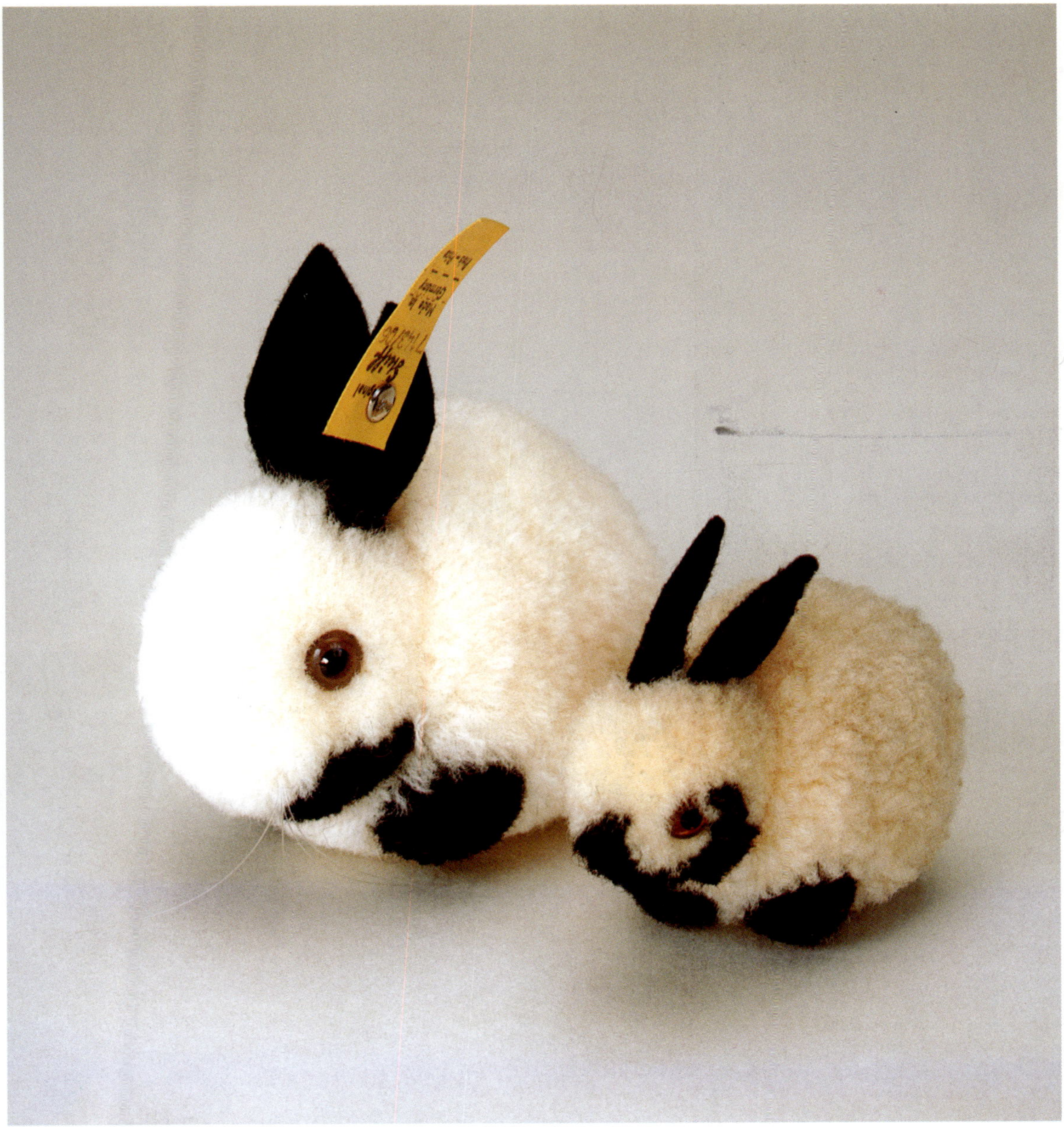

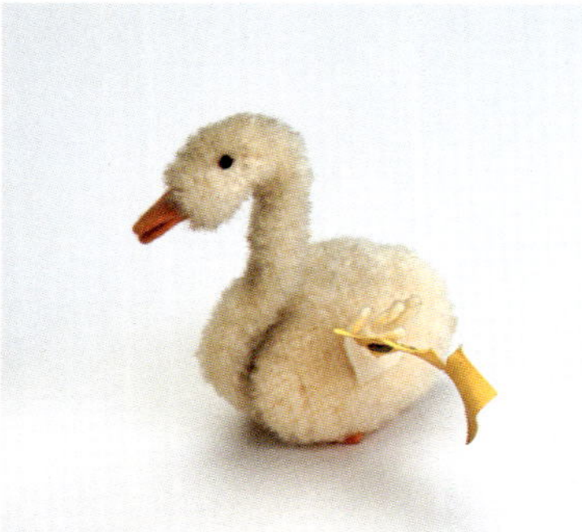

Woll-Gans - *Woolen Goose*

Wolle, Fluegel, Fuesse & Schnabel aus Filz, weiss, liegend - *wool, wings, feet & bill made of felt, white, lying*

SERIE	ART.-NO	PERIOD	PR.	INFO
870 874	**2505,44**	1963-1964	2	5 cm
722	**2505,44**	1965-1967	2	

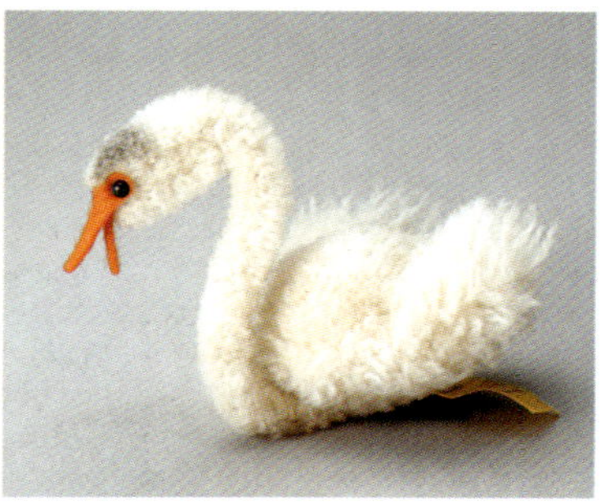

Woll-Schwan - *Woolen Swan*

Wolle, Fluegel, Fuesse & Schnabel aus Filz, weiss, liegend - *wool, wings, feet & bill made of felt, white, lying*

SERIE	ART.-NO	PERIOD	PR.	INFO
870 889	**2508,44**	1964-1964	2	8 cm
745	**2508,44**	1965-1967	2	
	7450/08	1968-1969	1-2	

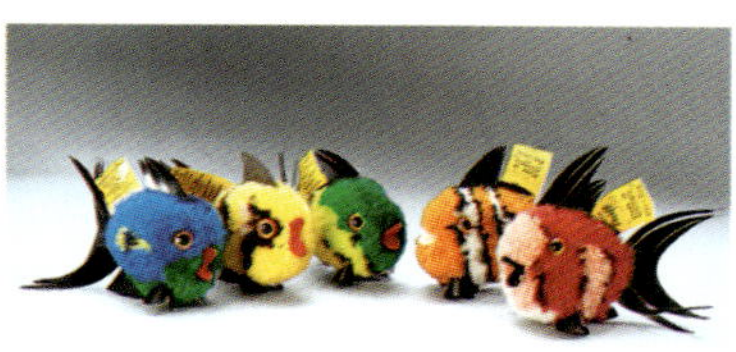

Woll-Korallenfisch - *Woolen Coral Reef Fish*

Nomotta-Wolle, 7 cm, Plastik-Flossen - *Nomotta wool, 7 cm, plastic fins*

SERIE	ART.-NO	PERIOD	PR.	INFO
736	**7507,41**	1967-1967	2	blau - *blue*
	7361/07	1968-1977	1-2	
736	**7507,42**	1967-1967	2	gelb - *yellow*
	7362/07	1968-1977	1-2	
736	**7507,43**	1967-1967	2	gruen - *green*
	7363/07	1968-1976	1-2	
736	**7507,44**	1967-1967	2	orange
	7364/07	1968-1977	1-2	
736	**7507,45**	1967-1967	2	rot - *red*
	7365/07	1968-1977	1-2	
736	**7507,46**	1967-1967	4	Sortiment, 10 Woll-Korallenfische im Karton - *assortment, 10 woolen coral reef fish per box*
	7366/07	1971-1972	3-4	

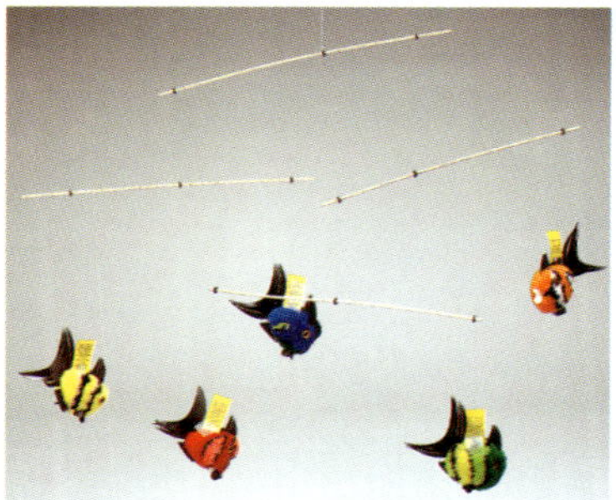

Woll-Korallenfisch-Mobile - *Woolen Coral Reef Fish Mobile*

Nomotta-Wolle, Plastik-Flossen, 5 Korallenfische in verschiedenen Farben als Mobile, in eckiger Klarsichtpackung, Artikel-Nr. nur fuer kpl. Mobile - *Nomotta wool, plastic fins, 5 coral reef fish of various colors as mobile, packed in square plastic, art.no. refers only to complete mobile*

SERIE	ART.-NO	PERIOD	PR.	INFO
	7367/07	1969-1975	4	7 cm

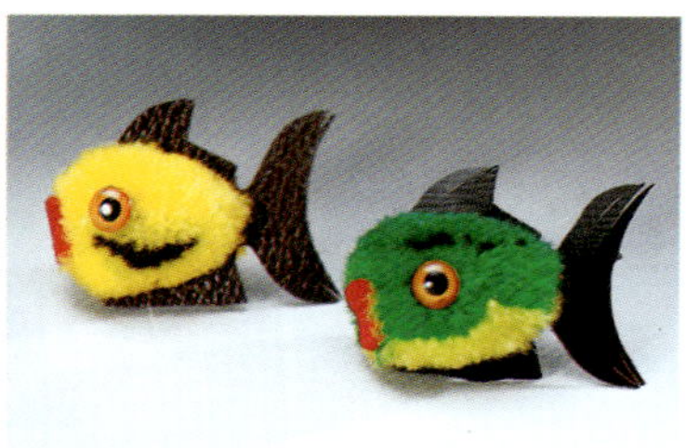

Woll-Korallenfisch-Mobile - *Woolen Coral Reef Fish Mobile*

Wolle, Plastikflossen, 5 Korallenfische, verschiedene Farben, als Mobile, in runder Klarsichtpackung, Artikel-Nr. nur fuer kpl. Mobile - *wool, plastic fins, 5 coral reef fish, various colors, as mobile, packed in round plastic package, art.no. refers only to complete mobile*

SERIE	ART.-NO	PERIOD	PR.	INFO
	7367/03	1970-1977	3-4	3 cm

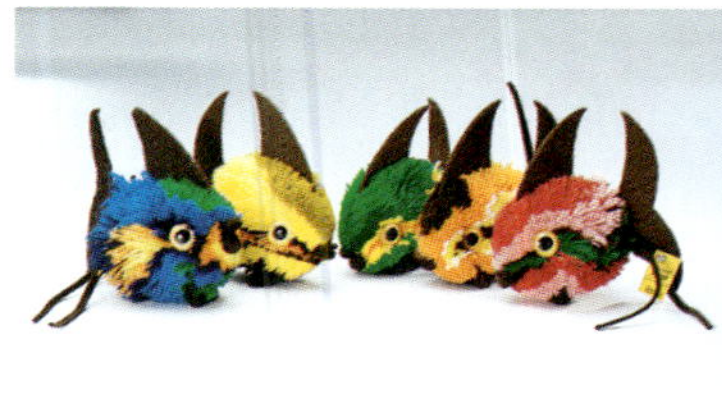

Wollfisch - *Woolen Fish*

Wolle, 9 cm, Flossen in braunem Filz - *wool, 9 cm, fins made of brown felt*

SERIE	ART.-NO	PERIOD	PR.	INFO
	7271/09	1977-1981	1-2	blau - *blue*
	7272/09	1977-1981	1-2	gelb - *yellow*
	7273/09	1977-1981	1-2	gruen - *green*
	7274/09	1977-1981	1-2	orange
	7275/09	1977-1981	1-2	rot - *red*

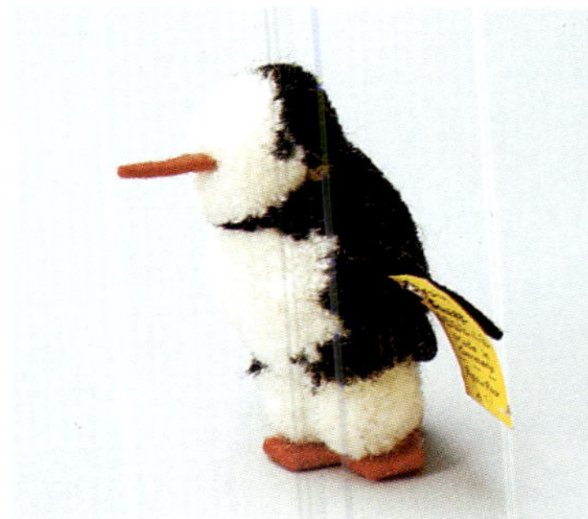

Woll-Pinguin - *Woolen Penguin*

Wolle, Filzfuesse, ab 1967 Plastikfuesse, schwarz/weiss/rot, aufwartend - *wool, feet made of felt, from 1967 plastic feet, black/white/red, sitting up*

SERIE	ART.-NO	PERIOD	PR.	INFO
870 887	**4508,46**	1964-1964	2-3	8 cm
739	**4508,46**	1965-1967	2-3	
	7390/08	1968-1977	2	
	7390/10	1973-1981	1-2	10 cm

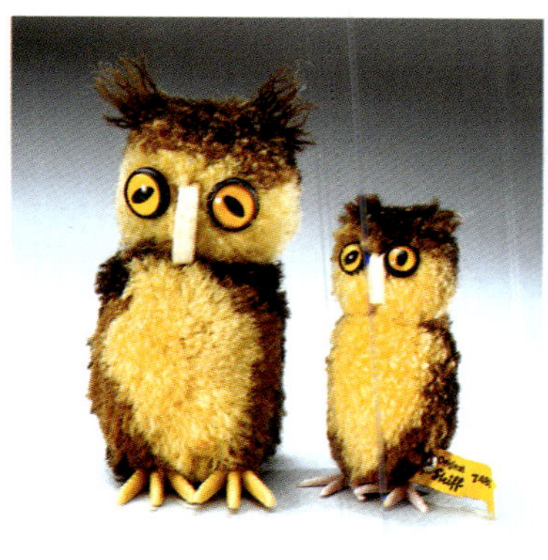

Woll-Eule - *Woolen Owl*

Wolle, Plastikfuesse, braun/gelb, stehend - *wool, plastic feet, brown/yellow, standing*

SERIE	ART.-NO	PERIOD	PR.	INFO
	7480/06	1971-1984	1-2	6 cm
	7480/09	1971-1984	1-2	9 cm

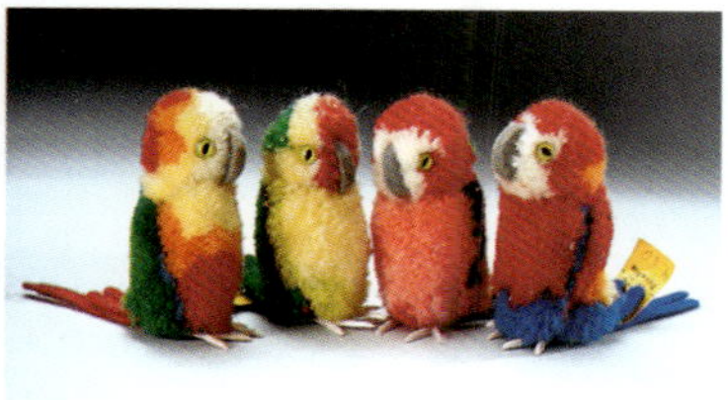

Woll-Papagei - *Woolen Parrot*

Wolle, 6 cm, stehend, Plastikfuesse, Mobile: 5 Papageien als Mobile in eckiger Klarsichtpackung, Sortiment: 10 Stueck im Karton, Artikel-Nr. nur fuer kpl. Mobile/Sortiment - *wool, 6 cm, standing, plastic feet, mobile: 5 parrots, packed as mobile unit in clear plastic package, assortment: 10 parrots per box, art.no. refer only to complete mobile/assortment*

SERIE	ART.-NO	PERIOD	PR.	INFO
	7481/06	1971-1975	2	blau - *blue*
	7482/06	1971-1975	2	gruen - *green*
	7483/06	1971-1975	2	hellgruen - *light green*
	7484/06	1971-1975	2	rosé - *rose*
	7485/06	1971-1975	2	rot - *red*
	7491/06	1971-1975	4	Mobile
	7490/06	1971-1975	4-5	Sortiment - *assortment*

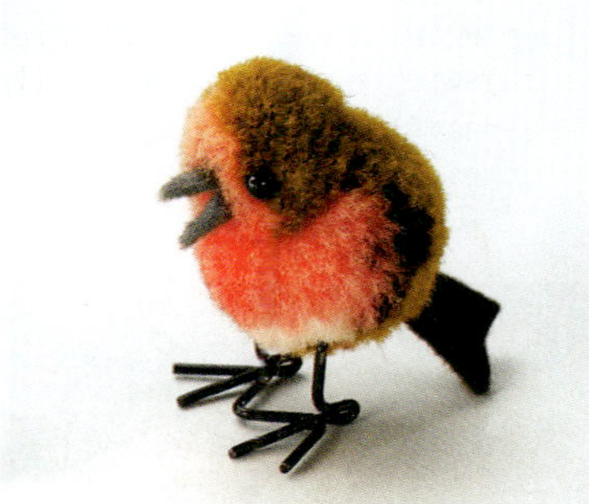

Woll-Vogel - *Woolen Bird*

bis 1950 Rotkehlchen, farbidentisch mit Modell bis 1940, gruen/rot, Wolle, Drahtbeine, ab 1956 Plastikbeine, Filzschwanz & -schnabel bzw. Plastikschnabel, stehend, Kopf drehbar, 4 cm: Gewicht 3 g, 8 cm: 6 g - *up to 1950 red robin, identical to model made prior to 1940, green & red, wool, wire legs, from 1956 plastic legs & feet, felt tail, beak felt or plastic, standing, head swivels, 4 cm: weight 3 g, 8 cm: 6 g*

SERIE	ART.-NO	PERIOD	PR.	INFO
71 5	**6504,1**	1949-1958	2	4 cm
870 871	**6504,41**	1959-1964	1-2	
710	**6504,41**	1965-1967	1-2	
	7101/04	1968-1978	1	

SERIE	ART.-NO	PERIOD	PR.	INFO
71 5	**6508,1**	1949-1958	2	8 cm
870 871	**6508,41**	1959-1964	1-2	
710	**6508,41**	1965-1967	1-2	
	7111/08	1968-1983	1	

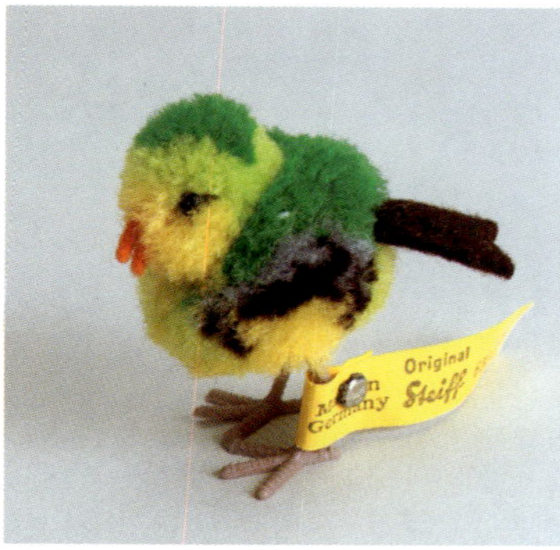

Woll-Vogel - *Woolen Bird*

bis 1950 Gruenspecht, farbidentisch mit Modell bis 1940, gelb/gruen/braun, Wolle, Drahtbeine, ab 1956 Plastikbeine, Filzschwanz & -schnabel bzw. Plastikschnabel, stehend, Kopf drehbar, 4 cm: Gewicht 3 g, 8 cm: 6 g - *up to 1950 green woodpecker, identical to model made prior to 1940, yellow, green & brown, wool, wire legs, from 1956 plastic legs & feet, felt tail, beak felt or plastic, standing, head swivels, 4 cm: weight 3 g, 8 cm: 6 g*

SERIE	ART.-NO	PERIOD	PR.	INFO
71 5	**6504,2**	1949-1958	2	4 cm
870 871	**6504,42**	1959-1964	1-2	
710	**6504,42**	1965-1967	1-2	
	7102/04	1968-1978	1	
71 5	**6508,2**	1949-1958	2	8 cm
870 871	**6508,42**	1959-1964	1-2	
710	**6508,42**	1965-1967	1-2	
	7112/08	1968-1983	1	

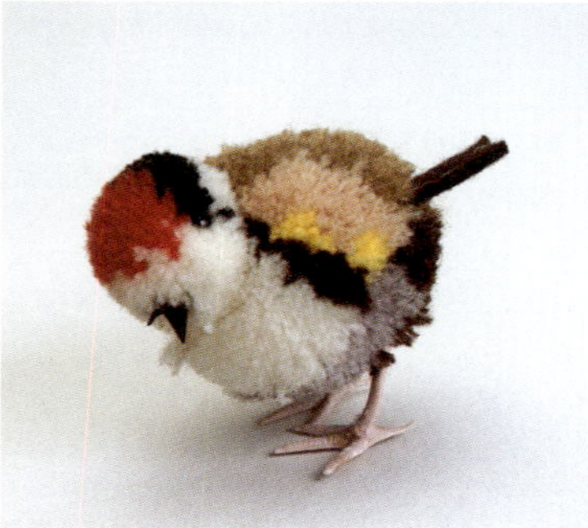

Woll-Vogel - *Woolen Bird*

bis 1950 Buntfink, weiss/braun/rot, Wolle, Drahtbeine, ab 1956 Plastikbeine, Filzschwanz & -schnabel bzw. Plastikschnabel, stehend, Kopf drehbar, 4 cm: Gewicht 3 g, 8 cm: 6 g - *up to 1950 bright colored finch, white, brown & red, wool, wire legs, from 1956 plastic legs & feet, felt tail, beak felt or plastic, standing, head swivels, 4 cm: weight 3 g, 8 cm: 6 g*

SERIE	ART.-NO	PERIOD	PR.	INFO
71 5	**6504,3**	1949-1958	2	4 cm
870 871	**6504,43**	1959-1964	1-2	
710	**6504,43**	1965-1967	1-2	
	7103/04	1968-1978	1	
71 5	**6508,3**	1949-1958	2	8 cm
870 871	**6508,43**	1959-1964	1-2	
710	**6508,43**	1965-1967	1-2	
	7113/08	1968-1983	1	

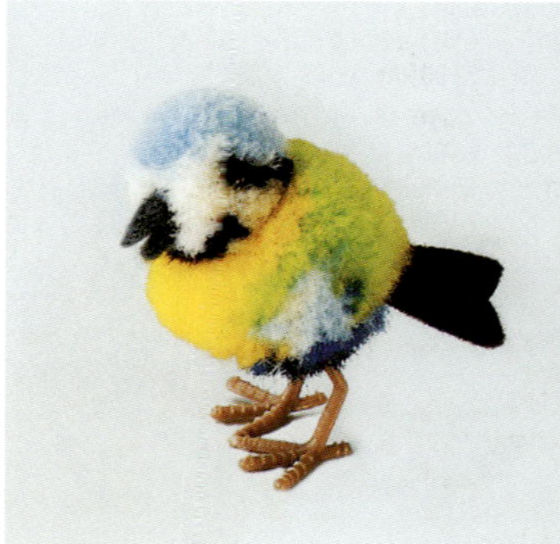

Wollvogel - *Woolen Bird*

bis 1950 Blaumeise, farbidentisch mit Modell bis 1940, gelb/hellgruen/hellblau, Wolle, Drahtbeine, ab 1956 Plastikbeine, Filzschwanz & -schnabel bzw. Plastikschnabel, stehend, Kopf drehbar, 4 cm: Gewicht 3 g, 8 cm: 6 g - *up to 1950 blue tit, identical to model made prior to 1940, yellow, light green & light blue, wool, wire legs, from 1956 plastic legs & feet, felt tail, beak felt or plastic, standing, head swivels, 4 cm: weight 3 g, 8 cm: 6 g*

SERIE	ART.-NO	PERIOD	PR.	INFO
71 5	**6504,4**	1949-1958	2	4 cm
870 871	**6504,44**	1959-1964	1-2	
710	**6504,44**	1965-1967	1-2	
	7104/04	1968-1978	1	
71 5	**6508,4**	1949-1958	2	8 cm
870 871	**6508,44**	1959-1964	1-2	
710	**6508,44**	1965-1967	1-2	
	7114/08	1968-1983	1	

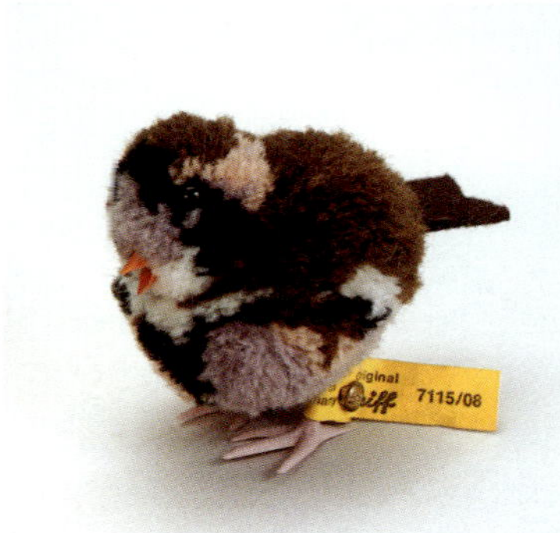

Woll-Vogel - *Woolen Bird*

bis 1950 Spatz, farbidentisch mit Modell bis 1940, braun/weiss, Wolle, Drahtbeine, ab 1956 Plastikbeine, Filzschwanz & -schnabel bzw. Plastikschnabel, stehend, Kopf drehbar, 4 cm: Gewicht 3 g, 8 cm: 6 g - *up to 1950 sparrow, identical to model made prior to 1940, brown/white, wool, wire legs, from 1956 plastic legs & feet, felt tail, beak felt or plastic, standing, head swivels, 4 cm: weight 3 g, 8 cm: 6 g*

SERIE	ART.-NO	PERIOD	PR.	INFO
71 5	**6504,5**	1949-1958	2	4 cm
870 871	**6504,45**	1959-1964	1-2	
710	**6504,45**	1965-1967	1-2	
	7105/04	1968-1978	1	
71 5	**6508,5**	1949-1958	2	8 cm
870 871	**6508,45**	1959-1964	1-2	
710	**6508,45**	1965-1967	1-2	
	7115/08	1968-1983	1	

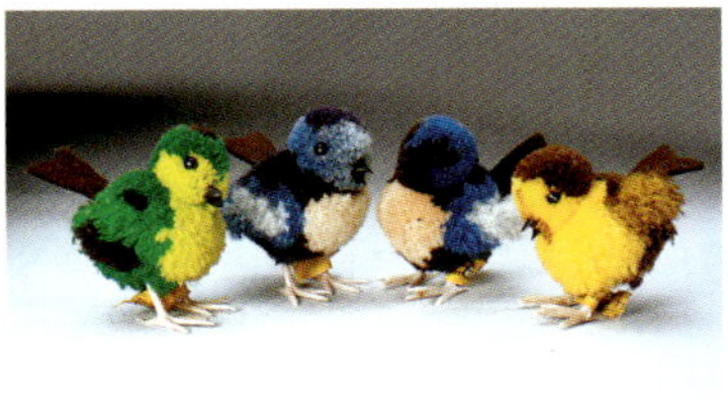

Woll-Vogel - *Woolen Bird*

Wolle, 9 cm, Plastikbeine, stehend - *wool, 9 cm, plastic feet, standing*

SERIE	ART.-NO	PERIOD	PR.	INFO
	7121/09	1968-1978	1	gruen - *green*
	7122/09	1968-1978	1	rot - *red*
	7123/09	1968-1977	1	blau - *blue*
	7124/09	1968-1978	1	gelb - *yellow*
	7125/09	1968-1978	1	rosa - *pink*

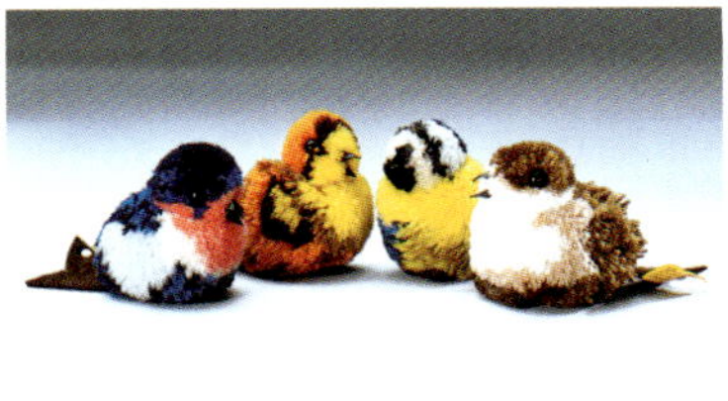

Wollvogel - *Woolen Bird*

Wolle/Filz, 10 cm, stehend, Halterung zur Befestigung an Zweigen etc. - *wool & felt, 10 cm, standing, with clamp attachment for fastening to branches, etc.*

SERIE	ART.-NO	PERIOD	PR.	INFO
	7081/10	1974-1981	1	blau - *blue*
	7082/10	1974-1980	1	gruen - *green*
	7083/10	1974-1981	1	orange
	7084/10	1974-1981	1	gelb - *yellow*
	7085/10	1974-1981	1	braun - *brown*

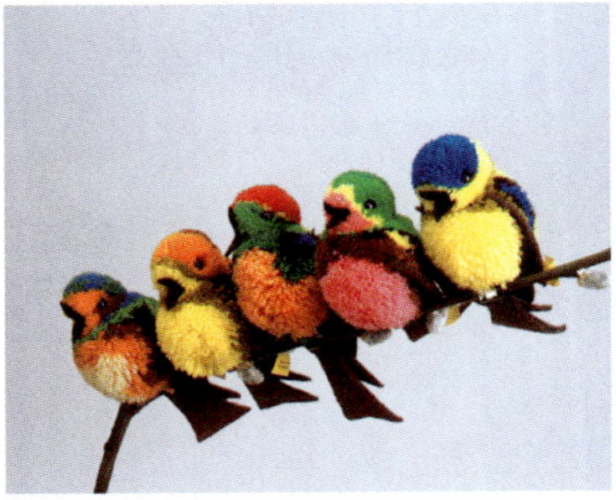

Wollvogel - *Woolen Bird*

Wollpluesch/Filz, 12 cm, Klemmhalterung zum Aufstecken an Zweigen etc. Set bestehend aus 5 Voegeln - *wool & felt, 12 cm, with clamp attachment to fasten to branches, etc., set with 5 birds*

SERIE	ART.-NO	PERIOD	PR.	INFO
	7091/12	1978-1981	1-2	rot - *red*
	7092/12	1978-1981	1-2	gruen - *green*
	7093/12	1978-1981	1-2	gelb - *yellow*
	7094/12	1978-1981	1-2	blau - *blue*
	7095/12	1978-1981	1-2	orange
	7088/07	1978-1982	3-4	Set

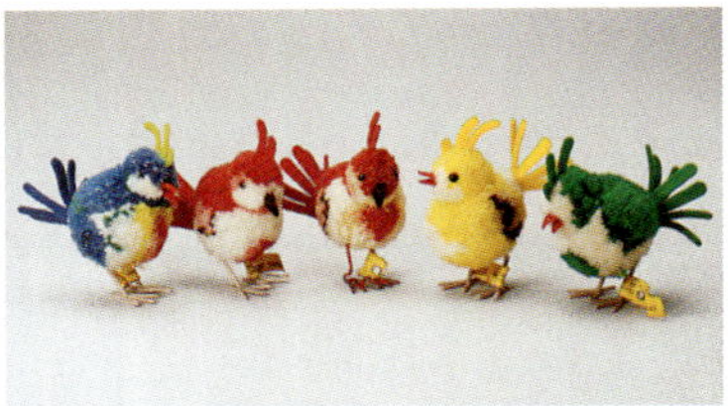

Woll-Exoten-Vogel - *Woolen Exotic Bird*

Wolle, Kopf- & Schwanzfedern aus Filz, Metall-Beine, ab 1956 Plastik-Beine, stehend - *wool, head & tail feathers felt, metal legs & feet, from 1956 plastic, standing*

SERIE	ART.-NO	PERIOD	PR.	INFO
71 5	**1509,1**	1953-1958	2	gelb/weiss - *yellow/white*
870 873	**1509,41**	1959-1963	1-2	
712	**1509,41**	1966-1966	1-2	
71 5	**1509,2**	1953-1958	2	blau/weiss - *blue/white*
870 873	**1509,42**	1959-1963	1-2	
712	**1509,42**	1966-1966	1-2	
71 5	**1509,3**	1953-1958	2	gruen/weiss - *green/white*
870 873	**1509,43**	1959-1963	1-2	
712	**1509,43**	1966-1966	1-2	
71 5	**1509,4**	1953-1958	2	rot/weiss - *red/white*
870 873	**1509,44**	1959-1963	1-2	
712	**1509,44**	1966-1966	1-2	

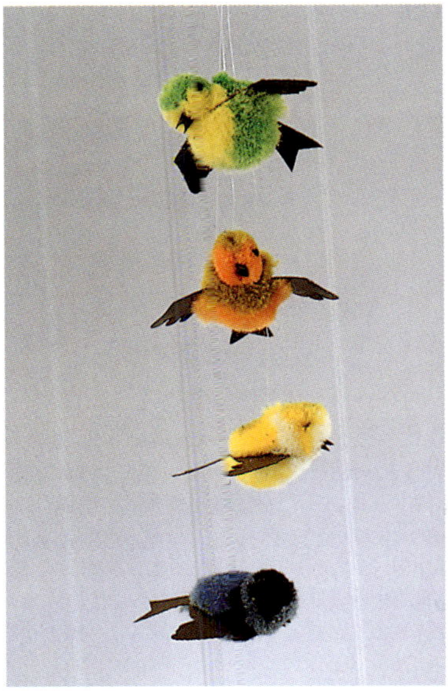

Woll-Kolibri - *Woolen Hummingbird*

Wolle, 3 cm, als Mobile oder Einzelvogel mit Anstecknadel, Mobile: 5 Kolibris als Mobile in runder Klarsichtpackung, Artikel-Nr. nur fuer kpl. Mobile - *wool, 3 cm, mobile or single bird with a pin for fastening, mobile: five hummingbirds as complete mobile unit in a round plastic package, art.no. refers only to complete mobile*

SERIE	ART.-NO	PERIOD	PR.	INFO
	7090/03	1969-1978	4	Mobile
	7091/03	1974-1976	1	rot - *red*
	7092/03	1974-1976	1	blau - *blue*
	7093/03	1974-1976	1	gelb - *yellow*
	7094/03	1974-1976	1	orange
	7095/03	1974-1976	1	gruen - *green*

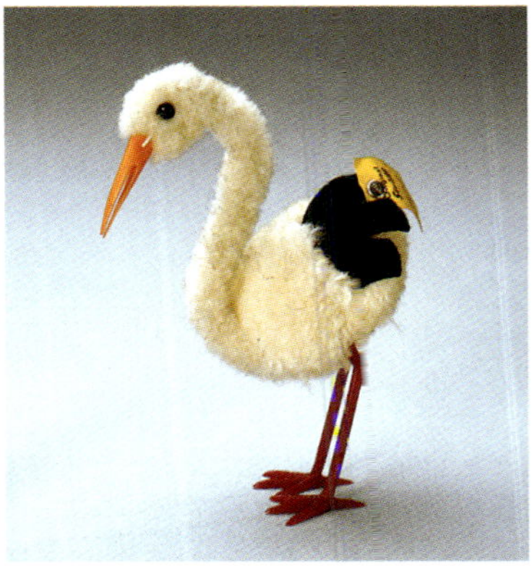

Woll-Storch - *Woolen Stork*

Wolle, Plastik-Beine, weiss/schwarz/rot, stehend - *wool, plastic legs & feet, white/black/red, standing*

SERIE	ART.-NO	PERIOD	PR.	INFO
	7460/11	1970-1977	2	11 cm

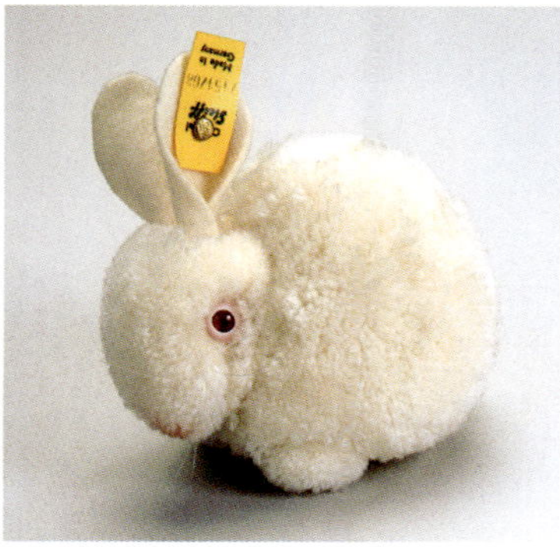

Woll-Hase - *Woolen Rabbit*

Wolle, Filzohren, liegend, Kopf drehbar, 4 cm: Gewicht 5 g, 6 cm: 10 g, weiss, Farbe identisch mit Modell bis 1940 - *wool, felt ears, lying, head swivels, 4 cm: weight 5 g, 6 cm: 10 g, white, colors identical to model prior to 1940*

SERIE	ART.-NO	PERIOD	PR.	INFO
71 36	**2504,1**	1949-1958	2	4 cm
870 875	**2504,41**	1959-1964	1-2	
714	**2504,41**	1965-1967	1-2	
	7131/04	1968-1984	1	
71 36	**2506,1**	1949-1958	2	6 cm
870 875	**2506,41**	1959-1964	1-2	
714	**2506,41**	1965-1967	1-2	
	7141/06	1968-1984	1	
714	**2508,41**	1967-1967	1-2	8 cm
	7151/08	1968-1984	1	

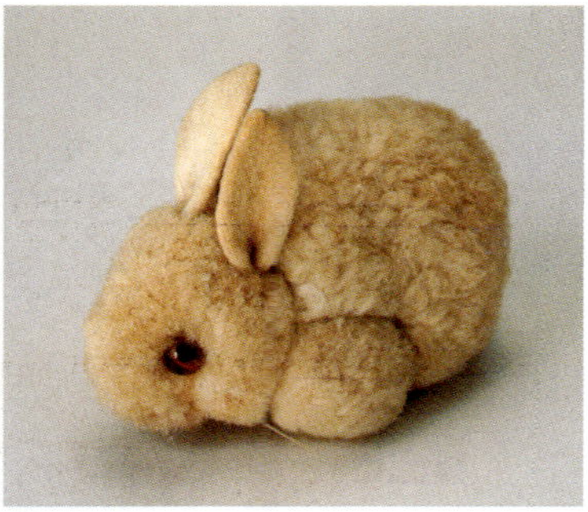

Woll-Hase - *Woolen Rabbit*

Wolle, Filzohren, liegend, Kopf drehbar, 4 cm: Gewicht 5 g, 6 cm: 10 g, weiss/beige, Farbe identisch mit Modell bis 1940 - *wool, felt ears, lying, head swivels, 4 cm: weight 5 g, 6 cm: 10 g, white/beige, colors identical to model prior to 1940*

SERIE	ART.-NO	PERIOD	PR.	INFO
71 36	**2504,2**	1949-1958	2	4 cm
870 875	**2504,42**	1959-1964	1-2	
714	**2504,42**	1965-1967	1-2	
	7132/04	1968-1984	1	
71 36	**2506,2**	1949-1958	2	6 cm
870 875	**2506,42**	1959-1964	1-2	
714	**2506,42**	1965-1967	1-2	
	7142/06	1968-1984	1	
714	**2508,42**	1967-1967	1-2	8 cm
	7152/08	1968-1984	1	

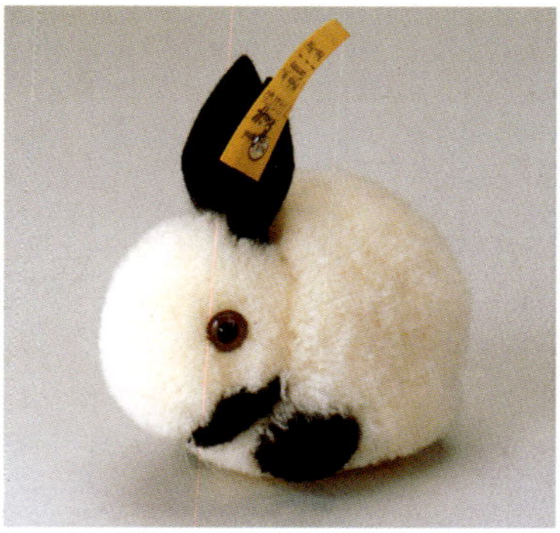

Woll-Hase - *Woolen Rabbit*

Wolle, Filzohren, liegend, Kopf drehbar, 4 cm: Gewicht 5 g, 6 cm: 10 g, weiss/schwarz, Farbe wie Modell ",4" bis 1940 - *wool, felt ears, lying, head swivels, 4 cm: weight 5 g, 6 cm: 10 g, white/black, colors identical to model ",4" prior to 1940*

SERIE	ART.-NO	PERIOD	PR.	INFO
71 36	**2504,3**	1949-1958	2	4 cm
870 875	**2504,43**	1959-1964	1-2	
714	**2504,43**	1965-1967	1-2	
	7133/04	1968-1984	1	
71 36	**2506,3**	1949-1958	2	6 cm
870 875	**2506,43**	1959-1964	1-2	
714	**2506,43**	1965-1967	1-2	
	7143/06	1968-1983	1	
714	**2508,43**	1967-1967	1-2	8 cm
	7153/08	1968-1984	1	

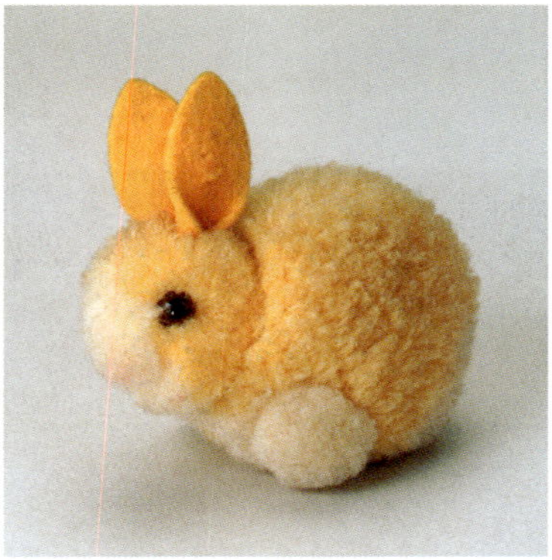

Woll-Hase - *Woolen Rabbit*

Wolle, Filzohren, liegend, Kopf drehbar, 4 cm: Gewicht 5 g, 6 cm: 10 g, hellbraun/weiss, Farbe wie Modell ",6" bis 1940 - *wool, felt ears, lying, head swivels, 4 cm: weight 5 g, 6 cm: 10 g, light brown/white, colors identical to model ",6" prior to 1940*

SERIE	ART.-NO	PERIOD	PR.	INFO
71 36	**2504,5**	1949-1950	2	4 cm
71 36	**2504,4**	1951-1958	2	
870 875	**2504,44**	1959-1964	1-2	
714	**2504,44**	1965-1967	1-2	
	7134/04	1968-1984	1	
71 36	**2506,5**	1949-1950	2	6 cm
71 36	**2506,4**	1951-1958	2	
870 875	**2506,44**	1959-1964	1-2	
714	**2506,44**	1965-1967	1-2	
	7144/06	1968-1984	1	
714	**2508,44**	1967-1967	1-2	8 cm
	7154/08	1968-1984	1	

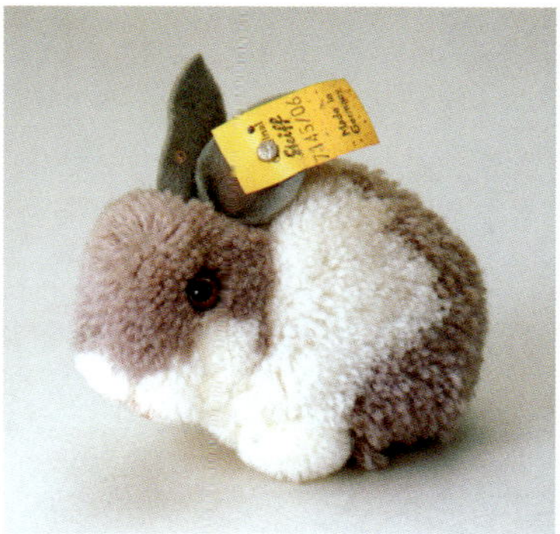

Woll-Hase - *Woolen Rabbit*

Wolle, Filzohren, liegend, Kopf drehbar, 4 cm: Gewicht 5 g, 6 cm: 10 g, grau/weiss, Farbe wie Modell ",5" bis 1940 - *wool, felt ears, lying, head swivels, 4 cm: weight 5 g, 6 cm: 10 g, grey/ white, colors identical to model ",5" prior to 1940*

SERIE	ART.-NO	PERIOD	PR.	INFO
71 36	**2504,4**	1949-1950	2	4 cm
71 36	**2504,5**	1951-1958	2	
870 875	**2504,45**	1959-1964	1-2	
714	**2504,45**	1965-1967	1-2	
	7135/04	1968-1984	1	
71 36	**2506,4**	1949-1950	2	6 cm
71 36	**2506,5**	1951-1958	2	
870 875	**2506,45**	1959-1964	1-2	
714	**2506,45**	1965-1967	1-2	
	7145/06	1968-1984	1	
714	**2508,45**	1967-1967	1-2	8 cm
	7155/08	1968-1984	1	

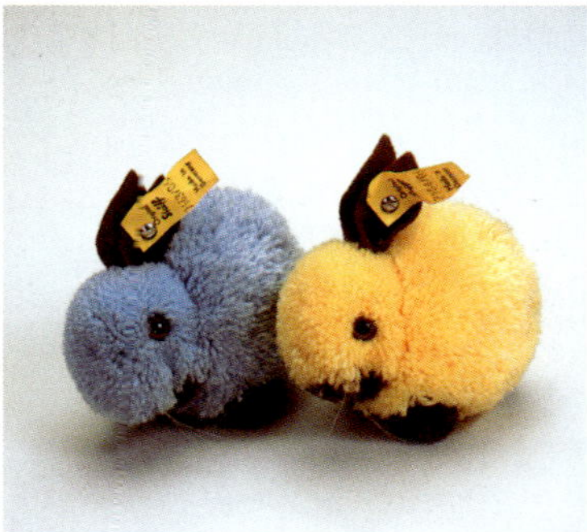

Woll-Hase - *Woolen Rabbit*

Wolle, 6 cm, Filzohren, sitzend - *wool, 6 cm, felt ears, sitting*

SERIE	ART.-NO	PERIOD	PR.	INFO
	7162/06	1973-1981	1-2	rot - *red*
	7163/06	1973-1981	1-2	blau - *blue*
	7164/06	1973-1981	1-2	gelb - *yellow*

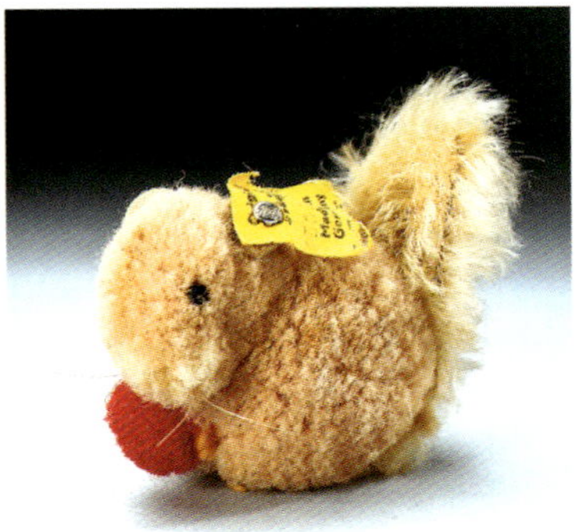

Woll-Eichhorn - *Woolen Squirrel*

Wolle, Filzfuesse, -pfoten & -ohren, Schwanz drahtverstaerkt, weiss/beige, rote Nuss, aufwartend - *wool, feet, paws, & ears made of felt, tail reinforced with wire, white/beige, holding red nut, sitting up*

SERIE	ART.-NO	PERIOD	PR.	INFO
71 19	**4505**	1954-1958	2-3	5 cm
870 876	**4505,43**	1959-1964	2	
716	**4505,43**	1965-1967	2	
	7160/05	1968-1978	1-2	

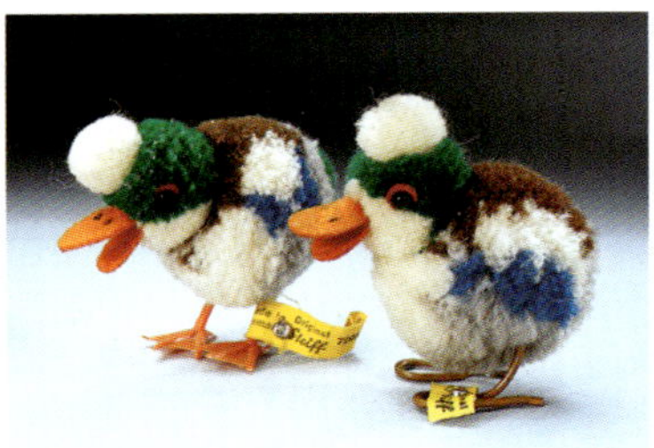

Woll-Erpel - *Woolen Drake*

Wolle, bunt, stehend, Metallbeine, ab 1971 Plastikbeine, Kopf drehbar, Gewicht 9 g - *wool, multi-colored, standing, metal legs & feet, from 1971 plastic, head swivels, weight: 9 g*

SERIE	ART.-NO	PERIOD	PR.	INFO
71 22	**1506** b	1949-1958	3	6 cm
870 877	**1506,47**	1959-1964	2-3	
720	**1506,47**	1965-1967	2-3	
	7205/06	1968-1976	2	

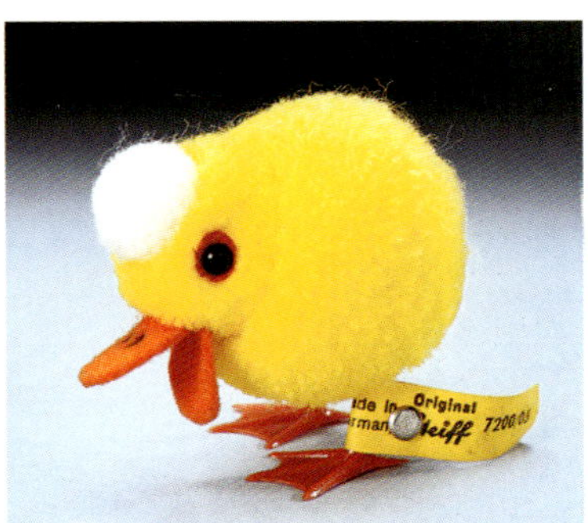

Woll-Ente - *Woolen Duck*

Wolle, gelb, stehend, Metallbeine, ab 1971 Plastikbeine, Kopf drehbar, Gewicht 9 g - *wool, yellow, standing, metal legs & feet, from 1971 plastic legs & feet, head swivels, weight 9 g*

SERIE	ART.-NO	PERIOD	PR.	INFO
71 22	**1506** g	1949-1958	3	6 cm
870 877	**1506,41**	1959-1964	2-3	
720	**1506,41**	1965-1967	2-3	
	7200/06	1968-1977	2	

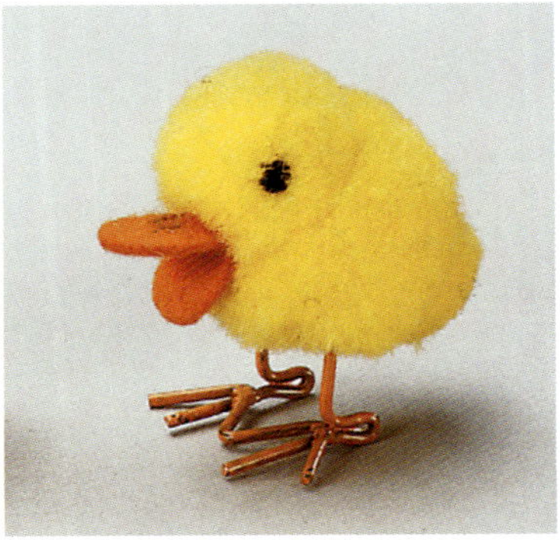

Woll-Entenkueken - *Woolen Duckling*

Wolle, gelb, stehend, Metallbeine, ab 1959 Plastikbeine, Kopf drehbar, Gewicht 3 g - *wool, yellow, standing, metal legs & feet, from 1959 plastic legs & feet, head swivels, weight 3 g*

SERIE	ART.-NO	PERIOD	PR.	INFO
71 22	**1504**	1949-1958	2-3	4 cm
870 877	**1504,41**	1959-1964	2	
720	**1504,41**	1965-1967	2	
	7200/04	1968-1976	1-2	

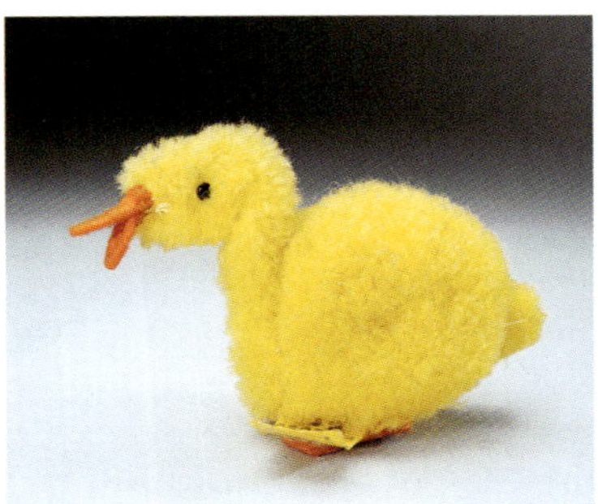

Woll-Ente - *Woolen Duck*

Wolle, gelb, liegend, Filzfuesse - *wool, yellow, lying, feet made of felt*

SERIE	ART.-NO	PERIOD	PR.	INFO
870 877	**2505,41**	1963-1964	2	5 cm
720	**2505,41**	1965-1967	2	

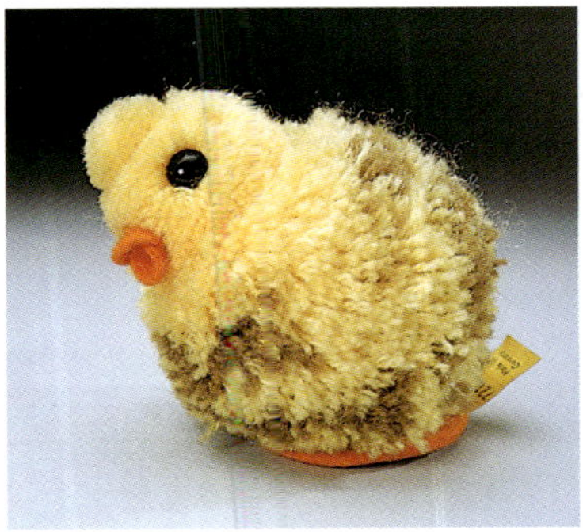

Woll-Ente - *Woolen Duck*

Wolle, mais/braun, liegend, Filzfuesse - *wool, corn yellow/brown, lying, feet made of felt*

SERIE	ART.-NO	PERIOD	PR.	INFO
	7210/08	1974-1978	1-2	8 cm

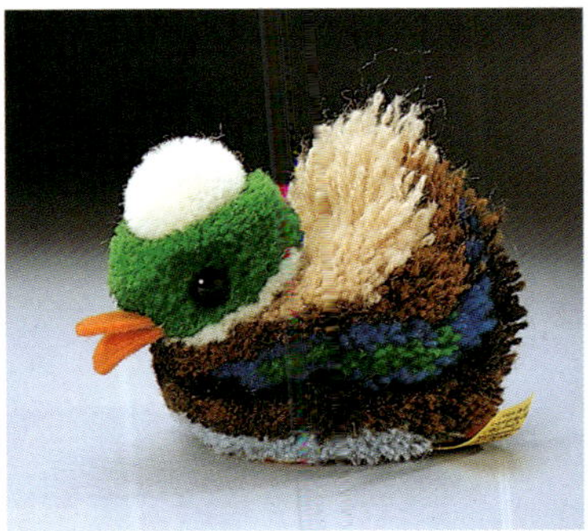

Woll-Erpel - *Woolen Drake*

Wolle, bunt, liegend, Filzfuesse - *wool, multi-colored, lying, feet are made of felt*

SERIE	ART.-NO	PERIOD	PR.	INFO
	7212/08	1976-1981	1-2	8 cm

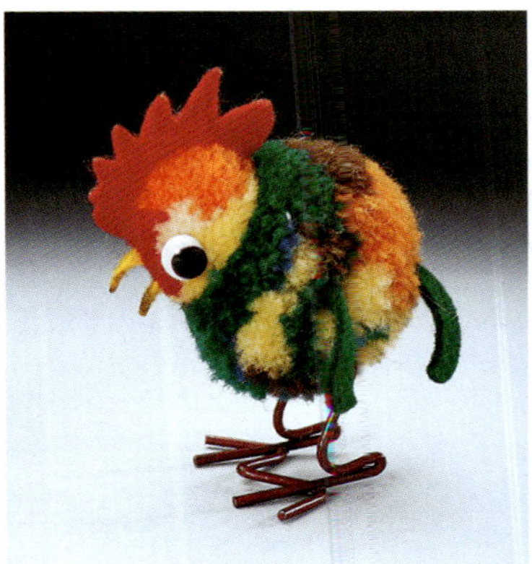

Woll-Hahn - *Woolen Rooster*

Wolle, Metallbeine, ab 1971 Plastikbeine, Filzkamm, bunt, Kopf drehbar, Gewicht 9 g - *wool, metal legs & feet, from 1971 plastic legs & feet, felt comb, multi-colored, head swivels, weight 9 g*

SERIE	ART.-NO	PERIOD	PR.	INFO
71 34	**1508**	1949-1958	3	8 cm
870 878	**1508,47**	1959-1964	2-3	
724	**1508,47**	1965-1967	2-3	
	7240/08	1968-1982	1-2	

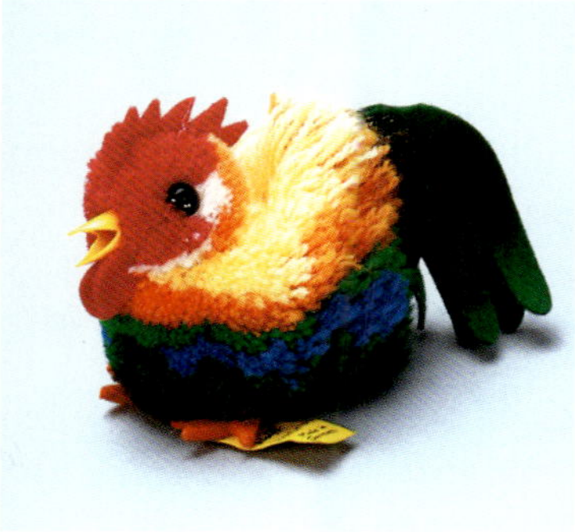

Woll-Hahn - *Woolen Rooster*

Wolle, bunt, liegend, Filzfuesse, -kamm & -schwanz, Plastikschnabel - *wool, multicolored, lying, felt feet, comb & tail, plastic beak*

SERIE	ART.-NO	PERIOD	PR.	INFO
	7245/08	1976-1983	1-2	8 cm

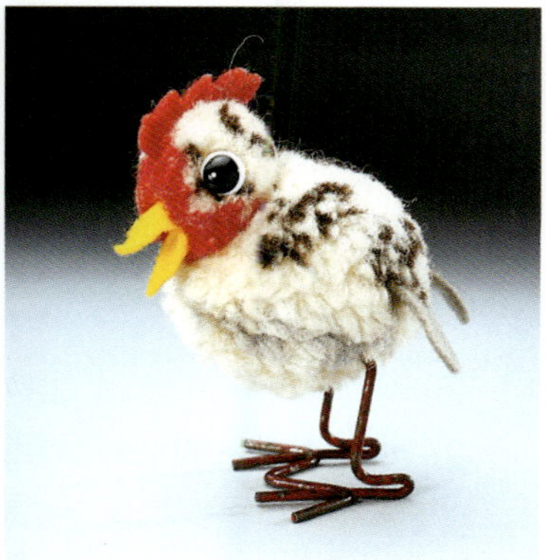

Woll-Henne - *Woolen Hen*

Wolle, Metallbeine, ab 1971 Plastikbeine, Filzkamm, weiss, hellbraun gefleckt, stehend, Kopf drehbar, Gewicht 9 g - *wool, metal legs & feet, from 1971 plastic legs & feet, felt comb, white, light brown speckles, standing, head swivels, weight 9 g*

SERIE	ART.-NO	PERIOD	PR.	INFO
71 35	**1508**	1949-1958	3	8 cm
870 879	**1508,44**	1959-1964	2-3	
725	**1508,44**	1965-1967	2-3	
	7250/08	1968-1982	1-2	

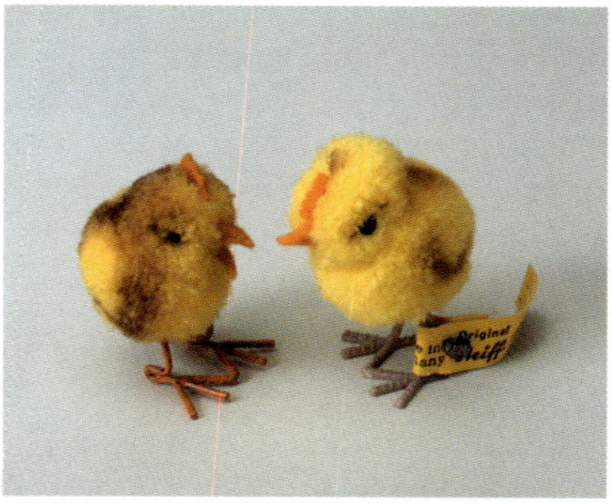

Woll-Kueken - *Woolen Chick*

Wolle, Metallbeine, ab 1959 Plastikbeine, Filzkamm, gelb, braun schattiert, stehend, Kopf drehbar - *wool, metal legs & feet, from 1959 plastic legs & feet, felt comb, yellow, brown shaded, standing, head swivels*

SERIE	ART.-NO	PERIOD	PR.	INFO
71 35	**1504**	1949-1958	2-3	4 cm
870 879	**1504,41**	1959-1964	2	
726	**1504,41**	1965-1967	2	
	7260/04	1968-1983	1-2	
71 35	**1506**	1953-1958	2-3	6 cm
870 879	**1506,41**	1959-1964	2	
726	**1506,41**	1965-1967	2	
	7260/06	1968-1984	1-2	

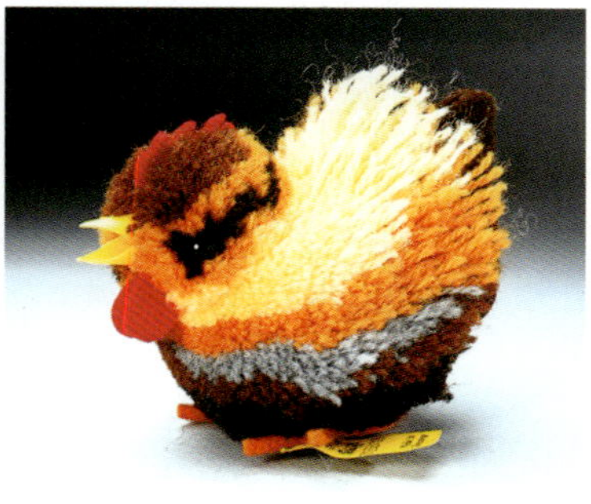

Woll-Henne - *Woolen Hen*

Wolle, bunt, liegend, Filzfuesse, -kamm & -schwanz, Plastikschnabel - *wool, multicolored, lying, felt feet, comb & tail, plastic beak*

SERIE	ART.-NO	PERIOD	PR.	INFO
	7255/08	1976-1984	1-2	8 cm

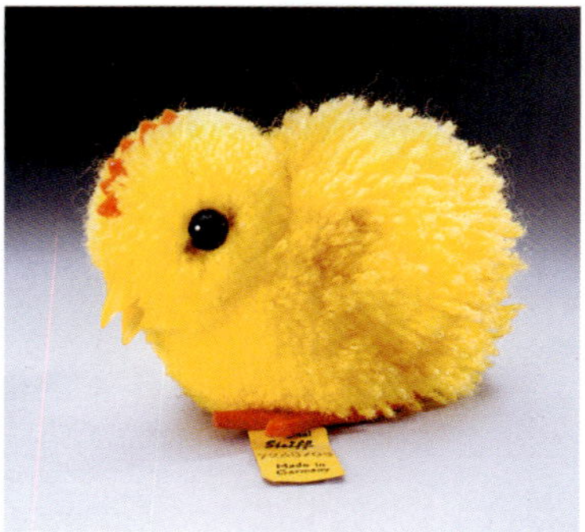

Woll-Kueken - *Woolen Chick*

Wolle, gelb, liegend, Filzfuesse & -kamm, Plastikschnabel - *wool, yellow, lying, felt feet & comb, plastic beak*

SERIE	ART.-NO	PERIOD	PR.	INFO
	7260/08	1976-1984	1-2	8 cm

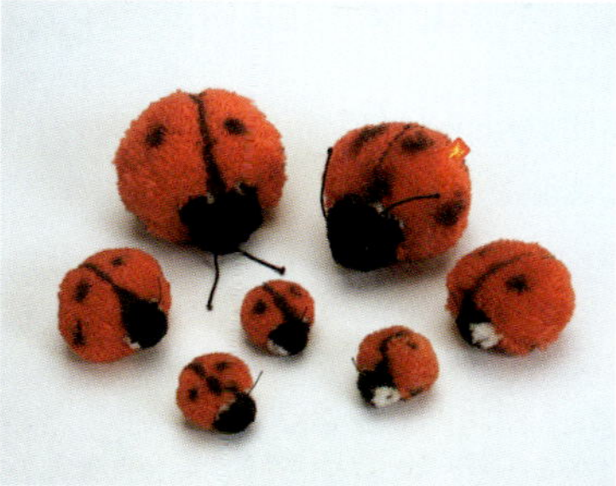

Woll-Marienkaefer - *Woolen Ladybird*

Wolle, rot/schwarz/weiss, stehend, ohne Steiff-Zeichen - *wool, red/black/white, standing, no Steiff labels*

SERIE	ART.-NO	PERIOD	PR.	INFO
71 39	**1503**	1953-1958	1	3 cm
870 880	**1503,40**	1959-1964	1	
737	**1503,40**	1965-1967	1	
	7370/03	1968-1982	1	
71 39	**1504**	1953-1958	1	4 cm
870 880	**1504,40**	1959-1964	1	
737	**1504,40**	1965-1967	1	
	7370/04	1968-1984	1	
	7370/06	1969-1984	1	6 cm
	7371/03	1976-1976	1-2	3 cm, mit Anstecknadel - *with pin*

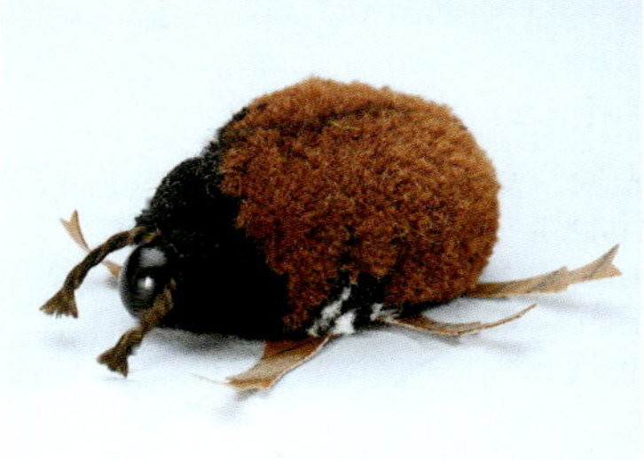

Woll-Maikaefer - *Woolen Cockchafer*

Wolle, Plastik-Fuesse, braun/schwarz, ohne Steiff-Zeichen - *wool, plastic feet, brown/black, no Steiff labels*

SERIE	ART.-NO	PERIOD	PR.	INFO
	7380/05	1969-1974	1-2	4 cm

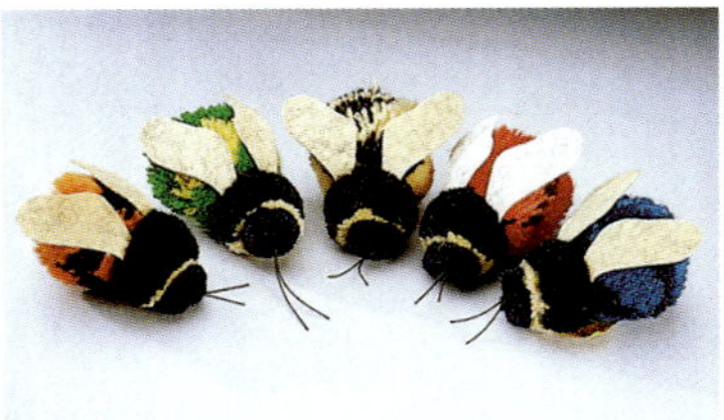

Woll-Hummel - *Woolen Bumble-Bee*

Wollpluesch, 6 cm - *wool plush, 6 cm*

Serie	Art.-No	Period	Pr.	Info
	7381/06	1975-1981	2-3	blau - *blue*
	7382/06	1975-1981	2-3	gelb - *yellow*
	7383/06	1975-1981	2-3	gruen - *green*
	7384/06	1975-1981	2-3	orange
	7385/06	1975-1981	2-3	rot - *red*

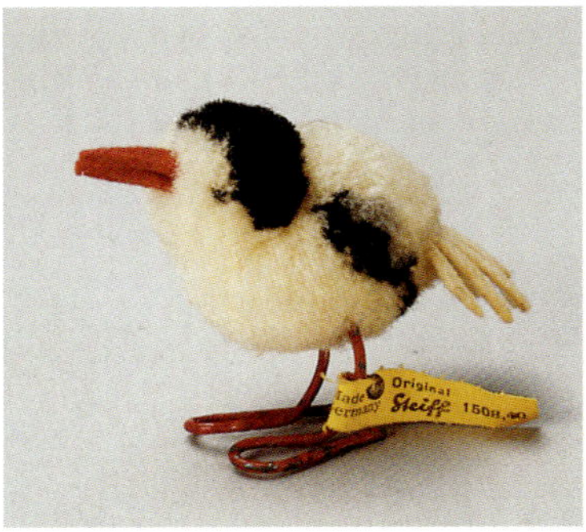

Woll-Moewe - *Woolen Seagull*

Wolle, schwarz/weiss, stehend, Metallbeine, ab 1962 Plastikbeine, Kopf drehbar - *wool, black/white, standing, metal legs & feet, from 1962 plastic, head swivels*

Serie	Art.-No	Period	Pr.	Info
71 49a	**1508**	1954-1957	3	8 cm
870 882	**1508,40**	1959-1963	2-3	

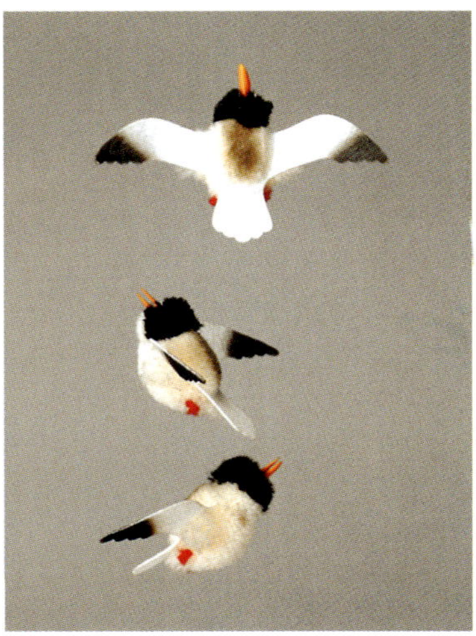

Woll-Moewen-Mobile - *Woolen Seagull Mobile*

Wollpluesch, in runder Klarsichtpackung, weiss/schwarz, 3 Wollmoewen mit ausgebreiteten Fluegeln als Mobile - *wool plush, packed in round clear plastic package, white/black, mobile of 3 woolen seagulls with expanded wings*

Serie	Art.-No	Period	Pr.	Info
	7098/03	1974-1976	4	3 x 3 cm

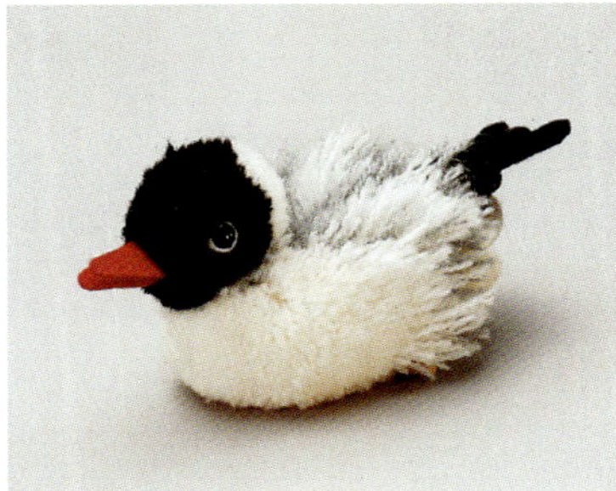

Woll-Moewe - *Woolen Seagull*

Wolle, weiss/schwarz/grau, liegend, Filzschnabel, -schwanz & -fuesse, Kopf drehbar - *wool, white/black/grey, lying, felt beak, tail & feet, head swivels*

Serie	Art.-No	Period	Pr.	Info
	7270/08	1976-1979	1-2	8 cm

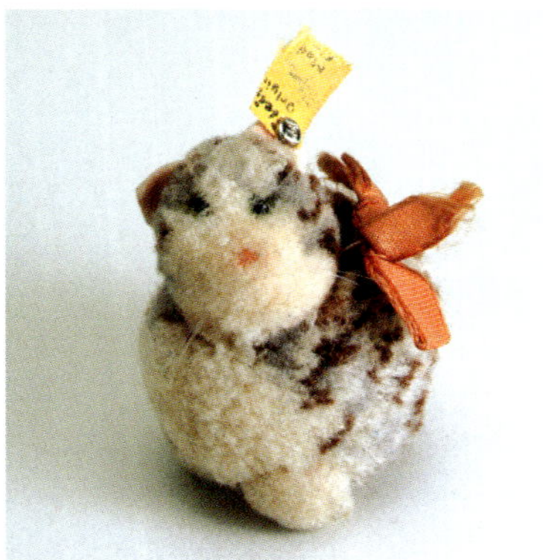

Woll-Katze - *Woolen Cat*

Wolle, weiss/braun/grau, Filzohren, sitzend - *wool, white/brown/grey, felt ears, sitting*

Serie	Art.-No	Period	Pr.	Info
71 44	**3505**	1954-1958	2-3	5 cm
870 884	**3505,40**	1959-1963	2	
729	**3505,40**	1966-1967	2	
	7290/05	1968-1978	1-2	

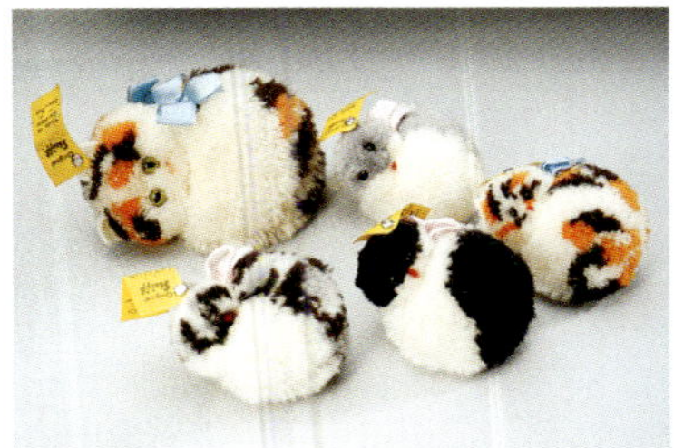

Woll-Katze - *Woolen Cat*

Wolle, Filzohren, liegend, Kopf drehbar, Grundfarbe weiss - *wool, felt ears, lying, head swivels, basic white*

Serie	Art.-No	Period	Pr.	Info
	7291/04	1970-1972	1-2	4 cm, weiss - *white*
	7301/06	1970-1973	1-2	6 cm
	7292/04	1970-1973	1-2	4 cm, grau/schwarzbraun - *grey/black-brown*
	7302/06	1970-1973	1-2	6 cm
	7293/04	1970-1973	1-2	4 cm, schwarz - *black*
	7303/06	1970-1972	1-2	6 cm
	7294/04	1970-1973	1-2	4 cm, orange/braun - *orange/brown*
	7304/06	1970-1973	1-2	6 cm
	7295/04	1970-1974	1-2	4 cm, grau - *grey*
	7305/06	1970-1974	1-2	6 cm

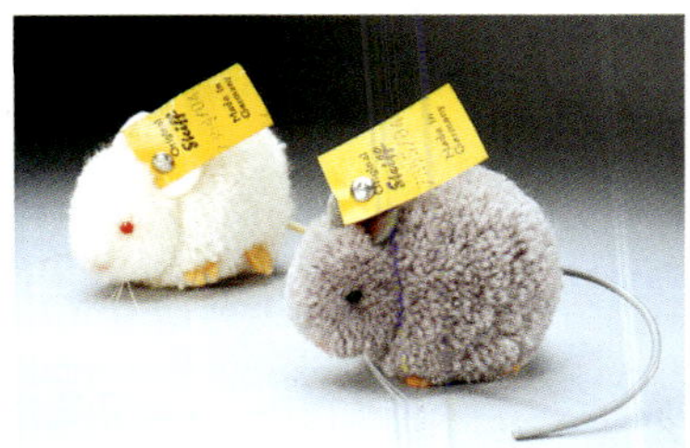

Woll-Maus - *Woolen Mouse*

Wolle, Filzfuesse & -ohren, liegend, Kopf drehbar, 4 cm, 5 g - *wool, felt feet & ears, lying, head swivels, 4 cm, weight 5 g*

Serie	Art.-No	Period	Pr.	Info
71 50	**2504** gr	1949-1951	2-3	grau - *grey*
71 50	**2504,1**	1952-1958	2-3	
870 886	**2504,44**	1959-1964	2	
735	**2504,44**	1965-1967	2	
	7354/04	1968-1984	1	
71 50	**2504** w	1949-1951	2-3	weiss - *white*
71 50	**2504,2**	1952-1958	2-3	
870 886	**2504,45**	1959-1964	2	
735	**2504,45**	1965-1967	2	
	7355/04	1968-1984	1	

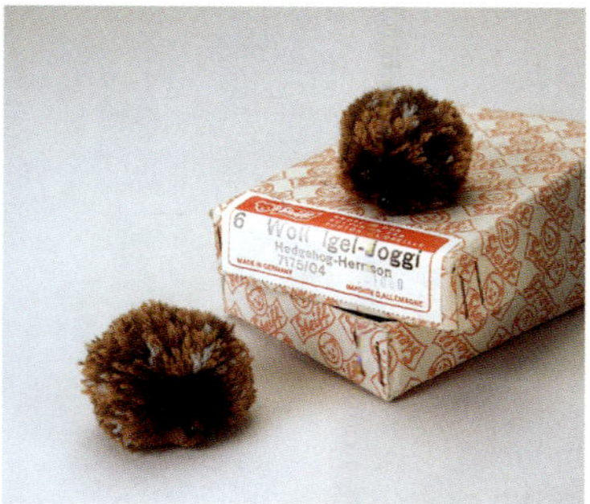

Woll-Igel Joggi - *Woolen Hedgehog Joggi*

Wolle, braun (Toene), Kunststoff-Augen & -Nase, ohne Steiff-Zeichen - *wool, brown, plastic-eyes & -nose, no Steiff labels*

Serie	Art.-No	Period	Pr.	Info
	7175/04	1970-1970	3	4 cm

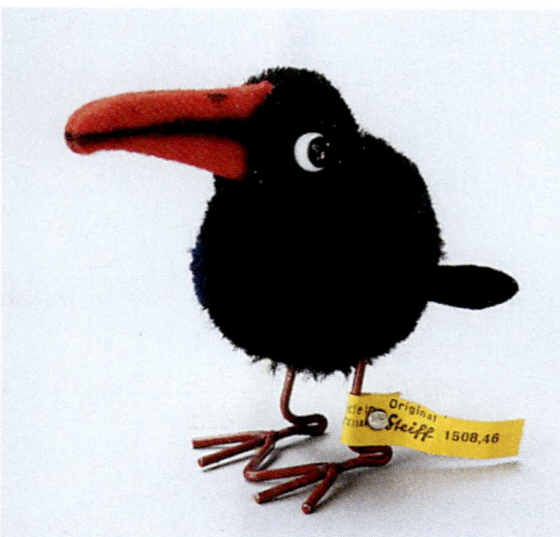

Woll-Rabe - *Woolen Raven*

Wolle, Drahtbeine, ab 1971 Plastik, schwarz/dunkelblau, Filzschnabel & -schwanzfedern, Kopf drehbar, stehend, Gewicht 9 g - *wool, wire legs & feet, from 1971 plastic, black/dark blue, felt beak & tail feathers, head swivels, standing, weight 9 g*

Serie	Art.-No	Period	Pr.	Info
71 62	**1508**	1949-1958	2-3	8 cm
870 888	**1508,46**	1959-1964	2	
743	**1508,46**	1965-1967	2	
	7430/03	1968-1984	1-2	

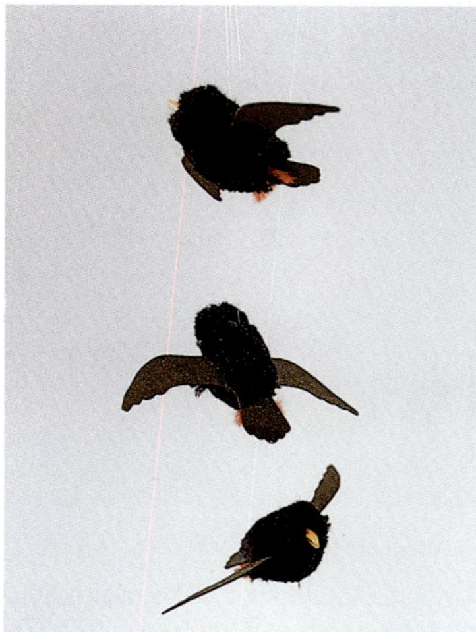

Woll-Raben-Mobile - *Woolen Raven Mobile*

Wollpluesch/Filz, in durchsichtiger Plastikroehre, schwarz, 3 Wollraben mit ausgebreiteten Filz-Fluegeln als Mobile - *wool plush & felt, packed in clear plastic tube, black, mobile includes 3 woolen ravens with expanded wings*

Serie	Art.-No	Period	Pr.	Info
	7087/03	1974-1976	4	3 x 3 cm

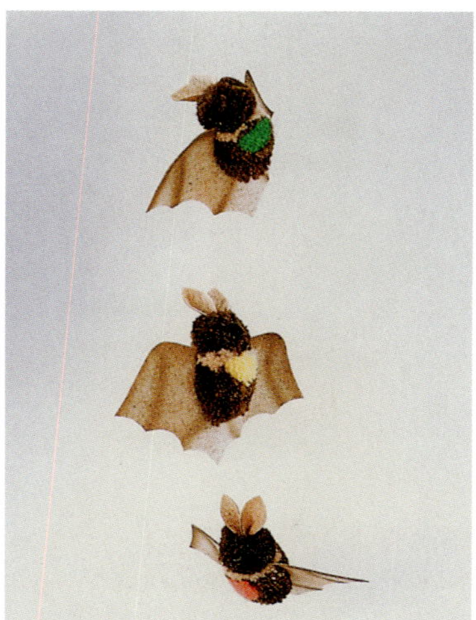

Woll-Fledermaus Mobile - *Woolen Bat Mobile*

Wollpluesch/Filz, in durchsichtiger Plastikroehre, braun, 3 Wollfledermaeuse mit ausgebreiteten Fluegeln als Mobile - *wool plush & felt, packed in clear plastic tube, brown, mobile with 3 woolen bats with expanded wings*

Serie	Art.-No	Period	Pr.	Info
	7088/05	1975-1976	4-5	3 x 3 cm

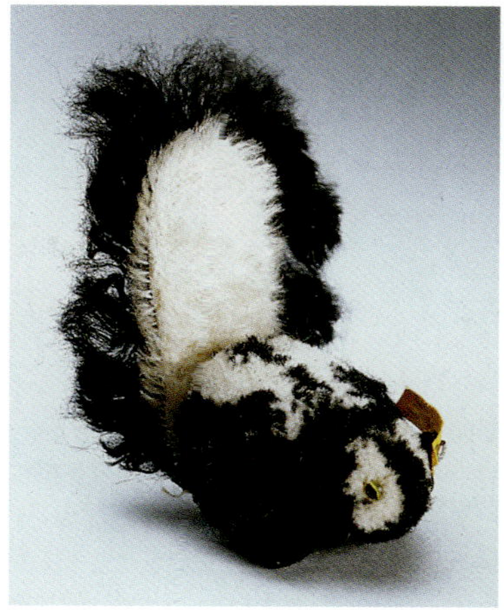

Wool-Skunk - *Woolen Skunk*

Wolle, schwarz/weiss, liegend, Schwanz drahtverstaerkt - *wool, black & white, lying, tail is reinforced with wire*

Serie	Art.-No	Period	Pr.	Info
71 45	**2506**	1955-1958	4	6 cm
870 890	**2506,40**	1959-1961	3-4	

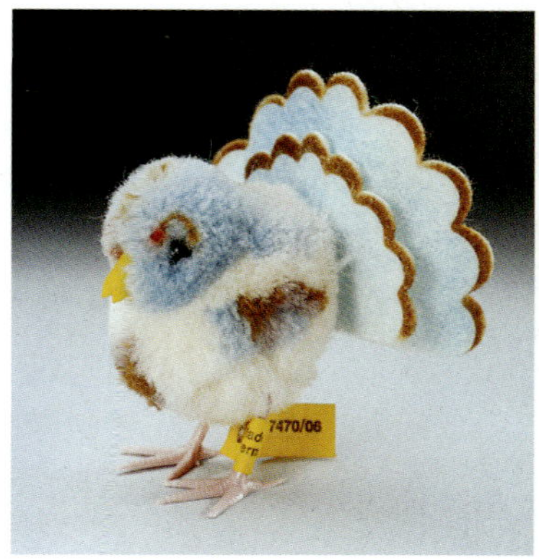

Woll-Taube - *Woolen Dove*

Wolle, Metallbeine, ab 1964 Plastik, Schwanzfedern aus Filz, Plastikschnabel, hellblau/weiss, stehend - *wool, metal legs & feet from 1964 plastic, felt tail feathers, plastic beak, light blue & white, standing*

Serie	Art.-No	Period	Pr.	Info
71 8	**1506**	1953-1958	3	6 cm
870 892	**1506,40**	1959-1963	2-3	
747	**1506,40**	1965-1967	2-3	
	7470/06	1968-1977	2	

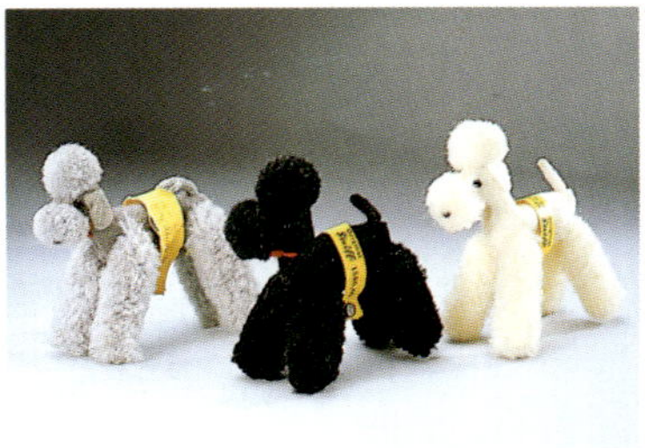

Woll-Pudel - *Woolen Poodle*

Wolle, 6 cm, weiss, grau oder schwarz, gegliedert - *wool, 6 cm, white, grey or black, jointed*

SERIE	ART.-NO	PERIOD	PR.	INFO
71 58	**1506** w	1955-1958	2	weiss - *white*
870 894	**1506,44**	1959-1964	1-2	
741	**1506,44**	1965-1967	1-2	
	7414/06	1968-1978	1	
71 58	**1506** gr	1955-1958	2	grau - *grey*
870 894	**1506,45**	1959-1964	1-2	
741	**1506,45**	1965-1967	1-2	
	7415/06	1968-1978	1	
71 58	**1506** s	1955-1958	2	schwarz - *black*
870 894	**1506,46**	1959-1964	1-2	
741	**1506,46**	1965-1967	1-2	
	7416/06	1968-1978	1	

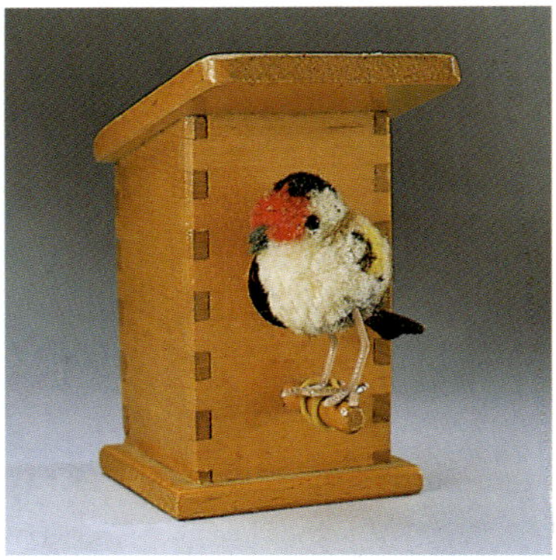

Starhaus - *Starling Birdhouse*

Hartholz, naturlackiert, 8 cm hoch, mit 4 cm grossem Wollvogel - *hardwood, naturally lacqered, 8 cm tall, with 4 cm large woolen bird*

SERIE	ART.-NO	PERIOD	PR.	INFO
71a	**807**	1951-1957	3	8 cm
870 896	**7807,40**	1961-1961	3	
757	**7807,40**	1966-1967	3	
	7570/07	1968-1974	2-3	

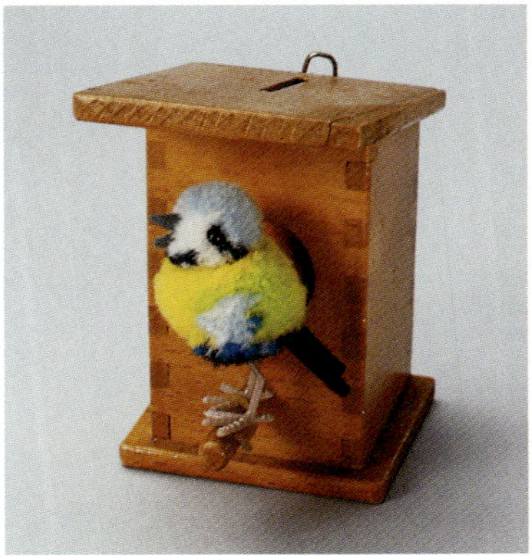

Starhaus als Spardose - *Starling Bank*

Hartholz, naturlackiert, Geldeinwurfschlitz im abnehmbaren Dach, Gesamthoehe 8 cm, mit 4 cm grossem Wollvogel - *hardwood, naturally lacquered, money slot is in the removable roof, total height 8 cm, with 4 cm large woolen bird*

SERIE	ART.-NO	PERIOD	PR.	INFO
71a	**807** S	1953-1957	3	8 cm
870 896	**7808,40**	1961-1961	3	
757	**7808,40**	1966-1967	3	
	7570/08	1968-1974	2-3	

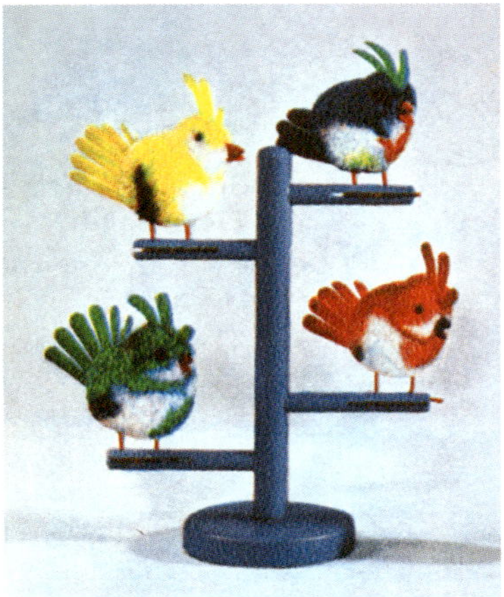

Vogelbaum - *Bird´s Tree*

Holz, im Karton, mit 4 Woll-Exoten-Voegeln - *wood, in box, with 4 woolen exotic birds*

SERIE	ART.-NO	PERIOD	PR.	INFO
71a	**5204** Ch	1953-1956	4-5	

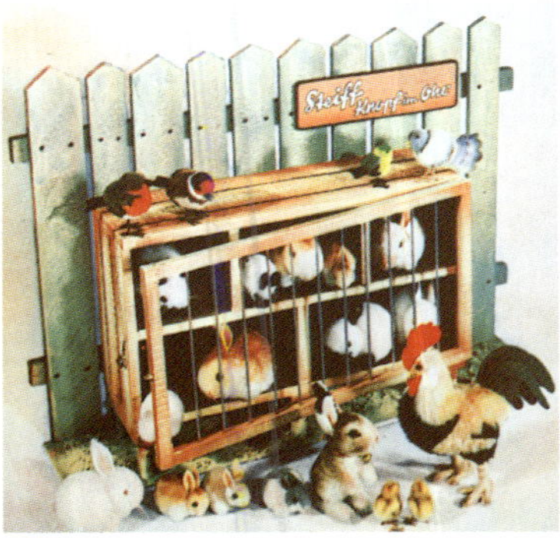

Hasenstall - *Rabbit Hutch*

Hasenstall, Holz, 24 x 34 cm, ganze Hoehe 38 cm, mit Zaun & 5 Wollhasen (3 x 36/2504 & 2 x 36/2506), als Ausstellungsstueck oder Verkaufs-Artikel - *rabbit hutch, wood, size 24 x 34 cm, total height 38 cm, with fence & 5 woolen rabbits (3 x 36/2504 & 2 x 36/2506), offered as a display piece or for sale*

SERIE	ART.-NO	PERIOD	PR.	INFO
71a	**5205** H	1953-1956	5	

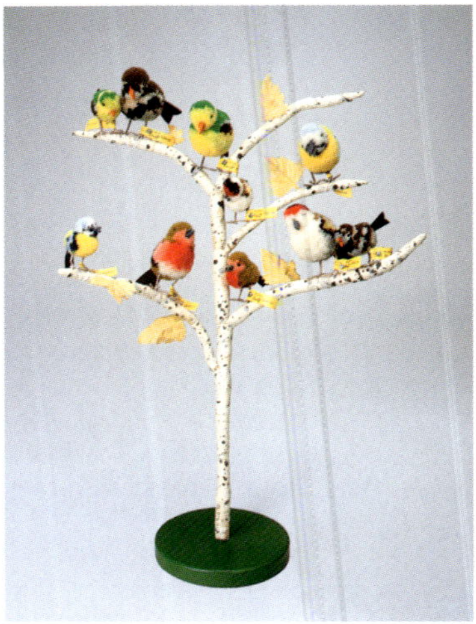

Vogelbaum - *Bird´s Tree*

Vogelbaum, imit. Birke, mit 12 oder 5 Woll-Voegeln - *bird´s tree made of birch imitation, with 12 or 5 woolen birds*

SERIE	ART.-NO	PERIOD	PR.	INFO
71a	**5640**	1957-1959	5	12 Voegel - *12 birds*
870	**1940,90**	1959-1959	5	
870	**1940,00**	1960-1960	5	
870	**1920,0**	1960-1960	4	5 Voegel - *5 birds*

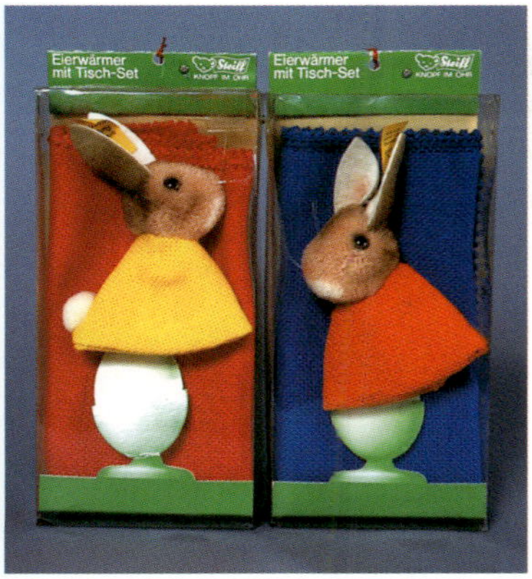

Eierwaermer-Set - *Egg Cozy Set*

Synthetik, Schaumstoff-kaschiert, blau/orange oder rot/gelb, Eierbecher & Filzwaermer mit Woll-Hasen-Kopf, abwaschbar - *synthetic, covered foam, blue/orange or red/yellow, egg cup & cozy with woolen rabbit head, surface washable*

SERIE	ART.-NO	PERIOD	PR.	INFO
	7157/10	1973-1974	2-3	blau/orange - *blue/orange*
	7157/11	1973-1974	2-3	rot/gelb - *red/yellow*

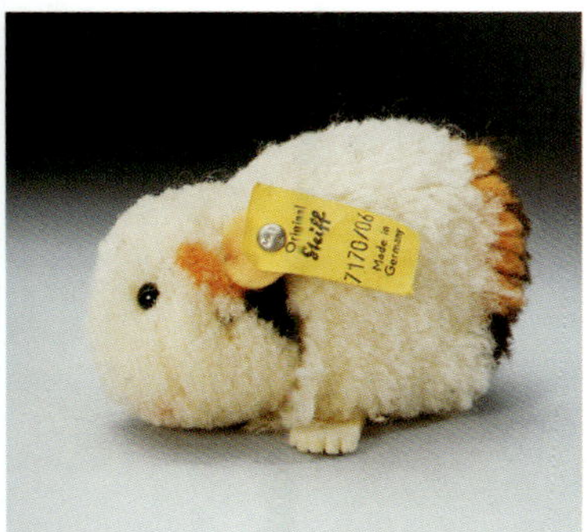

Woll-Meerschweinchen - *Woolen Guinea Pig*

Wolle, Filzfuesse & -ohren - *wool, felt feet & ears*

SERIE	ART.-NO	PERIOD	PR.	INFO
	7170/06	1973-1980	2	6 cm

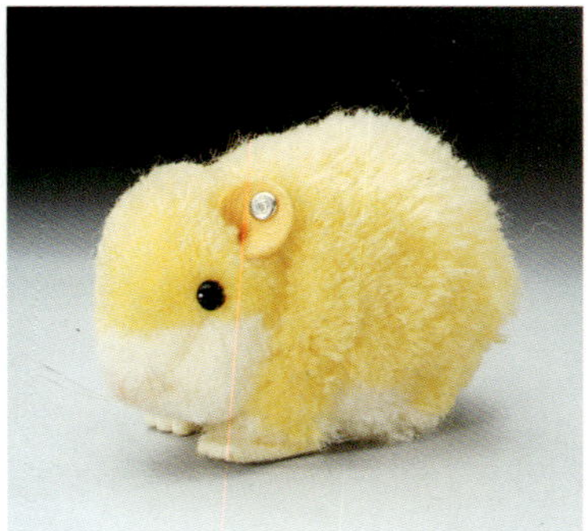

Woll-Hamster Goldi - *Woolen Hamster Goldi*

Wolle, Filzfuesse & -ohren - *wool, felt feet & ears*

SERIE	ART.-NO	PERIOD	PR.	INFO
	7173/06	1973-1979	2	6 cm

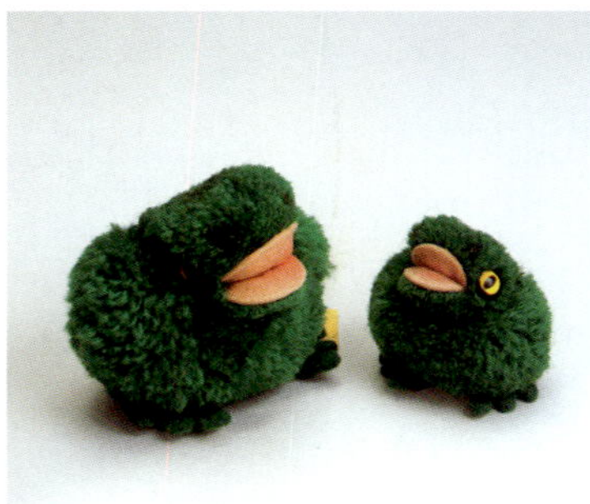

Woll-Frosch - *Woolen Frog*

Wolle, gruen, sitzend - *wool, green, sitting*

SERIE	ART.-NO	PERIOD	PR.	INFO
	7180/05	1972-1984	1	5 cm
	7180/07	1972-1983	1	7 cm

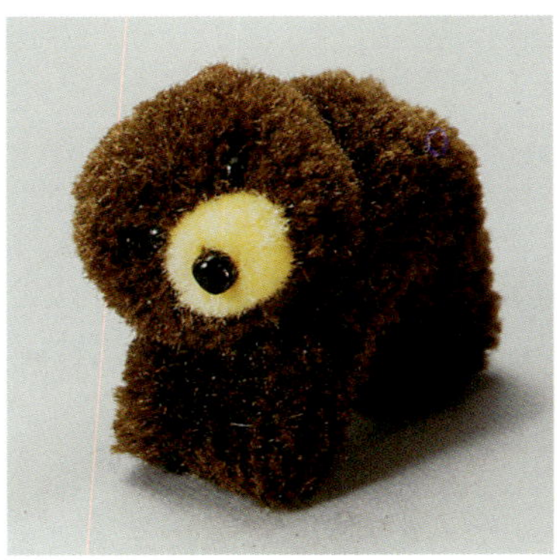

Pitty Baer - *Pitty Bear*

Wolle, braun - *wool, brown*

SERIE	ART.-NO	PERIOD	PR.	INFO
	7492/05	1977-1981	2	5 cm

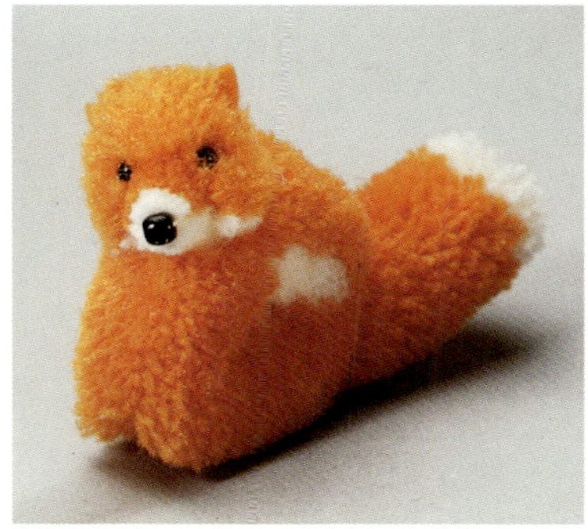

Pitty Fuchs - *Pitty Fox*

Wolle, orange - *wool, orange*

SERIE	ART.-NO	PERIOD	PR.	INFO
	7493/05	1977-1981	1-2	5 cm

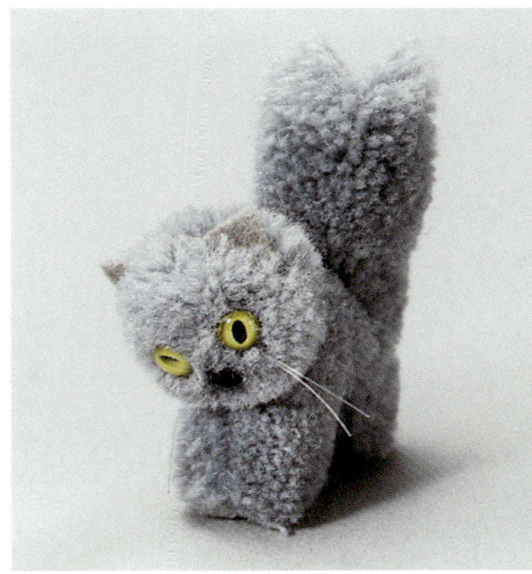

Pitty Katze - *Pitty Cat*

Wolle, grau - *wool, grey*

SERIE	ART.-NO	PERIOD	PR.	INFO
	7494/05	1977-1981	1-2	5 cm

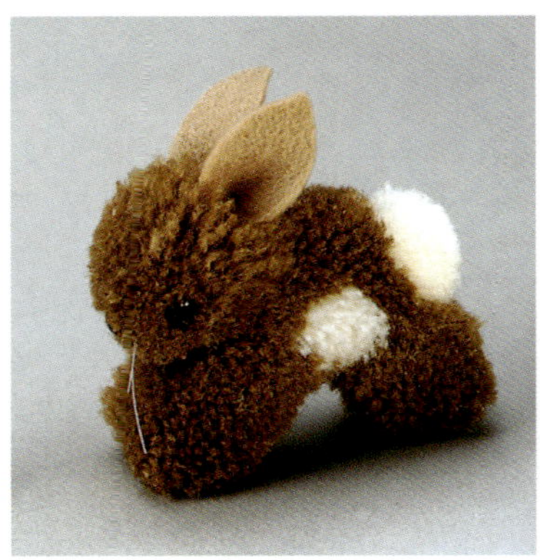

Pitty Hase - *Pitty Rabbit*

Wolle, braun - *wool, brown*

SERIE	ART.-NO	PERIOD	PR.	INFO
	7495/05	1977-1981	1-2	5 cm

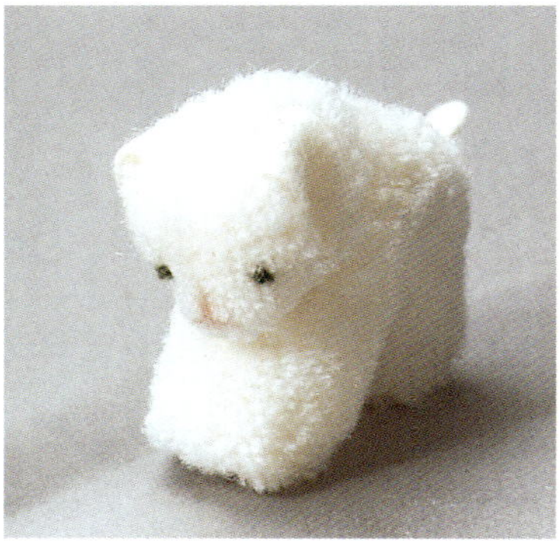

Pitty Lamm - *Pitty Lamb*

Wolle, weiss - *wool, white*

SERIE	ART.-NO	PERIOD	PR.	INFO
	7496/05	1977-1981	1-2	5 cm

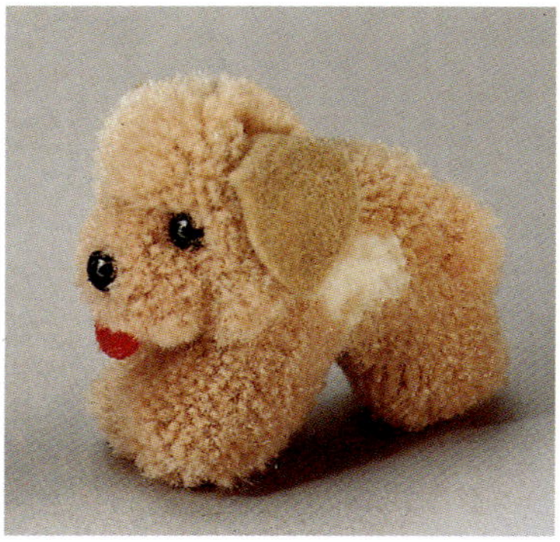

Pitty Hund - *Pitty Dog*

Wolle, beige - *wool, beige*

SERIE	ART.-NO	PERIOD	PR.	INFO
	7497/05	1977-1981	1-2	5 cm

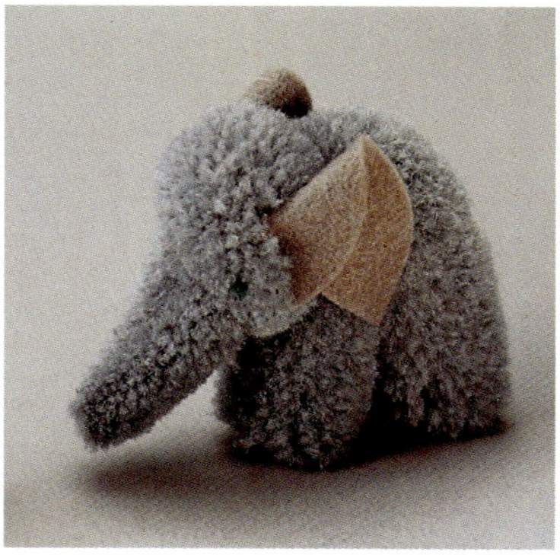

Pitty Elefant - *Pitty Elephant*

Wolle, grau, stehend - *wool, grey, standing*

SERIE	ART.-NO	PERIOD	PR.	INFO
	7500/05	1978-1981	1-2	5 cm

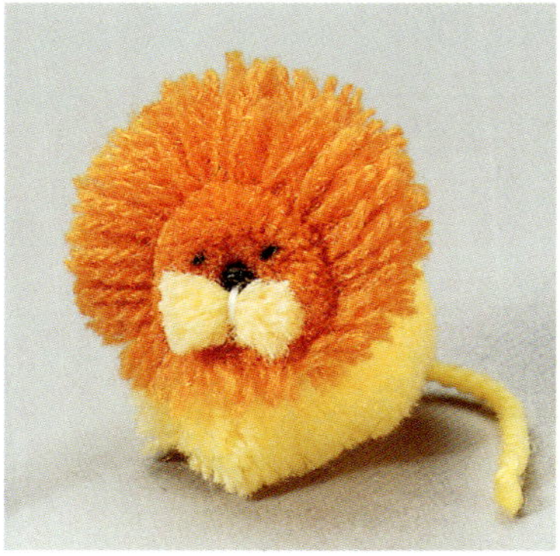

Pitty Loewe - *Pitty Lion*

Wolle, orange/gelb, sitzend - *wool, orange & yellow, sitting*

SERIE	ART.-NO	PERIOD	PR.	INFO
	7501/05	1978-1981	1-2	5 cm

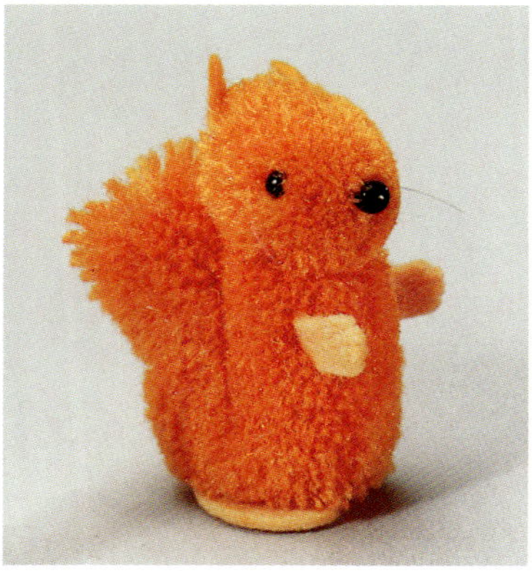

Pitty Eichhoernchen - *Pitty Squirrel*

Wolle, orange, aufwartend - *wool, orange, sitting up*

SERIE	ART.-NO	PERIOD	PR.	INFO
	7502/05	1978-1981	1-2	5 cm

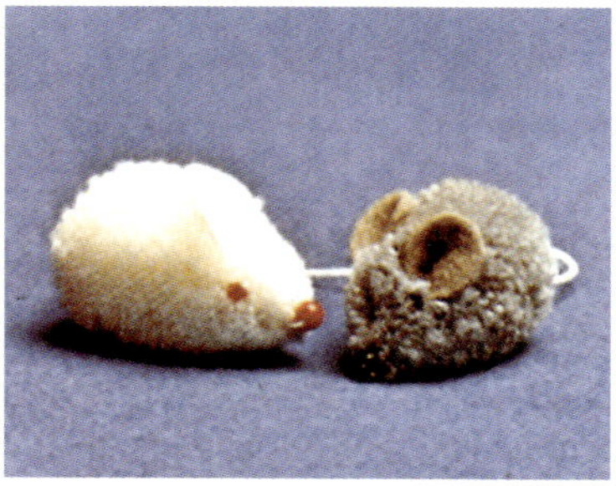

Pitty Maeuschen - *Pitty Mouse*

2 Stueck, Wolle, grau & weiss - *2 wool mice, grey & white*

SERIE	ART.-NO	PERIOD	PR.	INFO
	7503/05	1978-1981	1-2	5 cm

Handspielpuppen & -Tiere

Hand Puppets & Animals

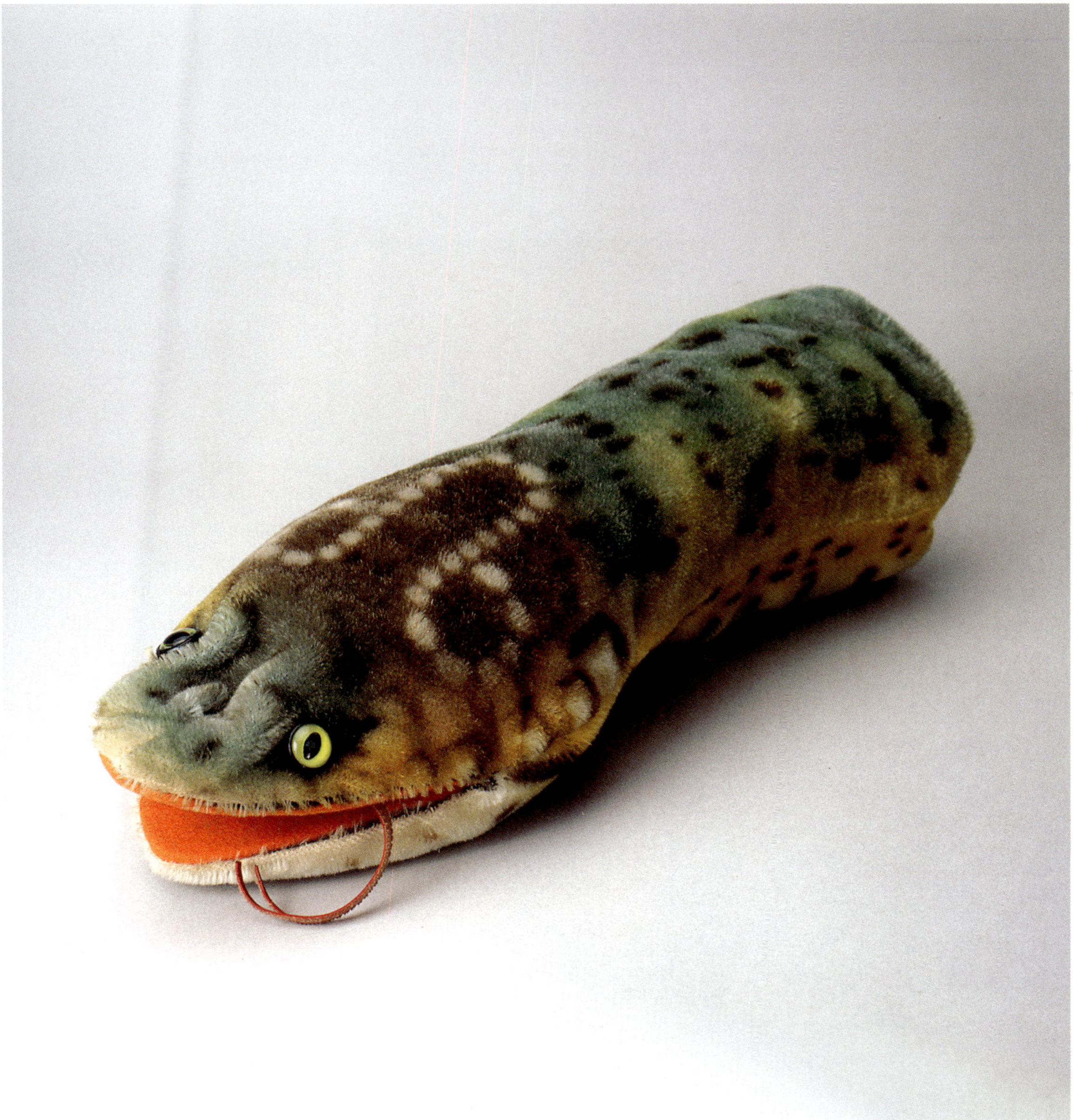

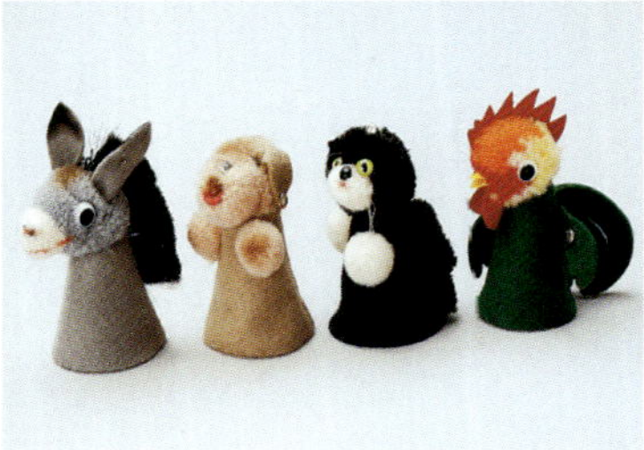

Fingerspieltiere "Bremer Stadtmusikanten" - *Finger Puppets "The Musicians of Bremen"*

Filz, Wolle, Sortiment bestehend aus Esel, Hund, Katze und Hahn, abwaschbar, in Klarsicht-Verpackung verschlossen mit drei Steiff-Knoepfen, davon 1x mit Fahne, die Artikel-Nr. gilt fuer das kpl. Sortiment - *felt & wool, the assortment consists of a donkey, a dog, a cat & a rooster, surface washable, packed in sealed clear plastic package with three Steiff buttons & one tag, art.-no. refers only to complete set*

SERIE	ART.-NO	PERIOD	PR.	INFO
	7080/06	1968-1974	3-4	Sortiment - *assortment*

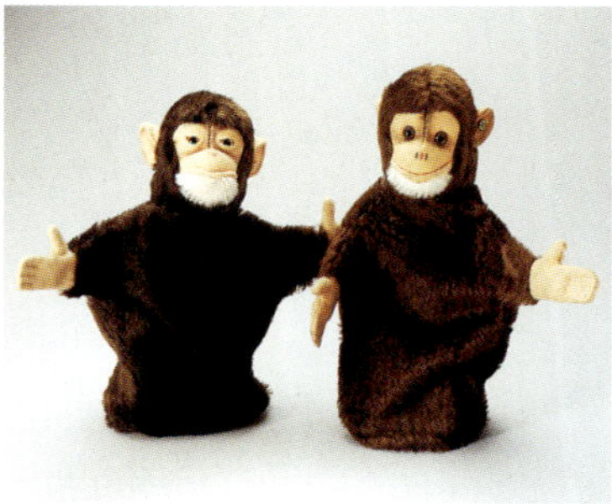

Hand-**Jocko** Schimpanse - *Hand-**Jocko** Chimpanzee*

Mohairpluesch, 1949 auch Seidenpluesch, 17 cm, braun - *mohair, in 1949 also silk plush, 17cm, brown*

SERIE	ART.-NO	PERIOD	PR.	INFO
79 9	**617**	1949-1949 Seidenpluesch - *silk plush*	4	
79 9	**317**	1949-1958 Mohairpluesch - *mohair*	4	
865 090	**0317,00**	1959-1964	3-4	
650	**0317,00**	1965-1967	3-4	
	6500/17	1968-1978	2-3	

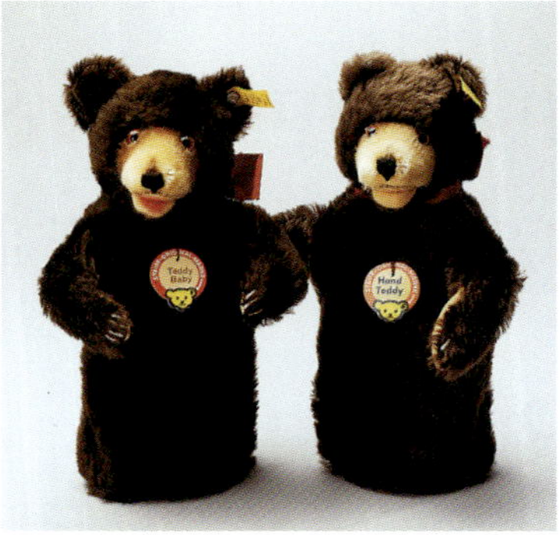

Hand-Teddy / Hand **Teddy Baby**

Mohairpluesch, 1949 auch Seidenpluesch, 17 cm, braun - *mohair, in 1949 also silk plush, 17cm, brown*

SERIE	ART.-NO	PERIOD	PR.	INFO
79 12	**617**	1949-1949 Seidenpluesch - *silk plush*	4	
79 12	**317**	1949-1958 Mohairpluesch - *mohair*	4	
865 120	**0317,00**	1959-1964	3-4	
656	**0317,00**	1965-1967	3-4	
	6560/17	1968-1978	3	

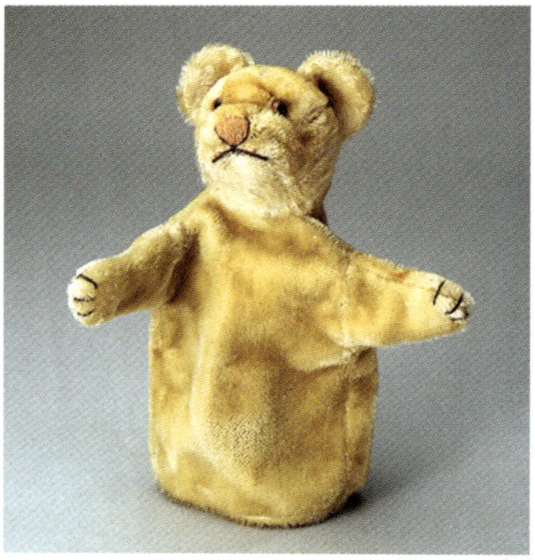

Hand-Jungloewe - *Young Lion Hand Puppet*

Wollpluesch, ab 1954 Mohair, 17 cm, gelbbraun getupft - *plush wool, from 1954 mohair, 17cm, tawny color-tipped*

SERIE	ART.-NO	PERIOD	PR.	INFO
79 48	**517**	1949-1954	4	Wollpluesch - *plush wool*
79 48	**317**	1954-1958 Mohairpluesch - *mohair*	4	
865 481	**0317,00**	1959-1961	3-4	

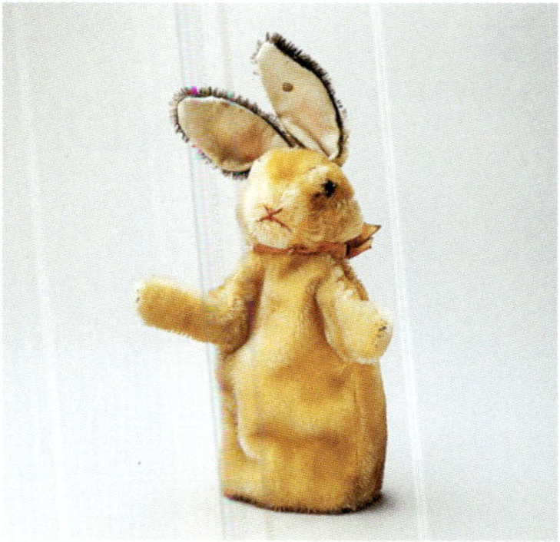

Hand-Hase - *Hand-Rabbit*

Mohairpluesch, hellbraun/weiss, bemalt - *mohair, light brown/white, painted*

SERIE	ART.-NO	PERIOD	PR.	INFO
79 36	**317**	1950-1958	4	17 cm
865 360	**0317,00**	1959-1964	3-4	
660	**0317,00**	1965-1967	3-4	
	6600/17	1968-1978	2-3	

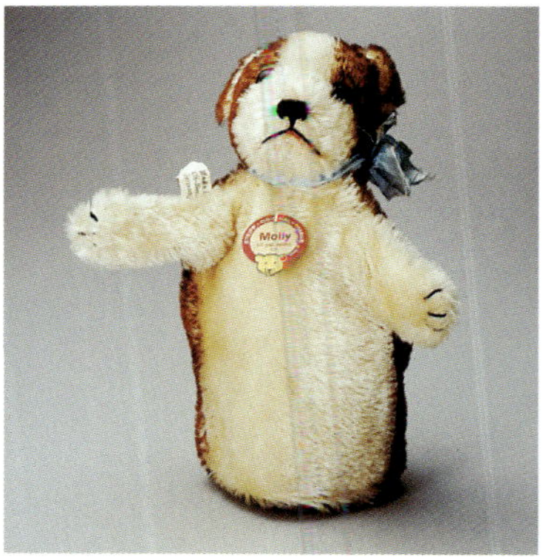

Hand-**Molly**

Mohairpluesch, braun gespitzt, weiss - *mohair, brown tipped, white*

SERIE	ART.-NO	PERIOD	PR.	INFO
79 68	**317**	1950-1958	4-5	17 cm
865 680	**0317,00**	1959-1962	4	

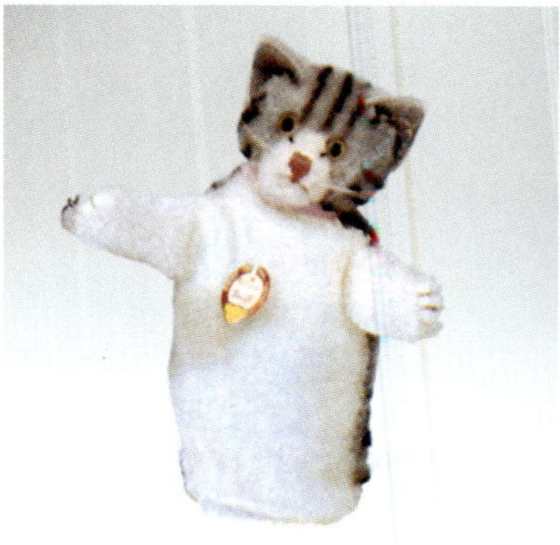

Hand-Katze - *Hand-Cat*

Mohairpluesch, grau gestromelt, weiss - *mohair, grey tabby, white*

Serie	Art.-No	Period	Pr.	Info
79 44	**317**	1950-1958	4	17 cm
865 440	**0317,00**	1959-1964	3-4	
666	**0317,00**	1965-1967	3-4	
	6660/17	1968-1978	2-3	

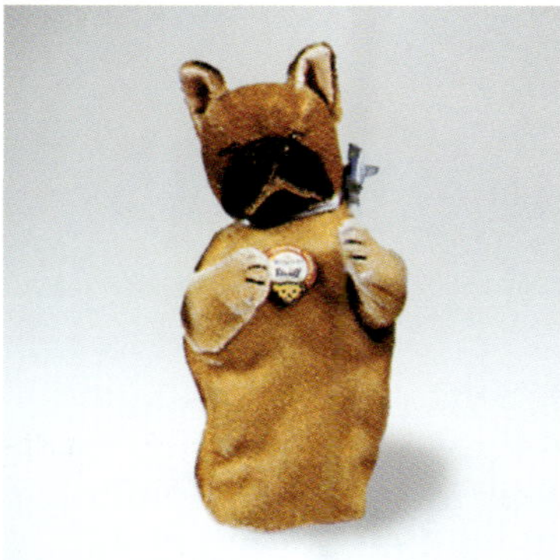

Hand-**Sarras** / Hand-**Boxer**

Mohair, braun/schwarz - *mohair, brown/ black*

Serie	Art.-No	Period	Pr.	Info
79 16	**317**	1951-1958	4	17 cm
865 160	**0317,00**	1959-1963	3-4	

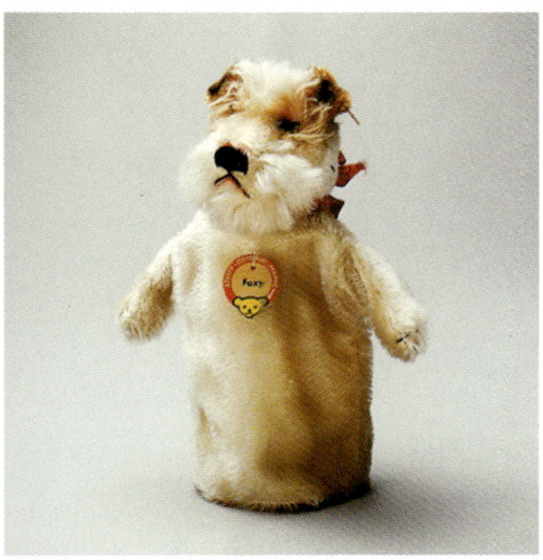

Hand-**Foxy** Foxterrier

Mohair, weiss, gefleckt - *mohair, white, spotted*

Serie	Art.-No	Period	Pr.	Info
79 26	**317**	1951-1958	4	17 cm
865 260	**0317,00**	1959-1963	3-4	
664	**0317,00**	1965-1967	3-4	
	6640/17	1968-1978	3	

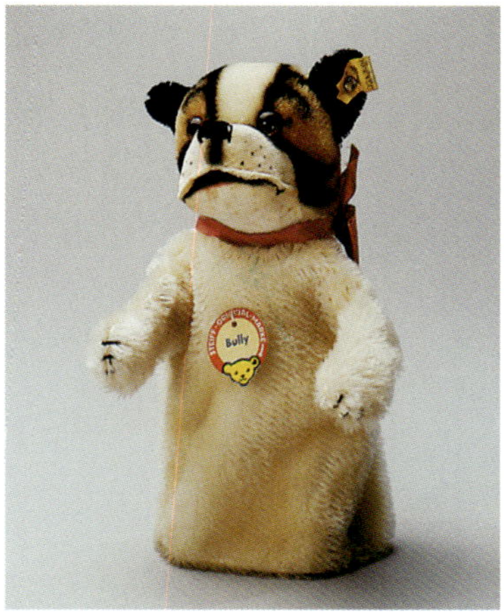

Hand-**Bully**

Mohair, weiss, gefleckt - *mohair, white, spotted*

Serie	Art.-No	Period	Pr.	Info
79 11	**317**	1952-1958	4-5	17 cm
865 110	**0317,00**	1959-1963	4	

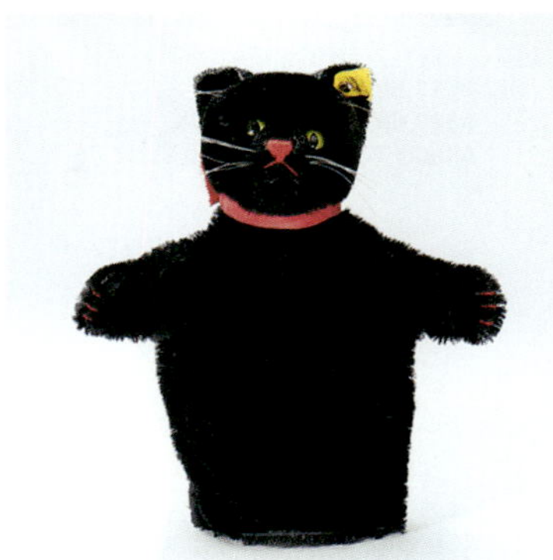

Hand-Kater - *Hand-Tom Cat*

Mohair, schwarz, rot bestickt - *mohair, black with red embroidery*

Serie	Art.-No	Period	Pr.	Info
79 44	**717**	1952-1958	4	17 cm
865 440	**0717,00**	1959-1964	3-4	
667	**0717,00**	1965-1967	3-4	
	6670/17	1968-1978	2-3	

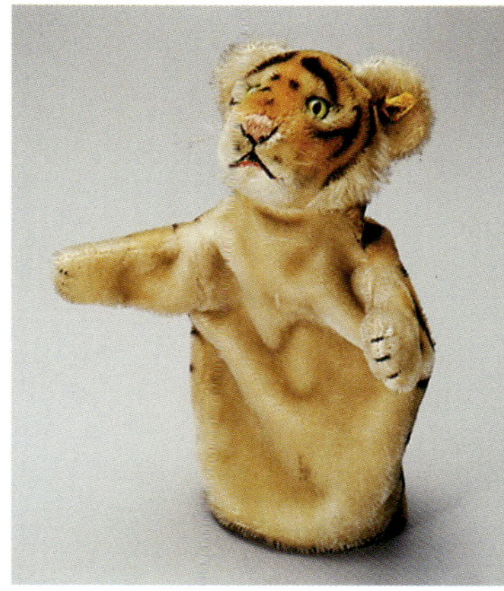

Hand-Tiger

Mohair, gelb/weiss, schwarz getigert - *mohair, tawny & white with black tiger stripes*

Serie	Art.-No	Period	Pr.	Info
79 70	**317**	1952-1958	4	17 cm
865 700	**0317,00**	1959-1963	3-4	
688	**0317,00**	1965-1967	3-4	
	6880/17	1968-1978	2-3	

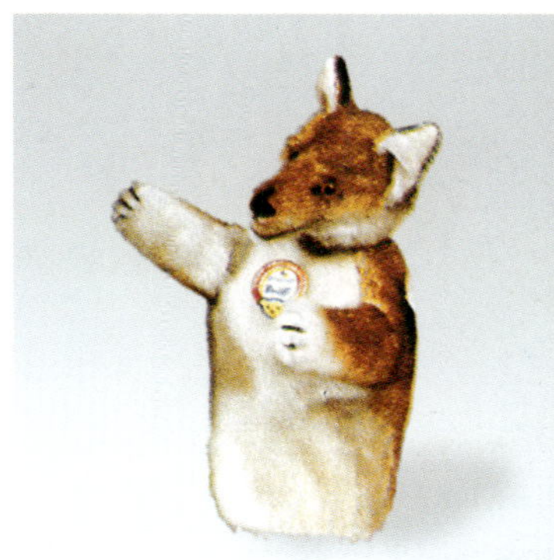

Hand-Fuchs - *Hand-Fox*

Mohair, rotbraun/weiss, offener Mund - *mohair, reddish-brown & white, open mouth*

Serie	Art.-No	Period	Pr.	Info
79 28	**317**	1952-1958	4	17 cm
865 280	**0317,00**	1959-1963	3-4	

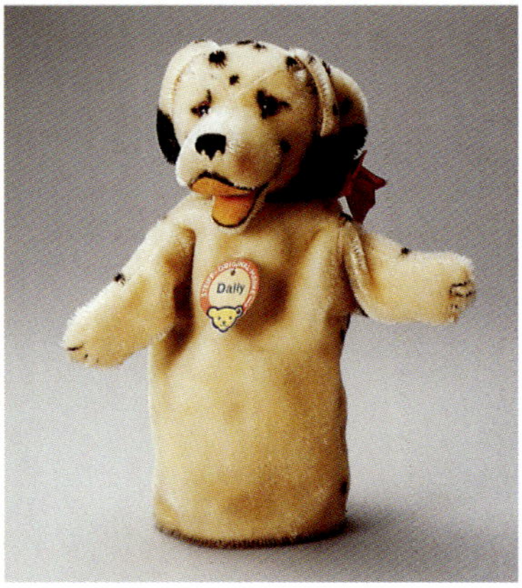

Hand-**Dally** Dalmatiner - *Hand-**Dally** Dalmation*

Mohair, weiss, schwarz getupft - *mohair, white with black spots*

SERIE	ART.-NO	PERIOD	PR.	INFO
79 15	**317**	1955-1956	5	17 cm

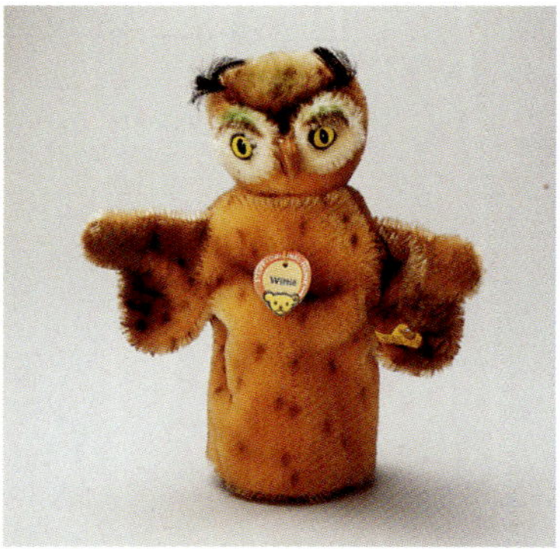

Hand-Uhu **Wittie** - *Hand-Owl **Wittie***

Mohairpluesch - *mohair*

SERIE	ART.-NO	PERIOD	PR.	INFO
79 67b	**317**	1955-1958	4	17 cm
865 674	**0317,00**	1959-1964	3-4	
671	**0317,00**	1965-1967	3-4	
	6710/17	1968-1978	2-3	

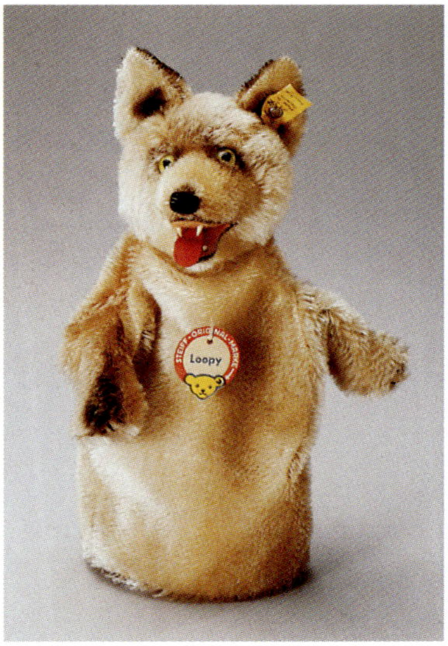

Hand-Wolf **Loopy**

Mohair, offenes Maul mit Zaehnen - *mohair, open mouth with teeth*

SERIE	ART.-NO	PERIOD	PR.	INFO
79 61a	**317**	1956-1958	4	17 cm
865 612	**0317,00**	1959-1964	3-4	
686	**0317,00**	1965-1967	3-4	
	6860/17	1968-1978	3	

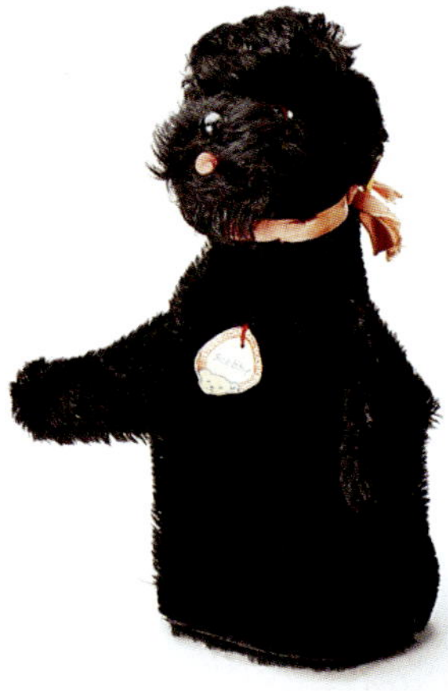

Hand-Pudel **Snobby** - *Hand-Poodle **Snobby***

Mohairpluesch, schwarz - *mohair, black*

SERIE	ART.-NO	PERIOD	PR.	INFO
79 58	**317**	1955-1958	4	17 cm
865 580	**0317,00**	1959-1964	3-4	
684	**0317,00**	1965-1966	3-4	

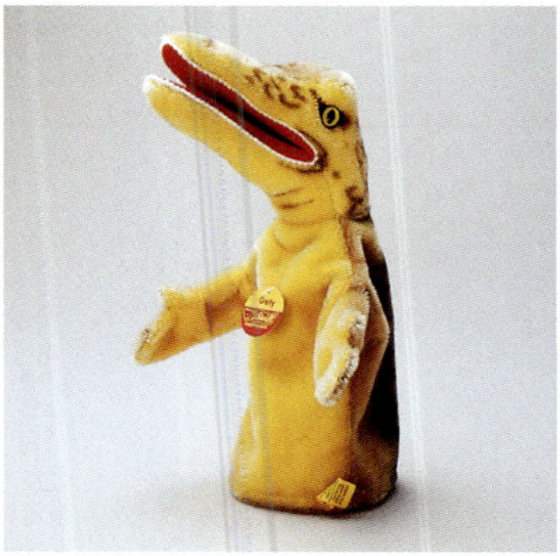

Hand-Krokodil **Gaty** - *Hand-Crocodile **Gaty***

Mohair, offenes Maul, Filzzaehne rundum - *mohair, open mouth with felt teeth*

SERIE	ART.-NO	PERIOD	PR.	INFO
79 41	**317**	1956-1958	4	17 cm
865 410	**0317,00**	1959-1964	3-4	
697	**0317,00**	1965-1967	3-4	
	6970/17	1968-1978	2-3	

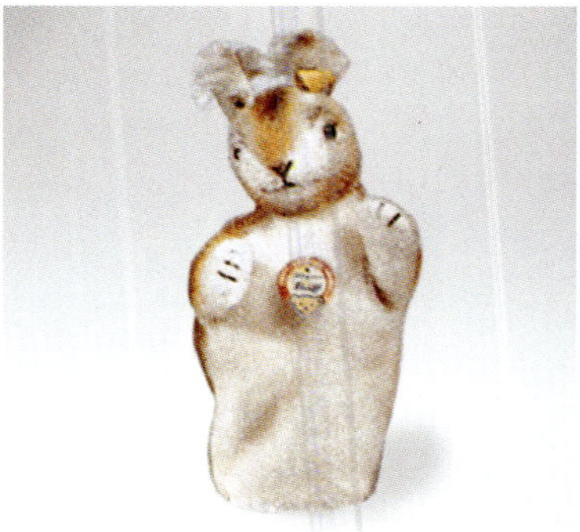

Hand-**Possy** Eichhorn - *Hand-**Possy** Squirrel*

Mohairpluesch, 17 cm, braun oder grau - *mohair, 17 cm, brown or grey*

SERIE	ART.-NO	PERIOD	PR.	INFO
79 19	**317**	1957-1958	4	braun - *brown*
865 190	**0317,01**	1959-1961	3-4	
865 190	**0317,05**	1959-1961	3-4	grau - *grey*

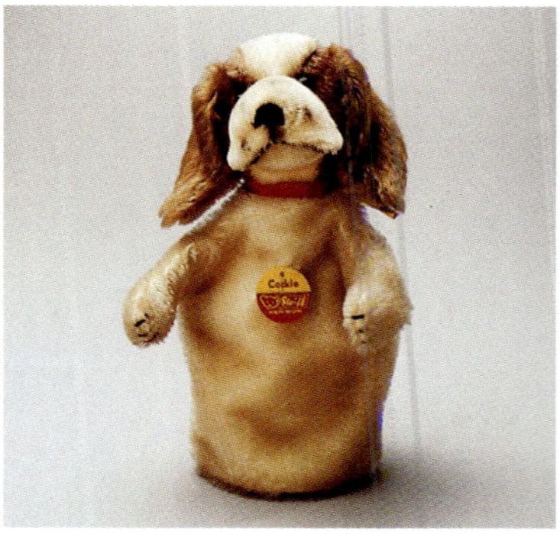

Hand-**Cockie**

Mohairpluesch, braun/weiss - *mohair, brown & white*

SERIE	ART.-NO	PERIOD	PR.	INFO
79 29	**317**	1957-1958	4	17 cm
865 290	**0317,00**	1959-1964	3-4	
680	**0317,00**	1965-1967	3-4	
	6800/17	1968-1978	2-3	

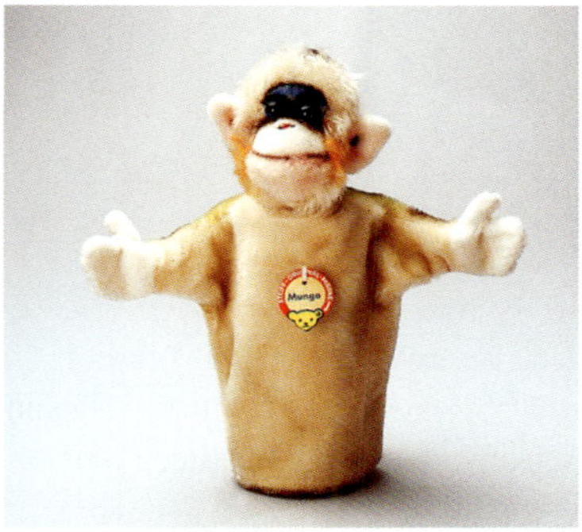

Hand-**Mungo** Buntaffe - *Hand-**Mungo** Monkey*

Mohairpluesch, mehrfarbig - *mohair, multi-colored*

SERIE	ART.-NO	PERIOD	PR.	INFO
79 9b	**318**	1958-1958	4	18 cm
865 102	**0318,00**	1959-1964	3-4	
652	**0318,00**	1965-1967	3-4	
	6520/18	1968-1978	2-3	

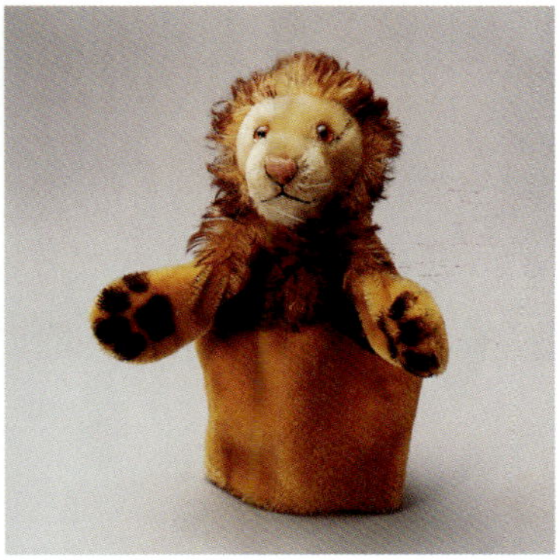

Hand-**Leo** Loewe - *Hand-**Leo** Lion*

Mohairpluesch, mit Maehne - *mohair, with mane*

SERIE	ART.-NO	PERIOD	PR.	INFO
79 48	**318**	1958-1958	4	18 cm
865 480	**0318,00**	1959-1964	3-4	
682	**0318,00**	1965-1967	3-4	
	6820/18	1968-1978	2-3	

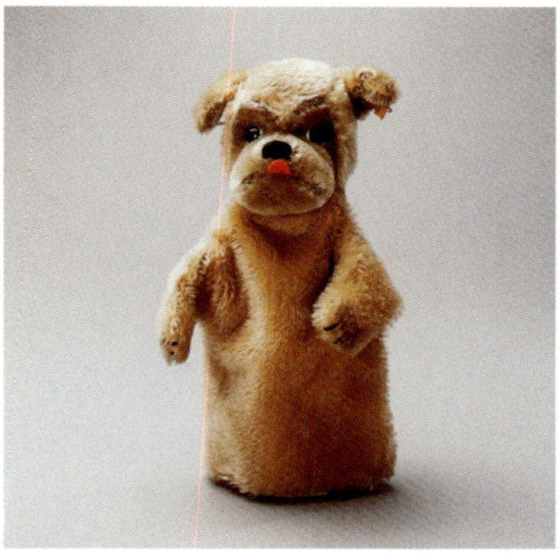

Hand-**Mopsy** Hund - *Hand-**Mopsy** Dog*

Mohairpluesch, braun - *mohair, brown*

SERIE	ART.-NO	PERIOD	PR.	INFO
865 113	**0317,00**	1960-1963	3	17 cm
662	**0317,00**	1965-1967	3	
	6620/17	1968-1978	2-3	

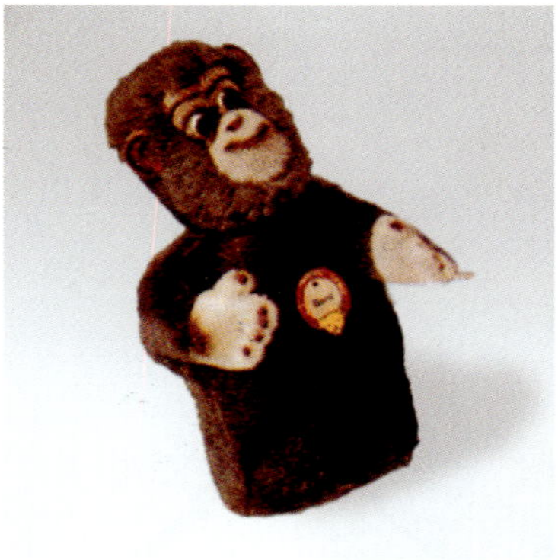

Hand-**Gora** Gorilla

Dralon, graubraun - *dralon, greyish-brown*

SERIE	ART.-NO	PERIOD	PR.	INFO
865 103	**0617,05**	1961-1964	3	17 cm

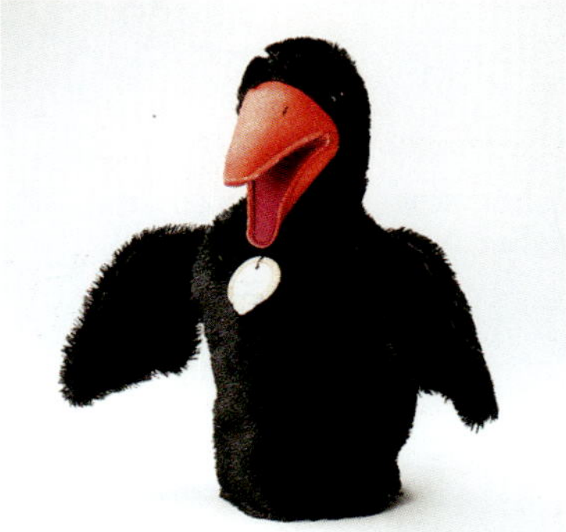

Hand-**Hucky** Rabe - *Hand-**Hucky** Raven*

Mohair, schwarz, Schnabel bewegbar durch Finger in Unterlippe - *mohair, black, beak is movable by finger in lower lip*

SERIE	ART.-NO	PERIOD	PR.	INFO
865 620	**0317,00**	1962-1964	3-4	17 cm
669	**0317,00**	1965-1967	3-4	
	6690/17	1968-1969	3	

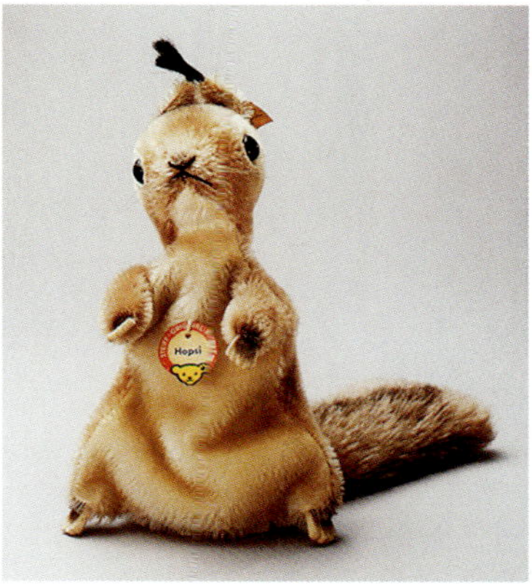

Hand-**Hopsi** Eichhorn - *Hand-**Hopsi** Squirrel*

Mohair, mit Schwanz, aus der Hopsi-Fibel, 1965-1967 auch mit Zusatz "im Steiff-Kinderbuch" - *mohair, with tail, taken from the Hopsi stories, 1965-1967 also with supplement ' im Steiff Kinderbuch"*

SERIE	ART.-NO	PERIOD	PR.	INFO
865 192	**0318,00**	1962-1964	3	18 cm
690	**0318,00**	1965-1967	3	
	6900/18	1968-1978	2-3	

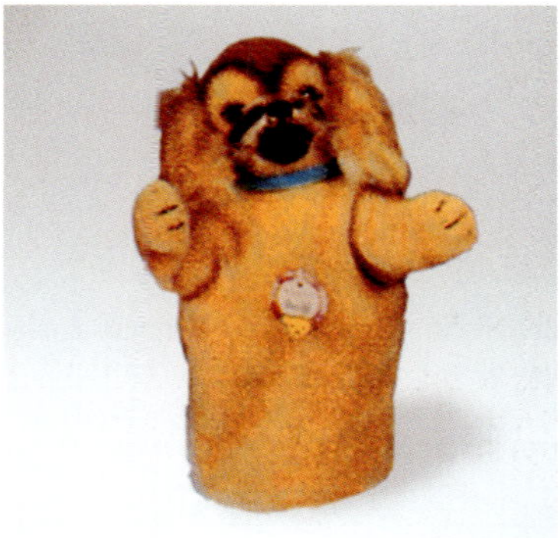

Hand-**Peky** Pekinese

Mohairpluesch, braun - *mohair, brown*

SERIE	ART.-NO	PERIOD	PR.	INFO
865 172	**0318,00**	1963-1964	3-4	18 cm

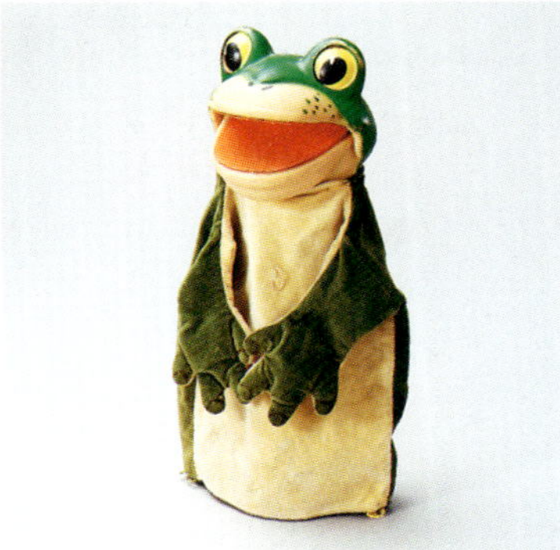

Hand-**Froggy**

Plastikkopf, gruen/gelber Samtrock, Maul beweglich - *plastic head, green & yellow, velvet body, mouth is movable*

SERIE	ART.-NO	PERIOD	PR.	INFO
865 310	**0417,00**	1963-1964	3-4	17 cm
658	**0417,00**	1965-1967	3	
	6580/17	1968-1978	3	

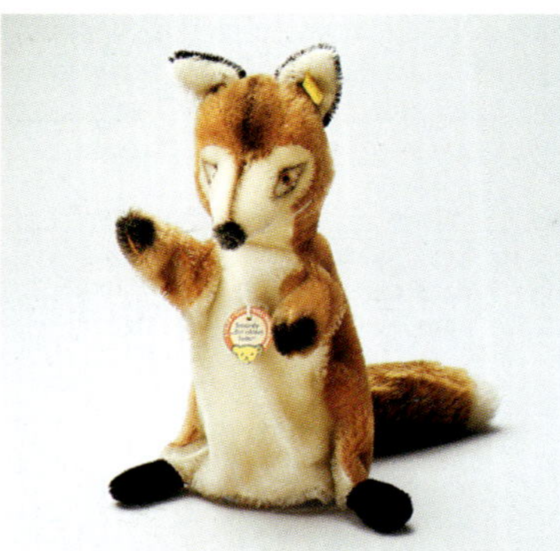

Hand-Fuchs **Smardy** - *Hand-Fox **Smardy***

Mohair, mit Schwanz, der schlaue Fuchs aus dem gleichnamigen Rechenbuch - *mohair, with tail, the crafty fox in the arithmetic book of the same name*

SERIE	ART.-NO	PERIOD	PR.	INFO
865 281	**0318,00**	1964-1964	3-4	18 cm
699	**0318,00**	1965-1967	3-4	
	6990/18	1968-1978	2-3	

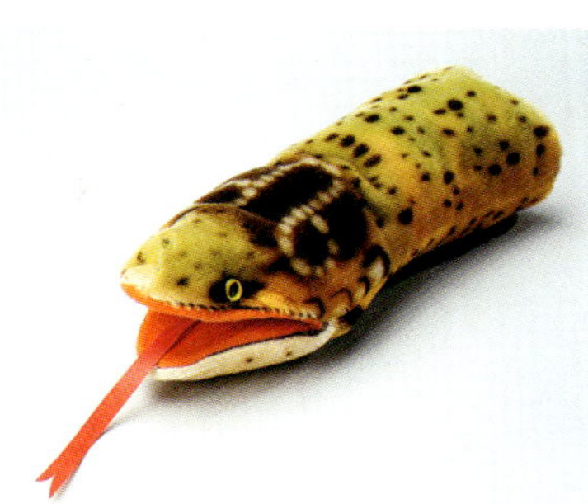

Hand-**Snaky** Schlange - *Hand-**Snaky** Snake*

Mohair, mit Klappmaul - *mohair, with snapping mouth*

SERIE	ART.-NO	PERIOD	PR.	INFO
678	**0320,00**	1965-1966	4-5	20 cm

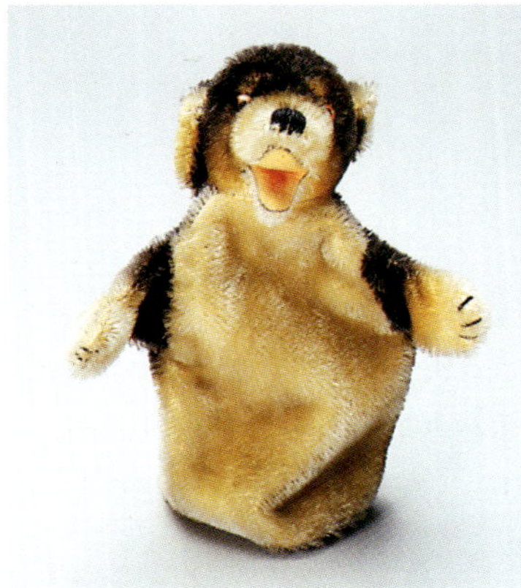

Hand-**Lumpi** Dackel - *Hand-**Lumpi** Dachshund*

Mohairpluesch, braun/schwarz - *mohair, brown & black*

SERIE	ART.-NO	PERIOD	PR.	INFO
696	**0317,06**	1965-1966	4	17 cm

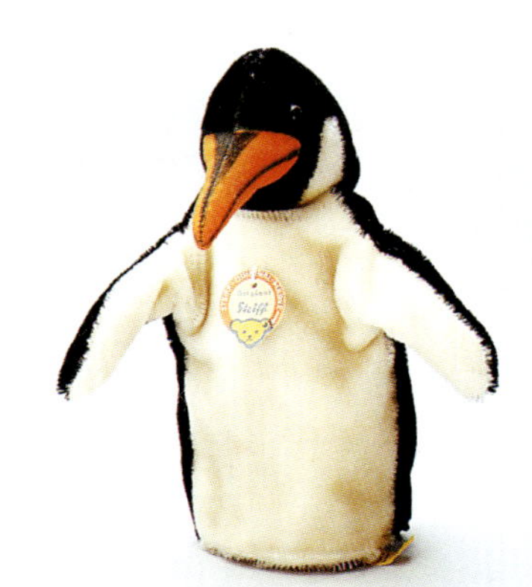

Hand-Pinguin - *Hand-Penguin*

Mohair, schwarz/weiss, roter Schnabel - *mohair, black & white, red beak*

SERIE	ART.-NO	PERIOD	PR.	INFO
668	**0317,00**	1967-1967	3-4	17 cm
	6680/17	1968-1976	2-3	

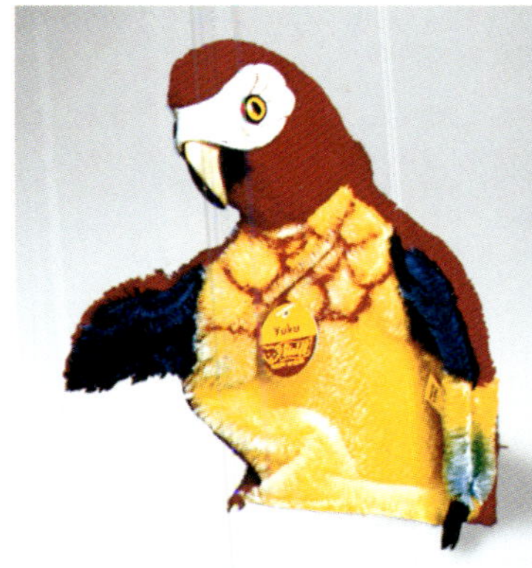

Hand-Papagei ab 1974 Hand-**Yuku** - *Hand-Parrot from 1974 Hand-**Yuku***

Mohair, Schnabel aus Plastik - *mohair, plastic beak*

SERIE	ART.-NO	PERIOD	PR.	INFO
668	**0317,07**	1967-1967	3-4	17 cm
	6685/17	1968-1977	2-3	

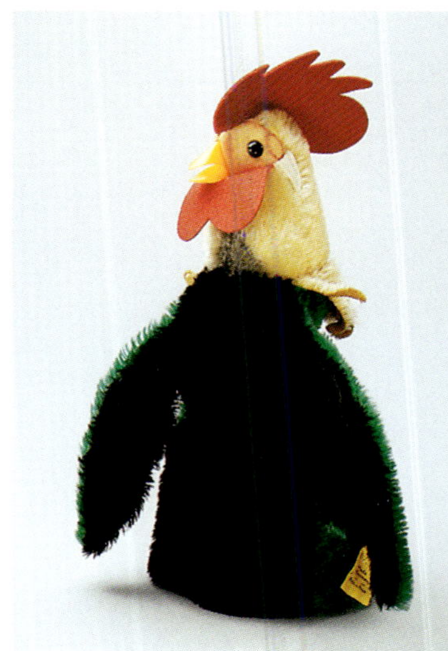

Hand-Hahn - *Hand-Rooster*

Mohair, Filzkamm, Plastikschnabel - *mohair, felt comb, plastic beak*

SERIE	ART.-NO	PERIOD	PR.	INFO
	6721/18	1968-1974	3-4	18 cm

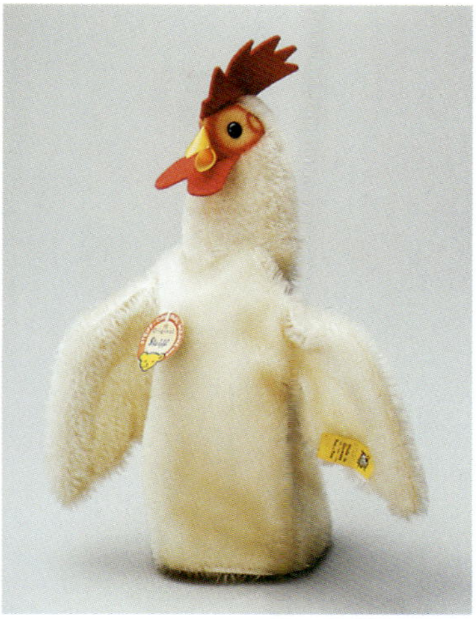

Hand-Henne - *Hand-Hen*

Mohair, Filzkamm, Plastikschnabel - *mohair, felt comb, plastic beak*

SERIE	ART.-NO	PERIOD	PR.	INFO
	6722/17	1968-1974	3-4	17 cm

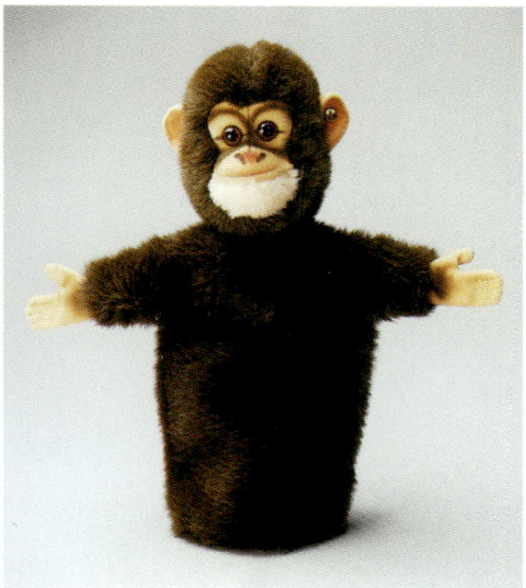

Hand-**Jocko** Schimpanse - *Hand-**Jocko** Chimpanzee*

Webpelz, Kopf formgeschaeumt - *woven fur, head is stuffed with pre-formed foam*

SERIE	ART.-NO	PERIOD	PR.	INFO
253027	**6991/30**	1978-1987	2	30 cm

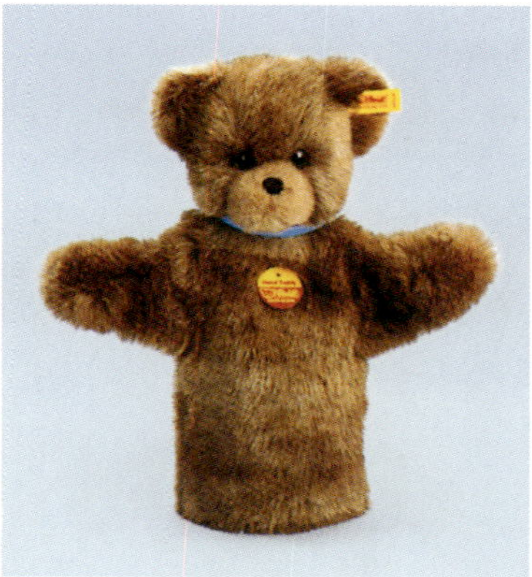

Hand-Teddy

Webpelz, Kopf formgeschaeumt - *woven fur, head is stuffed with pre-formed foam*

SERIE	ART.-NO	PERIOD	PR.	INFO
253126	**6992/30**	1978-1987	2	30 cm

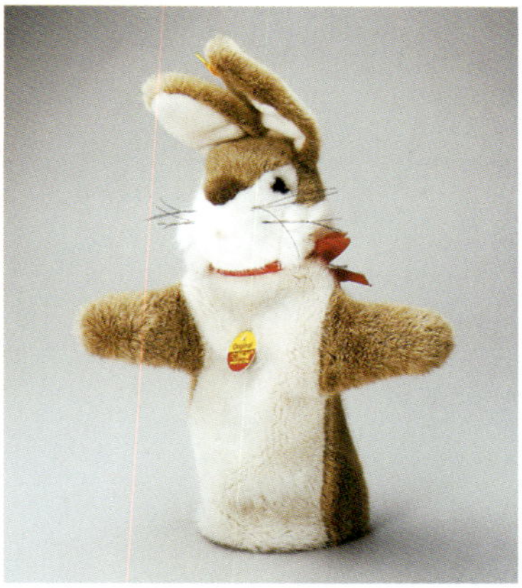

Hand-**Lausy** Hase - *Hand-**Lausy** Rabbit*

Webpelz, Kopf formgeschaeumt - *woven fur, head is stuffed with pre-formed foam*

SERIE	ART.-NO	PERIOD	PR.	INFO
253225	**6993/30**	1978-1987	2	30 cm

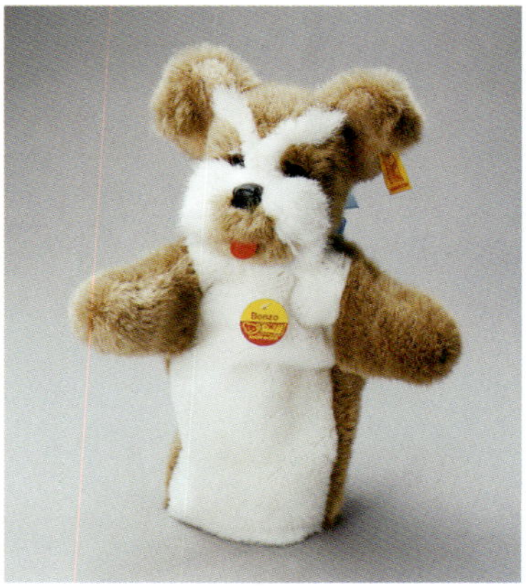

Hand-**Bonzo** Hund - *Hand-**Bonzo** Dog*

Webpelz, Kopf formgeschaeumt - *woven fur, head is stuffed with pre-formed foam*

SERIE	ART.-NO	PERIOD	PR.	INFO
253324	**6994/30**	1978-1987	2	30 cm

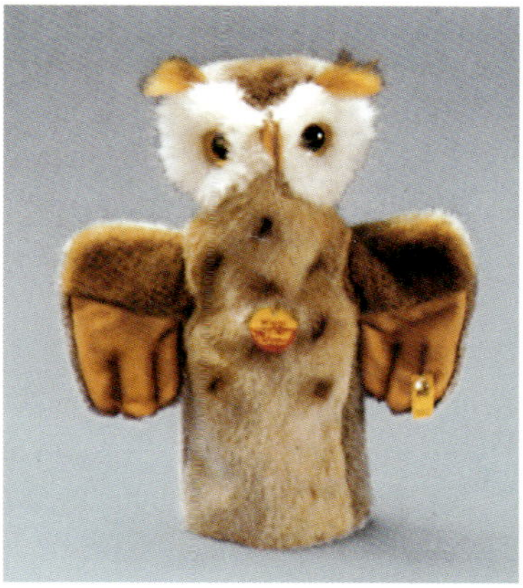

Hand-**Wiggi** Uhu - *Hand-**Wiggi** Owl*

Webpelz, Kopf formgeschaeumt - *woven fur, head is stuffed with pre-formed foam*

SERIE	ART.-NO	PERIOD	PR.	INFO
	6995/30	1978-1981	2	30 cm

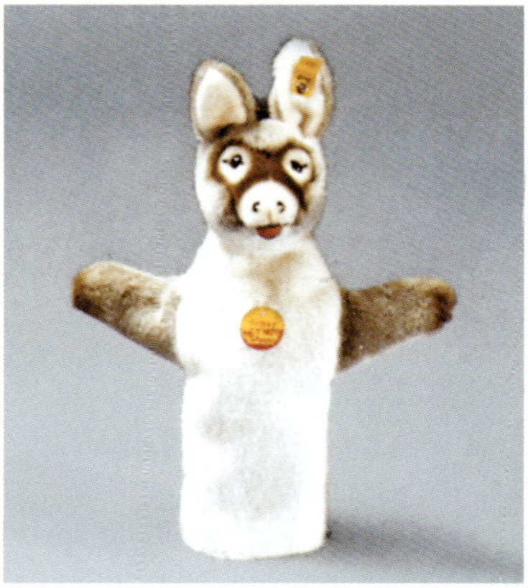

Hand-**Grissy** Esel - *Hand-**Grissy** Donkey*

Webpelz, Kopf formgeschaeumt - *woven fur, head is stuffed with pre-formed foam*

SERIE	ART.-NO	PERIOD	PR.	INFO
	6996/30	1978-1980	2	30 cm

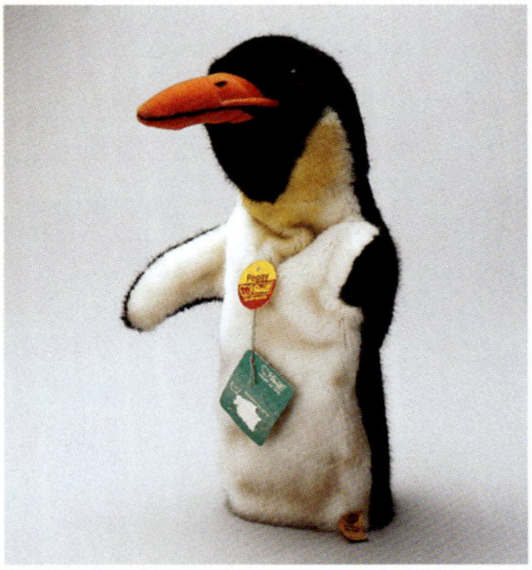

Hand-**Peggy** Pinguin - *Hand-**Peggy** Penguin*

Webpelz, Kopf formgeschaeumt - *woven fur, head is stuffed with pre-formed foam*

SERIE	ART.-NO	PERIOD	PR.	INFO
	6997/30	1978-1980	2	30 cm

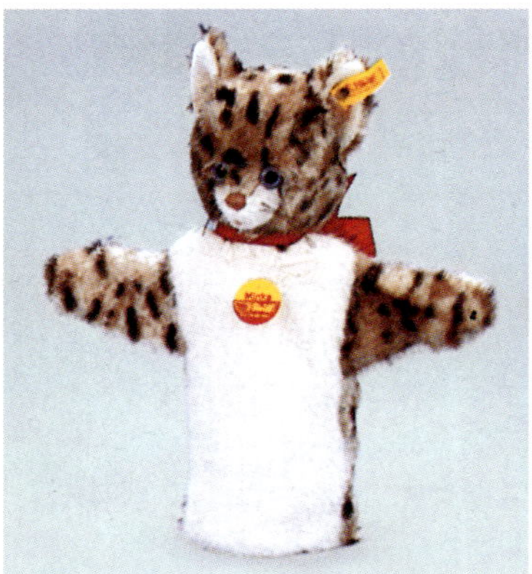

Hand-**Minka** Katze - *Hand-**Minka** Cat*

Webpelz, Kopf formgeschaeumt - *woven fur, head is stuffed with pre-formed foam*

SERIE	ART.-NO	PERIOD	PR.	INFO
	6998/30	1978-1984	2	30 cm

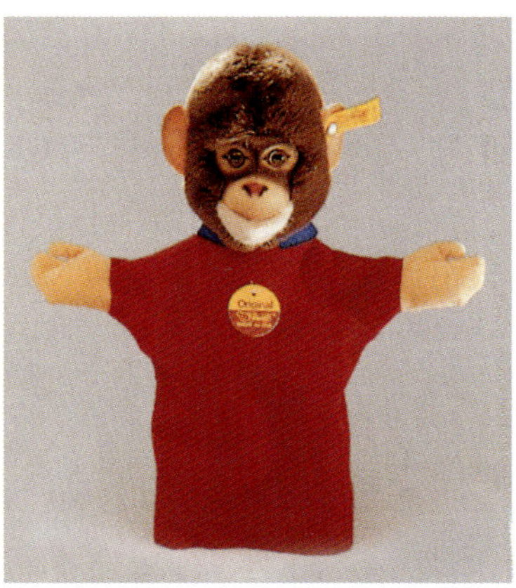

Hand-Schimpanse - *Hand-Chimpanzee*

Webpelz/Trevira-Samt - *woven fur/trevira velvet*

SERIE	ART.-NO	PERIOD	PR.	INFO
251306	**6460/27**	1979-1989	2	27 cm

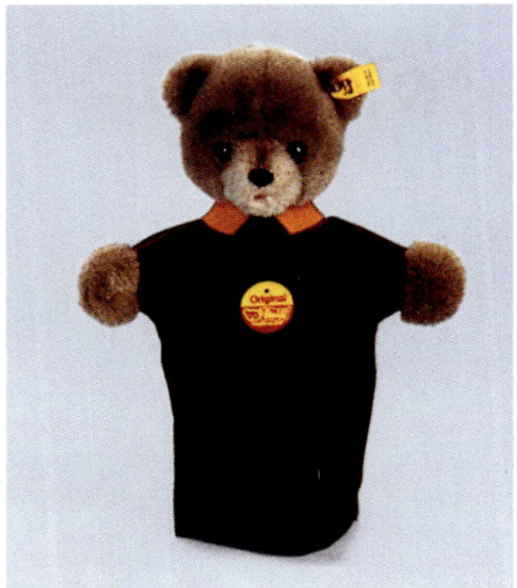

Hand-Baer - *Hand-Bear*

Webpelz/Trevira-Samt - *woven fur/trevira velvet*

SERIE	ART.-NO	PERIOD	PR.	INFO
	6461/27	1979-1985	2	27 cm

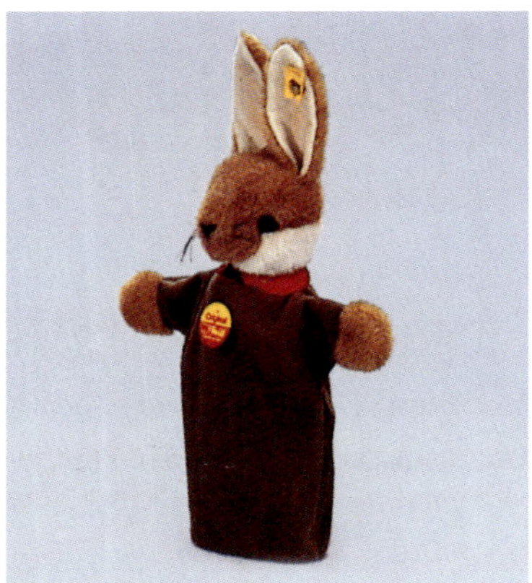

Hand-Hase - *Hand-Rabbit*

Webpelz/Trevira-Samt - *woven fur/trevira velvet*

SERIE	ART.-NO	PERIOD	PR.	INFO
	6463/27	1979-1985	2	27 cm

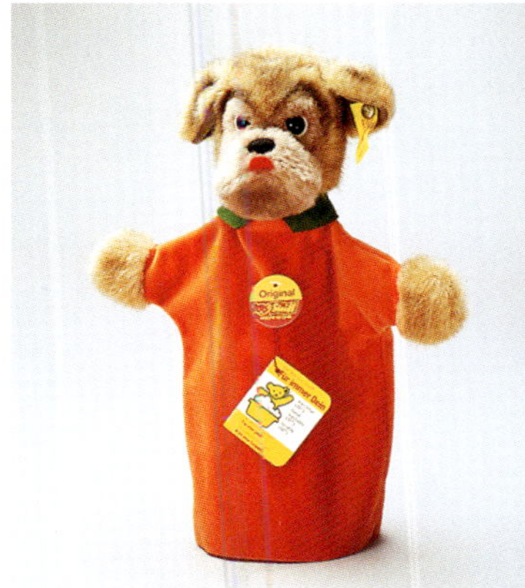

Hand-Hund - *Hand-Dog*

Webpelz/Trevira-Samt - *woven fur/trevira velvet*

SERIE	ART.-NO	PERIOD	PR.	INFO
	6464/27	1979-1985	2	27 cm

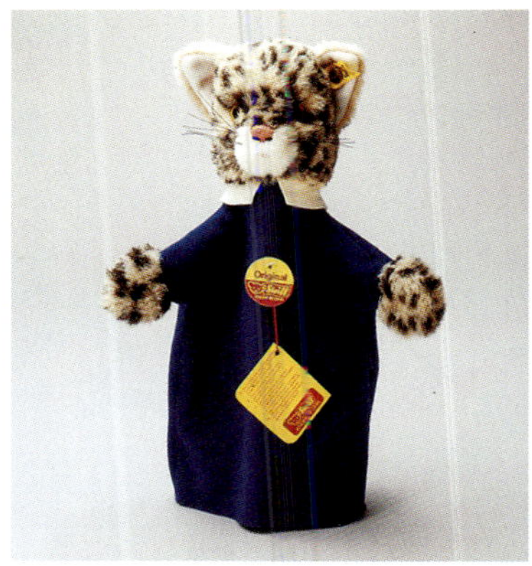

Hand-Katze - *Hand-Cat*

Webpelz/Trevira-Samt - *woven fur/trevira velvet*

SERIE	ART.-NO	PERIOD	PR.	INFO
	6466/27	1979-1983	2	27 cm

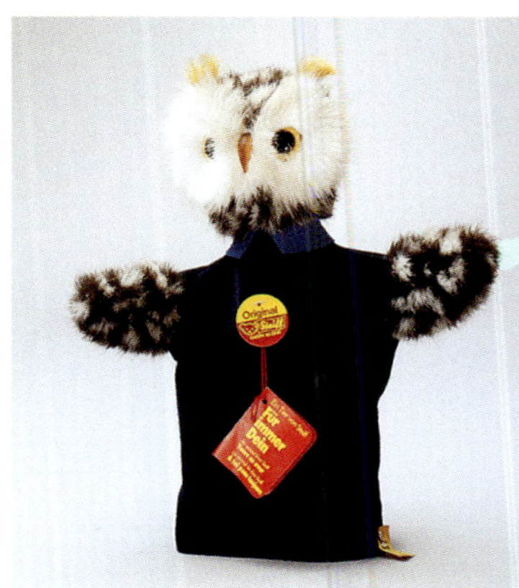

Hand-Uhu - *Hand-Owl*

Wirkpelz (1982 Webpelz)/Trevirasamt - *knitted fur (1982 woven fur)/trevira velvet*

SERIE	ART.-NO	PERIOD	PR.	INFO
	6470/27	1979-1982	2	27 cm

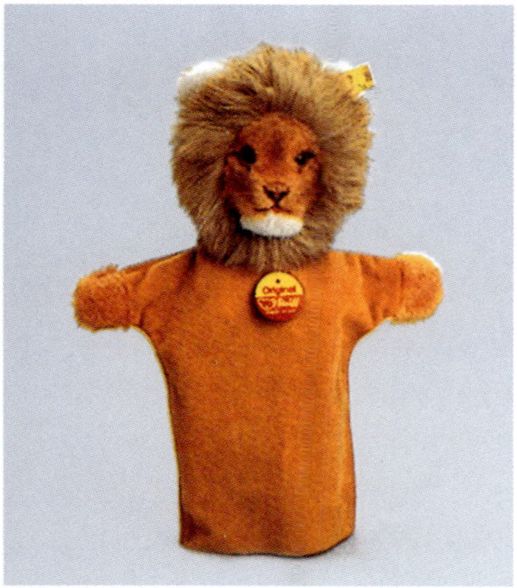

Hand-Loewe - *Hand-Lion*

Webpelz/Trevira-Samt - *woven fur/trevira velvet*

SERIE	ART.-NO	PERIOD	PR.	INFO
	6471/27	1979-1985	2	27 cm

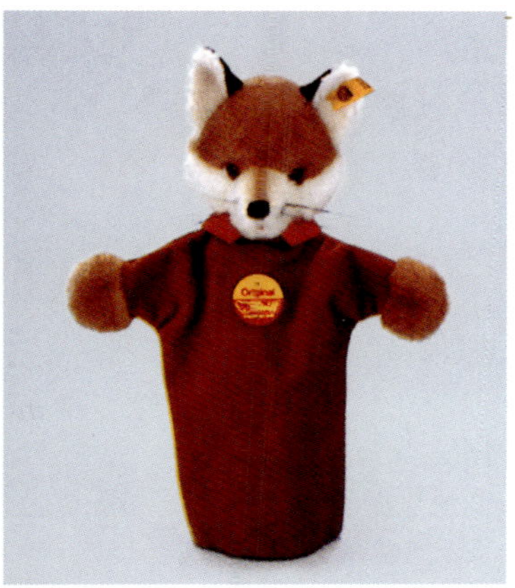

Hand-Fuchs - *Hand-Fox*

Webpelz/Trevira-Samt - *woven fur/trevira velvet*

SERIE	ART.-NO	PERIOD	PR.	INFO
	6472/27	1979-1985	2	27 cm

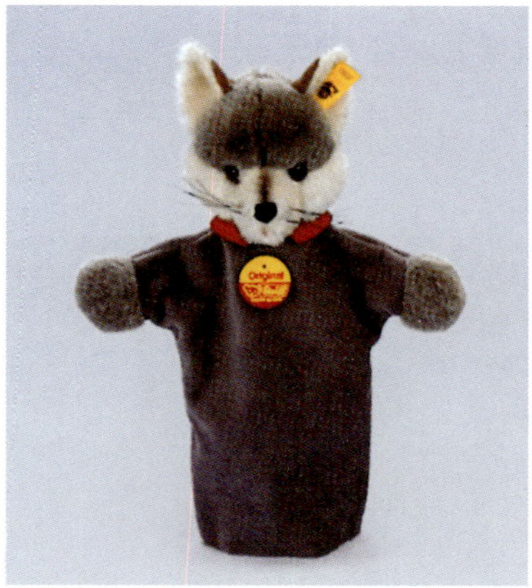

Hand-Wolf

Webpelz/Trevira-Samt - *woven fur/trevira velvet*

SERIE	ART.-NO	PERIOD	PR.	INFO
	6474/27	1979-1983	2	27 cm

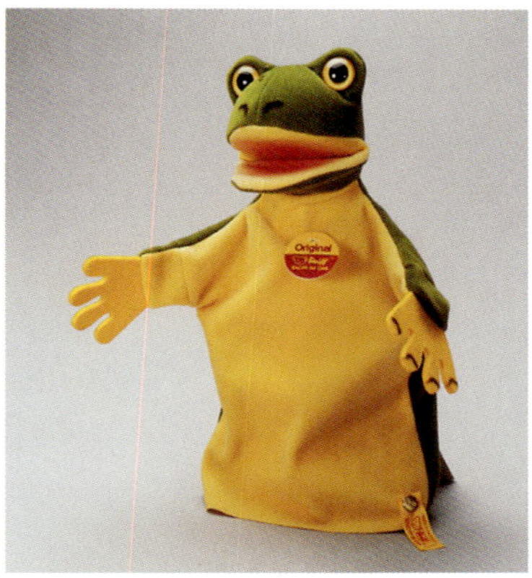

Hand-Frosch - *Hand-Frog*

Trevirasamt, bewegliches Maul - *trevira velvet, movable mouth*

SERIE	ART.-NO	PERIOD	PR.	INFO
251306	**6462/27**	1979-1990	2	27 cm
	251306	1991-1996	1-2	

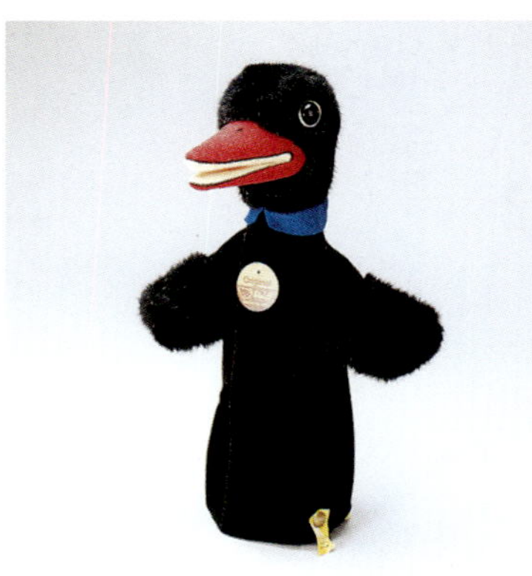

Hand-Rabe - *Hand-Raven*

Webpelz/Trevira-Samt, beweglicher Schnabel - *woven fur/trevira velvet, movable beak*

SERIE	ART.-NO	PERIOD	PR.	INFO
251559	**6468/27**	1979-1990	2	27 cm
	251559	1991-1997	1-2	

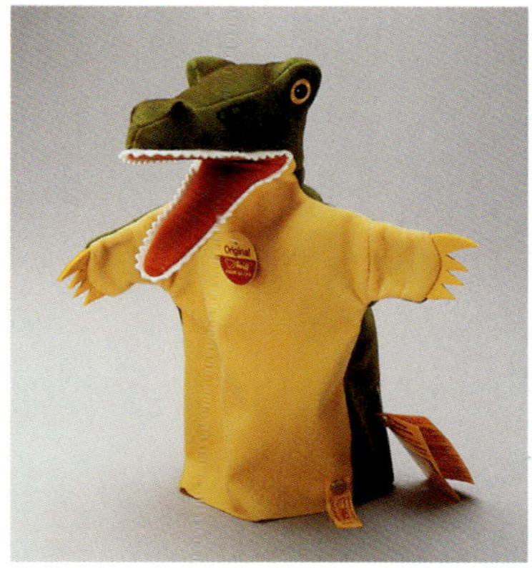

Hand-Krokodil - *Hand-Crocodile*

Webpelz/Trevirasamt, bewegliches Maul - *woven fur/trevira velvet, movable mouth*

SERIE	ART.-NO	PERIOD	PR.	INFO
251757	**6476/27**	1979-1990	2	27 cm
	251757	1991-1997	1-2	

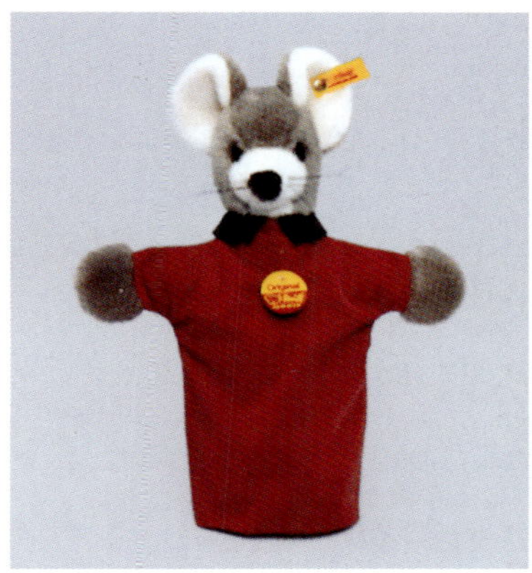

Hand-Maus - *Hand-Mouse*

Webpelz/Trevirasamt - *woven fur/trevira velvet*

SERIE	ART.-NO	PERIOD	PR.	INFO
251504	**6467/27**	1984-1987	2	27 cm

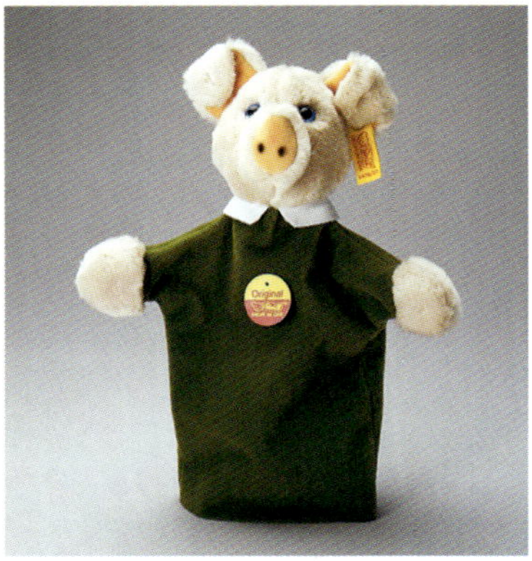

Hand-Schwein - *Hand-Pig*

Webpelz/Trevirasamt - *woven fur/trevira velvet*

Serie	Art.-No	Period	Pr.	Info
251603	**6470/27**	1984-1986	2	27 cm

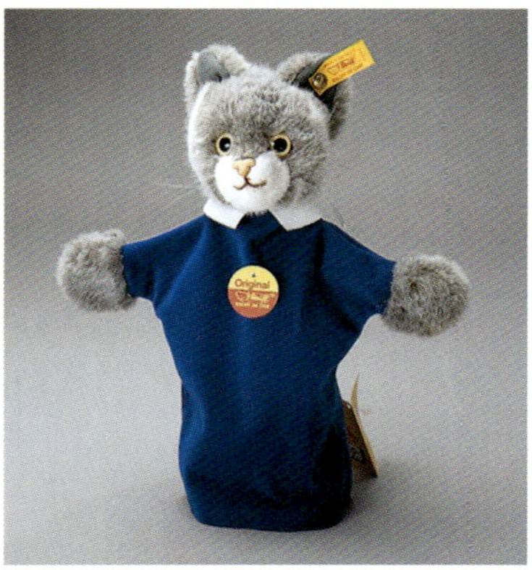

Hand-Katze - *Hand-Cat*

Webpelz/Trevirasamt - *woven fur/trevira velvet*

Serie	Art.-No	Period	Pr.	Info
251351	**6465/27**	1984-1990	2	27 cm
	251351	1991-1992	2	

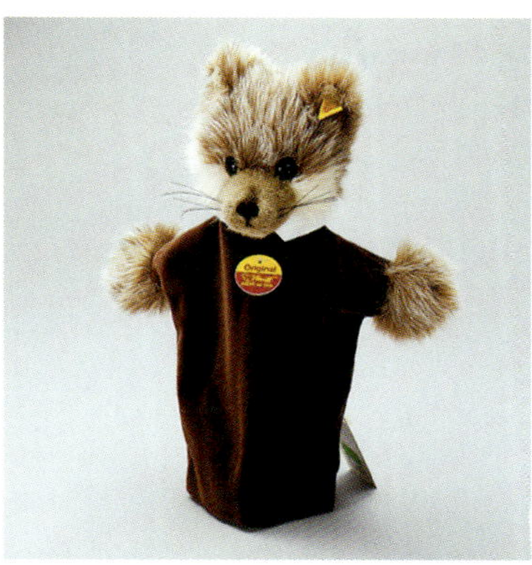

Hand-Wolf

Webpelz/Trevirasamt - *woven fur/trevira velvet*

Serie	Art.-No	Period	Pr.	Info
251658	**6473/27**	1984-1990	2	27 cm
	251658	1991-1997	2	

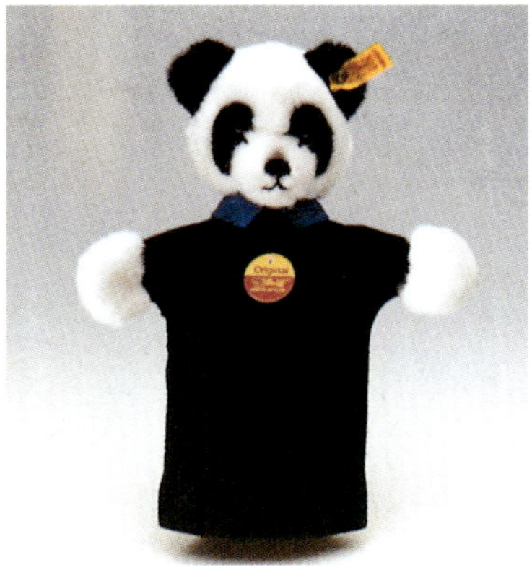

Hand-Panda

Webpelz/Trevirasamt - *woven fur/trevira velvet*

Serie	Art.-No	Period	Pr.	Info
251108	**6454/27**	1985-1988	2-3	27 cm

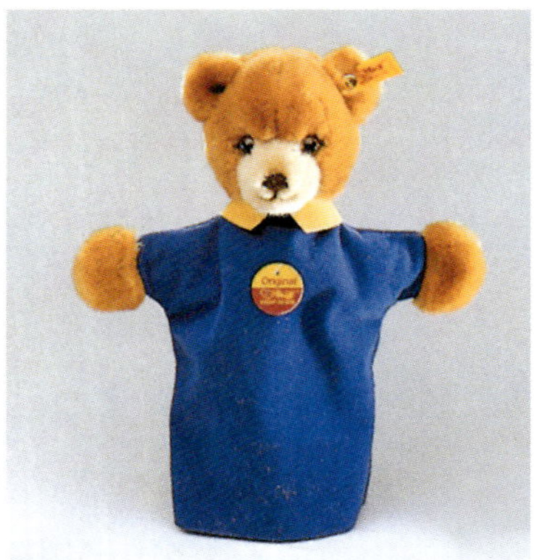

Hand-Baer - *Hand-Bear*

Webpelz/Trevirasamt - *woven fur/trevira velvet*

Serie	Art.-No	Period	Pr.	Info
251054	**6453/27**	1985-1990	2	27 cm
	251054	1991-1991	2	

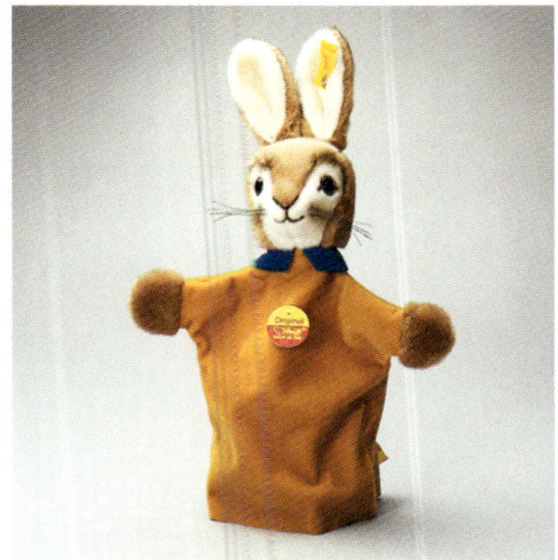

Hand-Hase - *Hand-Rabbit*

Webpelz/Trevirasamt - *woven fur/trevira velvet*

Serie	Art.-No	Period	Pr.	Info
251153	**6455/27**	1985-1990	2	27 cm

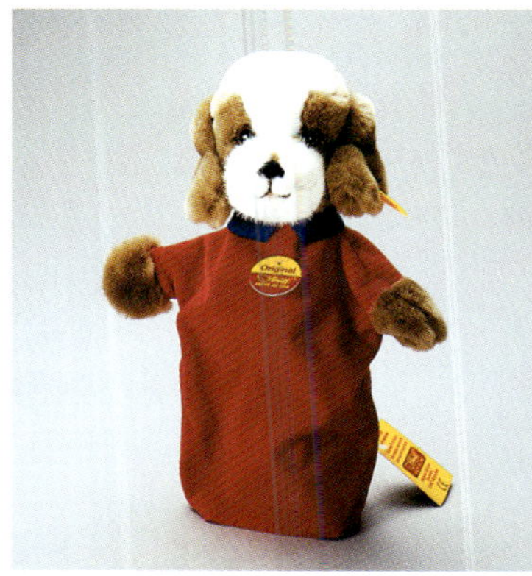

Hand-Hund - *Hand-Dog*

Webpelz/Trevirasamt - *woven fur/trevira velvet*

Serie	Art.-No	Period	Pr.	Info
251207	**6457/27**	1985-1990	2	27 cm
	251207	1991-1996	1-2	

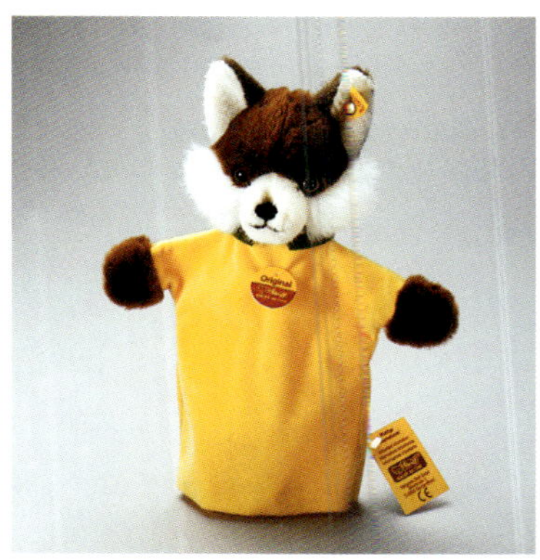

Hand-Fuchs - *Hand-Fox*

Webpelz/Trevirasamt - *woven fur/trevira velvet*

SERIE	ART.-NO	PERIOD	PR.	INFO
251702	**6475/27**	1985-1990	2	27 cm
	251702	1991-1997	1-2	

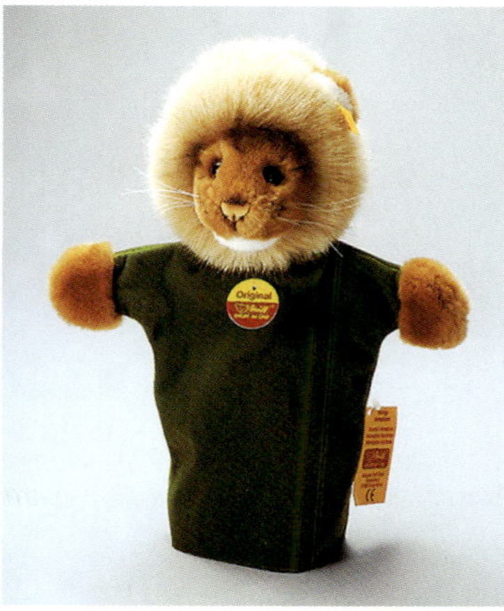

Hand-Loewe - *Hand-Lion*

Webpelz/Trevirasamt - *woven fur/trevira velvet*

SERIE	ART.-NO	PERIOD	PR.	INFO
251801	**6478/27**	1985-1990	2	27 cm
	251801	1991-1997	2	

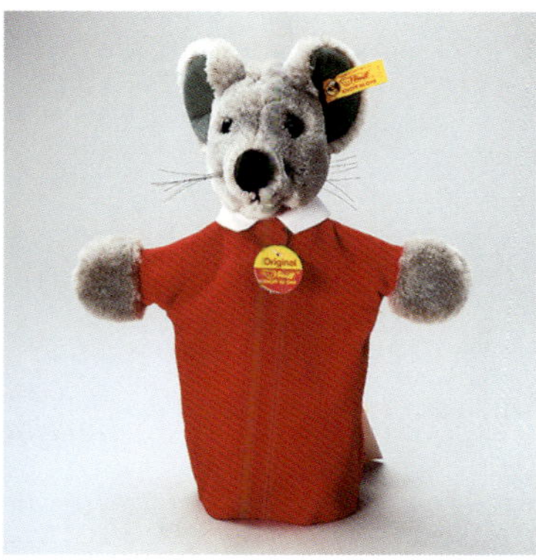

Hand-Maus - *Hand-Mouse*

Webpelz/Trevirasamt - *woven fur/trevira velvet*

SERIE	ART.-NO	PERIOD	PR.	INFO
251498	**6466/27**	1988-1990	2	27 cm
	251498	1991-1997	2	

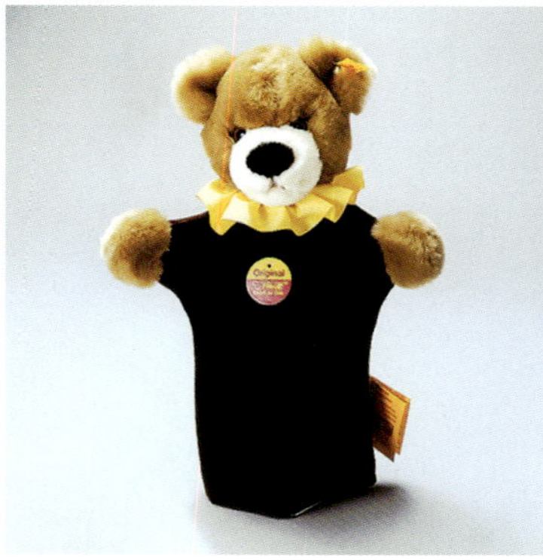

Hand-Baer - *Hand-Bear*

Webpelz/Trevirasamt - *woven fur/trevira velvet*

EAN-NO.	PERIOD	PR.	INFO
252006	1991-1993	2-3	28 cm

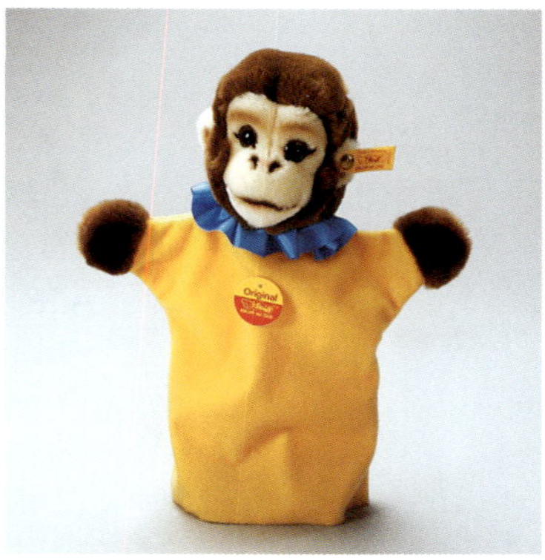

Hand-Affe - *Hand-Monkey*

Webpelz/Trevirasamt - *woven fur/trevira velvet*

EAN-NO.	PERIOD	PR.	INFO
252051	1991-1992	2	28 cm

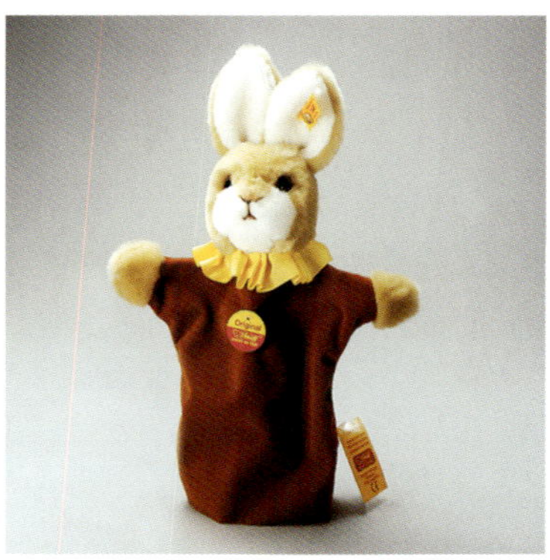

Hand-Hase - *Hand-Rabbit*

Webpelz/Trevirasamt - *woven fur/trevira velvet*

EAN-NO.	PERIOD	PR.	INFO
252105	1991-1994	2	28 cm

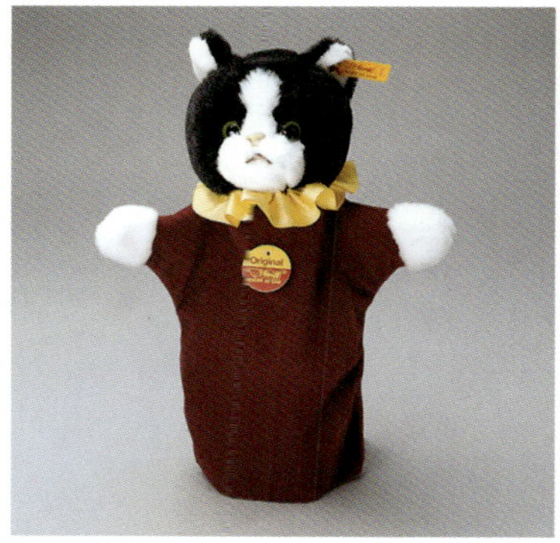

Hand-Kater - *Hand-Tom Cat*

Webpelz/Trevirasamt - *woven fur/trevira velvet*

EAN-NO.	PERIOD	PR.	INFO
252150	1991-1994	2	28 cm

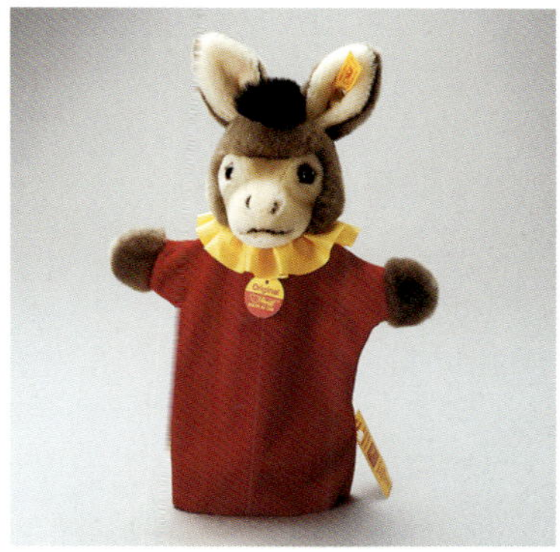

Hand-Esel - *Hand-Donkey*

Webpelz/Trevirasamt - *woven fur/trevira velvet*

EAN-NO.	PERIOD	PR.	INFO
252204	1991-1994	2	28 cm

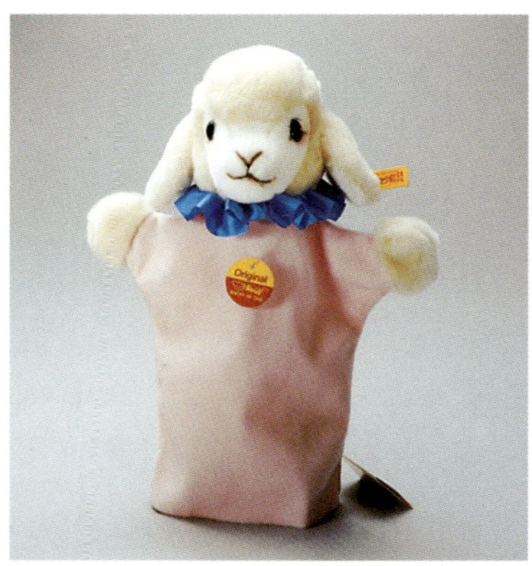

Hand-Lamm - *Hand-Lamb*

Webpelz/Trevirasamt - *woven fur/trevira velvet*

EAN-NO.	PERIOD	PR.	INFO
252259	1991-1993	2	28 cm

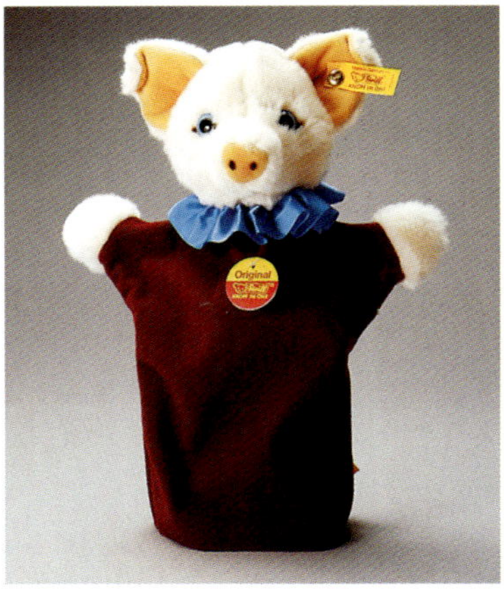

Hand-Schwein - *Hand-Pig*

Webpelz/Trevirasamt - *woven fur/trevira velvet*

EAN-No.	Period	Pr.	Info
252303	1991-1992	2	28 cm

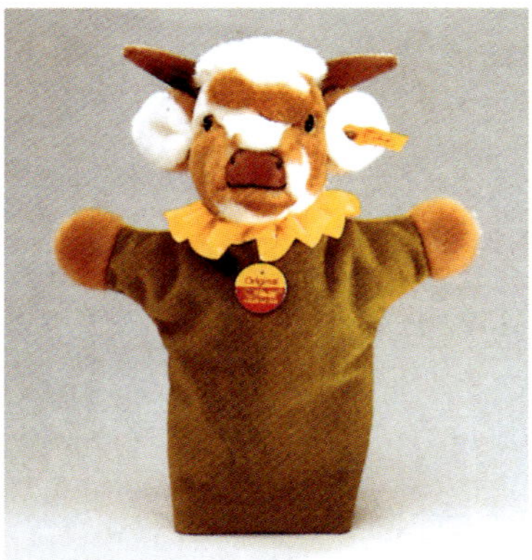

Hand-Kuh - *Hand-Cow*

Webpelz/Trevirasamt - *woven fur/trevira velvet*

EAN-No.	Period	Pr.	Info
252358	1991-1992	2-3	28 cm

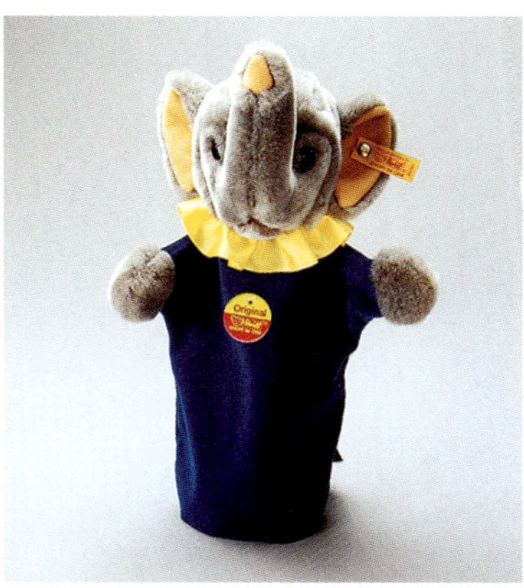

Hand-Elefant - *Hand-Elephant*

Webpelz/Trevirasamt - *woven fur/trevira velvet*

EAN-No.	Period	Pr.	Info
252402	1991-1993	2-3	28 cm

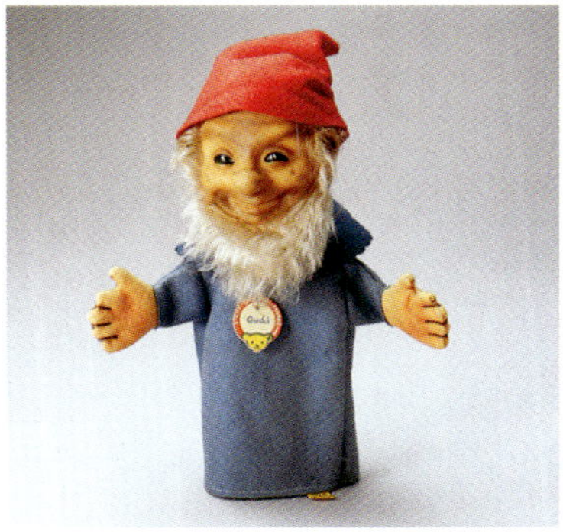

Hand-Zwerg **Gucki** - *Hand-Dwarf* ***Gucki***

Gummikopf (Plastik/PVC), Filzkleidung - *rubber head (plastic/PVC), felt clothing*

Serie	Art.-No	Period	Pr.	Info
79 88	**117**	1953-1958	4	17 cm
865 901	**0117,00**	1960-1963	3-4	
705	**0117,00**	1966-1967	3-4	
	7050/17	1968-1975	2-3	

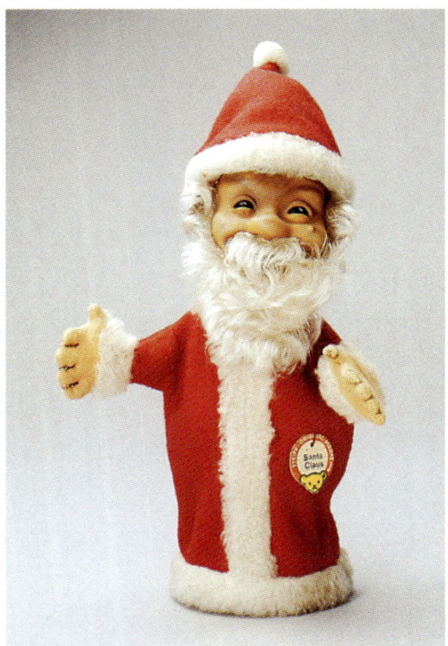

Hand-**Santa Claus**

Gummikopf (Plastik), Filzkleidung - *rubber head (plastic), felt clothing*

Serie	Art.-No	Period	Pr.	Info
79 88	**121**	1954-1958	4-5	21 cm
865 903	**0121,00**	1961-1961	4	

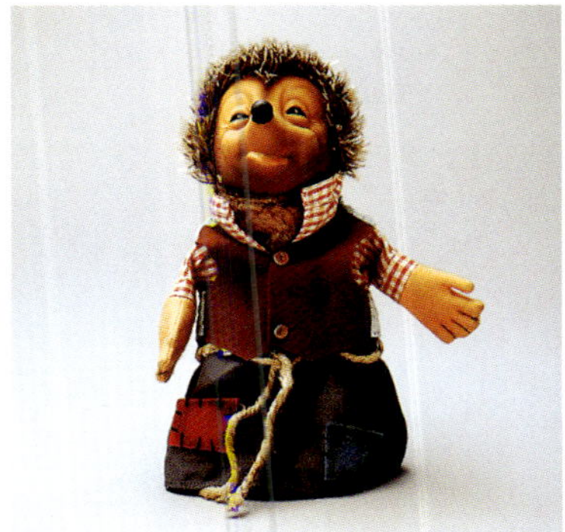

Hand-**Mecki**

Gummikopf (Plastik/PVC), Stoffkleidung - *rubber head (plastic/PVC), clothing made of fabric*

Serie	Art.-No	Period	Pr.	Info
79 88	**720**	1954-1958	4	20 cm
865 900	**0720,00**	1959-1963	3-4	
704	**0720,00**	1966-1967	3-4	
	7040/20	1968-1975	2-3	

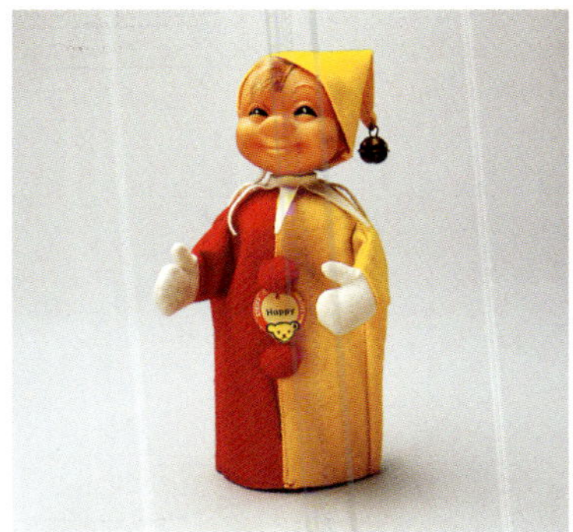

Hand-Kasper **Happy** - *Hand-Punch* ***Happy***

Plastikkopf (PVC), Filzkleidung - *plastic head (PVC), felt clothing*

Serie	Art.-No	Period	Pr.	Info
865 867	**0017,00**	1963-1964	3-4	17 cm
703	**0017,00**	1965-1967	3-4	
	7030/17	1968-1974	2-3	

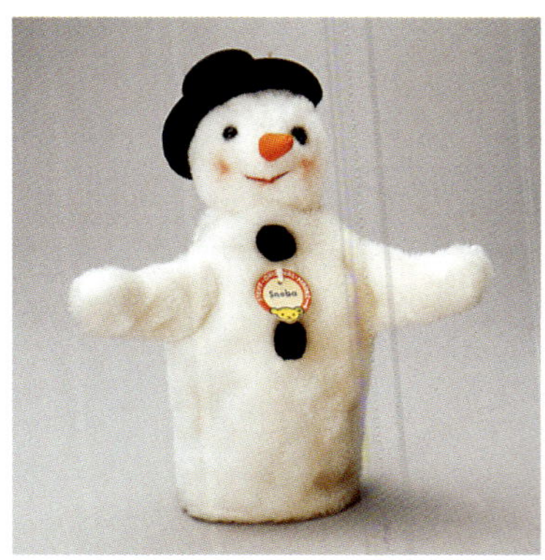

Hand-**Sneba**

Dralon, weiss, schwarzer Hut und Knoepfe - *dralon, white, a black hat, with buttons down the front*

SERIE	ART.-NO	PERIOD	PR.	INFO
935	**0617,00**	1964-1964	5	17 cm

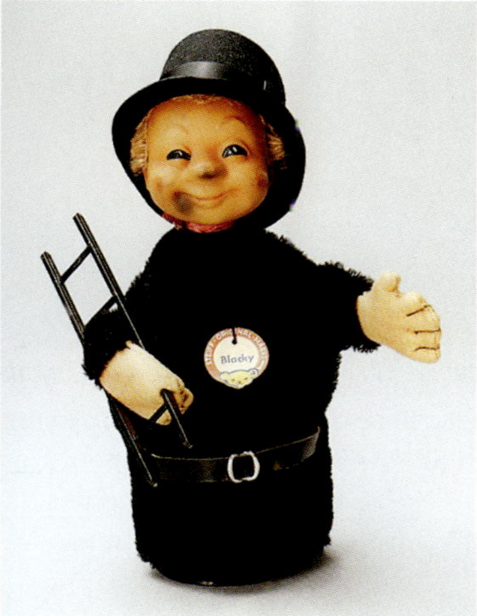

Hand-**Blacky** Kaminfeger - *Hand-**Blacky** Chimney Sweep*

Mohair, Kunststoffkopf, schwarz, mit Leiter - *mohair, synthetic head, black, equipped with a ladder*

SERIE	ART.-NO	PERIOD	PR.	INFO
865 936	**0317,00**	1964-1964	4-5	17 cm

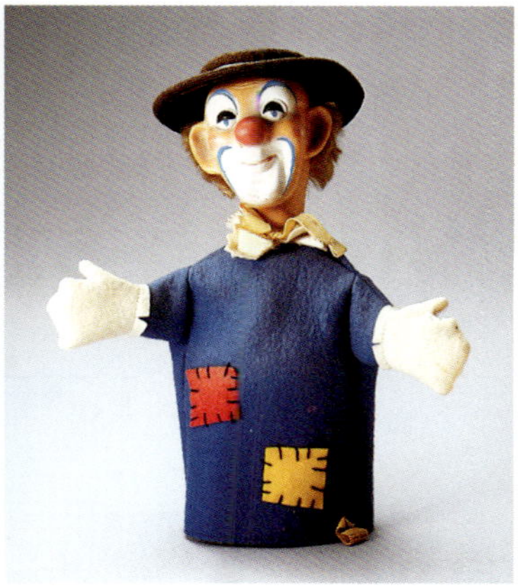

Hand-Clown

Plastikkopf (PVC), Filzrock - *plastic head (PVC), felt costume*

SERIE	ART.-NO	PERIOD	PR.	INFO
706	**0317,00**	1967-1967	3-4	17 cm
	7060/17	1968-1976	3	

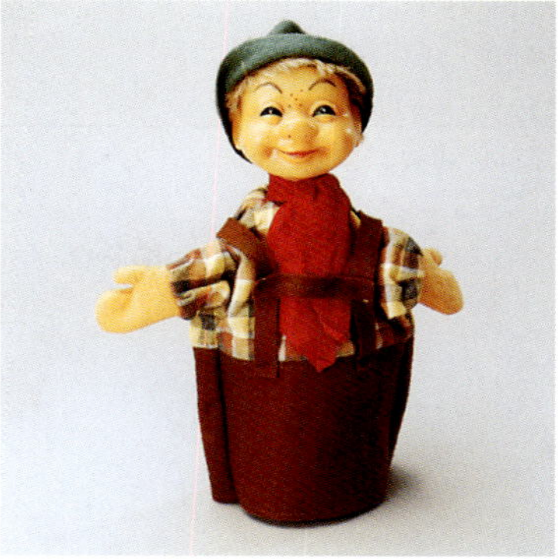

Hand-Haensel

PVC-Kopf, Stoff- & Filzkleidung - *PVC head, fabric & felt clothing*

SERIE	ART.-NO	PERIOD	PR.	INFO
	7071/17	1969-1978	2	17 cm

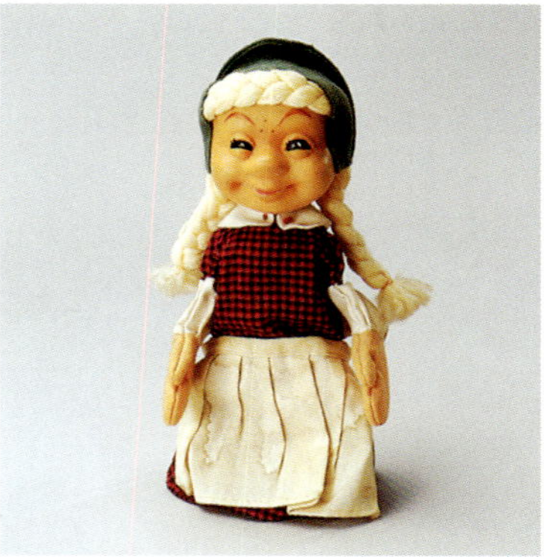

Hand-Gretel

PVC-Kopf, Stoff- & Filzkleidung - *PVC head, fabric & felt clothing*

SERIE	ART.-NO	PERIOD	PR.	INFO
	7072/17	1969-1978	2	17 cm

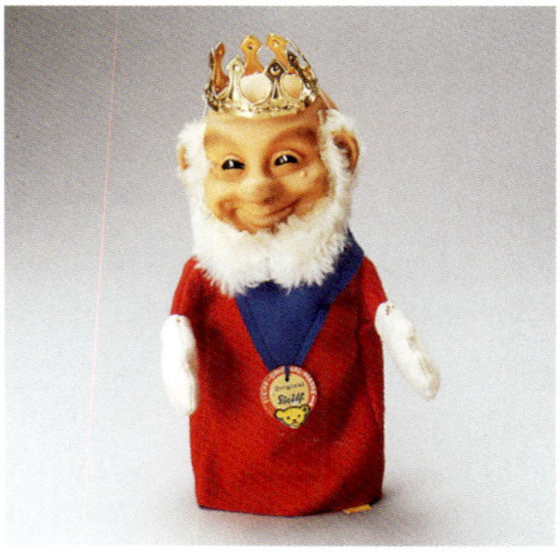

Hand-Koenig - *Hand-King*

PVC-Kopf, Stoff- & Filzkleidung - *PVC head, fabric & felt clothing*

SERIE	ART.-NO	PERIOD	PR.	INFO
	7073/17	1969-1978	2	17 cm

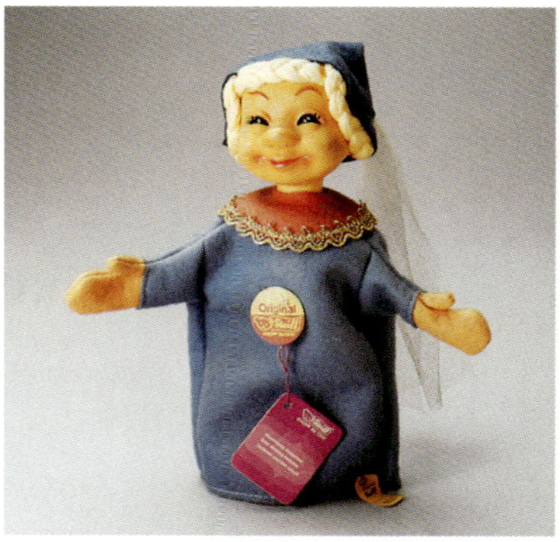

Hand-Prinzessin - *Hand-Princess*

PVC-Kopf, Stoff- & Filzkleidung - *PVC head, fabric & felt clothing*

SERIE	ART.-NO	PERIOD	PR.	INFO
	7074/17	1969-1977	2	17 cm

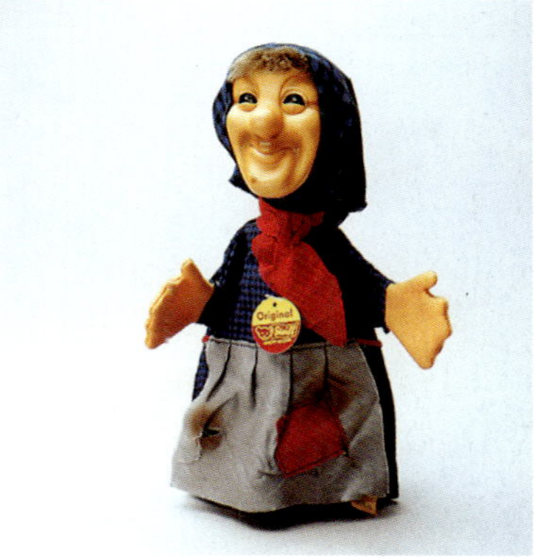

Hand-Hexe - *Hand-Witch*

PVC-Kopf, Stoff- & Filzkleidung - *PVC head, fabric & felt clothing*

SERIE	ART.-NO	PERIOD	PR.	INFO
	7075/17	1969-1977	2	17 cm

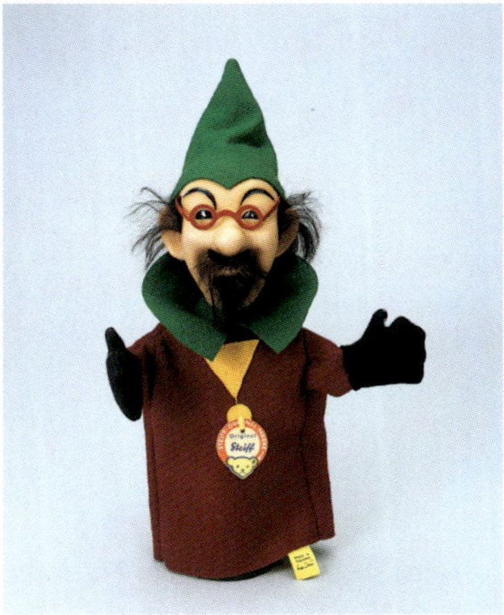

Hand-Zauberer ab 1974 Hand-**Faky** - *Hand-Magician from 1974 Hand-**Faky***

PVC-Kopf, Stoff- & Filzkleidung - *PVC head, fabric & felt clothing*

SERIE	ART.-NO	PERIOD	PR.	INFO
	7076/17	1969-1977	2	17 cm

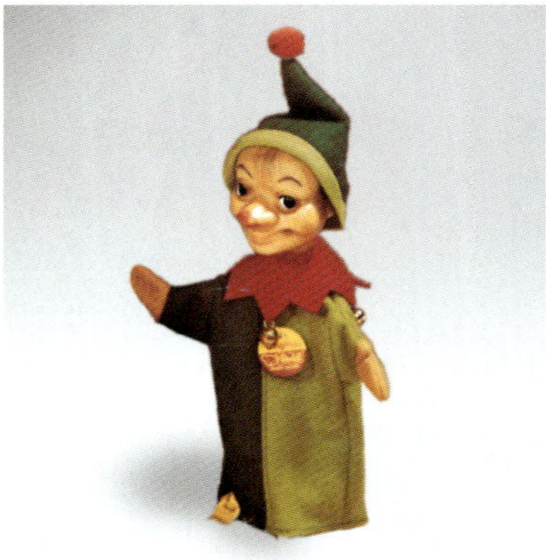

Hand-Kasper - *Hand-Punch*

PVC-Kopf, Stoff- & Filzkleidung - *PVC head, fabric & felt clothing*

SERIE	ART.-NO	PERIOD	PR.	INFO
	7077/17	1970-1978	2	17 cm

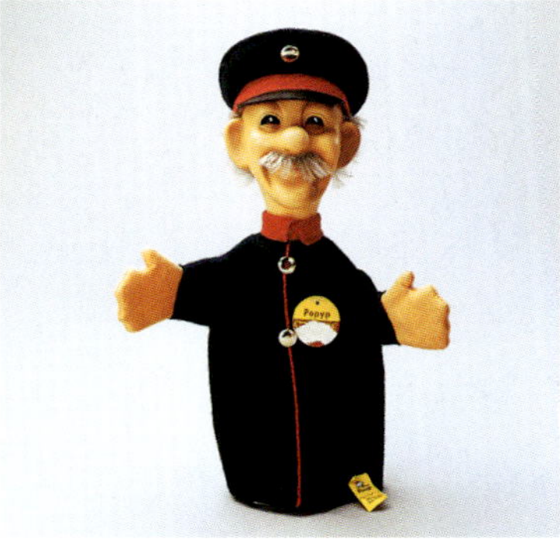

Hand-Polizist ab 1974 Hand-**Popyp** - *Hand-Policeman from 1974 Hand-**Popyp***

PVC-Kopf, blaue Filz-Kleidung - *PVC head, blue felt clothing*

SERIE	ART.-NO	PERIOD	PR.	INFO
	7010/17	1972-1978	2	17 cm

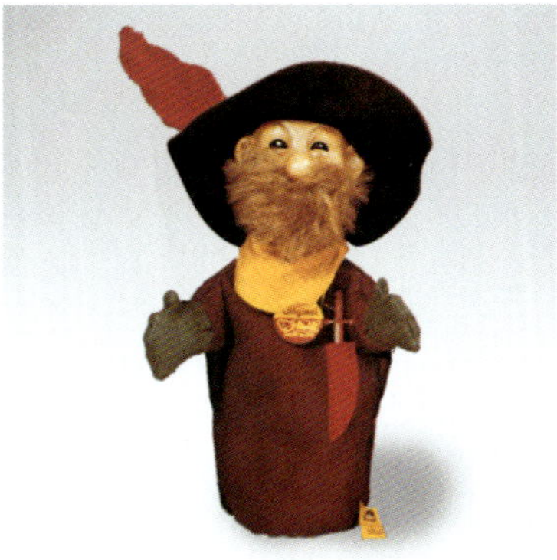

Hand-Raeuber - *Hand-Robber*

PVC-Kopf, braune Filz-Kleidung - *PVC head, brown felt clothing*

SERIE	ART.-NO	PERIOD	PR.	INFO
	7020/17	1972-1978	2	17 cm

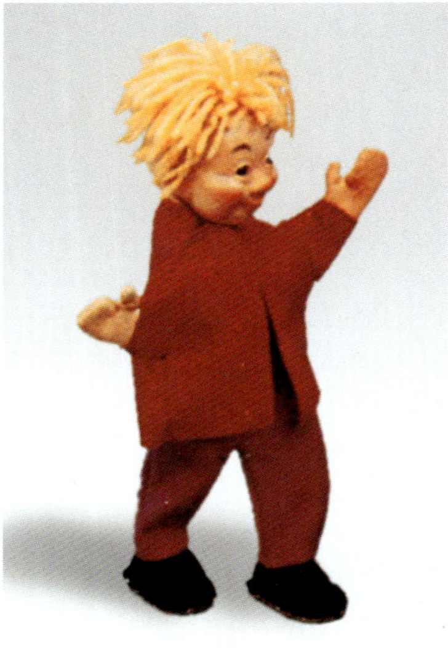

Lese-Peter - *Studious Peter*

PVC-Kopf, Filz, Schlenkerbeine - *PVC head, felt, floppy legs*

SERIE	ART.-NO	PERIOD	PR.	INFO
	7070/30	1972-1975	3	30 cm

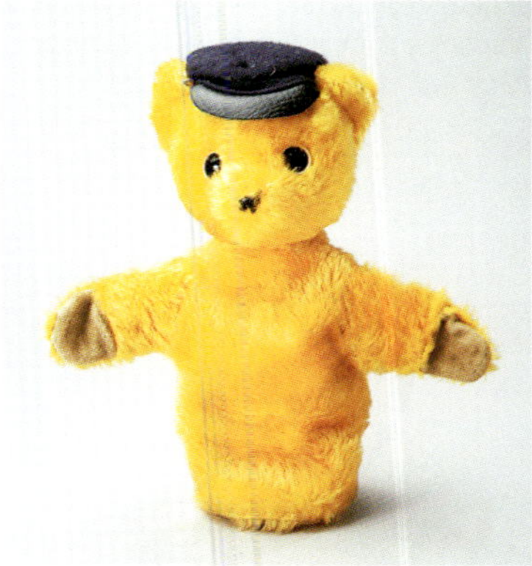

Hand-**Seebaer** - *Hand-Bear Sailor*

Mohairpluesch, Filzmuetze, Copyr. Wolfgang Buresch - *mohair, felt cap, Copyr. Wolfgang Buresch*

SERIE	ART.-NO	PERIOD	PR.	INFO
	7078/17	1972-1975	3	17 cm

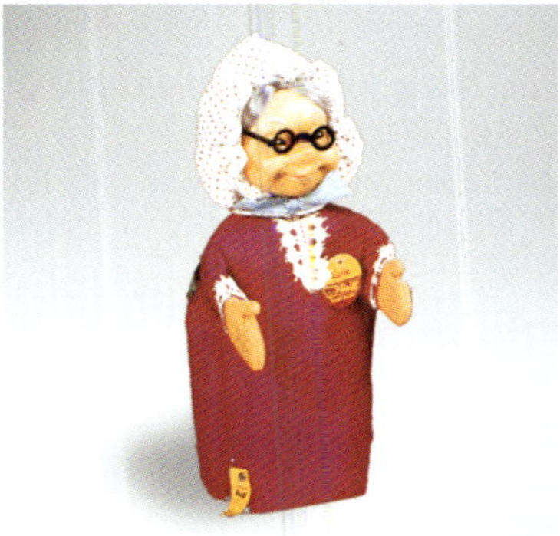

Hand-Grossmutter ab 1974 Hand-**Lulia** - *Hand-Grandmother from 1974 Hand-**Lulia***

PVC-Kopf, Filzkleidung - *PVC head, felt clothing*

SERIE	ART.-NO	PERIOD	PR.	INFO
	7067/17	1973-1978	2	17 cm

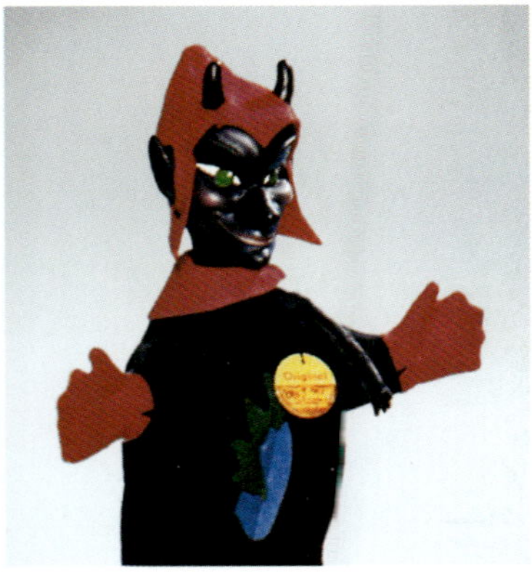

Hand-Teufel - *Hand-Devil*

PVC-Kopf, Filzkleidung - *PVC head, felt clothing*

SERIE	ART.-NO	PERIOD	PR.	INFO
	7068/17	1973-1975	2-3	17 cm

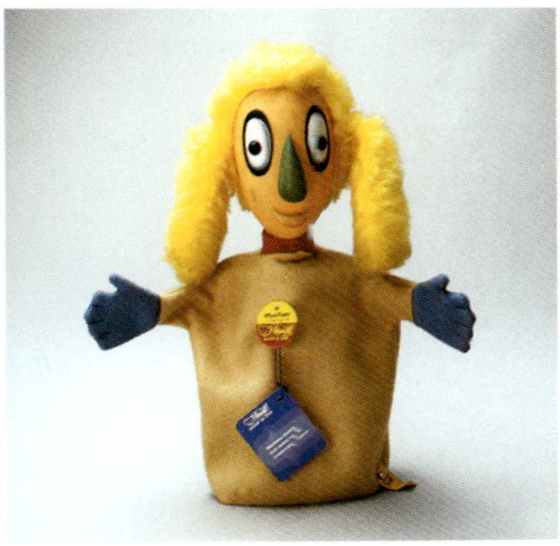

Maxifant

PVC-Kopf, Filz, blonde Haare - *PVC head, felt, blond hair*

SERIE	ART.-NO	PERIOD	PR.	INFO
	7002/25	1974-1976	2-3	25 cm

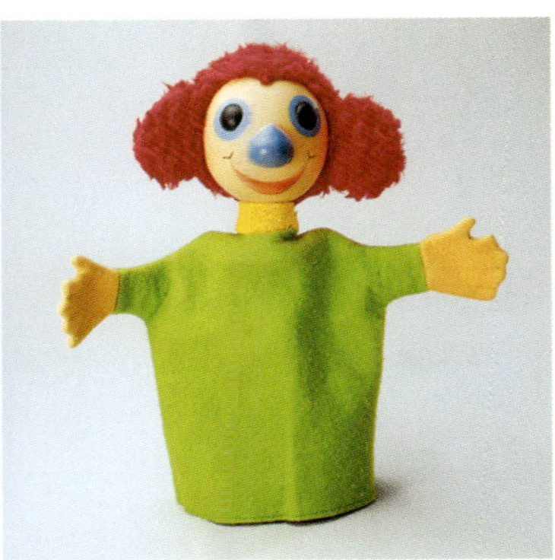

Minifant

PVC-Kopf, Filz, rote Haare - *PVC head, felt, red hair*

SERIE	ART.-NO	PERIOD	PR.	INFO
	7003/25	1974-1976	2-3	25 cm

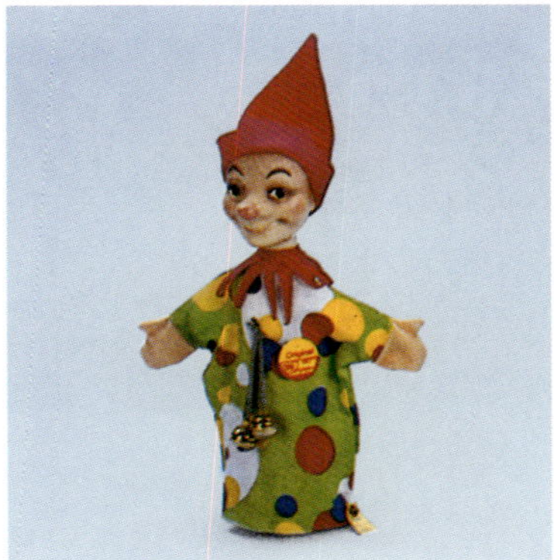

Hand-Kasper - *Hand-Punch*

PVC-Kopf, Stoffkleidung - *PVC head, clothing made of fabric*

SERIE	ART.-NO	PERIOD	PR.	INFO
	7001/27	1979-1983	2	27 cm

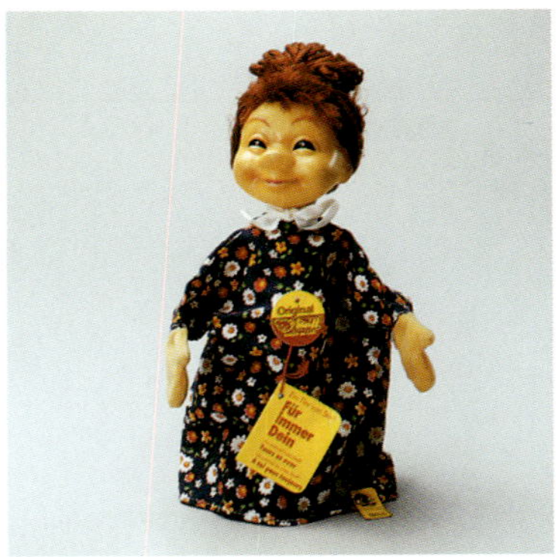

Hand-Grossmutter - *Hand-Grandmother*

PVC-Kopf, Stoffkleidung - *PVC head, clothing made of fabric*

SERIE	ART.-NO	PERIOD	PR.	INFO
	7003/27	1979-1983	2	27 cm

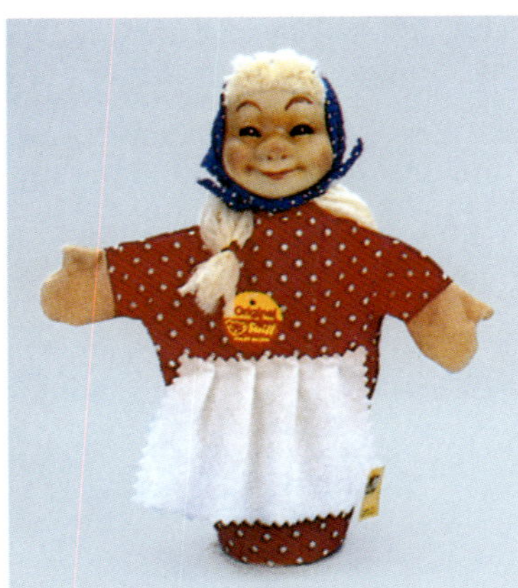

Hand-Maedel - *Hand-Girl*

PVC-Kopf, Stoffkleidung - *PVC head, clothing made of fabric*

SERIE	ART.-NO	PERIOD	PR.	INFO
	7005/27	1979-1983	2	27 cm

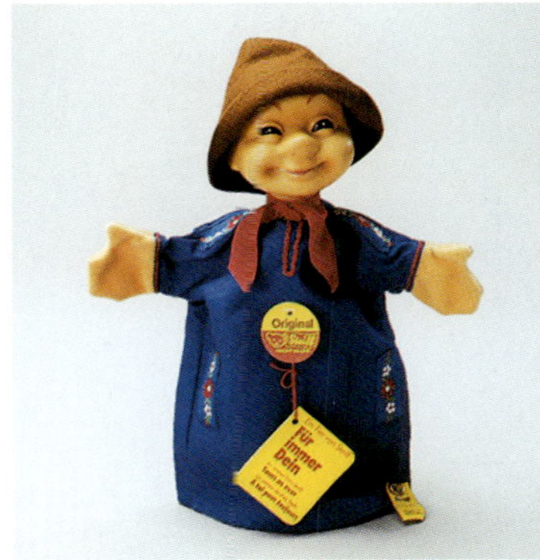

Hand-Bub - *Hand-Boy*

PVC-Kopf, Stoffkleidung - *PVC head, clothing made of fabric*

SERIE	ART.-NO	PERIOD	PR.	INFO
	7007/27	1979-1981	2	27 cm

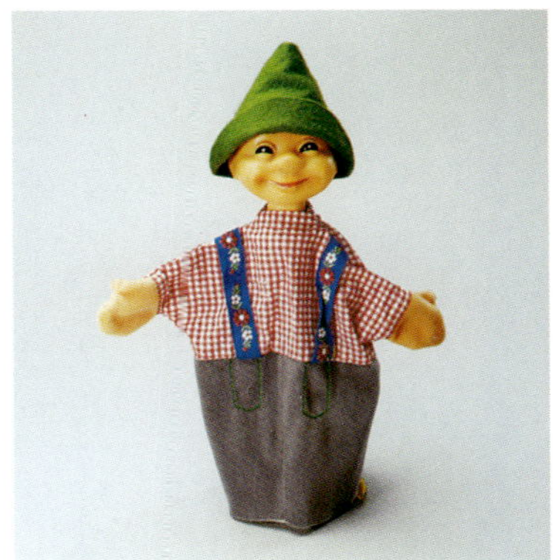

Hand-Sepp

PVC-Kopf, Stoffkleidung - *PVC head, clothing made of fabric*

SERIE	ART.-NO	PERIOD	PR.	INFO
	7011/27	1979-1983	2	27 cm

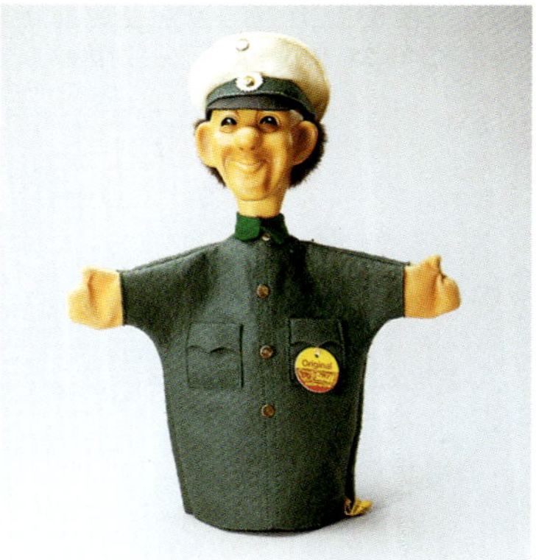

Hand-Polizist - *Hand-Policeman*

PVC-Kopf, Stoffkleidung - *PVC head, clothing made of fabric*

SERIE	ART.-NO	PERIOD	PR.	INFO
	7013/27	1979-1983	2	27 cm

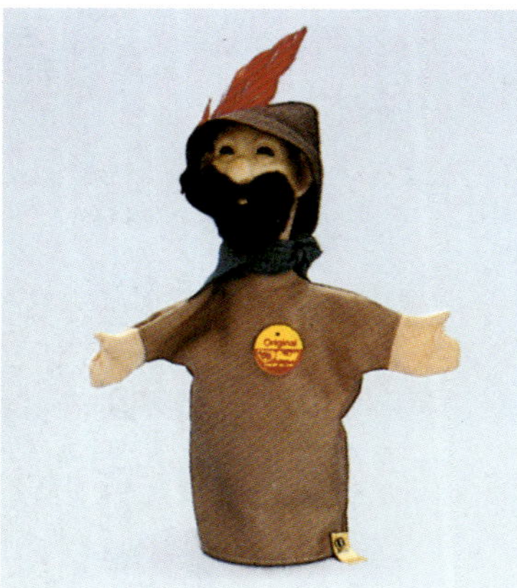

Hand-Raeuber - *Hand-Robber*

PVC-Kopf, Stoffkleidung - *PVC head, clothing made of fabric*

SERIE	ART.-NO	PERIOD	PR.	INFO
	7015/27	1979-1983	2	27 cm

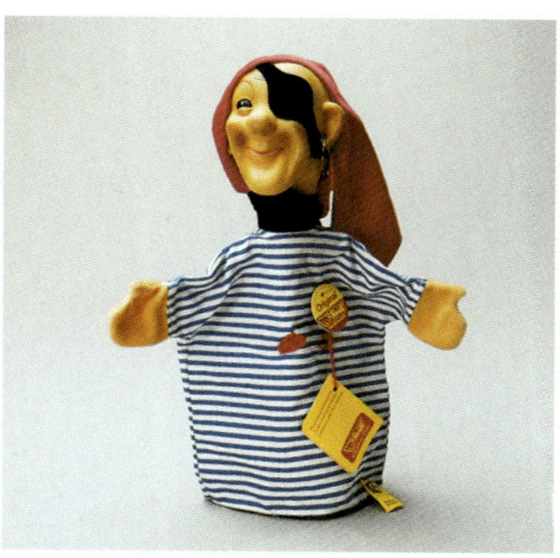

Hand-Seeraeuber - *Hand-Pirate*

PVC-Kopf, Stoffkleidung - *PVC head, clothing made of fabric*

SERIE	ART.-NO	PERIOD	PR.	INFO
	7017/27	1979-1983	2	27 cm

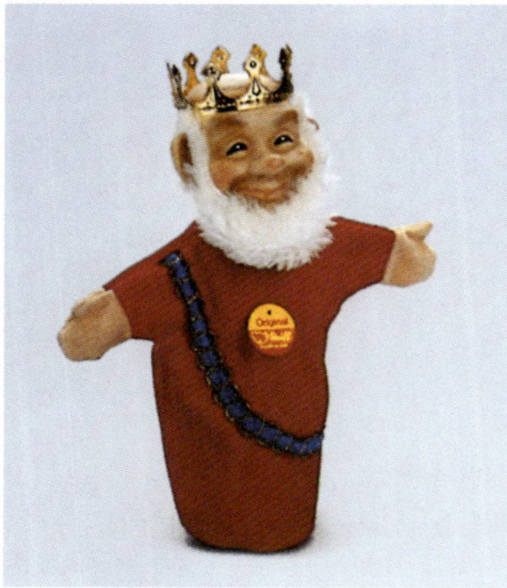

Hand-Koenig - *Hand-King*

PVC-Kopf, Stoffkleidung - *PVC head, clothing made of fabric*

SERIE	ART.-NO	PERIOD	PR.	INFO
	7021/27	1979-1983	2	27 cm

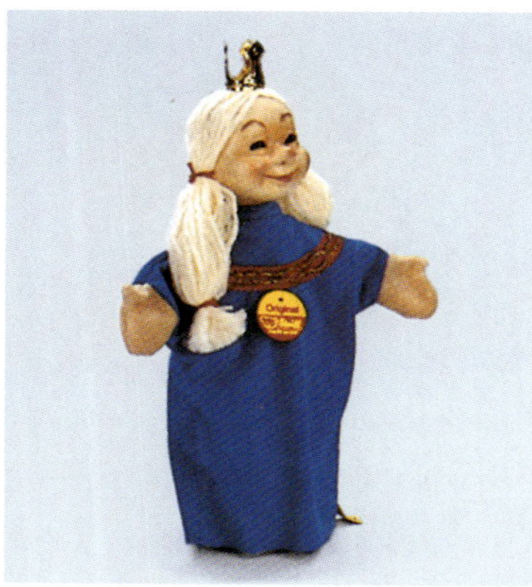

Hand-Prinzessin - *Hand-Princess*

PVC-Kopf, Stoffkleidung - *PVC head, clothing made of fabric*

SERIE	ART.-NO	PERIOD	PR.	INFO
	7023/27	1979-1983	2	27 cm

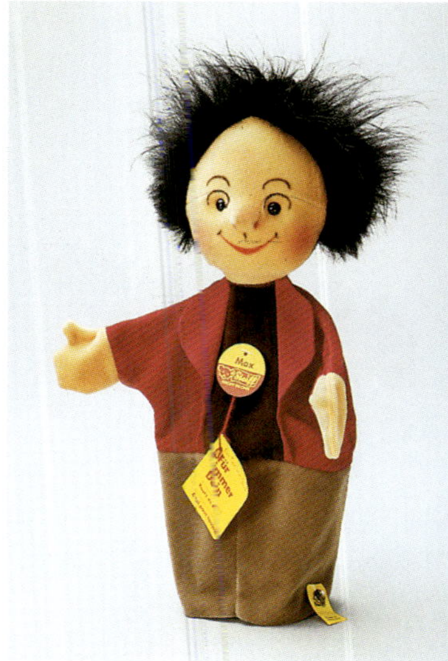

Hand-**Max**

Trevirasamt, waschbar - *trevira velvet, washable*

SERIE	ART.-NO	PERIOD	PR.	INFO
	7030/30	1979-1982	2-3	30 cm

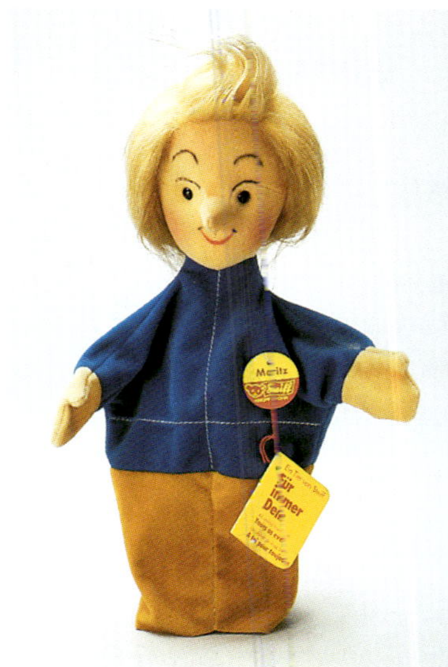

Hand-**Moritz**

Trevirasamt, waschbar - *trevira velvet, washable*

SERIE	ART.-NO	PERIOD	PR.	INFO
	7031/30	1979-1982	2-3	30 cm

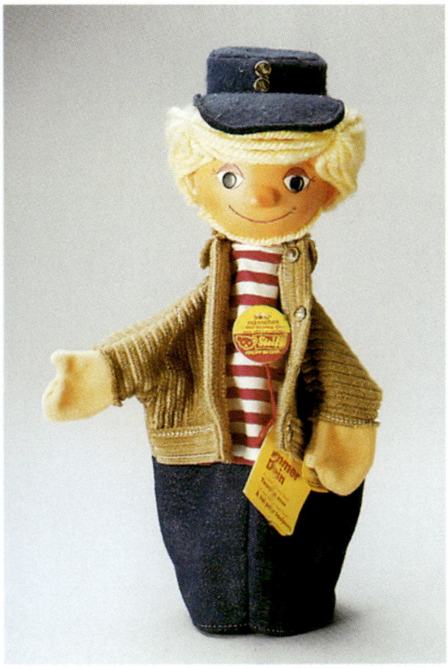

Hand-**Sandmaennchen** - *Hand-Sandman*

PVC-Kopf, Stoffkleidung, Copyr. NWF/St.Hmbg./Cinetrick/JBS Langenfeld - *PVC head, clothing made of fabric, Copyr. NWF/St.Hmbg./Cinetrick/JBS Langenfeld*

SERIE	ART.-NO	PERIOD	PR.	INFO
	7040/30	1979-1981	3	30 cm

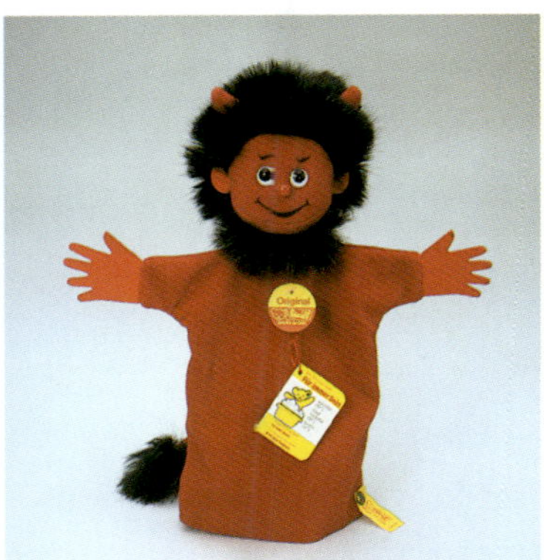

Hand-Teufel - *Hand-Devil*

Webpelz/Trevira - *woven fur/trevira*

SERIE	ART.-NO	PERIOD	PR.	INFO
	7025/27	1980-1983	2	27 cm

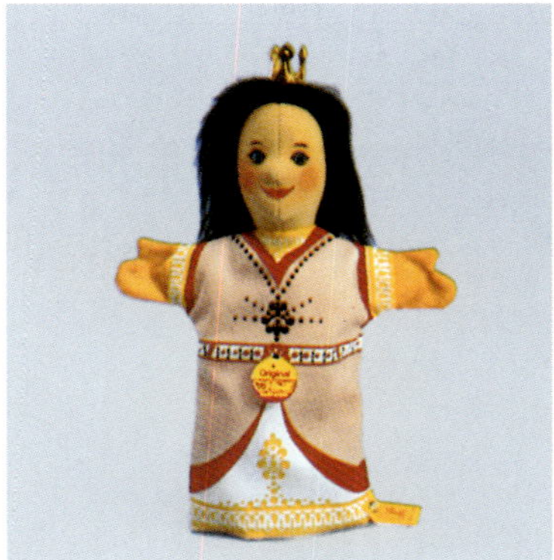

Hand-Prinzessin - *Hand-Princess*

Trevirasamt, schwarze Haare, abwaschbar - *trevira velvet, black hair, surface washable*

SERIE	ART.-NO	PERIOD	PR.	INFO
	7061/28	1984-1985	1-2	28 cm

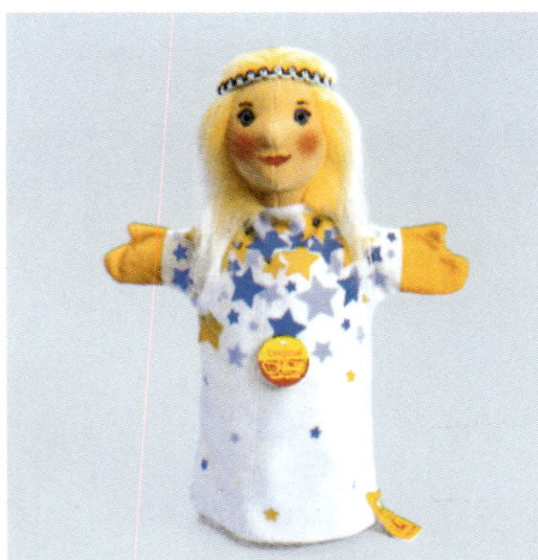

Hand-Fee - *Hand-Fairy*

Trevirasamt, abwaschbar - *trevira velvet, surface washable*

SERIE	ART.-NO	PERIOD	PR.	INFO
	7066/28	1984-1985	1-2	28 cm

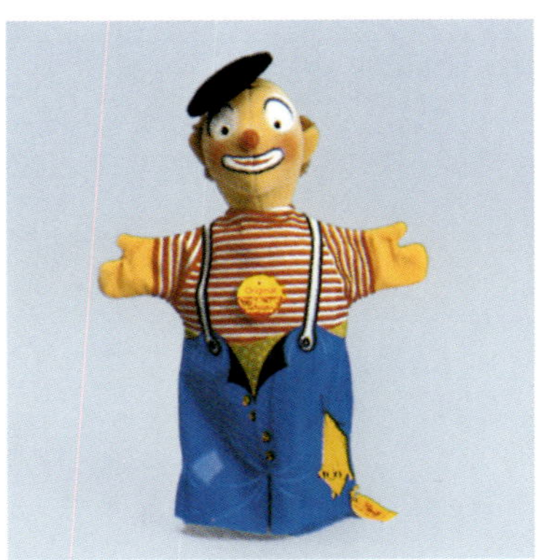

Hand-Clown

Trevirasamt, abwaschbar - *trevira velvet, surface washable*

SERIE	ART.-NO	PERIOD	PR.	INFO
255854	**7075/28**	1984-1987	1-2	28 cm

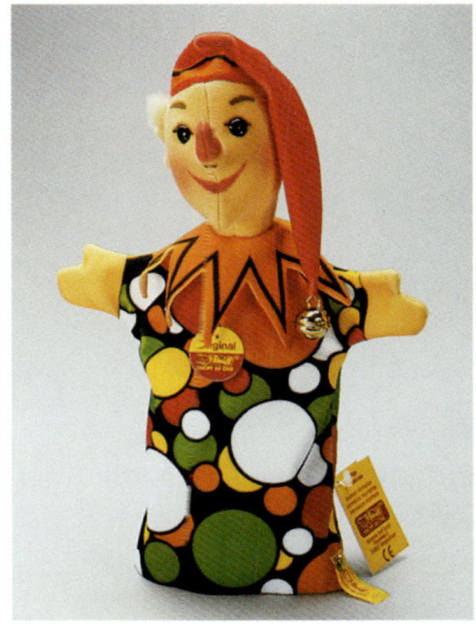

Hand-Kasper - *Hand-Punch*

Trevirasamt, abwaschbar - *trevira velvet, surface washable*

SERIE	ART.-NO	PERIOD	PR.	INFO
255007	**7051/28**	1984-1990	1-2	28 cm
	255007	1991-1997	1-2	

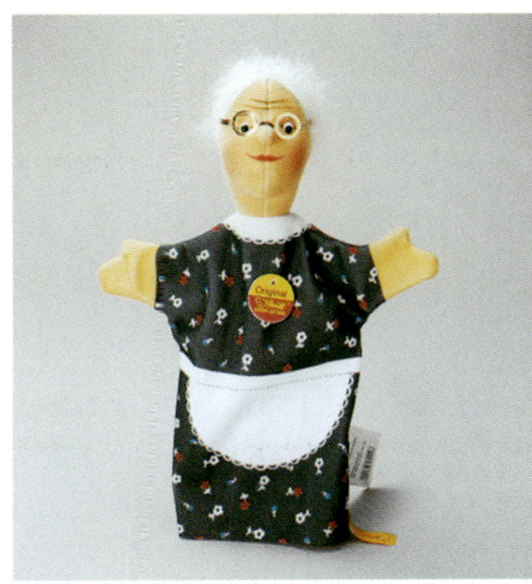

Hand-Grossmutter - *Hand-Grandmother*

Trevirasamt, abwaschbar - *trevira velvet, surface washable*

SERIE	ART.-NO	PERIOD	PR.	INFO
255106	**7052/28**	1984-1990	1-2	28 cm
	255106	1991-1997	1-2	

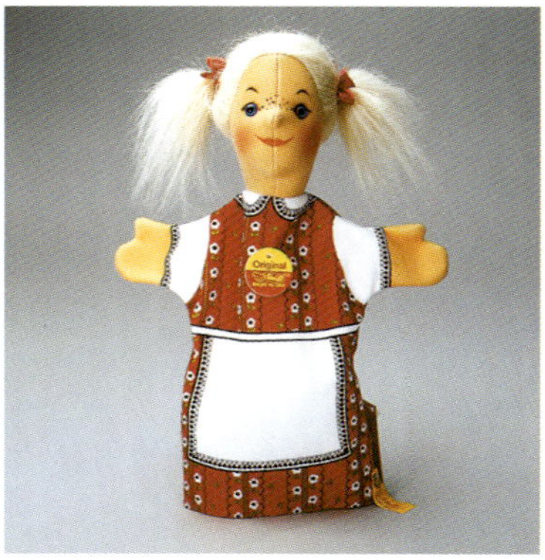

Hand-Gretel

Trevirasamt, abwaschbar - *trevira velvet, surface washable*

SERIE	ART.-NO	PERIOD	PR.	INFO
255151	**7053/28**	1984-1990	1-2	28 cm
	255151	1991-1993	1-2	

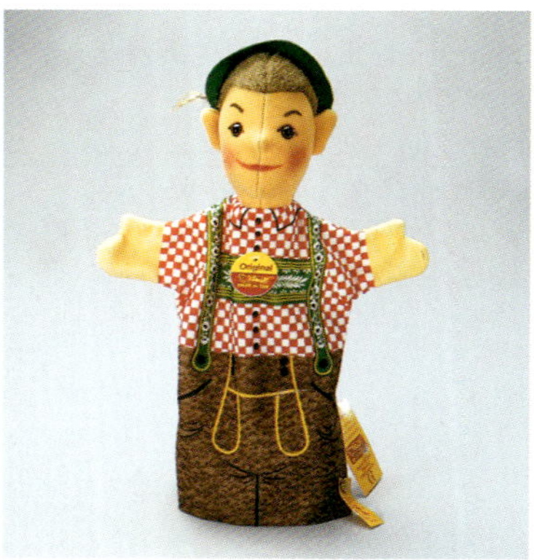

Hand-Seppl

Trevirasamt, abwaschbar - *trevira velvet, surface washable*

SERIE	ART.-NO	PERIOD	PR.	INFO
255205	**7054/28**	1984-1990	1-2	28 cm
	255205	1991-1997	1-2	

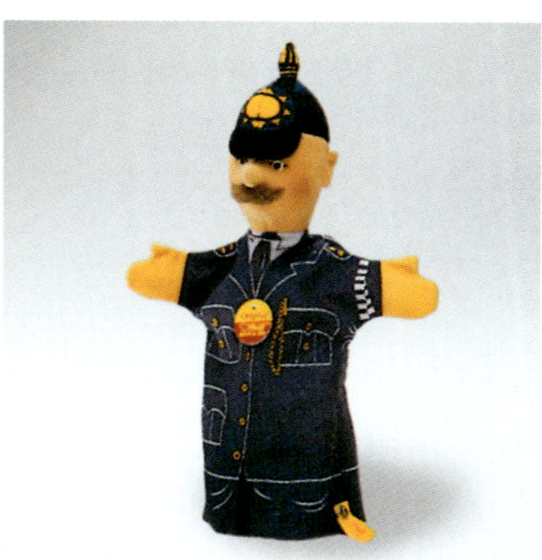

Hand-Polizist - *Hand-Policeman*

Trevirasamt, abwaschbar - *trevira velvet, surface washable*

SERIE	ART.-NO	PERIOD	PR.	INFO
255250	**7057/28**	1984-1990	1-2	28 cm
	255250	1991-1993	1-2	

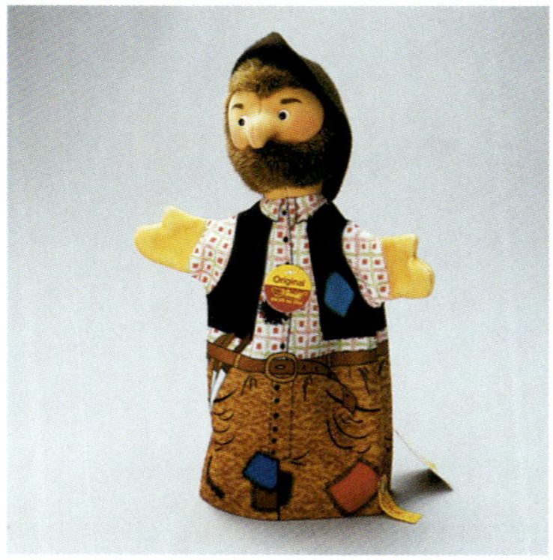

Hand-Raeuber - *Hand-Robber*

Trevirasamt, abwaschbar - *trevira velvet, surface washable*

SERIE	ART.-NO	PERIOD	PR.	INFO
255304	**7058/28**	1984-1990	1-2	28 cm
	255304	1991-1997	1-2	

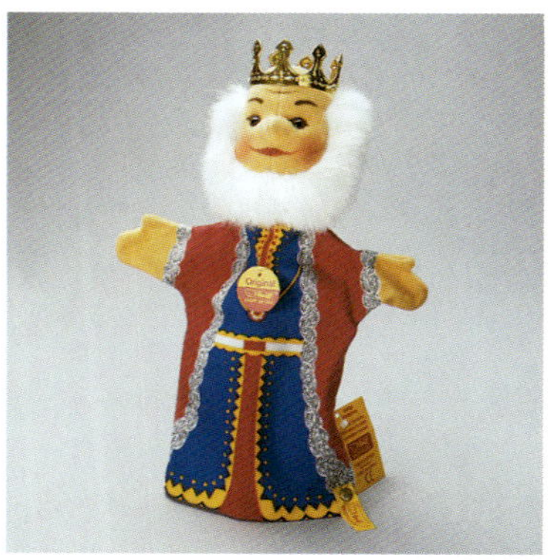

Hand-Koenig - *Hand-King*

Trevirasamt, abwaschbar - *trevira velvet, surface washable*

SERIE	ART.-NO	PERIOD	PR.	INFO
255359	**7060/28**	1984-1990	1-2	28 cm
	255359	1991-1997	1-2	

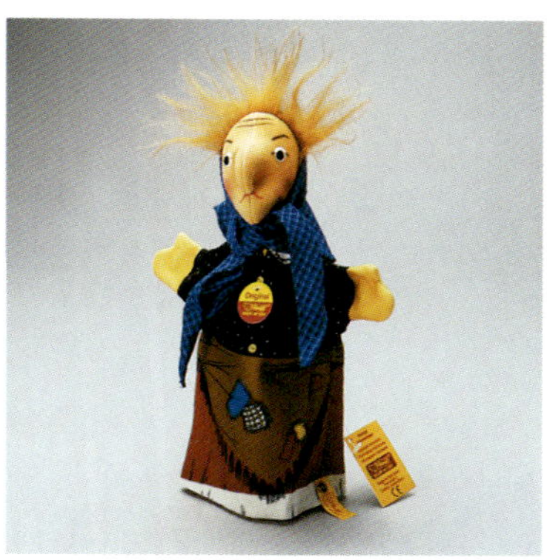

Hand-Hexe - *Hand-Witch*

Trevirasamt, abwaschbar - *trevira velvet, surface washable*

SERIE	ART.-NO	PERIOD	PR.	INFO
255458	**7065/28**	1984-1990	1-2	28 cm
	255458	1991-1997	1-2	

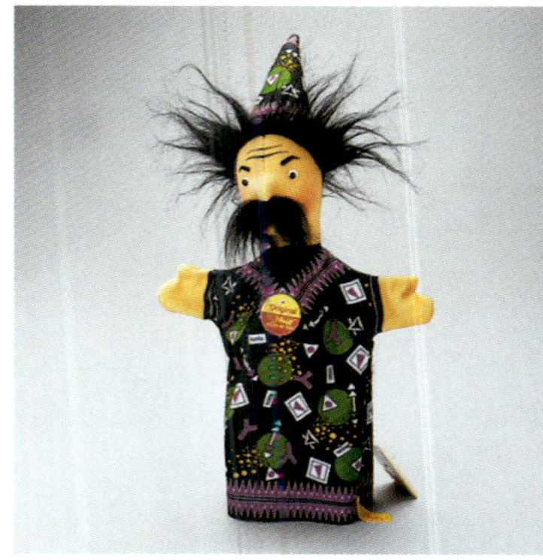

Hand-Zauberer - *Hand-Magician*

Trevirasamt, abwaschbar - *trevira velvet, surface washable*

SERIE	ART.-NO	PERIOD	PR.	INFO
255502	**7068/28**	1984-1990	1-2	28 cm
	255502	1991-1997	1-2	

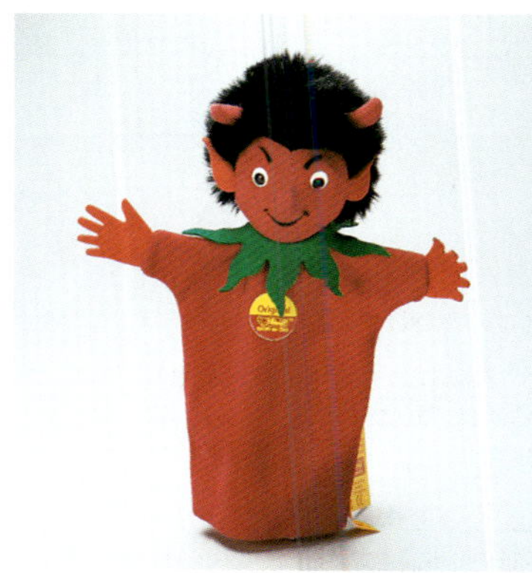

Hand-Teufel - *Hand-Devil*

Trevirasamt, abwaschbar - *trevira velvet, surface washable*

SERIE	ART.-NO	PERIOD	PR.	INFO
255557	**7070/28**	1984-1990	1-2	28 cm
	255557	1991-1997	1-2	

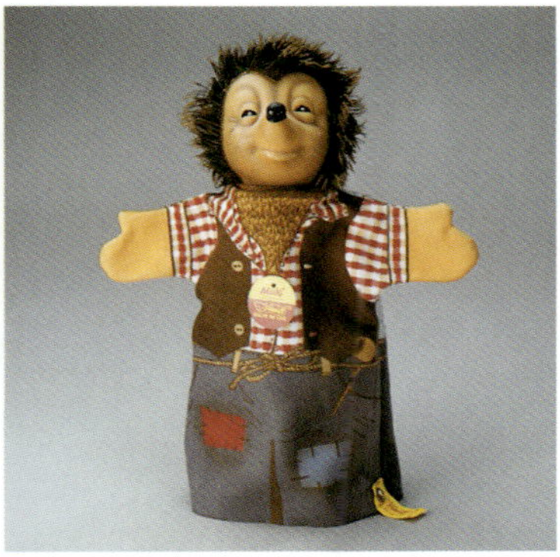

Hand-Mecki

Webpelz/Trevira-Samt, abwaschbar - *woven fur/trevira velvet, surface washable*

SERIE	ART.-NO	PERIOD	PR.	INFO
251979	**6490/28**	1985-1988	2	28 cm

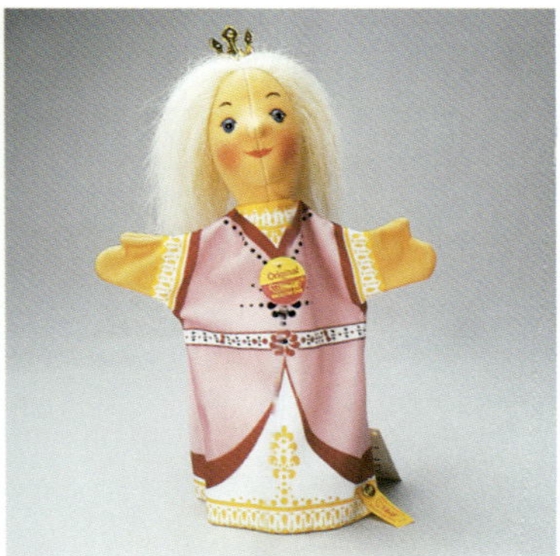

Hand-Prinzessin - *Hand-Princess*

Trevirasamt, blonde Haare, abwaschbar - *trevira velvet, blond hair, surface washable*

SERIE	ART.-NO	PERIOD	PR.	INFO
255403	**7062/28**	1986-1990	1-2	28 cm
	255403	1991-1994	1-2	

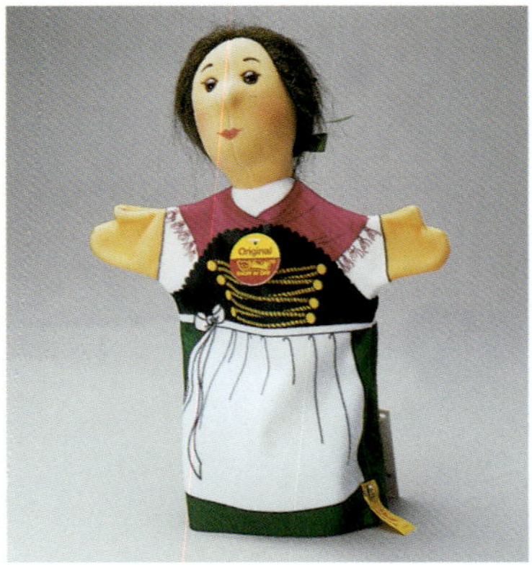

Handspiel-Gretel - *Hand-Puppet Gretel*

Trevirasamt, abwaschbar - *trevira velvet, surface washable*

EAN-NO.	PERIOD	PR.	INFO
255168	1994-1997	2	28 cm

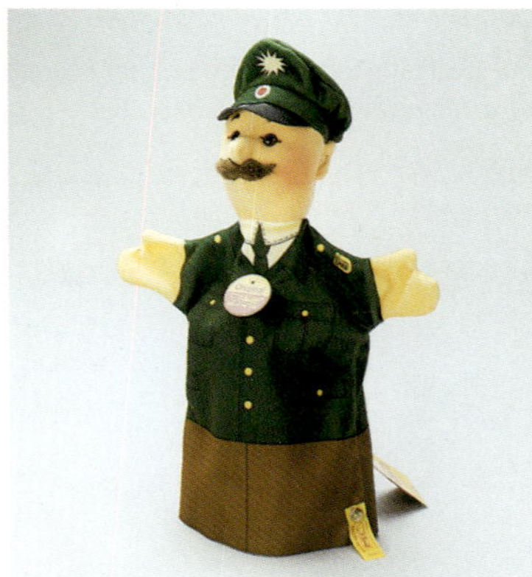

Handspiel-Polizist - *Hand-Puppet Policeman*

Trevirasamt, abwaschbar - *trevira velvet, surface washable*

EAN-NO.	PERIOD	PR.	INFO
255267	1994-1997	2	28 cm

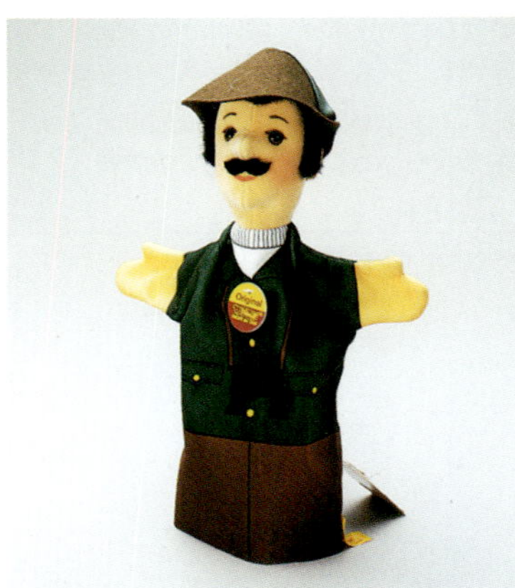

Handspiel-Jaeger - *Hand-Puppet Hunter*

Trevirasamt, abwaschbar - *trevira velvet, surface washable*

EAN-NO.	PERIOD	PR.	INFO
255335	1994-1997	2	28 cm

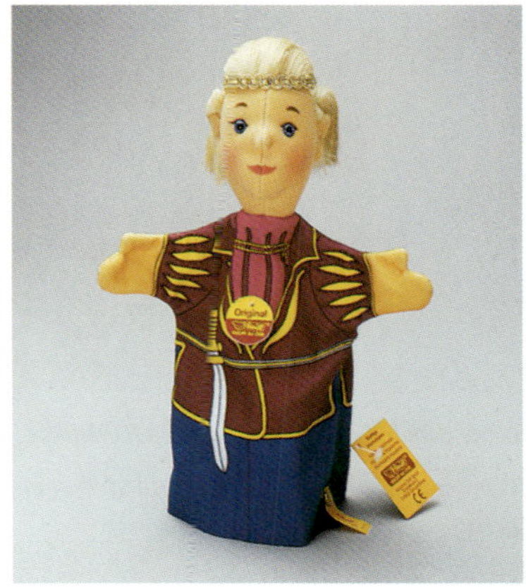

Handspiel-Prinz - *Hand-Puppet Prince*

Trevirasamt, abwaschbar - *trevira velvet, surface washable*

EAN-NO.	PERIOD	PR.	INFO
255434	1994-1997	2	28 cm

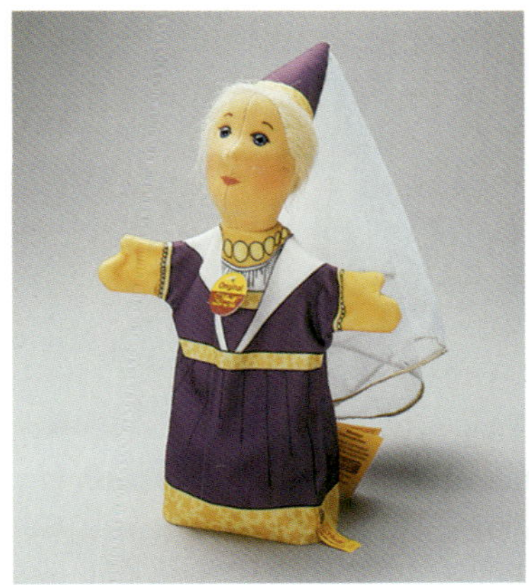

Handspiel-Fee - *Hand-Puppet Fairy*

Trevirasamt, abwaschbar - *trevira velvet, surface washable*

EAN-NO	PERIOD	PR.	INFO
255496	1994-1997	2	28 cm

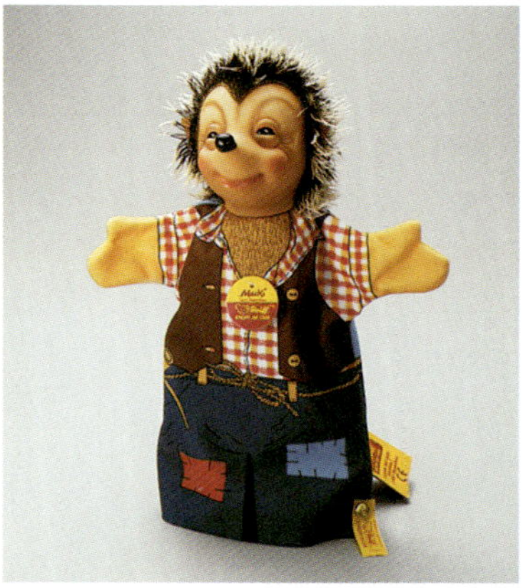

Handspiel-**Mecki** - *Hand-Puppet* ***Mecki***

Trevirasamt, abwaschbar - *trevira velvet, surface washable*

EAN-No.	Period	Pr.	Info
255984	1994-1997	2	28 cm

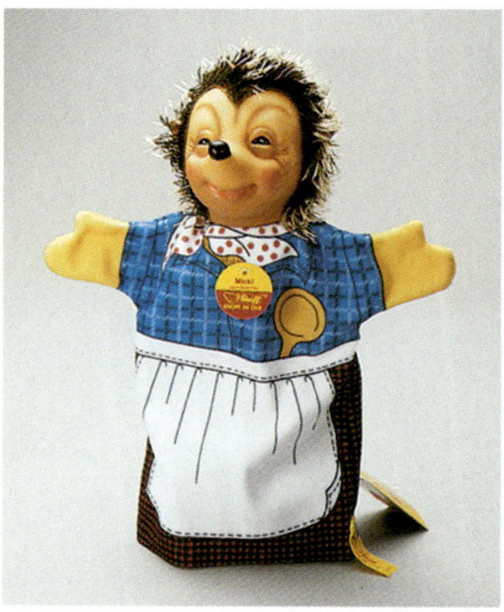

Handspiel-**Micki** - *Hand-Puppet* ***Micki***

Trevirasamt, abwaschbar - *trevira velvet, surface washable*

EAN-No.	Period	Pr.	Info
255991	1994-1997	2	28 cm

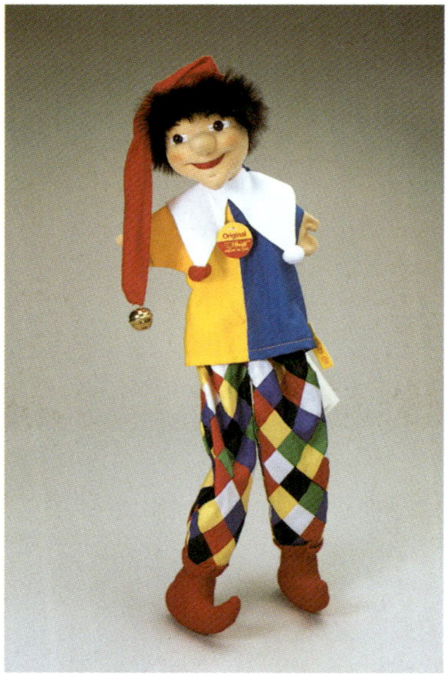

Hand-Kasper - *Punch glove puppet*

Kopf aus Polyestersamt, abwaschbar - *head: polyester velvet, surface washable*

EAN-No.	Period	Pr.	Info
255014	1998-1999	2	48 cm

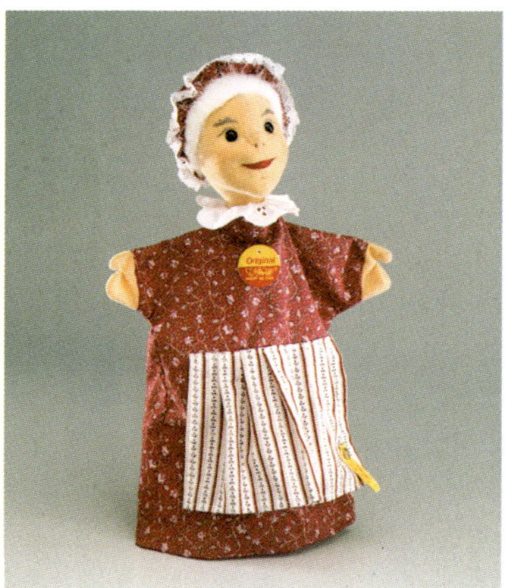

Hand-Grossmutter - *Grandma glove puppet*

Kopf aus Polyestersamt, abwaschbar - *head: polyester velvet, surface washable*

EAN-No.	Period	Pr.	Info
255113	1998-1999	2	32 cm

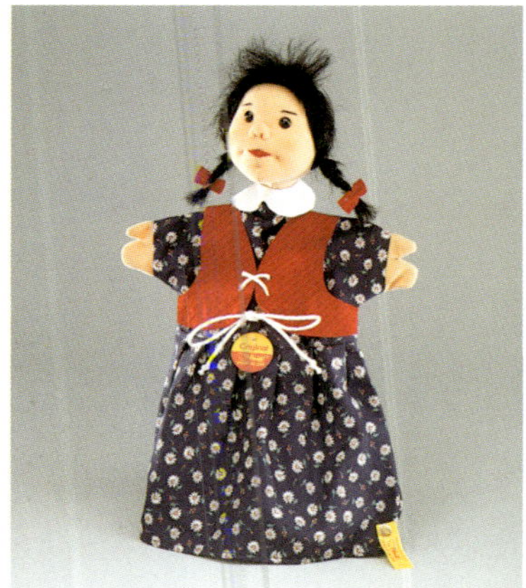

Hand-Gretl - *Gretl glove puppet*

Kopf aus Polyestersamt, abwaschbar - *head: polyester velvet, surface washable*

EAN-No.	Period	Pr.	Info
255175	1998-1999	2	32 cm

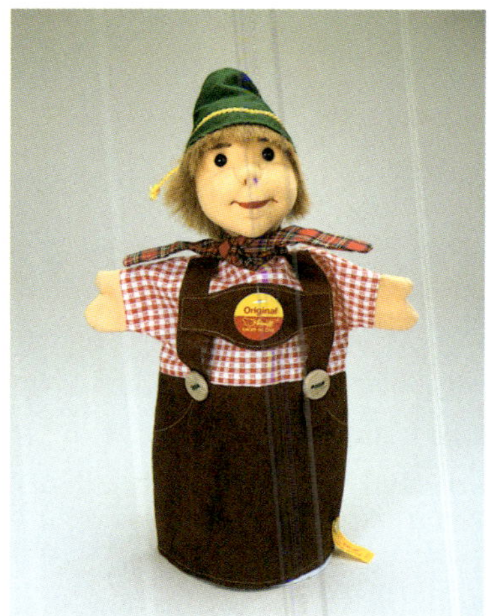

Hand-Seppl - *Seppl glove puppet*

Kopf aus Polyestersamt, abwaschbar - *head: polyester velvet, surface washable*

EAN-No.	Period	Pr.	Info
255212	1998-1999	2	32 cm

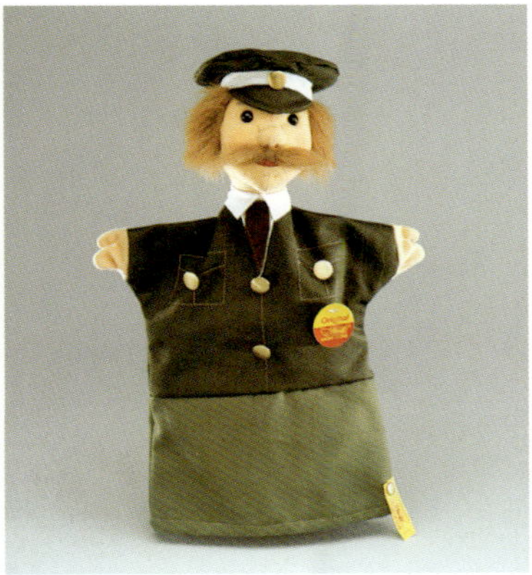

Hand-Polizist - *Policeman glove puppet*

Kopf aus Polyestersamt, abwaschbar - ***head:*** ***polyester velvet, surface washable***

EAN-No.	Period	Pr.	Info
255274	1998-1999	2	32 cm

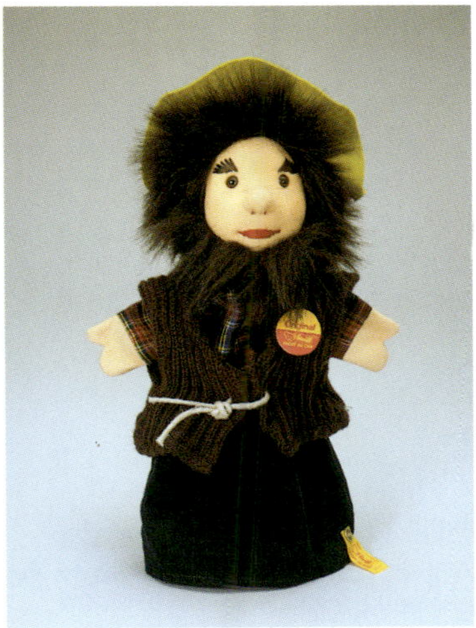

Hand-Raeuber - *Robber glove puppet*

Kopf aus Polyestersamt, abwaschbar - ***head:*** ***polyester velvet, surface washable***

EAN-No.	Period	Pr.	Info
255311	1998-1999	2	32 cm

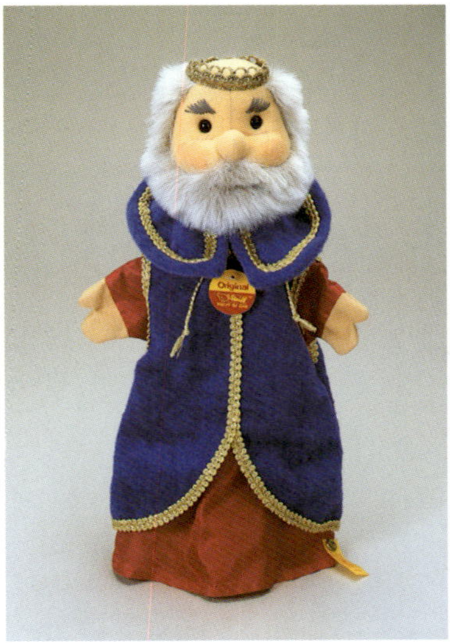

Hand-Koenig - *King glove puppet*

Kopf aus Polyestersamt, abwaschbar - ***head:*** ***polyester velvet, surface washable***

EAN-No.	Period	Pr.	Info
255366	1998-1999	2	32 cm

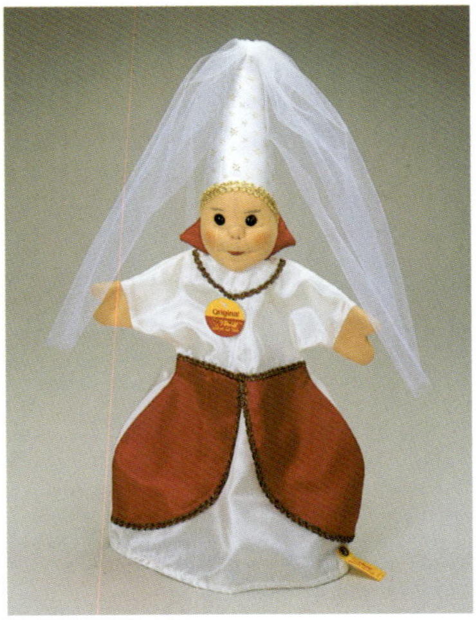

Hand-Prinzessin - *Princess glove puppet*

Kopf aus Polyestersamt, abwaschbar - ***head:*** ***polyester velvet, surface washable***

EAN-No.	Period	Pr.	Info
255410	1998-1999	2	32 cm

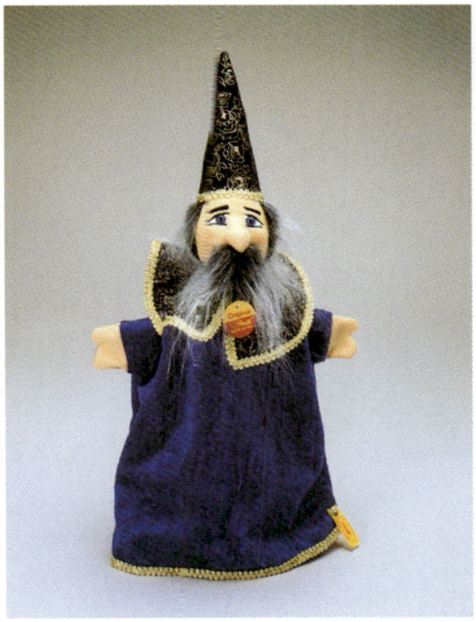

Hand-Zauberer - *Magician glove puppet*

Kopf aus Polyestersamt, abwaschbar - ***head:*** ***polyester velvet, surface washable***

EAN-No.	Period	Pr.	Info
255519	1998-1999	2	32 cm

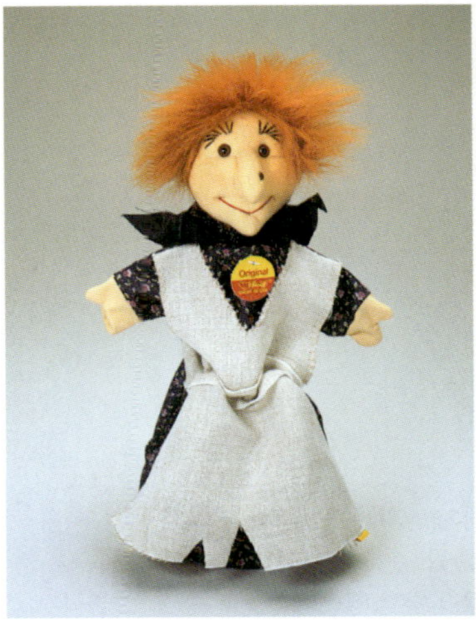

Hand-Hexe - *Witch glove puppet*

Kopf aus Polyestersamt, abwaschbar - ***head:*** ***polyester velvet, surface washable***

EAN-No.	Period	Pr.	Info
255465	1999-1999	2	32 cm

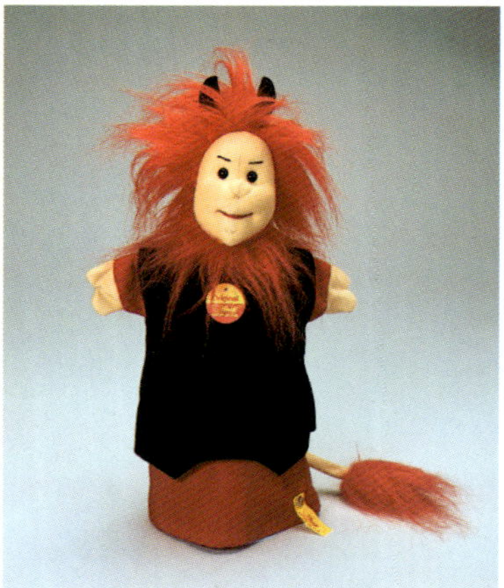

Hand-Teufel - *Devil glove puppet*

Kopf aus Polyestersamt, abwaschbar - *head: polyester velvet, surface washable*

EAN-No.	Period	Pr.	Info
255564	1999-1999	2	32 cm

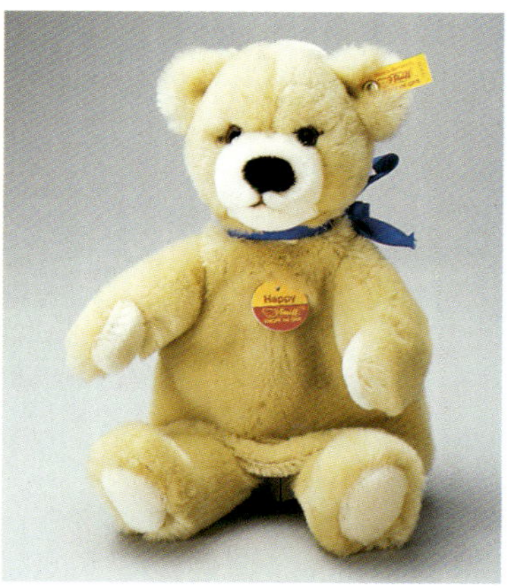

Happy Baer - ***Happy*** *Bear*

Webpelz, waschmaschinenfest - *woven fur, machine washable*

Serie	Art.-No	Period	Pr.	Info
253539	**6485/32**	1989-1990	2-3	32 cm
	253539	1991-1997	2-3	

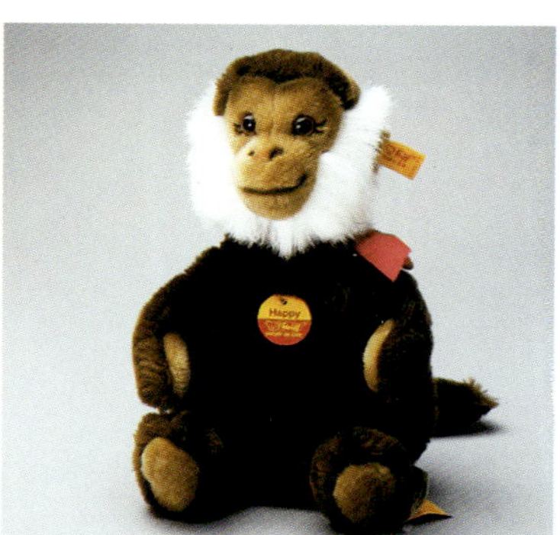

Happy Meerkatze - ***Happy*** *Meerkat*

Webpelz, waschmaschinenfest - *woven fur, machine washable*

Serie	Art.-No	Period	Pr.	Info
253577	**6488/32**	1989-1990	2-3	32 cm

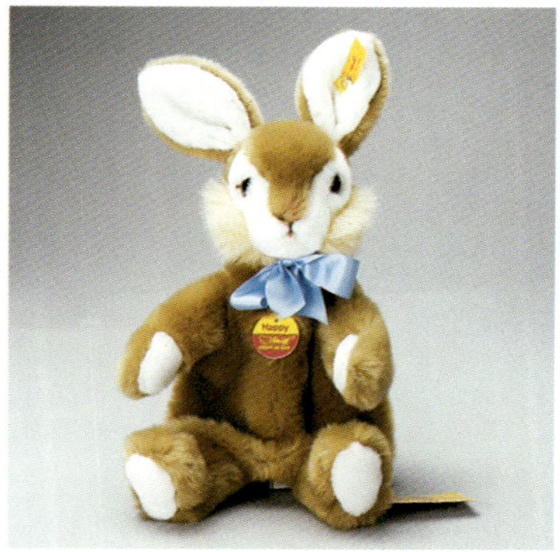

Happy Hase - ***Happy*** *Rabbit*

Webpelz, waschmaschinenfest - *woven fur, machine washable*

Serie	Art.-No	Period	Pr.	Info
253607	**6490/32**	1989-1990	2-3	32 cm
	253607	1991-1997	2-3	

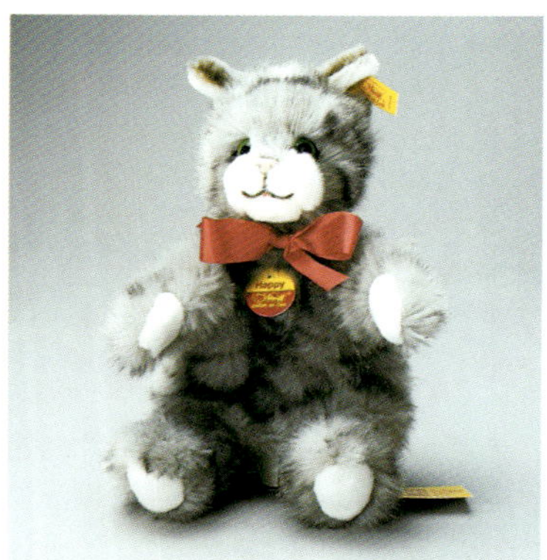

Happy Katze - ***Happy*** *Cat*

Webpelz, waschmaschinenfest - *woven fur, machine washable*

Serie	Art.-No	Period	Pr.	Info
253669	**6494/32**	1989-1990	2-3	32 cm
	253669	1991-1999	2-3	

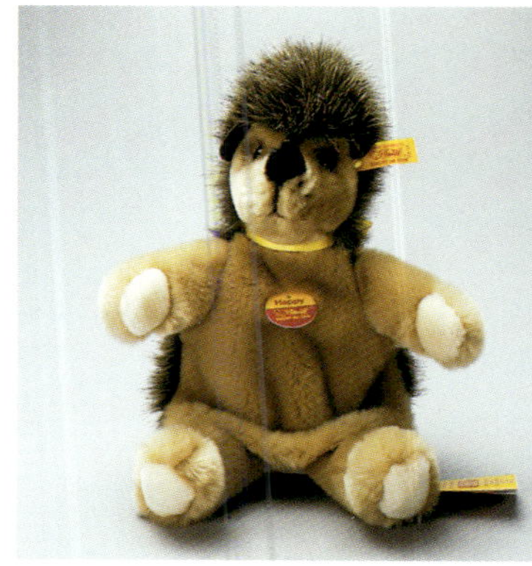

Happy Igel - ***Happy*** *Hedgehog*

Webpelz, waschmaschinenfest - *woven fur, machine washable*

Serie	Art.-No	Period	Pr.	Info
253713	**6496/32**	1989-1990	2-3	32 cm
	253713	1991-1999	2-3	

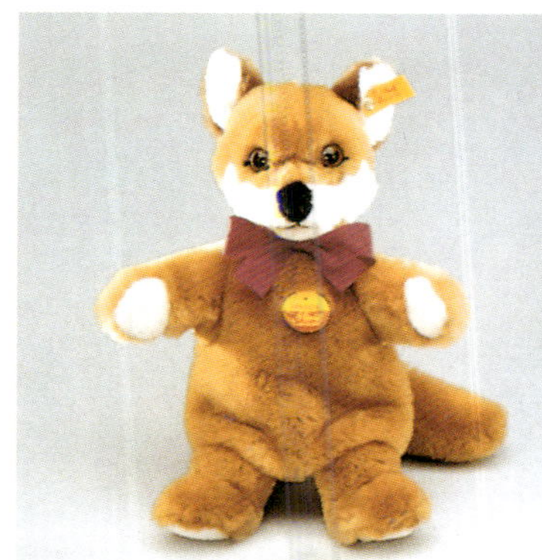

Happy Fuchs - ***Happy*** *Fox*

Webpelz, waschmaschinenfest - *woven fur, machine washable*

Serie	Art.-No	Period	Pr.	Info
253737	**6497/32**	1989-1990	2-3	32 cm
	253737	1991-1991	2-3	

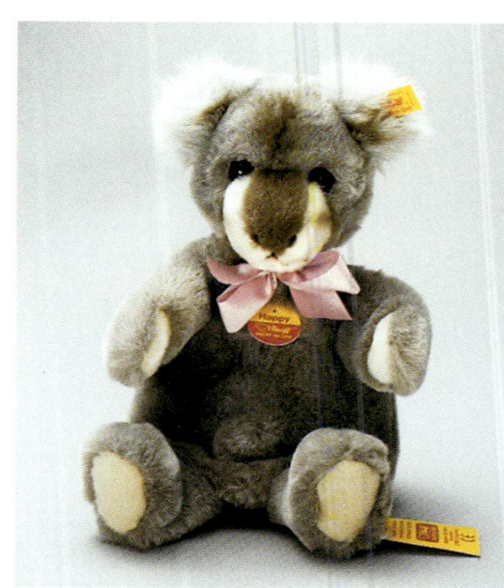

Happy Koala

Webpelz, waschmaschinenfest - *woven fur, machine washable*

EAN-No.	Period	Pr.	Info
253546	1992-1993	2-3	32 cm

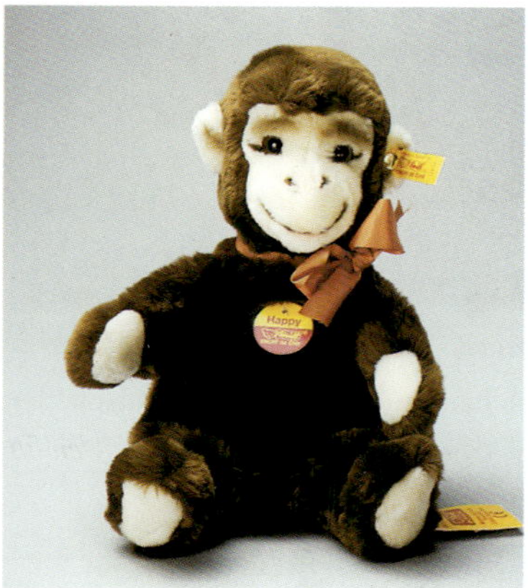

Happy Affe - ***Happy** Monkey*

Webpelz, waschmaschinenfest - *woven fur, machine washable*

EAN-No.	Period	Pr.	Info
253560	1992-1994	2-3	32 cm

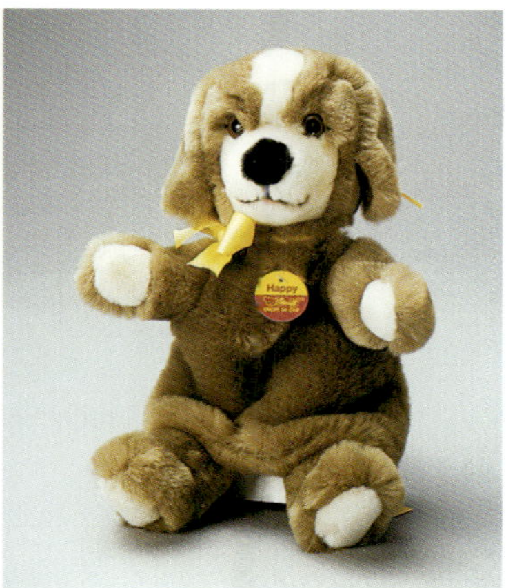

Happy Hund - ***Happy** Dog*

Webpelz, waschmaschinenfest - *woven fur, machine washable*

EAN-No.	Period	Pr.	Info
253638	1992-1994	2-3	32 cm

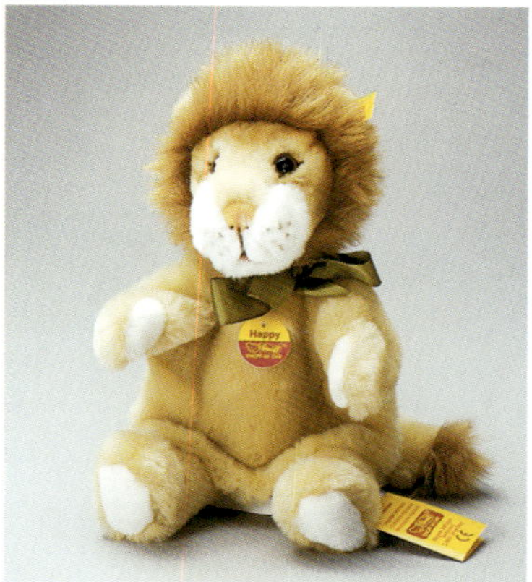

Happy Loewe - ***Happy** Lion*

Webpelz, waschmaschinenfest - *woven fur, machine washable*

EAN-No.	Period	Pr.	Info
253751	1992-1995	2-3	32 cm

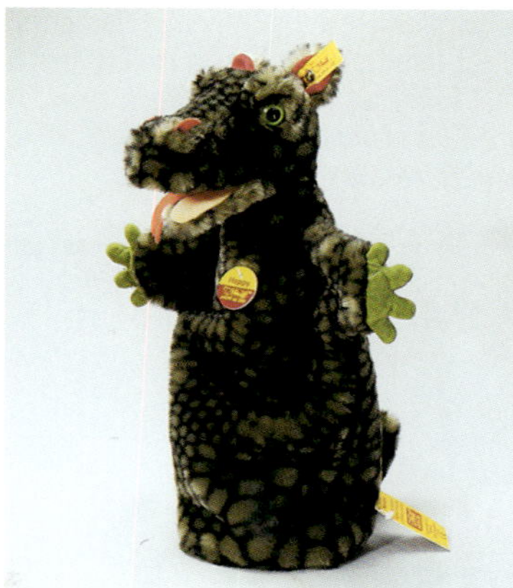

Happy Drache - ***Happy** Dragon*

Webpelz, abwaschbar - *woven fur, surface washable*

EAN-No.	Period	Pr.	Info
253836	1994-1997	2-3	28 cm

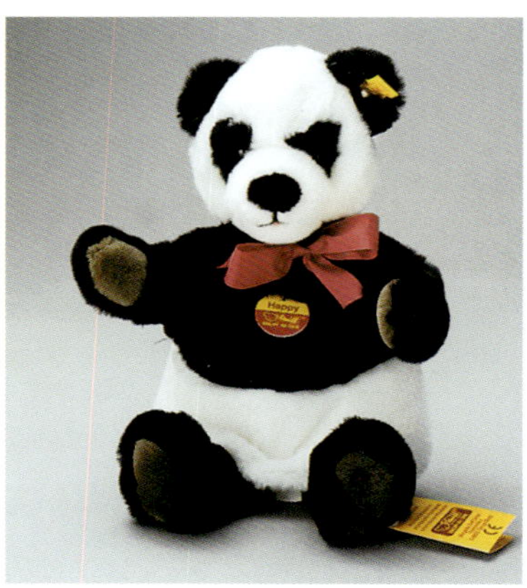

Happy Panda

Webpelz, waschmaschinenfest - *woven fur, machine washable*

EAN-No.	Period	Pr.	Info
253522	1995-1997	2-3	32 cm

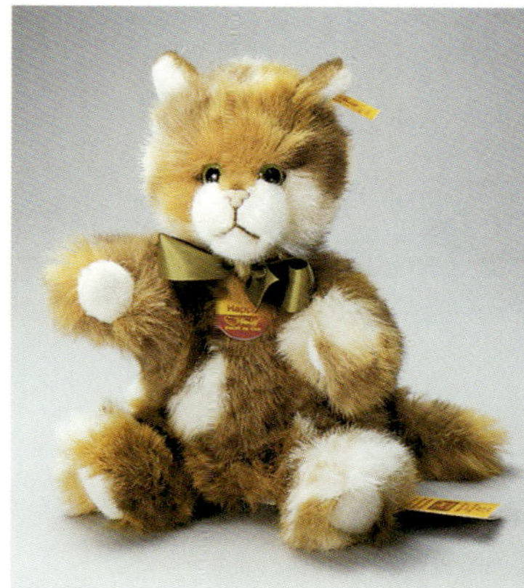

Happy Katze - ***Happy** Cat*

Webpelz, waschmaschinenfest - *woven fur, machine washable*

EAN-No.	Period	Pr.	Info
253676	1995-1997	2-3	32 cm

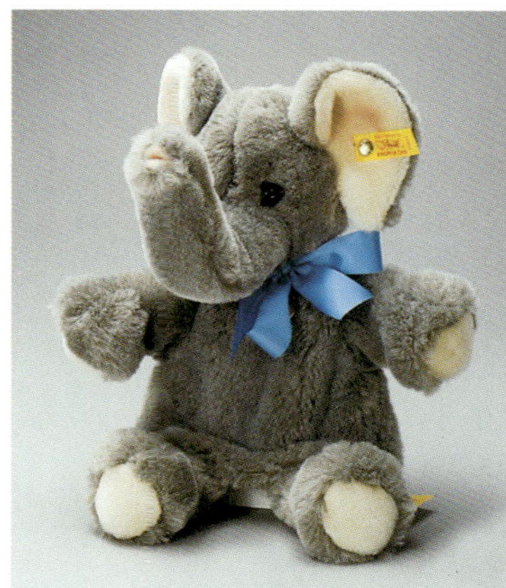

Happy Elefant - ***Happy** Elephant*

Webpelz, waschmaschinenfest - *woven fur, machine washable*

EAN-No.	Period	Pr.	Info
253867	1995-1997	2-3	32 cm

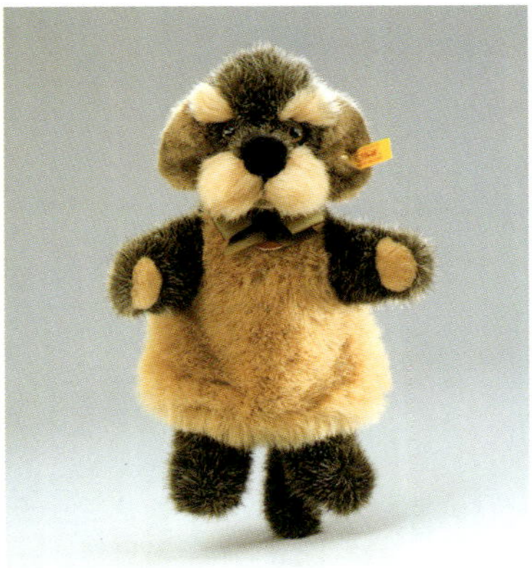

Happy Hund - ***Happy** Dog*

Webpelz, waschmaschinenfest - *woven fur, machine washable*

EAN-No.	Period	Pr.	Info
253645	1997-1999	2-3	32 cm

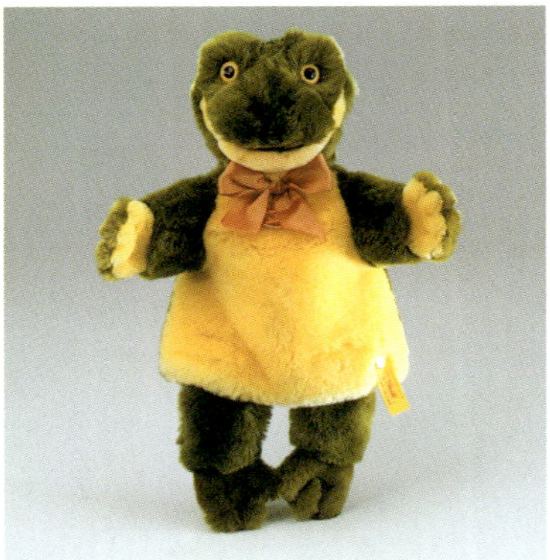

Happy Frosch - ***Happy** Frog*

Webpelz, waschmaschinenfest - *woven fur, machine washable*

EAN-No.	Period	Pr.	Info
253782	1997-1999	2-3	32 cm

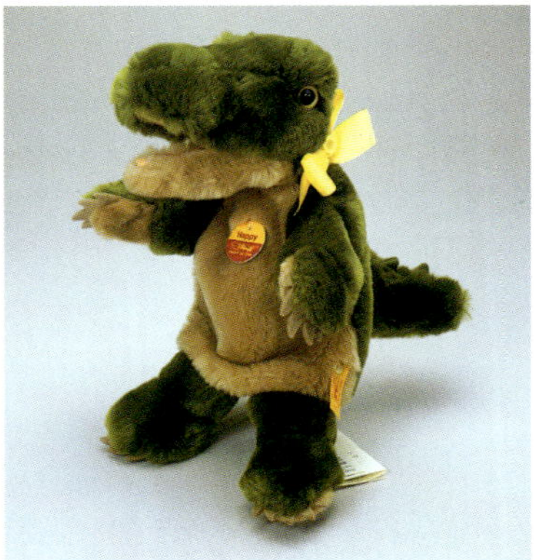

Happy Krokodil - ***Happy** Crocodile*

Webpelz, waschmaschinenfest - *woven fur, machine washable*

EAN-No.	Period	Pr.	Info
253805	1997-1999	2-3	32 cm

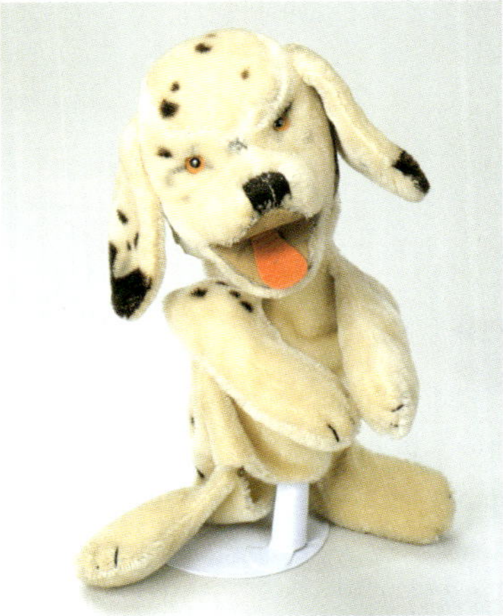

Mimic Dally Dalmatiner - ***Mimic Dally** Dalmation*

Mohairpluesch, weiss, schwarze Flecken, 5-Finger-Handspieltier, bewegt Pfoten, Kopf & Maul - *mohair, white with black spots, 5-finger hand puppet which moves its paws, head & muzzle*

Serie	Art.-No	Period	Pr.	Info
79a 15	**0328**	1958-1958	4	28 cm
866 150	**0328,00**	1959-1959	4-5	

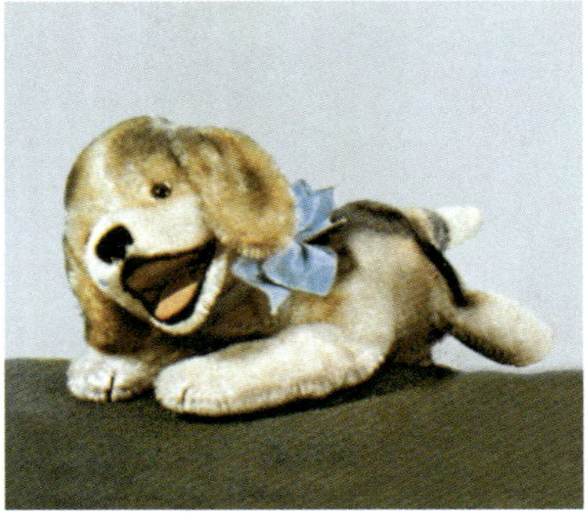

Mimic Biggie Beagle

Mohairpluesch, 5-Finger-Handspieltier, bewegt Pfoten, Kopf & Maul - *mohair, 5-finger hand puppet which moves its paws, head & muzzle*

Serie	Art.-No	Period	Pr.	Info
79a 23	**0328**	1958-1958	4-5	28 cm
866 230	**0328,00**	1959-1959	4	

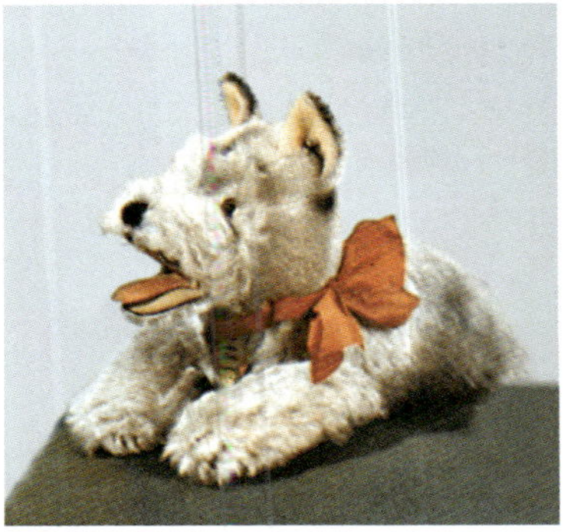

Mimic Tessie Schnauzer

Mohairpluesch, 5-Finger-Handspieltier, bewegt Pfoten, Kopf & Maul - *mohair, 5-finger hand puppet which moves its paws, head and muzzle*

Serie	Art.-No	Period	Pr.	Info
79a 47	**0328**	1958-1958	4-5	17 cm
866 470	**0328,00**	1959-1959	4	

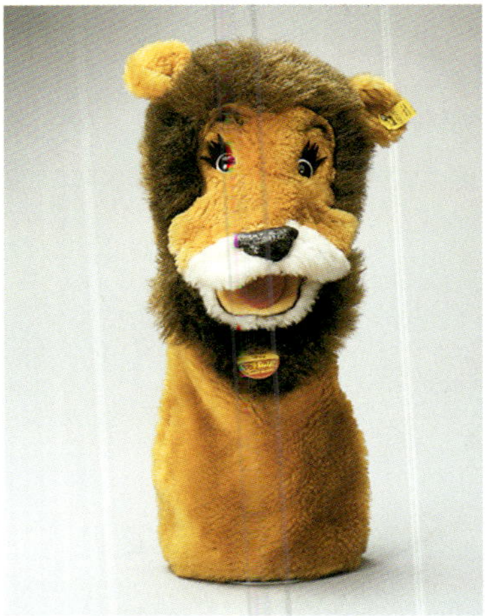

Mimic Loewe - *Mimic Lion*

Dralon, bewegliche Schnauze - *dralon, movable muzzle*

Serie	Art.-No	Period	Pr.	Info
	6481/35	1973-1977	3	35 cm
	6481/50	1972-1975	3	50 cm

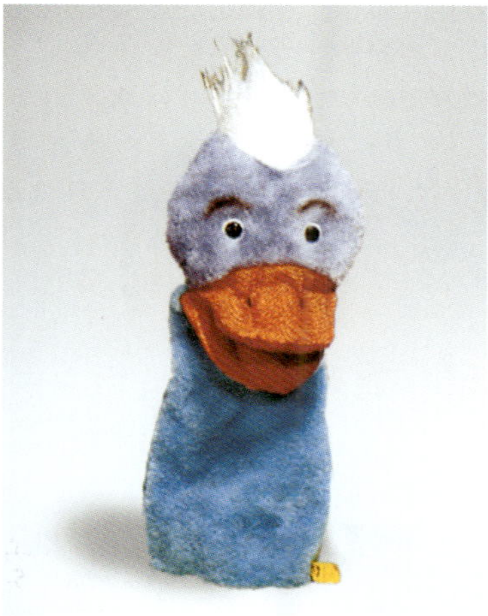

Mimic Ente ab 1975 Piccy - *Mimic Duck from 1975 Piccy*

Dralon, 50 cm weiss, 35 cm bunt, bewegliche Schnauze - *dralon, 50 cm white, 35 cm multi-colored, movable muzzle*

SERIE	ART.-NO	PERIOD	PR.	INFO
	6482/35	1973-1977	3	35 cm
	6482/50	1972-1975	3	50 cm

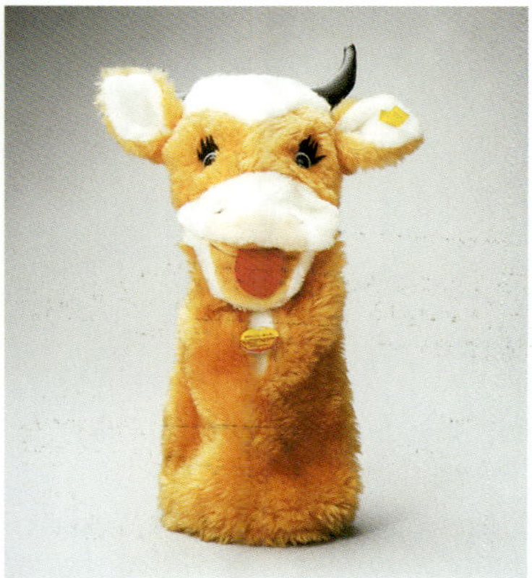

Mimic Kuh - *Mimic Cow*

Dralon, bewegliche Schnauze - *dralon, movable muzzle*

SERIE	ART.-NO	PERIOD	PR.	INFO
	6483/35	1973-1977	3	35 cm
	6483/50	1972-1975	3	50 cm

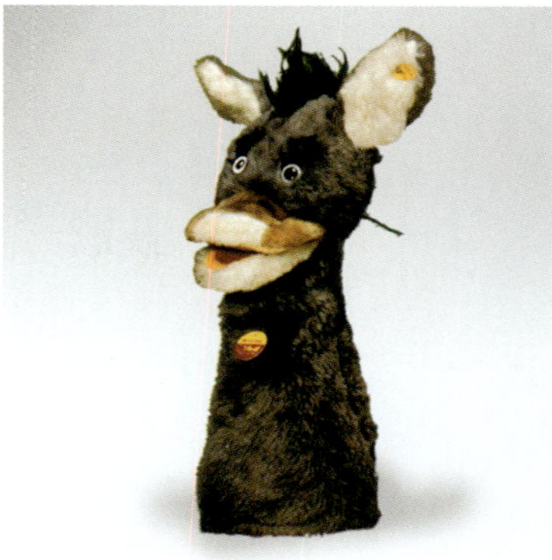

Mimic Esel - *Mimic Donkey*

Dralon, bewegliche Schnauze - *dralon, movable muzzle*

SERIE	ART.-NO	PERIOD	PR.	INFO
	6485/35	1973-1977	3	35 cm
	6485/50	1972-1975	3	50 cm

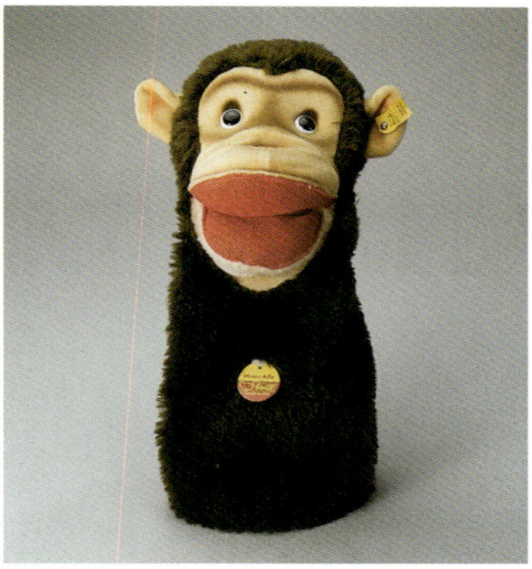

Mimic Affe - *Mimic Monkey*

Dralon, bewegliche Schnauze - *dralon, movable muzzle*

SERIE	ART.-NO	PERIOD	PR.	INFO
	6480/35	1973-1977	3	35 cm

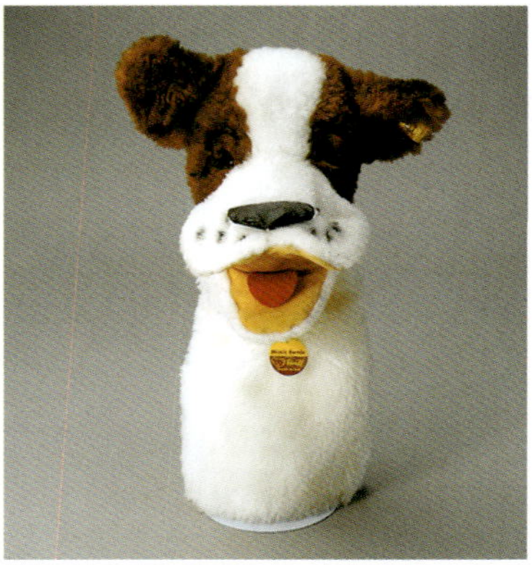

Mimic Bernie

Dralon, bewegliche Schnauze - *dralon, movable muzzle*

SERIE	ART.-NO	PERIOD	PR.	INFO
	6486/35	1973-1977	3	35 cm

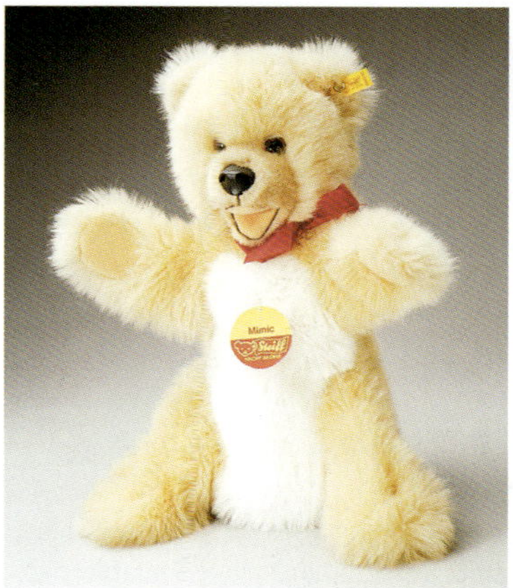

Mimic Baer - ***Mimic** Bear*

Webpelz, Maul beweglich, abwaschbar - *woven fur, movable snout, surface washable*

SERIE	ART.-NO	PERIOD	PR.	INFO
250309	**3490/45**	1983-1987	3	45 cm

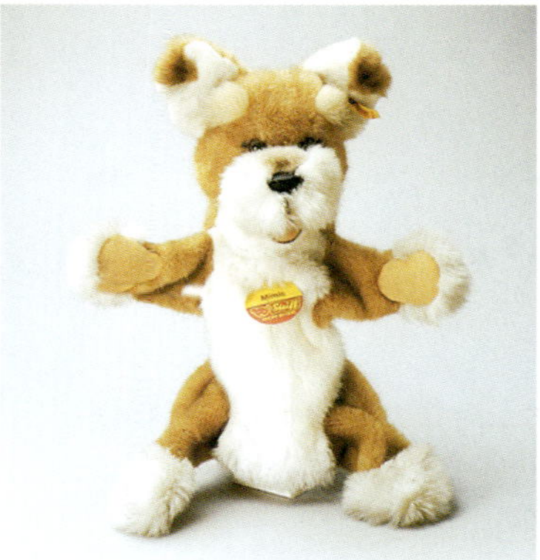

Mimic Hund - ***Mimic** Dog*

Webpelz, Maul beweglich, abwaschbar - *woven fur, movable snout, surface washable*

SERIE	ART.-NO	PERIOD	PR.	INFO
250354	**3492/45**	1983-1987	3	45 cm

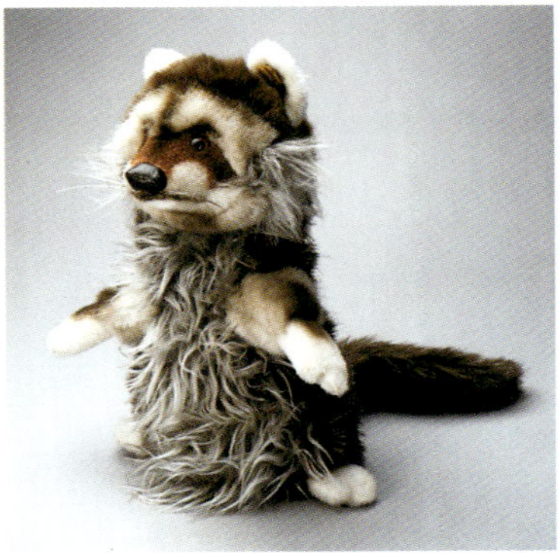

Jolly Raggy Waschbaer - ***Jolly Raggy*** *Raccoon*

Nerzimitation, ab 1978 Synthetik-Webpelz, supergrosses Handspiel-, Schlaftier oder Pyjama-Tasche, kuschelig weich, abwaschbar - *imitation mink, from 1978 synthetic woven fur, extra large hand puppet & sleeping animal - or pyjama pouch, very soft & cuddly, surface washable*

SERIE	ART.-NO	PERIOD	PR.	INFO
	3477/50	1973-1982	3	50 cm

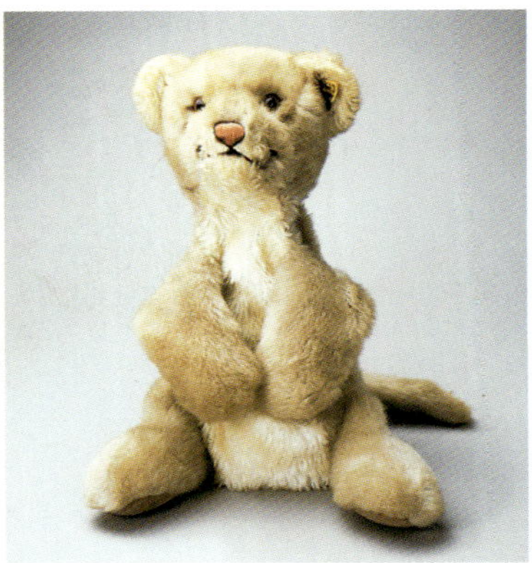

Jolly Puma

Nerz-Imitation, ab 1978 Synth.-Webpelz - *imitation mink, from 1978 synthetic woven fur*

SERIE	ART.-NO	PERIOD	PR.	INFO
	3478/50	1973-1981	3	50 cm

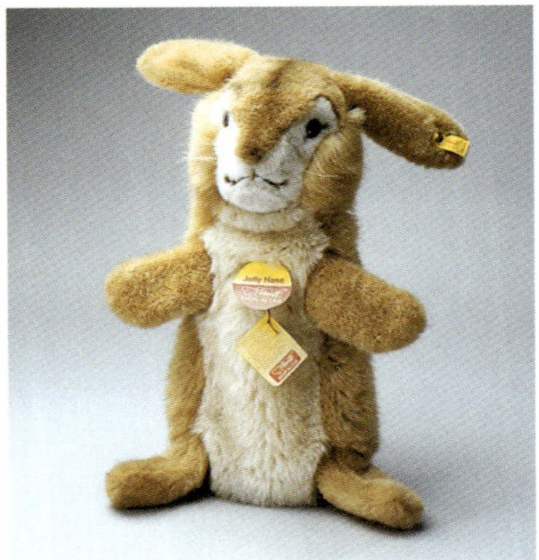

Jolly Hase - *Jolly Rabbit*

Pelz-Imitation, 40 cm, ab 1978 Synth.-Webpelz - *imitation fur, 40 cm, from 1978 synthetic woven fur*

SERIE	ART.-NO	PERIOD	PR.	INFO
250101	**3480/40**	1973-1986	3	grau - *grey*
250156	**3481/40**	1973-1986	3	braun - *brown*

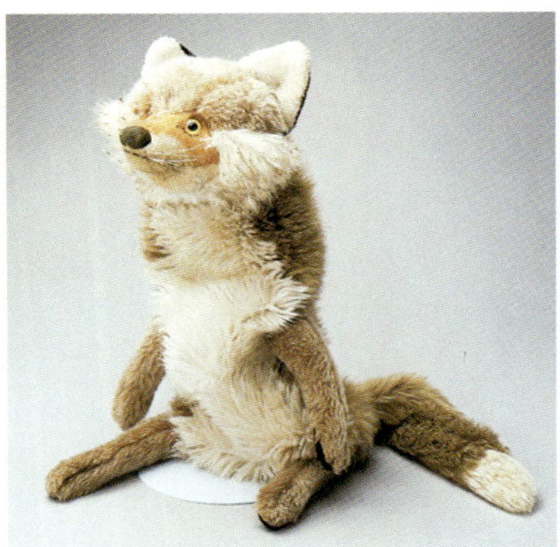

Jolly Fuchs - *Jolly Fox*

Pelz-Imitation, ab 1978 Synth.-Webpelz - *imitation fur, from 1978 synthetic woven fur*

SERIE	ART.-NO	PERIOD	PR.	INFO
	3482/50	1973-1978	3	50 cm

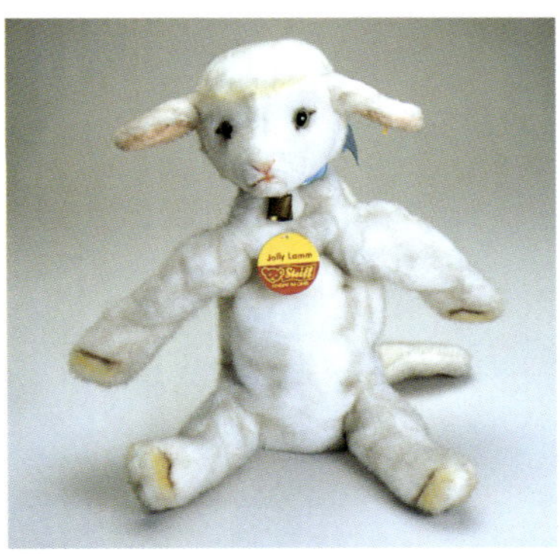

Jolly Lamm - *Jolly Lamb*

Pelz-Imitation, weiss - *imitation fur, white*

SERIE	ART.-NO	PERIOD	PR.	INFO
	3485/40	1973-1977	3	40 cm

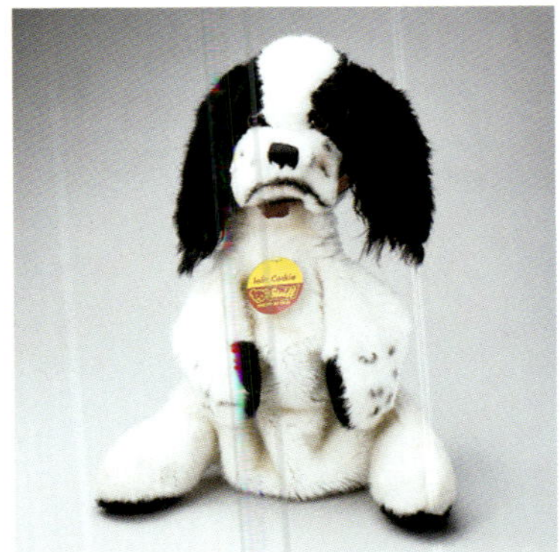

Jolly Cockie

Dralon-Pelz, ab 1975 Pelz-Imitation - *dralon fur, from 1975 imitation fur*

SERIE	ART.-NO	PERIOD	PR.	INFO
	3486/50	1973-1976	3	50 cm

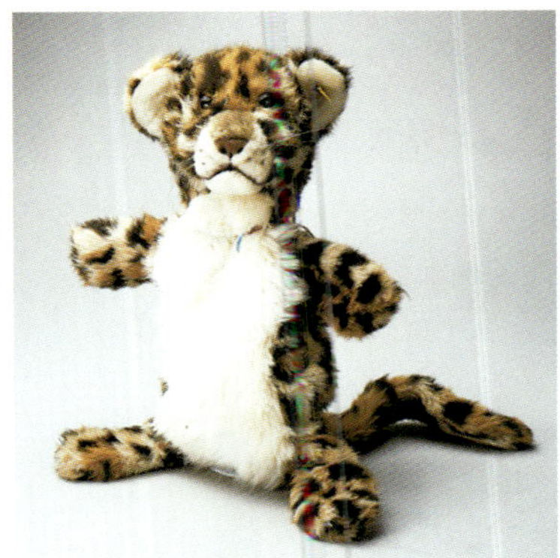

Jolly Taky Jungleopard - ***Jolly Taky*** *Leopard Cub*

Wirkpluesch, ab 1978 Synth.-Wirkpelz - *knitted plush, from 1978 synthetic knitted fur*

SERIE	ART.-NO	PERIOD	PR.	INFO
	3475/40	1977-1982	3	40 cm

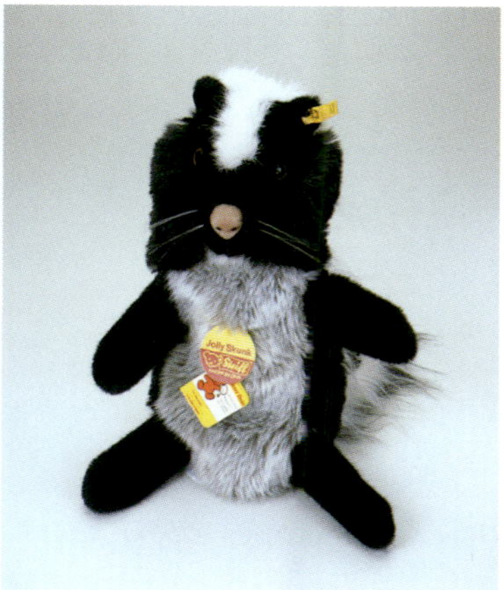

Jolly Skunk

Pelzimitation, ab 1978 Synthetik-Webpelz, grosses Handspiel-, Schlaftier oder Pyjama-Tasche, kuschelig weich, vollwaschbar - *imitation fur, from 1978 synthetic woven fur, large hand puppet & sleeping animal or pyjama pouch, very soft & cuddly, fully washable*

SERIE	ART.-NO	PERIOD	PR.	INFO
	3476/40	1977-1983	3	40 cm

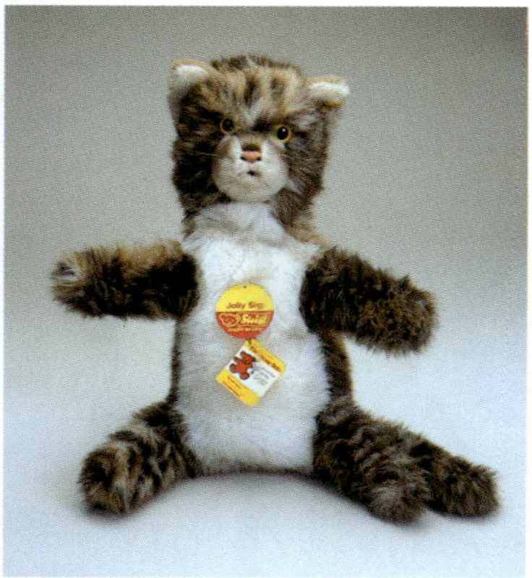

Jolly Sigi Katze - ***Jolly Sigi*** *Cat*

Wirkpluesch, ab 1978 Synth.-Wirkpelz - *knitted plush, from 1978 synthetic knitted fur*

SERIE	ART.-NO	PERIOD	PR.	INFO
	3483/40	1977-1981	3	40 cm

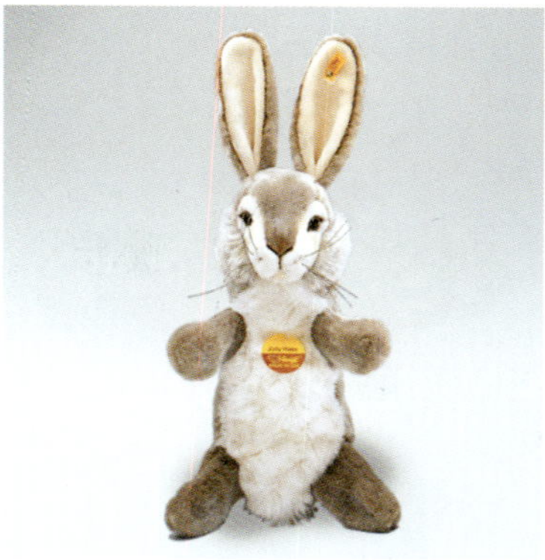

Jolly Hase - ***Jolly*** *Rabbit*

Webpelz, Kopf formgeschaeumt - *woven fur, head is stuffed with pre-formed foam*

SERIE	ART.-NO	PERIOD	PR.	INFO
254505	**7010/45**	1988-1990	2	45 cm

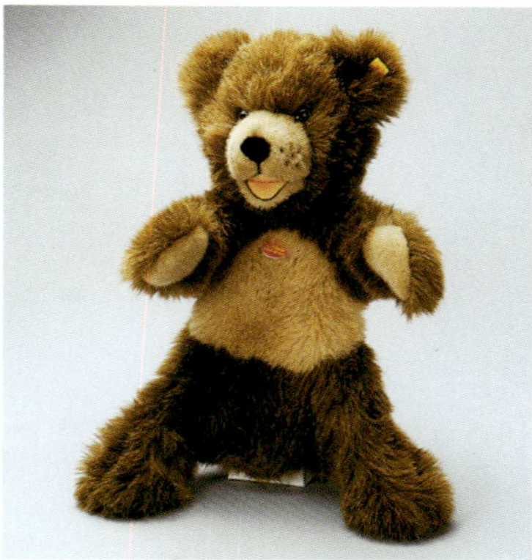

Jolly Baer - ***Jolly*** *Bear*

Webpelz - *woven fur*

EAN-NO.	PERIOD	PR.	INFO
254024	1994-1995	3	45 cm

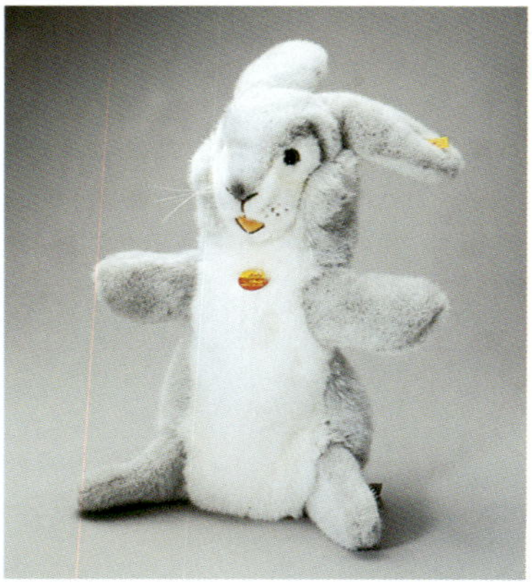

Jolly Hase - ***Jolly*** *Rabbit*

Webpelz - *woven fur*

EAN-NO.	PERIOD	PR.	INFO
254055	1994-1995	2	45 cm

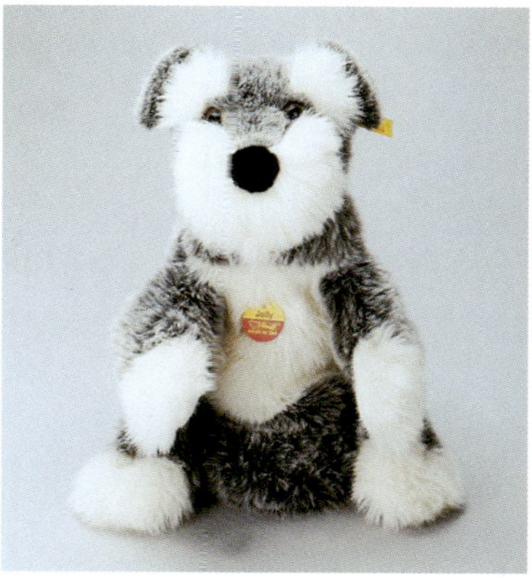

Jolly Hund - ***Jolly*** *Dog*

Webpelz - *woven fur*

EAN-NO.	PERIOD	PR.	INFO
254086	1994-1995	2	45 cm

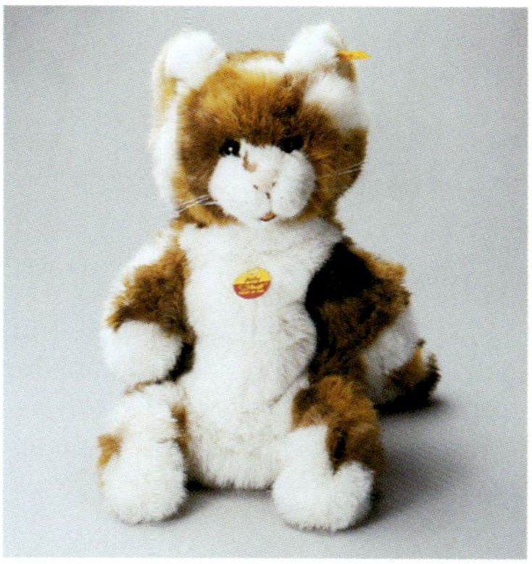

Jolly Katze - ***Jolly*** *Cat*

Webpelz - *woven fur*

EAN-NO.	PERIOD	PR.	INFO
254123	1994-1995	2	45 cm

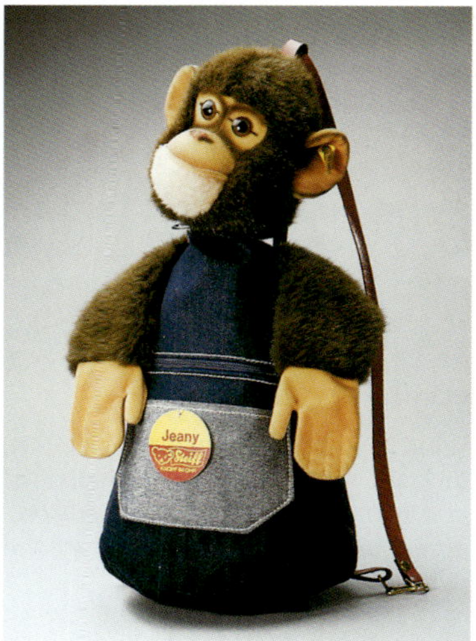

Jeany Schimpanse - ***Jeany*** *Chimpanzee*

Webpelz/Jeansstoff, formgeschaeumt, Rucksack oder Handspieltier, vollwaschbar - *woven fur/jeans fabric, stuffed with preformed foam, either a rucksack or a hand puppet, fully washable*

SERIE	ART.-NO	PERIOD	PR.	INFO
	6350/40	1978-1981	3	40 cm

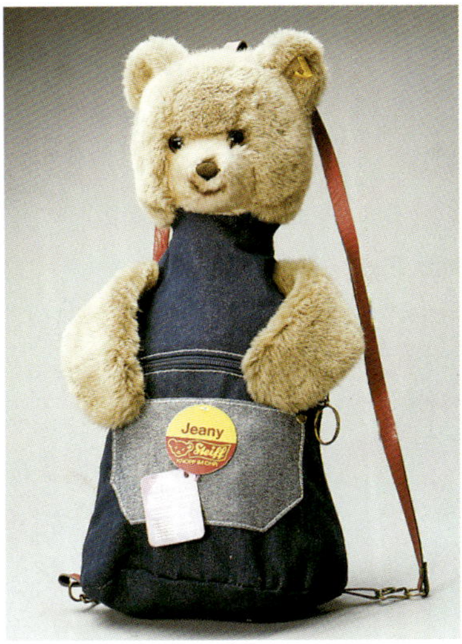

Jeany Baer - ***Jeany*** *Bear*

Webpelz/Jeansstoff, formgeschaeumt, Rucksack oder Handspieltier, vollwaschbar - *woven fur/jeans fabric, stuffed with preformed foam, either a rucksack or a hand puppet, fully washable*

SERIE	ART.-NO	PERIOD	PR.	INFO
	6351/40	1978-1981	3	40 cm

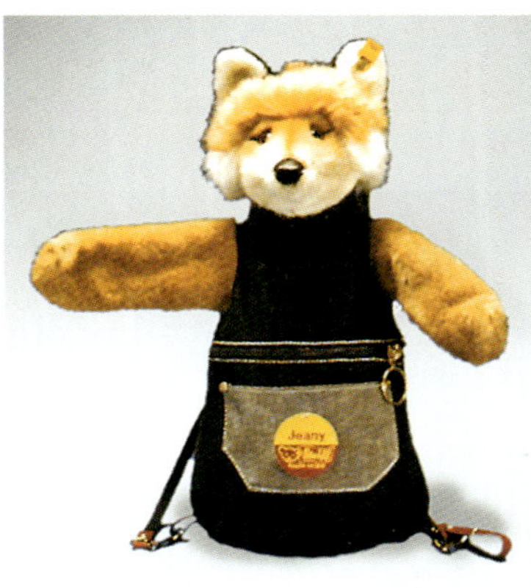

Jeany Fuchs - ***Jeany*** *Fox*

Webpelz/Jeansstoff, formgeschaeumt, Rucksack oder Handspieltier, vollwaschbar - *woven fur/jeans fabric, stuffed with preformed foam, either a rucksack or a hand puppet, fully washable*

SERIE	ART.-NO	PERIOD	PR.	INFO
	6352/40	1978-1980	3	40 cm

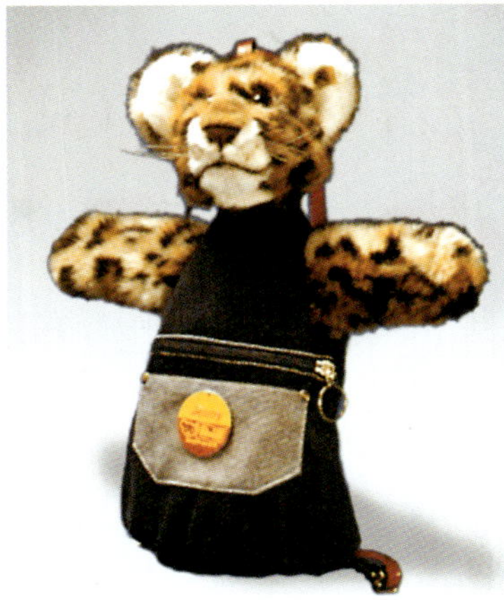

Jeany Leopard

Webpelz/Jeansstoff, formgeschaeumt, Rucksack oder Handspieltier, vollwaschbar - *woven fur/jeans fabric, stuffed with preformed foam, either a rucksack or a hand puppet, fully washable*

SERIE	ART.-NO	PERIOD	PR.	INFO
	6353/40	1978-1980	3	40 cm

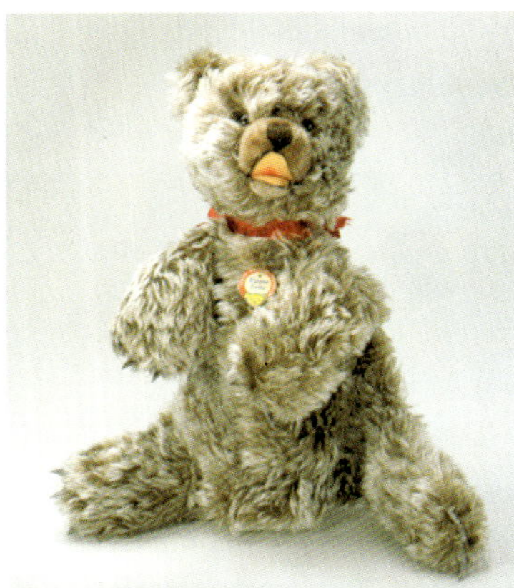

Zipper Zotty

Mohair, braun gespitzt, Koerper als Tasche mit Reissverschluss, zugl. Handspieltier - *mohair, brown tipped, body can be used as a bag with a zipper or also as a hand puppet*

SERIE	ART.-NO	PERIOD	PR.	INFO
121	**0330,00**	1964-1964	5-6	30 cm
588	**0330,00**	1966-1966	5-6	

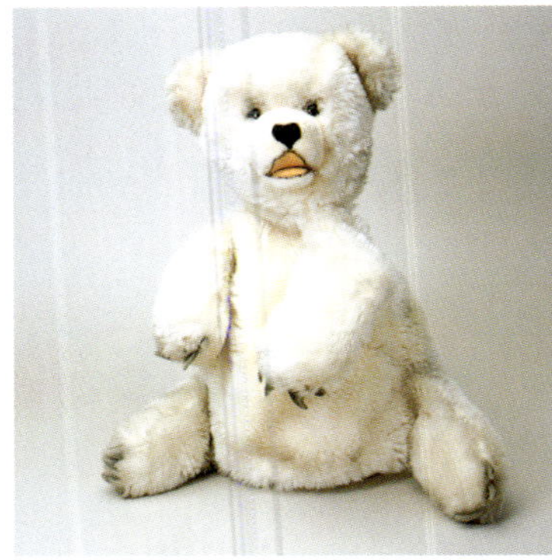

Zipper Nauty Eisbaer - ***Zipper Nauty*** *Polar Bear*

Dralon, Pfoten mit Krallen, weiss - *dralon, paws have claws, white*

SERIE	ART.-NO	PERIOD	PR.	INFO
130	**0630,00**	1964-1964	5	30 cm
589	**0630,00**	1965-1966	5	

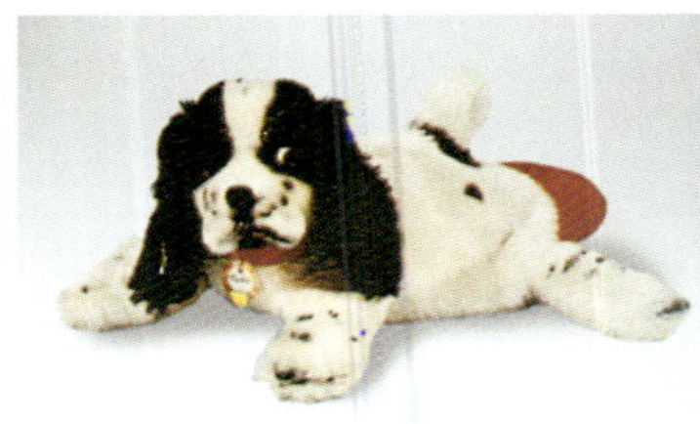

Zipper **Cockie**

Mohair, weiss/schwarz gefleckt - *mohair, white with black spots*

SERIE	ART.-NO	PERIOD	PR.	INFO
290	**0330,06**	1964-1964	5	30 cm

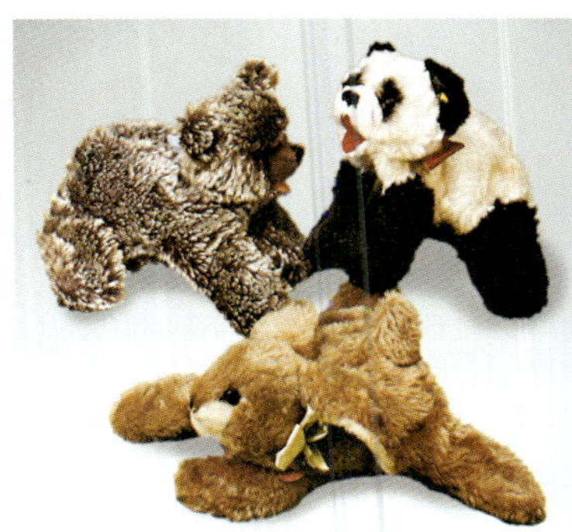

Zipper Tiere - *Zipper Animals*

Handspieltier oder Pyjama-Tasche, 30 cm, Dralon, mit Klettverschluss - *hand puppet or pyjama pouch, 30 cm, dralon, with Velcro seal*

SERIE	ART.-NO	PERIOD	PR.	INFO
	5910/30	1970-1976	3-4	Zotty
	5915/30	1970-1976	3-4	Panda
	5940/30	1970-1976	3-4	Hase - *Rabbit*

PUPPEN & FIGUREN

DOLLS & FIGURES

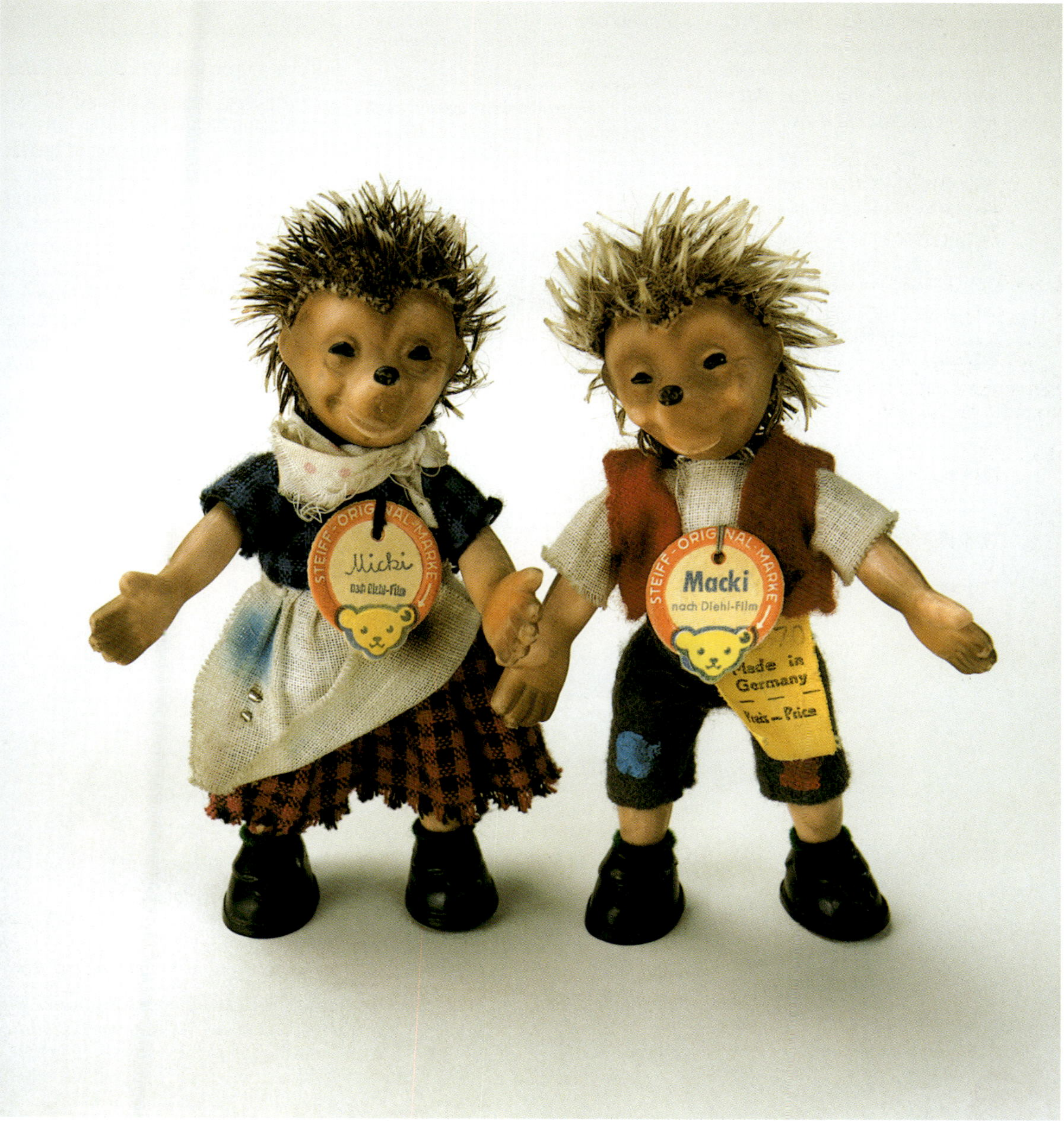

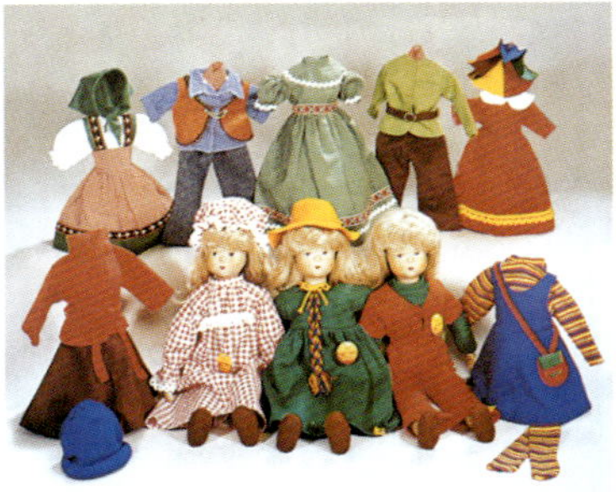

Ludenia Puppen & Bekleidung - *Ludenia dolls & clothing*

Hart-PVC, formgeschaeumt, 40 cm, Copyr. Ludenia, vollwaschbar, frisierbar, bekleidet, Kleidung kann beliebig fuer alle Ludenia Puppen verwendet werden - *Hard PVC, stuffed with pre-formed foam, 40 cm, Copyr. Ludenia, fully washable, hair can be combed, dressed, clothing is interchangeable for all Ludenia dolls*

SERIE	ART.-NO	PERIOD	PR.	INFO
	7900/40	1977-1978	3-4	**Steffi**
	7901/40	1977-1978	3-4	**Rosi**
	7902/40	1977-1978	3-4	**Susi**
	7910/40	1977-1978	1-2	Jeans Kombination - *jeans outfit*
	7911/40	1977-1978	1-2	Folklorekleid - *folkloric costume*
	7912/40	1977-1978	1-2	Kleid mit Blumenhut - *dress & flowered hat*
	7913/40	1977-1978	1-2	Maxi-Kombination - *maxi outfit*
	7914/40	1977-1978	1-2	Ringelpulli mit Traegerrock - *striped sweater & jumper dress*
	7915/40	1977-1978	1-2	Hosenanzug - *pants suit*
	7916/40	1977-1978	1-2	Dirndl Set

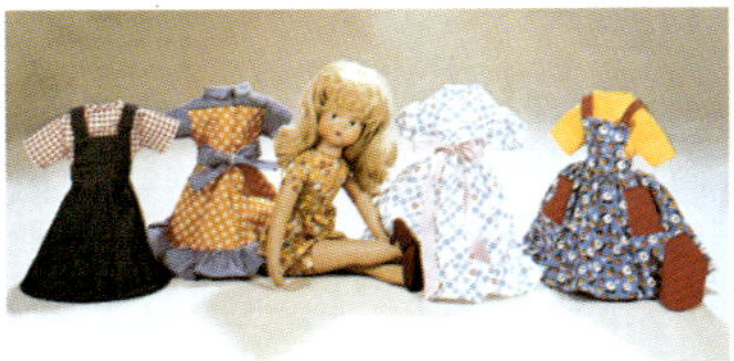

Ludenia Puppen & Bekleidung - *Ludenia dolls & clothing*

Beschreibung der Puppe wie oben, als Zubehoer wurde ein Schnittmusterbogen beigelegt - *see above for description of the doll, as an accessory, a cut-out paper pattern was included*

SERIE	ART.-NO	PERIOD	PR.	INFO
	7904/40	1978-1978	3-4	**Loni**
	7917/40	1978-1978	1-2	Jeans Rock Kombination - *jeans skirt outfit*
	7918/40	1978-1978	1-2	Latzrock Kombination - *pinafore outfit*
	7919/40	1978-1978	1-2	Rueschen Kleid - *ruffled dress*
	7920/40	1978-1978	1-2	Geburtstags-kleid - *birthday dress*

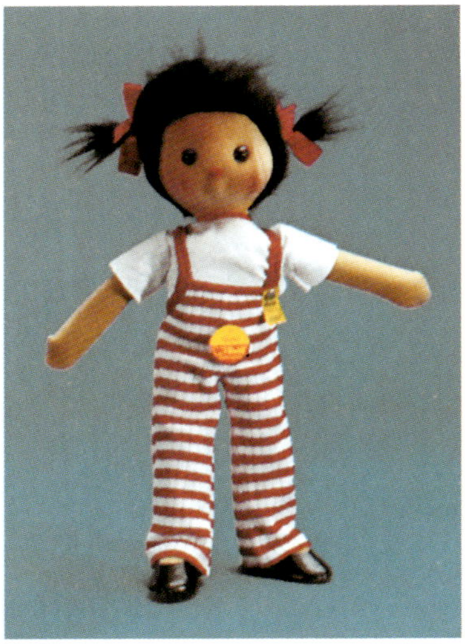

Schlenkerpuppe **Gabi** - *Floppy Doll **Gabi***

Synthetik-Haut, formgeschaeumt, ab 1978 Trevira-Samt, blau/rotes Kleid, rote Schuhe, ab 1973 rot/weiss gestreifte Latzhose, weisses Shirt, vollwaschbar - *synthetic skin, stuffed with pre-formed foam, from 1978 trevira velvet, blue/red dress, red shoes, from 1973 red/white striped bibbed trousers, white shirt, fully washable*

SERIE	ART.-NO	PERIOD	PR.	INFO
	7880/45	1972-1979	2-3	45 cm

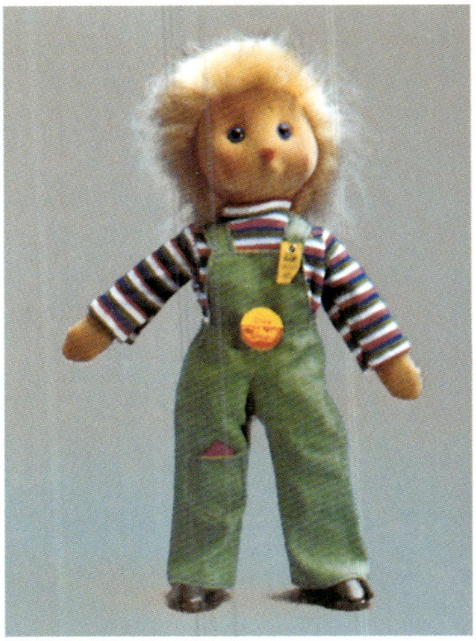

Schlenkerpuppe **Gitte** - *Floppy Doll **Gitte***

Synthetik-Haut, formgeschaeumt, ab 1978 Trevira-Samt, blond, rotes Kleid, schwarze Schuhe, ab 1973 Hosenanzug in tuerkis, rote Schuhe, blaukarierter Haenger, ab 1975 gruener Overall, bunter Ringelpullover, schwarze Schuhe, vollwaschbar - *synthetic skin, stuffed with pre-formed foam, from 1978 trevira velvet, blond, red dress, black shoes, from 1973 turquoise pants suit, red shoes, blue checked hanger, from 1975 green overall with multicolor striped sweater, black shoes, fully washable*

SERIE	ART.-NO	PERIOD	PR.	INFO
	7881/45	1972-1979	2-3	45 cm

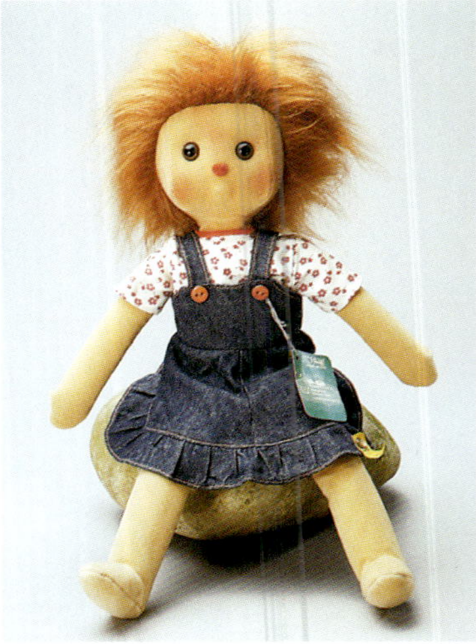

Schlenkerpuppe **Tina** - *Floppy Doll **Tina***

Synthetik-Haut, formgeschaeumt, ab 1978 Trevira-Samt, rote Haare, gruene Cord-Latzhose, Ringelpullover (variiert), 1979 Jeanskleid, weisse, kurzaermelige Bluse mit roten Blumen, vollwaschbar - *synthetic skin, stuffed with pre-formed foam, from 1978 trevira velvet, red hair, green corduroy bibbed trousers, striped sweater (varied), 1979 jeans dress, short sleeved white blouse with red flowers, fully washable*

SERIE	ART.-NO	PERIOD	PR.	INFO
	7882/45	1972-1979	2-3	45 cm

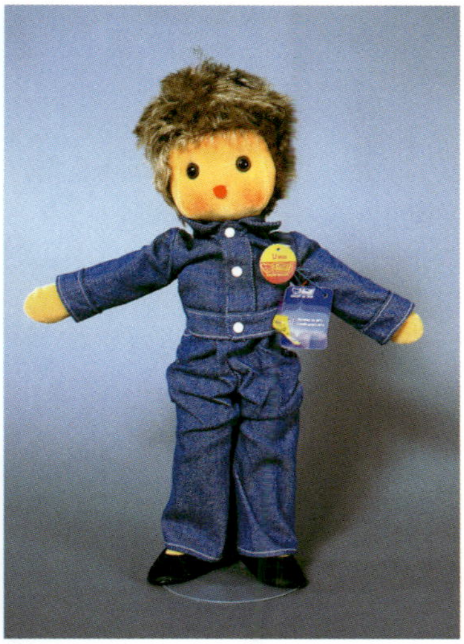

Schlenkerpuppe **Uwe** - *Floppy Doll* ***Uwe***

Synthetik-Haut, formgeschaeumt, ab 1978 Trevira-Samt, dunkelblauer Anzug, rot/weiss-kariertes Hemd, ab 1976 mittelblauer Freizeitanzug, vollwaschbar - *synthetic skin, stuffed with pre-formed foam, from 1978 trevira velvet, dark blue suit with a red & white checked shirt, from 1976 medium blue leisure outfit, fully washable*

SERIE	ART.-NO	PERIOD	PR.	INFO
	7883/45	1972-1979	2-3	45 cm

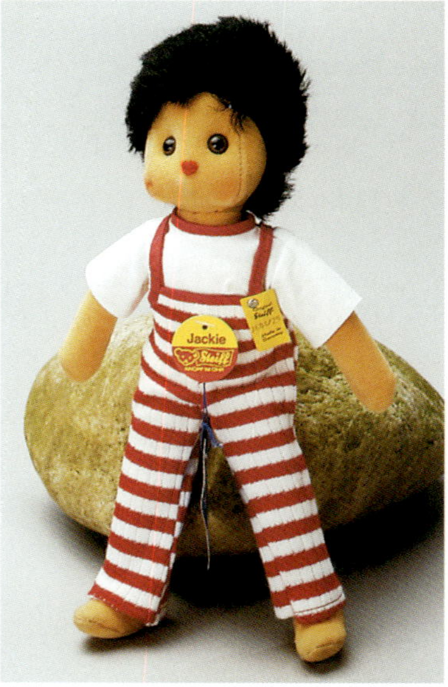

Schlenkerpuppe **Jackie** - *Floppy Doll* ***Jackie***

Synthetik-Haut, formgeschaeumt, ab 1978 Trevira-Samt, weisses Shirt, rot-weisse Hose, ab 1979 gruene Hose mit buntem Muster, vollwaschbar - *synthetic skin, stuffed with pre-formed foam, from 1978 trevira velvet, white shirt with red & white trousers, from 1979 green trousers with a bright pattern, fully washable*

SERIE	ART.-NO	PERIOD	PR.	INFO
	7884/28	1973-1981	2	28 cm

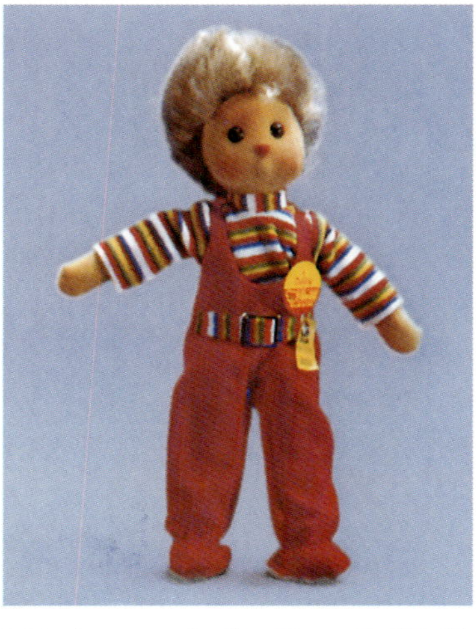

Schlenkerpuppe **Dolly** - *Floppy Doll* ***Dolly***

Synthetik-Haut, formgeschaeumt, ab 1978 Trevira-Samt, Schlafanzug rosa/weiss, ab 1979 rote Latzhose, gestreifter Pullover, vollwaschbar - *synthetic skin, stuffed with pre-formed foam, from 1978 trevira velvet, red/white pyjamas, from 1979 red bibbed trousers, striped sweater, fully washable*

SERIE	ART.-NO	PERIOD	PR.	INFO
	7885/28	1973-1981	2	28 cm

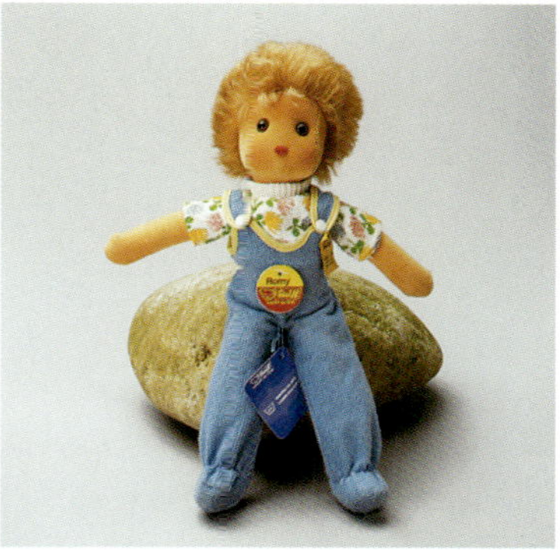

Schlenkerpuppe **Romy** - *Floppy Doll* ***Romy***

Synthetik-Haut, formgeschaeumt, ab 1978 Trevira-Samt, hellblauer Strampelanzug, ab 1979 bunt gemusterter Strampelanzug - *synthetic skin stuffed with pre-formed foam, from 1978 trevira velvet, light blue rompers, from 1979 brightly patterned rompers*

SERIE	ART.-NO	PERIOD	PR.	INFO
	7886/28	1973-1980	2	28 cm

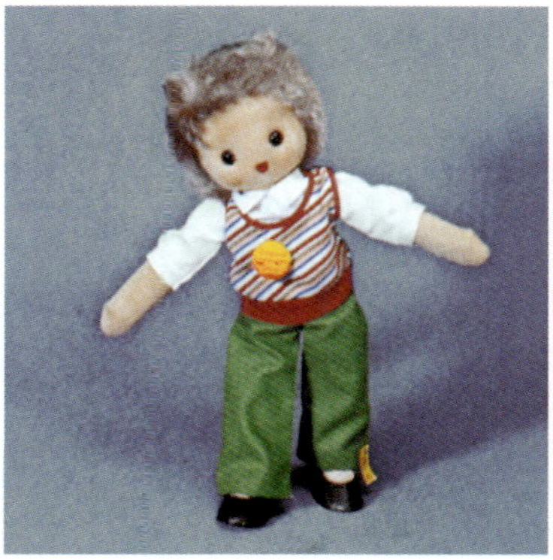

Schlenkerpuppe **Jim** - *Floppy Doll* ***Jim***

Trevirasamt, formgeschaeumt, vollwaschbar - *trevira velvet, stuffed with pre-formed foam, fully washable*

SERIE	ART.-NO	PERIOD	PR.	INFO
	7377/45	1975-1979	2-3	45 cm

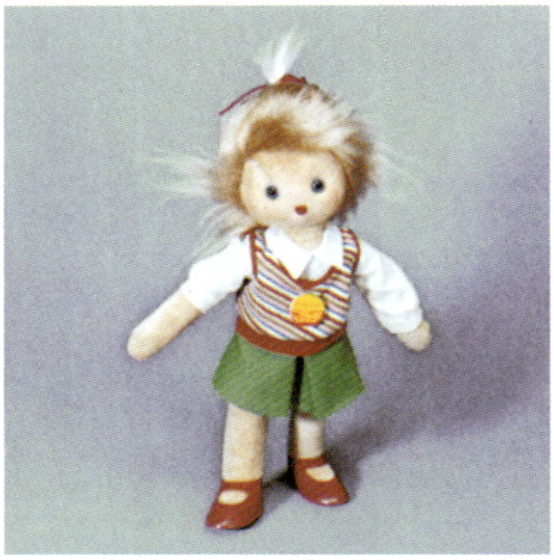

Schlenkerpuppe **Jenny** - *Floppy Doll* ***Jenny***

Trevirasamt, formgeschaeumt, vollwaschbar - *trevira velvet, stuffed with pre-formed foam, fully washable*

SERIE	ART.-NO	PERIOD	PR.	INFO
	7878/45	1975-1979	2-3	45 cm

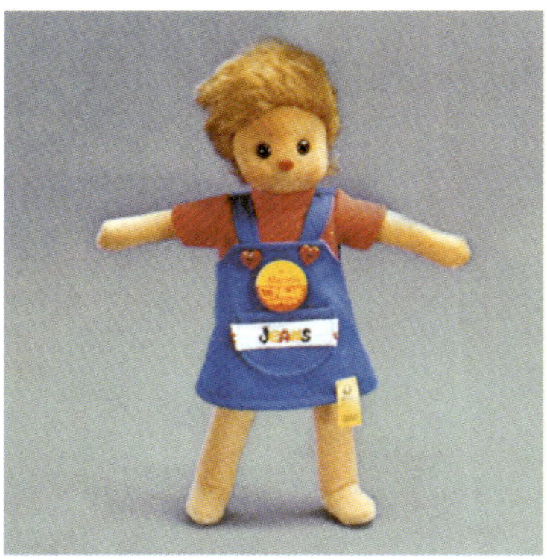

Schlenkerpuppe **Marion** - *Floppy Doll* ***Marion***

Trevirasamt, formgeschaeumt, waschbar - *trevira velvet, stuffed with pre-formed foam, washable*

SERIE	ART.-NO	PERIOD	PR.	INFO
	7871/28	1979-1983	2	28 cm

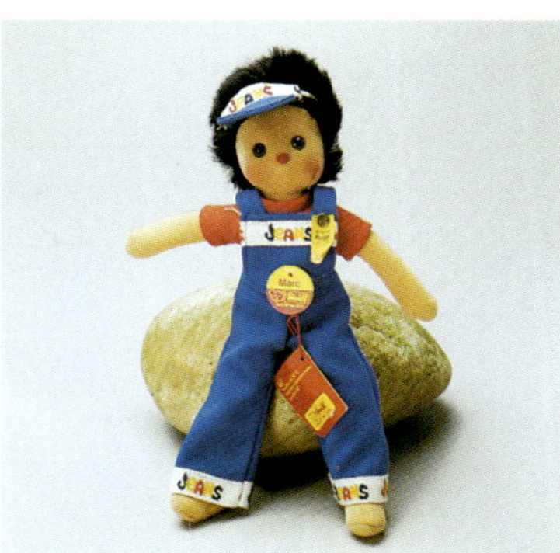

Schlenkerpuppe **Marc** - *Floppy Doll* ***Marc***

Trevirasamt, formgeschaeumt, waschbar - *trevira velvet, stuffed with pre-formed foam, washable*

SERIE	ART.-NO	PERIOD	PR.	INFO
	7872/28	1979-1983	2	28 cm

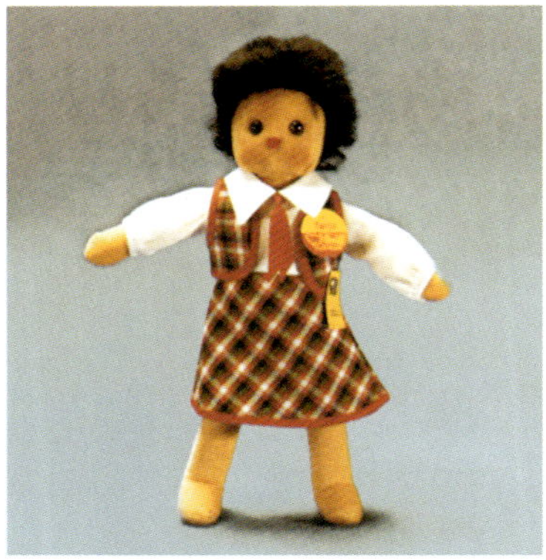

Schlenkerpuppe **Tanja** - *Floppy Doll* ***Tanja***

Trevirasamt, formgeschaeumt, waschbar - *trevira velvet, stuffed with pre-formed foam, washable*

SERIE	ART.-NO	PERIOD	PR.	INFO
	7873/28	1979-1983	2	28 cm

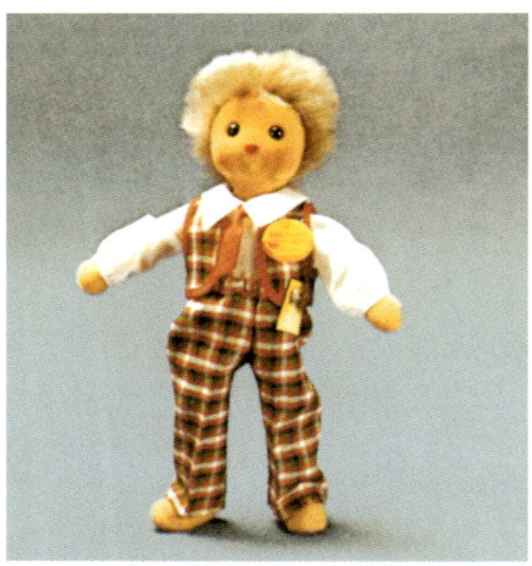

Schlenkerpuppe **Michael** - *Floppy Doll* ***Michael***

Trevirasamt, formgeschaeumt, waschbar - *trevira velvet, stuffed with pre-formed foam, washable*

SERIE	ART.-NO	PERIOD	PR.	INFO
	7874/28	1979-1982	2	28 cm

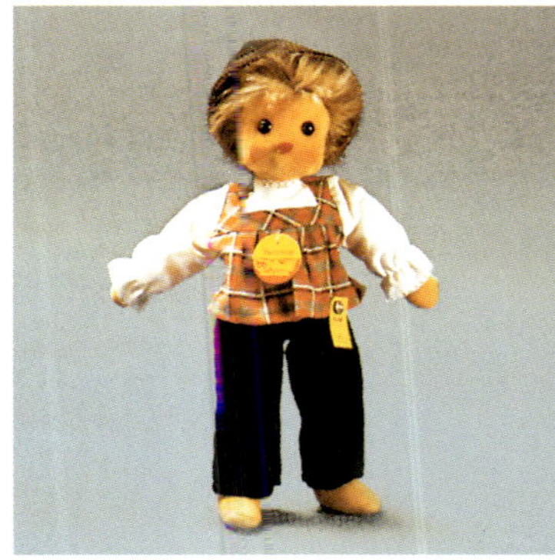

Schlenkerpuppe **Yvonne** - *Floppy Doll* ***Yvonne***

Trevirasamt, formgeschaeumt, waschbar - *trevira velvet, stuffed with pre-formed foam, washable*

SERIE	ART.-NO	PERIOD	PR.	INFO
	7875/28	1979-1982	2	28 cm

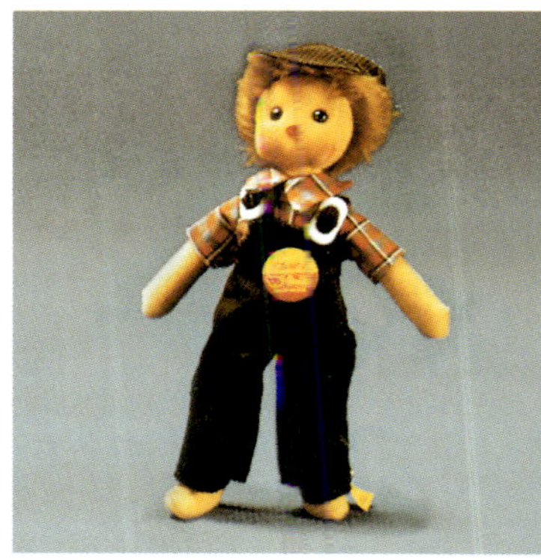

Schlenkerpuppe **Oliver** ab 1980 **Charly** - *Floppy Doll* ***Oliver*** *from 1980* ***Charly***

Trevirasamt, formgeschaeumt, waschbar - *trevira velvet, stuffed with pre-formed foam, washable*

SERIE	ART.-NO	PERIOD	PR.	INFO
	7876/28	1979-1981	2	28 cm

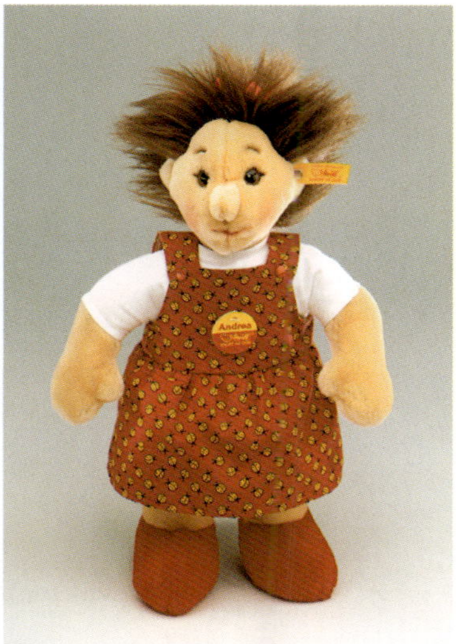

Andrea Schlenkerpuppe - *Dangling Doll **Andrea***

Webpelz, waschmaschinenfest - *woven fur, machine-washable*

EAN-No.	Period	Pr.	Info
704017	1999-1999	2-3	32 cm

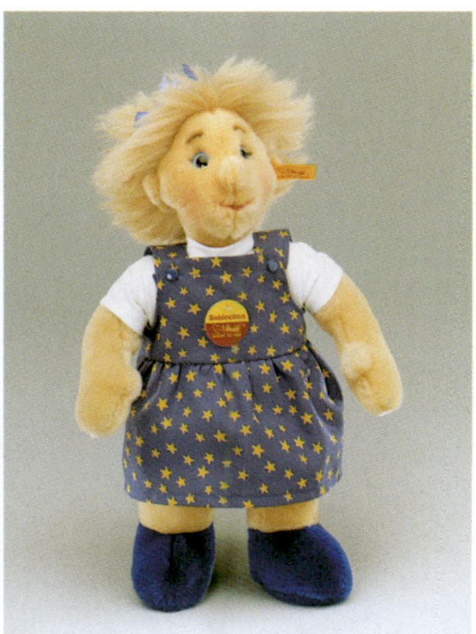

Babinchen Schlenkerpuppe - *Dangling Doll **Babinchen***

Webpelz, waschmaschinenfest - *woven fur, machine-washable*

EAN-No.	Period	Pr.	Info
704024	1999-1999	2-3	32 cm

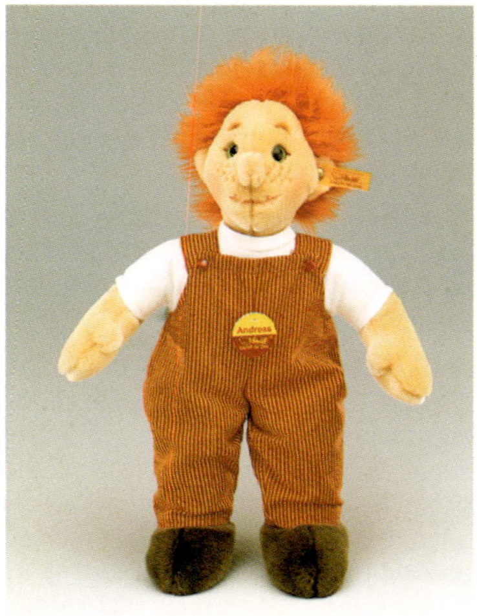

Andreas Schlenkerpuppe - *Dangling Doll **Andreas***

Webpelz, waschmaschinenfest - *woven fur, machine-washable*

EAN-No.	Period	Pr.	Info
704031	1999-1999	2-3	32 cm

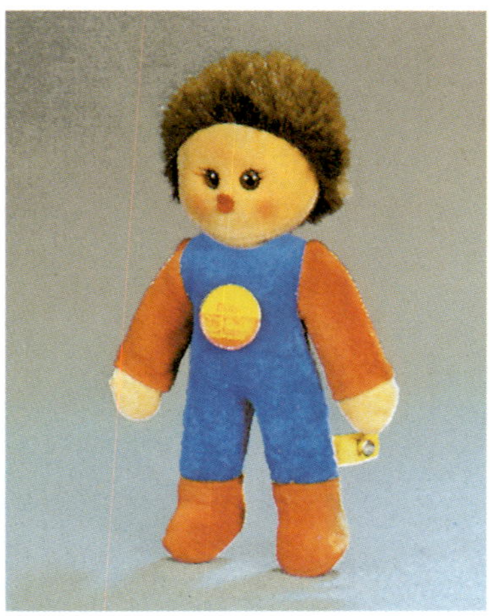

Bubi Werfpuppe - ***Bubi** Boy Doll*

Nicki-Stoff, Koerper formgeschaeumt, blau/rot, waschbar - *nicki velvet, body stuffed with pre-formed foam, blue/red, washable*

Serie	Art.-No	Period	Pr.	Info
	7850/25	1978-1981	1-2	25 cm

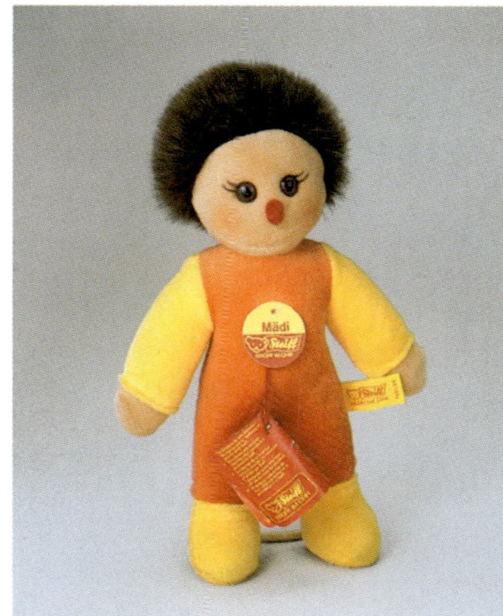

Maedi Werfpuppe - ***Maedi** Girl Doll*

Nicki-Stoff, Koerper formgeschaeumt, rot/gelb, waschbar - *nicki velvet, body stuffed with pre-formed foam, red/yellow, washable*

Serie	Art.-No	Period	Pr.	Info
	7851/25	1978-1982	1-2	25 cm

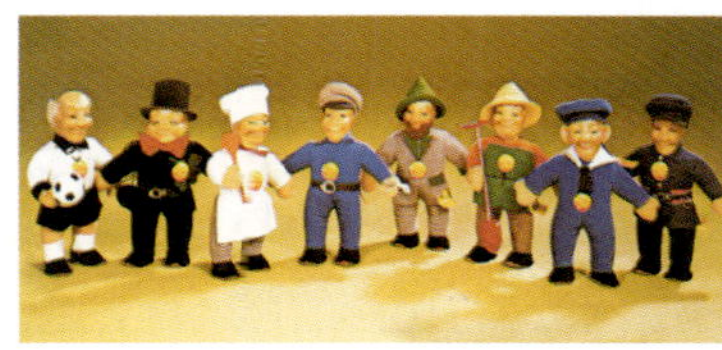

Puppen als Berufsgruppen - *Dolls in Business Clothes*

Synthetik-Samt/PVC, 20 cm, abwaschbar - *synthetic velvet/PVC, 20 cm, surface washable*

Serie	Art.-No	Period	Pr.	Info
	7665/20	1978-1978	3	**Jupp** Fussballer - ***Jupp** Soccer Player*
	7670/20	1978-1978	3	**Lucky** Koch - ***Lucky** Cook*
	7673/20	1978-1978	3	**Rusty** Kaminfeger - ***Rusty** Chimney Sweep*
	7675/20	1978-1978	3	**Hein** Matrose - ***Hein** Sailor*
	7677/20	1978-1978	3	**Rico** Mechaniker - ***Rico** Mechanic*
	7680/20	1978-1978	3	**Florian** Feuerwehrmann - ***Florian** Fireman*
	7685/20	1978-1978	3	**Hubert** Jaeger - ***Hubert** Hunter*
	7687/20	1978-1978	3	**Herby** Gaertner - ***Herby** Gardener*

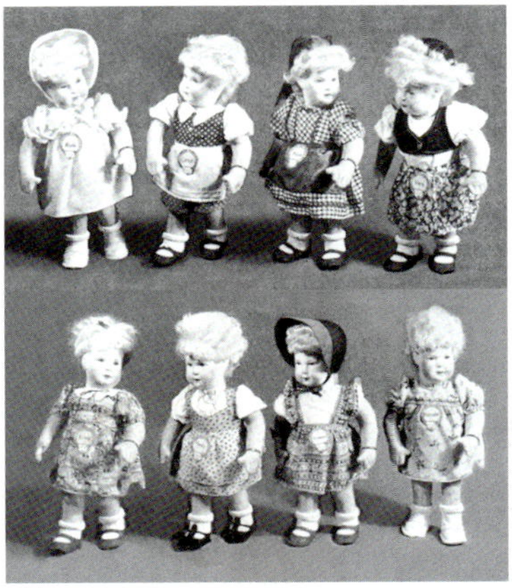

Steiff Puppen - *Steiff Dolls*

Kopf drehbar, nahtlos gepresst aus Wollfilz mit Glasaugen, Haare Mohairpluesch mit Lockenfrisur, Koerper aus Stoff, bewegl. Beine, Schlenkerarme, Kleidung ausziehbar, mit Unterkleidung, Struempfen und Schuhen, 35 cm, Gewicht 190 Gramm, im Einzelkarton - *head swivels, pressed seamlessly using wool felt, glass eyes, hair is mohair with a curly style, body made of fabric, legs are movable, arms floppy, clothing & underwear removable, socks & shoes, 35 cm, weight 190 Gramms, individual box*

Serie	Art.-No	Period	Pr.	Info
90	**35**	1949-1950	6	**Ruth**, Katalog D 49/50 **Otti** - ***Ruth**, catalog D 49/50 **Otti***
90	**35**	1949-1950	6	**Cenzi**
90	**35**	1949-1950	6	**Rosi**, Katalog D 49/50 **Mia** - ***Rosi**, catalog D 49/50 **Mia***
90	**35**	1949-1950	6	**Vera**
90	**35**	1949-1950	6	**Lissy**
90	**35**	1949-1950	6	**Hedy**
90	**35**	1949-1950	6	**Irmgard**
90	**35**	1949-1950	6	**Renate**, Katalog D 49/50 **Inge** - ***Renate**, catalog D 49/50 **Inge***

Die Beschreibung fuer die nun folgenden Puppen ist identisch und wird deshalb an dieser Stelle nur einmalig abgedruckt. Bei den betroffenen Puppen befindet sich ein entsprechender Verweis.

The description for the following dolls is identical and is therefore printed only once. Each doll concerned has a corresponding referring notice.

Stoffkoerper, Haut Maco-Baumwolle, Fuellung PU-Schaum, kaemmbare Echthaar-Peruecke, Gesicht & Augen handbemalt, Kopf durch Kugelgelenk in alle Richtungen beweglich, Arme frei beweglich, Beine drehbar angescheibt, hochwertige Bekleidungsmaterialien z.B. Lederschuhe, ab 1991 Kunststoffaugen & Kunsthaarperuecken - *body made of fabric, the skin is made of maco cotton, stuffed with PU foam, real hair wigs which can be combed, face & eyes are hand painted, the head swivels in any direction by means of a ball joint, arms are freely movable, the legs swivel, clothing is of high quality fabrics and materials - i.e. leather shoes, from 1991 plastic eyes and synthetic hair wig*

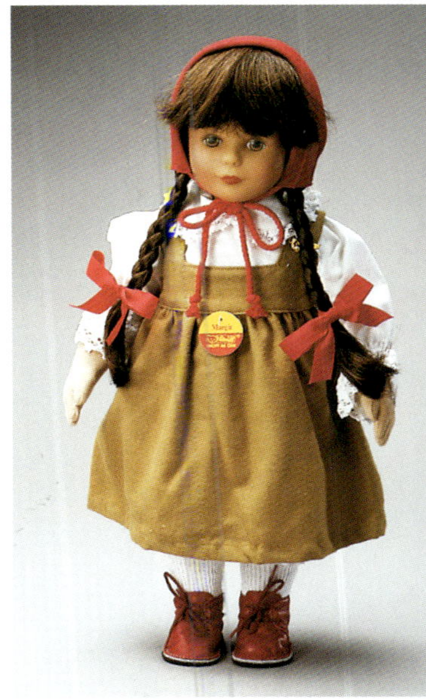

Margit

Beschreibung siehe Seite 340 - *for description refer to page 340*

Serie	Art.-No	Period	Pr.	Info
701061	**9204**/**42**	1987-1988	4-5	42 cm

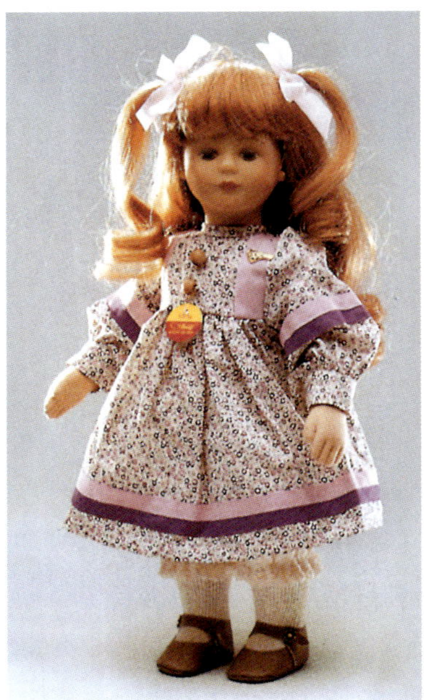

Silvia

Beschreibung siehe Seite 340 - *for description refer to page 340*

Serie	Art.-No	Period	Pr.	Info
701016	**9201**/**42**	1987-1988	4-5	42 cm

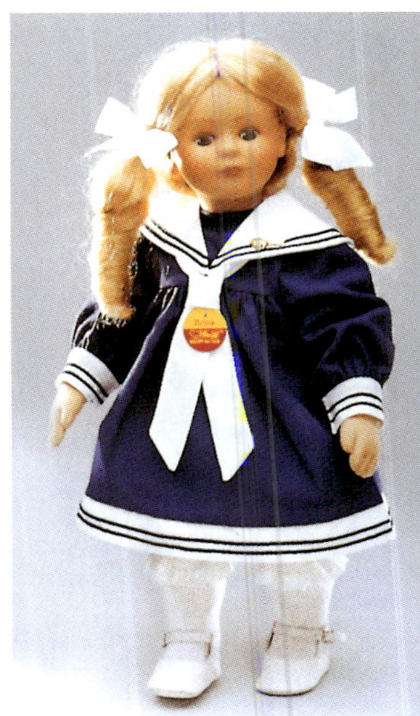

Bettina

Beschreibung siehe Seite 340 - *for description refer to page 340*

Serie	Art.-No	Period	Pr.	Info
701115	**9207**/**42**	1987-1988	4-5	42 cm

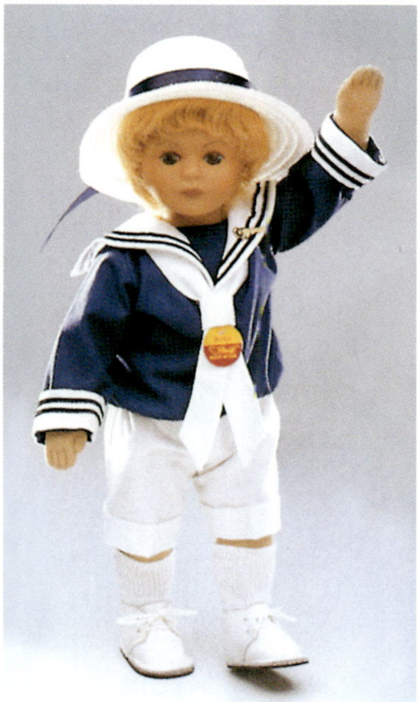

Bernd

Beschreibung siehe Seite 340 - *for description refer to page 340*

SERIE	ART.-NO	PERIOD	PR.	INFO
701160	**9210**/**42**	1987-1988	4-5	42 cm

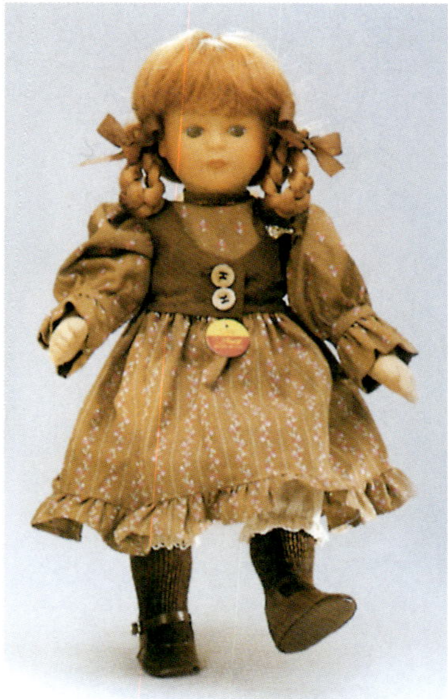

Gabi

Beschreibung siehe Seite 340 - *for description refer to page 340*

SERIE	ART.-NO	PERIOD	PR.	INFO
701269	**9216**/**42**	1987-1988	4-5	42 cm

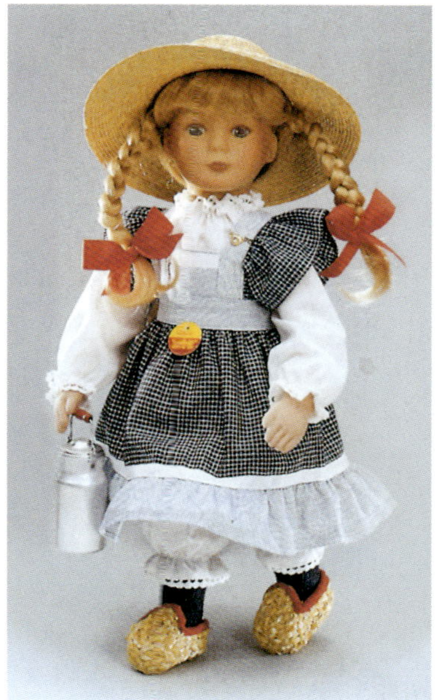

Babette

Beschreibung siehe Seite 340 - *for description refer to page 340*

SERIE	ART.-NO	PERIOD	PR.	INFO
702068	**9244**/**50**	1987-1988	5	50 cm

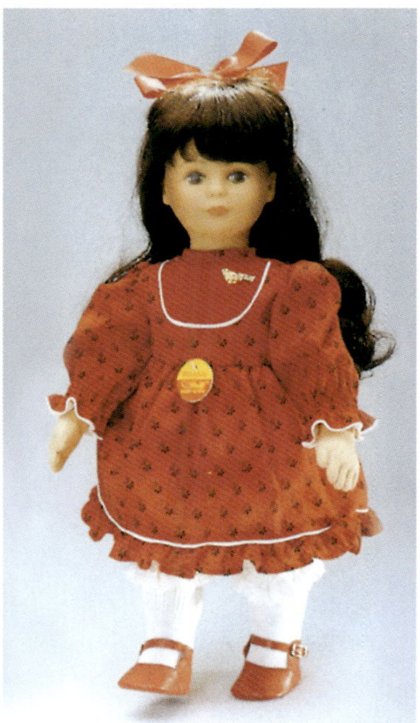

Piroschka

Beschreibung siehe Seite 340 - *for description refer to page 340*

SERIE	ART.-NO	PERIOD	PR.	INFO
701214	**9213**/**42**	1987-1988	4-5	42 cm

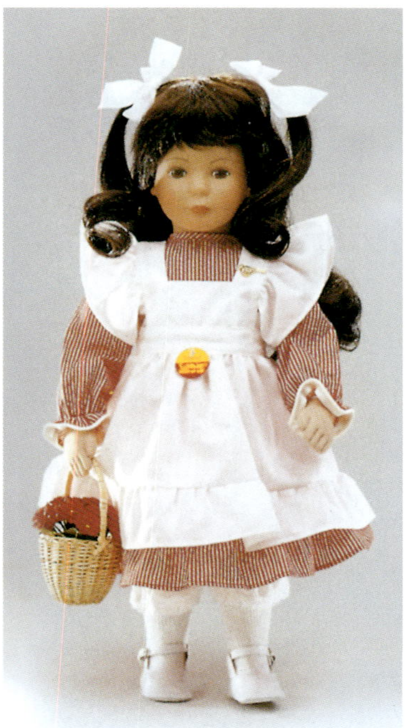

Mimmi

Beschreibung siehe Seite 340 - *for description refer to page 340*

SERIE	ART.-NO	PERIOD	PR.	INFO
702013	**9241**/**50**	1987-1988	5	50 cm

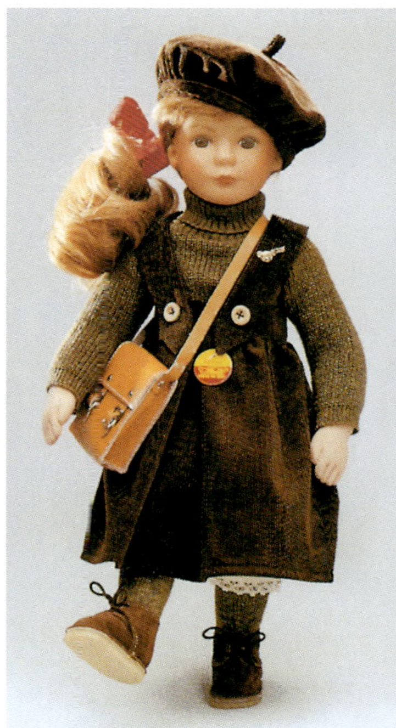

Andrea

Beschreibung siehe Seite 340 - *for description refer to page 340*

SERIE	ART.-NO	PERIOD	PR.	INFO
702112	**9247**/**50**	1987-1988	5	50 cm

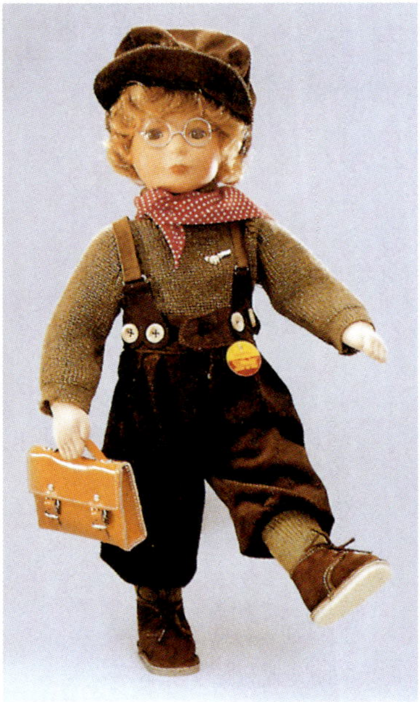

Andreas

Beschreibung siehe Seite 340 - *for description refer to page 340*

SERIE	ART.-NO	PERIOD	PR.	INFO
702167	**9250/50**	1987-1988	5	50 cm

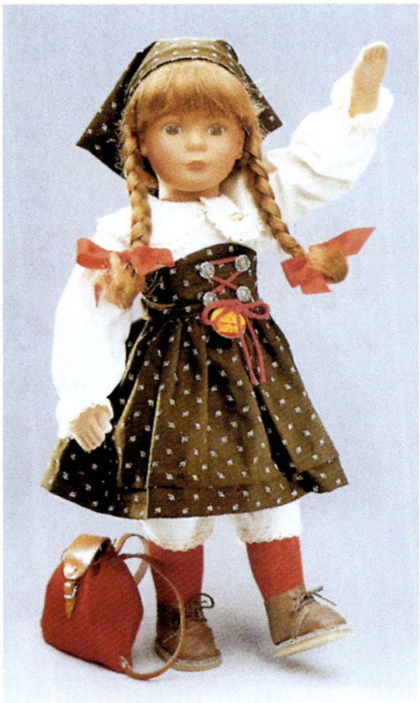

Ulla

Beschreibung siehe Seite 340 - *for description refer to page 340*

SERIE	ART.-NO	PERIOD	PR.	INFO
702266	**9256/50**	1987-1988	5	50 cm

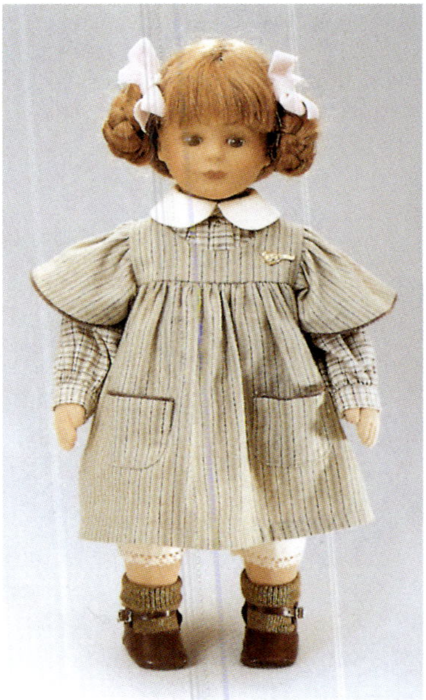

Bea

Beschreibung siehe Seite 340 - *for description refer to page 340*

SERIE	ART.-NO	PERIOD	PR.	INFO
701412	**9227/42**	1988-1989	4-5	42 cm

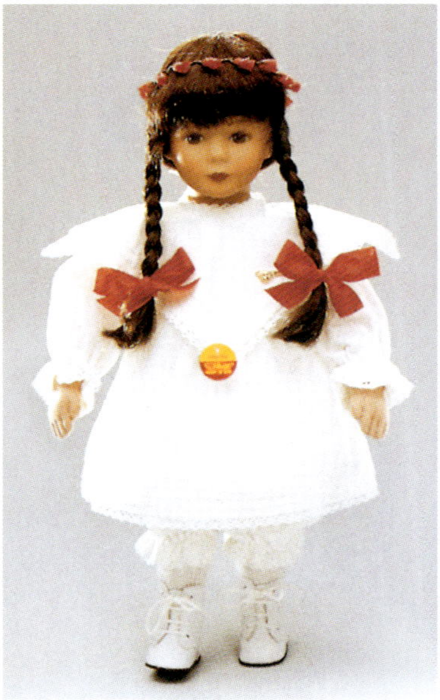

Anette

Beschreibung siehe Seite 340 - *for description refer to page 340*

SERIE	ART.-NO	PERIOD	PR.	INFO
702211	**9253/50**	1987-1988	5	50 cm

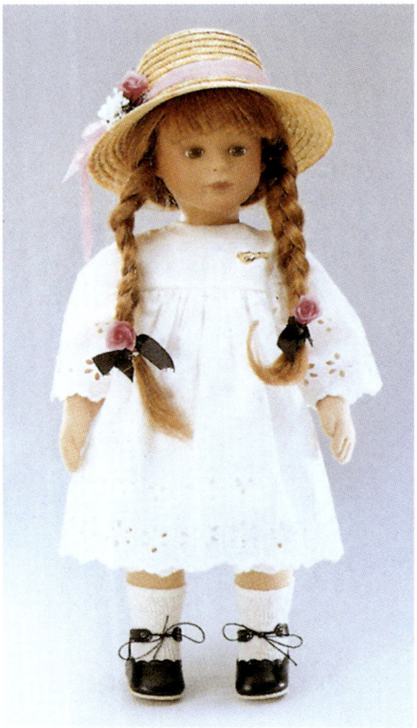

Susi

Beschreibung siehe Seite 340 - *for description refer to page 340*

SERIE	ART.-NO	PERIOD	PR.	INFO
701313	**9221/42**	1988-1989	4-5	42 cm

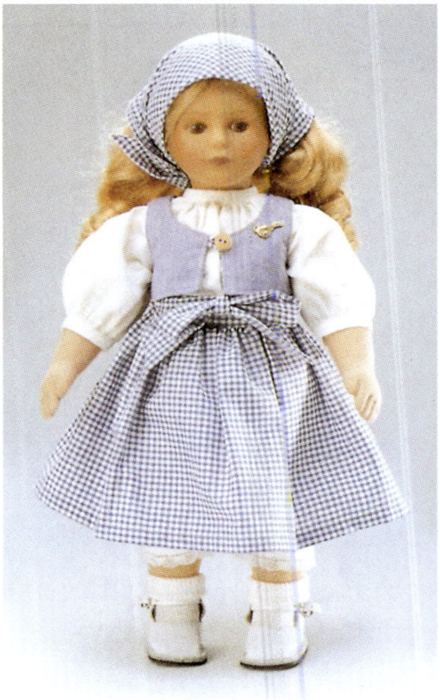

Resi

Beschreibung siehe Seite 340 - *for description refer to page 340*

SERIE	ART.-NO	PERIOD	PR.	INFO
701368	**9224/42**	1988-1990	4-5	42 cm

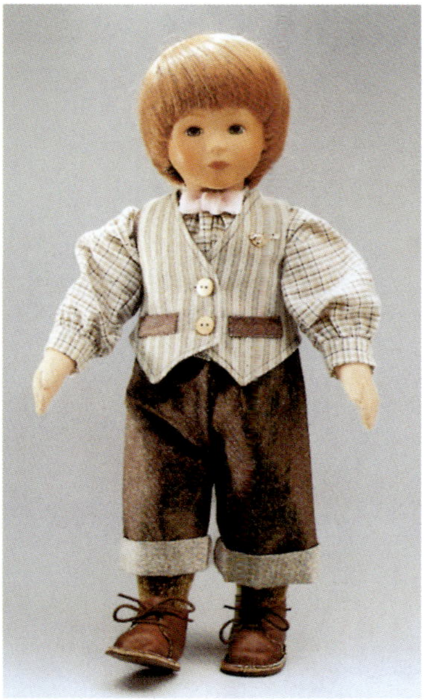

Bernie

Beschreibung siehe Seite 340 - *for description refer to page 340*

SERIE	ART.-NO	PERIOD	PR.	INFO
701467	**9230/42**	1988-1990	4-5	42 cm

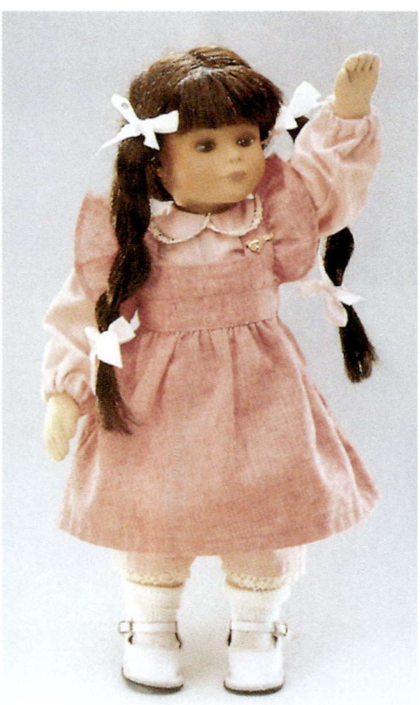

Barbara

Beschreibung siehe Seite 340 - *for description refer to page 340*

SERIE	ART.-NO	PERIOD	PR.	INFO
701511	**9233/42**	1988-1990	4-5	42 cm

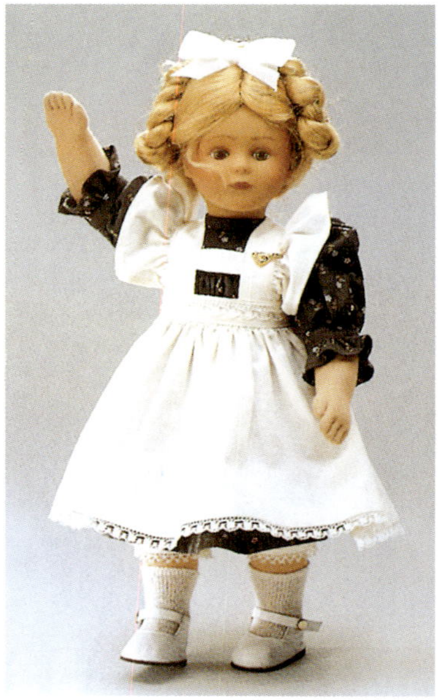

Marieluise

Beschreibung siehe Seite 340 - *for description refer to page 340*

SERIE	ART.-NO	PERIOD	PR.	INFO
701566	**9236/42**	1988-1990	4-5	42 cm

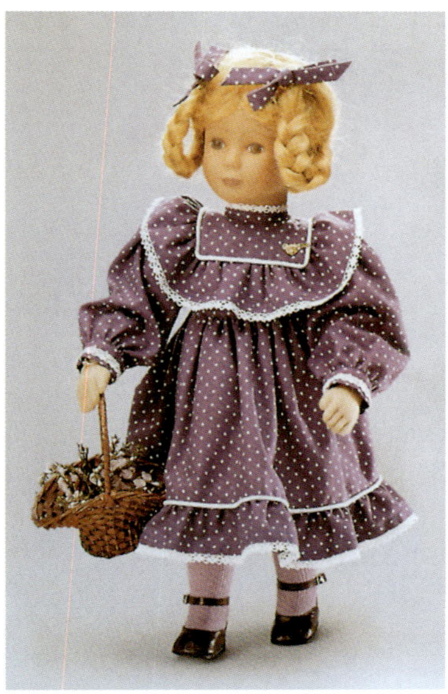

Lizzy

Beschreibung siehe Seite 340 - *for description refer to page 340*

SERIE	ART.-NO	PERIOD	PR.	INFO
702310	**9261/50**	1988-1990	5	50 cm

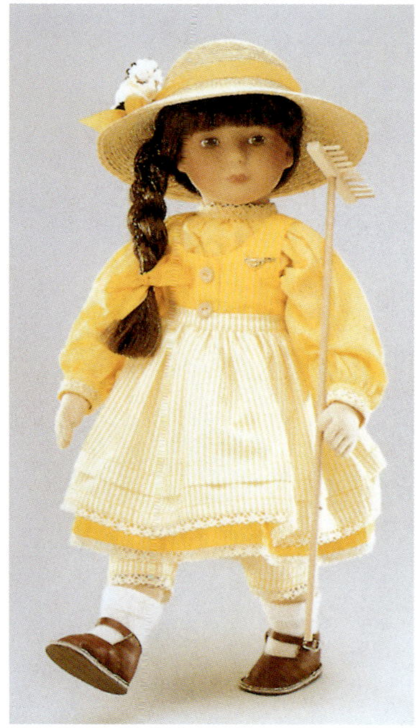

Linda

Beschreibung siehe Seite 340 - *for description refer to page 340*

SERIE	ART.-NO	PERIOD	PR.	INFO
702365	**9264/50**	1988-1990	5	50 cm

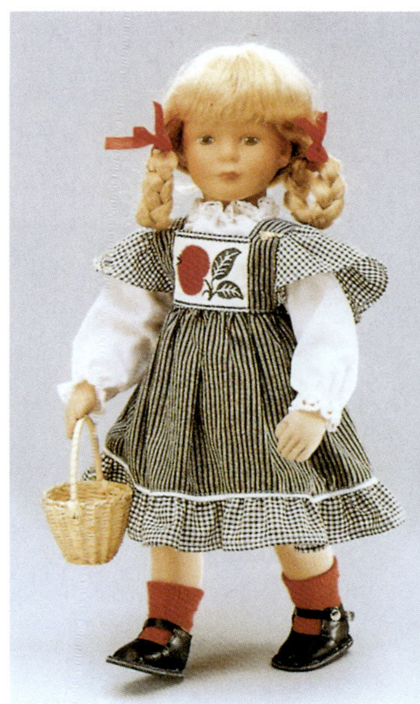

Siglinde

Beschreibung siehe Seite 340 - *for description refer to page 340*

SERIE	ART.-NO	PERIOD	PR.	INFO
702419	**9267/50**	1988-1990	5	50 cm

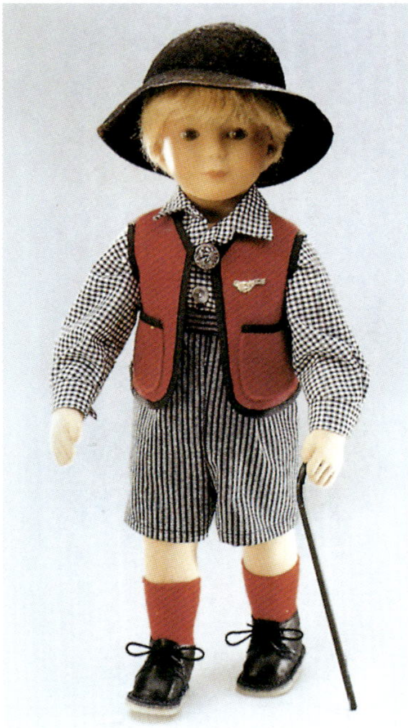

Sigi

Beschreibung siehe Seite 340 - *for description refer to page 340*

SERIE	ART.-NO	PERIOD	PR.	INFO
702464	**9270/50**	1988-1990	5	50 cm

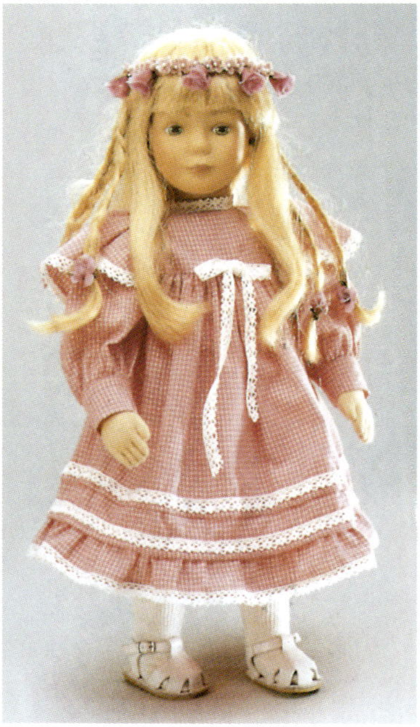

Claire

Beschreibung siehe Seite 340 - *for description refer to page 340*

SERIE	ART.-NO	PERIOD	PR.	INFO
702518	**9273/50**	1988-1990	5	50 cm

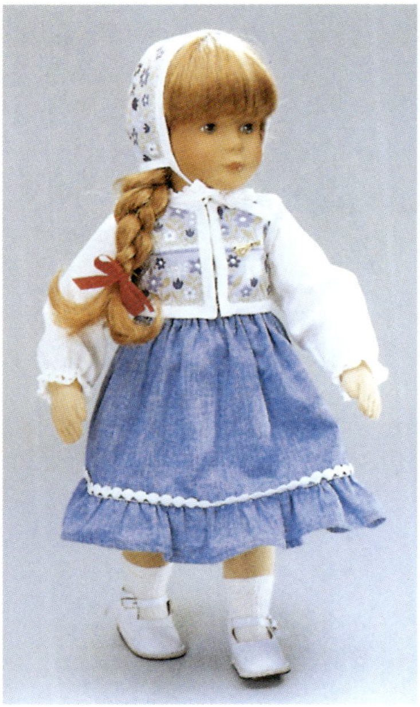

Kati

Beschreibung siehe Seite 340 - *for description refer to page 340*

SERIE	ART.-NO	PERIOD	PR.	INFO
702563	**9276/50**	1988-1990	5	50 cm

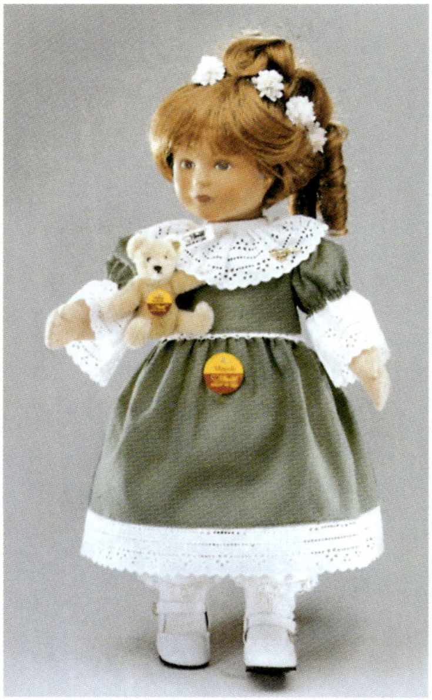

Minnie

mit 11 cm Original Teddy, lim. Auflage 1.000 Stueck, Beschreibung siehe Seite 340 - *with an 11cm Original Teddy Bear, ltd edition of 1,000, for description refer to page 340*

SERIE	ART.-NO	PERIOD	PR.	INFO
701627	**9240/43**	1989-1990	5	42 cm
	701627	1991-1992	5	

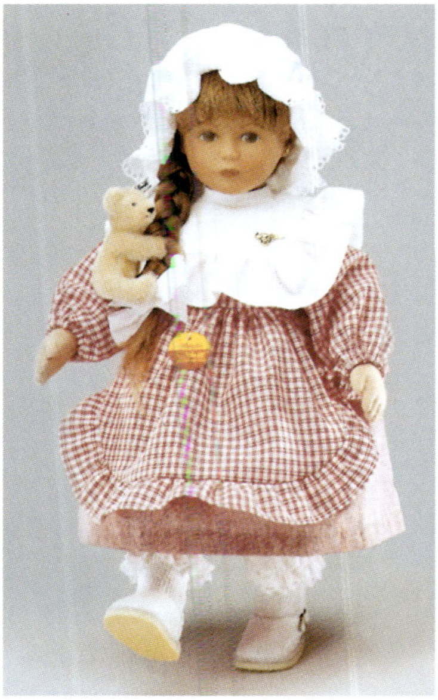

Magda

mit 11 cm Original Teddy, lim. Auflage 1.000 Stueck, Beschreibung siehe Seite 340 - *with an 11cm Original Teddy Bear, ltd edition of 1,000, for description refer to page 340*

SERIE	ART.-NO	PERIOD	PR.	INFO
701672	**9243/43**	1989-1990	5	42 cm
	701672	1991-1991	5	

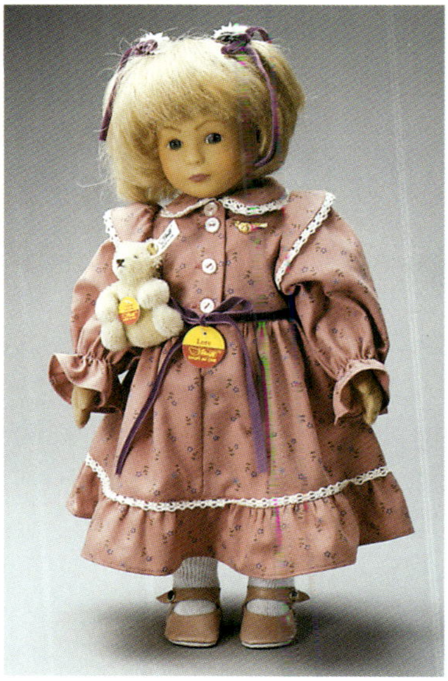

Lore

mit 11 cm Original Teddy, lim. Auflage 1.000 Stueck, Beschreibung siehe Seite 340 - *with an 11cm Original Teddy Bear, ltd edition of 1,000, for description refer to page 340*

SERIE	ART.-NO	PERIOD	PR.	INFO
701726	**9246/43**	1989-1990	5	42 cm
	701726	1991-1992	5	

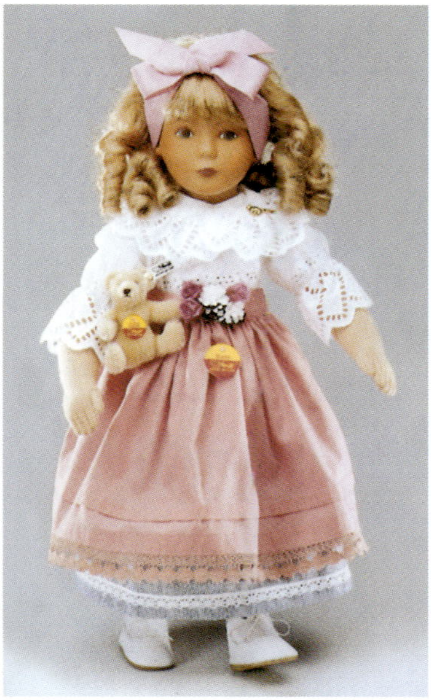

Bertha

mit 11 cm Original Teddy, lim. Auflage 1.000 Stueck, Beschreibung siehe Seite 340 - *with an 11cm Original Teddy Bear, ltd edition of 1,000, for description refer to page 340*

SERIE	ART.-NO	PERIOD	PR.	INFO
702624	**9280/51**	1989-1990	5	50 cm
	702624	1991-1991	5	

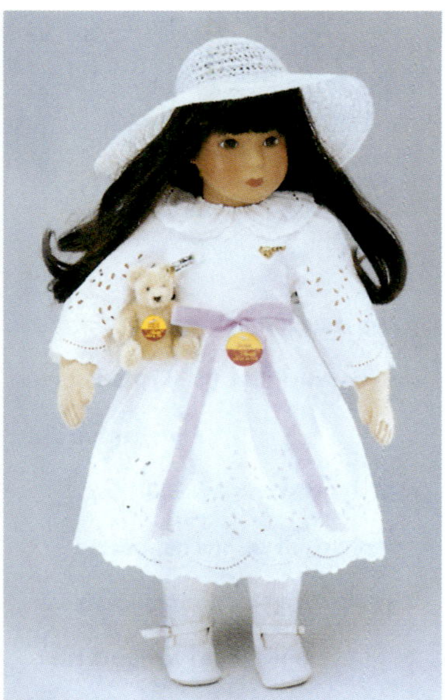

Irene

mit 11 cm Original Teddy, lim. Auflage 1.000 Stueck, Beschreibung siehe Seite 340 - *with an 11cm Original Teddy Bear, ltd edition of 1,000, for description refer to page 340*

SERIE	ART.-NO	PERIOD	PR.	INFO
702679	**9283/51**	1989-1990	5	50 cm
	702679	1991-1992	5	

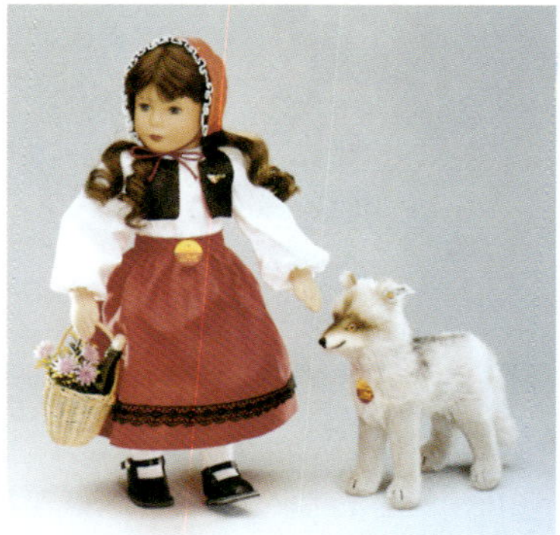

Rotkaeppchen - *Little Red Riding Hood*

mit Wolf, lim. Auflage 1.000 Stueck, Beschreibung siehe Seite 340 - *with wolf, ltd edition of 1,000, for description refer to page 340*

SERIE	ART.-NO	PERIOD	PR.	INFO
703010	**9291/55**	1989-1990	5	50 cm
	703010	1991-1991	5	

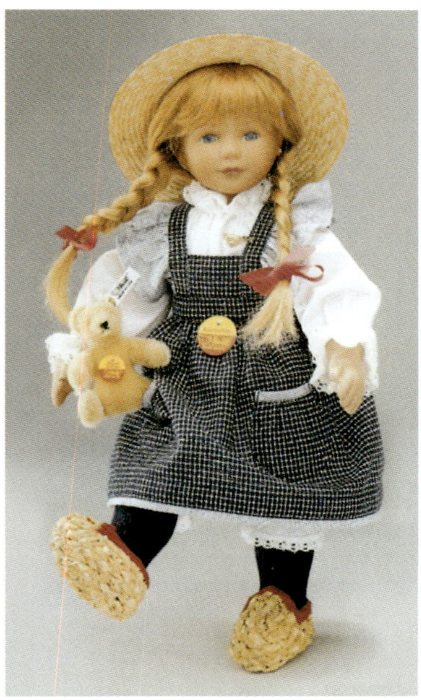

Babinchen

mit 11 cm Original Teddy, lim. Auflage 1.000 Stueck, Beschreibung siehe Seite 340 - *with an 11cm Original Teddy Bear, ltd edition of 1,000, for description refer to page 340*

SERIE	ART.-NO	PERIOD	PR.	INFO
701771	**9250/43**	1990-1990	5	43 cm
	701771	1991-1991	5	

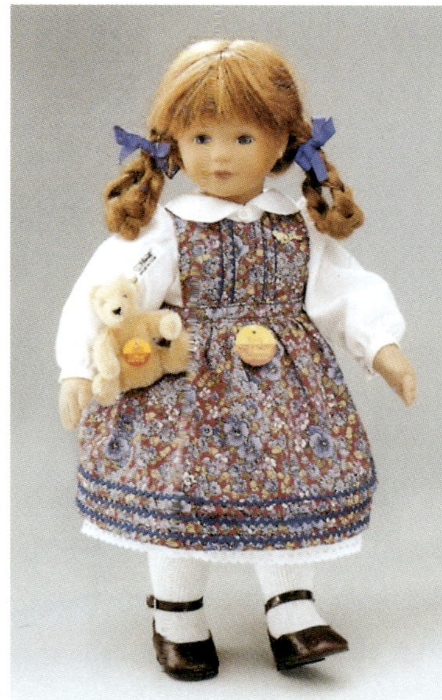

Dolly

mit 11 cm Original Teddy, lim. Auflage 1.000 Stueck, Beschreibung siehe Seite 340 - *with an 11cm Original Teddy Bear, ltd edition of 1,000, for description refer to page 340*

SERIE	ART.-NO	PERIOD	PR.	INFO
701825	**9253/43**	1990-1990	5	43 cm
	701825	1991-1992	5	

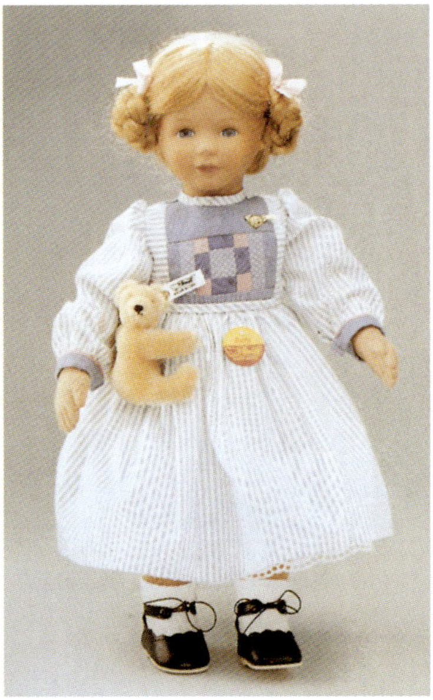

Patty

mit 11 cm Original Teddy, lim. Auflage 1.000 Stueck, Beschreibung siehe Seite 340 - *with an 11cm Original Teddy Bear, ltd edition of 1,000, for description refer to page 340*

Serie	Art.-No	Period	Pr.	Info
701870	**9256/43**	1990-1990	5	43 cm
	701870	1991-1991	5	

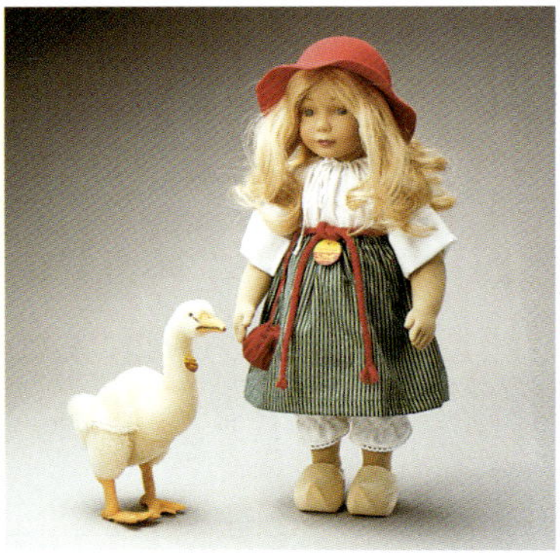

Gaenseliesel - *Little Goose Liesel*

mit Gans, lim. Auflage 1.000 Stueck, Beschreibung siehe Seite 340 - *with goose, ltd edition of 1,000, for description refer to page 340*

Serie	Art.-No	Period	Pr.	Info
703027	**9293/55**	1990-1990	5	55 cm
	703027	1991-1991	5	

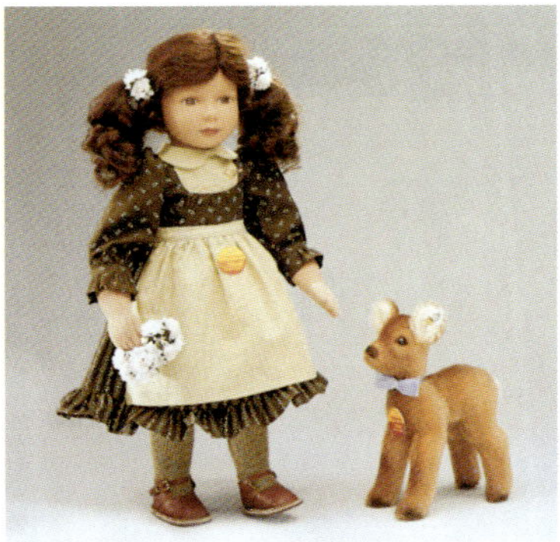

Schwesterchen - *Little Sister*

mit Reh, lim. Auflage 1.000 Stueck, Beschreibung siehe Seite 340 - *with deer, ltd edition of 1,000, for description refer to page 340*

Serie	Art.-No	Period	Pr.	Info
703034	**9295/55**	1990-1990	5	55 cm
	703034	1991-1992	5	

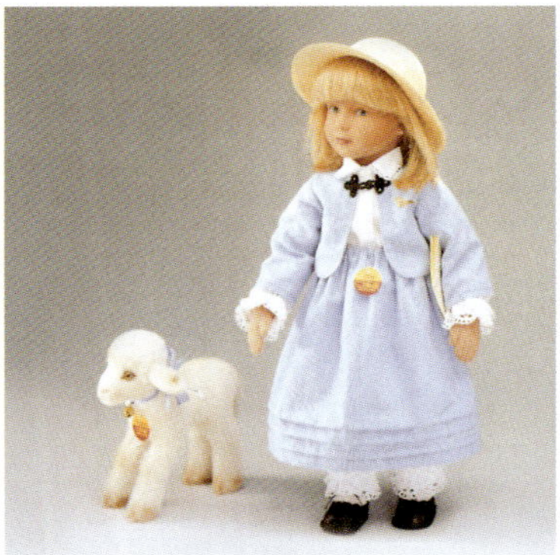

Mary

mit Lamm, lim. Auflage 1.000 Stueck, Beschreibung siehe Seite 340 - *with lamb, ltd edition of 1,000, for description refer to page 340*

Serie	Art.-No	Period	Pr.	Info
703218	**9297/55**	1990-1990	5	55 cm
	703218	1991-1992	5	

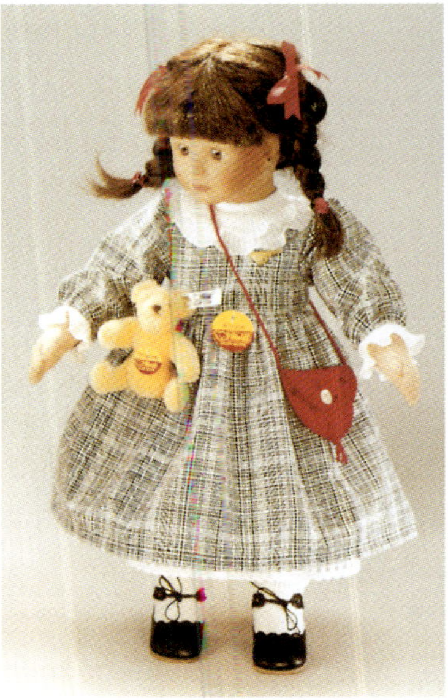

Nicole

mit 11 cm Original Teddy, lim. Auflage 1.000 Stueck, Beschreibung siehe Seite 340 - *with an 11cm Original Teddy Bear, ltd edition of 1,000, for description refer to page 340*

EAN-No.	Period	Pr.	Info
701924	1991-1992	5	43 cm

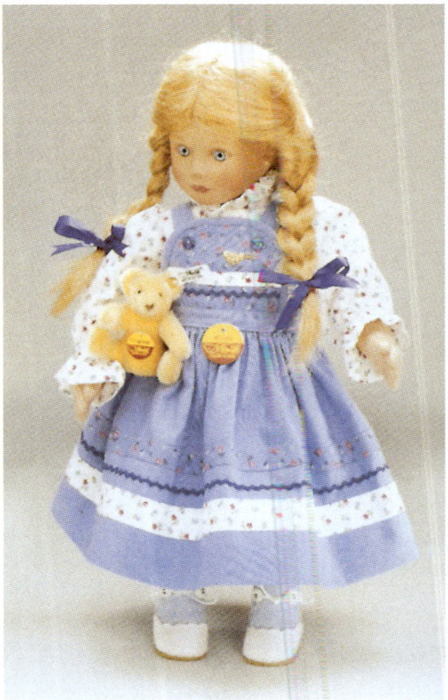

Hilde

mit 11 cm Original Teddy, lim. Auflage 1.000 Stueck, Beschreibung siehe Seite 340 - *with an 11cm Original Teddy Bear, ltd edition of 1,000, for description refer to page 340*

EAN-No.	Period	Pr.	Info
701979	1991-1992	5	43 cm

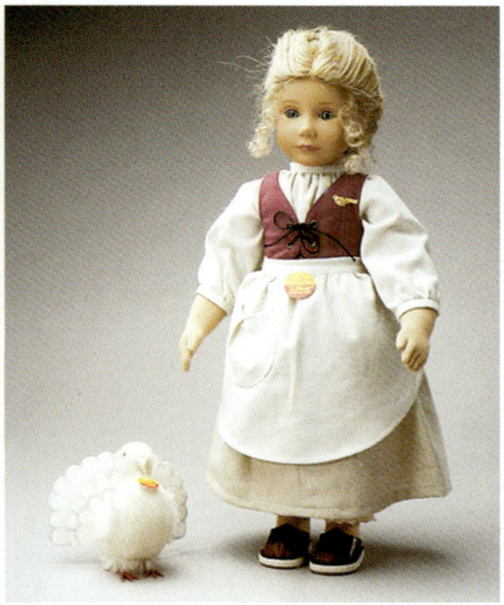

Aschenputtel mit Taube - *Cinderella with Dove*

mit Taube, lim. Auflage 1.000 Stueck, Beschreibung siehe Seite 340 - *with dove, ltd edition of 1,000, for description refer to page 340*

EAN-No.	Period	Pr.	Info
703041	1991-1992	5	50 cm

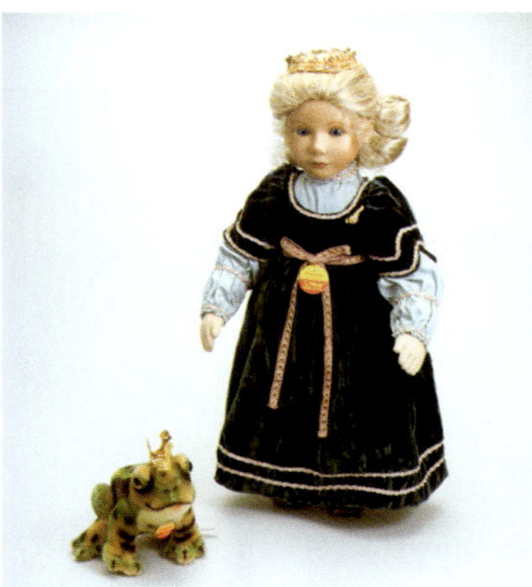

Prinzessin und Froschkoenig - *Princess and the Frog Prince*

mit Frosch, lim. Auflage 1.000 Stueck, Beschreibung siehe Seite 340 - *with frog, ltd edition of 1,000, for description refer to page 340*

EAN-No.	Period	Pr.	Info
703058	1991-1992	5	50 cm

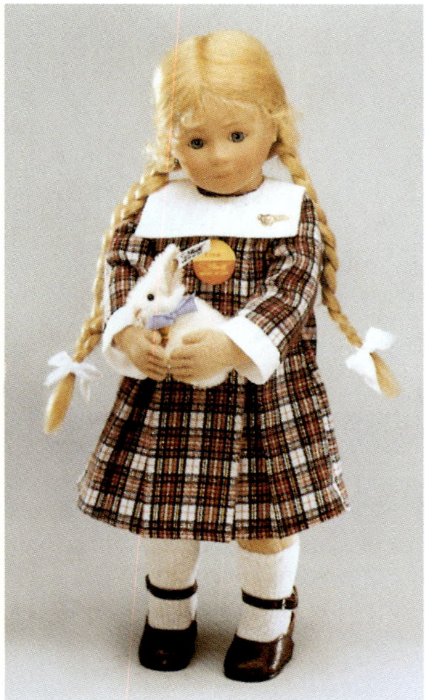

Else

mit Hase, lim. Auflage 500 Stueck, Beschreibung siehe Seite 340 - *with rabbit, ltd edition of 500, for description refer to page 340*

EAN-No.	Period	Pr.	Info
701030	1992-1992	5	43 cm

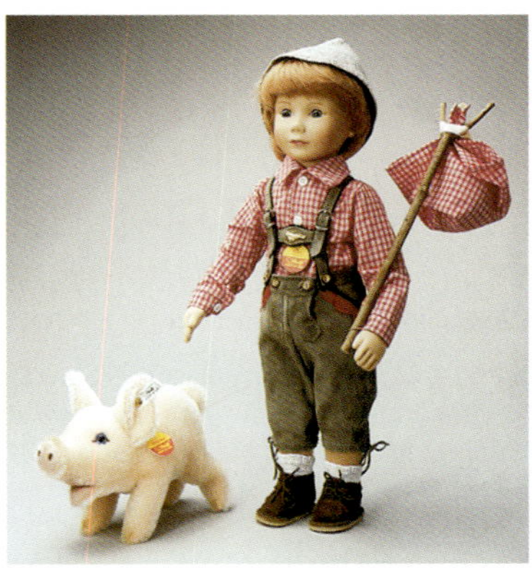

Hans im Glueck - *Lucky Hans*

mit Schwein, lim. Auflage 500 Stueck, Beschreibung siehe Seite 340 - *with pig, ltd edition of 500, for description refer to page 340*

EAN-No.	Period	Pr.	Info
702037	1992-1992	5	50 cm

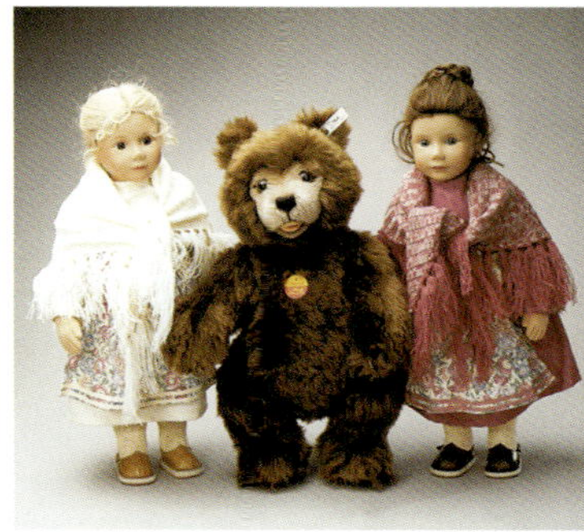

Schneeweisschen und **Rosenrot** - *Snow White and Rose Red*

mit Bär aus Mohair, gegliedert, lim. Auflage 1.200 Stueck, Beschreibung siehe Seite 340 - *with bear of mohair, jointed, ltd edition of 1,200, for description refer to page 340*

EAN-No.	Period	Pr.	Info
703157	1992-1992	5-6	kpl. Set - *compl. set*
J04098	1992-1992	5	50 cm, Baer - *bear*

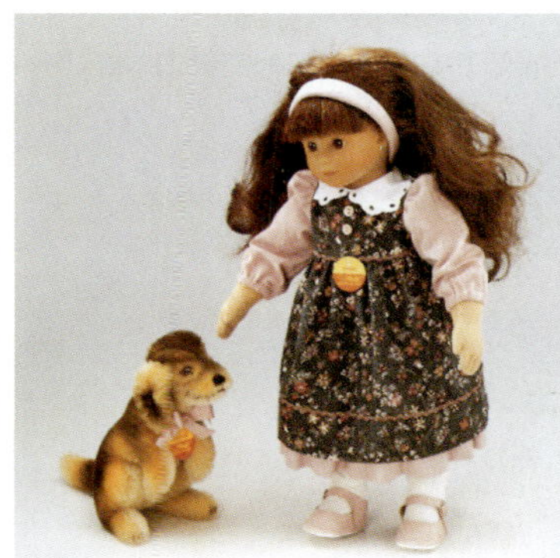

Anna

mit Hund, lim. Auflage 600 Stueck, Beschreibung siehe Seite 340 - *with dog, ltd edition of 600, for description refer to page 340*

EAN-No.	Period	Pr.	Info
701085	1993-1994	5	43 cm

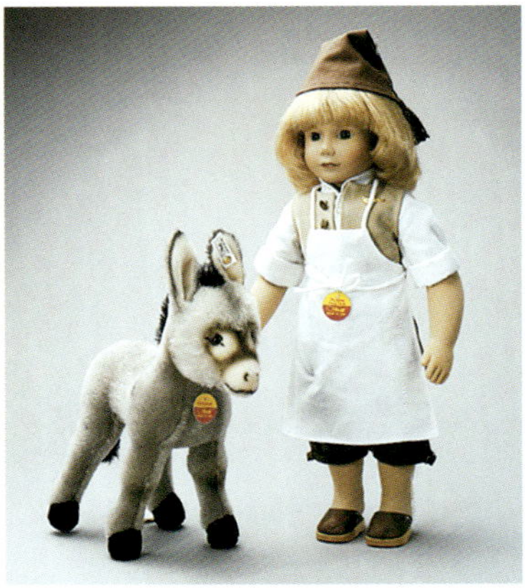

Tischlein deck dich mit Esel - *Magic Table*

mit Esel, lim. Auflage 600 Stueck, Beschreibung siehe Seite 340 - *with donkey, ltd edition of 600, for description refer to page 340*

EAN-No.	Period	Pr.	Info
703072	1993-1993	5	50 cm

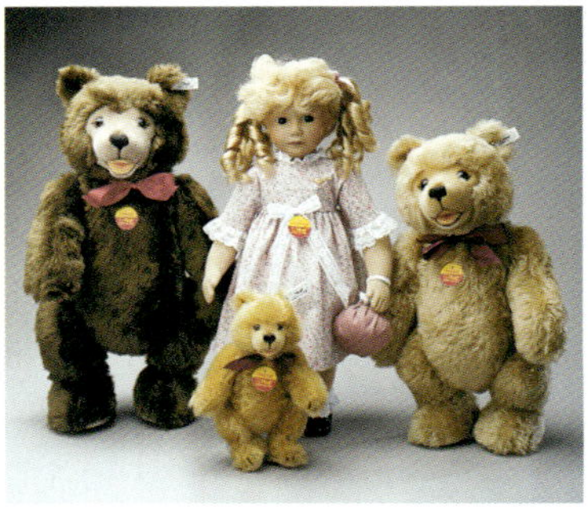

Goldilocks

mit Mama-, Papa- und Baby-Baer, Mohair, gegliedert, lim. Auflage 1.500 Stueck, Beschreibung siehe Seite 340 - *with Mama-, Papa- & Baby bear of mohair, ltd edition of 1,500, for description refer to page 340*

EAN-No.	Period	Pr.	Info
703164	1993-1995	6	kpl. Set - *compl. set*
J04074	1993-1995	5	42 cm, Mama-Baer - *Mama-bear*
J04191	1993-1995	5	50 cm, Papa-Baer - *Papa-Bear*
J04193	1993-1995	4-5	22 cm, Baby-Baer

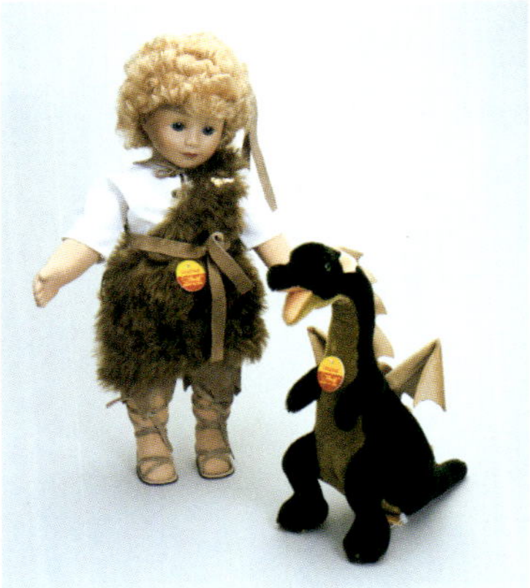

Siegfried

mit Drache (28 cm), lim. Auflage 600 Stueck, Beschreibung siehe Seite 340 - *with dragon (28 cm), ltd edition of 600, for description refer to page 340*

EAN-No.	Period	Pr.	Info
701139	1994-1995	5	43 cm

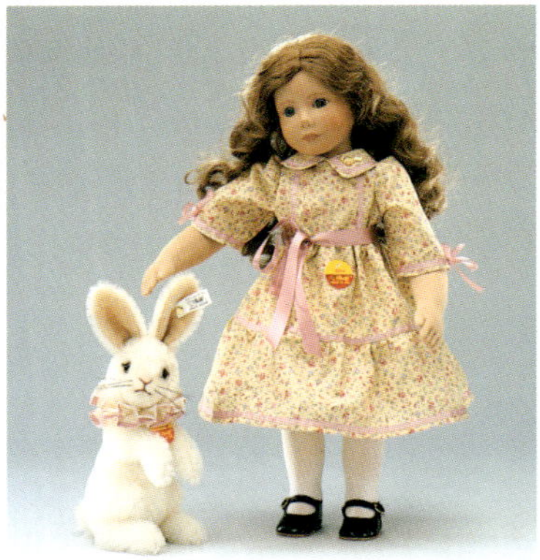

Alice

mit Hase (27 cm), lim. Auflage 600 Stueck, Beschreibung siehe Seite 340 - *with rabbit (27 cm), ltd edition of 600, for description refer to page 340*

EAN-No.	Period	Pr.	Info
703089	1994-1995	5	50 cm

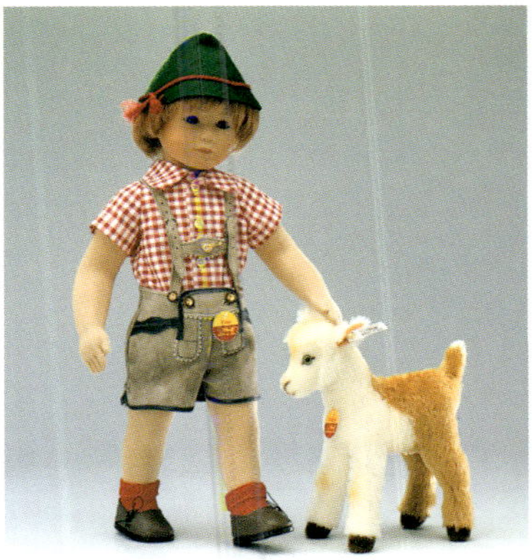

Peter

mit Ziege (25 cm), lim. Auflage 600 Stueck, Beschreibung siehe Seite 340 - *with goat (25 cm), ltd edition of 600, for description refer to page 340*

EAN-No.	Period	Pr.	Info
703096	1994-1995	5	50 cm

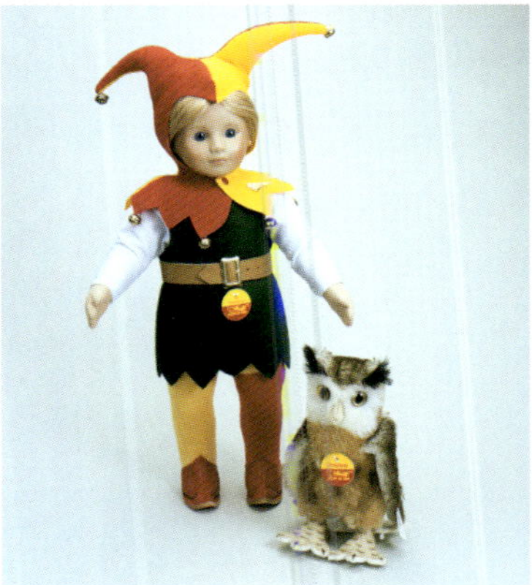

Till Eulenspiegel - *Tom Fool*

mit Eule (19 cm), lim. Auflage 600 Stueck, Beschreibung siehe Seite 340 - *with owl (19 cm), ltd edition of 600, for description refer to page 340*

EAN-No.	Period	Pr.	Info
701184	1995-1996	5	43 cm

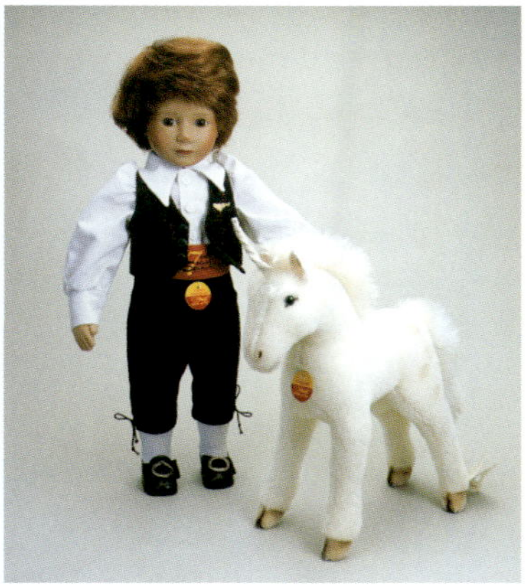

Tapferes Schneiderlein - *The Brave Little Tailor*

mit Einhorn (34 cm), lim. Auflage 600 Stueck, Beschreibung siehe Seite 340 - *with unicorn (34 cm), ltd edition of 600, for description refer to page 340*

EAN-No.	Period	Pr.	Info
703263	1995-1996	5	50 cm

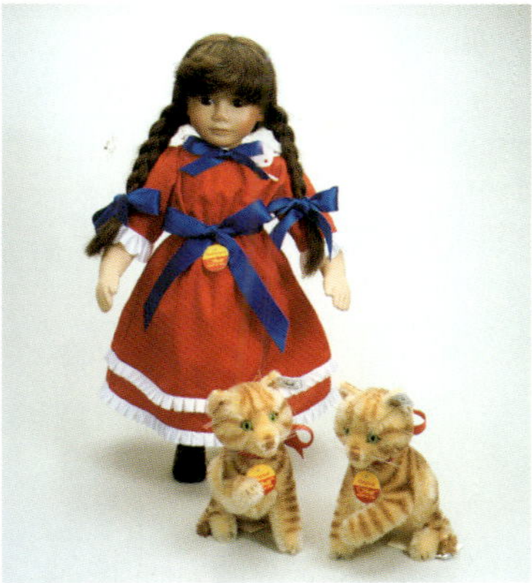

Paulinchen - *Little Paula*

mit 2 Katzen (je 17 cm), lim. Auflage 600 Stueck, Beschreibung siehe Seite 340 - *with two cats (17 cm each), ltd edition of 600, for description refer to page 340*

EAN-No.	Period	Pr.	Info
703270	1995-1997	5	50 cm

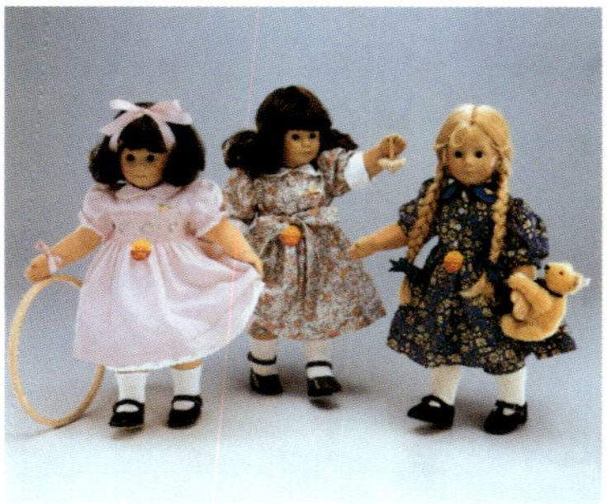

Margarete Steiff Puppen - *Margarete Steiff Doll*

Design der Puppenbekleidung von Caroline von Wrede, Babette mit Hula-Hopp-Reifen, Betina mit Kreisel, Babinchen mit Teddy blond 12 cm, Puppen 43 cm, limitierte Auflage 300 Stueck - *doll cloth design by Caroline von Wrede, Babette with Hula-Hopp, Betina with top, Babinchen with teddy blond 12 cm, dolls 43 cm, ltd edition of 300 each*

EAN-No.	Period	Pr.	Info
701337	1996-1996	5	Babette
701276	1996-1997	5	Betina
701382	1996-1997	5	Babinchen

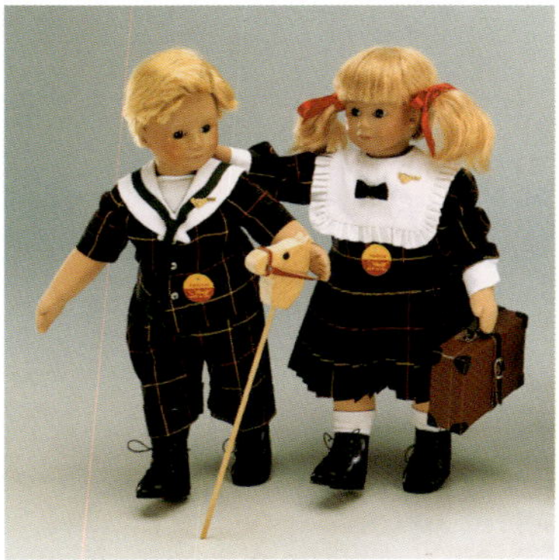

Margarete Steiff Puppen - *Margarete Steiff Doll*

Design der Puppenbekleidung von Caroline von Wrede, Andreas mit Steckenpferd, Andrea mit Koffer, Puppen 43 cm, limitierte Auflage 300 Stueck - *doll cloth design by Caroline von Wrede, Andreas with Hobby-Horse, Andrea with suitcase, dolls 43 cm, ltd edition of 300 each*

EAN-No.	Period	Pr.	Info
701481	1996-1997	5	Andreas
701436	1996-1997	5	Andrea

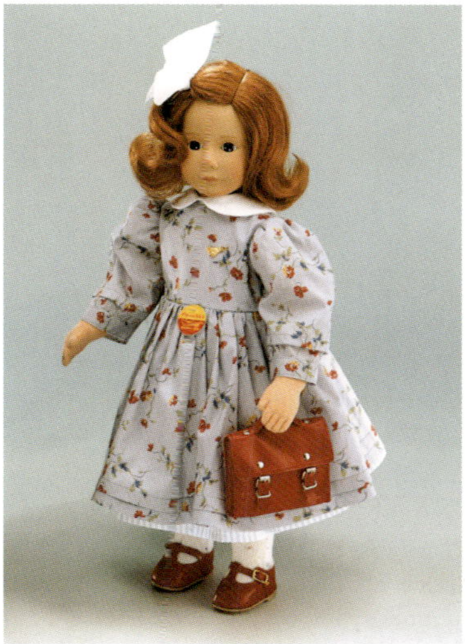

Piroschka

Design der Puppenbekleidung von Caroline von Wrede, mit roter Lederschultasche, limitierte Auflage 300 Stueck - *doll cloth design by Caroline von Wrede, with red leather schoolbag, ltd edition of 300*

EAN-No.	Period	Pr.	Info
703294	1996-1997	5	50 cm

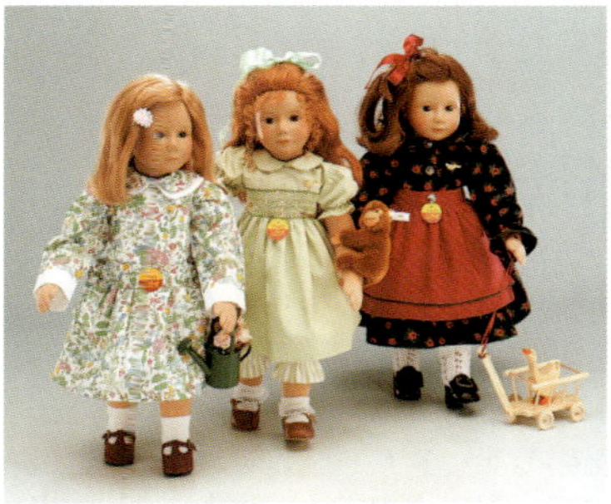

Margarete Steiff Puppen - *Margarete Steiff Doll*

Design der Puppenbekleidung von Caroline von Wrede, Flora mit Giesskanne, Magda mit Schimpanse, kupfer 13 cm, Anette mit Leiterwagen und Gans aus Holz, Puppen 50 cm, limitierte Auflage 300 Stueck - *doll cloth design by Caroline von Wrede, Flora with watering can, Magda with chimpanzee, copper 13 cm, Anette with wooden handcart and goose from wood, dolls 50 cm, ltd edition of 300 each*

EAN-No.	Period	Pr.	Info
703324	1996-1996	5	Flora
703317	1996-1997	5	Magda
703300	1996-1997	5	Anette

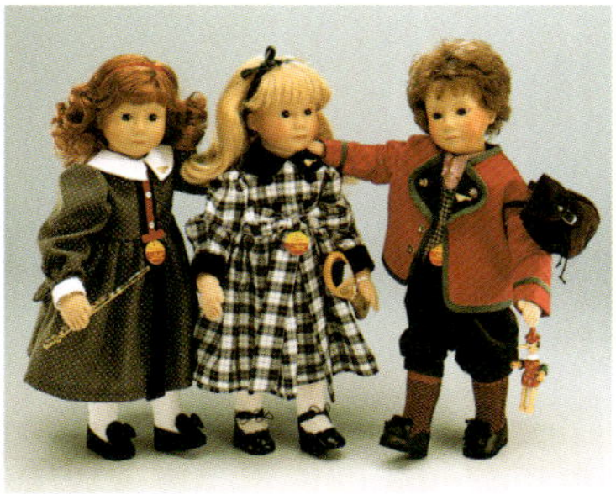

Margarete Steiff Puppen - *Margarete Steiff Doll*

Design der Puppenbekleidung von Caroline von Wrede, Marieluise mit Querfloete, Claire mit Handspiegel, Bernd mit Rucksack & Pinocchio, Puppen 50 cm, limitierte Auflage 300 Stueck - *doll cloth design by Caroline von Wrede, Marieluise with flute, Claire with hand mirror, Bernd with rucksack & Pinocchio, dolls 50 cm, ltd edition of 300 each*

EAN-No.	Period	Pr.	Info
703331	1996-1997	5	Marieluise
703348	1996-1997	5	Claire
703355	1996-1997	5	Bernd

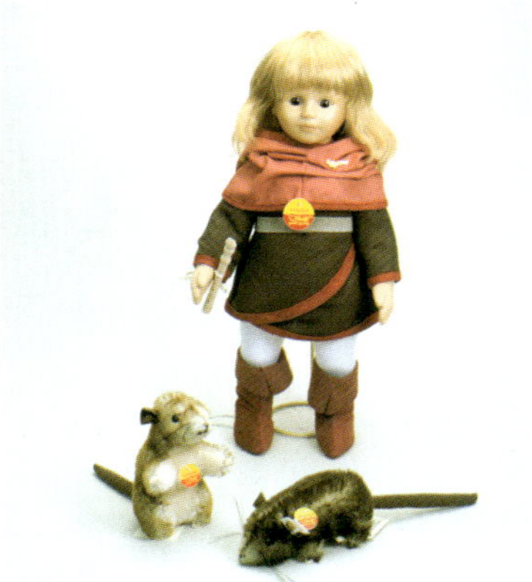

Rattenfaenger mit Ratten - *Pied Piper with Rats*

lim. Auflage 500 Stueck, mit 2 Ratten (je 12 cm) - *limited edition of 500, with 2 rats (12 cm each)*

EAN-No.	Period	Pr.	Info
701191	1997-1997	5	43 cm

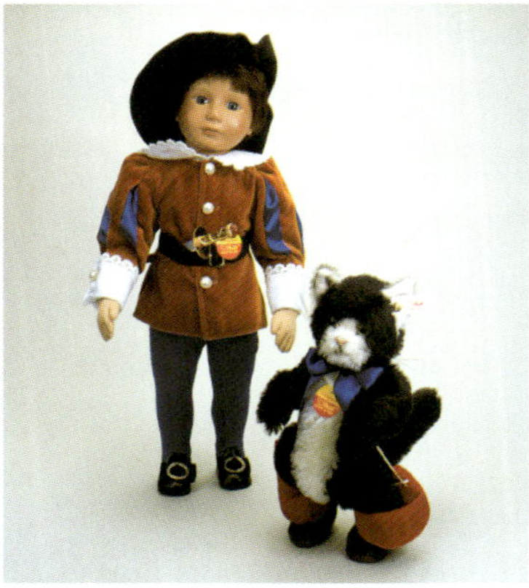

Puppe mit gestiefeltem Kater - *Doll with Puss in Boots*

lim. Auflage 500 Stueck mit Kater (25 cm) - *ltd edition of 500, with tomcat (25 cm)*

EAN-No.	Period	Pr.	Info
703256	1997-1997	5	50 cm

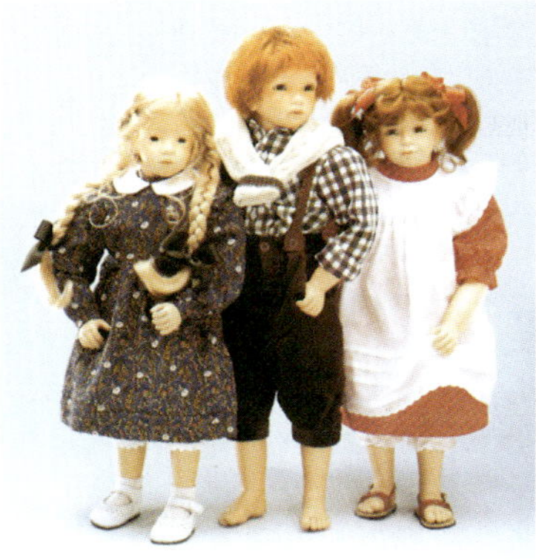

Kuenstlerpuppen von Rosa Adami - *Artist Dolls by Rosa Adami*

Kopf & Glieder Porzellan, Glasaugen, Koerper Ziegenleder, Echthaarperuecke, Markierung und Numerierung am Hals sowie Echtheits-Zertifikat am Handgelenk, lim. Aufl. 300 Stueck - *head & limbs porcelain, glass eyes, body covered with goat leather, real hair wigs, marked & numbered on the neck & a certificate of authenticity around the wrist, ltd edition of 300*

EAN-No.	Period	Pr.	Info
705014	1993-1996	6-7	60 cm, Monika
705021	1993-1994	6-7	64 cm, Michael
705038	1993-1996	6-7	56 cm, Verena

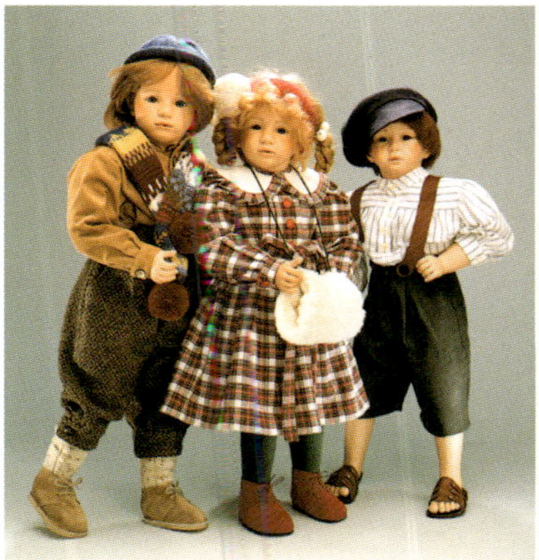

Kuenstlerpuppen von Rosa Adami - *Artist Dolls by Rosa Adami*

Kopf & Glieder Porzellan, Glasaugen, Koerper Ziegenleder, Echthaarperuecke, Markierung und Numerierung am Hals sowie Echtheits-Zertifikat am Handgelenk, lim. Aufl. 300 Stueck - *head & limbs porcelain, glass eyes, body covered with goat leather, real hair wigs, marked & numbered on the neck & a certificate of authenticity around the wrist, ltd edition of 300*

EAN-No.	Period	Pr.	Info
705045	1994-1996	6-7	60 cm, Viktor
705052	1994-1995	6-7	60 cm, Fanni
705069	1994-1995	6-7	65 cm, Felix

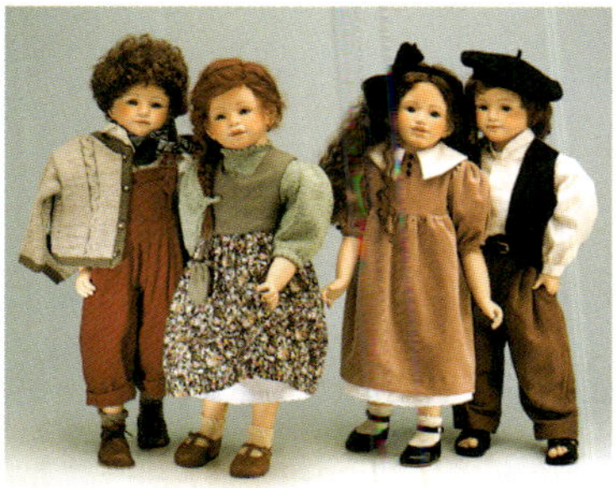

Kuenstlerpuppen von Rosa Adami - *Artist Dolls by Rosa Adami*

Kopf & Glieder Porzellan, Glasaugen, Koerper Ziegenleder, Echthaarperuecke, Markierung und Numerierung am Hals sowie Echtheits-Zertifikat am Handgelenk, lim. Aufl. 300 Stueck - *head & limbs porcelain, glass eyes, body covered with goat leather, real hair wigs, marked & numbered on the neck & a certificate of authenticity around the wrist, ltd edition of 300*

EAN-No.	Period	Pr.	Info
705083	1995-1997	6-7	65 cm, Arno
705090	1995-1997	6-7	60 cm, Anna
705106	1995-1996	6-7	60 cm, Sonja
705113	1995-1996	6-7	65 cm, Sebastian

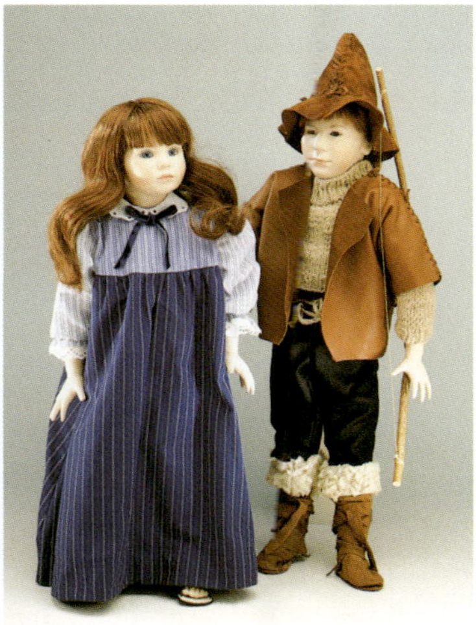

Kuenstlerpuppen von Christl Baust - *Artist Dolls by Christl Baust*

Kopf & Glieder Porzellan, Glasaugen, Koerper Ziegenleder, Echthaarperuecke, Markierung und Numerierung am Hals sowie Echtheits-Zertifikat am Handgelenk, lim. Aufl. 300 Stueck - *head & limbs porcelain, glass eyes, body covered with goat leather, real hair wigs, marked & numbered on the neck & a certificate of authenticity around the wrist, ltd edition of 300*

EAN-No.	Period	Pr.	Info
705502	1995-1995	5-7	65 cm, Marian
705519	1995-1995	6-7	70 cm, Robin

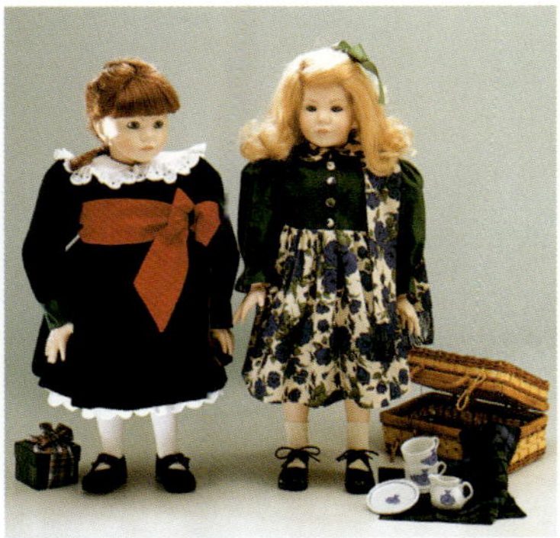

Kuenstlerpuppen von Christl Baust - *Artist Dolls by Christl Baust*

Kopf & Glieder Porzellan, mundgeblasene Glasaugen, Echthaarperuecke, Irene mit Geschenk, Lore mit Picknickkorb, limit. Auflage je 50 Stueck - *head & limbs porcelain, mouth blown glass eyes, genuine hair wig, Irene with present, Lore with picnic basket, ltd edition of 50 each*

EAN-No.	Period	Pr.	Info
705533	1995-1996	6-7	65 cm, Irene
705540	1996-1996	6-7	65 cm, Lore

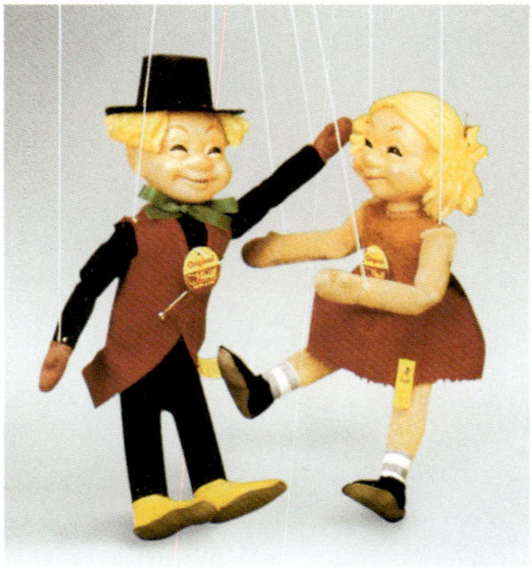

Marionette Bub / Maid - *Marionette Boy / Girl*

Bub: schwarz gekleidet, roter Frack, schwarzer Zylinder, blonde Haare, Maid: rotes Kleid, blonde Haare, 32 cm, mit je 4 Nylonfaeden, abwaschbar - *boy: dressed in black with a red tail coat & black top hat, blond hair, maid: wearing red dress, blond hair, 32 cm, each with four nylon strings attached. surface washable*

Serie	Art.-No	Period	Pr.	Info
	7720/32	1974-1975	3-4	Bub - *Boy*
	7721/32	1974-1975	3-4	Maid - *Girl*

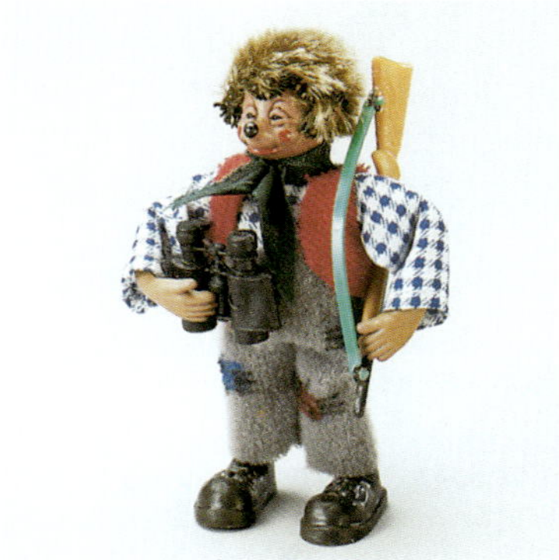

Macky Jaeger - *Macky Hunter*

Kunststoff, bekleidet, Plastikschachtel - *plastic, fully dressed, plastic box*

Serie	Art.-No	Period	Pr.	Info
	7630/10	1978-1978	2-3	10 cm

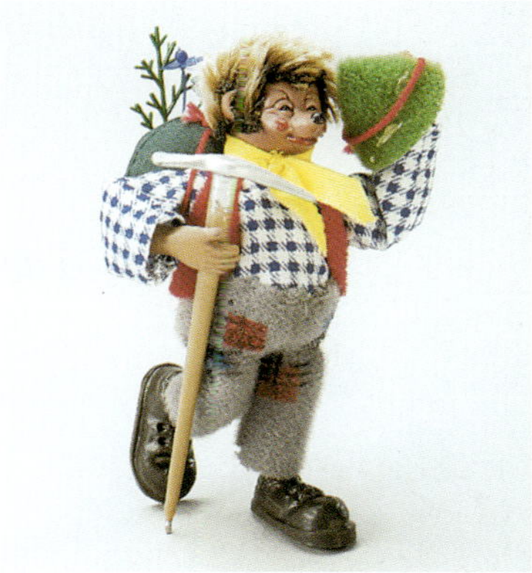

Macky Wanderer - *Macky Hobo*

Kunststoff, bekleidet, Plastikschachtel - *plastic, fully dressed, plastic box*

Serie	Art.-No	Period	Pr.	Info
	7631/10	1978-1978	2-3	10 cm

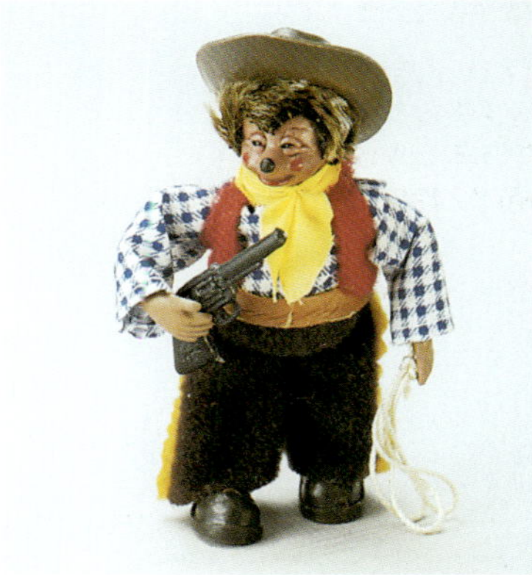

Macky Cowboy

Kunststoff, bekleidet, Plastikschachtel - *plastic, fully dressed, plastic box*

Serie	Art.-No	Period	Pr.	Info
	7632/10	1978-1978	2-3	10 cm

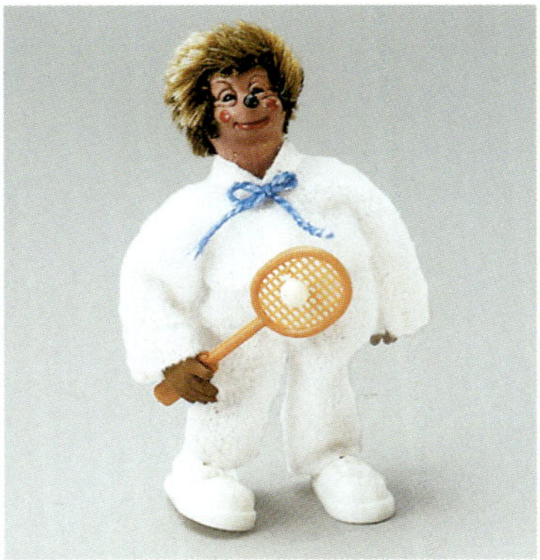

Macky Tennisspieler - *Macky Tennis Player*

Kunststoff, bekleidet, Plastikschachtel - *plastic, fully dressed, plastic box*

Serie	Art.-No	Period	Pr.	Info
	7633/10	1978-1978	2-3	10 cm

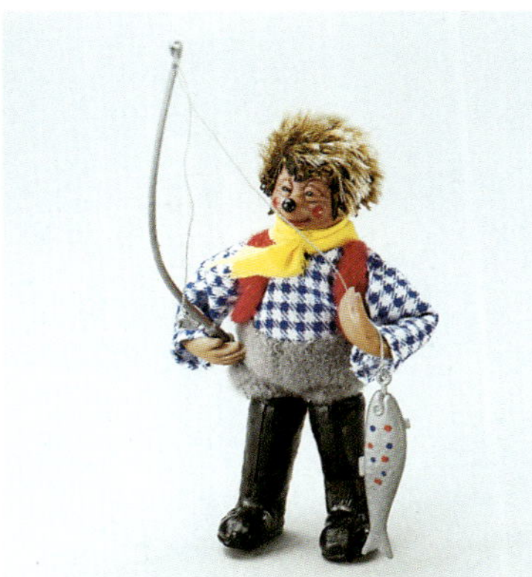

Macky Angler - *Macky Fisherman*

Kunststoff, bekleidet, Plastikschachtel - *plastic, fully dressed, plastic box*

Serie	Art.-No	Period	Pr.	Info
	7634/10	1978-1978	2-3	10 cm

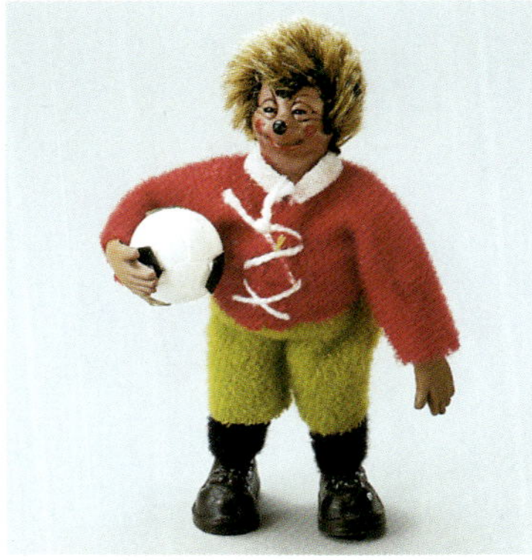

Macky Fussballspieler - *Macky Soccer Player*

Kunststoff, bekleidet, Plastikschachtel - *plastic, fully dressed, plastic box*

Serie	Art.-No	Period	Pr.	Info
	7635/10	1978-1978	2-3	10 cm

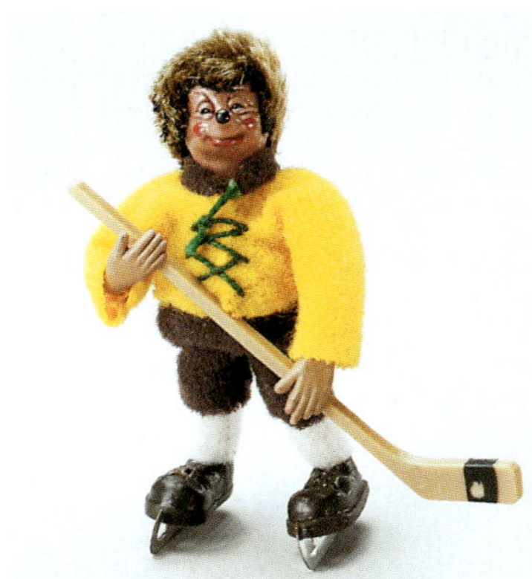

Macky Eishockeyspieler - *Macky Ice Hockey Player*

Kunststoff, bekleidet, Plastikschachtel - *plastic, fully dressed, plastic box*

Serie	Art.-No	Period	Pr.	Info
	7636/10	1978-1978	2-3	10 cm

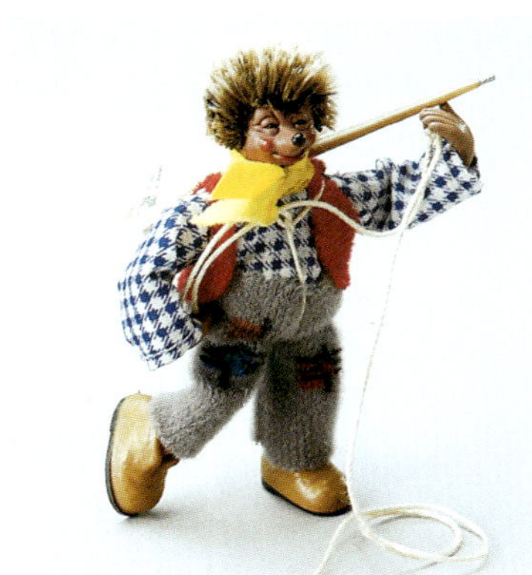

Macky Kletterer - *Macky Mountain Climber*

Kunststoff, bekleidet, Plastikschachtel - *plastic, fully dressed, plastic box*

Serie	Art.-No	Period	Pr.	Info
	7637/10	1978-1978	2-3	10 cm

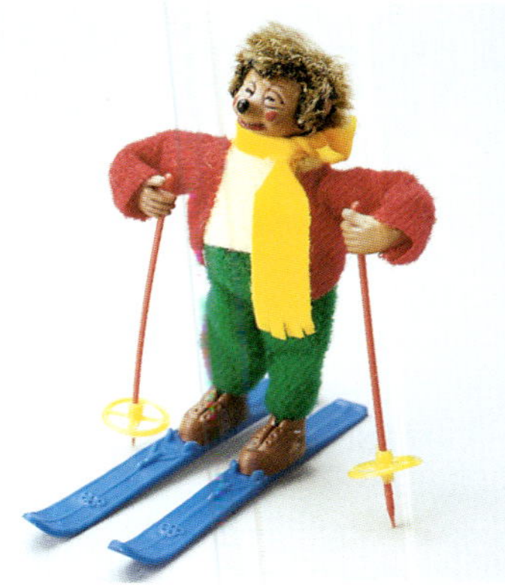

Macky Skifahrer - *Macky the Skier*

Kunststoff, bekleidet, Plastikschachtel - *plastic, fully dressed, plastic box*

Serie	Art.-No	Period	Pr.	Info
	7638/10	1978-1978	2-3	10 cm

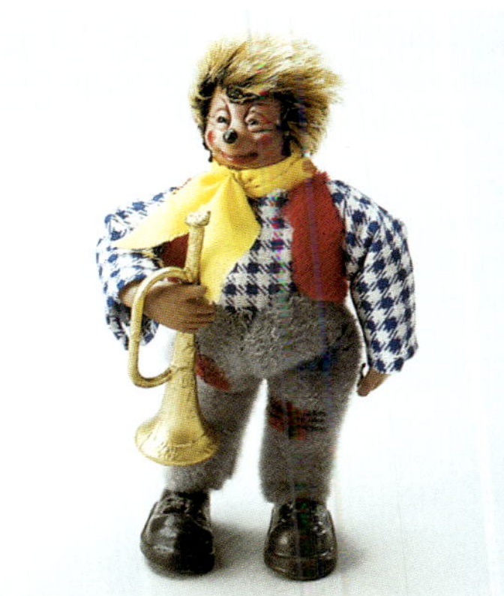

Macky Trompeter - *Macky Trumpeter*

Kunststoff, bekleidet, Plastikschachtel - *plastic, fully dressed, plastic box*

Serie	Art.-No	Period	Pr.	Info
	7640/10	1978-1978	2-3	10 cm

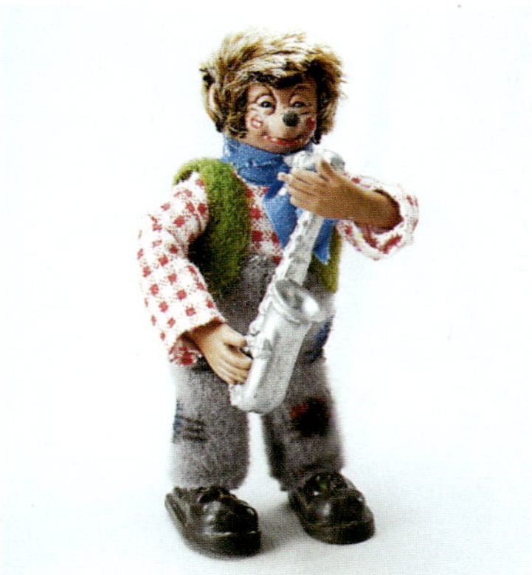

Macky Saxophonist - *Macky Saxophone Player*

Kunststoff, bekleidet, Plastikschachtel - *plastic, fully dressed, plastic box*

SERIE	ART.-NO	PERIOD	PR.	INFO
	7641/10	1978-1978	2-3	10 cm

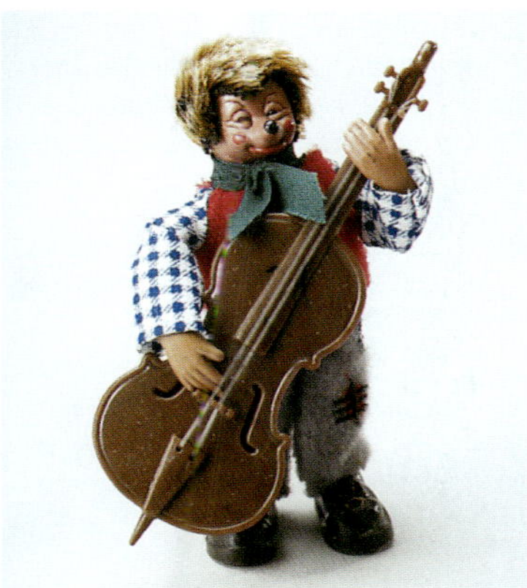

Macky Bassgeigenspieler - *Macky Double Bass Player*

Kunststoff, bekleidet, Plastikschachtel - *plastic, fully dressed, plastic box*

SERIE	ART.-NO	PERIOD	PR.	INFO
	7642/10	1978-1978	2-3	10 cm

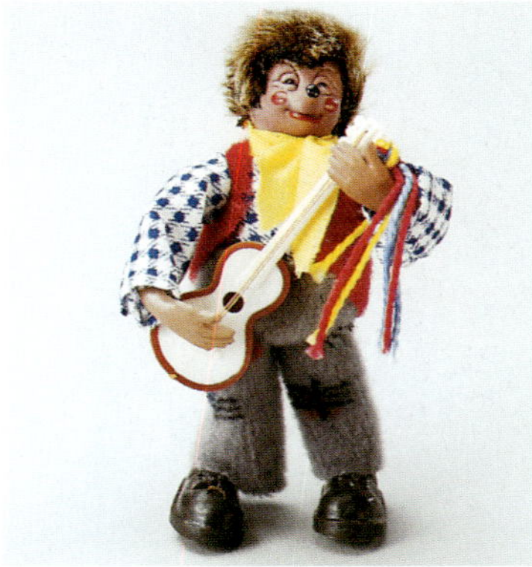

Macky Gitarrist - *Macky Guitarist*

Kunststoff, bekleidet, Plastikschachtel - *plastic, fully dressed, plastic box*

SERIE	ART.-NO	PERIOD	PR.	INFO
	7643/10	1978-1978	2-3	10 cm

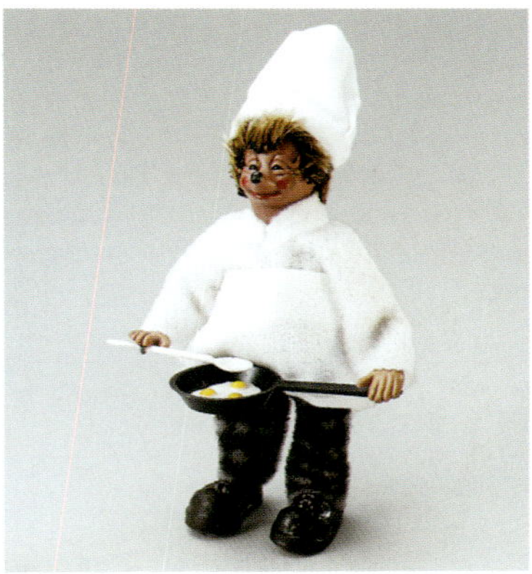

Macky Koch - *Macky Chef*

Kunststoff, bekleidet, Plastikschachtel - *plastic, fully dressed, plastic box*

SERIE	ART.-NO	PERIOD	PR.	INFO
	7644/10	1978-1978	2-3	10 cm

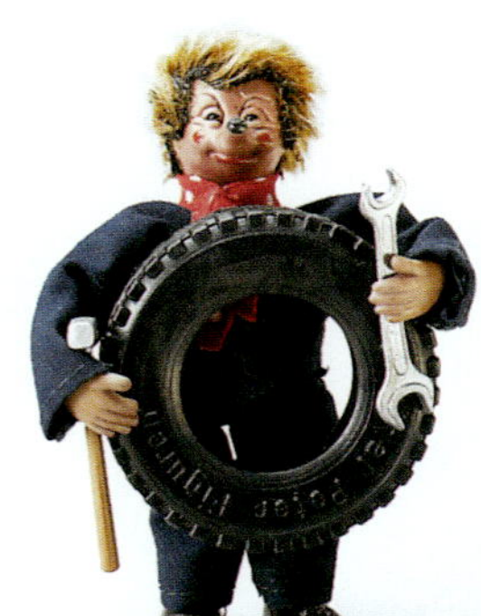

Macky Mechaniker - *Macky Mechanic*

Kunststoff, bekleidet, Plastikschachtel - *plastic, fully dressed, plastic box*

SERIE	ART.-NO	PERIOD	PR.	INFO
	7645/10	1978-1978	2-3	10 cm

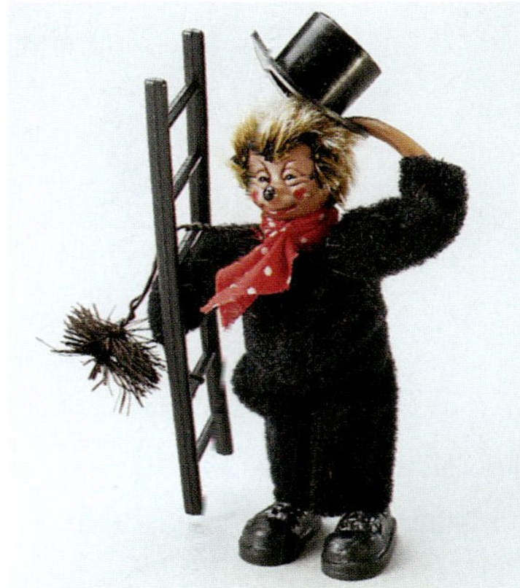

Macky Schornsteinfeger - *Macky Chimney Sweep*

Kunststoff, bekleidet, Plastikschachtel - *plastic, fully dressed, plastic box*

SERIE	ART.-NO	PERIOD	PR.	INFO
	7646/10	1978-1978	2-3	10 cm

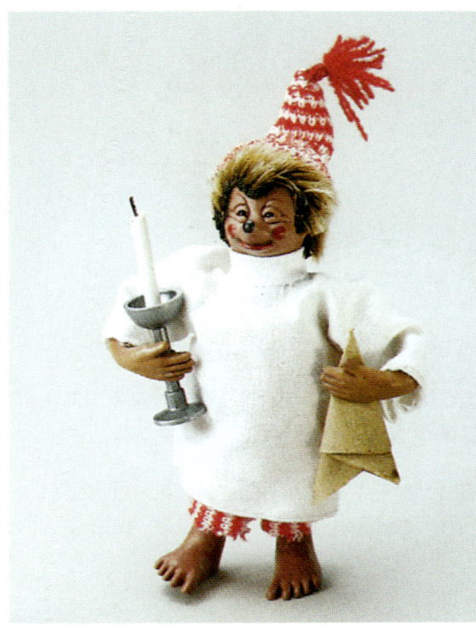

Macky Schlafwandler - *Macky Sleepwalker*

Kunststoff, bekleidet, Plastikschachtel - *plastic, fully dressed, plastic box*

SERIE	ART.-NO	PERIOD	PR.	INFO
	7647/10	1978-1978	2-3	10 cm

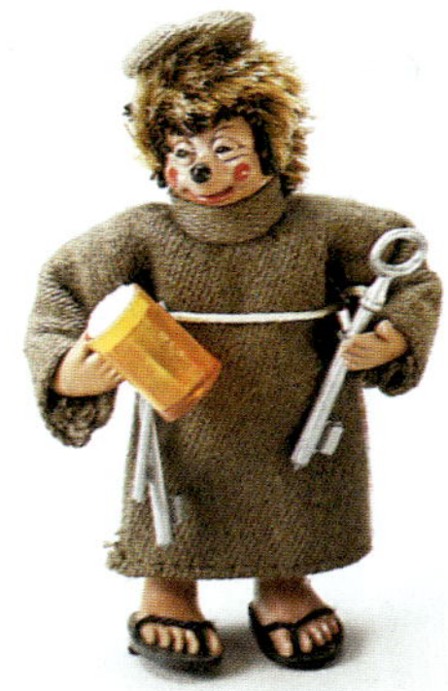

Macky Moench - *Macky Monk*

Kunststoff, bekleidet, Plastikschachtel - *plastic, fully dressed, plastic box*

SERIE	ART.-NO	PERIOD	PR.	INFO
	7648/10	1978-1978	2-3	10 cm

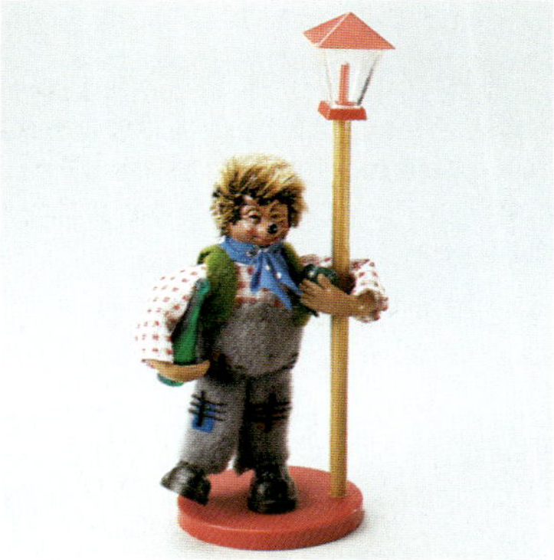

Macky Trinker - *Macky Drunkard*

Kunststoff, bekleidet, Plastikschachtel - *plastic, fully dressed, plastic box*

SERIE	ART.-NO	PERIOD	PR.	INFO
	7650/10	1978-1978	2-3	10 cm

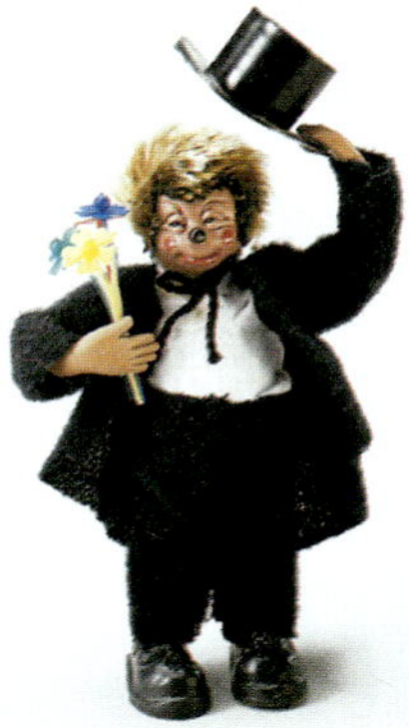

Macky Gratulant - *Macky Well-Wisher*

Kunststoff, bekleidet, Plastikschachtel - *plastic, fully dressed, plastic box*

SERIE	ART.-NO	PERIOD	PR.	INFO
	7652/10	1978-1978	2-3	10 cm

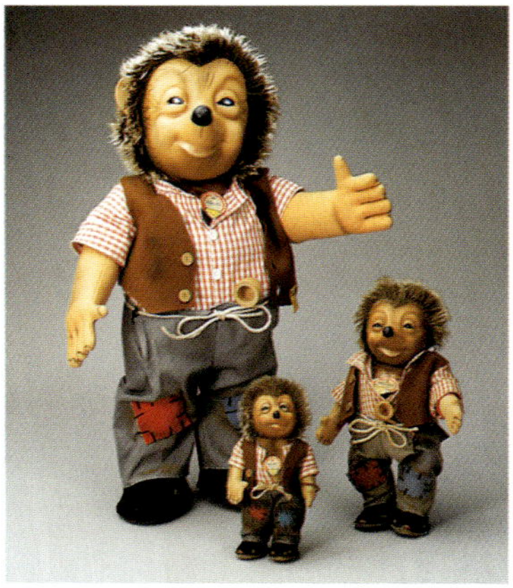

Mecki

Gummikopf, Ende 50er-Jahre Plastikkopf, ab 1979 PVC-Kopf, Stoff-/Filzkoerper, Redaktionsigel der HOER ZU, Copyr. Diehl-Film, rot/weiss kariertes Hemd, braune Weste, blaue Hose, Pfeife, 100 cm, Schaustueck - *rubber head, end of the 50´s plastic head, from 1979 PVC head, body made of fabric & felt, editor´s logo from "HOER ZU" magazine, Copyr. Diehl-Film, red/white checkered shirt, brown vest, blue trousers, with a pipe, 100 cm display piece*

SERIE	ART.-NO	PERIOD	PR.	INFO
88	**717** B	1952-1958	3-4	17 cm
900	**8717,70**	1959-1964	3	
762	**8717,70**	1965-1967	3	
350108	**7627/17**	1968-1990	2-3	
	350108	1991-1999	2-3	
88	**728** B	1951-1958	4	28 cm
900	**8728,70**	1959-1964	3-4	
762	**8728,70**	1965-1967	3-4	
350153	**7627/28**	1968-1990	3	
	350153	1991-1999	3	
88	**750** B	1952-1957	5	50 cm
900	**8750,70**	1959-1964	4-5	
762	**8750,70**	1965-1967	4-5	
350306	**7627/50**	1968-1990	4	
	350306	1991-1999	4	
	7629/10	1967-1967	6	100 cm

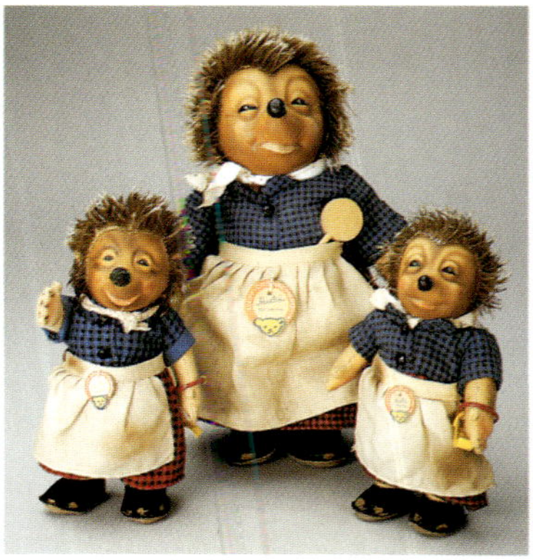

Micki

Gummikopf, Ende 50er-Jahre Plastikkopf, ab 1979 PVC-Kopf, Stoff-/Filzkoerper, Redaktionsigel der HOER ZU, Copyr. Diehl-Film, blau/schwarz karierte Bluse, blau/rot karierter Rock, beige Schuerze, Kochloeffel - *rubber head, end of the 50´s plastic head, from 1979 PVC head, body made of fabric & felt, editor´s logo from "HOER ZU" magazine, Copyr. Diehl-Film, blue & black checkered blouse, blue & red checkered skirt, beige apron, with a cooking spoon*

SERIE	ART.-NO	PERIOD	PR.	INFO
88	**717** M	1952-1958	3-4	17 cm
900	**8717,80**	1959-1964	3	
762	**8717,80**	1965-1967	3	
350603	**7628/17**	1968-1990	2-3	
	350603	1991-1999	2-3	
88	**728** M	1951-1958	4	28 cm
900	**8728,80**	1959-1964	3-4	
762	**8728,80**	1965-1967	3-4	
350658	**7628/28**	1968-1990	3	
	350658	1991-1999	3	
88	**750** M	1952-1957	5	50 cm
900	**8750,80**	1959-1964	4-5	
762	**8750,80**	1965-1967	4-5	
350801	**7628/50**	1968-1990	4	
	350801	1991-1999	4	

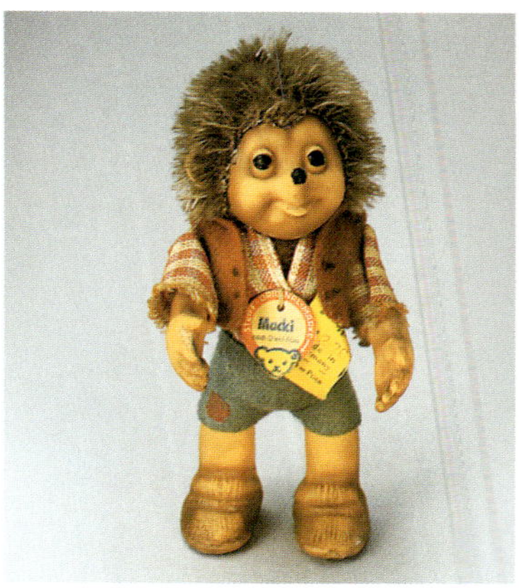

Macki (Bub) - ***Macki*** *(Boy)*

Gummigesicht, Vinylkoerper, ab Ende 50er-Jahre Kopf & Koerper Plastik, ab 1978 PVC, rot/weiss kariertes Hemd, braune Weste, blaue Hose, Redaktionsigel der HOER ZU, Copyr. Diehl-Film - *rubber face, body made of vinyl, end of the 50´s head & body plastic, from 1978 PVC, red/white checkered shirt, brown vest, blue trousers, editor´s logo from "HOER ZU" magazine, Copyr. Diehl-Film*

Serie	Art.-No	Period	Pr.	Info
88	**712** B	1953-1958	3	12 cm
900	**8712,70**	1959-1964	2-3	
762	**8712,70**	1965-1967	2-3	
350054	**7627/12**	1968-1990	1-2	
	350054	1991-1999	1-2	

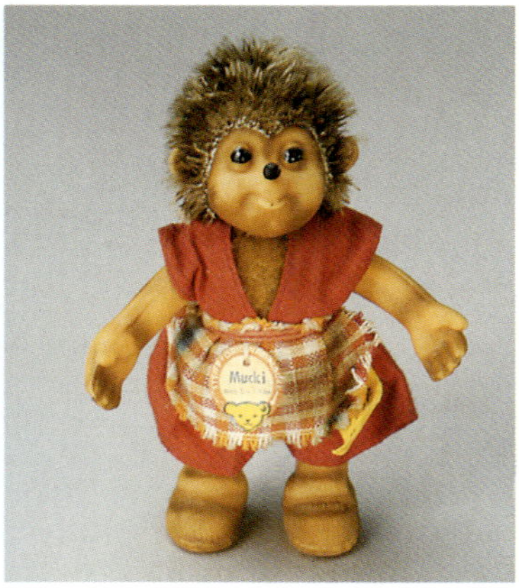

Mucki (Maid) - ***Mucki*** *(Girl)*

Gummigesicht, Vinylkoerper, ab Ende 50er-Jahre Kopf & Koerper Plastik, ab 1978 PVC, rotes Kleid, rot/weiss karierte Schuerze, Redaktionsigel der HOER ZU, Copyr. Diehl-Film - *rubber face, body made of vinyl, end of the 50´s head & body plastic, from 1978 PVC, red dress & red/white checkered apron, editor´s logo from "HOER ZU" magazine, Copyr. Diehl-Film*

Serie	Art.-No	Period	Pr.	Info
88	**712** M	1953-1958	3	12 cm
900	**8712,80**	1959-1964	2-3	
762	**8712,80**	1965-1967	2-3	
350559	**7628/12**	1968-1990	1-2	
	350559	1991-1999	1-2	

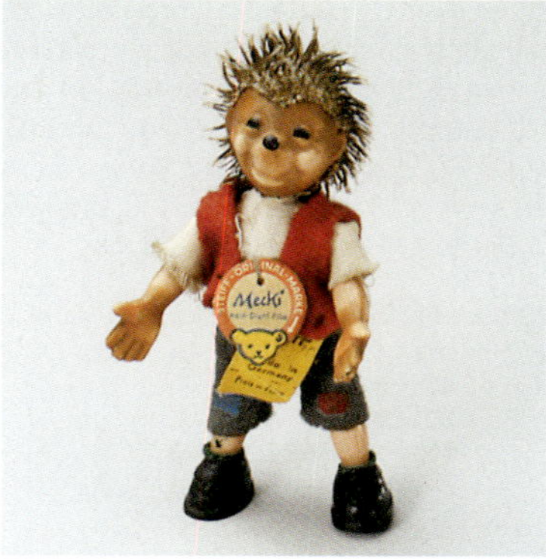

Miniatur **Mecki** Bub - *Miniature Boy* ***Mecki***

Kopf & Koerper aus Plastik, Biegefigur, Copyr. Diehl-Film - *head & body plastic, flexible body, Copyr. Diehl-Film*

Serie	Art.-No	Period	Pr.	Info
900	**8709,70**	1961-1964	3-4	9 cm

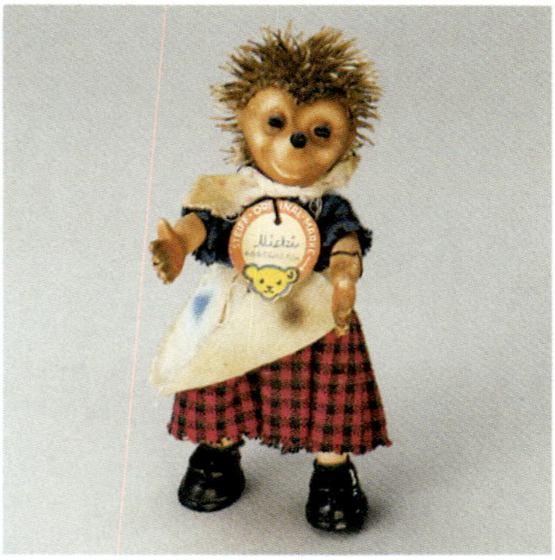

Miniatur **Micki** Maedel - *Miniature Girl* ***Micki***

Kopf & Koerper aus Plastik, Biegefigur, Copyr. Diehl-Film - *head & body plastic, flexible body, Copyr. Diehl-Film*

Serie	Art.-No	Period	Pr.	Info
900	**8709,80**	1961-1964	3-4	9 cm

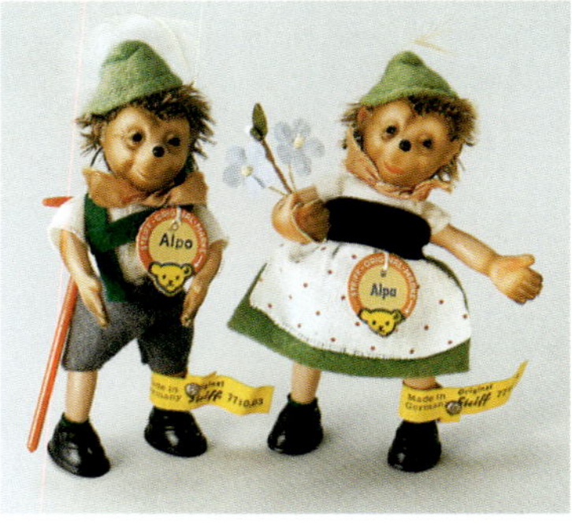

Alpo / Alpa

Bergler & Berglerin aus Miniatur-Mecki-Sortiment, Plastik, Biegefiguren, Copyr. Diehl-Film - *alpine Alpo & Alpa from the Miniature Mecki assortment, plastic, flexible bodies, Copyr. Diehl-Film*

Serie	Art.-No	Period	Pr.	Info
900	**7710,03**	1964-1964	4	10 cm, Alpo
900	**7710,04**	1964-1964	4	10 cm, Alpa

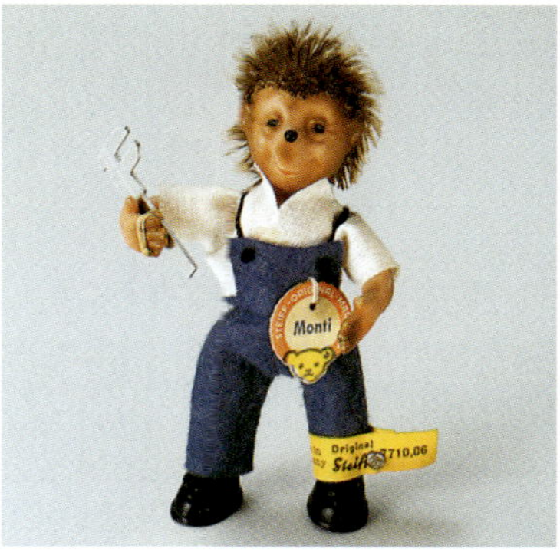

Monti

Monteur aus Miniatur-Mecki-Sortiment, Plastik, Biegefigur, Copyr. Diehl-Film - *mechanic from the Miniature Mecki assortment, plastic, flexible body, Copyr. Diehl-Film*

Serie	Art.-No	Period	Pr.	Info
900	**7710,06**	1964-1964	4	10 cm

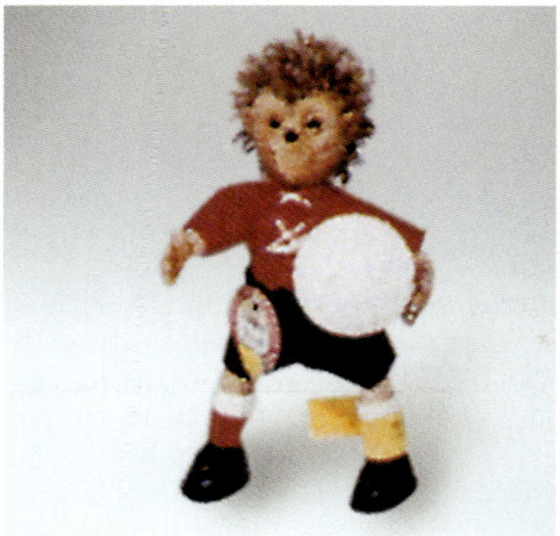

Fuba

Fussballer aus Miniatur-Mecki-Sortiment, Plastik, Biegefigur, Copyr. Diehl-Film - *soccer player from the Miniature Mecki assortment, plastic, flexible body, Copyr. Diehl-Film*

Serie	Art.-No	Period	Pr.	Info
900	**7710,05**	1964-1964	4	10 cm

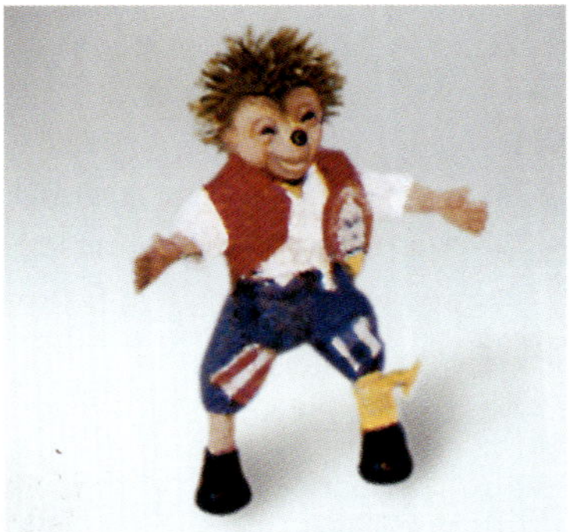

Mini **Mecki** Bub - *Mini **Mecki** Boy*

aus Miniatur-Mecki-Sortiment, Plastik, Biegefigur, Copyr. Diehl-Film - *from the Miniature Mecki assortment, plastic, flexible body, Copyr. Diehl-Film*

Serie	Art.-No	Period	Pr.	Info
900	**7710,01**	1964-1964	3-4	10 cm
760	**7710,01**	1965-1965	3-4	

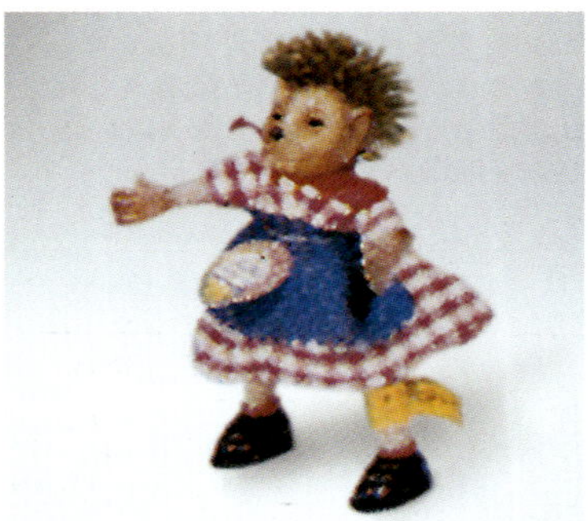

Mini **Micki** Maid

aus Miniatur-Mecki-Sortiment, Plastik, Biegefigur, Copyr. Diehl-Film - *from the Miniature Mecki assortment, plastic, flexible body, Copyr. Diehl-Film*

Serie	Art.-No	Period	Pr.	Info
900	**7710,02**	1964-1964	3-4	10 cm
760	**7710,02**	1965-1965	3-4	

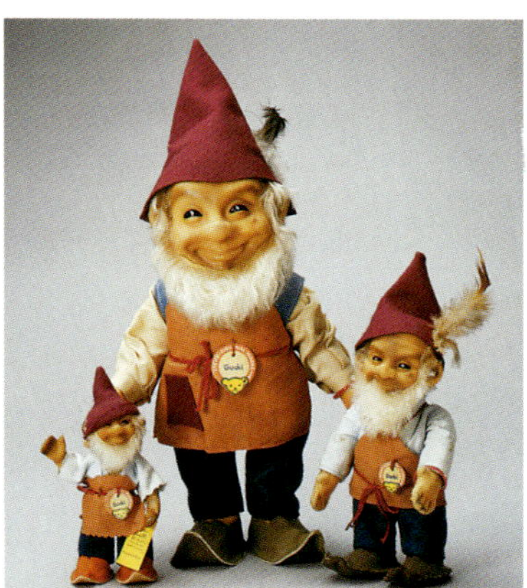

Zwerg **Gucki** - *Dwarf **Gucki***

Gummikopf, ab Ende 50er-Jahre Kunststoffkopf, ab 18 cm Filzkoerper mit beweglichen Armen & Beinen, Filzkleidung, 115 cm Schaustueck - *rubber head, from the end of the 50´s synthetic head, from 18 cm felt body with movable arms & legs, felt clothing, 115 cm display piece*

Serie	Art.-No	Period	Pr.	Info
88	**713,1**	1954-1958	3-4	13 cm
901	**8713,01**	1959-1964	3	
765	**8713,01**	1965-1967	3	
	7650/13	1968-1973	2-3	
88	**718,1**	1954-1958	3-4	18 cm
901	**8718,01**	1959-1964	3	
765	**8718,01**	1965-1967	3	
	7650/18	1968-1972	2-3	
88	**730,1**	1953-1958	4	30 cm
901	**8730,01**	1959-1964	3-4	
765	**8730,01**	1965-1967	3-4	
	7650/30	1968-1973	3	
88	**755,1**	1953-1957	4-5	55 cm
901	**8755,01**	1959-1964	4	
765	**8755,01**	1966-1967	4	
	7650/55	1968-1968	4	
901	**8115,91**	1960-1960	5-6	115 cm
	7659/12	1967-1967	5-6	

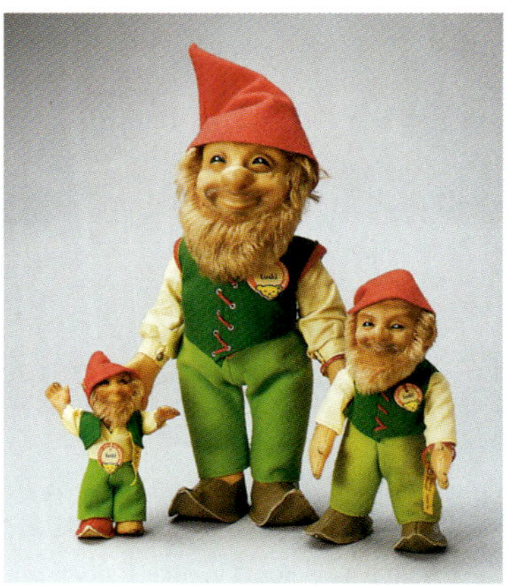

Zwerg **Lucki** - *Dwarf **Lucki***

Gummikopf, ab Ende 50er-Jahre Kunststoffkopf, ab 18 cm Filzkoerper mit beweglichen Armen & Beinen, Filzkleidung, 115 cm Schaustueck - *rubber head, from the end of the 50´s synthetic head, from 18 cm felt body with movable arms & legs, felt clothing, 115 cm display piece*

Serie	Art.-No	Period	Pr.	Info
88	**713,2**	1954-1958	3-4	13 cm
901	**8713,02**	1959-1964	3	
766	**8713,02**	1965-1967	3	
	7660/13	1968-1971	2-3	
88	**718,2**	1954-1958	3-4	18 cm
901	**8718,02**	1959-1964	3	
766	**8718,02**	1965-1967	3	
	7660/18	1968-1971	2-3	
88	**730,2**	1953-1958	4	30 cm
901	**8730,02**	1959-1964	3-4	
766	**8730,02**	1965-1967	3-4	
	7660/30	1968-1973	3	
88	**755,2**	1953-1957	4-5	55 cm
901	**8755,02**	1959-1964	4	
766	**8755,02**	1966-1967	4	
	7660/55	1968-1968	4	
901	**8115,92**	1960-1960	5-6	115 cm
	7669/12	1967-1967	5-6	

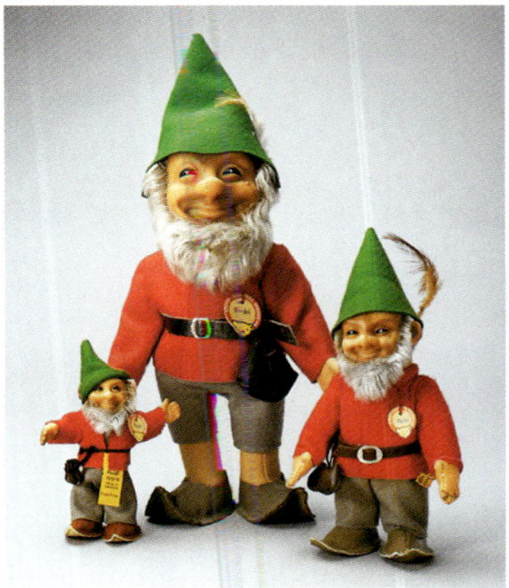

Zwerg **Pucki** - *Dwarf **Pucki***

Gummikopf, ab Ende 50er-Jahre Kunststoffkopf, ab 18 cm Filzkoerper mit beweglichen Armen & Beinen, Filzkleidung, 115 cm Schaustueck - *rubber head, from the end of the 50´s synthetic head, from 18 cm felt body with movable arms & legs, felt clothing, 115 cm display piece*

Serie	Art.-No	Period	Pr.	Info
88	**713,3**	1954-1958	3-4	13 cm
901	**8713,03**	1959-1964	3	
767	**8713,03**	1965-1967	3	
	7670/13	1968-1974	2-3	
88	**718,3**	1954-1958	3-4	18 cm
901	**8718,03**	1959-1964	3	
767	**8718,03**	1965-1967	3	
	7670/18	1968-1974	2-3	
88	**730,3**	1953-1958	4	30 cm
901	**8730,03**	1959-1964	3-4	
767	**8730,03**	1965-1967	3-4	
	7670/30	1968-1974	3	
88	**755,3**	1953-1957	4-5	55 cm
901	**8755,03**	1959-1964	4	
767	**8755,03**	1966-1967	4	
	7670/55	1968-1974	4	
901	**8115,93**	1960-1960	5-6	115 cm
	7679/12	1967-1967	5-6	

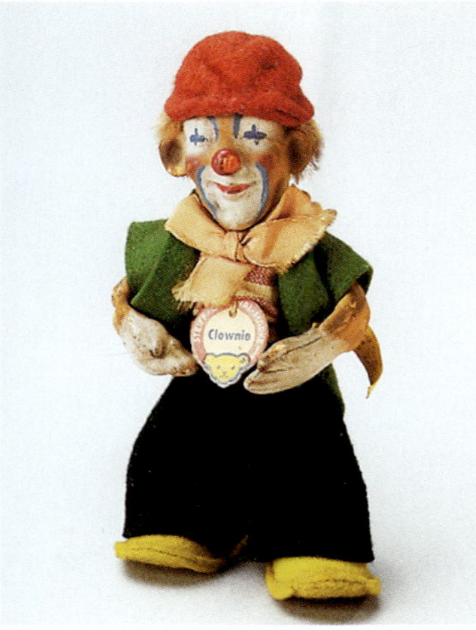

Clownie

14 cm Gummikopf und -koerper, 19 cm Gummikopf, Filzkoerper mit beweglichen Armen & Beinen, Filzkleidung - *14 cm size rubber head & body, 19 cm size rubber head & felt body with movable arms & legs, felt clothing*

SERIE	ART.-NO	PERIOD	PR.	INFO
88	**714**	1954-1955	5-6	14 cm
88	**719**	1954-1955	5-6	19 cm

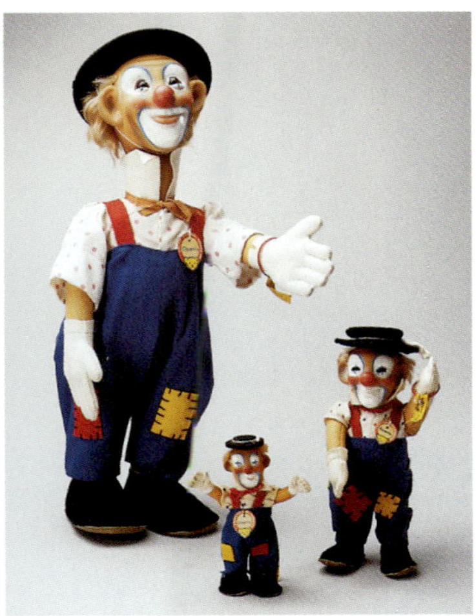

Clownie

Gummikopf & -koerper, ab Ende 50er-Jahre Kunststoffkopf, ab 19 cm Stoffkoerper mit beweglichen Armen, Filzkleidung - *rubber head & body, end of the 50´s synthetic head, from 19 cm body made of fabric with movable arms, felt clothing*

SERIE	ART.-NO	PERIOD	PR.	INFO
88	**714**	1956-1957	4	14 cm
902	**8714,00**	1959-1964	3-4	
770	**8714,00**	1965-1967	3-4	
	7700/14	1968-1975	3	
88	**719**	1956-1958	4-5	19 cm
902	**8719,00**	1959-1964	4	
770	**8719,00**	1965-1967	4	
	7700/19	1968-1975	3-4	
88	**743**	1953-1957	5-6	43 cm
902	**8743,00**	1959-1964	5	
770	**8743,00**	1965-1967	5	
	7700/43	1968-1975	4-5	
88	**7120**	1953-1953	6-7	120 cm, Schaustueck - *display piece*
902	**8120,90**	1960-1960	6	
	7709/12	1967-1967	6	

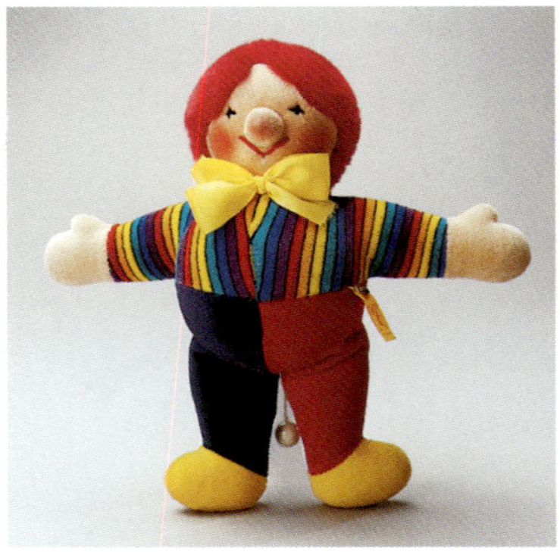

Musik Clown - *Musical Clown*

Nicki-Stoff, formgeschaeumt, Musikwerk austauschbar - *nicki velvet, stuffed with pre-formed foam, music box can be exchanged*

SERIE	ART.-NO	PERIOD	PR.	INFO
232305	**6362/26**	1986-1990	2-3	26 cm
	232305	1991-1996	2-3	

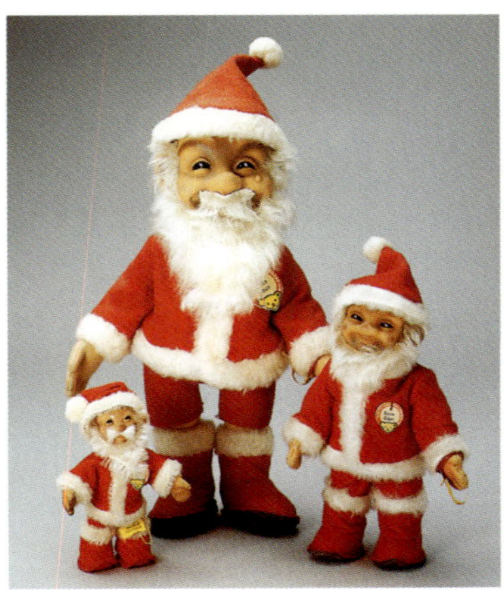

Santa Claus

Gummikopf, Filzkoerper mit beweglichen Armen & Beinen, Filzkleidung - *rubber head, felt body with movable arms & legs, felt clothing*

SERIE	ART.-NO	PERIOD	PR.	INFO
88	**113**	1954-1957	5-6	13 cm
903	**8013,08**	1961-1963	5	
88	**118**	1955-1957	5-6	18 cm
903	**8018,08**	1961-1963	5	
88	**731**	1953-1957	6	31 cm
903	**8031,08**	1961-1963	5-6	
903	**8150,90**	1960-1960	6-7	150 cm, Schaustueck - *display piece*
	7729/15	1967-1967	6-7	

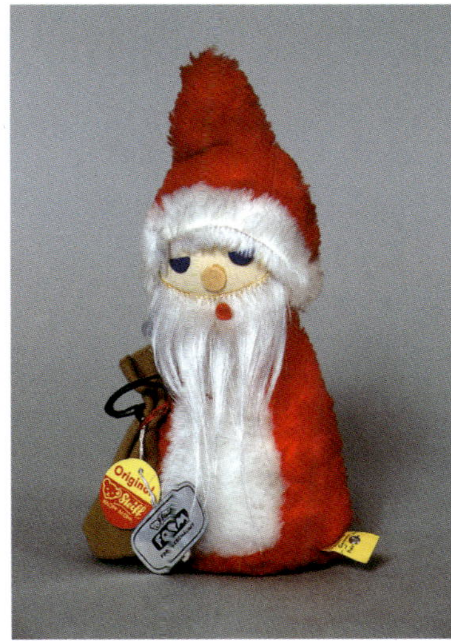

Buzzel Nico Nikolaus - *Buzzel Nico Santa Claus*

Dralon (Orlon), formgeschaeumt, superweich, vollwaschbar - *dralon (orlon), stuffed with pre-formed foam, super soft, fully washable*

SERIE	ART.-NO	PERIOD	PR.	INFO
	6175/20	1972-1974	2	20 cm

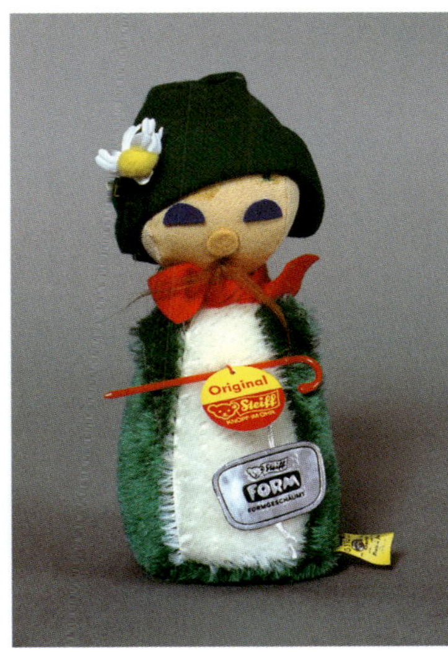

Buzzel Sepp

Dralon, formgeschaeumt, gruen/weiss, superweich, vollwaschbar - *dralon, stuffed with pre-formed foam, green/white, super soft, fully washable*

SERIE	ART.-NO	PERIOD	PR.	INFO
	6176/20	1972-1974	2	20 cm

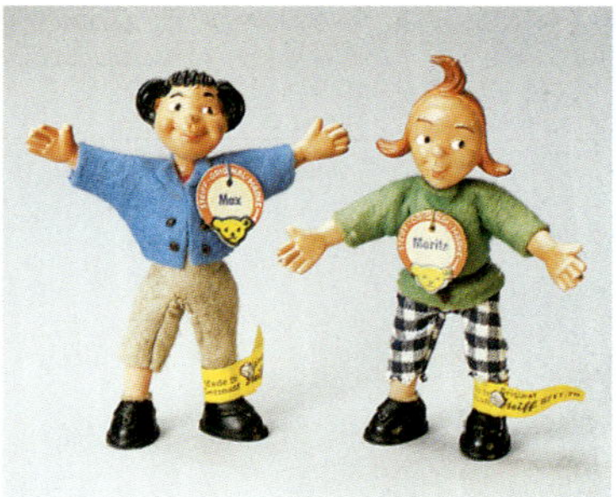

Max / **Moritz**

Biegefiguren, Plastikkoerper, Filzkleidung - *flexible figures, plastic bodies, felt clothing*

SERIE	ART.-NO	PERIOD	PR.	INFO
906	**8710,70**	1962-1963	3-4	10 cm, Max
774	**8710,70**	1965-1967	3-4	
906	**8711,70**	1962-1963	3-4	10 cm, Moritz
774	**8711,70**	1965-1967	3-4	

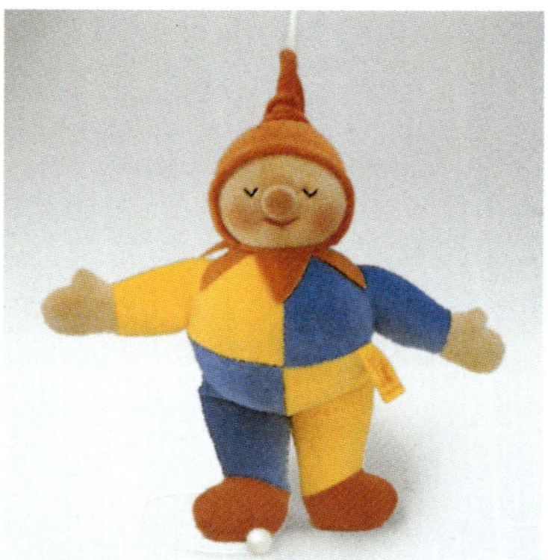

Musik Hampelmann - *Musical Puppet*

Nicki-Stoff, formgeschaeumt, Musikwerk austauschbar - *nicki velvet, stuffed with pre-formed foam, music box can be exchanged*

SERIE	ART.-NO	PERIOD	PR.	INFO
232107	**6360/26**	1986-1988	2	26 cm

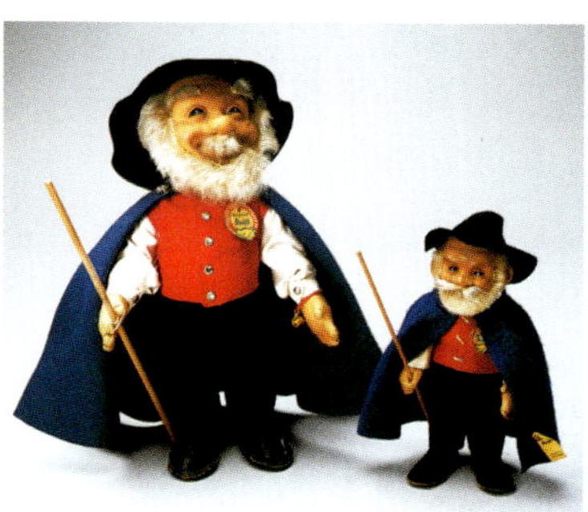

Schaefer - *Shepherd*

Gummi-, ab ca. 1960 Plastikkopf, Filzkoerper mit beweglichen Armen & Beinen, Filzkleidung, Schaeferstab aus Holz - *rubber-, from approx. 1960 plastic head, felt body with movable arms & legs, felt clothing, wooden shepherd´s staff*

SERIE	ART.-NO	PERIOD	PR.	INFO
	7750/19	1969-1974	3-4	19 cm
88	**735**	1958-1958	5	35 cm
920	**8735,00**	1959-1964	4-5	
775	**8735,00**	1965-1967	4-5	
	7750/35	1968-1974	4	
775	**8165,90**	1966-1966	6	165 cm, Schaustueck - *display piece*
	7759/17	1967-1967	6	

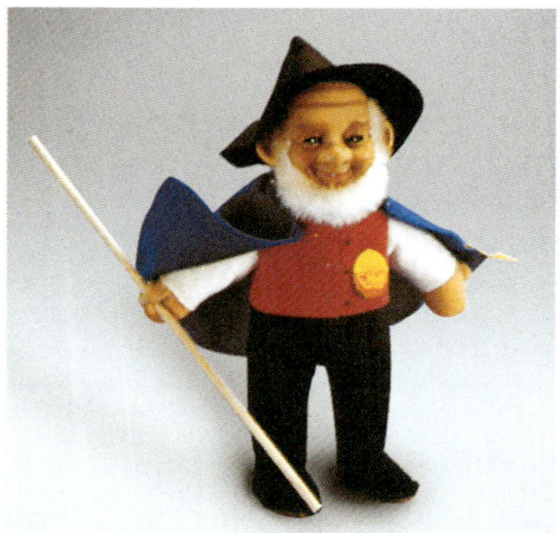

Vincenz Schaefer - ***Vincenz*** *Shepherd*

PVC-Kopf, Trevira-Samt, abwaschbar - *PVC head, trevira velvet, surface washable*

SERIE	ART.-NO	PERIOD	PR.	INFO
	7690/20	1978-1981	2-3	20 cm

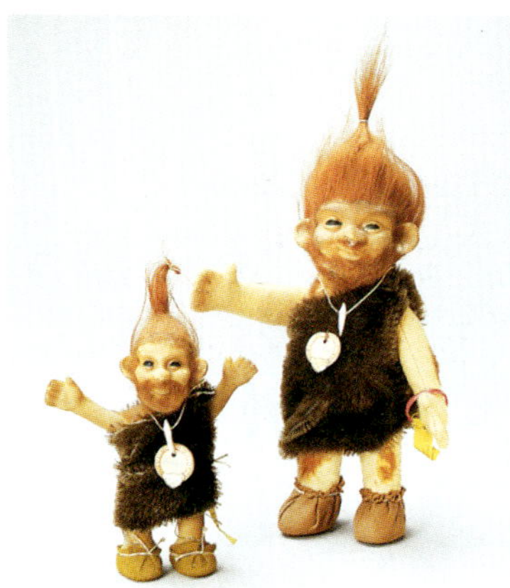

Urmensch **Neander** - *Caveman* ***Neander***

13 cm Plastikkopf (drehbar) & -koerper, 19 cm Plastikkopf & Filzkoerper mit beweglichem Kopf & Armen, Fell aus Mohair - *13 cm plastic head (swivels) & body, 19 cm plastic head & felt body with movable arms & head, mohair animal skin*

SERIE	ART.-NO	PERIOD	PR.	INFO
	7755/13	1968-1973	4	13 cm
	7755/19	1968-1974	4-5	19 cm

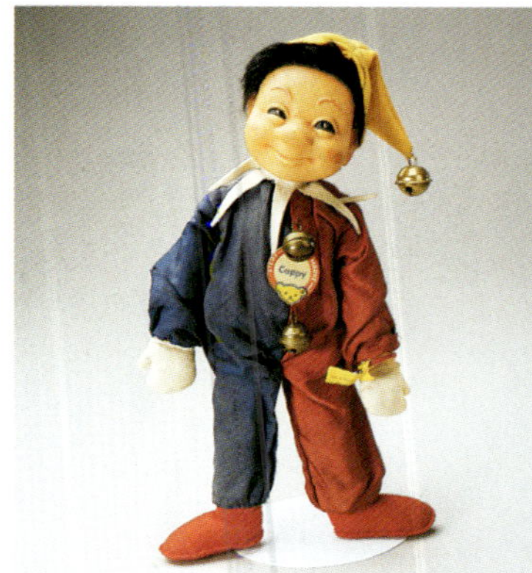

Cappy Schlenkerpuppe - ***Cappy*** *Floppy Doll*

Plastikkopf, Kleidung Kunstseidenstoff - *plastic head, artificial silk clothing*

SERIE	ART.-NO	PERIOD	PR.	INFO
925	**8728,70**	1963-1964	3	28 cm
776	**8728,70**	1965-1967	3	
	7760/28	1968-1974	3	

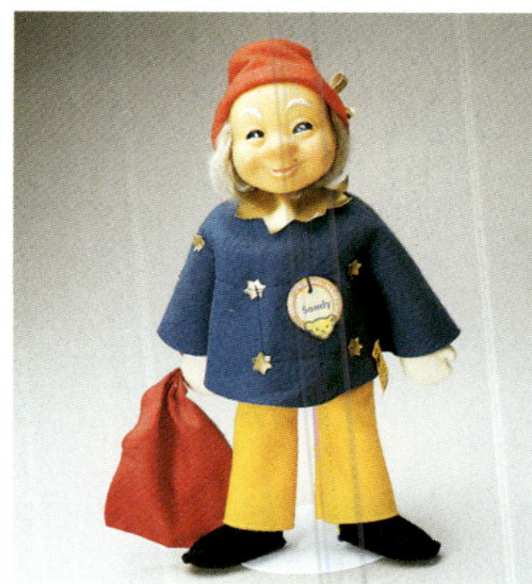

Sandmaennchen **Sandy** - *Sandman* ***Sandy***

Plastikkopf, Filzkleidung, mit rotem Sack, abwaschbar - *plastic head, felt clothing, with a red sack, surface washable*

SERIE	ART.-NO	PERIOD	PR.	INFO
776	**8729,70**	1965-1967	3	29 cm
	7760/29	1968-1974	3	

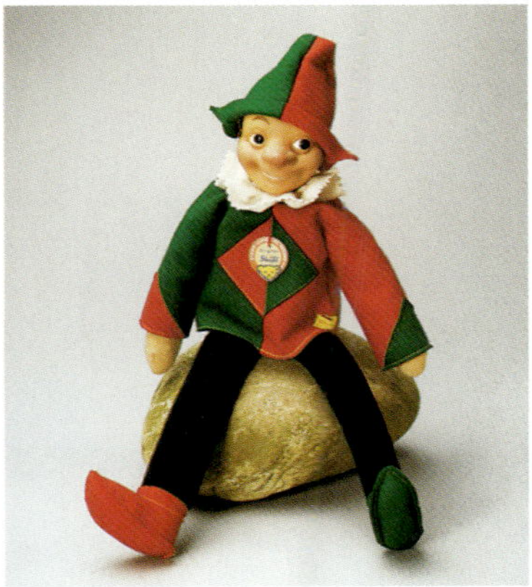

Schlenker-Harlekin - *Floppy Harlequin*

PVC-Kopf, Filz, Schlenkerglieder, abwaschbar - *PVC head, felt, floppy joints, surface washable*

SERIE	ART.-NO	PERIOD	PR.	INFO
	7760/40	1970-1974	3	40 cm

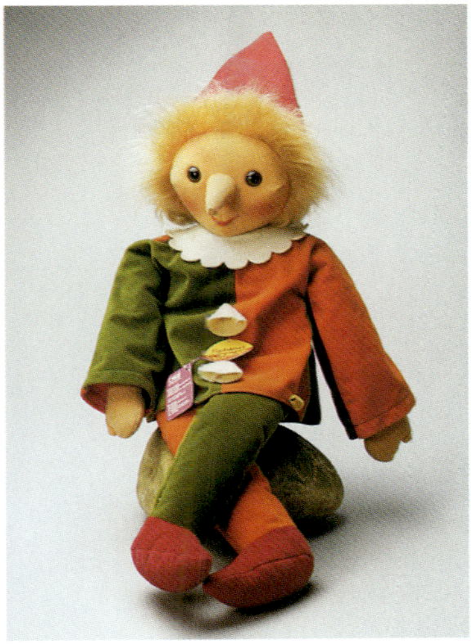

Schlori Kasper - ***Schlori** Punch*

Synthetik-Samt, ab 1979 Trevira-Samt, Schlenkerglieder, abwaschbar - *synthetic velvet, from 1979 trevira velvet, floppy joints, surface washable*

SERIE	ART.-NO	PERIOD	PR.	INFO
	7890/70	1978-1980	3-4	70 cm

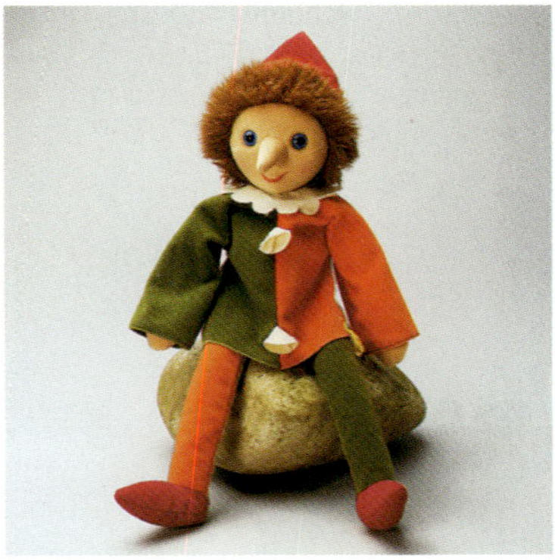

Lari Kasper - ***Lari** Punch*

Synthetik-Samt, ab 1979 Trevira-Samt, rot/gruen, Schlenkerglieder, abwaschbar - *synthetic velvet, from 1979 trevira velvet, red/green, floppy joints, surface washable*

SERIE	ART.-NO	PERIOD	PR.	INFO
	7891/40	1978-1980	2-3	40 cm

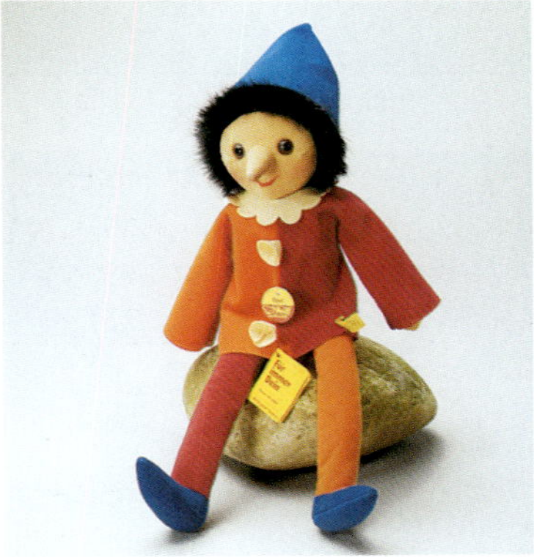

Fari Kasper - ***Fari** Punch*

Synthetik-Samt, ab 1979 Trevira-Samt, rot/blau, Schlenkerglieder, abwaschbar - *synthetic velvet, from 1979 trevira velvet, red/blue, floppy joints, surface washable*

SERIE	ART.-NO	PERIOD	PR.	INFO
	7892/40	1978-1982	2-3	40 cm

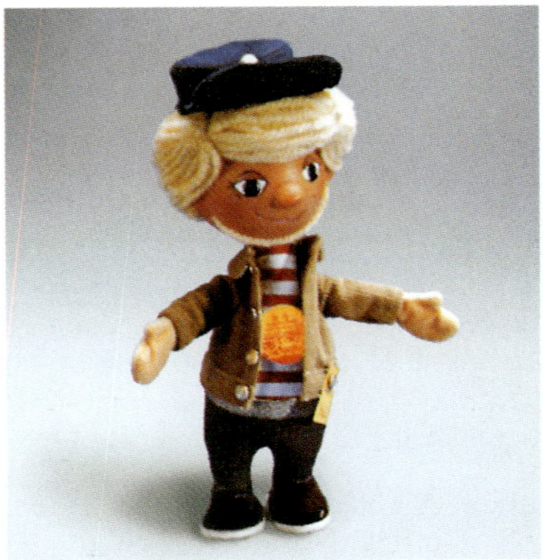

Sandmaennchen - *Sandman*

PVC-Kopf, abwaschbar - *PVC head, surface washable*

SERIE	ART.-NO	PERIOD	PR.	INFO
	7853/25	1979-1981	4	25 cm

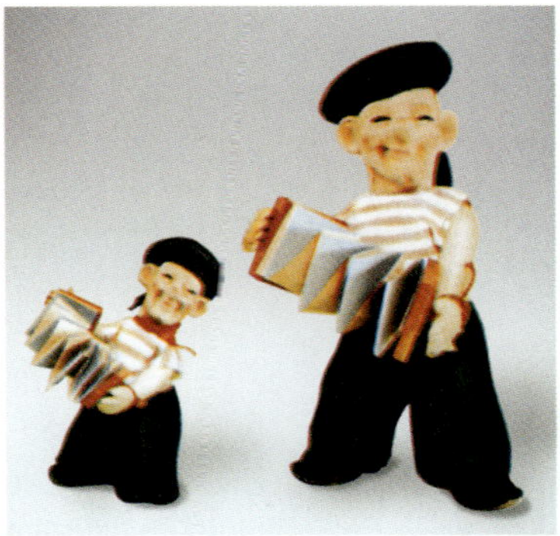

Mat Matrose - ***Mat** Sailor*

Gummikopf, rot/weiss gestreiftes Hemd - *rubber head, red & white striped shirt*

SERIE	ART.-NO	PERIOD	PR.	INFO
88	**114**	1954-1954	5-6	14 cm
88	**119**	1954-1954	6	19 cm

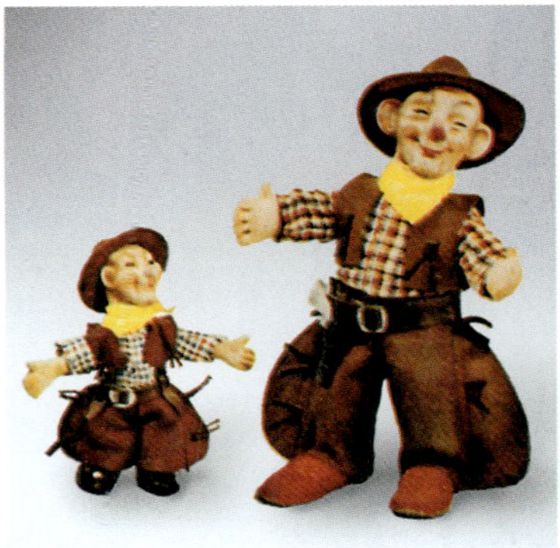

Boy Cowboy

Presskopf, Plastik-/Stoffkoerper, Filzkleidung - *molded head, body made of plastic & fabric, felt clothing*

SERIE	ART.-NO	PERIOD	PR.	INFO
88	**112**	1954-1957	5-6	12 cm
88	**117**	1954-1957	6	17 cm

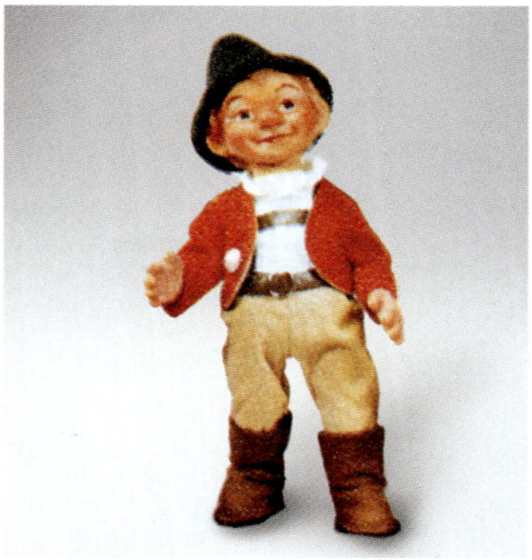

Larifari

Kinderbuchfigur, Anzug in rot/gelb/gruen, Copyr. Diehl - *character from a children´s book, dressed in red/yellow/green, Copyr. Diehl*

SERIE	ART.-NO	PERIOD	PR.	INFO
88	**732**	1955-1957	6	32 cm

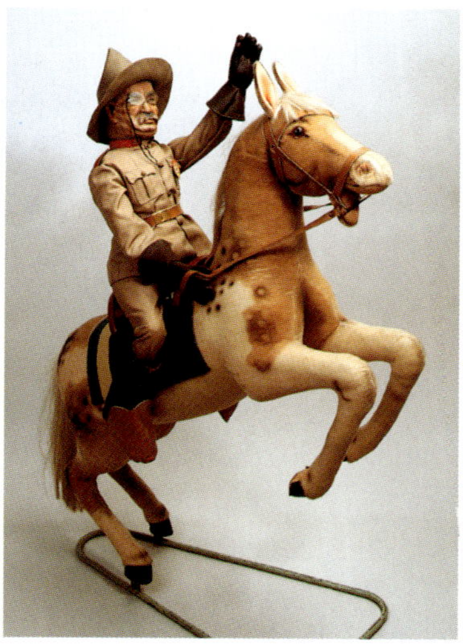

Teddy Roosevelt mit Pferd - *Teddy Roosevelt with horse*

Filz / Mohair, Schaustueck anlaesslich des 100. Geburtstages von Theodor (Teddy) Roosevelt, Gesamthoehe ca. 100 cm, Puppe 70 cm, Filzkoerper & Gummikopf, Lederhandschuhe & -stiefel, Holzsattel, ein Metalldorn verbindet Pferd, Sattel und Puppe - *felt / mohair, exhibition piece, produced on the occasion of Theodore (Teddy) Roosevelt 100th birthday, total size appr. 100 cm, doll 70 cm, felt body & rubber head, gloves & boots of leather, wooden saddle, a metal spike connects doll, saddle & horse*

EAN-NO.	PERIOD	PR.	INFO
	1958-1958	9	100 cm

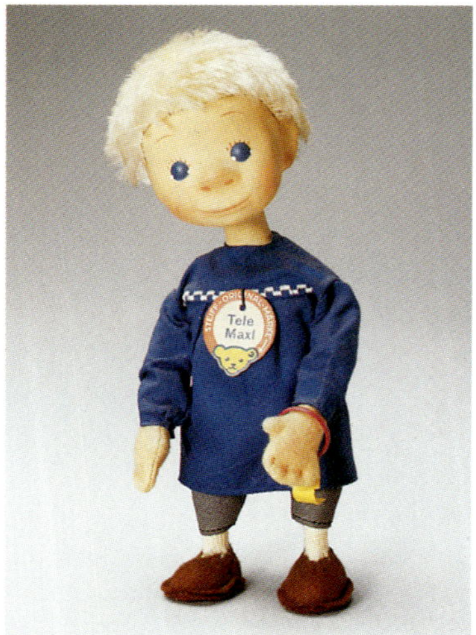

Tele-Maxl

Presskopf, blaues Hemd, blonde Haare, Fernseh-Figur - *molded head, blue shirt, blond hair, TV figure*

SERIE	ART.-NO	PERIOD	PR.	INFO
88	**720**	1958-1958	4	20 cm

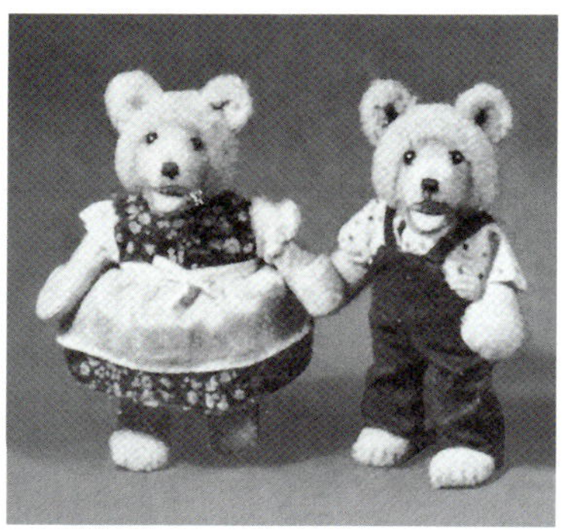

Puppbaer Maedel / Bub - *Doll Bear Girl / Boy*

Kopf Wollpluesch, mais, weicher Stoffkoerper, feste Beine, freistehend, Drehkopf, offener Mund, Schlenkerarme, Stimme - *plush wool head, corn yellow, soft fabric body, fixed legs, free-standing, head swivels, open mouth, floppy arms, voice*

SERIE	ART.-NO	PERIOD	PR.	INFO
91 12	**525,4**	1949-1950	6-7	25 cm
91 12	**525,8**	1949-1950	6-7	25 cm

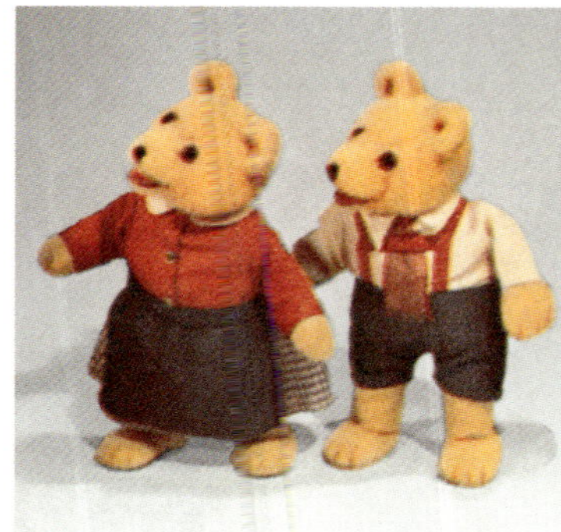

Puppbaer Maedel / Bub 1954 Teddyli - *Doll Bear Girl / Boy 1954 Teddyli*

Kopf aus Wollpluesch, Stoffkoerper, mais, freistehend, offener Mund, Kopf drehbar - *plush wool head, body made of fabric, corn yellow, free-standing, open mouth, head swivels*

SERIE	ART.-NO	PERIOD	PR.	INFO
91 12	**525** B	1951-1954	6-7	25 cm
91 12	**525** M	1951-1954	6-7	25 cm

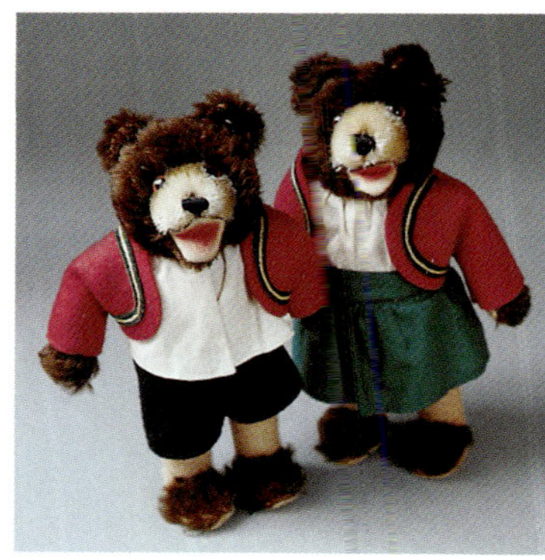

Puppbaer Maedel / Bub 1954 Teddyli - *Doll Bear Girl / Boy 1954 Teddyli*

Kopf aus Mohairpluesch, Stoffkoerper, braun, freistehend, Kopf drehbar, offener Mund - *mohair head, body made of fabric, brown, free-standing, head swivels, open mouth*

SERIE	ART.-NO	PERIOD	PR.	INFO
91 12	**325** B	1950-1957	6-7	25 cm
91 12	**325** M	1950-1957	6-7	25 cm

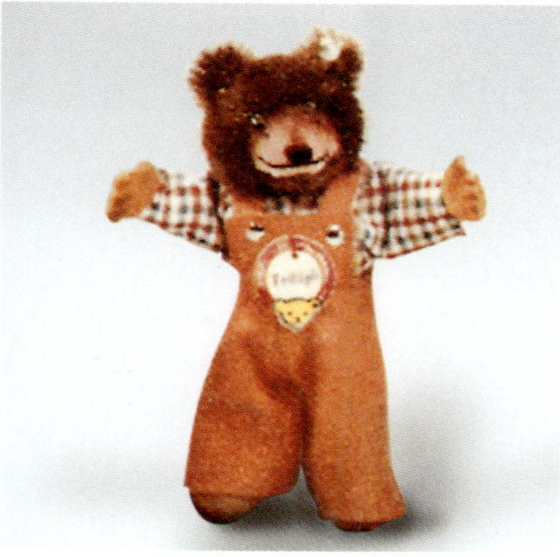

Teddyli

Gummikoerper, Plueschkopf, braun, freistehend, geschlossener Mund - *rubber body, plush head, brown, free-standing, mouth closed*

SERIE	ART.-NO	PERIOD	PR.	INFO
91 12	**712**	1955-1957	5-6	12 cm

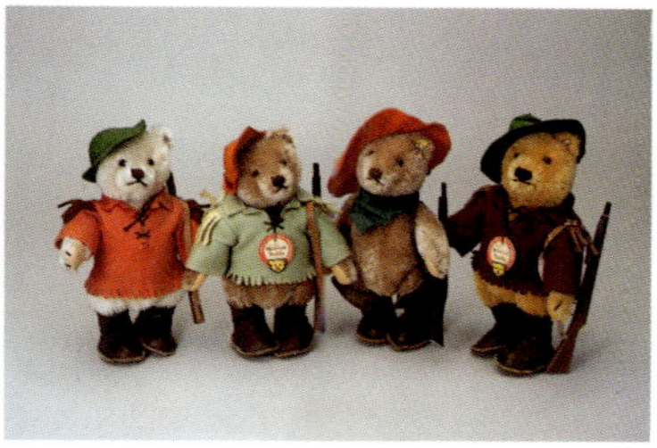

Nimrod Teddy

Original Teddybaer 5322,2 bzw. 5350,2 in verschiedenen Farben, als Jaeger bekleidet, braune Lederstiefel, Holzgewehr - *Original Teddybear 5322,2 or 5350,2 in different colors, dressed as a hunter, brown leather boots, wooden rifle*

SERIE	ART.-NO	PERIOD	PR.	INFO
12	**5322,2** N	1953-1954	6	22 cm, weiss, oranges Hemd, hellgruene Muetze - *white, orange shirt, light green cap*
12	**5350,2** N	1953-1953	8	50 cm
12	**5322,2** N	1953-1954	6	22 cm, gold, braunes Hemd, gruener Hut - *gold, brown shirt, green hat*
12	**5322,2** N	1953-1954	6	22 cm, caramel, hellgruenes Hemd, orange Muetze - *caramel, light green shirt, orange cap*
12	**5322,2** N	1953-1954	6	22 cm, caramel, gruenes Halstuch, oranger Hut - *caramel, green scarf, orange hat*

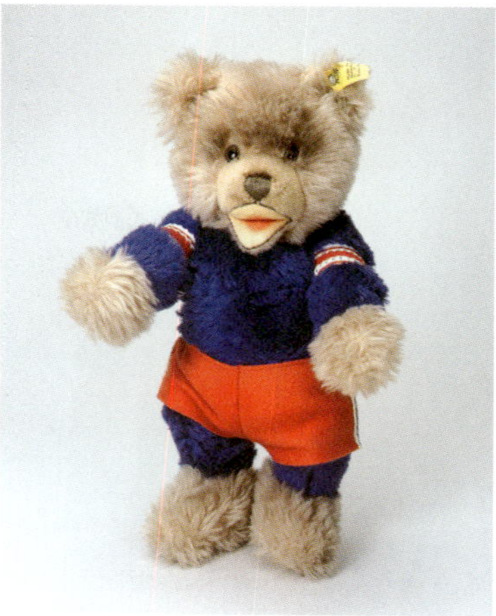

Hockey-Spieler Baer - *Hockey Player Bear*

Dolan, mit Sportdress, abwaschbar - *dolan, with Sport dress, surface washable*

SERIE	ART.-NO	PERIOD	PR.	INFO
	7824/30	1972-1975	3	30 cm

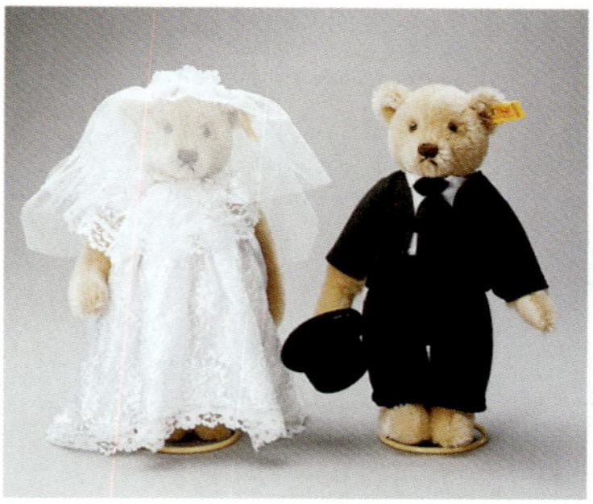

Teddybaer als Braut / Braeutigam - *Teddybear Bride / Groom*

Mohair Webpelz, gegliedert, abwaschbar - *mohair woven fur, jointed, surface washable*

SERIE	ART.-NO	PERIOD	PR.	INFO
010101	**0270/28**	1986-1988	3-4	28 cm, Braut - *bride*
010125	**0271/28**	1986-1988	3-4	28 cm, Braeutigam - *groom*

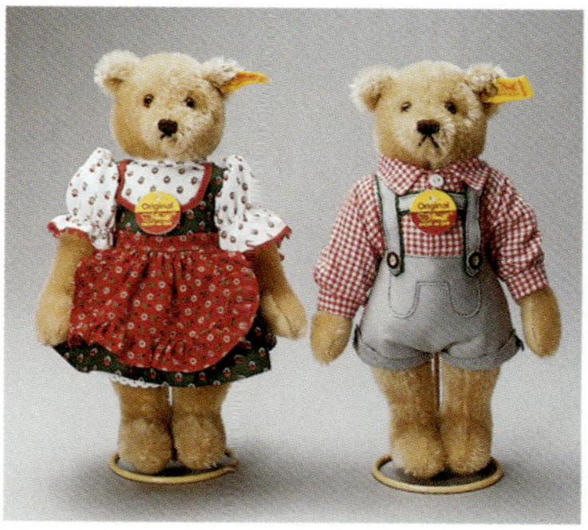

Teddybaer mit Dirndl / Lederhose - *Teddybear in Dirndl Dress / Leather Shorts*

Mohair Webpelz, gegliedert, abwaschbar - *mohair woven fur, jointed, surface washable*

SERIE	ART.-NO	PERIOD	PR.	INFO
010156	**0275/28**	1986-1988	3	28 cm, mit Dirndl - *Dirndl dress*
010170	**0276/28**	1986-1989	3	28 cm, mit Lederhose - *leather shorts*

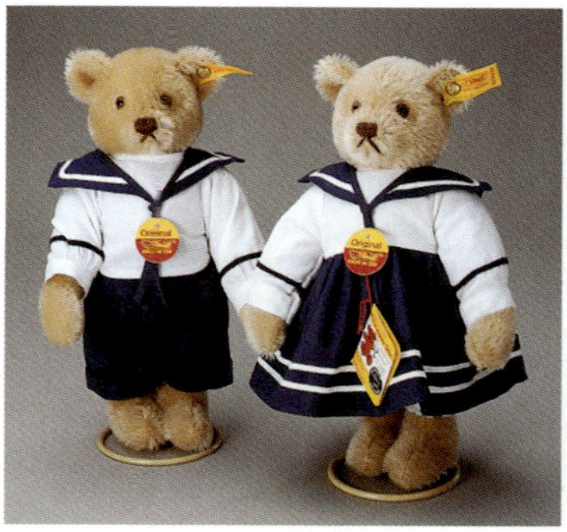

Teddybaer mit Matrosenkleid / -Anzug - *Teddybear with Sailor Dress / -Suit*

Mohair Webpelz, gegliedert, abwaschbar - *mohair woven fur, jointed, surface washable*

SERIE	ART.-NO	PERIOD	PR.	INFO
010200	**0280/28**	1986-1989	3	28 cm, Mann - *male*
010224	**0281/28**	1986-1989	3	28 cm, Frau - *female*

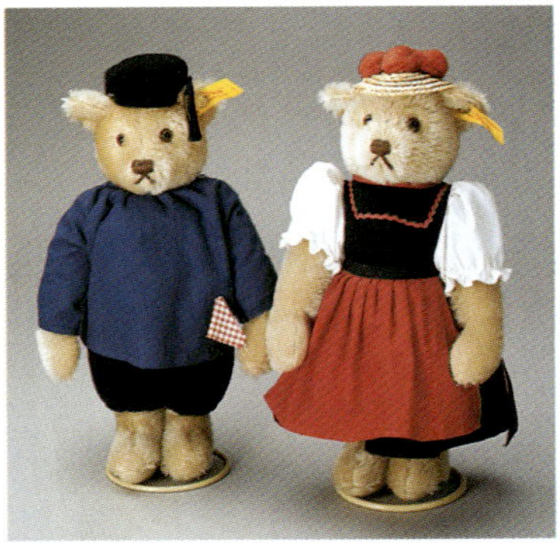

Teddybaer mit Schwarzwaldtracht / Bauerntracht - *Teddybear in Black Forest Costume / Farmer´s Outfit*

Mohair Webpelz, gegliedert, abwaschbar - *mohair woven fur, jointed, surface washable*

Serie	Art.-No	Period	Pr.	Info
010255	**0283/28**	1987-1987	3-4	28 cm, Frau - *female*
010279	**0284/28**	1987-1987	3-4	28 cm, Mann - *male*

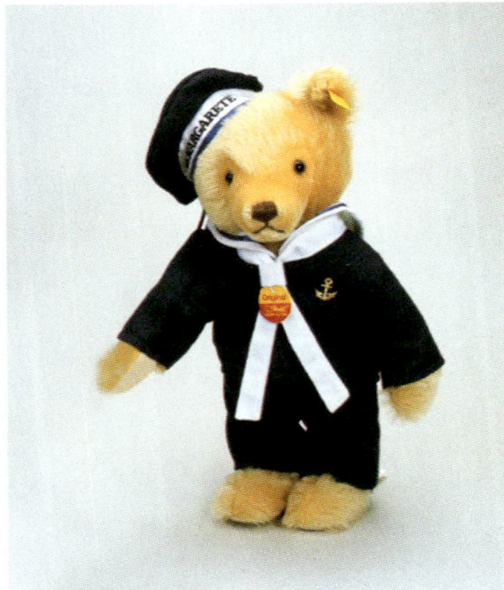

Teddybaer Matrose - *Teddybear Sailor*

Mohair-Webpelz, blond, gegliedert, abwaschbar, Brumm-Stimme, bekleidet - *mohair woven fur, blond, jointed, surface washable, growler, dressed*

EAN-No.	Period	Pr.	Info
028519	1997-1999	3	35 cm

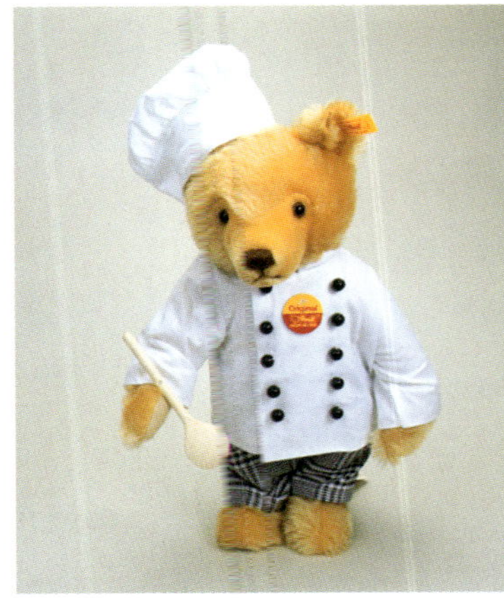

Teddybaer Koch - *Teddybear Chef*

Mohair-Webpelz, blond, gegliedert, abwaschbar, Brumm-Stimme, bekleidet - *mohair woven fur, blond, jointed, surface washable, growler, dressed*

EAN-No.	Period	Pr.	Info
028557	1997-1999	3-4	35 cm

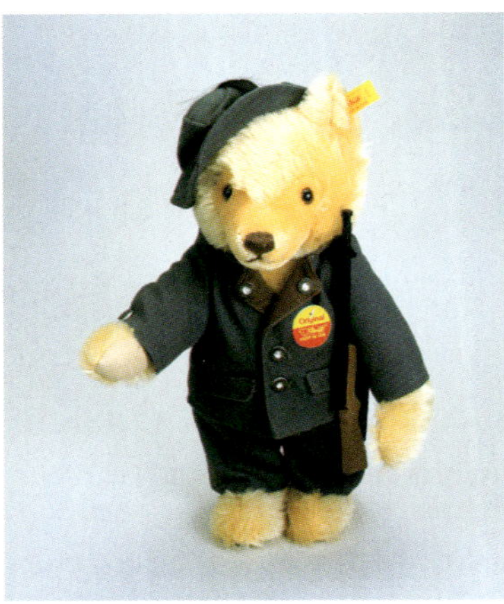

Teddybaer Jaeger - *Teddybear Hunter*

Mohair-Webpelz, blond, gegliedert, abwaschbar, Brumm-Stimme, bekleidet - *mohair woven fur, blond, jointed, surface washable, growler, dressed*

EAN-No.	Period	Pr.	Info
028502	1997-1999	3-4	35 cm

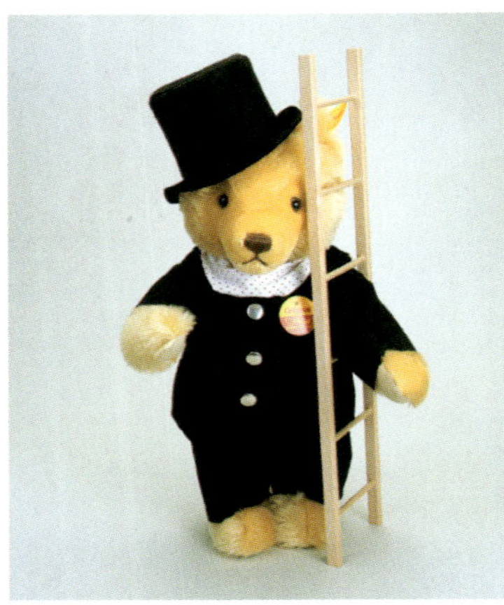

Teddybaer Kaminfeger - *Teddybear Chimney Sweep*

Mohair-Webpelz, blond, gegliedert, abwaschbar, Brumm-Stimme, bekleidet - *mohair woven fur, blond, jointed, surface washable, growler, dressed*

EAN-No.	Period	Pr.	Info
028540	1997-1999	3-4	35 cm

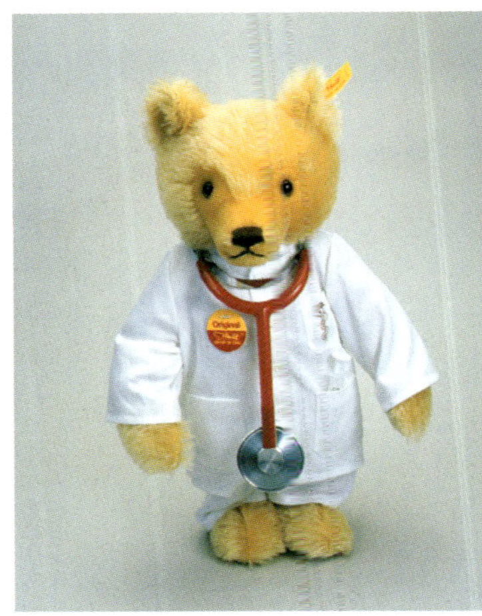

Teddybaer Arzt - *Teddybear Doctor*

Mohair-Webpelz, blond, gegliedert, abwaschbar, Brumm-Stimme, bekleidet - *mohair woven fur, blond, jointed, surface washable, growler, dressed*

EAN-No.	Period	Pr.	Info
028564	1998-1999	3-4	35 cm

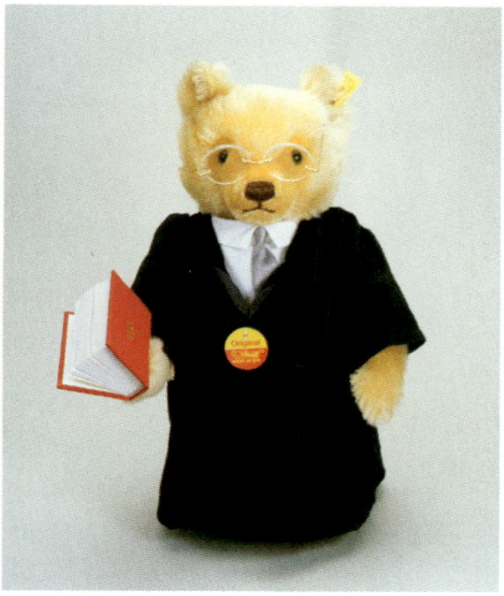

Teddybaer Anwalt - *Teddybear Attorney*

Mohair-Webpelz, blond, gegliedert, abwaschbar, Brumm-Stimme, bekleidet - *mohair woven fur, blond, jointed, surface washable, growler, dressed*

EAN-No.	Period	Pr.	Info
028571	1998-1999	3-4	35 cm

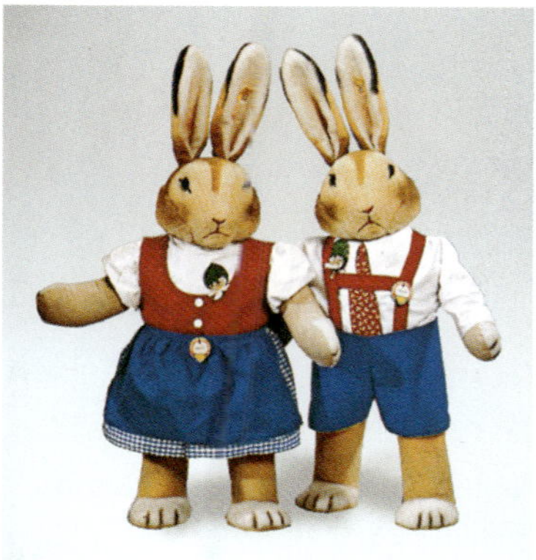

Pupphase Bub / Maedel ab 1954 **Hansili** - *Rabbit Doll Boy / Girl from 1954* ***Hansili***

Kopf Wollpluesch, weicher Koerper, feste Beine, freistehend, Drehkopf, Schlenkerarme, Stimme, 60 cm Schautier - *plush wool head, soft body, fixed legs, free-standing, head swivels, floppy arms, voice, 60 cm. display animal*

Serie	Art.-No	Period	Pr.	Info
91 36	**525** B	1949-1955	6	25 cm, Bub - *boy*
91 36	**560** B	1951-1957	6-7	60 cm
930	**8760,70**	1961-1961	6	
780	**8760,70**	1965-1966	6	
91 36	**525** M	1949-1955	6	25 cm, Maedel - *girl*
91 36	**560** M	1951-1957	6-7	60 cm
930	**8760,80**	1961-1961	6	
780	**8760,80**	1965-1966	6	

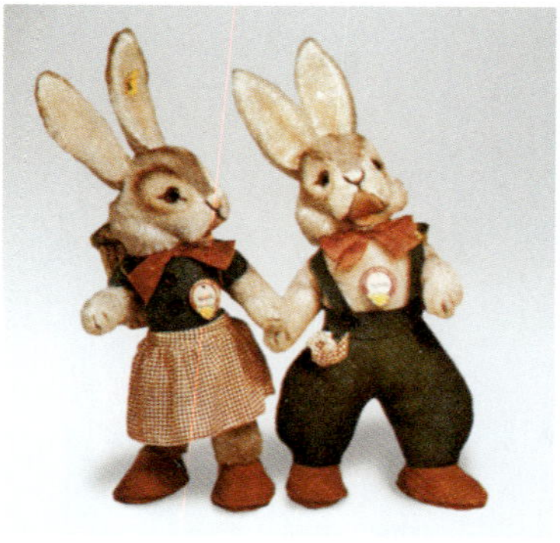

Pupphase Bub / Maedel ab 1954 **Nikili** - *Rabbit Doll Boy / Girl from 1954* ***Nikili***

Kopf Mohairpluesch, weicher Koerper, weiss/grau schattiert, freistehend, Kopf drehbar, mit Kiepe - *mohair head, soft body, white, grey shaded, free-standing, head swivels, with wicker basket*

Serie	Art.-No	Period	Pr.	Info
91 36	**725** B	1951-1957	6	25 cm, Bub - *boy*
91 36	**735** B	1953-1957	6-7	35 cm
91 36	**725** M	1951-1957	6	25 cm, Maedel - *girl*
91 36	**735** M	1953-1957	6-7	35 cm

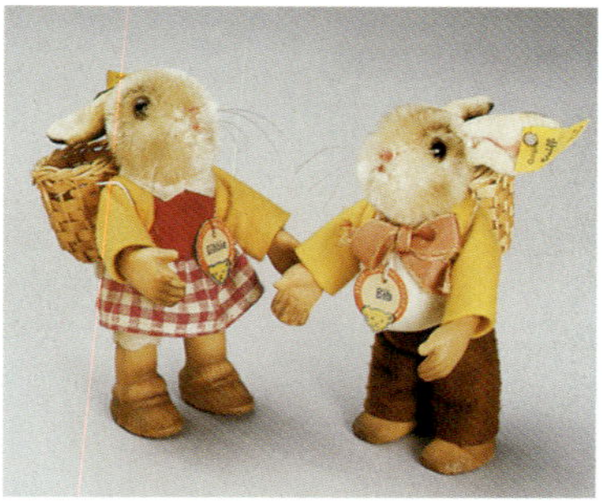

Bib & **Bibbie**

Kopf Mohairpluesch, Gummikoerper, weiss/braun, freistehend, mit Kiepe - *mohair head, rubber body, white/brown, free-standing, with wicker basket*

Serie	Art.-No	Period	Pr.	Info
91 36	**312** B	1954-1958	5-6	12 cm, Bib
931	**8312,70**	1959-1964	5-6	
91 36	**312** M	1954-1958	5-6	12 cm, Bibbie
931	**8312,80**	1959-1964	5-6	

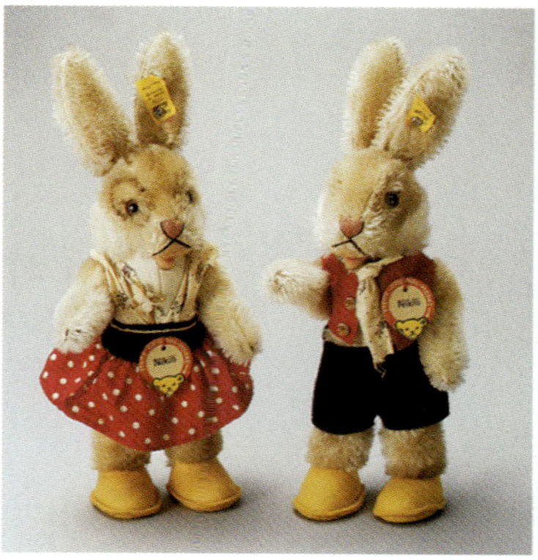

Nikili Hase Bub / Maedel - ***Nikili*** *Rabbit Boy / Girl*

Kopf, Arme & Beine Mohair, Stoffkoerper, freistehend, Kopf drehbar, Arme gegliedert, Druckstimme - *mohair head, arms & legs, body is made of fabric, free-standing, head swivels, arms jointed, press voice*

Serie	Art.-No	Period	Pr.	Info
91 36	**726** B	1958-1958	5-6	26 cm, Bub - *boy*
930	**8726,70**	1959-1963	5-6	
91 36	**736** B	1958-1958	6-7	36 cm
930	**8736,70**	1959-1962	6	
91 36	**726** M	1958-1958	5-6	26 cm, Maedel - *girl*
930	**8726,80**	1959-1963	5-6	
91 36	**736** M	1958-1958	6-7	36 cm
930	**8736,80**	1959-1962	6	

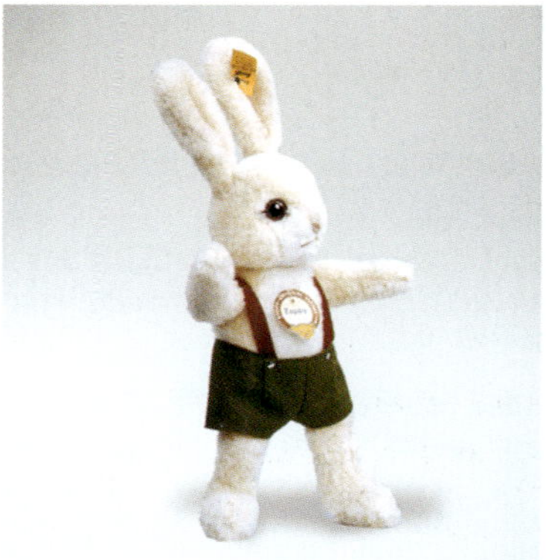

Zappy Pupphase - ***Zappy*** *Doll Rabbit*

Dralon, weiss, Filzhose, Schlenkerglieder, Kopf drehbar, sehr weich, abwaschbar - *dralon, white, felt trousers, floppy joints, head swivels, very soft, surface washable*

Serie	Art.-No	Period	Pr.	Info
780	**8625,00**	1966-1967	3	25 cm
	7800/25	1968-1974	3	

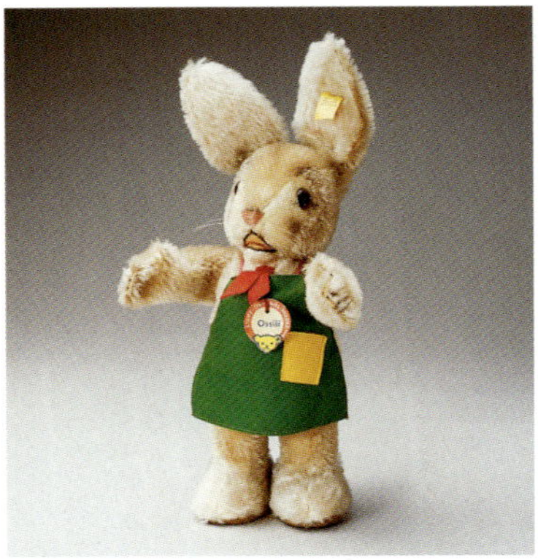

Ossili Hase - ***Ossili** Rabbit*

Mohair, Filzkleidung, weich, Kopf drehbar, abwaschbar - *mohair, felt clothing, soft, head swivels, surface washable*

SERIE	ART.-NO	PERIOD	PR.	INFO
930 360	**8730,70**	1962-1964	3-4	30 cm
780	**8730,70**	1965-1967	3-4	
	7800/30	1968-1974	3	

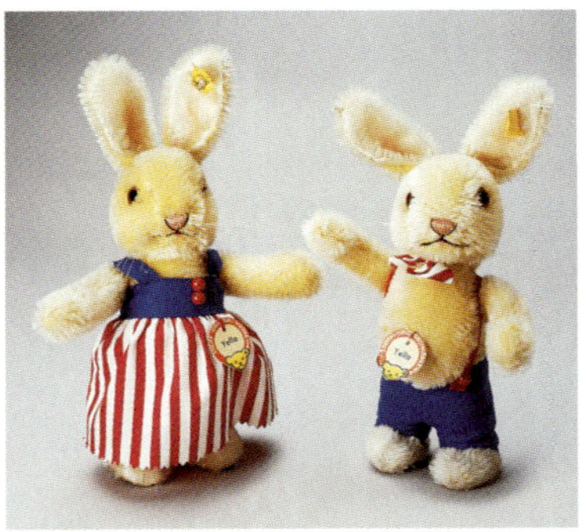

Yello / **Yella** Hase - ***Yello** / **Yella** Rabbit*

Mohairpluesch, weiss/gelb, freistehend, Kopf drehbar, Filz- & Stoffkleidung - *mohair, white/yellow, free-standing, head swivels, felt & fabric clothing*

SERIE	ART.-NO	PERIOD	PR.	INFO
930	**8720,70**	1964-1964	5	20 cm, Yello
780	**8720,70**	1965-1967	5	
930	**8720,80**	1964-1964	5	20 cm, Yella
780	**8720,80**	1965-1967	5	

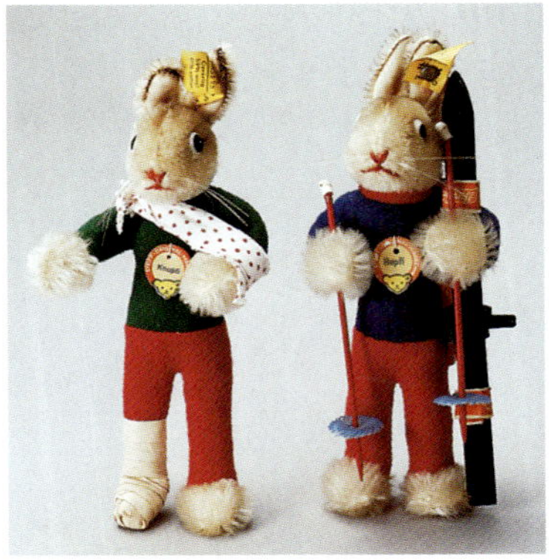

Ski-Hase **Knupfi** / **Hupfi** - *Ski Bunnies* ***Knupfi** / **Hupfi***

Mohair, Filz- & Perlonvelours, Knupfi mit einem Skistock und bandagiertem Fuss, Hupfi mit 2 Skiern und 2 Skistoecken - *mohair, felt & perlon velvet, Knupfi has one ski pole & a bandaged leg, Hupfi has two skis & two ski poles*

SERIE	ART.-NO	PERIOD	PR.	INFO
	7810/18	1968-1971	4-5	18 cm, Knupfi
	7811/18	1968-1970	4-5	18 cm, Hupfi

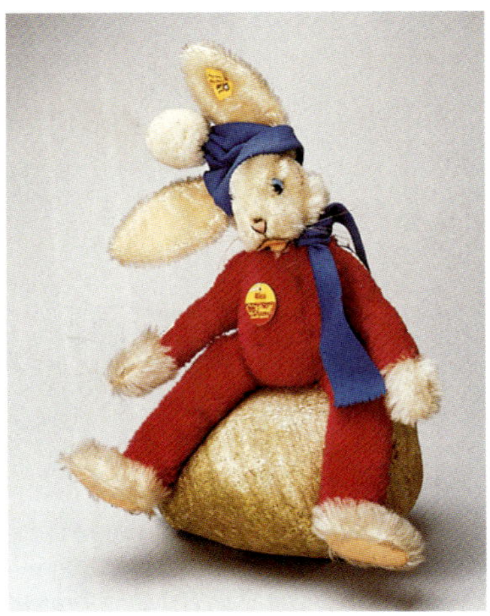

Rico-Hase - ***Rico** Rabbit*

Kopf Mohair, Koerper Dralon in rot, Schal & Zipfelmuetze in blau, Schlenkerglieder - *mohair head, red dralon body, blue scarf & peaked cap, floppy joints*

SERIE	ART.-NO	PERIOD	PR.	INFO
	7828/43	1972-1974	3	43 cm

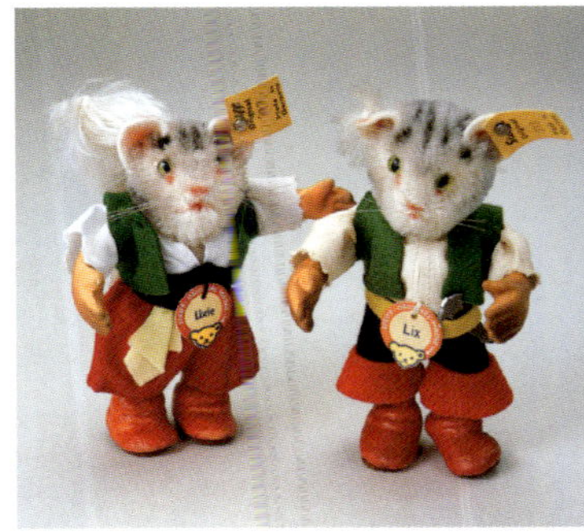

Lix / **Lixie**

Gestiefelter Kater, Kopf & Schwanz Mohairpluesch, grau, schwarz gestromelt, Gummikoerper, freistehend, Lix mit Plastikschwert - *puss inboots, head & tail mohair, grey tabby markings, rubber body, free-standing, Lix has plastic sword*

SERIE	ART.-NO	PERIOD	PR.	INFO
91 44	**313** B	1954-1957	6	13 cm, Lix
91 44	**313** M	1954-1957	6	13 cm, Lixie

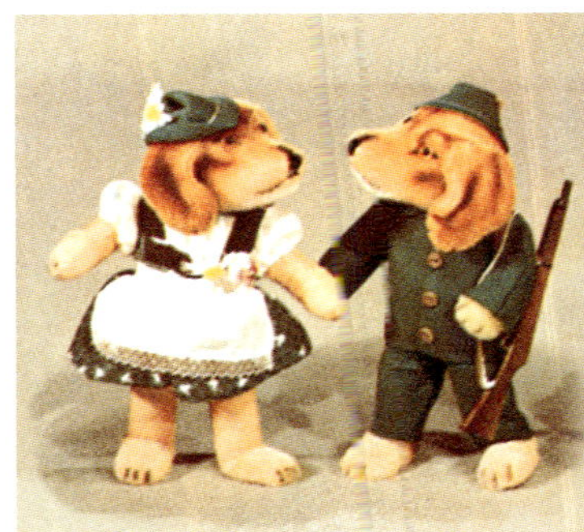

Pupp-Bazi Bube / Maedel 1954 **Bazili** - *Bazi Doll Boy / Girl 1954* ***Bazili***

Kopf aus Mohairpluesch, braun, freistehend, 25 cm, Bube als Jaeger mit Gewehr, Maedel als Trachtenmaedel - *head is mohair, brown, free-standing, 25 cm, boy is hunter with rifle, girl is wearing peasant costume*

SERIE	ART.-NO	PERIOD	PR.	INFO
91 18	**325** B	1950-1954	6-7	Bub - *boy*
91 18	**325** M	1950-1954	6-7	Maedel - *girl*

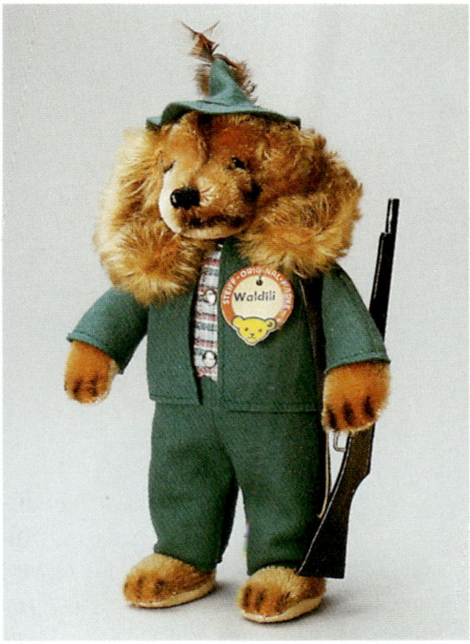

Pupp-Waldi als Jäger ab 1954 **Waldili** - *Waldi Doll as Hunter from 1954* ***Waldili***

Kopf, Haende & Fuesse Mohairpluesch, braun, Koerper & Kleidung aus Filz, freistehend, Kopf drehbar, mit Gewehr - *head, hands & feet are mohair, brown, body & clothing are felt, free-standing, head swivels, with rifle*

SERIE	ART.-NO	PERIOD	PR.	INFO
91 18	**326** B	1950-1957	4-5	26 cm
930	**8326,70**	1960-1961	4	
777	**8326,70**	1966-1967	4	
	7770/26	1968-1974	4	

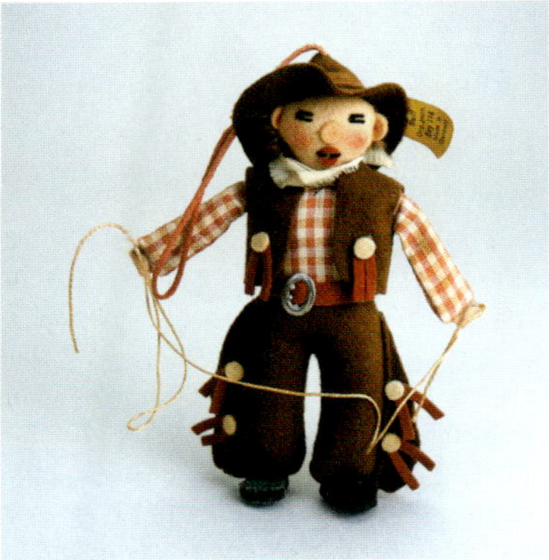

Boy

Filz, zum Aufhaengen im Auto - *felt, for hanging in your car*

SERIE	ART.-NO	PERIOD	PR.	INFO
92 Boy	**114**	1951-1951	6	14 cm
92 Boy	**20**	1951-1951	6	20 cm

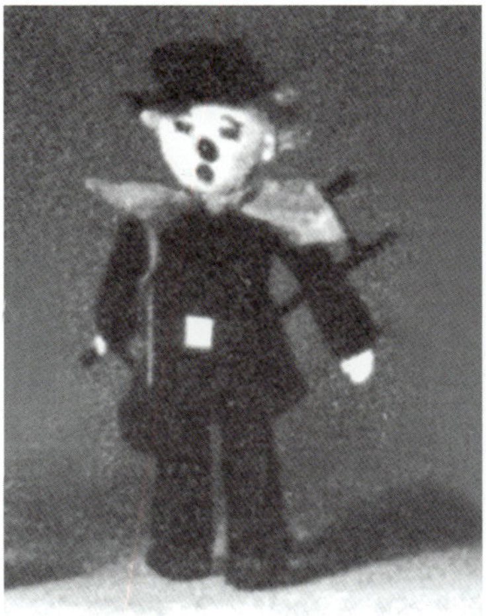

Feger - *Chimney Sweep*

Samt, zum Aufhaengen im Auto - *velvet, for hanging in the car*

SERIE	ART.-NO	PERIOD	PR.	INFO
92 Feg	**20**	1951-1951	6	20 cm

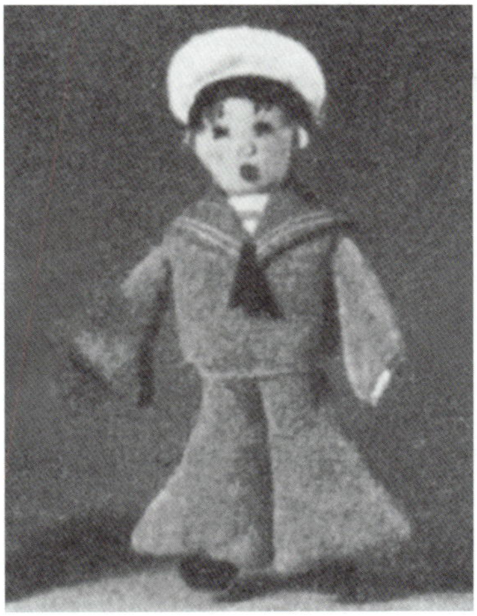

Matrose - *Sailor*

Samt, zum Aufhaengen im Auto - *velvet, for hanging in the car*

SERIE	ART.-NO	PERIOD	PR.	INFO
92 Mat	**20**	1951-1951	6	20 cm

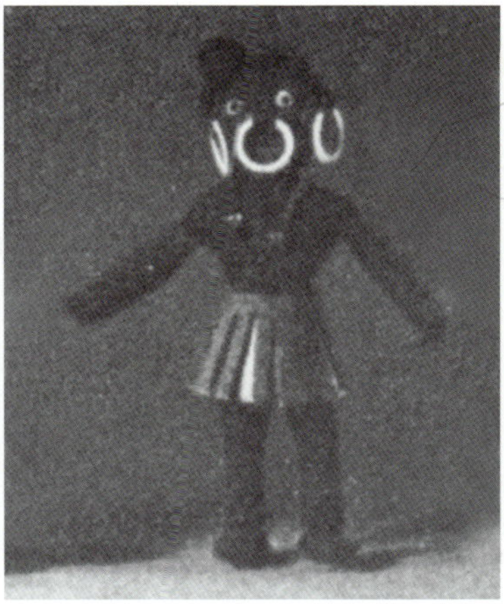

Neger - *Black Man*

Filz, zum Aufhaengen im Auto - *felt, for hanging in your car*

SERIE	ART.-NO	PERIOD	PR.	INFO
92 Neg	**20**	1951-1951	6	20 cm

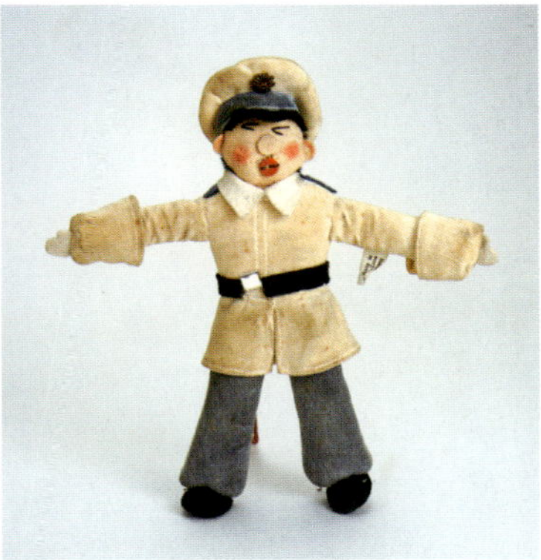

Polizist - *Policeman*

Samt, zum Aufhaengen im Auto - *velvet, for hanging in the car*

SERIE	ART.-NO	PERIOD	PR.	INFO
92 Pol	**20**	1951-1951	6	20 cm

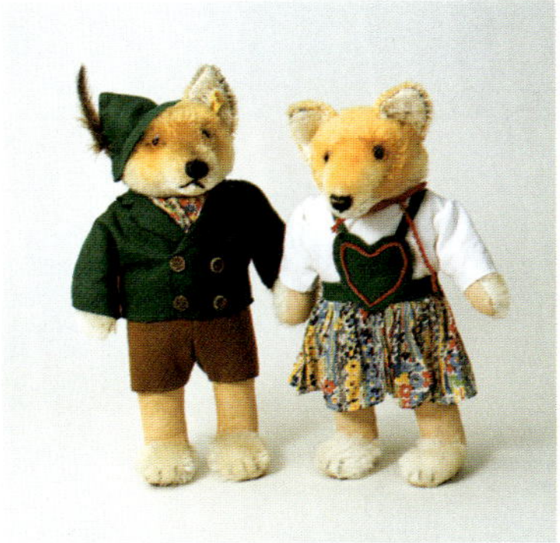

Pupp-Fuchs Bube / Maedel 1954 **Fixili** - *Fox Doll Boy / Girl 1954* ***Fixili***

Kopf aus Mohairpluesch, braun/weiss, freistehend, 25 cm, in Trachtenkleidung - *head is mohair, brown & white, free-standing, 25 cm, peasant costumes*

SERIE	ART.-NO	PERIOD	PR.	INFO
91 28	**325** B	1950-1954	6-7	Bub - *boy*
91 28	**325** M	1950-1954	6-7	Maedel - *girl*

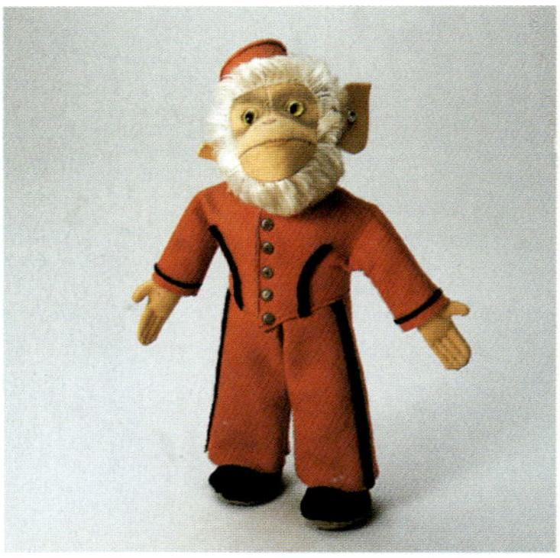

Pupp-Coco ab 1954 **Cocoli** - *Doll Coco from 1954* ***Cocoli***

Kopf Mohairpluesch, Stoffkoerper, Filzgesicht & -kleidung, freistehend, Pavian Coco als Liftboy - *head is mohair, body is fabric, face & clothing are felt, free-standing, Coco Baboon as Bell-Boy*

SERIE	ART.-NO	PERIOD	PR.	INFO
91 9a	**328** B	1952-1957	6	28 cm

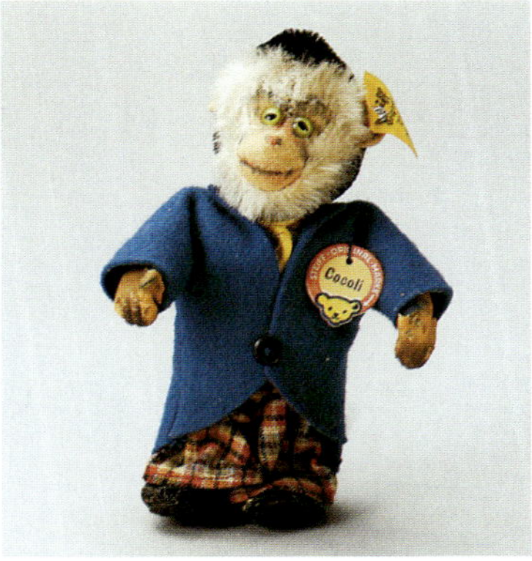

Cocoli Pavian - ***Cocoli*** *Baboon*

Gummikoerper, Filzkopf, Haare aus Mohair, freistehend - *rubber body, felt head, hair made of mohair, free-standing*

SERIE	ART.-NO	PERIOD	PR.	INFO
91 9a	**712**	1955-1957	5-6	12 cm

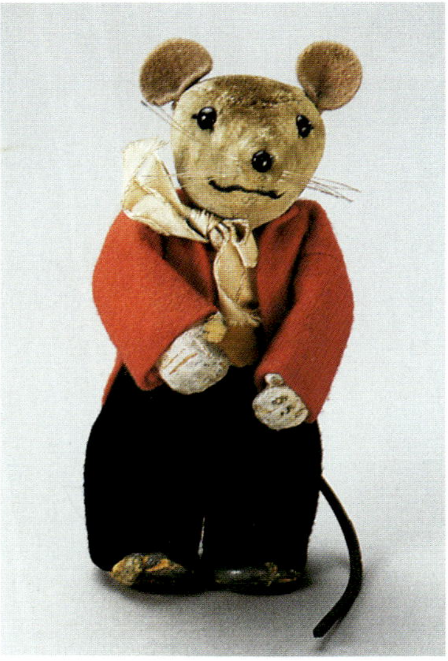

Pippy Maus - ***Pippy*** *Mouse*

Gummikoerper, Plueschkopf, grau, freistehend - *rubber body, plush head, grey, free-standing*

SERIE	ART.-NO	PERIOD	PR.	INFO
91 50	**712**	1955-1958	5-6	12 cm
931	**8314,00**	1959-1959	5-6	

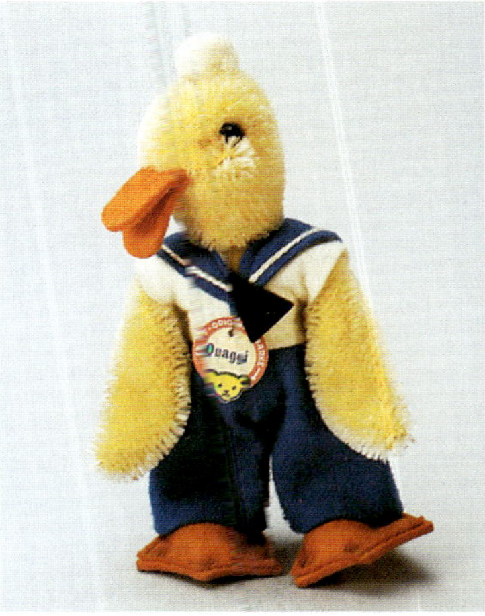

Quaggi Ente - ***Quaggi*** *Duck*

Gummikoerper, Kopf & Arme Mohairpluesch, gelb, Fuesse & Schnabel Filz, orange - *rubber body, mohair head & arms, yellow, orange felt feet & bill*

SERIE	ART.-NO	PERIOD	PR.	INFO
91 22	**712**	1955-1958	5-6	12 cm
931	**8311,00**	1959-1959	5-6	

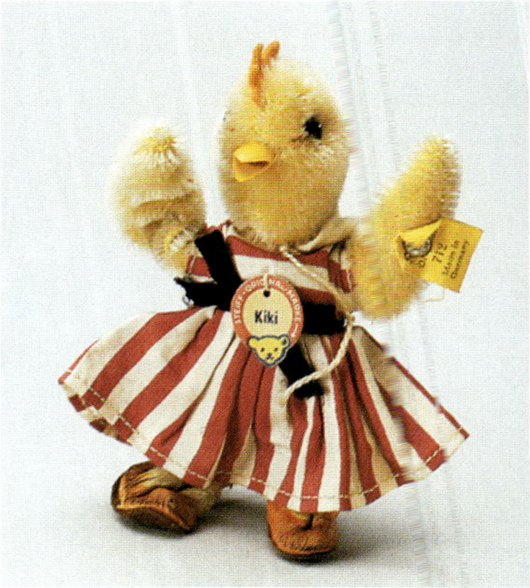

Kiki Kueken - ***Kiki*** *Chick*

Gummikoerper, Kopf und Arme Mohairpluesch, gelb, freistehend, oranger Filzkamm, gelber Plastikschnabel - *rubber body, mohair head & arms, yellow, orange felt comb, yellow plastic beak*

SERIE	ART.-NO	PERIOD	PR.	INFO
91 35	**712**	1955-1958	5-6	12 cm
931	**8313,00**	1959-1959	5-6	

WERBE- & FILMTIERE

PROMOTIONAL & FILM ANIMALS

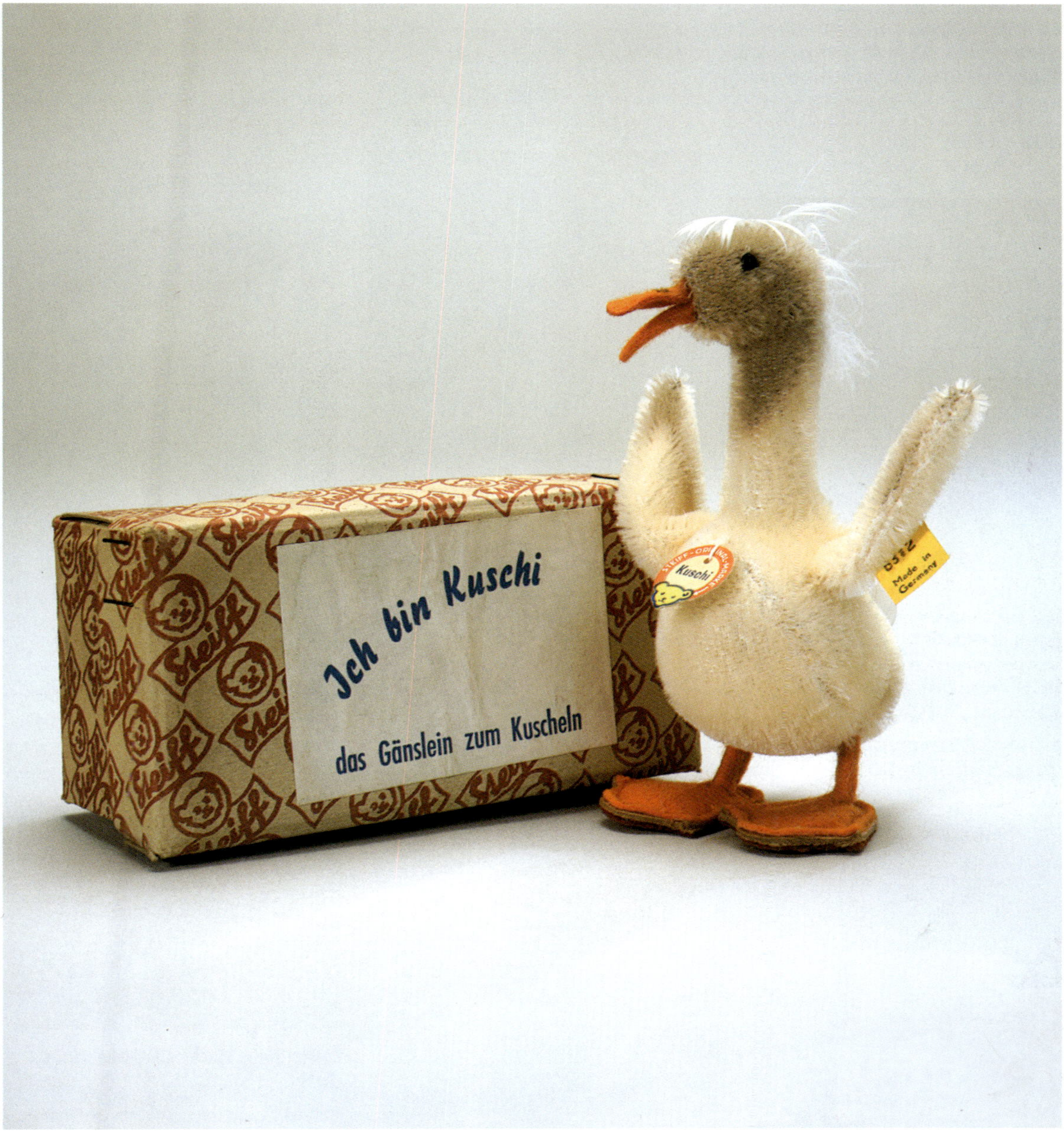

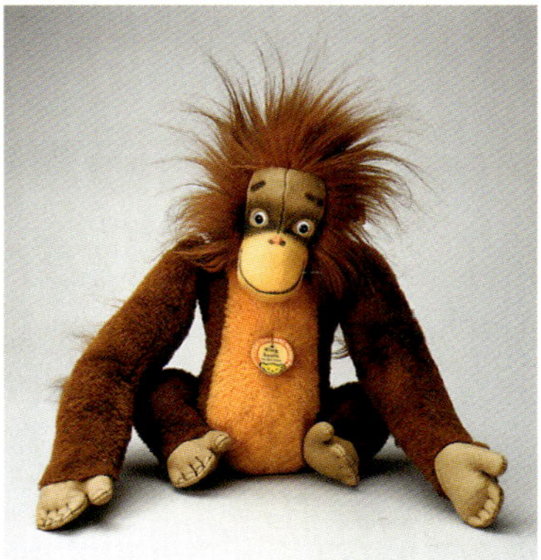

Affe **King Louie** - *Ape* ***King Louie***

Crylor, braun, Copyr. W. Disney Prod., Kopf drehbar, Schlenkerarme, abwaschbar - *crylor, brown, Copyr. W. Disney Productions, head swivels, floppy arms, surface washable*

Serie	Art.-No	Period	Pr.	Info
	0050/25	1968-1974	4	25 cm

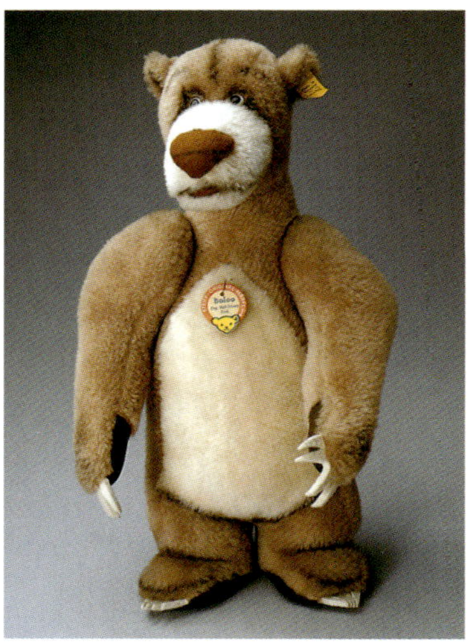

Baer **Baloo** - *Bear* ***Baloo***

Dralon, beige, Copyr. W. Disney Prod., Kopf & Arme drehbar - *dralon, beige, Copyr. W Disney Productions, head & arms swivels*

Serie	Art.-No	Period	Pr.	Info
	0360/40	1968-1974	6	40 cm

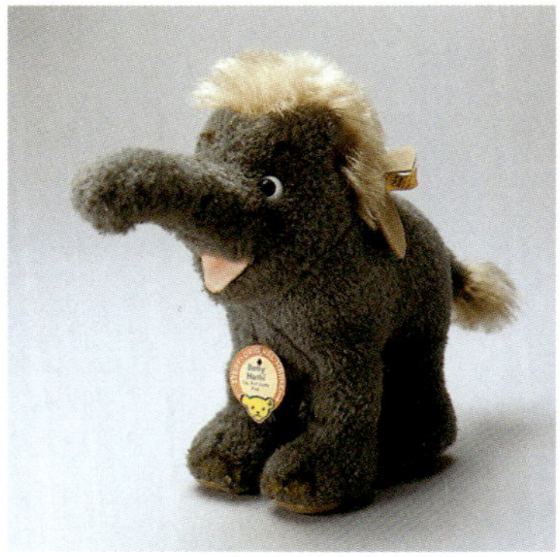

Elefant **Baby Hathi** - *Elephant* ***Baby Hathi***

Dralon, grau, stehend, Copyr. W. Disney Productions - *dralon, grey, standing, Copyr. W. Disney Productions*

Serie	Art.-No	Period	Pr.	Info
	0530/20	1968-1976	4	20 cm

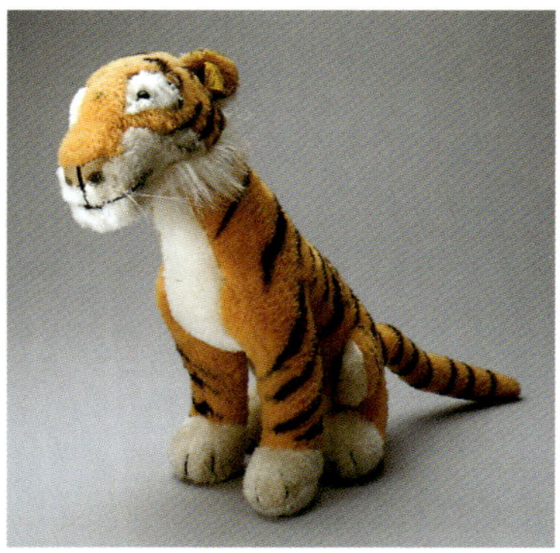

Tiger **Shere Khan**

Dralon, gelb/weiss, schwarz getigert, sitzend, Copyr. W. Disney Prod., Kopf drehbar - *dralon, yellow & white, black tiger stripes, sitting, Copyr. W. Disney Productions, head swivels*

Serie	Art.-No	Period	Pr.	Info
	0920/35	1968-1974	4-5	35 cm

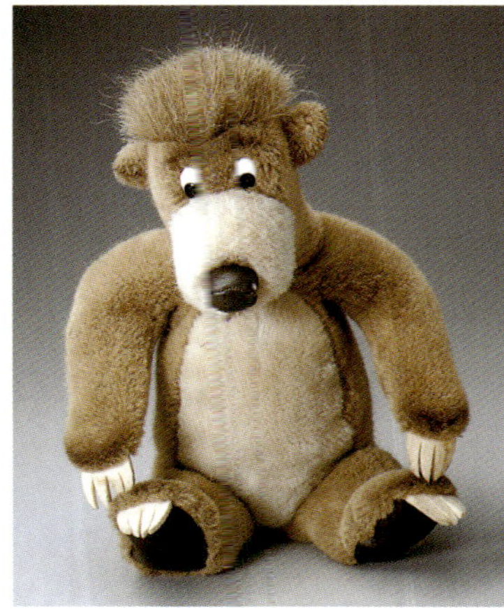

Baloo Baer - ***Baloo*** *Bear*

Webpelz, beige, sitzend, abwaschbar, aus dem Film "Dschungelbuch" - *woven fur, beige, sitting, surface washable, from the film "Jungle Book"*

Serie	Art.-No	Period	Pr.	Info
	0380/28	1979-1981	5-6	28 cm

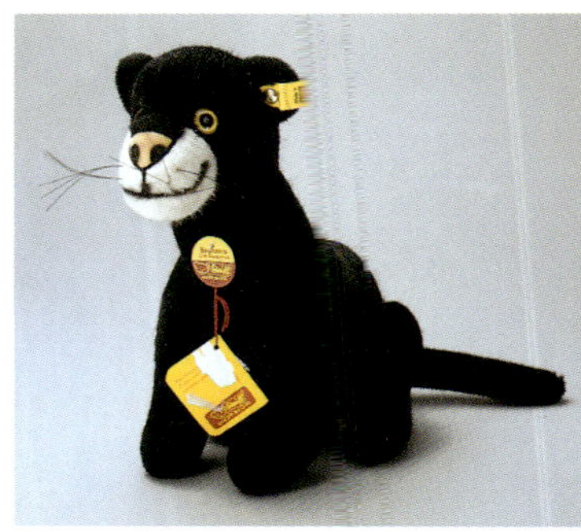

Bagheera Panther

Webpelz, schwarz, sitzend, abwaschbar, aus dem Film "Dschungelbuch" - *woven fur, black, sitting, surface washable, from the film "Jungle Book"*

Serie	Art.-No	Period	Pr.	Info
	0381/25	1979-1982	4	25 cm

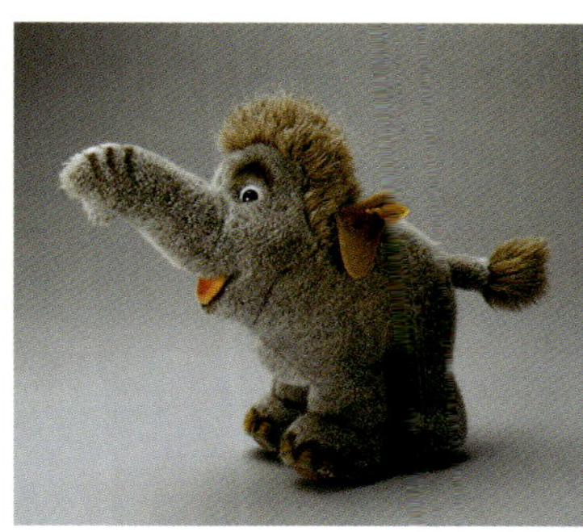

Elefant **Baby Hathi** - *Elephant* ***Baby Hathi***

Webpelz, grau, stehend, abwaschbar, aus

dem Film "Dschungelbuch" - *woven fur, grey, standing, surface washable, from the film "Jungle Book"*

SERIE	ART.-NO	PERIOD	PR.	INFO
	0382/22	1979-1982	4	22 cm

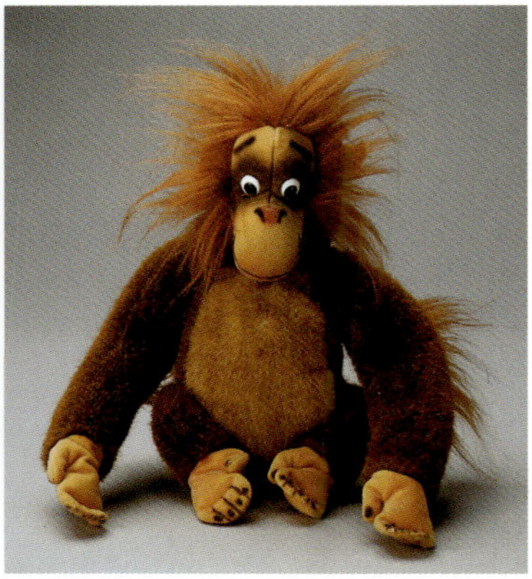

King Louie Affe - ***King Louie** Ape*

Webpelz, rotbraun, Schlenkerarme, sitzend, abwaschbar, aus dem Film "Dschungelbuch" - *woven fur, rusty brown, floppy arms, sitting, surface washable, from the film "Jungle Book"*

SERIE	ART.-NO	PERIOD	PR.	INFO
	0383/22	1979-1982	4	22 cm

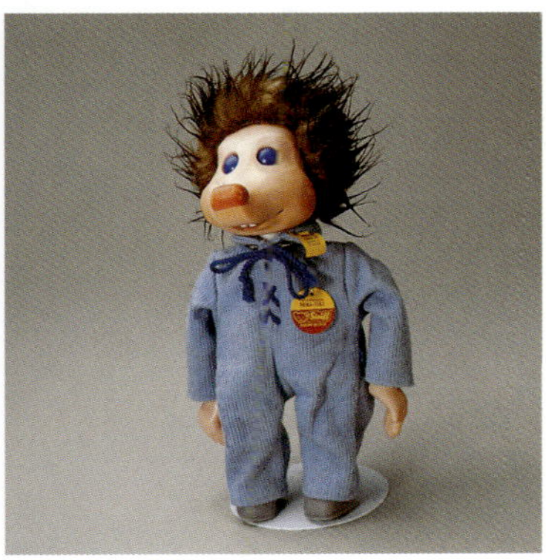

Niki-Tiki

Fernsehpuppe des Schweizer Fernsehens, Plastikkopf & -haende, Dralon - *dralon, plastic head & hands, TV doll of the Swiss TV network*

SERIE	ART.-NO	PERIOD	PR.	INFO
	7680/30	1973-1973	4	30 cm

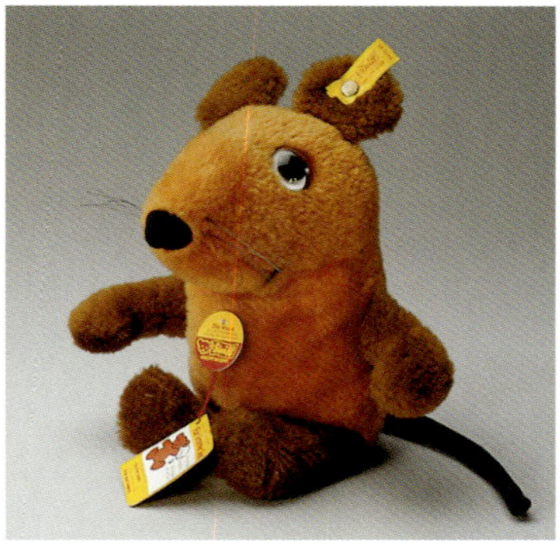

Die Maus - *The Mouse*

Dralon, aus dem deutschen Fernsehen, Copyr. I. Schmitt-Menzel - Lizenz-Agentur Becker, Wiesbaden - *dralon, figure from German TV, Copyr. I. Schmitt-Menzel - Licensed Agency Becker, Wiesbaden*

SERIE	ART.-NO	PERIOD	PR.	INFO
	7855/28	1980-1984	4	28 cm

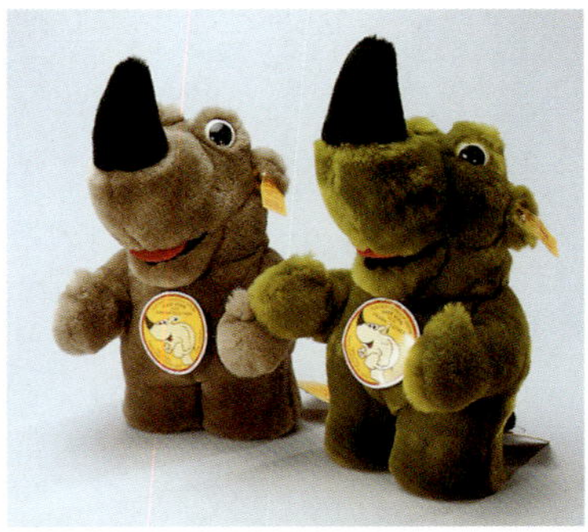

Nasevornhoernchen - *Nose Up Rhinoceros*

Webpelz, stehend, waschmaschinenfest, aus der Fernseh-Show "Nase vorn" - *woven fur, standing, machine washable, from the German TV show "Nase Vorn"*

SERIE	ART.-NO	PERIOD	PR.	INFO
352126	**7502/20**	1989-1990	1-2	20 cm, rot - *red*
	352126	1991-1991	1-2	
352157	**7502/30**	1989-1990	1-2	30 cm
	352157	1991-1991	1-2	
352324	**7504/20**	1989-1990	1-2	20 cm, gelb - *yellow*
	352324	1991-1991	1-2	
352355	**7504/30**	1989-1990	1-2	30 cm
	352355	1991-1991	1-2	
352423	**7505/20**	1989-1990	1-2	20 cm, gruen - *green*
	352423	1991-1991	1-2	
352454	**7505/30**	1989-1990	1-2	30 cm
	352454	1991-1991	1-2	
352522	**7506/20**	1989-1990	1-2	20 cm, blau - *blue*
	352522	1991-1991	1-2	
352553	**7506/30**	1989-1990	1-2	30 cm
	352553	1991-1991	1-2	
352720	**7508/20**	1989-1990	1-2	20 cm, grau - *grey*
	352720	1991-1991	1-2	
352751	**7508/30**	1989-1990	1-2	30 cm
	352751	1991-1991	1-2	
352003	**7500/00**	1989-1990	4-5	kpl. Sortiment - *assortment*
	352003	1991-1991	4-5	

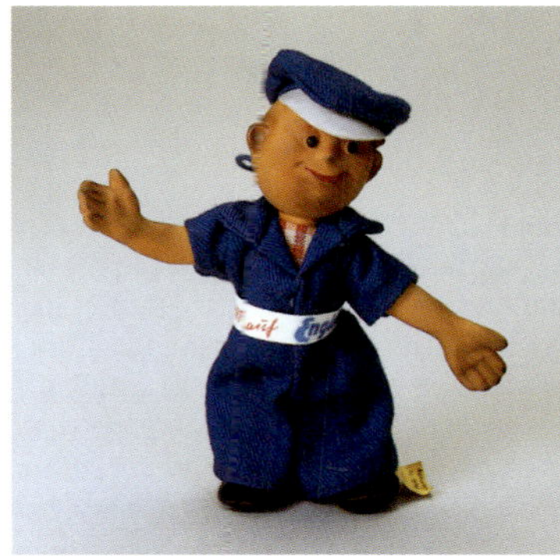

Gummibert

Gummi, stehend, blauer Overall & Schirmmuetze, weisser Plastikguertel mit Aufschrift "GUTE FAHRT auf Englebert J55", Werbeartikel fuer Fa. Englebert, Aachen - *rubber, standing, blue overall & peaked cap, white plastic belt with inscription "GUTE FAHRT auf Englebert J55", promotional item for Englebert, Aachen, a tyre manufactorer*

SERIE	ART.-NO	PERIOD	PR.	INFO
	712	1954-1954	4-5	12 cm

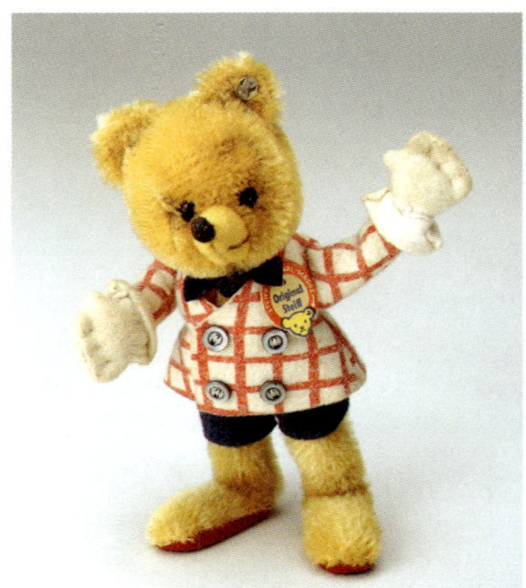

Breuni Baer - *Breuni Bear*

Mohair/Filz, gegliedert, Kaufhaus Breuninger, Stuttgart - *mohair & felt, jointed, Breuninger Department Store, Stuttgart*

SERIE	ART.-NO	PERIOD	PR.	INFO
	714	1956-1957	7	14 cm

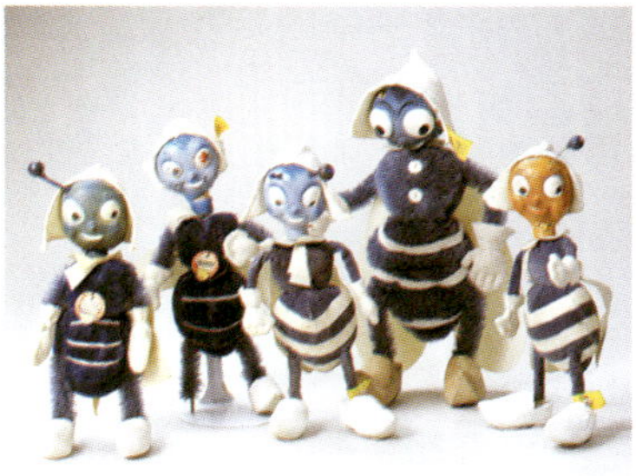

Trokky

Mohair, blau, stehend, Werbeartikel fuer die Fa. Paul Bendix, Hersteller von Baumwollhandtuechern, mit weissen Streifen aus Perlgarn, Gummikopf, Filzhandschuhe, Holzschuhe, Leinenhaube & -kragen - *mohair, blue, standing, promotional item for Paul Bendix, a producer of cotton towels, with white stripes of yarn, rubber head, felt gloves, wooden shoes, linen hood & collar*

SERIE	ART.-NO	PERIOD	PR.	INFO
	7312	1953-1953	8-9	12 cm
	0720	1953-1953	8-9	20 cm
	7320	1953-1953	8-9	

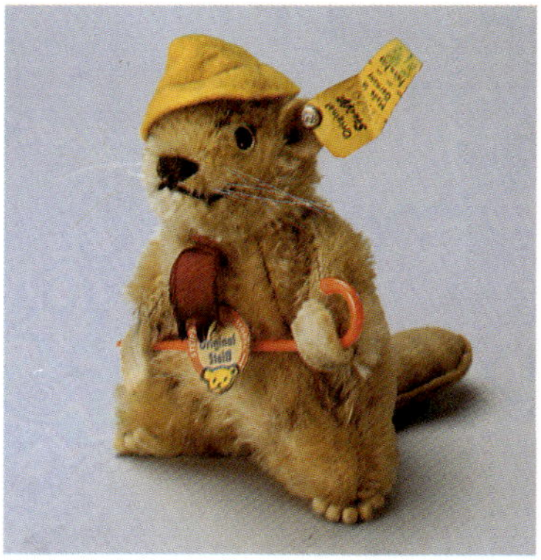

Biber - *Beaver*

Werbeartikel fuer CANADA Airlines, Mohair, aufwartend - *promotional item for CANADA airlines, mohair, sitting up*

SERIE	ART.-NO	PERIOD	PR.	INFO
	2129/01	1968-1970	4	10 cm

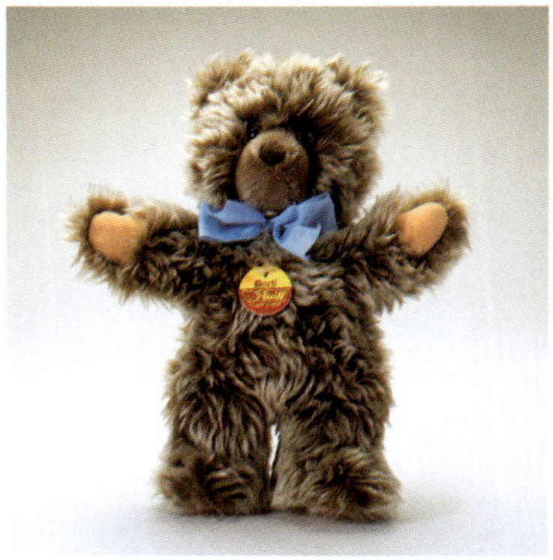

Berti Baer - ***Berti*** *Bear*

Dralon, braun gespitzt, stehend, Werbeartikel fuer Bertelsmann - *dralon, brown tipped, standing, promotional item for Bertelsmann*

SERIE	ART.-NO	PERIOD	PR.	INFO
	7972/25	1978-1978	4	25 cm

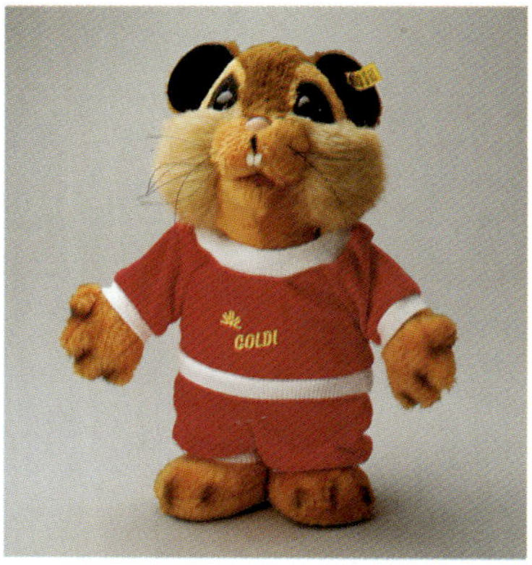

Hamster **Goldi** - *Guinea Pig* ***Goldi***

Dralon, stehend, weich, Werbeartikel für die Commerzbank - *dralon, standing, soft, promotional item for Commerce Bank*

SERIE	ART.-NO	PERIOD	PR.	INFO
	7955/32	1978-1980	2-3	32 cm

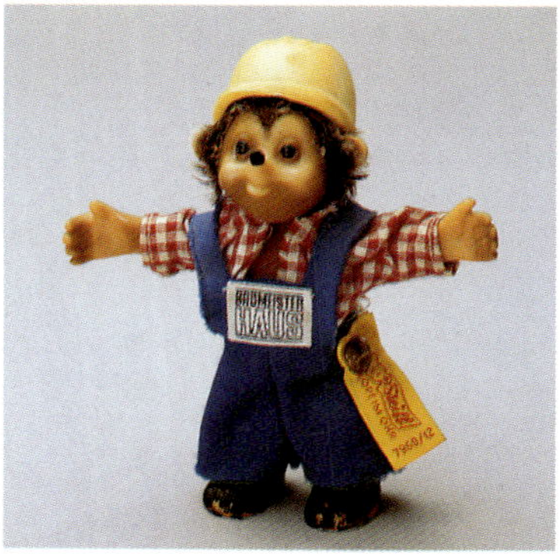

Mecki

Kunststoff, stehend, Werbeartikel fuer Baumeister Haus - *plastic, standing, promotional item for Baumeister Haus Company*

SERIE	ART.-NO	PERIOD	PR.	INFO
	7960/12	1984-1984	3	12 cm

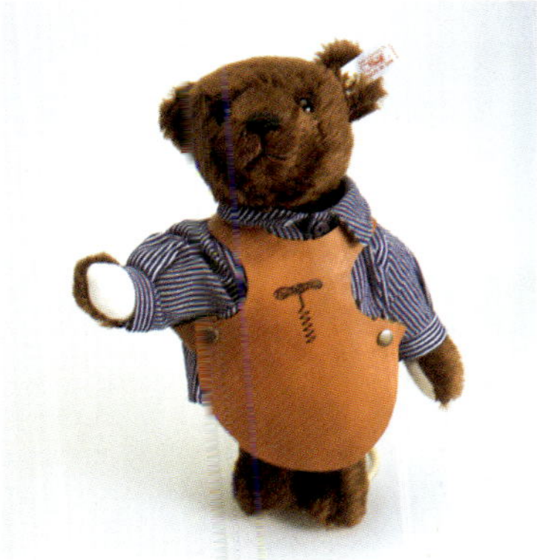

Kellermeister Baer - *Cellarman Bear*

Mohair, braun, gegliedert, limit. Auflage 1.500 Stueck fuer das Weingut Buergerspital zum hl. Geist, Wuerzburg - *mohair, brown, jointed, ltd edition of 1,500 for wine-cellars Buergerspital zum hl. Geist, Wuerzburg*

EAN-NO.	PERIOD	PR.	INFO
998621	1997-1997	4	25 cm

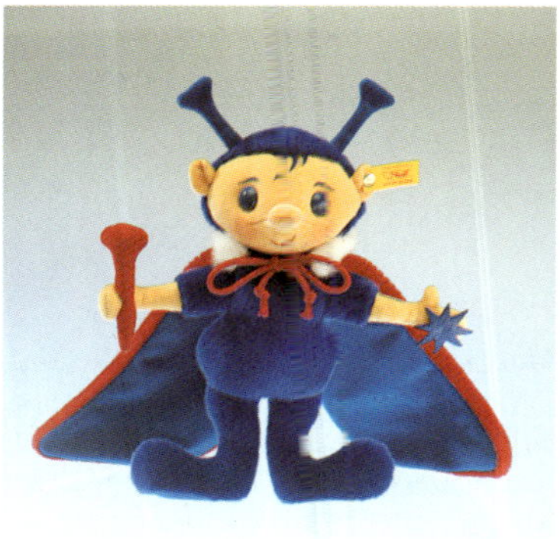

Maari

Webpelz, blau, stehend, Marienkaefer-Prinz, Maskottchen der Deutschen Kinder-Krebshilfe, fuer die Deutsche Krebshilfe, Bonn - *woven fur, blue, standing, ladybug-prince, mascot of the German children´s cancer charity, for the German cancer aid, Bonn*

EAN-NO.	PERIOD	PR.	INFO
998812	1997-1997	3	25 cm

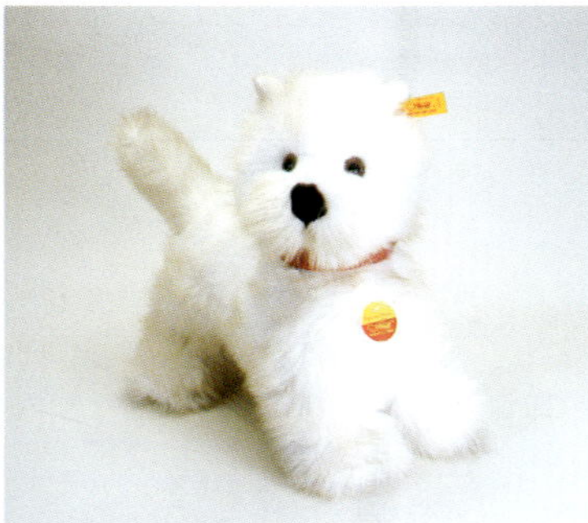

Taps von Cesar - *Taps from Cesar*

Webpelz, weiss, stehend, waschmaschinenfest, Werbeartikel fuer Cesar Hundefutter - *woven fur, white, standing, machine washable, promotional item for Cesar dog food*

EAN-No.	Period	Pr.	Info
999598	1997-1997	3	25 cm

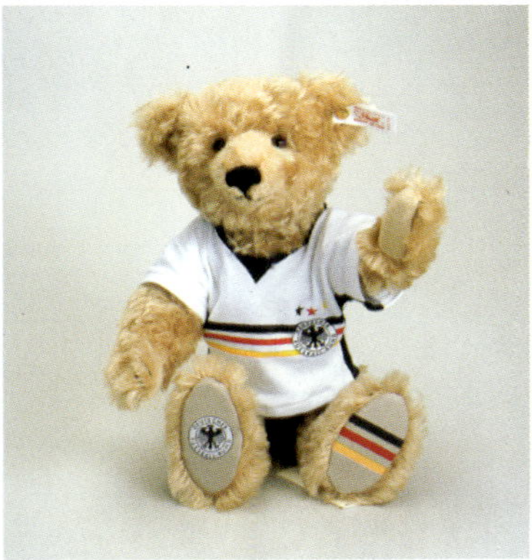

DFB Baer - *DFB Bear*

Mohair, blond, gegliedert, abwaschbar, Sonderbaer fuer den Deutschen Fussball Bund (DFB) anlaesslich der Fussballweltmeisterschaft in Frankreich, limitierte Auflage 1.998 Stueck - *mohair, blond, jointed, surface washable, special bear for the German Football Association (DFB) on the occasion of the Soccer Worldcup in France, ltd edition of 1,998*

EAN-No.	Period	Pr.	Info
996733	1998-1998	3-4	32 cm

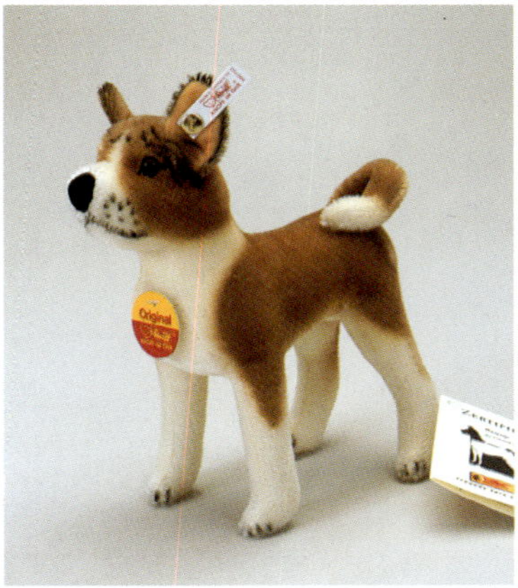

Basenji

Mohair-Pluesch, braun/weiss, stehend, limit. Auflage 1.500 Stueck fuer den Deutschen Basenji Club - *mohair-plush, brown/white, standing, ltd. edition of 1,500 for the German Basenji Club*

EAN-No.	Period	Pr.	Info
996702	1998-1998	3	22 cm

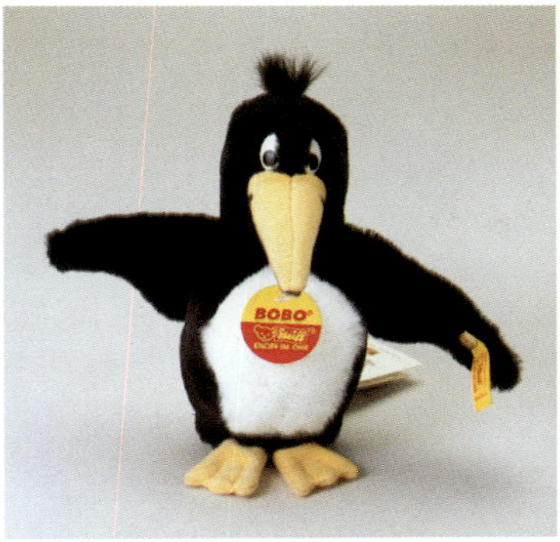

Bobo Pinguin - ***Bobo** Penguin*

Webpelz, stehend, waschmaschinenfest - *woven fur, standing, machine washable*

EAN-No.	Period	Pr.	Info
354045	1999-1999	2	15 cm

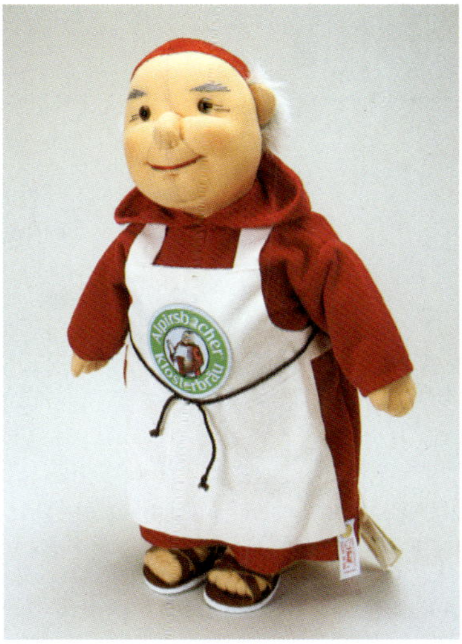

Moench - *Monk*

Trevirasamt, stehend, abwaschbar, rote Kutte, hellbeige Schuerze, Sandalen, Werbeartikel für Alpirsbacher Klosterbraeu, lim. Auflage 1.500 Stueck - *Trevira velvet, standing, surface washable, red cowl, beige apron, leather sandals, promotional item for Alpirsbacher monastery brewery, ltd edition of 1,500*

EAN-No.	Period	Pr.	Info
996245	1999-1999	3	35 cm

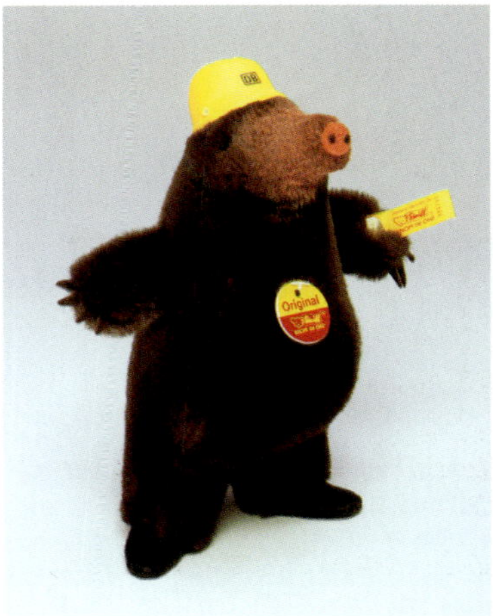

Max Maulwurf - *Max Mole*

Webpelz, braun, aufwartend, gelber Helm mit DB-Logo, Werbeartikel für die Deutsche Bahn - *woven fur, brown, sitting up, yellow helmet with DB logo, promotional item for the German Railway*

EAN-No.	Period	Pr.	Info
996740	1999-1999	3	15 cm

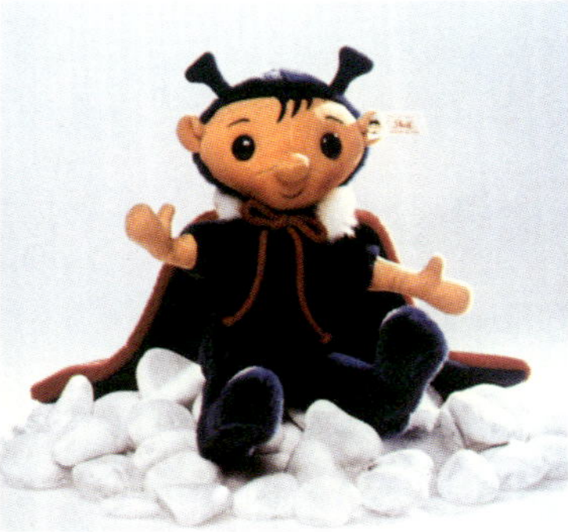

Maari

Webpelz, blau, sitzend, Marienkaefer-Prinz, Maskottchen der Deutschen Kinder-Krebshilfe, lim. Auflage 2.000 Stueck fuer die Deutsche Krebshilfe, Bonn - *woven fur, blue, sitting, ladybug-prince, mascot of the German Children´s Cancer Charity, ltd edition of 2,000 for the German cancer aid, Bonn*

EAN-No.	Period	Pr.	Info
996092	1999-1999	2-3	25 cm

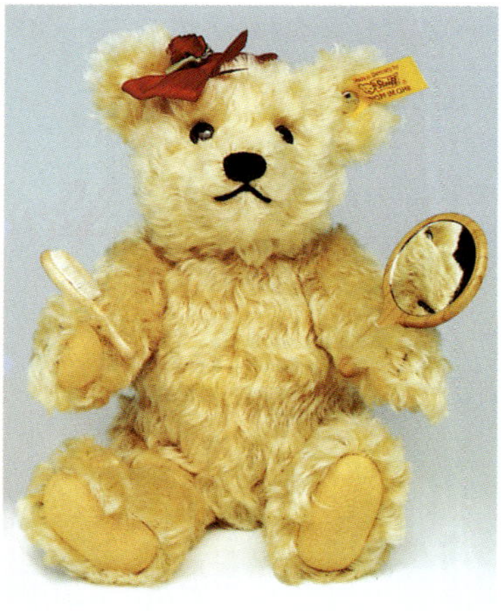

Teddybaer Montag - *Teddybear Monday*

Mohair, blond, gegliedert, abwaschbar, fuer Danbury Mint, aus der Serie der sogenannten Wochentagsbaeren - *mohair, blond, jointed, surface washable, for Danbury Mint, part of a series so called Bears of the Week*

EAN-No.	Period	Pr.	Info
654596	1999-1999	4	23 cm

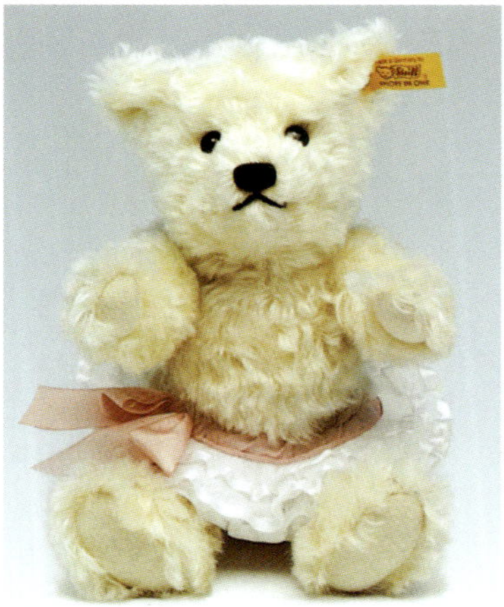

Teddybaer Dienstag - *Teddybear Tuesday*

Mohair, weiss, gegliedert, abwaschbar, fuer Danbury Mint, aus der Serie der sogenannten Wochentagsbaeren - *mohair, white, jointed, surface washable, for Danbury Mint, part of a series so called Bears of the Week*

EAN-No.	Period	Pr.	Info
654602	1999-1999	4	23 cm

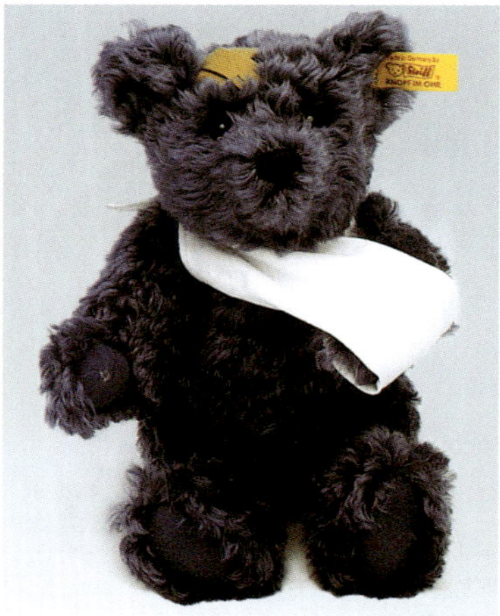

Teddybaer Mittwoch - *Teddybear Wednesday*

Mohair, blau, gegliedert, abwaschbar, fuer Danbury Mint, aus der Serie der sogenannten Wochentagsbaeren - *mohair, blue, jointed, surface washable, for Danbury Mint, part of a series so called Bears of the Week*

EAN-No.	Period	Pr.	Info
654619	1999-1999	4	23 cm

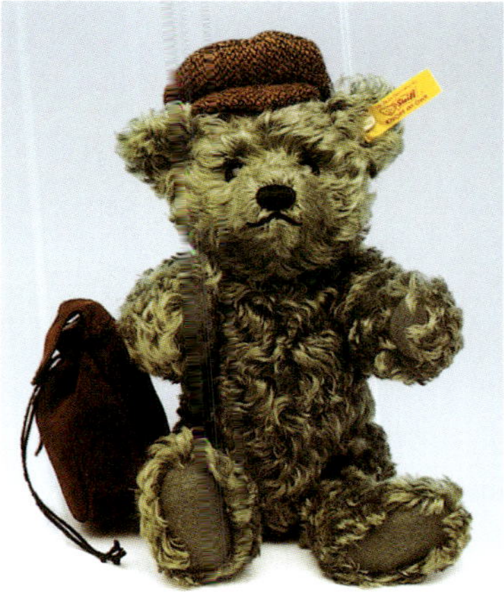

Teddybaer Donnerstag - *Teddybear Thursday*

Mohair, gruen, gegliedert, abwaschbar, fuer Danbury Mint, aus der Serie der sogenannten Wochentagsbaeren - *mohair, green, jointed, surface washable, for Danbury Mint, part of a series so called Bears of the Week*

EAN-No.	Period	Pr.	Info
654626	1999-1999	4	23 cm

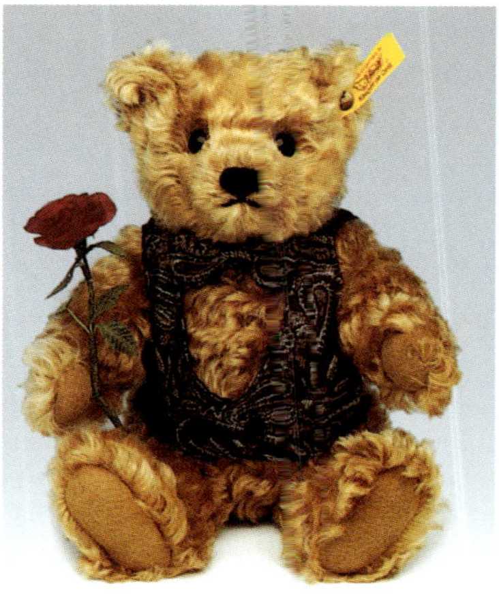

Teddybaer Freitag - *Teddybear Friday*

Mohair, zimt, gegliedert, abwaschbar, fuer Danbury Mint, aus der Serie der sogenannten Wochentagsbaeren - *mohair, cinnamon, jointed, surface washable, for Danbury Mint, part of a series so called Bears of the Week*

EAN-No.	Period	Pr.	Info
654633	1999-1999	4	23 cm

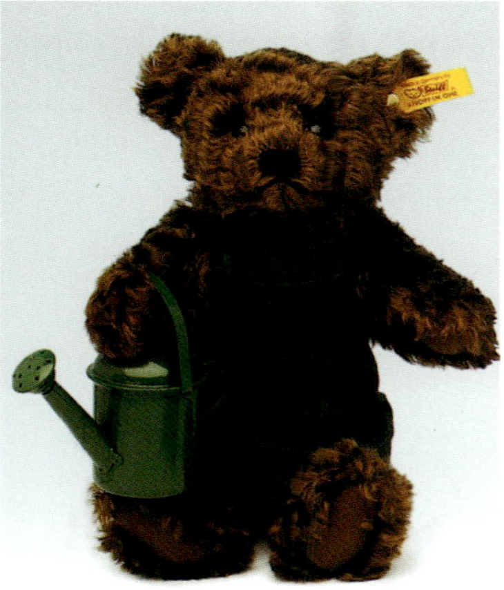

Teddybaer Samstag - *Teddybear Saturday*

Mohair, dunkelbraun, gegliedert, abwaschbar, fuer Danbury Mint, aus der Serie der sogenannten Wochentagsbaeren - *mohair, dark brown, jointed, surface washable, for Danbury Mint, part of a series so called Bears of the Week*

EAN-No.	Period	Pr.	Info
654640	1999-1999	4	23 cm

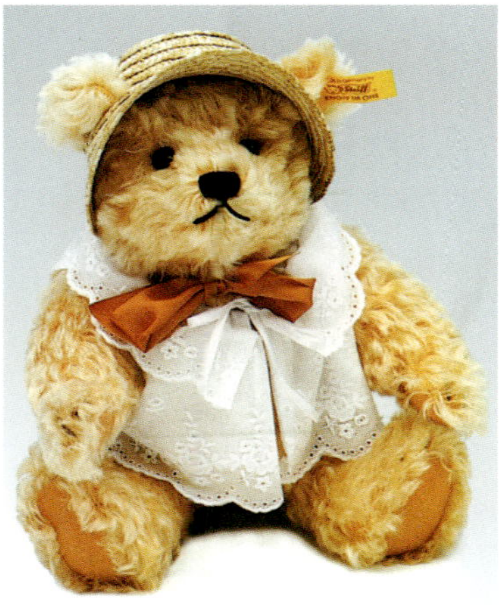

Teddybaer Sonntag - *Teddybear Sunday*

Mohair, lachs, gegliedert, abwaschbar, fuer Danbury Mint, aus der Serie der sogenannten Wochentagsbaeren - *mohair, salmon, jointed, surface washable, for Danbury Mint, part of a series so called Bears of the Week*

EAN-No.	Period	Pr.	Info
654657	1999-1999	4	23 cm

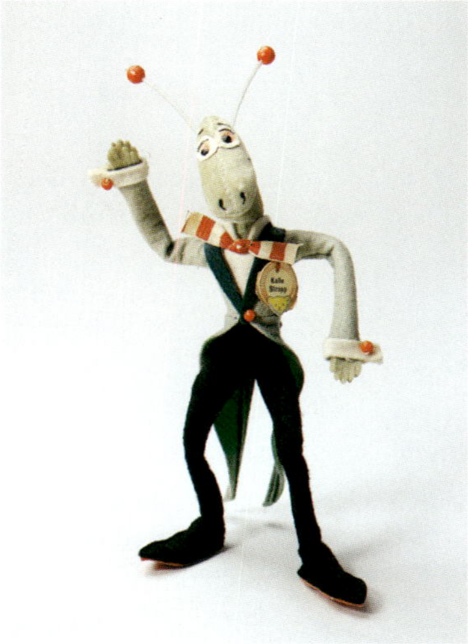

Grashuepfer **Kalle Stropp** - *Grasshopper* ***Kalle Stropp***

Samt/Filz, stehend, Kopf drehbar, aus einer Dänischen Kindergeschichte - *velvet & felt, standing, head swivels, from a Danish fairy tale*

Serie	Art.-No	Period	Pr.	Info
	114	1956-1956	9	18 cm

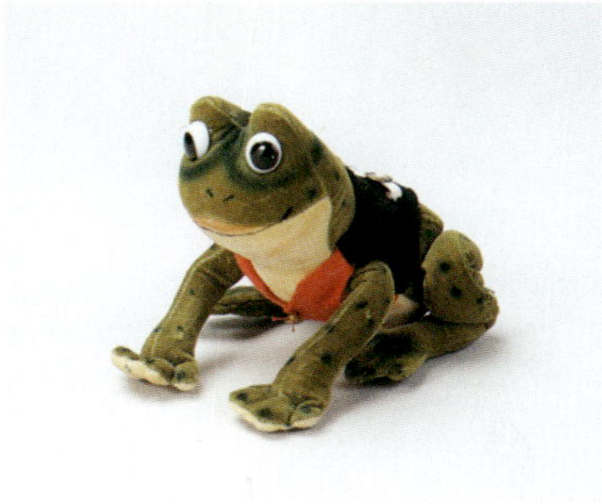

Grodan Boll

Kroete, Samt, gruen/gelb, sitzend, schwarz-rote Filzweste, zusammen mit Kalle Stropp Titelfigur aus einer Dänischen Kindergeschichte - *toad, velvet, green/yellow, sitting, waistcoat of felt in red & black, from a Danish fairy tale named Kalle Stropp*

EAN-No.	Period	Pr.	Info
	1956-1956	7	14 cm

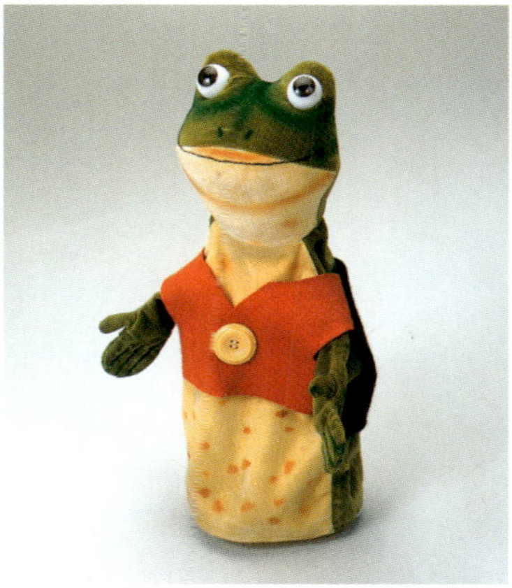

Handpuppe **Grodan Boll** - *Glove Puppet* ***Grodan Boll***

Kroete als Handpuppe, Samt, gruen/gelb, schwarz-rote Filzweste, zusammen mit Kalle StroppTitelfigur aus einer Daenischen Kindergeschichte - *toad as glove puppet, velvet, green/yellow, waistcoat of felt in red & black, from a Danish fairy tale named Kalle Stropp*

Serie	Art.-No	Period	Pr.	Info
	417W	1956-1956	7	17 cm

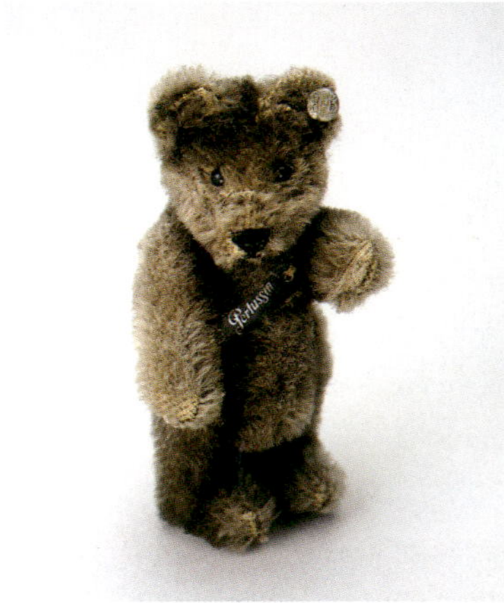

Pertussin Baer - *Pertussin Bear*

Mohair, braun, gegliedert, Werbeartikel fuer gleichnamigen Hustensaft, Fa. Fink - *mohair, brown, jointed, promotional item for a cough syrup with the same name from a company with the name Fink*

EAN-No.	Period	Pr.	Info
	1960-1960	6	10 cm

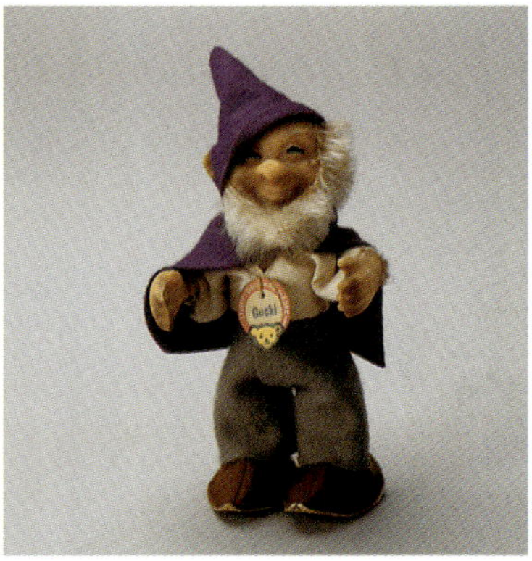

Zwerg **Gucki** - *Dwarf **Gucki***

Zweck unbekannt, Kunststoff, lila Umhang - *purpose unknown, synthetic figure, lavender cape*

EAN-No.	Period	Pr.	Info
	1960-1962	3-4	13 cm

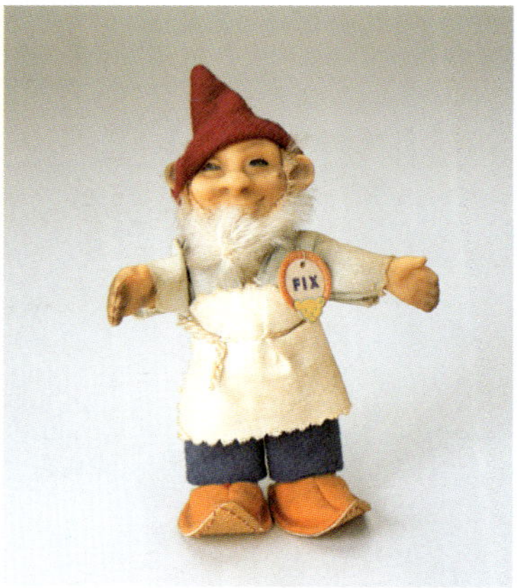

Zwerg **Fix** - *Dwarf **Fix***

Kunststoff, stehend, Zweck unbekannt, hell-beige Schürze mit Gürtel aus Kordel - *synthetic, standing, purpuse unknown, apron in light beige with a belt of cord*

EAN-No.	Period	Pr.	Info
	1962-1962	4	13 cm

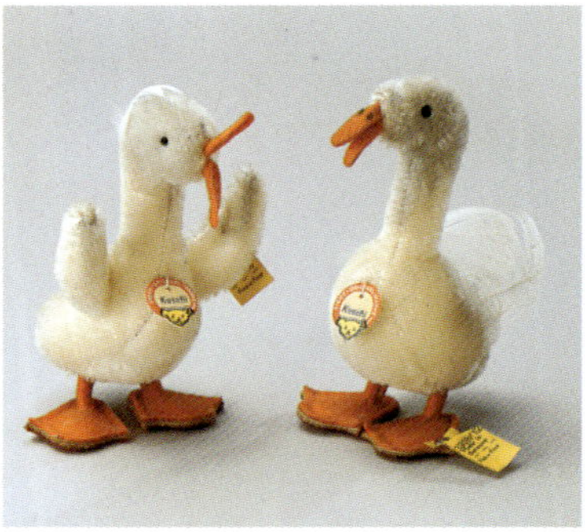

Kuschi Gans - ***Kuschi** Goose*

Gans, Bettfedern-Reklame, Mohair/Daune/Filz, stehend - *promotion for goose down, mohair/down & felt, standing*

Serie	Art.-No	Period	Pr.	Info
	6312,90	1965-1967	3-4	12 cm
	3309/12	1968-1970	3-4	

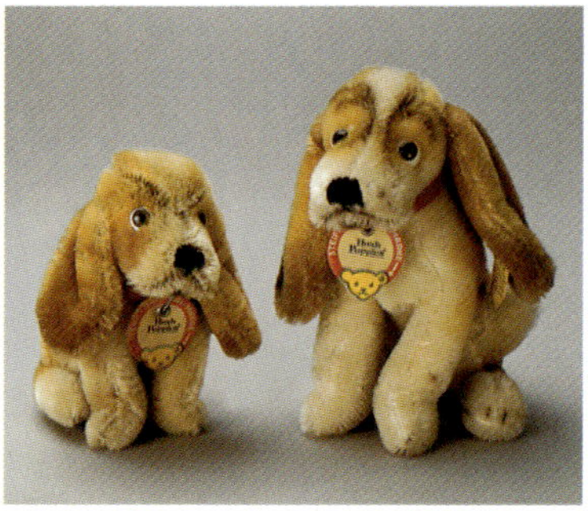

Basset **Hush Puppies**

Werbeartikel für Schuhhersteller, Mohair, sitzend - *promotional item for shoe manufacturer Hush Puppies, mohair, sitting*

Serie	Art.-No	Period	Pr.	Info
	4080/12	1970-1972	4	12 cm
	4080/14	1970-1972	4	14 cm

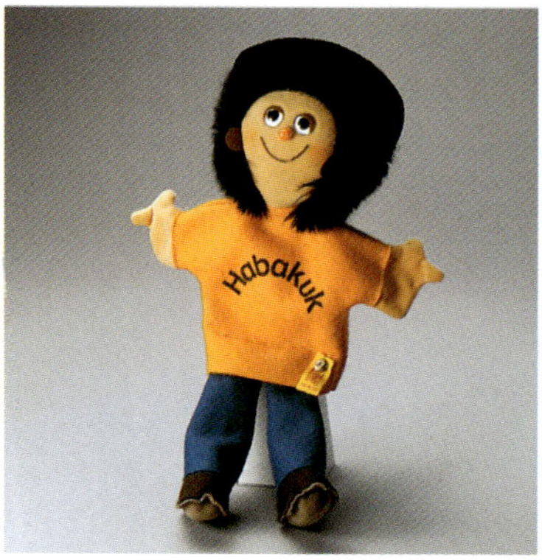

Habakuk

Trevira/Filz, Handspielpuppe, nach dem Schuelerbuch "Lies mit Habakuk", Diesterweg Verlag - *trevira/felt, hand puppet, taken from the school book "Read with Habakuk", Diesterweg Publishing House*

Serie	Art.-No	Period	Pr.	Info
	7954/30	1980-1980	3	30 cm

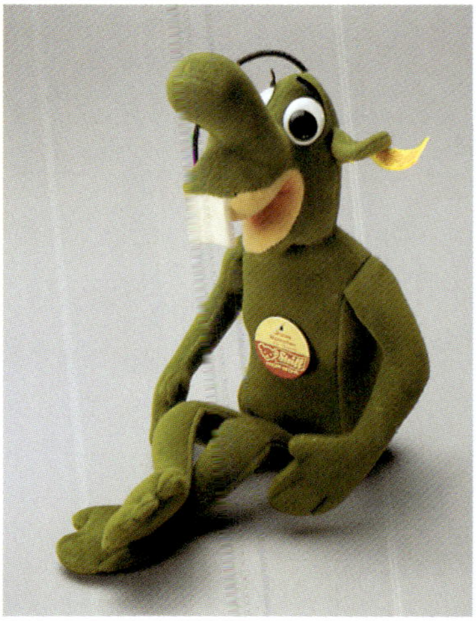

Gruenes Maennchen - *Little Green Man*

Trevirasamt, gruen, gestaltet vom belg. Kuenstler Mallet, abwaschbar - *trevira velvet, green, created by the Belgian artist Mallet, surface washable*

Serie	Art.-No	Period	Pr.	Info
	7885/35	1982-1984	5	35 cm

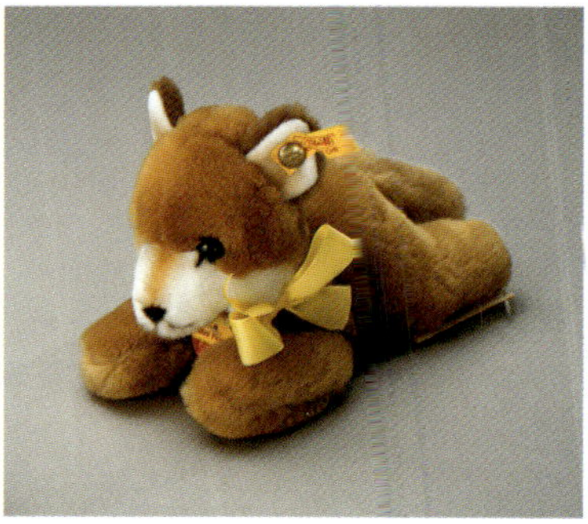

Fuchs - *Fox*

Webpelz, liegend, weich, Zweck unbekannt - *woven fur, lying, soft, purpose unknown*

Serie	Art.-No	Period	Pr.	Info
999512	**5678/17**	1988-1990	2	17 cm

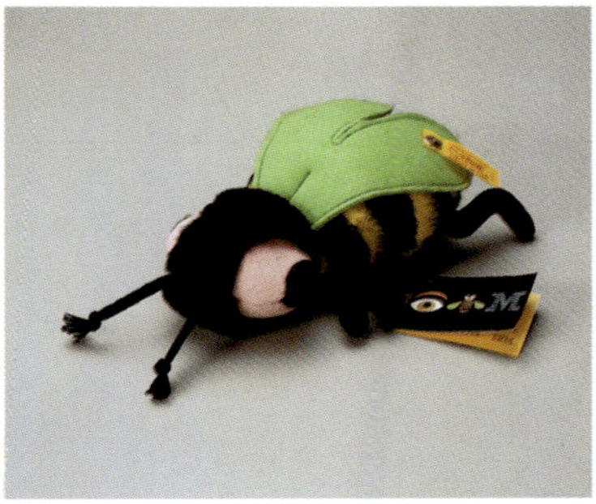

Biene - *Bee*

Webpelz, Filz, Werbeartikel für IBM - *woven fur, felt, promotional item for IBM*

EAN-No.	PERIOD	PR.	INFO
999741	1990-1990	3	17 cm

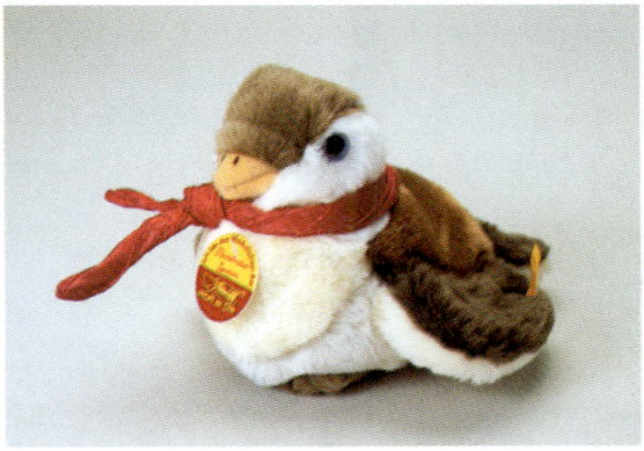

Kastelruther Spatz - *Kastelruther Sparrow*

Webpelz, mehrfarbig, Maskottchen der Volksmusikgruppe Kastelruther Spatzen - *woven fur, multi-colored, mascot of the folkloristic music group Kastelruther Spatzen*

EAN-No.	PERIOD	PR.	INFO
999864	1995-1995	2	15 cm

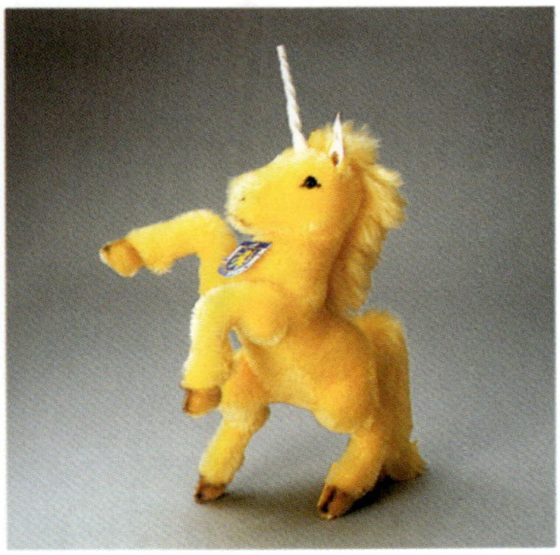

Einhorn - *Unicorn*

Mohair, aufwartend, Wappentier der Stadt Giengen, lim. Auflage 3.000 Stueck - *mohair, rearing, heraldic figure of the city of Giengen´s coat of arms, ltd edition of 3,000*

EAN-No.	PERIOD	PR.	INFO
999086	1995-1995	3	27 cm

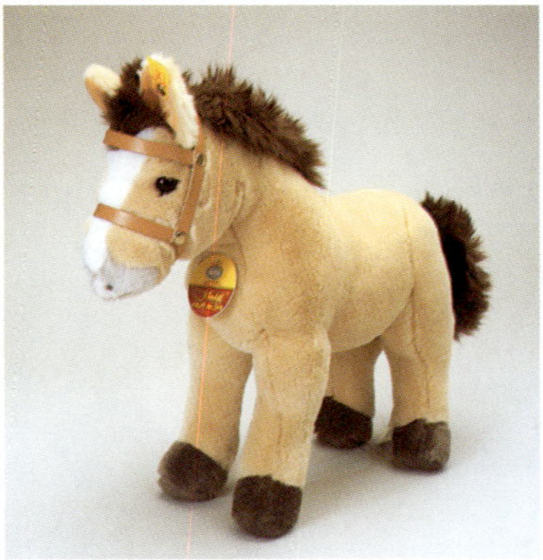

Pferd - *Horse*

Webpelz, stehend, fuer die Serie Brittany´s Club der Fa. Goetz - *woven fur, standing, for the series Brittany´s Club offered by Goetz company*

EAN-No.	PERIOD	PR.	INFO
998836	1996-1999	3-4	37 cm

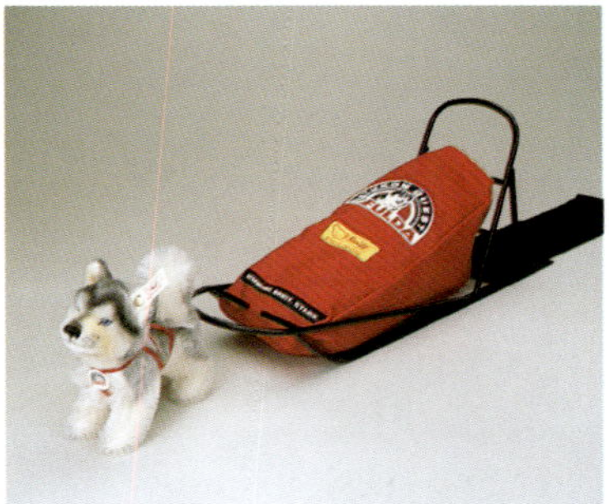

Husky-Schlitten-Set - *Husky-Sledge-Set*

Mohair Webpelz, abwaschbar, rotes Geschirr, Metall-Schlitten mit Schlittensack, in Zusammenarbeit mit Fa. Fulda, limitierte Auflage 3.000 Stueck - *mohair woven fur, surface washable, with red harness & sledge made of metal with sledge-basket, ltd edition of 3,000, in cooperation with Fulda Tyres*

EAN-No.	PERIOD	PR.	INFO
038617	1998-1998	4	15 cm

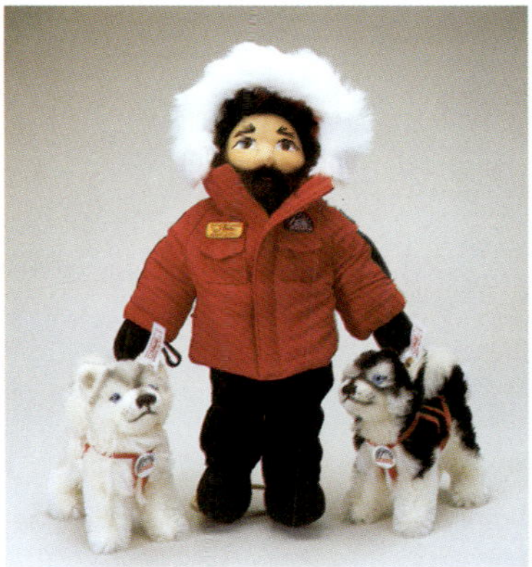

Husky-Set mit Musher - *Husky-Set with Musher*

2 Husky´s Mohair Webpelz, schwarz/weiss & weiss, stehend, abwaschbar & Musher, Polyestersamt, limitierte Auflage 3.000 Stueck in Zusammenarbeit mit Fulda Reifen - *husky´s mohair woven fur, 15 cm, black/white & white, standing, surface washable and musher, polyester velvet, ltd edition of 3,000 in cooperation with FULDA tyres*

EAN-No.	PERIOD	PR.	INFO
038624	1999-1999	4-5	kpl. Set - *cpl. set*
J04281	1999-1999	3-4	weiss - *white*
J04282	1999-1999	3-4	schwarz/weiss - *black/white*

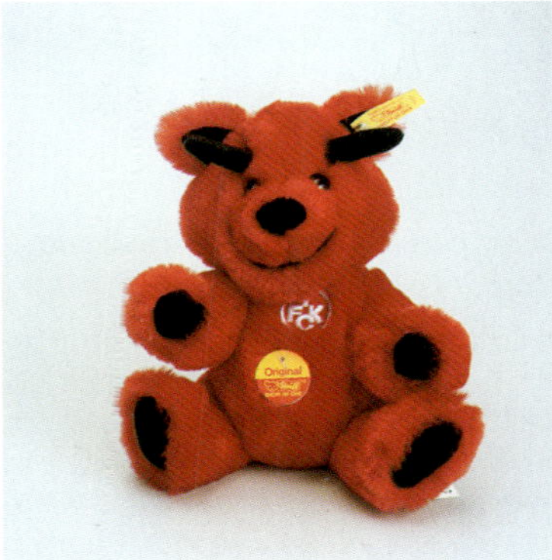

Betzi

Webpelz, rot, abwaschbar, Teufel, Maskottchen des Fussballclubs 1. FC Kaiserslautern - *woven fur, red, surface washable, devil, mascot of German soccer club 1. FC Kaiserslautern*

EAN-No.	PERIOD	PR.	INFO
998652	1998-1998	3	25 cm

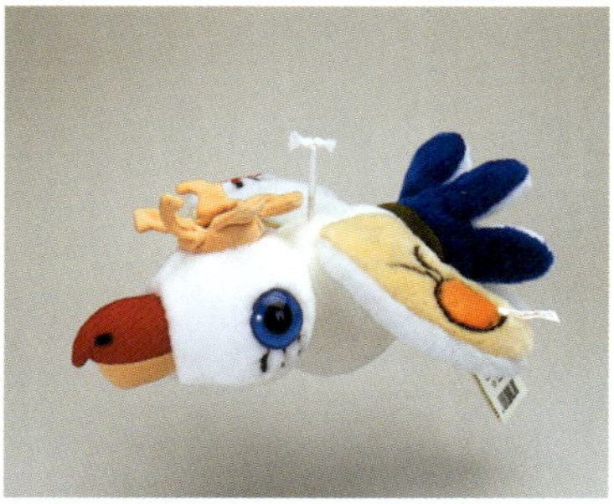

Otmar Alt Taube - *Otmar Alt Pigeon*

Webpelz/Trevirasamt, mehrfarbig, fliegend, bewegliche Krone, drehbarer Schwanz, nach Zeichnungen von Otmar Alt, zur Unterstuetzung der Arbeit des Juedischen Nationalfonds, limit. Auflage 1.818 Stueck - *woven fur/trevira velvet, multi-colored, flying, movable crown & rotating tail, from drawings of Otmar Alt, to support the work of the Jewish National Fund, ltd edition of 1,818*

EAN-No.	Period	Pr.	Info
996504	1998-1998	3	30 cm

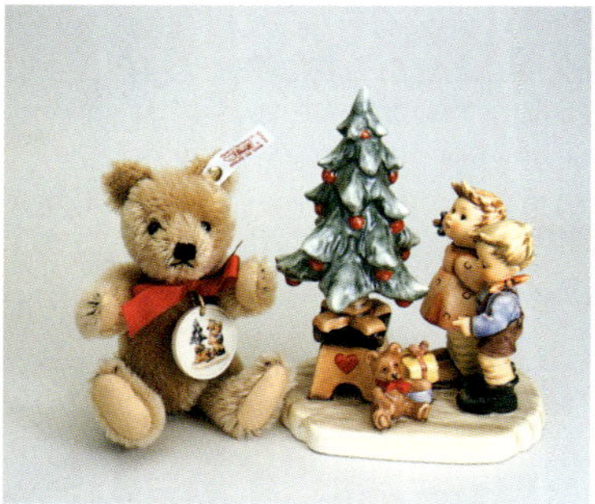

Steiff / Goebel Set Am Weihnachtsbaum - *Steiff / Goebel Set Wonder of Christmas*

Mohair bzw. Keramik, zimt bzw. mehrfarbig, Baer gegliedert und mit Keramik-Medaillon, zusammen mit Hummel-Figur, limit. Auflage 20.000 Stueck fuer Fa. Goebel - *mohair or ceramics, cinnemon or multi-colored, bear jointed and with ceramics-locket, together with a Hummel figurine, ltd edition of 20,000 for Goebel*

EAN-No.	Period	Pr.	Info
996535	1998-1998	5	kpl. Set - *compl. set*
996535	1998-1998	4	18 cm, zimt - *cinnamon*

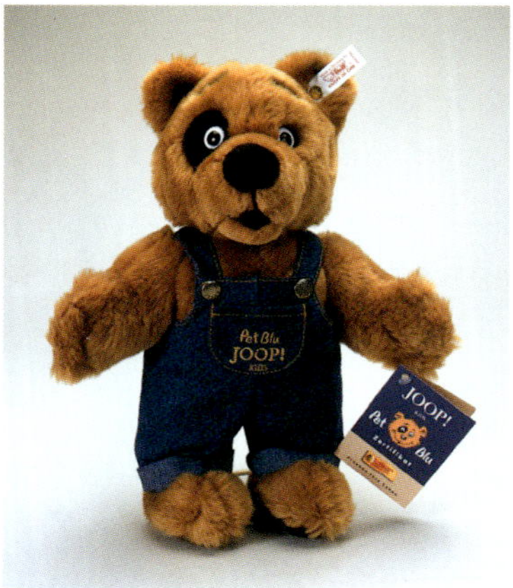

Pet Blu Teddy

Webpelz, dunkelblau, mit Joop Jeans Pet Blu fuer Kids, limit. Auflage 1.555 Stueck - *woven fur, dark blue, with Joop Jeans Pet Blu for Kids, ltd edition of 1,555*

EAN-No.	Period	Pr.	Info
996788	1998-1998	3	32 cm

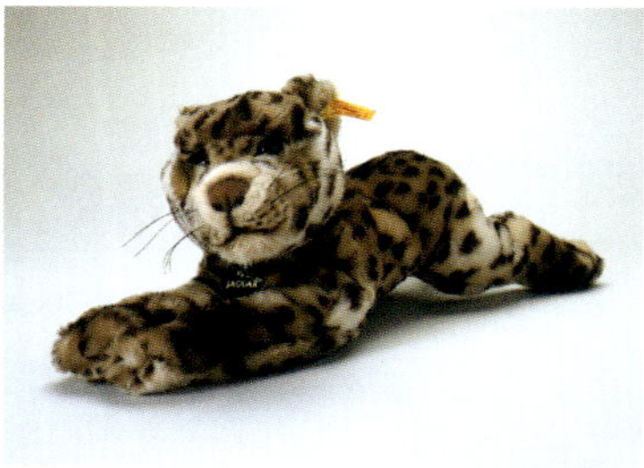

Jaguar

Webpelz, naturfarben, liegend, abwaschbar, Werbeartikel fuer Jaguar Fahrzeuge - *woven fur, natural color, lying, surface washable, promotional item for Jaguar car company*

EAN-No.	Period	Pr.	Info
998539	1999-1999	3	45 cm

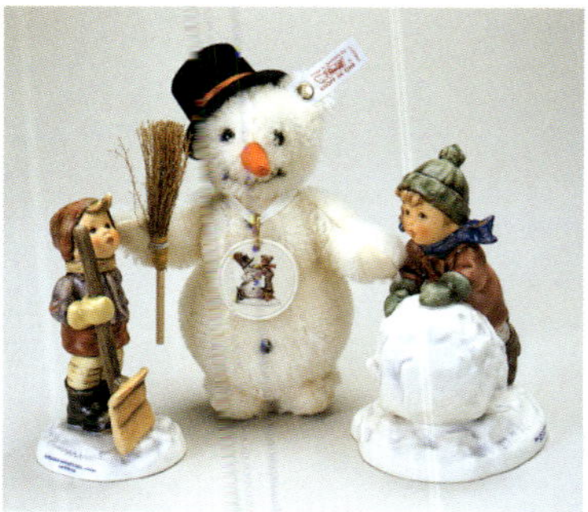

Steiff / Goebel Set Winterzauber - *Steiff / Goebel Set Frosty Friends*

Mohair bzw. Keramik, weiss bzw. mehrfarbig, gegliedert, Schneemann mit Keramik-Medaillon, zusammen mit 2 Hummel-Figuren, limit. Auflage 20.000 Stueck fuer Fa. Goebel - *mohair or ceramics, white or multi-colored, jointed, snowman with ceramics-locket, together with 2 Hummel figurines, ltd edition of 20,000 for Goebel*

EAN-No.	Period	Pr.	Info
996207	1999-1999	5-6	kpl. Set - *compl. set*
996207	1999-1999	4-5	18 cm, weiss - *white*

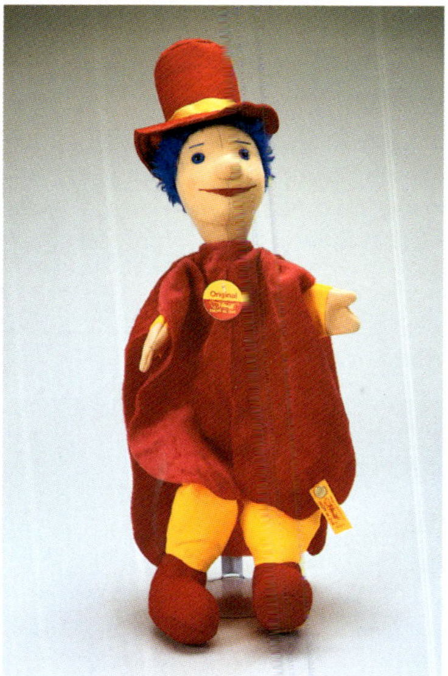

Zauberer Nono - *Magician Nono*

Trevira/Filz, mehrfarbig, Handspielpuppe, roter Umhang & Hut, blaue Haare, gelber Anzug, Werbeartikel fuer den Ernst Klett Verlag - *Trevira/felt, multi-colored, glove puppet, red cape & hat, blue hair, yellow suit, promotional item for Ernst Klett publishing house*

EAN-No.	Period	Pr.	Info
996443	1999-1999	3	45 cm

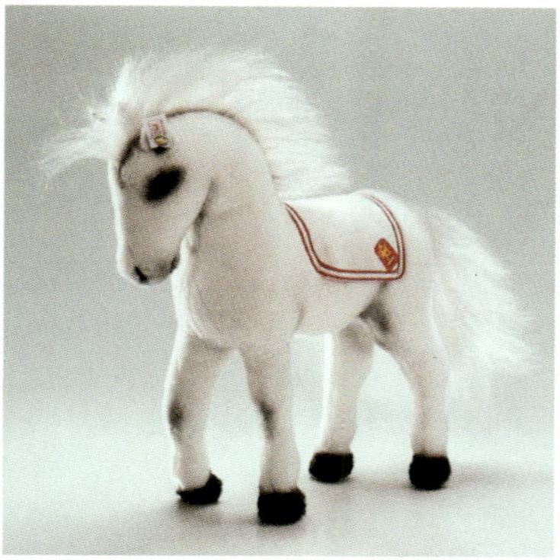

Lipizzaner

Synthetik-Webpelz, Schweif & Maehne aus Mohair, weiss, stehend, mit Satteldecke, Werbeartikel fuer Koeflach, Partnerstadt der Stadt Giengen, limit. Auflage 3.000 Stueck - *synthetic woven fur, tail & mane of mohair, white, standing, saddle blanket, promotional piece for Koeflach in Austria, twin town to the city of Giengen, ltd edition of 3,000*

EAN-No.	Period	Pr.	Info
996481	1999-1999	3-4	30 cm

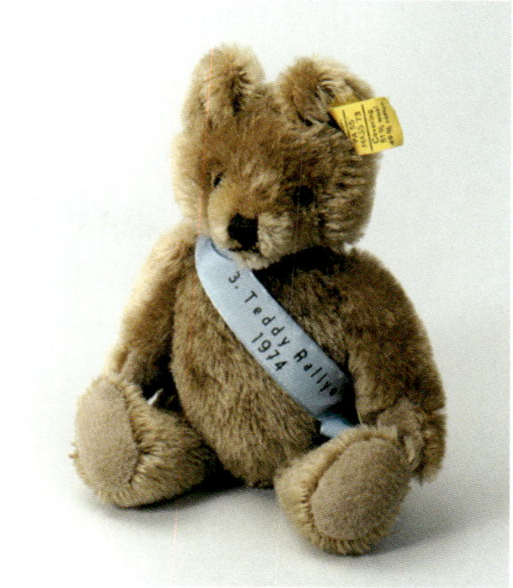

Original Teddy

Mohair, caramel, gegliedert, Sonderbaer zur 3. Teddy Rallye Giengen (Brenz) 1974, mit bedruckter Schaerpe - *mohair, caramel, jointed, special bear for 3rd Teddy Rallye in Giengen (Brenz) 1974, with imprinted sash*

Serie	Art.-No	Period	Pr.	Info
	0202/19	1974-1974	4	19 cm

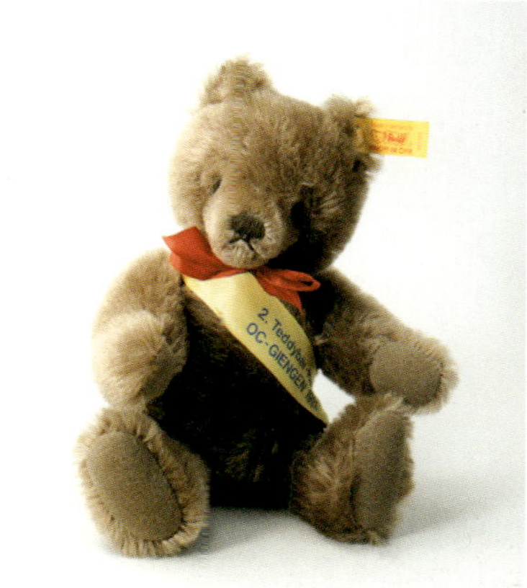

Original Teddy

Mohair, caramel, gegliedert, Sonderbaer zur 2. Teddybaer Rallye OC Giengen 1993, mit bedruckter Schaerpe - *mohair, caramel, jointed, special bear for 2nd Teddybaer Rallye OC Giengen 1993, sash with imprint*

EAN-No.	Period	Pr.	Info
002205	1993-1993	3-4	26 cm

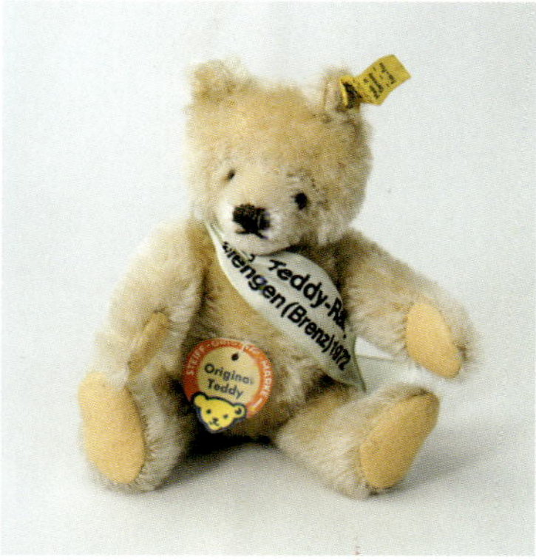

Original Teddy

Mohair, honig, gegliedert, Sonderbaer zur 1. Teddy Rallye Giengen (Brenz) 1972, mit bedruckter Schaerpe - *mohair, honey, jointed, special bear for 1st Teddy Rallye in Giengen (Brenz) 1972, with imprinted sash*

Serie	Art.-No	Period	Pr.	Info
	5319,01	1972-1972	4	19 cm

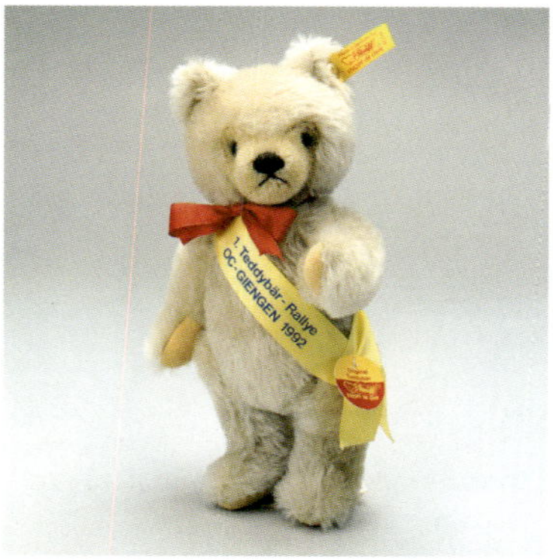

Original Teddy

Mohair, honig, gegliedert, Sonderbaer zur 1. Teddybaer Rallye OC Giengen 1992, mit bedruckter Schaerpe - *mohair woven fur, honey, jointed, special bear for 1st Teddybaer Rallye OC Giengen 1992, sash with imprint*

EAN-No.	Period	Pr.	Info
001208	1992-1992	4	26 cm

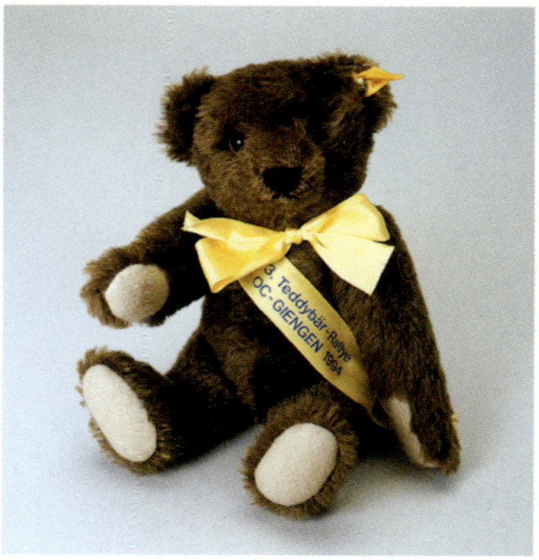

Original Teddy

Mohair, dunkelbraun, gegliedert, Sonderbaer zur 3. Teddybaer Rallye OC Giengen 1994, mit bedruckter Schaerpe - *mohair, dark brown, jointed, special bear for 3rd Teddybaer Rallye OC Giengen 1994, sash with imprint*

EAN-No.	Period	Pr.	Info
000423	1994-1994	3-4	26 cm

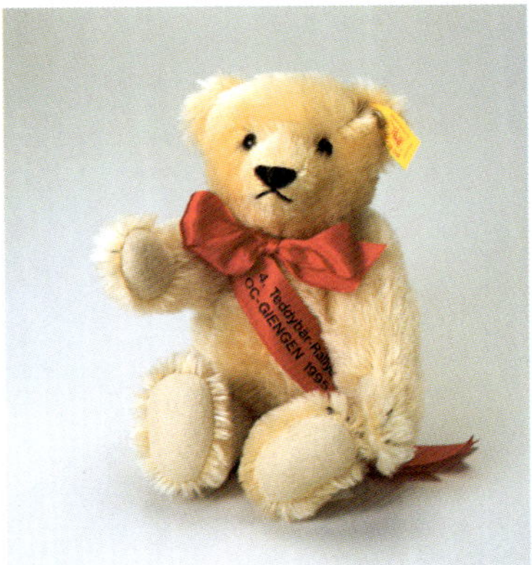

Original Teddy

Mohair, blond, gegliedert, Sonderbaer zur 4. Teddybaer Rallye OC Giengen 1995, mit bedruckter Schaerpe - *mohair, blond, jointed, special bear for 4th Teddybaer Rallye OC Giengen 1995, sash with imprint*

EAN-No.	Period	Pr.	Info
000355	1995-1995	3-4	26 cm

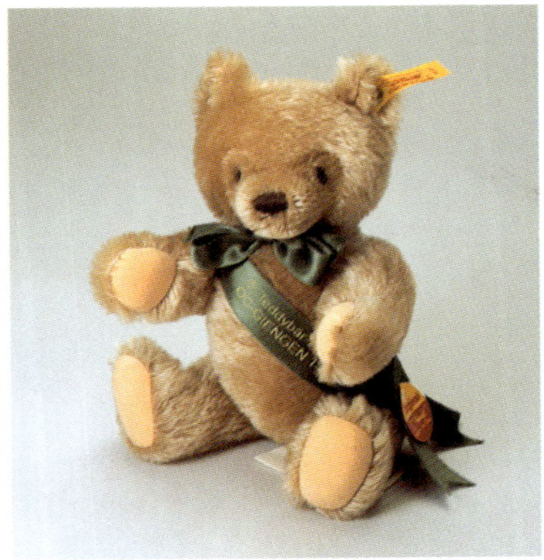

Original Teddy

Mohair, zimt, gegliedert, Sonderbaer zur 6. Teddybaer Rallye OC Giengen 1997, mit bedruckter Schaerpe - *mohair, cinnamon, jointed, special bear for 6th Teddybaer Rallye OC Giengen 1997, sash with imprint*

EAN-No.	Period	Pr.	Info
998607	1997-1997	3	26 cm

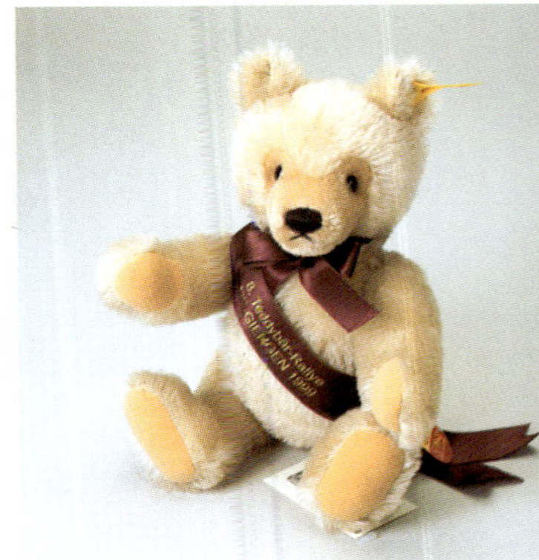

Original Teddy

Mohair, honig, gegliedert, Sonderbaer zur 8. Teddybaer Rallye OC Giengen 1999, mit bedruckter Schaerpe - *mohair, honey, jointed, special bear for 8th Teddybaer Rallye OC Giengen 1999, sash with imprint*

EAN-No.	Period	Pr.	Info
996108	1999-1999	3	26 cm

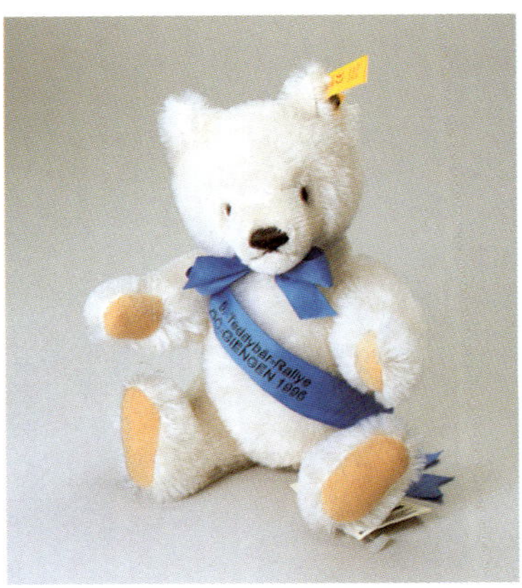

Original Teddy

Mohair, weiss, gegliedert, Sonderbaer zur 5. Teddybaer Rallye OC Giengen 1996, mit bedruckter Schaerpe - *mohair, white, jointed, special bear for 5th Teddybaer Rallye OC Giengen 1996, sash with imprint*

EAN-No.	Period	Pr.	Info
998874	1996-1996	3	26 cm

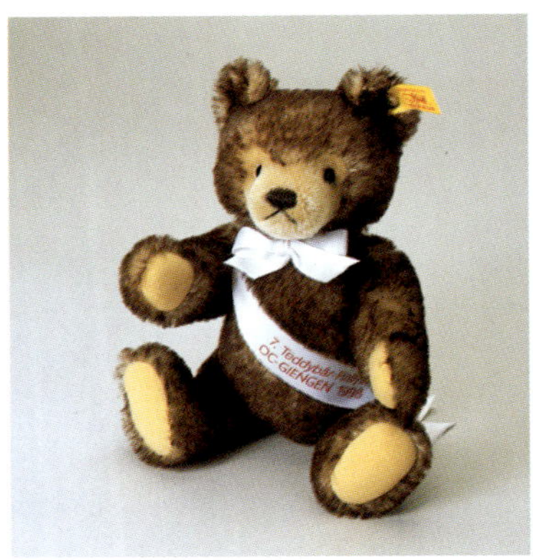

Original Teddy

Mohair, braun gespitzt, gegliedert, Sonderxbaer zur 7. Teddybaer Rallye OC Giengen 1998, mit bedruckter Schaerpe - *mohair, brown tipped, jointed, special bear for 7th Teddybaer Rallye OC Giengen 1998, sash with imprint*

EAN-No.	Period	Pr.	Info
996559	1998-1998	3	26 cm

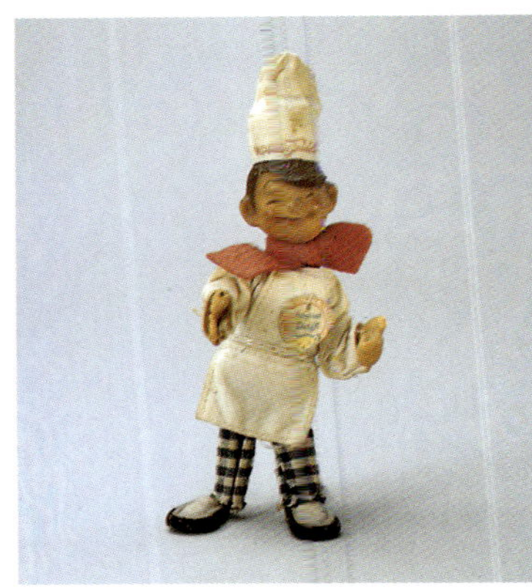

Maggi Fridolin

Werbeartikel für Fa. Maggi, Gummifigur, stehend - *promotional item for the Maggi Company, rubber figure, standing*

Serie	Art.-No	Period	Pr.	Info
	713	1958-1958	5	13 cm

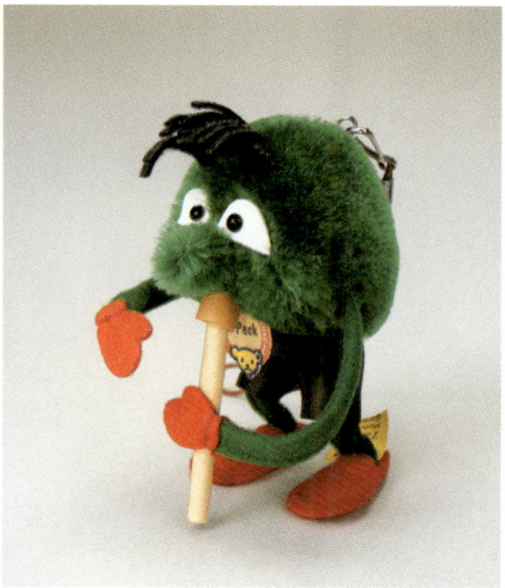

Peck

Blattlaus, Werbeartikel für Fa. Merck, Mohair/Filz/Gummi, stehend - *greenfly, promotional item for the Merck Company, mohair/felt/rubber, standing*

SERIE	ART.-NO	PERIOD	PR.	INFO
	7312	1959-1959	7	12 cm

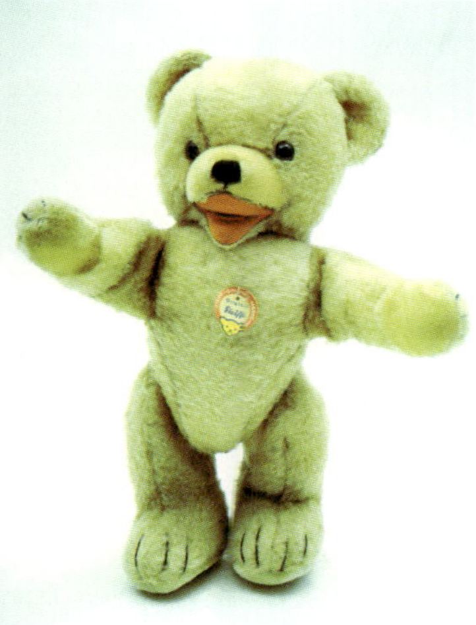

Baeren-Marke Baer - *Baeren-Marke Bear*

Wollpluesch, hellbraun, Beine & Kopf gegliedert, Werbeartikel fuer die gleichnamige Dosenmilch - *plush wool, light brown, legs & head jointed, promotional item for tinned milk with the same name*

SERIE	ART.-NO	PERIOD	PR.	INFO
	7535,90	1960-1960	6-7	35 cm

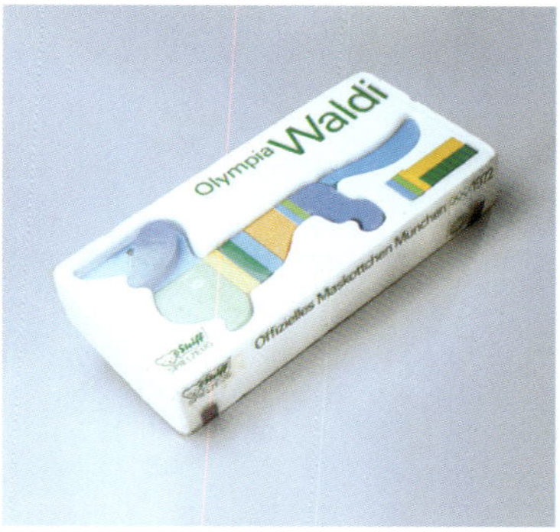

Olympia Waldi - *Olympic Waldi*

17 Holzteile, lackiert, offizielles Maskottchen der olymp. Spiele 1972, Muenchen - *17 wooden pieces, painted, official mascot of the 1972 Olympic Games, Munich Germany*

SERIE	ART.-NO	PERIOD	PR.	INFO
	8320/15	1971-1972	3	15 cm

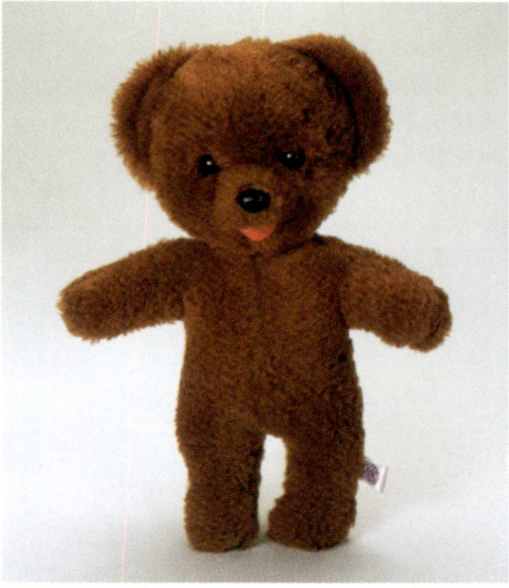

Baeren-Marke Baer - *Baeren-Marke Bear*

Wollpluesch, braun, stehend, Werbeartikel fuer die gleichnamige Dosenmilch - *plush wool, brown, standing, promotional item for tinned milk with the same name*

SERIE	ART.-NO	PERIOD	PR.	INFO
	7951/25	1977-1977	3	25 cm

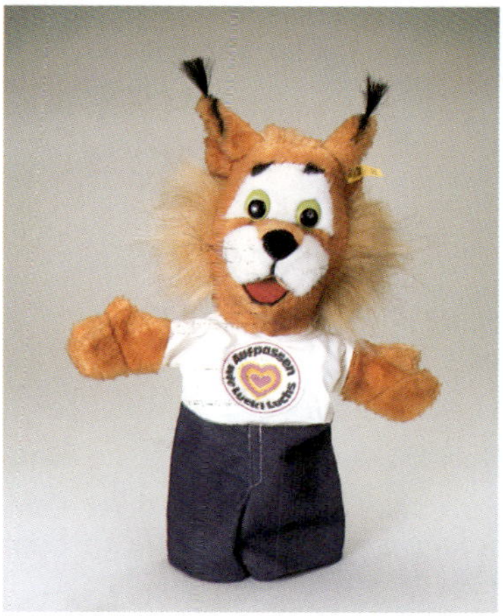

Lucki Luchs - *Lucky Lynx*

Dralon, Handspieltier, diente zur Verkehrerziehung von Kindern - *dralon, hand puppet, for traffic school & education purposes*

SERIE	ART.-NO	PERIOD	PR.	INFO
	7956/35	1978-1980	3	30 cm

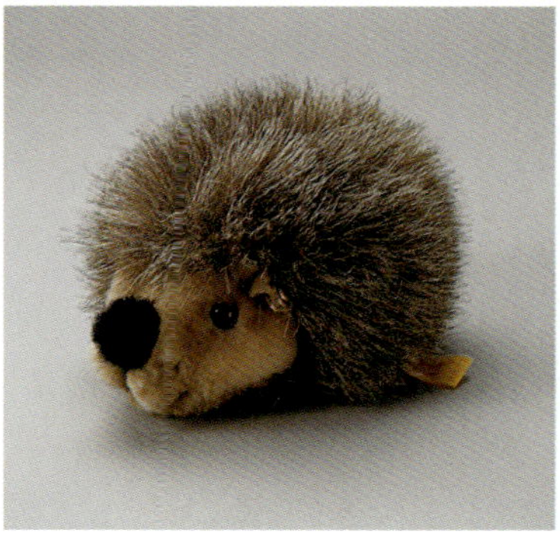

Igel Joggi - *Hedgehog Joggi*

Webpelz, graubraun, für Lufthansa Bordverkauf - *woven fur, grey-brown, sold on bord Lufthansa aircraft*

SERIE	ART.-NO	PERIOD	PR.	INFO
	1675/13	1980-1980	2	12 cm

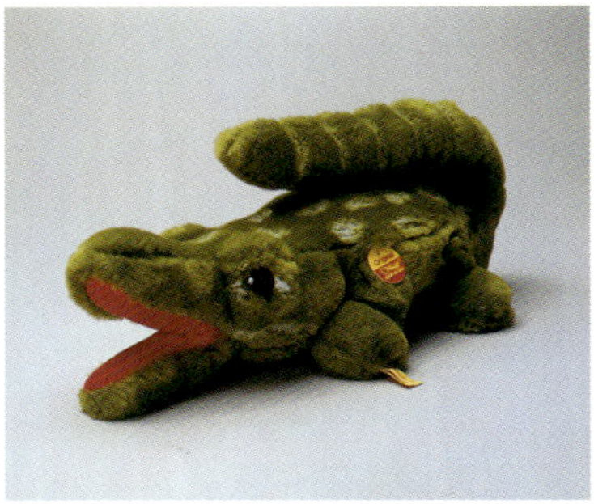

Krokodil - *Crocodile*

Werbeartikel für Fa. LaCoste, Webpelz, stehend - *promotional item for LaCoste Company, woven fur, standing*

SERIE	ART.-NO	PERIOD	PR.	INFO
	7961/45	1984-1984	3-4	45 cm
	999383	1993-1993	5	

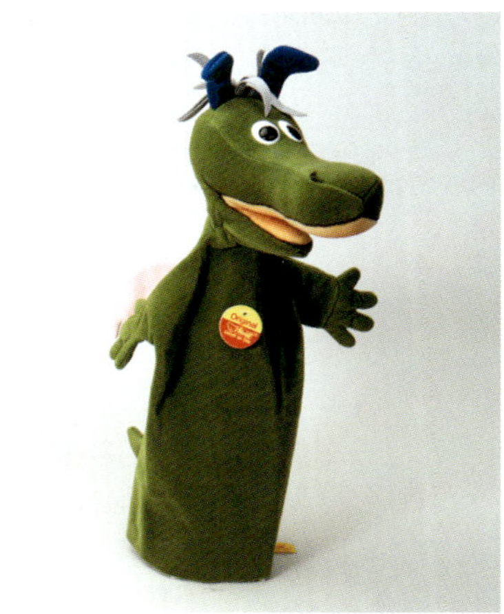

Hand-Drache - *Hand-Dragon*

Trevirasamt, gruen, Werbeartikel fuer Oldenburg Verlag - *trevira velvet, green, promotional item for Oldenburg Publishing House*

EAN-NO.	PERIOD	PR.	INFO
999666	1991-1991	3-4	35 cm

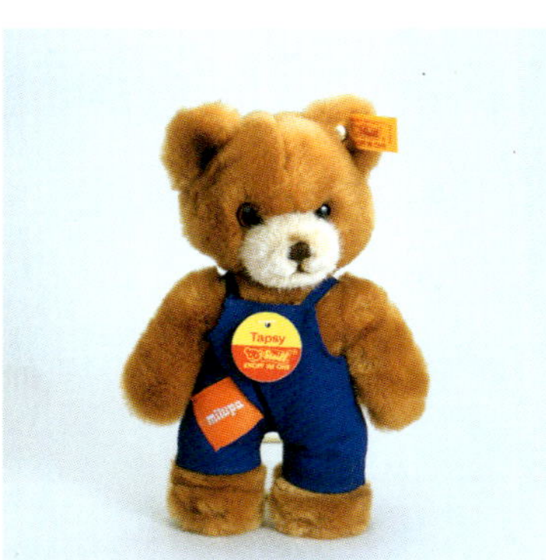

Tapsy Baer - ***Tapsy** Bear*

Werbeartikel für Milupa, Webpelz - *promotional item for the Milupa Company, woven fur*

EAN-NO.	PERIOD	PR.	INFO
999413	1991-1991	2-3	20 cm

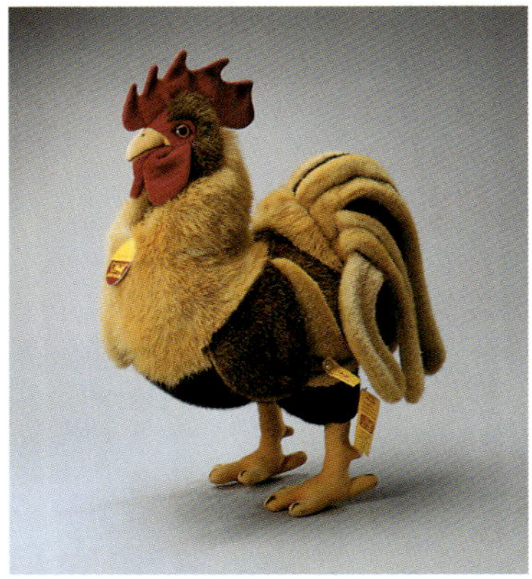

Der Hahn - *The Rooster*

Werbeartikel für Pohl Boskamp (Chloraldurat), Webpelz-Mohair, stehend - *promotional item for the Pohl Boskamp Company (Chloraldurat), woven fur, mohair, standing*

EAN-NO.	PERIOD	PR.	INFO
999772	1992-1992	4	40 cm

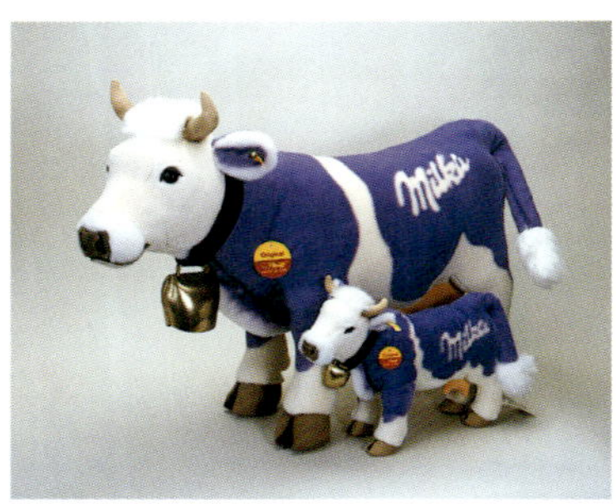

Milka Kuh - *Milka Cow*

Synthetik-Webpelz, lila/weiss, stehend, abwaschbar, Lederhalsband mit Glocke, Werbeartikel in Zusammenarbeit mit der Fa. Kraft Jacobs Suchard - *woven fur, lilac/white, standing, surface washable, leather collar & bell, promotional item in cooperation with the Kraft Jacobs Suchard Company*

EAN-NO.	PERIOD	PR.	INFO
354014	1998-1999	3-4	32 cm
998546	1997-1997	5	100 cm

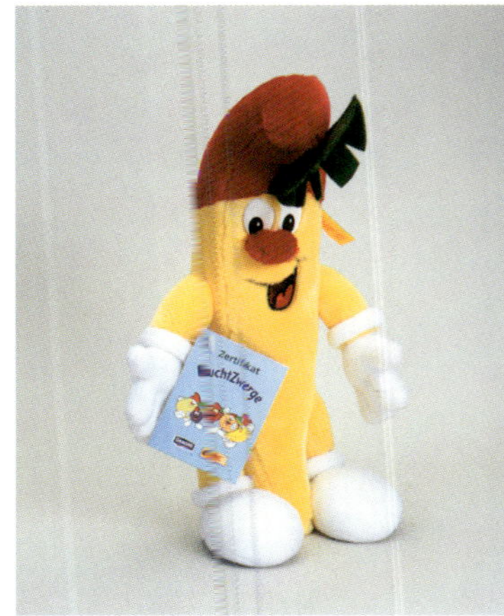

Danone Banane *Danone Banana*

Synthetik-Webpelz, gelb, aufwartend, personifiziert, Werbeartikel fuer Danone Joghurt, Fa. Nestlé - *synthetic woven fur, yellow, sitting up, humanized, promotional item for Danone Yoghurt, the Nestlé Company*

EAN-NO.	PERIOD	PR.	INFO
999840	1995-1995	3-4	32 cm

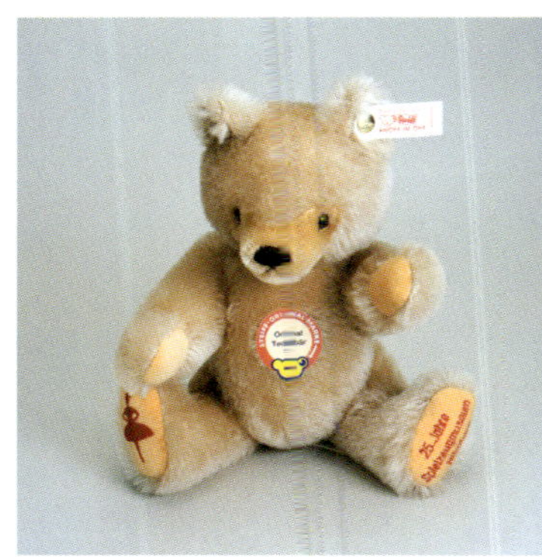

Original Teddybaer - *Original Teddybear*

Mohair, blond, gegliedert, limit. Auflage 3.000 Stueck zum 25jaehrigen Jubilaeum des Nuernberger Spielzeugmuseum - *mohair, blond, jointed, ltd edition of 3,000 for the 25th anniversary of the Nuremberg Toy Museum*

EAN-NO.	PERIOD	PR.	INFO
998928	1996-1996	4	2[illegible] cm

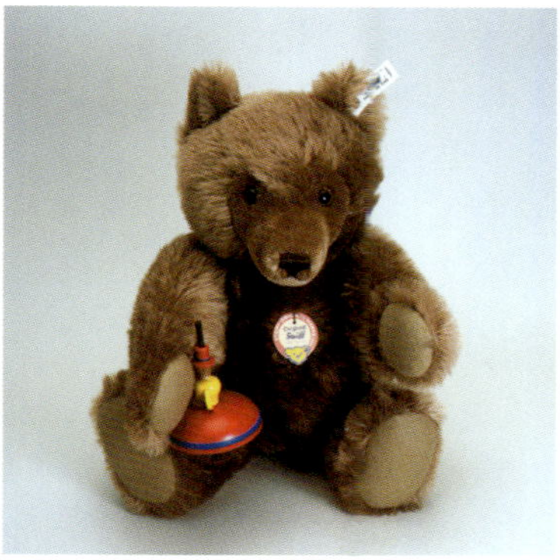

Teddybaer - *Teddybear*

Mohair, caramel, gegliedert, limit. Auflage 3.000 Stueck zum 25jaehrigen Jubilaeum des Nuernberger Spielzeugmuseum - *mohair, caramel, jointed, ltd edition of 3,000 for the 25th anniversary of the Nuremberg Toy Museum*

EAN-No.	Period	Pr.	Info
998935	1996-1996	4	41 cm

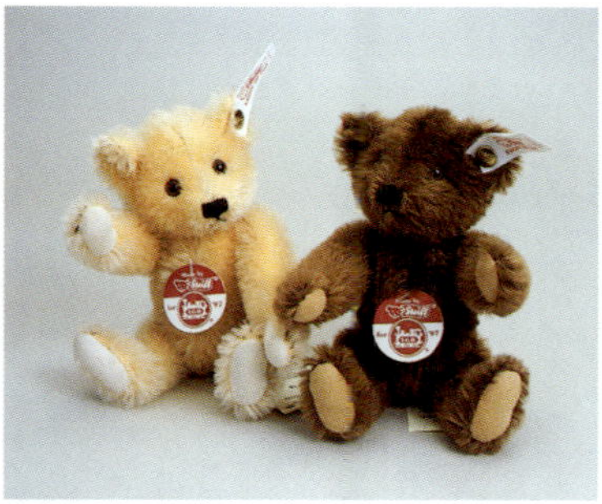

LGB Baerenpaar - *LGB Bear-Couple*

Mohair Webpelz, braun bzw. blond, gegliedert, mit LGB Eisenbahnwagen, limitierte Auflage 3.800 Stueck, Werbeartikel fuer LGB - *mohair, brown or blond, jointed, with LGB railway wagon, ltd edition of 3,800, promotional item for LGB Company*

EAN-No.	Period	Pr.	Info
998751	1997-1997	4-5	kpl. Set - *compl. Set*
	1997-1997	3-4	16 cm, braun - *brown*
	1997-1997	3-4	16 cm, blond

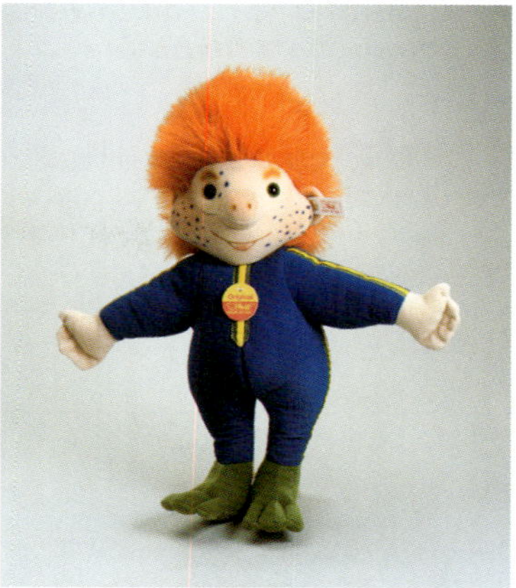

Sams

Webpelz, blau, stehend, Kinderbuchfigur des Autors Paul Maar, limit. Auflage 2.000 Stueck fuer Oetinger Verlag - *woven fur, blue, standing, children´s book figure from the author Paul Maar, ltd edition of 2,000 for Oetinger Publishing House*

EAN-No.	Period	Pr.	Info
998782	1997-1997	2-3	25 cm

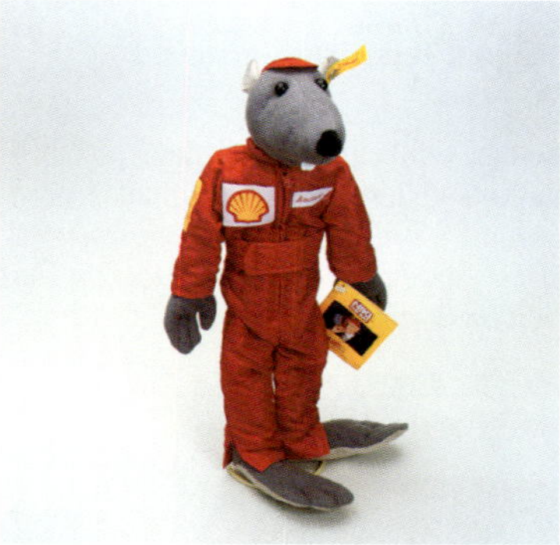

NIKI THE RAT

Baumwolle, rot, der oesterreichische Autorennfahrer Niki Lauda stand Pate fuer diese karikierte Ratte, bekleidet mit einem rotem Rennanzug (ausziehbar) mit Lauda-Air, Shell und Steiff-Stickern, mit typischer Niki Lauda Muetze - *cotton, red, Austrian race driver Niki Lauda was the model for this caricature rat, dressed with a red race-overall (can be removed) with Lauda-Air, Shell & Steiff stickers, with typical Niki Lauda cap*

EAN-No.	Period	Pr.	Info
998881	1997-1997	2-3	37 cm

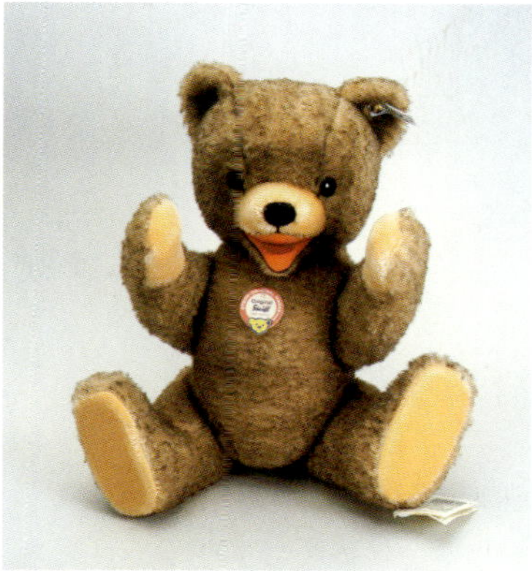

Baeren-Marke Baer - *Baeren-Marke Bear*

Wollpluesch, hellbraun, gegliedert, Werbeartikel fuer die gleichnamige Dosenmilch, limit. Auflage 1.500 Stueck fuer Fa. Nestlé - *plush wool, light brown, jointed, promotional item for tinned milk with the same name, ltd edition of 1,500 for the Nestlé Company*

EAN-No.	Period	Pr.	Info
999000	1997-1997	5	35 cm

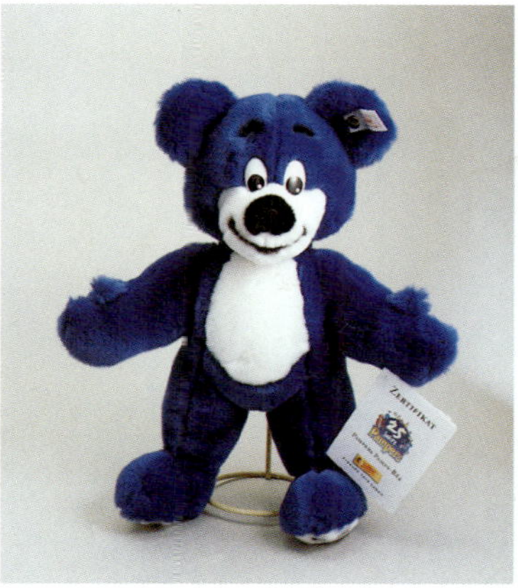

Pampy Baer - *Pampy Bear*

Webpluesch, blau/weiss, abwaschbar, zum 25. Geburtstag von Pampers, limitierte Auflage 5.000 Stueck fuer Procter & Gamble - *woven fur, blue/white, surface washable, to celebrate the 25th birthday of Pampers, ltd edition of 5,000 for Procter & Gamble*

EAN-No.	Period	Pr.	Info
996767	1998-1998	3	30 cm

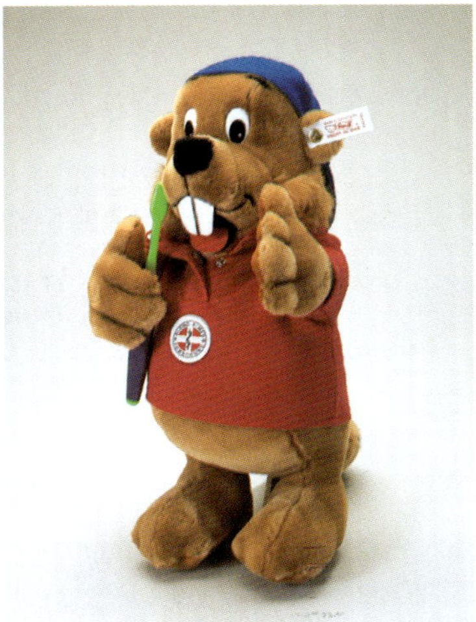

Blendi Biber - *Blendi Beaver*

Webpelz, braun, aufwartend, abwaschbar, Maskottchen fuer blend-a-med, mit Zahnbuerste, limitierte Auflage 3.000 Stueck fuer Procter & Gamble - *woven fur, brown, sitting up, surface washable, maskot for blend-a-med, with tooth-brush, ltd edition of 3,000 for Procter & Gamble*

EAN-No.	Period	Pr.	Info
996405	1999-1999	3	28 cm

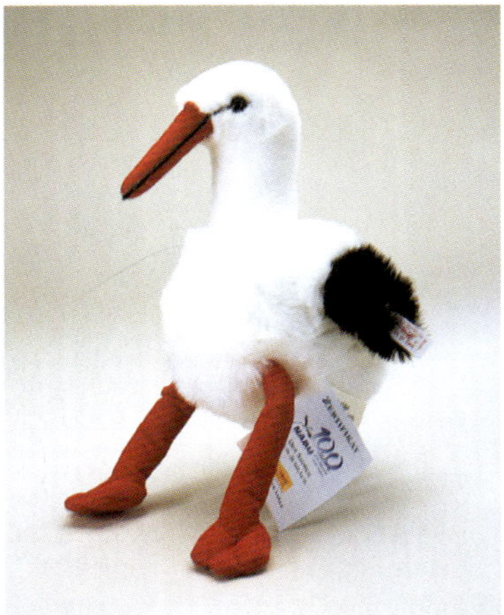

Storch Nabu - *Stork Nabu*

Webpelz, waschmaschinenfest, zum 100. Geburtstag des Naturschutzbund Deutschland e.V. - *woven fur, machine washable, to celebrate the 100th birthday of the German Nature Conservation Union*

EAN-No.	Period	Pr.	Info
354038	1999-1999	3	30 cm

kein Bild vorhanden -
no picture available

Original Teddybaer

Mohair, honig, gegliedert, abwaschbar, Werbegeschenk fuer die Nuernberger Spielwaren Messe, limit. Auflage 250 Stueck - *mohair, honey, jointed, surface washable, promotional gift for Nuremberg Toy Fair, ltd edition of 250*

EAN-No.	Period	Pr.	Info
995934	1999-1999	3	10 cm

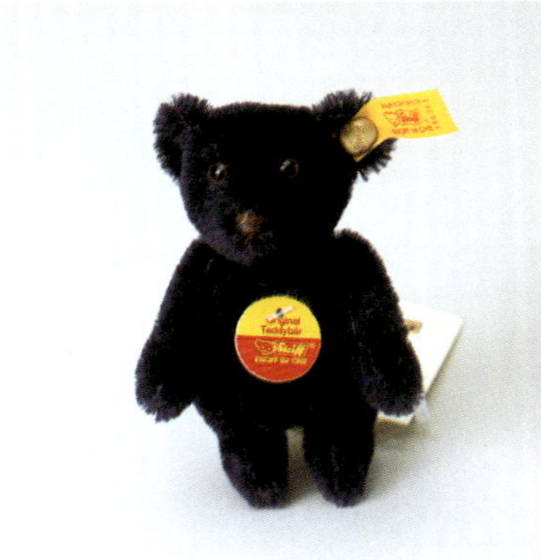

Original Teddybaer - *Original Teddybear*

Mohair, dunkelblau, gegliedert, abwaschbar, ausschliesslich fuer Lufthansa Bordverkauf - *mohair, dark blue, jointed, surface washable, exclusively sold on bord Lufthansa aircraft*

EAN-No.	Period	Pr.	Info
996351	1999-1999	2-3	10 cm

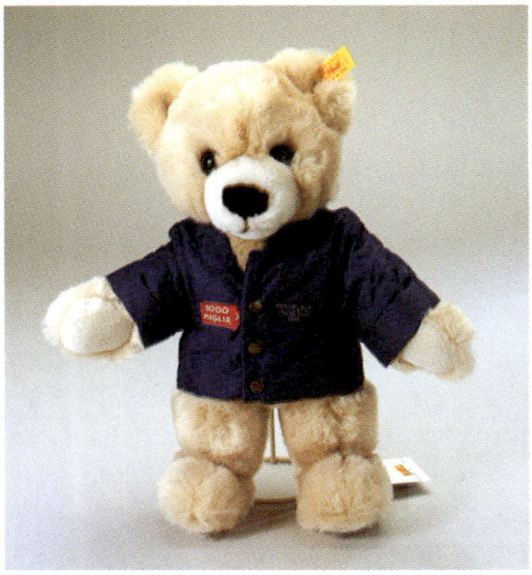

Mercedes-Benz Teddybaer - *Mercedes-Benz Teddybear*

Webpelz, blond, waschmaschinenfest, Werbeartikel "Mercedes-Benz Classic Team 1999" - *woven fur, blond, promotional item "Mercedes-Benz Classic Team 1999"*

EAN-No.	Period	Pr.	Info
996177	1999-1999	3	32 cm

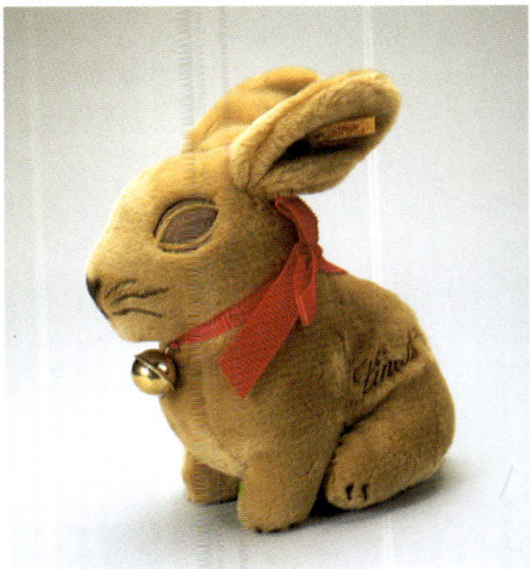

Goldhase - *Gold Rabbit*

Webpelz, hellbraun, sitzend, gestickte Augen, linke Körperseite mit Lindt-Schriftzug und -Firmenzeichen, Werbeartikel für Lindt - *woven fur, light brown, sitting, eyes embroidered, Lindt in writing & logo on the left, promotional item for Lindt*

EAN-No.	Period	Pr.	Info
996320	1999-1999	3-4	25 cm

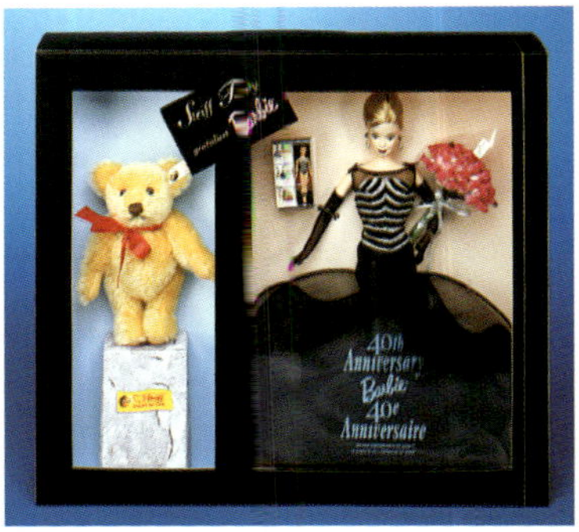

Steiff / Barbie Set

Mohair, blond, gegliedert, Baer & Barbie Puppe, zum 40. Geburtstag der Barbie, limit. Auflage 1.500 Stueck fuer Fa. Mattel - *mohair, blond, jointed, bear & Barbie doll, to celebrate the 40th birthday of Barbie, ltd edition of 1,500 for Mattel*

EAN-No.	Period	Pr.	Info
996115	1999-1999	4	15 cm

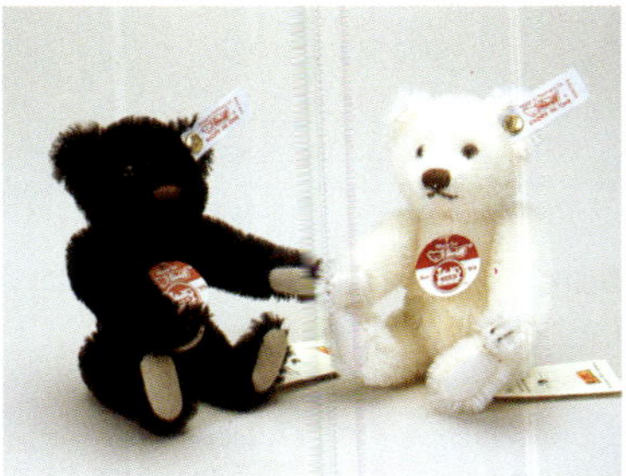

LGB Baerenpaar - *LGB Bear-Couple*

Mohair, schwarz bzw. weiss, gegliedert, mit LGB Eisenbahnwagen, limitierte Auflage 2.900 Stueck, Werbeartikel fuer LGB - *mohair, black or white, jointed, with LGB railway wagon, ltd edition of 2,900, promotional item for LGB Company*

EAN-No.	Period	Pr.	Info
996764	1999-1999	4-5	kpl. Set - *compl. Set*
J04000	1999-1999	3-4	16 cm, schwarz - *black*
J04001	1999-1999	3-4	16 cm, weiss - *white*

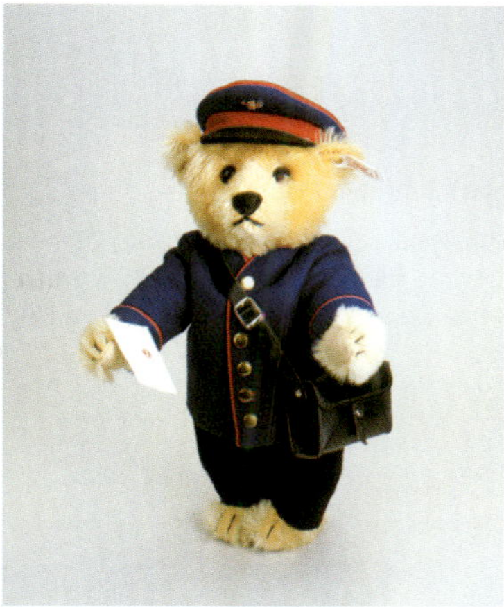

Johannes der Brieftraeger - *Johannes the Postman*

Mohair, blond, gegliedert, limit. Auflage 1.500 Stueck fuer das Postmuseum - *mohair, blond, jointed, ltd edition of 1,500 for the German Post Museum*

EAN-No.	Period	Pr.	Info
999062	1995-1995	5	32 cm

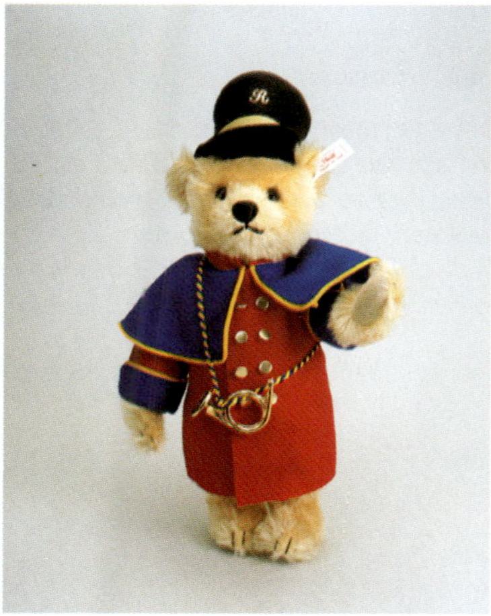

Heinrich der Postillion - *Heinrich the Postman*

Mohair, blond, gegliedert, limit. Auflage 2.000 Stueck fuer das Postmuseum - *mohair, blond, jointed, ltd edition of 2,000 for the German Post Museum*

EAN-No.	Period	Pr.	Info
998959	1996-1996	5	32 cm

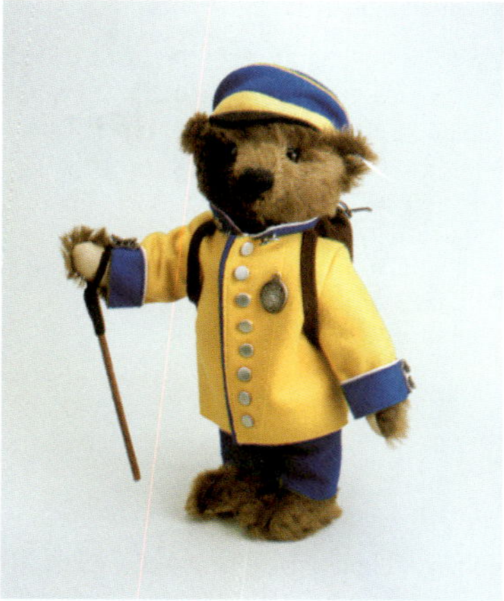

Moritz

Mohair, braun, gegliedert, hist. Uniform der saechsischen Landbrieftraeger, limit. Auflage 1.500 Stueck fuer das Postmuseum - *mohair, brown, jointed, hist. uniform of a Saxony Postman, ltd edition of 1,500 for the German Post Museum*

EAN-No.	Period	Pr.	Info
998744	1997-1997	4-5	32 cm

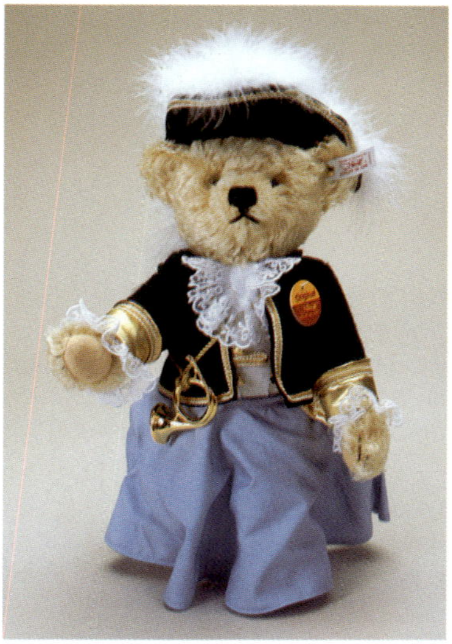

Christel von der Post - *Christel from the Post*

Teddybaer, Mohair, blond, gegliedert, Musikwerk "Christel von der Post", limit. Auflage 2.000 Stueck fuer das Postmuseum - *Teddybear, mohair, blond, jointed, with musicbox playing "Christel von der Post", ltd edition of 2,000 for the German Post Museum*

EAN-No.	Period	Pr.	Info
996627	1998-1998	4-5	32 cm

kein Bild vorhanden -
no picture available

Maximilian der Postillion - *Maximilian the Postman*

Mohair, blond, gegliedert, Koeniglich Bayerische Post Uniform um 1850, limit. Auflage 1.500 Stueck fuer das Postmuseum - *mohair, blond, jointed, Royal Bavarian Post uniform from 1850, ltd edition of 1,500 for the German Post Museum*

EAN-No.	Period	Pr.	Info
	1999-1999	4	32 cm

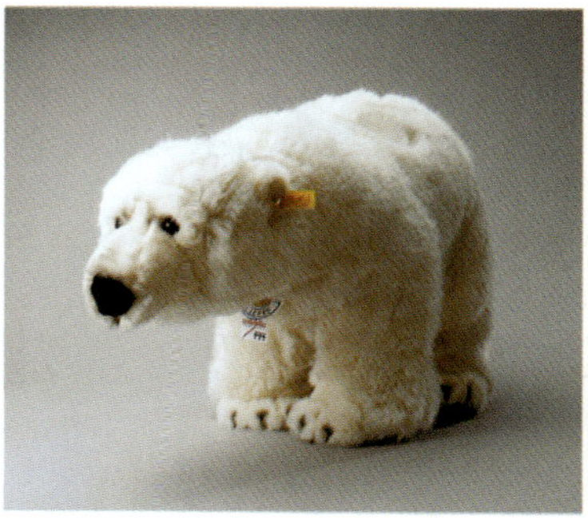

Eisbaer - *Ice Bear*

Webpelz, 70 Jahre "The Alaska Railroad", Werbeartikel fuer Fa. Maerklin - *woven fur, to celebrate 70 years "The Alaska Railroad", promotional item for Maerklin Company*

EAN-No.	Period	Pr.	Info
999758	1994-1994	4-5	30 cm

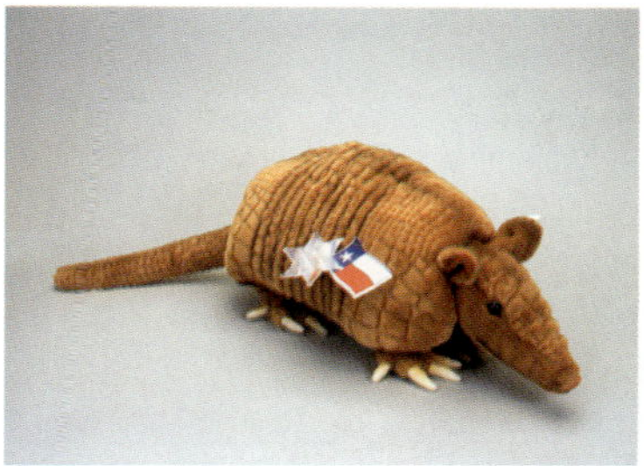

Guerteltier - *Armadillo*

Webpelz, braun, stehend, Filzfuesse, Werbetier fuer Maerklin-Texaszug, limit. Auflage 3.500 Stueck - *woven fur, brown, standing, felt feet, promotional item for the Maerklin Texas Train, ltd edition of 3,500*

EAN-No.	Period	Pr.	Info
999147	1995-1995	3-4	34 cm

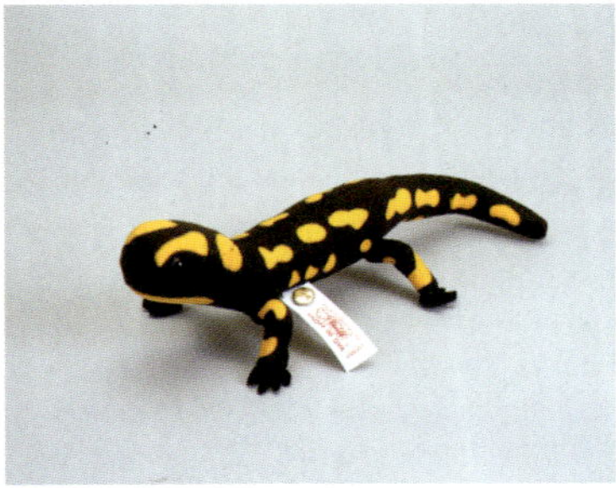

Salamander-Set

Trevirasamt, schwarz/gelb, stehend, zusammen mit 2 H0 Gueterwagen der koeniglich wuerttembergischen Staatseisenbahn, Werbeartikel fuer Fa. Maerklin - *trevira velvet, black/yellow, standing, complete with 2 H0 railroad cars of the Royal Wurttemberg Railway, promotional item for Maerklin*

EAN-No.	Period	Pr.	Info
488061	1995-1995	3-4	22 cm

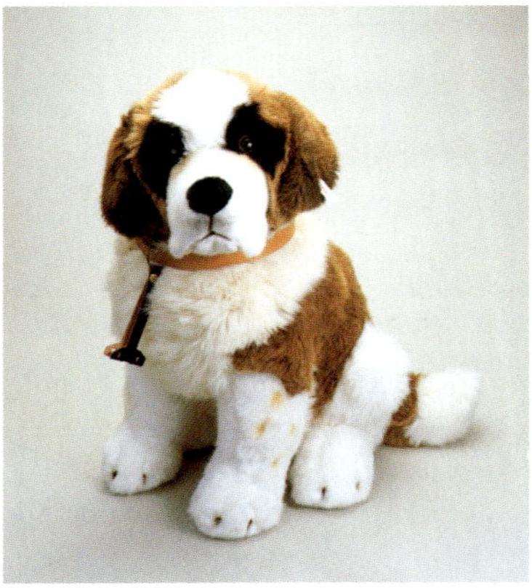

St. Bernhard

Webpelz, weiss/braun, sitzend, limitierte Auflage 2.400 Stueck fuer Fa. Maerklin - *woven fur, white/brown, sitting, ltd edition of 2,400 for Maerklin*

EAN-No.	Period	Pr.	Info
998577	1997-1997	4	48 cm

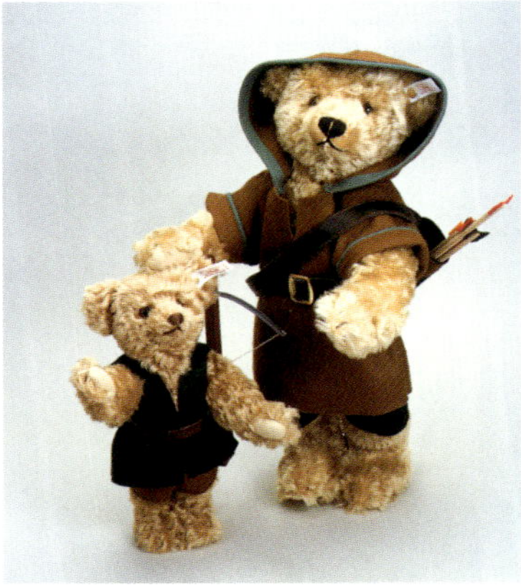

Wilhelm Tell & Sohn - *Wilhelm Tell & Son*

Mohair Webpelz, hellbraun, gegliedert, limitierte Auflage 1.100 Stueck, Werbeartikel fuer Fa. Maerklin - *mohair woven fur, light brown, jointed, ltd edition of 1,100 for Maerklin*

EAN-No.	Period	Pr.	Info
996528	1998-1998	5	42/26 cm

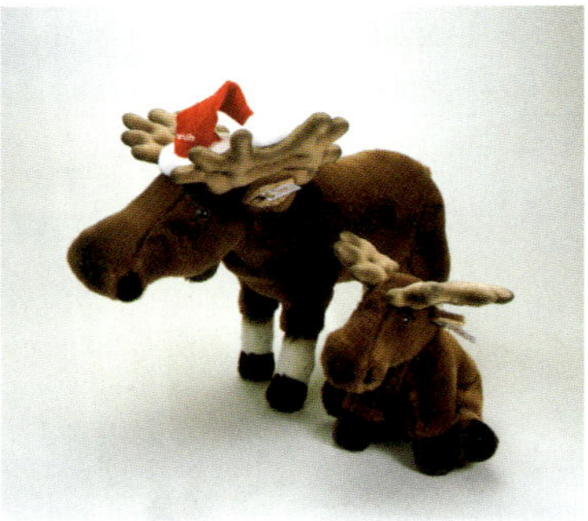

Elchpaar - *Elk-Couple*

Webpelz, braun, stehend bzw. sitzend, limitierte Auflage 1.500 Stueck, Werbeartikel fuer Fa. Maerklin - *woven fur, brown, standing and sitting, ltd edition of 1,500 for Maerklin*

EAN-No.	Period	Pr.	Info
996566	1999-1999	4-5	45/25 cm

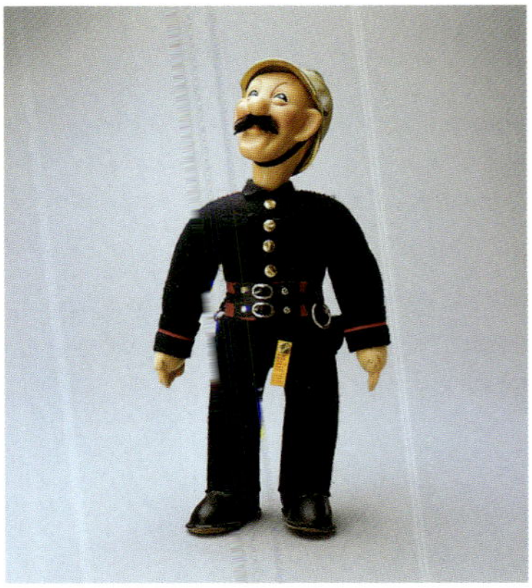

Feuerwehrmann - *Fireman*

Kunststoff, stehend Werbeartikel fuer Fa. Ziegler, Giengen - *synthetic, standing, promotional item for the Ziegler Company*

Serie	Art.-No	Period	Pr.	Info
999369	**7889/05**	1968-1990	3	32 cm
	999369	1991-1999	2-3	

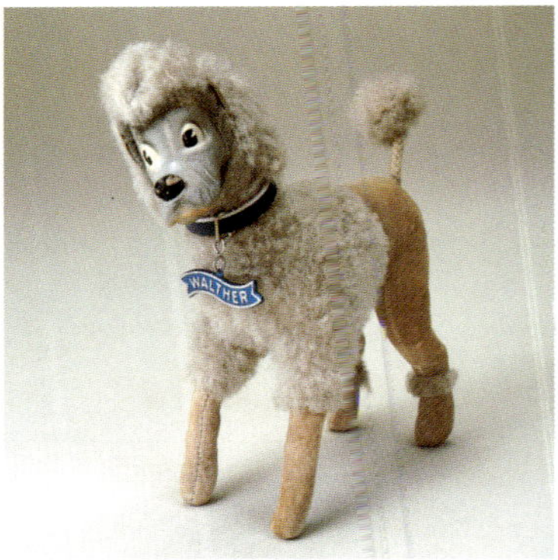

Pudel - *Poodle*

Wollpluesch/Samt, Gummigesicht, stehend, Werbeartikel für Fa. Walther - *plush wool & velvet, rubber face, standing, promotional item for the Walther Company*

Serie	Art.-No	Period	Pr.	Info
	7517	1955-1955	5	17 cm
	7540	1955-1955	6	40 cm

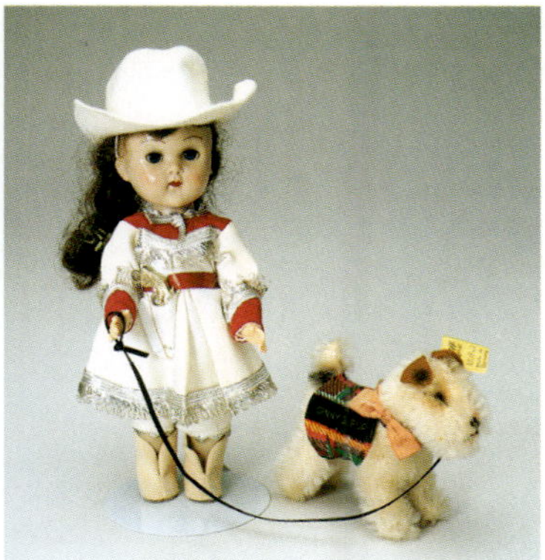

Ginny´s Pup Foxterrier mit Puppe - *Ginny´s Pup Foxterrier with Doll*

Mohair, weiss, schwarz/gelb gefleckt, stehend, Körperdecke mit der Aufschrift GINNY´S PUP und Hundeleine, zusammen mit Ginny Puppe als Werbeartikel fuer die Firma Vogue Dolls Inc. - *mohair, white, black/yellow spotted, standing, with body rug inscribed GINNY´S PUP and dog lead, together with a Ginny doll as a promotional piece for the company Vogue Dolls Inc.*

SERIE	ART.-NO	PERIOD	PR.	INFO
	1308,0	1956-1956	5	8 cm

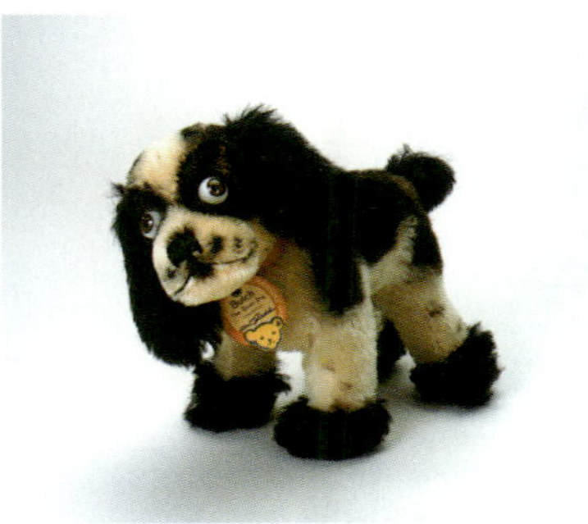

Butch The Cover Dog

Mohair, schwarz/weiss, stehend, Werbeartikel fuer die Saturday Evening Post nach Zeichnungen von Albert Staehle - *mohair, black/white, standing, promotional item for the Saturday Evening Post from drawings of Albert Staehle*

SERIE	ART.-NO	PERIOD	PR.	INFO
	1317,0	1958-1958	6	17 cm

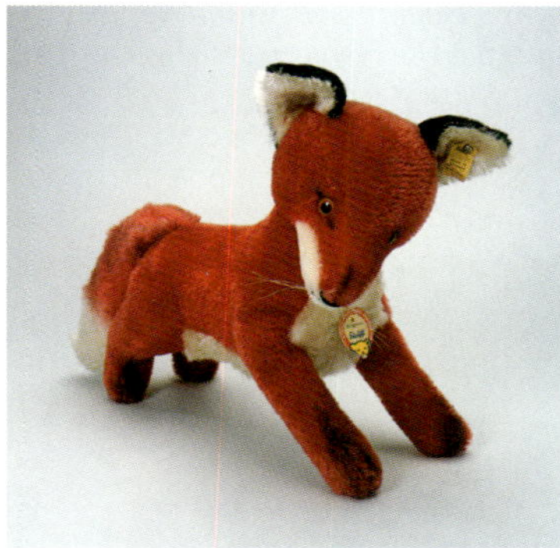

Fuchs - *Fox*

Mohair, rot, stehend, Zweck unbekannt, vermutlich Werbeartikel - *mohair, red, standing, purpose unknown, probably promotional item*

SERIE	ART.-NO	PERIOD	PR.	INFO
	1329,98	1958-1958	6	29 cm

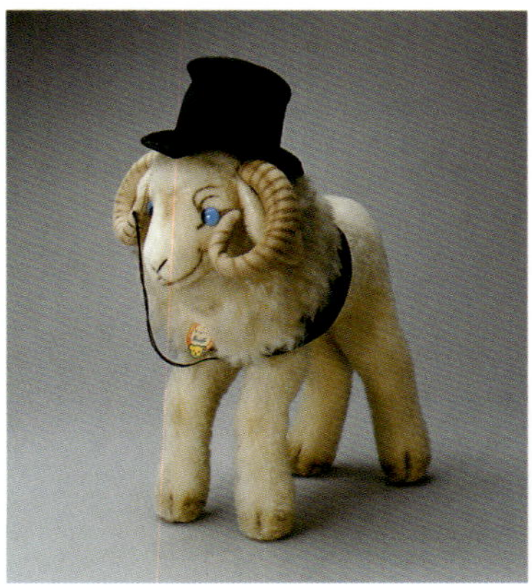

Ziegenbock - *Billy-Goat*

Wollpluesch/Filz, stehend, Zweck unbekannt - *plush wool & felt, standing, purpose unknown*

SERIE	ART.-NO	PERIOD	PR.	INFO
	6535,90	1959-1959	6-7	35 cm

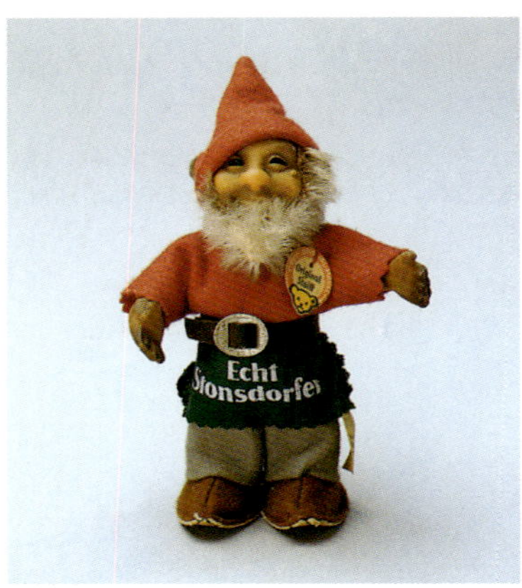

Zwerg - *Dwarf*

Echt Stonsdorfer, Magenbitter, Kunststoff, stehend, Werbeartikel fuer Fa. Stonsdorfer - *synthetic, standing, promotional item for the Stonsdorfer Magenbitter Company*

SERIE	ART.-NO	PERIOD	PR.	INFO
	8713,93	1960-1960	4	13 cm

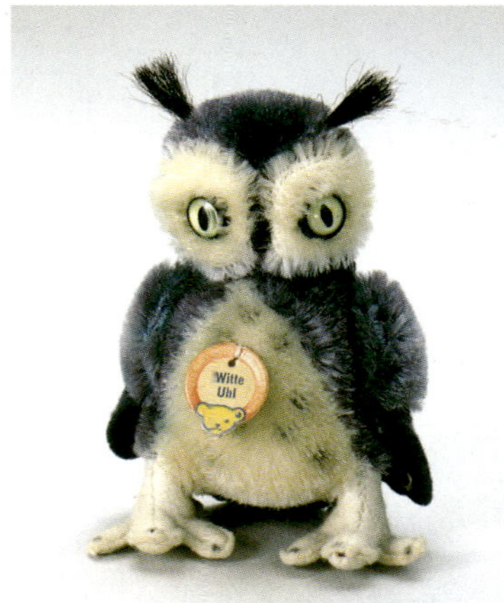

Witte Uhl

Mohair/Filz, stehend, Werbeartkel für Weisse Eule - *mohair & felt, standing, promotional item for Weiße Eule*

SERIE	ART.-NO	PERIOD	PR.	INFO
	4310,94	1960-1960	5-6	10 cm

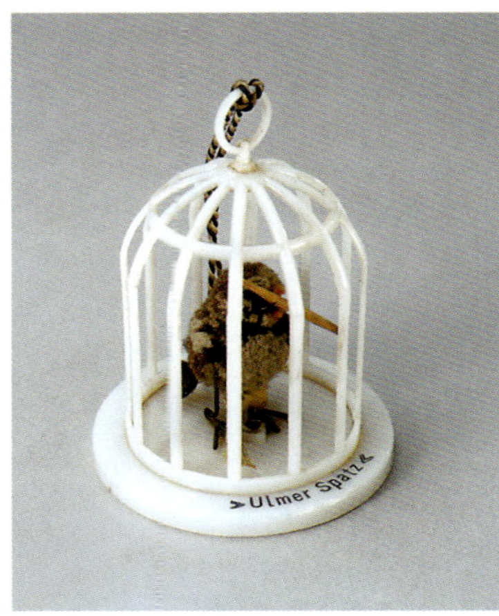

Ulmer Spatz - *Ulm Sparrow*

Wolle, Metallbeine, im Plastikkaefig, Werbetier der Stadt Ulm - *wool, metal legs, in plastic cage, promotional item for the City of Ulm*

EAN-NO.	PERIOD	PR.	INFO
	1961-1961	3	8 cm

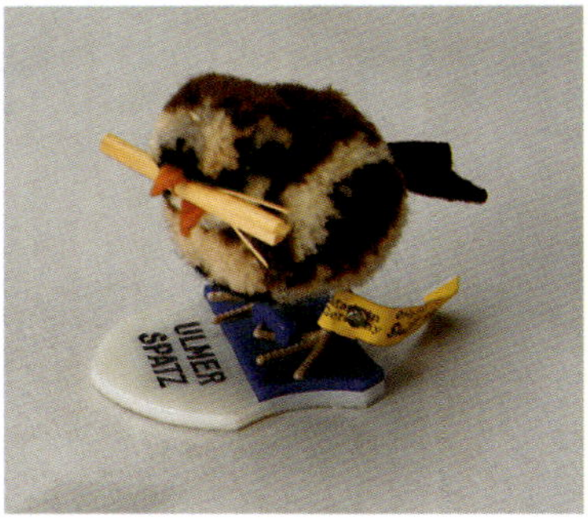

Ulmer Spatz - *Ulm Sparrow*

Wolle, Plastikuntersatz, mit Strohhalm, Werbetier der Stadt Ulm - *wool, plastic base, with straw in its beak, promotional item for the City of Ulm*

SERIE	ART.-NO	PERIOD	PR.	INFO
	6508,45	1965-1965	2-3	8 cm

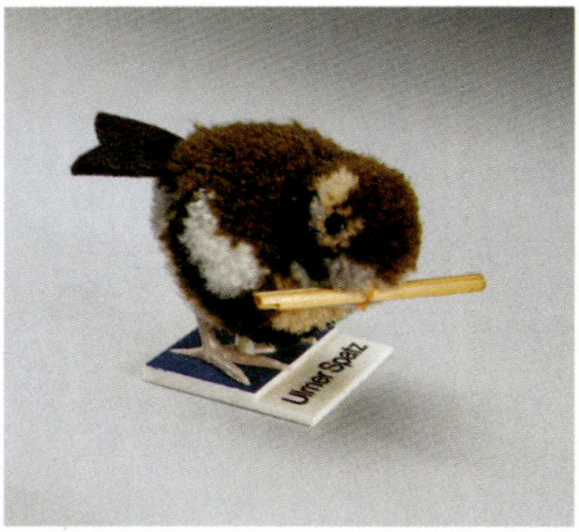

Ulmer Spatz - *Ulm Sparrow*

Wolle, Plastikuntersatz, mit Strohhalm, Werbetier der Stadt Ulm - *wool, plastic base, with straw in its beak, promotional item for the City of Ulm*

SERIE	ART.-NO	PERIOD	PR.	INFO
	7109/01	1971-1971	2-3	4 cm
	7119/01	1971-1971	2-3	8 cm

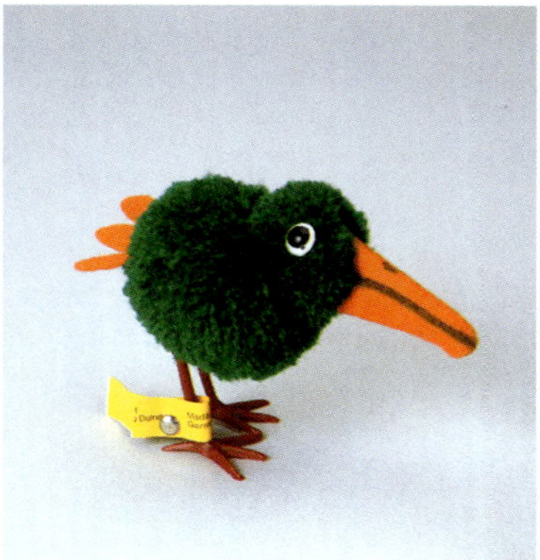

Rabe - *Raven*

Wolle, gruen, stehend, Werbeartikel für Venoruton-Gel macht schwere Beine federleicht - *wool, green, standing, promotional item for "Venoruton Gel makes tired legs light as a feather"*

SERIE	ART.-NO	PERIOD	PR.	INFO
	7439/08	1970-1970	3	8 cm

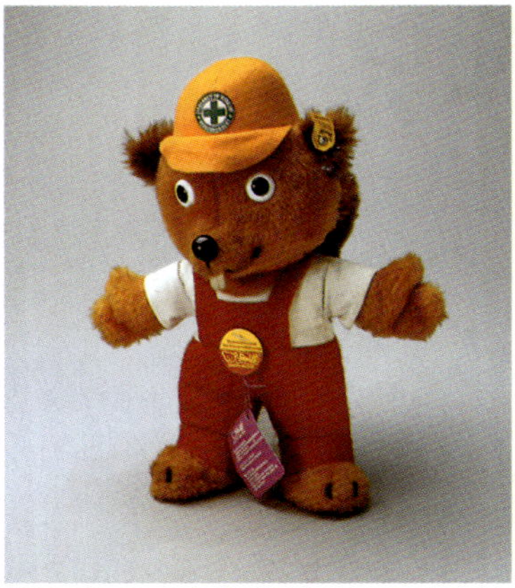

Verkehrshoernchen - *Little Traffic Horn*

des Kinderverkehrsclub der Verkehrswacht, Dralonpluesch, abwaschbar - *of the children´s traffic club, dralon, surface washable*

SERIE	ART.-NO	PERIOD	PR.	INFO
	7832/30	1978-1980	2	30 cm

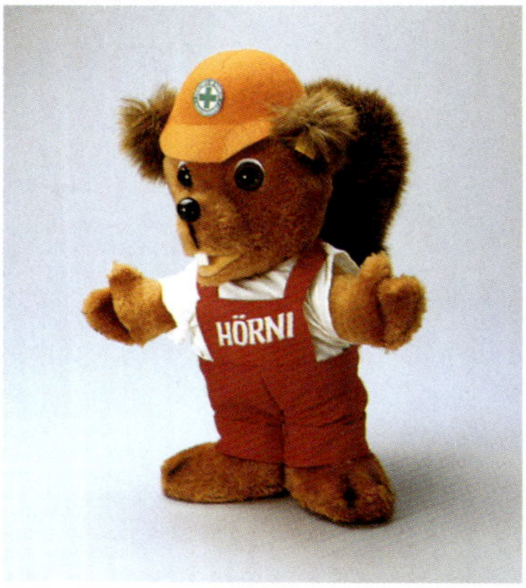

Verkehrshoernchen Hoerni - *Little Traffic Horn Hoerni*

der Verkehrswacht, Dralonpluesch, abwaschbar - *of the traffic authority, dralon, surface washable*

SERIE	ART.-NO	PERIOD	PR.	INFO
	7832/32	1978-1980	2-3	32 cm

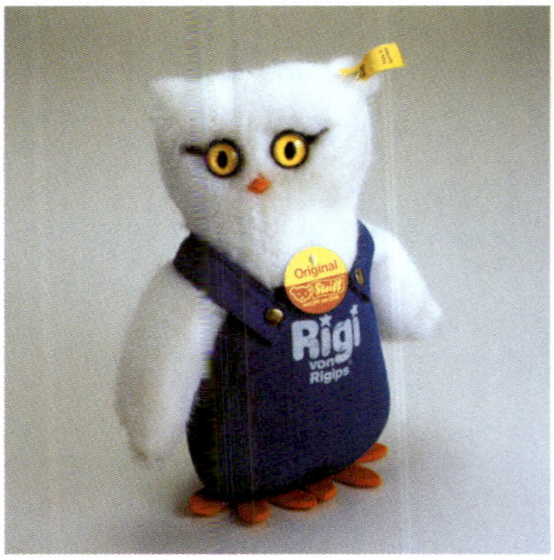

Rigi von Rigips - *Rigi from Rigips*

Webpelz, weiss, stehend, abwaschbar, Eule, Werbefigur fuer die Fa. Rigips, bekleidet mit blauem Trevira-Overall, die Traeger werden von je einem Steiff-Knopf gehalten, orange Filzfuesse und -schnabel - *woven fur, white, standing, surface washable, owl, promotional item for Rigips, dressed with a blue trevira-overall, straps are held in place by two Steiff-buttons, orange felt feet & beak*

SERIE	ART.-NO	PERIOD	PR.	INFO
	7952/20	1979-1979	4	20 cm

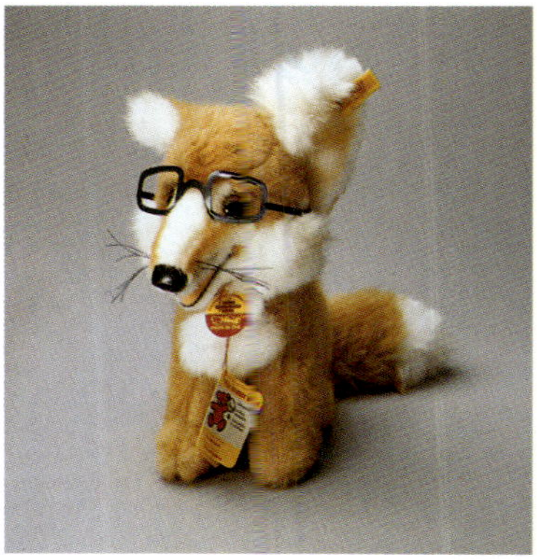

Fuchs - *Fox*

Webpelz, sitzend, Werbetier für die Bausparkasse Schwaebisch Hall - *woven fur, sitting, promotional item for Bausparkasse Schwaebisch Hall*

SERIE	ART.-NO	PERIOD	PR.	INFO
	7957/22	1979-1980	2-3	22 cm

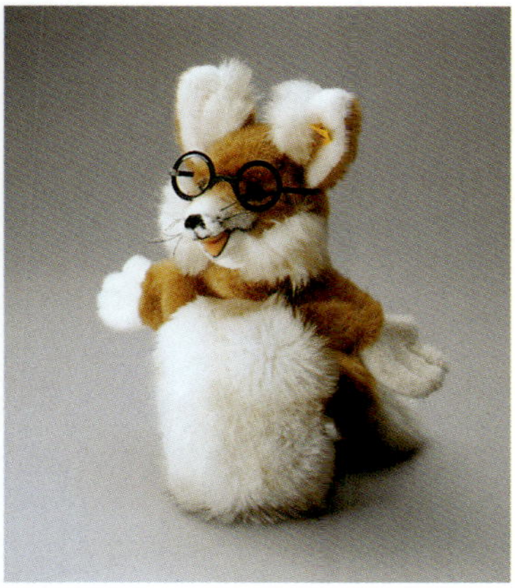

Hand-Fuchs - *Hand-Fox*

Webpelz, Handspieltier, Werbetier für die Bausparkasse Schwaebisch Hall - *woven fur, hand puppet, promotional item for Bausparkasse Schwaebisch Hall*

SERIE	ART.-NO	PERIOD	PR.	INFO
	7958/30	1979-1980	2-3	30 cm

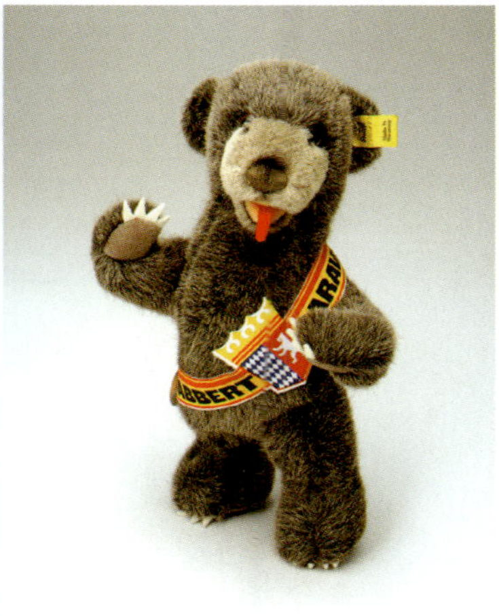

Tabby Baer - *Tabby Bear*

Webpelz, braun, stehend, Filzkrallen an Pfoten & Fuessen, Schaerpe mit Werbeaufdruck Tabbert Caravan - *woven fur, brown, standing, felt claws on paws & feet, sash with advertising message Tabbert Caravan*

SERIE	ART.-NO	PERIOD	PR.	INFO
	7960/23	1980-1980	6	23 cm

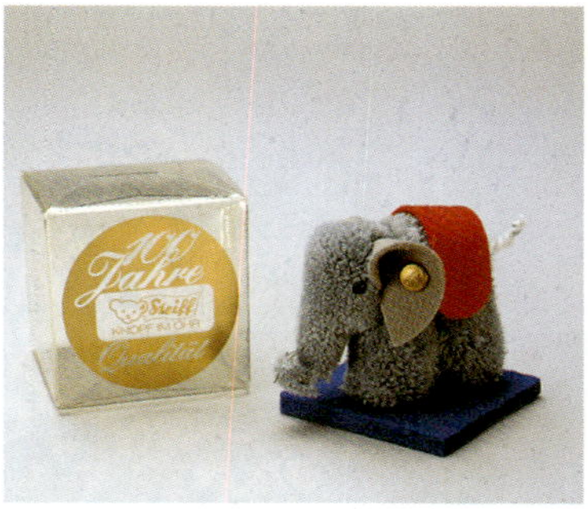

Elefant - *Elephant*

Wolle/Filz, anlaesslich 100 Jahre Margarete Steiff GmbH - *wool & felt, to celebrate 100 Years of the Margarete Steiff Company*

EAN-NO.	PERIOD	PR.	INFO
	1980-1980	3-4	4 cm

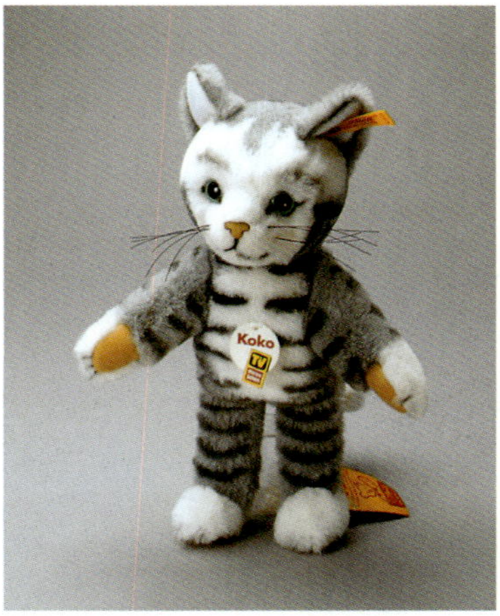

Koko Katze - *Koko Cat*

Wirkpelz, waschmaschinenfest, Maskottchen aus "TV Hoeren und Sehen" - *knitted fur, machine washable, mascot for the TV magazine "Hearing & Seeing"*

SERIE	ART.-NO	PERIOD	PR.	INFO
351006	**7610/28**	1988-1988	3	28 cm

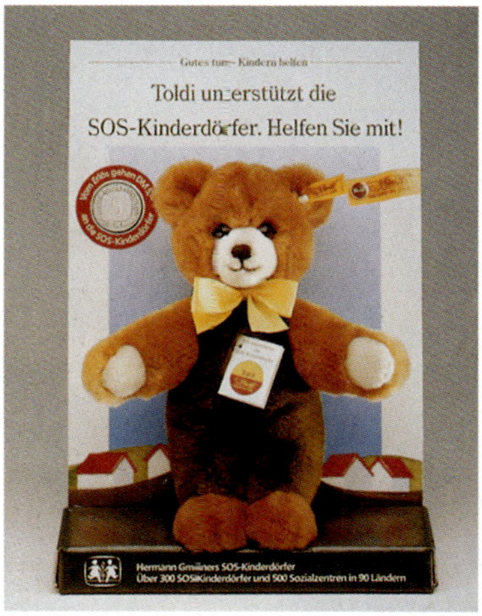

Toldi Baer - ***Toldi** Bear*

SOS-Kinderdorf Toldi Baer, Webpelz, Pieps-Stimme, waschmaschinenfest - *SOS-Kinderdorf Toldi bear, woven fur, squeaker, machine washable*

SERIE	ART.-NO	PERIOD	PR.	INFO
351105	**7580/27**	1989-1990	3	27 cm
	351105	1991-1991	3	

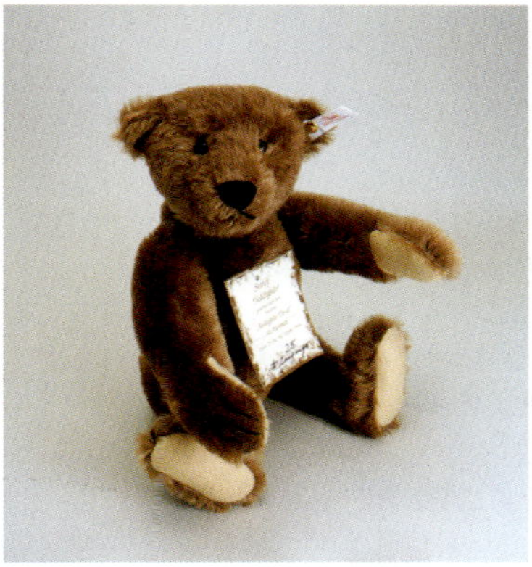

Teddybaer - *Teddybear*

Mohair, braun, gegliedert, limit. Auflage 40 Stueck fuer Messe Teddy Total, Hennef - *mohair, brown, jointed, ltd edition of 40 for Teddy Total, Hennef*

EAN-NO.	PERIOD	PR.	INFO
	1995-1995	5	25 cm

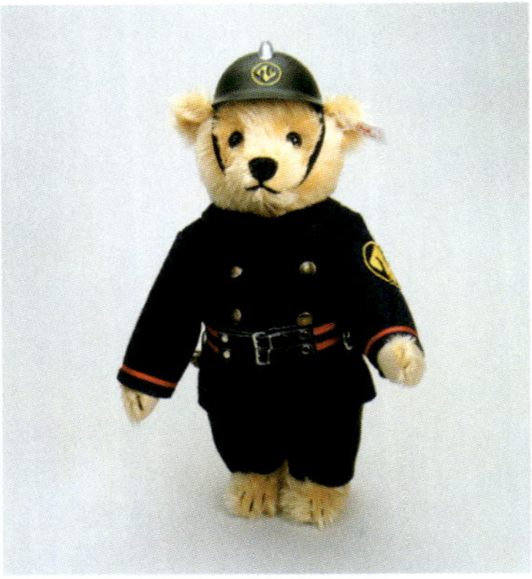

Feuerwehr Baer - *Firebrigade Bear*

Mohair, blond, gegliedert, limit. Auflage 3.000 Stueck fuer Fa. Ziegler, Giengen - *mohair, blond, jointed, ltd edition of 3,000 for Ziegler, Giengen*

EAN-No.	Period	Pr.	Info
999161	1996-1996	4	34 cm

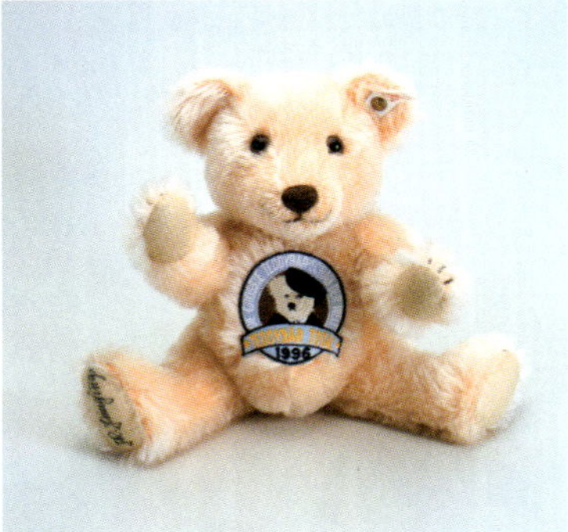

Teddybaer - *Teddybear*

Mohair, apricot, gegliedert, limit. Auflage 500 Stueck fuer Messe Teddy Total, Hennef - *mohair, apricot, jointed, ltd edition of 500 for Teddy Total, Hennef*

EAN-No.	Period	Pr.	Info
655265	1996-1996	4-5	28 cm

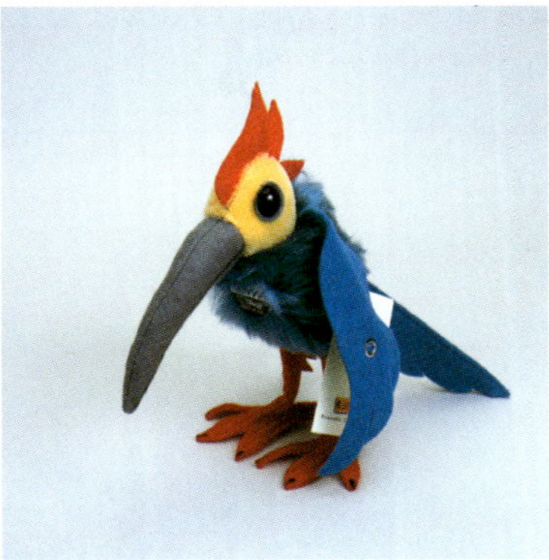

YaYa Paradiesvogel - *YaYa Paradise Bird*

Filz/Mohair, mehrfarbig, stehend, Werbeartikel fuer YaYa Bike Project, Bergisch Gladbach, limit. Auflage 1.500 Stueck - *felt/mohair, multi-colored, standing, promotional item for YaYa Bike Project, Bergisch Gladbach, ltd edition of 1,500*

EAN-No.	Period	Pr.	Info
998645	1997-1997	4	17 cm

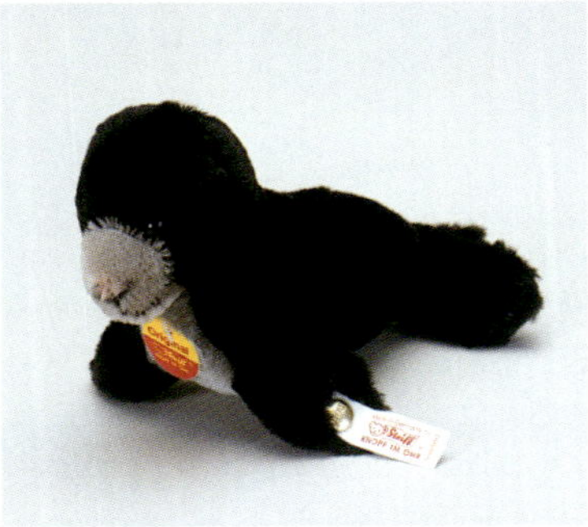

Moenchsrobbe - *Monastic Seal*

Webpelz/Schnauze aus Mohair, schwarz/grau, waschbar, Werbeartikel fuer Zeulenroda, Partnerstadt der Stadt Giengen, limit. Auflage 1.500 Stueck - *woven fur/muzzle of mohair, black/grey, washable, promotional item for Zeulenroda, twin town to the city of Giengen, ltd edition of 1,500*

EAN-No.	Period	Pr.	Info
998560	1997-1997	2	15 cm

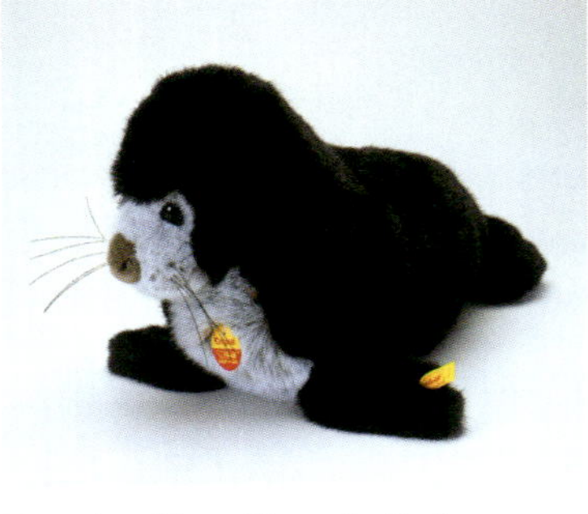

Moenchsrobbe - *Monastic Seal*

Webpelz, schwarz/grau, waschbar, Werbeartikel fuer Zeulenroda, Partnerstadt der Stadt Giengen - *woven fur, black/grey, washable, promotional item for Zeulenroda, twin town to the city of Giengen*

EAN-No.	Period	Pr.	Info
998706	1997-1997	3	34 cm

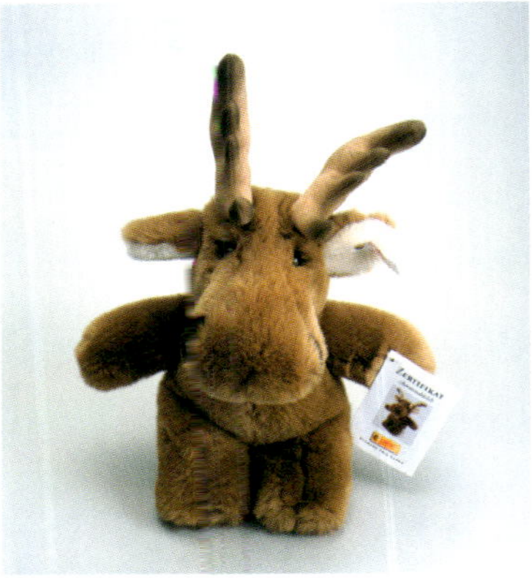

Schwarzwaldelch - *Blackwood Forest Elk*

Webpelz, hellbraun, aufwartend, Brummstimme, Sondermalsmarke mit Logo des SWF3-Club, fuer Radiosender SWF3, Jahreslimitierung 1998 - 3.000 Stueck - *woven fur, light brown, sitting up, growler, chest-tag with logo of SWF3-Club, for Radio Station SWF3, ltd edition of 3,000*

EAN-No.	Period	Pr.	Info
996672	1998-1998	3-4	32 cm

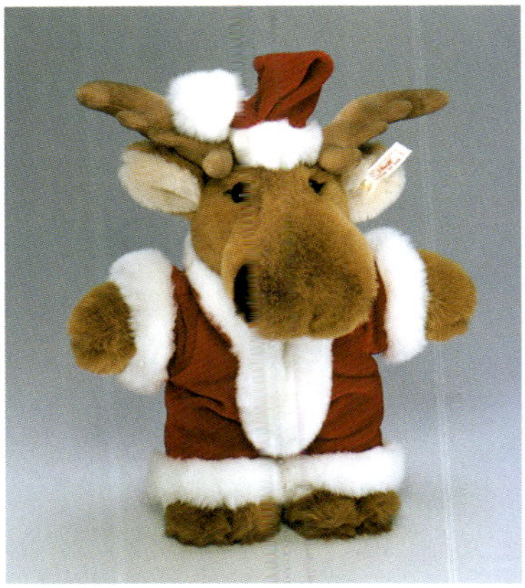

Weihnachts-Schwarzwaldelch - *Christmas Blackwood Forest Elk*

Webpelz, hellbraun, aufwartend, Brummstimme, rote Muetze & Anzug mit weissem Besatz, fuer Radiosender SWF3, lim. Auflage 1.500 Stueck - *woven fur, light brown, sitting up, growler, red cap & suit with white trimmings, for Radio Station SWF3, ltd edition of 1,500*

EAN-No.	Period	Pr.	Info
996375	1998-1998	3	32 cm

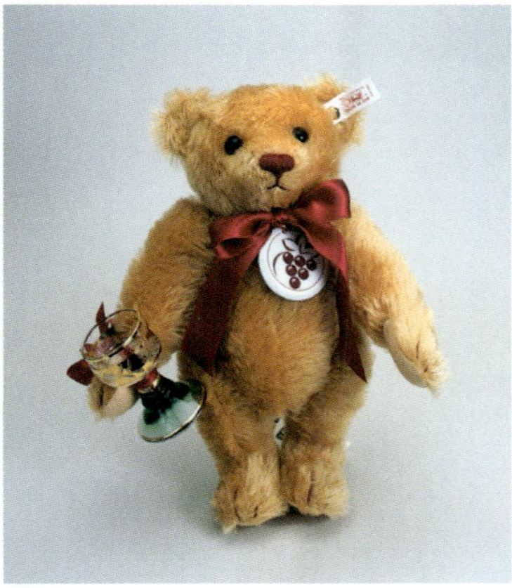

Wein-Geniesser Baer - *Wine Bon Vivant Bear*

Mohair Webpelz, blond, gegliedert, abwaschbar, limit. Auflage 1.500 Stueck fuer WIF Langenlohnsheim - *mohair, blond, gegliedert, jointed, ltd edition of 1,500 for WIF Langenlohnsheim*

EAN-No.	Period	Pr.	Info
996580	1998-1998	4	33 cm

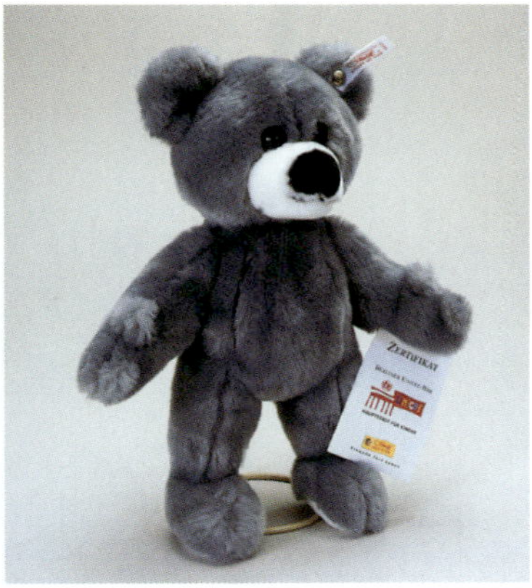

Berliner UNICEF Baer - *Berlin UNICEF Bear*

Webpelz, blaugrau, gegliedert, anlaesslich Berlin in 1999 als UNICEF-Partnerstadt, Jahreslimitierung 1999 - *woven fur, blue-grey, jointed, for the occasion of Berlin beeing the UNICEF-partner-city in 1999, ltd edition for the year 1999 only*

EAN-No.	Period	Pr.	Info
996337	1999-1999	2-3	26 cm

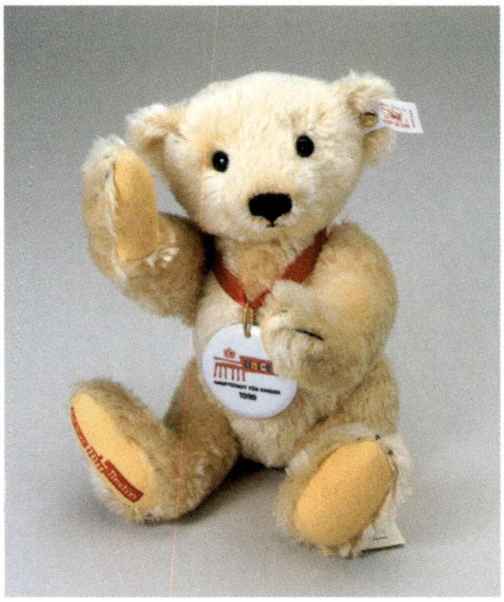

Berliner UNICEF Baer - *Berlin UNICEF Bear*

Mohair, blond, gegliedert, Porzellanhalsmarke, anlaesslich Berlin in 1999 als UNICEF-Partnerstadt, Jahreslimitierung 1999 - *mohair, blond, jointed, porcelain chest tag, for the occasion of Berlin beeing the UNICEF-partner-city in 1999, ltd edition for the year 1999 only*

EAN-No.	Period	Pr.	Info
996344	1999-1999	3	28 cm

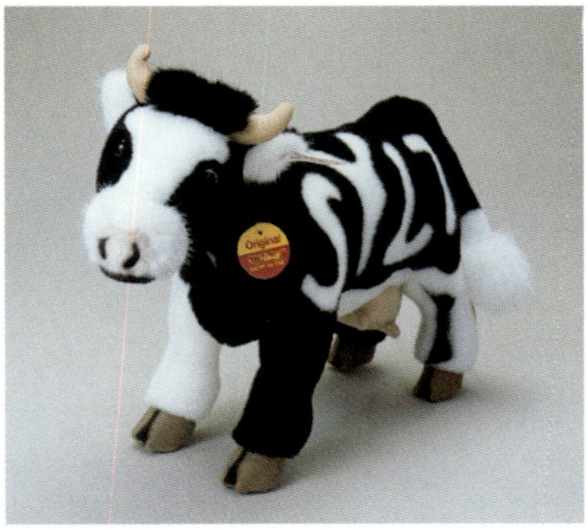

Sylter Kuh - *Sylt Cow*

Webpelz, schwarz/weiss, stehend, Werbeartikel fuer die Insel Sylt, lim. Auflage 1.500 Stueck - *woven fur, black/white, standing, promotional piece for the island Sylt, ltd edition of 1,500*

EAN-No.	Period	Pr.	Info
996467	1999-1999	4	32 cm

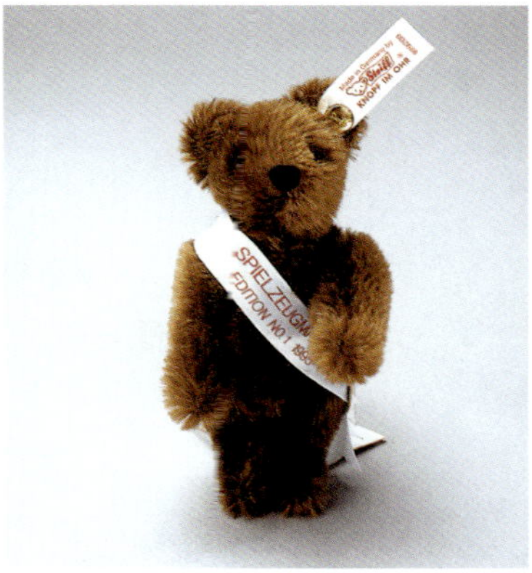

Original Teddy

Mohair, braun, gegliedert, limit. Auflage 170 Stueck fuer Zeitschrift Spielzeugmarkt - *mohair, brown, jointed, limited edition of 170 for the magazine Spielzeugmarkt, Germany*

EAN-No.	Period	Pr.	Info
999208	1995-1995	4-5	12 cm

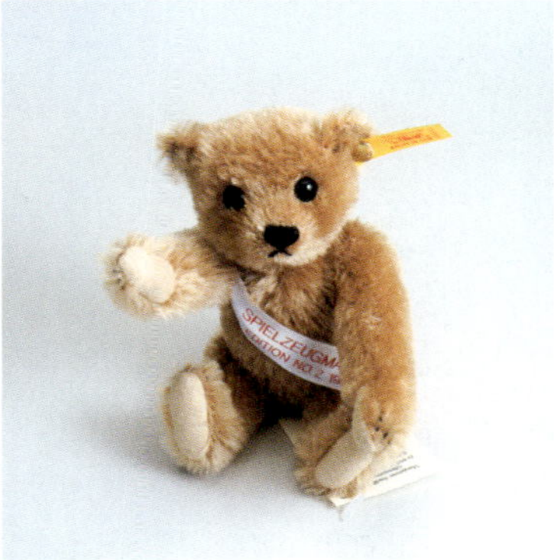

Original Teddy

Mohair, hellbraun, gegliedert, limit. Auflage 170 Stueck fuer Zeitschrift Spielzeugmarkt - *mohair, light brown, jointed, limited edition of 170 for the magazine Spielzeugmarkt, Germany*

EAN-No.	Period	Pr.	Info
998942	1996-1996	4	16 cm

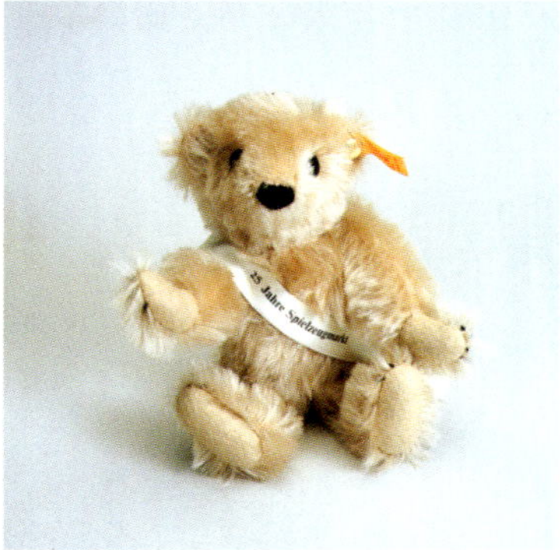

Teddybaer - *Teddybear*

Mohair, blond, gegliedert, limit. Auflage 200 Stueck fuer Zeitschrift Spielzeugmarkt zum 25jaehrigen Jubilaeum - *mohair, blond, jointed, limited edition of 200 on the occasion of the 25th anniversary of the magazine Spielzeugmarkt, Germany*

EAN-No.	Period	Pr.	Info
998690	1997-1997	4	15 cm

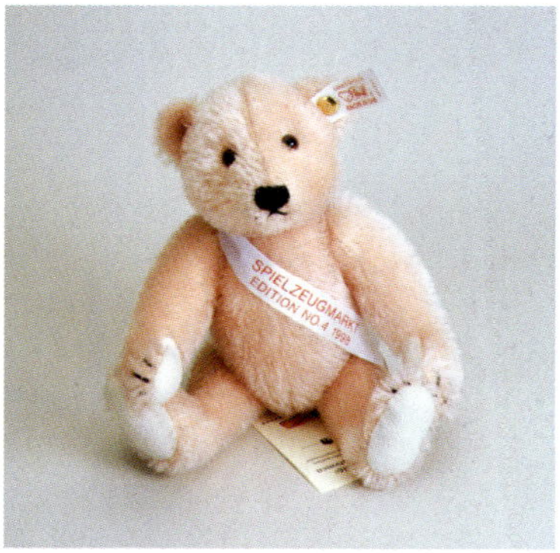

Teddybaer - *Teddybear*

Mohair, rosa, gegliedert, Auflage 150 Stueck fuer Zeitschrift Spielzeugmarkt - *mohair, rose, jointed, edition of 150 for the magazine Spielzeugmarkt, Germany*

EAN-No.	Period	Pr.	Info
665202	1998-1998	3-4	22 cm

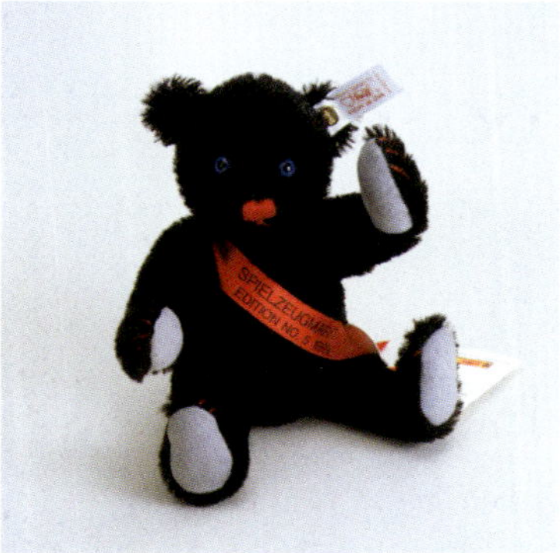

Teddybaer - *Teddybear*

Mohair, schwarz, gegliedert, Auflage 150 Stueck fuer Zeitschrift Spielzeugmarkt - *mohair, black, jointed, edition of 150 for the magazine Spielzeugmarkt, Germany*

EAN-No.	Period	Pr.	Info
670312	1999-1999	3-4	22 cm

HOLZ- & BLECHSPIELZEUG HOLZFAHRZEUGE

WOODEN & METAL TOYS WOODEN VEHICLES

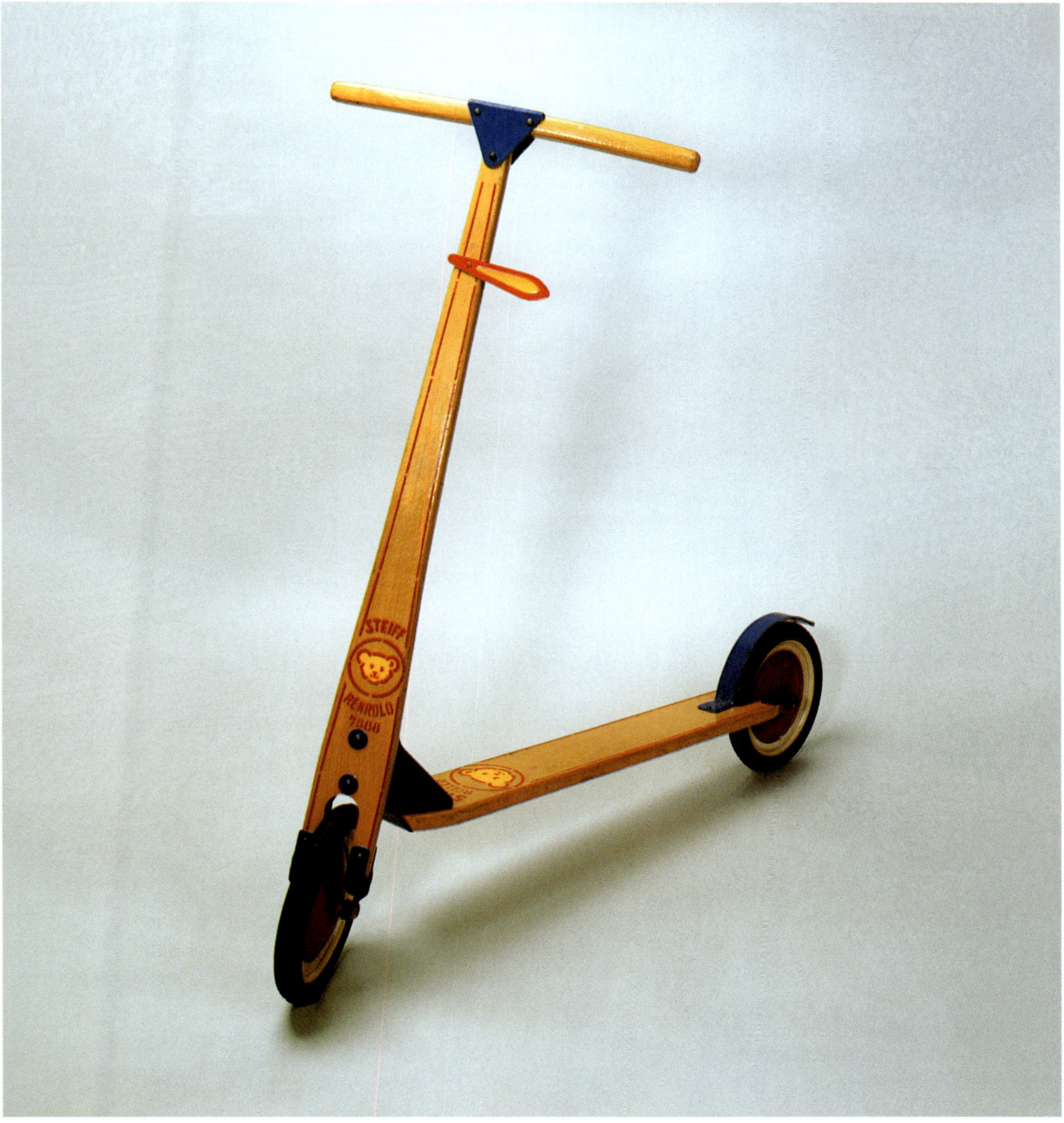

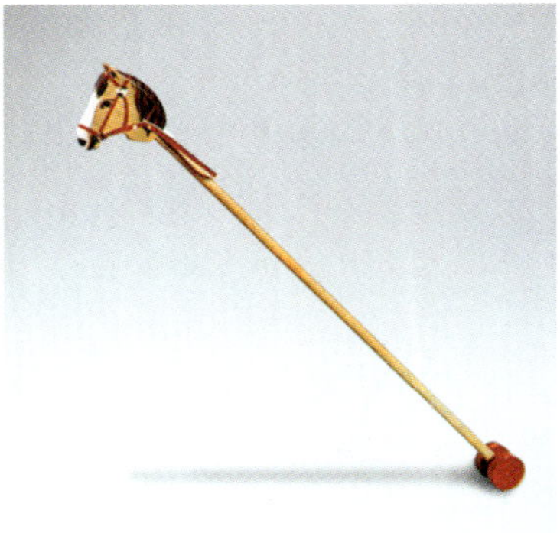

Steckenpferd - *Hobby Horse*

Holz, Lederzuegel, naturlackiert, 2 Laufrollen - *wood, leather reins, naturally stained, with two rollers*

SERIE	ART.-NO	PERIOD	PR.	INFO
56	**895**	1949-1957	3-4	100 cm
561	**7899,00**	1961-1961	3	
379	**7899,00**	1966-1967	3	
	3782/99	1968-1973	3	

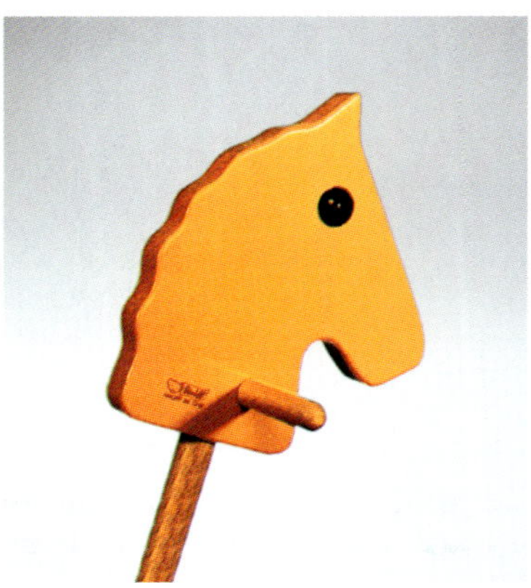

Steckenpferd - *Hobby Horse*

Holz, gelb lackiert - *wood, painted yellow*

SERIE	ART.-NO	PERIOD	PR.	INFO
	8495/99	1975-1977	2-3	100 cm

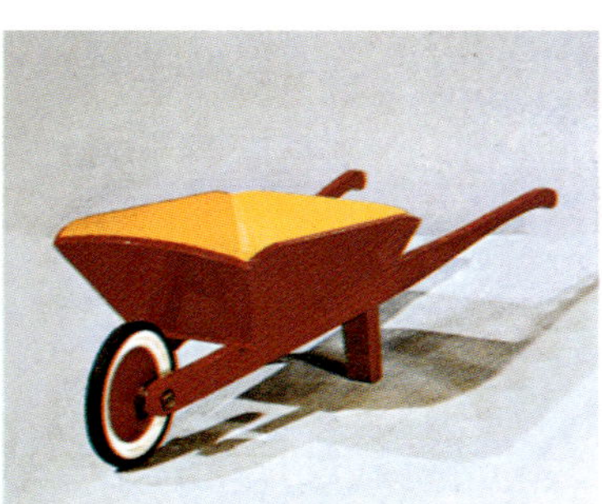

Schubkarre - *Wheelbarrow*

Holz, gelb & rot lackiert, gummibereifte Metallfelge - *wood, painted yellow & red, metal rim with rubber tire*

SERIE	ART.-NO	PERIOD	PR.	INFO
127	**8090**	1951-1958	3-4	85 cm
970	**1890,00**	1959-1963	3-4	

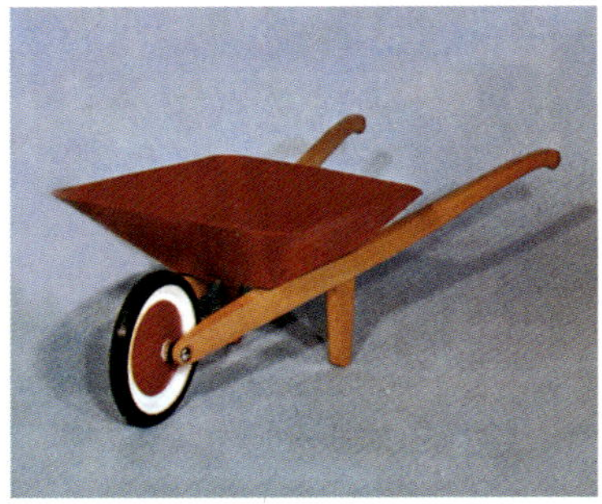

Schubkarre - *Wheelbarrow*

Holz, naturlackiert, Plastikwanne, rot, Scheibenrad mit Gummi 17 cm - *wood, naturally stained, plastic trough, red, disc wheel with rubber tire 17 cm*

SERIE	ART.-NO	PERIOD	PR.	INFO
970	**1785,00**	1964-1964	2-3	85 cm
850	**1785,00**	1965-1967	2-3	
	8500/85	1968-1970	2-3	

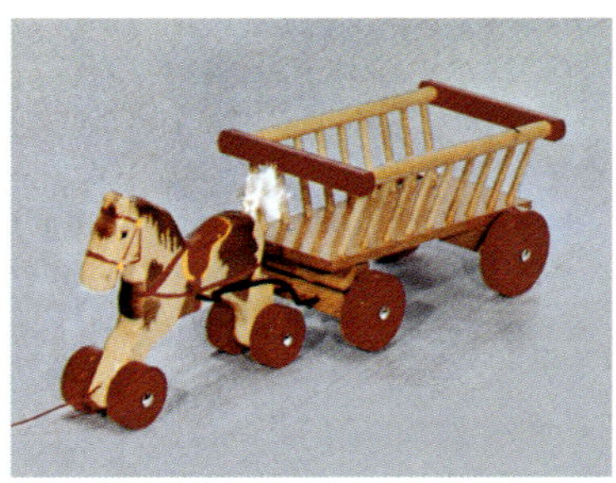

Leiterwagen-Gespann - *Horse Drawn Cradle Wagon*

Holz, naturlackiert, rot & schwarz bemalt - *wood, naturally stained, painted red & black*

SERIE	ART.-NO	PERIOD	PR.	INFO
128	**4812** L	1949-1958	3-4	35 cm
975	**4812,10**	1959-1964	3-4	
855	**4812,10**	1965-1967	3-4	
	8550/12	1968-1968	3-4	
128	**4817** L	1951-1958	4	55 cm
975	**4817,10**	1959-1964	4	
855	**4817,10**	1965-1967	4	
	8550/17	1968-1968	4	

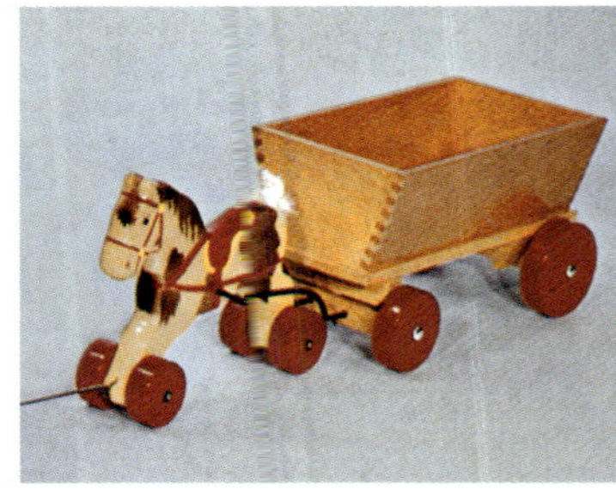

Kastenwagen-Gespann - *Horse Drawn Box Type Wagon*

Holz, naturlackiert, rot & schwarz bemalt - *wood, naturally stained, painted red & black*

SERIE	ART.-NO	PERIOD	PR.	INFO
128	**4813** K	1949-1958	3-4	35 cm
975	**4813,10**	1959-1964	3-4	
856	**4813,10**	1965-1967	3-4	
	8560/13	1968-1968	3-4	
128	**4818** K	1951-1958	4	55 cm
975	**4818,10**	1959-1964	4	
856	**4818,10**	1965-1967	4	
	8560/18	1968-1968	4	

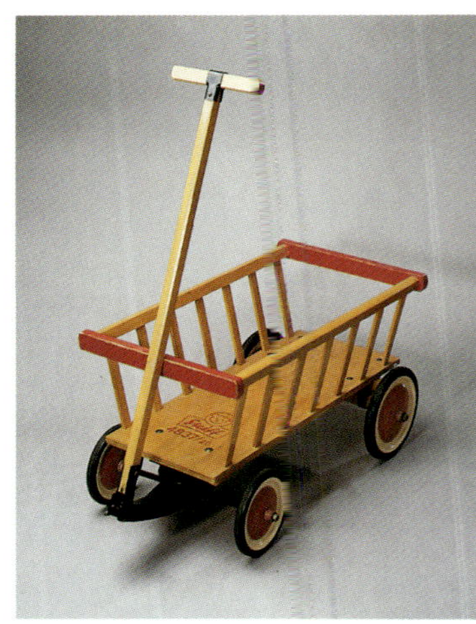

Hand-Leiterwagen - *Manual Cradle Wagon*

Holz, naturlackiert, rot, verschiedene Ausfuehrungen - *wood, naturally stained, red, different versions*

SERIE	ART.-NO	PERIOD	PR.	INFO
128	**4835** L	1949-1951	4-5	63 cm
128	**4837** L	1952-1958	4-5	63 cm
975	**4837,20**	1959-1964	4-5	
862	**4837,20**	1965-1967	4-5	
	8620/37	1968-1970	4-5	
128	**4850** L	1948-1949	4-5	77 cm
128	**4857** L	1948-1948	4-5	94 cm

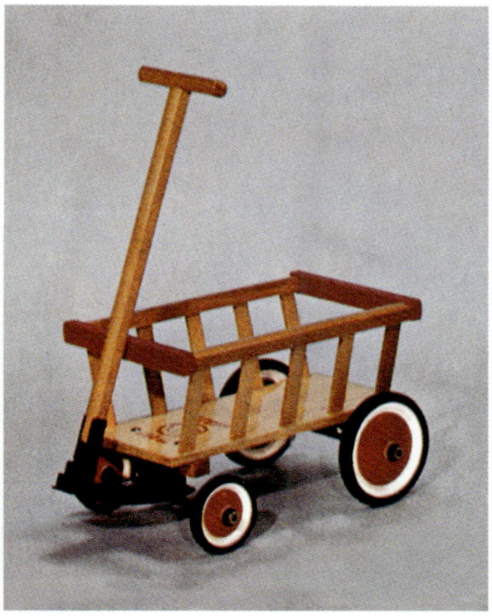

Spiel-Leiterwagen - *Playing Cradle Wagon*

Holz, verschiedene Ausfuehrungen, naturlackiert, rot - *wood, naturally stained, red, different versions*

SERIE	ART.-NO	PERIOD	PR.	INFO
128	**4822** L	1951-1951	4	36 cm
128	**4824** L	1953-1958	4	36 cm
975	**4824,10**	1959-1964	4	
860	**4824,10**	1965-1967	4	
	8600/24	1968-1968	4	

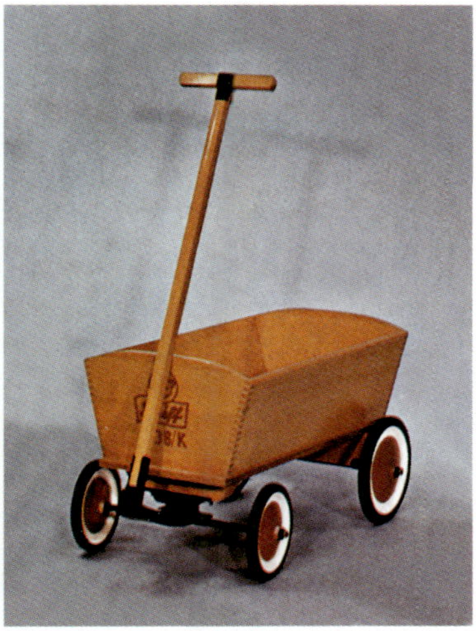

Hand-Kastenwagen - *Manual Box-Type Wagon*

Holz, naturlackiert, verschiedene Ausfuehrungen, Tragkraft 50 kg - *wood, naturally stained, different versions, capacity 50 kg*

SERIE	ART.-NO	PERIOD	PR.	INFO
128	**4836** K	1951-1951	4-5	63 cm
128	**4838** K	1953-1958	4-5	63 cm
975	**4838,20**	1959-1964	4-5	
862	**4838,20**	1965-1967	4-5	
	8620/38	1968-1970	4-5	

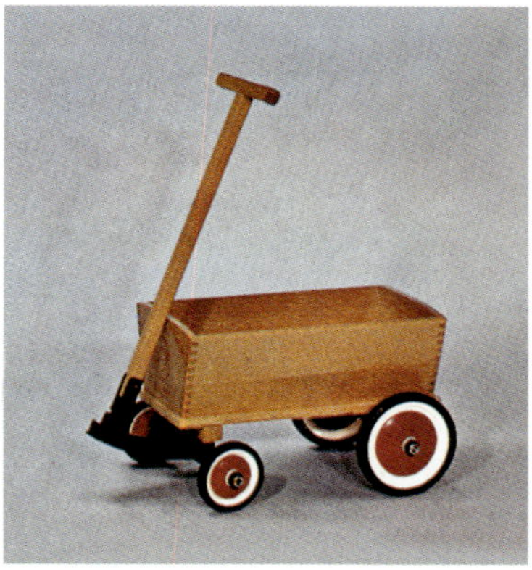

Spiel-Kastenwagen - *Box Type Wagon for Playing*

Holz, naturlackiert, verschiedene Ausfuehrungen - *wood, naturally stained, different versions*

SERIE	ART.-NO	PERIOD	PR.	INFO
128	**4823** K	1951-1951	4	36 cm
128	**4825** K	1952-1958	4	36 cm
975	**4825,10**	1959-1964	4	
860	**4825,10**	1965-1967	4	
	8600/25	1968-1968	4	

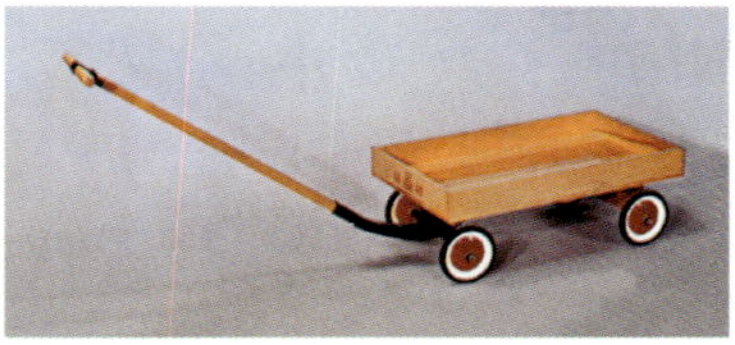

Brueckenwagen - *Open Wagon*

Hartholz, Scheibenraeder mit Gummireifen, ab 1967 Plastik, Tragkraft 50 kg - *hardwood, disc wheels with rubber tires, from 1967 plastic, capacity 50 kg*

SERIE	ART.-NO	PERIOD	PR.	INFO
975	**4840,20**	1960-1964	4	38 x 63cm
862	**4840,20**	1965-1967	4	
	8620/40	1968-1969	4	

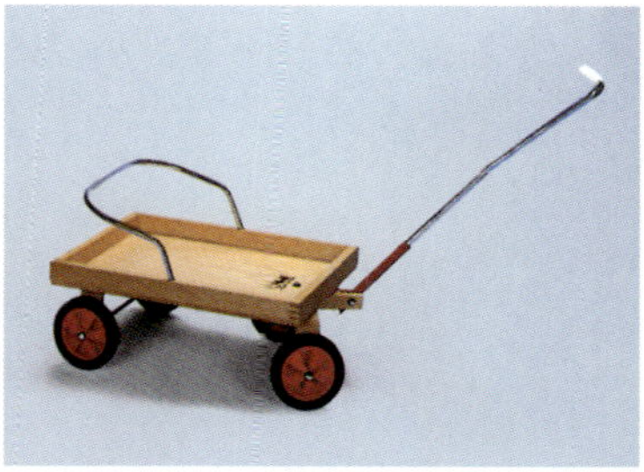

Handwagen - *Manual Wagon*

Holz, natur, PVC Raeder, mit Deichsel, Vorderachse lenkbar, Lehne aus Stahlrohr - *natural wood, PVC wheels, with shaft, front axle can be steered, steel tube backrest*

SERIE	ART.-NO	PERIOD	PR.	INFO
483509	**8430/55**	1979-1986	2-3	55 cm
483523	**8431/55**	1979-1986	1	Lehne - *backrest*

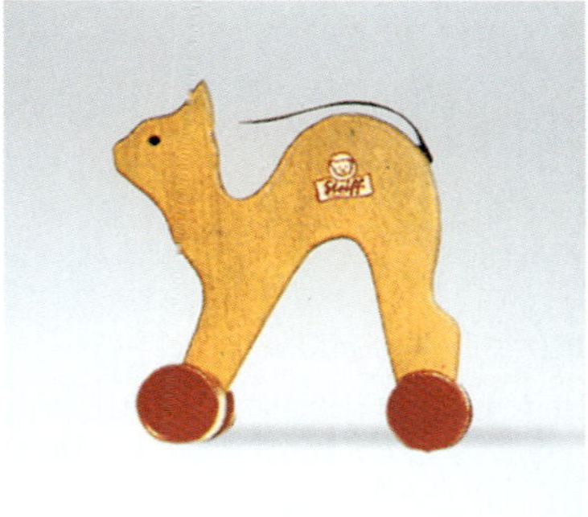

Holz-Kater - *Wooden Tom Cat*

geschliffenes Buchenholz, natur, Raeder rot - *sanded natural beech wood, red wheels*

SERIE	ART.-NO	PERIOD	PR.	INFO
	8310/17	1968-1968	2	17/12 cm

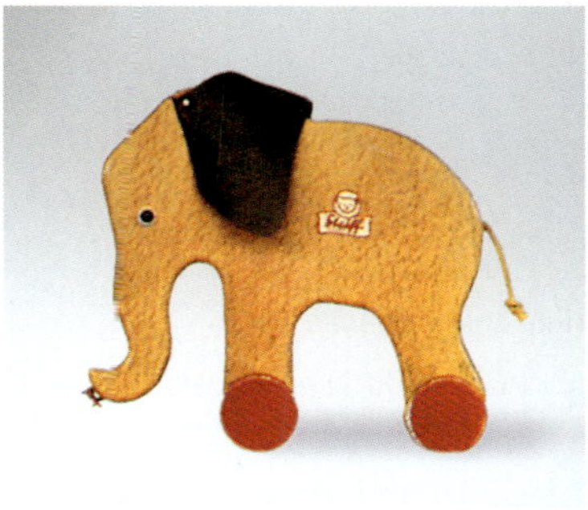

Holz-Ele Elefant - *Wooden Ele Elephant*

geschliffenes Buchenholz, natur, Raeder rot - *sanded natural beech wood, red wheels*

SERIE	ART.-NO	PERIOD	PR.	INFO
	8310/18	1968-1968	2	20/19 cm

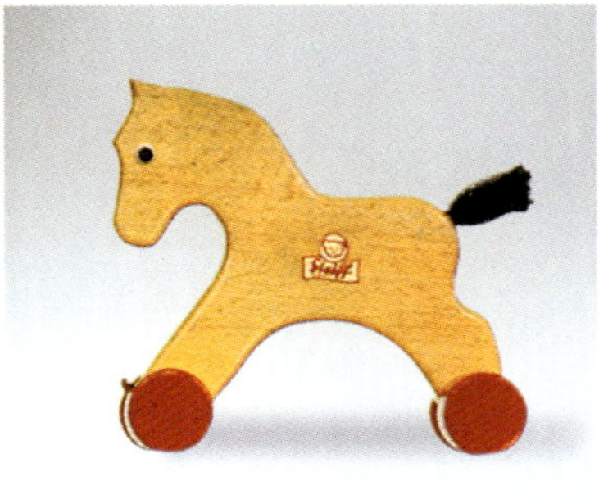

Holz-Pferd - *Wooden Horse*

geschliffenes Buchenholz, natur, Raeder rot - *sanded natural beech wood, red wheels*

Serie	Art.-No	Period	Pr.	Info
	8310/23	1968-1968	2	17/23 cm

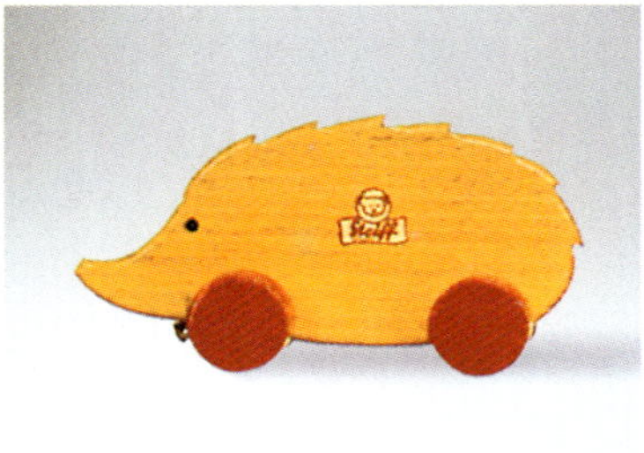

Holz-Igel - *Wooden Hedgehog*

geschliffenes Buchenholz, natur, Raeder rot - *sanded natural beech wood, red wheels*

Serie	Art.-No	Period	Pr.	Info
	8320/10	1968-1968	2	21/11 cm

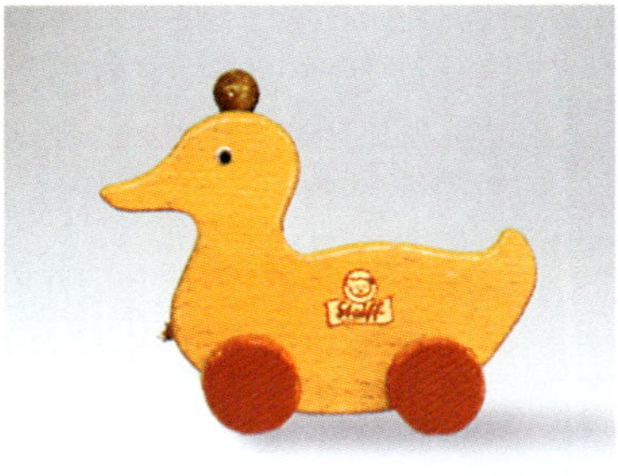

Holz-Ente - *Wooden Duck*

geschliffenes Buchenholz, natur, Raeder rot - *sanded natural beech wood, red wheels*

Serie	Art.-No	Period	Pr.	Info
	8320/12	1968-1968	2	18/14 cm

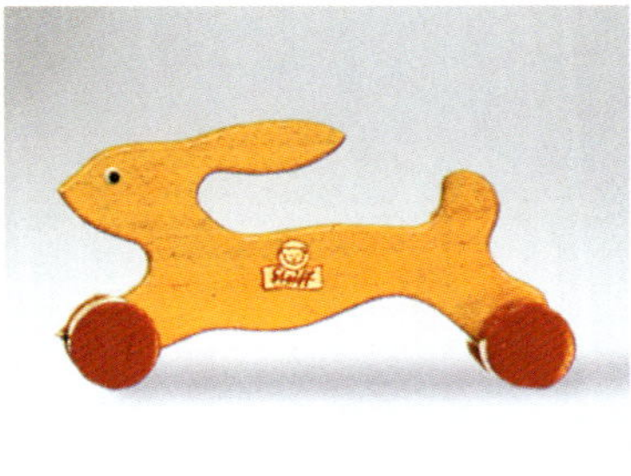

Holz-Hase - *Wooden Rabbit*

geschliffenes Buchenholz, natur, Raeder rot - *sanded natural beech wood, red wheels*

Serie	Art.-No	Period	Pr.	Info
	8320/13	1968-1968	2	22/13 cm

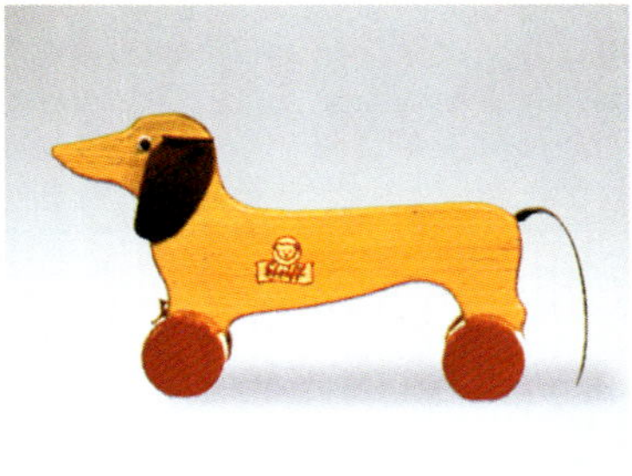

Holz-Dackel - *Wooden Dachshund*

geschliffenes Buchenholz, natur, Raeder rot - *sanded natural beech wood, red wheels*

Serie	Art.-No	Period	Pr.	Info
	8320/14	1968-1968	2	23/14 cm

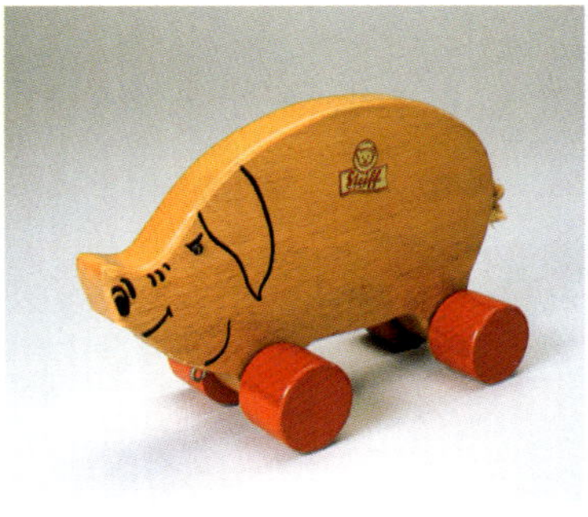

Holz-Schwein - *Wooden Pig*

geschliffenes Buchenholz, natur, Raeder rot - *sanded natural beech wood, red wheels*

Serie	Art.-No	Period	Pr.	Info
	8320/15	1968-1968	2	20/12 cm

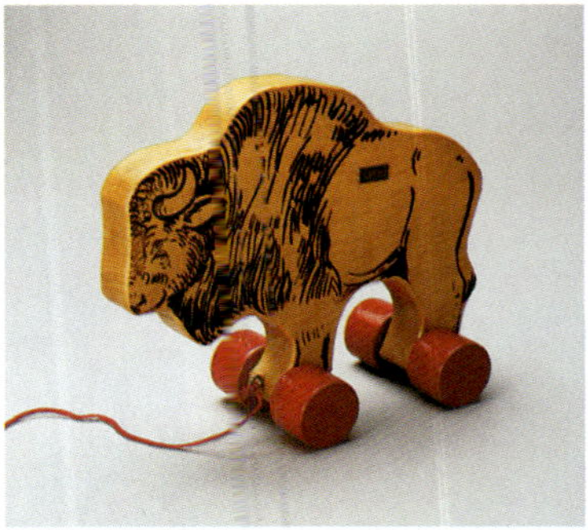

Holz-Wisent - *Wooden Bison*

geschliffenes Buchenholz, eingebrannte Zeichnung - *sanded beech wood, burned in markings*

Serie	Art.-No	Period	Pr.	Info
	8350/19	1959-1974	1-2	23/18 cm

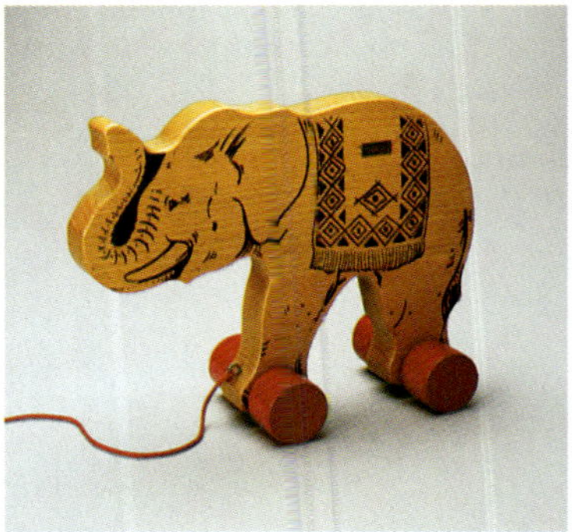

Holz-Elefant - *Wooden Elephant*

geschliffenes Buchenholz, eingebrannte Zeichnung - *sanded beech wood, burned in markings*

Serie	Art.-No	Period	Pr.	Info
	8350/20	1969-1974	1-2	25/19 cm

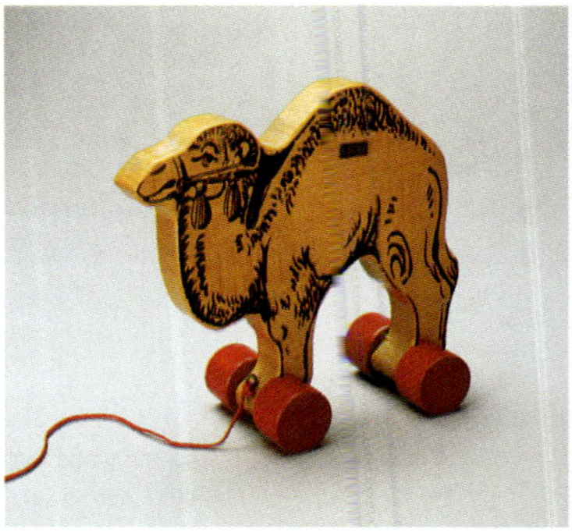

Holz-Dromedar - *Wooden Dromedary*

geschliffenes Buchenholz, eingebrannte Zeichnung - *sanded beech wood, burned in markings*

Serie	Art.-No	Period	Pr.	Info
	8350/21	1969-1974	1-2	23/21 cm

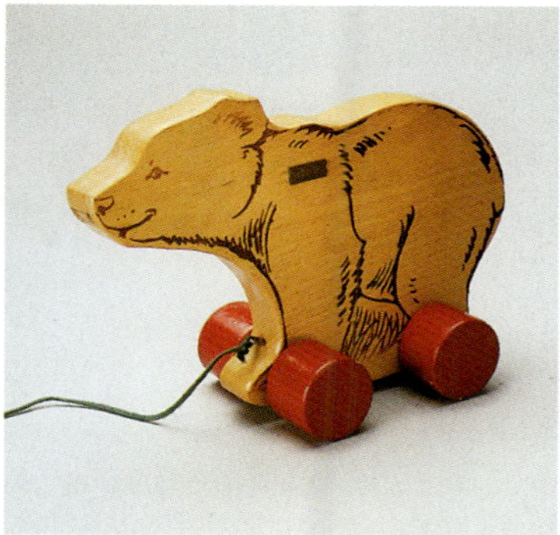

Holz-Baer - *Wooden Bear*

geschliffenes Buchenholz, eingebrannte Zeichnung - *sanded beech wood, burned in markings*

SERIE	ART.-NO	PERIOD	PR.	INFO
	8360/15	1969-1974	1-2	22/16 cm

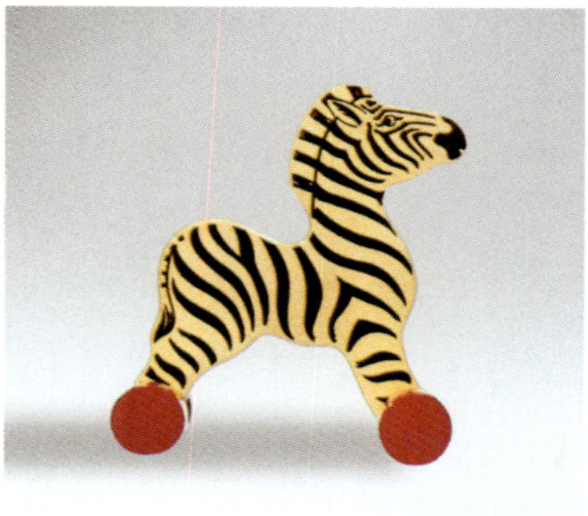

Holz-Zebra - *Wooden Zebra*

geschliffenes Buchenholz, eingebrannte Zeichnung - *sanded beech wood, burned in markings*

SERIE	ART.-NO	PERIOD	PR.	INFO
	8360/18	1969-1974	1-2	18/20 cm

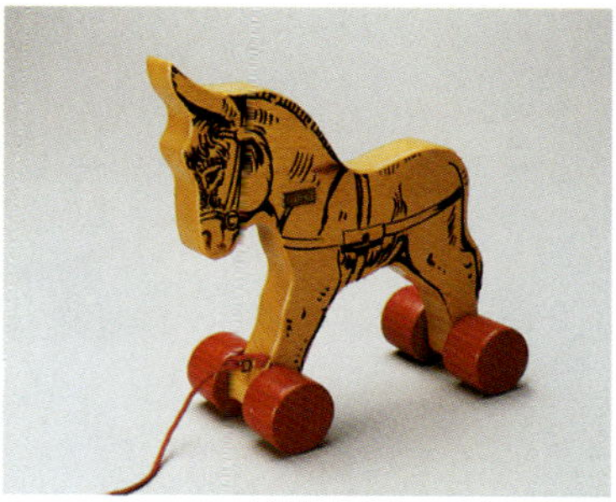

Holz-Esel - *Wooden Donkey*

geschliffenes Buchenholz, eingebrannte Zeichnung - *sanded beech wood, burned in markings*

SERIE	ART.-NO	PERIOD	PR.	INFO
	8360/21	1969-1974	1-2	19/20 cm

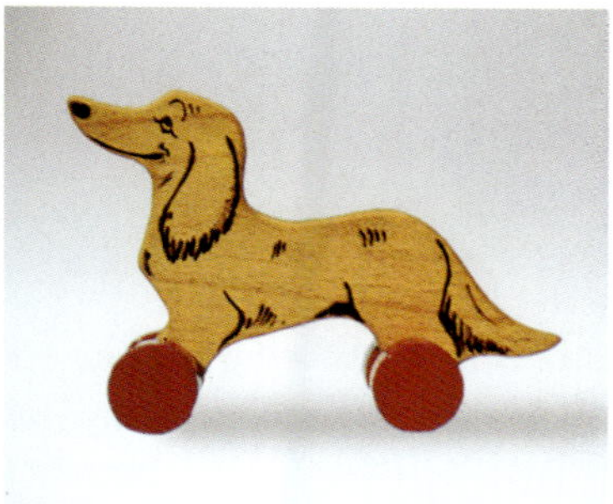

Holz-Dackel - *Wooden Dachshund*

geschliffenes Buchenholz, eingebrannte Zeichnung - *sanded beech wood, burned in markings*

SERIE	ART.-NO	PERIOD	PR.	INFO
	8360/16	1969-1974	1-2	22/15 cm

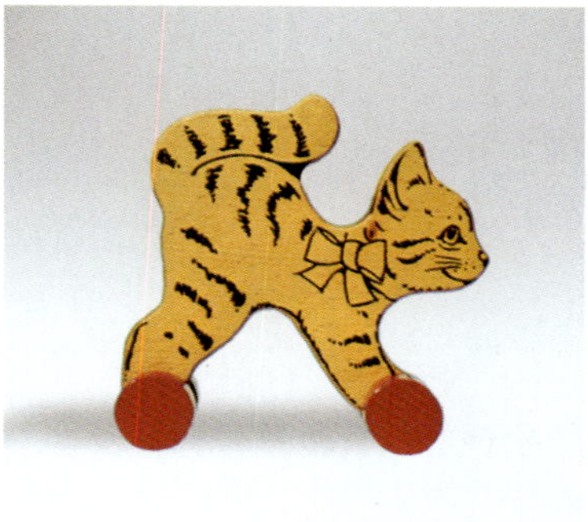

Holz-Katze - *Wooden Cat*

geschliffenes Buchenholz, eingebrannte Zeichnung - *sanded beech wood, burned in markings*

SERIE	ART.-NO	PERIOD	PR.	INFO
	8360/19	1969-1974	1-2	16/18 cm

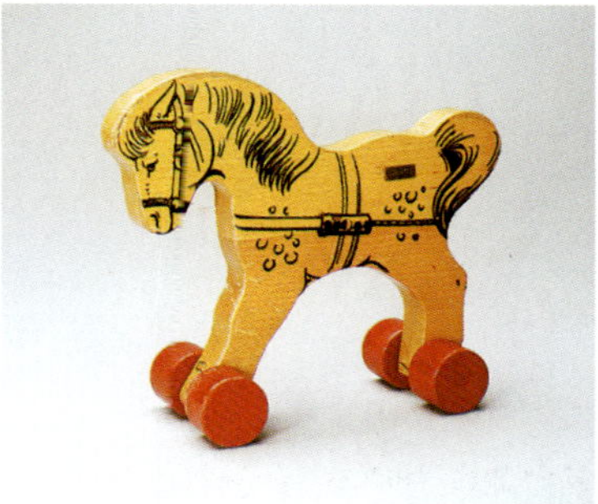

Holz-Pferd - *Wooden Horse*

geschliffenes Buchenholz, eingebrannte Zeichnung - *sanded beech wood, burned in markings*

SERIE	ART.-NO	PERIOD	PR.	INFO
	8360/22	1969-1974	1-2	24/20 cm

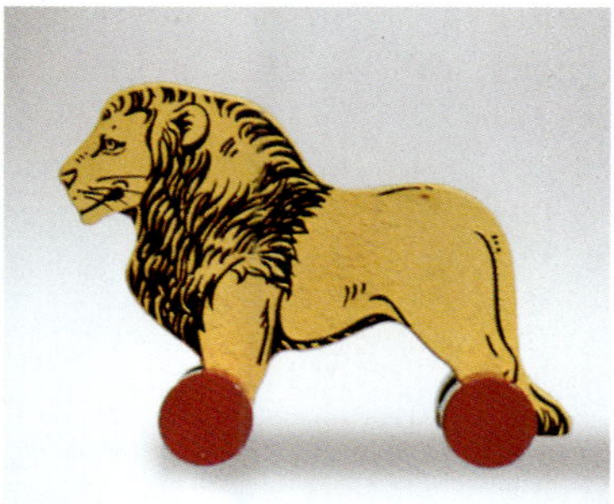

Holz-Loewe - *Wooden Lion*

geschliffenes Buchenholz, eingebrannte Zeichnung - *sanded beech wood, burned in markings*

SERIE	ART.-NO	PERIOD	PR.	INFO
	8360/17	1969-1974	1-2	20/16 cm

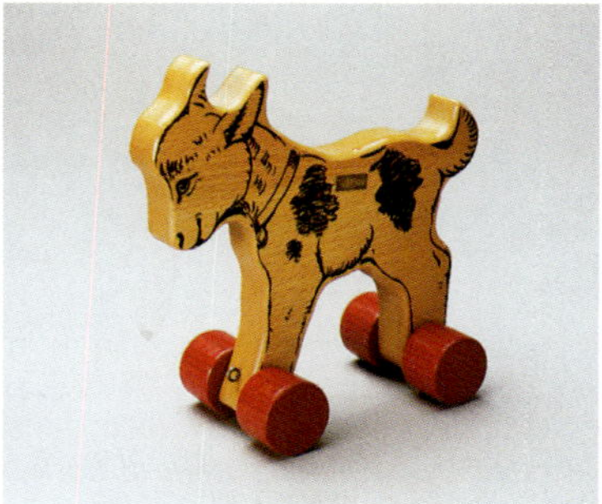

Holz-Ziege - *Wooden Goat*

geschliffenes Buchenholz, eingebrannte Zeichnung - *sanded beech wood, burned in markings*

SERIE	ART.-NO	PERIOD	PR.	INFO
	8360/20	1969-1974	1-2	20/20 cm

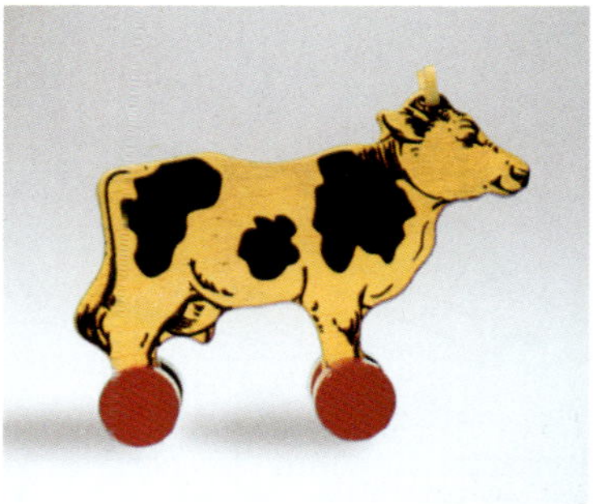

Holz-Kuh - *Wooden Cow*

geschliffenes Buchenholz, eingebrannte Zeichnung - *sanded beech wood, burned in markings*

SERIE	ART.-NO	PERIOD	PR.	INFO
	8360/23	1969-1970	1-2	22/18 cm

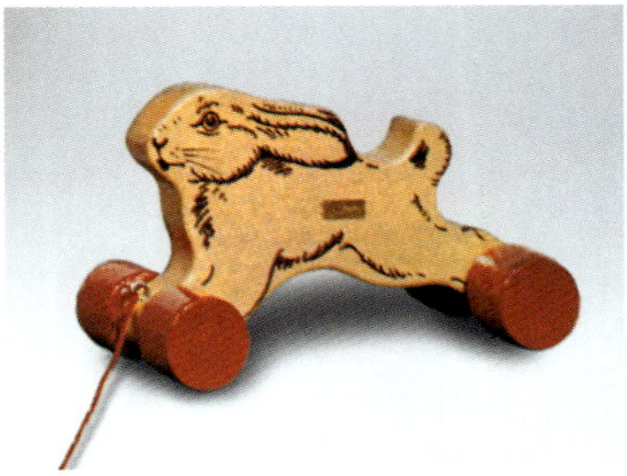

Holz-Hase - *Wooden Rabbit*

geschliffenes Buchenholz, eingebrannte Zeichnung - *sanded beech wood, burned in markings*

SERIE	ART.-NO	PERIOD	PR.	INFO
	8361/12	1970-1974	1-2	19 cm

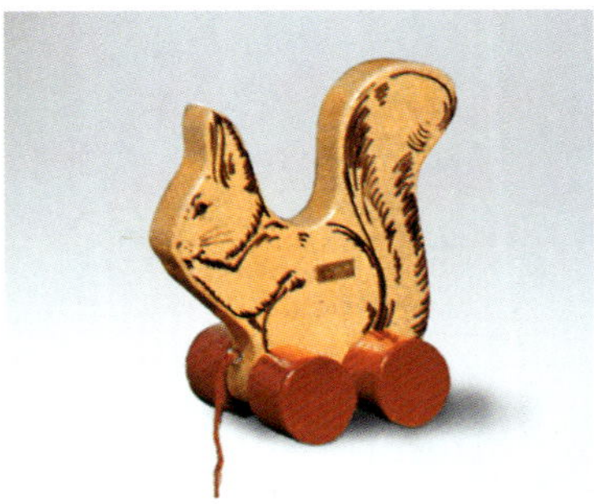

Holz-Eichhorn - *Wooden Squirrel*

geschliffenes Buchenholz, eingebrannte Zeichnung - *sanded beech wood, burned in markings*

SERIE	ART.-NO	PERIOD	PR.	INFO
	8361/16	1970-1974	1-2	13 cm

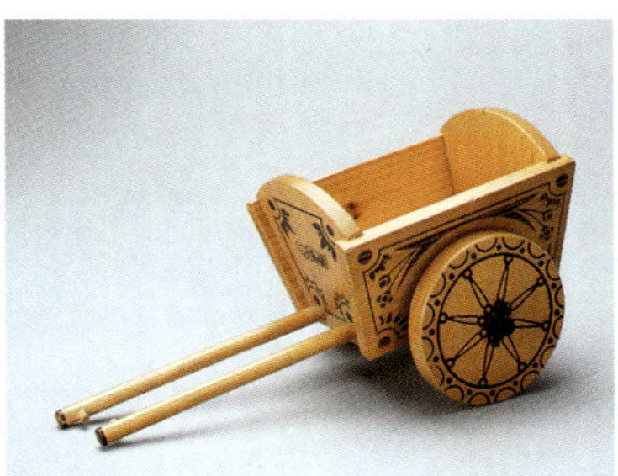

Radkarren sizilianisch - *Sicilian 2-Wheel Cart*

geschliffenes Buchenholz, eingebrannte Zeichnung - *sanded beech wood, burned in markings*

SERIE	ART.-NO	PERIOD	PR.	INFO
	8380/12	1969-1974	1-2	14 cm

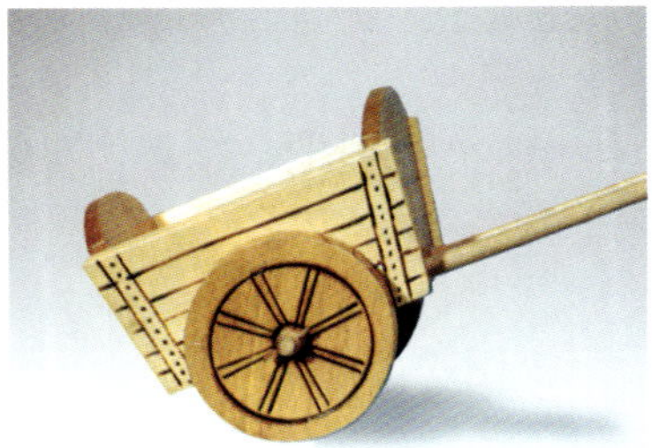

Radkarren rustikal - *Rustic 2- Wheel Cart*

geschliffenes Buchenholz, eingebrannte Zeichnung - *sanded beech wood, burned in markings*

SERIE	ART.-NO	PERIOD	PR.	INFO
	8380/13	1969-1974	1-2	14 cm

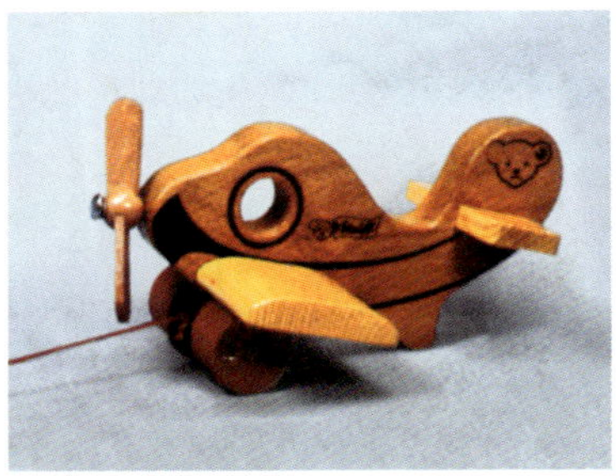

Flugzeug - *Airplane*

geschliffenes Holz, naturfarben, holzgebrannt - *sanded wood, natural, burned in markings*

SERIE	ART.-NO	PERIOD	PR.	INFO
	8430/12	1969-1974	2	23/12 cm

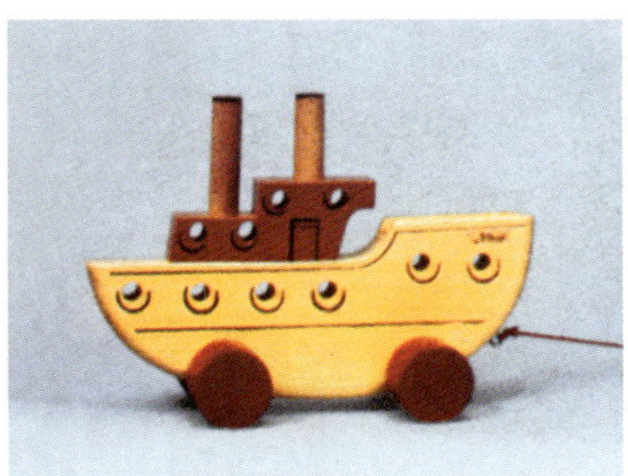

Schiff - *Ship*

geschliffenes Holz, naturfarben, holzgebrannt - *sanded wood, natural, burned in markings*

SERIE	ART.-NO	PERIOD	PR.	INFO
	8435/17	1969-1974	2	25/17 cm

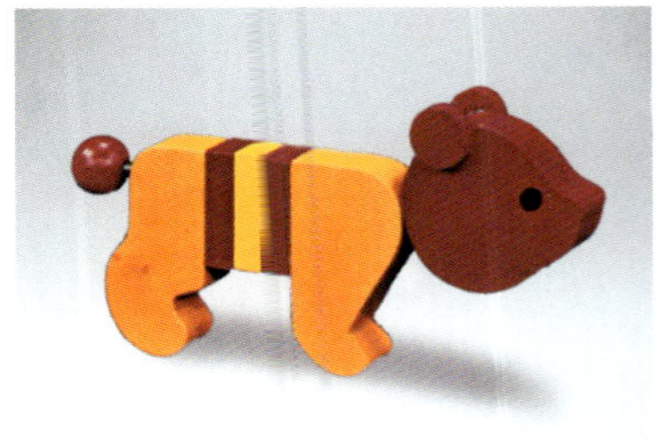

Steck-Baer - *Connecting Bear*

Holz, Kunststoff-Hohlstaebe, gelb/rot lakkiert - *wood, hollow plastic connectors, yellow/red painted*

SERIE	ART.-NO	PERIOD	PR.	INFO
	8330/09	1972-1974	2	8 Teile - *8 pieces*

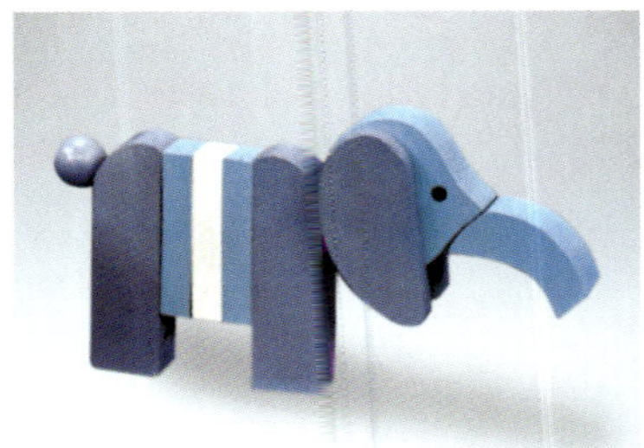

Steck-Elefant - *Connecting Elephant*

Holz, Kunststoff-Hohlstaebe, blau/weiss lakkiert - *wood, hollow plastic connectors, blue/white painted*

SERIE	ART.-NO	PERIOD	PR.	INFO
	8332/11	1972-1974	2	13 Teile - *13 pieces*

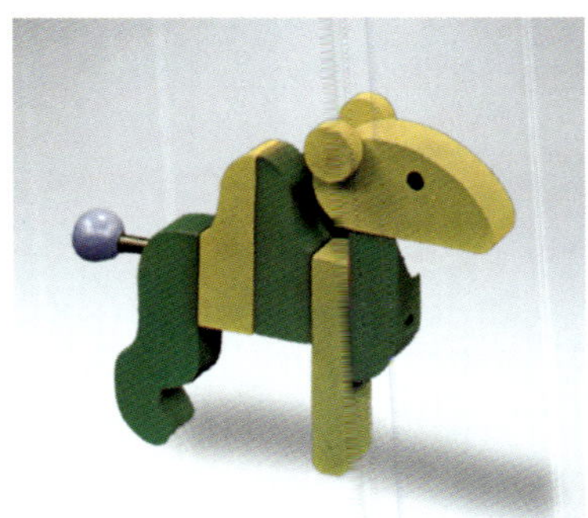

Steck-Dromedar - *Connecting Dromedary*

Holz, Kunststoff-Hohlstaebe, gruen lackiert - *wood, hollow plastic connectors, green painted*

SERIE	ART.-NO	PERIOD	PR.	INFO
	8333/12	1972-1974	2	9 Teile - *9 pieces*

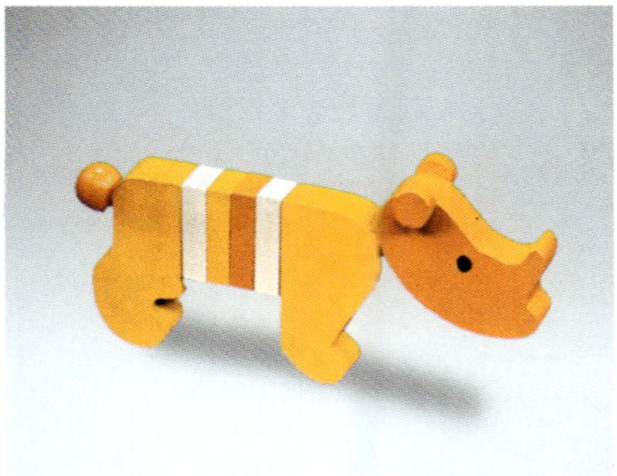

Steck-Nashorn - *Connecting Rhinoceros*

Holz, Kunststoff-Hohlstaebe, gelb/weiss lakkiert - *wood, hollow plastic connectors, yellow/white painted*

SERIE	ART.-NO	PERIOD	PR.	INFO
	8335/09	1972-1974	2	9 Teile - *9 pieces*

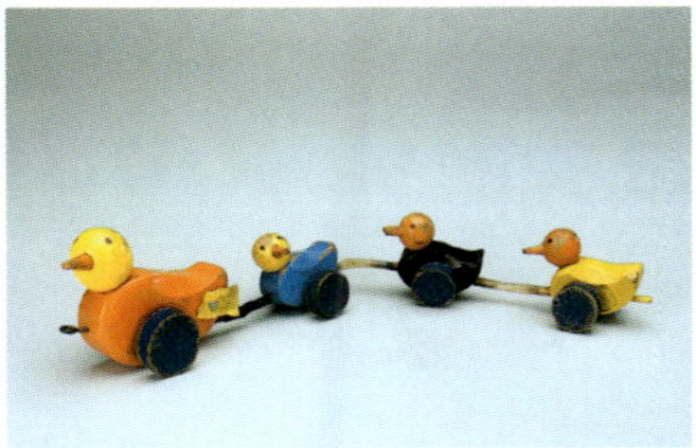

Entkette - *Duck Chain*

Hartholz, 4-farbig lackiert, 4-teilig, Entenkoepfe drehbar, plastische Form, auf Exzenterraedern, in farbigem Karton - *hardwood, in four colors, 4-piece set, duck heads swivel, plastic shapes, on eccentric wheels, packed in a colored box*

SERIE	ART.-NO	PERIOD	PR.	INFO
130	**808/4**	1949-1949	3	32 cm
132	**808/4**	1950-1958	3	
985	**8808,17**	1959-1959	3	
985	**7808,17**	1960-1964	2-3	
840	**7808,17**	1966-1966	2-3	

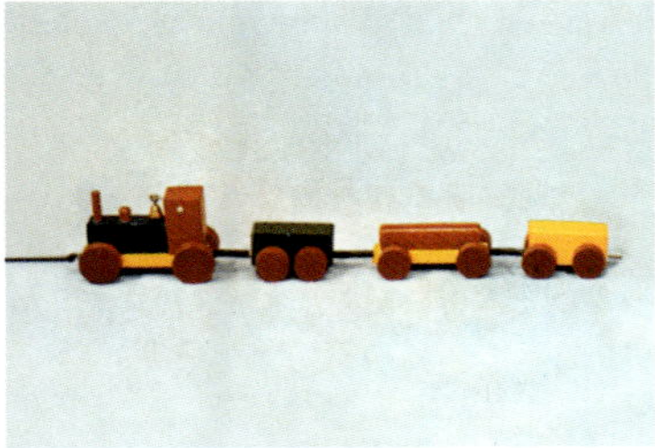

Bimmelbahn - *Small Train*

Hartholz, bunt lackiert, 4-teilig, Wackelbahn auf Exzenterraedern, mit Glocke, in farbigem Karton - *hardwood, painted in bright colors, 4-piece set, eccentric wheels, bell, brightly colored box*

SERIE	ART.-NO	PERIOD	PR.	INFO
128	**4205** ex	1949-1950	3	35 cm
132	**4205** ex	1951-1958	3	
985	**4805,17**	1959-1959	3	
985	**7804,17**	1960-1964	2-3	
840	**7804,17**	1965-1966	2-3	

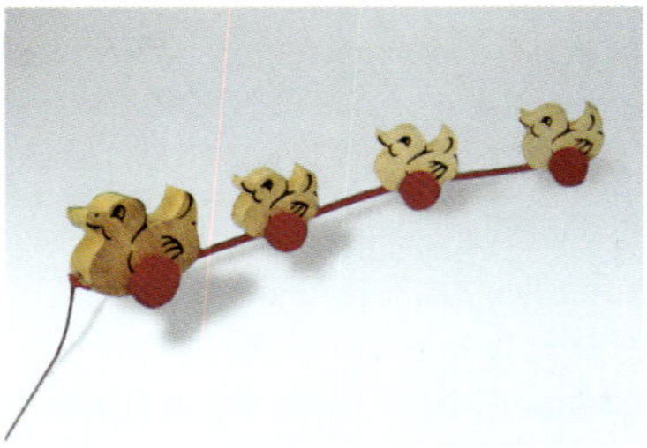

Entenkette - *Duck Chain*

geschliffenes Buchenholz, eingebrannte Zeichnung - *sanded beech wood, burned in markings*

SERIE	ART.-NO	PERIOD	PR.	INFO
	8410/08	1969-1973	2	38 cm

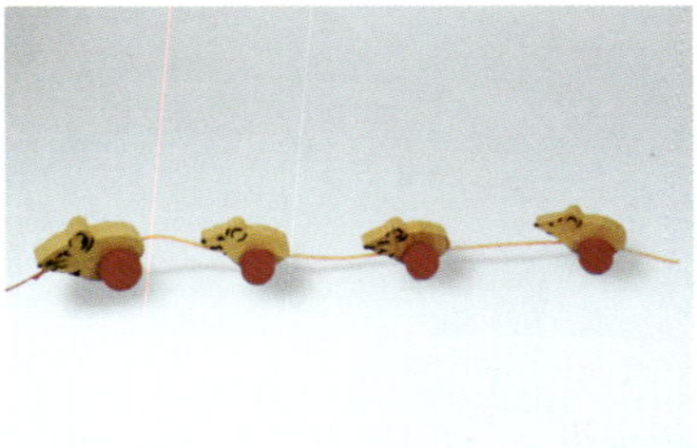

Mauskette - *Mouse Chain*

geschliffenes Buchenholz, eingebrannte Zeichnung - *sanded beech wood, burned in markings*

SERIE	ART.-NO	PERIOD	PR.	INFO
	8410/05	1969-1974	2	38 cm

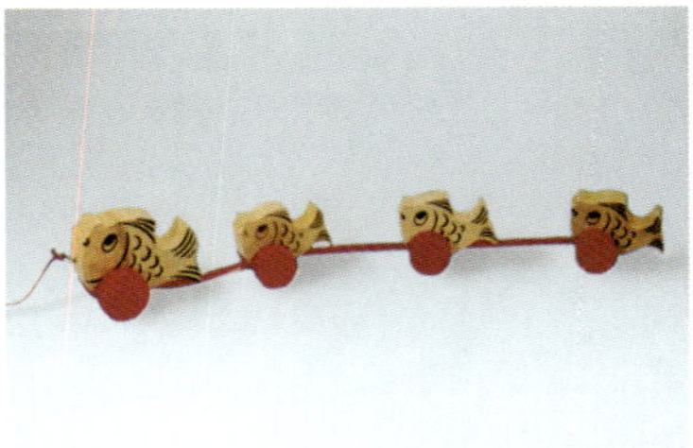

Fischkette - *Fish Chain*

geschliffenes Buchenholz, eingebrannte Zeichnung - *sanded beech wood, burned in markings*

SERIE	ART.-NO	PERIOD	PR.	INFO
	8410/06	1969-1973	2	38 cm

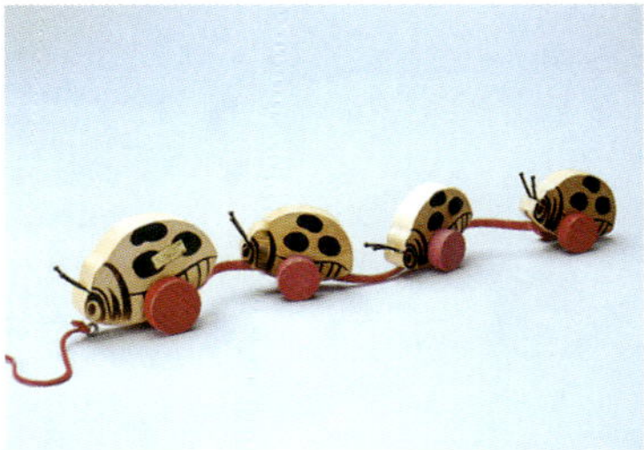

Marienkaeferkette - *Ladybird Chain*

geschliffenes Buchenholz, eingebrannte Zeichnung - *sanded beech wood, burned in markings*

SERIE	ART.-NO	PERIOD	PR.	INFO
	8410/07	1969-1973	2	38 cm

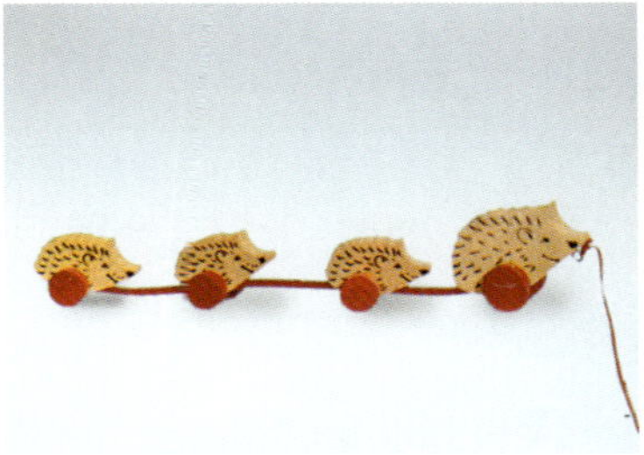

Igel-Kette - *Hedgehog Chain*

geschliffenes Buchenholz, eingebrannte Zeichnung - *sanded beech wood, burned in markings*

SERIE	ART.-NO	PERIOD	PR.	INFO
	8410/09	1970-1974	2	38 cm

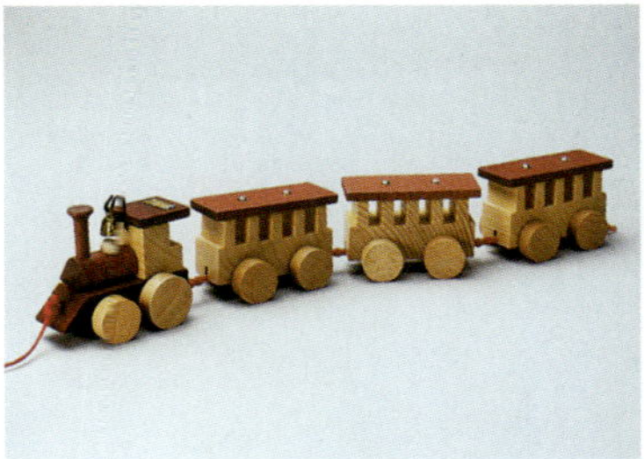

Kleinbahn - *Light Train*

geschliffenes Holz, naturfarben, Bimmelglocke - *sanded natural wood, with tinkling bell*

SERIE	ART.-NO	PERIOD	PR.	INFO
	8420/06	1969-1973	2	40 cm

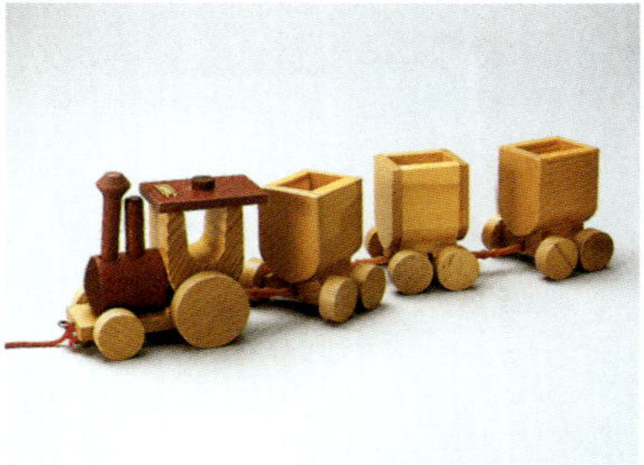

Lorenbahn - *Trolley Train*

geschliffenes Holz, naturfarben, Wagen abhaengbar - *sanded natural wood, rail cars are removable*

SERIE	ART.-NO	PERIOD	PR.	INFO
	8420/08	1969-1973	2	32 cm

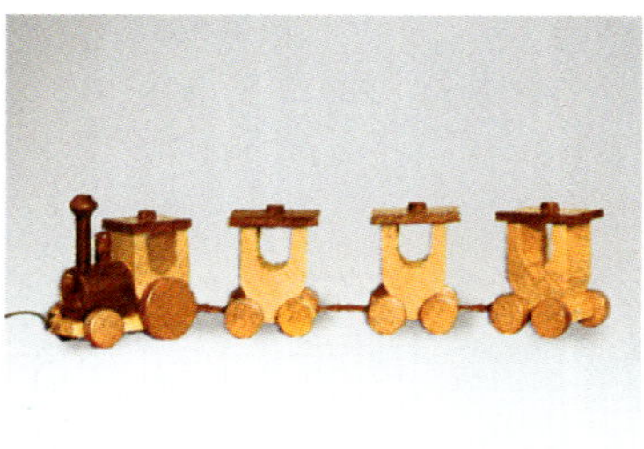

Groteskbahn - *Grotesque Train*

geschliffenes Holz, naturfarben, Wagen abhaengbar - *sanded natural wood, rail cars are removable*

SERIE	ART.-NO	PERIOD	PR.	INFO
	8420/09	1969-1974	2	32 cm

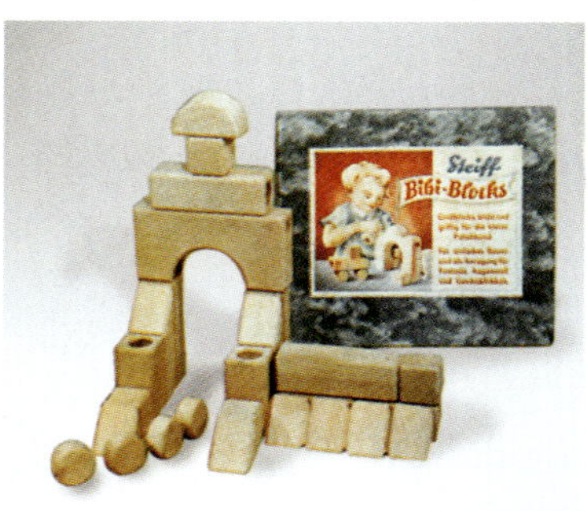

Bibi Blocks Baukasten - *Bibi Blocks Construction Set*

Hartholz, fein geschliffen, unlackiert - *hardwood, finely sanded, unpainted*

SERIE	ART.-NO	PERIOD	PR.	INFO
132	**8030**	1951-1954	4	25x29 cm

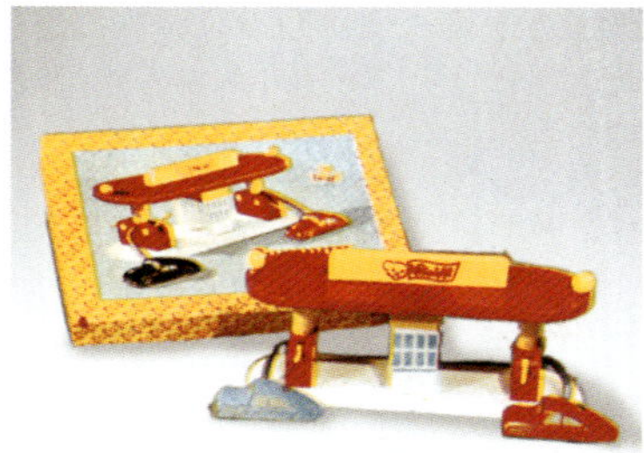

Tankstellen Baukasten Pumpax - *Pumpax Gas Station Construction Set*

Hartholz, lackiert, in farbigem Kasten - *hardwood, painted, in brightly colored box*

SERIE	ART.-NO	PERIOD	PR.	INFO
132	**8028**	1952-1954	4-5	20x28 cm

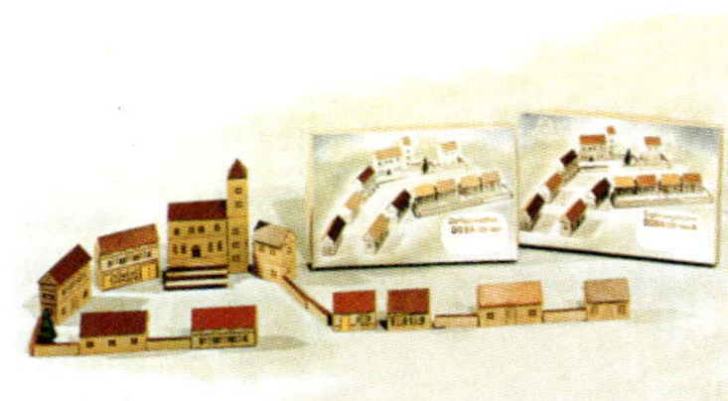

Doba Dorfbaukasten - *Doba Village Construction Set*

Hartholz, lackiert & bemalt, eingeschossige Blocks mit je zwei verschiedenen Haustypen von Dorfhaeusern, im Karton - *hardwood, painted & lacquered, single story blocks with two different house models included, packed in its box*

SERIE	ART.-NO	PERIOD	PR.	INFO
130	**1805**	1954-1957	4	Baukasten - *Construction Set*
130	**1805** A	1954-1956	3	Ergaenzungskasten - *Construction Set Supplement*

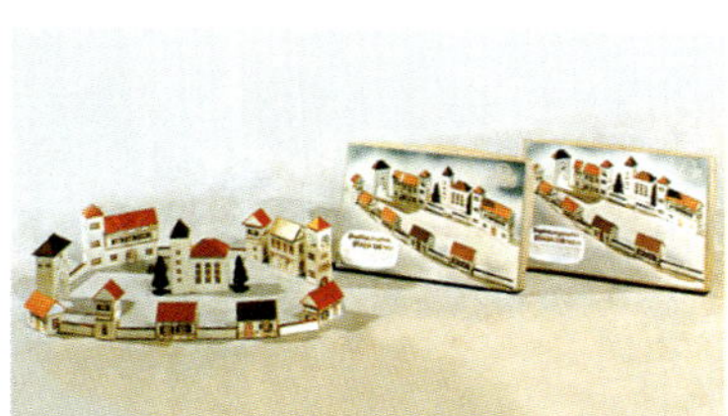

Staba Stadtbaukasten - *Staba City Construction Set*

Hartholz, lackiert & bemalt, eingeschossige Blocks mit je zwei verschiedenen Haustypen alter Staedte, im Karton - *hardwood, painted & lacquered, single story blocks with two different house models of old cities, packed in its box*

SERIE	ART.-NO	PERIOD	PR.	INFO
130	**1806**	1954-1957	4	Baukasten - *Construction Set*
130	**1806** A	1954-1956	3	Ergaenzungskasten - *Construction Set Supplement*

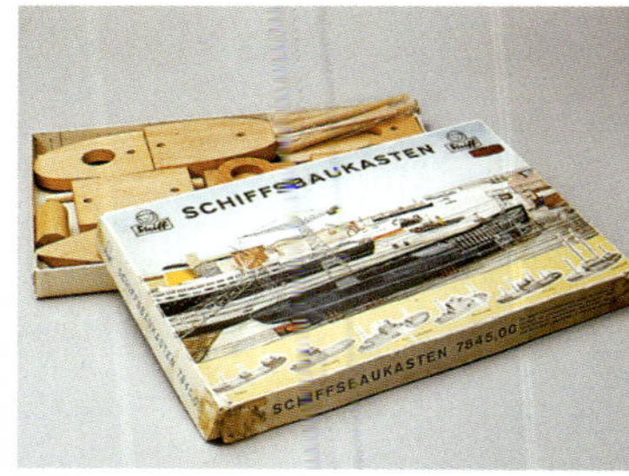

Sibauka Schiffsbaukasten - *Sibauka Ship Construction Set*

Hartholz, natur, unlackiert, 30 Teile im Karton - *natural hardwood, unpainted, 30-piece set in box*

SERIE	ART.-NO	PERIOD	PR.	INFO
985	**7846,00**	1963-1964	3	25x38 cm
845	**7846,00**	1965-1967	3	
	8450/46	1968-1969	3	

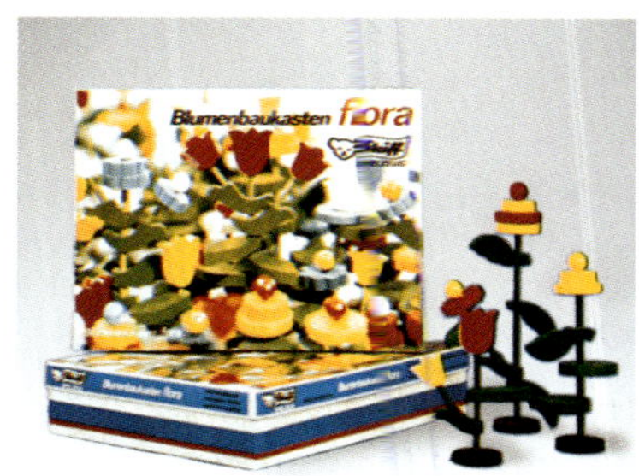

Blumenbaukasten Flora - *Flower Construction Set*

Holz, farbig lackierte Blumenbauteile - *wooden brightly painted flower building blocks*

SERIE	ART.-NO	PERIOD	PR.	INFO
	8461/05	1969-1974	3	Groesse I - *Size I*
	8462/05	1969-1974	3	Groesse II - *Size II*
	8463/05	1969-1974	3	Groesse III - *Size III*

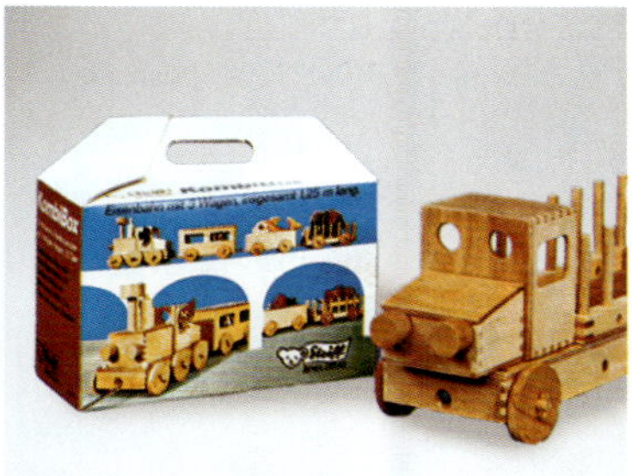

Kombibox Eisenbahn - *Combination Box Train*

Holz, naturfarben, diverse Baumoeglichkeiten - *wood, natural color, different variations possible*

SERIE	ART.-NO	PERIOD	PR.	INFO
	8470/20	1969-1973	3	28x18 cm

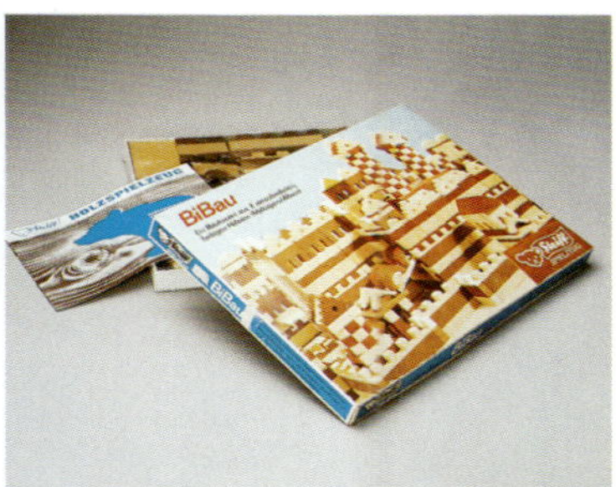

BiBaukasten - *BiBau Construction Set*

Ahorn und Mahagoniholz, verleimt - *maple & mahogany wood, bonded*

SERIE	ART.-NO	PERIOD	PR.	INFO
	8481/04	1969-1974	3	Groesse I - *Size I*
	8482/04	1969-1974	3	Groesse II - *Size II*

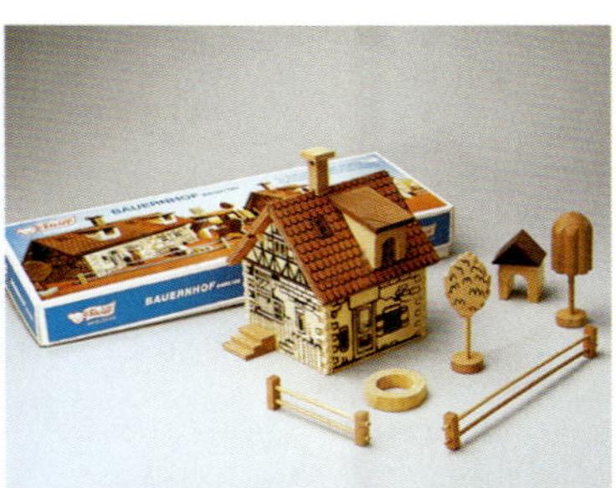

Bauernhof-Baukasten - *Farm Construction Set*

geschliffenes Holz, eingebrannte Zeichnung - *sanded wood, burned in design*

SERIE	ART.-NO	PERIOD	PR.	INFO
	8450/05	1970-1973	3	50x19 cm

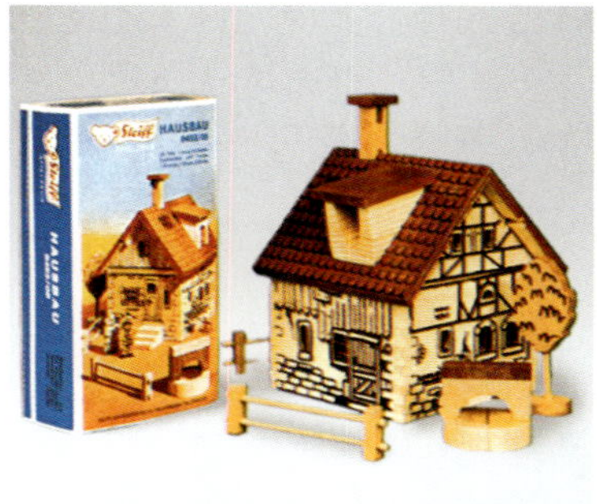

Hausbau-Baukasten - *House Construction Set*

geschliffenes Holz, eingebrannte Zeichnung - *sanded wood, burned in design*

SERIE	ART.-NO	PERIOD	PR.	INFO
	8453/05	1970-1974	3	20x12 cm

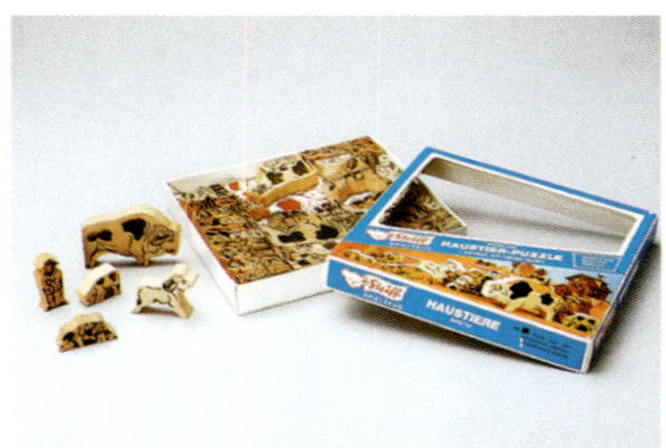

Haustier-Puzzle - *House Animal Puzzle*

geschliffenes Holz, eingebrannte Zeichnung - *sanded wood, burned in design*

SERIE	ART.-NO	PERIOD	PR.	INFO
	8458/04	1970-1974	3	40 Teile - *40 pieces*

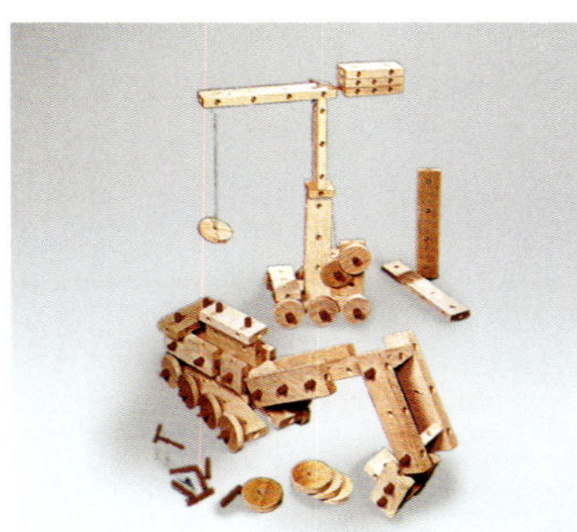

Steck-Baukasten - *Plug Type Building Blocks*

Holz, natur - *natural wood*

SERIE	ART.-NO	PERIOD	PR.	INFO
	8487/05	1973-1973	3	

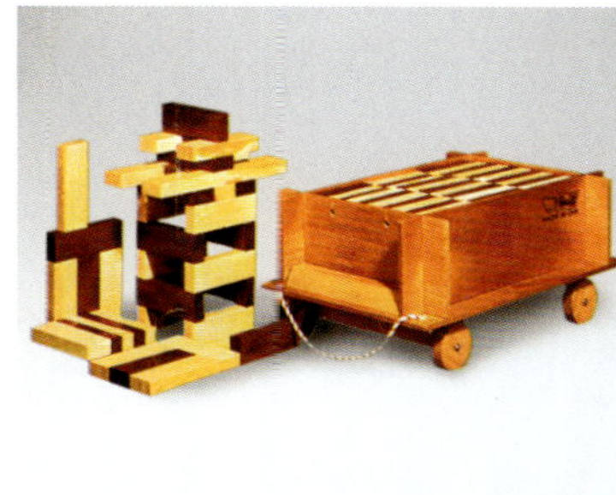

Holzbaukasten - *Wooden Building Blocks*

Holz, naturfarben, Baukloetze 2x4x12cm in zerlegbarem Kasten mit Raedern - *natural wood, building blocks are 2x4x12cm, packed in their own box with wheels which can be dismantled*

SERIE	ART.-NO	PERIOD	PR.	INFO
	8485/45	1974-1975	3	90 Stueck - *90 pieces*

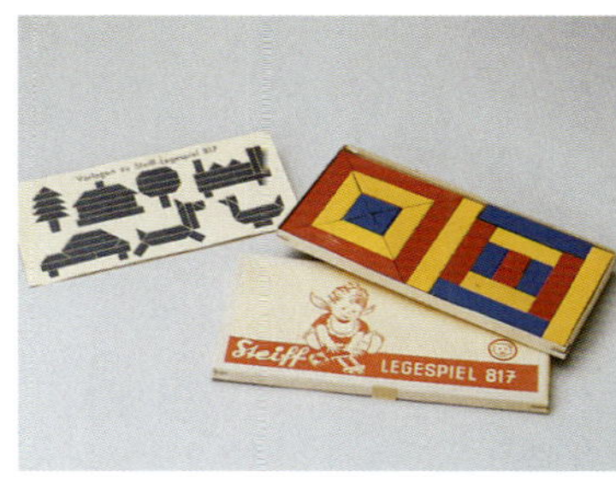

Legespiel - *Wooden Block Game*

Holz, farbig lackiert - *wood, painted in bright colors*

SERIE	ART.-NO	PERIOD	PR.	INFO
132	**817**	1947-1948	4	16/18 cm

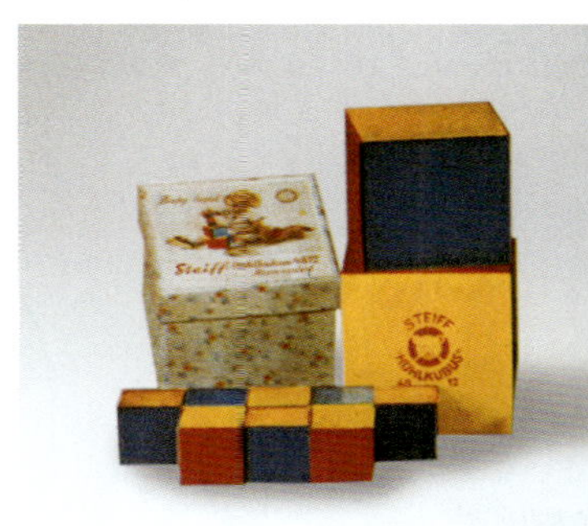

Hohlkubus / Wuerfelkubus - *Hollow Cube / Cubes within a Cube*

Holz, 2 grosse Wuerfel enthalten 8 kleine Wuerfel - *wood, two large cubes contain 8 small cubes*

SERIE	ART.-NO	PERIOD	PR.	INFO
132	**4812**	1949-1958	4	4,5/12 cm
985	**7812,07**	1960-1961	4	

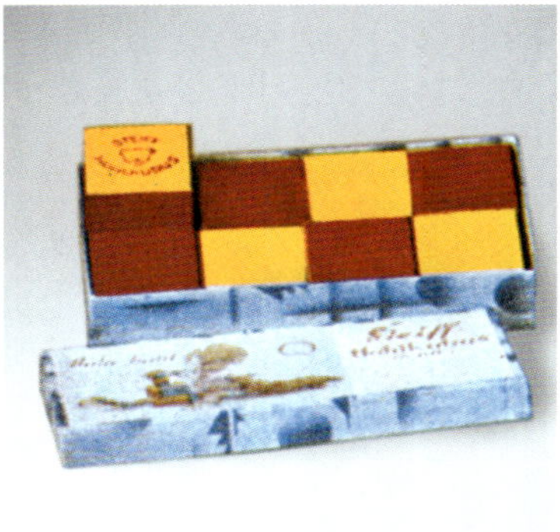

Hohlkubus / Rasselkubus - *Hollow Cube / Rattling Cube*

Holz, 8 Wuerfel mit Rassel, Geschenkpakkung - *wood, 8 cubes with rattles, packed in a gift box*

SERIE	ART.-NO	PERIOD	PR.	INFO
132	**805**	1949-1958	4	22 cm
985	**7805,07**	1959-1961	4	

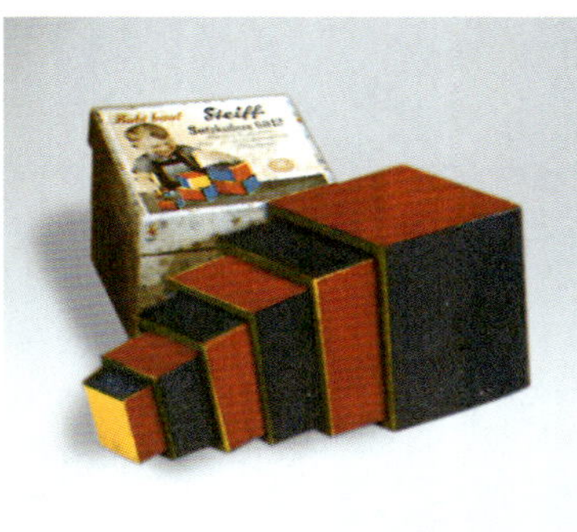

Satz- / Pyramiden-Kubus - *Set of Pyramid Cubes*

Holz, 6 sich verjuengende Kubusse ineinander - *wood, a set of 6 cubes graduating in size from small to large, each fitting inside the next*

SERIE	ART.-NO	PERIOD	PR.	INFO
132	**6812**	1949-1958	4	bis 12 cm

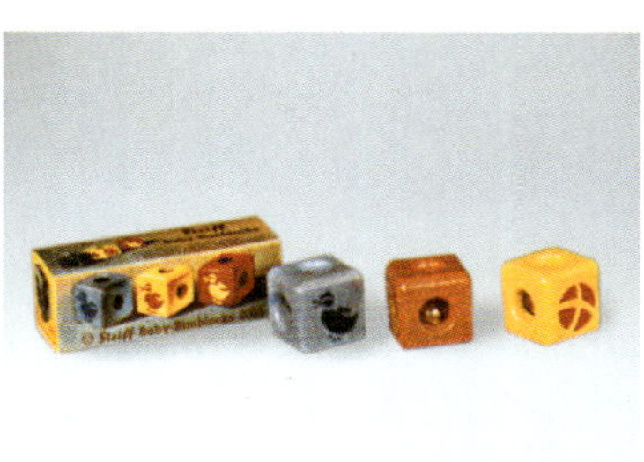

Glockenwuerfel Bimblock - *Bimblock Bell Cubes*

Holz, 3 Wuerfel mit Glocke, Geschenkkarton - *wood, 3 cubes with bells packed in a gift box*

SERIE	ART.-NO	PERIOD	PR.	INFO
132	**8005**	1949-1958	4	3 Stueck - *3 pieces*
985	**7806,07**	1959-1961	3-4	
840	**7806,07**	1966-1966	3-4	

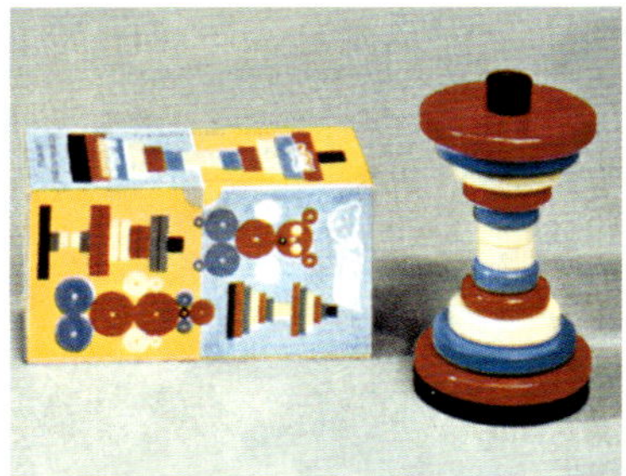

Multiform Scheibenbauturm - *Multiform Disc Buliding Tower*

Hartholz, farbig lackiert - *hardwood, painted in multiple colors*

SERIE	ART.-NO	PERIOD	PR.	INFO
132	**8013**	1949-1958	4	13 Teile - *13 pieces*
985	**7813,07**	1959-1961	4	

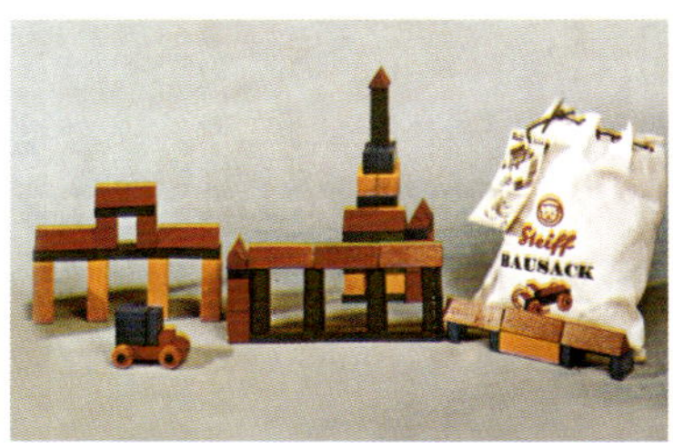

Bausack - *Building Bag*

Holz, farbig gewachste Bausteine & ein Auto - *wood, colored building blocks & one car*

SERIE	ART.-NO	PERIOD	PR.	INFO
132	**8100**	1951-1958	4	100 Stueck - *100 pieces*
985	**8100,00**	1959-1964	3-4	
845	**8100,00**	1965-1966	3-4	

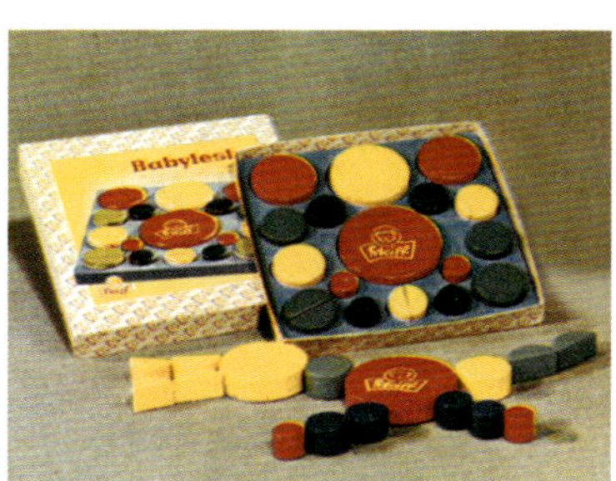

Babytest - *Baby Test*

Holz, lackiert, auch Bau- und Legespiel - *wood, painted, the game can be laid out or used to build something*

SERIE	ART.-NO	PERIOD	PR.	INFO
132	**8020**	1952-1954	4	

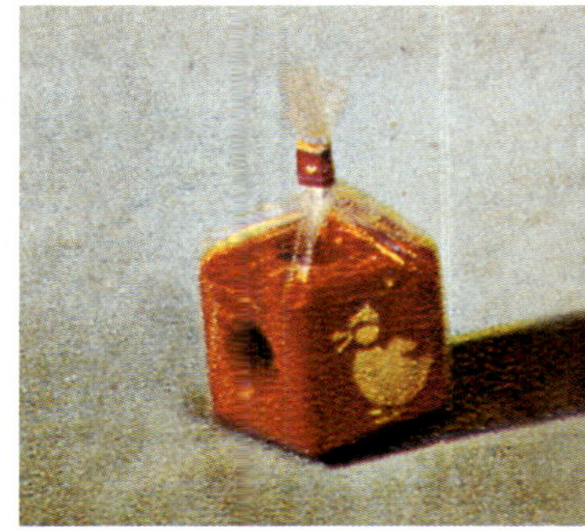

Glockenwuerfel - *Bell Cube*

Holz, Wuerfel mit Glocke einzeln im Plastikbeutel - *wood, single cube with bell packed in a plastic bag*

SERIE	ART.-NO	PERIOD	PR.	INFO
985	**7807,08**	1959-1961	1-2	1 Stueck - *1 piece*
840	**7807,08**	1966-1966	1-2	

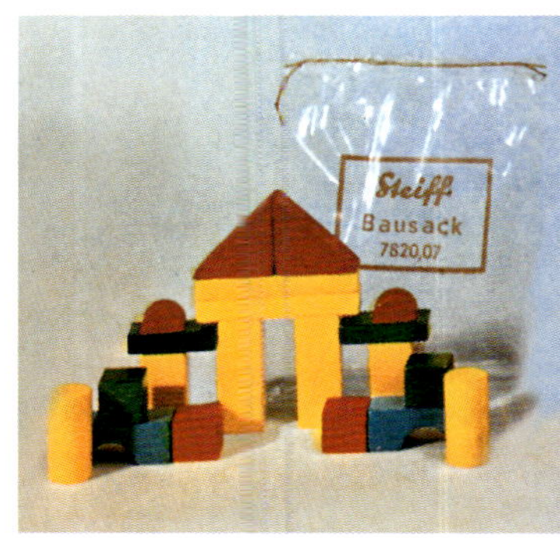

Bausack - *Building Bag*

farbig gewachste Holzbausteine im Plastik-Sack - *colored wooden building blocks packed in plastic bag*

SERIE	ART.-NO	PERIOD	PR.	INFO
985	**7820,07**	1961-1963	3	20 Stueck - *20 pieces*

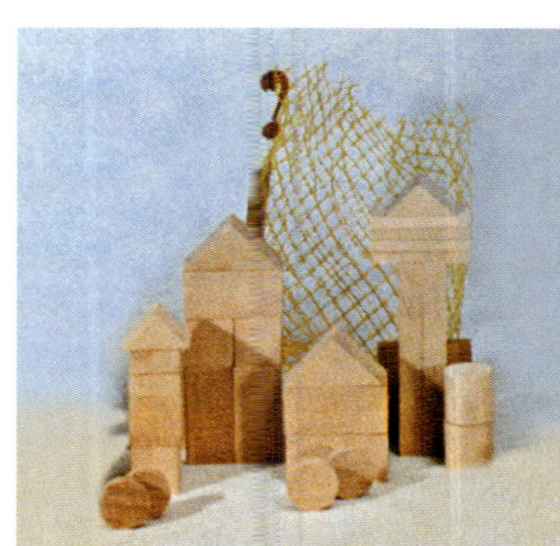

Bausack Babyblocks - *Baby Blocks Building Bag*

Holz, natur, geschliffene Bloecke - *sanded natural wood blocks*

Serie	Art.-No	Period	Pr.	Info
985	**7830,00**	1962-1964	2-3	30 Stueck - *30 pieces*
845	**7830,00**	1965-1966	2-3	

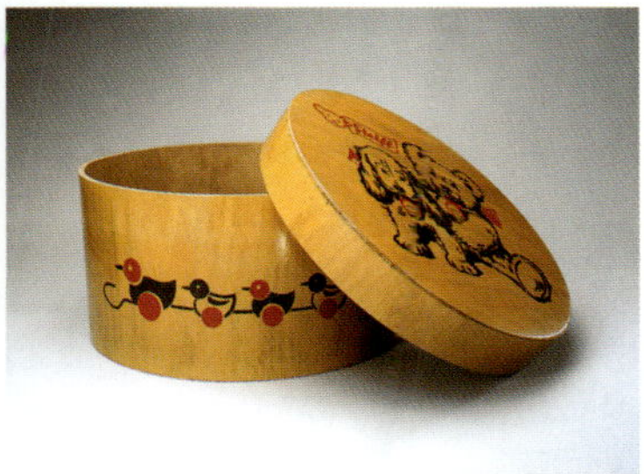

Spielzeugschachtel - *Toy Box*

Hartholz, naturlackiert, bemalt - *hardwood, naturally painted & lacquered*

Serie	Art.-No	Period	Pr.	Info
985	**7845,00**	1960-1964	4-5	45x24 cm
849	**7845,00**	1965-1967	4-5	
	8490/45	1968-1969	4-5	

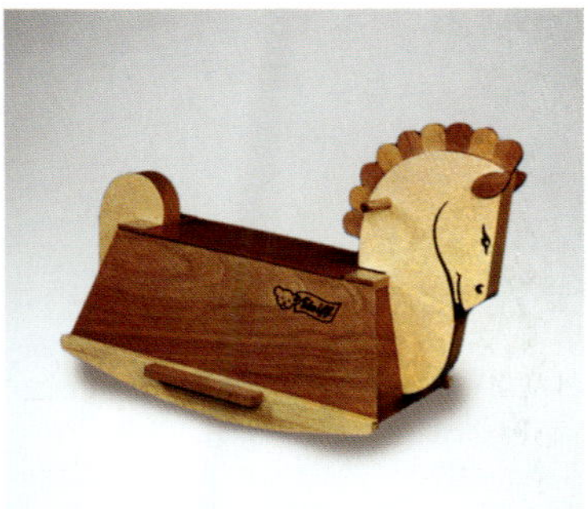

Spielzeugkiste Troja - *Trojan Toy Box*

Holz-Schaukelpferd als Spielzeugtruhe, naturfarben, hell & dunkelbraun, lackiert, am Pferderuecken zu oeffnen - *wooden rocking horse toy box, natural dark & light wood, lacquered, the horse´s back opens up*

Serie	Art.-No	Period	Pr.	Info
	8491/45	1970-1975	4-5	65x35x90 cm

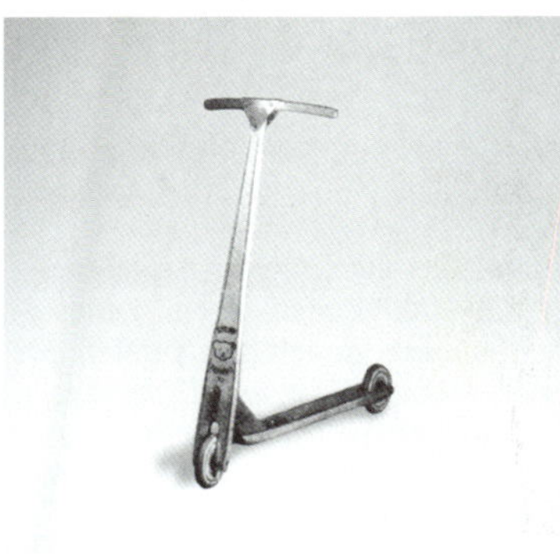

Tramro

Hartholz, Holzrad mit Gleitnabe 10,5 cm und Gummi, naturlackiert, 74 cm hoch, gebogener Lenkgriff - *hardwood, 10.5 cm wooden wheels with sliding hub & rubber, stained naturally, 74 cm tall, curved handle bars*

Serie	Art.-No	Period	Pr.	Info
	70	1949-1949	4	74 cm

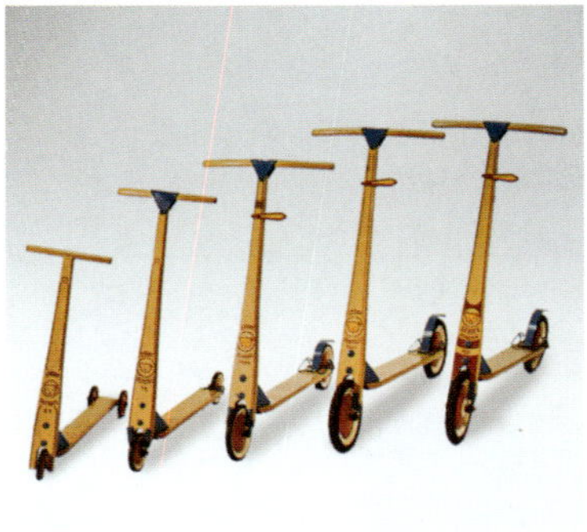

Steiff Baerkopf Roller - *Steiff Bearhead Scooter*

Hartholz, naturlackiert, gebogener Lenkgriff, alle Modelle mit Bremse, Staender & Richtungsanzeiger (ausser Tritrott), Metallscheibenraeder mit Gummireifen, ab 1967 Plastik, Modelle: Tritrott Dreiradroller, 62 cm, Raeder 8 cm / Flitzro, 74 cm, Raeder 10 cm / Renrogi, 80 cm, Raeder 15 cm / Renrolo, 88 cm, Raeder 20 cm / Rollux, 90 cm, Raeder 20 cm - *hardwood, naturally stained, curved handle bars, all modells equipped with brakes, stand & direction indicator (except Tritrott), metal disc wheels with rubber tires, plastic from 1967, models: Tritrott 3-wheel scooter, 62 cm, 8 cm wheels / Flitzro, 74 cm, 10 cm wheels / Renrogi, 80 cm, 15 cm wheels / Renrolo, 88 cm, 20 cm wheels / Rollux, 90 cm, 20 cm wheels*

Serie	Art.-No	Period	Pr.	Info
139	**61**	1950-1953	3	Tritrott
139	**62**	1954-1958	3	
995	**3862,30**	1959-1964	3	
890	**3862,30**	1965-1967	3	
	8910/62	1968-1969	3	
139	**73**	1949-1958	4	Flitzro
995	**2873,30**	1959-1964	4	
891	**2873,30**	1965-1967	4	
	8910/73	1968-1969	4	
139	**7884**	1949-1958	4	Renrogi
995	**2884,30**	1959-1964	4	
891	**2884,30**	1965-1967	4	
	8910/84	1968-1969	4	
139	**7887**	1949-1952	4	Renrolo
139	**7888**	1953-1958	4	
995	**2888,30**	1959-1963	4	
139	**7890**	1950-1951	4	Rollux
139	**7891**	1952-1958	4	
995	**2891,30**	1959-1963	4	

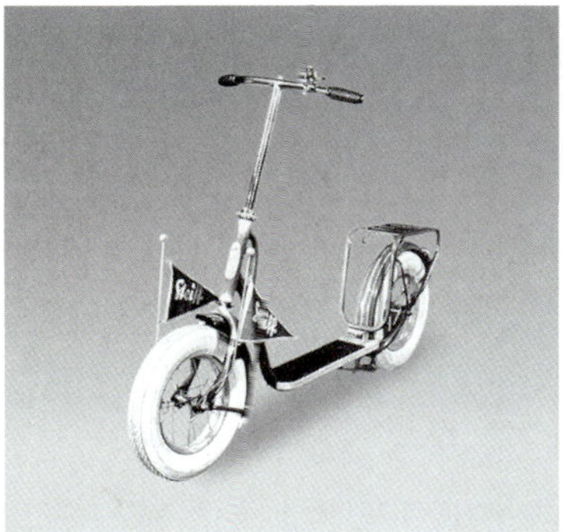

Ballonroller Avus - *Balloon Scooter Avus*

Stahlrohr-Rahmen geschweisst, Speichenraeder mit Ballonreifen 33 cm & Kugellager, Laufbrett mit Gummiauflage, Gepaecktraeger mit Federbuegel zugleich Kippstaender, Hoehe 83 cm, Laenge 124 cm, 7,8 kg, Fussbremse am Hinterrad - *welded steel tubular frame, spoke wheels with 33 cm balloon tires & ball bearings, running board has rubber coating layer, luggage rack by means of a bar with springs which also functions as a kick stand, 83 cm tall, 124 cm long, 7.8 kg, pedal brakes on rear wheel*

Serie	Art.-No	Period	Pr.	Info
139	**7994**	1953-1953	5-6	124 cm

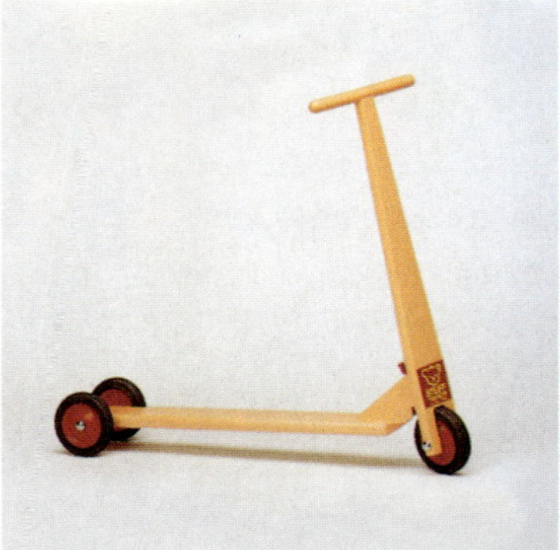

Tritrott

Dreiradroller, Holz, PVC Raeder, farblos lackiert - *three-wheel scooter, wood, PVC wheels, painted with clear lacquer*

Serie	Art.-No	Period	Pr.	Info
483103	**8410/55**	1979-1990	1-2	55 cm

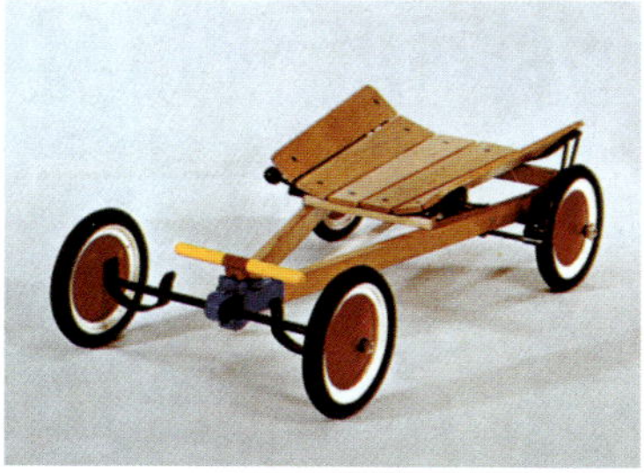

Ruderrenner - *Rudder Racer*

Kindersportfahrzeug, Hartholz, naturlackiert, verschiedene Modellaenderungen innerhalb der angegebenen Katalogzeiten - *children´s racing vehicle, made of hardwood, naturally varnished, various model modifications within the catalog periods listed*

SERIE	ART.-NO	PERIOD	PR.	INFO
139	**2596**	1949-1951	4-5	95/85 cm
139	**2585**	1951-1952	4-5	
139	**2587**	1953-1958	4-5	
995	**4887,30**	1959-1964	4	
895	**4887,30**	1965-1967	4	
	8950/87	1968-1970	4	
	8995/87	1971-1971	4	

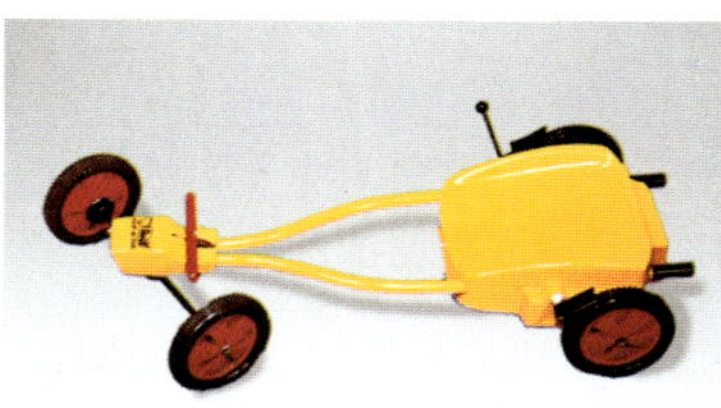

Ruderrenner - *Rudder Racer*

Stahlrohrrahmen, Kunststoffsitz (Duromer) - *steel tubular frame with plastic seat (Duromer)*

SERIE	ART.-NO	PERIOD	PR.	INFO
	8996/87	1972-1974	3	95 cm

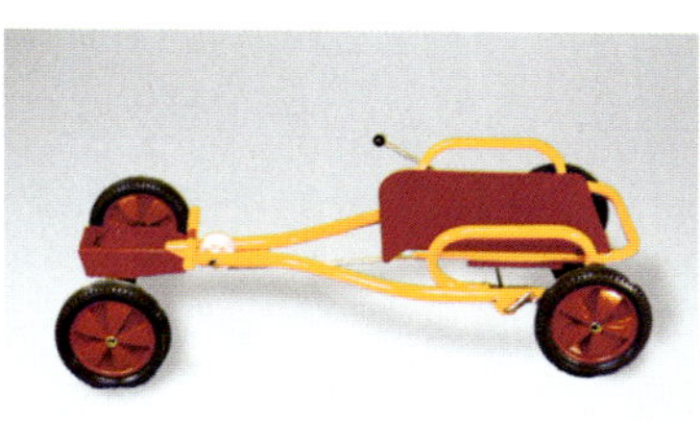

Ruderrenner - *Rudder Racer*

Hartholz, naturlackiert, bemalt - *hardwood, naturally varnished, painted*

SERIE	ART.-NO	PERIOD	PR.	INFO
	8998/99	1975-1979	3	102 cm

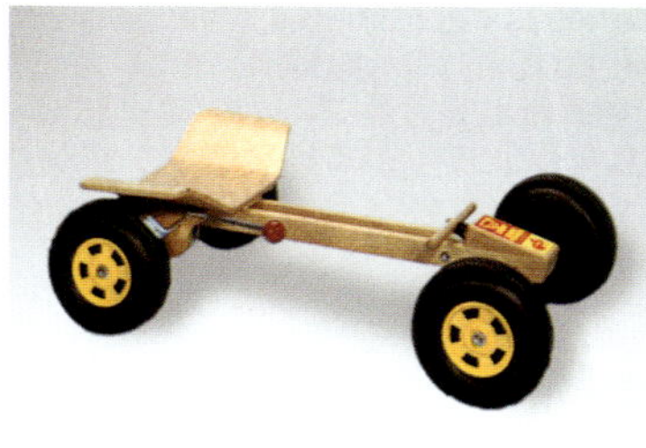

Ruderrenner - *Rudder Racer*

Holzkonstruktion, Sitz verstellbar - *wooden structure with adjustable seat*

SERIE	ART.-NO	PERIOD	PR.	INFO
483301	**8420/94**	1981-1987	3	94 cm

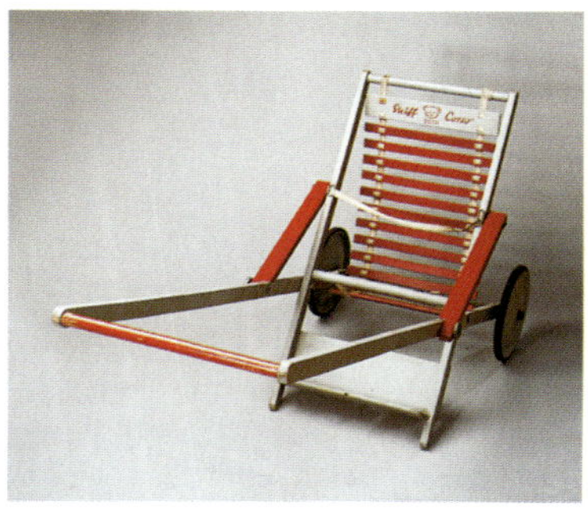

Corso Klapp-Sportwagen - *Corso Collapsible Sports Vehicle*

Hartholz, Metallscheibenraeder 20 cm - *hardwood, 20 cm metal disc wheels*

SERIE	ART.-NO	PERIOD	PR.	INFO
139	**2870**	1947-1950	5	112 cm

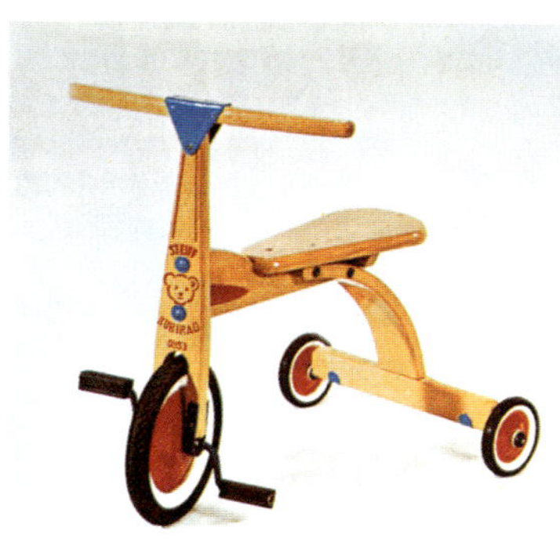

Bubirad - *Bubi-Cycle*

Dreirad fuer 2-5 Jahre, Hartholz, Gummipedale, verschiedene Modellaenderungen - *tricycle for children between 2 & 5 years, hardwood, rubber pedals, various model modifications*

SERIE	ART.-NO	PERIOD	PR.	INFO
139	**6850**	1949-1952	4	52/63 cm
139	**6853**	1953-1958	4	
995	**3853,30**	1959-1962	3-4	
139	**6865**	1951-1951	4	64/78 cm

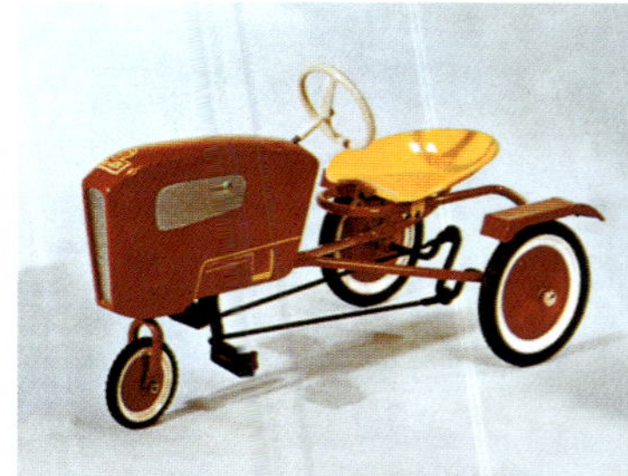

Selbstfahr-Traktor - *Self-Driven Tractor*

Stahlrohrrahmen, Gummipedale & -reifen - *tubular steel frame, rubber pedals, rubber tires*

SERIE	ART.-NO	PERIOD	PR.	INFO
139	**3980**	1953-1958	5	
995	**3880,30**	1959-1959	5	
995	**3980,30**	1960-1961	5	

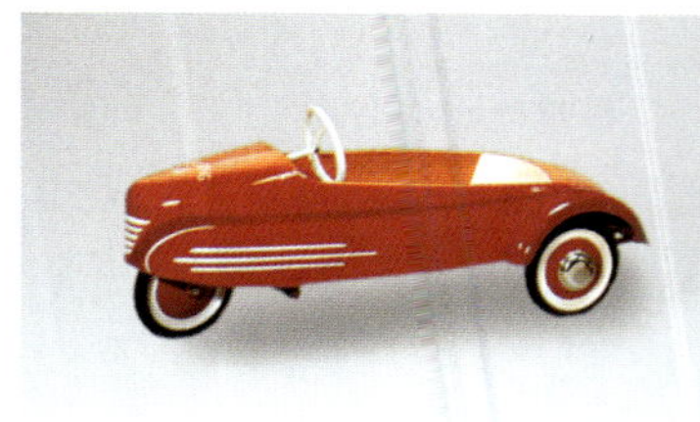

Touring Car I

Dreirad-Auto, Blechkoerper, Scheibenraeder mit Gummireifen 20 cm, Zahnsegmentlenkung, Nadellager, verstellbare Pedale - *three-wheel car, metal vehicle body, 20 cm disc wheels with rubber tires, gear type segment steering, needle bearing, adjustable pedals*

SERIE	ART.-NO	PERIOD	PR.	INFO
140	**3940**	1954-1958	5-6	100/45 cm
997	**3940,38**	1959-1959	5-6	

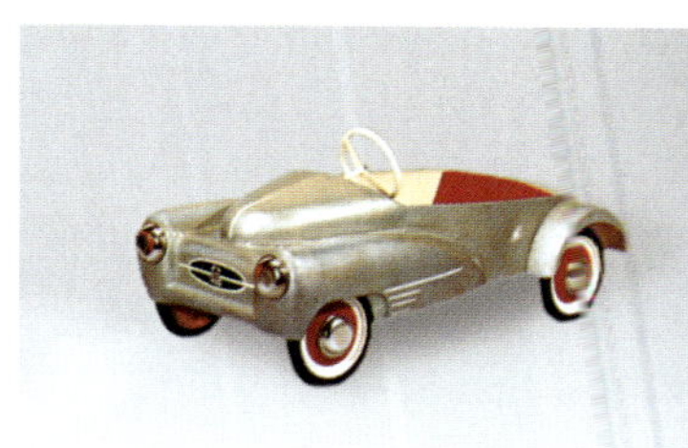

Touring Car II

Vierrad-Auto, Blechkoerper, Scheibenraeder mit Gummireifen 20 cm, Zahnsegmentlenkung, Nadellager, verstellbare Pedale - *four-wheel car, metal vehicle body, 20 cm disc wheels with rubber tires, gear type segment steering, needle bearing, adjustable pedals*

SERIE	ART.-NO	PERIOD	PR.	INFO
140	**4945**	1955-1958	5-6	109/45 cm
997	**4945,38**	1959-1959	5-6	

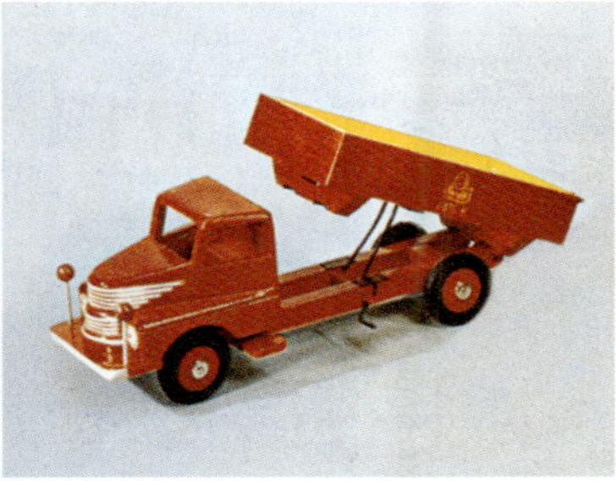

Kipplaster - *Dump Truck*

Holz, Gummireifen, mit Kippmechanik - *wood, rubber tires, with tipping mechanism*

SERIE	ART.-NO	PERIOD	PR.	INFO
129	**4816** K	1953-1957	5	45 cm

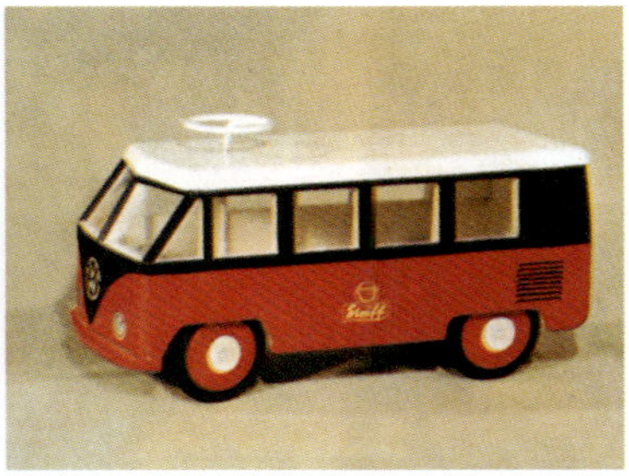

Lenk-Bus - *Steerable Mini-Van*

Hartholz, Gummireifen, Cellon Scheiben - *hardwood, rubber tires, cellon disc brakes*

SERIE	ART.-NO	PERIOD	PR.	INFO
129	**4823** B	1953-1954	5	60 cm

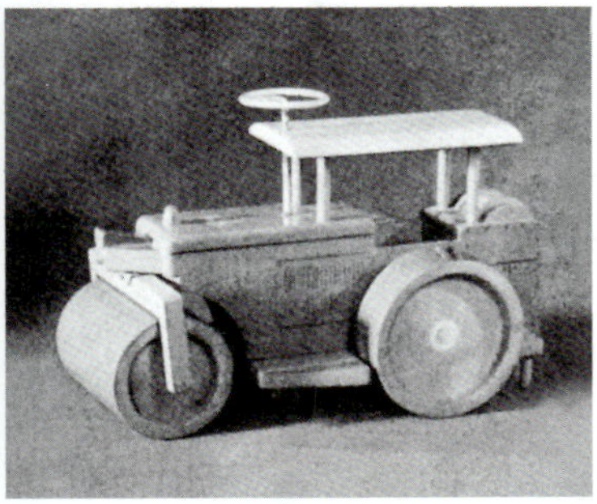

Lenk-Walze - *Steerable Roller*

Holz, gruen/rot/gelb lackiert - *wood, painted green/red/yellow*

SERIE	ART.-NO	PERIOD	PR.	INFO
129	**4834** W	1953-1953	5	60 cm

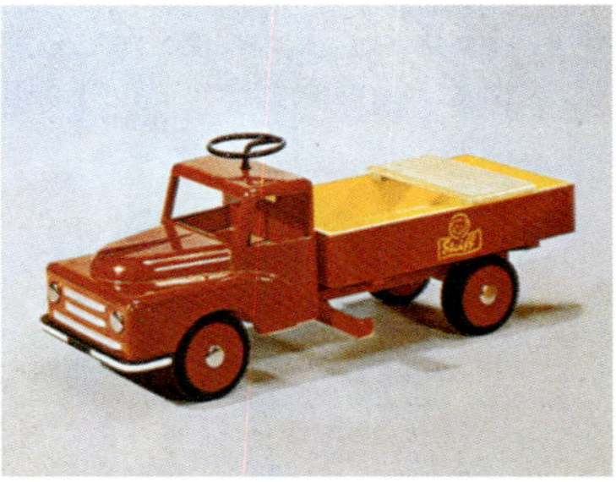

Lenk-Laster - *Steerable Truck*

Holz, Gummireifen, Fussrasten, Steuerrad - *wood, rubber tires, foot rests, steering wheel*

SERIE	ART.-NO	PERIOD	PR.	INFO
129	**4835** L	1953-1958	5	75 cm
978	**4835,20**	1959-1963	5	

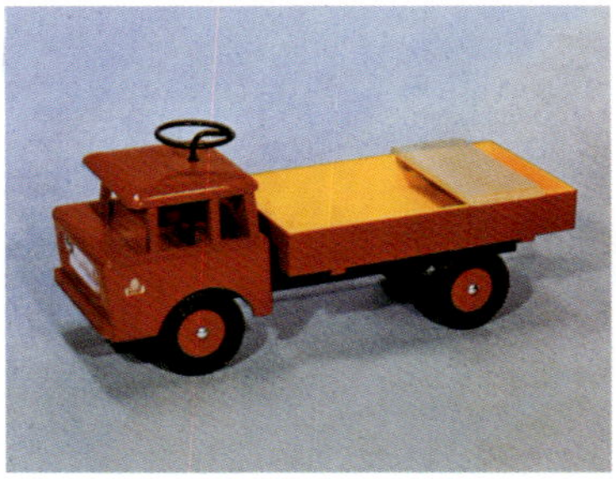

Lenk-Laster - *Steerable Truck*

Holz, Gummireifen, Fussrasten, Steuerrad - *wood, rubber tires, foot rests, steering wheel*

SERIE	ART.-NO	PERIOD	PR.	INFO
978	**4870,20**	1964-1964	5	75 cm
851	**4870,20**	1965-1967	5	
	8510/70	1968-1970	5	

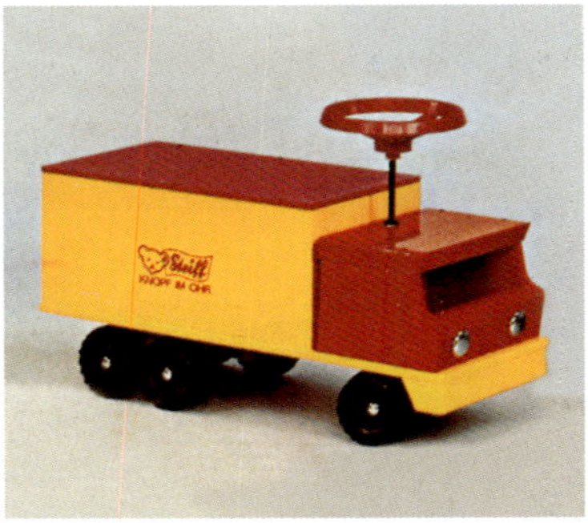

Lenklaster "Kasten" - *Steerable Box Truck*

Holz, lenkbar, zum Draufsitzen - *wood, steerable, to sit on & drive*

SERIE	ART.-NO	PERIOD	PR.	INFO
	8510/30	1971-1980	3-4	55 cm

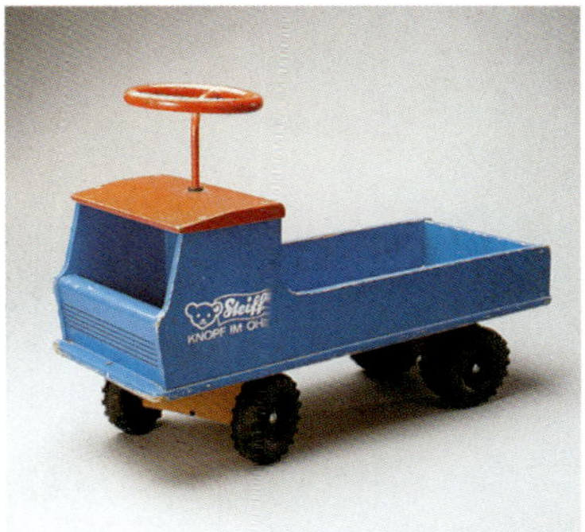

Lenklaster "offen" - *Steerable Open Pick Up Truck*

Holz, lenkbar, zum Draufsitzen - *wood, steerable, to sit on & drive*

SERIE	ART.-NO	PERIOD	PR.	INFO
	8511/30	1971-1977	3-4	55 cm

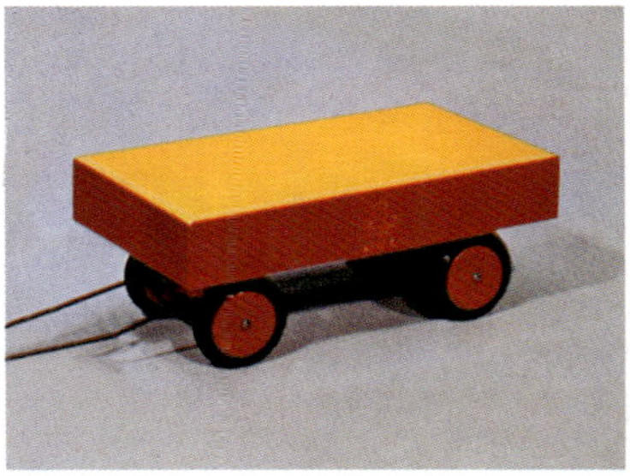

Anhaenger - *Trailer*

Hartholz, Gummireifen, lenkbar - *hardwood, rubber tires, steerable*

SERIE	ART.-NO	PERIOD	PR.	INFO
129	**4810** A	1953-1958	3-4	25 cm
978	**4810,10**	1959-1964	3-4	
870	**4810,10**	1965-1966	3-4	

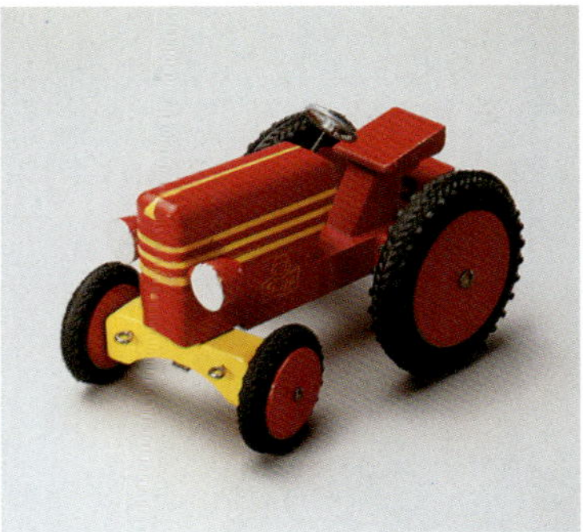

Traktor - *Tractor*

Holz, Gummireifen, mit Lenkrad-Steuerung - *wood, rubber tires, with steering wheel*

SERIE	ART.-NO	PERIOD	PR.	INFO
129	**4811** T	1953-1958	4	20 cm
978	**4811,10**	1959-1964	4	
870	**4811,10**	1965-1966	4	

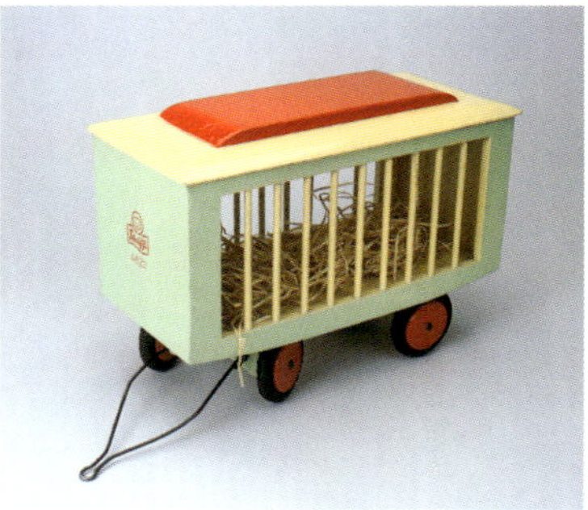

Kaefigwagen - *Animal Cage Wagon*

Holz, Gummireifen, Dach abnehmbar - *wood, rubber tires, roof is removable*

SERIE	ART.-NO	PERIOD	PR.	INFO
129	**4820**	1955-1958	4	28 cm
978	**4820,10**	1959-1964	4	

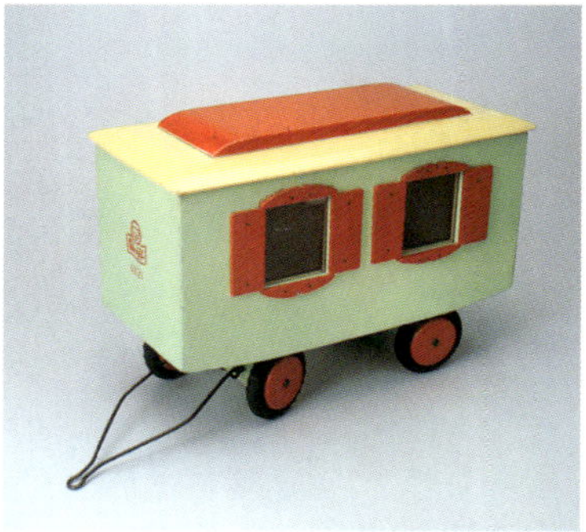

Wohnwagen - *Caravan*

Holz, Gummireifen, Dach abnehmbar - *wood, rubber tires, roof is removable*

SERIE	ART.-NO	PERIOD	PR.	INFO
129	**4821**	1955-1958	4	28 cm
978	**4821,10**	1959-1964	4	

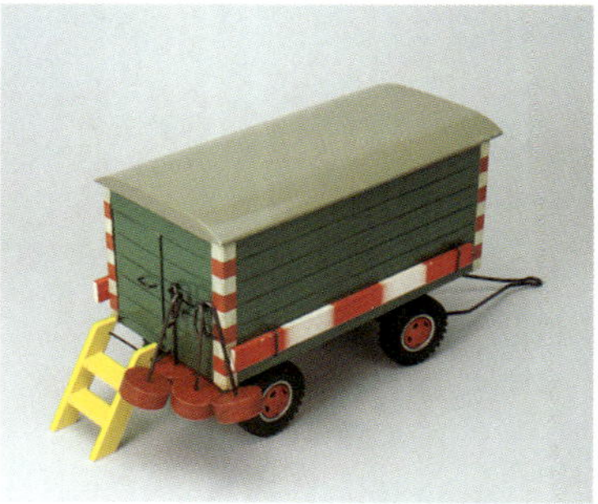

Bauwagen (1:20) - *Construction Trailer (1:20)*

Holz, Dach abnehmbar, Absperrschranken, Treppe, Tuer, lenkbar - *wood, roof is removable, barrier, stairs, door, steerable*

SERIE	ART.-NO	PERIOD	PR.	INFO
978	**4815,10**	1959-1964	4	20cm
880	**4815,10**	1965-1967	4	
	8825/15	1968-1978	3-4	

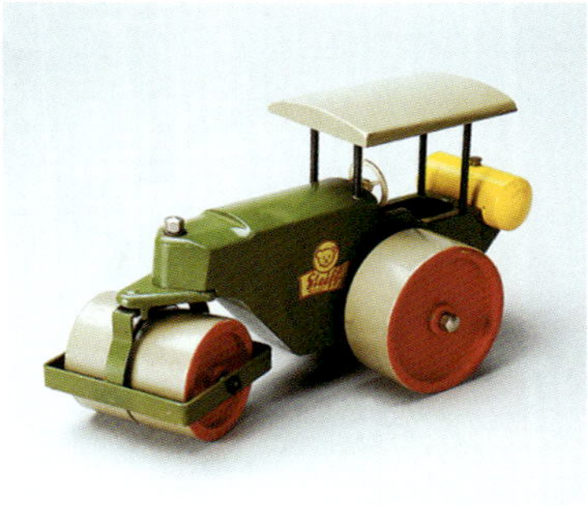

Strassenwalze - *Road Roller*

Holz, Schiebelenkung - *wood, push type steering*

SERIE	ART.-NO	PERIOD	PR.	INFO
978	**4814,10**	1959-1963	5	22cm

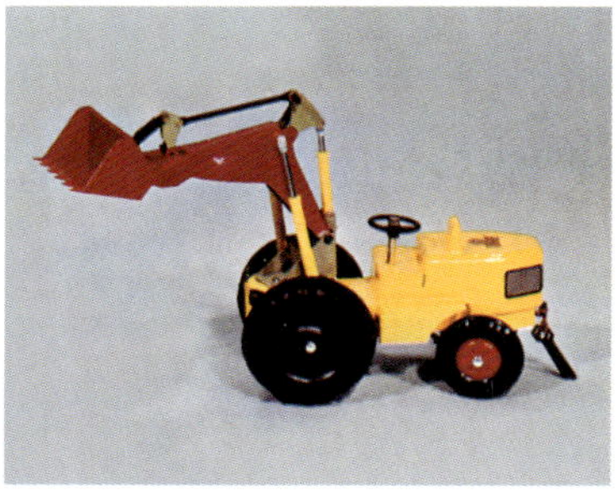

Schaufelbagger (1:20) - *Shovel Digger (1:20)*

Holz/Blech/Plastik, lenkbar - *wood/metal/plastic, steerable*

SERIE	ART.-NO	PERIOD	PR.	INFO
978	**4829,10**	1961-1964	4	40 cm
870	**4829,10**	1965-1967	4	
	8740/29	1968-1970	4	

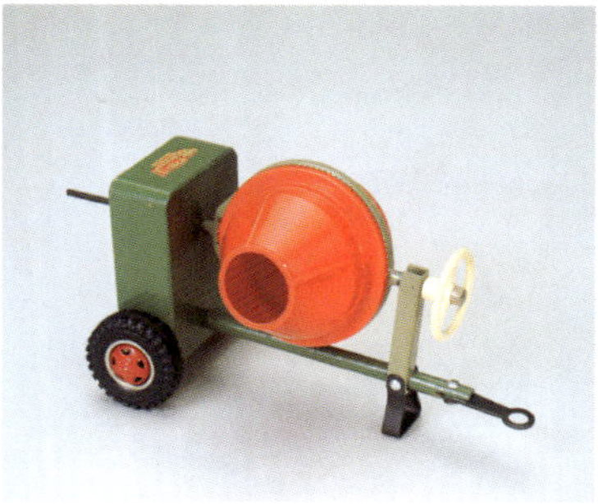

Beton-Mischer (1:20) - *Concrete Mixer (1:20)*

Holz, Plastiktrommel, Anhaengebuegel - *wood, plastic drum, tow bar*

SERIE	ART.-NO	PERIOD	PR.	INFO
978	**2812,10**	1961-1964	4	24 cm
870	**2812,10**	1965-1967	4	
	8710/12	1968-1980	3	

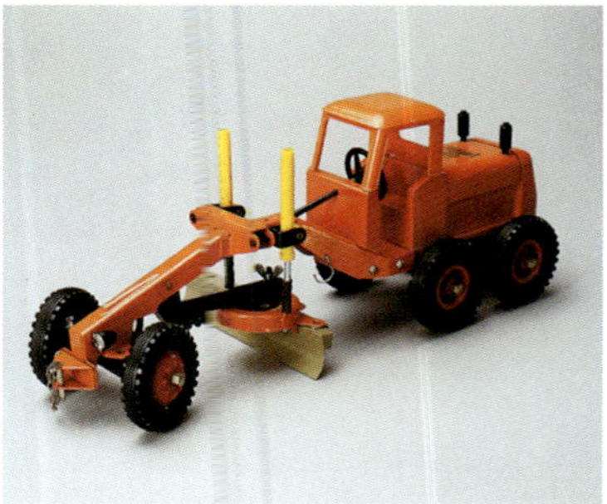

Grader (1:20)

Holz, Metall, Plastikdach, verstellbar - *wood, metal, plastic roof, adjustable*

SERIE	ART.-NO	PERIOD	PR.	INFO
978	**6816,0**	1962-1964	5	36cm
870	**6816,10**	1965-1966	5	

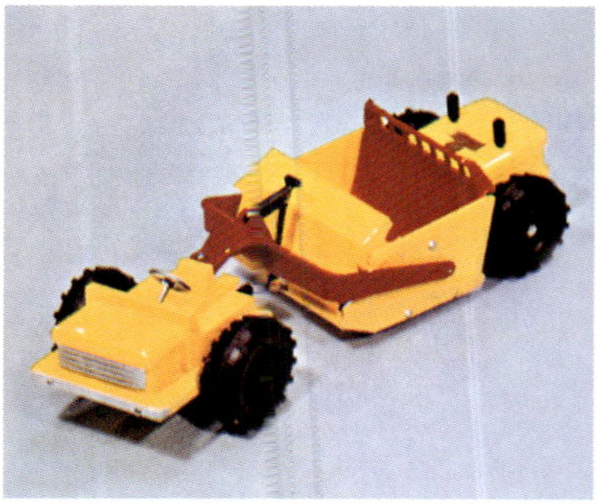

Schuerfer (1:20) - *Scraper (1:20)*

Metall, Holz, Plastik, lenkbar, Be- & Entladen mit Fingerdruck - *metal, wood, plastic, steerable, loading & unloading activated by pushing with your finger*

SERIE	ART.-NO	PERIOD	PR.	INFO
978	**4935,10**	1963-1964	4-5	35 cm
870	**4935,10**	1965-1966	4-5	

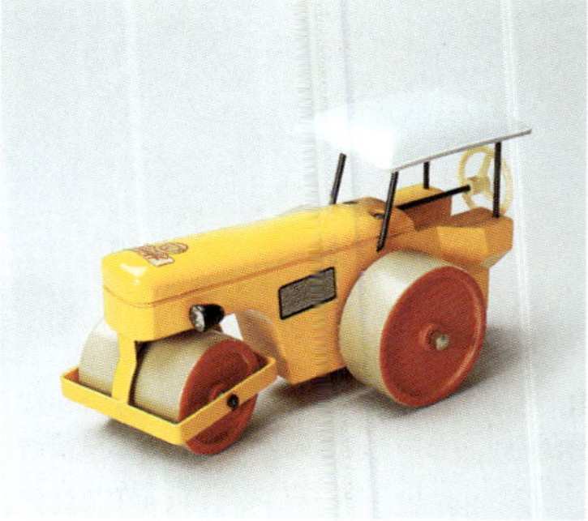

Strassenwalze (1:20) - *Road Roller (1:20)*

Holz, Plastikdach, lenkbar - *wood, plastic roof, steerable*

SERIE	ART.-NO	PERIOD	PR.	INFO
978	**3813,10**	1964-196[illegible]	3	22 cm
880	**3813,10**	1965-196[illegible]	3	
	8815/13	1968-197[illegible]	3	

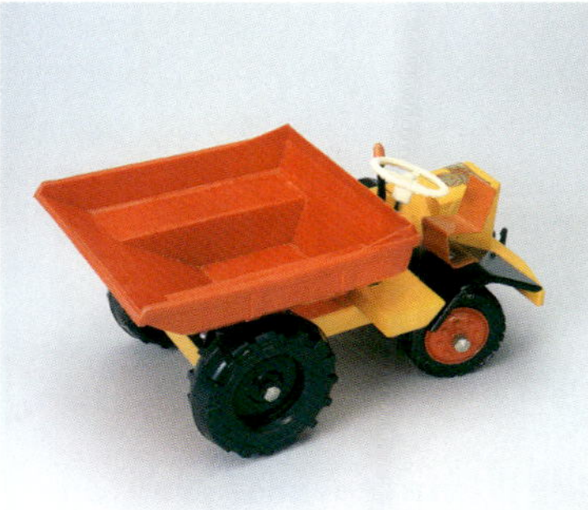

Auto-Schuetter (1:20) - *Dumper (1:20)*

Holz, Plastikwanne, Metall, lenkbar - *wood, plastic trough, metal, steerable*

SERIE	ART.-NO	PERIOD	PR.	INFO
880	**4822,10**	1965-1967	3	22 cm
	8830/22	1968-1970	3	

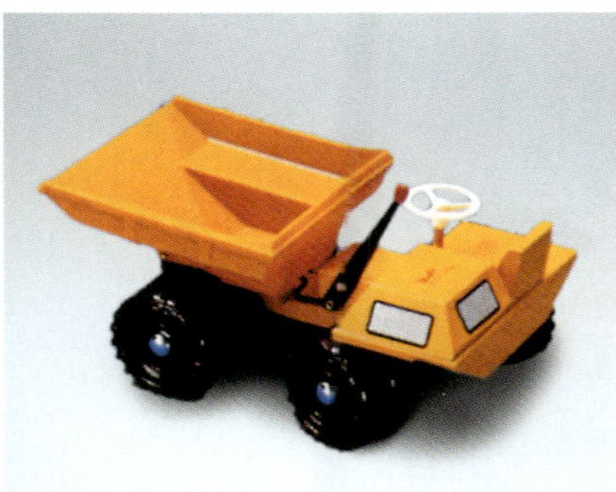

Autoschuetter - *Dumper*

Plastik, lenkbar - *plastic, steerable*

SERIE	ART.-NO	PERIOD	PR.	INFO
	8830/23	1971-1980	3	23 cm

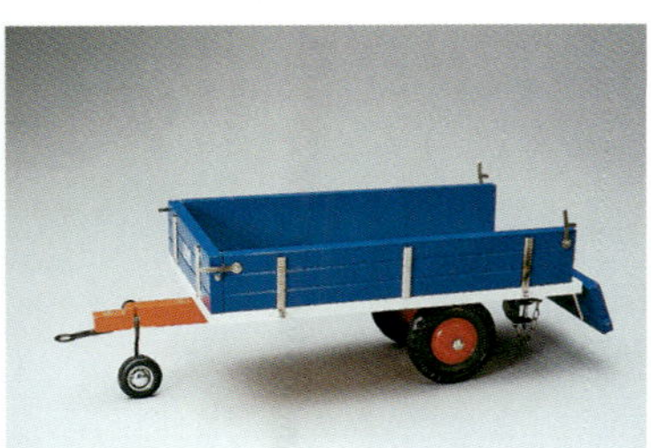

Allzweckwagen (1:20) - *All Purpose Trailer (1:20)*

Holz, Blech, Plastikreifen, Stuetzrad und Fallen klappbar - *wood, metal, plastic tires, supporting wheel & drop are collapsible*

SERIE	ART.-NO	PERIOD	PR.	INFO
880	**3914,10**	1966-1967	3	35cm
	8820/14	1968-1974	3	

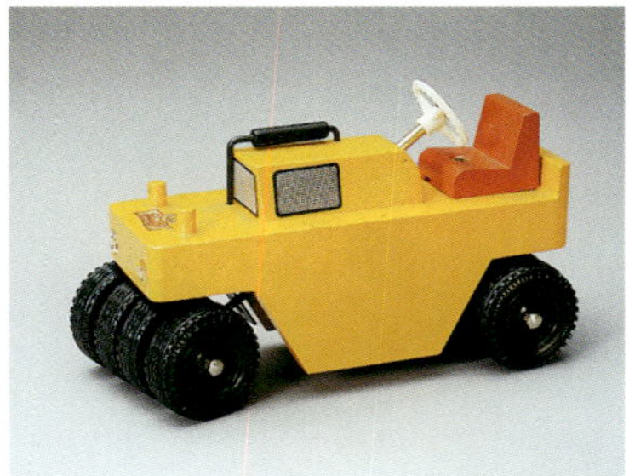

Gummiwalze - *Road Roller with Rubber Wheels*

Holz, Plastikreifen, lenkbar, 8 fach bereift - *wood, plastic tires, steerable, with 8 wheels*

SERIE	ART.-NO	PERIOD	PR.	INFO
870	**8822,10**	1967-1967	3	22 cm
	8770/22	1968-1970	3	

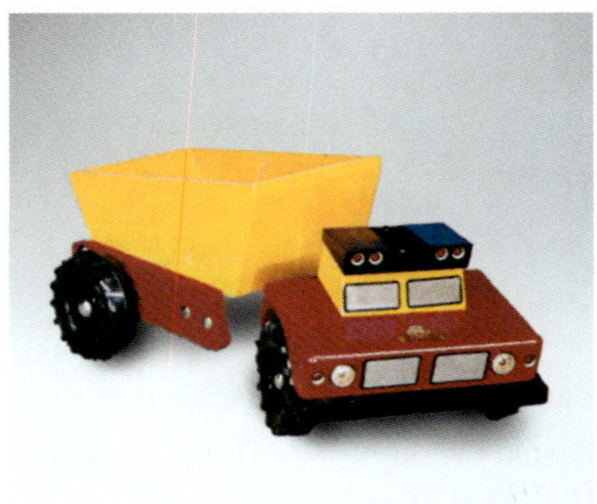

Sattelkipper - *Dump Semi-Trailer*

Holz, Plastikreifen, robustes Sandspielzeug, lenkbar, Mulde kippbar - *wood, plastic tires, very robust toy for playing in the sand, steerable, the skip can be tipped*

SERIE	ART.-NO	PERIOD	PR.	INFO
870	**4832,10**	1967-1967	3	32 cm
	8750/32	1968-1974	3	

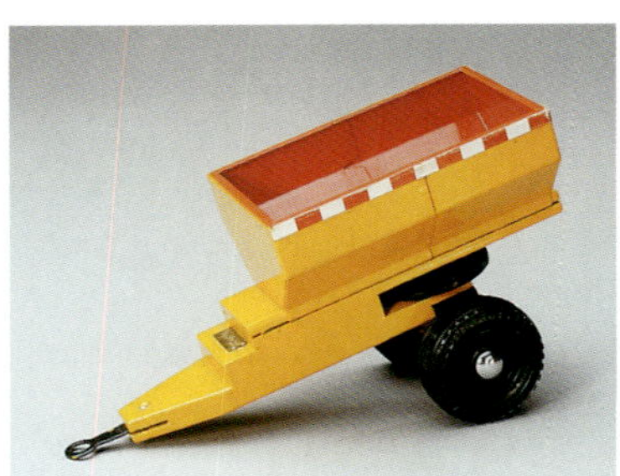

Streuwagen - *Gritting Trailer*

Hartholz, Blechwanne, PVC Reifen - *hardwood, metal trough, PVC tires*

SERIE	ART.-NO	PERIOD	PR.	INFO
	8808/12	1969-1974	3	22 cm

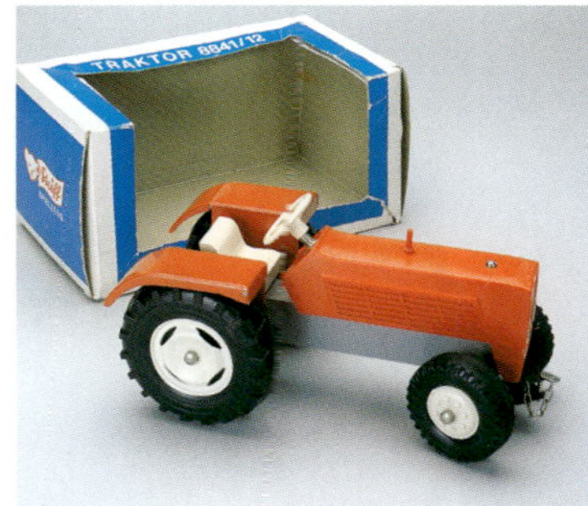

Traktor - *Tractor*

Holz, Metall, Bereifung PVC - *wood, metal, PVC tires*

SERIE	ART.-NO	PERIOD	PR.	INFO
	8841/12	1970-1978	4	24cm

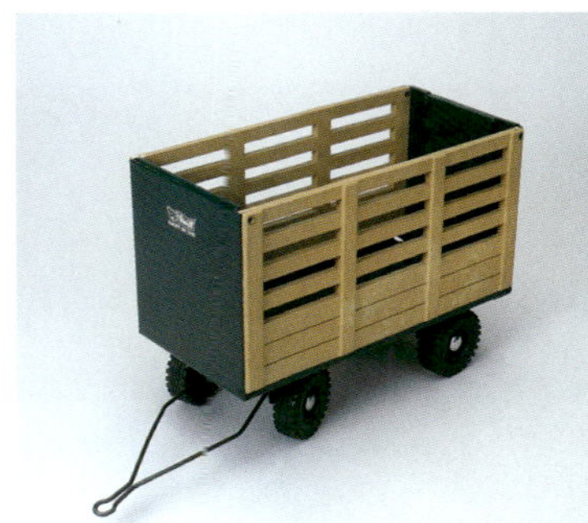

Tiertransporter - *Animal Trailer*

Metallaufbau, Kunststoffgitter, PVC Reifen, Heckklappe zum oeffnen, lenkbar - *metal structure, synthetic lattice-work, PVC tires, rear door can be opened, steerable*

SERIE	ART.-NO	PERIOD	PR.	INFO
	8827/20	1971-1978	3	20 cm

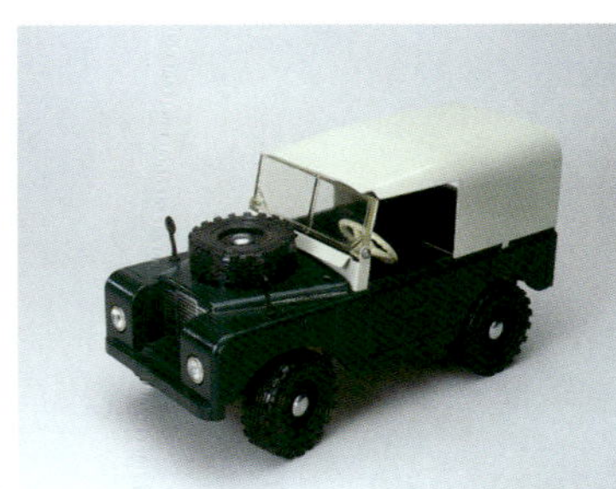

Safari-Wagen - *Safari Vehicle*

Kunststoffunterbau, PVC Reifen, gruen, hellbeige, ab 1977 beige, Dach abnehmbar, lenkbar, Frontscheibe klappbar - *synthetic sub-structure, PVC tires, green & light beige, from 1977 beige, roof is removable, steerable, front window is hinged*

SERIE	ART.-NO	PERIOD	PR.	INFO
	8857/25	1971-1978	3	25 cm

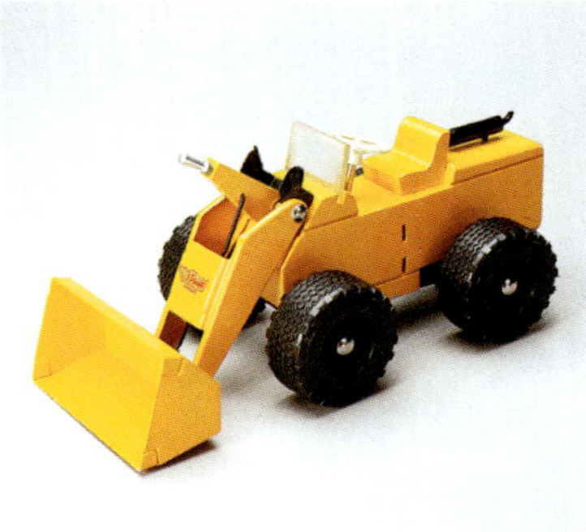

Schaufellader - *Front End Loader*

Kunststoffkoerper, Schaufel & Mechanik Metall, lenkbar - *plastic body, shovel & mechanisms are metal, steerable*

SERIE	ART.-NO	PERIOD	PR.	INFO
	8745/30	1971-1973	3-4	31 cm

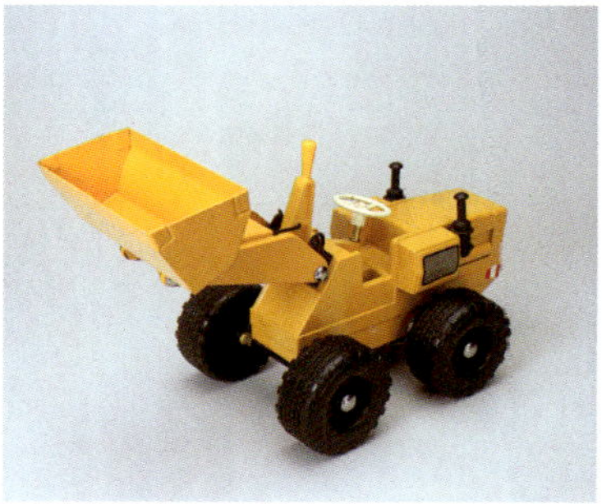

Radlader - *Wheel Loader*

Holz, Plastik - *wood, plastic*

SERIE	ART.-NO	PERIOD	PR.	INFO
	8746/30	1974-1978	3-4	31 cm

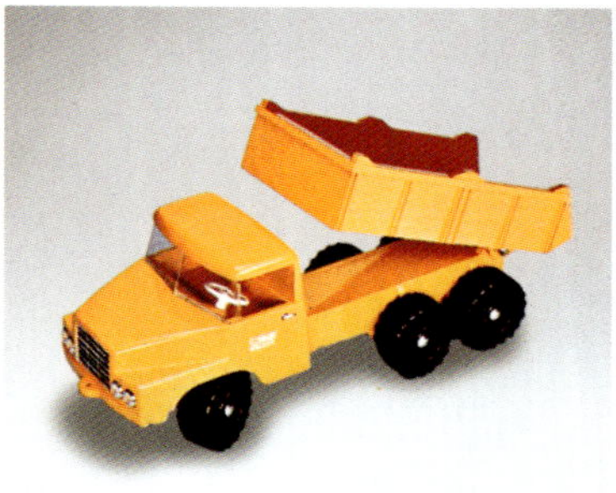

Lastwagen - *Truck*

Plastikreifen (6 fach), Ladeflaeche zum Kippen - *plastic tires (6), loading surface can be tipped*

SERIE	ART.-NO	PERIOD	PR.	INFO
	8858/45	1973-1981	4	45 cm

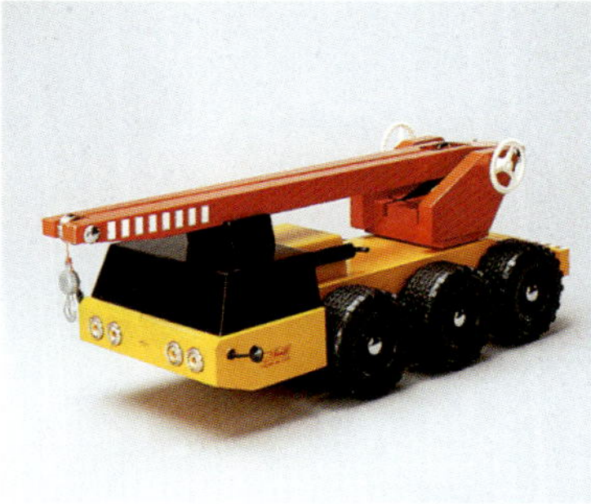

Schwerlastkran - *Heavy Duty Crane*

Holz, Plastikreifen - *wood, plastic tires*

SERIE	ART.-NO	PERIOD	PR.	INFO
	8817/14	1975-1981	4	41 cm

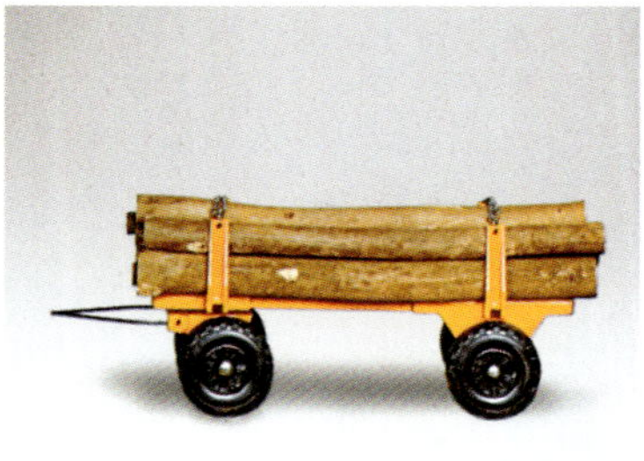

Langholzwagen - *Long Timber Trailer*

Plastik, PVC Raeder, mit Ladung - *plastic, PVC wheels, complete with load*

SERIE	ART.-NO	PERIOD	PR.	INFO
	8848/15	1975-1978	3	34 cm

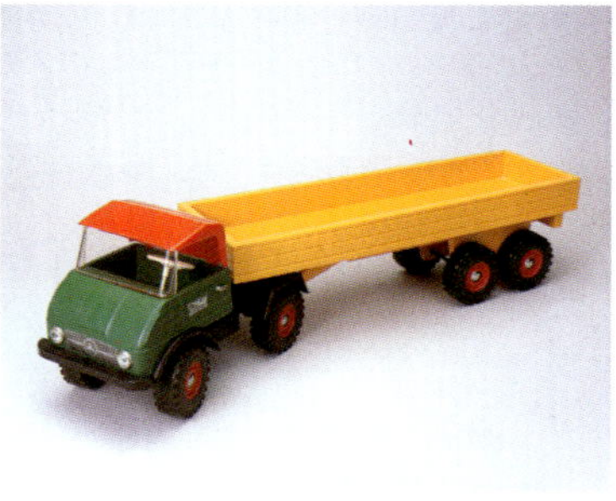

Unimog-Sattel-Aufleger - *Unimog Semi-Trailer*

Holz, Plastikreifen - *wood, plastic tires*

SERIE	ART.-NO	PERIOD	PR.	INFO
	8851/16	1975-1981	3	57 cm

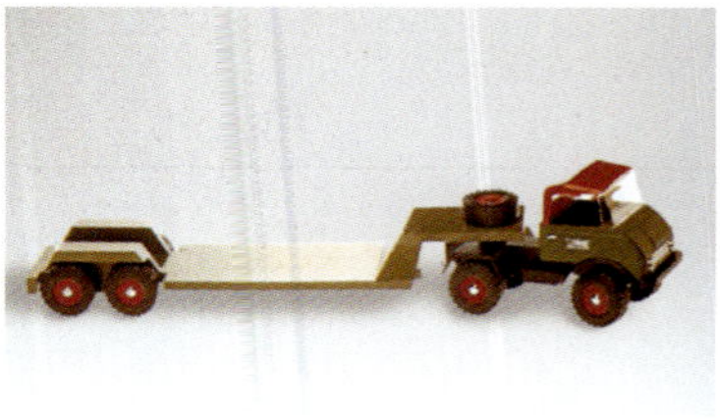

Unimog-Tieflader - *Unimog Low-Boy Trailer*

Holz, Plastikreifen - *wood, plastic tires*

SERIE	ART.-NO	PERIOD	PR.	INFO
	8852/16	1975-1981	3	69 cm

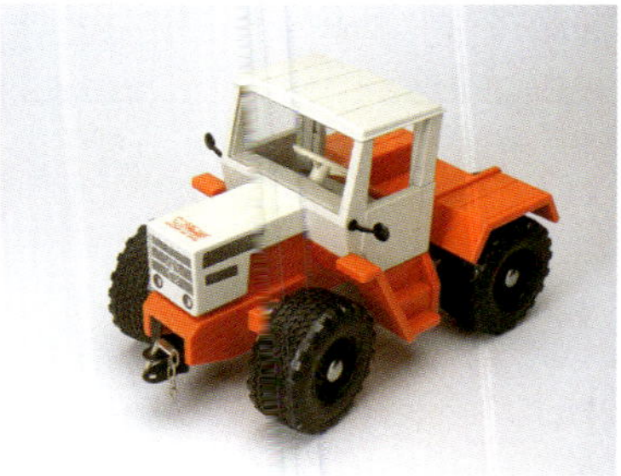

TRAC Schlepper - *TRAC Tractor*

Plastik, PVC-Reifen - *plastic, PVC tires*

SERIE	ART.-NO	PERIOD	PR.	INFO
	8842/16	197[illegible]-1978	3	26 cm

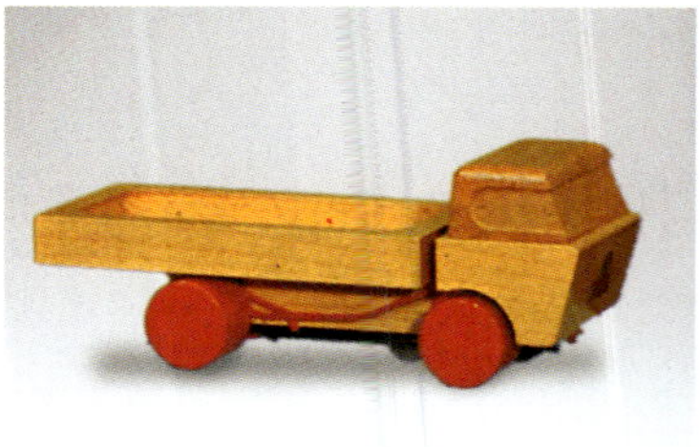

Lastwagen - *Truck*

Hartholz, naturlackiert - *hardwood, naturally stained*

SERIE	ART.-NO	PERIOD	PR.	INFO
	8700/08	1968-19[illegible]9	2	20 cm
	8700/10	1968-19[illegible]9	2	26 cm

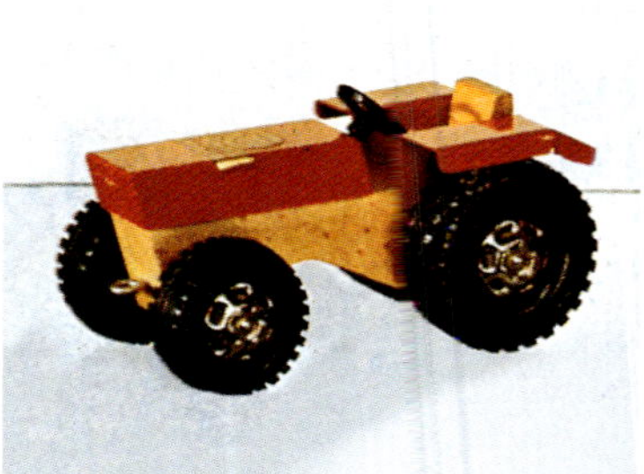

Traktor - *Tractor*

Holz, Metall, Plastikreifen - *wood, metal, plastic tires*

Serie	Art.-No	Period	Pr.	Info
	8840/05	1968-1970	2	11 cm

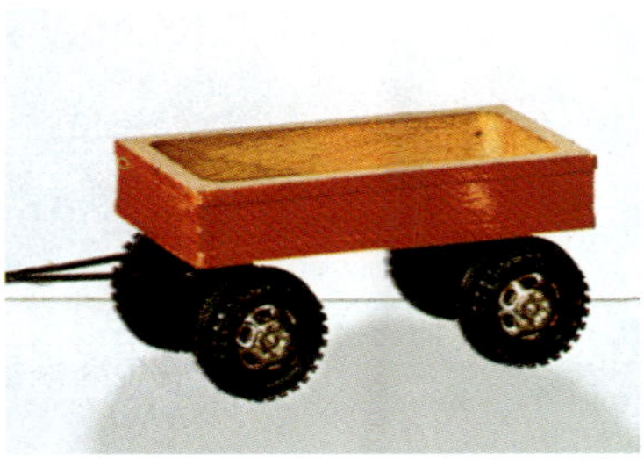

Anhaenger - *Trailer*

Holz, Metall, PVC Reifen, lenkbar - *wood, metal, PVC tires, steerable*

Serie	Art.-No	Period	Pr.	Info
	8845/06	1968-1970	2	12 cm

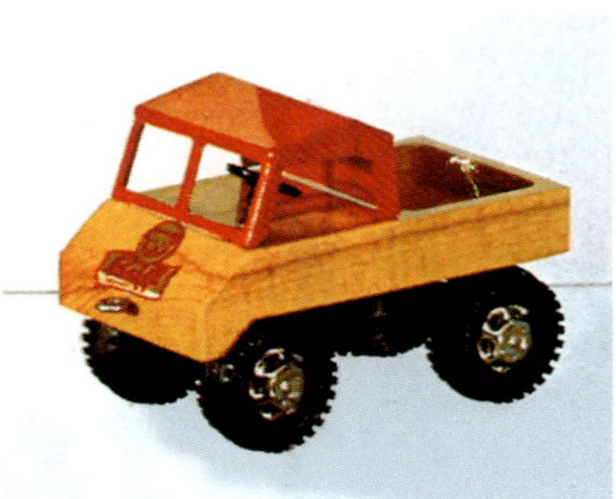

Unimog

Holz, Metall, PVC Bereifung - *wood, metal, PVC tires*

Serie	Art.-No	Period	Pr.	Info
	8855/07	1968-1970	2-3	13 cm

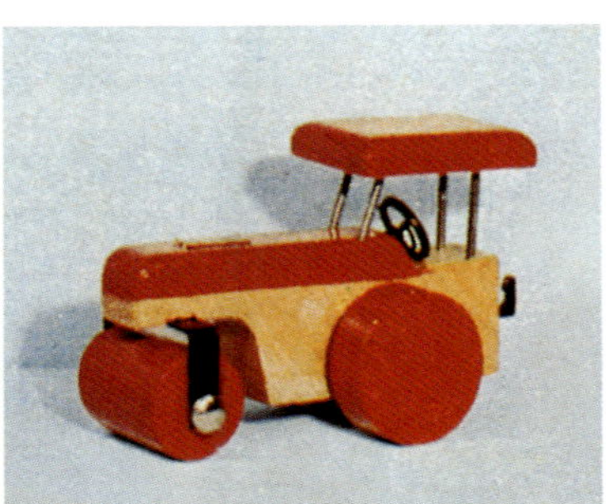

Strassenwalze - *Road Roller*

Holz, mit Anhaengehaken - *wood, with tow hook*

Serie	Art.-No	Period	Pr.	Info
	8815/09	1969-1970	2	14 cm

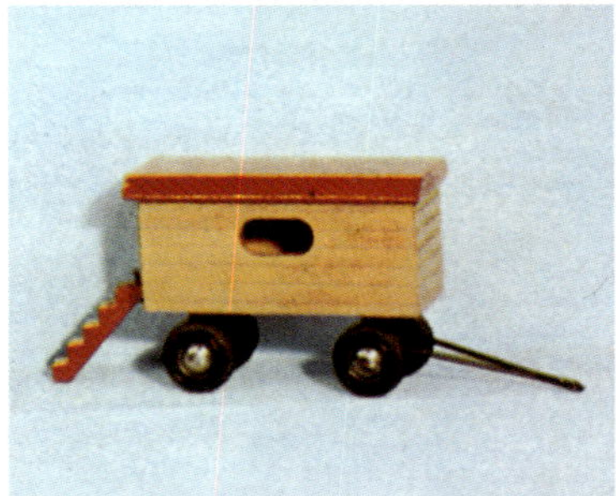

Bauwagen - *Construction Trailer*

Holz, Dach abnehmbar, Treppe, lenkbar - *wood, roof is removable, steps, steerable*

Serie	Art.-No	Period	Pr.	Info
	8825/08	1969-1970	2	16 cm

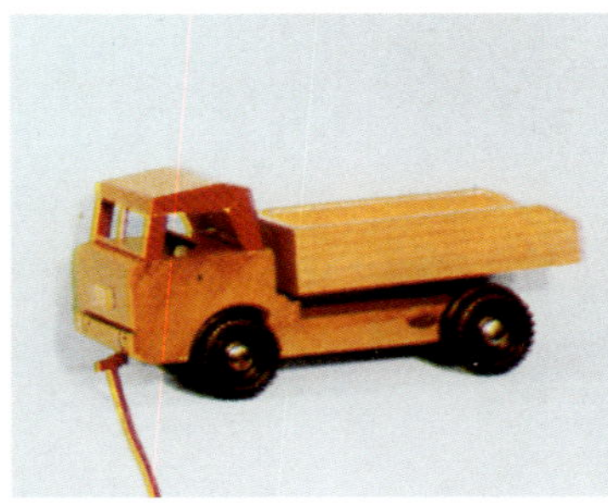

Lastwagen - *Truck*

Holz, 4 fach bereift, Ladeflaeche kippbar - *wood, 4 tires, loading surface can be tipped*

Serie	Art.-No	Period	Pr.	Info
	8858/09	1969-1970	2	18 cm

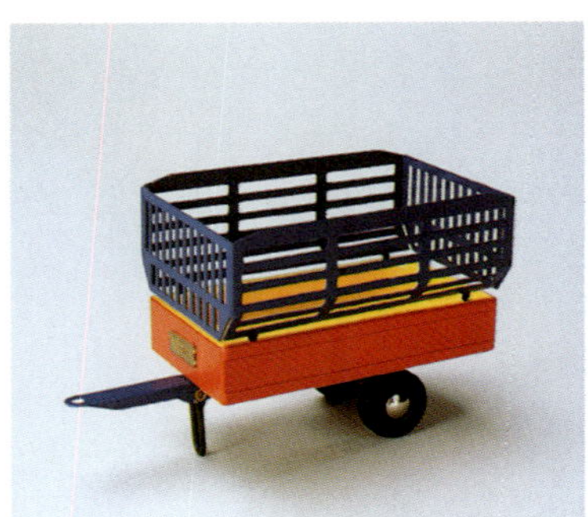

Allzweckwagen / Ladegitter - *Multi-Purpose Trailer / Load Grid*

Holz, Plastikreifen, zum Anhaengen an Unimog & Traktor, Stuetze klappbar, rot, ab 1971 innen gelb lackiert - Ladegitter, 11 cm, Metall, blau lackiert, zum Aufstecken - *wood, plastic tires, for appending to Unimog & Tractor, support is collapsible, red, from 1971 painted yellow on the inside - loading grid, 11 cm, metal, painted blue, can be removed or snapped into place*

Serie	Art.-No	Period	Pr.	Info
	8820/06	1970-1970	2	16 cm
	8920/06	1971-1976	1	
	8890/12	1970-1973	1	11 cm

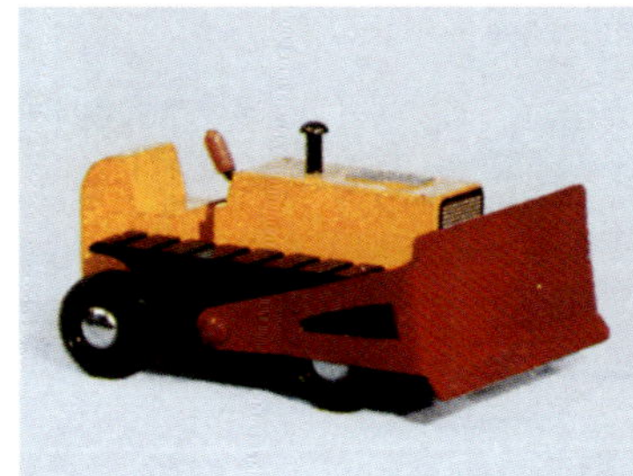

Planierraupe - *Bulldozer*

Holz, mit bewegl. Planierschild - *wood, with movable skimmer*

Serie	Art.-No	Period	Pr.	Info
	8828/06	1970-1970	2	12 cm

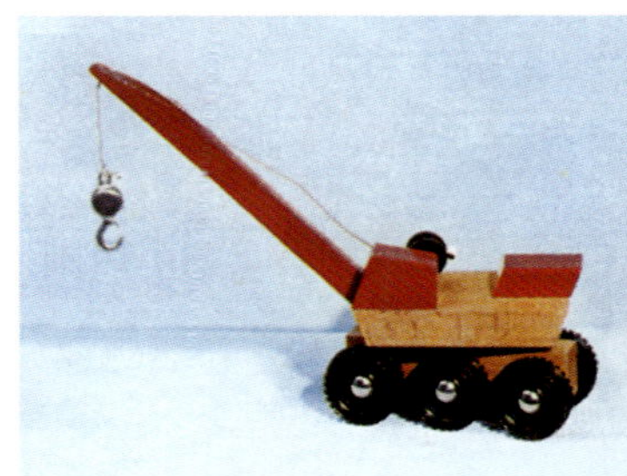

Mobilkran - *Mobile Crane*

Holz, Plastikreifen (6 fach) - *wood, 6 plastic tires*

Serie	Art.-No	Period	Pr.	Info
	8875/08	1970-1970	2	20 cm

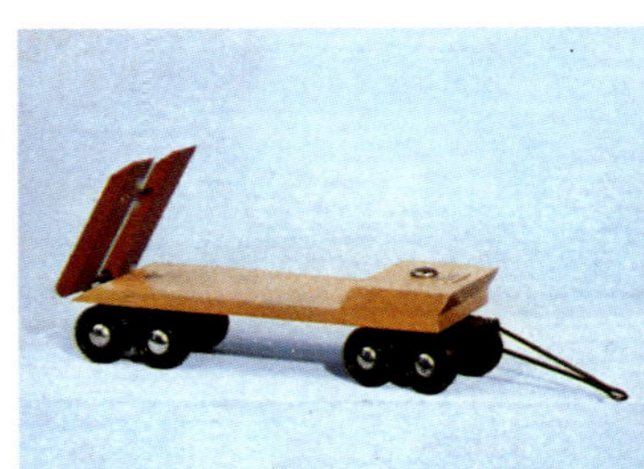

Tieflader - *Low Boy Trailer*

Holz, Plastikreifen (8 fach) - *wood, 8 plastic tires*

Serie	Art.-No	Period	Pr.	Info
	8885/08	1970-1970	2-3	31 cm

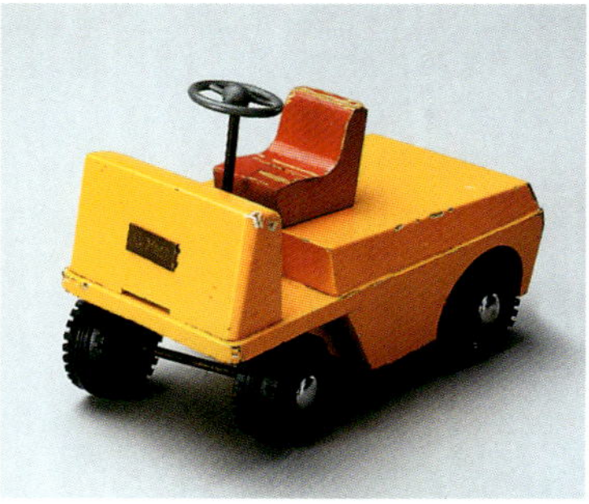

Ameise - *Towing Vehicle*

Holz, lenkbar, Zugfahrzeug - *wood, steerable, towing vehicle*

SERIE	ART.-NO	PERIOD	PR.	INFO
	8705/15	1971-1974	2-3	13 cm

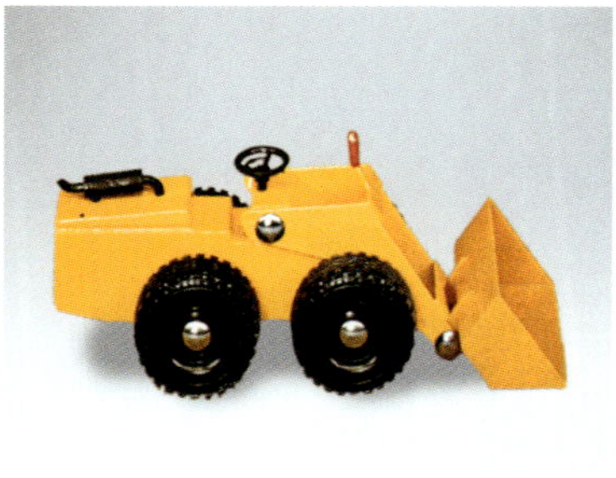

Schaufellader - *Front End Loader*

Holz, Metall, PVC Bereifung - *wood, metal, PVC tires*

SERIE	ART.-NO	PERIOD	PR.	INFO
	8905/08	1971-1977	3	19 cm

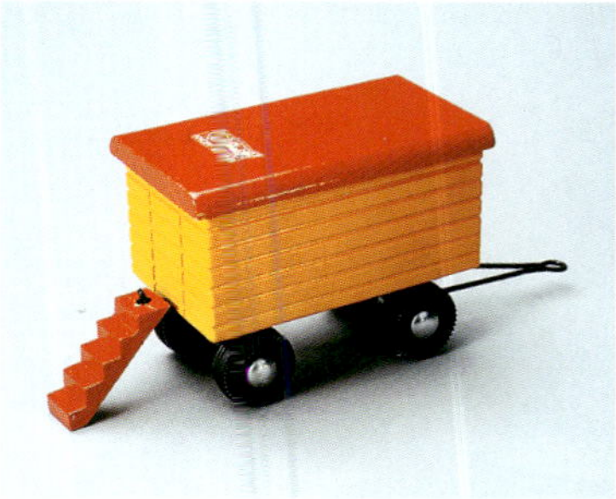

Bauwagen - *Construction Trailer*

Holz, Dach abnehmbar, mit Treppe - *wood, roof is removable, with steps*

SERIE	ART.-NO	PERIOD	PR.	INFO
	8925/08	1971-1980	2	13 cm

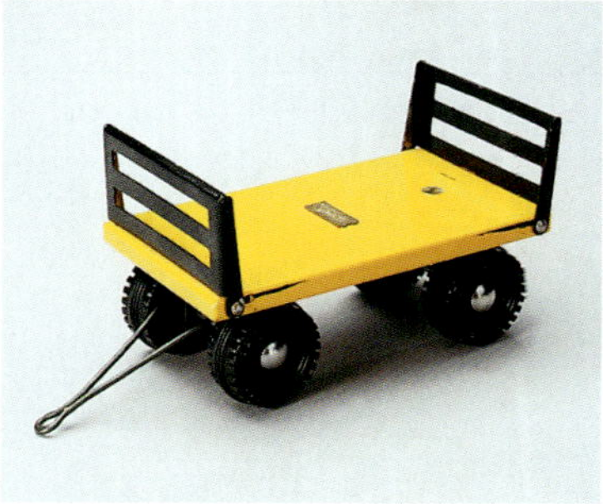

Anhaenger - *Trailer*

Holz, passend zu Ameise 8705/15 - *wood, fits the towing vehicle no. 8705/15*

SERIE	ART.-NO	PERIOD	PR.	INFO
	8705/16	1971-1974	2	13 cm

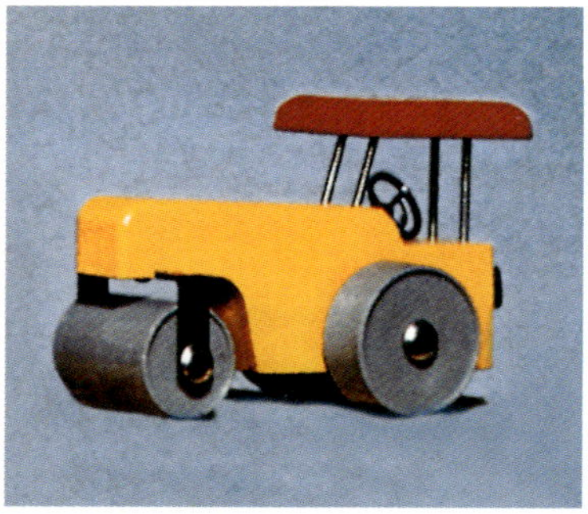

Strassenwalze - *Road Roller*

Holz, mit Anhaengehaken - *wood, with tow hook*

SERIE	ART.-NO	PERIOD	PR.	INFO
	8915/09	1971-1980	2	14 cm

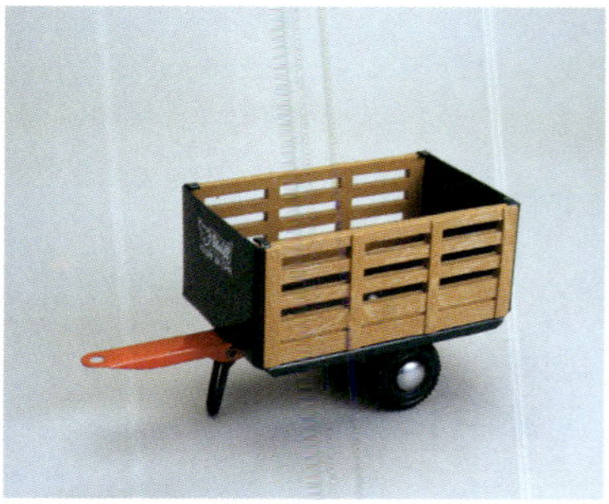

Tiertransporter - *Animal Trailer*

Kunststoff, Metall, PVC Reifen - *synthetic with metal & PVC tires*

SERIE	ART.-NO	PERIOD	PR.	INFO
	8927/07	1971-1977	2	14 cm

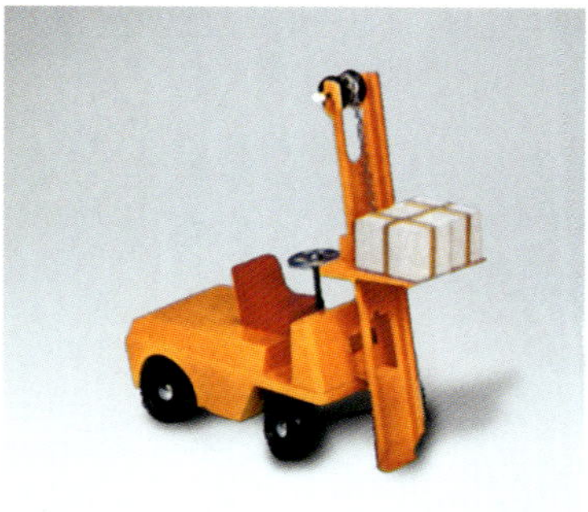

Stapler - *Forklift*

Holz, Zusatzgeraet zu Ameise 8705/15 - *wood, supplementary equipment for towing vehicle no. 8705/15*

SERIE	ART.-NO	PERIOD	PR.	INFO
	8890/18	1971-1974	2	19 cm

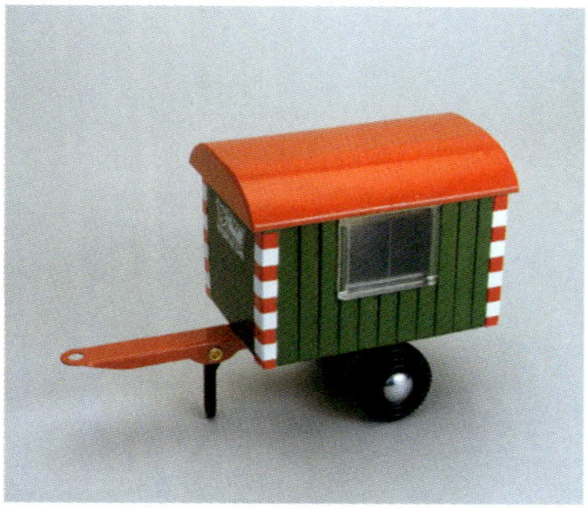

Einachsbauwagen - *Single Axle Construction Trailer*

Holz, gruen/rot, rot/weisse Ecken - *wood, green/red, with red/white striped corners*

SERIE	ART.-NO	PERIOD	PR.	INFO
	8924/09	1971-1978	2	13 cm

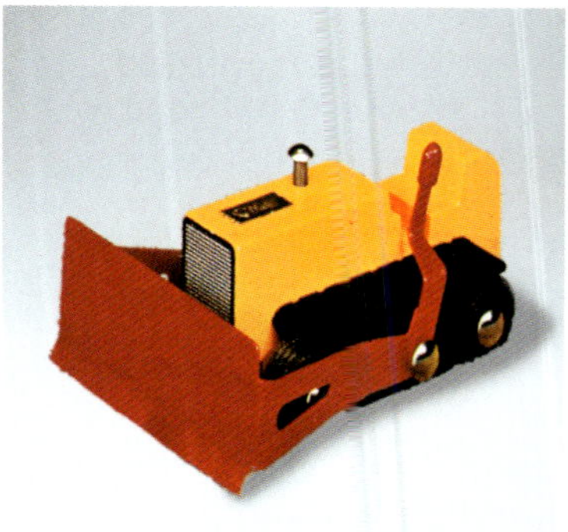

Planierraupe - *Bulldozer*

Holz, bewegl. Planierschild - *wood, with movable skimmer*

SERIE	ART.-NO	PERIOD	PR.	INFO
	8928/06	1971-1977	2	12 cm

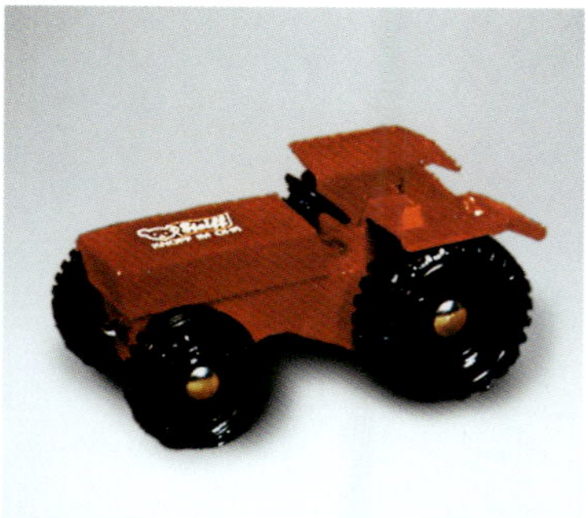

Traktor - *Tractor*

Holz, Metall, PVC Reifen - *wood, metal, PVC tires*

SERIE	ART.-NO	PERIOD	PR.	INFO
	8940/05	1971-1978	2-3	11 cm

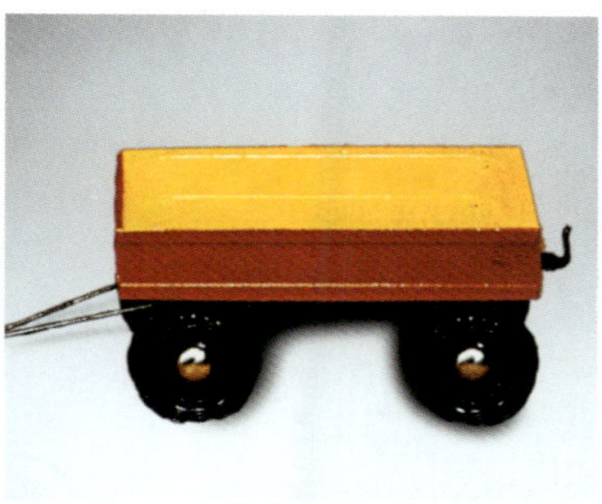

Anhaenger - *Trailer*

Holz, Metall, PVC Reifen - *wood, metal, PVC tires*

SERIE	ART.-NO	PERIOD	PR.	INFO
	8945/06	1971-1978	2	12 cm

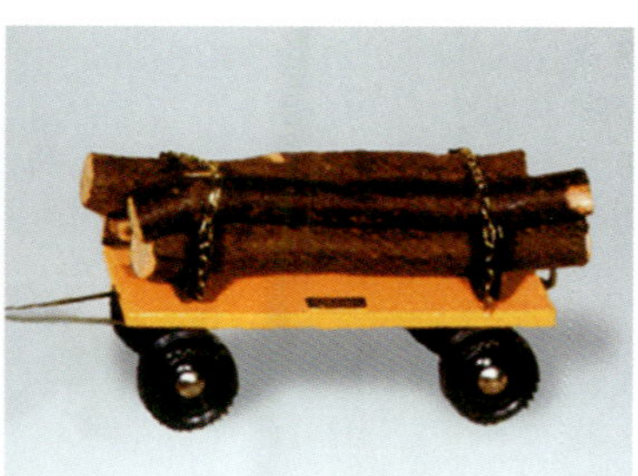

Langholzwagen - *Long Timber Trailer*

Holz, Metall, PVC Reifen, mit Ladung - *wood, metal, PVC tires, complete with load*

SERIE	ART.-NO	PERIOD	PR.	INFO
	8950/08	1971-1975	2	14 cm

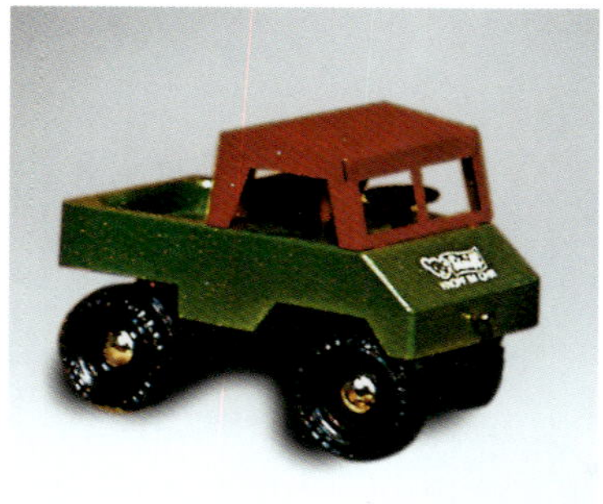

Unimog

Holz, Metall, PVC Reifen - *wood, metal, PVC tires*

SERIE	ART.-NO	PERIOD	PR.	INFO
	8955/07	1971-1978	2	13 cm

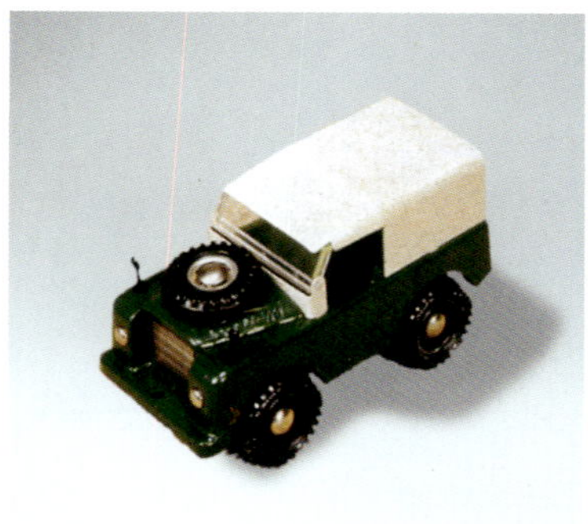

Safari-Wagen - *Safari Vehicle*

Kunststoff, Metall, PVC Reifen - *wood, metal, PVC tires*

SERIE	ART.-NO	PERIOD	PR.	INFO
	8957/08	1971-1977	2	14,5 cm

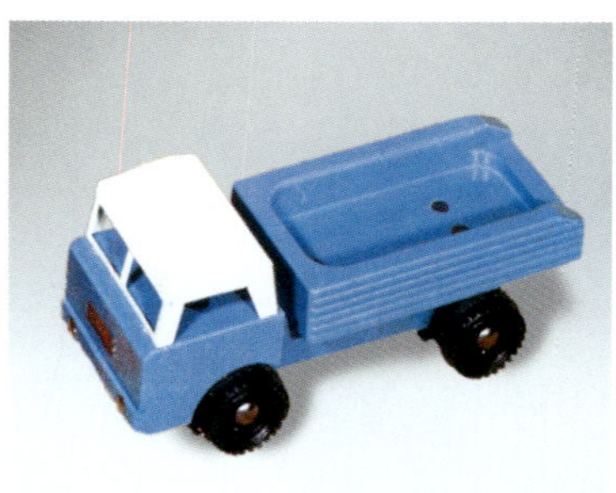

Lastwagen - *Truck*

Holz, Ladeflaeche kippbar, Anhaengevorrichtung - *wood, load surface tips, towing device*

SERIE	ART.-NO	PERIOD	PR.	INFO
	8958/09	1971-1974	2	18 cm

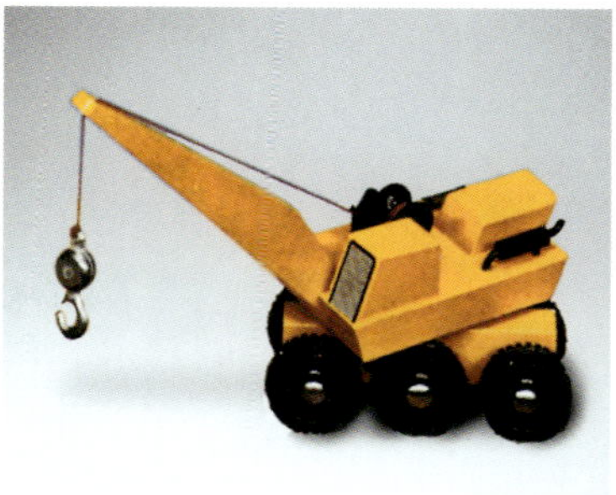

Mobilkran - *Mobile Crane*

Holz, Plastikreifen, Oberteil schwenkbar - *wood, plastic tires, upper section swivels*

SERIE	ART.-NO	PERIOD	PR.	INFO
	8975/08	1971-1977	2-3	20 cm

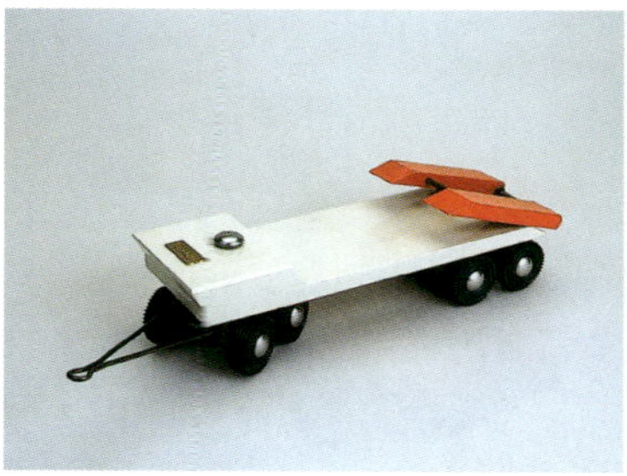

Tieflader - *Low Boy Trailer*

Holz, Plastikreifen, Rampen klappbar - *wood, plastic tires, ramp folds up*

SERIE	ART.-NO	PERIOD	PR.	INFO
	8985/09	1971-1978	2	25 cm

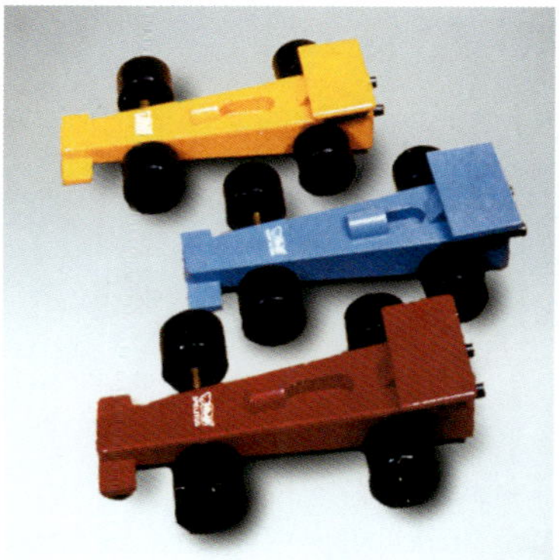

Rennwagen - *Racing Car*

Holz, 20 cm, rot, blau oder gelb, schwarze Raeder - *wood, 20 cm, red, blue or yellow, black wheels*

SERIE	ART.-NO	PERIOD	PR.	INFO
	8720/20	1973-1974	1-2	rot - *red*
	8721/20	1973-1974	1-2	blau - *blue*
	8722/20	1973-1974	1-2	gelb - *yellow*

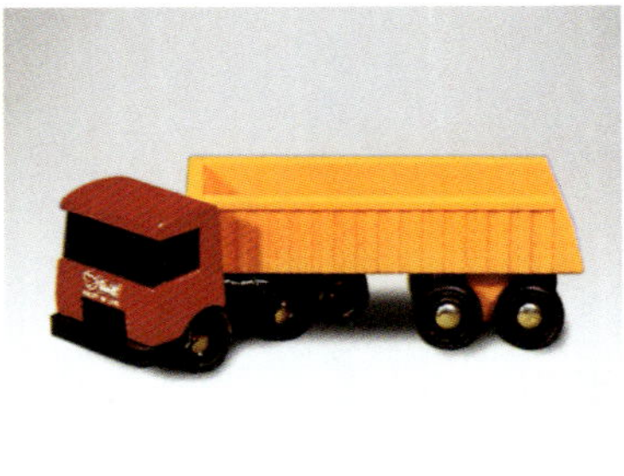

Mini-Sattelschlepper - *Mini Truck Tractor for Semi-Trailers*

Kunststoff, Metall - *plastic, metal*

SERIE	ART.-NO	PERIOD	PR.	INFO
	8892/07	1975-1977	2	20 cm

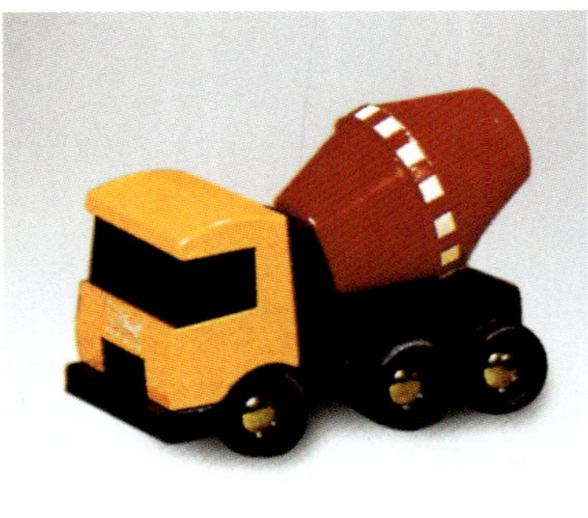

Mini-Mischer - *Mini Cement Mixer*

Kunststoff, Metall - *plastic, metal*

SERIE	ART.-NO	PERIOD	PR.	INFO
	8893/07	1975-1977	2	12 cm

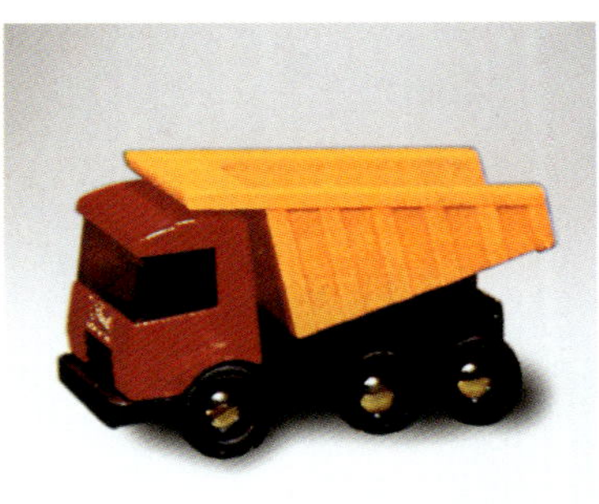

Mini-Mulden-Kipper - *Mini Earth Moving Vehicle*

Kunststoff, Metall - *plastic, metal*

SERIE	ART.-NO	PERIOD	PR.	INFO
	8894/07	1975-1977	2	13 cm

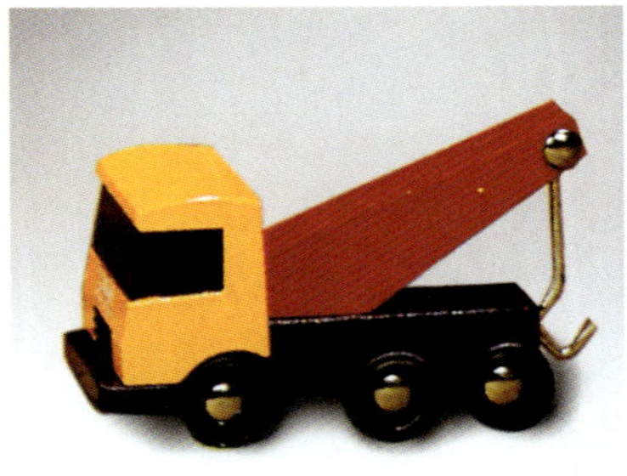

Mini-Abschleppwagen - *Mini Tow Truck*

Kunststoff, Metall - *plastic, metal*

SERIE	ART.-NO	PERIOD	PR.	INFO
	8895/07	1975-1977	2	14 cm

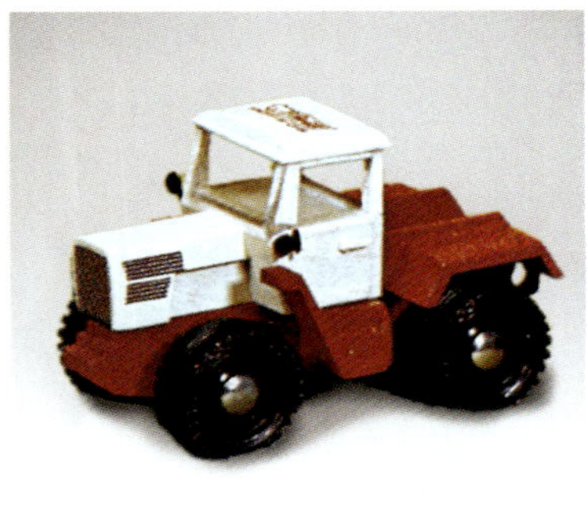

TRAC Schlepper - *TRAC Tractor*

Kunststoff, Metall - *plastic, metal*

SERIE	ART.-NO	PERIOD	PR.	INFO
	8941/07	1976-1978	2	11 cm

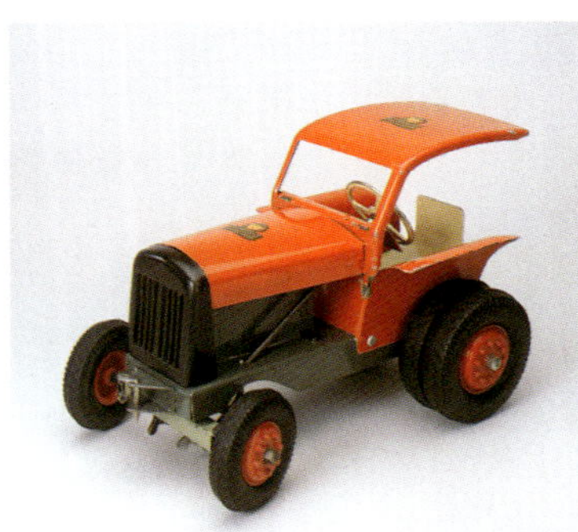

Traktor (1:20) - *Tractor (1:20)*

starkes Blech, Gummireifen 75 und 82 mm, zerlegbar - *thick metal, rubber tires 75 & 82 mm sizes, can be dismantled*

SERIE	ART.-NO	PERIOD	PR.	INFO
135	**4912**	1954-1958	5	24 cm
990	**4912,10**	1959-1961	5	

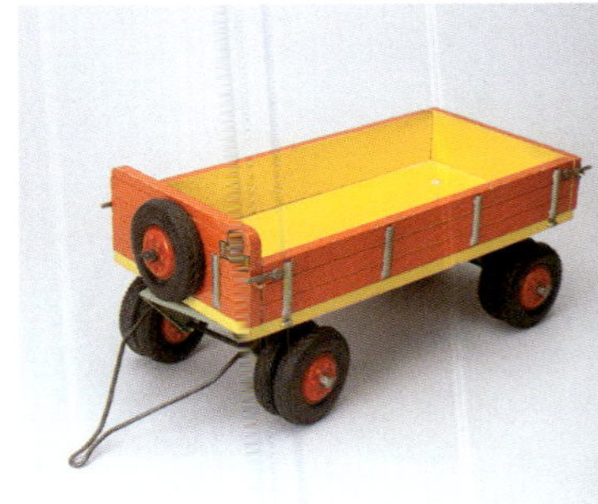

Kasten-Anhaenger (1:20) - *Box Trailer (1:20)*

Sperrholz, Gummireifen, starkes Blech, 8-fach bereift & Reserverad, verschiedene Aenderungen, ab 1974 komplett veraendert - *plywood, rubber tires, thick metal, 8 tires & spare wheel, various changes introduced, 1974 completely modified*

SERIE	ART.-NO	PERIOD	PR.	INFO
135	**4913**	1954-1958	4	30 cm
990	**4913,10**	1959-1964	4	
880	**4913,10**	1965-1967	4	
	8845/13	1968-1978	2-4	

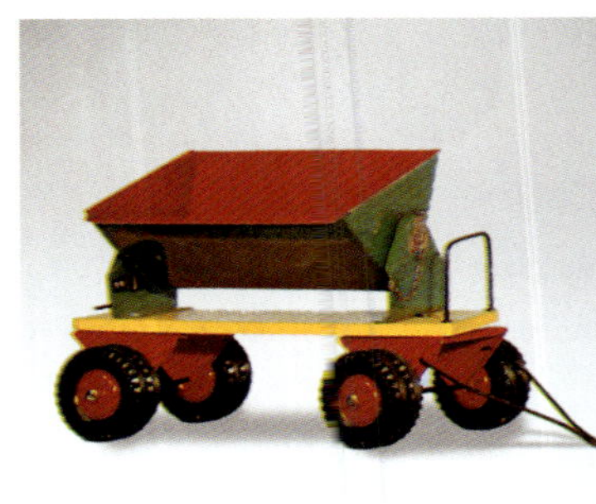

Muldenkipper (1:20) - *Hauling Unit with Trough (1:20)*

Blech, 8-fach bereift, Kippen durch Kurbel, ab 1974 geaendertes Modell - *metal, 8 tires, crank operated tipping function, modified model from 1974*

SERIE	ART.-NO	PERIOD	PR.	INFO
135	**4917**	1954-1958	4	28 cm
990	**4917,10**	1959-1964	4	
880	**4917,10**	1965-1967	4	
	8860/17	1968-198	2-4	

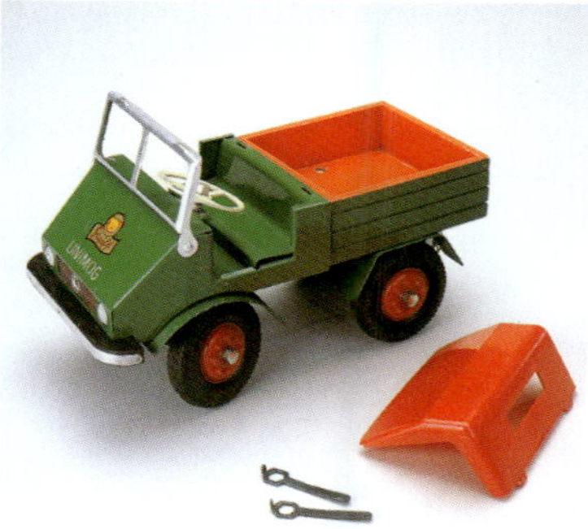

Unimog (1:20)

Holz/Blech/Plastik, 4-fach bereift & Reserverad, 1973 & 1979 geaenderte Modelle - *wood/metal/plastic, 4 tires & spare wheel, 1973 & 1979 models were modified*

SERIE	ART.-NO	PERIOD	PR.	INFO
135	**4916**	1956-1958	4-5	23 cm
990	**4916,10**	1959-1964	4-5	
880	**4916,10**	1965-1967	4-5	
	8855/16	1968-1981	3-5	

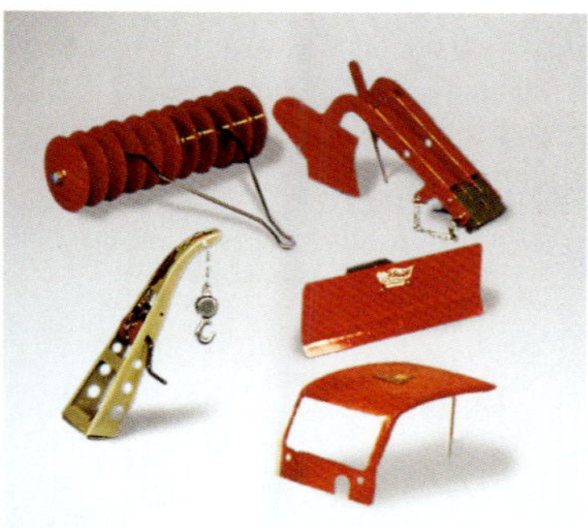

Zusatzgeraete fuer Unimog & Traktor - *Accessory for Unimog & Tractor*

Metall, lackiert - *Painted metal*

SERIE	ART.-NO	PERIOD	PR.	INFO
135	**913**	1954-1957	1	13 cm, Scheibenegge - *disc barrow*
990	**5913,50**	1961-1961	1	
882	**5913,50**	1966-1967	1	
	8890/13	1968-1979	1	
135	**914**	1954-1957	1	14 cm, Wechselpflug - *plow*
990	**5914,50**	1961-1961	1	
882	**5914,50**	1966-1967	1	
	8890/14	1968-1979	1	
135	**915**	1954-1957	1	Kran - *crane*
990	**5915,50**	1961-1961	1	
882	**5915,50**	1966-1967	1	
	8890/15	1968-1977	1	
135	**916**	1954-1957	1	Traktor Schutzdach - *roof for tractor*
990	**5916,50**	1961-1961	1	
135	**917**	1954-1957	1	17 cm, Raeumblech - *snow plow*
990	**5917,50**	1961-1961	1	
882	**5917,50**	1966-1967	1	
	8890/17	1968-1981	1	

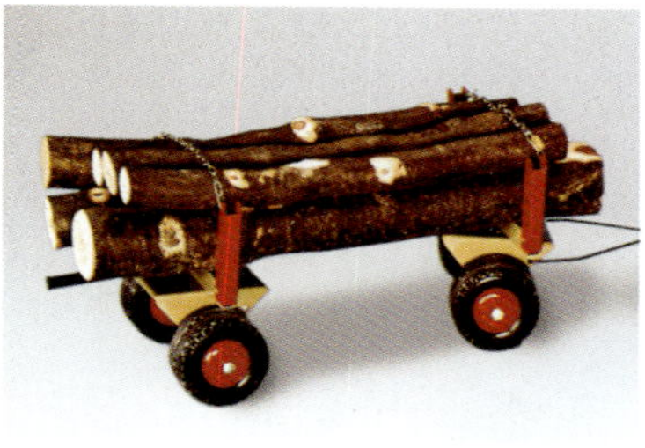

Langholz-Wagen (1:20) - *Long Timber Trailer (1:20)*

Holz, Blech, 8-fach bereift, mit Ladung - *wood, metal, 8 tires, complete with load*

SERIE	ART.-NO	PERIOD	PR.	INFO
135	**4915**	1954-1957	3	36 cm
990	**4915,10**	1961-1964	3	
880	**4915,10**	1965-1967	3	
	8850/15	1968-1975	3	

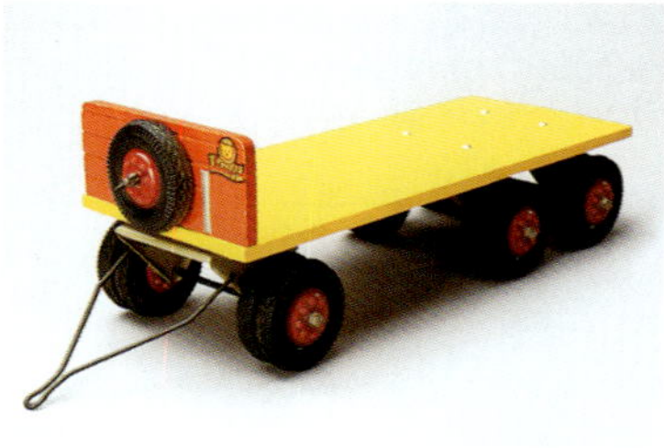

Dreiachs-Wagen (1:20) - *Three Axle Trailer (1:20)*

Holz, Blech, 12 Raeder & Ersatzrad, Gummireifen - *wood, metal , 12 wheels & spare wheel, rubber tires*

SERIE	ART.-NO	PERIOD	PR.	INFO
135	**6914**	1954-1957	4	36 cm
990	**6914,10**	1961-1961	4	

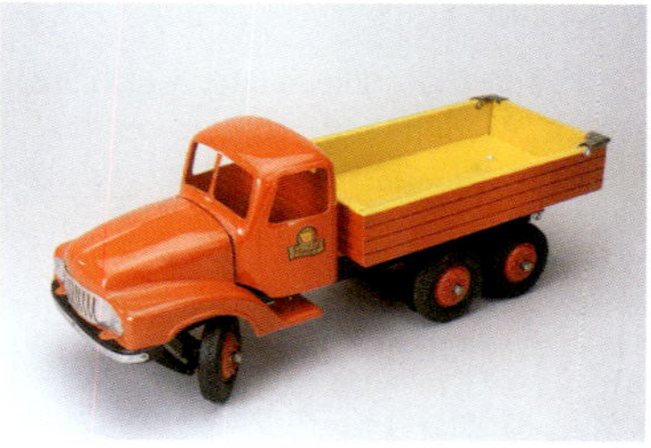

Schwingachsen-Laster - *Three-Axle Truck*

Blech, Gummireifen, 10-fach bereift, Plastik-Fuehrerhaus steuert Schiebelenkung - *metal, 10 rubber tires, steered by means of the cab*

SERIE	ART.-NO	PERIOD	PR.	INFO
135	**6918**	1956-1958	5	38 cm
990	**6918,10**	1959-1961	5	

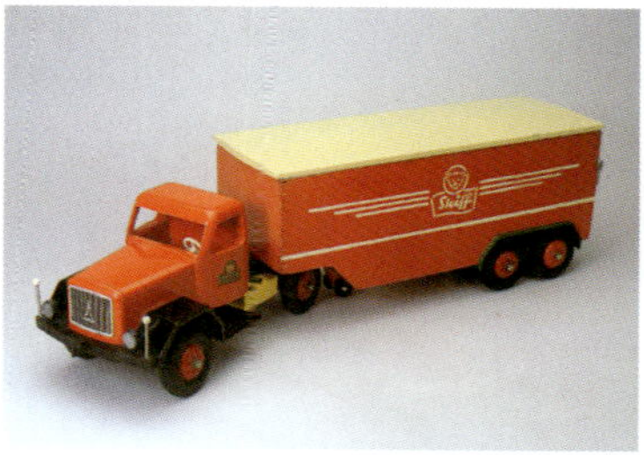

Sattelschlepper / -anhaenger (1:20) - *Semi-Trailer Truck / Trailer (1:20)*

Blech, 4-fach bereift, Schlepper: 25 cm, lenkbar durch Drehen des Fuehrerhauses, Anhaenger: 38 cm, Rueckwand zum Herunterklappen, Dach abnehmbar - *metal, 4 wheels, truck: 25 cm, steered by turning the cab, trailer: 38 cm, rear wall folds down, roof is removable*

SERIE	ART.-NO	PERIOD	PR.	INFO
135	**4919**	1958-1958	4	25 cm
990	**4919,10**	1959-1961	4	
135	**4939**	1958-1958	4	38 cm
990	**4939,10**	1959-1961	4	

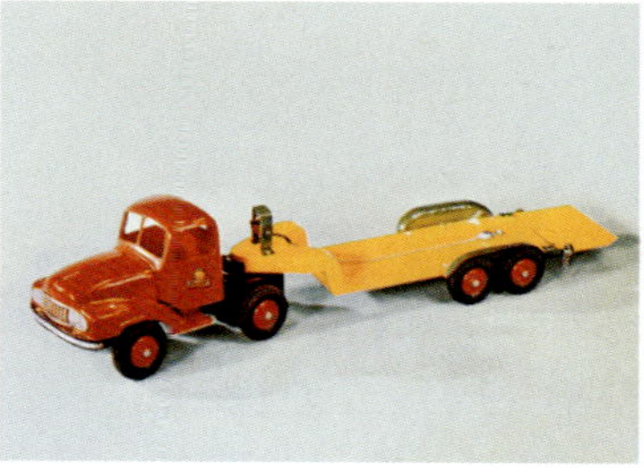

Tieflader (1:20) - *Low Boy Trailer (1:20)*

Holz/Blech/Plastik, 4-fach bereift, Kettenwinde, herunterklappbare Rampe - *wood/metal/plastic, 4 tires, chain winch, ramp drops down*

SERIE	ART.-NO	PERIOD	PR.	INFO
135	**4940**	1958-1958	4	46 cm
990	**4940,10**	1961-1961	4	

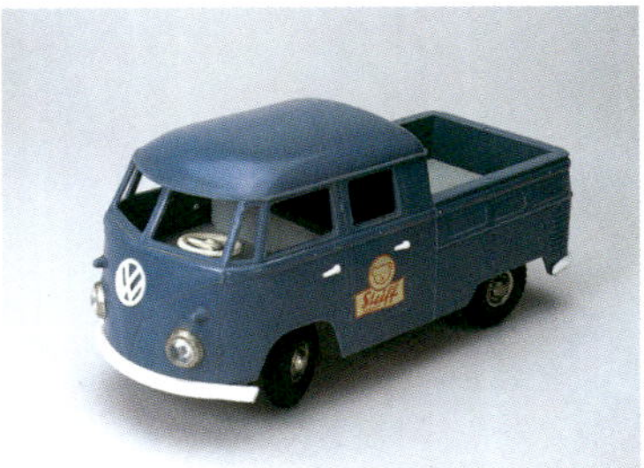

VW-Transporter (1:20) - *VW Hauling Vehicle (1:20)*

Blech, Plastikaufbau, Gummireifen, Schiebelenkung - *metal, plastic structure, rubber tires, push-type steering*

SERIE	ART.-NO	PERIOD	PR.	INFO
990	**4920,10**	1960-1964	3-4	21cm
880	**4920,10**	1965-1967	3-4	
	8865/20	1968-1972	3-4	

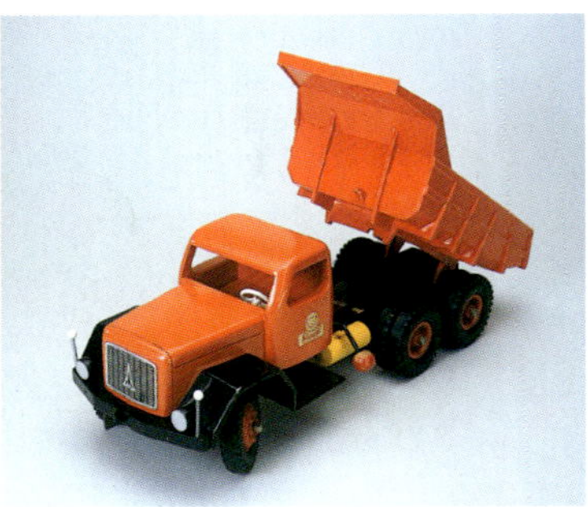

Hinterkipper (1:20) - *Rear-Dump Truck (1:20)*

Blech, Plastikaufbau, Gummireifen, 10-fach bereift, Kippmechanik - *metal, plastic structure, 10 rubber tires, dumping mechanism*

SERIE	ART.-NO	PERIOD	PR.	INFO
990	**4925,10**	1960-1964	4	40 cm
880	**4925,10**	1965-1967	4	
	8870/25	1968-1970	4	

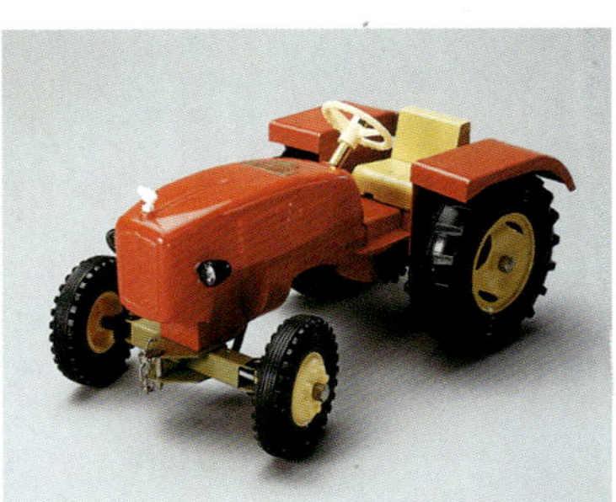

Traktor (1:20) - *Tractor (1:20)*

Blech, Plastik, Baerenkopf als Kuehlerfigur, Lenkradlenkung - 4911,00 = Bausatz - *metal & plastic, bear´s head figure mounted on the radiator, steered by the steering wheel, 4911,00 = in kit form*

SERIE	ART.-NO	PERIOD	PR.	INFO
990	**4911,10**	1960-1964	4-5	22 cm
880	**4911,10**	1965-1967	4-5	
	8840/11	1968-1970	4-5	
880	**4911,00**	1966-1966	4-5	Bausatz - *Kit*

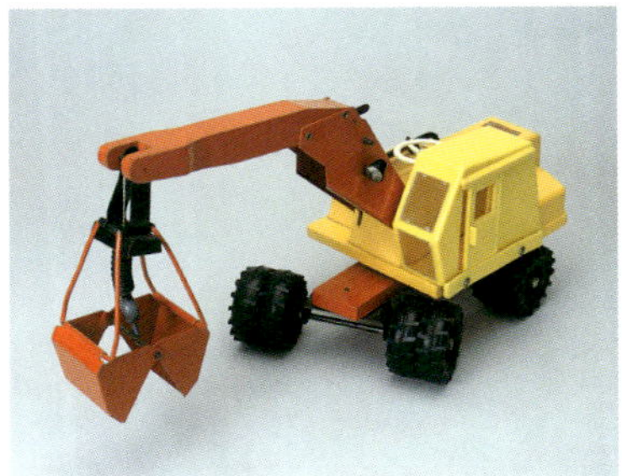

Mobilkran (1:20) - *Mobile Crane (1:20)*

Plastik, Metall, Holz, 6-fach bereift, Greifbagger mit Lenkradlenkung, drehbar - *plastic, metal, wood, twin wheels (6 tires), grabbing crane steered by the steering wheel, vehicle swivels*

SERIE	ART.-NO	PERIOD	PR.	INFO
990	**4926,10**	1964-1964	4-5	38 cm
880	**4926,10**	1965-1967	4-5	
	8875/26	1968-1969	4-5	

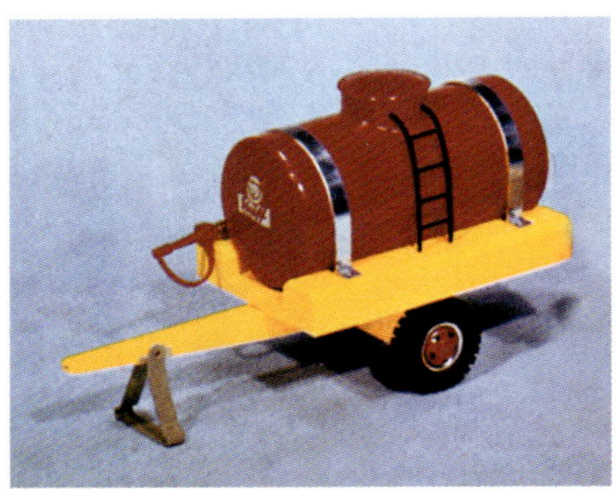

Tankwagen (1:20) - *Fuel Dispenser (1:20)*

Blech, Sperrholz, Plastiktank & -schlauch, versch. Modellaenderungen - *metal & plywood, plastic tank & hose, various model modifications*

SERIE	ART.-NO	PERIOD	PR.	INFO
990	**2621,10**	1964-1964	3	25 cm
880	**2621,10**	1965-1967	3	
	8805/21	1968-1977	3	

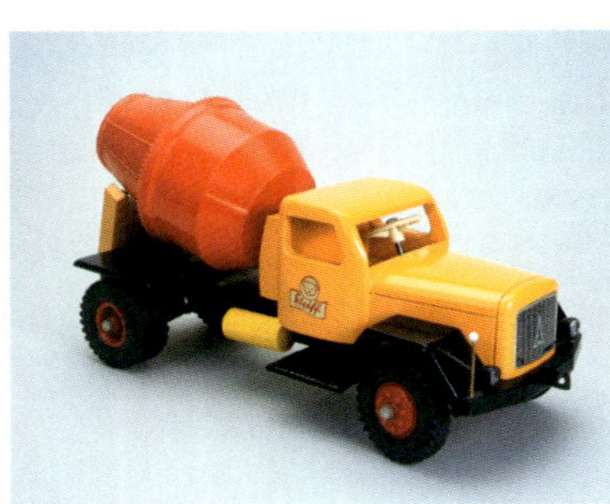

Transport-Mischer (1:20) - *Ready-Mix Concrete Mixer (1:20)*

rotierende Plastiktrommel zum Kippen, 6-fach bereift, lenkbar - *rotating plastic drum tiltable, 6 tires, steerable*

SERIE	ART.-NO	PERIOD	PR.	INFO
880	**6836,10**	1965-1967	4	36 cm
	8880/36	1968-1969	4	

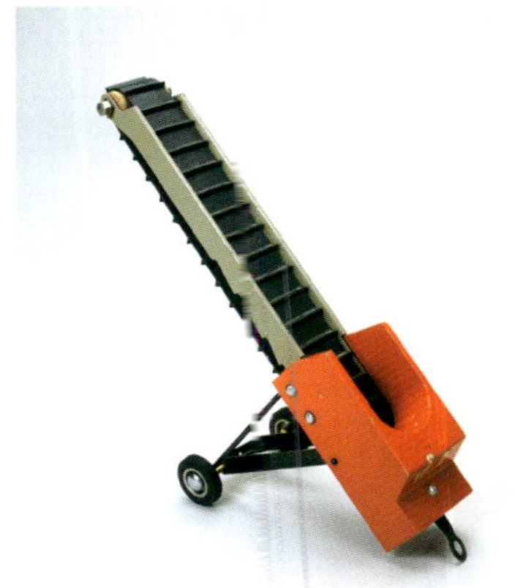

Foerderband (1:20) - *Conveyor Belt (1:20)*

Metall, Plastikreifen & -band, Foerderhoehe verstellbar - *metal, plastic tires & belt, conveyor height is adjustable*

SERIE	ART.-NO	PERIOD	PR.	INFO
880	**2830,10**	1966-1967	3	30 cm
	8810/30	1968-1980	3	

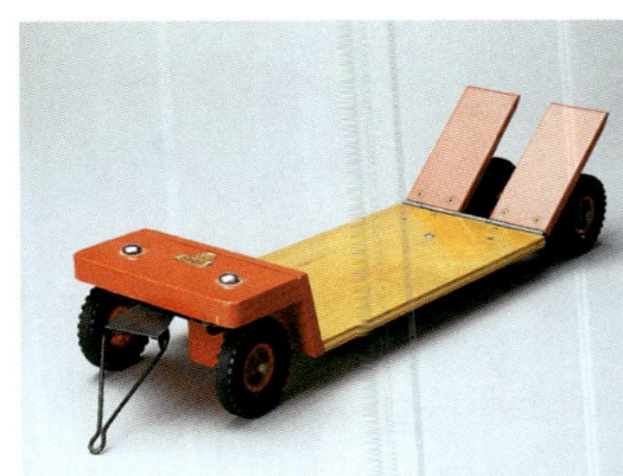

Tieflader - *Low Boy Trailer*

Holz, Plastikreifen, 6-fach bereift, lenkbar, Reifen zum Beladen ausschwenkbar - *wood, plastic tires, 6 tires, steerable, tires can be swiveled outwards for loading*

SERIE	ART.-NO	PERIOD	PR.	INFO
880	**6842,10**	1967-1967	3	42 cm
	8885/42	1968-1971	3	

REPLIKEN & SONDERSERIEN

REPLICA & SPECIAL EDITION

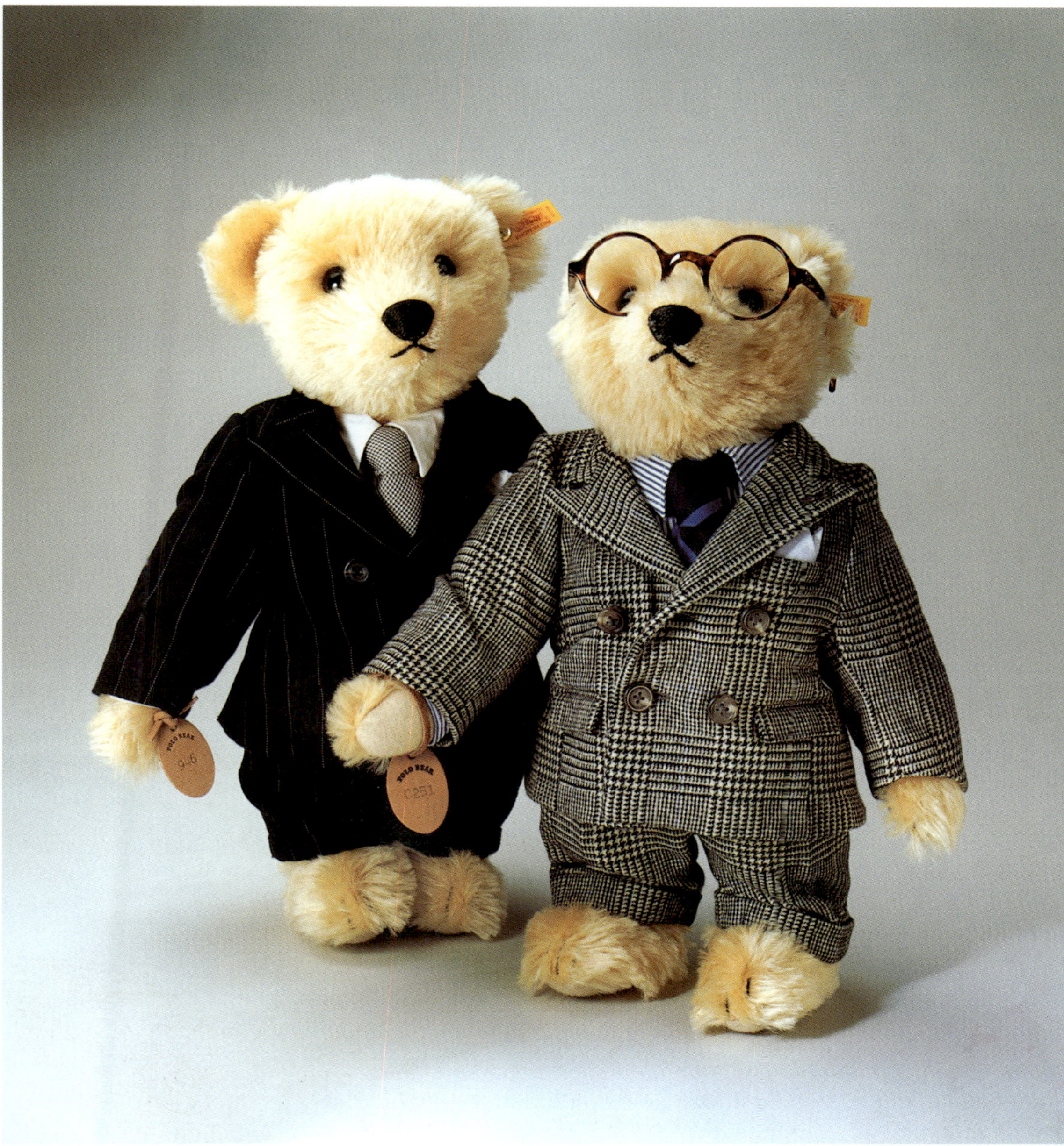

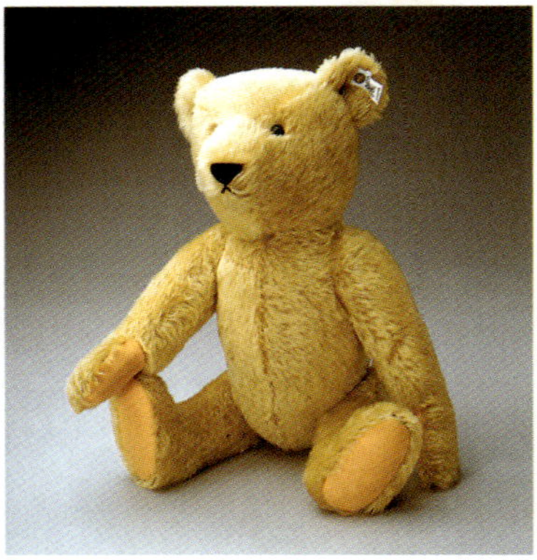

Steiff Original Teddy

Mohair, gegliedert, Replik des 1. Steiff Teddys zum 100. Geburtstag der Fa. Steiff, limit. Auflage 11.000 Stueck - *mohair woven fur, jointed, replica of the 1st Steiff Teddy to celebrate the 100th anniversary, ltd edition of 11,000*

SERIE	ART.-NO	PERIOD	PR.	INFO
	0153/43	1980-1980	6	43 cm

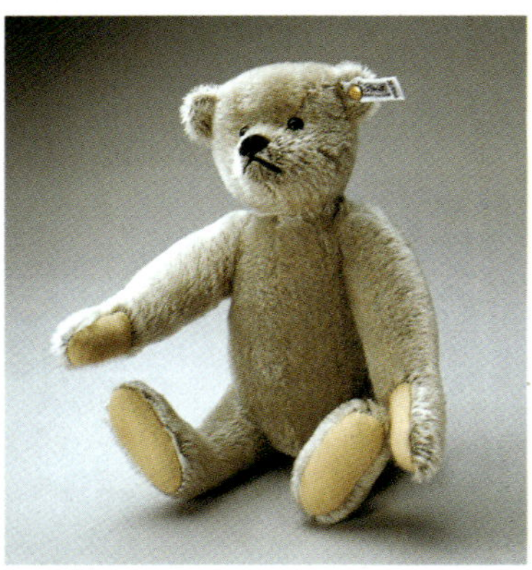

Richard Steiff Teddy

Mohair Webpelz, gegliedert, Replica anlaesslich des 80. Teddy-Geburtstages - *mohair woven fur, jointed, replica for the occasion of the 80th Birthday of the Teddy*

SERIE	ART.-NO	PERIOD	PR.	INFO
	0150/32	1983-1983	5-6	32 cm

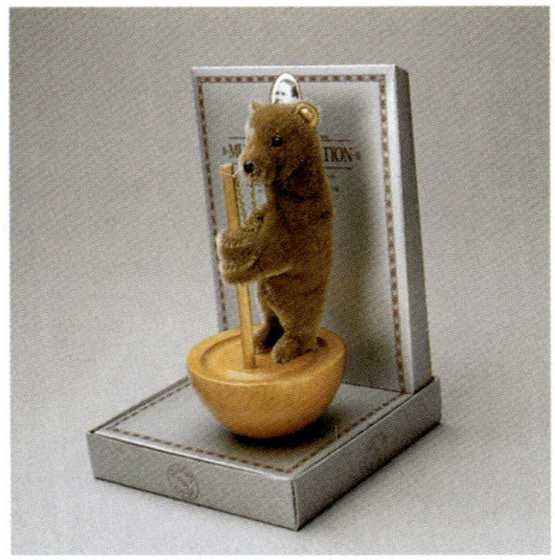

Stehaufbaer Replica 1894 - *1894 Tumbler Bear Replica*

Mohair Webpelz, limit. Auflage 9.000 Stueck - *mohair woven fur, ltd edition of 9,000*

SERIE	ART.-NO	PERIOD	PR.	INFO
400247	**0082/20**	1984-1987	4-5	20 cm

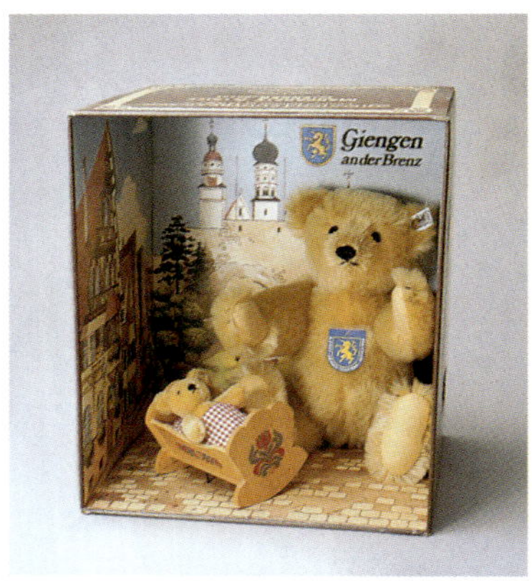

Giengen Teddy Set

Replica 1906, Mohair, Baeren gegliedert, limit. Auflage 16.000 Stueck - *1906 replica, mohair woven fur, bears jointed, ltd edition of 16,000*

SERIE	ART.-NO	PERIOD	PR.	INFO
405808	**0162/00**	1984-1987	5	32 cm/10 cm

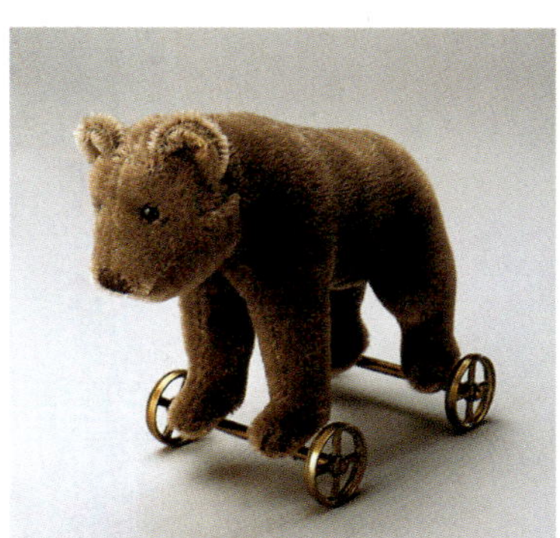

Baer auf Raedern Replica 1905 - *1905 Replica of Bear on Wheels*

Mohair Webpelz, limit. Auflage 12.000 Stueck - *mohair woven fur, ltd edition of 12,000*

SERIE	ART.-NO	PERIOD	PR.	INFO
400377	**0085/12**	1985-1987	4-5	12 cm

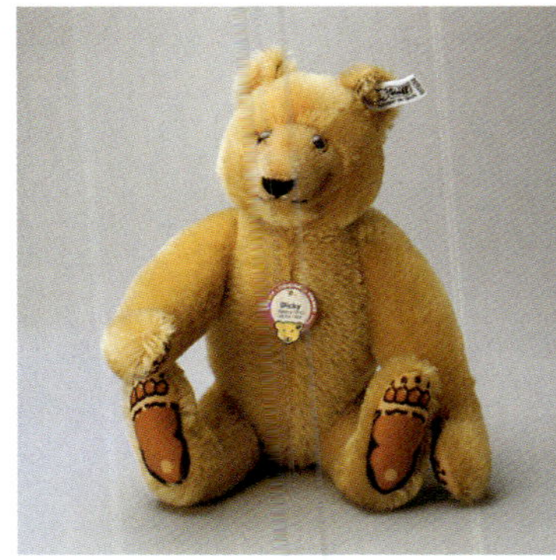

Dicky Baer Replica 1930 - *Dicky Bear Replica 1930*

Mohair Webpelz, blond, gegliedert, limit. Auflage 20.000 Stueck - *mohair woven fur, blond, jointed, ltd edition of 20,000*

SERIE	ART.-NO	PERIOD	PR.	INFO
407505	**0172/32**	1985-1988	5	34 cm

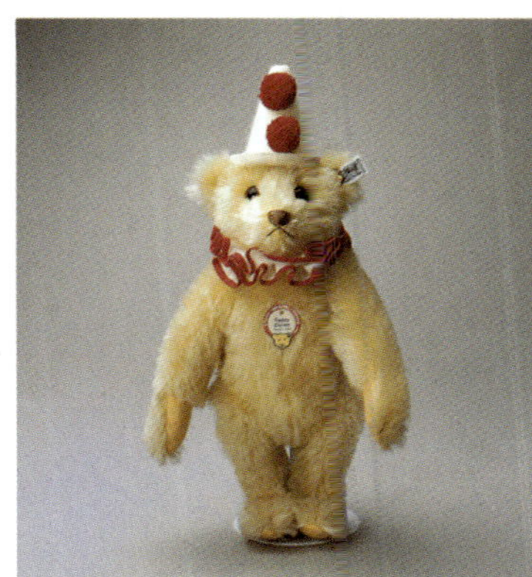

Teddy Clown Replica 1926

Replica 1926, Mohair Webpelz, gegliedert, Druckstimme, limit. Auflage 10.000 Stueck - *1926 replica, mohair woven fur, jointed, press voice, ltd edition of 10,000*

SERIE	ART.-NO	PERIOD	PR.	INFO
407253	**0170/32**	1986-1986	5-6	32 cm

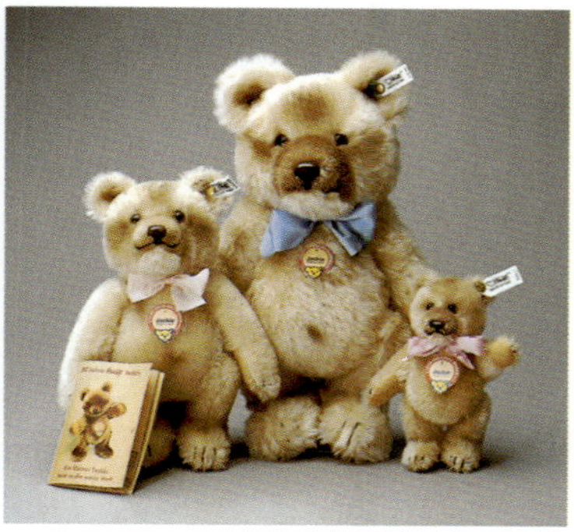

Jackie Baer Replica 1953 - *Jackie Bear Replica 1953*

Mohair Webpelz, gegliedert, Stimme, limit. Auflage 17 cm 12.000, 25 cm 10.000 & 35 cm 4.000 Stueck - *mohair woven fur, jointed, press voice, 17 cm ltd edition of 12,000, 25 cm 10,000 & 35 cm size 4,000*

SERIE	ART.-NO	PERIOD	PR.	INFO
408496	**0190/17**	1989-1990	4	17 cm
408502	**0190/25**	1986-1987	4-5	25 cm
408526	**0190/35**	1988-1989	5-6	35 cm

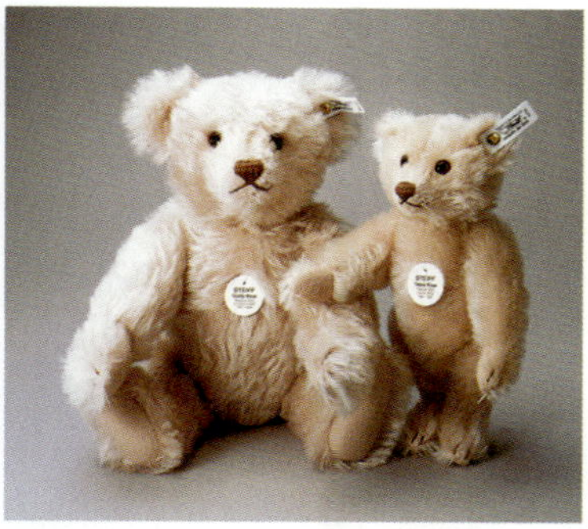

Teddy Rosé Replica 1925 - *Teddy Rose Replica 1925*

Mohair Webpelz, gegliedert, Stimme, limit. Auflage 25 cm 8.000 & 41 cm 10.000 Stueck - *mohair woven fur, jointed, press voice, ltd edition of 8,000 25 cm size, 10,000 41 cm size*

SERIE	ART.-NO	PERIOD	PR.	INFO
407154	**0171/25**	1990-1990	4-5	25 cm
407208	**0171/41**	1987-1989	5-6	41 cm

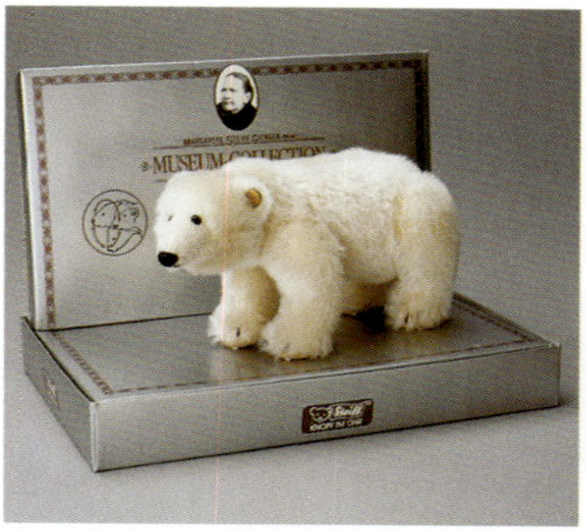

Polarbaer Replica 1909 - *1909 Polar Bear Replica*

Mohair Webpelz, Beine gegliedert, mit Halsmechanik, limit. Auflage 3.000 Stueck - *mohair woven fur, legs are jointed, neck mechanism, ltd edition of 3,000*

SERIE	ART.-NO	PERIOD	PR.	INFO
400568	**0090/11**	1987-1987	5	11 cm

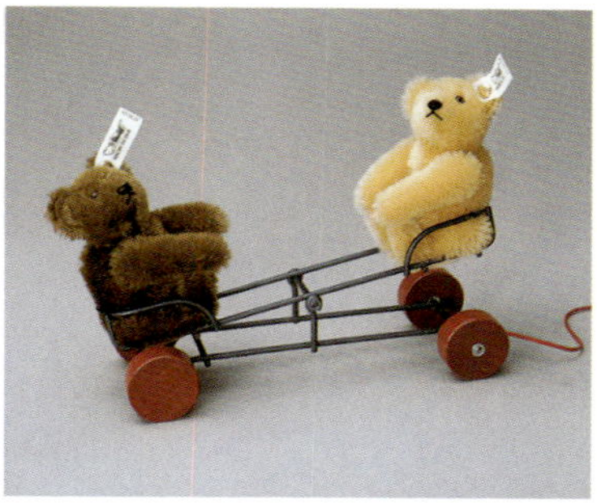

Wiwag mit Teddybaeren - *Teddy Bears with Seesaw*

Replica 1924, Mohair Webpelz, Baeren gegliedert, limit. Auflage 4.000 Stueck - *1924 replica, mohair woven fur, bears are jointed, ltd edition of 4,000*

SERIE	ART.-NO	PERIOD	PR.	INFO
400858	**0132/24**	1988-1989	5	11 cm

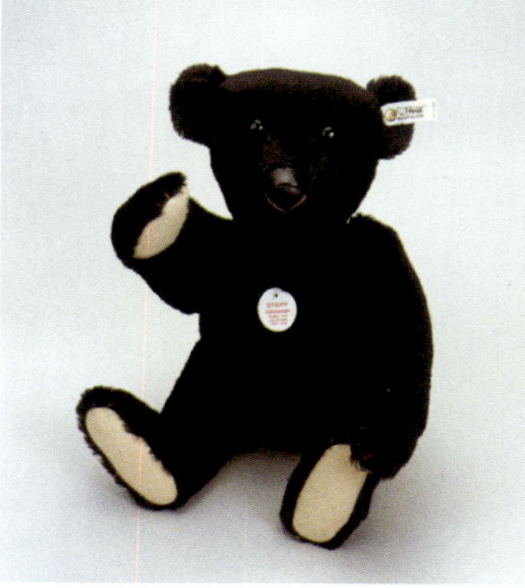

Schwarzbaer Replica 1907 - *1907 Black Bear Replica*

Mohair Webpelz, gegliedert, Brummstimme, limit. Auflage 4.000 Stueck - *mohair woven fur, jointed, growler, ltd edition of 4,000*

SERIE	ART.-NO	PERIOD	PR.	INFO
406003	**0173/40**	1988-1989	6	40 cm

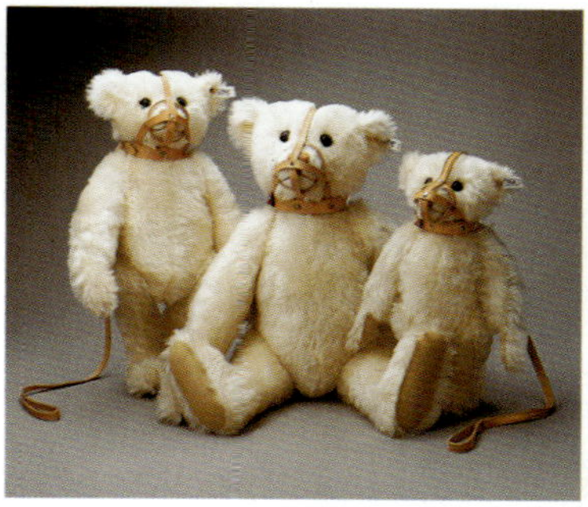

Teddybaer mit Maulkorb - *Teddy Bear with Muzzle*

Replica 1908, Mohair Webpelz, gegliedert, Stimme, limit. Auflage 35 cm 6.000, 46 cm 5.000 & 60 cm 2.650 Stueck, 46 & 60 cm nur USA - *1908 replica, mohair woven fur, jointed, voice, limited edtion of 6,000 35 cm size, 5,000 46 cm size, and 2,650 60 cm size, 46 & 60 cm exclusively sold in the USA*

SERIE	ART.-NO	PERIOD	PR.	INFO
406126	**0174/35**	1990-1990	4-5	35 cm
	0174/46	1988-1990	5	46 cm
	0174/60	1989-1990	6	60 cm

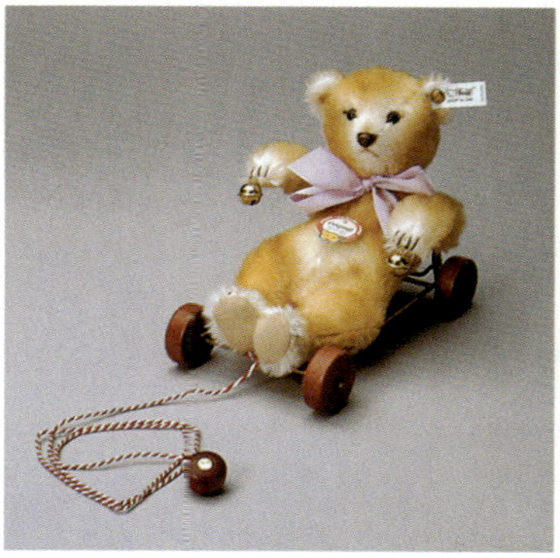

Baby-Baer auf Wagen - *Baby Bear with Wagon*

Replica 1939, Mohair Webpelz, Kopf & Arme gegliedert, limit. Auflage 4.000 Stueck - *1939 replica, mohair woven fur, head & arms jointed, ltd edition of 4,000*

SERIE	ART.-NO	PERIOD	PR.	INFO
401602	**0135/20**	1989-1990	4-5	20 cm

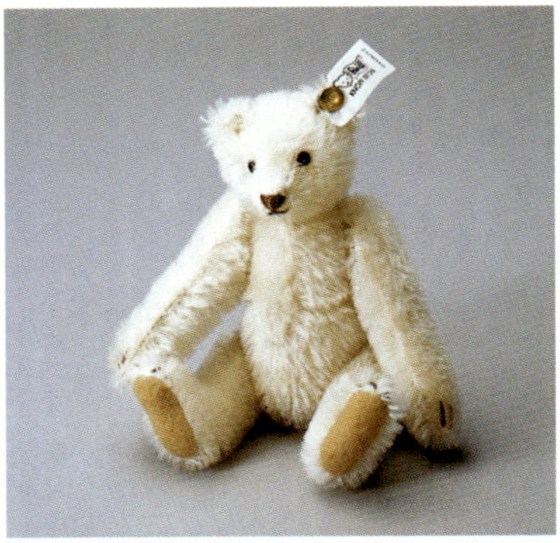

Druckknopfteddy - *Press Button Teddy*

Replica 1909, Mohair Webpelz, Glieder & Kopf mit Druckknoepfen am Koerper befestigt, abnehmbar, limit. Auflage 5.000 Stueck - *1909 replica, mohair woven fur, limbs & head fastened to the body with press buttons, removable, ltd edition of 5,000*

SERIE	ART.-NO	PERIOD	PR.	INFO
406607	**0158/17**	1989-1990	5	17 cm
	406607	1991-1991	5	

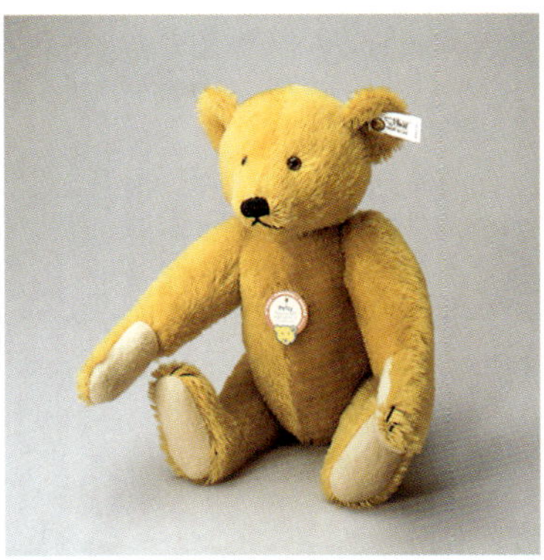

Petsy Messing Replica 1927 - *1927 Brass Color **Petsy** Replica*

Mohair, gegliedert, Druckstimme, Mittelnaht, limit. Auflage 5.000 Stueck - *mohair woven fur, jointed, press voice, center seam, ltd edition of 5,000*

SERIE	ART.-NO	PERIOD	PR.	INFO
407376	**0181/35**	1989-1990	4-5	35 cm

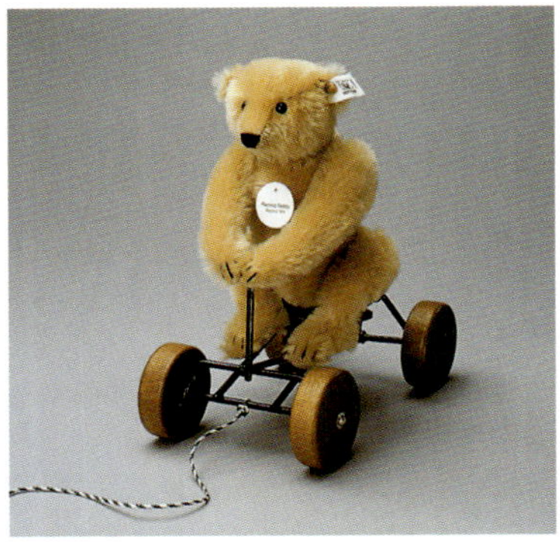

Record Teddy Replica 1913

Mohair Webpelz, gegliedert, Druckbalgstimme, limit. Auflage 4.000 Stueck - *mohair woven fur, jointed, squeaker at the car, ltd edition of 4,000*

SERIE	ART.-NO	PERIOD	PR.	INFO
400698	**0116/25**	1990-1990	4-5	25 cm

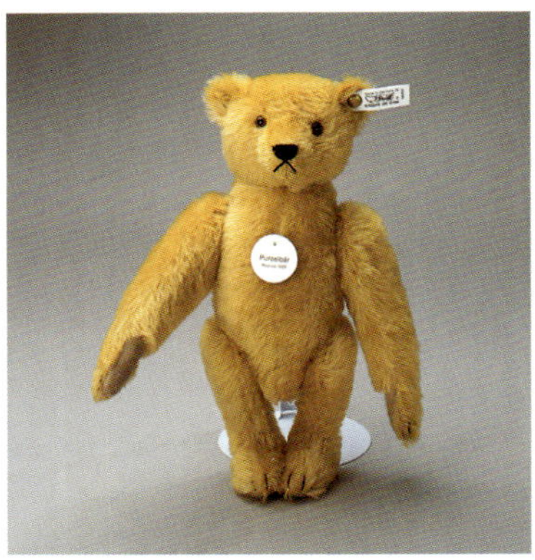

Purzelbaer Replica 1909 - *1909 Somersault Bear Replica*

Mohair Webpelz, Uhrwerk-Antrieb, an den Armen aufzuziehen, limit. Auflage 5.000 Stueck - *mohair woven fur, clockwork driven, winding mechanism in the arms, ltd edition of 5,000*

SERIE	ART.-NO	PERIOD	PR.	INFO
406553	**0164/29**	1990-1990	5-6	29 cm
	406553	1991-1991	5-6	

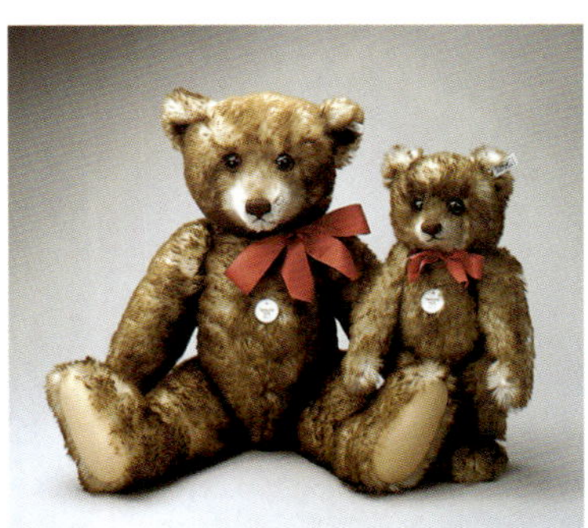

Teddybaer Replica 1926

Mohair Webpelz, graubraun, gegliedert, Brummstimme, limit. Auflage 40 cm 6.000 & 65 cm 5.000 Stueck - *mohair woven fur, greyish-brown, jointed, growler, ltd edition of 6,000 40 cm size & 5,000 65 cm size*

SERIE	ART.-NO	PERIOD	PR.	INFO
	407215	1991-1991	4-5	40 cm
407239	**0169/65**	1990-1990	5-6	65 cm

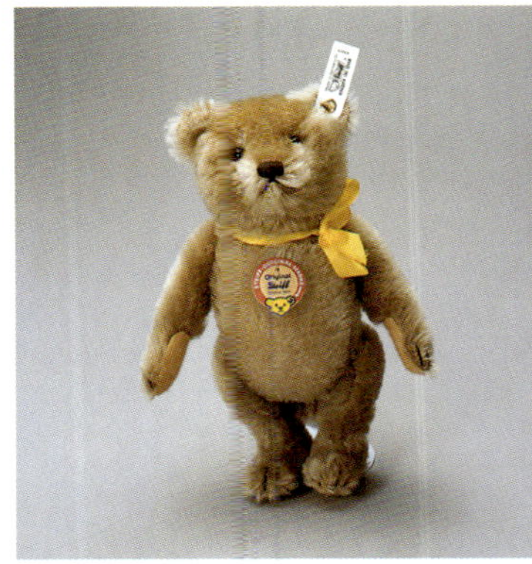

Teddybaer mit Halsmechanik - *Teddy Bear with Neck Mechanism*

Replica 1955, Mohair Webpelz, gegliedert, limit. Auflage 4.000 Stueck - *1955 replica, mohair woven fur, jointed, ltd edition of 4,000*

SERIE	ART.-NO	PERIOD	PR.	INFO
408854	**0188/25**	1990-1990	4-5	25 cm
	408854	1991-1991	4-5	

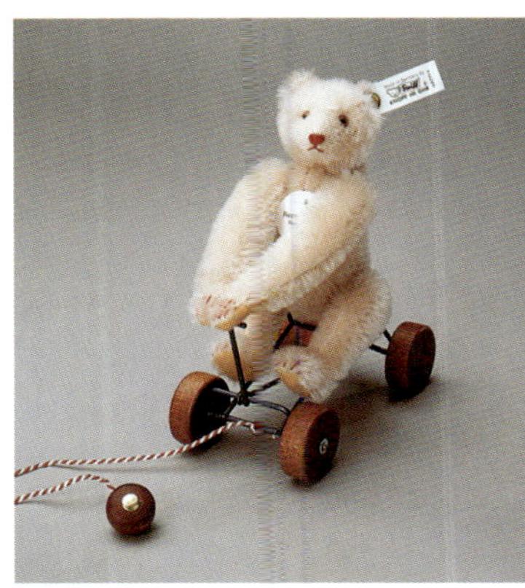

Record Teddy Rose - ***Record Teddy** Rose*

Repl. 1913, Mohair Webpelz, gegliedert, Druckbalgstimme, limit. Auflage 4.000 Stueck - *1913 replica, mohair woven fur, jointed, squeaker at the car, ltd edition of 4,000*

EAN-NO.	PERIOD	PR.	INFO
400704	1991-1992	4-5	20 cm

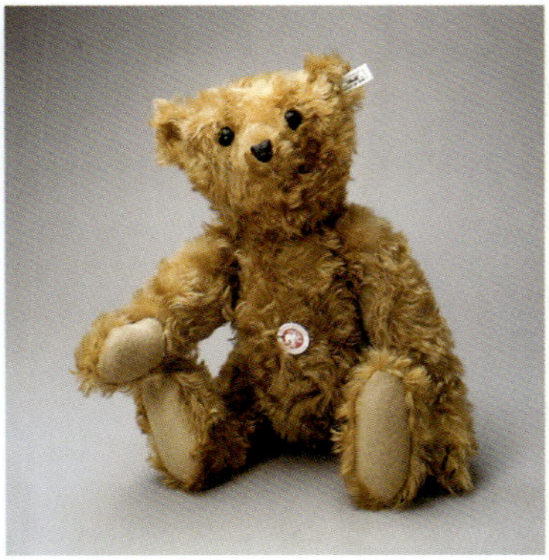

Teddybaer 35 PB (Baerle) - *35 PB Teddy Bear Baerle*

Replica 1904, Mohair Webpelz, gegliedert, Bindfaden-Anscheibung, limit. Auflage 6.000 Stueck - *1904 replica, mohair woven fur, jointed with string, ltd edition of 6000*

EAN-No.	Period	Pr.	Info
404108	1991-1991	5	50 cm

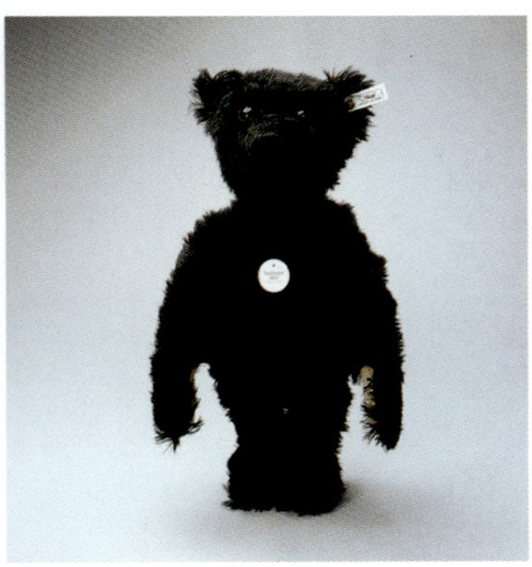

Teddybaer Replica 1912 - *1912 Teddy Bear Replica*

Mohair Webpelz, schwarz, gegliedert, limit. Auflage 7.000 Stueck - *mohair woven fur, black, jointed, ltd edition of 7,000*

EAN-No.	Period	Pr.	Info
406805	1992-1992	4-5	40 cm

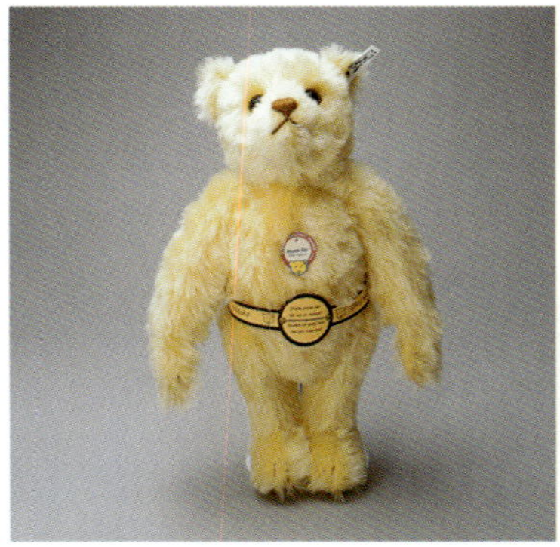

Musik Baer Replica 1928 - *1928 Musical Bear Replica*

Mohair Webpelz, gelb, gegliedert, Musikwerk, limit. Auflage 8.000 Stueck - *mohair woven fur, yellow, jointed, music box, ltd edition of 8,000*

EAN-No.	Period	Pr.	Info
407482	1992-1992	4-5	40 cm

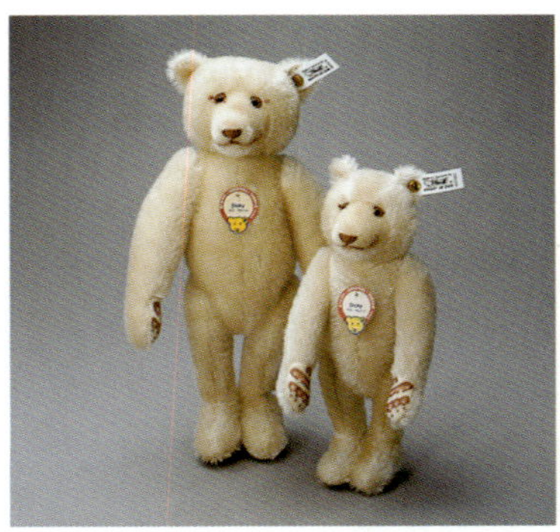

Dicky Baer Replica 1930 - *Dicky Bear Replica 1930*

Mohair Webpelz, weiss, gegliedert, limit. Auflage 25 cm 9.000, 33 cm 7.000 Stueck - *mohair woven fur, white, jointed, 25 cm size ltd edition of 9,000, 33 cm 7,000*

EAN-No.	Period	Pr.	Info
407550	1992-1993	4	25 cm
407574	1992-1992	4-5	33 cm

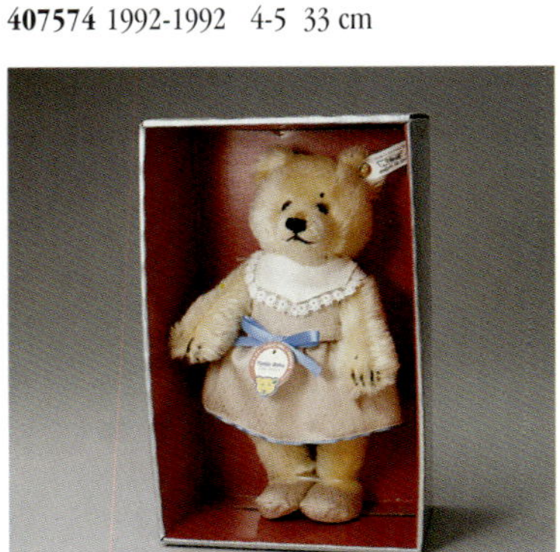

Teddy Baby Maid

Replica 1930, Mohair Webpelz, gegliedert, limit. Auflage 7.000 Stueck - *1930 replica, mohair woven fur, jointed, ltd edition of 7,000*

EAN-No.	Period	Pr.	Info
407512	1993-1993	4-5	25 cm

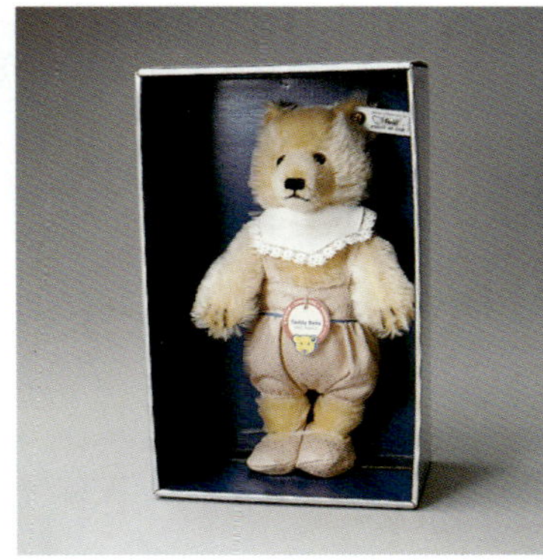

Teddy Baby Bub - ***Teddy Baby*** *Boy*

Replica 1930, Mohair Webpelz, gegliedert, limit. Auflage 7.000 Stueck - *1930 replica, mohair woven fur, jointed, ltd edition of 7,000*

EAN-No.	Period	Pr.	Info
407529	1993-1993	4-5	25 cm

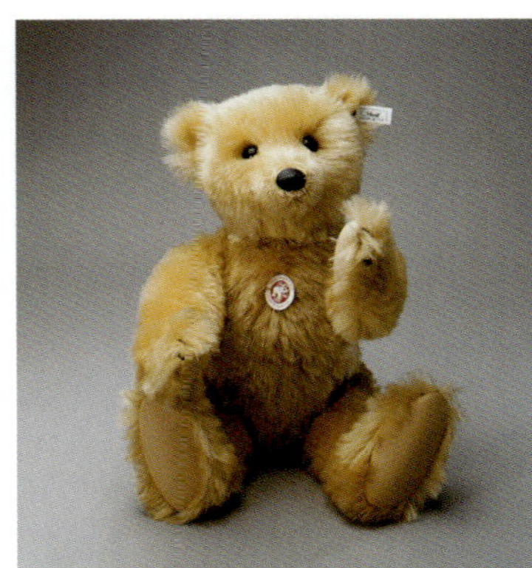

Baerle 35 PAB Replica 1905

Mohair Webpelz, gegliedert, Scheibengelenke, limit. Auflage 6.000 Stueck - *mohair woven fur, jointed, disc joints, ltd edition of 6,000*

EAN-No.	Period	Pr.	Info
404207	1993-1993	5	50 cm

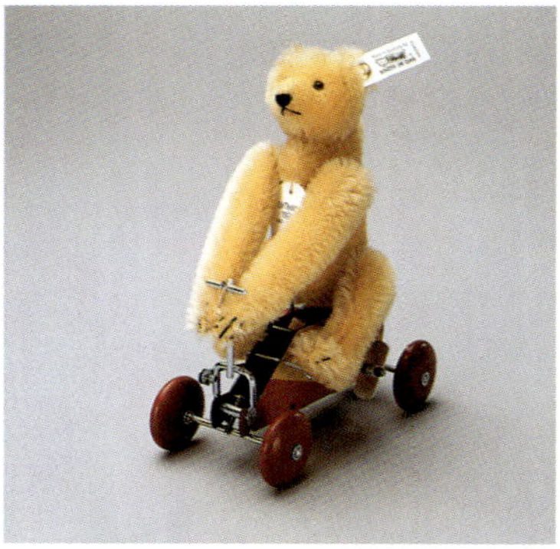

Ur-Teddy Replica 1926 - *1926 Grand Teddy Replica*

Mohair Webpelz, Uhrwerk-Spielzeug, hellbraun, limit. Auflage 4.000 Stueck - *mohair woven fur, clockwork toy, light brown, ltd edition of 4,000*

EAN-No.	Period	Pr.	Info
400919	1993-1993	4-5	20 cm

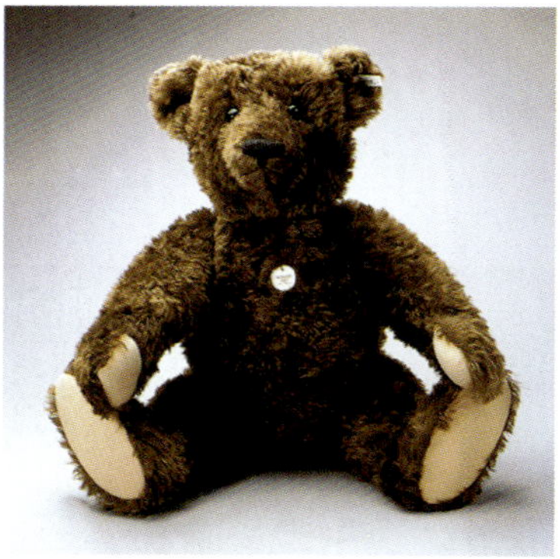

Teddybaer 1907 Replica - *1907 Teddy Bear Replica*

Mohair Webpelz, braun, gegliedert, limit. Auflage 5.000 Stueck - *mohair woven fur, brown, jointed, ltd edition of 5,000*

EAN-No.	Period	Pr.	Info
406010	1993-1993	5-6	70 cm

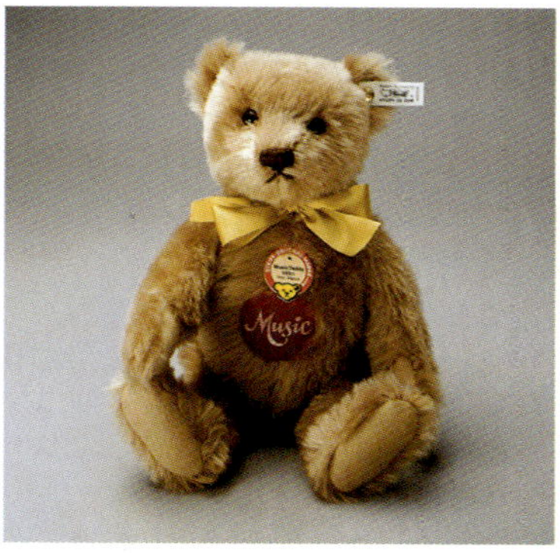

Musikteddy Replica 1951 - *1951 Musical Teddy Replica*

Mohair Webpelz, gegliedert, Musikwerk, limit. Auflage 7.000 Stueck - *mohair woven fur, jointed, music box, ltd edition of 7,000*

EAN-No.	Period	Pr.	Info
408458	1993-1993	4-5	35 cm

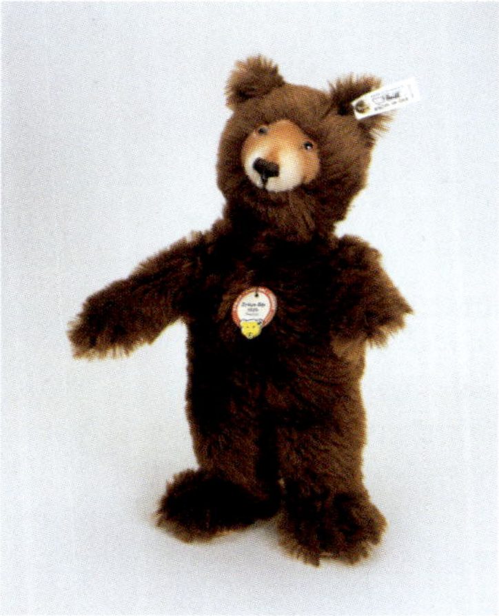

Zirkus-Baer 1935 - *1935 Circus Bear*

Mohair Webpelz, 2fach gegliedert, Schnappglieder in den Beinen, Stimme, Halsmechanik, limit. Auflage 4000 Stueck - *mohair woven fur, double jointed with spring joints in the legs, voice, neck mechanism, ltd edition of 4,000*

EAN-No.	Period	Pr.	Info
401534	1994-1995	4-5	32 cm

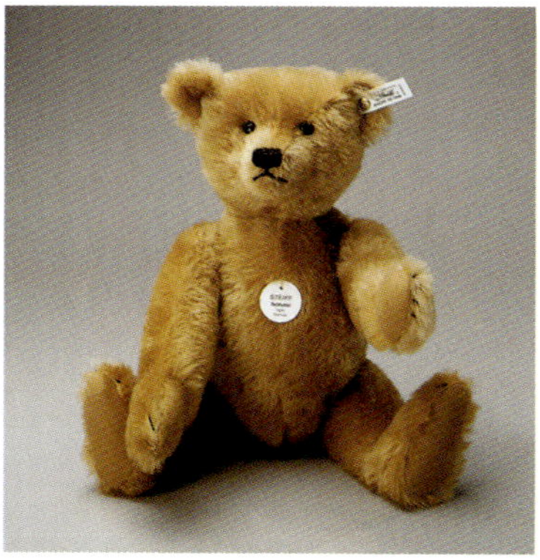

Teddybaer 1906 - *1906 Teddy Bear*

Mohair Webpelz, gegliedert, Druckstimme, Mittelnaht, limit. Auflage 5.000 Stueck - *mohair woven fur, jointed, press voice, center seam, ltd edition of 5,000*

EAN-No.	Period	Pr.	Info
405891	1994-1994	4-5	43 cm

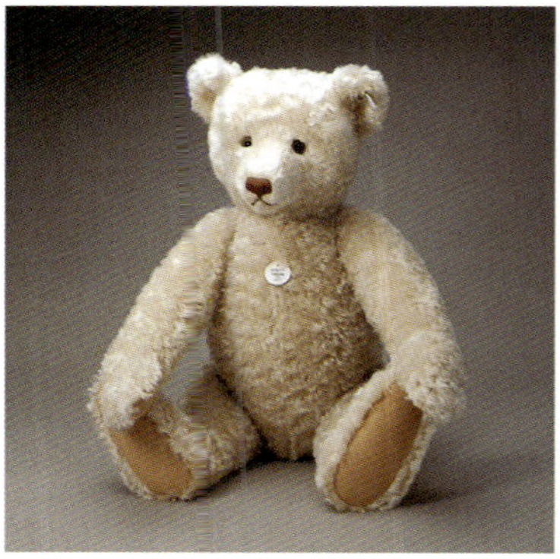

Teddybaer 1908 - *1908 Teddy Bear*

Mohair Webpelz weiss, gegliedert, Brummstimme, limit. Auflage 7.000 Stueck - *mohair woven fur, white, jointed, growler, ltd edition of 7,000*

EAN-No.	Period	Pr.	Info
406041	1994-1994	5-6	65 cm

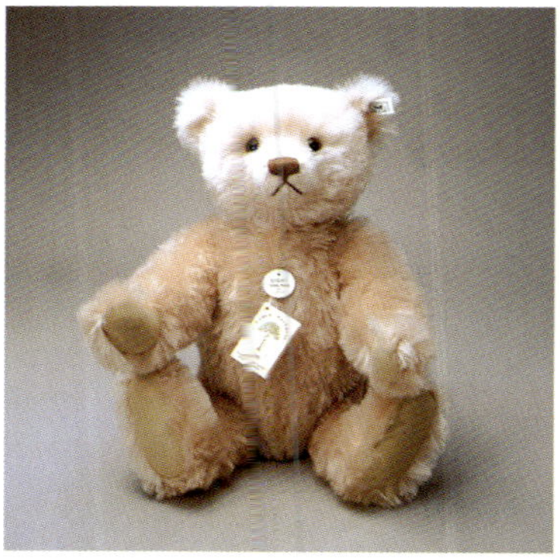

Teddybaer Rosé 1927 - *1927 Rose Teddy Bear*

Mohair Webpelz, gegliedert, Brummstimme, limit. Auflage 7.000 Stueck - *mohair woven fur, jointed, growler, ltd edition of 7,000*

EAN-No.	Period	Pr.	Info
407192	1994-1994	5	48 cm

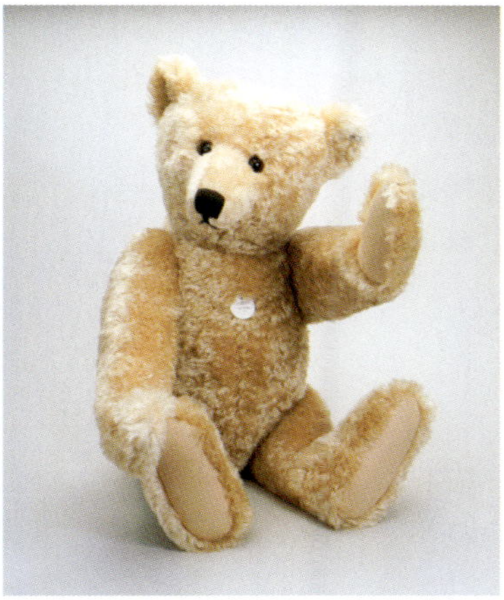

Teddybaer 1909 - *1909 Teddy Bear*

Mohair Webpelz, blond, limit. Auflage 5.000 Stueck - *mohair woven fur, blond, ltd edition of 5,000*

EAN-No.	Period	Pr.	Info
406058	1995-1995	5-6	65 cm

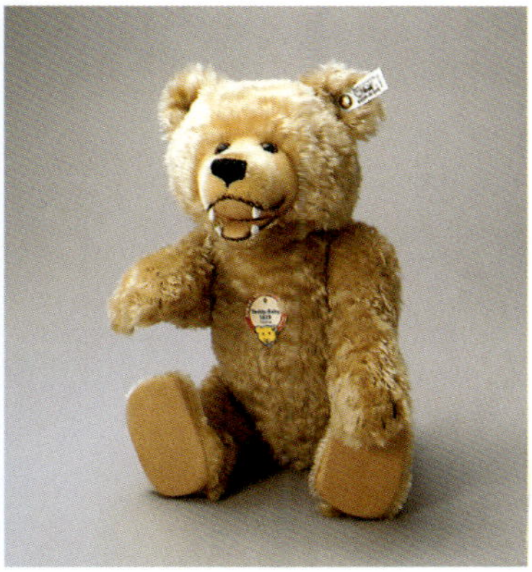

Teddy Baby 1929

mit Zaehnen, Mohair Webpelz, blond, gegliedert, limit. Auflage 3.000 Stueck - *with teeth, mohair woven fur, blond, jointed, ltd edition of 3,000*

EAN-No.	Period	Pr.	Info
408175	1995-1995	4-5	35 cm

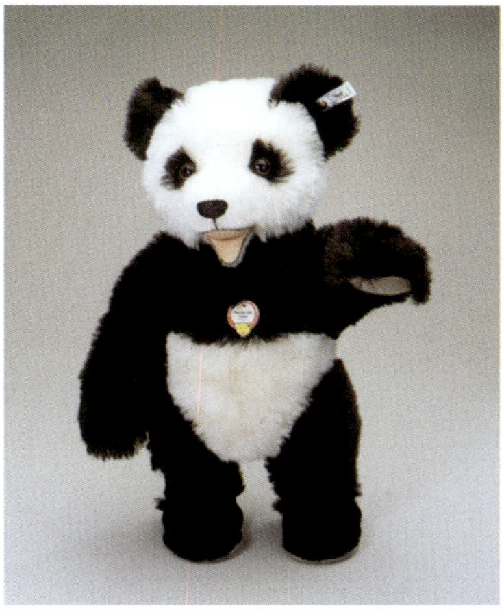

Panda Baer 1951 - *1951 Panda Bear*

Mohair Webpelz, gegliedert, schwarz/weiss, limit. Auflage 3.000 Stueck - *mohair woven fur, jointed, black/white, ltd edition of 3,000*

EAN-No.	Period	Pr.	Info
408335	1995-1995	5	50 cm

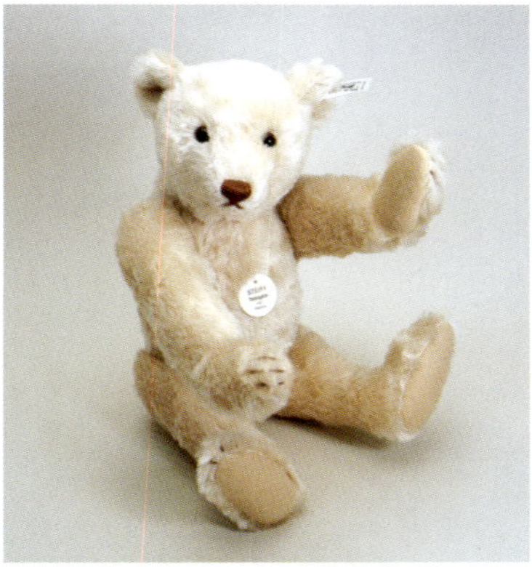

Teddybaer 1921 Replica - *Teddybear 1921 Replica*

Mohair Webpelz, weiss, gegliedert, abwaschbar, Brummstimme, Stopfung Holzwolle, limit. Auflage 4.000 Stueck - *mohair woven fur, white, jointed, surface washable, growler, excelsior stuffing, ltd edition of 4,000*

EAN-No.	Period	Pr.	Info
407123	1996-1996	5	40 cm

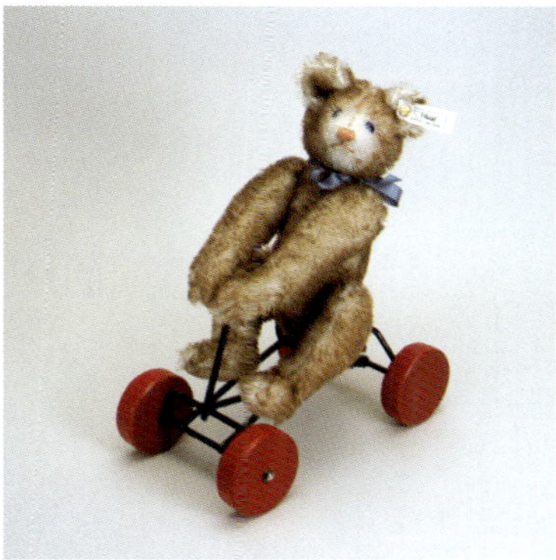

Record Petsy 1928 Replica

Mohair Webpelz, gegliedert, abwaschbar, mit Fahrwagen, Druckstimme am Fahrwagen, Stopfung Holzwolle, limit. Auflage 4.000 Stueck - *mohair woven fur, jointed, surface washable, with car, squeaker at the car, excelsior stuffing, ltd edition of 4,000*

EAN-No.	Period	Pr.	Info
407468	1996-1998	4-5	25 cm

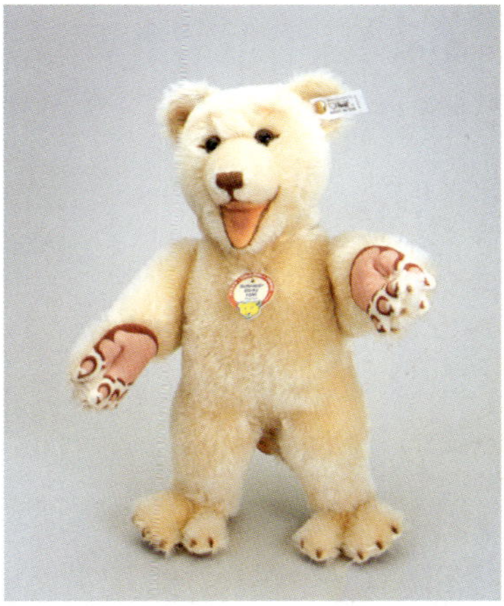

Schnapp Dicky 1936 Replica - *Snap Dicky 1936 Replica*

Mohair Webpelz, blond, abwaschbar, mit Halsmechanik und Schnappgliedern, Stopfung Holzwolle, limit. Auflage 5.000 Stueck - *mohair woven fur, blond, surface washable, neck mechanism and spring joints, excelsior stuffing, ltd edition of 5,000*

EAN-No.	Period	Pr.	Info
408243	1996-1997	4-5	32 cm

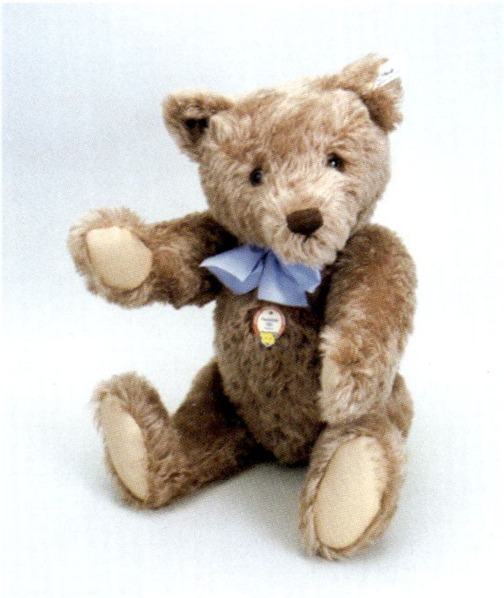

Teddybaer 1951 Replica - *Teddybear 1951 Replica*

Mohair Webpelz, caramel, gegliedert, abwaschbar, Brummstimme, Stopfung Holzwolle, limit. Auflage 5.000 Stueck - *mohair woven fur, caramel, jointed, surface washable, growler, excelsior stuffing, ltd edition of 5,000*

EAN-No.	Period	Pr.	Info
408427	1996-1996	5	50 cm

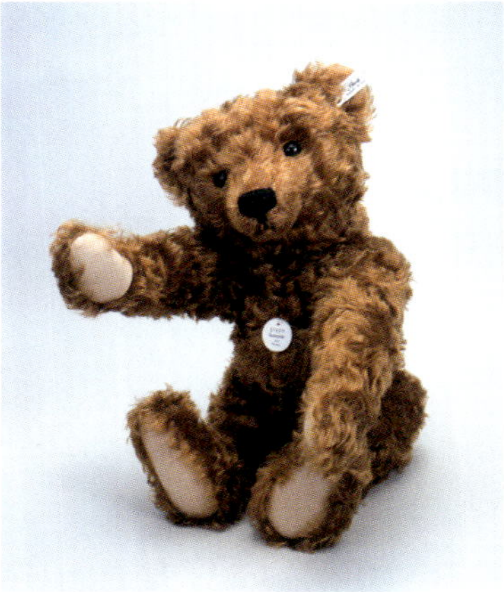

Teddybaer Replica 1905 - *Teddybear Replica 1905*

Mohair Webpelz, rotbraun, gegliedert, abwaschbar, Druckstimme, limit. Auflage 6.000 Stueck - *mohair woven fur, redbrown, jointed, surface washable, press voice, ltd edition of 6,000*

EAN-No.	Period	Pr.	Info
404306	1997-1997	5	50 cm

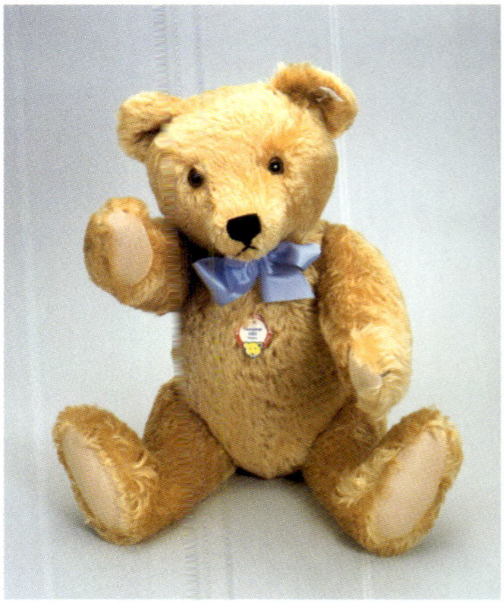

Teddybaer Replica 1951 - *Teddybear Replica 1951*

Mohair Webpelz, blond, gegliedert, abwaschbar, Brummstimme, limit. Auflage 4.000 Stueck - *mohair woven fur, blond, jointed, surface washable, growler, ltd edition of 4,000*

EAN-No.	Period	Pr.	Info
408434	1997-1997	5	50 cm

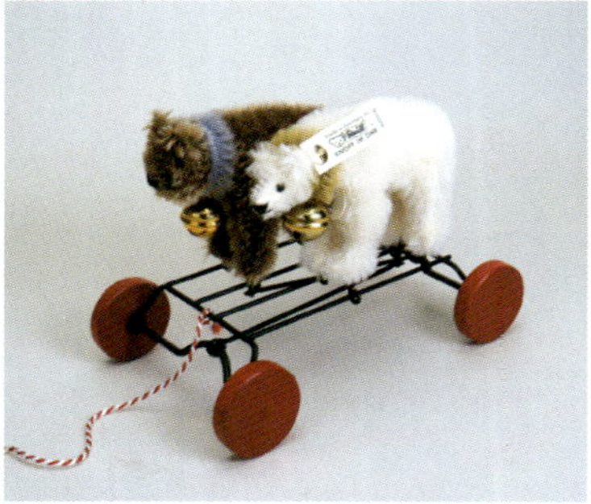

Galop-Teddy Replica 1926

Mohair Webpelz, abwaschbar, Braunbaer & Eisbaer auf Fahrwagen, farbige Plueschhalskrausen & Gloeckchen, limit. Auflage 2.500 Stueck - *mohair woven fur, surface washable, brown bear & ice bear with car, plush neck collar & little bell, ltd edition of 2,500*

EAN-No.	Period	Pr.	Info
400926	1997-1997	4-5	12 cm

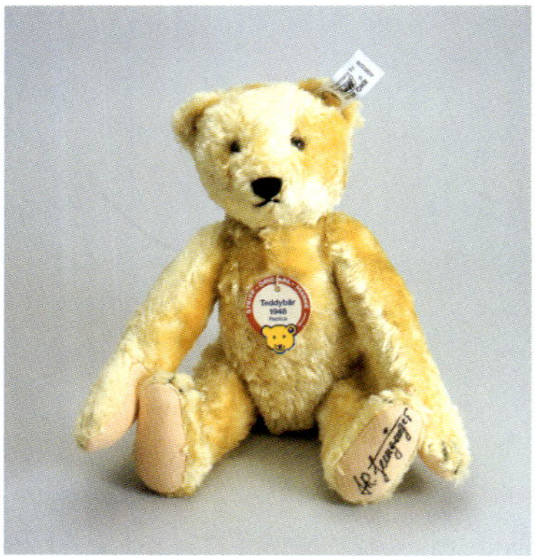

Teddybaer Replica 1948 - *Teddybear Replica 1948*

Viscose Webpelz, blond, gegliedert, abwaschbar, Druckstimme, limit. Auflage 5.000 Stueck - *viscose woven fur, blond, jointed, surface washable, press voice, ltd edition of 5,000*

EAN-No.	Period	Pr.	Info
408328	1997-1997	4	25 cm

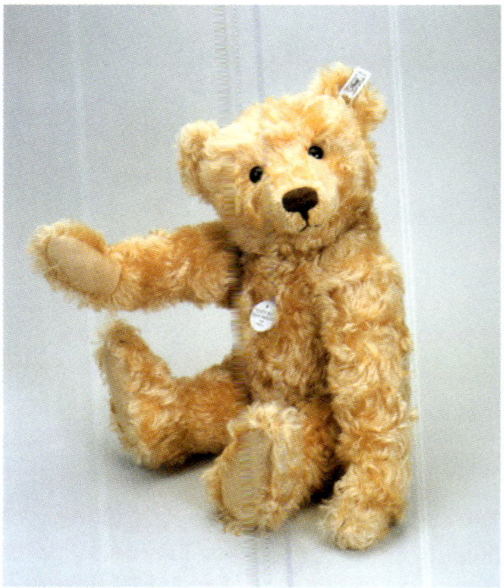

Teddy Boy Replica 1905

Mohair Webpelz, hellblond, gegliedert, abwaschbar, Druckstimme, limit. Auflage 6.000 Stueck - *mohair woven fur, light blond, jointed, surface washable, growler, ltd edition of 6,000*

EAN-No.	Period	Pr.	Info
404320	1998-1998	5	50 cm

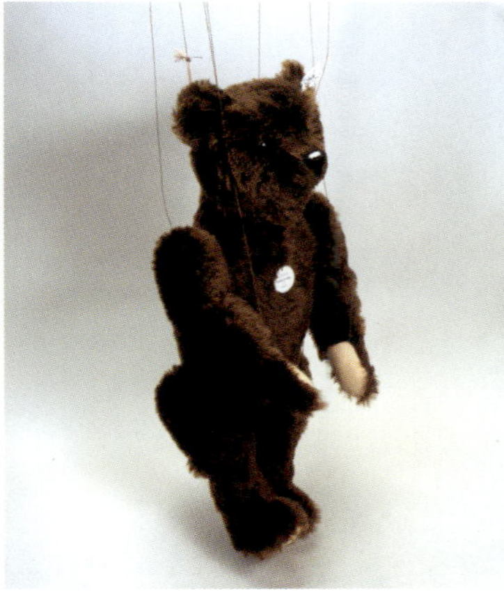

Pantom-Baer Replica 1910 - *Pantom-Bear Replica 1910*

Mohair Webpelz, dunkelbraun, gegliedert, abwaschbar, Zugstimme, mit Spielkreuz aus Holz, limit. Auflage 4.000 Stueck - *mohair woven fur, dark brown, jointed, surface washable, pull-voice, wooden puppet mechanism, ltd edition of 4,000*

EAN-No.	Period	Pr.	Info
406614	1998-1998	5	55 cm

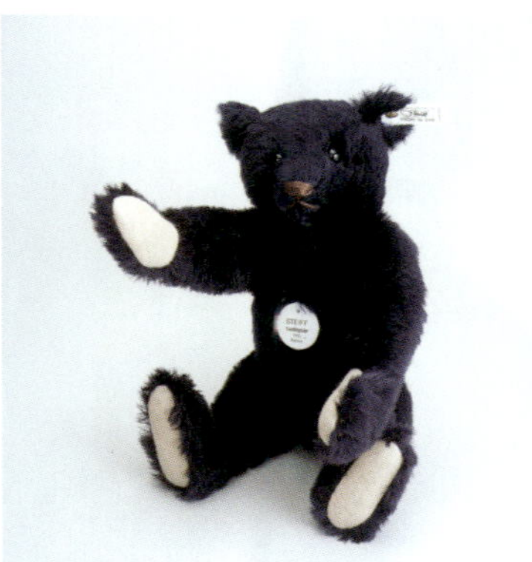

Teddybaer Replica 1909 - *Teddybear Replica 1909*

Mohair Webpelz, dunkelblau, gegliedert, abwaschbar, Brummstimme, limit. Auflage 7.000 Stueck - *mohair woven fur, dark blue, jointed, surface washable, growler, ltd edition of 7,000*

EAN-No.	Period	Pr.	Info
406508	1998-1998	4-5	35 cm

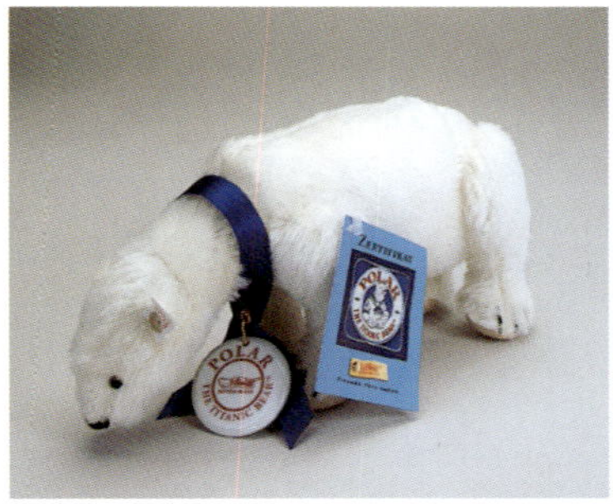

Titanic Polarbaer - *Polar the Titanic Bear*

Mohair, weiss, gegliedert, Halsmechanik, aus der Geschichte eines kleinen Jungen, der den Untergang der Titanic zusammen mit seinem Steiff Polarbaeren ueberlebte, Porzellanmarke an blauem Satinband, limit. Auflage 5.000 Stueck - *mohair, white, jointed, neck mechanism, from the story of a little child, who survived, together with his Steiff ice bear, the disaster of the Titanic, porcelain medallion with blue satin ribbon, ltd edition of 5,000*

EAN-No.	Period	Pr.	Info
670299	1998-1998	4-5	25 cm

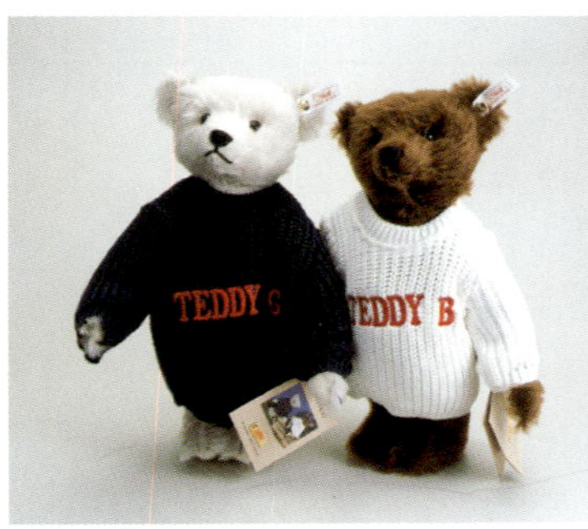

Teddy B / Teddy G

Mohair, 33 cm, gegliedert, Druckstimme, zum 140. Geburtstag Teddy Roosevelts, B steht fuer braun, G fuer grau, TEDDY B bzw. G aufgestickt auf dem weissen bzw. dunkelblauen Strickpullover, Jahreslimitation fuer 1998 - *mohair woven fur, 33 cm, jointed, press voice, on the occasion of Teddy Roosevelts 140th birthday, B means brown, G means grey, TEDDY B or G is embroidered on the white or dark-blue pullovers, limitation for 1998 only*

EAN-No.	Period	Pr.	Info
670275	1998-1998	4-5	dunkelbraun, 3.220 Stueck - *dark brown, 3,220 pc*
670282	1998-1998	4-5	rohweiss, 3.341 Stueck - *raw white, 3,341 pc*

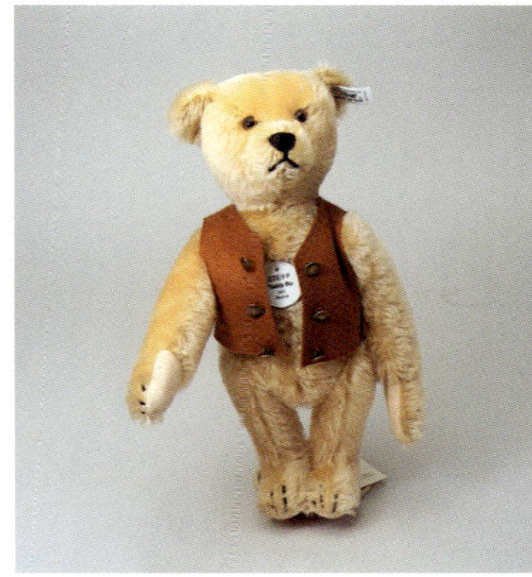

Teddy Bu 1925

Mohair Webpelz, blond, gegliedert, abwaschbar, teakfarbene Filzweste, Holzwollstopfung, limit. Auflage 4.000 Stueck - *mohair woven fur, blond, jointed, surface washable, teak-coloured felt waistcoat, excelsior stuffed, ltd edition of 4,000*

EAN-No.	Period	Pr.	Info
407161	1999-1999	4	30 cm

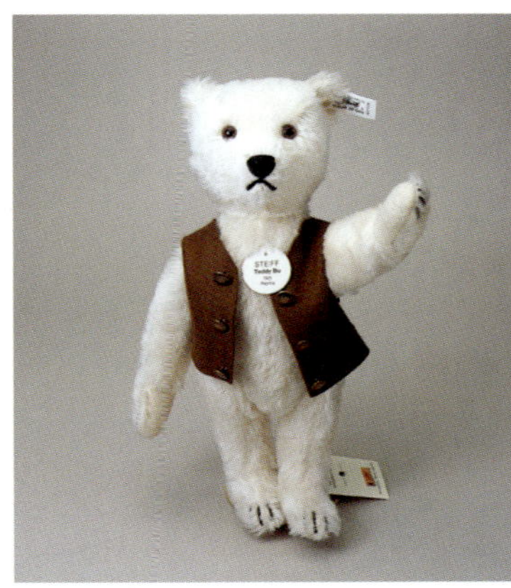

Teddy Bu 1925

Mohair Webpelz, weiss, gegliedert, abwaschbar, tabakfarbene Filzweste, Holzwollstopfung, limit. Auflage 4.000 Stueck - *mohair woven fur, white, jointed, surface washable, snuff-coloured felt waistcoat, excelsior stuffed, ltd edition of 4,000*

EAN-No.	Period	Pr.	Info
407178	1999-1999	4	30 cm

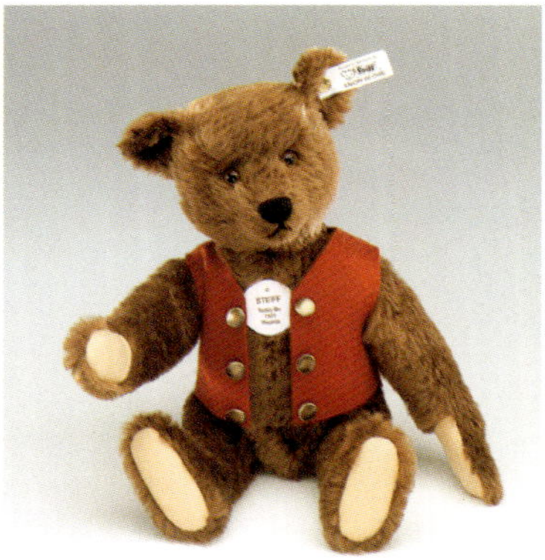

Teddy Bu 1925

Mohair Webpelz, braun, gegliedert, abwaschbar, kupferfarbene Filzweste, Holzwollstopfung, limit. Auflage 4.000 Stueck - *mohair woven fur, brown, jointed, surface washable, copper-coloured felt waistcoat, excelsior stuffed, ltd edition of 4,000*

EAN-No.	Period	Pr.	Info
407185	1999-1999	4	30 cm

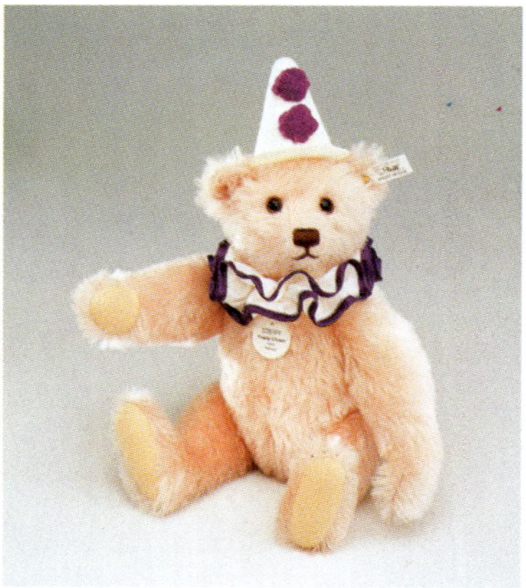

Teddy Clown 1926

Mohair Webpelz, rosè, gegliedert, abwaschbar, Clownhut & Halskrause, Holzwollstopfung, limit. Auflage 5.000 Stueck - *mohair woven fur, rose, jointed, surface washable, clown´s & and ruff, excelsior stuffed, ltd edition of 5,000*

EAN-No.	Period	Pr.	Info
407260	1999-1999	4	33 cm

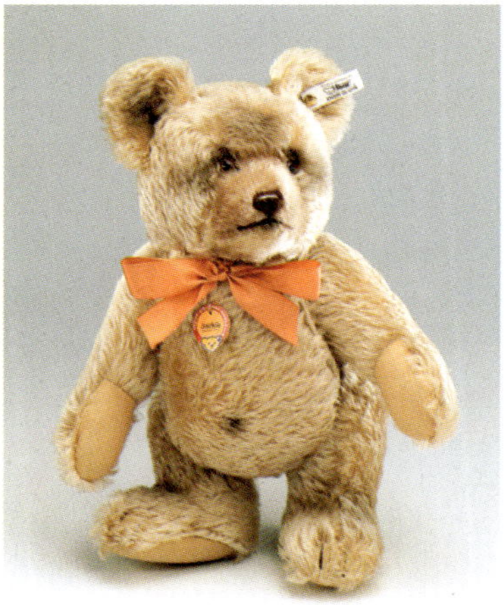

Teddybaer **Jackie** Replica 1953 - *Teddybear **Jackie** Replica 1953*

Mohair Webpelz, honig, gegliedert, abwaschbar, echt vergoldeter Knopf im Ohr, Holzwollstopfung, limit. Auflage 1.000 Stueck - *mohair woven fur, honey, jointed, surface washable, genuine gold plated button in ear, excelsior stuffed, ltd edition of 1,000*

EAN-No.	Period	Pr.	Info
408533	1999-1999	6	75 cm

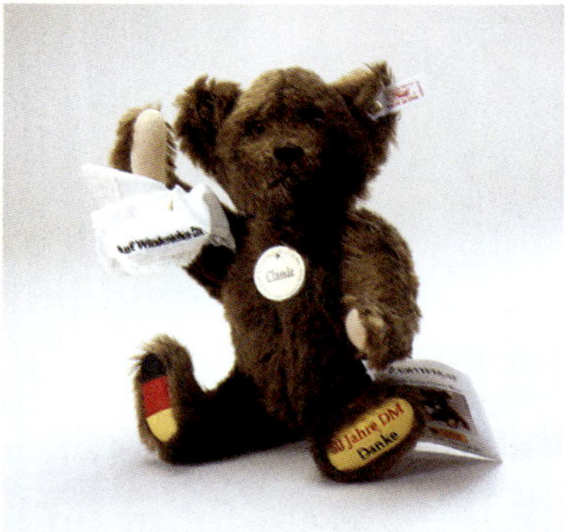

DM-Abschieds-Baer - *Goodbye DM Bear*

Mohair Webpelz, dunkelbraun, gegliedert, abwaschbar, Taschentuch & Sohlen bestickt, Zeitlimitierung bis Ende 1999 - *mohair woven fur, dark brown, jointed, surface washable, embroidered handkerchief & soles, limited availability up to 31.12.1999*

EAN-No.	Period	Pr.	Info
028403	1999-1999	3	28 cm

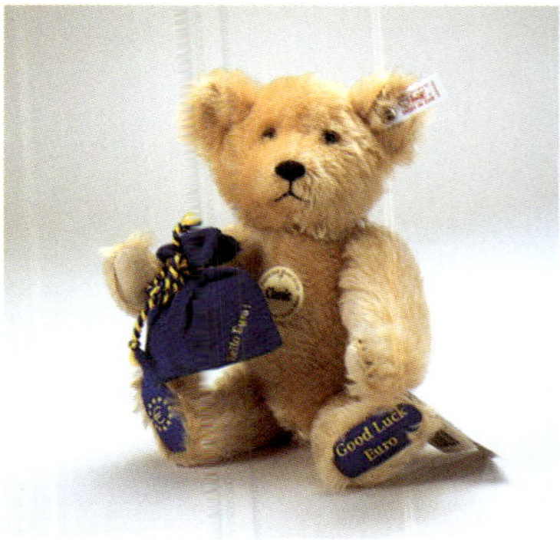

Euro-Begruessungs-Baer - *Hello EURO Bear*

Mohair Webpelz, blond, gegliedert, abwaschbar, Geldsaeckchen & Sohlen bestickt, Zeitlimitierung bis Ende 1999 - *mohair woven fur, blond, jointed, surface washable, embroidered money bag & soles, limited availability up to 31.12.1999*

EAN-No.	Period	Pr.	Info
028410	1999-1999	3	28 cm

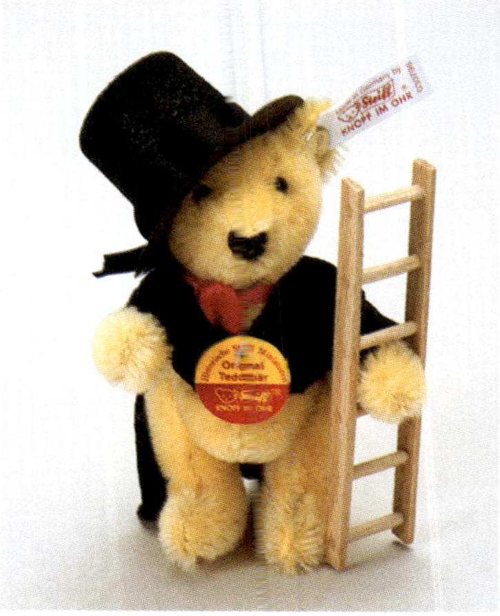

Gluecksbringer-Kaminfeger **Original Teddybaer** - *Teddybear Lucky Chimney Sweep*

Mohair Webpelz, gold, gegliedert, abwaschbar, Jacken-Ruecken bestickt mit "Happy 2000", Zeitlimitierung bis Ende 1999 - *mohair woven fur, gold, jointed, surface washable, embroidered with "HAPPY 2000" on the backside of the jacket, limited availability up to 31.12.1999*

EAN-No.	Period	Pr.	Info
030796	1999-1999	2-3	10 cm

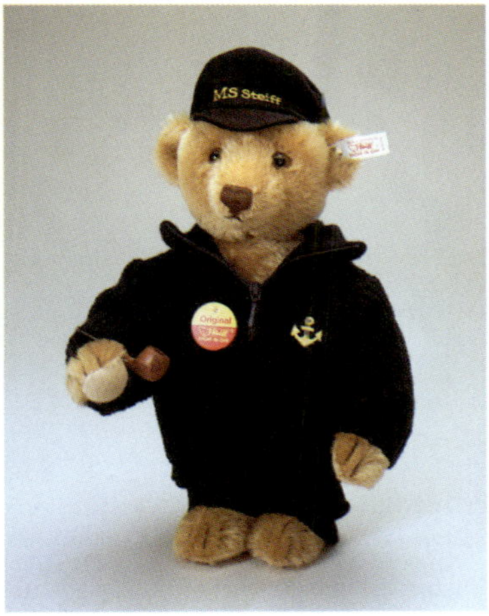

Teddybaer Fischer - *Teddybear Fisherman*

Mohair Webpelz, beige, gegliedert, abwaschbar, Kippstimme, limit. Auflage 2.000 Stueck - *mohair woven fur, beige, jointed, surface washable, tilt-me voice, ltd edition of 2,000*

EAN-No.	Period	Pr.	Info
670114	1999-1999	4	35 cm

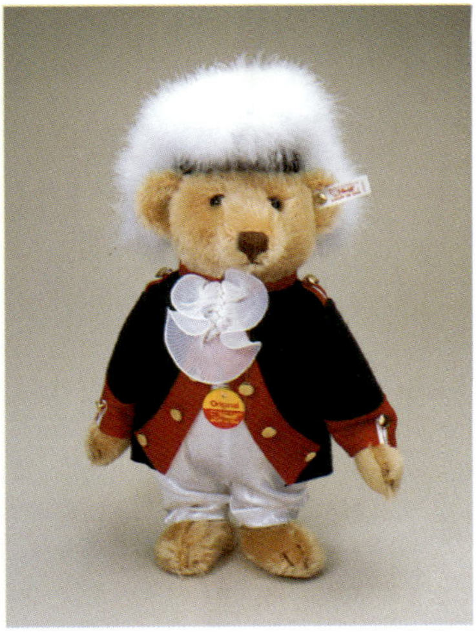

Teddybaer Stadtsoldat - *Teddybear Town Soldier*

Mohair Webpelz, honigblond, gegliedert, abwaschbar, Kippstimme, limit. Auflage 2.000 Stueck - *mohair woven fur, honey blond, jointed, surface washable, tilt-me voice, ltd edition of 2,000*

EAN-No.	Period	Pr.	Info
670251	1999-1999	4	35 cm

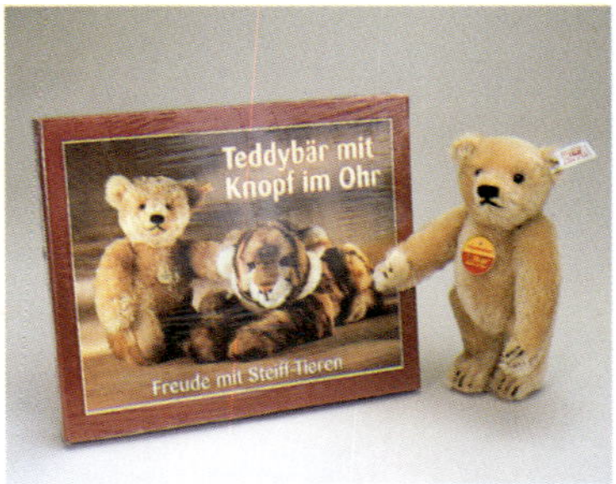

Teddybaer **Celebration** - *Teddybear **Celebration***

Mohair Webpelz, blond, gegliedert, abwaschbar, mit Buch "Steiff Design", limit. Auflage 4.000 Stueck, 1.000 in Deutsch, 3.000 in Englisch - *mohair woven fur, blond, jointed, surface washable, with book "Teddybär mit Knopf im Ohr", ltd edition of 4,000, 1,000 German, 3,000 English*

EAN-No.	Period	Pr.	Info
670176	1999-1999	4	22 cm

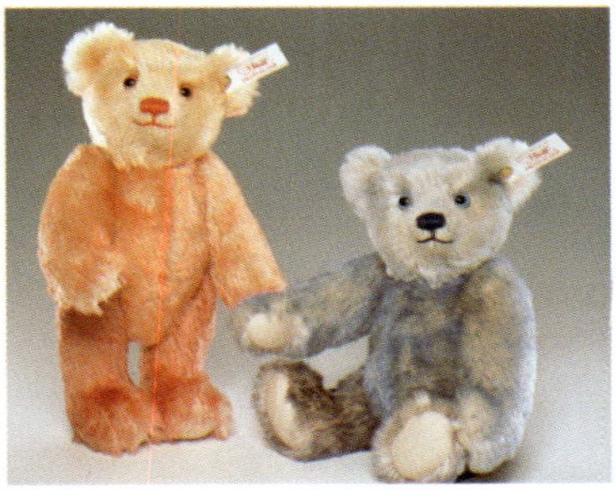

Hallo / Good-Bye Baerenset - *Hallo / Good-Bye Bear-Set*

Mohair Webpelz, hellblau bzw. apricot, gegliedert, abwaschbar, Jahreslimitierung bis 31.12.2000 - *mohair woven fur, light blue or apricot, jointed, surface washable, limited availability up to 31.12.2000*

EAN-No.	Period	Pr.	Info
670367	1999-2000	4-5	kpl. Set - *compl. set*
	1999-2000	3-4	22 cm, hellblau - *light blue*
	1999-2000	3-4	22 cm, apricot

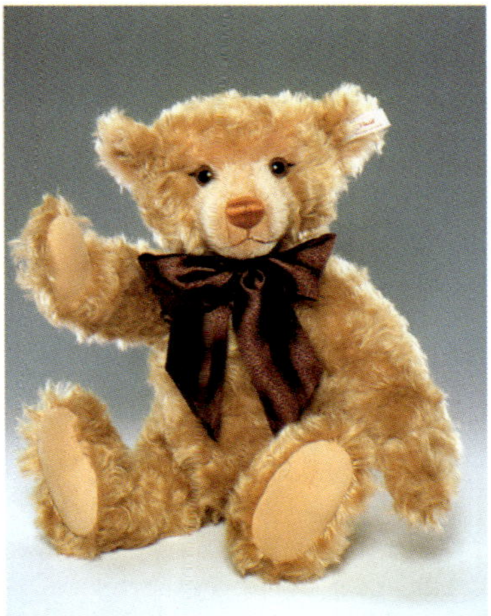

Jahrtausend Teddybaer - *Millenium Teddybear*

Mohair Webpelz, dunkelblond, gegliedert, abwaschbar, mit vergoldetem Knopf im Ohr, Jahreslimitierung bis 31.12.2000 - *mohair woven fur, dark blond, jointed, surface washable, genuine gold plated button in ear, limited availability up to 31.12.2000*

EAN-No.	Period	Pr.	Info
670374	1999-2000	4	43 cm

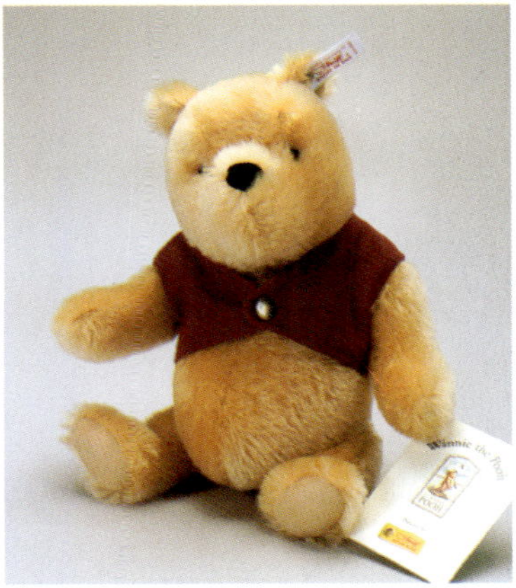

Winnie the Pooh

Mohair Webpelz, blond, gegliedert, abwaschbar, mit roter Weste, Lizenzartikel Walt Disney, limit. Auflage 10.000 Stueck - *mohair woven fur, blond, jointed, surface washable, red waistcoat, in cooperation with Walt Disney Company, ltd edition of 10,000*

EAN-No.	Period	Pr.	Info
651489	1999-1999	4	27 cm

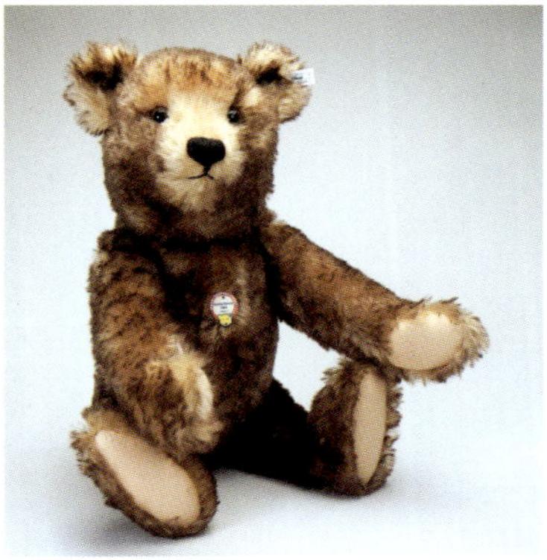

Teddy Peace

Mohair, braun gespitzt, gegliedert, abwaschbar, Replik des Bären von 1925, der auf dem 1. Steiff Festival fuer DM 189.550,00 versteigert wurde, limit. Auflage 1.500 Stueck - *mohair, brown tipped, jointed, surface washable, reproduction of the 1925 bear, sold in the auction of the 1st Steiff Festival for DM 189,550.00, ltd edition of 1,500*

EAN-No.	Period	Pr.	Info
675249	1999-1999	6	65 cm

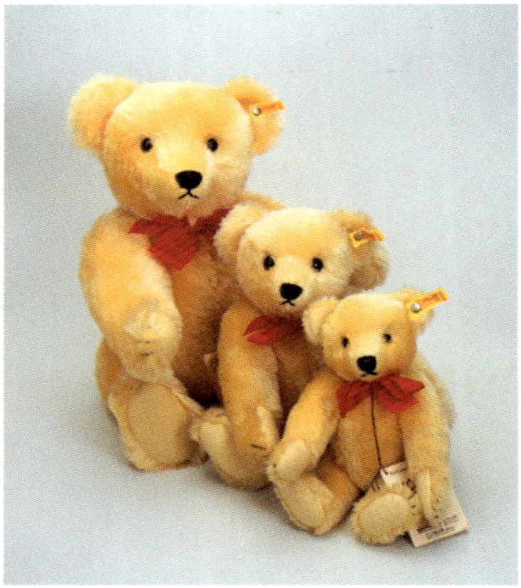

Teddybaer Replica 1909 - *1909 Teddy Bear Replica*

Mohair Webpelz, Filzpfoten, gestickte Krallen, gold, gegliedert, Brummstimme, 28 & 60 cm nur in USA, 38 & 51 cm 1983 nur USA - ab 1984 weltweit, abwaschbar - *mohair woven fur, felt paws with claws embroidered, gold, jointed, growler, 28 & 60 cm exclusively for USA, 38 & 51 cm in 1983 exclusively for USA, from 1984 worldwide. surface washable*

Serie	Art.-No	Period	Pr.	Info
	0165/28	1984-1986	4-5	28 cm
406331	**0165/38**	1983-1988	4	38 cm
406379	**0165/51**	1983-1988	5	51 cm
	0165/60	1984-1986	5-6	60 cm

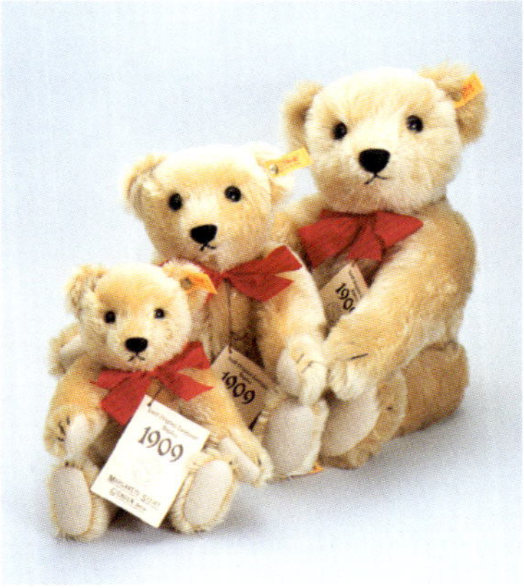

Classic 1909 Teddybaer - *Classic 1909 Teddybear*

Mohair Webpelz, Filzpfoten, gestickte Krallen, blond, gegliedert, 25 cm Druck-, ab 35 cm Brummstimme, abwaschbar - *mohair woven fur, felt paws, embroidered claws, blond, jointed, 25 cm press voice, from 35 cm growler, surface washable*

Serie	Art.-No	Period	Pr.	Info
406201	**0166/25**	1988-1990	3	25 cm
	406201	1991-1992	3	
	000355	1993-1999	3	
406225	**0166/35**	1988-1990	3	35 cm
	406225	1991-1992	3	
	000379	1993-1999	3	
406256	**0166/43**	1988-1990	3-4	43 cm
	406256	1991-1992	3-4	
	000393	1993-1999	3-4	

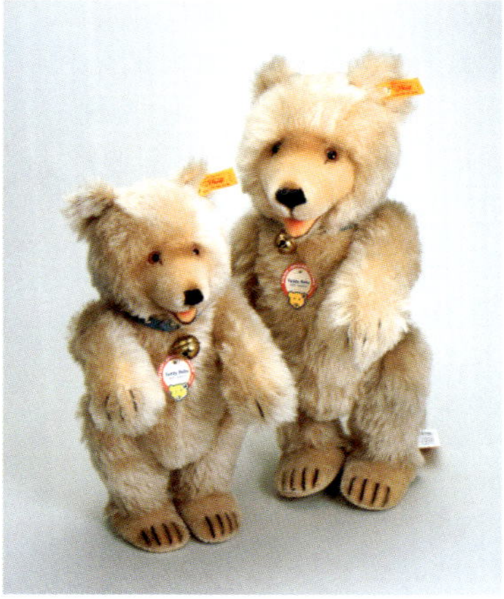

Teddy Baby Replica 1930

Mohair Webpelz, gegliedert, verziertes Lederhalsband, blond, Stimme - *mohair woven fur, jointed, decorated collar, blond, voice*

EAN-No.	Period	Pr.	Info
407833	1992-1996	3	29 cm
407857	1992-1993	4	35 cm

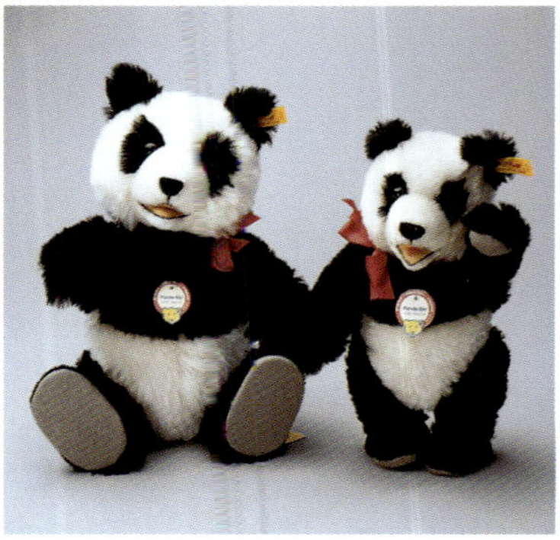

Panda Baer Replica 1938 - *1938 Panda Bear Replica*

Mohair Webpelz, schwarz/weiss, gegliedert - *mohair woven fur, black/white, jointed*

EAN-No.	Period	Pr.	Info
408304	1992-1998	3	29 cm
408311	1992-1998	3	35 cm

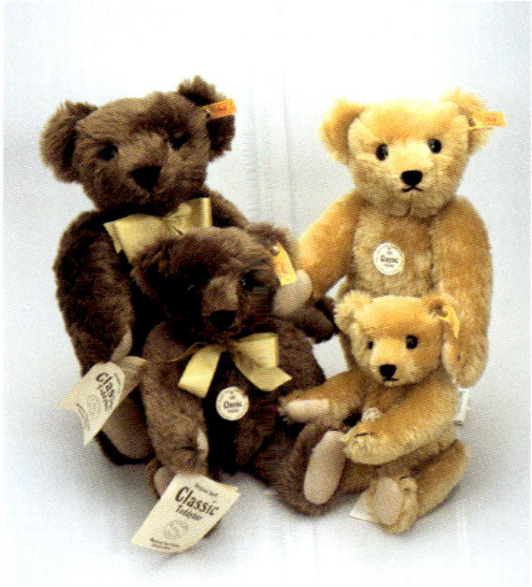

Classic 1909 Teddybaer - *Classic 1909 Teddy Bear*

Mohair Webpelz, gegliedert, 25 cm Druck-, ab 35 cm Brummstimme - *mohair woven fur, jointed, 25 cm press voice, from 35 cm growler*

EAN-No.	Period	Pr.	Info
000423	1993-1999	3	25 cm, dunkelbraun - *dark brown*
000447	1993-1999	3	35 cm
000461	1993-1999	3-4	43 cm
000492	1998-1999	3	25 cm, messing - *brass*
000508	1998-1999	3	35 cm
000515	1999-1999	3-4	43 cm

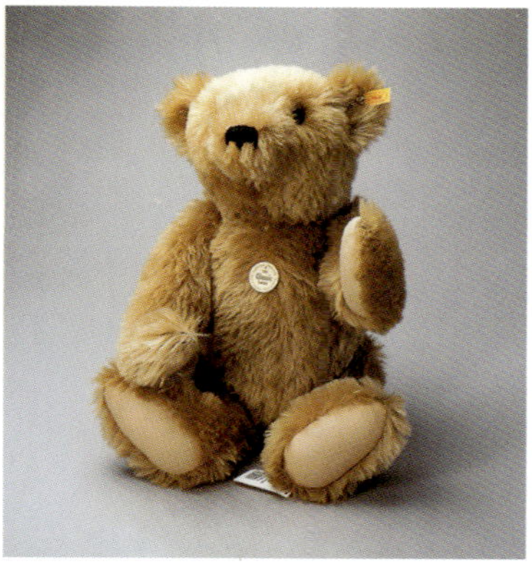

Classic Teddybaer - *Classic Teddy Bear*

Mr. Cinnamon, Mohair Webpelz, zimt, gegliedert, Druckstimme - *Mr. Cinnamon, mohair woven fur, cinnamon, jointed, press voice*

EAN-No.	Period	Pr.	Info
000201	1993-1999	4	55 cm

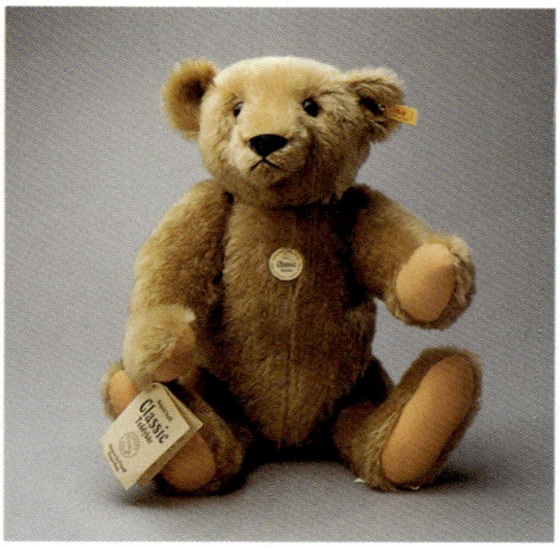

Classic 1906 Teddybaer - *Classic 1906 Teddy Bear*

Mohair Webpelz, beige, gegliedert, Brummstimme - *mohair woven fur, beige, jointed, growler, surface washable*

EAN-No.	Period	Pr.	Info
000256	1993-1999	4	51 cm

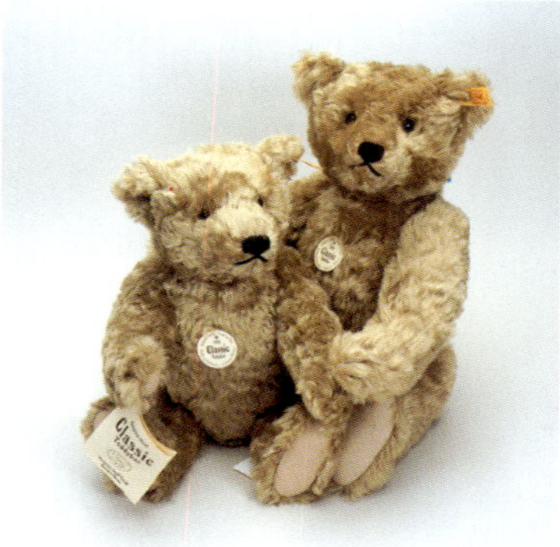

Classic 1920 Teddybaer - *Classic 1920 Teddy Bear*

Mohair Webpelz, hellbraun, gegliedert, ab 35 cm mit Brummstimme - *mohair woven fur, light brown, jointed, from 35 cm growler*

EAN-No.	Period	Pr.	Info
000713	1996-1999	3	25 cm
000737	1994-1999	3-4	35 cm
000751	1993-1999	3-4	42 cm

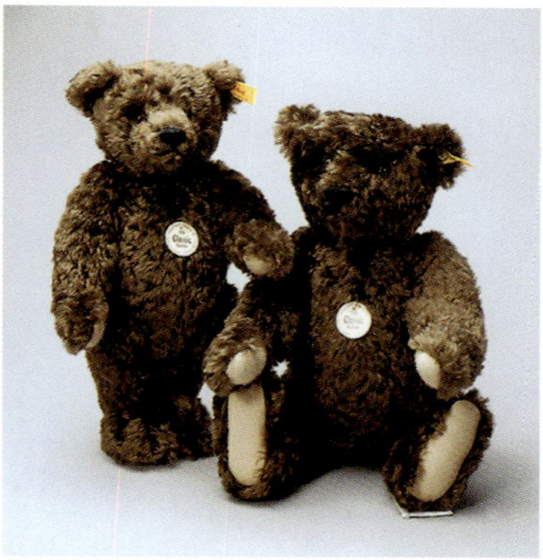

Classic 1920 Teddybaer - *Classic 1920 Teddy Bear*

Mohair Webpelz, dunkelbraun, ab 35 cm Brummstimme, gegliedert - *mohair woven fur, dark brown, jointed, from 35 cm growler*

EAN-No.	Period	Pr.	Info
000829	1994-1999	3	25 cm
000836	1994-1999	3-4	35 cm
000850	1993-1999	3-4	42 cm

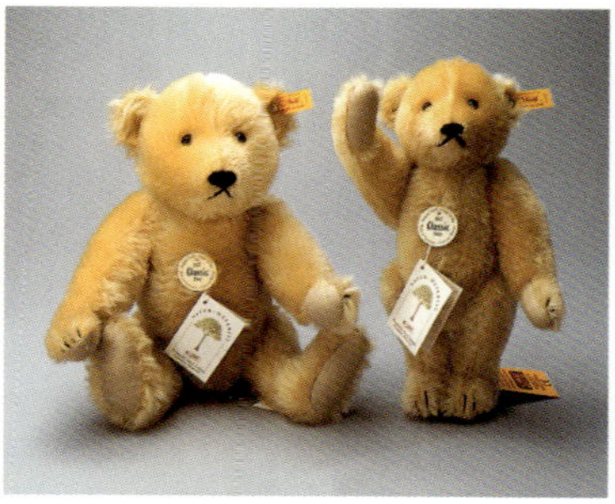

Classic 1927 Petsy

Mohair Webpelz, gelb, gegliedert, 28 cm Druck-, 35 cm Brummstimme - *mohair woven fur, yellow, jointed, 28 cm press voice, 35 cm growler*

EAN-No.	Period	Pr.	Info
000911	1994-1997	3	28 cm
000935	1994-1997	3	35 cm

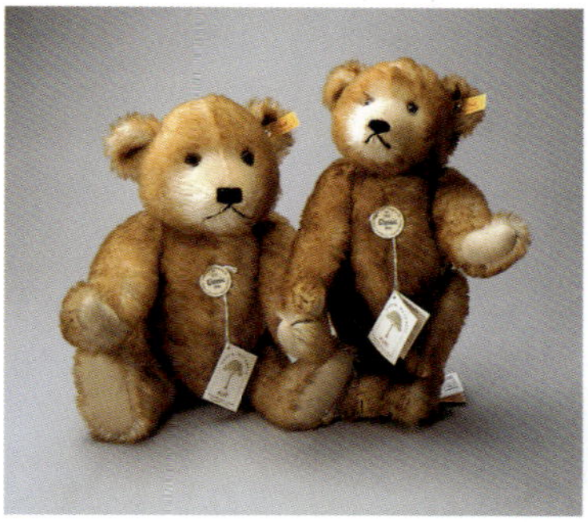

Classic 1928 Petsy

Mohair Webpelz, gespitzt, gegliedert, Brummstimme - *mohair woven fur, tipped fur, jointed, growler*

EAN-No.	Period	Pr.	Info
000966	1995-1997	3-4	35 cm
000980	1995-1999	4	43 cm

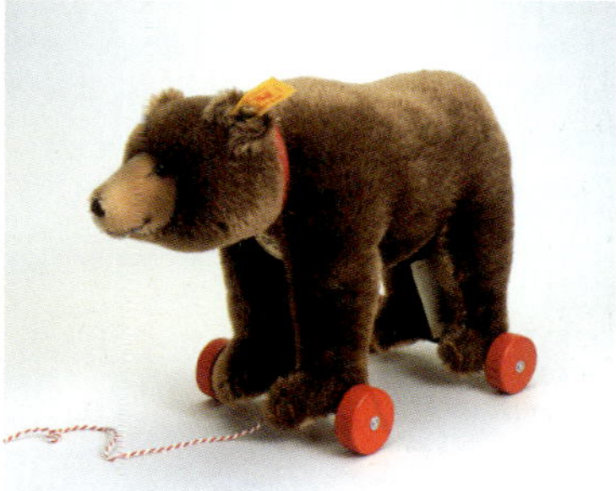

Classic 1938 Baer auf Raedern - *Classic 1938 Bear on Wheels*

Mohair Webpelz, braun, stehend auf Raedern, Kopf drehbar - *mohair woven fur, brown, mounted on wheels, head swivels*

EAN-No.	Period	Pr.	Info
036064	1995-1999	3-4	30 cm

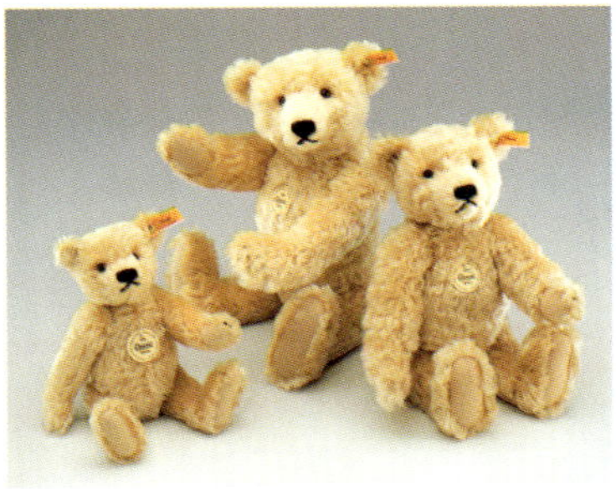

Classic 1920 Teddybaer - *Classic 1920 Teddybear*

Mohair Webpelz, hellblond, gegliedert, ab 35 cm Brummstimme, abwaschbar - *mohair woven fur, light blond, jointed, from 35 cm growler, surface washable*

EAN-No.	Period	Pr.	Info
000645	1996-1999	3	25 cm
000669	1996-1999	3-4	35 cm
000683	1996-1999	3-4	42 cm

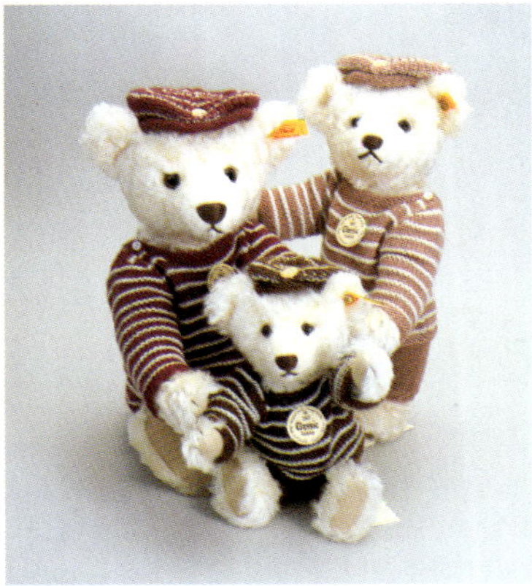

Classic 1907 Teddybaer - *Classic 1907 Teddybear*

Mohair Webpelz, rohweiss, gegliedert, abwaschbar, Druckstimme, Strickbekleidung - *mohair woven fur, raw white, jointed, surface washable, press voice, dressed in knitted wear*

EAN-No.	Period	Pr.	Info
027550	1996-1997	3-4	26 cm, dunkelbraun - *dark brown*
027567	1996-1997	3-4	33 cm, rosa - *pink*
027574	1996-1997	4	40 cm, brombeer - *blackberry*

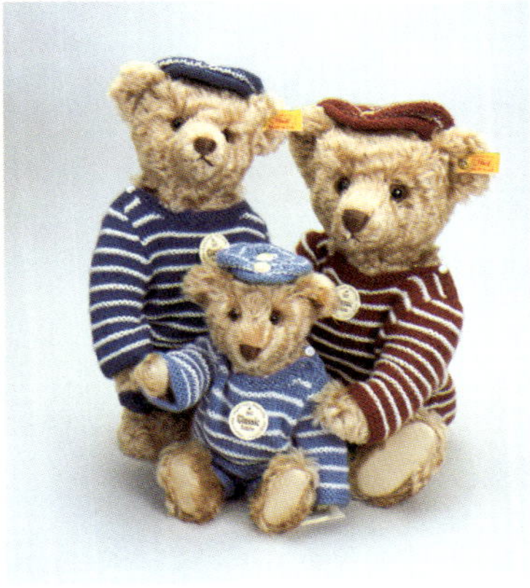

Classic 1907 Teddybaer - *Classic 1907 Teddybear*

Mohair Webpelz, zimt, gegliedert, abwaschbar, Druckstimme, Strickbekleidung - *mohair woven fur, cinnamon, jointed, surface washable, press voice, dressed in knitted wear*

EAN-No.	Period	Pr.	Info
027659	1996-1997	3-4	26 cm, hellblau - *light blue*
027666	1996-1997	3-4	33 cm, dunkelblau - *dark blue*
027673	1996-1997	4	40 cm, rost - *rusty*

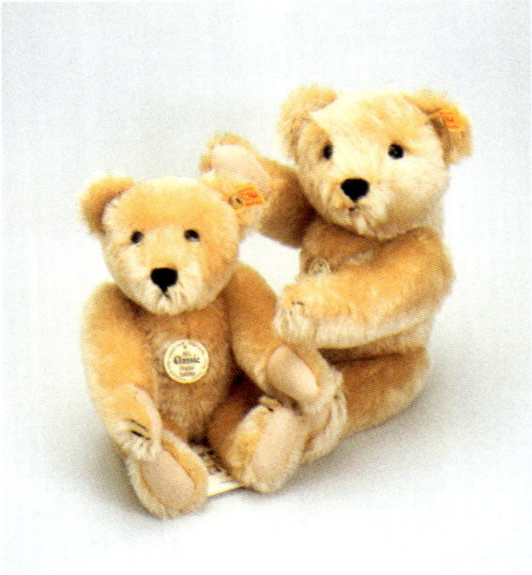

Classic 1951 Teddybaer - *Classic 1951 Teddybear*

Mohair Webpelz, blond, gegliedert, abwaschbar, Druckstimme - *mohair woven fur, blond, jointed, surface washable, press voice*

EAN-No.	Period	Pr.	Info
000874	1997-1999	3	22 cm
000881	1997-1999	3	25 cm
000898	1997-1999	3	32 cm

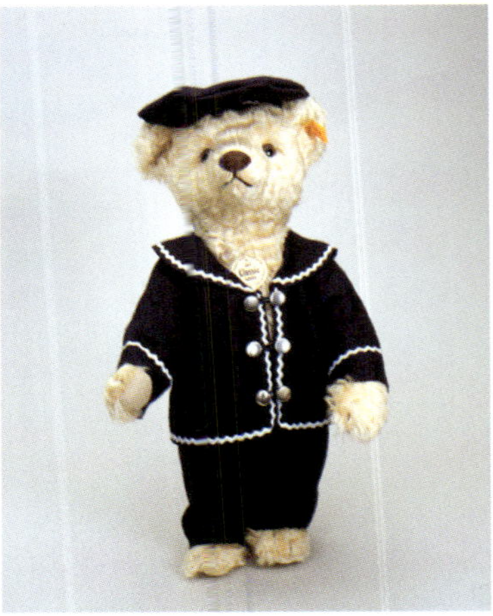

Classic 1907 Teddybaer - *Classic 1907 Teddybear*

Mohair Webpelz, hellblond, gegliedert, abwaschbar, Brummstimme, Filzbekleidung - *mohair woven fur, light blond, jointed, surface washable, growler, felt clothing*

EAN-No.	Period	Pr.	Info
027758	1997-1997	[illegible]	40 cm

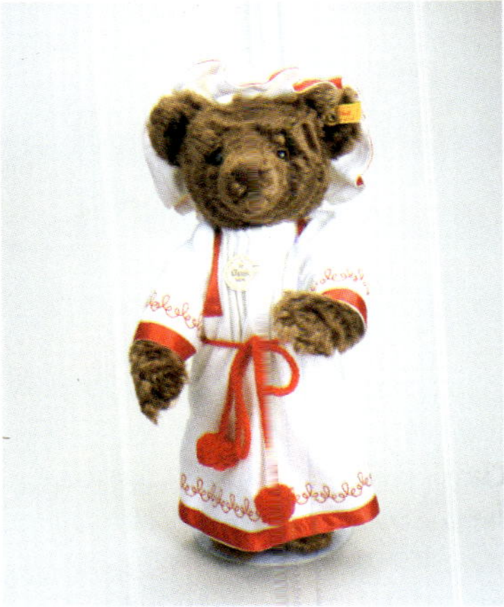

Classic 1907 Teddybaer - *Classic 1907 Teddybear*

Mohair Webpelz, rotbraun, gegliedert, abwaschbar, Brummstimme, Filzbekleidung - *mohair woven fur, redbrown, jointed, surface washable, growler, felt clothing*

EAN-No.	Period	Pr.	Info
027802	1997-1997	4	40 cm

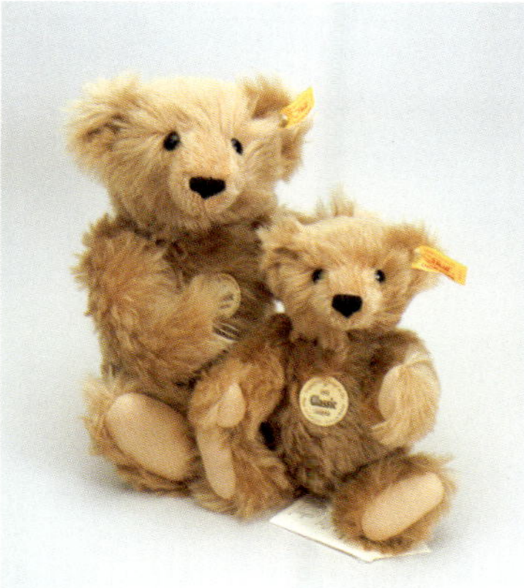

Classic 1903 Mr. Cinnamon

Mohair Webpelz, zimt, gegliedert, abwaschbar, 22 cm Druckstimme, 30 cm Brummstimme - *mohair woven fur, cinnamon, jointed, surface washable, 22 cm press voice, 30 cm tilt-me voice*

EAN-No.	Period	Pr.	Info
000171	1998-1999	3	22 cm
000188	1998-1999	3	30 cm

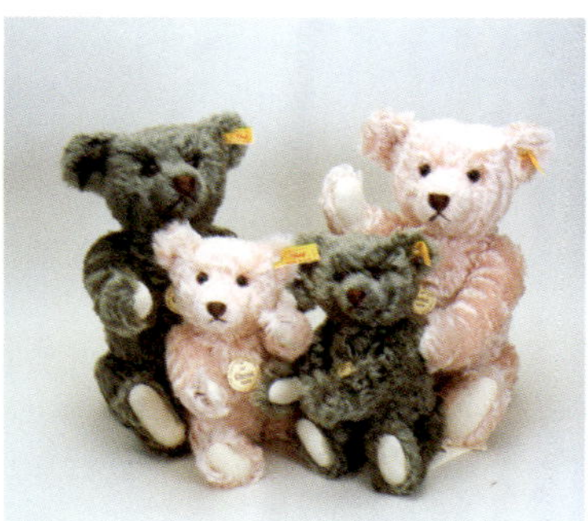

Classic 1907 Teddybaer - *Classic 1907 Teddybear*

Mohair Webpelz, gegliedert, abwaschbar, 25 cm mit Druck-, 35 cm Brummstimme - *mohair woven fur, jointed, surface washable, 25 cm press voice, 35 cm tilt-me voice*

EAN-No.	Period	Pr.	Info
000263	1998-1999	3	25 cm, rosè - *rose*
000270	1998-1999	3-4	35 cm
000300	1998-1999	3	25 cm, moosgruen - *moss-green*
000317	1998-1999	3-4	35 cm

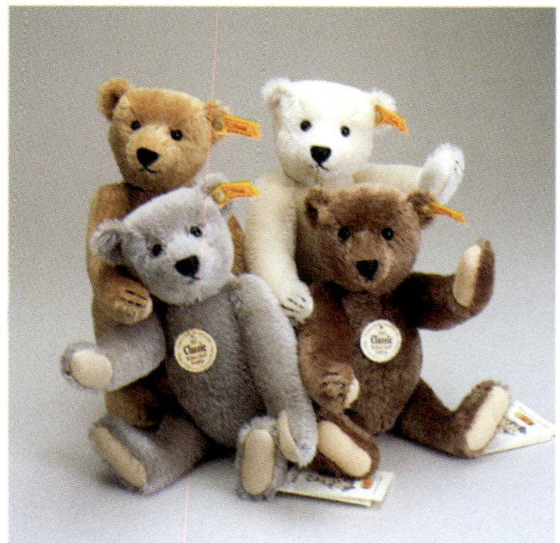

Classic 1905 Richard Steiff Teddybaer - *Classic 1905 Richard Steiff Teddybear*

Mohair Webpelz, 25 cm, gegliedert, abwaschbar - *mohair woven fur, 25 cm, jointed, surface washable*

EAN-No.	Period	Pr.	Info
001604	1999-1999	3	weiss - *white*
001666	1999-1999	3	grau - *grey*
001727	1999-1999	3	beige
001789	1999-1999	3	caramel

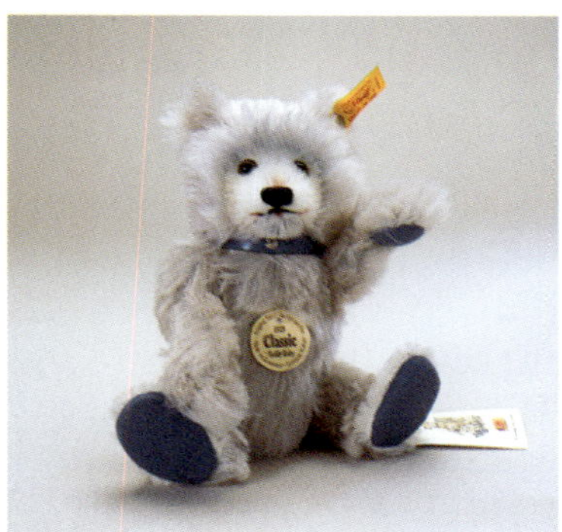

Classic 1929 Teddy Baby

Mohair Webpelz, blau, gegliedert, abwaschbar, Lederhalsband - *mohair woven fur, blue, jointed, surface washable, leather collar*

EAN-No.	Period	Pr.	Info
006425	1999-1999	3	22 cm

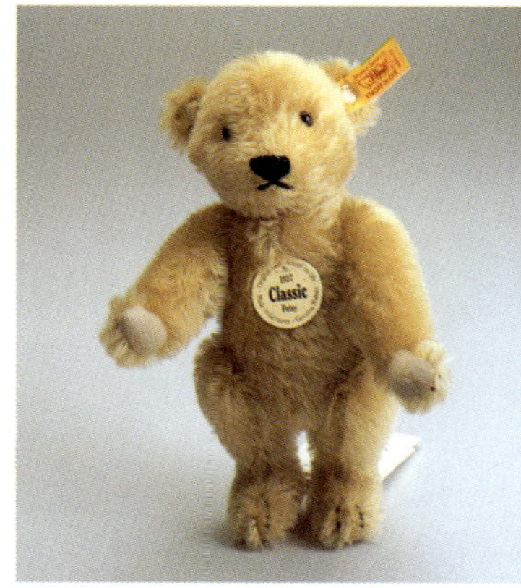

Classic 1927 Teddy Petsy

Mohair Webpelz, messing, gegliedert, abwaschbar - *mohair woven fur, brass, jointed, surface washable*

EAN-No.	Period	Pr.	Info
006432	1999-1999	3	22 cm

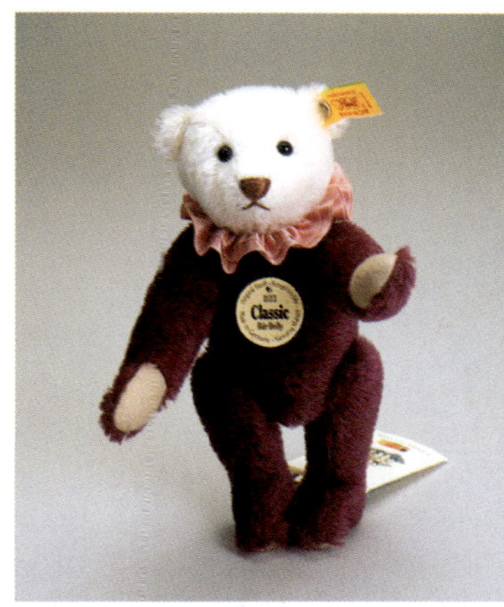

Classic 1913 Baer Dolly - *Classic 1913 Bear Dolly*

Mohair Webpelz, weiss/violett, gegliedert, abwaschbar, Halskrause - *mohair woven fur, white/violet, jointed, surface washable, ruff*

EAN-No.	Period	Pr.	Info
006401	1999-1999	3	22 cm

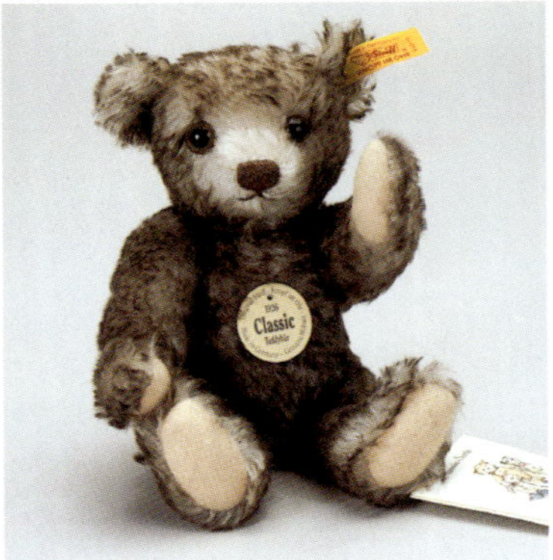

Classic 1926 Teddybaer - *Classic 1926 Teddybear*

Mohair Webpelz, braun gespitzt, gegliedert, abwaschbar - *mohair woven fur, brown tipped, jointed, surface washable*

EAN-No.	Period	Pr.	Info
006418	1999-1999	3	22 cm

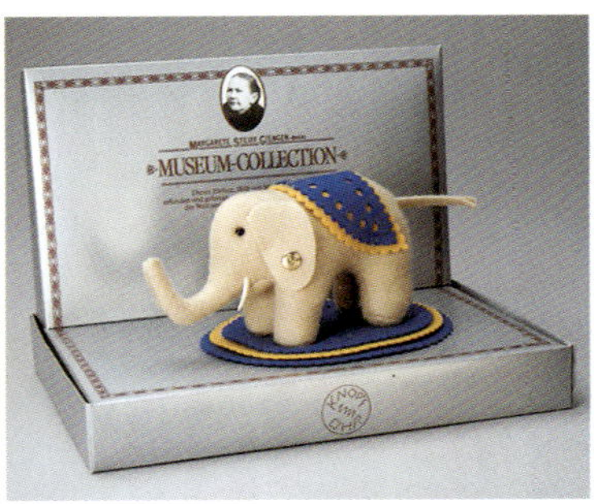

Filzelefant Replica 1880 - *1880 Felt Elephant Replica*

Wollfilz, limit. Auflage 10.000 Stueck - *wool felt, ltd edition of 10,000*

Serie	Art.-No	Period	Pr.	Info
400025	0080/08	1984-1987	3-4	8 cm

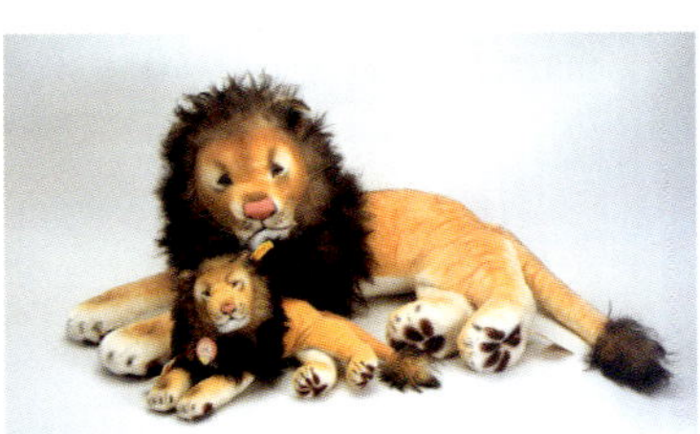

Leo Loewe Replica 1956 - *1956 Leo Lion Replica*

Mohair-Webpelz, liegend, 50 cm limit. Auflage 4.000 Stueck - *mohair woven fur, lying, size 50 cm ltd edition of 4,000*

Serie	Art.-No	Period	Pr.	Info
402425	**0111/21**	1984-1986	3-4	21 cm
402449	**0111/35**	1984-1986	4	35 cm
	402463	1992-1998	4-5	50 cm

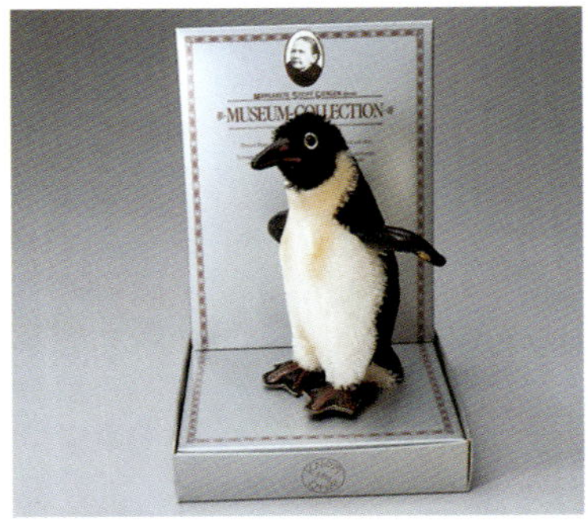

Pinguin Replica 1928 - *1928 Penguin Replica*

Mohair Webpelz, stehend, limit. Auflage 8.000 Stueck - *mohair woven fur, standing, ltd edition of 8,000*

Serie	Art.-No	Period	Pr.	Info
401251	0105/17	1985-1987	3-4	17 cm

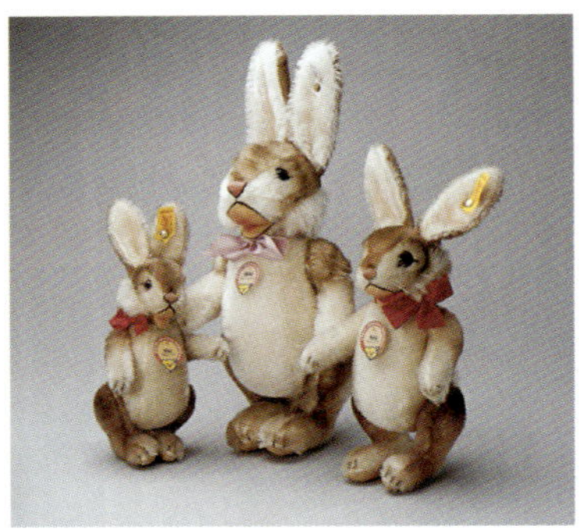

Niki Replica 1952

Mohair Webpelz, gegliedert, 35 cm limit. Auflage 5.000 Stueck - *mohair woven fur, jointed, size 35 cm ltd edition of 5,000*

Serie	Art.-No	Period	Pr.	Info
	0134/22	1985-1985	3	22 cm
	0134/28	1985-1985	3-4	28 cm
	402159	1992-1998	3-4	35 cm

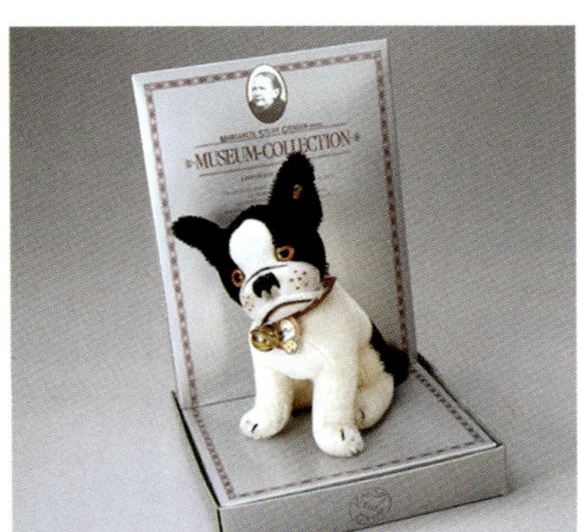

Bully Replica 1927

Mohair Webpelz, sitzend, limit. Auflage 6.000 Stueck - *mohair woven fur, sitting, ltd edition of 6,000*

Serie	Art.-No	Period	Pr.	Info
400957	0101/14	1986-1987	4	14 cm

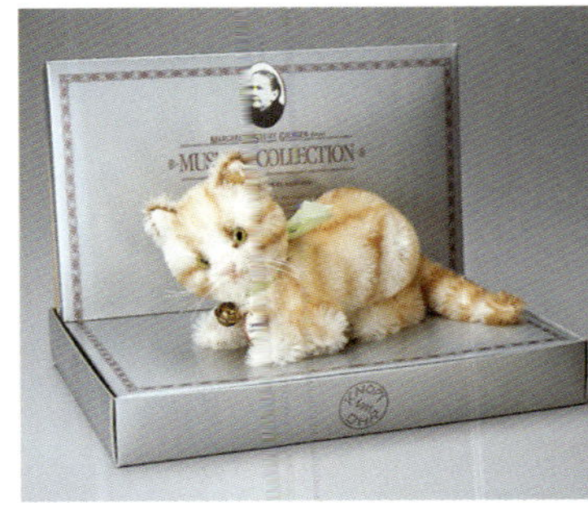

Tabby Replica 1928

Mohair Webpelz, liegend, limit. Auflage 6.000 Stueck - *mohair woven fur, lying, ltd edition of 6,000*

Serie	Art.-No	Period	Pr.	Info
401237	0104/10	1986-1988	3-4	10 cm

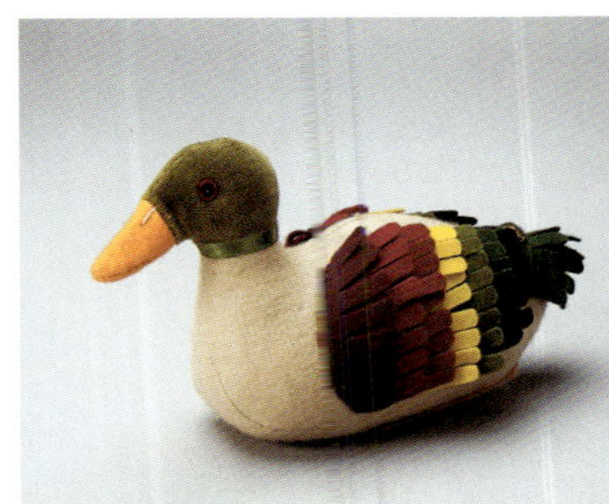

Ente Replica 1892 - *1892 Duck Replica*

Wollfilz, limit. Auflage 4.000 Stueck - *wool felt, ltd edition of 4,000*

Serie	Art.-No	Period	Pr.	Info
400186	0081/14	1988-1989	3	14 cm

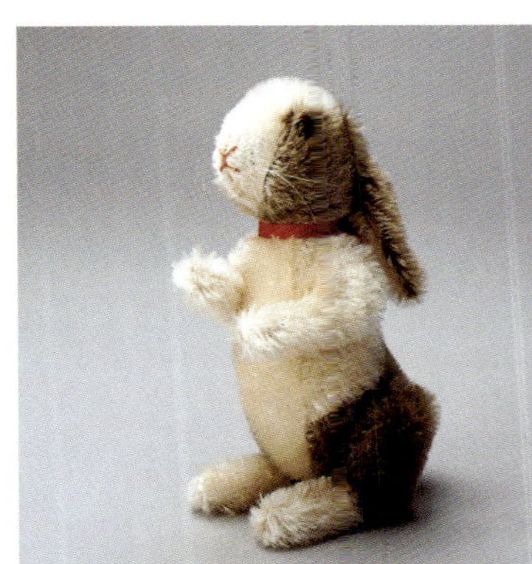

Hollaender Hase Replica 1911 - *1911 Dutch Rabbit Replica*

Mohair Webpelz, Kopf, Arme, Beine & Ohren gegliedert, limit. Auflage 4.000 Stueck - *mohair woven fur, head, arms, legs & ears jointed, ltd edition of 4,000*

SERIE	ART.-NO	PERIOD	PR.	INFO
400605	**0095/17**	1988-1988	4	17 cm

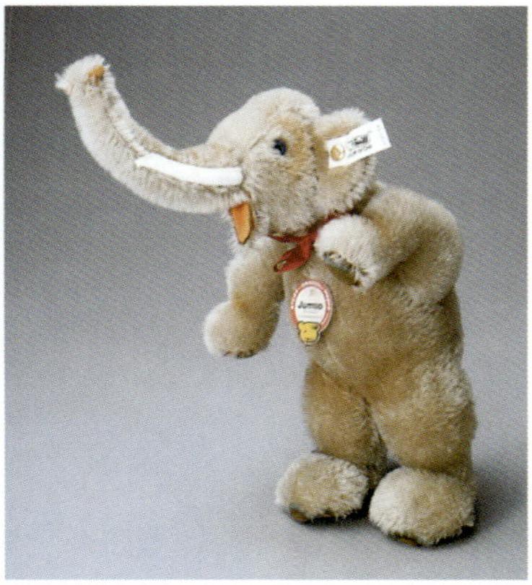

Jumbo Elefant Replica 1932 - ***Jumbo*** *1932 Elephant Replica*

Mohair, Vorderbeine & Ruessel gegliedert, Halsmechanik, limit. Auflage 4.000 Stueck - *mohair, front legs & trunk are jointed, neck mechanism, ltd edition of 4,000*

SERIE	ART.-NO	PERIOD	PR.	INFO
401404	**0125/24**	1988-1989	4	24 cm

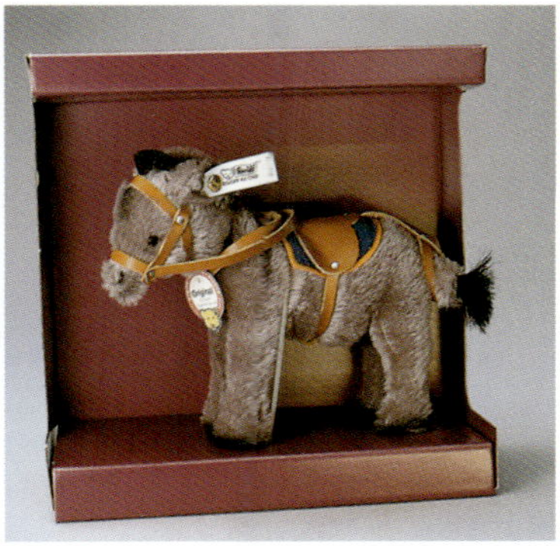

Esel Replica 1931 - *1931 Donkey Replica*

Mohair, stehend, Halsmechanik, limit. Auflage 4.000 Stueck - *mohair, standing, neck mechanism, ltd edition of 4,000*

SERIE	ART.-NO	PERIOD	PR.	INFO
401350	**0126/20**	1988-1989	3-4	20 cm

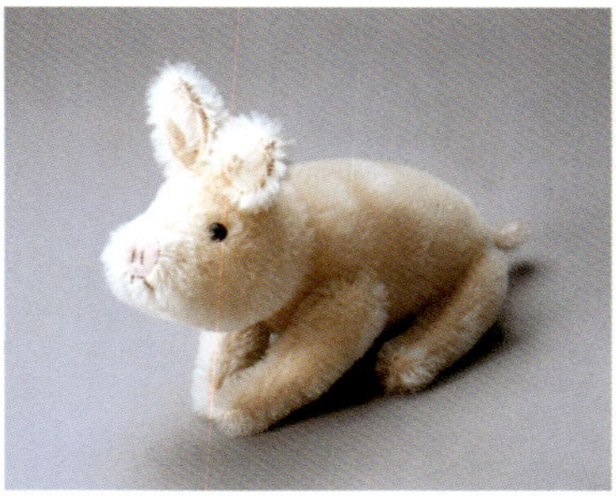

Schwein Replica 1909 - *1909 Pig Replica*

Mohair-Webpelz, Halsmechanik, limit. Auflage 4.000 Stueck - *mohair woven fur, neck mechanism, ltd edition of 4,000*

SERIE	ART.-NO	PERIOD	PR.	INFO
400551	0091/14	1989-1990	3-4	14 cm
	400551	1991-1992	3-4	

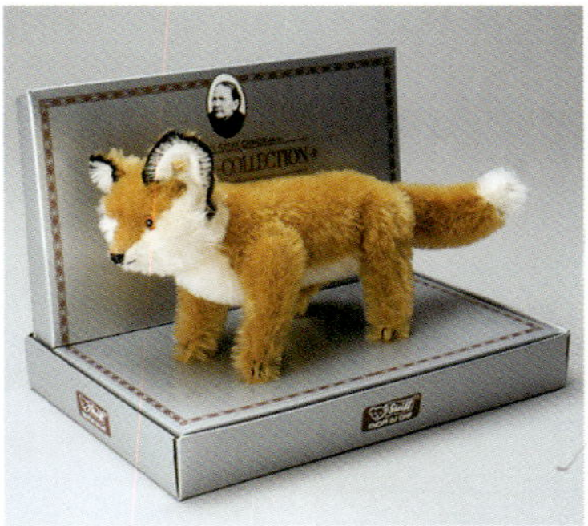

Fuchs Replica 1910 - *1910 Fox Replica*

Mohair-Webpelz, gegliedert, limit. Auflage 4.000 Stueck - *mohair woven fur, jointed, ltd edition of 4,000*

SERIE	ART.-NO	PERIOD	PR.	INFO
400582	0093/12	1989-1990	3-4	12 cm
	400582	1991-1992	3-4	

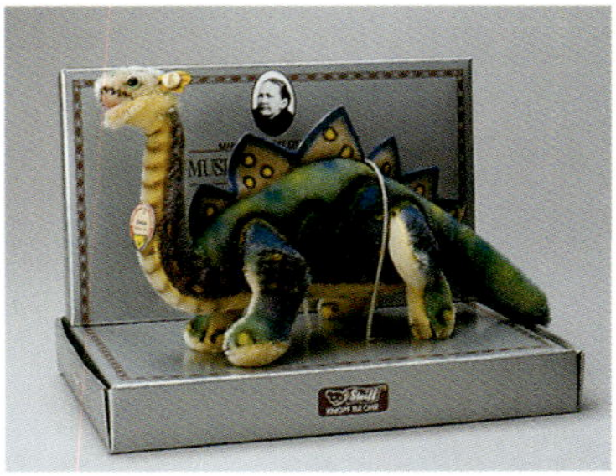

Dinos Replica 1959

Mohair Webpelz, limit. Auflage 4.000 Stueck - *mohair woven fur, ltd edition of 4,000*

SERIE	ART.-NO	PERIOD	PR.	INFO
401701	0050/28	1990-1990	4	28 cm
	401701	1991-1991	4	

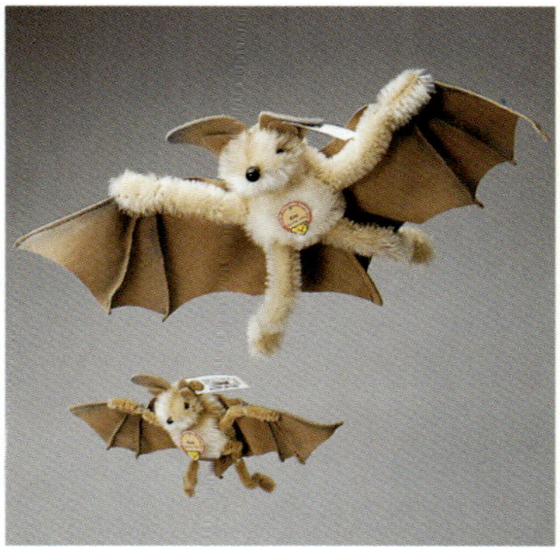

Eric Replica 1959

Mohair Webpelz, limit. Auflage 4.000 Stueck - *mohair woven fur, ltd edition of 4,000*

SERIE	ART.-NO	PERIOD	PR.	INFO
401800	**0055/00**	1990-1990	4-5	12/17 cm
	401800	1991-1991	4-5	

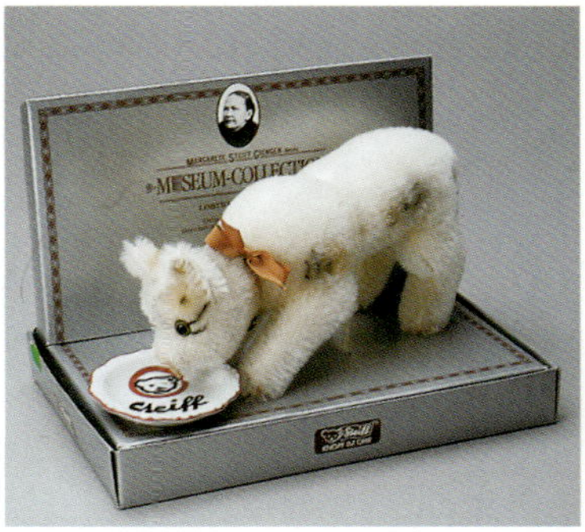

Trink-Katze Replica 1933 - *1933 Drinking Cat Replica*

Mohair Webpelz, limit. Auflage 4.000 Stueck, trinkt durch Gummibalg im Inneren der Katze - *mohair woven fur, drinks by means of rubber sack inside the cat, ltd edition of 4,000*

SERIE	ART.-NO	PERIOD	PR.	INFO
401459	0108/14	1990-1990	3-4	14 cm

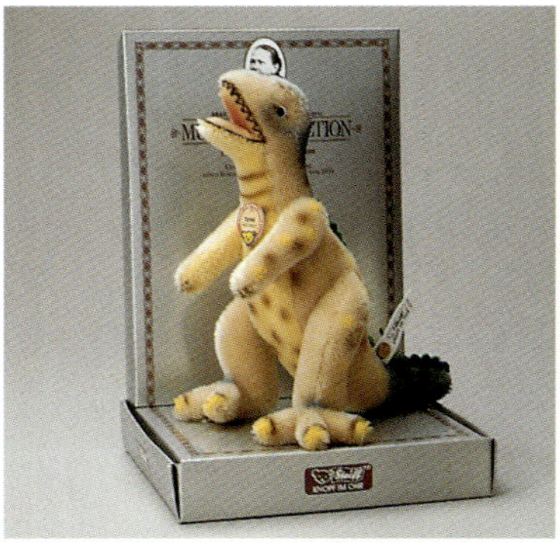

Tyros Replica 1959

Mohair, Arme gegliedert, limit. Auflage 4.000 Stueck - *mohair, arms jointed, ltd edition of 4,000*

EAN-No.	Period	Pr.	Info
401718	1991-1992	4	20 cm

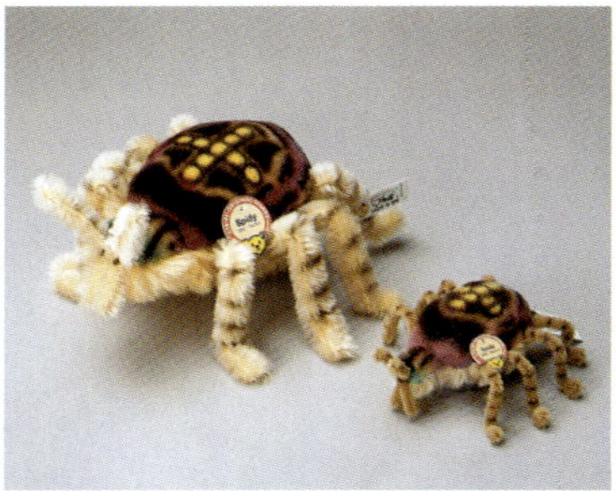

Spidy Replica 1960 Set

Mohair Webpelz, limit. Auflage 4.000 Stueck - *mohair woven fur, ltd edition of 4,000*

EAN-No.	Period	Pr.	Info
401732	1991-1992	4-5	13/23 cm

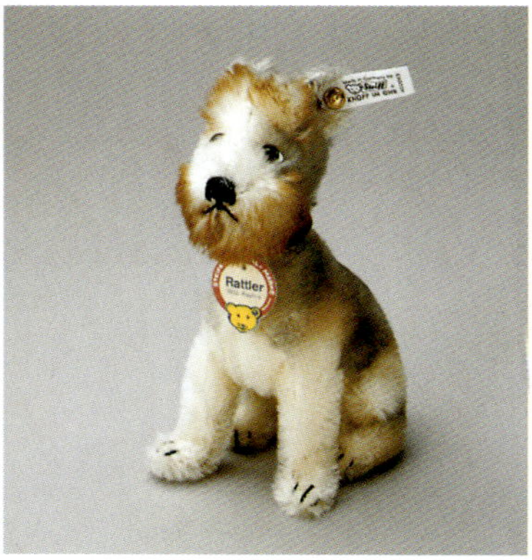

Rattler Replica 1930

Mohair Webpelz, Halsmechanik, limit. Auflage 4.000 Stueck - *mohair woven fur, neck mechanism, ltd edition of 4,000*

EAN-No.	Period	Pr.	Info
402043	1992-1992	4	17 cm

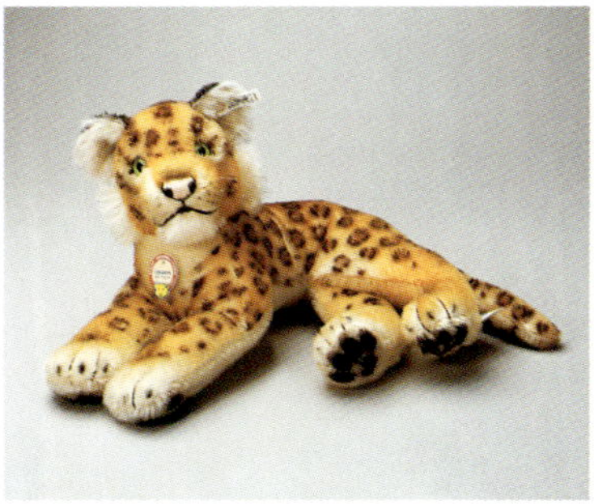

Leopard Replica 1953

Mohair Webpelz, liegend, limit. Auflage 4.000 Stueck - *mohair woven fur, lying, ltd edition of 4,000*

EAN-No.	Period	Pr.	Info
402357	1992-1997	3-4	28 cm

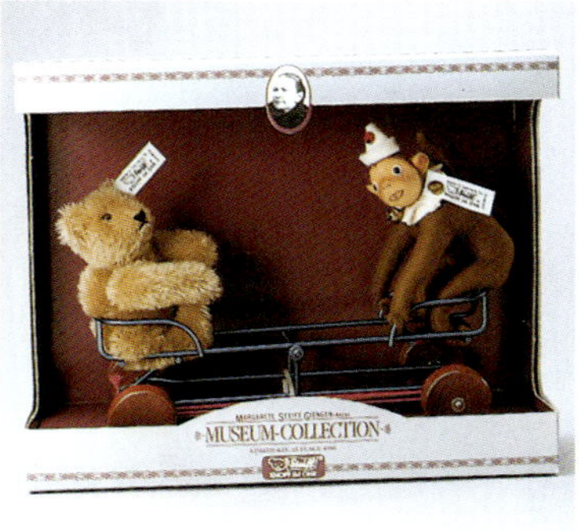

Wiwag mit Affe Replica 1924 - *1924 Seesaw with Monkey Replica*

Mohair Webpelz, limit. Auflage 4.000 Stueck - *mohair woven fur, ltd edition of 4,000*

EAN-No.	Period	Pr.	Info
400872	1992-1992	3	24 cm

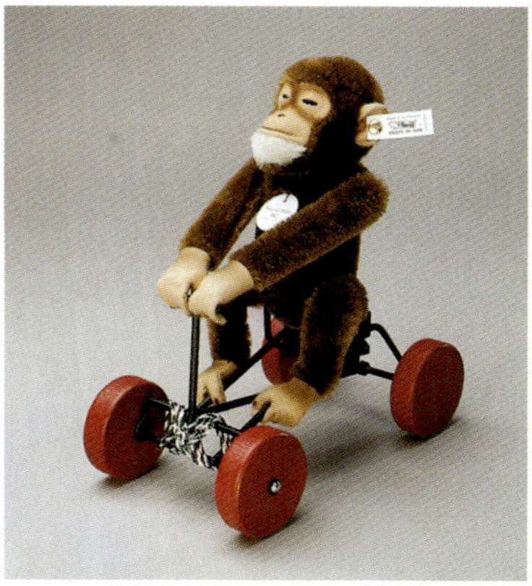

Record Peter Replica 1921

Mohair Webpelz, limit. Auflage 4.000 Stueck - *mohair woven fur, ltd edition of 4,000*

EAN-No.	Period	Pr.	Info
400759	1993-1993	3	25 cm

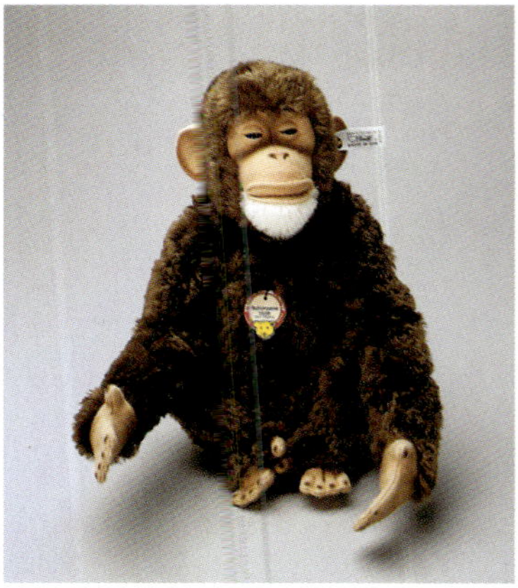

Schimpanse Replica 1928 - *1928 Chimpanzee Replica*

Mohair Webpelz, gegliedert, limit. Auflage 4.000 Stueck - *mohair woven fur, jointed, ltd edition of 4,000*

EAN-No.	Period	Pr.	Info
401213	1993-1993	[illegible]	40 cm

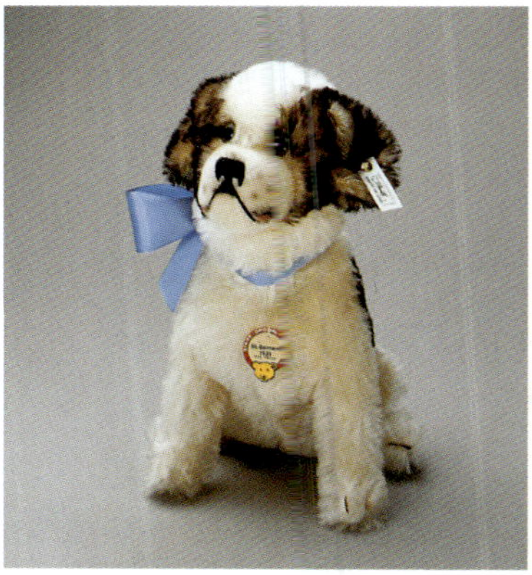

St. Bernhard Replica 1931

Mohair Webpelz, sitzend, Halsmechanik, limit. Auflage 4.000 Stueck - *mohair woven fur, sitting, neck mechanism, ltd edition of 4,000*

EAN-No.	Period	Pr.	Info
401367	1993-1993	4	28 cm

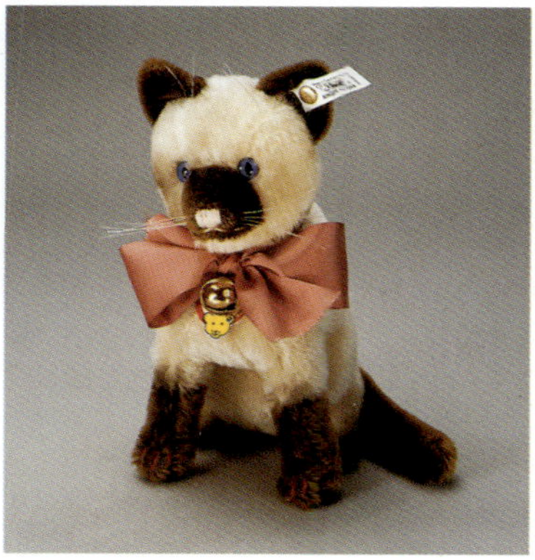

Siamy 1930 Replica

Mohair Webpelz, sitzend, Kopf drehbar, limit. Auflage 4.000 Stueck - *mohair woven fur, sitting, head swivels, ltd edition of 4,000*

EAN-No.	Period	Pr.	Info
400810	1994-1994	4	22 cm

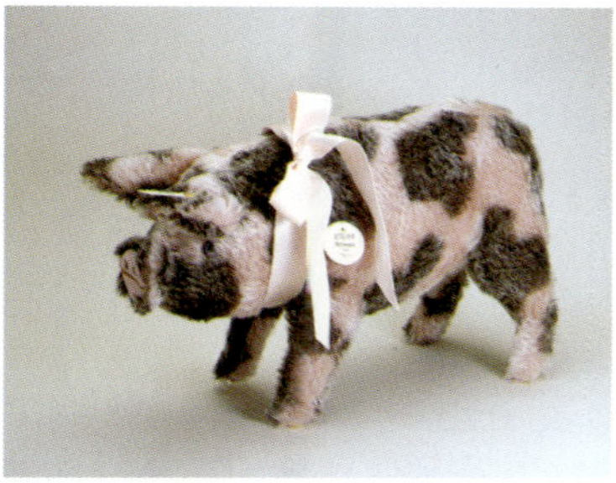

Schwein 1926 Replica - *1926 Pig Replica*

Mohair Webpelz, Druckbalgstimme, rosa, schwarz gefleckt, limit. Auflage 3.000 Stueck - *mohair woven fur, squeeze voice, pink, black spots, ltd edition of 3,000*

EAN-No.	Period	Pr.	Info
401190	1995-1996	4	35 cm

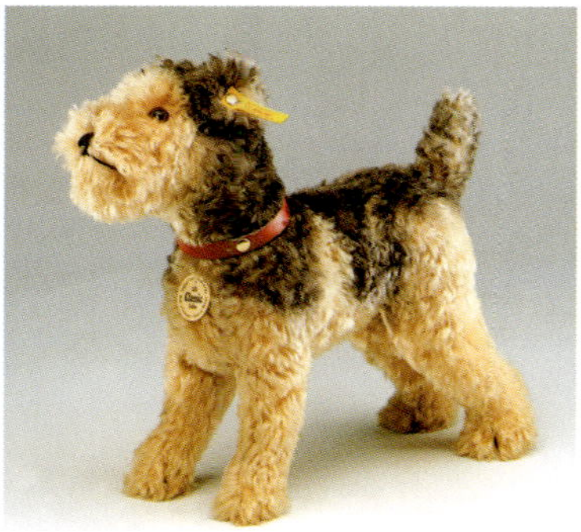

Classic 1935 Fellow

Schnauzer, Mohair Webpelz, Lederhalsband, stehend - *Schnauzer, mohair woven fur, leather collar, standing*

EAN-No.	Period	Pr.	Info
035012	1995-1999	3	30 cm

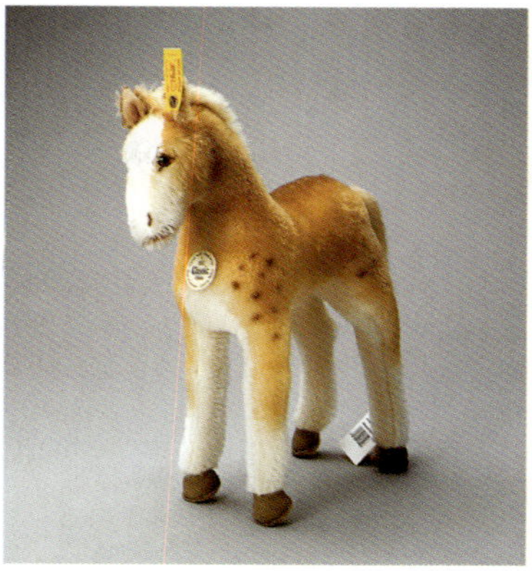

Classic 1932 Fohlen - *1932 Classic Foal*

Mohair Webpelz, hellbraun, stehend - *mohair woven fur, light brown, standing*

EAN-No.	Period	Pr.	Info
034503	1995-1997	3	33 cm

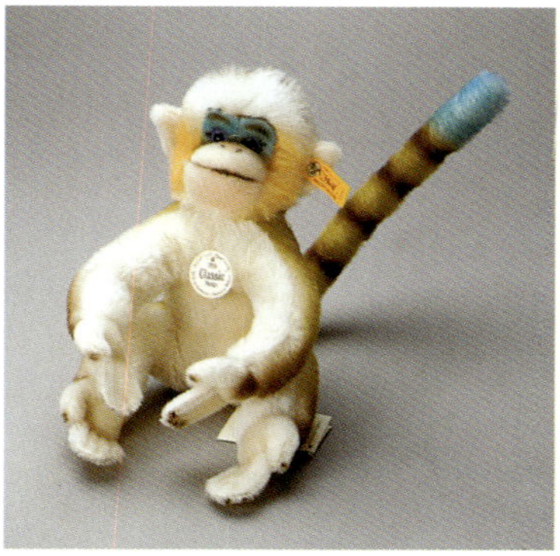

Classic 1958 Mungo

Buntaffe, Mohair Webpelz, sitzend, Kopf drehbar - *multi-colored monkey, mohair woven fur, sitting, head swivels*

EAN-No.	Period	Pr.	Info
034053	1995-1998	3	22 cm

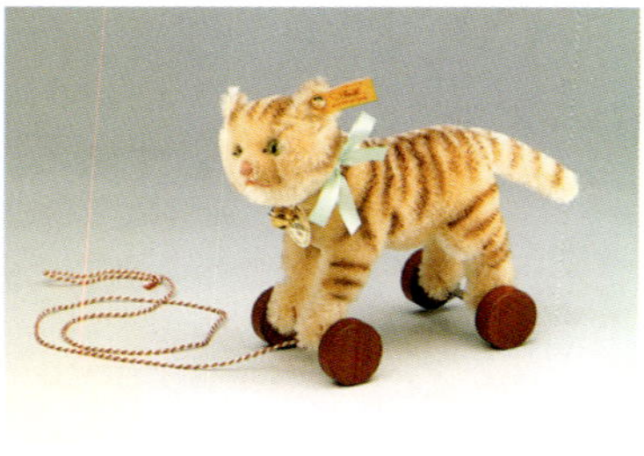

Classic 1928 Tabby

Katze auf Raedern, Mohair Webpelz, Holzraeder & Zugschnur, Kopf drehbar - *cat on wheels, mohair woven fur, wooden wheels with pull cord, head swivels*

EAN-No.	Period	Pr.	Info
036200	1995-1998	3-4	20 cm

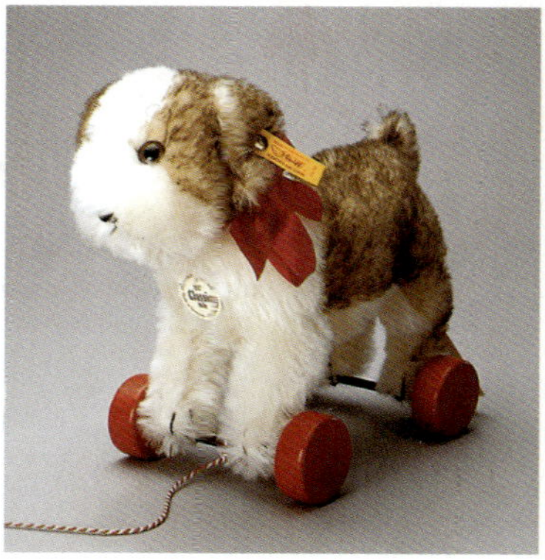

Classic 1927 Molly

Hund auf Exzenterraedern, Mohair Webpelz, Kopf drehbar - *dog on eccentric wheels, mohair woven fur, head swivels*

EAN-No.	Period	Pr.	Info
036354	1995-1996	3-4	25 cm

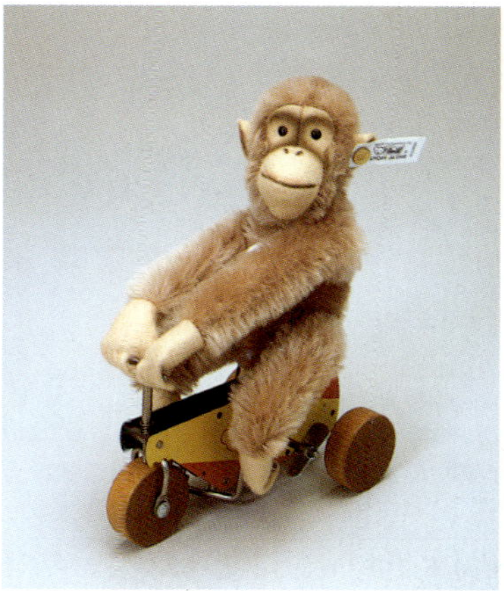

Urfips Replica 1926

Mohair Webpelz, braun, gegliedert, abwaschbar, auf Dreirad, Stopfung Holzwolle, limit. Auflage 3.000 Stueck - *mohair woven fur, brown, jointed, surface washable, on a tricycle, excelsior stuffed, ltd edition of 3,000*

EAN-No.	Period	Pr.	Info
400896	1996-1998	4	18 cm

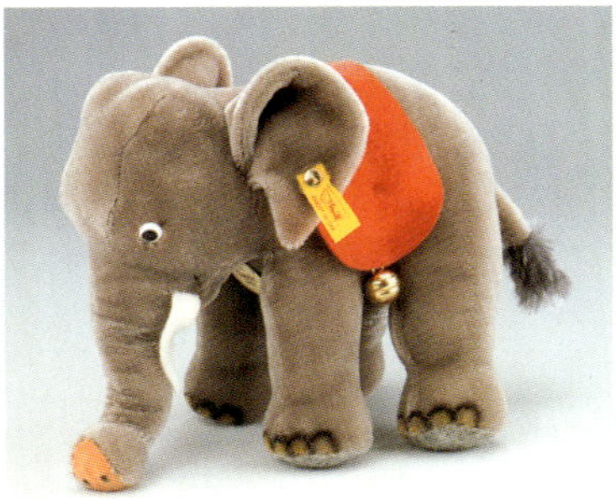

Classic 1952 Elefant - *Classic 1952 Elephant*

Mohair Webpelz, abwaschbar, Filzschabracke - *mohair woven fur, surface washable, felt saddlecloth*

EAN-No.	Period	Pr.	Info
034152	1997-1998	3	22 cm

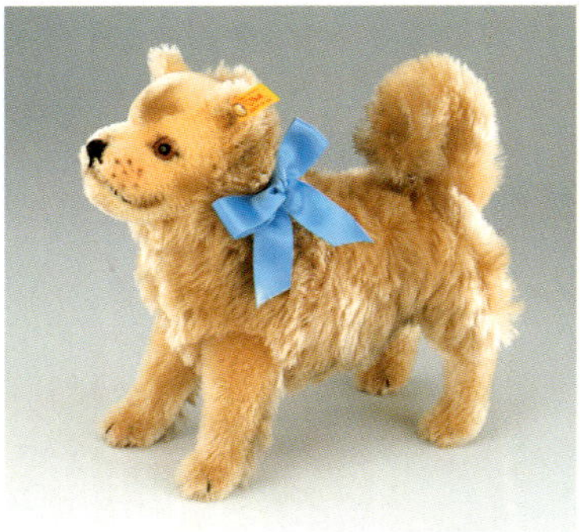

Classic 1928 Chow Chow

Mohair Webpelz, abwaschbar, Druckstimme - *mohair woven fur, surface washable, press voice*

EAN-No.	Period	Pr.	Info
035036	1997-1999	3-4	28 cm

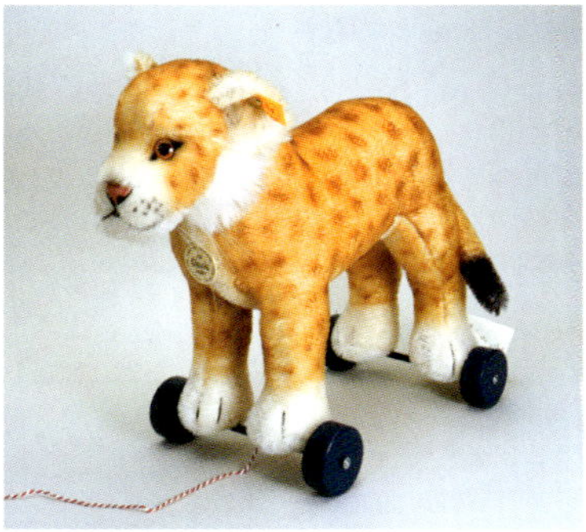

Classic 1939 Jungloewe auf Raedern - *Classic 1939 Lion Cub on Wheels*

Mohair Webpelz, abwaschbar, Fahrgestell - *mohair woven fur, surface washable, on wooden wheels*

EAN-No.	Period	Pr.	Info
036286	1997-1997	4	29 cm

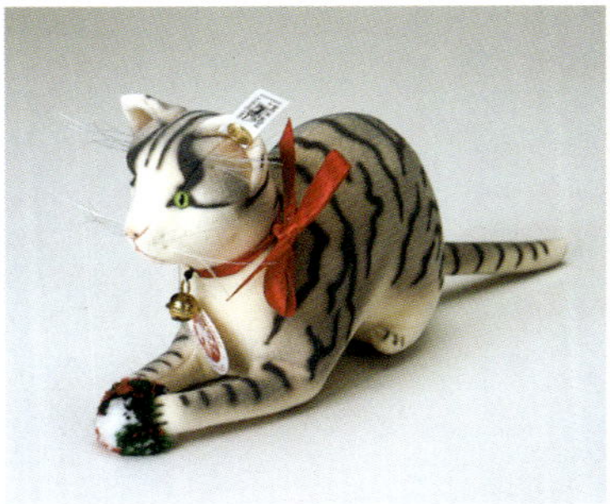

Katze 1901 Replica - *Cat 1901 Replica*

Samt, grau gestromelt, abwaschbar, Satinband & Gloeckchen, limit. Auflage 2.500 Stueck - *velvet, grey tabby, surface washable, satin ribbon & little bell, ltd edition of 2,500*

EAN-No.	Period	Pr.	Info
400339	1997-1997	3	18 cm

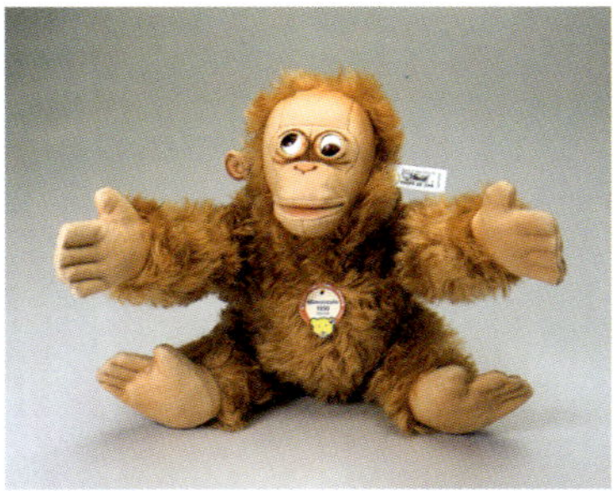

Orang Utan **Mimocculo Replica 1930**

Mohair Webpelz, rostbraun, gegliedert, abwaschbar, Druckstimme, Augen vom Ohr aus drehbar, limit. Auflage 3.000 Stueck - *mohair woven fur, rust-brown, jointed, surface washable, press voice, turnable eyes, ltd edition of 3,000*

EAN-No.	Period	Pr.	Info
401312	1998-1998	4-5	25 cm

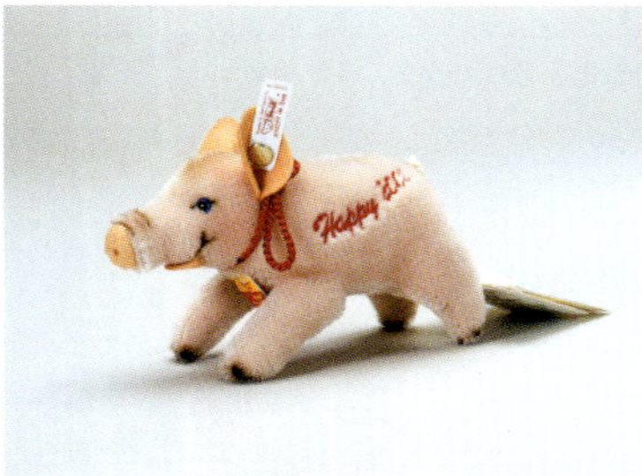

Gluecksschwein Happy 2000 - *Lucky Pig Happy 2000*

Mohair Webpelz, rosa, stehend, abwaschbar, Bestickung "Happy 2000", Zeitlimitierung bis Ende 1999 - *mohair woven fur, pink, standing, surface washable, embroidered with "Happy 2000", limited availability up to 31.12.1999*

EAN-No.	Period	Pr.	Info
033278	1999-1999	2	10 cm

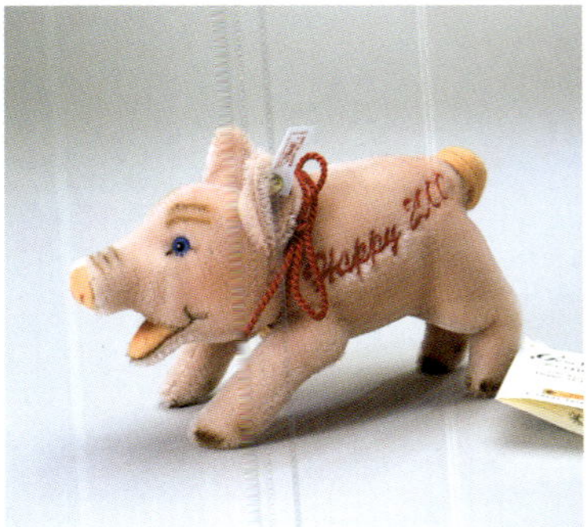

Gluecksschwein Happy 2000 - *Lucky Pig Happy 2000*

Mohair Webpelz, rosa, stehend, abwaschbar, Bestickung "Happy 2000", Zeitlimitierung bis Ende 1999 - *mohair woven fur, pink, standing, surface washable, embroidered with "Happy 2000", limited availability up to 31.12.1999*

EAN-No.	Period	Pr.	Info
035197	1999-1999	2-3	17 cm

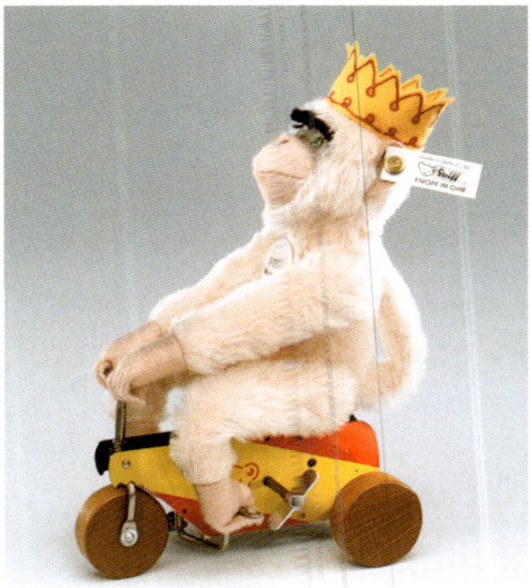

Monk King Replica 1925

Mohair Webpelz, weiss, gegliedert, abwaschbar, holzwollgestopft, auf Dreirad, limit. Auflage 1.200 Stueck - *mohair woven fur, white, jointed, surface washable, excelsior stuffed, riding a tricycle, ltd edition of 1,200*

EAN-No.	Period	Pr.	Info
400933	1999-1999	4	19 cm

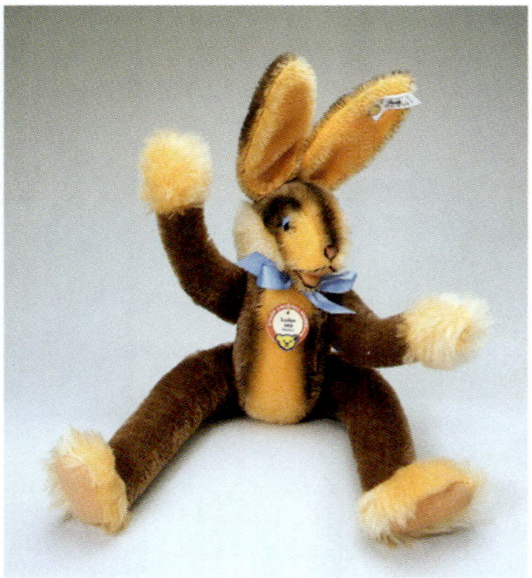

Lulac 1952 Hase Replica - *Lulac Rabbit Replica 1952*

Mohair Webpelz, caramel, gegliedert, abwaschbar, hellblaue Halsschleife, limit. Auflage 1.500 Stueck - *mohair woven fur, caramel, jointed, surface washable, light blue bow, ltd edition of 1,500*

EAN-No.	Period	Pr.	Info
402166	1999-1999	3-4	43 cm

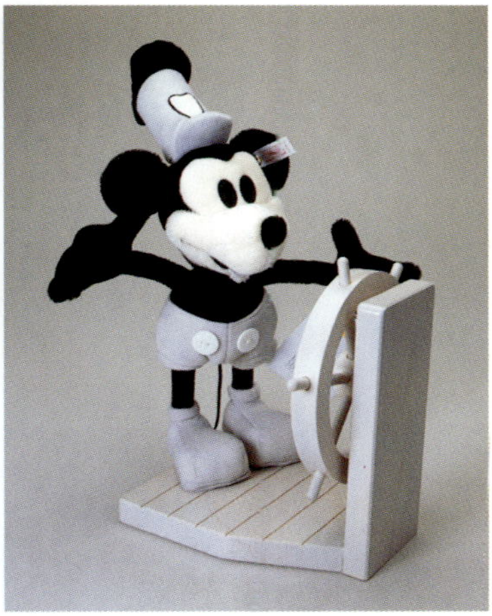

Steamboat Willie

Mohair Webpelz, schwarz/weiss, stehend, abwaschbar, Schuhe, Hose & Hut aus Trevirasamt, Lizenzartikel, limit. Auflage 10.000 Stueck - *mohair woven fur, black/white, standing, surface washable, shoes, trousers & hat of trevira velvet, in cooperation with Walt Disney Company, ltd edition of 10,000*

EAN-No.	Period	Pr.	Info
651472	1999-1999	4-5	22 cm

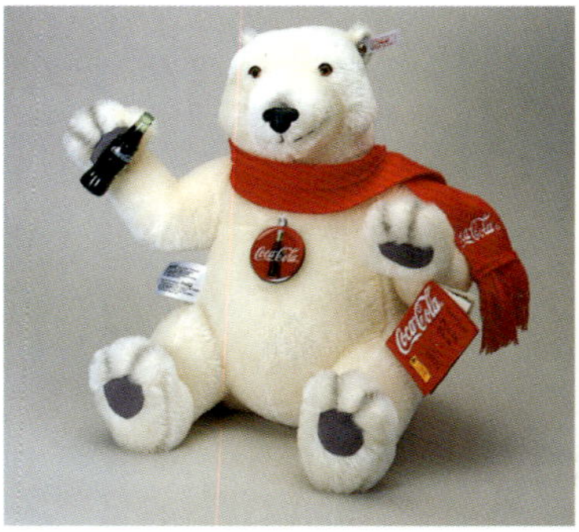

COCA-COLA Eisbaer - *COCA-COLA Polarbear*

Mohair Webpelz, weiss, sitzend, abwaschbar, Arme gegliedert, mit COCA-COLA Flasche, Lizenzartikel, limit. Auflage 10.000 Stueck - *mohair woven fur, white, sitting, surface washable, arms jointed, with COCA-COLA bottle, in cooperation with The Coca-Cola Company, ltd edition of 10,000*

EAN-No.	Period	Pr.	Info
670336	1999-1999	4-5	35 cm

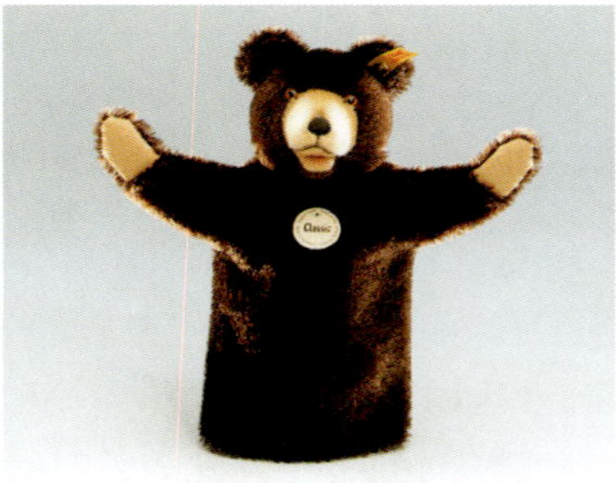

Classic Hand Baer - ***Classic** Hand Bear*

Mohair Webpelz, abwaschbar, Kopf formgeschaeumt - *Mohair Webpelz, abwaschbar, head stuffed with preformed foam*

EAN-No.	Period	Pr.	Info
250118	1996-1996	2-3	27 cm

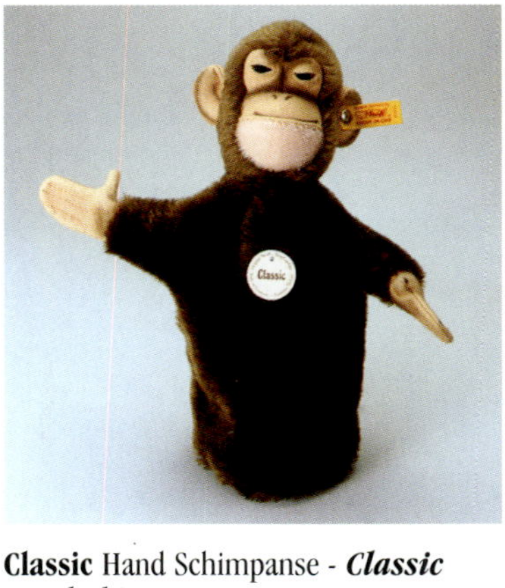

Classic Hand Schimpanse - ***Classic** Hand Chimpanzee*

Mohair Webpelz, abwaschbar, Kopf formgeschaeumt - *mohair woven fur, surface washable, head stuffed with preformed foam*

EAN-No.	Period	Pr.	Info
250163	1996-1996	2-3	27 cm

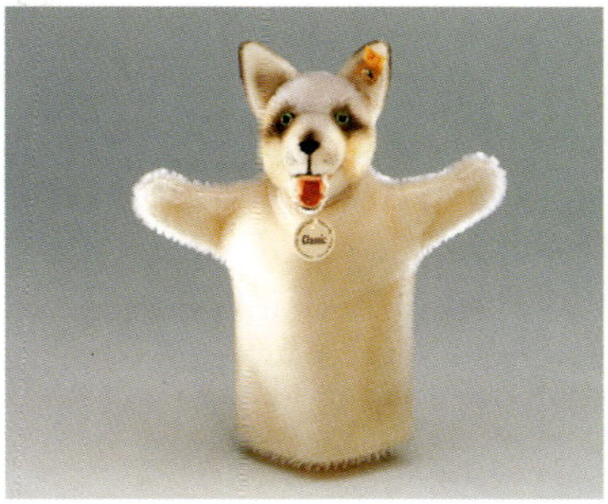

Classic Hand Wolf

Mohair Webpelz, abwaschbar, Kopf formgeschaeumt - *mohair woven fur, surface washable, head stuffed with preformed foam*

EAN-No.	Period	Pr.	Info
250217	1996-1996	2-3	27 cm

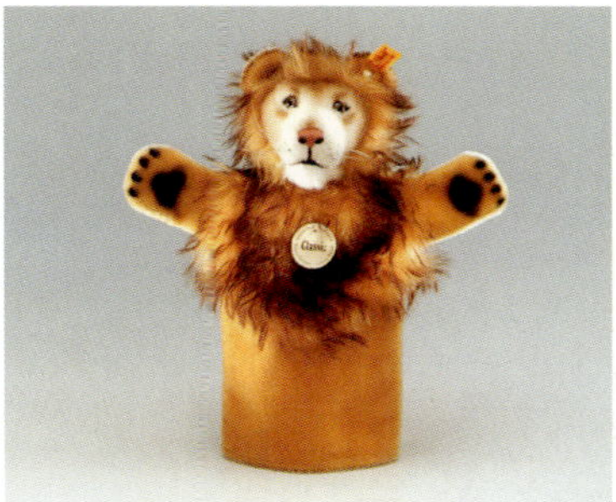

Classic Hand Loewe - ***Classic** Hand Lion*

Mohair Webpelz, abwaschbar, Kopf formgeschaeumt - *mohair woven fur, surface washable, head stuffed with preformed foam*

EAN-No.	Period	Pr.	Info
250262	1996-1996	2-3	27 cm

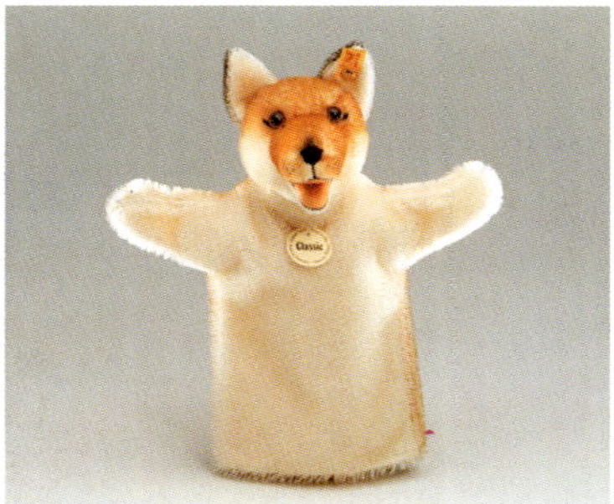

Classic Hand Fuchs - ***Classic** Hand Fox*

Mohair Webpelz, abwaschbar, Kopf formgeschaeumt - *mohair woven fur, surface washable, head stuffed with preformed foam*

EAN-No.	Period	Pr.	Info
250316	1996-1996	2-3	27 cm

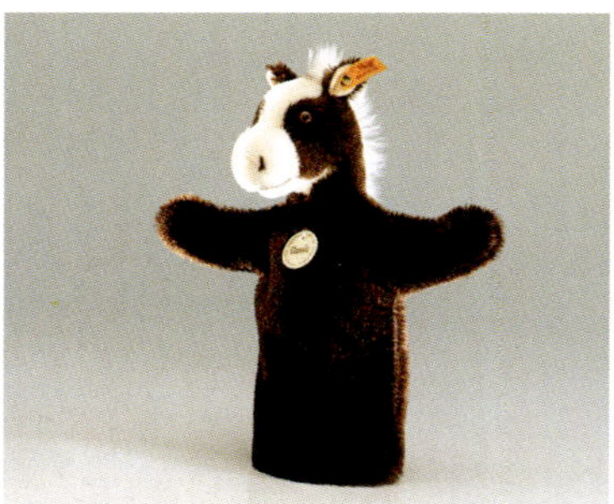

Classic Hand Pferd - ***Classic** Hand Horse*

Mohair Webpelz, abwaschbar, Kopf formgeschaeumt - *mohair woven fur, surface washable, head stuffed with preformed foam*

EAN-No.	Period	Pr.	Info
250361	1996-1996	2-3	27 cm

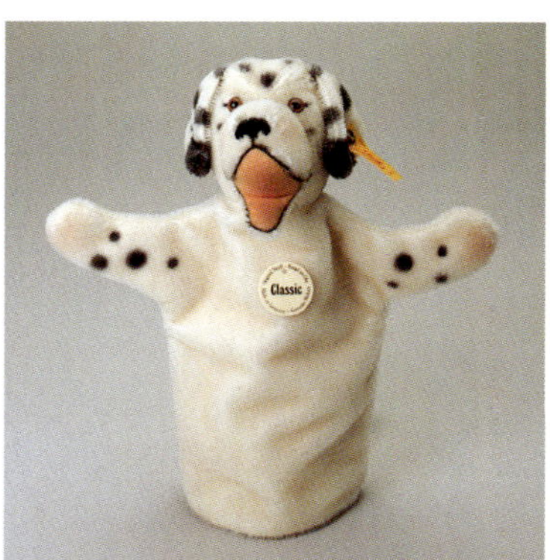

Classic Hand Dally

Mohair Webpelz, abwaschbar, Kopf formgeschaeumt - *mohair woven fur, surface washable, head stuffed with preformed foam*

EAN-No.	Period	Pr.	Info
250415	1996-1996	2-3	27 cm

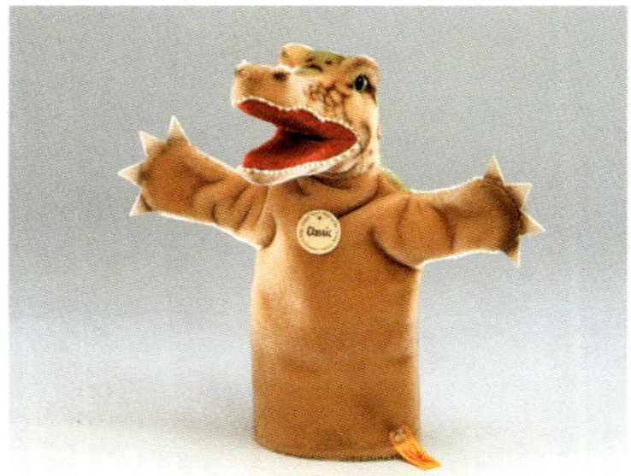

Classic Hand Krokodil - ***Classic** Hand Crocodile*

Mohair Webpelz, abwaschbar, Kopf formgeschaeumt - *mohair woven fur, surface washable, head stuffed with preformed foam*

EAN-No.	Period	Pr.	Info
250460	1996-1996	2-3	27 cm

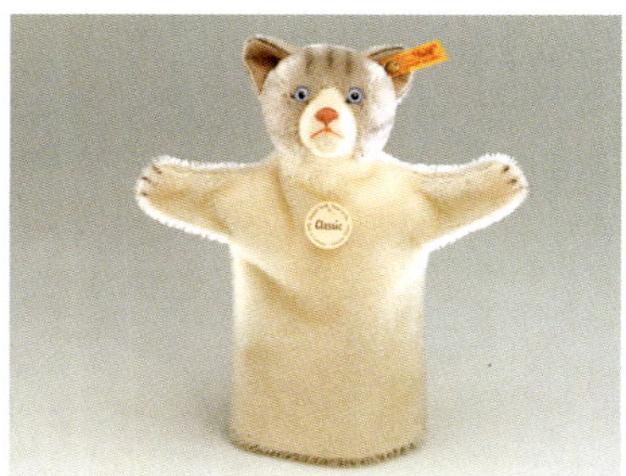

Classic Hand Katze - ***Classic** Hand Cat*

Mohair Webpelz, abwaschbar, Kopf formgeschaeumt - *mohair woven fur, surface washable, head stuffed with preformed foam*

EAN-No.	Period	Pr.	Info
250514	1996-1996	2-3	27 cm

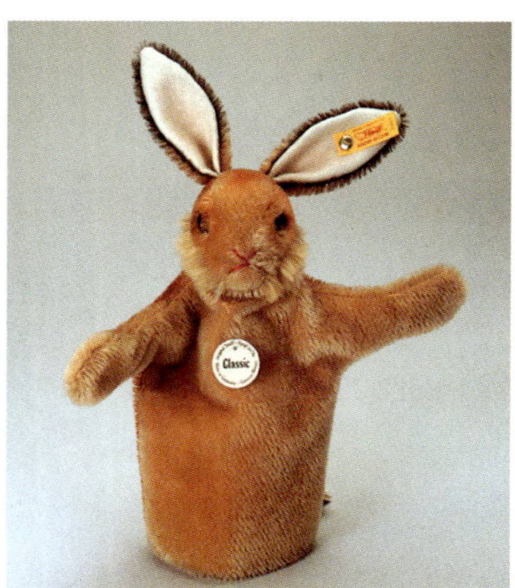

Classic Hand Hase - ***Classic** Hand Rabbit*

Mohair Webpelz, abwaschbar, Kopf formgeschaeumt - *mohair woven fur, surface washable, head stuffed with preformed foam*

EAN-No.	Period	Pr.	Info
250569	1996-1996	2-3	27 cm

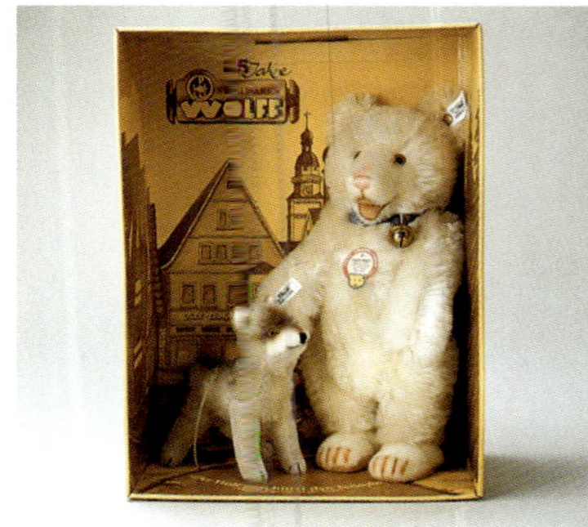

Teddy Baby & Wolf

Set, Mohair, Teddy gegliedert, limit. Auflage 1.000 Stueck, zum 85jaehrigen Jubilaeum der Fa. Paul Wolff, Giengen - *set, mohair, Teddy jointed, ltd edition of 1,000 to celebrate 85 Year Jubilee of the Paul Wolff Company of Giengen, Germany*

Serie	Art.-No	Period	Pr.	Info
	0177/00	1988-1988	5-6	28 cm

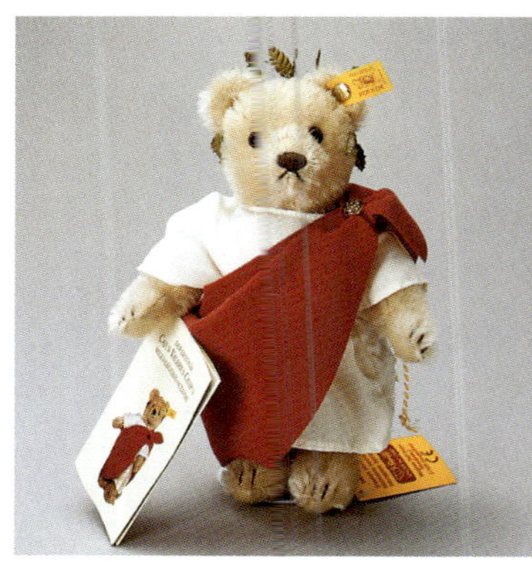

Roemer Baeren - *Roman Bears*

Mohair, gegliedert, auf der Rueckseite ist der jeweilige Name aufgebracht, Zertifikat mit Kurzgeschichte zum Namen - *mohair, jointed, the bear´s name is on the reverse side of the bear, certificate with a short explanation about the name*

EAN-No.	Period	Pr.	Info
650390	1992-1992	3-4	Ursulus, Feldhaus, Koeln - *Ursulus, Feldhaus, Cologne*
650611	1993-1993	3-4	Severus Alexander, Behle, Frankfurt/M.
650628	1993-1993	3-4	Titus Julius Saturninus, Spielzeugmuseum Trier - *Titus Julius Saturninus, Toy Museum of Trier*

650635	1993-1993	3-4	Imperator Caracalla, Abele, Aachen
650642	1993-1993	3-4	Cajus Valerius Crispus, Spielwaren am Markt, Wiesbaden - *Cajus Valerius Crispus, Toy Shop on the Market, Wiesbaden*
650659	1993-1993	3-4	Caius Fulvius Lupus, Puppenkoenig, Bonn
650666	1993-1993	3-4	Imperator Vespasian, Wolff, Giengen
650673	1993-1993	3-4	Baccharus, Stiehl, Bacharach
650697	1993-1993	3-4	Drusus, Joosten & Kloeden, Neuss
650772	1993-1993	3-4	Bocvoc, Teddy Bears of Whitney

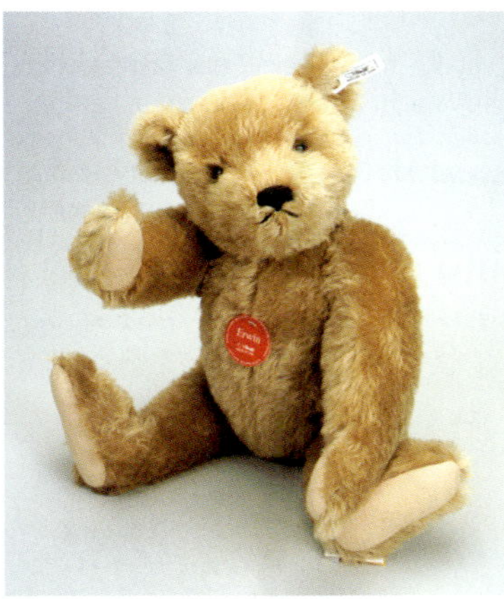

Erwin Teddybaer - ***Erwin*** *Teddy Bear*

Mohair, gegliedert, limit. Auflage 7.777 Stueck fuer Arbeitsgem. Kinderkrebsnachsorge - *mohair, jointed, ltd edition of 7,777 for the Children´s Post Cancer Care Work Group*

EAN-No.	Period	Pr.	Info
650888	1993-1993	5	43 cm

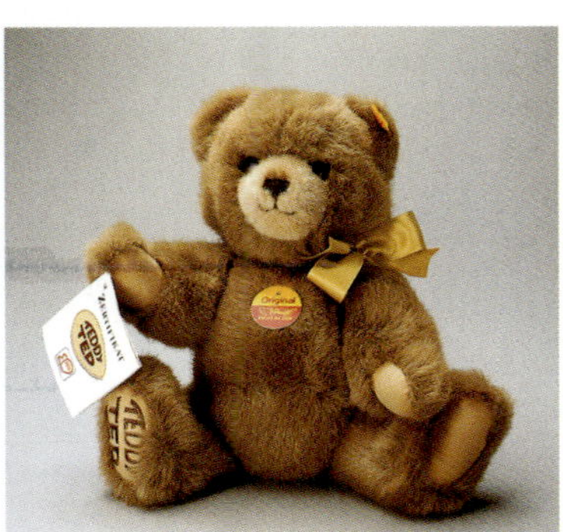

Teddy Ted

Webpelz, braun, gegliedert, limit. Auflage 3.333 Stueck fuer Idee + Spiel - *woven fur, brown, jointed, ltd edition of 3,333 for "Idee + Spiel"*

EAN-No.	Period	Pr.	Info
650855	1993-1993	3-4	43 cm

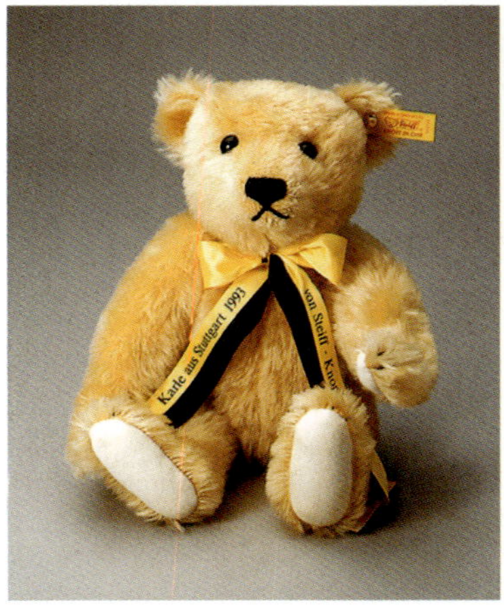

Karle aus Stuttgart - *Karle from Stuttgart*

Teddy Replica 1909, Mohair, blond, gegliedert, mit Musikwerk "Let me be your Teddybear", Auflage ca. 200 St. fuer Breuninger - *1909 Teddy replica, mohair, blond, jointed, music box "Let me be your Teddybear", edition of approx. 200 for Breuninger Store*

EAN-No.	Period	Pr.	Info
999789	1993-1993	4-5	30 cm

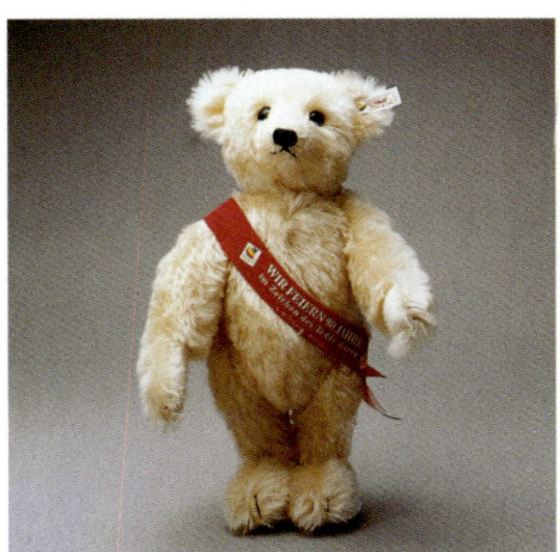

Teddybaer - *Teddy Bear*

Mohair, blond, gegliedert, Brummstimme, limit. Auflage 6.000 Stueck fuer Vedes - *mohair, blond, jointed, growler, ltd edition of 6,000 for Vedes*

EAN-No.	Period	Pr.	Info
650901	1994-1994	4-5	40 cm

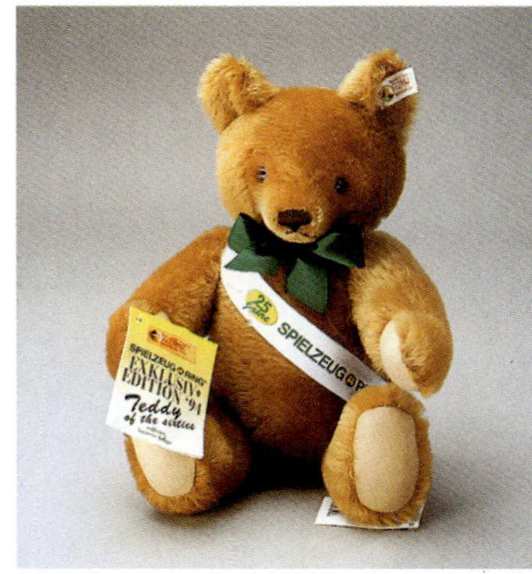

Original Teddybaer - *Original Teddy Bear*

Mohair, rotblond, gegliedert, Brummstimme, limit. Auflage 3.000 Stueck fuer Spielzeugring - *mohair, auburn, jointed, growler, ltd edition of 3,000 for Spielzeugring store*

EAN-No.	Period	Pr.	Info
650918	1994-1994	4-5	36 cm

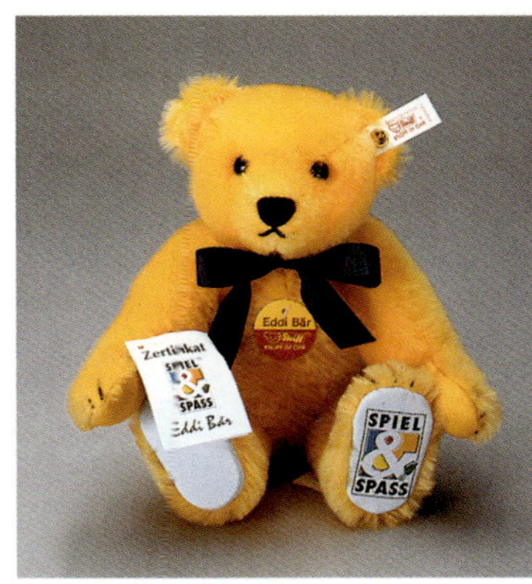

Eddi Baer - *Eddi Bear*

Mohair, gold, gegliedert, limit. Auflage 2.000 Stueck fuer Spiel & Spass - *mohair, gold, jointed, ltd edition of 2,000 for Spiel & Spass store*

EAN-No.	Period	Pr.	Info
650925	1994-1994	4-5	27 cm

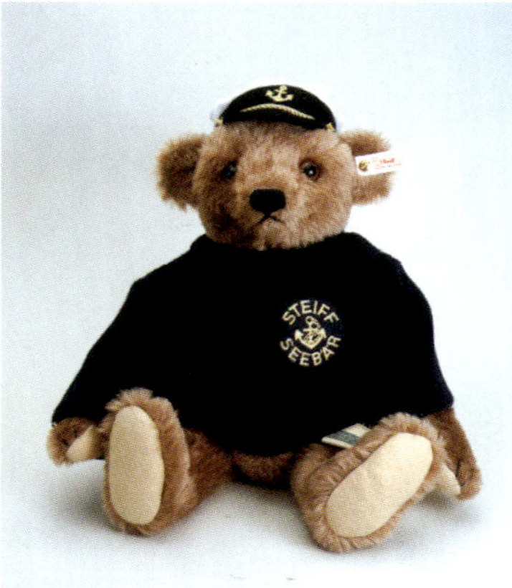

Seebaer - *Sea Bear*

Mohair, hellbraun, gegliedert, abwaschbar, limit. Auflage 450 Stueck fuer Karstadt, Hamburg - *mohair, light brown, jointed, surface washable, ltd edition of 450 for Karstadt, Hamburg*

EAN-No.	Period	Pr.	Info
655067	1994-1994	5-6	42 cm

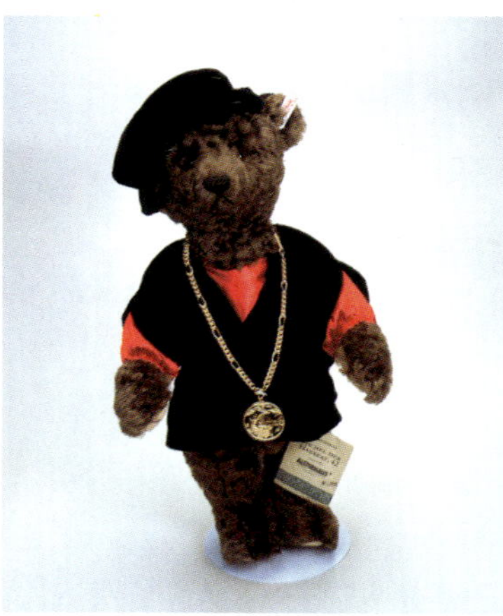

Michel der Hanseat - *Michel the Hanseat*

Mohair, braun, gegliedert, limit. Auflage 300 Stueck fuer Alsterhaus, Hamburg - *mohair, brown, jointed, ltd edition of 300 for Alsterhaus, Hamburg*

EAN-No.	Period	Pr.	Info
655104	1994-1994	5-6	42 cm

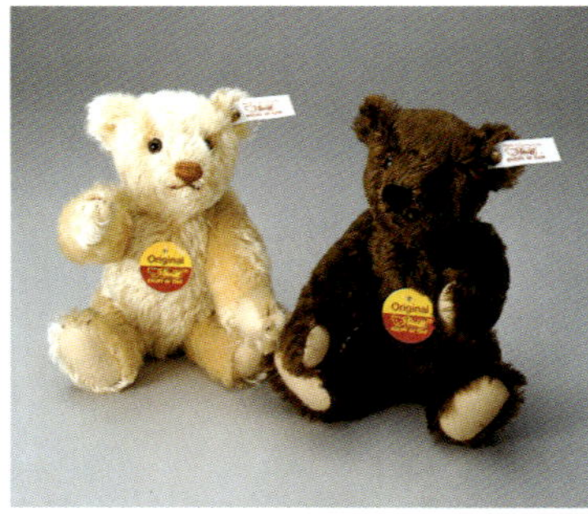

Teddy braun & beige - *Teddy Brown & Beige*

Mohair, gegliedert, limit. Auflage, paarweise zusammen mit einem Exemplar des Buches "Steiff-Teddybaeren eine Liebe fuers Leben", die angegebene Preisgruppe gilt fuer ein komplettes Set - *mohair, jointed, ltd edition, in pairs together with the book "Steiff Teddy Bears - a Love for Life", the price group named refers to a complete set*

EAN-No.	Period	Pr.	Info
J04075	1995-1995	4-5	22 cm
J04076	1995-1995	4-5	22 cm, Setpreis Baeren & Buch - *price per set of 2 bears & book*

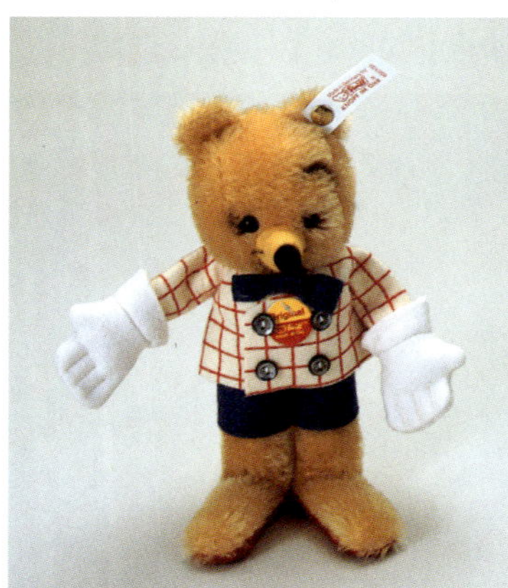

Breuni Baer - *Breuni Bear*

Mohair, stehend, abwaschbar, bekleidet, limit. Auflage 1.500 Stueck fuer Kaufhaus Breuninger - *mohair, standing, surface washable, dressed with felt clothes, ltd edition of 1,500 for Breuninger Store*

EAN-No.	Period	Pr.	Info
655135	1995-1995	4-5	20 cm

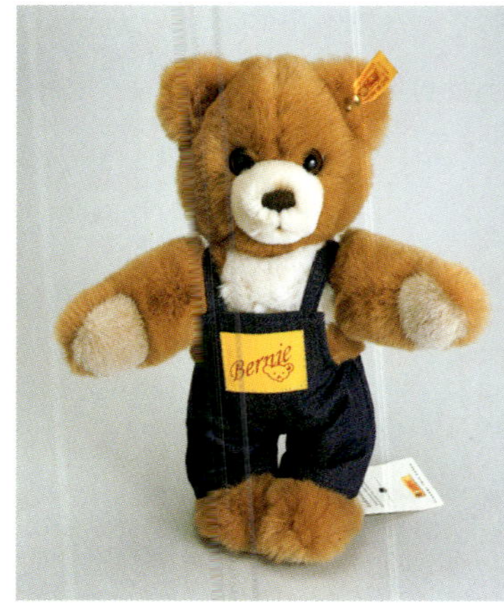

Teddy Bernie

Webpelz, braun/beige, mit Jeans-Overall, sehr weich, Sonderartikel fuer Kaufhof - *woven fur, brown/beige, wearing jeans-overall, very soft, exclusive for Kaufhof*

EAN-No.	Period	Pr.	Info
655173	1995-1995	3	26 cm

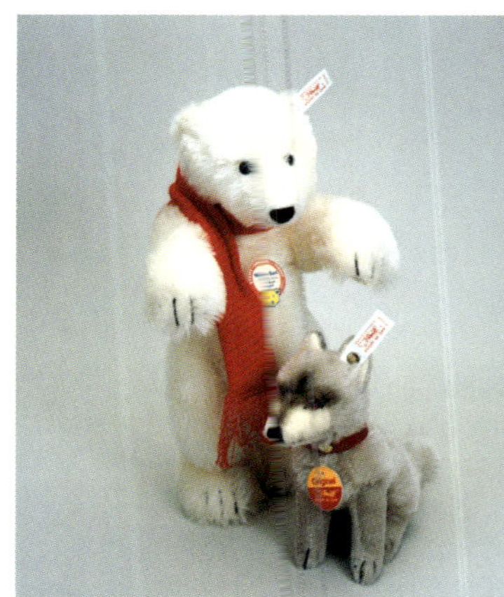

Polarbaer und Wolf - *Polarbear and Wolf*

Mohair, weiss/grau, aufwartend/sitzend, abwaschbar, Baer gegliedert 32 cm, Hund 16 cm, limit. Auflage 2.000 Stueck fuer Fa. Paul Wolff, Giengen - *mohair, white/grey, begging/sitting, surface washable, bear jointed, size 32 cm, dog 16 cm, ltd edition of 2,000 for Paul Wolff Company, Giengen*

EAN-No.	Period	Pr.	Info
655098	1995-1995	4-5	32 und 16 cm - *32 and 16 cm*

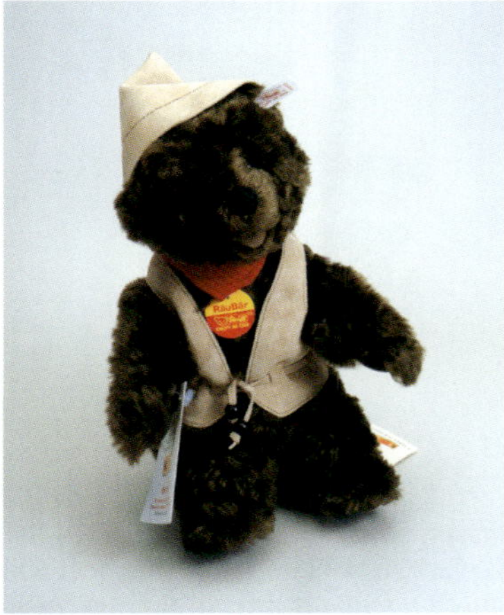

RaeuBaer - *RaeuBear*

Mohair, braun, gegliedert, limit. Auflage 3.000 Stueck fuer Idee & Spiel - *mohair, brown, jointed, ltd edition of 3,000 for Idee & Spiel*

EAN-No.	Period	Pr.	Info
650956	1995-1995	4-5	25 cm

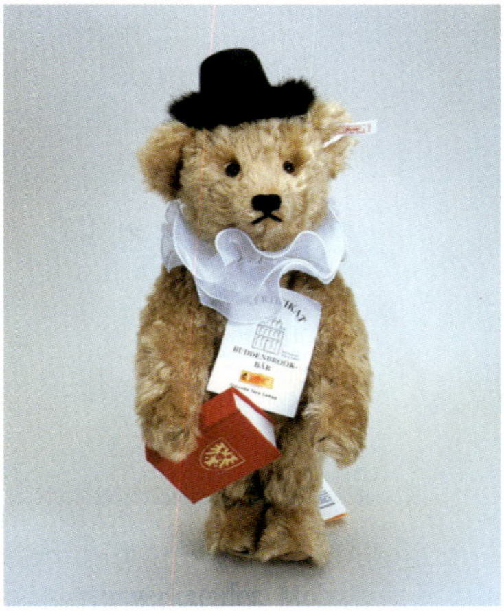

Buddenbrook Baer - *Buddenbrook Bear*

Mohair, blond, gegliedert, limit. Auflage 2.000 Stueck fuer Morgenroth, Luebeck - *mohair, blond, jointed, ltd edition of 2,000 for Morgenroth, Luebeck*

EAN-No.	Period	Pr.	Info
655050	1995-1995	4-5	33 cm

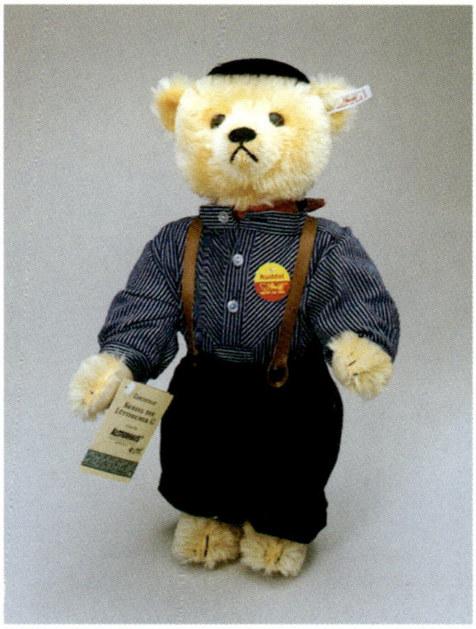

Kuddel der Luettfischer - *Fisher* ***Kuddel***

Mohair, blond, gegliedert, limit. Auflage 400 Stueck fuer Alsterhaus, Hamburg - *mohair, blond, jointed, ltd edition of 400 for Alsterhaus, Hamburg*

EAN-No.	Period	Pr.	Info
655166	1995-1995	5	42 cm

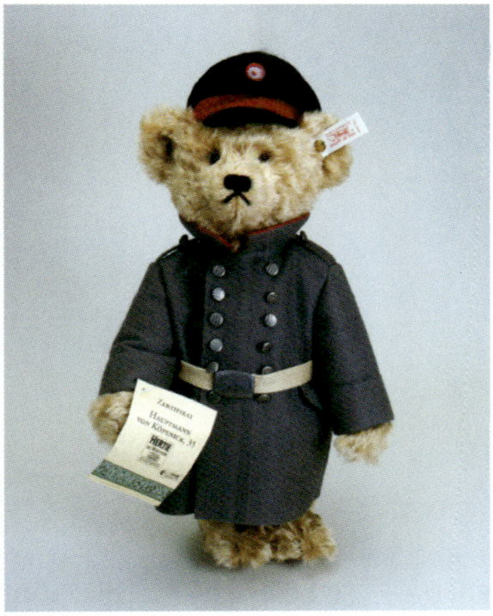

Hauptmann von Koepenick - *Officer of Koepenick*

Mohair, hellbraun, gegliedert, limit. Auflage 450 Stueck fuer Wertheim, Berlin - *mohair, light brown, jointed, ltd edition of 450 for Wertheim, Berlin*

EAN-No.	Period	Pr.	Info
655180	1995-1995	6	35 cm

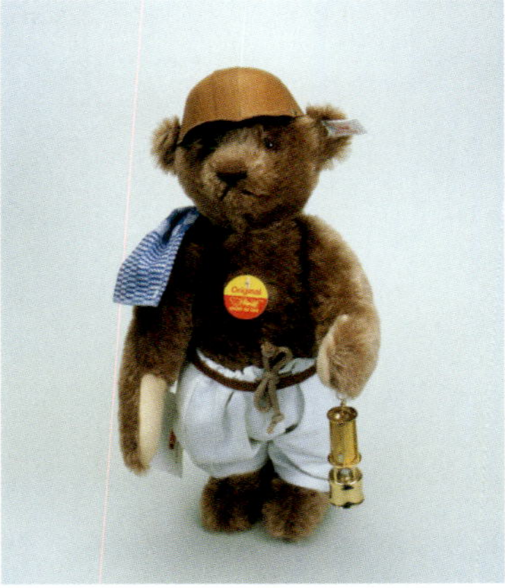

Steiger Anton - *Pit Foreman Anton*

Mohair, braun, stehend, abwaschbar, limit. Auflage 490 Stueck fuer Luethgenau, Dortmund - *mohair, brown, standing, surface washable, ltd edition of 490 for Luethgenau, Dortmund*

EAN-No.	Period	Pr.	Info
655111	1995-1995	4-5	35 cm

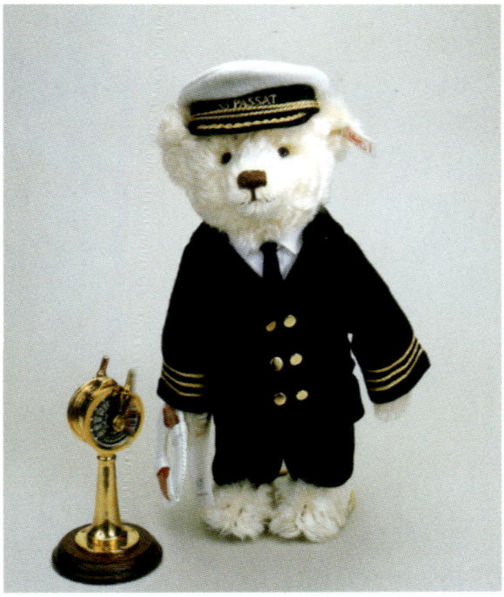

Passat Baer - *Passat Bear*

Mohair, weiss, gegliedert, limit. Auflage 1.500 Stueck fuer Fa. Morgenroth, Luebeck - *mohair, white, jointed, ltd edition of 1,500 for Morgenroth, Luebeck*

EAN-No.	Period	Pr.	Info
655272	1996-1996	4-5	35 cm

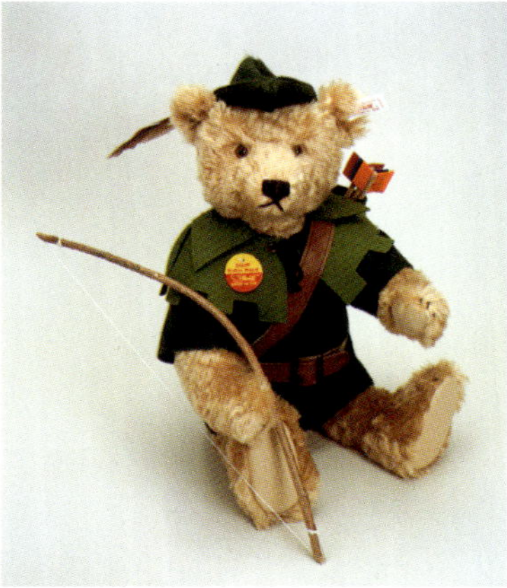

Robin Hood Baer - *Robin Hood Bear*

Mohair, blond, gegliedert, limit. Auflage 1.500 Stueck fuer Hertie/Karstadt - *mohair, blond, jointed, ltd edition of 1,500 for Hertie/Karstadt stores*

EAN-No.	Period	Pr.	Info
655203	1996-1996	5	42 cm

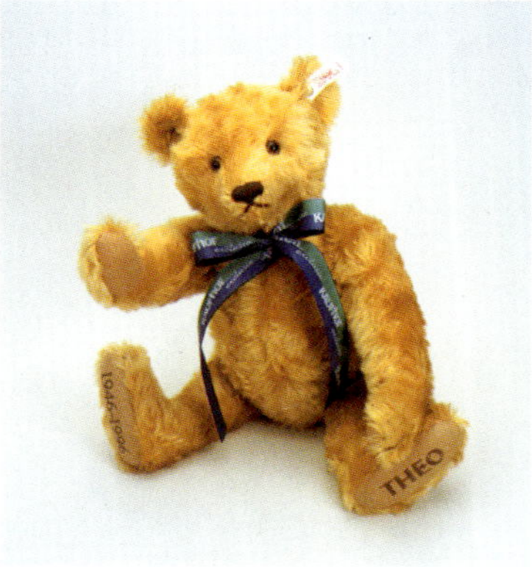

Teddy Theo

Mohair, blond, gegliedert, limit. Auflage 1.946 Stueck fuer Kaufhof/Horten zum 50jaehrigen Bestehen - *mohair, blond, jointed, ltd edition of 1,946 for Kaufhof/ Horten stores to celebrate the 50th anniversary*

EAN-No.	Period	Pr.	Info
655227	1996-1996	4-5	43 cm

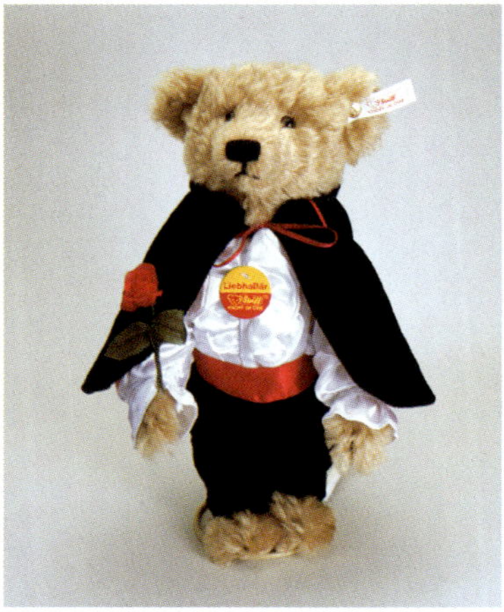

LiebhaBaer - *LiebhaBear*

Mohair, hellbraun, gegliedert, limit. Auflage 2.550 Stueck fuer Idee & Spiel - *mohair, light brown, jointed, ltd edition of 2,550 for Idee & Spiel*

EAN-No.	Period	Pr.	Info
650970	1996-1996	4-5	32 cm

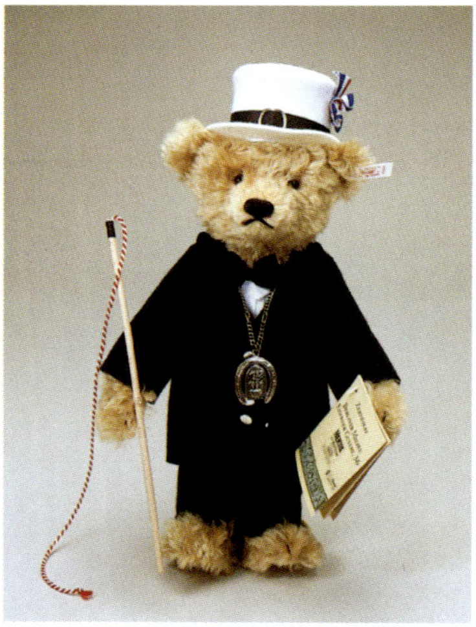

Eiserner Gustav - *Iron Gustav*

Mohair, hellbraun, gegliedert, limit. Auflage 1.500 Stueck fuer Wertheim, Berlin - *mohair, light brown, jointed, ltd edition of 1, 500 for Wertheim store, Berlin*

EAN-No.	Period	Pr.	Info
655241	1996-1996	5-6	35 cm

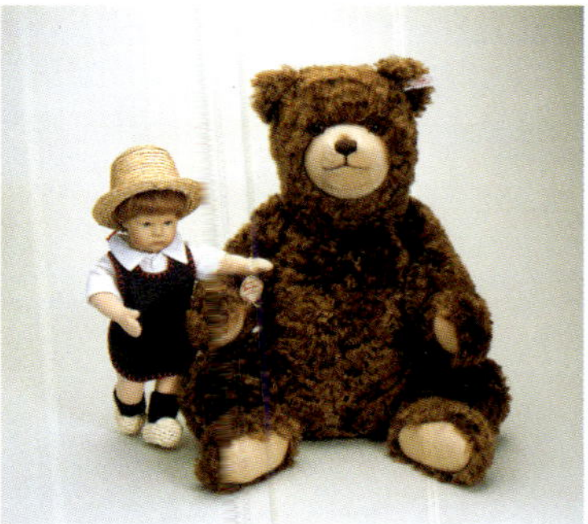

Fritzl und Hein - *Fritzl and Hein*

Mohair, braun, gegliedert, zusammen mit Kaethe Kruse Puppe, limit. Auflage 2.500 Stueck - *mohair, brown, jointed, bear together with Kaethe Kruse doll, ltd edition of 2,500*

EAN-No.	Period	Pr.	Info
655234	1996-1996	5	43 cm

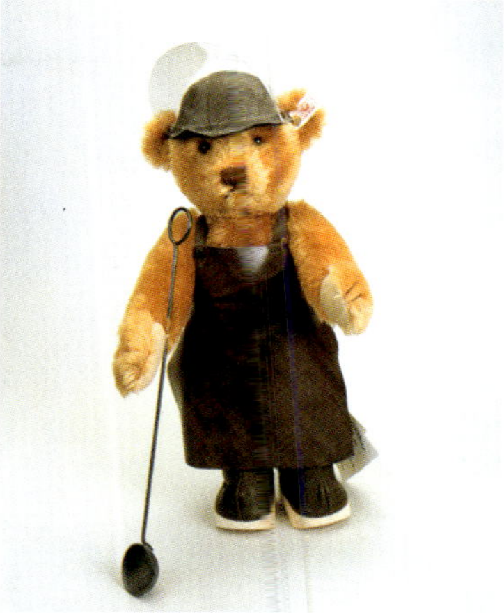

Stahlkocher Willi - *Steelworker Willi*

Mohair, braun, stehend, abwaschbar, limit. Auflage 1.500 Stueck fuer Luethgenau, Dortmund - *mohair, brown, standing, surface washable, ltd edition of 1,500 for Luethgenau, Dortmund*

EAN-No.	Period	Pr.	Info
655289	1996-1996	4	35 cm

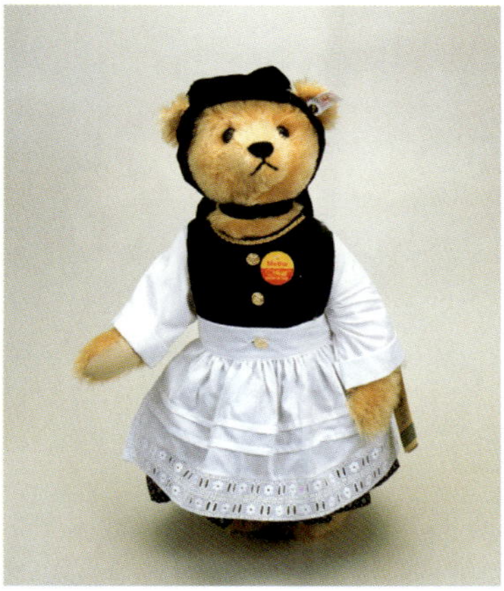

Finkenwerder Fischerin **Metha** - *Finkenwerder Fisher´s Wife **Metha***

Mohair, blond, gegliedert, limit. Auflage 1.500 Stueck fuer Alsterhaus, Hamburg - *mohair, blond, jointed, ltd edition of 1,500 for Alsterhaus, Hamburg*

EAN-No.	Period	Pr.	Info
655210	1996-1996	4-5	42 cm

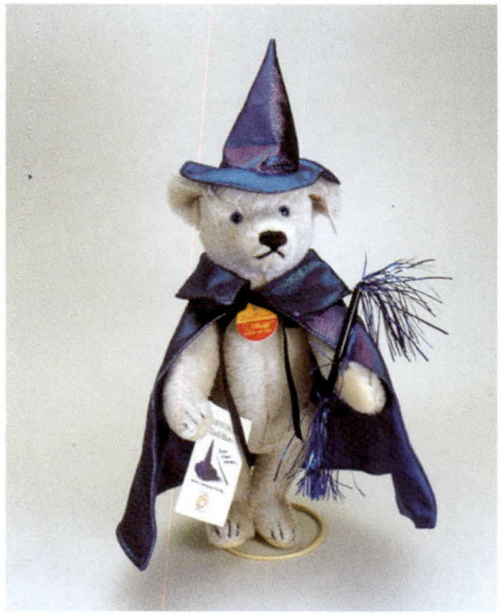

ZauBaerer Baer - *Magician Bear*

Mohair, blond, gegliedert, limit. Auflage 2.000 Stueck fuer Idee & Spiel - *mohair, blond, jointed, ltd edition of 2,000 for Idee & Spiel stores*

EAN-No.	Period	Pr.	Info
651007	1997-1997	4	32 cm

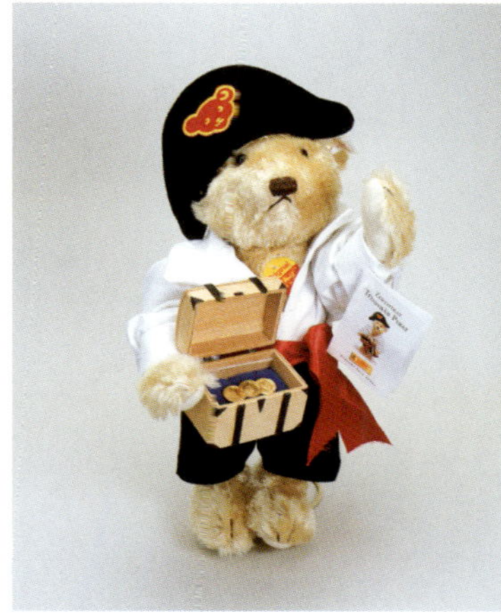

Pirat - *Pirate*

Mohair, hellblond, gegliedert, limit. Auflage 1.500 Stueck fuer Morgenroth, Luebeck - *mohair, light blond, jointed, ltd edition of 1,500 for Morgenroth, Luebeck*

EAN-No.	Period	Pr.	Info
655371	1997-1997	4	38 cm

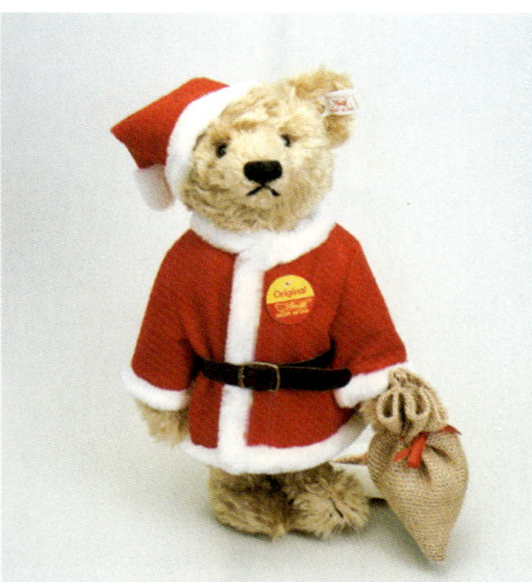

Weihnachtsmann Baer - *Santa Claus Bear*

Mohair, blond, gegliedert, limit. Auflage 1.500 Stueck fuer Spielzeugring - *mohair, blond, jointed, ltd edition of 1,500 for Spielzeugring*

EAN-No.	Period	Pr.	Info
650963	1996-1996	4	32 cm

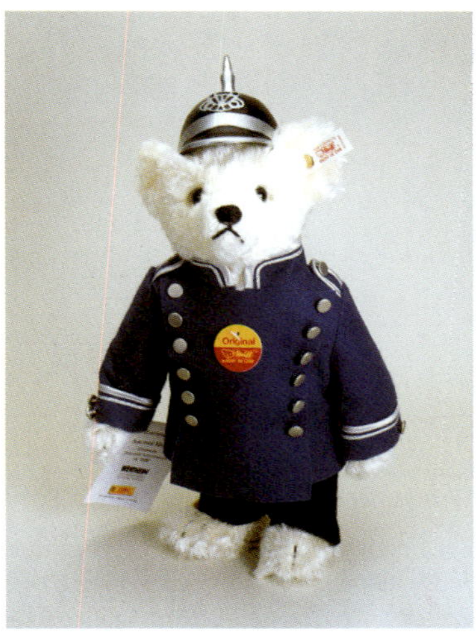

Berliner Schutzmann Baer - *Berlin Policeman Bear*

Mohair, weiss, gegliedert, hist. Uniform um 1900, limit. Auflage 1.500 Stueck fuer Wertheim, Berlin - *mohair, white, jointed, historical uniform from the beginning of the 20th century, ltd edition of 1,500 for Wertheim stores, Berlin*

EAN-No.	Period	Pr.	Info
655364	1997-1997	4	32 cm

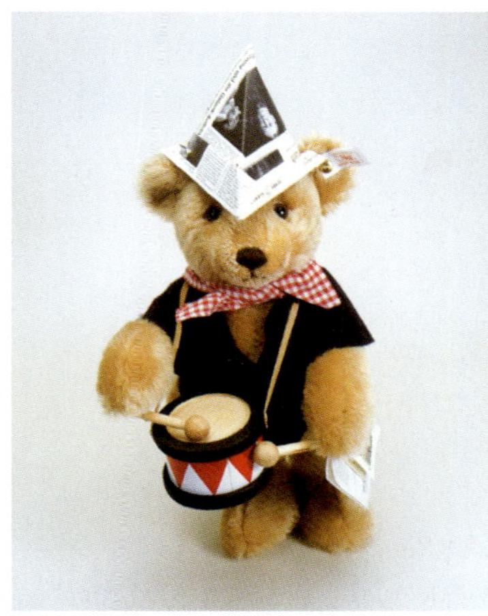

Trommler Baer - *Drummer Bear*

Mohair, blond, gegliedert, limit. Auflage 2.000 Stueck fuer Spielzeugring - *mohair, blond, jointed, ltd edition of 2,000 for Spielzeugring stores*

EAN-No.	Period	Pr.	Info
651021	1997-1997	4	33 cm

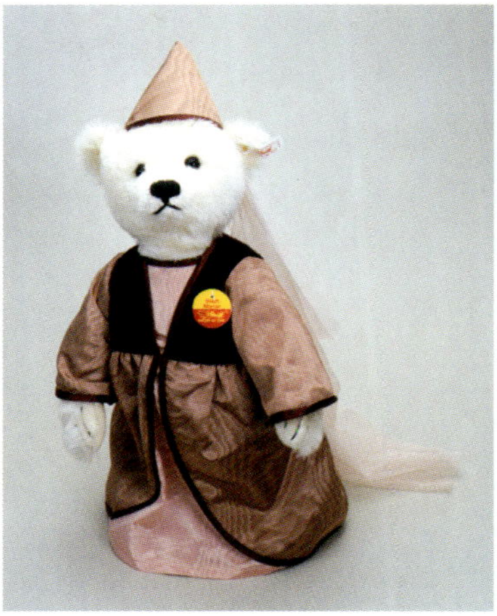

Baer Marian - *Bear Marian*

Mohair, weiss, gegliedert, limit. Auflage 1.500 Stueck fuer Hertie/Karstadt - *mohair, white, jointed, ltd edition of 1,500 for Hertie/Karstadt stores*

EAN-No.	Period	Pr.	Info
655357	1997-1997	4	44 cm

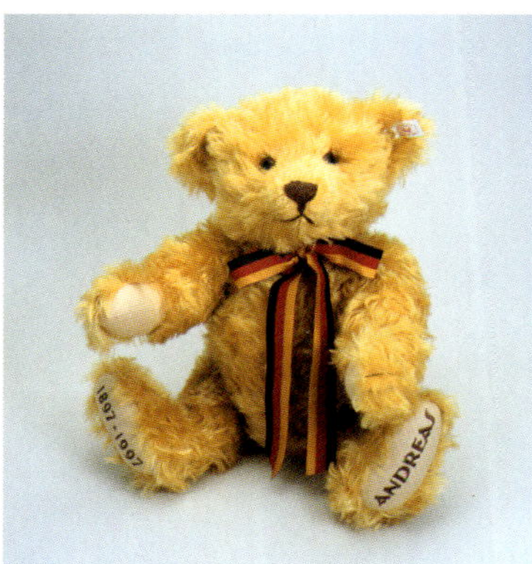

Andreas

Mohair, blond, gegliedert, limit. Auflage 1.997 Stueck fuer Kaufhof AG zum 100jaehrigen Jubilaeum - *mohair, blond, jointed, ltd edition of 1,997 for Kaufhof AG to celebrate the 100th anniversary*

EAN-No.	Period	Pr.	Info
655302	1997-1997	4	40 cm

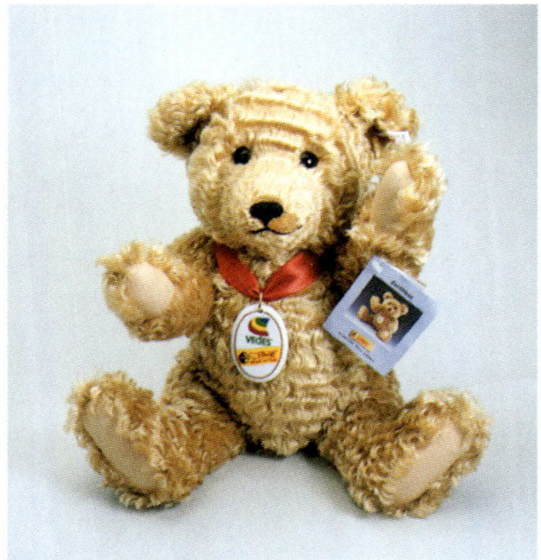

Teddybaer - *Teddybear*

Mohair, dunkelblond, gegliedert, limit. Auflage 3.000 Stueck fuer Vedes - *mohair, dark blond, jointed, ltd edition of 1,500 for Vedes stores*

EAN-No.	Period	Pr.	Info
651014	1997-1997	4	40 cm

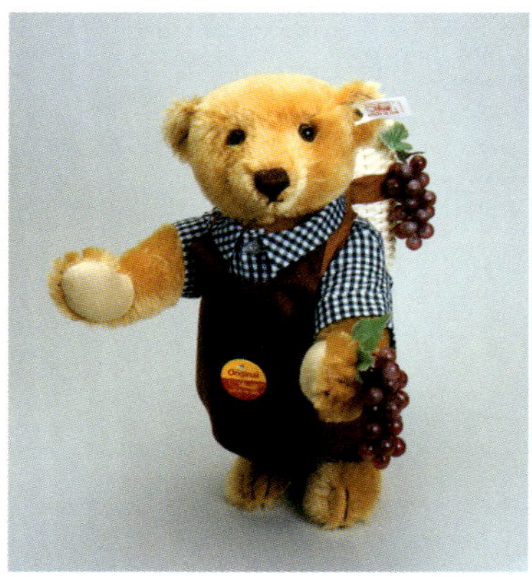

Teddybaer Winzer - *Teddybear Winegrower*

Mohair, rotblond, gegliedert, exclusiv fuer Deutschland, limit. Auflage 2.000 Stueck - *mohair, strawberry blond, jointed, German exclusive, ltd edition of 2,000*

EAN-No.	Period	Pr.	Info
670091	1997-1997	4	32 cm

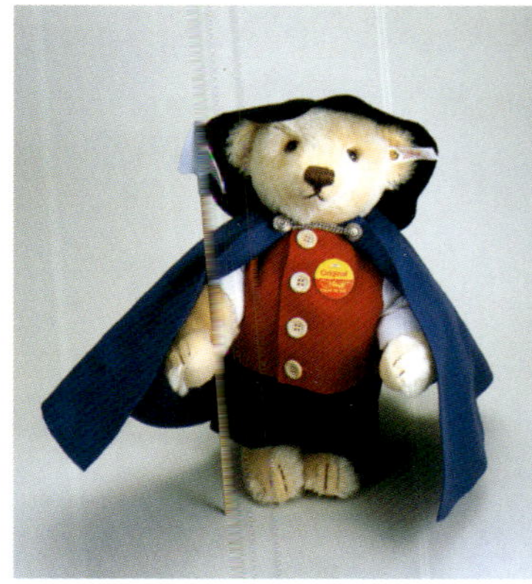

Teddybaer Heideschaefer - *Teddybear Heath Shepherd*

Mohair, blond, gegliedert, exclusiv fuer Deutschland, limit. Auflage 2.000 Stueck - *mohair, blond, jointed, German exclusive, ltd edition of 2,000*

EAN-No.	Period	Pr.	Info
670107	1997-1997	3-4	35 cm

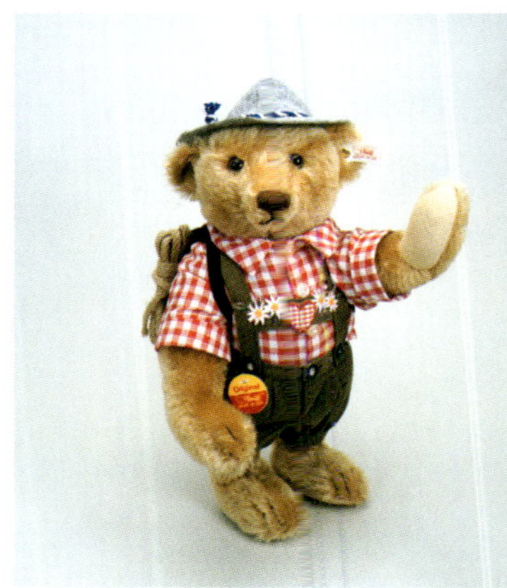

Teddybaer Gipfelstuermer - *Teddybear Mountain Climber*

Mohair, zimt, gegliedert, exclusiv fuer Deutschland, limit. Auflage 2.000 Stueck - *mohair, cinnamon, jointed, German exclusive, ltd edition of 2,000*

EAN-No.	Period	Pr.	Info
670121	1997-1997	3-4	35 cm

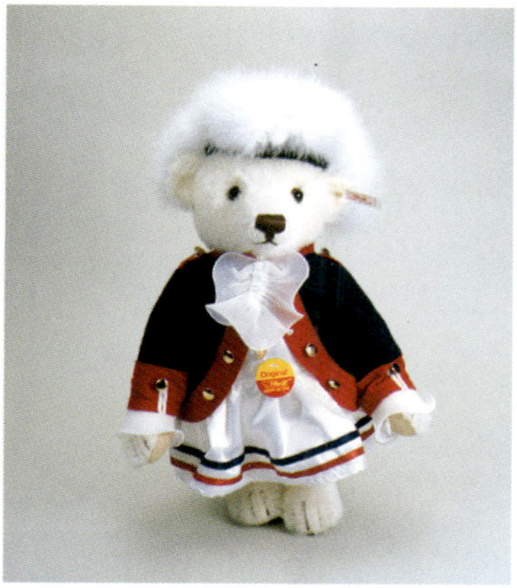

Teddybaer Funkenmariechen - *Teddybear Carnival Mariechen*

Mohair, weiss, gegliedert, exclusiv fuer Deutschland, limit. Auflage 2.000 Stueck - *mohair, white, jointed, German exclusive, ltd edition of 2,000*

EAN-No.	Period	Pr.	Info
670169	1997-1997	3-4	35 cm

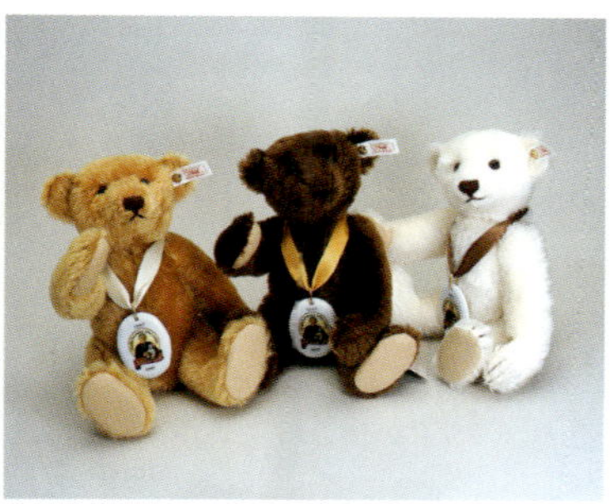

Geburtstagsbaer - *Birthday Bear*

Mohair, 28 cm, gegliedert, zum 150. Geburtstag von Margarete Steiff, mit Porzellanplakette an Satinband, Jahreslimitierungen 1997 - *mohair, 28 cm, jointed, to celebrate the 150th birthday of Margarete Steiff, porcelain medallion with satin ribbon, ltd edition for 1997 only*

EAN-No.	Period	Pr.	Info
670183	1997-1997	4	weiss, 9.272 Stueck - *white, 9,272 pc*
670190	1997-1997	4	blond, 9.061 Stueck - *blond, 9,061 pc*
670206	1997-1997	4	dunkelbraun, 7.459 Stueck - *dark brown, 7,459 pc*

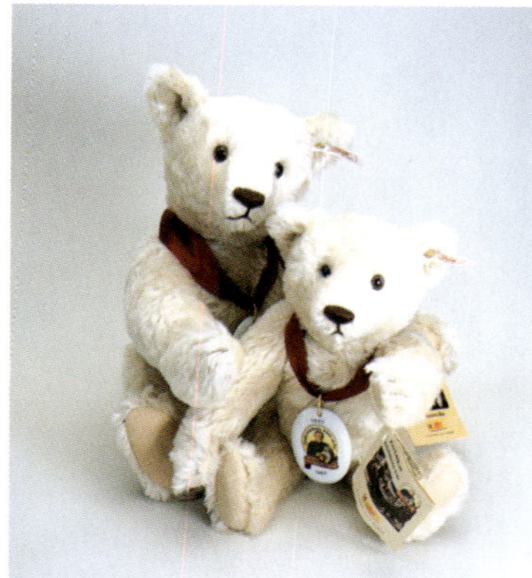

Jubilaeumsbaer - *Jubilee Bear*

Mohair, rohweiss, gegliedert, anlaesslich der Feierlichkeiten zum 150. Geburtstag von Margarete Steiff in Giengen an der Brenz, mit Porzellanplakette an Satinband, 40 cm als limit. Auflage mit 3.999 Stueck, 30 cm als limit. Auflage mit 300 Stueck, aus Schaufertigung anlaesslich des 1. Steiff-Festival´s, 55 cm Auflage nur 15 Stueck, die weltweit ausschliesslich zu wohltaetigen Zwecken versteigert wurden - *mohair, raw white, jointed, to celebrate the 150th birthday of Margarete Steiff in Giengen at the Brenz, porcelain medallion with satin ribbon, 40 cm ltd edition of 3,999, 30 cm ltd edition of 300, from exhibition manufactoring during 1st Steiff Festival, 55 cm ltd edition of 15, all auctioned for charity purposes*

EAN-No.	Period	Pr.	Info
670152	1997-1997	5	40 cm
670220	1997-1997	5-6	30 cm
	1997-1997	9	55 cm

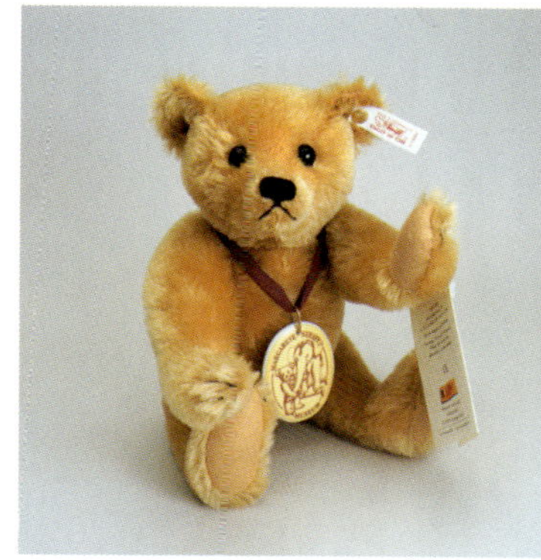

Steiff Museumsbaer - *Steiff Museum Bear*

Mohair, blond, gegliedert, mit Porzellanplakette, exclusiv nur fuer Besucher des Steiff Museums in Giengen, Jahreslimitierung 1998 - 3.050 Stueck - *mohair, blond, jointed, porcelain medallion, exclusive for visitors of the Steiff Museum in Giengen, ltd edition 1998 only - manufactured - 3,050 pieces*

EAN-No.	Period	Pr.	Info
670084	1998-1998	4	30 cm

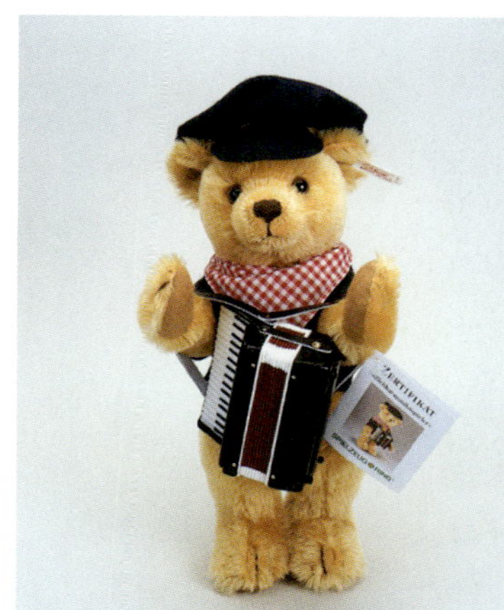

Teddybaer - *Teddybear*

Mohair, goldblond, gegliedert, Druckstimme, als Ziehharmonikaspieler, limit. Auflage 1.500 Stueck fuer Spielzeugring - *mohair, gold-blond, jointed, press voice, accordion player, ltd edition of 1,500 for Spielzeugring stores*

EAN-No	Period	Pr.	Info
651069	1998-1998	4	30 cm

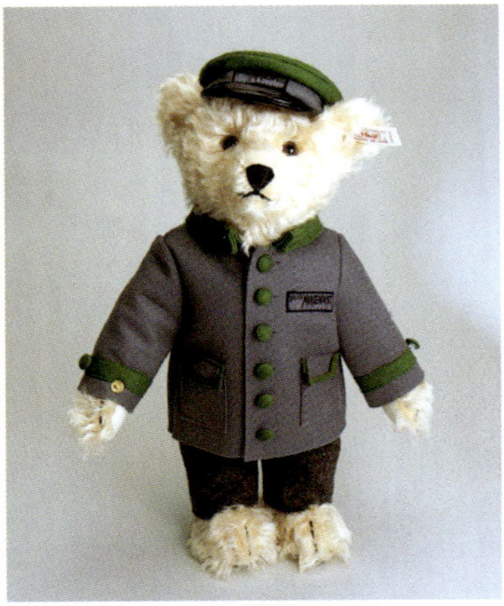

Morgenpostbaer - *Morning Post Bear*

Mohair, blond, gegliedert, Brummstimme, bekleidet als Zeitungsjunge der Berliner Morgenpost, limit. Auflage 1.500 Stueck fuer Berlin - *mohair, blond, jointed, growler, dressed as a newsboy of the Berlin Morning Post, ltd edition of 1,500, exclusive for stores in Berlin*

EAN-No.	Period	Pr.	Info
655425	1998-1998	4	32 cm

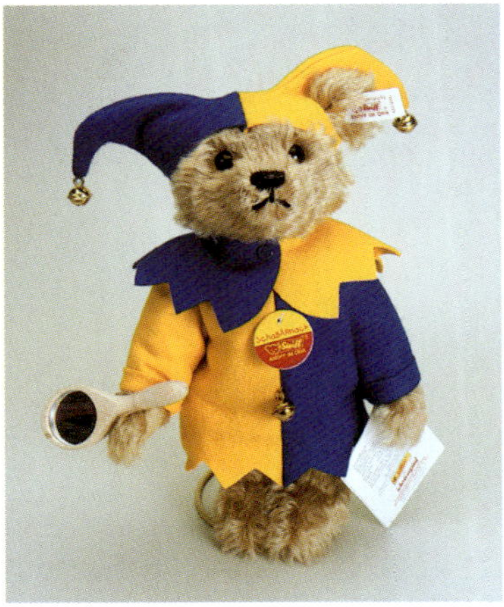

SchaBAERnack

Mohair, zimt, gegliedert, mit Narrenkappe und -jacke in blau/gelb, limit. Auflage 1.500 Stueck fuer idee+spiel - *mohair, cinnamon, jointed, with fool´s-cap and suit in blue/yellow, ltd edition of 1,500 for idee+spiel stores*

EAN-No.	Period	Pr.	Info
651076	1998-1998	4	26 cm

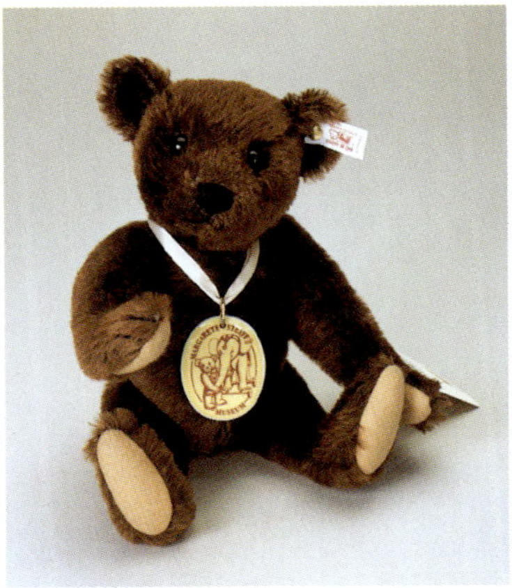

Steiff Museumsbaer - *Steiff Museum Bear*

Mohair, rotbraun, gegliedert, mit Porzellanplakette, exclusiv nur fuer Besucher des Steiff Museums in Giengen, Jahreslimitierung 1999 - *mohair, red-brown, jointed, porcelain medallion, exclusive for visitors of the Steiff Museum in Giengen, ltd edition 1999 only*

EAN-No.	Period	Pr.	Info
670343	1999-1999	3	30 cm

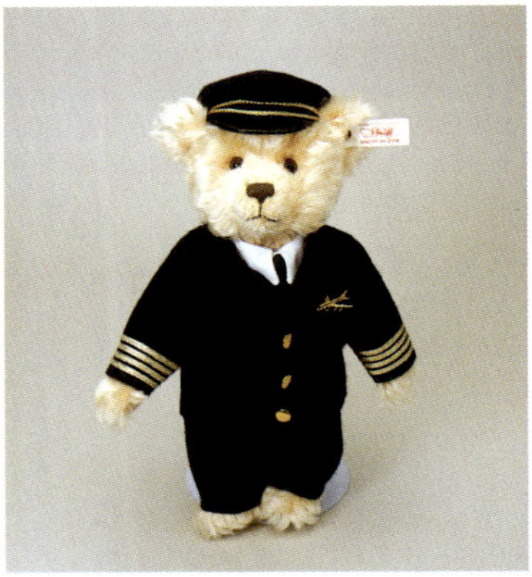

Teddybaer Pilot - *Teddybear Pilot*

Mohair, hellblond, gegliedert, limit. Auflage 1.500 Stueck fuer Vedes - *mohair, light blond, jointed, ltd edition of 1,500 for Vedes*

EAN-No.	Period	Pr.	Info
651120	1999-1999	4	27 cm

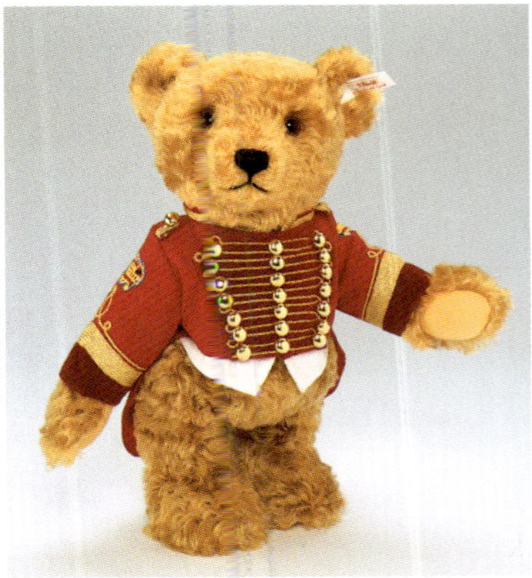

Teddybaer Zirkusdirektor - *Teddybear Ringmaster*

Mohair, gold, gegliedert, Uniformjacke des Zirkus Roncalli, limit. Auflage 1.999 Stueck fuer Karstadt/Hertie - *mohair, gold, jointed, uniform-jacket of Roncalli Circus, ltd edition of 1,999 for Karstadt/Hertie*

EAN-No.	Period	Pr.	Info
655416	1999-1999	[illegible]	30 cm

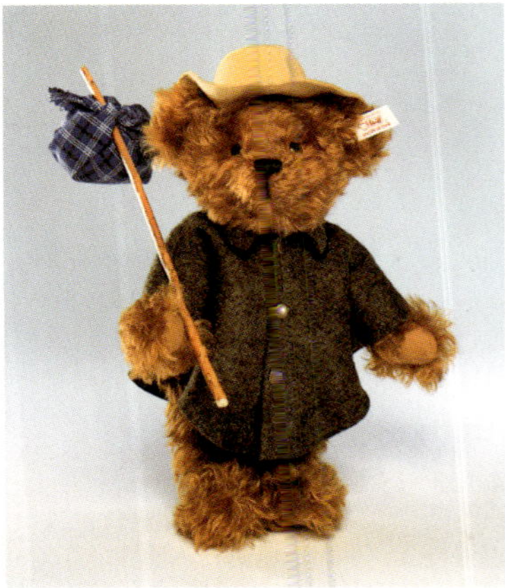

RumtreiBAER

Mohair, mittelbraun, gegliedert, ausgestattet wie ein Vagabund, limit. Auflage 1.500 Stueck fuer idee+spiel - *mohair, medium brown, jointed, equipped & dressed like a tramp, ltd edition of 1,500 for idee+spiel stores*

EAN-No.	Period	Pr.	Info
653113	1999-1999	3-4	27 cm

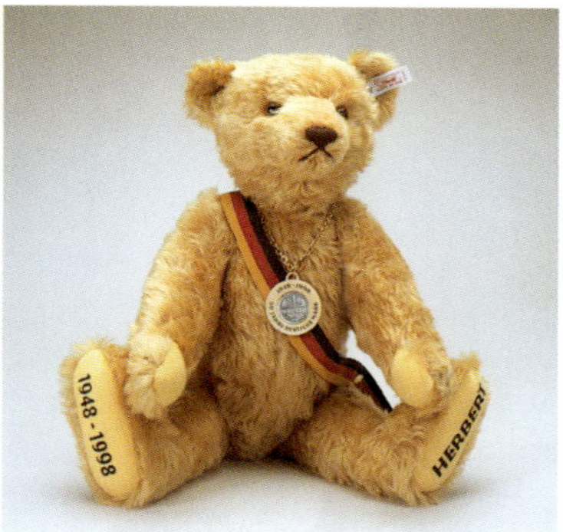

Herbert

Mohair, goldbraun, gegliedert, limit. Auflage 1.500 Stueck fuer Kaufhof AG zum 50jaehrigen Jubilaeum der DM im Jahr 1998, Muenzanhaenger mit der Praegung eines 1 DM Stuecks von 1948 - *mohair, gold-brown, jointed, ltd edition of 1,500 for Kaufhof AG to celebrate the 50th anniversary of the DM in the year 1998, pendant with a 1 DM coin from 1948*

EAN-No.	Period	Pr.	Info
655395	1999-1999	3-4	45 cm

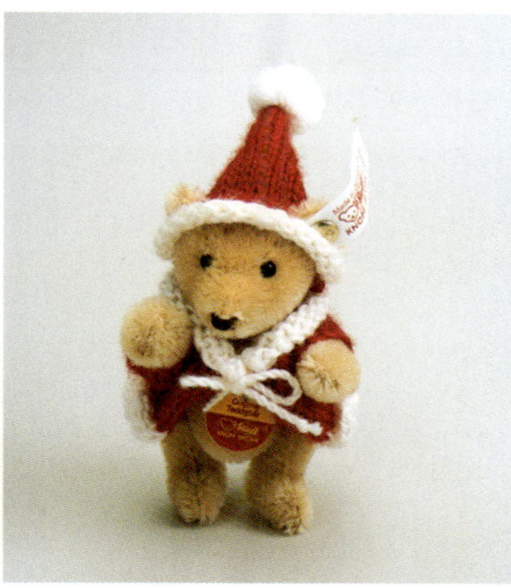

Weihnachtsbaum Baer - *Christmas Tree Bear*

Mohair, blond, gegliedert, als Christbaumschmuck, limit. Auflage 5.000 Stueck - *mohair, blond, jointed, as christmas tree ornament, ltd edition of 5,000*

EAN-No.	Period	Pr.	Info
655296	1996-1996	4	10 cm

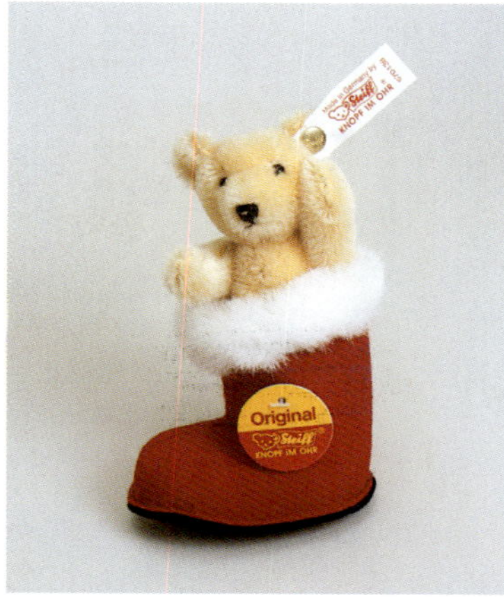

Weihnachtsbaum Baer - *Christmas Tree Bear*

Mohair, blond, gegliedert, in rotem Stiefel mit weissem Plueschbesatz, als Christbaumschmuck, limit. Auflage 5.000 Stueck - *mohair, blond, jointed, in a red boot with white plush trimmings, as christmas tree ornament, ltd edition of 5,000*

EAN-No.	Period	Pr.	Info
670138	1997-1997	3-4	10 cm

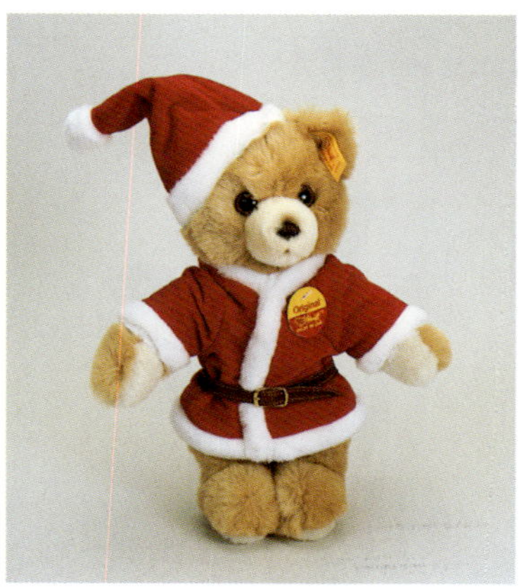

Weihnachts Teddybaer - *Santa Claus Teddybear*

Mohair, blond, stehend, abwaschbar, roter Mantel & Muetze aus Trevirasamt mit weissem Plueschbesatz, brauner Lederguertel - *mohair, blond, standing, surface washable, red coat & cap of trevira-velvet with white trimmings of plush, brown belt*

EAN-No.	Period	Pr.	Info
670145	1997-1997	3	26 cm

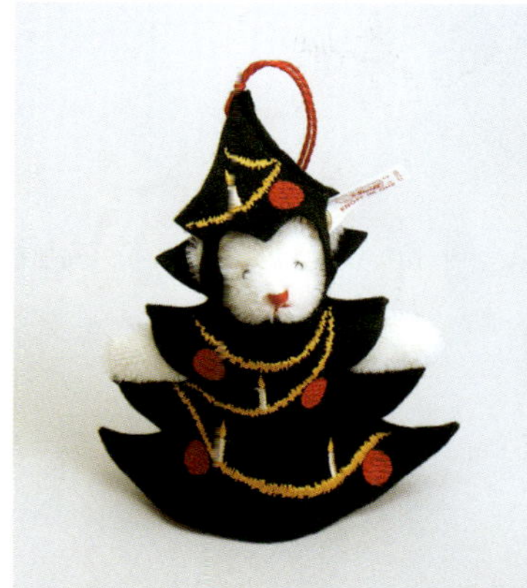

Weihnachtsbaum Baer - *Christmas Tree Bear*

Mohair, weiss, in gruenem Filz-Weihnachtsbaum, als Christbaumschmuck, limit. Auflage 5.000 Stueck - *mohair, white, in a green christmas tree of felt, as christmas tree ornament, ltd edition of 5,000*

EAN-No.	Period	Pr.	Info
670329	1998-1998	3	12 cm

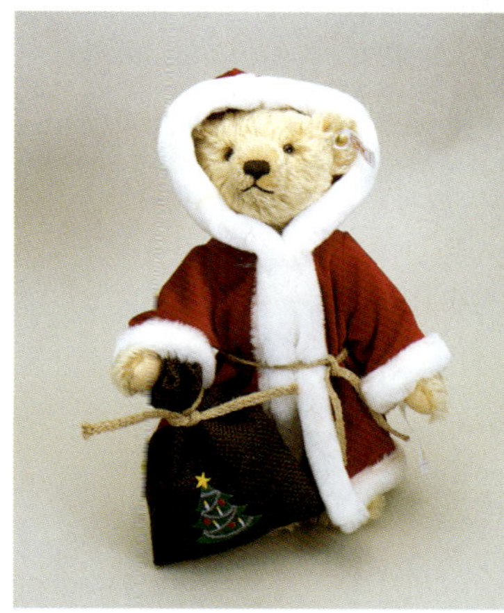

Nikolaus Teddybaer - *Santa Claus Teddybear*

Mohair, blond, gegliedert, roter Samtmantel & Jutesack, keine Krallenbestickung, limit. Auflage 3.000 Stueck - *mohair, blond, jointed, red coat of velvet & sack of jute, no claws, ltd edition of 3,000*

EAN-No.	Period	Pr.	Info
670268	1998-1998	3-4	32 cm

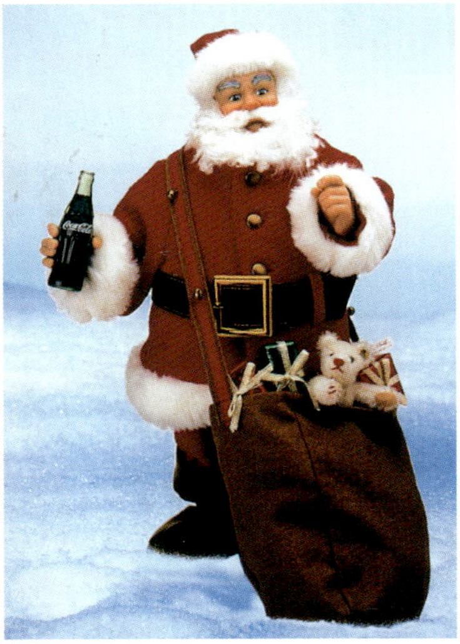

COCA COLA Santa mit Baer - *COCA COLA Santa & Bear*

PVC bzw. Mohair, gegliedert, abwaschbar, Santa: Kopf & Arme gegliedert, roter Mantel, Muetze, Lederguertel & -stiefel, Coca Cola Flasche, Sack mit Gloeckchen & 6 cm Teddy in weiss, limit. Auflage 10.000 Stueck - *PVC / mohair, jointed, surface washable, Santa: head & arms jointed, red coat, cap, leather-belt & -boots, Coca Cola bottle, sack with bell and a 6 cm Teddy in white, ltd edition of 10,000*

EAN-No.	Period	Pr.	Info
670350	1999-1999	4-5	35/6 cm

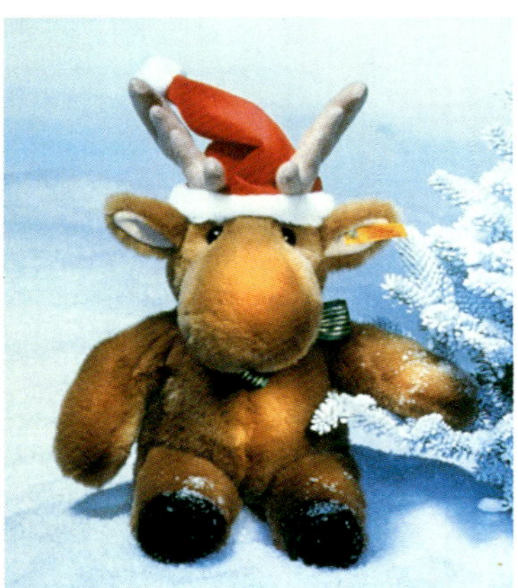

Weihnachtselch - *Christmas Elk*

Webpelz, braun, waschmaschinenfest, Schlenkertier, rote Samtmuetze mit weissem Plueschbesatz - *woven fur, brown, machine washable, dangling animal, red cap of velvet with white trimmings of plush*

EAN-No.	Period	Pr.	Info
670411	1999-1999	3	32 cm

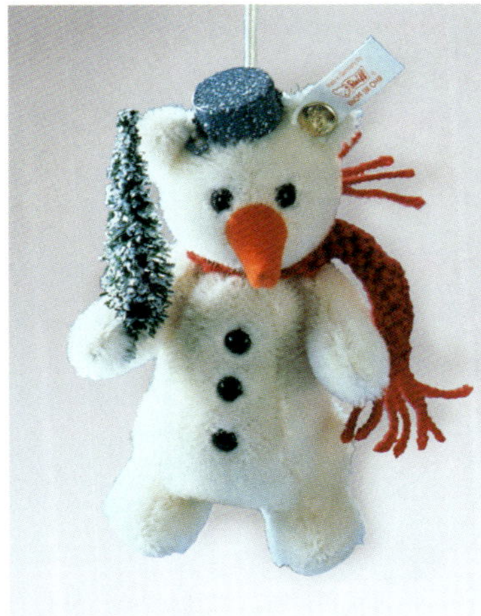

Weihnachtsbaum Schneemann - *Christmas Tree Snowman*

Mohair, weiss, stehend, abwaschbar, Kopf & Arme gegliedert, blaugrauer Topfhut aus Email, Christbaumschmuck, limit. Auflage 5.000 Stueck - *mohair, white, standing, surface washable, head & arms jointed, blue-grey hat of enamel, christmas tree ornament, ltd edition of 5,000*

EAN-No.	Period	Pr.	Info
670428	1999-1999	3	12 cm

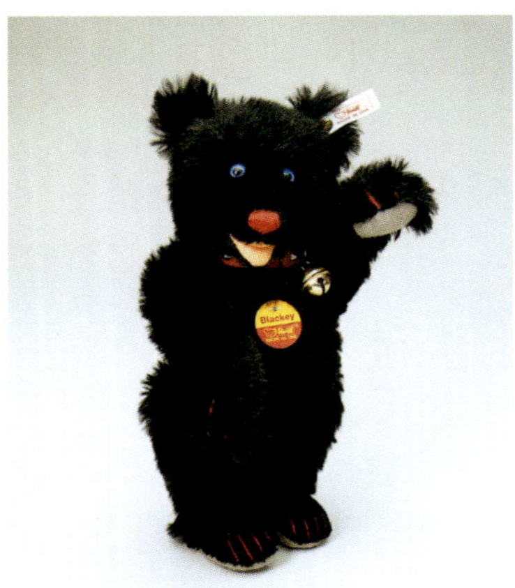

Blackey

Mohair, schwarz, gegliedert, abwaschbar, Sonderbaer zum 1. Steiff Festival 1997 in Giengen an der Brenz, Lederhalsband mit Gloeckchen, autom. Brummstimme, limit. Auflage 3.000 Stueck - *mohair, black, jointed, surface washable, special bear for 1st Steiff Festival 1997 in Giengen at the Brenz, leather collar with bell, growler, ltd edition of 3,000*

EAN-No.	Period	Pr.	Info
655333	1997-1997	6	28 cm

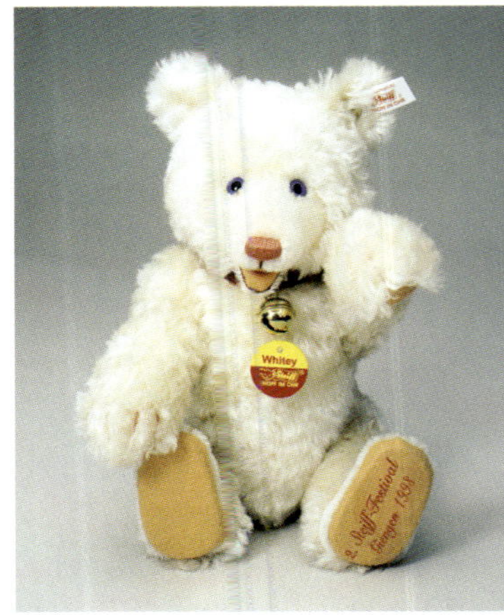

Whitey

Mohair, weiss, gegliedert, abwaschbar, Sonderbaer zum 2. Steiff Festival 1998 in Giengen an der Brenz, Lederhalsband mit Gloeckchen, autom. Brummstimme, limit. Auflage 3.000 Stueck - *mohair, white, jointed, surface washable, special bear for 2nd Steiff Festival 1998 in Giengen at the Brenz, leather collar with bell, growler, ltd edition of 3,000*

EAN-No.	Period	Pr.	Info
655340	1998-1998	5	28 cm

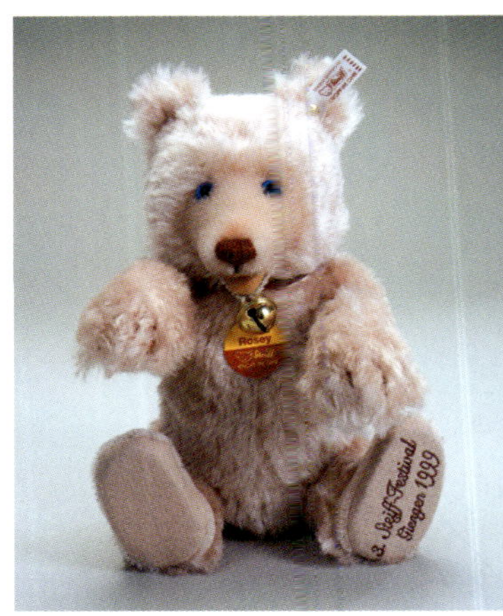

Rosey

Mohair, rosé, gegliedert, abwaschbar, Sonderbaer zum 3. Steiff Festival 1999 in Giengen an der Brenz, Lederhalsband mit Gloeckchen, autom. Brummstimme, limit. Auflage 3.000 Stueck - *mohair, rose, jointed, surface washable, special bear for 3rd Steiff Festival 1999 in Giengen at the Brenz, leather collar with bell, growler, ltd edition of 3,000*

EAN-No.	Period	Pr.	Info
655487	1999-1999	5-6	29 cm

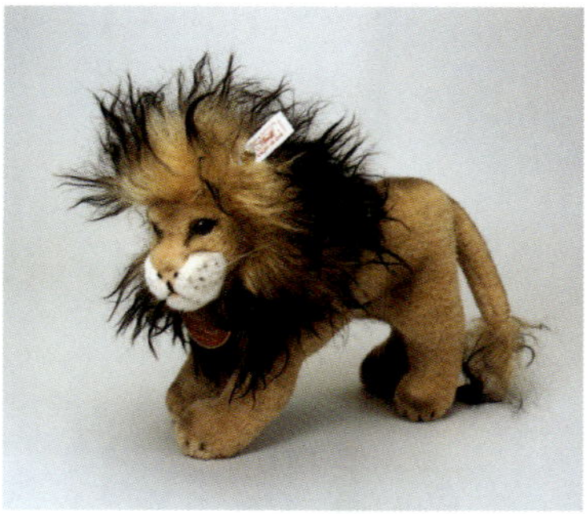

Loewe King Leo - *Lion King Leo*

Webpelz, hellbraun, stehend, abwaschbar, limit. Auflage 3.000 Stueck fuer Idee & Spiel - *woven fur, light brown, standing, surface washable, ltd edition of 3,000 for Idee + Spiel stores*

EAN-No.	Period	Pr.	Info
650932	1994-1994	3-4	22 cm

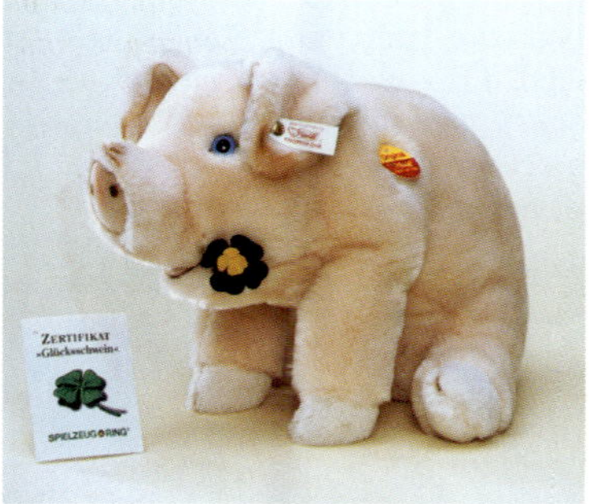

Gluecksschwein - *Lucky Pig*

Webpelz, rosa, sitzend, abwaschbar, limit. Auflage 3.000 Stueck fuer Spielzeugring - *woven fur, pink, sitting, surface washable, ltd edition of 3,000 for Spielzeugring*

EAN-No.	Period	Pr.	Info
650949	1995-1995	3	30 cm

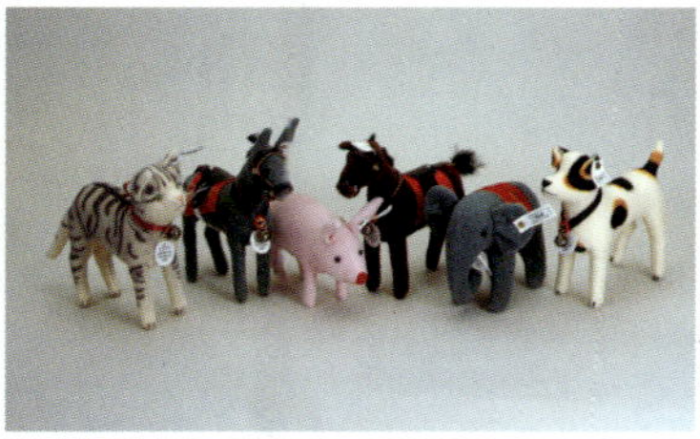

Jubilaeumssortiment 1997 - *Jubilee Assortment 1997*

Samt, abwaschbar, zum 150. Geburtstag der Margarete Steiff, 6 Tiere - Elefant, Esel, Schwein, Pferd, Katze & Hund - im Karton, limit. Auflage 1.847 Stueck - *velvet, surface washable, on the occasion of the 150th birthday of Margarete Steiff, 6 animals - elephant, donkey, pig, horse, cat & dog - in a box, ltd edition of 1,847*

EAN-No.	Period	Pr.	Info
400285	1997-1997	5	kpl. Set - *compl.set*
J04220	1997-1997	2-3	Esel - *donkey*
J04221	1997-1997	2-3	Hund - *dog*
J04222	1997-1997	2-3	Elefant - *elephant*
J04223	1997-1997	2-3	Pferd - *horse*
J04224	1997-1997	2-3	Katze - *cat*
J04225	1997-1997	2-3	Schwein - *pig*

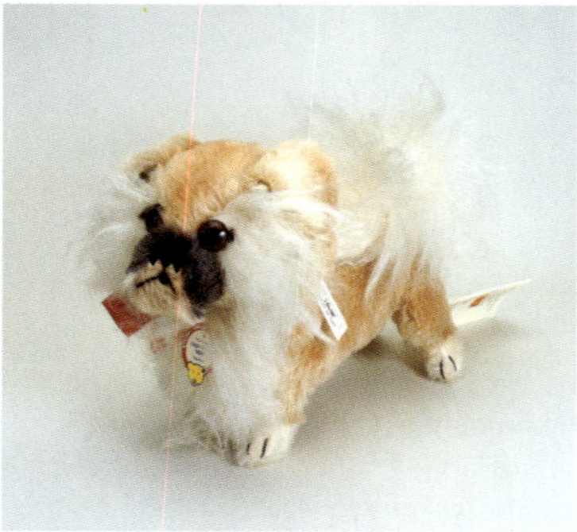

Pekinese **Chin Chin**

Mohair, hellbraun, stehend, abwaschbar, limit. Auflage 300 Stueck, aus Schaufertigung anlaesslich des 2. Steiff-Festival´s - *mohair, light brown, standing, surface washable, ltd edition of 300, from exhibition manufacturing during 2nd Steiff Festival*

EAN-No.	Period	Pr.	Info
670305	1998-1998	4	20 cm

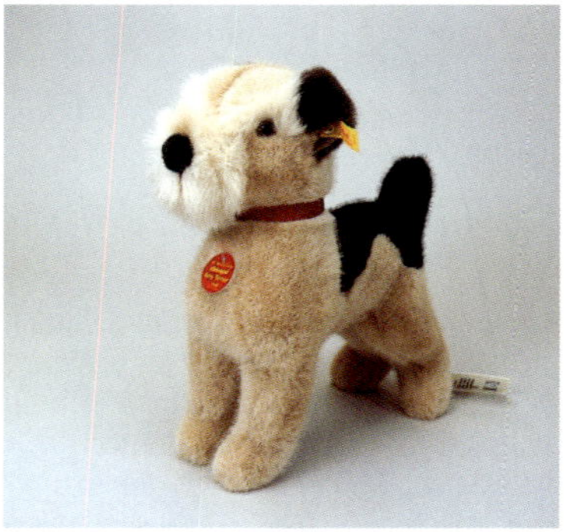

Arry Terrier

Webpelz, hellbraun/schwarz, stehend, abwaschbar, zum 20. Geburtstag von Idee & Spiel - *woven fur, light brown/black, standing, surface washable, to celebrate the 20th birthday of Idee & Spiel*

EAN-No.	Period	Pr.	Info
651038	1998-1998	3-4	28 cm

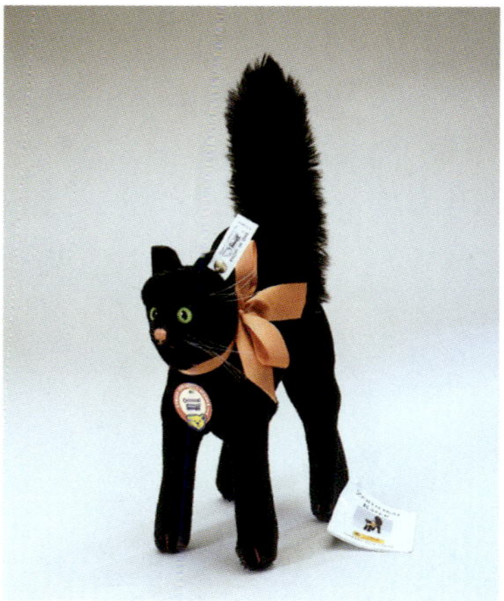

Kater Repl. 1950 - *Tomcat Repl. 1950*

Mohair, schwarz, stehend, abwaschbar, Holzwolle-Stopfung, limit. Auflage 300 Stueck, aus Schaufertigung anlaesslich des 3. Steiff-Festival´s - *mohair, black, standing, surface washable, excelsior-stuffed, ltd edition of 300, from exhibition manufacturing during 3rd Steiff Festival*

EAN-No.	Period	Pr.	Info
670404	1999-1999	4-5	22 cm

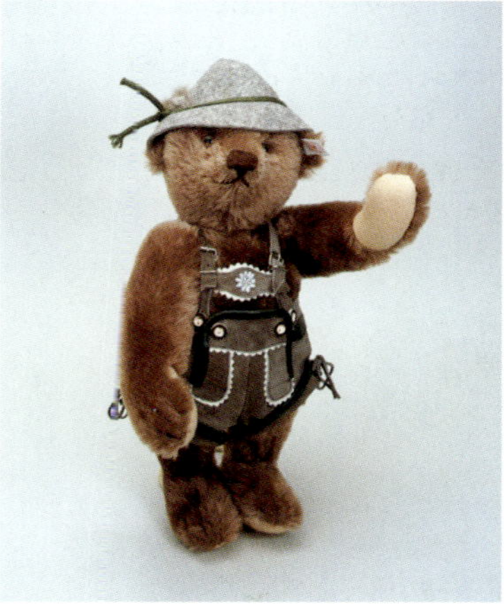

Teddybaer - *Teddybear*

Mohair Webpelz, caramel, gegliedert, Brummstimme, limit. Auflage 1.500 Stueck fuer Oesterreich - *mohair woven fur, caramel, jointed, growler, ltd edition of 1,500 for Austria*

EAN-No	Period	Pr.	Info
650871	1995-1995	4	32 cm

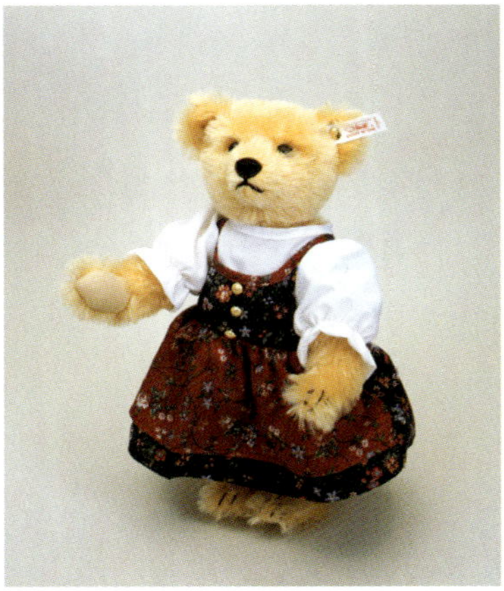

Teddybaer - *Teddybear*

Mohair Webpelz, blond, gegliedert, mit Dirndl, Druckstimme, limit. Auflage 1.500 Stueck fuer Oesterreich - *mohair woven fur, blond, jointed, with dirndl, press voice, ltd edition of 1,500 for Austria*

EAN-No.	Period	Pr.	Info
659850	1996-1996	4	32 cm

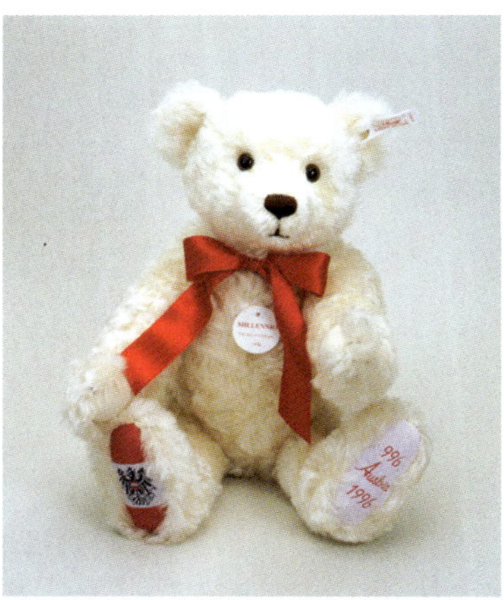

Teddybaer **Millennio** - *Teddybear **Millennio***

Mohair Webpelz, weiss, gegliedert, Brummstimme, limit. Auflage 1.500 Stueck zum 1000. Jahrestag Oesterreichs - *mohair woven fur, white, jointed, growler, ltd edition of 1,500 on the occasion of the 1000th anniversary of Austria*

EAN-No.	Period	Pr.	Info
659898	1996-1996	4	35 cm

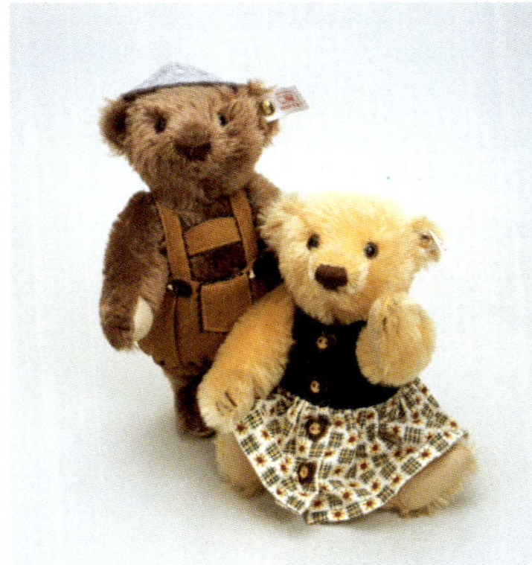

Teddy Geschwisterpaar - *Teddy Brother & Sister*

Mohair Webpelz, braun / blond, gegliedert, bekleidet mit Lederhose bzw. Dirndl, limit. Auflage 1.847 Stueck fuer Oesterreich - *mohair woven fur, brown / blond, jointed, dressed with leather trousers and dirndl, ltd edition of 1,847 for Austria*

EAN-No.	Period	Pr.	Info
659911	1997-1997	4-5	25 cm

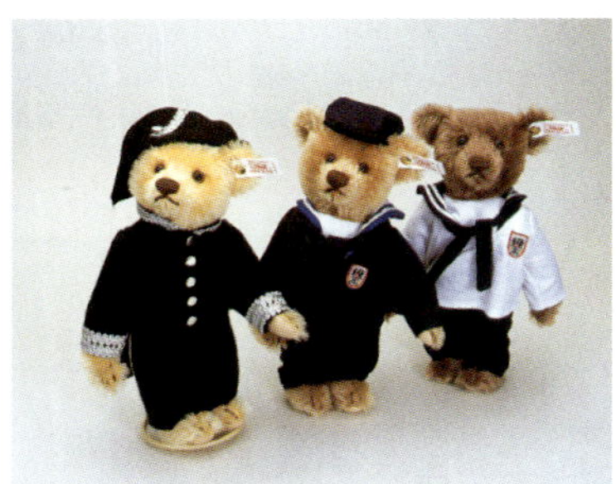

Teddybaeren Wiener Saengerknaben - *Vienna Chorus Boys Teddybears*

Mohair Webpelz, zimt, caramel & blond, gegliedert, 3 Baeren, je 26 cm, bekleidet als Wiener Saengerknaben, zum 500. Jubilaeum, limit. Auflage 1.847 Stueck fuer Oesterreich - *mohair woven fur, cinnamon, caramel & blond, jointed, 3 bears, 26 cm each, dressed like the Vienna Chorus Boys, to celebrate the 500th anniversary, ltd edition of 1,847*

EAN-No.	Period	Pr.	Info
659966	1998-1998	4	kpl. Set - *compl. set*
	1998-1998	3	26 cm, zimt - *cinnamon*
	1998-1998	3	26 cm, caramel
	1998-1998	3	26 cm, blond

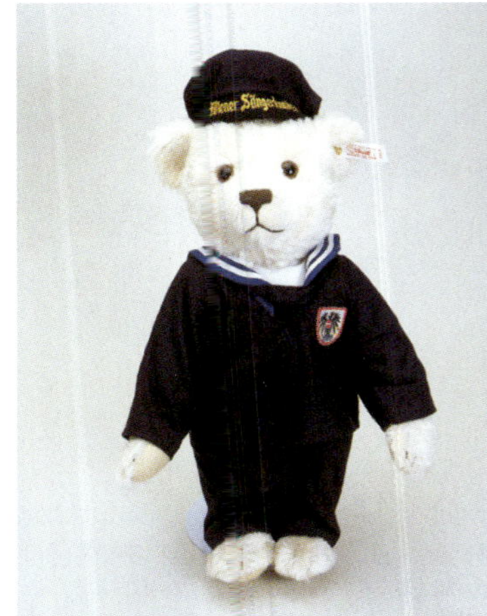

Teddy Wiener Saengerknabe - *Vienna Chorus Boy Teddybear*

Mohair Webpelz, weiss, gegliedert, bekleidet als Wiener Saengerknabe, zum 500. Jubilaeum, limit. Auflage 3.000 Stueck, mit Musik-CD - *mohair woven fur, white, jointed, dressed like a Vienna Chorus Boy, to celebrate the 500th anniversary, ltd edition of 3,000, with a music CD*

EAN-No.	Period	Pr.	Info
996634	1998-1998	3-4	33 cm

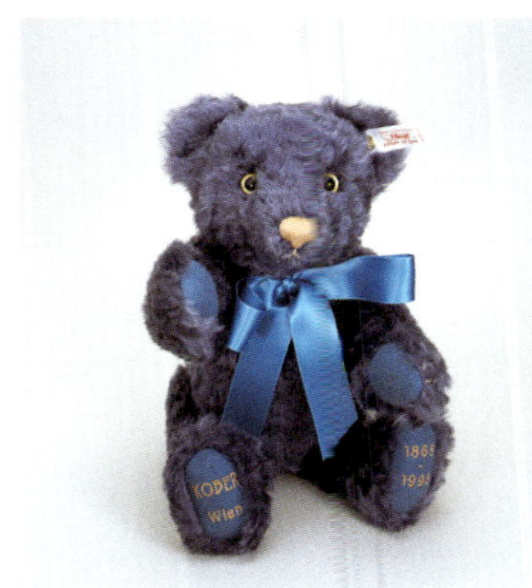

Teddybaer - *Teddybear*

Mohair Webpelz, dunkelblau, gegliedert, Druckstimme, zum 130. Jubilaeum der Fa. Kober, Wien, limit. Auflage 1.500 Stueck - *mohair woven fur, dark blue, jointed, press voice, to celebrate the 130th anniversary of Kober, Vienna, ltd edition of 1,500*

EAN-No.	Period	Pr.	Info
658013	1998-1998	4	30 cm

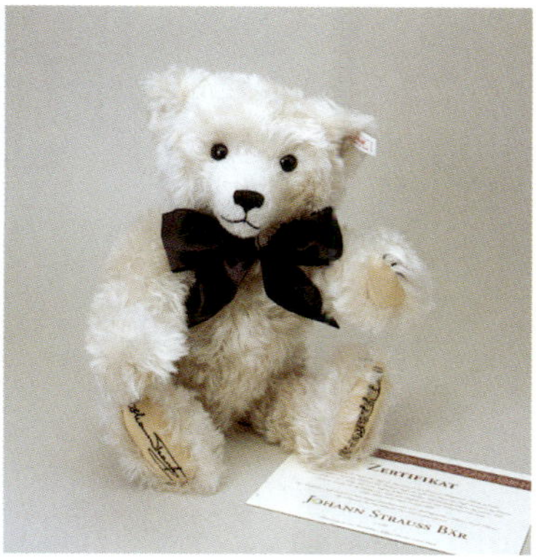

Johann Strauss Baer - *Johann Strauss Bear*

Mohair, silbergrau, gegliedert, zum 100. Todestag des Johann Strauss, mit Musikwerk "An der schoenen blauen Donau", limit. Auflage 1.847 Stueck fuer Oesterreich - *mohair, silver grey, jointed, to honour the 100th day of death of Johann Strauss, with music box playing "An der schoenen blauen Donau", ltd edition of 1,847 for Austria*

EAN-No.	Period	Pr.	Info
660030	1999-1999	4-5	40 cm

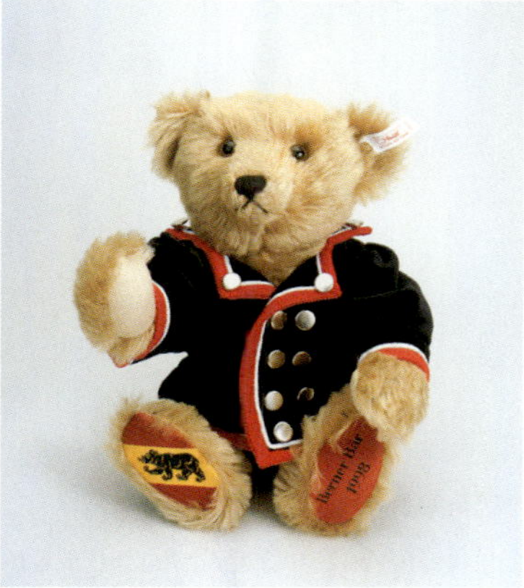

Berner Baer - *Bern Bear*

Mohair, zimt, gegliedert, abwaschbar, bestickte Fusssohlen, limit. Auflage 1.847 Stueck fuer die Schweiz - *mohair, cinnamon, jointed, surface washable, embroidered soles, ltd edition of 1,847 for Switzerland*

EAN-No.	Period	Pr.	Info
659928	1998-1998	4	32 cm

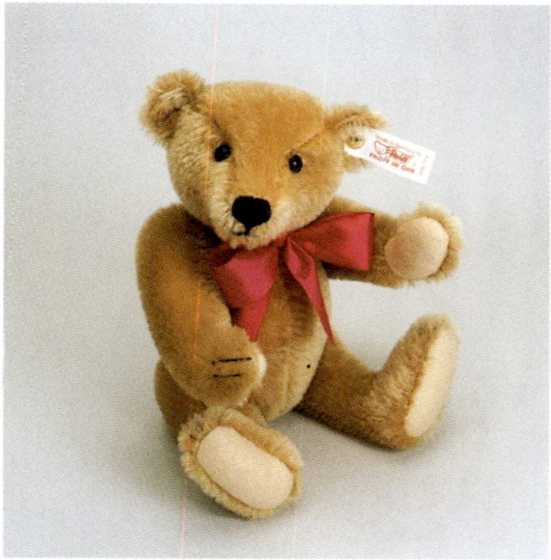

Logo Baer - *Logo Bear*

Mohair, blond, gegliedert, limit. Auflage 1.500 Stueck fuer das Puppenhausmuseum, Basel - *mohair, blond, jointed, ltd edition of 1,500 for the Basle Doll´s House Museum*

EAN-No.	Period	Pr.	Info
998713	1998-1998	4	25 cm

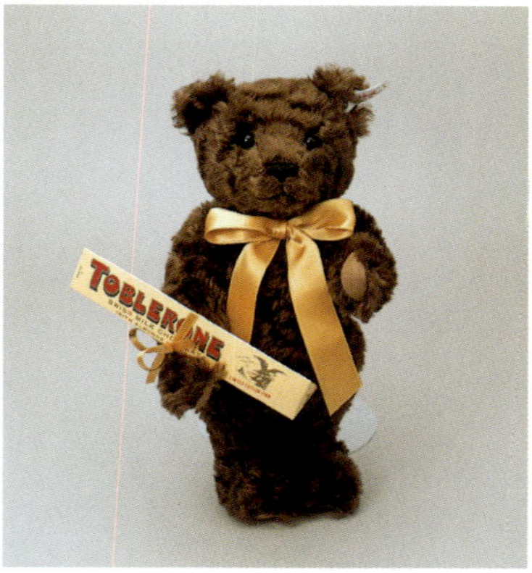

Schoggi Baer - *Schoggi Bear*

Mohair, schokoladenbraun, gegliedert, abwaschbar, Baer nach dem Schnitt von 1908, mit Toblerone Schachtel Originaldesign 1908, limit. Auflage 1.847 Stueck fuer die Schweiz - *mohair, chocolate, jointed, surface washable, produced from the pattern of the 1908 bear, with Toblerone box identical to the original from 1908, ltd edition of 1,847 for Switzerland*

EAN-No.	Period	Pr.	Info
660054	1999-1999	4	30 cm

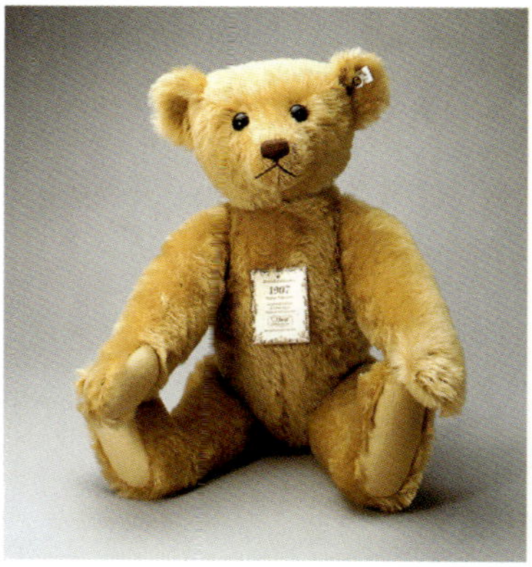

British Collector´s

Teddybaer Repl. 1907, Mohair, blond, gegliedert, Brummstimme, limit. Auflage 2.000 Stueck - *1907 Teddy bear replica, mohair, blond jointed, growler, ltd edition of 2,000*

Serie	Art.-No	Period	Pr.	Info
406104	**0174/61**	1989-1989	6	61 cm

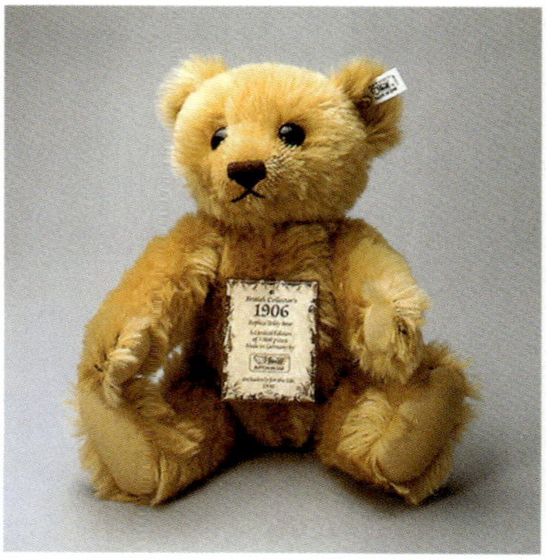

British Collector´s

Teddybaer Repl. 1906, Mohair, blond, gegliedert, Brummstimme, limit. Auflage 3.000 Stueck - *1906 Teddy bear replica, mohair, blond, jointed, growler, ltd edition of 3,000*

Serie	Art.-No	Period	Pr.	Info
406096	**0174/33**	1990-1990	4-5	33 cm

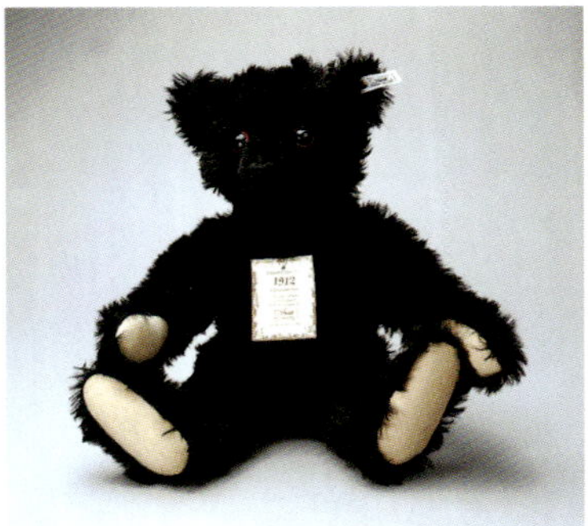

British Collector´s

Teddybaer Repl. 1912, Mohair Webpelz, gegliedert, Brummstimme, limit. Auflage 3.000 Stueck - *1912 Teddy bear replica, mohair woven fur, jointed, growler, ltd edition of 3,000*

EAN-No.	Period	Pr.	Info
406829	1991-1991	5-6	48 cm

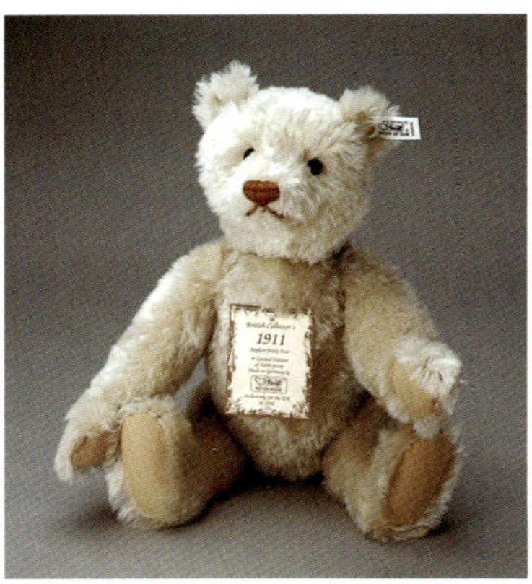

British Collector´s

Teddybaer Repl. 1911, Mohair, weiss, gegliedert, Brummstimme, limit. Auflage 3.000 Stueck - *1911 Teddy bear replica, mohair, white, jointed, growler, ltd edition of 3,000*

EAN-No.	Period	Pr.	Info
406645	1992-1992	5	42 cm

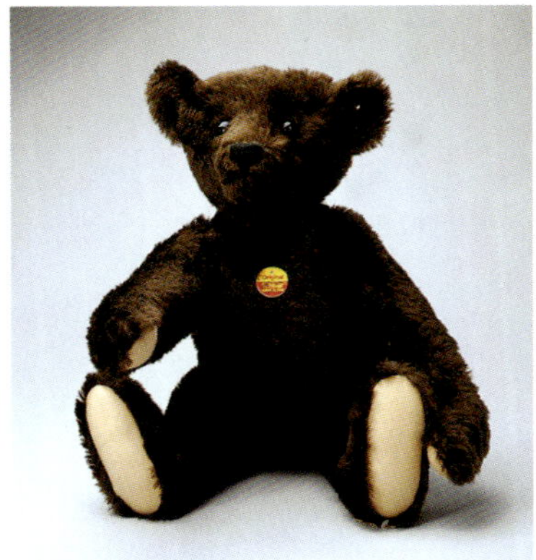

British Collector´s

Teddybaer Repl. 1907, Mohair Webpelz, gegliedert, Brummstimme, limit. Auflage 3.000 Stueck - *1907 Teddy bear replica, mohair woven fur, jointed, growler, ltd edition of 3,000*

EAN-No.	Period	Pr.	Info
406065	1993-1993	5	60 cm

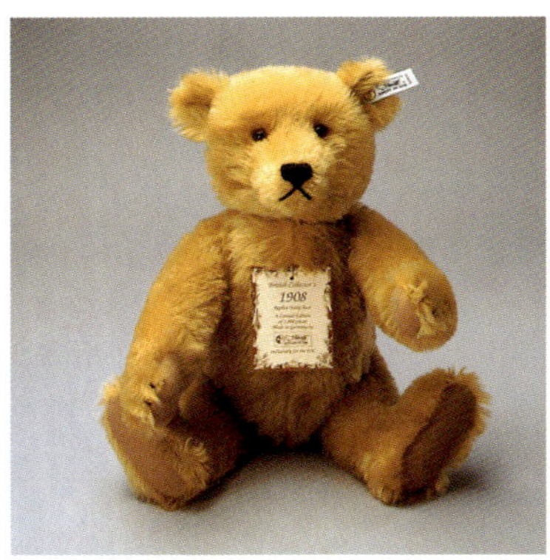

British Collector´s

Teddybaer Repl. 1908, Mohair Webpelz, gegliedert, Brummstimme, limit. Auflage 3.000 Stueck - *1908 Teddy bear replica, mohair woven fur, jointed, growler, ltd edition of 3,000*

EAN-No.	Period	Pr.	Info
406072	1994-1994	4-5	40 cm

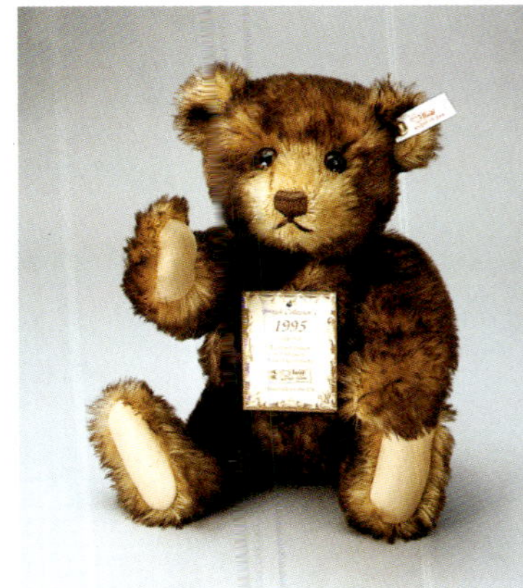

British Collector´s

Teddybaer, Mohair Webpelz, braun gespitzt, gegliedert, Brummstimme, limit. Auflage 3.000 Stueck - *Teddy bear, mohair woven fur, brown tipped, jointed, growler, ltd edition of 3,000*

EAN-No.	Period	Pr.	Info
654404	1995-1995	4	35 cm

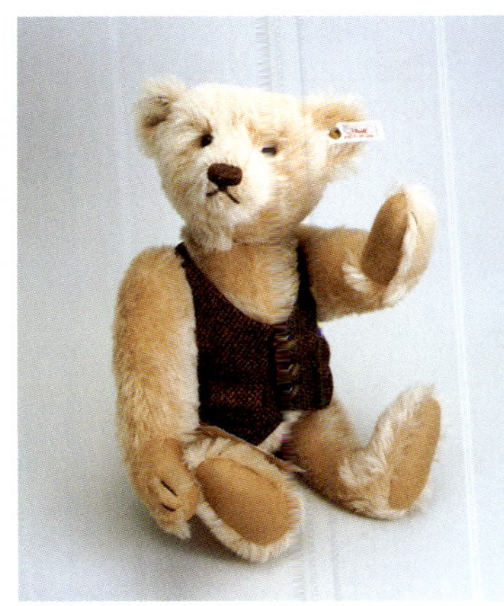

British Collector´s

Teddybaer, Mohair Webpelz, blond, gegliedert, Brummstimme, mit rot-brauner Tweed-Weste, limit. Auflage 3.000 Stueck - *Teddy bear, mohair woven fur, blond, jointed, growler, red-brown waistcoat, ltd edition of 3,000*

EAN-No.	Period	Pr.	Info
654411	1996-1996	4	43 cm

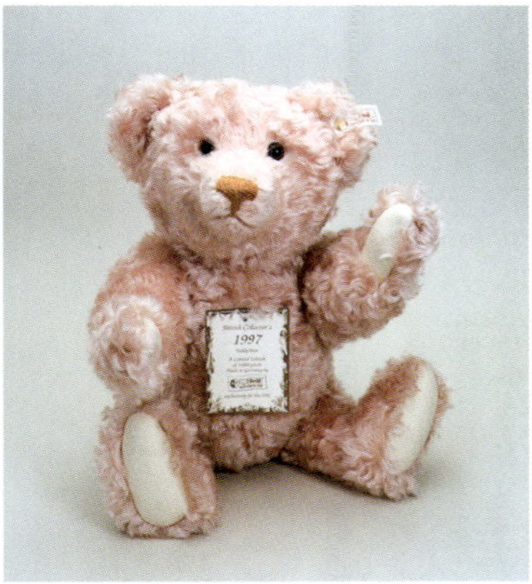

British Collector´s

Teddybaer, Mohair Webpelz, rosè, gegliedert, limit. Auflage 3.000 Stueck - *Teddy bear, mohair woven fur, rose, jointed, ltd edition of 3,000*

EAN-No.	Period	Pr.	Info
654480	1997-1997	4	38 cm

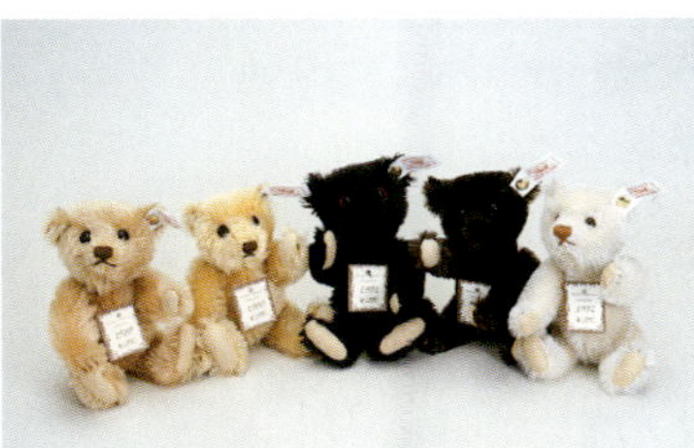

British Collector´s Set

Mohair Webpelz, gegliedert, Reproduktionen der British Collectors Baeren von 1989 bis 1993, je 16 cm, limit. Auflage 1.847 Stueck - *mohair woven fur, jointed, smaller reproductions of British Collector´s bears from 1989 to 1993, 16 cm each, ltd edition of 1,847 sets*

EAN-No.	Period	Pr.	Info
654497	1997-1997	5	kpl. Set - *compl. set*
J04210	1997-1997	3	1989, blond
J04211	1997-1997	3	1990, blond
J04212	1997-1997	3	1991, schwarz - *1991, black*
J04213	1997-1997	3	1992, weiss - *1992, white*
J04214	1997-1997	3	1993, dunkelbraun - *1993, dark brown*

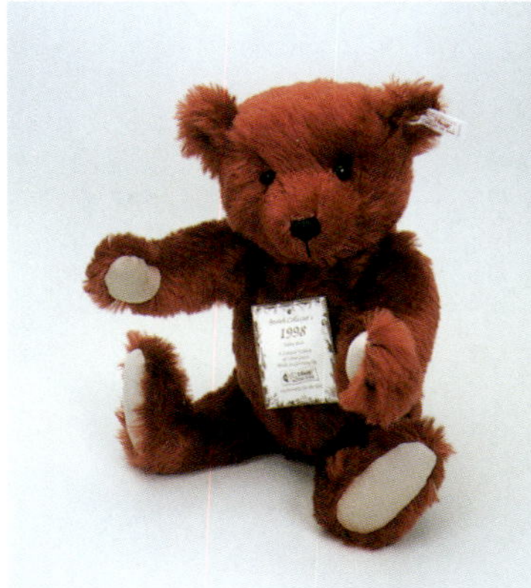

British Collector´s

Teddybaer, Mohair, burgunderrot, gegliedert, Brummstimme, limit. Auflage 3.000 Stueck - *Teddy bear, mohair woven fur, burgundy, jointed, growler, ltd edition of 3,000*

EAN-No.	Period	Pr.	Info
659973	1998-1998	4	40 cm

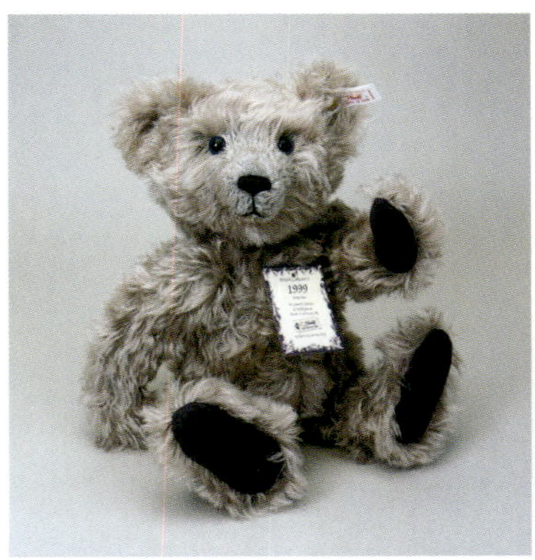

British Collector´s

Teddybaer, Mohair, lila, gegliedert, limit. Auflage 3.000 Stueck - *Teddy bear, lilac, jointed, ltd edition of 3,000*

EAN-No.	Period	Pr.	Info
660047	1999-1999	4	36 cm

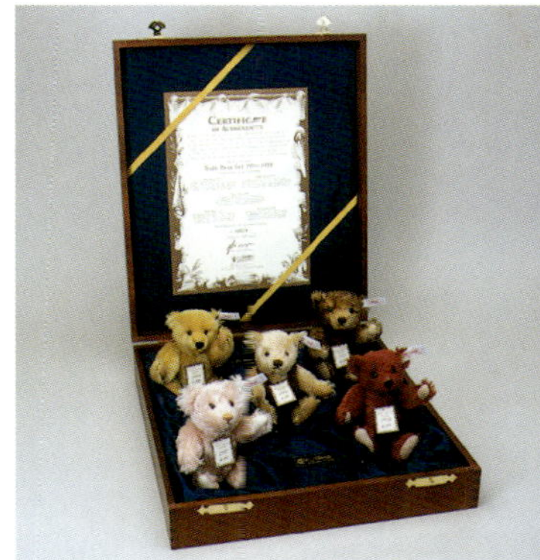

British Collector´s Set

Mohair Webpelz, gegliedert, Reproduktionen der British Collectors Baeren von 1994 bis 1998, je 16 cm, limit. Auflage 1.847 Stueck - *mohair woven fur, jointed, smaller reproductions of British Collector´s bears from 1994 to 1998, 16 cm each, ltd edition of 1,847 sets*

EAN-No.	Period	Pr.	Info
654695	1999-1999	5	kpl. Set - *compl. set*
	1999-1999	3	1994, blond
	1999-1999	3	1995, braun gespitzt - *1995, brown tipped*
	1999-1999	3	1996, blond
	1999-1999	3	1997, rosè - *1997, rose*
	1999-1999	3	1998, burgunderrot - *1998, burgundy*

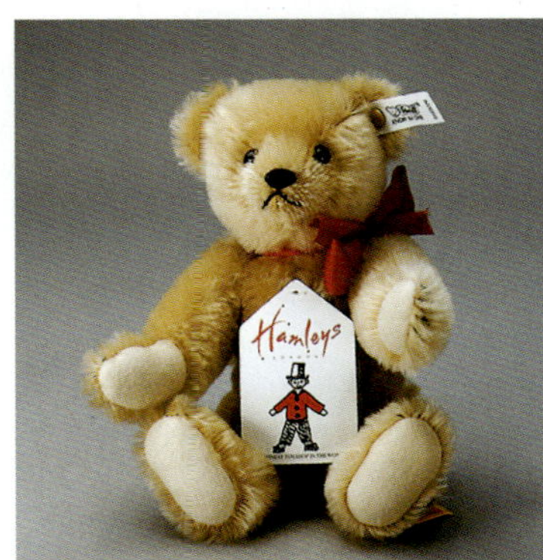

Hamleys Baer - *Hamleys Bear*

Mohair, blond, gegliedert, limit. Auflage 2.000 Stueck fuer Hamleys, London - *mohair, blond, jointed, ltd edition of 2,000 for Hamleys, London*

Serie	Art.-No	Period	Pr.	Info
650291	**0163/26**	1988-1988	4-5	26 cm

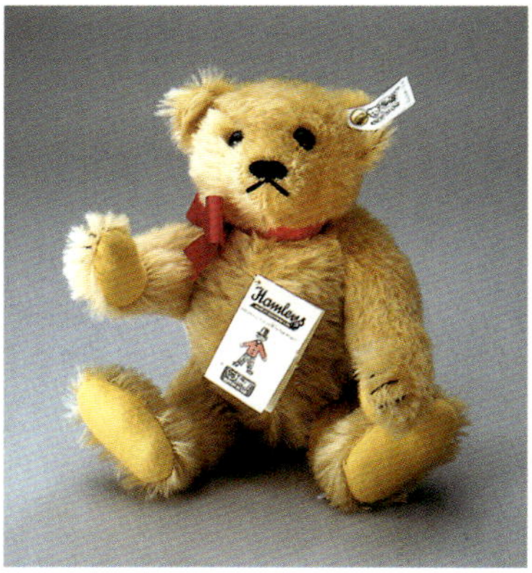

Hamleys Baer - *Hamleys Bear*

Mohair, hellblond, gegliedert, limit. Auflage 2.000 Stueck fuer Hamleys, London - *mohair, light blond, jointed, ltd edition of 2,000 for Hamleys, London*

SERIE	ART.-NO	PERIOD	PR.	INFO
650284	**0168/28**	1989-1989	4-5	29 cm

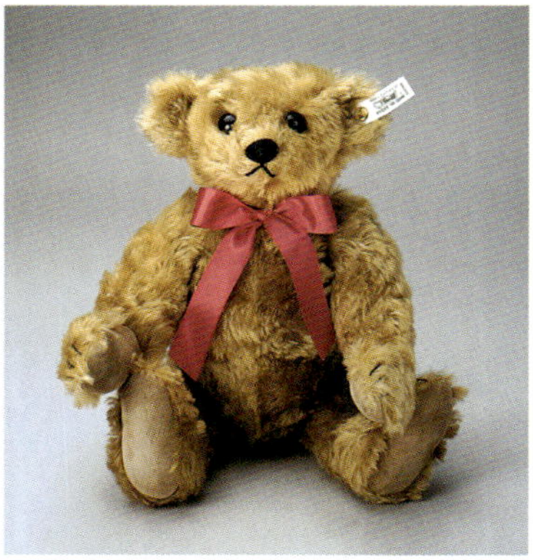

Hamleys Baer Tobias - *Hamleys Bear Tobias*

Mohair, dunkelblond, gegliedert, limit. Auflage 2.000 Stueck fuer Hamleys, London - *mohair, dark blond, jointed, ltd edition of 2,000 for Hamleys, London*

EAN-NO.	PERIOD	PR.	INFO
011948	1992-1992	4-5	38 cm

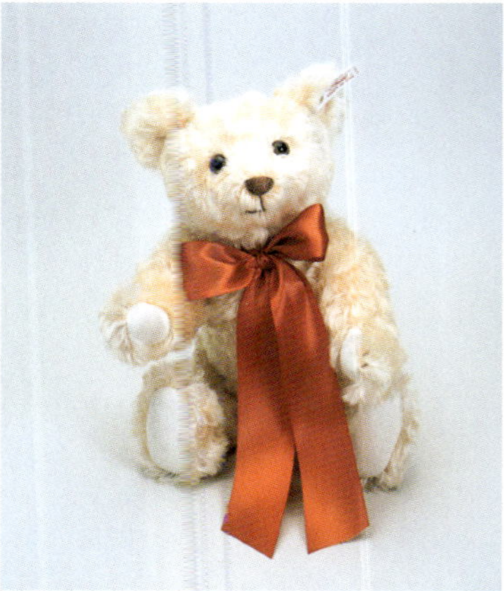

Hamleys Baer Chester - *Hamleys Bear Chester*

Mohair, apricot, gegliedert, limit. Auflage 2.000 Stueck fuer Hamleys, London - *mohair, apricot, jointed, ltd edition of 2,000 for Hamleys, London*

EAN-NO.	PERIOD	PR.	INFO
652820	1996-1996	4	32 cm

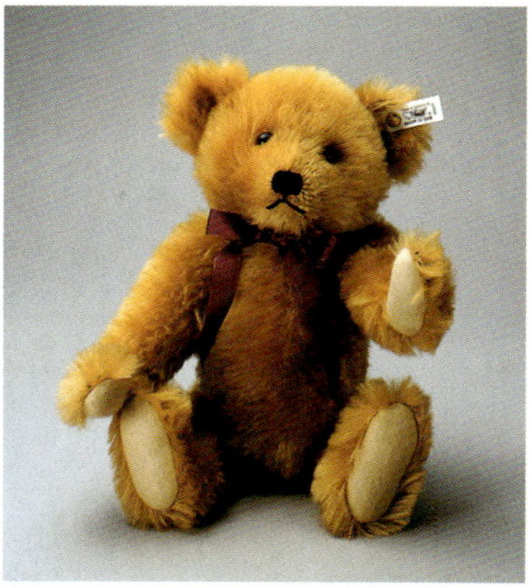

Hamleys Baer Oliver - *Hamleys Bear Oliver*

Mohair, blond, gegliedert, Brummstimme, limit. Auflage 2.000 Stueck fuer Hamleys, London - *mohair, blond, jointed, growler, ltd edition of 2,000 for Hamleys, London*

SERIE	ART.-NO	PERIOD	PR.	INFO
650277	**0181/36**	1990-1990	4-5	36 cm

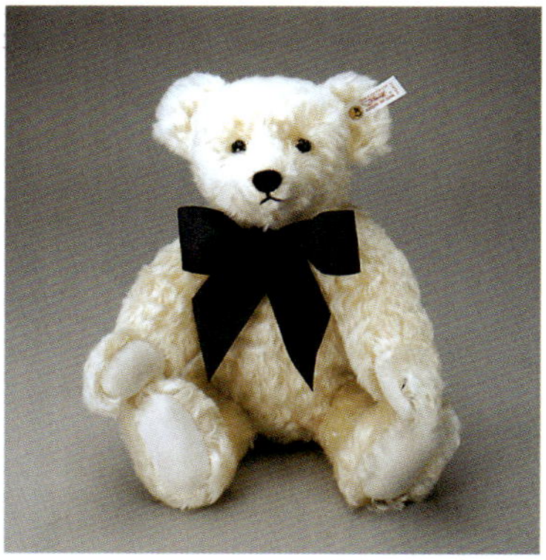

Hamleys Baer Charlotte - *Hamleys Bear Charlotte*

Mohair, weiss, gegliedert, Brummstimme, limit. Auflage 2.000 Stueck fuer Hamleys, London - *mohair, white, jointed, growler, ltd edition of 2,000 for Hamleys, London*

EAN-NO.	PERIOD	PR.	INFO
652813	1994-1994	4-5	35 cm

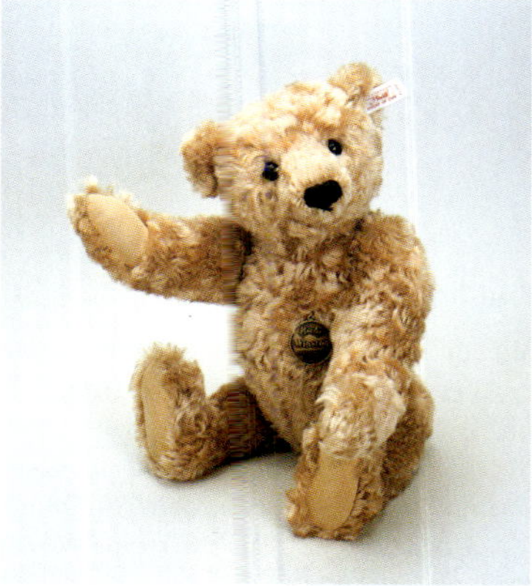

Hamleys Baer Winston - *Hamleys Bear Winston*

Mohair, hellbraun, gegliedert, limit. Auflage 1.500 Stueck fuer Hamleys, London - *mohair, light brown, jointed, ltd edition of 1,500 for Hamleys, London*

EAN-NO.	PERIOD	PR.	INFO
652837	1997-1997	[illegible]	38 cm

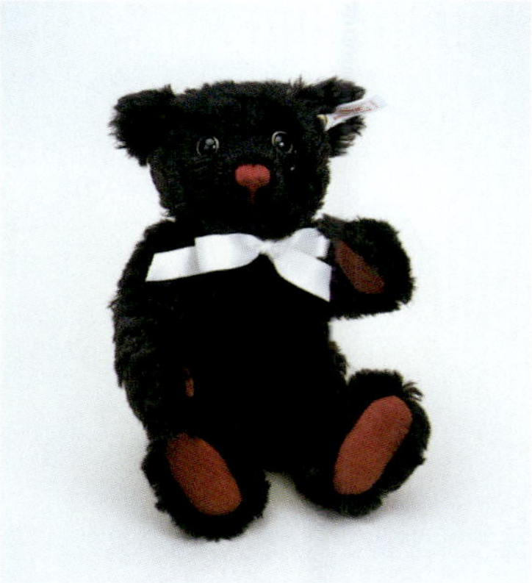

Hamleys Baer Dominic - *Hamleys Bear Dominic*

Mohair, schwarz, gegliedert, Pfoten & Fusssohlen aus Velorslederimitat, limit. Auflage 1.500 Stueck fuer Hamleys, London - *mohair, black, jointed, paws & feet of suede imitation, ltd edition of 1,500 for Hamleys, London*

EAN-No.	Period	Pr.	Info
652844	1998-1998	4	28 cm

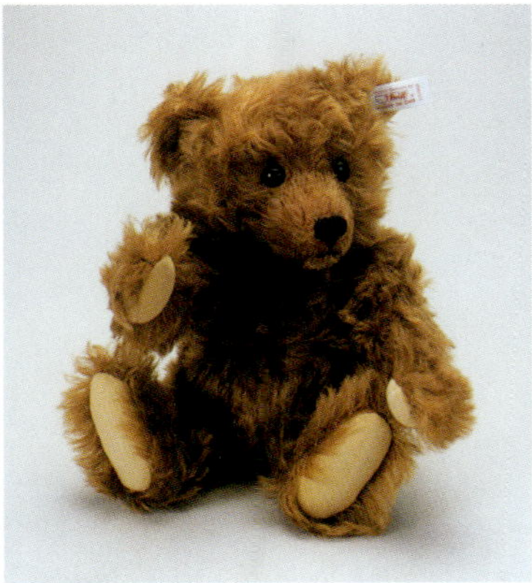

Hamleys Baer Jeremy - *Hamleys Bear Jeremy*

Mohair, rotbraun, gegliedert, Pfoten & Fusssohlen aus Velorslederimitat, limit. Auflage 1.500 Stueck fuer Hamleys, London - *mohair, reddish brown, jointed, paws & feet of suede imitation, ltd edition of 1,500 for Hamleys, London*

EAN-No.	Period	Pr.	Info
652868	1999-1999	4	28 cm

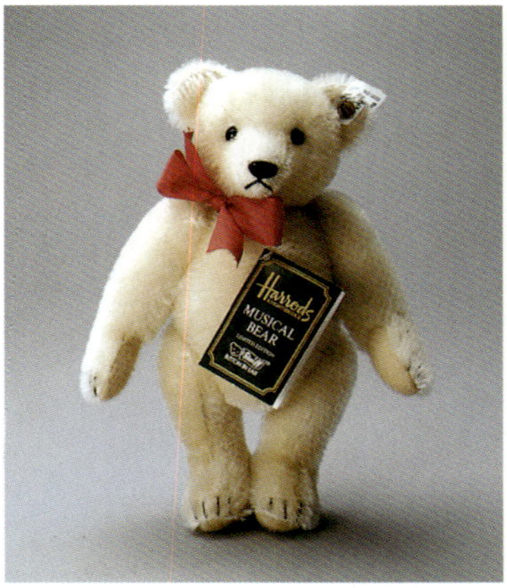

Harrods Musik Baer 1909 - *Harrods Musical Bear 1909*

Mohair, gegliedert, Musikwerk "Brahms Wiegenlied", limit. Auflage 2.000 Stueck fuer Harrods - *mohair, jointed, music box "Brahms Lullabye", ltd edition of 2,000 for Harrods, London*

Serie	Art.-No	Period	Pr.	Info
011917	**0291/26**	1989-1990	5	26 cm

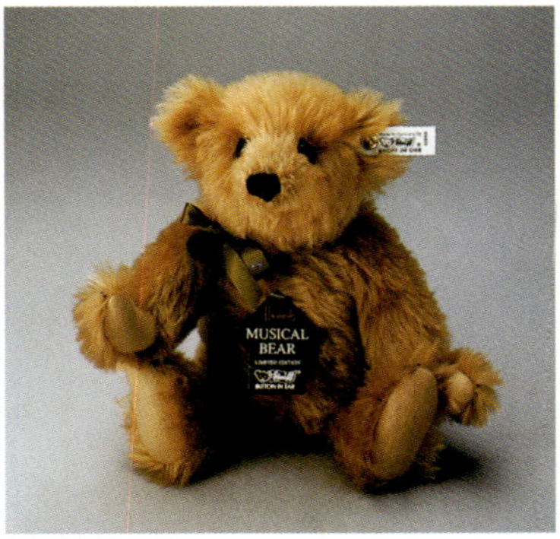

Harrods Musik Baer 1904/5 - *Harrods Musical Bear 1904/5*

Mohair, gegliedert, "Wiegenlied" von Mozart, limit. Auflage 2.000 Stueck fuer Harrods, London - *mohair, jointed, "Mozart´s Lullabye", ltd edition of 2,000 for Harrods, London*

Serie	Art.-No	Period	Pr.	Info
650369	**0151/27**	1990-1990	4-5	27 cm

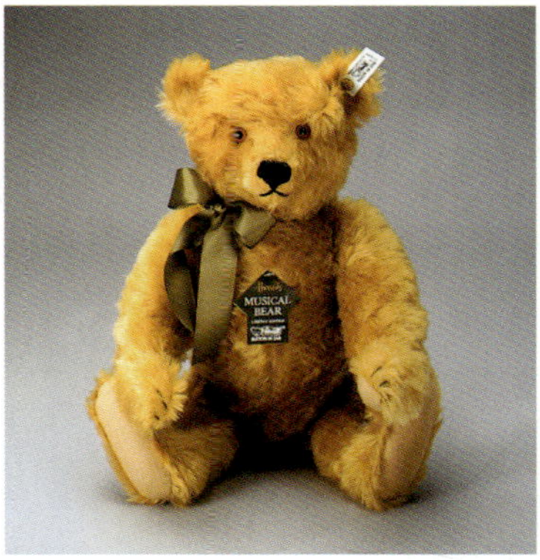

Harrods Musik Baer 1920 - *Harrods Musical Bear 1920*

Mohair, gegliedert, Beethoven "Fuer Elise", limit. Auflage 2.000 Stueck fuer Harrods, London - *mohair, jointed, Beethoven "Fuer Elise", ltd edition of 2,000 for Harrods, London*

Serie	Art.-No	Period	Pr.	Info
011924	**0294/42**	1991-1991	5	42 cm

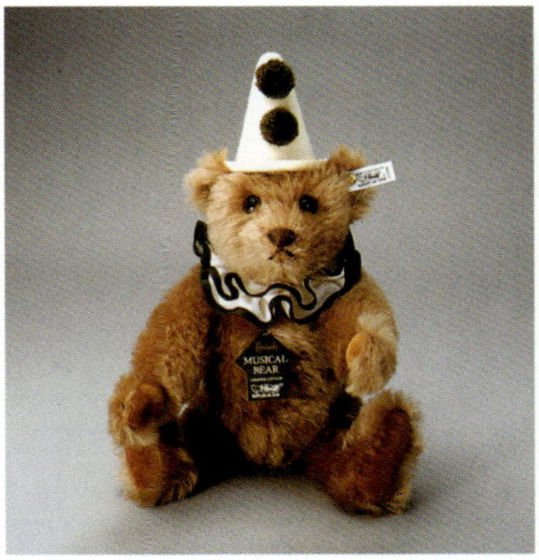

Harrods Musik Baer 1926 - *Harrods Musical Bear 1926*

Mohair, caramel, gegliedert, "The Entertainer" (Joplin), limit. Auflage 2.000 Stueck fuer Harrods - *mohair, caramel, jointed, "The Entertainer" (Joplin), ltd edition of 2,000 for Harrods, London*

EAN-No.	Period	Pr.	Info
011894	1992-1992	5	36 cm

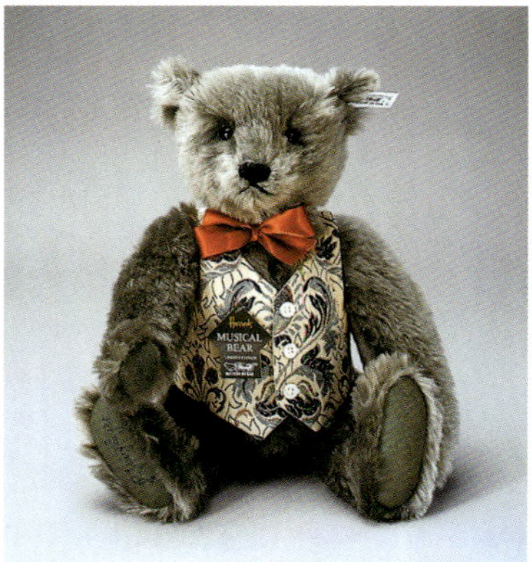

Harrods Musik Baer 1926 - *Harrods Musical Bear 1926*

Mohair, gegliedert, "Die diebische Elster" (Rossini), limit. Auflage 2.000 Stueck fuer Harrods, London - *mohair, jointed, "Die diebische Elster" (Rossini), ltd edition of 2,000 for Harrods, London*

EAN-No.	Period	Pr.	Info
650680	1993-1993	5	42 cm

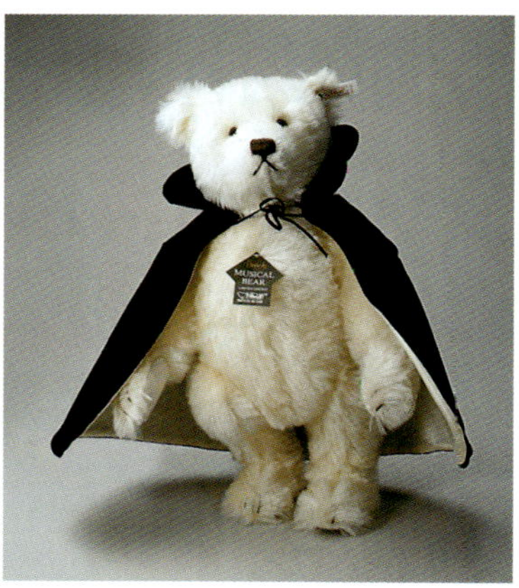

Harrods Musik Baer - *Harrods Musical Bear*

Mohair, gegliedert, "All I ask of you" (A.L. Webber), limit. Auflage 2.000 Stueck fuer Harrods - *mohair, jointed, "All I ask of you" (A.L. Webber), ltd edition of 2,000 for Harrods, London*

EAN-No.	Period	Pr.	Info
653131	1994-1994	5	42 cm

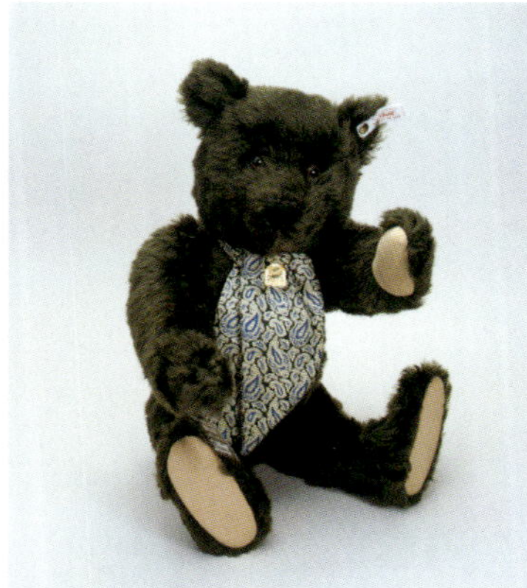

Harrods Musik Baer - *Harrods Musical Bear*

Mohair, olivgruen, gegliedert, abwaschbar, "Anniversary Waltz" (J. Ivanovici), limit. Auflage 2.000 Stueck fuer Harrods, London - *mohair, olive-green, jointed, surface washable, "Anniversary Waltz" (J. Ivanovici), ltd edition of 2,000 for Harrods, London*

EAN-No.	Period	Pr.	Info
653148	1995-1995	4-5	44 cm

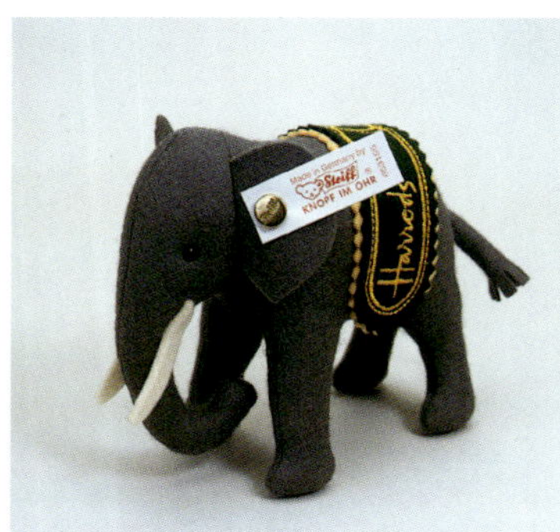

Elefant - *Elephant*

Filz, grau, stehend, anlaesslich 100 Jahre Harrods / Steiff, gruene Satteldecke, gelb bestickt, limit. Auflage 2.000 Stueck fuer Harrods, London - *felt, grey, standing, on the occasion of 100 years of cooperation between Harrods & Steiff, green saddle cloth, yellow embroidered, ltd edition of 2,000 for Harrods, London*

EAN-No.	Period	Pr.	Info
653155	1995-1995	3	12 cm

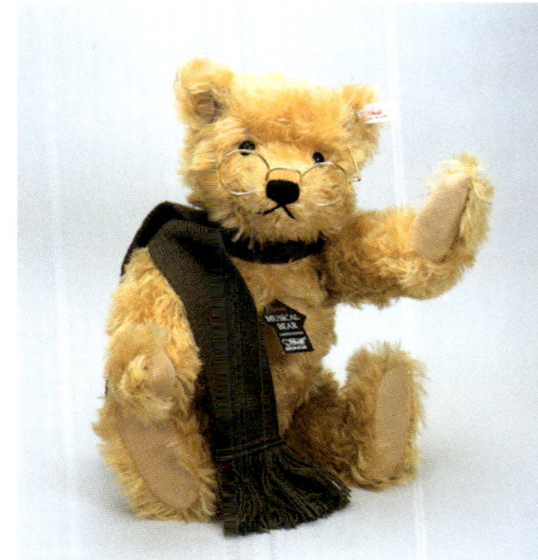

Harrods Musik Baer - *Harrods Musical Bear*

Mohair, gold, gegliedert, "Toy Symphony" (Haydn), limit. Auflage 2.000 Stueck fuer Harrods, London - *mohair, gold, jointed, "Toy Symphony" (Haydn), ltd edition of 2,000 for Harrods, London*

EAN-No.	Period	Pr.	Info
653162	1996-1996	4	44 cm

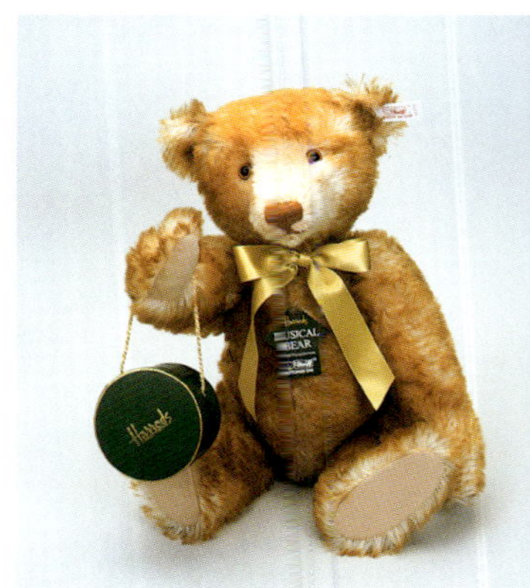

Harrods Musik Baer - *Harrods Musical Bear*

Mohair, rotbraun gespitzt, gegliedert, The Extravagance Bear, "Big Spender" (S. Bassey), limit. Auflage 2.000 Stueck fuer Harrods, London - *mohair, red-brown tipped, jointed, The Extravagance Bear, "Big Spender" (S. Bassey), ltd edition of 2,000 for Harrods, London*

EAN-No.	Period	Pr.	Info
653179	1997-1997	4-5	42 cm

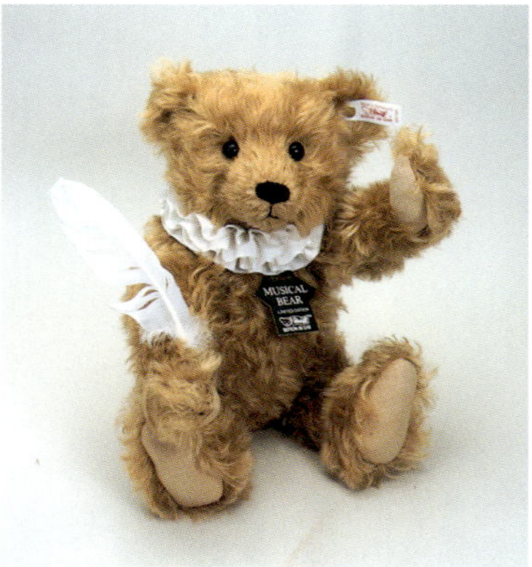

Harrods Musik Baer - *Harrods Musical Bear*

Mohair, braun, gegliedert, Poet Bear, "Gavotte D" (J. S. Bach), Pfoten & Fusssohlen aus Alcantara, limit. Auflage 2.000 Stueck fuer Harrods, London - *mohair, caramel, jointed, Poet Bear, "Gavotte D" (J. S. Bach), paws & feet of alcantara, ltd edition of 2,000 for Harrods, London*

EAN-No.	Period	Pr.	Info
653186	1998-1998	4	34 cm

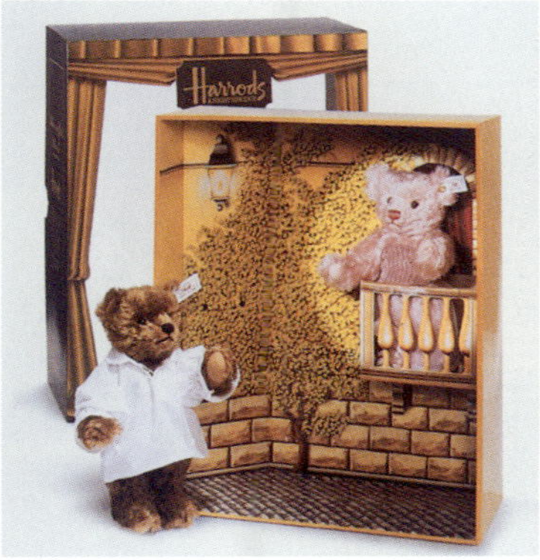

Harrods Romeo & Julia Teddy Set

Mohair, Romeo 22 cm, dunkelbraun / Julia 20 cm, rosé, gegliedert, aufwendige Verpackung mit Musikwerk, Baeren ohne Stimme, bekleidet, limit. Auflage 2.000 Stueck fuer Harrods, London - *mohair, Romeo 22 cm, dark brown / Julia 20 cm, rose, jointed, in decoration packaging with music-box, bears without voice, ltd edition of 2,000 for Harrods, London*

EAN-No.	Period	Pr.	Info
653193	1999-1999	4-5	kpl. Set - *set*
	1999-1999	4	Romeo, 22 cm
	1999-1999	4	Julia, 20 cm

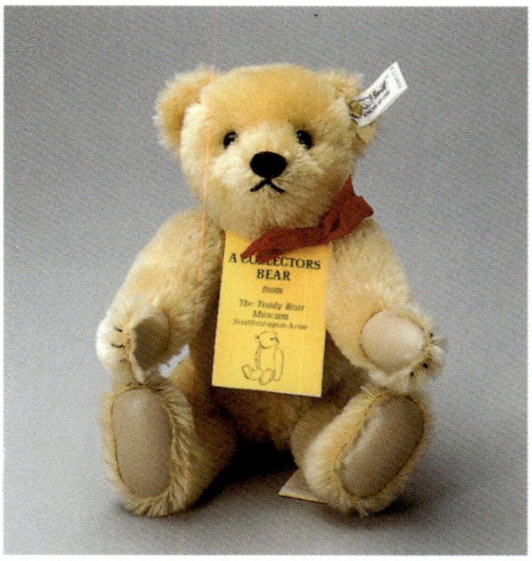

William Shakespeare Baer - *William Shakespeare Bear*

Mohair, blond, wie Teddybaer 1909, gegliedert, limit. Auflage 2.000 Stueck fuer Grossbritannien - *mohair, blond, like the1909 Teddy bear, jointed, ltd edition of 2,000 for Great Britain*

Serie	Art.-No	Period	Pr.	Info
	0166/29	1987-1987	4-5	29 cm

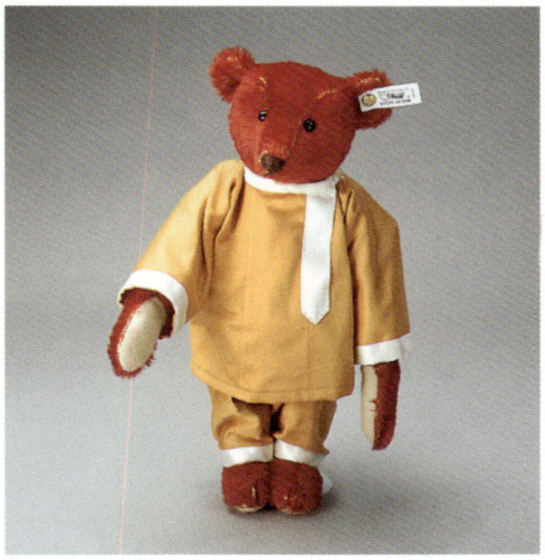

Alfonzo Teddybaer - *Alfonzo Teddy Bear*

Mohair, rot, gegliedert, limit. Auflage 5.000 Stueck fuer Teddy Bears of Whitney - *mohair, red, jointed, ltd edition of 5,000 for Teddy Bears of Whitney*

Serie	Art.-No	Period	Pr.	Info
406195	**0184/35**	1990-1990	5-6	35 cm

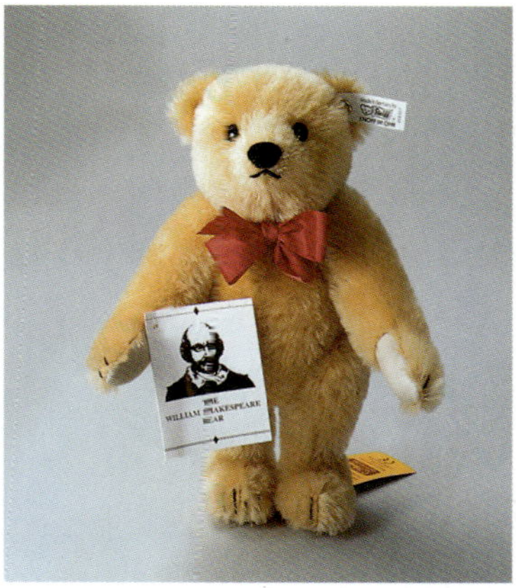

William Shakespeare Baer - *William Shakespeare Bear*

Mohair, blond, wie Teddybaer 1909, gegliedert, fuer Grossbritannien - *mohair, blond, like 1909 teddy bear, jointed, exclusive for Great Britain*

EAN-No.	Period	Pr.	Info
650307	1992-1992	4	29 cm

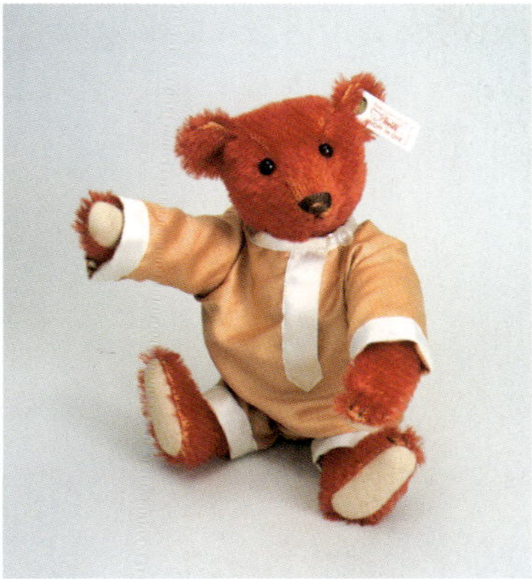

Alfonzo

Mohair, rot, gegliedert, limit. Auflage 5.000 Stueck fuer Teddy Bears of Whitney - *mohair, red, jointed, ltd edition of 5,000 for Teddy Bears of Whitney*

EAN-No.	Period	Pr.	Info
653773	1995-1995	4	24 cm

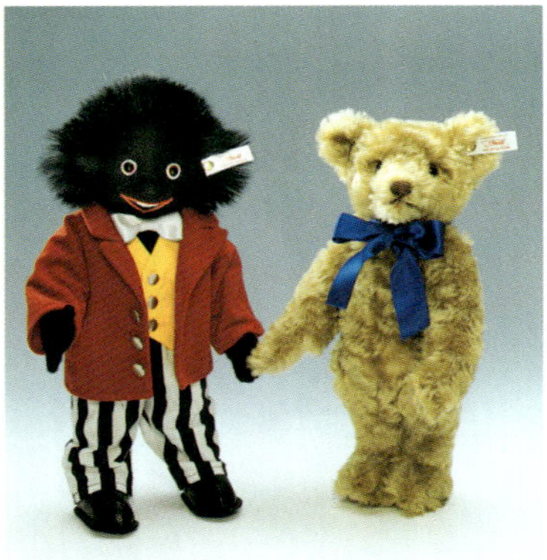

Jolly Golly & Baer - *Jolly Golly & Bear*

Jolly Golly: Filz, schwarz, stehend, Baer: Mohair, blond, gegliedert, limit. Auflage 1.500 Stueck fuer Dolly Land, Grossbritannien - *Jolly Golly: felt, black, standing, bear: mohair, blond, jointed, ltd edition of 1,500 sets for Dolly Land, Great Britain*

EAN-No.	Period	Pr.	Info
654428	1996-1996	4-5	34/24 cm - Set
	1996-1996	3-4	34 cm, Jolly Golly
J04113	1996-1996	3	24 cm, Baer - *bear*

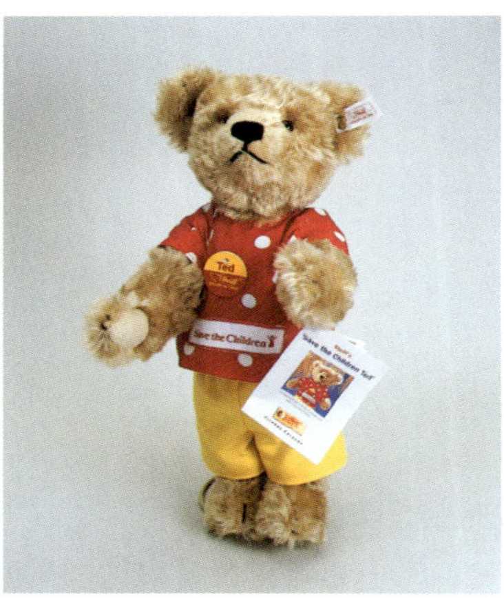

Ted

Mohair, blond, gegliedert, bekleidet, limit. Auflage 3.000 Stueck fuer Save the Children, Grossbritannien - *mohair, blond, jointed, dressed, ltd edition of 3,000 for Save the Children, Great Britain*

EAN-No.	Period	Pr.	Info
654442	1996-1996	3	32 cm

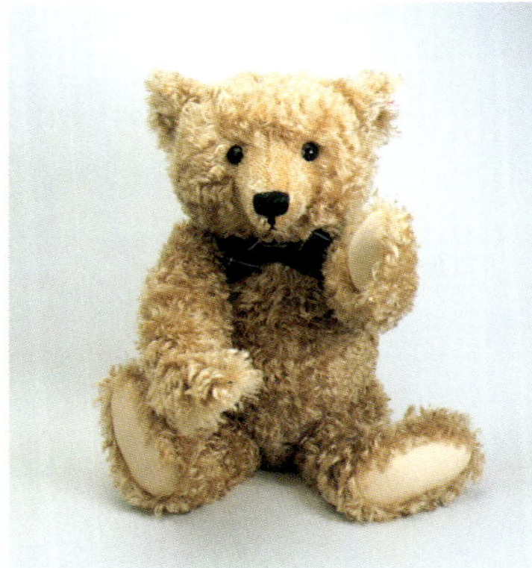

Henderson

Teddybaer, Mohair, dunkelblond, gegliedert, Mittelnaht, limit. Auflage 2.000 Stueck fuer Teddy Bears of Whitney zu Ehren von Colonel Bob Henderson - *Teddy bear, mohair, dark blond, jointed, center seam, ltd edition of 2,000 for Teddy Bears of Whitney in honour of Colonel Bob Henderson*

EAN-No.	Period	Pr.	Info
653780	1997-1997	5	55 cm

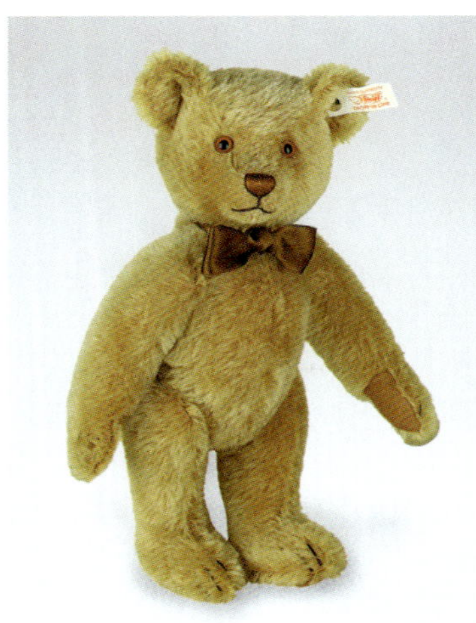

Teddy George

Mohair, gold, gegliedert, Holzwolle gestopft, die braun gestickte Nase ist mit schwarz umsaeumt, limit. Auflage 2.000 Stueck fuer Teddy Bears of Whitney - *mohair, gold, jointed, excelsior stuffed, black thread around the dark amber nose, ltd edition of 2,000 for Teddy Bears of Whitney*

EAN-No.	Period	Pr.	Info
654749	2000-2000	4	30 cm

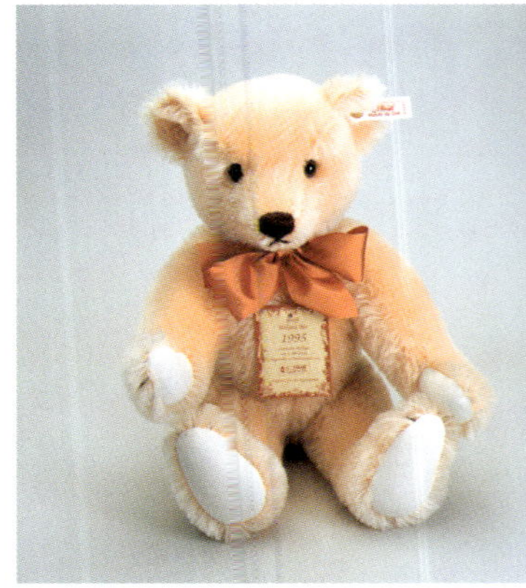

Teddybaer - *Teddy Bear*

Mohair Webpelz, lachsfarben, gegliedert, Brummstimme, limit. Auflage 1.500 Stueck fuer Holland - *mohair woven fur, salmon color, jointed, growler, ltd edition of 1,500 for Holland*

EAN-No.	Period	Pr.	Info
650857	1995-1995	4-5	40 cm

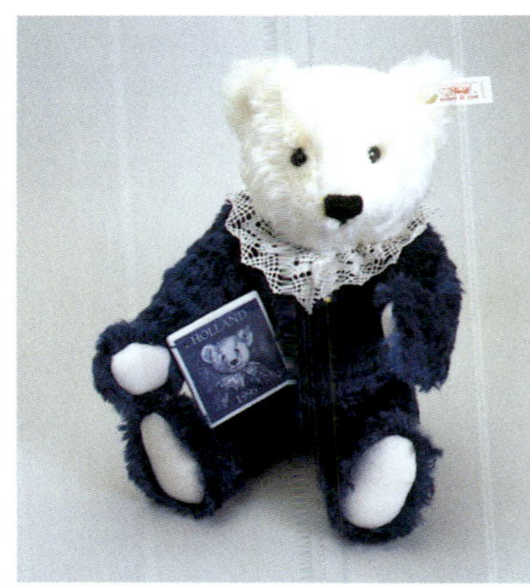

Teddybaer - *Teddy Bear*

Mohair Webpelz, blau/weiss, gegliedert, Druckstimme, Pfoten & Fusssohlen aus weissem Kunstleder, limit. Auflage 1.500 Stueck fuer Holland - *mohair woven fur, blue/white, jointed, press voice, paws & feet of white artificial leather, ltd edition of 1,500 for Holland*

EAN-No.	Period	Pr.	Info
659843	1996-1996	4-5	33 cm

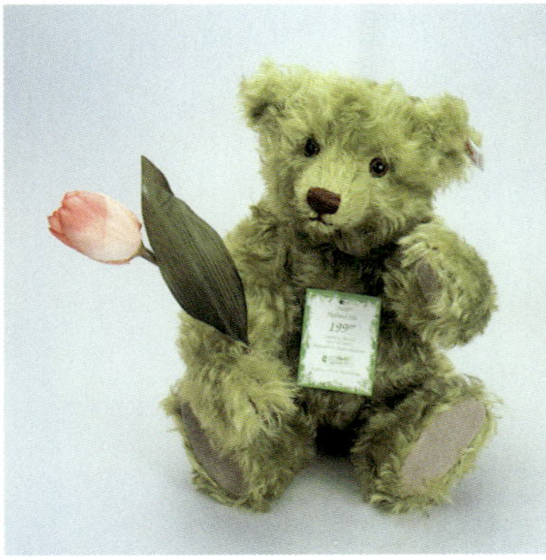

Teddybaer - *Teddy Bear*

Mohair Webpelz, gruen, gegliedert, limit. Auflage 1.847 Stueck fuer Holland - *mohair woven fur, green, jointed, ltd edition of 1,847 for Holland*

EAN-No.	Period	Pr.	Info
659935	1997-1997	4-5	35 cm

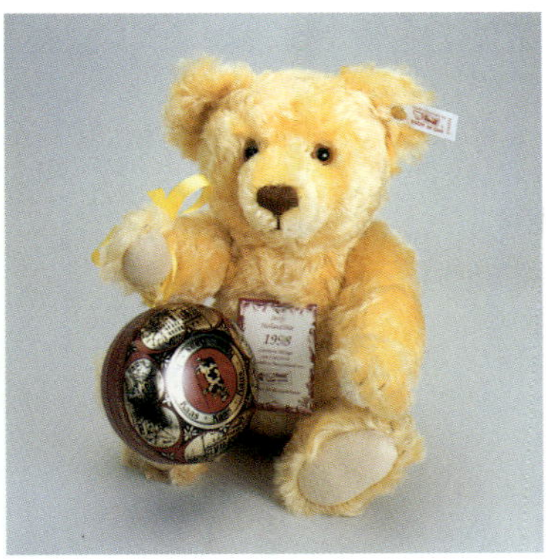

Kaas Baer - *Cheese Bear*

Mohair Webpelz, gold, gegliedert, abwaschbar, limit. Auflage 1.847 Stueck fuer Holland - *mohair woven fur, gold, jointed, surface washable, ltd edition of 1,847 for Holland*

EAN-No.	Period	Pr.	Info
659959	1998-1998	4	30 cm

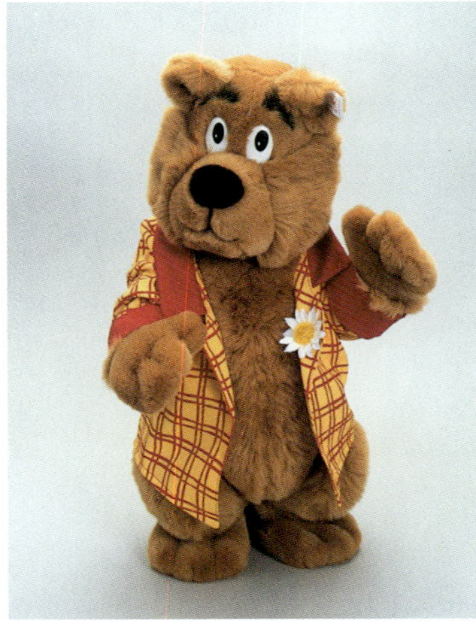

Oliver B. Bommel

Mohair Webpelz, hellbraun, stehend, abwaschbar, Characterfigur von Marten Toonder, limit. Auflage 3.000 Stueck fuer Holland - *mohair woven fur, light brown, jointed, surface washable, character from Marten Toonder, ltd edition of 3,000 for Holland*

EAN-No.	Period	Pr.	Info
657955	1998-1998	4	40 cm

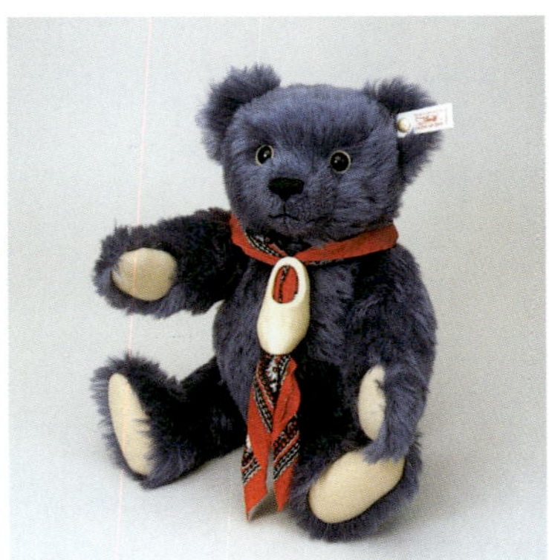

De Boer Beer

Mohair, blau, gegliedert, limit. Auflage 1.847 Stueck fuer Holland - *mohair, blue, jointed, ltd edition of 1,847 for Holland*

EAN-No.	Period	Pr.	Info
660078	1999-1999	4	36 cm

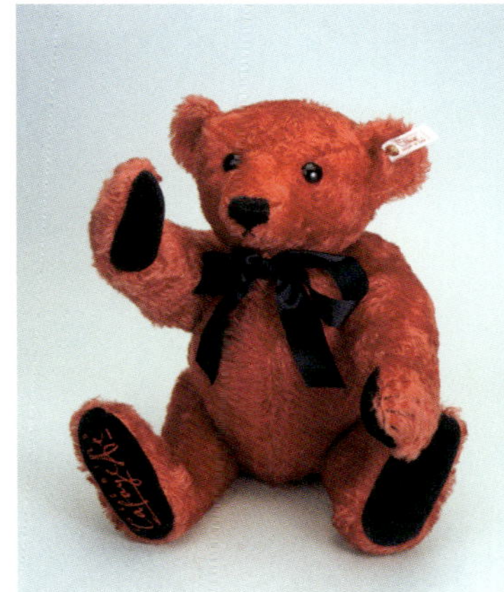

Teddybaer - *Teddybear*

Mohair Webpelz, himbeer, gegliedert, abwaschbar, bestickte Fusssohle, limit. Auflage 1.500 Stueck fuer Galeries Lafayette, Paris - *mohair woven fur, raspberry, jointed, surface washable, embroidered sole, ltd edition of 1,500 for Galeries Lafayette, Paris*

EAN-No.	Period	Pr.	Info
657931	1995-1995	4-5	42 cm

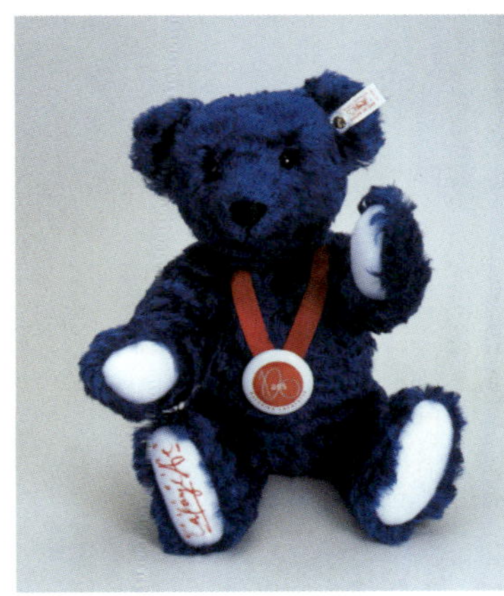

Teddybaer - *Teddybear*

Mohair Webpelz, blau, gegliedert, abwaschbar, bestickte Fusssohle, limit. Auflage 1.500 Stueck fuer Galeries Lafayette, Paris, zum 100jaehrigen Bestehen - *mohair woven fur, blue, jointed, surface washable, embroidered sole, ltd edition of 1,500 on the occasion of the 100th birthday of Galeries Lafayette, Paris*

EAN-No.	Period	Pr.	Info
657948	1996-1996	4-5	38 cm

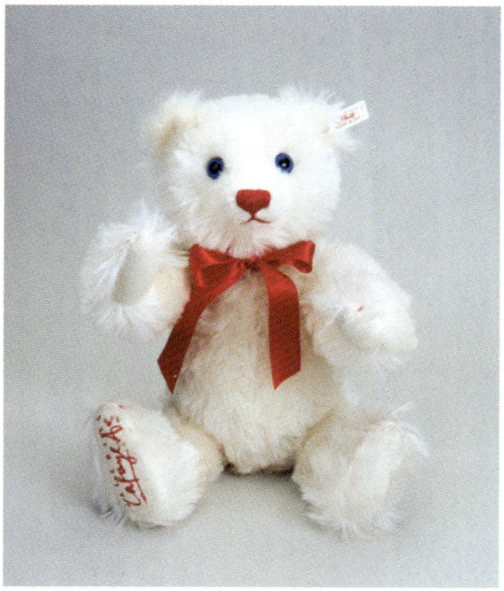

Tricolore-Teddybaer - *Tricolore-Teddybear*

Mohair, weiss, blaue Augen, rotes Halsband, gegliedert, abwaschbar, bestickte Fusssohle, limit. Auflage 1.500 Stueck fuer Galeries Lafayette, Paris - *mohair, white, blue eyes, red collar, jointed, surface washable, embroidered sole, ltd edition of 1,500 for Galeries Lafayette, Paris*

EAN-No.	Period	Pr.	Info
657986	1997-1997	4-5	30 cm

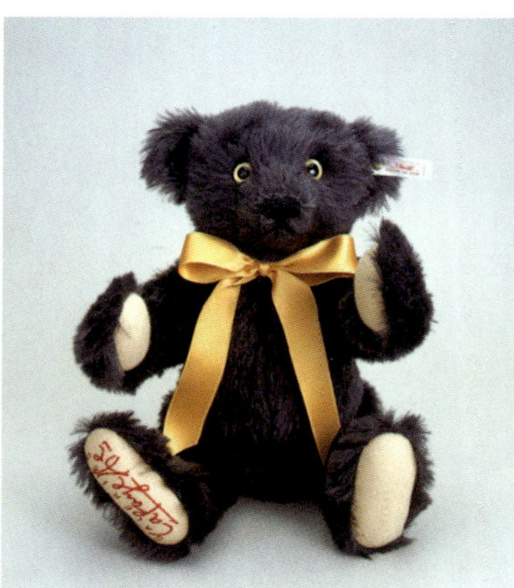

Teddybaer - *Teddybear*

Mohair Webpelz, anthrazit, gegliedert, abwaschbar, mit Eiffelturm-Miniatur, gelbe Schleife, bestickte Fusssohle, limit. Auflage 1.500 Stueck fuer Galeries Lafayette, Paris - *mohair woven fur, anthracite, jointed, surface washable, with miniature of Eiffel Tower, yellow ribbon, embroidered sole, ltd edition of 1,500 for Galeries Lafayette, Paris*

EAN-No.	Period	Pr.	Info
658044	1998-1998	4	34 cm

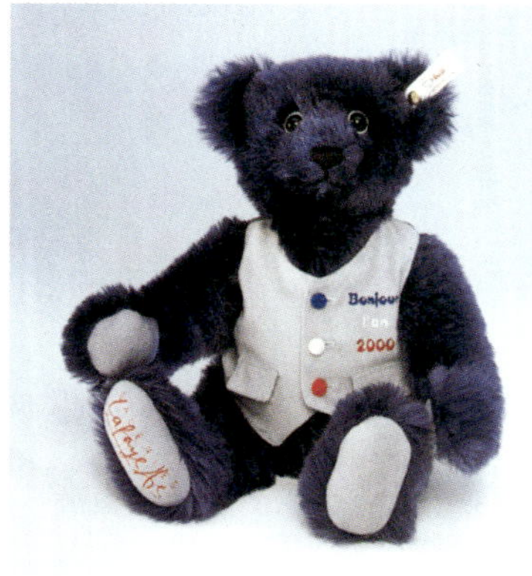

Teddybaer - *Teddybear*

Mohair, blau, gegliedert, abwaschbar, Weste aus Samt/Satin, bestickte Fusssohle, limit. Auflage 1.500 Stueck fuer Galeries Lafayette, Paris - *mohair, blue, jointed, surface washable, vest of velvet/satin, embroidered sole, ltd edition of 1,500 for Galeries Lafayette, Paris*

EAN-No.	Period	Pr.	Info
658075	1999-1999	4	34 cm

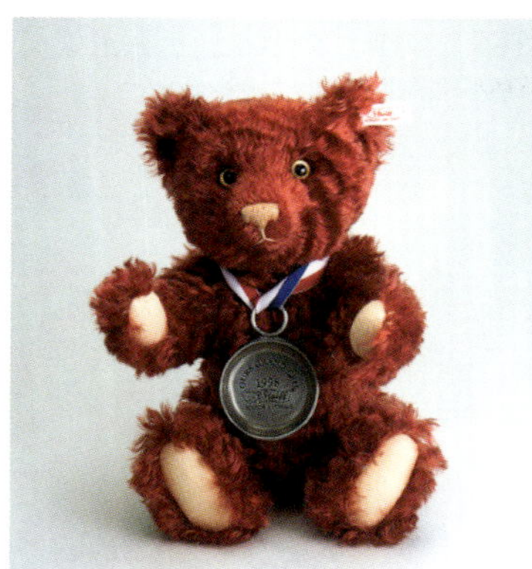

Teddybaer Grand Cru - *Teddybear Grand Cru*

Mohair Webpelz, burgunder, gegliedert, abwaschbar, am Halsband in den franzoesischen Nationalfarben haengt eine kleine Weinprobierpfanne, limit. Auflage 1.500 Stueck exklusiv fuer Frankreich - *mohair woven fur, burgundy, jointed, surface washable, ribbon in the colours of the Tricolore with a little wine tasting pan, ltd edition of 1,500 for France*

EAN-No.	Period	Pr.	Info
660009	1998-1998	4	38 cm

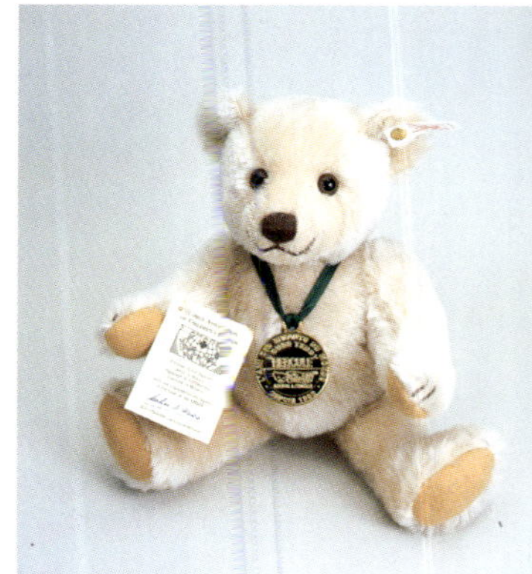

Teddybaer Hercule - *Hercule the Teddy Bear*

Mohair Webpelz, cremefarben, gegliedert, limit. Auflage 3.000 Stueck fuer AMADE , Monaco - *mohair woven fur, cream, jointed, ltd edition of 3,000 for AMADE, Monaco*

EAN-No.	Period	Pr.	Info
999079	1995-1995	4	28 cm

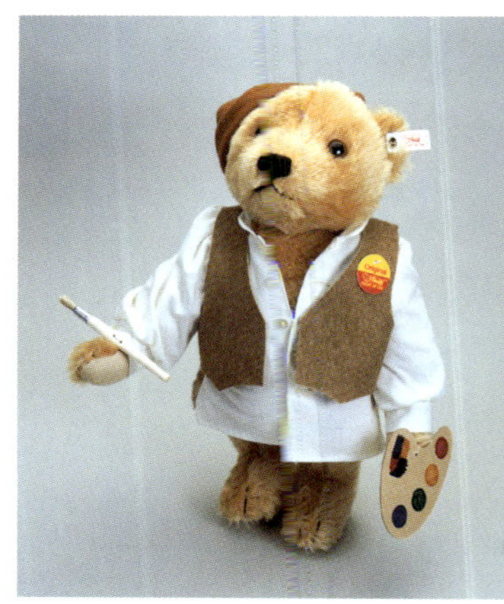

Breughel Baer - *Breughel Bear*

Mohair Webpelz, blond, gegliedert, abwaschbar, mit Pinsel & Palette, limit. Auflage 1.847 Stueck fuer Belgien - *mohair woven fur, blond, jointed, surface washable, with brush & palette, ltd edition of 1,847 for Belgium*

EAN-No.	Period	Pr.	Info
659942	1997-1997	4	42 cm

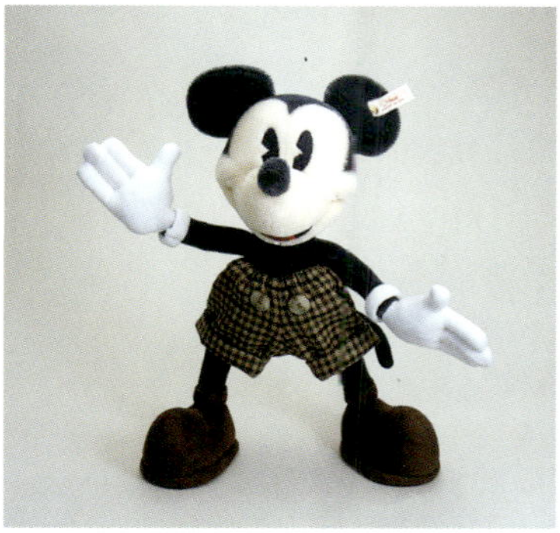

Mickey Mouse

Mohair Webpelz, blau/weiss, stehend, abwaschbar, limit. Auflage 2.000 Stueck fuer Donaldson Blue Production S.A., Belgien - *mohair woven fur, blue/white, standing, surface washable, ltd edition of 2,000 for Donaldson Blue Production S.A., Belgium*

EAN-No.	Period	Pr.	Info
657962	1997-1997	4	35 cm

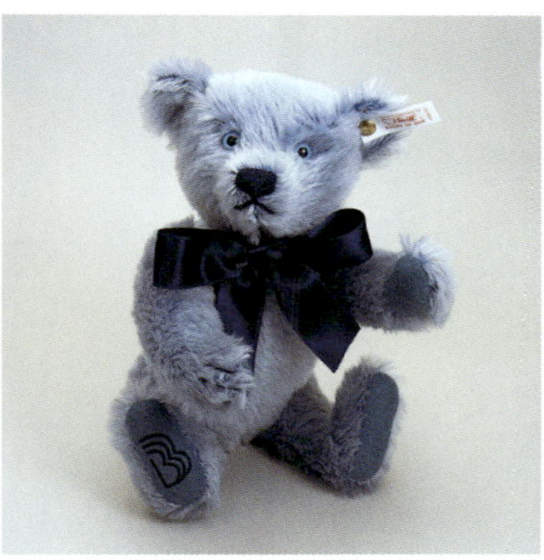

Beach Baer - *Beach Bear*

Mohair Webpelz, hellblau, gegliedert, abwaschbar, limit. Auflage 1.500 Stueck fuer Belgien - *mohair woven fur, light blue, jointed, surface washable, ltd edition of 1,500 for Belgium*

EAN-No.	Period	Pr.	Info
658037	1998-1998	4	28 cm

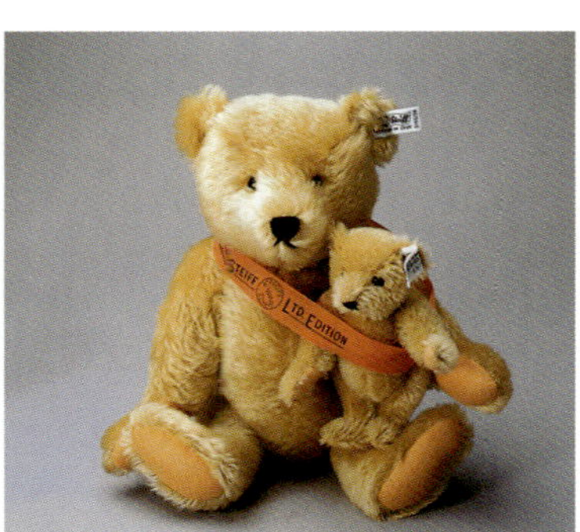

Mama & Baby Set

Replica, Mohair, gegliedert, USA-Artikel, limit. Auflage 8.000 Stueck, Babys Fahne ohne Art.-Nr. - *replica, mohair, jointed, USA exclusive, ltd edition of 8,000, baby´s tag has no art.-no.*

Serie	Art.-No	Period	Pr.	Info
	0155/38	1981-1981	5-6	38/15 cm

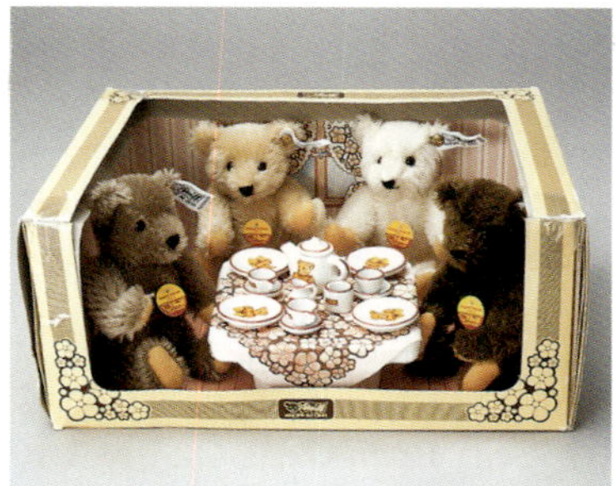

Tee Party Set - *Tea Party Set*

4 Teddy´s in honig, caramel, weiss & dunkelbraun, Mohair, gegliedert, alle mit gleicher Art.-Nr., Porzellangeschirr, limit. Auflage 10.000 Stueck, nur fuer USA - *4 Teddys in honey, caramel, white & dark brown, mohair, jointed, all have the same article number, porcelain crockery, ltd edition of 10,000, USA exclusive*

Serie	Art.-No	Period	Pr.	Info
	0204/16	1982-1985	5-6	je 16 cm - *each*

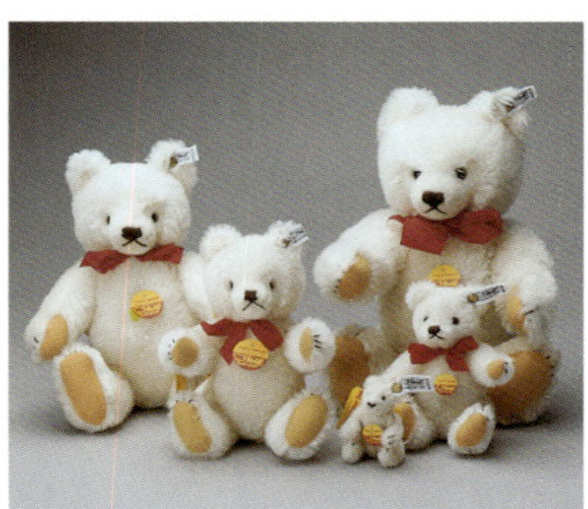

Original Teddybaer Set - *Original Teddy Bear Set*

Mohair, weiss, 11 cm Kopf drehbar, ab 18 cm gegliedert, USA Sammlerausgabe 1982 - *mohair, white, 11 cm swivel head, from 18 cm jointed, USA collector´s edition 1982*

Serie	Art.-No	Period	Pr.	Info
	0203/00	1982-1982	5-6	kpl. Set - *compl. set*
	0203/11	1982-1982	3	11 cm
	0203/18	1982-1982	3	18 cm
	0203/26	1982-1982	3-4	26 cm
	0203/36	1982-1982	4	36 cm
	0203/41	1982-1982	4	41 cm

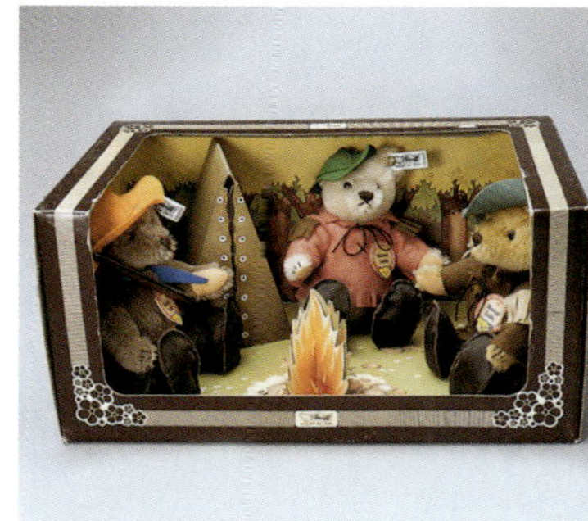

Nimrod Teddy Set

3 Teddybaeren in gold, weiss & caramel, gegliedert, Mohair, zum 80. Geburtstag des Teddybaeren & zum 125. Geburtstag von Theodor (Teddy) Roosevelt, limit. Auflage 10.000 Stueck. USA-Artikel - *3 Teddy bears in gold, white & caramel, jointed, mohair, to celebrate the 80th anniversary of the Teddy Bear & the 125th birthday of Theodore (Teddy) Roosevelt, ltd edition of 10,000, USA exclusive*

Serie	Art.-No	Period	Pr.	Info
	0210/22	1983-1983	5	je 22 cm - *each*

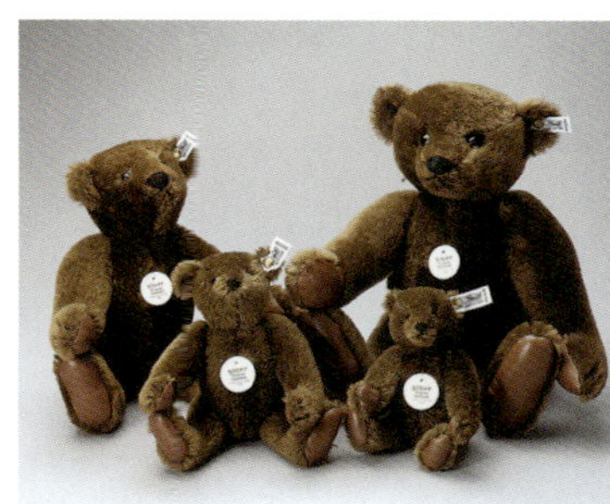

Margaret Strong Baer Set - *Margaret Strong Bear Set*

Mohair, gegliedert, Kunstlederpfoten & -fuesse, 18 & 26 cm Druckstimme, ab 32 cm Brummstimme, USA-Sammler-Ausgabe 1983, limit. Auflage 2.000 Sets - *mohair, jointed, artificial leather paws & feet, 18 & 26 cm press voice, from 32 cm growler, USA collector´s edition 1983, ltd edition of 2,000 sets*

Serie	Art.-No	Period	Pr.	Info
	0160/00	1983-1983	5-6	kpl. Set - *compl. set*
	0160/18	1983-1983	3-4	18 cm
	0160/26	1983-1983	4	26 cm
	0160/32	1983-1983	4	32 cm
	0160/42	1983-1983	5	42 cm

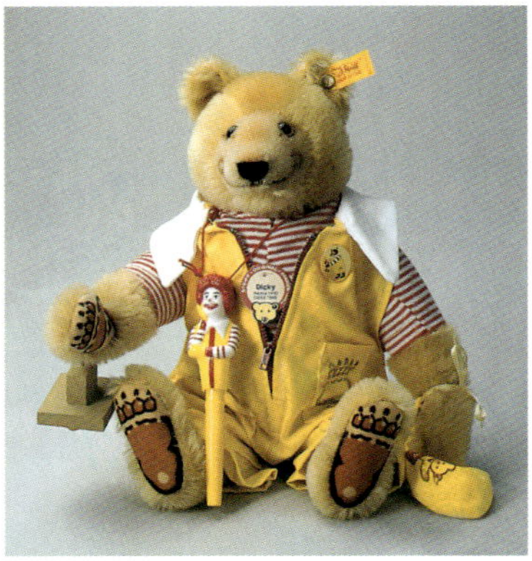

Dicky "Clowns Around"

Mohair, blond, gegliedert, Dicky Baer Replica 1930, Brustschild wie Replik von 1985, gelbe oder weisse Ohrfahne, bekleidet in Amerika fuer Ronald Mc Donald House, limit. Auflage 100 Stueck - *mohair, blond, jointed, 1930 replica of Dicky Bear, chest label is like the replica from 1985, yellow or white ear tag, dressed in USA for Ronald McDonald´s, ltd edition of 100*

SERIE	ART.-NO	PERIOD	PR.	INFO
	0172/32	1984-1986	8	32 cm

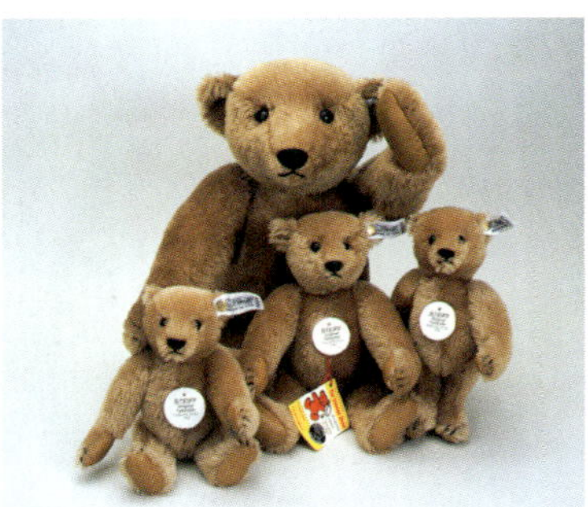

Margaret Strong Baer Set - *Margaret Strong Bear Set*

Mohair, gegliedert, Kunstlederpfoten & -fuesse, 18 & 26 cm Druckstimme, ab 32 cm Brummstimme, USA-Sammler-Ausgabe 1984, limit. Auflage 2.000 Sets - *mohair, jointed, artificial leather paws & feet, 18 & 26 cm press voice, from 32 cm growler, USA collector´s edition 1984, ltd edition of 2,000 sets*

SERIE	ART.-NO	PERIOD	PR.	INFO
	0156/00	1984-1984	5-6	kpl. Set - *compl. set*
	0156/18	1984-1984	3-4	18 cm
	0156/26	1984-1984	4	26 cm
	0156/32	1984-1984	4-5	32 cm
	0156/42	1984-1984	5	42 cm

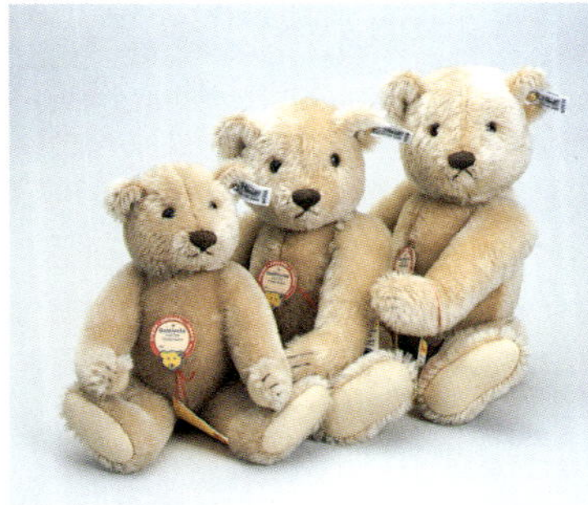

Goldilocks Baeren - ***Goldilocks*** *Baers*

Mohair, cremefarben, gegliedert, Mama-, Papa- & Baby-Baer im Set mit einer Suzanne Gibson Puppe, Bekleidung fehlt auf Abbildung, limit. Auflage 2.000 Stueck fuer Reeves International, USA - *mohair, cream, jointed, Mama-, Papa- & Baby-Bear as set together with a Suzanne Gibson doll, clothes are not shown in this photograph, ltd edition of 2,000 for Reeves International, USA*

SERIE	ART.-NO	PERIOD	PR.	INFO
	0173/25	1984-1984	4	25 cm
	0173/30	1984-1984	4	30 cm
	0173/32	1984-1984	4	32 cm

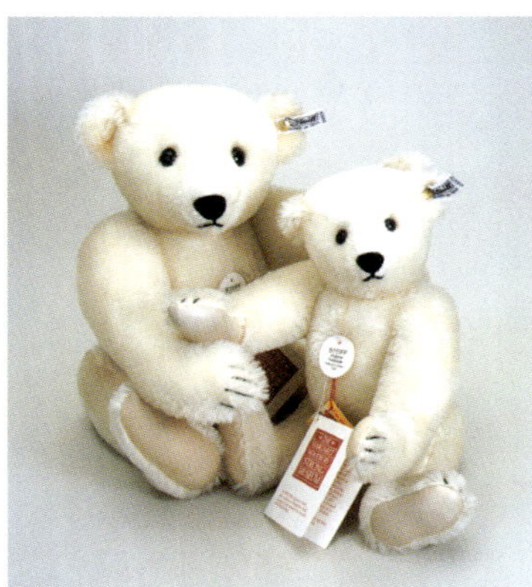

Margaret Strong Baer - *Margaret Strong Bear*

Mohair, gegliedert, weiss, Lederpfoten & -fuesse, Brummstimme, USA-Artikel, limit. Auflage - *mohair, jointed, white, leather paws & feet, growler, USA exclusive, ltd edition*

SERIE	ART.-NO	PERIOD	PR.	INFO
	0158/25	1985-1988	4-5	25 cm, 3.000 Stueck - *3,000 pieces*
	0158/31	1985-1988	5	31 cm, 2.500 Stueck - *2,500 pieces*
	0158/41	1985-1988	5-6	41 cm, 2.000 Stueck - *2,000 pieces*
	0158/50	1986-1986	7	50 cm, 750 Stueck - *750 pieces*

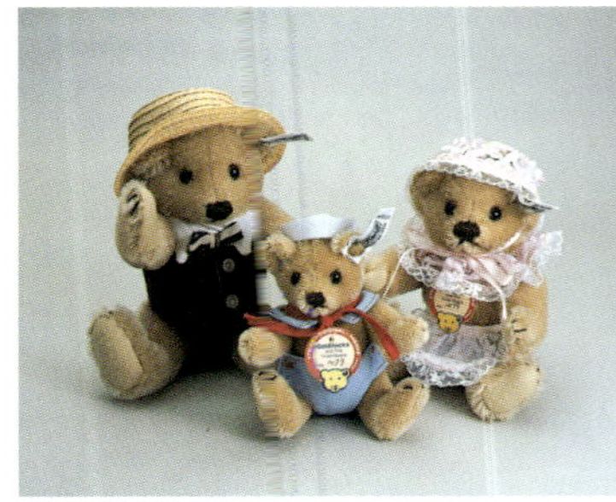

Goldilocks Baeren - ***Goldilocks*** *Baers*

Mohair, blond, gegliedert, Mama-, Papa- & Baby-Baer im Set mit einer Suzanne Gibson Puppe, limit. Auflage 5.000 Stueck fuer Reeves International, USA - *mohair, blond, jointed, Mama-, Papa- & Baby-Bear as set together with a Suzanne Gibson doll, ltd edition of 5,000 for Reeves International, USA*

SERIE	ART.-NO	PERIOD	PR.	INFO
	0173/14	1985-1985	3-4	14 cm
	0173/18	1985-1985	3-4	18 cm
	0173/22	1985-1985	3-4	22 cm

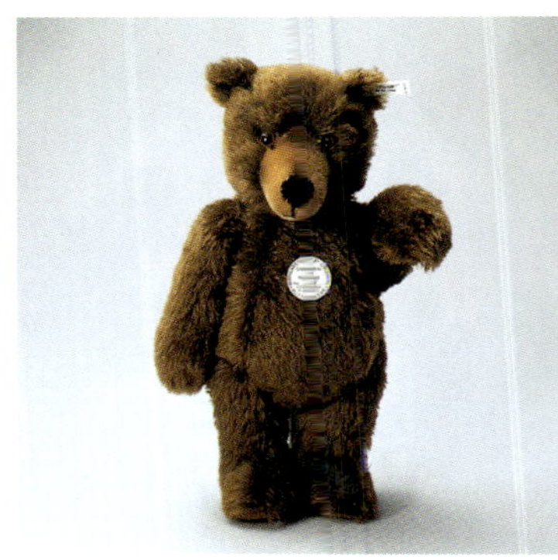

Baer - *Bear*

Mohair, braun, gegliedert, aus amerikanischem Schneeweisschen & Rosenrot-Set, Brummstimme, limit. Auflage 2.000 Stueck fuer Reeves International, USA - *mohair, brown, jointed, from the American "Snow White & Rose Red" set, growler, ltd edition of 2,000 for Reeves International, USA*

SERIE	ART.-NO	PERIOD	PR.	INFO
	0128/33	1986-1986	5	33 cm

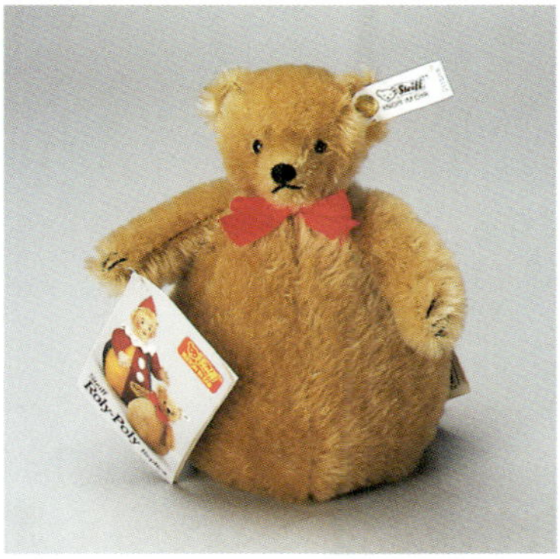

Rolly Polly Baer - *Rolly Polly Bear*

Replica 1908, Mohair, Arme & Kopf gegliedert, USA-Artikel - *1908 replica, mohair, arms & head jointed, USA exclusive*

SERIE	ART.-NO	PERIOD	PR.	INFO
	0115/18	1988-1989	4-5	18 cm

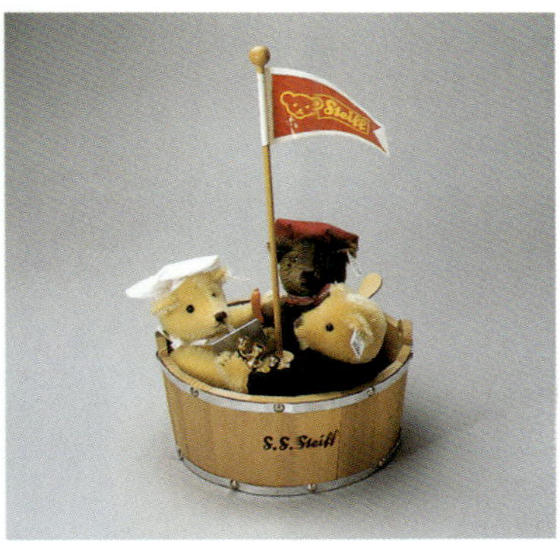

Rub-A-Dub-Dub-Set

3 Teddy-Baeren, 23 cm, Mohair in gelb, messing & braun, als Baecker, Kerzenmacher & Metzger, im Holzzuber, USA-Artikel, limit. Auflage 2.000 Stueck - *3 Teddy Bears, 23 cm mohair in yellow, brass color & brown, dressed as baker, candlestick maker & butcher, in a wooden tub, ltd edition of 2,000 sets, USA exclusive*

SERIE	ART.-NO	PERIOD	PR.	INFO
	0131/00	1988-1988	5-6	kpl. Set - *compl. set*
	0131/23	1988-1988	3-4	gelb - *yellow*
	0131/24	1988-1988	3-4	messing - *brass color*
	0131/25	1988-1988	3-4	braun - *brown*

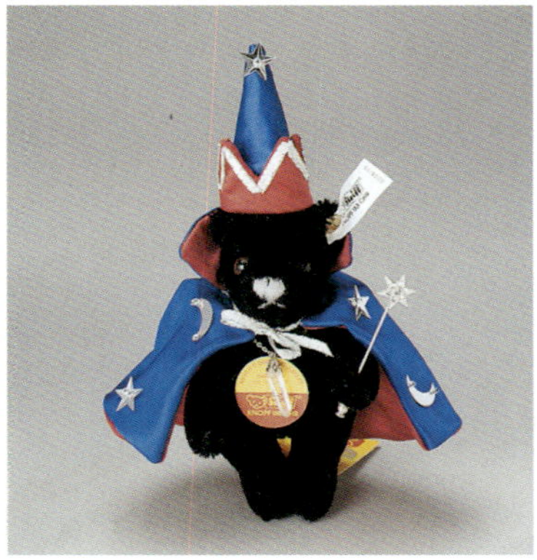

Teddybaer - *Teddy Bear*

Mohair, schwarz, gegliedert, limit. Auflage 1.000 Stueck fuer Meyer´s Diamond Jubilee - *mohair, black, jointed, ltd edition of 1,000 for Meyer´s Diamond Jubilee*

SERIE	ART.-NO	PERIOD	PR.	INFO
009624	**0208/15**	1989-1989	4-5	15 cm

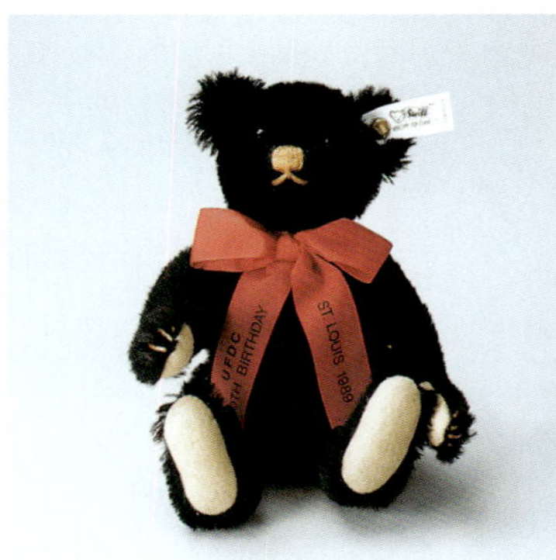

Teddybaer - *Teddy Bear*

Mohair, schwarz, gegliedert, limit. Auflage 360 Stueck zum 4. Geburtstag der UFDC - *mohair, black, jointed, ltd edition of 360 to celebrate the 4th birthday of the UFDC*

SERIE	ART.-NO	PERIOD	PR.	INFO
	0167/23	1989-1989	5	23 cm

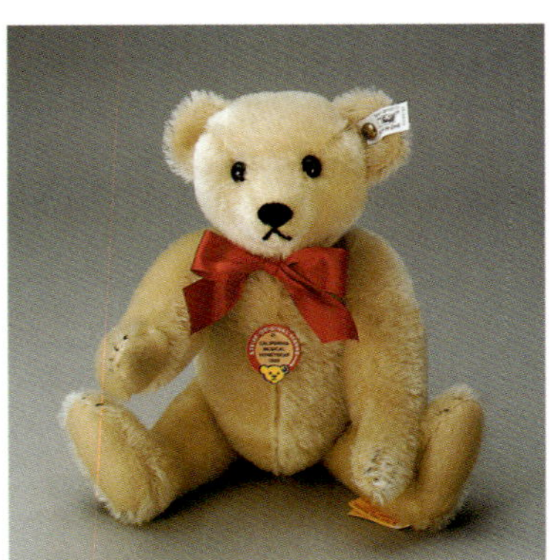

California Musical Honey Bear

Mohair, honig, gegliedert, limit. Auflage 2.000 Stueck, USA-Artikel - *mohair, honey, jointed, ltd edition of 2,000, USA exclusive*

SERIE	ART.-NO	PERIOD	PR.	INFO
011931	**0293/32**	1989-1989	5-6	32 cm

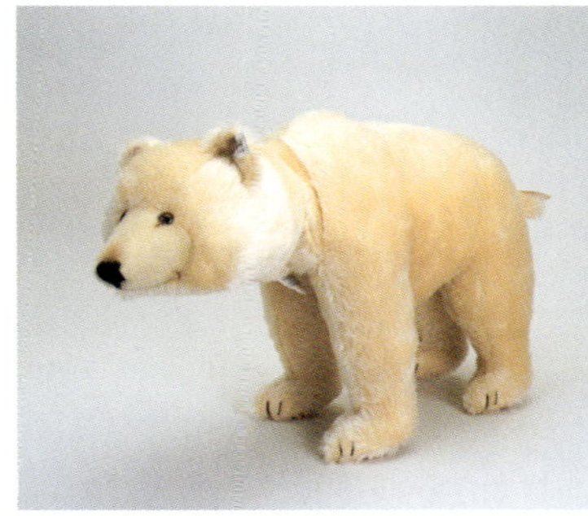

Baer Replica 1931 - *Bear Replica 1931*

Mohair, beige, auf 4 Fuessen stehend, Halsmechanik, limit. Auflage 3.000 Stueck, USA-Artikel - *mohair, beige, standing on 4 feet, neck mechanism, ltd edition of 3,000, USA exclusive*

SERIE	ART.-NO	PERIOD	PR.	INFO
	0130/28	1989-1990	5-6	28 cm

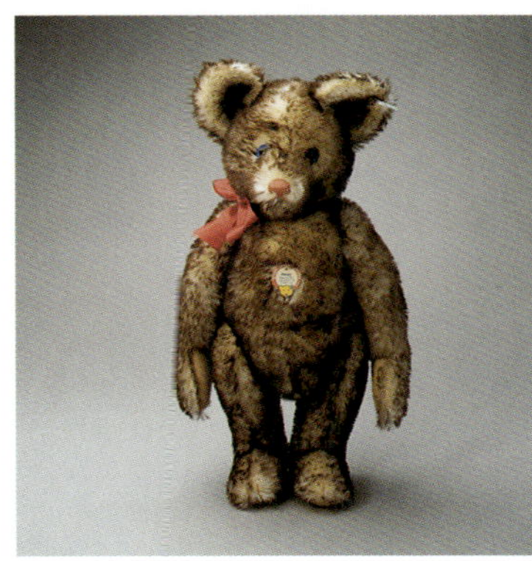

Petsy Replica 1927

Mohair, braun gespitzt, gegliedert, limit. Auflage 5.000 Stueck, USA-Artikel - *mohair, brown tipped, jointed, ltd edition of 5,000, USA exclusive*

SERIE	ART.-NO	PERIOD	PR.	INFO
407307	**0130/50**	1989-1990	5-6	50 cm
	407307	1991-1991	5-6	

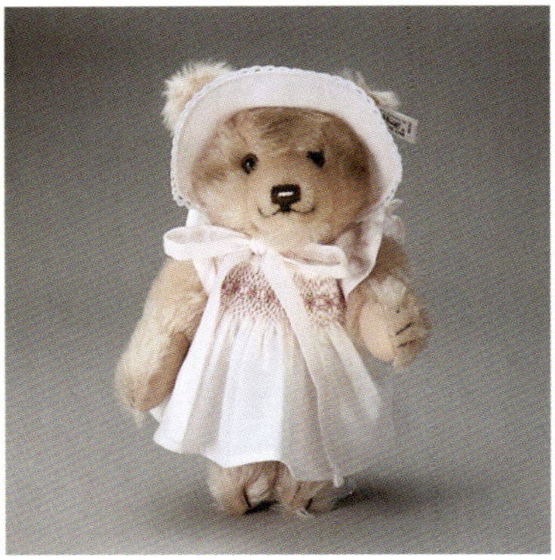

Jackie Baer - *Jackie Bear*

Mohair, rosé, gegliedert, limit. Auflage 1.000 Stueck fuer Doll House Southern Bear - *mohair, rose, jointed, ltd edition of 1,000 for Doll House Southern Bear*

SERIE	ART.-NO	PERIOD	PR.	INFO
650352	**0260/25**	1990-1990	5	25 cm

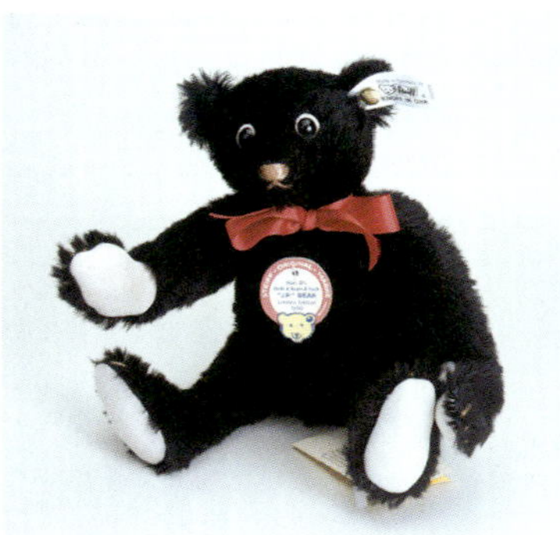

Teddy J.P. Baer - *Teddy **J.P. Bear***

Mohair, schwarz, gegliedert, limit. Auflage 1.000 Stueck fuer Mary D´s Dolls & Bears & Such - *mohair, black, jointed, ltd edition of 1,000 for Mary D´s Dolls & Bears & Such*

SERIE	ART.-NO	PERIOD	PR.	INFO
650376	**0159/26**	1990-1990	4-5	26 cm

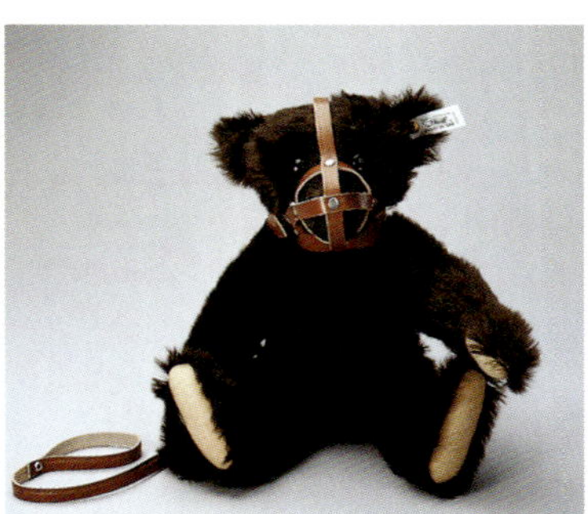

Maulkorb Baer - *Muzzle Bear*

Replica 1908, Mohair Webpelz, gegliedert, dunkelbraun, Ledermaulkorb & -halsband, Brummstimme, limit. Auflage 5.000 Stueck, USA-Artikel - *1908 replica, mohair woven fur, jointed, dark brown, leather muzzle & collar, growler, ltd edition of 5,000 for the USA*

EAN-NO.	PERIOD	PR.	INFO
406119	1991-1991	4-5	35 cm

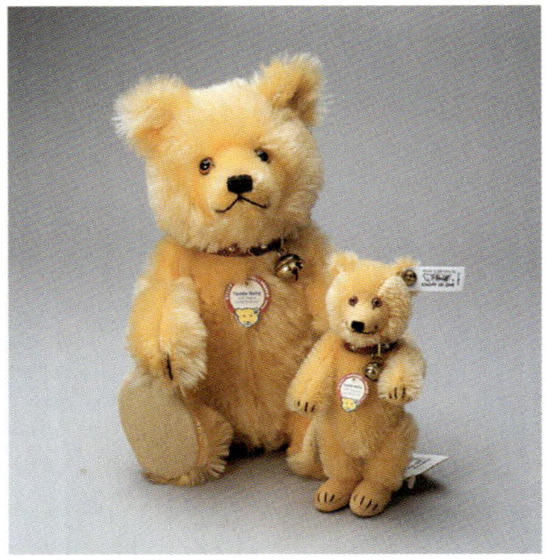

Teddy Baby Replica 1931

Mohair, mais, gegliedert, Lederhalsband, USA-Artikel, limit. Auflage je 5.000 Stueck - *mohair, corn yellow, jointed, leather collar, USA exclusive, ltd edition of 5,000 each*

EAN-NO.	PERIOD	PR.	INFO
408113	1991-1991	4	15 cm
408144	1991-1991	5	32 cm

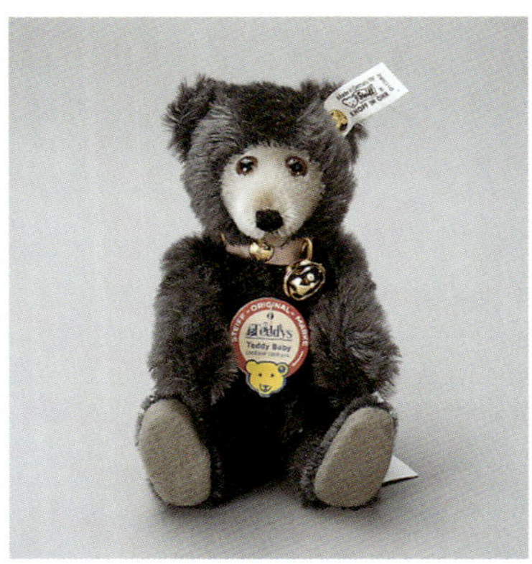

Teddy Baby

Mohair, Lederhalsband, anthrazit, gegliedert, Druckstimme, limit. Auflage 1.000 Stueck fuer "Teddys" - *mohair, leather collar, anthracite, jointed, press voice, ltd edition of 1,000 for "Teddys"*

EAN-NO.	PERIOD	PR.	INFO
011382	1991-1991	5	19 cm

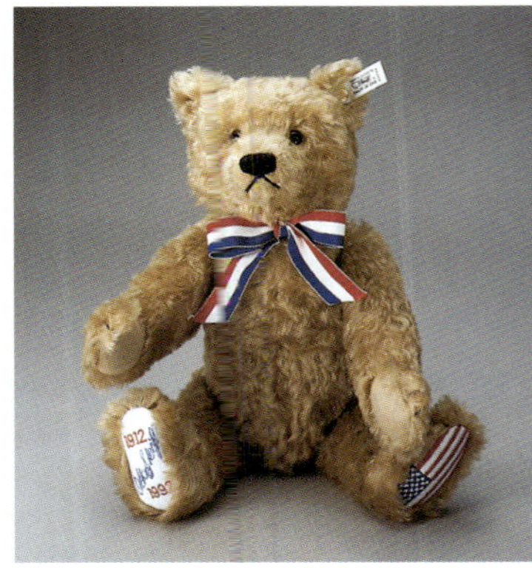

Otto Steiff Teddy Baer - *Otto Steiff Teddy Bear*

Mohair, dunkelblond, gegliedert, zur Gruendung einer Steiff Niederlassung in USA, 1912, limit. Auflage 5.000 Stueck - *mohair, dark blond, jointed, on the occasion of founding a Steiff subsidiary in the USA in 1912, ltd edition of 5,000*

EAN-NO.	PERIOD	PR.	INFO
406744	1992-1992	5	40 cm

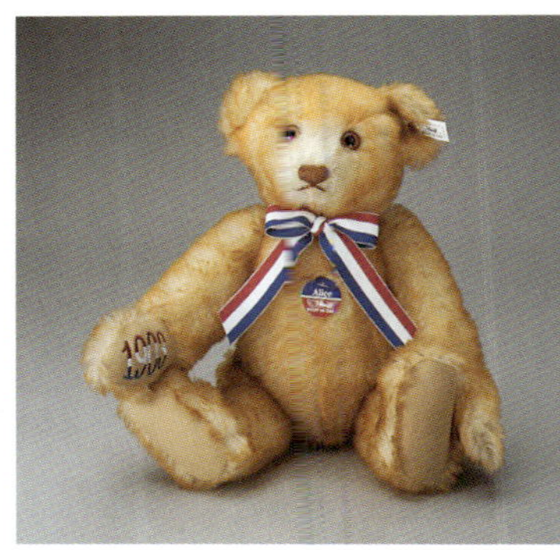

Alice

Teddy 1903 - 1993, Mohair, gespitzt, gegliedert, USA-Artikel, limit. Auflage 5.000 Stueck - *Teddy 1903 - 1993, mohair, tipped, jointed, ltd edition of 5,000, USA exclusive*

EAN-NO.	PERIOD	PR.	INFO
650574	1993-1993	5	40 cm

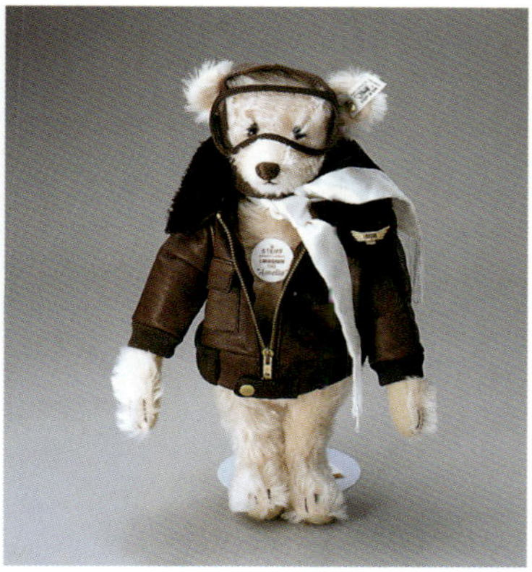

Teddy Rosé **Amelia** - *Teddy Rose **Amelia***

Mohair, rosé, gegliedert, limit. Auflage 1.000 Stueck davon 650 im Fliegerdress fuer I. Magnin, Rest 350 Stueck unbekleidet - *mohair, rose, jointed, ltd edition of 1,000, 650 are in pilot dress for I. Magnin, the remaining 350 are not dressed*

EAN-No.	Period	Pr.	Info
999765	1993-1993	5-6	35 cm

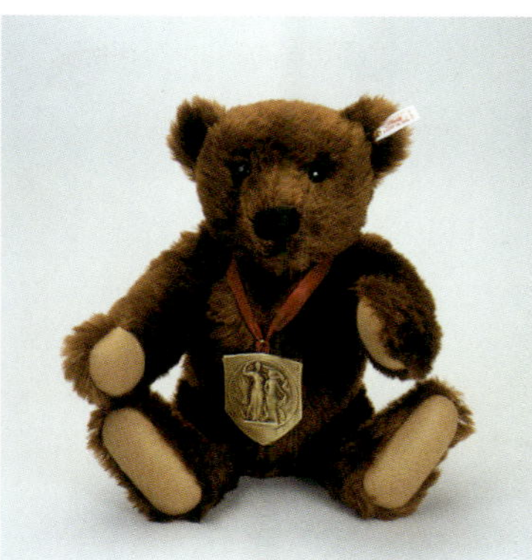

Louis Teddybaer - *Louis Teddy Bear*

Mohair, dunkelbraun, gegliedert, USA-Artikel, limit. Auflage 3.500 Stueck - *mohair, dark brown, jointed, ltd edition of 3,500, USA exclusive*

EAN-No.	Period	Pr.	Info
650789	1994-1994	5	44 cm

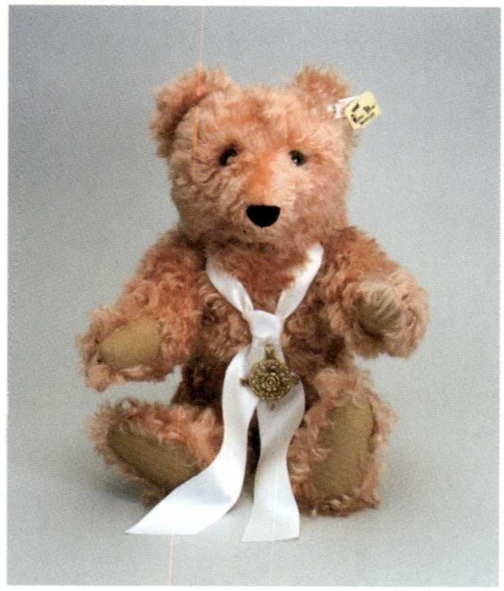

Teddybaer - *Teddy Bear*

Mohair, rosenholzfarben, gegliedert, USA-Artikel, limit. Auflage 3.500 Stueck - *mohair, rosewood-color, jointed, ltd edition of 3,500, USA exclusive*

EAN-No.	Period	Pr.	Info
650819	1995-1995	5	44 cm

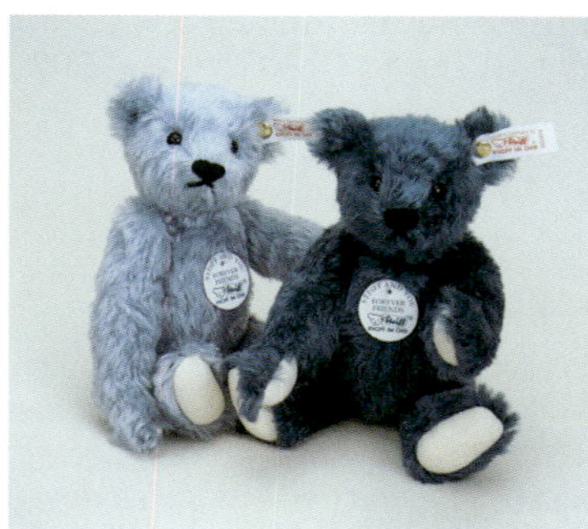

Forever Friends Baerenpaar - ***Forever Friends** Bear Couple*

Mohair Webpelz, eisblau bzw. petrol, gegliedert, limit. Auflage 4.000 Paare fuer Amerika - *mohair woven fur, ice blue and petrol, jointed, ltd edition of 4,000 sets exclusive for the USA*

EAN-No.	Period	Pr.	Info
665059	1996-1996	5	kpl. Set - *compl. set*
J04079	1996-1996	4	23 cm, eisblau - *ice blue*
J04080	1996-1996	4	23 cm, petrol

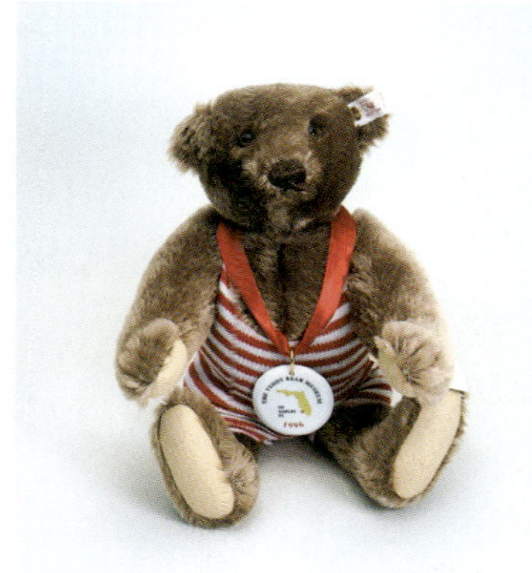

Teddybaer Wiggins - *Teddybear Wiggins*

Mohair Webpelz, braun, gegliedert, abwaschbar, rot/weiss gestreifter Badeanzug, Porzellanplakette, limit. Auflage 500 Stueck fuer das Teddybaer Museum Naples, Florida - *mohair woven fur, brown, jointed, surface washable, red/white striped swimshirt, porcelain medaillon, ltd edition of 500 for the Teddybear Museum Naples, Florida*

EAN-No.	Period	Pr.	Info
665158	1996-1996	4-5	28 cm

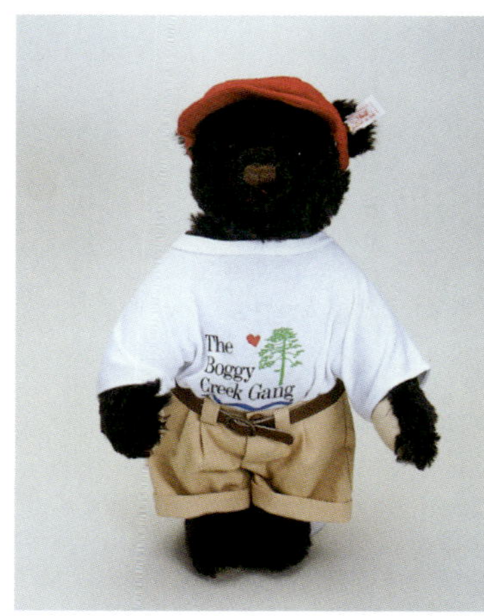

Boggy Creek Bob Baer - *Boggy Creek Bob Bear*

Mohair, schwarz, gegliedert, Maskottchen der Boggy Creek Gang, ein Camp fuer lebensbedrohlich erkrankte Kinder, limit. Auflage 3.000 Stueck fuer Amerika - *mohair, black, jointed, mascot of the Boggy Creek Gang, a camp for kids with life-threatening illnesses, ltd edition of 3,000 for the USA*

EAN-No.	Period	Pr.	Info
665110	1996-1996	4	28 cm

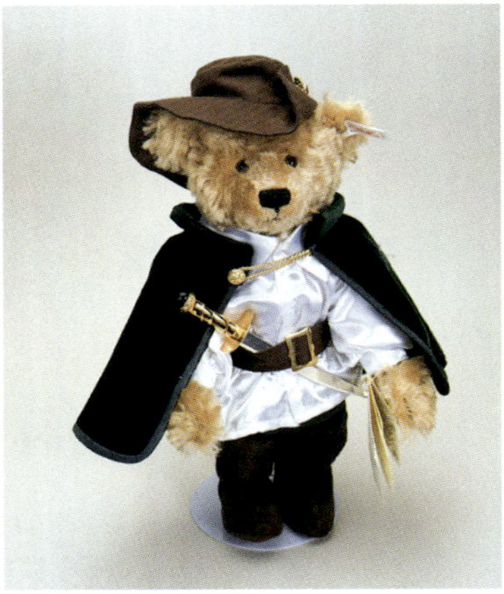

Buccaneer Baer - *Buccaneer Bear*

Mohair, blond, gegliedert, Musketier, limit. Auflage 500 Stueck, USA-Artikel - *mohair, blond, jointed, buccaneer, ltd edition of 500 exclusive for the USA*

EAN-No.	Period	Pr.	Info
665141	1996-1996	5	35 cm

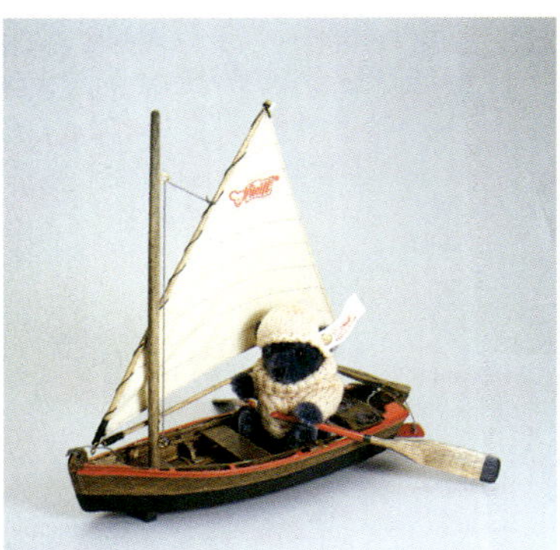

Boatswain Baer - *Boatswain Bear*

Mohair, dunkelblau, gegliedert, Strickbekleidung, mit Ruder im Segelboot, limit. Auflage 3.500 Stueck fuer Amerika - *mohair, dark blue, jointed, dressed with knitwear, with oar in a sailing boat, ltd edition of 3,500 exclusive for the USA*

EAN-No.	Period	Pr.	Info
665127	1996-1996	4-5	10 cm

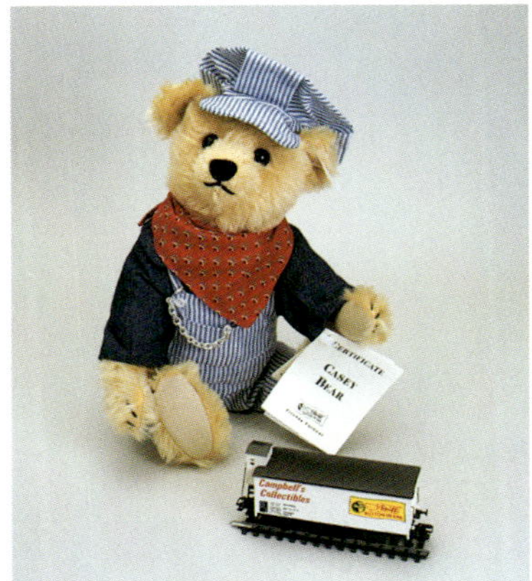

Casey Baer - *Casey Bear*

Mohair Webpelz, blond, gegliedert, mit Maerklin-Wagen, limit. Auflage 500 Stueck fuer Campbell´s Collectibles, USA - *mohair woven fur, blond, jointed, with a Maerklin railroad car, ltd edition of 500 for Campbell´s Collectibles, USA*

EAN-No.	Period	Pr.	Info
665134	1996-1996	4-5	33 cm

kein Bild vorhanden
no picture available

Teddybaer - *Teddybear*

Mohair Webpelz, blond, gegliedert, Beautiful Children, limit. Auflage 365 Stueck fuer UFDC, USA - *mohair woven fur, blond, jointed, Beautiful Children, ltd edition of 365 for UFDC, USA*

EAN-No.	Period	Pr.	Info
665042	1996-1996	4-5	

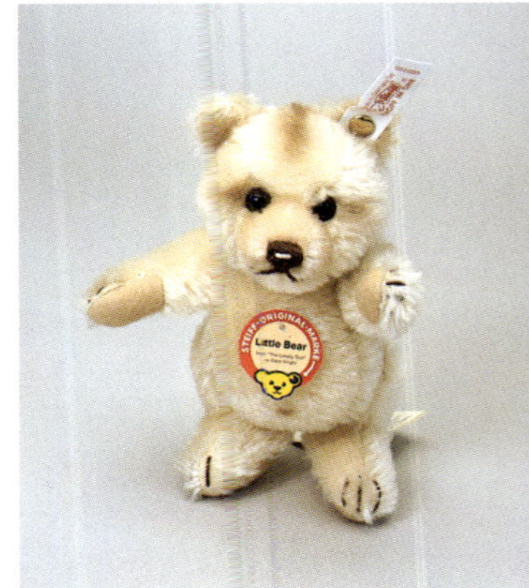

Kleiner Baer - *Little Bear*

Mohair Webpelz, honig, gegliedert, limit. Auflage 750 Stueck fuer The Toy Shoppe, USA - *mohair woven fur, honey, jointed, ltd edition of 750 for The Toy Shoppe, USA*

EAN-No.	Period	Pr.	Info
665165	1996-1996	4	18 cm

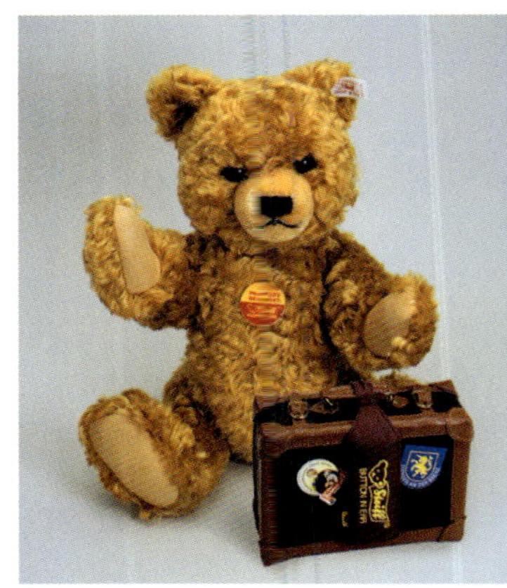

Passport Baer 1997 - ***Passport Bear 1997***

Mohair, blond, gegliedert, Lederkoffer mit T-Shirt, Shorts & Ausweis, limit. Auflage 3.500 Stueck, USA-Artikel - *mohair, blond, jointed, leather suitcase with t-shirt, shorts & passport, ltd edition of 3,500 exclusive for the USA*

EAN-No.	Period	Pr.	Info
665318	1997-1997	4-5	30 cm

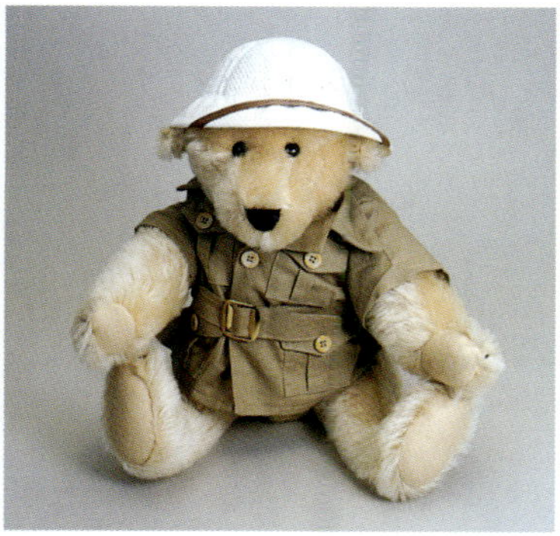

Teddybaer Reggie - *Teddybear Reggie*

Mohair Webpelz, blond, gegliedert, mit Safari-Jacke & Tropenhelm, als Luxusedition auch mit Originalrucksack der Fa. Ghurka & Baerenjournal Safari (Sonderauflage 250 Stueck), limit. Gesamtauflage 3.500 Stueck, USA-Artikel - *mohair woven fur, blond, jointed, with khaki safari jacket & bush hat, also as luxury edition with authentic Ghurka backpack & the bear´s journal Safari (special edition of 250 only), ltd edition of 3,500 exclusive for the USA*

EAN-No.	Period	Pr.	Info
665219	1997-1997	5	32 cm

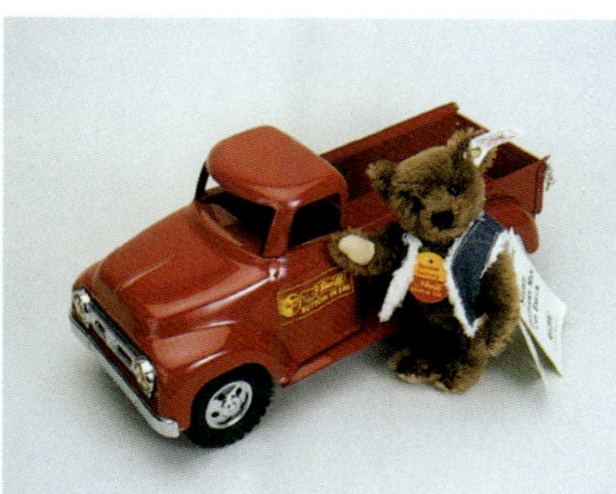

Special Delivery Bear

Mohair, dunkelbraun, gegliedert, zusammen mit rot lackiertem Lieferwagen aus Metall, limit. Auflage 3.500 Stueck, USA-Artikel - *mohair, dark brown, jointed, together with a red steel truck, ltd edition of 3,500 exclusive for the USA*

EAN-No.	Period	Pr.	Info
665226	1997-1997	5	16 cm

kein Bild vorhanden
no picture available

Teddybaer Braut - *Teddybear Bride*

Mohair, weiss, gegliedert, limit. Auflage 365 Stueck für UFDC, USA - *mohair, white, jointed, ltd edition of 365 for UFDC*

EAN-No.	Period	Pr.	Info
665400	1997-1997	4	23 cm

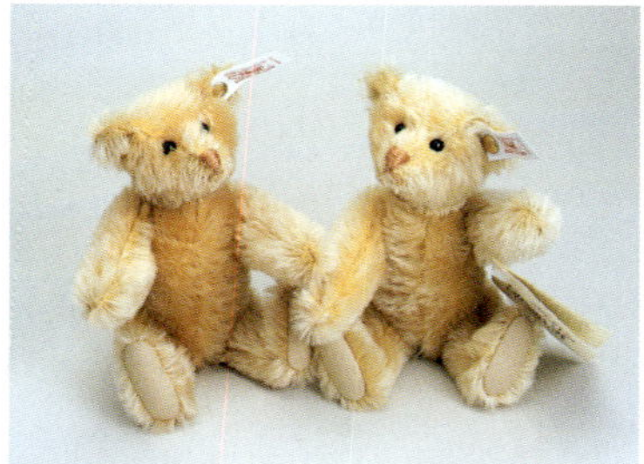

Zwillingsbaeren - *Twin Bears*

Mohair, cremefarben, gegliedert, Reproduktionen von Steiff Baeren aus 1905 vom Strong Museum, auf der Rueckseite der Fahne mit 18 bl. A bzw. B zu unterscheiden, Pfoten ohne Filzeinsatz, limit. Auflage 5.000 Paare, USA Artikel - *mohair, cream, jointed, reproductions of Steiff bears from 1905, originals are in the Strong Museum, the backside of the ear tag shows either 18 bl. A or B, upper limbs with no felt paw pads, ltd edition of 5,000 pairs exclusive for the USA*

EAN-No.	Period	Pr.	Info
665370	1998-1998	4-5	kpl. Set - *compl.set*
665370	1998-1998	3-4	18 cm, A
665370	1998-1998	3-4	18 cm, B

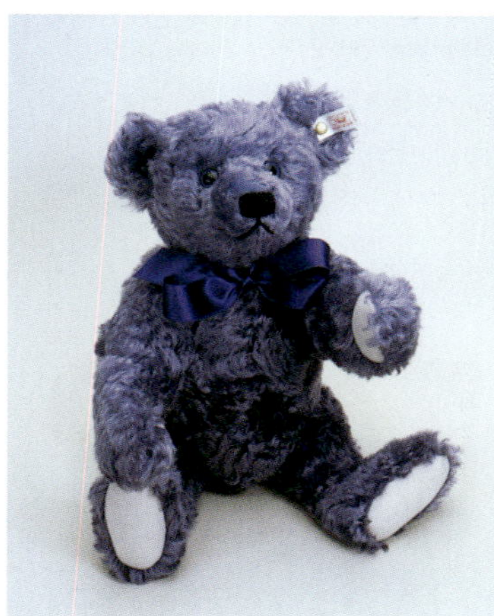

Lavender Blue Baer - *Lavender Blue Bear*

Mohair, lavendelblau, gegliedert, limit. Auflage 3.500 Stueck fuer Amerika - *mohair, lavender blue, jointed, ltd edition of 3,500 exclusive for the USA*

EAN-No.	Period	Pr.	Info
665479	1998-1998	5	42 cm

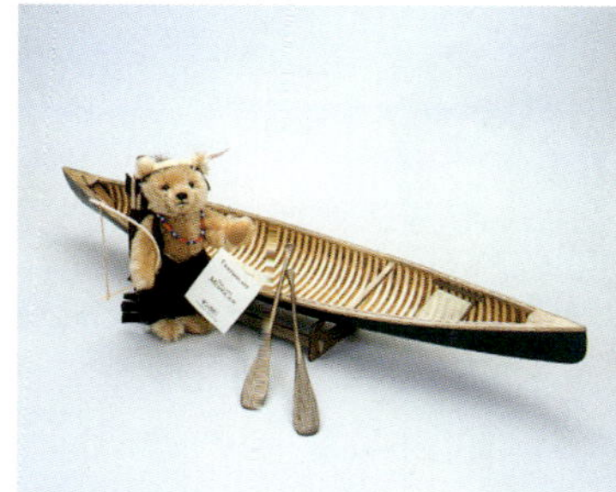

Der letzte Mohikaner - *The Last Mohican*

Mohair, blond, gegliedert, Baer als Indianer mit Bogen & Pfeilen sowie einem Holzkanu, limit. Auflage 3.000 Stueck fuer Amerika - *mohair, blond, jointed, bear dressed like a Native American carries a bow & a quiver of arrows, wooden canoe, ltd edition of 3,000 exclusive for the USA*

EAN-No.	Period	Pr.	Info
665509	1998-1998	4-5	20 cm

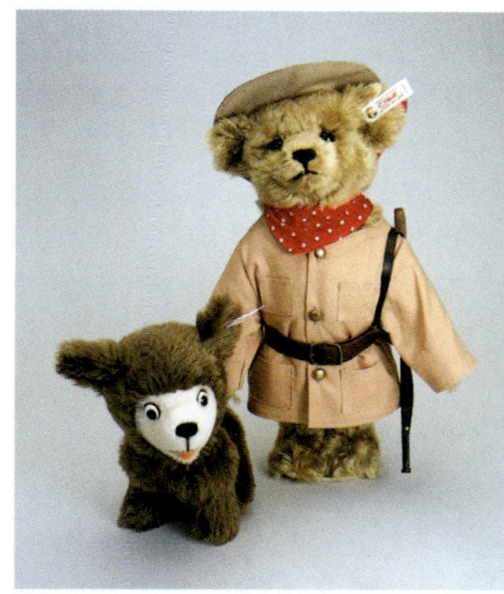

Teddy Roosevelt & Jungbaer - *Teddy Roosevelt & Cub*

Mohair, blond bzw. braun, gegliedert bzw. sitzend, Teddy Roosevelt mit Gewehr, nach der Karikatur von John Berryman, limit. Auflage 4.000 Stueck fuer Amerika - *mohair, T.R.: blond, jointed, with rifle, Cub: brown, sitting, from the political cartoon of John Berryman, ltd edition of 4,000 exclusive for the USA*

EAN-No.	Period	Pr.	Info
665615	1998-1998	5	34/18 cm - kpl. Set - *compl. set*
	1998-1998	4	34 cm, Teddy Roosevelt
	1998-1998	4	18 cm, Jungbaer - *cub*

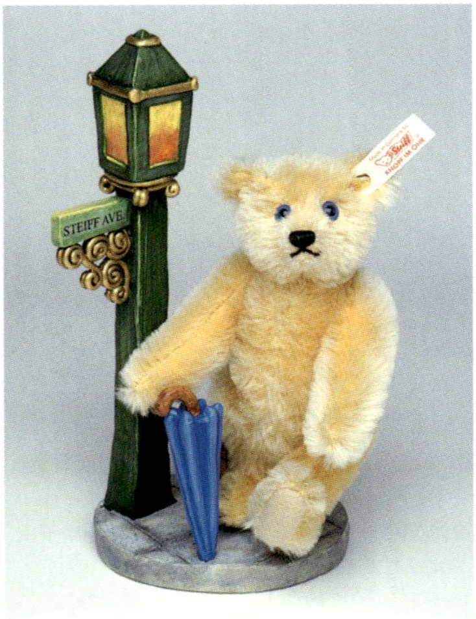

Splash Teddybaer - *Splash Teddybear*

Mohairpluesch, blond, gegliedert, mit Strassenlaterne "Steiff Ave." & blauem Regenschirm, keine Krallenbestickung, limit. Auflage 4.000 Stueck fuer Amerika - *mohair, blond, jointed, leans on a lamppost "Steiff Ave." & carries a blue umbrella, ltd edition of 4,000 for America*

EAN-No.	Period	Pr.	Info
665998	1999-1999	4	18 cm

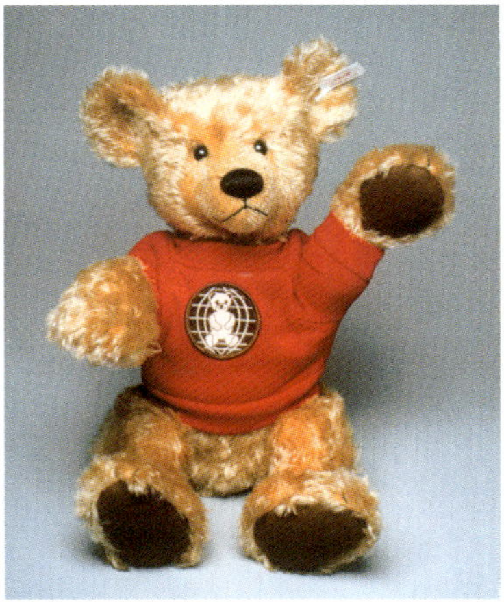

Teddybaer Gulliver - *Teddybear Gulliver*

Mohairpluesch, blond, gegliedert, Pfoten & Fussohlen aus braunem Filz, rotes T-Shirt mit Logo "Good Bears of the World", limit. Auflage 5.000 Stueck fuer Amerika - *mohair, blond, jointed, paws & soles of brown felt, red T-Shirt with "Good Bears of the World" logo, ltd edition of 5,000 for America*

EAN-No.	Period	Pr.	Info
665936	1999-1999	5	40 cm

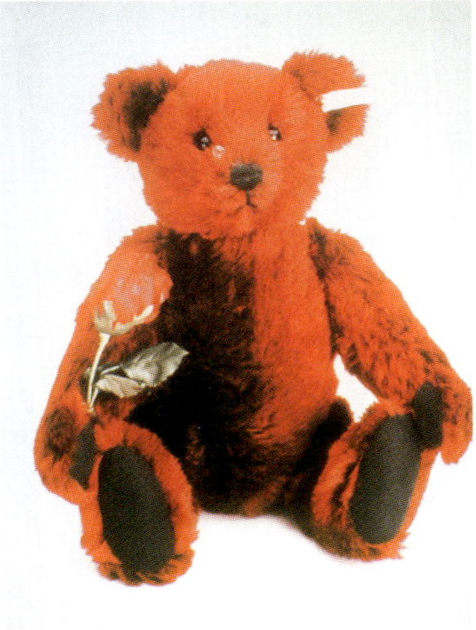

Tautropfenbär - *Dew Drop Rose Bear*

Mohairpluesch, dunkelrot, gegliedert, mit Tautropfen aus Swarovski-Kristall & roter Rose aus Samt, Sohlen & Pfoten schwarz, limit. Auflage 3.500 Stueck fuer Amerika - *mohair, burgundy, jointed, with an Austrian Crystal dew drop on her cheek & a dark red velvet rose, black pades & soles, ltd edition of 3,500 for America*

EAN-No.	Period	Pr.	Info
665844	1999-1999	4-5	40 cm

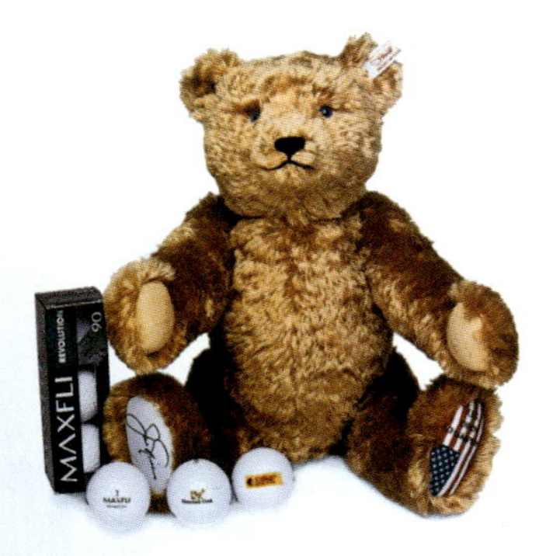

Jack Nicklaus Baer - *Jack Nicklaus Bear*

Mohairpluesch, gold, gegliedert, zu Ehren des Golfers Jack Nicklaus, mit 3 Golfbaellen, limit. Auflage 2.000 Stueck fuer Amerika - *mohair, gold, jointed, in honor to the golfer Jack Nicklaus, with 3 golf balls, ltd edition of 2,000 for America*

EAN-No.	Period	Pr.	Info
665943	1999-1999	5	40 cm

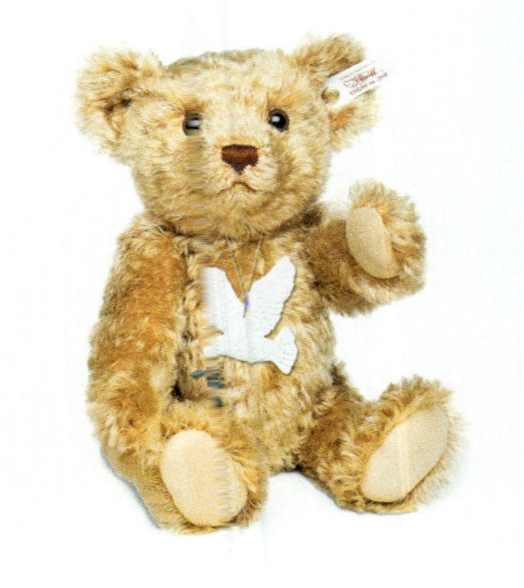

Frieden Baer - *Peace Bear*

Mohairpluesch, blond, gegliedert, Friedensbaer mit weisser Friedenstaube als Medaillon, limit. Auflage 3.000 Stueck fuer Amerika - *mohair, blond, jointed, wearing a white dove medallion, ltd edition of 3,000 for America*

EAN-No.	Period	Pr.	Info
665981	1999-1999	4	28 cm

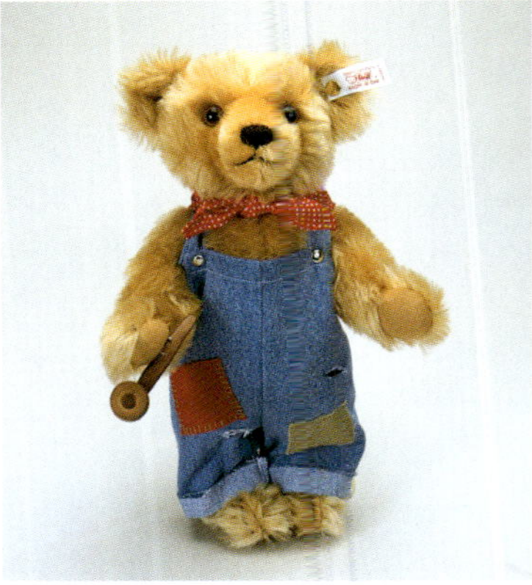

Huckleberry Finn Baer - *Huckleberry Finn Bear*

Mohairpluesch, blond, gegliedert, nach dem Romanhelden von Mark Twain, limit. Auflage 1.500 Stueck fuer Amerika - *mohair, blond, jointed, from Mark Twains novel Tom Sawyer, ltd edition of 1,500 for America*

EAN-No.	Period	Pr.	Info
665851	1999-1999	4-5	28 cm

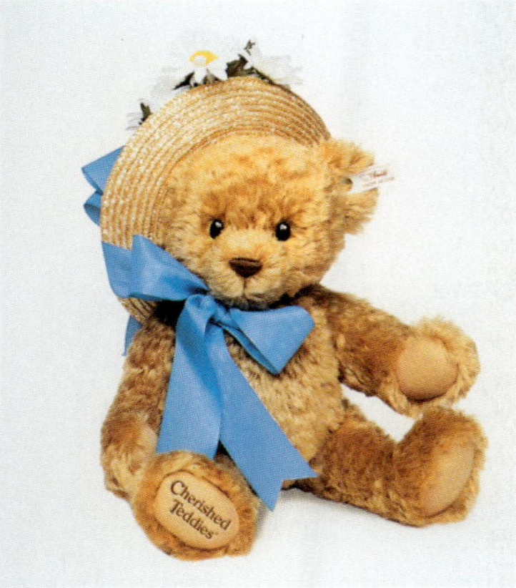

Teddy Daisy

Mohairpluesch, gold, gegliedert, in Zusammenarbeit mit Enesco, nach dem Vorbild der Cherished Teddies, limit. Auflage 5.000 Stueck fuer Amerika - *mohair, gold, jointed, created in collaboration with Enesco, based on the classic Cherished Teddies figurines, ltd edition of 5,000 for America*

EAN-No.	Period	Pr.	Info
665905	1999-1999	4-5	30 cm

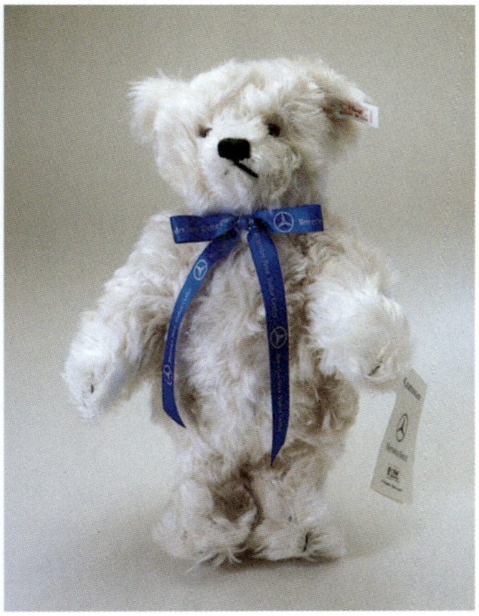

Mercedes-Benz Steiff Baer - *Mercedes-Benz Steiff Bear*

Mohairpluesch, silber, gegliedert, limit. Auflage 1.500 Stueck fuer das Besucher-Zentrum von Mercedes-Benz U.S. International - *mohair, silver, jointed, ltd edition of 1,500, exclusively for the Visitor Center at Mercedes-Benz U.S. International*

EAN-No.	Period	Pr.	Info
665837	1999-1999	5	35 cm

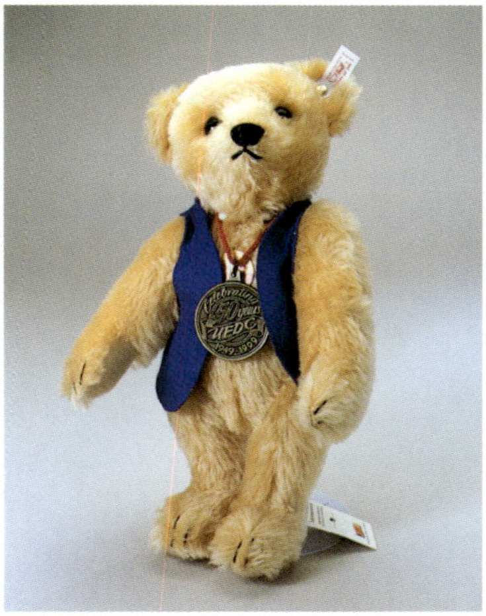

Teddybaer - *Teddybear*

Mohair, blond, gegliedert, limit. Auflage 1.500 Stueck für UFDC, USA - *mohair, blond, jointed, ltd edition of 1,500 for UFDC*

EAN-No.	Period	Pr.	Info
665974	1999-1999	4	35 cm

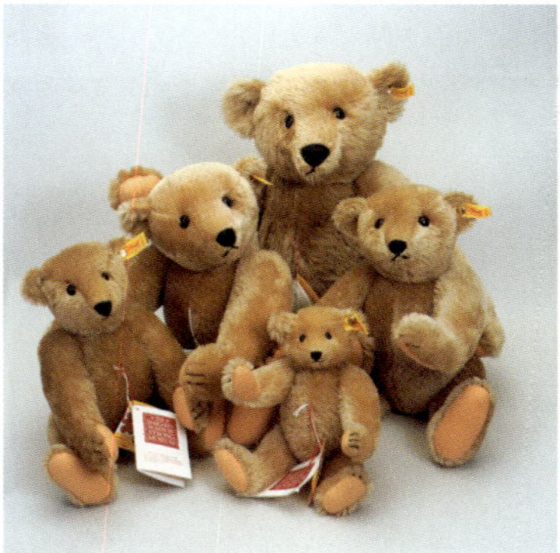

Margaret Strong Baer - *Margaret Strong Bear*

Replica 1904, Mohair, gegliedert, gold, 26 cm mit Druckstimme, ab 32 cm Brummstimme, USA-Artikel - *1904 replica, mohair, jointed, gold, 26 cm press voice, from 32 cm growler, USA exclusive*

Serie	Art.-No	Period	Pr.	Info
404597	**0155/26**	1982-1990	3	26 cm
	404597	1991-1991	3	
404627	**0155/32**	1982-1990	3-4	32 cm
	404627	1991-1991	3-4	
404832	**0155/42**	1983-1990	4	42 cm
	404832	1991-1991	4	
404863	**0155/51**	1984-1990	5	51 cm
	404863	1991-1991	5	
404894	**0155/60**	1984-1990	5-6	60 cm
	404894	1991-1991	5-6	

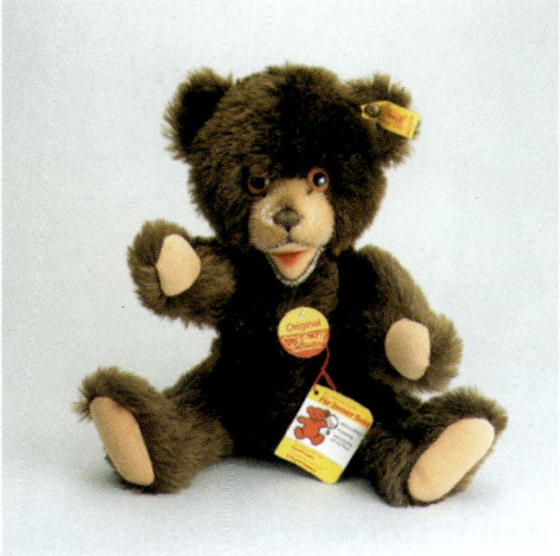

Teddy Bruno

Mohair, dunkelbraun, gegliedert, USA-Artikel - *mohair, dark brown, jointed, USA exclusive*

Serie	Art.-No	Period	Pr.	Info
	0223/30	1982-1984	4-5	30 cm

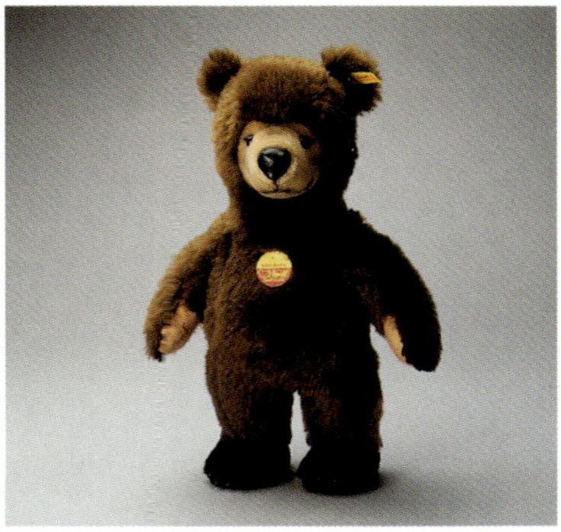

Klein Archie - *Little Archie*

Mohair, dunkelbraun, stehend, limit. Auflage 2.500 Stueck fuer Enchanted Dollhouse, Vermont - *mohair, dark brown, standing ltd edition of 2,500 for Enchanted Doll House*

Serie	Art.-No	Period	Pr.	Info
	0140/38	1983-1983	5	38 cm

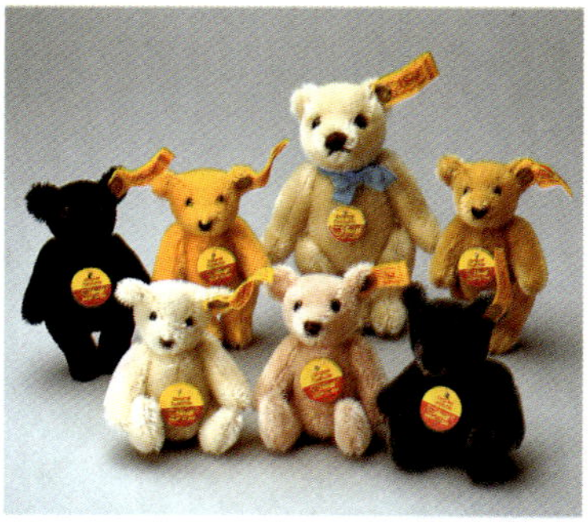

Original Teddybaer - *Original Teddy Bear*

Mohair, gegliedert, USA-Artikel - *mohair, jointed, exclusive for the USA*

SERIE	ART.-NO	PERIOD	PR.	INFO
	0201/10	1984-1985	3	10 cm, beige
	0201/14	1983-1985	3-4	14 cm
	0202/10	1984-1985	3	10 cm, caramel
	0202/14	1983-1985	3-4	14 cm
	0203/10	1984-1985	3	10 cm, weiss - *white*
	0203/14	1983-1986	3-4	14 cm
	0206/10	1984-1985	3	10 cm, dunkelbraun - *dark brown*
	0206/14	1984-1986	3-4	14 cm
	0207/10	1985-1986	3	10 cm, grau - *grey*
	0207/14	1985-1985	3-4	14 cm
	0208/10	1985-1986	3	10 cm, schwarz - *black*
	0208/14	1985-1985	3-4	14 cm
	0210/10	1986-1986	3	10 cm, blond
	0212/10	1986-1986	3	10 cm, creme - *cream*
	0213/10	1986-1986	3	10 cm, zimt - *cinnamon*
	0214/10	1986-1986	3	10 cm, gold
	0211/10	1990-1990	3	10 cm, rosé - *rose*
030567	**0212/10**	1991-1991	3	10 cm, anthrazit - *anthracite*

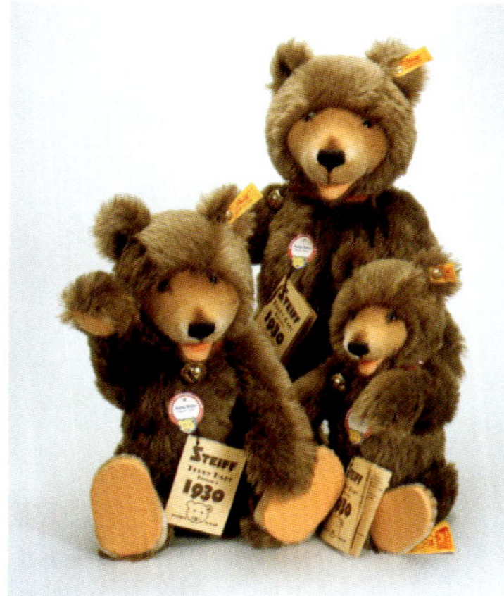

Teddy Baby Replica 1930

Mohair, dunkelbraun, gegliedert, Lederhalsband, USA-Artikel - *mohair, dark brown, jointed, leather collar, article for USA*

SERIE	ART.-NO	PERIOD	PR.	INFO
	0175/29	1984-1989	4-5	29 cm
407758	**0175/35**	1984-1990	4-5	35 cm
	407758	1991-1991	4-5	
	0175/42	1984-1989	5	42 cm

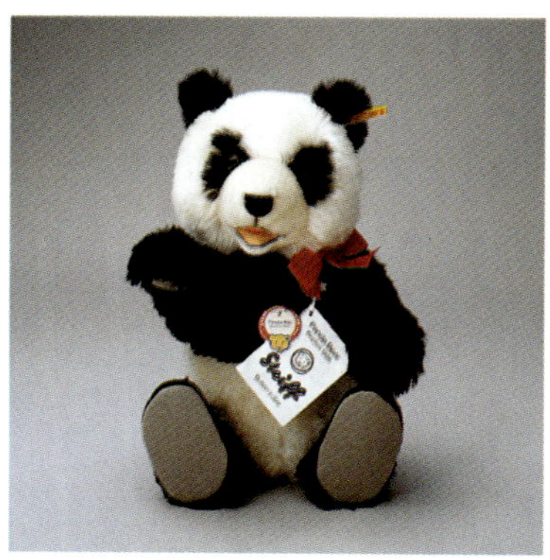

Panda Baer Replica 1938 - *Panda Bear Replica 1938*

Mohair-Webpelz, gegliedert, USA-Artikel - *mohair woven fur, jointed, article for USA*

SERIE	ART.-NO	PERIOD	PR.	INFO
	0178/29	1984-1985	4-5	29 cm
	0178/35	1984-1985	5	35 cm

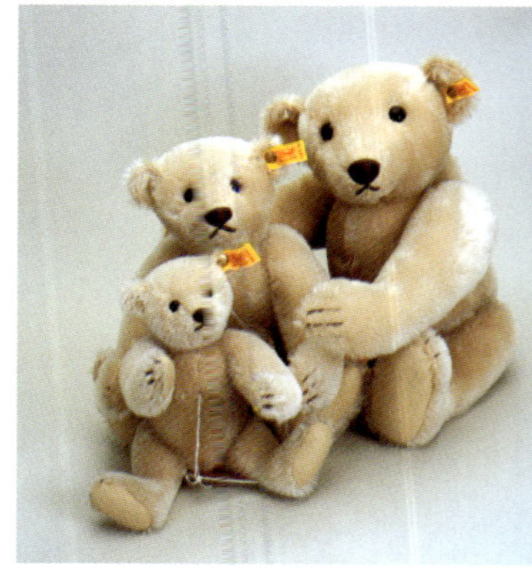

Margaret Strong Baer - *Margaret Strong Bear*

Replica 1904, Mohair, gegliedert, cremefarben, 26 cm mit Druckstimme, ab 32 cm Brummstimme, USA-Artikel - *1904 replica, mohair, jointed, cream, 26 cm press voice, from 32 cm growler, article for USA*

SERIE	ART.-NO	PERIOD	PR.	INFO
	0157/26	1984-1986	4	26 cm
	0157/32	1984-1986	5	32 cm
	0157/42	198[illegible]-1986	5	42 cm
	0157/51	1985-1986	5-6	51 cm
	0157/60	1985-1986	6	60 cm

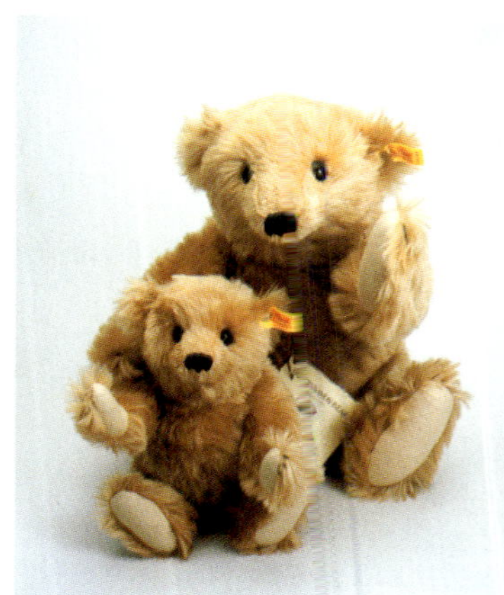

Mr. Cinnamon Baer - *Mr. Cinnamon Bear*

Replica 1903, Langhaar-Mohair, gegliedert, Stimme, USA-Artikel - *1903 replica, longhair mohair, jointed, press voice, article for USA*

SERIE	ART.-NO	PERIOD	PR.	INFO
	0151/25	1984-1986	4-5	25 cm
	0151/32	1984-1986	[illegible]	32 cm
	0151/40	1984-1986	5-6	40 cm

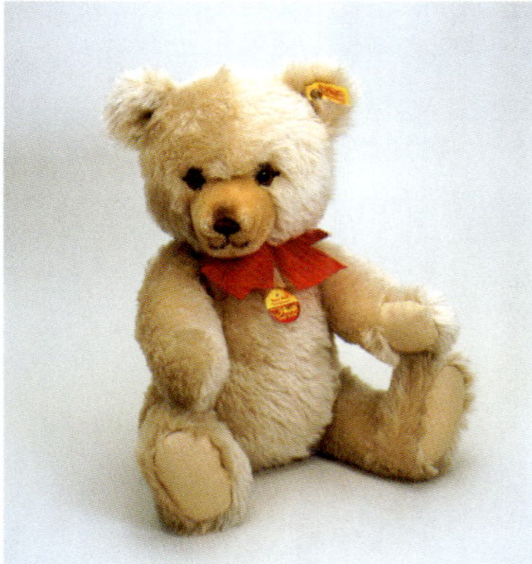

Baby Soft Teddy Baer - *Baby Soft Teddy Bear*

Webpelz, beige, formgeschaeumt, gegliedert, Stimme, USA-Artikel - *woven fur, beige, stuffed with pre-formed foam, jointed, press voice, article for USA*

Serie	Art.-No	Period	Pr.	Info
	0237/28	1984-1987	2-3	28 cm
	0237/35	1984-1987	3	35 cm
	0237/45	1984-1987	3-4	45 cm

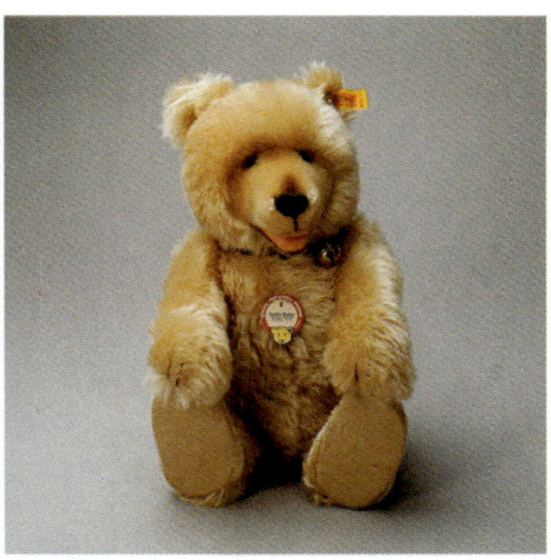

Teddy Baby Replica 1930

Mohair, mais, gegliedert, Lederhalsband, USA-Artikel - *mohair, corn yellow, jointed, leather collar, article for USA*

Serie	Art.-No	Period	Pr.	Info
	0176/29	1985-1986	4-5	29 cm
	0176/35	1985-1986	4-5	35 cm
	0176/42	1985-1986	5	42 cm

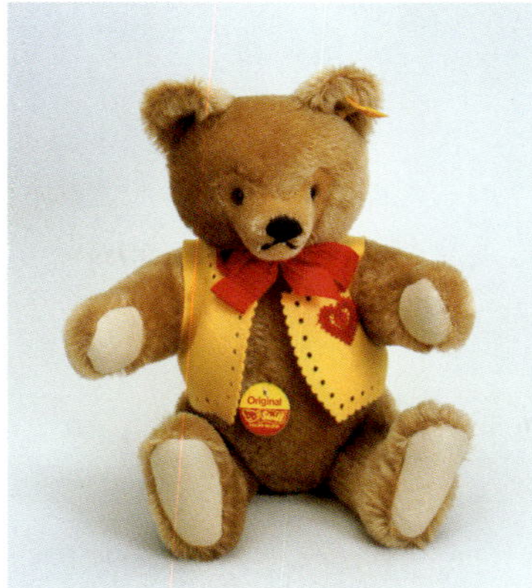

Luv Bear-er

Original Teddy mit Filzweste, Mohair, zimt, gegliedert, Stimme, USA-Artikel - *Original Teddy, felt vest, mohair, cinnamon, jointed, press voice, article for USA*

Serie	Art.-No	Period	Pr.	Info
	0211/26	1985-1986	4	26 cm
	0211/36	1985-1986	4-5	36 cm

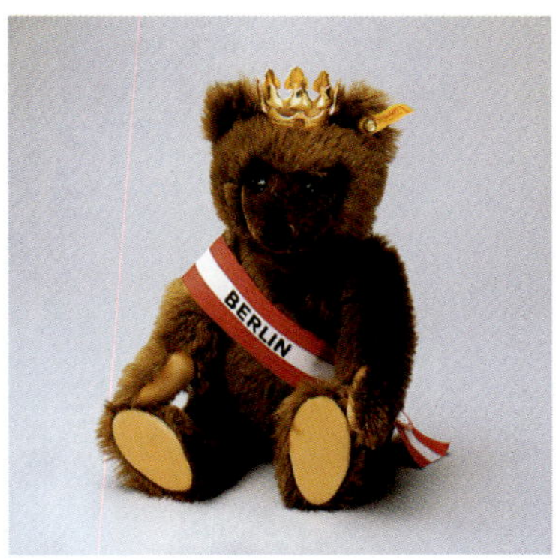

Berlin Baer - *Berlin Bear*

Original Teddy mit Berlin-Schaerpe & Krone, Mohair, dunkelbraun, gegliedert, Brummstimme, USA-Artikel - *Original Teddy with Berlin sash & crown, mohair, dark brown, jointed, growler, article for USA*

Serie	Art.-No	Period	Pr.	Info
	0251/34	1985-1987	4-5	34 cm

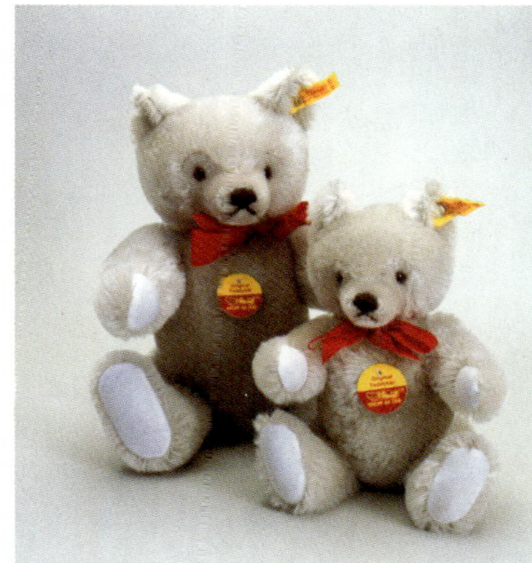

Original Teddybaer - *Original Teddy Bear*

Mohair, grau, 26 cm Druck-, ab 36 cm Brummstimme, gegliedert, USA Artikel - *mohair, grey, 26 cm press voice, from 36 cm growler, jointed, article for the USA*

Serie	Art.-No	Period	Pr.	Info
007200	**0207/26**	1986-1990	3	26 cm
	007200	1991-1991	3	
	0207/36	1986-1989	4	36 cm
007241	**0207/41**	1986-1990	4-5	41 cm
	007241	1991-1991	4-5	

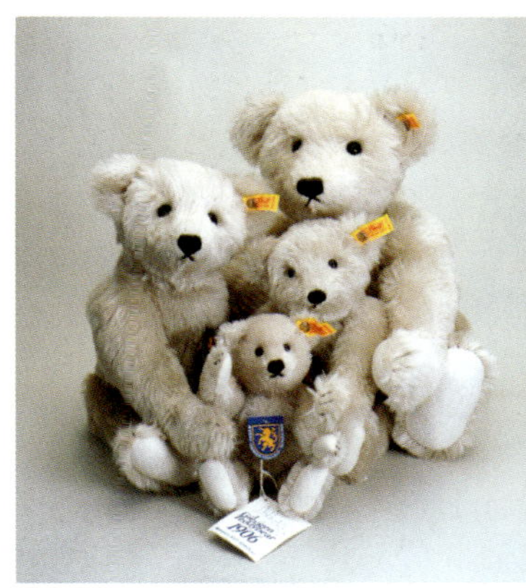

Giengen Teddy Baer - *Giengen Teddy Bear*

Replica 1906. Mohair, grau, gegliedert, Stimme, USA-Artikel - *1906 replica, mohair, grey, jointed, press voice, article for USA*

Serie	Art.-No	Period	Pr.	Info
	0167/22	1986-1990	4	22 cm
	0167/32	1985-1989	4-5	32 cm
	0167/42	1985-1989	5	42 cm
	0167/52	1986-1989	5-6	52 cm

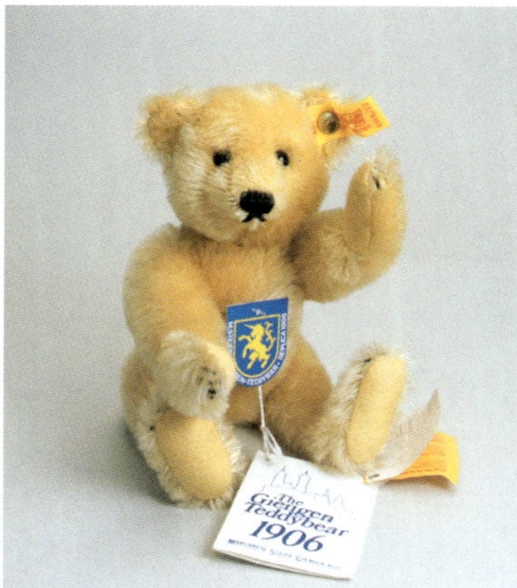

Giengen Teddy Baer - *Giengen Teddy Bear*

Replica 1906, Mohair, blond gegliedert, Stimme, USA-Artikel - *1906 replica, mohair, blond, jointed, press voice, article for USA*

SERIE	ART.-NO	PERIOD	PR.	INFO
	0168/22	1986-1988	4-5	22 cm
	0168/42	1986-1988	5	42 cm

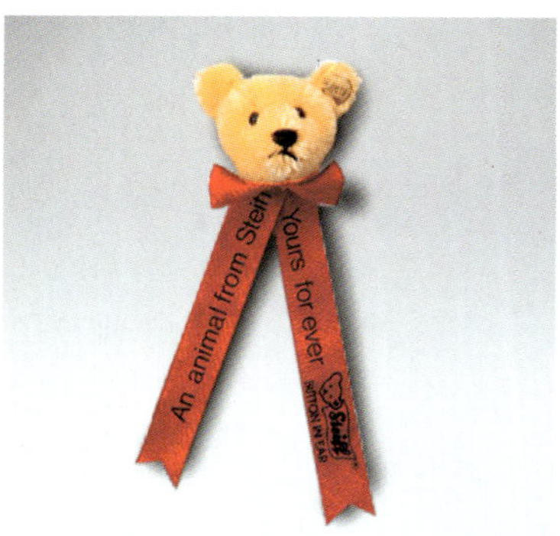

Teddy Pin

Mohair, Teddykopf mit rotem Band, zum Anstecken, USA-Artikel - *mohair, teddy head with red ribbon, stick pin, article for USA*

SERIE	ART.-NO	PERIOD	PR.	INFO
	8494/03	1986-1988	3-4	33 cm

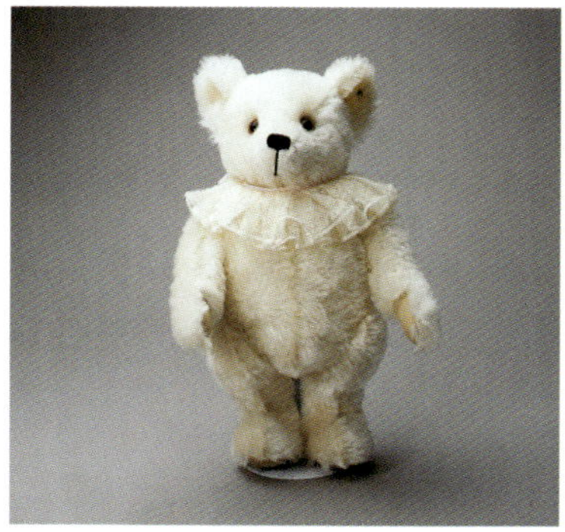

Ophelia Baer - *Ophelia Bear*

Mohair, weiss, gegliedert, USA-Artikel, designed von Michele Durkson Clise - *mohair, white, jointed, article for USA, designed by Michele Durkson Clise*

SERIE	ART.-NO	PERIOD	PR.	INFO
	0225/42	1984-1989	5	42 cm

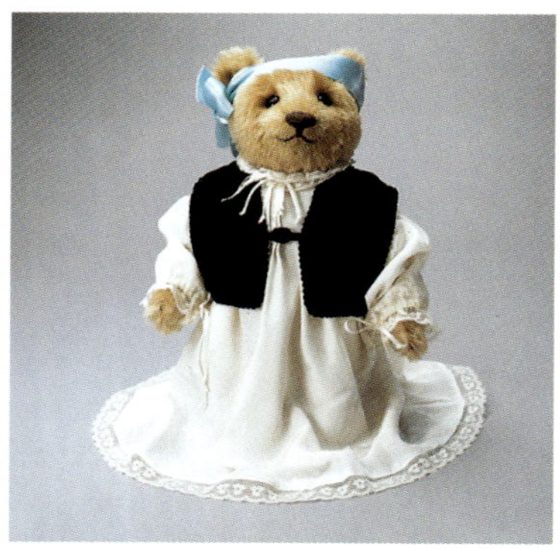

Schnuffy Baer - *Schnuffy Bear*

Mohair, blond, gegliedert, Brummstimme, Partner von Ophelia, USA-Artikel - *mohair, blond, jointed, growler, partner to Ophelia, article for USA*

SERIE	ART.-NO	PERIOD	PR.	INFO
	0227/33	1987-1989	5	33 cm

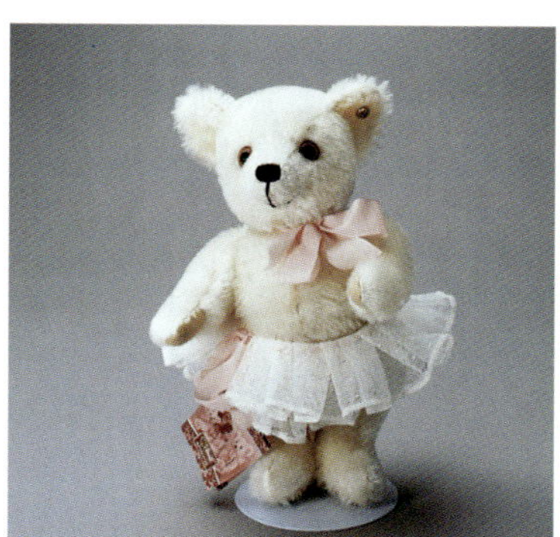

Baby Ophelia

Mohair, weiss, gegliedert, USA-Artikel, begleitet Ophelia & Schnuffi Baer - *mohair, white, jointed article for USA, accompanied by Ophelia & Schnuffi Bears*

SERIE	ART.-NO	PERIOD	PR.	INFO
	0225/27	1988-1990	5	27 cm

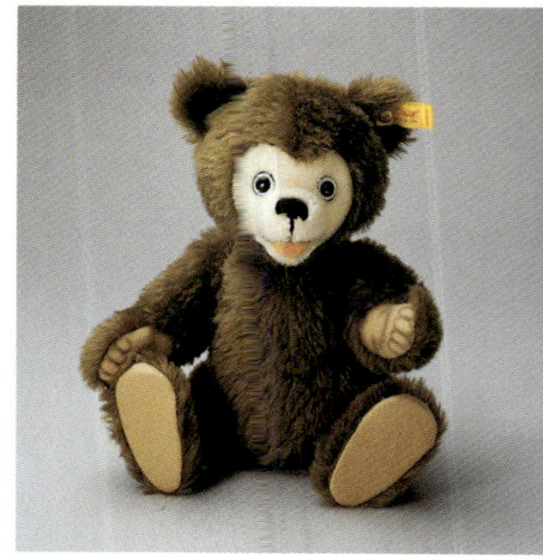

Clifford Berryman Baer - *Clifford Berryman Bear*

Mohair, gegliedert, USA-Artikel, nach einem Karrikaturisten der Washington Post - *mohair, jointed, article for USA, after a caricaturist from the Washington Post*

SERIE	ART.-NO	PERIOD	PR.	INFO
	0255/35	1987-1989	5	35 cm

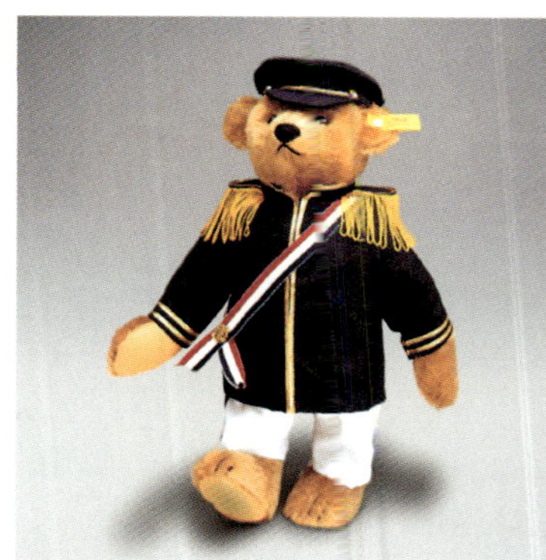

Captain Strong Baer - *Captain Strong Bear*

Mohair, blond, gegliedert, USA-Artikel - *mohair, blond, jointed, article for USA*

SERIE	ART.-NO	PERIOD	PR.	INFO
	0156/34	1988-1989	5	34 cm

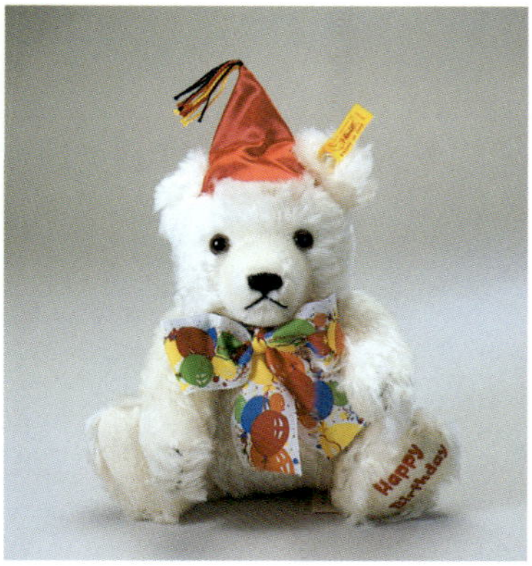

Geburtstags Baer - *Birthday Bear*

Mohairpluesch, weiss, gegliedert, roter Clownhut & bunte Schleife aus Satin, linke Sohle bestickt mit "Happy Birthday", Musikwerk "Happy Birthday to you", USA-Artikel - *mohair, white, jointed, red clown hat & multi-color ribbon of silk, left foot pad embroidered with 'Happy Birthday", music box playing 'Happy Birthday to you", North American exclusive*

EAN-No.	Period	Pr.	Info
665547	1999-1999	4	25 cm

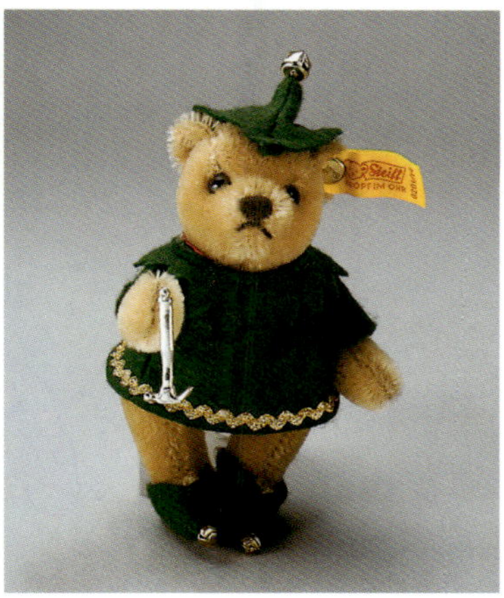

Hans Helfer - *Hans Helper*

Mohair, blond, gegliedert, limit. Auflage 200 Stueck, fuer Steiff Sammler Club Hobby Center Toys - *mohair, jointed, ltd edition of 200, for Steiff collector´s club Hobby Center Toys, Toledo*

Serie	Art.-No	Period	Pr.	Info
	0201/14	1987-1987	5	14 cm

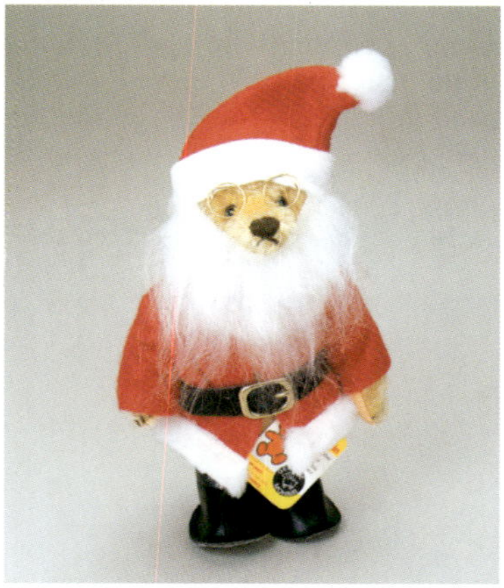

Nikolaus Baer - *Mr. Santa*

Mohair, blond, gegliedert, Nikolausmantel & -muetze, Stiefel, Guertel & Brille, ohne Artikel-Nr., limit. Auflage 300 Stueck fuer Steiff Sammler Club Hobby Center Toys - *mohair, blond, jointed, Santa Claus coat & hat, boots, belt & glasses, without art.-no., ltd edition of 300 for Steiff collector´s club Hobby Center Toys, Toledo*

EAN-No.	Period	Pr.	Info
	1987-1987	5-6	22 cm

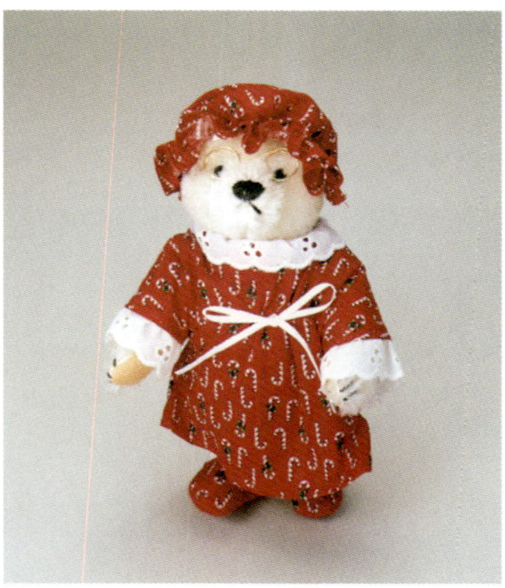

Frau Nikolaus - *Mrs. Santa*

Mohair, weiss, gegliedert, ohne Artikel-Nr., limit. Auflage 150 Stueck fuer Steiff Sammler Club Hobby Center Toys - *mohair, white, jointed, without art.-no., ltd edition of 150 for Steiff collector´s club Hobby Center Toys, Toledo*

EAN-No.	Period	Pr.	Info
	1987-1987	5-6	22 cm

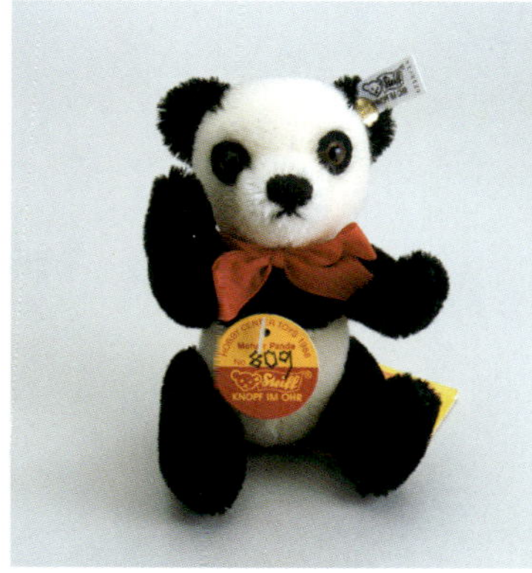

Panda Baer - *Panda Bear*

Mohair, gegliedert, fuer Hobby-Center Toys, limit. Auflage 1.000 Stueck - *mohair, jointed, for Hobby Center Toys, ltd edition of 1,000*

Serie	Art.-No	Period	Pr.	Info
	0218/14	1988-1988	5	14 cm

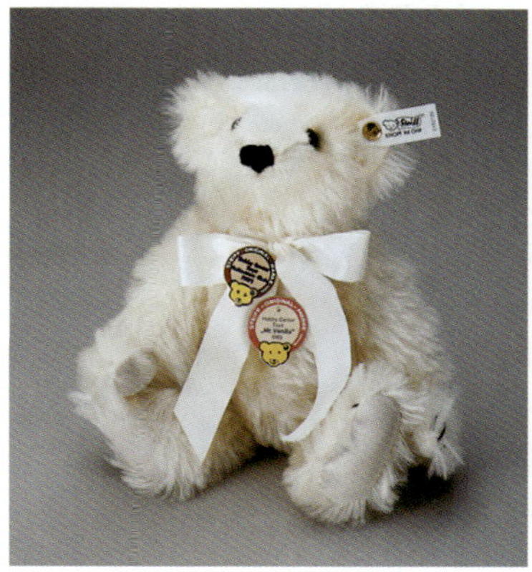

Mr. Vanilla Baer - *Mr. Vanilla Bear*

Mohair, weiss, gegliedert, limit. Auflage 1.000 Stueck fuer Hobby Center Toys - *mohair, white, jointed, ltd edition of 1,000 for Hobby Center Toys*

Serie	Art.-No	Period	Pr.	Info
011412	**0152/25**	1989-1989	6	25 cm

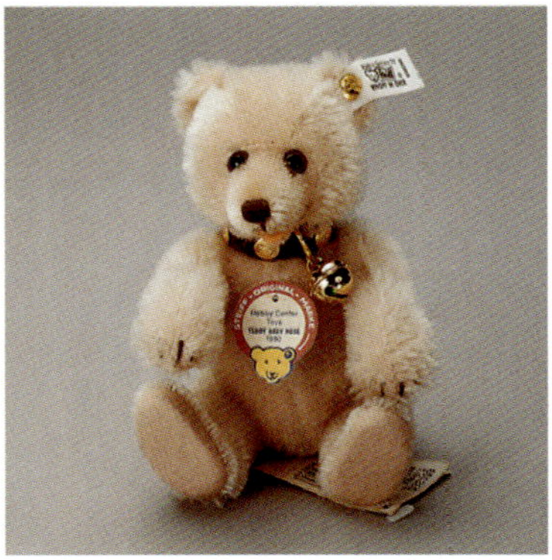

Teddy Baby Rosé - *Teddy Baby Rose*

Mohair, gegliedert, Stimme, Lederhalsband, limit. Auflage 1.000 Stueck fuer The Toy Store - *mohair, jointed, press voice, leather collar, ltd edition of 1,000 for The Toy Store*

SERIE	ART.-NO	PERIOD	PR.	INFO
650260	**0179/19**	1990-1990	5	19 cm

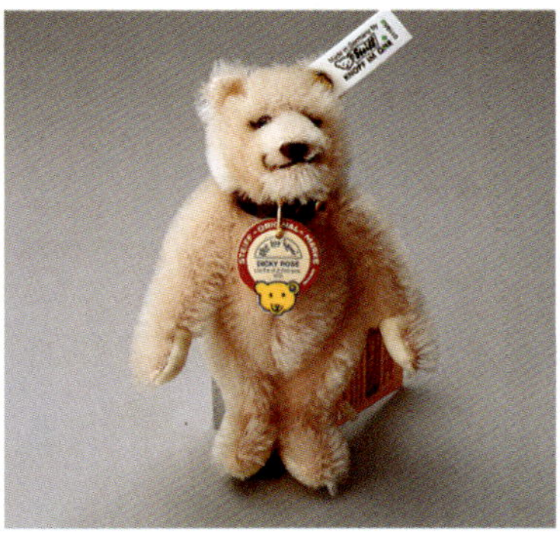

Dicky Rosé - *Dicky Rose*

Mohair, gegliedert, Lederhalsband, limit. Auflage 2.000 Stueck fuer The Toy Store, Toledo/Ohio - *mohair, jointed, leather collar, ltd edition of 2,000 for The Toy Store, Toledo, Ohio*

EAN-NO.	PERIOD	PR.	INFO
011955	1991-1991	5	16 cm

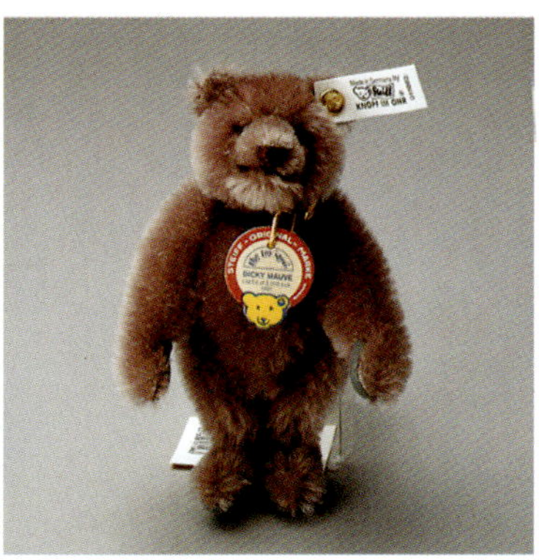

Dicky Mauve

Mohair, gegliedert, Lederhalsband, limit. Auflage 2.000 Stueck fuer The Toy Store, Toledo/Ohio - *mohair, jointed, leather collar, ltd edition of 2,000 for The Toy Store, Toledo, Ohio*

EAN-NO.	PERIOD	PR.	INFO
011962	1991-1991	5	16 cm

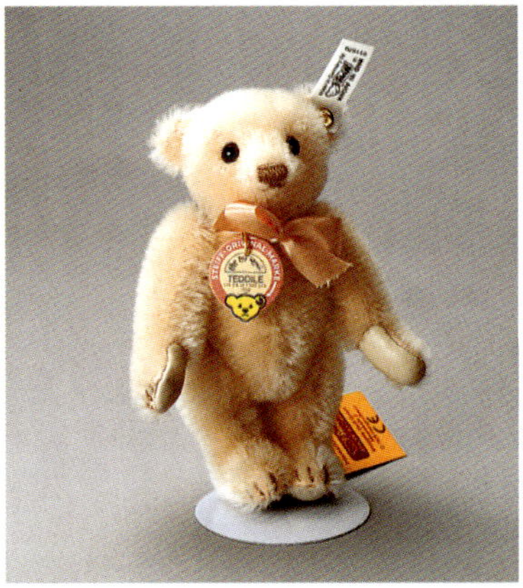

Teddile

Mohair, Lederpfoten, rosa, gegiedert., Stimme, limit. Auflage 1.500 Stueck fuer The Toy Store, Toledo/Ohio - *mohair, leather paws, pink, jointed, press voice, ltd edition of 1,500 for The Toy Store, Toledo, Ohio*

EAN-NO.	PERIOD	PR.	INFO
011979	1992-1992	5	19 cm

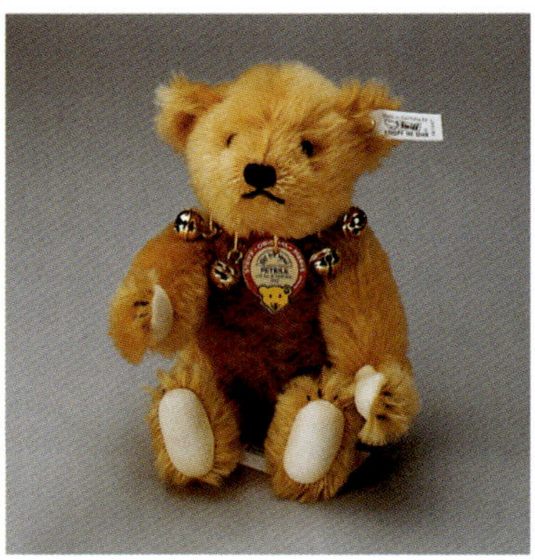

Petsile

Mohair, blond, gegliedert, Druckstimme, limit. Auflage 1.500 Stueck fuer The Toy Store, Toledo/Ohio - *mohair, blond, jointed, press voice, ltd edition of 1,500 for The Toy Store, Toledo, Ohio*

EAN-NO.	PERIOD	PR.	INFO
651847	1993-1993	5	19 cm

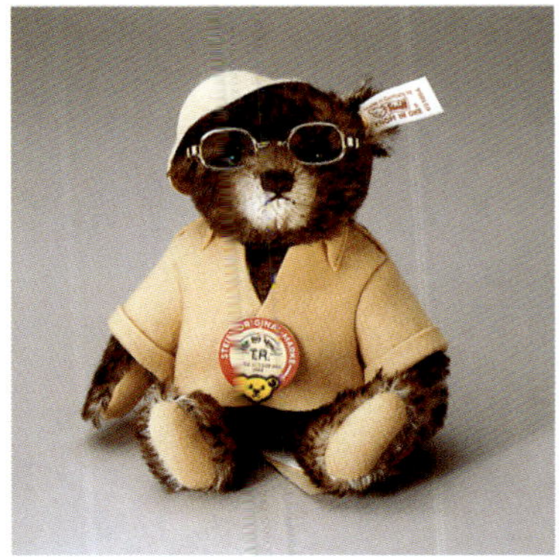

Safari Teddy Baer - *Safari Teddy Bear*

Mohair, braun gespitzt, gegliedert, limit. Auflage 1.500 Stueck fuer The Toy Store, Toledo/Ohio - *mohair, brown tipped, jointed, ltd edition of 1,500 for The Toy Store, Toledo, Ohio*

EAN-NO.	PERIOD	PR.	INFO
651854	1994-1994	4-5	19 cm

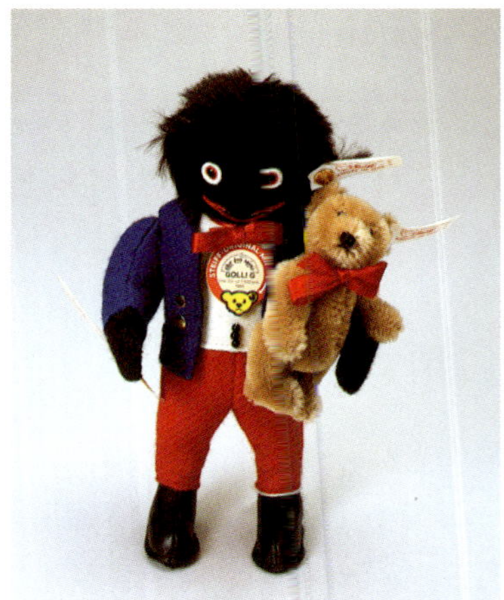

Golli G. & Teddi B.

Golli aus Filz, schwarz, stehend, Kopf & Arme gegliedert, Teddi aus Mohair, hellbraun, gegliedert, limit. Auflage 1.500 Stueck fuer The Toy Store, Toledo, USA - *Golli: felt, black, standing, head & arms jointed, Teddi: mohair, light brown, jointed, ltd edition of 1,500 for The Toy Store, Toledo, USA*

EAN-NO.	PERIOD	PR.	INFO
651861	1995-1995	4	kpl. Set - *compl. set*
J04104	1995-1995	3-4	24 cm, Golli G.
J04082	1995-1995	3	10 cm, Teddi B.

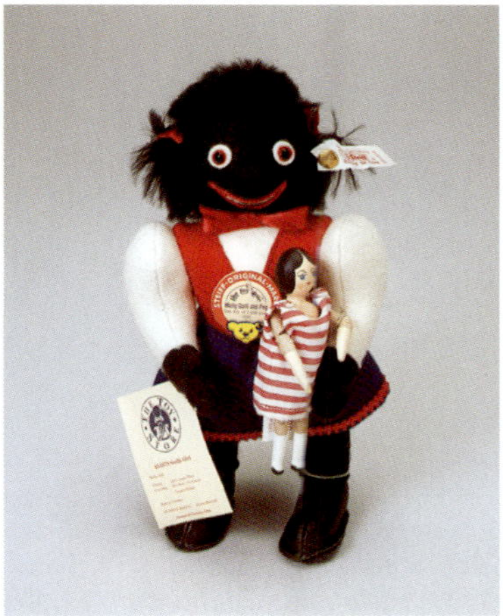

Molly Golli and Peg

Filz, schwarz, stehend, Kopf & Arme gegliedert, mit kleiner Puppe aus Holz, limit. Auflage 2.500 Stueck fuer The Toy Store, Toledo, USA - *felt, black, standing, head & arms jointed, with a little wooden doll, ltd edition of 2,500 for The Toy Store, Toledo, USA*

EAN-No.	Period	Pr.	Info
651878	1996-1996	4	22 cm

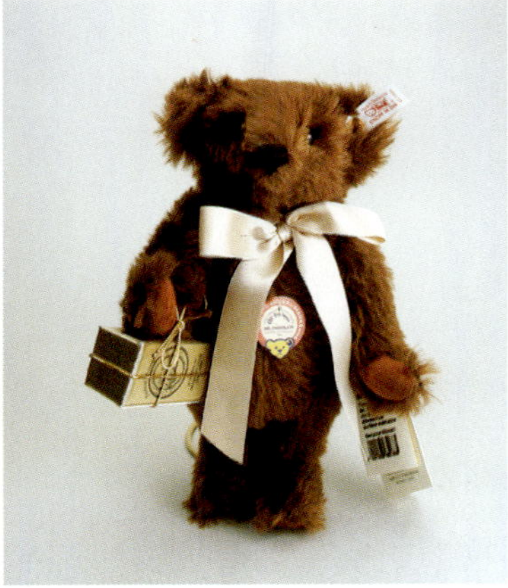

Mr. Chocolate Baer - ***Mr. Chocolate Bear***

Mohair, dunkelbraun, gegliedert, limit. Auflage 2.000 Stueck fuer The Toy Store, Toledo, USA - *mohair, dark brown, jointed, ltd edition of 2,000 for The Toy Store, Toledo, USA*

EAN-No.	Period	Pr.	Info
651885	1997-1997	4-5	25 cm

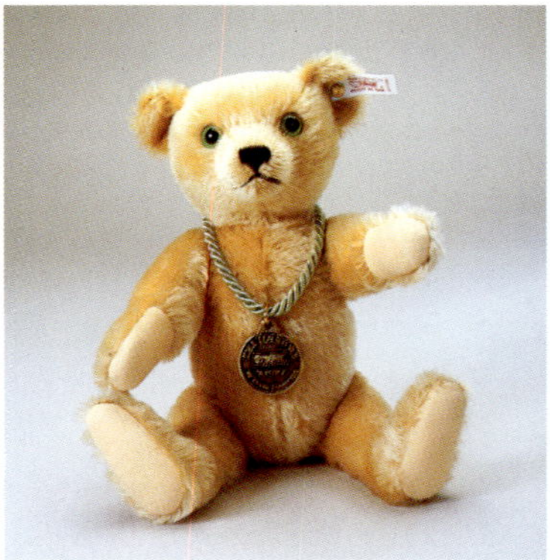

Teddybaer Anno - *Teddybear Anno*

Mohair, blond, gegliedert, limit. Auflage 1.500 Stueck fuer The Toy Store, Toledo, USA - *mohair, blond, jointed, ltd edition of 1,500 for The Toy Store, Toledo, USA*

EAN-No.	Period	Pr.	Info
651908	1999-1999	4	32 cm

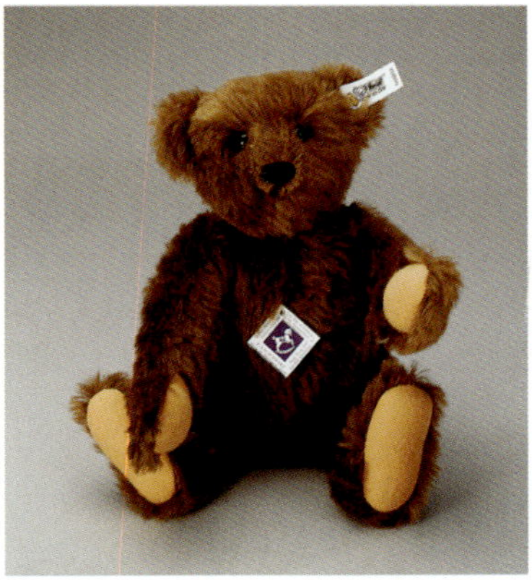

Teddy Baer 1906 - *1906 Teddy Bear*

Mohair, braun, gegliedert, limit. Auflage 1.000 Stueck fuer FAO Schwarz zum 125jaehrigen Jubilaeum - *mohair, brown, jointed, ltd edition of 1,000 for FAO Schwarz, USA, to celebrate 125th anniversary*

Serie	Art.-No	Period	Pr.	Info
	0162/33	1987-1987	6	33 cm

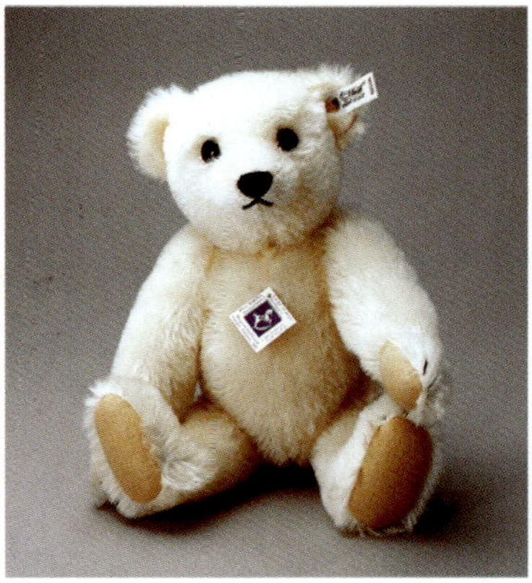

Teddy Baer 1909 - *1909 Teddy Bear*

Mohair, weiss, gegliedert, Brummstimme, limit. Auflage 2.000 Stueck fuer FAO Schwarz - *mohair, white, jointed, growler, ltd edition of 2000 for FAO Schwarz, USA*

Serie	Art.-No	Period	Pr.	Info
	0163/34	1988-1988	5-6	34 cm

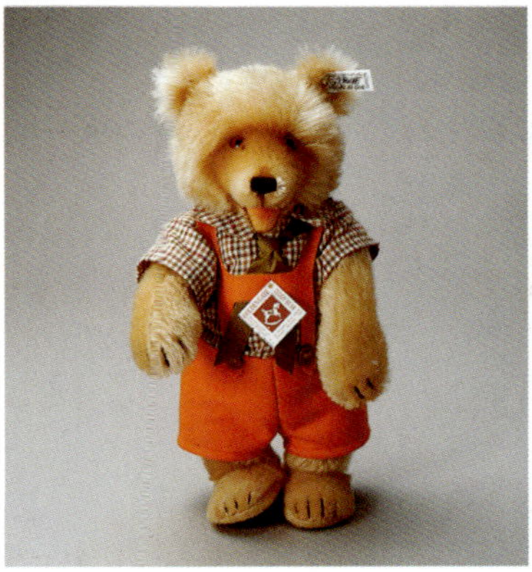

Golden Gate Baer - *Golden Gate Bear*

Mohair, mais, gegliedert, limit. Auflage 2.000 Stueck fuer FAO Schwarz - *mohair, corn yellow, jointed, ltd edition of 2,000 for FAO Schwarz, USA*

Serie	Art.-No	Period	Pr.	Info
	0285/29	1989-1989	5	29 cm

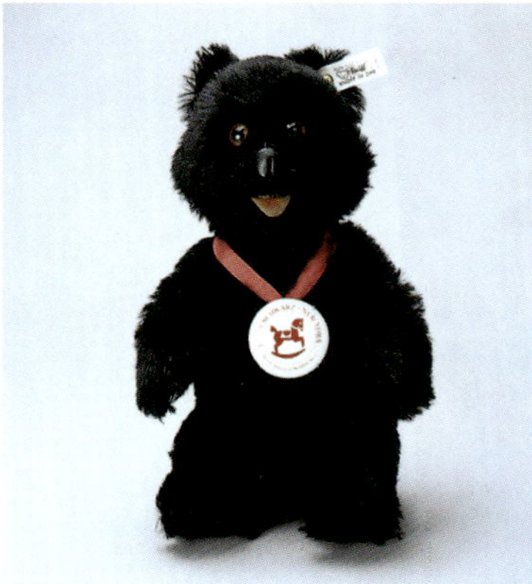

Schwarzbaer Baby - *Mohair Soft Black Bear*

Mohair, schwarz, sehr weich, 1. Ausgabe fuer North American Wildlife Series, FAO Schwarz, limit. Auflage 2.000 Stueck - *mohair, black, very soft, 1st issue for the North American Wildlife Series, FAO Schwarz, USA, ltd edition of 2,000*

Serie	Art.-No	Period	Pr.	Info
652059	**1232/25**	1990-1990	4-5	25 cm

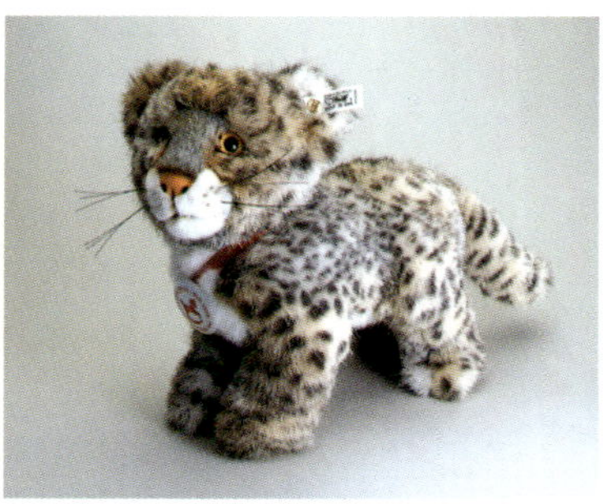

Schneeleopard Baby - *Snow Leopard Cub*

Acryl-Webpelz, stehend, Endangered Wildlife Series, limit. Auflage 1.000 Stueck fuer FAO Schwarz - *acrylic fur, standing, Endangered Wildlife Series, ltd edition of 1,000 for FAO Schwarz, USA*

EAN-No.	Period	Pr.	Info
652066	1991-1991	4	25 cm

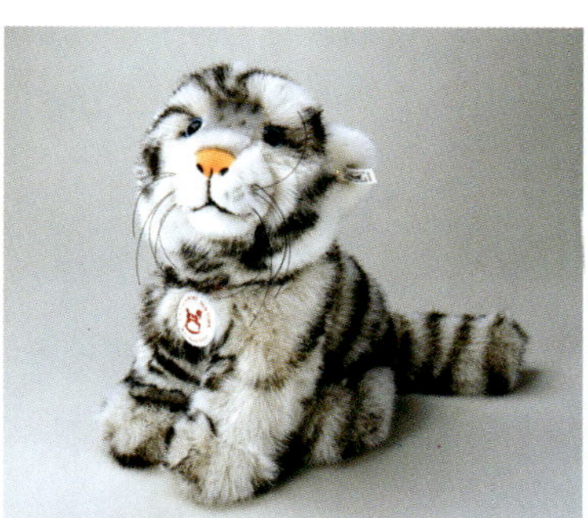

Weisser Jungtiger - *White Tiger Cub*

Webpelz, grau/weiss, sitzend, Rare Breed Series, limit. Auflage 2.000 Stueck fuer FAO Schwarz - *woven fur, grey/white, sitting, Rare Breed Series, ltd edition of 2,000 for FAO Schwarz, USA*

EAN-No.	Period	Pr.	Info
652073	1992-1993	4	25 cm

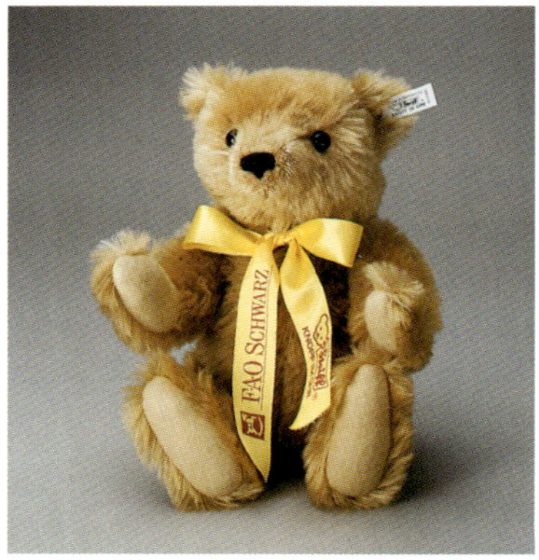

Musikteddy - *Musical Teddy*

Mohair, blond, gegliedert, mit Musikwerk "Welcome to our World of Toys", limit. Auflage 2.000 Stueck fuer FAO Schwarz - *mohair, blond, jointed, with music box "Welcome to our World of Toys", ltd edition of 2,000 for FAO Schwarz, USA*

EAN-No.	Period	Pr.	Info
652080	1993-1993	4-5	33 cm

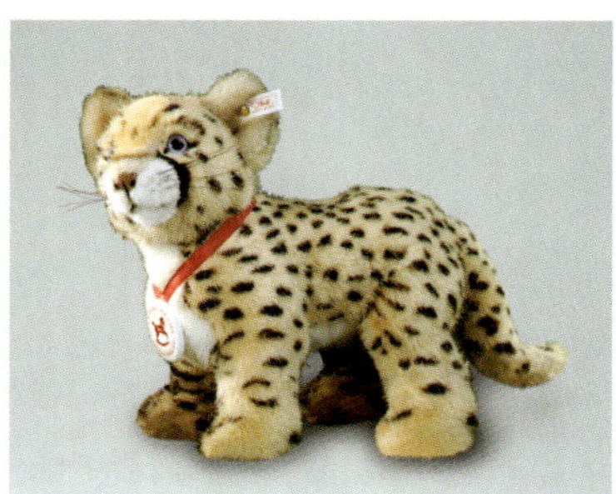

Florida Panther

Mohair, stehend, limit. Auflage 2.000 Stueck fuer FAO Schwarz, USA - *mohair, standing, ltd edition of 2,000 for FAO Schwarz, USA*

EAN-No.	Period	Pr.	Info
652103	1994-1994	4	25 cm

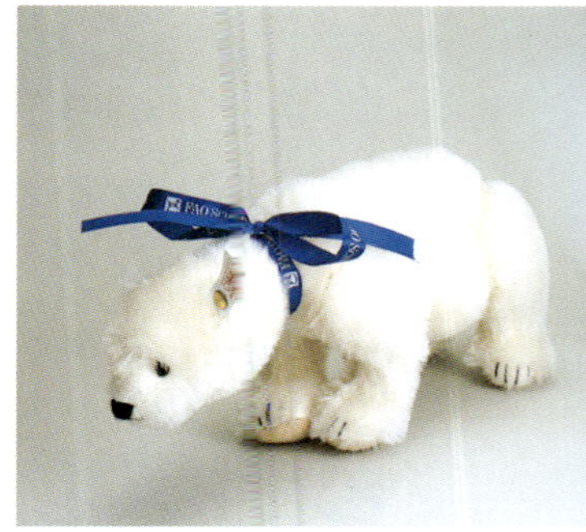

Polarbaer - *Polarbear*

Mohair, weiss, gegliedert, limit. Auflage 1.000 Stueck fuer FAO Schwarz, USA - *mohair, white, jointed, ltd edition of 1,000 for FAO Schwarz, USA*

EAN-No.	Period	Pr.	Info
652110	1995-1995	4	27 cm

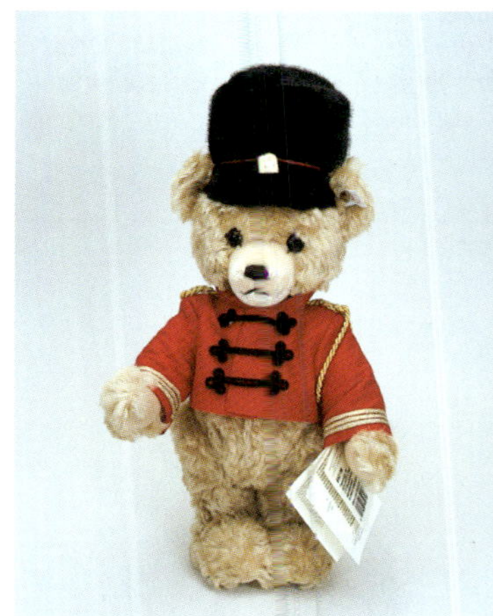

Toy Soldier Teddybaer - *Toy Soldier Teddybear*

Mohair Webpelz, blond, gegliedert, mit Musikwerk "Come to our World of Toy", limit. Auflage 2.000 Stueck fuer FAO Schwarz - *mohair woven fur, blond, jointed, with music box "Come to our World of Toy", ltd edition of 2,000 for FAO Schwarz, USA*

EAN-No.	Period	Pr.	Info
652158	1996-1996	4-5	35 cm

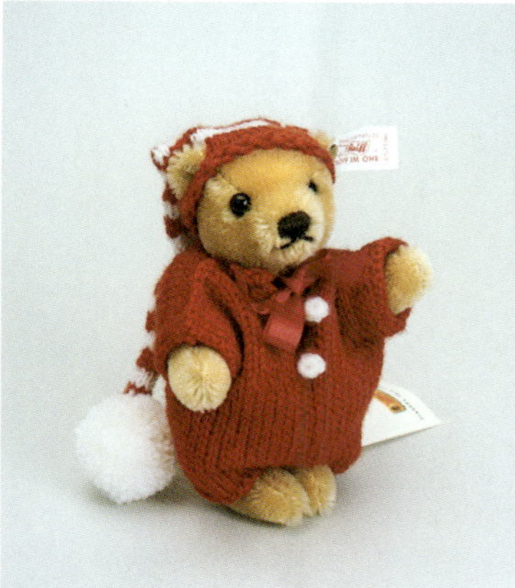

Original Teddybaer - *Original Teddybear*

Mohair, blond, gegliedert, als Christbaumschmuck, rote Strickbekleidung, limit. Auflage 2.000 Stueck fuer FAO Schwarz, USA - *mohair, blond, jointed, christmas tree ornament, dressed in red knitwear, ltd edition of 2,000 for FAO Schwarz, USA*

EAN-No.	Period	Pr.	Info
652196	1997-1997	4	13 cm

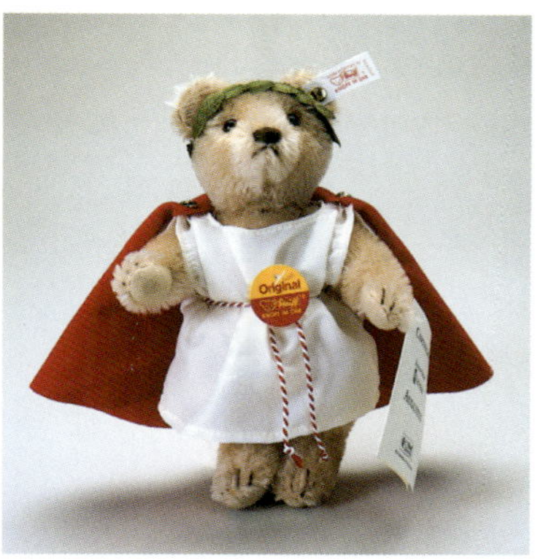

Roemer Baer Augustus - *Roman Bear Augustus*

Mohair, blond, gegliedert, mit rotem Umhang, zur Eroeffnung des FAO Schwarz Geschaeftes in Las Vegas, USA - *mohair, blond, jointed, red cape, to the occasion of opening a FAO Schwarz store in Las Vegas, USA*

EAN-No.	Period	Pr.	Info
652172	1997-1997	4	22 cm

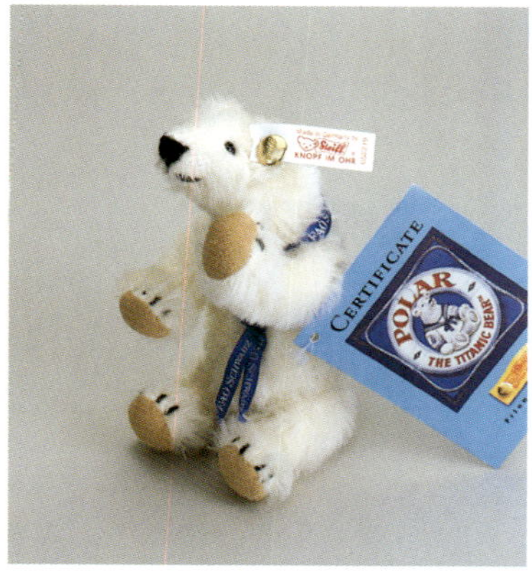

Polar der Titanic Baer - *Polar the Titanic Bear*

Mohair, weiss, gegliedert, Replik des Polarbaeren von 1909, aus der Geschichte des kleinen Jungen, der den Untergang der Titanic zusammen mit seinem Steiff Polarbaeren ueberlebte, limit. Auflage 2.000 Stueck fuer FAO Schwarz - *mohair, white, jointed, replica of the 1909 polar bear, from the story of the little boy, who survived, together with his Steiff ice bear, the disaster of the Titanic, ltd edition of 2,000 for FAO Schwarz, USA*

EAN-No.	Period	Pr.	Info
652219	1998-1998	4	12 cm

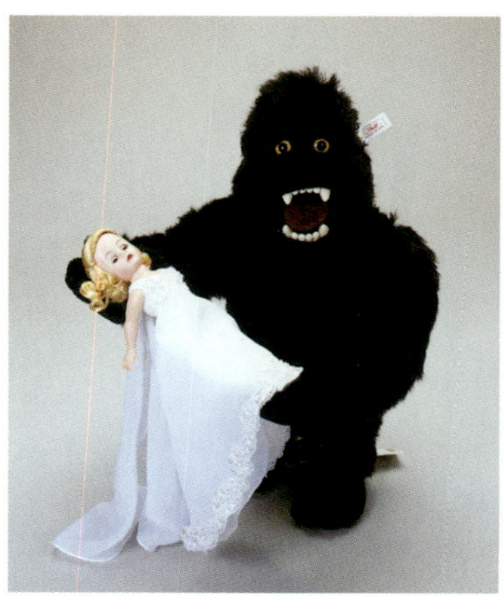

King Kong

Mohair, dunkelbraun, gegliedert, mit Madame Alexander Puppe Fay Wray, limit. Auflage 500 Stueck fuer FAO Schwarz, USA - *mohair, dark brown, jointed, together with Madame Alexander doll Fay Wray, ltd edition of 500 for FAO Schwarz, USA*

EAN-No.	Period	Pr.	Info
200493	1998-1999	5	48 cm

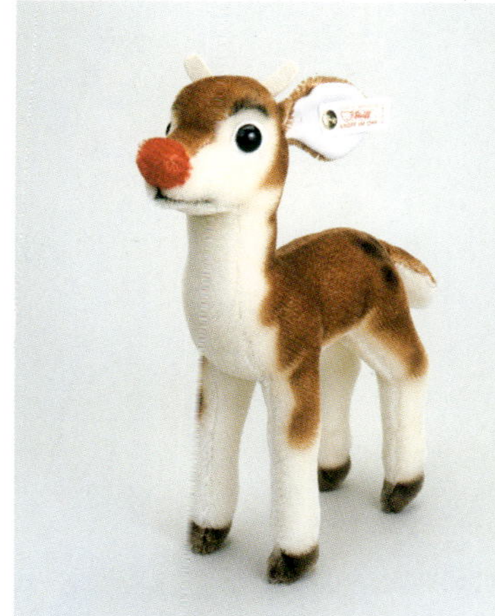

Rudolph Red-Nosed Reinder - *Rudolph Red-Nosed Reindeer*

Mohair, braun/weiss, stehend, Rudolph, das Rentier mit der roten Nase, Lizenzartikel, limit. Auflage 2.000 Stueck fuer FAO Schwarz, USA - *mohair, brown/white, standing, Rudolph, the reindeer with the red nose, licensed article, ltd edition of 2,000 for FAO Schwarz, USA*

EAN-No.	Period	Pr.	Info
652141	1998-1998	4	18 cm

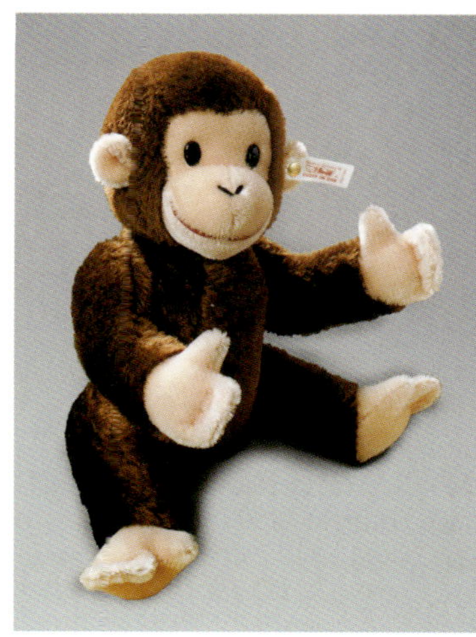

Curious George

Schimpanse, Mohair, braun, gegliedert, limit. Auflage 2.000 Stueck fuer FAO Schwarz, USA - *chimpanzee, mohair, brown, jointed, ltd edition of 2,000 for FAO Schwarz, USA*

EAN-No.	Period	Pr.	Info
652165	1998-1999	4	33 cm

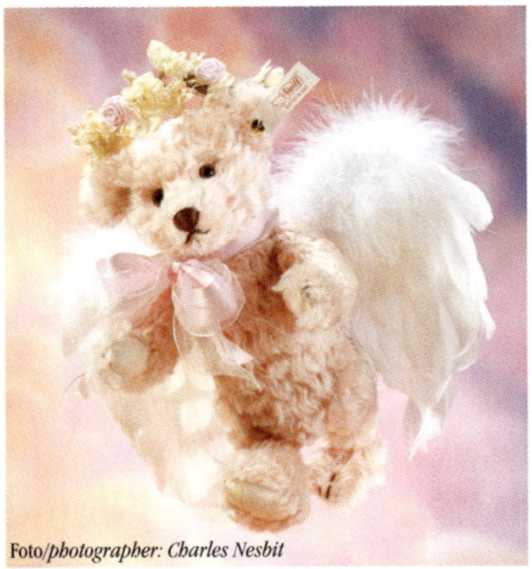

Foto/*photographer: Charles Nesbit*

Engel Baer - *Angel Bear*

Mohair, rosa, gegliedert, mit Fluegeln aus Federn, limit. Auflage 2.000 Stueck fuer FAO Schwarz, USA - *mohair, pink, jointed, with wings of feathers, ltd edition of 2,000 for FAO Schwarz, USA*

EAN-No.	Period	Pr.	Info
	1999-1999	5	25 cm

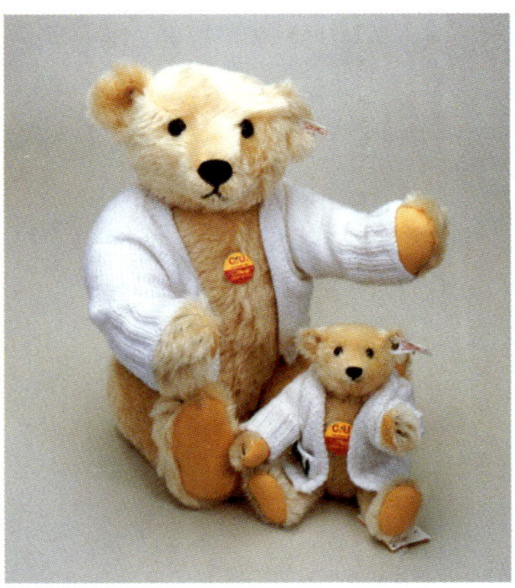

C. U. Teddy Baer - ***C. U.** Teddy Bear*

Mohair, blond, gegliedert, limit. Auflage 26 cm 650 & 52 cm 165 Stueck fuer "Collectors United Gathering 1995", USA - *mohair, blond, jointed, ltd edition of 650 in 26 cm & 165 in 52 cm for the "Collectors United Gathering 1995", USA*

EAN-No.	Period	Pr.	Info
405259	1995-1995	4-5	26 cm
405279	1995-1995	5-6	52 cm

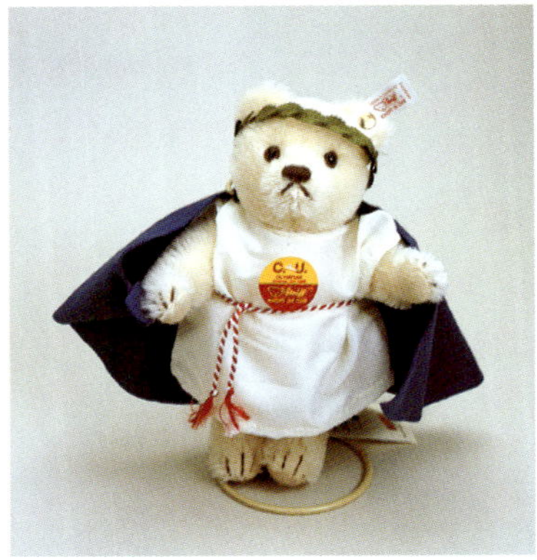

C. U. Olympian Teddy

Mohair, hellblond, gegliedert, limit. Auflage 26 cm 650 & 52 cm 165 Stueck fuer "Collectors United Gathering, Atlanta 1996", USA - *mohair, light blond, jointed, ltd edition of 650 in 26 cm & 165 in 52 cm for "Collectors United Gathering, Atlanta 1996", USA*

EAN-No.	Period	Pr.	Info
665073	1996-1996	4	26 cm
665080	1996-1996	5-6	52 cm

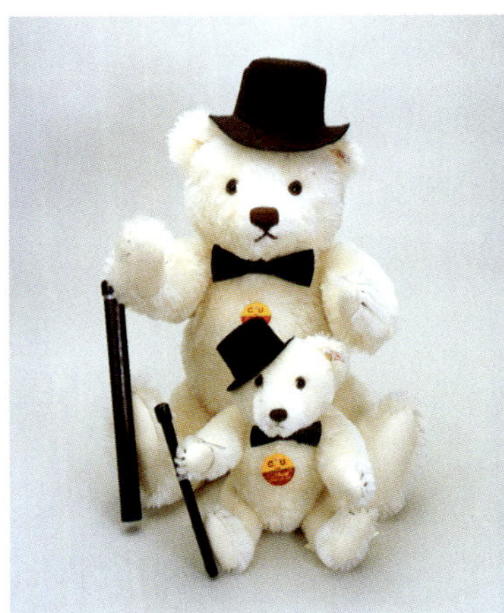

C. U. Teddybaer - ***C. U.** Teddybear*

Mohair, weiss, gegliedert, "Salut to Broadway", limit. Auflage 26 cm 650 & 52 cm 140 Stueck fuer "Collectors United Gathering 1997", USA - *mohair, white, jointed, "Salut to Broadway", ltd edition of 650 in 26 cm & 140 in 52 cm for "Collectors United Gathering 1997", USA*

EAN-No.	Period	Pr.	Info
665387	1997-1997	4-5	26 cm
665394	1997-1997	6	52 cm

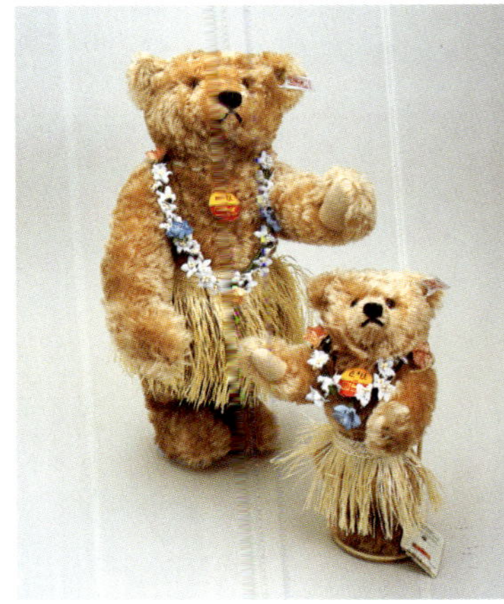

C. U. Teddybaer - ***C. U.** Teddybear*

Mohair, gold, gegliedert, "Hawaiian Girl", limit. Auflage 26 cm 550 & 42 cm 166 Stueck fuer "Collectors United Gathering 1998", USA - *mohair, gold, jointed, "Hawaiian Girl", ltd edition of 550 in 26 cm & 166 in 42 cm for "Collectors United Gathering 1998", USA*

EAN-No.	Period	Pr	Info
665646	1998-1998	4-5	26 cm
665653	1998-1998	6	42 cm

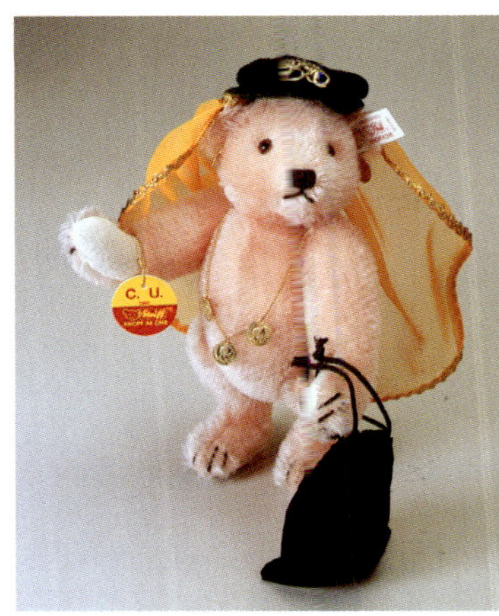

C. U. Teddybaer - ***C. U.** Teddybear*

Mohair, rosé, gegliedert, limit. Auflage 400 Stueck fuer Collectors United Gathering 1999, USA - *mohair, rose, jointed, ltd edition of 400 for Collectors United Gathering 1999, USA*

EAN-No.	Period	Pr.	Info
665202	1999-1999	4	22 cm

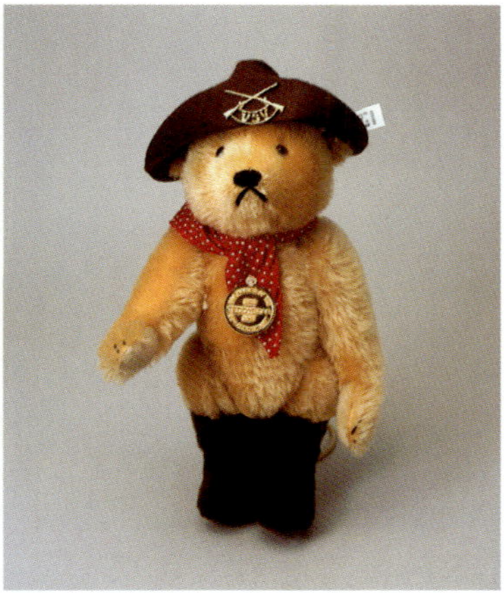

Teddybaer - *Teddybear*

Mohair, blond, gegliedert, Rough Rider, mit Hut & Stiefeln, limit. Auflage 1.906 Stueck fuer QVC, USA - *mohair, blond, jointed, Rough Rider, with hat & boots, ltd edition of 1,906 for QVC, USA*

EAN-No.	Period	Pr.	Info
665028	1996-1996	4	28 cm

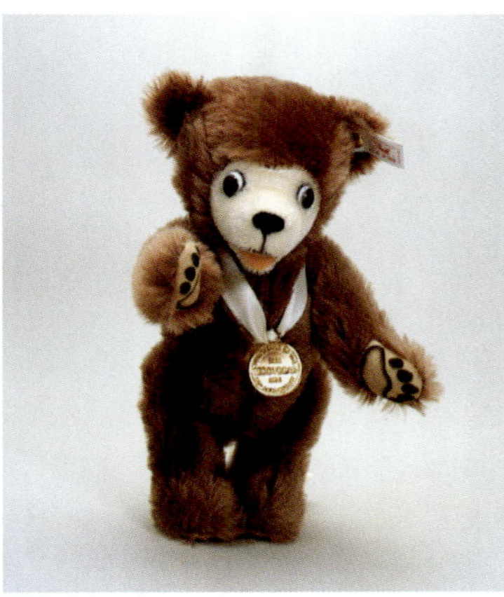

Clifford Berryman Baer - *Clifford Berryman Bear*

Mohair, dunkelbraun, gegliedert, Gesichtsmaske in hellem Kurzmohair, limit. Auflage 7.000 Stueck fuer QVC, USA - *mohair, dark brown, jointed, face in light short-mohair, ltd edition of 7,000 for QVC, USA*

EAN-No.	Period	Pr.	Info
665097	1997-1997	4-5	28 cm

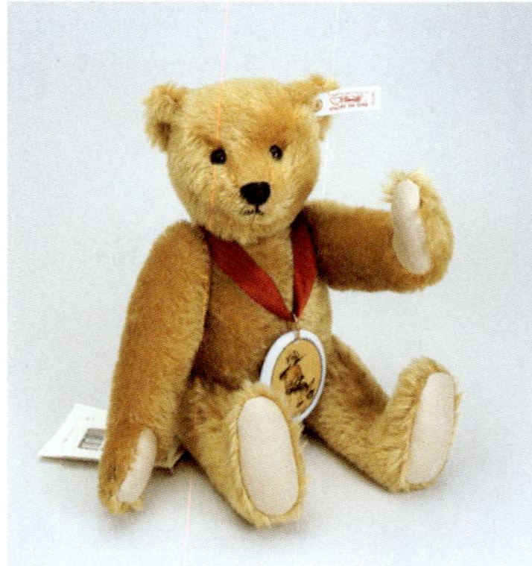

Teddybaer - *Teddybear*

Mohair, blond, gegliedert, mit Porzellanplakette, limit. Auflage 7.500 Stueck fuer QVC, USA - *mohair, blond, jointed, with porcelain medaillon, ltd edition of 7,500 for QVC, USA*

EAN-No.	Period	Pr.	Info
665363	1997-1997	4-5	24 cm

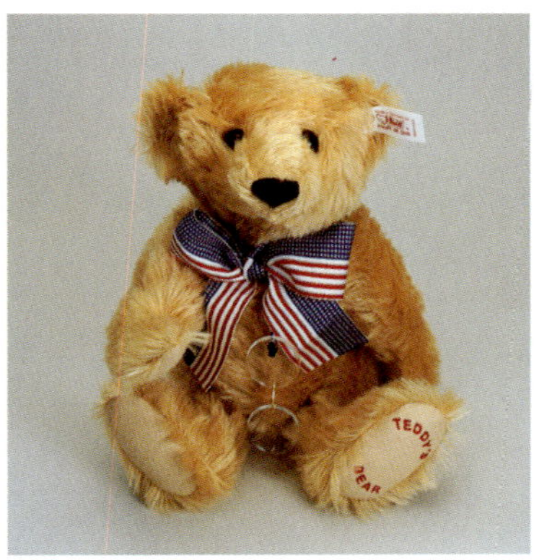

Teddy´s Baer - *Teddy´s Bear*

Mohair, blond, gegliedert, zum 140. Geburtstag von Theodor Roosevelt, mit Buch Teddy Bear Man, limit. Auflage 7.500 Stueck fuer QVC, USA - *mohair, blond, jointed, to celebrate the 140th birthday of Theodor Roosevelt, with book "Teddy Bear Man", ltd edition of 7,500 for QVC, USA*

EAN-No.	Period	Pr.	Info
665462	1998-1998	4	30 cm

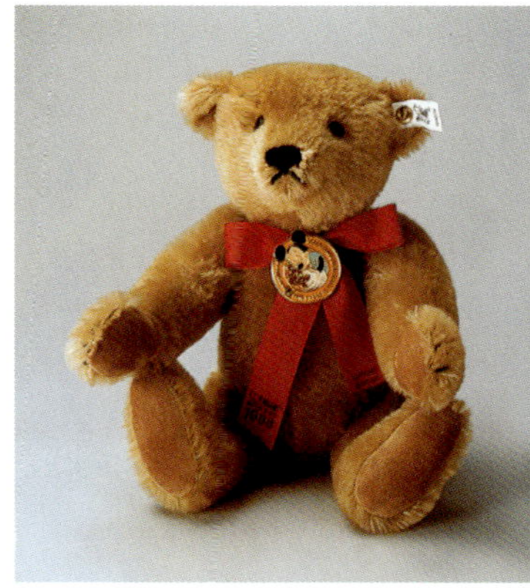

Antik Teddy - *Antique Teddy*

Mohair, dunkelblond, gegliedert, limit. Auflage 1.000 Stueck fuer 1. Teddy Bear & Doll Convention, Walt Disney World - *mohair, dark blond, jointed, ltd edition of 1,000 for Walt Disney World*

Serie	Art.-No	Period	Pr.	Info
	0243/32	1988-1988	6	32 cm

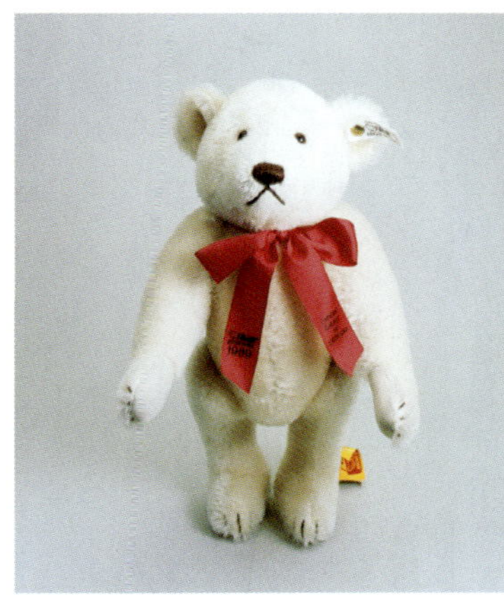

Petsy Baer - *Petsy Bear*

Mohair, weiss, gegliedert, limit. Auflage 1.000 Stueck fuer 2. Teddy Bear & Doll Convention, Walt Disney World - *mohair, white, jointed, ltd edition of 1,000 for Walt Disney World*

Serie	Art.-No	Period	Pr.	Info
011443	**0244/35**	1989-1989	6	35 cm

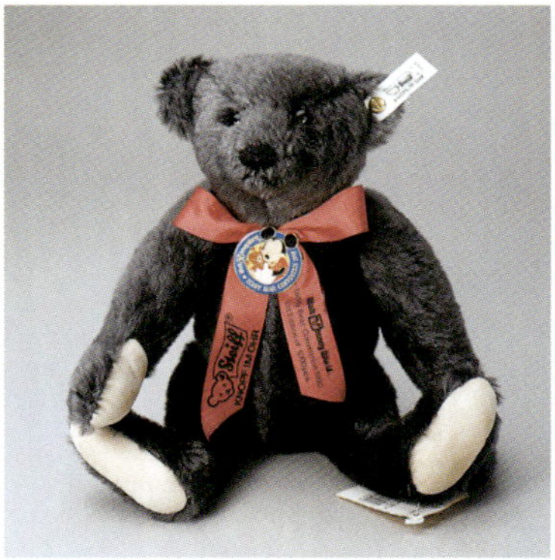

Antik Teddy - *Antique Teddy*

Mohair, anthrazit, gegliedert, limit. Auflage 1.000 Stueck fuer 3. Teddy Bear & Doll Convention, Walt Disney World - *mohair, anthracite, jointed, ltd edition of 1,000 for Walt Disney World*

SERIE	ART.-NO	PERIOD	FR.	INFO
011429	**0245/32**	1990-1990	5-6	32 cm

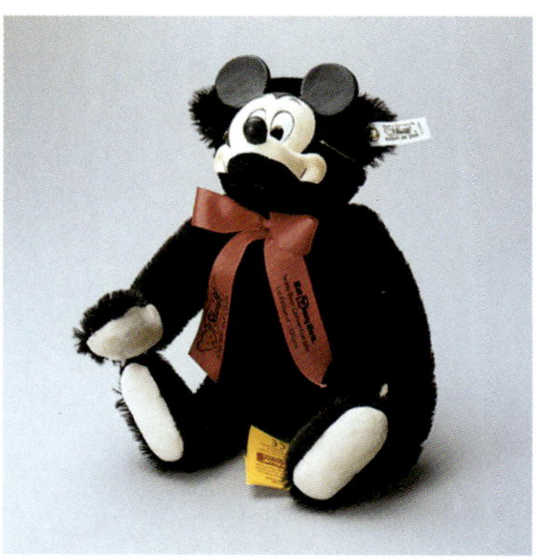

Antik Teddy - *Antique Teddy*

Mohair, schwarz, Mickey Mouse Maske, gegliedert, limit. Auflage 1.500 Stueck fuer 4. Teddy Bear & Doll Convention, Walt Disney World - *mohair, black, with Mickey Mouse mask, jointed, ltd edition of 1,500 for Walt Disney World*

EAN-NO.	PERIOD	PR.	INFO
011269	1991-1991	6	32 cm

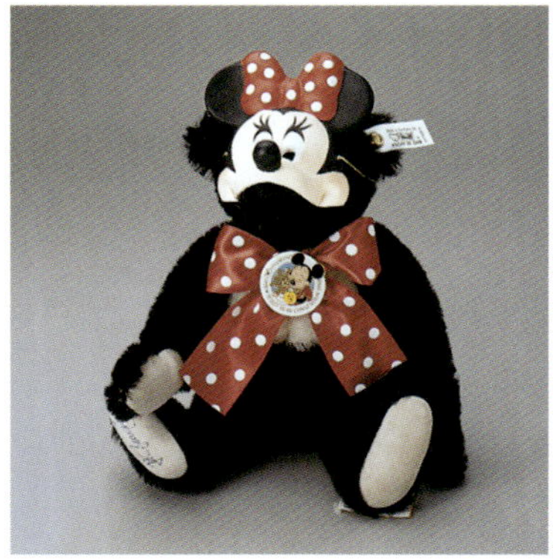

Antik Teddy - *Antique Teddy*

Mohair, schwarz/weiss, Minnie Mouse Maske, gegliedert, limit. Auflage 1.500 Stueck fuer 5. Teddy Bear & Doll Convention, Walt Disney World - *mohair, black/white, with Minnie Mouse mask, jointed, ltd edition of 1,500 for Walt Disney World*

EAN-NO.	PERIOD	PR.	INFO
011863	1992-1992	6	30 cm

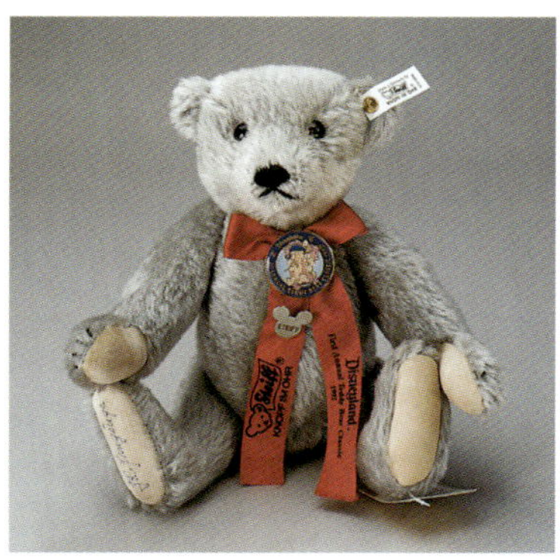

Antik Teddy - *Antique Teddy*

Mohair, grau, gegliedert, limit. Auflage 2.000 Stueck fuer 1. Teddy Bear Classic 1992, Disneyland California - *mohair, grey, jointed, ltd edition of 2,000 for the 1st Annual Teddy Bear Classic 1992, Disneyland, California*

EAN-NO.	PERIOD	PR.	INFO
011986	1992-1992	5	32 cm

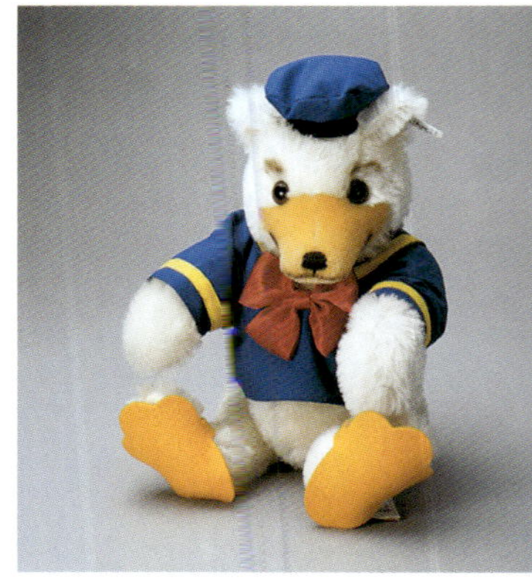

Teddy Donald

Mohair, weiss, gegliedert, limit. Auflage 1.500 Stueck fuer 6. Teddy Bear & Doll Convention, Walt Disney World - *mohair, white, jointed, ltd edition of 1,500 for Walt Disney World*

EAN-NO.	PERIOD	FR.	INFO
651205	1993-1993	5-6	30 cm

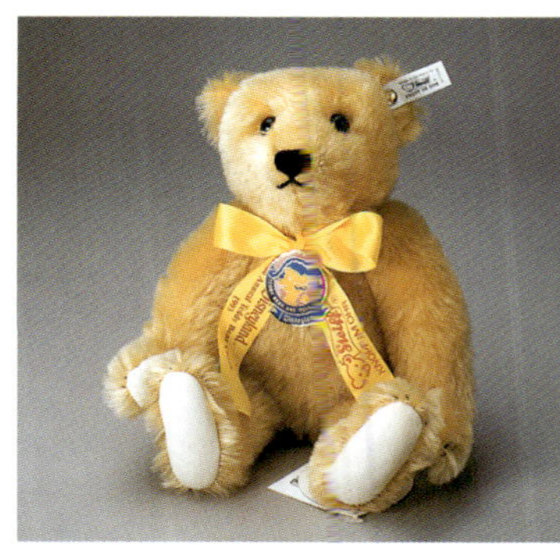

Teddybaer - *Teddy Bear*

Mohair, blond, gegliedert, limit. Auflage 1.500 Stueck fuer 2. Teddy Bear Classic, Disneyland California - *mohair, blond, jointed, ltd edition of 1,500 for the 2nd Annual Teddy Bear Classic 1993, Disneyland, California*

EAN-NO.	PERIOD	PR.	INFO
651526	1993-1993	5	30 cm

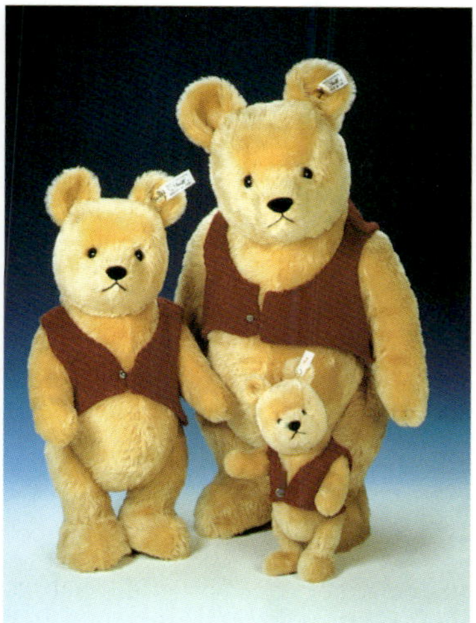

Winnie the Pooh

Mohair, blond, gegliedert, limit. Auflage 2.500 Stueck (60 cm 25 & 80 cm 2 Stueck) fuer 7. Teddy Bear & Doll Convention, Walt Disney World - *mohair, blond, jointed, ltd edition of 2,500 (60 cm - 25 & 80 cm - 2) for Walt Disney World*

EAN-No.	Period	Pr.	Info
651243	1994-1994	6	30 cm

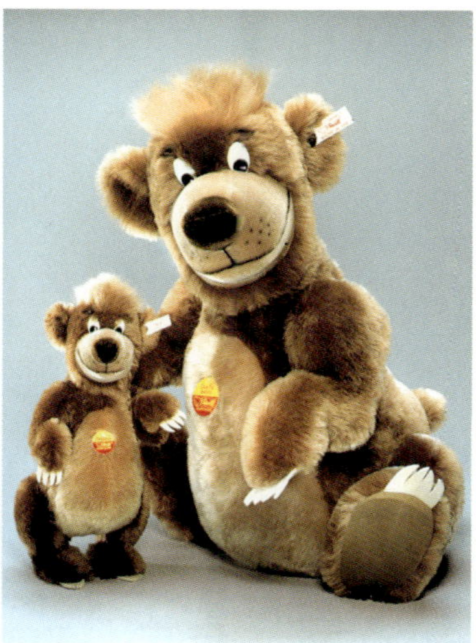

Baloo

Mohair, hellbraun, gegliedert, limit. Auflage 2.500 Stueck (60 cm - 25 & 80 cm - 5 Stueck) fuer 8. Teddy Bear & Doll Convention, Walt Disney World - *mohair, light brown, jointed, ltd edition of 2,500 (60 cm - 25 & 80 cm - 5) for Walt Disney World*

EAN-No.	Period	Pr.	Info
651274	1995-1995	5-6	35 cm
	1995-1995	7	60 cm
	1995-1995	7	80 cm

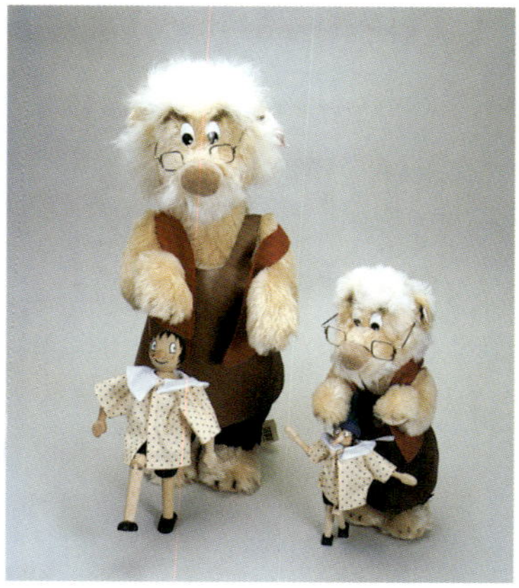

Gepetto & Pinocchio

Mohair, hellbraun, gegliedert, mit Pinocchio als Holzpuppe, limit. Auflage 1.500 Stueck (60 cm - 25 & 80 cm - 5 Stueck) fuer 9. Teddy Bear Convention, Walt Disney World - *mohair, light brown, jointed, with wooden puppet Pinocchio, ltd edition of 1,500 (60 cm - 25 & 80 cm - 5) for Walt Disney World*

EAN-No.	Period	Pr.	Info
651311	1996-1996	5-6	35 cm
	1996-1996	7	60 cm
	1996-1996	7	80 cm

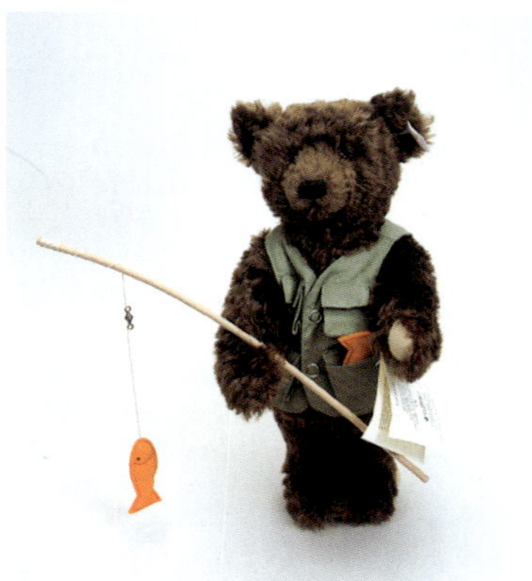

Fischerbaer - *Fisher Bear*

Mohair, dunkelbraun, gegliedert, limit. Auflage 1.500 Stueck fuer 9. Teddy Bear Convention, Walt Disney World - *mohair, dark brown, jointed, ltd edition of 1,500 for Walt Disney World*

EAN-No.	Period	Pr.	Info
651342	1996-1996	4-5	32 cm

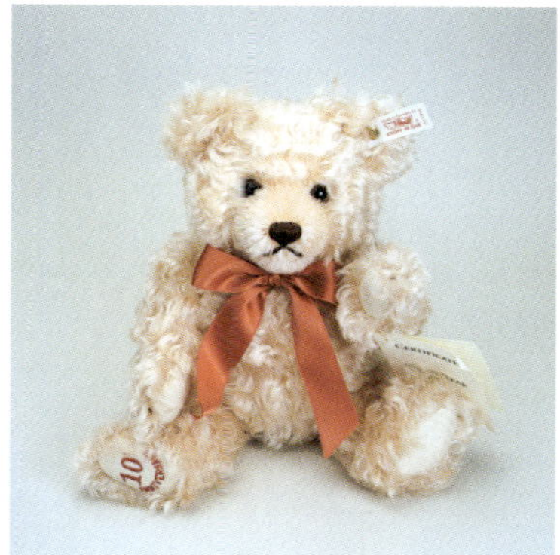

Teddybaer - *Teddybear*

Mohair, pfirsichfarben, gegliedert, limit. Auflage 2.000 Stueck (60 cm - 25 & 80 cm - 5 Stueck) fuer 10. Teddy Bear Convention, Walt Disney World - *mohair, peach-colour, jointed, ltd edition of 2,000 (60 cm - 25 & 80 cm - 5) for Walt Disney World*

EAN-No.	Period	Pr.	Info
651359	1997-1997	5	28 cm
651366	1997-1997	7	60 cm
651373	1997-1997	7	80 cm

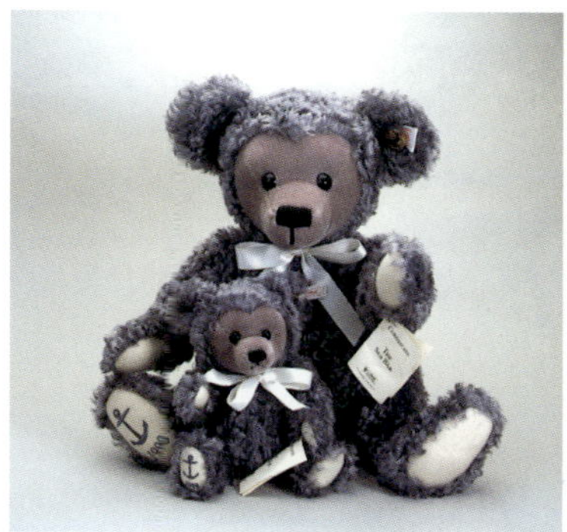

Teddybaer See Baer - *Teddybear Sea Bear*

Mohair, graublau, gegliedert, limit. Auflage 2.000 Stueck (60 cm - 25 & 80 cm - 5 Stueck) fuer 11. Teddy Bear Convention, Walt Disney World - *mohair, grey-blue, jointed, ltd edition of 2,000 (60 cm - 25 & 80 cm - 5) for Walt Disney World*

EAN-No.	Period	Pr.	Info
651380	1998-1998	5	28 cm
651397	1998-1998	7	60 cm
651403	1998-1998	7	80 cm

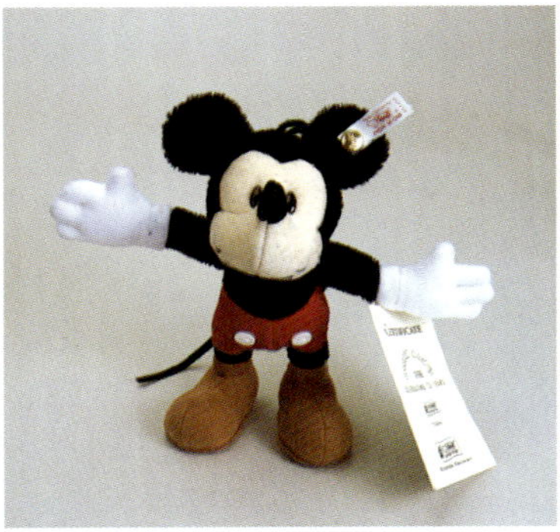

Mickey Mouse Ornament

Mohair/Trevirasamt, schwarz/weiss, stehend, zum 70. Geburtstag der Mickey Mouse, limit. Auflage 1.928 Stueck fuer Walt Disney Companies - *mohair/Trevira velvet, black/white, standing, to celebrate the 70th birthday of Mickey Mouse, ltd edition of 1,928 for Walt Disney Companies*

EAN-No.	Period	Pr.	Info
651410	1998-1998	4	14 cm

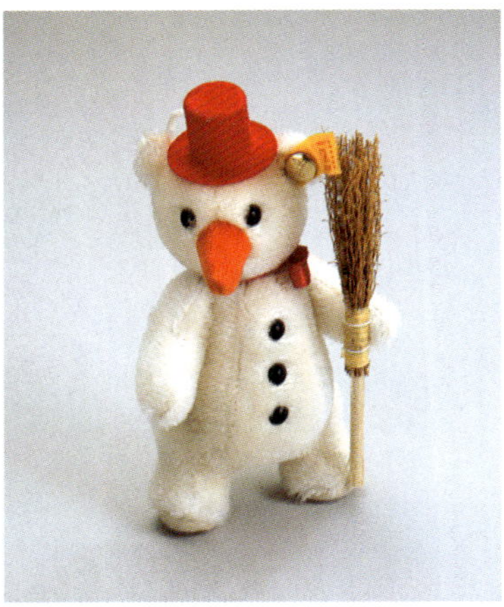

Schneemann - *Snowman*

Mohair, weiss, stehend, Kopf & Arme gegliedert, als Christbaumschmuck, mit rotem Zylinder & Reiserbesen, Zertifikat & Button, anlaesslich der 1. Christmas Collectibles Convention, Walt Disney World - *mohair, white, standing, head & arms jointed, christmas tree ornament, with red top hat & broom, certificat & button, for 1st Christmas Collectibles Convention, Walt Disney World*

EAN-No.	Period	Pr.	Info
651427	1998-1998	4	12 cm

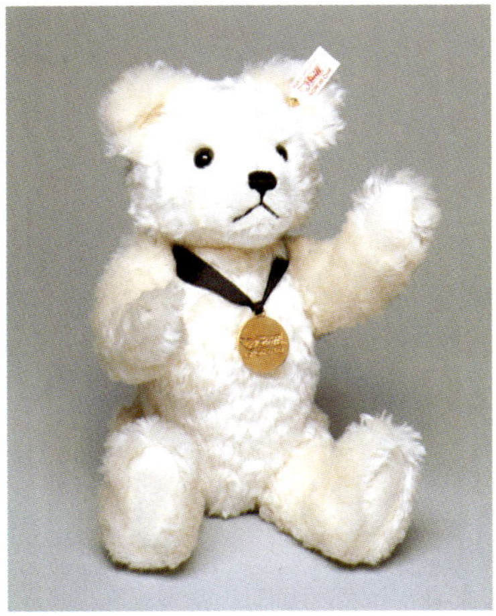

Teddybaer Dawn - *Teddybear Dawn*

Mohair, weiss, gegliedert, "Dawn of the New Millenium", limit. Auflage 1.500 Stueck (60 cm - 25 & 80 cm - 5 Stueck) fuer 12. Teddy Bear Convention, Walt Disney World - *mohair, white, jointed, "Dawn of the New Millenium", ltd edition of 1,500 (60 cm - 25 & 80 cm - 5) for Walt Disney World*

EAN-No.	Period	Pr.	Info
651434	1999-1999	5	32 cm
	1999-1999	6	60 cm
	1999-1999	6-7	80 cm

kein Bild vorhanden
no picture available

Minney Mouse Ornament

Mohair/Trevirasamt, schwarz/weiss, stehend, limit. Auflage 1.928 Stueck fuer Walt Disney Companies - *mohair/Trevira velvet, black/white, standing, ltd edition of 1,928 for Walt Disney Companies*

EAN-No.	Period	Pr.	Info
651649	1999-1999	3-4	15 cm

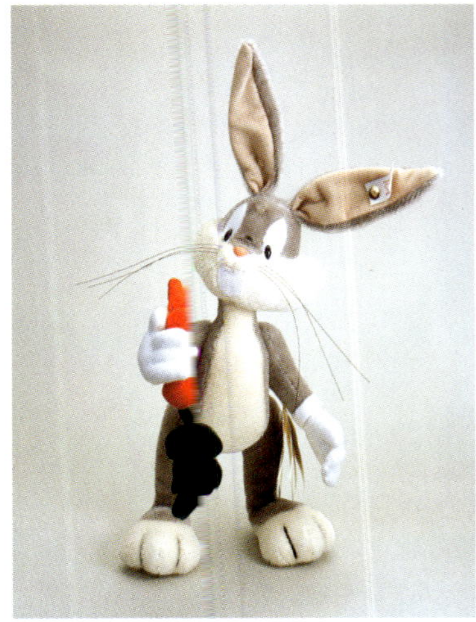

Bugs Bunny

Mohairpluesch/Trevirasamt, grau/weiss, gegliedert, Comicfigur aus Zeichentrickfilmen, limit. Auflage 2.500 Stueck fuer Warner Bros. - *mohair woven fur/trevira velvet, grey/white, jointed, cartoon character, ltd edition of 2,500 for Warner Bros.*

EAN-No.	Period	Pr.	Info
665789	1996-1996	5	32 cm

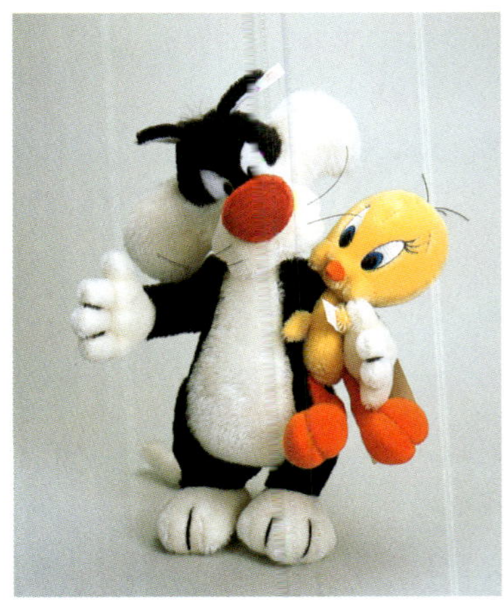

Sylvester & Tweety

Mohairpluesch, schwarz/weiss bzw. gelb, gegliedert, Comicfiguren aus Zeichentrickfilmen von Looney Tunes, limit. Auflage 2.500 Stueck fuer Warner Bros. - *mohair woven fur, black/white and yellow, jointed, cartoon characters from Looney Tunes, ltd edition of 2.500 for Warner Bros.*

EAN-No.	Period	Pr.	Info
665448	1998-1998	5-6	32/14 cm
	1998-1998	5	32 cm, Sylvester
	1998-1998	4-5	14 cm, Tweety

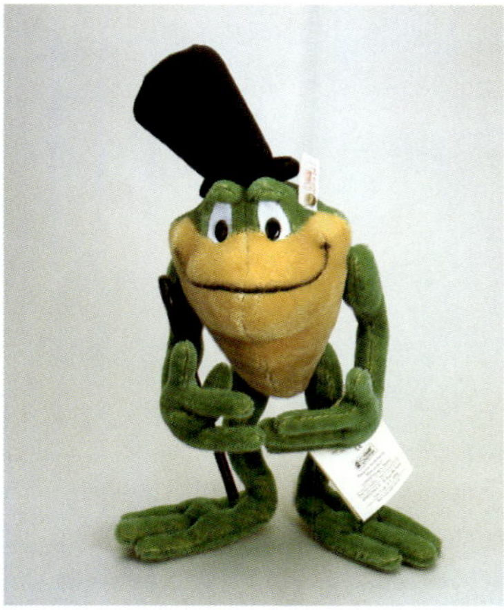

Michigan J. Frog

Mohairpluesch, gruen/gelb, gegliedert, Zeichentrickfilm-Figur, mit Zylinder & Stock, limit. Auflage 2.500 Stueck fuer Warner Bros. - *mohair woven fur, green/yellow, jointed, cartoon character, with top hat & stick, ltd edition of 2,500 for Warner Bros.*

EAN-No.	Period	Pr.	Info
665820	1999-1999	5	30 cm

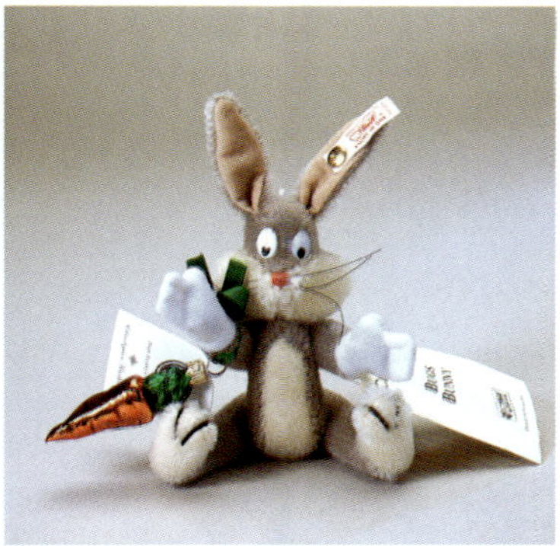

Bugs Bunny

Mohairpluesch, grau/weiss, gegliedert, Comicfigur aus Zeichentrickfilmen von Looney Tunes, mit Karotte aus Glas von Christopher Radko, limit. Auflage 2.500 Stueck fuer Warner Bros. - *mohair, grey/white, jointed, cartoon character from Looney Tunes, with a hand-blown carrot of glass from Christopher Radko, ltd edition of 2,500 for Warner Bros.*

EAN-No.	Period	Pr.	Info
665455	1999-1999	4	15 cm

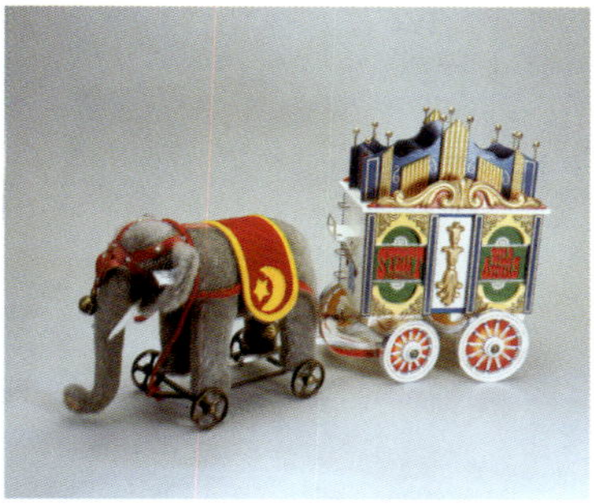

Elefant auf Raedern mit 1. Zirkuswagen - *Elephant on Wheels with Lead Circus Wagon*

1. Zirkuswagen, mit Elefant, Zirkuswagen Handarbeit, USA-Artikel, limit. Auflage 5.000 Stueck - *1st circus wagon, with elephant, the circus wagon is hand-made, article for the USA, ltd edition of 5,000*

Serie	Art.-No	Period	Pr.	Info
	0100/86	1986-1986	5-6	

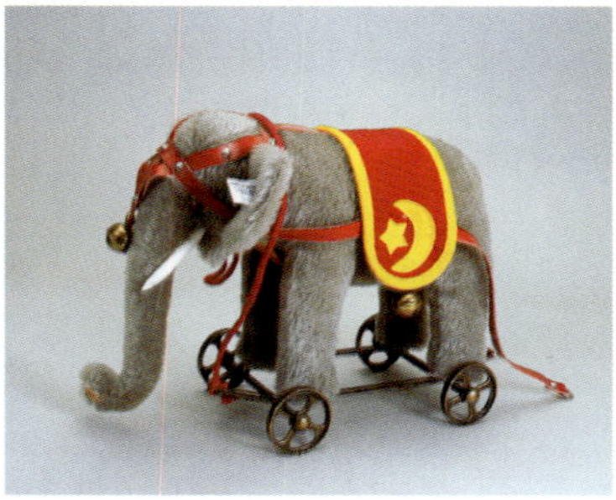

Elefant auf Raedern - *Elephant on Wheels*

Elefant aus 1. Zirkuswagen, Mohair, grau, stehend, auf Metallraedern - *elephant from the 1st circus wagon, mohair, grey, standing, on metal wheels*

Serie	Art.-No	Period	Pr.	Info
	0135/22	1986-1986	5	22 cm

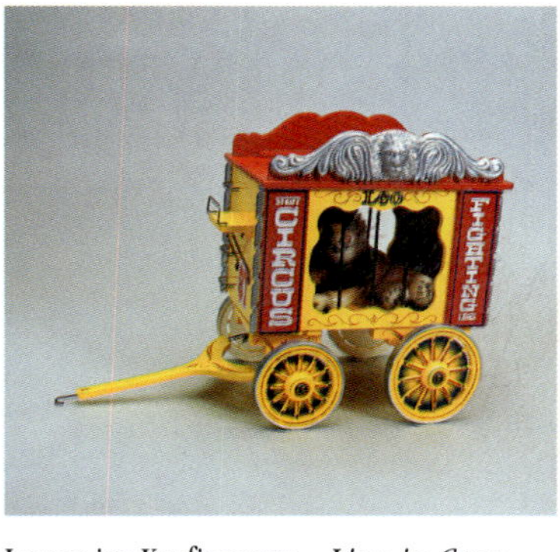

Loewe im Kaefigwagen - *Lion in Cage Wagon*

2. Zirkuswagen, mit Loewe, Zirkuswagen Handarbeit, USA-Artikel, limit. Auflage 5.000 Stueck - *2nd circus wagon, with lion, the circus wagon is hand-made, article for the USA, ltd edition of 5,000*

Serie	Art.-No	Period	Pr.	Info
	0100/87	1987-1987	5	

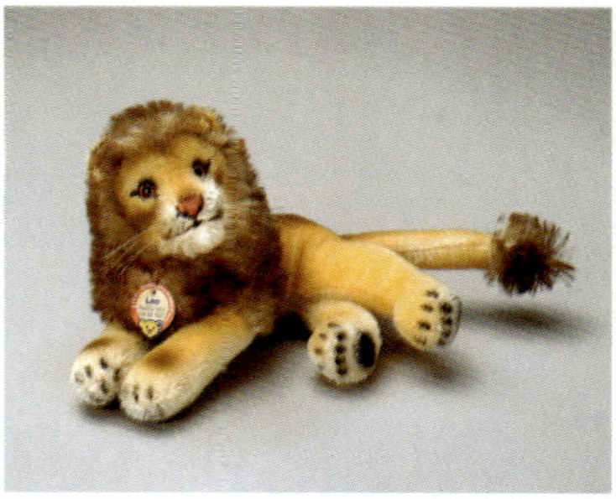

Loewe - *Lion*

Loewe aus 2. Zirkuswagen, Mohair, braun, liegend - *lion in the 2nd circus wagon, mohair, brown, lying*

Serie	Art.-No	Period	Pr.	Info
	0136/15	1987-1987	3-4	15 cm

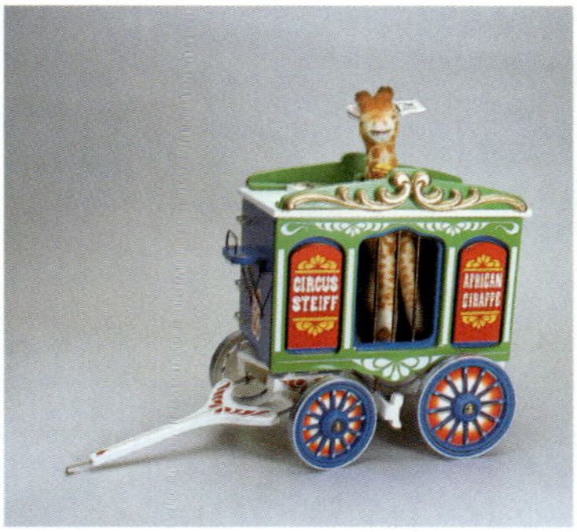

Zirkuswagen mit Giraffe - *Circus Wagon with Giraffe*

3. Zirkuswagen, mit Giraffe, Zirkuswagen Handarbeit, USA-Artikel, limit. Auflage 5.000 Stueck - *3rd circus wagon, with giraffe, circus wagon is hand-made, article for the USA, ltd edition of 5,000*

Serie	Art.-No	Period	Pr.	Info
	0100/88	1988-1988	5	

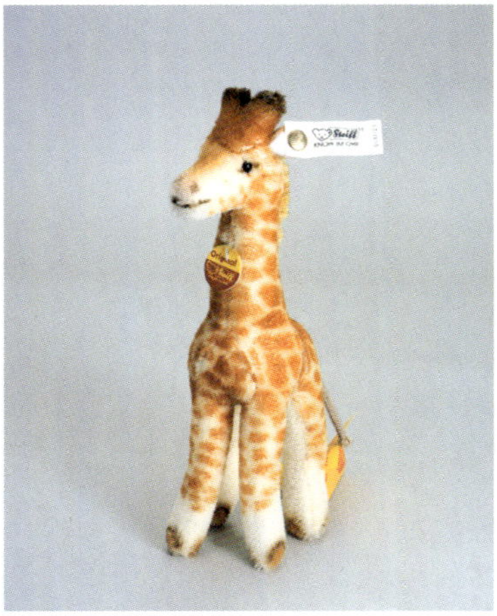

Giraffe

Giraffe aus 3. Zirkuswagen, Mohair, gelb, braun gefleckt, stehend - *giraffe in the 3rd circus wagon, mohair, yellow, brown spotted, standing*

SERIE	ART.-NO	PERIOD	PR.	INFO
	0137/28	1988-1988	3-4	28 cm

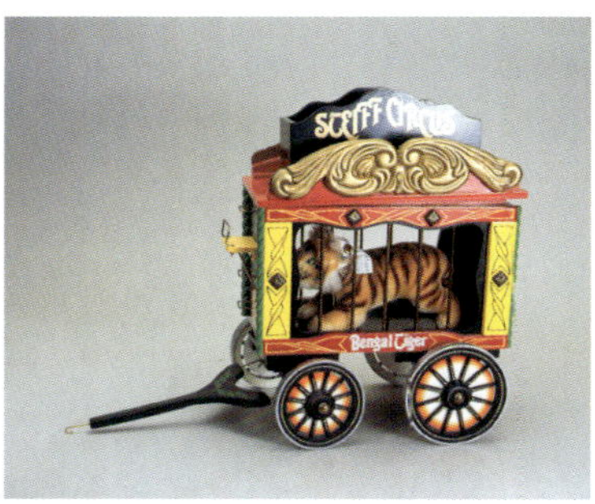

Zirkuswagen mit Tiger - *Circus Wagon with Tiger*

4. Zirkuswagen, mit Tiger, Zirkuswagen Handarbeit, USA-Artikel, limit. Auflage 5.000 Stueck - *4th circus wagon, with tiger, circus wagon is hand-made, article for the USA ltd edition of 5,000*

SERIE	ART.-NO	PERIOD	PR.	INFO
	0100/89	1989-1989	5	

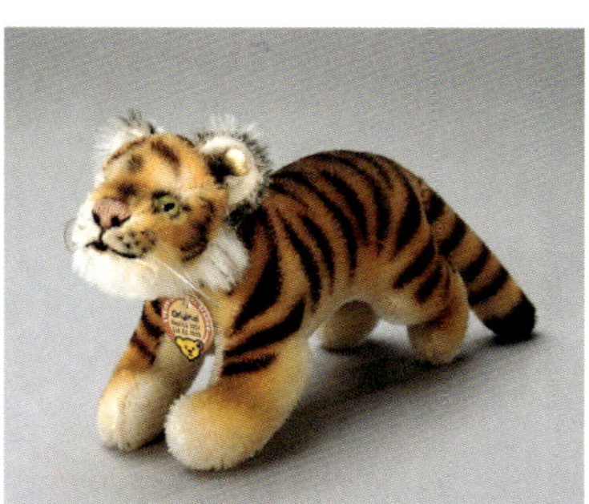

Tiger

Tiger aus 4. Zirkuswagen, Mohair, gelb, braun gestreift, stehend - *tiger in the 4th circus wagon, mohair, yellow, brown striped, standing*

SERIE	ART.-NO	PERIOD	PR.	INFO
	0138/10	1989-1989	3-4	10 cm

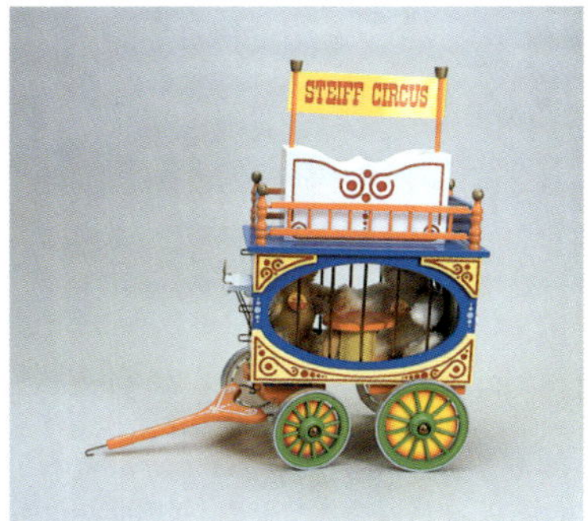

Zirkuswagen mit Baeren - *Circus Wagon with Bears*

5. Zirkuswagen, mit Dicky-Baeren, Zirkuswagen Handarbeit, USA-Artikel, limit. Auflage 5.000 Stueck - *5th circus wagon, with Dicky bears, circus wagon is hand-made, article for the USA, ltd edition of 5,000*

SERIE	ART.-NO	PERIOD	PR.	INFO
	0100/90	1990-1990	5	

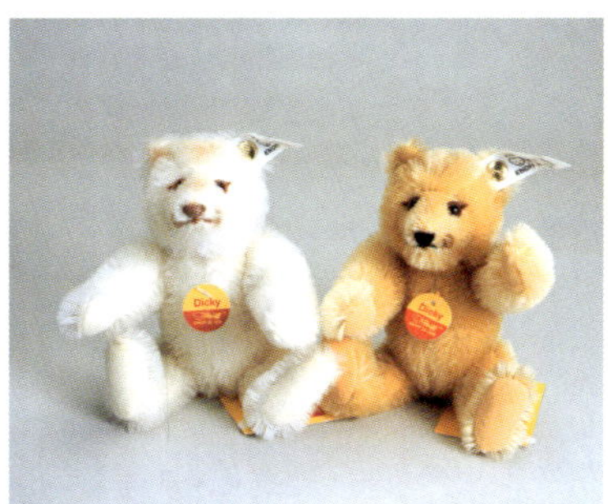

Dicky Baer - *Dicky Bear*

Dicky Baeren aus 5. Zirkuswagen, Mohair, weiss bzw. blond, gegliedert - *Dicky bears in the 5th circus wagon, mohair, white or blond, jointed*

SERIE	ART.-NO	PERIOD	PR.	INFO
650505	**0172/16**	1990-1990	4	16 cm
650512	**0172/17**	1990-1990	4	17 cm

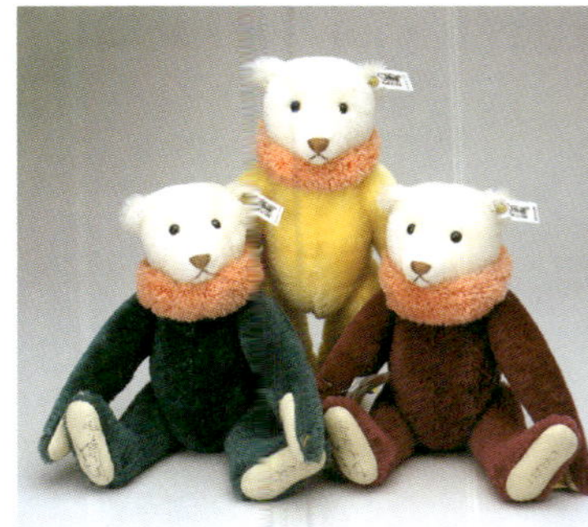

Circus Dolly Baer - *Circus Dolly Bear*

Replica 1913, USA-Artikel, Mohair, gegliedert, Brummstimme, gelb, gruen oder violett, die Farbe blassgelb enstand durch einen Produktionsfehler und wurde deshalb durch gelb ersetzt - *replica 1913, article for the USA, mohair, jointed, growler, yellow, green or violet, the color pale yellow results out of a production mistake and has been replaced with the correct yellow*

SERIE	ART.-NO	PERIOD	PR.	INFO
	0164/30	1987-1987	5	32 cm, blassgelb - *pale yellow*
	0164/31	1987-1989	4-5	gelb - *yellow*
	0164/32	1987-1989	4-5	gruen - *green*
	0164/34	1987-1989	4-5	violett - *violet*

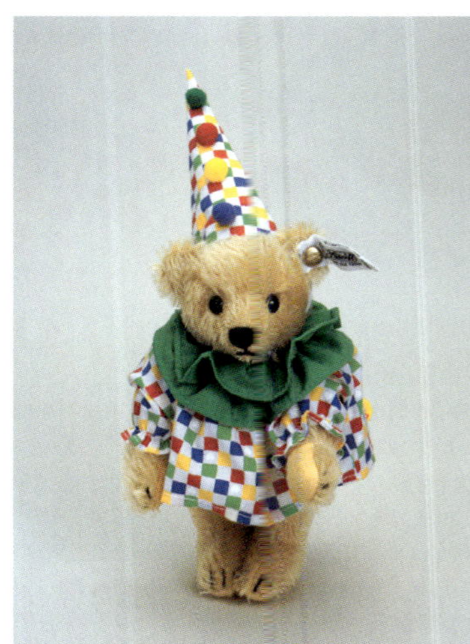

Teddy Clown Junior

Mohair, gegliedert, USA-Artikel, limit. Auflage 5.000 Stueck - *mohair, jointed, article for the USA, ltd edition of 5,000*

SERIE	ART.-NO	PERIOD	PR.	INFO
	0163/19	1987-1987	5	19 cm

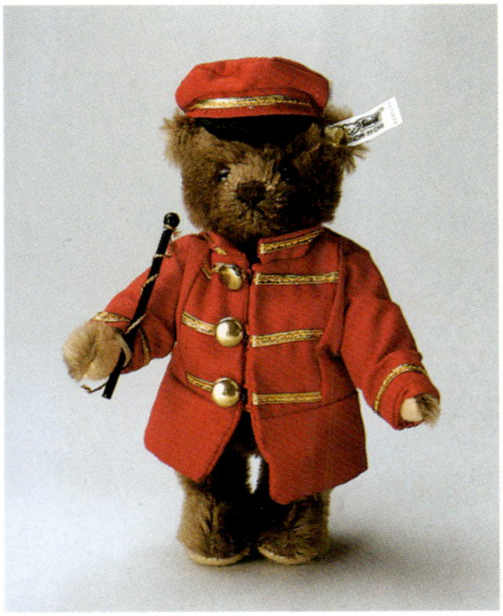

Baer mit Taktstock - *Bear Bandmaster with Baton*

Mohair, gegliedert, bekleidet mit Zirkus-Musiker-Uniform, USA-Artikel, limit. Auflage 5.000 Stueck - *mohair, jointed, fully dressed in circus musician uniform, article for the USA, ltd edition of 5,000*

SERIE	ART.-NO	PERIOD	PR.	INFO
	0120/19	1988-1989	5	19 cm

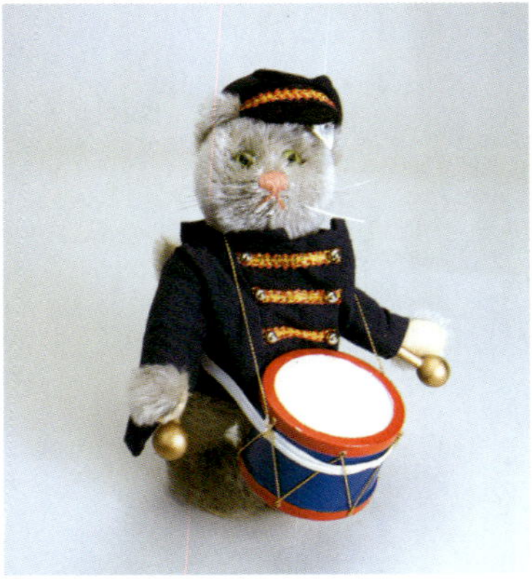

Katze mit Trommel - *Cat Bandsman with Drum*

Mohair, gegliedert, bekleidet mit Zirkus-Musiker-Uniform, USA-Artikel, limit. Auflage 5.000 Stueck - *mohair, jointed, fully dressed in circus musician uniform, article for the USA, ltd edition of 5,000*

SERIE	ART.-NO	PERIOD	PR.	INFO
	0122/19	1988-1989	4-5	19 cm

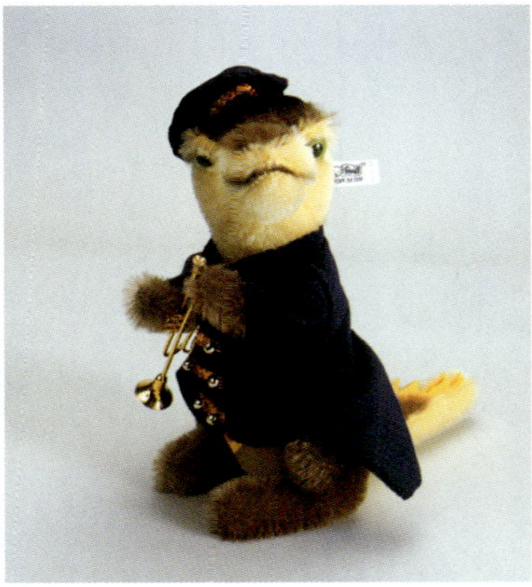

Krokodil mit Trompete - *Crocodile Bandsman with Trumpet*

Mohair, gegliedert, bekleidet mit Zirkus-Musiker-Uniform, USA-Artikel, limit. Auflage 5.000 Stueck - *mohair, jointed, fully dressed in circus musician uniform, article for the USA, ltd edition of 5,000*

SERIE	ART.-NO	PERIOD	PR.	INFO
	0124/19	1988-1989	4-5	19 cm

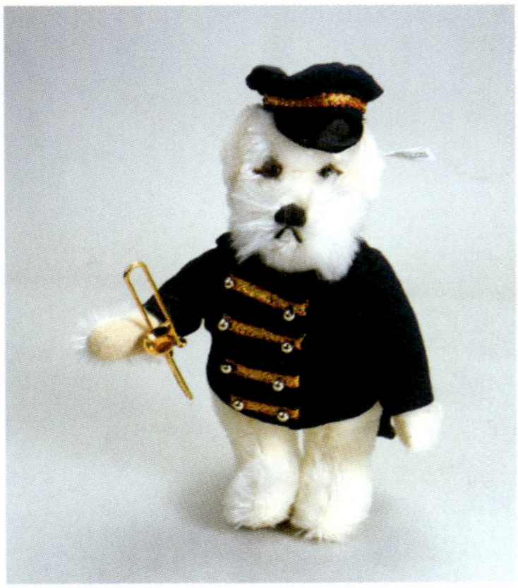

Hund mit Posaune - *Dog Bandsman with Trombone*

Mohair, gegliedert, bekleidet mit Zirkus-Musiker-Uniform, USA-Artikel, limit. Auflage 5.000 Stueck - *mohair, jointed, fully dressed in circus musician uniform, article for the USA, ltd edition of 5,000*

SERIE	ART.-NO	PERIOD	PR.	INFO
	0121/19	1988-1989	4-5	19 cm

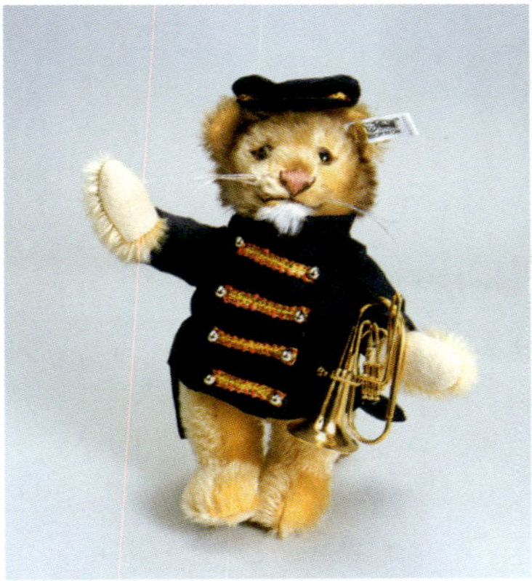

Loewe mit Tuba - *Lion Bandsman with Tuba*

Mohair, gegliedert, bekleidet mit Zirkus-Musiker-Uniform, USA-Artikel, limit. Auflage 5.000 Stueck - *mohair, jointed, fully dressed in circus musician uniform, article for the USA, ltd edition of 5,000*

SERIE	ART.-NO	PERIOD	PR.	INFO
	0123/19	1988-1989	4-5	19 cm

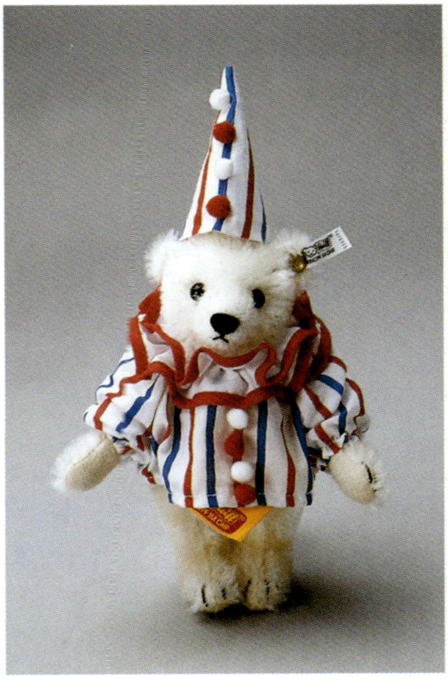

Teddy Clown

Mohair, gegliedert, USA-Artikel, limit. Auflage 5.000 Stueck - *mohair, jointed, article for the USA, ltd edition of 5,000*

SERIE	ART.-NO	PERIOD	PR.	INFO
	0163/20	1989-1989	5	19 cm

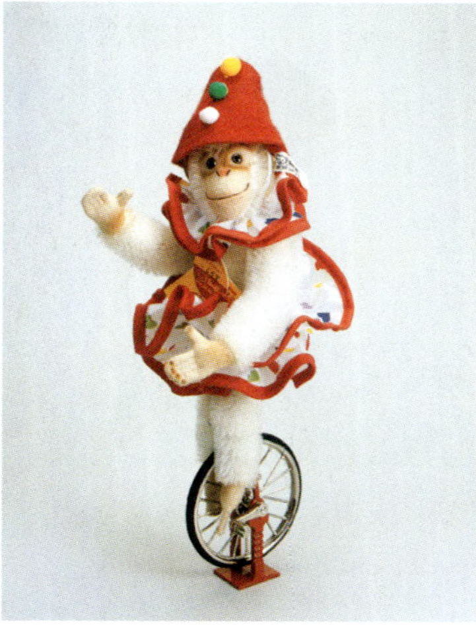

Schimpanse auf Einrad - *Chimp on Unicycle*

Mohair, gegliedert, USA-Artikel, limit. Auflage 5.000 Stueck - *mohair, jointed, article for the USA, ltd edition of 5,000*

SERIE	ART.-NO	PERIOD	PR.	INFO
	0143/19	1989-1989	4	19 cm

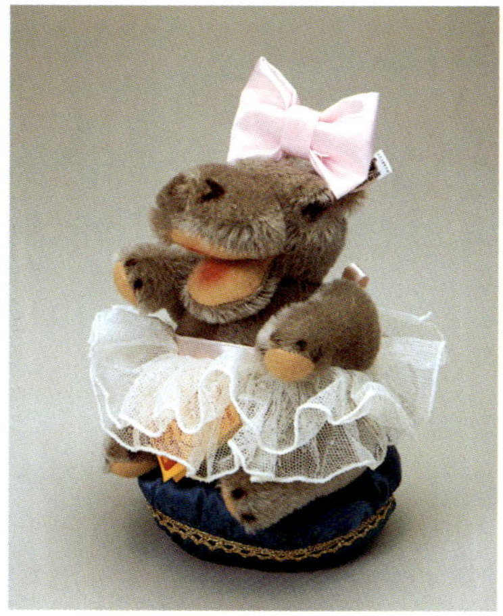

Flusspferd - *Hippo Fat Lady*

mit TuTu auf Kissen, Mohair, gegliedert, USA-Artikel, limit. Auflage 5.000 Stück - *wearing a TuTu & sitting on a cushion, mohair, jointed, article for the USA, ltd edition of 5,000*

SERIE	ART.-NO	PERIOD	PR.	INFO
	0146/19	1989-1990	4	19 cm

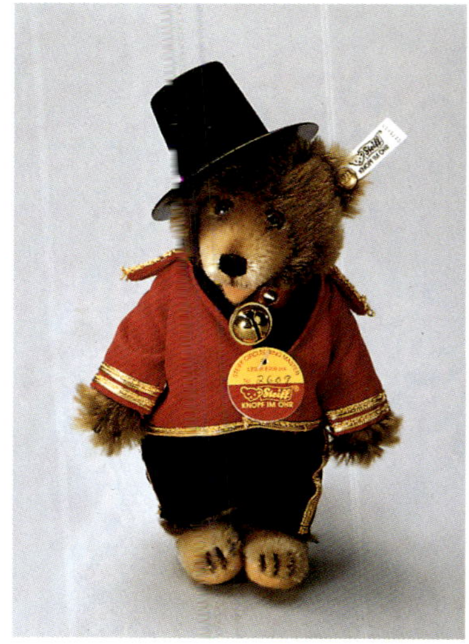

Teddy Baby - *Ringmaster Teddy Baby*

als Zirkusdirektor, Mohair, gegliedert, USA-Artikel, limit. Auflage 5.000 Stück - *Teddy Baby dressed as a circus director, mohair, jointed, article for the USA, ltd edition of 5,000*

SERIE	ART.-NO	PERIOD	PR.	INFO
	0175/19	1989-1990	4-5	19 cm

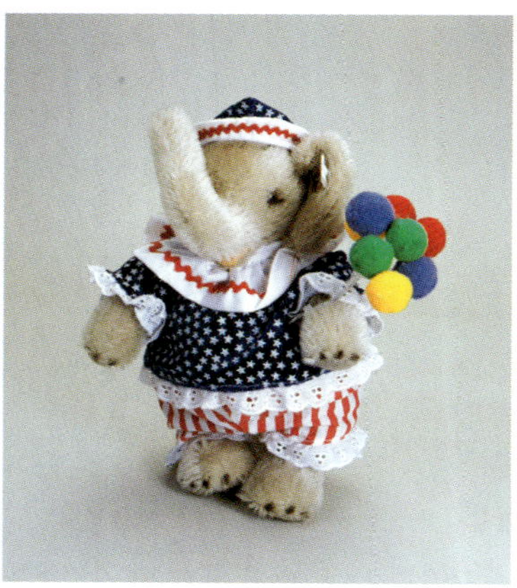

Baby Elefant - *Baby Elephant Balloon Seller*

als Ballonverkaeufer, Mohair, gegliedert, USA-Artikel, limit. Auflage 5.000 Stück - *dressed as a balloon sales elephant, mohair, jointed, article for the USA, ltd edition of 5,000*

SERIE	ART.-NO	PERIOD	PR.	INFO
	0145/19	1989-1990	4	19 cm

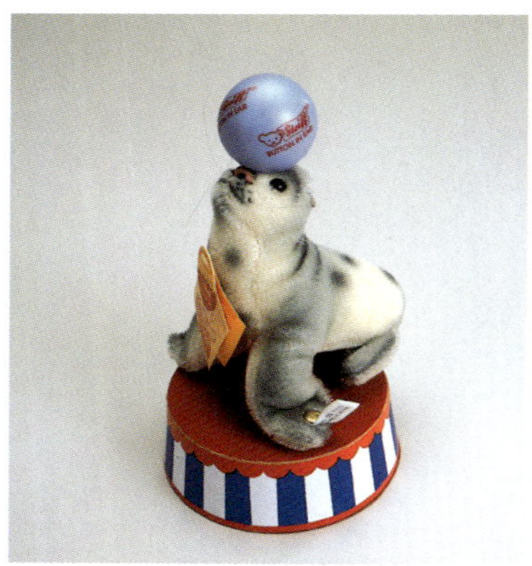

Robbe - *Seal with Ball on Stand*

mit Ball, auf Zirkuspodest, Mohair, USA-Artikel, limit. Auflage 5.000 Stück - *seal with ball, positioned on circus pedestal, mohair, article for the USA, ltd edition of 5,000*

SERIE	ART.-NO	PERIOD	PR.	INFO
650444	**0147/12**	1989-1990	4	12 cm
	650444	1991-1991	4	

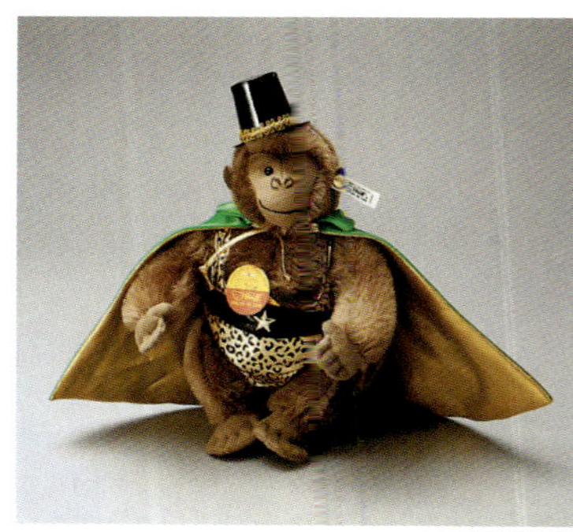

Gorilla - *Strong Man Gorilla*

als "Starker Mann", Mohair, gegliedert, USA-Artikel, limit. Auflage 5.000 Stueck - *gorilla dressed as a "strong man", mohair, jointed, article for the USA, ltd edition of 5,000*

SERIE	ART.-NO	PERIOD	PR.	INFO
650482	**0144/19**	1990-1990	4	19 cm
	650482	1991-1991	4	

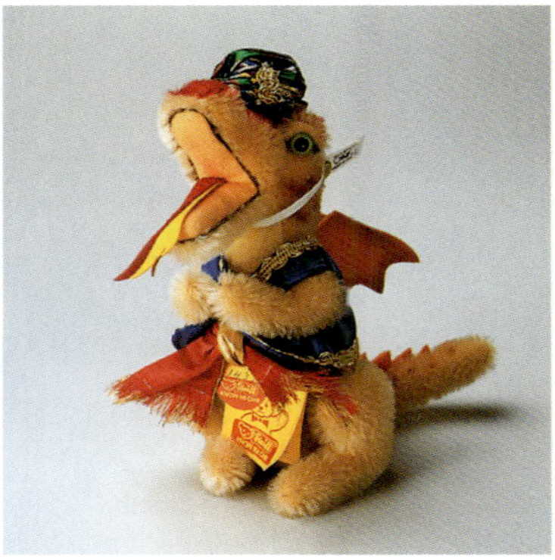

Drache - *Fire Eater Dragon*

als Feuerschlucker, Mohair, Arme gegliedert, USA-Artikel, limit. Auflage 5.000 Stueck - *dragon dressed as a "Fire-Eater", mohair, arms jointed, article for the USA, ltd edition of 5,000*

SERIE	ART.-NO	PERIOD	PR.	INFO
650475	**0149/19**	1990-1990	4	19 cm
	650475	1991-1991	4	

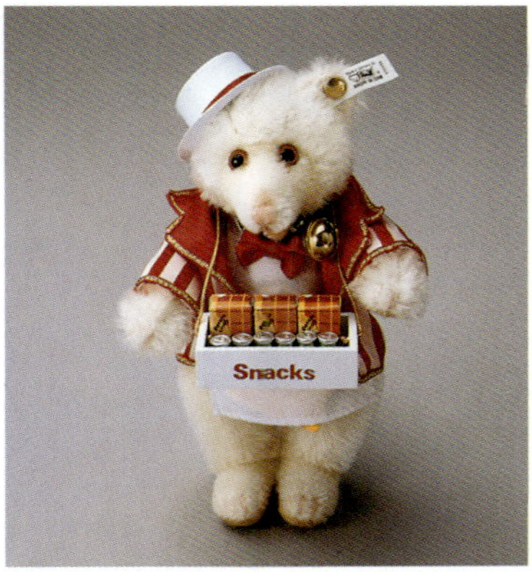

Teddy Baby - *Teddy Baby Food Vendor*

mit Bauchladen, Mohair, gegliedert, USA-Artikel, limit. Auflage 5.000 Stueck - *equipped with a snack tray, mohair, jointed, article for the USA, ltd edition of 5,000*

SERIE	ART.-NO	PERIOD	PR.	INFO
	0177/19	1990-1990	4-5	19 cm

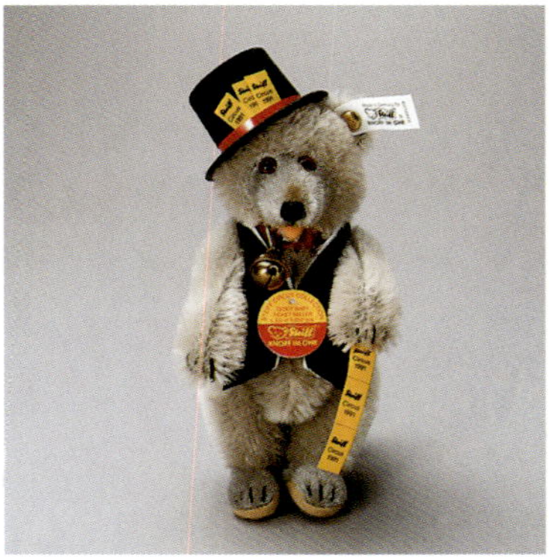

Teddy Baby - *Teddy Baby Ticket Seller*

als Kartenverkaeufer, Mohair, gegliedert, USA-Artikel, limit. Auflage 5.000 Stueck - *dressed as a ticket salesman, mohair, jointed, article for the USA, ltd edition of 5,000*

EAN-NO.	PERIOD	PR.	INFO
650529	1991-1991	4-5	19 cm

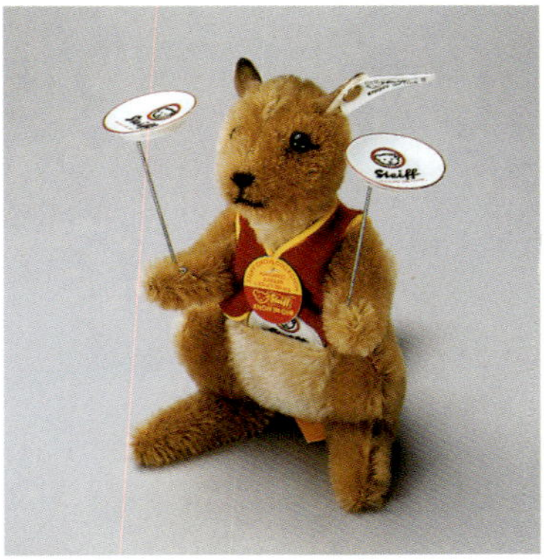

Kaenguruh - *Kangaroo Juggler*

als Jongleur, Mohair, Kopf & Arme gegliedert, USA-Artikel, limit. Auflage 5.000 Stueck - *dressed as a juggler, mohair, head & arms are jointed, article for the USA, ltd edition of 5,000*

EAN-NO.	PERIOD	PR.	INFO
650536	1991-1991	4	19 cm

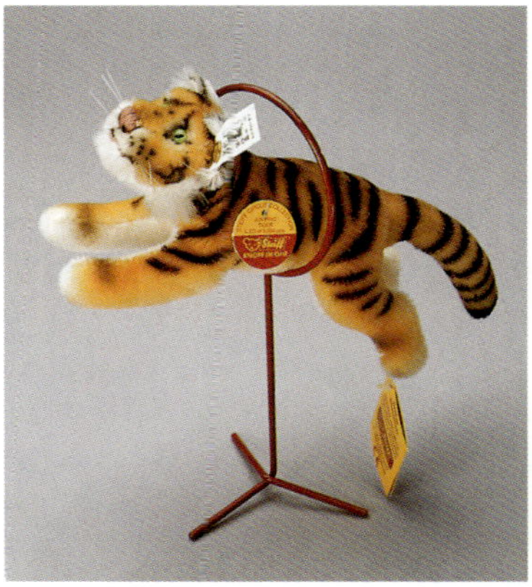

Tiger - *Tiger Jumping Through Hoop*

durch Reifen springend, Mohair, USA-Artikel, limit. Auflage 5.000 Stueck - *jumping through a ring, mohair, article for the USA, ltd edition of 5,000*

EAN-NO.	PERIOD	PR.	INFO
650543	1991-1991	4	23 cm

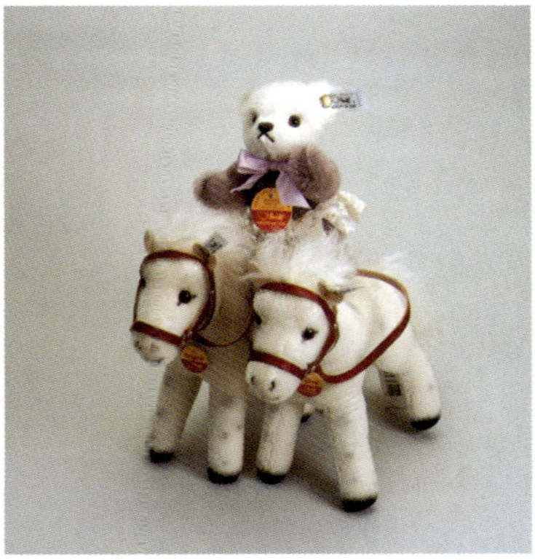

Dolly Baer auf 2 Pferden - *Bearback Rider Set*

Mohair, Baer gegliedert, 15 cm, Pferde 18 cm, USA-Artikel, limit. Auflage 5.000 Stueck - *mohair, bear jointed, 15 cm, horses are 18 cm, article for the USA, ltd edition of 5,000*

EAN-NO.	PERIOD	PR.	INFO
650550	1991-1991	5	3-tlg. Set - *3-piece set*

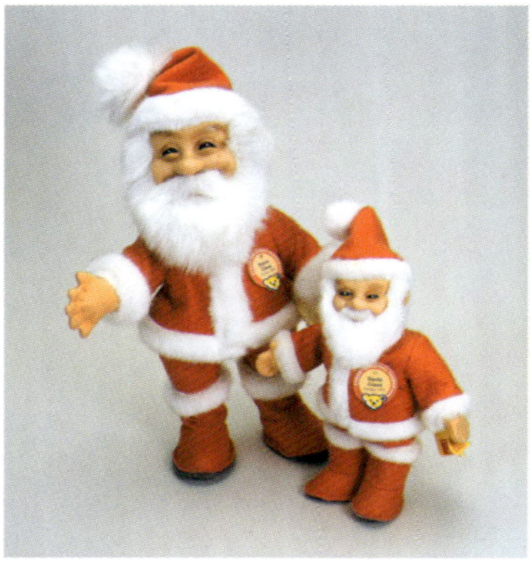

Santa Claus

Kunststoff/Filz, gegliedert, USA-Artikel, limit. Auflage je 1.200 Stück - *synthetic material/ felt, jointed, article for the USA, ltd edition of 1,200 each*

Serie	Art.-No	Period	Pr.	Info
	7635/19	1985-1988	4	19 cm
	7635/28	1984-1988	4	28 cm

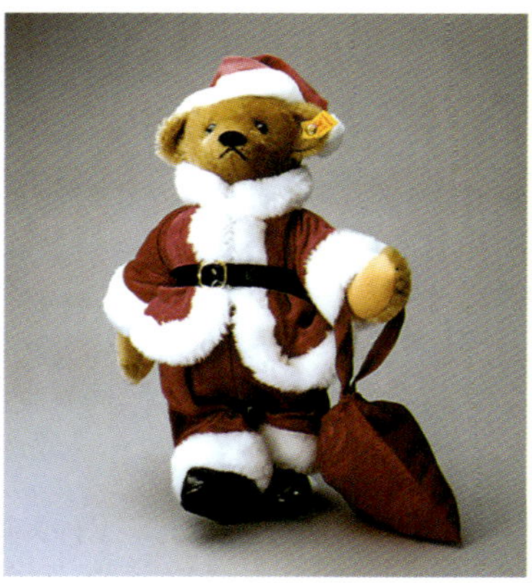

Nikolaus - *Santa*

Mohair, gegliedert, Sack mit Geschenken, USA-Artikel - *mohair, jointed, holding a sack with gifts, article for the USA*

Serie	Art.-No	Period	Pr.	Info
	0155/38	1986-1989	5	38 cm

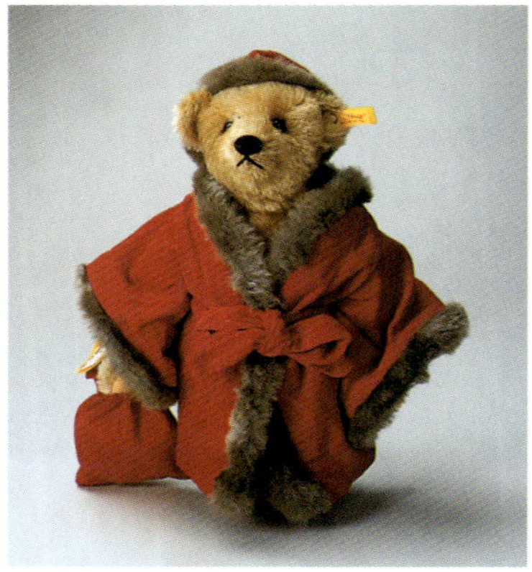

St. Nicholas Baer - *St. Nicholas Bear*

Margaret Strong Baer, Mohair, gegliedert, USA-Artikel, limit. Auflage 5.000 Stueck - *Margaret Strong Bear, mohair, jointed, article for the USA, ltd edition of 5,000*

Serie	Art.-No	Period	Pr.	Info
	0156/38	1987-1989	5	38 cm

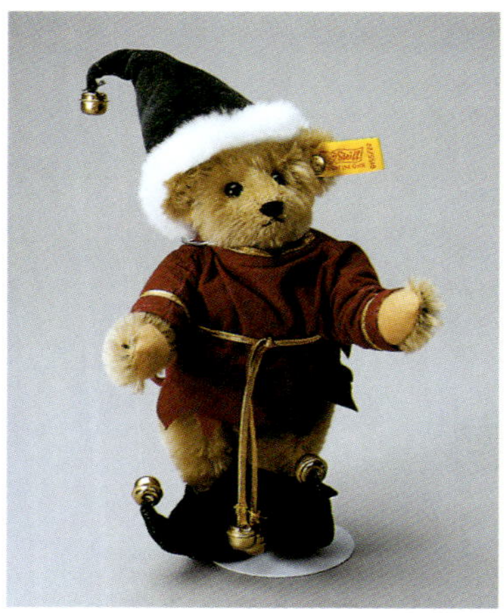

Santa´s Elf

Helfer des Nikolaus, Mohair, gegliedert, USA-Artikel - *Santa´s helper, mohair, jointed, article for the USA*

Serie	Art.-No	Period	Pr.	Info
	0155/22	1988-1988	4-5	22 cm

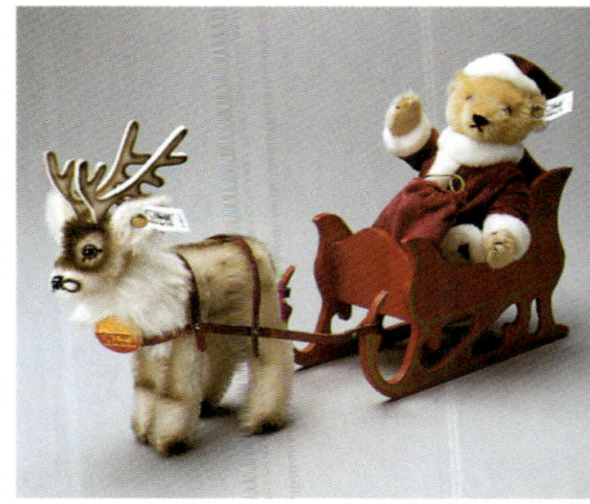

Schlitten mit Rentier und Nikolaus - *Sleigh, Reindeer and Santa Teddy*

Nikolaus-Teddy und Rentier Mohair, 43 cm Gesamtlaenge, Baer gegliedert, USA-Artikel, limit. Auflage 6.000 Stueck, Rentier auch einzeln erhaeltlich, mit Anschlussteil als Erweiterung des Schlittens, limit. Auflage 4.000 Stueck - *St. Nicholas Teddy & reindeer are mohair, the bear is jointed, article for the USA, ltd edition of 6,000, reindeer also available individually, together with connecting piece to extend the sleigh, ltd edition of 4,000*

Serie	Art.-No	Period	Pr.	Info
660101	0118/00	1989-1990	5	kpl. Set - *compl. set*
	660101	1991-1991	5	
	0118/18	1989-1990	4	18 cm, Nikolaus - *St. Claus*
660115	**0118/17**	1990-1990	4	17 cm, Rentier - *reindeer*
	660115	1991-1991	4	

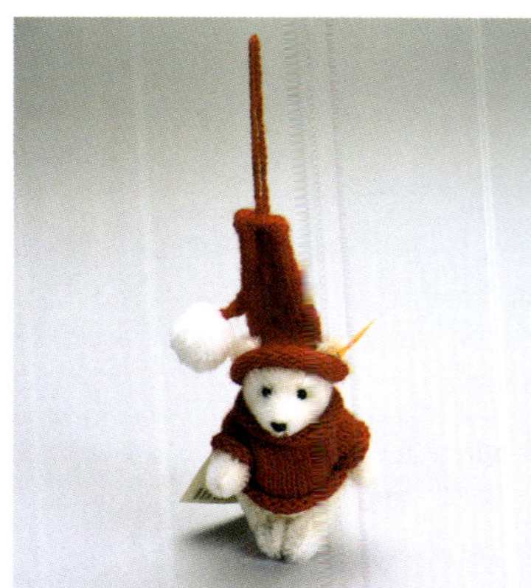

Original Teddybaer Tinsel - *Original Teddybear Tinsel*

Mohair, weiss, gegliedert, als Christbaumschmuck, rote Strickbekleidung, limit. Auflage 2.500 Stueck fuer Amerika, mit Steiff USA Zertifikat - *mohair, white, jointed, christmas tree ornament, red knitwear clothes, ltd edition of 2,500 for the USA, with Steiff USA certificat*

EAN-No.	Period	Pr.	Info
650802	1994-1994	4-5	10 cm

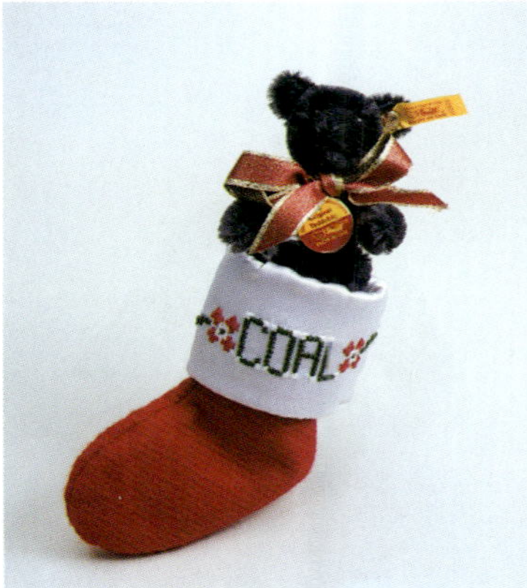

Original Teddybaer Coal - *Original Teddybear Coal*

Mohair, anthrazit, gegliedert, als Christbaumschmuck, im rot-weissen Filzstiefel, limit. Auflage 3.500 Stueck fuer Amerika, mit Steiff USA Zertifikat - *mohair, anthracite, jointed, christmas tree ornament, in a red-white boot of felt, ltd edition of 3,500 for the USA, with Steiff USA certificat*

EAN-No.	Period	Pr.	Info
650833	1995-1995	4	10 cm

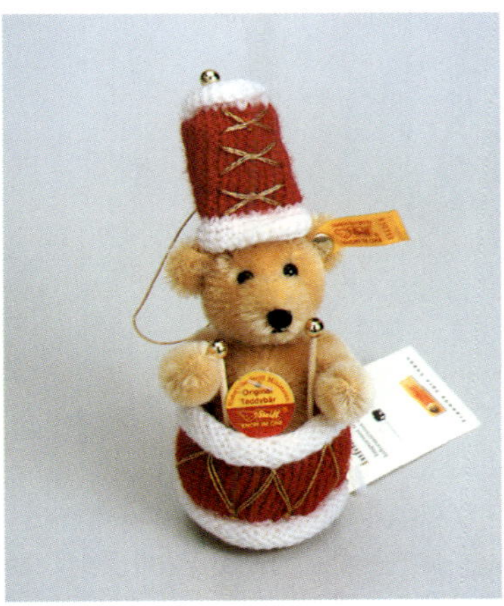

Original Teddybaer Percussion - *Original Teddybear Percussion*

Mohair, honig, gegliedert, als Christbaumschmuck, rot/weisse Strickbekleidung, limit. Auflage 3.500 Stueck fuer Amerika, mit Steiff USA Zertifikat - *mohair, honey, jointed, christmas tree ornament, red/white knitwear, ltd edition of 3,500 for the USA, with Steiff USA certificat*

EAN-No.	Period	Pr.	Info
665066	1996-1996	4	10 cm

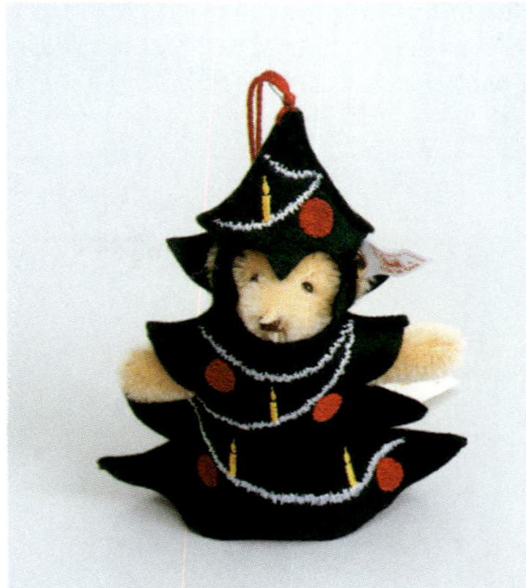

Weihnachtsbaum Baer - *Christmas Tree Bear Evergreen*

Mohair, blond, als Christbaumschmuck, im gruenen Filz-Weihnachtsbaum, limit. Auflage 4.000 Stueck fuer Amerika - *mohair, blond, christmas tree ornament, in a green christmas tree of felt, ltd edition of 4,000 for the USA*

EAN-No.	Period	Pr.	Info
665417	1997-1997	3-4	12 cm

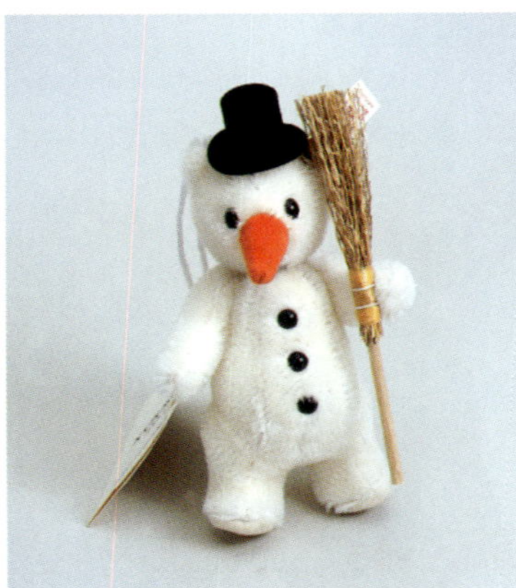

Schneemann - *Snowman*

Mohair, weiss, stehend, Kopf & Arme gegliedert, als Christbaumschmuck, mit schwarzem Zylinder & Reiserbesen, limit. Auflage 5.000 Stueck fuer Amerika - *mohair, white, standing, head & arms jointed, christmas tree ornament, black top hat & broom, ltd edition of 5,000 for the USA*

EAN-No.	Period	Pr.	Info
665592	1998-1998	3-4	13 cm

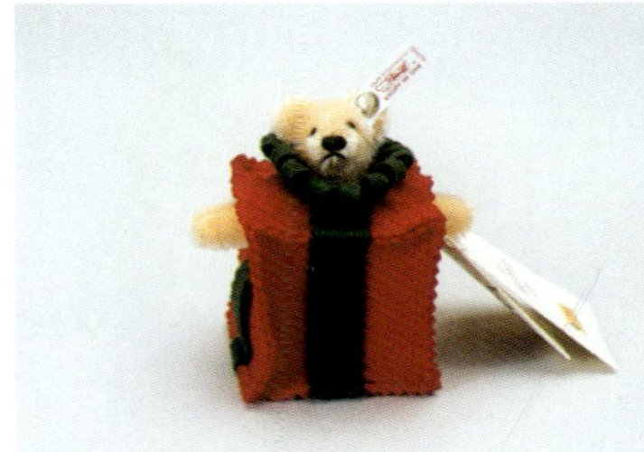

Weihnachtsbaum Baer - *All Wrapped Up*

Mohair, blond, als Christbaumschmuck, im Weihnachtspaket, nur Kopf und Arme sind sichtbar, limit. Auflage 5.000 Stueck fuer Amerika - *mohair, blond, christmas tree ornament, bear poking out of a tiny gift package, ltd edition of 5,000 for America*

EAN-No.	Period	Pr.	Info
665882	1999-1999	3-4	10 cm

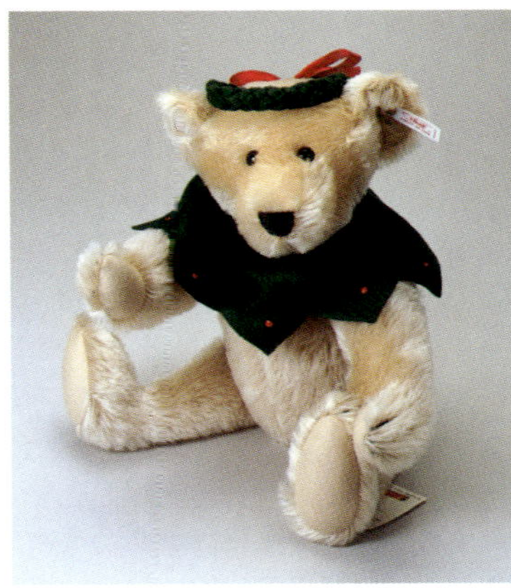

Baer Noel - *Bear Noel*

Mohair, blond, gegliedert, mit weihnachtlichem Kragen & Kopfschmuck, limit. Auflage 1.500 Stueck fuer Amerika - *mohair, blond, jointed, wearing Christmas colors and an advent wreath headdress, ltd edition of 1,500 for America*

EAN-No.	Period	Pr.	Info
666025	1999-1999	4-5	40 cm

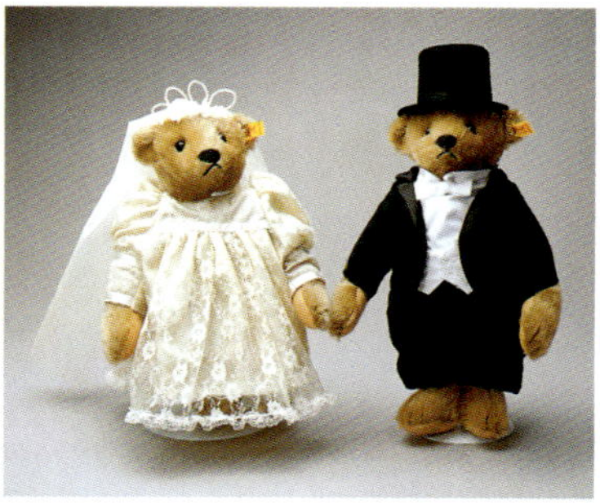

Braut / Braeutigam - *Bride / Groom*

Margaret Strong Baeren, Mohair, gegliedert, 36 / 37 cm, Brummstimme, USA-Artikel - *Margaret Strong bears, mohair, jointed, 36 / 37 cm, growler, article for the USA*

SERIE	ART.-NO	PERIOD	PR.	INFO
	0155/36	1984-1989	5	Braut - *Bride*
	0155/37	1984-1989	5	Braeutigam - *Groom*

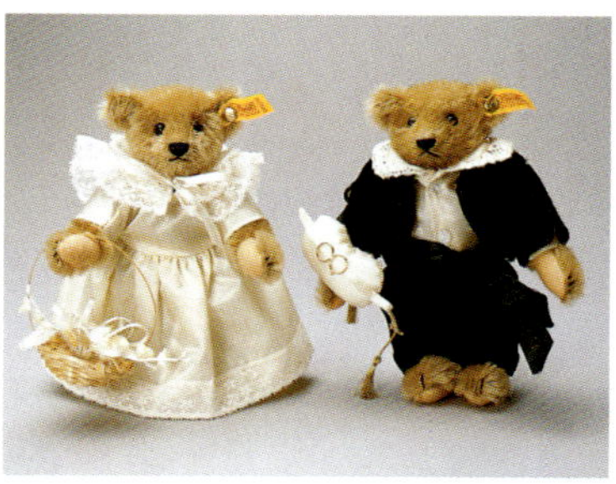

Blumenmaedchen / Ringtraeger - *Flower Bear-er / Ring Bear-er*

Margaret Strong Baeren, Mohair, gegliedert, 22 / 23 cm, Druckstimme, USA-Artikel - *Margaret Strong bears, mohair, jointed, 22 / 23 cm, press voice, article for the USA*

SERIE	ART.-NO	PERIOD	PR.	INFO
	0155/22	1985-1987	4-5	Blumen-maedchen - *Flower Girl*
	0155/23	1985-1987	4-5	Ringtraeger - *Ring Bearer*

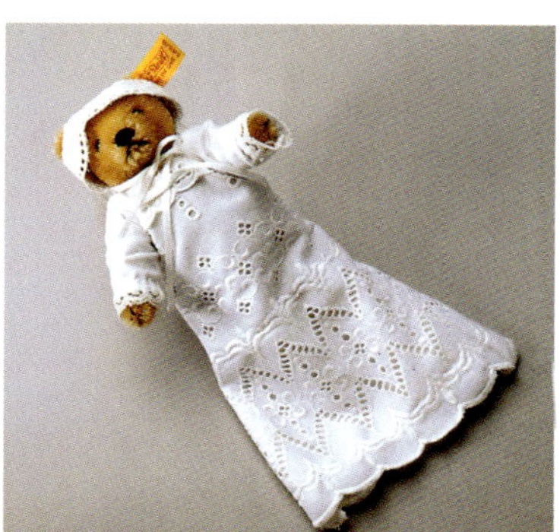

Taufbaby - *Christening Bear*

Margaret Strong Baer, Mohair, gegliedert, USA-Artikel - *Margaret Strong bear, mohair, jointed, article for the USA*

SERIE	ART.-NO	PERIOD	PR.	INFO
	0155/15	1986-1987	4-5	15 cm

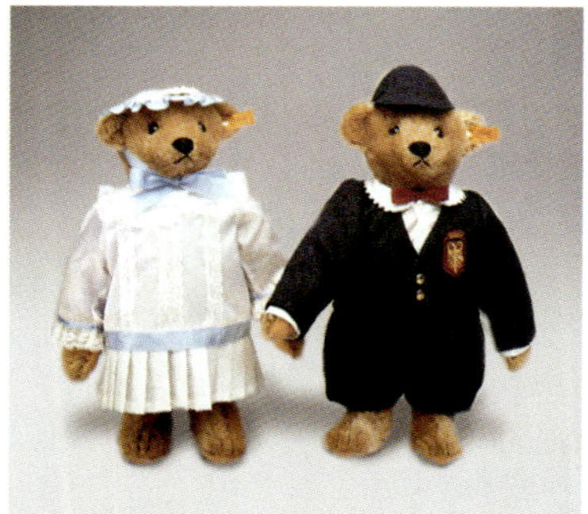

Victorian. Maedchen / Junge - *Victorian Girl / Victorian Boy*

Margaret Strong Baeren, Mohair, gegliedert, 34 / 35 cm, Brummstimme, USA-Artikel - *Margaret Strong bears, mohair, jointed, 34 / 35 cm, growler, article for the USA*

SERIE	ART.-NO	PERIOD	PR.	INFO
	0155/34	1986-1986	5	Maedchen - *Girl*
	0155/35	1986-1986	5	Junge - *Boy*

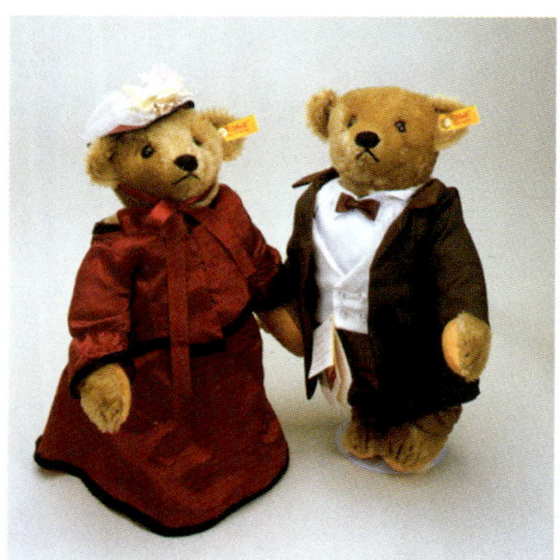

Victorian. Herr / Dame - *Victorian Lady / Victorian Gentlemen*

Margaret Strong Baeren, Mohair, gegliedert, 36 / 37 cm, Brummstimme, USA-Artikel - *Margaret Strong bears, mohair, jointed, 36 / 37 cm, growler, article for the USA*

SERIE	ART.-NO	PERIOD	PR.	INFO
	0156/36	1987-1989	5	Dame - *Lady*
	0156/37	1987-1989	5	Herr - *Gentleman*

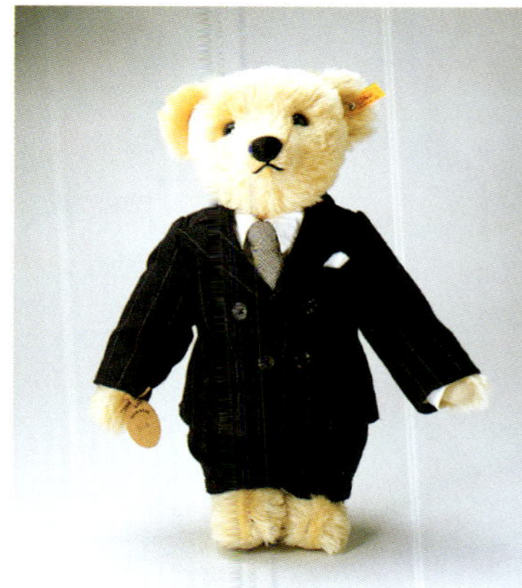

Chairman I Baer - *Chairman I Bear*

Mohair Webpelz, blond, gegliedert, abwaschbar, limit. Auflage 1.000 Stueck fuer Ralph Lauren - *mohair woven fur, blond, jointed, surface washable, ltd edition of 1,000 for Ralph Lauren*

EAN-NO.	PERIOD	PR.	INFO
650598	1992-1992	5	43 cm

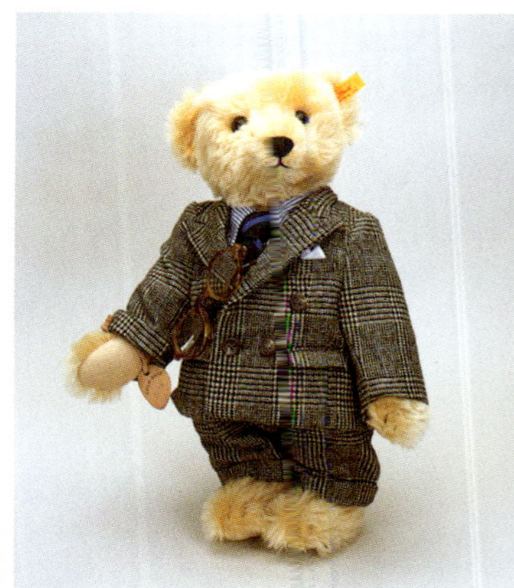

Chairman II Baer - *Chairman II Bear*

Mohair Webpelz, blond, gegliedert, abwaschbar, limit. Auflage 1.500 Stueck fuer Ralph Lauren - *mohair woven fur, blond, jointed, surface washable, ltd edition of 1,500 for Ralph Lauren*

EAN-NO.	PERIOD	PR.	INFO
027079	1993-1993	5-6	43 cm

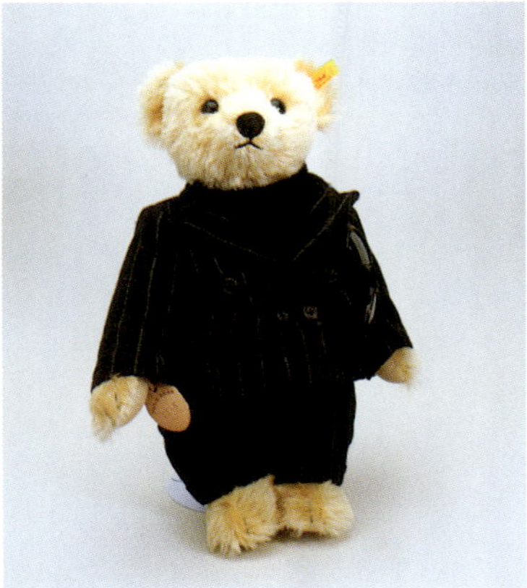

Producer Baer - *Producer Bear*

Mohair Webpelz, blond, gegliedert, abwaschbar, limit. Auflage 1.500 Stueck fuer Ralph Lauren - *mohair woven fur, blond, jointed, surface washable, ltd edition of 1,500 for Ralph Lauren*

EAN-No.	Period	Pr.	Info
027093	1993-1993	5-6	43 cm

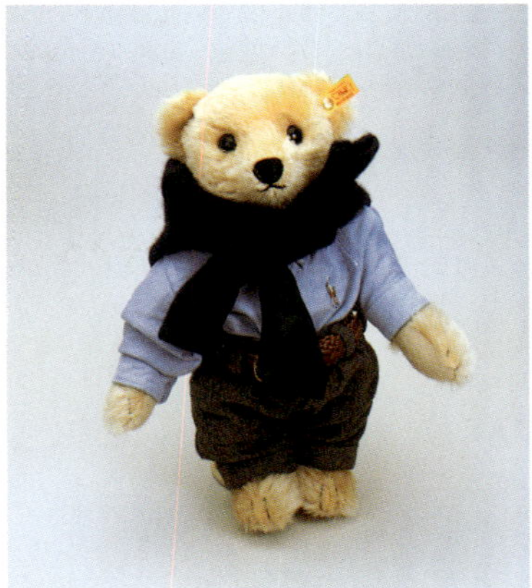

Preppy Baer - *Preppy Bear*

Mohair Webpelz, blond, gegliedert, abwaschbar, Sonderartikel fuer Ralph Lauren - *mohair woven fur, blond, jointed, surface washable, exclusive for Ralph Lauren*

EAN-No.	Period	Pr.	Info
027062	1993-1993	5-6	35 cm

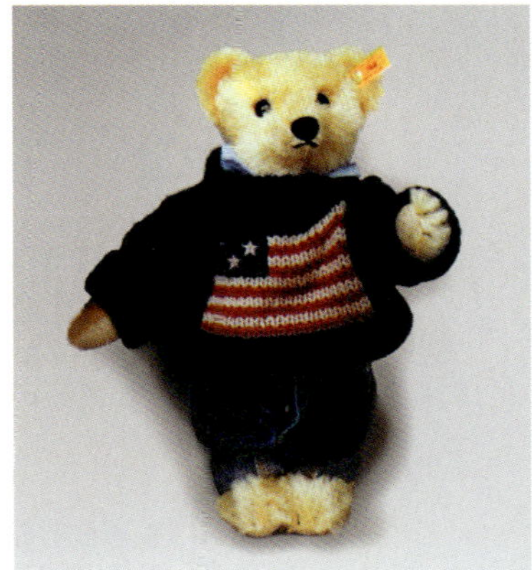

American Flag Baer - *American Flag Bear*

Mohair Webpelz, blond, gegliedert, abwaschbar, limit. Auflage 3.500 Stueck fuer Ralph Lauren - *mohair woven fur, blond, jointed, surface washable, ltd edition of 3,500 for Ralph Lauren*

EAN-No.	Period	Pr.	Info
	1993-1993	6	35 cm

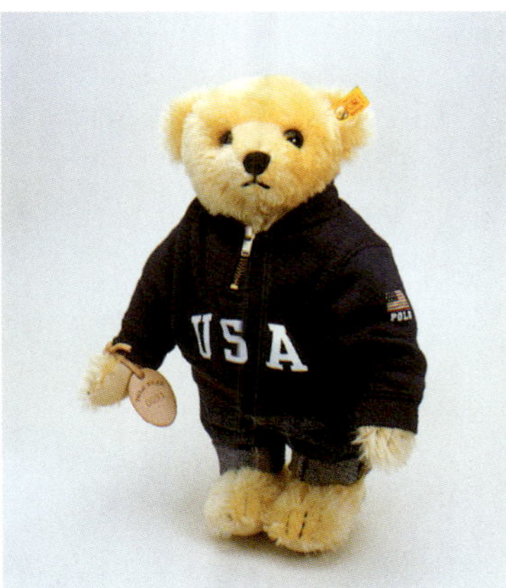

Varsity Baer - *Varsity Bear*

Mohair Webpelz, blond, gegliedert, abwaschbar, limit. Auflage 3.500 Stueck fuer Ralph Lauren - *mohair woven fur, blond, jointed, surface washable, ltd edition of 3,500 for Ralph Lauren*

EAN-No.	Period	Pr.	Info
027086	1993-1993	5-6	35 cm

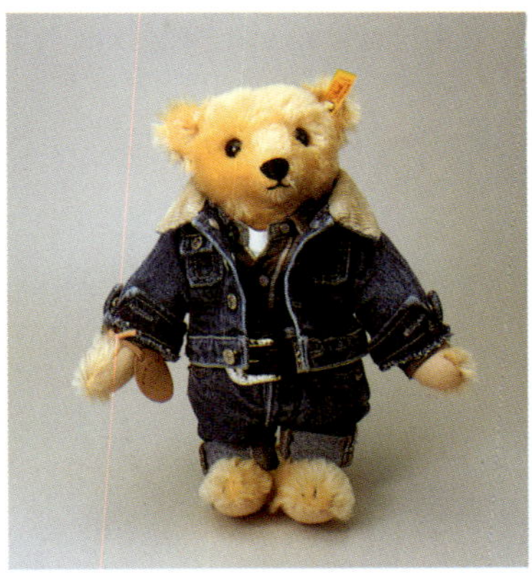

Ranch Baer - *Ranch Bear*

Mohair Webpelz, blond, gegliedert, abwaschbar, limit. Auflage 3.500 Stueck fuer Ralph Lauren - *mohair woven fur, blond, jointed, surface washable, ltd edition of 3,500 for Ralph Lauren*

EAN-No.	Period	Pr.	Info
027055	1993-1993	5-6	35 cm

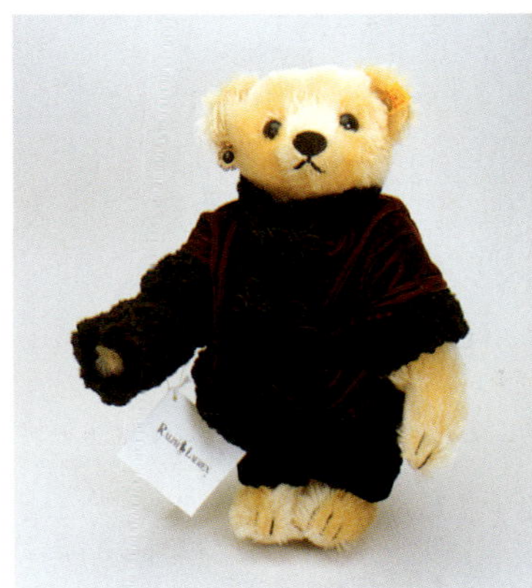

Russian Girl Baer - *Russian Girl Bear*

Mohair Webpelz, blond, gegliedert, abwaschbar, limit. Auflage 1.100 Stueck fuer Ralph Lauren - *mohair woven fur, blond, jointed, surface washable, ltd edition of 1,100 for Ralph Lauren*

EAN-No.	Period	Pr.	Info
650581	1994-1994	5-6	35 cm

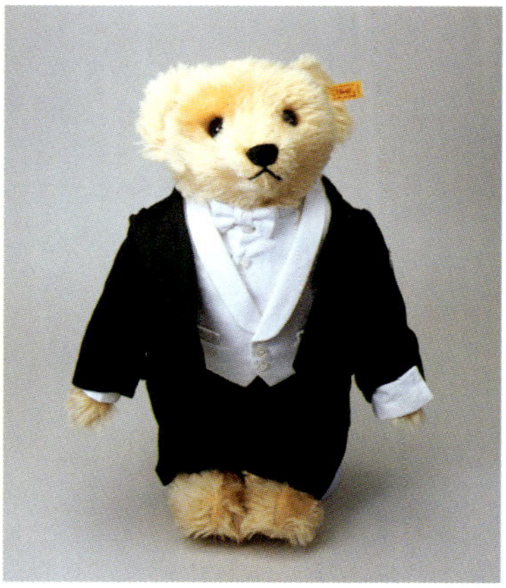

Martini Baer - *Martini Bear*

Mohair Webpelz, blond, gegliedert, abwaschbar, Sonderartikel fuer Ralph Lauren - *mohair woven fur, blond, jointed, surface washable, exclusive for Ralph Lauren*

EAN-No.	Period	Pr.	Info
650598	1994-1994	6	43 cm

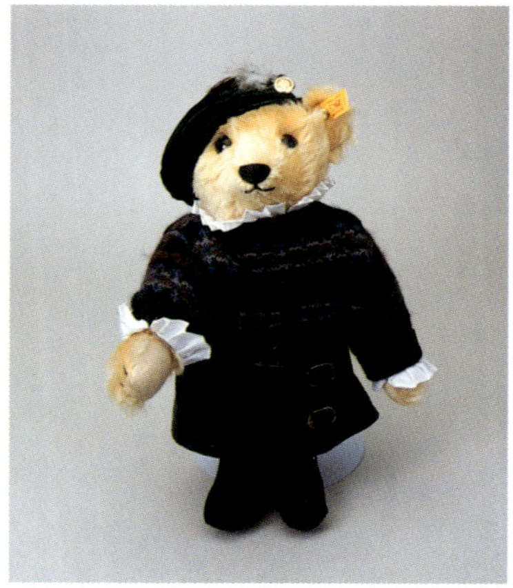

New Romantic Girl

Mohair Webpelz, blond, gegliedert, abwaschbar, limit. Auflage 1.500 Stueck fuer Ralph Lauren - *mohair woven fur, blond, jointed, surface washable, ltd edition of 1,500 for Ralph Lauren*

EAN-No.	Period	Pr.	Info
027147	1995-1995	5-6	35 cm

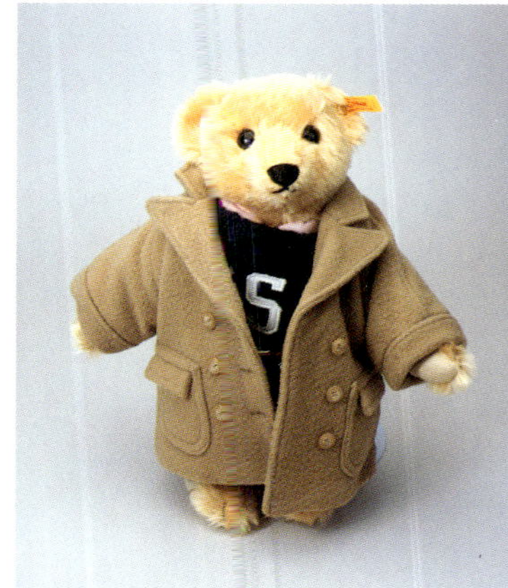

Collegiate Baer - *Collegiate Bear*

Mohair Webpelz, blond, gegliedert, abwaschbar, limit. Auflage 1.000 Stueck fuer Ralph Lauren - *mohair woven fur, blond, jointed, surface washable, ltd edition of 1,000 for Ralph Lauren*

EAN-No.	Period	Pr.	Info
027154	1996-1996	5-5	35 cm

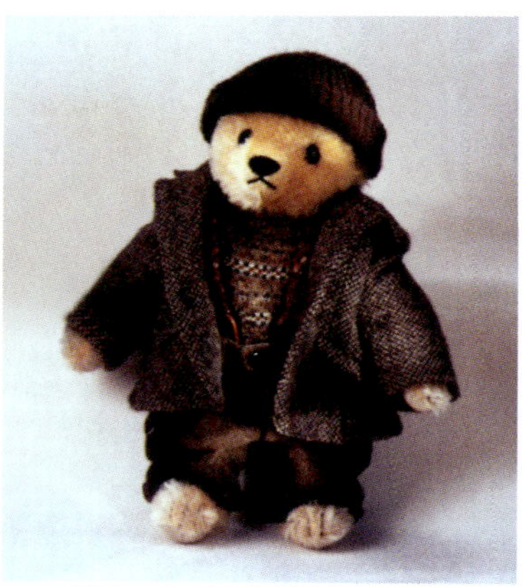

Wellington Baer - *Wellington Bear*

Mohair Webpelz, blond, gegliedert, abwaschbar, limit. Auflage 1.070 Stueck fuer Ralph Lauren - *mohair woven fur, blond, jointed, surface washable, ltd edition of 1,070 for Ralph Lauren*

EAN-No.	Period	Pr.	Info
027116	1994-1994	6	35 cm

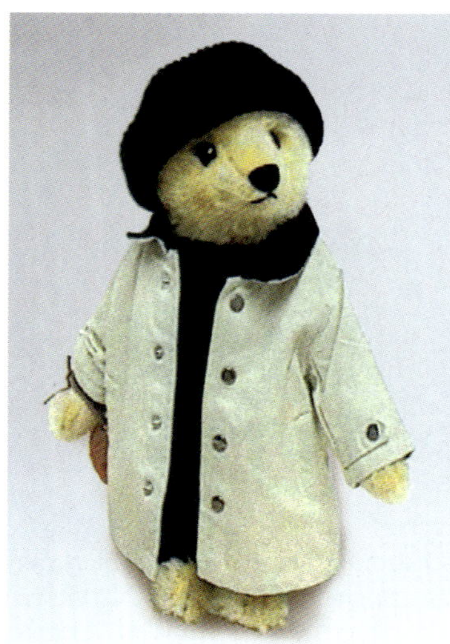

Nauticman Baer - *Nauticman Bear*

Mohair Webpelz, blond, gegliedert, abwaschbar, limit. Auflage 1.500 Stueck fuer Ralph Lauren - *mohair woven fur, blond, jointed, surface washable, ltd edition of 1,500 for Ralph Lauren*

EAN-No.	Period	Pr.	Info
027008	1995-1995	6	35 cm

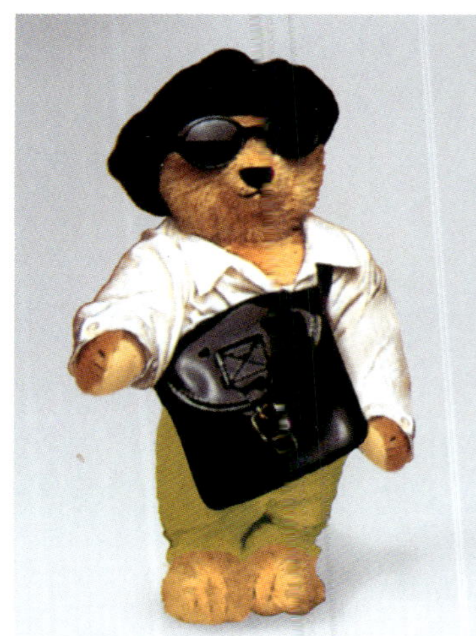

Racy Baer - *Racy Bear*

Mohair Webpelz, blond gegliedert, abwaschbar, limit. Auflage 800 Stueck fuer Ralph Lauren - *mohair woven fur, blond, jointed, surface washable, ltd edition of 800 for Ralph Lauren*

EAN-No.	Period	Pr.	Info
027004	1996-1996	6	35 cm

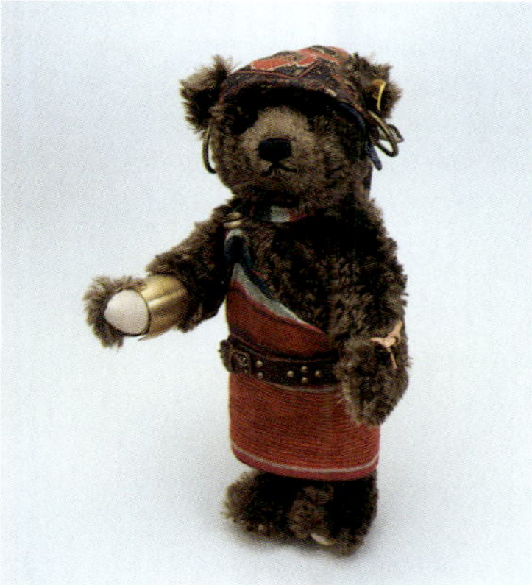

Safari Girl Baer - *Safari Girl Bear*

Mohair Webpelz, braun, gegliedert, abwaschbar, limit. Auflage 500 Stueck fuer Ralph Lauren - *mohair woven fur, brown, jointed, surface washable, ltd edition of 500 for Ralph Lauren*

EAN-No.	Period	Pr.	Info
665431	1997-1997	5-6	35 cm

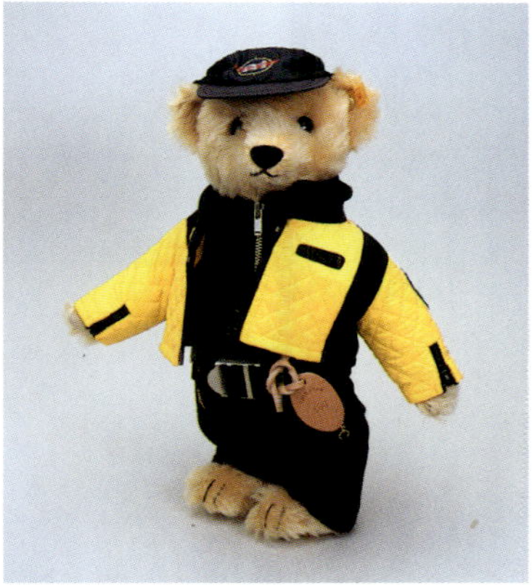

Racer Baer - *Racer Bear*

Mohair Webpelz, blond, gegliedert, abwaschbar, limit. Auflage 1.000 Stueck fuer Ralph Lauren - *mohair woven fur, blond, jointed, surface washable, ltd edition of 1,000 for Ralph Lauren*

EAN-No.	Period	Pr.	Info
665424	1997-1997	5-6	35 cm

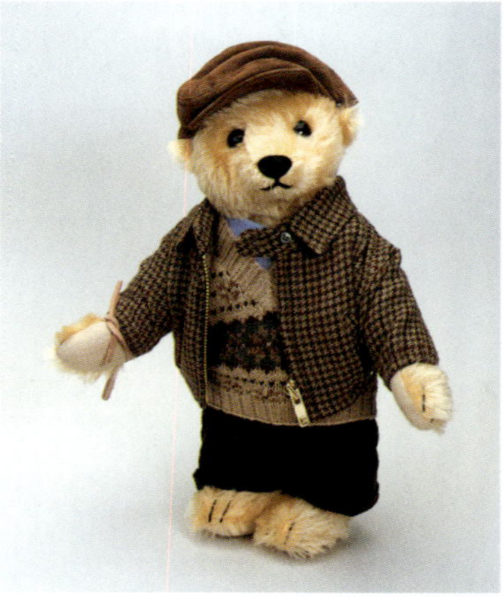

Highland Golf Baer - *Highland Golf Bear*

Mohair Webpelz, blond, gegliedert, abwaschbar, limit. Auflage 500 Stueck fuer Ralph Lauren - *mohair, blond, jointed, surface washable, ltd edition of 500 for Ralph Lauren*

EAN-No.	Period	Pr.	Info
000379	1999-1999	5-6	35 cm

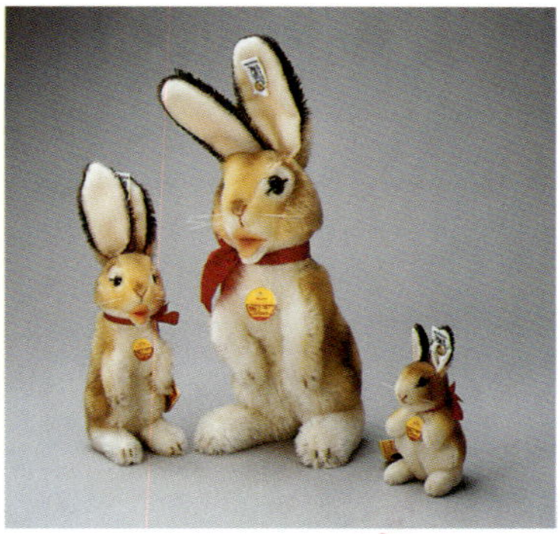

Manni Hase Set - ***Manni** Rabbit Set*

Mohair, aufwartend, 20 & 30 cm Kopf drehbar, USA-Sammler-Ausgabe 1983 - *mohair, sitting up, head swivels on 20 & 30 cm sizes, USA Collector´s edition 1983*

Serie	Art.-No	Period	Pr.	Info
	3020/00	1983-1985	4-5	kpl. Set - *compl. set*
	3020/10	1983-1985	3	10 cm
	3020/20	1983-1985	3	20 cm
	3020/30	1983-1985	3-4	30 cm

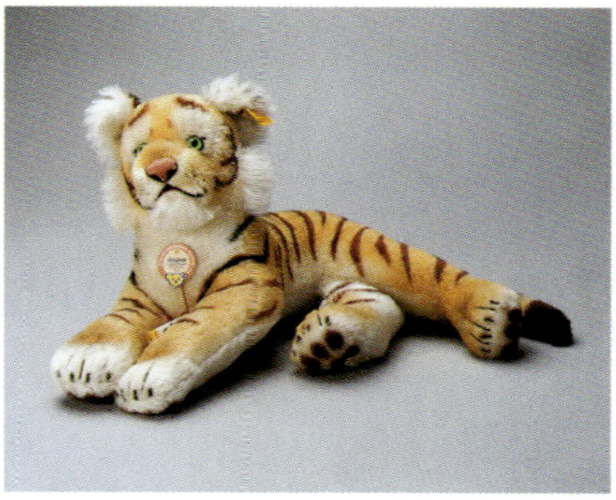

Tiger

Replica, Mohair-Webpelz, liegend, USA-Sammler-Ausgabe 1983, limit. Auflage 2.000 Stueck - *replica, mohair woven fur, lying, USA Collector´s edition 1983, ltd edition of 2,000 each*

Serie	Art.-No	Period	Pr.	Info
	0112/17	1983-1987	4	17 cm
	0112/28	1983-1987	4	28 cm

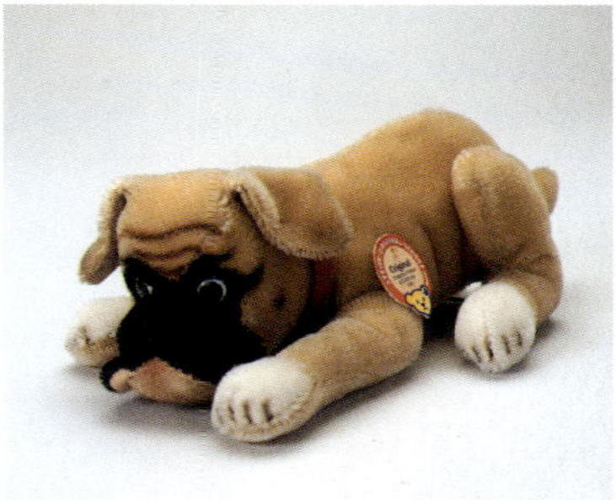

Boxer

Mohair, liegend, limit. Auflage 2.000 Stueck fuer Amerika - *mohair, lying, ltd edition of 2,000, USA exclusive*

Serie	Art.-No	Period	Pr.	Info
	0118/25	1983-1987	4	25 cm

kein Bild vorhanden
no picture available

Rotkaeppchen & der Wolf - *Red Riding Hood & Wolf Mask*

Mohair, graubraun, Wolfsmaske aus Set mit 2 Suzanne Gibson Puppen (Rotkaeppchen & Grossmutter), limit. Auflage 3.000 Stueck fuer Reeves International, USA - *mohair, grey-brown, mask of the wolf´s head together with 2 Suzanne Gibson dolls (Red Riding Hood & Grandma), ltd edition of 3,000 for Reeves International, USA*

Serie	Art.-No	Period	Pr.	Info
	7980/20	1983-1983	4	20 cm

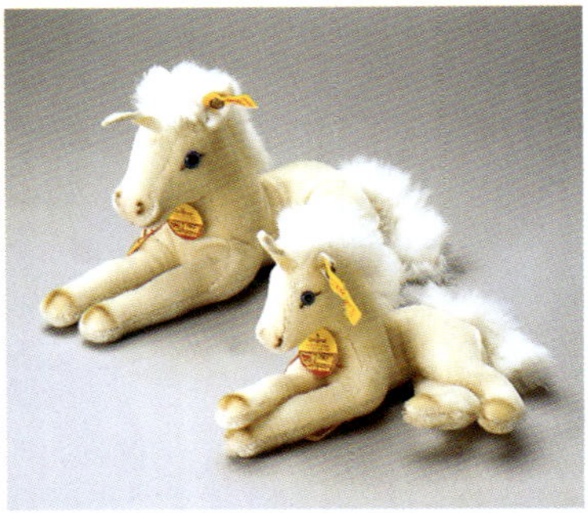

Einhorn - *Unicorn*

Mohair, liegend, weiss, USA-Sammler-Ausgabe 1983, limit. Auflage je 2.000 Stueck - *mohair, lying, white, USA Collector´s edition 1983, ltd edition of 2,000 each*

SERIE	ART.-NO	PERIOD	PR.	INFO
	0130/17	1983-1984	4	17 cm
	0130/27	1983-1984	5	27 cm

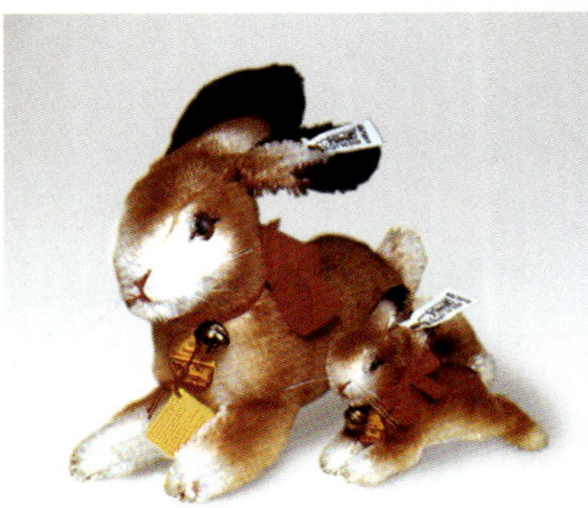

Hoppy Hase Set - ***Hoppy** Rabbit Set*

Mohair, springend, USA-Sammler-Ausgabe 1984 - *mohair, hopping, USA Collector´s edition 1984*

SERIE	ART.-NO	PERIOD	PR.	INFO
	0155/00	1984-1984	4-5	kpl. Set - *compl. set*
	0155/08	1984-1984	2-3	8 cm
	0155/14	1984-1984	3	14 cm
	0155/17	1984-1984	3-4	17 cm

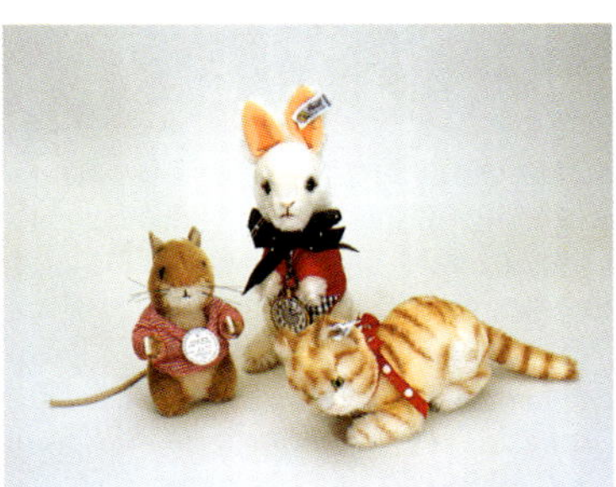

Alice & Freunde - ***Alice & Her Friends***

Set, Mohair, bestehend aus Katze, Hase & Maus mit Suzanne Gibson Puppe, limit. Auflage 3.000 Stueck fuer Reeves International, USA - *set, mohair, cat, rabbit & mouse with Suzanne Gibson doll, ltd edition of 3,000 for Reeves International, USA*

SERIE	ART.-NO	PERIOD	PR.	INFO
	0146/13	1986-1986	3-4	13 cm, Katze - *cat*
	0147/20	1986-1986	3-4	20 cm, Hase - *rabbit*
	0148/13	1986-1986	3-4	13 cm, Maus - *mouse*

kein Bild vorhanden
no picture available

Lamm - *Lamb*

Mohair, weiss, stehend, aus Set "Mary & ihr kleines Lamm" mit Suzanne Gibson Puppe, limitierte Auflage 2.000 Stueck fuer Reeves International, USA - *mohair, white, standing, part of "Mary had a little Lamb" set with a Suzanne Gibson doll, ltd edition of 2,000 for Reeves International, USA*

EAN-NO.	PERIOD	PR.	INFO
	1986-1986	4	12 cm

kein Bild vorhanden
no picture available

Rotkaeppchen & der Wolf - *Red Riding Hood & Wolf*

Mohair, grau, stehend, aus Set mit Suzanne Gibson Puppe, limitierte Auflage 2.000 Stueck fuer Reeves International, USA - *mohair, grey, standing, in a set together with a Suzanne Gibson doll, ltd edition of 2,000 for Reeves International, USA*

SERIE	ART.-NO	PERIOD	PR.	INFO
	0127/12	1987-1987	4	12 cm

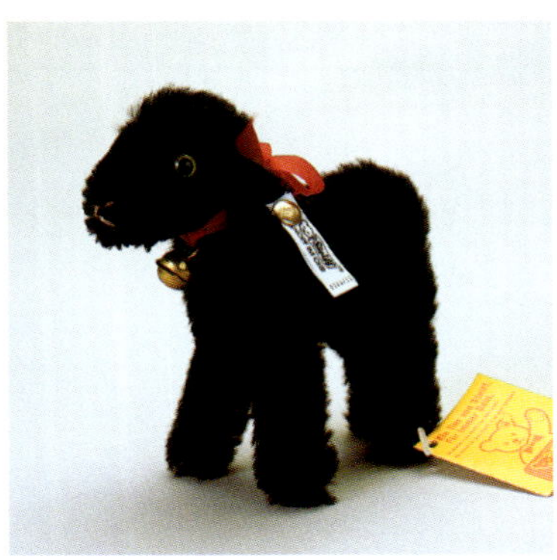

Baa Baa Schwarzes Schaf - *Baa Baa Black Sheep*

Mohair, schwarz, stehend, aus Set mit Suzanne Gibson Puppe, limit. Auflage 1988 fuer Reeves International, USA - *mohair, black, standing, in a set together with a Suzanne Gibson doll, ltd edition in 1988 for Reeves International, USA*

SERIE	ART.-NO	PERIOD	PR.	INFO
650055	**0144/12**	1988-1988	4	12 cm

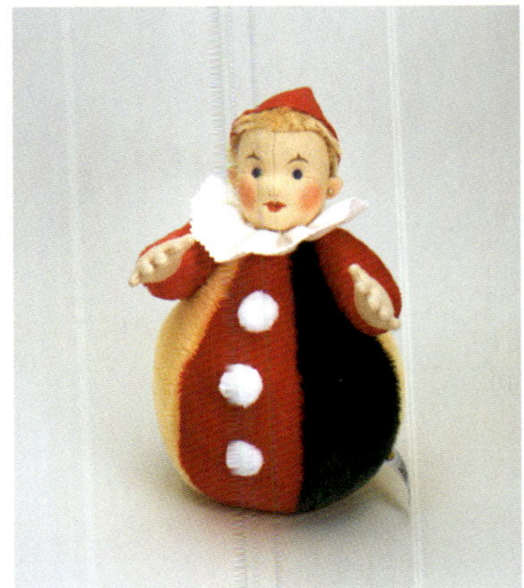

Rolly Polly Clown

Replica 1909, Mohair, Arme gegliedert, mit Rassel, USA-Artikel - *1909 replica, mohair, arms jointed, with rattle, article for the USA*

SERIE	ART.-NO	PERIOD	PR.	INFO
	0116/28	1983-1989	4	28 cm

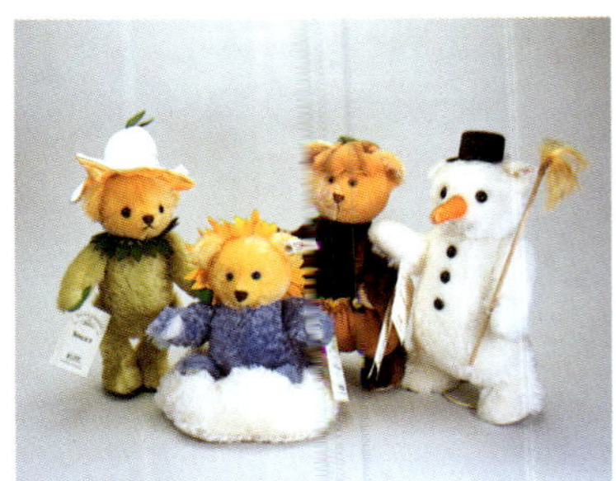

Vier Jahreszeiten - *Four Seasons*

Fruehling, Sommer, Herbst & Winter, Mohair Webpelz, limit. Auflage je 5.000 Stueck fuer USA - *spring, summer, autumn & winter, mohair woven fur, ltd edition of 5,000 each, exclusive for the USA*

EAN-NO.	PERIOD	PR.	INFO
665172	1996-1998	4-5	36 cm, Schneemann - *Snowman*
665271	1997-1998	4-5	31 cm, Fruehlingstrieb - *Sprout*
665288	1997-1998	4-5	25 cm, Sonnenstrahl - *Sunbeam*
665295	1997-1998	4-5	32 cm, Kuerbis - *Pumpkin*

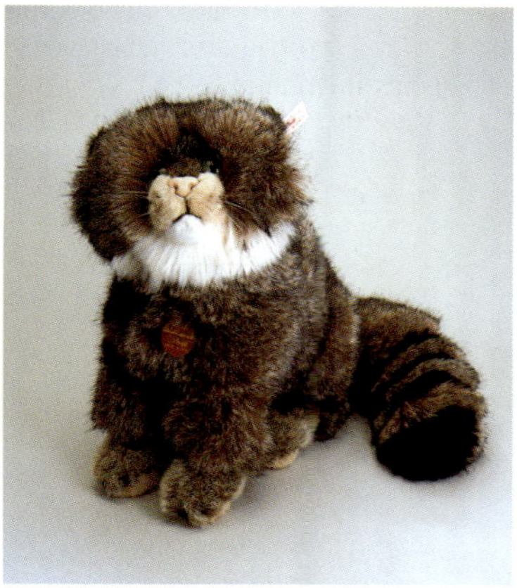

Pallas Katze - *Pallas Cat*

Acryl-Webpelz, naturfarben, stehend, limit. Auflage 2.500 Stueck fuer Smithonian´s, USA - *acrylic fur, natural color, standing, ltd edition of 2,500 for Smithonian´s, USA*

EAN-No.	Period	Pr.	Info
665356	1997-1998	4	32 cm

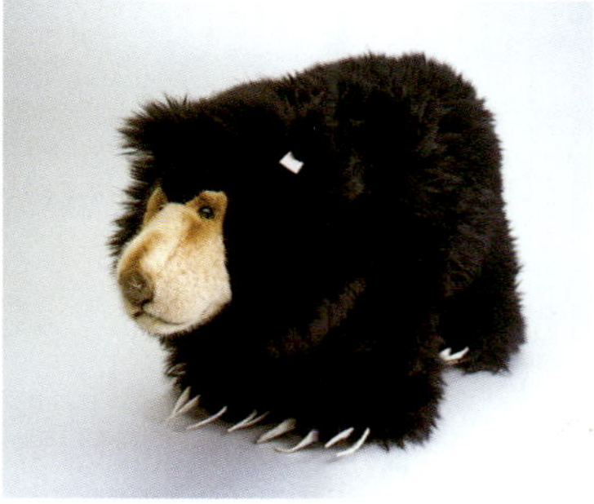

Sloth Baer - *Sloth Bear*

Webpelz, schwarz, stehend, limit. Auflage 2.500 Stueck fuer Smithonian's, USA - *woven fur, black, standing, ltd edition of 2,500 for Smithonian´s, USA*

EAN-No.	Period	Pr.	Info
665523	1998-1998	4	26 cm

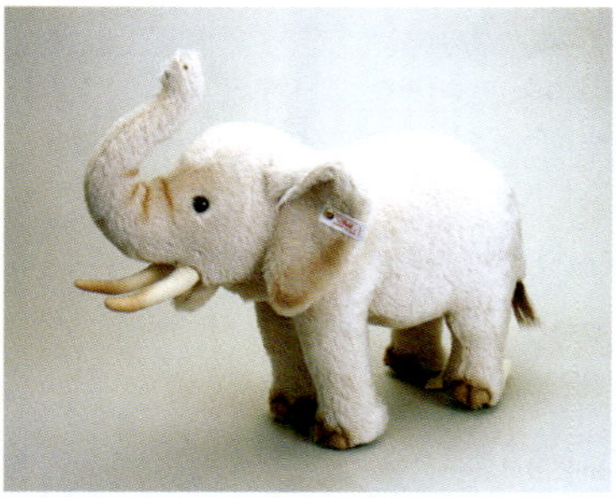

Afrikanischer Elefant - *African Elephant*

Mohair Webpelz, grau, stehend, limit. Auflage 1.500 Stueck in Zusammenarbeit mit Discovery Channel / Animal Planet, Amerika - *mohair woven fur, grey, standing, ltd edition of 1,500 in cooperation with Discovery Channel / Animal Planet, USA*

EAN-No.	Period	Pr.	Info
665301	1998-1998	4-5	40 cm

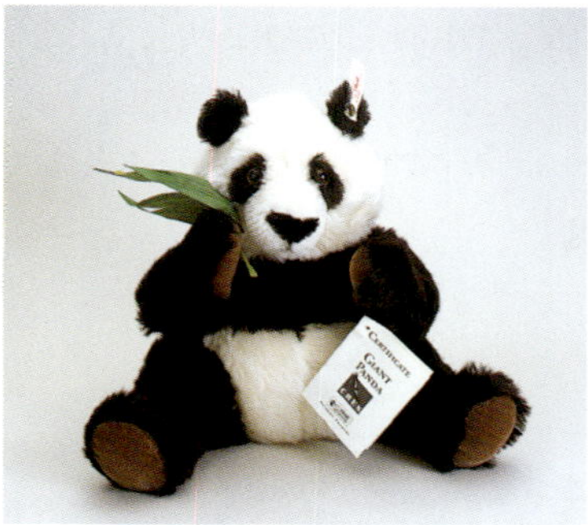

Riesen-Panda - *Giant Panda*

Mohair Webpelz, schwarz/weiss, gegliedert, limit. Auflage 1.500 Stueck fuer Zoological Society of San Diego, USA - *mohair woven fur, black/white, jointed, ltd edition of 1,500 for Zoological Society of San Diego, USA*

EAN-No.	Period	Pr.	Info
665332	1998-1998	4-5	25 cm

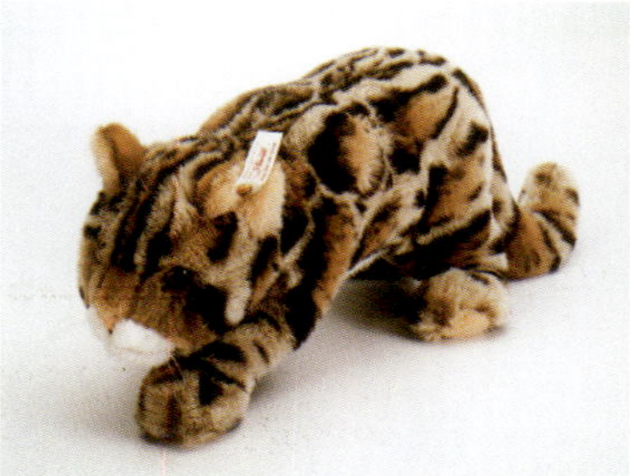

Clouded Leopard

Webpelz, gefleckt, stehend, limit. Auflage 1.500 Stueck fuer Smithonian's, USA - *woven fur, spotted, standing, ltd edition of 1,500 for Smithonian's, USA*

EAN-No.	Period	Pr.	Info
665875	1999-1999	4	35 cm

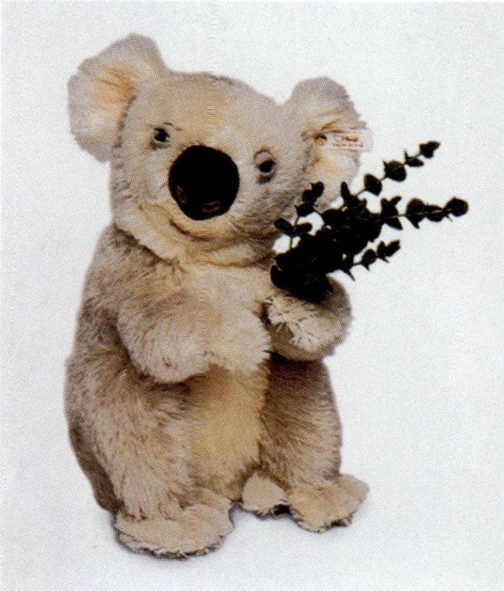

Koala

Mohair Webpelz, beige, stehend, limit. Auflage 1.500 Stueck fuer Zoological Society of San Diego, USA - *mohair woven fur, beige, sitting up, ltd edition of 1,500 for Zoological Society of San Diego, USA*

EAN-No.	Period	Pr.	Info
665967	1999-1999	4-5	30 cm

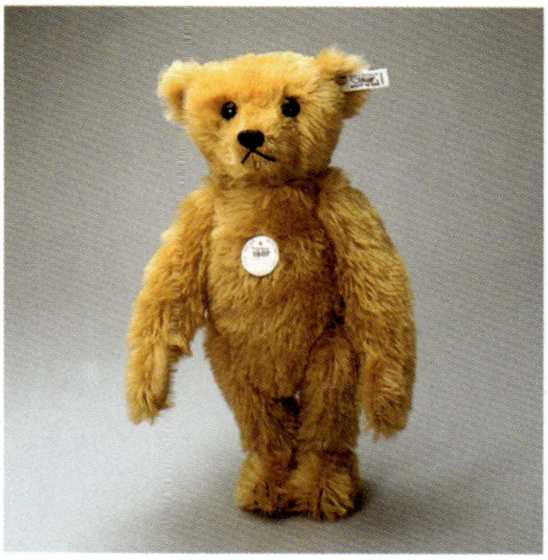

Teddybaer 1907 - *Teddy Bear 1907*

"Japanbaer", Mohair, blond, gegliedert, Brummstimme, limit. Auflage 5.000 Stueck - *"Japanese Bear", mohair, blond, jointed, growler, ltd edition of 5,000*

Serie	Art.-No	Period	Pr.	Info
406034	**0174/34**	1991-1991	4-5	34 cm

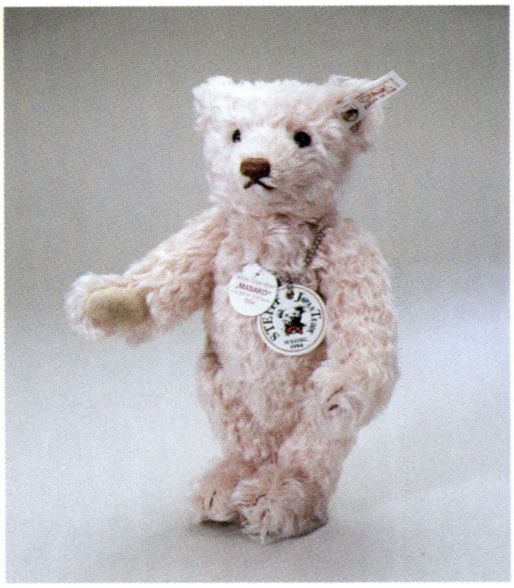

Teddybaer Masako - *Teddybear Masako*

Mohair, rosé, gegliedert, abwaschbar, limit. Auflage 1.500 Stueck fuer Japan - *mohair, rose, jointed, surface washable, ltd edition of 1,500 for Japan*

EAN-No.	Period	Pr.	Info
650797	1994-1994	7	25 cm

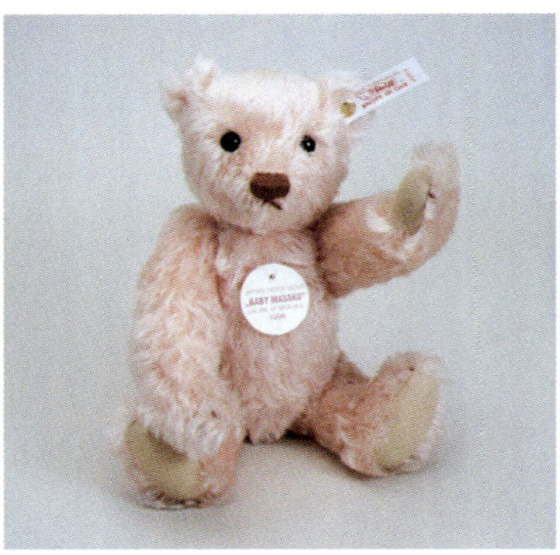

Baby Masako

Mohair, rosé, gegliedert, abwaschbar, limit. Auflage 3.000 Stueck fuer Japan - *mohair, rose, jointed, surface washable, ltd edition of 3,000 for Japan*

EAN-No.	Period	Pr.	Info
652516	1996-1996	5-6	23 cm

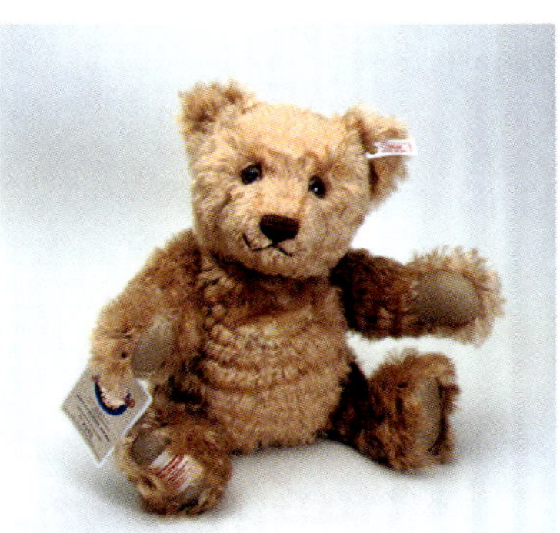

Teddybaer Chooky - *Teddybear Chooky*

Mohair, braun, gegliedert, abwaschbar, limit. Auflage 2.000 Stueck fuer Japan - *mohair, brown, jointed, surface washable, growler, ltd edition of 2,000 for Japan*

EAN-No.	Period	Pr.	Info
650840	1995-1995	5-6	39 cm

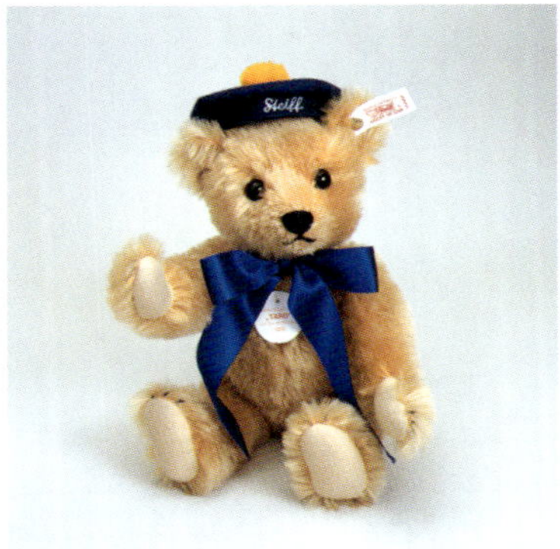

Teddybaer **Taro** - *Teddybear **Taro***

Mohair, goldbraun, gegliedert, abwaschbar, blaue Muetze & Schleife, limit. Auflage 2.000 Stueck fuer Japan - *mohair, gold-brown, jointed, surface washable, blue hat & ribbon, ltd edition of 2,000 for Japan*

EAN-No.	Period	Pr.	Info
650864	1995-1995	5	28 cm

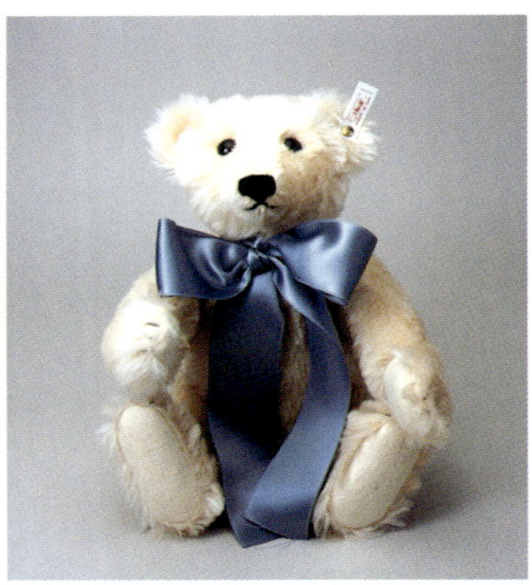

Teddy Victoria

Mohair, hellbraun, gegliedert, abwaschbar, limit. Auflage 500 Stueck fuer Japan - *mohair, light brown, jointed, surface washable, ltd edition of 500 for Japan*

EAN-No.	Period	Pr.	Info
652509	1995-1995	6	40 cm

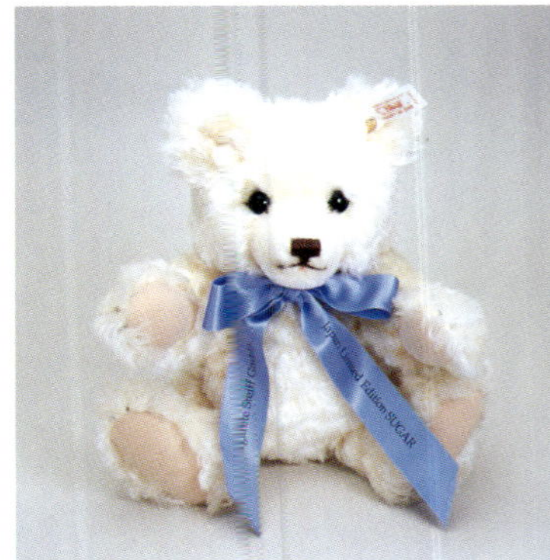

Teddy Sugar

Mohair, weiss, gegliedert, abwaschbar, limit. Auflage 3.000 Stueck fuer Japan - *mohair, white, jointed, surface washable, ltd edition of 3,000 for Japan*

EAN-No.	Period	Pr.	Info
652547	1996-1996	5	25 cm

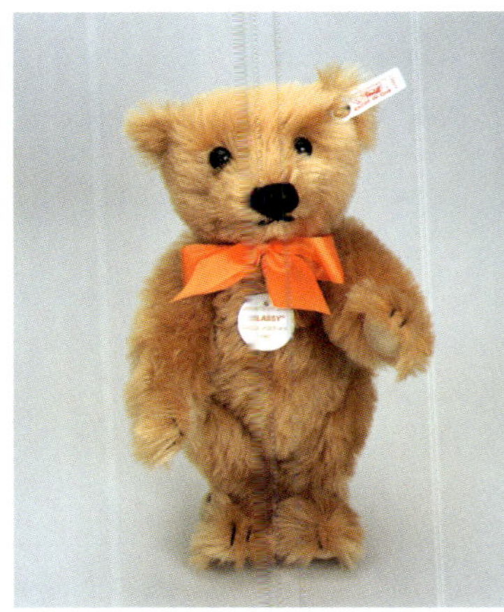

Teddy **Classy**

Mohair, rotblond, gegliedert, abwaschbar, limit. Auflage 3.000 Stueck fuer Japan - *mohair, red-blond, jointed, surface washable, ltd edition of 3,000 for Japan*

EAN-No.	Period	Pr.	Info
659867	1996-1996	5	26 cm

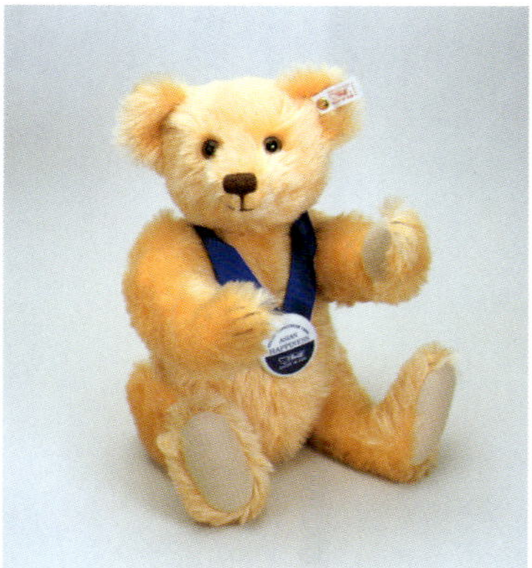

Asian Happiness

Mohair, apricot, gegliedert, abwaschbar, limit. Auflage 3.000 Stueck fuer Asien - *mohair, apricot, jointed, surface washable, ltd edition of 3.000 for Asia*

EAN-No.	Period	Pr.	Info
659874	1996-1996	5	40 cm

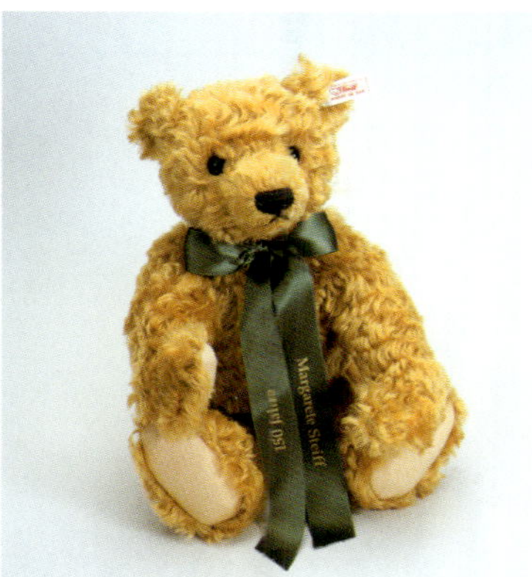

Margarete Steiff Teddy

Mohair, blond, gegliedert, abwaschbar, zum 150. Geburtstag von Margarete Steiff, limit. Auflage 3.000 Stueck fuer Japan - *mohair, blond, jointed, surface washable, on the occasion of the 150. Birthday of Margarete Steiff, ltd edition of 3,000 for Japan*

EAN-No.	Period	Pr.	Info
652608	1997-1997	5	35 cm

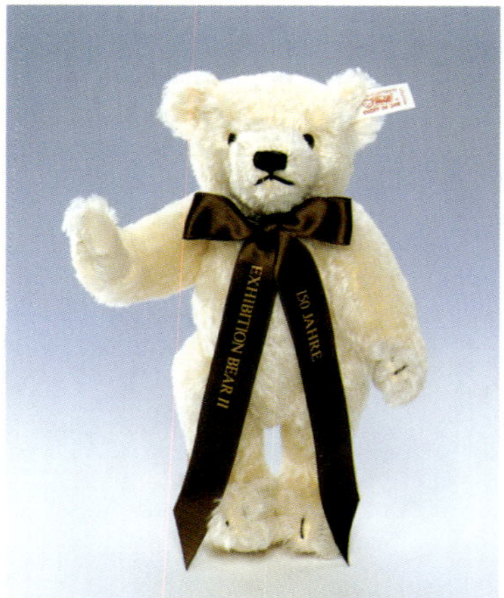

Teddybaer - *Teddybear*

Mohair, weiss, gegliedert, zur Wanderausstellung in Japan anlaesslich des 150. Geburtstags von Margarete Steiff, limit. Auflage 1.500 Stueck fuer Japan - *mohair, white, jointed, for the touring exhibition in Japan on the occasion of the 150. Birthday of Margarete Steiff, ltd edition of 1,500 for Japan*

EAN-No.	Period	Pr.	Info
652707	1997-1997	5	26 cm

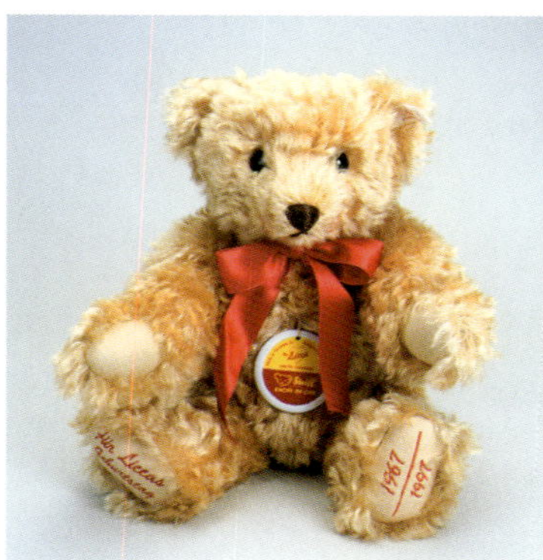

Teddybaer - *Teddybear*

Mohair, blond, gegliedert, abwaschbar, zum 30. Geburtstag von Licca, limit. Auflage 3.000 Stueck fuer Japan - *mohair, blond, jointed, surface washable, to celebrate the 30th birthday of Licca, ltd edition of 3,000 for Japan*

EAN-No.	Period	Pr.	Info
652585	1997-1997	4-5	35 cm

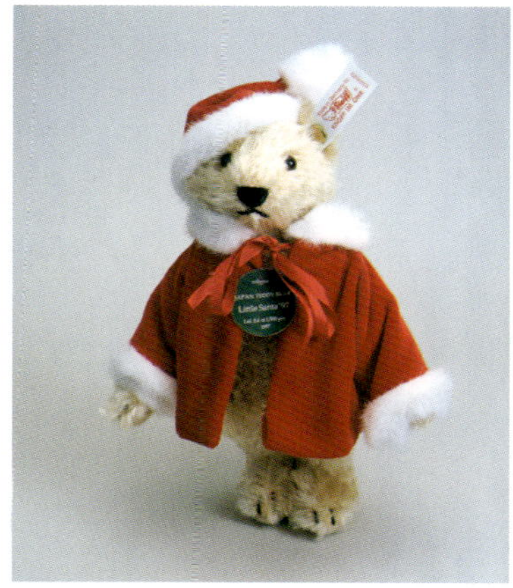

Little Santa

Mohair, blond, gegliedert, abwaschbar, limit. Auflage 2.500 Stueck fuer Japan - *mohair, blond, jointed, surface washable, ltd edition of 2,500 for Japan*

EAN-No.	Period	Pr.	Info
652622	1997-1997	4-5	20 cm

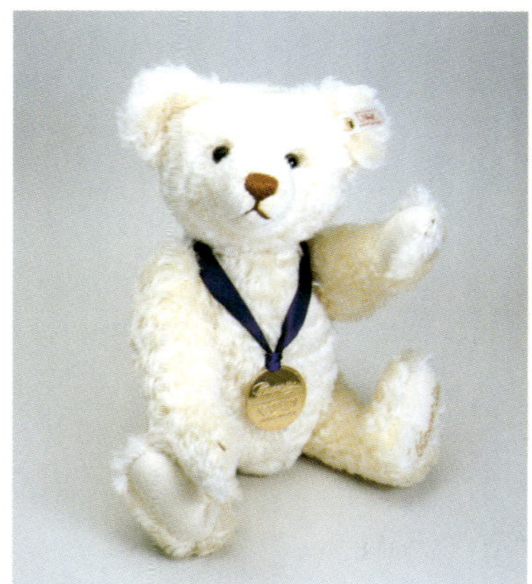

Prosperity Teddy

Mohair, weiss, gegliedert, abwaschbar, limit. Auflage 1.847 Stueck fuer Asien - *mohair, white, jointed, surface washable, ltd edition of 1,847 for Asia*

EAN-No.	Period	Pr.	Info
652561	1997-1997	5	35 cm

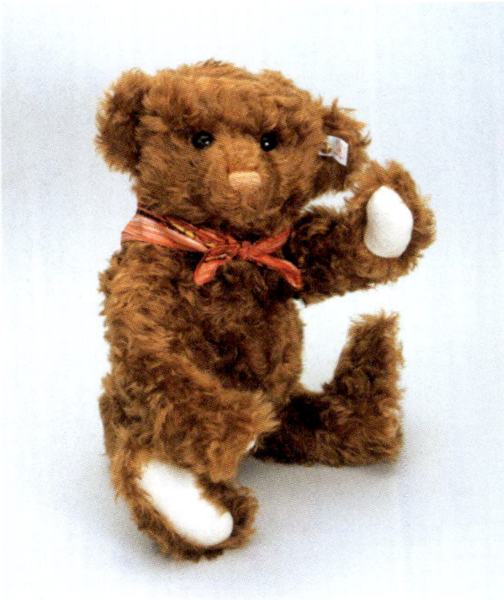

Teddy Raffles

Mohair, dunkelbraun, gegliedert, abwaschbar, limit. Auflage 1.500 Stueck fuer Singapur - *mohair, dark brown, jointed, surface washable, ltd edition of 1,500 for Singapore*

EAN-No.	Period	Pr.	Info
652578	1997-1997	5	43 cm

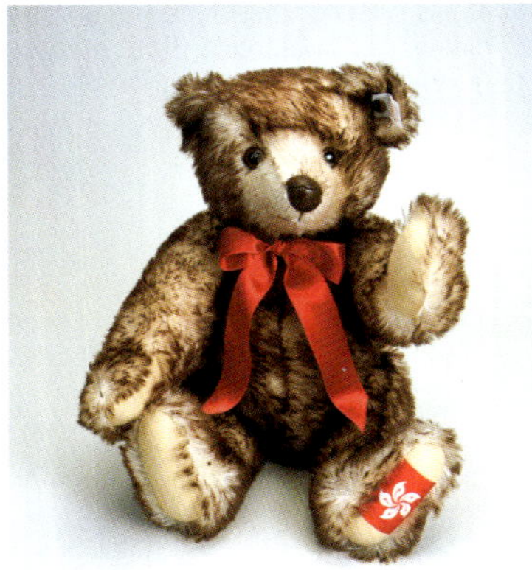

Harmony Teddy

Mohair, braun gespitzt, gegliedert, abwaschbar, limit. Auflage 1.997 Stueck fuer Hong Kong / China - *mohair, brown tipped, jointed, surface washable, ltd edition of 1.997 for Hong Kong / China*

EAN-No.	Period	Pr.	Info
652615	1997-1997	5	35 cm

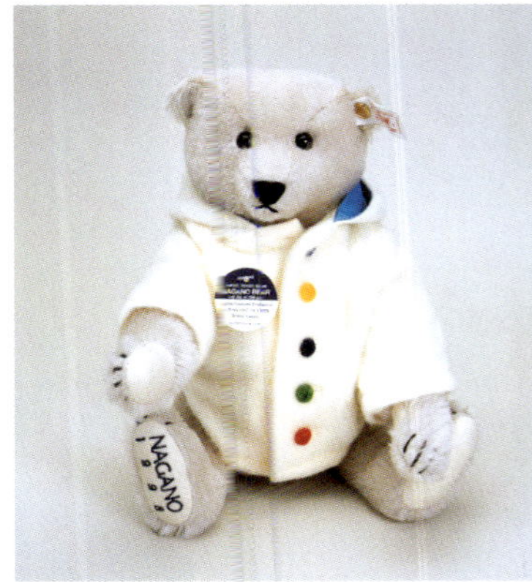

Nagano Teddybaer - ***Nagano** Teddybear*

Mohair, hellgrau, gegliedert, Ausgabe anlaesslich der olympischen Winterspiele 1998 in Nagano, limit. Auflage 2.500 Stueck fuer Japan - *mohair, light grey, jointed, on the occasion of the 1998 Olympic Games (winter) in Nagano, ltd edition of 2,500 for Japan*

EAN-No.	Period	Pr.	Info
652592	1998-1998	6-7	30 cm

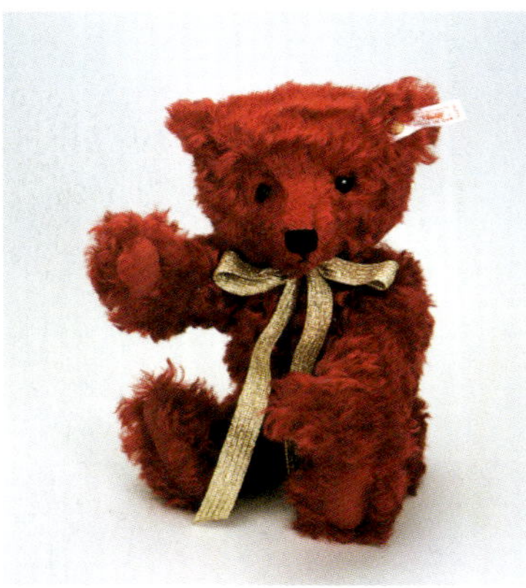

Romantic Baer - *Romantic Bear*

Mohair, himbeerrot, gegliedert, abwaschbar, limit. Auflage 2.000 Stueck fuer Hong Kong - *mohair, raspberry, jointed, surface washable, ltd edition of 2,000 for Hong Kong*

EAN-No.	Period	Pr.	Info
652530	1997-1997	5	28 cm

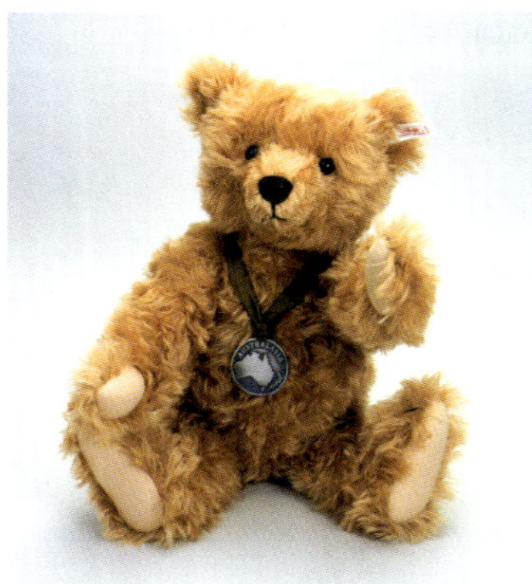

Captain James Teddy

Mohair, hellbraun, gegliedert, abwaschbar, Australasia-Baer, limit. Auflage 1.500 Stueck - *mohair, light brown, jointed, surface washable, Australasia-Bear, ltd edition of 1,500*

EAN-No.	Period	Pr.	Info
659904	1997-1997	5-6	42 cm

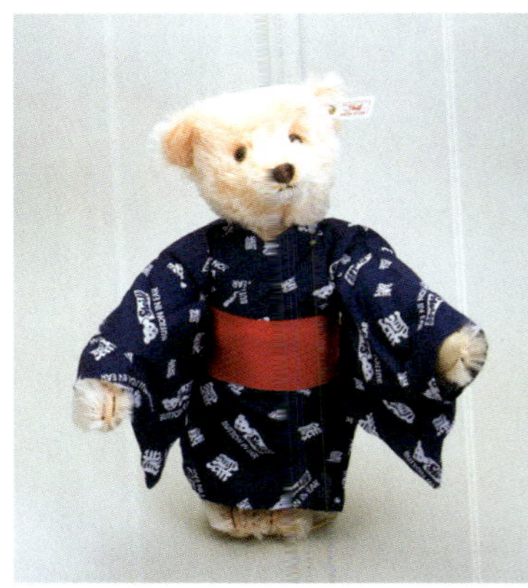

Yukata Teddybaer - *Yukata Teddybear*

Mohair, apricot, gegliedert, limit. Auflage 1.500 Stueck fuer Japan Teddy Baer Vereinigung - *mohair, apricot, jointed, ltd edition of 1,500 for Japan Teddy Bear Association*

EAN-No.	Period	Pr.	Info
652790	1998-1998	5	30 cm

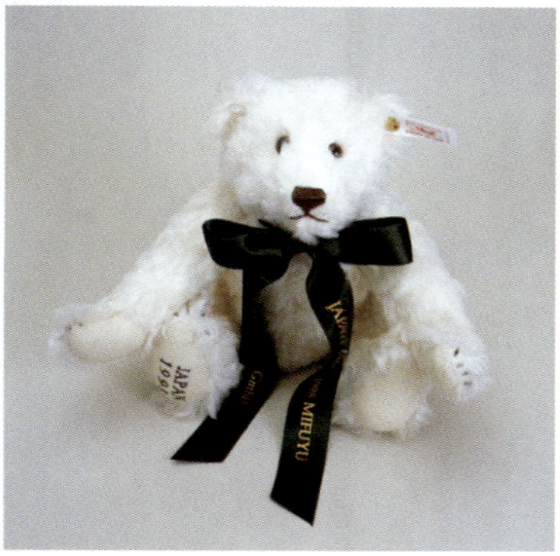

Mifuyu Teddybaer - *Mifuyu Teddybear*

Mohair, weiss, gegliedert, limit. Auflage 3.000 Stueck fuer Japan - *mohair, white, jointed, ltd edition of 3,000 for Japan*

EAN-No.	Period	Pr.	Info
652721	1998-1998	4-5	28 cm

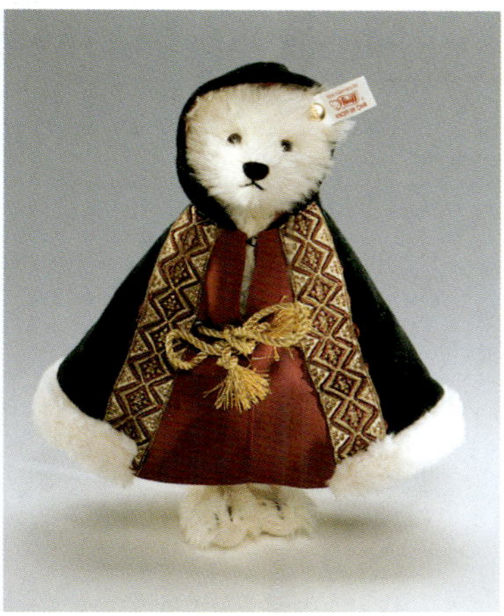

Little Santa

Mohair, weiss, gegliedert, limit. Auflage 2.500 Stueck fuer Japan - *mohair, white, jointed, ltd edition of 2,500 for Japan*

EAN-No.	Period	Pr.	Info
652776	1998-1998	4-5	23 cm

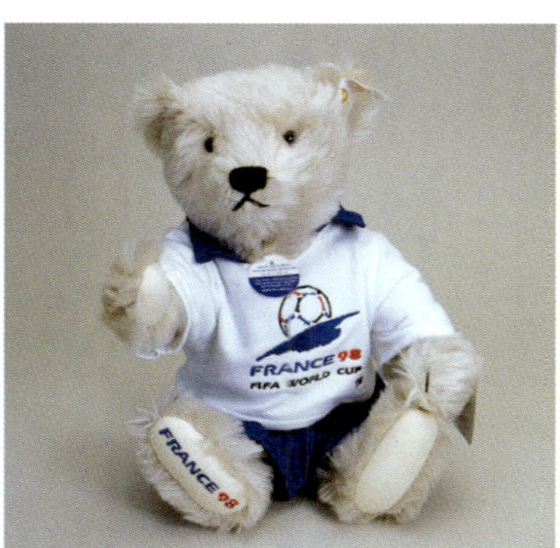

Fussball Teddy - *Soccer Teddy*

Mohair, hellgrau, gegliedert, anlaesslich der Fussball-WM in Frankreich, limit. Auflage 2.000 Stueck fuer Japan - *mohair, light grey, jointed, on the occasion of the 1998 Soccer World Championship in France, ltd edition of 2,000 for Japan*

EAN-No.	Period	Pr.	Info
652783	1998-1998	4-5	35 cm

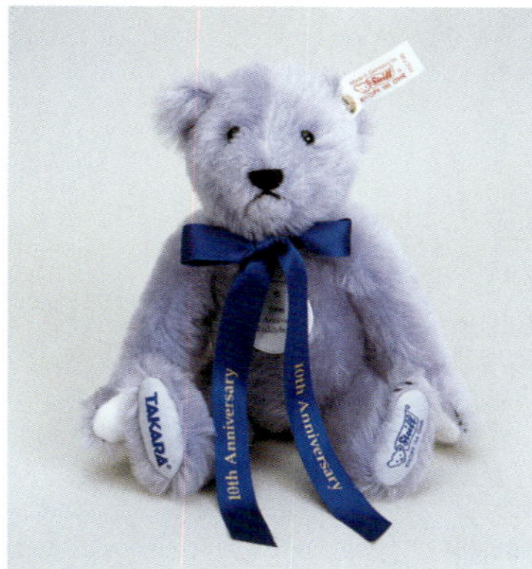

Takara Teddy

Mohair, hellblau, gegliedert, anlaesslich 10 Jahre Takara / Steiff, limit. Auflage 1.500 Stueck fuer Japan - *mohair, light blue, jointed, on the occasion of 10 years cooperation between Steiff & Takara, ltd edition of 1,500 for Japan*

EAN-No.	Period	Pr.	Info
652738	1998-1998	4-5	21 cm

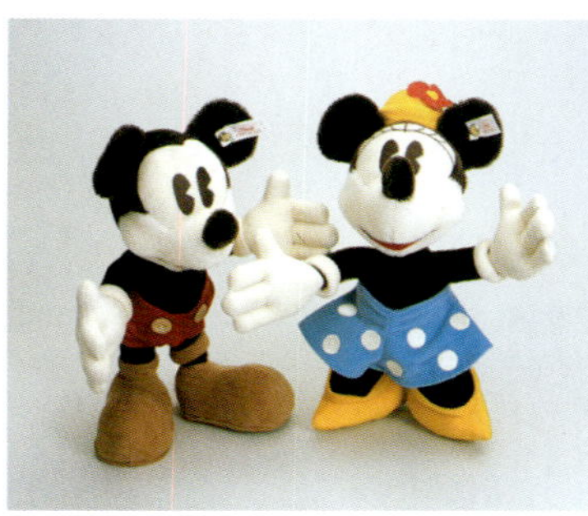

Mickey & Minnie Set

Mohair, schwarz/weiss, stehend, 28 cm, limit. Auflage 3.000 Stueck fuer Japan - *mohair, black/white, standing, 28 cm, ltd edition of 3,000 for Japan*

EAN-No.	Period	Pr.	Info
652769	1998-1998	5	kpl. Set - *compl.set*
J04260	1998-1998	4	Mickey
J04261	1998-1998	4	Minnie

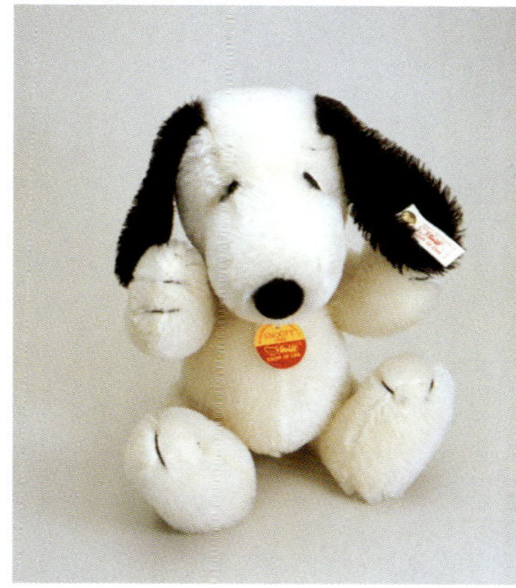

Snoopy

Mohair, weiss/schwarz, gegliedert, aus der Serie Peanuts, Copyright United Feature Syndicate, Inc., limit. Auflage 1.500 Stueck fuer Japan - *mohair, white/black, jointed, from the cartoon Peanuts, Copyright United Feature Syndicate, Inc., ltd edition of 1,500 for Japan*

EAN-No.	Period	Pr.	Info
652714	1998-1998	5	26 cm

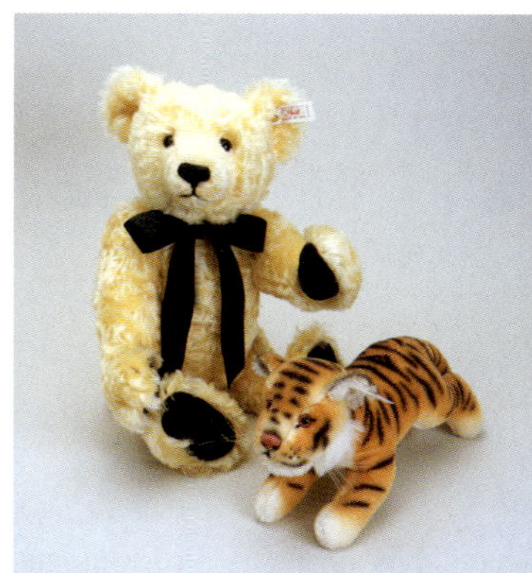

Tiger & Baer Set - *Tiger & Bear Set*

Mohair, 38/22 cm, gelb bzw. orange/schwarz, gegliedert bzw. stehend, nach dem chinesischen Kalender, limit. Auflage 1.500 Stueck fuer Hong Kong / China - *mohair, 38/22 cm, yellow and orange/black, jointed and standing, taken from the Chinese calendar, ltd edition of 1,500 sets for Hong Kong / China*

EAN-No.	Period	Pr.	Info
652639	1998-1998	5	kpl. Set - *compl. set*
	1998-1998	4-5	38 cm, Baer - *bear*
	1998-1998	3	22 cm, Tiger

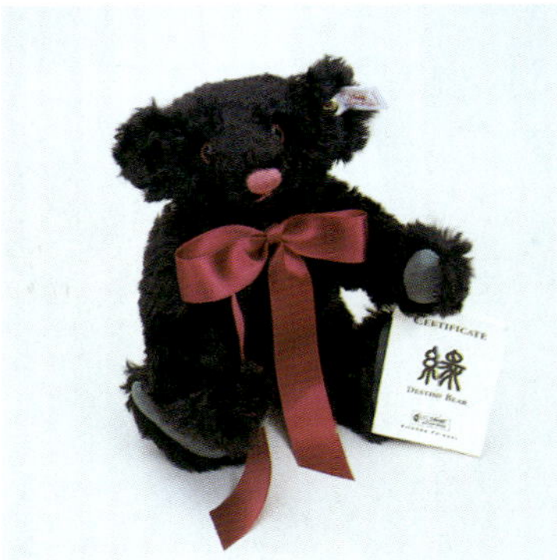

Destiny Baer - *Destiny Bear*

Mohair, schwarz, gegliedert, Druckstimme, zum 10jaehrigen Bestehen von Animal Kingom Ltd., Hong Kong, limit. Auflage 1.500 Stueck - *mohair, black, jointed, press voice, on the occasion of 10 years Animal Kingdom Ltd, Hong Kong, ltd edition of 1,500*

EAN-No.	Period	Pr.	Info
652691	1998-1998	4-5	27 cm

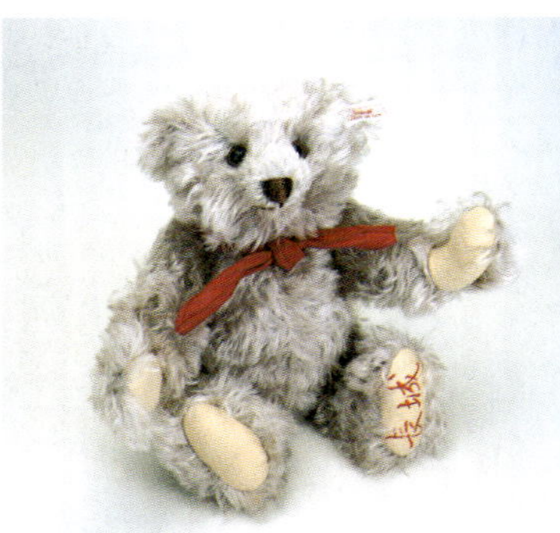

Great Wall Baer - *Great Wall Bear*

Mohair, grau, gegliedert, Druckstimme, limit. Auflage 1.500 Stueck fuer Hong Kong / China - *mohair, grey, jointed, press voice, ltd edition of 1,500 for Hong Kong / China*

EAN-No.	Period	Pr.	Info
652677	1998-1998	4-5	30 cm

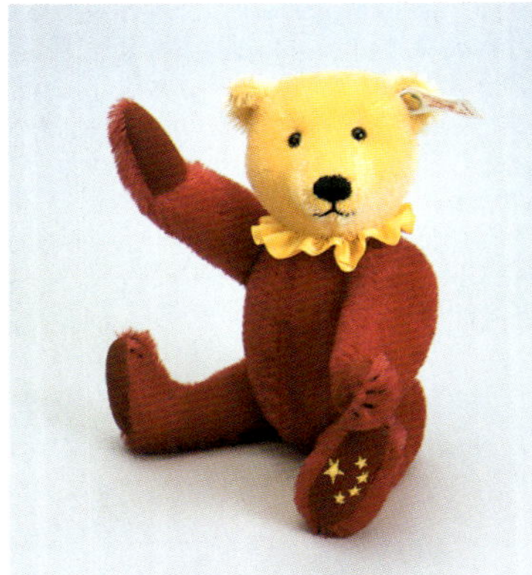

Stary Baer - *Stary Bear*

Mohair, rot/gelb, gegliedert, limit. Auflage 1.500 Stueck fuer Hong Kong / China - *mohair, red/yellow, jointed, ltd edition of 1,500 for Hong Kong / China*

EAN-No.	Period	Pr.	Info
652684	1998-1998	4-5	24 cm

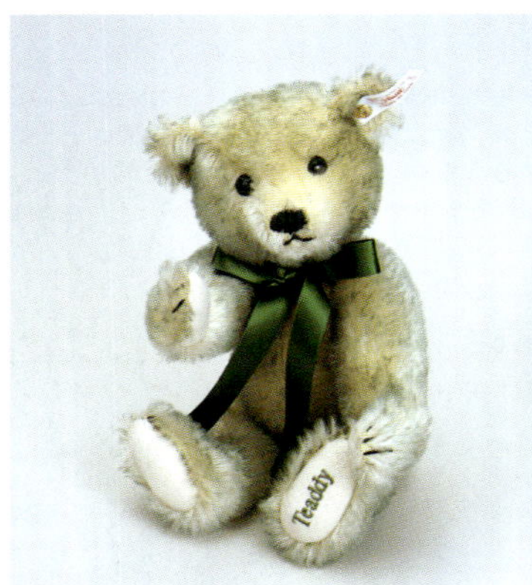

Teaddy Baer - *Teaddy Bear*

Mohair, gruen gespitzt, gegliedert, limit. Auflage 1.500 Stueck fuer Taiwan - *mohair, green tipped, jointed, ltd edition of 1,500 for Taiwan*

EAN-No.	Period	Pr.	Info
652646	1998-1998	4-5	28 cm

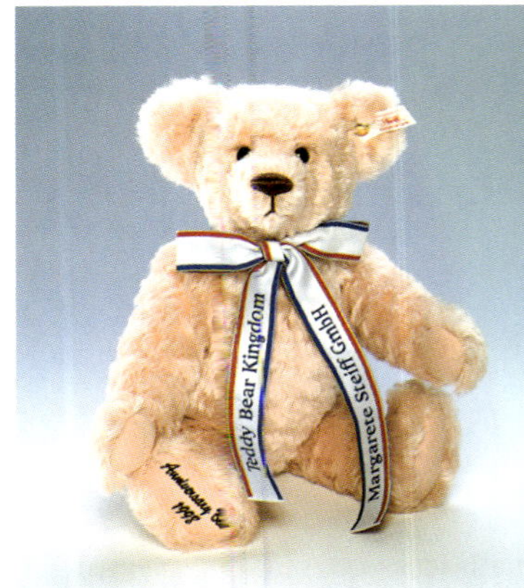

Teddy Baer Kingdom - *Teddy Bear Kingdom*

Mohair, zartrosa, gegliedert, zum 1. Geburtstag des Teddy Bear Kingdom Vergnuegungspark / Museum, Japan, limit. Auflage 1.500 Stueck - *mohair, pale-rose, jointed, on the occasion of the 1st birthday of the Kingdom amusement park / museum in Japan, ltd edition of 1,500*

EAN-No.	Period	Pr.	Info
675201	1998-1998	5	33 cm

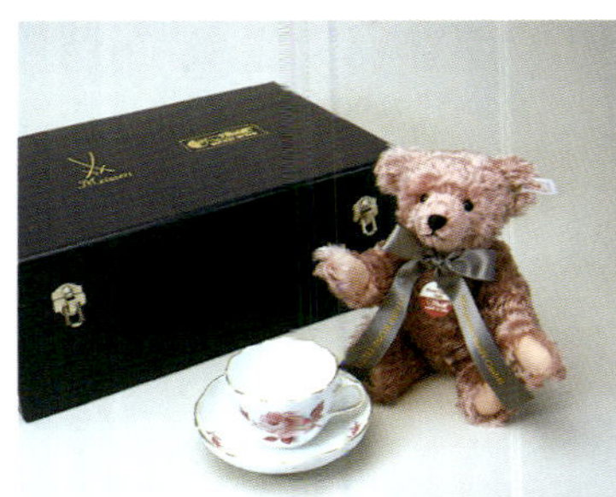

Meissen / Steiff Teddy

Mohair, rosa, gegliedert, abwaschbar, zusammen mit einer Meissner Tasse mit Untertasse, limit. Auflage 1.500 Stueck fuer Japan - *mohair, pink, jointed, with a cup of Meissen porcelain, ltd edition of 1,500 for Japan*

EAN-No.	Period	Pr.	Info
675232	1999-1999	5-6	28 cm

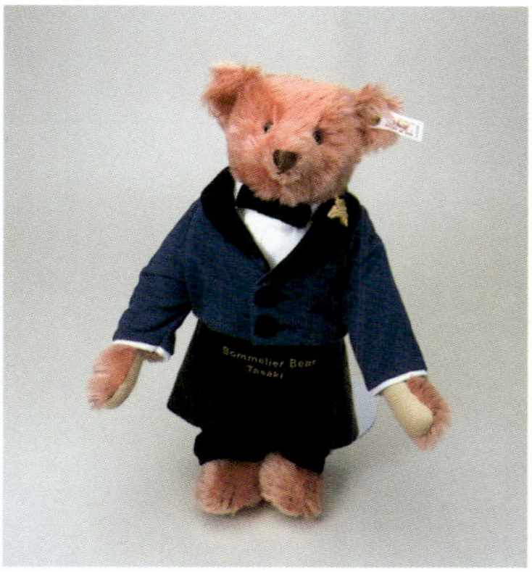

Sommelier Baer - *Sommelier Bear*

Mohair, rosenholz, gegliedert, abwaschbar, zu Ehren des Sommeliers Tasaki, limit. Auflage 1.500 Stueck fuer Japan - *mohair woven fur, rosewood, jointed, surface washable, to honor the Sommelier Tasaki, ltd. edition of 1500 for Japan*

EAN-No.	Period	Pr.	Info
675300	1999-1999	5	33 cm

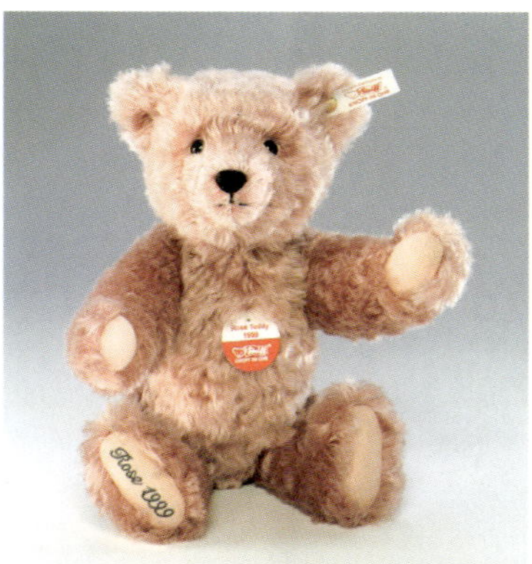

Rosé Teddy - *Rose Teddy*

Mohair, rosé, gegliedert, abwaschbar, limit. Auflage 2.500 Stueck fuer Japan - *mohair, rose, jointed, ltd edition of 2,500 for Japan*

EAN-No.	Period	Pr.	Info
675270	1999-1999	5	40 cm

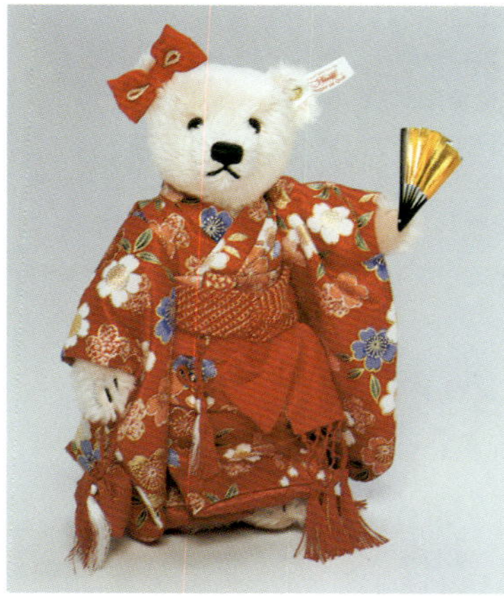

Teddy Hatsuhime

Mohair, rosé, gegliedert, abwaschbar, vergoldeter Steiff-Knopf, limit. Auflage 2.000 Stueck fuer Japan - *mohair, rose, jointed, surface washable, gold-plated Steiff button, ltd edition of 2,000 for Japan*

EAN-No.	Period	Pr.	Info
675287	1999-1999	4-5	28 cm

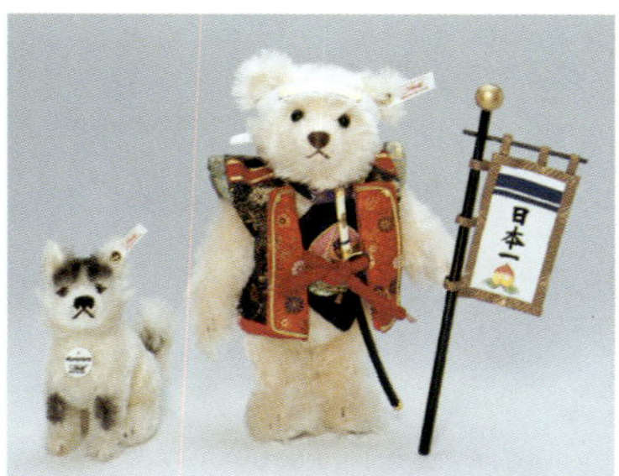

Momotaro mit Hund - *Momotaro and Dog*

Teddybaer & Hund, Mohair, pfirsichfarben / weiss, gegliedert / sitzend, limit. Auflage 2.000 Stueck fuer Japan - *Teddybear & dog, mohair, peach color / white, jointed / sitting, ltd edition of 2,000 for Japan*

EAN-No.	Period	Pr.	Info
675294	1999-1999	5	kpl. Set - *compl. set*
J04292	1999-1999	4	27 cm, Momotaro
J04291	1999-1999	3-4	14 cm, Hund - *dog*

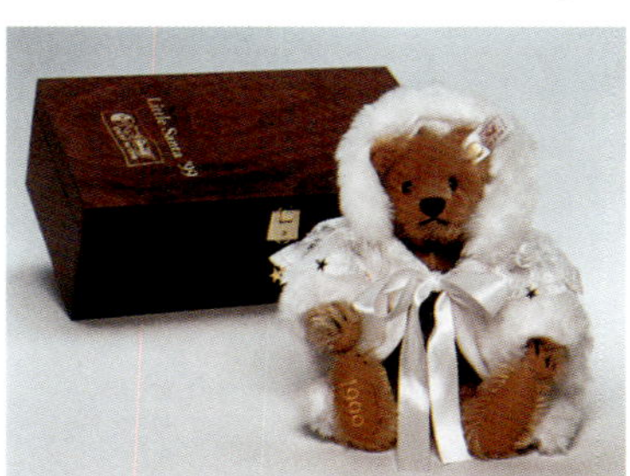

Little Santa

Mohair, zimt, gegliedert, weisser Kapuzenmantel aus Samt mit Plueschbesatz & Spitzenkragen, limit. Auflage 2.500 Stueck fuer Japan - *mohair, cinnamon, jointed, white coat of velvet with hood, plush trimming & lace collar, ltd edition of 2,500 for Japan*

EAN-No.	Period	Pr.	Info
675317	1999-1999	4	20 cm

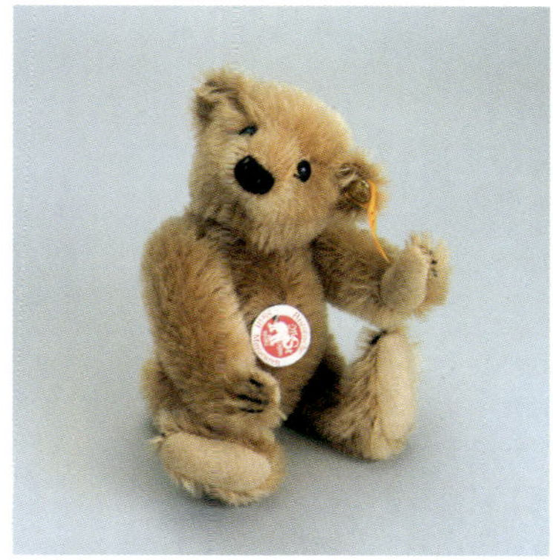

Cinnamon Baer - *Cinnamon Bear*

Mohair Webpelz, zimt, gegliedert - *mohair woven fur, cinnamon, jointed*

EAN-No.	Period	Pr.	Info
029073	1992-1997	2-3	16 cm

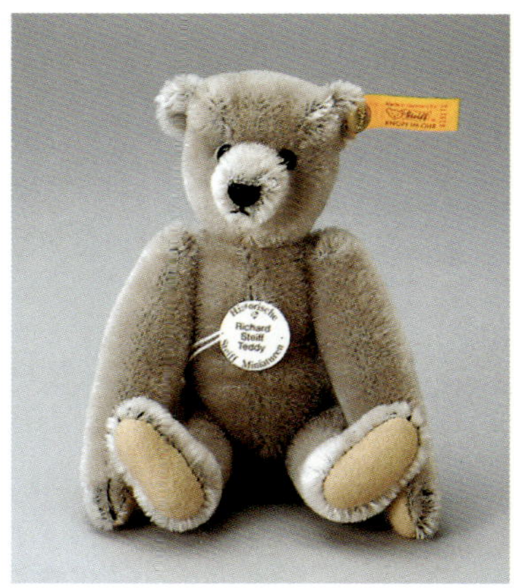

Richard Steiff Teddy

Mohair Webpelz, grau, gegliedert - *mohair woven fur, grey, jointed*

EAN-No.	Period	Pr.	Info
029172	1992-1997	2-3	16 cm

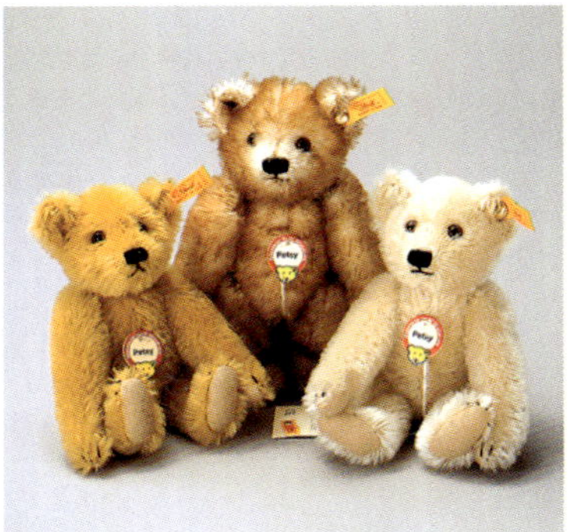

Petsy

Mohair Webpelz, 16 cm, gegliedert - *mohair woven fur, 16 cm, jointed*

EAN-No.	Period	Pr.	Info
029424	1992-1999	2-3	messing - *brass color*
029479	1992-1997	2-3	altgold - *old gold*
029523	1992-1995	2-3	fahlgold - *fawn gold*
029561	1995-1999	2-3	gespitzt - *tipped*

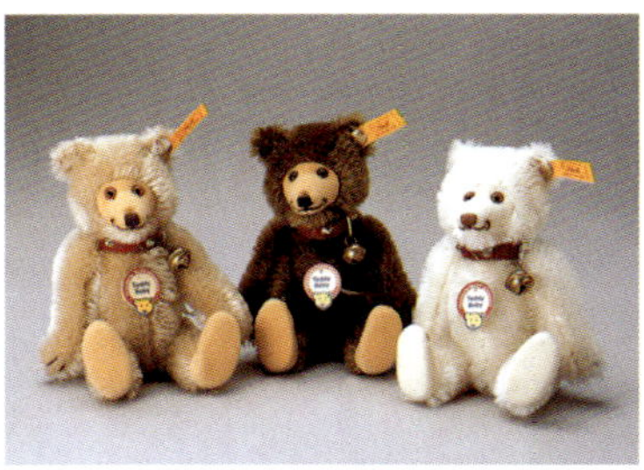

Teddy Baby

Mohair Webpelz, verziertes Lederhalsband, 16 cm, gegliedert - *mohair woven fur, leather collar, 16 cm, jointed*

EAN-No.	Period	Pr.	Info
029622	1992-1998	2-3	weiss - *white*
029677	1992-1998	2-3	hellmais - *pale corn yellow*
029721	1992-1998	2-3	braun - *brown*

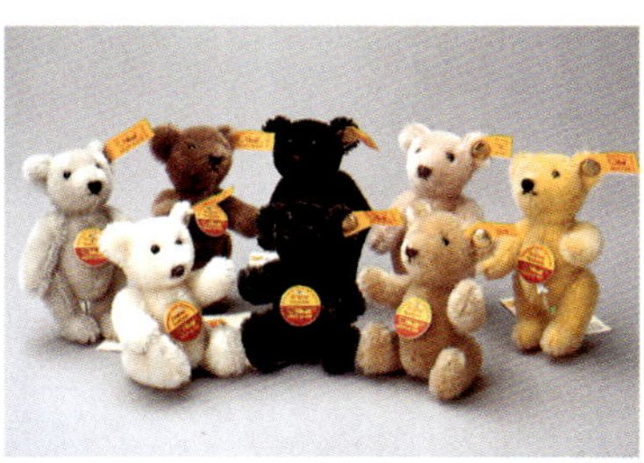

Original Teddybaer - *Original Teddy Bear*

Mohair Webpelz, gegliedert, 10 cm - *mohair woven fur, jointed, 10 cm*

EAN-No.	Period	Pr.	Info
030000	1992-1999	2	weiss - *white*
030055	1992-1999	2	honig - *honey*
030109	1992-1999	2	caramel
030505	1992-1999	2	schwarz - *black*
030406	1993-1999	2	rosé - *rose*
030307	1993-1998	2	grau - *grey*
030567	1993-1999	2	anthrazit - *anthracite*
030574	1993-1999	2	gold

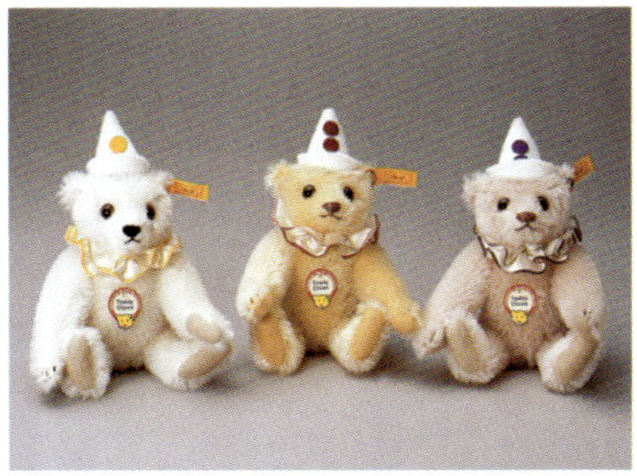

Teddy Clown

Mohair Webpelz, 16 cm, gegliedert - *mohair woven fur, 16 cm, jointed*

EAN-No.	Period	Pr.	Info
029387	1993-1997	2-3	gelb - *yellow*
029394	1993-1997	2-3	rosa - *pink*
029400	1993-1996	2-3	weiss - *white*

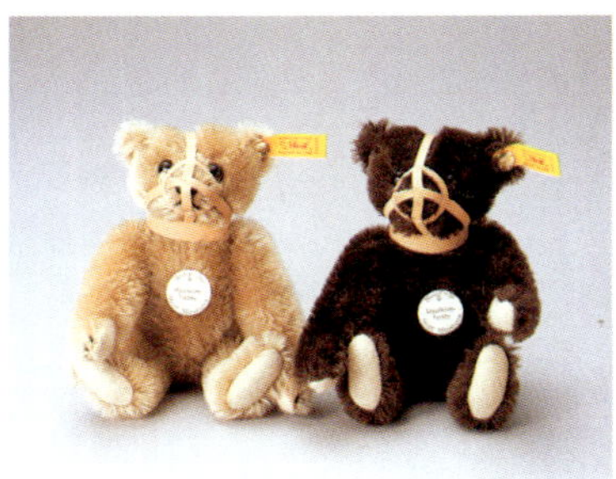

Maulkorb Teddy - *Teddy with Muzzle*

Mohair Webpelz, Maulkorb aus Leder, 16 cm, gegliedert - *mohair woven fur, leather muzzle, 16 cm, jointed*

EAN-No.	Period	Pr.	Info
029189	1993-1994	2-3	dunkelbraun - *dark brown*
029196	1993-1995	2-3	hellbraun - *light brown*

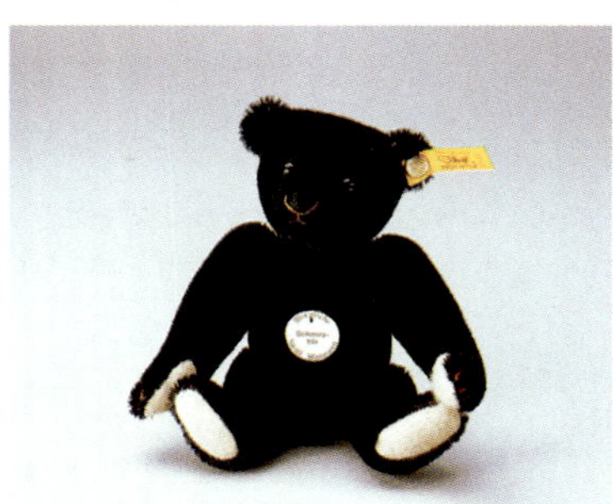

Schwarzbaer - *Black Bear*

Mohair Webpelz, gegliedert - *mohair woven fur, jointed*

EAN-No.	Period	Pr.	Info
029202	1993-1995	2-3	16 cm

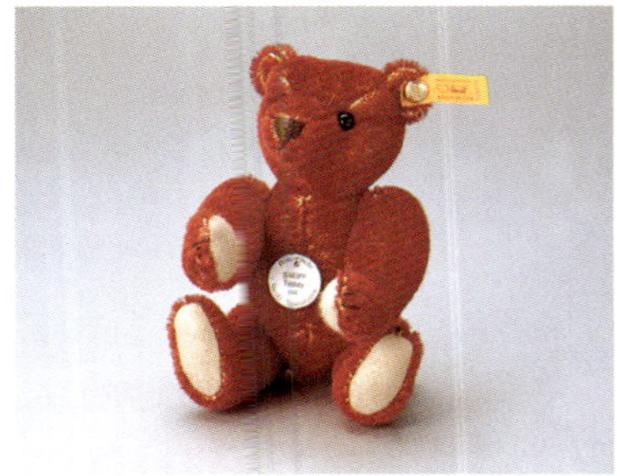

Steiff Teddy rot - *Teddy Red*

Mohair Webpelz, gegliedert - *mohair woven fur, jointed*

EAN-No.	Period	Pr.	Info
029226	1993-1999	2-3	16 cm

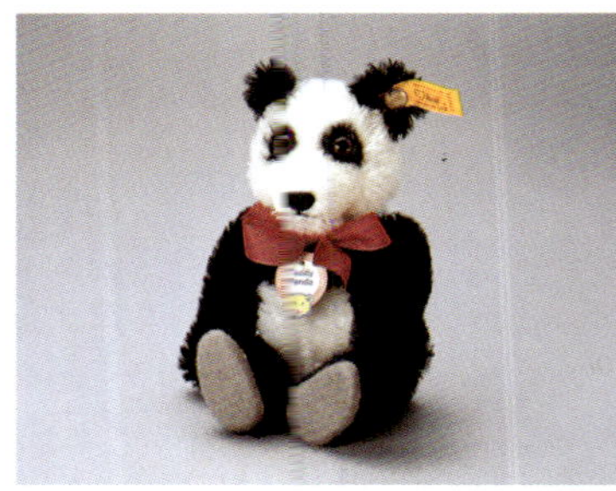

Teddy Panda

Mohair Webpelz, schwarz/weiss, gegliedert - *mohair woven fur, black/white, jointed*

EAN-No.	Period	Pr.	Info
029905	1993-1996	2-3	16 cm

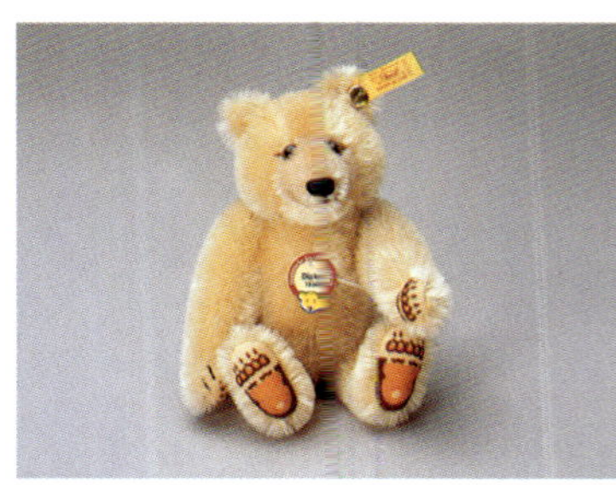

Dicky 1930

Mohair Webpelz, blond, gegliedert - *mohair woven fur, blond, jointed*

EAN-No.	Period	Pr.	Info
029783	1994-1995	2-3	16 cm

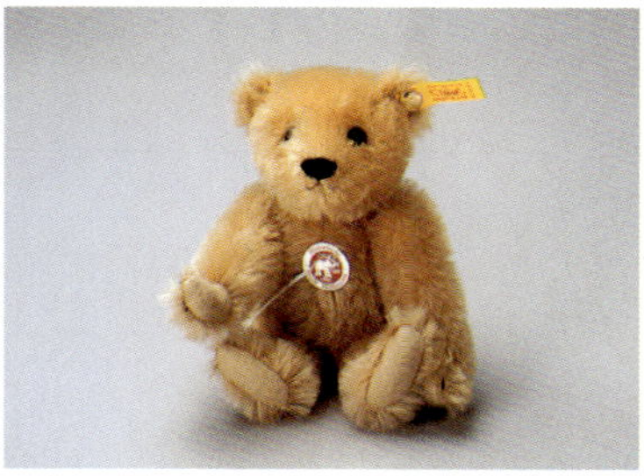

Baerle PAB

Mohair Webpelz, gegliedert - *mohair woven fur, jointed*

EAN-No.	Period	Pr.	Info
029097	1994-1997	2-3	16 cm

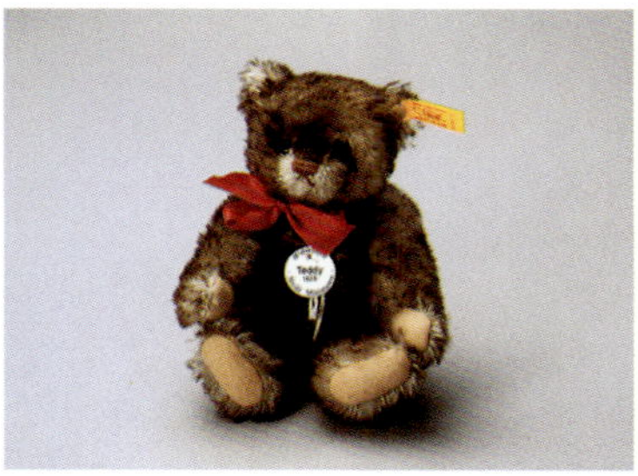

Teddy 1926

Mohair Webpelz, gespitzt, gegliedert - *mohair woven fur, tipped, jointed*

EAN-No.	Period	Pr.	Info
029271	1994-1999	2-3	16 cm

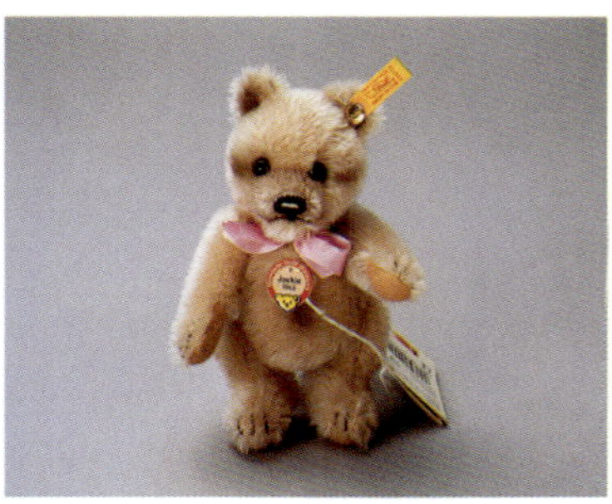

Jackie 1953

Mohair Webpelz, honig, gegliedert - *mohair woven fur, honey, jointed*

EAN-No.	Period	Pr.	Info
029929	1994-1999	2-3	16 cm

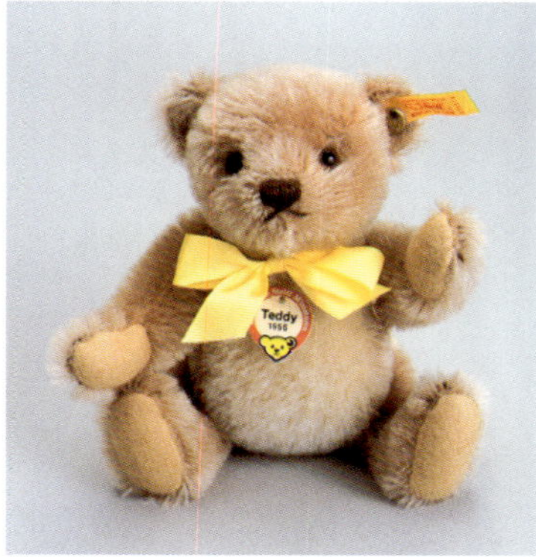

Teddy 1955

Mohair Webpelz, caramel, gegliedert - *mohair woven fur, caramel, jointed*

EAN-No.	Period	Pr.	Info
029974	1995-1997	2-3	16 cm

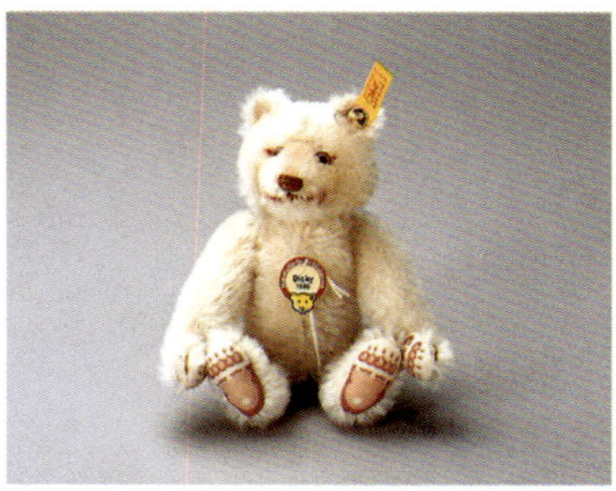

Dicky 1930

Mohair Webpelz, weiss, gegliedert - *mohair woven fur, white, jointed*

EAN-No.	Period	Pr.	Info
029776	1995-1996	2-3	16 cm

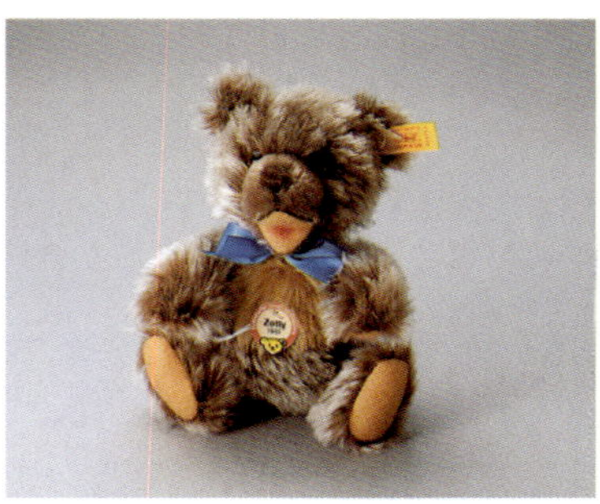

Zotty 1951

Mohair Webpelz, caramel/weiss gespitzt, gegliedert - *mohair woven fur, caramel, white tipped, jointed*

EAN-No.	Period	Pr.	Info
029950	1995-1999	2-3	16 cm

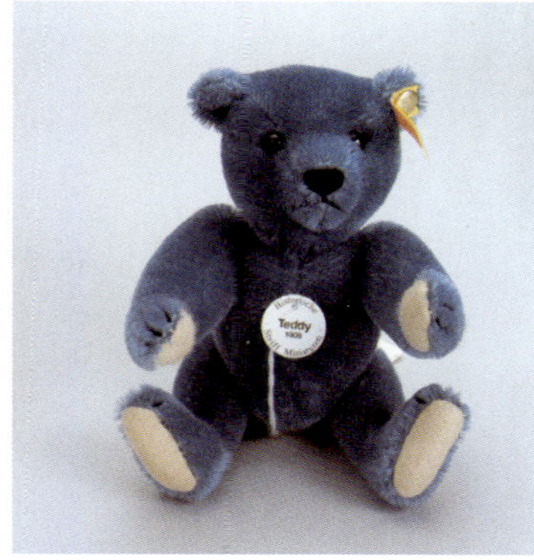

Teddy 1908

Mohair Webpelz, blau, gegliedert - *mohair woven fur, blue, jointed*

EAN-No.	Period	Pr.	Info
029233	1996-1999	2-3	16 cm

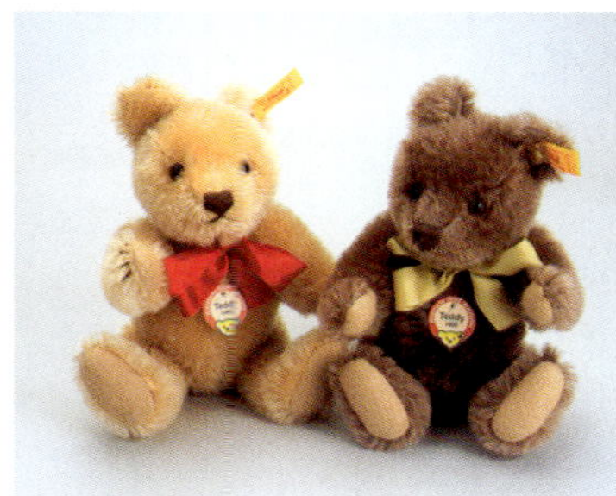

Teddy 1960

Mohair Webpelz, 18 cm, gegliedert - *mohair woven fur, 18 cm, jointed*

EAN-No.	Period	Pr.	Info
029936	1996-1999	2-3	blond
029943	1996-1998	2-3	caramel

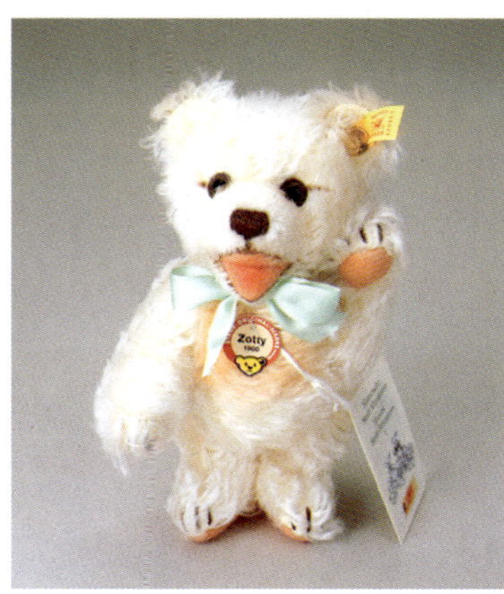

Zotty 1960

Mohair Webpelz, weiss, gegliedert - *mohair woven fur, white, jointed*

EAN-No.	Period	Pr.	Info
029967	1996-1999	2-3	16 cm

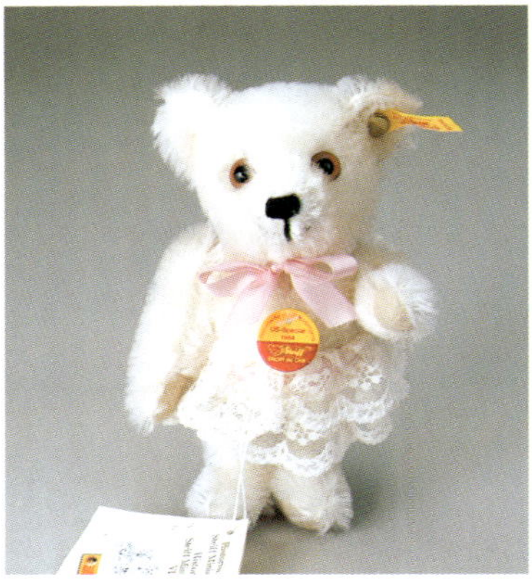

Teddybaer Ophelia **US-Special 1984** - *Teddybear Ophelia **US-Special 1984***

Mohair Webpelz, weiss, gegliedert, Spitzenroeckchen, Copyr. Michele D. Clise - *mohair woven fur, white, jointed, little lace skirt, Copyr. Michele D. Clise*

EAN-No.	Period	Pr.	Info
029288	1997-1998	2-3	16 cm

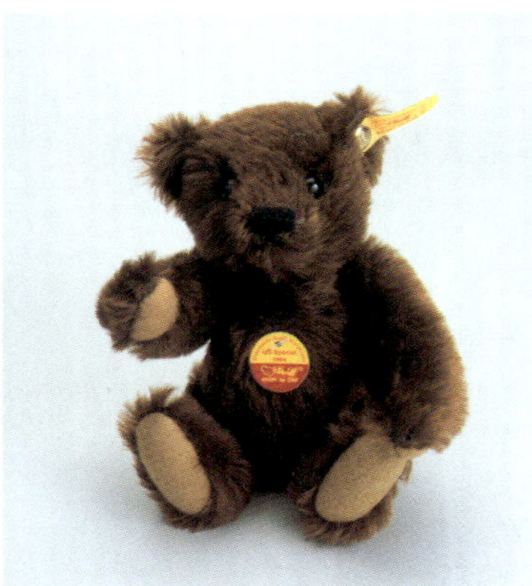

Teddybaer **US-Special 1994** - *Teddybear **US-Special 1994***

Mohair Webpelz, rotbraun, gegliedert - *mohair woven fur, red-brown, jointed*

EAN-No.	Period	Pr.	Info
029295	1997-1998	2-3	18 cm

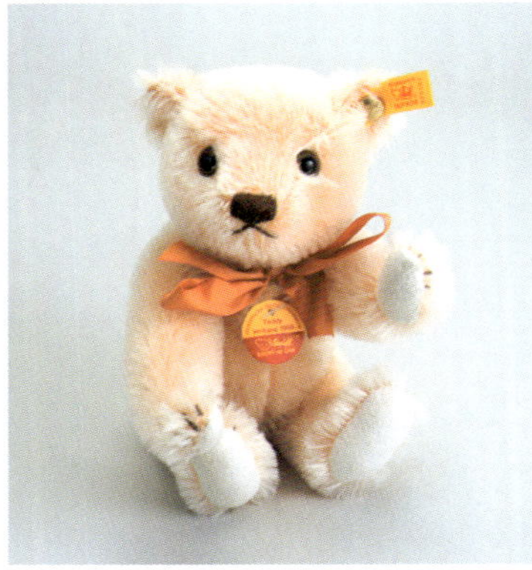

Teddy Holland 1995

Mohair Webpelz, lachs, gegliedert - *mohair woven fur, salmon-pink, jointed*

EAN-No.	Period	Pr.	Info
029301	1997-1999	2-3	16 cm

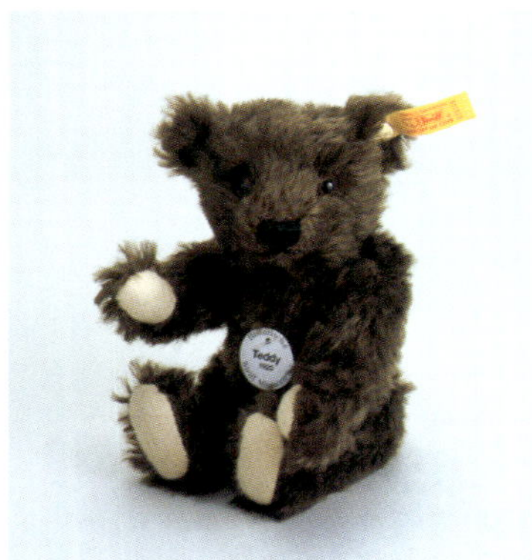

Teddybaer 1920 - *Teddybear 1920*

Mohair Webpelz, dunkelbraun, gegliedert - *mohair woven fur, dark brown, jointed*

EAN-No.	Period	Pr.	Info
029349	1997-1999	2-3	16 cm

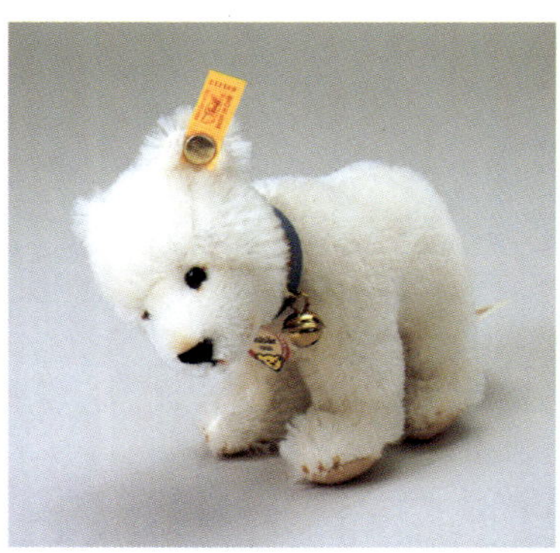

Eisbaer 1950 - *Polar Bear 1950*

Mohair Webpelz, stehend, Kopf drehbar, blaues Lederhalsband & Gloeckchen - *mohair woven fur, standing, head turnable, blue leather collar & bell*

EAN-No.	Period	Pr.	Info
031212	1997-1999	2	15 cm

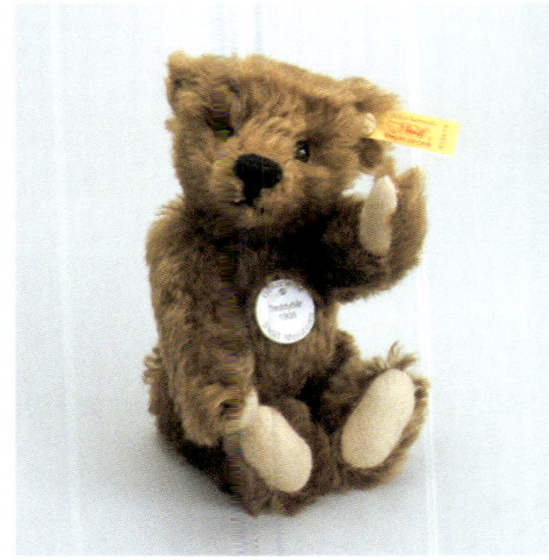

Teddybaer 1905 - *Teddybear 1905*

Mohair Webpelz, rotbraun, gegliedert - *mohair woven fur, red-brown, jointed*

EAN-No.	Period	Pr.	Info
029578	1998-1999	2-3	16 cm

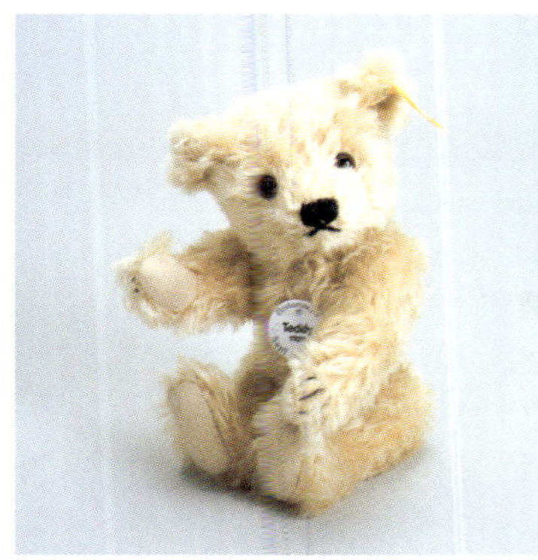

Teddy 1920

Mohair Webpelz, blond, gegliedert - *mohair woven fur, blond, jointed*

EAN-No.	Period	Pr.	Info
029585	1998-1999	2-3	16 cm

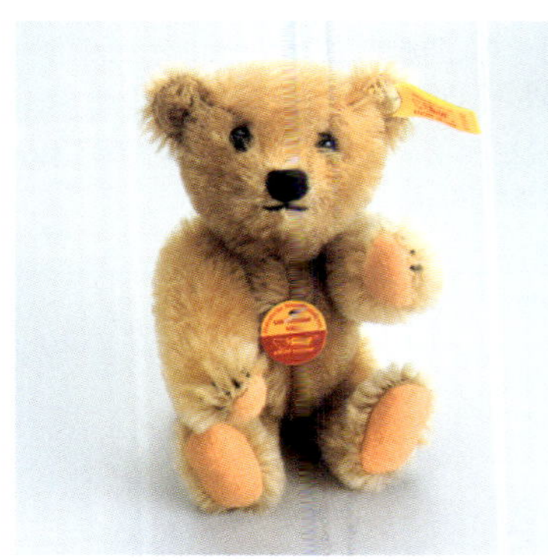

Teddybaer **US-Special 1983** - *Teddybear **US-Special 1983***

Mohair Webpelz, beige, gegliedert - *mohair woven fur, beige, jointed*

EAN-No.	Period	Pr.	Info
029592	1998-1999	2-3	16 cm

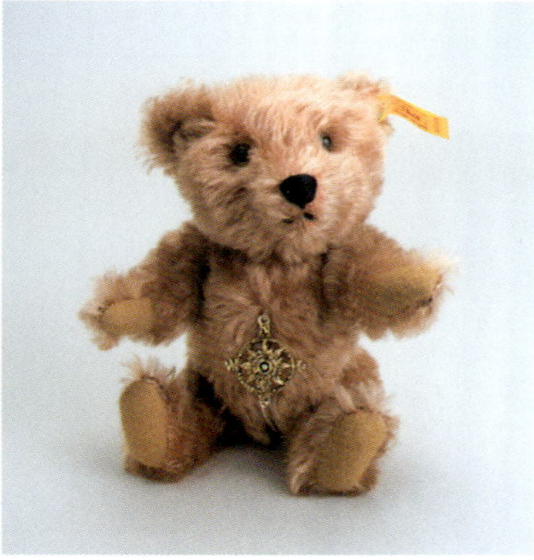

Teddybaer US-Special 1995 - *Teddybear US-Special 1995*

Mohair Webpelz, rosenholz, gegliedert, Compass mit Metall-Rose - *mohair woven fur, rosewood, jointed, metal compass rose*

EAN-No.	Period	Pr.	Info
029608	1998-1999	2-3	16 cm

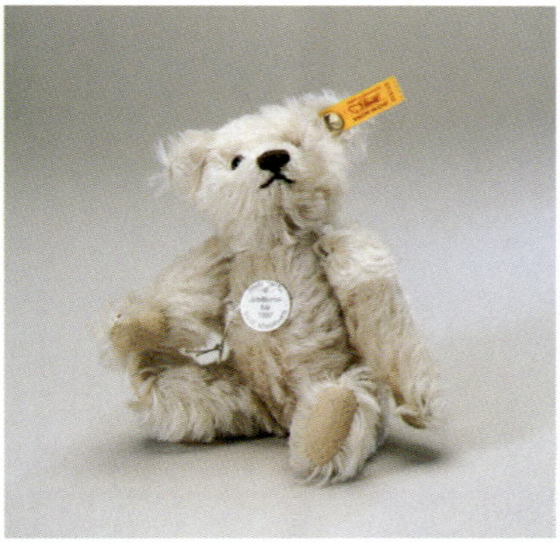

Jubilaeumsbaer 1997 - *Anniversary Baer 1997*

Mohair Webpelz, rohweiss, gegliedert - *mohair woven fur, off-white, jointed*

EAN-No.	Period	Pr	Info
029240	1999-1999	2-3	16 cm

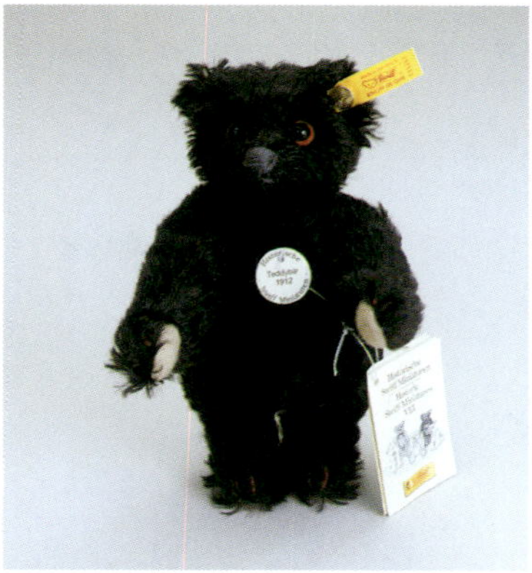

Teddybaer 1912 - *Teddybear 1912*

Mohair Webpelz, schwarz, gegliedert - *mohair woven fur, black, jointed*

EAN-No.	Period	Pr.	Info
029257	1999-1999	2-3	16 cm

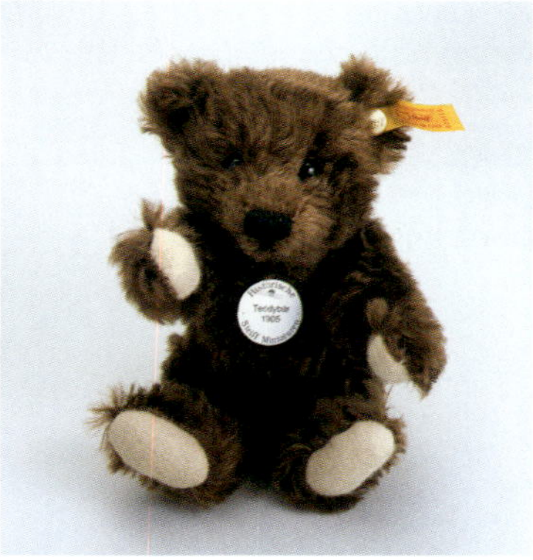

Teddybaer 1905 - *Teddybear 1905*

Mohair Webpelz, dunkelbraun, gegliedert - *mohair woven fur, dark brown, jointed*

EAN-No.	Period	Pr.	Info
029615	1999-1999	2-3	16 cm

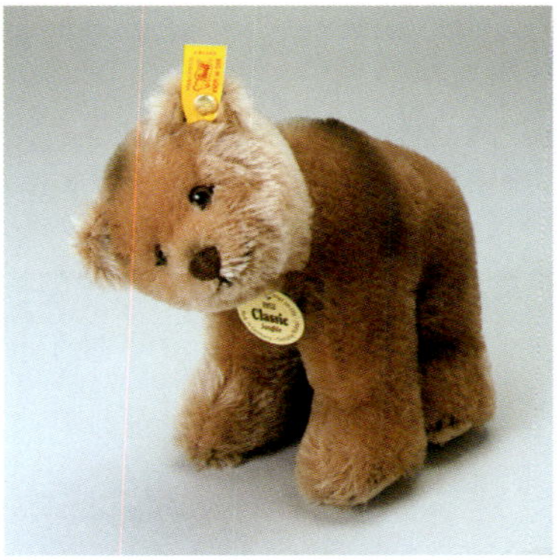

Classic 1952 Jungbaer - *Classic 1952 Bear Cub*

Mohair Webpelz, stehend - *mohair woven fur, standing*

EAN-No.	Period	Pr.	Info
034305	1999-1999	2-3	17 cm

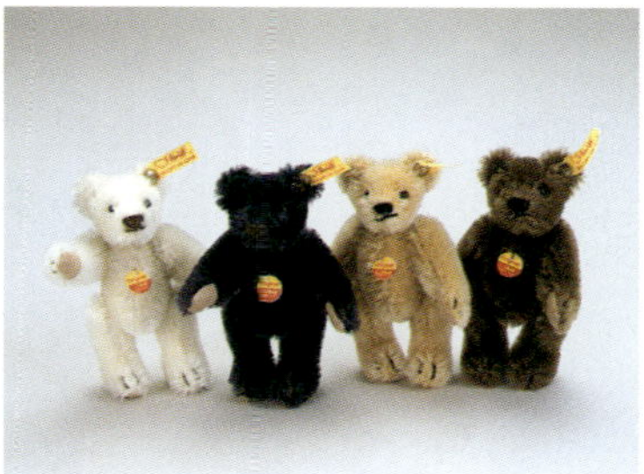

Mini Teddybaer Replica 1909 - *Mini Teddybear Replica 1909*

Mohair Webpelz 6 cm, gegliedert, abwaschbar - *mohair woven fur, 6 cm, jointed, surface washable*

EAN-No.	Period	Pr.	Info
039010	1998-1999	2-3	messing - *brass color*
039027	1998-1999	2-3	dunkelbraun - *dark brown*
039034	1998-1999	2-3	weiss - *white*
039041	1999-1999	2-3	dunkelblau - *dark blue*

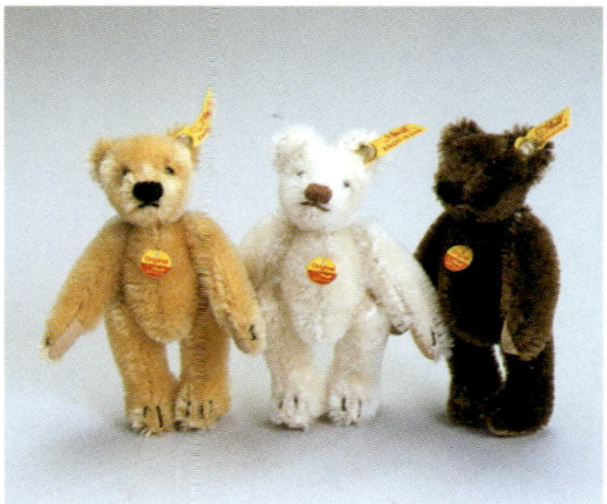

Mini Teddybaer Replica 1921 - *Mini Teddybear Replica 1921*

Mohair Webpelz, 6 cm, gegliedert, abwaschbar - *mohair woven fur, 6 cm, jointed, surface washable*

EAN-No.	Period	Pr.	Info
039119	1998-1999	2-3	hellblond - *light blond*
039126	1998-1999	2-3	rohweiss - *off-white*
039133	1998-1999	2-3	dunkelbraun - *dark brown*

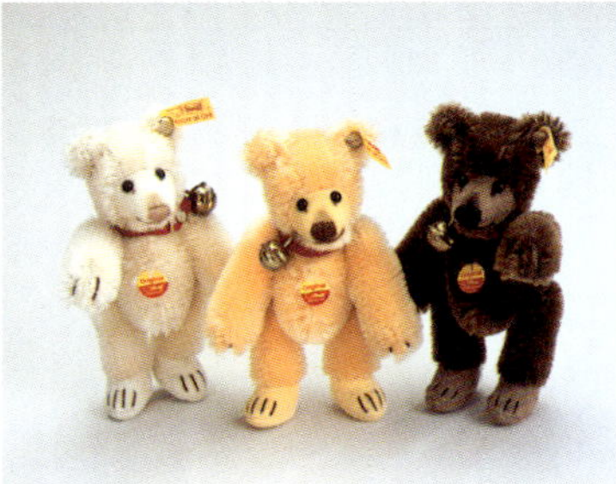

Mini Teddy Baby Replica 1930

Mohair Webpelz, 6 cm, gegliedert, abwaschbar, Lederhalsband mit Glocke - *mohair woven fur, 6 cm, jointed, surface washable, leather collar with bell*

EAN-No.	Period	Pr.	Info
039218	1998-1999	2-3	blond
039225	1998-1999	2-3	mais - *maize*
039232	1998-1999	2-3	braun - *brown*

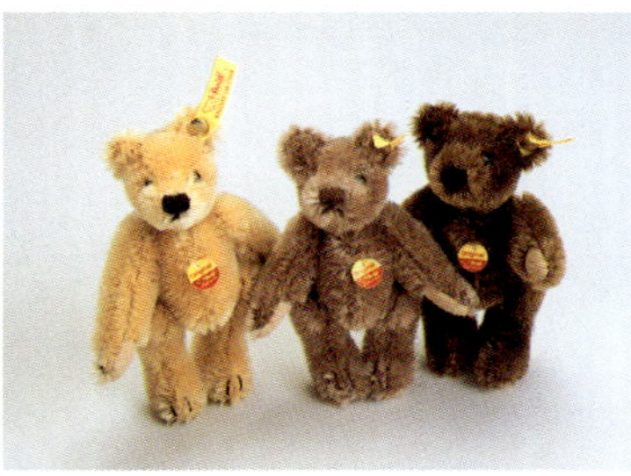

Mini Teddybaer Replica 1951 - *Mini Teddybear Replica 1951*

Mohair Webpelz, 6 cm, gegliedert, abwaschbar - *mohair woven fur, 6 cm, jointed, surface washable*

EAN-No.	Period	Pr.	Info
039317	1998-1999	2-3	blond
039324	1998-1999	2-3	caramel
039331	1998-1999	2-3	dunkelbraun - *dark brown*

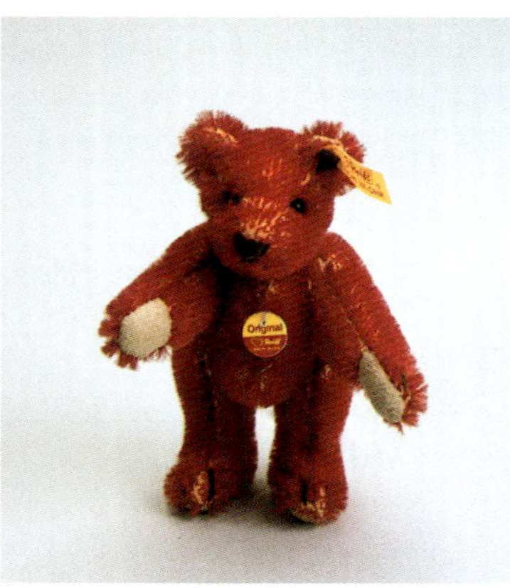

Mini Teddybaer Replica 1908 - *Mini Teddybear Replica 1908*

Mohair Webpelz, rot, gegliedert, abwaschbar - *mohair woven fur, red, jointed, surface washable*

EAN-No.	Period	Pr.	Info
039058	1999-1999	2-3	6 cm

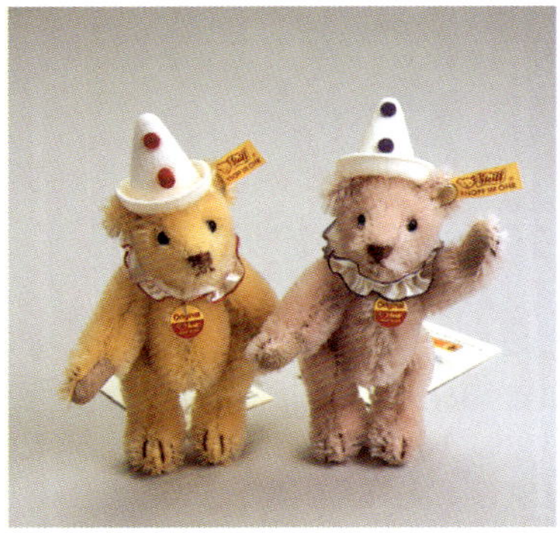

Mini Teddy Clown Replica 1926

Mohair Webpelz, 6 cm, gegliedert, abwaschbar, Clownhut & Halskrause - *mohair woven fur, 6 cm, jointed, surface washable, clown hat & neck frill*

EAN-No.	Period	Pr.	Info
039065	1999-1999	2-3	gelb - *yellow*
039072	1999-1999	2-3	rosè - *rose*

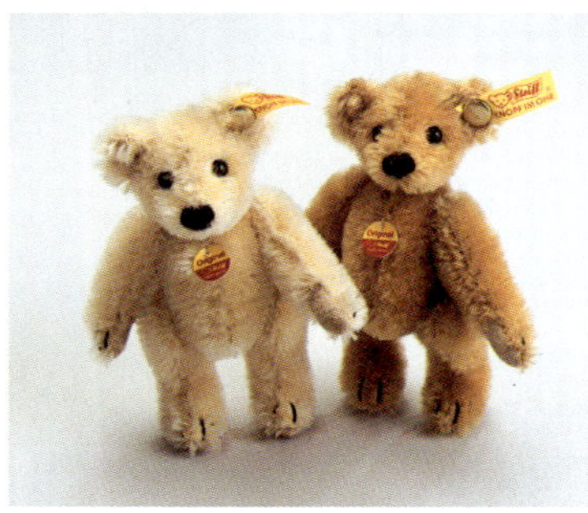

Mini Teddy Petsy Replica 1927

Mohair Webpelz, 6 cm, gegliedert, abwaschbar - *mohair woven fur, 6 cm, jointed, surface washable*

EAN-No.	Period	Pr.	Info
039140	1999-1999	2-3	hellbeige - *light beige*
039164	1999-1999	2-3	goldblond - *gold-blond*

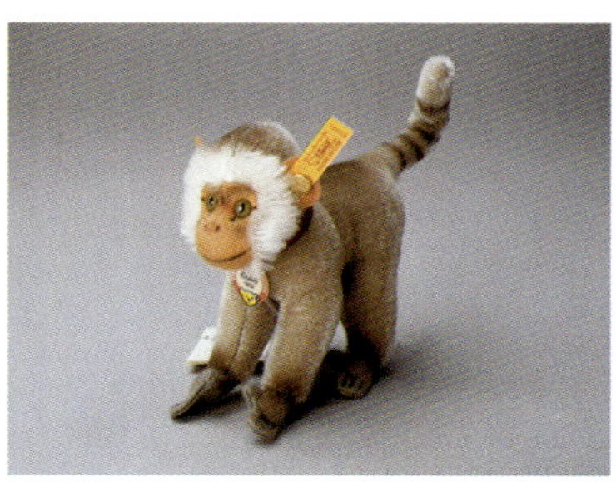

Coco 1952

Pavian, Mohair Webpelz, Kopf drehbar, Lederhalsband - *baboon, mohair woven fur, head swivels*

EAN-No.	Period	Pr.	Info
030901	1994-1998	2-3	12 cm

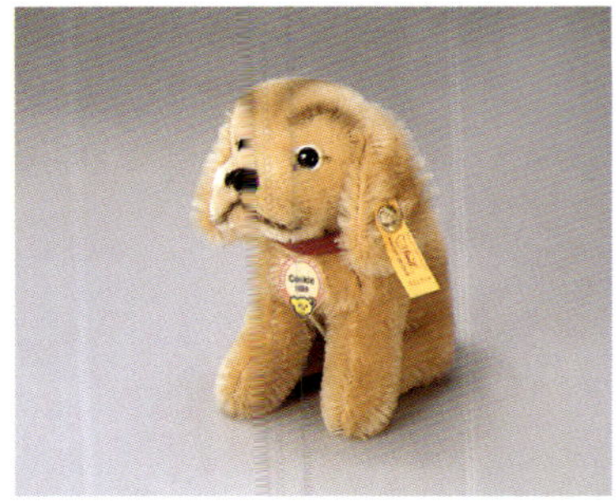

Cockie 1959

Mohair Webpelz, sitzend, Kopf drehbar - *mohair woven fur, sitting, head swivels*

EAN-No.	Period	Pr.	Info
031564	1994-1995	2	12 cm

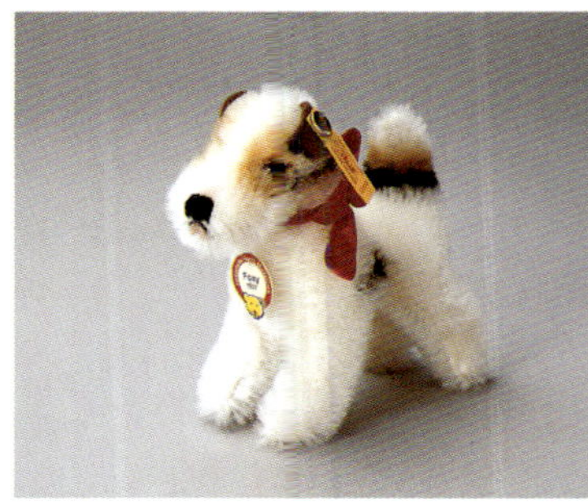

Foxy 1937

Mohair Webpelz, stehend - *mohair woven fur, standing*

EAN-No.	Period	Pr.	Info
031601	1994-1996	2	12 cm

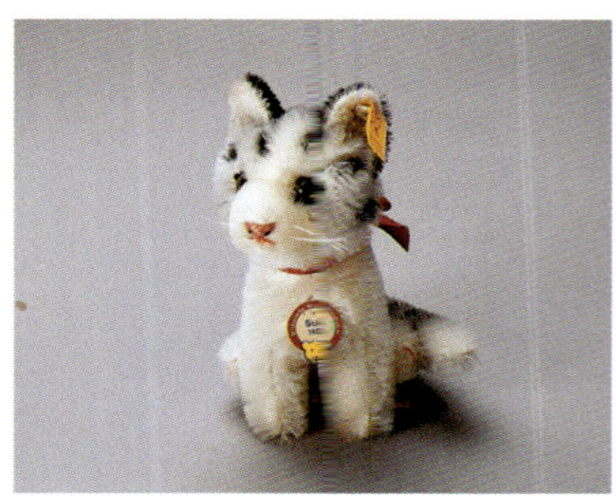

Susi 1936

Mohair Webpelz, Kopf drehbar, Druckstimme - *mohair woven fur, head swivels, press voice*

EAN-No.	Period	Pr.	Info
031748	1994-1996	2	12 cm

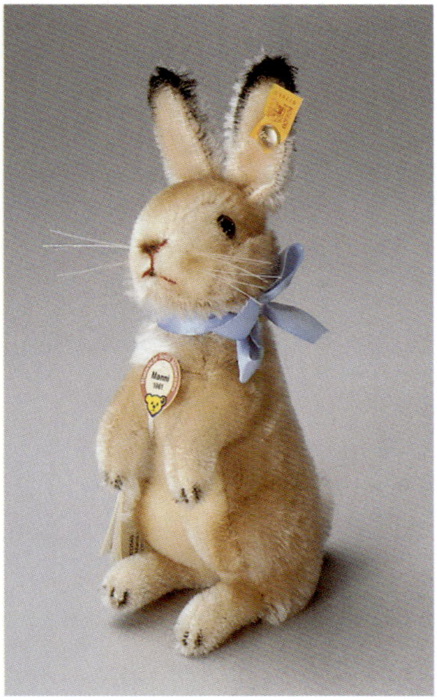

Manni 1961

Mohair Webpelz, aufwartend, Kopf drehbar - *mohair woven fur, sitting up, head swivels*

EAN-No.	Period	Pr.	Info
032660	1994-1995	2	15 cm

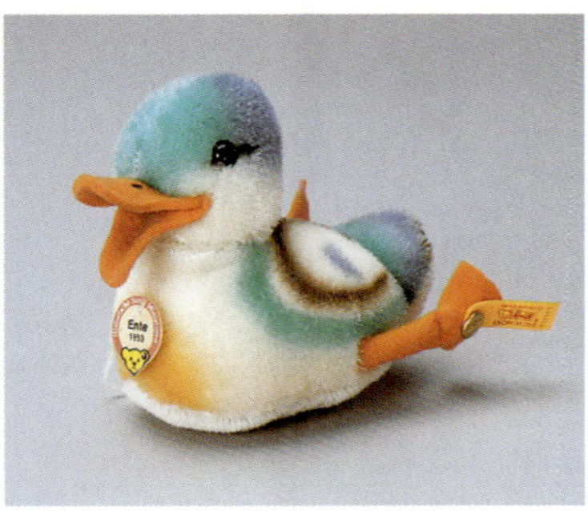

Ente 1953 - *Duck 1953*

Mohair Webpelz, blau, Druckstimme - *mohair woven fur, blue, press voice*

EAN-No.	Period	Pr.	Info
032905	1994-1995	2	12 cm

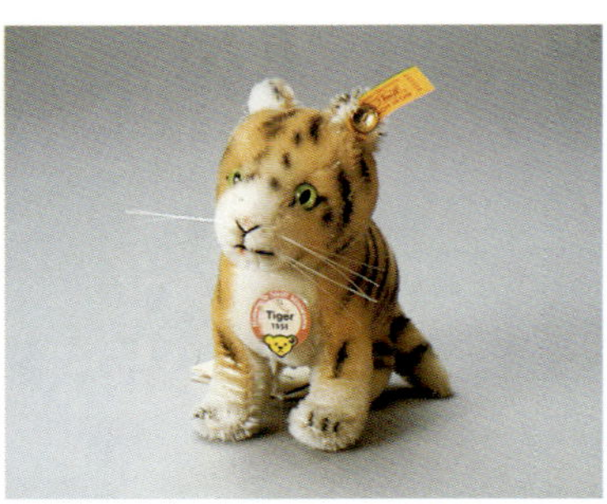

Tiger 1951

Mohair Webpelz, sitzend, Kopf drehbar - *mohair woven fur, sitting, head swivels*

EAN-No.	Period	Pr.	Info
031007	1995-1998	2	13 cm

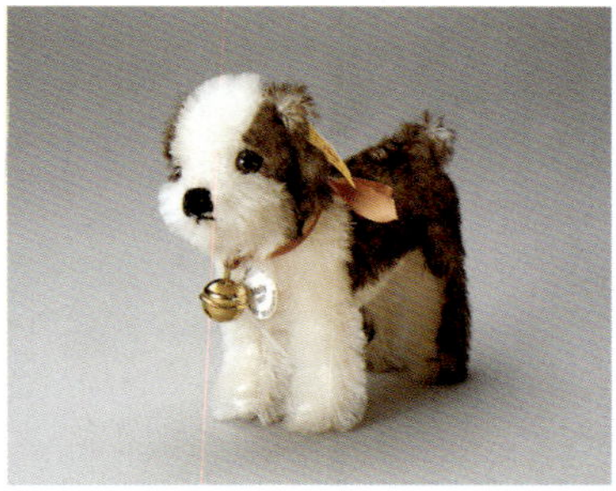

Molly 1927

Mohair Webpelz, weiss/braun, Kopf drehbar - *mohair woven fur, white/brown, head swivels*

EAN-No.	Period	Pr.	Info
031458	1995-1996	2	16 cm

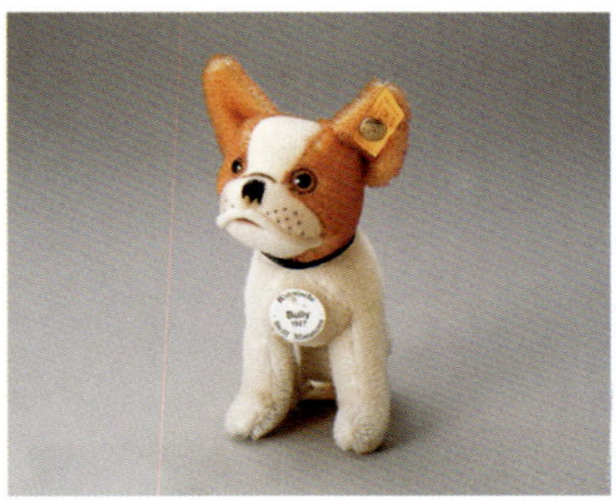

Bully 1927

Mohair Webpelz, orange/weiss, sitzend, Kopf drehbar - *mohair woven fur, orange/white, sitting, head swivels*

EAN-No.	Period	Pr.	Info
031496	1995-1996	2-3	14 cm

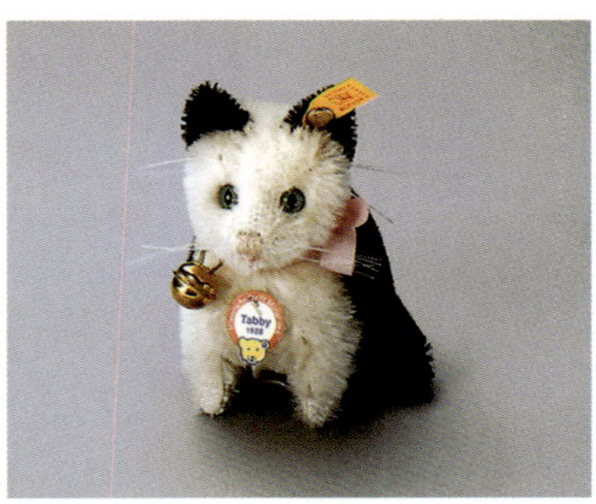

Tabby 1928

Mohair Webpelz, schwarz/weiss, Kopf drehbar - *mohair woven fur, black & white, head swivels*

EAN-No.	Period	Pr.	Info
031823	1995-1996	2	12 cm

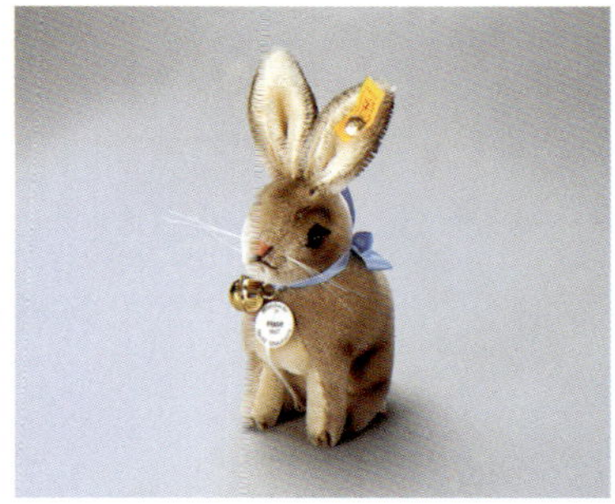

Hase 1927 - *Rabbit 1927*

Mohair Webpelz, hellgrau, Kopf drehbar - *mohair woven fur, light grey, head swivels*

EAN-No.	Period	Pr.	Info
032622	1995-1996	2-3	16 cm

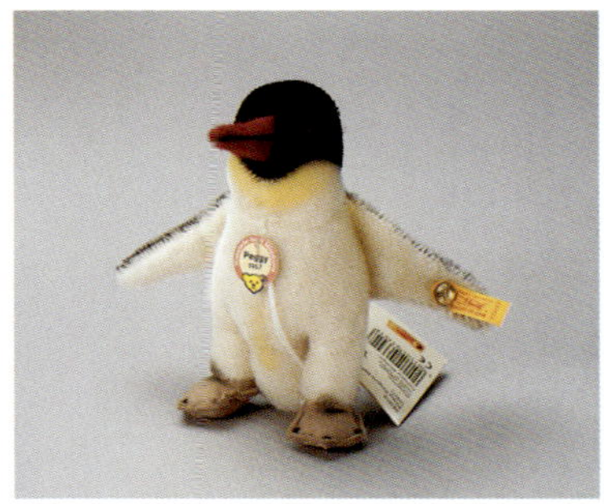

Peggy 1957

Mohair Webpelz, hellgrau, offene Fluegel - *mohair woven fur, light grey, wings extended*

EAN-No.	Period	Pr.	Info
033018	1995-1997	2	13 cm

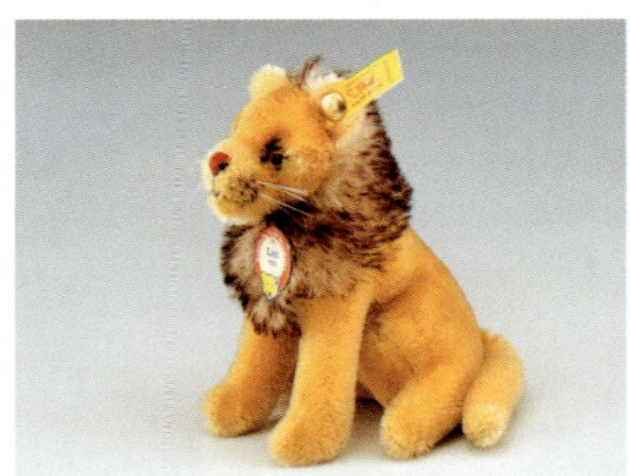

Leo 1932

Mohair Webpelz, sitzend, abwaschbar - *mohair woven fur, sitting, surface washable*

EAN-No.	Period	Pr.	Info
030956	1996-1997	2	12 cm

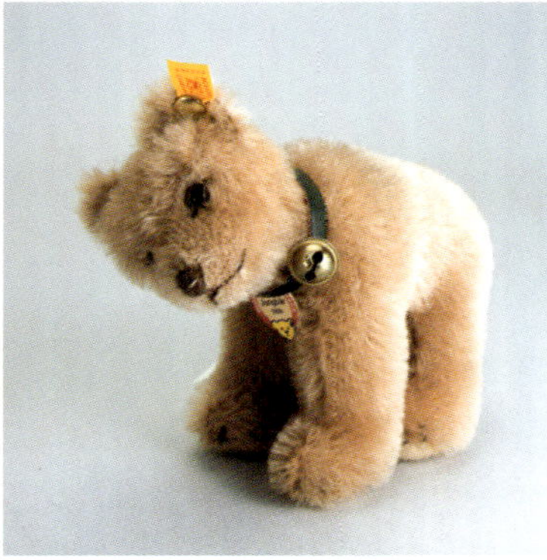

Jungbaer 1950 - *Bear Cub 1950*

Mohair Webpelz, hellbraun, stehend, abwaschbar, Kopf drehbar, Lederhalsband & Glocke - *mohair woven fur, light brown, standing, surface washable, head swivels, leather collar with bell*

EAN-No.	Period	Pr.	Info
031205	1996-1997	2-3	15 cm

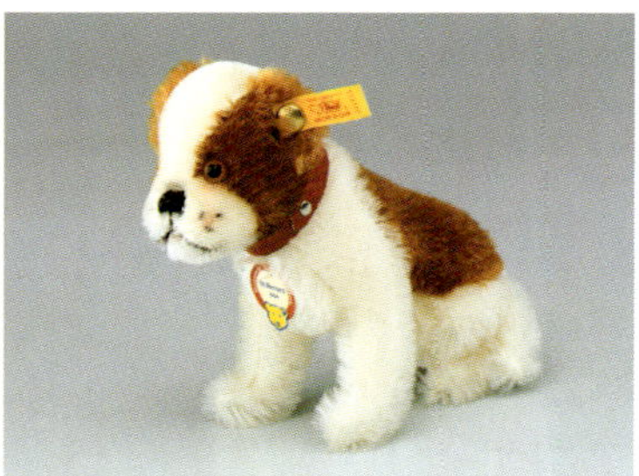

St. Bernhard 1934

Mohair Webpelz, sitzend, abwaschbar, Kopf drehbar, Lederhalsband - *mohair woven fur, sitting, surface washable, head swivels, leather collar*

EAN-No.	Period	Pr.	Info
031625	1996-1997	2	13 cm

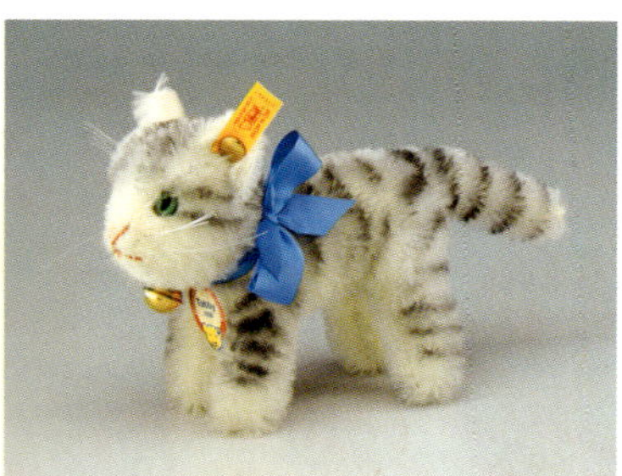

Tabby 1936

Mohair Webpelz, grau/weiss, stehend, abwaschbar, Taftband & Gloeckchen - *mohair woven fur, grey/white, standing, surface washable, taffeta collar with bell*

EAN-No.	Period	Pr.	Info
031847	1996-1997	2	12 cm

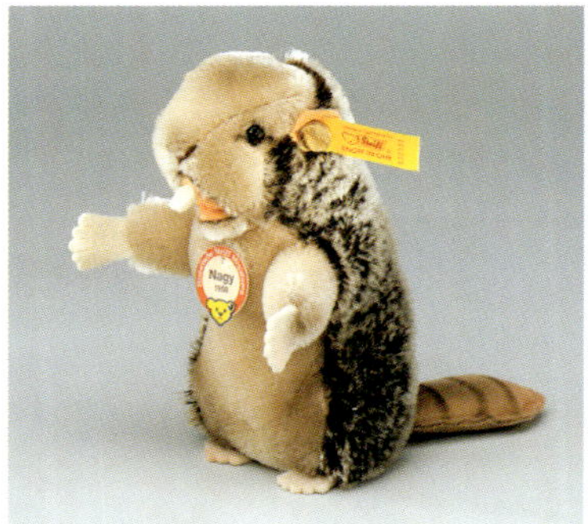

Nagy 1958

Biber, Mohair Webpelz, aufwartend, abwaschbar - *beaver, mohair woven fur, sitting up, surface washable*

EAN-No.	Period	Pr.	Info
032332	1996-1998	2	12 cm

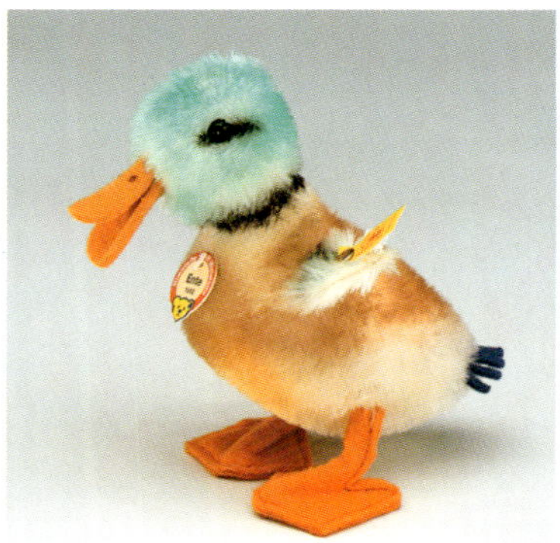

Ente 1952 - *Duck 1952*

Mohair Webpelz, stehend, abwaschbar - *mohair woven fur, standing, surface washable*

EAN-No.	Period	Pr.	Info
032936	1996-1998	2	13 cm

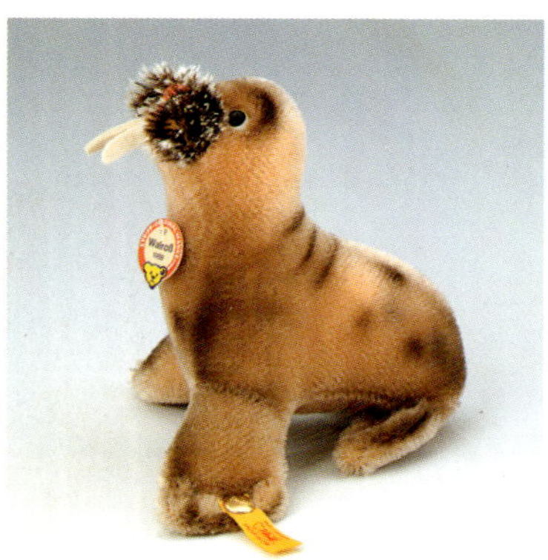

Walross 1959 - *Walrus 1959*

Mohair Webpelz, aufwartend, abwaschbar - *mohair woven fur, sitting up, surface washable*

EAN-No.	Period	Pr.	Info
031267	1997-1998	2	10 cm

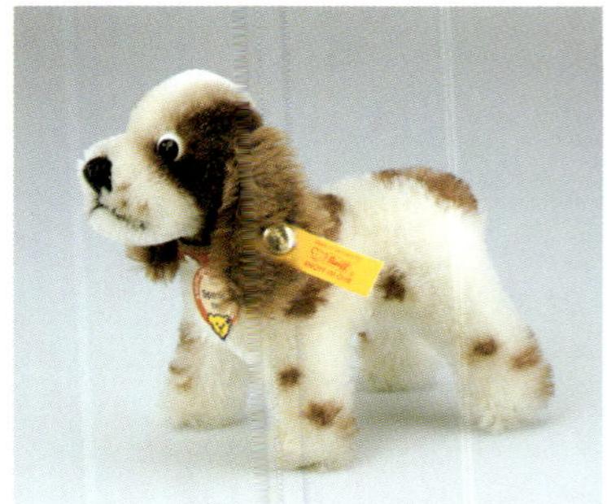

Spaniel 1960

Mohair Webpelz, braun/weiss, stehend, abwaschbar, Lederhalsband - *mohair woven fur, brown/white, standing, surface washable, leather collar*

EAN-No.	Period	Pr.	Info
031571	1997-1998	2	12 cm

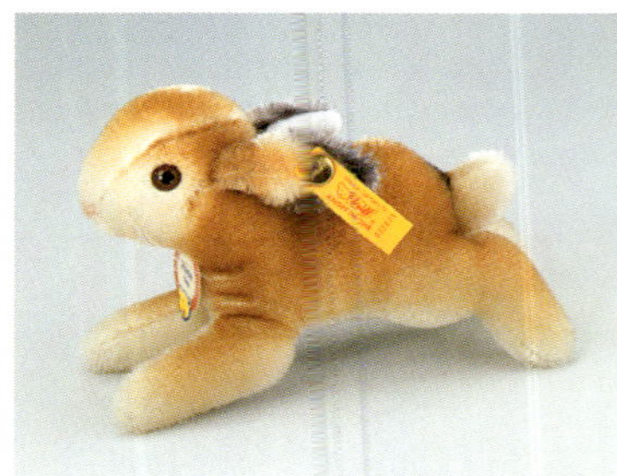

Hase 1948 - *Rabbit 1948*

Mohair Webpelz, springend, abwaschbar, Taftband & Gloeckchen - *mohair woven fur, jumping, surface washable, taffeta collar with bell*

EAN-No.	Period	Pr.	Info
032639	1997-1998	2	14 cm

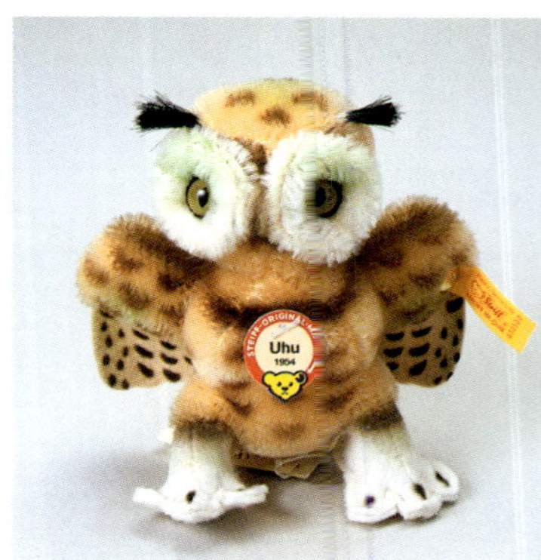

Uhu 1954 - *Eagle-owl 1954*

Mohair Webpelz, abwaschbar - *mohair woven fur, surface washable*

EAN-No.	Period	Pr.	Info
033100	1997-1999	2	10 cm

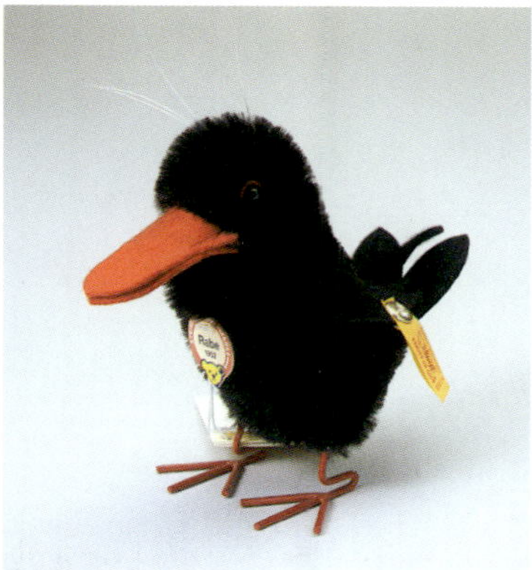

Rabe 1952 - *Raven 1952*

Mohair Webpelz, stehend, abwaschbar, Metallfuesse - *mohair woven fur, standing, surface washable, metal feet*

EAN-No.	Period	Pr.	Info
033124	1997-1999	2	10 cm

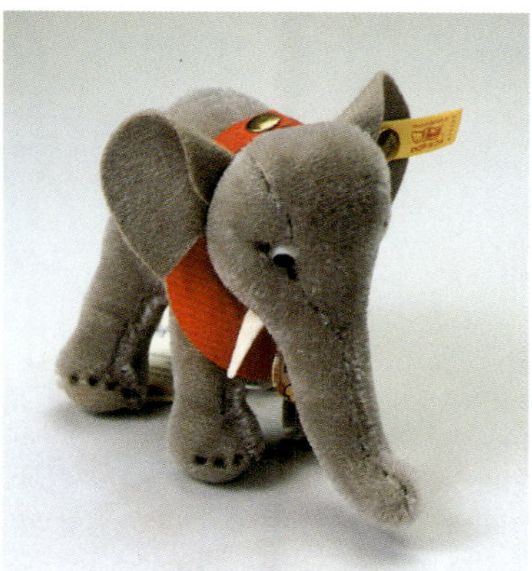

Elefant 1950 - *Elephant 1950*

Mohair Webpelz, grau, abwaschbar, Filzhalskrause - *mohair woven fur, grey, surface washable, felt-frill*

EAN-No.	Period	Pr.	Info
031137	1998-1999	2	10 cm

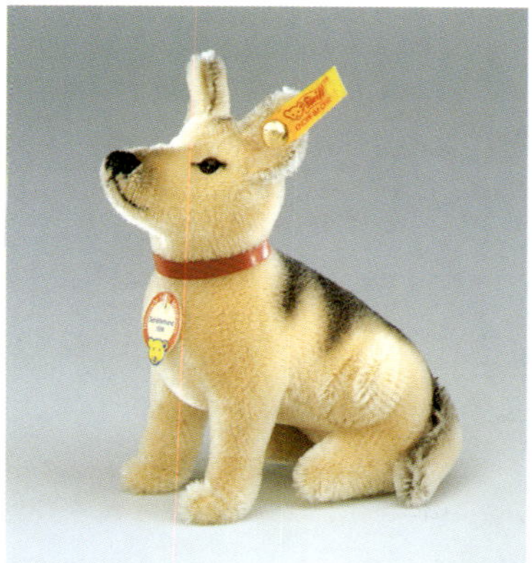

Schaeferhund 1936 - *Alsation Dog 1936*

Mohair Webpelz, sitzend, abwaschbar, Lederhalsband - *mohair woven fur, sitting, surface washable, leather collar*

EAN-No.	Period	Pr.	Info
031649	1998-1998	2-3	14 cm

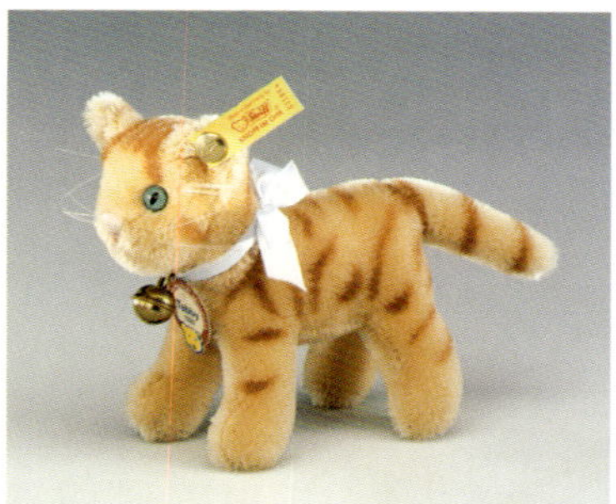

Tabby 1929

Mohair Webpelz, hellbraun gestromelt, stehend, abwaschbar, Taftband mit Gloeckchen - *mohair woven fur, light brown tabby, standing, surface washable, taffeta collar with bell*

EAN-No.	Period	Pr.	Info
031854	1998-1998	2	10 cm

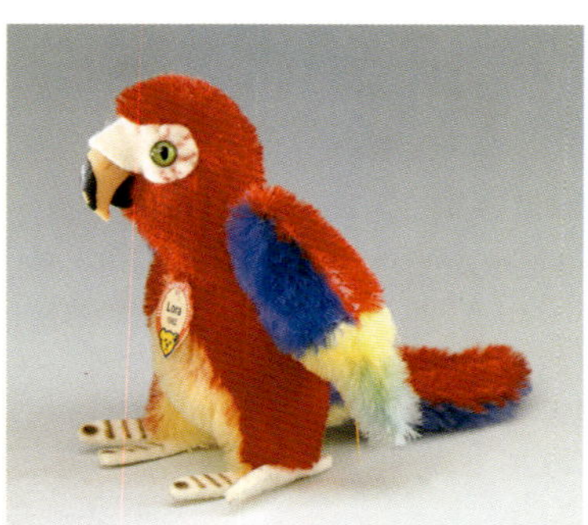

Lora 1962

Mohair Webpelz, stehend, abwaschbar - *mohair woven fur, standing, surface washable*

EAN-No.	Period	Pr.	Info
033148	1998-1999	2-3	12 cm

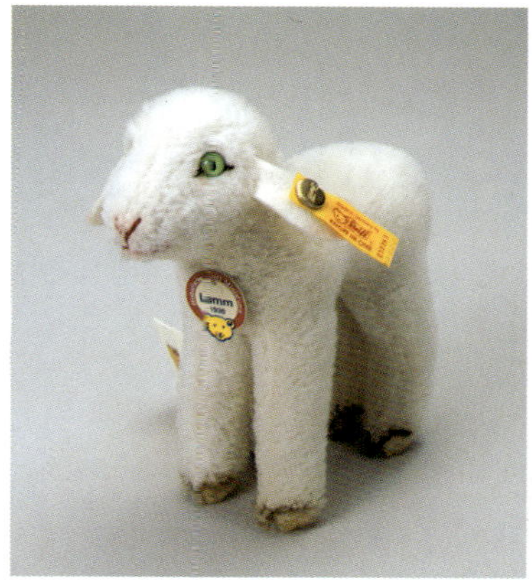

Lamm 1936 - *Lamb 1936*

Mohair Webpelz, weiss, stehend, abwaschbar - *mohair woven fur, white, standing, surface washable*

EAN-No.	Period	Pr.	Info
033353	1999-1999	2	14 cm

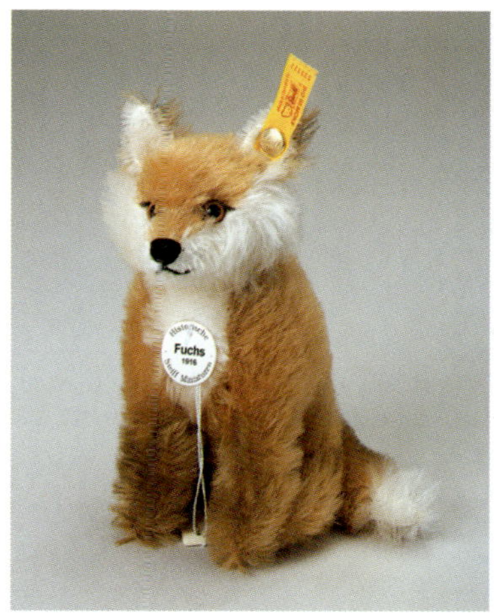

Fuchs 1916 - *Fox 1916*

Mohair Webpelz, sitzend, abwaschbar - *mohair woven fur, sitting, surface washable*

EAN-No.	Period	Pr.	Info
033322	1999-1999	2	14 cm

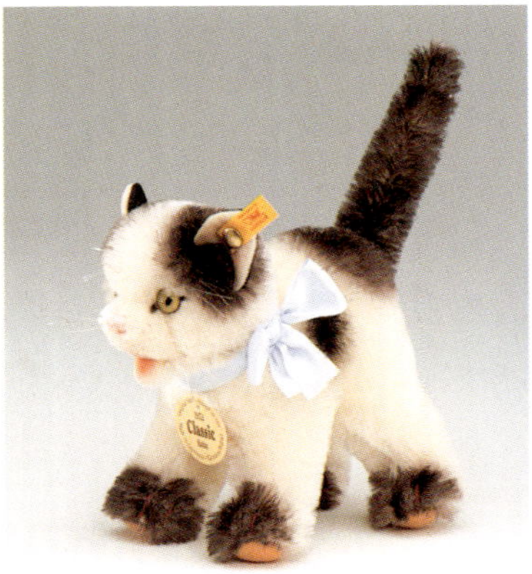

Classic 1952 Katze - *Classic 1952 Cat*

Mohair Webpelz, schwarz/weiss, stehend, abwaschbar - *mohair woven fur, black/white, standing, surface washable*

EAN-No.	Period	Pr.	Info
034701	1999-1999	2-3	17 cm

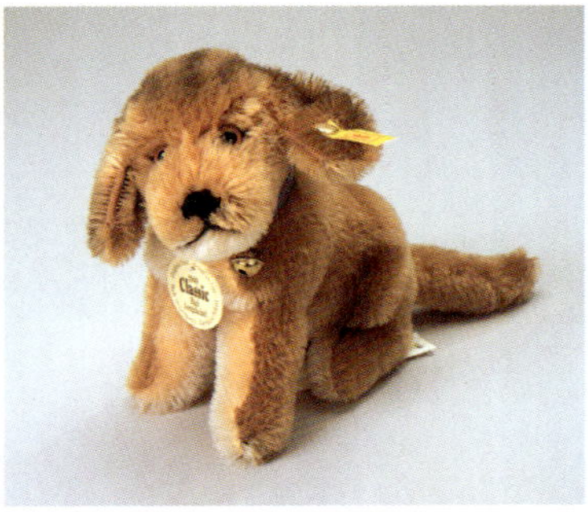

Classic 1949 Bazi Jungdackel - *Classic 1949 Bazi dachshund*

Mohair Webpelz, abwaschbar, Lederhalsband - *mohair woven fur, surface washable, leather collar*

EAN-No.	Period	Pr.	Info
035050	1999-1999	2-3	17 cm

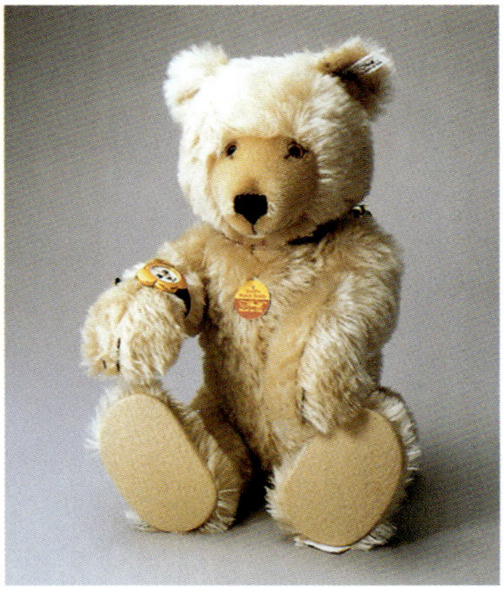

Steiff´s Watch Teddy

Mohair Webpelz, gegliedert, hellbraun, limit. Auflage 2.000 Stueck - *mohair woven fur, jointed, light brown, ltd edition of 2,000*

Serie	Art.-No	Period	Pr.	Info
	8530/43	1991-1991	5	43 cm

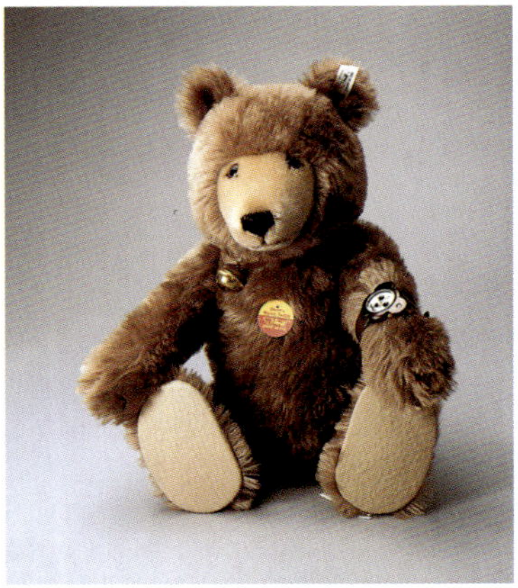

Steiff´s Watch Teddy

Mohair Webpelz, gegliedert, dunkelbraun, limit. Auflage 2.000 Stueck - *mohair woven fur, jointed, dark brown, ltd edition of 2,000*

Serie	Art.-No	Period	Pr.	Info
	8530/44	1991-1992	4-5	43 cm

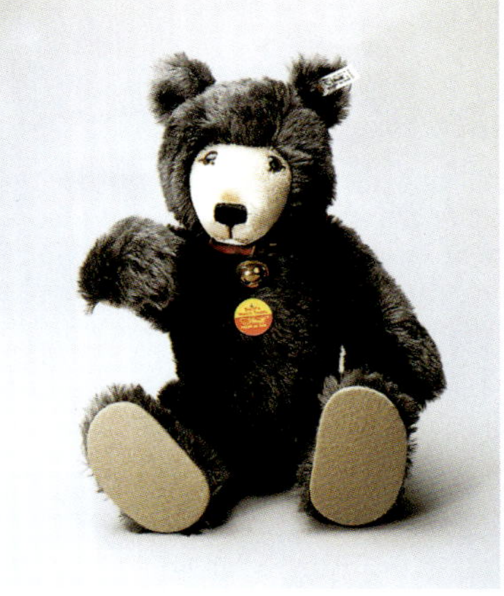

Steiff´s Watch Teddy

Mohair Webpelz, gegliedert, grau, limit. Auflage 4.000 Stueck - *mohair woven fur, jointed, grey, ltd edition of 4,000*

EAN-No.	Period	Pr.	Info
606304	1992-1992	4	43 cm

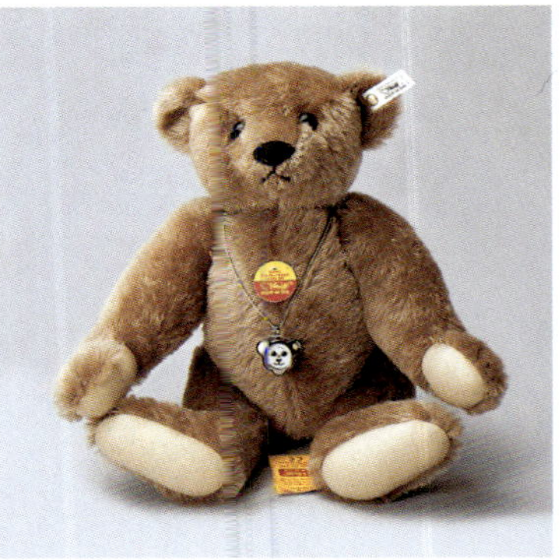

Steiff´s Pendant Watch Teddy

Mohair Webpelz, gegliedert, caramel, limit. Auflage 3.000 Stueck - *mohair woven fur, jointed, caramel, ltd edition of 3,000*

EAN-No.	Period	Pr.	Info
606502	1993-1993	4	43 cm

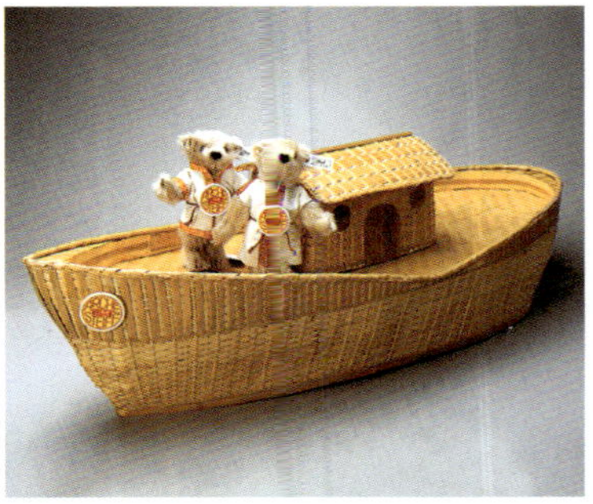

Steiff-Arche - *Steiff Ark*

mit Teddy Noah & Frau, Arche: Korbgeflecht 100 cm, Teddy´s Mohair-Webpelz, 20 cm, limit. Auflage 8.000 Stueck - *with Teddy Noah & wife, ark: wicker work, 100 cm, Teddys: mohair woven fur, 20 cm, limited edition of 8,000*

EAN-No.	Period	Pr	Info
038006	1992-1997	3	100/20 cm

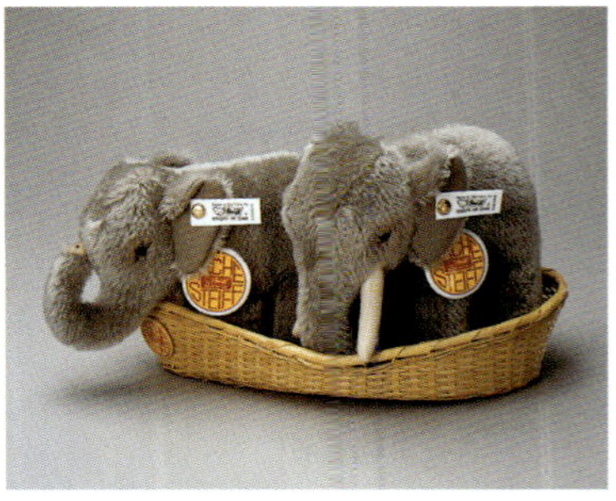

Arche Elefanten-Set - *Elephant Ark Set*

Beiboot: Korbgeflecht 30 cm, Elefanten: Mohair Webpelz 17 & 15 cm, limit. Auflage 8.000 Stueck - *long boat: 30 cm, wicker work, elephants: mohair woven fur, 17 & 15 cm, limited edition of 8,000*

EAN-No.	Period	Pr.	Info
038303	1992-1997	3	30/17/15 cm

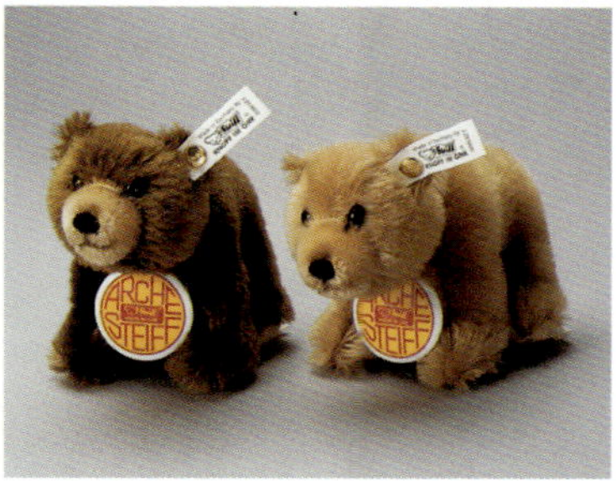

Arche Braunbaeren-Set - *Brown Bear Ark Set*

Baer & Baerin je 12 cm, Kopf drehbar, limit. Auflage 8.000 Stueck - *mohair woven fur, 12 cm each, their heads swivel, ltd edition of 8,000*

EAN-No.	Period	Pr.	Info
038327	1993-1996	3	12 cm

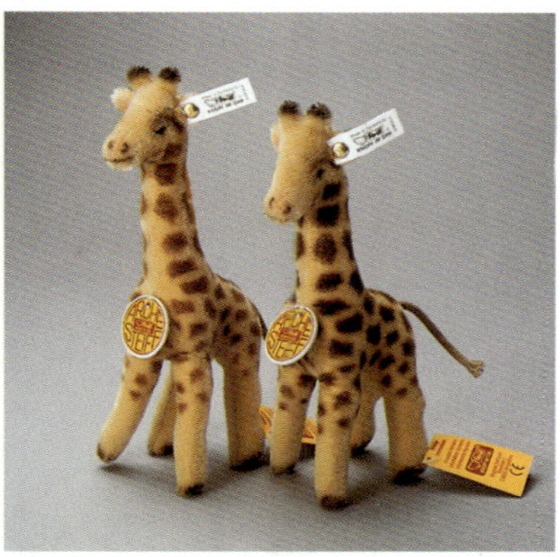

Arche Giraffen-Set - *Giraffe Ark Set*

mit Rampe, Mohair Webpelz, Giraffen-Bulle 20 cm, -Kuh 18 cm, limit. Auflage 8.000 Stueck - *with their own ramp, mohair woven fur, giraffe bull 20 cm, giraffe cow 18 cm, ltd edition of 8,000*

EAN-No.	Period	Pr.	Info
038341	1993-1995	3	20/18 cm

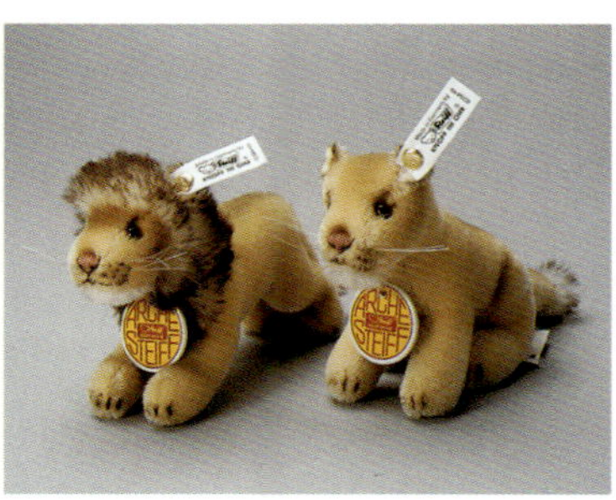

Arche Loewen-Set - *Lion Ark Set*

Mohair Webpelz, Loewin: sitzend 12 cm, Loewe: stehend 10 cm, limit. Auflage 8.000 Stueck - *mohair woven fur, lioness: sitting 12 cm, lion: standing 10 cm, ltd edition of 8,000*

EAN-No.	Period	Pr.	Info
038440	1994-1996	3	12/10 cm

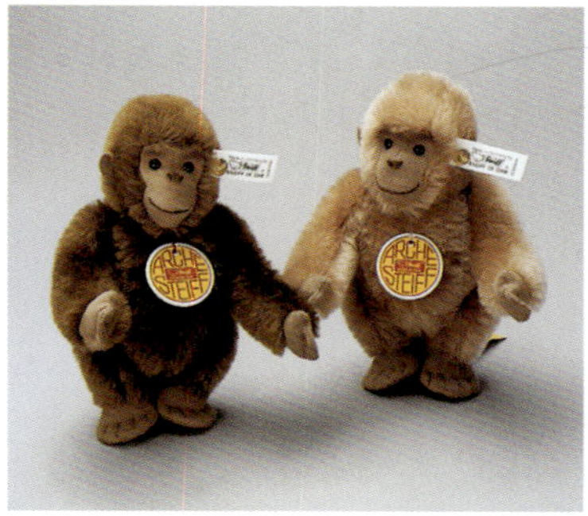

Arche Gorilla-Set - *Gorilla Ark Set*

Mohair Webpelz, Gorilla-Frau caramel, Mann dunkelbraun, je 18 cm, gegliedert, limit. Auflage 8.000 Stueck - *mohair woven fur, female gorilla is caramel, the male is dark brown, 18 cm each, jointed, ltd edition of 8,000*

EAN-No.	Period	Pr.	Info
038464	1994-1995	3	18 cm

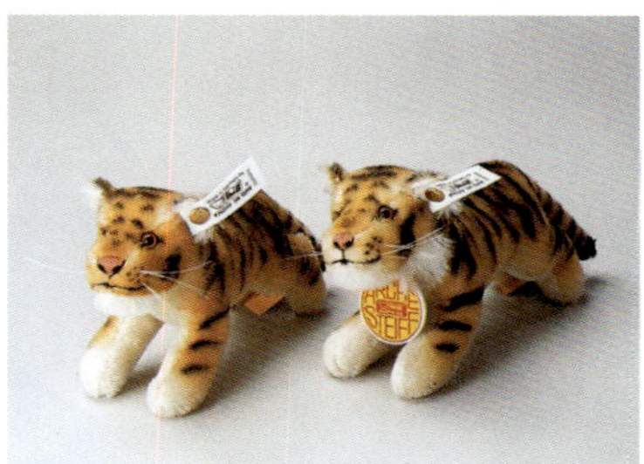

Arche Tiger-Set - *Tiger Ark Set*

Mohair Webpelz, Tiger 12, Tigerin 10 cm, stehend, limit. Auflage 8.000 Stueck - *mohair woven fur, male tiger 12 cm, tigress 10 cm, standing, ltd edition of 8,000*

EAN-No.	Period	Pr.	Info
038488	1995-1997	3	12/10 cm

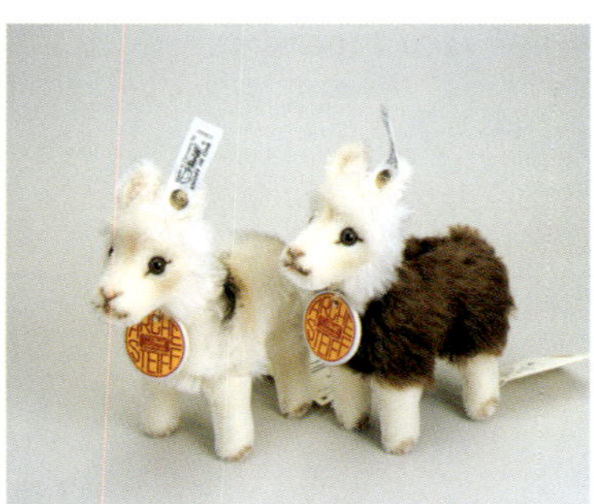

Arche Lama-Set - *Llama Ark Set*

Mohair Webpelz, weiss & weiss/braun, je 16 cm, stehend, limit. Auflage 8.000 Stueck - *mohair woven fur, white/brown & white, 16 cm each, standing, ltd edition of 8,000*

EAN-No.	Period	Pr.	Info
038501	1995-1995	3	16 cm

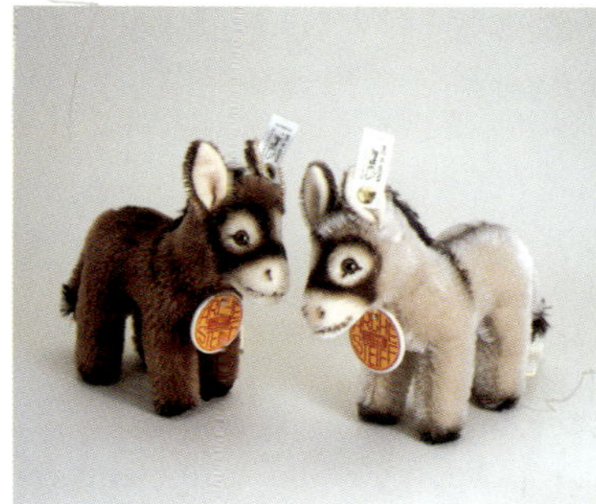

Arche Esel Set - *Donkey Ark Set*

Mohair Webpelz, grau bzw. braun, stehend, abwaschbar, limit. Auflage 8.000 Stueck - *mohair woven fur, grey and brown, standing, surface washable, ltd edition of 8,000*

EAN-No.	Period	Pr.	Info
038525	1996-1997	3	16 cm

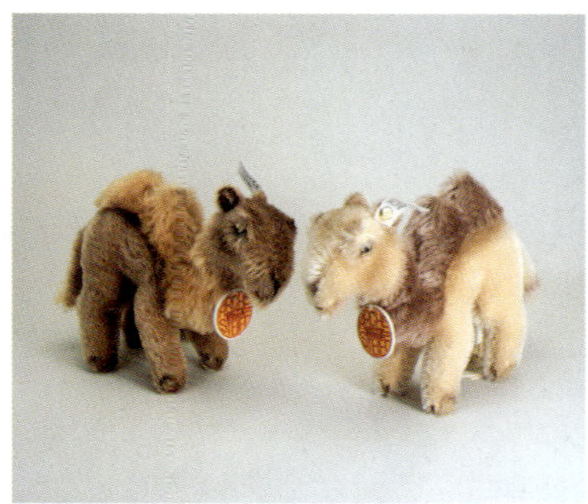

Arche Kamel Set - *Camel Ark Set*

Mohair Webpelz, hellsand bzw. zimt, stehend, abwaschbar, limit. Auflage 8.000 Stueck - *mohair woven fur, light-sand and cinnamon, standing, surface washable, ltd edition of 8,000*

EAN-No.	Period	Pr.	Info
038549	1996-1997	3	16 cm

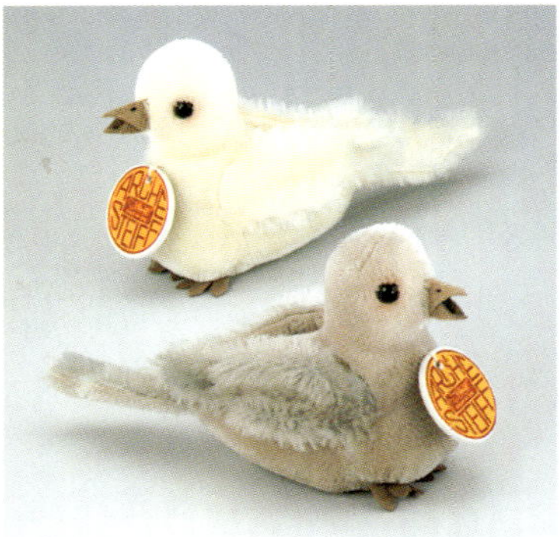

Arche Tauben Set - *Pigeon Ark Set*

Mohair Webpelz, grau bzw. weiss, abwaschbar, limit. Auflage 8.000 Stueck - *mohair woven fur, grey and white, surface washable, ltd edition of 8,000*

EAN-No.	Period	Pr.	Info
038563	1997-1997	3	10 cm

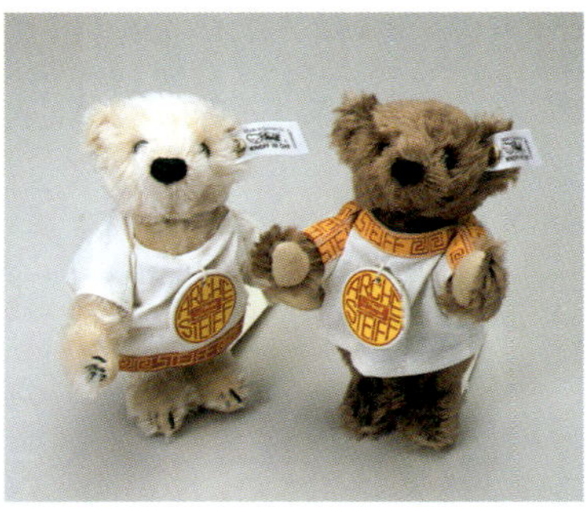

Arche Teddy Kinder Set - *Teddy Children Ark Set*

Mohair Webpelz, je 15 cm, blond bzw. caramel, gegliedert, abwaschbar, limit. Auflage 8.000 Stueck - *mohair woven fur, 15 cm each, blond and caramel, jointed, surface washable, ltd edition of 8,000*

EAN-No.	Period	Pr.	Info
038587	1997-1997	3-4	kpl. Set - *compl.set*
J06020	1997-1997	3	blond
J06021	1997-1997	3	caramel

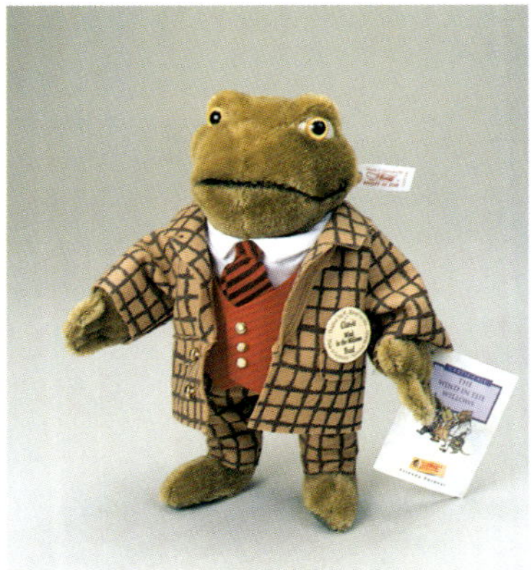

Classic Kroete **Toad** - *Classic **Toad***

Mohair Webpelz, gruen, gegliedert, abwaschbar, Anzug, Weste & Krawatte aus Filz, Hemd aus Baumwolle, limit. Auflage 4000 Stueck - *mohair woven fur, green, jointed, surface washable, suit, waistcoat & tie: felt, cotton shirt, ltd edition of 4,000*

EAN-No.	Period	Pr.	Info
037016	1998-1999	4	25 cm

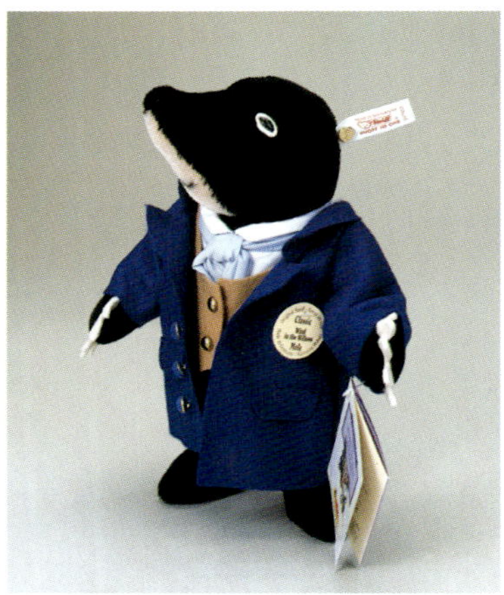

Classic Maulwurf **Mole** - *Classic **Mole***

Mohair Webpelz, schwarz, gegliedert, abwaschbar, Anzug & Weste aus Filz, Hemd & Halstuch aus Baumwolle, limit. Auflage 4000 Stueck - *mohair woven fur, black, jointed, surface washable, suit & waistcoat: felt, shirt & scarf: cotton, ltd edition of 4,000*

EAN-No.	Period	Pr.	Info
037023	1998-1999	4	25 cm

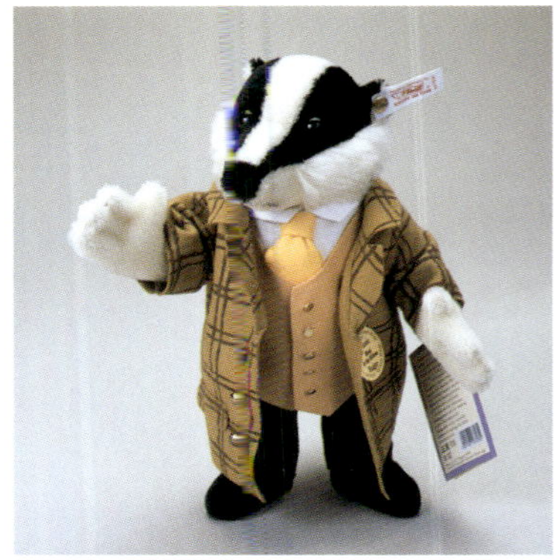

Classic Dachs **Badger** - *Classic **Badger***

Mohair Webpelz, schwarz/weiss, gegliedert, abwaschbar, Jacke, Hose & Krawatte aus Filz, Hemd aus Baumwolle, limit. Auflage 4000 Stueck - *mohair woven fur, black/white, jointed, surface washable, jacket, trousers & tie: felt, cotton shirt, ltd edition of 4,000*

EAN-No.	Period	Pr.	Info
037030	1999-1999	4	28 cm

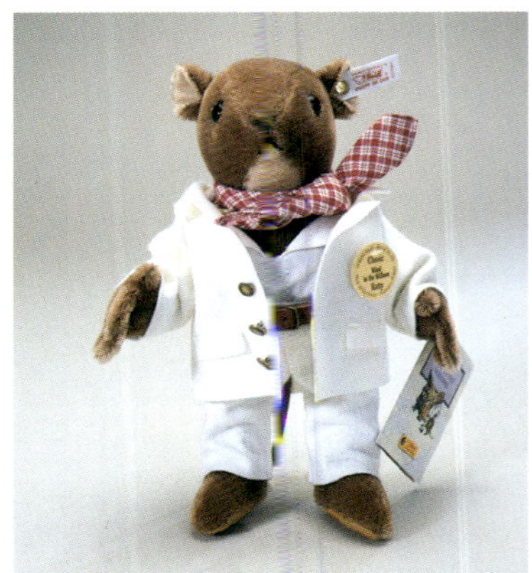

Classic Ratte **Ratty** - *Classic **Ratty***

Mohair Webpelz, graubraun, gegliedert, abwaschbar, Jacke & Hose aus Filz, Hemd & Halstuch aus Baumwolle, limit. Auflage 4000 Stueck - *mohair woven fur, grey-brown, jointed, surface washable, jacket & trousers: felt, shirt & scarf: cotton, ltd edition of 4,000*

EAN-No.	Period	Pr.	Info
037047	1999-1999	4	25 cm

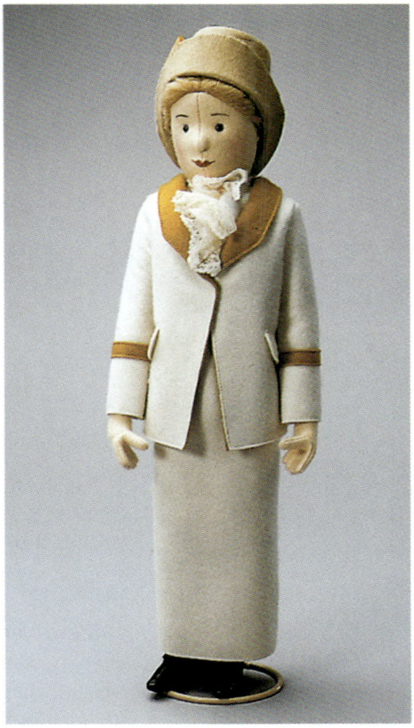

Betty Tennisdame, Replica 1913 - *Betty the Tennis Lady Replica 1913*

Wollfilz, limit. Auflage 3.000 Stueck - *wool felt, ltd edition of 3,000*

SERIE	ART.-NO	PERIOD	PR.	INFO
412301	**9100/45**	1987-1990	4	45 cm

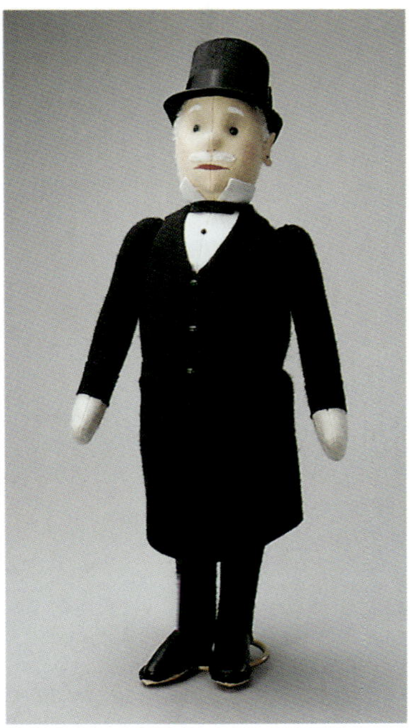

Herr im Gehrock, Replica 1914 - *Gentleman in Frock Coat Replica 1914*

Wollfilz, limit. Auflage 3.000 Stueck - *wool felt, ltd edition of 3,000*

SERIE	ART.-NO	PERIOD	PR.	INFO
412400	**9102/50**	1987-1990	4	50 cm

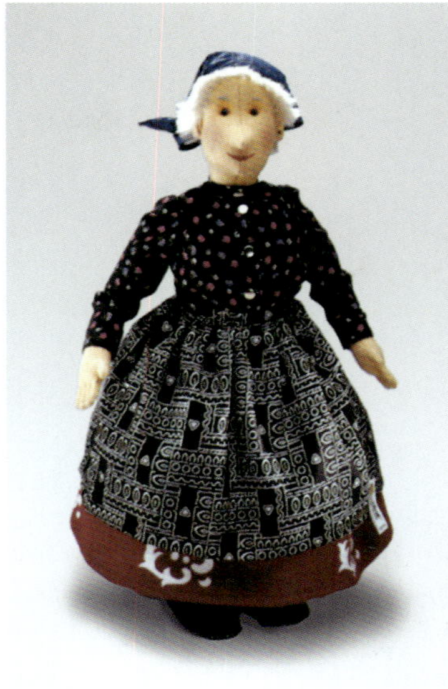

Baeuerin Replica 1912 - *Peasant Lady Replica 1912*

Wollfilz, limit. Auflage 3.000 Stueck - *wool felt, ltd edition of 3,000*

SERIE	ART.-NO	PERIOD	PR.	INFO
412202	**9110/43**	1987-1990	4	43 cm

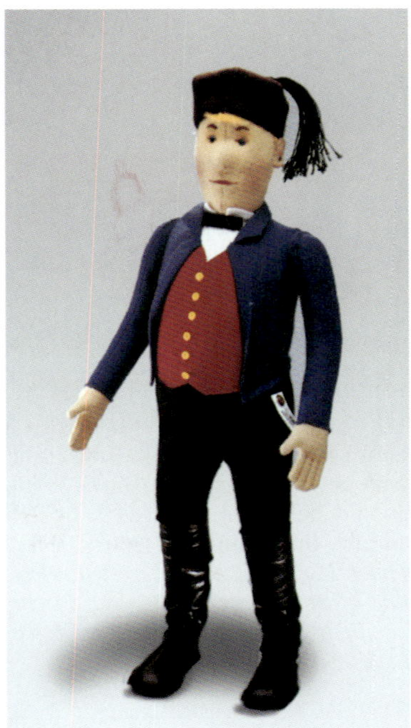

Bauer Joerg Replica 1915 - *Peasant Man Joerg Replica 1915*

Wollfilz, limit. Auflage 3.000 Stueck - *wool felt, ltd edition of 3,000*

SERIE	ART.-NO	PERIOD	PR.	INFO
412509	**9112/45**	1987-1990	4	45 cm

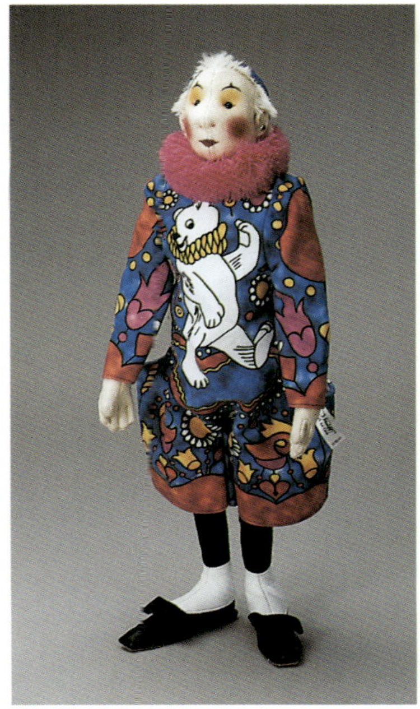

Coloro Clown Replica 1911

Wollfilz, limit. Auflage 3.000 Stueck - *wool felt, ltd edition of 3,000*

SERIE	ART.-NO	PERIOD	PR.	INFO
412189	**9130/43**	1988-1990	4	43 cm

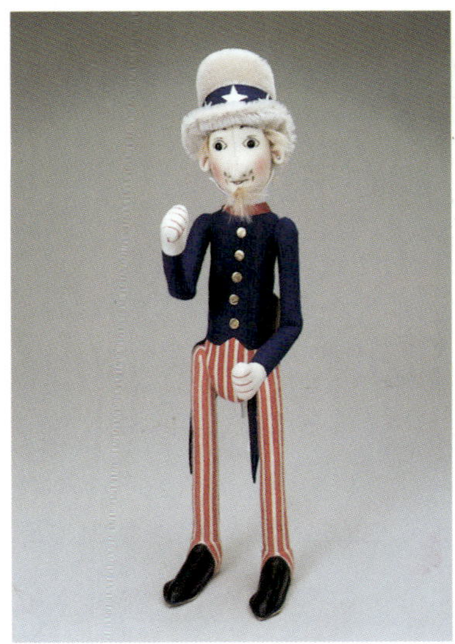

Filzpuppe Onkel Sam 1904 - *1904 Uncle Sam Felt Doll*

Filz/Trevirasamt, gegliedert, limit. Auflage 1.000 Stueck - *felt/trevira velvet, jointed, ltd edition of 1,000*

EAN-NO.	PERIOD	PR.	INFO
411601	1994-1994	4-5	50 cm

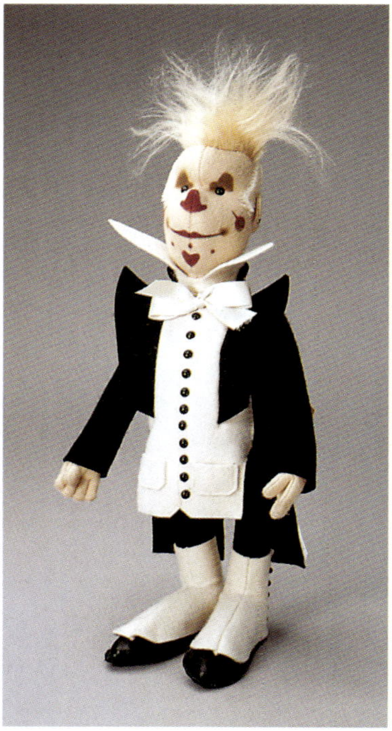

Filzpuppe Gusto 1911 - *1911 Gusto Felt Doll*

Wollfilz/Mohair, gegliedert, limit. Auflage 1.000 Stueck - *wool felt/mohair, jointed, ltd edtion of 1,000*

EAN-No.	Period	Pr.	Info
412011	1994-1994	4-5	31 cm

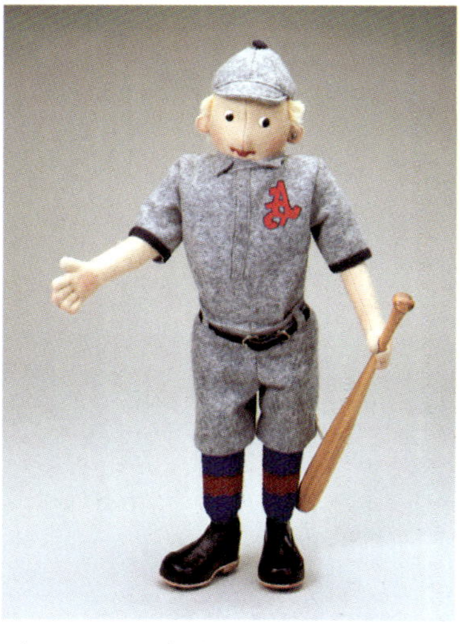

Filzpuppe Baseballspieler - *Baseball Player Felt Doll*

Wollfilz/Mohair, gegliedert, limit. Auflage 1.200 Stueck - *wool felt & mohair, jointed, ltd edition of 1,200*

EAN-No.	Period	Pr.	Info
411656	1995-1998	4-5	45 cm

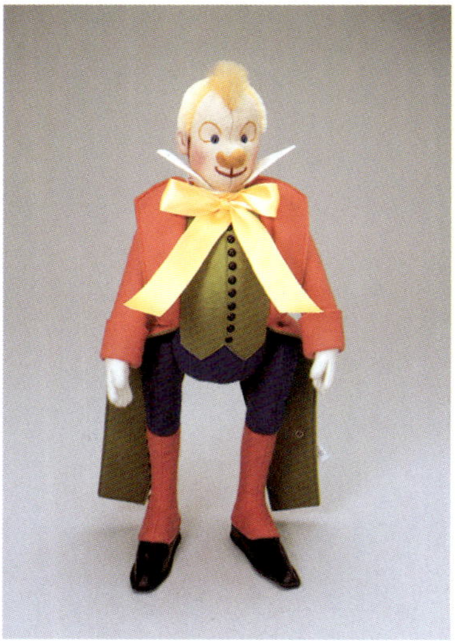

Filzpuppe Clown Noso - *Clown Noso Felt Doll*

Wollfilz/Mohair, gegliedert, limit. Auflage 1.200 Stueck - *wool felt/mohair, jointed, ltd edition of 1,200*

EAN-No.	Period	Pr.	Info
412042	1995-1995	4-5	42 cm

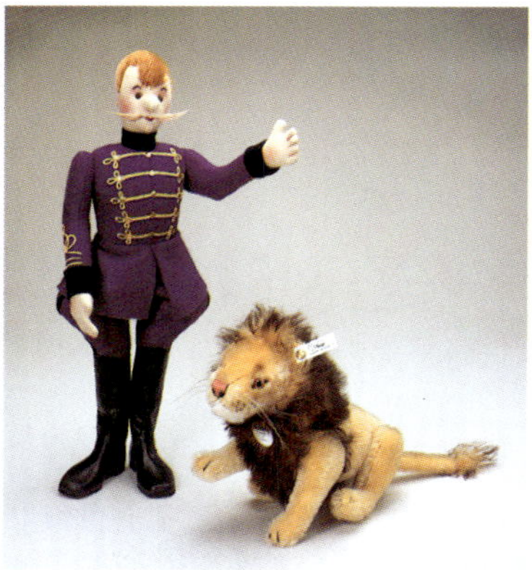

Filzpuppe Dompteur mit Loewe - *Animal Trainer Felt Doll with Lion*

Replica 1911, Puppe: 50 cm, Trevirasamt, Haare aus Mohair, gegliedert, Loewe: 20 cm, Mohair, hellbraun, gegliedert, Druckstimme, limit. Auflage 1.200 Stueck - *replica 1911, doll: 50 cm, trevira velvet, hair of mohair, jointed, lion: 20 cm, mohair, light brown, jointed, press voice, ltd edition of 1,200*

EAN-No.	Period	Pr.	Info
412073	1995-1995	5	kpl. Set - *compl. set*
	1995-1995	4	Puppe - *doll*
J04099	1995-1995	3-4	Loewe - *lion*

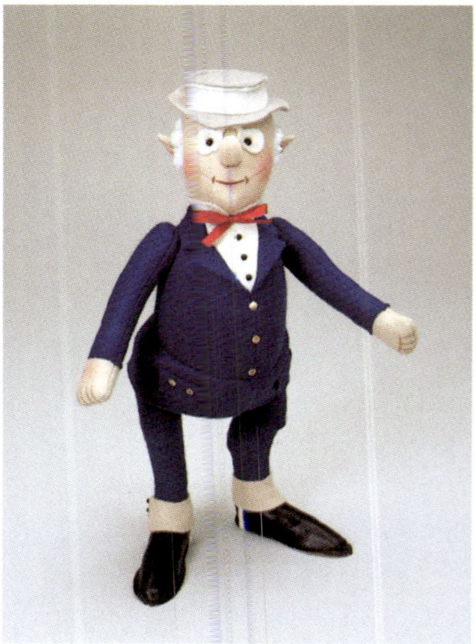

Filzpuppe Grandpa Foxy 1906 - *Felt Doll Grandpa Foxy 1906*

Wollfilz/Webpelz, gegliedert, abwaschbar, Druckstimme im Hut, limit. Auflage 1.200 Stueck - *wool felt/woven fur, jointed, surface washable, with squeaker in hat, ltd edition of 1,200*

EAN-No.	Period	Pr.	Info
411687	1996-1998	4	35 cm

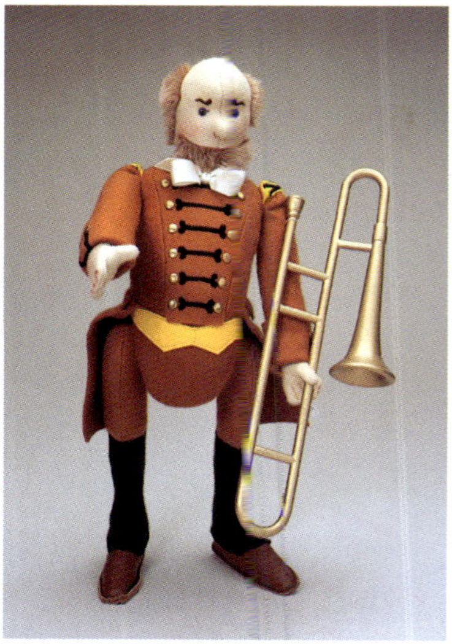

Filzpuppe Musiker Brown 1911 - *Felt Doll Musician Brown 1911*

Wollfilz/Mohair Webpelz, gegliedert, abwaschbar, mit Posaune, limit. Auflage 1.200 Stueck - *wool felt/mohair woven fur, jointed, surface washable, with trumpet, ltd edition of 1,200*

EAN-No.	Period	Pr.	Info
411908	1996-1998	4-5	43 cm

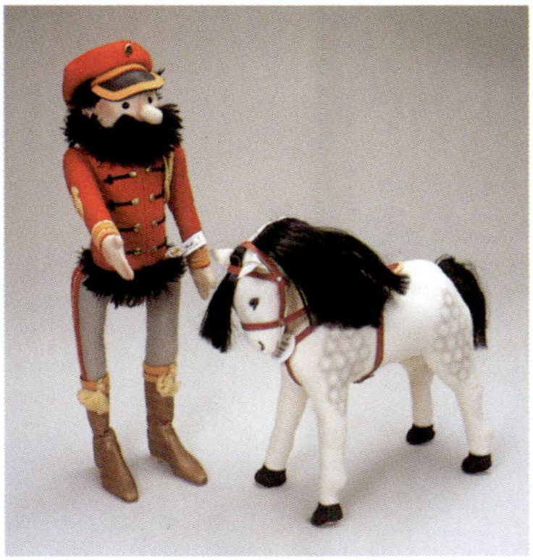

Filzpuppe Ungar mit Pferd 1912 - *Felt Doll Hungarian with Horse 1912*

Wollfilz/Wirkpelz, abwaschbar, Puppe: 43 cm, gegliedert, Pferd: 28 cm, stehend, Ledersattel & Zaumzeug, limit. Auflage 1.200 Stueck - *wool felt, knitted fur, surface washable, doll: 43 cm, jointed, horse: 28 cm, wool felt, leather saddle & bridle, ltd edition of 1,200*

EAN-No.	Period	Pr.	Info
411984	1996-1998	5	kpl. Set - *compl. set*
	1996-1998	4-5	Puppe - *doll*
J04108	1996-1998	3-4	Pferd - *horse*

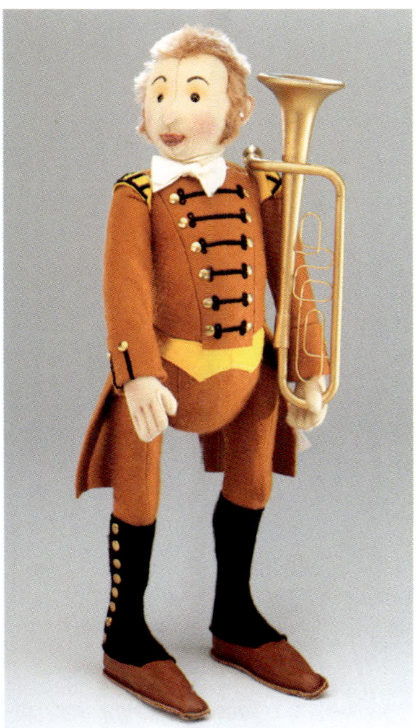

Filzpuppe Musiker Brown 1911 - *Felt Doll Musician Brown 1911*

Wollfilz/Mohair Webpelz, gegliedert, abwaschbar, mit Tenorhorn, limit. Auflage 1.200 Stueck - *wool felt/mohair woven fur, jointed, surface washable, with tenor horn, ltd edition of 1,200*

EAN-No.	Period	Pr.	Info
411915	1997-1998	4-5	43 cm

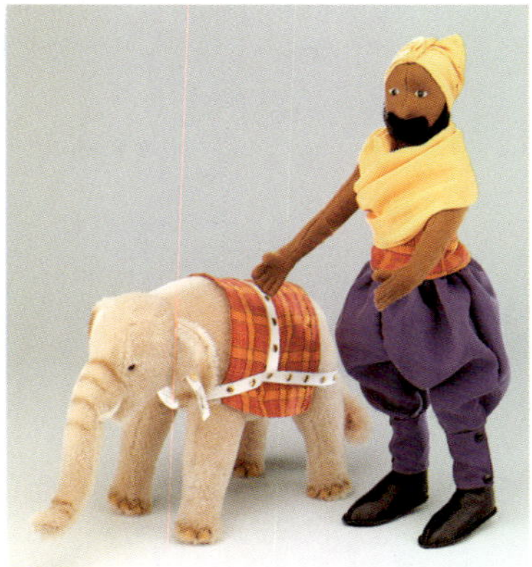

Filzpuppe Inder mit Elefant 1911 - *Felt Doll Indian with Elephant 1911*

Wollfilz / Mohair, abwaschbar, Puppe: 43 cm, gegliedert, Elefant: 30 cm, Satteldecke & Ledergeschirr, limit. Auflage 1.200 Stueck - *wool felt / mohair woven fur, surface washable, doll: 43 cm, jointed, elephant: 30 cm, saddlecloth & leather harness, ltd edition of 1,200*

EAN-No.	Period	Pr.	Info
412080	1997-1998	5-6	43 / 30 cm

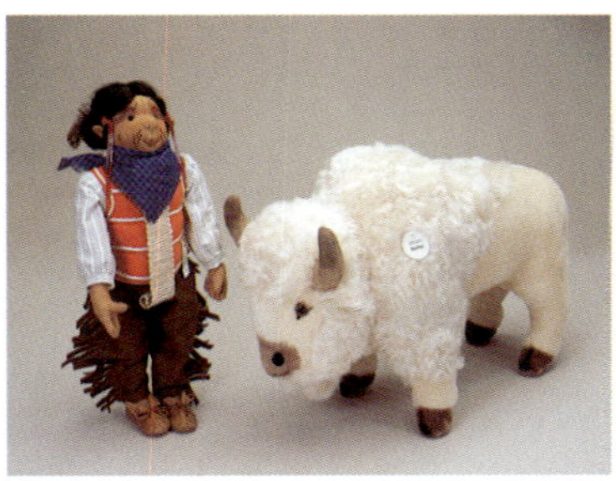

Filzpuppe Indianer mit Bueffel 1911 - *Felt Doll Indian with Buffalo 1911*

Puppe: 43 cm, Wollfilz/Webpelz, gegliedert, Bueffel: 45 cm, Mohair Webpelz, weiss, stehend, beide abwaschbar, limit. Auflage 750 Stueck - *doll: 43 cm, wool felt/woven fur, jointed, buffalo: 45 cm, mohair woven fur, white, standing, both surface washable, ltd edition of 750*

EAN-No.	Period	Pr.	Info
411762	1998-1998	5-6	kpl. Set - *compl. set*
	1998-1998	4-5	Puppe - *doll*
J04255	1998-1998	4-5	Bueffel - *buffalo*

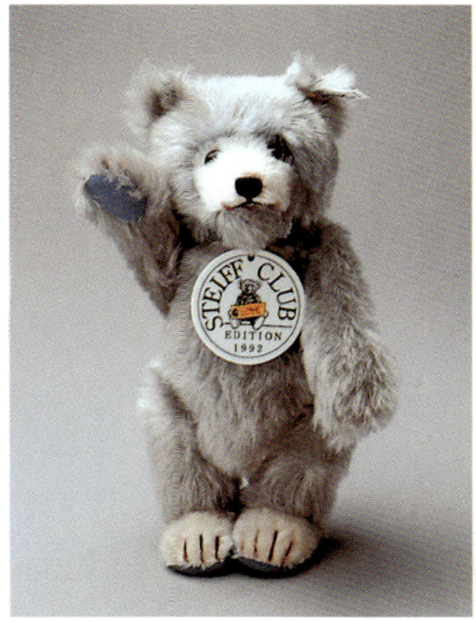

Teddy Baby Blau - *Blue Teddy Baby*

Steiff Club Edition 1992, Mohair, gegliedert, limit. Auflage 7.959 Stueck (nur fuer Europa) - *1992 Steiff Club Edition, mohair, jointed, ltd edition of 7,959 (exclusively for Europe)*

EAN-No.	Period	Pr.	Info
420016	1992-1992	5-6	28 cm

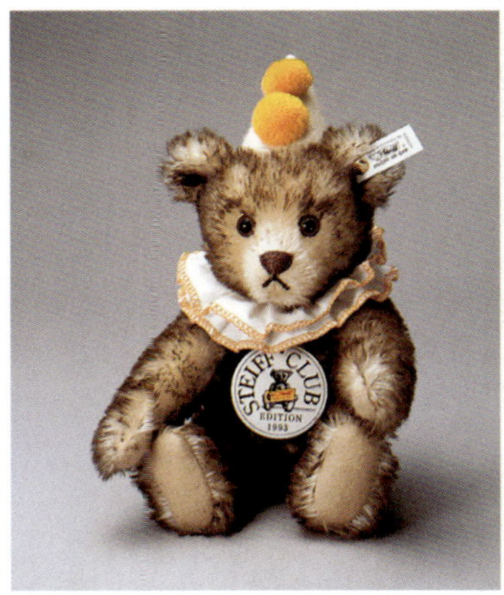

Teddy Clown 1928

Steiff Club Edition 1993, Mohair, gegliedert, limit. Auflage 11.020 Stueck (nur fuer Europa) - *1993 Steiff Club Edition, mohair, jointed, ltd edition of 11,020 (exclusively for Europe)*

EAN-No.	Period	Pr.	Info
420023	1993-1993	4-5	28 cm

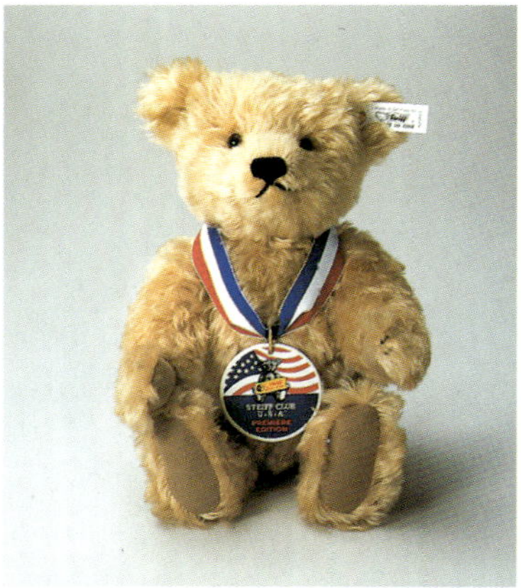

Teddy Sam

Steiff Club USA Edition 1993, Mohair, gegliedert, limit. Auflage nur fuer Mitglieder des Steiff Club USA - *1993 Steiff Club USA Edition. mohair, jointed, ltd edition only for members of Steiff-Club USA*

EAN-No.	Period	Pr.	Info
420801	1993-1993	5	28 cm

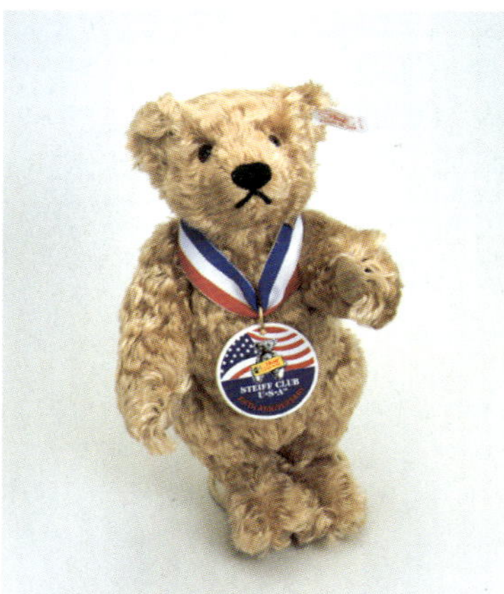

Teddy Sammi

Mohair, blond, gegliedert, nur fuer Mitglieder des Steiff Club USA - *mohair, blond, jointed, only for members of Steiff-Club USA*

EAN-No.	Period	Pr.	Info
665196	1998-1998	4	22 cm

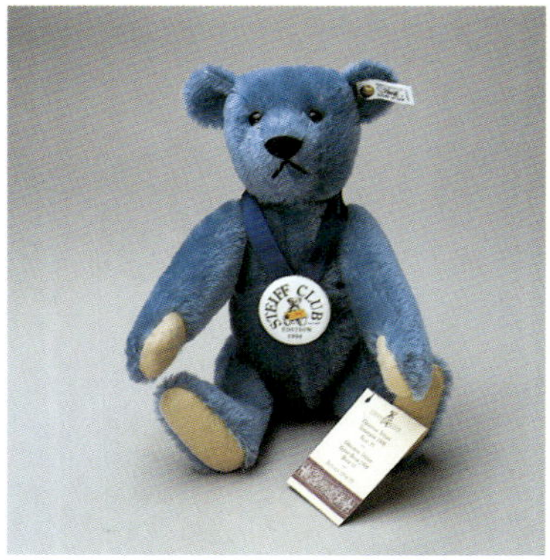

Original Teddybaer 1908 - *Original Teddy Bear 1908*

Steiff Club Edition 1994, Mohair, gegliedert, limit. Auflage 14.910 Stueck (weltweit) - *1994 Steiff Club Edition, mohair, jointed, ltd edition of 14,910 (worldwide)*

EAN-No.	Period	Pr.	Info
420047	1994-1994	4	35 cm

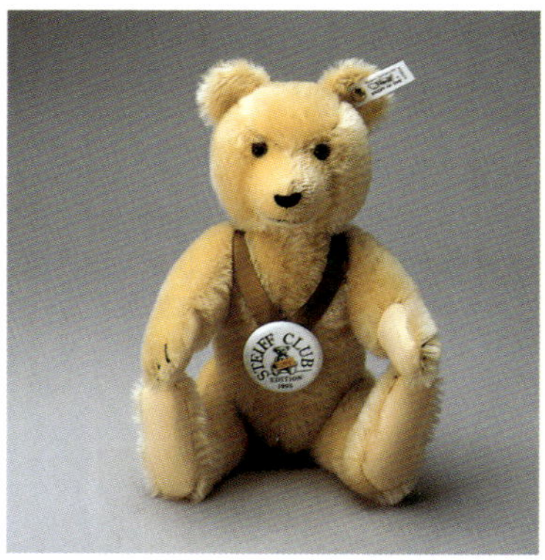

Baby Baer 1946 - *Baby Bear 1946*

Steiff Club Edition 1995, Mohair, blond, gegliedert, limit. Auflage 10.880 Stueck - *1995 Steiff Club Edition, mohair, blond, jointed, ltd edition of 10,880*

EAN-No.	Period	Pr.	Info
420054	1995-1995	4	35 cm

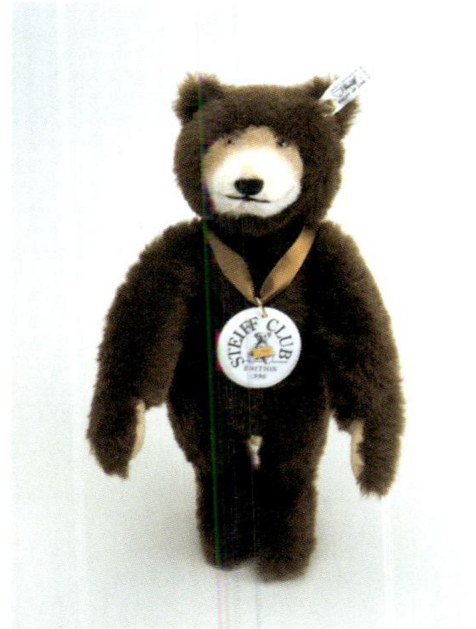

Dicky 1935

Steiff Club Edition 1996, Wollpluesch, dunkelbraun, gegliedert, Druckstimme, limit. Auflage 7.965 Stueck - *1996 Steiff Club Edition, wool plush, dark brown, jointed, press voice, ltd edition of 7,965*

EAN-No.	Period	Pr.	Info
420078	1996-1996	4	32 cm

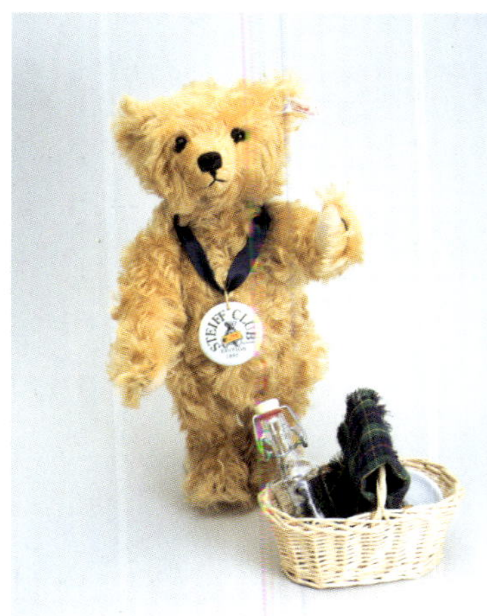

Picknick Baer - *Picknick Bear*

Steiff Club Edition 1997, Mohair Webpelz, goldblond, gegliedert, Brummstimme, Korb mit Glasflasche & zwei Porzellantellern - jeweils mit Club-Logo - und blau-gruen karierter Picknick-Decke, limit. Auflage 9.888 Stueck - *1997 Steiff Club Edition, mohair woven fur, gold-blond, jointed, growler, basket with bottle and two plates made of porcelain - all with Club logo - and blue-green chequered Picknick blanket, ltd edition of 9.888*

EAN-No.	Period	Pr.	Info
420108	1997-1997	4	34 cm

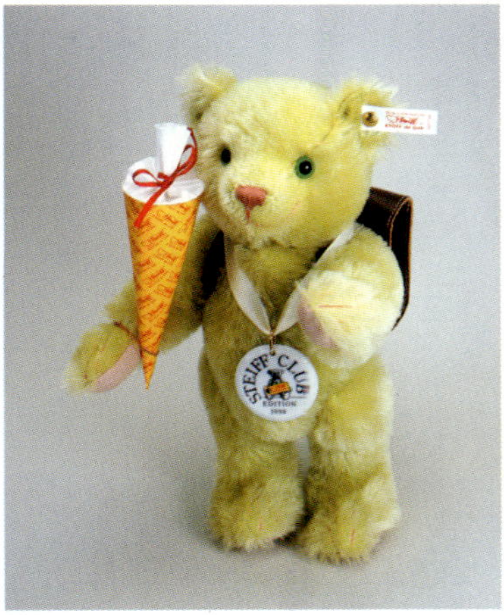

Schulanfaenger Baer - *School Beginner Bear*

Steiff Club Edition 1998, Mohair, hellgruen, gegliedert, Druckstimme, mit Leder-Schulranzen & Schultuete, limit. Auflage 8.730 Stueck - *1998 Steiff Club Edition, mohair, light green, jointed, press voice, with leather satchel and beginners paper bag, ltd edition of 8,730*

EAN-No.	Period	Pr.	Info
420139	1998-1998	4	30 cm

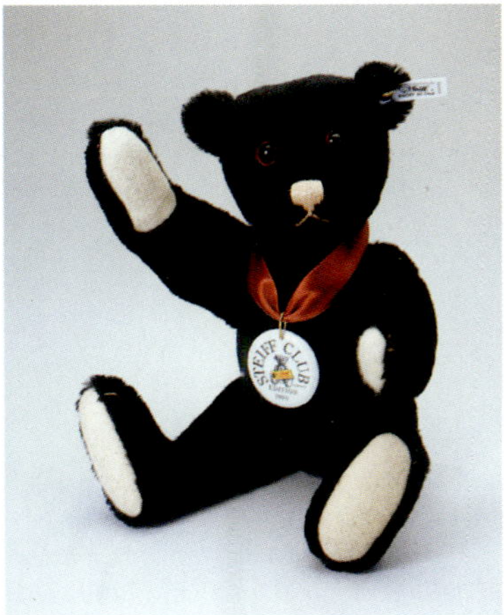

Teddybaer 1912 - *Teddybear 1912*

Steiff Club Edition 1999, Mohair, schwarz, gegliedert, Kippstimme, limit. Auflage gebunden an Bestellungen von Club-Mitgliedern bis 31.3.2000 - *1999 Steiff Club Edition, mohair, black, jointed, tilt-me voice, ltd edition depending on Club member orders up to 31.3.2000*

EAN-No.	Period	Pr.	Info
420160	1999-1999	4	35 cm

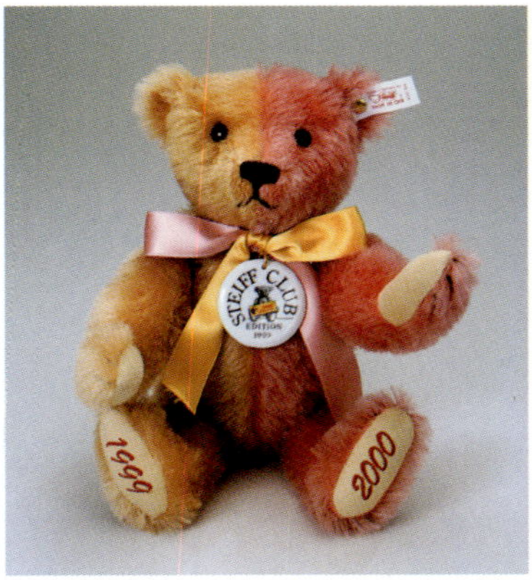

Jahrtausendwechsel-Baer - *Millenium Bear*

2\. Steiff Club Edition 1999, Mohairplüsch, goldbraun/altrosé, gegliedert, Stopfung Acrylfaser, limit. Auflage gebunden an Bestellungen von Club-Mitgliedern bis 31.3.2000 - *2nd Steiff Club Edition 1999, mohair, gold-brown/rose, jointed, ltd edition depending on Club member orders up to 31.3.2000*

EAN-No.	Period	Pr.	Info
420184	1999-1999	3-4	32 cm

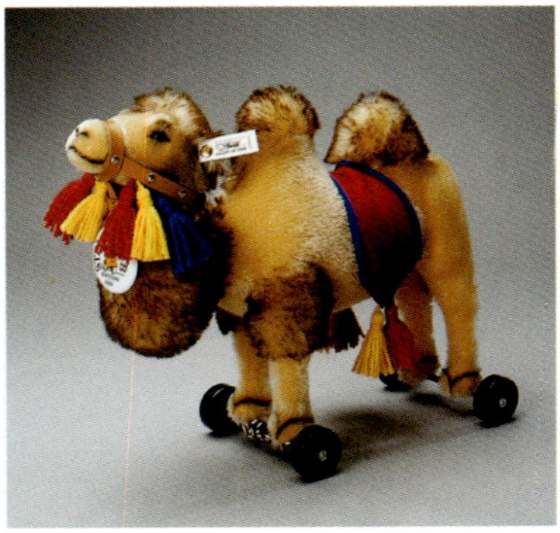

Kamel auf Raedern - *Camel on Wheels*

Steiff Club Edition II 1995, Mohair Webpelz, sandfarben, Eisen-Innengestell, Holzraeder, Leder-Kopfgeschirr, Filzschabracke, limit. Auflage 1.770 Stueck - *Steiff Club Edition II 1995, mohair woven fur, sandy colored, iron frame, wooden wheels, leather halter, felt saddle cloth, ltd edition of 1,770*

EAN-No.	Period	Pr.	Info
420061	1995-1995	5	35 cm

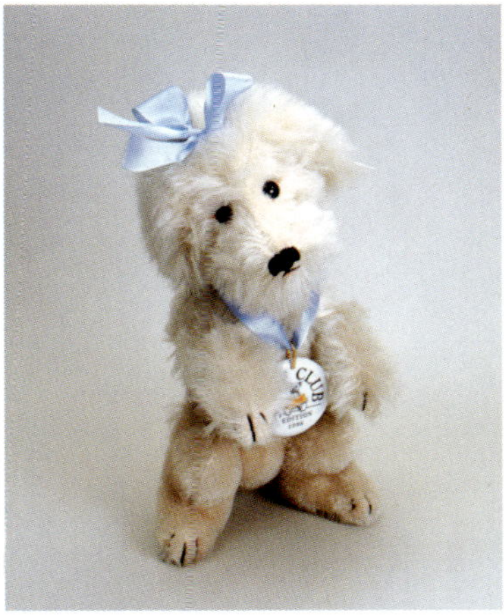

Pudel 1931 - *Poodle 1931*

Steiff Club Edition II 1996, Mohair, weiss, aufwartend, Halsmechanik, Druckstimme, limit. Auflage 3.545 Stueck - *Steiff Club Edition II 1996, mohair, white, sitting up, neck mechanism, press voice, ltd edition of 3,545*

EAN-No.	Period	Pr.	Info
420085	1996-1996	4	28 cm

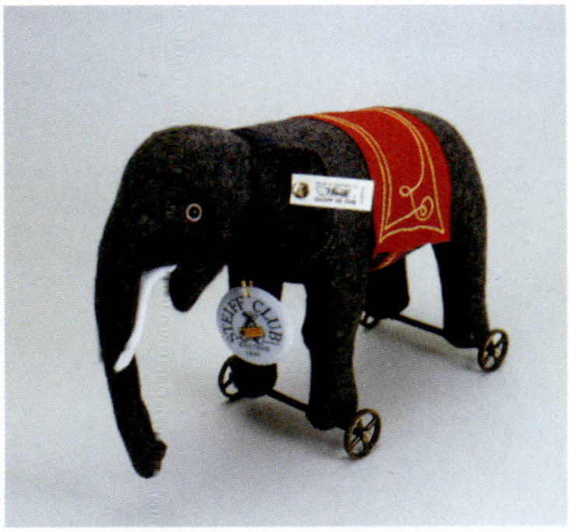

Elefant auf Raedern 1914 - *Elephant on wheels 1914*

Steiff Club Edition II 1997, Filz, grau, stehend, auf Metallraedern, rote Filz-Satteldekke, limit. Auflage 3.236 Stueck - *Steiff Club Edition II 1997, felt, grey, standing, on metal wheels, red felt saddle-cloth, ltd edition of 3,236*

EAN-No.	Period	Pr.	Info
420115	1997-1997	4	22 cm

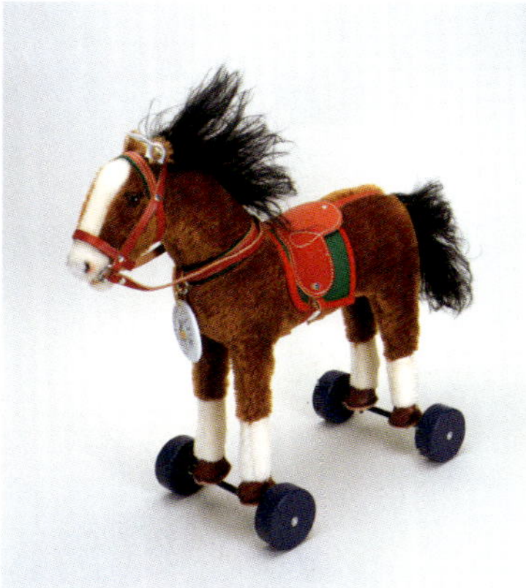

Pferd auf Raedern 1929 - *Horse on wheels 1929*

Steiff Club Edition II 1998, Mohair Webpelz, braun, stehend, auf Holzraedern, Filz-Satteldecke, Ledergeschirr & Sattel, limit. Auflage 2.020 Stueck - *Steiff Club Edition II 1998, mohair woven fur, brown, standing, on wooden wheels, felt saddle-cloth, leather bridle and saddle, ltd edition of 2,020*

EAN-No.	Period	Pr.	Info
420146	1998-1998	4-5	35 cm

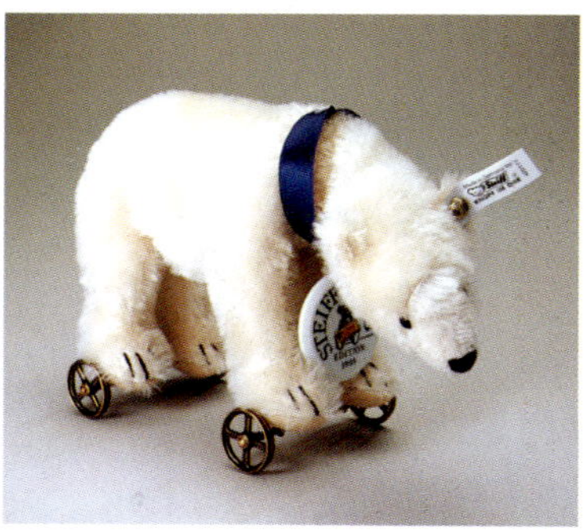

Eisbaer 1910 - *Polar Bear 1910*

Steiff Club Edition II 1999, Mohairpluesch, weiss, stehend, auf Metallraedern, limit. Auflage gebunden an Bestellungen von Club-Mitgliedern bis 31.3.2000 - *Steiff Club Edition II 1999, mohair woven fur, white, standing, on metal wheels, ltd edition depending on Club member orders up to 31.3.2000*

EAN-No.	Period	Pr.	Info
420177	1999-1999	4	22 cm

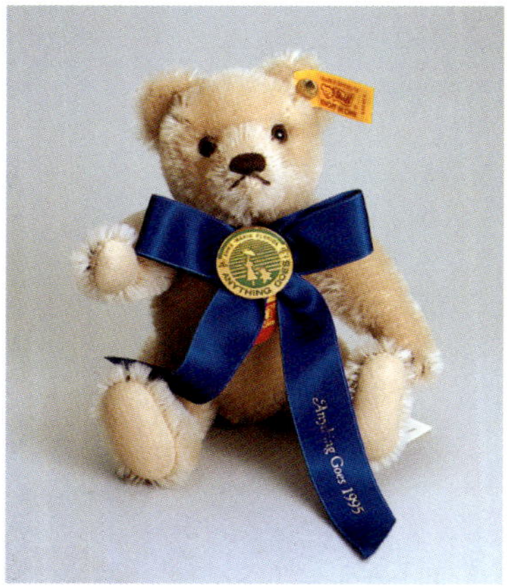

Teddybaer - *Teddybear*

Mohair, honig, gegliedert, fuer USA Steiff-Events des Jahres 1995 - *mohair woven fur, honey, jointed, for USA Steiff-Events in 1995 only*

EAN-No.	Period	Pr.	Info
650826	1995-1995	4	22 cm

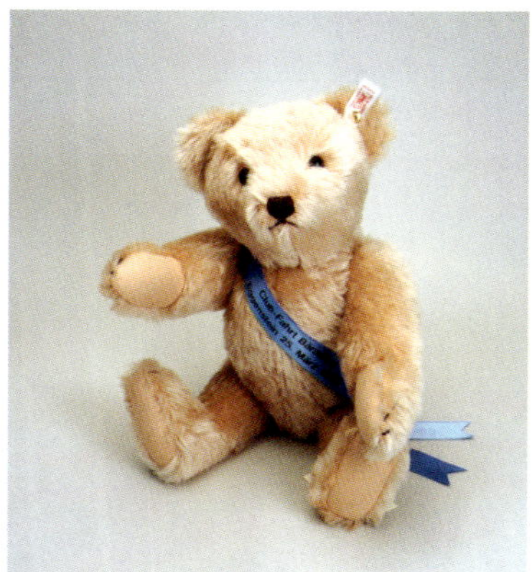

Teddybaer - *Teddybear*

Mohair, blond, gegliedert, limit. Auflage 3.000 Stueck, nur fuer Steiff-Club-Events im Jahr 1996 - *mohair woven fur, blond, jointed, ltd edition of 3,000, for Steiff Club-Events in 1996 only*

EAN-No.	Period	Pr.	Info
655258	1996-1996	4	25 cm

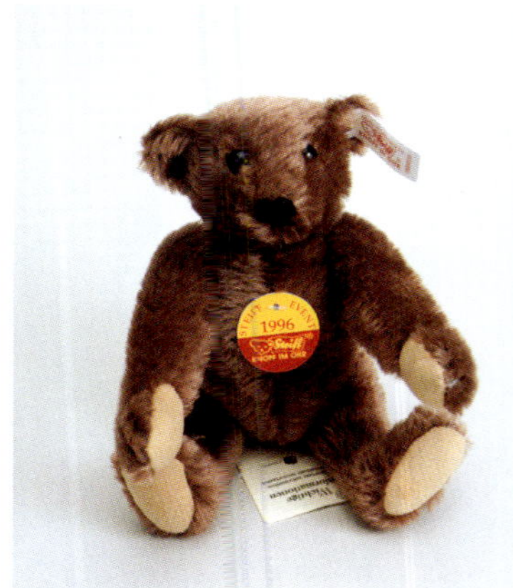

Teddybaer - *Teddybear*

Mohair, braun, gegliedert, limit. Auflage 1.000 Stueck, nur fuer USA Steiff-Club-Events des Jahres 1996 - *mohair woven fur, brown, jointed, ltd edition of 1,000 for USA Steiff-Club-Events in 1996 only*

EAN-No.	Period	Pr.	Info
665035	1996-1996	4	25 cm

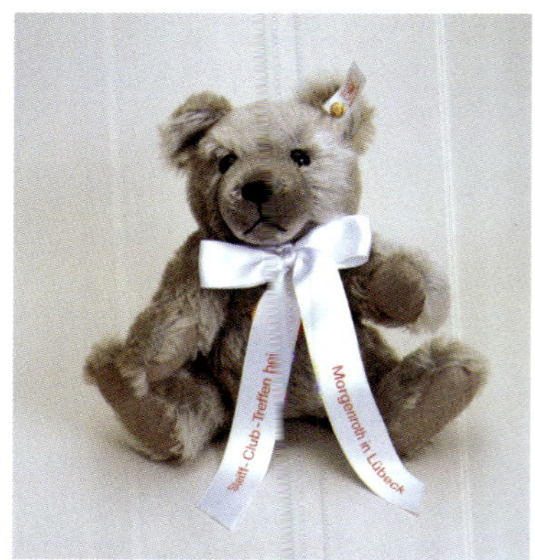

Teddybaer - *Teddybear*

Mohair, grau, gegliedert, limit. Auflage 3.000 Stueck, nur fuer Steiff-Club-Events des Jahres 1997 - *mohair woven fur, grey, jointed, ltd edition of 3,000 for Steiff-Club-Events in 1997 only*

EAN-No.	Period	Pr.	Info
670213	1997-1997	4	25 cm

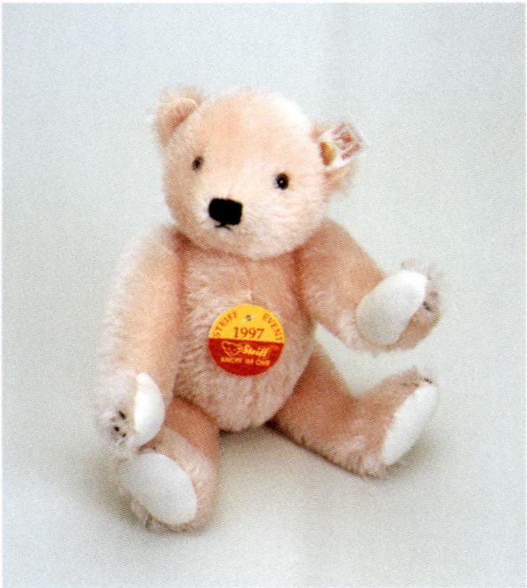

Teddybaer - *Teddybear*

Mohair, rosé, gegliedert, limit. Auflage 2.000 Stueck, nur fuer USA Steiff-Club-Events des Jahres 1997 - *mohair woven fur, rose, jointed, ltd edition of 2,000 for USA Steiff-Club-Events in 1997 only*

EAN-No.	Period	Pr.	Info
665202	1997-1997	3-4	22 cm

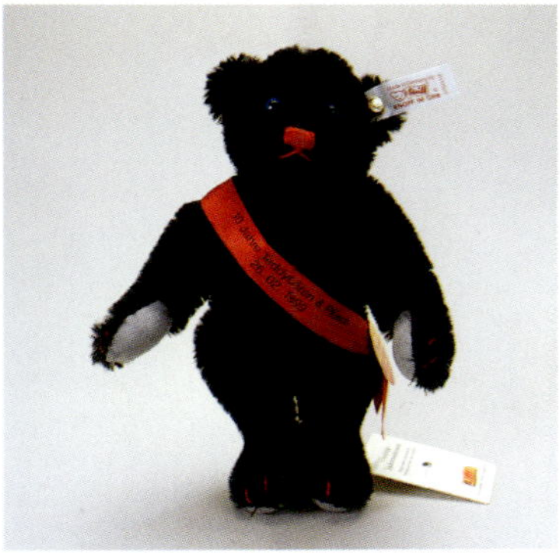

Teddybaer - *Teddybear*

Mohair, schwarz, gegliedert, limit. Auflage 2.000 Stueck, nur fuer Steiff-Club-Events der Jahre 1998 & 1999 - *mohair, black, jointed, ltd edition of 2,000 for Steiff-Club-Events in 1998 & 1999 only*

EAN-No.	Period	Pr.	Info
670312	1998-1999	3	22 cm

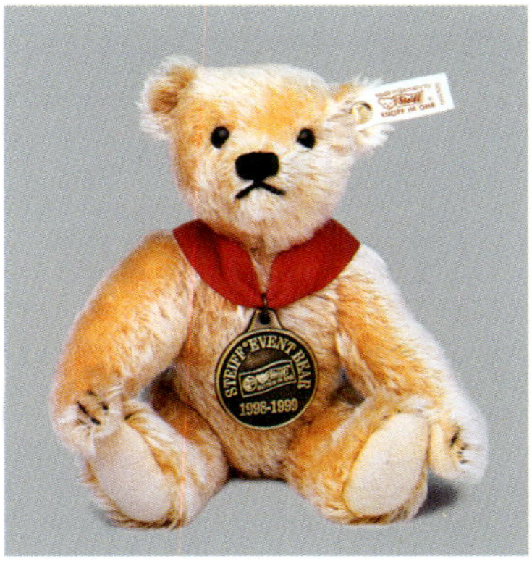

Teddybaer - *Teddybear*

Mohair, blond, gegliedert, limit. Auflage 3.000 Stueck, nur fuer USA Steiff-Club-Events der Jahre 1998 & 1999, zusammen mit Buch "A Celebration of Steiff" - *mohair, blond, jointed, ltd edition of 3,000 for USA Steiff-Club-Events in 1998 & 1999 only, with book "A Celebration of Steiff"*

EAN-No.	Period	Pr.	Info
665325	1998-1999	4	22 cm

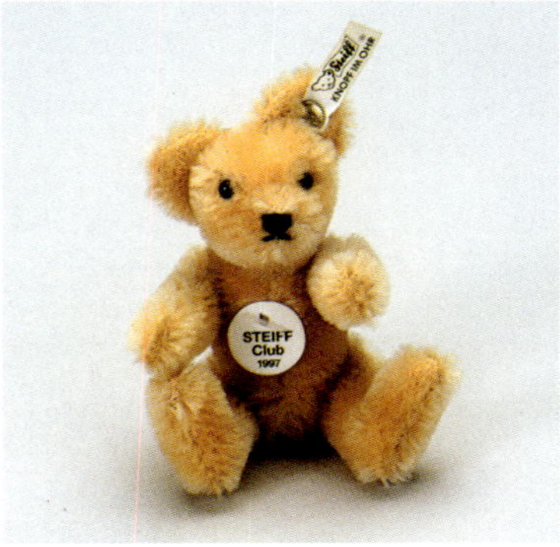

Teddybaer - *Teddybear*

Mohair, blond, gegliedert, Groesse sitzend gemessen, Club Geschenk fuer neue Mitglieder, weisses Brustschild mit Aufschrift "STEIFF Club" & Jahreszahl - *mohair, blond, jointed, Club gift for new members, size measured sitting, white chest tag with inscription "STEIFF Club" & the year*

EAN-No.	Period	Pr.	Info
420092	1997-1999	2-3	7 cm

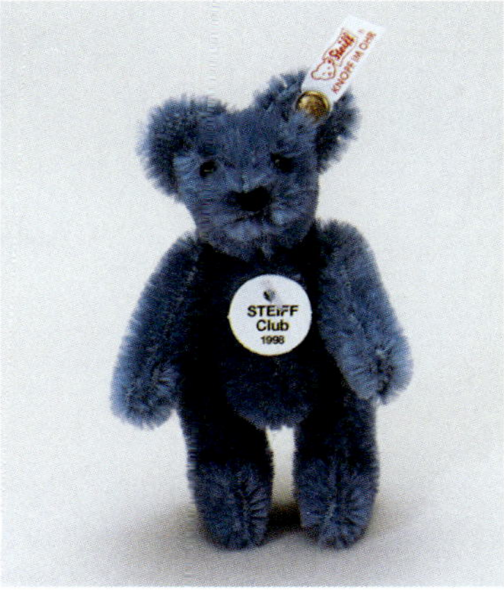

Teddybaer - *Teddybear*

Mohair, blau, gegliedert, Groesse sitzend gemessen, Club Treue-Geschenk, weisses Brustschild mit Aufschrift "STEIFF Club 1998" - *mohair, blue, jointed, Club loyalty gift, size measured sitting, white chest tag with inscription "STEIFF Club 1998"*

EAN-No.	Period	Pr.	Info
420122	1998-1998	3	7 cm

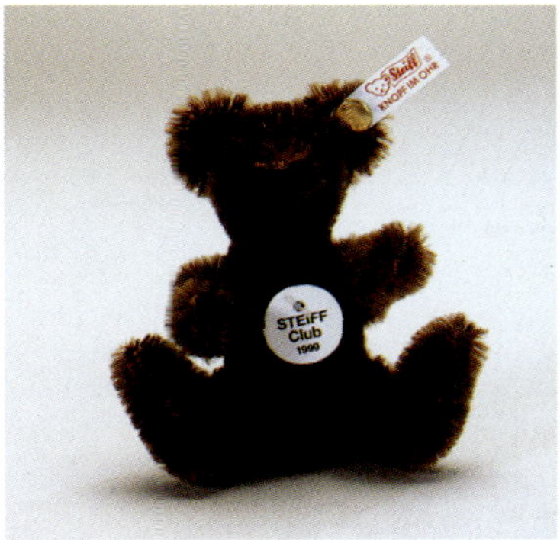

Teddybaer - *Teddybear*

Mohair, dunkelbraun, gegliedert, Groesse sitzend gemessen, Club Treue-Geschenk, weisses Brustschild mit Aufschrift "STEIFF Club 1999' - *mohair, dark brown, jointed, Club loyalty gift, size measured sitting, white chest tag with inscription "STEIFF Club 1999"*

EAN-No.	Period	Pr.	Info
420153	1999-1999	2-3	7 cm

USA Sonderserien bis 1980

US Special Editions up to 1980

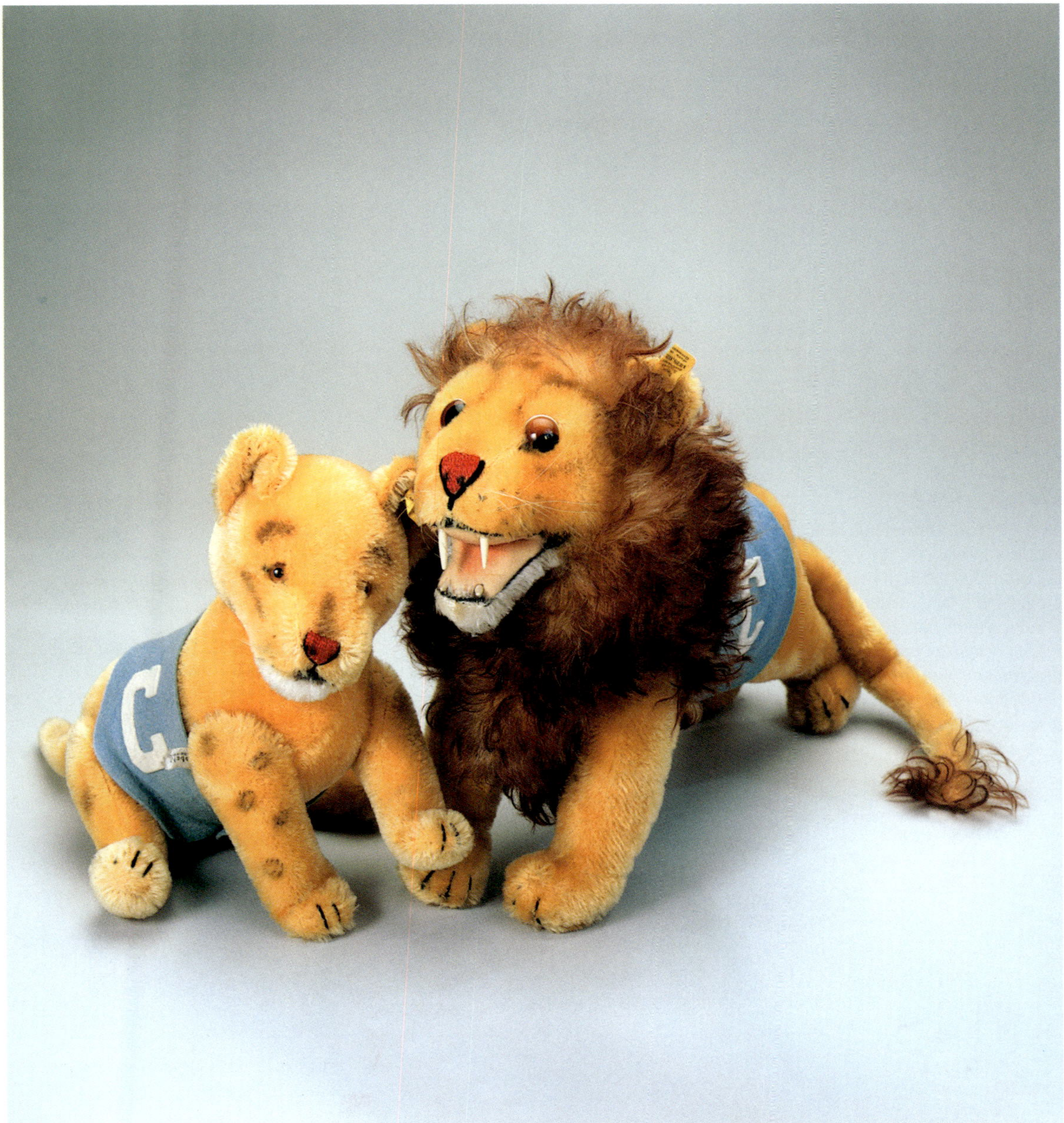

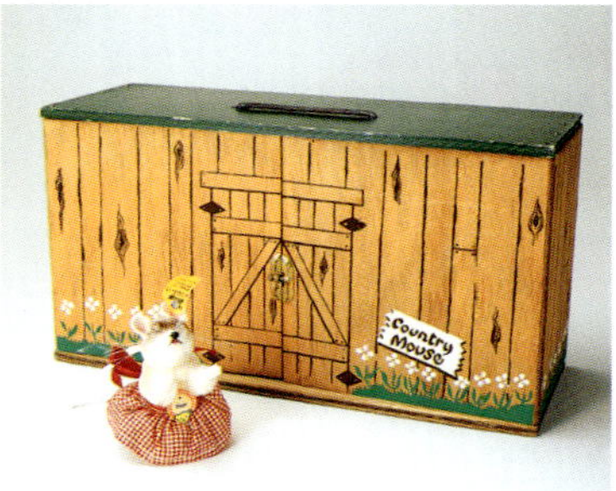

Landmaus - *Country Mouse*

Mohair, grau, aufwartend, Maus Pieps bekleidet und mit aufklappbarem Haus aus Sperrholz, eingerichtet im Landhausstil, Sonderartikel fuer FAO Schwarz, USA - *mohair, grey, begging, mouse Pieps dressed, with a house from plywood, furnished like a country house, special piece for FAO Schwarz, USA*

SERIE	ART.-NO	PERIOD	PR.	INFO
	4308.05	1962-1967	5-6	8 cm
	2175/08	1968-1972	5-6	

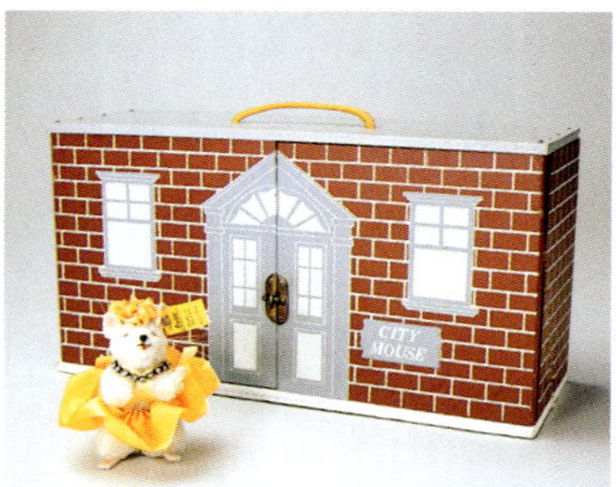

Stadtmaus - *City Mouse*

Mohair, weiss, aufwartend, Maus Pieps bekleidet mit blauem, ab 1965 gelbem, Satin, mit aufklappbarem Haus aus Sperrholz, eingerichtet als vornehmes Stadthaus, Sonderartikel fuer FAO Schwarz, USA - *mohair, white, begging, mouse Pieps dressed with blue, from 1965 yellow, satin, with a house from plywood, furnished like a noble city house, special piece for FAO Schwarz, USA*

SERIE	ART.-NO	PERIOD	PR.	INFO
	4308.04	1962-1967	5-6	8 cm
	2174/08	1968-1972	5-6	

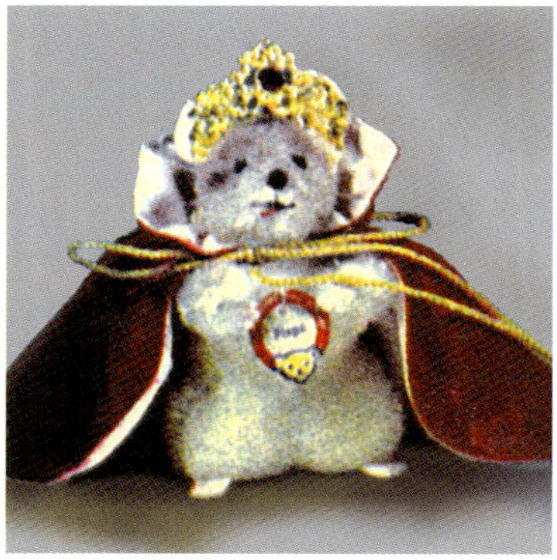

Royal Maus - *Royal Mouse*

Mohair, weiss, aufwartend, Maus Pieps bekleidet, Sonderartikel fuer FAO Schwarz, USA - *mohair, white, begging, mouse "Pieps" dressed, exclusive for FAO Schwarz, USA*

SERIE	ART.-NO	PERIOD	PR.	INFO
	4308,04	1965-1966	4	8 cm

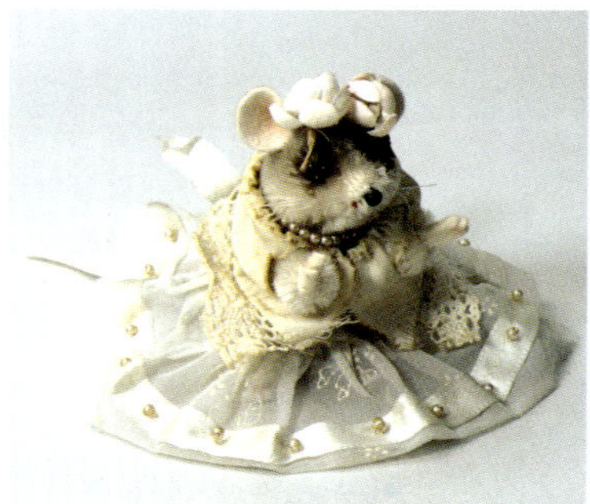

Ballerina Maus - *Ballerina Mouse*

Mohair, weiss, aufwartend, Maus Pieps bekleidet, Ballerina gibt es mit und ohne Seidenschleife am Tutu, Sonderartikel fuer FAO Schwarz, USA - *mohair, white, begging, mouse "Pieps" dressed, versions of "Ballerina" with and without silk ribbon on the Tutu, exclusive for FAO Schwarz, USA*

SERIE	ART.-NO	PERIOD	PR.	INFO
	4308,04	1965-1967	4	8 cm
	2174/08	1968-1971	4	

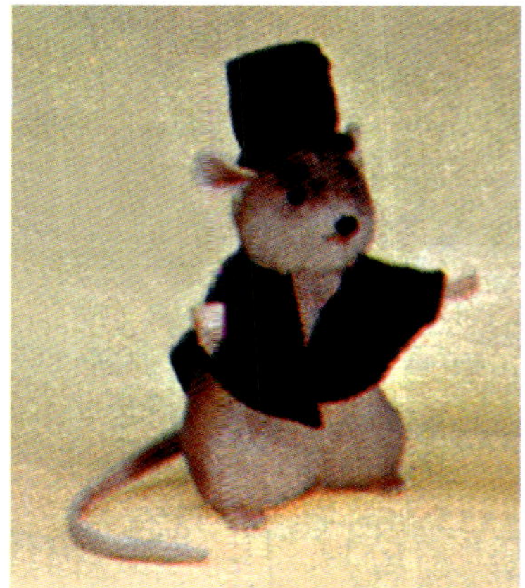

Braeutigam Maus - *Groom Mouse*

Mohair, weiss, aufwartend, Maus Pieps bekleidet, Sonderartikel fuer FAO Schwarz, USA - *mohair, white, begging, mouse "Pieps" dressed, exclusive for FAO Schwarz, USA*

SERIE	ART.-NO	PERIOD	PR.	INFO
	4308.04	1965-1967	4	8 cm

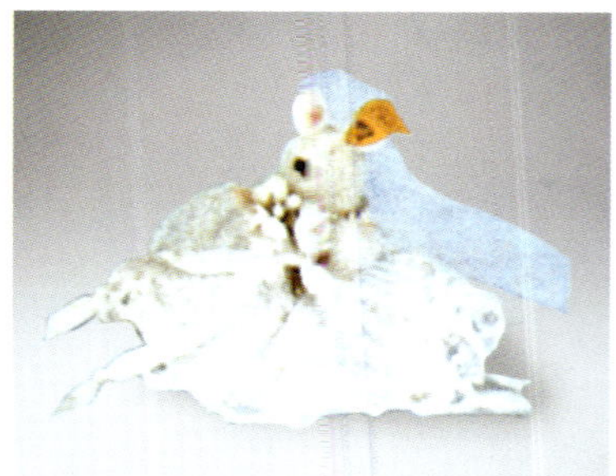

Braut Maus - *Bride Mouse*

Mohair, weiss, aufwartend, Maus Pieps bekleidet, Sonderartikel fuer FAO Schwarz, USA - *mohair, white, begging, mouse "Pieps" dressed, exclusive for FAO Schwarz, USA*

SERIE	ART.-NO	PERIOD	PR.	INFO
	4308.04	1966-1967	4	8 cm
	2174/08	1968-1972	4	

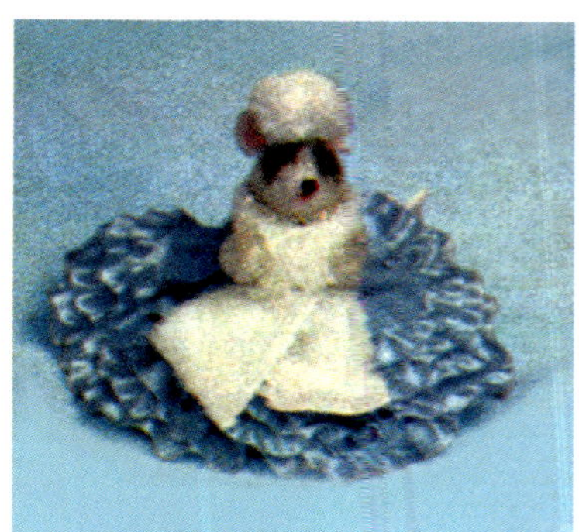

Princess Royal Maus - *Princess Royal Mouse*

Mohair, weiss, aufwartend, Maus Pieps bekleidet, Sonderartikel fuer FAO Schwarz, USA - *mohair, white, begging, mouse "Pieps" dressed, exclusive for FAO Schwarz, USA*

SERIE	ART.-NO	PERIOD	PR.	INFO
	4308,04	1967-1967	4	8 cm

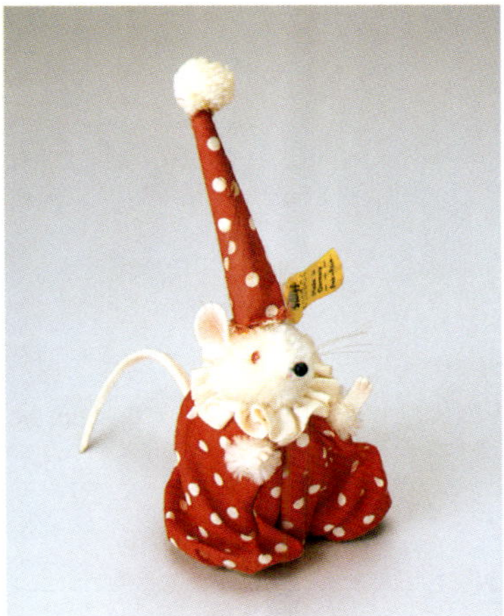

Clownie Maus - *Clownie Mouse*

Mohair, weiss, aufwartend, Maus Pieps bekleidet, Sonderartikel fuer FAO Schwarz, USA - *mohair, white, begging, mouse "Pieps" dressed, exclusive for FAO Schwarz, USA*

SERIE	ART.-NO	PERIOD	PR.	INFO
	4308,04	1967-1967	4	8 cm
	2174/08	1968-1969	4	

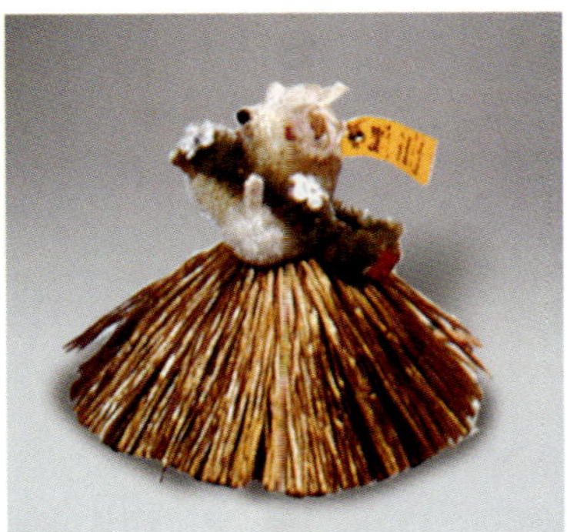

Hawaiian Maus - *Hawaiian Mouse*

Mohair, weiss, aufwartend, Maus Pieps bekleidet, Sonderartikel fuer FAO Schwarz, USA - *mohair, white, begging, mouse "Pieps" dressed, exclusive for FAO Schwarz, USA*

SERIE	ART.-NO	PERIOD	PR.	INFO
	2174/08	1968-1970	4	8 cm

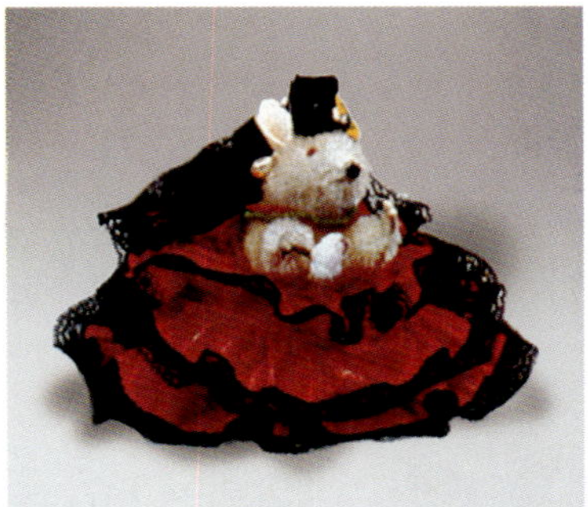

Senorita Maus - *Senorita Mouse*

Mohair, weiss, aufwartend, Maus Pieps bekleidet, Sonderartikel fuer FAO Schwarz, USA - *mohair, white, begging, mouse "Pieps" dressed, exclusive for FAO Schwarz, USA*

SERIE	ART.-NO	PERIOD	PR.	INFO
	2174/08	1969-1970	4	8 cm

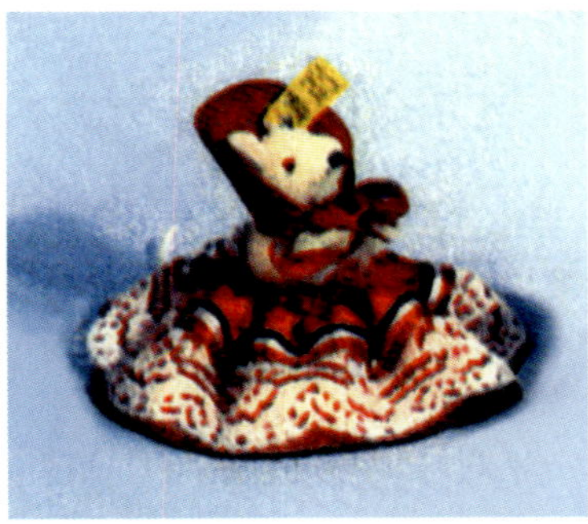

Ballkoenigin Maus - *Queen of the Ball Mouse*

Mohair, weiss, aufwartend, Maus Pieps bekleidet, Sonderartikel fuer FAO Schwarz, USA - *mohair, white, begging, mouse "Pieps" dressed, exclusive for FAO Schwarz, USA*

SERIE	ART.-NO	PERIOD	PR.	INFO
	2174/08	1970-1971	4	8 cm

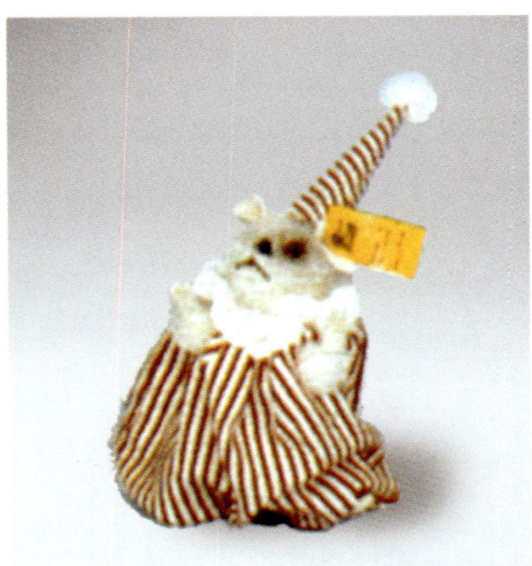

Polka Dot Clown Maus - *Polka Dot Clown Mouse*

Mohair, weiss, aufwartend, Maus Pieps bekleidet, Sonderartikel fuer FAO Schwarz, USA - *mohair, white, begging, mouse "Pieps" dressed, exclusive for FAO Schwarz, USA*

SERIE	ART.-NO	PERIOD	PR.	INFO
	2174/08	1970-1972	4	8 cm

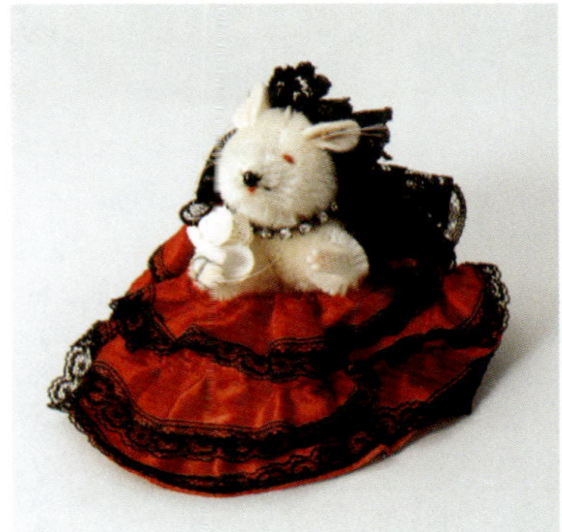

Spanish Senorita Maus - *Spanish Senorita Mouse*

Mohair, weiss, aufwartend, Maus Pieps bekleidet, Sonderartikel fuer FAO Schwarz, USA - *mohair, white, begging, mouse "Pieps" dressed, exclusive for FAO Schwarz, USA*

SERIE	ART.-NO	PERIOD	PR.	INFO
	2174/08	1972-1972	4	8 cm

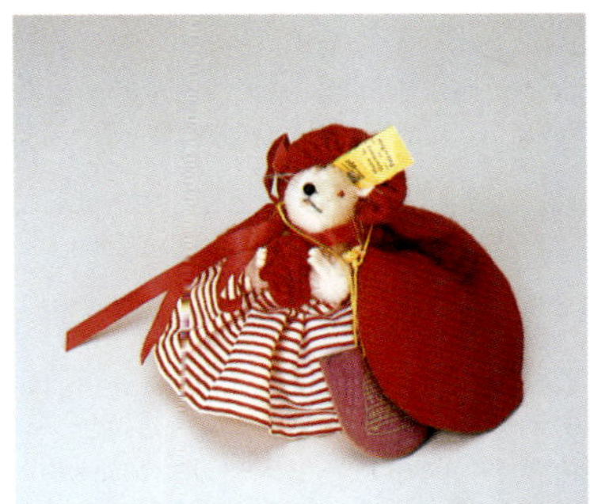

Rotkaeppchen Maus - *Red Ridinghood Mouse*

Mohair, weiss, aufwartend, Maus Pieps bekleidet, Sonderartikel fuer FAO Schwarz, USA - *mohair, white, begging, mouse "Pieps" dressed, exclusive for FAO Schwarz, USA*

SERIE	ART.-NO	PERIOD	PR.	INFO
	2174/08	1972-1973	4	8 cm

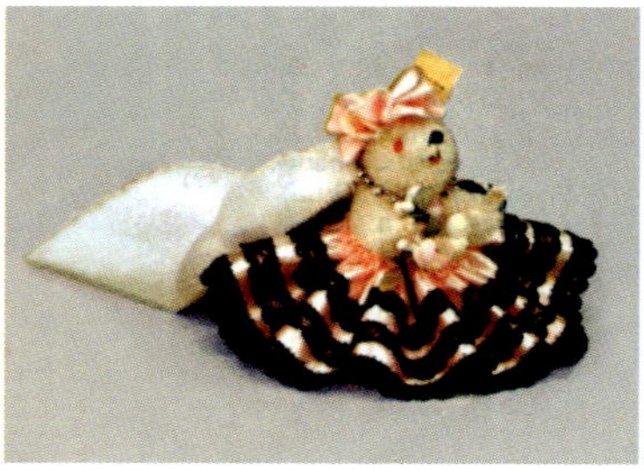

Miss America Maus - *Miss America Mouse*

Mohair, weiss, aufwartend, Maus Pieps bekleidet, Sonderartikel fuer FAO Schwarz, USA - *mohair, white, begging, mouse "Pieps" dressed, exclusive for FAO Schwarz, USA*

SERIE	ART.-NO	PERIOD	PR.	INFO
	2174/08	1972-1973	4	8 cm

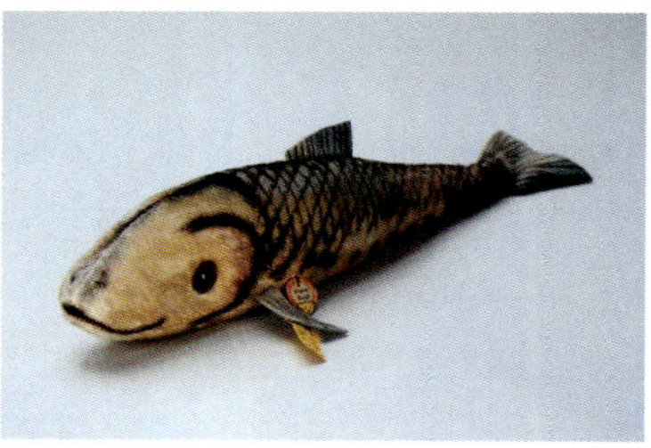

Forelle - *Trout*

Seidenpluesch, Filzflossen, USA Artikel - *silk plush, fin of felt, USA exclusive*

SERIE	ART.-NO	PERIOD	PR.	INFO
	2610,90	1950-1950	6	40 cm

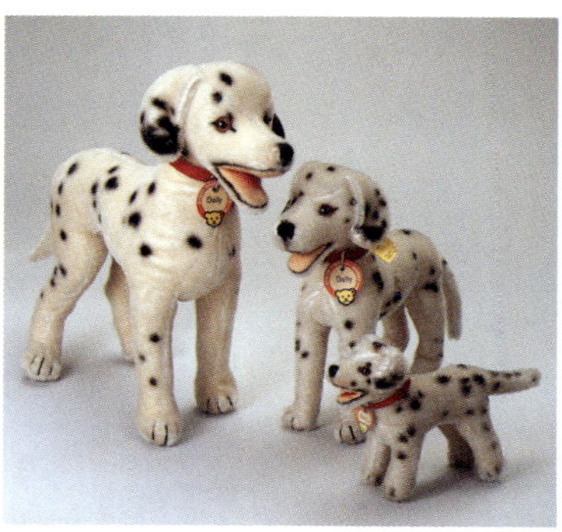

Dally

Mohair, weiss/schwarz, stehend, offener Mund, Lederhalsband, ab 22 cm Druckstimme, Sonderartikel fuer FAO Schwarz, USA - *mohair, white/black, standing, open mouth, leather collar, from 22 cm press voice, exclusive for FAO Schwarz, USA*

SERIE	ART.-NO	PERIOD	PR.	INFO
	1311	1953-1953	6	11 cm
	1322,0	1955-1955	6	22 cm
	1328,02	1955-1955	6	28 cm

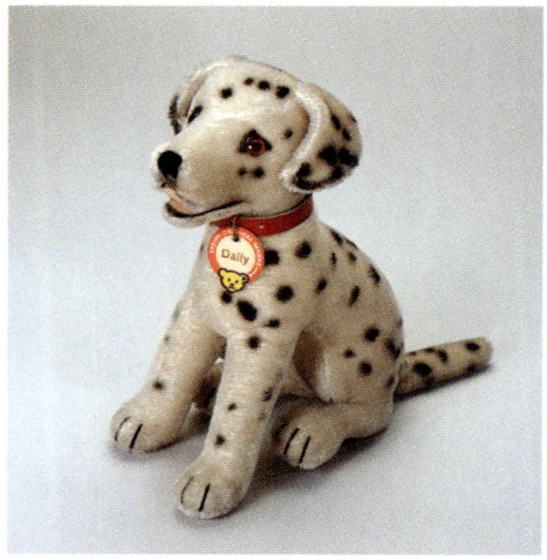

Dally

Mohair, weiss/schwarz, sitzend, offener Mund, Lederhalsband, Druckstimme, Sonderartikel fuer FAO Schwarz, USA - *mohair, white/black, sitting, open mouth, leather collar, press voice, exclusive for FAO Schwarz, USA*

SERIE	ART.-NO	PERIOD	PR.	INFO
	3323	1953-1953	6	23 cm

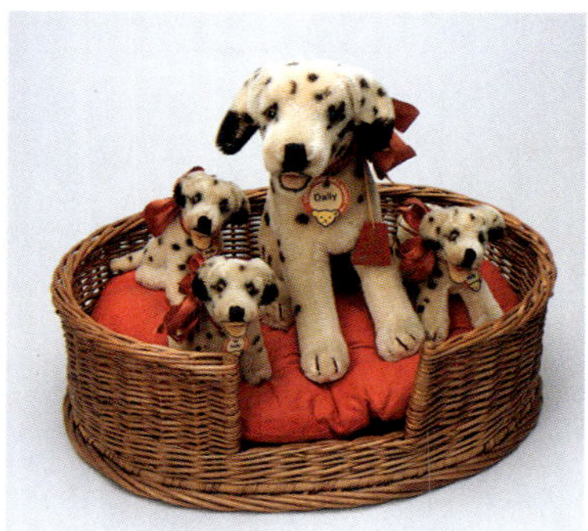

Dally Familie - ***Dally*** *Family*

Mohair, weiss/schwarz, sitzend, Dally 23 cm mit drei Jungen 10 cm, im Weidenkorb mit weichem Kissen, Sonderartikel fuer FAO Schwarz, USA - *mohair, white/black, sitting, Dally 23 cm & three puppies 10 cm, in a basket with a soft pillow, exclusive for FAO Schwarz, USA*

EAN-NO.	PERIOD	PR.	INFO
	1953-1953	6-7	

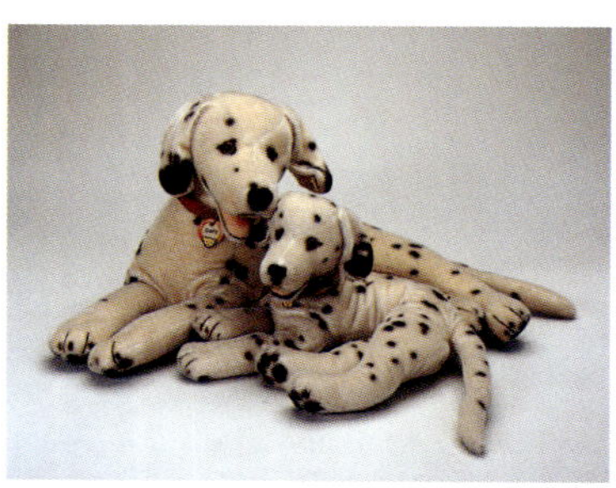

Dally

Mohair, weiss/schwarz, liegend, offener Mund, Lederhalsband, Druckstimme, Sonderartikel fuer FAO Schwarz, USA - *mohair, white/black, lying, open mouth, leather collar, press voice, exclusive for FAO Schwarz, USA*

SERIE	ART.-NO	PERIOD	PR.	INFO
	2328,1	1956-1956	5-6	28 cm
	2343,1	1956-1956	5-6	43 cm

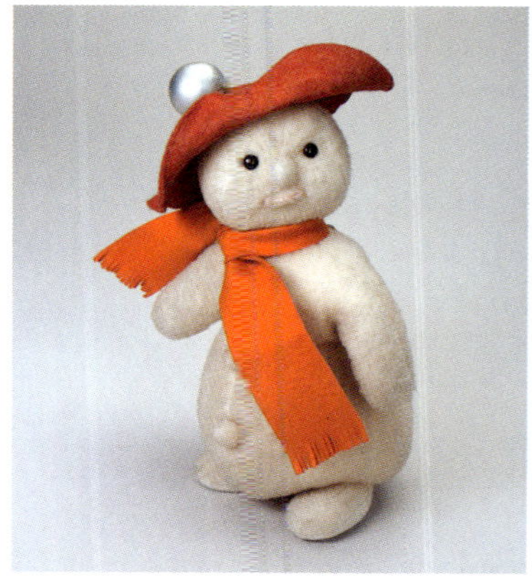

Schneemann - *Snowman*

Wollpluesch, weiss, stehend, roter Filzhut mit Holzkugel, oranger Schal, mit Tannenbaum (fehlt auf Abbildung), vermutlich USA Artikel - *wool plush, white, standing, red felt hat with wooden ball, orange felt scarf, holding a christmas tree (missing on photo), probably USA exclusive*

SERIE	ART.-NO	PERIOD	PR.	INFO
	7525	1955-1955	7	25 cm

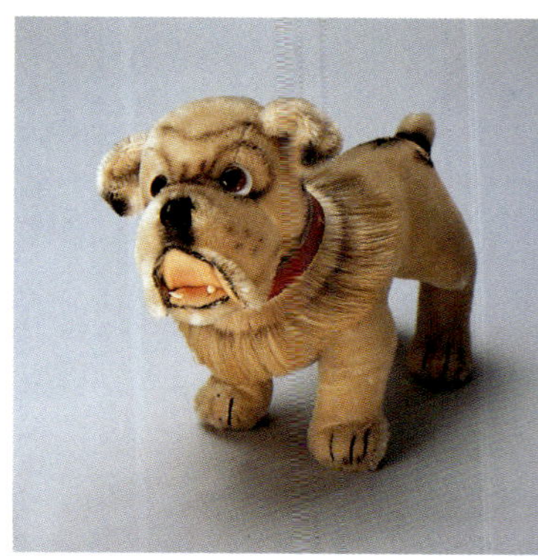

Englische Bulldogge - *English Bulldogg*

Mohair, beige, schwarz gezeichnet, stehend, Halsband mit Haarkranz, USA Artikel - *mohair, beige, black marking, standing, with hair-ruff, USA exclusive*

EAN-NO.	PERIOD	PR.	INFO
	1960-1960	6	[illegible]5 cm

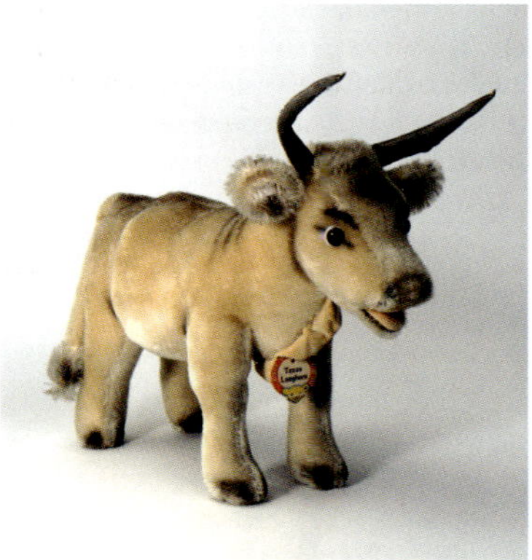

Texas Longhorn

Rind, Mohair, hellbraun, stehend, lange Hörner aus Leder, USA Artikel für FAO Schwarz - *bull, mohair, light brown, standing, long horns of leather, exclusive for FAO Schwarz, USA*

SERIE	ART.-NO	PERIOD	PR.	INFO
	1325,90	1960-1960	6	25 cm

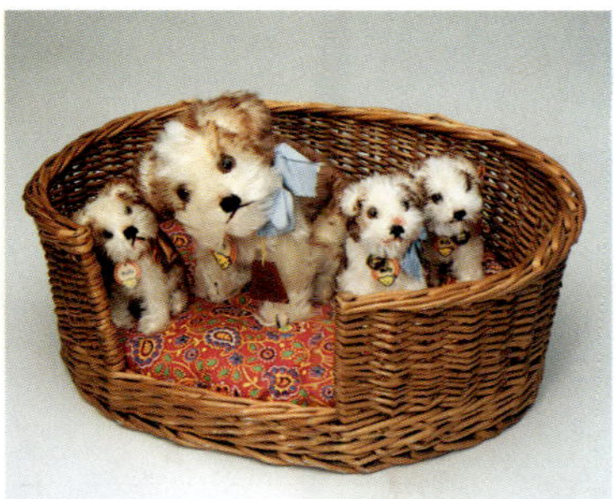

Molly Familie - ***Molly** Family*

Mohair, braun, weiss gespitzt, sitzend, Molly 17 cm zusammen mit drei Jungen 10 cm, im Weidenkorb mit weichem Kissen, Sonderartikel fuer FAO Schwarz, USA - *mohair, brown, white tipped, sitting, Molly 17 cm & three puppies 10 cm, in a basket with a soft pillow, exclusive for FAO Schwarz, USA*

EAN-NO.	PERIOD	PR.	INFO
	1961-1961	6	

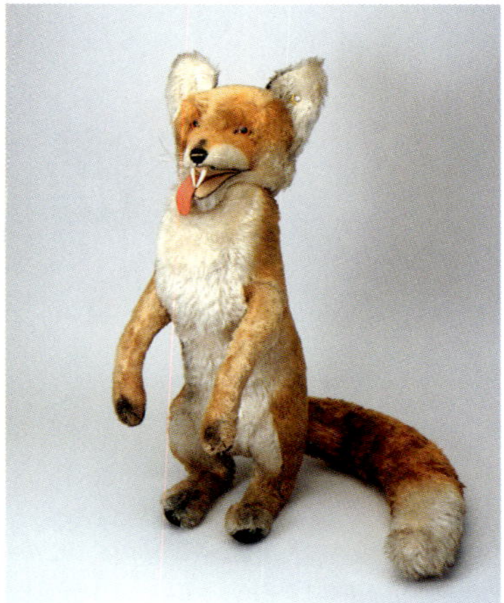

Rotfuchs - *Fox*

Mohair, aufwartend, Kopf drehbar, offener Mund mit Filzzunge & Zaehnen, Sonderartikel fuer FAO Schwarz, USA - *mohair, sitting up, head swivels, mouth open with felt tongue & teeth, exclusive for FAO Schwarz, USA*

SERIE	ART.-NO	PERIOD	PR.	INFO
28	**4355**	1962-1971	6	55 cm

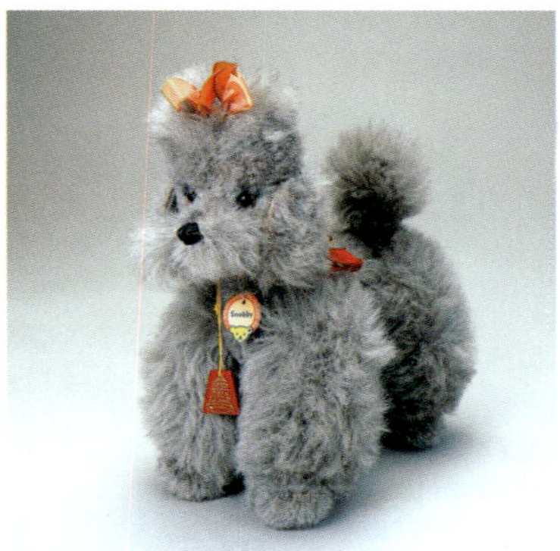

Snobby Pudel - ***Snobby** Poodle*

Wollpluesch, grau, gegliedert, franzoesische Schur, Ledernase, Sonderartikel fuer FAO Schwarz, USA - *wool plush, grey, jointed, french trim, leather nose, exclusive for FAO Schwarz, USA*

SERIE	ART.-NO	PERIOD	PR.	INFO
	5528,95	1962-1968	4-5	28 cm
	5535,95	1962-1968	4-5	35 cm

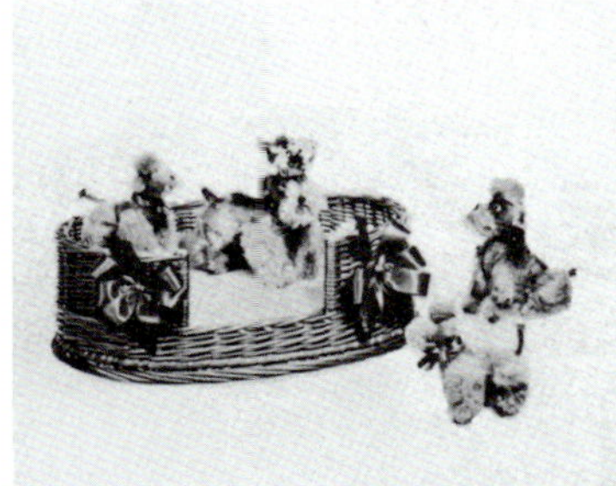

Snobby Familie - ***Snobby** Family*

Mohair, grau, gegliedert, Pudelvater (nur 1962, ab 1963 mit nur drei Hunden) und -mutter je 14 cm und zwei Pudeljunge 10 cm, Pudelmutter mit Blumenkranz, alle mit roten Schleifen, im Weidenkorb mit weichem Kissen, Sonderartikel fuer FAO Schwarz, USA - *mohair, grey, jointed, poodle male (only 1962, from 1963 only three dogs) & -female 14 cm each, two poodle-baby´s 10 cm, poodle-female with flower slide, all with red ribbons in a basket with a soft pillow, exclusive for FAO Schwarz, USA*

EAN-NO.	PERIOD	PR.	INFO
	1962-1963	5	

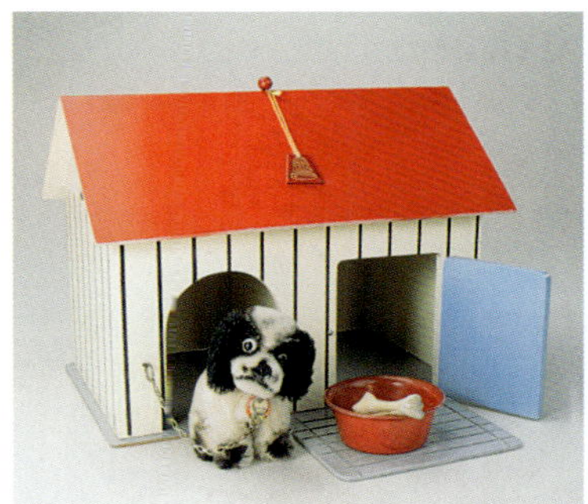

Cockie Cocker Spaniel

Mohair, schwarz/weiss, sitzend, mit rot/weiss lackierter Hundehuette, Zugstimme am Dach Futterschuessel & Knochen, Sonderartikel fuer FAO Schwarz, USA - *mohair, black/white, sitting, with red & white laquered kennel, pull voice on the roof, food bowl & bone, exclusive for FAO Schwarz, USA*

SERIE	ART.-NO	PERIOD	PR.	INFO
	3312,96	1962-1966	5-6	12 cm

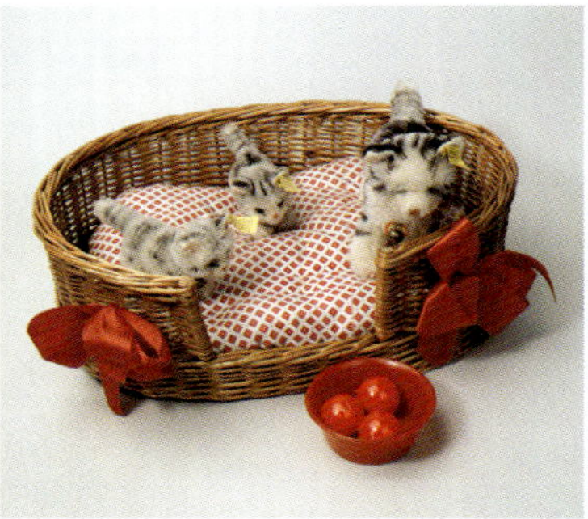

Katzenfamilie - *Cat Family*

Mohair, grau gestromelt, gegliedert, Katzenvater (nur 1962, ab 1963 mit nur drei Katzen) und -mutter je ca. 15 cm und zwei Katzenjunge ca. 12 cm, es wurden die Katzen Susi, Kitty & Tabby verwendet, Katzenmutter mit Blumenkranz, alle mit Schleifen, im Weidenkorb mit weichem Kissen, Sonderartikel fuer FAO Schwarz, USA - *mohair, grey tabby, jointed, cat father (only 1962, from 1963 only three cats) & -mother 15 cm each, two cat-baby´s 12 cm, the Steiff cats Susi, Kitty & Tabby have been used, cat-female with flower slide, all with ribbons in a basket with a soft pillow, exclusive for FAO Schwarz, USA*

EAN-No.	Period	Pr.	Info
	1962-1972	5	

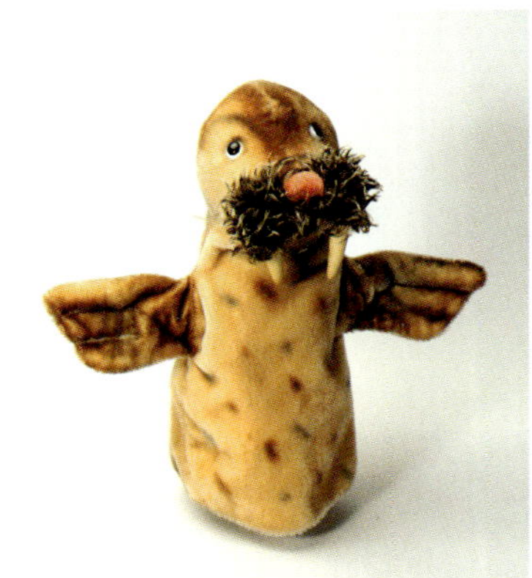

Hand-Walross - *Hand-Walrus*

Mohair, braun gefleckt, Sonderartikel fuer FAO Schwarz, USA - *mohair, brown spotted, exclusive for FAO Schwarz, USA*

EAN-No.	Period	Pr.	Info
	1962-1962	5	20 cm

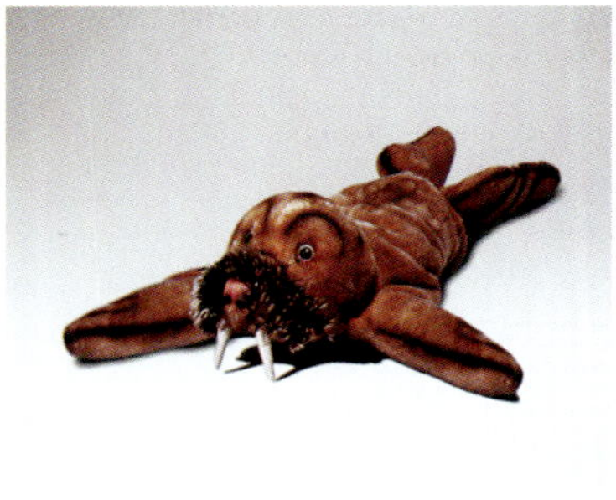

Walross - *Walrus*

Mohair, braun gefleckt, als Schlafanzugtasche mit Reissverschluss, Sonderartikel fuer FAO Schwarz, USA - *mohair, brown spotted, pyjama bag with zip, exclusive for FAO Schwarz, USA*

Serie	Art.-No	Period	Pr.	Info
	2345,00	1962-1972	5	45 cm

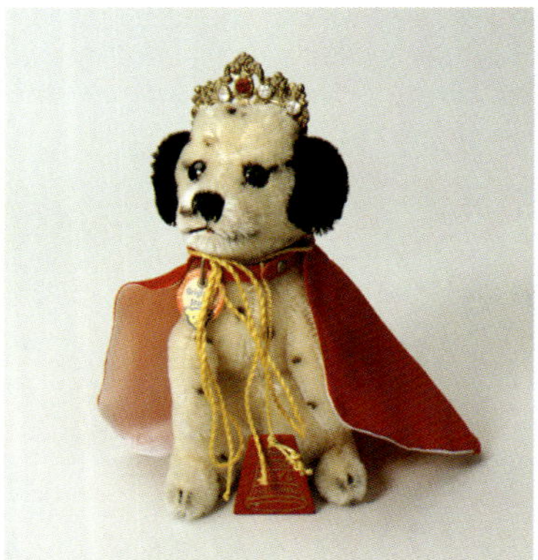

Royal Dalmation Dally

Mohair, weiss, schwarz gefleckt, aufwartend, Kopf drehbar, mit Krone & Umhang, Sonderartikel fuer FAO Schwarz, USA - *mohair, white, black spotted, sitting up, head swivels, with crown & cape, exclusive for FAO Schwarz, USA*

EAN-No.	Period	Pr.	Info
	1963-1963	6	15 cm

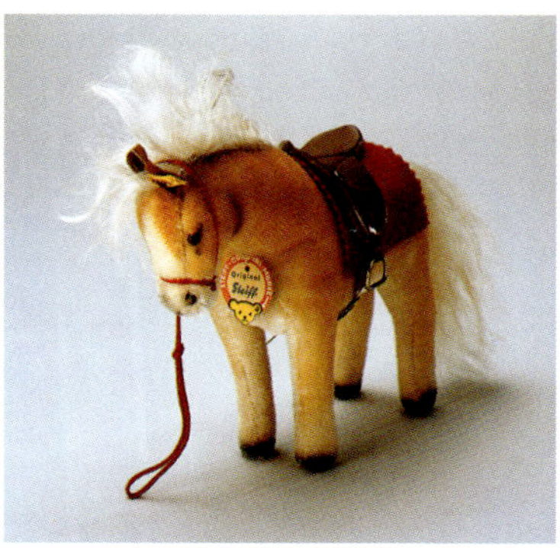

Pony

Mohair, weiss/hellbraun, stehend, mit Sattel, Steigbuegel, Zaumzeug & Satteldecke, Sonderartikel fuer FAO Schwarz, USA - *mohair, white/light brown, standing, with saddle, stirrup, bridle & saddle blanket, exclusive for FAO Schwarz, USA*

Serie	Art.-No	Period	Pr.	Info
	3759/02	1963-1972	5	20 cm

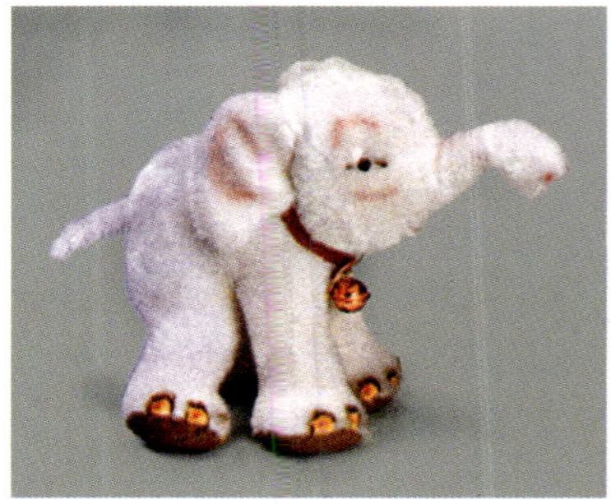

Baby Elefant - *Baby Elephant*

Dralon, weiss, stehend, waschbar, Halsband & Glocke, Sonderartikel fuer FAO Schwarz, USA - *dralon, white, standing, washable, ribbon & bell, exclusive for FAO Schwarz, USA*

EAN-No.	Period	Pr.	Info
	1965-1967	4	20 cm

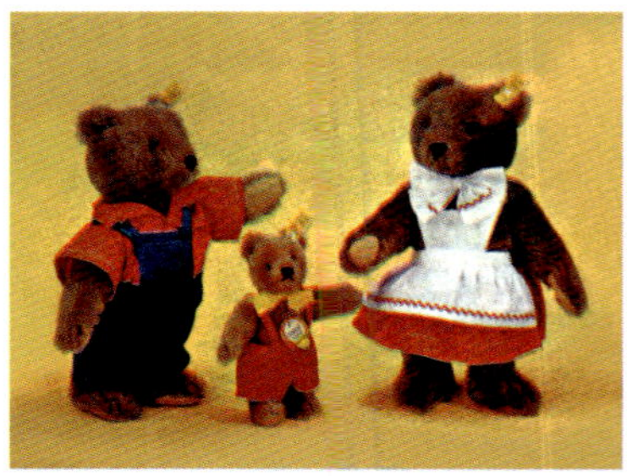

Baeren Familie - *Bear Family*

Original Teddybaeren, Mohair, caramel, gegliedert, bekleidet, Familie bestehend aus Mama, Papa & Baby Baer, Sonderartikel fuer FAO Schwarz, USA - *Original Teddybears, mohair, caramel, jointed, dressed, family members are Mama, Papa & Baby Bear, exclusive for FAO Schwarz, USA*

Serie	Art.-No	Period	Pr.	Info
	5328,02	1965-1966	5	28 cm, Mama Baer - *Mama Bear*
	5328,02	1965-1966	5	28 cm, Papa Baer - *Papa Bear*
	5318,02	1965-1966	4-5	18 cm, Baby Baer - *Baby Bear*

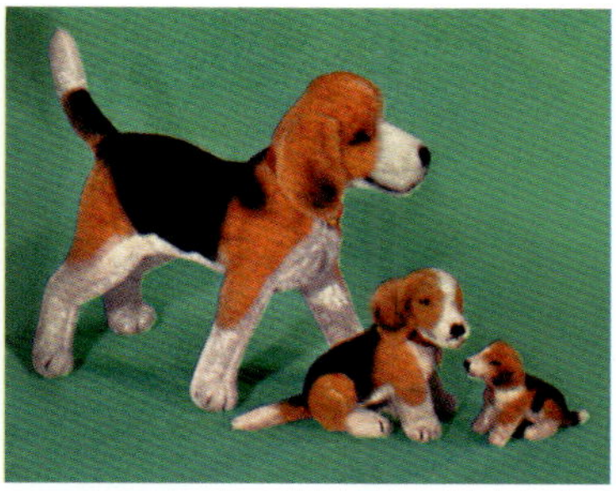

Beagle

Mohair, braun/weiss/schwarz, stehend, Studiotier, Sonderartikel fuer FAO Schwarz, USA - *mohair, brown/white/black, standing, display animal, exclusive for FAO Schwarz, USA*

EAN-No.	Period	Pr.	Info
	1965-1966	5	46 cm

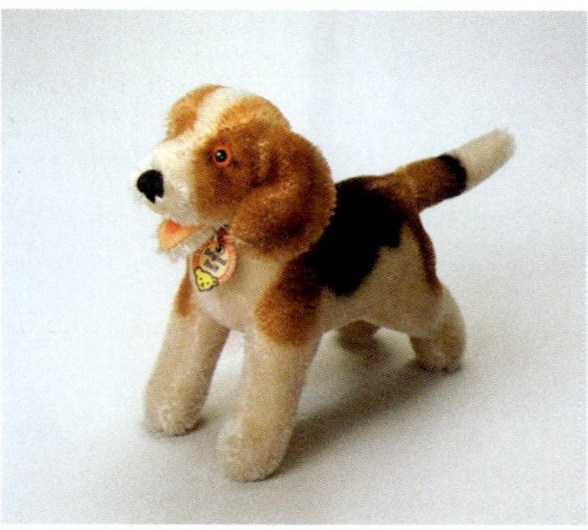

Beagle

Mohair, braun/weiss/schwarz, stehend, offenes Maul, Sonderartikel fuer FAO Schwarz, USA - *mohair, brown/white/black, standing, open mouth, exclusive for FAO Schwarz, USA*

Serie	Art.-No	Period	Pr.	Info
	1314,00	1965-1966	4-5	15 cm

kein Bild vorhanden -
no picture available

Beagle Familie - *Beagle Family*

Mohair, braun/weiss, gegliedert, Beaglemutter ca. 15 cm und zwei Beaglejunge 10 cm, im Weidenkorb mit weichem Kissen, Sonderartikel fuer FAO Schwarz, USA - *mohair, brown/white, jointed, beagle-mother 15 cm and two puppies 10 cm, in a basket with a soft pillow, exclusive for FAO Schwarz, USA*

EAN-No.	Period	Pr.	Info
	1966-1966	5-6	

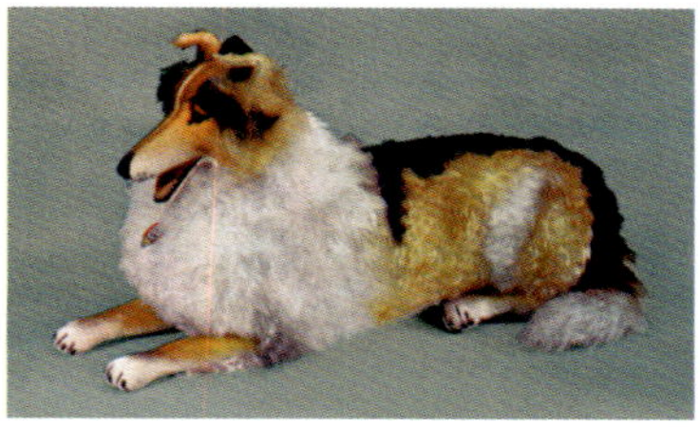

Collie

Mohair, braun/weiss/schwarz, liegend, Studiotier, Sonderartikel fuer FAO Schwarz, USA - *mohair, brown/white/black, lying, display animal, exclusive for FAO Schwarz, USA*

EAN-No.	Period	Pr.	Info
	1966-1966	6	135 cm

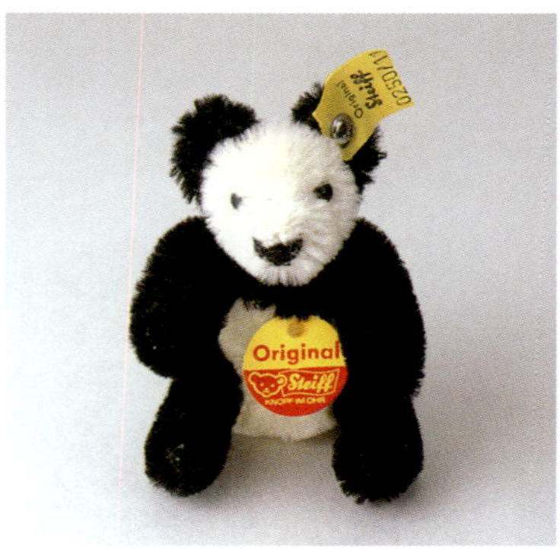

Panda Baer - *Panda Bear*

Mohair, schwarz/weiss, Biegeglieder, Sonderartikel USA - *mohair, black/white, flexible limbs, exclusive for USA*

Serie	Art.-No	Period	Pr.	Info
	0250/11	1968-1972	4-5	11 cm

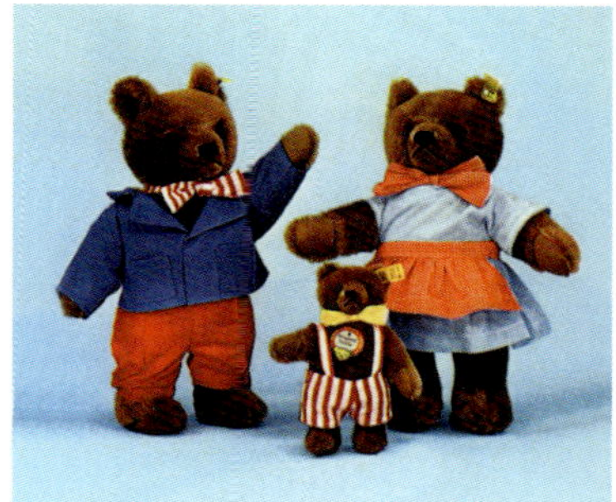

Baeren Familie - *Bear Family*

Maskenbaeren, Mohair, caramel, gegliedert, bekleidet, Familie bestehend aus Mama, Papa & Baby Baer, Sonderartikel fuer FAO Schwarz, USA - *Masked Bears, mohair, caramel, jointed, family members are Mama, Papa & Baby Bear, exclusive for FAO Schwarz, USA*

Serie	Art.-No	Period	Pr.	Info
	5336,02	1967-1967	4	36 cm, Mama Baer - *Mama Bear*
	0201/36	1968-1968	4	
	5336,02	1967-1967	4	36 cm, Papa Baer - *Papa Bear*
	0201/36	1968-1968	4	
	5319,02	1967-1967	4	19 cm, Baby Baer - *Baby Bear*
	0201/19	1968-1968	4	

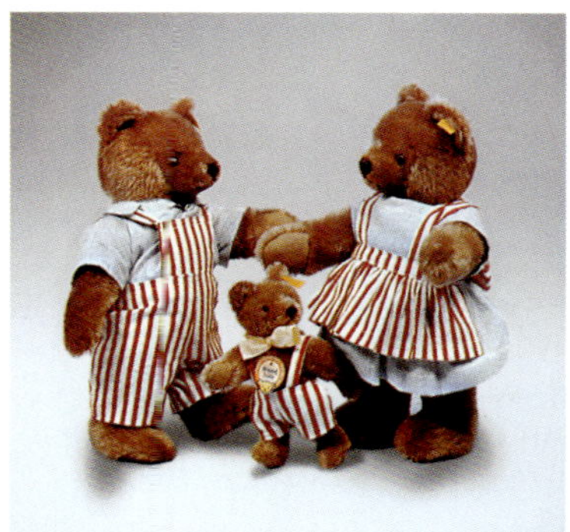

Baeren Familie - *Bear Family*

Maskenbaeren, Mohair, caramel, gegliedert, bekleidet, Familie bestehend aus Mama, Papa & Baby Baer (identisch mit Baby Baer aus 1967er-Familie), Sonderartikel fuer FAO Schwarz, USA - *Masked Bears, mohair, caramel, jointed, family members are Mama, Papa & Baby Bear (dressed like Baby Bear from the 1967 family), exclusive for FAO Schwarz, USA*

Serie	Art.-No	Period	Pr.	Info
	0201/36	1969-1972	4	36 cm, Mama Baer - *Mama Bear*
	0201/36	1969-1972	4	36 cm, Papa Baer - *Papa Bear*
	0201/19	1969-1972	4	19 cm, Baby Baer - *Baby Bear*

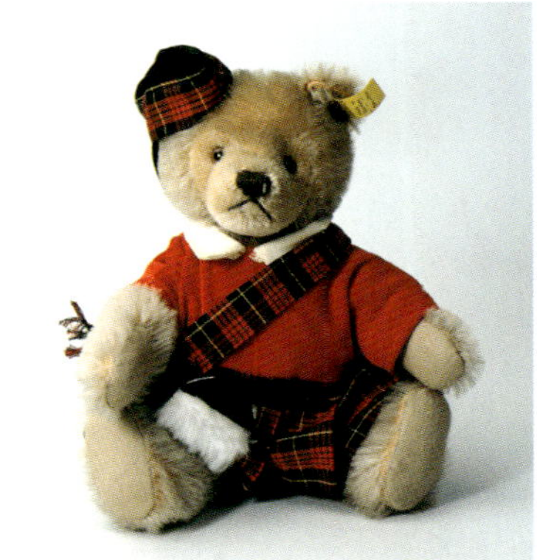

Scotty Baer - *Scotty Bear*

Mohair, honig, gegliedert, bekleideter Maskenbaer mit schottischer Tracht, Sonderartikel fuer FAO Schwarz, USA - *mohair, honey, jointed, Masked Bear, dressed in Scottish traditional costume, exclusive for FAO Schwarz, USA*

Serie	Art.-No	Period	Pr.	Info
	5326,01	1967-1967	4-5	26 cm
	0201/26	1968-1972	4	

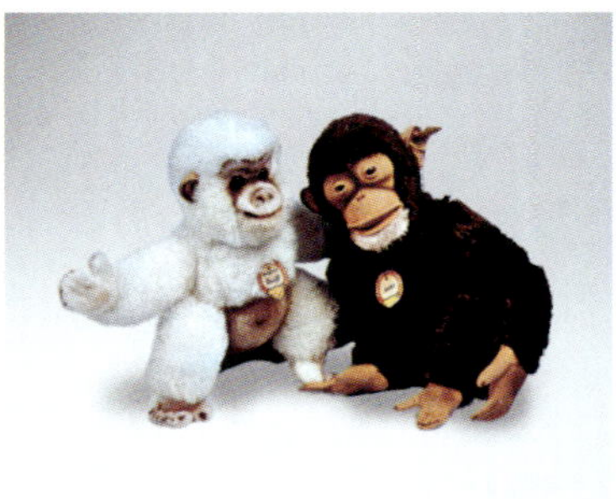

Gorilla

Dralon, weiss, sitzend, Sonderartikel fuer FAO Schwarz, USA - *dralon, white, sitting, exclusive for FAO Schwarz, USA*

Serie	Art.-No	Period	Pr.	Info
	6625,94	1967-1971	4-5	25 cm

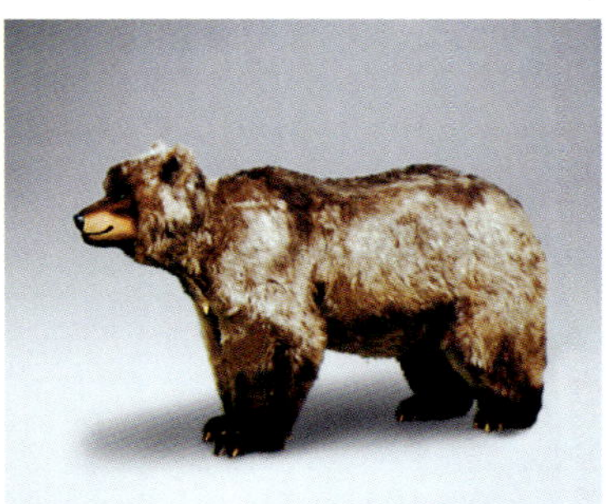

Studio Baer - *Studio Bear*

Pelzimitation, braun, stehend, wurde mit Studio- & Jungbaer (s. Kapitel Baeren & Teddybaeren) als Baerenfamilie von FAO Schwarz in USA angeboten - *imitation fur, brown, standing, was offered through FAO Schwarz together with Studio & Young Bear as Bear Family, exclusive for the USA*

EAN-No.	Period	Pr.	Info
	1972-1972	5-6	110 cm

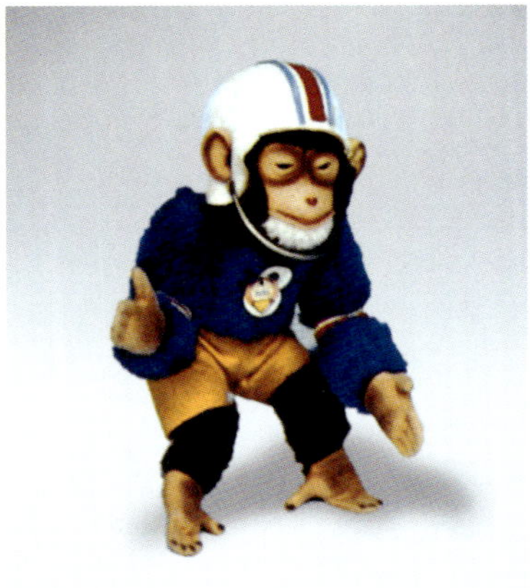

Jocko Schimpanse - ***Jocko*** *Chimpanzee*

Dralon, braun/blau, als Football Hero, mit Helm, Sonderartikel fuer FAO Schwarz, USA - *dralon, brown/blue, dressed as "football star", with helmet, exclusive for FAO Schwarz, USA*

Serie	Art.-No	Period	Pr.	Info
	7820/25	1972-1973	4-5	25 cm

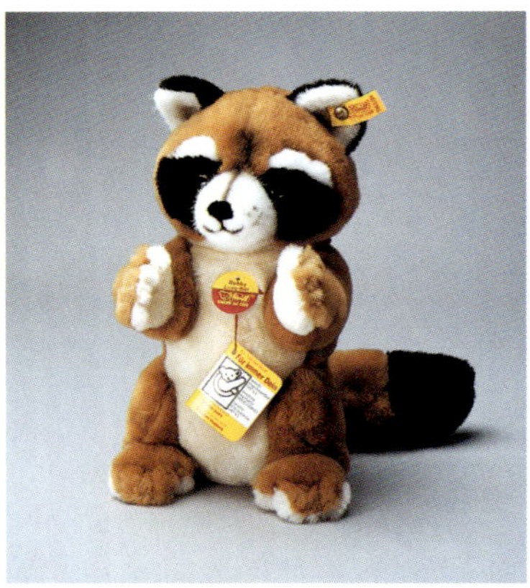

Bobby Luv´s Baer - *Bobby Luv´s Bear*

Waschbaer, Webpelz, aufwartend, USA-Artikel, kein Katalognachweis bekannt - *racoon, woven fur, sitting up, exclusive for the USA, no catalog information available*

Serie	Art.-No	Period	Pr.	Info
	7962/26	1983-1983	3-4	26 cm

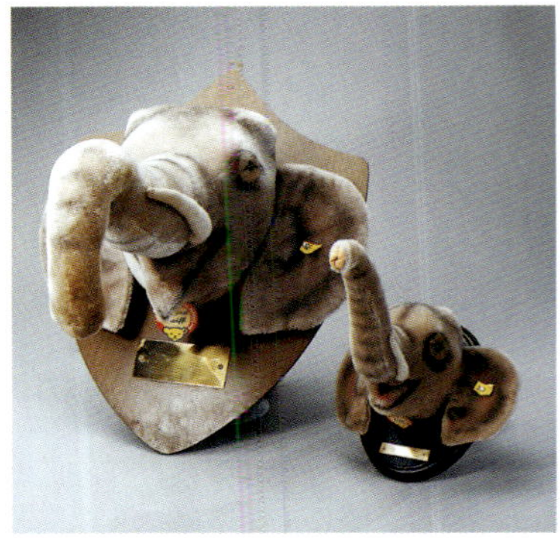

Elefanten Trophaee - *Elephant Trophy*

Mohair, grau, Tierkopf als Jagdtrophaee auf Holzbrett montiert, mit Holzwolle gestopft, USA Artikel - *mohair, grey, animal head mounted as "hunting trophy" on a wooden disc, excelsior stuffed, exclusive for the USA*

Serie	Art.-No	Period	Pr.	Info
	28	1958-1958	5	28 cm
	60	1958-1958	5-6	60 cm

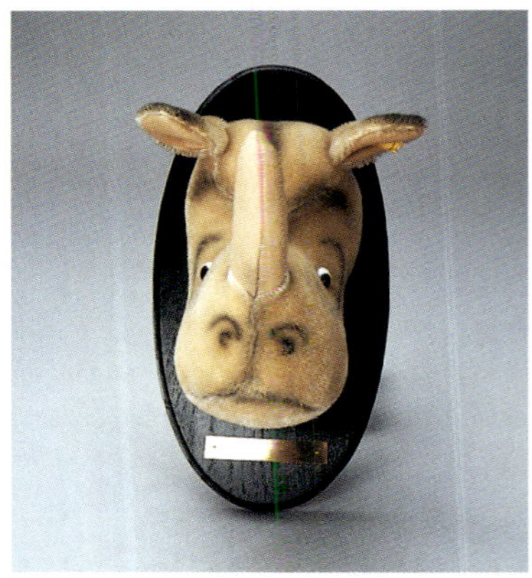

Nashorn Trophaee - *Rhinoceros Trophy*

Mohair, grau, Tierkopf als Jagdtrophaee auf Holzbrett montiert, mit Holzwolle gestopft, USA Artikel - *mohair, grey, animal head mounted as "hunting trophy" on a wooden disc, excelsior stuffed, exclusive for the USA*

Serie	Art.-No	Period	Pr.	Info
	28	1958-1958	5	28 cm
	60	1958-1958	5-6	60 cm

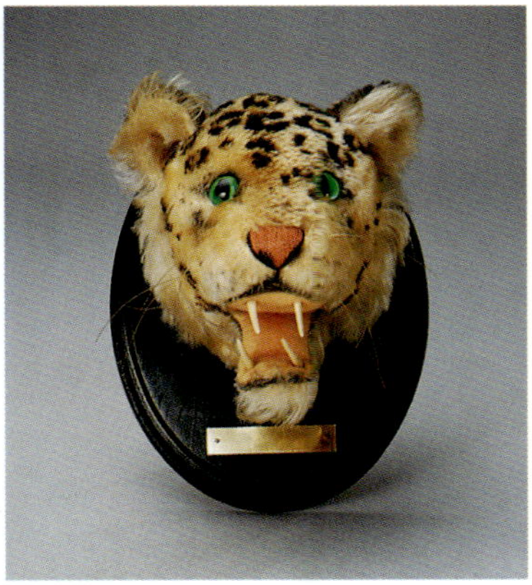

Leoparden Trophaee - *Leopard Trophy*

Mohair, blond, schwarz gefleckt, Tierkopf als Jagdtrophaee auf Holzbrett montiert, mit Holzwolle gestopft, USA Artikel - *mohair, blond, black spotted, animal head mounted as "hunting trophy" on a wooden disc, excelsior stuffed, exclusive for the USA*

SERIE	ART.-NO	PERIOD	PR.	INFO
	28	1958-1958	5	28 cm
	60	1958-1958	5-6	60 cm

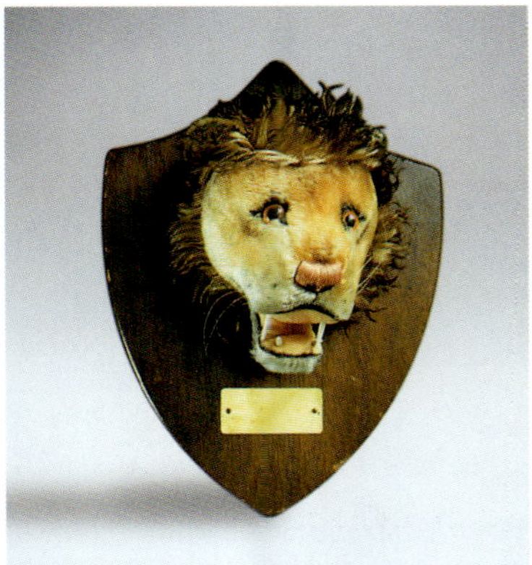

Loewen Trophaee - *Lion Trophy*

Mohair, blond, dunkelblonde Maehne, Tierkopf als Jagdtrophaee auf Holzbrett montiert, mit Holzwolle gestopft, USA Artikel - *mohair, blond, dark blond mane, animal head mounted as "hunting trophy" on a wooden disc, excelsior stuffed, exclusive for the USA*

SERIE	ART.-NO	PERIOD	PR.	INFO
	28	1958-1958	5	28 cm
	60	1958-1958	5-6	60 cm

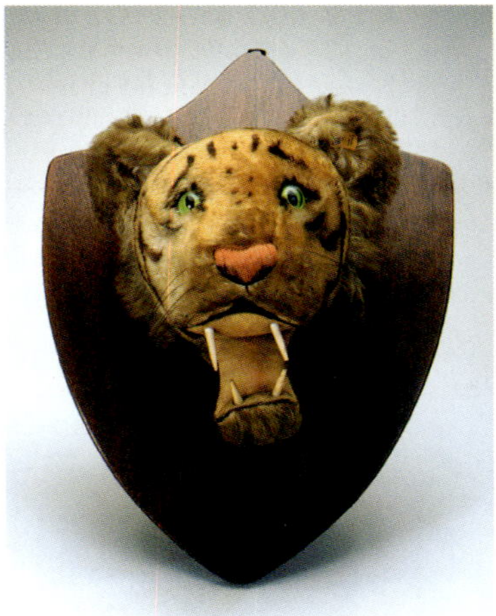

Tiger Trophaee - *Tiger Trophy*

Mohair, blond, schwarz gestreift, Tierkopf als Jagdtrophaee auf Holzbrett montiert, mit Holzwolle gestopft, USA Artikel - *mohair, blond, black striped, animal head mounted as "hunting trophy" on a wooden disc, excelsior stuffed, exclusive for the USA*

SERIE	ART.-NO	PERIOD	PR.	INFO
	28	1958-1958	5	28 cm
	60	1958-1958	5-6	60 cm

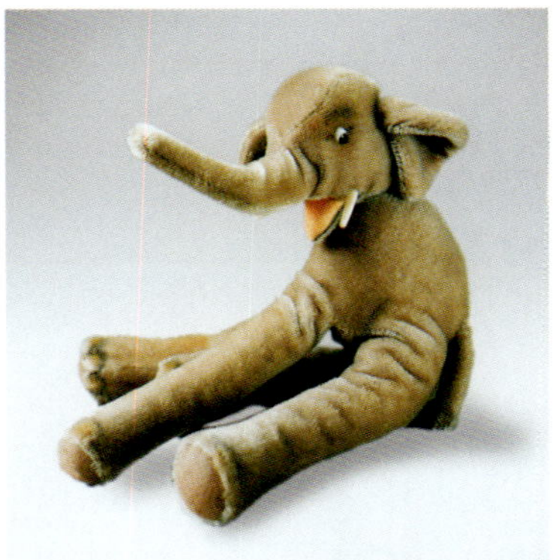

Lulac Elefant - *Lulac Elephant*

Mohair, grau, Schlenkerbeine, Kopf drehbar, USA Artikel - *mohair, grey, floppy legs, head swivels, exclusive for the USA*

EAN-NO.	PERIOD	PR.	INFO
	1958-1958	6	40 cm

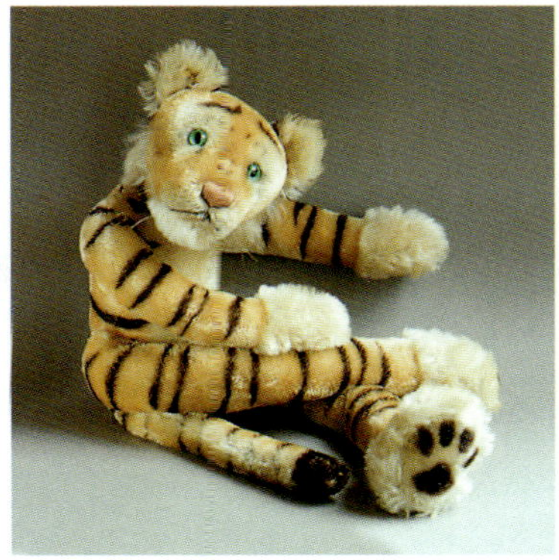

Lulac Tiger

Mohair, blond, schwarz gestreift, gegliedert, Schlenkerglieder, USA Artikel - *mohair, blond, black striped, jointed, floppy legs, exclusive for the USA*

EAN-NO.	PERIOD	PR.	INFO
	1958-1958	6-7	90 cm

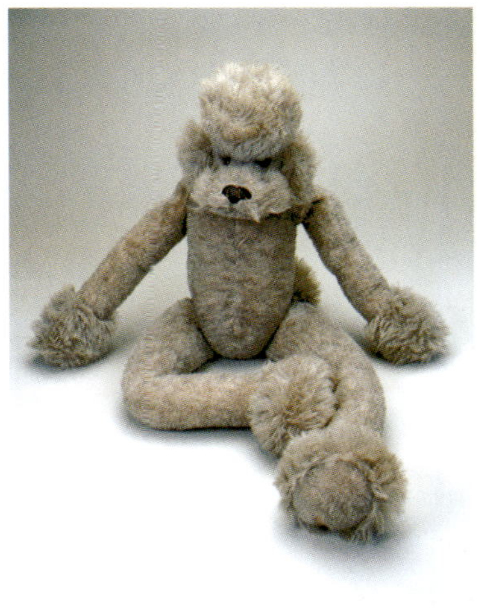

Snobbylac Pudel - *Snobbylac Poodle*

Wollplueschm, grau, gegliedert, Schlenkerglieder, USA Artikel - *wool plush, grey, jointed, floppy legs, exclusive for the USA*

EAN-NO.	PERIOD	PR.	INFO
	1958-1958	5-6	80 cm

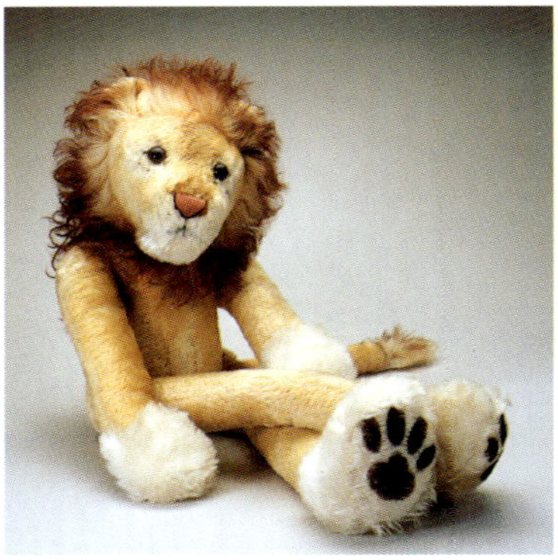

Lulac Loewe - *Lulac Lion*

Mohair, hellbraun, gegliedert, Schlenkerglieder, USA Artikel - *mohair, light brown, jointed, floppy legs, exclusive for the USA*

EAN-No.	Period	Pr.	Info
	1958-1958	6-7	80 cm

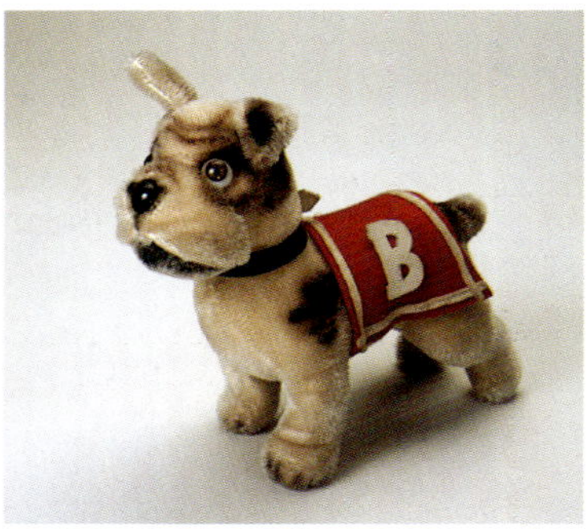

Bulldogge - *Bulldog*

Mohair, weiss, gefleckt, stehend, Googly Glasaugen, schwarze Nase aus Glas, mit roter Filzdecke und dem Buchstaben "B", Maskottchen der Brown University, USA - *mohair, white, spotted, standing, googly glass-eyes, black nose of glass, red felt blanket with a white "B", mascot of Brown University, USA*

Serie	Art.-No	Period	Pr.	Info
	1314,0	1957-1957	6	14 cm

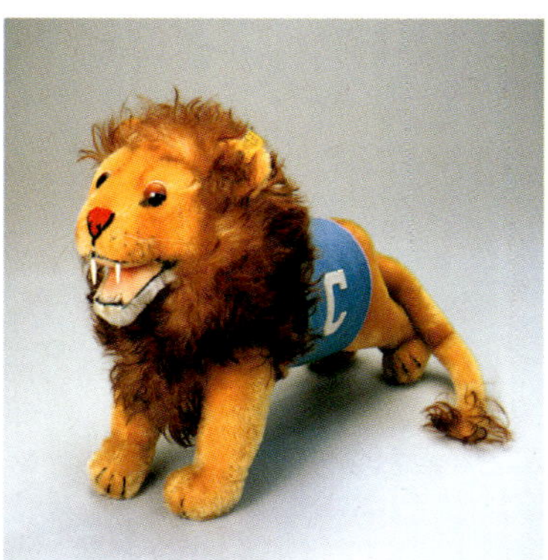

Loewe - *Lion*

Mohair, gelbbraun, springend, offener Mund mit Zaehnen, braun-schwarze Schielaugen aus Glas, mit hellblauer Filzdecke und dem Buchstaben "C", Maskottchen der Columbia University, USA - *mohair, yellow-brown, leaping, open mouth with teeth, brown-black squint eyes made of glass, light-blue felt blanket with a white "C", mascot of Columbia University, USA*

Serie	Art.-No	Period	Pr.	Info
	1328,02	1952-1952	6-7	28 cm

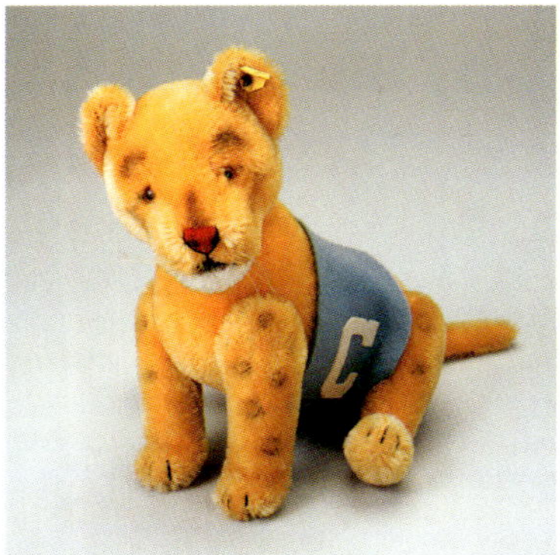

Loewin - *Lioness*

Mohair, gelbbraun, gegliedert, mit hellblauer Filzdecke und dem Buchstaben "C", Maskottchen der Columbia University, USA - *mohair, yellow-brown, jointed, light-blue felt blanket with a white "C", mascot of Columbia University, USA*

Serie	Art.-No	Period	Pr.	Info
	5321,2	1952-1952	6-7	21 cm

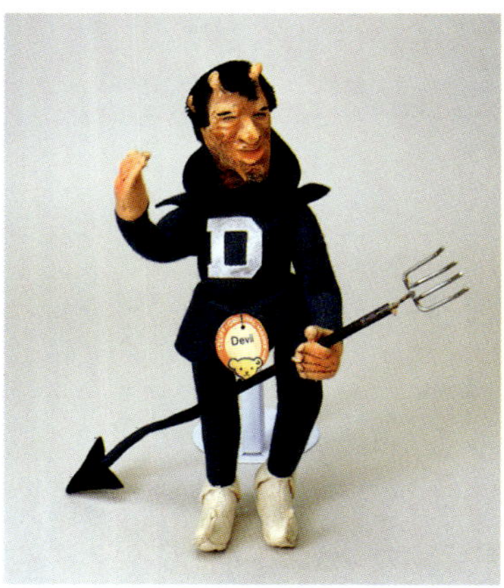

Teufel - *Devil*

Filzkoerper/Gummikopf, blau, gegliedert, mit Dreizack, weisses "D" auf dem blauen Filzanzug, Maskottchen der Duke University, USA - *felt body/rubber head, blue, jointed, with trident, white "D" on the blue felt suit, mascot of Duke University, USA*

Serie	Art.-No	Period	Pr.	Info
	7128	1954-1954	6-7	28 cm

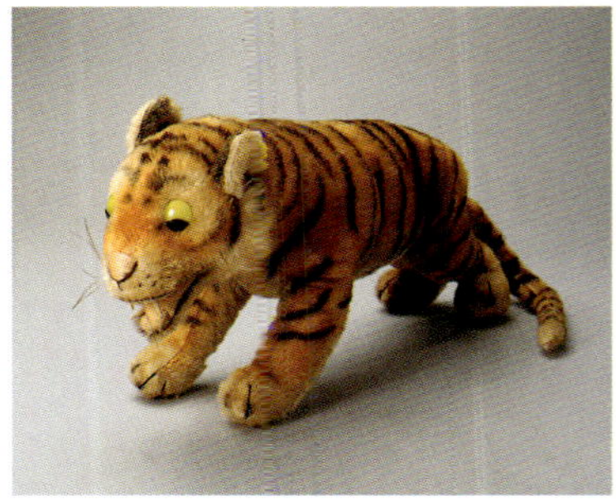

Tiger

Mohair, gelbbraun weiss, schwarz gestreift, stehend, offener Mund mit Zaehnen, gruen-schwarze Schielaugen aus Glas, Maskottchen der Princeton University, USA - *mohair, yellow-brown, white, black striped, standing, open mouth with teeth, green-black squint eyes made of glass, mascot of Princeton University, USA*

EAN-No.	Period	Pr.	Info
	1952-1952	6	25 cm

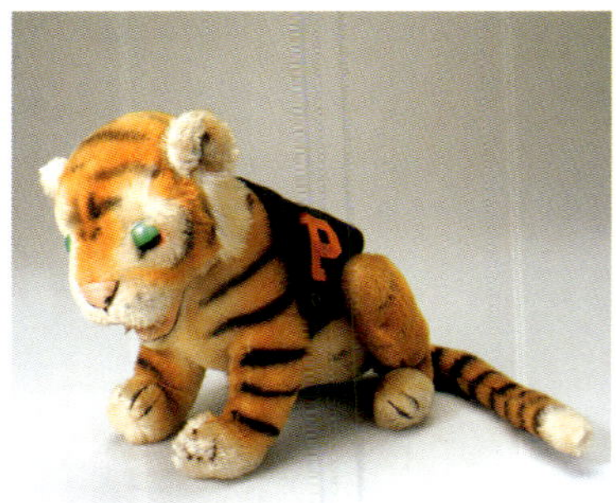

Tiger

Mohair, gelbbraun, weiss, schwarz gestreift, sitzend, Kopf drehbar, offener Mund mit Zaehnen, gruen-schwarze Schielaugen aus Glas, schwarze Filzdecke mit rotem "P", Maskottchen der Princeton University, USA - *mohair, yellow-brown, white, black striped, sitting, head swivels, open mouth with teeth, green-black squint eyes made of glass, black felt blanket with a red "P", mascot of Princeton University, USA*

EAN-No.	Period	Pr.	Info
	1952-1952	6	25 cm

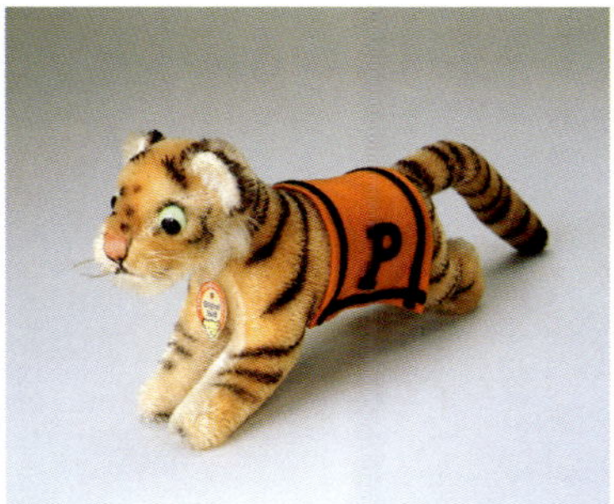

Tiger

Mohair, gelbbraun, weiss, schwarz gestreift, stehend, gruen-schwarze Schielaugen aus Glas, orangerote Filzdecke mit schwarzem "P" (auch mit dunkelblauer Filzdecke & weissem "P" bekannt), Maskottchen der Princeton University, USA - *mohair, yellow-brown, white, black striped, standing, green-black squint eyes made of glass, orange-red felt blanket with a black "P" (also known with dark-blue felt blanket & a white "P"), mascot of Princeton University, USA*

EAN-No.	Period	Pr.	Info
	1957-1958	5	10 cm

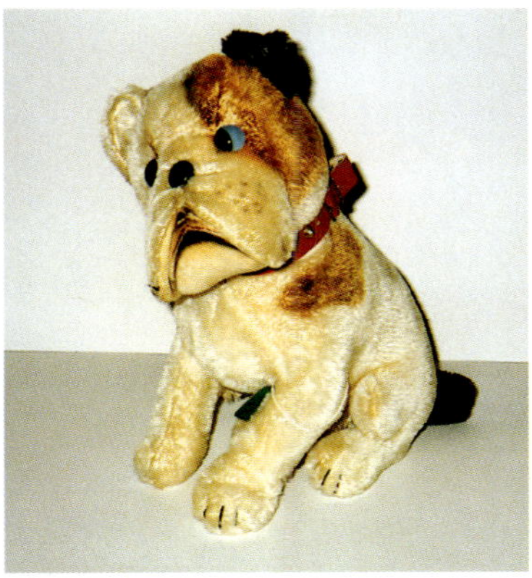

Bulldogge - *Bulldog*

Mohair, weiss, gefleckt, sitzend, Kopf drehbar, Samtschnauze, blau-schwarze Schielaugen & schwarze Nase aus Glas, Druckstimme, mit blauer Filzdecke und weissem "Y", Maskottchen der Yale University, USA - *mohair, white, spotted, sitting, head swivels, velvet snout, blue-black squint eyes & a black nose made of glass, press voice, blue felt blanket with a white "Y", mascot of Yale University, USA*

Serie	Art.-No	Period	Pr.	Info
	3328,2	1952-1952	6	28 cm

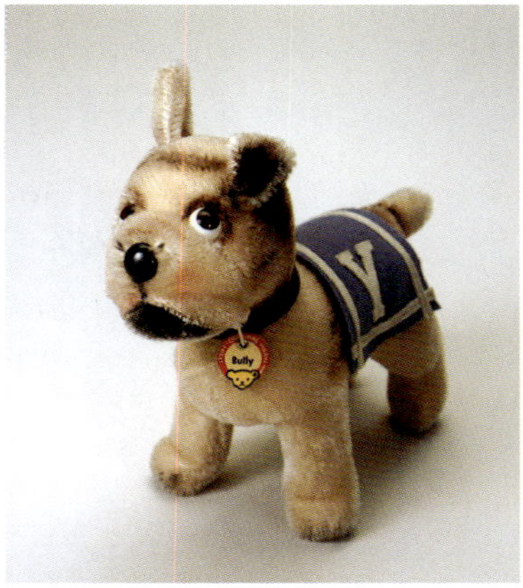

Bulldogge - *Bulldog*

Mohair, weiss, gefleckt, stehend, Googly Glasaugen, schwarze Nase aus Glas, mit blauer Filzdecke und weissem "Y", Maskottchen der Yale University, USA - *mohair, white, spotted, standing, googly glass-eyes, black nose of glass, blue felt blanket with a white "Y", mascot of Yale University, USA*

Serie	Art.-No	Period	Pr.	Info
	1314,0	1957-1957	5-6	14 cm

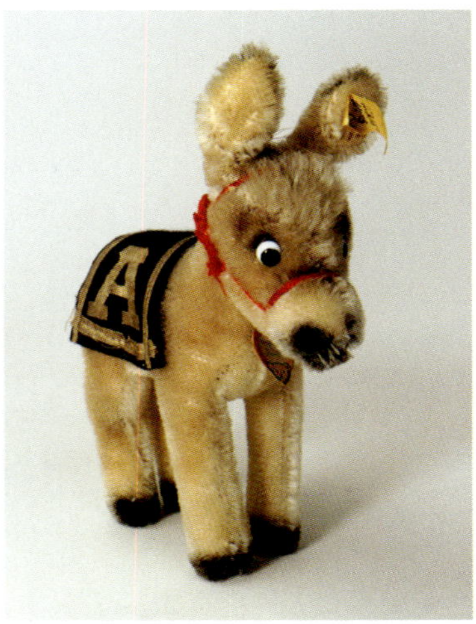

Esel - *Donkey*

12 cm Samt, 14 cm Mohair, grau, stehend, Army Mule, Googly Glasaugen, gelbe oder blaue Filzdecke mit dem Buchstaben "A" in gold oder weiss, Maskottchen der amerikanischen Army, USA - *12 cm velvet, 14 cm mohair, grey, standing, Army Mule, googly glass-eyes, yellow or blue felt blanket with a golden or white "A", mascot of the American Army, USA*

Serie	Art.-No	Period	Pr.	Info
	1412,0	1957-1957	5	12 cm
	1314,0	1957-1957	5-6	14 cm

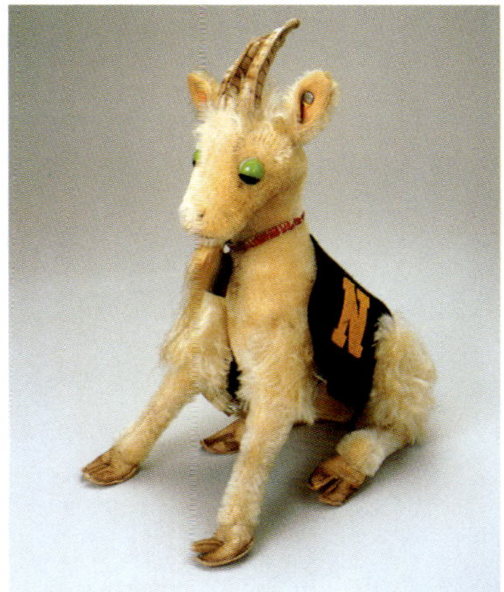

Ziege - *Goat*

Mohair, weiss, sitzend, Navy Goat, Lederhufe & -hoerner, Lederhalsband mit Glocke, gruen-schwarze Schielaugen aus Glas, mit blauer Filzdecke und gelbem "N", Maskottchen der amerikanischen Navy, USA - *mohair, white, sitting, Navy Goat, leather hooves & horns, leather collar with bell, green-black squint eyes made of glass, blue felt blanket with a yellow "N", mascot of the American Navy, USA*

Serie	Art.-No	Period	Pr.	Info
	7928	1952-1952	6	28 cm

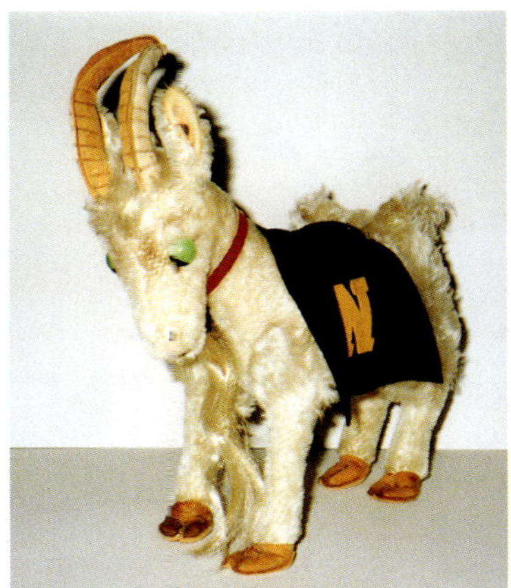

Ziege - *Goat*

Mohair, weiss, stehend, Navy Goat, Lederhufe & -hoerner, Lederhalsband mit Glokke, gruen-schwarze Schielaugen aus Glas, mit blauer Filzdecke und gelbem "N", Maskottchen der amerikanischen Navy, USA - *mohair, white, standing, Navy Goat, leather hooves & horns, leather collar with bell, green-black squint eyes made of glass, blue felt blanket with a yellow "N", mascot of the American Navy, USA*

EAN-No.	Period	Pr.	Info
	1952-1952	6	25 cm

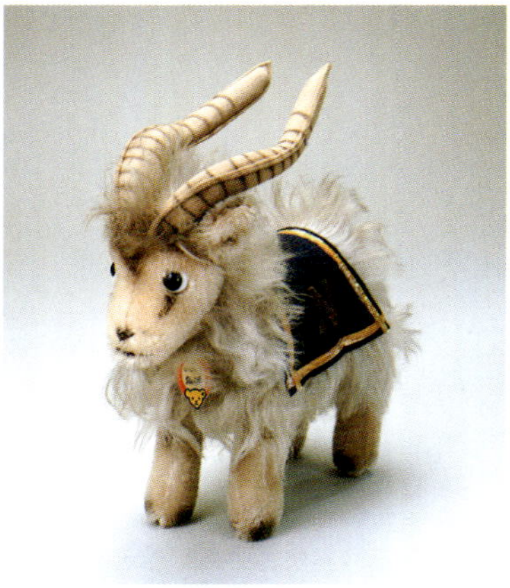

Ziege - *Goat*

Mohair, hellgrau, stehend, Navy Goat, Googly Glasaugen (auch mit gruen-schwarzen Schielaugen aus Glas bekannt), Filzhörner, mit blauer Filzdecke und "N" in gold, Maskottchen der U.S. Naval Academies, USA - *mohair, light grey, standing, Navy Goat, googly glass-eyes (also known with green-black squint eyes of glass), felt horns, blue felt blanket with a golden "N", mascot of the U.S. Naval Academies, USA*

SERIE	ART.-NO	PERIOD	PR.	INFO
	7315,90	1957-1957	5	15 cm
	7325,90	1957-1960	5-6	25 cm

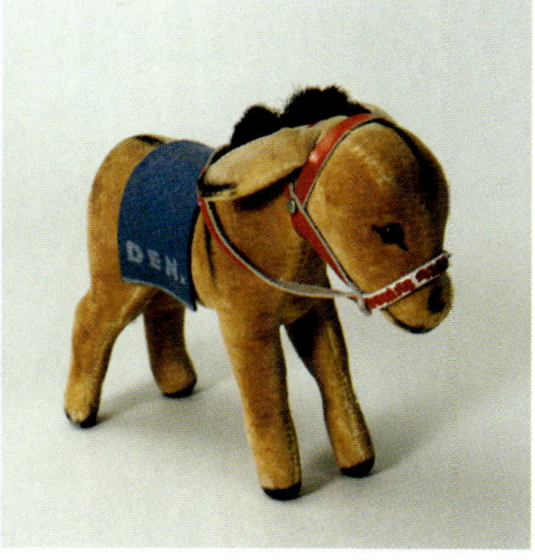

Esel - *Donkey*

Samt, grau, stehend, schwarze Glasaugen, mit blauer Filzdecke und den Buchstaben "DEM", Maskottchen für die amerikanische Democratic Party, USA - *velvet, grey, standing, black glass-eyes, blue felt blanket with "DEM" in white, mascot for the American Democratic Party*

EAN-NO.	PERIOD	PR.	INFO
	1957-1957	5	12 cm

Sonstiges

Miscellaneous

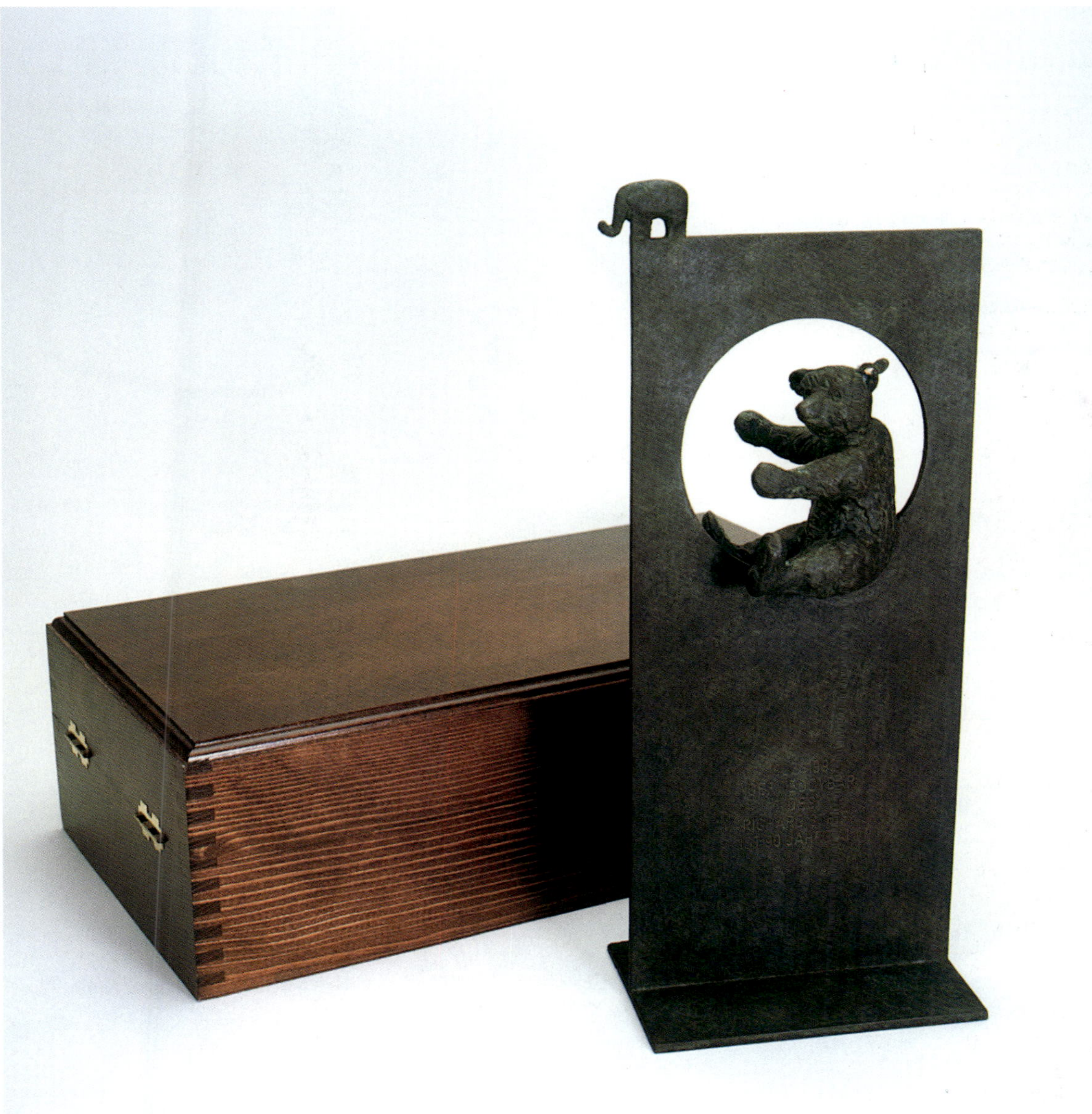

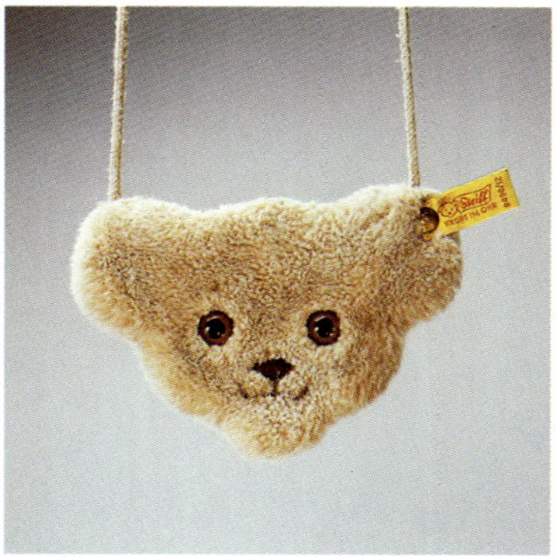

Teddy Tasche - *Teddy Bag*

Teddykopf als Tragebeutel, Geldboerse oder Tasche, Webpelz, waschbar - *Teddy bear´s head for use as a bag, money purse or hand bag, woven fur, washable*

SERIE	ART.-NO	PERIOD	PR.	INFO
	6360/12	1978-1983	1	12 cm, Beutelchen - *bag*
600050	**8490/12**	1984-1990	1	
	600050	1991-1999	1	
	6361/12	1978-1982	1	12 cm, Teddyboerse, ohne Kordel - *teddy money purse without cord strap*
	6365/26	1978-1983	1	26 cm, Tasche - *hand bag*
600104	**8492/26**	1984-1990	1	
	600104	1991-1999	1	

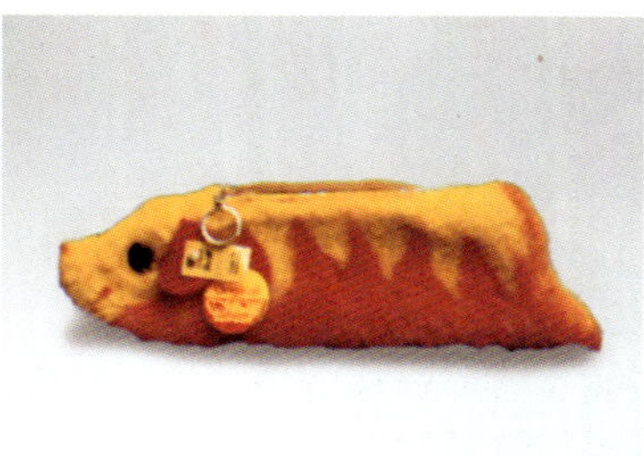

Schlampermaeppchen - *Accessory Case*

Wirkpelz, abwaschbar - *knitted fur, surface washable*

SERIE	ART.-NO	PERIOD	PR.	INFO
	6355/23	1979-1979	2	23 cm
	6355/25	1980-1981	2	

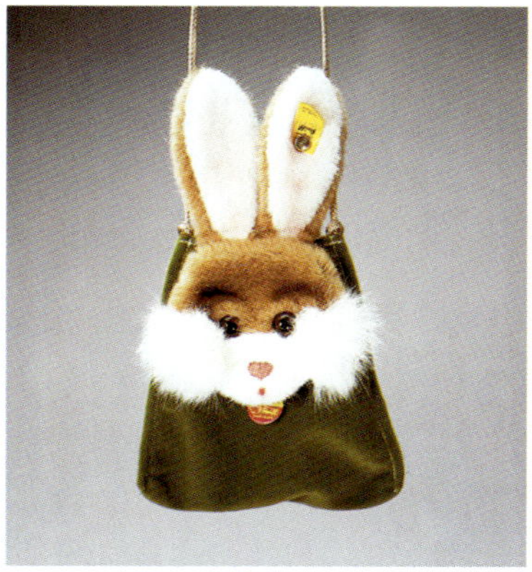

Hasen-Taeschchen - *Little Rabbit Purse*

Webpelz/Trevira-Samt, vollwaschbar - *woven fur/Trevira-velvet, fully washable*

SERIE	ART.-NO	PERIOD	PR.	INFO
	6367/26	1979-1983	3	26 cm

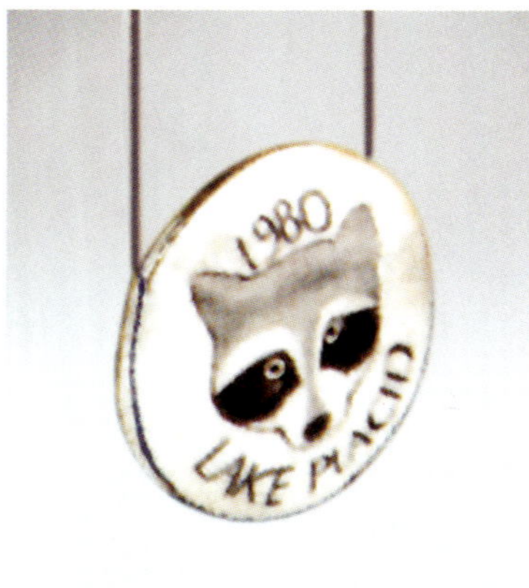

Lake-Placid-Tasche - *Lake Placid Purse*

Disco-Bag, weiss, rund, mit schwarzem Waschbaerenkopf und Aufschrift "1980 Lake-Placid" - *disco purse, white, round, with black raccoon´s face & "1980 Lake Placid" on the front*

SERIE	ART.-NO	PERIOD	PR.	INFO
	6354/18	1979-1979	3	18 cm

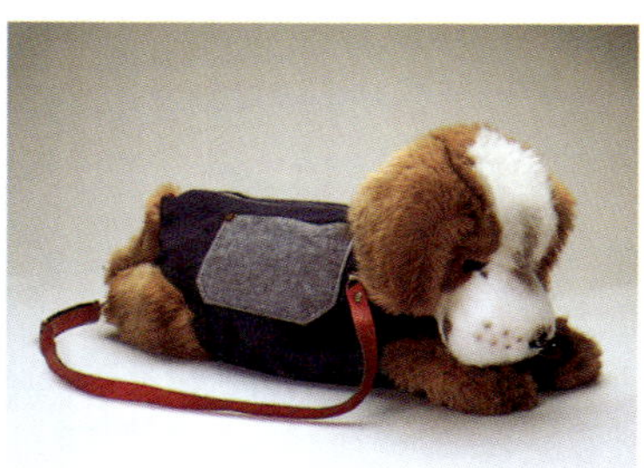

Barry Spieltasche - *Barry Play Bag*

Webpelz/Jeansstoff, vollwaschbar - *woven fur & denim fabric, fully washable*

SERIE	ART.-NO	PERIOD	PR.	INFO
	6357/50	1980-1980	3	50 cm

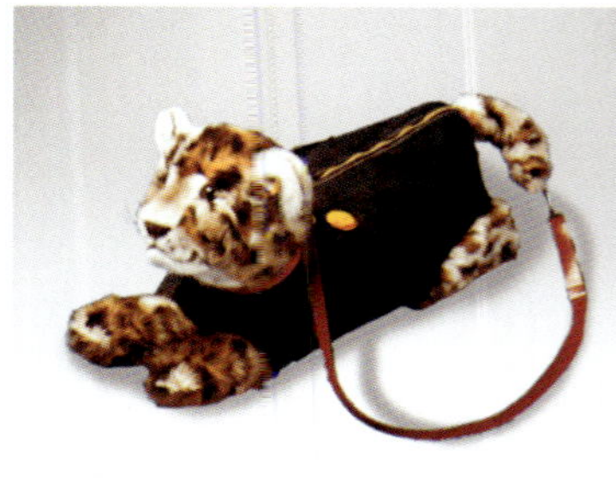

Lommy Spieltasche - *Lommy Play Bag*

Webpelz/Jeansstoff, vollwaschbar - *woven fur & denim fabric, fully washable*

SERIE	ART.-NO	PERIOD	PR.	INFO
	6358/50	1980-1980	3	50 cm

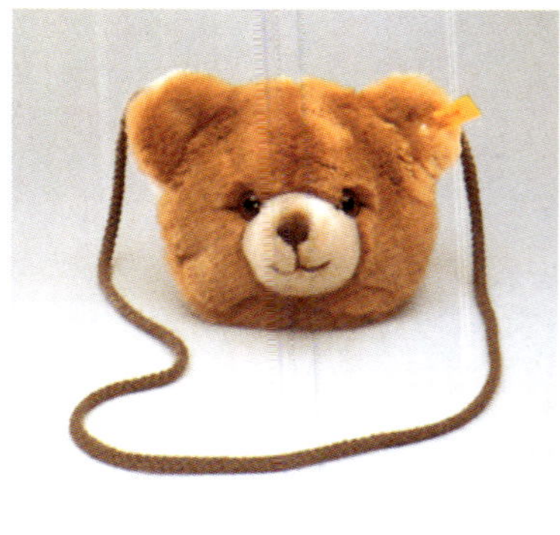

Teeny-Tasche Baer - *Teeny Bear Purse*

Webpelz, waschmaschinenfest - *woven fur, machine washable*

SERIE	ART.-NO	PERIOD	PR.	INFO
600203	**8470/17**	1987-1988	3	17 cm

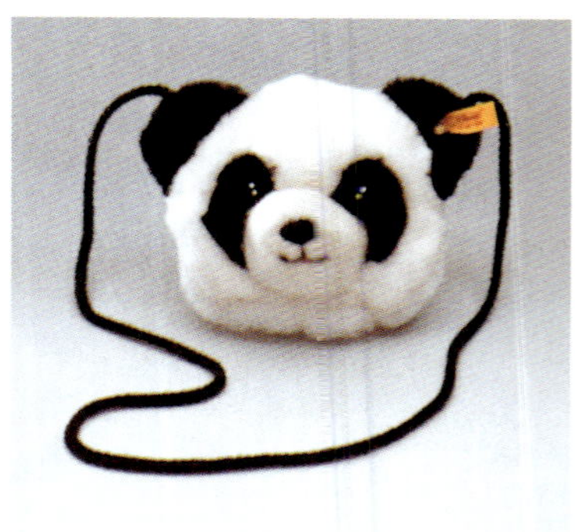

Teeny-Tasche Panda - *Teeny Panda Purse*

Webpelz, waschmaschinenfest - *woven fur, machine washable*

SERIE	ART.-NO	PERIOD	PR.	INFO
600258	**8472/17**	1987-1988	3	17 cm

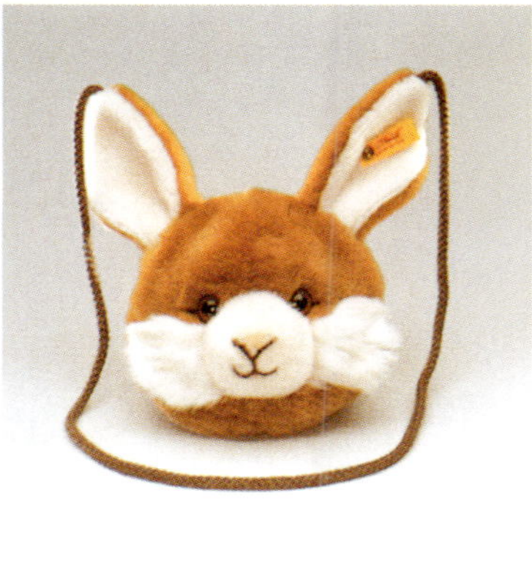

Teeny-Tasche Hase - *Teeny Rabbit Purse*

Webpelz, waschmaschinenfest - *woven fur, machine washable*

SERIE	ART.-NO	PERIOD	PR.	INFO
600302	**8474/17**	1987-1988	3	17 cm

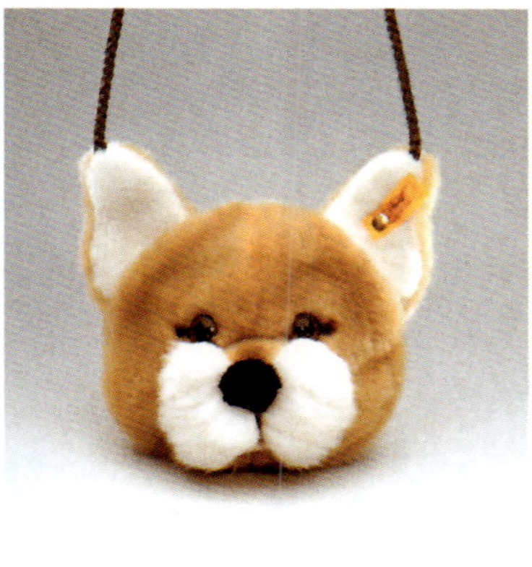

Teeny-Tasche Hund - *Teeny Dog Purse*

Webpelz, waschmaschinenfest - *woven fur, machine washable*

SERIE	ART.-NO	PERIOD	PR.	INFO
600357	**8476/17**	1987-1988	3	17 cm

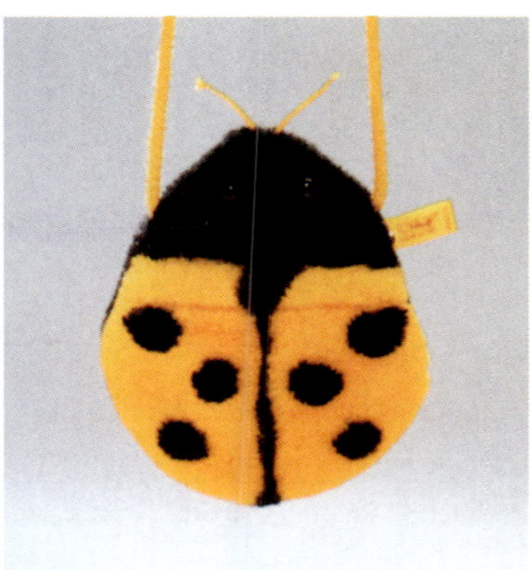

Marienkaefer Tasche - *Ladybird Purse*

Webpelz, 18 cm, waschmaschinenfest - *woven fur, 18 cm, machine washable*

SERIE	ART.-NO	PERIOD	PR.	INFO
600500	**8480/18**	1988-1990	2	rot - *red*
	600500	1991-1991	2	
600524	**8481/18**	1988-1989	2	gelb - *yellow*

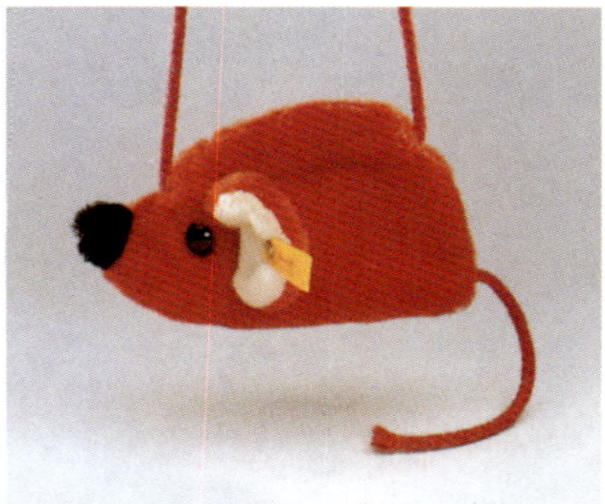

Maus Tasche - *Mouse Purse*

Webpelz, 18 cm, waschmaschinenfest - *woven fur, 18 cm, machine washable*

SERIE	ART.-NO	PERIOD	PR.	INFO
600609	**8482/18**	1988-1989	2	rot - *red*
600623	**8483/18**	1988-1988	2	gelb - *yellow*

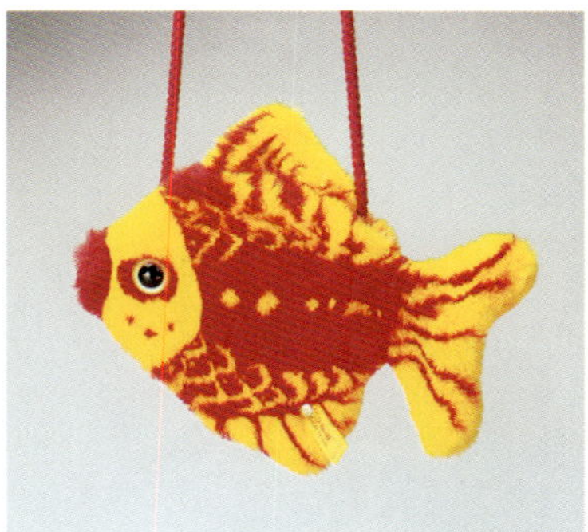

Fisch Tasche - *Fish Purse*

Webpelz, 18 cm, waschmaschinenfest - *woven fur, 18 cm, machine washable*

SERIE	ART.-NO	PERIOD	PR.	INFO
600708	**8487/18**	1988-1988	2	rot - *red*
600746	**8488/18**	1988-1988	2	blau - *blue*

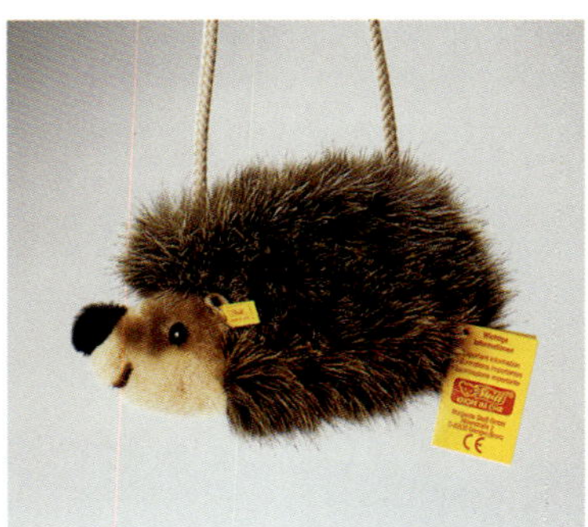

Igel Tasche - *Hedgehog Purse*

Webpelz, waschmaschinenfest - *woven fur, machine washable*

SERIE	ART.-NO	PERIOD	PR.	INFO
600906	**8485/18**	1988-1990	1	18 cm
	600906	1991-1997	1	

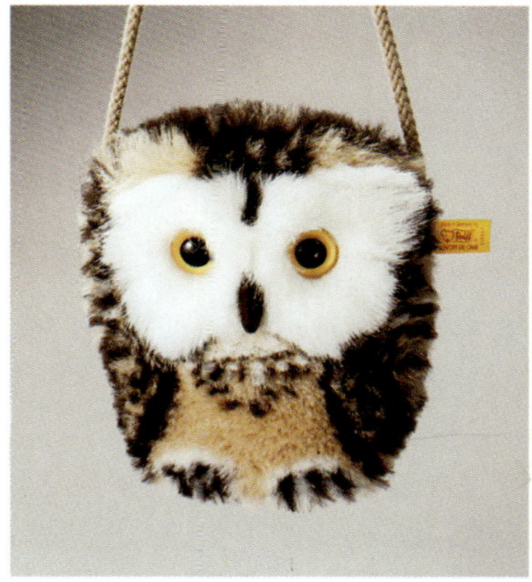

Uhu Tasche - *Owl Purse*

Wirkpelz, waschmaschinenfest - *knitted fur, machine washable*

SERIE	ART.-NO	PERIOD	PR.	INFO
600937	**8486/18**	1988-1990	1-2	18 cm
	600937	1991-1997	1-2	

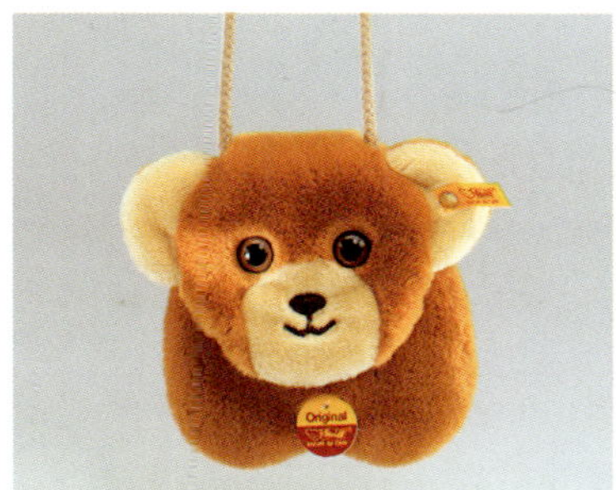

Teddy-Tasche - *Teddy Purse*

Webpelz, waschmaschinenfest - *woven fur, machine washable*

EAN-NO.	PERIOD	PR.	INFO
601019	1996-1999	1-2	16 cm

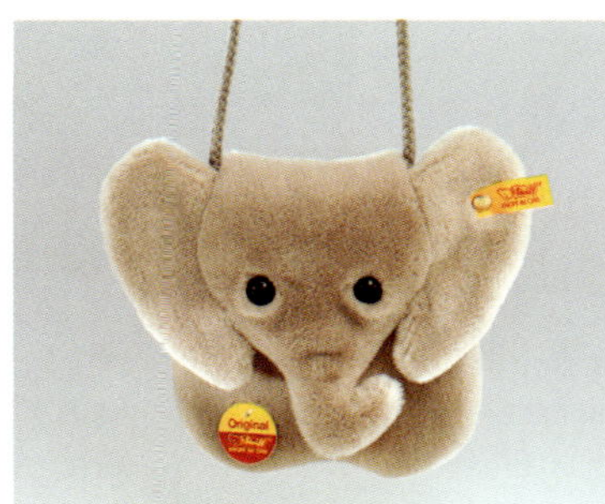

Elefanten-Tasche - *Elephant Purse*

Webpelz, waschmaschinenfest - *woven fur, machine washable*

EAN-NO.	PERIOD	PR.	INFO
601064	1996-1999	1-2	16 cm

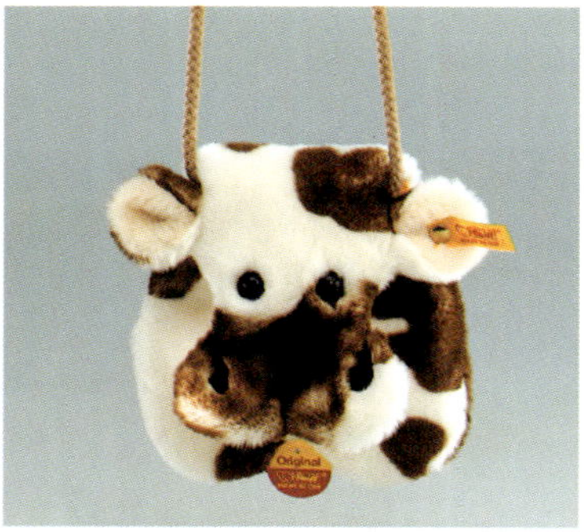

Kuh-Tasche - *Cow Purse*

Webpelz, waschmaschinenfest - *woven fur, machine washable*

EAN-No.	Period	Pr.	Info
601118	1996-1997	1-2	16 cm

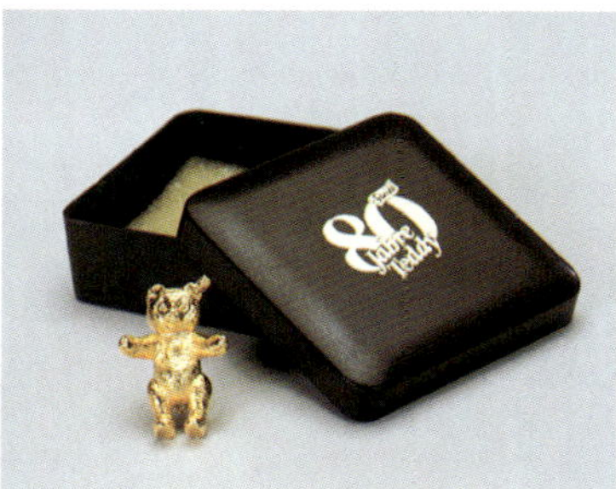

Ansteckteddy - *Teddy Pin*

vergoldet - *gold plated*

Serie	Art.-No	Period	Pr.	Info
	8500/03	1984-1985	2	3 cm

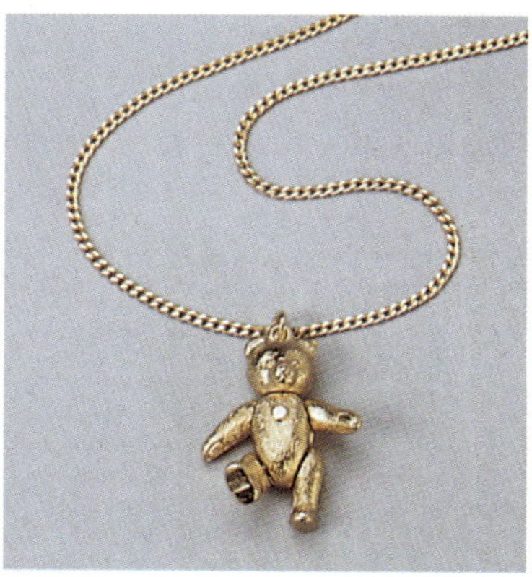

Teddy Anhaenger - *Teddy Pendant*

mit Kette 45 cm, vergoldet - *with chain 45 cm, gold plated*

Serie	Art.-No	Period	Pr.	Info
605154	8510/02	1984-1990	1	2 cm
	605154	1991-1999	1	

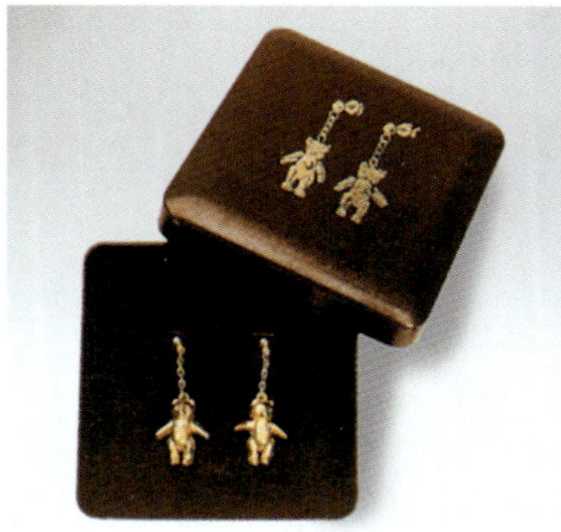

Teddy Ohrstecker - *Teddy pierced Earrings*

2 Stueck - *2 pieces*

Serie	Art.-No	Period	Pr.	Info
605109	8505/01	1985-1989	1	
605406	8511/00	1985-1987	4	Set mit: 4 Teddy Ohrstecker 8505/01, 6 Teddy Halskettchen 8510/02, 4 Ansteckteddys 8500/03 - *Set: includes 4 Teddy earrings (pierced) 8505/01, 6 Teddy necklaces 8510/02, 4 Teddy pins 8500/03*

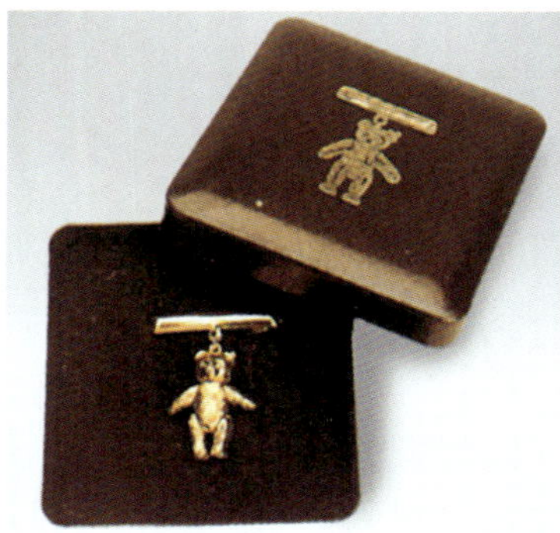

Teddy Brosche - *Teddy Brooch*

vergoldet, gegliederter Teddy - *gold plated, jointed teddy*

Serie	Art.-No	Period	Pr.	Info
605031	8501/02	1986-1988	1	2 cm

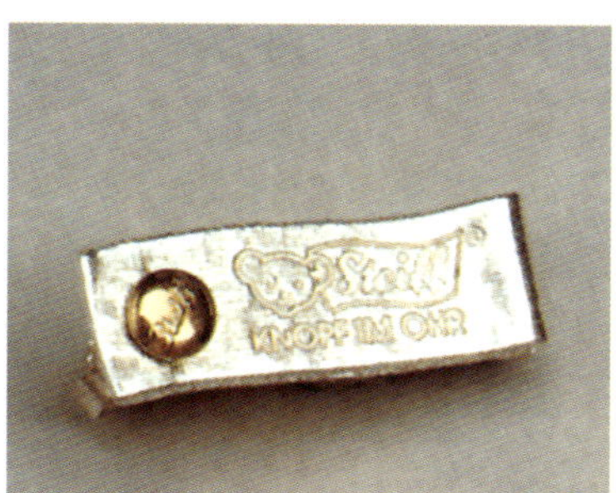

Ohrstecker - *Pierced Earring*

"Knopf im Ohr" - "*Button in Ear*"

EAN-No.	Period	Pr.	Info
605628	1992-1992	1	1 Stueck - *one only*

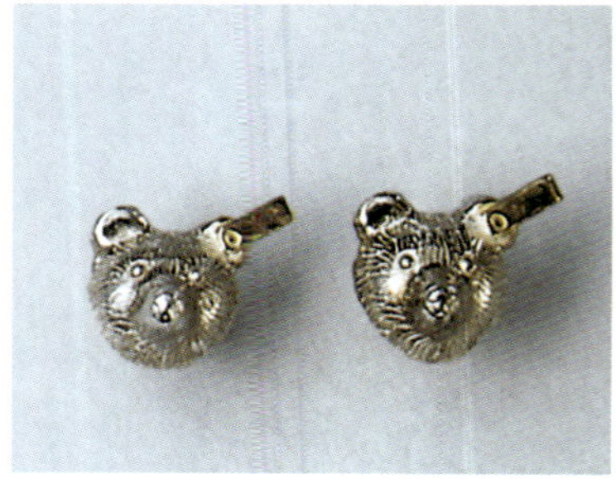

Ohrstecker - *Pierced Earrings*

"Teddykoepfchen" - "*Teddy Bear Head*"

EAN-No.	Period	Pr.	Info
605642	1992-1992	1	2 Stueck - *2 earrings*

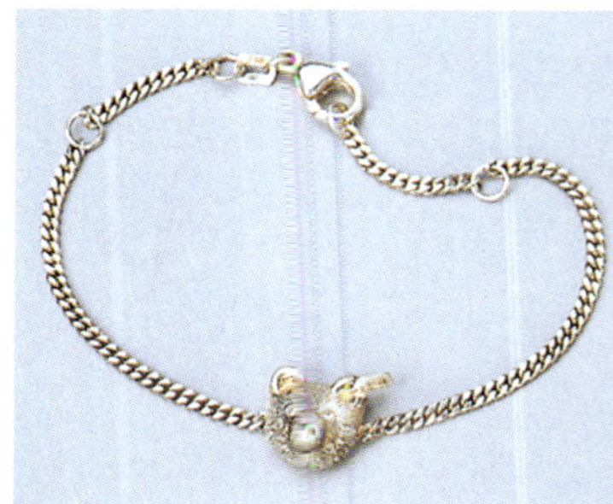

Armkettchen - *Bracelet*

"Teddykoepfchen" - "*Teddy Bear Head*"

EAN-No.	Period	Pr.	Info
605666	1992-1992	1	14 cm

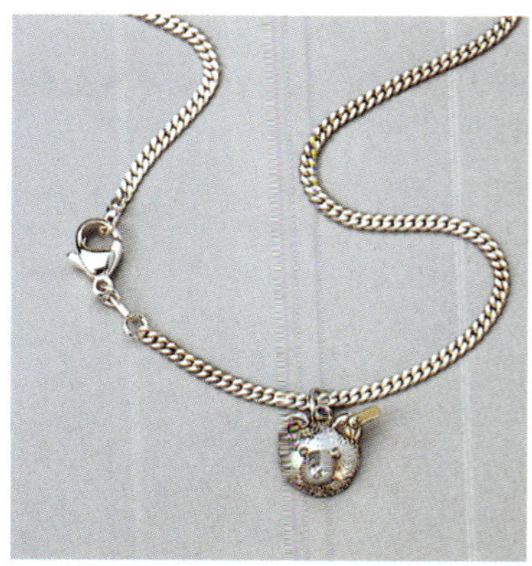

Collier - *Necklace*

"Teddykoepfchen" - "*Teddy Bear Head*"

EAN-No.	Period	Pr.	Info
605680	1992-1992	1	38 cm

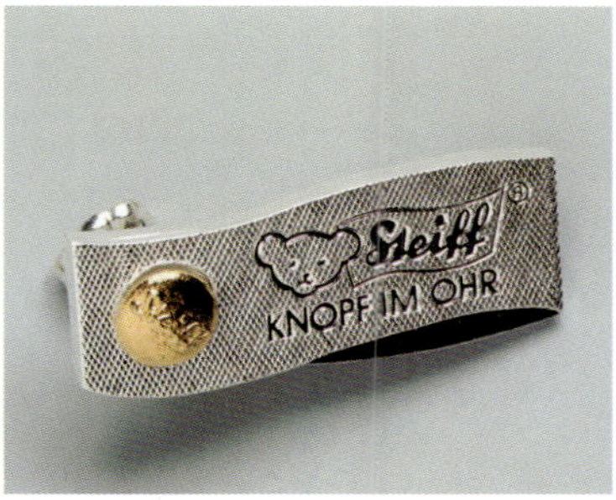

Ohrstecker - *Pierced Earring*

"Knopf im Ohr", 925 Silber - *"Button in Ear", 925 Sterling Silver*

EAN-No.	Period	Pr.	Info
605529	1993-1998	1	1 Stueck - *one only*

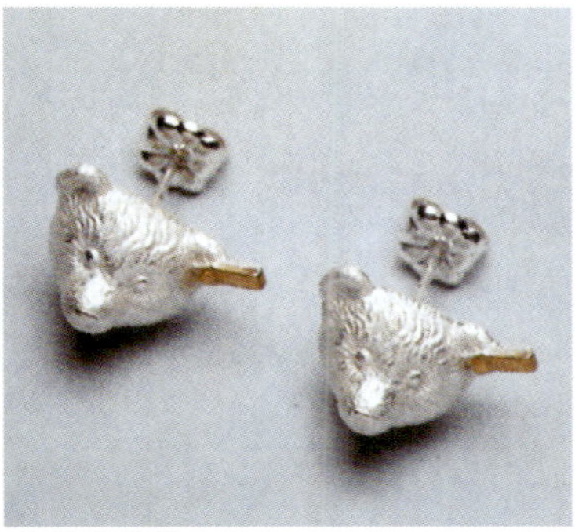

Ohrstecker - *Pierced Earrings*

"Teddykoepfchen", 925 Silber - *"Teddy Bear Head", 925 Sterling Silver*

EAN-No.	Period	Pr.	Info
605536	1993-1994	1	2 Stueck - *2 earrings*

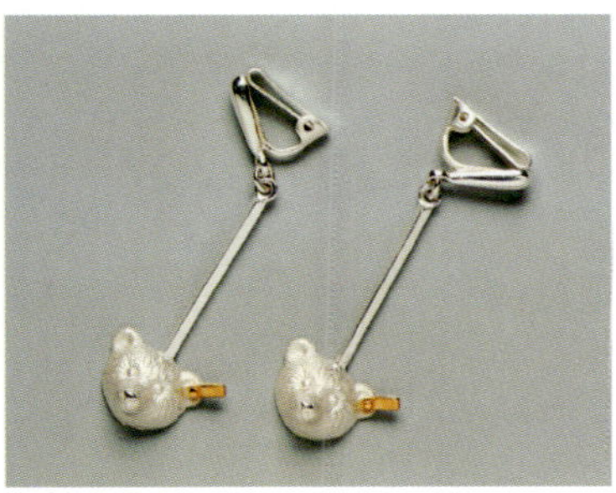

Ohrclip - *Ear Clips*

"Teddykoepfchen", 925 Silber - *"Teddy Bear Head", 925 Sterling Silver*

EAN-No.	Period	Pr.	Info
605543	1993-1996	1	2 Stueck - *2 earrings*

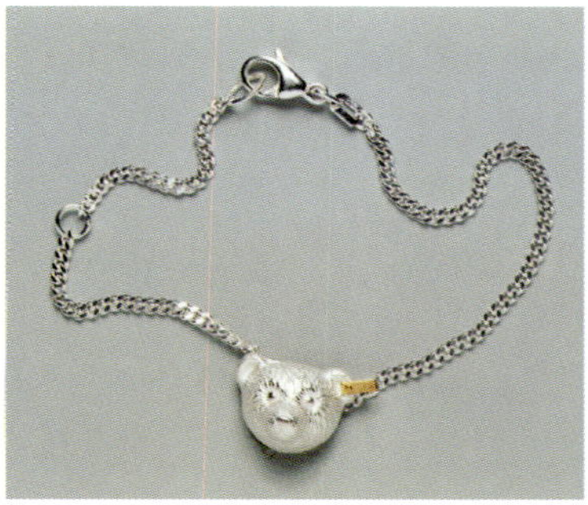

Armkettchen - *Bracelet*

"Teddykoepfchen", 925 Silber - *"Teddy Bear Head", 925 Sterling Silver*

EAN-No.	Period	Pr.	Info
605550	1993-1998	1	18 cm

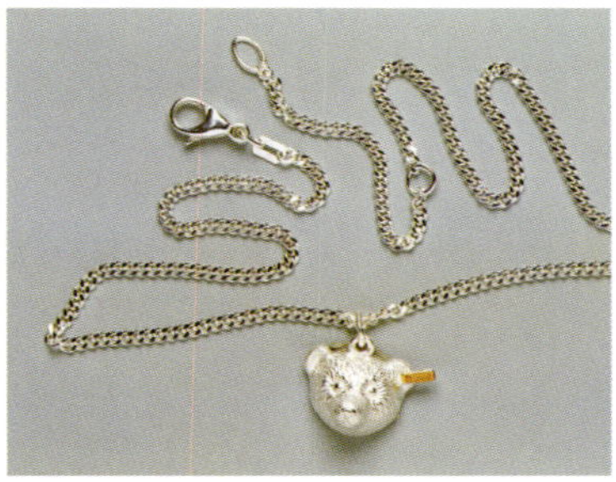

Collier - *Necklace*

"Teddykoepfchen", 925 Silber - *"Teddy Bear Head", 925 Sterling Silver*

EAN-No.	Period	Pr.	Info
605567	1993-1996	1	42 cm

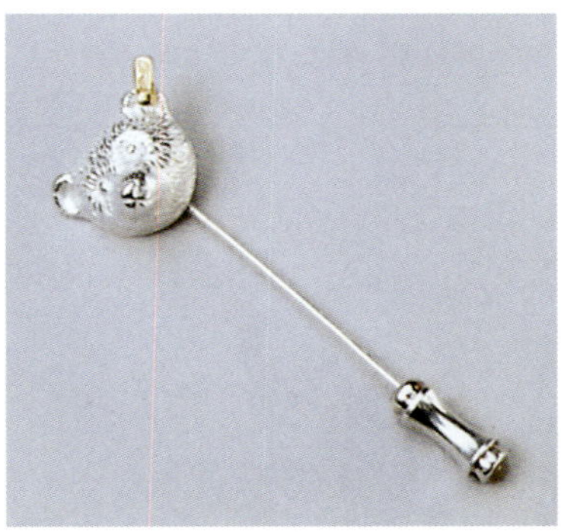

Anstecknadel - *Stick Pin*

"Teddykoepfchen", 925 Silber - *"Teddy Bear Head", 925 Sterling Silver*

EAN-No.	Period	Pr.	Info
605581	1993-1998	1	

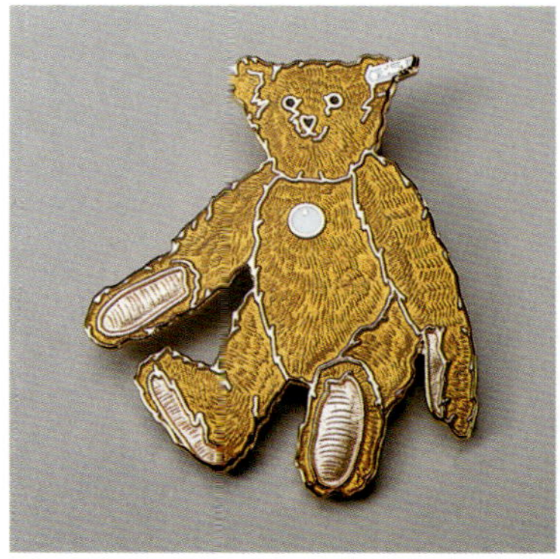

Steiff Pin

Baerle 35 PB 1904, Lasuremaille - *1904 Baerle 35 PB, glazed enamel*

EAN-No.	Period	Pr.	Info
605802	1993-1996	1	5 cm

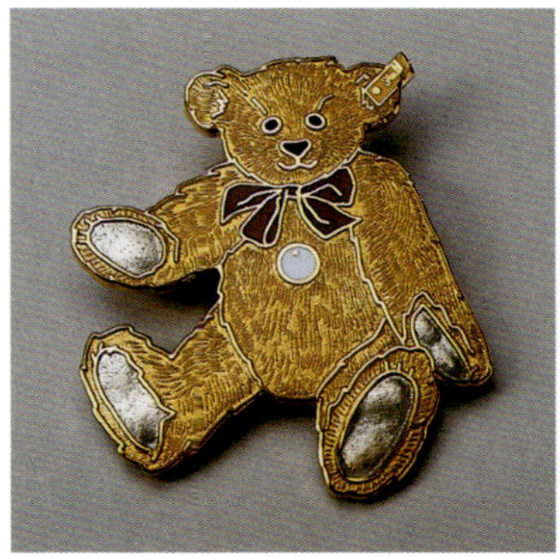

Steiff Pin

Classic 1909 Teddybaer, Lasuremaille - *Classic 1909 Teddy bear, glazed enamel*

EAN-No.	Period	Pr.	Info
605819	1993-1996	1	5 cm

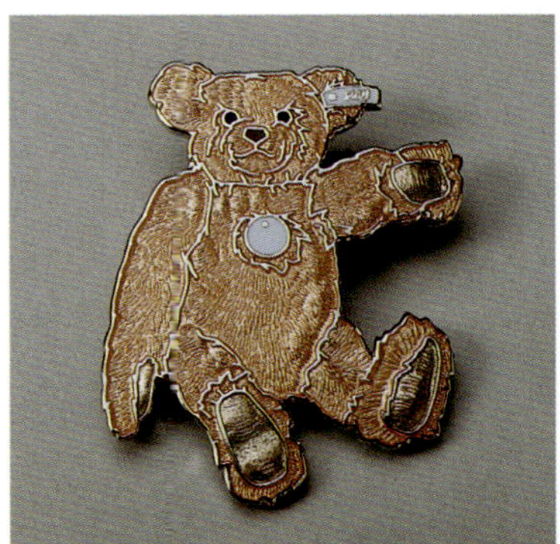

Steiff Pin

Teddy Rose 1925, Lasuremaille - *1925 Teddy Rose, glazed enamel*

EAN-No.	Period	Pr.	Info
605826	1993-1996	1	5 cm

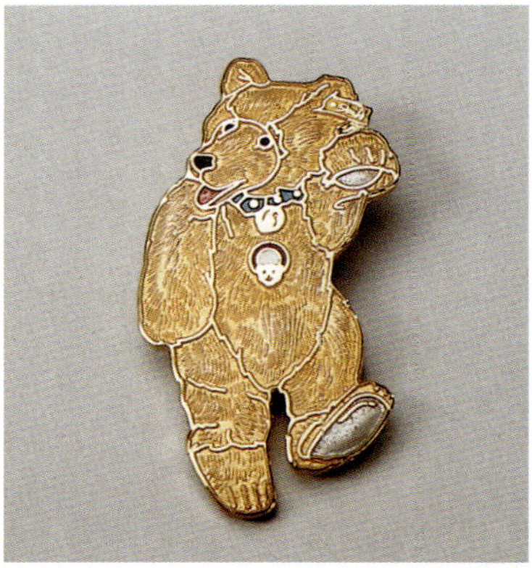

Steiff Pin

Teddy Baby 1930, Lasuremaille - *1930 Teddy Baby, glazed enamel*

EAN-No.	Period	Pr.	Info
605833	1993-1996	1	5 cm

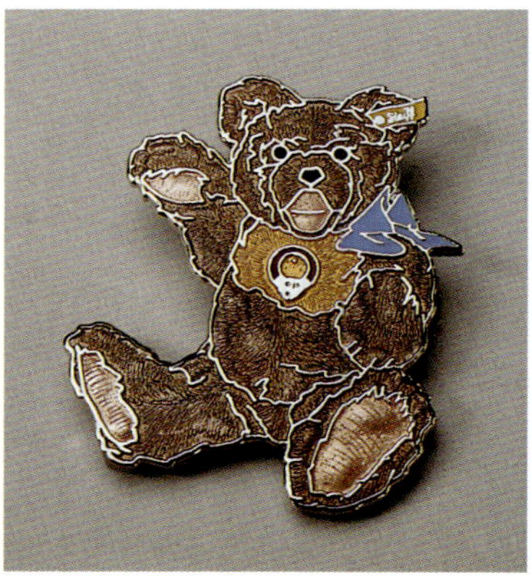

Steiff Pin

Zotty 1951, Lasuremaille - *1951 Zotty, glazed enamel*

EAN-No.	Period	Pr.	Info
605840	1993-1996	1	5 cm

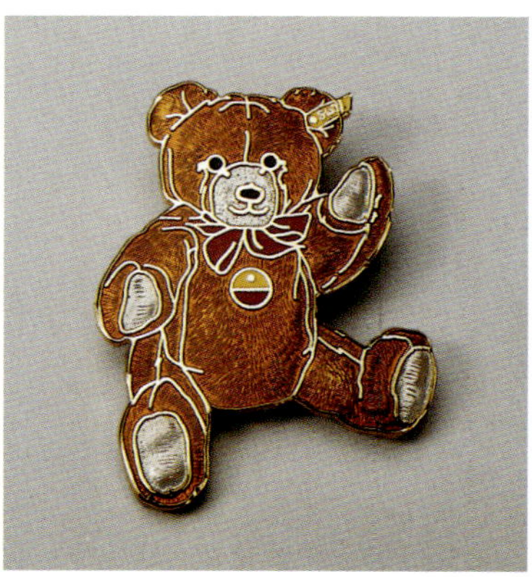

Steiff Pin

Teddy Petsy 1984, Lasuremaille - *1984 Teddy Petsy, glazed enamel*

EAN-No.	Period	Pr.	Info
605857	1993-1996	1	5 cm

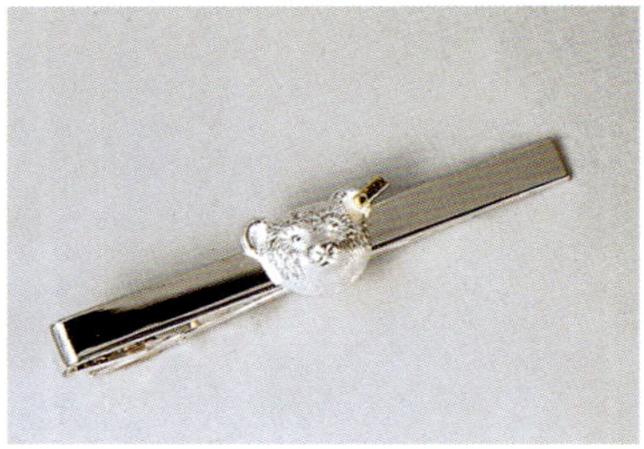

Krawattenklammer - *Tie Clip*

mit Teddykoepfchen, versilbert - *tie clip with teddy bear´s head, silver-plated*

EAN-No.	Period	Pr.	Info
605048	1994-1995	1	6 cm

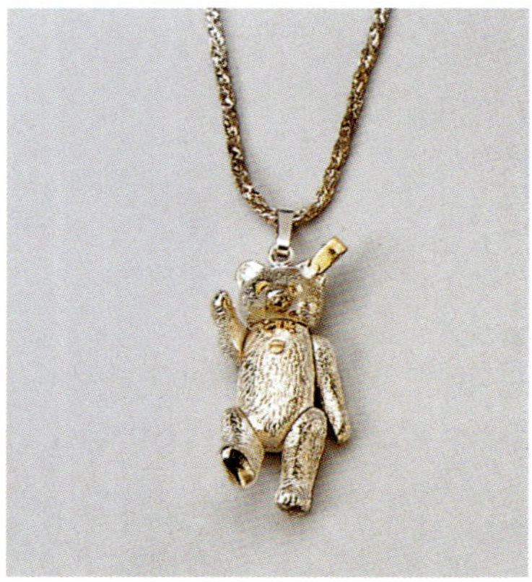

Collier Teddybaer - *Teddy Bear Necklace*

Teddy 3 cm, gegliedert, Kette 50 cm - *3 cm teddy, jointed, with 50 cm long chain*

EAN-No.	Period	Pr.	Info
605253	1994-1995	2	925 Silber - *925 silver*

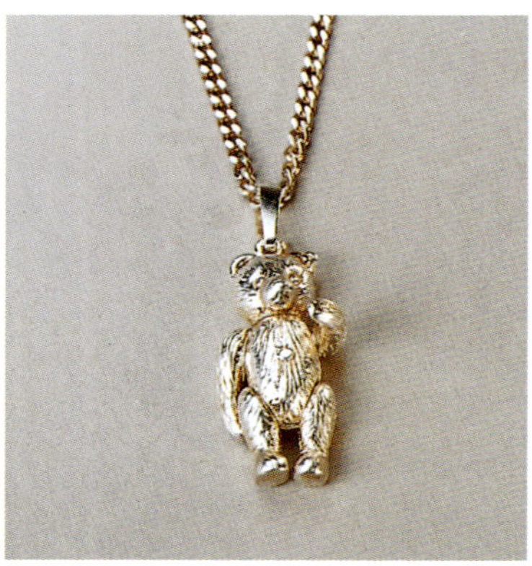

Teddy-Anhaenger - *Teddy Pendant*

Teddy 2 cm, mit Kette 42 cm - *2 cm teddy with 42 cm chain*

EAN-No.	Period	Pr.	Info
605277	1995-1997	2	925 Silber - *925 silver*

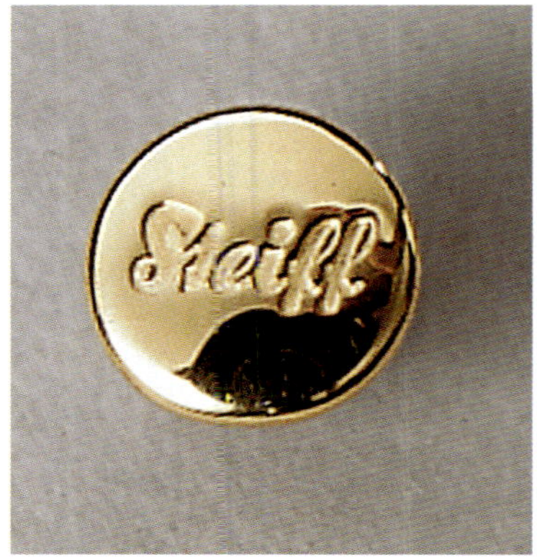

Ohrstecker - *Pierced Earring*

"Knopf im Ohr", 585 Gold - *"Button in Ear", 14 K gold*

EAN-No.	Period	Pr.	Info
605468	1995-1997	2	1 Stueck - *one only*

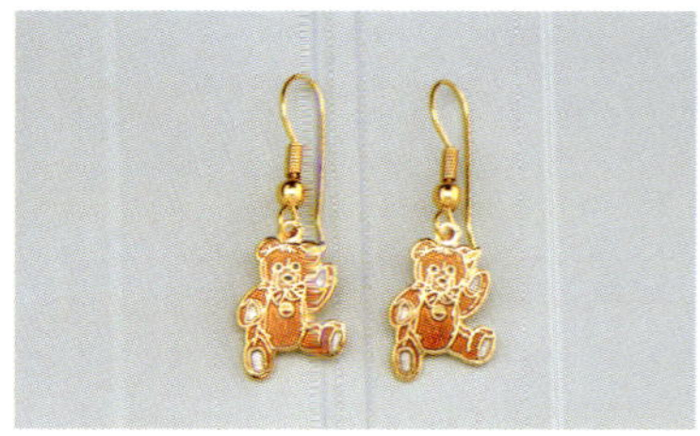

Email-Ohrring - *Enamel Earring*

Lasuremaille, vergoldet - *glazed enamel, gold plated*

EAN-No.	Period	Pr.	Info
605475	1995-1996	1	1 Paar - *1 pair*

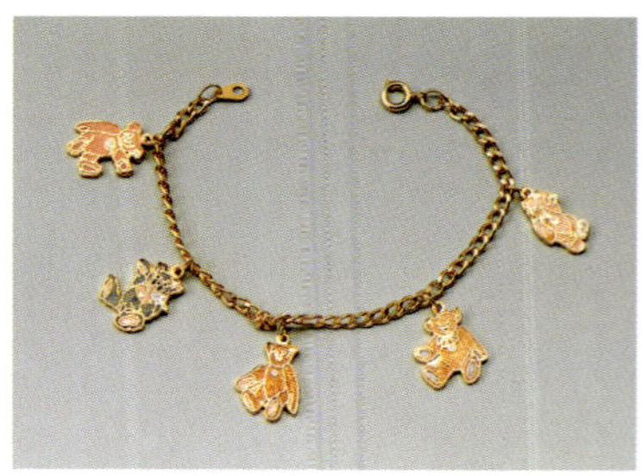

Armkettchen - *Bracelet*

Lasuremaille, vergoldet, mit Baerenanhaengern 2 cm, Kettchen 16 cm - *bracelet with glazed enamel charms, bear charms are 2 cm in size, bracelet 16 cm*

EAN-No.	Period	Pr.	Info
605673	1995-1997	1	vergoldet - *gold plated*

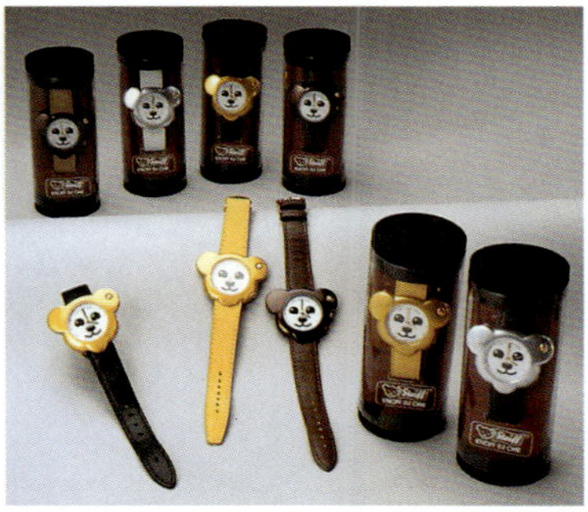

Steiff Teddys Watch

Metallgehaeuse, Quarzwerk, vergoldeter Steiff-Knopf im Ohr, Gehaeuse in blank, gelb oder braun, Armband in schwarz, weiss, gelb, dunkelbraun oder beige - *metal housing, quartz movement, gold-plated Steiff Button in Ear, available in polished metal, yellow or brown, watch strap available in black, white, yellow, dark brown or beige*

EAN-No.	Period	Pr.	Info
606113	1991-1991	1-2	blank/schwarz - *polished metal/black*
606120	1991-1991	1-2	blank/weiss - *polished metal/white*
606168	1991-1991	1-2	gelb/schwarz - *yellow/black*
606175	1991-1991	1-2	gelb/gelb - *yellow/yellow*
606212	1991-1991	1-2	braun/dunkelbraun - *brown/dark brown*
606229	1991-1991	1-2	braun/beige - *brown/beige*

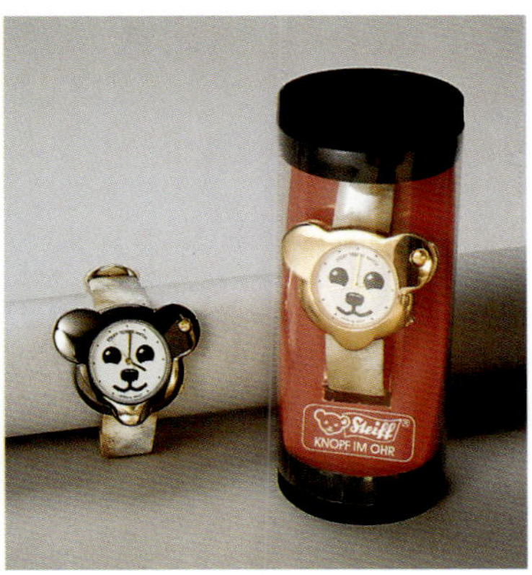

Steiff Teddys Watch 1992

Metallgehaeuse, Quarzwerk, vergoldeter Steiff-Knopf im Ohr, Gehaeuse in chrom, grau oder goldfarbig, Armband in schwarz, grau, graubraun oder aubergine (meliert) - *metal housing, quartz movement, gold-plated Steiff Button in Ear, available in chrome, grey or gold-color, watch strap available in black, grey, greyish-brown or aubergine (mottled)*

EAN-No.	Period	Pr.	Info
606311	1992-1993	1-2	chrom/schwarz - *chrome/black*
606328	1992-1993	1-2	chrom/grau - *chrome/grey*
606366	1992-1993	1-2	grau/schwarz - *grey/black*
606373	1992-1995	1-2	grau/graubraun - *grey/greyish brown*
606410	1992-1995	1-2	gold/aubergine
606427	1992-1995	1-2	gold/graubraun - *gold/greyish brown*

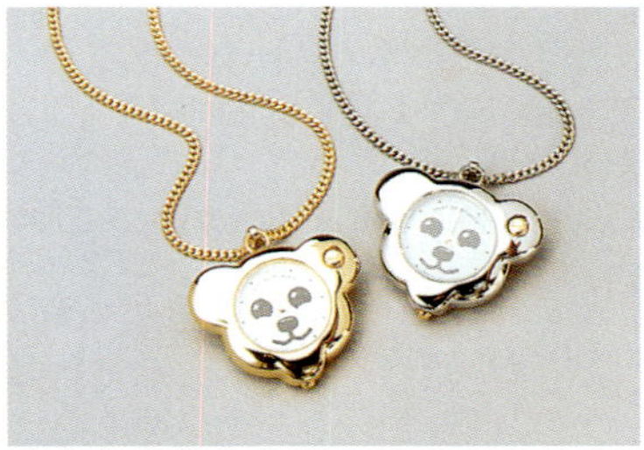

Steiff Teddys Pendant Watch

Metallgehaeuse in chrom, grau, gelb-gold oder rot-gold, Quarzwerk, vergoldeter Steiff-Knopf im Ohr, Kette 60 cm - *metal housing in chrome, grey, yellow gold or red gold, quartz movement, gold-plated Steiff Button in Ear, 60 cm long chain*

EAN-No.	Period	Pr.	Info
606519	1993-1996	1	chrom - *chrome*
606564	1993-1996	1	grau - *grey*
606618	1993-1996	1	gelb-gold - *yellow gold*
606663	1993-1996	1	rot-gold - *red gold*

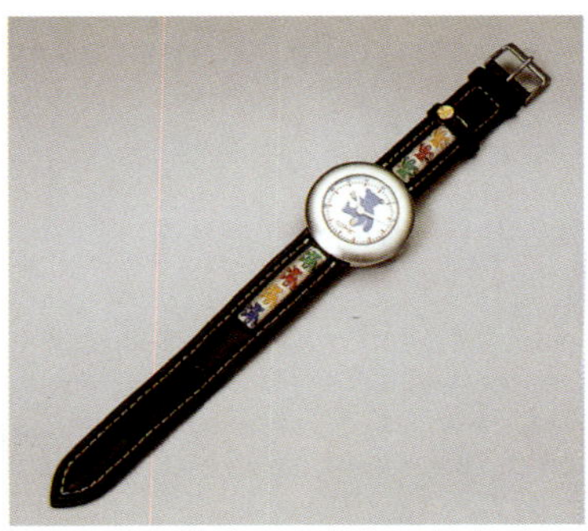

Armbanduhr - *wrist-watch*

Motiv "Teddybaer 1908 blau", Leder/Metall, Lederarmband mit Steiff-Knopf - *motive "teddy bear 1908 blue", leather/metal, leather bracelet with Steiff button*

EAN-No.	Period	Pr.	Info
606755	1998-1999	2	Gehaeuse gold, Armband dunkelbraun - *case gold, dark brown bracelet*
606762	1998-1999	2	Gehaeuse silber, Armband schwarz - *case silver, black bracelet*

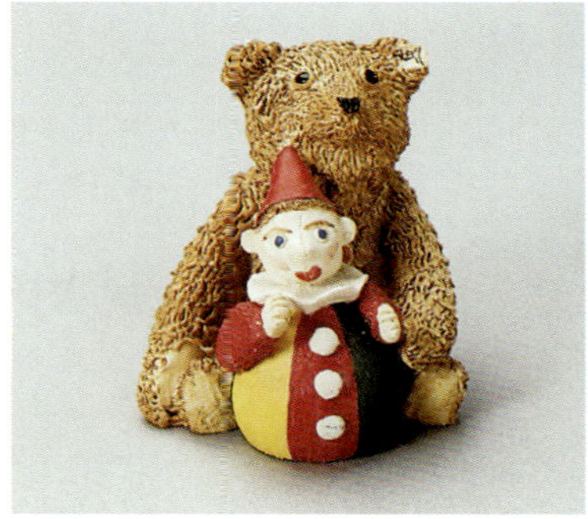

Ceramic Miniatur

Baerle 35 PB (1904) & Roly Poly (1909), Keramik - *Baerle 35 PB (1904) & Roly Poly (1909), in ceramic*

EAN-No.	Period	Pr.	Info
612657	1994-1996	1	5,5 cm

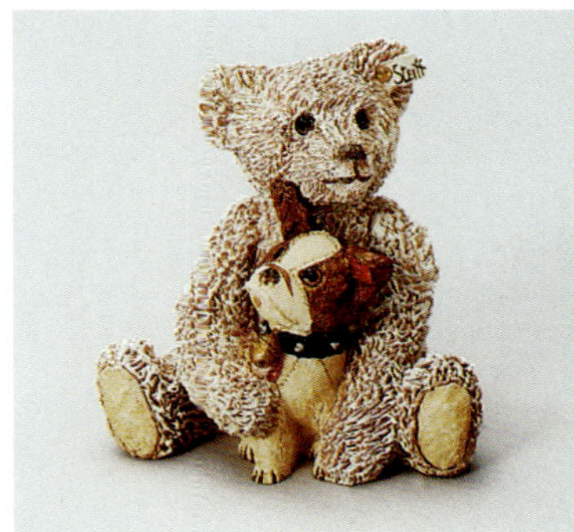

Ceramic Miniatur

Teddy rosé (1925) & Bully Hund (1927), Keramik - *Teddy Rose (1924) & Bully Dog (1927) in ceramic*

EAN-No.	Period	Pr.	Info
612671	1994-1996	1	5,5 cm

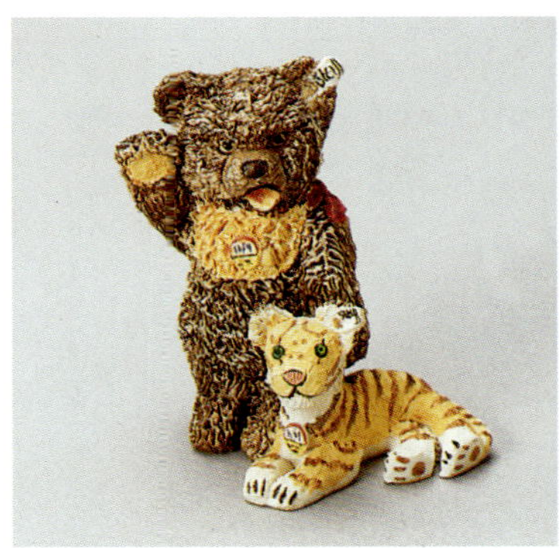

Ceramic Miniatur

Zotty Zottelbaer (1951) & Tiger (1955), Keramik - *Zotty Zottelbaer (1951) & Tiger (1955), in ceramic*

EAN-No.	Period	Pr.	Info
612701	1994-1996	1	6,5 cm

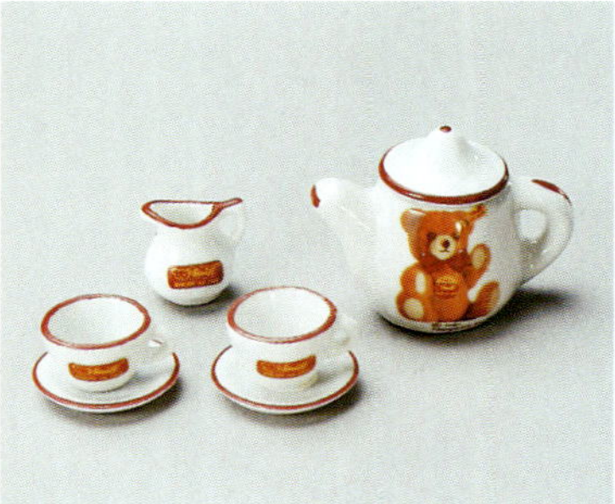

Mini Porzellan Set - *Miniature Porcelain Set*

Mini Porzellan Service, 6-teilig, Dekor Petsy - *miniature 6-piece porcelain service, Petsy design*

SERIE	ART.-NO	PERIOD	PR.	INFO
613005	8601/06	1988-1989	2	6 cm

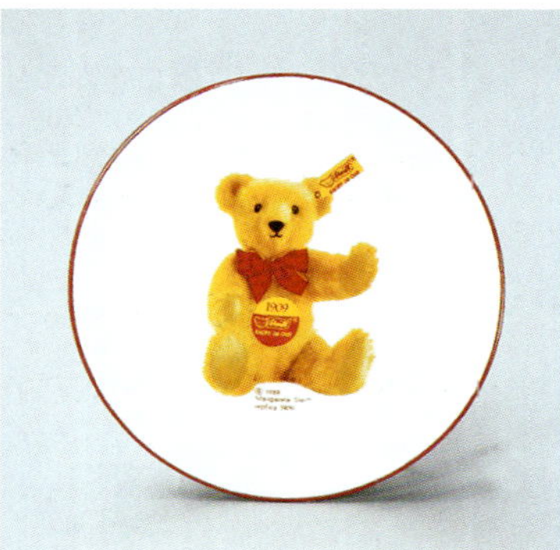

Porzellan Service Teile - *Porcelain Service Parts*

Wandteller/Mini Porzellan Set/Puppen Porzellan Service, Dekor Teddybaer 1909 - *wall plate/miniature porcelain set/doll´s porcelain service, 1909 Teddy Bear design*

SERIE	ART.-NO	PERIOD	PR.	INFO
613104	8605/01	1989-1990	1	10 cm
613111	8605/06	1989-1989	1-2	6-teilig - *6-piece set*
613173	8605/15	1989-1989	2	15-teilig - *15-piece set*

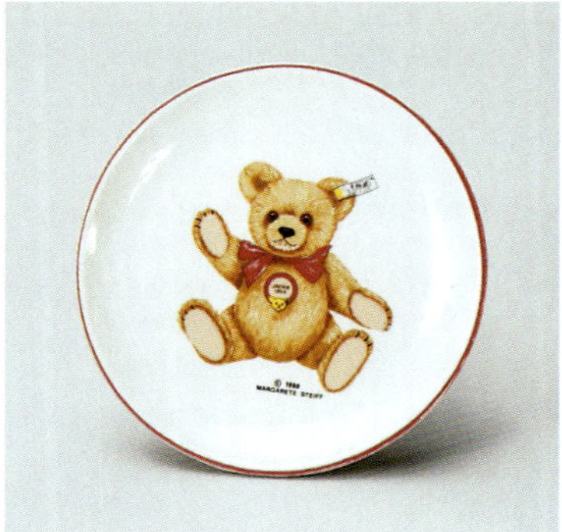

Porzellan Service Teile - *Porcelain Service Parts*

Wandteller/Mini Porzellan Set/Puppen Porzellan Service, Dekor Jackie - *wall plate/miniature porcelain set/doll´s porcelain service, Jackie design*

SERIE	ART.-NO	PERIOD	PR.	INFO
613203	8606/02	1990-1990	1	10 cm
	613203	1991-1991	1	
613234	8606/08	1990-1990	1-2	8-teilig - *8-piece set*
	613234	1991-1991	1-2	
613272	8606/15	1990-1990	2	15-teilig - *15-piece set*
	613272	1991-1991	2	

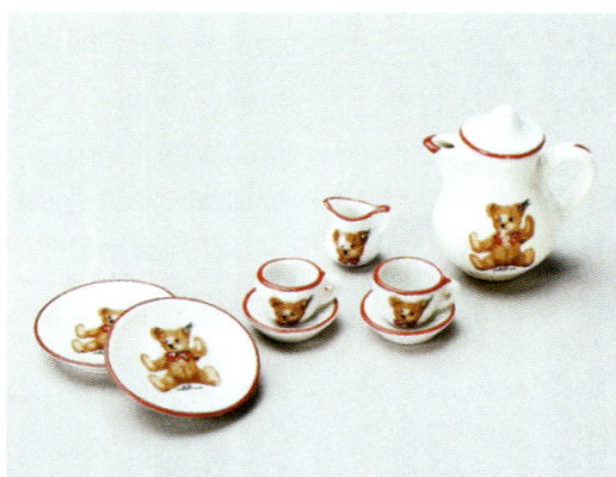

Porzellan Service Teile - *Porcelain Service Parts*

Wandteller/Mini Porzellan Set/Puppen Porzellan Service, Dekor Teddybaer 1926 - *wall plate/miniature porcelain set/doll´s porcelain service, 1926 Teddy Bear design*

EAN-NO.	PERIOD	PR.	INFO
613302	1991-1992	1	10 cm
613333	1991-1992	1-2	8-teilig - *8-piece set*
613371	1991-1992	2	15-teilig - *15-piece set*

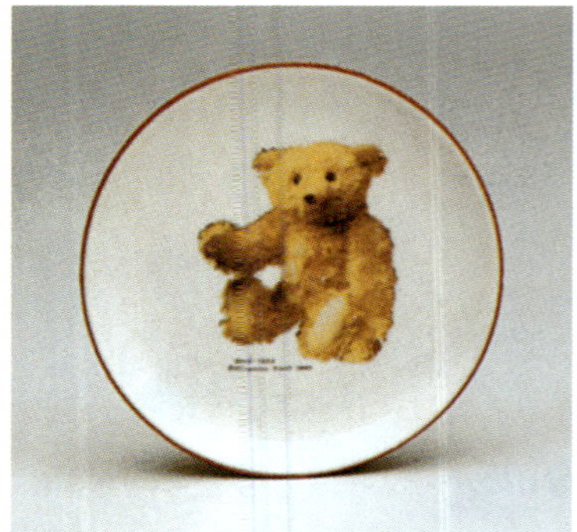

Porzellan Service Teile - *Porcelain Service Parts*

Wandteller/Mini Porzellan Set/Puppen Porzellan Service, Dekor Baerle - *wall plate/miniature porcelain set/doll´s porcelain service, Baerle design*

EAN-NO.	PERIOD	PR.	INFO
613401	1992-1993	1	10 cm
613432	1992-1993	1-2	8-teilig - *8-piece set*
613470	1992-1993	2	15-teilig - *15-piece set*

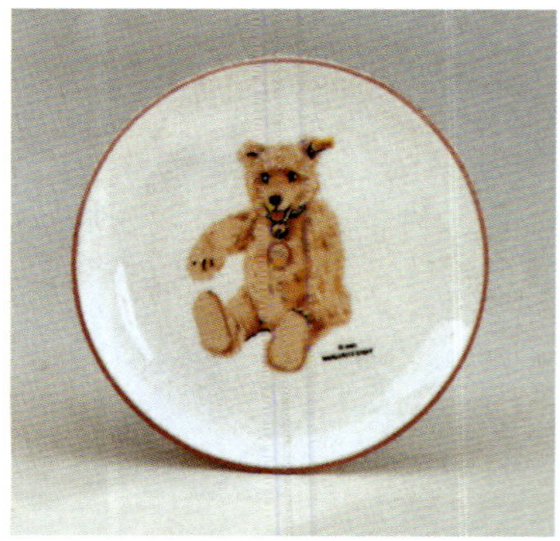

Porzellan Service Teile - *Porcelain Service Parts*

Wandteller/Mini Porzellan Set/Puppen Porzellan Service, Dekor Teddy Baby - *wall plate/miniature porcelain set/doll´s porcelain service, Teddy Baby design*

EAN-NO.	PERIOD	PR.	INFO
613500	1993-1994	1	10 cm
613531	1993-1994	1-2	9-teilig - *9-piece set*
613579	1993-1994	2	15-teilig - *15-piece set*

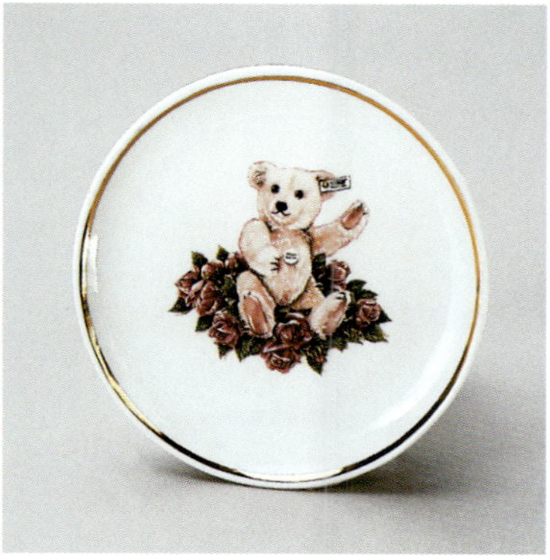

Porzellan Service Teile - *Porcelain Service Parts*

Wandteller/Mini Porzellan Set/Puppen Porzellan Service, Dekor Teddy Rosé - *wall plate/miniature porcelain set/doll´s porcelain service, Teddy Rose design*

EAN-No.	Period	Pr.	Info
613609	1994-1995	1	10 cm
613630	1994-1995	1-2	9-teilig - *9-piece set*
613678	1994-1995	2	12-teilig - *12-piece set*

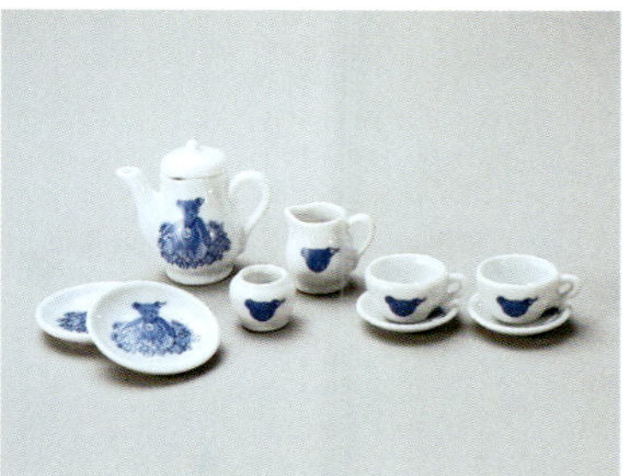

Porzellan Service Teile - *Porcelain Service Parts*

Wandteller/Mini Porzellan Set/Puppen Porzellan Service, Dekor Teddy blau - *wall plate/miniature porcelain set/doll´s porcelain service, Teddy Blue design*

EAN-No.	Period	Pr.	Info
613692	1995-1996	1	10 cm
613708	1995-1996	1	9-teilig - *9-piece set*
613715	1995-1996	1-2	12-teilig - *12-piece set*

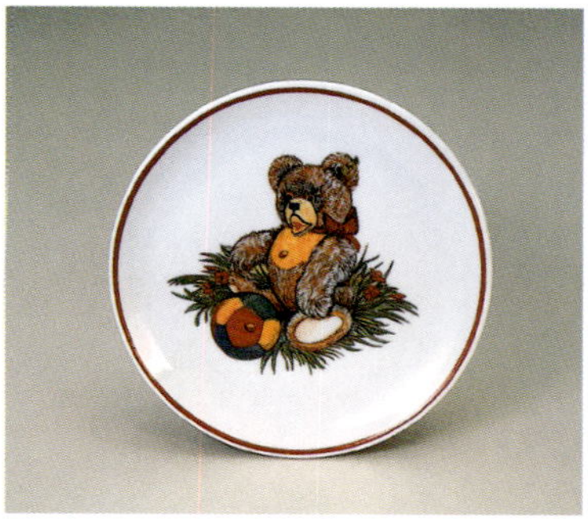

Porzellan Service Teile - *Porcelain Service Parts*

Wandteller/Mini Porzellan Set/Puppen Porzellan Service, Dekor Zotty - *wall plate/miniature porcelain set/doll´s porcelain service, Zotty design*

EAN-No.	Period	Pr.	Info
613739	1996-1997	1	10 cm
613746	1996-1997	1	10-teilig - *10-piece set*
613753	1996-1998	2	12-teilig - *12-piece set*

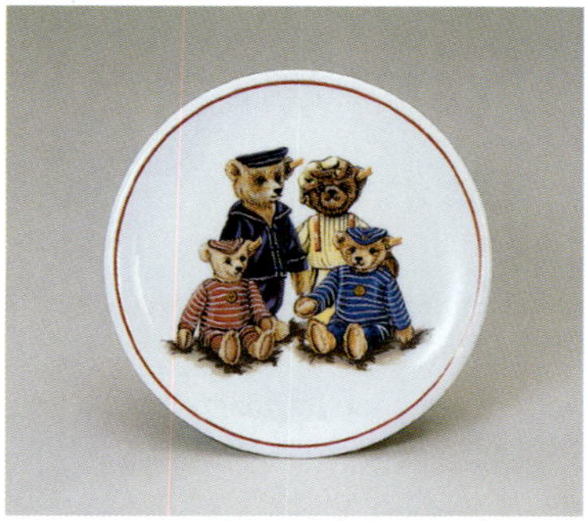

Porzellan Service Teile - *Porcelain Service Parts*

Wandteller/Mini Porzellan Set/Puppen Porzellan Service, Dekor Teddys mit Bekleidung - *wall plate/miniature porcelain set/doll´s porcelain service, Teddies with Clothing design*

EAN-No.	Period	Pr.	Info
613777	1997-1997	1	10 cm
613784	1997-1997	1	10-teilig - *10-piece set*
613791	1997-1997	2	12-teilig - *12-piece set*

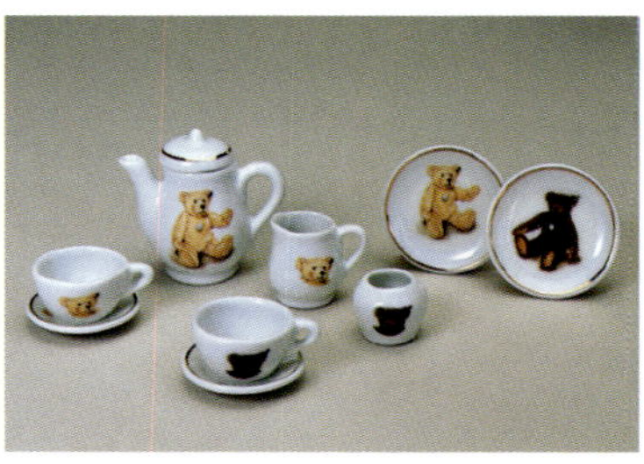

Porzellan Service Teile - *Porcelain Service Parts*

Wandteller/Mini Porzellan Set/Puppen Porzellan Service, Dekor Teddybaeren 1905 - *wall plate/miniature porcelain set/doll´s porcelain service, 1905 Teddy Bear design*

EAN-No.	Period	Pr.	Info
613814	1998-1998	1	10 cm
613821	1998-1998	1	10-teilig - *10-piece set*
613838	1998-1998	2	12-teilig - *12-piece set*

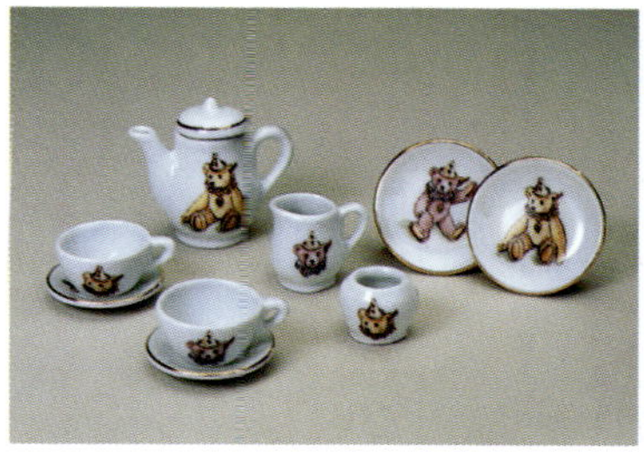

Porzellan Service Teile - *Porcelain Service Parts*

Wandteller/Mini Porzellan Set/Puppen Porzellan Service, Dekor Teddy Clown Rosé - *wall plate/miniature porcelain set/doll´s porcelain service, Teddy Clown Rose design*

EAN-No.	Period	Pr.	Info
613852	1999-1999	1	10 cm
613869	1999-1999	1	10-teilig - *10-piece set*
613876	1999-1999	2	12-teilig - *12-piece set*

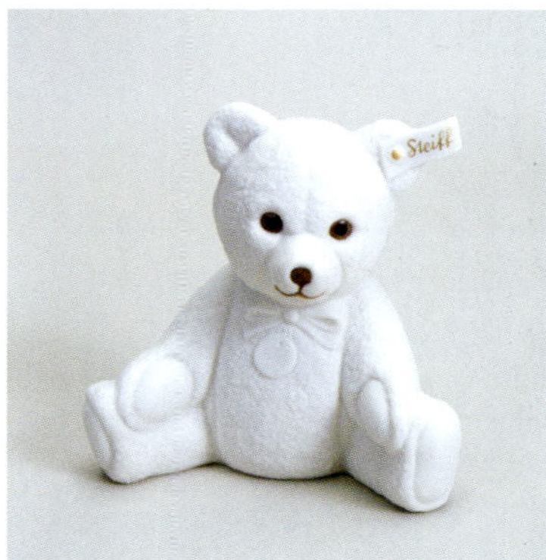

Porzellanfigur Petsy - *Porcelain Petsy Figurine*

Hutschenreuther Edelbisquit-Porzellan, limitierte Auflage 5.000 Stueck - *Hutschenreuther high quality biscuit porcelain, ltd edition of 5.000*

EAN-No.	Period	Pr.	Info
614200	1995-1996	2-3	9 cm

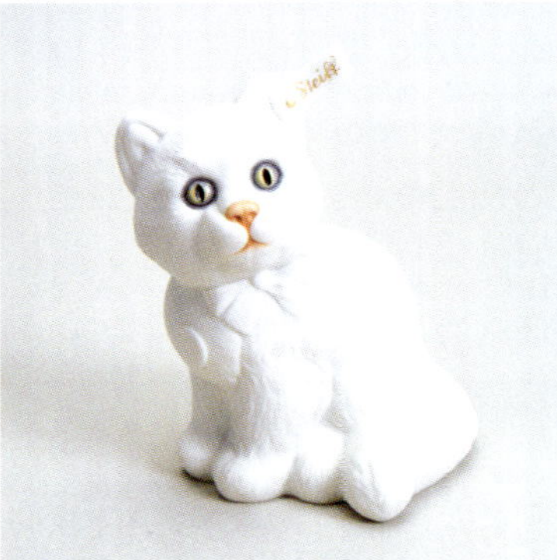

Porzellanfigur Katze - *Porcelain Cat Figurine*

Hutschenreuther Edelbisquit-Porzellan, limitierte Auflage 5.000 Stueck - *Hutschenreuther high quality biscuit porcelain, ltd edition of 5,000*

EAN-No.	Period	Pr.	Info
614217	1995-1996	2-3	10 cm

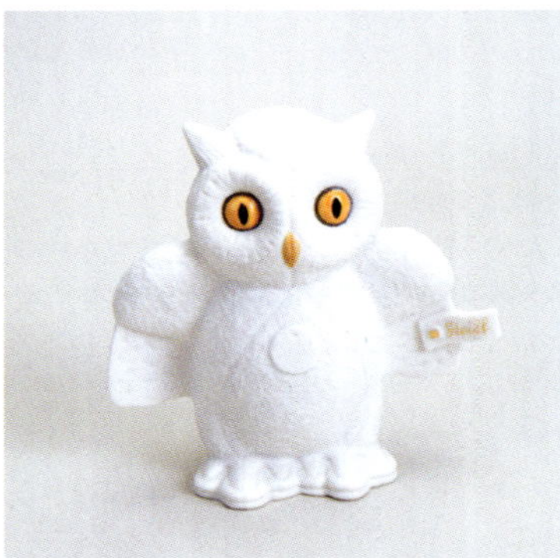

Porzellanfigur Uhu - *Porcelain Owl Figurine*

Hutschenreuther Edelbisquit-Porzellan, limitierte Auflage 5.000 Stueck - *Hutschenreuther high quality biscuit porcelain, ltd edition of 5,000*

EAN-No.	Period	Pr.	Info
614224	1995-1996	2-3	9 cm

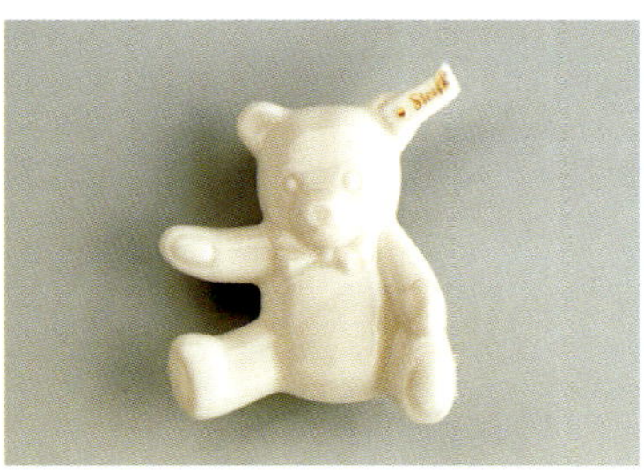

Porzellanbrosche Baer - *Porcelain Bear Brooch*

Hutschenreuther Hartporzellan, weiss - *Hutschenreuther hard porcelain, white*

EAN-No.	Period	Pr.	Info
614507	1995-1996	1-2	5 cm

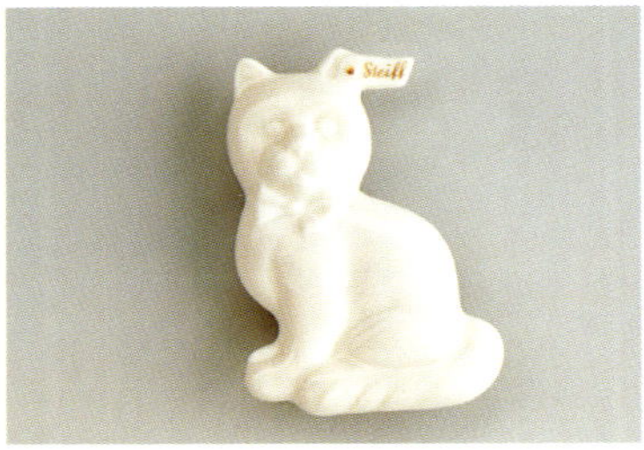

Porzellanbrosche Katze - *Porcelain Cat Brooch*

Hutschenreuther Hartporzellan, weiss - *Hutschenreuther hard porcelain, white*

EAN-No.	Period	Pr.	Info
614514	1995-1996	1-2	5 cm

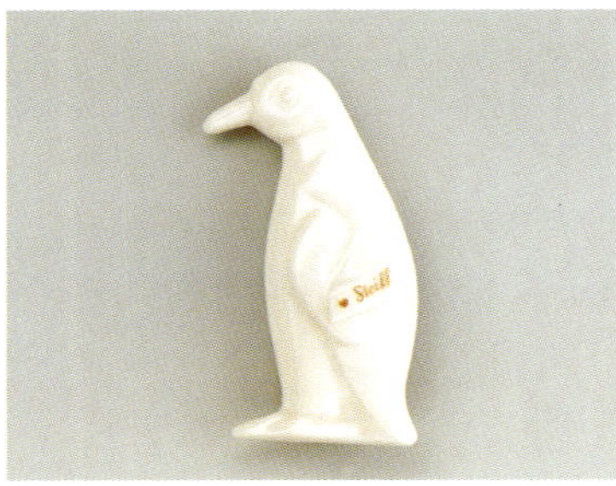

Porzellanbrosche Pinguin - *Porcelain Penguin Brooch*

Hutschenreuther Hartporzellan, weiss - *Hutschenreuther hard porcelain, white*

EAN-No.	Period	Pr.	Info
614521	1995-1996	1-2	6 cm

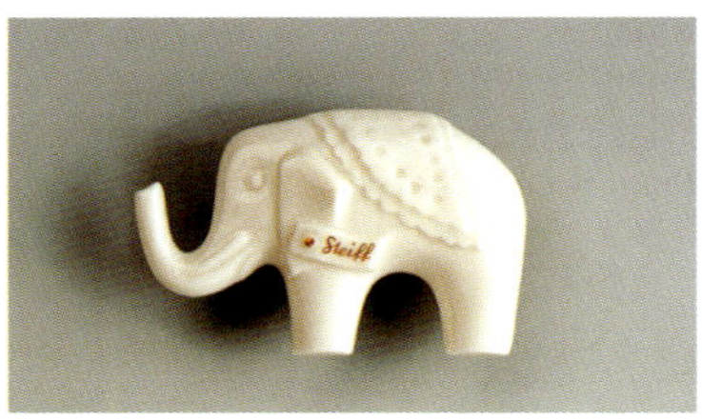

Porzellanbrosche Elefant - *Porcelain Elephant Brooch*

Hutschenreuther Hartporzellan, weiss - *Hutschenreuther hard porcelain, white*

EAN-No.	Period	Pr.	Info
614538	1995-1996	1-2	5 cm

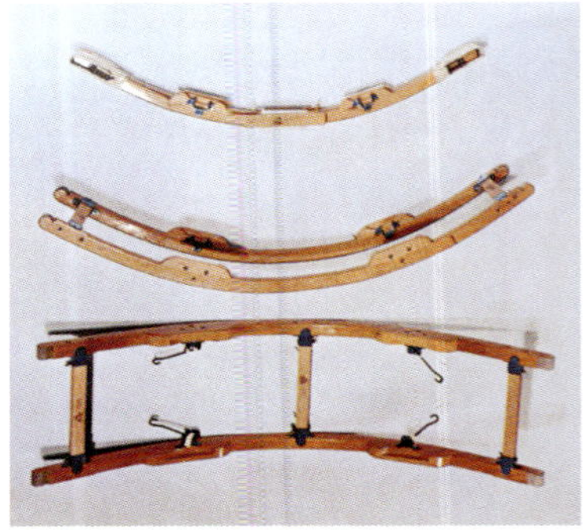

Wiegenlaeufel - *Rocker*

Zubehoer fuer Reittiere, Hartholz, natur - *accessories for riding animals made of natural hardwood*

Serie	Art.-No	Period	Pr.	Info
73	843	1950-1954	3	fuer Reittiere der Groesse 43 - *for size 43 riding animals*
73	9843	1956-1958	3	
750	9843,00	1959-1964	3	
820	9843,00	1965-1967	3	
	8200/43	1968-1968	3	
73	850	1950-1954	3	fuer Reittiere der Groesse 50 - *for size 50 riding animals*
73	9850	1956-1958	3	
750	9850,00	1959-1964	3	
820	9850,00	1965-1967	3	
	8200/50	1968-1968	3	
73	860	1950-1954	3	fuer Reittiere der Groesse 60 - *for size 60 riding animals*
73	9860	1956-1958	3	
750	9860,00	1959-1964	3	
820	9860,00	1965-1967	3	
	8200/60	1968-1968	3	
73	880	1950-1954	3	fuer Reittiere der Groesse 80 - *for size 80 riding animals*
73	9880	1955-1957	3	
750	9880,00	1961-1961	3	
820	9880,00	1965-1967	3	
	8200/80	1963-1968	3	

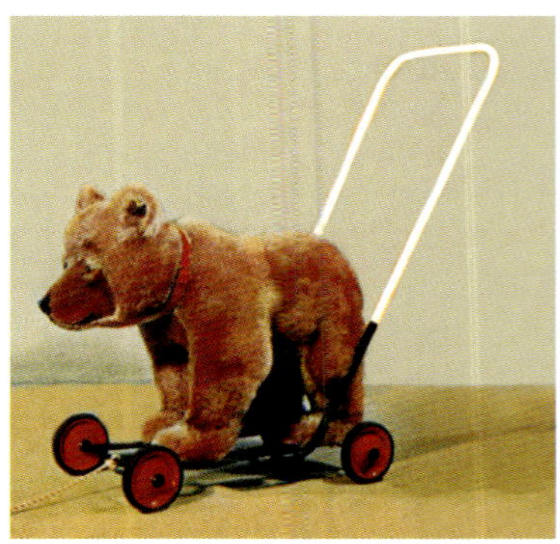

Schiebegriff fuer Reittiere - *Push Handle for Riding Animals*

mittels Schrauben an Reittiere 1343 - 60 anzubringen - *to be fastened to the riding animals 1343 - 60 by means of screws*

SERIE	ART.-NO	PERIOD	PR.	INFO
73	985	1951-1956	3	

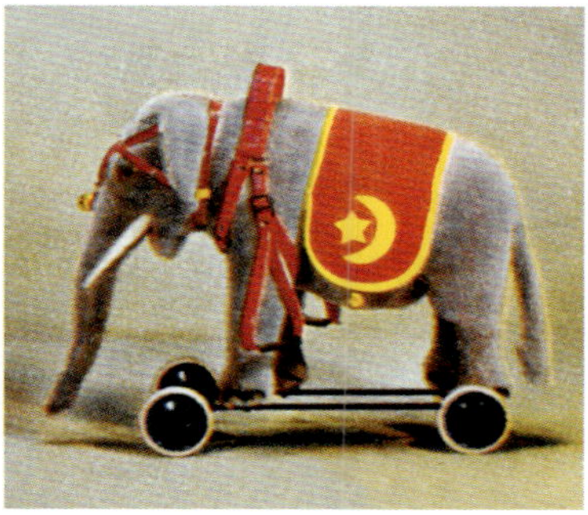

Paar Steigbuegel / Reitgriff - *Pair of Stirrups / Grip Handle*

Steigbuegel: nur in Verbindung mit Reitgriff verwendbar, Reitgriff: fuer Reittiere 1343,2, 1350,2, 1360,2 & 1380,2, mit Steigbuegeln, zum Festschnallen mit Riemen - *stirrups: may only be used in conjunction with grip handle / grip handle: for riding animals 1343,2, 1350,2, 1360,2 & 1380,2, complete with stirrups, fasten tight with straps*

SERIE	ART.-NO	PERIOD	PR.	INFO
73	917	1953-1954	2	
73	916/4	1953-1954	3	
73	916/6	1953-1954	3	
73	625/2	1955-1957	3	

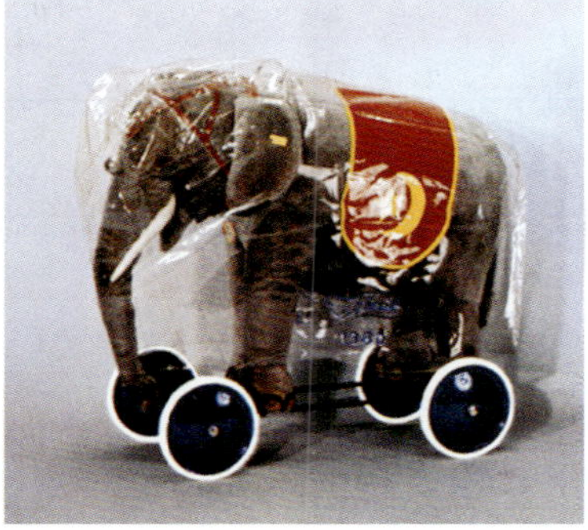

Plastik-Huelle - *Plastic Cover*

Plastik, glasklar, zur Schonung fuer alle Reittiere 1343, 1350, 1360 & 1380 - *clear plastic cover as protective for riding animals 1343, 1350, 1360, & 1380*

SERIE	ART.-NO	PERIOD	PR.	INFO
73	043	1957-1957	1	1343
826	0743,00	1966-1966	1	
73	050	1957-1957	1	1350
826	0750,00	1966-1966	1	
73	060	1957-1957	1	1360
826	0760,00	1966-1966	1	
73	080	1957-1957	1	1380
826	0780,00	1966-1966	1	

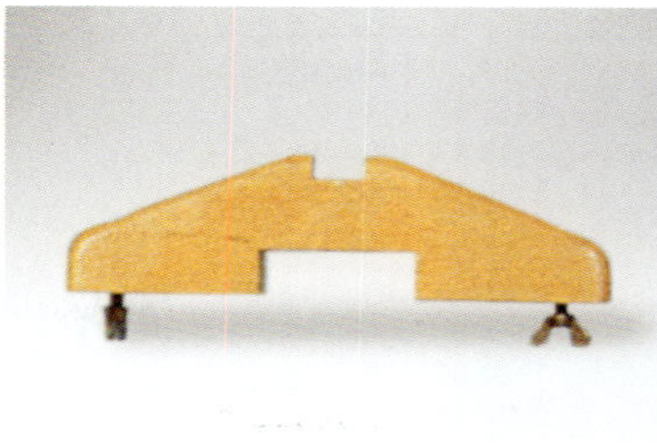

Zusatzsteg Wiegenlaeufel - *Additional Crosspiece for Rocker*

Holz, natur, fuer Reit-Fisch (Wiege 50 cm) - *natural wood, to be used for riding fish (rocker 50 cm)*

SERIE	ART.-NO	PERIOD	PR.	INFO
820	9855,00	1965-1967	1	
	8200/55	1968-1968	1	

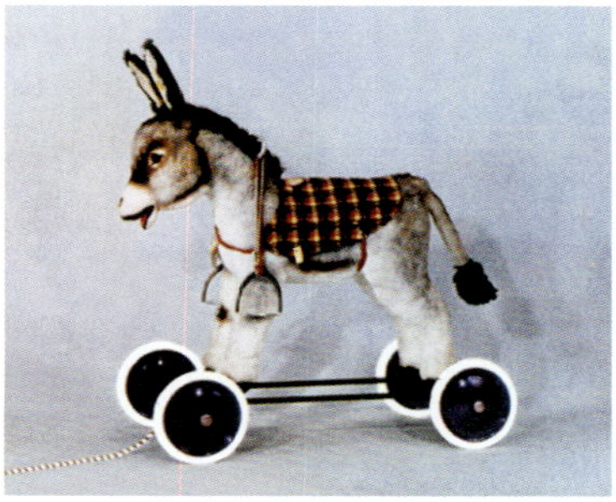

Satteldecke - *Saddlecloth*

dicker Stoff, mit Schnallriemen, Schondecke fuer Reittiere 1343, 1350 & 1360 - *saddlecloth of thick fabric, with fastening straps, as protective cover for riding animals 1343, 1350 & 1360*

SERIE	ART.-NO	PERIOD	PR.	INFO
824	7643,00	1966-1967	3	1343
	8240/43	1968-1968	3	
824	7650,60	1966-1967	3	1350 & 1360
	8240/50	1968-1968	3	

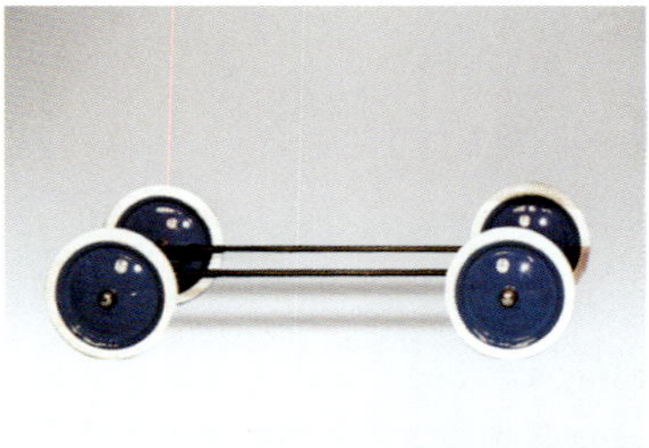

Wechsel-Rahmen - *Exchangeable Frame*

fuer Wiegen-Esel & -Pony zur Umwandlung in ein Reittier auf Raedern - *for rocking donkey & rocking pony, so they can be used as riding animals on wheels*

SERIE	ART.-NO	PERIOD	PR.	INFO
822	4955,50	1966-1967	3	
	8220/55	1968-1968	3	

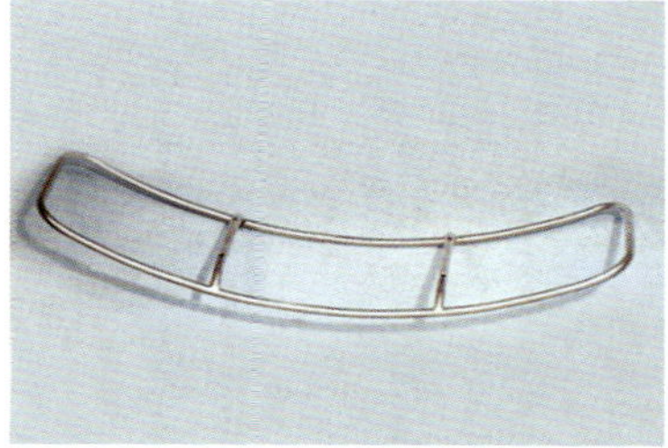

Wechselwiege - *Exchangeable Rocker*

fuer Reit-Esel & -Pony zur Umwandlung in ein Wiegentier - *for riding donkey & riding pony, so they can be used as rocking animals*

SERIE	ART.-NO	PERIOD	PR.	INFO
	8220/60	1968-1968	2	

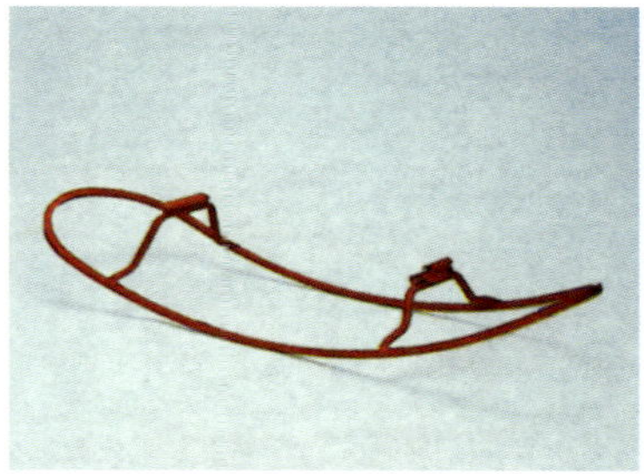

Stahlwiege - *Steel Rocker*

Stahlrohr, rot fuer Reittiere Groesse /30, /40, /43, /50, /60 & /80 - *red steel tube for riding animals in the following sizes: /30, /40, /43, /50, /60 & /80*

SERIE	ART.-NO	PERIOD	PR.	INFO
	8210/43	1969-1984	2	30/40/43
	8210/50	1969-1983	2	50
	8210/60	1969-1983	2	60
	8210/30	1970-1975	2	80

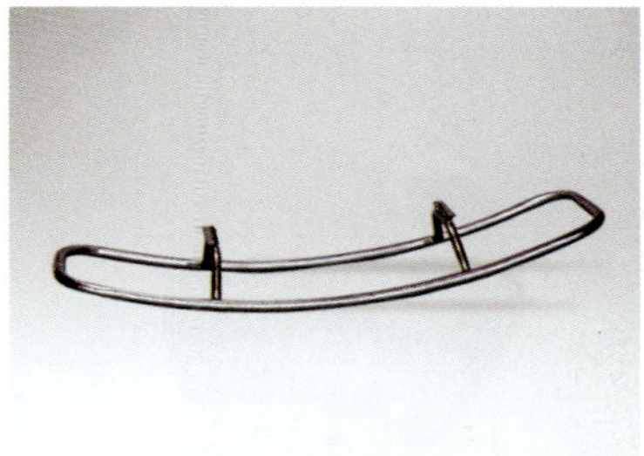

Stahlrohr-Wiege - *Steel Tube Rocker*

chromfarben, fuer Reittiere 1399,20 - *chrome-color, for riding animals 1399,20*

SERIE	ART.-NO	PERIOD	PR.	INFO
750	9999,00	1964-1964	2	
820	9999,00	1966-1966	2	

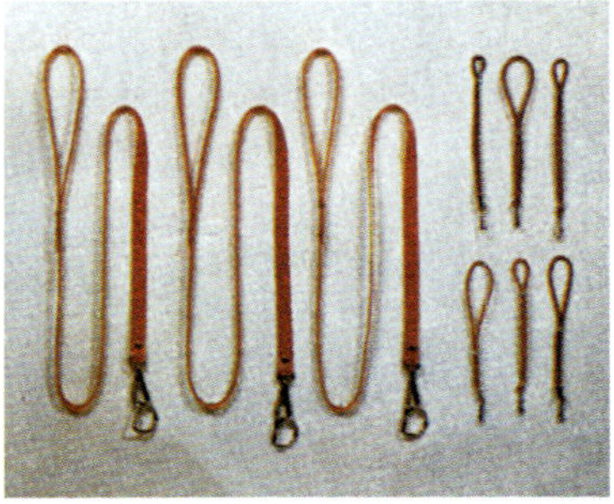

Mascot Band - *Mascot Leashes*

Gummikordel mit Schieber & Karabiner - *rubber cords with slide & swivel clip*

SERIE	ART.-NO	PERIOD	PR.	INFO
73	12	1956-1957	1	12 cm
752	7712,00	1961-1961	1	
828	7712,00	1966-1967	1	
	8280/12	1968-1971	1	

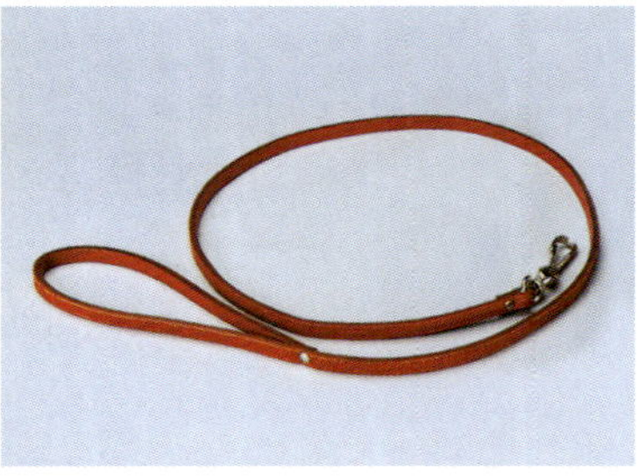

Hundeleine - *Dog Leash*

Plastik, mit Karabiner, rot, gruen oder gelb - *plastic dog leash with swivel clip in either red, green or yellow*

SERIE	ART.-NO	PERIOD	PR.	INFO
73	675	1955-1957	1	75 cm
754	7775,08	1961-1961	1	
829	7775,08	1966-1967	1	
	8290/75	1968-1970	1	

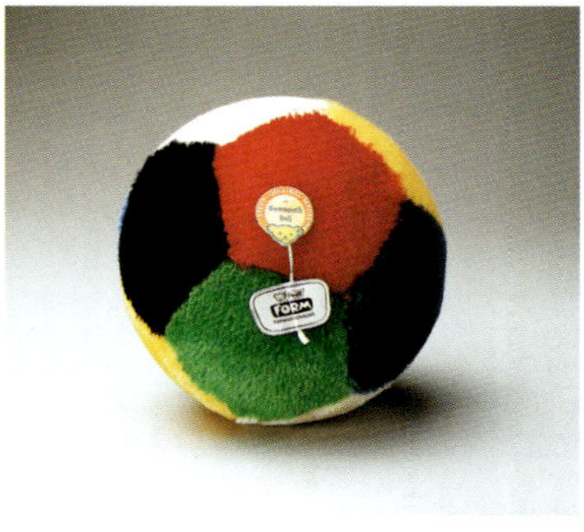

Gymnastik Ball - *Gymnastics Ball*

Mohairpluesch, Spezialfuellung, ab 1976 formgeschaeumt, Mosaikball in 6 Farben, abwaschbar - *mohair, special stuffing, from 1976 stuffed with pre-formed foam, mosaic pattern in 6 colors, surface washable*

SERIE	ART.-NO	PERIOD	PR.	INFO
87	**315**	1950-1958	3	15 cm
855	**7315,07**	1959-1964	2-3	
640	**7315,07**	1965-1967	2-3	
	6400/15	1968-1982	2	
87	**317**	1950-1954	3-4	17 cm
87	**320**	1950-1958	3	20 cm
855	**7320,07**	1959-1964	2-3	
640	**7320,07**	1965-1967	2-3	
	6400/20	1968-1982	2	
87	**322**	1950-1954	3-4	22 cm
87	**325**	1950-1958	3-4	25 cm
855	**7325,07**	1959-1964	3	
640	**7325,07**	1965-1967	3	
	6400/25	1968-1968	3	
	6407/25	1969-1977	2-3	

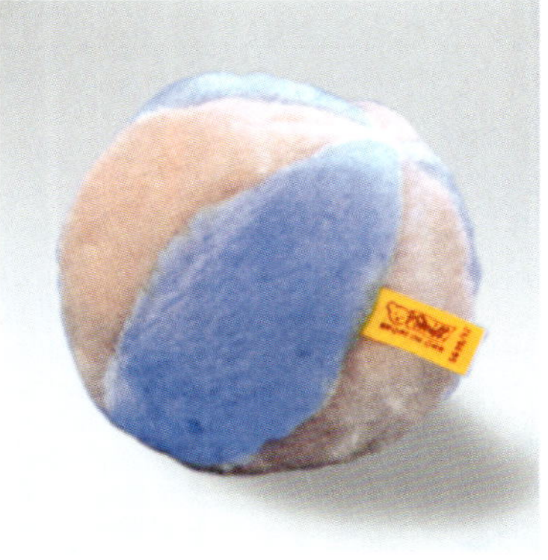

Baby Ball

Webpelz, blau/rosa, waschmaschinenfest - *woven fur, blue & pink, machine washable*

SERIE	ART.-NO	PERIOD	PR.	INFO
201790	**5698/12**	1983-1987	1	12 cm

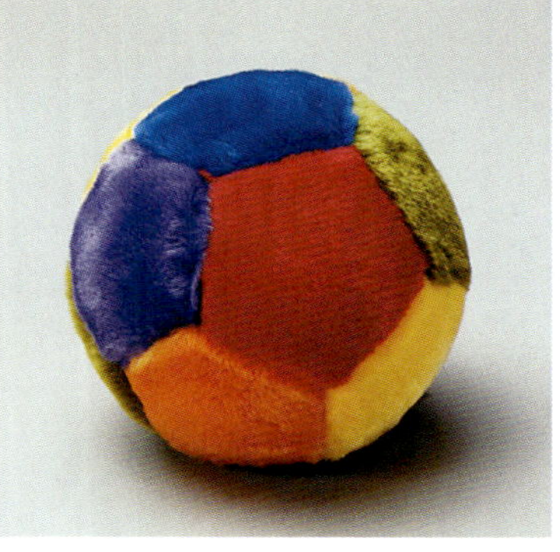

Ball

Webpelz, formgeschaeumt, waschmaschinenfest - *woven fur, stuffed with pre-formed foam, machine washable*

SERIE	ART.-NO	PERIOD	PR.	INFO
205224	**6450/15**	1983-1990	1-2	15 cm
	205224	1991-1999	1-2	
205255	**6450/20**	1983-1990	1-2	20 cm
	205255	1991-1993	1-2	

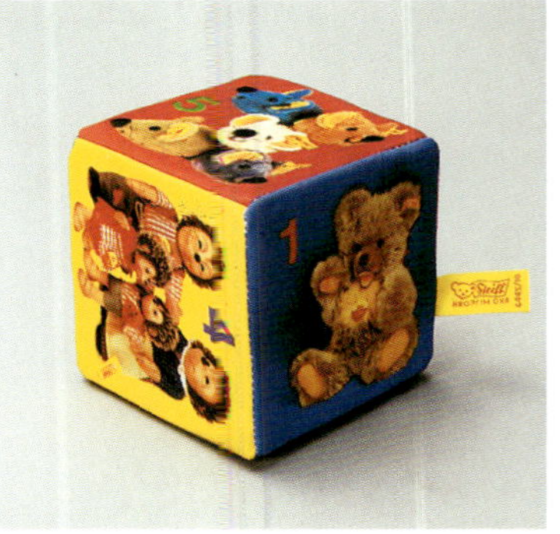

Wuerfel - *Cube*

Trevirasamt, waschmaschinenfest - *trevira velvet, machine washable*

SERIE	ART.-NO	PERIOD	PR.	INFO
205170	**6445/10**	1982-1986	2	10 cm

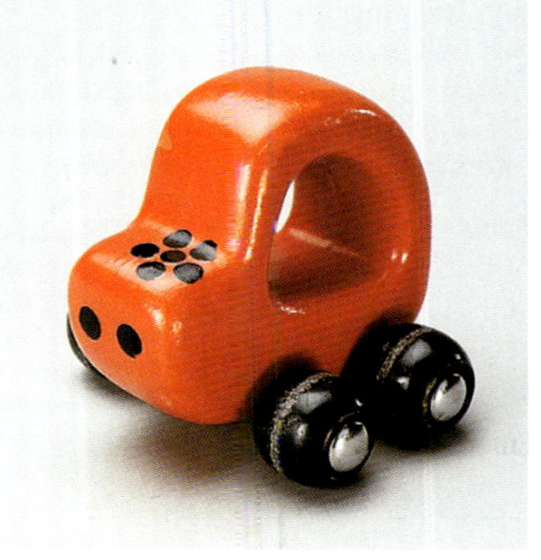

Baby Roll

Auto, babygerecht - *baby-size car*

SERIE	ART.-NO	PERIOD	PR.	INFO
	8340/08	1975-1982	1	8 cm

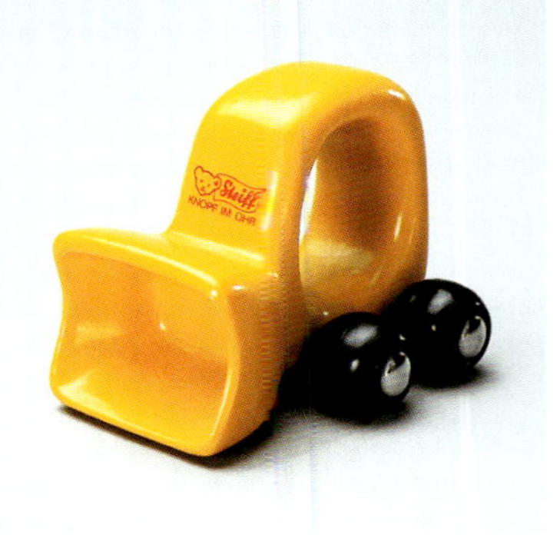

Baby Digg

Radlader, babygerecht - *baby-size digger*

SERIE	ART.-NO	PERIOD	PR.	INFO
	8341/08	1975-1978	1	8 cm

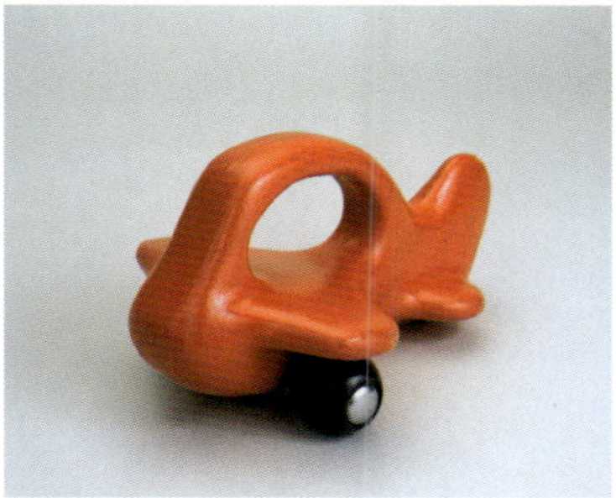

Baby Jet

Flugzeug, babygerecht - *baby-size airplane*

SERIE	ART.-NO	PERIOD	PR.	INFO
	8342/08	1975-1982	1	8 cm

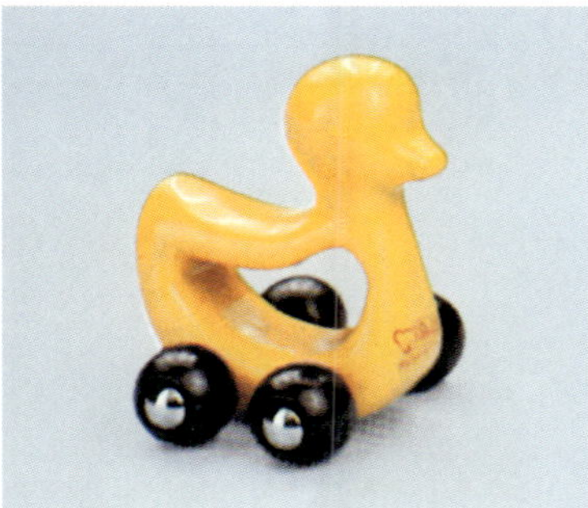

Baby Ente - *Baby Duck*

Ente, babygerecht - *baby-size duck*

SERIE	ART.-NO	PERIOD	PR.	INFO
	8343/08	1975-1983	1	8 cm

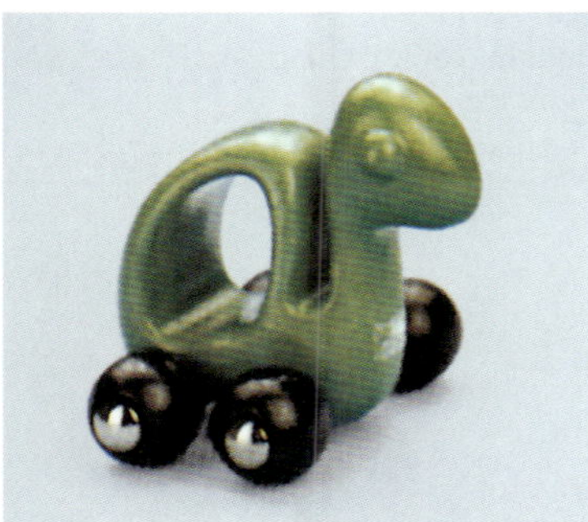

Baby Slo

Schildkroete, babygerecht - *baby-size turtle*

SERIE	ART.-NO	PERIOD	PR.	INFO
	8344/08	1975-1984	1	8 cm

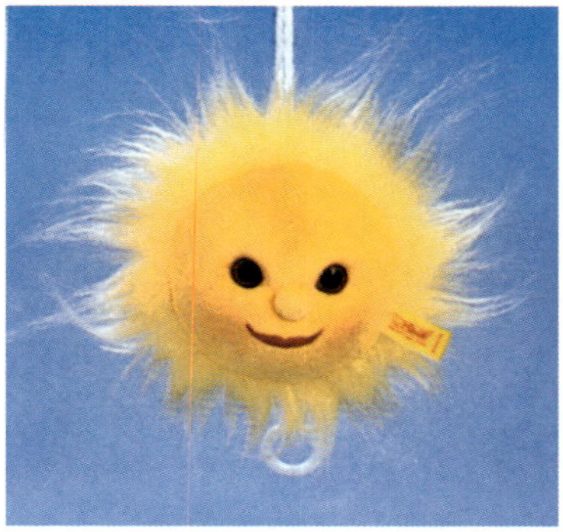

Musik-Sonne - *Musical Sun*

Nicki-Stoff, formgeschaeumt, Musikwerk austauschbar - *nicki fabric, stuffed with pre-formed foam, music box is exchangeable*

SERIE	ART.-NO	PERIOD	PR.	INFO
233937	**6384/18**	1978-1987	2	18 cm

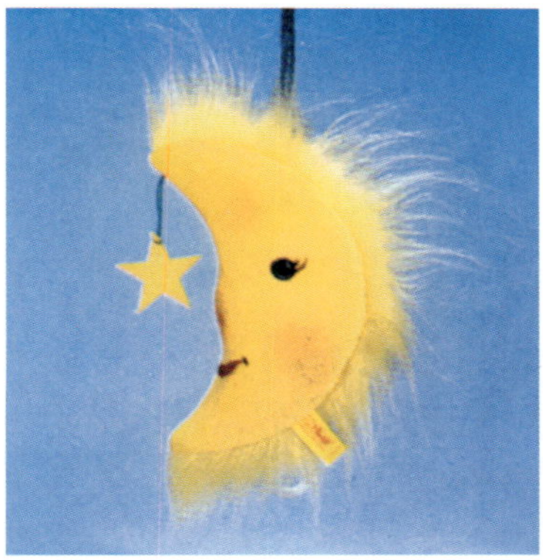

Musik-Mond - *Musical Moon*

Nicki-Stoff, formgeschaeumt, Musikwerk austauschbar - *nicki fabric, stuffed with pre-formed foam, music box is exchangeable*

SERIE	ART.-NO	PERIOD	PR.	INFO
233951	**6385/18**	1978-1988	2	18 cm

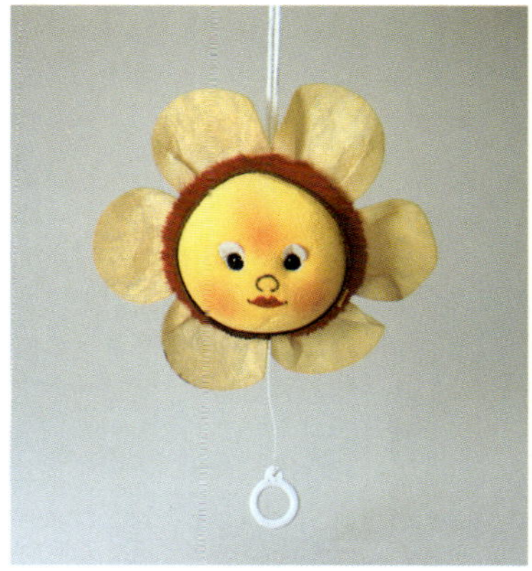

Musik-Bluete - *Musical Flower*

Nicki-Stoff, formgeschaeumt, Musikwerk austauschbar - *nicki fabric, stuffed with pre-formed foam, music box is exchangeable*

SERIE	ART.-NO	PERIOD	PR.	INFO
233975	**6387/18**	1978-1986	2	18 cm

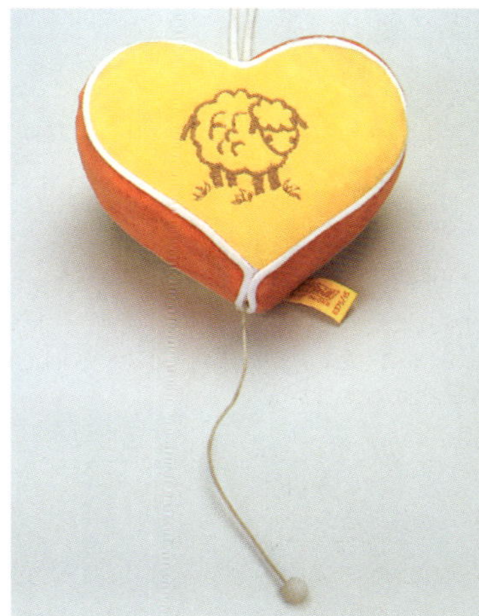

Musik Herz - *Musical Heart*

Nicki-Stoff, blau/gelb oder gelb/orange, Musikwerk austauschbar - *nicki fabric, blue/yellow or yellow/orange, music box is exchangeable*

SERIE	ART.-NO	PERIOD	PR.	INFO
233371	**6374/15**	1981-1988	2	blau/gelb - *blue/yellow*
233388	**6375/15**	1981-1988	2	gelb/orange - *yellow/orange*

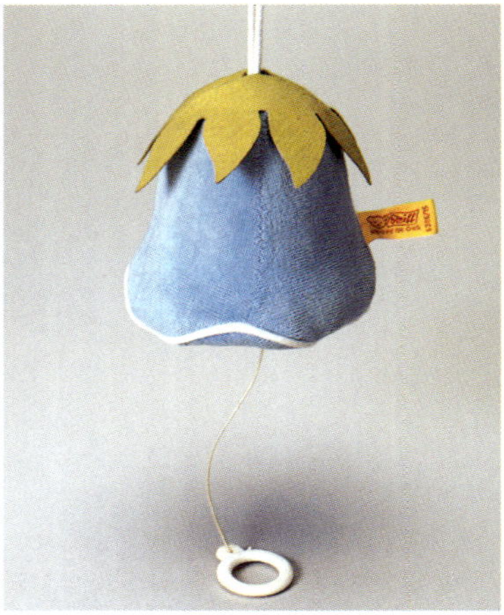

Musik Glockenblume - *Musical Bluebell Flower*

Nicki-Stoff, formgeschaeumt, rot oder blau, Musikwerk austauschbar - *nicki fabric, stuffed with pre-formed foam, red or blue, music box is exchangeable*

Serie	Art.-No	Period	Pr.	Info
	6386/14	1983-1984	2	14 cm, rot - *red*
	6386/15	1982-1984	2	15 cm, blau - *blue*

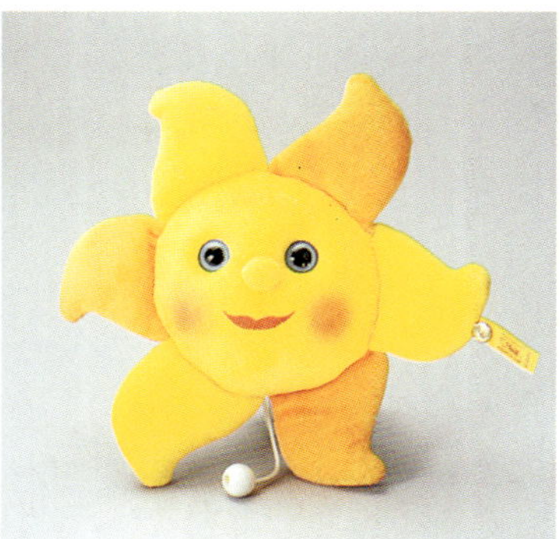

Musik Sonne - *Musical Sun*

Nicki-Stoff, formgeschaeumt, Musikwerk austauschbar - *nicki fabric, stuffed with pre-formed foam, music box is exchangeable*

Serie	Art.-No	Period	Pr.	Info
233920	**6384/20**	1988-1990	2	20 cm
	233920	1991-1999	2	

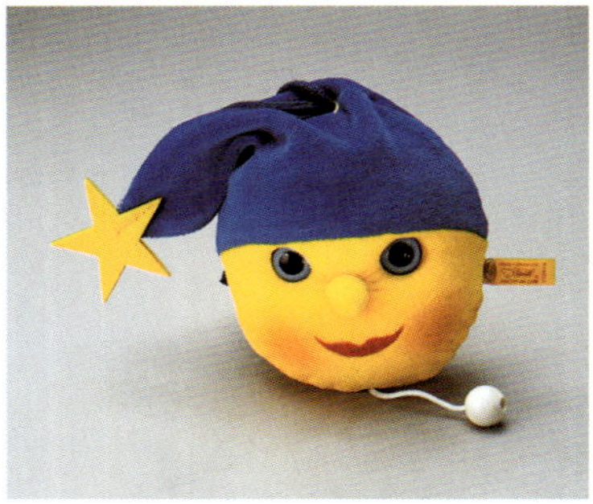

Musik Mond - *Musical Moon*

Nicki-Stoff, formgeschaeumt, Musikwerk austauschbar - *nicki fabric, stuffed with pre-formed foam, music box is exchangeable*

Serie	Art.-No	Period	Pr.	Info
233944	**6385/20**	1988-1990	2	20 cm
	233944	1991-1999	2	

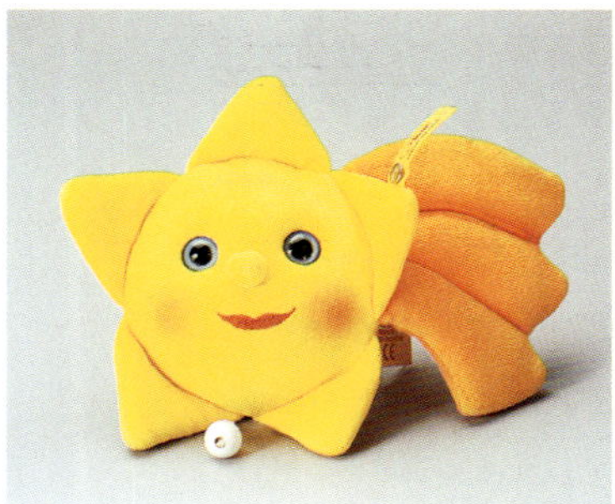

Musik Stern - *Musical Star*

Nicki-Stoff, formgeschaeumt, Musikwerk austauschbar - *nicki fabric, stuffed with pre-formed foam, music box is exchangeable*

EAN-No.	Period	Pr.	Info
233876	1994-1996	2	25 cm

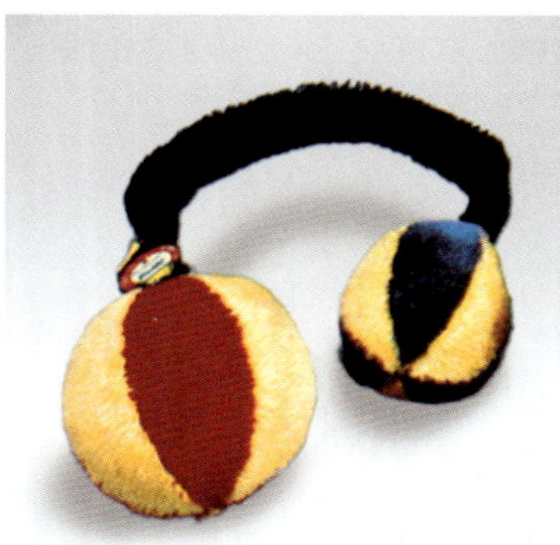

Doppelball - *Double Balls*

Mohair, 2 zusammenhaengende Baelle - *mohair, 2 balls connected together*

Serie	Art.-No	Period	Pr.	Info
	6410/12	1970-1974	2-3	12 cm

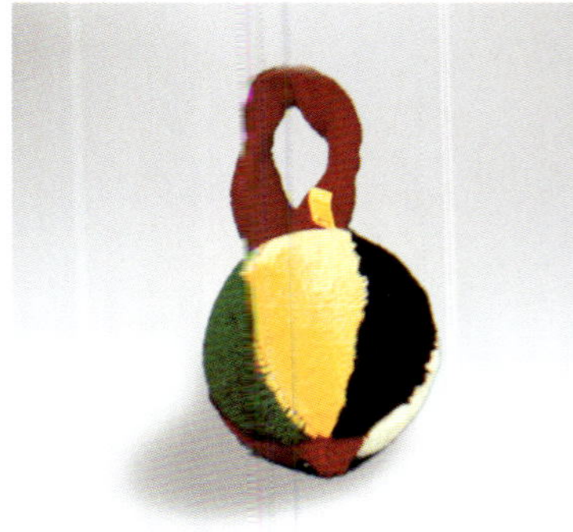

Schleuderball - *Swinging Ball*

Mohair, formgeschaeumt, mit Laeutwerk - *mohair, stuffed with pre-formed foam, with bell sound*

Serie	Art.-No	Period	Pr.	Info
	6411/12	1970-1973	2	12 cm
	6412/15	1970-1977	2	15 cm

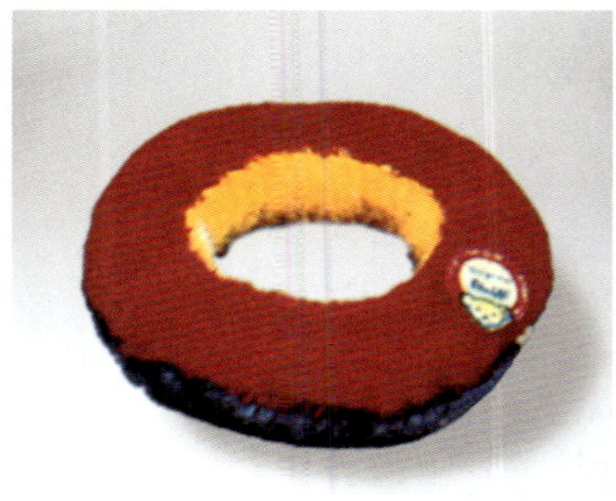

Spielring - *Play Ring*

Mohair, vollwaschbar - *mohair, fully washable*

Serie	Art.-No	Period	Pr.	Info
	6413/16	1970-1974	2	16 cm

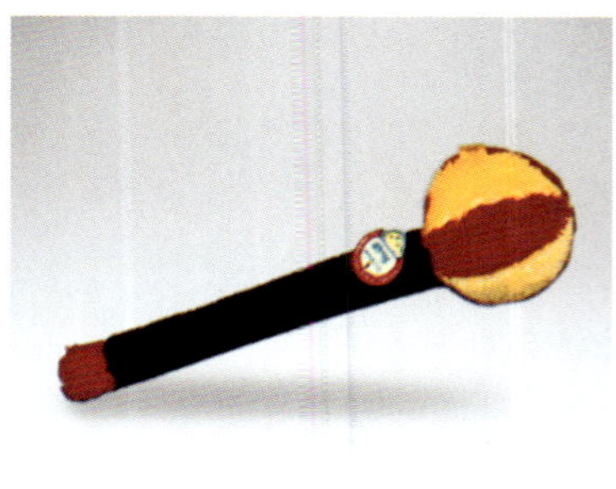

Trommelschlegel - *Drum Stick*

Mohair, vollwaschbar - *mohair, fully washable*

Serie	Art.-No	Period	Pr.	Info
	6414/30	1970-1974	2-3	30 cm

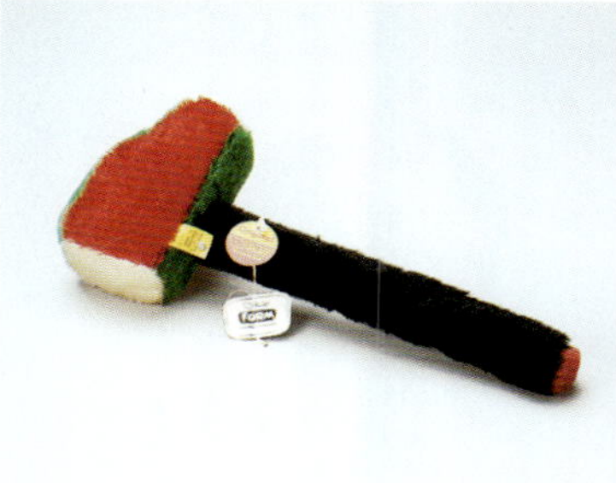

Hammer

Mohair, vollwaschbar - *mohair, fully washable*

SERIE	ART.-NO	PERIOD	PR.	INFO
	6415/30	1970-1974	2-3	30 cm

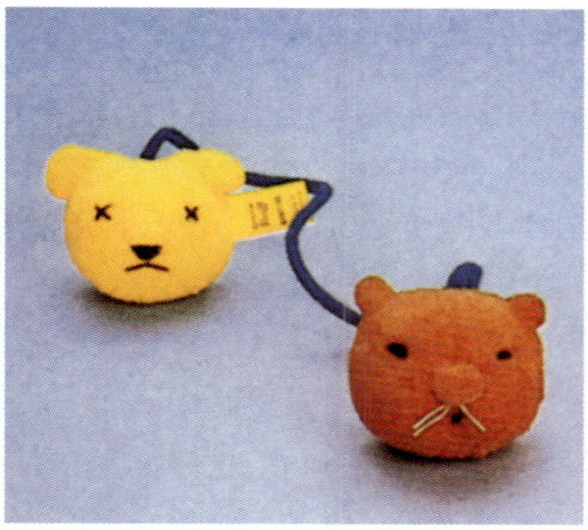

Wiegengehaenge - *Crib Decoration*

Nicki-Stoff, formgeschaeumt, mit Schellen - *nicki fabric, stuffed with pre-formed foam, with bells*

SERIE	ART.-NO	PERIOD	PR.	INFO
	6407/10	1980-1984	2	10 cm

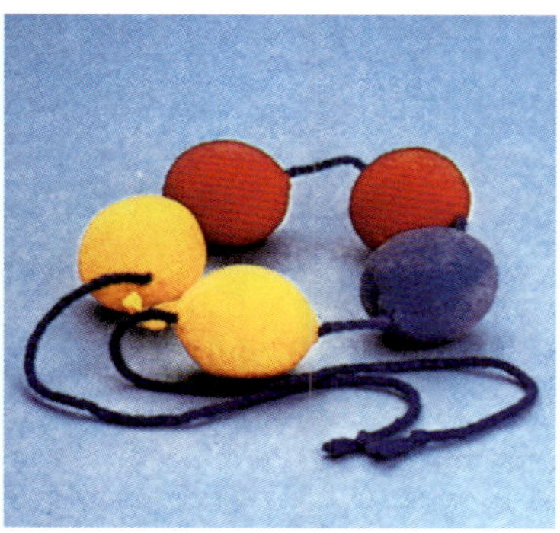

Wagenkette - *Pram Toy*

Nicki-Stoff, formgeschaeumt, mit Schellen - *nicki fabric, stuffed with pre-formed foam, with bells*

SERIE	ART.-NO	PERIOD	PR.	INFO
	6408/30	1980-1985	1	30 cm

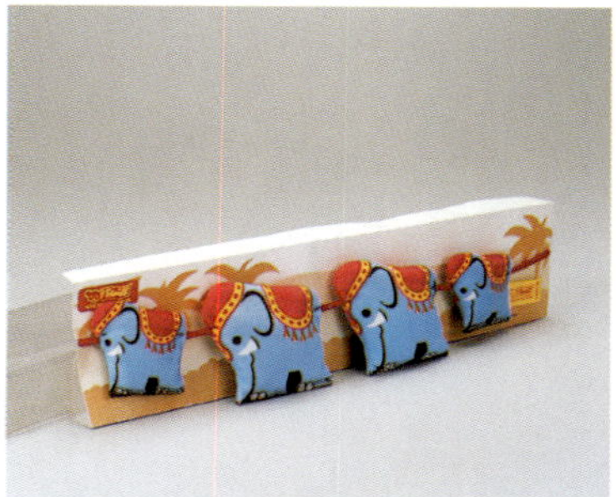

Wagenkette Elefanten - *Elephant Pram Toy*

Trevirasamt, mit Schellen, waschmaschinenfest - *trevira velvet, with bells, machine washable*

SERIE	ART.-NO	PERIOD	PR.	INFO
	6406/30	1982-1985	2	30 cm

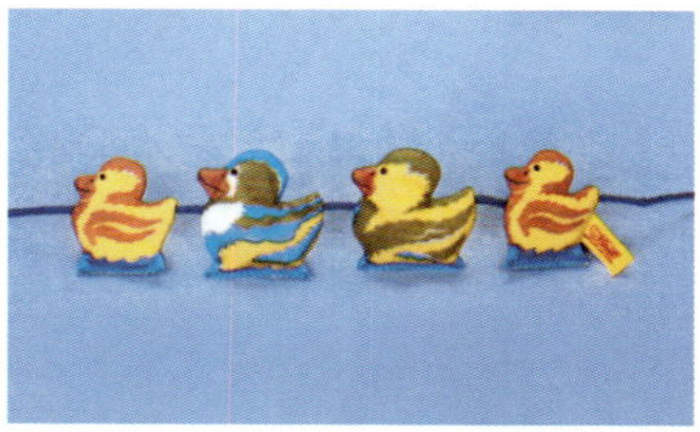

Wagenkette Enten - *Duck Pram Toy*

Trevirasamt, mit Schellen, waschmaschinenfest - *trevira velvet, with bells, machine washable*

SERIE	ART.-NO	PERIOD	PR.	INFO
	6406/32	1982-1985	2	30 cm

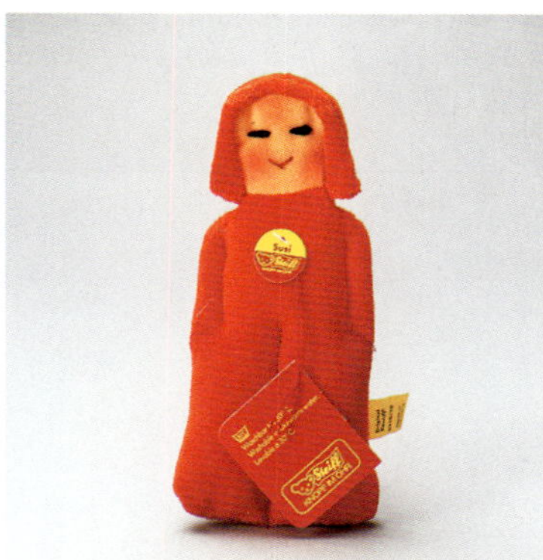

Susi Puppe - ***Susi** Doll*

Nicki-Stoff, vollwaschbar - *nicki fabric, fully washable*

SERIE	ART.-NO	PERIOD	PR.	INFO
	6416/19	1980-1981	1	19 cm

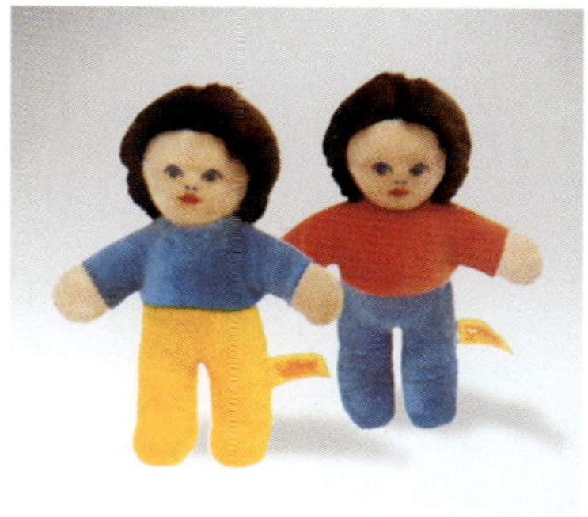

Baby Puppe - *Baby Doll*

Nicki-Stoff, formgeschaeumt, 18 cm, rot/blau oder blau/gelb, waschmaschinenfest - *nicki fabric, stuffed with pre-formed foam, 18 cm, red & blue or yellow & blue, machine washable*

SERIE	ART.-NO	PERIOD	PR.	INFO
	6417/18	1981-1981	2	rot/blau - *red/blue*
	6418/18	1981-1981	2	blau/gelb - *blue/yellow*

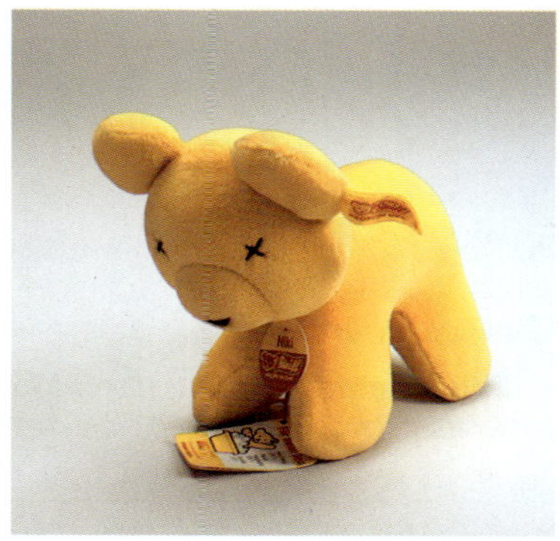

Niki-Baer - ***Niki** Bear*

Nicki-Stoff, formgeschaeumt, gelb - *nicki fabric, stuffed with pre-formed foam, yellow*

SERIE	ART.-NO	PERIOD	PR.	INFO
	7840/14	1976-1985	1	14 cm

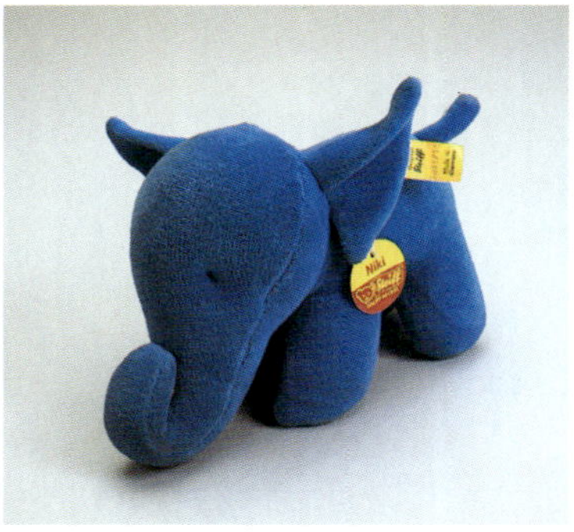

Niki-Elefant - ***Niki** Elephant*

Nicki-Stoff, formgeschaeumt, blau - *nicki fabric, stuffed with pre-formed foam, blue*

SERIE	ART.-NO	PERIOD	PR.	INFO
205422	**7841/14**	1976-1986	1	14 cm

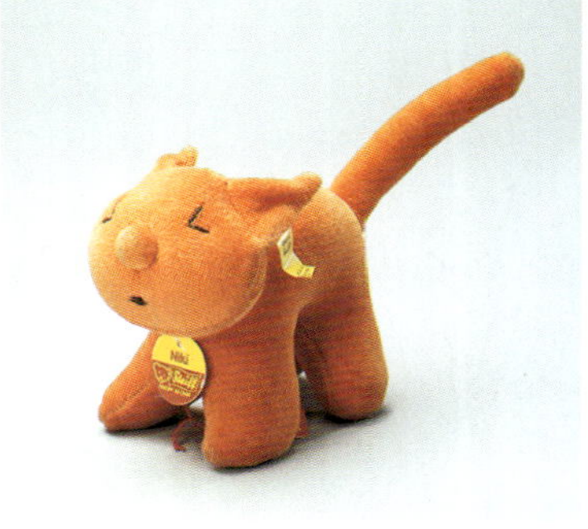

Niki-Katze - ***Niki** Cat*

Nicki-Stoff, formgeschaeumt, rot - *nicki fabric, stuffed with pre-formed foam, red*

SERIE	ART.-NO	PERIOD	PR.	INFO
205446	**7842/14**	1976-1986	1	14 cm

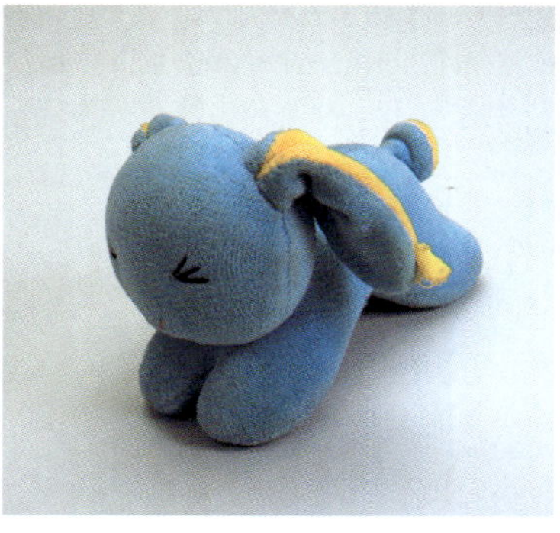

Niki-Hase - ***Niki** Rabbit*

Nicki-Stoff, formgeschaeumt, blau - *nicki fabric, stuffed with pre-formed foam, blue*

SERIE	ART.-NO	PERIOD	PR.	INFO
205460	**7843/14**	1976-1986	1	14 cm

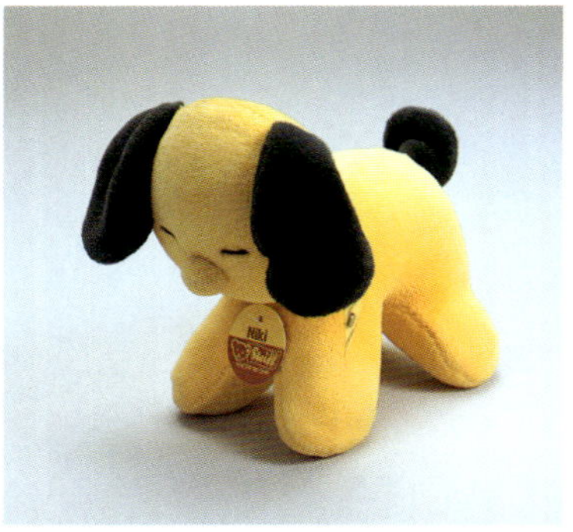

Niki-Hund - ***Niki** Dog*

Nicki-Stoff, formgeschaeumt, gelb - *nicki fabric, stuffed with pre-formed foam, yellow*

SERIE	ART.-NO	PERIOD	PR.	INFO
	7844/14	1976-1983	1	14 cm

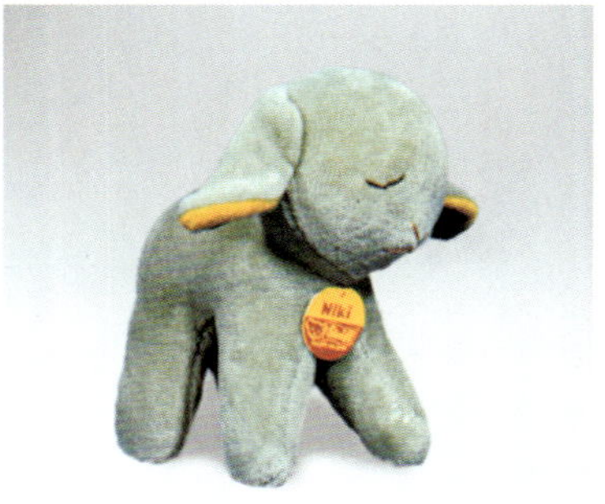

Niki-Lamm - ***Niki** Lamb*

Nicki-Stoff, formgeschaeumt, hellgruen - *nicki fabric, stuffed with pre-formed foam, light green*

SERIE	ART.-NO	PERIOD	PR.	INFO
	7845/14	1976-1979	1	14 cm

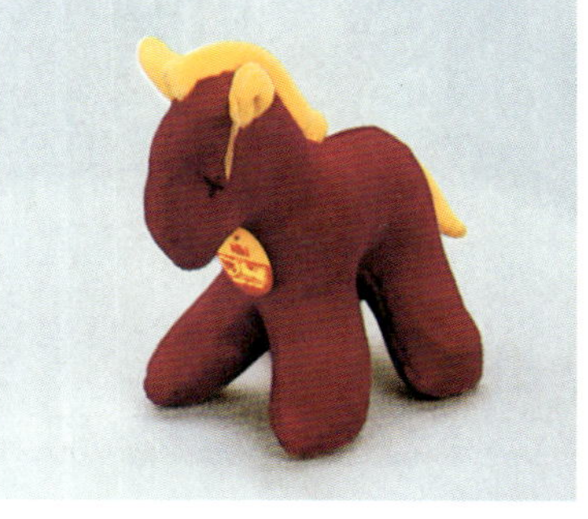

Niki-Pony - ***Niki** Pony*

Nicki-Stoff, formgeschaeumt, rotbraun - *nicki fabric, stuffed with pre-formed foam, reddish-brown*

SERIE	ART.-NO	PERIOD	PR.	INFO
205484	**7846/14**	1976-1986	1	14 cm

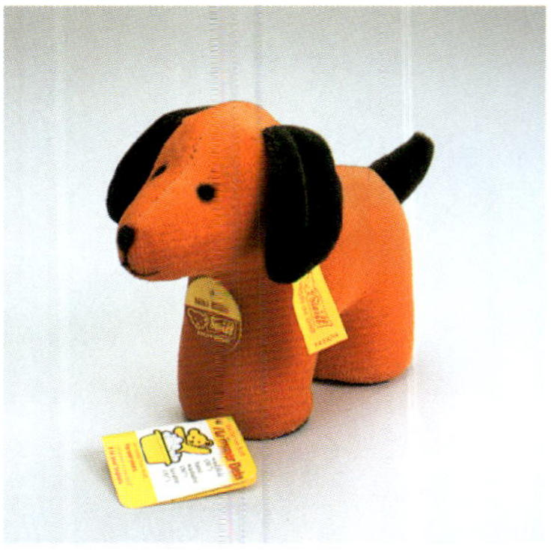

Niki Bello

Nicki-Stoff, formgeschaeumt, waschbar - *nicki fabric, stuffed with pre-formed foam, washable*

SERIE	ART.-NO	PERIOD	PR.	INFO
	7834/14	1980-1983	1	14 cm

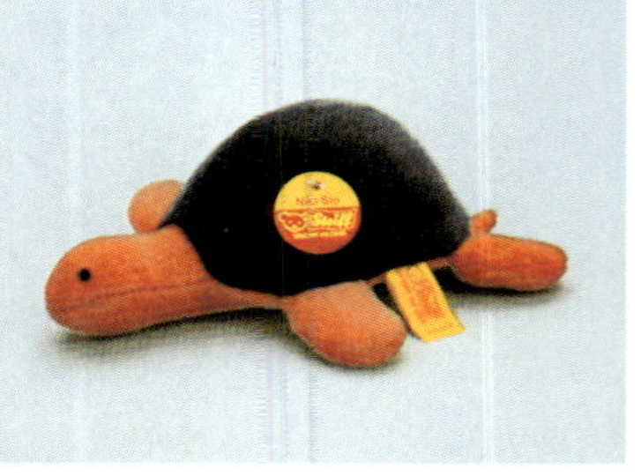

Niki Slo Schildkroete - ***Niki Slo** Turtle*

Nicki-Stoff, formgeschaeumt, waschbar - *nicki fabric, stuffed with pre-formed foam, washable*

SERIE	ART.-NO	PERIOD	PR.	INFO
	7835/12	1980-1984	1	12 cm

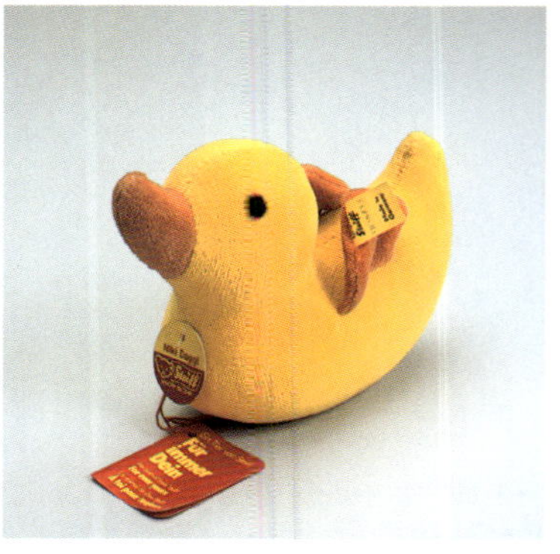

Niki Daggi Ente - ***Niki Daggi** Duck*

Nicki-Stoff, formgeschaeumt, waschbar - *nicki fabric, stuffed with pre-formed foam, washable*

SERIE	ART.-NO	PERIOD	PR.	INFO
	7836/12	1980-1985	1	12 cm

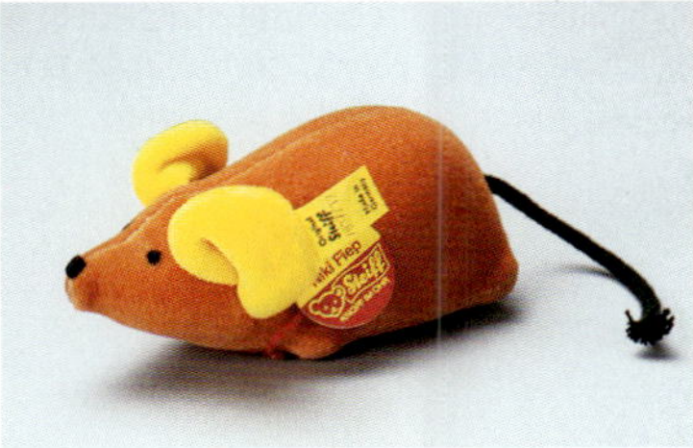

Niki Fiep Maus - ***Niki Fiep*** *Mouse*

Nicki-Stoff, formgeschaeumt, waschbar - *nicki fabric, stuffed with pre-formed foam, washable*

Serie	Art.-No	Period	Pr.	Info
	7837/12	1980-1982	1	12 cm

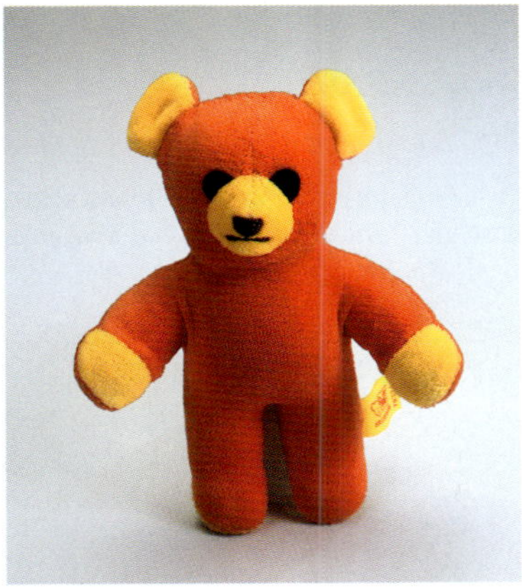

Niki Teddy

Nicki-Stoff, formgeschaeumt, 15 cm, waschbar - *nicki fabric, stuffed with pre-formed foam, 15 cm, washable*

Serie	Art.-No	Period	Pr.	Info
	7833/15	1982-1985	1	braun - *brown*
	7833/16	1982-1983	1	rot - *red*

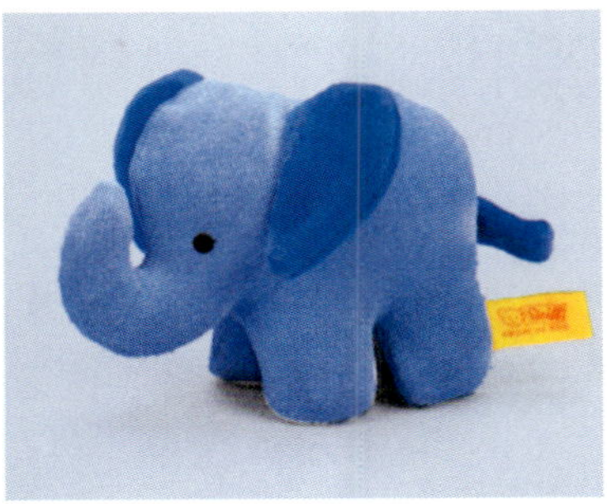

Niki Baby Elefant - *Niki Baby Elephant*

Nicki-Stoff, formgeschaeumt, waschbar - *nicki fabric, stuffed with pre-formed foam, washable*

Serie	Art.-No	Period	Pr.	Info
	6430/13	1983-1985	1	13 cm

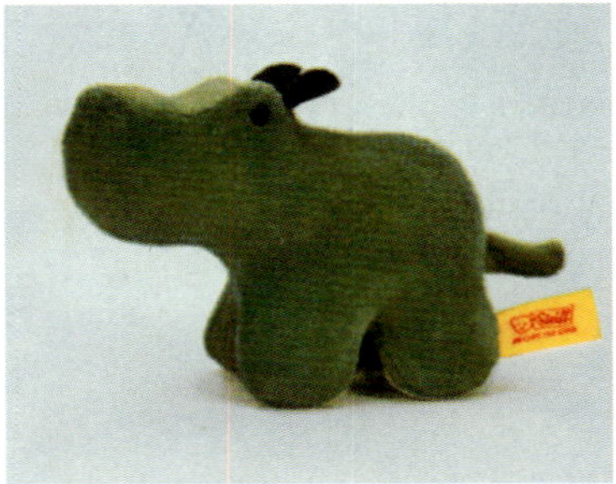

Niki Baby Nilpferd - *Niki Baby Hippo*

Nicki-Stoff, formgeschaeumt, waschbar - *nicki fabric, stuffed with pre-formed foam, washable*

Serie	Art.-No	Period	Pr.	Info
	6431/13	1983-1985	1	13 cm

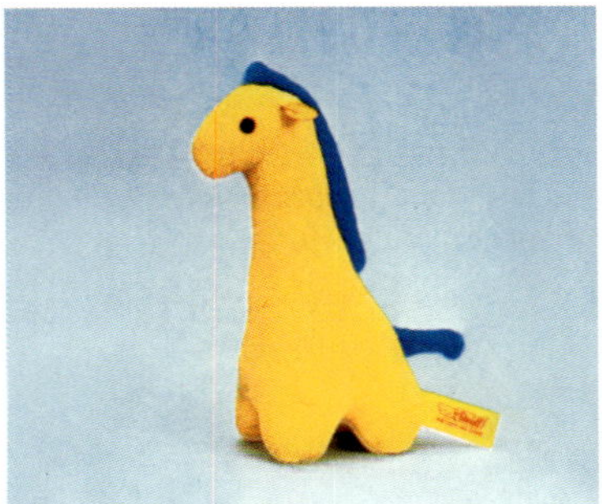

Niki Baby Giraffe

Nicki-Stoff, formgeschaeumt, waschbar - *nicki fabric, stuffed with pre-formed foam, washable*

Serie	Art.-No	Period	Pr.	Info
	6432/13	1983-1985	1	13 cm

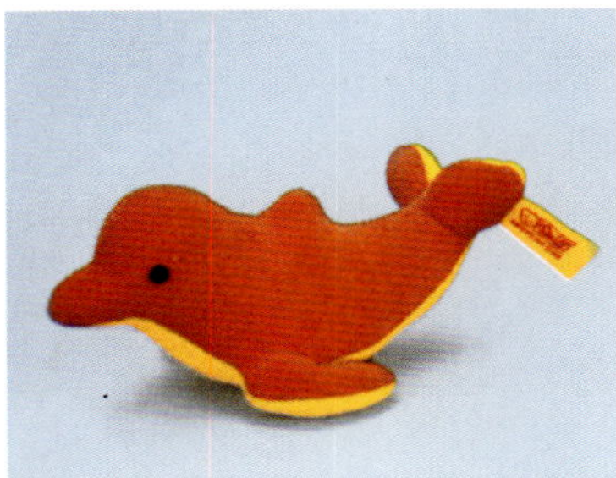

Niki Baby Delphin - *Niki Baby Dolphin*

Nicki-Stoff, formgeschaeumt, waschbar - *nicki fabric, stuffed with pre-formed foam, washable*

Serie	Art.-No	Period	Pr.	Info
	6434/13	1983-1985	1	13 cm

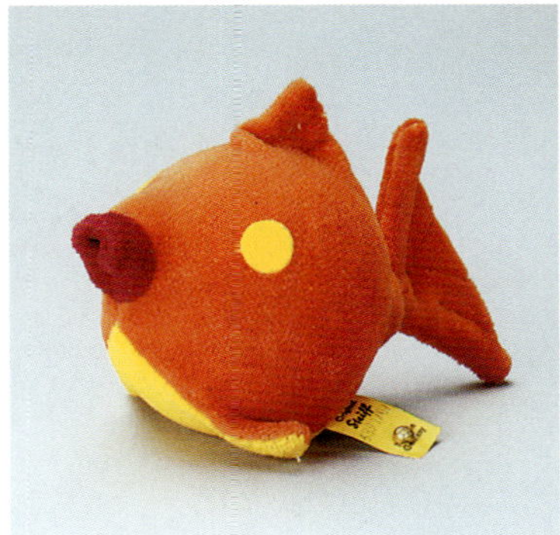

Rollo Fisch - *Rollo Fish*

Nicki Stoff, Koerper formgeschaeumt, 7 cm rot oder blau, mit Schellen, waschbar - *nicki fabric, stuffed with pre-formed foam, 7 cm, red or blue, with bells, washable*

Serie	Art.-No	Period	Pr.	Info
	6391/07	1978-1984	1	rot - *red*
	6392/07	1978-1984	1	blau - *blue*

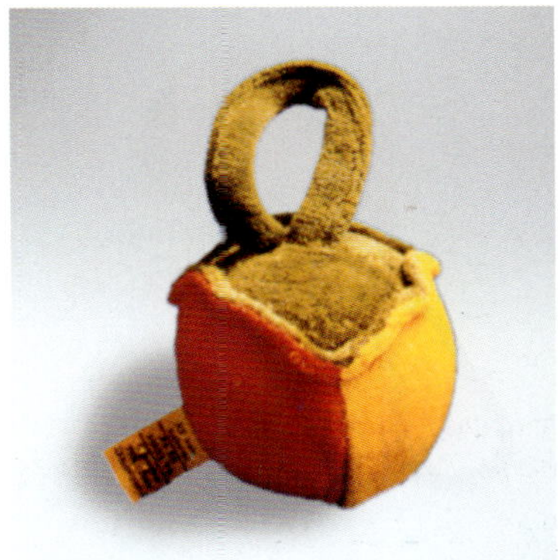

Rollo Beere - *Rollo Berry*

Nicki Stoff, formgeschaeumt, mit Schellen, vollwaschbar - *nicki fabric, stuffed with pre-formed foam, with bells, fully washable*

Serie	Art.-No	Period	Pr.	Info
	6395/06	1978-1980	1	6 cm

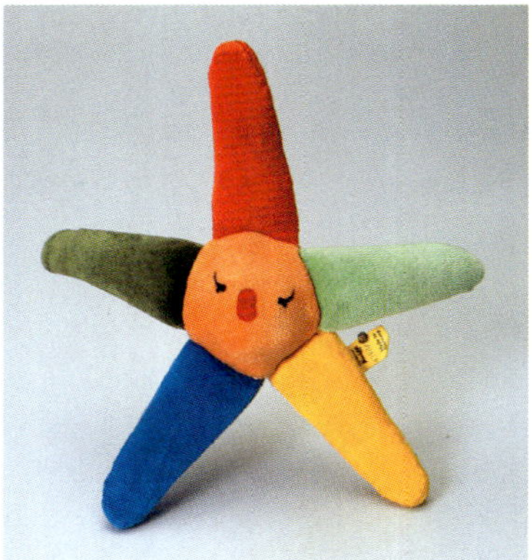

Rollo Stern - *Rollo Star*

Nicki Stoff, formgeschaeumt, mit Schellen, waschbar - *nicki fabric, stuffed with pre-formed foam, with bells, washable*

SERIE	ART.-NO	PERIOD	PR.	INFO
205033	**6390/10**	1978-1990	1	10 cm
	205033	1991-1992	1	

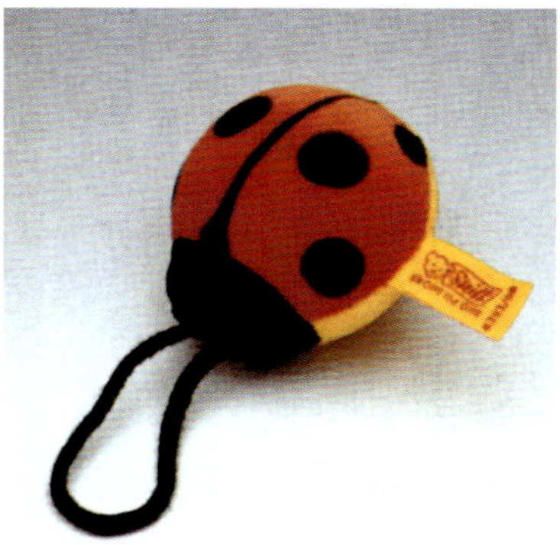

Rollo Marienkaefer - *Rollo Ladybird*

Nicki Stoff, formgeschaeumt, mit Schellen, waschbar - *nicki fabric, stuffed with pre-formed foam, with bells, washable*

SERIE	ART.-NO	PERIOD	PR.	INFO
205064	**6393/06**	1978-1990	1	6 cm
	205064	1991-1992	1	

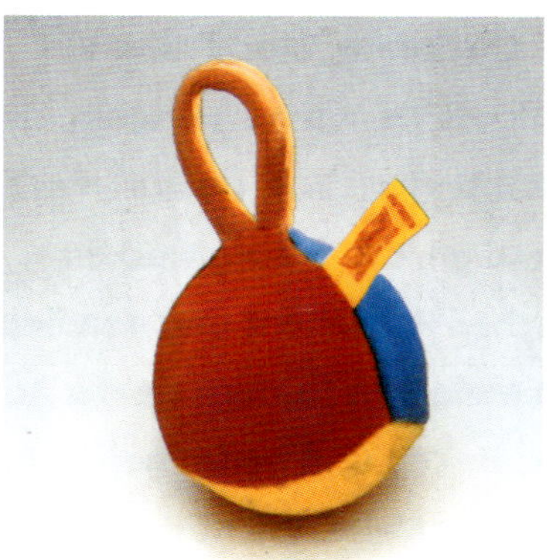

Rollo Ball

Nicki Stoff, formgeschaeumt, mit Schellen und Schlinge, waschbar - *nicki fabric, stuffed with pre-formed foam, with bells & loop handle, washable*

SERIE	ART.-NO	PERIOD	PR.	INFO
205088	**6396/07**	1978-1990	1	7 cm
	205088	1991-1992	1	

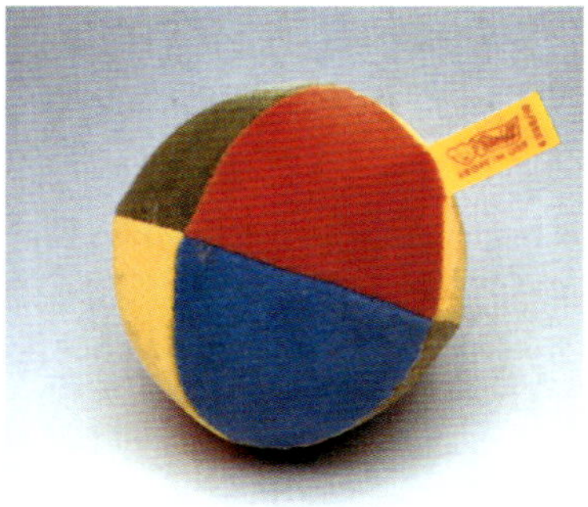

Rollo Ball

Nicki Stoff, formgeschaeumt, mit Schellen, waschbar - *nicki fabric, stuffed with pre-formed foam, with bells, washable*

SERIE	ART.-NO	PERIOD	PR.	INFO
205101	**6398/10**	1978-1990	1	10 cm
	205101	1991-1992	1	

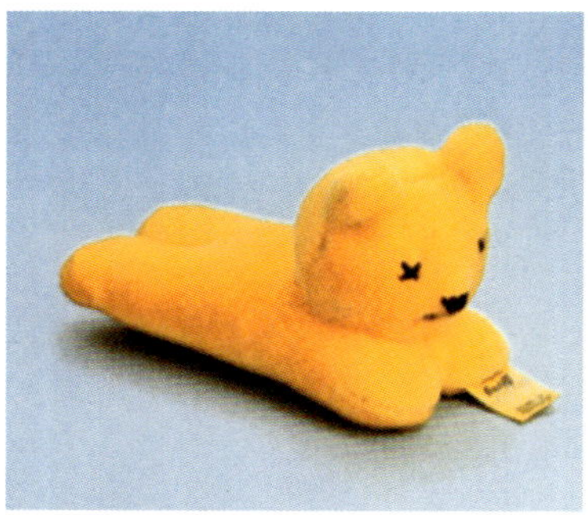

Rollo Baer - *Rollo Bear*

Nicki Stoff, formgeschaeumt, mit Schellen, waschbar - *nicki fabric, stuffed with pre-formed foam, with bells, washable*

SERIE	ART.-NO	PERIOD	PR.	INFO
	6403/08	1980-1982	1	8 cm

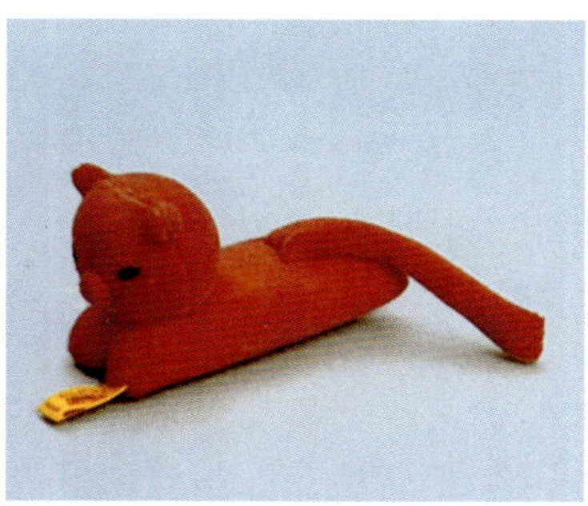

Rollo Katze - *Rollo Cat*

Nicki Stoff, formgeschaeumt, mit Schellen, waschbar - *nicki fabric, stuffed with pre-formed foam, with bells, washable*

SERIE	ART.-NO	PERIOD	PR.	INFO
	6404/08	1980-1984	1	8 cm

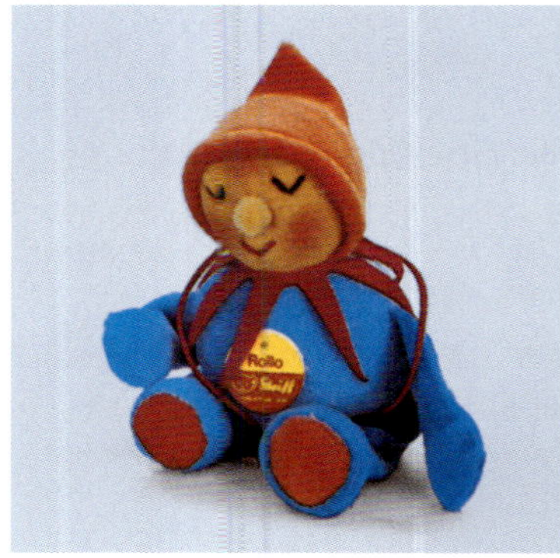

Rollo Hampelmann - *Rollo Jumping Jack*

Nicki Stoff, formgeschaeumt, mit Schellen, waschbar - *nicki fabric, stuffed with pre-formed foam, with bells, washable*

SERIE	ART.-NO	PERIOD	PR.	INFO
205156	**6405/20**	1980-1986	2	20 cm

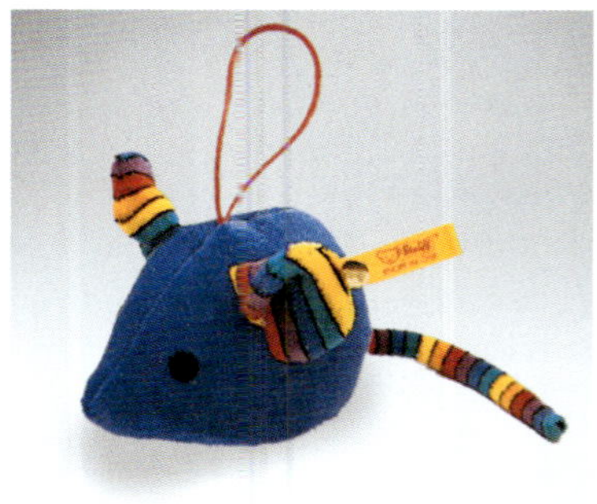

Rollo Maus - *Rollo Mouse*

Nicki-Stoff, formgeschaeumt, rot oder blau, 8 cm, mit Rassel, waschbar - *nicki fabric, stuffed with pre-formed foam, red or blue, 8 cm, with rattle, washable*

SERIE	ART.-NO	PERIOD	PR.	INFO
206313	**6316/08**	1987-1989	1	rot - *red*
206351	**6318/08**	1987-1989	1	blau - *blue*

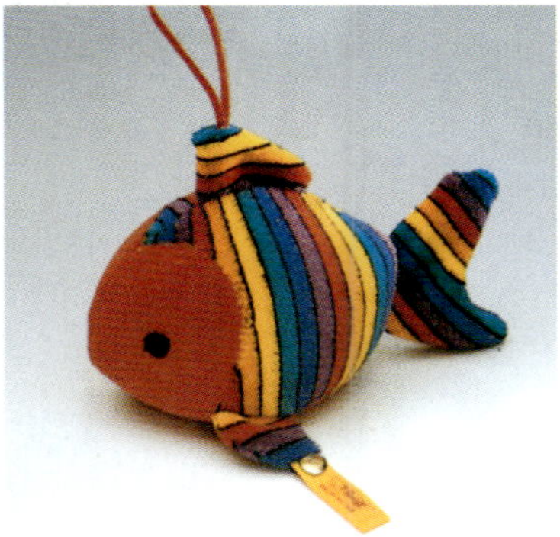

Rollo Fisch - *Rollo Fish*

Nicki-Stoff, formgeschaeumt, rot oder gelb, 9 cm, mit Rassel, waschbar - *nicki fabric, stuffed with pre-formed foam, red or yellow, 9 cm, with rattle, washable*

SERIE	ART.-NO	PERIOD	PR.	INFO
206511	**6322/09**	1987-1989	1	rot - *red*
206535	**6323/09**	1987-1988	1	gelb - *yellow*

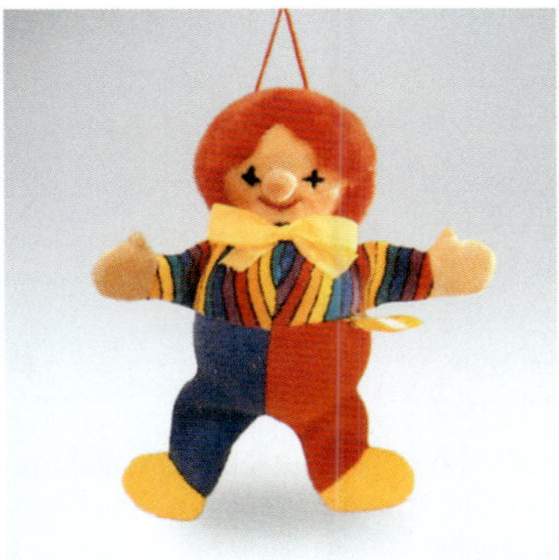

Rollo Clown

Nicki-Stoff, formgeschaeumt, rot oder gelb, 18 cm, mit Rassel, waschbar - *nicki fabric, stuffed with pre-formed foam, red or yellow, 18 cm, with rattle, washable*

SERIE	ART.-NO	PERIOD	PR.	INFO
207211	**6342/18**	1987-1988	1-2	rot - *red*
207235	**6343/18**	1987-1988	1-2	gelb - *yellow*

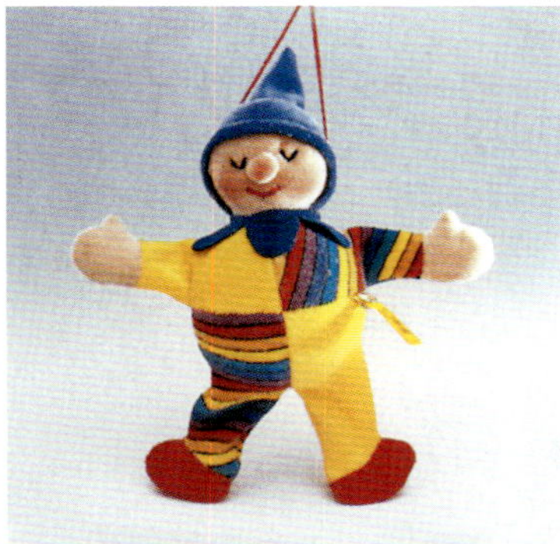

Rollo Hampelmann - *Rollo Jumping Jack*

Nicki-Stoff, formgeschaeumt, orange oder gelb, 18 cm, mit Rassel, waschbar - *nicki fabric, stuffed with pre-formed foam, orange or yellow, 18 cm, with rattle, washable*

SERIE	ART.-NO	PERIOD	PR.	INFO
207426	**6346/18**	1987-1988	1-2	orange
207433	**6347/18**	1987-1990	1-2	gelb - *yellow*

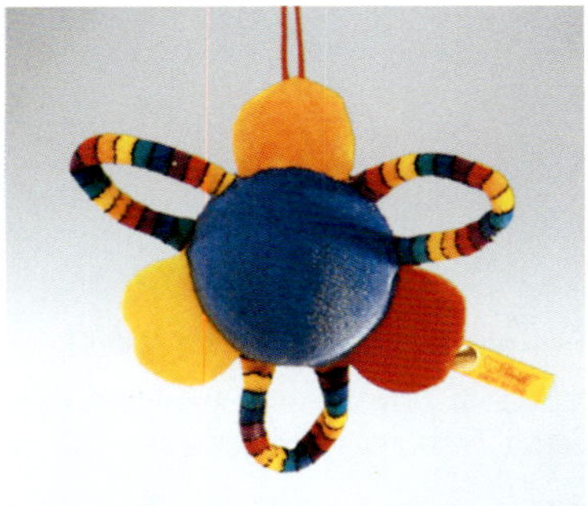

Rollo Blume - *Rollo Flower*

Nicki-Stoff, formgeschaeumt, gelb oder blau, 12 cm, mit Rassel, waschbar - *nicki fabric, stuffed with pre-formed foam, yellow or blue, 12 cm, with rattle, washable*

SERIE	ART.-NO	PERIOD	PR.	INFO
206139	**6313/12**	1987-1990	1	gelb - *yellow*
	206139	1991-1992	1	
206153	**6314/12**	1987-1990	1	blau - *blue*
	206153	1991-1992	1	

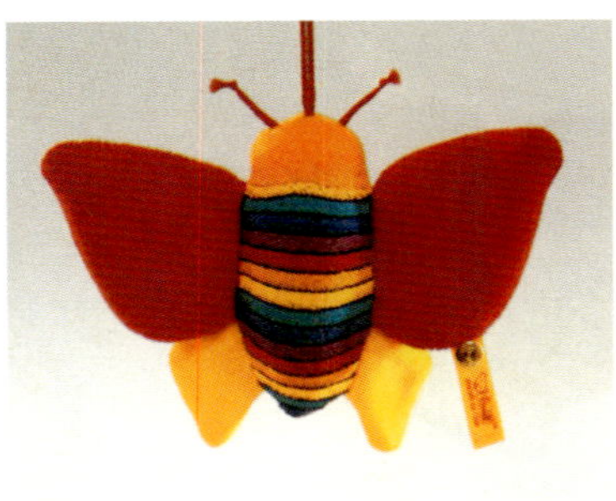

Rollo Schmetterling - *Rollo Butterfly*

Nicki-Stoff, formgeschaeumt, rot oder blau, 11 cm, mit Rassel, waschbar - *nicki fabric, stuffed with pre-formed foam, red or blue, 11 cm, with rattle, washable*

SERIE	ART.-NO	PERIOD	PR.	INFO
206719	**6326/11**	1987-1990	1	rot - *red*
	206719	1991-1992	1	
206757	**6328/11**	1987-1990	1	blau - *blue*
	206757	1991-1992	1	

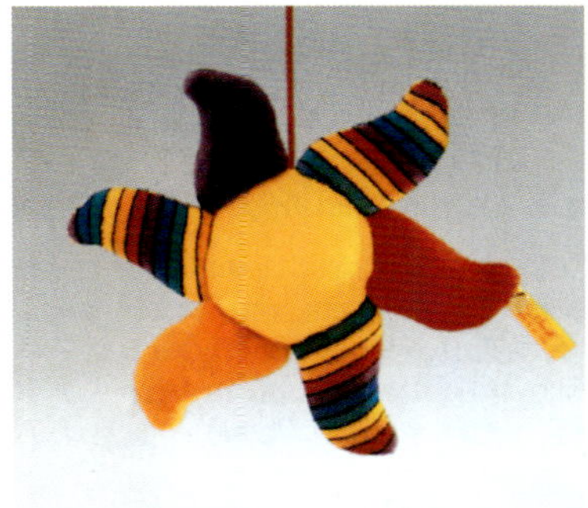

Rollo Seestern - *Rollo Starfish*

Nicki-Stoff, formgeschaeumt, rot oder gelb, 16 cm, mit Rassel, waschbar - *nicki fabric, stuffed with pre- formed foam, red or yellow, 16 cm, with rattle, washable*

SERIE	ART.-NO	PERIOD	PR.	INFO
206917	**6332/16**	1987-1990	1	rot - *red*
	206917	1991-1991	1	
206931	**6333/16**	1987-1990	1	gelb - *yellow*
	206931	1991-1991	1	

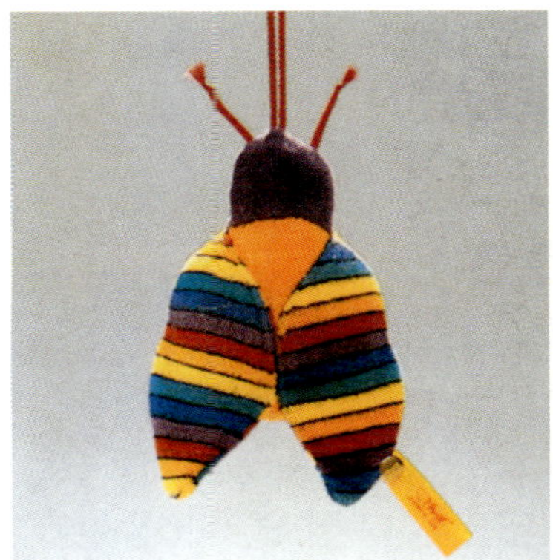

Rollo Kaefer - *Rollo Beetle*

Nicki-Stoff, formgeschaeumt, rot oder orange, 11 cm, mit Rassel, waschbar - *nicki fabric, stuffed with pre-formed foam, red or orange, 11 cm, with rattle, washable*

SERIE	ART.-NO	PERIOD	PR.	INFO
206214	**6306/11**	1988-1989	1	rot - *red*
206221	**6307/11**	1988-1989	1	orange

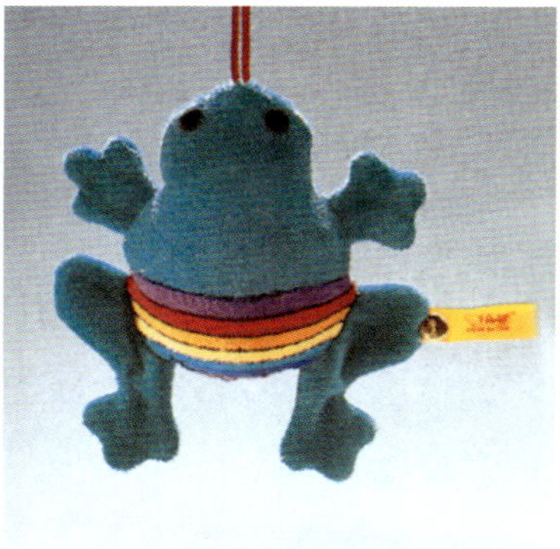

Rollo Frosch - *Rollo Frog*

Nicki-Stoff, formgeschaeumt, rot, orange oder gruen, 12 cm, mit Rassel, handwaschbar - *nicki fabric, stuffed with pre-formed foam, red, orange or green, 12 cm, with rattle, hand washable*

SERIE	ART.-NO	PERIOD	PR.	INFO
206818	**6335/12**	1988-1988	1	rot - *red*
206825	**6336/12**	1988-1988	1	orange
206849	**6338/12**	1988-1988	1	gruen - *green*

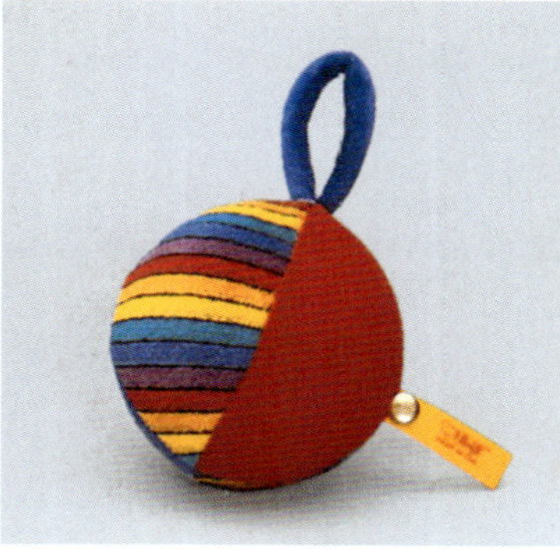

Rollo Ball

Nicki-Stoff, formgeschaeumt, gelb oder blau, 8 cm, mit Schlinge & Rassel, waschbar - *nicki fabric, stuffed with pre-formed foam, yellow or blue, 8 cm, with loop handle & rattle, washable*

SERIE	ART.-NO	PERIOD	PR.	INFO
206030	**6303/08**	1988-1990	1	gelb - *yellow*
	206030	1991-1992	1	
206054	**6304/08**	1988-1990	1	blau - *blue*
	206054	1991-1991	1	

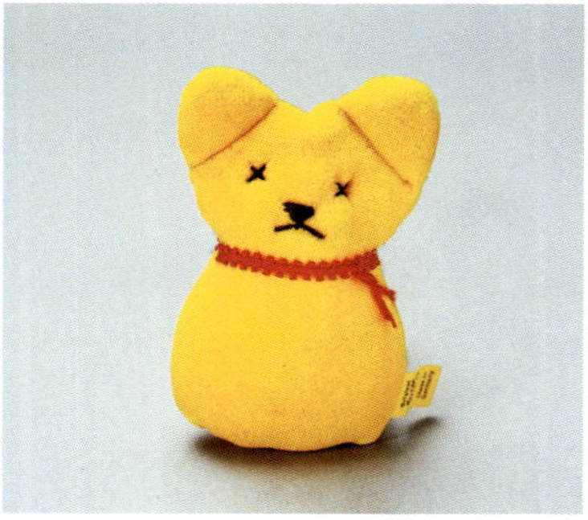

Steiff Pieps Baer - *Steiff Pieps Bear*

Nicki-Stoff, Druckstimme, waschbar - *nicki fabric, press voice, washable*

SERIE	ART.-NO	PERIOD	PR.	INFO
	6410/13	1980-1984	1	13 cm

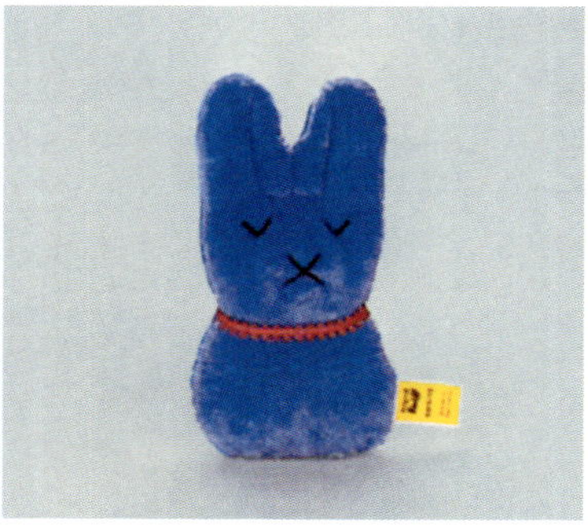

Steiff Pieps Hase - *Steiff Pieps Rabbit*

Nicki-Stoff, Druckstimme, waschbar - *nicki fabric, press voice, washable*

SERIE	ART.-NO	PERIOD	PR.	INFO
	6411/13	1980-1984	1	13 cm

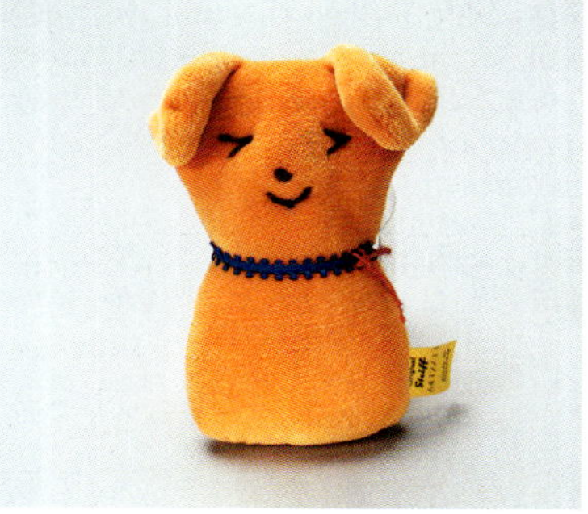

Steiff Pieps Hund - *Steiff Pieps Dog*

Nicki-Stoff, Druckstimme, waschbar - *nicki fabric, press voice, washable*

SERIE	ART.-NO	PERIOD	PR.	INFO
	6412/13	1980-1981	1	13 cm

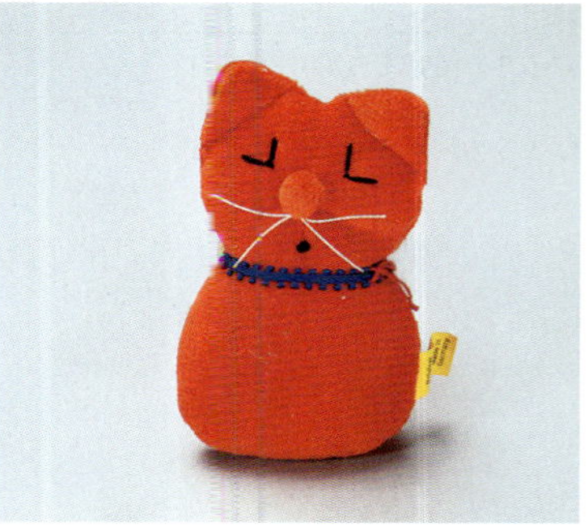

Steiff Pieps Katze - *Steiff Pieps Cat*

Nicki-Stoff, Druckstimme, waschbar - *nicki fabric, press voice, washable*

SERIE	ART.-NO	PERIOD	PR.	INFO
	6413/13	1980-1984	1	13 cm

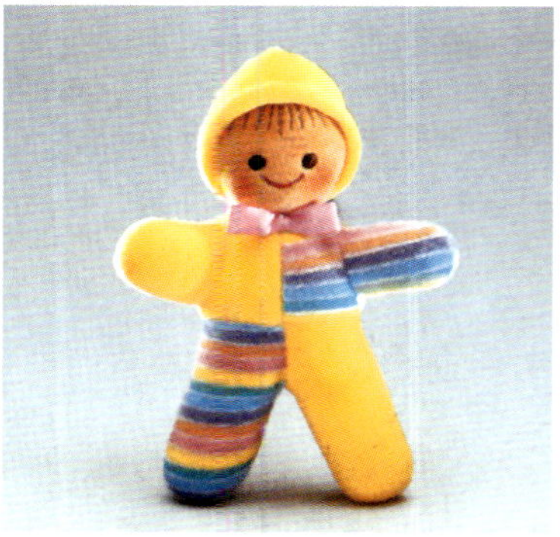

Baby Happy

Nicki-Stoff, 15 cm, Rassel, waschmaschinenfest - *nicki fabric, 15 cm, with rattle, machine washable*

SERIE	ART.-NO	PERIOD	PR.	INFO
208034	**6405/15**	1990-1990	1	gelb - *yellow*
208072	**6407/15**	1990-1990	1	rosé - *rose*

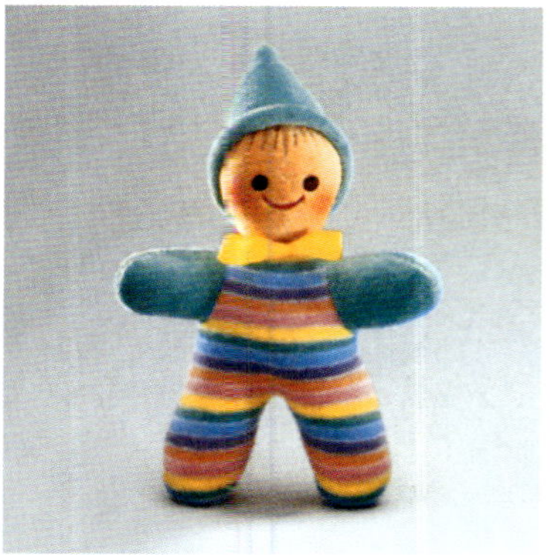

Baby Cappy

Nicki-Stoff, 15 cm, Rassel, waschmaschinenfest - *nicki fabric, 15 cm, with rattle, machine washable*

SERIE	ART.-NO	PERIOD	PR.	INFO
208188	**6409/15**	1990-1990	1	mint - *mint green*
208195	**6411/15**	1990-1990	1	bleu - *soft blue*

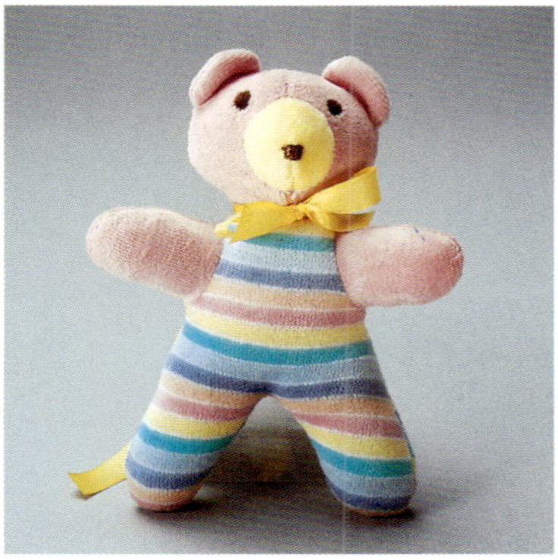

Baby Teddy

Nicki-Stoff, 15 cm, Rassel, waschmaschinenfest - *nicki fabric, 15 cm, with rattle, machine washable*

SERIE	ART.-NO	PERIOD	PR.	INFO
208539	**6413/15**	1990-1990	1	gelb - *yellow*
208577	**6415/15**	1990-1990	1	rosé - *rose*
208584	**6417/15**	1990-1990	1	mint - *mint green*
208591	**6419/15**	1990-1990	1	bleu - *soft blue*

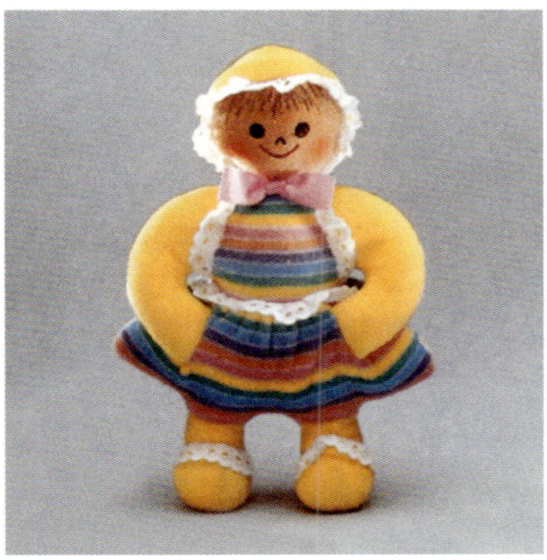

Baby Maidi

Nicki-Stoff, 20 cm, Rassel, waschmaschinenfest - *nicki fabric, 20 cm, with rattle, machine washable*

SERIE	ART.-NO	PERIOD	PR.	INFO
209031	**6422/20**	1990-1990	1-2	gelb - *yellow*
209079	**6424/20**	1990-1990	1-2	rosé - *rose*

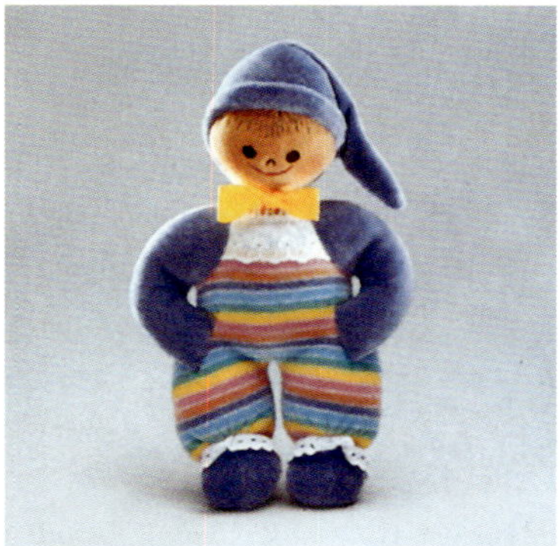

Baby Bubi

Nicki-Stoff, 20 cm, Rassel, waschmaschinenfest - *nicki fabric, 20 cm, with rattle, machine washable*

SERIE	ART.-NO	PERIOD	PR.	INFO
209185	**6426/20**	1990-1990	1-2	mint - *mint green*
209192	**6428/20**	1990-1990	1-2	bleu - *soft blue*

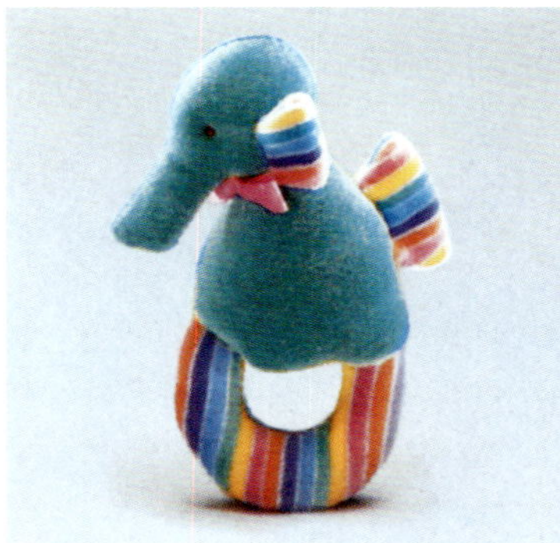

Baby Seepferdchen - *Baby Seahorse*

Nicki-Stoff, 14 cm, Rassel, waschmaschinenfest - *nicki fabric, 14 cm, with rattle, machine washable*

SERIE	ART.-NO	PERIOD	PR.	INFO
209932	**6448/14**	1990-1990	1	gelb - *yellow*
209987	**6449/14**	1990-1990	1	mint - *mint green*

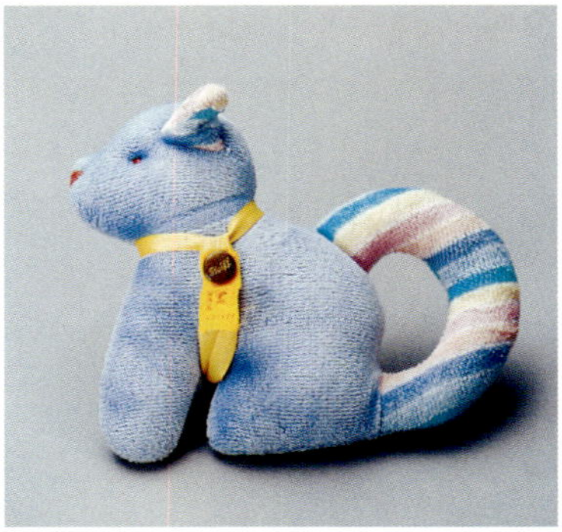

Baby Katze - *Baby Cat*

Nicki-Stoff, 14 cm, Rassel, waschmaschinenfest - *nicki fabric, 14 cm, with rattle, machine washable*

SERIE	ART.-NO	PERIOD	PR.	INFO
209635	**6436/14**	1990-1990	1	gelb - *yellow*
209697	**6438/14**	1990-1990	1	bleu - *soft blue*

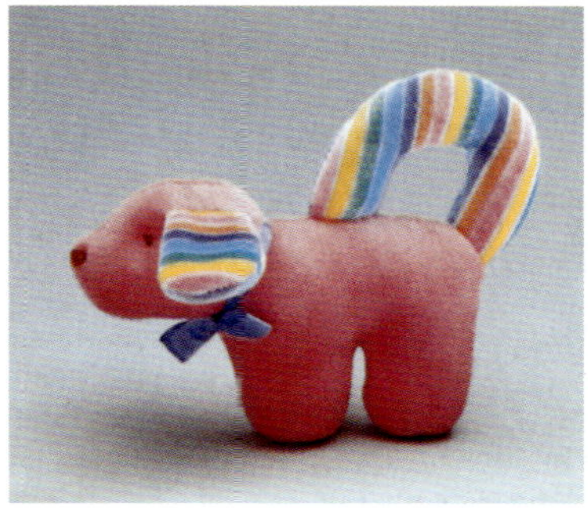

Baby Hund - *Baby Dog*

Nicki-Stoff, 14 cm, Rassel, waschmaschinenfest - *nicki fabric, 14 cm, with rattle, machine washable*

SERIE	ART.-NO	PERIOD	PR.	INFO
209772	**6440/14**	1990-1990	1	rosé - *rose*
209789	**6442/14**	1990-1990	1	mint - *mint green*

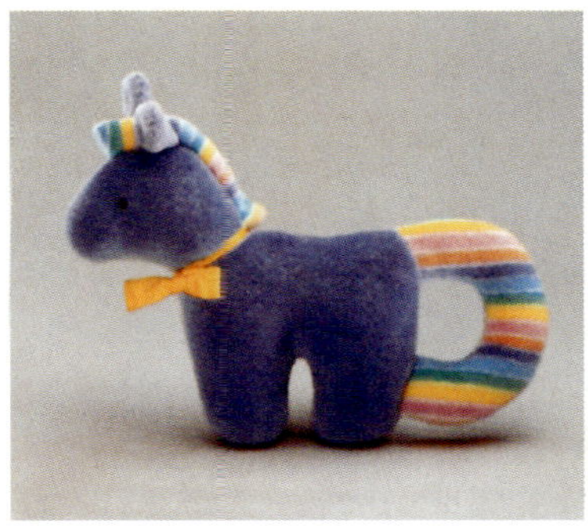

Baby Pony

Nicki-Stoff, 14 cm, Rassel, waschmaschinenfest - *nicki fabric, 14 cm, with rattle, machine washable*

SERIE	ART.-NO	PERIOD	PR.	INFO
209833	**6444/14**	1990-1990	1	gelb - *yellow*
209895	**6446/14**	1990-1990	1	bleu - *soft blue*

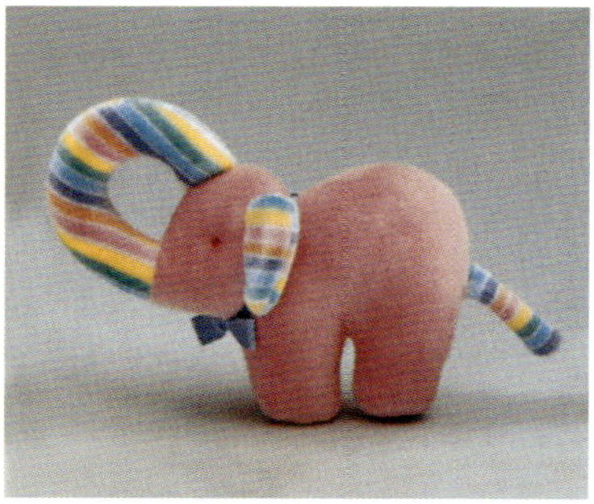

Baby Elefant - *Baby Elephant*

Nicki-Stoff, 14 cm, Rassel, waschmaschinenfest - *nicki fabric, 14 cm, with rattle, machine washable*

SERIE	ART.-NO	PERIOD	PR.	INFO
209574	**6432/14**	1990-1990	1	rosé - *rose*
209598	**6434/14**	1990-1990	1	bleu - *soft blue*

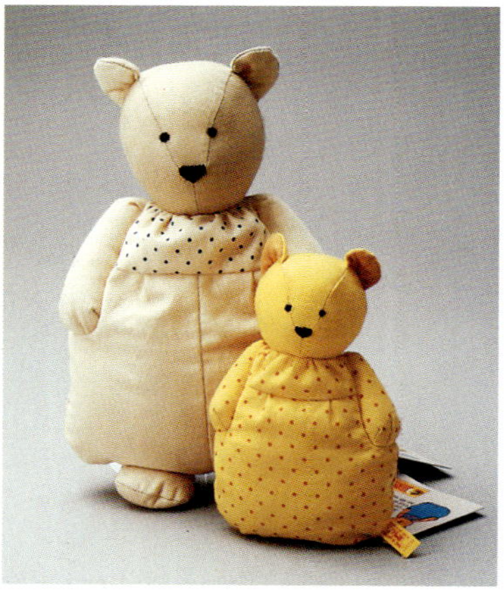

Knoepfchen Baer - *Little Button Bear*

Baumwolle, waschmaschinenfest - *cotton, machine washable*

EAN-NO.	PERIOD	PR.	INFO
203114	1992-1996	1	18 cm, rot - *red*
203138	1992-1996	1	gelb - *yellow*
203152	1992-1996	1	blau - *blue*
203619	1992-1995	1	24 cm, rot - *red*
203657	1992-1995	1	blau - *blue*
203688	1992-1996	1	beige

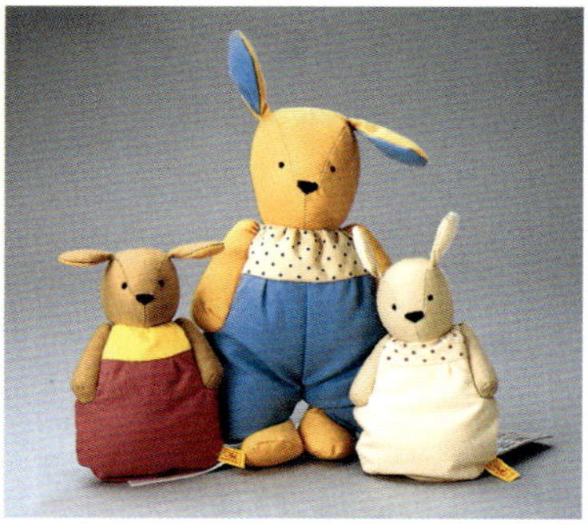

Knoepfchen Hase - *Little Button Rabbit*

Baumwolle, waschmaschinenfest - *cotton, machine washable*

EAN-NO.	PERIOD	PR.	INFO
203213	1992-1996	1	18 cm, rot - *red*
203251	1992-1996	1	blau - *blue*
203282	1992-1996	1	beige
203718	1992-1995	1	24 cm, rot - *red*
203756	1992-1995	1	blau - *blue*
203787	1992-1996	1	beige

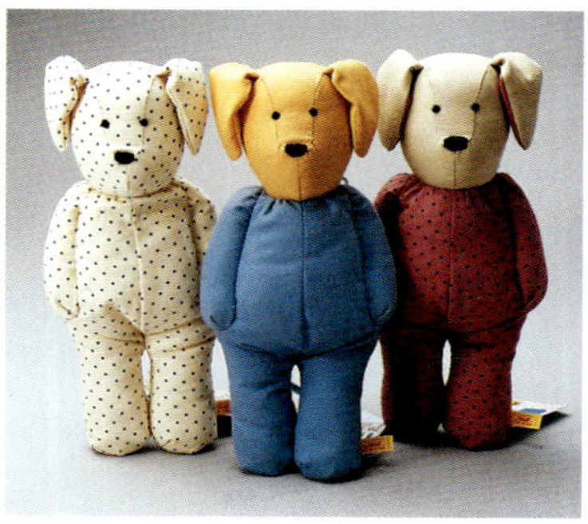

Knoepfchen Hund - *Little Button Dog*

Baumwolle, waschmaschinenfest - *cotton, machine washable*

EAN-NO.	PERIOD	PR.	INFO
203312	1992-1996	1	18 cm, rot - *red*
203350	1992-1996	1	blau - *blue*
203381	1992-1996	1	beige
203817	1992-1996	1	24 cm, rot - *red*
203855	1992-1996	1	blau - *blue*
203886	1992-1996	1	beige

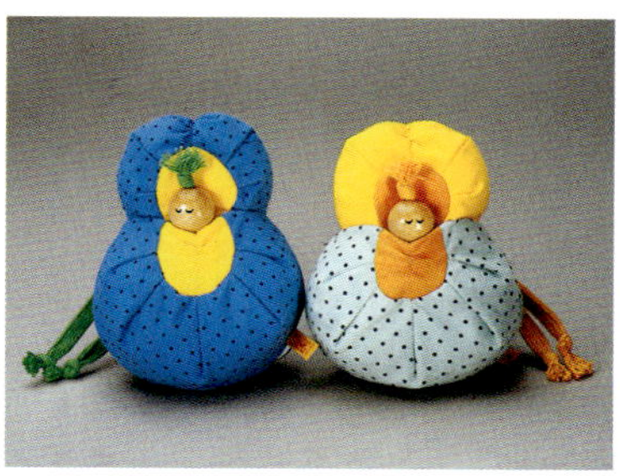

Knoepfchen Kissenpueppchen - *Little Button Cushion Dolls*

Baumwolle, 14 cm, handwaschbar - *cotton, 14 cm, hand washable*

EAN-NO.	PERIOD	PR.	INFO
204241	1992-1996	1	gruen - *green*
204258	1992-1996	1	blau - *blue*
204289	1992-1996	1	beige

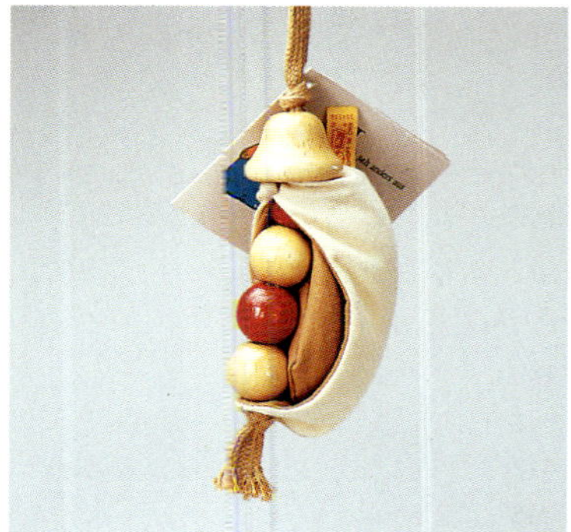

Knoepfchen Schote - *Little Button Pod*

Baumwolle, 14 cm, handwaschbar - *cotton, 14 cm, hand washable*

EAN-NO.	PERIOD	PR.	INFO
204111	1992-1996	1	rot - *red*
204135	1992-1996	1	gelb - *yellow*
204180	1992-1996	1	beige

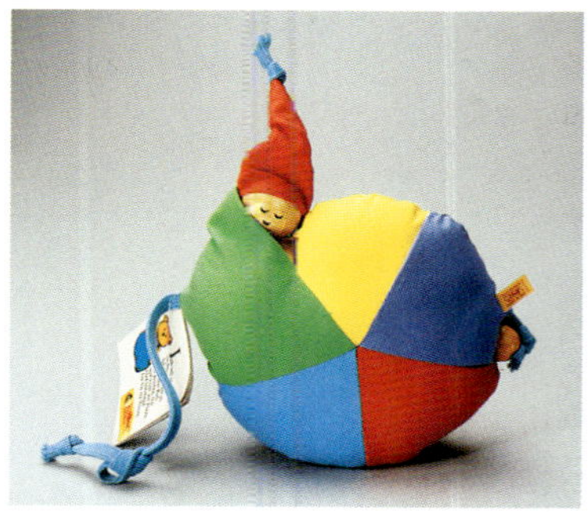

Knoepfchen Musik-Schnecke - *Little Button Musical Snail*

Baumwolle, 18 cm, handwaschbar - *cotton, 18 cm, hand washable*

EAN-NO.	PERIOD	PR.	INFO
204708	1992-1996	1	bunt - *multi-color*
204739	1992-1996	1	gelb - *yellow*
204753	1992-1996	1	blau - *blue*

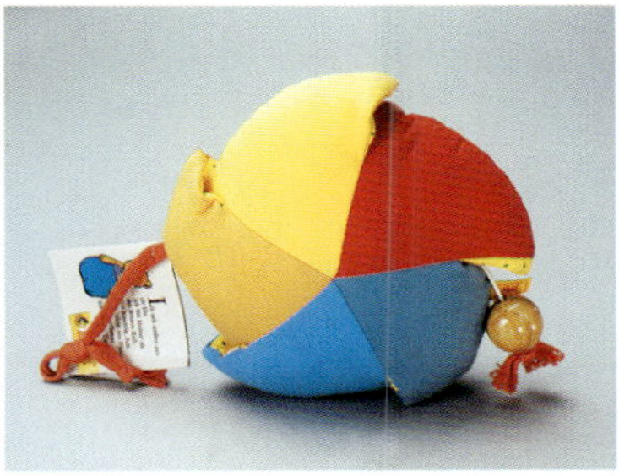

Knoepfchen Musik-Sonnenrad - *Little Button Musical Sun Wheel*

Baumwolle, 18 cm, handwaschbar - *cotton, 18 cm, hand washable*

EAN-No.	Period	Pr.	Info
204807	1992-1996	1	bunt - *multi-color*
204852	1992-1996	1	blau - *blue*
204883	1992-1996	1	beige

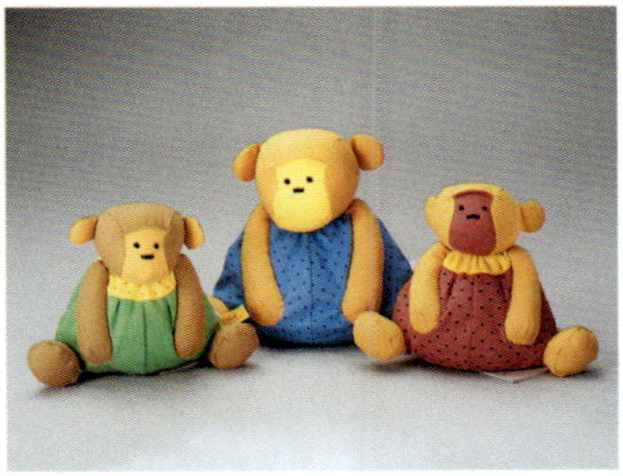

Knoepfchen Affe - *Little Button Monkey*

Baumwolle, waschmaschinenfest - *cotton, machine washable*

EAN-No.	Period	Pr.	Info
203411	1993-1995	1	18 cm, rot - *red*
203442	1993-1995	1	gruen - *green*
203480	1993-1996	1	beige
203947	1993-1996	1	24 cm, gruen - *green*
203954	1993-1996	1	blau - *blue*
203985	1993-1995	1	beige

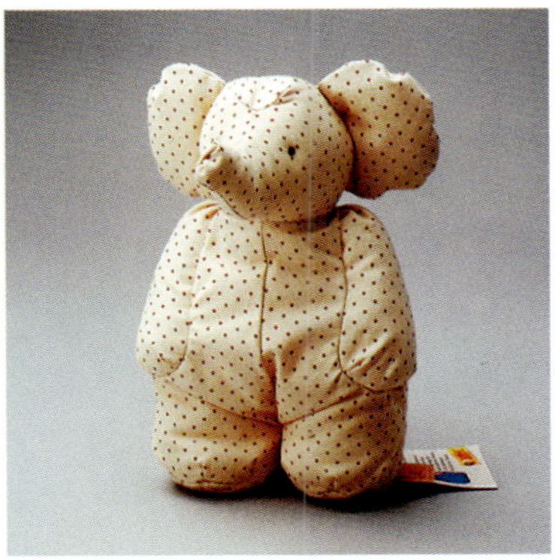

Knoepfchen Elefant - *Little Button Elephant*

Baumwolle, waschmaschinenfest - *cotton, machine washable*

EAN-No.	Period	Pr.	Info
203510	1993-1996	1	18 cm, rot - *red*
203541	1993-1996	1	gruen - *green*
203589	1993-1996	1	beige
204012	1993-1995	1	24 cm, rot - *red*
204050	1993-1995	1	blau - *blue*
204081	1993-1996	1	beige

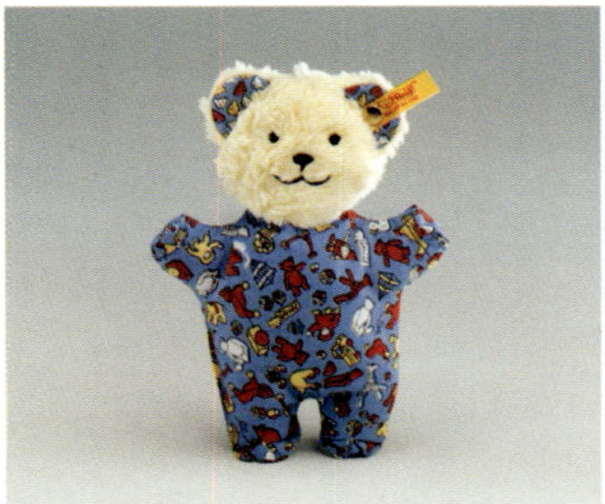

Baby Baer - *Baby Bear*

Baumwolle, Baumwollpluesch, rot oder blau, 18 cm, waschmaschinenfest, Gesicht bestickt, mit Rassel (nur rot) - *cotton, cotton plush, red or blue, 18 cm, machine washable, face embroidered, with rattle (only red)*

EAN-No.	Period	Pr.	Info
200502	1996-1996	1	rot - *red*
200557	1996-1996	1	blau - *blue*

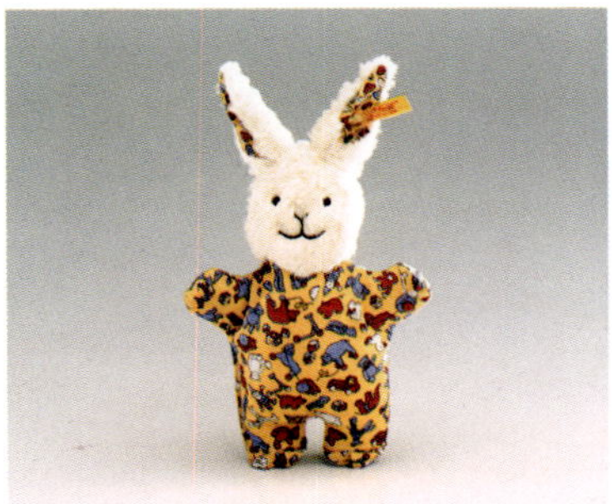

Baby Hase - *Baby Rabbit*

Baumwolle, Baumwollpluesch, gruen oder gelb, 18 cm, waschmaschinenfest, Gesicht bestickt, mit Rassel (nur gruen) - *cotton, cotton plush, green or yellow, 18 cm, machine washable, face embroidered, with rattle (only green)*

EAN-No.	Period	Pr.	Info
200601	1996-1996	1	gruen - *green*
200656	1996-1996	1	gelb - *yellow*

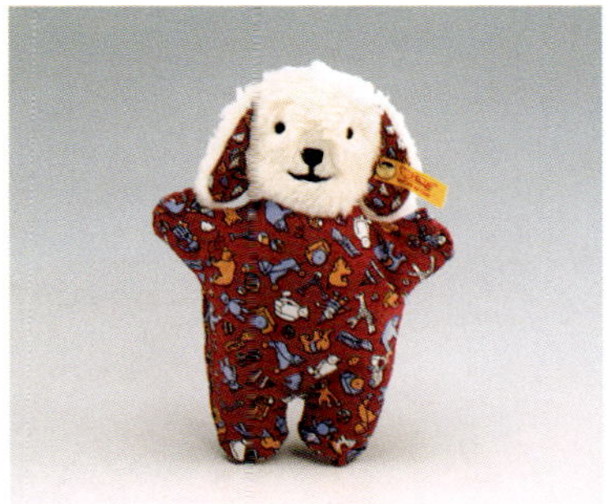

Baby Hund - *Baby Dog*

Baumwolle, Baumwollpluesch, rot oder gruen, 18 cm, waschmaschinenfest, Gesicht bestickt, mit Rassel (nur rot) - *cotton, cotton plush, red or green, 18 cm, machine washable, face embroidered, with rattle (only red)*

EAN-No.	Period	Pr.	Info
200700	1996-1996	1	rot - *red*
200755	1996-1996	1	gruen - *green*

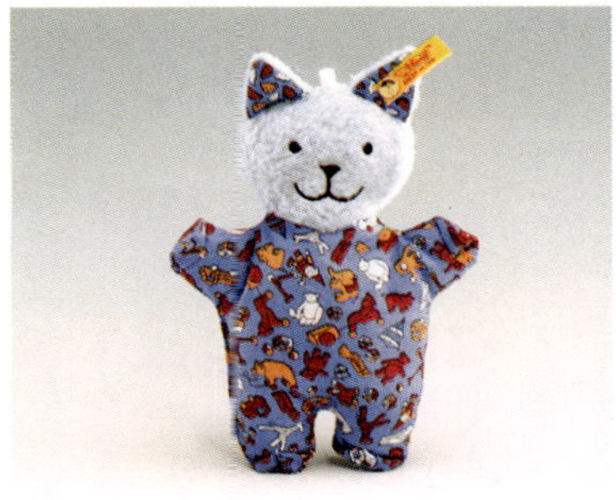

Baby Katze - *Baby Cat*

Baumwolle, Baumwollpluesch, blau oder rot, 18 cm, waschmaschinenfest, Gesicht bestickt, mit Rassel (nur blau) - *cotton, cotton plush, blue or red, 18 cm, machine washable, face embroidered, with rattle (only blue)*

EAN-No.	Period	Pr.	Info
200809	1996-1996	1	blau - *blue*
200854	1996-1996	1	rot - *red*

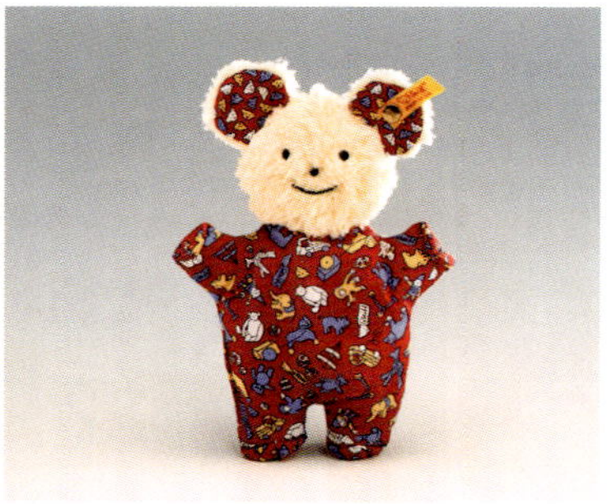

Baby Maus - *Baby Mouse*

Baumwolle, Baumwollpluesch, blau oder rot, 18 cm, waschmaschinenfest, Gesicht bestickt, mit Rassel (nur blau) - *cotton, cotton plush, blue or red, 18 cm, machine washable, face embroidered, with rattle (only blue)*

EAN-No.	Period	Pr.	Info
200908	1996-1996	1	blau - *blue*
200953	1996-1996	1	rot - *red*

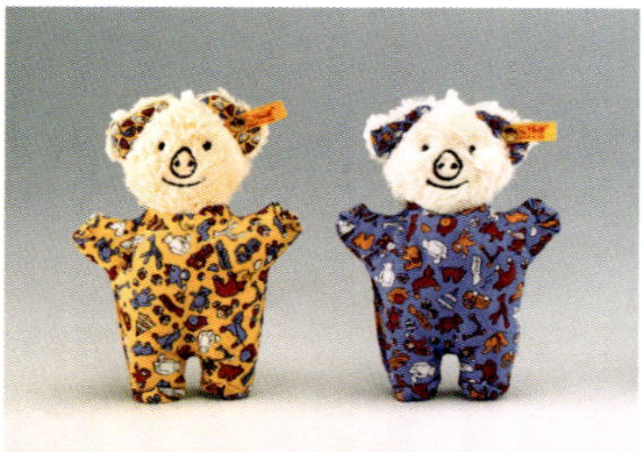

Baby Schwein - *Baby Pig*

Baumwolle, Baumwollpluesch, gelb oder blau, 18 cm, waschmaschinenfest. Gesicht bestickt, mit Rassel (nur gelb) - *cotton, cotton plush, blue or yellow, 18 cm, machine washable, face embroidered, with rattle (only yellow)*

EAN-No.	Period	Pr.	Info
201004	1996-1996	1	gelb - *yellow*
201042	1996-1996	1	blau - *blue*

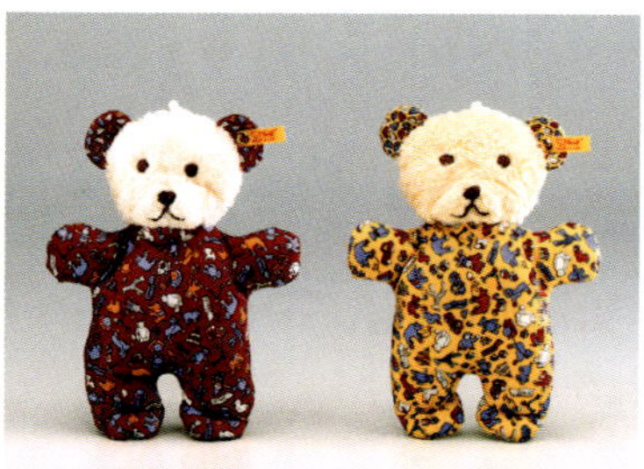

Baby Baer - *Baby Bear*

Baumwolle, Baumwollpluesch, rot oder gelb, 22 cm, waschmaschinenfest, Gesicht bestickt, mit Rassel (nur rot) - *cotton, cotton plush, red or yellow, 22 cm, machine washable, face embroidered, with rattle (only red)*

EAN-No.	Period	Pr.	Info
201202	1996-1996	1	rot - *red*
201257	1996-1996	1	gelb - *yellow*

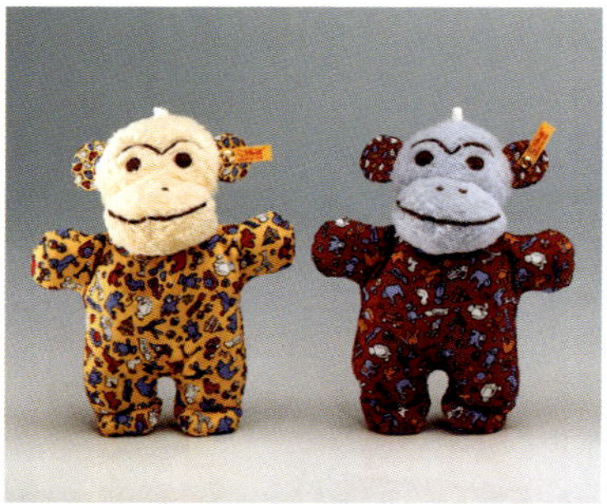

Baby Affe - *Baby Monkey*

Baumwolle, Baumwollpluesch, gelb oder rot, 22 cm, waschmaschinenfest, Gesicht bestickt, mit Rassel (nur gelb) - *cotton, cotton plush, red or yellow, 22 cm, machine washable, face embroidered, with rattle (only yellow)*

EAN-No.	Period	Pr.	Info
201301	1996-1996	1	gelb - *yellow*
201356	1996-1996	1	rot - *red*

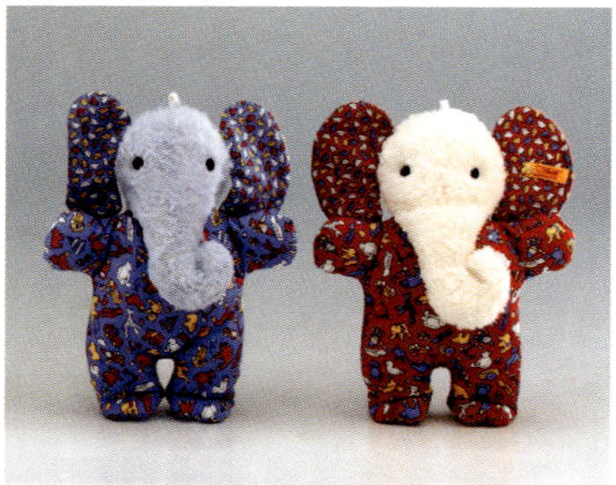

Baby Elefant - *Baby Elephant*

Baumwolle, Baumwollpluesch, blau oder rot, 22 cm, waschmaschinenfest, Gesicht bestickt, mit Rassel (nur blau) - *cotton, cotton plush, red or blue, 22 cm, machine washable, face embroidered, with rattle (only blue)*

EAN-No.	Period	Pr.	Info
201400	1996-1996	1	blau - *blue*
201455	1996-1996	1	rot - *red*

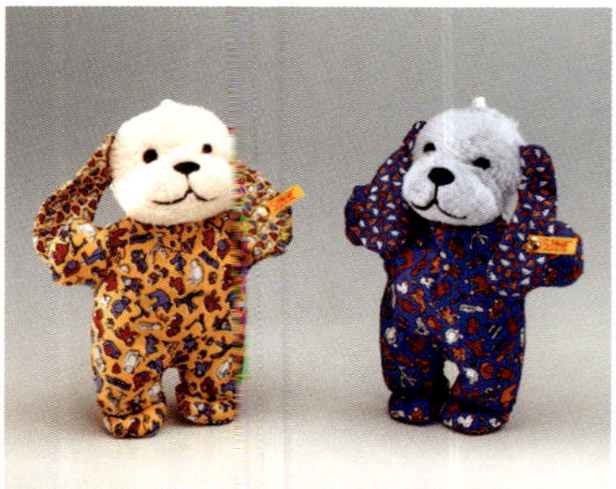

Baby Hund - *Baby Dog*

Baumwolle, Baumwollpluesch, gelb oder blau, 22 cm, waschmaschinenfest, Gesicht bestickt, mit Rassel (nur gelb) - *cotton, cotton plush, blue or yellow, 22 cm, machine washable, face embroidered, with rattle (only yellow)*

EAN-No.	Period	Pr.	Info
201509	1996-1996	1	gelb - *yellow*
201554	1996-1996	1	blau - *blue*

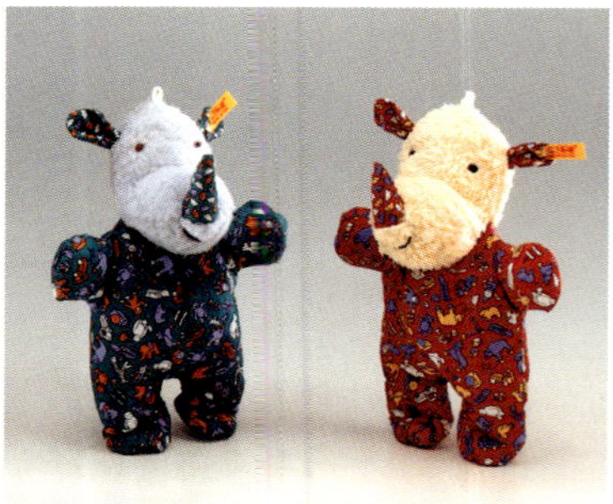

Baby Nashorn - *Baby Rhinoceros*

Baumwolle, Baumwollpluesch, gruen oder rot, 22 cm, waschmaschinenfest, Gesicht bestickt, mit Rassel (nur gruen) - *cotton, cotton plush, red or green, 22 cm, machine washable, face embroidered, with rattle (only green)*

EAN-No.	Period	Pr.	Info
201608	1996-1996	1	gruen - *green*
201653	1996-1996	1	rot - *red*

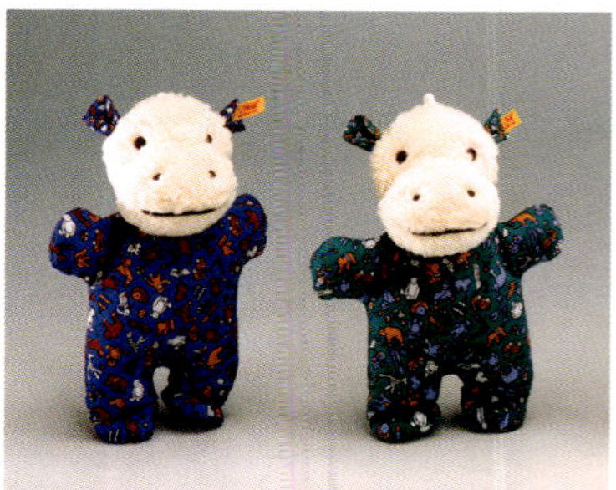

Baby Nilpferd - *Baby Hippopotamus*

Baumwolle, Baumwollpluesch, blau oder gruen, 22 cm, waschmaschinenfest, Gesicht bestickt, mit Rassel (nur blau) - *cotton, cotton plush, blue or green, 22 cm, machine washable, face embroidered, with rattle (only blue)*

EAN-No.	Period	Pr.	Info
201707	1996-1996	1	blau - *blue*
201752	1996-1996	1	gruen - *green*

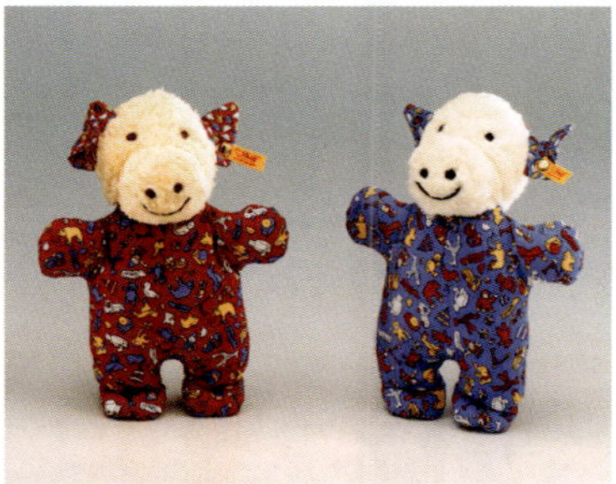

Baby Schwein - *Baby Pig*

Baumwolle, Baumwollpluesch, rot oder blau, 22 cm, waschmaschinenfest, Gesicht bestickt, mit Rassel (nur rot) - *cotton, cotton plush, red or blue, 22 cm, machine washable, face embroidered, with rattle (only red)*

EAN-No.	Period	Pr.	Info
201806	1996-1996	1	rot - *red*
201851	1996-1996	1	blau - *blue*

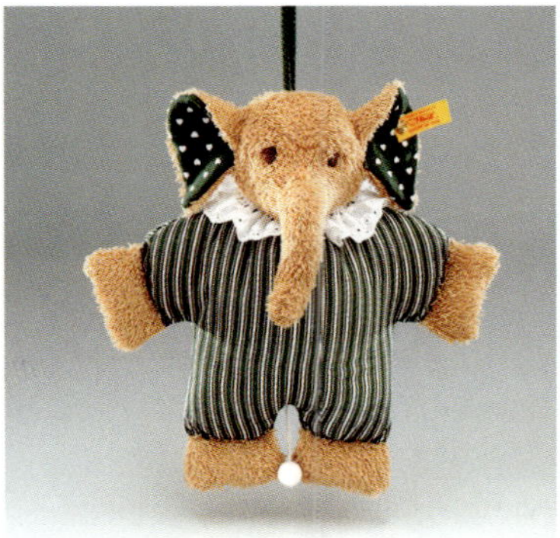

Elefant - *Elephant*

Baumwolle, beige/gruen, abwaschbar, Musikwerk (Schlaf, Kindlein, Schlaf) - *cotton, beige/green, surface washable, music box (Sleep, baby, sleep)*

EAN-No.	Period	Pr.	Info
210402	1998-1998	2	30 cm

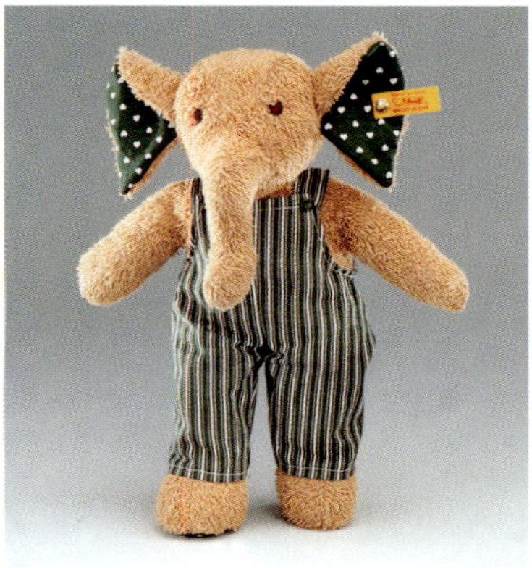

Elefant - *Elephant*

Baumwolle, beige/gruen, waschmaschinenfest, gruene Latzhose - *cotton, beige/green, machine washable, green dungarees*

EAN-No.	Period	Pr.	Info
210419	1998-1999	2	35 cm

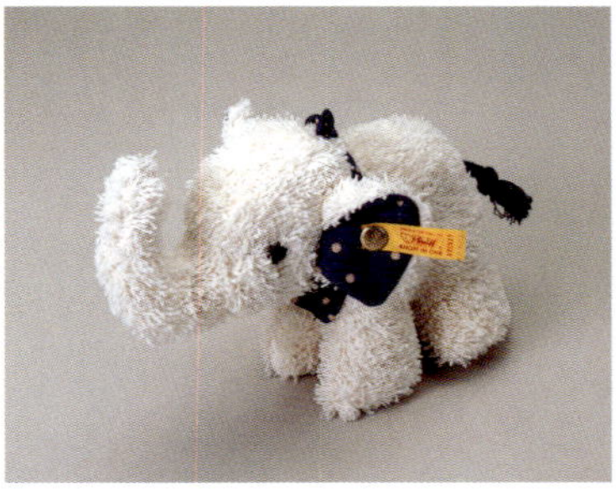

Elefant - *Elephant*

Baumwolle, weiss/blau, waschmaschinenfest, Rassel, Halstuch - *cotton, white/blue, machine washable, rattle, scarf*

EAN-No.	Period	Pr.	Info
221927	1999-1999	1-2	16 cm

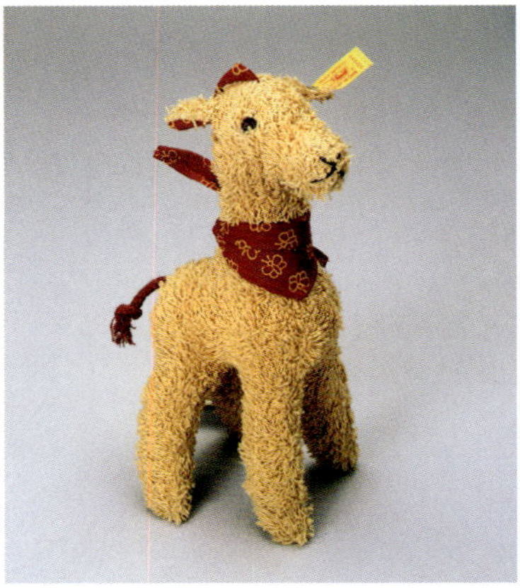

Giraffe

Baumwolle, honig/rot, waschmaschinenfest, Rassel, Halstuch - *cotton, honey/red, machine washable, rattle, scarf*

EAN-No.	Period	Pr.	Info
222085	1999-1999	1-2	21 cm

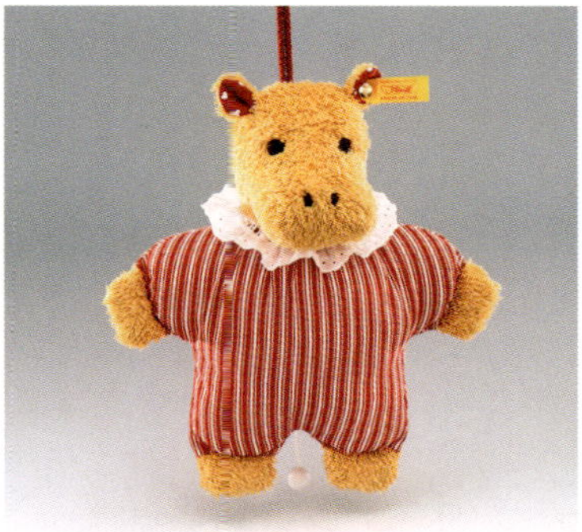

Nilpferd - *Hippopotamus*

Baumwolle, honig/rot, abwaschbar, Musikwerk (Schlafe mein Prinzchen) - *cotton, honey/red, surface washable, music box (Sleep my little prince)*

EAN-No.	Period	Pr.	Info
210501	1998-1998	2	30 cm

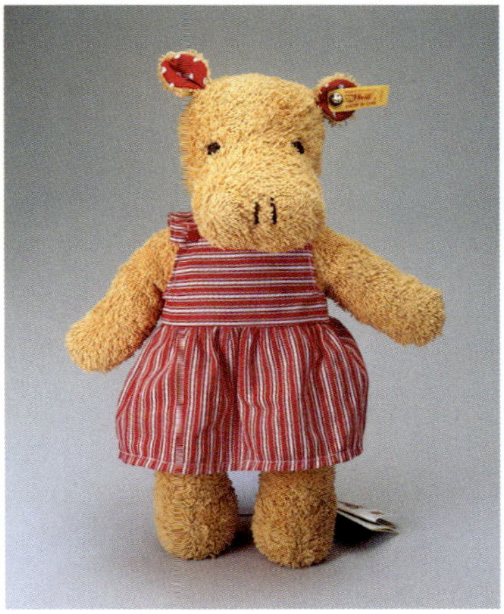

Nilpferd - *Hippopotamus*

Baumwolle, honig/rot, waschmaschinenfest, rotes Kleid - *cotton, honey/red, machine washable, red dress*

EAN-No.	Period	Pr.	Info
210518	1998-1999	2	35 cm

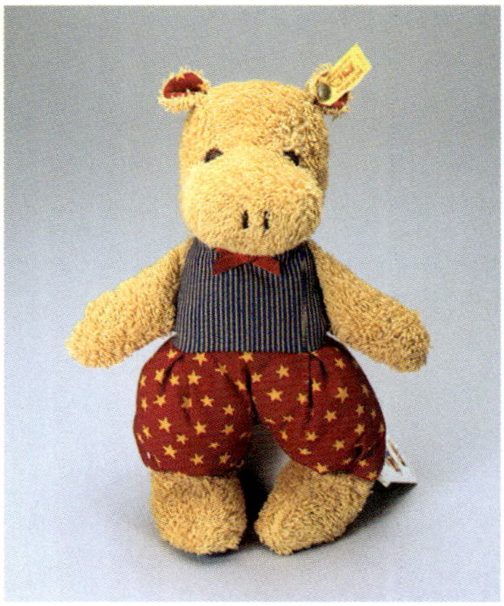

Nilpferd (Bub) - *Hippopotamus (Boy)*

Baumwolle, honig/rot, waschmaschinenfest - *cotton, honey/red, machine washable*

EAN-No.	Period	Pr.	Info
217104	1998-1999	2	30 cm

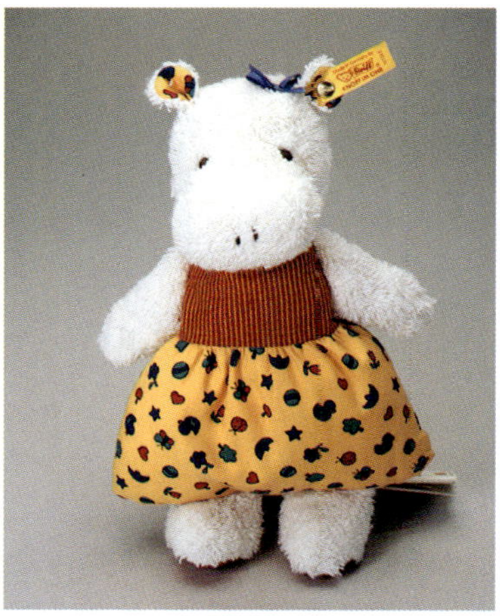

Nilpferd (Maedi) - *Hippopotamus (Girl)*

Baumwolle, weiss/gelb, waschmaschinenfest - *cotton, white/yellow, machine washable*

EAN-No.	Period	Pr.	Info
217159	1998-1999	2	30 cm

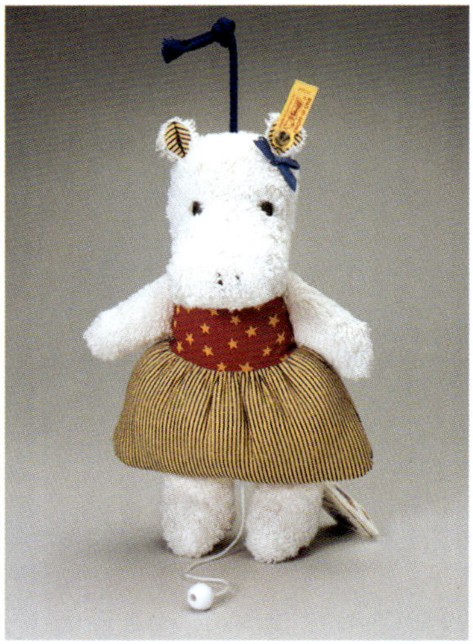

Nilpferd (Maedi) - *Hippopotamus (Girl)*

Baumwolle, weiss/gelb, abwaschbar, Musikwerk (Schlafe mein Prinzchen) - *cotton, white/yellow, surface washable, music box (Sleep my little prince)*

EAN-No.	Period	Pr.	Info
217166	1998-1999	2	30 cm

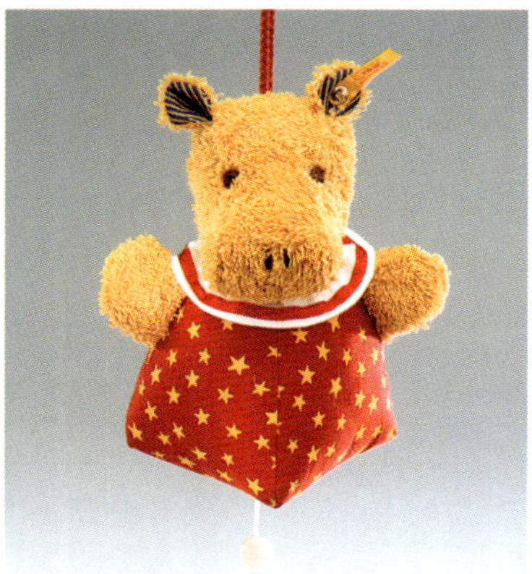

Baby-Nilpferd - *Baby Hippopotamus*

Baumwolle, honig/rot, waschmaschinenfest, Musikwerk (Weisst Du wieviel Sternlein ...) - *cotton, honey/red, machine washable, music box (Count the Stars)*

EAN-No.	Period	Pr.	Info
212994	1999-1999	2	17 cm

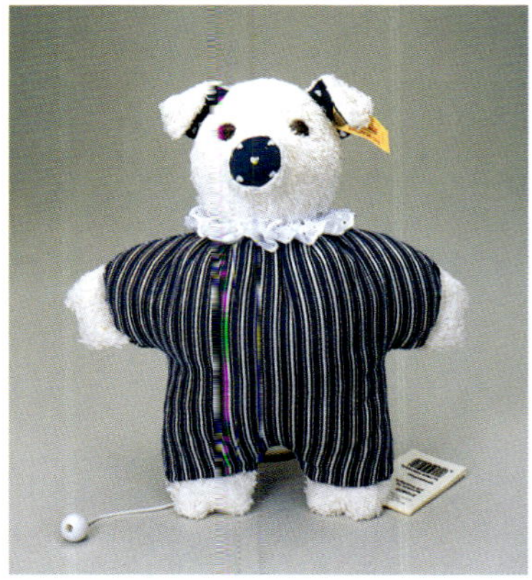

Schwein - *Pig*

Baumwolle, weiss/blau, abwaschbar, Musikwerk (Weisst Du wieviel Sternlein) - *cotton, white/blue, surface washable, music box (Count the Stars)*

EAN-No.	Period	Pr.	Info
210600	1998-1998	2	30 cm

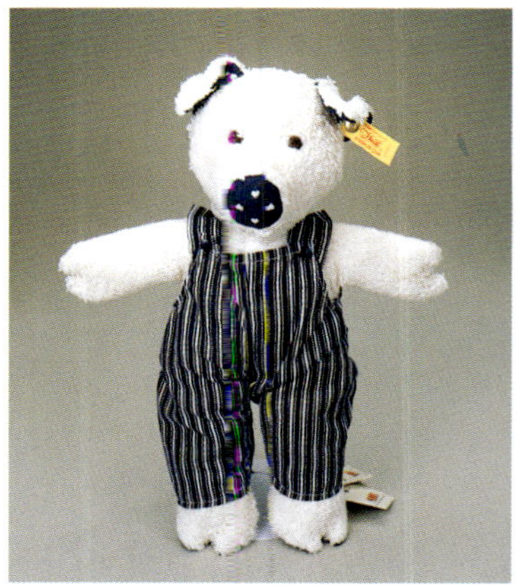

Schwein - *Pig*

Baumwolle, weiss/blau, waschmaschinenfest, blaue Latzhose - *cotton, white/blue, machine washable, blue dungarees*

EAN-No.	Period	Pr.	Info
210617	1998-1999	2	35 cm

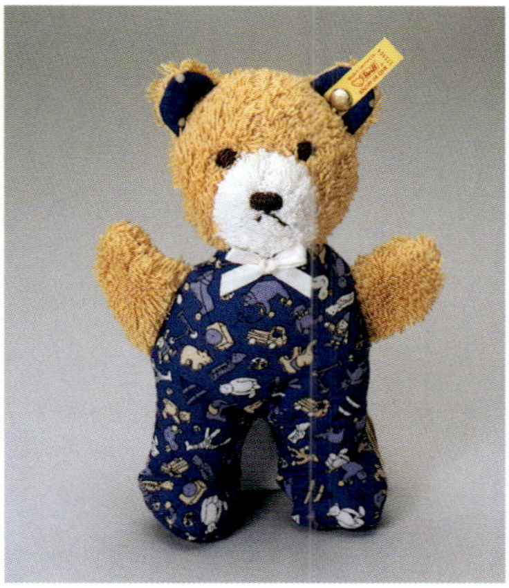

Baer - *Bear*

Baumwolle, 22 cm, waschmaschinenfest - *cotton, 22 cm, machine washable*

EAN-No.	Period	Pr.	Info
211904	1998-1999	1-2	honig/blau - *honey/blue*
214202	1998-1999	1-2	braun/rot - *brown/red*
214301	1998-1999	1-2	honig/blau, gelbe Sterne - *honey/blue, yellow stars*

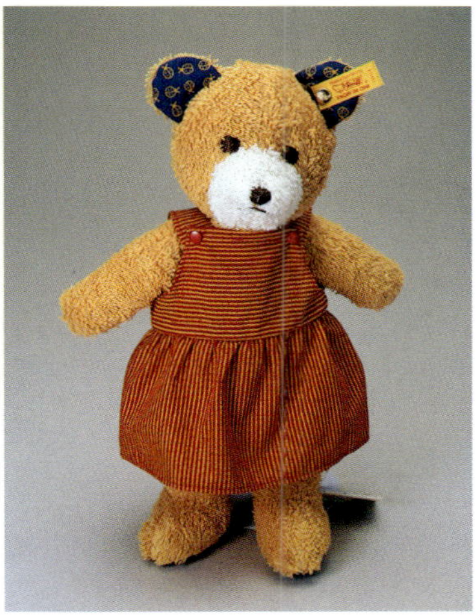

Baer - *Bear*

Baumwolle, 35 cm, waschmaschinenfest, mit Kleid - *cotton, 35 cm, machine washable, with dress*

EAN-No.	Period	Pr.	Info
211911	1998-1999	2	braun/ocker - *brown/ochre*
214318	1998-1999	2	honig/blau - *honey/blue*

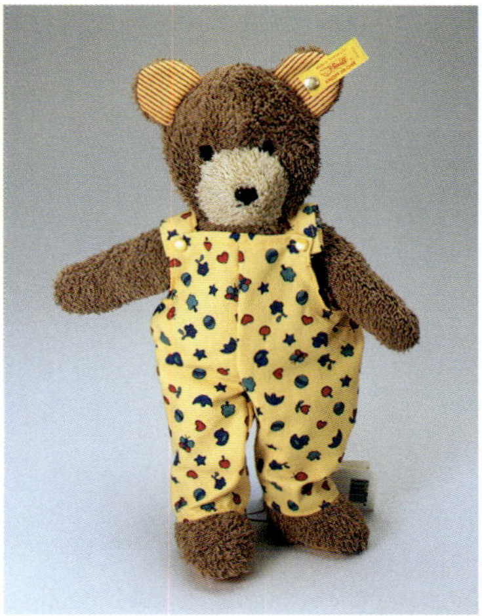

Baer - *Bear*

Baumwolle, braun/gelb, waschmaschinenfest, gelbe Latzhose - *cotton, brown/yellow, machine washable, yellow dungarees*

EAN-No.	Period	Pr.	Info
214219	1998-1999	2	35 cm

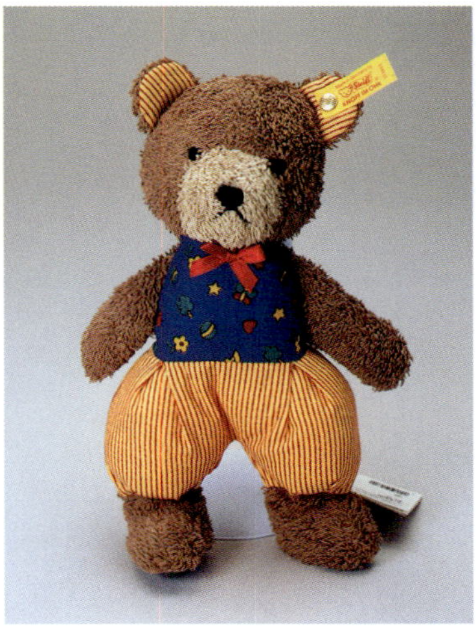

Baer (Bub) - *Bear (Boy)*

Baumwolle, braun/gelb, waschmaschinenfest - *cotton, brown/yellow, machine washable*

EAN-No.	Period	Pr.	Info
216800	1998-1999	2	30 cm

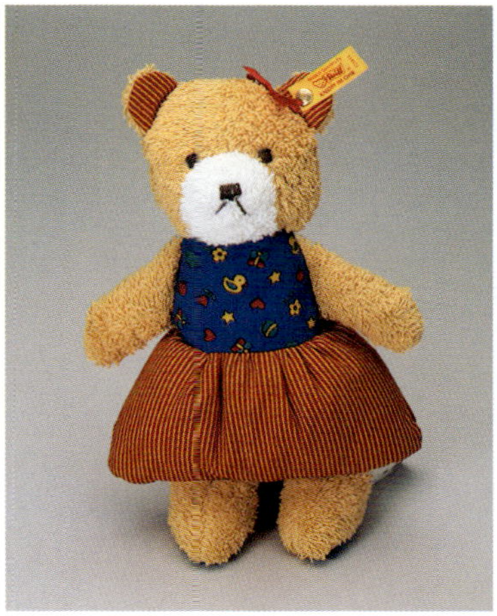

Baer (Maedi) - *Bear (Girl)*

Baumwolle, honig/rot, waschmaschinenfest - *cotton, honey/red, machine washable*

EAN-No.	Period	Pr.	Info
216855	1998-1999	2	30 cm

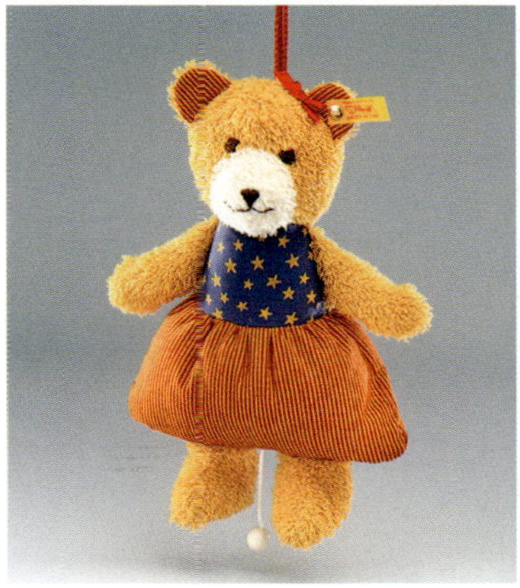

Baer (Maedi) - *Bear (Girl)*

Baumwolle, honig/rot, abwaschbar, Musikwerk (Weisst Du wieviel Sternlein) - *cotton, honey/red, surface washable, music box (Count the Stars)*

EAN-No.	Period	Pr.	Info
216862	1998-1999	2	30 cm

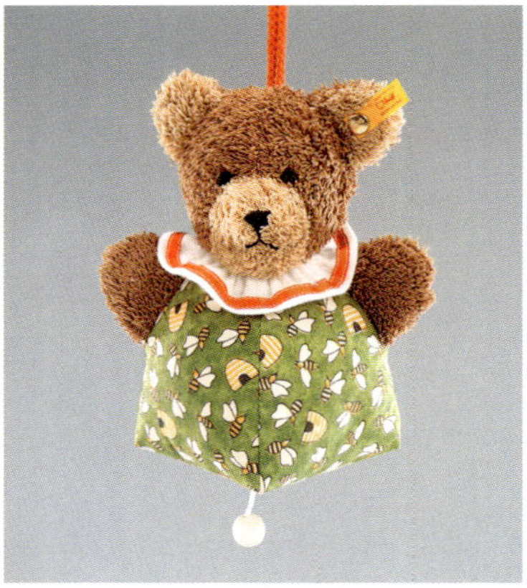

Baby-Baer - *Baby-Bear*

Baumwolle, braun/gruen, waschmaschinenfest, Musikwerk (Schubert´s Sandmaennchen) - *cotton, brown/green, machine washable, music box (Schubert´s Lullaby)*

EAN-No.	Period	Pr.	Info
211959	1999-1999	2	17 cm

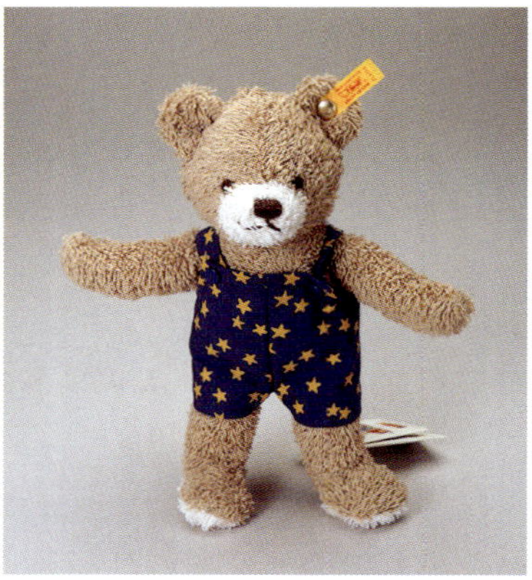

Baer - *Bear*

Baumwolle, beige, waschmaschinenfest, blaue Latzhose - *cotton, beige, machine washable, blue dungarees*

EAN-No.	Period	Pr.	Info
214325	1999-1999	1-2	22 cm

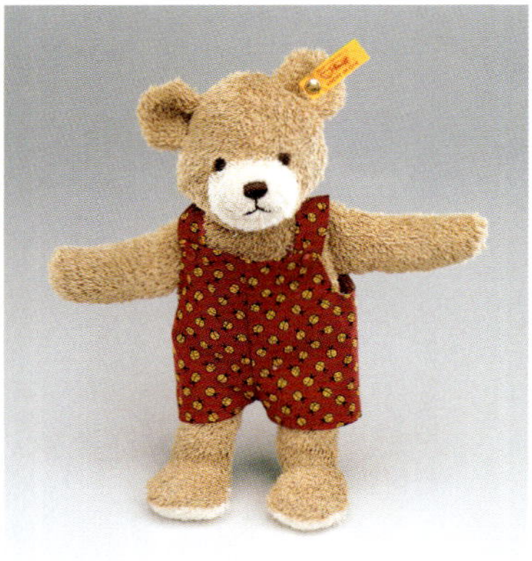

Baer - *Bear*

Baumwolle, beige, waschmaschinenfest, rote Latzhose - *cotton, beige, machine washable, red dungarees*

EAN-No.	Period	Pr.	Info
214332	1999-1999	2	28 cm

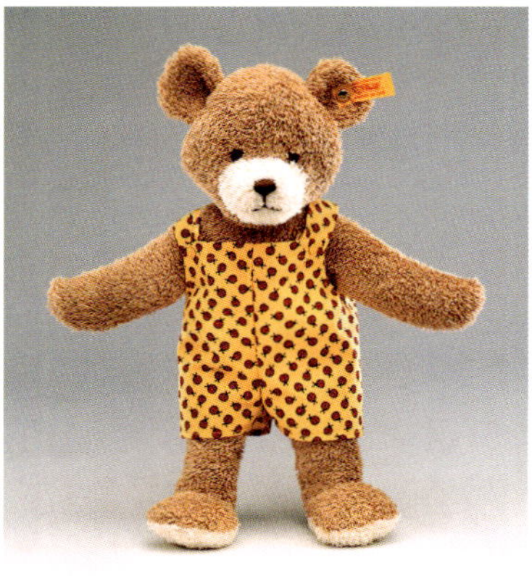

Baer - *Bear*

Baumwolle, beige, waschmaschinenfest, gelbe Latzhose - *cotton, beige, machine washable, yellow dungarees*

EAN-No.	Period	Pr.	Info
214349	1999-1999	2	35 cm

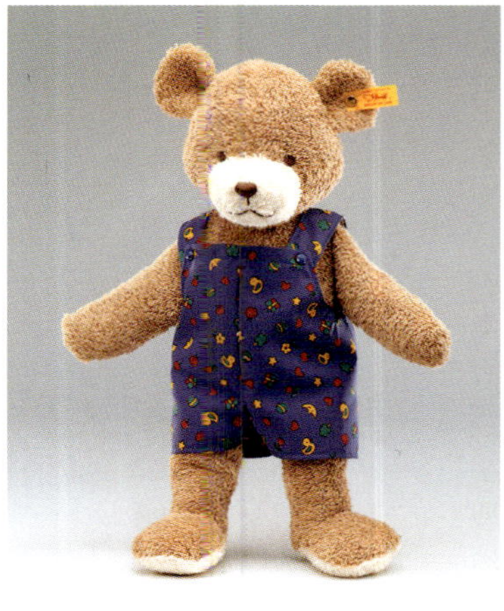

Baer - *Bear*

Baumwolle, beige, waschmaschinenfest, blaue Latzhose - *cotton, beige, machine washable, blue dungarees*

EAN-No.	Period	Pr.	Info
214356	1999-1999	2-3	40 cm

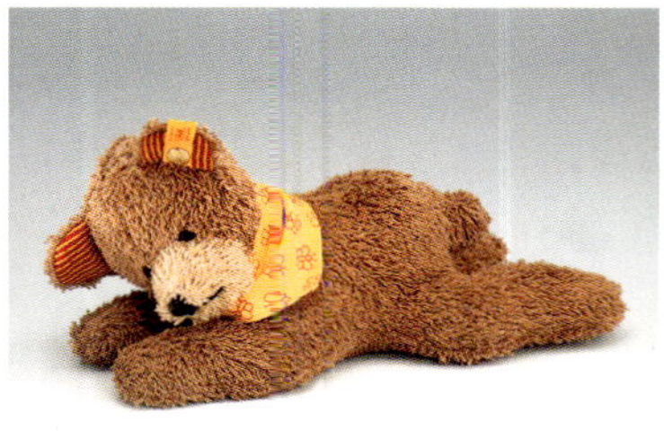

Baer - *Bear*

Baumwolle, braun/rot, liegend, waschmaschinenfest, Halstuch - *cotton, brown/red, lying, machine washable, scarf*

EAN-No.	Period	Pr.	Info
221132	1999-1999	1-2	22 cm

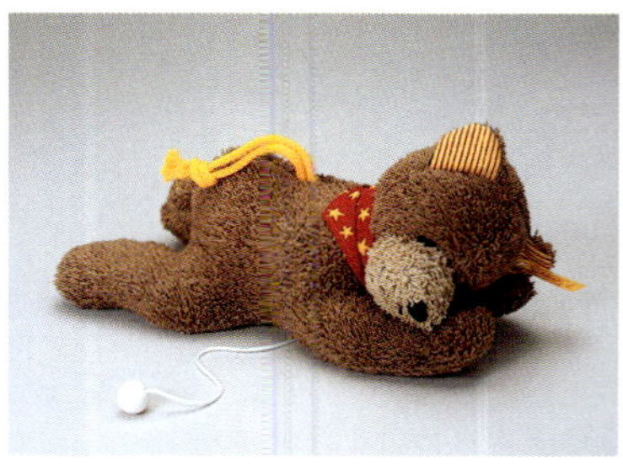

Baer - *Bear*

Baumwolle, braun/gelb, liegend, waschmaschinenfest, Halstuch, Musikwerk (Schlafe mein Prinzchen) - *cotton, brown/yellow, lying, machine washable, scarf, music box (Sleep my little prince)*

EAN-No.	Period	Pr.	Info
221149	1999-1999	2	28 cm

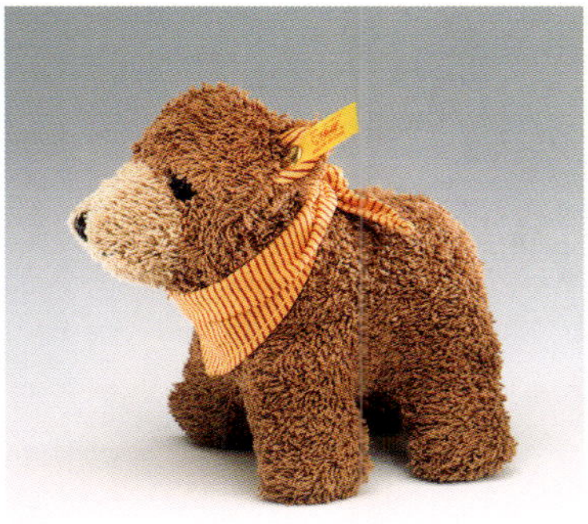

Baer - *Bear*

Baumwolle, braun/gelb, waschmaschinenfest, Rassel, Halstuch - *cotton, brown/yellow, machine washable, rattle, scarf*

EAN-No.	Period	Pr.	Info
221767	1999-1999	1-2	16 cm

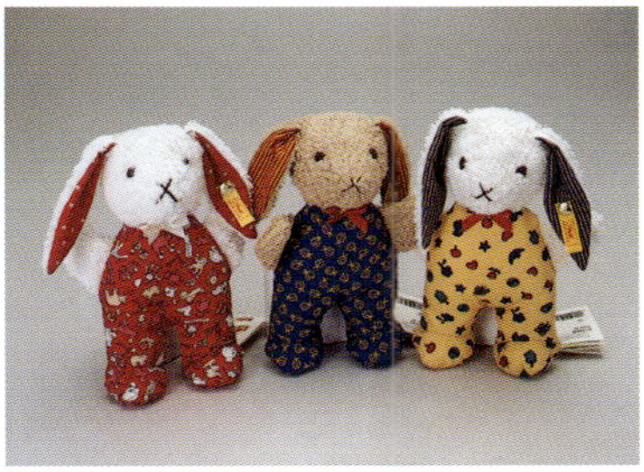

Hase - *Rabbit*

Baumwolle, 22 cm, waschmaschinenfest - *cotton, 22 cm, machine washable*

EAN-No.	Period	Pr.	Info
212109	1998-1999	1-2	weiss/rot - *white/red*
214608	1998-1999	1-2	weiss/gelb - *white/yellow*
214707	1998-1999	1-2	beige/blau - *beige/blue*

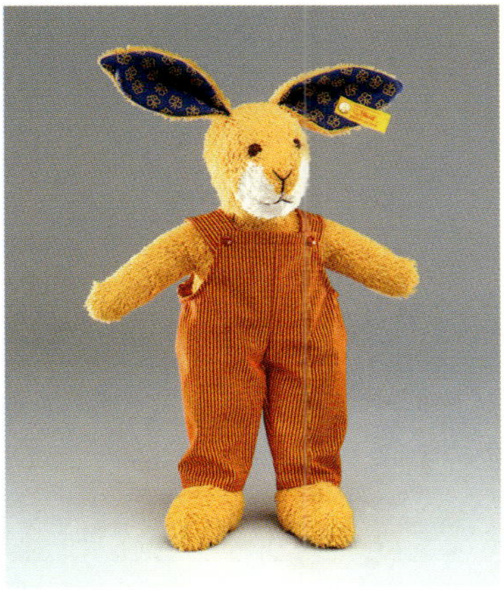

Hase - *Rabbit*

Baumwolle, 35 cm, waschmaschinenfest, mit Latzhose - *cotton, 35 cm, machine washable, with dungarees*

EAN-No.	Period	Pr.	Info
212116	1998-1999	2	honig/blau, blaue Latzhose - *honey/blue, blue dungarees*
214714	1998-1999	2	honig/blau, rote Latzhose - *honey/blue, red dungarees*

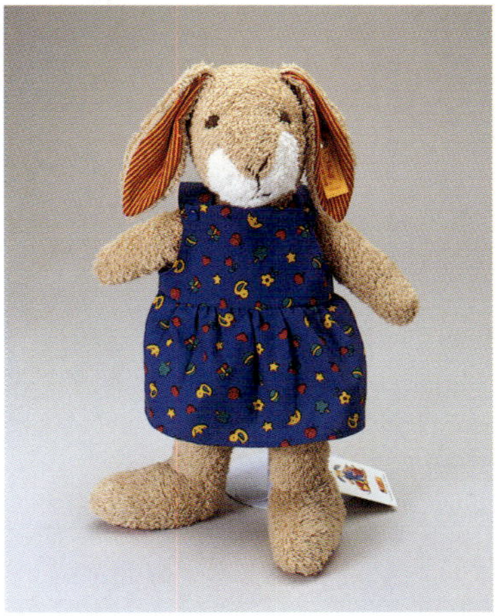

Hase - *Rabbit*

Baumwolle, beige/rot, waschmaschinenfest, blaues Kleid - *cotton, beige/red, machine washable, blue dress*

EAN-No.	Period	Pr.	Info
214615	1998-1999	2	35 cm

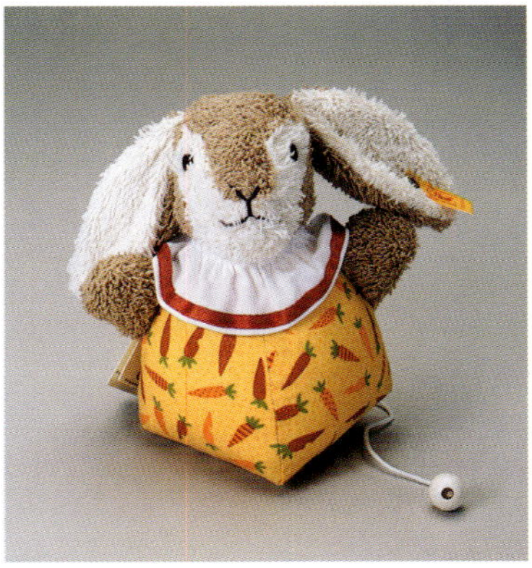

Baby-Hase - *Baby-Rabbit*

Baumwolle, beige/gelb, waschmaschinenfest, Musikwerk (Schlaf, Kindlein, schlaf) - *cotton, beige/yellow, machine washable, music box (Sleep, baby, sleep)*

EAN-No.	Period	Pr.	Info
212154	1999-1999	2	17 cm

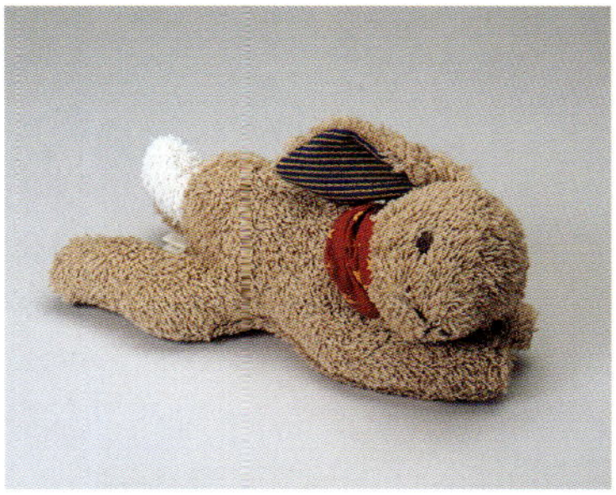

Hase - *Rabbit*

Baumwolle, beige/blau, liegend, waschmaschinenfest, Halstuch - *cotton, beige/blue, lying, machine washable, scarf*

EAN-No.	Period	Pr.	Info
221255	1999-1999	1-2	22 cm

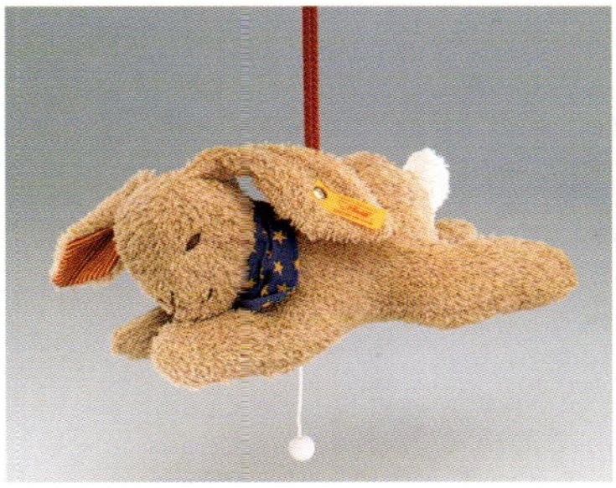

Hase - *Rabbit*

Baumwolle, beige/rot, liegend, waschmaschinenfest, Halstuch, Musikwerk (Guten Abend, gute Nacht) - *cotton, beige/red, lying, machine washable, scarf, music box (Brahm´s Lullaby)*

EAN-No.	Period	Pr.	Info
221262	1999-1999	2	28 cm

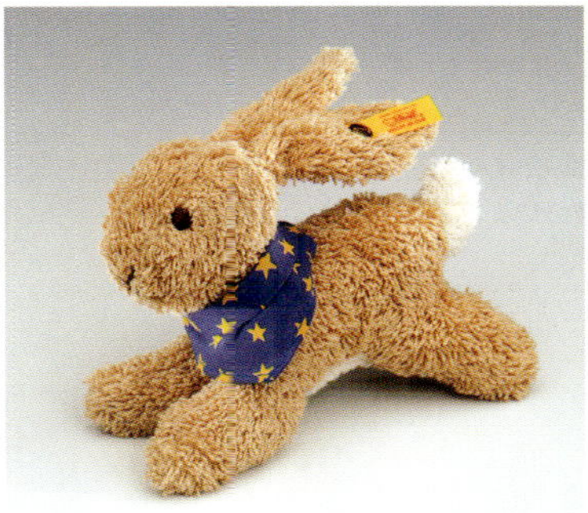

Hase - *Rabbit*

Baumwolle, beige/blau, waschmaschinenfest, Rassel, Halstuch - *cotton, beige/blue, machine washable, rattle, scarf*

EAN-No.	Period	Pr.	Info
222726	1999-1999	1-2	16 cm

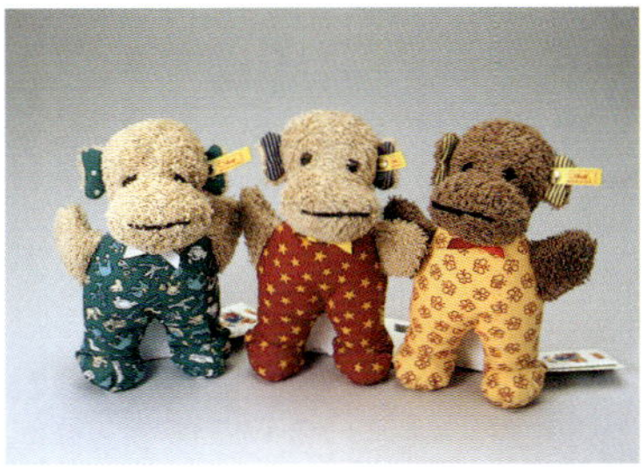

Affe - *Monkey*

Baumwolle, 22 cm, waschmaschinenfest - *cotton, 22 cm, machine washable*

EAN-No.	Period	Pr.	Info
212307	1998-1999	1-2	beige/gruen - *beige/green*
215001	1998-1999	1-2	braun/gelb - *brown/yellow*
215100	1998-1999	1-2	beige/rot - *beige/red*

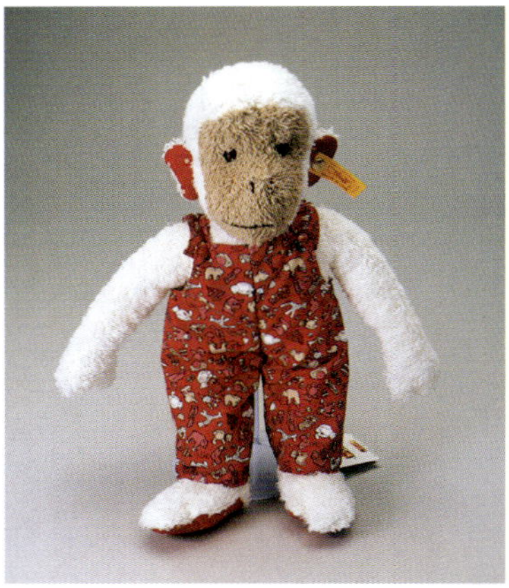

Affe - *Monkey*

Baumwolle, 35 cm, waschmaschinenfest, mit Latzhose - *cotton, 35 cm, machine washable, with dungarees*

EAN-No.	Period	Pr.	Info
212314	1998-1999	2	weiss/rot - *white/red*
215117	1998-1999	2	weiss/blau - *white/blue*

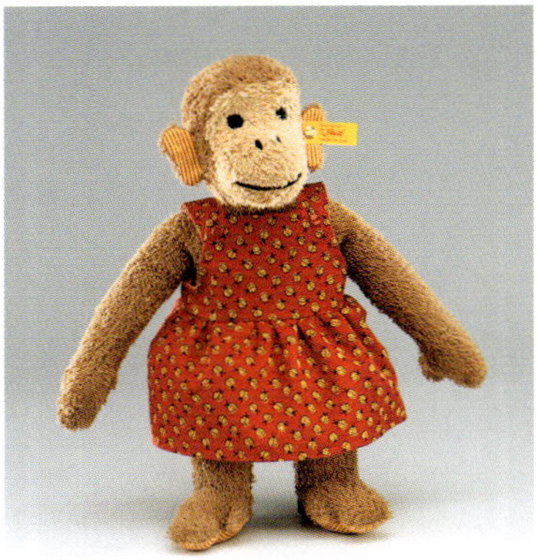

Affe - *Monkey*

Baumwolle, braun/gelb, waschmaschinenfest, rotes Kleid - *cotton, brown/yellow, machine washable, red dress*

EAN-No.	Period	Pr.	Info
215018	1998-1999	2	35 cm

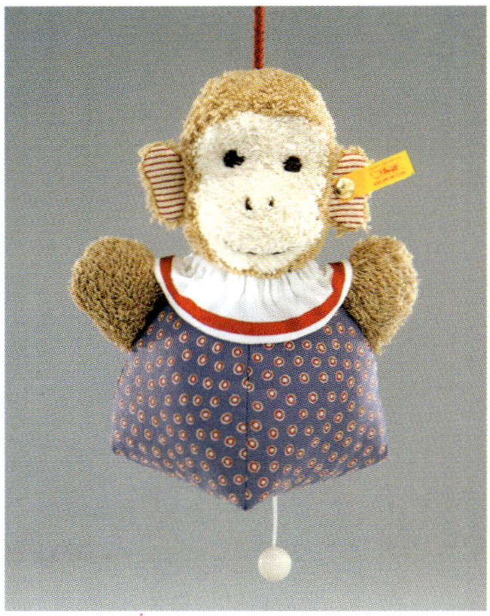

Baby-Affe - *Baby-Monkey*

Baumwolle, beige/blau, waschmaschinenfest, Musikwerk (Guten Abend, gute Nacht) - *cotton, beige/blue, machine washable, scarf, music box (Brahm´s Lullaby)*

EAN-No.	Period	Pr.	Info
212352	1999-1999	2	17 cm

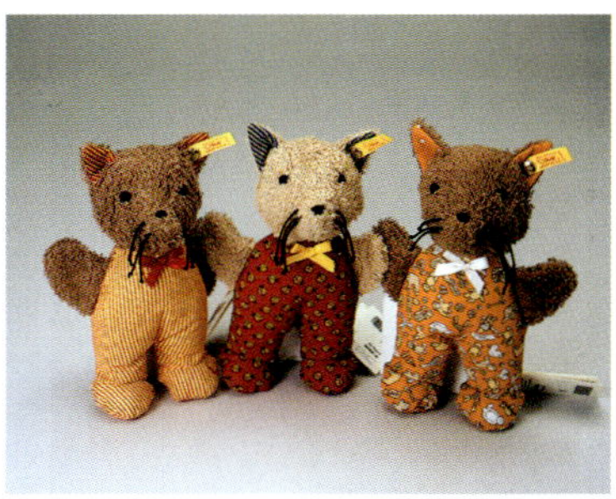

Katze - *Cat*

Baumwolle, 22 cm, waschmaschinenfest - *cotton, 22 cm, machine washable*

EAN-No.	Period	Pr.	Info
212505	1998-1999	1-2	braun/ocker - *brown/ochre*
215407	1998-1999	1-2	braun/gelb - *brown/yellow*
215506	1998-1999	1-2	beige/rot - *beige/red*

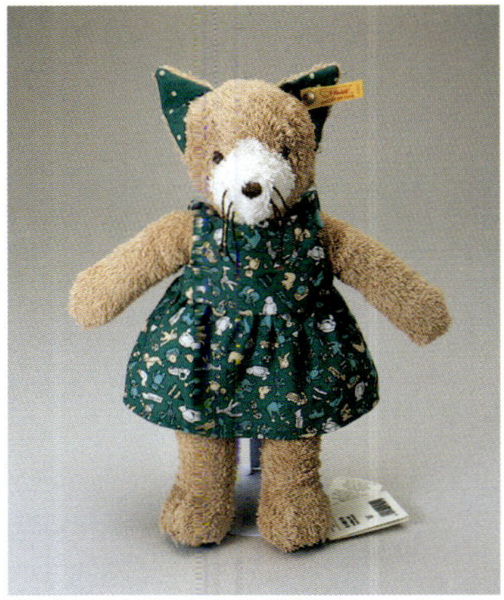

Katze - *Cat*

Baumwolle, 35 cm, waschmaschinenfest, mit Kleid - *cotton, 22 cm, machine washable, with dress*

EAN-No.	Period	Pr.	Info
212512	1998-1999	2	beige/gruen - *beige/green*
215414	1998-1999	2	beige/rot - *beige/red*

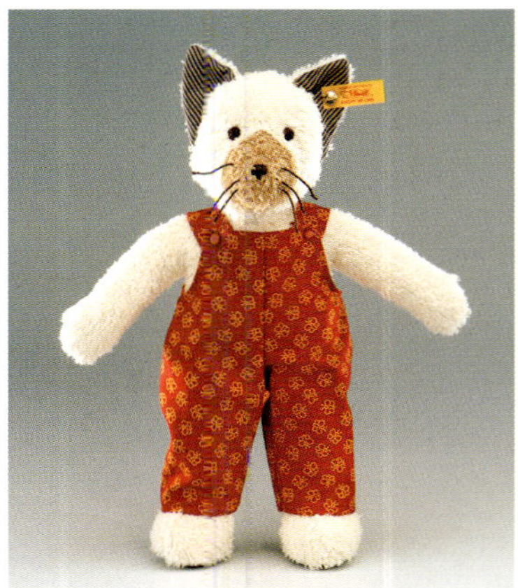

Katze - *Cat*

Baumwolle, weiss/blau, waschmaschinenfest, rote Latzhose - *cotton, white/blue, machine washable, red dungarees*

EAN-No.	Period	Pr.	Info
215513	1998-1999	2	35 cm

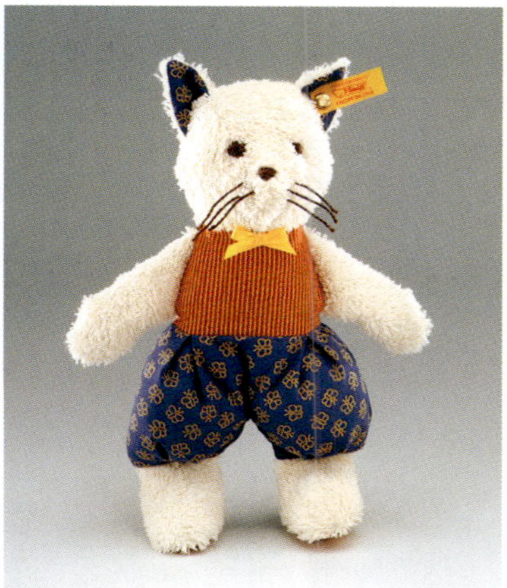

Katze (Bub) - *Cat (Boy)*

Baumwolle, weiss/blau, waschmaschinenfest - *cotton, white/blue, machine washable*

EAN-No.	Period	Pr.	Info
217708	1998-1999	2	30 cm

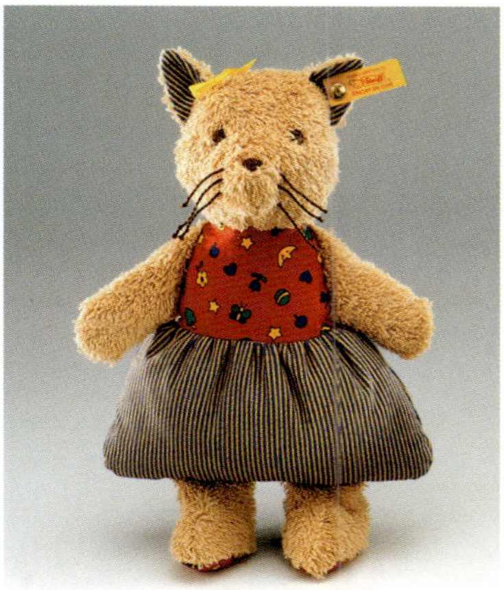

Katze (Maedi) - *Cat (Girl)*

Baumwolle, beige/blau, waschmaschinenfest - *cotton, beige/blue, machine washable*

EAN-No.	Period	Pr.	Info
217753	1998-1999	2	30 cm

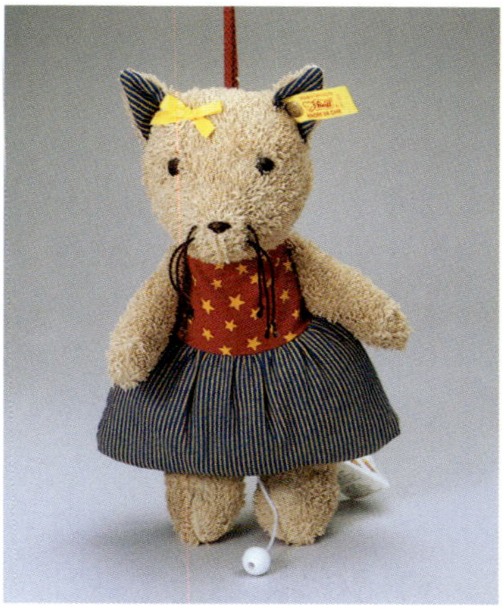

Katze (Maedi) - *Cat (Girl)*

Baumwolle, beige/blau, abwaschbar, Musikwerk (Guter Mond) - *cotton, beige/blue, surface washable, music box (Good moon)*

EAN-No.	Period	Pr.	Info
217760	1998-1999	2	30 cm

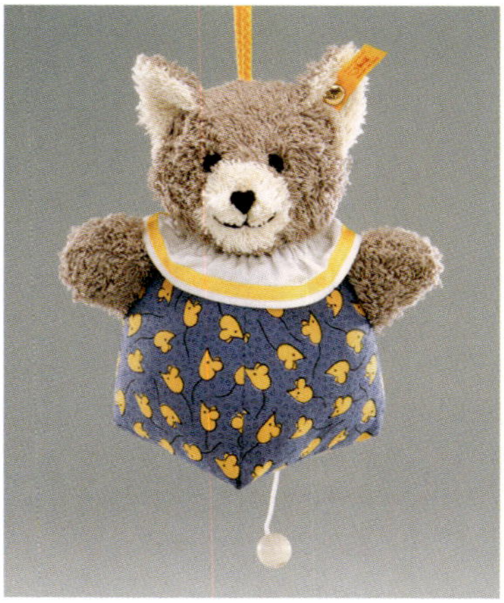

Baby-Katze - *Baby-Cat*

Baumwolle, grau/blau, waschmaschinenfest, Musikwerk (La Le Lu) - *cotton, gray/blue, machine washable, music box (La Le Lu)*

EAN-No.	Period	Pr.	Info
212550	1999-1999	2	17 cm

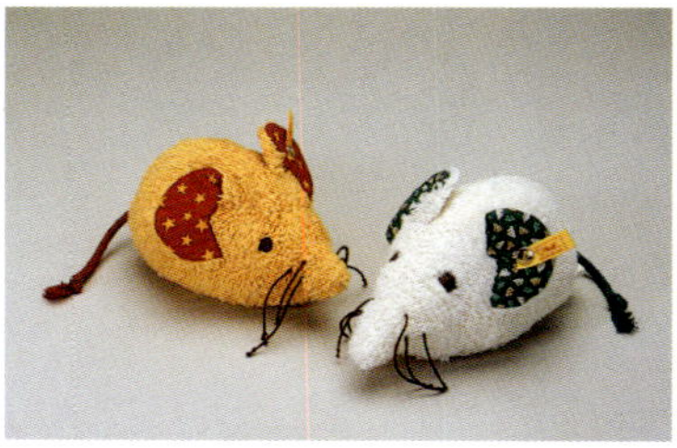

Maus - *Mouse*

Baumwolle, 16 cm, waschmaschinenfest, Pieps-Stimme - *cotton, 16 cm, machine washable, squeaker*

EAN-No.	Period	Pr.	Info
212703	1998-1999	1	weiss/gruen - *white/green*
212710	1998-1999	1	beige/blau - *beige/blue*
219009	1998-1999	1	honig/rot - *honey/red*
219054	1998-1999	1	weiss/blau - *white/blue*

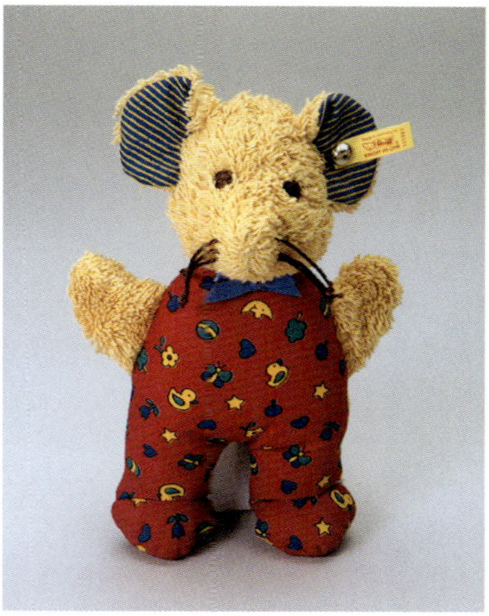

Maus - *Mouse*

Baumwolle, 22 cm, waschmaschinenfest - *cotton, 22 cm, machine washable*

EAN-No.	Period	Pr.	Info
215803	1998-1999	1-2	weiss/blau - *white/blue*
215902	1998-1999	1-2	honig/rot - *honey/red*

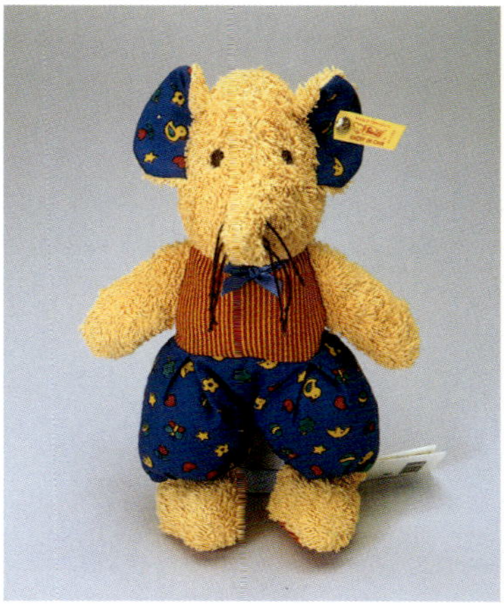

Maus (Bub) - *Mouse (Boy)*

Baumwolle, honig/blau, waschmaschinenfest - *cotton, honey/blue, machine washable*

EAN-No.	Period	Pr.	Info
217401	1998-1999	2	30 cm

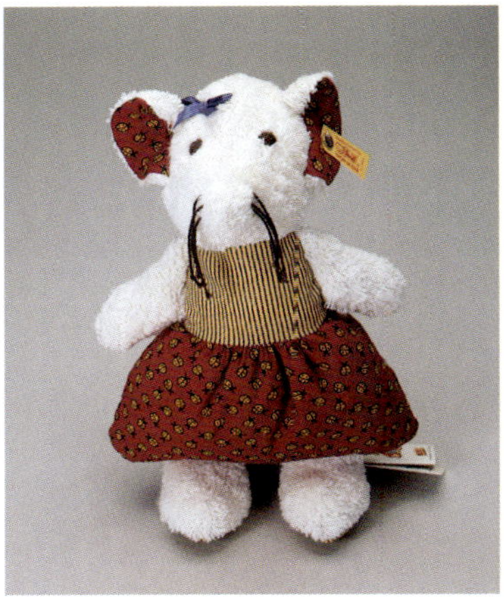

Maus (Maedi) - *Mouse (Girl)*

Baumwolle, weiss/rot, waschmaschinenfest - *cotton, white/red, machine washable*

EAN-No.	Period	Pr.	Info
217456	1998-1999	2	30 cm

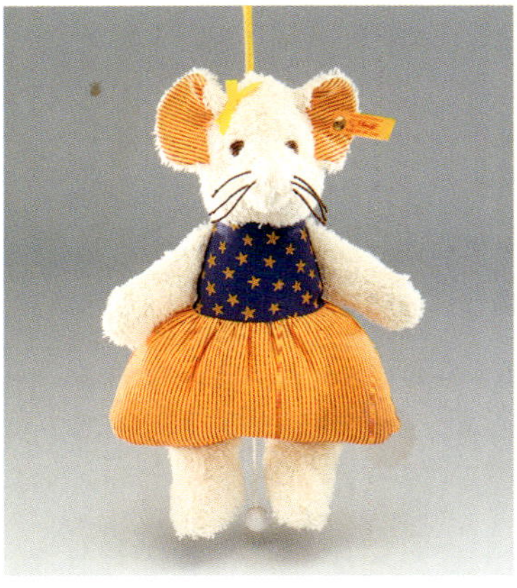

Maus (Maedi) - *Mouse (Girl)*

Baumwolle, weiss/gelb, abwaschbar, Musikwerk (Schlaf, Kindlein, schlaf) - *cotton, white/yellow, surface washable, music box (Sleep, baby, sleep)*

EAN-No.	Period	Pr.	Info
217463	1998-1999	2	30 cm

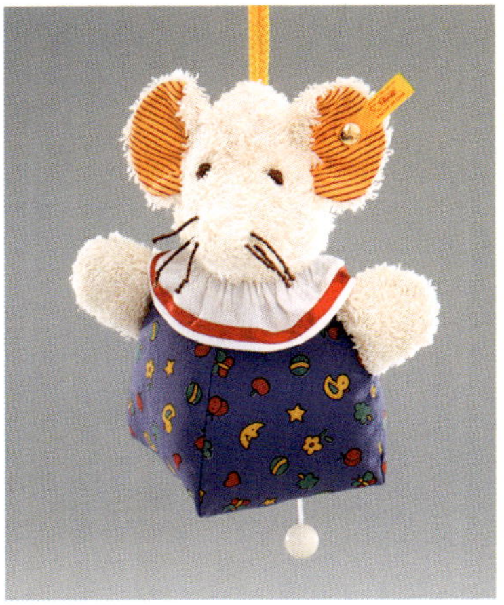

Baby-Maus - *Baby-Mouse*

Baumwolle, weiss/blau, waschmaschinenfest, Musikwerk (Schlaf, Kindlein, schlaf) - *cotton, white/yellow, machine washable, music box (sleep, baby, sleep)*

EAN-No.	Period	Pr.	Info
212758	1999-1999	2	17 cm

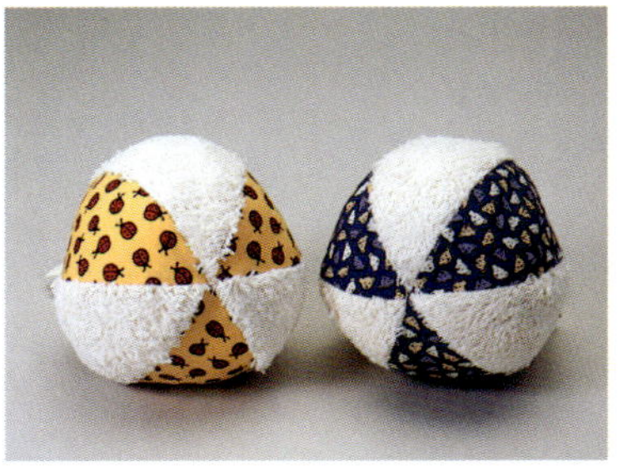

Ball

Baumwolle, 10 cm, waschmaschinenfest, mit Rassel - *cotton, 10 cm, machine washable, with rattle*

EAN-No.	Period	Pr.	Info
213601	1998-1999	1	weiss/blau - *white/blue*
221002	1998-1999	1	weiss/gelb - *white/yellow*

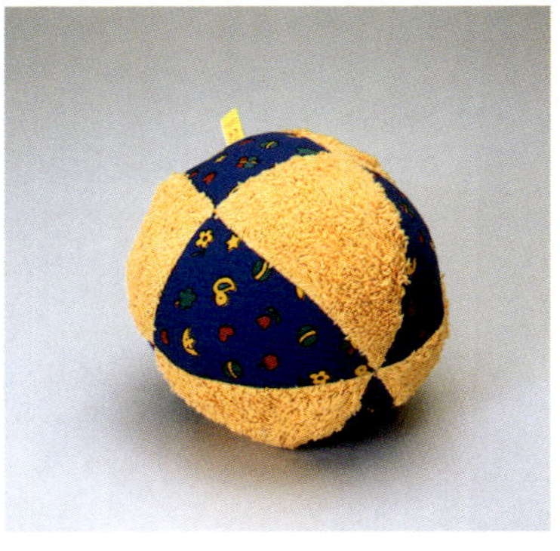

Ball

Baumwolle, 15 cm, waschmaschinenfest, Rassel - *cotton, 15 cm, machine washable, rattle*

EAN-No.	Period	Pr.	Info
213618	1998-1999	1	honig/rot - *honey/red*
221101	1998-1999	1	honig/blau - *honey/blue*

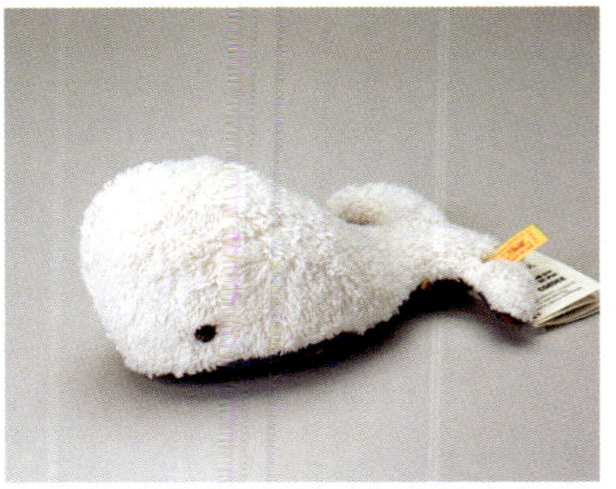

Wal - *Whale*

Baumwolle, weiss/blau, waschmaschinenfest, Pieps-Stimme - *cotton, white/blue, machine washable, squeaker*

EAN-No.	Period	Pr.	Info
220203	1998-1999	1	20 cm

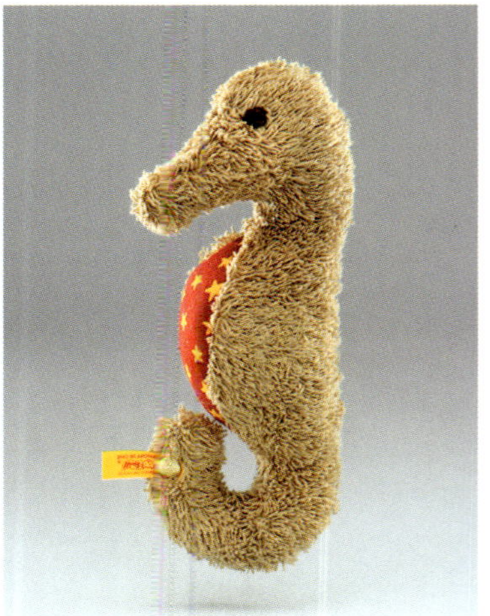

Seepferdchen - *Seahorse*

Baumwolle, beige/rot, waschmaschinenfest, Rassel - *cotton, beige/red, machine washable, rattle*

EAN-No.	Period	Pr.	Info
220302	1998-1999	1	20 cm

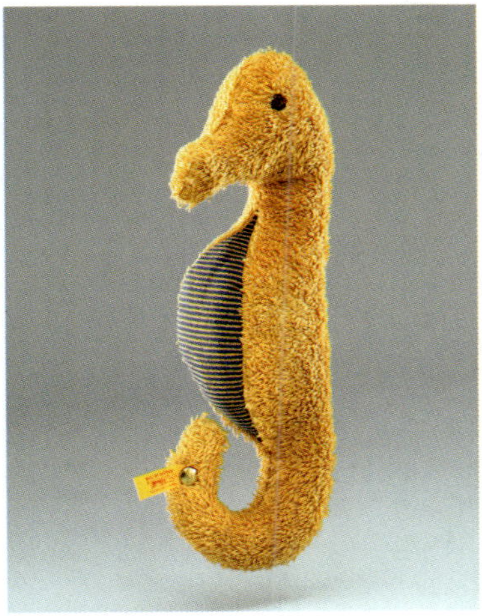

Seepferdchen - *Seahorse*

Baumwolle, 25 cm, waschmaschinenfest, Pieps-Stimme - *cotton, 25 cm, machine washable, squeaker*

EAN-No.	Period	Pr.	Info
220326	1998-1999	1	honig/blau - *honey/blue*
220340	1999-1999	1	beige/creme

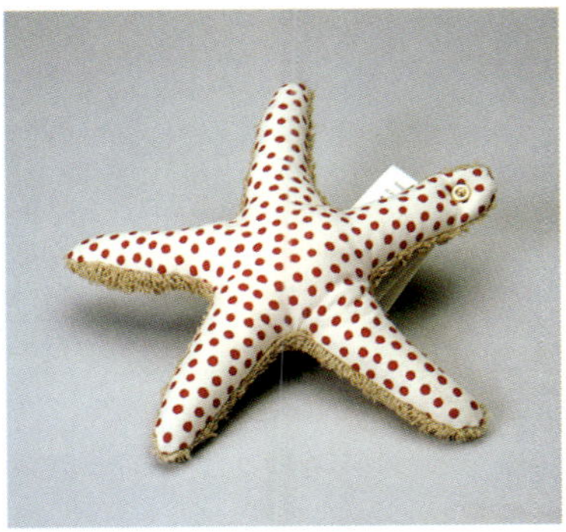

Seestern - *Starfish*

Baumwolle, 20 cm, waschmaschinenfest, Pieps-Stimme - *cotton, 20 cm, machine washable, squeaker*

EAN-No.	Period	Pr.	Info
220500	1998-1999	1	honig/rot - *honey/red*
220555	1998-1999	1	beige/blau - *beige/blue*
220579	1999-1999	1	beige/creme - *beige/cream*

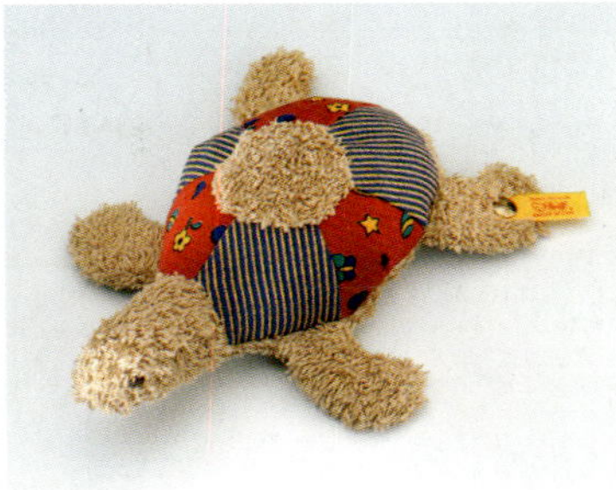

Schildkroete - *Turtle*

Baumwolle, 15 cm, waschmaschinenfest, Rassel - *cotton, 15 cm, machine washable, squeaker*

EAN-No.	Period	Pr.	Info
219900	1999-1999	1	beige/rot - *beige/red*
219917	1999-1999	1	braun/blau - *brown/blue*

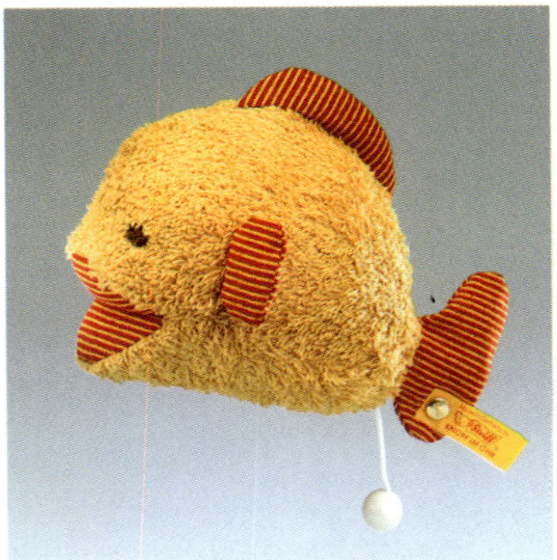

Fisch - *Fish*

Baumwolle, honig/rot, waschmaschinenfest, Musikwerk (Schlaf, Kindlein, schlaf) - *cotton, honey/red, machine washable, music box (Sleep, baby, sleep)*

EAN-No.	Period	Pr.	Info
219986	1999-1999	1-2	15 cm

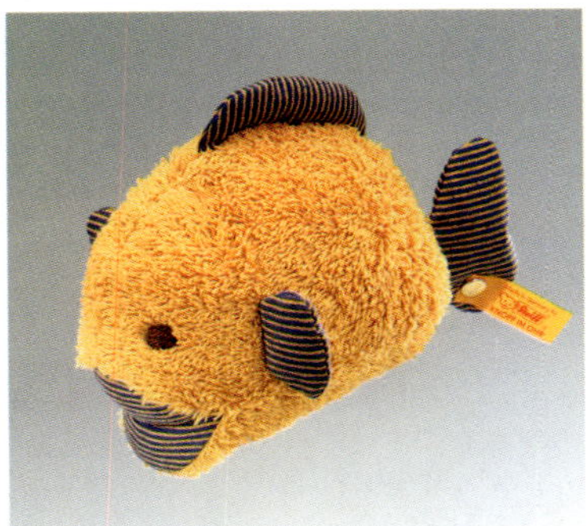

Fisch - *Fish*

Baumwolle, honig/blau, waschmaschinenfest, Druckstimme - *cotton, honey/blue, machine washable, press voice*

EAN-No.	Period	Pr.	Info
219993	1999-1999	1	15 cm

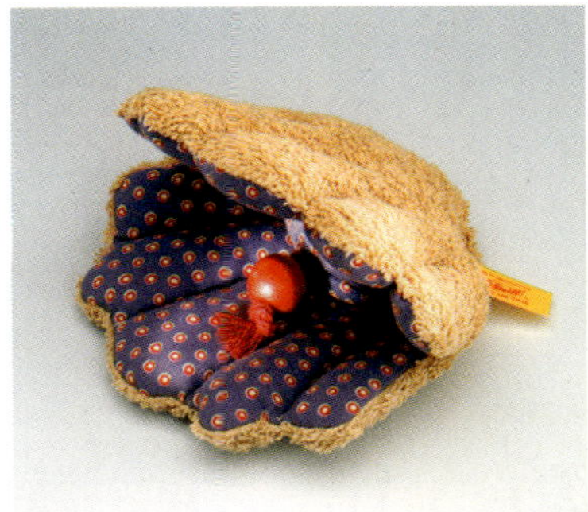

Muschel - *Shell*

Baumwolle, 15 cm, waschmaschinenfest, Holzperle - *cotton, 15 cm, machine washable, wooden pearl*

EAN-No.	Period	Pr.	Info
220654	1999-1999	1	beige/blau - *beige/blue*
220661	1999-1999	1	weiss/rot - *white/red*

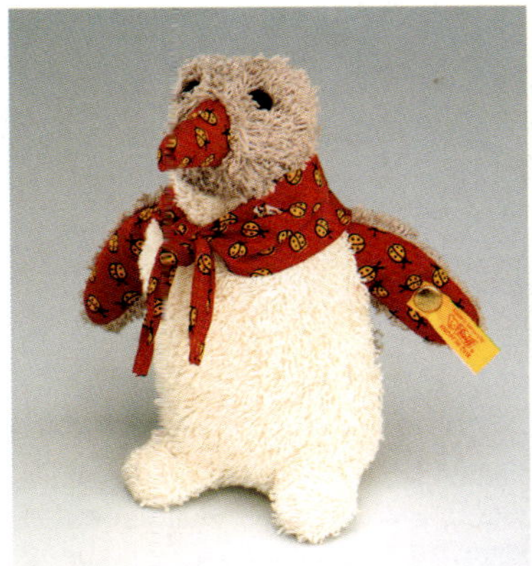

Pinguin - *Penguin*

Baumwolle, grau/rot, waschmaschinenfest, Rassel, Halstuch - *cotton, grey/red, machine washable, rattle, scarf*

EAN-No.	Period	Pr.	Info
223365	1999-1999	1	16 cm

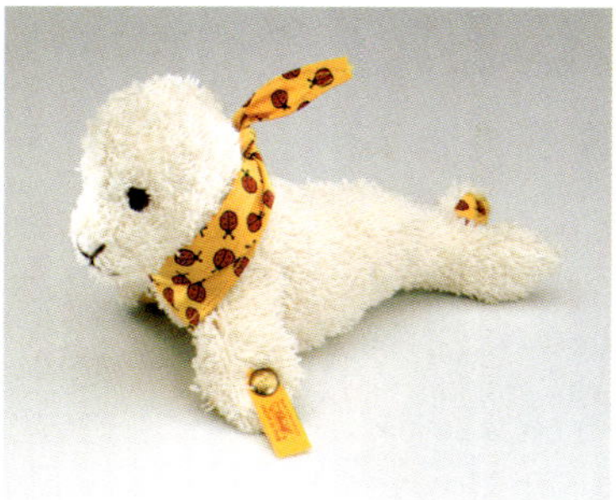

Seehund - *Seal*

Baumwolle, weiss/gelb, waschmaschinenfest, Rassel, Halstuch - *cotton, white/yellow, machine washable, rattle, scarf*

EAN-No.	Period	Pr.	Info
223525	1999-1999	1	16 cm

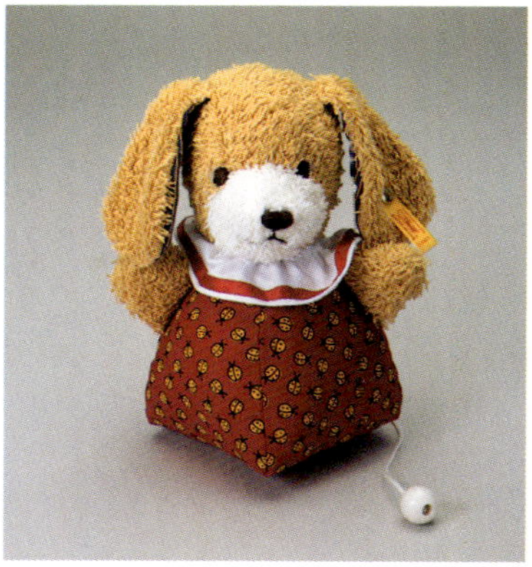

Baby-Hund - *Baby-Dog*

Baumwolle, honig/rot, waschmaschinenfest, Musikwerk (Guter Mond) - *cotton, honey/red, machine washable, music box (Good moon)*

EAN-No.	Period	Pr.	Info
212659	1999-1999	2	17 cm

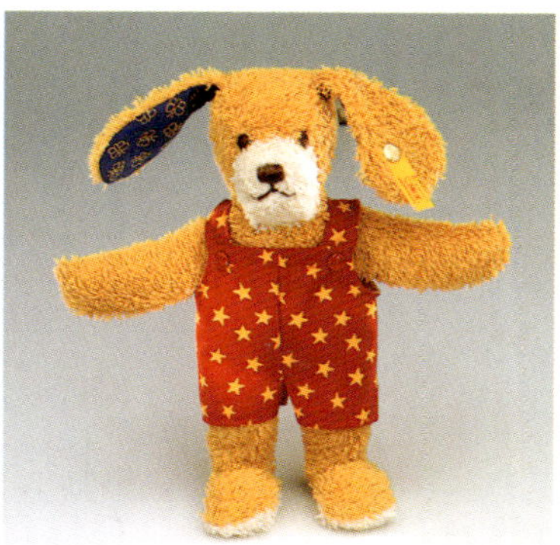

Hund - *Dog*

Baumwolle, honig/blau, waschmaschinenfest, rote Latzhose - *cotton, honey/blue, machine washable, red bibbed trousers*

EAN-No.	Period	Pr.	Info
215575	1999-1999	1-2	22 cm

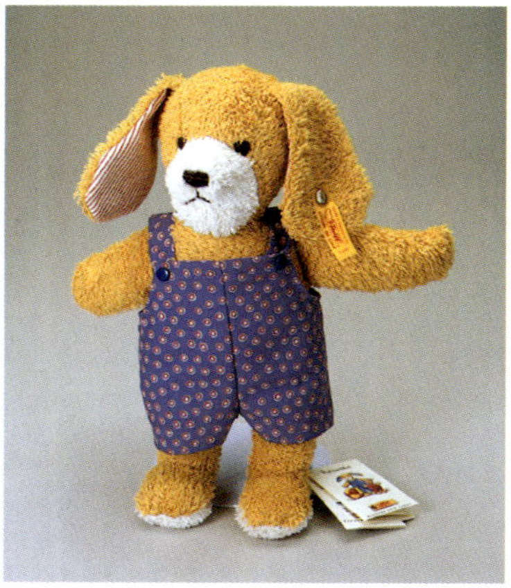

Hund - *Dog*

Baumwolle, honig/weiss, waschmaschinenfest, blaue Latzhose - *cotton, honey/white, machine washable, blue bibbed trousers*

EAN-No.	Period	Pr.	Info
215582	1999-1999	2	28 cm

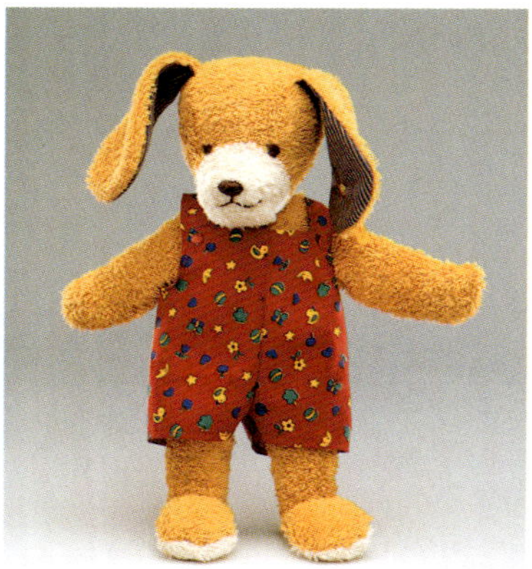

Hund - *Dog*

Baumwolle, honig/blau, waschmaschinenfest, rote Latzhose - *cotton, honey/blue, machine washable, red bibbed trousers*

EAN-No.	Period	Pr.	Info
215599	1999-1999	2	35 cm

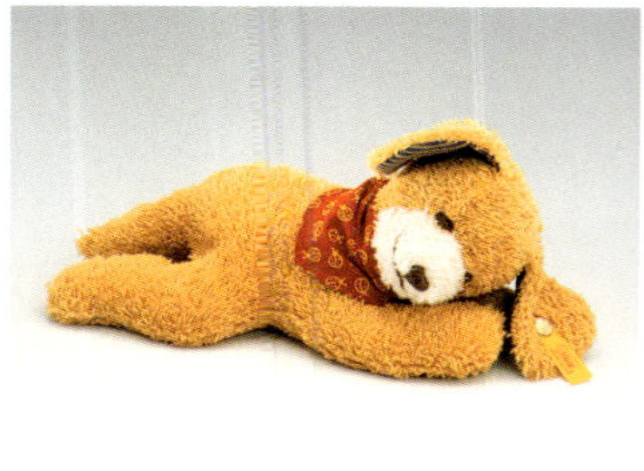

Hund - *Dog*

Baumwolle, honig/blau, liegend, waschmaschinenfest, Halstuch - *cotton, honey/blue, lying, machine washable, scarf*

EAN-No.	Period	Pr.	Info
221194	1999-1999	1-2	22 cm

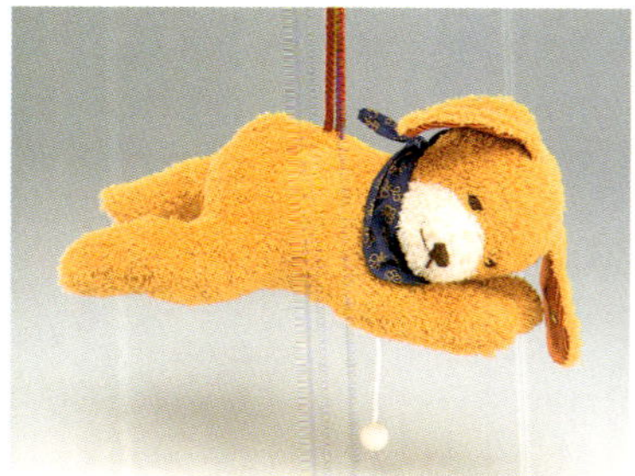

Hund - *Dog*

Baumwolle, honig/rot, liegend, waschmaschinenfest, Halstuch, Musikwerk (Schubert`s Sandmaennchen) - *cotton, honey/red, lying, machine washable, scarf, music box (Schubert`s Lullaby)*

EAN-No.	Period	Pr	Info
221200	1999-1999	2	28 cm

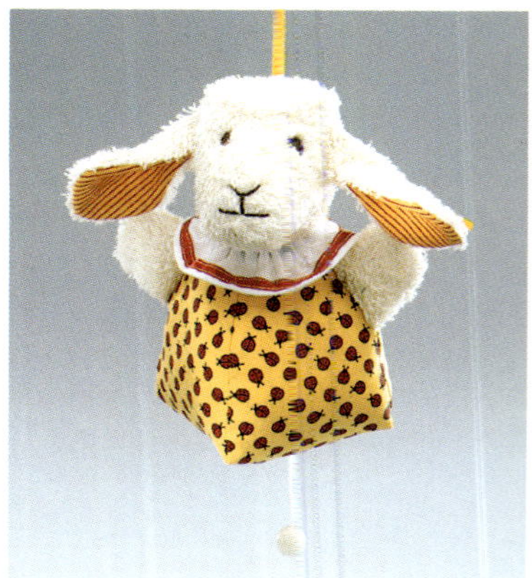

Baby-Lamm - *Baby Lamb*

Baumwolle, weiss/gelb, waschmaschinenfest, Musikwerk (La Le Lu) - *cotton, white/yellow, machine washable, music box (La Le Lu)*

EAN-No.	Period	Pr.	Info
212895	1999-1999	2	17 cm

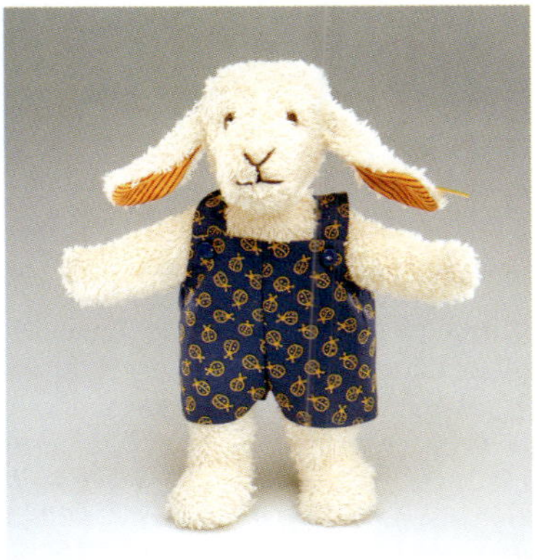

Lamm - *Lamb*

Baumwolle, weiss/gelb, waschmaschinenfest, blaue Latzhose - *cotton, white/yellow, machine washable, blue dungarees*

EAN-No.	Period	Pr.	Info
215674	1999-1999	1-2	22 cm

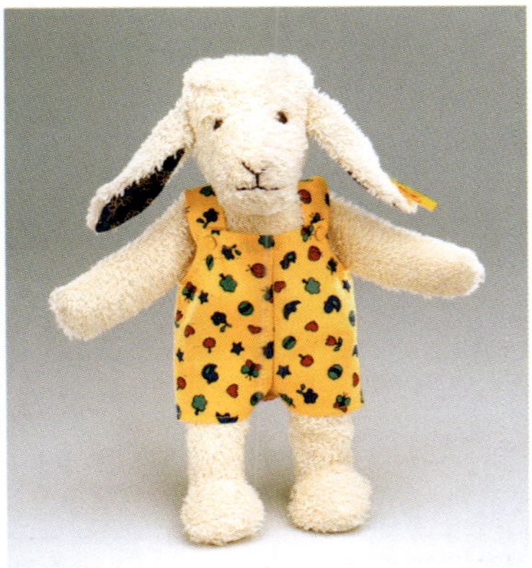

Lamm - *Lamb*

Baumwolle, weiss/blau, waschmaschinenfest, gelbe Latzhose - *cotton, white/blue, machine washable, yellow dungarees*

EAN-No.	Period	Pr.	Info
215681	1999-1999	2	28 cm

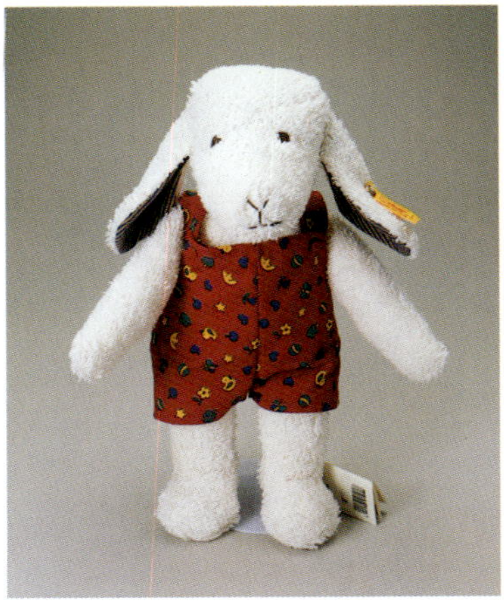

Lamm - *Lamb*

Baumwolle, weiss/blau, waschmaschinenfest, rote Latzhose - *cotton, white/blue, machine washable, red dungarees*

EAN-No.	Period	Pr.	Info
215698	1999-1999	2	35 cm

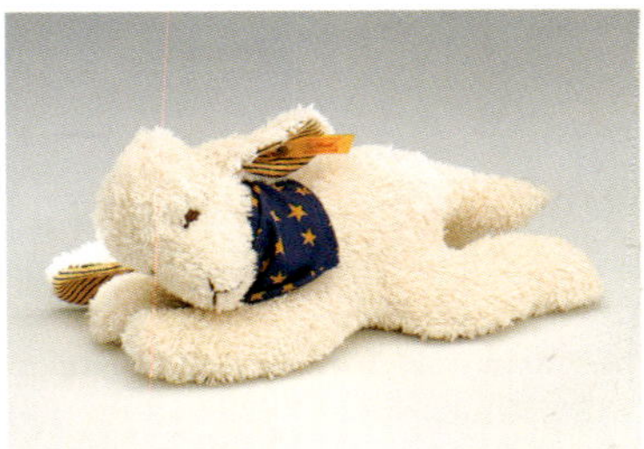

Lamm - *Lamb*

Baumwolle, weiss/gelb, liegend, waschmaschinenfest, Halstuch - *cotton, white/yellow, lying, machine washable, scarf*

EAN-No.	Period	Pr.	Info
221316	1999-1999	1-2	22 cm

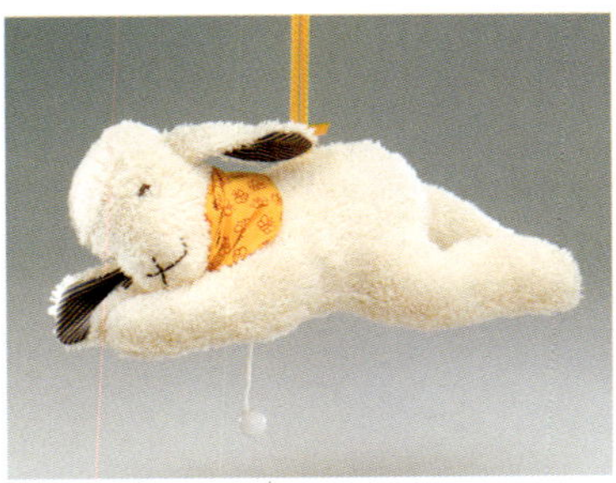

Lamm - *Lamb*

Baumwolle, weiss/blau, liegend, waschmaschinenfest, Halstuch, Musikwerk (La Le Lu) - *cotton, white/blue, lying, machine washable, scarf, music box (La Le Lu)*

EAN-No.	Period	Pr.	Info
221323	1999-1999	2	28 cm

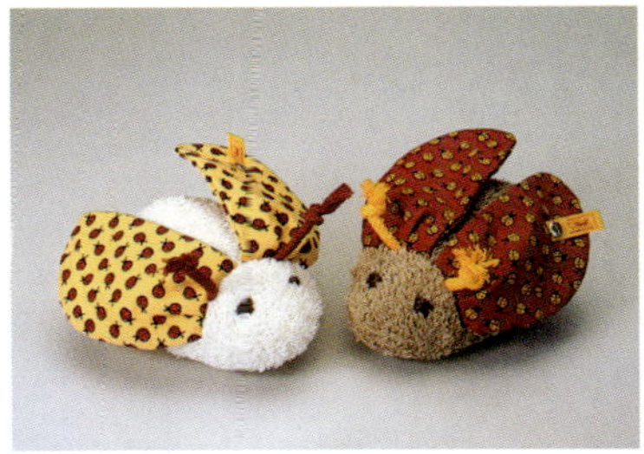

Kaefer - *Beetle*

Baumwolle, 15 cm, waschmaschinenfest, Druck-Stimme - *cotton, 15 cm, machine washable, press voice*

EAN-No.	Period	Pr.	Info
219528	1999-1999	1	beige/rot - *beige/red*
219535	1999-1999	1	weiss/gelb - *white/yellow*

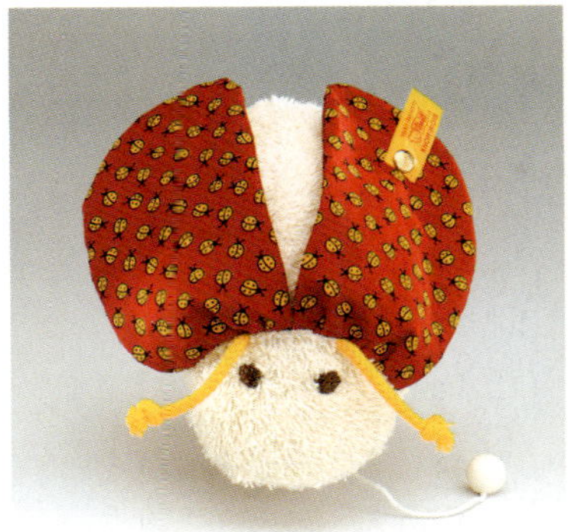

Kaefer - *Beetle*

Baumwolle, weiss/rot, waschmaschinenfest, Musikwerk (La Le Lu) - *cotton, white/red, machine washable, music box (La Le Lu)*

EAN-No.	Period	Pr.	Info
219542	1999-1999	1-2	17 cm

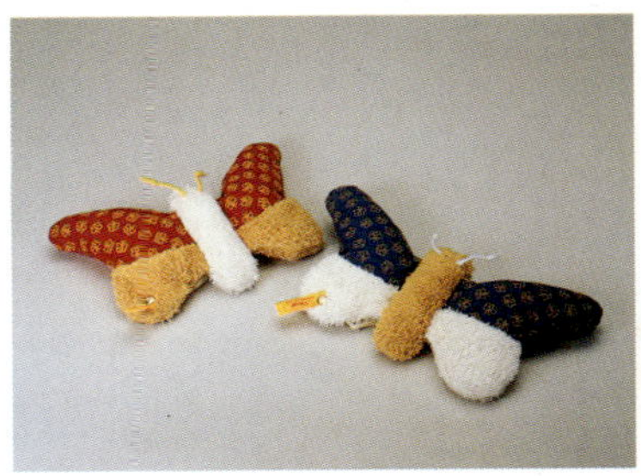

Schmetterling - *Butterfly*

Baumwolle, 25 cm, waschmaschinenfest - *cotton, 25 cm, machine washable*

EAN-No.	Period	Pr.	Info
219665	1999-1999	1	honig/rot - *honey/red*
219672	1999-1999	1	weiss/blau - *white/blue*

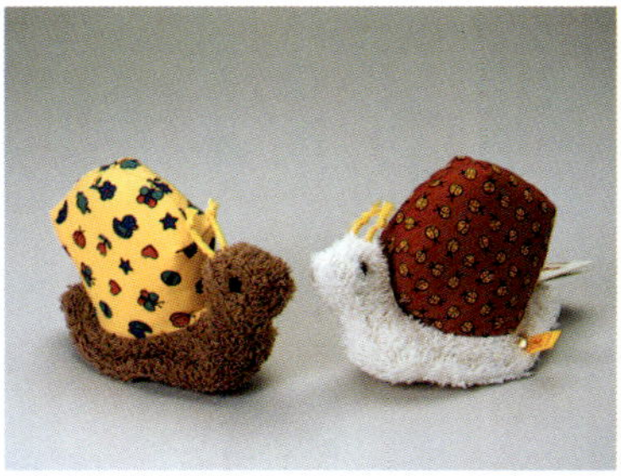

Schnecke - *Snail*

Baumwolle, 15 cm, waschmaschinenfest, Druck-Stimme - *cotton, 15 cm, machine washable, press voice*

EAN-No.	Period	Pr.	Info
219849	1999-1999	1	weiss/rot - *white/red*
219856	1999-1999	1	braun/gelb - *brown/yellow*

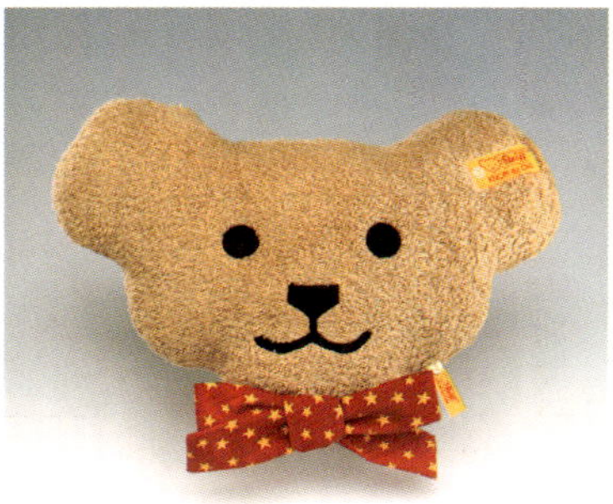

Kissen Teddykopf - *Teddy Head Cushion*

Baumwolle, beige/rot, waschmaschinenfest - *cotton, beige/red, machine washable*

EAN-No.	Period	Pr.	Info
224966	1999-1999	2	35 cm

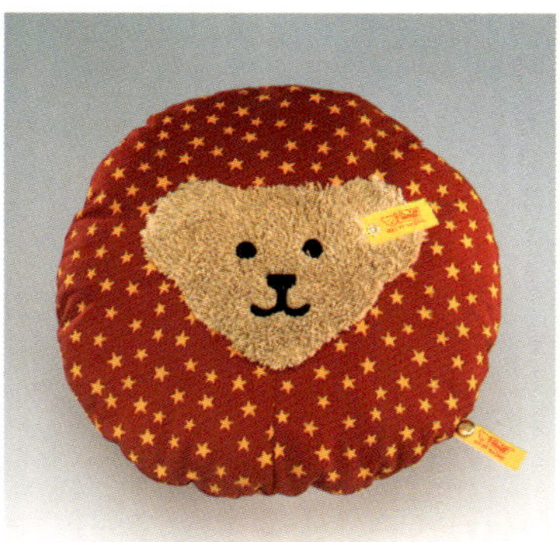

Rundkissen - *Round Cushion*

Baumwolle, beige/rot, waschmaschinenfest, Teddykoepfchen - *cotton, beige/red, machine washable, Teddy head*

EAN-No.	Period	Pr.	Info
224973	1999-1999	1-2	25 cm

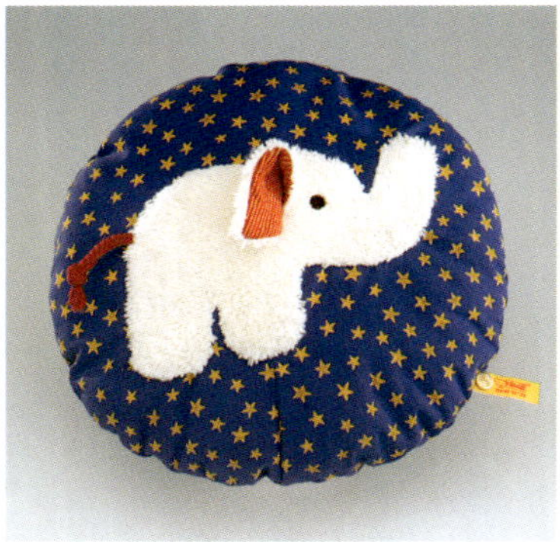

Rundkissen - *Round Cushion*

Baumwolle, weiss/blau, waschmaschinenfest, Elefant - *cotton, white/blue, machine washable, elephant*

EAN-No.	Period	Pr.	Info
224980	1999-1999	1-2	25 cm

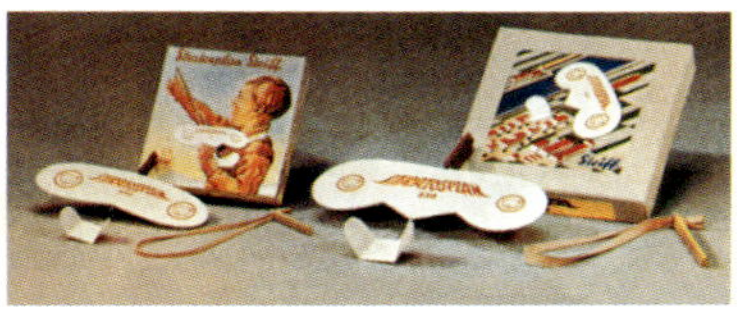

Stratosplan Schleuderflugzeug - *Stratosplan Sling-Shot Glider*

Katapultflieger, Gerippe aus rostfreiem Stahldraht mit Gummistoff D.R.P., weiss/rot, wasserfeste Tragflaechen, federndes Stahlgerippe, hohe Flugleistung, mit Schleuder, farbige Einzelpackung, Schleuder als Ersatz erhaeltlich - *catapult-type glider plane, framework made of stainless steel wire with rubber fabric D.R.P., white/red, water resistant wings, springy steel framework, high flight performance, with catapult sling, packed in a colorful individual package, catapult sling available as spare part*

Serie	Art.-No	Period	Pr.	Info
120	520	1950-1957	4	20 cm
		Spannweite - *wing span*		
120	530	1952-1957	4	30 cm
		Spannweite - *wing span*		

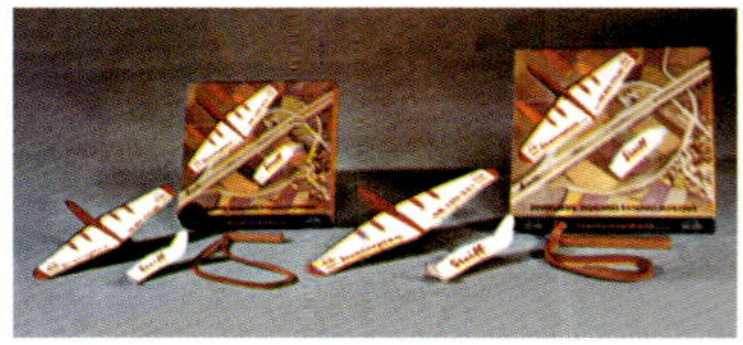

Stratosplan

Schleuderflieger, weiss/rot, mit Schleuder, farbige Einzelpackung, Schleuder als Ersatz erhaeltlich - *catapult-type glider plane, white/red, with catapult sling, packed in a colorful individual package, catapult sling available as spare part*

Serie	Art.-No	Period	Pr.	Info
120	521	1957-1958	4	20 cm
		Spannweite - *wing span*		
950	1721,00	1959-1962	4	
120	531	1957-1958	4	30 cm
		Spannweite - *wing span*		
950	1731,00	1959-1962	4	
120	1201	1950-1951	1	Ersatz-
		schleuder - *Catapult Sling Spare Part*		
120	520 S	1952-1956	1	
120	530 S	1956-1956	1	

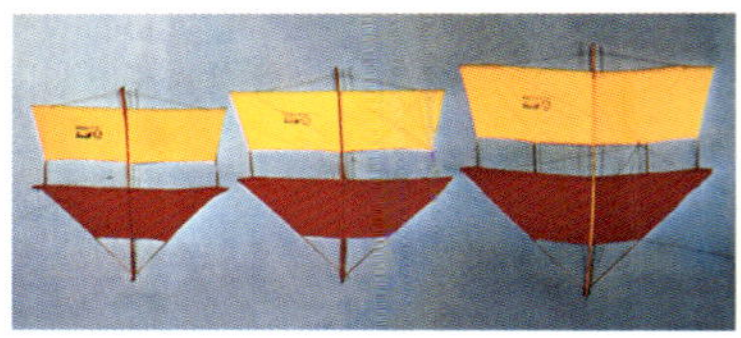

Roloplan

schwanzloser Stoffdrachen, gelb/rot, mit 2 Stoff-Flaechen, zusammenlegbar zum Verpacken in Stoffsack, mit Gebrauchsanweisung - *cloth kite without a tail, yellow/red, with two cloth surfaces, collapsible - to be packed into a cloth bag, with operating instructions*

Serie	Art.-No	Period	Pr.	Info
125	90/2	1950-1958	4	90 cm
		Spannweite - *wing span*		
960	7090,00	1959-1964	4	
800	7090,00	1965-1967	4	
	8000/09	1968-1968	4	
125	100/2	1950-1958	4	100 cm
		Spannweite - *wing span*		
960	7100,00	1959-1964	4	
800	7100,00	1965-1967	4	
	8000/10	1968-1968	4	
125	120/2	1950-1953	4	120 cm
		Spannweite - *wing span*		
960	7120,00	1959-1964	4	
800	7120,00	1965-1967	4	
	8000/12	1968-1968	4	

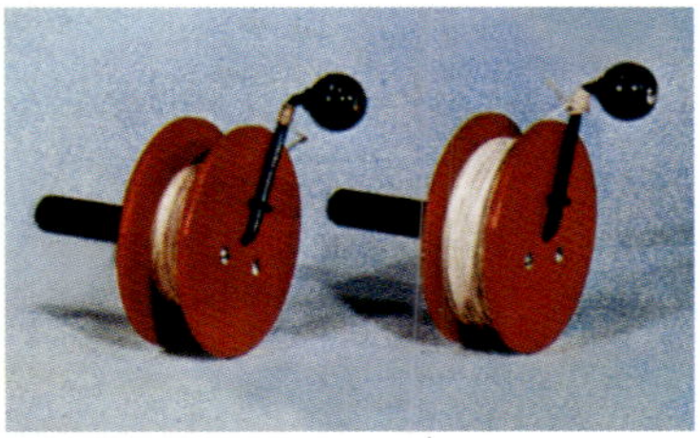

Schnurspule - *String Reel*

Schnurspule mit oder ohne Schnur fuer verschiedene Drachen - *reel with or without string, for various kites*

SERIE	ART.-NO	PERIOD	PR.	INFO
125	812	1950-1956	1	ohne Schnur, fuer Roloplan 90, 100 & 120 cm & Adlerdrachen - *without string, for Roloplan 90, 100 & 120cm & eagle kite*
812	7812,00	1966-1967	1	
	8120/12	1968-1968	1	
	8090/08	1969-1971	1	ohne Schnur, fuer Roloplan 90 cm - *without string, for Roloplan 90 cm*
125	812/10/90	1950-1956	1	mit 100 m Schnur, fuer Roloplan 90 & 100 cm & Adlerdrachen - *with 100 m string, for Roloplan 90 & 100 cm & eagle kite*
812	2090,10	1966-1967	1	
	8091/08	1969-1971	1	
125	812/10/120	1950-1956	1	mit 100 m Schnur, fuer Roloplan 120 cm - *with 100 m string, for Roloplan 120 cm*
125	812/15/90	1950-1956	1	mit 150 m Schnur, fuer Roloplan 90 & 100 cm & Adlerdrachen - *with 150 m string, for Roloplan 90 & 100 cm & eagle kite*
812	2090,15	1966-1967	1	
125	812/15/120	1950-1956	1	mit 150 m Schnur, fuer Roloplan 120 cm - *with 150 m string, for Roloplan 120 cm*
812	2120,15	1967-1967	1	

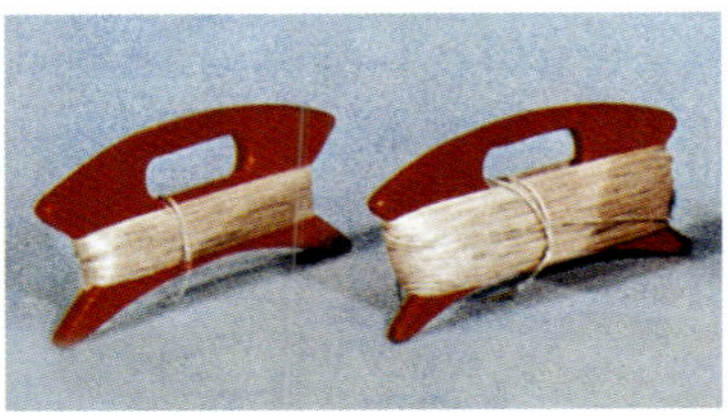

Bretthaspel - *String Winder*

Haspel mit oder ohne Schnur fuer verschiedene Drachen - *string winder with or without string, for various kites*

SERIE	ART.-NO	PERIOD	PR.	INFO
125	824	1950-1956	1	ohne Schnur - *without string*
810	7824,00	1966-1966	1	
125	824/10/90	1950-1956	1	mit 100 m Schnur, fuer Roloplan 90 & 100 cm & Adlerdrachen - *with 100 m string, for Roloplan 90 & 100 cm & eagle kite*
810	4090,10	1966-1967	1	
125	824/10/120	1950-1956	1	mit 100 m Schnur, Roloplan 120 cm - *with 100 m string, Roloplan120 cm*
125	824/15/90	1950-1956	1	mit 150 m Schnur, fuer Roloplan 90 & 100 cm & Adlerdrachen - *with 150 m string, for Roloplan 90 & 100 cm & eagle kite*
810	4090,15	1966-1967	1	
125	824/15/120	1950-1956	1	mit 150 m Schnur, Roloplan 120 cm - *with 150 m string, Roloplan120 cm*
810	4120,15	1966-1967	1	

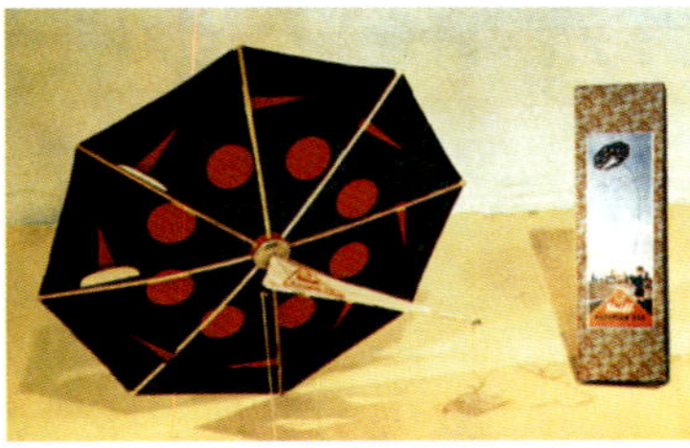

Rotaplan-Duesendrachen - *Rotaplan Jet Kite*

Rumpf: Metallrahmen mit Achse fuer die rotierende Tragflaeche, Tragflaeche: 55 cm, transparente Plastik-Folie in blau/rot, Wind stroemt durch die 8 Duesen der Tragflaeche und setzt diese in rasche Drehung, wodurch sich der Rotaplan in die Luft erhebt - *fuselage is a metal frame with a shaft for the rotating airfoil, the airfoil consists of a 55 cm transparent plastic foil in blue/red, the wind flows through the 8 jets of the airfoil & causes it to rotate quickly, so that the Rotaplan can then elevate itself into the atmosphere*

SERIE	ART.-NO	PERIOD	PR.	INFO
125	555	1953-1954	4	55 cm

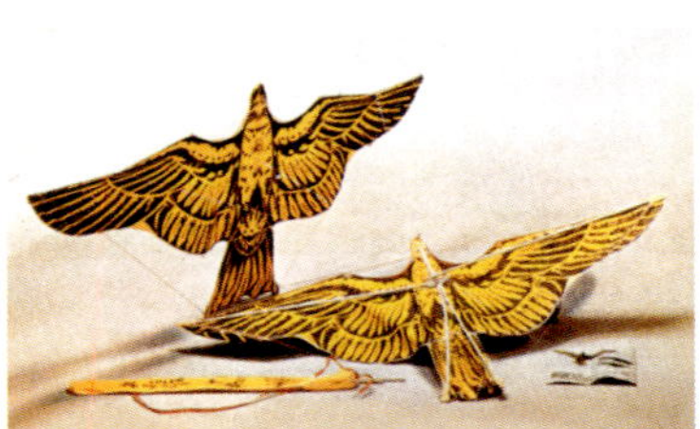

Adlerdrachen - *Eagle Kite*

Stoffdrachen, schwarz/gelb, farbig bemalt, 120 cm Spannweite, in Stoffsack verpackt, wird wie ein Schirm aufgespannt, mit Gebrauchsanweisung - *cloth kite, black/yellow, 120 cm wing span, packed in a cloth bag, it opens like an umbrella, comes with a set of instructions*

SERIE	ART.-NO	PERIOD	PR.	INFO
125	122 A	1954-1958	4	120 cm Spannweite - *wing span*
960	7122,00	1959-1964	4	
802	7122,00	1965-1967	4	
	8020/22	1968-1968	3-4	

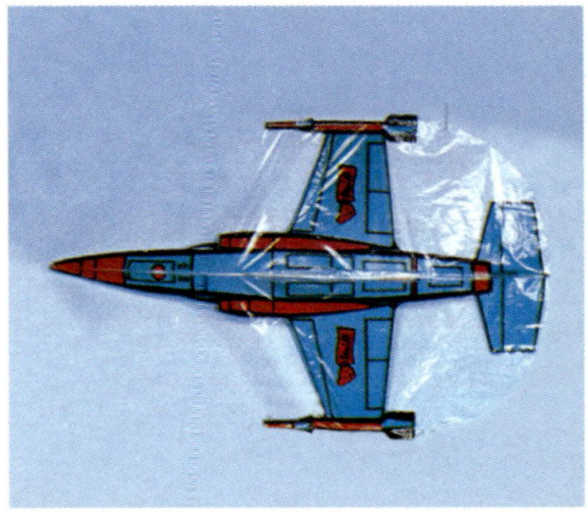

Flugzeug-Drachen - *Airplane Kite*

Klarsicht-Polyaethylen-Folie, Kunststoff-Mittelstueck, bedruckt, Laenge 1,31 m - *clear polyethylene foil, center section made of plastic, imprinted, length 1.31 meters*

SERIE	ART.-NO	PERIOD	PR.	INFO
	8040/12	1968-1970	3	85 cm

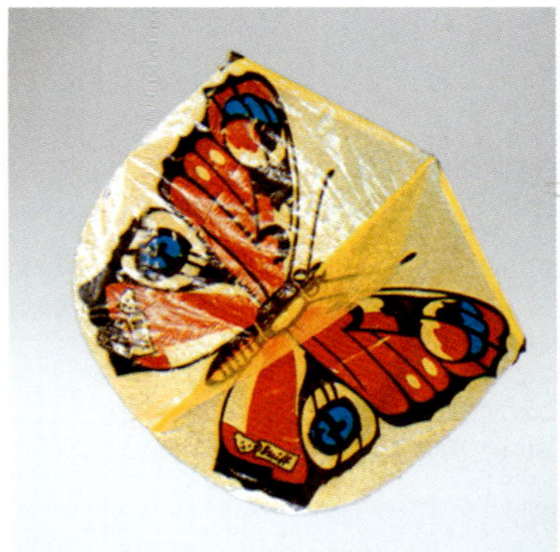

Schmetterling-Drachen - *Butterfly Kite*

farbige Polyaethylen-Folie, bedruckt, Kunststoff-Mittelstueck, Laenge 75 cm - *brightly colored polyethylene foil, imprinted, plastic center section, length 75 cm*

SERIE	ART.-NO	PERIOD	PR.	INFO
	8045/07	1968-1971	3	85 cm

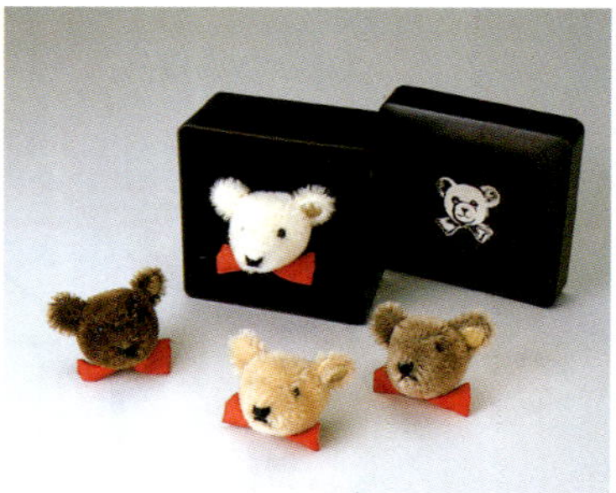

Ansteck-Teddykopf - *Teddy Head Pin*

Mohair, 3 cm, mit Anstecknadel, in Kunststoff-Schachtel - *mohair, 3 cm, with pin, in a plastic box*

SERIE	ART.-NO	PERIOD	PR.	INFO
600401	8495/03	1984-1986	2-3	honig - *honey*
600425	8496/03	1984-1986	2-3	caramel
600449	8497/03	1984-1986	2-3	weiss - *white*
600463	8498/03	1984-1988	2-3	braun - *brown*

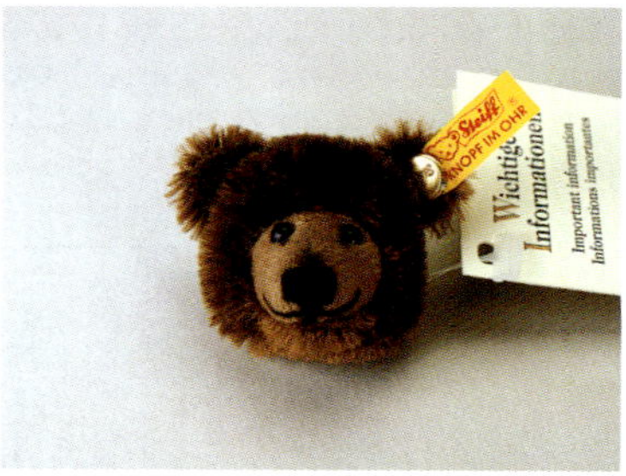

Anstecker Teddykoepfchen Teddy Baby - *Teddy Head Brooch Teddy Baby*

Mohair Webpelz, dunkelbraun, abwaschbar - *mohair woven fur, dark brown, surface washable*

EAN-NO.	PERIOD	PR.	INFO
601507	1999-1999	1-2	4 cm

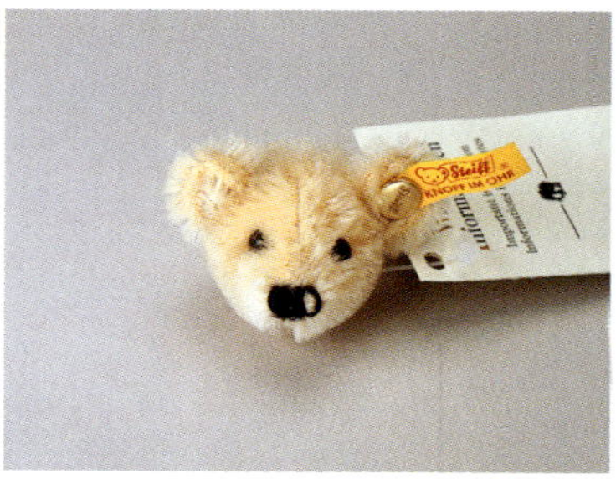

Anstecker Teddykoepfchen Teddy Petsy - *Teddy Head Brooch Teddy Petsy*

Mohair Webpelz, blond, abwaschbar - *mohair woven fur, blond, surface washable*

EAN-NO.	PERIOD	PR.	INFO
601514	1999-1999	1-2	4 cm

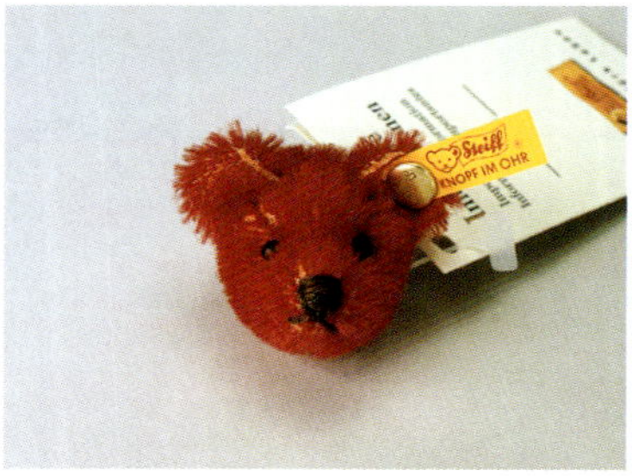

Anstecker Teddykoepfchen Teddy Rot - *Teddy Head Brooch Teddy Red*

Mohair Webpelz, rot, abwaschbar - *mohair woven fur, red, surface washable*

EAN-NO.	PERIOD	PR.	INFO
601521	1999-1999	1-2	4 cm

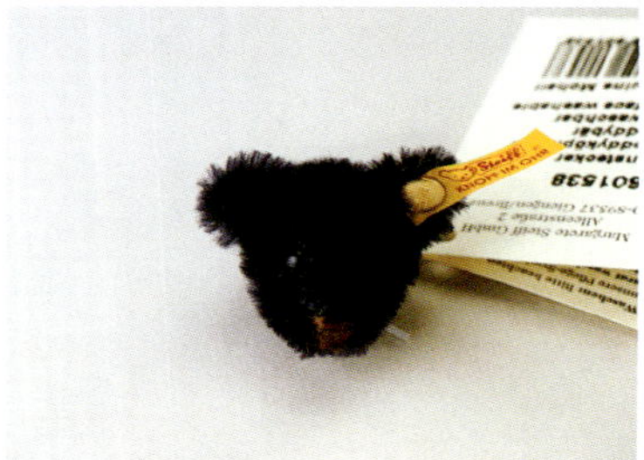

Anstecker Teddykoepfchen Teddy Blau - *Teddy Head Brooch Teddy Blue*

Mohair Webpelz, blau, abwaschbar - *mohair woven fur, blue, surface washable*

EAN-NO.	PERIOD	PR.	INFO
601538	1999-1999	1-2	4 cm

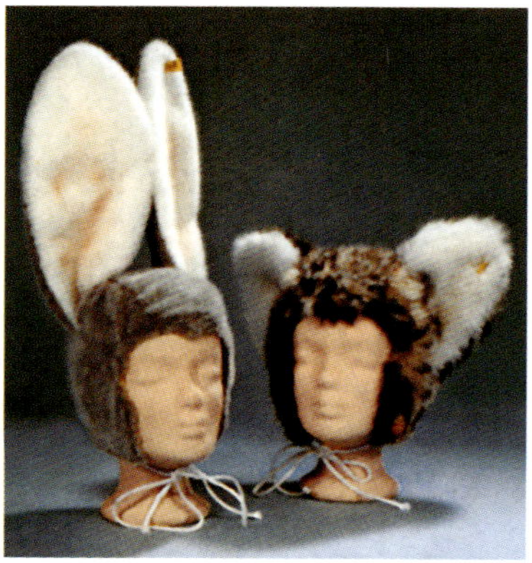

Katzen- / Hasen-Peruecke - *Cat- / Rabbit-Wig*

Kopfhaube mit Ohren, 30 cm, Wirkpelz (Katze), Webpelz (Hase), vollwaschbar - *cap with ears, 30 cm, knitted fur (cat), woven fur (rabbit), fully washable*

SERIE	ART.-NO	PERIOD	PR.	INFO
	7941/30	1978-1978	3-4	Katze - *cat*
	7942/30	1978-1978	3-4	Hase - *rabbit*

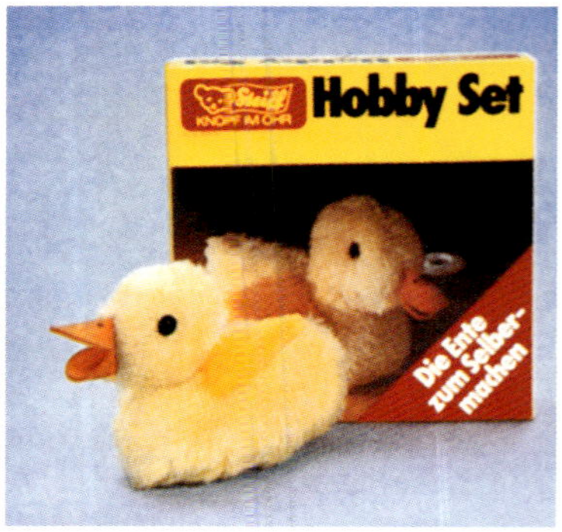

Hobby Set Ente - *Duck Hobby Set*

Dralon, gelb, Spieltier zum Selbermachen - *dralon, yellow, toy must be assembled*

SERIE	ART.-NO	PERIOD	PR.	INFO
	8110/16	1980-1983	1	16 cm

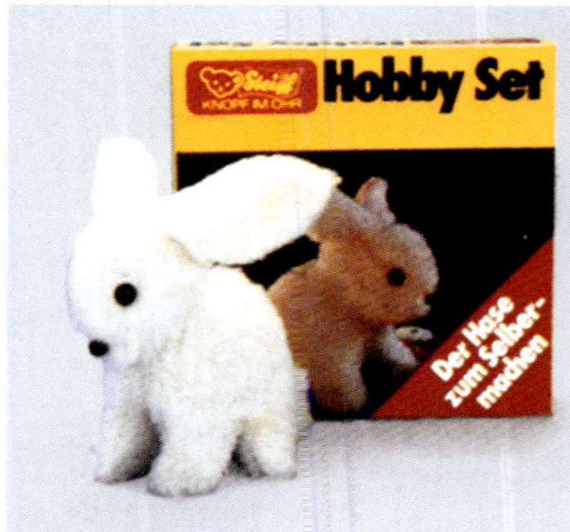

Hobby Set Hase - *Rabbit Hobby Set*

Dralon, weiss, Spieltier zum Selbermachen - *dralon, white, toy must be assembled*

SERIE	ART.-NO	PERIOD	PR.	INFO
	8112/16	1980-1983	1	16 cm

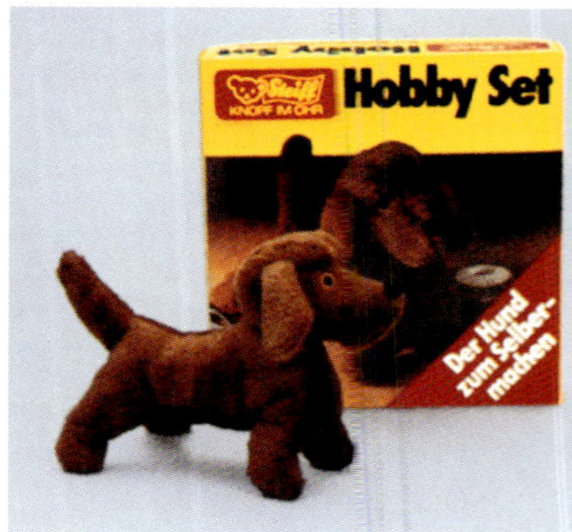

Hobby Set Hund - *Dog Hobby Set*

Dralon, braun, Spieltier zum Selbermachen - *dralon, brown, toy must be assembled*

SERIE	ART.-NO	PERIOD	PR.	INFO
	8114/16	1980-1983	1	16 cm

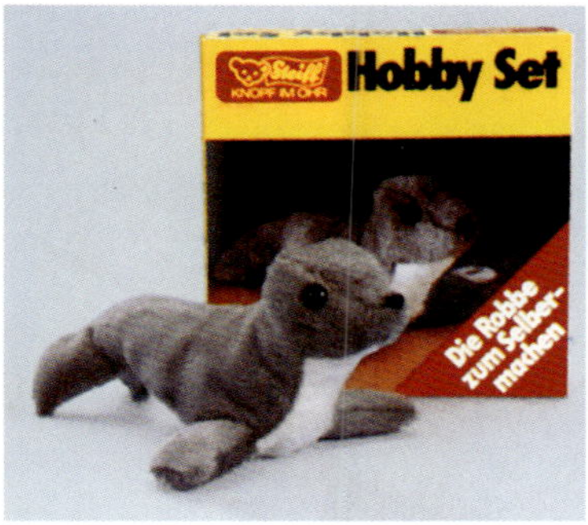

Hobby Set Robbe - *Seal Hobby Set*

Dralon, grau, Spieltier zum Selbermachen - *dralon, grey, toy must be assembled*

SERIE	ART.-NO	PERIOD	PR.	INFO
	8116/16	1980-1983	1	16 cm

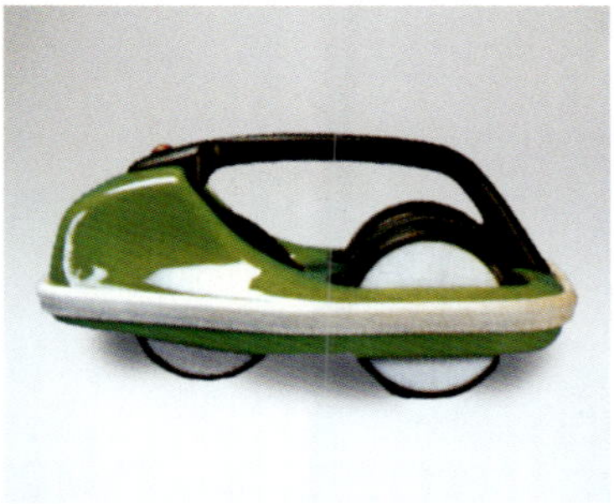

Super-Roll

Spielmoeglichkeiten auf ebenen Flaechen: Weit-, Ziel-, Hindernisschiessen usw - *for games on flat surfaces i.e. long distance shooting, & shooting at targets & obstacles*

SERIE	ART.-NO	PERIOD	PR.	INFO
	8360/50	1980-1980	2-3	

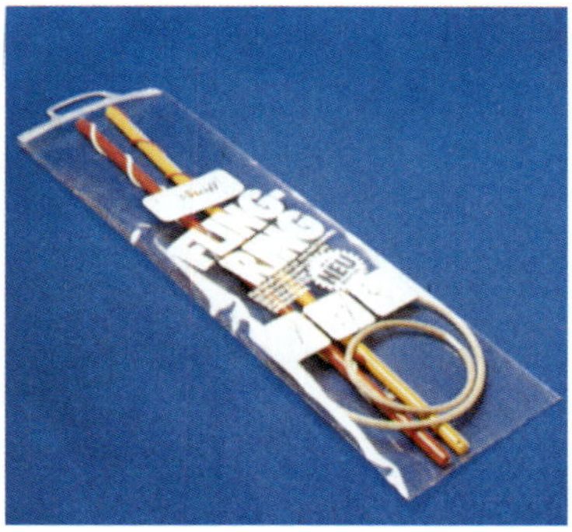

Steiff-Flingring

Abziehen, fliegen, auffangen: ein lustiges Spiel fuer Gross und Klein - *an enjoyable game for the whole family - pull it, throw it, catch it*

SERIE	ART.-NO	PERIOD	PR.	INFO
	8370/50	1980-1981	2-3	

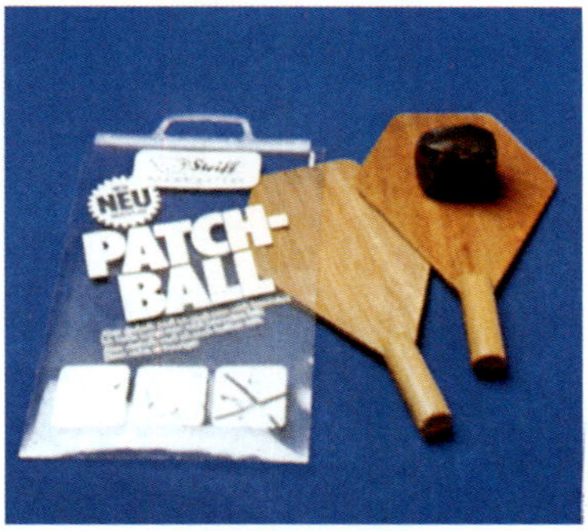

Steiff-Patchball

Ballspiel fuer jung und alt, fuer drinnen und draussen - *a ball game for young & old, which can be be played either indoors or outdoors*

SERIE	ART.-NO	PERIOD	PR.	INFO
	8380/50	1980-1981	2	

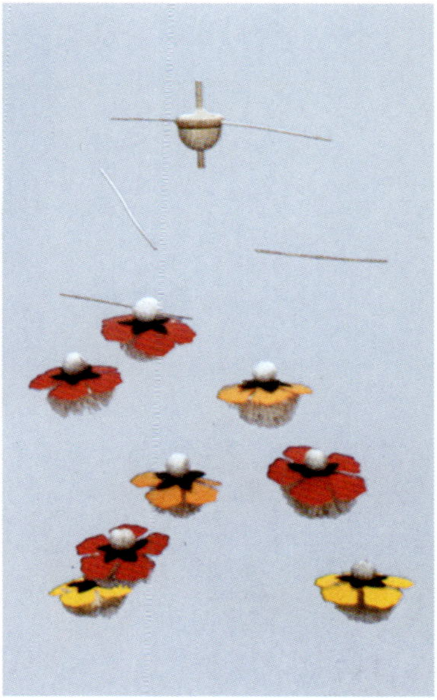

Blumenmobile - *Flower Mobile*

mit Antriebskreisel fuer Bewegung ohne Wind, zum Selbermachen - *equipped with a drive rotor to ensure movement even without a breeze, a do-it-yourself mobile*

SERIE	ART.-NO	PERIOD	PR.	INFO
	8140/24	1981-1985	3	24 cm

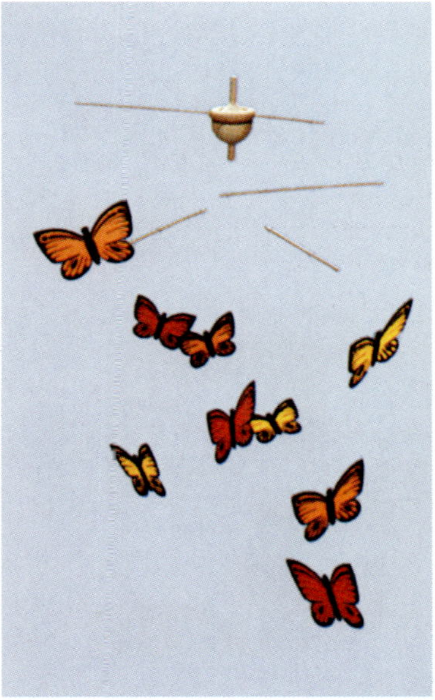

Schmetterlingsmobile - *Butterfly Mobile*

mit Antriebskreisel fuer Bewegung ohne Wind, zum Selbermachen - *equipped with a drive rotor to ensure movement even without a breeze, a do-it-yourself mobile*

SERIE	ART.-NO	PERIOD	PR.	INFO
	8141/24	1981-1984	3	24 cm

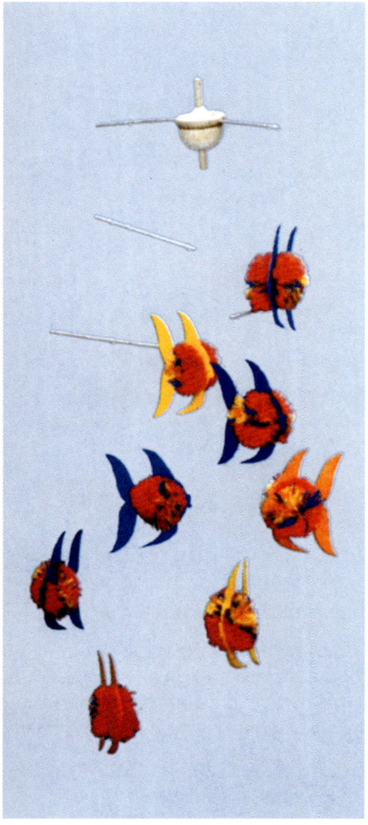

Fischmobile - *Fish Mobile*

mit Antriebskreisel fuer Bewegung ohne Wind, zum Selbermachen - *equipped with a drive rotor to ensure movement even without a breeze, a do-it-yourself mobile*

SERIE	ART.-NO	PERIOD	PR.	INFO
	8142/24	1981-1985	3	24 cm

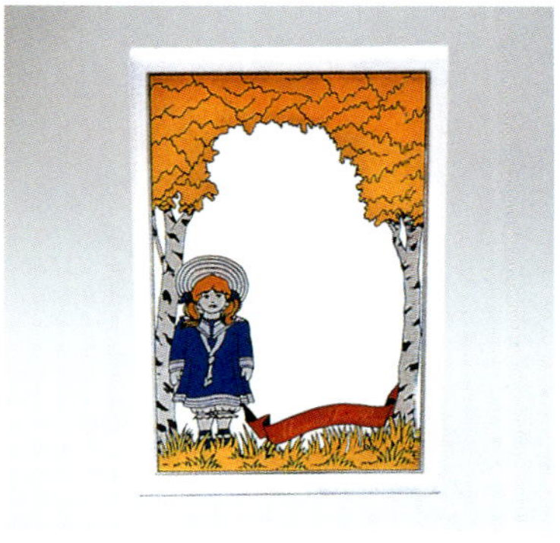

Spiegel - *Mirror*

mit Puppenmotiv, gestaltet wie Oberseite der Puppen-Verpackung - *mirror with doll decor, like the front of the doll package*

SERIE	ART.-NO	PERIOD	PR.	INFO
749056	9470/21	1987-1989	2	21 cm

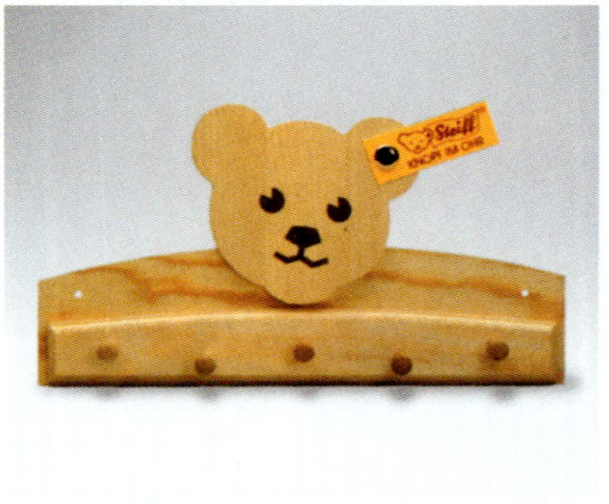

Steiff-Kleiderhaken - *Clothes Hook*

Holz, natur, Boutique-Artikel - *natural wood, boutique article*

SERIE	ART.-NO	PERIOD	PR.	INFO
614002	8630/50	1988-1990	2	50 cm

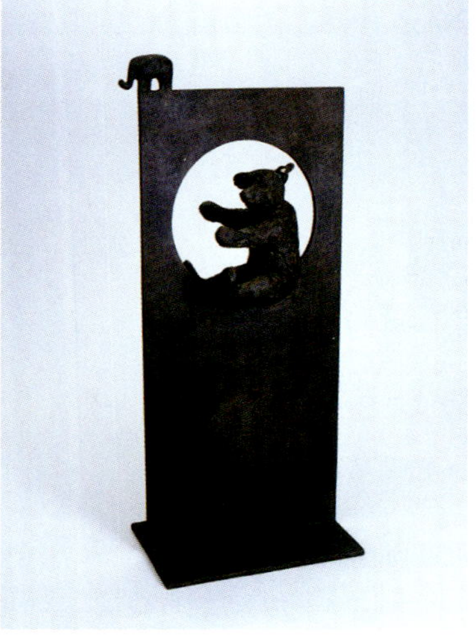

Kleinbronze - *Small Bronze*

Bronze, Miniatur des vor dem Steiff-Werk stehenden Bronzedenkmals zum 90. Geburtstag des von Richard Steiff erschaffenen Teddybaeren, limit. Auflage 499 Stueck fuer Steiff Club Mitglieder - *bronze, miniature of the bronze memorial for the 90th birthday of the Teddy Bear created by Richard Steiff, the original is standing in front of the Steiff factory, ltd edition of 499, exclusive for Steiff Club members*

EAN-NO.	PERIOD	PR.	INFO
420030	1992-1992	6	33 cm

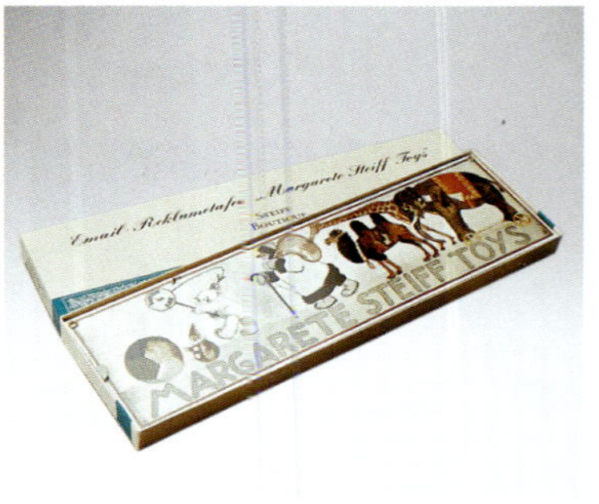

Emailschild - *Enamel Sign*

"Margarete Steiff Toys", Boutique-Artikel - *"Margarete Steiff Toys", boutique article*

EAN-NO.	PERIOD	PR.	INFO
615016	1995-1999	1	48 x 13,8 cm

INDEX

D

I

J

K

L

M

T

U

Steiff Sortiment im Internet

Steiff Articles in the Internet

Seit Juni 1999 gibt es das Steiff Sortiment auch im Internet!

Es stellt die ideale Ergänzung zum vorliegenden Buch dar, da wir Sie damit permanent über alle Neuheiten und Veränderungen im Bereich der bereits bekannten Artikel, informieren können.

Sie finden unsere Homepage unter der Adresse:

http://www.gaf-pfeiffer.com

Auf dieser Seite befindet sich auch die Umschaltmöglichkeit für die deutsche bzw. englische Version.

Der Knopf „STEIFF ARCHIV" führt Sie zur Datenbank.

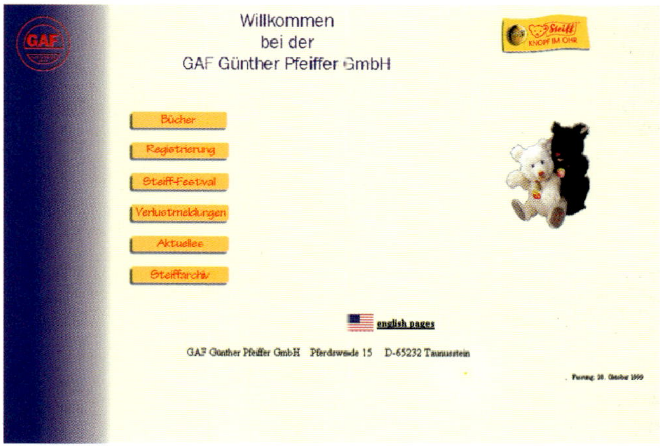

Steiff lovers and collectors have also been able to admire Steiff products in the Internet since June 1999!

This is a perfect compliment to the new edition of the book, as it offers us a means of informing you about new articles and any changes that have taken place among items that you are already familiar with.

You can call up our home page at the following address: http://www.gaf-pfeiffer.com

This page also contains the button to select the German or English version.

You can use the "STEIFF ARCHIVE" button to open the database.

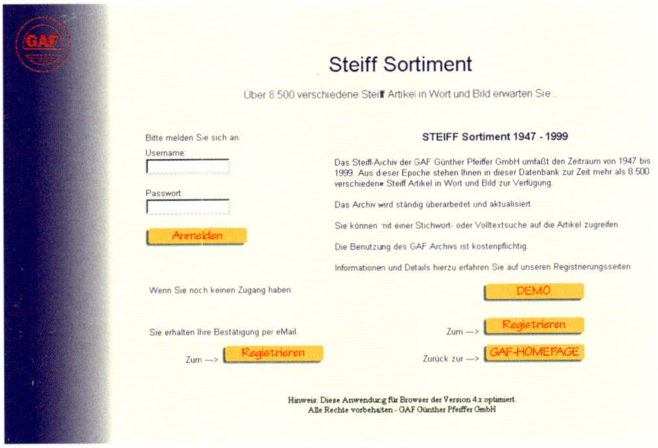

Es bedarf jetzt nur noch Ihrer persönlichen Anmeldung und Sie haben Zugriff auf die Steiff Daten.

Sind Sie bereits in der Datenbank registriert, genügt die Angabe Ihres Benutzernamens und Passwortes. Handelt es sich um Ihren ersten Besuch – folgen Sie bitte den Schritten zur Erstanmeldung. Selbstverständlich bewegen Sie sich bei Angabe aller persönlichen Daten auf geschütztem, d.h. speziell verschlüsselten, Seiten.

Die Bezahlung erfolgt per Kreditkarte oder innerhalb Deutschlands auch per Lastschrift.

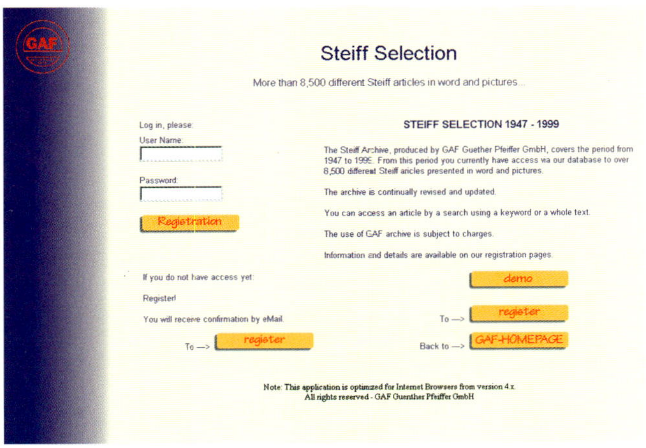

All you now have to do to access the Steiff data is to enter your personal information for registration.

If you have already been registered in the database, you will only have to enter your user name and password. If you are visiting the database for the first time, just follow the instructions for registration. It goes without saying that your personal data is being entered into secure pages that have been encrypted in a special way.

Payment may be made by credit card (or by direct debit inside Germany).

Mit Ihrer Eingabe in die Suchmaske wählen Sie die oder den gewünschten Artikel aus.

Sie können z. B. über die Artikel-Nr. oder den Namen direkt einen speziellen Steiff-Artikel auswählen.

Bei der Eingabe einer Tierkategorie und des Erscheinungsjahres, werden alle im gewünschten Zeitraum hergestellten Artikel, angezeigt.

Oder Sie lassen sich alle Teile, die aus z. B. Mohair gefertigt sind, aufrufen.

Die Suche ist völlig flexibel.

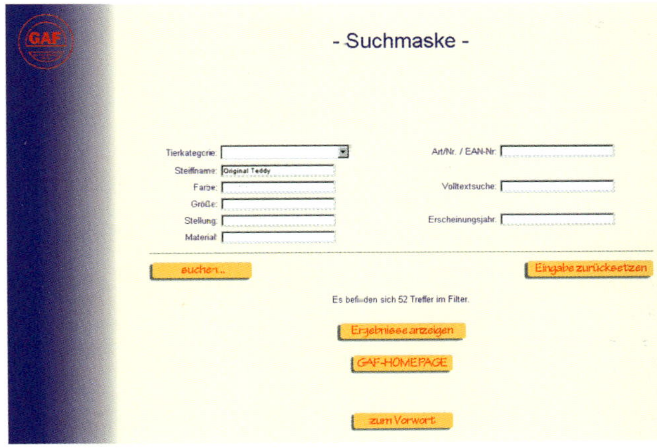

Select the article(s) of your choice by entering the relevant data in the search mask.

Select a specific Steiff product by entering the article number or the name, for example.

If you enter an animal category and the year of production, the program will output all of the corresponding articles to the screen.

Or you can call up all of the items made of mohair, for example.

The search function is completely flexible.

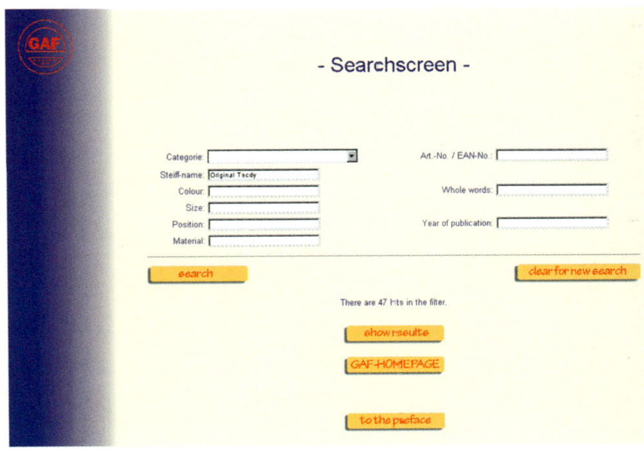

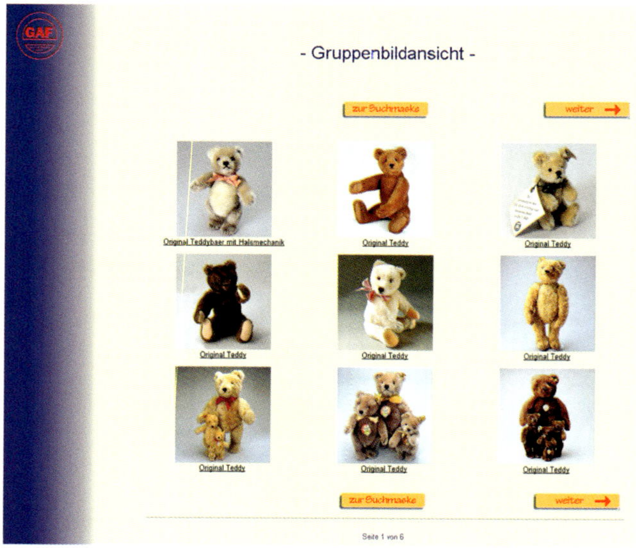

In der „Gruppenbildansicht“ werden nun die Ergebnisse Ihrer Suche im Bild dargestellt. Pro Bildschirm erscheinen maximal 9 Artikel.

Gibt es zu Ihrem Suchbegriff mehr als 9 Ergebnisse, schauen Sie einfach die nächsten Anzeige-Seiten an.

Wollen Sie mehr über einen der Artikel wissen, klicken Sie einfach darauf.

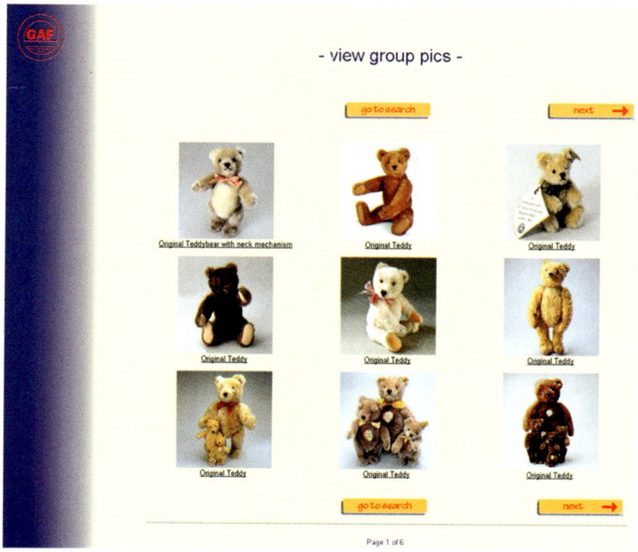

The „Group view“ display shows the results of your search on the screen. Each display contains up to 9 articles. If the program has found more than 9 items that match the search criteria, simply go on to the next page.

If you want to find out more about one of the displayed items, simply click onto it with the mouse button.

Sie erhalten dann in der „Gruppeninformation“ alle Informationen zu der ausgewählten Artikelgruppe. Die Darstellung entspricht dem Aufbau im Buch.

Wenn Sie noch mehr zu einem Artikel oder zu einem bestimmten Produktionszeitraum erfahren möchten, klicken Sie einfach die entsprechende Zeile an.

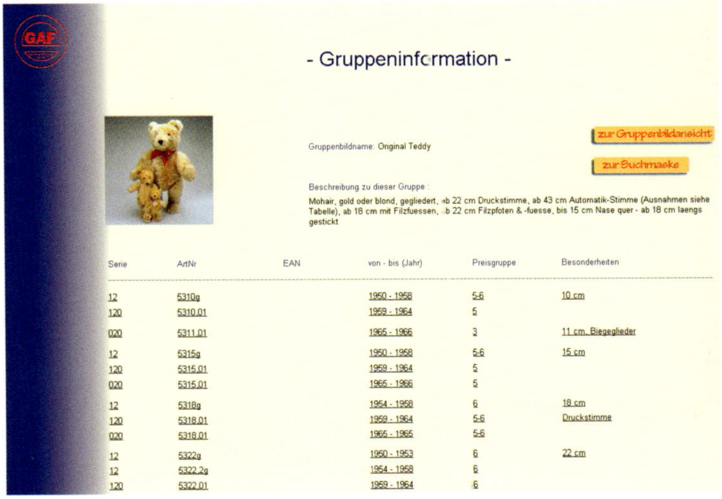

The "Group information" display contains all of the relevant information concerning the selected group of articles. The information is displayed according to the same format as the book.

If you want to find out more about a specific article or a particular production period, simply click onto the relevant line with the mouse button.

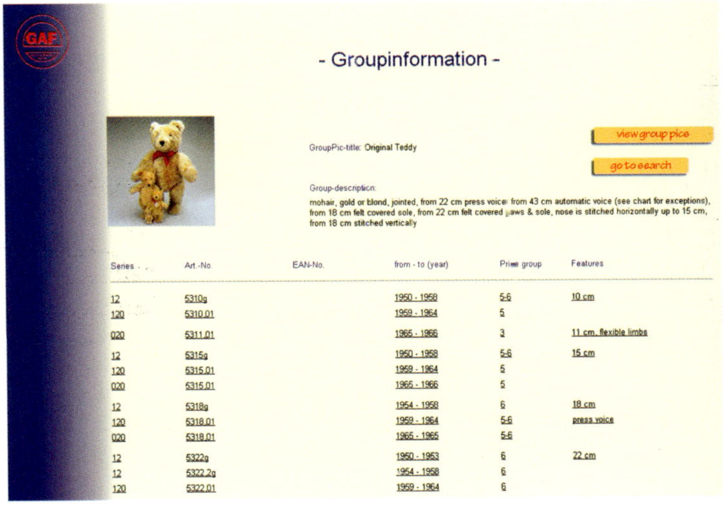

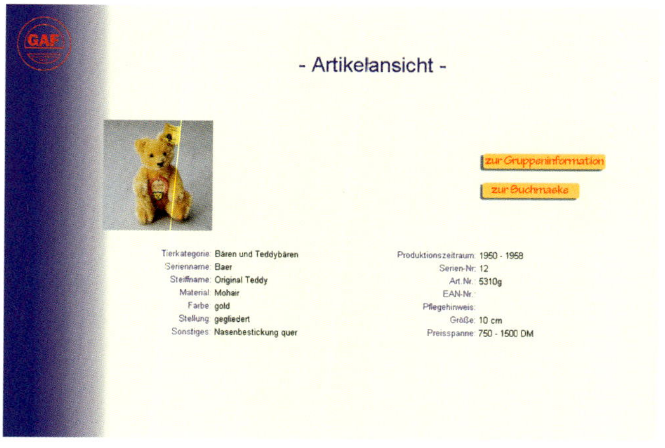

Sie erhalten dann die „Artikelansicht“. Diese Seite beinhaltet alle Details zu diesem von Ihnen ausgewählten Artikel.

Allein für die hier gezeigten Bilder, haben wir einige tausend neue Fotos gemacht. Wenn es interessant ist, zeigen wir Ihnen sogar die Rückseite oder Detailansichten zu den Artikeln.

Hier liegt, neben der permanenten Aktualität, der zweite große Vorzug des Mediums Internet. All diese zusätzlichen Abbildungen können wir, im Rahmen dieses Buches, natürlich nicht zeigen.

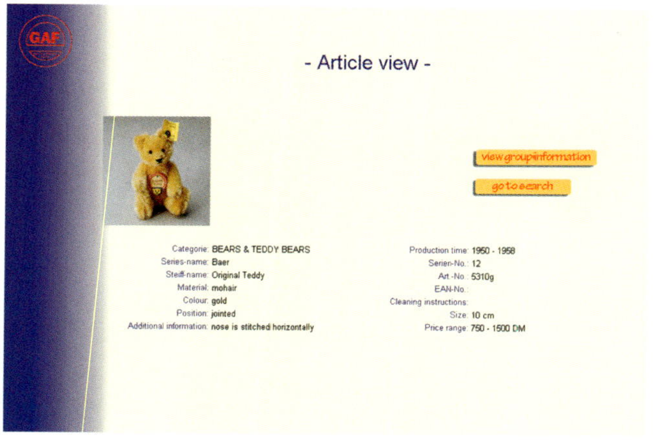

The „Article view“ display then appears on the screen. This page contains all of the details for your selected article.

We have taken several thousand photographs for the pictures displayed in this section alone. If it is of special interest, we can also show you the articles from behind or in detail.

Apart from always being up to date, this is the other great advantage of Internet as a medium. We would, of course, be unable to print all of these additional images in the book.

Alle Abbildungen der Datenbank können Sie sich per „Mausklick" im Großformat anzeigen lassen.

Selbstverständlich können Sie alle Informationen, im Rahmen der Copyright-Bestimmungen und ausschließlich für den privaten Gebrauch, auch auf Ihren PC herunterladen bzw. ausdrucken.

So können Sie dieses Buch, bis zum Erscheinen der nächsten Aktualisierung, immer auf dem aktuellen Stand halten.

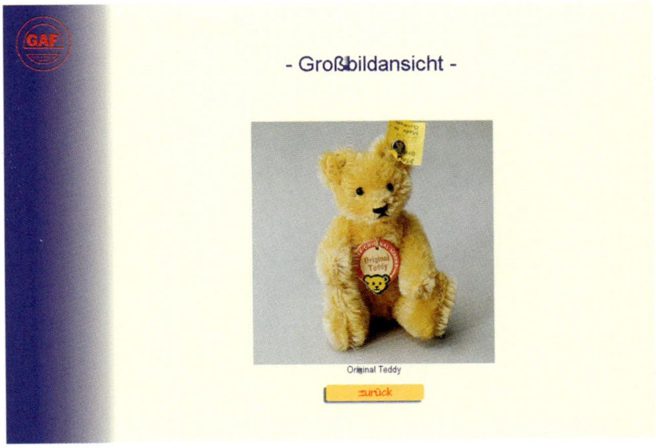

Clicking onto the picture with the mouse button calls up a large-scale image of the selected article to the screen.

It goes without saying that you can download all of this information to your own PC and print it exclusively for your own private use, as long as you comply with the stipulations of the copyright laws.

This offers you a means of keeping your copy of the book up to date until the next edition is issued.

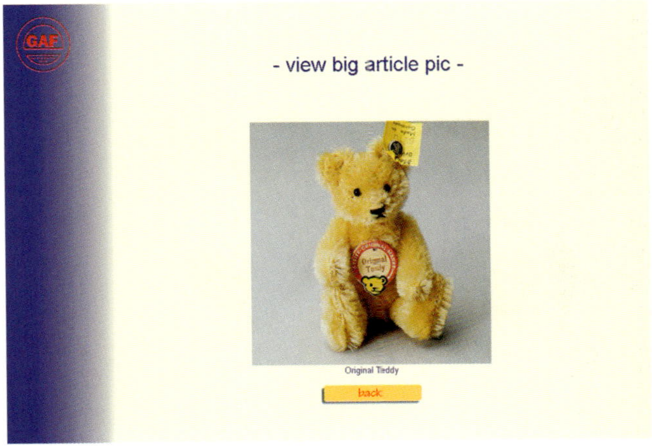

Zum Schluss einige Abbildungen von wunderschönen Steiff Artikeln aus der Frühzeit.

In conclusion, a few pictures of some wonderful Steiff articles from the early days.

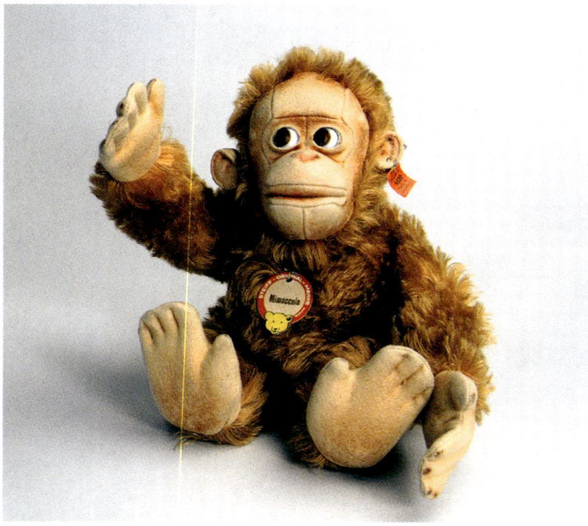

Orang Utan Mimocculo, 22 cm, ca. 1930, Art.-Nr. 5322

Reproduziert 1998, siehe Seite 432

Orang Utan Mimocculo, 22 cm, around 1930, Art. No. 5322

Reproduced in 1998, refer to page 432

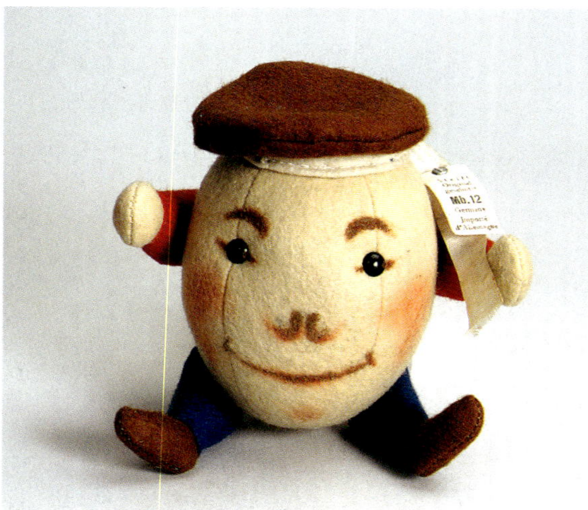

Marsbewohner, 12 cm, ca. 1910,

Art.-Nr. Mb. 12

Humpty Dumpty, 12 cm, around 1910, Art. No. Mb. 12

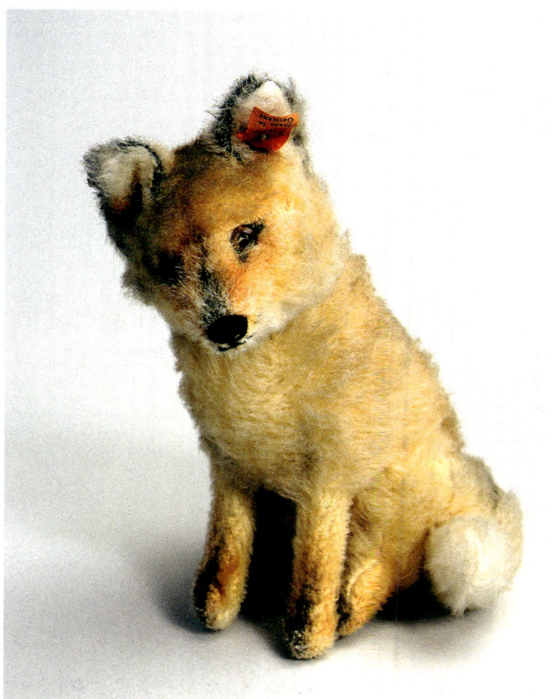

Fuchs, 14 cm, Anfang 30er-Jahre, Art.-Nr. 3514

Fox, 14 cm, early 1930s, Art. No. 3514

Haben Sie Geschmack gefunden an diesen wunderschönen Stücken?

Bei dem jährlich in Giengen an der Brenz stattfindenden Steiff Festival können Sie viele solcher Schätze bewundern und erwerben. Steiff Händler aus der ganzen Welt bieten dort ausschließlich hochwertige Steiff Erzeugnisse an. Aus der Frühzeit bis hin zu aktuellen Stücken, d. h. Sie finden wirklich alles was Steiff zu bieten hatte und hat aus mehr als 100 Jahren Produktionszeit.

Gleichzeitig werden im Rahmen der Raritätenausstellung Exponate aus Privatbesitz gezeigt.

Ein Ereignis, das Sammlerherzen höher schlagen lässt stellt der jährliche Festivalbär dar. Falls Sie Blackey, Whitey und Rosey, unsere Bären aus 1997 bis 1999 noch nicht kennen, schauen Sie auf Seite 444.

Have we whetted your appetite with these wonderful pieces?

Held every year in Giengen, the Steiff Festival provides an opportunity to admire and acquire many treasures like these. Steiff dealers from all over the world offer high-quality Steiff products exclusively at this festival. Items that date back to the very early days and those currently available in the shops, i.e. you will find everything that Steiff had to offer and still has, from over 100 years of production.

Special exhibits from private collections are also on show within the framework of the exhibition of rare items.

The annual festival bear is another occurrence that makes collectors' hearts beat just that little bit faster. If you have not yet made acquaintance with Blackey, Whitey or Rosey, the Steiff Festival bears from 1997 to 1999, take a look at page 444.

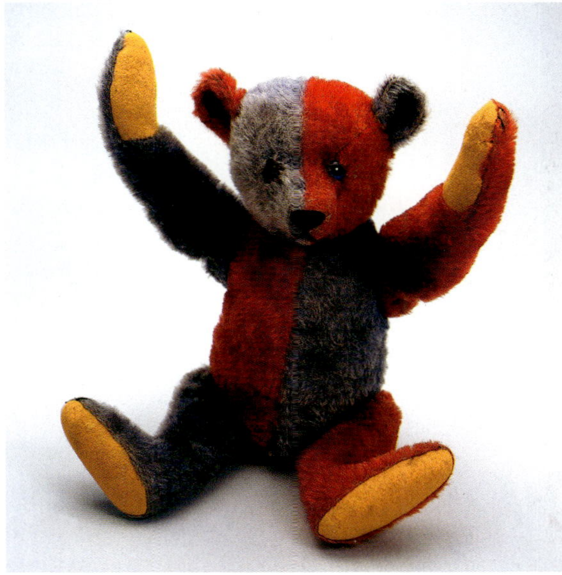

Auch diesen Bär gab es nur auf dem Steiff Festival zu sehen. Er wurde auf der im Rahmenprogramm stattfindenden Steiff Sonderauktion für DM 189.720,00 versteigert.

This bear is another item that was only on show during the Steiff Festival. He was sold during the Steiff special auction held as part of the supporting program and fetched DM 189,720.

You can find out more about the festival on our pages in the Internet.

If you consult our Internet pages, you will also be informed of the completion of our book covering Steiff articles dating back to before 1947. We are working very hard to get it finished, but we cannot give you details of the forthcoming publication date yet.

We would also be delighted to send you information by post, of course. Please address any queries to:

Mehr über das Festival erfahren Sie ebenfalls auf unseren Seiten im Internet.

Sie werden dort auch sofort informiert, wenn unser Buch über die Steiff Artikel aus der Zeit vor 1947 fertiggestellt ist. Wir arbeiten fleißig daran. Einen Erscheinungstermin können wir Ihnen aber noch nicht nennen.

Selbstverständlich senden wir Ihnen auch gern weitere Informationen per Post. Unsere Anschrift lautet:

GAF Günther Pfeiffer GmbH

GAF Günther Pfeiffer GmbH, Pferdsweide 15, 65232 Taunusstein, Germany.

DANKSAGUNG

An dieser Stelle möchte ich mich noch einmal ganz herzlich bei allen bedanken, die mich bei der Zusammenstellung der Daten für dieses Buch unterstützt haben.

Mein Dank gilt allen genannten Personen und Firmen – unabhängig von der Art und dem Ausmaß der Unterstützung – gleichermaßen, denn das Gelingen eines solchen Werkes hängt auch und gerade von den kleinsten Details ab. Die Auflistung erfolgt in alphabetischer Reihenfolge.

A WORD OF THANKS

At this point, I would like to express my heartfelt thanks to all of the people who have given me their support in compiling the data for this book.

I am equally grateful to all of the individuals and companies mentioned below - irrespective of the nature and scope of their support - because the success of such a work of reference as this also depends on the finest details and these are what can make and break it. The names are listed in alphabetical order.

Auktionshaus Arnold, Frankfurt am Main

Klaus und Barbara Bildt, Krefeld

Stephan Ebert

Birgit Glöckler, Bäradies, Fürstenfeldbruck

Klaus Hartmann, Teddybären & Plüsch, Heidelberg

Jaguar Deutschland GmbH, Kronberg

Ernst Klett Verlag, Stuttgart

Sylvia Kühn

Ernst Paul Lehmann, Patentwerk, Nürnberg

Jochen und Susanne Mencke, Wingst

Manon Motulsky, Spielwarenhaus am Markt, Wiesbaden

Elizabeth Neitz, Old-Timers' Antiques, West Palm Beach, Florida

Erwin und Gisela Pfeiffer, Wiesbaden

Martina Pfeifle, Karlsruhe

Thomas Pilgrim, Essen

Ian Pout, Teddybears of Witney, Oxfordshire

Albert und Waltraud Rast, Karben

Astrid Reinshagen, Bochum

Norbert Scharmann

Margarete Steiff GmbH, Giengen/Brenz

Steiff USA, L.P., New York

Siegfried Treide, Oldtimer Club, Giengen/Brenz

www.gaf-pfeiffer.com

.steiff.de